THE NEW

LIFE
APPLICATION®
BIBLE FOR
Students

KING JAMES VERSION

Tyndale House Publishers, Inc.
WHEATON, ILLINOIS

The publisher gratefully acknowledges the role of Youth for Christ/USA in preparing the Life Application Notes and Bible Helps.

The Bible text used in this *Life Application Bible for Students* is the New King James Version .

Book opening illustrations copyright © 1991 by Janet Cameron

Ultimate Issues photos: Paul Brackley, page 900; Werner Braun, page 224; Ron Byers, pages 152, 1226; Camerique, pages 78, 170, 428, 544; Michael Chickey, page 6; Dave DeJong, pages 606, 702, 1124; Kenneth DeJong, page 512; Mimi Forsyth, pages 300, 490, 1032; Luke Golobitsh, page 1070; Bill Koechling, pages 110, 204, 910; Jean-Claude LeJeune, page 262; Darrold D. McCurdy, page 734; Cheryl and Leo Meyer, page 636; Jonathan A. Meyers, pages 710, 840; Kenneth C. Poertner, page 980; H. Armstrong Roberts, pages 782, 1222; Vernon Sigl, page 612; Jim Steere, pages 250, 924, 938, 1088, 1148.

Library of Congress Cataloging-in-Publication Data

Bible. English. New King James. 1994.
  Life application Bible for students : the New King James Version.
      p.   cm.
  Includes indexes.
    ISBN 0-8423-2845-9 (HC). — ISBN 0-8423-2846-7 (SC)
    I. Tyndale House Publishers. II. Title.
BS551.2.B47427 1994
220.5′208—dc20   93-13867

ISBN 0-8423-2845-9 Hardcover
ISBN 0-8423-2904-8 Hardcover, indexed
ISBN 0-8423-2846-7 Softcover
ISBN 0-8423-2848-3 Amethyst (purple) Bonded Leather
ISBN 0-8423-2903-x Black Bonded Leather
ISBN 0-8423-2901-3 Burgundy Bonded Leather

Printed in the United States of America
01   00
8   7   6   5   4

CONTRIBUTORS

Design Team
Dr. Bruce B. Barton
Ron Beers
Dr. James Galvin
LaVonne Neff
David R. Veerman

Senior Editor
David R. Veerman

Associate Editor
Karen Ball

Assistant Editors
Linda Taylor
Karen Voke
Derrick Blanchette

Graphic Design
Timothy R. Botts
Janet Cameron
Dan Beery
Tan Nguyen

WRITERS

Richard R. Dunn
Chairman, Department of Youth Ministry
Trinity College, Deerfield, Illinois

Terry Prisk
Youth Communicator/Consultant
Executive Director of Contemporary
  Communication
Detroit, Michigan

Kent Keller
Director of Single Adult Ministry
Key Biscayne Presbyterian Church
Miami, Florida

Jared Reed
Minister of Youth
Key Biscayne Presbyterian Church
Miami, Florida

Len Woods
Former Editor of *Youthwalk*
Minister to Students, Christ Community Church
Ruston, Louisiana

Greg Johnson
Editor, *Breakaway*
Focus on the Family
Colorado Springs, Colorado

Byron Emmert
Speaker and seminar leader
Youth for Christ
Mt. Lake, Minnesota

Diane Eble
Associate Editor, *Campus Life* magazine
Wheaton, Illinois

Neil Wilson
Pastor, Eureka United Methodist Church
Omro, Wisconsin

Bill Sanders
Author and speaker
Kalamazoo, Michigan

David R. Veerman
Veteran youth worker and author
Vice President, Livingstone Corporation
Naperville, Illinois

Thank you to the young people from the following youth groups for their invaluable assistance with this project.
Southern Gables Church (Denver, Colorado)
Spring Hill Camps (Evart, Michigan)
Pekin Bible Church (Pekin, Illinois)
Ward Presbyterian Church (Livonia, Michigan)
First Baptist Church (Holdrege, Nebraska)
Naperville Presbyterian Church (Naperville, Illinois)

NOTES AND FEATURES

Book Introductions
Jared Reed
Len Woods
David R. Veerman

Personality Profiles
Neil Wilson

Moral Dilemma Notes
Len Woods

"I Wonder" Notes
Greg Johnson

"Here's What I Did" Notes
Terry Prisk
Diane Eble

Megathemes and Discussion Questions
Richard R. Dunn
Dr. Bruce B. Barton

Ultimate Issues
Kent Keller

Life-Changer Index
Bill Sanders
Linda Taylor

Maps
Adapted from the *Life Application Bible*

Charts
Adapted from the *Life Application Bible*
Tan Nguyen

Memory Verses
Timothy R. Botts
Tan Nguyen
David R. Veerman
Karen Ball

Bible Reading Plan
Neil Wilson

Follow-Up/Appointments with God
Byron Emmert

Life Application Notes
Adapted from the *Life Application Bible*
David R. Veerman

OLD TESTAMENT

NEW TESTAMENT

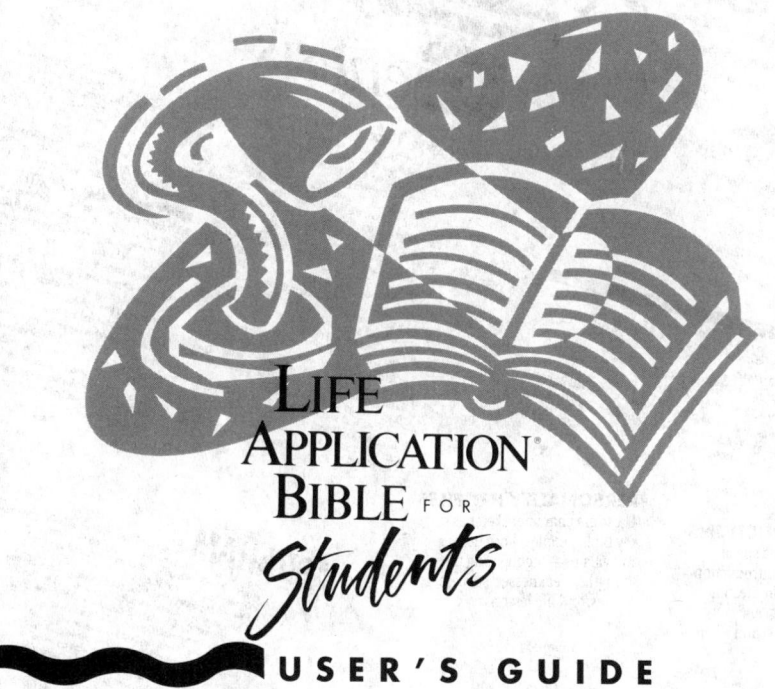

LIFE APPLICATION® BIBLE FOR Students

USER'S GUIDE

Welcome to the *Life Application Bible for Students*. God gave us his Word to tell us about himself and his plan for our life. When we read the Bible, we see God's love in action and we learn about what he wants us to do. "All Scripture *is* given by inspiration of God, and *is* profitable for doctrine, for reproof, for correction, for instruction in righteousness, that the man of God may be complete, thoroughly equipped for every good work" (2 Timothy 3:16-17).

You can see that reading the Bible is very important. In addition to reading, however, we should be studying the Bible. Then we can discover what God wants us to do and do it. That's what the word *application* means—putting into practice, obeying, *doing* biblical principles.

That's why the *Life Application Bible for Students* was written—to help you understand and apply God's Word. It is easy to use and packed with helpful notes and other features. You will find the notes within the text, at the beginnings and endings of books, and at the back of the Bible. These special features *are not* God's Word—only the Bible text itself speaks with God's authority. The notes and other features *are* a valuable help in understanding God's truth and seeing how the biblical principles apply to life, your life, today.

The following spread is a quick look at each of the special features.

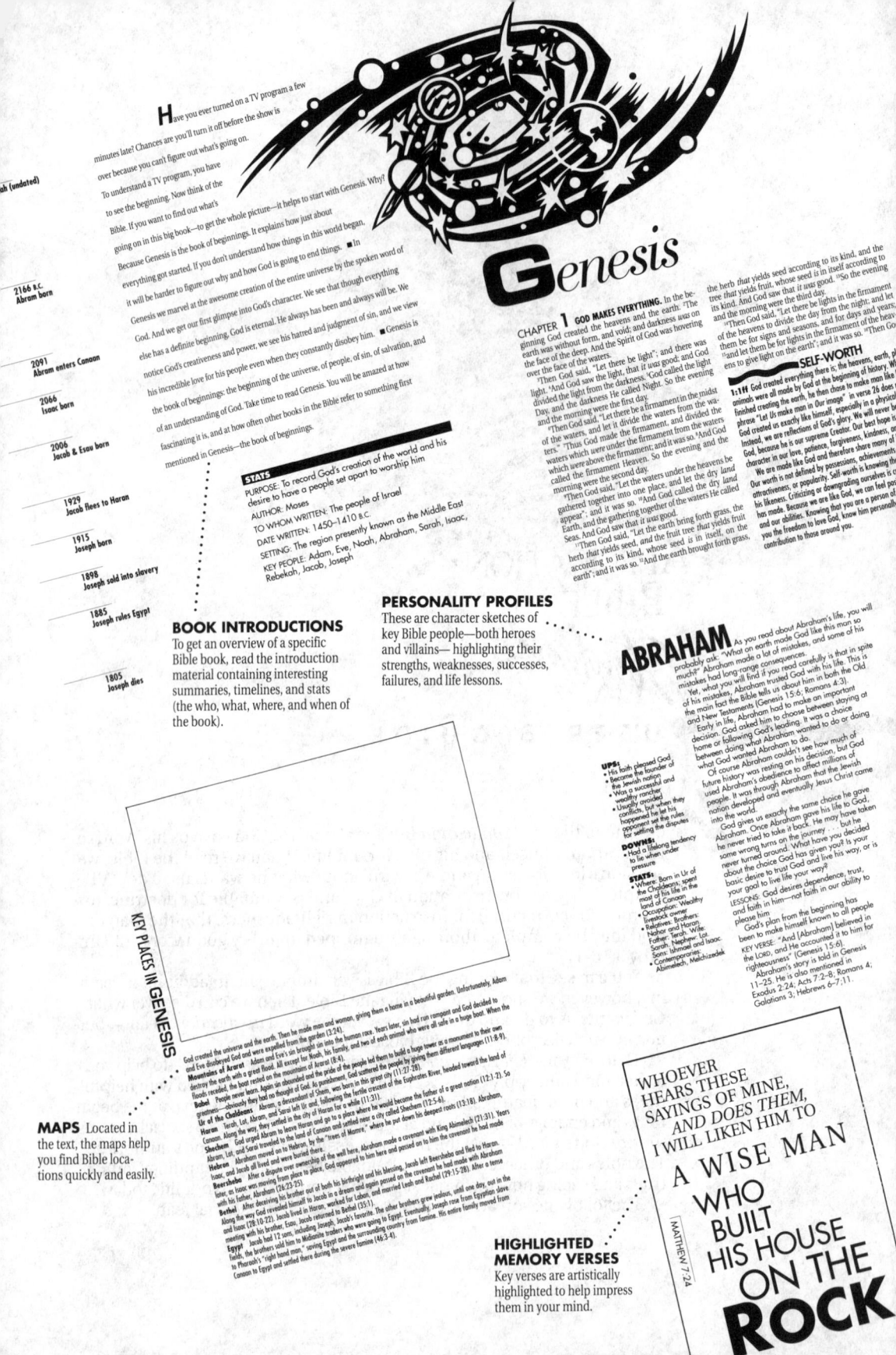

ah (undated)

2166 B.C.
Abram born

2091
Abram enters Canaan

2066
Isaac born

2006
Jacob & Esau born

1929
Jacob flees to Haran

1915
Joseph born

1898
Joseph sold into slavery

1885
Joseph rules Egypt

1805
Joseph dies

Have you ever turned on a TV program a few minutes late? Chances are you'll turn it off before the show is over because you can't figure out what's going on.

To understand a TV program, you have to see the beginning. Now think of the Bible. If you want to find out what's going on in this big book—to get the whole picture—it helps to start with Genesis. Why? Because Genesis is the book of beginnings. It explains how just about everything got started. If you don't understand how things in this world began, it will be harder to figure out why and how God is going to end things. ■ In Genesis we marvel at the awesome creation of the entire universe by the spoken word of God. And we get our first glimpse into God's character. We see that though everything else has a definite beginning, God is eternal. He always has been and always will be. We notice God's creativeness and power, we see his hatred and judgment of sin, and we view his incredible love for his people even when they constantly disobey him. ■ Genesis is the book of beginnings. Take time to read the book of Genesis. You will be amazed at how often other books in the Bible refer to something first mentioned in Genesis—the book of beginnings.

STATS
PURPOSE: To record God's creation of the world and his desire to have a people set apart to worship him
AUTHOR: Moses
TO WHOM WRITTEN: The people of Israel
DATE WRITTEN: 1450–1410 B.C.
SETTING: The region presently known as the Middle East
KEY PEOPLE: Adam, Eve, Noah, Abraham, Sarah, Isaac, Rebekah, Jacob, Joseph

Genesis

CHAPTER 1 **GOD MAKES EVERYTHING.** In the beginning God created the heavens and the earth. The earth was without form, and void; and darkness was on the face of the deep. And the Spirit of God was hovering over the face of the waters.

Then God said, "Let there be light"; and there was light. And God saw the light, that it was good; and God divided the light from the darkness. God called the light Day, and the darkness He called Night. So the evening and the morning were the first day.

Then God said, "Let there be a firmament in the midst of the waters, and let it divide the waters from the waters." Thus God made the firmament, and divided the waters which were under the firmament from the waters which were above the firmament; and it was so. And God called the firmament Heaven. So the evening and the morning were the second day.

Then God said, "Let the waters under the heavens be gathered together into one place, and let the dry land appear"; and it was so. And God called the dry land Earth, and the gathering together of the waters He called Seas. And God saw that it was good.

Then God said, "Let the earth bring forth grass, the herb that yields seed, and the fruit tree that yields fruit according to its kind, whose seed is in itself, on the earth"; and it was so. And the earth brought forth grass,

the herb that yields seed according to its kind, and the tree that yields fruit, whose seed is in itself according to its kind. And God saw that it was good. So the evening and the morning were the third day.

Then God said, "Let there be lights in the firmament of the heavens to divide the day from the night; and let them be for signs and seasons, and for days and years; and let them be for lights in the firmament of the heavens to give light on the earth"; and it was so. Then God

SELF-WORTH

1:1H God created everything there is; the heavens, earth, plants, animals were all made by God at the beginning of history. When finished creating the earth, he then chose to make man like himself. "Let Us make man in our image" in verse 26 does not phrase God created a man in our image", especially in a physical Instead, we are reflections of God's glory. We will never be as God, because he is our supreme Creator. Our best hope is to character in our love, patience, forgiveness, kindness, and

We are made like God and therefore share many of his...
Our worth is not defined by possessions, achievements...
attractiveness, or popularity. Self-worth is knowing that...
his likeness. Criticizing or downgrading ourselves is cri...
has made. Knowing that we are like God, we can feel posi...
and our abilities. Knowing that you are a person of ...
you the freedom to love God, know him personally...
contribution to those around you.

BOOK INTRODUCTIONS
To get an overview of a specific Bible book, read the introduction material containing interesting summaries, timelines, and stats (the who, what, where, and when of the book).

PERSONALITY PROFILES
These are character sketches of key Bible people—both heroes and villains— highlighting their strengths, weaknesses, successes, failures, and life lessons.

ABRAHAM

As you read about Abraham's life, you will probably ask, "What on earth made God like this man so much?" Abraham made a lot of mistakes, and some of his mistakes had long-range consequences.

Yet, what you will find if you read carefully is that in spite of his mistakes, Abraham trusted God with his life. This is the main fact the Bible tells us about him in both the Old and New Testaments (Genesis 15:6; Romans 4:3).

Early in life, Abraham had to make an important decision. God asked him to choose between staying at home or following God's leading. It was a choice between doing what Abraham wanted to do or doing what God wanted Abraham to do.

Of course Abraham couldn't see how much of future history was resting on his decision, but God used Abraham's obedience to affect millions of people. It was through Abraham that the Jewish nation developed and eventually Jesus Christ came into the world.

God gives us exactly the same choice he gave Abraham. Once Abraham gave his life to God; he never tried to take it back. He may have taken some wrong turns on the journey . . . but he never turned around. What have you decided about the choice God has given you? Is your basic desire to trust God and live his way, or is your goal to live life your way?

LESSONS: God desires dependence, trust, and faith in him—not faith in our ability to please him

God's plan from the beginning has been to make himself known to all people

KEY VERSE: "And it [Abraham] believed in the LORD, and He accounted it to him for righteousness" (Genesis 15:6).

Abraham's story is told in Genesis 11–25. He is also mentioned in Exodus 2:24; Acts 7:2–8; Romans 4; Galatians 3; Hebrews 6–7;11.

UPS:
• His faith pleased God
• Became the founder of the Jewish nation
• Was a successful and wealthy rancher
• Usually avoided conflicts, but when they happened he let his opponent set the rules in settling the disputes

DOWNS:
• Had a tendency to lie when under pressure

STATS:
• Where: Born in Ur of the Chaldeans; spent most of his life in the land of Canaan
• Occupation: Wealthy livestock owner
• Relatives: Brothers: Nahor and Haran. Father: Terah. Wife: Sarah. Nephew: Lot. Sons: Ishmael and Isaac.
• Contemporaries: Abimelech, Melchizedek

KEY PLACES IN GENESIS

God created the universe and the earth. Then he made man and woman, giving them a home in a beautiful garden. Unfortunately, Adam and Eve disobeyed God and were expelled from the garden (3:24).

As time went on, the human race. Years later, sin had run rampant and God decided to destroy the earth with a great flood. All except for Noah, his family, and two of each animal who were all safe in a huge boat. When the floods receded, the boat rested on the **Mountains of Ararat** (8:4).

Babel People never learn. Again sin abounded and the pride of the people led them to build a huge tower as a monument to their own greatness. God was obviously they had no thoughts of God. As punishment, God scattered the people by giving them different languages (11:27-28).

Ur of the Chaldeans Terah, Lot, Abram, and Sarai left Ur and, following the call of God, headed toward the land of Canaan. Along the way they settled in the city of Haran for a while (11:31).

Haran After Terah died, Abram, a descendant of Shem, was born in the great city (12:1-2). So Abram, Lot, and Sarai traveled to the land of Canaan and settled near a city called Shechem (12:5-6).

Shechem God appeared to Abram here and confirmed the fertile crescent of the Euphrates River, promising he would become the father of a great nation (12:1-7). Abram moved on to Hebron, by the "trees of Mamre," where he put down his deepest roots (13:18). Abraham, Isaac, and Jacob all lived and were buried there.

Hebron After a dispute over ownership of the well here, Abraham made a covenant with King Abimelech (21:31). Years later, as Isaac was moving from place to place, God appeared to him here and posted on to him the covenant he had made.

Beersheba After deceiving his brother out of Isaac's birthright and his blessing, Jacob left Beersheba and fled to Haran, with his father, Abraham (26:23-25).

Bethel After deceiving his brother out of Jacob in a dream and again passed on the covenant he had made with Abraham and Isaac (28:10-22). Jacob lived in Haran, worked for Laban, and married Leah and Rachel (29:15-28). After a tense meeting with his brother, Esau, Jacob returned to Bethel (35:1).

Along the way God revealed himself to Jacob. The other brothers grew jealous, until one day, out in the fields, they sold him to Midianite traders who were going to Egypt. Eventually, Joseph rose from Egyptian slave to **Egypt** Jacob had 12 sons, including Joseph, Jacob's favorite. The entire family moved from Pharaoh's "right hand man," saving Egypt and the surrounding country from famine. His entire family moved to Canaan to Egypt and settled there during the severe famine (46:3-4).

MAPS
Located in the text, the maps help you find Bible locations quickly and easily.

WHOEVER
HEARS THESE
SAYINGS OF MINE,
AND DOES THEM,
I WILL LIKEN HIM TO

A WISE MAN

WHO
BUILT
HIS HOUSE
ON THE
ROCK

MATTHEW 7:24

HIGHLIGHTED MEMORY VERSES
Key verses are artistically highlighted to help impress them in your mind.

DAYS OF CREATION

DAY 1 LIGHT so there was light and darkness

DAY 2 SKY AND WATER vapors separated

DAY 3 SEA AND EARTH waters gathered

DAY 4 SUN, MOON, AND STARS to preside over day and night, to bring about the seasons, and to mark days and years

DAY 5 FISH AND BIRDS to fill the waters and the sky

DAY 6 ANIMALS to fill the earth MAN AND WOMAN to care for the earth and commune with God

DAY 7 GOD RESTED AND WAS PLEASED

CHARTS These compare, contrast, and list important information to help you visualize difficult concepts or pull together related Bible facts.

ULTIMATE ISSUE notes An "ultimate issue" is a tough question about life or God. These full-page notes bring up difficult questions and then give clear and helpful answers.

RAL DILEMMA notes These are real-life case ..es, situations where kids like you had to make impor- ..ecisions. In each of these notes, you will be told ... to find a Bible passage that will help you under- ...what God has to say about the situations you face.

"Here's what I did..."

I used to struggle a lot with doubt. Was God real? Did he really care about what happens to me? Is the Bible relevant? Then someone challenged me to actively try to apply a passage from the Bible every day for two weeks and see if that made any difference. I did. I read some of the psalms and found that they were wonderfully relevant. When I felt lonely and had no one to turn to, I found that David's words perfectly expressed my feelings. Another passage I came across reminded me that God has promised never to leave us. Then when I came across Jesus' words in Matthew 7:24-27, I realized that it's only through obeying and applying God's Word that we know he's real. His Word is the only solid thing we have to build our lives on. The Matthew passage, and my two-week experiment, motivated me to try to live out what I read more and more every day.

Laura AGE 17

VIOLENCE On Friday nights at seven o'clock you're practi- cally guaranteed to find Derek and Steve in one of two places. Check first at Derek's. If they're not there, munching pizza and watching horror movies on video, try the mall. There probably will be standing in line at the movie theater, anxiously waiting for the chance to purchase tickets for the newest cinematic tale of gore. In the last couple of years, these guys have seen hundreds of violent movies. It doesn't matter what the plot is—deranged killers on the loose, murderous monsters on the rampage, savage mutants from outer space—as long as there are some gruesome torture scenes, lots of mutilated bodies, and gallons of blood and guts, Derek and Steve are satisfied.

"That one scene was so weak," Steve complains as he ejects a video one Friday.
"Which one?" Derek responds.
"You know, the one where he shoved the girl into that giant meat grinder. . . .
I mean, the blood didn't even look real."
"Yeah, that one," Derek agrees. "Every scene in the whole movie was just ripped off from another movie."
"Want to watch Babies with Rabies now?"
"Sure. But let me go get some more cherry soda first."
See how God feels about individuals and societies that are tolerant of violence—Genesis 6:11-13.

THE ORIGIN OF MAN

"It is now commonly accepted in scientific circles that man has become what he is today as a result of millions of years of evolution. Beginning as a one-celled animal. . . ." So reads the textbook used in biology classes in many public high schools today. "In the beginning God created the heavens and the earth. The earth was without form, and void. . . ." So begins the book of Genesis. The Christian student faces a conflict: Who does he believe? Probably no other issue has drawn a sharper dividing line between religious and nonreligious thought in our society than that of the origin of man. Were we, as Genesis 1 and 2 state, placed here by special divine creation? Or did we, as many contemporary educators, philosophers, and others tell us, evolve from nothing into one-celled animals and on up the zoological chain into Homo sapiens? Or perhaps a third option—God created man, using the process of evolution as his "laboratory." Many young people feel the uneasy tension that exists between these views. Their spiritual authorities—the Bible, the church, the pastor or youth minister—stand firmly in the creationist camp, while the public educational system, their biology teachers, and probably the majority of their peers lean heavily toward the evolutionist viewpoint. Who's right? Unfortunately, the Bible doesn't spell out in precise detail how human beings came to be. It does, however, give us some basic truths. First and foremost, human beings, like all the rest of the universe, are creations of God. The Bible states that fact in the clearest of terms—God is mentioned performing some part of his creative work 31 times in Genesis 1 alone. The idea that we simply materialized out of nothingness is a logical and scientific impossibility. The first law of thermodynamics, this is an insurmountable dilemma. If only natural causes are involved, how did nothing turn into something? And then, how did that something become something personal—with intelligence, morality, personality, and spirituality? By chance? Impossible. Absolutely, God did it. It is a simple but utterly profound rationale. "In the beginning God created the heavens and the earth. The Christian, then, turns to the supernatural—God did it and that sums it up. It does not rule out the possibility of some kind of God-directed evolution; neither does it give it any support. And frankly, the honest evolutionist will admit that his beliefs involve as much faith and speculation—if not more—as the creationist's. Nobel Prize winner Ernst Chain said in 1970: "To postulate that the development and survival of the fittest is entirely irreconcilable with the facts. . . . it amazes me that [classical evolutionary theories] are swallowed so uncritically and readily, and for such a long time, by so many scientists without a murmur of protest." So the Bible, and Genesis in particular, gives us one bedrock fact about the origin of humanity. God created us in his own image. Exactly how he did that remains a matter of faith, open to investigation by scientific inquiry. But the creationist position is as intellectually respectable as any of the alternatives. Every Christian can draw strength and confidence—and awe for his or her Creator—from knowing that.

"HERE'S WHAT I DID" notes After interviewing tons of kids, we took some of their stories and included them here. These notes tell how other young people used the principles of God's Word in specific situations in their life.

"I WONDER" notes If you've ever wondered about what the Bible has to say about something, or about some aspect of the Christian life, you'll probably find your questions repeated in these notes. And you'll also find in- teresting and thoughtful answers.

I WONDER

...hat does God really expect from me? ...hear so much from so ...many people that I ...almost feel over- ...whelmed. I feel like ...I have to give up ...a lot in order to ...make God ...happy.

One essential quality about God is that he is very personal with each individual Christian. Although he chooses not to treat everyone alike, he does have expectations of his kids. Some Christians may tell you about God's expectations based on where they are in their walk with him. If too many people are giving you advice, it does not mean though God expects way too much. This does not mean that you should quit listening to sincere Christians who want to help. It does mean, however, that if you are feeling overwhelmed, you are probably listening too much to others and not enough to God. So what do you do? How do you please God? The example from the story of Cain and Abel (see Genesis 4) gives a significant piece to the puzzle. Both of these men brought something to God, but only Abel's sacrifice pleased God. One reason was because Cain's heart was not really in it. He tried to please God out of obligation instead of love. The key to pleasing God is found in our heart or our motivation. Do we really want to make God happy, or are we going through the motions because someone told us we should? The second key to pleasing God is obedience. "He who has My commandments and keeps them, it is he who loves Me. And he who loves Me will be loved by My Father, and I will love him and manifest Myself to him" (John 14:21). Good parents want their children to obey them in the essentials of how to live, how to avoid situations that will lead to pain or scars, and how to treat other people. God is no different. But he is the perfect Father. He does not overload us with too many rules, because he knows we would get discouraged. Obedience to God is loving him enough to listen to ...he says, then following him...

MEGA Themes

BEGINNINGS Genesis introduces God as Creator of all that exists: the universe, water, and all of life, including man, who was created in God's own image. When God finished creating, he described all of creation as being "good." When sin entered this flawless creation, God began his plan of salvation to restore the lost perfection. All of creation was created to glorify God. Human beings are unique in their ability to bring God glory because they are created in God's image. Because sin broke man's good relationship with God, each person must look to God for a restoration of that lost fellowship.

1. What have you learned about the character of God from reading Genesis 1-38
2. What does it mean to be created in the image of the God who is Lord of all?
3. How do you feel about yourself when you think about being created in God's image?
4. How should the fact that each person is truly created in God's image affect the way you act toward people who appear to be different than you (i.e., skin color, physical disability, unusual habits)?

5. As a person who is created in God's image, how can you glorify God in your relationships with others? With nature? With God?

SIN AND DISOBEDIENCE Sin is destructive. It destroys the goodness of God's creation, ruining the life God intended. Sin results from human beings choosing to go their own way rather than obeying God. Only God can reverse the consequences of sinful choices. No person escapes the effects of sin. Without God providing salvation, we would all be condemned to death because of sin. God offers life that is good and glorifying to himself. When a person chooses not to obey God, he or she misses out on the goodness and glory of God.

1. What are some of the changes that happened because of Adam and Eve's sin?
2. How did sinful choices affect the people in Genesis (i.e., builders of the tower of Babel, Lot and his family, Joseph's brothers)?
3. Does a person ever "get away with" sin? Explain.
4. What are some of the reasons that people who know God still choose to sin?
5. What are some reasons that you would choose to

WORRYWART

7:16 Many have wondered how this animal kingdom roundup happened. Did Noah and his sons spend years collecting them? In reality, the creation, along with Noah, was doing just as God had commanded. There seemed to be no problem gathering the animals—God took care of the details of that job while Noah was doing his part by building the ark. Often we do just the opposite of Noah. We worry about details, lives over which we have no control, while neglecting specific area... as attitudes, relationships, responsibilities) that are under our co... Like Noah, concentrate on what God has given you to do, and le... rest to him.

LIFE APPLICATION notes On just about every page you'll find these concise mini- lessons. Each note helps explain a specific Bible passage and then tells ways you can put it into practice.

MEGATHEMES At the end of each Bible book the main themes are presented. With each theme there is a set of questions that can be used for individual or group study.

At the back of the Bible you will discover . . .

BIBLE READING PLAN By following this simple plan, you will read all the major biblical themes and stories in a year.

FOLLOW-THROUGH COURSE This course takes new believers through the basics of the Christian faith. Use it yourself or share it with a friend.

LIFE CHANGER INDEX More than 100 topics are listed in this index. Each topic has a selection of relevant Bible passages and the notes that relate. (The Scripture references listed for the notes in this section are given only to help you find the note. It may or may not actually relate to the Scripture listed.)

INDEXES FOR MORAL DILEMMA, "I WONDER," AND ULTIMATE ISSUE NOTES; CHARTS; PERSONALITY PROFILES; MAPS; AND "HERE'S WHAT I DID" NOTES Again, Scripture references listed for these notes are to help you locate the notes easily. The notes may or may not actually relate to the Scripture listed.

"WHERE TO FIND IT" INDEX More than 70 of the best-known Bible stories are listed in this index, along with Jesus' parables and miracles. Use either the Scripture references or the page numbers to find the story, parable, or miracle you want quickly and easily.

It's all here. Just about everything you will need to help you understand and apply God's Word. The next step—actually taking time to read and study the Bible—is yours. *GO FOR IT!*

OLD Testament

Noah (undated)

2166 B.C.
Abram born

2091
Abram enters Canaan

2066
Isaac born

2006
Jacob & Esau born

1929
Jacob flees to Haran

1915
Joseph born

1898
Joseph sold into slavery

1885
Joseph rules Egypt

1805
Joseph dies

Have you ever turned on a TV program a few minutes late? Chances are you'll turn it off before the show is over because you can't figure out what's going on. To understand a TV program, you have to see the beginning. Now think of the Bible. If you want to find out what's going on in this big book—to get the whole picture—it helps to start with Genesis. Why? Because Genesis is the book of beginnings. It explains how just about everything got started. If you don't understand how things in this world began, it will be harder to figure out why and how God is going to end things. ■ In Genesis we marvel at the awesome creation of the entire universe by the spoken word of God. And we get our first glimpse into God's character. We see that though everything else has a definite beginning, God is eternal. He always has been and always will be. We notice God's creativeness and power, we see his hatred and judgment of sin, and we view his incredible love for his people even when they constantly disobey him. ■ Genesis is the book of beginnings: the beginning of the universe, of people, of sin, of salvation, and of an understanding of God. Take time to read Genesis. You will be amazed at how fascinating it is, and at how often other books in the Bible refer to something first mentioned in Genesis—the book of beginnings.

STATS

PURPOSE: To record God's creation of the world and his desire to have a people set apart to worship him
AUTHOR: Moses
TO WHOM WRITTEN: The people of Israel
DATE WRITTEN: 1450–1410 B.C.
SETTING: The region presently known as the Middle East
KEY PEOPLE: Adam, Eve, Noah, Abraham, Sarah, Isaac, Rebekah, Jacob, Joseph

Genesis

CHAPTER **1** **GOD MAKES EVERYTHING.** In the beginning God created the heavens and the earth. [2]The earth was without form, and void; and darkness *was* on the face of the deep. And the Spirit of God was hovering over the face of the waters.

[3]Then God said, "Let there be light"; and there was light. [4]And God saw the light, that *it was* good; and God divided the light from the darkness. [5]God called the light Day, and the darkness He called Night. So the evening and the morning were the first day.

[6]Then God said, "Let there be a firmament in the midst of the waters, and let it divide the waters from the waters." [7]Thus God made the firmament, and divided the waters which *were* under the firmament from the waters which *were* above the firmament; and it was so. [8]And God called the firmament Heaven. So the evening and the morning were the second day.

[9]Then God said, "Let the waters under the heavens be gathered together into one place, and let the dry *land* appear"; and it was so. [10]And God called the dry *land* Earth, and the gathering together of the waters He called Seas. And God saw that *it was* good.

[11]Then God said, "Let the earth bring forth grass, the herb *that* yields seed, *and* the fruit tree *that* yields fruit according to its kind, whose seed *is* in itself, on the earth"; and it was so. [12]And the earth brought forth grass,

the herb *that* yields seed according to its kind, and the tree *that* yields fruit, whose seed *is* in itself according to its kind. And God saw that *it was* good. [13]So the evening and the morning were the third day.

[14]Then God said, "Let there be lights in the firmament of the heavens to divide the day from the night; and let them be for signs and seasons, and for days and years; [15]and let them be for lights in the firmament of the heavens to give light on the earth"; and it was so. [16]Then God

SELF-WORTH

1:1ff God created everything there is; the heavens, earth, plants, and animals were all made by God at the beginning of history. When God finished creating the earth, he then chose to make man like himself. The phrase "Let *Us* make man in *Our* image" in verse 26 does not mean that God created us exactly like himself, especially in a physical sense. Instead, we are reflections of God's glory. We will never be totally like God, because he is our supreme Creator. Our best hope is to reflect his character in our love, patience, forgiveness, kindness, and faithfulness.

We are made like God and therefore share many of his characteristics. Our worth is not defined by possessions, achievements, physical attractiveness, or popularity. Self-worth is knowing that God created us in his likeness. Criticizing or downgrading ourselves is criticizing what God has made. Because we are like God, we can feel positive about ourselves and our abilities. Knowing that you are a person of infinite worth gives you the freedom to love God, know him personally, and make a valuable contribution to those around you.

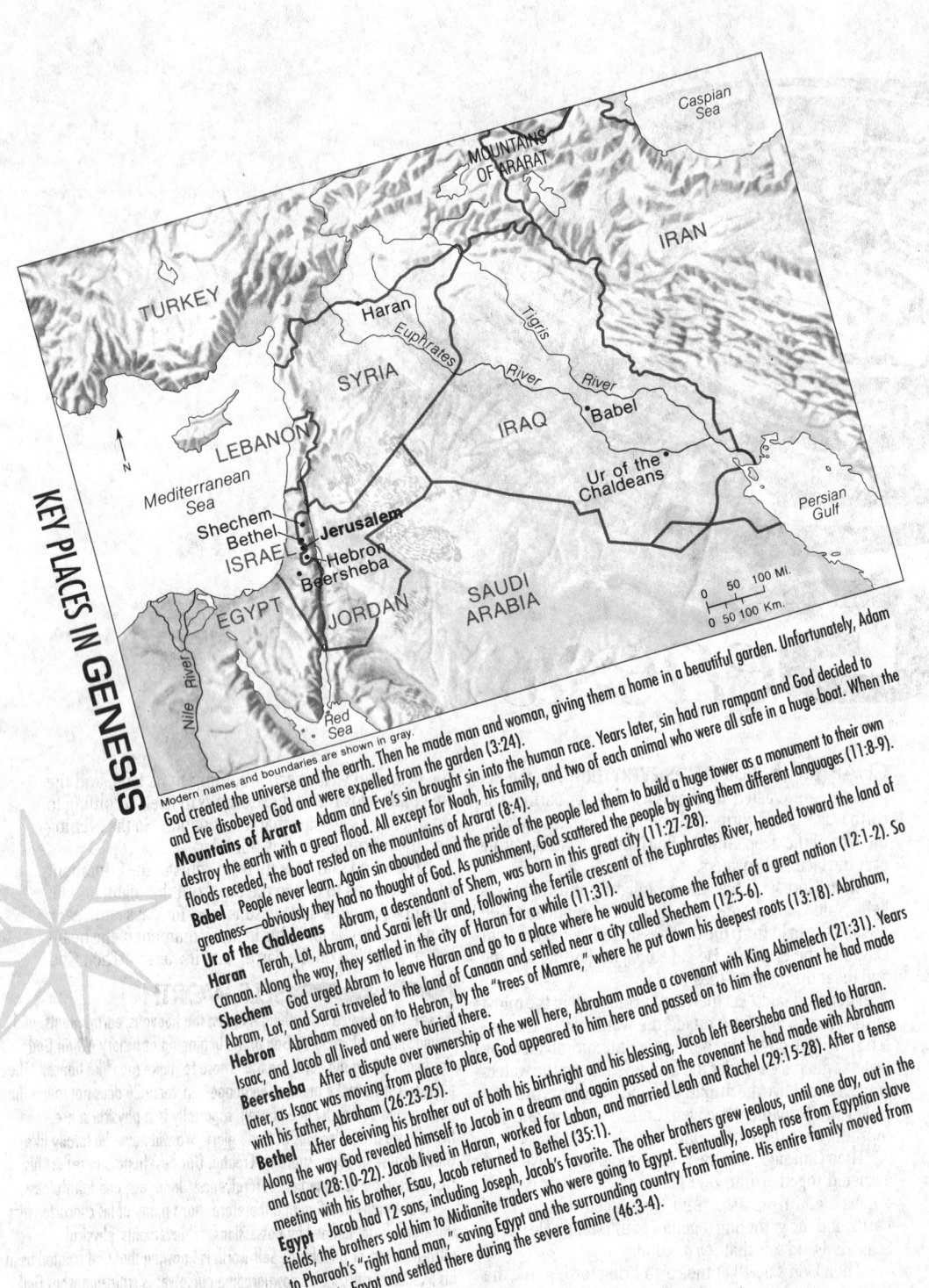

KEY PLACES IN GENESIS

Modern names and boundaries are shown in gray.

God created the universe and the earth. Then he made man and woman, giving them a home in a beautiful garden. Unfortunately, Adam and Eve disobeyed God and were expelled from the garden (3:24).

Mountains of Ararat Adam and Eve's sin brought sin into the human race. Years later, sin had run rampant and God decided to destroy the earth with a great flood. All except for Noah, his family, and two of each animal who were all safe in a huge boat. When the floods receded, the boat rested on the mountains of Ararat (8:4).

Babel People never learn. Again sin abounded and the pride of the people led them to build a huge tower as a monument to their own greatness—obviously they had no thought of God. As punishment, God scattered the people by giving them different languages (11:8-9).

Ur of the Chaldeans Abram, a descendant of Shem, was born in this great city (11:27-28).

Haran Terah, Lot, Abram, and Sarai left Ur and, following the fertile crescent of the Euphrates River, headed toward the land of Canaan. Along the way, they settled in the city of Haran for a while (11:31).

Shechem God urged Abram to leave Haran and go to a place where he would become the father of a great nation (12:1-2). So Abram, Lot, and Sarai traveled to the land of Canaan and settled near a city called Shechem (12:5-6).

Hebron Abraham moved on to Hebron, by the "trees of Mamre," where he put down his deepest roots (13:18). Abraham, Isaac, and Jacob all lived and were buried there.

Beersheba After a dispute over ownership of the well here, Abraham made a covenant with King Abimelech (21:31). Years later, as Isaac was moving from place to place, God appeared to him here and passed on to him the covenant he had made with his father, Abraham (26:23-25).

Bethel After deceiving his brother out of both his birthright and his blessing, Jacob left Beersheba and fled to Haran. Along the way God revealed himself to Jacob in a dream and again passed on the covenant he had made with Abraham and Isaac (28:10-22). Jacob lived in Haran, worked for Laban, and married Leah and Rachel (29:15-28). After a tense meeting with his brother, Esau, Jacob returned to Bethel (35:1).

Egypt Jacob had 12 sons, including Joseph, Jacob's favorite. The other brothers grew jealous, until one day, out in the fields, the brothers sold him to Midianite traders who were going to Egypt. Eventually, Joseph rose from Egyptian slave to Pharaoh's "right hand man," saving Egypt and the surrounding country from famine. His entire family moved from Canaan to Egypt and settled there during the severe famine (46:3-4).

Lamech were seven hundred and seventy-seven years; and he died.

³²And Noah was five hundred years old, and Noah begot Shem, Ham, and Japheth.

CHAPTER **6** **NOAH BUILDS THE ARK.** Now it came to pass, when men began to multiply on the face of the earth, and daughters were born to them, ²that the sons of God saw the daughters of men, that they *were* beautiful; and they took wives for themselves of all whom they chose.

³And the LORD said, "My Spirit shall not strive with man forever, for he *is* indeed flesh; yet his days shall be one hundred and twenty years." ⁴There were giants on the earth in those days, and also afterward, when the sons of God came in to the daughters of men and they bore *children* to them. Those *were* the mighty men who *were* of old, men of renown.

VIOLENCE

On Friday nights at seven o'clock you're practically guaranteed to find Derek and Steve in one of two places. Check first at Derek's. If they're not there, munching pizza and watching horror movies on video, try the mall. They probably will be standing in line at the movie theater, anxiously waiting for the chance to purchase tickets for the newest cinematic tale of gore.

In the last couple of years, these guys have seen hundreds of violent movies. It doesn't matter what the plot is—deranged killers on the loose, murderous monsters on the rampage, savage mutants from outer space—as long as there are some gruesome torture scenes, lots of mutilated bodies, and gallons of blood and guts, Derek and Steve are satisfied.

"That one scene was so weak," Steve complains as he ejects a video one Friday.

"Which one?" Derek responds.

"You know, the one where he shoved the girl into that giant meat grinder. . . . I mean, the blood didn't even look real."

"Tell me about it!" Derek agrees. "Every scene in the whole movie was just ripped off from another movie."

"Want to watch *Babies with Rabies* now?"

"Sure. But let me go get some more cherry soda first."

See how God feels about individuals and societies that are tolerant of violence—Genesis 6:11-13.

⁵Then the LORD saw that the wickedness of man *was* great in the earth, and *that* every intent of the thoughts of his heart *was* only evil continually. ⁶And the LORD was sorry that He had made man on the earth, and He was grieved in His heart. ⁷So the LORD said, "I will destroy man whom I have created from the face of the earth, both man and beast, creeping thing and birds of the air, for I am sorry that I have made them." ⁸But Noah found grace in the eyes of the LORD.

⁹This is the genealogy of Noah. Noah was a just man, perfect in his generations. Noah walked with God. ¹⁰And Noah begot three sons: Shem, Ham, and Japheth.

¹¹The earth also was corrupt before God, and the earth

7:16 Many have wondered how this animal kingdom roundup happened. Did Noah and his sons spend years collecting them? In reality the creation, along with Noah, was doing just as God had commanded. There seemed to be no problem gathering the animals—God took care of the details of that job while Noah was doing his part by building the ark. Often we do just the opposite of Noah. We worry about details in our lives over which we have no control, while neglecting specific areas (such as attitudes, relationships, responsibilities) that *are* under our control. Like Noah, concentrate on what God has given you to do, and leave the rest to him.

was filled with violence. ¹²So God looked upon the earth, and indeed it was corrupt; for all flesh had corrupted their way on the earth.

¹³And God said to Noah, "The end of all flesh has come before Me, for the earth is filled with violence through them; and behold, I will destroy them with the earth. ¹⁴Make yourself an ark of gopherwood; make rooms in the ark, and cover it inside and outside with pitch. ¹⁵And this is how you shall make it: The length of the ark *shall be* three hundred cubits, its width fifty cubits, and its height thirty cubits. ¹⁶You shall make a window for the ark, and you shall finish it to a cubit from above; and set the door of the ark in its side. You shall make it *with* lower, second, and third *decks*. ¹⁷And behold, I Myself am bringing floodwaters on the earth, to destroy from under heaven all flesh in which *is* the breath of life; everything that *is* on the earth shall die. ¹⁸But I will establish My covenant with you; and you shall go into the ark—you, your sons, your wife, and your sons' wives with you. ¹⁹And of every living thing of all flesh you shall bring two of every *sort* into the ark, to keep *them* alive with you; they shall be male and female. ²⁰Of the birds after their kind, of animals after their kind, and of every creeping thing of the earth after its kind, two of every *kind* will come to you to keep *them* alive. ²¹And you shall take for yourself of all food that is eaten, and you shall gather *it* to yourself; and it shall be food for you and for them."

²²Thus Noah did; according to all that God commanded him, so he did.

CHAPTER **7** **GOD SENDS THE GREAT FLOOD.** Then the LORD said to Noah, "Come into the ark, you and all your household, because I have seen *that* you *are* righteous before Me in this generation. ²You shall take with you seven each of every clean animal, a male and his female; two each of animals that *are* unclean, a male and his female; ³also seven each of birds of the air, male and female, to keep the species alive on the face of all the earth. ⁴For after seven more days I will cause it to rain on the earth forty days and forty nights, and I will destroy from the face of the earth all living things that I have made." ⁵And Noah did according to all that the LORD commanded him. ⁶Noah *was* six hundred years old when the floodwaters were on the earth.

⁷So Noah, with his sons, his wife, and his sons' wives, went into the ark because of the waters of the flood. ⁸Of clean animals, of animals that *are* unclean, of birds, and of everything that creeps on the earth, ⁹two by two they went into the ark to Noah, male and female, as God had commanded Noah. ¹⁰And it came to pass after seven days

[25]And Adam knew his wife again, and she bore a son and named him Seth, "For God has appointed another seed for me instead of Abel, whom Cain killed." [26]And as for Seth, to him also a son was born; and he named him Enosh. Then *men* began to call on the name of the LORD.

CHAPTER 5 ADAM'S FAMILY. This is the book of
the genealogy of Adam. In the day that God created man, He made him in the likeness of God. [2]He created them male and female, and blessed them and called them Mankind in the day they were created. [3]And Adam lived one hundred and thirty years, and begot *a son* in his own likeness, after his image, and named him Seth. [4]After he begot Seth, the days of Adam were eight hundred years; and he had sons and daughters. [5]So all the days that Adam lived were nine hundred and thirty years; and he died.

[6]Seth lived one hundred and five years, and begot Enosh. [7]After he begot Enosh, Seth lived eight hundred and seven years, and had sons and daughters. [8]So all the days of Seth were nine hundred and twelve years; and he died.

[9]Enosh lived ninety years, and begot Cainan. [10]After he begot Cainan, Enosh lived eight hundred and fifteen years, and had sons and daughters. [11]So all the days of Enosh were nine hundred and five years; and he died.

[12]Cainan lived seventy years, and begot Mahalalel. [13]After he begot Mahalalel, Cainan lived eight hundred and forty years, and had sons and daughters. [14]So all the days of Cainan were nine hundred and ten years; and he died.

[15]Mahalalel lived sixty-five years, and begot Jared. [16]After he begot Jared, Mahalalel lived eight hundred and thirty years, and had sons and daughters. [17]So all the days of Mahalalel were eight hundred and ninety-five years; and he died.

[18]Jared lived one hundred and sixty-two years, and begot Enoch. [19]After he begot Enoch, Jared lived eight hundred years, and had sons and daughters. [20]So all the days of Jared were nine hundred and sixty-two years; and he died.

[21]Enoch lived sixty-five years, and begot Methuselah. [22]After he begot Methuselah, Enoch walked with God three hundred years, and had sons and daughters. [23]So all the days of Enoch were three hundred and sixty-five years. [24]And Enoch walked with God; and he *was* not, for God took him.

[25]Methuselah lived one hundred and eighty-seven years, and begot Lamech. [26]After he begot Lamech, Methuselah lived seven hundred and eighty-two years, and had sons and daughters. [27]So all the days of Methuselah were nine hundred and sixty-nine years; and he died.

[28]Lamech lived one hundred and eighty-two years, and had a son. [29]And he called his name Noah, saying, "This *one* will comfort us concerning our work and the toil of our hands, because of the ground which the LORD has cursed." [30]After he begot Noah, Lamech lived five hundred and ninety-five years, and had sons and daughters. [31]So all the days of

ADAM & EVE

were the only two humans who never experienced being young. Depending on how you feel, they may or may not have missed a lot! But try to imagine starting out life as an adult—no memories, no mistakes, no past little lessons to help you make adult decisions. . . . Most of us don't realize how much we learn or fail to learn during our growing years until it's too late.

For instance, we have many opportunities to learn as children that while there are some trustworthy people in our lives, not everyone can be trusted. We learn not to immediately trust new advice. We discover it is often helpful to compare it to wisdom we already have, or even to ask someone who has been trustworthy to evaluate the new advice. Eve got some new information: "The fruit is great. . . God's being selfish. . . you will be like him." She trusted new advice even though it went against what had been trustworthy. She ate the fruit. She failed to trust the One who had never failed her. Adam made the same mistake. New advice, no questions, no checking . . . he ate the fruit. Both of them disobeyed God. The result was death!

Like Adam and Eve, we often have to live with the painful consequences of accepting bad advice. But consequences are reminders of hard lessons. They are not excuses to give up or to repeat the same mistakes.

How do you evaluate new advice? Are your past mistakes and successes helping you make better decisions? How often do you seriously consider the source as well as the advice?

LESSONS: As Adam and Eve's descendants, we all reflect to some degree the image of God The basic tendency to sin goes back to the beginning of the human race

God wants people who are free to sin to choose instead to trust and love him God's design for marriage was part of God's creation

KEY VERSE: "So God created man in His own image; in the image of God He created him; male and female He created them" (Genesis 1:27).

Adam and Eve's story is told in Genesis 1:26–4:26. They are also mentioned in 1 Chronicles 1:1; Job 31:33; Luke 3:38; Romans 5:14; 1 Corinthians 15:22,45; 1 Timothy 2:13-14.

UPS:
- The first male and female, husband and wife, human beings
- First to be made in the image of God
- First caretakers of creation
- First to know God personally

DOWNS:
- Both tended to handle mistakes and sin by excuses or blaming others
- Acted without considering consequences
- Together they brought sin into the creation

STATS:
- Where: Garden of Eden
- Occupation: Husband and wife, caretakers of Eden
- Relatives: Sons: Cain, Abel, Seth. Numerous other children.

Doubt	Makes you question God's Word and his goodness
Discouragement	Makes you look at your problems rather than at God
Diversion	Makes the wrong things seem attractive so you want them more than the right things
Defeat	Makes you feel like a failure, so you don't even try
Delay	Makes you put off doing something so it never gets done

¹⁷Then to Adam He said, "Because you have heeded the voice of your wife, and have eaten from the tree of which I commanded you, saying, 'You shall not eat of it':

"Cursed *is* the ground for your sake;
In toil you shall eat *of* it
All the days of your life.
¹⁸ Both thorns and thistles it shall bring forth for you,
And you shall eat the herb of the field.
¹⁹ In the sweat of your face you shall eat bread
Till you return to the ground,
For out of it you were taken;
For dust you *are*,
And to dust you shall return."

²⁰And Adam called his wife's name Eve, because she was the mother of all living.

²¹Also for Adam and his wife the LORD God made tunics of skin, and clothed them.

²²Then the LORD God said, "Behold, the man has become like one of Us, to know good and evil. And now, lest he put out his hand and take also of the tree of life, and eat, and live forever"—²³therefore the LORD God sent him out of the garden of Eden to till the ground from which he was taken. ²⁴So He drove out the man; and He placed cherubim at the east of the garden of Eden, and a flaming sword which turned every way, to guard the way to the tree of life.

CHAPTER **4** **CAIN KILLS ABEL.** Now Adam knew Eve his wife, and she conceived and bore Cain, and said, "I have acquired a man from the LORD." ²Then she bore again, this time his brother Abel. Now Abel was a keeper of sheep, but Cain was a tiller of the ground. ³And in the process of time it came to pass that Cain brought an offering of the fruit of the ground to the LORD. ⁴Abel also brought of the firstborn of his flock and of their fat. And

the LORD respected Abel and his offering, ⁵but He did not respect Cain and his offering. And Cain was very angry, and his countenance fell.

⁶So the LORD said to Cain, "Why are you angry? And why has your countenance fallen? ⁷If you do well, will you not be accepted? And if you do not do well, sin lies at the door. And its desire *is* for you, but you should rule over it."

⁸Now Cain talked with Abel his brother; and it came to pass, when they were in the field, that Cain rose up against Abel his brother and killed him.

⁹Then the LORD said to Cain, "Where *is* Abel your brother?"

He said, "I do not know. *Am* I my brother's keeper?"

¹⁰And He said, "What have you done? The voice of your brother's blood cries out to Me from the ground. ¹¹So now you *are* cursed from the earth, which has opened its mouth to receive your brother's blood from your hand. ¹²When you till the ground, it shall no longer yield its strength to you. A fugitive and a vagabond you shall be on the earth."

¹³And Cain said to the LORD, "My punishment *is* greater than I can bear! ¹⁴Surely You have driven me out this day from the face of the ground; I shall be hidden from Your face; I shall be a fugitive and a vagabond on the earth, and it will happen *that* anyone who finds me will kill me."

¹⁵And the LORD said to him, "Therefore, whoever kills Cain, vengeance shall be taken on him sevenfold." And the LORD set a mark on Cain, lest anyone finding him should kill him.

¹⁶Then Cain went out from the presence of the LORD and dwelt in the land of Nod on the east of Eden. ¹⁷And Cain knew his wife, and she conceived and bore Enoch. And he built a city, and called the name of the city after the name of his son—Enoch. ¹⁸To Enoch was born Irad; and Irad begot Mehujael, and Mehujael begot Methushael, and Methushael begot Lamech.

¹⁹Then Lamech took for himself two wives: the name of one *was* Adah, and the name of the second *was* Zillah. ²⁰And Adah bore Jabal. He was the father of those who dwell in tents and have livestock. ²¹His brother's name *was* Jubal. He was the father of all those who play the harp and flute. ²²And as for Zillah, she also bore Tubal-Cain, an instructor of every craftsman in bronze and iron. And the sister of Tubal-Cain *was* Naamah.

²³Then Lamech said to his wives:

"Adah and Zillah, hear my voice;
Wives of Lamech, listen to my speech!
For I have killed a man for wounding me,
Even a young man for hurting me.
²⁴ If Cain shall be avenged sevenfold,
Then Lamech seventy-sevenfold."

BAD APPLE

4:8-10 Adam and Eve's disobedience brought sin into the human race. They may have thought their sin (eating a "harmless" piece of fruit) wasn't very bad, but notice how quickly their sinful nature developed in the lives of their children. Simple disobedience degenerated into outright murder. Adam and Eve acted only against God, but Cain acted against both God and man. A small sin has a way of growing out of control. Let God help you with your little sins before they turn into tragedies.

SUN, MOON, AND STARS to preside over day and night, to bring about the seasons, and to mark days and years	FISH AND BIRDS to fill the waters and the sky	ANIMALS to fill the earth MAN AND WOMAN to care for the earth and commune with God	GOD RESTED AND WAS PLEASED
DAY **4**	DAY **5**	DAY **6**	DAY **7**

the whole land of Havilah, where *there is* gold. ¹²And the gold of that land *is* good. Bdellium and the onyx stone *are* there. ¹³The name of the second river *is* Gihon; it *is* the one which goes around the whole land of Cush. ¹⁴The name of the third river *is* Hiddekel; it *is* the one which goes toward the east of Assyria. The fourth river *is* the Euphrates.

¹⁵Then the LORD God took the man and put him in the garden of Eden to tend and keep it. ¹⁶And the LORD God commanded the man, saying, "Of every tree of the garden you may freely eat; ¹⁷but of the tree of the knowledge of good and evil you shall not eat, for in the day that you eat of it you shall surely die."

¹⁸And the LORD God said, "*It is* not good that man should be alone; I will make him a helper comparable to him." ¹⁹Out of the ground the LORD God formed every beast of the field and every bird of the air, and brought *them* to Adam to see what he would call them. And whatever Adam called each living creature, that *was* its name. ²⁰So Adam gave names to all cattle, to the birds of the air, and to every beast of the field. But for Adam there was not found a helper comparable to him.

²¹And the LORD God caused a deep sleep to fall on Adam, and he slept; and He took one of his ribs, and closed up the flesh in its place. ²²Then the rib which the LORD God had taken from man He made into a woman, and He brought her to the man.

²³And Adam said:

"This *is* now bone of my bones
And flesh of my flesh;
She shall be called Woman,
Because she was taken out of Man."

²⁴Therefore a man shall leave his father and mother and be joined to his wife, and they shall become one flesh.

²⁵And they were both naked, the man and his wife, and were not ashamed.

CHAPTER **3** ADAM AND EVE ARE TEMPTED. Now the serpent was more cunning than any beast of the field which the LORD God had made. And he said to the woman, "Has God indeed said, 'You shall not eat of every tree of the garden'?"

²And the woman said to the serpent, "We may eat the fruit of the trees of the garden; ³but of the fruit of the tree which *is* in the midst of the garden, God has said, 'You shall not eat it, nor shall you touch it, lest you die.'"

⁴Then the serpent said to the woman, "You will not surely die. ⁵For God knows that in the day you eat of it

your eyes will be opened, and you will be like God, knowing good and evil."

⁶So when the woman saw that the tree *was* good for food, that it *was* pleasant to the eyes, and a tree desirable to make *one* wise, she took of its fruit and ate. She also gave to her husband with her, and he ate. ⁷Then the eyes of both of them were opened, and they knew that they *were* naked; and they sewed fig leaves together and made themselves coverings.

⁸And they heard the sound of the LORD God walking in the garden in the cool of the day, and Adam and his wife hid themselves from the presence of the LORD God among the trees of the garden.

⁹Then the LORD God called to Adam and said to him, "Where *are* you?"

¹⁰So he said, "I heard Your voice in the garden, and I was afraid because I was naked; and I hid myself."

¹¹And He said, "Who told you that you *were* naked? Have you eaten from the tree of which I commanded you that you should not eat?"

¹²Then the man said, "The woman whom You gave *to be* with me, she gave me of the tree, and I ate."

¹³And the LORD God said to the woman, "What *is* this you have done?"

The woman said, "The serpent deceived me, and I ate."

¹⁴So the LORD God said to the serpent:

"Because you have done this,
You *are* cursed more than all cattle,
And more than every beast of the field;
On your belly you shall go,
And you shall eat dust
All the days of your life.
¹⁵ And I will put enmity
Between you and the woman,
And between your seed and her Seed;
He shall bruise your head,
And you shall bruise His heel."

¹⁶To the woman He said:

"I will greatly multiply your sorrow and your
    conception;
In pain you shall bring forth children;
Your desire *shall be* for your husband,
And he shall rule over you."

▰▰▰▰▰▰▰▰ **MARRIAGE**

2:18-24 God's creative work was not complete until he made woman. He could have made her from the dust of the ground, as he made man. God chose, however, to make her from the man's flesh and bone. In so doing, he illustrated that in marriage man and woman symbolically become one flesh. This is a mystical union of the couple's hearts and lives. Throughout the Bible, God treats this special partnership seriously. If you are planning to be married, are you willing to keep the commitment that makes the two of you one? The goal in marriage should be more than friendship; it should be oneness.

**DAYS OF
CREATION**

LIGHT
so there
was light
and darkness

SKY AND
WATER
vapors
separated

SEA AND
EARTH
waters
gathered

DAY 1

DAY 2

DAY 3

THE ORIGIN OF MAN

"It is now commonly accepted in scientific circles that man has become what he is today as a result of millions of years of evolution. Beginning as a one-celled animal. . . ." So reads the textbook used in biology classes in many public high schools today. "In the beginning God created the heavens and the earth. The earth was without form, and void. . . ." So begins the book of Genesis. The Christian student faces a conflict: Who does he believe? Probably no other issue has drawn a sharper dividing line between religious and nonreligious thought in our society than that of the origin of man. Were we, as Genesis 1 and 2 state, placed here by special divine creation? Or did we, as many contemporary educators, philosophers, and others tell us, evolve from nothing into one-celled animals and on up the zoological chain into Homo sapiens? Or perhaps a third option—God created man, using the process of evolution as his "laboratory." Many young people feel the uneasy tension that exists between these views. Their spiritual authorities—the Bible, the church, the pastor or youth minister—stand firmly in the creationist camp, while the public educational system, their biology teachers, and probably the majority of their peers lean heavily toward the evolutionist viewpoint. Who's right?

Unfortunately, the Bible doesn't spell out in precise detail how human beings came to be. It does, however, give us some basic truths. First and foremost, human beings, like all the rest of the universe, are creations of God. The Bible states that fact in the clearest of terms—God is mentioned performing some part of his creative work 31 times in Genesis 1 alone. The idea that we simply materialized out of nothingness is a logical and scientific impossibility. The first law of thermodynamics tells us matter can neither be created nor destroyed by natural causes. For the strict naturalist/evolutionist, this is an insurmountable dilemma. If only natural causes are involved, how did nothing turn into something? And then, how did that something become something personal—with intelligence, morality, personality, and spirituality? By chance? Impossible. Absolutely, scientifically, intellectually, and logically impossible. "In the beginning God created the heavens and the earth . . ." It is a simple but utterly profound rationale. It does not rule out the possibility of some kind of God-directed evolution; neither does it give it any support. And frankly, the honest evolutionist will admit that his beliefs involve as much faith and speculation—if not more—as the creationist's. Nobel Prize winner Ernst Chain said in 1970: "To postulate that the development and survival of the fittest is entirely a consequence of chance mutations seems to me a hypothesis based on no evidence and entirely irreconcilable with the facts. . . . it amazes me that [classical evolutionary theories] are swallowed so uncritically and readily, and for such a long time, by so many scientists without a murmur of protest." So the Bible, and Genesis in particular, gives us one bedrock fact about the origin of humanity: God created us in his own image. Exactly how he did that remains a matter of faith, open to investigation by scientific inquiry. But the creationist position is as intellectually respectable as any of the alternatives. Every Christian can draw strength and confidence—and awe for his or her Creator—from knowing that.

made two great lights: the greater light to rule the day, and the lesser light to rule the night. *He made* the stars also. ¹⁷God set them in the firmament of the heavens to give light on the earth, ¹⁸and to rule over the day and over the night, and to divide the light from the darkness. And God saw that *it was* good. ¹⁹So the evening and the morning were the fourth day.

²⁰Then God said, "Let the waters abound with an abundance of living creatures, and let birds fly above the earth across the face of the firmament of the heavens." ²¹So God created great sea creatures and every living thing that moves, with which the waters abounded, according to their kind, and every winged bird according to its kind. And God saw that *it was* good. ²²And God blessed them, saying, "Be fruitful and multiply, and fill the waters in the seas, and let birds multiply on the earth." ²³So the evening and the morning were the fifth day.

²⁴Then God said, "Let the earth bring forth the living creature according to its kind: cattle and creeping thing and beast of the earth, *each* according to its kind"; and it was so. ²⁵And God made the beast of the earth according to its kind, cattle according to its kind, and everything that creeps on the earth according to its kind. And God saw that *it was* good.

²⁶Then God said, "Let Us make man in Our image, according to Our likeness; let them have dominion over the fish of the sea, over the birds of the air, and over the cattle, over all the earth and over every creeping thing that creeps on the earth." ²⁷So God created man in His *own* image; in the image of God He created him; male and female He created them. ²⁸Then God blessed them, and God said to them, "Be fruitful and multiply; fill the earth and subdue it; have dominion over the fish of the sea, over the birds of the air, and over every living thing that moves on the earth."

²⁹And God said, "See, I have given you every herb *that* yields seed which *is* on the face of all the earth, and every tree whose fruit yields seed; to you it shall be for food. ³⁰Also, to every beast of the earth, to every bird of the air, and to everything that creeps on the earth, in which *there* is life, *I have given* every green herb for food"; and it was so. ³¹Then God saw everything that He had made, and indeed *it was* very good. So the evening and the morning were the sixth day.

CHAPTER 2 GOD MAKES ADAM AND EVE.

Thus the heavens and the earth, and all the host of them, were finished. ²And on the seventh day God ended His work which He had done, and He rested on the seventh day from all His work which He had done. ³Then God blessed the seventh day and sanctified it, because in it He rested from all His work which God had created and made.

⁴This *is* the history of the heavens and the earth when they were created, in the day that the LORD God made the earth and the heavens, ⁵before any plant of the field was in the earth and before any herb of the field had grown. For the LORD God had not caused it to rain on the earth, and *there was* no man to till the ground; ⁶but a mist went up from the earth and watered the whole face of the ground.

⁷And the LORD God formed man *of* the dust of the ground, and breathed into his nostrils the breath of life; and man became a living being.

⁸The LORD God planted a garden eastward in Eden, and there He put the man whom He had formed. ⁹And out of the ground the LORD God made every tree grow that is pleasant to the sight and good for food. The tree of life *was* also in the midst of the garden, and the tree of the knowledge of good and evil.

¹⁰Now a river went out of Eden to water the garden, and from there it parted and became four riverheads. ¹¹The name of the first *is* Pishon; it *is* the one which skirts

When I read about creation and miracles in the Bible, I get confused. How do science and the Bible relate?

I WONDER...

The Bible and science debate has raged for many years. Conflicts arise when we look for spiritual answers from science or for scientific answers in the Bible.

A former Vietnam POW told of the time he was allowed to send a cassette tape home to his family. Realizing that it might be the last communication he would ever have with those that he loved, he took extensive notes on what he would cover before he began to make the tape. His goal was to communicate the most important things that his family should know. To his wife, he talked of insurance, mortgages, child-rearing, and relatives. To the kids, he personalized each message so that he touched on unique situations they would face the next few years as they grew up without him. To all of them he made sure that they knew how much he loved them.

This is exactly the purpose behind the Bible. God put 66 books together to let his creation know the most important things about life, about what to do in certain situations, and especially about the extent of his love for them.

For some reason he chose to leave out dinosaurs, fusion, and gravity (among other significant discoveries). Instead he included stories of real people with real struggles who faced hardship and trials, many of whom conquered fears and circumstances because they realized that if God was for them, who could be against them! Many other stories are included of those who rejected God and then experienced tragic consequences.

Most of these biblical examples tell us much more about living, surviving, and prospering in a complicated society than science could ever hope to promise.

Your mind matters to God—he wants you to think. Never be afraid to ask tough questions about the Bible or the Christian faith. But also consider the appropriateness of each question. Is this the kind of question the Bible should answer? And do the same with science, asking the right questions.

Creation and the resurrection of Jesus Christ are two of the most important tenets of the Christian faith. Although neither can be duplicated in a laboratory, they also cannot be proven to be false by science.

If God can create life from nothing, as well as raise a man from the dead, he can lead us through this life and the next. We can trust him.

that the waters of the flood were on the earth. [11]In the six hundredth year of Noah's life, in the second month, the seventeenth day of the month, on that day all the fountains of the great deep were broken up, and the windows of heaven were opened. [12]And the rain was on the earth forty days and forty nights.

[13]On the very same day Noah and Noah's sons, Shem, Ham, and Japheth, and Noah's wife and the three wives of his sons with them, entered the ark— [14]they and every beast after its kind, all cattle after their kind, every creeping thing that creeps on the earth after its kind, and every bird after its kind, every bird of every sort. [15]And they went into the ark to Noah, two by two, of all flesh in which *is* the breath of life. [16]So those that entered, male and female of all flesh, went in as God had commanded him; and the LORD shut him in.

[17]Now the flood was on the earth forty days. The waters increased and lifted up the ark, and it rose high above the earth. [18]The waters prevailed and greatly increased on the earth, and the ark moved about on the surface of the waters. [19]And the waters prevailed exceedingly on the earth, and all the high hills under the whole heaven were covered. [20]The waters prevailed fifteen cubits upward, and the mountains were covered. [21]And all flesh died that moved on the earth: birds and cattle and beasts and every creeping thing that creeps on the earth, and every man. [22]All in whose nostrils *was* the breath of the spirit of life, all that *was* on the dry *land*, died. [23]So He destroyed all living things which were on the face of the ground: both man and cattle, creeping thing and bird of the air. They were destroyed from the earth. Only Noah and those who *were* with him in the ark remained *alive*. [24]And the waters prevailed on the earth one hundred and fifty days.

CHAPTER 8 Then God remembered Noah, and every living thing, and all the animals that *were* with him in the ark. And God made a wind to pass over the earth, and the waters subsided. [2]The fountains of the deep and the windows of heaven were also stopped, and the rain from heaven was restrained. [3]And the waters receded continually from the earth. At the end of the hundred and fifty days the waters decreased. [4]Then the ark rested in the seventh month, the seventeenth day of the month, on the mountains of Ararat. [5]And the waters decreased continually until the tenth month. In the tenth *month*, on the first *day* of the month, the tops of the mountains were seen.

[6]So it came to pass, at the end of forty days, that Noah opened the window of the ark which he had made. [7]Then he sent out a raven, which kept going to and fro until the waters had dried up from the earth. [8]He also sent out from himself a dove, to see if the waters had receded from the face of the ground. [9]But the dove found no resting place for the sole of her foot, and she returned into the ark to him, for the waters *were* on the face of the whole earth. So he put out his hand and took her, and drew her into the ark to himself. [10]And he waited yet another seven days, and again he sent the dove out from the ark. [11]Then the dove came to him in the evening, and behold, a freshly plucked olive leaf *was* in her mouth; and Noah knew that the waters had receded from the earth. [12]So he waited yet another seven days and sent out the dove, which did not return again to him anymore.

[13]And it came to pass in the six hundred and first year, in the first *month*, the first *day* of the month, that the waters were dried up from the earth; and Noah removed the covering of the ark and looked, and indeed the surface of the ground was dry. [14]And in the second month, on the twenty-seventh

ABEL

No matter what parents do, their kids don't always get along. In most cases, all the loving and fighting that goes on eventually creates a strong bond between brothers and sisters. We love them even when we hate them. Sometimes, though, we find it's easier to hurt than to help. The death of Adam and Eve's son Abel shows us how bad this can get.

Abel was the second child born into the world, but the first one to obey God. He worshiped in a way that pleased God. That really bothered his brother Cain. We don't know how Abel felt, but he must have known Cain was angry at him. Brothers and sisters know things like that about each other. Yet Abel trusted his brother even when Cain suggested they go out to the field together. Abel was the kind of brother worth having. Once in a while we need to let our brothers and sisters know we think they're worth having and trusting.

The Bible doesn't tell us why God liked Abel's gift and disliked Cain's, but both brothers knew what God expected. Only Abel obeyed. He is remembered for his obedience and faith (Hebrews 11:4), and he is called "righteous" (Matthew 23:35). When we know what God wants, we need to obey like Abel, no matter what the cost, and trust God to make things work out right.

LESSONS: God hears those who come to him with a right heart
God recognizes the innocent person, and sooner or later he judges the guilty

KEY VERSE: "By faith Abel offered to God a more excellent sacrifice than Cain, through which he obtained witness that he was righteous, God testifying of his gifts; and through it he being dead still speaks" (Hebrews 11:4).
Abel's story is told in Genesis 4:1-8. He is also mentioned in Matthew 23:35; Luke 11:51; Hebrews 11:4; 12:24.

UPS:
- First member of the Hall of Faith in Hebrews 11:4
- First shepherd
- First martyr for truth (Matthew 23:35)

STATS:
- Where: Just outside of Eden
- Occupation: Shepherd
- Relatives: Parents: Adam and Eve. Brother: Cain.

day of the month, the earth was dried.

¹⁵Then God spoke to Noah, saying, ¹⁶"Go out of the ark, you and your wife, and your sons and your sons' wives with you. ¹⁷Bring out with you every living thing of all flesh that *is* with you: birds and cattle and every creeping thing that creeps on the earth, so that they may abound on the earth, and be fruitful and multiply on the earth." ¹⁸So Noah went out, and his sons and his wife and his sons' wives with him. ¹⁹Every animal, every creeping thing, every bird, *and* whatever creeps on the earth, according to their families, went out of the ark.

²⁰Then Noah built an altar to the LORD, and took of every clean animal and of every clean bird, and offered burnt offerings on the altar. ²¹And the LORD smelled a soothing aroma. Then the LORD said in His heart, "I will never again curse the ground for man's sake, although the imagination of man's heart *is* evil from his youth; nor will I again destroy every living thing as I have done.

²² "While the earth remains,
Seedtime and harvest,
Cold and heat,
Winter and summer,
And day and night
Shall not cease."

CHAPTER 9 So God blessed Noah and his sons, and said to them: "Be fruitful and multiply, and fill the earth. ²And the fear of you and the dread of you shall be on every beast of the earth, on every bird of the air, on all that move *on* the earth, and on all the fish of the sea. They are given into your hand. ³Every moving thing that lives shall be food for you. I have given you all things, even as the green herbs. ⁴But you shall not eat flesh with its life, *that is*, its blood. ⁵Surely for your lifeblood I will demand *a reckoning;* from the hand of every beast I will require it, and from the hand of man. From the hand of every man's brother I will require the life of man.

MURDERERS

9:5-6 Here God explains why murder is so wrong: to kill a person is to kill one made like God. Because human beings are made in God's image, all people possess the qualities that distinguish us from animals: morality, reason, creativity, and self-worth. When we interact with others, we are interacting with beings made by God, beings to whom God offers eternal life. God wants us to recognize these special qualities in all people.

⁶ "Whoever sheds man's blood,
By man his blood shall be shed;
For in the image of God
He made man.
⁷ And as for you, be fruitful and multiply;
Bring forth abundantly in the earth
And multiply in it."

⁸Then God spoke to Noah and to his sons with him, saying: ⁹"And as for Me, behold, I establish My covenant with you and with your descendants after you, ¹⁰and with every living creature that *is* with you: the birds, the cattle, and every beast of the earth with you, of all that go out of the ark, every beast of the earth. ¹¹Thus I establish My covenant with you: Never again shall all flesh be cut off by the waters of the flood; never again shall there be a flood to destroy the earth."

¹²And God said: "This *is* the sign of the covenant which I make between Me and you, and every living creature that *is* with you, for perpetual generations: ¹³I set My rainbow in the cloud, and it shall be for the sign of the covenant between Me and the earth. ¹⁴It shall be, when I bring a cloud over the earth, that the rainbow shall be seen in the cloud; ¹⁵and I will remember My covenant which *is* between Me and you and every living creature of all flesh; the waters shall never again become a flood to destroy all flesh. ¹⁶The rainbow shall be in the cloud, and I will look on it to remember the everlasting covenant between God and every living creature of all flesh that *is* on the earth." ¹⁷And God said to Noah, "This *is* the sign of the covenant which I have established between Me and all flesh that *is* on the earth."

¹⁸Now the sons of Noah who went out of the ark were Shem, Ham, and Japheth. And Ham *was* the father of Canaan. ¹⁹These three *were* the sons of Noah, and from these the whole earth was populated.

²⁰And Noah began *to be* a farmer, and he planted a vineyard. ²¹Then he drank of the wine and was drunk, and became uncovered in his tent. ²²And Ham, the father of Canaan, saw the nakedness of his father, and told his two brothers outside. ²³But Shem and Japheth took a garment, laid *it* on both their shoulders, and went backward and covered the nakedness of their father. Their faces *were* turned away, and they did not see their father's nakedness.

²⁴So Noah awoke from his wine, and knew what his younger son had done to him. ²⁵Then he said:

"Cursed *be* Canaan;
A servant of servants
He shall be to his brethren."

²⁶And he said:

"Blessed *be* the LORD,
The God of Shem,
And may Canaan be his servant.
²⁷ May God enlarge Japheth,
And may he dwell in the tents of Shem;
And may Canaan be his servant."

²⁸And Noah lived after the flood three hundred and fifty years. ²⁹So all the days of Noah were nine hundred and fifty years; and he died.

CHAPTER 10 NOAH'S FAMILY. Now this *is* the genealogy of the sons of Noah: Shem, Ham, and Japheth. And sons were born to them after the flood.

²The sons of Japheth *were* Gomer, Magog, Madai, Javan, Tubal, Meshech, and Tiras. ³The sons of Gomer *were* Ashkenaz, Riphath, and Togarmah. ⁴The sons of Javan *were* Elishah, Tarshish, Kittim, and Dodanim. ⁵From these the coastland *peoples* of the Gentiles were separated into their lands, everyone according to his language, according to their families, into their nations.

⁶The sons of Ham *were* Cush, Mizraim, Put, and Ca-

naan. 7The sons of Cush *were* Seba, Havilah, Sabtah, Raamah, and Sabtechah; and the sons of Raamah *were* Sheba and Dedan.

8Cush begot Nimrod; he began to be a mighty one on the earth. 9He was a mighty hunter before the LORD; therefore it is said, "Like Nimrod the mighty hunter before the LORD." 10And the beginning of his kingdom was Babel, Erech, Accad, and Calneh, in the land of Shinar. 11From that land he went to Assyria and built Nineveh, Rehoboth Ir, Calah, 12and Resen between Nineveh and Calah (that *is* the principal city).

13Mizraim begot Ludim, Anamim, Lehabim, Naphtuhim, 14Pathrusim, and Casluhim (from whom came the Philistines and Caphtorim).

15Canaan begot Sidon his firstborn, and Heth; 16the Jebusite, the Amorite, and the Girgashite; 17the Hivite, the Arkite, and the Sinite; 18the Arvadite, the Zemarite, and the Hamathite. Afterward the families of the Canaanites were dispersed. 19And the border of the Canaanites was from Sidon as you go toward Gerar, as far as Gaza; then as you go toward Sodom, Gomorrah, Admah, and Zeboiim, as far as Lasha. 20These *were* the sons of Ham, according to their families, according to their languages, in their lands *and* in their nations.

21And *children* were born also to Shem, the father of all the children of Eber, the brother of Japheth the elder. 22The sons of Shem *were* Elam, Asshur, Arphaxad, Lud, and Aram. 23The sons of Aram *were* Uz, Hul, Gether, and Mash. 24Arphaxad begot Salah, and Salah begot Eber. 25To Eber were born two sons: the name of one *was* Peleg, for in his days the earth was divided; and his brother's name *was* Joktan. 26Joktan begot Almodad, Sheleph, Hazarmaveth, Jerah, 27Hadoram, Uzal, Diklah, 28Obal, Abimael, Sheba, 29Ophir, Havilah, and Jobab. All these *were* the sons of Joktan. 30And their dwelling place was from Mesha as you go toward Sephar, the mountain of the east. 31These *were* the sons of Shem, according to their families, according to their languages, in their lands, according to their nations.

32These *were* the families of the sons of Noah, according to their generations, in their nations; and from these the nations were divided on the earth after the flood.

CHAPTER 11 BUILDING A TOWER TO THE SKY.

Now the whole earth had one language and one speech. 2And it came to pass, as they journeyed from the east, that they found a plain in the land of Shinar, and they dwelt there. 3Then they said to one another, "Come, let us make bricks and bake *them* thoroughly." They had brick for stone, and they had asphalt for mortar. 4And they said, "Come, let us build ourselves a city, and a tower whose top *is* in the heavens; let us make a name for ourselves, lest we be scattered abroad over the face of the whole earth."

TOWERING PRIDE

11:4 The tower of Babel was a great human achievement, a wonder of the world. But it was a monument to the people themselves rather than to God. We often build monuments to ourselves (expensive clothes, big house, fancy car, important job) to call attention to our achievements. These may not be wrong in themselves, but when we use them to give us identity and self-worth, they take God's place in our lives. We are free to develop in many areas, but we are not free to think we have replaced God. What "monuments" are in your life?

5But the LORD came down to see the city and the tower which the sons of men had built. 6And the LORD said, "Indeed the people *are* one and they all have one language, and this is what they begin to

NOAH

The story of Noah's life involved not one, but two great and tragic floods. The first was a flood of evil. The world had become so bad that there was only one person left who remembered the God of creation, perfection, and love. Noah was the last of God's people.

God's response to this flood of evil was a 120-year-long last chance. During those years, he had Noah build a large advertisement of what God was going to do. Nothing like a huge boat built on dry land to make a point! Of course, everyone thought Noah was crazy. Despite the jeers of his friends and neighbors, Noah continued to build. When the flood came, no one could say they hadn't been warned. For Noah, obedience to God meant a long-term courageous commitment to a project.

Many of us have trouble sticking to any project, whether or not it is directed by God. Or we back off when opposition occurs. Noah obeyed God and worked on one project longer than we even expect to live. The only project we have that is like Noah's is our life. Maybe this is the biggest lesson and challenge Noah's life can give us: we should live, depending on God's help, an entire lifetime of obedience.

LESSONS: God is faithful to those who obey him. God does not always protect us from trouble, but cares for us in spite of trouble. Obedience is a long-term commitment. A man may be faithful, but his sinful nature always travels with him.

KEY VERSE: "Thus Noah did; according to all that God commanded him, so he did" (Genesis 6:22).

Noah's story is told in Genesis 5:29–10:32. He is also mentioned in 1 Chronicles 1:4; Isaiah 54:9; Ezekiel 14:14,20; Matthew 24:37-38; Luke 3:36; 17:26-27; Hebrews 11:7; 1 Peter 3:20; 2 Peter 2:5.

UPS:
• Only follower of God left in his generation
• Second father of the human race
• Man of patience, consistency, and obedience
• First major shipbuilder in history

STATS:
• Where: We're not told how far from the Garden of Eden people had settled
• Occupation: Farmer, shipbuilder, preacher
• Relatives: Grandfather: Methuselah. Father: Lamech. Sons: Ham, Shem, and Japheth.

12:2 God promised to bless Abram and make him great, but there was one condition. Abram had to do what God wanted him to do. This meant leaving his home and friends and traveling to a new land where God promised to build a great nation from Abram's family. Abram obeyed, leaving his home for God's promise of even greater blessings in the future. God may be trying to lead you to a place of greater service and usefulness for him. Don't let the comfort and security of your present position make you miss God's plan for you.

do; now nothing that they propose to do will be withheld from them. [7]Come, let Us go down and there confuse their language, that they may not understand one another's speech." [8]So the LORD scattered them abroad from there over the face of all the earth, and they ceased building the city. [9]Therefore its name is called Babel, because there the LORD confused the language of all the earth; and from there the LORD scattered them abroad over the face of all the earth.

[10]This *is* the genealogy of Shem: Shem *was* one hundred years old, and begot Arphaxad two years after the flood. [11]After he begot Arphaxad, Shem lived five hundred years, and begot sons and daughters.

[12]Arphaxad lived thirty-five years, and begot Salah. [13]After he begot Salah, Arphaxad lived four hundred and three years, and begot sons and daughters.

[14]Salah lived thirty years, and begot Eber. [15]After he begot Eber, Salah lived four hundred and three years, and begot sons and daughters.

[16]Eber lived thirty-four years, and begot Peleg. [17]After he begot Peleg, Eber lived four hundred and thirty years, and begot sons and daughters.

[18]Peleg lived thirty years, and begot Reu. [19]After he begot Reu, Peleg lived two hundred and nine years, and begot sons and daughters.

[20]Reu lived thirty-two years, and begot Serug. [21]After he begot Serug, Reu lived two hundred and seven years, and begot sons and daughters.

[22]Serug lived thirty years, and begot Nahor. [23]After he begot Nahor, Serug lived two hundred years, and begot sons and daughters.

[24]Nahor lived twenty-nine years, and begot Terah. [25]After he begot Terah, Nahor lived one hundred and nineteen years, and begot sons and daughters.

[26]Now Terah lived seventy years, and begot Abram, Nahor, and Haran.

[27]This *is* the genealogy of Terah: Terah begot Abram, Nahor, and Haran. Haran begot Lot. [28]And Haran died before his father Terah in his native land, in Ur of the Chaldeans. [29]Then Abram and Nahor took wives: the name of Abram's wife *was* Sarai, and the name of Nahor's wife, Milcah, the daughter of Haran the father of Milcah and the father of Iscah. [30]But Sarai was barren; she had no child.

[31]And Terah took his son Abram and his grandson Lot, the son of Haran, and his daughter-in-law Sarai, his son Abram's wife, and they went out with them from Ur of the Chaldeans to go to the land of Canaan; and they came to Haran and dwelt there. [32]So the days of Terah were two hundred and five years, and Terah died in Haran.

CHAPTER 12 ABRAM MOVES TO NEW LANDS.

Now the LORD had said to Abram:

"Get out of your country,
From your family
And from your father's house,
To a land that I will show you.
[2] I will make you a great nation;
I will bless you
And make your name great;
And you shall be a blessing.
[3] I will bless those who bless you,
And I will curse him who curses you;
And in you all the families of the earth shall be blessed."

[4]So Abram departed as the LORD had spoken to him, and Lot went with him. And Abram *was* seventy-five years old when he departed from Haran. [5]Then Abram took Sarai his wife and Lot his brother's son, and all their possessions that they had gathered, and the people whom they had acquired in Haran, and they departed to go to the land of Canaan. So they came to the land of Canaan. [6]Abram passed through the land to the place of Shechem, as far as the terebinth tree of Moreh. And the Canaanites *were* then in the land.

[7]Then the LORD appeared to Abram and said, "To your descendants I will give this land." And there he built an altar to the LORD, who had appeared to him. [8]And he moved from there to the mountain east of Bethel, and he pitched his tent *with* Bethel on the west and Ai on the east; there he built an altar to the LORD and called on the name of the LORD. [9]So Abram journeyed, going on still toward the South.

[10]Now there was a famine in the land, and Abram went down to Egypt to dwell there, for the famine *was* severe in the land. [11]And it came to pass, when he was close to entering Egypt, that he said to Sarai his wife, "Indeed I know that you *are* a woman of beautiful countenance. [12]Therefore it will happen, when the Egyptians see you, that they will say, 'This *is* his wife'; and they will kill me, but they will let you live. [13]Please say you *are* my sister, that it may be well with me for your sake, and that I may live because of you."

[14]So it was, when Abram came into Egypt, that the Egyptians saw the woman, that she *was* very beautiful. [15]The princes of Pharaoh also saw her and commended her to Pharaoh. And the woman was taken to Pharaoh's house. [16]He treated Abram well for her sake. He had sheep, oxen, male donkeys, male and female servants, female donkeys, and camels.

[17]But the LORD plagued Pharaoh and his house with great plagues because of Sarai, Abram's wife. [18]And Pharaoh called Abram and said, "What *is* this you have done to me? Why did you not tell me that she *was* your wife? [19]Why did you say, 'She *is* my sister'? I might have taken her as my wife. Now therefore, here is your wife; take *her* and go your way." [20]So Pharaoh commanded *his* men concerning him; and they sent him away, with his wife and all that he had.

CHAPTER **13** LOT LEAVES ABRAM.

Then Abram went up from Egypt, he and his wife and all that he had, and Lot with him, to the South. ²Abram *was* very rich in livestock, in silver, and in gold. ³And he went on his journey from the South as far as Bethel, to the place where his tent had been at the beginning, between Bethel and Ai, ⁴to the place of the altar which he had made there at first. And there Abram called on the name of the LORD.

⁵Lot also, who went with Abram, had flocks and herds and tents. ⁶Now the land was not able to support them, that they might dwell together, for their possessions were so great that they could not dwell together. ⁷And there was strife between the herdsmen of Abram's livestock and the herdsmen of Lot's livestock. The Canaanites and the Perizzites then dwelt in the land.

⁸So Abram said to Lot, "Please let there be no strife between you and me, and between my herdsmen and your herdsmen; for we *are* brethren. ⁹*Is* not the whole land before you? Please separate from me. If *you take* the left, then I will go to the right; or, if *you go* to the right, then I will go to the left."

¹⁰And Lot lifted his eyes and saw all the plain of Jordan, that it *was* well watered everywhere (before the LORD destroyed Sodom and Gomorrah) like the garden of the LORD, like the land of Egypt as you go toward Zoar. ¹¹Then Lot chose for himself all the plain of Jordan, and Lot journeyed east. And they separated from each other. ¹²Abram dwelt in the land of Canaan, and Lot dwelt in the cities of the plain and pitched *his* tent even as far as Sodom. ¹³But the men of Sodom *were* exceedingly wicked and sinful against the LORD.

¹⁴And the LORD said to Abram, after Lot had separated from him: "Lift your eyes now and look from the place where you are—northward, southward, eastward, and westward; ¹⁵for all the land which you see I give to you and your descendants forever. ¹⁶And I will make your descendants as the dust of the earth; so that if a man could number the dust of the earth, *then* your descendants also could be numbered. ¹⁷Arise, walk in the land through its length and its width, for I give it to you."

¹⁸Then Abram moved *his* tent, and went and dwelt by the terebinth trees of Mamre, which *are* in Hebron, and built an altar there to the LORD.

CHAPTER **14** ABRAM RESCUES LOT.

And it came to pass in the days of Amraphel king of Shinar, Arioch king of Ellasar, Chedorlaomer king of Elam, and Tidal king of nations, ²*that* they made war with Bera king of Sodom, Birsha king of Gomorrah, Shinab king of Admah, Shemeber king of Zeboiim, and the king of Bela (that is, Zoar).

◣〰〰〰 FAMILY FEUD

13:5-9 Facing a potential conflict with his nephew Lot, Abram took the initiative in settling the dispute. He gave Lot first choice and showed a willingness to risk being cheated. Abram's example shows us how to respond to difficult family situations: (1) take the initiative in resolving conflicts; (2) let others have first choice, even if that means not getting what we want; (3) put family peace above personal desires.

³All these joined together in the Valley of Siddim (that is, the Salt Sea). ⁴Twelve years they served Chedorlaomer, and in the thirteenth year they rebelled.

⁵In the fourteenth year Chedorlaomer and the kings that *were* with him came and attacked the Rephaim in Ashteroth Karnaim, the Zuzim in Ham, the Emim

ABRAHAM

As you read about Abraham's life, you will probably ask: "What on earth made God like this man so much?" Abraham made a lot of mistakes, and some of his mistakes had long-range consequences.

Yet, what you will find if you read carefully is that in spite of his mistakes, Abraham trusted God with his life. This is the main fact the Bible tells us about him in both the Old and New Testaments (Genesis 15:6; Romans 4:3).

Early in life, Abraham had to make an important decision. God asked him to choose between staying at home or following God's leading. It was a choice between doing what Abraham wanted to do or doing what God wanted Abraham to do.

Of course Abraham couldn't see how much of future history was resting on his decision, but God used Abraham's obedience to affect millions of people. It was through Abraham that the Jewish nation developed and eventually Jesus Christ came into the world.

God gives us exactly the same choice he gave Abraham. Once Abraham gave his life to God, he never tried to take it back. He may have taken some wrong turns on the journey . . . but he never turned around. What have you decided about the choice God has given you? Is your basic desire to trust God and live his way, or is your goal to live life your way?

LESSONS: God desires dependence, trust, and faith in him—not faith in our ability to please him

God's plan from the beginning has been to make himself known to all people

KEY VERSE: "And [Abraham] believed in the LORD, and He accounted it to him for righteousness" (Genesis 15:6).

Abraham's story is told in Genesis 11–25. He is also mentioned in Exodus 2:24; Acts 7:2–8; Romans 4; Galatians 3; Hebrews 6–7;11.

UPS:
- His faith pleased God
- Became the founder of the Jewish nation
- Was a successful and wealthy rancher
- Usually avoided conflicts, but when they happened he let his opponent set the rules for settling the disputes

DOWNS:
- Had a lifelong tendency to lie when under pressure

STATS:
- Where: Born in Ur of the Chaldeans; spent most of his life in the land of Canaan
- Occupation: Wealthy livestock owner
- Relatives: Brothers: Nahor and Haran. Father: Terah. Wife: Sarah. Nephew: Lot. Sons: Ishmael and Isaac.
- Contemporaries: Abimelech, Melchizedek

in Shaveh Kiriathaim, ⁶and the Horites in their mountain of Seir, as far as El Paran, which *is* by the wilderness. ⁷Then they turned back and came to En Mishpat (that *is*, Kadesh), and attacked all the country of the Amalekites, and also the Amorites who dwelt in Hazezon Tamar.

⁸And the king of Sodom, the king of Gomorrah, the king of Admah, the king of Zeboiim, and the king of Bela (that *is*, Zoar) went out and joined together in battle in the Valley of Siddim ⁹against Chedorlaomer king of Elam, Tidal king of nations, Amraphel king of Shinar, and Arioch king of Ellasar—four kings against five. ¹⁰Now the Valley of Siddim *was full of* asphalt pits; and the kings of Sodom and Gomorrah fled; *some* fell there, and the remainder fled to the mountains. ¹¹Then they took all the goods of Sodom and Gomorrah, and all their provisions, and went their way. ¹²They also took Lot, Abram's brother's son who dwelt in Sodom, and his goods, and departed.

¹³Then one who had escaped came and told Abram the Hebrew, for he dwelt by the terebinth trees of Mamre the Amorite, brother of Eshcol and brother of Aner; and they *were* allies with Abram. ¹⁴Now when Abram heard that his brother was taken captive, he armed his three hundred and eighteen trained *servants* who were born in his own house, and went in pursuit as far as Dan. ¹⁵He divided his forces against them by night, and he and his servants attacked them and pursued them as far as Hobah, which *is* north of Damascus. ¹⁶So he brought back all the goods, and also brought back his brother Lot and his goods, as well as the women and the people.

¹⁷And the king of Sodom went out to meet him at the Valley of Shaveh (that *is*, the King's Valley), after his return from the defeat of Chedorlaomer and the kings who *were* with him.

¹⁸Then Melchizedek king of Salem brought out bread and wine; he *was* the priest of God Most High. ¹⁹And he blessed him and said:

"Blessed be Abram of God Most High,
Possessor of heaven and earth;
²⁰ And blessed be God Most High,
Who has delivered your enemies into your hand."

And he gave him a tithe of all.

²¹Now the king of Sodom said to Abram, "Give me the persons, and take the goods for yourself."

²²But Abram said to the king of Sodom, "I have raised my hand to the LORD, God Most High, the Possessor of heaven and earth, ²³that I *will take* nothing, from a thread to a sandal strap, and that I will not take anything that *is* yours, lest you should say, 'I have made Abram rich'— ²⁴except only what the young men have eaten, and the portion of the men who went with me: Aner, Eshcol, and Mamre; let them take their portion."

CHAPTER 15 GOD MAKES A PROMISE TO ABRAM.

After these things the word of the LORD came to Abram in a vision, saying, "Do not be afraid, Abram. I *am* your shield, your exceedingly great reward."

²But Abram said, "Lord GOD, what will You give me, seeing I go childless, and the heir of my house *is* Eliezer

GETTING IT RIGHT

15:6 Although Abram had been demonstrating his faith through his actions, it was believing in the Lord, not actions, that made Abram right with God (Romans 4:1-5). We too can have a right relationship with God by trusting him with our lives. Our outward actions—church attendance, prayer, good deeds—will not by themselves make us right with God. A right relationship is based on faith—the heartfelt inner confidence that God is who he says he is and does what he says he will do. Right actions follow naturally as by-products.

of Damascus?" ³Then Abram said, "Look, You have given me no offspring; indeed one born in my house is my heir!"

⁴And behold, the word of the LORD *came* to him, saying, "This one shall not be your heir, but one who will come from your own body shall be your heir." ⁵Then He brought him outside and said, "Look now toward heaven, and count the stars if you are able to number them." And He said to him, "So shall your descendants be."

⁶And he believed in the LORD, and He accounted it to him for righteousness.

⁷Then He said to him, "I *am* the LORD, who brought you out of Ur of the Chaldeans, to give you this land to inherit it."

⁸And he said, "Lord GOD, how shall I know that I will inherit it?"

⁹So He said to him, "Bring Me a three-year-old heifer, a three-year-old female goat, a three-year-old ram, a turtledove, and a young pigeon." ¹⁰Then he brought all these to Him and cut them in two, down the middle, and placed each piece opposite the other; but he did not cut the birds in two. ¹¹And when the vultures came down on the carcasses, Abram drove them away.

¹²Now when the sun was going down, a deep sleep fell upon Abram; and behold, horror *and* great darkness fell upon him. ¹³Then He said to Abram: "Know certainly that your descendants will be strangers in a land *that is* not theirs, and will serve them, and they will afflict them four hundred years. ¹⁴And also the nation whom they serve I will judge; afterward they shall come out with great possessions. ¹⁵Now as for you, you shall go to your fathers in peace; you shall be buried at a good old age. ¹⁶But in the fourth generation they shall return here, for the iniquity of the Amorites *is* not yet complete."

¹⁷And it came to pass, when the sun went down and it was dark, that behold, there appeared a smoking oven and a burning torch that passed between those pieces. ¹⁸On the same day the LORD made a covenant with Abram, saying:

"To your descendants I have given this land, from the river of Egypt to the great river, the River Euphrates— ¹⁹the Kenites, the Kenezzites, the Kadmonites, ²⁰the Hittites, the Perizzites, the Rephaim, ²¹the Amorites, the Canaanites, the Girgashites, and the Jebusites."

RUNAWAY

16:8 As Hagar was running away from her mistress and her problem, the Angel of the Lord gave her this advice: (1) return and face Sarai, the cause of her problem, and (2) act as she should. Hagar needed to work on her attitude toward Sarai, no matter how justified it may have been. Running away from our problems rarely solves them. It is wise to face our problems squarely, accept God's promise of help, correct our attitudes, and act as we should.

CHAPTER 16 SARAI BECOMES JEALOUS. Now Sarai, Abram's wife, had borne him no *children*. And she had an Egyptian maidservant whose name was Hagar. ²So Sarai said to Abram, "See now, the LORD has restrained me from bearing *children*. Please, go in to my maid; perhaps I shall obtain children by her." And Abram heeded the voice of Sarai. ³Then Sarai, Abram's wife, took Hagar her maid, the Egyptian, and gave her to her husband Abram to be his wife, after Abram had dwelt ten years in the land of Canaan. ⁴So he went in to Hagar, and she conceived. And when she saw that she had conceived, her mistress became despised in her eyes.

⁵Then Sarai said to Abram, "My wrong *be* upon you! I gave my maid into your embrace; and when she saw that she had conceived, I became despised in her eyes. The LORD judge between you and me."

⁶So Abram said to Sarai, "Indeed your maid *is* in your hand; do to her as you please." And when Sarai dealt harshly with her, she fled from her presence.

⁷Now the Angel of the LORD found her by a spring of water in the wilderness, by the spring on the way to Shur. ⁸And He said, "Hagar, Sarai's maid, where have you come from, and where are you going?"

She said, "I am fleeing from the presence of my mistress Sarai."

⁹The Angel of the LORD said to her, "Return to your mistress, and submit yourself under her hand." ¹⁰Then the Angel of the LORD said to her, "I will multiply your descendants exceedingly, so that they shall not be counted for multitude."

¹¹And the Angel of the LORD said to her:

"Behold, you *are* with child,
And you shall bear a son.
You shall call his name Ishmael,
Because the LORD has heard
    your affliction.
¹² He shall be a wild man;
His hand *shall be* against every
    man,
And every man's hand against him.
And he shall dwell in the presence of
    all his brethren."

¹³Then she called the name of the LORD who spoke to her, You-Are-the-God-Who-Sees; for she said, "Have I also here seen Him who sees me?" ¹⁴Therefore the well was called Beer Lahai Roi; observe, *it is* between Kadesh and Bered.

¹⁵So Hagar bore Abram a son; and Abram named his son, whom Hagar bore, Ishmael. ¹⁶Abram *was* eighty-six years old when Hagar bore Ishmael to Abram.

CHAPTER 17 GOD'S COVENANT WITH ABRAM. When Abram was ninety-nine years old, the LORD appeared to Abram and said to him, "I *am* Almighty God; walk before Me and be blameless. ²And I will make My covenant between Me and you, and will multiply you exceedingly." ³Then Abram fell on his face, and God talked with him, saying: ⁴"As for Me, behold, My covenant

REASON ENOUGH

17:1 The Lord told Abram, "I *am* Almighty God; walk before Me and be blameless." God has the same message for us today. We are to obey him because he is God—that is reason enough. If you don't think the benefits are worth it, consider who God is—the only one with the power and ability to meet your every need.

is with you, and you shall be a father of many nations. ⁵No longer shall your name be called Abram, but your name shall be Abraham; for I have made you a father of many nations. ⁶I will make you exceedingly fruitful; and I will make nations of you, and kings shall come from you. ⁷And I will establish

SARAH

Sadly, some women who really want to be mothers are not able to have children. Sometimes doctors can't figure out what's wrong, and the waiting can be terrible. Usually, a woman begins to feel hopelessness and desperation. That's how Abraham's wife, Sarah, was feeling.

Then Sarah was told she was going to have a baby. She burst out laughing. She was 90 years old. Have you ever laughed out loud because you thought something was funny, only to discover that what you heard wasn't supposed to be funny? Then you know how Sarah felt. God had to gently teach her how to laugh at the right things. Maybe God is trying to teach you the same lesson.

God also got the last laugh. Sarah laughed because she thought God's plan to make a 90-year-old mother was impossible. So, God had her name the baby Isaac, which means "laughter." God likes to do the impossible! Sarah discovered that it's much more fun to laugh with God than at him.

LESSONS: God responds to faith even in the midst of failures

God is not bound by what usually happens. He can stretch the limits and cause unheard-of events to occur.

KEY VERSE: "By faith Sarah herself also received strength to conceive seed, and she bore a child when she was past the age, because she judged Him faithful who had promised" (Hebrews 11:11). Sarah's story is told in Genesis 11–25. She is also mentioned in Isaiah 51:1; Romans 4:19; 9:9; Hebrews 11:11; 1 Peter 3:6.

UPS:
• Was intensely loyal to her own child
• Became the mother of a nation and an ancestor of Jesus
• Was a woman of faith. She is the first woman listed in the Hall of Faith in Hebrews 11.

DOWNS:
• Had trouble believing God's promises to her
• Attempted to work problems out on her own, without consulting God
• Tried to cover her own faults by blaming others

STATS:
• Where: Married Abram in Ur of the Chaldeans, then moved with him to Canaan
• Occupation: Wife, mother, household manager
• Relatives: Father: Terah. Husband: Abraham. Brothers: Nahor and Haran. Nephew: Lot. Son: Isaac.

18:15 Sarah lied because she was afraid of being discovered. Fear is the most common motive for lying. We are afraid that our inner thoughts and emotions will be exposed or our wrongdoings discovered. But lying causes greater complications than telling the truth and brings even more problems. If God can't be trusted with our innermost thoughts and fears, we are in greater trouble than we first imagined.

My covenant between Me and you and your descendants after you in their generations, for an everlasting covenant, to be God to you and your descendants after you. ⁸Also I give to you and your descendants after you the land in which you are a stranger, all the land of Canaan, as an everlasting possession; and I will be their God."

⁹And God said to Abraham: "As for you, you shall keep My covenant, you and your descendants after you throughout their generations. ¹⁰This *is* My covenant which you shall keep, between Me and you and your descendants after you: Every male child among you shall be circumcised; ¹¹and you shall be circumcised in the flesh of your foreskins, and it shall be a sign of the covenant between Me and you. ¹²He who is eight days old among you shall be circumcised, every male child in your generations, he who is born in your house or bought with money from any foreigner who is not your descendant. ¹³He who is born in your house and he who is bought with your money must be circumcised, and My covenant shall be in your flesh for an everlasting covenant. ¹⁴And the uncircumcised male child, who is not circumcised in the flesh of his foreskin, that person shall be cut off from his people; he has broken My covenant."

¹⁵Then God said to Abraham, "As for Sarai your wife, you shall not call her name Sarai, but Sarah *shall be* her name. ¹⁶And I will bless her and also give you a son by her; then I will bless her, and she shall be *a mother of* nations; kings of peoples shall be from her."

¹⁷Then Abraham fell on his face and laughed, and said in his heart, "Shall *a child* be born to a man who is one hundred years old? And shall Sarah, who is ninety years old, bear *a child?*" ¹⁸And Abraham said to God, "Oh, that Ishmael might live before You!"

¹⁹Then God said: "No, Sarah your wife shall bear you a son, and you shall call his name Isaac; I will establish My covenant with him for an everlasting covenant, *and* with his descendants after him. ²⁰And as for Ishmael, I have heard you. Behold, I have blessed him, and will make him fruitful, and will multiply him exceedingly. He shall beget twelve princes, and I will make him a great nation. ²¹But My covenant I will establish with Isaac, whom Sarah shall bear to you at this set time next year." ²²Then He finished talking with him, and God went up from Abraham.

²³So Abraham took Ishmael his son, all who were born in his house and all who were bought with his money, every male among the men of Abraham's house, and circumcised the flesh of their foreskins that very same day, as God had said to him. ²⁴Abraham *was* ninety-nine years old when he was circumcised in the flesh of his foreskin. ²⁵And Ishmael his son *was* thirteen years old when he was circumcised in the flesh of his foreskin. ²⁶That very same day Abraham was circumcised, and his son Ishmael; ²⁷and all the men of his house, born in the house or bought with money from a foreigner, were circumcised with him.

CHAPTER 18 ANGELS VISIT ABRAHAM. Then the LORD appeared to him by the terebinth trees of Mamre, as he was sitting in the tent door in the heat of the day. ²So he lifted his eyes and looked, and behold, three men were standing by him; and when he saw *them*, he ran from the tent door to meet them, and bowed himself to the ground, ³and said, "My Lord, if I have now found favor in Your sight, do not pass on by Your servant. ⁴Please let a little water be brought, and wash your feet, and rest yourselves under the tree. ⁵And I will bring a morsel of bread, that you may refresh your hearts. After that you may pass by, inasmuch as you have come to your servant."

They said, "Do as you have said."

⁶So Abraham hurried into the tent to Sarah and said, "Quickly, make ready three measures of fine meal; knead *it* and make cakes." ⁷And Abraham ran to the herd, took a tender and good calf, gave *it* to a young man, and he hastened to prepare it. ⁸So he took butter and milk and the calf which he had prepared, and set *it* before them; and he stood by them under the tree as they ate.

⁹Then they said to him, "Where *is* Sarah your wife?"

So he said, "Here, in the tent."

¹⁰And He said, "I will certainly return to you according to the time of life, and behold, Sarah your wife shall have a son."

(Sarah was listening in the tent door which *was* behind him.) ¹¹Now Abraham and Sarah were old, well advanced in age; *and* Sarah had passed the age of childbearing. ¹²Therefore Sarah laughed within herself, saying, "After I have grown old, shall I have pleasure, my lord being old also?"

¹³And the LORD said to Abraham, "Why did Sarah laugh, saying, 'Shall I surely bear *a child*, since I am old?' ¹⁴Is anything too hard for the LORD? At the appointed time I will return to you, according to the time of life, and Sarah shall have a son."

¹⁵But Sarah denied *it*, saying, "I did not laugh," for she was afraid.

And He said, "No, but you did laugh!"

¹⁶Then the men rose from there and looked toward Sodom, and Abraham went with them to send them on the way. ¹⁷And the LORD said, "Shall I hide from Abraham

IS aNyThIng TOO hard for THE LORD?

GENESIS 18:14

what I am doing, [18]since Abraham shall surely become a great and mighty nation, and all the nations of the earth shall be blessed in him? [19]For I have known him, in order that he may command his children and his household after him, that they keep the way of the LORD, to do righteousness and justice, that the LORD may bring to Abraham what He has spoken to him." [20]And the LORD said, "Because the outcry against Sodom and Gomorrah is great, and because their sin is very grave, [21]I will go down now and see whether they have done altogether according to the outcry against it that has come to Me; and if not, I will know."

[22]Then the men turned away from there and went toward Sodom, but Abraham still stood before the LORD. [23]And Abraham came near and said, "Would You also destroy the righteous with the wicked? [24]Suppose there were fifty righteous within the city; would You also destroy the place and not spare *it* for the fifty righteous that were in it? [25]Far be it from You to do such a thing as this, to slay the righteous with the wicked, so that the righteous should be as the wicked; far be it from You! Shall not the Judge of all the earth do right?"

[26]So the LORD said, "If I find in Sodom fifty righteous within the city, then I will spare all the place for their sakes."

[27]Then Abraham answered and said, "Indeed now, I who *am but* dust and ashes have taken it upon myself to speak to the Lord: [28]Suppose there were five less than the fifty righteous; would You destroy all of the city for *lack of* five?"

So He said, "If I find there forty-five, I will not destroy *it*."

[29]And he spoke to Him yet again and said, "Suppose there should be forty found there?"

So He said, "I will not do *it* for the sake of forty."

[30]Then he said, "Let not the Lord be angry, and I will speak: Suppose thirty should be found there?"

So He said, "I will not do *it* if I find thirty there."

[31]And he said, "Indeed now, I have taken it upon myself to speak to the Lord: Suppose twenty should be found there?"

So He said, "I will not destroy *it* for the sake of twenty."

[32]Then he said, "Let not the Lord be angry, and I will speak but once more: Suppose ten should be found there?"

And He said, "I will not destroy *it* for the sake of ten." [33]So the LORD went His way as soon as He had finished speaking with Abraham; and Abraham returned to his place.

CHAPTER 19 GOD DESTROYS SODOM. Now the two angels came to Sodom in the evening, and Lot was sitting in the gate of Sodom. When Lot saw *them*, he rose to meet them, and he bowed himself with his face toward the ground. [2]And he said, "Here now, my lords, please turn in to your servant's house and spend the night, and wash your feet; then you may rise early and go on your way."

And they said, "No, but we will spend the night in the open square."

[3]But he insisted strongly; so they turned in to him and entered his house. Then he made them a feast, and baked unleavened bread, and they ate.

[4]Now before they lay down, the men of the city, the men of Sodom, both old and young, all the people from every quarter, surrounded the house. [5]And they called to Lot and said to him, "Where are the men who came to you tonight? Bring them out to us that we may know them *carnally*."

[6]So Lot went out to them through the doorway,

LOT

Some people simply drift through life. They don't really make choices; they just take the easiest way. Usually, that choice turns out to be the wrong way. Lot, Abram's nephew, was a person like this. His life can help keep us from being drifters.

While still young, Lot lost his father. This must have been a difficult time for him, but he was loved and cared for by his grandfather Terah and his uncle Abram. Though they were good examples, Lot's life was full of unwise decisions. Despite Abram's attention and God's help, Lot went his own way.

By the time Lot drifted out of the picture, his life had taken an ugly turn. He had become so blended into the culture of his day that he did not want to leave it. His wife was killed during Lot's narrow escape, and his daughters committed incest with him. His drifting finally led him to destruction.

God gives us hope by showing us how he can bring good even out of failure and evil. The New Testament describes Lot as a righteous man (2 Peter 2:7-8). Even though he didn't do much about the evil surrounding him, it still bothered him deeply. And Ruth—a descendant of Moab, a child born from the incest between Lot and one of his daughters—was an ancestor of Jesus Christ.

What is the direction of your life? Are you headed toward God or away from him? If you find it easy to drift, the choice to live for God may seem difficult, but it is the one choice that makes life fit together.

LESSONS: God wants us to do more than drift through life; he wants people to be an influence for him

KEY VERSE: "And while [Lot] lingered, the men took hold of his hand" (Genesis 19:16).

Lot's story is told in Genesis 11–14; 19. He is also mentioned in Deuteronomy 2:9; Luke 17:28-32; 2 Peter 2:7-8.

UPS:
- He was a successful businessman
- Peter calls him a righteous man (2 Peter 2:7-8)

DOWNS:
- When faced with decisions, he tended to put off deciding, then chose the easiest course of action
- When given a choice, his first reaction was to think of himself

STATS:
- **Where:** Lived first in Ur of the Chaldeans, then moved to Canaan with Abram
- **Occupation:** Wealthy sheep and cattle rancher, city official
- **Relatives:** Father: Haran. Adopted by Abram when his father died. The name of his wife, who turned into a pillar of salt, is not mentioned.

shut the door behind him, [7]and said, "Please, my brethren, do not do so wickedly! [8]See now, I have two daughters who have not known a man; please, let me bring them out to you, and you may do to them as you wish; only do nothing to these men, since this is the reason they have come under the shadow of my roof."

[9]And they said, "Stand back!" Then they said, "This one came in to stay *here*, and he keeps acting as a judge; now we will deal worse with you than with them." So they pressed hard against the man Lot, and came near to break down the door. [10]But the men reached out their hands and pulled Lot into the house with them, and shut the door. [11]And they struck the men who *were* at the doorway of the house with blindness, both small and great, so that they became weary *trying* to find the door.

[12]Then the men said to Lot, "Have you anyone else here? Son-in-law, your sons, your daughters, and whomever you have in the city—take *them* out of this place! [13]For we will destroy this place, because the outcry against them has grown great before the face of the LORD, and the LORD has sent us to destroy it."

◢◤ CHAMELEON

19:14 Lot had lived so long, and was so content among ungodly people that he was no longer a believable witness for God. He had allowed his environment to shape him, rather than he shaping his environment. Do those who know you see you as a witness for God, or are you just one of the crowd, blending in unnoticed? Lot had compromised to the point that he was almost useless to God. When he finally made a stand, nobody listened. Have you also become useless to God because you are too much like your environment? To make a difference, you must first decide to be different in what you believe and how you act.

[14]So Lot went out and spoke to his sons-in-law, who had married his daughters, and said, "Get up, get out of this place; for the LORD will destroy this city!" But to his sons-in-law he seemed to be joking.

[15]When the morning dawned, the angels urged Lot to hurry, saying, "Arise, take your wife and your two daughters who are here, lest you be consumed in the punishment of the city." [16]And while he lingered, the men took hold of his hand, his wife's hand, and the hands of his two daughters, the LORD being merciful to him, and they brought him out and set him outside the city. [17]So it came to pass, when they had brought them outside, that he said, "Escape for your life! Do not look behind you nor stay anywhere in the plain. Escape to the mountains, lest you be destroyed."

[18]Then Lot said to them, "Please, no, my lords! [19]Indeed now, your servant has found favor in your sight, and you have increased your mercy which you have shown me by saving my life; but I cannot escape to the mountains, lest some evil overtake me and I die. [20]See now, this city *is* near *enough* to flee to, and it *is* a little one; please let me escape there (*is* it not a little one?) and my soul shall live."

[21]And he said to him, "See, I have favored you concerning this thing also, in that I will not overthrow this city for which you have spoken. [22]Hurry, escape there. For I cannot do anything until you arrive there."

Therefore the name of the city was called Zoar.

[23]The sun had risen upon the earth when Lot entered

21:7 After repeated promises, a visit by two angels, and the appearance of the Lord himself, Sarah finally cried out with surprise and joy at the birth of her son. Because of her doubt, worry, and fear, she had forfeited the peace she could have felt in God's wonderful promise to her. The way to have peace of mind is to focus on God's promises. Trust him to do what he says.

Zoar. [24]Then the LORD rained brimstone and fire on Sodom and Gomorrah, from the LORD out of the heavens. [25]So He overthrew those cities, all the plain, all the inhabitants of the cities, and what grew on the ground.

[26]But his wife looked back behind him, and she became a pillar of salt.

[27]And Abraham went early in the morning to the place where he had stood before the LORD. [28]Then he looked toward Sodom and Gomorrah, and toward all the land of the plain; and he saw, and behold, the smoke of the land which went up like the smoke of a furnace. [29]And it came to pass, when God destroyed the cities of the plain, that God remembered Abraham, and sent Lot out of the midst of the overthrow, when He overthrew the cities in which Lot had dwelt.

[30]Then Lot went up out of Zoar and dwelt in the mountains, and his two daughters were with him; for he was afraid to dwell in Zoar. And he and his two daughters dwelt in a cave. [31]Now the firstborn said to the younger, "Our father *is* old, and *there is* no man on the earth to come in to us as is the custom of all the earth. [32]Come, let us make our father drink wine, and we will lie with him, that we may preserve the lineage of our father." [33]So they made their father drink wine that night. And the firstborn went in and lay with her father, and he did not know when she lay down or when she arose.

[34]It happened on the next day that the firstborn said to the younger, "Indeed I lay with my father last night; let us make him drink wine tonight also, and you go in *and* lie with him, that we may preserve the lineage of our father." [35]Then they made their father drink wine that night also. And the younger arose and lay with him, and he did not know when she lay down or when she arose.

[36]Thus both the daughters of Lot were with child by their father. [37]The firstborn bore a son and called his name Moab; he *is* the father of the Moabites to this day. [38]And the younger, she also bore a son and called his name Ben-Ammi; he *is* the father of the people of Ammon to this day.

CHAPTER 20 ABRAHAM TRICKS THE KING. And Abraham journeyed from there to the South, and dwelt between Kadesh and Shur, and stayed in Gerar. [2]Now Abraham said of Sarah his wife, "She *is* my sister." And Abimelech king of Gerar sent and took Sarah.

[3]But God came to Abimelech in a dream by night, and said to him, "Indeed you *are* a dead man because of the woman whom you have taken, for she *is* a man's wife."

[4]But Abimelech had not come near her; and he said, "Lord, will You slay a righteous nation also? [5]Did he not say to me, 'She *is* my sister'? And she, even she herself said, 'He *is* my brother.' In the integrity of my heart and innocence of my hands I have done this."

[6]And God said to him in a dream, "Yes, I know that you did this in the integrity of your heart. For I also withheld

you from sinning against Me; therefore I did not let you touch her. ⁷Now therefore, restore the man's wife; for he *is* a prophet, and he will pray for you and you shall live. But if you do not restore *her,* know that you shall surely die, you and all who *are* yours."

⁸So Abimelech rose early in the morning, called all his servants, and told all these things in their hearing; and the men were very much afraid. ⁹And Abimelech called Abraham and said to him, "What have you done to us? How have I offended you, that you have brought on me and on my kingdom a great sin? You have done deeds to me that ought not to be done." ¹⁰Then Abimelech said to Abraham, "What did you have in view, that you have done this thing?"

¹¹And Abraham said, "Because I thought, surely the fear of God *is* not in this place; and they will kill me on account of my wife. ¹²But indeed *she is* truly my sister. She *is* the daughter of my father, but not the daughter of my mother; and she became my wife. ¹³And it came to pass, when God caused me to wander from my father's house, that I said to her, 'This *is* your kindness that you should do for me: in every place, wherever we go, say of me, "He *is* my brother." ' "

¹⁴Then Abimelech took sheep, oxen, and male and female servants, and gave *them* to Abraham; and he restored Sarah his wife to him. ¹⁵And Abimelech said, "See, my land *is* before you; dwell where it pleases you." ¹⁶Then to Sarah he said, "Behold, I have given your brother a thousand *pieces* of silver; indeed this vindicates you before all who *are* with you and before everybody." Thus she was rebuked.

¹⁷So Abraham prayed to God; and God healed Abimelech, his wife, and his female servants. Then they bore *children;* ¹⁸for the LORD had closed up all the wombs of the house of Abimelech because of Sarah, Abraham's wife.

CHAPTER **21** ISAAC IS BORN. And the LORD visited Sarah as He had said, and the LORD did for Sarah as He had spoken. ²For Sarah conceived and bore Abraham a son in his old age, at the set time of which God had spoken to

him. ³And Abraham called the name of his son who was born to him—whom Sarah bore to him—Isaac. ⁴Then Abraham circumcised his son Isaac when he was eight days old, as God had commanded him. ⁵Now Abraham was one hundred years old when his son Isaac was born to him. ⁶And Sarah said, "God has made me laugh, *and* all who hear will laugh with me." ⁷She also said, "Who would have said to Abraham that Sarah would nurse children? For I have borne *him* a son in his old age."

⁸So the child grew and was weaned. And Abraham made a great feast on the same day that Isaac was weaned.

⁹And Sarah saw the son of Hagar the Egyptian, whom she had borne to Abraham,

ISAAC

Like it or not, your name is powerful. It sets you apart. It triggers memories of you in other people's minds. When you hear your name said you almost have to look. When people heard Isaac's name, they almost had to laugh!

Isaac's name means "laughter." As with many Bible characters, there were several reasons Isaac got that name. Isaac's name reminded his parents of their first reaction of shocked laughter when God told them they would have a son though they were quite old. At other times, his name must have reminded them of the great joy they had when Isaac was born. His name also was a reminder of God's presence, for God had told Isaac's parents to give their child that name.

In a family of active leaders, Isaac was the quiet, "mind-my-own-business" type unless he had to be involved. He was the protected only child until Abraham arranged his marriage to Rebekah. Then Isaac allowed his wife to run their family. He rarely stood his ground and found it easier to compromise or lie in order to avoid confrontations.

In spite of these problems, Isaac was part of God's plan. Isaac learned the importance of faith in the one true God from his father. God's promise to Abraham to create a great nation through which he would bless the world was passed on to Isaac and to his twin sons.

From time to time you may feel like Isaac—like you just go along or find it hard to stand on your own in a crowd. But remember, God works through people in spite of their shortcomings. Tell God you're available to him, weaknesses and all. You will discover that his willingness to use you is even greater than your desire to be used.

UPS:
- Was the miracle child born to 90-year-old Sarah and 100-year-old Abraham
- The first descendant in fulfillment of God's promise to Abraham
- Seems to have been a caring and consistent husband, at least until his sons were born
- Demonstrated great patience

DOWNS:
- Under pressure he tended to imitate his father and lie
- In conflict he tried to avoid confrontation by bargaining
- He played favorites between his sons and alienated his wife

STATS:
- Where: The area called Negev, or "the South," in the southern part of Palestine, between Kadesh and Shur (Genesis 20:1)
- Occupation: Wealthy livestock owner
- Relatives: Parents: Abraham and Sarah. Half brother: Ishmael. Wife: Rebekah. Twin sons: Esau and Jacob.

LESSONS: Patience often brings rewards. Both God's plans and his promises are larger than people

God keeps his promises! He remains faithful though we are often faithless

KEY VERSE: "Sarah your wife shall bear you a son, and you shall call his name Isaac; I will establish My covenant with him for an everlasting covenant, and with his descendants after him" (Genesis 17:19).

Isaac's story is told in Genesis 17:15—35:29. He is also mentioned in Romans 9:7-8; Hebrews 11:17-20; James 2:21-24.

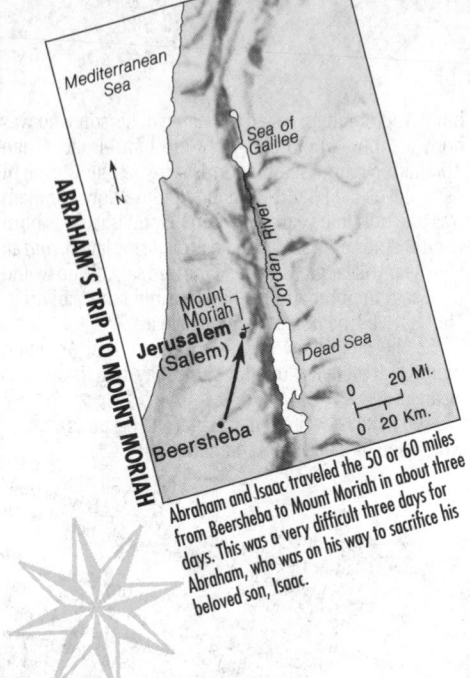

ABRAHAM'S TRIP TO MOUNT MORIAH

Mediterranean Sea

Sea of Galilee

Jordan River

Mount Moriah

Jerusalem (Salem)

Dead Sea

Beersheba

N

0   20 Mi.

0   20 Km.

Abraham and Isaac traveled the 50 or 60 miles from Beersheba to Mount Moriah in about three days. This was a very difficult three days for Abraham, who was on his way to sacrifice his beloved son, Isaac.

scoffing. ¹⁰Therefore she said to Abraham, "Cast out this bondwoman and her son; for the son of this bondwoman shall not be heir with my son, *namely* with Isaac." ¹¹And the matter was very displeasing in Abraham's sight because of his son.

¹²But God said to Abraham, "Do not let it be displeasing in your sight because of the lad or because of your bondwoman. Whatever Sarah has said to you, listen to her voice; for in Isaac your seed shall be called. ¹³Yet I will also make a nation of the son of the bondwoman, because he *is* your seed."

¹⁴So Abraham rose early in the morning, and took bread and a skin of water; and putting *it* on her shoulder, he gave *it* and the boy to Hagar, and sent her away. Then she departed and wandered in the Wilderness of Beersheba. ¹⁵And the water in the skin was used up, and she placed the boy under one of the shrubs. ¹⁶Then she went and sat down across from *him* at a distance of about a bowshot; for she said to herself, "Let me not see the death of the boy." So she sat opposite *him*, and lifted her voice and wept.

¹⁷And God heard the voice of the lad. Then the angel of God called to Hagar out of heaven, and said to her, "What ails you, Hagar? Fear not, for God has heard the voice of the lad where he *is*. ¹⁸Arise, lift up the lad and hold him with your hand, for I will make him a great nation."

¹⁹Then God opened her eyes, and she saw a well of water. And she went and filled the skin with water, and gave the lad a drink. ²⁰So God was with the lad; and he grew and dwelt in the wilderness, and became an archer. ²¹He dwelt in the Wilderness of Paran; and his mother took a wife for him from the land of Egypt.

²²And it came to pass at that time that Abimelech and Phichol, the commander of his army, spoke to Abraham, saying, "God *is* with you in all that you do. ²³Now therefore, swear to me by God that you will not deal falsely with me, with my offspring, or with my posterity; but that

according to the kindness that I have done to you, you will do to me and to the land in which you have dwelt."

²⁴And Abraham said, "I will swear."

²⁵Then Abraham rebuked Abimelech because of a well of water which Abimelech's servants had seized. ²⁶And Abimelech said, "I do not know who has done this thing; you did not tell me, nor had I heard *of it* until today." ²⁷So Abraham took sheep and oxen and gave them to Abimelech, and the two of them made a covenant. ²⁸And Abraham set seven ewe lambs of the flock by themselves.

²⁹Then Abimelech asked Abraham, "What *is the meaning of* these seven ewe lambs which you have set by themselves?"

³⁰And he said, "You will take *these* seven ewe lambs from my hand, that they may be my witness that I have dug this well." ³¹Therefore he called that place Beersheba, because the two of them swore an oath there.

³²Thus they made a covenant at Beersheba. So Abime-

TESTS

22:1 God gave Abraham a test, not to trip him and watch him fall, but to deepen his capacity to obey God and thus to develop his character. Just as fire refines ore to extract precious metals, God refines us through difficult circumstances. When we are tested we can complain, or we can try to see how God is stretching us to develop our character.

lech rose with Phichol, the commander of his army, and they returned to the land of the Philistines. ³³Then *Abraham* planted a tamarisk tree in Beersheba, and there called on the name of the LORD, the Everlasting God. ³⁴And Abraham stayed in the land of the Philistines many days.

CHAPTER **22** ABRAHAM OFFERS ISAAC. Now it came to pass after these things that God tested Abraham, and said to him, "Abraham!"

And he said, "Here I am."

²Then He said, "Take now your son, your only *son* Isaac, whom you love, and go to the land of Moriah, and offer him there as a burnt offering on one of the mountains of which I shall tell you."

³So Abraham rose early in the morning and saddled his donkey, and took two of his young men with him, and Isaac his son; and he split the wood for the burnt offering, and arose and went to the place of which God had told him. ⁴Then on the third day Abraham lifted his eyes and saw the place afar off. ⁵And Abraham said to his young men, "Stay here with the donkey; the lad and I will go yonder and worship, and we will come back to you."

⁶So Abraham took the wood of the burnt offering and laid *it* on Isaac his son; and he took the fire in his hand,

PERFECT TIMING

22:7-8 Why did God ask Abraham to perform human sacrifice? Heathen nations practiced human sacrifice, but God condemned this as a terrible sin (Leviticus 20:1-5). God did not want Isaac to die, but he wanted Abraham to prove that he loved God more than he loved his promised and long-awaited son. God was testing Abraham. The purpose of testing is to strengthen our character and deepen our commitment to God and his perfect timing. Through this difficult experience, Abraham strengthened his commitment to obey God. He also learned about God's ability to provide.

and a knife, and the two of them went together. ⁷But Isaac spoke to Abraham his father and said, "My father!"

And he said, "Here I am, my son."

Then he said, "Look, the fire and the wood, but where *is* the lamb for a burnt offering?"

⁸And Abraham said, "My son, God will provide for Himself the lamb for a burnt offering." So the two of them went together.

⁹Then they came to the place of which God had told him. And Abraham built an altar there and placed the wood in order; and he bound Isaac his son and laid him on the altar, upon the wood. ¹⁰And Abraham stretched out his hand and took the knife to slay his son.

¹¹But the Angel of the LORD called to him from heaven and said, "Abraham, Abraham!"

So he said, "Here I am."

¹²And He said, "Do not lay your hand on the lad, or do anything to him; for now I know that you fear God, since you have not withheld your son, your only *son*, from Me."

¹³Then Abraham lifted his eyes and looked, and there behind *him was* a ram caught in a thicket by its horns. So Abraham went and took the ram, and offered it up for a burnt offering instead of his son. ¹⁴And Abraham called the name of the place, The-LORD-Will-Provide; as it is said *to* this day, "In the Mount of the LORD it shall be provided."

¹⁵Then the Angel of the LORD called to Abraham a second time out of heaven, ¹⁶and said: "By Myself I have sworn, says the LORD, because you have done this thing, and have not withheld your son, your only *son*— ¹⁷blessing I will bless you, and multiplying I will multiply your descendants as the stars of the heaven and as the sand which *is* on the seashore; and your descendants shall possess the gate of their enemies. ¹⁸In your seed all the nations of the earth shall be blessed, because you have obeyed My voice." ¹⁹So Abraham returned to his young men, and they rose and went together to Beersheba; and Abraham dwelt at Beersheba.

²⁰Now it came to pass after these things that it was told Abraham, saying, "Indeed Milcah also has borne children to your brother Nahor: ²¹Huz his firstborn, Buz his brother, Kemuel the father of Aram, ²²Chesed, Hazo, Pildash, Jidlaph, and Bethuel." ²³And Bethuel begot Rebekah. These eight Milcah bore to Nahor, Abraham's brother. ²⁴His concubine, whose name was Reumah, also bore Tebah, Gaham, Thahash, and Maachah.

CHAPTER **23** SARAH DIES. Sarah lived one hundred and twenty-seven years; *these were* the years of the life of Sarah. ²So Sarah died in Kirjath Arba (that *is*, Hebron) in the land of Canaan, and Abraham came to mourn for Sarah and to weep for her.

³Then Abraham stood up from before his dead, and spoke to the sons of Heth, saying, ⁴"I *am* a foreigner and a visitor among you. Give me property for a burial place among you, that I may bury my dead out of my sight."

⁵And the sons of Heth answered Abraham, saying to him, ⁶"Hear us, my lord: You *are* a mighty prince among us; bury your dead in the choicest of our burial places.

None of us will withhold from you his burial place, that you may bury your dead."

⁷Then Abraham stood up and bowed himself to the people of the land, the sons of Heth. ⁸And he spoke with them, saying, "If it is your wish that I bury my dead out of my sight, hear me, and meet with Ephron the son of Zohar for me, ⁹that he may give me the cave of Machpelah which he has, which *is* at the end of his field. Let him

What does God really expect from me? I hear so much from so many people that I almost feel overwhelmed. I feel like I have to give up a lot in order to make God happy.

I WONDER . . .

One essential quality about God is that he is very personal with each individual Christian. Although he chooses not to treat everyone alike, he does have expectations of his kids.

Some Christians may tell you about God's expectations based on where they are in their walk with him. If too many people are giving you advice, it could seem as though God expects way too much. This does not mean that you should quit listening to sincere Christians who want to help. It does mean, however, that if you are feeling overwhelmed, you are probably listening too much to others and not enough to God.

So what do you do? How do you please God?

The example from the story of Cain and Abel (see Genesis 4) gives a significant piece to the puzzle. Both of these men brought something to God, but only Abel's sacrifice pleased God. One reason was because Cain's heart was not really in it. He tried to please God out of obligation instead of love.

The first key to pleasing God is found in our heart or our motivation. Do we really want to make God happy, or are we going through the motions because someone told us we should?

The second key to pleasing God is obedience: "He who has My commandments and keeps them, it is he who loves Me. And he who loves Me will be loved by My Father, and I will love him and manifest Myself to him" (John 14:21).

Good parents want their children to obey them in the essentials of how to live, how to avoid situations that will lead to pain or scars, and how to treat other people. God is no different. But he is the perfect Father. He does not overload us with too many rules, because he knows we would get discouraged.

Obedience to God is loving him enough to listen to what he says, then following through on what we know he is telling us.

This is why reading the Bible every day is so important. We cannot obey what we do not know. All that God wants us to know is written very plainly in his Word.

Through the Holy Spirit, God speaks to us as we come to him with willing hearts. He gently shows us areas in our lives that we need to examine and change according to his timetable, not someone else's.

GETTING MARRIED

24:4 Abraham wanted Isaac to marry a relative. This was a common and acceptable practice that had the added advantage of avoiding intermarriage with heathen neighbors. A son's wife was usually chosen by the parents. It was common for a woman to be married in her early teens, although Rebekah was probably older.

give it to me at the full price, as property for a burial place among you."

¹⁰Now Ephron dwelt among the sons of Heth; and Ephron the Hittite answered Abraham in the presence of the sons of Heth, all who entered at the gate of his city, saying, ¹¹"No, my lord, hear me: I give you the field and the cave that *is* in it; I give it to you in the presence of the sons of my people. I give it to you. Bury your dead!"

¹²Then Abraham bowed himself down before the people of the land; ¹³and he spoke to Ephron in the hearing of the people of the land, saying, "If you *will give it,* please hear me. I will give you money for the field; take *it* from me and I will bury my dead there."

¹⁴And Ephron answered Abraham, saying to him, ¹⁵"My lord, listen to me; the land *is worth* four hundred shekels of silver. What *is* that between you and me? So bury your dead." ¹⁶And Abraham listened to Ephron; and Abraham weighed out the silver for Ephron which he had named in the hearing of the sons of Heth, four hundred shekels of silver, currency of the merchants.

¹⁷So the field of Ephron which *was* in Machpelah, which *was* before Mamre, the field and the cave which *was* in it, and all the trees that *were* in the field, which *were* within all the surrounding borders, were deeded ¹⁸to Abraham as a possession in the presence of the sons of Heth, before all who went in at the gate of his city.

¹⁹And after this, Abraham buried Sarah his wife in the cave of the field of Machpelah, before Mamre (that *is,* Hebron) in the land of Canaan. ²⁰So the field and the cave that *is* in it were deeded to Abraham by the sons of Heth as property for a burial place.

CHAPTER **24** ISAAC GETS MARRIED. Now Abraham was old, well advanced in age; and the LORD had blessed Abraham in all things. ²So Abraham said to the oldest servant of his house, who ruled over all that he had, "Please, put your hand under my thigh, ³and I will make you swear by the LORD, the God of heaven and the God of the earth, that you will not take a wife for my son from the daughters of the Canaanites, among whom I dwell; ⁴but you shall go to my country and to my family, and take a wife for my son Isaac."

⁵And the servant said to him, "Perhaps the woman will not be willing to follow me to this land. Must I take your son back to the land from which you came?"

⁶But Abraham said to him, "Beware that you do not take my son back there. ⁷The LORD God of heaven, who took me from my father's house and from the land of my family, and who spoke to me and swore to me, saying, 'To your descendants I give this land,' He will send His angel before you, and you shall take a wife for my son from there. ⁸And if the woman is not willing to follow you, then you will be released from this oath; only do not take my son back there." ⁹So the servant put his hand under the

thigh of Abraham his master, and swore to him concerning this matter.

¹⁰Then the servant took ten of his master's camels and departed, for all his master's goods *were in* his hand. And he arose and went to Mesopotamia, to the city of Nahor. ¹¹And he made his camels kneel down outside the city by a well of water at evening time, the time when women go out to draw *water.* ¹²Then he said, "O LORD God of my master Abraham, please give me success this day, and show kindness to my master Abraham. ¹³Behold, *here* I stand by the well of water, and the daughters of the men of the city are coming out to draw water. ¹⁴Now let it be that the young woman to whom I say, 'Please let down your pitcher that I may drink,' and she says, 'Drink, and I will also give your camels a drink'—*let* her *be the one* You have appointed for Your servant Isaac. And by this I will know that You have shown kindness to my master."

BEAUTY

24:15-16 Rebekah had physical beauty, but the servant was looking for a sign of inner beauty. Our appearance is important to us, and we spend time and money improving it. But how do we develop our inner beauty? Patience, kindness, and joy are the beauty treatments that help us become truly lovely—on the inside.

¹⁵And it happened, before he had finished speaking, that behold, Rebekah, who was born to Bethuel, son of Milcah, the wife of Nahor, Abraham's brother, came out with her pitcher on her shoulder. ¹⁶Now the young woman *was* very beautiful to behold, a virgin; no man had known her. And she went down to the well, filled her pitcher, and came up. ¹⁷And the servant ran to meet her and said, "Please let me drink a little water from your pitcher."

¹⁸So she said, "Drink, my lord." Then she quickly let her pitcher down to her hand, and gave him a drink. ¹⁹And when she had finished giving him a drink, she said, "I will draw *water* for your camels also, until they have finished drinking." ²⁰Then she quickly emptied her pitcher into the trough, ran back to the well to draw *water,* and drew for all his camels. ²¹And the man, wondering at her, remained silent so as to know whether the LORD had made his journey prosperous or not.

²²So it was, when the camels had finished drinking, that the man took a golden nose ring weighing half a shekel, and two bracelets for her wrists weighing ten *shekels* of gold, ²³and said, "Whose daughter *are* you? Tell me, please, is there room *in* your father's house for us to lodge?"

²⁴So she said to him, "I *am* the daughter of Bethuel, Milcah's son, whom she bore to Nahor." ²⁵Moreover she said to him, "We have both straw and feed enough, and room to lodge."

²⁶Then the man bowed down his head and worshiped the LORD. ²⁷And he said, "Blessed *be* the LORD God of my master Abraham, who has not forsaken His mercy and His truth toward my master. As for me, being on the way, the LORD led me to the house of my master's brethren." ²⁸So the young woman ran and told her mother's household these things.

²⁹Now Rebekah had a brother whose name *was* Laban, and Laban ran out to the man by the well. ³⁰So it came to pass, when he saw the nose ring, and the bracelets on his sister's wrists, and when he heard the words of his sister Rebekah, saying, "Thus the man spoke to me," that he went to the man. And there he stood by the camels at the well. ³¹And he said, "Come in, O blessed of the LORD! Why do you stand outside? For I have prepared the house, and a place for the camels."

³²Then the man came to the house. And he unloaded the camels, and provided straw and feed for the camels, and water to wash his feet and the feet of the men who *were* with him. ³³*Food* was set before him to eat, but he said, "I will not eat until I have told about my errand."

And he said, "Speak on."

³⁴So he said, "I *am* Abraham's servant. ³⁵The LORD has blessed my master greatly, and he has become great; and He has given him flocks and herds, silver and gold, male and female servants, and camels and donkeys. ³⁶And Sarah my master's wife bore a son to my master when she was old; and to him he has given all that he has. ³⁷Now my master made me swear, saying, 'You shall not take a wife for my son from the daughters of the Canaanites, in whose land I dwell; ³⁸but you shall go to my father's house and to my family, and take a wife for my son.' ³⁹And I said to my master, 'Perhaps the woman will not follow me.' ⁴⁰But he said to me, 'The LORD, before whom I walk, will send His angel with you and prosper your way; and you shall take a wife for my son from my family and from my father's house. ⁴¹You will be clear from this oath when you arrive among my family; for if they will not give *her* to you, then you will be released from my oath.'

⁴²"And this day I came to the well and said, 'O LORD God of my master Abraham, if You will now prosper the way in which I go, ⁴³behold, I stand by the well of water; and it shall come to pass that when the virgin comes out to draw *water*, and I say to her, "Please give me a little water from your pitcher to drink," ⁴⁴and she says to me, "Drink, and I will draw for your camels also,"—*let* her *be* the woman whom the LORD has appointed for my master's son.'

⁴⁵"But before I had finished speaking in my heart, there was Rebekah, coming out with her pitcher on her shoulder; and she went down to the well and drew *water*. And I said to her, 'Please let me drink.' ⁴⁶And she made haste and let her pitcher down from her *shoulder*, and said, 'Drink, and I will give your camels a drink also.' So I drank, and she gave the camels a drink also. ⁴⁷Then I asked her, and said, 'Whose daughter *are* you?' And she said, 'The daughter of Bethuel, Nahor's son, whom Milcah bore to him.' So I put the nose ring on her nose and the bracelets on her wrists. ⁴⁸And I bowed my head and worshiped the LORD, and blessed the LORD God of my master Abraham, who had led me in the way of truth to take the daughter of my master's brother for his son. ⁴⁹Now if you will deal kindly and truly with my master, tell me. And if not, tell me, that I may turn to the right hand or to the left."

⁵⁰Then Laban and Bethuel answered and said, "The thing comes from the LORD; we cannot speak to you either bad or good.

REBEKAH

Some people know how to get things started. They're initiators. Like Rebekah, they naturally make the first moves. When she saw something that needed to be done, she took action—even though her actions weren't always right.

Look at what she did at the well near her home. She gave a drink to Eliezer, Abraham's servant who was looking for a wife for Isaac. That was kind. Then she offered to give a drink to his 10 thirsty camels. That really caught his attention! Often, a person's helpfulness makes a deeper impression than his or her appearance.

Other times, though, Rebekah acted without such good results. She had a favorite between her two boys—Jacob. She found ways to help him do better than his brother, Esau. But since Esau was the oldest, Rebekah's husband, Isaac, gave him more attention. This created a situation in which Rebekah ended up deceiving her husband into giving to Jacob a special blessing that was meant for Esau. She tried to accomplish God's plan her way—and made a mess.

Most of the time we try to think of good reasons for the things we choose to do. Often we even want to add God's approval to our actions. While it is true that our actions will not spoil God's plan, it is also true that we are responsible for what we do. Before we take action we need to be truthful about our real motives. Asking this question can help: "Am I sure God wants me to do this, or do I just want his approval on what I've decided to do anyway?" Your actions will bring great results when they are controlled by God's wisdom.

LESSONS: Our actions must be guided by God's Word

God even makes use of our mistakes in his plan

Parental favoritism hurts a family

KEY VERSE: "Then Isaac brought her into his mother Sarah's tent; and he took Rebekah and she became his wife, and he loved her. So Isaac was comforted after his mother's death" (Genesis 24:67).

Rebekah's story is told in Genesis 24–27. She is also mentioned in Romans 9:10.

UPS:
- When confronted with a need she took immediate action
- She was persistent in her plans

DOWNS:
- Her initiative was not always balanced by wisdom
- She favored one of her sons
- She deceived her husband

STATS:
- Where: Haran, Canaan
- Occupation: Wife, mother, household manager
- Relatives: Parents: Bethuel and Milcah. Husband: Isaac. Brother: Laban. Twin sons: Esau and Jacob.

⁵¹Here *is* Rebekah before you; take *her* and go, and let her be your master's son's wife, as the LORD has spoken."

⁵²And it came to pass, when Abraham's servant heard their words, that he worshiped the LORD, *bowing himself* to the earth. ⁵³Then the servant brought out jewelry of silver, jewelry of gold, and clothing, and gave *them* to Rebekah. He also gave precious things to her brother and to her mother.

IMPULSE BUYING

25:32-33 Esau traded the lasting benefits of his birthright for the immediate pleasure of food. We can fall into the same trap. When we see something we want, our first impulse is to get it. But immediate pleasure often loses sight of the future.

Esau exaggerated his hunger. "I *am* about to die," he said. This thought made his choice much easier, because if he was starving, what good was an inheritance anyway? The pressure of the moment distorted his perspective and made his decision seem urgent. We sometimes feel such great pressure in one area that nothing else seems to matter, and we lose our perspective. We can avoid making Esau's mistake by comparing the short-term satisfaction with its long-range consequences before we act.

⁵⁴And he and the men who *were* with him ate and drank and stayed all night. Then they arose in the morning, and he said, "Send me away to my master."

⁵⁵But her brother and her mother said, "Let the young woman stay with us *a few* days, at least ten; after that she may go."

⁵⁶And he said to them, "Do not hinder me, since the LORD has prospered my way; send me away so that I may go to my master."

⁵⁷So they said, "We will call the young woman and ask her personally." ⁵⁸Then they called Rebekah and said to her, "Will you go with this man?"

And she said, "I will go."

⁵⁹So they sent away Rebekah their sister and her nurse, and Abraham's servant and his men. ⁶⁰And they blessed Rebekah and said to her:

"Our sister, *may* you *become*
The mother of thousands of ten thousands;
And may your descendants possess
The gates of those who hate them."

⁶¹Then Rebekah and her maids arose, and they rode on the camels and followed the man. So the servant took Rebekah and departed.

⁶²Now Isaac came from the way of Beer Lahai Roi, for he dwelt in the South. ⁶³And Isaac went out to meditate in the field in the evening; and he lifted his eyes and looked, and there, the camels *were* coming. ⁶⁴Then Rebekah lifted her eyes, and when she saw Isaac she dismounted from her camel; ⁶⁵for she had said to the servant, "Who *is* this man walking in the field to meet us?"

The servant said, "It *is* my master." So she took a veil and covered herself.

⁶⁶And the servant told Isaac all the things that he had done. ⁶⁷Then Isaac brought her into his mother Sarah's tent; and he took Rebekah and she became his wife, and he loved her. So Isaac was comforted after his mother's *death.*

CHAPTER **25 ABRAHAM DIES.** Abraham again took a wife, and her name *was* Keturah. ²And she bore him Zimran, Jokshan, Medan, Midian, Ishbak, and Shuah. ³Jokshan begot Sheba and Dedan. And the sons of Dedan were Asshurim, Letushim, and Leummim. ⁴And the sons of Midian *were* Ephah, Epher, Hanoch, Abidah, and Eldaah. All these *were* the children of Keturah.

⁵And Abraham gave all that he had to Isaac. ⁶But Abraham gave gifts to the sons of the concubines which Abraham had; and while he was still living he sent them eastward, away from Isaac his son, to the country of the east.

⁷This *is* the sum of the years of Abraham's life which he lived: one hundred and seventy-five years. ⁸Then Abraham breathed his last and died in a good old age, an old man and full *of years,* and was gathered to his people. ⁹And his sons Isaac and Ishmael buried him in the cave of Machpelah, which *is* before Mamre, in the field of Ephron the son of Zohar the Hittite, ¹⁰the field which Abraham purchased from the sons of Heth. There Abraham was buried, and Sarah his wife. ¹¹And it came to pass, after the death of Abraham, that God blessed his son Isaac. And Isaac dwelt at Beer Lahai Roi.

¹²Now this *is* the genealogy of Ishmael, Abraham's son, whom Hagar the Egyptian, Sarah's maidservant, bore to Abraham. ¹³And these *were* the names of the sons of Ishmael, by their names, according to their generations: The firstborn of Ishmael, Nebajoth; then Kedar, Adbeel, Mibsam, ¹⁴Mishma, Dumah, Massa, ¹⁵Hadar, Tema, Jetur, Naphish, and Kedemah. ¹⁶These *were* the sons of Ishmael and these *were* their names, by their towns and their settlements, twelve princes

WHAT THE BIBLE SAYS ABOUT MARRIAGE

Genesis 2:18-24 Marriage is God's idea

Genesis 24:58-60 Commitment is essential to a successful marriage

Genesis 29:10-11 Romance is important

Jeremiah 33:10-11 Marriage holds times of great joy

Malachi 2:14-15 Marriage creates the best environment for raising children

Matthew 5:32 Unfaithfulness breaks the bond of trust, the foundation of all relationships

Matthew 19:6 Marriage is permanent

Romans 7:2-3 Ideally, only death should dissolve marriage

Ephesians 5:21-33 Marriage is based on the principled practice of love, not on feelings

Ephesians 5:23,32 Marriage is a living symbol of Christ and the church

Hebrews 13:4 Marriage is good and honorable

JEALOUSY

26:12-16 God kept his promise to bless Isaac. The neighboring Philistines grew jealous because everything Isaac did seemed to go right. So they stopped up his wells and tried to get rid of him. Jealousy is a dividing force strong enough to tear apart the mightiest of nations or the closest of friends. When you find yourself becoming jealous of others, try thanking God for their good fortune. Before striking out in anger, consider what you could lose.

sister"; for he was afraid to say, "*She is* my wife," *because he thought,* "lest the men of the place kill me for Rebekah, because she *is* beautiful to behold." ⁸Now it came to pass, when he had been there a long time, that Abimelech king of the Philistines looked through a window, and saw, and there was Isaac, showing endearment to Rebekah his wife. ⁹Then Abimelech called Isaac and said, "Quite obviously she *is* your wife; so how could you say, 'She *is* my sister'?"

Isaac said to him, "Because I said, 'Lest I die on account of her.' "

¹⁰And Abimelech said, "What *is* this you have done to us? One of the people might soon have lain with your wife, and you would have brought guilt on us." ¹¹So Abimelech charged all *his* people, saying, "He who touches this man or his wife shall surely be put to death."

¹²Then Isaac sowed in that land, and reaped in the same year a hundredfold; and the LORD blessed him. ¹³The man began to prosper, and continued prospering until he became very prosperous; ¹⁴for he had possessions of flocks and possessions of herds and a great number of servants. So the Philistines envied him. ¹⁵Now the Philistines had stopped up all the wells which his father's servants had dug in the days of Abraham his father, and they had filled them with earth. ¹⁶And Abimelech said to Isaac, "Go away from us, for you are much mightier than we."

¹⁷Then Isaac departed from there and pitched his tent in the Valley of Gerar, and dwelt there. ¹⁸And Isaac dug again the wells of water which they had dug in the days of Abraham his father, for the Philistines had stopped them up after the death of Abraham. He called them by the names which his father had called them.

¹⁹Also Isaac's servants dug in the valley, and found a well of running water there. ²⁰But the herdsmen of Gerar quarreled with Isaac's herdsmen, saying, "The water *is* ours." So he called the name of the well Esek, because they

PARENTS

26:34-35 Esau married heathen women, and this really upset his parents. Most parents have a wealth of good advice because they have a lifetime of insight into their children's character. You may not agree with everything your parents say, but at least talk with them and listen carefully. This will help avoid the hard feelings Esau experienced.

quarreled with him. ²¹Then they dug another well, and they quarreled over that *one* also. So he called its name Sitnah. ²²And he moved from there and dug another well, and they did not quarrel over it. So he called its name Rehoboth, because he said, "For now the LORD has made room for us, and we shall be fruitful in the land."

²³Then he went up from there to Beersheba. ²⁴And the LORD appeared to him the same night and said, "I *am* the God of your father Abraham; do not fear, for I *am* with

you. I will bless you and multiply your descendants for My servant Abraham's sake." ²⁵So he built an altar there and called on the name of the LORD, and he pitched his tent there; and there Isaac's servants dug a well.

²⁶Then Abimelech came to him from Gerar with Ahuzzath, one of his friends, and Phichol the commander of his army. ²⁷And Isaac said to them, "Why have you come to me, since you hate me and have sent me away from you?"

²⁸But they said, "We have certainly seen that the LORD is with you. So we said, 'Let there now be an oath between us, between you and us; and let us make a covenant with you, ²⁹that you will do us no harm, since we have not touched you, and since we have done nothing to you but good and have sent you away in peace. You *are* now the blessed of the LORD.' "

³⁰So he made them a feast, and they ate and drank. ³¹Then they arose early in the morning and swore an oath with one another; and Isaac sent them away, and they departed from him in peace.

³²It came to pass the same day that Isaac's servants came and told him about the well which they had dug, and said to him, "We have found water." ³³So he called it Shebah. Therefore the name of the city *is* Beersheba to this day.

GOOD GOALS

27:5-10 When Rebekah learned that Isaac was preparing to bless Esau, she quickly devised a plan to trick him into blessing Jacob instead. Although God had already told her that Jacob would become the family leader (25:23-26), Rebekah took matters into her own hands. She resorted to doing something wrong to try to bring about what God had already said would happen. For Rebekah, the end justified the means. No matter how good we think our goals are, we should not attempt to achieve them by doing what is wrong.

³⁴When Esau was forty years old, he took as wives Judith the daughter of Beeri the Hittite, and Basemath the daughter of Elon the Hittite. ³⁵And they were a grief of mind to Isaac and Rebekah.

CHAPTER **27** JACOB DECEIVES ISAAC. Now it came to pass, when Isaac was old and his eyes were so dim that he could not see, that he called Esau his older son and said to him, "My son."

And he answered him, "Here I am."

²Then he said, "Behold now, I am old. I do not know the day of my death. ³Now therefore, please take your weapons, your quiver and your bow, and go out to the field and hunt game for me. ⁴And make me savory food, such as I love, and bring *it* to me that I may eat, that my soul may bless you before I die."

⁵Now Rebekah was listening when Isaac spoke to Esau

WARNING!

27:11-12 How we react to a moral dilemma often exposes our real motives. Frequently we are more worried about getting caught than about doing what is right. Jacob did not seem concerned about the deceitfulness of his mother's plan; instead he was afraid of getting in trouble while carrying it out. If you are worried about getting caught, you are probably in a position that is less than honest. Let your fear of getting caught be a warning to do right. Jacob paid a huge price for carrying out this dishonest plan.

according to their nations. [17]These *were* the years of the life of Ishmael: one hundred and thirty-seven years; and he breathed his last and died, and was gathered to his people. [18](They dwelt from Havilah as far as Shur, which *is* east of Egypt as you go toward Assyria.) He died in the presence of all his brethren.

[19]This *is* the genealogy of Isaac, Abraham's son. Abraham begot Isaac. [20]Isaac was forty years old when he took Rebekah as wife, the daughter of Bethuel the Syrian of Padan Aram, the sister of Laban the Syrian. [21]Now Isaac pleaded with the LORD for his wife, because she *was* barren; and the LORD granted his plea, and Rebekah his wife conceived. [22]But the children struggled together within her; and she said, "If *all is* well, why *am I* like this?" So she went to inquire of the LORD.

[23]And the LORD said to her:

"Two nations *are* in your womb,
Two peoples shall be separated from your body;
One people shall be stronger
   than the other,
And the older shall
   serve the
   younger."

[24]So when her days were fulfilled *for her* to give birth, indeed *there were* twins in her womb. [25]And the first came out red. *He was* like a hairy garment all over; so they called his name Esau. [26]Afterward his brother came out, and his hand took hold of Esau's heel; so his name was called Jacob. Isaac *was* sixty years old when she bore them.

[27]So the boys grew. And Esau was a skillful hunter, a man of the field; but Jacob was a mild man, dwelling in tents. [28]And Isaac loved Esau because he ate *of his* game, but Rebekah loved Jacob.

[29]Now Jacob cooked a stew; and Esau came in from the field, and he *was* weary. [30]And Esau said to Jacob, "Please feed me with that same red *stew,* for I *am* weary." Therefore his name was called Edom.

[31]But Jacob said, "Sell me your birthright as of this day."

[32]And Esau said, "Look, I *am* about to die; so what *is* this birthright to me?"

[33]Then Jacob said, "Swear to me as of this day."

So he swore to him, and sold his birthright to Jacob. [34]And Jacob gave Esau bread and stew of lentils; then he ate and drank, arose, and went his way. Thus Esau despised *his* birthright.

CHAPTER **26** **ISAAC TRICKS THE KING.** There was a famine in the land, besides the first famine that was in the days of Abraham. And Isaac went to Abimelech king of the Philistines, in Gerar.

[2]Then the LORD appeared to him and said: "Do not go down to Egypt; live in the land of which I shall tell you. [3]Dwell in this land, and I will be with you and bless you; for to you and your descendants I give all these lands, and I will perform the oath which I swore to Abraham your father. [4]And I will make your descendants multiply as the stars of heaven; I will give to your descendants all these lands; and in your seed all the nations of the earth shall be blessed; [5]because Abraham obeyed My voice and kept My charge, My commandments, My statutes, and My laws."

[6]So Isaac dwelt in Gerar. [7]And the men of the place asked about his wife. And he said, "She *is* my

ESAU

UPS:
• Ancestor of the Edomites
• Known for his archery skill
• Able to forgive after explosive anger

DOWNS:
• When faced with important decisions, tended to choose according to the immediate need rather than the long-range effect
• Angered his parents by poor marriage choices

STATS:
• Where: Canaan
• Occupation: Skillful hunter
• Relatives: Parents: Isaac and Rebekah. Brother: Jacob. Wives: Judith, Basemath, and Mahalath.

You probably have had people tell you to use common sense. Have they ever explained what they meant? "Using common sense" means refusing to do something that you know will bring results you won't like. Esau had a real problem with common sense. He made many wrong decisions because he didn't stop to think about what would happen. He wanted things right away without figuring out what he would have to pay later. Trading his birthright for a bowl of stew was one example of this problem. He also chose wives in direct opposition to his parents' wishes.

What are you willing to trade for the things you want? Do you find yourself willing at times to give anything—even your family, friendships, reputation, body, or soul—to get what you feel you need now? Maybe, like Esau, you haven't been using common sense.

If so, your first response, also like Esau, may be to get angry. That isn't necessarily wrong, as long as you direct the energy of that anger toward finding a solution and not toward punishing yourself or others. Your greatest need probably is to find a new way to measure how important things are to you. Up until now, your only measurement may have been to ask, "Do I need this now?" But the best measurement of value comes from God and his Word. In other words, you should ask: "Is this what God wants?" A relationship with him will not only give an ultimate purpose to your life, but will also be a daily guideline for real commonsense living.

LESSONS: God allows certain events in our lives to accomplish his overall purposes, but we are still responsible for our actions
Consequences are important to consider
It is possible to have great anger and yet not sin

KEY VERSE: "For you know that afterward, when [Esau] wanted to inherit the blessing, he was rejected, for he found no place for repentance, though he sought it diligently with tears" (Hebrews 12:17).

Esau's story is told in Genesis 25–36. He is also mentioned in Malachi 1:2; Romans 9:13; Hebrews 12:16-17.

his son. And Esau went to the field to hunt game and to bring *it.* 6So Rebekah spoke to Jacob her son, saying, "Indeed I heard your father speak to Esau your brother, saying, 7'Bring me game and make savory food for me, that I may eat it and bless you in the presence of the LORD before my death.' 8Now therefore, my son, obey my voice according to what I command you. 9Go now to the flock and bring me from there two choice kids of the goats, and I will make savory food from them for your father, such as he loves. 10Then you shall take *it* to your father, that he may eat *it,* and that he may bless you before his death."

11And Jacob said to Rebekah his mother, "Look, Esau my brother *is* a hairy man, and I *am* a smooth-*skinned* man. 12Perhaps my father will feel me, and I shall seem to be a deceiver to him; and I shall bring a curse on myself and not a blessing."

13But his mother said to him, "*Let* your curse *be* on me, my son; only obey my voice, and go, get *them* for me." 14And he went and got *them* and brought *them* to his mother, and his mother made savory food, such as his father loved. 15Then Rebekah took the choice clothes of her elder son Esau, which *were* with her in the house, and put them on Jacob her younger son. 16And she put the skins of the kids of the goats on his hands and on the smooth part of his neck. 17Then she gave the savory food and the bread, which she had prepared, into the hand of her son Jacob.

18So he went to his father and said, "My father."

And he said, "Here I am. Who *are* you, my son?"

19Jacob said to his father, "I *am* Esau your firstborn; I have done just as you told me; please arise, sit and eat of my game, that your soul may bless me."

20But Isaac said to his son, "How *is it* that you have found *it* so quickly, my son?"

And he said, "Because the LORD your God brought *it* to me."

21Isaac said to Jacob, "Please come near, that I may feel you, my son, whether you *are* really my son Esau or not." 22So Jacob went near to Isaac his father, and he felt him and said, "The voice *is* Jacob's voice, but the hands *are* the hands of Esau." 23And he did not recognize him,

because his hands were hairy like his brother Esau's hands; so he blessed him.

24Then he said, "*Are* you really my son Esau?"

He said, "I *am.*"

25He said, "Bring *it* near to me, and I will eat of my son's game, so that my soul may bless you." So he brought *it* near to him, and he ate; and he brought him wine, and he drank. 26Then his father Isaac said to him, "Come near now and kiss me, my son." 27And he came near and kissed him; and he smelled the smell of his clothing, and blessed him and said:

JACOB

was the third person in God's plan to start the nation of Israel from Abraham's family. But sometimes Jacob just seemed to get in the way of the plan. God used his life anyway. God works in the same way, even though we don't cooperate perfectly. God is willing to use people like us even though we don't cooperate perfectly. He is willing to use people

Jacob's name means "Usurper," or "Grabber," and he certainly lived up to it. He got the name by grabbing his twin brother Esau's heel while they were being born. Later, when he grabbed his brother's birthright and blessing, he had to run for his life.

While Jacob was running away from home, God appeared to him. God let Jacob know he was real and that he planned to work through Jacob's life. Shortly after this, Jacob had to live with his uncle Laban who was just as big a grabber! Jacob got 20 years' worth of patience lessons with his uncle, but he realized he was where God wanted him to be. When Jacob did leave Laban, he had become a different kind of grabber. This time, by the Jordan River, he grabbed on to God and wouldn't let go. He realized now that everything he had grabbed in life could be taken away except for God's presence and blessing. God had changed Jacob, so he also changed his name—to Israel. Jacob had learned the lesson that no one or nothing can take God's place in our lives. By the time Jacob (Israel) was an old man, he wasn't so much a grabber as someone who had been grabbed by God. He no longer made plans without including God.

At what times and places has God made himself known to you? Are you more like the young Jacob, forcing God to track you down in the wilderness of your own plans and mistakes? Or are you more like the Jacob who placed his desires and plans before God for his approval before taking any action?

LESSONS: Security doesn't come from filling your life with things

All human intentions and actions—for good or for evil—are woven by God into his ongoing plan

KEY VERSE: "Behold, I am with you and will keep you wherever you go, and will bring you back to this land; for I will not leave you until I have done what I have spoken to you" (Genesis 28:15).

Jacob's story is told in Genesis 25—50. He is also mentioned in Hosea 12:2-5; Matthew 1:2; 22:32; Acts 3:13; 7:46; Romans 9:11-13; Hebrews 11:9,20-21.

UPS:
- Father of the 12 tribes of Israel
- Third in the Abrahamic line of God's plan
- Determined; willing to work long and hard for what he wanted
- Successful livestock owner

DOWNS:
- When faced with conflict, he relied on his own resources rather than going to God for help
- Wanted to fill his life with things

STATS:
- Where: Canaan
- Occupation: Shepherd, livestock owner
- Relatives: Parents: Isaac and Rebekah. Brother: Esau. Father-in-law: Laban. Wives: Rachel and Leah. Twelve sons and one daughter are named in the Bible.

"Surely, the smell of my son
Is like the smell of a field
Which the LORD has blessed.
28 Therefore may God give you
Of the dew of heaven,
Of the fatness of the earth,
And plenty of grain and wine.
29 Let peoples serve you,
And nations bow down to you.
Be master over your brethren,
And let your mother's sons bow down to you.
Cursed be everyone who curses you,
And blessed be those who bless you!"

30Now it happened, as soon as Isaac had finished blessing Jacob, and Jacob had scarcely gone out from the presence of Isaac his father, that Esau his brother came in from his hunting. 31He also had made savory food, and brought it to his father, and said to his father, "Let my father arise and eat of his son's game, that your soul may bless me."

32And his father Isaac said to him, "Who are you?"

So he said, "I am your son, your firstborn, Esau."

33Then Isaac trembled exceedingly, and said, "Who? Where is the one who hunted game and brought it to me? I ate all of it before you came, and I have blessed him—and indeed he shall be blessed."

34When Esau heard the words of his father, he cried with an exceedingly great and bitter cry, and said to his father, "Bless me—me also, O my father!"

35But he said, "Your brother came with deceit and has taken away your blessing."

36And Esau said, "Is he not rightly named Jacob? For he has supplanted me these two times. He took away my birthright, and now look, he has taken away my blessing!" And he said, "Have you not reserved a blessing for me?"

37Then Isaac answered and said to Esau, "Indeed I have made him your master, and all his brethren I have given to him as servants; with grain and wine I have sustained him. What shall I do now for you, my son?"

38And Esau said to his father, "Have you only one blessing, my father? Bless me—me also, O my father!" And Esau lifted up his voice and wept.

39Then Isaac his father answered and said to him:

"Behold, your dwelling shall be of the fatness of the earth,
And of the dew of heaven from above.
40 By your sword you shall live,
And you shall serve your brother;
And it shall come to pass, when you become restless,
That you shall break his yoke from your neck."

41So Esau hated Jacob because of the blessing with which his father blessed him, and Esau said in his heart, "The days of mourning for my father are at hand; then I will kill my brother Jacob."

42And the words of Esau her older son were told to Rebekah. So she sent and called Jacob her younger son, and said to him, "Surely your brother Esau comforts himself concerning you by intending to kill you. 43Now therefore, my son, obey my voice: arise, flee to my brother Laban in Haran. 44And stay with him a few days, until your brother's fury turns away, 45until your brother's anger turns away from you, and he forgets what you have done to him; then I will send and bring you from there.

PERSONALIZED FAITH

28:10-15 God's covenant promise to Abraham and Isaac was offered to Jacob as well. But it was not enough to be Abraham's grandson; Jacob had to establish his own personal relationship with God. God has no grandchildren; each of us must have a personal relationship with him. It is not enough to hear wonderful stories about Christians in your family. You need to become part of the story yourself (see Galatians 3:6-7).

Why should I be bereaved also of you both in one day?"

46And Rebekah said to Isaac, "I am weary of my life because of the daughters of Heth; if Jacob takes a wife of the daughters of Heth, like these who are the daughters of the land, what good will my life be to me?"

CHAPTER **28** JACOB IS SENT TO FIND A WIFE.
Then Isaac called Jacob and blessed him, and charged him, and said to him: "You shall not take a wife from the daughters of Canaan. 2Arise, go to Padan Aram, to the house of Bethuel your mother's father; and take yourself a wife from there of the daughters of Laban your mother's brother.

3 "May God Almighty bless you,
And make you fruitful and multiply you,
That you may be an assembly of peoples;
4 And give you the blessing of Abraham,
To you and your descendants with you,
That you may inherit the land
In which you are a stranger,
Which God gave to Abraham."

5So Isaac sent Jacob away, and he went to Padan Aram, to Laban the son of Bethuel the Syrian, the brother of Rebekah, the mother of Jacob and Esau.

6Esau saw that Isaac had blessed Jacob and sent him away to Padan Aram to take himself a wife from there, and that as he blessed him he gave him a charge, saying, "You shall not take a wife from the daughters of Canaan," 7and that Jacob had obeyed his father and his mother and had gone to Padan Aram. 8Also Esau saw that the daughters of Canaan did not please his father Isaac. 9So Esau went to Ishmael and took Mahalath the daughter of Ishmael, Abraham's son, the sister of Nebajoth, to be his wife in addition to the wives he had.

10Now Jacob went out from Beersheba and went toward Haran. 11So he came to a certain place and stayed there all night, because the sun had set. And he took one of the stones of that place and put it at his head, and he lay down in that place to sleep. 12Then he dreamed, and behold, a ladder was set up on the earth, and its top reached to heaven; and there the angels of God were ascending and descending on it.

13And behold, the LORD stood above it and said: "I am the LORD God of Abraham your father and the God of Isaac; the land on which you lie I will give to you and your

serve me for nothing? Tell me, what *should* your wages *be?* " [16]Now Laban had two daughters: the name of the elder *was* Leah, and the name of the younger *was* Rachel. [17]Leah's eyes *were* delicate, but Rachel was beautiful of form and appearance.

[18]Now Jacob loved Rachel; so he said, "I will serve you seven years for Rachel your younger daughter."

[19]And Laban said, "*It is* better that I give her to you than that I should give her to another man. Stay with me." [20]So Jacob served seven years for Rachel, and they seemed *only* a few days to him because of the love he had for her.

[21]Then Jacob said to Laban, "Give *me* my wife, for my days are fulfilled, that I may go in to her." [22]And Laban gathered together all the men of the place and made a feast. [23]Now it came to pass in the evening, that he took Leah his daughter and brought her to Jacob; and he went in to her. [24]And Laban gave his maid Zilpah to his daughter Leah *as* a maid. [25]So it came to pass in the morning, that behold, it *was* Leah. And he said to Laban, "What is this you have done to me? Was it not for Rachel that I served you? Why then have you deceived me?"

[26]And Laban said, "It must not be done so in our country, to give the younger before the firstborn. [27]Fulfill her week, and we will give you this one also for the service which you will serve with me still another seven years."

[28]Then Jacob did so and fulfilled her week. So he gave him his daughter Rachel as wife also. [29]And Laban gave his maid Bilhah to his daughter Rachel as a maid. [30]Then *Jacob* also went in to Rachel, and he also loved Rachel more than Leah. And he served with Laban still another seven years.

[31]When the LORD saw that Leah *was* unloved, He opened her womb; but Rachel *was* barren. [32]So Leah conceived and bore a son, and she called his name Reuben; for she said, "The LORD has surely looked on my affliction. Now therefore, my husband will love me." [33]Then she conceived again and bore a son, and said, "Because the LORD has heard that I *am* unloved, He has therefore given me this *son* also." And she called his name Simeon. [34]She conceived again and bore a son, and said, "Now this time my husband will become attached to me, because I have borne him three sons." Therefore his name was called Levi. [35]And she conceived again and bore a son, and said, "Now I will praise the LORD." Therefore she called his name Judah. Then she stopped bearing.

CHAPTER **30** Now when Rachel saw that she bore Jacob no children, Rachel envied her sister, and said to Jacob, "Give me children, or else I die!"

[2]And Jacob's anger was aroused against Rachel, and he said, "*Am* I in the place of God, who has withheld from you the fruit of the womb?"

[3]So she said, "Here is my maid Bilhah; go in to her, and she will bear *a child* on my knees, that I also may have children by her." [4]Then she gave him Bilhah her maid as wife, and Jacob went in to her. [5]And Bilhah conceived and bore Jacob a son. [6]Then Rachel said, "God has judged my case; and He has also heard my voice and given me a

son." Therefore she called his name Dan. [7]And Rachel's maid Bilhah conceived again and bore Jacob a second son. [8]Then Rachel said, "With great wrestlings I have wrestled with my sister, *and* indeed I have prevailed." So she called his name Naphtali.

◤ WORTH THE WAIT

29:20-28 People often wonder if waiting a long time for something they want is worth it. Jacob waited seven years to marry Rachel. After being tricked, he agreed to work seven more years for her! The most important goals and desires are worth working and waiting for. Movies and television have created the illusion that people have to wait only about an hour to solve their problems or get what they want. Don't be trapped into thinking the same is true in real life. Patience is hardest when we need it the most, but it is the key to achieving our goals.

[9]When Leah saw that she had stopped bearing, she took Zilpah her maid and gave her to Jacob as wife. [10]And Leah's maid Zilpah bore Jacob a son. [11]Then Leah said, "A troop comes!" So she called his name Gad. [12]And Leah's maid Zilpah bore Jacob a second son. [13]Then Leah said, "I am happy, for the daughters will call me blessed." So she called his name Asher.

[14]Now Reuben went in the days of wheat harvest and found mandrakes in the field, and brought them to his mother Leah. Then Rachel said to Leah, "Please give me *some* of your son's mandrakes."

◤ BABY CONTEST

30:4-12 Rachel and Leah were locked in a cruel contest. In their race to have more children, they both gave their servant girls to Jacob as concubines. Jacob would have been wise to refuse, even though this was an accepted custom of the day. The fact that a custom is socially acceptable does not mean it is wise or right. You will be spared much heartbreak if you look at the potential consequences—to you or others—of your actions. Are you doing anything now that might cause future problems?

[15]But she said to her, "*Is it* a small matter that you have taken away my husband? Would you take away my son's mandrakes also?"

And Rachel said, "Therefore he will lie with you tonight for your son's mandrakes."

[16]When Jacob came out of the field in the evening, Leah went out to meet him and said, "You must come in to me, for I have surely hired you with my son's mandrakes." And he lay with her that night.

[17]And God listened to Leah, and she conceived and bore Jacob a fifth son. [18]Leah said, "God has given me my wages, because I have given my maid to my husband." So she called his name Issachar. [19]Then Leah conceived again and bore Jacob a sixth son. [20]And Leah said, "God has endowed me *with* a good endowment; now my husband will dwell with me, because I have borne him six sons." So she called his name Zebulun. [21]Afterward she bore a daughter, and called her name Dinah.

[22]Then God remembered Rachel, and God listened to her and opened her womb. [23]And she conceived and bore a son, and said, "God has taken away my reproach." [24]So

descendants. ¹⁴Also your descendants shall be as the dust of the earth; you shall spread abroad to the west and the east, to the north and the south; and in you and in your seed all the families of the earth shall be blessed. ¹⁵Behold, I *am* with you and will keep you wherever you go, and will bring you back to this land; for I will not leave you until I have done what I have spoken to you."

¹⁶Then Jacob awoke from his sleep and said, "Surely the LORD is in this place, and I did not know *it*." ¹⁷And he was afraid and said, "How awesome *is* this place! This *is* none other than the house of God, and this *is* the gate of heaven!"

¹⁸Then Jacob rose early in the morning, and took the stone that he had put at his head, set it up as a pillar, and poured oil on top of it. ¹⁹And he called the name of that place Bethel; but the name of that city had been Luz previously. ²⁰Then Jacob made a vow, saying, "If God will be with me, and keep me in this way that I am going, and give me bread to eat and clothing to put on, ²¹so that I come back to my father's house in peace, then the LORD shall be my God. ²²And this stone which I have set as a pillar shall be God's house, and of all that You give me I will surely give a tenth to You."

CHAPTER 29
JACOB MEETS RACHEL.

So Jacob went on his journey and came to the land of the people of the East. ²And he looked, and saw a well in the field; and behold, there *were* three flocks of sheep lying by it; for out of that well they watered the flocks. A large stone *was* on the well's mouth. ³Now all the flocks would be gathered there; and they would roll the stone from the well's mouth, water the sheep, and put the stone back in its place on the well's mouth.

⁴And Jacob said to them, "My brethren, where *are* you from?"

And they said, "We *are* from Haran."

⁵Then he said to them, "Do you know Laban the son of Nahor?"

And they said, "We know him."

⁶So he said to them, "Is he well?"

And they said, "*He is* well. And look, his daughter Rachel is coming with the sheep."

⁷Then he said, "Look, *it is* still high day; *it is* not time for the cattle to be gathered together. Water the sheep, and go and feed *them*."

⁸But they said, "We cannot until all the flocks are gathered together, and they have rolled the stone from the well's mouth; then we water the sheep."

⁹Now while he was still speaking with them, Rachel came with her father's sheep, for she was a shepherdess. ¹⁰And it came to pass, when Jacob saw Rachel the daughter of Laban his mother's brother, and the sheep of Laban his mother's brother, that Jacob went near and rolled the stone from the well's mouth, and watered the flock of Laban his mother's brother. ¹¹Then Jacob kissed Rachel, and lifted up his voice and wept. ¹²And Jacob told Rachel that he *was* her father's relative and that he *was* Rebekah's son. So she ran and told her father.

¹³Then it came to pass, when Laban heard the report about Jacob his sister's son, that he ran to meet him, and embraced him and kissed him, and brought him to his house. So he told Laban all these things. ¹⁴And Laban said to him, "Surely you *are* my bone and my flesh." And he stayed with him for a month.

¹⁵Then Laban said to Jacob, "Because you *are* my relative, should you therefore

RACHEL

For Rachel's family, the town well at Haran was an important place. Someone had to go there for water every day. Some great things happened at the well. There Rebekah met Eliezer, Abraham's servant, who had come to find a wife for Isaac. Some 40 years later, Rebekah's son Jacob met his cousin Rachel at the same well. The relationship that quickly grew between them not only reminds us that romance is not a modern invention, but also teaches us a few lessons about real love.

Jacob's love for Rachel was both patient and practical. Jacob had the patience to wait seven years for her, but he kept busy in the meantime. His faithfulness to Rachel created a strong loyalty to him in her. But Rachel was also frustrated. At first, she couldn't have children. She felt she was competing with her sister, Leah, for Jacob's affection. But she missed the point: Jacob had already freely given her his devoted love.

Sometimes we make the same mistake, thinking we can "earn" love and friendship. We even think we can somehow earn God's love. But we can't earn what God has already given us. He loves us! His love had no beginning and is incredibly patient. All we need to do is respond to God's love, which he has offered freely to us.

God's Word says in many ways, "I do love you. I have demonstrated my love by all I've done for you. I have even sacrificed my Son, Jesus, to pay the price for your sins. Now live because of my love. Respond to me; love me with your whole being; give yourself to me in thanks, not as payment. Live life fully, in the freedom of knowing you are loved."

LESSONS: Loyalty must be controlled by what is true and right

Love is accepted, not earned

KEY VERSE: "So Jacob served seven years for Rachel, and they seemed only a few days to him because of the love he had for her" (Genesis 29:20).

Rachel's story is told in Genesis 29:6–35:20. She is also mentioned in Ruth 4:11.

UPS:
- Showed great loyalty to her family
- Mothered Joseph and Benjamin after being barren for many years

DOWNS:
- Her envy and competitiveness marred her relationship with her sister, Leah
- Was capable of dishonesty by taking her loyalty too far
- Failed to recognize that Jacob's devotion was not dependent on her ability to have children

STATS:
- Where: Haran
- Occupation: Shepherdess, homemaker
- Relatives: Father: Laban. Aunt: Rebekah. Sister: Leah. Husband: Jacob. Sons: Joseph and Benjamin.

she called his name Joseph, and said, "The LORD shall add to me another son."

²⁵And it came to pass, when Rachel had borne Joseph, that Jacob said to Laban, "Send me away, that I may go to my own place and to my country. ²⁶Give *me* my wives and my children for whom I have served you, and let me go; for you know my service which I have done for you."

²⁷And Laban said to him, "Please *stay*, if I have found favor in your eyes, *for* I have learned by experience that the LORD has blessed me for your sake." ²⁸Then he said, "Name me your wages, and I will give *it*."

²⁹So *Jacob* said to him, "You know how I have served you and how your livestock has been with me. ³⁰For what you had before I *came was* little, and it has increased to a great amount; the LORD has blessed you since my coming. And now, when shall I also provide for my own house?"

³¹So he said, "What shall I give you?"

And Jacob said, "You shall not give me anything. If you will do this thing for me, I will again feed and keep your flocks: ³²Let me pass through all your flock today, removing from there all the speckled and spotted sheep, and all the brown ones among the lambs, and the spotted and speckled among the goats; and *these* shall be my wages. ³³So my righteousness will answer for me in time to come, when the subject of my wages comes before you: every one that *is* not speckled and spotted among the goats, and brown among the lambs, will be considered stolen, if *it is* with me."

³⁴And Laban said, "Oh, that it were according to your word!" ³⁵So he removed that day the male goats that were speckled and spotted, all the female goats that were speckled and spotted, every one that had *some* white in it, and all the brown ones among the lambs, and gave *them* into the hand of his sons. ³⁶Then he put three days' journey between himself and Jacob, and Jacob fed the rest of Laban's flocks.

³⁷Now Jacob took for himself rods of green poplar and of the almond and chestnut trees, peeled white strips in them, and exposed the white which *was* in the rods. ³⁸And the rods which he had peeled, he set before the flocks in the gutters, in the watering troughs where the flocks came to drink, so that they should conceive when they came to drink. ³⁹So the flocks conceived before the rods, and the flocks brought forth streaked, speckled, and spotted. ⁴⁰Then Jacob separated the lambs, and made the flocks face toward the streaked and all the brown in the flock of Laban; but he put his own flocks by themselves and did not put them with Laban's flock.

⁴¹And it came to pass, whenever the stronger livestock conceived, that Jacob placed the rods before the eyes of the livestock in the gutters, that they might conceive among the rods. ⁴²But when the flocks were feeble, he did not put *them* in; so the feebler were Laban's and the stronger Jacob's. ⁴³Thus the man became exceedingly prosperous, and had large flocks, female and male servants, and camels and donkeys.

CHAPTER **31** JACOB LEAVES LABAN. Now *Jacob*
heard the words of Laban's sons, saying, "Jacob has taken away all that was our father's, and from what was our father's he has acquired all this wealth." ²And Jacob saw the countenance of Laban, and indeed it *was* not *favorable* toward him as before. ³Then the LORD said to Jacob, "Return to the land of your fathers and to your family, and I will be with you."

WAIT FOR GOD

30:22-24 Eventually God answered Rachel's prayers and gave her a child of her own. In the meantime, however, she had given her servant girl to Jacob. Trusting God when nothing seems to happen is difficult. But it is harder still to live with the consequences of taking matters into our own hands. Resist the temptation to think God has forgotten you. Have patience and courage to wait for God to act.

⁴So Jacob sent and called Rachel and Leah to the field, to his flock, ⁵and said to them, "I see your father's countenance, that it *is* not *favorable* toward me as before; but the God of my father has been with me. ⁶And you know that with all my might I have served your father. ⁷Yet your father has deceived me and changed my wages ten times, but God did not allow him to hurt me. ⁸If he said thus: 'The speckled shall be your wages,' then all the flocks bore speckled. And if he said thus: 'The streaked shall be your wages,' then all the flocks bore streaked. ⁹So God has taken away the livestock of your father and given *them* to me.

¹⁰"And it happened, at the time when the flocks conceived, that I lifted my eyes and saw in a dream, and behold, the rams which leaped upon the flocks *were* streaked, speckled, and gray-spotted. ¹¹Then the Angel of God spoke to me in a dream, saying, 'Jacob.' And I said, 'Here I am.' ¹²And He said, 'Lift your eyes now and see, all the rams which leap on the flocks *are* streaked, speckled, and gray-spotted; for I have seen all that Laban is doing to you. ¹³I *am* the God of Bethel, where you anointed the pillar *and* where you made a vow to Me. Now arise, get out of this land, and return to the land of your family.'"

¹⁴Then Rachel and Leah answered and said to him, "Is there still any portion or inheritance for us in our father's house? ¹⁵Are we not considered strangers by him? For he has sold us, and also completely consumed our money. ¹⁶For all these riches which God has taken from our father are *really* ours and our children's; now then, whatever God has said to you, do it."

¹⁷Then Jacob rose and set his sons and his wives on camels. ¹⁸And he carried away all his livestock and all his possessions which he had gained, his acquired livestock which he had gained in Padan Aram, to go to his father Isaac in the land of Canaan. ¹⁹Now Laban had gone to shear his sheep, and Rachel had stolen the household idols that were her father's. ²⁰And Jacob stole away, unknown to Laban the Syrian, in that he did not tell him that he intended to flee. ²¹So he fled with all that he had. He arose and crossed the river, and headed toward the mountains of Gilead.

²²And Laban was told on the third day that Jacob had fled. ²³Then he took his brethren with him and pursued him for seven days' journey, and he overtook him in the mountains of Gilead. ²⁴But God had come to Laban the

Syrian in a dream by night, and said to him, "Be careful that you speak to Jacob neither good nor bad."

²⁵So Laban overtook Jacob. Now Jacob had pitched his tent in the mountains, and Laban with his brethren pitched in the mountains of Gilead.

²⁶And Laban said to Jacob: "What have you done, that you have stolen away unknown to me, and carried away my daughters like captives *taken* with the sword? ²⁷Why did you flee away secretly, and steal away from me, and not tell me; for I might have sent you away with joy and songs, with timbrel and harp? ²⁸And you did not allow me to kiss my sons and my daughters. Now you have done foolishly in *so* doing. ²⁹It is in my power to do you harm, but the God of your father spoke to me last night, saying, 'Be careful that you speak to Jacob neither good nor bad.' ³⁰And now you have surely gone because you greatly long for your father's house, *but* why did you steal my gods?"

³¹Then Jacob answered and said to Laban, "Because I was afraid, for I said, 'Perhaps you would take your daughters from me by force.' ³²With whomever you find your gods, do not let him live. In the presence of our brethren, identify what I have of yours and take *it* with you." For Jacob did not know that Rachel had stolen them.

▶ THE PAYOFF

31:38-42 Jacob made it a habit to do more than was expected of him. When his flocks were attacked, he took the losses rather than splitting them with Laban. He worked hard even after several pay cuts. His diligence eventually paid off; his flocks began to multiply. Making a habit of doing more than is expected can pay off. It (1) pleases God, (2) earns recognition and advancement, (3) enhances your reputation, (4) builds others' confidence in you, (5) gives you more experience and knowledge, and (6) develops your spiritual maturity.

³³And Laban went into Jacob's tent, into Leah's tent, and into the two maids' tents, but he did not find *them*. Then he went out of Leah's tent and entered Rachel's tent. ³⁴Now Rachel had taken the household idols, put them in the camel's saddle, and sat on them. And Laban searched all about the tent but did not find *them*. ³⁵And she said to her father, "Let it not displease my lord that I cannot rise before you, for the manner of women *is* with me." And he searched but did not find the household idols.

³⁶Then Jacob was angry and rebuked Laban, and Jacob answered and said to Laban: "What *is* my trespass? What *is* my sin, that you have so hotly pursued me? ³⁷Although you have searched all my things, what part of your household things have you found? Set *it* here before my brethren and your brethren, that they may judge between us both! ³⁸These twenty years I *have been* with you; your ewes and your female goats have not miscarried their young, and I have not eaten the rams of your flock. ³⁹That which was torn *by beasts* I did not bring to you; I bore the loss of it. You required it from my hand, *whether* stolen by day or stolen by night. ⁴⁰*There* I was! In the day the drought consumed me, and the frost by night, and my sleep departed from my eyes. ⁴¹Thus I have been in your house twenty years; I served you fourteen years for your two daughters, and six years for your flock, and you have changed my wages ten times. ⁴²Unless the God of

my father, the God of Abraham and the Fear of Isaac, had been with me, surely now you would have sent me away empty-handed. God has seen my affliction and the labor of my hands, and rebuked *you* last night."

⁴³And Laban answered and said to Jacob, "*These* daughters *are* my daughters, and *these* children *are* my children, and *this* flock *is* my flock; all that you see *is* mine. But what can I do this day to these my daughters or to their children whom they have borne? ⁴⁴Now therefore, come, let us make a covenant, you and I, and let it be a witness between you and me."

⁴⁵So Jacob took a stone and set it up *as* a pillar. ⁴⁶Then Jacob said to his brethren, "Gather stones." And they took stones and made a heap, and they ate there on the heap. ⁴⁷Laban called it Jegar Sahadutha, but Jacob called it Galeed. ⁴⁸And Laban said, "This heap *is* a witness between you and me this day." Therefore its name was called Galeed, ⁴⁹also Mizpah, because he said, "May the LORD watch between you and me when we are absent one from another. ⁵⁰If you afflict my daughters, or if you take *other* wives besides my daughters, *although* no man *is* with us—see, God *is* witness between you and me!"

⁵¹Then Laban said to Jacob, "Here is this heap and here is *this* pillar, which I have placed between you and me. ⁵²This heap *is* a witness, and *this* pillar *is* a witness, that I will not pass beyond this heap to you, and you will not pass beyond this heap and this pillar to me, for harm. ⁵³The God of Abraham, the God of Nahor, and the God of their father judge between us." And Jacob swore by the Fear of his father Isaac. ⁵⁴Then Jacob offered a sacrifice on the mountain, and called his brethren to eat bread. And they ate bread and stayed all night on the mountain. ⁵⁵And early in the morning Laban arose, and kissed his sons and daughters and blessed them. Then Laban departed and returned to his place.

CHAPTER 32 JACOB MEETS ESAU.

So Jacob went on his way, and the angels of God met him. ²When Jacob saw them, he said, "This *is* God's camp." And he called the name of that place Mahanaim.

³Then Jacob sent messengers before him to Esau his brother in the land of Seir, the country of Edom. ⁴And he commanded them, saying, "Speak thus to my lord Esau, 'Thus your servant Jacob says: "I have dwelt with Laban and stayed there until now. ⁵I have oxen, donkeys, flocks, and male and female servants; and I have sent to tell my lord, that I may find favor in your sight." ' "

⁶Then the messengers returned to Jacob, saying, "We came to your brother Esau, and he also is coming to meet you, and four hundred men *are* with him." ⁷So Jacob was greatly afraid and distressed; and he divided the people that *were* with him, and the flocks and herds and camels, into two companies. ⁸And he said, "If Esau comes to the one company and attacks it, then the other company which is left will escape."

⁹Then Jacob said, "O God of my father Abraham and God of my father Isaac, the LORD who said to me, 'Return to your country and to your family, and I will deal well with you': ¹⁰I am not worthy of the least of all the mercies and of all the truth which You have shown Your servant;

she called his name Joseph, and said, "The LORD shall add to me another son."

²⁵And it came to pass, when Rachel had borne Joseph, that Jacob said to Laban, "Send me away, that I may go to my own place and to my country. ²⁶Give *me* my wives and my children for whom I have served you, and let me go; for you know my service which I have done for you."

²⁷And Laban said to him, "Please *stay,* if I have found favor in your eyes, *for* I have learned by experience that the LORD has blessed me for your sake." ²⁸Then he said, "Name me your wages, and I will give *it.*"

²⁹So *Jacob* said to him, "You know how I have served you and how your livestock has been with me. ³⁰For what you had before I *came was* little, and it has increased to a great amount; the LORD has blessed you since my coming. And now, when shall I also provide for my own house?"

³¹So he said, "What shall I give you?"

And Jacob said, "You shall not give me anything. If you will do this thing for me, I will again feed and keep your flocks: ³²Let me pass through all your flock today, removing from there all the speckled and spotted sheep, and all the brown ones among the lambs, and the spotted and speckled among the goats; and *these* shall be my wages. ³³So my righteousness will answer for me in time to come, when the subject of my wages comes before you: every one that *is* not speckled and spotted among the goats, and brown among the lambs, will be considered stolen, if *it is* with me."

³⁴And Laban said, "Oh, that it were according to your word!" ³⁵So he removed that day the male goats that were speckled and spotted, all the female goats that were speckled and spotted, every one that had *some* white in it, and all the brown ones among the lambs, and gave *them* into the hand of his sons. ³⁶Then he put three days' journey between himself and Jacob, and Jacob fed the rest of Laban's flocks.

³⁷Now Jacob took for himself rods of green poplar and of the almond and chestnut trees, peeled white strips in them, and exposed the white which *was* in the rods. ³⁸And the rods which he had peeled, he set before the flocks in the gutters, in the watering troughs where the flocks came to drink, so that they should conceive when they came to drink. ³⁹So the flocks conceived before the rods, and the flocks brought forth streaked, speckled, and spotted. ⁴⁰Then Jacob separated the lambs, and made the flocks face toward the streaked and all the brown in the flock of Laban; but he put his own flocks by themselves and did not put them with Laban's flock.

⁴¹And it came to pass, whenever the stronger livestock conceived, that Jacob placed the rods before the eyes of the livestock in the gutters, that they might conceive among the rods. ⁴²But when the flocks were feeble, he did not put *them* in; so the feebler were Laban's and the stronger Jacob's. ⁴³Thus the man became exceedingly prosperous, and had large flocks, female and male servants, and camels and donkeys.

CHAPTER 31 JACOB LEAVES LABAN. Now *Jacob*
heard the words of Laban's sons, saying, "Jacob has taken away all that was our father's, and from what was our father's he has acquired all this wealth." ²And Jacob saw the countenance of Laban, and indeed it *was* not *favorable* toward him as before. ³Then the LORD said to Jacob, "Return to the land of your fathers and to your family, and I will be with you."

◣▬▬▬▬▬WAIT FOR GOD

30:22-24 Eventually God answered Rachel's prayers and gave her a child of her own. In the meantime, however, she had given her servant girl to Jacob. Trusting God when nothing seems to happen is difficult. But it is harder still to live with the consequences of taking matters into our own hands. Resist the temptation to think God has forgotten you. Have patience and courage to wait for God to act.

⁴So Jacob sent and called Rachel and Leah to the field, to his flock, ⁵and said to them, "I see your father's countenance, that it *is* not *favorable* toward me as before; but the God of my father has been with me. ⁶And you know that with all my might I have served your father. ⁷Yet your father has deceived me and changed my wages ten times, but God did not allow him to hurt me. ⁸If he said thus: 'The speckled shall be your wages,' then all the flocks bore speckled. And if he said thus: 'The streaked shall be your wages,' then all the flocks bore streaked. ⁹So God has taken away the livestock of your father and given *them* to me.

¹⁰"And it happened, at the time when the flocks conceived, that I lifted my eyes and saw in a dream, and behold, the rams which leaped upon the flocks *were* streaked, speckled, and gray-spotted. ¹¹Then the Angel of God spoke to me in a dream, saying, 'Jacob.' And I said, 'Here I am.' ¹²And He said, 'Lift your eyes now and see, all the rams which leap on the flocks *are* streaked, speckled, and gray-spotted; for I have seen all that Laban is doing to you. ¹³I *am* the God of Bethel, where you anointed the pillar *and* where you made a vow to Me. Now arise, get out of this land, and return to the land of your family.' "

¹⁴Then Rachel and Leah answered and said to him, "Is there still any portion or inheritance for us in our father's house? ¹⁵Are we not considered strangers by him? For he has sold us, and also completely consumed our money. ¹⁶For all these riches which God has taken from our father are *really* ours and our children's; now then, whatever God has said to you, do it."

¹⁷Then Jacob rose and set his sons and his wives on camels. ¹⁸And he carried away all his livestock and all his possessions which he had gained, his acquired livestock which he had gained in Padan Aram, to go to his father Isaac in the land of Canaan. ¹⁹Now Laban had gone to shear his sheep, and Rachel had stolen the household idols that were her father's. ²⁰And Jacob stole away, unknown to Laban the Syrian, in that he did not tell him that he intended to flee. ²¹So he fled with all that he had. He arose and crossed the river, and headed toward the mountains of Gilead.

²²And Laban was told on the third day that Jacob had fled. ²³Then he took his brethren with him and pursued him for seven days' journey, and he overtook him in the mountains of Gilead. ²⁴But God had come to Laban the

descendants. [14]Also your descendants shall be as the dust of the earth; you shall spread abroad to the west and the east, to the north and the south; and in you and in your seed all the families of the earth shall be blessed. [15]Behold, I *am* with you and will keep you wherever you go, and will bring you back to this land; for I will not leave you until I have done what I have spoken to you."

[16]Then Jacob awoke from his sleep and said, "Surely the LORD is in this place, and I did not know *it*." [17]And he was afraid and said, "How awesome *is* this place! This *is* none other than the house of God, and this *is* the gate of heaven!"

[18]Then Jacob rose early in the morning, and took the stone that he had put at his head, set it up as a pillar, and poured oil on top of it. [19]And he called the name of that place Bethel; but the name of that city had been Luz previously. [20]Then Jacob made a vow, saying, "If God will be with me, and keep me in this way that I am going, and give me bread to eat and clothing to put on, [21]so that I come back to my father's house in peace, then the LORD shall be my God. [22]And this stone which I have set as a pillar shall be God's house, and of all that You give me I will surely give a tenth to You."

CHAPTER 29
JACOB MEETS RACHEL.

So Jacob went on his journey and came to the land of the people of the East. [2]And he looked, and saw a well in the field; and behold, there *were* three flocks of sheep lying by it; for out of that well they watered the flocks. A large stone *was* on the well's mouth. [3]Now all the flocks would be gathered there; and they would roll the stone from the well's mouth, water the sheep, and put the stone back in its place on the well's mouth.

[4]And Jacob said to them, "My brethren, where *are* you from?"

And they said, "We *are* from Haran."

[5]Then he said to them, "Do you know Laban the son of Nahor?"

And they said, "We know him."

[6]So he said to them, "Is he well?"

And they said, "*He is* well. And look, his daughter Rachel is coming with the sheep."

[7]Then he said, "Look, *it is* still high day; *it is* not time for the cattle to be gathered together. Water the sheep, and go and feed *them*."

[8]But they said, "We cannot until all the flocks are gathered together, and they have rolled the stone from the well's mouth; then we water the sheep."

[9]Now while he was still speaking with them, Rachel came with her father's sheep, for she was a shepherdess. [10]And it came to pass, when Jacob saw Rachel the daughter of Laban his mother's brother, and the sheep of Laban his mother's brother, that Jacob went near and rolled the stone from the well's mouth, and watered the flock of Laban his mother's brother. [11]Then Jacob kissed Rachel, and lifted up his voice and wept. [12]And Jacob told Rachel that he *was* her father's relative and that he *was* Rebekah's son. So she ran and told her father.

[13]Then it came to pass, when Laban heard the report about Jacob his sister's son, that he ran to meet him, and embraced him and kissed him, and brought him to his house. So he told Laban all these things. [14]And Laban said to him, "Surely you *are* my bone and my flesh." And he stayed with him for a month.

[15]Then Laban said to Jacob, "Because you *are* my relative, should you therefore

RACHEL

For Rachel's family, the town well at Haran was an important place. Someone had to go there for water every day. Some great things happened at the well. There Rebekah met Eliezer, Abraham's servant, who had come to find a wife for Isaac. Some 40 years later, Rebekah's son Jacob met his cousin Rachel at the same well. The relationship that quickly grew between them not only reminds us that romance is not a modern invention, but also teaches us a few lessons about real love.

Jacob's love for Rachel was both patient and practical. Jacob had the patience to wait seven years for her, but he kept busy in the meantime. His faithfulness to Rachel created a strong loyalty to him in her. But Rachel was also frustrated. At first, she couldn't have children. She felt she was competing with her sister, Leah, for Jacob's affection. But she missed the point: Jacob had already freely given her his devoted love.

Sometimes we make the same mistake, thinking we can "earn" love and friendship. We even think we can somehow earn God's love. But we can't earn what God has already given us. He loves us! His love had no beginning and is incredibly patient. All we need to do is respond to God's love, which he has offered freely to us.

God's Word says in many ways, "I do love you. I have demonstrated my love by all I've done for you. I have even sacrificed my Son, Jesus, to pay the price for your sins. Now live because of my love. Respond to me; love me with your whole being; give yourself to me in thanks, not as payment. Live life fully, in the freedom of knowing you are loved."

LESSONS: Loyalty must be controlled by what is true and right

Love is accepted, not earned

KEY VERSE: "So Jacob served seven years for Rachel, and they seemed only a few days to him because of the love he had for her" (Genesis 29:20).

Rachel's story is told in Genesis 29:6–35:20. She is also mentioned in Ruth 4:11.

UPS:
• Showed great loyalty to her family
• Mothered Joseph and Benjamin after being barren for many years

DOWNS:
• Her envy and competitiveness marred her relationship with her sister, Leah
• Was capable of dishonesty by taking her loyalty too far
• Failed to recognize that Jacob's devotion was not dependent on her ability to have children

STATS:
• Where: Haran
• Occupation: Shepherdess, homemaker
• Relatives: Father: Laban. Aunt: Rebekah. Sister: Leah. Husband: Jacob. Sons: Joseph and Benjamin.

serve me for nothing? Tell me, what *should* your wages *be?*" ¹⁶Now Laban had two daughters: the name of the elder *was* Leah, and the name of the younger *was* Rachel. ¹⁷Leah's eyes *were* delicate, but Rachel was beautiful of form and appearance.

¹⁸Now Jacob loved Rachel; so he said, "I will serve you seven years for Rachel your younger daughter."

¹⁹And Laban said, "*It is* better that I give her to you than that I should give her to another man. Stay with me." ²⁰So Jacob served seven years for Rachel, and they seemed *only* a few days to him because of the love he had for her.

²¹Then Jacob said to Laban, "Give *me* my wife, for my days are fulfilled, that I may go in to her." ²²And Laban gathered together all the men of the place and made a feast. ²³Now it came to pass in the evening, that he took Leah his daughter and brought her to Jacob; and he went in to her. ²⁴And Laban gave his maid Zilpah to his daughter Leah *as* a maid. ²⁵So it came to pass in the morning, that behold, it *was* Leah. And he said to Laban, "What is this you have done to me? Was it not for Rachel that I served you? Why then have you deceived me?"

²⁶And Laban said, "It must not be done so in our country, to give the younger before the firstborn. ²⁷Fulfill her week, and we will give you this one also for the service which you will serve with me still another seven years."

²⁸Then Jacob did so and fulfilled her week. So he gave him his daughter Rachel as wife also. ²⁹And Laban gave his maid Bilhah to his daughter Rachel as a maid. ³⁰Then *Jacob* also went in to Rachel, and he also loved Rachel more than Leah. And he served with Laban still another seven years.

³¹When the LORD saw that Leah *was* unloved, He opened her womb; but Rachel *was* barren. ³²So Leah conceived and bore a son, and she called his name Reuben; for she said, "The LORD has surely looked on my affliction. Now therefore, my husband will love me." ³³Then she conceived again and bore a son, and said, "Because the LORD has heard that I *am* unloved, He has therefore given me this *son* also." And she called his name Simeon. ³⁴She conceived again and bore a son, and said, "Now this time my husband will become attached to me, because I have borne him three sons." Therefore his name was called Levi. ³⁵And she conceived again and bore a son, and said, "Now I will praise the LORD." Therefore she called his name Judah. Then she stopped bearing.

CHAPTER 30 Now when Rachel saw that she bore Jacob no children, Rachel envied her sister, and said to Jacob, "Give me children, or else I die!"

²And Jacob's anger was aroused against Rachel, and he said, "*Am* I in the place of God, who has withheld from you the fruit of the womb?"

³So she said, "Here is my maid Bilhah; go in to her, and she will bear *a child* on my knees, that I also may have children by her." ⁴Then she gave him Bilhah her maid as wife, and Jacob went in to her. ⁵And Bilhah conceived and bore Jacob a son. ⁶Then Rachel said, "God has judged my case; and He has also heard my voice and given me a

son." Therefore she called his name Dan. ⁷And Rachel's maid Bilhah conceived again and bore Jacob a second son. ⁸Then Rachel said, "With great wrestlings I have wrestled with my sister, *and* indeed I have prevailed." So she called his name Naphtali.

▸ WORTH THE WAIT

29:20-28 People often wonder if waiting a long time for something they want is worth it. Jacob waited seven years to marry Rachel. After being tricked, he agreed to work seven more years for her! The most important goals and desires are worth working and waiting for. Movies and television have created the illusion that people have to wait only about an hour to solve their problems or get what they want. Don't be trapped into thinking the same is true in real life. Patience is hardest when we need it the most, but it is the key to achieving our goals.

⁹When Leah saw that she had stopped bearing, she took Zilpah her maid and gave her to Jacob as wife. ¹⁰And Leah's maid Zilpah bore Jacob a son. ¹¹Then Leah said, "A troop comes!" So she called his name Gad. ¹²And Leah's maid Zilpah bore Jacob a second son. ¹³Then Leah said, "I am happy, for the daughters will call me blessed." So she called his name Asher.

¹⁴Now Reuben went in the days of wheat harvest and found mandrakes in the field, and brought them to his mother Leah. Then Rachel said to Leah, "Please give me *some* of your son's mandrakes."

▸ BABY CONTEST

30:4-12 Rachel and Leah were locked in a cruel contest. In their race to have more children, they both gave their servant girls to Jacob as concubines. Jacob would have been wise to refuse, even though this was an accepted custom of the day. The fact that a custom is socially acceptable does not mean it is wise or right. You will be spared much heartbreak if you look at the potential consequences—to you or others—of your actions. Are you doing anything now that might cause future problems?

¹⁵But she said to her, "*Is it* a small matter that you have taken away my husband? Would you take away my son's mandrakes also?"

And Rachel said, "Therefore he will lie with you tonight for your son's mandrakes."

¹⁶When Jacob came out of the field in the evening, Leah went out to meet him and said, "You must come in to me, for I have surely hired you with my son's mandrakes." And he lay with her that night.

¹⁷And God listened to Leah, and she conceived and bore Jacob a fifth son. ¹⁸Leah said, "God has given me my wages, because I have given my maid to my husband." So she called his name Issachar. ¹⁹Then Leah conceived again and bore Jacob a sixth son. ²⁰And Leah said, "God has endowed me *with* a good endowment; now my husband will dwell with me, because I have borne him six sons." So she called his name Zebulun. ²¹Afterward she bore a daughter, and called her name Dinah.

²²Then God remembered Rachel, and God listened to her and opened her womb. ²³And she conceived and bore a son, and said, "God has taken away my reproach." ²⁴So

for I crossed over this Jordan with my staff, and now I have become two companies. [11]Deliver me, I pray, from the hand of my brother, from the hand of Esau; for I fear him, lest he come and attack me *and* the mother with the children. [12]For You said, 'I will surely treat you well, and make your descendants as the sand of the sea, which cannot be numbered for multitude.' "

[13]So he lodged there that same night, and took what came to his hand as a present for Esau his brother: [14]two hundred female goats and twenty male goats, two hundred ewes and twenty rams, [15]thirty milk camels with their colts, forty cows and ten bulls, twenty female donkeys and ten foals. [16]Then he delivered *them* to the hand of his servants, every drove by itself, and said to his servants, "Pass over before me, and put some distance between successive droves." [17]And he commanded the first one, saying, "When Esau my brother meets you and asks you, saying, 'To whom do you belong, and where are you going? Whose *are* these in front of you?' [18]then you shall say, 'They *are* your servant Jacob's. It *is* a present sent to my lord Esau; and behold, he also *is* behind us.' " [19]So he commanded the second, the third, and all who followed the droves, saying, "In this manner you shall speak to Esau when you find him; [20]and also say, 'Behold, your servant Jacob *is* behind us.' " For he said, "I will appease him with the present that goes before me, and afterward I will see his face; perhaps he will accept me." [21]So the present went on over before him, but he himself lodged that night in the camp.

[22]And he arose that night and took his two wives, his two female servants, and his eleven sons, and crossed over the ford of Jabbok. [23]He took them, sent them over the brook, and sent over what he had. [24]Then Jacob was left alone; and a Man wrestled with him until the breaking of day. [25]Now when He saw that He did not prevail against him, He touched the socket of his hip; and the socket of Jacob's hip was out of joint as He wrestled with him. [26]And He said, "Let Me go, for the day breaks."

But he said, "I will not let You go unless You bless me!"

[27]So He said to him, "What *is* your name?"

He said, "Jacob."

[28]And He said, "Your name shall no longer be called Jacob, but Israel; for you have struggled with God and with men, and have prevailed."

[29]Then Jacob asked, saying, "Tell *me* Your name, I pray."

And He said, "Why *is* it *that* you ask about My name?" And He blessed him there.

[30]So Jacob called the name of the place Peniel: "For I have seen God face to face, and my life is preserved." [31]Just as he crossed over Penuel the sun rose on him, and he limped on his hip. [32]Therefore to this day the children of Israel do not eat the muscle that shrank, which *is* on the hip socket, because He touched the socket of Jacob's hip in the muscle that shrank.

CHAPTER 33 Now Jacob lifted his eyes and looked, and there, Esau was coming, and with him were four hundred men. So he divided the children among Leah, Rachel, and the two maidservants. [2]And he put the maidservants and their children in front, Leah and her children behind, and Rachel and Joseph last. [3]Then he crossed over before them and bowed himself to the ground seven times, until he came near to his brother.

[4]But Esau ran to meet him, and embraced him, and fell on his neck and kissed him, and they wept. [5]And he lifted his eyes and saw the women and children, and said, "Who *are* these with you?"

▶ FRANTIC WITH FEAR

32:9-12 How would you feel knowing you were about to meet the person you had cheated out of his most precious possession? Jacob had taken Esau's birthright (25:33) and his blessings (27:27-40). Now he was about to meet this brother for the first time in 20 years, and he was frantic with fear. He collected his thoughts, however, and decided to pray. When we face a difficult conflict, we can run about frantically or we can pause to pray. Which approach will be more effective?

So he said, "The children whom God has graciously given your servant." [6]Then the maidservants came near, they and their children, and bowed down. [7]And Leah also came near with her children, and they bowed down. Afterward Joseph and Rachel came near, and they bowed down.

[8]Then Esau said, "What *do* you *mean by* all this company which I met?"

And he said, "*These are* to find favor in the sight of my lord."

[9]But Esau said, "I have enough, my brother; keep what you have for yourself."

[10]And Jacob said, "No, please, if I have now found favor in your sight, then receive my present from my hand, inasmuch as I have seen your face as though I had seen the face of God, and you were pleased with me. [11]Please, take my blessing that is brought to you, because God has dealt graciously with me, and because I have enough." So he urged him, and he took *it*.

[12]Then Esau said, "Let us take our journey; let us go, and I will go before you."

[13]But Jacob said to him, "My lord knows that the children *are* weak, and the flocks and herds which are nursing *are* with me. And if the men should drive them hard one day, all the flock will die. [14]Please let my lord go on ahead before his servant. I will lead on slowly at a pace which the livestock that go before me, and the children, are able to endure, until I come to my lord in Seir."

[15]And Esau said, "Now let me leave with you *some* of the people who *are* with me."

But he said, "What need is there? Let me find favor in the sight of my lord." [16]So Esau returned that day on his way to Seir. [17]And Jacob journeyed to Succoth, built him-

▶ BITTERNESS

33:1-11 It is refreshing to see Esau's change of heart when the two brothers meet again. The bitterness over losing his birthright and blessing (25:29-34) seems gone. Instead Esau is content with what he has. Jacob even exclaims how great it is to see his brother obviously pleased with him (33:10). Life can deal us some bad situations. We can feel cheated, as Esau did, but we don't have to remain bitter. We can remove bitterness from our lives by honestly expressing our feelings to God, forgiving those who have wronged us, and being content with what we have.

self a house, and made booths for his livestock. Therefore the name of the place is called Succoth.

¹⁸Then Jacob came safely to the city of Shechem, which *is* in the land of Canaan, when he came from Padan Aram; and he pitched his tent before the city. ¹⁹And he bought the parcel of land, where he had pitched his tent, from the children of Hamor, Shechem's father, for one hundred pieces of money. ²⁰Then he erected an altar there and called it El Elohe Israel.

CHAPTER 34 JACOB'S SONS TAKE REVENGE.

Now Dinah the daughter of Leah, whom she had borne to Jacob, went out to see the daughters of the land. ²And when Shechem the son of Hamor the Hivite, prince of the country, saw her, he took her and lay with her, and violated her. ³His soul was strongly attracted to Dinah the daughter of Jacob, and he loved the young woman and spoke kindly to the young woman. ⁴So Shechem spoke to his father Hamor, saying, "Get me this young woman as a wife."

PASSION

34:1-4 Shechem may have been a victim of "love at first sight," but his actions were impulsive and evil. Not only did he sin against Dinah; he sinned against the entire family (34:6-7). The consequences of his deed were severe both for his family and for Jacob's (34:25-31). Even Shechem's declared love for Dinah could not excuse the evil he did by raping her. Don't allow sexual passion to boil over into evil actions. Passion must be controlled.

⁵And Jacob heard that he had defiled Dinah his daughter. Now his sons were with his livestock in the field; so Jacob held his peace until they came. ⁶Then Hamor the father of Shechem went out to Jacob to speak with him. ⁷And the sons of Jacob came in from the field when they heard *it;* and the men were grieved and very angry, because he had done a disgraceful thing in Israel by lying with Jacob's daughter, a thing which ought not to be done. ⁸But Hamor spoke with them, saying, "The soul of my son Shechem longs for your daughter. Please give her to him as a wife. ⁹And make marriages with us; give your daughters to us, and take our daughters to yourselves. ¹⁰So you shall dwell with us, and the land shall be before you. Dwell and trade in it, and acquire possessions for yourselves in it."

¹¹Then Shechem said to her father and her brothers, "Let me find favor in your eyes, and whatever you say to me I will give. ¹²Ask me ever so much dowry and gift, and I will give according to what you say to me; but give me the young woman as a wife."

¹³But the sons of Jacob answered Shechem and Hamor his father, and spoke deceitfully, because he had defiled Dinah their sister. ¹⁴And they said to them, "We cannot do this thing, to give our sister to one who is uncircumcised, for that *would be* a reproach to us. ¹⁵But on this *condition* we will consent to you: If you will become as we *are,* if every male of you is circumcised, ¹⁶then we will give our daughters to you, and we will take your daughters to us; and we will dwell with you, and we will become one people. ¹⁷But if you will not heed us and be circumcised, then we will take our daughter and be gone."

¹⁸And their words pleased Hamor and Shechem, Hamor's son. ¹⁹So the young man did not delay to do the thing, because he delighted in Jacob's daughter. He *was* more honorable than all the household of his father.

²⁰And Hamor and Shechem his son came to the gate of their city, and spoke with the men of their city, saying: ²¹"These men *are* at peace with us. Therefore let them dwell in the land and trade in it. For indeed the land *is* large enough for them. Let us take their daughters to us as wives, and let us give them our daughters. ²²Only on this *condition* will the men consent to dwell with us, to be one people: if every male among us is circumcised as they *are* circumcised. ²³*Will* not their livestock, their property, and every animal of theirs *be* ours? Only let us consent to them, and they will dwell with us." ²⁴And all who went out of the gate of his city heeded Hamor and Shechem his son; every male was circumcised, all who went out of the gate of his city.

²⁵Now it came to pass on the third day, when they were in pain, that two of the sons of Jacob, Simeon and Levi, Dinah's brothers, each took his sword and came boldly upon the city and killed all the males. ²⁶And they killed Hamor and Shechem his son with the edge of the sword, and took Dinah from Shechem's house, and went out. ²⁷The sons of Jacob came upon the slain, and plundered the city, because their sister had been defiled. ²⁸They took their sheep, their oxen, and their donkeys, what *was* in the city and what *was* in the field, ²⁹and all their wealth. All their little ones and their wives they took captive; and they plundered even all that *was* in the houses. ³⁰Then Jacob said to Simeon and Levi, "You have troubled me by making me obnoxious among the inhabitants of the land, among the Canaanites and the Perizzites; and since I *am* few in number, they will gather themselves together against me and kill me. I shall be destroyed, my household and I." ³¹But they said, "Should he treat our sister like a harlot?"

CHAPTER 35 RACHEL AND ISAAC DIE.

Then God said to Jacob, "Arise, go up to Bethel and dwell there; and make an altar there to God, who appeared to you when you fled from the face of Esau your brother."

²And Jacob said to his household and to all who *were* with him, "Put away the foreign gods that *are* among you, purify yourselves, and change your garments. ³Then let us arise and go up to Bethel; and I will make an altar there to God, who answered me in the day of my distress and has been with me in the way which I have gone." ⁴So they gave Jacob all the foreign gods which *were* in their hands, and the earrings which *were* in their ears; and Jacob hid them under the terebinth tree which *was* by Shechem.

⁵And they journeyed, and the terror of God was upon the cities that *were* all around them, and they did not pursue the sons of Jacob. ⁶So Jacob came to Luz (that *is,* Bethel), which *is* in the land of Canaan, he and all the people who *were* with him. ⁷And he built an altar there and called the place El Bethel, because there God appeared to him when he fled from the face of his brother.

⁸Now Deborah, Rebekah's nurse, died, and she was

buried below Bethel under the terebinth tree. So the name of it was called Allon Bachuth.

⁹Then God appeared to Jacob again, when he came from Padan Aram, and blessed him. ¹⁰And God said to him, "Your name *is* Jacob; your name shall not be called Jacob anymore, but Israel shall be your name." So He called his name Israel. ¹¹Also God said to him: "I *am* God Almighty. Be fruitful and multiply; a nation and a company of nations shall proceed from you, and kings shall come from your body. ¹²The land which I gave Abraham and Isaac I give to you; and to your descendants after you I give this land." ¹³Then God went up from him in the place where He talked with him. ¹⁴So Jacob set up a pillar in the place where He talked with him, a pillar of stone; and he poured a drink offering on it, and he poured oil on it. ¹⁵And Jacob called the name of the place where God spoke with him, Bethel.

¹⁶Then they journeyed from Bethel. And when there was but a little distance to go to Ephrath, Rachel labored *in childbirth,* and she had hard labor. ¹⁷Now it came to pass, when she was in hard labor, that the midwife said to her, "Do not fear; you will have this son also." ¹⁸And so it was, as her soul was departing (for she died), that she called his name Ben-Oni; but his father called him Benjamin. ¹⁹So Rachel died and was buried on the way to Ephrath (that *is,* Bethlehem). ²⁰And Jacob set a pillar on her grave, which *is* the pillar of Rachel's grave to this day.

²¹Then Israel journeyed and pitched his tent beyond the tower of Eder. ²²And it happened, when Israel dwelt in that land, that Reuben went and lay with Bilhah his father's concubine; and Israel heard *about it.*

Now the sons of Jacob were twelve: ²³the sons of Leah *were* Reuben, Jacob's firstborn, and Simeon, Levi, Judah, Issachar, and Zebulun; ²⁴the sons of Rachel *were* Joseph and Benjamin; ²⁵the sons of Bilhah, Rachel's maidservant, *were* Dan and Naphtali; ²⁶and the sons of Zilpah, Leah's maidservant, *were* Gad and Asher. These *were* the sons of Jacob who were born to him in Padan Aram.

²⁷Then Jacob came to his father Isaac at Mamre, or Kirjath Arba (that *is,* Hebron), where Abraham and Isaac had dwelt. ²⁸Now the days of Isaac were one hundred and eighty years. ²⁹So Isaac breathed his last and died, and was gathered to his people, *being* old and full of days. And his sons Esau and Jacob buried him.

CHAPTER **36** **ESAU'S FAMILY.** Now this *is* the genealogy of Esau, who is Edom. ²Esau took his wives from the daughters of Canaan: Adah the daughter of Elon the Hittite; Aholibamah the daughter of Anah, the daughter of Zibeon the Hivite; ³and Basemath, Ishmael's daughter, sister of Nebajoth. ⁴Now Adah bore Eliphaz to Esau, and Basemath bore Reuel. ⁵And Aholibamah bore Jeush, Jaalam, and Korah. These *were* the sons of Esau who were born to him in the land of Canaan.

⁶Then Esau took his wives, his sons, his daughters, and all the persons of his household, his cattle and all his animals, and all his goods which he had gained in the land of Canaan, and went to a country away from the presence of his brother Jacob. ⁷For their possessions were too great for them to dwell together, and the land where they were

strangers could not support them because of their livestock. ⁸So Esau dwelt in Mount Seir. Esau *is* Edom.

⁹And this *is* the genealogy of Esau the father of the Edomites in Mount Seir. ¹⁰These *were* the names of Esau's sons: Eliphaz the son of Adah the wife of Esau, and Reuel the son of Basemath the wife of Esau. ¹¹And the sons of Eliphaz were Teman, Omar, Zepho, Gatam, and Kenaz.

¹²Now Timna was the concubine of Eliphaz, Esau's

▸▸▸ WINNING OUT

35:10 God reminded Jacob of his new name, Israel, which meant "one who prevails with God." Although Jacob's life was littered with difficulties and trials, his new name was a tribute to his desire to stay close to God despite life's disappointments. Many people believe that Christianity should offer a problem-free life. Consequently, as life gets tough, they draw back disappointed. Instead, they should determine to stick close to God through life's storms. Problems and difficulties are painful but inevitable; you might as well see them as opportunities for growth. You can't prevail with God unless you have troubles to prevail over.

son, and she bore Amalek to Eliphaz. These *were* the sons of Adah, Esau's wife.

¹³These *were* the sons of Reuel: Nahath, Zerah, Shammah, and Mizzah. These were the sons of Basemath, Esau's wife.

¹⁴These were the sons of Aholibamah, Esau's wife, the daughter of Anah, the daughter of Zibeon. And she bore to Esau: Jeush, Jaalam, and Korah.

¹⁵These *were* the chiefs of the sons of Esau. The sons of Eliphaz, the firstborn *son* of Esau, were Chief Teman, Chief Omar, Chief Zepho, Chief Kenaz, ¹⁶Chief Korah, Chief Gatam, *and* Chief Amalek. These *were* the chiefs of Eliphaz in the land of Edom. They *were* the sons of Adah.

¹⁷These *were* the sons of Reuel, Esau's son: Chief Nahath, Chief Zerah, Chief Shammah, and Chief Mizzah. These *were* the chiefs of Reuel in the land of Edom. These *were* the sons of Basemath, Esau's wife.

¹⁸And these *were* the sons of Aholibamah, Esau's wife: Chief Jeush, Chief Jaalam, and Chief Korah. These *were* the chiefs *who descended* from Aholibamah, Esau's wife, the daughter of Anah. ¹⁹These *were* the sons of Esau, who is Edom, and these *were* their chiefs.

²⁰These *were* the sons of Seir the Horite who inhabited the land: Lotan, Shobal, Zibeon, Anah, ²¹Dishon, Ezer, and Dishan. These *were* the chiefs of the Horites, the sons of Seir, in the land of Edom.

²²And the sons of Lotan were Hori and Hemam. Lotan's sister *was* Timna.

²³These *were* the sons of Shobal: Alvan, Manahath, Ebal, Shepho, and Onam.

▸▸▸ INHERITANCE

35:22 Reuben's sin was costly, although not right away. As the oldest son, he stood to receive a double portion of the family inheritance and a place of leadership among his people. Reuben may have thought he got away with his sin. No more is mentioned of it until Jacob, on his deathbed, assembled his family for the final blessing. Suddenly Jacob took away Reuben's double portion and gave it to someone else (49:4). Sin's consequences can plague us long after the sin is committed. When we do something wrong we may think we can escape unnoticed, only to discover later that the sin has been quietly breeding serious consequences.

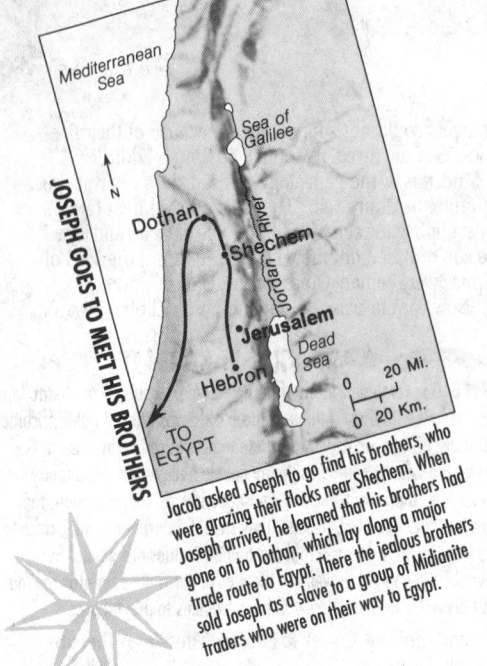

JOSEPH GOES TO MEET HIS BROTHERS

Jacob asked Joseph to go find his brothers, who were grazing their flocks near Shechem. When Joseph arrived, he learned that his brothers had gone on to Dothan, which lay along a major trade route to Egypt. There the jealous brothers sold Joseph as a slave to a group of Midianite traders who were on their way to Egypt.

²⁴These *were* the sons of Zibeon: both Ajah and Anah. This *was the* Anah who found the water in the wilderness as he pastured the donkeys of his father Zibeon. ²⁵These *were* the children of Anah: Dishon and Aholibamah the daughter of Anah.

²⁶These *were* the sons of Dishon: Hemdan, Eshban, Ithran, and Cheran. ²⁷These *were* the sons of Ezer: Bilhan, Zaavan, and Akan. ²⁸These *were* the sons of Dishan: Uz and Aran.

◣ BRAGGING

37:6-11 Joseph's brothers were already angry over the possibility of being ruled by their little brother. Joseph then fueled the fire with his immature attitude and boastful manner. No one enjoys a braggart. Joseph learned his lesson the hard way. His angry brothers sold him into slavery to get rid of him. After several years of hardship, Joseph learned an important lesson: because our talents and knowledge come from God, it is more appropriate to thank him for them than to brag about them. Later, Joseph gives God the credit (41:16).

²⁹These *were* the chiefs of the Horites: Chief Lotan, Chief Shobal, Chief Zibeon, Chief Anah, ³⁰Chief Dishon, Chief Ezer, and Chief Dishan. These *were* the chiefs of the Horites, according to their chiefs in the land of Seir.

³¹Now these *were* the kings who reigned in the land of Edom before any king reigned over the children of Israel: ³²Bela the son of Beor reigned in Edom, and the name of his city *was* Dinhabah. ³³And when Bela died, Jobab the son of Zerah of Bozrah reigned in his place. ³⁴When Jobab died, Husham of the land of the Temanites reigned in his place. ³⁵And when Husham died, Hadad the son of Bedad, who attacked Midian in the field of Moab, reigned in his place. And the name of his city *was* Avith. ³⁶When Hadad died, Samlah of Masrekah reigned in his place. ³⁷And when Samlah died, Saul of Rehoboth-*by*-the-River reigned in his place. ³⁸When Saul died, Baal-Hanan the son of Achbor reigned in his place. ³⁹And when Baal-Hanan the son of Achbor died, Hadar reigned in his place; and the name of

his city *was* Pau. His wife's name *was* Mehetabel, the daughter of Matred, the daughter of Mezahab.

⁴⁰And these *were* the names of the chiefs of Esau, according to their families and their places, by their names: Chief Timnah, Chief Alvah, Chief Jetheth, ⁴¹Chief Aholibamah, Chief Elah, Chief Pinon, ⁴²Chief Kenaz, Chief Teman, Chief Mibzar, ⁴³Chief Magdiel, and Chief Iram. These *were* the chiefs of Edom, according to their dwelling places in the land of their possession. Esau *was* the father of the Edomites.

CHAPTER 37 JOSEPH'S STRANGE DREAMS.

Now Jacob dwelt in the land where his father was a stranger, in the land of Canaan. ²This *is* the history of Jacob.

Joseph, *being* seventeen years old, was feeding the flock with his brothers. And the lad *was* with the sons of Bilhah and the sons of Zilpah, his father's wives; and Joseph brought a bad report of them to his father.

³Now Israel loved Joseph more than all his children, because he *was* the son of his old age. Also he made him a tunic of *many* colors. ⁴But when his brothers saw that their father loved him more than all his brothers, they hated him and could not speak peaceably to him.

⁵Now Joseph had a dream, and he told *it* to his brothers; and they hated him even more. ⁶So he said to them, "Please hear this dream which I have dreamed: ⁷There we were, binding sheaves in the field. Then behold, my sheaf arose and also stood upright; and indeed your sheaves stood all around and bowed down to my sheaf."

⁸And his brothers said to him, "Shall you indeed reign over us? Or shall you indeed have dominion over us?" So they hated him even more for his dreams and for his words.

⁹Then he dreamed still another dream and told it to his brothers, and said, "Look, I have dreamed another dream. And this time, the sun, the moon, and the eleven stars bowed down to me."

¹⁰So he told *it* to his father and his brothers; and his father rebuked him and said to him, "What *is* this dream that you have dreamed? Shall your mother and I and your brothers indeed come to bow down to the earth before you?" ¹¹And his brothers envied him, but his father kept the matter *in mind*.

¹²Then his brothers went to feed their father's flock in Shechem. ¹³And Israel said to Joseph, "Are not your brothers feeding *the flock* in Shechem? Come, I will send you to them."

So he said to him, "Here I am."

¹⁴Then he said to him, "Please go and see if it is well

◣ UGLY RAGE

37:19-20 Could jealousy ever make you feel like killing someo[ne] Before saying, "Of course not," look at what happened in this stor[y] men were willing to kill their youngest brother over a tunic and a [?] reported dreams. Their deep jealousy had grown into ugly rage, b[?] them completely to what was right. Jealousy can be hard to recog[nize] because our reasons for it seem to make sense. But left unchecked[,] jealousy grows quickly and leads to serious sins. The longer you c[??] jealous feelings, the harder it is to uproot them. The time to deal w[ith] jealousy is when you notice yourself keeping score of what others

with your brothers and well with the flocks, and bring back word to me." So he sent him out of the Valley of Hebron, and he went to Shechem.

¹⁵Now a certain man found him, and there he was, wandering in the field. And the man asked him, saying, "What are you seeking?"

¹⁶So he said, "I am seeking my brothers. Please tell me where they are feeding *their flocks*."

¹⁷And the man said, "They have departed from here, for I heard them say, 'Let us go to Dothan.' " So Joseph went after his brothers and found them in Dothan.

¹⁸Now when they saw him afar off, even before he came near them, they conspired against him to kill him. ¹⁹Then they said to one another, "Look, this dreamer is coming! ²⁰Come therefore, let us now kill him and cast him into some pit; and we shall say, 'Some wild beast has devoured him.' We shall see what will become of his dreams!"

²¹But Reuben heard *it,* and he delivered him out of their hands, and said, "Let us not kill him." ²²And Reuben said to them, "Shed no blood, *but* cast him into this pit which *is* in the wilderness, and do not lay a hand on him"—that he might deliver him out of their hands, and bring him back to his father.

²³So it came to pass, when Joseph had come to his brothers, that they stripped Joseph *of* his tunic, the tunic of *many* colors that *was* on him. ²⁴Then they took him and cast him into a pit. And the pit *was* empty; *there was* no water in it.

²⁵And they sat down to eat a meal. Then they lifted their eyes and looked, and there was a company of Ishmaelites, coming from Gilead with their camels, bearing spices, balm, and myrrh, on their way to carry *them* down to Egypt. ²⁶So Judah said to his brothers, "What profit *is there* if we kill our brother and conceal his blood? ²⁷Come and let us sell him to the Ishmaelites, and let not our hand be upon him, for he *is* our brother *and* our flesh." And his brothers listened. ²⁸Then Midianite traders passed by; so *the brothers* pulled Joseph up and lifted him out of the pit, and sold him to the Ishmaelites for twenty *shekels* of silver. And they took Joseph to Egypt.

²⁹Then Reuben returned to the pit, and indeed Joseph *was* not in the pit; and he tore his clothes. ³⁰And he returned to his brothers and said, "The lad *is* no *more;* and I, where shall I go?"

³¹So they took Joseph's tunic, killed a kid of the goats, and dipped the tunic in the blood. ³²Then they sent the tunic of *many* colors, and they brought *it* to their father and said, "We have found this. Do you know whether it *is* your son's tunic or not?"

³³And he recognized it and said, "*It is* my son's tunic. A wild beast has devoured him. Without doubt Joseph is torn to pieces." ³⁴Then Jacob tore his clothes, put sackcloth on his waist, and mourned for his son many days. ³⁵And all his sons and all his daughters arose to comfort

ME FIRST

37:30 Reuben returned to the pit to find Joseph, but his little brother was gone. His first response, in effect, was "What is going to happen to me?" rather than "What is going to happen to Joseph?" In a tough situation, are you always concerned first about yourself? Consider the person most affected by the problem, and you are more likely to find a solution for it.

him; but he refused to be comforted, and he said, "For I shall go down into the grave to my son in mourning." Thus his father wept for him.

³⁶Now the Midianites had sold him in Egypt to Potiphar, an officer of Pharaoh *and* captain of the guard.

CHAPTER 38 JUDAH AND TAMAR. It came to pass at that time that Judah departed from his brothers, and visited a certain Adullamite whose name *was* Hirah. ²And Judah saw there a daughter of a certain Canaanite whose name *was* Shua,

REUBEN

Parents are usually the best judges of their children's character. Jacob summarized the personality of his son Reuben by comparing him to wild waves. Except when frozen, water has no stable shape of its own. It always shapes itself to its container or environment. Reuben usually wanted to do the right thing, but seemed unable to stand against a crowd. His instability made him hard to trust. He had both private and public values, but they contradicted each other. He went along with his brothers in their actions against Joseph while hoping he could counteract the evil in private. His plan failed.

Compromise has a way of destroying convictions. Without convictions, there is no direction. And lack of direction will destroy life. In Reuben's case, his early mistakes led to a real mess later on in life. Are you the same person on the inside that you are on the outside? We may want to keep our private and public lives separate, but we can't deny that they affect each other. What convictions are present in your life at all times? How often does Jacob's description of his son, "unstable as the wild waves," fit your life?

LESSONS: Public and private lives must show the same integrity, or one will destroy the other

Punishment for sin may not be immediate, but it is certain

KEY VERSE: "Unstable as water, you shall not excel, because you went up to your father's bed; then you defiled it" (Genesis 49:4).

Reuben's story is told in Genesis 29—50.

UPS:
- Saved Joseph's life by talking the other brothers out of murder
- Showed intense love for his father by offering his own sons as a guarantee that Benjamin's life would be safe

DOWNS:
- Gave in quickly to group pressure
- Did not directly protect Joseph from his brothers, although as eldest son he had the authority to do so
- Slept with his father's concubine

STATS:
- Where: Canaan, Egypt
- Occupation: Shepherd
- Relatives: Parents: Jacob and Leah. Eleven brothers, one sister.

²⁷Now it came to pass, at the time for giving birth, that behold, twins *were* in her womb. ²⁸And so it was, when she was giving birth, that *the one* put out *his* hand; and the midwife took a scarlet *thread* and bound it on his hand, saying, "This one came out first." ²⁹Then it happened, as he drew back his hand, that his brother came out unexpectedly; and she said, "How did you break through? *This* breach *be* upon you!" Therefore his name was called Perez. ³⁰Afterward his brother came out who had the scarlet *thread* on his hand. And his name was called Zerah.

CHAPTER **39** **POTIPHAR BUYS JOSEPH.** Now Joseph had been taken down to Egypt. And Potiphar, an officer of Pharaoh, captain of the guard, an Egyptian, bought him from the Ishmaelites who had taken him down there. ²The LORD was with Joseph, and he was a successful man; and he was in the house of his master the Egyptian. ³And his master saw that the LORD *was* with him and that the LORD made all he did to prosper in his hand.

⁴So Joseph found favor in his sight, and served him. Then he made him overseer of his house, and all *that* he had he put under his authority. ⁵So it was, from the time *that* he had made him overseer of his house and all that he had, that the LORD blessed the Egyptian's house for Joseph's sake; and the blessing of the LORD was on all that he had in the house and in the field. ⁶Thus he left all that he had in Joseph's hand, and he did not know what he had except for the bread which he ate.

Now Joseph was handsome in form and appearance.

⁷And it came to pass after these things that his master's wife cast longing eyes on Joseph, and she said, "Lie with me."

⁸But he refused and said to his master's wife, "Look, my master does not know what *is* with me in the house, and he has committed all that he has to my hand. ⁹*There is* no one greater in this house than I, nor has he kept back anything from me but you, because you *are* his wife. How then can I do this great wickedness, and sin against God?"

¹⁰So it was, as she spoke to Joseph day by day, that he did not heed her, to lie with her *or* to be with her.

¹¹But it happened about this time, when Joseph went into the house to do his work, and none of the men of the house *was* inside, ¹²that she caught him by his garment, saying, "Lie with me." But he left his garment in her hand, and fled and ran outside. ¹³And so it was, when she saw that he had left his garment in her hand and fled outside, ¹⁴that she called to the men of her house and spoke to them, saying, "See, he has brought in to us a Hebrew to mock us. He came in to me to lie with me, and I cried out with a loud voice. ¹⁵And it happened, when he heard that I lifted my voice and cried out, that he left his garment with me, and fled and went outside."

¹⁶So she kept his garment with her until his master came home. ¹⁷Then she spoke to him with words like these, saying, "The Hebrew servant whom you brought to us came in to me to mock me; ¹⁸so it happened, as I lifted my voice and cried out, that he left his garment with me and fled outside."

JOSEPH

Some people think they can be or do anything! That was Joseph. He was naturally self-confident. He was also Jacob's favorite son. God had given Joseph a strong sense that there were great plans for his life. Sometimes, though, he wasn't very sensitive of others' feelings. All this made Joseph's brothers jealous and angry. Eventually they tried to get rid of him.

As he grew, Joseph learned. His self-confidence was changed by the painful experiences in his life into a quiet but powerful confidence in God. He was able to survive and do well where most people would have failed. He added practical wisdom to his confidence and won the hearts of almost everyone who got to know him—Potiphar, the jailer, other prisoners, the king, and after many years even those 10 older brothers.

Perhaps you can identify with one or more of these hardships Joseph experienced—he was betrayed and deserted by his family, exposed to sexual temptation, punished for doing the right thing, imprisoned for a long time, and forgotten by those he helped. As you read his story, note what Joseph did in each case. His positive response transformed each setback into a step forward. He didn't spend much time asking why. His approach was, what shall I do now? Those who watched his life were aware that wherever Joseph went and whatever he did, God was with him. The next time things go wrong, try the Joseph approach. Start by reminding yourself God is with you. There is nothing like knowing he is there to help you work things out.

LESSONS: What matters is not so much the events or circumstances of life, but our responses to them

With God's help, any situation can be used for good, even when others intend it for evil

KEY VERSE: "Pharaoh said to his servants, 'Can we find such a one as this, a man in whom *is* the Spirit of God?'" (Genesis 41:38).

Joseph's story is told in Genesis 37–50. He is also mentioned in Hebrews 11:22.

UPS:
• Rose in power from slave to ruler of Egypt
• Was known for his personal integrity
• Was a man of spiritual sensitivity
• Prepared a nation to survive a famine

DOWNS:
• His youthful pride caused friction with his brothers

STATS:
• Where: Canaan, Egypt
• Occupation: Shepherd, slave, convict, ruler
• Relatives: Parents: Jacob and Rachel. Eleven brothers, one sister. Wife: Asenath. Sons: Manasseh and Ephraim.

and he married her and went in to her. ³So she conceived and bore a son, and he called his name Er. ⁴She conceived again and bore a son, and she called his name Onan. ⁵And she conceived yet again and bore a son, and called his name Shelah. He was at Chezib when she bore him.

⁶Then Judah took a wife for Er his firstborn, and her name *was* Tamar. ⁷But Er, Judah's firstborn, was wicked in the sight of the LORD, and the LORD killed him. ⁸And Judah said to Onan, "Go in to your brother's wife and marry her, and raise up an heir to your brother." ⁹But Onan knew that the heir would not be his; and it came to pass, when he went in to his brother's wife, that he emitted on the ground, lest he should give an heir to his brother. ¹⁰And

◣ SEDUCTION

39:9 Potiphar's wife failed to seduce Joseph, who resisted this temptation by saying it would be a sin against God. Joseph didn't say, "I'd be hurting you," or "I'd be sinning against Potiphar," or "I'd be sinning against myself." Under pressure, such excuses are easily rationalized away. Remember that sexual sin is not just between two consenting adults. It is an act of disobedience to God.

the thing which he did displeased the LORD; therefore He killed him also.

¹¹Then Judah said to Tamar his daughter-in-law, "Remain a widow in your father's house till my son Shelah is grown." For he said, "Lest he also die like his brothers." And Tamar went and dwelt in her father's house.

¹²Now in the process of time the daughter of Shua, Judah's wife, died; and Judah was comforted, and went up to his sheepshearers at Timnah, he and his friend Hirah the Adullamite. ¹³And it was told Tamar, saying, "Look, your father-in-law is going up to Timnah to shear his sheep." ¹⁴So she took off her widow's garments, covered *herself* with a veil and wrapped herself, and sat in an open place which *was* on the way to Timnah; for she saw that Shelah was grown, and she was not given to him as a wife. ¹⁵When Judah saw her, he thought she *was* a harlot, because she had covered her face. ¹⁶Then he turned to her by the way, and said, "Please let me come in to

◣ TURN AND RUN

39:10-15 Joseph avoided Potiphar's wife as much as possible. He refused her advances and finally *ran* from her. Sometimes merely trying to avoid temptation is not enough. We must turn and run, especially when the temptations seem very strong, as is often the case in sexual temptations.

you"; for he did not know that she *was* his daughter-in-law.

So she said, "What will you give me, that you may come in to me?"

¹⁷And he said, "I will send a young goat from the flock." So she said, "Will you give *me* a pledge till you send *it*?"

¹⁸Then he said, "What pledge shall I give you?"

So she said, "Your signet and cord, and your staff that *is* in your hand." Then he gave *them* to her, and went in to her, and she conceived by him. ¹⁹So she arose and went away, and laid aside her veil and put on the garments of her widowhood.

²⁰And Judah sent the young goat by the hand of his

WOMEN IN JESUS' FAMILY TREE

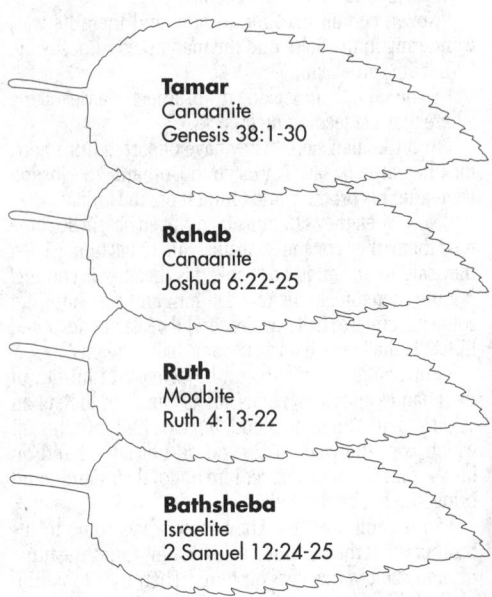

Tamar
Canaanite
Genesis 38:1-30

Rahab
Canaanite
Joshua 6:22-25

Ruth
Moabite
Ruth 4:13-22

Bathsheba
Israelite
2 Samuel 12:24-25

friend the Adullamite, to receive *his* pledge from the woman's hand, but he did not find her. ²¹Then he asked the men of that place, saying, "Where is the harlot who *was* openly by the roadside?"

And they said, "There was no harlot in this *place*."

²²So he returned to Judah and said, "I cannot find her. Also, the men of the place said there was no harlot in this *place*."

²³Then Judah said, "Let her take *them* for herself, lest we be shamed; for I sent this young goat and you have not found her."

²⁴And it came to pass, about three months after, that Judah was told, saying, "Tamar your daughter-in-law has played the harlot; furthermore she *is* with child by harlotry."

So Judah said, "Bring her out and let her be burned!"

²⁵When she *was* brought out, she sent to her father-in-law, saying, "By the man to whom these belong, I *am* with child." And she said, "Please determine whose these *are*—the signet and cord, and staff."

²⁶So Judah acknowledged *them* and said, "She has been more righteous than I, because I did not give her to Shelah my son." And he never knew her again.

◣ POSITIVE ATTITUDE

39:21-23 As a prisoner and slave, Joseph could have seen his situation as hopeless. Instead, he did his best with each small task him. His diligence and positive attitude were soon noticed by the of the prison, who promoted him to prison administrator. Are you midst of a seemingly hopeless predicament? At work, at home, or school, follow Joseph's example by taking each small task and do your best. Remember how God turned Joseph's situation around. see your efforts and can reverse even overwhelming odds.

40:8 When the subject of dreams came up, Joseph focused everyone's attention on God. Rather than using the situation to make himself look good, he turned it into a powerful witness for the Lord. One secret of effective witnessing is to recognize opportunities to relate God to the other person's experience. When the opportunity arises, we must have the courage to speak, as Joseph did.

¹⁹So it was, when his master heard the words which his wife spoke to him, saying, "Your servant did to me after this manner," that his anger was aroused. ²⁰Then Joseph's master took him and put him into the prison, a place where the king's prisoners *were* confined. And he was there in the prison. ²¹But the LORD was with Joseph and showed him mercy, and He gave him favor in the sight of the keeper of the prison. ²²And the keeper of the prison committed to Joseph's hand all the prisoners who *were* in the prison; whatever they did there, it was his doing. ²³The keeper of the prison did not look into anything *that was* under *Joseph's* authority, because the LORD was with him; and whatever he did, the LORD made *it* prosper.

CHAPTER 40 JOSEPH EXPLAINS TWO DREAMS.

It came to pass after these things *that* the butler and the baker of the king of Egypt offended their lord, the king of Egypt. ²And Pharaoh was angry with his two officers, the chief butler and the chief baker. ³So he put them in custody in the house of the captain of the guard, in the prison, the place where Joseph *was* confined. ⁴And the captain of the guard charged Joseph with them, and he served them; so they were in custody for a while.

⁵Then the butler and the baker of the king of Egypt, who *were* confined in the prison, had a dream, both of them, each man's dream in one night *and* each man's dream with its *own* interpretation. ⁶And Joseph came in to them in the morning and looked at them, and saw that they *were* sad. ⁷So he asked Pharaoh's officers who *were* with him in the custody of his lord's house, saying, "Why do you look *so* sad today?"

⁸And they said to him, "We each have had a dream, and *there is* no interpreter of it."

So Joseph said to them, "Do not interpretations belong to God? Tell *them* to me, please."

⁹Then the chief butler told his dream to Joseph, and said to him, "Behold, in my dream a vine *was* before me, ¹⁰and in the vine *were* three branches; it *was* as though it budded, its blossoms shot forth, and its clusters brought forth ripe grapes. ¹¹Then Pharaoh's cup *was* in my hand; and I took the grapes and pressed them into Pharaoh's cup, and placed the cup in Pharaoh's hand."

¹²And Joseph said to him, "This *is* the interpretation of it: The three branches *are* three days. ¹³Now within three days Pharaoh will lift up your head and restore you to your place, and you will put Pharaoh's cup in his hand according to the former manner, when you were his butler. ¹⁴But remember me when it is well with you, and please show kindness to me; make mention of me to Pharaoh, and get me out of this house. ¹⁵For indeed I was stolen away from the land of the Hebrews; and also I have done nothing here that they should put me into the dungeon."

¹⁶When the chief baker saw that the interpretation was good, he said to Joseph, "I also *was* in my dream, and there *were* three white baskets on my head. ¹⁷In the uppermost basket *were* all kinds of baked goods for Pharaoh, and the birds ate them out of the basket on my head."

¹⁸So Joseph answered and said, "This *is* the interpretation of it: The three baskets *are* three days. ¹⁹Within three days Pharaoh will lift off your head from you and hang you on a tree; and the birds will eat your flesh from you."

²⁰Now it came to pass on the third day, *which was* Pharaoh's birthday, that he made a feast for all his servants; and he lifted up the head of the chief butler and of the chief baker among his servants. ²¹Then he restored the chief butler to his butlership again, and he placed the cup in Pharaoh's hand. ²²But he hanged the chief baker, as Joseph had interpreted to them. ²³Yet the chief butler did not remember Joseph, but forgot him.

CHAPTER 41 JOSEPH BECOMES THE RULER.

Then it came to pass, at the end of two full years, that Pharaoh had a dream; and behold, he stood by the river. ²Suddenly there came up out of the river seven cows, fine looking and fat; and they fed in the meadow. ³Then behold, seven other cows came up after them out of the river, ugly and gaunt, and stood by the *other* cows on the bank of the river. ⁴And the ugly and gaunt cows ate up the seven fine looking and fat cows. So Pharaoh awoke. ⁵He slept and dreamed a second time; and suddenly seven heads of grain came up on one stalk, plump and good. ⁶Then behold, seven thin heads, blighted by the east wind, sprang up after them. ⁷And the seven thin heads devoured the seven plump and full heads. So Pharaoh awoke, and indeed, *it was* a dream. ⁸Now it came to pass in the morning that his spirit was troubled, and he sent and called for all the magicians of Egypt and all its wise men. And Pharaoh told them his dreams, but *there was* no one who could interpret them for Pharaoh.

⁹Then the chief butler spoke to Pharaoh, saying: "I remember my faults this day. ¹⁰When Pharaoh was angry with his servants, and put me in custody in the house of the captain of the guard, *both* me and the chief baker, ¹¹we each had a dream in one night, he and I. Each of us dreamed according to the interpretation of his *own* dream. ¹²Now there *was* a young Hebrew man with us there, a servant of the captain of the guard. And we told him, and he interpreted our dreams for us; to each man he interpreted according to his *own* dream. ¹³And it came to pass, just as he interpreted for us, so it happened. He restored me to my office, and he hanged him."

¹⁴Then Pharaoh sent and called Joseph, and they brought him quickly out of the dungeon; and he shaved,

41:14 Our most important opportunities may come when we lea[st] expect them. Joseph was brought hastily from the dungeon and pu[t] before Pharaoh. Did he have time to prepare? Yes and no. He had [no] warning that he suddenly would be pulled from prison and questio[ned by] the king. Yet Joseph was ready for almost anything because of his [close] relationship with God. It was not Joseph's knowledge of dreams th[at] helped him interpret their meaning. It was his knowledge of God. [Be] ready for opportunities by getting to know more about God. Then [you] will be ready to take on almost anything that comes your way.

changed his clothing, and came to Pharaoh. ¹⁵And Pharaoh said to Joseph, "I have had a dream, and *there is* no one who can interpret it. But I have heard it said of you *that* you can understand a dream, to interpret it."

¹⁶So Joseph answered Pharaoh, saying, "*It is* not in me; God will give Pharaoh an answer of peace."

¹⁷Then Pharaoh said to Joseph: "Behold, in my dream I stood on the bank of the river. ¹⁸Suddenly seven cows came up out of the river, fine looking and fat; and they fed in the meadow. ¹⁹Then behold, seven other cows came up after them, poor and very ugly and gaunt, such ugliness as I have never seen in all the land of Egypt. ²⁰And the gaunt and ugly cows ate up the first seven, the fat cows. ²¹When they had eaten them up, no one would have known that they had eaten them, for they *were* just as ugly as at the beginning. So I awoke. ²²Also I saw in my dream, and suddenly seven heads came up on one stalk, full and good. ²³Then behold, seven heads, withered, thin, *and* blighted by the east wind, sprang up after them. ²⁴And the thin heads devoured the seven good heads. So I told *this* to the magicians, but *there was* no one who could explain *it* to me."

²⁵Then Joseph said to Pharaoh, "The dreams of Pharaoh *are* one; God has shown Pharaoh what He *is* about to do: ²⁶The seven good cows *are* seven years, and the seven good heads *are* seven years; the dreams *are* one. ²⁷And the seven thin and ugly cows which came up after them *are* seven years, and the seven empty heads blighted by the east wind are seven years of famine. ²⁸This *is* the thing which I have spoken to Pharaoh. God has shown Pharaoh what He *is* about to do. ²⁹Indeed seven years of great plenty will come throughout all the land of Egypt; ³⁰but after them seven years of famine will arise, and all the plenty will be forgotten in the land of Egypt; and the famine will deplete the land. ³¹So the plenty will not be known in the land because of the famine following, for it *will be* very severe. ³²And the dream was repeated to Pharaoh twice because the thing *is* established by God, and God will shortly bring it to pass.

³³"Now therefore, let Pharaoh select a discerning and wise man, and set him over the land of Egypt. ³⁴Let Pharaoh do *this*, and let him appoint officers over the land, to collect one-fifth *of the produce* of the land of Egypt in the seven plentiful years. ³⁵And let them gather all the food of those good years that are coming, and store up grain under the authority of Pharaoh, and let them keep food in the cities. ³⁶Then that food shall be as a reserve for the land for the seven years of famine which shall be in the land of Egypt, that the land may not perish during the famine."

³⁷So the advice was good in the eyes of Pharaoh and in the eyes of all his servants. ³⁸And Pharaoh said to his servants, "Can we find *such a one* as this, a man in whom *is* the Spirit of God?"

³⁹Then Pharaoh said to Joseph, "Inasmuch as God has shown you all this, *there is* no one as discerning and wise as you. ⁴⁰You shall be over my house, and all my people shall be ruled according to your word; only in regard to the throne will I be greater than you." ⁴¹And Pharaoh said to Joseph, "See, I have set you over all the land of Egypt." ⁴²Then Pharaoh took his signet ring off his hand and

put it on Joseph's hand; and he clothed him in garments of fine linen and put a gold chain around his neck. ⁴³And he had him ride in the second chariot which he had; and they cried out before him, "Bow the knee!" So he set him over all the land of Egypt. ⁴⁴Pharaoh also said to Joseph, "I *am* Pharaoh, and without your consent no man may lift his hand or foot in all the land of Egypt." ⁴⁵And Pharaoh called Joseph's name Zaphnath-Paaneah. And he gave him as a wife Asenath, the daughter of Poti-Pherah priest of On. So Joseph went out over *all* the land of Egypt.

◣◥◤ TRAINING PROGRAM

41:38-40 Joseph rose quickly to the top, from prison walls to Pharaoh's palace. His training for this important position involved being first a slave and then a prisoner. In each situation he learned the importance of serving God and others. Whatever your situation, no matter how undesirable, consider it part of your training program for serving God.

⁴⁶Joseph was thirty years old when he stood before Pharaoh king of Egypt. And Joseph went out from the presence of Pharaoh, and went throughout all the land of Egypt. ⁴⁷Now in the seven plentiful years the ground brought forth abundantly. ⁴⁸So he gathered up all the food of the seven years which were in the land of Egypt, and laid up the food in the cities; he laid up in every city the food of the fields which surrounded them. ⁴⁹Joseph gathered very much grain, as the sand of the sea, until he stopped counting, for it *was* immeasurable.

⁵⁰And to Joseph were born two sons before the years of famine came, whom Asenath, the daughter of Poti-Pherah priest of On, bore to him. ⁵¹Joseph called the name of the firstborn Manasseh: "For God has made me forget all my toil and all my father's house." ⁵²And the name of the second he called Ephraim: "For God has caused me to be fruitful in the land of my affliction."

⁵³Then the seven years of plenty which were in the land of Egypt ended, ⁵⁴and the seven years of famine began to come, as Joseph had said. The famine was in all lands, but in all the land of Egypt there was bread. ⁵⁵So when all the land of Egypt was famished, the people cried to Pharaoh for bread. Then Pharaoh said to all the Egyptians, "Go to Joseph; whatever he says to you, do." ⁵⁶The famine was over all the face of the earth, and Joseph opened all the storehouses and sold to the Egyptians. And the famine became severe in the land of Egypt. ⁵⁷So all countries came to Joseph in Egypt to buy *grain*, because the famine was severe in all lands.

CHAPTER 42 JOSEPH'S BROTHERS BUY GRAIN.

When Jacob saw that there was grain in Egypt, Jacob said to his sons, "Why do you look at one another?" ²And he said, "Indeed I have heard that there is grain in Egypt; go down to that place and buy for us there, that we may live and not die."

³So Joseph's ten brothers went down to buy grain in Egypt. ⁴But Jacob did not send Joseph's brother Benjamin with his brothers, for he said, "Lest some calamity befall him." ⁵And the sons of Israel went to buy *grain* among

those who journeyed, for the famine was in the land of Canaan.

⁶Now Joseph *was* governor over the land; and it was he who sold to all the people of the land. And Joseph's brothers came and bowed down before him with *their* faces to the earth. ⁷Joseph saw his brothers and recognized them, but he acted as a stranger to them and spoke roughly to them. Then he said to them, "Where do you come from?"

And they said, "From the land of Canaan to buy food."

◀ BAD MEMORIES

42:7 Joseph could have revealed his identity to his brothers at once. But Joseph's last memory of them was of staring in horror at their faces as slave traders carried him away. Were his brothers still evil and treacherous, or had they changed over the years? Joseph decided to put them through a few tests to find out.

⁸So Joseph recognized his brothers, but they did not recognize him. ⁹Then Joseph remembered the dreams which he had dreamed about them, and said to them, "You *are* spies! You have come to see the nakedness of the land!"

¹⁰And they said to him, "No, my lord, but your servants have come to buy food. ¹¹We *are* all one man's sons; we *are* honest *men;* your servants are not spies."

¹²But he said to them, "No, but you have come to see the nakedness of the land."

¹³And they said, "Your servants *are* twelve brothers, the sons of one man in the land of Canaan; and in fact, the youngest *is* with our father today, and one *is* no more."

¹⁴But Joseph said to them, "It *is* as I spoke to you, saying, 'You *are* spies!' ¹⁵In this *manner* you shall be tested: By the life of Pharaoh, you shall not leave this place unless your youngest brother comes here. ¹⁶Send one of you, and let him bring your brother; and you shall be kept in prison, that your words may be tested to see whether *there is* any truth in you; or else, by the life of Pharaoh, surely you *are* spies!" ¹⁷So he put them all together in prison three days.

¹⁸Then Joseph said to them the third day, "Do this and live, *for* I fear God: ¹⁹If you *are* honest *men,* let one of your brothers be confined to your prison house; but you, go and carry grain for the famine of your houses. ²⁰And bring your youngest brother to me; so your words will be verified, and you shall not die."

And they did so. ²¹Then they said to one another, "We *are* truly guilty concerning our brother, for we saw the anguish of his soul when he pleaded with us, and we would not hear; therefore this distress has come upon us."

²²And Reuben answered them, saying, "Did I not speak to you, saying, 'Do not sin against the boy'; and you would not listen? Therefore behold, his blood is now required of us." ²³But they did not know that Joseph understood *them,* for he spoke to them through an interpreter. ²⁴And he turned himself away from them and wept. Then he returned to them again, and talked with them. And he took Simeon from them and bound him before their eyes.

²⁵Then Joseph gave a command to fill their sacks with grain, to restore every man's money to his sack, and to give them provisions for the journey. Thus he did for them. ²⁶So they loaded their donkeys with the grain and departed from there. ²⁷But as one *of them* opened his sack to give his donkey feed at the encampment, he saw his money; and there it was, in the mouth of his sack. ²⁸So he said to his brothers, "My money has been restored, and there it is, in my sack!" Then their hearts failed *them* and they were afraid, saying to one another, "What *is* this *that* God has done to us?"

²⁹Then they went to Jacob their father in the land of Canaan and told him all that had happened to them, saying: ³⁰"The man *who is* lord of the land spoke roughly to us, and took us for spies of the country. ³¹But we said to him, 'We *are* honest *men;* we are not spies. ³²We *are* twelve brothers, sons of our father; one *is* no *more,* and the youngest *is* with our father this day in the land of Canaan.' ³³Then the man, the lord of the country, said to us, 'By this I will know that you *are* honest *men:* Leave one of your brothers *here* with me, take *food for* the famine of your households, and be gone. ³⁴And bring your youngest brother to me; so I shall know that you *are* not spies, but *that* you *are* honest *men.* I will grant your brother to you, and you may trade in the land.' "

³⁵Then it happened as they emptied their sacks, that surprisingly each man's bundle of money *was* in his sack; and when they and their father saw the bundles of money, they were afraid. ³⁶And Jacob their father said to them, "You have bereaved me: Joseph is no *more,* Simeon is no *more,* and you want to take Benjamin. All these things are against me."

³⁷Then Reuben spoke to his father, saying, "Kill my two sons if I do not bring him *back* to you; put him in my hands, and I will bring him back to you."

³⁸But he said, "My son shall not go down with you, for his brother is dead, and he is left alone. If any calamity should befall him along the way in which you go, then you would bring down my gray hair with sorrow to the grave."

CHAPTER **43** JOSEPH'S BROTHERS RETURN.

Now the famine *was* severe in the land. ²And it came to pass, when they had eaten up the grain which they had brought from Egypt, that their father said to them, "Go back, buy us a little food."

³But Judah spoke to him, saying, "The man solemnly warned us, saying, 'You shall not see my face unless your brother *is* with you.' ⁴If you send our brother with us, we will go down and buy you food. ⁵But if you will not send *him,* we will not go down; for the man said to us, 'You shall not see my face unless your brother *is* with you.' "

⁶And Israel said, "Why did you deal *so* wrongfully with me *as* to tell the man whether you had still *another* brother?"

⁷But they said, "The man asked us pointedly about ourselves and our family, saying, '*Is* your father still alive? Have you *another* brother?' And we told him according to these words. Could we possibly have known that he would say, 'Bring your brother down'?"

⁸Then Judah said to Israel his father, "Send the lad with

me, and we will arise and go, that we may live and not die, both we and you *and* also our little ones. ⁹I myself will be surety for him; from my hand you shall require him. If I do not bring him *back* to you and set him before you, then let me bear the blame forever. ¹⁰For if we had not lingered, surely by now we would have returned this second time."

¹¹And their father Israel said to them, "If *it must be* so, then do this: Take some of the best fruits of the land in your vessels and carry down a present for the man—a little balm and a little honey, spices and myrrh, pistachio nuts and almonds. ¹²Take double money in your hand, and take back in your hand the money that was returned in the mouth of your sacks; perhaps it was an oversight. ¹³Take your brother also, and arise, go back to the man. ¹⁴And may God Almighty give you mercy before the man, that he may release your other brother and Benjamin. If I am bereaved, I am bereaved!"

¹⁵So the men took that present and Benjamin, and they took double money in their hand, and arose and went down to Egypt; and they stood before Joseph. ¹⁶When Joseph saw Benjamin with them, he said to the steward of his house, "Take *these* men to my home, and slaughter an animal and make ready; for *these* men will dine with me at noon." ¹⁷Then the man did as Joseph ordered, and the man brought the men into Joseph's house.

¹⁸Now the men were afraid because they were brought into Joseph's house; and they said, "*It is* because of the money, which was returned in our sacks the first time, that we are brought in, so that he may make a case against us and seize us, to take us as slaves with our donkeys."

¹⁹When they drew near to the steward of Joseph's house, they talked with him at the door of the house, ²⁰and said, "O sir, we indeed came down the first time to buy food; ²¹but it happened, when we came to the encampment, that we opened our sacks, and there, *each* man's money *was* in the mouth of his sack, our money in full weight; so we have brought it back in our hand. ²²And we have brought down other money in our hands to buy food. We do not know who put our money in our sacks."

²³But he said, "Peace *be* with you, do not be afraid. Your God and the God of your father has given you treasure in your sacks; I had your money." Then he brought Simeon out to them.

²⁴So the man brought the men into Joseph's house and gave *them* water, and they washed their feet; and he gave their donkeys feed. ²⁵Then they made the present ready for Joseph's coming at noon, for they heard that they would eat bread there.

²⁶And when Joseph came home, they brought him the present which *was* in their hand into the house, and bowed down before him to the earth. ²⁷Then he asked them about *their* well-being, and said, "*Is* your father well, the old man of whom you spoke? *Is* he still alive?"

²⁸And they answered, "Your servant our father *is* in good health; he *is* still alive." And they bowed their heads down and prostrated themselves.

²⁹Then he lifted his eyes and saw his brother Benjamin, his mother's son, and said, "*Is* this your younger brother of whom you spoke to me?" And he said, "God be gracious to you, my son." ³⁰Now his heart yearned for his brother; so Joseph made haste and sought *somewhere* to weep. And he went into *his* chamber and wept there. ³¹Then he washed his face and came out; and he restrained himself, and said, "Serve the bread."

◣◣◣ FULL RESPONSIBILITY

43:9 Judah accepted full responsibility for Benjamin's safety. He did not know what that might mean for him, but he was determined to carry it out. In the end it was Judah's stirring words that caused Joseph to break down and reveal himself to his brothers (44:18-34). Accepting and fulfilling responsibilities is difficult, but it builds character and confidence, earns others' respect, and motivates us to complete our work. When you have been given an assignment to complete or a responsibility to fulfill, commit yourself to seeing it through.

³²So they set him a place by himself, and them by themselves, and the Egyptians who ate with him by themselves; because the Egyptians could not eat food with the Hebrews, for that *is* an abomination to the Egyptians. ³³And they sat before him, the firstborn according to his birthright and the youngest according to his youth; and the men looked in astonishment at one another. ³⁴Then he took servings to them from before him, but Benjamin's serving was five times as much as any of theirs. So they drank and were merry with him.

CHAPTER **44** JOSEPH TESTS HIS BROTHERS.

And he commanded the steward of his house, saying, "Fill the men's sacks with food, as much as they can carry, and put each man's money in the mouth of his sack. ²Also put my cup, the silver cup, in the mouth of the sack of the youngest, and his grain money." So he did according to the word that Joseph had spoken. ³As soon as the morning dawned, the men were sent away, they and their donkeys. ⁴When they had gone out of the city, *and* were not *yet* far off, Joseph said to his steward, "Get up, follow the men; and when you overtake them, say to them, 'Why have you repaid evil for good? ⁵*Is* not this *the one* from which my lord drinks, and with which he indeed practices divination? You have done evil in so doing.' "

⁶So he overtook them, and he spoke to them these same words. ⁷And they said to him, "Why does my lord say these words? Far be it from us that your servants should do such a thing. ⁸Look, we brought back to you from the land of Canaan the money which we found in the mouth of our sacks. How then could we steal silver or gold from your lord's house? ⁹With whomever of your servants it is found, let him die, and we also will be my lord's slaves."

¹⁰And he said, "Now also *let* it *be* according to your words; he with whom it is found shall be my slave, and you shall be blameless." ¹¹Then each man speedily let down his sack to the ground, and each opened his sack. ¹²So he searched. He began with the oldest and left off with the youngest; and the cup was found in Benjamin's sack. ¹³Then they tore their clothes, and each man loaded his donkey and returned to the city.

¹⁴So Judah and his brothers came to Joseph's house,

CHANGED LIFE

44:16-34 When Judah was younger, he showed no regard for his brother Joseph or his father, Jacob. First he convinced his brothers to sell Joseph as a slave (37:27); then he joined his brothers in lying to his father about Joseph's fate (37:32). But what a change had taken place in Judah! The man who sold one favored little brother into slavery now offered to become a slave himself to save another favored little brother. He was so concerned for his father and younger brother that he was willing to die for them. When you are ready to give up hope on yourself or others, remember that God can change even the most selfish personality.

and he *was* still there; and they fell before him on the ground. ¹⁵And Joseph said to them, "What deed *is* this you have done? Did you not know that such a man as I can certainly practice divination?"

¹⁶Then Judah said, "What shall we say to my lord? What shall we speak? Or how shall we clear ourselves? God has found out the iniquity of your servants; here we are, my lord's slaves, both we and *he* also with whom the cup was found."

¹⁷But he said, "Far be it from me that I should do so; the man in whose hand the cup was found, he shall be my slave. And as for you, go up in peace to your father."

¹⁸Then Judah came near to him and said: "O my lord, please let your servant speak a word in my lord's hearing, and do not let your anger burn against your servant; for you *are* even like Pharaoh. ¹⁹My lord asked his servants, saying, 'Have you a father or a brother?' ²⁰And we said to my lord, 'We have a father, an old man, and a child of *his* old age, *who is* young; his brother is dead, and he alone

INTENTIONS

45:4-8 Although Joseph's brothers had wanted to get rid of him, God used even their evil actions to fulfill his ultimate plan. He sent Joseph ahead to preserve their lives, save Egypt, and prepare the way for the beginning of the nation of Israel. God is in control. His plans are not dictated by human actions. When others intend evil toward you, remember that they are only God's tools. As Joseph said to his brothers, "You meant evil against me; *but* God meant it for good, in order to bring it about as *it is* this day, to save many people alive" (50:20).

is left of his mother's children, and his father loves him.' ²¹Then you said to your servants, 'Bring him down to me, that I may set my eyes on him.' ²²And we said to my lord, 'The lad cannot leave his father, for *if* he should leave his father, *his father* would die.' ²³But you said to your servants, 'Unless your youngest brother comes down with you, you shall see my face no more.'

²⁴"So it was, when we went up to your servant my father, that we told him the words of my lord. ²⁵And our father said, 'Go back *and* buy us a little food.' ²⁶But we said, 'We cannot go down; if our youngest brother is with us, then we will go down; for we may not see the man's face unless our youngest brother *is* with us.' ²⁷Then your servant my father said to us, 'You know that my wife bore me two sons; ²⁸and the one went out from me, and I said, "Surely he is torn to pieces"; and I have not seen him since. ²⁹But if you take this one also from me, and calamity befalls him, you shall bring down my gray hair with sorrow to the grave.'

³⁰"Now therefore, when I come to your servant my

father, and the lad *is* not with us, since his life is bound up in the lad's life, ³¹it will happen, when he sees that the lad *is* not *with us,* that he will die. So your servants will bring down the gray hair of your servant our father with sorrow to the grave. ³²For your servant became surety for the lad to my father, saying, 'If I do not bring him *back* to you, then I shall bear the blame before my father forever.' ³³Now therefore, please let your servant remain instead of the lad as a slave to my lord, and let the lad go up with his brothers. ³⁴For how shall I go up to my father if the lad *is* not with me, lest perhaps I see the evil that would come upon my father?"

CHAPTER 45 JOSEPH FORGIVES HIS BROTHERS.

Then Joseph could not restrain himself before all those who stood by him, and he cried out, "Make everyone go out from me!" So no one stood with him while Joseph made himself known to his brothers. ²And he wept aloud, and the Egyptians and the house of Pharaoh heard *it.*

³Then Joseph said to his brothers, "I *am* Joseph; does my father still live?" But his brothers could not answer him, for they were dismayed in his presence. ⁴And Joseph said to his brothers, "Please come near to me." So they came near. Then he said: "I *am* Joseph your brother, whom you sold into Egypt. ⁵But now, do not therefore be grieved or angry with yourselves because you sold me here; for God sent me before you to preserve life. ⁶For these two years the famine *has been* in the land, and *there are* still five years in which *there will be* neither plowing nor harvesting. ⁷And God sent me before you to preserve a posterity for you in the earth, and to save your lives by a great deliverance. ⁸So now *it was* not you *who* sent me here, but God; and He has made me a father to Pharaoh, and lord of all his house, and a ruler throughout all the land of Egypt.

⁹"Hurry and go up to my father, and say to him, 'Thus says your son Joseph: "God has made me lord of all Egypt; come down to me, do not tarry. ¹⁰You shall dwell in the land of Goshen, and you shall be near to me, you and your children, your children's children, your flocks and your herds, and all that you have. ¹¹There I will provide for you, lest you and your household, and all that you have, come to poverty; for *there are* still five years of famine." '

¹²"And behold, your eyes and the eyes of my brother Benjamin see that *it is* my mouth that speaks to you. ¹³So you shall tell my father of all my glory in Egypt, and of all that you have seen; and you shall hurry and bring my father down here."

¹⁴Then he fell on his brother Benjamin's neck and wept, and Benjamin wept on his neck. ¹⁵Moreover he kissed all his brothers and wept over them, and after that his brothers talked with him.

¹⁶Now the report of it was heard in Pharaoh's house,

STRANGE PLACES

46:3-4 God told Jacob to leave his home and travel to a strange faraway land. But God reassured him by promising to go with him, take care of him. When new situations or surroundings frighten or you, recognize that experiencing fear is normal. To be paralyzed however, is an indication that you question God's ability to take ca you.

saying, "Joseph's brothers have come." So it pleased Pharaoh and his servants well. ¹⁷And Pharaoh said to Joseph, "Say to your brothers, 'Do this: Load your animals and depart; go to the land of Canaan. ¹⁸Bring your father and your households and come to me; I will give you the best of the land of Egypt, and you will eat the fat of the land. ¹⁹Now you are commanded—do this: Take carts out of the land of Egypt for your little ones and your wives; bring your father and come. ²⁰Also do not be concerned about your goods, for the best of all the land of Egypt *is* yours.' "

²¹Then the sons of Israel did so; and Joseph gave them carts, according to the command of Pharaoh, and he gave them provisions for the journey. ²²He gave to all of them, to each man, changes of garments; but to Benjamin he gave three hundred *pieces* of silver and five changes of garments. ²³And he sent to his father these *things:* ten donkeys loaded with the good things of Egypt, and ten female donkeys loaded with grain, bread, and food for his father for the journey.

²⁴So he sent his brothers away, and they departed; and he said to them, "See that you do not become troubled along the way."

²⁵Then they went up out of Egypt, and came to the land of Canaan to Jacob their father. ²⁶And they told him, saying, "Joseph *is* still alive, and he *is* governor over all the land of Egypt." And Jacob's heart stood still, because he did not believe them. ²⁷But when they told him all the words which Joseph had said to them, and when he saw the carts which Joseph had sent to carry him, the spirit of Jacob their father revived. ²⁸Then Israel said, "*It is* enough. Joseph my son *is* still alive. I will go and see him before I die."

CHAPTER **46** JACOB MOVES TO EGYPT.

So Israel took his journey with all that he had, and came to Beersheba, and offered sacrifices to the God of his father Isaac. ²Then God spoke to Israel in the visions of the night, and said, "Jacob, Jacob!"

And he said, "Here I am."

³So He said, "I *am* God, the God of your father; do not fear to go down to Egypt, for I will make of you a great nation there. ⁴I will go down with you to Egypt, and I will also surely bring you up *again;* and Joseph will put his hand on your eyes."

⁵Then Jacob arose from Beersheba; and the sons of Israel carried their father Jacob, their little ones, and their wives, in the carts which Pharaoh had sent to carry him. ⁶So they took their livestock and their goods, which they had acquired in the land of Canaan, and went to Egypt, Jacob and all his descendants with him. ⁷His sons and his sons' sons, his daughters and his sons' daughters, and all his descendants he brought with him to Egypt.

⁸Now these *were* the names of the children of Israel, Jacob and his sons, who went to Egypt: Reuben *was* Jacob's firstborn. ⁹The sons of Reuben *were* Hanoch, Pallu, Hezron, and Carmi. ¹⁰The sons of Simeon *were* Jemuel, Jamin, Ohad, Jachin, Zohar, and Shaul, the son of a Canaanite woman. ¹¹The sons of Levi *were* Gershon, Kohath, and Merari. ¹²The sons of Judah *were* Er, Onan, Shelah, Perez, and Zerah (but Er and Onan died in the

JUDAH

People who are leaders stand out at the right time. They don't necessarily act or look a certain way until the need for action comes along. Among their skills are the abilities to speak up, make decisions, take action, or take control. Leaders can use their skills for great good or great evil.

Jacob's fourth son, Judah, was a natural leader. His life included many opportunities to exercise his skills. Unfortunately, Judah's decisions were often shaped more by the pressures of the moment than by a desire to cooperate with God's plan. But when he did recognize his mistakes, he was willing to admit them. His experience with Tamar and the final confrontation with Joseph are both examples of Judah's willingness to take responsibility for his sins when confronted. That quality was a strength Judah passed on to his descendant David.

Whether or not we have natural leadership qualities like Judah, we do have just as hard a time as he did seeing our own sins. When we do discover we've done something wrong, we usually are not eager to admit it. From Judah we can learn that it is not wise to wait until our sins force us to admit we've done wrong. It is better to openly admit our mistakes, shoulder the blame, and seek forgiveness.

LESSONS: God is in control far beyond the immediate situation

Procrastination often brings about a worse result

Judah's offer to substitute his life for Benjamin's is a picture of what his descendant Jesus would do for all men

KEY VERSES: "Judah, you are he whom your brothers shall praise; your hand shall be on the neck of your enemies; your father's children shall bow down before you. Judah is a lion's whelp; from the prey, my son, you have gone up. He bows down, he lies down as a lion; and as a lion, who shall rouse him?" (Genesis 49:8-9).

Judah's story is told in Genesis 29:35–50:26. He is also mentioned in 1 Chronicles 2:4.

UPS:
• Was a natural leader—outspoken and decisive
• Thought clearly and took action in pressure situations
• Was willing to stand by his word and put himself on the line when necessary
• Was the fourth son of 12, and the one through whom God would eventually bring King David and Jesus, the Messiah

DOWNS:
• Suggested to his brothers they sell Joseph into slavery
• Failed to keep his promise to his daughter-in-law, Tamar

STATS:
• Where: Canaan, Egypt
• Occupation: Shepherd
• Relatives: Parents: Jacob and Leah. Wife: the daughter of Shua (1 Chronicles 2:3). Daughter-in-law: Tamar. Eleven brothers, one sister, and at least five sons (Genesis 29:31–30:24; 38:3-5, 27-30).

land of Canaan). The sons of Perez were Hezron and Hamul. ¹³The sons of Issachar *were* Tola, Puvah, Job, and Shimron. ¹⁴The sons of Zebulun *were* Sered, Elon, and Jahleel. ¹⁵These *were* the sons of Leah, whom she bore to Jacob in Padan Aram, with his daughter Dinah. All the persons, his sons and his daughters, *were* thirty-three.

¹⁶The sons of Gad *were* Ziphion, Haggi, Shuni, Ezbon, Eri, Arodi, and Areli. ¹⁷The sons of Asher *were* Jimnah, Ishuah, Isui, Beriah, and Serah, their sister. And the sons of Beriah *were* Heber and Malchiel. ¹⁸These *were* the sons of Zilpah, whom Laban gave to Leah his daughter; and these she bore to Jacob: sixteen persons.

¹⁹The sons of Rachel, Jacob's wife, *were* Joseph and Benjamin. ²⁰And to Joseph in the land of Egypt were born Manasseh and Ephraim, whom Asenath, the daughter of Poti-Pherah priest of On, bore to him. ²¹The sons of Benjamin *were* Belah, Becher, Ashbel, Gera, Naaman, Ehi, Rosh, Muppim, Huppim, and Ard. ²²These *were* the sons of Rachel, who were born to Jacob: fourteen persons in all.

²³The son of Dan *was* Hushim. ²⁴The sons of Naphtali *were* Jahzeel, Guni, Jezer, and Shillem. ²⁵These *were* the sons of Bilhah, whom Laban gave to Rachel his daughter, and she bore these to Jacob: seven persons in all.

²⁶All the persons who went with Jacob to Egypt, who came from his body, besides Jacob's sons' wives, *were* sixty-six persons in all. ²⁷And the sons of Joseph who were born to him in Egypt *were* two persons. All the persons of the house of Jacob who went to Egypt were seventy.

²⁸Then he sent Judah before him to Joseph, to point out before him *the way* to Goshen. And they came to the land of Goshen. ²⁹So Joseph made ready his chariot and went up to Goshen to meet his father Israel; and he presented himself to him, and fell on his neck and wept on his neck a good while.

³⁰And Israel said to Joseph, "Now let me die, since I have seen your face, because you *are* still alive." ³¹Then Joseph said to his brothers and to his father's household, "I will go up and tell Pharaoh, and say to him, 'My brothers and those of my father's house, who *were* in the land of Canaan, have come to me. ³²And the men *are* shepherds, for their occupation has been to feed livestock; and they have brought their flocks, their herds, and all that they have.' ³³So it shall be, when Pharaoh calls you and says, 'What is your occupation?' ³⁴that you shall say, 'Your servants' occupation has been with livestock from our youth even till now, both we *and* also our fathers,' that you may dwell in the land of Goshen; for every shepherd *is* an abomination to the Egyptians."

CHAPTER 47

Then Joseph went and told Pharaoh, and said, "My father and my brothers, their flocks and their herds and all that they possess, have come from the land of Canaan; and indeed they *are* in the land of Goshen." ²And he took five men from among his brothers and presented them to Pharaoh. ³Then Pharaoh said to his brothers, "What *is* your occupation?"

And they said to Pharaoh, "Your servants *are* shepherds, both we *and* also our fathers." ⁴And they said to Pharaoh, "We have come to dwell in the land, because your servants have no pasture for their flocks, for the famine *is* severe in the land of Canaan. Now therefore, please let your servants dwell in the land of Goshen."

⁵Then Pharaoh spoke to Joseph, saying, "Your father and your brothers have come to you. ⁶The land of Egypt *is* before you. Have your father and brothers dwell in the best of the land; let them dwell in the land of Goshen. And if you know *any* competent men among them, then make them chief herdsmen over my livestock."

KEEP THE FAITH

47:1-6 The faithfulness of Joseph affected his entire family. Whe was in prison, Joseph must have wondered about his future. Instea despairing, he faithfully obeyed God and did what was right. Here one of the exciting results. We may not always see the effects of ou faith, but we can be sure that God will honor faithfulness.

⁷Then Joseph brought in his father Jacob and set him before Pharaoh; and Jacob blessed Pharaoh. ⁸Pharaoh said to Jacob, "How old *are* you?"

⁹And Jacob said to Pharaoh, "The days of the years of my pilgrimage *are* one hundred and thirty years; few and evil have been the days of the years of my life, and they have not attained to the days of the years of the life of my fathers in the days of their pilgrimage." ¹⁰So Jacob blessed Pharaoh, and went out from before Pharaoh.

¹¹And Joseph situated his father and his brothers, and gave them a possession in the land of Egypt, in the best of the land, in the land of Rameses, as Pharaoh had commanded. ¹²Then Joseph provided his father, his brothers, and all his father's household with bread, according to the number in *their* families.

¹³Now *there was* no bread in all the land; for the famine *was* very severe, so that the land of Egypt and the land of Canaan languished because of the famine. ¹⁴And Joseph gathered up all the money that was found in the land of Egypt and in the land of Canaan, for the grain which they bought; and Joseph brought the money into Pharaoh's house.

¹⁵So when the money failed in the land of Egypt and in the land of Canaan, all the Egyptians came to Joseph and said, "Give us bread, for why should we die in your presence? For the money has failed."

¹⁶Then Joseph said, "Give your livestock, and I will give you *bread* for your livestock, if the money is gone." ¹⁷So they brought their livestock to Joseph, and Joseph gave them bread *in exchange* for the horses, the flocks, the cattle of the herds, and for the donkeys. Thus he fed them with bread *in exchange* for all their livestock that year.

¹⁸When that year had ended, they came to him the next year and said to him, "We will not hide from my lord that our money is gone; my lord also has our herds of

KEEPING YOUR WOR

47:29-31 Jacob had Joseph promise to bury him in his homela things were written in this culture, so a person's word then carried much force as a written contract today. People today seem to find to say, "I didn't mean what I said." God's people, however, are to the truth and live the truth. Let your words be as binding as a wri contract.

livestock. There is nothing left in the sight of my lord but our bodies and our lands. ¹⁹Why should we die before your eyes, both we and our land? Buy us and our land for bread, and we and our land will be servants of Pharaoh; give *us* seed, that we may live and not die, that the land may not be desolate."

²⁰Then Joseph bought all the land of Egypt for Pharaoh; for every man of the Egyptians sold his field, because the famine was severe upon them. So the land became Pharaoh's. ²¹And as for the people, he moved them into the cities, from *one* end of the borders of Egypt to the *other* end. ²²Only the land of the priests he did not buy; for the priests had rations *allotted to them* by Pharaoh, and they ate their rations which Pharaoh gave them; therefore they did not sell their lands.

²³Then Joseph said to the people, "Indeed I have bought you and your land this day for Pharaoh. Look, *here is* seed for you, and you shall sow the land. ²⁴And it shall come to pass in the harvest that you shall give one-fifth to Pharaoh. Four-fifths shall be your own, as seed for the field and for your food, for those of your households and as food for your little ones."

²⁵So they said, "You have saved our lives; let us find favor in the sight of my lord, and we will be Pharaoh's servants." ²⁶And Joseph made it a law over the land of Egypt to this day, *that* Pharaoh should have one-fifth, except for the land of the priests only, *which* did not become Pharaoh's.

²⁷So Israel dwelt in the land of Egypt, in the country of Goshen; and they had possessions there and grew and multiplied exceedingly. ²⁸And Jacob lived in the land of Egypt seventeen years. So the length of Jacob's life was one hundred and forty-seven years. ²⁹When the time drew near that Israel must die, he called his son Joseph and said to him, "Now if I have found favor in your sight, please put your hand under my thigh, and deal kindly and truly with me. Please do not bury me in Egypt, ³⁰but let me lie with my fathers; you shall carry me out of Egypt and bury me in their burial place."

And he said, "I will do as you have said."

³¹Then he said, "Swear to me." And he swore to him. So Israel bowed himself on the head of the bed.

CHAPTER **48** JACOB BLESSES JOSEPH'S SONS.

Now it came to pass after these things that Joseph was told, "Indeed your father *is* sick"; and he took with him his two sons, Manasseh and Ephraim. ²And Jacob was told, "Look, your son Joseph is coming to you"; and Israel strengthened himself and sat up on the bed. ³Then Jacob said to Joseph: "God Almighty appeared to me at Luz in the land of Canaan and blessed me, ⁴and said to me, Behold, I will make you fruitful and multiply you, and I will make of you a multitude of people, and give this land to your descendants after you *as* an everlasting possession.' ⁵And now your two sons, Ephraim and Manasseh, who were born to you in the land of Egypt before I came to you in Egypt, *are* mine; as Reuben and Simeon, they shall be mine. ⁶Your offspring whom you beget after them shall be yours; they will be called by the name of their brothers in their inheritance. ⁷But as for me, when I

came from Padan, Rachel died beside me in the land of Canaan on the way, when *there was* but a little distance to go to Ephrath; and I buried her there on the way to Ephrath (that is, Bethlehem)."

Bad things seem to happen all the time. Does God care about what is happening in the world?

I WONDER . . .

There are bad things that happen, and then there are tragedies. At some time in life everyone will experience both of these. Let's cover them one at a time.

The person who flunks a math test had something bad happen to him. Did he learn that it is important to keep up with assignments and study before a test? Hopefully.

A 10-year-old boy races out from behind a parked car and is almost hit by a car. He is scared to death, realizing that he could have been killed! Did he learn a lesson about not darting into the street? He better have; he may not get another chance!

In each case the person probably was not happy about what happened. But each situation in life, good or bad, is a learning experience.

Does God care that we learn important lessons about studying and safety? He cares very much!

Ask your folks about the five worst things that have happened to them. Then ask what they learned from these bad experiences. Finally, ask them if they were thankful that these occurred.

Going through tough times is bad only when you don't learn something when it's over.

Now let's discuss tragedy.

Unfortunately, no one is immune from what we believe is the ultimate tragedy—death. Even Jesus went through the loss of someone he loved (see John 11). It is the timing of death (especially when someone dies young), and how it occurs (like an innocent victim killed by a drunk driver), that makes us wonder if God really cares.

When Adam and Eve disobeyed God in the Garden of Eden, their punishment was separation from God. This incident also set in motion the life cycle, ending in death. But the good news is that Jesus Christ's death on the cross killed death! Not physical death, but spiritual death for all those who receive his gift of forgiveness.

The curse brought on the human race by Adam was physical death. Since that time people have discovered ways to make death happen in some pretty ugly ways (nuclear bombs, lung cancer, AIDS, and many others).

Still, as terrible as those may be, God knows that spiritual death is far worse than physical death. That's why he focused his attention on taking care of the real penalty for our sin—spiritual death! (See Romans 6:23.) God also knows how tragedy can point us to him and his purposes: "And we know that all things work together for good to those who love God (Romans 8:28).

Although God is not in heaven pushing buttons to make people die young, he can use any situation for good. And remember, whatever happens to you, God cares. He loves you and wants to work out his purposes in your life.

GOD'S SURPRISES

48:8-20 Jacob gave Ephraim the greater blessing, instead of his older brother Manasseh. When Joseph objected, Jacob refused to listen, because God had told him that Ephraim would become greater. God often works in unexpected ways. When he chooses people to fulfill his plans, he always goes deeper than appearance, tradition, or position. He sometimes surprises us by choosing the less obvious person. God can use you to carry out his plans, even if you don't think you have all the qualifications.

⁸Then Israel saw Joseph's sons, and said, "Who *are* these?"

⁹Joseph said to his father, "They *are* my sons, whom God has given me in this *place*."

And he said, "Please bring them to me, and I will bless them." ¹⁰Now the eyes of Israel were dim with age, *so that* he could not see. Then Joseph brought them near him, and he kissed them and embraced them. ¹¹And Israel said to Joseph, "I had not thought to see your face; but in fact, God has also shown me your offspring!"

NEVER SO BAD

48:11 When Joseph became a slave, Jacob thought he was dead and wept in despair (37:34). But eventually God's plan allowed Jacob to regain not only his son, but his grandchildren as well. Circumstances are never so bad that they are beyond God's help. Jacob regained his son. Job got a new family (Job 42:10-17). Mary regained her brother Lazarus (John 11:1-44). We need never despair because we belong to a loving God. We never know what good he will bring out of a seemingly hopeless situation.

¹²So Joseph brought them from beside his knees, and he bowed down with his face to the earth. ¹³And Joseph took them both, Ephraim with his right hand toward Israel's left hand, and Manasseh with his left hand toward Israel's right hand, and brought *them* near him. ¹⁴Then Israel stretched out his right hand and laid *it* on Ephraim's head, who *was* the younger, and his left hand on Manasseh's head, guiding his hands knowingly, for Manasseh *was* the firstborn. ¹⁵And he blessed Joseph, and said:

"God, before whom my fathers Abraham and Isaac walked,
The God who has fed me all my life long to this day,
¹⁶ The Angel who has redeemed me from all evil,
Bless the lads;
Let my name be named upon them,
And the name of my fathers Abraham and Isaac;
And let them grow into a multitude in the midst of the earth."

¹⁷Now when Joseph saw that his father laid his right hand on the head of Ephraim, it displeased him; so he took hold of his father's hand to remove it from Ephraim's head to Manasseh's head. ¹⁸And Joseph said to his father, "Not so, my father, for this *one is* the firstborn; put your right hand on his head."

¹⁹But his father refused and said, "I know, my son, I know. He also shall become a people, and he also shall be

great; but truly his younger brother shall be greater than he, and his descendants shall become a multitude of nations."

²⁰So he blessed them that day, saying, "By you Israel will bless, saying, 'May God make you as Ephraim and as Manasseh!' " And thus he set Ephraim before Manasseh.

²¹Then Israel said to Joseph, "Behold, I am dying, but God will be with you and bring you back to the land of your fathers. ²²Moreover I have given to you one portion above your brothers, which I took from the hand of the Amorite with my sword and my bow."

CHAPTER 49 JACOB TALKS ABOUT HIS SONS

And Jacob called his sons and said, "Gather together, that I may tell you what shall befall you in the last days:

² "Gather together and hear, you sons of Jacob,
And listen to Israel your father.

³ "Reuben, you are my firstborn,
My might and the beginning of my strength,
The excellency of dignity and the excellency of power.
⁴ Unstable as water, you shall not excel,
Because you went up to your father's bed;
Then you defiled *it*—
He went up to my couch.

⁵ "Simeon and Levi *are* brothers;
Instruments of cruelty *are in* their dwelling place.
⁶ Let not my soul enter their council;
Let not my honor be united to their assembly;
For in their anger they slew a man,
And in their self-will they hamstrung an ox.
⁷ Cursed *be* their anger, for *it is* fierce;
And their wrath, for it is cruel!
I will divide them in Jacob
And scatter them in Israel.

⁸ "Judah, you *are he* whom your brothers shall praise;
Your hand *shall be* on the neck of your enemies;
Your father's children shall bow down before you.
⁹ Judah *is* a lion's whelp;
From the prey, my son, you have gone up.
He bows down, he lies down as a lion;
And as a lion, who shall rouse him?
¹⁰ The scepter shall not depart from Judah,
Nor a lawgiver from between his feet,
Until Shiloh comes;
And to Him *shall be* the obedience of the people.
¹¹ Binding his donkey to the vine,
And his donkey's colt to the choice vine,
He washed his garments in wine,

FUTURE CHOICE

49:3-28 Jacob blessed each of his sons and then made a prediction about each one's future. The way the men had lived played an important part in Jacob's blessing and prophecy. Our past also affects our present and future. By sunrise tomorrow, our actions of today will have become part of the past. Yet they will already have begun to shape the future. What actions can you choose or avoid in order to positively shape your future?

And his clothes in the blood of grapes.
12 His eyes *are* darker than wine,
And his teeth whiter than milk.

13 "Zebulun shall dwell by the haven of the sea;
He *shall become* a haven for ships,
And his border shall adjoin Sidon.

14 "Issachar is a strong donkey,
Lying down between two burdens;
15 He saw that rest *was* good,
And that the land *was* pleasant;
He bowed his shoulder to bear *a burden,*
And became a band of slaves.

16 "Dan shall judge his people
As one of the tribes of Israel.
17 Dan shall be a serpent by the way,
A viper by the path,
That bites the horse's heels
So that its rider shall fall backward.

18 I have waited for your salvation, O LORD!

19 "Gad, a troop shall tramp upon him,
But he shall triumph at last.

20 "Bread from Asher *shall be* rich,
And he shall yield royal dainties.

21 "Naphtali *is* a deer let loose;
He uses beautiful words.

22 "Joseph *is* a fruitful bough,
A fruitful bough by a well;
His branches run over the wall.
23 The archers have bitterly grieved him,
Shot *at him* and hated him.
24 But his bow remained in strength,
And the arms of his hands were made strong
By the hands of the Mighty *God* of Jacob
(From there *is* the Shepherd, the Stone of Israel),
25 By the God of your father who will help you,
And by the Almighty who will bless you
With blessings of heaven above,
Blessings of the deep that lies beneath,
Blessings of the breasts and of the womb.
26 The blessings of your father
Have excelled the blessings of my ancestors,
Up to the utmost bound of the everlasting hills.
They shall be on the head of Joseph,
And on the crown of the head of him who was
separate from his brothers.

27 "Benjamin is a ravenous wolf;
In the morning he shall devour the prey,
And at night he shall divide the spoil."

28All these *are* the twelve tribes of Israel, and this *is* what their father spoke to them. And he blessed them; he blessed each one according to his own blessing.

29Then he charged them and said to them: "I am to be gathered to my people; bury me with my fathers in the cave that *is* in the field of Ephron the Hittite, 30in the cave that *is* in the field of Machpelah, which *is* before Mamre in the land of Canaan, which Abraham bought with the field of Ephron the Hittite as a possession for a burial place. 31There they buried Abraham and Sarah his wife, there they buried Isaac and Rebekah his wife, and there I buried Leah. 32The field and the cave that *is* there *were* purchased from the sons of Heth." 33And when Jacob had finished commanding his sons, he drew his feet up into the bed and breathed his last, and was gathered to his people.

CHAPTER **50** **JACOB DIES AND IS BURIED.** Then Joseph fell on his father's face and wept over him, and kissed him. 2And Joseph commanded his servants the physicians to embalm his father. So the physicians embalmed Israel. 3Forty days were required for him, for such are the days required for those who are embalmed; and the Egyptians mourned for him seventy days.

> ◣▬▬▬▬▬**GOOD GRIEF**
>
> **50:1-11** When Jacob died at the age of 147, Joseph wept and mourned for months. When someone close to us dies, we need a long period of time to work through our grief. Crying and sharing our feelings with others helps us recover and go on with life. Allow yourself and others the freedom to grieve over the loss of a loved one, and give yourself time enough to complete your grieving process.

4Now when the days of his mourning were past, Joseph spoke to the household of Pharaoh, saying, "If now I have found favor in your eyes, please speak in the hearing of Pharaoh, saying, 5My father made me swear, saying, "Behold, I am dying; in my grave which I dug for myself in the land of Canaan, there you shall bury me." Now therefore, please let me go up and bury my father, and I will come back.' "

6And Pharaoh said, "Go up and bury your father, as he made you swear."

7So Joseph went up to bury his father; and with him went up all the servants of Pharaoh, the elders of his house, and all the elders of the land of Egypt, 8as well as all the house of Joseph, his brothers, and his father's house. Only their little ones, their flocks, and their herds they left in the land of Goshen. 9And there went up with him both chariots and horsemen, and it was a very great gathering.

10Then they came to the threshing floor of Atad, which *is* beyond the Jordan, and they mourned there with a great and very solemn lamentation. He observed seven days of mourning for his father. 11And when the inhabitants of the land, the Canaanites, saw the mourning at the threshing floor of Atad, they said, "This *is* a deep mourning of the Egyptians." Therefore its name was called Abel Mizraim, which *is* beyond the Jordan.

> ◣▬▬▬▬▬**RELIABLE**
>
> **50:5** Joseph had proven himself trustworthy as Pharaoh's adviser. Because of his good record, Pharaoh was sure that he would return to Egypt as promised after burying his father in Canaan. Privileges and freedom often result when we have demonstrated our trustworthiness. Because trust must be built gradually over time, take every opportunity to prove your reliability even in minor matters.

MUSCLE BUILDING

50:24 Joseph was ready to die. He had no doubts that God would keep his promise and one day bring the Israelites back to their homeland. What a tremendous example! The secret of that kind of faith is a lifetime of trusting God. Your faith is like a muscle—it grows with exercise, gaining strength over time. After a lifetime of exercising trust, your faith can be as strong as Joseph's. Then at your death, you can be confident that God will fulfill all his promises to you and to all those faithful to him who may live after you.

[12]So his sons did for him just as he had commanded them. [13]For his sons carried him to the land of Canaan, and buried him in the cave of the field of Machpelah, before Mamre, which Abraham bought with the field from Ephron the Hittite as property for a burial place. [14]And after he had buried his father, Joseph returned to Egypt, he and his brothers and all who went up with him to bury his father.

[15]When Joseph's brothers saw that their father was dead, they said, "Perhaps Joseph will hate us, and may actually repay us for all the evil which we did to him." [16]So they sent *messengers* to Joseph, saying, "Before your father died he commanded, saying, [17]'Thus you shall say to Joseph: "I beg you, please forgive the trespass of your brothers and their sin; for they did evil to you." ' Now, please, forgive the trespass of the servants of the God of your father." And Joseph wept when they spoke to him.

[18]Then his brothers also went and fell down before his face, and they said, "Behold, we *are* your servants."

[19]Joseph said to them, "Do not be afraid, for *am* I in the place of God? [20]But as for you, you meant evil against me; *but* God meant it for good, in order to bring it about as *it is* this day, to save many people alive. [21]Now therefore, do not be afraid; I will provide for you and your little ones." And he comforted them and spoke kindly to them.

[22]So Joseph dwelt in Egypt, he and his father's household. And Joseph lived one hundred and ten years. [23]Joseph saw Ephraim's children to the third *generation*. The children of Machir, the son of Manasseh, were also brought up on Joseph's knees.

[24]And Joseph said to his brethren, "I am dying; but God will surely visit you, and bring you out of this land to the land of which He swore to Abraham, to Isaac, and to Jacob." [25]Then Joseph took an oath from the children of Israel, saying, "God will surely visit you, and you shall carry up my bones from here." [26]So Joseph died, *being* one hundred and ten years old; and they embalmed him, and he was put in a coffin in Egypt.

MEGA *Themes*

BEGINNINGS Genesis introduces God as Creator of all that exists: the universe, water, and all of life, including man, who was created in God's own image. When God finished creating, he described all of creation as being "good." When sin entered this flawless creation, God began his plan of salvation to restore the lost perfection.

All of creation was created to glorify God. Human beings are unique in their ability to bring God glory because they are created in God's image. Because sin broke man's good relationship with God, each person must look to God for a restoration of that lost fellowship.

1. What have you learned about the character of God from reading Genesis 1–3?

2. What does it mean to be created in the image of the God who is Lord of all?

3. How do you feel about yourself when you think about being created in God's image?

4. How should the fact that each person is truly created in God's image affect the way you act toward people who appear to be different than you (i.e., skin color, physical disability, unusual habits)?

5. As a person who is created in God's image, how can you glorify God in your relationships with others? With nature? With God?

SIN AND DISOBEDIENCE Sin is destructive. It destroys the goodness of God's creation, ruining the life God intended. Sin results from human beings choosing to go their own way rather than obeying God. Only God can reverse the consequences of sinful choices.

No person escapes the effects of sin. Without God providing salvation, we would all be condemned to death because of sin. God offers life that is good and glorifying to himself. When a person chooses not to obey God, he or she misses out on the goodness and glory of God.

1. What are some of the changes that happened because of Adam and Eve's sin?

2. How did sinful choices affect the people in Genesi (i.e., builders of the tower of Babel, Lot and his family, Joseph's brothers)?

3. Does a person ever "get away with" sin? Explain.

4. What are some of the reasons that people who know God still choose to sin?

5. What are some reasons that you would choose to

do God's will even when you felt like being disobedient?

PROMISES God promised to protect and provide for his people. He specifically made promises in the form of what is known as a "covenant," or a binding agreement. God made a covenant with his people as a guarantee of what they could expect from him.

God is a God of Truth; he can be trusted to keep his promises. He has not left us in the dark about who he is and what his plans are. While we may not always know all of the details of what God will do, we can be confident that he will do what he has promised.

1. What was God's covenant with Noah following the flood?

2. What was God's covenant with Abraham?

3. What do you learn about God from reading these covenants?

4. What are some of God's promises that you know from other passages of Scripture? Write out these promises in this form: "Because God has said so, I know that he _____."

OBEDIENCE AND PROSPERITY Choosing to obey God results in enjoying his goodness and glory. Everyone who makes the choice to obey will prosper. A person who prospers does not necessarily have the nicest possessions money can buy, or is involved in the most popular social group. Rather, true prosperity is living life as God created it to be lived—in the fullness of his blessings.

If a person truly wants to "choose life," that person must put his or her faith in God. To put one's faith in God means obeying him and trusting that he will provide for all of life's needs. God is not boring, nor is he a spoiler of fun. He created life to be enjoyed and really *lived!* Successful living, therefore, requires living in God's will.

1. In what ways was Joseph a truly successful person? What are some of the choices Joseph made that resulted in his success?

2. Joseph had to choose what to do with his hurt and bitterness from being rejected by his brothers. Based on Genesis 45:1-8, how do you think he dealt with these feelings?

3. When you are elderly, what would you want to be able to say about the life you had lived? What do you think would be a sign that your life was successful?

4. What difference will it make in your life whether or not you obey God in your youth?

5. Describe a successful teenager.

I promise!" she exclaimed. But soon her words were forgotten in the rush and excitement of school. ■ Remember when you promised to do something for a friend, but then forgot? Or what about when someone made an important promise to you and then didn't come through? Promises are part of life—from innocent childhood pledges to earnest, romantic commitments. We promise to do something, be somewhere, or give something. And when others make promises to us, we expect them to keep their word. If not, we become angry, disappointed, and even heartbroken. ■ The book of Exodus is all about promises: God's promises to his people. We too are God's people. Just as God was faithful to Israel in keeping promises he made to them, he will keep every promise he has made to us: promises to love us no matter what, to care for and protect us, to help with temptation we can't handle, to comfort and teach us, and to bring us to heaven someday. ■ Do you know the promises of God? Do you realize the things God has said he will do for you and to you? If you do, you understand how incredible those promises are. If you don't, you may have no idea of the many ways God has promised to be there for you. Each and every promise God makes, he keeps. To the Israelites and to you.

STATS

PURPOSE: To record the events of Israel's deliverance from Egypt and development as a nation

AUTHOR: Moses

DATE WRITTEN: 1450–1410 B.C., approximately the same as Genesis

WHERE WRITTEN: In the wilderness during Israel's wanderings, somewhere in the Sinai Peninsula

SETTING: Egypt. God's people, once highly favored in the land, are now slaves. A God of great miracles is about to set them free.

KEY PEOPLE: Moses, Miriam, Pharaoh, Pharaoh's daughter, Jethro, Aaron, Joshua, Bezalel

KEY PLACES: Egypt, Goshen, Nile River, Land of Midian, Red Sea, Sinai Peninsula, Mount Sinai

SPECIAL FEATURES: Exodus relates more miracles than any other Old Testament book and is noted for containing the Ten Commandments

the land." ¹¹Therefore they set taskmasters over them to afflict them with their burdens. And they built for Pharaoh supply cities, Pithom and Raamses. ¹²But the more they afflicted them, the more they multiplied and grew. And they were in dread of the children of Israel. ¹³So the Egyptians made the children of Israel serve with rigor. ¹⁴And they made their lives bitter with hard bondage—in mortar, in brick, and in all manner of service in the field. All their service in which they made them serve *was* with rigor.

¹⁵Then the king of Egypt spoke to the Hebrew midwives, of whom the name of one *was* Shiphrah and the name of the other Puah; ¹⁶and he said, "When you do the duties of a midwife for the Hebrew women, and see *them* on the birthstools, if it *is* a son, then you shall kill him; but if it *is* a daughter, then she shall live." ¹⁷But the midwives feared God, and did not do as the king of Egypt commanded them, but saved the male children alive. ¹⁸So the king of Egypt called for the midwives and said to them, "Why have you done this thing, and saved the male children alive?"

¹⁹And the midwives said to Pharaoh, "Because the Hebrew women *are* not like the Egyptian women; for they *are* lively and give birth before the midwives come to them."

²⁰Therefore God dealt well with the midwives, and the people multiplied and grew very mighty. ²¹And so it was, because the midwives feared God, that He provided households for them.

²²So Pharaoh commanded all his people, saying, "Every son who is born you shall cast into the river, and every daughter you shall save alive."

CHAPTER 2 MOSES IS BORN. And a man of the house of Levi went and took *as wife* a daughter of Levi. ²So the woman conceived and bore a son. And when she

CHAPTER 1 THE HEBREWS BECOME SLAVES. Now these *are* the names of the children of Israel who came to Egypt; each man and his household came with Jacob: ²Reuben, Simeon, Levi, and Judah; ³Issachar, Zebulun, and Benjamin; ⁴Dan, Naphtali, Gad, and Asher. ⁵All those who were descendants of Jacob were seventy persons (for Joseph was in Egypt *already*). ⁶And Joseph died, all his brothers, and all that generation. ⁷But the children of Israel were fruitful and increased abundantly, multiplied and grew exceedingly mighty; and the land was filled with them.

⁸Now there arose a new king over Egypt, who did not know Joseph. ⁹And he said to his people, "Look, the people of the children of Israel *are* more and mightier than we; ¹⁰come, let us deal shrewdly with them, lest they multiply, and it happen, in the event of war, that they also join our enemies and fight against us, and *so* go up out of

◥◣◢ FOREIGNERS

1:1 Jacob's family had moved to Egypt at the invitation of Joseph, one of Jacob's sons, who had become a great ruler under Pharaoh. Jacob's family grew into a large nation. But, as foreigners and newcomers, their lives were quite different from the lives of the Egyptians. The Hebrews worshiped one God; the Egyptians worshiped many gods. The Hebrews were wanderers; the Egyptians had a deeply rooted culture. The Hebrews were shepherds; the Egyptians were builders. The Hebrews were also physically separated from the rest of the Egyptians: they lived in Goshen, north of the great Egyptian cultural centers.

KEY PLACES IN **EXODUS**

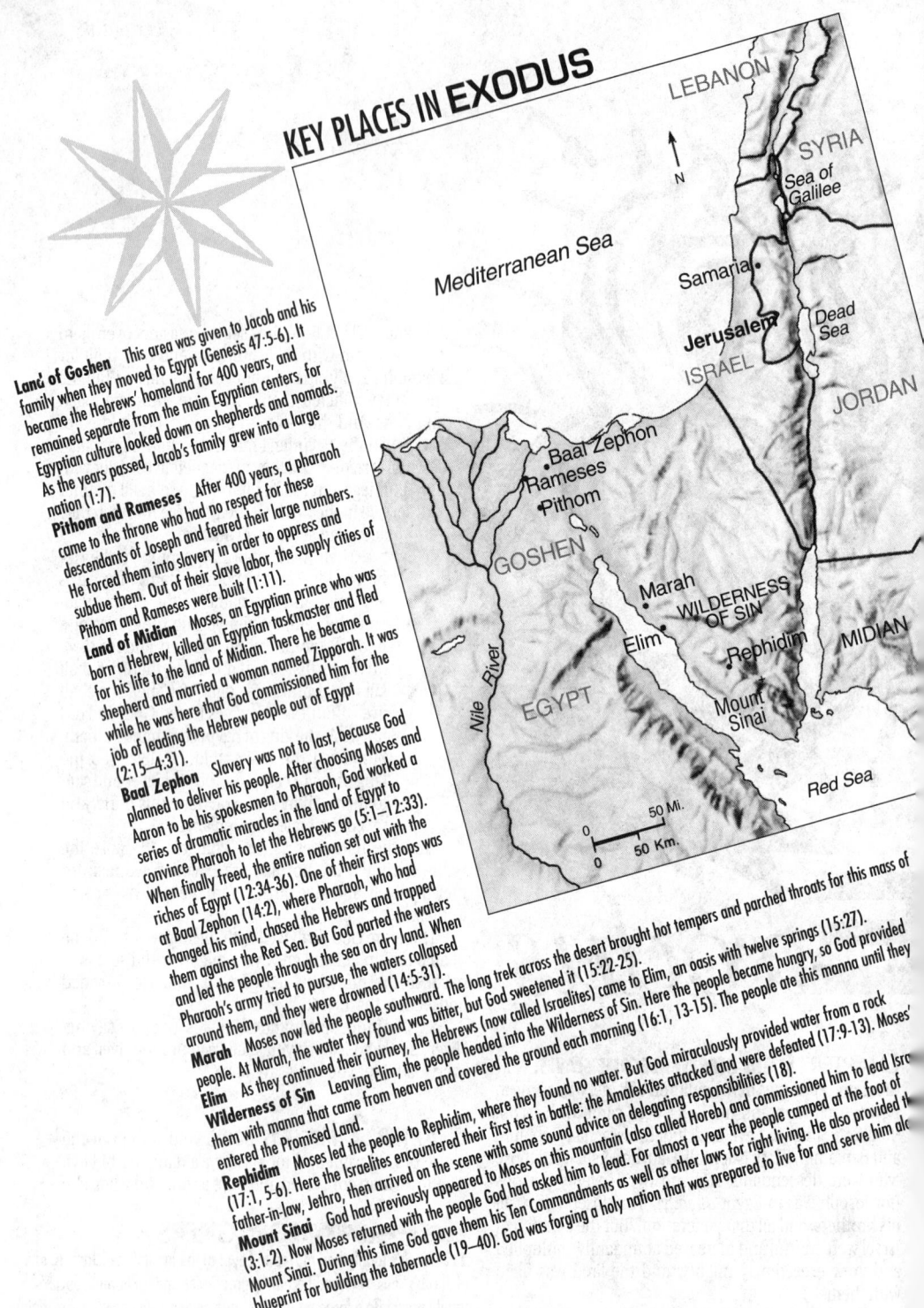

Land of Goshen This area was given to Jacob and his family when they moved to Egypt (Genesis 47:5-6). It became the Hebrews' homeland for 400 years, and remained separate from the main Egyptian centers, for Egyptian culture looked down on shepherds and nomads. As the years passed, Jacob's family grew into a large nation (1:7).

Pithom and Rameses After 400 years, a pharaoh came to the throne who had no respect for these descendants of Joseph and feared their large numbers. He forced them into slavery in order to oppress and subdue them. Out of their slave labor, the supply cities of Pithom and Rameses were built (1:11).

Land of Midian Moses, an Egyptian prince who was born a Hebrew, killed an Egyptian taskmaster and fled for his life to the land of Midian. There he became a shepherd and married a woman named Zipporah. It was while he was leading the Hebrew people out of Egypt (2:15–4:31).

Baal Zephon Slavery was not to last, because God planned to deliver his people. After choosing Moses and Aaron to be his spokesmen to Pharaoh, God worked a series of dramatic miracles in the land of Egypt to convince Pharaoh to let the Hebrews go (5:1—12:33). When finally freed, the entire nation set out with the riches of Egypt (12:34-36). One of their first stops was at Baal Zephon (14:2), where Pharaoh, who had changed his mind, chased the Hebrews and trapped them against the Red Sea. But God parted the waters and led the people through the sea on dry land. When Pharaoh's army tried to pursue, the waters collapsed around them, and they were drowned (14:5:31).

Marah Moses now led the people southward. The long trek across the desert brought hot tempers and parched throats for this mass of people. At Marah, the water they found was bitter, but God sweetened it (15:22-25).

Elim As they continued their journey, the Hebrews (now called Israelites) came to Elim, an oasis with twelve springs (15:27). Leaving Elim, the people headed into the Wilderness of Sin (16:1, 13-15). The people ate this manna until they entered the Promised Land.

Wilderness of Sin Moses led the people southward. The long trek across the desert brought hot tempers and parched throats for this mass of people became hungry, so God provided them with manna that came from heaven and covered the ground each morning (16:1, 13-15). The people ate this manna until they entered the Promised Land.

Rephidim Moses led the people to Rephidim, where they found no water. But God miraculously provided water from a rock (17:1, 5-6). Here the Israelites encountered their first test in battle: the Amalekites attacked and were defeated (17:9-13). Moses' father-in-law, Jethro, then arrived on the scene with some sound advice on delegating responsibilities (18).

Mount Sinai God had previously appeared to Moses on this mountain (also called Horeb) and commissioned him to lead Isr[...] (3:1-2). Now Moses returned with the people God had asked him to lead. For almost a year the people camped at the foot of Mount Sinai. During this time God gave them his Ten Commandments as well as other laws for right living. He also provided th[...] blueprint for building the tabernacle (19–40). God was forging a holy nation that was prepared to live for and serve him al[...]

saw that he *was* a beautiful *child*, she hid him three months. ³But when she could no longer hide him, she took an ark of bulrushes for him, daubed it with asphalt and pitch, put the child in it, and laid *it* in the reeds by the river's bank. ⁴And his sister stood afar off, to know what would be done to him.

⁵Then the daughter of Pharaoh came down to bathe at the river. And her maidens walked along the riverside; and when she saw the ark among the reeds, she sent her maid to get it. ⁶And when she opened *it,* she saw the child, and behold, the baby wept. So she had compassion on him, and said, "This is one of the Hebrews' children."

⁷Then his sister said to Pharaoh's daughter, "Shall I go and call a nurse for you from the Hebrew women, that she may nurse the child for you?"

⁸And Pharaoh's daughter said to her, "Go." So the maiden went and called the child's mother. ⁹Then Pharaoh's daughter said to her, "Take this child away and nurse him for me, and I will give *you* your wages." So the woman took the child and nursed him. ¹⁰And the child grew, and she brought him to Pharaoh's daughter, and he became her son. So she called his name Moses, saying, "Because I drew him out of the water."

¹¹Now it came to pass in those days, when Moses was grown, that he went out to his brethren and looked at their burdens. And he saw an Egyptian beating a Hebrew, one of his brethren. ¹²So he looked this way and that way, and when he saw no one, he killed the Egyptian and hid him in the sand. ¹³And when he went out the second day, behold, two Hebrew men were fighting, and he said to the one who did the wrong, "Why are you striking your companion?"

¹⁴Then he said, "Who made you a prince and a judge over us? Do you intend to kill me as you killed the Egyptian?"

So Moses feared and said, "Surely this thing is known!" ¹⁵When Pharaoh heard of this matter, he sought to kill Moses. But Moses fled from the face of Pharaoh and dwelt in the land of Midian; and he sat down by a well.

¹⁶Now the priest of Midian had seven daughters. And they came and drew water, and they filled the troughs to water their father's flock. ¹⁷Then the shepherds came and drove them away; but Moses stood up and helped them, and watered their flock.

¹⁸When they came to Reuel their father, he said, "How *is it that* you have come so soon today?"

¹⁹And they said, "An Egyptian delivered us from the hand of the shepherds, and he also drew enough water for us and watered the flock."

²⁰So he said to his daughters, "And where *is* he? Why *is* it *that* you have left the man? Call him, that he may eat bread."

◢ FIGHT EVIL

2:3ff Moses' mother knew how wrong it would be to destroy her child. But there was little she could do to change Pharaoh's new law. Her only alternative was to hide the child and later place him in a tiny basket on the river. God used her courageous act to place her son, the Hebrew of his choice, in the house of Pharaoh. Do you sometimes feel surrounded by evil and frustrated by how little you can do about it? When faced with evil, look for ways to act against it. Then trust God to use your effort, however small it seems, in his war against evil.

²¹Then Moses was content to live with the man, and he gave Zipporah his daughter to Moses. ²²And she bore *him* a son. He called his name Gershom, for he said, "I have been a stranger in a foreign land."

²³Now it happened in the process of time that the king of Egypt died. Then the children of Israel groaned because of the bondage, and they cried out; and their cry came up to God because of the bondage.

MIRIAM

Ask older brothers or sisters what their greatest test in life is and they will often answer, "My younger brother (or sister)!" This is especially true when the younger one seems more successful than the older. At such times, the bonds of family loyalty can be stretched to the breaking point.

When we first meet Miriam, she is involved in one of history's most unusual baby-sitting jobs: She is watching her infant brother float down the Nile River in a waterproof cradle. When the baby is found, Miriam's quick thinking saves her brother and even allows him to be raised by his own mother. But it isn't long before the little brother she had protected grows into a great man—and their relationship changes. Moses had needed her; now, she needed him. The change wasn't easy for Miriam.

Instead of appreciating what God was doing in her brother's life, Miriam chose to criticize. Sound familiar? God had to teach Miriam and her other brother Aaron that each had a unique part in his plans. Being jealous of one another was wrong. The same lesson applies to our families, too.

What difference would it make in your family if every criticism was changed into an encouraging or loving statement? Does God want you to start the new trend?

LESSONS: The motives behind criticism are often more important to deal with than the criticism itself

KEY VERSE: "And Miriam answered them: 'Sing to the LORD, for He has triumphed gloriously!'" (Exodus 15:21).

Miriam's story is told in Exodus 2 and 15; Numbers 12 and 20:1. She is also mentioned in Deuteronomy 24:9; 1 Chronicles 6:3; Micah 6:4.

UPS:
• Quick thinker under pressure
• Able leader
• Songwriter
• Prophetess

DOWNS:
• Was jealous of Moses' authority
• Openly criticized Moses' leadership

STATS:
• Where: Egypt, Sinai Peninsula
• Relatives: Brothers: Aaron and Moses

²⁴So God heard their groaning, and God remembered His covenant with Abraham, with Isaac, and with Jacob. ²⁵And God looked upon the children of Israel, and God acknowledged *them*.

CHAPTER **3** **THE BURNING BUSH.** Now Moses was tending the flock of Jethro his father-in-law, the priest of Midian. And he led the flock to the back of the desert, and came to Horeb, the mountain of God. ²And the Angel of the LORD appeared to him in a flame of fire from the midst of a bush. So he looked, and behold, the bush was burning with fire, but the bush *was* not consumed. ³Then Moses said, "I will now turn aside and see this great sight, why the bush does not burn."

EXTRAORDINARY

4:2-4 A shepherd's rod was commonly a three- to six-foot wooden staff with a curved hook at the top. The shepherd used it for walking, guiding his sheep, killing snakes, and many other tasks. Still, it was just a stick. But God used the simple shepherd's rod Moses carried to teach him an important lesson. God sometimes takes joy in using ordinary things for extraordinary purposes. What are the ordinary things in your life—your voice, a pen, a hammer, a broom, a musical instrument? It is easy to assume that God can use only special skills, but he can also use your everyday contributions. Little did Moses imagine the power his simple rod would wield when it became the rod of God.

⁴So when the LORD saw that he turned aside to look, God called to him from the midst of the bush and said, "Moses, Moses!"

And he said, "Here I am."

⁵Then He said, "Do not draw near this place. Take your sandals off your feet, for the place where you stand *is* holy ground." ⁶Moreover He said, "I *am* the God of your father—the God of Abraham, the God of Isaac, and the God of Jacob." And Moses hid his face, for he was afraid to look upon God.

⁷And the LORD said: "I have surely seen the oppression of My people who *are* in Egypt, and have heard their cry because of their taskmasters, for I know their sorrows. ⁸So I have come down to deliver them out of the hand of the Egyptians, and to bring them up from that land to a good and large land, to a land flowing with milk and honey, to the place of the Canaanites and the Hittites and the Amorites and the Perizzites and the Hivites and the Jebusites. ⁹Now therefore, behold, the cry of the children of Israel has come to Me, and I have also seen the oppression with which the Egyptians oppress them. ¹⁰Come now, therefore, and I will send you to Pharaoh that you may bring My people, the children of Israel, out of Egypt."

¹¹But Moses said to God, "Who *am* I that I should go to Pharaoh, and that I should bring the children of Israel out of Egypt?"

¹²So He said, "I will certainly be with you. And this *shall be* a sign to you that I have sent you: When you have brought the people out of Egypt, you shall serve God on this mountain."

¹³Then Moses said to God, "Indeed, *when* I come to the children of Israel and say to them, 'The God of your fathers has sent me to you,' and they say to me, 'What *is* His name?' what shall I say to them?"

¹⁴And God said to Moses, "I AM WHO I AM." And He said, "Thus you shall say to the children of Israel, 'I AM has sent me to you.'" ¹⁵Moreover God said to Moses, "Thus you shall say to the children of Israel: 'The LORD God of your fathers, the God of Abraham, the God of Isaac, and the God of Jacob, has sent me to you. This *is* My name forever, and this *is* My memorial to all generations.' ¹⁶Go and gather the elders of Israel together, and say to them, 'The LORD God of your fathers, the God of Abraham, of Isaac, and of Jacob, appeared to me, saying, "I have surely visited you and *seen* what is done to you in Egypt; ¹⁷and I have said I will bring you up out of the affliction of Egypt to the land of the Canaanites and the Hittites and the Amorites and the Perizzites and the Hivites and the Jebusites, to a land flowing with milk and honey." ' ¹⁸Then they will heed your voice; and you shall come, you and the elders of Israel, to the king of Egypt; and you shall say to him, 'The LORD God of the Hebrews has met with us; and now, please, let us go three days' journey into the wilderness, that we may sacrifice to the LORD our God.' ¹⁹But I am sure that the king of Egypt will not let you go, no, not even by a mighty hand. ²⁰So I will stretch out My hand and strike Egypt with all My wonders which I will do in its midst; and after that he will let you go. ²¹And I will give this people favor in the sight of the Egyptians; and it shall be, when you go, that you shall not go empty-handed. ²²But every woman shall ask of her neighbor, namely, of her who dwells near her house, articles of silver, articles of gold, and clothing; and you shall put *them* on your sons and on your daughters. So you shall plunder the Egyptians."

CHAPTER **4** Then Moses answered and said, "But suppose they will not believe me or listen to my voice; suppose they say, 'The LORD has not appeared to you.'"

²So the LORD said to him, "What *is* that in your hand?" He said, "A rod."

³And He said, "Cast it on the ground." So he cast it on the ground, and it became a serpent; and Moses fled from it. ⁴Then the LORD said to Moses, "Reach out your hand and take *it* by the tail" (and he reached out his hand

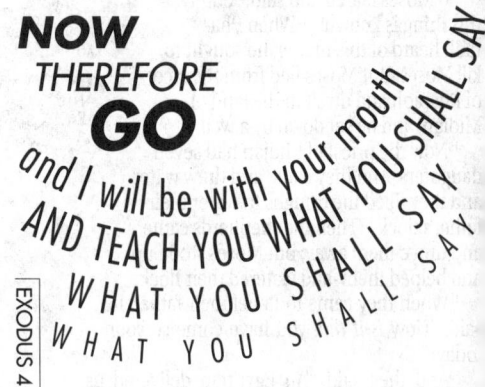

NOW THEREFORE GO and I will be with your mouth AND TEACH YOU WHAT YOU SHALL SAY WHAT YOU SHALL SAY WHAT YOU SHALL SAY

EXODUS 4:12

and caught it, and it became a rod in his hand), ⁵"that they may believe that the LORD God of their fathers, the God of Abraham, the God of Isaac, and the God of Jacob, has appeared to you."

⁶Furthermore the LORD said to him, "Now put your hand in your bosom." And he put his hand in his bosom, and when he took it out, behold, his hand *was* leprous, like snow. ⁷And He said, "Put your hand in your bosom again." So he put his hand in his bosom again, and drew it out of his bosom, and behold, it was restored like his *other* flesh. ⁸"Then it will be, if they do not believe you, nor heed the message of the first sign, that they may believe the message of the latter sign. ⁹And it shall be, if they do not believe even these two signs, or listen to your voice, that you shall take water from the river and pour *it* on the dry *land.* The water which you take from the river will become blood on the dry *land.*"

¹⁰Then Moses said to the LORD, "O my Lord, I *am* not eloquent, neither before nor since You have spoken to Your servant; but I *am* slow of speech and slow of tongue."

¹¹So the LORD said to him, "Who has made man's mouth? Or who makes the mute, the deaf, the seeing, or the blind? *Have* not I, the LORD? ¹²Now therefore, go, and I will be with your mouth and teach you what you shall say."

¹³But he said, "O my Lord, please send by the hand of whomever *else* You may send."

¹⁴So the anger of the LORD was kindled against Moses, and He said: "Is not Aaron the Levite your brother? I know that he can speak well. And look, he is also coming out to meet you. When he sees you, he will be glad in his heart. ¹⁵Now you shall speak to him and put the words in his mouth. And I will be with your mouth and with his mouth, and I will teach you what you shall do. ¹⁶So he shall be your spokesman to the people. And he himself shall be as a mouth for you, and you shall be to him as God. ¹⁷And you shall take this rod in your hand, with which you shall do the signs."

¹⁸So Moses went and returned to Jethro his father-in-law, and said to him, "Please let me go and return to my brethren who *are* in Egypt, and see whether they are still alive."

And Jethro said to Moses, "Go in peace."

¹⁹Now the LORD said to Moses in Midian, "Go, return to Egypt; for all the men who sought your life are dead." ²⁰Then Moses took his wife and his sons and set them on a donkey, and he returned to the land of Egypt. And Moses took the rod of God in his hand.

²¹And the LORD said to Moses, "When you go back to Egypt, see that you do all those wonders before Pharaoh which I have put in your hand. But I will harden his heart, so that he will not let the people go. ²²Then you shall say to Pharaoh, 'Thus says the LORD: "Israel *is* My son, My firstborn. ²³So I say to you, let My son go that he may serve Me. But if you refuse to let him go, indeed I will kill your son, your firstborn." ' "

²⁴And it came to pass on the way, at the encampment, that the LORD met him and sought to kill him. ²⁵Then Zipporah took a sharp stone and cut off the foreskin of her son and cast *it* at *Moses'* feet, and said, "Surely you *are*

a husband of blood to me!" ²⁶So He let him go. Then she said, "*You are* a husband of blood!"—because of the circumcision.

²⁷And the LORD said to Aaron, "Go into the wilderness to meet Moses." So he went and met him on the mountain of God, and kissed him. ²⁸So Moses told Aaron all the words of the LORD who had sent him, and all the signs which He had commanded him. ²⁹Then Moses and Aaron went and gathered together all the elders of the children of Israel. ³⁰And Aaron spoke all the words which the LORD had spoken to Moses. Then he did the signs in the sight of the people. ³¹So the people believed; and when they heard that the LORD had visited the children of Israel and that He had looked on their affliction, then they bowed their heads and worshiped.

I am having trouble letting other people know I am a Christian. I'm afraid they will laugh at me or ask a question I can't answer.

I WONDER . . .

The Bible is filled with examples of people who faced the choice of either being courageous or letting their fears tell them how to act. Learning about the courage of people in the Bible is one good reason to read it every day. The examples we find in the Bible can give us the strength to step out in faith and do things that may at first seem very frightening.

In Exodus 3, God had just finished speaking with Moses through a burning bush. Although this was an incredible miracle, Exodus 4 relates how Moses was afraid people wouldn't believe that God had actually spoken to him! He had to choose between giving in to his fears or facing them head on. Eventually, Moses chose to draw courage from God and completed the task God had given him.

Character and skill are developed by repeating an action until you can do it well enough to enjoy it. This is true with everything from skiing to skateboarding—and it is true in telling your best friends on earth about your Friend in heaven.

God does not expect you to know all the answers. When the apostle Peter was confronted by the hostile religious leaders of the day who told him to stop talking about Jesus, he answered, "We cannot but speak the things which we have seen and heard" (Acts 4:20). He had learned the joy of sharing his faith in Christ so much that he couldn't help but share what he knew!

You have the privilege and the responsibility of sharing what you have learned and what God has done in your life. If you don't know the answer, you can always say, "That's a good question. Can I find out the answer and get back with you tomorrow?"

The key to Moses' decision to obey God's command to be his spokesman for the Israelites was remembering when God first spoke to him. The burning bush experience and God's continuing miracles gave Moses the courage to face incredible obstacles.

Rely on what God has done for you and daily lean on your growing relationship with Christ to strengthen you.

CHAPTER 5 MAKING BRICKS WITHOUT STRAW.

Afterward Moses and Aaron went in and told Pharaoh, "Thus says the LORD God of Israel: 'Let My people go, that they may hold a feast to Me in the wilderness.' "

²And Pharaoh said, "Who *is* the LORD, that I should obey His voice to let Israel go? I do not know the LORD, nor will I let Israel go."

³So they said, "The God of the Hebrews has met with us. Please, let us go three days' journey into the desert and sacrifice to the LORD our God, lest He fall upon us with pestilence or with the sword."

⁴Then the king of Egypt said to them, "Moses and Aaron, why do you take the people from their work? Get *back* to your labor." ⁵And Pharaoh said, "Look, the people of the land *are* many now, and you make them rest from their labor!"

⁶So the same day Pharaoh commanded the taskmasters of the people and their officers, saying, ⁷"You shall no longer give the people straw to make brick as before. Let them go and gather straw for themselves. ⁸And you shall lay on them the quota of bricks which they made before. You shall not reduce it. For they are idle; therefore they cry out, saying, 'Let us go *and* sacrifice to our God.' ⁹Let more work be laid on the men, that they may labor in it, and let them not regard false words."

◗REJECTION

5:3 Pharaoh would not listen to Moses and Aaron because he did not know or respect God. People who do not know God may not listen to his word or his messengers. Like Moses and Aaron, we need to persist. When others reject you or your faith, don't be surprised or discouraged. Continue to tell them about God, trusting him to open closed minds and soften stubborn hearts.

¹⁰And the taskmasters of the people and their officers went out and spoke to the people, saying, "Thus says Pharaoh: 'I will not give you straw. ¹¹Go, get yourselves straw where you can find it; yet none of your work will be reduced.' " ¹²So the people were scattered abroad throughout all the land of Egypt to gather stubble instead of straw. ¹³And the taskmasters forced *them* to hurry, saying, "Fulfill your work, *your* daily quota, as when there was straw." ¹⁴Also the officers of the children of Israel, whom Pharaoh's taskmasters had set over them, were beaten *and* were asked, "Why have you not fulfilled your task in making brick both yesterday and today, as before?"

¹⁵Then the officers of the children of Israel came and cried out to Pharaoh, saying, "Why are you dealing thus with your servants? ¹⁶There is no straw given to your servants, and they say to us, 'Make brick!' And indeed your servants *are* beaten, but the fault *is* in your *own* people."

¹⁷But he said, "You *are* idle! Idle! Therefore you say, 'Let us go *and* sacrifice to the LORD.' ¹⁸Therefore go now *and* work; for no straw shall be given you, yet you shall deliver the quota of bricks." ¹⁹And the officers of the children of Israel saw *that* they *were* in trouble after it was said, "You shall not reduce *any* bricks from your daily quota."

²⁰Then, as they came out from Pharaoh, they met Moses and Aaron who stood there to meet them. ²¹And they said to them, "Let the LORD look on you and judge, because you have made us abhorrent in the sight of Pharaoh and in the sight of his servants, to put a sword in their hand to kill us."

²²So Moses returned to the LORD and said, "Lord, why have You brought trouble on this people? Why *is* it You have sent me? ²³For since I came to Pharaoh to speak in Your name, he has done evil to this people; neither have You delivered Your people at all."

CHAPTER 6 THE HEBREWS WON'T LISTEN.

Then the LORD said to Moses, "Now you shall see what I will do to Pharaoh. For with a strong hand he will let them go, and with a strong hand he will drive them out of his land."

²And God spoke to Moses and said to him: "I *am* the LORD. ³I appeared to Abraham, to Isaac, and to Jacob, as God Almighty, but *by* My name LORD I was not known to them. ⁴I have also established My covenant with them, to give them the land of Canaan, the land of their pilgrimage, in which they were strangers. ⁵And I have also heard the groaning of the children of Israel whom the Egyptians keep in bondage, and I have remembered My covenant. ⁶Therefore say to the children of Israel: 'I *am* the LORD; I will bring you out from under the burdens of the Egyptians, I will rescue you from their bondage, and I will redeem you with an outstretched arm and with great judgments. ⁷I will take you as My people, and I will be your God. Then you shall know that I *am* the LORD your God who brings you out from under the burdens of the Egyptians. ⁸And I will bring you into the land which I swore to give to Abraham, Isaac, and Jacob; and I will give it to you *as* a heritage: I *am* the LORD.' " ⁹So Moses spoke thus to the children of Israel; but they did not heed Moses, because of anguish of spirit and cruel bondage.

¹⁰And the LORD spoke to Moses, saying, ¹¹"Go in, tell Pharaoh king of Egypt to let the children of Israel go out of his land."

¹²And Moses spoke before the LORD, saying, "The children of Israel have not heeded me. How then shall Pharaoh heed me, for I *am* of uncircumcised lips?"

¹³Then the LORD spoke to Moses and Aaron, and gave them a command for the children of Israel and for Pharaoh king of Egypt, to bring the children of Israel out of the land of Egypt.

¹⁴These *are* the heads of their fathers' houses: The sons of Reuben, the firstborn of Israel, *were* Hanoch, Pallu, Hezron, and Carmi. These are the families of Reuben. ¹⁵And the sons of Simeon *were* Jemuel, Jamin, Ohad, Jachin, Zohar, and Shaul the son of a Canaanite woman. These *are* the families of Simeon. ¹⁶These *are* the names of the sons of Levi according to their generations: Gershon, Kohath, and Merari. And the years of the life of Levi *were* one hundred and thirty-seven. ¹⁷The sons of Gershon *were* Libni and Shimi according to their families. ¹⁸And the sons of Kohath *were* Amram, Izhar, Hebron, and Uzziel. And the years of the life of Kohath *were* one hundred and thirty-three. ¹⁹The sons of Merari *were* Mahli and Mushi. These *are* the families of Levi according to their generations.

²⁰Now Amram took for himself Jochebed, his father's sister, as wife; and she bore him Aaron and Moses. And the years of the life of Amram *were* one hundred and thirty-seven. ²¹The sons of Izhar *were* Korah, Nepheg, and Zichri. ²²And the sons of Uzziel *were* Mishael, Elzaphan, and Zithri. ²³Aaron took to himself Elisheba, daughter of Amminadab, sister of Nahshon, as wife; and she bore him Nadab, Abihu, Eleazar, and Ithamar. ²⁴And the sons of Korah *were* Assir, Elkanah, and Abiasaph. These are the families of the Korahites. ²⁵Eleazar, Aaron's son, took for himself one of the daughters of Putiel as wife; and she bore him Phinehas. These *are* the heads of the fathers' houses of the Levites according to their families.

²⁶These *are the same* Aaron and Moses to whom the LORD said, "Bring out the children of Israel from the land of Egypt according to their armies." ²⁷These *are* the ones who spoke to Pharaoh king of Egypt, to bring out the children of Israel from Egypt. These *are the same* Moses and Aaron.

²⁸And it came to pass, on the day the LORD spoke to Moses in the land of Egypt, ²⁹that the LORD spoke to Moses, saying, "I *am* the LORD. Speak to Pharaoh king of Egypt all that I say to you."

³⁰But Moses said before the LORD, "Behold, I *am* of uncircumcised lips, and how shall Pharaoh heed me?"

CHAPTER 7 AARON'S ROD BECOMES A SNAKE.

So the LORD said to Moses: "See, I have made you *as* God to Pharaoh, and Aaron your brother shall be your prophet. ²You shall speak all that I command you. And Aaron your brother shall tell Pharaoh to send the children of Israel out of his land. ³And I will harden Pharaoh's heart, and multiply My signs and My wonders in the land of Egypt. ⁴But Pharaoh will not heed you, so that I may lay My hand on Egypt and bring My armies *and* My people, the children of Israel, out of the land of Egypt by great judgments. ⁵And the Egyptians shall know that I *am* the LORD, when I stretch out My hand on Egypt and bring out the children of Israel from among them."

⁶Then Moses and Aaron did *so;* just as the LORD commanded them, so they did. ⁷And Moses *was* eighty years old and Aaron eighty-three years old when they spoke to Pharaoh.

⁸Then the LORD spoke to Moses and Aaron, saying, ⁹"When Pharaoh speaks to you, saying, 'Show a miracle for yourselves,' then you shall say to Aaron, 'Take your rod and cast *it* before Pharaoh, *and* let it become a serpent.' " ¹⁰So Moses and Aaron went in to Pharaoh, and they did so, just as the LORD commanded. And Aaron cast down his rod before Pharaoh and before his servants, and it became a serpent.

¹¹But Pharaoh also called the wise men and the sorcerers; so the magicians of Egypt, they also did in like manner with their enchantments. ¹²For every man threw down his rod, and they became serpents. But Aaron's rod swallowed up their rods. ¹³And Pharaoh's heart grew hard, and he did not heed them, as the LORD had said.

¹⁴So the LORD said to Moses: "Pharaoh's heart *is* hard; he refuses to let the people go. ¹⁵Go to Pharaoh in the morning, when he goes out to the water, and you shall

stand by the river's bank to meet him; and the rod which was turned to a serpent you shall take in your hand. ¹⁶And you shall say to him, 'The LORD God of the Hebrews has sent me to you, saying, "Let My people go, that they may serve Me in the wilderness"; but indeed, until now you would not hear! ¹⁷Thus says the LORD: "By this you shall know that I *am* the LORD. Behold, I will strike the waters which *are* in the river with the rod that *is* in my hand, and they shall be turned to blood. ¹⁸And the fish that *are* in the river shall die, the river shall stink, and the Egyptians will loathe to drink the water of the river." ' "

◆◆◆◆◆ AMBASSADOR

7:1 God made Moses his representative; he was "*as* God to Pharaoh." We are each God's representatives—showing the world that Christians are a different people with a different life-style. Much of the world knows nothing about God except what it sees in the lives of God's people. What kind of God would they think you represent? Taking note of how you come across to others gives you a good indication of how well you are representing God.

¹⁹Then the LORD spoke to Moses, "Say to Aaron, 'Take your rod and stretch out your hand over the waters of Egypt, over their streams, over their rivers, over their ponds, and over all their pools of water, that they may become blood. And there shall be blood throughout all the land of Egypt, both in *buckets of* wood and *pitchers of* stone.' " ²⁰And Moses and Aaron did so, just as the LORD commanded. So he lifted up the rod and struck the waters that *were* in the river, in the sight of Pharaoh and in the sight of his servants. And all the waters that *were* in the river were turned to blood. ²¹The fish that *were* in the river died, the river stank, and the Egyptians could not drink the water of the river. So there was blood throughout all the land of Egypt.

²²Then the magicians of Egypt did so with their enchantments; and Pharaoh's heart grew hard, and he did not heed them, as the LORD had said. ²³And Pharaoh turned and went into his house. Neither was his heart moved by this. ²⁴So all the Egyptians dug all around the river for water to drink, because they could not drink the water of the river. ²⁵And seven days passed after the LORD had struck the river.

CHAPTER 8 PHARAOH LEARNS ABOUT GOD'S

POWER. And the LORD spoke to Moses, "Go to Pharaoh and say to him, 'Thus says the LORD: "Let My people go, that they may serve Me. ²But if you refuse to let *them* go, behold, I will smite all your territory with frogs. ³So the river shall bring forth frogs abundantly, which shall go up and come into your house, into your bedroom, on your bed, into the houses of your servants, on your people,

◆◆◆◆◆ TRICKERY

7:11 How were these sorcerers and magicians able to duplicate Moses' miracles? Some of their feats involved trickery or illusion. But some may have used satanic power, since worshiping gods of the underworld was part of the Egyptians' religion. Ironically, whenever the sorcerers duplicated one of Moses' plagues, it only made matters worse. If the magicians had been as powerful as God, they would have reversed the plagues, not added to them.

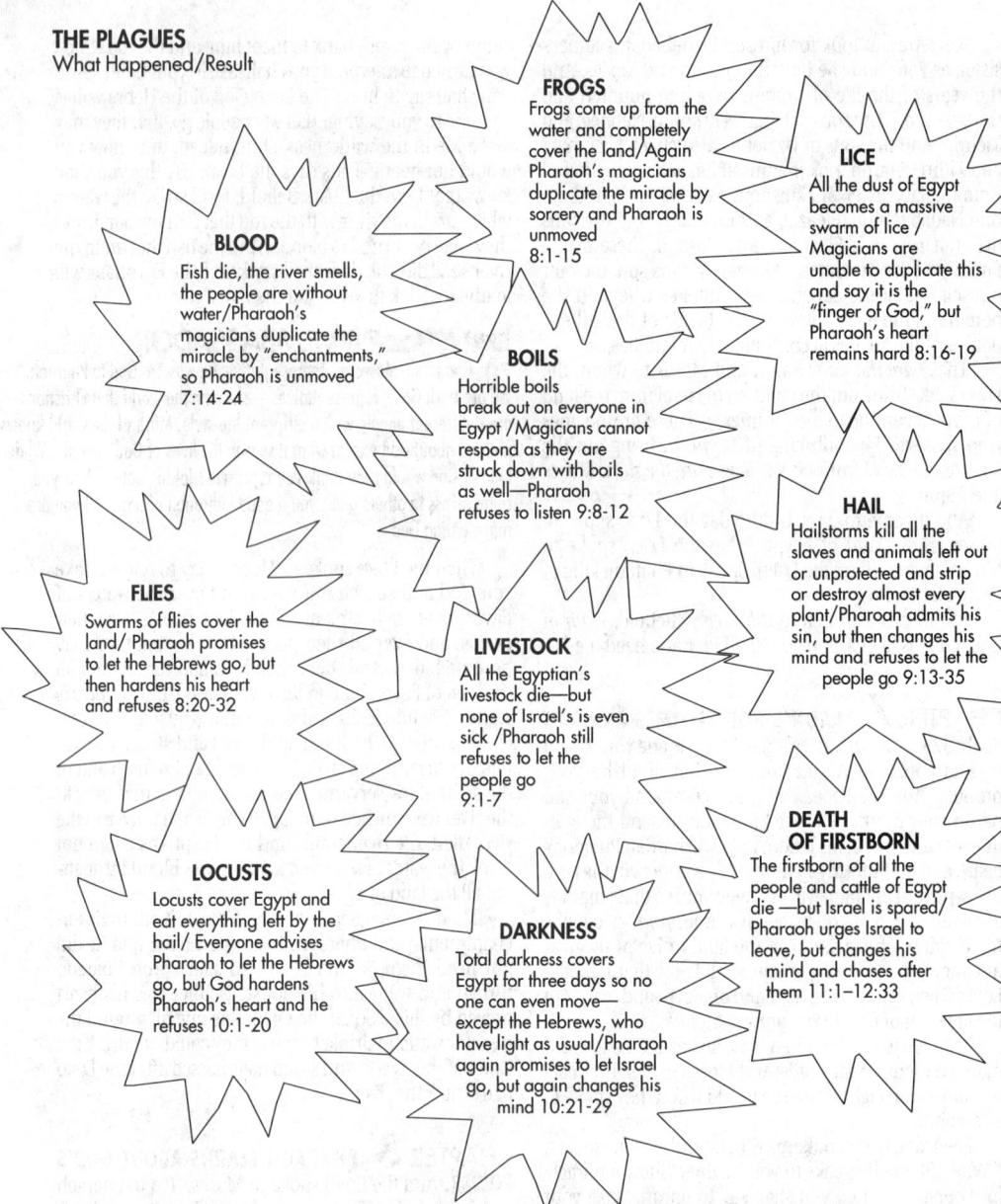

THE PLAGUES
What Happened/Result

FROGS
Frogs come up from the water and completely cover the land/Again Pharaoh's magicians duplicate the miracle by sorcery and Pharaoh is unmoved 8:1-15

LICE
All the dust of Egypt becomes a massive swarm of lice / Magicians are unable to duplicate this and say it is the "finger of God," but Pharaoh's heart remains hard 8:16-19

BLOOD
Fish die, the river smells, the people are without water/Pharaoh's magicians duplicate the miracle by "enchantments," so Pharaoh is unmoved 7:14-24

BOILS
Horrible boils break out on everyone in Egypt /Magicians cannot respond as they are struck down with boils as well—Pharaoh refuses to listen 9:8-12

HAIL
Hailstorms kill all the slaves and animals left out or unprotected and strip or destroy almost every plant/Pharoah admits his sin, but then changes his mind and refuses to let the people go 9:13-35

FLIES
Swarms of flies cover the land/ Pharaoh promises to let the Hebrews go, but then hardens his heart and refuses 8:20-32

LIVESTOCK
All the Egyptian's livestock die—but none of Israel's is even sick /Pharaoh still refuses to let the people go 9:1-7

DEATH OF FIRSTBORN
The firstborn of all the people and cattle of Egypt die —but Israel is spared/ Pharaoh urges Israel to leave, but changes his mind and chases after them 11:1–12:33

LOCUSTS
Locusts cover Egypt and eat everything left by the hail/ Everyone advises Pharaoh to let the Hebrews go, but God hardens Pharaoh's heart and he refuses 10:1-20

DARKNESS
Total darkness covers Egypt for three days so no one can even move—except the Hebrews, who have light as usual/Pharaoh again promises to let Israel go, but again changes his mind 10:21-29

into your ovens, and into your kneading bowls. ⁴And the frogs shall come up on you, on your people, and on all your servants." ' "

⁵Then the LORD spoke to Moses, "Say to Aaron, 'Stretch out your hand with your rod over the streams, over the rivers, and over the ponds, and cause frogs to come up on the land of Egypt.' " ⁶So Aaron stretched out his hand over the waters of Egypt, and the frogs came up and covered the land of Egypt. ⁷And the magicians did so with their enchantments, and brought up frogs on the land of Egypt.

⁸Then Pharaoh called for Moses and Aaron, and said, "Entreat the LORD that He may take away the frogs from me and from my people; and I will let the people go, that they may sacrifice to the LORD."

⁹And Moses said to Pharaoh, "Accept the honor of saying when I shall intercede for you, for your servants, and for your people, to destroy the frogs from you and your houses; *that* they may remain in the river only."

¹⁰So he said, "Tomorrow." And he said, "*Let it be* according to your word, that you may know that *there is* no one like the LORD our God. ¹¹And the frogs shall depart from you, from your houses, from your servants, and from your people. They shall remain in the river only."

¹²Then Moses and Aaron went out from Pharaoh. And Moses cried out to the LORD concerning the frogs which

He had brought against Pharaoh. [13]So the LORD did according to the word of Moses. And the frogs died out of the houses, out of the courtyards, and out of the fields. [14]They gathered them together in heaps, and the land stank. [15]But when Pharaoh saw that there was relief, he hardened his heart and did not heed them, as the LORD had said.

[16]So the LORD said to Moses, "Say to Aaron, 'Stretch out your rod, and strike the dust of the land, so that it may become lice throughout all the land of Egypt.' " [17]And they did so. For Aaron stretched out his hand with his rod and struck the dust of the earth, and it became lice on man and beast. All the dust of the land became lice throughout all the land of Egypt.

[18]Now the magicians so worked with their enchantments to bring forth lice, but they could not. So there were lice on man and beast. [19]Then the magicians said to Pharaoh, "This *is* the finger of God." But Pharaoh's heart grew hard, and he did not heed them, just as the LORD had said.

[20]And the LORD said to Moses, "Rise early in the morning and stand before Pharaoh as he comes out to the water. Then say to him, 'Thus says the LORD: "Let My people go, that they may serve Me. [21]Or else, if you will not let My people go, behold, I will send swarms *of flies* on you and your servants, on your people and into your houses. The houses of the Egyptians shall be full of swarms *of flies*, and also the ground on which they *stand*. [22]And in that day I will set apart the land of Goshen, in which My people dwell, that no swarms *of flies* shall be there, in order that you may know that I *am* the LORD in the midst of the land. [23]I will make a difference between My people and your people. Tomorrow this sign shall be." ' " [24]And the LORD did so. Thick swarms *of flies* came into the house of Pharaoh, *into* his servants' houses, and into all the land of Egypt. The land was corrupted because of the swarms *of flies*.

[25]Then Pharaoh called for Moses and Aaron, and said, "Go, sacrifice to your God in the land."

[26]And Moses said, "It is not right to do so, for we would be sacrificing the abomination of the Egyptians to the LORD our God. If we sacrifice the abomination of the Egyptians before their eyes, then will they not stone us? [27]We will go three days' journey into the wilderness and sacrifice to the LORD our God as He will command us."

[28]So Pharaoh said, "I will let you go, that you may sacrifice to the LORD your God in the wilderness; only you shall not go very far away. Intercede for me."

[29]Then Moses said, "Indeed I am going out from you, and I will entreat the LORD, that the swarms *of flies* may depart tomorrow from Pharaoh, from his servants, and from his people. But let Pharaoh not deal deceitfully anymore in not letting the people go to sacrifice to the LORD."

[30]So Moses went out from Pharaoh and entreated the LORD. [31]And the LORD did according to the word of Moses; He removed the swarms *of flies* from Pharaoh, from his servants, and from his people. Not one remained. [32]But Pharaoh hardened his heart at this time also; neither would he let the people go.

CHAPTER 9 Then the LORD said to Moses, "Go in to Pharaoh and tell him, 'Thus says the LORD God of the Hebrews: "Let My people go, that they may serve Me. [2]For if you refuse to let *them* go, and still hold them, [3]behold, the hand of the LORD will be on your cattle in the field, on the horses, on the donkeys, on the camels, on the oxen, and on the sheep—a very severe pestilence. [4]And the LORD will make a difference between the livestock of Israel and the livestock of Egypt. So nothing shall die of all *that* belongs to the children of Israel." ' " [5]Then the LORD appointed a set time, saying, "Tomorrow the LORD will do this thing in the land."

▸ STUBBORN

8:19 Some people think, "If only I could see a miracle, I would believe in God." God gave Pharaoh just such an opportunity. When lice infested Egypt, even the magicians agreed that this was God's work ("the finger of God") —but still Pharaoh refused to believe. He was stubborn, and stubbornness can blind a person to the truth. When you rid yourself of stubbornness, you may be surprised to discover abundant evidence of God's hand in your life.

[6]So the LORD did this thing on the next day, and all the livestock of Egypt died; but of the livestock of the children of Israel, not one died. [7]Then Pharaoh sent, and indeed, not even one of the livestock of the Israelites was dead. But the heart of Pharaoh became hard, and he did not let the people go.

[8]So the LORD said to Moses and Aaron, "Take for yourselves handfuls of ashes from a furnace, and let Moses scatter it toward the heavens in the sight of Pharaoh. [9]And it will become fine dust in all the land of Egypt, and it will cause boils that break out in sores on man and beast throughout all the land of Egypt." [10]Then they took ashes from the furnace and stood before Pharaoh, and Moses scattered *them* toward heaven. And *they* caused boils that break out in sores on man and beast. [11]And the magicians could not stand before Moses because of the boils, for the boils were on the magicians and on all the Egyptians. [12]But the LORD hardened the heart of Pharaoh; and he did not heed them, just as the LORD had spoken to Moses.

▸ PERSISTENT

9:1 This was the fifth time God sent Moses back to Pharaoh with the demand to let his people go! Moses may have been tired and discouraged by this time, but he continued to obey. Is there a difficult conflict you must face again and again? Don't give up when you know what is right to do. As Moses discovered, persistence is rewarded.

[13]Then the LORD said to Moses, "Rise early in the morning and stand before Pharaoh, and say to him, 'Thus says the LORD God of the Hebrews: "Let My people go, that they may serve Me, [14]for at this time I will send all My plagues to your very heart, and on your servants and on your people, that you may know that *there is* none like Me in all the earth. [15]Now if I had stretched out My hand and struck you and your people with pestilence, then you would have been cut off from the earth. [16]But indeed for this *purpose* I have raised you up, that I may show My power *in* you, and that My name may be declared in all

the earth. ¹⁷As yet you exalt yourself against My people in that you will not let them go. ¹⁸Behold, tomorrow about this time I will cause very heavy hail to rain down, such as has not been in Egypt since its founding until now. ¹⁹Therefore send now *and* gather your livestock and all that you have in the field, for the hail shall come down on every man and every animal which is found in the field and is not brought home; and they shall die.' ' "

²⁰He who feared the word of the LORD among the servants of Pharaoh made his servants and his livestock flee to the houses. ²¹But he who did not regard the word of the LORD left his servants and his livestock in the field.

²²Then the LORD said to Moses, "Stretch out your hand toward heaven, that there may be hail in all the land of Egypt—on man, on beast, and on every herb of the field, throughout the land of Egypt." ²³And Moses stretched out his rod toward heaven; and the LORD sent thunder and hail, and fire darted to the ground. And the LORD rained hail on the land of Egypt. ²⁴So there was hail, and fire mingled with the hail, so very heavy that there was none like it in all the land of Egypt since it became a nation. ²⁵And the hail struck throughout the whole land of Egypt, all that *was* in the field, both man and beast; and the hail struck every herb of the field and broke every tree of the field. ²⁶Only in the land of Goshen, where the children of Israel *were*, there was no hail.

²⁷And Pharaoh sent and called for Moses and Aaron, and said to them, "I have sinned this time. The LORD *is* righteous, and my people and I *are* wicked. ²⁸Entreat the LORD, that there may be no *more* mighty thundering and hail, for *it is* enough. I will let you go, and you shall stay no longer."

²⁹So Moses said to him, "As soon as I have gone out of the city, I will spread out my hands to the LORD; the thunder will cease, and there will be no more hail, that you may know that the earth *is* the LORD's. ³⁰But as for you and your servants, I know that you will not yet fear the LORD God."

³¹Now the flax and the barley were struck, for the barley *was* in the head and the flax *was* in bud. ³²But the wheat and the spelt were not struck, for they *are* late crops.

³³So Moses went out of the city from Pharaoh and spread out his hands to the LORD; then the thunder and the hail ceased, and the rain was not poured on the earth. ³⁴And when Pharaoh saw that the rain, the hail, and the thunder had ceased, he sinned yet more; and he hardened his heart, he and his servants. ³⁵So the heart of Pharaoh was hard; neither would he let the children of Israel go, as the LORD had spoken by Moses.

CHAPTER **10** **THE LONGEST NIGHT.** Now the LORD said to Moses, "Go in to Pharaoh; for I have hardened his heart and the hearts of his servants, that I may show these signs of Mine before him, ²and that you may tell in the hearing of your son and your son's son the mighty things I have done in Egypt, and My signs which I have done among them, that you may know that I *am* the LORD."

³So Moses and Aaron came in to Pharaoh and said to him, "Thus says the LORD God of the Hebrews: 'How long

will you refuse to humble yourself before Me? Let My people go, that they may serve Me. ⁴Or else, if you refuse to let My people go, behold, tomorrow I will bring locusts into your territory. ⁵And they shall cover the face of the earth, so that no one will be able to see the earth; and they shall eat the residue of what is left, which remains to you from the hail, and they shall eat every tree which grows up for you out of the field. ⁶They shall fill your houses, the houses of all your servants, and the houses of all the Egyptians—which neither your fathers nor your fathers' fathers have seen, since the day that they were on the earth to this day.' " And he turned and went out from Pharaoh.

⁷Then Pharaoh's servants said to him, "How long shall this man be a snare to us? Let the men go, that they may serve the LORD their God. Do you not yet know that Egypt is destroyed?"

⁸So Moses and Aaron were brought again to Pharaoh, and he said to them, "Go, serve the LORD your God. Who *are* the ones that are going?"

⁹And Moses said, "We will go with our young and our old; with our sons and our daughters, with our flocks and our herds we will go, for we must hold a feast to the LORD."

¹⁰Then he said to them, "The LORD had better be with you when I let you and your little ones go! Beware, for evil is ahead of you. ¹¹Not so! Go now, you *who are* men, and serve the LORD, for that is what you desired." And they were driven out from Pharaoh's presence.

¹²Then the LORD said to Moses, "Stretch out your hand over the land of Egypt for the locusts, that they may come upon the land of Egypt, and eat every herb of the land— all that the hail has left." ¹³So Moses stretched out his rod over the land of Egypt, and the LORD brought an east wind on the land all that day and all *that* night. When it was morning, the east wind brought the locusts. ¹⁴And the locusts went up over all the land of Egypt and rested on all the territory of Egypt. *They were* very severe; previously there had been no such locusts as they, nor shall there be such after them. ¹⁵For they covered the face of the whole earth, so that the land was darkened; and they ate every herb of the land and all the fruit of the trees which the hail had left. So there remained nothing green on the trees or on the plants of the field throughout all the land of Egypt.

¹⁶Then Pharaoh called for Moses and Aaron in haste, and said, "I have sinned against the LORD your God and against you. ¹⁷Now therefore, please forgive my sin only this once, and entreat the LORD your God, that He may take away from me this death only." ¹⁸So he went out from Pharaoh and entreated the LORD. ¹⁹And the LORD turned a very strong west wind, which took the locusts away and blew them into the Red Sea. There remained not one locust in all the territory of Egypt. ²⁰But the LORD hardened Pharaoh's heart, and he did not let the children of Israel go.

²¹Then the LORD said to Moses, "Stretch out your hand toward heaven, that there may be darkness over the land of Egypt, darkness *which* may even be felt." ²²So Moses stretched out his hand toward heaven, and there was thick darkness in all the land of Egypt three days. ²³The

did not see one another; nor did anyone rise from his place for three days. But all the children of Israel had light in their dwellings.

²⁴Then Pharaoh called to Moses and said, "Go, serve the LORD; only let your flocks and your herds be kept back. Let your little ones also go with you."

²⁵But Moses said, "You must also give us sacrifices and burnt offerings, that we may sacrifice to the LORD our God. ²⁶Our livestock also shall go with us; not a hoof shall be left behind. For we must take some of them to serve the LORD our God, and even we do not know with what we must serve the LORD until we arrive there."

²⁷But the LORD hardened Pharaoh's heart, and he would not let them go. ²⁸Then Pharaoh said to him, "Get away from me! Take heed to yourself and see my face no more! For in the day you see my face you shall die!"

²⁹So Moses said, "You have spoken well. I will never see your face again."

CHAPTER 11 EGYPT'S FIRSTBORN WILL DIE. And

the LORD said to Moses, "I will bring one more plague on Pharaoh and on Egypt. Afterward he will let you go from here. When he lets *you* go, he will surely drive you out of here altogether. ²Speak now in the hearing of the people, and let every man ask from his neighbor and every woman from her neighbor, articles of silver and articles of gold." ³And the LORD gave the people favor in the sight of the Egyptians. Moreover the man Moses *was* very great in the land of Egypt, in the sight of Pharaoh's servants and in the sight of the people.

⁴Then Moses said, "Thus says the LORD: 'About midnight I will go out into the midst of Egypt; ⁵and all the firstborn in the land of Egypt shall die, from the firstborn of Pharaoh who sits on his throne, even to the firstborn of the female servant who *is* behind the handmill, and all the firstborn of the animals. ⁶Then there shall be a great cry throughout all the land of Egypt, such as was not like it *before*, nor shall be like it again. ⁷But against none of the children of Israel shall a dog move its tongue, against man or beast, that you may know that the LORD does make a difference between the Egyptians and Israel.' ⁸And all these your servants shall come down to me and bow down to me, saying, 'Get out, and all the people who follow you!' After that I will go out." Then he went out from Pharaoh in great anger.

⁹But the LORD said to Moses, "Pharaoh will not heed you, so that My wonders may be multiplied in the land of Egypt." ¹⁰So Moses and Aaron did all these wonders before Pharaoh; and the LORD hardened Pharaoh's heart, and he did not let the children of Israel go out of his land.

CHAPTER 12 THE FIRST PASSOVER. Now the LORD

spoke to Moses and Aaron in the land of Egypt, saying, ²"This month *shall be* your beginning of months; it *shall be* the first month of the year to you. ³Speak to all the congregation of Israel, saying: 'On the tenth of this month every man shall take for himself a lamb, according to the house of *his* father, a lamb for a household. ⁴And if the household is too small for the lamb, let him and his neighbor next to his house take *it* according to

the number of the persons; according to each man's need you shall make your count for the lamb. ⁵Your lamb shall be without blemish, a male of the first year. You may take *it* from the sheep or from the goats. ⁶Now you shall keep it until the fourteenth day of the same month. Then the whole assembly of the congregation of Israel shall kill it at twilight. ⁷And they shall take *some* of the blood and put *it* on the two doorposts and on the lintel of the houses where they eat it. ⁸Then they shall eat the flesh on that night; roasted in fire, with unleavened bread *and* with bitter *herbs* they shall eat it. ⁹Do not eat it raw, nor boiled at all with water, but roasted in fire—its head with its legs and its entrails. ¹⁰You shall let none of it remain until morning, and what remains of it until morning you shall burn with fire. ¹¹And thus you shall eat it: *with* a belt on your waist, your sandals on your feet, and your staff in your hand. So you shall eat it in haste. It *is* the LORD's Passover.

¹²'For I will pass through the land of Egypt on that night, and will strike all the firstborn in the land of Egypt, both man and beast; and against all the gods of Egypt I will execute judgment: I *am* the LORD. ¹³Now the blood shall be a sign for you on the houses where you *are*. And when I see the blood, I will pass over you; and the plague shall not be on you to destroy *you* when I strike the land of Egypt.

◢◣◤▬▬▬**HARD-HEARTED**

11:10 Did God really harden Pharaoh's heart and force him to do wrong? Before the 10 plagues began, Moses and Aaron announced what God would do if Pharaoh didn't let the people go. But their message only made Pharaoh stubborn—he was hardening his own heart. In so doing, he defied both God and his messengers. Through the first six plagues, Pharaoh's heart grew even more stubborn. After the sixth plague, God passed judgment. Sooner or later, evil people will be punished for their sins. When it became evident he wouldn't change, God confirmed Pharaoh's prideful decision and set the painful consequences of his actions in motion. God didn't force Pharaoh to reject him; rather, he gave him every opportunity to change his mind. In Ezekiel 33:11, God says, "I have no pleasure in the death of the wicked."

¹⁴'So this day shall be to you a memorial; and you shall keep it as a feast to the LORD throughout your generations. You shall keep it as a feast by an everlasting ordinance. ¹⁵Seven days you shall eat unleavened bread. On the first day you shall remove leaven from your houses. For whoever eats leavened bread from the first day until the seventh day, that person shall be cut off from Israel. ¹⁶On the first day *there shall be* a holy convocation, and on the seventh day there shall be a holy convocation for you. No manner of work shall be done on them; but *that* which everyone must eat—that only may be prepared by you. ¹⁷So you shall observe *the Feast of* Unleavened Bread, for on this same day I will have brought your armies out of the land of Egypt. Therefore you shall observe this day throughout your generations as an everlasting ordinance. ¹⁸In the first *month*, on the fourteenth day of the month at evening, you shall eat unleavened bread, until the twenty-first day of the month at evening. ¹⁹For seven days no leaven shall be found in your houses,

since whoever eats what is leavened, that same person shall be cut off from the congregation of Israel, whether *he is* a stranger or a native of the land. ²⁰You shall eat nothing leavened; in all your dwellings you shall eat unleavened bread.' "

²¹Then Moses called for all the elders of Israel and said to them, "Pick out and take lambs for yourselves according to your families, and kill the Passover *lamb*. ²²And you shall take a bunch of hyssop, dip *it* in the blood that *is* in the basin, and strike the lintel and the two doorposts with the blood that *is* in the basin. And none of you shall go out of the door of his house until morning. ²³For the

▶ SUBSTITUTE

12:23ff Every firstborn child of the Egyptians died, but the Israelite children were spared because the blood of the lamb had been placed on their doorposts. So begins the story of redemption, the central theme of the Bible.

Redemption means "to buy back." We must recognize that if we want to be freed from the deadly consequences of our sins, a tremendous price must be paid. But we don't have to pay it. Jesus Christ, our substitute, has already redeemed us by his death on the cross. Our part is to trust him and accept his gift of eternal life (Titus 2:14; Hebrews 9:13-15,23-26).

LORD will pass through to strike the Egyptians; and when He sees the blood on the lintel and on the two doorposts, the LORD will pass over the door and not allow the destroyer to come into your houses to strike *you*. ²⁴And you shall observe this thing as an ordinance for you and your sons forever. ²⁵It will come to pass when you come to the land which the LORD will give you, just as He promised, that you shall keep this service. ²⁶And it shall be, when your children say to you, 'What do you mean by this service?' ²⁷that you shall say, 'It *is* the Passover sacrifice of the LORD, who passed over the houses of the children of Israel in Egypt when He struck the Egyptians and delivered our households.' " So the people bowed their heads and worshiped. ²⁸Then the children of Israel went away and did *so;* just as the LORD had commanded Moses and Aaron, so they did.

²⁹And it came to pass at midnight that the LORD struck all the firstborn in the land of Egypt, from the firstborn of Pharaoh who sat on his throne to the firstborn of the captive who *was* in the dungeon, and all the firstborn of livestock. ³⁰So Pharaoh rose in the night, he, all his servants, and all the Egyptians; and there was a great cry in Egypt, for *there was* not a house where *there was* not one dead.

³¹Then he called for Moses and Aaron by night, and said, "Rise, go out from among my people, both you and the children of Israel. And go, serve the LORD as you have said. ³²Also take your flocks and your herds, as you have said, and be gone; and bless me also."

³³And the Egyptians urged the people, that they might send them out of the land in haste. For they said, "We *shall* all *be* dead." ³⁴So the people took their dough before it was leavened, having their kneading bowls bound up in their clothes on their shoulders. ³⁵Now the children of Israel had done according to the word of Moses, and they had asked from the Egyptians articles of silver, articles of

gold, and clothing. ³⁶And the LORD had given the people favor in the sight of the Egyptians, so that they granted them *what they requested*. Thus they plundered the Egyptians.

³⁷Then the children of Israel journeyed from Rameses to Succoth, about six hundred thousand men on foot, besides children. ³⁸A mixed multitude went up with them also, and flocks and herds—a great deal of livestock. ³⁹And they baked unleavened cakes of the dough which they had brought out of Egypt; for it was not leavened, because they were driven out of Egypt and could not wait, nor had they prepared provisions for themselves.

⁴⁰Now the sojourn of the children of Israel who lived in Egypt *was* four hundred and thirty years. ⁴¹And it came to pass at the end of the four hundred and thirty years—on that very same day—it came to pass that all the armies of the LORD went out from the land of Egypt. ⁴²It *is* a night of solemn observance to the LORD for bringing them out of the land of Egypt. This *is* that night of the LORD, a solemn observance for all the children of Israel throughout their generations.

⁴³And the LORD said to Moses and Aaron, "This *is* the ordinance of the Passover: No foreigner shall eat it. ⁴⁴But every man's servant who is bought for money, when you have circumcised him, then he may eat it. ⁴⁵A sojourner and a hired servant shall not eat it. ⁴⁶In one house it shall be eaten; you shall not carry any of the flesh outside the house, nor shall you break one of its bones. ⁴⁷All the congregation of Israel shall keep it. ⁴⁸And when a stranger dwells with you *and wants* to keep the Passover to the LORD, let all his males be circumcised, and then let him come near and keep it; and he shall be as a native of the land. For no uncircumcised person shall eat it. ⁴⁹One law shall be for the native-born and for the stranger who dwells among you."

⁵⁰Thus all the children of Israel did; as the LORD commanded Moses and Aaron, so they did. ⁵¹And it came to pass, on that very same day, that the LORD brought the children of Israel out of the land of Egypt according to their armies.

CHAPTER **13** FIRSTBORN DEDICATED TO GOD.

Then the LORD spoke to Moses, saying, ²"Consecrate to Me all the firstborn, whatever opens the womb among the children of Israel, *both* of man and beast; it is Mine."

³And Moses said to the people: "Remember this day in which you went out of Egypt, out of the house of bondage; for by strength of hand the LORD brought you out of this *place*. No leavened bread shall be eaten. ⁴On this day you are going out, in the month Abib. ⁵And it shall be,

▶ BRANDED

13:9 The Feast of Unleavened Bread marked the Hebrews as a u people—as though they were branded on their hands and foreh What do you do that marks you as a follower of God? Think abou way you act at school, demonstrate love for others, show concern social outcast, and treat your family—what you do in these areas leave visible marks for all to see. While certain nationalities are m by customs and traditions, Christians are marked by loving one ar (John 13:34-35).

THE HEBREW CALENDAR

A Hebrew month begins in the middle of a month on our calendar today. Crops are planted in November and December and harvested in March and April.

Month	Today's Calendar	Bible Reference	Israel's Holidays
1 Nisan (Abib)	March–April	Exodus 13:4; 23:15; 34:18; Deuteronomy 16:1	Passover (Leviticus 23:5); Unleavened Bread (Leviticus 23:6); Firstfruits (Leviticus 23:10)
2 Iyyar (Ziv)	April–May	1 Kings 6:1,37	
3 Sivan	May–June	Esther 8:9	Pentecost (Leviticus 23:15)
4 Tammuz	June–July		
5 Ab	July–August		
6 Elul	August–September	Nehemiah 6:15	
7 Tishri (Ethanim)	September–October	1 Kings 8:2	Trumpets (Leviticus 23:24; Numbers 29:1); Day of Atonement (Leviticus 23:27); Tabernacles (Leviticus 23:34)
8 Marchesvan (Bul)	October–November	1 Kings 6:38	
9 Chislev (Kislev)	November–December	Nehemiah 1:1	Dedication (John 10:22)
10 Tebeth	December–January	Esther 2:16	
11 Shebat	January–February	Zechariah 1:7	
12 Adar	February–March	Esther 3:7	Purim (Esther 9:24-32)

when the LORD brings you into the land of the Canaanites and the Hittites and the Amorites and the Hivites and the Jebusites, which He swore to your fathers to give you, a land flowing with milk and honey, that you shall keep this service in this month. ⁶Seven days you shall eat unleavened bread, and on the seventh day *there shall be* a feast to the LORD. ⁷Unleavened bread shall be eaten seven days. And no leavened bread shall be seen among you, nor shall leaven be seen among you in all your quarters. ⁸And you shall tell your son in that day, saying, '*This is done* because of what the LORD did for me when I came up from Egypt.' ⁹It shall be as a sign to you on your hand and as a memorial between your eyes, that the LORD's law may be in your mouth; for with a strong hand the LORD has brought you out of Egypt. ¹⁰You shall therefore keep this ordinance in its season from year to year.

¹¹"And it shall be, when the LORD brings you into the land of the Canaanites, as He swore to you and your fathers, and gives it to you, ¹²that you shall set apart to the LORD all that open the womb, that is, every firstborn that comes from an animal which you have; the males *shall be* the LORD's. ¹³But every firstborn of a donkey you shall redeem with a lamb; and if you will not redeem *it*, then you shall break its neck. And all the firstborn of man among your sons you shall redeem. ¹⁴So it shall be, when your son asks you in time to come, saying, 'What *is* this?'

that you shall say to him, 'By strength of hand the LORD brought us out of Egypt, out of the house of bondage. ¹⁵And it came to pass, when Pharaoh was stubborn about letting us go, that the LORD killed all the firstborn in the land of Egypt, both the firstborn of man and the firstborn of beast. Therefore I sacrifice to the LORD all males that open the womb, but all the firstborn of my sons I redeem.' ¹⁶It shall be as a sign on your hand and as frontlets between your eyes, for by strength of hand the LORD brought us out of Egypt."

OBSTACLES

13:17-18 God doesn't always work in the way that seems best to us. Instead of guiding the Israelites along the direct route from Egypt to the Promised Land, he took them by a longer route to avoid fighting with the Philistines. If God does not lead you along the shortest path to your goal, don't complain or resist. Follow him willingly and trust him to lead you safely around unseen obstacles. He can see the end of your journey from the beginning, and he knows the safest and best route.

¹⁷Then it came to pass, when Pharaoh had let the people go, that God did not lead them *by* way of the land of the Philistines, although that *was* near; for God said, "Lest perhaps the people change their minds when they see war, and return to Egypt." ¹⁸So God led the people around *by* way of the wilderness of the Red Sea. And the

children of Israel went up in orderly ranks out of the land of Egypt.

[19]And Moses took the bones of Joseph with him, for he had placed the children of Israel under solemn oath, saying, "God will surely visit you, and you shall carry up my bones from here with you."

[20]So they took their journey from Succoth and camped in Etham at the edge of the wilderness. [21]And the LORD went before them by day in a pillar of cloud to lead the way, and by night in a pillar of fire to give them light, so as to go by day and night. [22]He did not take away the pillar of cloud by day or the pillar of fire by night *from* before the people.

CHAPTER 14 CROSSING THE RED SEA. Now the

LORD spoke to Moses, saying: [2]"Speak to the children of Israel, that they turn and camp before Pi Hahiroth, between Migdol and the sea, opposite Baal Zephon; you shall camp before it by the sea. [3]For Pharaoh will say of the children of Israel, 'They *are* bewildered by the land; the wilderness has closed them in.' [4]Then I will harden Pharaoh's heart, so that he will pursue them; and I will gain honor over Pharaoh and over all his army, that the Egyptians may know that I *am* the LORD." And they did so.

[5]Now it was told the king of Egypt that the people had fled, and the heart of Pharaoh and his servants was turned against the people; and they said, "Why have we done this, that we have let Israel go from serving us?" [6]So he made ready his chariot and took his people with him. [7]Also, he took six hundred choice chariots, and all the chariots of Egypt with captains over every one of them. [8]And the LORD hardened the heart of Pharaoh king of Egypt, and he pursued the children of Israel; and the children of Israel went out with boldness. [9]So the Egyptians pursued them, all the horses *and* chariots of Pharaoh, his horsemen and his army, and overtook them camping by the sea beside Pi Hahiroth, before Baal Zephon.

[10]And when Pharaoh drew near, the children of Israel lifted their eyes, and behold, the Egyptians marched after them. So they were very afraid, and the children of Israel cried out to the LORD. [11]Then they said to Moses, "Because *there were* no graves in Egypt, have you taken us away to die in the wilderness? Why have you so dealt with us, to bring us up out of Egypt? [12]*Is* this not the word that we told you in Egypt, saying, 'Let us alone that we may serve the Egyptians'? For *it would have been* better for us to serve the Egyptians than that we should die in the wilderness."

[13]And Moses said to the people, "Do not be afraid. Stand still, and see the salvation of the LORD, which He will accomplish for you today. For the Egyptians whom you see today, you shall see again no more forever. [14]The LORD will fight for you, and you shall hold your peace."

[15]And the LORD said to Moses, "Why do you cry to Me? Tell the children of Israel to go forward. [16]"But lift up your rod, and stretch out your hand over the sea and divide it. And the children of Israel shall go on dry *ground* through the midst of the sea. [17]And I indeed will harden the hearts

GET MOVING!

14:15 God told Moses to stop praying and get moving! Prayer deser[ves] a vital place in our life, but there is also a place for action. Sometimes [we] know what to do, but we pray for more guidance as an excuse to postpone doing it. If you know what you should do, then it is time to g[et] moving.

of the Egyptians, and they shall follow them. So I will gain honor over Pharaoh and over all his army, his chariots, and his horsemen. [18]Then the Egyptians shall know that I *am* the LORD, when I have gained honor for Myself over Pharaoh, his chariots, and his horsemen."

[19]And the Angel of God, who went before the camp of Israel, moved and went behind them; and the pillar of cloud went from before them and stood behind them. [20]So it came between the camp of the Egyptians and the camp of Israel. Thus it was a cloud and darkness *to the one*, and it gave light by night *to the other*, so that the one did not come near the other all that night.

[21]Then Moses stretched out his hand over the sea; and the LORD caused the sea to go *back* by a strong east wind all that night, and made the sea into dry *land*, and the waters were divided. [22]So the children of Israel went into the midst of the sea on the dry *ground*, and the waters *were* a wall to them on their right hand and on their left. [23]And the Egyptians pursued and went after them into the midst of the sea, all Pharaoh's horses, his chariots, and his horsemen.

[24]Now it came to pass, in the morning watch, that the LORD looked down upon the army of the Egyptians through the pillar of fire and cloud, and He troubled the army of the Egyptians. [25]And He took off their chariot wheels, so that they drove them with difficulty; and the Egyptians said, "Let us flee from the face of Israel, for the LORD fights for them against the Egyptians."

[26]Then the LORD said to Moses, "Stretch out your hand over the sea, that the waters may come back upon the Egyptians, on their chariots, and on their horsemen." [27]And Moses stretched out his hand over the sea; and

Do not be afraid. STAND STILL AND SEE THE SALVATION OF THE LORD WHICH He will accomplish for you TODAY.

EXODUS 14:13

when the morning appeared, the sea returned to its full depth, while the Egyptians were fleeing into it. So the LORD overthrew the Egyptians in the midst of the sea. 28Then the waters returned and covered the chariots, the horsemen, *and* all the army of Pharaoh that came into the sea after them. Not so much as one of them remained. 29But the children of Israel had walked on dry *land* in the midst of the sea, and the waters *were* a wall to them on their right hand and on their left.

30So the LORD saved Israel that day out of the hand of the Egyptians, and Israel saw the Egyptians dead on the seashore. 31Thus Israel saw the great work which the LORD had done in Egypt; so the people feared the LORD, and believed the LORD and His servant Moses.

CHAPTER 15 SONGS TO THE LORD. Then Moses and the children of Israel sang this song to the LORD, and spoke, saying:

"I will sing to the LORD,
For He has triumphed gloriously!
The horse and its rider
He has thrown into the sea!
2 The LORD *is* my strength and song,
And He has become my salvation;
He *is* my God, and I will praise Him;
My father's God, and I will exalt Him.
3 The LORD *is* a man of war;
The LORD *is* His name.
4 Pharaoh's chariots and his army He has cast into the sea;
His chosen captains also are drowned in the Red Sea.
5 The depths have covered them;
They sank to the bottom like a stone.

6 "Your right hand, O LORD, has become glorious in power;
Your right hand, O LORD, has dashed the enemy in pieces.
7 And in the greatness of Your excellence
You have overthrown those who rose against You;
You sent forth Your wrath;
It consumed them like stubble.
8 And with the blast of Your nostrils
The waters were gathered together;
The floods stood upright like a heap;
The depths congealed in the heart of the sea.
9 The enemy said, 'I will pursue,
I will overtake,
I will divide the spoil;
My desire shall be satisfied on them.
I will draw my sword,
My hand shall destroy them.'
10 You blew with Your wind,

The sea covered them;
They sank like lead in the mighty waters.

11 "Who *is* like You, O LORD, among the gods?
Who *is* like You, glorious in holiness,
Fearful in praises, doing wonders?
12 You stretched out Your right hand;
The earth swallowed them.
13 You in Your mercy have led forth
The people whom You have redeemed;
You have guided *them* in Your strength
To Your holy habitation.

14 "The people will hear *and* be afraid;
Sorrow will take hold of the inhabitants of Philistia.
15 Then the chiefs of Edom will be dismayed;
The mighty men of Moab,
Trembling will take hold of them;
All the inhabitants of Canaan will melt away.
16 Fear and dread will fall on them;
By the greatness of Your arm
They will be *as* still as a stone,
Till Your people pass over, O LORD,
Till the people pass over
Whom You have purchased.
17 You will bring them in and plant them
In the mountain of Your inheritance,
In the place, O LORD, *which* You have made
For Your own dwelling,
The sanctuary, O LORD, *which* Your hands have established.
18 "The LORD shall reign forever and ever."

19For the horses of Pharaoh went with his chariots and his horsemen into the sea, and the LORD brought back the waters of the sea upon them. But the children of Israel went on dry *land* in the midst of the sea.

"Here's what I did..."

Whenever I get discouraged because I can't persuade a friend of the truth of the gospel, I remind myself that we are never going to convince those who don't want to be convinced. This has been a tough thing for me to accept; there are some people I want so badly to become Christians. But I find solace in the story of Moses and Pharaoh. Nothing would convince Pharaoh that Moses represented the one true God . . . not plagues, not miracles, not even the death of Egypt's firstborn. If calamities of this magnitude couldn't move Pharaoh to repent, I am no longer surprised that the daily witness of faithful Christians fails to make a dent in the hearts of many people in our society.

However, I am convinced that the best tactic is the slow, steady work of Christ in our lives, coupled with prayer and our attempts to live the Christian life. I'm learning to place the rest in God's hands.

Richard

AGE 18

FAMOUS SONGS IN THE BIBLE

Where	Purpose of Song
Exodus 15:1-21	Moses' song of victory and praise after God led Israel out of Egypt and saved them by parting the Red Sea; Miriam joined in the singing, too
Numbers 21:17-18	Israel's song of praise to God for giving them water in the wilderness
Deuteronomy 32:1-43	Moses' song of Israel's history with thanksgiving and praise as the Hebrews were about to enter the Promised Land
Judges 5:2-31	Deborah and Barak's song of praise thanking God for Israel's victory over King Jabin's army at Mount Tabor
2 Samuel 22:1-51	David's song of thanks and praise to God for rescuing him from Saul and his other enemies
Song of Solomon	Solomon's song of love celebrating the union of husband and wife
Isaiah 26:1	Isaiah's prophetic song about how the redeemed will sing in the new Jerusalem
Ezra 3:11	Israel's song of praise at the completion of the temple's foundation
Luke 1:46-55	Mary's song of praise to God for the conception of Jesus
Luke 1:68-79	Zacharias's song of praise for the promise of a son
Acts 16:25	Paul and Silas sang hymns in prison
Revelation 5:9-10	The "new song" of the 24 elders acclaiming Christ as worthy to break the seven seals of God's scroll
Revelation 14:3	The song of the 144,000 redeemed from the earth
Revelation 15:3-4	The song of all the redeemed in praise of the Lamb who redeemed them

²⁰Then Miriam the prophetess, the sister of Aaron, took the timbrel in her hand; and all the women went out after her with timbrels and with dances. ²¹And Miriam answered them:

"Sing to the LORD,
For He has triumphed gloriously!
The horse and its rider
He has thrown into the sea!"

²²So Moses brought Israel from the Red Sea; then they went out into the Wilderness of Shur. And they went three days in the wilderness and found no water. ²³Now when they came to Marah, they could not drink the waters of Marah, for they *were* bitter. Therefore the name of it was called Marah. ²⁴And the people complained against Moses, saying, "What shall we drink?" ²⁵So he cried out to the LORD, and the LORD showed him a tree. When he cast *it* into the waters, the waters were made sweet.

There He made a statute and an ordinance for them, and there He tested them, ²⁶and said, "If you diligently heed the voice of the LORD your God and do what is right in His sight, give ear to His commandments and keep all His statutes, I will put none of the diseases on you which I have brought on the Egyptians. For I *am* the LORD who heals you."

DISEASES

15:26 God promised that if the people obeyed him they would b[e] from the diseases that plagued the Egyptians. Little did they know many of the moral laws he later gave them were designed to keep free from sickness. For example, following God's law against prost[itution] would keep them free of venereal disease. God's laws for us are of designed to keep us from harm. Men and women are complex bei[ngs] Our physical, emotional, and spiritual lives are intertwined. Moder[n] medicine is now acknowledging what these laws assumed. If we w[ant] to care for us, we need to submit to his directions for living.

²⁷Then they came to Elim, where there *were* twelve wells of water and seventy palm trees; so they camped there by the waters.

CHAPTER 16 GOD SENDS MANNA AND QUAIL

And they journeyed from Elim, and all the congregation of the children of Israel came to the Wilderness of Sin which is between Elim and Sinai, on the fifteenth day o[f] the second month after they departed from the land of Egypt. ²Then the whole congregation of the children of Israel complained against Moses and Aaron in the wilderness. ³And the children of Israel said to them, "Oh, that we had died by the hand of the LORD in the land of Egypt, when we sat by the pots of meat *and* when we ate bread to the full! For you have brought us out into this wilderness to kill this whole assembly with hunger."

⁴Then the LORD said to Moses, "Behold, I will rain bread from heaven for you. And the people shall go out and gather a certain quota every day, that I may test them, whether they will walk in My law or not. ⁵And it shall be on the sixth day that they shall prepare what they bring in, and it shall be twice as much as they gather daily."

⁶Then Moses and Aaron said to all the children of Israel, "At evening you shall know that the LORD has brought you out of the land of Egypt. ⁷And in the morning you shall see the glory of the LORD; for He hears your complaints against the LORD. But what *are* we, that you complain against us?" ⁸Also Moses said, "*This shall be seen* when the LORD gives you meat to eat in the evening, and in the morning bread to the full; for the LORD hears your complaints which you make against Him. And what *are* we? Your complaints *are* not against us but against the LORD."

⁹Then Moses spoke to Aaron, "Say to all the congregation of the children of Israel, 'Come near before the LORD, for He has heard your complaints.' " ¹⁰Now it came to pass, as Aaron spoke to the whole congregation of the children of Israel, that they looked toward the wilderness, and behold, the glory of the LORD appeared in the cloud.

¹¹And the LORD spoke to Moses, saying, ¹²"I have heard the complaints of the children of Israel. Speak to them, saying, 'At twilight you shall eat meat, and in the morning you shall be filled with bread. And you shall know that I *am* the LORD your God.' "

¹³So it was that quails came up at evening and covered the camp, and in the morning the dew lay all around the camp. ¹⁴And when the layer of dew lifted, there, on the surface of the wilderness, was a small round substance, *as* fine as frost on the ground. ¹⁵So when the children of Israel saw *it*, they said to one another, "What is it?" For they did not know what it *was*.

And Moses said to them, "This *is* the bread which the LORD has given you to eat. ¹⁶This is the thing which the LORD has commanded: 'Let every man gather it according to each one's need, one omer for each person, *according to the* number of persons; let every man take for *those* who *are* in his tent.' "

¹⁷Then the children of Israel did so and gathered, some more, some less. ¹⁸So when they measured *it* by omers, he who gathered much had nothing left over, and he who gathered little had no lack. Every man had gathered according to each one's need. ¹⁹And Moses said, "Let no one leave any of it till morning." ²⁰Notwithstanding they did not heed Moses. But some of them left part of it until morning, and it bred worms and stank. And Moses was angry with them. ²¹So they gathered it every morning,

every man according to his need. And when the sun became hot, it melted.

²²And so it was, on the sixth day, *that* they gathered twice as much bread, two omers for each one. And all the rulers of the congregation came and told Moses. ²³Then he said to them, "This *is what* the LORD has said: 'Tomorrow *is* a Sabbath rest, a holy Sabbath to the LORD. Bake what you will bake *today*, and boil what you will boil; and

STRESSED OUT

16:2 It happened again. As the Israelites encountered danger, shortages, and inconvenience, they complained bitterly and longed to be back in Egypt. But as always, God provided for their needs. Difficult circumstances often lead to stress, and complaining is a natural response. The Israelites didn't really want to be back in Egypt; they just wanted life to get a little easier. In the pressure of the moment, they could not focus on the cause of their stress (in this case, lack of trust in God); they could only think about the quickest way of escape. When pressure comes your way, resist the temptation to make a quick escape. Instead, focus on God's power and wisdom to help you deal with the cause of your stress.

lay up for yourselves all that remains, to be kept until morning.' " ²⁴So they laid it up till morning, as Moses commanded; and it did not stink, nor were there any worms in it. ²⁵Then Moses said, "Eat that today, for today *is* a Sabbath to the LORD; today you will not find it in the field. ²⁶Six days you shall gather it, but on the seventh day, the Sabbath, there will be none."

SCHEDULING

16:23 The Israelites were not supposed to work on the Sabbath—not even to cook food. Why? God knew that the busy routine of daily living could distract people from worshiping him. It is so easy to let school, friends, and other activities crowd our schedules so tightly that we don't spend regular time with God. Carefully guard your time with God.

²⁷Now it happened *that some* of the people went out on the seventh day to gather, but they found none. ²⁸And the LORD said to Moses, "How long do you refuse to keep My commandments and My laws? ²⁹See! For the LORD has given you the Sabbath; therefore He gives you on the sixth day bread for two days. Let every man remain in his place; let no man go out of his place on the seventh day." ³⁰So the people rested on the seventh day.

³¹And the house of Israel called its name Manna. And it *was* like white coriander seed, and the taste of it *was* like wafers *made* with honey. ³²Then Moses said, "This *is* the thing which the LORD has commanded: 'Fill an omer with it, to be kept for your generations, that they may see the bread with which I fed you in the wilderness, when I brought you out of the land of Egypt.' " ³³And Moses said to Aaron, "Take a pot and put an omer of manna in it, and lay it up before the LORD, to be kept for your generations." ³⁴As the LORD commanded Moses, so Aaron laid it up before the Testimony, to be kept. ³⁵And the children of Israel ate manna forty years, until they came to an inhabited land; they ate manna until they came to the border of the land of Canaan. ³⁶Now an omer *is* one-tenth of an ephah.

CHAPTER **17** **WATER FROM A ROCK.** Then all the congregation of the children of Israel set out on their journey from the Wilderness of Sin, according to the commandment of the LORD, and camped in Rephidim; but *there was* no water for the people to drink. ²Therefore the people contended with Moses, and said, "Give us water, that we may drink."

So Moses said to them, "Why do you contend with me? Why do you tempt the LORD?"

³And the people thirsted there for water, and the people complained against Moses, and said, "Why *is* it you have brought us up out of Egypt, to kill us and our children and our livestock with thirst?"

⁴So Moses cried out to the LORD, saying, "What shall I do with this people? They are almost ready to stone me!"

⁵And the LORD said to Moses, "Go on before the people, and take with you some of the elders of Israel. Also take in your hand your rod with which you struck the river, and go. ⁶Behold, I will stand before you there on the rock in Horeb; and you shall strike the rock, and water will come out of it, that the people may drink."

And Moses did so in the sight of the elders of Israel. ⁷So he called the name of the place Massah and Meribah, because of the contention of the children of Israel, and because they tempted the LORD, saying, "Is the LORD among us or not?"

⁸Now Amalek came and fought with Israel in Rephidim. ⁹And Moses said to Joshua, "Choose us some men and go out, fight with Amalek. Tomorrow I will stand on the top of the hill with the rod of God in my hand." ¹⁰So Joshua did as Moses said to him, and fought with Amalek. And Moses, Aaron, and Hur went up to the top of the hill. ¹¹And so it was, when Moses held up his hand, that Israel prevailed; and when he let down his hand, Amalek prevailed. ¹²But Moses' hands *became* heavy; so they took a stone and put *it* under him, and he sat on it. And Aaron and Hur supported his hands, one on one side, and the other on the other side; and his hands were steady until the going down of the sun. ¹³So Joshua defeated Amalek and his people with the edge of the sword.

¹⁴Then the LORD said to Moses, "Write this *for* a memorial in the book and recount *it* in the hearing of Joshua, that I will utterly blot out the remembrance of Amalek from under heaven." ¹⁵And Moses built an altar and called its name, The-LORD-Is-My-Banner; ¹⁶for he said, "Because the LORD has sworn: the LORD *will have* war with Amalek from generation to generation."

CHAPTER **18** **JETHRO VISITS MOSES.** And Jethro, the priest of Midian, Moses' father-in-law, heard of all that God had done for Moses and for Israel His people—that the LORD had brought Israel out of Egypt. ²Then Jethro, Moses' father-in-law, took Zipporah, Moses' wife, after he had sent her back, ³with her two sons, of whom the name of one *was* Gershom (for he said, "I have been a stranger in a foreign land") ⁴and the name of the other *was* Eliezer (for *he said*, "The God of my father *was* my help, and delivered me from the sword of Pharaoh"); ⁵and Jethro, Moses' father-in-law, came with his sons and his wife to Moses in the wilderness, where he was en-

camped at the mountain of God. ⁶Now he had said to Moses, "I, your father-in-law Jethro, am coming to you with your wife and her two sons with her."

⁷So Moses went out to meet his father-in-law, bowed down, and kissed him. And they asked each other about *their* well-being, and they went into the tent. ⁸And Moses told his father-in-law all that the LORD had done to Pharaoh and to the Egyptians for Israel's sake, all the hardship that had come upon them on the way, and *how* the

► **RELATIVES**

18:8-11 Moses told his father-in-law all that God had done, convir him that the Lord was greater than any other god. Our relatives are the hardest people to tell about God. Yet we should look for opportu to tell them what God is doing in our life, because we can have an important influence on them.

LORD had delivered them. ⁹Then Jethro rejoiced for all the good which the LORD had done for Israel, whom He had delivered out of the hand of the Egyptians. ¹⁰And Jethro said, "Blessed *be* the LORD, who has delivered you out of the hand of the Egyptians and out of the hand of Pharaoh, *and* who has delivered the people from under the hand of the Egyptians. ¹¹Now I know that the LORD *is* greater than all the gods; for in the very thing in which they behaved proudly, *He was* above them." ¹²Then Jethro, Moses' father-in-law, took a burnt offering and *other* sacrifices *to offer* to God. And Aaron came with all the elders of Israel to eat bread with Moses' father-in-law before God.

¹³And so it was, on the next day, that Moses sat to judge the people; and the people stood before Moses from morning until evening. ¹⁴So when Moses' father-in-law saw all that he did for the people, he said, "What *is* this thing that you are doing for the people? Why do you alone sit, and all the people stand before you from morning until evening?"

¹⁵And Moses said to his father-in-law, "Because the people come to me to inquire of God. ¹⁶When they have a difficulty, they come to me, and I judge between one and another; and I make known the statutes of God and His laws."

¹⁷So Moses' father-in-law said to him, "The thing that you do *is* not good. ¹⁸Both you and these people who *are* with you will surely wear yourselves out. For this thing *is* too much for you; you are not able to perform it by yourself. ¹⁹Listen now to my voice; I will give you counsel, and God will be with you: Stand before God for the people, so that you may bring the difficulties to God ²⁰And you shall teach them the statutes and the laws, and show them the way in which they must walk and th work they must do. ²¹Moreover you shall select from a the people able men, such as fear God, men of truth hating covetousness; and place *such* over them *to b* rulers of thousands, rulers of hundreds, rulers of fifties and rulers of tens. ²²And let them judge the people at a times. Then it will be *that* every great matter they sha bring to you, but every small matter they themselve shall judge. So it will be easier for you, for they will be *the burden* with you. ²³If you do this thing, and God s

commands you, then you will be able to endure, and all this people will also go to their place in peace."

²⁴So Moses heeded the voice of his father-in-law and did all that he had said. ²⁵And Moses chose able men out of all Israel, and made them heads over the people: rulers of thousands, rulers of hundreds, rulers of fifties, and rulers of tens. ²⁶So they judged the people at all times; the hard cases they brought to Moses, but they judged every small case themselves.

²⁷Then Moses let his father-in-law depart, and he went his way to his own land.

CHAPTER 19 GOD TALKS TO MOSES. In the third month after the children of Israel had gone out of the land of Egypt, on the same day, they came *to* the Wilderness of Sinai. ²For they had departed from Rephidim, had come *to* the Wilderness of Sinai, and camped in the wilderness. So Israel camped there before the mountain.

³And Moses went up to God, and the LORD called to him from the mountain, saying, "Thus you shall say to the house of Jacob, and tell the children of Israel: ⁴'You have seen what I did to the Egyptians, and *how* I bore you on eagles' wings and brought you to Myself. ⁵Now therefore, if you will indeed obey My voice and keep My covenant, then you shall be a special treasure to Me above all people; for all the earth *is* Mine. ⁶And you shall be to Me a kingdom of priests and a holy nation.' These *are* the words which you shall speak to the children of Israel."

⁷So Moses came and called for the elders of the people, and laid before them all these words which the LORD commanded him. ⁸Then all the people answered together and said, "All that the LORD has spoken we will do." So Moses brought back the words of the people to the LORD. ⁹And the LORD said to Moses, "Behold, I come to you in the thick cloud, that the people may hear when I speak with you, and believe you forever."

So Moses told the words of the people to the LORD.

¹⁰Then the LORD said to Moses, "Go to the people and consecrate them today and tomorrow, and let them wash their clothes. ¹¹And let them be ready for the third day. For on the third day the LORD will come down upon Mount Sinai in the sight of all the people. ¹²You shall set bounds for the people all around, saying, 'Take heed to yourselves *that* you do *not* go up to the mountain or touch its base. Whoever touches the mountain shall

surely be put to death. ¹³Not a hand shall touch him, but he shall surely be stoned or shot *with an arrow;* whether man or beast, he shall not live.' When the trumpet sounds long, they shall come near the mountain."

¹⁴So Moses went down from the mountain to the people and sanctified the people, and they washed their clothes. ¹⁵And he said to the people, "Be ready for the third day; do not come near *your* wives."

¹⁶Then it came to pass on the third day, in the morning, that there were thunderings and lightnings, and a thick cloud on the mountain; and the sound of the trumpet was very loud, so that all the people who *were* in the camp trembled. ¹⁷And Moses brought the people out of the camp to meet with God, and they stood at the foot of the mountain. ¹⁸Now Mount Sinai *was* completely in smoke, because the LORD descended upon it in fire. Its smoke ascended like the smoke of a furnace, and the whole mountain quaked greatly. ¹⁹And when the blast of the trumpet sounded long and became louder and louder, Moses spoke, and God answered him by voice. ²⁰Then the LORD came down upon Mount Sinai, on the top of the mountain. And the LORD called Moses to the top of the mountain, and Moses went up.

MOSES

Some people can't stay out of trouble. Moses was that kind of person. He wasn't a troublemaker; he was usually trying to do the right thing. When he saw something wrong, he tried to make it right—and he often ended up in trouble. But doing the right thing is worth it, even if we do get in trouble.

Moses was a reactor. When there was action, he reacted. Whether checking out a burning bush that didn't burn, or defending a Hebrew slave, or trying to stop a fight, Moses reacted to the world around him. God changed Moses—he helped Moses learn to react correctly. When God changes us, he works with the good qualities he gave us at the start—and he forgives and straightens us out.

Moses became a great leader because he learned to react the right way. He wasn't perfect—he even made a mistake that kept him out of the Promised Land—but God shaped and used his life anyway. God didn't change who or what Moses was; he worked on how Moses used what he'd been given. God wants to change us in the same way. He will make the best version of us there could ever be, if we ask him and let him.

UPS:
• Egyptian education; wilderness training
• Greatest Jewish leader; set the Exodus in motion
• Prophet and lawgiver; recorder of the Ten Commandments

DOWNS:
• Failed to enter the Promised Land because of disobedience to God
• Did not always recognize and use the talents of others

STATS:
• Where: Egypt, Midian, Wilderness of Sinai
• Occupation: Prince, shepherd, leader of the Israelites
• Relatives: Sister: Miriam. Brother: Aaron. Wife: Zipporah. Sons: Gershom and Eliezer.

LESSONS: God prepares, and his timetable is life-sized

God does his greatest work through frail people

KEY VERSES: "By faith Moses, when he became of age, refused to be called the son of Pharaoh's daughter, choosing rather to suffer affliction with the people of God than to enjoy the passing pleasures of sin" (Hebrews 11:24-25).

Moses' story is told in the books of Exodus through Deuteronomy. He is also mentioned in Acts 7:20-41; Hebrews 11:23-29.

²¹And the LORD said to Moses, "Go down and warn the people, lest they break through to gaze at the LORD, and many of them perish. ²²Also let the priests who come near the LORD consecrate themselves, lest the LORD break out against them."

²³But Moses said to the LORD, "The people cannot come up to Mount Sinai; for You warned us, saying, 'Set bounds around the mountain and consecrate it.' "

²⁴Then the LORD said to him, "Away! Get down and then come up, you and Aaron with you. But do not let the priests and the people break through to come up to the LORD, lest He break out against them." ²⁵So Moses went down to the people and spoke to them.

CHAPTER 20 THE TEN COMMANDMENTS. And God spoke all these words, saying:

² "I *am* the LORD your God, who brought you out of the land of Egypt, out of the house of bondage.

³ "You shall have no other gods before Me.

⁴ "You shall not make for yourself a carved image—any likeness *of anything* that *is* in heaven above, or that *is* in the earth beneath, or that *is* in the water under the earth; ⁵you shall not bow down to them nor serve them. For I, the LORD your God, *am* a jealous God, visiting the iniquity of the fathers upon the children to the third and fourth *generations* of those who hate Me, ⁶but showing mercy to thousands, to those who love Me and keep My commandments.

◤◢◤◢GOD'S NAME
20:7 God's name is special because it carries his personal identity. Using it frivolously or in a curse is so common today that we may fail to realize how serious it is. The way we use God's name conveys how we really feel about him. We should respect his name and use it appropriately, speaking it in praise or worship rather than in curse or jest.

⁷ "You shall not take the name of the LORD your God in vain, for the LORD will not hold *him* guiltless who takes His name in vain.

⁸ "Remember the Sabbath day, to keep it holy. ⁹Six days you shall labor and do all your work, ¹⁰but the seventh day *is* the Sabbath of the LORD your God. *In it* you shall do no work: you, nor your son, nor your daughter, nor your male servant, nor your female servant, nor your cattle, nor your stranger who *is* within your gates. ¹¹For *in* six days the LORD made the heavens and the earth, the sea, and all that *is* in them, and rested the seventh day. Therefore the LORD blessed the Sabbath day and hallowed it.

¹² "Honor your father and your mother, that your days may be long upon the land which the LORD your God is giving you.

¹³ "You shall not murder.

¹⁴ "You shall not commit adultery.

¹⁵ "You shall not steal.

¹⁶ "You shall not bear false witness against your neighbor.

¹⁷ "You shall not covet your neighbor's house; you shall not covet your neighbor's wife, nor his male ser-

◤◢◤◢PARENTS' PLACE
20:12 This is the first commandment with a promise attached. To live peace for generations in the Promised Land, the Israelites would need respect authority and build strong families. But what does it mean to "honor" parents? Partly, it means speaking well of them and politely t them. It also means acting in a way that shows them courtesy and resp (but not to obey them if this means disobedience to God). It means following their teaching and their example of putting God first. Parent have a special place in God's sight. Even those who find it difficult to g along with their parents are still commanded to honor them.

vant, nor his female servant, nor his ox, nor his donkey, nor anything that *is* your neighbor's."

¹⁸Now all the people witnessed the thunderings, the lightning flashes, the sound of the trumpet, and the mountain smoking; and when the people saw *it,* they trembled and stood afar off. ¹⁹Then they said to Moses, "You speak with us, and we will hear; but let not God speak with us, lest we die."

²⁰And Moses said to the people, "Do not fear; for God has come to test you, and that His fear may be before you, so that you may not sin." ²¹So the people stood afar off, but Moses drew near the thick darkness where God *was.*

²²Then the LORD said to Moses, "Thus you shall say to the children of Israel: 'You have seen that I have talked with you from heaven. ²³You shall not make *anything to be* with Me—gods of silver or gods of gold you shall not make for yourselves. ²⁴An altar of earth you shall make for Me, and you shall sacrifice on it your burnt offerings and your peace offerings, your sheep and your oxen. In every place where I record My name I will come to you, and I will bless you. ²⁵And if you make Me an altar of stone, you shall not build it of hewn stone; for if you use your tool on it, you have profaned it. ²⁶Nor shall you go up by steps to My altar, that your nakedness may not be exposed on it.'

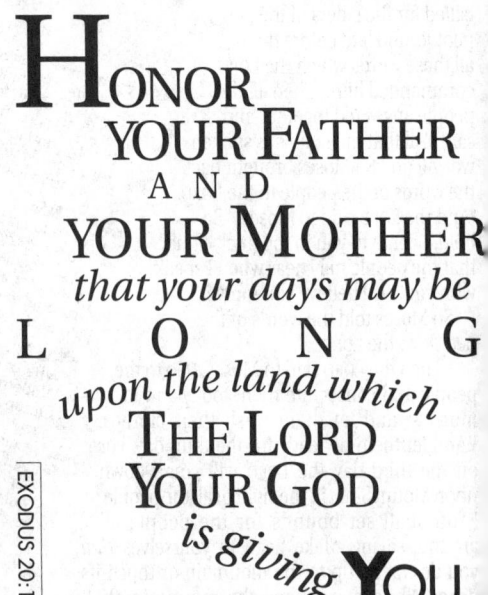

HONOR YOUR FATHER AND YOUR MOTHER *that your days may be* L O N G *upon the land which* THE LORD YOUR GOD *is giving* YOU.

CHAPTER **21** **LAWS ABOUT PEOPLE.** "Now these *are* the judgments which you shall set before them: ²If you buy a Hebrew servant, he shall serve six years; and in the seventh he shall go out free and pay nothing. ³If he comes in by himself, he shall go out by himself; if he *comes in* married, then his wife shall go out with him. ⁴If his master has given him a wife, and she has borne him sons or daughters, the wife and her children shall be her master's, and he shall go out by himself. ⁵But if the servant plainly says, 'I love my master, my wife, and my children; I will not go out free,' ⁶then his master shall bring him to the judges. He shall also bring him to the door, or to the doorpost, and his master shall pierce his ear with an awl; and he shall serve him forever.

⁷"And if a man sells his daughter to be a female slave, she shall not go out as the male slaves do. ⁸If she does not please her master, who has betrothed her to himself, then he shall let her be redeemed. He shall have no right to sell her to a foreign people, since he has dealt deceitfully with her. ⁹And if he has betrothed her to his son, he shall deal with her according to the custom of daughters. ¹⁰If he takes another *wife,* he shall not diminish her food, her clothing, and her marriage rights. ¹¹And if he does not do these three for her, then she shall go out free, without *paying* money.

¹²"He who strikes a man so that he dies shall surely be put to death. ¹³However, if he did not lie in wait, but God delivered *him* into his hand, then I will appoint for you a place where he may flee.

¹⁴"But if a man acts with premeditation against his neighbor, to kill him by treachery, you shall take him from My altar, that he may die.

¹⁵"And he who strikes his father or his mother shall surely be put to death.

¹⁶"He who kidnaps a man and sells him, or if he is found in his hand, shall surely be put to death.

¹⁷"And he who curses his father or his mother shall surely be put to death.

¹⁸"If men contend with each other, and one strikes the other with a stone or with *his* fist, and he does not die but is confined to *his* bed, ¹⁹if he rises again and walks about outside with his staff, then he who struck *him* shall be acquitted. He shall only pay *for* the loss of his time, and shall provide *for him* to be thoroughly healed.

²⁰"And if a man beats his male or female servant with a rod, so that he dies under his hand, he shall surely be punished. ²¹Notwithstanding, if he remains alive a day or two, he shall not be punished; for he *is* his property.

²²"If men fight, and hurt a woman with child, so that she gives birth prematurely, yet no harm follows, he shall surely be punished accordingly as the woman's husband

imposes on him; and he shall pay as the judges *determine.* ²³But if *any* harm follows, then you shall give life for life, ²⁴eye for eye, tooth for tooth, hand for hand, foot for foot, ²⁵burn for burn, wound for wound, stripe for stripe.

²⁶"If a man strikes the eye of his male or female servant, and destroys it, he shall let him go free for the sake of his eye. ²⁷And if he knocks out the tooth of his male or female servant, he shall let him go free for the sake of his tooth.

²⁸"If an ox gores a man or a woman to death, then the ox shall surely be stoned, and its flesh shall not be eaten; but the owner of the ox *shall be* acquitted. ²⁹But if the ox tended to thrust with its horn in times past, and it has been made known to his owner, and he has not kept it confined, so that it has killed a man or a woman, the ox shall be stoned and its owner also shall be put to death. ³⁰If there is imposed on him a sum of money, then he

I loved ballet. I learned how to dance when I was 5 years old and had been doing it ever since. I practiced every day, took lessons at least once a week. I dreamed of someday joining the American Ballet Company. By the time I got to high school, ballet had become my life. Everything revolved around my dancing—even my social life. If I had a recital, I dropped out of every other activity in order to practice. And I was obsessed with my weight, unwilling to gain even a few extra ounces that might jeopardize my figure.

When I became a Christian, I never dreamed it would affect my ballet. But one day in church the sermon was on the first commandment. The pastor talked about how certain things can become gods to us if we let them become more important than God. I thought about the amount of time I spent practicing my ballet compared to the amount of time I spent reading the Bible and praying. Had ballet become my idol?

I began to pray about it, and God showed me that I had let ballet become more important than him. I decided to spend no more time practicing than I did reading the Bible and praying. I cut down on my dancing lessons and got involved in our church's youth group. It's been difficult to let up on dancing, but now it's OK that dancing is my second love. Because my first love is Jesus.

Kristy

AGE 16

shall pay to redeem his life, whatever is imposed on him. ³¹Whether it has gored a son or gored a daughter, according to this judgment it shall be done to him. ³²If the ox gores a male or female servant, he shall give to their master thirty shekels of silver, and the ox shall be stoned.

³³"And if a man opens a pit, or if a man digs a pit and does not cover it, and an ox or a donkey falls in it, ³⁴the owner of the pit shall make *it* good; he shall give money to their owner, but the dead *animal* shall be his.

³⁵"If one man's ox hurts another's, so that it dies, then they shall sell the live ox and divide the money from it; and the dead *ox* they shall also divide. ³⁶Or if it was known

that the ox tended to thrust in time past, and its owner has not kept it confined, he shall surely pay ox for ox, and the dead animal shall be his own.

CHAPTER 22 LAWS ABOUT PROPERTY.
"If a man steals an ox or a sheep, and slaughters it or sells it, he shall restore five oxen for an ox and four sheep for a sheep. ²If the thief is found breaking in, and he is struck so that he dies, *there shall be* no guilt for his bloodshed. ³If the sun has risen on him, *there shall be* guilt for his bloodshed. He should make full restitution; if he has nothing, then he shall be sold for his theft. ⁴If the theft is certainly found alive in his hand, whether it is an ox or donkey or sheep, he shall restore double.

PEER PRESSURE
Mike and Kenny stare in horror at the wrecked family room—stacks of greasy pizza boxes, mud and beer stains on the carpet, a broken lamp. In the downstairs bathroom, Mike is sickened by the sight and smell of vomit. The toilet is clogged and overflowing.

Upstairs, it's even worse: a leaking waterbed, liquor spilled everywhere, a framed print knocked down and broken, a trashed bathroom.

"I'm history," Mike groans. "My parents will be back tomorrow."

"Don't panic. We can clean all night. Your folks will never know we had a party."

Mike gives his friend a you-must-be-brain-dead look. "Come on, Kenny! It would take five maids and a construction crew a week to fix this mess."

How did this disaster happen? Kenny and some friends talked Mike into throwing a "Party for Profit" while his parents were away. They could get a couple of kegs, invite about 50 friends, and charge them each $10. It was a guaranteed success!

Mike refused at first, but soon he gave in. "OK," he finally said. "But only a few people!" Well, the "few" turned into more than 100, and the low-key party quickly turned into a wild nightmare.

Suppose Mike had listened to the advice of Exodus 23:2 instead of the counsel of his friends?

⁵"If a man causes a field or vineyard to be grazed, and lets loose his animal, and it feeds in another man's field, he shall make restitution from the best of his own field and the best of his own vineyard.

⁶"If fire breaks out and catches in thorns, so that stacked grain, standing grain, or the field is consumed, he who kindled the fire shall surely make restitution.

⁷"If a man delivers to his neighbor money or articles to keep, and it is stolen out of the man's house, if the thief is found, he shall pay double. ⁸If the thief is not found, then the master of the house shall be brought to the judges *to see* whether he has put his hand into his neighbor's goods.

⁹"For any kind of trespass, *whether it concerns* an ox, a donkey, a sheep, or clothing, *or* for any kind of lost thing which *another* claims to be his, the cause of both parties shall come before the judges; *and* whomever the judges condemn shall pay double to his neighbor. ¹⁰If a man delivers to his neighbor a donkey, an ox, a sheep, or any

PAYING UP
22:3ff Throughout chapter 22 we find examples of the principle of restitution— making wrongs right. For example, if a man stole an animal, he had to repay double the beast's market value. If you have done someone wrong, perhaps you should go beyond what is expected to make things right. This will (1) help ease any pain you've caused, (2) help the other person to be more forgiving, and (3) make you more likely to think before you do it again.

animal to keep, and it dies, is hurt, or driven away, no one seeing *it*, ¹¹then an oath of the LORD shall be between them both, that he has not put his hand into his neighbor's goods; and the owner of it shall accept *that*, and he shall not make *it* good. ¹²But if, in fact, it is stolen from him, he shall make restitution to the owner of it. ¹³If it is torn to pieces *by a beast, then* he shall bring it as evidence, *and* he shall not make good what was torn.

¹⁴"And if a man borrows *anything* from his neighbor, and it becomes injured or dies, the owner of it not *being* with it, he shall surely make *it* good. ¹⁵If its owner *was* with it, he shall not make *it* good; if it *was* hired, it came for its hire.

¹⁶"If a man entices a virgin who is not betrothed, and lies with her, he shall surely pay the bride-price for her *to be* his wife. ¹⁷If her father utterly refuses to give her to him, he shall pay money according to the bride-price of virgins.

¹⁸"You shall not permit a sorceress to live.

¹⁹"Whoever lies with an animal shall surely be put to death.

²⁰"He who sacrifices to *any* god, except to the LORD only, he shall be utterly destroyed.

²¹"You shall neither mistreat a stranger nor oppress him, for you were strangers in the land of Egypt.

²²"You shall not afflict any widow or fatherless child. ²³If you afflict them in any way, *and* they cry at all to Me, I will surely hear their cry; ²⁴and My wrath will become hot, and I will kill you with the sword; your wives shall be widows, and your children fatherless.

²⁵"If you lend money to *any of* My people *who are* poor among you, you shall not be like a moneylender to him; you shall not charge him interest. ²⁶If you ever take your neighbor's garment as a pledge, you shall return it to him before the sun goes down. ²⁷For that *is* his only covering, it *is* his garment for his skin. What will he sleep in? And it will be that when he cries to Me, I will hear, for I *am* gracious.

²⁸"You shall not revile God, nor curse a ruler of your people.

²⁹"You shall not delay *to offer* the first of your ripe produce and your juices. The firstborn of your sons you shall give to Me. ³⁰Likewise you shall do with your oxen *and* your sheep. It shall be with its mother seven days; on the eighth day you shall give it to Me.

³¹"And you shall be holy men to Me: you shall not eat meat torn *by beasts* in the field; you shall throw it to the dogs.

STRANGERS
22:21 God warned the Israelites not to treat strangers unfairly, because they themselves were once strangers in Egypt. It is not easy coming to a new environment where you feel alone and out of place. Are there strangers in your corner of the world? New arrivals at school? Immigrants from another country? Be sensitive to their struggles and express God's love by your kindness and generosity.

CHAPTER 23 "You shall not circulate a false report. Do not put your hand with the wicked to be an unrighteous witness. ²You shall not follow a crowd to do evil; nor shall you testify in a dispute so as to turn aside after many to pervert *justice.* ³You shall not show partiality to a poor man in his dispute.

⁴"If you meet your enemy's ox or his donkey going astray, you shall surely bring it back to him again. ⁵If you see the donkey of one who hates you lying under its burden, and you would refrain from helping it, you shall surely help him with it.

⁶"You shall not pervert the judgment of your poor in his dispute. ⁷Keep yourself far from a false matter; do not kill the innocent and righteous. For I will not justify the wicked. ⁸And you shall take no bribe, for a bribe blinds the discerning and perverts the words of the righteous.

⁹"Also you shall not oppress a stranger, for you know the heart of a stranger, because you were strangers in the land of Egypt.

¹⁰"Six years you shall sow your land and gather in its produce, ¹¹but the seventh *year* you shall let it rest and lie fallow, that the poor of your people may eat; and what they leave, the beasts of the field may eat. In like manner you shall do with your vineyard *and* your olive grove. ¹²Six days you shall do your work, and on the seventh day you shall rest, that your ox and your donkey may rest, and the son of your female servant and the stranger may be refreshed.

¹³"And in all that I have said to you, be circumspect and make no mention of the name of other gods, nor let it be heard from your mouth.

¹⁴"Three times you shall keep a feast to Me in the year: ¹⁵You shall keep the Feast of Unleavened Bread (you shall eat unleavened bread seven days, as I commanded you, at the time appointed in the month of Abib, for in it you came out of Egypt; none shall appear before Me empty); ¹⁶and the Feast of Harvest, the firstfruits of your labors which you have sown in the field; and the Feast of Ingathering at the end of the year, when you have gathered in *the fruit of* your labors from the field. ¹⁷Three times in the year all your males shall appear before the Lord GOD.

¹⁸"You shall not offer the blood of My sacrifice with leavened bread; nor shall the fat of My sacrifice remain until morning. ¹⁹The first of the firstfruits of your land you shall bring into the house of the LORD your God. You shall not boil a young goat in its mother's milk.

²⁰"Behold, I send an Angel before you to keep you in the way and to bring you into the place which I have prepared. ²¹Beware of Him and obey His voice; do not provoke Him, for He will not pardon your transgressions; for My name *is* in Him. ²²But if you indeed obey His voice and do all that I speak, then I will be an enemy to your enemies and an adversary to your adversaries. ²³For My Angel will go before you and bring you in to the Amorites and the Hittites and the Perizzites and the Canaanites and the Hivites and the Jebusites; and I will cut them off. ²⁴You shall not bow down to their gods, nor serve them, nor do according to their works; but you shall utterly overthrow them and completely break down their *sacred* pillars.

²⁵"So you shall serve the LORD your God, and He will bless your bread and your water. And I will take sickness away from the midst of you. ²⁶No one shall suffer miscarriage or be barren in your land; I will fulfill the number of your days.

²⁷"I will send My fear before you, I will cause confusion among all the people to whom you come, and will make all your enemies turn *their* backs to you. ²⁸And I will send hornets before you, which shall drive out the Hivite, the Canaanite, and the Hittite from before you. ²⁹I will not drive them out from before you in one year, lest the land become desolate and the beasts of the field become too numerous for you. ³⁰Little by little I will drive them out from before you, until you have increased, and you inherit the land. ³¹And I will set your bounds from the Red

━━━━━━━━━**GOSSIP**

23:1 Making up or passing along untrue reports was strictly forbidden by God. Gossip, slander, and false witnessing undermined families, strained neighborhood cooperation, and made chaos of the justice system. Destructive gossip still causes problems. Even if you do not initiate a lie, you become responsible if you pass it along. Don't circulate rumors; squelch them.

Sea to the sea, Philistia, and from the desert to the River. For I will deliver the inhabitants of the land into your hand, and you shall drive them out before you. ³²You shall make no covenant with them, nor with their gods. ³³They shall not dwell in your land, lest they make you sin against Me. For *if* you serve their gods, it will surely be a snare to you."

CHAPTER 24 THE PEOPLE PROMISE TO OBEY.
Now He said to Moses, "Come up to the LORD, you and Aaron, Nadab and Abihu, and seventy of the elders of Israel, and worship from afar. ²And Moses alone shall come near the LORD, but they shall not come near; nor shall the people go up with him."

³So Moses came and told the people all the words of the LORD and all the judgments. And all the people answered with one voice and said, "All the words which the LORD has said we will do." ⁴And Moses wrote all the words of the LORD. And he rose early in the morning, and built an altar at the foot of the mountain, and twelve pillars according to the twelve tribes of Israel. ⁵Then he sent young men of the children of Israel, who offered burnt offerings and sacrificed peace offerings of oxen to the LORD. ⁶And Moses took half the blood and put *it* in basins, and half the blood he sprinkled on the altar. ⁷Then he took the Book of the Covenant and read in the hearing of the people. And they said, "All that the LORD has said we will do, and be obedient." ⁸And Moses took the blood, sprinkled *it* on the people, and said, "This is the blood of the covenant which the LORD has made with you according to all these words."

⁹Then Moses went up, also Aaron, Nadab, and Abihu, and seventy of the elders of Israel, ¹⁰and they saw the God of Israel. And *there was* under His feet as it were a paved work of sapphire stone, and it was like the very heavens in *its* clarity. ¹¹But on the nobles of the children of Israel

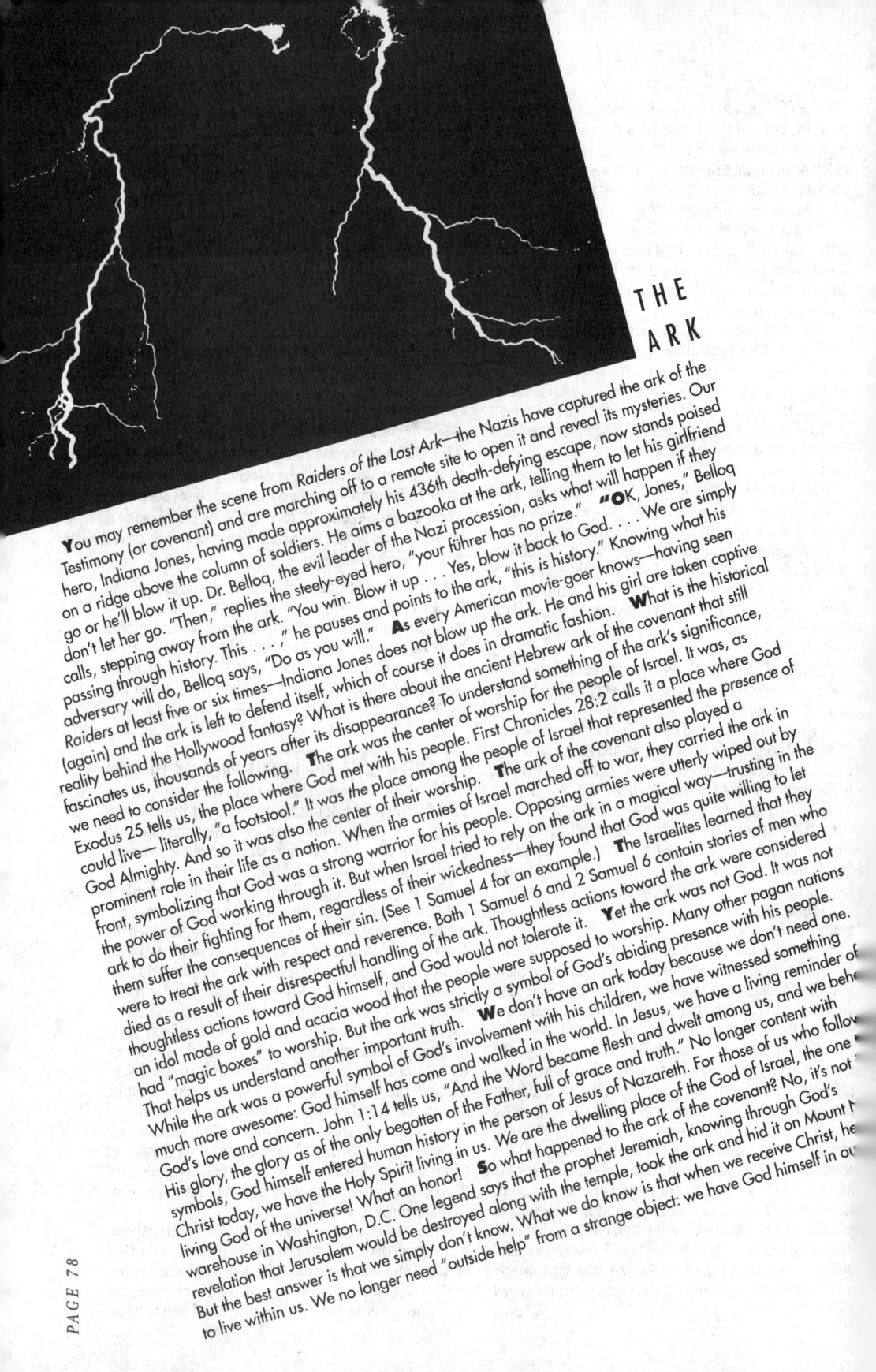

You may remember the scene from *Raiders of the Lost Ark*—the Nazis have captured the ark of the Testimony (or covenant) and are marching off to a remote site to open it and reveal its mysteries. Our hero, Indiana Jones, having made approximately his 436th death-defying escape, now stands poised on a ridge above the column of soldiers. He aims a bazooka at the ark, telling them to let his girlfriend go or he'll blow it up. Dr. Belloq, the evil leader of the Nazi procession, asks what will happen if they don't let her go. "Then," replies the steely-eyed hero, "your führer has no prize." **"O**K, Jones," Belloq calls, stepping away from the ark. "You win. Blow it up . . . Yes, blow it back to God. . . . We are simply passing through history. This . . . ," he pauses and points to the ark, "this is history." Knowing what his adversary will do, Belloq says, "Do as you will." **A**s every American movie-goer knows—having seen *Raiders* at least five or six times—Indiana Jones does not blow up the ark. He and his girl are taken captive (again) and the ark is left to defend itself. What is there about the ancient Hebrew ark of the covenant that still fascinates us, thousands of years after its disappearance? To understand something of the ark's significance, we need to consider the following. **T**he ark was the center of worship for the people of Israel. It was, as Exodus 25 tells us, the place where God met with his people. First Chronicles 28:2 calls it a place where God could live—literally, "a footstool." It was the place among the people of Israel that represented the presence of God Almighty. And so it was also the center of their worship. **T**he ark of the covenant also played a prominent role in their life as a nation. When the armies of Israel marched off to war, they carried the ark in front, symbolizing that God was a strong warrior for his people. Opposing armies were utterly wiped out by the power of God working through it. But when Israel tried to rely on the ark in a magical way—trusting in the ark to do their fighting for them, regardless of their wickedness—they found that God was quite willing to let them suffer the consequences of their sin. (See 1 Samuel 4 for an example.) **T**he Israelites learned that they were to treat the ark with respect and reverence. Both 1 Samuel 6 and 2 Samuel 6 contain stories of men who died as a result of their disrespectful handling of the ark. Thoughtless actions toward the ark were considered thoughtless actions toward God himself, and God would not tolerate it. **Y**et the ark was not God. It was not an idol made of gold and acacia wood. But the ark was strictly a symbol of God's abiding presence with his people. That helps us understand another important truth. **W**e don't have an ark today because we don't need one. While the ark was a powerful symbol of God's involvement with his children, we have witnessed something much more awesome: God himself has come and walked in the world. In Jesus, we have a living reminder of God's love and concern. John 1:14 tells us, "And the Word became flesh and dwelt among us, and we behe[ld] His glory, the glory as of the only begotten of the Father, full of grace and truth." No longer content with symbols, God himself entered human history in the person of Jesus of Nazareth. For those of us who follow Christ today, we have the Holy Spirit living in us. We are the dwelling place of the God of Israel, the one living God of the universe! What an honor! **S**o what happened to the ark of the covenant? No, it's not in a warehouse in Washington, D.C. One legend says that the prophet Jeremiah, knowing through God's revelation that Jerusalem would be destroyed along with the temple, took the ark and hid it on Mount N[ebo]. But the best answer is that we simply don't know. What we do know is that when we receive Christ, he[ ]to live within us. We no longer need "outside help" from a strange object: we have God himself in ou[r]

He did not lay His hand. So they saw God, and they ate and drank.

¹²Then the LORD said to Moses, "Come up to Me on the mountain and be there; and I will give you tablets of stone, and the law and commandments which I have written, that you may teach them."

¹³So Moses arose with his assistant Joshua, and Moses went up to the mountain of God. ¹⁴And he said to the elders, "Wait here for us until we come back to you. Indeed, Aaron and Hur *are* with you. If any man has a difficulty, let him go to them." ¹⁵Then Moses went up into the mountain, and a cloud covered the mountain.

¹⁶Now the glory of the LORD rested on Mount Sinai, and the cloud covered it six days. And on the seventh day He called to Moses out of the midst of the cloud. ¹⁷The sight of the glory of the LORD *was* like a consuming fire on the top of the mountain in the eyes of the children of Israel. ¹⁸So Moses went into the midst of the cloud and went up into the mountain. And Moses was on the mountain forty days and forty nights.

CHAPTER 25 HOW TO BUILD THE TABERNACLE.

Then the LORD spoke to Moses, saying: ²"Speak to the children of Israel, that they bring Me an offering. From everyone who gives it willingly with his heart you shall take My offering. ³And this *is* the offering which you shall take from them: gold, silver, and bronze; ⁴blue, purple, and scarlet *thread*, fine linen, and goats' *hair*; ⁵ram skins dyed red, badger skins, and acacia wood; ⁶oil for the light, and spices for the anointing oil and for the sweet incense; ⁷onyx stones, and stones to be set in the ephod and in the breastplate. ⁸And let them make Me a sanctuary, that I may dwell among them. ⁹According to all that I show you, *that is*, the pattern of the tabernacle and the pattern of all its furnishings, just so you shall make *it*.

¹⁰"And they shall make an ark of acacia wood; two and a half cubits *shall be* its length, a cubit and a half its width, and a cubit and a half its height. ¹¹And you shall overlay it with pure gold, inside and out you shall overlay it, and shall make on it a molding of gold all around. ¹²You shall cast four rings of gold for it, and put *them* in its four corners; two rings *shall be* on one side, and two rings on the other side. ¹³And you shall make poles *of* acacia wood, and overlay them with gold. ¹⁴You shall put the poles into the rings on the sides of the ark, that the ark may be carried by them. ¹⁵The poles shall be in the rings of the ark; they shall not be taken from it. ¹⁶And you shall put into the ark the Testimony which I will give you.

¹⁷"You shall make a mercy seat of pure gold; two and a half cubits *shall be* its length and a cubit and a half its width. ¹⁸And you shall make two cherubim of gold; of hammered work you shall make them at the two ends of the mercy seat. ¹⁹Make one cherub at one end, and the other cherub at the other end; you shall make the cherubim at the two ends of it *of one piece* with the mercy seat. ²⁰And the cherubim shall stretch out *their* wings above, covering the mercy seat with their wings, and they shall face one another; the faces of the cherubim *shall be* toward the mercy seat. ²¹You shall put the mercy seat on top of the ark, and in the ark you shall put the Testimony

that I will give you. ²²And there I will meet with you, and I will speak with you from above the mercy seat, from between the two cherubim which *are* on the ark of the Testimony, about everything which I will give you in commandment to the children of Israel.

²³"You shall also make a table of acacia wood; two cubits *shall be* its length, a cubit its width, and a cubit and a half its height. ²⁴And you shall overlay it with pure gold, and make a molding of gold all around. ²⁵You shall make for it a frame of a handbreadth all around, and you shall make a gold molding for the frame all around. ²⁶And you shall make for it four rings of gold, and put the rings on the four corners that *are* at its four legs. ²⁷The rings shall be close to the frame, as holders for the poles to bear the table. ²⁸And you shall make the poles of acacia wood, and overlay them with gold, that the table may be carried with them. ²⁹You shall make its dishes, its pans, its pitchers, and its bowls for pouring. You shall make them of pure gold. ³⁰And you shall set the showbread on the table before Me always.

³¹"You shall also make a lampstand of pure gold; the lampstand shall be of hammered work. Its shaft, its branches, its bowls, its *ornamental* knobs, and flowers shall be *of one piece*. ³²And six branches shall come out of its sides: three branches of the lampstand out of one side, and three branches of the lampstand out of the other side. ³³Three bowls *shall be* made like almond *blossoms* on one branch, *with* an *ornamental* knob and a flower, and three bowls made like almond *blossoms* on the other branch, *with* an *ornamental* knob and a flower—and so for the six branches that come out of the lampstand. ³⁴On the lampstand itself four bowls *shall be made like almond blossoms, each with* its *ornamental* knob and flower. ³⁵And *there shall be* a knob under the *first* two branches of the same, a knob under the *second* two branches of the same, and a knob under the *third* two branches of the same, according to the six branches that extend from the lampstand. ³⁶Their knobs and their branches *shall be of one piece;* all of it *shall be* one hammered piece of pure gold. ³⁷You shall make seven lamps for it, and they shall arrange its lamps so that they give light in front of it. ³⁸And its wick-trimmers and their trays *shall be* of pure gold. ³⁹It shall be made of a talent of pure gold, with all these utensils. ⁴⁰And see to it that you make *them* according to the pattern which was shown you on the mountain.

CHAPTER 26 THE TENT.

"Moreover you shall make the tabernacle *with* ten curtains *of* fine woven linen and blue, purple, and scarlet *thread;* with artistic designs of cherubim you shall weave them. ²The length of each curtain *shall be* twenty-eight cubits, and the width of each curtain four cubits. And every one of the curtains shall have the same measurements. ³Five curtains shall be coupled to one another, and *the other* five curtains *shall be* coupled to one another. ⁴And you shall make loops of blue *yarn* on the edge of the curtain on the selvedge of *one* set, and likewise you shall do on the outer edge of *the other* curtain of the second set. ⁵Fifty loops you shall make in the one curtain, and fifty loops you

26:31 This veil, or curtain, separated the two sacred rooms in the tabernacle—the holy place and the Most Holy. The priest entered the holy place each day to commune with God and tend to the altar of incense, the lampstand, and the table of the showbread. The Most Holy was where God himself dwelt, his presence resting on the mercy seat, which covered the ark of the covenant. Only the high priest could enter the Most Holy. Even he could do so only once a year (on the Day of Atonement) to make atonement for the sins of the nation as a whole. When Jesus Christ died on the cross, the curtain in the temple (which had replaced the tabernacle) tore from top to bottom (Mark 15:38), symbolizing our free access to God because of Jesus' death. No longer do people have to approach God through priests and sacrifices.

shall make on the edge of the curtain that *is* on the end of the second set, that the loops may be clasped to one another. ⁶And you shall make fifty clasps of gold, and couple the curtains together with the clasps, so that it may be one tabernacle.

⁷"You shall also make curtains of goats' *hair,* to be a tent over the tabernacle. You shall make eleven curtains. ⁸The length of each curtain *shall be* thirty cubits, and the width of each curtain four cubits; and the eleven curtains shall all have the same measurements. ⁹And you shall couple five curtains by themselves and six curtains by themselves, and you shall double over the sixth curtain at the forefront of the tent. ¹⁰You shall make fifty loops on the edge of the curtain that is outermost in *one* set, and fifty loops on the edge of the curtain of the second set. ¹¹And you shall make fifty bronze clasps, put the clasps into the loops, and couple the tent together, that it may be one. ¹²The remnant that remains of the curtains of the tent, the half curtain that remains, shall hang over the back of the tabernacle. ¹³And a cubit on one side and a cubit on the other side, of what remains of the length of the curtains of the tent, shall hang over the sides of the tabernacle, on this side and on that side, to cover it. ¹⁴"You shall also make a covering of ram skins dyed red for the tent, and a covering of badger skins above that.

¹⁵"And for the tabernacle you shall make the boards of acacia wood, standing upright. ¹⁶Ten cubits *shall be* the length of a board, and a cubit and a half *shall be* the width of each board. ¹⁷Two tenons *shall be* in each board for binding one to another. Thus you shall make for all the boards of the tabernacle. ¹⁸And you shall make the boards for the tabernacle, twenty boards for the south side. ¹⁹You shall make forty sockets of silver under the twenty boards: two sockets under each of the boards for its two tenons. ²⁰And for the second side of the tabernacle, the north side, *there shall be* twenty boards ²¹and their forty sockets of silver: two sockets under each of the boards. ²²For the far side of the tabernacle, westward, you shall make six boards. ²³And you shall also make two boards for the two back corners of the tabernacle. ²⁴They shall be coupled together at the bottom and they shall be coupled together at the top by one ring. Thus it shall be for both of them. They shall be for the two corners. ²⁵So there shall be eight boards with their sockets of silver—sixteen sockets—two sockets under each of the boards.

²⁶"And you shall make bars of acacia wood: five for the boards on one side of the tabernacle, ²⁷five bars for the boards on the other side of the tabernacle, and five bars for the boards of the side of the tabernacle, for the far side westward. ²⁸The middle bar shall pass through the midst of the boards from end to end. ²⁹You shall overlay the boards with gold, make their rings of gold *as* holders for the bars, and overlay the bars with gold. ³⁰And you shall raise up the tabernacle according to its pattern which you were shown on the mountain.

³¹"You shall make a veil woven of blue, purple, and scarlet *thread,* and fine woven linen. It shall be woven with an artistic design of cherubim. ³²You shall hang it upon the four pillars of acacia *wood* overlaid with gold. Their hooks *shall be* gold, upon four sockets of silver. ³³And you shall hang the veil from the clasps. Then you shall bring the ark of the Testimony in there, behind the veil. The veil shall be a divider for you between the holy *place* and the Most Holy. ³⁴You shall put the mercy seat upon the ark of the Testimony in the Most Holy. ³⁵You shall set the table outside the veil, and the lampstand across from the table on the side of the tabernacle toward the south; and you shall put the table on the north side.

³⁶"You shall make a screen for the door of the tabernacle, *woven of* blue, purple, and scarlet *thread,* and fine woven linen, made by a weaver. ³⁷And you shall make for the screen five pillars of acacia *wood,* and overlay them with gold; their hooks *shall be* gold, and you shall cast five sockets of bronze for them.

CHAPTER **27** **THE ALTAR.** "You shall make an altar of acacia wood, five cubits long and five cubits wide—the altar shall be square—and its height *shall be* three cubits. ²You shall make its horns on its four corners; its horns shall be of one piece with it. And you shall overlay it with bronze. ³Also you shall make its pans to receive its ashes, and its shovels and its basins and its forks and its firepans; you shall make all its utensils of bronze. ⁴You shall make a grate for it, a network of bronze; and on the network you shall make four bronze rings at its four corners. ⁵You shall put it under the rim of the altar beneath, that the network may be midway up the altar. ⁶And you shall make poles for the altar, poles of acacia wood, and overlay them with bronze. ⁷The poles shall be put in the rings, and the poles shall be on the two sides of the altar to bear it. ⁸You shall make it hollow with boards; as it was shown you on the mountain, so shall they make *it.*

⁹"You shall also make the court of the tabernacle. For the south side *there shall be* hangings for the court *made of* fine woven linen, one hundred cubits long for one side. ¹⁰And its twenty pillars and their twenty sockets *shall be* bronze. The hooks of the pillars and their bands *shall be* silver. ¹¹Likewise along the length of the north side *there shall be* hangings one hundred *cubits* long, with its twenty pillars and their twenty sockets of bronze, and the hooks of the pillars and their bands of silver.

¹²"And along the width of the court on the west side *shall be* hangings of fifty cubits, with their ten pillars and their ten sockets. ¹³The width of the court on the east side *shall be* fifty cubits. ¹⁴The hangings on *one* side *of the gate* *shall be* fifteen cubits, *with* their three pillars and their three sockets. ¹⁵And on the other side *shall be* hangings o-

ifteen *cubits, with* their three pillars and their three ockets.

¹⁶"For the gate of the court *there shall be* a screen wenty cubits long, *woven of* blue, purple, and scarlet *hread,* and fine woven linen, made by a weaver. It *shall have* four pillars and four sockets. ¹⁷All the pillars around he court shall have bands of silver; their hooks *shall be* of silver and their sockets of bronze. ¹⁸The length of the ourt *shall be* one hundred cubits, the width fifty hroughout, and the height five cubits, *made of* fine voven linen, and its sockets of bronze. ¹⁹All the utensils of the tabernacle for all its service, all its pegs, and all the egs of the court, *shall be* of bronze.

²⁰"And you shall command the children of Israel that hey bring you pure oil of pressed olives for the light, to ause the lamp to burn continually. ²¹In the tabernacle of neeting, outside the veil which *is* before the Testimony, aron and his sons shall tend it from evening until morn-ng before the LORD. *It shall be* a statute forever to their enerations on behalf of the children of Israel.

CHAPTER **28** CLOTHES FOR THE PRIESTS. "Now ake Aaron your brother, and his sons with him, from mong the children of Israel, that he may minister to Me s priest, Aaron *and* Aaron's sons: Nadab, Abihu, Eleazar, nd Ithamar. ²And you shall make holy garments for aron your brother, for glory and for beauty. ³So you shall peak to all *who are* gifted artisans, whom I have filled vith the spirit of wisdom, that they may make Aaron's arments, to consecrate him, that he may minister to Me s priest. ⁴And these *are* the garments which they shall nake: a breastplate, an ephod, a robe, a skillfully woven unic, a turban, and a sash. So they shall make holy arments for Aaron your brother and his sons, that he nay minister to Me as priest.

⁵"They shall take the gold, blue, purple, and scarlet *hread,* and the fine linen, ⁶and they shall make the phod of gold, blue, purple, *and* scarlet *thread,* and fine voven linen, artistically worked. ⁷It shall have two shoul-ler straps joined at its two edges, and *so* it shall be joined ogether. ⁸And the intricately woven band of the ephod, vhich *is* on it, shall be of the same workmanship, *made of* gold, blue, purple, and scarlet *thread,* and fine woven nen.

⁹"Then you shall take two onyx stones and engrave on hem the names of the sons of Israel: ¹⁰six of their names n one stone and six names on the other stone, in order f their birth. ¹¹With the work of an engraver in stone, *like* he engravings of a signet, you shall engrave the two tones with the names of the sons of Israel. You shall set hem in settings of gold. ¹²And you shall put the two tones on the shoulders of the ephod *as* memorial stones or the sons of Israel. So Aaron shall bear their names efore the LORD on his two shoulders as a memorial. You shall also make settings of gold, ¹⁴and you shall nake two chains of pure gold like braided cords, and asten the braided chains to the settings.

¹⁵"You shall make the breastplate of judgment. Artisti-ally woven according to the workmanship of the ephod ou shall make it: of gold, blue, purple, and scarlet

thread, and fine woven linen, you shall make it. ¹⁶It shall be doubled into a square: a span *shall be* its length, and a span *shall be* its width. ¹⁷And you shall put settings of stones in it, four rows of stones: *The first* row *shall be* a sardius, a topaz, and an emerald; *this shall be* the first row; ¹⁸the second row *shall be* a turquoise, a sapphire, and a diamond; ¹⁹the third row, a jacinth, an agate, and an amethyst; ²⁰and the fourth row, a beryl, an onyx, and a jasper. They shall be set in gold settings. ²¹And the stones shall have the names of the sons of Israel, twelve accord-ing to their names, *like* the engravings of a signet, each one with its own name; they shall be according to the twelve tribes.

²²"You shall make chains for the breastplate at the end, like braided cords of pure gold. ²³And you shall make two rings of gold for the breastplate, and put the two rings on the two ends of the breastplate. ²⁴Then you shall put the two braided *chains* of gold in the two rings which are on the ends of the breastplate; ²⁵and the *other* two ends of the two braided *chains* you shall fasten to the two set-tings, and put them on the shoulder straps of the ephod in the front.

²⁶"You shall make two rings of gold, and put them on the two ends of the breastplate, on the edge of it, which is on the inner side of the ephod. ²⁷And two *other* rings of gold you shall make, and put them on the two shoulder straps, underneath the ephod toward its front, right at the seam above the intricately woven band of the ephod. ²⁸They shall bind the breastplate by means of its rings to the rings of the ephod, using a blue cord, so that it is above the intricately woven band of the ephod, and so that the breastplate does not come loose from the ephod.

²⁹"So Aaron shall bear the names of the sons of Israel on the breastplate of judgment over his heart, when he goes into the holy *place,* as a memorial before the LORD continually. ³⁰And you shall put in the breastplate of judgment the Urim and the Thummim, and they shall be over Aaron's heart when he goes in before the LORD. So Aaron shall bear the judgment of the children of Israel over his heart before the LORD continually.

³¹"You shall make the robe of the ephod all of blue. ³²There shall be an opening for his head in the middle of it; it shall have a woven binding all around its opening, like the opening in a coat of mail, so that it does not tear. ³³And upon its hem you shall make pomegranates of blue, purple, and scarlet, all around its hem, and bells of gold between them all around: ³⁴a golden bell and a pomegranate, a golden bell and a pomegranate, upon the hem of the robe all around. ³⁵And it shall be upon Aaron when he ministers, and its sound will be heard when he goes into the holy *place* before the LORD and when he comes out, that he may not die.

³⁶"You shall also make a plate of pure gold and engrave on it, *like* the engraving of a signet:

HOLINESS TO THE LORD.

³⁷And you shall put it on a blue cord, that it may be on the turban; it shall be on the front of the turban. ³⁸So it shall be on Aaron's forehead, that Aaron may bear the iniquity of the holy things which the children of Israel hallow in

all their holy gifts; and it shall always be on his forehead, that they may be accepted before the LORD.

³⁹"You shall skillfully weave the tunic of fine linen *thread,* you shall make the turban of fine linen, and you shall make the sash of woven work.

⁴⁰"For Aaron's sons you shall make tunics, and you shall make sashes for them. And you shall make hats for them, for glory and beauty. ⁴¹So you shall put them on Aaron your brother and on his sons with him. You shall anoint them, consecrate them, and sanctify them, that they may minister to Me as priests. ⁴²And you shall make for them linen trousers to cover their nakedness; they shall reach from the waist to the thighs. ⁴³They shall be on Aaron and on his sons when they come into the tabernacle of meeting, or when they come near the altar to minister in the holy *place,* that they do not incur iniquity and die. *It shall be* a statute forever to him and his descendants after him.

CHAPTER 29 HOW TO DEDICATE THE PRIESTS.

"And this is what you shall do to them to hallow them for ministering to Me as priests: Take one young bull and two rams without blemish, ²and unleavened bread, unleavened cakes mixed with oil, and unleavened wafers anointed with oil (you shall make them of wheat flour). ³You shall put them in one basket and bring them in the basket, with the bull and the two rams.

⁴"And Aaron and his sons you shall bring to the door of the tabernacle of meeting, and you shall wash them with water. ⁵Then you shall take the garments, put the tunic on Aaron, and the robe of the ephod, the ephod, and the breastplate, and gird him with the intricately woven band of the ephod. ⁶You shall put the turban on his head, and put the holy crown on the turban. ⁷And you shall take the anointing oil, pour *it* on his head, and anoint him. ⁸Then you shall bring his sons and put tunics on them. ⁹And you shall gird them with sashes, Aaron and his sons, and put the hats on them. The priesthood shall be theirs for a perpetual statute. So you shall consecrate Aaron and his sons.

¹⁰"You shall also have the bull brought before the tabernacle of meeting, and Aaron and his sons shall put their hands on the head of the bull. ¹¹Then you shall kill the bull before the LORD, *by* the door of the tabernacle of meeting. ¹²You shall take *some* of the blood of the bull and put *it* on the horns of the altar with your finger, and pour all the blood beside the base of the altar. ¹³And you shall take all the fat that covers the entrails, the fatty lobe *attached* to the liver, and the two kidneys and the fat that *is* on them, and burn *them* on the altar. ¹⁴But the flesh of the bull, with its skin and its offal, you shall burn with fire outside the camp. It *is* a sin offering.

¹⁵"You shall also take one ram, and Aaron and his sons shall put their hands on the head of the ram; ¹⁶and you shall kill the ram, and you shall take its blood and sprinkle *it* all around on the altar. ¹⁷Then you shall cut the ram in pieces, wash its entrails and its legs, and put *them* with its pieces and with its head. ¹⁸And you shall burn the whole ram on the altar. It *is* a burnt offering to the LORD; it *is* a sweet aroma, an offering made by fire to the LORD.

¹⁹"You shall also take the other ram, and Aaron and his sons shall put their hands on the head of the ram. ²⁰Then you shall kill the ram, and take some of its blood and put *it* on the tip of the right ear of Aaron and on the tip of the right ear of his sons, on the thumb of their right hand and on the big toe of their right foot, and sprinkle the blood all around on the altar. ²¹And you shall take some of the blood that is on the altar, and some of the anointing oil, and sprinkle *it* on Aaron and on his garments, on his sons and on the garments of his sons with him; and he and his garments shall be hallowed, and his sons and his sons' garments with him.

²²"Also you shall take the fat of the ram, the fat tail, the fat that covers the entrails, the fatty lobe *attached to* the liver, the two kidneys and the fat on them, the right thigh (for it *is* a ram of consecration), ²³one loaf of bread, one cake *made with* oil, and one wafer from the basket of the unleavened bread that *is* before the LORD; ²⁴and you shall put all these in the hands of Aaron and in the hands of his sons, and you shall wave them *as* a wave offering before the LORD. ²⁵You shall receive them back from their hands and burn *them* on the altar as a burnt offering, as a sweet aroma before the LORD. It *is* an offering made by fire to the LORD.

²⁶"Then you shall take the breast of the ram of Aaron's consecration and wave it *as* a wave offering before the LORD; and it shall be your portion. ²⁷And from the ram of the consecration you shall consecrate the breast of the wave offering which is waved, and the thigh of the heave offering which is raised, of *that* which *is* for Aaron and of *that* which is for his sons. ²⁸It shall be from the children of Israel *for* Aaron and his sons by a statute forever. For it is a heave offering; it shall be a heave offering from the children of Israel from the sacrifices of their peace offerings, *that is,* their heave offering to the LORD.

²⁹"And the holy garments of Aaron shall be his sons after him, to be anointed in them and to be consecrated in them. ³⁰That son who becomes priest in his place shal put them on for seven days, when he enters the tabernacle of meeting to minister in the holy *place.*

³¹"And you shall take the ram of the consecration an boil its flesh in the holy place. ³²Then Aaron and his son shall eat the flesh of the ram, and the bread that *is* in th basket, *by* the door of the tabernacle of meeting. ³³The shall eat those things with which the atonement wa made, to consecrate *and* to sanctify them; but an out sider shall not eat *them,* because they *are* holy. ³⁴And any of the flesh of the consecration offerings, or of th bread, remains until the morning, then you shall bur

the remainder with fire. It shall not be eaten, because it *is* holy.

³⁵"Thus you shall do to Aaron and his sons, according to all that I have commanded you. Seven days you shall consecrate them. ³⁶And you shall offer a bull every day *as* a sin offering for atonement. You shall cleanse the altar when you make atonement for it, and you shall anoint it to sanctify it. ³⁷Seven days you shall make atonement for the altar and sanctify it. And the altar shall be most holy. Whatever touches the altar must be holy.

³⁸"Now this *is* what you shall offer on the altar: two lambs of the first year, day by day continually. ³⁹One lamb you shall offer in the morning, and the other lamb you shall offer at twilight. ⁴⁰With the one lamb shall be one-tenth *of an ephah* of flour mixed with one-fourth of a hin of pressed oil, and one-fourth of a hin of wine *as* a drink offering. ⁴¹And the other lamb you shall offer at twilight; and you shall offer with it the grain offering and the drink offering, as in the morning, for a sweet aroma, an offering made by fire to the LORD. ⁴²*This shall be* a continual burnt offering throughout your generations *at* the door of the tabernacle of meeting before the LORD, where I will meet you to speak with you. ⁴³And there I will meet with the children of Israel, and *the tabernacle* shall be sanctified by My glory. ⁴⁴So I will consecrate the tabernacle of meeting and the altar. I will also consecrate both Aaron and his sons to minister to Me as priests. ⁴⁵I will dwell among the children of Israel and will be their God. ⁴⁶And they shall know that I *am* the LORD their God, who brought them up out of the land of Egypt, that I may dwell among them. I *am* the LORD their God.

CHAPTER **30** PREPARATIONS FOR WORSHIP.

"You shall make an altar to burn incense on; you shall make it of acacia wood. ²A cubit *shall be* its length and a cubit its width—it shall be square—and two cubits *shall be* its height. Its horns *shall be* of one piece with it. ³And you shall overlay its top, its sides all around, and its horns with pure gold; and you shall make for it a molding of gold all around. ⁴Two gold rings you shall make for it, under the molding on both its sides. You shall place *them* on its two sides, and they will be holders for the poles with which to bear it. ⁵You shall make the poles of acacia wood, and overlay them with gold. ⁶And you shall put it before the veil that *is* before the ark of the Testimony, before the mercy seat that *is* over the Testimony, where I will meet with you.

⁷"Aaron shall burn on it sweet incense every morning; when he tends the lamps, he shall burn incense on it. ⁸And when Aaron lights the lamps at twilight, he shall burn incense on it, a perpetual incense before the LORD throughout your generations. ⁹You shall not offer strange incense on it, or a burnt offering, or a grain offering; nor shall you pour a drink offering on it. ¹⁰And Aaron shall make atonement upon its horns once a year with the blood of the sin offering of atonement; once a year he shall make atonement upon it throughout your generations. It *is* most holy to the LORD."

¹¹Then the LORD spoke to Moses, saying: ¹²"When you take the census of the children of Israel for their number,

then every man shall give a ransom for himself to the LORD, when you number them, that there may be no plague among them when *you* number them. ¹³This is what everyone among those who are numbered shall give: half a shekel according to the shekel of the sanctuary (a shekel *is* twenty gerahs). The half-shekel *shall be* an offering to the LORD. ¹⁴Everyone included among those who are numbered, from twenty years old and above, shall give an offering to the LORD. ¹⁵The rich shall not give more and the poor shall not give less than half a shekel, when *you* give an offering to the LORD, to make atonement for yourselves. ¹⁶And you shall take the atonement money of the children of Israel, and shall appoint it for the service of the tabernacle of meeting, that it may be a memorial for the children of Israel before the LORD, to make atonement for yourselves."

►►►►►►►BUY OFF GOD?

30:11-16 The atonement money was like a census tax. It continued the principle that all the people belonged to God and therefore needed to be redeemed by a sacrifice. Whenever a census took place, everyone, both rich and poor, was required to pay a ransom. God does not discriminate between people (see Acts 10:34; Galatians 3:28). All of us need mercy and forgiveness because of our sinful thoughts and actions. There is no way the rich person can buy off God, and no way the poor can avoid paying. God's demand is that all of us come humbly before him to be forgiven and brought into his family.

¹⁷Then the LORD spoke to Moses, saying: ¹⁸"You shall also make a laver of bronze, with its base also of bronze, for washing. You shall put it between the tabernacle of meeting and the altar. And you shall put water in it, ¹⁹for Aaron and his sons shall wash their hands and their feet in water from it. ²⁰When they go into the tabernacle of meeting, or when they come near the altar to minister, to burn an offering made by fire to the LORD, they shall wash with water, lest they die. ²¹So they shall wash their hands and their feet, lest they die. And it shall be a statute forever to them—to him and his descendants throughout their generations."

²²Moreover the LORD spoke to Moses, saying: ²³"Also take for yourself quality spices—five hundred *shekels* of liquid myrrh, half as much sweet-smelling cinnamon (two hundred and fifty *shekels*), two hundred and fifty *shekels* of sweet-smelling cane, ²⁴five hundred *shekels* of cassia, according to the shekel of the sanctuary, and a hin of olive oil. ²⁵And you shall make from these a holy anointing oil, an ointment compounded according to the art of the perfumer. It shall be a holy anointing oil. ²⁶With it you shall anoint the tabernacle of meeting and the ark of the Testimony; ²⁷the table and all its utensils, the lampstand and its utensils, and the altar of incense; ²⁸the altar of burnt offering with all its utensils, and the laver and its base. ²⁹You shall consecrate them, that they may be most holy; whatever touches them must be holy. ³⁰And you shall anoint Aaron and his sons, and consecrate them, that *they* may minister to Me as priests.

³¹"And you shall speak to the children of Israel, saying: 'This shall be a holy anointing oil to Me throughout your generations. ³²It shall not be poured on man's flesh; nor

shall you make *any other* like it, according to its composition. It *is* holy, *and* it shall be holy to you. ³³Whoever compounds *any* like it, or whoever puts *any* of it on an outsider, shall be cut off from his people.' "

³⁴And the LORD said to Moses: "Take sweet spices, stacte and onycha and galbanum, and pure frankincense with *these* sweet spices; there shall be equal amounts of each. ³⁵You shall make of these an incense, a compound according to the art of the perfumer, salted, pure, *and* holy. ³⁶And you shall beat *some* of it very fine, and put some of it before the Testimony in the tabernacle of meeting where I will meet with you. It shall be most holy to you. ³⁷But *as for* the incense which you shall make, you shall not make any for yourselves, according to its composition. It shall be to you holy for the LORD. ³⁸Whoever makes *any* like it, to smell it, he shall be cut off from his people."

CHAPTER 31 WORKMEN GIVEN SPECIAL SKILL.

Then the LORD spoke to Moses, saying: ²"See, I have called by name Bezalel the son of Uri, the son of Hur, of the tribe of Judah. ³And I have filled him with the Spirit of God, in wisdom, in understanding, in knowledge, and in all *manner of* workmanship, ⁴to design artistic works, to work in gold, in silver, in bronze, ⁵in cutting jewels for setting, in carving wood, and to work in all *manner of* workmanship.

IDOLS

32:1-10 Idols again! Even though Israel had seen the invisible God in action, they still wanted the familiar gods they could see and shape into whatever image they desired. How like them we are! Our great temptation is still to shape God to our liking, to make him convenient to obey or ignore. God responds in great anger when his mercy is trampled on. The gods we create blind us to the love God wants to shower on us. God cannot work in us when we elevate anyone or anything above him. What idols do you have in your life?

⁶"And I, indeed I, have appointed with him Aholiab the son of Ahisamach, of the tribe of Dan; and I have put wisdom in the hearts of all the gifted artisans, that they may make all that I have commanded you: ⁷the tabernacle of meeting, the ark of the Testimony and the mercy seat that *is* on it, and all the furniture of the tabernacle— ⁸the table and its utensils, the pure *gold* lampstand with all its utensils, the altar of incense, ⁹the altar of burnt offering with all its utensils, and the laver and its base— ¹⁰the garments of ministry, the holy garments for Aaron the priest and the garments of his sons, to minister as priests, ¹¹and the anointing oil and sweet incense for the holy *place.* According to all that I have commanded you they shall do."

¹²And the LORD spoke to Moses, saying, ¹³"Speak also to the children of Israel, saying: 'Surely My Sabbaths you shall keep, for it *is* a sign between Me and you throughout your generations, that *you* may know that I *am* the LORD who sanctifies you. ¹⁴You shall keep the Sabbath, therefore, for *it is* holy to you. Everyone who profanes it shall surely be put to death; for whoever does *any* work on it, that person shall be cut off from among his people.

¹⁵Work shall be done for six days, but the seventh *is* the Sabbath of rest, holy to the LORD. Whoever does *any* work on the Sabbath day, he shall surely be put to death. ¹⁶Therefore the children of Israel shall keep the Sabbath, to observe the Sabbath throughout their generations *as* a perpetual covenant. ¹⁷It *is* a sign between Me and the children of Israel forever; for *in* six days the LORD made the heavens and the earth, and on the seventh day He rested and was refreshed.' "

¹⁸And when He had made an end of speaking with him on Mount Sinai, He gave Moses two tablets of the Testimony, tablets of stone, written with the finger of God.

CHAPTER 32 THE GOLDEN CALF.

Now when the people saw that Moses delayed coming down from the mountain, the people gathered together to Aaron, and said to him, "Come, make us gods that shall go before us; for *as for* this Moses, the man who brought us up out of the land of Egypt, we do not know what has become of him."

²And Aaron said to them, "Break off the golden earrings which *are* in the ears of your wives, your sons, and your daughters, and bring *them* to me." ³So all the people broke off the golden earrings which *were* in their ears, and brought *them* to Aaron. ⁴And he received *the gold* from their hand, and he fashioned it with an engraving tool, and made a molded calf.

Then they said, "This *is* your god, O Israel, that brought you out of the land of Egypt!"

⁵So when Aaron saw *it*, he built an altar before it. And Aaron made a proclamation and said, "Tomorrow *is* a feast to the LORD." ⁶Then they rose early on the next day, offered burnt offerings, and brought peace offerings; and the people sat down to eat and drink, and rose up to play.

⁷And the LORD said to Moses, "Go, get down! For your people whom you brought out of the land of Egypt have corrupted *themselves.* ⁸They have turned aside quickly out of the way which I commanded them. They have made themselves a molded calf, and worshiped it and sacrificed to it, and said, 'This *is* your god, O Israel, that brought you out of the land of Egypt!' " ⁹And the LORD said to Moses, "I have seen this people, and indeed it *is* a stiff-necked people! ¹⁰Now therefore, let Me alone, that My wrath may burn hot against them and I may consume them. And I will make of you a great nation."

¹¹Then Moses pleaded with the LORD his God, and said: "LORD, why does Your wrath burn hot against Your people whom You have brought out of the land of Egypt with great power and with a mighty hand? ¹²Why should the Egyptians speak, and say, 'He brought them out to harm them, to kill them in the mountains, and to consume them from the face of the earth'? Turn from Your

PRAYER POWER

32:9-14 God was ready to destroy the whole nation because of people's sin. But Moses pleaded for mercy, and God spared them. one of the countless examples in Scripture of how prayer can ma difference. Don't neglect prayer because the situation seems irre Make a daily prayer list and spend time praying for others. Pray change things.

fierce wrath, and relent from this harm to Your people. [13]Remember Abraham, Isaac, and Israel, Your servants, to whom You swore by Your own self, and said to them, 'I will multiply your descendants as the stars of heaven; and all this land that I have spoken of I give to your descendants, and they shall inherit *it* forever.' " [14]So the LORD relented from the harm which He said He would do to His people.

[15]And Moses turned and went down from the mountain, and the two tablets of the Testimony *were* in his hand. The tablets *were* written on both sides; on the one *side* and on the other they were written. [16]Now the tablets *were* the work of God, and the writing *was* the writing of God engraved on the tablets.

[17]And when Joshua heard the noise of the people as they shouted, he said to Moses, "*There is* a noise of war in the camp."

[18]But he said:

"*It is* not the noise of the shout of victory,
Nor the noise of the cry of defeat,
But the sound of singing I hear."

[19]So it was, as soon as he came near the camp, that he saw the calf *and* the dancing. So Moses' anger became hot, and he cast the tablets out of his hands and broke them at the foot of the mountain. [20]Then he took the calf which they had made, burned *it* in the fire, and ground *it* to powder; and he scattered *it* on the water and made the children of Israel drink *it*. [21]And Moses said to Aaron, "What did this people do to you that you have brought *so* great a sin upon them?"

[22]So Aaron said, "Do not let the anger of my lord become hot. You know the people, that they *are set* on evil. [23]For they said to me, 'Make us gods that shall go before us; *as for* this Moses, the man who brought us out of the land of Egypt, we do not know what has become of him.' [24]And I said to them, 'Whoever has any gold, let them break *it* off.' So they gave *it* to me, and I cast it into the fire, and this calf came out."

[25]Now when Moses saw that the people *were* unrestrained (for Aaron had not restrained them, to *their* shame among their enemies), [26]then Moses stood in the entrance of the camp, and said, "Whoever *is* on the LORD's side—*come* to me!" And all the sons of Levi gathered themselves together to him. [27]And he said to them, "Thus says the LORD God of Israel: 'Let every man put his sword on his side, and go in and out from entrance to entrance throughout the camp, and let every man kill his brother, every man his companion, and every man his neighbor.' " [28]So the sons of Levi did according to the word of Moses. And about three thousand men of the people fell that day. [29]Then Moses said, "Consecrate yourselves today to the LORD, that He may bestow on you a blessing this day, for every man has opposed his son and his brother."

[30]Now it came to pass on the next day that Moses said to the people, "You have committed a great sin. So now I will go up to the LORD; perhaps I can make atonement for your sin." [31]Then Moses returned to the LORD and said, "Oh, these people have committed a great sin, and have made for themselves a god of gold! [32]Yet now, if You will

forgive their sin—but if not, I pray, blot me out of Your book which You have written."

[33]And the LORD said to Moses, "Whoever has sinned against Me, I will blot him out of My book. [34]Now therefore, go, lead the people to *the place* of which I have spoken to you. Behold, My Angel shall go before you. Nevertheless, in the day when I visit for punishment, I will visit punishment upon them for their sin."

[35]So the LORD plagued the people because of what they did with the calf which Aaron made.

CHAPTER **33** **THE PEOPLE ARE SORRY.** Then the LORD said to Moses, "Depart *and* go up from here, you and the people whom you have brought out of the land of Egypt, to the land of which I swore to Abraham, Isaac, and Jacob, saying, 'To your descendants I will give it.' [2]And I will send *My* Angel before you, and I will drive out the Canaanite and the Amorite and the Hittite and the Perizzite and the Hivite and the Jebusite. [3]*Go up* to a land flowing with milk and honey; for I will not go up in your midst, lest I consume you on the way, for you *are* a stiff-necked people."

[4]And when the people heard this bad news, they mourned, and no one put on his ornaments. [5]For the LORD had said to Moses, "Say to the children of Israel, 'You *are* a stiff-necked people. I could come up into your midst in one moment and consume you. Now therefore, take off your ornaments, that I may know what to do to you.' " [6]So the children of Israel stripped themselves of their ornaments by Mount Horeb.

◄▬▬▬ FRIENDS

33:11 God and Moses talked like two friends. Why did Moses find such favor with God? It certainly was not because he was perfect, gifted, or powerful. Moses was God's friend because friends trust each other, talk to each other, and have common interests. No one can drive wedges between them. Moses never knew where he was going with God, and it didn't matter. He knew with whom he was going, and that was all that mattered.

[7]Moses took his tent and pitched it outside the camp, far from the camp, and called it the tabernacle of meeting. And it came to pass *that* everyone who sought the LORD went out to the tabernacle of meeting which *was* outside the camp. [8]So it was, whenever Moses went out to the tabernacle, *that* all the people rose, and each man stood *at* his tent door and watched Moses until he had gone into the tabernacle. [9]And it came to pass, when Moses entered the tabernacle, that the pillar of cloud descended and stood *at* the door of the tabernacle, and *the* LORD talked with Moses. [10]All the people saw the pillar of cloud standing *at* the tabernacle door, and all the people rose and worshiped, each man *in* his tent door. [11]So the LORD spoke to Moses face to face, as a man speaks to his friend. And he would return to the camp, but his servant Joshua the son of Nun, a young man, did not depart from the tabernacle.

[12]Then Moses said to the LORD, "See, You say to me, 'Bring up this people.' But You have not let me know whom You will send with me. Yet You have said, 'I know

you by name, and you have also found grace in My sight.' ¹³Now therefore, I pray, if I have found grace in Your sight, show me now Your way, that I may know You and that I may find grace in Your sight. And consider that this nation *is* Your people."

¹⁴And He said, "My Presence will go *with you,* and I will give you rest."

¹⁵Then he said to Him, "If Your Presence does not go *with us,* do not bring us up from here. ¹⁶For how then will it be known that Your people and I have found grace in Your sight, except You go with us? So we shall be separate, Your people and I, from all the people who *are* upon the face of the earth."

◣▬▬▬▬▬▬**WONDERFUL MERCY**

34:6-7 Moses had asked to see God's glory (33:18), and this was God's response. What is God's glory? It is his character, his nature, his way of relating to his creatures. Notice that God did not give Moses a vision of his power and majesty, but rather of his love. God's glory is revealed in his mercy, grace, compassion, faithfulness, forgiveness, and justice. God's love and mercy are truly wonderful, and we benefit from them. We can respond and give glory to God when our character resembles his.

¹⁷So the LORD said to Moses, "I will also do this thing that you have spoken; for you have found grace in My sight, and I know you by name."

¹⁸And he said, "Please, show me Your glory."

¹⁹Then He said, "I will make all My goodness pass before you, and I will proclaim the name of the LORD before you. I will be gracious to whom I will be gracious, and I will have compassion on whom I will have compassion." ²⁰But He said, "You cannot see My face; for no man shall see Me, and live." ²¹And the LORD said, "Here is a place by Me, and you shall stand on the rock. ²²So it shall be, while My glory passes by, that I will put you in the cleft of the rock, and will cover you with My hand while I pass by. ²³Then I will take away My hand, and you shall see My back; but My face shall not be seen."

CHAPTER **34** **MOSES TALKS WITH GOD.** And the LORD said to Moses, "Cut two tablets of stone like the first *ones,* and I will write on *these* tablets the words that were on the first tablets which you broke. ²So be ready in the morning, and come up in the morning to Mount Sinai, and present yourself to Me there on the top of the mountain. ³And no man shall come up with you, and let no man be seen throughout all the mountain; let neither flocks nor herds feed before that mountain."

⁴So he cut two tablets of stone like the first *ones.* Then Moses rose early in the morning and went up Mount Sinai, as the LORD had commanded him; and he took in his hand the two tablets of stone.

⁵Now the LORD descended in the cloud and stood with him there, and proclaimed the name of the LORD. ⁶And the LORD passed before him and proclaimed, "The LORD, the LORD God, merciful and gracious, longsuffering, and abounding in goodness and truth, ⁷keeping mercy for thousands, forgiving iniquity and transgression and sin, by no means clearing *the guilty,* visiting the iniquity of

the fathers upon the children and the children's children to the third and the fourth generation."

⁸So Moses made haste and bowed his head toward the earth, and worshiped. ⁹Then he said, "If now I have found grace in Your sight, O Lord, let my Lord, I pray, go among us, even though we *are* a stiff-necked people; and pardon our iniquity and our sin, and take us as Your inheritance."

¹⁰And He said: "Behold, I make a covenant. Before all your people I will do marvels such as have not been done in all the earth, nor in any nation; and all the people among whom you *are* shall see the work of the LORD. For it *is* an awesome thing that I will do with you. ¹¹Observe what I command you this day. Behold, I am driving out from before you the Amorite and the Canaanite and the Hittite and the Perizzite and the Hivite and the Jebusite. ¹²Take heed to yourself, lest you make a covenant with the inhabitants of the land where you are going, lest it be a snare in your midst. ¹³But you shall destroy their altars, break their *sacred* pillars, and cut down their wooden images ¹⁴(for you shall worship no other god, for the LORD, whose name *is* Jealous, *is* a jealous God), ¹⁵lest you make a covenant with the inhabitants of the land, and they play the harlot with their gods and make sacrifice to their gods, and *one of them* invites you and you eat of his sacrifice, ¹⁶and you take of his daughters for your sons, and his daughters play the harlot with their gods and make your sons play the harlot with their gods.

◣▬▬▬▬▬▬**LOYALTY**

34:12-14 God told the Israelites not to compromise with the sin[ful] people around them, but to give their absolute loyalty and exclusiv[e] devotion to him. When we compromise, our sensitivity to sin becom[es] dulled. Are you beginning to accept lower standards regarding the [things] you do or think about? This could lead to a downhill slide you won['t be] able to stop. The way you act shows where your true allegiance is.

¹⁷"You shall make no molded gods for yourselves.

¹⁸"The Feast of Unleavened Bread you shall keep. Seven days you shall eat unleavened bread, as I commanded you, in the appointed time of the month of Abib; for in the month of Abib you came out from Egypt.

¹⁹"All that open the womb *are* Mine, and every male firstborn among your livestock, *whether* ox or sheep. ²⁰But the firstborn of a donkey you shall redeem with a lamb. And if you will not redeem *him,* then you shall break his neck. All the firstborn of your sons you shall redeem.

"And none shall appear before Me empty-handed.

²¹"Six days you shall work, but on the seventh day you shall rest; in plowing time and in harvest you shall rest.

²²"And you shall observe the Feast of Weeks, of the firstfruits of wheat harvest, and the Feast of Ingathering at the year's end.

²³"Three times in the year all your men shall appea[r] before the Lord, the LORD God of Israel. ²⁴For I will cas[t] out the nations before you and enlarge your borders; neither will any man covet your land when you go up t[o] appear before the LORD your God three times in the yea[r].

²⁵"You shall not offer the blood of My sacrifice wit[h]

leaven, nor shall the sacrifice of the Feast of the Passover be left until morning.

²⁶"The first of the firstfruits of your land you shall bring to the house of the LORD your God. You shall not boil a young goat in its mother's milk."

²⁷Then the LORD said to Moses, "Write these words, for according to the tenor of these words I have made a covenant with you and with Israel." ²⁸So he was there with the LORD forty days and forty nights; he neither ate bread nor drank water. And He wrote on the tablets the words of the covenant, the Ten Commandments.

²⁹Now it was so, when Moses came down from Mount Sinai (and the two tablets of the Testimony *were* in Moses' hand when he came down from the mountain), that Moses did not know that the skin of his face shone while he talked with Him. ³⁰So when Aaron and all the children of Israel saw Moses, behold, the skin of his face shone, and they were afraid to come near him. ³¹Then Moses called to them, and Aaron and all the rulers of the congregation returned to him; and Moses talked with them. ³²Afterward all the children of Israel came near, and he gave them as commandments all that the LORD had spoken with him on Mount Sinai. ³³And when Moses had finished speaking with them, he put a veil on his face. ³⁴But whenever Moses went in before the LORD to speak with Him, he would take the veil off until he came out; and he would come out and speak to the children of Israel whatever he had been commanded. ³⁵And whenever the children of Israel saw the face of Moses, that the skin of Moses' face shone, then Moses would put the veil on his face again, until he went in to speak with Him.

CHAPTER 35 GIFTS FOR THE TABERNACLE. Then Moses gathered all the congregation of the children of Israel together, and said to them, "These *are* the words which the LORD has commanded *you* to do: ²Work shall be done for six days, but the seventh day shall be a holy day for you, a Sabbath of rest to the LORD. Whoever does any work on it shall be put to death. ³You shall kindle no fire throughout your dwellings on the Sabbath day."

POCKETBOOKS

35:21 Those whose hearts were stirred by God gave cheerfully to the tabernacle. They gave with great enthusiasm because they knew how important their giving was to the completion of God's house. Airline pilots and computer operators can push test buttons to see if their equipment is functioning properly. God has a quick test button he can push to see the level of our commitment— our pocketbook. Generous people aren't necessarily faithful to God. But faithful people are always generous.

⁴And Moses spoke to all the congregation of the children of Israel, saying, "This *is* the thing which the LORD commanded, saying: ⁵'Take from among you an offering to the LORD. Whoever *is* of a willing heart, let him bring it as an offering to the LORD: gold, silver, and bronze; ⁶blue, purple, and scarlet *thread*, fine linen, and goats' *hair*; ⁷ram skins dyed red, badger skins, and acacia wood; ⁸oil for the light, and spices for the anointing oil and for the sweet incense; ⁹onyx stones, and stones to be set in the ephod and in the breastplate.

¹⁰'All *who are* gifted artisans among you shall come and make all that the LORD has commanded: ¹¹the tabernacle, its tent, its covering, its clasps, its boards, its bars, its pillars, and its sockets; ¹²the ark and its poles, *with* the mercy seat, and the veil of the covering; ¹³the table and its poles, all its utensils, and the showbread; ¹⁴also the lampstand for the light, its utensils, its lamps, and the oil for the light; ¹⁵the incense altar, its poles, the anointing oil, the sweet incense, and the screen for the door at the entrance of the tabernacle; ¹⁶the altar of burnt offering with its bronze grating, its poles, all its utensils, *and* the laver and its base; ¹⁷the hangings of the court, its pillars, their sockets, and the screen for the gate of the court; ¹⁸the pegs of the tabernacle, the pegs of the court, and their cords; ¹⁹the garments of ministry, for ministering in the holy *place*—the holy garments for Aaron the priest and the garments of his sons, to minister as priests.' "

²⁰And all the congregation of the children of Israel departed from the presence of Moses. ²¹Then everyone came whose heart was stirred, and everyone whose spirit was willing, *and* they brought the LORD's offering for the work of the tabernacle of meeting, for all its service, and for the holy garments. ²²They came, both men and women, as many as had a willing heart, *and* brought earrings and nose rings, rings and necklaces, all jewelry of gold, that is, every man who *made* an offering of gold to the LORD. ²³And every man, with whom was found

WORK SHALL BE DONE FOR SIX DAYS
FOR SIX DAYS
FOR SIX DAYS
FOR SIX DAYS
FOR SIX DAYS
FOR SIX DAYS

BUT THE **7**TH DAY *shall be* A HOLY DAY FOR **YOU** A SABBATH OF R E S T TO **THE LORD.**

blue, purple, and scarlet *thread*, fine linen, goats' *hair*, red skins of rams, and badger skins, brought *them*. ²⁴Everyone who offered an offering of silver or bronze brought the LORD's offering. And everyone with whom was found acacia wood for any work of the service, brought *it*. ²⁵All the women *who were* gifted artisans spun yarn with their hands, and brought what they had spun, of blue, purple, *and* scarlet, and fine linen. ²⁶And all the women whose hearts stirred with wisdom spun yarn of goats' *hair*. ²⁷The rulers brought onyx stones, and the stones to be set in the ephod and in the breastplate, ²⁸and spices and oil for the light, for the anointing oil, and for the sweet incense. ²⁹The children of Israel brought a freewill offering to the LORD, all the men and women whose hearts were willing to bring *material* for all kinds of work which the LORD, by the hand of Moses, had commanded to be done.

◣■■■■ TEAMWORK

36:8-9 Making cloth (spinning and weaving) took a great deal of time in Moses' day. To own more than two or three changes of clothing was a sign of wealth! As you can imagine, the effort involved in making enough cloth for a building like the tabernacle was staggering. It demonstrated a tremendous community effort. Churches and neighborhoods today often require this same kind of community teamwork. Without it, many essential services just wouldn't get done. What part can you play in your church or community "team"?

³⁰And Moses said to the children of Israel, "See, the LORD has called by name Bezalel the son of Uri, the son of Hur, of the tribe of Judah; ³¹and He has filled him with the Spirit of God, in wisdom and in understanding, in knowledge and all manner of workmanship, ³²to design artistic works, to work in gold and silver and bronze, ³³in cutting jewels for setting, in carving wood, and to work in all manner of artistic workmanship.

³⁴"And He has put in his heart the ability to teach, *in* him and Aholiab the son of Ahisamach, of the tribe of Dan. ³⁵He has filled them with skill to do all manner of work of the engraver and the designer and the tapestry maker, in blue, purple, and scarlet *thread*, and fine linen, and of the weaver—those who do every work and those who design artistic works.

CHAPTER 36   BUILDING THE TABERNACLE.

"And Bezalel and Aholiab, and every gifted artisan in whom the LORD has put wisdom and understanding, to know how to do all manner of work for the service of the sanctuary, shall do according to all that the LORD has commanded."

²Then Moses called Bezalel and Aholiab, and every gifted artisan in whose heart the LORD had put wisdom, everyone whose heart was stirred, to come and do the work. ³And they received from Moses all the offering which the children of Israel had brought for the work of the service of making the sanctuary. So they continued bringing to him freewill offerings every morning. ⁴Then all the craftsmen who were doing all the work of the sanctuary came, each from the work he was doing, ⁵and they spoke to Moses, saying, "The people bring much

more than enough for the service of the work which the LORD commanded *us* to do."

⁶So Moses gave a commandment, and they caused it to be proclaimed throughout the camp, saying, "Let neither man nor woman do any more work for the offering of the sanctuary." And the people were restrained from bringing, ⁷for the material they had was sufficient for all the work to be done—indeed too much.

⁸Then all the gifted artisans among them who worked on the tabernacle made ten curtains woven of fine linen, and of blue, purple, and scarlet thread; *with* artistic designs of cherubim they made them. ⁹The length of each curtain *was* twenty-eight cubits, and the width of each curtain four cubits; the curtains *were* all the same size. ¹⁰And he coupled five curtains to one another, and *the other* five curtains he coupled to one another. ¹¹He made loops of blue *yarn* on the edge of the curtain on the selvedge of one set; likewise he did on the outer edge of *the other* curtain of the second set. ¹²Fifty loops he made on one curtain, and fifty loops he made on the edge of the curtain on the end of the second set; the loops held one *curtain* to another. ¹³And he made fifty clasps of gold, and coupled the curtains to one another with the clasps, that it might be one tabernacle.

¹⁴He made curtains of goats' *hair* for the tent over the tabernacle; he made eleven curtains. ¹⁵The length of each curtain *was* thirty cubits, and the width of each curtain four cubits; the eleven curtains *were* the same size. ¹⁶He coupled five curtains by themselves and six curtains by themselves. ¹⁷And he made fifty loops on the edge of the curtain that is outermost in one set, and fifty loops he made on the edge of the curtain of the second set. ¹⁸He also made fifty bronze clasps to couple the tent together, that it might be one. ¹⁹Then he made a covering for the tent of ram skins dyed red, and a covering of badger skins above *that*.

²⁰For the tabernacle he made boards of acacia wood, standing upright. ²¹The length of each board *was* ten cubits, and the width of each board a cubit and a half. ²²Each board had two tenons for binding one to another. Thus he made for all the boards of the tabernacle. ²³And he made boards for the tabernacle, twenty boards for the south side. ²⁴Forty sockets of silver he made to go under the twenty boards: two sockets under each of the boards for its two tenons. ²⁵And for the other side of the tabernacle, the north side, he made twenty boards ²⁶and their forty sockets of silver: two sockets under each of the boards. ²⁷For the west side of the tabernacle he made six boards. ²⁸He also made two boards for the two back corners of the tabernacle. ²⁹And they were coupled at the bottom and coupled together at the top by one ring. Thus he made both of them for the two corners. ³⁰So there were eight boards and their sockets—sixteen sockets of silver—two sockets under each of the boards.

³¹And he made bars of acacia wood: five for the boards on one side of the tabernacle, ³²five bars for the boards on the other side of the tabernacle, and five bars for the boards of the tabernacle on the far side westward. ³³And he made the middle bar to pass through the boards from one end to the other. ³⁴He overlaid the boards with gold,

made their rings of gold *to be* holders for the bars, and overlaid the bars with gold.

³⁵And he made a veil of blue, purple, and scarlet *thread,* and fine woven linen; it was worked *with* an artistic design of cherubim. ³⁶He made for it four pillars of acacia *wood,* and overlaid them with gold, with their hooks of gold; and he cast four sockets of silver for them. ³⁷He also made a screen for the tabernacle door, of blue, purple, and scarlet *thread,* and fine woven linen, made by a weaver, ³⁸and its five pillars with their hooks. And he overlaid their capitals and their rings with gold, but their five sockets *were* bronze.

CHAPTER **37** **MAKING THE ARK.** Then Bezalel made the ark of acacia wood; two and a half cubits *was* its length, a cubit and a half its width, and a cubit and a half its height. ²He overlaid it with pure gold inside and outside, and made a molding of gold all around it. ³And he cast for it four rings of gold *to be set* in its four corners: two rings on one side, and two rings on the other side of it. ⁴He made poles of acacia wood, and overlaid them with gold. ⁵And he put the poles into the rings at the sides of the ark, to bear the ark. ⁶He also made the mercy seat of pure gold; two and a half cubits *was* its length and a cubit and a half its width. ⁷He made two cherubim of beaten gold; he made them of one piece at the two ends of the mercy seat: ⁸one cherub at one end on this side, and the other cherub at the *other* end on that side. He made the cherubim at the two ends *of one piece* with the mercy seat. ⁹The cherubim spread out *their* wings above, *and* covered the mercy seat with their wings. They faced one another; the faces of the cherubim were toward the mercy seat.

¹⁰He made the table of acacia wood; two cubits *was* its length, a cubit its width, and a cubit and a half its height. ¹¹And he overlaid it with pure gold, and made a molding of gold all around it. ¹²Also he made a frame of a handbreadth all around it, and made a molding of gold for the frame all around it. ¹³And he cast for it four rings of gold, and put the rings on the four corners that *were* at its four legs. ¹⁴The rings were close to the frame, as holders for the poles to bear the table. ¹⁵And he made the poles of acacia wood to bear the table, and overlaid them with gold. ¹⁶He made of pure gold the utensils which were on the table: its dishes, its cups, its bowls, and its pitchers for pouring.

¹⁷He also made the lampstand of pure gold; of hammered work he made the lampstand. Its shaft, its branches, its bowls, its *ornamental* knobs, and its flowers were of the same piece. ¹⁸And six branches came out of its sides: three branches of the lampstand out of one side, and three branches of the lampstand out of the other side. ¹⁹There were three bowls made like almond *blossoms* on one branch, with an *ornamental* knob and a flower, and three bowls made like almond *blossoms* on the other branch, with an *ornamental* knob and a flower—and so for the six branches coming out of the lampstand. ²⁰And on the lampstand itself *were* four bowls made like almond *blossoms, each with* its *ornamental* knob and flower. ²¹*There was* a knob under the *first* two branches of the same, a knob under the *second* two

branches of the same, and a knob under the *third* two branches of the same, according to the six branches extending from it. ²²Their knobs and their branches were of one piece; all of it *was* one hammered piece of pure gold. ²³And he made its seven lamps, its wick-trimmers, and its trays of pure gold. ²⁴Of a talent of pure gold he made it, with all its utensils.

²⁵He made the incense altar of acacia wood. Its length *was* a cubit and its width a cubit—*it was* square—and two cubits *was* its height. Its horns were *of one piece* with it. ²⁶And he overlaid it with pure gold: its top, its sides all around, and its horns. He also made for it a molding of gold all around it. ²⁷He made two rings of gold for it under its molding, by its two corners on both sides, as holders for the poles with which to bear it. ²⁸And he made the poles of acacia wood, and overlaid them with gold.

²⁹He also made the holy anointing oil and the pure incense of sweet spices, according to the work of the perfumer.

CHAPTER **38** **MAKING THE BURNT OFFERING ALTAR.** He made the altar of burnt offering of acacia wood; five cubits *was* its length and five cubits its width—*it was* square—and its height *was* three cubits. ²He made its horns on its four corners; the horns were *of one piece* with it. And he overlaid it with bronze. ³He made all the utensils for the altar: the pans, the shovels, the basins, the forks, and the firepans; all its utensils he made of bronze. ⁴And he made a grate of bronze network for the altar, under its rim, midway from the bottom. ⁵He cast four rings for the four corners of the bronze grating, *as* holders for the poles. ⁶And he made the poles of acacia wood, and overlaid them with bronze. ⁷Then he put the poles into the rings on the sides of the altar, with which to bear it. He made the altar hollow with boards.

⁸He made the laver of bronze and its base of bronze, from the bronze mirrors of the serving women who assembled at the door of the tabernacle of meeting.

⁹Then he made the court on the south side; the hangings of the court *were of* fine woven linen, one hundred cubits long. ¹⁰There *were* twenty pillars for them, with twenty bronze sockets. The hooks of the pillars and their bands *were* silver. ¹¹On the north side *the hangings were* one hundred cubits *long,* with twenty pillars and their twenty bronze sockets. The hooks of the pillars and their bands *were* silver. ¹²And on the west side *there were* hangings of fifty cubits, with ten pillars and their ten sockets. The hooks of the pillars and their bands *were* silver. ¹³For the east side *the hangings were* fifty cubits. ¹⁴The hangings of one side *of the gate were* fifteen cubits *long, with* their three pillars and their three sockets, ¹⁵and the same for the other side of the court gate; on this side and that *were* hangings of fifteen cubits, *with* their three pillars and their three sockets. ¹⁶All the hangings of the court all around *were of* fine woven linen. ¹⁷The sockets for the pillars *were* bronze, the hooks of the pillars and their bands *were* silver, and the overlay of their capitals *was* silver; and all the pillars of the court had bands of silver. ¹⁸The screen for the gate of the court *was* woven of blue, purple, and scarlet *thread,* and of fine woven linen. The

length *was* twenty cubits, and the height along its width *was* five cubits, corresponding to the hangings of the court. [19]And *there were* four pillars *with* their four sockets of bronze; their hooks *were* silver, and the overlay of their capitals and their bands *was* silver. [20]All the pegs of the tabernacle, and of the court all around, *were* bronze.

BE YOURSELF!

38:21 In building the tabernacle, Moses laid out the steps, but Ithamar supervised the project. We all have different talents and abilities. God didn't ask Moses to build the tabernacle but to motivate the experts to do it. Look for the areas where God has gifted you and then seek opportunities to allow God to use them.

[21]This is the inventory of the tabernacle, the tabernacle of the Testimony, which was counted according to the commandment of Moses, for the service of the Levites, by the hand of Ithamar, son of Aaron the priest. [22]Bezalel the son of Uri, the son of Hur, of the tribe of Judah, made all that the LORD had commanded Moses. [23]And with him *was* Aholiab the son of Ahisamach, of the tribe of Dan, an engraver and designer, a weaver of blue, purple, and scarlet *thread*, and of fine linen. [24]All the gold that was used in all the work of the holy *place*, that is, the gold of the offering, was twenty-nine talents and seven hundred and thirty shekels, according to the shekel of the sanctuary. [25]And the silver from those who were numbered of the congregation *was* one hundred talents and one thousand seven hundred and seventy-five shekels, according to the shekel of the sanctuary: [26]a bekah for each man (*that is,* half a shekel, according to the shekel of the sanctuary), for everyone included in the numbering from twenty years old and above, for six hundred and three thousand, five hundred and fifty *men.* [27]And from the hundred talents of silver were cast the sockets of the sanctuary and the bases of the veil: one hundred sockets from the hundred talents, one talent for each socket. [28]Then from the one thousand seven hundred and seventy-five *shekels* he made hooks for the pillars, overlaid their capitals, and made bands for them. [29]The offering of bronze *was* seventy talents and two thousand four hundred shekels. [30]And with it he made the sockets for the door of the tabernacle of meeting, the bronze altar, the bronze grating for it, and all the utensils for the altar, [31]the sockets for the court all around, the bases for the court gate, all the pegs for the tabernacle, and all the pegs for the court all around.

CHAPTER 39 MAKING THE PRIEST'S CLOTHING.

Of the blue, purple, and scarlet *thread* they made garments of ministry, for ministering in the holy *place*, and made the holy garments for Aaron, as the LORD had commanded Moses.

[2]He made the ephod of gold, blue, purple, and scarlet *thread*, and of fine woven linen. [3]And they beat the gold into thin sheets and cut *it into* threads, to work *it* in *with* the blue, purple, and scarlet *thread*, and the fine linen, *into* artistic designs. [4]They made shoulder straps for it to couple *it* together; it was coupled together at its two edges. [5]And the intricately woven band of his ephod that *was* on it *was* of the same workmanship, *woven of* gold, blue, purple, and scarlet *thread*, and of fine woven linen, as the LORD had commanded Moses.

[6]And they set onyx stones, enclosed in settings of gold; they were engraved, as signets are engraved, with the names of the sons of Israel. [7]He put them on the shoulders of the ephod *as* memorial stones for the sons of Israel, as the LORD had commanded Moses.

[8]And he made the breastplate, artistically woven like the workmanship of the ephod, of gold, blue, purple, and scarlet *thread*, and of fine woven linen. [9]They made the breastplate square by doubling it; a span *was* its length and a span its width when doubled. [10]And they set in it four rows of stones: a row with a sardius, a topaz, and an emerald was the first row; [11]the second row, a turquoise, a sapphire, and a diamond; [12]the third row, a jacinth, an agate, and an amethyst; [13]the fourth row, a beryl, an onyx, and a jasper. *They were* enclosed in settings of gold in their mountings. [14]*There were* twelve stones according to the names of the sons of Israel: according to their names, *engraved like* a signet, each one with its own name according to the twelve tribes. [15]And they made chains for the breastplate at the ends, like braided cords of pure gold. [16]They also made two settings of gold and two gold

DETAILS

39:32 The tabernacle was finally complete to the last detail. God keenly interested in every minute part. The Creator of the universe concerned about even the little things. Matthew 10:30 says that Go knows the number of hairs on our head. This shows that God is grea interested in you. Don't be afraid to talk with him about any of you concerns—no matter how small or unimportant they might seem.

rings, and put the two rings on the two ends of the breastplate. [17]And they put the two braided *chains* of gold in the two rings on the ends of the breastplate. [18]The two ends of the two braided *chains* they fastened in the two settings, and put them on the shoulder straps of the ephod in the front. [19]And they made two rings of gold and put *them* on the two ends of the breastplate, on the edge of it, which *was* on the inward side of the ephod. [20]They made two *other* gold rings and put them on the two shoulder straps, underneath the ephod toward its front, right at the seam above the intricately woven band of the ephod. [21]And they bound the breastplate by means of its rings to the rings of the ephod with a blue cord, so that it would be above the intricately woven band of the ephod and that the breastplate would not come loose from the ephod, as the LORD had commanded Moses.

[22]He made the robe of the ephod of woven work, all o blue. [23]And *there was* an opening in the middle of the robe, like the opening in a coat of mail, *with* a wove binding all around the opening, so that it would not tea [24]They made on the hem of the robe pomegranates o blue, purple, and scarlet, and of fine woven *linen*. [25]An they made bells of pure gold, and put the bells betwee the pomegranates on the hem of the robe all aroun between the pomegranates: [26]a bell and a pomegranate

a bell and a pomegranate, all around the hem of the robe to minister in, as the LORD had commanded Moses.

[27]They made tunics, artistically woven of fine linen, for Aaron and his sons, [28]a turban of fine linen, exquisite hats of fine linen, short trousers of fine woven linen, [29]and a sash of fine woven linen with blue, purple, and scarlet *thread*, made by a weaver, as the LORD had commanded Moses.

[30]Then they made the plate of the holy crown of pure gold, and wrote on it an inscription *like* the engraving of a signet:

HOLINESS TO THE LORD.

[31]And they tied to it a blue cord, to fasten *it* above on the turban, as the LORD had commanded Moses.

[32]Thus all the work of the tabernacle of the tent of meeting was finished. And the children of Israel did according to all that the LORD had commanded Moses; so they did. [33]And they brought the tabernacle to Moses, the tent and all its furnishings: its clasps, its boards, its bars, its pillars, and its sockets; [34]the covering of ram skins dyed red, the covering of badger skins, and the veil of the covering; [35]the ark of the Testimony with its poles, and the mercy seat; [36]the table, all its utensils, and the showbread; [37]the pure *gold* lampstand with its lamps (the lamps set in order), all its utensils, and the oil for light; [38]the gold altar, the anointing oil, and the sweet incense; the screen for the tabernacle door; [39]the bronze altar, its grate of bronze, its poles, and all its utensils; the laver with its base; [40]the hangings of the court, its pillars and its sockets, the screen for the court gate, its cords, and its pegs; all the utensils for the service of the tabernacle, for the tent of meeting; [41]and the garments of ministry, to minister in the holy *place:* the holy garments for Aaron the priest, and his sons' garments, to minister as priests.

[42]According to all that the LORD had commanded Moses, so the children of Israel did all the work. [43]Then Moses looked over all the work, and indeed they had done it; as the LORD had commanded, just so they had done it. And Moses blessed them.

CHAPTER **40** THE TABERNACLE IS BUILT. Then

the LORD spoke to Moses, saying: [2]"On the first day of the first month you shall set up the tabernacle of the tent of meeting. [3]You shall put in it the ark of the Testimony, and partition off the ark with the veil. [4]You shall bring in the table and arrange the things that are to be set in order on it; and you shall bring in the lampstand and light its lamps. [5]You shall also set the altar of gold for the incense before the ark of the Testimony, and put up the screen for the door of the tabernacle. [6]Then you shall set the altar of the burnt offering before the door of the tabernacle of the tent of meeting. [7]And you shall set the laver between the tabernacle of meeting and the altar, and put water in it. [8]You shall set up the court all around, and hang up the screen at the court gate.

[9]"And you shall take the anointing oil, and anoint the tabernacle and all that *is* in it; and you shall hallow it and all its utensils, and it shall be holy. [10]You shall anoint the

altar of the burnt offering and all its utensils, and consecrate the altar. The altar shall be most holy. [11]And you shall anoint the laver and its base, and consecrate it.

[12]"Then you shall bring Aaron and his sons to the door of the tabernacle of meeting and wash them with water. [13]You shall put the holy garments on Aaron, and anoint him and consecrate him, that he may minister to Me as priest. [14]And you shall bring his sons and clothe them with tunics. [15]You shall anoint them, as you anointed their father, that they may minister to Me as priests; for their anointing shall surely be an everlasting priesthood throughout their generations."

[16]Thus Moses did; according to all that the LORD had commanded him, so he did.

◣▬▬▬FOLLOW-UP

39:43 Moses inspected the finished work, saw that it was done the way God wanted, and then blessed the people. A good leader follows up on assigned tasks and gives rewards for good work. In whatever responsible position you find yourself, follow up to make sure tasks are completed as intended, and show your appreciation to the people who have helped.

[17]And it came to pass in the first month of the second year, on the first *day* of the month, *that* the tabernacle was raised up. [18]So Moses raised up the tabernacle, fastened its sockets, set up its boards, put in its bars, and raised up its pillars. [19]And he spread out the tent over the tabernacle and put the covering of the tent on top of it, as the LORD had commanded Moses. [20]He took the Testimony and put *it* into the ark, inserted the poles through the rings of the ark, and put the mercy seat on top of the ark. [21]And he brought the ark into the tabernacle, hung up the veil of the covering, and partitioned off the ark of the Testimony, as the LORD had commanded Moses.

◣▬▬▬DIRTY WORK

40:17-33 The physical care of the tabernacle required a long list of tasks, and each was important to the work of God's house. This principle is important to remember today. There are many seemingly unimportant tasks that must be done to keep your church building maintained. Washing dishes, painting walls, or shoveling snow may not seem very spiritual, but they are vital to the ministry of the church and have an important role in our worship of God.

[22]He put the table in the tabernacle of meeting, on the north side of the tabernacle, outside the veil; [23]and he set the bread in order upon it before the LORD, as the LORD had commanded Moses. [24]He put the lampstand in the tabernacle of meeting, across from the table, on the south side of the tabernacle; [25]and he lit the lamps before the LORD, as the LORD had commanded Moses. [26]He put the gold altar in the tabernacle of meeting in front of the veil; [27]and he burned sweet incense on it, as the LORD had commanded Moses. [28]He hung up the screen *at* the door of the tabernacle. [29]And he put the altar of burnt offering *before* the door of the tabernacle of the tent of meeting, and offered upon it the burnt offering and the grain offering, as the LORD had commanded Moses. [30]He set the laver between the tabernacle of meeting and the altar,

and put water there for washing; ³¹and Moses, Aaron, and his sons would wash their hands and their feet *with water* from it. ³²Whenever they went into the tabernacle of meeting, and when they came near the altar, they washed, as the LORD had commanded Moses. ³³And he raised up the court all around the tabernacle and the altar, and hung up the screen of the court gate. So Moses finished the work.

³⁴Then the cloud covered the tabernacle of meeting, and the glory of the LORD filled the tabernacle. ³⁵And Moses was not able to enter the tabernacle of meeting, because the cloud rested above it, and the glory of the LORD filled the tabernacle. ³⁶Whenever the cloud was taken up from above the tabernacle, the children of Israel would go onward in all their journeys. ³⁷But if the cloud was not taken up, then they did not journey till the day that it was taken up. ³⁸For the cloud of the LORD *was* above the tabernacle by day, and fire was over it by night, in the sight of all the house of Israel, throughout all their journeys.

MEGA *Themes*

SLAVERY The Israelites were slaves for 400 years. Pharaoh, the king of Egypt, mistreated them cruelly.

Physical slavery is like slavery to sin. The longer you are a slave, the more difficult it becomes to break free. Gaining freedom from sin requires God's power and the guidance of godly leaders.

1. How did the Hebrews feel about being enslaved to the Egyptians?
2. What are some examples of how people become enslaved to specific sins in their lives?
3. When you look at your own life, what types of things have the potential to become your master?
4. How does God's power enable you to live in freedom?
5. What can you do to avoid becoming a slave to sin?

RESCUE/REDEMPTION God rescued Israel through the leader Moses and through mighty miracles. The Passover celebration was given by God as an annual reminder of their escape from slavery.

All of us need to experience the deliverance from sin that God provides. Jesus Christ celebrated the Passover with his disciples at the Last Supper and then completed God's plan for our redemption by dying in our place.

1. Describe the characteristics that were required for a Passover lamb.
2. Why was the lamb important?
3. In what way can Jesus be described as our Passover Lamb? (Check John 1:29.)
4. If someone were to ask you, "Why did Jesus have to die?" how would you respond?
5. From what has God rescued you through the sacrifice of Jesus?
6. In what ways has being redeemed by Christ affected the way you live? How do you plan to allow this truth to affect your future?

GUIDANCE God guided Israel out of slavery by using the plagues, Moses' heroic courage, the miracle of the Red Sea, and the Ten Commandments.

God demonstrates his power in our life through the guidance of wise leaders and the group effort of Christian friends working together. He can be trusted to give us the guidance we need to follow his will.

1. At first, Moses had difficulty following God's guidance. What questions did Moses have for God when he was spoken to through the burning bush? What were God's responses?
2. Think about a time when you, like Moses, felt inadequate or unwilling to obey God's will in your life. What decisions did you make? If God had spoken to you in that situation, what do you think he would have said?
3. What resources has God provided to help you learn how to follow his will for you?
4. What decisions are you facing now or in the near future that will require you to rely on these resources in order to obey him?
5. What are some specific ways that you can seek God's guidance as you get ready to make the right decisions?

TEN COMMANDMENTS God's law system had three interwoven parts. The Ten Commandments were the first part, containing the absolutes of spiritual and moral life. The civil law was the second part, giving the people rules to manage their lives. The ceremonial law was the third part, showing them patterns for building the tabernacle and for regular worship.

God was teaching Israel the importance of choice and responsibility. When they obeyed the conditions of the law, he blessed them; if they forgot or disobeyed, he punished them or allowed disasters to come upon them. God's moral laws, as given in

Exodus, have been reflected in the legal systems of many great countries, past and present.

1. The law was given to Israel to show them their sin and their need for redemption. How does the law point us to Christ?

2. There were some very severe and immediate consequences for those who disobeyed the law. What are some of the long-term consequences facing young people who go against God's moral law (the Ten Commandments)?

3. Why does God want you to obey his moral law?

THE NATION God established the nation of Israel to be the source of truth and salvation to all the world. His relationship to his people was loving, yet firm. God was their direct leader in government, social concerns, and worship.

Israel's newly formed nation models for us the need to depend upon God. Whether we are rebellious or obedient, God remains our only source of absolute, eternal truth and life.

1. Describe the qualities you find in God's leadership of the Israelites.

2. Which of these qualities are most important to you in your relationship with God at this time in your life?

3. In what specific areas do you need to depend on God in your relationships at home? At school? With close friends?

4. Based on God's relationship to Israel in Exodus, how can you know that God can be trusted in these important areas?

*J*ason was the coach's kid. At practice he tried hard to pay attention, but one day he knew he was doomed. Patti, the cutest girl on the cheerleading squad, stopped by. Soon she sat next to Jason on the grass, and they began to whisper together—until Jason's dad looked their way. Jason paid attention for a few minutes, but soon they were whispering again. ■ The rest of the world faded away. It was just the two of them . . . until Jason's father intruded. "Jason!" he demanded. "You are the coach's son, and I expect you to pay attention!" Jason understood. He remained attentive for the rest of the practice. ■ The coach expected Jason to listen during practice. Not because he was different than the other players, but because Jason was his son. He felt Jason's actions were a reflection on his father, so Jason should pay attention—even if no one else did. ■ The Israelites were in a similar situation. God demanded they "pay attention" because they were his chosen people, his children. God told them, "You shall be holy, for I the LORD your God *am* holy" (19:2). *Holy* means "set apart, good, and different." That's why God gave them the book of Leviticus. It contains laws of holiness, things they needed to do to remain holy. God also gave them the Day of Atonement so they could be forgiven. ■ The book of Leviticus is important to us, too. Our day of atonement is the day Jesus died. Because of him we can be "holy" before God even though we disobey him. Jesus' death covers everything we do wrong. ■ As you read Leviticus, consider your relationship with God. And, where it's needed, ask Christ for forgiveness.

STATS

PURPOSE: A handbook for the Levites outlining their priestly duties in worship, and a guidebook of holy living for the Hebrews

AUTHOR: Moses

DATE OF EVENTS: 1445–1444 B.C.

SETTING: At the foot of Mount Sinai. God teaches the Israelites how to live as holy people.

KEY PEOPLE: Moses, Aaron, Nadab, Abihu, Eleazar, Ithamar

SPECIAL FEATURE: Holiness is mentioned more often (152 times) than in any other book of the Bible

_eviticus

burn all on the altar as a burnt sacrifice, an offering made by fire, a sweet aroma to the LORD.

¹⁰'If his offering *is* of the flocks—of the sheep or of the goats—as a burnt sacrifice, he shall bring a male without blemish. ¹¹He shall kill it on the north side of the altar before the LORD; and the priests, Aaron's sons, shall sprinkle its blood all around on the altar. ¹²And he shall cut it into its pieces, with its head and its fat; and the priest shall lay them in order on the wood that *is* on the fire upon the altar; ¹³but he shall wash the entrails and the legs with water. Then the priest shall bring *it* all and burn *it* on the altar; it *is* a burnt sacrifice, an offering made by fire, a sweet aroma to the LORD.

¹⁴'And if the burnt sacrifice of his offering to the LORD *is* of birds, then he shall bring his offering of turtledoves or young pigeons. ¹⁵The priest shall bring it to the altar, wring off its head, and burn *it* on the altar; its blood shall be drained out at the side of the altar. ¹⁶And he shall remove its crop with its feathers and cast it beside the altar on the east side, into the place for ashes. ¹⁷Then he shall split it at its wings, *but* shall not divide *it* completely; and the priest shall burn it on the altar, on the wood that *is* on the fire. It *is* a burnt sacrifice, an offering made by fire, a sweet aroma to the LORD.

CHAPTER 1 HOW TO GIVE A BURNT OFFERING.
Now the LORD called to Moses, and spoke to him from the tabernacle of meeting, saying, ²"Speak to the children of Israel, and say to them: 'When any one of you brings an offering to the LORD, you shall bring your offering of the livestock—of the herd and of the flock.

³'If his offering *is* a burnt sacrifice of the herd, let him offer a male without blemish; he shall offer it of his own free will at the door of the tabernacle of meeting before the LORD. ⁴Then he shall put his hand on the head of the burnt offering, and it will be accepted on his behalf to make atonement for him. ⁵He shall kill the bull before the LORD; and the priests, Aaron's sons, shall bring the blood and sprinkle the blood all around on the altar that *is by* the door of the tabernacle of meeting. ⁶And he shall skin the burnt offering and cut it into its pieces. ⁷The sons of Aaron the priest shall put fire on the altar, and lay the wood in order on the fire. ⁸Then the priests, Aaron's sons, shall lay the parts, the head, and the fat in order on the wood that *is* on the fire upon the altar; ⁹but he shall wash its entrails and its legs with water. And the priest shall

THE COST OF SIN

1:1 Animal sacrifices were practiced in many cultures in the Middle East. God used the form of sacrifice to teach his people about faith. Sin needed to be taken seriously. When people saw the sacrificial animals being killed, they were sensitized to the importance of their sin and guilt. Our culture's casual attitude toward doing wrong ignores the cost of sin and the need for repentance and restoration. Although many of the rituals of Leviticus were fitted to the culture of the day, their purpose was to reveal a high and holy God who should be loved, obeyed, and worshiped. God's laws and sacrifices were intended to bring out true devotion of the heart. The ceremonies and rituals were the best way for the Israelites to focus their hearts on God.

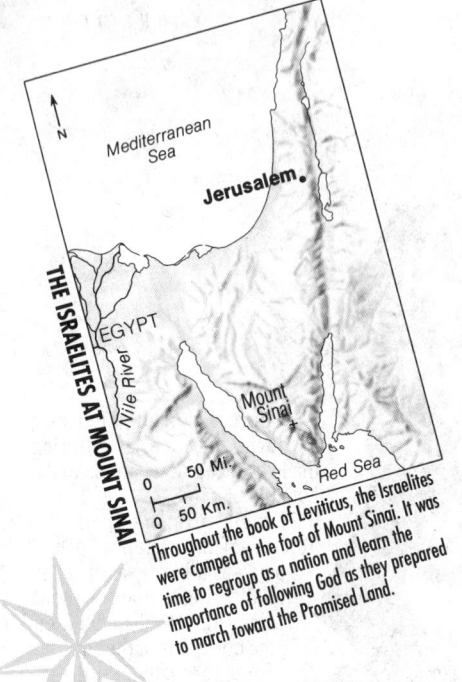

THE ISRAELITES AT MOUNT SINAI

Throughout the book of Leviticus, the Israelites were camped at the foot of Mount Sinai. It was time to regroup as a nation and learn the importance of following God as they prepared to march toward the Promised Land.

the covenant of your God to be lacking from your grain offering. With all your offerings you shall offer salt.

¹⁴If you offer a grain offering of your firstfruits to the LORD, you shall offer for the grain offering of your firstfruits green heads of grain roasted on the fire, grain beaten from full heads. ¹⁵And you shall put oil on it, and lay frankincense on it. It *is* a grain offering. ¹⁶Then the priest shall burn the memorial portion: *part* of its beaten grain and *part* of its oil, with all the frankincense, as an offering made by fire to the LORD.

CHAPTER 3 HOW TO GIVE A PEACE OFFERING.

¹When his offering *is* a sacrifice of a peace offering, if he offers *it* of the herd, whether male or female, he shall offer it without blemish before the LORD. ²And he shall lay his hand on the head of his offering, and kill it *at* the door of the tabernacle of meeting; and Aaron's sons, the priests, shall sprinkle the blood all around on the altar. ³Then he shall offer from the sacrifice of the peace offering an offering made by fire to the LORD. The fat that covers the entrails and all the fat that *is* on the entrails, ⁴the two kidneys and the fat that *is* on them by the flanks, and the fatty lobe *attached* to the liver above the kidneys, he shall remove; ⁵and Aaron's sons shall burn it on the altar upon the burnt sacrifice, which *is* on the wood that *is* on the fire, *as* an offering made by fire, a sweet aroma to the LORD.

⁶If his offering as a sacrifice of a peace offering to the LORD *is* of the flock, *whether* male or female, he shall offer it without blemish. ⁷If he offers a lamb as his offering, then he shall offer it before the LORD. ⁸And he shall lay his hand on the head of his offering, and kill it before the tabernacle of meeting; and Aaron's sons shall sprinkle its blood all around on the altar.

SALT

2:13 The offerings were seasoned with salt as a reminder of the people's covenant (contract) with God. Salt is a good symbol of God's activity in a person's life, because it penetrates, preserves, and aids healing. God wants to be active in your life. Let him become part of penetrating every aspect of your life, preserving you from the evil around, and healing you of your sins and shortcomings.

⁹Then he shall offer from the sacrifice of the peace offering, as an offering made by fire to the LORD, its fat *and* the whole fat tail which he shall remove close to the backbone. And the fat that covers the entrails and all the fat that *is* on the entrails, ¹⁰the two kidneys and the fat that *is* on them by the flanks, and the fatty lobe *attached* to the liver above the kidneys, he shall remove; ¹¹and the priest shall burn *them* on the altar *as* food, an offering made by fire to the LORD.

¹²And if his offering *is* a goat, then he shall offer *it* before the LORD. ¹³He shall lay his hand on its head and kill it before the tabernacle of meeting; and the sons of Aaron shall sprinkle its blood all around on the altar. ¹⁴Then he shall offer from it his offering, as an offering made by fire to the LORD. The fat that covers the entrails and all the fat that *is* on the entrails, ¹⁵the two kidneys and the fat that *is* on them by the flanks, and the fatty lobe

CHAPTER 2 HOW TO GIVE A GRAIN OFFERING.

¹When anyone offers a grain offering to the LORD, his offering shall be *of* fine flour. And he shall pour oil on it, and put frankincense on it. ²He shall bring it to Aaron's sons, the priests, one of whom shall take from it his handful of fine flour and oil with all the frankincense. And the priest shall burn *it as* a memorial on the altar, an offering made by fire, a sweet aroma to the LORD. ³The rest of the grain offering *shall be* Aaron's and his sons'. *It is* most holy of the offerings to the LORD made by fire.

⁴And if you bring as an offering a grain offering baked in the oven, *it shall be* unleavened cakes of fine flour mixed with oil, or unleavened wafers anointed with oil. ⁵But if your offering *is* a grain offering *baked* in a pan, *it shall be of* fine flour, unleavened, mixed with oil. ⁶You shall break it in pieces and pour oil on it; it *is* a grain offering.

⁷If your offering *is* a grain offering *baked* in a covered pan, it shall be made *of* fine flour with oil. ⁸You shall bring the grain offering that is made of these things to the LORD. And when it is presented to the priest, he shall bring it to the altar. ⁹Then the priest shall take from the grain offering a memorial portion, and burn *it* on the altar. *It is* an offering made by fire, a sweet aroma to the LORD. ¹⁰And what is left of the grain offering *shall be* Aaron's and his sons'. *It is* most holy of the offerings to the LORD made by fire.

¹¹No grain offering which you bring to the LORD shall be made with leaven, for you shall burn no leaven nor any honey in any offering to the LORD made by fire. ¹²As for the offering of the firstfruits, you shall offer them to the LORD, but they shall not be burned on the altar for a sweet aroma. ¹³And every offering of your grain offering you shall season with salt; you shall not allow the salt of

	Burnt Offering (Lev. 1— voluntary)	Grain Offering (Lev. 2— voluntary)	Peace Offering (Lev. 3— voluntary)	Sin Offering (Lev. 4— required)	Trespass Offering (Lev. 5— required)
Purpose	To make payment for sins in general	To show honor and respect to God in worship	To express gratitude to God	To make payment for unintentional sins of uncleanness, neglect, or thoughtlessness	To make payment for sins against God and others. A sacrifice was made to God and the injured person repaid or compensated.
Significance	Showed a person's devotion to God	Acknowledged that everything we have belongs to God	Symbolized peace and fellowship with God	Restored the sinner to fellowship with God; showed seriousness of sin	Provided compensation for injured parties
Christ, the Perfect Offering	Christ's death was the perfect offering	Christ was the perfect man, who gave all of himself to God and others	Christ is the only way to fellowship with God	Christ's death restores our fellowship with God	Christ's death takes away the deadly consequences of sin

(left margin label: Offering)

THE OFFERINGS

Listed here are the five key offerings the Israelites made to God. The Jews made these offerings in order to have their sins forgiven and to restore their fellowship with God. The death of Jesus Christ made these sacrifices unnecessary. Because of Jesus' death our sins are completely forgiven and fellowship with God has been restored.

attached to the liver above the kidneys, he shall remove; [16]and the priest shall burn them on the altar *as* food, an offering made by fire for a sweet aroma; all the fat *is* the LORD's.

[17]"*This shall be* a perpetual statute throughout your generations in all your dwellings: you shall eat neither fat nor blood.' "

CHAPTER 4 HOW TO GIVE A SIN OFFERING. Now

the LORD spoke to Moses, saying, [2]"Speak to the children of Israel, saying: 'If a person sins unintentionally against any of the commandments of the LORD *in anything* which ought not to be done, and does any of them, [3]if the anointed priest sins, bringing guilt on the people, then let him offer to the LORD for his sin which he has sinned a young bull without blemish as a sin offering. [4]He shall bring the bull to the door of the tabernacle of meeting before the LORD, lay his hand on the bull's head, and kill the bull before the LORD. [5]Then the anointed priest shall

take some of the bull's blood and bring it to the tabernacle of meeting. [6]The priest shall dip his finger in the blood and sprinkle some of the blood seven times before the LORD, in front of the veil of the sanctuary. [7]And the priest shall put some of the blood on the horns of the altar of sweet incense before the LORD, which is in the tabernacle of meeting; and he shall pour the remaining blood of the bull at the base of the altar of the burnt offering, which is at the door of the tabernacle of meeting. [8]He shall take from it all the fat of the bull as the sin offering. The fat that covers the entrails and all the fat which *is* on the entrails, [9]the two kidneys and the fat that *is* on them by the flanks, and the fatty lobe *attached* to the liver above the kidneys, he shall remove, [10]as it was taken from the bull of the sacrifice of the peace offering; and the priest shall burn them on the altar of the burnt offering. [11]But the bull's hide and all its flesh, with its head and legs, its entrails and offal— [12]the whole bull he shall carry outside the camp to a clean place, where the ashes are poured

4:1ff Have you ever done something wrong without realizing it until later? Although your sin was unintentional, it was still sin. One of the purposes of God's law was to make the Israelites aware of their unintentional sins so they would not repeat them and so they could be forgiven for them. Leviticus 4 and 5 mention some of these unintentional sins and the way the Israelites could be forgiven for them. As you read more of God's laws, keep in mind that they were meant to teach and guide the people. Let them help you become more aware of sin in your life.

out, and burn it on wood with fire; where the ashes are poured out it shall be burned.

¹³'Now if the whole congregation of Israel sins unintentionally, and the thing is hidden from the eyes of the assembly, and they have done *something against* any of the commandments of the LORD *in anything* which should not be done, and are guilty; ¹⁴when the sin which they have committed becomes known, then the assembly shall offer a young bull for the sin, and bring it before the tabernacle of meeting. ¹⁵And the elders of the congregation shall lay their hands on the head of the bull before the LORD. Then the bull shall be killed before the LORD. ¹⁶The anointed priest shall bring some of the bull's blood to the tabernacle of meeting. ¹⁷Then the priest shall dip his finger in the blood and sprinkle *it* seven times before the LORD, in front of the veil. ¹⁸And he shall put *some* of the blood on the horns of the altar which *is* before the LORD, which *is* in the tabernacle of meeting; and he shall pour the remaining blood at the base of the altar of burnt offering, which is at the door of the tabernacle of meeting. ¹⁹He shall take all the fat from it and burn *it* on the altar. ²⁰And he shall do with the bull as he did with the bull as a sin offering; thus he shall do with it. So the priest shall make atonement for them, and it shall be forgiven them. ²¹Then he shall carry the bull outside the camp, and burn it as he burned the first bull. It *is* a sin offering for the assembly.

²²'When a ruler has sinned, and done *something* unintentionally *against* any of the commandments of the LORD his God *in anything* which should not be done, and is guilty, ²³or if his sin which he has committed comes to his knowledge, he shall bring as his offering a kid of the goats, a male without blemish. ²⁴And he shall lay his hand on the head of the goat, and kill it at the place where they kill the burnt offering before the LORD. It *is* a sin offering. ²⁵The priest shall take some of the blood of the sin offering with his finger, put *it* on the horns of the altar of burnt offering, and pour its blood at the base of the altar of burnt offering. ²⁶And he shall burn all its fat on the altar, like the fat of the sacrifice of the peace offering. So the priest shall make atonement for him concerning his sin, and it shall be forgiven him.

²⁷'If anyone of the common people sins unintentionally by doing *something against* any of the commandments of the LORD *in anything* which ought not to be done, and is guilty, ²⁸or if his sin which he has committed comes to his knowledge, then he shall bring as his offering a kid of the goats, a female without blemish, for his sin which he has committed. ²⁹And he shall lay his hand on the head of the sin offering, and kill the sin offering at the place of the burnt offering. ³⁰Then the priest shall take *some* of its blood with his finger, put *it* on the horns

of the altar of burnt offering, and pour all *the remaining* blood at the base of the altar. ³¹He shall remove all its fat, as fat is removed from the sacrifice of the peace offering; and the priest shall burn it on the altar for a sweet aroma to the LORD. So the priest shall make atonement for him, and it shall be forgiven him.

³²'If he brings a lamb as his sin offering, he shall bring a female without blemish. ³³Then he shall lay his hand on the head of the sin offering, and kill it as a sin offering at the place where they kill the burnt offering. ³⁴The priest shall take *some* of the blood of the sin offering with his finger, put *it* on the horns of the altar of burnt offering, and pour all *the remaining* blood at the base of the altar. ³⁵He shall remove all its fat, as the fat of the lamb is removed from the sacrifice of the peace offering. Then the priest shall burn it on the altar, according to the offerings made by fire to the LORD. So the priest shall make atonement for his sin that he has committed, and it shall be forgiven him.

CHAPTER 5 WHAT TO GIVE IF ONE IS POOR. 'If a person sins in hearing the utterance of an oath, and *is* a witness, whether he has seen or known *of the matter*—if he does not tell *it*, he bears guilt.

²'Or if a person touches any unclean thing, whether *it is* the carcass of an unclean beast, or the carcass of unclean livestock, or the carcass of unclean creeping things, and he is unaware of it, he also shall be unclean and guilty. ³Or if he touches human uncleanness—whatever uncleanness with which a man may be defiled, and he is unaware of it—when he realizes *it*, then he shall be guilty.

■▬▬▬**SELF-CONTROL**

5:4 Have you ever sworn to do or not do something and then real[ized] what a foolish thing you had done? God's people are called to keep [their] word, even if they make promises that are tough to keep. Our wor[d] should be enough. To feel we need to strengthen a promise with a v[ow] shows that something is wrong. The only promises we ought not to [keep] are promises that lead to sin. A wise and self-controlled person avo[ids] making rash vows.

⁴'Or if a person swears, speaking thoughtlessly with *his* lips to do evil or to do good, whatever *it is* that a man may pronounce by an oath, and he is unaware of it— when he realizes *it*, then he shall be guilty in any of these *matters*.

⁵'And it shall be, when he is guilty in any of these *matters*, that he shall confess that he has sinned in that *thing*; ⁶and he shall bring his trespass offering to the LORD for his sin which he has committed, a female from the flock, a lamb or a kid of the goats as a sin offering. So the priest shall make atonement for him concerning his sin.

⁷'If he is not able to bring a lamb, then he shall bring to the LORD, for his trespass which he has committed, two turtledoves or two young pigeons: one as a sin offer[ing] and the other as a burnt offering. ⁸And he shall bring them to the priest, who shall offer *that* which *is* for the si[n] offering first, and wring off its head from its neck, bu[t] shall not divide *it* completely. ⁹Then he shall sprinkl[e] *some* of the blood of the sin offering on the side of th[e]

altar, and the rest of the blood shall be drained out at the base of the altar. It *is* a sin offering. [10]And he shall offer the second *as* a burnt offering according to the prescribed manner. So the priest shall make atonement on his behalf for his sin which he has committed, and it shall be forgiven him.

[11]'But if he is not able to bring two turtledoves or two young pigeons, then he who sinned shall bring for his offering one-tenth of an ephah of fine flour as a sin offering. He shall put no oil on it, nor shall he put frankincense on it, for it *is* a sin offering. [12]Then he shall bring it to the priest, and the priest shall take his handful of it as a memorial portion, and burn *it* on the altar according to the offerings made by fire to the LORD. It *is* a sin offering. [13]The priest shall make atonement for him, for his sin that he has committed in any of these matters; and it shall be forgiven him. *The rest* shall be the priest's as a grain offering.' "

[14]Then the LORD spoke to Moses, saying: [15]"If a person commits a trespass, and sins unintentionally in regard to the holy things of the LORD, then he shall bring to the LORD as his trespass offering a ram without blemish from the flocks, with your valuation in shekels of silver according to the shekel of the sanctuary, as a trespass offering. [16]And he shall make restitution for the harm that he has done in regard to the holy thing, and shall add one-fifth to it and give it to the priest. So the priest shall make atonement for him with the ram of the trespass offering, and it shall be forgiven him.

[17]"If a person sins, and commits any of these things which are forbidden to be done by the commandments of the LORD, though he does not know *it*, yet he is guilty and shall bear his iniquity. [18]And he shall bring to the priest a ram without blemish from the flock, with your valuation, as a trespass offering. So the priest shall make atonement for him regarding his ignorance in which he erred and did not know *it*, and it shall be forgiven him. [19]It is a trespass offering; he has certainly trespassed against the LORD."

CHAPTER 6 BURNT AND GRAIN OFFERINGS. And

the LORD spoke to Moses, saying: [2]"If a person sins and commits a trespass against the LORD by lying to his neighbor about what was delivered to him for safekeeping, or about a pledge, or about a robbery, or if he has extorted from his neighbor, [3]or if he has found what was lost and lies concerning it, and swears falsely—in any one of these things that a man may do in which he sins: [4]then it shall be, because he has sinned and is guilty, that he shall restore what he has stolen, or the thing which he has extorted, or what was delivered to him for safekeeping, or the lost thing which he found, [5]or all that about which he has sworn falsely. He shall restore its full value, add one-fifth more to it, *and* give it to whomever it belongs, on the day of his trespass offering. [6]And he shall bring his trespass offering to the LORD, a ram without blemish from the flock, with your valuation, as a trespass offering, to the priest. [7]So the priest shall make atonement for him before the LORD, and he shall be forgiven

for any one of these things that he may have done in which he trespasses."

[8]Then the LORD spoke to Moses, saying, [9]"Command Aaron and his sons, saying, 'This *is* the law of the burnt offering: The burnt offering *shall be* on the hearth upon the altar all night until morning, and the fire of the altar shall be kept burning on it. [10]And the priest shall put on his linen garment, and his linen trousers he shall put on his body, and take up the ashes of the burnt offering which the fire has consumed on the altar, and he shall put them beside the altar. [11]Then he shall take off his garments, put on other garments, and carry the ashes outside the camp to a clean place. [12]And the fire on the altar shall be kept burning on it; it shall not be put out. And the priest shall burn wood on it every morning, and lay the burnt offering in order on it; and he shall burn on it the fat of the peace offerings. [13]A fire shall always be burning on the altar; it shall never go out.

◆◆◆◆◆◆◆ STEALING

6:1-7 Here we discover that stealing involves more than just taking from someone. Finding something and not returning it, or refusing to return something borrowed are other forms of stealing. These are sins against God and not just your neighbor, a stranger, or a business. If you have gotten something deceitfully, then confess your sin to God, apologize to the owner, and return the stolen items.

[14]"This *is* the law of the grain offering: The sons of Aaron shall offer it on the altar before the LORD. [15]He shall take from it his handful of the fine flour of the grain offering, with its oil, and all the frankincense which *is* on the grain offering, and shall burn *it* on the altar *for* a sweet aroma, as a memorial to the LORD. [16]And the remainder of it Aaron and his sons shall eat; with unleavened bread it shall be eaten in a holy place; in the court of the tabernacle of meeting they shall eat it. [17]It shall not be baked with leaven. I have given it *as* their portion of My offerings made by fire; it *is* most holy, like the sin offering and the trespass offering. [18]All the males among the children of Aaron may eat it. *It shall be* a statute forever in your generations concerning the offerings made by fire to the LORD. Everyone who touches them must be holy.' "

[19]And the LORD spoke to Moses, saying, [20]"This *is* the offering of Aaron and his sons, which they shall offer to the LORD, *beginning* on the day when he is anointed: one-tenth of an ephah of fine flour as a daily grain offering, half of it in the morning and half of it at night. [21]It shall be made in a pan with oil. *When it is* mixed, you shall bring it in. The baked pieces of the grain offering you shall offer *for* a sweet aroma to the LORD. [22]The priest from among his sons, who is anointed in his place, shall offer it. *It is* a statute forever to the LORD. It shall be wholly burned. [23]For every grain offering for the priest shall be wholly burned. It shall not be eaten."

[24]Also the LORD spoke to Moses, saying, [25]"Speak to Aaron and to his sons, saying, 'This *is* the law of the sin offering: In the place where the burnt offering is killed, the sin offering shall be killed before the LORD. It *is* most holy. [26]The priest who offers it for sin shall eat it. In a holy place it shall be eaten, in the court of the tabernacle of

7:29 God told the people of Israel to bring their peace offerings personally, with their own hands. They were to take time and effort to express thanks to God. You are the only person who can express your gratitude to God and to others. Take time to express thanks both to God and to others who have helped and blessed you.

meeting. [27]Everyone who touches its flesh must be holy. And when its blood is sprinkled on any garment, you shall wash that on which it was sprinkled, in a holy place. [28]But the earthen vessel in which it is boiled shall be broken. And if it is boiled in a bronze pot, it shall be both scoured and rinsed in water. [29]All the males among the priests may eat it. It *is* most holy. [30]But no sin offering from which *any* of the blood is brought into the tabernacle of meeting, to make atonement in the holy *place*, shall be eaten. It shall be burned in the fire.

CHAPTER 7 TRESPASS AND PEACE OFFERINGS.

'Likewise this *is* the law of the trespass offering (it *is* most holy): [2]In the place where they kill the burnt offering they shall kill the trespass offering. And its blood he shall sprinkle all around on the altar. [3]And he shall offer from it all its fat. The fat tail and the fat that covers the entrails, [4]the two kidneys and the fat that *is* on them by the flanks, and the fatty lobe *attached* to the liver above the kidneys, he shall remove; [5]and the priest shall burn them on the altar *as* an offering made by fire to the LORD. It *is* a trespass offering. [6]Every male among the priests may eat it. It shall be eaten in a holy place. It *is* most holy. [7]The trespass offering *is* like the sin offering; *there is* one law for them both: the priest who makes atonement with it shall have *it*. [8]And the priest who offers anyone's burnt offering, that priest shall have for himself the skin of the burnt offering which he has offered. [9]Also every grain offering that is baked in the oven and all that is prepared in the covered pan, or in a pan, shall be the priest's who offers it. [10]Every grain offering, *whether* mixed with oil or dry, shall belong to all the sons of Aaron, to one *as much* as the other.

[11]'This *is* the law of the sacrifice of peace offerings which he shall offer to the LORD: [12]If he offers it for a thanksgiving, then he shall offer, with the sacrifice of thanksgiving, unleavened cakes mixed with oil, unleavened wafers anointed with oil, or cakes of blended flour mixed with oil. [13]Besides the cakes, *as* his offering he shall offer leavened bread with the sacrifice of thanksgiving of his peace offering. [14]And from it he shall offer one cake from each offering *as* a heave offering to the LORD. It shall belong to the priest who sprinkles the blood of the peace offering.

[15]'The flesh of the sacrifice of his peace offering for thanksgiving shall be eaten the same day it is offered. He shall not leave any of it until morning. [16]But if the sacrifice of his offering *is* a vow or a voluntary offering, it shall be eaten the same day that he offers his sacrifice; but on the next day the remainder of it also may be eaten; [17]the remainder of the flesh of the sacrifice on the third day must be burned with fire. [18]And if *any* of the flesh of the sacrifice of his peace offering is eaten at all on the third day, it shall not be accepted, nor shall it be imputed to him; it shall be an abomination *to* him who offers it, and the person who eats of it shall bear guilt.

[19]'The flesh that touches any unclean thing shall not be eaten. It shall be burned with fire. And as for the *clean* flesh, all who are clean may eat of it. [20]But the person who eats the flesh of the sacrifice of the peace offering that *belongs* to the LORD, while he is unclean, that person shall be cut off from his people. [21]Moreover the person who touches any unclean thing, *such as* human uncleanness, *an* unclean animal, or any abominable unclean thing, and who eats the flesh of the sacrifice of the peace offering that *belongs* to the LORD, that person shall be cut off from his people.' "

[22]And the LORD spoke to Moses, saying, [23]"Speak to the children of Israel, saying: 'You shall not eat any fat, of ox or sheep or goat. [24]And the fat of an animal that dies *naturally*, and the fat of what is torn by wild beasts, may be used in any other way; but you shall by no means eat it. [25]For whoever eats the fat of the animal of which men offer an offering made by fire to the LORD, the person who eats *it* shall be cut off from his people. [26]Moreover you shall not eat any blood in any of your dwellings, *whether* of bird or beast. [27]Whoever eats any blood, that person shall be cut off from his people.' "

[28]Then the LORD spoke to Moses, saying, [29]"Speak to the children of Israel, saying: 'He who offers the sacrifice of his peace offering to the LORD shall bring his offering to the LORD from the sacrifice of his peace offering. [30]His own hands shall bring the offerings made by fire to the LORD. The fat with the breast he shall bring, that the breast may be waved *as* a wave offering before the LORD. [31]And the priest shall burn the fat on the altar, but the breast shall be Aaron's and his sons'. [32]Also the right thigh you shall give to the priest *as* a heave offering from the sacrifices of your peace offerings. [33]He among the sons of Aaron, who offers the blood of the peace offering and the fat, shall have the right thigh for *his* part. [34]For the breast of the wave offering and the thigh of the heave offering I have taken from the children of Israel, from the sacrifices of their peace offerings, and I have given them to Aaron the priest and to his sons from the children of Israel by a statute forever.' "

[35]This *is* the consecrated portion for Aaron and his sons, from the offerings made by fire to the LORD, on the day when *Moses* presented them to minister to the LORD as priests. [36]The LORD commanded this to be given to them by the children of Israel, on the day that He anointed them, *by* a statute forever throughout their generations.

[37]This *is* the law of the burnt offering, the grain offering, the sin offering, the trespass offering, the consecrations, and the sacrifice of the peace offering, [38]which the LORD commanded Moses on Mount Sinai, on the day when He commanded the children of Israel to offer their offerings to the LORD in the Wilderness of Sinai.

WORSHIP

7:38 God gave his people many rituals and instructions to follo[w] the rituals in Leviticus were meant to teach the people valuable l[essons] But over time, the people became indifferent to the meanings of rituals and they began to lose touch with God. When your church[seems] to be conducting dry, meaningless rituals, try rediscovering the [deeper] meaning and purpose behind each, and your worship will come [alive]

CHAPTER **8** **AARON AND HIS SONS.** And the LORD spoke to Moses, saying: ²"Take Aaron and his sons with him, and the garments, the anointing oil, a bull as the sin offering, two rams, and a basket of unleavened bread; ³and gather all the congregation together at the door of the tabernacle of meeting."

⁴So Moses did as the LORD commanded him. And the congregation was gathered together at the door of tabernacle of meeting. ⁵And Moses said to the congregation, "This *is* what the LORD commanded to be done."

⁶Then Moses brought Aaron and his sons and washed them with water. ⁷And he put the tunic on him, girded him with the sash, clothed him with the robe, and put the ephod on him; and he girded him with the intricately woven band of the ephod, and with it tied *the ephod* on him. ⁸Then he put the breastplate on him, and he put the Urim and the Thummim in the breastplate. ⁹And he put the turban on his head. Also on the turban, on its front, he put the golden plate, the holy crown, as the LORD had commanded Moses.

¹⁰Also Moses took the anointing oil, and anointed the tabernacle and all that *was* in it, and consecrated them. ¹¹He sprinkled some of it on the altar seven times, anointed the altar and all its utensils, and the laver and its base, to consecrate them. ¹²And he poured some of the anointing oil on Aaron's head and anointed him, to consecrate him.

¹³Then Moses brought Aaron's sons and put tunics on them, girded them with sashes, and put hats on them, as the LORD had commanded Moses.

¹⁴And he brought the bull for the sin offering. Then Aaron and his sons laid their hands on the head of the bull for the sin offering, ¹⁵and Moses killed *it.* Then he took the blood, and put *some* on the horns of the altar all around with his finger, and purified the altar. And he poured the blood at the base of the altar, and consecrated it, to make atonement for it. ¹⁶Then he took all the fat that *was* on the entrails, the fatty lobe *attached to* the liver, and the two kidneys with their fat, and Moses burned *them* on the altar. ¹⁷But the bull, its hide, its flesh, and its offal, he burned with fire outside the camp, as the LORD had commanded Moses.

¹⁸Then he brought the ram as the burnt offering. And Aaron and his sons laid their hands on the head of the ram, ¹⁹and Moses killed *it.* Then he sprinkled the blood all around on the altar. ²⁰And he cut the ram into pieces; and Moses burned the head, the pieces, and the fat. ²¹Then he washed the entrails and the legs in water. And Moses burned the whole ram on the altar. It *was* a burnt sacrifice for a sweet aroma, an offering made by fire to the LORD, as the LORD had commanded Moses.

²²And he brought the second ram, the ram of consecration. Then Aaron and his sons laid their hands on the head of the ram, ²³and Moses killed *it.* Also he took *some* of its blood and put it on the tip of Aaron's right ear, on the thumb of his right hand, and on the big toe of his right foot. ²⁴Then he brought Aaron's sons. And Moses put *some* of the blood on the tips of their right ears, on the thumbs of their right hands, and on the big toes of their right feet. And Moses sprinkled the blood all around on the altar. ²⁵Then he took the fat and the fat tail, all the fat that *was* on the entrails, the fatty lobe *attached to* the liver, the two kidneys and their fat, and the right thigh; ²⁶and from the basket of unleavened bread that was before the LORD he took one unleavened cake, a cake of bread *anointed with* oil, and one wafer, and put *them* on the fat and on the right thigh; ²⁷and he put all *these* in Aaron's hands and in his sons' hands, and waved them *as* a wave offering before the LORD. ²⁸Then Moses took them from their hands and burned *them* on the altar, on the burnt offering. They *were* consecration offerings for a sweet aroma. That *was* an offering made by fire to the LORD. ²⁹And Moses took the breast and waved it *as* a wave offering before the LORD. It was Moses' part of the ram of consecration, as the LORD had commanded Moses.

³⁰Then Moses took some of the anointing oil and some of the blood which *was* on the altar, and sprinkled *it* on Aaron, on his garments, on his sons, and on the garments of his sons with him; and he consecrated Aaron, his garments, his sons, and the garments of his sons with him.

TOTALLY HOLY

8:36 Aaron and his sons did all that the Lord told them to do. Considering the many detailed lists of Leviticus, that was a remarkable feat. They knew what God wanted, how he wanted it done, and with what attitude it was to be carried out. This shows how carefully we ought to obey God. God wants us to be thoroughly holy people, not a rough approximation of the way his followers should be.

³¹And Moses said to Aaron and his sons, "Boil the flesh *at* the door of the tabernacle of meeting, and eat it there with the bread that *is* in the basket of consecration offerings, as I commanded, saying, 'Aaron and his sons shall eat it.' ³²What remains of the flesh and of the bread you shall burn with fire. ³³And you shall not go outside the door of the tabernacle of meeting *for* seven days, until the days of your consecration are ended. For seven days he shall consecrate you. ³⁴As he has done this day, *so* the LORD has commanded to do, to make atonement for you. ³⁵Therefore you shall stay *at* the door of the tabernacle of meeting day and night for seven days, and keep the charge of the LORD, so that you may not die; for so I have been commanded." ³⁶So Aaron and his sons did all the things that the LORD had commanded by the hand of Moses.

CHAPTER **9** **THE PRIESTS BEGIN THEIR WORK.** It came to pass on the eighth day that Moses called Aaron and his sons and the elders of Israel. ²And he said to Aaron, "Take for yourself a young bull as a sin offering and a ram as a burnt offering, without blemish, and offer *them* before the LORD. ³And to the children of Israel you shall speak, saying, 'Take a kid of the goats as a sin offering, and a calf and a lamb, *both* of the first year, without blemish, as a burnt offering, ⁴also a bull and a ram as peace offerings, to sacrifice before the LORD, and a grain offering mixed with oil; for today the LORD will appear to you.' "

⁵So they brought what Moses commanded before the tabernacle of meeting. And all the congregation drew near and stood before the LORD. ⁶Then Moses said, "This

10:2 Aaron's sons were careless about following the laws for sacrifices. In response, God destroyed them with a blast of fire. Performing the sacrifices was an act of obedience. Doing them correctly showed respect for God. It is easy for us to grow careless about obeying God, to live our way instead of his. But if one way were just as good as another, God would not command us to live his way. He always has good reasons for his commands, and we always place ourselves in danger when we consciously or carelessly disobey them.

is the thing which the LORD commanded you to do, and the glory of the LORD will appear to you." [7]And Moses said to Aaron, "Go to the altar, offer your sin offering and your burnt offering, and make atonement for yourself and for the people. Offer the offering of the people, and make atonement for them, as the LORD commanded."

[8]Aaron therefore went to the altar and killed the calf of the sin offering, which *was* for himself. [9]Then the sons of Aaron brought the blood to him. And he dipped his finger in the blood, put *it* on the horns of the altar, and poured the blood at the base of the altar. [10]But the fat, the kidneys, and the fatty lobe from the liver of the sin offering he burned on the altar, as the LORD had commanded Moses. [11]The flesh and the hide he burned with fire outside the camp.

[12]And he killed the burnt offering; and Aaron's sons presented to him the blood, which he sprinkled all around on the altar. [13]Then they presented the burnt offering to him, with its pieces and head, and he burned *them* on the altar. [14]And he washed the entrails and the legs, and burned *them* with the burnt offering on the altar.

[15]Then he brought the people's offering, and took the goat, which *was* the sin offering for the people, and killed it and offered it for sin, like the first one. [16]And he brought the burnt offering and offered it according to the prescribed manner. [17]Then he brought the grain offering, took a handful of it, and burned *it* on the altar, besides the burnt sacrifice of the morning.

[18]He also killed the bull and the ram *as* sacrifices of peace offerings, which *were* for the people. And Aaron's sons presented to him the blood, which he sprinkled all around on the altar, [19]and the fat from the bull and the ram—the fatty tail, what covers *the entrails* and the kidneys, and the fatty lobe *attached to* the liver; [20]and they put the fat on the breasts. Then he burned the fat on the altar; [21]but the breasts and the right thigh Aaron waved *as* a wave offering before the LORD, as Moses had commanded.

[22]Then Aaron lifted his hand toward the people, blessed them, and came down from offering the sin offering, the burnt offering, and peace offerings. [23]And Moses and Aaron went into the tabernacle of meeting, and came out and blessed the people. Then the glory of the LORD appeared to all the people, [24]and fire came out from before the LORD and consumed the burnt offering and the fat on the altar. When all the people saw *it*, they shouted and fell on their faces.

CHAPTER 10 TWO PRIESTS ARE KILLED BY FIRE.
Then Nadab and Abihu, the sons of Aaron, each took his censer and put fire in it, put incense on it, and offered profane fire before the LORD, which He had not com-

manded them. [2]So fire went out from the LORD and devoured them, and they died before the LORD. [3]And Moses said to Aaron, "This is what the LORD spoke, saying:

'By those who come near Me
I must be regarded as holy;
And before all the people
I must be glorified.' "

So Aaron held his peace.

[4]Then Moses called Mishael and Elzaphan, the sons of Uzziel the uncle of Aaron, and said to them, "Come near, carry your brethren from before the sanctuary out of the camp." [5]So they went near and carried them by their tunics out of the camp, as Moses had said.

[6]And Moses said to Aaron, and to Eleazar and Ithamar, his sons, "Do not uncover your heads nor tear your clothes, lest you die, and wrath come upon all the people. But let your brethren, the whole house of Israel, bewail the burning which the LORD has kindled. [7]You shall not go out from the door of the tabernacle of meeting, lest you die, for the anointing oil of the LORD *is* upon you." And they did according to the word of Moses.

[8]Then the LORD spoke to Aaron, saying: [9]"Do not drink wine or intoxicating drink, you, nor your sons with you, when you go into the tabernacle of meeting, lest you die. *It shall be* a statute forever throughout your generations, [10]that you may distinguish between holy and unholy, and between unclean and clean, [11]and that you may teach the children of Israel all the statutes which the LORD has spoken to them by the hand of Moses."

[12]And Moses spoke to Aaron, and to Eleazar and Ithamar, his sons who were left: "Take the grain offering that remains of the offerings made by fire to the LORD, and eat it without leaven beside the altar; for it *is* most holy. [13]You shall eat it in a holy place, because it *is* your due and your sons' due, of the sacrifices made by fire to the LORD; for so I have been commanded. [14]The breast of the wave offering and the thigh of the heave offering you shall eat in a clean place, you, your sons, and your daughters with you; for *they are* your due and your sons' due, *which* are given from the sacrifices of peace offerings of the children of Israel. [15]The thigh of the heave offering and the breast of the wave offering they shall bring with the offerings of fat made by fire, to offer *as* a wave offering before the LORD. And it shall be yours and your sons' with you, by a statute forever, as the LORD has commanded."

[16]Then Moses made careful inquiry about the goat of the sin offering, and there it was—burned up. And he was angry with Eleazar and Ithamar, the sons of Aaron *who were* left, saying, [17]"Why have you not eaten the sin offering in a holy place, since it *is* most holy, and *God* has given it to you to bear the guilt of the congregation, to make atonement for them before the LORD? [18]See! Its blood was not brought inside the holy *place;* indeed you should have eaten it in a holy *place,* as I commanded."

[19]And Aaron said to Moses, "Look, this day they have offered their sin offering and their burnt offering before the LORD, and such things have befallen me! *If* I had eaten the sin offering today, would it have been accepted in the sight of the LORD?" [20]So when Moses heard *that,* he was content.

CHAPTER **11** **CLEAN AND UNCLEAN ANIMALS.** Now the LORD spoke to Moses and Aaron, saying to them, [2]"Speak to the children of Israel, saying, 'These *are* the animals which you may eat among all the animals that *are* on the earth: [3]Among the animals, whatever divides the hoof, having cloven hooves *and* chewing the cud— that you may eat. [4]Nevertheless these you shall not eat among those that chew the cud or those that have cloven hooves: the camel, because it chews the cud but does not have cloven hooves, is unclean to you; [5]the rock hyrax, because it chews the cud but does not have cloven hooves, *is* unclean to you; [6]the hare, because it chews the cud but does not have cloven hooves, *is* unclean to you; [7]and the swine, though it divides the hoof, having cloven hooves, yet does not chew the cud, *is* unclean to you. [8]Their flesh you shall not eat, and their carcasses you shall not touch. They *are* unclean to you.

[9]These you may eat of all that *are* in the water: whatever in the water has fins and scales, whether in the seas or in the rivers—that you may eat. [10]But all in the seas or in the rivers that do not have fins and scales, all that move in the water or any living thing which *is* in the water, they *are* an abomination to you. [11]They shall be an abomination to you; you shall not eat their flesh, but you shall regard their carcasses as an abomination. [12]Whatever in the water does not have fins or scales—that *shall be* an abomination to you.

[13]And these you shall regard as an abomination among the birds; they shall not be eaten, they *are* an abomination: the eagle, the vulture, the buzzard, [14]the kite, and the falcon after its kind; [15]every raven after its kind, [16]the ostrich, the short-eared owl, the sea gull, and the hawk after its kind; [17]the little owl, the fisher owl, and the screech owl; [18]the white owl, the jackdaw, and the carrion vulture; [19]the stork, the heron after its kind, the hoopoe, and the bat.

[20]All flying insects that creep on *all* fours *shall be* an abomination to you. [21]Yet these you may eat of every flying insect that creeps on *all* fours: those which have jointed legs above their feet with which to leap on the earth. [22]These you may eat: the locust after its kind, the destroying locust after its kind, the cricket after its kind, and the grasshopper after its kind. [23]But all *other* flying insects which have four feet *shall be* an abomination to you.

[24]By these you shall become unclean; whoever touches the carcass of any of them shall be unclean until evening; [25]whoever carries part of the carcass of any of them shall wash his clothes and be unclean until evening: [26]*The carcass* of any animal which divides the foot, but is not cloven-hoofed or does not chew the cud, *is* unclean to you. Everyone who touches it shall be unclean. [27]And whatever goes on its paws, among all kinds of animals that go on *all* fours, those *are* unclean to you. Whoever touches any such carcass shall be unclean until evening. [28]Whoever carries *any such* carcass shall wash his clothes and be unclean until evening. It *is* unclean to you.

[29]These also *shall be* unclean to you among the creeping things that creep on the earth: the mole, the mouse, and the large lizard after its kind; [30]the gecko, the monitor lizard, the sand reptile, the sand lizard, and the chameleon. [31]These *are* unclean to you among all that creep. Whoever touches them when they are dead shall be unclean until evening. [32]Anything on which *any* of them falls, when they are dead shall be unclean, whether *it is* any item of wood or clothing or skin or sack, whatever item *it is*, in which *any* work is done, it must be put in water. And it shall be unclean until evening; then it shall be clean. [33]Any earthen vessel into which *any* of them falls you shall break; and whatever *is* in it shall be unclean: [34]in such a vessel, any edible food upon which

RATIONALIZING

11:8 God had strictly forbidden eating the meat of certain animals; to make sure, he forbade even touching them. He wanted the people to be totally separated from those things he had forbidden. Often we flirt with temptation, rationalizing that at least we are technically keeping the commandment not to commit the sin. But God wants us to separate ourselves completely from all sin and tempting situations.

water falls becomes unclean, and any drink that may be drunk from it becomes unclean. [35]And everything on which *a part* of *any such* carcass falls shall be unclean; *whether it is* an oven or cooking stove, it shall be broken down; *for* they *are* unclean, and shall be unclean to you. [36]Nevertheless a spring or a cistern, *in which there is* plenty of water, shall be clean, but whatever touches any such carcass becomes unclean. [37]And if a part of *any such* carcass falls on any planting seed which is to be sown, it *remains* clean. [38]But if water is put on the seed, and if *a part* of *any such* carcass falls on it, it *becomes* unclean to you.

[39]And if any animal which you may eat dies, he who touches its carcass shall be unclean until evening. [40]He who eats of its carcass shall wash his clothes and be unclean until evening. He also who carries its carcass shall wash his clothes and be unclean until evening.

[41]And every creeping thing that creeps on the earth *shall be* an abomination. It shall not be eaten. [42]Whatever crawls on its belly, whatever goes on *all* fours, or whatever has many feet among all creeping things that creep on the earth—these you shall not eat, for they *are* an abomination. [43]You shall not make yourselves abominable with any creeping thing that creeps; nor shall you make yourselves unclean with them, lest you be defiled by them. [44]For I *am* the LORD your God. You shall therefore consecrate yourselves, and you shall be holy; for I *am* holy. Neither shall you defile yourselves with any creeping thing that creeps on the earth. [45]For I *am* the LORD who brings you up out of the land of Egypt, to be your God. You shall therefore be holy, for I *am* holy.

PREPARED

11:25 To worship, people need to be prepared. Certain things could ceremonially defile a person, thus disqualifying him from worship. This chapter describes the things that made people "unclean" until they were "cleansed" or straightened out. Similarly, we cannot live any way we want during the week then rush into God's presence on Sunday. Our relationship with him must be one of constant repentance and cleansing so that we are prepared to worship him and his holiness.

◣◣ HOLY DESIGN

11:44-45 There is more to this chapter than eating right. These verses provide a key to understanding all the laws and regulations in Leviticus. God wanted his people to be *holy* (set apart, different, unique), just as he is holy. He knew they had only two options: to be separate and holy, or to compromise with their heathen neighbors and become corrupt. That is why he called them out of idolatrous Egypt and set them apart as a unique nation, dedicated to worshiping him alone and leading moral lives. That is also why he designed laws and restrictions to help them remain separate—both socially and spiritually—from the wicked heathen nations they would encounter in Canaan.

Christians also are called to be holy (1 Peter 1:15). Like the Israelites, we are to remain spiritually separate from the world's wickedness, even though, unlike them, we rub shoulders with unbelievers every day. It is no easy task to be holy in an unholy world, but God doesn't ask you to accomplish this on your own. Through the death of his Son, he will present you holy and blameless before him (Colossians 1:22).

⁴⁶'This *is* the law of the animals and the birds and every living creature that moves in the waters, and of every creature that creeps on the earth, ⁴⁷to distinguish between the unclean and the clean, and between the animal that may be eaten and the animal that may not be eaten.' "

CHAPTER 12 MOTHERS AND CHILDBIRTH. Then

the LORD spoke to Moses, saying, ²"Speak to the children of Israel, saying: 'If a woman has conceived, and borne a male child, then she shall be unclean seven days; as in the days of her customary impurity she shall be unclean. ³And on the eighth day the flesh of his foreskin shall be circumcised. ⁴She shall then continue in the blood of *her* purification thirty-three days. She shall not touch any hallowed thing, nor come into the sanctuary until the days of her purification are fulfilled.

⁵'But if she bears a female child, then she shall be unclean two weeks, as in her customary impurity, and she shall continue in the blood of *her* purification sixty-six days.

⁶'When the days of her purification are fulfilled, whether for a son or a daughter, she shall bring to the priest a lamb of the first year as a burnt offering, and a young pigeon or a turtledove as a sin offering, to the door of the tabernacle of meeting. ⁷Then he shall offer it before the LORD, and make atonement for her. And she shall be clean from the flow of her blood. This *is* the law for her who has borne a male or a female.

⁸'And if she is not able to bring a lamb, then she may bring two turtledoves or two young pigeons—one as a burnt offering and the other as a sin offering. So the priest shall make atonement for her, and she will be clean.' "

CHAPTER 13 RULES ABOUT LEPROSY. And the

LORD spoke to Moses and Aaron, saying: ²"When a man has on the skin of his body a swelling, a scab, or a bright spot, and it becomes on the skin of his body *like* a leprous sore, then he shall be brought to Aaron the priest or to one of his sons the priests. ³The priest shall examine the sore on the skin of the body; and if the hair on the sore has turned white, and the sore appears *to be* deeper than the skin of his body, it *is* a leprous sore. Then the priest

shall examine him, and pronounce him unclean. ⁴But if the bright spot *is* white on the skin of his body, and does not appear *to be* deeper than the skin, and its hair has not turned white, then the priest shall isolate *the one who ha* the sore seven days. ⁵And the priest shall examine him on the seventh day; and indeed *if* the sore appears to be as it was, *and* the sore has not spread on the skin, then the priest shall isolate him another seven days. ⁶Then the priest shall examine him again on the seventh day; and indeed *if* the sore has faded, *and* the sore has not spread on the skin, then the priest shall pronounce him clean; if *is only* a scab, and he shall wash his clothes and be clean. ⁷But if the scab should at all spread over the skin, after he has been seen by the priest for his cleansing, he shall be seen by the priest again. ⁸And *if* the priest sees that the scab has indeed spread on the skin, then the priest shall pronounce him unclean. It *is* leprosy.

⁹"When the leprous sore is on a person, then he shall be brought to the priest. ¹⁰And the priest shall examine *him;* and indeed *if* the swelling on the skin *is* white, and it has turned the hair white, and *there is* a spot of raw flesh in the swelling, ¹¹it *is* an old leprosy on the skin of his body. The priest shall pronounce him unclean, and shall not isolate him, for he *is* unclean.

¹²"And if leprosy breaks out all over the skin, and the leprosy covers all the skin of *the one who has* the sore from his head to his foot, wherever the priest looks, ¹³then the priest shall consider; and indeed *if* the leprosy has covered all his body, he shall pronounce *him* clean *who has* the sore. It has all turned white. He *is* clean. ¹⁴But when raw flesh appears on him, he shall be unclean. ¹⁵And the priest shall examine the raw flesh and pronounce him to be unclean; *for* the raw flesh *is* unclean. It *is* leprosy. ¹⁶Or if the raw flesh changes and turns white again, he shall come to the priest. ¹⁷And the priest shall examine him; and indeed *if* the sore has turned white, then the priest shall pronounce *him* clean *who has* the sore. He *is* clean.

◣◣ RIGHT RITES

12:1-4 *Unclean* did not mean "sinful," implying that sex or chi dirty. Instead, it meant "not appropriate to make sacrifice." In Ca prostitution and fertility rites were part of worship. By contrast, in anything related to sex was avoided when worshiping God. Again doesn't mean that sex is unclean. It just means that there are ap (and inappropriate) times and places for everything.

¹⁸"If the body develops a boil in the skin, and it i healed, ¹⁹and in the place of the boil there comes a whit swelling or a bright spot, reddish-white, then it shall be shown to the priest; ²⁰and *if,* when the priest sees it, i indeed *appears* deeper than the skin, and its hair ha turned white, the priest shall pronounce him unclean It *is* a leprous sore which has broken out of the boil ²¹But if the priest examines it, and indeed *there are* n white hairs in it, and it *is* not deeper than the skin, bu has faded, then the priest shall isolate him seven days ²²and if it should at all spread over the skin, then th priest shall pronounce him unclean. It *is* a leprous sore ²³But if the bright spot stays in one place, *and* has no

spread, it *is* the scar of the boil; and the priest shall pronounce him clean.

²⁴"Or if the body receives a burn on its skin by fire, and the raw *flesh* of the burn becomes a bright spot, reddish-white or white, ²⁵then the priest shall examine it; and indeed *if* the hair of the bright spot has turned white, and it appears deeper than the skin, it *is* leprosy broken out in the burn. Therefore the priest shall pronounce him unclean. It *is* a leprous sore. ²⁶But if the priest examines it, and indeed *there are* no white hairs in the bright spot, and it *is* not deeper than the skin, but has faded, then the priest shall isolate him seven days. ²⁷And the priest shall examine him on the seventh day. If it has at all spread over the skin, then the priest shall pronounce him unclean. It *is* a leprous sore. ²⁸But if the bright spot stays in one place, *and* has not spread on the skin, but has faded, it *is* a swelling from the burn. The priest shall pronounce him clean, for it *is* the scar from the burn.

²⁹"If a man or a woman has a sore on the head or the beard, ³⁰then the priest shall examine the sore; and indeed if it appears deeper than the skin, *and there is* in it thin yellow hair, then the priest shall pronounce him unclean. It *is* a scaly leprosy of the head or beard. ³¹But if the priest examines the scaly sore, and indeed it does not appear deeper than the skin, and *there is* no black hair in it, then the priest shall isolate *the one who has* the scale seven days. ³²And on the seventh day the priest shall examine the sore; and indeed *if* the scale has not spread, and there is no yellow hair in it, and the scale does not appear deeper than the skin, ³³he shall shave himself, but the scale he shall not shave. And the priest shall isolate *the one who has* the scale another seven days. ³⁴On the seventh day the priest shall examine the scale; and indeed *if* the scale has not spread over the skin, and does not appear deeper than the skin, then the priest shall pronounce him clean. He shall wash his clothes and be clean. ³⁵But if the scale should at all spread over the skin after his cleansing, ³⁶then the priest shall examine him; and indeed *if* the scale has spread over the skin, the priest need not seek for yellow hair. He *is* unclean. ³⁷But if the scale appears to be at a standstill, and there is black hair grown up in it, the scale has healed. He *is* clean, and the priest shall pronounce him clean.

³⁸"If a man or a woman has bright spots on the skin of the body, *specifically* white bright spots, ³⁹then the priest shall look; and indeed *if* the bright spots on the skin of the body *are* dull white, it *is* a white spot *that* grows on the skin. He *is* clean.

⁴⁰"As for the man whose hair has fallen from his head, he *is* bald, *but* he *is* clean. ⁴¹He whose hair has fallen from his forehead, he *is* bald on the forehead, *but* he *is* clean. ⁴²And if there is on the bald head or bald forehead a reddish-white sore, it *is* leprosy breaking out on his bald head or his bald forehead. ⁴³Then the priest shall examine it; and indeed *if* the swelling of the sore *is* reddish-white on his bald head or on his bald forehead, as the appearance of leprosy on the skin of the body, ⁴⁴he is a leprous man. He *is* unclean. The priest shall surely pronounce him unclean; his sore *is* on his head.

⁴⁵"Now the leper on whom the sore *is*, his clothes shall be torn and his head bare; and he shall cover his mus-tache, and cry, 'Unclean! Unclean!' ⁴⁶He shall be unclean. All the days he has the sore he shall be unclean. He *is* unclean, and he shall dwell alone; his dwelling *shall be* outside the camp.

⁴⁷"Also, if a garment has a leprous plague in it, *whether it is* a woolen garment or a linen garment, ⁴⁸whether *it is* in the warp or woof of linen or wool, whether in leather or in anything made of leather, ⁴⁹and if the plague is greenish or reddish in the garment or in the leather, whether in the warp or in the woof, or in anything made of leather, it *is* a leprous plague and shall be shown to the priest. ⁵⁰The priest shall examine the plague and isolate *that which has* the plague seven days. ⁵¹And he shall examine the plague on the seventh day. If the plague has spread in the garment, either in the warp or in the woof, in the leather *or* in anything made of leather, the plague *is* an active leprosy. It *is* unclean. ⁵²He shall therefore burn that garment in which is the plague, whether warp or woof, in wool or in linen, or anything of leather, for it *is* an active leprosy; *the garment* shall be burned in the fire.

⁵³"But if the priest examines *it*, and indeed the plague has not spread in the garment, either in the warp or in the woof, or in anything made of leather, ⁵⁴then the priest shall command that they wash *the thing* in which *is* the plague; and he shall isolate it another seven days. ⁵⁵Then the priest shall examine the plague after it has been washed; and indeed *if* the plague has not changed its color, though the plague has not spread, it *is* unclean, and you shall burn it in the fire; it continues eating away, *whether* the damage *is* outside or inside. ⁵⁶If the priest examines *it*, and indeed the plague has faded after washing it, then he shall tear it out of the garment, whether out of the warp or out of the woof, or out of the leather. ⁵⁷But if it appears again in the garment, either in the warp or in the woof, or in anything made of leather, it *is* a spreading *plague;* you shall burn with fire that in which is the plague. ⁵⁸And if you wash the garment, either warp or woof, or whatever is made of leather, if the plague has disappeared from it, then it shall be washed a second time, and shall be clean.

⁵⁹"This *is* the law of the leprous plague in a garment of wool or linen, either in the warp or woof, or in anything made of leather, to pronounce it clean or to pronounce it unclean."

CHAPTER **14** Then the LORD spoke to Moses, saying, ²"This shall be the law of the leper for the day of his cleansing: He shall be brought to the priest. ³And the priest shall go out of the camp, and the priest shall examine *him;* and indeed, *if* the leprosy is healed in the leper, ⁴then the priest shall command to take for him who is to be cleansed two living *and* clean birds, cedar wood, scarlet, and hyssop. ⁵And the priest shall command that one of the birds be killed in an earthen vessel over running water. ⁶As for the living bird, he shall take it, the cedar wood and the scarlet and the hyssop, and dip them and the living bird in the blood of the bird *that was* killed over the running water. ⁷And he shall sprinkle it seven times on him who is to be cleansed from the leprosy, and shall pronounce him clean, and shall let the living bird loose in the open field. [8]He who is to be cleansed shall wash his clothes, shave off all his hair, and wash himself in water, that he may be clean. After that he shall come into the camp, and shall stay outside his tent seven days. [9]But on the seventh day he shall shave all the hair off his head and his beard and his eyebrows—all his hair he shall shave off. He shall wash his clothes and wash his body in water, and he shall be clean.

[10]"And on the eighth day he shall take two male lambs without blemish, one ewe lamb of the first year without blemish, three-tenths *of an ephah* of fine flour mixed with oil as a grain offering, and one log of oil. [11]Then the priest who makes *him* clean shall present the man who is to be made clean, and those things, before the LORD, *at* the door of the tabernacle of meeting. [12]And the priest shall take one male lamb and offer it as a trespass offering, and the log of oil, and wave them *as* a wave offering before the LORD. [13]Then he shall kill the lamb in the place where he kills the sin offering and the burnt offering, in a holy place; for as the sin offering *is* the priest's, so *is* the trespass offering. It *is* most holy. [14]The priest shall take *some* of the blood of the trespass offering, and the priest shall put *it* on the tip of the right ear of him who is to be cleansed, on the thumb of his right hand, and on the big toe of his right foot. [15]And the priest shall take *some* of the log of oil, and pour *it* into the palm of his own left hand. [16]Then the priest shall dip his right finger in the oil that *is* in his left hand, and shall sprinkle some of the oil with his finger seven times before the LORD. [17]And of the rest of the oil in his hand, the priest shall put *some* on the tip of the right ear of him who is to be cleansed, on the thumb of his right hand, and on the big toe of his right foot, on the blood of the trespass offering. [18]The rest of the oil that *is* in the priest's hand he shall put on the head of him who is to be cleansed. So the priest shall make atonement for him before the LORD.

[19]"Then the priest shall offer the sin offering, and make atonement for him who is to be cleansed from his uncleanness. Afterward he shall kill the burnt offering. [20]And the priest shall offer the burnt offering and the grain offering on the altar. So the priest shall make atonement for him, and he shall be clean.

[21]"But if he *is* poor and cannot afford it, then he shall take one male lamb *as* a trespass offering to be waved, to make atonement for him, one-tenth *of an ephah* of fine flour mixed with oil as a grain offering, a log of oil, [22]and two turtledoves or two young pigeons, such as he is able to afford: one shall be a sin offering and the other a burnt offering. [23]He shall bring them to the priest on the eighth day for his cleansing, to the door of the tabernacle of meeting, before the LORD. [24]And the priest shall take the lamb of the trespass offering and the log of oil, and the priest shall wave them *as* a wave offering before the LORD. [25]Then he shall kill the lamb of the trespass offering, and the priest shall take *some* of the blood of the trespass offering and put *it* on the tip of the right ear of him who is to be cleansed, on the thumb of his right hand, and on the big toe of his right foot. [26]And the priest shall pour some of the oil into the palm of his own left hand. [27]Then the priest shall sprinkle with his right finger *some* of the oil that *is* in his left hand seven times before

the LORD. [28]And the priest shall put *some* of the oil that *is* in his hand on the tip of the right ear of him who is to be cleansed, on the thumb of the right hand, and on the big toe of his right foot, on the place of the blood of the trespass offering. [29]The rest of the oil that *is* in the priest's hand he shall put on the head of him who is to be cleansed, to make atonement for him before the LORD. [30]And he shall offer one of the turtledoves or young pigeons, such as he can afford— [31]such as he is able to afford, the one *as* a sin offering and the other *as* a burnt offering, with the grain offering. So the priest shall make atonement for him who is to be cleansed before the LORD. [32]This *is* the law *for one* who had a leprous sore, who cannot afford the usual cleansing."

FUNGUS

14:33-53 Could leprosy really infect one's clothing or house? The Hebrew word for leprosy included a variety of skin diseases as well as other molds and fungi. The "leprosy" found on clothing or house wall was more like a mold, fungus, or bacteria. Like mildew, this fungus c spread rapidly and promote disease. It was therefore important to ch its spread as soon as possible. Is there anything in your life—an act or relationship—that has a similar, destructive effect on you or your faith?

[33]And the LORD spoke to Moses and Aaron, saying: [34]"When you have come into the land of Canaan, which I give you as a possession, and I put the leprous plague in a house in the land of your possession, [35]and he who owns the house comes and tells the priest, saying, 'It seems to me that *there is* some plague in the house,' [36]then the priest shall command that they empty the house, before the priest goes *into it* to examine the plague, that all that *is* in the house may not be made unclean; and afterward the priest shall go in to examine the house. [37]And he shall examine the plague; and indeed *if* the plague *is* on the walls of the house with ingrained streaks, greenish or reddish, which appear to be deep in the wall, [38]then the priest shall go out of the house, to the door of the house, and shut up the house seven days. [39]And the priest shall come again on the seventh day and look; and indeed *if* the plague has spread on the walls of the house, [40]then the priest shall command that they take away the stones in which *is* the plague, and they shall cast them into an unclean place outside the city. [41]And he shall cause the house to be scraped inside, all around, and the dust that they scrape off they shall pour out in an unclean place outside the city. [42]Then they shall take other stones and put *them* in the place of *those* stones, and he shall take other mortar and plaster the house.

[43]"Now if the plague comes back and breaks out in the house, after he has taken away the stones, after he has scraped the house, and after it is plastered, [44]then the priest shall come and look; and indeed *if* the plague has spread in the house, it *is* an active leprosy in the house. It is unclean. [45]And he shall break down the house, its stones, its timber, and all the plaster of the house, and he shall carry *them* outside the city to an unclean place. [46]Moreover he who goes into the house at all while it is shut up shall be unclean until evening. [47]And he who lies

down in the house shall wash his clothes, and he who eats in the house shall wash his clothes.

48"But if the priest comes in and examines *it,* and indeed the plague has not spread in the house after the house was plastered, then the priest shall pronounce the house clean, because the plague is healed. 49And he shall take, to cleanse the house, two birds, cedar wood, scarlet, and hyssop. 50Then he shall kill one of the birds in an earthen vessel over running water; 51and he shall take the cedar wood, the hyssop, the scarlet, and the living bird, and dip them in the blood of the slain bird and in the running water, and sprinkle the house seven times. 52And he shall cleanse the house with the blood of the bird and the running water and the living bird, with the cedar wood, the hyssop, and the scarlet. 53Then he shall let the living bird loose outside the city in the open field, and make atonement for the house, and it shall be clean.

54"This *is* the law for any leprous sore and scale, 55for the leprosy of a garment and of a house, 56for a swelling and a scab and a bright spot, 57to teach when *it is* unclean and when *it is* clean. This *is* the law of leprosy."

CHAPTER 15 RULES OF HEALTH FOR MEN AND WOMEN.

And the LORD spoke to Moses and Aaron, saying, 2"Speak to the children of Israel, and say to them: When any man has a discharge from his body, his discharge *is* unclean. 3And this shall be his uncleanness in regard to his discharge—whether his body runs with his discharge, or his body is stopped up by his discharge, it *is* his uncleanness. 4Every bed is unclean on which he who has the discharge lies, and everything on which he sits shall be unclean. 5And whoever touches his bed shall wash his clothes and bathe in water, and be unclean until evening. 6He who sits on anything on which he who has the discharge sat shall wash his clothes and bathe in water, and be unclean until evening. 7And he who touches the body of him who has the discharge shall wash his clothes and bathe in water, and be unclean until evening. 8If he who has the discharge spits on him who is clean, then he shall wash his clothes and bathe in water, and be unclean until evening. 9Any saddle on which he who has the discharge rides shall be unclean. 10Whoever touches anything that was under him shall be unclean until evening. He who carries *any of* those things shall wash his clothes and bathe in water, and be unclean until evening. 11And whomever the one who has the discharge touches, and has not rinsed his hands in water, he shall wash his clothes and bathe in water, and be unclean until evening. 12The vessel of earth that he who has the discharge touches shall be broken, and every vessel of wood shall be rinsed in water.

13"And when he who has a discharge is cleansed of his discharge, then he shall count for himself seven days for his cleansing, wash his clothes, and bathe his body in running water; then he shall be clean. 14On the eighth day he shall take for himself two turtledoves or two young pigeons, and come before the LORD, to the door of the tabernacle of meeting, and give them to the priest. 15Then the priest shall offer them, the one *as* a sin offering and the other *as* a burnt offering. So the priest shall make atonement for him before the LORD because of his discharge.

16"If any man has an emission of semen, then he shall wash all his body in water, and be unclean until evening. 17And any garment and any leather on which there is semen, it shall be washed with water, and be unclean until evening. 18Also, when a woman lies with a man, and *there is* an emission of semen, they shall bathe in water, and be unclean until evening.

19"If a woman has a discharge, *and* the discharge from her body is blood, she shall be set apart seven days; and whoever touches her shall be unclean until evening. 20Everything that she lies on during her impurity shall be unclean; also everything that she sits on shall be unclean. 21Whoever touches her bed shall wash his clothes and bathe in water, and be unclean until evening. 22And whoever touches anything that she sat on shall wash his clothes and bathe in water, and be unclean until evening. 23If *anything* is on *her* bed or on anything on which she sits, when he touches it, he shall be unclean until evening. 24And if any man lies with her at all, so that her impurity is on him, he shall be unclean seven days; and every bed on which he lies shall be unclean.

25"If a woman has a discharge of blood for many days, other than at the time of her *customary* impurity, or if it runs beyond her *usual time of* impurity, all the days of her unclean discharge shall be as the days of her *customary* impurity. She *shall be* unclean. 26Every bed on which she lies all the days of her discharge shall be to her as the bed of her impurity; and whatever she sits on shall be unclean, as the uncleanness of her impurity. 27Whoever touches those things shall be unclean; he shall wash his clothes and bathe in water, and be unclean until evening.

28"But if she is cleansed of her discharge, then she shall count for herself seven days, and after that she shall be clean. 29And on the eighth day she shall take for herself two turtledoves or two young pigeons, and bring them to the priest, to the door of the tabernacle of meeting. 30Then the priest shall offer the one *as* a sin offering and the other *as* a burnt offering, and the priest shall make atonement for her before the LORD for the discharge of her uncleanness.

31"Thus you shall separate the children of Israel from their uncleanness, lest they die in their uncleanness when they defile My tabernacle that *is* among them. 32This *is* the law for one who has a discharge, and *for him* who emits semen and is unclean thereby, 33and for her who is indisposed because of her *customary* impurity, and for one who has a discharge, either man or woman, and for him who lies with her who is unclean.' "

━━━━━━━━━━SEX

15:18 This verse is not implying that sex is dirty or disgusting. God created sex, both for the enjoyment of married couples and for continuing the race and the covenant. Everything must be seen and done with a view toward God's love and control. Sex is not separate from spirituality and God's care. God is concerned about our sexual habits. We tend to separate our physical and spiritual lives, but there is an inseparable intertwining. God must be Lord over our whole self—including our private life.

Old System of Sacrifice

Was temporary
(Hebrews 7:21)

Aaron first high priest
(Leviticus 16:32)

From tribe of Levi
(Hebrews 7:16)

Ministered on earth
(Hebrews 8:4)

Used blood of animals
(Leviticus 16:15)

Required many sacrifices
(Hebrews 10:1-3)

Needed perfect animals
(Leviticus 22:19)

Required careful approach
to tabernacle (Leviticus 16:2)

Looked forward to new system
(Hebrews 10:1)

New System of Sacrifice

Is permanent
(Hebrews 7:21)

Jesus only high priest
(Leviticus 4:14)

From tribe of Judah
(Hebrews 7:14)

Ministers in heaven
(Hebrews 8:12)

Uses blood of Christ
(Hebrews 10:4-12)

Requires one sacrifice
(Hebrews 9:28)

Needs perfect life
(Hebrews 5:9)

Encourages bold approach
to throne (Hebrews 4:16)

Cancels old system
(Hebrews 10:9)

CHAPTER **16** **THE DAY OF ATONEMENT.** Now the LORD spoke to Moses after the death of the two sons of Aaron, when they offered *profane fire* before the LORD, and died; ²and the LORD said to Moses: "Tell Aaron your brother not to come at *just* any time into the Holy *Place* inside the veil, before the mercy seat which *is* on the ark, lest he die; for I will appear in the cloud above the mercy seat.

³"Thus Aaron shall come into the Holy *Place:* with *the blood of* a young bull as a sin offering, and *of* a ram as a burnt offering. ⁴He shall put the holy linen tunic and the linen trousers on his body; he shall be girded with a linen sash, and with the linen turban he shall be attired. These *are* holy garments. Therefore he shall wash his body in water, and put them on. ⁵And he shall take from the congregation of the children of Israel two kids of the goats as a sin offering, and one ram as a burnt offering.

⁶"Aaron shall offer the bull as a sin offering, which *is* for himself, and make atonement for himself and for his house. ⁷He shall take the two goats and present them before the LORD *at* the door of the tabernacle of meeting. ⁸Then Aaron shall cast lots for the two goats: one lot for the LORD and the other lot for the scapegoat. ⁹And Aaron shall bring the goat on which the LORD's lot fell, and offer it *as* a sin offering. ¹⁰But the goat on which the lot fell to be the scapegoat shall be presented alive before the LORD, to make atonement upon it, *and* to let it go as the scapegoat into the wilderness.

¹¹"And Aaron shall bring the bull of the sin offering, which is for himself, and make atonement for himself and for his house, and shall kill the bull as the sin offering which *is* for himself. ¹²Then he shall take a censer full of burning coals of fire from the altar before the LORD, with his hands full of sweet incense beaten fine, and bring *it* inside the veil. ¹³And he shall put the incense on the fire before the LORD, that the cloud of incense may cover the mercy seat that *is* on the Testimony, lest he die. ¹⁴He shall take some of the blood of the bull and sprinkle *it* with his finger on the mercy seat on the east *side;* and before the mercy seat he shall sprinkle some of the blood with his finger seven times.

¹⁵"Then he shall kill the goat of the sin offering, which *is* for the people, bring its blood inside the veil, do with that blood as he did with the blood of the bull, and sprinkle it on the mercy seat and before the mercy seat. ¹⁶So he shall make atonement for the Holy *Place*, because of the uncleanness of the children of Israel, and because of their transgressions, for all their sins; and so he shall do for the tabernacle of meeting which remains among them in the midst of their uncleanness. ¹⁷There shall be no man in the tabernacle of meeting when he goes in to make atonement in the Holy *Place*, until he comes out, that he may make atonement for himself, for his household, and for all the assembly of Israel. ¹⁸And he shall go out to the altar that *is* before the LORD, and make atone-

GET READY

16:1-25 Aaron had to spend hours preparing himself to meet we can approach God anytime (Hebrews 4:16). What a privilege offered easier access to God than the high priests of Old Testame Still, we must never forget that God is holy or let this privilege co approach God carelessly. The way to God has been opened to us Christ. But easy access to God does not eliminate our need to pre hearts as we draw near in prayer.

ment for it, and shall take some of the blood of the bull and some of the blood of the goat, and put it on the horns of the altar all around. ¹⁹Then he shall sprinkle some of the blood on it with his finger seven times, cleanse it, and consecrate it from the uncleanness of the children of Israel.

²⁰"And when he has made an end of atoning for the Holy *Place*, the tabernacle of meeting, and the altar, he shall bring the live goat. ²¹Aaron shall lay both his hands on the head of the live goat, confess over it all the iniquities of the children of Israel, and all their transgressions, concerning all their sins, putting them on the head of the goat, and shall send *it* away into the wilderness by the hand of a suitable man. ²²The goat shall bear on itself all their iniquities to an uninhabited land; and he shall release the goat in the wilderness.

²³"Then Aaron shall come into the tabernacle of meeting, shall take off the linen garments which he put on when he went into the Holy *Place*, and shall leave them there. ²⁴And he shall wash his body with water in a holy place, put on his garments, come out and offer his burnt offering and the burnt offering of the people, and make atonement for himself and for the people. ²⁵The fat of the sin offering he shall burn on the altar. ²⁶And he who released the goat as the scapegoat shall wash his clothes and bathe his body in water, and afterward he may come into the camp. ²⁷The bull *for* the sin offering and the goat *for* the sin offering, whose blood was brought in to make atonement in the Holy *Place*, shall be carried outside the camp. And they shall burn in the fire their skins, their flesh, and their offal. ²⁸Then he who burns them shall wash his clothes and bathe his body in water, and afterward he may come into the camp.

²⁹"*This* shall be a statute forever for you: In the seventh month, on the tenth *day* of the month, you shall afflict your souls, and do no work at all, *whether* a native of your own country or a stranger who dwells among you. ³⁰For on that day *the priest* shall make atonement for you, to cleanse you, *that* you may be clean from all your sins before the Lᴏʀᴅ. ³¹It *is* a sabbath of solemn rest for you, and you shall afflict your souls. *It is* a statute forever. ³²And the priest, who is anointed and consecrated to minister as priest in his father's place, shall make atonement, and put on the linen clothes, the holy garments; ³³then he shall make atonement for the Holy Sanctuary, and he shall make atonement for the tabernacle of meeting and for the altar, and he shall make atonement for the priests and for all the people of the assembly. ³⁴This shall be an everlasting statute for you, to make atonement for the children of Israel, for all their sins, once a year." And he did as the Lᴏʀᴅ commanded Moses.

CHAPTER **17** WARNING AGAINST SACRIFICING WRONGLY. And the Lᴏʀᴅ spoke to Moses, saying, ²"Speak to Aaron, to his sons, and to all the children of Israel, and say to them, 'This *is* the thing which the Lᴏʀᴅ has commanded, saying: ³"Whatever man of the house of Israel who kills an ox or lamb or goat in the camp, or who kills *it* outside the camp, ⁴and does not bring it to the door of the tabernacle of meeting to offer an offering to the Lᴏʀᴅ

before the tabernacle of the Lᴏʀᴅ, the guilt of bloodshed shall be imputed to that man. He has shed blood; and that man shall be cut off from among his people, ⁵to the end that the children of Israel may bring their sacrifices which they offer in the open field, that they may bring them to the Lᴏʀᴅ at the door of the tabernacle of meeting, to the priest, and offer them *as* peace offerings to the Lᴏʀᴅ. ⁶And the priest shall sprinkle the blood on the altar of the Lᴏʀᴅ *at* the door of the tabernacle of meeting, and burn the fat for a sweet aroma to the Lᴏʀᴅ. ⁷They shall no more offer their sacrifices to demons, after whom they have played the harlot. This shall be a statute forever for them throughout their generations." '

◤▬▬▬▬▬▬▬▬ **WHAT'S RIGHT?**
17:3-9 God had established specific times and places for sacrifices, and each occasion was filled with symbolism. If people sacrificed on their own, not only would it demonstrate a callous disregard for God, but it also would encourage people to add to or subtract from God's laws to fit their own life-style. It is interesting that whenever the Israelites slipped into idolatry, it was because "everyone did *what was* right in his own eyes" (Judges 17:6).

⁸"Also you shall say to them: 'Whatever man of the house of Israel, or of the strangers who dwell among you, who offers a burnt offering or sacrifice, ⁹and does not bring it to the door of the tabernacle of meeting, to offer it to the Lᴏʀᴅ, that man shall be cut off from among his people.

¹⁰"And whatever man of the house of Israel, or of the strangers who dwell among you, who eats any blood, I will set My face against that person who eats blood, and will cut him off from among his people. ¹¹For the life of the flesh *is* in the blood, and I have given it to you upon the altar to make atonement for your souls; for it *is* the blood *that* makes atonement for the soul.' ¹²Therefore I said to the children of Israel, 'No one among you shall eat blood, nor shall any stranger who dwells among you eat blood.'

¹³"Whatever man of the children of Israel, or of the strangers who dwell among you, who hunts and catches any animal or bird that may be eaten, he shall pour out its blood and cover it with dust; ¹⁴for *it is* the life of all flesh. Its blood sustains its life. Therefore I said to the children of Israel, 'You shall not eat the blood of any flesh, for the life of all flesh is its blood. Whoever eats it shall be cut off.'

¹⁵"And every person who eats what died *naturally* or what was torn *by beasts, whether he is* a native of your own country or a stranger, he shall both wash his clothes and bathe in water, and be unclean until evening. Then he shall be clean. ¹⁶But if he does not wash *them* or bathe his body, then he shall bear his guilt."

CHAPTER **18** WRONG SEXUAL RELATIONSHIPS. Then the Lᴏʀᴅ spoke to Moses, saying, ²"Speak to the children of Israel, and say to them: 'I am the Lᴏʀᴅ your God. ³According to the doings of the land of Egypt, where you dwelt, you shall not do; and according to the doings of the land of Canaan, where I am bringing you, you shall not do; nor shall you walk in their ordinances. ⁴You shall observe My judgments and keep My ordinances, to walk

THE LAW

It's universal: You see a sign that says Wet Paint; you want to touch it. Walk by a sign in a pet shop window that says, Do Not Tap on Glass! and what do you do? Tap on the glass. It's a law of human nature: rules are made to be broken. Something inside makes us wonder, "What happens if I cross the line?"

God's people are not immune to this temptation. The Old Testament seems like a series of stories about God giving Israel rules—obedience meant blessing; disobedience meant punishment. They always seemed to disobey. They would just get over one "whipping" from God and they'd be finding new ways to be disobedient. So what is the role of the law for Christians today? Are we, like the people of Moses' time, obligated to obey the law or are we free of it? There are several different views on this. First, the law can be divided into three branches: ceremonial, judicial, and moral. Ceremonial laws related to sacrifices, cleansing rituals, festivals, etc. Judicial laws dealt with the government—what kind of king Israel needed, criminal codes, etc. The moral law concerned how people interacted with each other and with God. (The Ten Commandments are the best-known section of the moral law.) There is some sharp disagreement as to how we are to view each branch; the judicial laws applied to the nation of Israel alone (although these principles are the foundation for laws in the United States and other Western nations); and the moral laws are true for all people, everywhere, at all times. Now, what does the law do? It acts as:

- A mirror: If you had a three-year-old draw a line on a chalkboard, you'd probably get a crooked line. If you drew a line next to it and compared them, you might think, My line really is straight, especially compared to little Sally's. But if someone else drew a line next to yours using a straightedge, you'd see all the imperfections in your line. It wasn't straight at all; it only looked good next to a crooked one. That's what the law does for us. It's tempting to look at bad people (by human standards) and think, I'm a pretty good dude/dudette. But when compared to God's perfect standard—the law—we see our sins. We see what we look like from God's point of view; and frankly, it's not a pretty sight.

- An instructor: Though nobody likes instructors, we all need them. Paul wrote, "The law was our tutor to bring us to Christ, that we might be justified by faith" (Galatians 3:24). The law taught the Israelites how to live before a holy God who set high standards and expected his people to live up to them: "You shall be holy, for I the LORD your God am holy" (Leviticus 19:2). Those other nations might worship idols; practice child sacrifice; wink at sexual immorality, divorce, dishonesty, etc. But not Israel. They were held to a higher standard. Often a law served simply to make a distinction between Israel and other nations. With God's law, God's law also set Israel apart from pagan nations. as instructor, there was no "grading on the curve."

- An encourager: The law gave Abraham's descendants guidelines for living in a manner worthy of God. Think of the law as training wheels. When you first try to ride a bike, you wobble and then fall over. With God's law, you have something to keep you straight—like training wheels. They help you stay upright until you "get the hang of it." The law does that, too—it shows you how to walk uprightly before a holy God. When you read about God's laws, don't just see pointless rules and regulations designed to make our lives rough. The law shows us who we are—sinners in need of a Savior. It shows us how to live before a holy, righteous and how to please that awesome God—by obeying his commandments. Most important, the law points people of the Old Testament toward a coming Savior, who would fulfill the law and set his people free. We don't need a law to guide us until he comes—he has come already and written his law on our hearts.

in them: I *am* the LORD your God. ⁵You shall therefore keep My statutes and My judgments, which if a man does, he shall live by them: I *am* the LORD.

⁶'None of you shall approach anyone who is near of kin to him, to uncover his nakedness: I *am* the LORD. ⁷The nakedness of your father or the nakedness of your mother you shall not uncover. She *is* your mother; you shall not uncover her nakedness. ⁸The nakedness of your father's wife you shall not uncover; it *is* your father's nakedness. ⁹The nakedness of your sister, the daughter of your father, or the daughter of your mother, *whether* born at home or elsewhere, their nakedness you shall not uncover. ¹⁰The nakedness of your son's daughter or your daughter's daughter, their nakedness you shall not uncover; for theirs *is* your own nakedness. ¹¹The nakedness of your father's wife's daughter, begotten by your father—she *is* your sister—you shall not uncover her nakedness. ¹²You shall not uncover the nakedness of your father's sister; she *is* near of kin to your father. ¹³You shall not uncover the nakedness of your mother's sister, for she *is* near of kin to your mother. ¹⁴You shall not uncover the nakedness of your father's brother. You shall not approach his wife; she *is* your aunt. ¹⁵You shall not uncover the nakedness of your daughter-in-law—she *is* your son's wife—you shall not uncover her nakedness. ¹⁶You shall not uncover the nakedness of your brother's wife; it *is* your brother's nakedness. ¹⁷You shall not uncover the nakedness of a woman and her daughter, nor shall you take her son's daughter or her daughter's daughter, to uncover her nakedness. They *are* near of kin to her. It *is* wickedness. ¹⁸Nor shall you take a woman as a rival to her sister, to uncover her nakedness while the other is alive.

¹⁹'Also you shall not approach a woman to uncover her nakedness as long as she is in her *customary* impurity. ²⁰Moreover you shall not lie carnally with your neighbor's wife, to defile yourself with her. ²¹And you shall not let any of your descendants pass through *the fire* to Molech, nor shall you profane the name of your God: I *am* the LORD. ²²You shall not lie with a male as with a woman. It *is* an abomination. ²³Nor shall you mate with any animal, to defile yourself with it. Nor shall any woman stand before an animal to mate with it. It *is* perversion.

²⁴'Do not defile yourselves with any of these things; for by all these the nations are defiled, which I am casting out before you. ²⁵For the land is defiled; therefore I visit the punishment of its iniquity upon it, and the land vomits out its inhabitants. ²⁶You shall therefore keep My statutes and My judgments, and shall not commit *any* of these abominations, *either* any of your own nation or any stranger who dwells among you ²⁷(for all these abominations the men of the land have done, who *were* before you, and thus the land is defiled), ²⁸lest the land vomit you out also when you defile it, as it vomited out the nations that *were* before you. ²⁹For whoever commits any of these abominations, the persons who commit *them* shall be cut off from among their people.

³⁰'Therefore you shall keep My ordinance, so that *you* do not commit *any* of these abominable customs which were committed before you, and that you do not defile yourselves by them: I *am* the LORD your God.' "

CHAPTER **19** **COMMANDS FOR DAILY LIFE.** And the LORD spoke to Moses, saying, ²"Speak to all the congregation of the children of Israel, and say to them: 'You shall be holy, for I the LORD your God *am* holy.

³'Every one of you shall revere his mother and his father, and keep My Sabbaths: I *am* the LORD your God.

⁴'Do not turn to idols, nor make for yourselves molded gods: I *am* the LORD your God.

⟩⟩⟩CULTURE

18:3 The Israelites moved from one idol-infested country to another. As God helped them form a new culture, he warned them to leave all aspects of their heathen background behind. He also warned them how easy it would be to slip into the heathen culture of Canaan, where they were going. Canaan's society and religions appealed to carnal desires, especially sexual immorality and drunkenness. The Israelites were to keep themselves pure and set apart for God. God did not want his people absorbed in the surrounding culture and environment. Society may pressure us to conform to its way of life and thought, but yielding to that pressure will (1) create confusion as to which side we should be on, and (2) eliminate our effectiveness in serving God. Follow God, and don't let the culture around you mold your thoughts and actions.

⁵'And if you offer a sacrifice of a peace offering to the LORD, you shall offer it of your own free will. ⁶It shall be eaten the same day you offer *it*, and on the next day. And if any remains until the third day, it shall be burned in the fire. ⁷And if it is eaten at all on the third day, it *is* an abomination. It shall not be accepted. ⁸Therefore *everyone* who eats it shall bear his iniquity, because he has profaned the hallowed *offering* of the LORD; and that person shall be cut off from his people.

⁹'When you reap the harvest of your land, you shall not wholly reap the corners of your field, nor shall you gather the gleanings of your harvest. ¹⁰And you shall not glean your vineyard, nor shall you gather *every* grape of your vineyard; you shall leave them for the poor and the stranger: I *am* the LORD your God.

¹¹'You shall not steal, nor deal falsely, nor lie to one another.¹²And you shall not swear by My name falsely, nor shall you profane the name of your God: I *am* the LORD.

¹³'You shall not cheat your neighbor, nor rob *him*. The wages of him who is hired shall not remain with you all night until morning. ¹⁴You shall not curse the deaf, nor put a stumbling block before the blind, but shall fear your God: I *am* the LORD.

¹⁵'You shall do no injustice in judgment. You shall not be partial to the poor, nor honor the person of the mighty. In righteousness you shall judge your neighbor. ¹⁶You shall not go about *as* a talebearer among your people; nor shall you take a stand against the life of your neighbor: I *am* the LORD.

¹⁷'You shall not hate your brother in your heart. You

⟩⟩⟩DON'T

19:18 Don't, don't, don't. Some people think the Bible is nothing but a book of don'ts. But Jesus neatly summarized all these rules when he said to love God with all your heart, and your neighbor as yourself. He called these the greatest commandments (or rules) of all (Matthew 22:34-40). By carrying out Jesus' simple commands, we find ourselves following all of God's other laws as well.

shall surely rebuke your neighbor, and not bear sin because of him. [18]You shall not take vengeance, nor bear any grudge against the children of your people, but you shall love your neighbor as yourself: I *am* the LORD.

[19]'You shall keep My statutes. You shall not let your livestock breed with another kind. You shall not sow your field with mixed seed. Nor shall a garment of mixed linen and wool come upon you.

[20]'Whoever lies carnally with a woman who *is* betrothed to a man as a concubine, and who has not at all been redeemed nor given her freedom, for this there shall be scourging; *but* they shall not be put to death, because she was not free. [21]And he shall bring his trespass offering to the LORD, to the door of the tabernacle of

STEALING

Kelli and Sandra work together at Quackers, the newest fast-food restaurant in town. It's not such a bad job. The hours are good, the uniforms—surprise!—don't look like circus costumes, and the pay is more than minimum wage. Besides, the girls have great fun (and a lot of laughs) checking out the tons of cute guys from a rival high school who frequent the place on weekends.

Today, however, when the girls come to work, there is a terse note from the boss: "I want to talk to both of you. It's very important!"

Kelli's heart drops to her shoes, and Sandra's stomach does a cartwheel. What could it mean? A raise? A promotion? Not likely. In fact, the girls are expecting the worst. See, they've been giving away free food and Quackers T-shirts to certain male customers. And Sandra took a whole box of burgers from the freezer late last Friday night to use at her Saturday pool party.

"We're dead!" Kelli moans. "We've done everything but actually take money out of the cash register!"

"No—I even did that one night."

"Sandra! You didn't! How much did you take?"

"Ten bucks."

"Oh no! What are we gonna say?"

See how Kelli and Sandra could have avoided this whole horrible headache—Leviticus 19:11.

meeting, a ram as a trespass offering. [22]The priest shall make atonement for him with the ram of the trespass offering before the LORD for his sin which he has committed. And the sin which he has committed shall be forgiven him.

[23]'When you come into the land, and have planted all kinds of trees for food, then you shall count their fruit as uncircumcised. Three years it shall be as uncircumcised to you. *It* shall not be eaten. [24]But in the fourth year all its fruit shall be holy, a praise to the LORD. [25]And in the fifth year you may eat its fruit, that it may yield to you its increase: I *am* the LORD your God.

[26]'You shall not eat *anything* with the blood, nor shall you practice divination or soothsaying. [27]You shall not shave around the sides of your head, nor shall you disfigure the edges of your beard. [28]You shall not make any cuttings in your flesh for the dead, nor tattoo any marks on you: I *am* the LORD.

[29]'Do not prostitute your daughter, to cause her to be a harlot, lest the land fall into harlotry, and the land become full of wickedness.

[30]'You shall keep My Sabbaths and reverence My sanctuary: I *am* the LORD.

[31]'Give no regard to mediums and familiar spirits; do not seek after them, to be defiled by them: I *am* the LORD your God.

[32]'You shall rise before the gray headed and honor the presence of an old man, and fear your God: I *am* the LORD.

[33]'And if a stranger dwells with you in your land, you shall not mistreat him. [34]The stranger who dwells among you shall be to you as one born among you, and you shall love him as yourself; for you were strangers in the land of Egypt: I *am* the LORD your God.

[35]'You shall do no injustice in judgment, in measurement of length, weight, or volume. [36]You shall have honest scales, honest weights, an honest ephah, and an honest hin: I *am* the LORD your God, who brought you out of the land of Egypt.

[37]'Therefore you shall observe all My statutes and all My judgments, and perform them: I *am* the LORD.' "

CHAPTER 20 PUNISHMENTS FOR SIN. Then the LORD spoke to Moses, saying, [2]"Again, you shall say to the children of Israel: 'Whoever of the children of Israel, or of the strangers who dwell in Israel, who gives *any* of his descendants to Molech, he shall surely be put to death. The people of the land shall stone him with stones. [3]I will set My face against that man, and will cut him off from his people, because he has given *some* of his descendants to Molech, to defile My sanctuary and profane My holy name. [4]And if the people of the land should in any way hide their eyes from the man, when he gives *some* of his descendants to Molech, and they do not kill him, [5]then I will set My face against that man and against his family and I will cut him off from his people, and all who prostitute themselves with him to commit harlotry with Molech.

[6]'And the person who turns to mediums and familiar spirits, to prostitute himself with them, I will set My face against that person and cut him off from his people. [7]Consecrate yourselves therefore, and be holy, for I *am* the LORD your God. [8]And you shall keep My statutes, and perform them: I *am* the LORD who sanctifies you.

[9]'For everyone who curses his father or his mother shall surely be put to death. He has cursed his father or his mother. His blood *shall be* upon him.

[10]'The man who commits adultery with *another* man's

OCCULT

20:6 Everyone is interested in what the future holds, and we of to others for guidance. But God warned about looking to the occu advice. Mediums and spiritists were outlawed because God was n source of their information. At best, occult practitioners are fakes predictions cannot be trusted. At worst, they are in contact with ev and are thus extremely dangerous. We don't need to look to the for information about the future. God has given us the Bible so th may obtain all the information we need—and the Bible's teachin trustworthy.

I THE LORD *who sanctify* YOU

AM HOLY
HOLY
HOLY
HOLY

wife, *he* who commits adultery with his neighbor's wife, the adulterer and the adulteress, shall surely be put to death. [11]The man who lies with his father's wife has uncovered his father's nakedness; both of them shall surely be put to death. Their blood *shall be* upon them. [12]If a man lies with his daughter-in-law, both of them shall surely be put to death. They have committed perversion. Their blood *shall be* upon them. [13]If a man lies with a male as he lies with a woman, both of them have committed an abomination. They shall surely be put to death. Their blood *shall be* upon them. [14]If a man marries a woman and her mother, it *is* wickedness. They shall be burned with fire, both he and they, that there may be no wickedness among you. [15]If a man mates with an animal, he shall surely be put to death, and you shall kill the animal. [16]If a woman approaches any animal and mates with it, you shall kill the woman and the animal. They shall surely be put to death. Their blood *is* upon them.

[17]'If a man takes his sister, his father's daughter or his mother's daughter, and sees her nakedness and she sees his nakedness, it *is* a wicked thing. And they shall be cut off in the sight of their people. He has uncovered his sister's nakedness. He shall bear his guilt. [18]If a man lies with a woman during her sickness and uncovers her nakedness, he has exposed her flow, and she has uncovered the flow of her blood. Both of them shall be cut off from their people.

[19]'You shall not uncover the nakedness of your mother's sister nor of your father's sister, for that would uncover his near of kin. They shall bear their guilt. [20]If a man lies with his uncle's wife, he has uncovered his uncle's nakedness. They shall bear their sin; they shall die childless. [21]If a man takes his brother's wife, it *is* an unclean thing. He has uncovered his brother's nakedness. They shall be childless.

[22]'You shall therefore keep all My statutes and all My judgments, and perform them, that the land where I am bringing you to dwell may not vomit you out. [23]And you shall not walk in the statutes of the nation which I am casting out before you; for they commit all these things, and therefore I abhor them. [24]But I have said to you, "You

shall inherit their land, and I will give it to you to possess, a land flowing with milk and honey." I *am* the LORD your God, who has separated you from the peoples. [25]You shall therefore distinguish between clean animals and unclean, between unclean birds and clean, and you shall not make yourselves abominable by beast or by bird, or by any kind of living thing that creeps on the ground, which I have separated from you as unclean. [26]And you shall be holy to Me, for I the LORD *am* holy, and have separated you from the peoples, that you should be Mine.

[27]'A man or a woman who is a medium, or who has familiar spirits, shall surely be put to death; they shall stone them with stones. Their blood *shall be* upon them.' "

CHAPTER 21 RULES FOR THE PRIESTS.

And the LORD said to Moses, "Speak to the priests, the sons of Aaron, and say to them: 'None shall defile himself for the dead among his people, [2]except for his relatives who are nearest to him: his mother, his father, his son, his daughter, and his brother; [3]also his virgin sister who is near to him, who has had no husband, for her he may defile himself. [4]*Otherwise* he shall not defile himself, *being* a chief man among his people, to profane himself.

[5]'They shall not make any bald *place* on their heads, nor shall they shave the edges of their beards nor make any cuttings in their flesh. [6]They shall be holy to their God and not profane the name of their God, for they offer the offerings of the LORD made by fire, *and* the bread of their God; therefore they shall be holy. [7]They shall not take a wife *who is* a harlot or a defiled woman, nor shall they take a woman divorced from her husband; for *the priest* is holy to his God. [8]Therefore you shall consecrate him, for he offers the bread of your God. He shall be holy to you, for I the LORD, who sanctify you, *am* holy. [9]The daughter of any priest, if she profanes herself by playing the harlot, she profanes her father. She shall be burned with fire.

[10]'He who is the high priest among his brethren, on whose head the anointing oil was poured and who is consecrated to wear the garments, shall not uncover his head nor tear his clothes; [11]nor shall he go near any dead body, nor defile himself for his father or his mother; [12]nor shall he go out of the sanctuary, nor profane the sanctuary of his God; for the consecration of the anointing oil of his God *is* upon him: I *am* the LORD. [13]And he shall take a wife in her virginity. [14]A widow or a divorced woman or a defiled woman *or* a harlot—these he shall not marry; but he shall take a virgin of his own people as wife. [15]Nor

SELF-DESTRUCTING

20:22-23 God gave many rules to his people—but not without reason. He did not withhold good from them; he only prohibited those acts that would bring them to ruin. All of us understand God's physical laws of nature. For example, jumping off a 10-story building means death because of the law of gravity. But some of us don't understand how God's spiritual laws work. God forbids us to do certain things because he wants to keep us from self-destruction. Next time you feel like doing something that you know is wrong, remember that the consequences might be suffering and separation from the God who is trying to help you.

22:19-25 Animals with defects were not acceptable as sacrifices because they did not represent God's holy nature. Furthermore, the animal had to be without blemish to symbolize the perfect, sinless life of Jesus Christ. When we give our best time, talent, and treasure to God, rather than giving him something tarnished or common, we show the true meaning of worship and testify to God's supreme worth.

shall he profane his posterity among his people, for I the LORD sanctify him.' "

¹⁶And the LORD spoke to Moses, saying, ¹⁷"Speak to Aaron, saying: 'No man of your descendants in *succeeding* generations, who has *any* defect, may approach to offer the bread of his God. ¹⁸For any man who has a defect shall not approach: a man blind or lame, who has a marred *face* or any *limb* too long, ¹⁹a man who has a broken foot or broken hand, ²⁰or is a hunchback or a dwarf, or *a man* who has a defect in his eye, or eczema or scab, or is a eunuch. ²¹No man of the descendants of Aaron the priest, who has a defect, shall come near to offer the offerings made by fire to the LORD. He has a defect; he shall not come near to offer the bread of his God. ²²He may eat the bread of his God, *both* the most holy and the holy; ²³only he shall not go near the veil or approach the altar, because he has a defect, lest he profane My sanctuaries; for I the LORD sanctify them.' "

²⁴And Moses told *it* to Aaron and his sons, and to all the children of Israel.

CHAPTER 22 Then the LORD spoke to Moses, saying, ²"Speak to Aaron and his sons, that they separate themselves from the holy things of the children of Israel, and that they do not profane My holy name *by* what they dedicate to Me: I *am* the LORD. ³Say to them: 'Whoever of all your descendants throughout your generations, who goes near the holy things which the children of Israel dedicate to the LORD, while he has uncleanness upon him, that person shall be cut off from My presence: I *am* the LORD.

⁴'Whatever man of the descendants of Aaron, who *is* a leper or has a discharge, shall not eat the holy offerings until he is clean. And whoever touches anything made unclean *by* a corpse, or a man who has had an emission of semen, ⁵or whoever touches any creeping thing by which he would be made unclean, or any person by whom he would become unclean, whatever his uncleanness may be— ⁶the person who has touched any such thing shall be unclean until evening, and shall not eat the holy *offerings* unless he washes his body with water. ⁷And when the sun goes down he shall be clean; and afterward he may eat the holy *offerings*, because it *is* his food. ⁸Whatever dies *naturally* or is torn *by beasts* he shall not eat, to defile himself with it: I *am* the LORD.

⁹'They shall therefore keep My ordinance, lest they bear sin for it and die thereby, if they profane it: I the LORD sanctify them.

¹⁰'No outsider shall eat the holy *offering;* one who dwells with the priest, or a hired servant, shall not eat the holy thing. ¹¹But if the priest buys a person with his money, he may eat it; and one who is born in his house may eat his food. ¹²If the priest's daughter is married to an outsider, she may not eat of the holy offerings. ¹³But if the priest's daughter is a widow or divorced, and has no child, and has returned to her father's house as in her youth, she may eat her father's food; but no outsider shall eat it.

¹⁴'And if a man eats the holy *offering* unintentionally, then he shall restore a holy *offering* to the priest, and add one-fifth to it. ¹⁵They shall not profane the holy *offerings* of the children of Israel, which they offer to the LORD, ¹⁶or allow them to bear the guilt of trespass when they eat their holy *offerings;* for I the LORD sanctify them.' "

¹⁷And the LORD spoke to Moses, saying, ¹⁸"Speak to Aaron and his sons, and to all the children of Israel, and say to them: 'Whatever man of the house of Israel, or of the strangers in Israel, who offers his sacrifice for any of his vows or for any of his freewill offerings, which they offer to the LORD as a burnt offering— ¹⁹*you shall offer* of your own free will a male without blemish from the cattle, from the sheep, or from the goats. ²⁰Whatever has a defect, you shall not offer, for it shall not be acceptable on your behalf. ²¹And whoever offers a sacrifice of a peace offering to the LORD, to fulfill *his* vow, or a freewill offering from the cattle or the sheep, it must be perfect to be accepted; there shall be no defect in it. ²²Those *that are* blind or broken or maimed, or have an ulcer or eczema or scabs, you shall not offer to the LORD, nor make an offering by fire of them on the altar to the LORD. ²³Either a bull or a lamb that has any limb too long or too short you may offer *as* a freewill offering, but for a vow it shall not be accepted.

²⁴'You shall not offer to the LORD what is bruised or crushed, or torn or cut; nor shall you make *any offering of them* in your land. ²⁵Nor from a foreigner's hand shall you offer any of these as the bread of your God, because their corruption *is* in them, *and* defects *are* in them. They shall not be accepted on your behalf.' "

²⁶And the LORD spoke to Moses, saying: ²⁷"When a bull or a sheep or a goat is born, it shall be seven days with its mother; and from the eighth day and thereafter it shall be accepted as an offering made by fire to the LORD. ²⁸*Whether it is* a cow or ewe, do not kill both her and her young on the same day. ²⁹And when you offer a sacrifice of thanksgiving to the LORD, offer *it* of your own free will. ³⁰On the same day it shall be eaten; you shall leave none of it until morning: I *am* the LORD.

³¹"Therefore you shall keep My commandments, and perform them: I *am* the LORD. ³²You shall not profane My holy name, but I will be hallowed among the children of Israel. I *am* the LORD who sanctifies you, ³³who brought you out of the land of Egypt, to be your God: I *am* the LORD."

CHAPTER 23 **SPECIAL DAYS.** And the LORD spoke to Moses, saying, ²"Speak to the children of Israel, and say to them: 'The feasts of the LORD, which you shall proclaim *to be* holy convocations, these *are* My feasts.

³'Six days shall work be done, but the seventh day *is* a

TRADITIONS

23:1-4 God established several national holidays each year for celebration, fellowship, and worship. Much can be learned about by observing the holidays they celebrate and the way they celebrate them. What do your holiday traditions say about your values?

THE FEASTS

Besides enjoying one Sabbath day of rest each week, the Israelites also enjoyed 19 days when national holidays were celebrated.

Feast	What It Celebrated	Its Importance
Passover One day (Lev. 23:5)	When God spared the lives of Israel's firstborn children in Egypt and freed the Hebrews from slavery	Reminded the people of God's deliverance
Unleavened Bread Seven days (Lev. 23:6-8)	The exodus from Egypt	Reminded the people they were leaving the old life behind and entering a new way of living
Firstfruits One day (Lev. 23:9-14)	The first crops of the barley harvest	Reminded the people how God provided for them
Pentecost (Weeks) One day (Lev. 23:15-22)	The end of the barley harvest and beginning of the wheat harvest	Showed joy and thanksgiving over the bountiful harvest
Trumpets One day (Lev. 23:23-25)	The beginning of the seventh month (civil new year)	Expressed joy and thanksgiving to God
Day of Atonement One day (Lev. 23:26-32)	The removal of sin from the people and the nation	Restored fellowship with God
Tabernacles Seven days (Lev. 23:33-43)	God's protection and guidance in the wilderness	Renewed Israel's commitment to God and trust in his guidance and protection

Sabbath of solemn rest, a holy convocation. You shall do no work *on it;* it *is* the Sabbath of the LORD in all your dwellings.

⁴"These *are* the feasts of the LORD, holy convocations which you shall proclaim at their appointed times. ⁵On the fourteenth *day* of the first month at twilight *is* the LORD's Passover. ⁶And on the fifteenth day of the same month *is* the Feast of Unleavened Bread to the LORD; seven days you must eat unleavened bread. ⁷On the first day you shall have a holy convocation; you shall do no customary work on it. ⁸But you shall offer an offering made by fire to the LORD for seven days. The seventh day *shall be* a holy convocation; you shall do no customary work *on it.*' "

⁹And the LORD spoke to Moses, saying, ¹⁰"Speak to the children of Israel, and say to them: 'When you come into the land which I give to you, and reap its harvest, then you shall bring a sheaf of the firstfruits of your harvest to the priest. ¹¹He shall wave the sheaf before the LORD, to be accepted on your behalf; on the day after the Sabbath the priest shall wave it. ¹²And you shall offer on that day, when you wave the sheaf, a male lamb of the first year, without blemish, as a burnt offering to the LORD. ¹³Its grain offering *shall be* two-tenths *of an ephah* of fine flour mixed with oil, an offering made by fire to the LORD, for a sweet aroma; and its drink offering *shall be* of wine, one-fourth of a hin. ¹⁴You shall eat neither bread nor parched grain nor fresh grain until the same day that you have brought an offering to your God; *it shall be* a statute

forever throughout your generations in all your dwellings.

¹⁵'And you shall count for yourselves from the day after the Sabbath, from the day that you brought the sheaf of the wave offering: seven Sabbaths shall be completed. ¹⁶Count fifty days to the day after the seventh Sabbath; then you shall offer a new grain offering to the LORD. ¹⁷You shall bring from your dwellings two wave *loaves* of two-tenths *of an ephah.* They shall be of fine flour; they shall be baked with leaven. *They are* the firstfruits to the LORD. ¹⁸And you shall offer with the bread seven lambs of the first year, without blemish, one young bull, and two rams. They shall be *as* a burnt offering to the LORD, with their grain offering and their drink offerings, an offering made by fire for a sweet aroma to the LORD. ¹⁹Then you shall sacrifice one kid of the goats as a sin offering, and two male lambs of the first year as a sacrifice of a peace offering. ²⁰The priest shall wave them with the bread of the firstfruits *as* a wave offering before the LORD, with the two lambs. They shall be holy to the LORD for the priest. ²¹And you shall proclaim on the same day *that* it is a holy convocation to you. You shall do no customary work *on it. It shall be* a statute forever in all your dwellings throughout your generations.

²²'When you reap the harvest of your land, you shall not wholly reap the corners of your field when you reap, nor shall you gather any gleaning from your harvest. You shall leave them for the poor and for the stranger: I *am* the LORD your God.' "

²³Then the LORD spoke to Moses, saying, ²⁴"Speak to the children of Israel, saying: 'In the seventh month, on the first *day* of the month, you shall have a sabbath-*rest,* a memorial of blowing of trumpets, a holy convocation. ²⁵You shall do no customary work *on it;* and you shall offer an offering made by fire to the LORD.' "

²⁶And the LORD spoke to Moses, saying: ²⁷"Also the tenth *day* of this seventh month *shall be* the Day of Atonement. It shall be a holy convocation for you; you shall afflict your souls, and offer an offering made by fire to the LORD. ²⁸And you shall do no work on that same day, for it *is* the Day of Atonement, to make atonement for you before the LORD your God. ²⁹For any person who is not afflicted *in soul* on that same day shall be cut off from his people. ³⁰And any person who does any work on that same day, that person I will destroy from among his people. ³¹You shall do no manner of work; *it shall be* a statute forever throughout your generations in all your dwellings. ³²It *shall be* to you a sabbath of *solemn* rest, and you shall afflict your souls; on the ninth *day* of the month at evening, from evening to evening, you shall celebrate your sabbath."

³³Then the LORD spoke to Moses, saying, ³⁴"Speak to the children of Israel, saying: 'The fifteenth day of this seventh month *shall be* the Feast of Tabernacles *for* seven days to the LORD. ³⁵On the first day *there shall be* a holy convocation. You shall do no customary work *on it.* ³⁶*For* seven days you shall offer an offering made by fire to the LORD. On the eighth day you shall have a holy convocation, and you shall offer an offering made by fire to the LORD. It *is* a sacred assembly, *and* you shall do no customary work *on it.*

³⁷'These *are* the feasts of the LORD which you shall proclaim *to be* holy convocations, to offer an offering made by fire to the LORD, a burnt offering and a grain offering, a sacrifice and drink offerings, everything on its day— ³⁸besides the Sabbaths of the LORD, besides your gifts, besides all your vows, and besides all your freewill offerings which you give to the LORD.

³⁹'Also on the fifteenth day of the seventh month, when you have gathered in the fruit of the land, you shall keep the feast of the LORD *for* seven days; on the first day *there shall be* a sabbath-*rest,* and on the eighth day a sabbath-*rest.* ⁴⁰And you shall take for yourselves on the first day the fruit of beautiful trees, branches of palm trees, the boughs of leafy trees, and willows of the brook; and you shall rejoice before the LORD your God for seven days. ⁴¹You shall keep it as a feast to the LORD for seven days in the year. *It shall be* a statute forever in your generations. You shall celebrate it in the seventh month. ⁴²You shall dwell in booths for seven days. All who are native Israelites shall dwell in booths, ⁴³that your generations may know that I made the children of Israel dwell in booths when I brought them out of the land of Egypt: I *am* the LORD your God.' "

⁴⁴So Moses declared to the children of Israel the feasts of the LORD.

CHAPTER 24 THE MEMORIAL OFFERING. Then the LORD spoke to Moses, saying: ²"Command the chil-

dren of Israel that they bring to you pure oil of pressed olives for the light, to make the lamps burn continually. ³Outside the veil of the Testimony, in the tabernacle of meeting, Aaron shall be in charge of it from evening until morning before the LORD continually; *it shall be* a statute forever in your generations. ⁴He shall be in charge of the lamps on the pure *gold* lampstand before the LORD continually.

⁵"And you shall take fine flour and bake twelve cakes with it. Two-tenths *of an ephah* shall be in each cake. ⁶You shall set them in two rows, six in a row, on the pure *gold* table before the LORD. ⁷And you shall put pure frankincense on *each* row, that it may be on the bread for a memorial, an offering made by fire to the LORD. ⁸Every Sabbath he shall set it in order before the LORD continually, *being taken* from the children of Israel by an everlasting covenant. ⁹And it shall be for Aaron and his sons, and they shall eat it in a holy place; for it *is* most holy to him from the offerings of the LORD made by fire, by a perpetual statute."

¹⁰Now the son of an Israelite woman, whose father *was* an Egyptian, went out among the children of Israel; and this Israelite *woman's* son and a man of Israel fought each other in the camp. ¹¹And the Israelite woman's son blasphemed the name *of the* LORD and cursed; and so they brought him to Moses. (His mother's name *was* Shelomith the daughter of Dibri, of the tribe of Dan.) ¹²Then they put him in custody, that the mind of the LORD might be shown to them.

¹³And the LORD spoke to Moses, saying, ¹⁴"Take outside the camp him who has cursed; then let all who heard *him* lay their hands on his head, and let all the congregation stone him.

¹⁵"Then you shall speak to the children of Israel, saying: 'Whoever curses his God shall bear his sin. ¹⁶And whoever blasphemes the name of the LORD shall surely be put to death. All the congregation shall certainly stone him, the stranger as well as him who is born in the land. When he blasphemes the name *of the* LORD, he shall be put to death.

¹⁷'Whoever kills any man shall surely be put to death. ¹⁸Whoever kills an animal shall make it good, animal for animal.

¹⁹'If a man causes disfigurement of his neighbor, as he has done, so shall it be done to him— ²⁰fracture for fracture, eye for eye, tooth for tooth; as he has caused disfigurement of a man, so shall it be done to him. ²¹And whoever kills an animal shall restore it; but whoever kills a man shall be put to death. ²²You shall have the same law for the stranger and for one from your own country; for *I am* the LORD your God.' "

²³Then Moses spoke to the children of Israel; and they took outside the camp him who had cursed, and stoned him with stones. So the children of Israel did as the LORD commanded Moses.

CHAPTER 25 REST FOR THE LAND. And the LORD spoke to Moses on Mount Sinai, saying, ²"Speak to the children of Israel, and say to them: 'When you come into the land which I give you, then the land shall keep

sabbath to the LORD. ³Six years you shall sow your field, and six years you shall prune your vineyard, and gather its fruit; ⁴but in the seventh year there shall be a sabbath of solemn rest for the land, a sabbath to the LORD. You shall neither sow your field nor prune your vineyard. ⁵What grows of its own accord of your harvest you shall not reap, nor gather the grapes of your untended vine, *for* it is a year of rest for the land. ⁶And the sabbath *produce* of the land shall be food for you: for you, your male and female servants, your hired man, and the stranger who dwells with you, ⁷for your livestock and the beasts that *are* in your land—all its produce shall be for food.

⁸'And you shall count seven sabbaths of years for yourself, seven times seven years; and the time of the seven sabbaths of years shall be to you forty-nine years. ⁹Then you shall cause the trumpet of the Jubilee to sound on the tenth *day* of the seventh month; on the Day of Atonement you shall make the trumpet to sound throughout all your land. ¹⁰And you shall consecrate the fiftieth year, and proclaim liberty throughout *all* the land to all its inhabitants. It shall be a Jubilee for you; and each of you shall return to his possession, and each of you shall return to his family. ¹¹That fiftieth year shall be a Jubilee to you; in it you shall neither sow nor reap what grows of its own accord, nor gather *the grapes* of your untended vine. ¹²For it *is* the Jubilee; it shall be holy to you; you shall eat its produce from the field.

¹³'In this Year of Jubilee, each of you shall return to his possession. ¹⁴And if you sell anything to your neighbor or buy from your neighbor's hand, you shall not oppress one another. ¹⁵According to the number of years after the Jubilee you shall buy from your neighbor, and according to the number of years of crops he shall sell to you. ¹⁶According to the multitude of years you shall increase its price, and according to the fewer number of years you shall diminish its price; for he sells to you *according* to the number *of the years* of the crops. ¹⁷Therefore you shall not oppress one another, but you shall fear your God; for I *am* the LORD your God.

¹⁸'So you shall observe My statutes and keep My judgments, and perform them; and you will dwell in the land in safety. ¹⁹Then the land will yield its fruit, and you will eat your fill, and dwell there in safety. ²⁰'And if you say, "What shall we eat in the seventh year, since we shall not sow nor gather in our produce?" ²¹Then I will command My blessing on you in the sixth year, and it will bring forth produce enough for three years. ²²And you shall sow in the eighth year, and eat old produce until the ninth year; until its produce comes in, you shall eat of the old *harvest.*

²³'The land shall not be sold permanently, for the land *is* Mine; for you *are* strangers and sojourners with Me. ²⁴And in all the land of your possession you shall grant redemption of the land.

²⁵'If one of your brethren becomes poor, and has sold *some* of his possession, and if his redeeming relative comes to redeem it, then he may redeem what his brother sold. ²⁶Or if the man has no one to redeem it, but he himself becomes able to redeem it, ²⁷then let him count the years since its sale, and restore the remainder to the man to whom he sold it, that he may return to his possession. ²⁸But if he is not able to have *it* restored to himself, then what was sold shall remain in the hand of him who bought it until the Year of Jubilee; and in the Jubilee it shall be released, and he shall return to his possession.

²⁹'If a man sells a house in a walled city, then he may redeem it within a whole year after it is sold; *within* a full year he may redeem it. ³⁰But if it is not redeemed within the space of a full year, then the house in the walled city shall belong permanently to him who bought it, throughout his generations. It shall not be released in the Jubilee. ³¹However the houses of villages which have no wall around them shall be counted as the fields of the country. They may be redeemed, and they shall be released in the Jubilee. ³²Nevertheless the cities of the Levites, *and* the houses in the cities of their possession, the Levites may redeem at any time. ³³And if a man purchases a house from the Levites, then the house that was sold in the city of his possession shall be released in the Jubilee; for the houses in the cities of the Levites *are* their possession among the children of Israel. ³⁴But the field of the common-land of their cities may not be sold, for it *is* their perpetual possession.

³⁵'If one of your brethren becomes poor, and falls into poverty among you, then you shall help him, like a stranger or a sojourner, that he may live with you. ³⁶Take no usury or interest from him; but fear your God, that your brother may live with you. ³⁷You shall not lend him your money for usury, nor lend him your food at a profit. ³⁸I *am* the LORD your God, who brought you out of the land of Egypt, to give you the land of Canaan *and* to be your God.

³⁹'And if *one of* your brethren *who dwells* by you becomes poor, and sells himself to you, you shall not compel him to serve as a slave. ⁴⁰As a hired servant *and* a sojourner he shall be with you, *and* shall serve you until the Year of Jubilee. ⁴¹And *then* he shall depart from you—

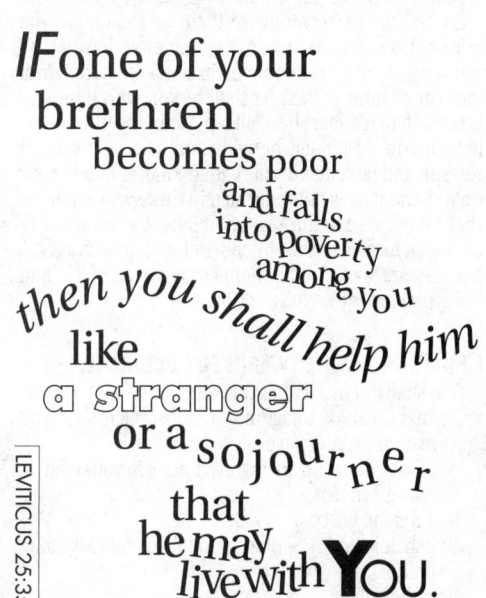

IF one of your brethren becomes poor and falls into poverty among you then you shall help him like a stranger or a sojourner that he may live with YOU.

26:1 The people of the Old Testament were warned over and over against worshiping idols. We wonder how they could deceive themselves with these objects of wood and stone. Yet God could give us the same warning, because we often put idols before him. Idolatry is making anything more important than God, and our lives are full of that temptation. Money, looks, success, reputation, security, popularity—these are today's idols. As you look at these false gods that promise everything you want but nothing you need, does idolatry seem so far removed from your experience?

he and his children with him—and shall return to his own family. He shall return to the possession of his fathers. [42]For they *are* My servants, whom I brought out of the land of Egypt; they shall not be sold as slaves. [43]You shall not rule over him with rigor, but you shall fear your God. [44]And as for your male and female slaves whom you may have—from the nations that are around you, from them you may buy male and female slaves. [45]Moreover you may buy the children of the strangers who dwell among you, and their families who are with you, which they beget in your land; and they shall become your property. [46]And you may take them as an inheritance for your children after you, to inherit *them as* a possession; they shall be your permanent slaves. But regarding your brethren, the children of Israel, you shall not rule over one another with rigor.

[47]'Now if a sojourner or stranger close to you becomes rich, and *one of* your brethren *who dwells* by him becomes poor, and sells himself to the stranger *or* sojourner close to you, or to a member of the stranger's family, [48]after he is sold he may be redeemed again. One of his brothers may redeem him; [49]or his uncle or his uncle's son may redeem him; or *anyone* who is near of kin to him in his family may redeem him; or if he is able he may redeem himself. [50]Thus he shall reckon with him who bought him: The price of his release shall be according to the number of years, from the year that he was sold to him until the Year of Jubilee; *it shall be* according to the time of a hired servant for him. [51]If *there are* still many years *remaining,* according to them he shall repay the price of his redemption from the money with which he was bought. [52]And if there remain but a few years until the Year of Jubilee, then he shall reckon with him, *and* according to his years he shall repay him the price of his redemption. [53]He shall be with him as a yearly hired servant, and he shall not rule with rigor over him in your sight. [54]And if he is not redeemed in these *years,* then he shall be released in the Year of Jubilee—he and his children with him. [55]For the children of Israel *are* servants to Me; they *are* My servants whom I brought out of the land of Egypt: I *am* the LORD your God.

CHAPTER 26 REWARDS FOR OBEDIENCE.

'You shall not make idols for yourselves;
neither a carved image nor a *sacred* pillar shall you
rear up for yourselves;
nor shall you set up an engraved stone in your land, to
bow down to it;
for I *am* the LORD your God.
[2] You shall keep My Sabbaths and reverence My sanctuary:
I *am* the LORD.

[3] 'If you walk in My statutes and keep My commandments, and perform them,
[4] then I will give you rain in its season, the land shall yield its produce, and the trees of the field shall yield their fruit.
[5] Your threshing shall last till the time of vintage, and the vintage shall last till the time of sowing;
you shall eat your bread to the full, and dwell in your land safely.
[6] I will give peace in the land, and you shall lie down and none will make *you* afraid;
I will rid the land of evil beasts,
and the sword will not go through your land.
[7] You will chase your enemies, and they shall fall by the sword before you.
[8] Five of you shall chase a hundred, and a hundred of you shall put ten thousand to flight;
your enemies shall fall by the sword before you.

26:40-45 These verses show what God meant when he said he long-suffering (Exodus 34:6). Even if the Israelites chose to disob and were scattered among the heathen, God would still give them opportunity to repent and return to him. His purpose was not to them, but to help them grow. Our day-to-day experiences and hardships are sometimes overwhelming; unless we can see that G purpose is to bring about continual growth in us, we may give up retain hope while we suffer shows we understand God's merciful of relating to his people. (See Jeremiah 29:11 too.)

[9] 'For I will look on you favorably and make you fruitful, multiply you and confirm My covenant with you.
[10] You shall eat the old harvest, and clear out the old because of the new.
[11] I will set My tabernacle among you, and My soul shall not abhor you.
[12] I will walk among you and be your God, and you shall be My people.
[13] I *am* the LORD your God, who brought you out of the land of Egypt, that *you* should not be their slaves
I have broken the bands of your yoke and made you walk upright.

[14] 'But if you do not obey Me, and do not observe all these commandments,
[15] and if you despise My statutes, or if your soul abhors My judgments, so that you do not perform all My commandments, *but* break My covenant,
[16] I also will do this to you:
I will even appoint terror over you, wasting disease and fever which shall consume the eyes and cause sorrow of heart.
And you shall sow your seed in vain, for your enemies shall eat it.
[17] I will set My face against you, and you shall be defeated by your enemies.
Those who hate you shall reign over you, and you shall flee when no one pursues you.

18 'And after all this, if you do not obey Me, then I will punish you seven times more for your sins.

19 I will break the pride of your power;
I will make your heavens like iron and your earth like bronze.

20 And your strength shall be spent in vain;
for your land shall not yield its produce, nor shall the trees of the land yield their fruit.

21 'Then, if you walk contrary to Me, and are not willing to obey Me, I will bring on you seven times more plagues, according to your sins.

22 I will also send wild beasts among you, which shall rob you of your children, destroy your livestock, and make you few in number;
and your highways shall be desolate.

23 'And if by these things you are not reformed by Me, but walk contrary to Me,

24 then I also will walk contrary to you, and I will punish you yet seven times for your sins.

25 And I will bring a sword against you that will execute the vengeance of the covenant;
when you are gathered together within your cities I will send pestilence among you;
and you shall be delivered into the hand of the enemy.

26 When I have cut off your supply of bread, ten women shall bake your bread in one oven, and they shall bring back your bread by weight, and you shall eat and not be satisfied.

27 'And after all this, if you do not obey Me, but walk contrary to Me,

28 then I also will walk contrary to you in fury;
and I, even I, will chastise you seven times for your sins.

29 You shall eat the flesh of your sons, and you shall eat the flesh of your daughters.

30 I will destroy your high places, cut down your incense altars, and cast your carcasses on the lifeless forms of your idols;
and My soul shall abhor you.

31 I will lay your cities waste and bring your sanctuaries to desolation, and I will not smell the fragrance of your sweet aromas.

32 I will bring the land to desolation, and your enemies who dwell in it shall be astonished at it.

33 I will scatter you among the nations and draw out a sword after you;
your land shall be desolate and your cities waste.

34 Then the land shall enjoy its sabbaths as long as it lies desolate and you *are* in your enemies' land;

then the land shall rest and enjoy its sabbaths.

35 As long as *it* lies desolate it shall rest—
for the time it did not rest on your sabbaths when you dwelt in it.

36 'And as for those of you who are left, I will send faintness into their hearts in the lands of their enemies;
the sound of a shaken leaf shall cause them to flee;
they shall flee as though fleeing from a sword, and they shall fall when no one pursues.

37 They shall stumble over one another, as it were before a sword, when no one pursues;
and you shall have no *power* to stand before your enemies.

"Here's what I did..."

I know that most people, especially kids, don't usually read Leviticus for devotions, and I won't pretend that that's what I was doing. But I was involved in a read-through-the-Bible-in-a-year program, and so I had to read every word of this book. What hit me most as I read all this stuff about laws and sacrifices was how seriously God takes the way his people obey or disobey him. And he stated it so clearly for the Israelites. For example, in chapter 26 God says that obedience will bring prosperity in the Promised Land, but disobedience will bring nothing but trouble. *How could the people be so stupid,* I thought as I read. *Why would they ever disobey?* But then I thought of how I have even more evidence of God's love than those people had and *all* of his Word; and yet, I take God for granted and even disobey him on purpose at times. Then I thought of what I knew God wanted me to do that day (for one thing, I needed to apologize to my mom for something I had said). So I asked God to forgive me and went to talk with Mom. God takes obedience seriously, and so should I.

Kara

AGE 15

38 You shall perish among the nations, and the land of your enemies shall eat you up.

39 And those of you who are left shall waste away in their iniquity in your enemies' lands;
also in their fathers' iniquities, which are with them, they shall waste away.

40 'But if they confess their iniquity and the iniquity of their fathers, with their unfaithfulness in which they were unfaithful to Me, and that they also have walked contrary to Me,

41 and *that* I also have walked contrary to them and have brought them into the land of their enemies;
if their uncircumcised hearts are humbled, and they accept their guilt—

42 then I will remember My covenant with Jacob, and My covenant with Isaac and My covenant with Abraham I will remember;
I will remember the land.

43 The land also shall be left empty by them, and will enjoy its sabbaths while it lies desolate without them;

they will accept their guilt, because they despised My judgments and because their soul abhorred My statutes.

44 Yet for all that, when they are in the land of their enemies, I will not cast them away, nor shall I abhor them, to utterly destroy them and break My covenant with them;

for I *am* the LORD their God.

45 But for their sake I will remember the covenant of their ancestors, whom I brought out of the land of Egypt in the sight of the nations, that I might be their God:

I *am* the LORD.' "

46These *are* the statutes and judgments and laws which the LORD made between Himself and the children of Israel on Mount Sinai by the hand of Moses.

CHAPTER 27 PAYMENTS TO THE LORD.

Now the LORD spoke to Moses, saying, 2"Speak to the children of Israel, and say to them: 'When a man consecrates by a vow certain persons to the LORD, according to your valuation, 3if your valuation is of a male from twenty years old up to sixty years old, then your valuation shall be fifty shekels of silver, according to the shekel of the sanctuary. 4If it *is* a female, then your valuation shall be thirty shekels; 5and if from five years old up to twenty years old, then your valuation for a male shall be twenty shekels, and for a female ten shekels; 6and if from a month old up to five years old, then your valuation for a male shall be five shekels of silver, and for a female your valuation shall be three shekels of silver; 7and if from sixty years old and above, if *it is* a male, then your valuation shall be fifteen shekels, and for a female ten shekels.

8'But if he is too poor to pay your valuation, then he shall present himself before the priest, and the priest shall set a value for him; according to the ability of him who vowed, the priest shall value him.

9'If *it is* an animal that men may bring as an offering to the LORD, all that *anyone* gives to the LORD shall be holy. 10He shall not substitute it or exchange it, good for bad or bad for good; and if he at all exchanges animal for animal, then both it and the one exchanged for it shall be holy. 11If *it is* an unclean animal which they do not offer as a sacrifice to the LORD, then he shall present the animal before the priest; 12and the priest shall set a value for it, whether it is good or bad; as you, the priest, value it, so it shall be. 13But if he *wants* at all *to* redeem it, then he must add one-fifth to your valuation.

14'And when a man dedicates his house *to be* holy to the LORD, then the priest shall set a value for it, whether it is good or bad; as the priest values it, so it shall stand. 15If he who dedicated it *wants to* redeem his house, then he must add one-fifth of the money of your valuation to it, and it shall be his.

16'If a man dedicates to the LORD *part* of a field of his possession, then your valuation shall be according to the seed for it. A homer of barley seed *shall be valued* at fifty shekels of silver. 17If he dedicates his field from the Year of Jubilee, according to your valuation it shall stand. 18But if he dedicates his field after the Jubilee, then the priest shall reckon to him the money due according to the years that remain till the Year of Jubilee, and it shall be deducted from your valuation. 19And if he who dedicated the field ever wishes to redeem it, then he must add one-fifth of the money of your valuation to it, and it shall belong to him. 20But if he does not want to redeem the field, or if he has sold the field to another man, it shall not be redeemed anymore; 21but the field, when it is released in the Jubilee, shall be holy to the LORD, as a devoted field; it shall be the possession of the priest.

22'And if a man dedicates to the LORD a field which he has bought, which is not the field of his possession, 23then the priest shall reckon to him the worth of your valuation, up to the Year of Jubilee, and he shall give your valuation on that day *as* a holy *offering* to the LORD. 24In the Year of Jubilee the field shall return to him from whom it was bought, to the one who *owned* the land as a possession. 25And all your valuations shall be according to the shekel of the sanctuary: twenty gerahs to the shekel.

26'But the firstborn of the animals, which should be the LORD's firstborn, no man shall dedicate; whether *it is* an ox or sheep, it *is* the LORD's. 27And if *it is* an unclean animal, then he shall redeem *it* according to your valuation, and shall add one-fifth to it; or if it is not redeemed, then it shall be sold according to your valuation.

28'Nevertheless no devoted *offering* that a man may devote to the LORD of all that he has, *both* man and beast, or the field of his possession, shall be sold or redeemed; every devoted *offering is* most holy to the LORD. 29No person under the ban, who may become doomed to destruction among men, shall be redeemed, *but* shall surely be put to death. 30And all the tithe of the land, *whether* of the seed of the land *or* of the fruit of the tree, *is* the LORD's. It *is* holy to the LORD. 31If a man wants at all to redeem *any* of his tithes, he shall add one-fifth to it. 32And concerning the tithe of the herd or the flock, of whatever passes under the rod, the tenth one shall be holy to the LORD. 33He shall not inquire whether it is good or bad, nor shall he exchange it; and if he exchanges it at all, then both it and the one exchanged for it shall be holy; it shall not be redeemed.' "

34These *are* the commandments which the LORD commanded Moses for the children of Israel on Mount Sinai.

TODAY AND FOREVER

27:34 The book of Leviticus is filled with the commands God gave his people at the foot of Mount Sinai. From these commands we can learn much about God's nature and character. At first glance, Leviticus seems irrelevant to our high-tech world. But digging a little deeper, we find that the book still speaks to us today, because God has not changed and his principles are for all times. As people and society change, we must constantly to search for ways to apply the principles of God's law to present circumstances. God was the same in Leviticus as he is today and will be forever (Hebrews 13:8).

MEGA *Themes*

SACRIFICE/OFFERING There are five kinds of offerings that fulfill two main purposes. One purpose is to show praise, thankfulness, and devotion. The other purpose is atonement, the covering and removal of sin.

Sacrifices (offerings) fulfilled two functions: worship, and forgiveness of sins. Through them we learn that sin has a great cost. Because men and women cannot remove their own sins, God requires that a life be given for the cleansing of each person. Until Christ, this cleansing (atonement) was accomplished through the sacrifice of an animal. Jesus' death, however, did away with this temporary system by permanently paying the penalty for our sin.

1. What differences are there between the sacrifices found in the book of Leviticus and the sacrifice provided by Jesus? (Check the book of Hebrews in the New Testament for a detailed study of the contrast of the old and new provisions of God.)
2. The worship offerings focused on praise, thankfulness, and devotion. In what ways can you bring offerings of worship to God?
3. What are some of the aspects of God that you feel are worthy of worship?
4. How does Christ's sacrifice help you worship God freely?
5. What will you do this week to bring God an offering of worship?

HEALTH God gave civil rules for handling food, disease, and sex. God called Israel to obey him and to be different from the surrounding nations. Through these rules, God preserved them from disease and genetic problems as well as teaching them spiritual principles.

We still are to be different morally and spiritually from the unbelievers around us. Principles for healthy living are as important today as in the day of Moses. God is concerned not just about our inner spirit but also about our outer body because it, too, was made to glorify him.

1. What are some ways that people you know abuse their body?
2. Based on what you have learned about God's view of our body, why is he against such abuse?
3. What are some of the biblical principles for taking care of your body?
4. How would following these principles improve your health?
5. Do you agree or disagree with this statement: "Taking care of your body's health is an important part of Christian discipleship"? Explain your answer.

6. Based on your answer to number five, what changes do you need to make in how you take care of your body?

HOLINESS *Holy* means "separated" or "devoted." God removed his people from Egypt, then he had to remove Egypt from his people. God called his people to be committed to his ways, leaving behind the old life-style they had lived in Egypt.

God calls us to devote every area of our life to him. This requires learning to live in obedience to him daily so that we reflect his holiness in the world. While we may not be required to worship as the Israelites did, we are to be committed to leaving behind those things "which belong to Egypt" in our life-styles.

1. How do you think most of your friends at school would describe a "holy" person?
2. What in their ideas is similar to and what is different from the definition of holiness that you are learning in the Scriptures?
3. What would it mean to live a holy life in your school?
4. What areas of your life still "belong to Egypt" and keep you from personal holiness? What are some specific ways to increase your devotion to God and become a clearer reflection of his holiness?

LEVITES The Levites and priests taught the people how to worship. They were ministers who regulated the moral, civil, and ceremonial laws of the people and supervised the health, justice, and welfare of the nation.

The Levites were servants who showed Israel the way to God. Understanding their role enables us to comprehend more of Jesus as our High Priest and our own rules through the priesthood of all believers.

1. What type of attitude would you expect the people to have toward the Levites?
2. The high priest was the one who brought the community of God's people into God's presence. In what ways does Jesus fulfill our need for a high priest?
3. Based on your responses to the first two questions, what do we learn about Jesus who, although holding a position of reverence, chose to be our servant?
4. In what ways do you need Jesus in your life today? What do you need from him as your minister, servant, and Lord?
5. How can you spend some time with the Lord today so that he can meet you right where you are?

*A*t noon, two weary travelers who had been walking all day wanted to get out of the heat and rest. They noticed a huge tree with branches that formed a canopy of shade. They stumbled to the shade of the tree, threw down their packs, spread their blankets, and soon were blissfully asleep. When they awoke, one of the travelers, feeling refreshed and a little arrogant, gazed into the tree and complained: "What a useless tree. There's no fruit!" He had forgotten about the tree's wonderful shade. That traveler was a lot like Israel. ■ The Israelites seemed to be sitting in God's "shade." The future looked great. God himself was leading them and they were about to enter the Promised Land. Then the people began to complain about everything. They decided they would rather be back in Egypt as slaves than where they were. Finally God got fed up and banished them to the wilderness, refusing to let them enter the Promised Land. Though God still considered these complainers his people, he was no longer ready to give them all he had promised. ■ Are we much different from the complaining Israelites? God has done, is doing, and will do so much for us. Yet we complain. "God, what are you doing?" "God, you don't care!" "God, I hate you!" We don't trust him although he has proven himself trustworthy. Do you trust God, or do you complain? You are sitting under the "shade" of God's love. Don't complain. God was leading the Israelites even when they thought he wasn't, and he is leading you.

STATS

PURPOSE: To tell the story of how Israel prepared to enter the Promised Land, how they sinned and were punished, and how they prepared to try again

AUTHOR: Moses

TO WHOM WRITTEN: The people of Israel

DATE WRITTEN: 1450–1410 B.C.

SETTING: The vast wilderness of the Sinai region, as well as lands just south and east of Canaan

KEY PEOPLE: Moses, Aaron, Miriam, Joshua, Caleb, Eleazar, Korah, Balaam

KEY PLACES: Mount Sinai, Promised Land (Canaan), Kadesh, Mount Hor, plains of Moab

Numbers

CHAPTER 1 **THE PEOPLE ARE COUNTED.** Now the LORD spoke to Moses in the Wilderness of Sinai, in the tabernacle of meeting, on the first *day* of the second month, in the second year after they had come out of the land of Egypt, saying: 2"Take a census of all the congregation of the children of Israel, by their families, by their fathers' houses, according to the number of names, every male individually, 3from twenty years old and above—all who *are able to* go to war in Israel. You and Aaron shall number them by their armies. 4And with you there shall be a man from every tribe, each one the head of his father's house.

5"These are the names of the men who shall stand with you: from Reuben, Elizur the son of Shedeur; 6from Simeon, Shelumiel the son of Zurishaddai; 7from Judah, Nahshon the son of Amminadab; 8from Issachar, Nethanel the son of Zuar; 9from Zebulun, Eliab the son of Helon; 10from the sons of Joseph: from Ephraim, Elishama the son of Ammihud; from Manasseh, Gamaliel the son of Pedahzur; 11from Benjamin, Abidan the son of Gideoni; 12from Dan, Ahiezer the son of Ammishaddai; 13from Asher, Pagiel the son of Ocran; 14from Gad, Eliasaph the son of Deuel; 15from Naphtali, Ahira the son of Enan." 16These *were* chosen from the congregation, leaders of their fathers' tribes, heads of the divisions in Israel.

17Then Moses and Aaron took these men who had been mentioned by name, 18and they assembled all the congregation together on the first *day* of the second month; and they recited their ancestry by families, by their fathers' houses, according to the number of names, from twenty years old and above, each one individually. 19As the LORD commanded Moses, so he numbered them in the Wilderness of Sinai.

20Now the children of Reuben, Israel's oldest son, their genealogies by their families, by their fathers' house, according to the number of names, every male individually, from twenty years old and above, all who *were able to* go to war: 21those who were numbered of the tribe of Reuben *were* forty-six thousand five hundred.

22From the children of Simeon, their genealogies by their families, by their fathers' house, of those who were numbered, according to the number of names, every male individually, from twenty years old and above, all who *were able to* go to war: 23those who were numbered of the tribe of Simeon *were* fifty-nine thousand three hundred.

24From the children of Gad, their genealogies by their families, by their fathers' house, according to the number of names, from twenty years old and above, all who *were able to* go to war: 25those who were numbered of the tribe of Gad *were* forty-five thousand six hundred and fifty.

26From the children of Judah, their genealogies by their families, by their fathers' house, according to the number of names, from twenty years old and above, all who *were able to* go to war: 27those who were numbered of the tribe of Judah *were* seventy-four thousand six hundred.

28From the children of Issachar, their genealogies by their families, by their fathers' house, according to the number of names, from twenty years old and above, all who *were able to* go to war: 29those who were numbered of the tribe of Issachar *were* fifty-four thousand four hundred.

30From the children of Zebulun, their genealogies by their families, by their fathers' house, according to the number of names, from twenty years old and above, all who *were able to* go to war: 31those who were numbered

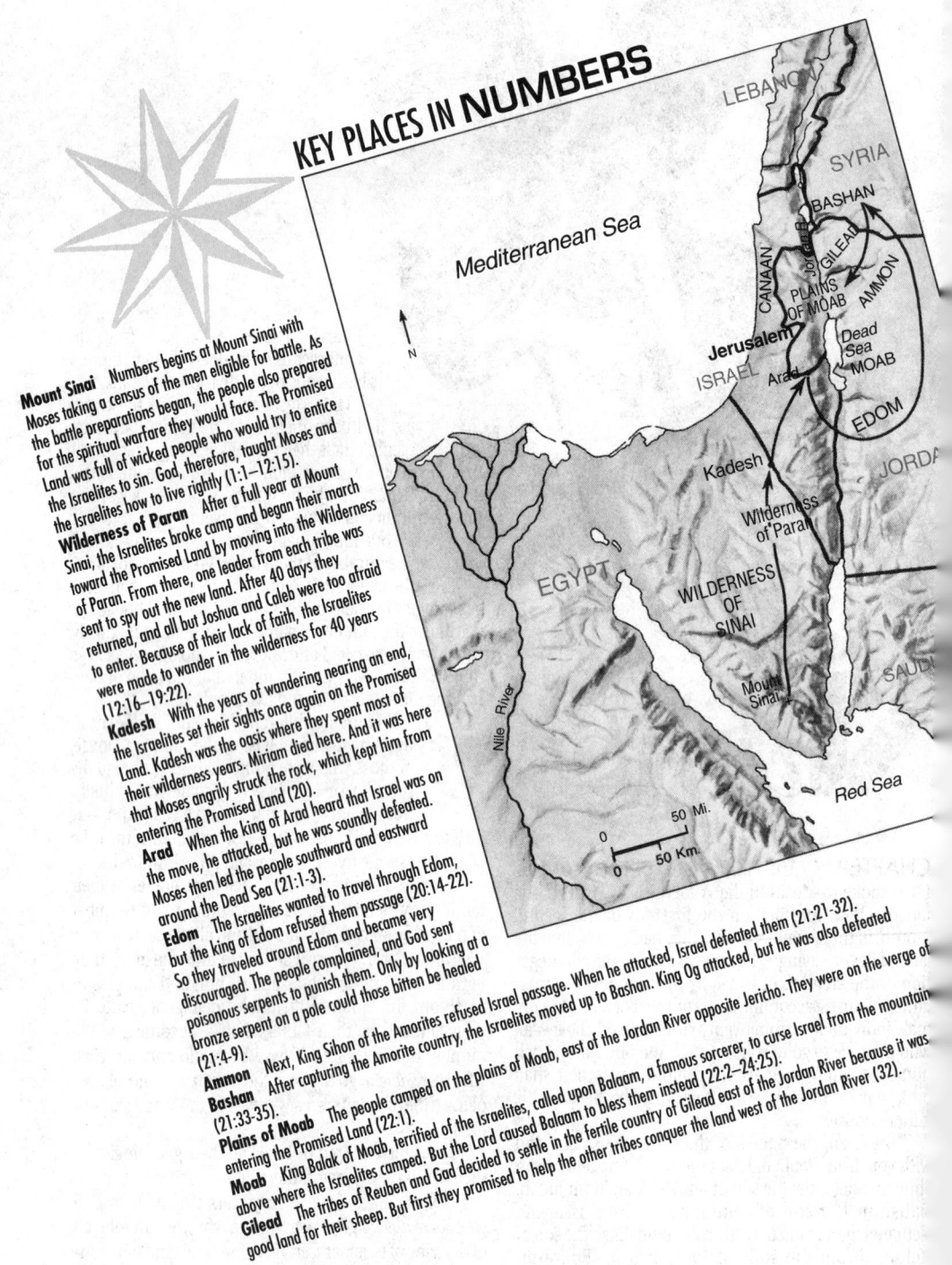

KEY PLACES IN NUMBERS

Mediterranean Sea

LEBANON

SYRIA

BASHAN

CANAAN

GILEAD

Jordan River

PLAINS OF MOAB

AMMON

Dead Sea

Jerusalem

ISRAEL

Arad

MOAB

EDOM

JORDAN

Kadesh

Wilderness of Paran

EGYPT

WILDERNESS OF SINAI

Mount Sinai

SAUDI

Nile River

Red Sea

N

0   50 Mi.

0   50 Km

Mount Sinai   Numbers begins at Mount Sinai with Moses taking a census of the men eligible for battle. As the battle preparations began, the people also prepared for the spiritual warfare they would face. The Promised Land was full of wicked people who would try to entice the Israelites to sin. God, therefore, taught Moses and the Israelites how to live rightly (1:1–12:15).

Wilderness of Paran   After a full year at Mount Sinai, the Israelites broke camp and began their march toward the Promised Land by moving into the Wilderness of Paran. From there, one leader from each tribe was sent to spy out the new land. After 40 days they returned, and all but Joshua and Caleb were too afraid to enter. Because of their lack of faith, the Israelites were made to wander in the wilderness for 40 years (12:16–19:22).

Kadesh   With the years of wandering nearing an end, the Israelites set their sights once again on the Promised Land. Kadesh was the oasis where they spent most of their wilderness years. Miriam died here. And it was here that Moses angrily struck the rock, which kept him from entering the Promised Land (20).

Arad   When the king of Arad heard that Israel was on the move, he attacked, but he was soundly defeated. Moses then led the people southward and eastward around the Dead Sea (21:1-3).

Edom   The Israelites wanted to travel through Edom, but the king of Edom refused them passage (20:14-22). So they traveled around Edom and became very discouraged. The people complained, and God sent poisonous serpents to punish them. Only by looking at a bronze serpent on a pole could those bitten be healed (21:4-9).

Ammon   Next, King Sihon of the Amorites refused Israel passage. When he attacked, Israel defeated them (21:21-32).

Bashan   After capturing the Amorite country, the Israelites moved up to Bashan. King Og attacked, but he was also defeated (21:33-35).

Plains of Moab   The people camped on the plains of Moab, east of the Jordan River opposite Jericho. They were on the verge of entering the Promised Land (22:1).

Moab   King Balak of Moab, terrified of the Israelites, called upon Balaam, a famous sorcerer, to curse Israel from the mountain above where the Israelites camped. But the Lord caused Balaam to bless them instead (22:2–24:25).

Gilead   The tribes of Reuben and Gad decided to settle in the fertile country of Gilead east of the Jordan River because it was good land for their sheep. But first they promised to help the other tribes conquer the land west of the Jordan River (32).

of the tribe of Zebulun *were* fifty-seven thousand four hundred.

³²From the sons of Joseph, the children of Ephraim, their genealogies by their families, by their fathers' house, according to the number of names, from twenty years old and above, all who *were able to* go to war: ³³those who were numbered of the tribe of Ephraim *were* forty thousand five hundred.

³⁴From the children of Manasseh, their genealogies by their families, by their fathers' house, according to the number of names, from twenty years old and above, all who *were able to* go to war: ³⁵those who were numbered of the tribe of Manasseh *were* thirty-two thousand two hundred.

³⁶From the children of Benjamin, their genealogies by their families, by their fathers' house, according to the number of names, from twenty years old and above, all who *were able to* go to war: ³⁷those who were numbered of the tribe of Benjamin *were* thirty-five thousand four hundred.

³⁸From the children of Dan, their genealogies by their families, by their fathers' house, according to the number of names, from twenty years old and above, all who *were able to* go to war: ³⁹those who were numbered of the tribe of Dan *were* sixty-two thousand seven hundred.

⁴⁰From the children of Asher, their genealogies by their families, by their fathers' house, according to the number of names, from twenty years old and above, all who *were able to* go to war: ⁴¹those who were numbered of the tribe of Asher *were* forty-one thousand five hundred.

⁴²From the children of Naphtali, their genealogies by their families, by their fathers' house, according to the number of names, from twenty years old and above, all who *were able to* go to war: ⁴³those who were numbered of the tribe of Naphtali *were* fifty-three thousand four hundred.

⁴⁴These are the ones who were numbered, whom Moses and Aaron numbered, with the leaders of Israel, twelve men, each one representing his father's house. ⁴⁵So all who were numbered of the children of Israel, by their fathers' houses, from twenty years old and above, all who *were able to* go to war in Israel— ⁴⁶all who were numbered were six hundred and three thousand five hundred and fifty.

⁴⁷But the Levites were not numbered among them by their fathers' tribe; ⁴⁸for the LORD had spoken to Moses, saying: ⁴⁹"Only the tribe of Levi you shall not number, nor take a census of them among the children of Israel; ⁵⁰but you shall appoint the Levites over the tabernacle of the Testimony, over all its furnishings, and over all things that belong to it; they shall carry the tabernacle and all its furnishings; they shall attend to it and camp around the tabernacle. ⁵¹And when the tabernacle is to go forward, the Levites shall take it down; and when the tabernacle is to be set up, the Levites shall set it up. The outsider who comes near shall be put to death. ⁵²The children of Israel shall pitch their tents, everyone by his own camp, everyone by his own standard, according to their armies; ⁵³but the Levites shall camp around the tabernacle of the Testimony, that there may be no wrath on the congregation

of the children of Israel; and the Levites shall keep charge of the tabernacle of the Testimony."

⁵⁴Thus the children of Israel did; according to all that the LORD commanded Moses, so they did.

CHAPTER **2** **WHERE THE TRIBES CAMPED.** And the LORD spoke to Moses and Aaron, saying: ²"Everyone of the children of Israel shall camp by his own standard, beside the emblems of his father's house; they shall camp some distance from the tabernacle of meeting. ³On the east side, toward the rising of the sun, those of the standard of the forces with Judah shall camp according to their armies; and Nahshon the son of Amminadab *shall be* the leader of the children of Judah." ⁴And his army was numbered at seventy-four thousand six hundred.

⁵"Those who camp next to him *shall be* the tribe of Issachar, and Nethanel the son of Zuar *shall be* the leader of the children of Issachar." ⁶And his army was numbered at fifty-four thousand four hundred.

⁷"Then *comes* the tribe of Zebulun, and Eliab the son of Helon *shall be* the leader of the children of Zebulun." ⁸And his army was numbered at fifty-seven thousand four hundred. ⁹All who were numbered according to their armies of the forces with Judah, one hundred and eighty-six thousand four hundred—these shall break camp first.

¹⁰"On the south side *shall be* the standard of the forces with Reuben according to their armies, and the leader of the children of Reuben *shall be* Elizur the son of Shedeur." ¹¹And his army was numbered at forty-six thousand five hundred.

¹²"Those who camp next to him *shall be* the tribe of Simeon, and the leader of the children of Simeon *shall be* Shelumiel the son of Zurishaddai." ¹³And his army was numbered at fifty-nine thousand three hundred.

¹⁴"Then *comes* the tribe of Gad, and the leader of the children of Gad *shall be* Eliasaph the son of Reuel." ¹⁵And his army was numbered at forty-five thousand six hundred and fifty. ¹⁶All who were numbered according to their armies of the forces with Reuben, one hundred and fifty-one thousand four hundred and fifty—they shall be the second to break camp.

¹⁷"And the tabernacle of meeting shall move out with the camp of the Levites in the middle of the camps; as they camp, so they shall move out, everyone in his place, by their standards.

¹⁸"On the west side *shall be* the standard of the forces with Ephraim according to their armies, and the leader of the children of Ephraim *shall be* Elishama the son of Ammihud." ¹⁹And his army was numbered at forty thousand five hundred.

²⁰"Next to him *comes* the tribe of Manasseh, and the leader of the children of Manasseh *shall be* Gamaliel the son of Pedahzur." ²¹And his army was numbered at thirty-two thousand two hundred.

²²"Then *comes* the tribe of Benjamin, and the leader of the children of Benjamin *shall be* Abidan the son of Gideoni." ²³And his army was numbered at thirty-five thousand four hundred. ²⁴"All who were numbered according to their armies of the forces with Ephraim, one hundred

and eight thousand one hundred—they shall be the third to break camp.

²⁵"The standard of the forces with Dan *shall be* on the north side according to their armies, and the leader of the children of Dan *shall be* Ahiezer the son of Ammishaddai." ²⁶And his army was numbered at sixty-two thousand seven hundred.

²⁷"Those who camp next to him *shall be* the tribe of Asher, and the leader of the children of Asher *shall be* Pagiel the son of Ocran." ²⁸And his army was numbered at forty-one thousand five hundred.

²⁹"Then *comes* the tribe of Naphtali, and the leader of the children of Naphtali *shall be* Ahira the son of Enan." ³⁰And his army was numbered at fifty-three thousand four hundred. ³¹"All who were numbered of the forces with Dan, one hundred and fifty-seven thousand six hundred—they shall break camp last, with their standards."

³²These *are* the ones who were numbered of the children of Israel by their fathers' houses. All who were numbered according to their armies of the forces *were* six hundred and three thousand five hundred and fifty. ³³But the Levites were not numbered among the children of Israel, just as the LORD commanded Moses.

◣◣◣◣◣CONTRAST

2:34 This must have been one of the biggest campsites the world has ever seen! It would have taken about 12 square miles to set up tents for just the 600,000 fighting men—not to mention the women and children. Moses must have had a difficult time managing such a group. In the early stages of the journey and at Mount Sinai, the people were generally obedient to both God and Moses. But when the people left Mount Sinai and traveled across the rugged wilderness, they began to complain, grumble, and disobey. Soon problems erupted, and Moses could no longer effectively manage the Israelites. The books of Exodus, Leviticus, and Numbers present a striking contrast between how much we can accomplish when we obey God, and how little we can accomplish when we don't.

³⁴Thus the children of Israel did according to all that the LORD commanded Moses; so they camped by their standards and so they broke camp, each one by his family, according to their fathers' houses.

CHAPTER **3** **WHAT THE LEVITES DID.** Now these *are* the records of Aaron and Moses when the LORD spoke with Moses on Mount Sinai. ²And these *are* the names of the sons of Aaron: Nadab, the firstborn, and Abihu, Eleazar, and Ithamar. ³These *are* the names of the sons of Aaron, the anointed priests, whom he consecrated to minister as priests. ⁴Nadab and Abihu had died before the LORD when they offered profane fire before the LORD in the Wilderness of Sinai; and they had no children. So Eleazar and Ithamar ministered as priests in the presence of Aaron their father.

⁵And the LORD spoke to Moses, saying: ⁶"Bring the tribe of Levi near, and present them before Aaron the priest, that they may serve him. ⁷And they shall attend to his needs and the needs of the whole congregation before the tabernacle of meeting, to do the work of the tabernacle. ⁸Also they shall attend to all the furnishings of the tabernacle of meeting, and to the needs of the children of Israel, to do the work of the tabernacle. ⁹And you shall give the Levites to Aaron and his sons; they *are* given entirely to him from among the children of Israel. ¹⁰So you shall appoint Aaron and his sons, and they shall attend to their priesthood; but the outsider who comes near shall be put to death."

¹¹Then the LORD spoke to Moses, saying: ¹²"Now behold, I Myself have taken the Levites from among the children of Israel instead of every firstborn who opens the womb among the children of Israel. Therefore the Levites shall be Mine, ¹³because all the firstborn *are* Mine. On the day that I struck all the firstborn in the land of Egypt, I sanctified to Myself all the firstborn in Israel, both man and beast. They shall be Mine: I *am* the LORD."

¹⁴Then the LORD spoke to Moses in the Wilderness of Sinai, saying: ¹⁵"Number the children of Levi by their fathers' houses, by their families; you shall number every male from a month old and above."

¹⁶So Moses numbered them according to the word of the LORD, as he was commanded. ¹⁷These were the sons of Levi by their names: Gershon, Kohath, and Merari. ¹⁸And these *are* the names of the sons of Gershon by their families: Libni and Shimei. ¹⁹And the sons of Kohath by their families: Amram, Izehar, Hebron, and Uzziel. ²⁰And the sons of Merari by their families: Mahli and Mushi. These *are* the families of the Levites by their fathers' houses.

²¹From Gershon *came* the family of the Libnites and the family of the Shimites; these *were* the families of the Gershonites. ²²Those who were numbered, according to the number of all the males from a month old and above—of those who were numbered *there were* seven thousand five hundred. ²³The families of the Gershonites were to camp behind the tabernacle westward. ²⁴And the leader of the father's house of the Gershonites *was* Eliasaph the son of Lael. ²⁵The duties of the children of Gershon in the tabernacle of meeting *included* the tabernacle, the tent with its covering, the screen for the door of the tabernacle of meeting, ²⁶the screen for the door of the court, the hangings of the court which *are* around the tabernacle and the altar, and their cords according to all the work relating to them.

²⁷From Kohath *came* the family of the Amramites, the family of the Izharites, the family of the Hebronites, and the family of the Uzzielites; these *were* the families of the Kohathites. ²⁸According to the number of all the males from a month old and above, *there were* eight thousand six hundred keeping charge of the sanctuary. ²⁹The families of the children of Kohath were to camp on the south side of the tabernacle. ³⁰And the leader of the father's house of the families of the Kohathites *was* Elizaphan the son of Uzziel. ³¹Their duty *included* the ark, the table, the lampstand, the altars, the utensils of the sanctuary with which they ministered, the screen, and all the work relating to them.

³²And Eleazar the son of Aaron the priest *was to b* chief over the leaders of the Levites, *with* oversight *o* those who kept charge of the sanctuary.

³³From Merari *came* the family of the Mahlites and th

amily of the Mushites; these *were* the families of Merari. And those who were numbered, according to the number of all the males from a month old and above, *were* six thousand two hundred. [35]The leader of the fathers' house of the families of Merari *was* Zuriel the son of Abihail. These *were* to camp on the north side of the tabernacle. And the appointed duty of the children of Merari *included* the boards of the tabernacle, its bars, its pillars, its sockets, its utensils, all the work relating to them, [37]and the pillars of the court all around, with their sockets, their pegs, and their cords.

[38]Moreover those who were to camp before the tabernacle on the east, before the tabernacle of meeting, *were* Moses, Aaron, and his sons, keeping charge of the sanctuary, to meet the needs of the children of Israel; but the outsider who came near was to be put to death. [39]All who were numbered of the Levites, whom Moses and Aaron numbered at the commandment of the LORD, by their families, all the males from a month old and above, *were* twenty-two thousand.

[40]Then the LORD said to Moses: "Number all the firstborn males of the children of Israel from a month old and above, and take the number of their names. [41]And you shall take the Levites for Me—I *am* the LORD—instead of all the firstborn among the children of Israel, and the livestock of the Levites instead of all the firstborn among the livestock of the children of Israel." [42]So Moses numbered all the firstborn among the children of Israel, as the LORD commanded him. [43]And all the firstborn males, according to the number of names from a month old and above, of those who were numbered of them, were twenty-two thousand two hundred and seventy-three.

[44]Then the LORD spoke to Moses, saying: [45]"Take the Levites instead of all the firstborn among the children of Israel, and the livestock of the Levites instead of their livestock. The Levites shall be Mine: I *am* the LORD. [46]And for the redemption of the two hundred and seventy-three of the firstborn of the children of Israel, who are more than the number of the Levites, [47]you shall take five shekels for each one individually; you shall take *them* in the currency of the shekel of the sanctuary, the shekel of twenty gerahs. [48]And you shall give the money, with which the excess number of them is redeemed, to Aaron and his sons."

[49]So Moses took the redemption money from those who were over and above those who were redeemed by the Levites. [50]From the firstborn of the children of Israel he took the money, one thousand three hundred and sixty-five *shekels*, according to the shekel of the sanctuary. [51]And Moses gave their redemption money to Aaron and his sons, according to the word of the LORD, as the LORD commanded Moses.

CHAPTER 4 JOBS FOR THE KOHATH CLAN. Then

the LORD spoke to Moses and Aaron, saying: [2]"Take a census of the sons of Kohath from among the children of Levi, by their families, by their fathers' house, [3]from thirty years old and above, even to fifty years old, all who enter the service to do the work in the tabernacle of meeting.

[4]"This *is* the service of the sons of Kohath in the tabernacle of meeting, *relating to* the most holy things: [5]When the camp prepares to journey, Aaron and his sons shall come, and they shall take down the covering veil and cover the ark of the Testimony with it. [6]Then they shall put on it a covering of badger skins, and spread over *that* a cloth entirely of blue; and they shall insert its poles.

[7]"On the table of showbread they shall spread a blue cloth, and put on it the dishes, the pans, the bowls, and the pitchers for pouring; and the showbread shall be on it. [8]They shall spread over them a scarlet cloth, and cover the same with a covering of badger skins; and they shall insert its poles. [9]And they shall take a blue cloth and cover the lampstand of the light, with its lamps, its wicktrimmers, its trays, and all its oil vessels, with which they service it. [10]Then they shall put it with all its utensils in a covering of badger skins, and put *it* on a carrying beam.

[11]"Over the golden altar they shall spread a blue cloth, and cover it with a covering of badger skins; and they shall insert its poles. [12]Then they shall take all the utensils of service with which they minister in the sanctuary, put *them* in a blue cloth, cover them with a covering of badger skins, and put *them* on a carrying beam. [13]Also they shall take away the ashes from the altar, and spread a purple cloth over it. [14]They shall put on it all its implements with which they minister there—the firepans, the forks, the shovels, the basins, and all the utensils of the altar—and they shall spread on it a covering of badger skins, and insert its poles. [15]And when Aaron and his sons have finished covering the sanctuary and all the furnishings of the sanctuary, when the camp is set to go, then the sons of Kohath shall come to carry *them;* but they shall not touch any holy thing, lest they die.

"These *are* the things in the tabernacle of meeting which the sons of Kohath are to carry.

[16]"The appointed duty of Eleazar the son of Aaron the priest *is* the oil for the light, the sweet incense, the daily grain offering, the anointing oil, the oversight of all the tabernacle, of all that *is* in it, with the sanctuary and its furnishings."

[17]Then the LORD spoke to Moses and Aaron, saying: [18]"Do not cut off the tribe of the families of the Kohathites from among the Levites; [19]but do this in regard to them, that they may live and not die when they approach the most holy things: Aaron and his sons shall go in and appoint each of them to his service and his task. [20]But they shall not go in to watch while the holy things are being covered, lest they die."

[21]Then the LORD spoke to Moses, saying: [22]"Also take a census of the sons of Gershon, by their fathers' house, by their families. [23]From thirty years old and above, even to fifty years old, you shall number them, all who enter to perform the service, to do the work in the tabernacle of meeting. [24]This *is* the service of the families of the Gershonites, in serving and carrying: [25]They shall carry the curtains of the tabernacle and the tabernacle of meeting *with* its covering, the covering of badger skins that *is* on it, the screen for the door of the tabernacle of meeting, [26]the screen for the door of the gate of the court, the hangings of the court which *are* around the tabernacle and altar, and their cords, all the furnishings for their

service and all that is made for these things: so shall they serve.

²⁷"Aaron and his sons shall assign all the service of the sons of the Gershonites, all their tasks and all their service. And you shall appoint to them all their tasks as their duty. ²⁸This *is* the service of the families of the sons of Gershon in the tabernacle of meeting. And their duties *shall be* under the authority of Ithamar the son of Aaron the priest.

²⁹"*As for* the sons of Merari, you shall number them by their families and by their fathers' house. ³⁰From thirty years old and above, even to fifty years old, you shall number them, everyone who enters the service to do the work of the tabernacle of meeting. ³¹And this *is* what they must carry as all their service for the tabernacle of meeting: the boards of the tabernacle, its bars, its pillars, its sockets, ³²and the pillars around the court with their sockets, pegs, and cords, with all their furnishings and all their service; and you shall assign *to each man* by name the items he must carry. ³³This *is* the service of the families of the sons of Merari, as all their service for the tabernacle of meeting, under the authority of Ithamar the son of Aaron the priest."

◣▬▬▬▬▬SET THINGS RIGHT

5:5-8 God included restitution, a unique concept for that day, as part of his law for Israel. When someone was robbed, the guilty person was required to restore to the victim what had been taken and pay an additional interest penalty. When we have wronged someone, we should look for ways to set things right and, if possible, leave the victim even better off than before we harmed him or her. When we have been wronged, we should seek restoration rather than striking out in revenge.

³⁴And Moses, Aaron, and the leaders of the congregation numbered the sons of the Kohathites by their families and by their fathers' house, ³⁵from thirty years old and above, even to fifty years old, everyone who entered the service for work in the tabernacle of meeting; ³⁶and those who were numbered by their families were two thousand seven hundred and fifty. ³⁷These *were* the ones who were numbered of the families of the Kohathites, all who might serve in the tabernacle of meeting, whom Moses and Aaron numbered according to the commandment of the LORD by the hand of Moses.

³⁸And those who were numbered of the sons of Gershon, by their families and by their fathers' house, ³⁹from thirty years old and above, even to fifty years old, everyone who entered the service for work in the tabernacle of meeting— ⁴⁰those who were numbered by their families, by their fathers' house, were two thousand six hundred and thirty. ⁴¹These *are* the ones who were numbered of the families of the sons of Gershon, of all who might serve in the tabernacle of meeting, whom Moses and Aaron numbered according to the commandment of the LORD.

⁴²Those of the families of the sons of Merari who were numbered, by their families, by their fathers' house, ⁴³from thirty years old and above, even to fifty years old, everyone who entered the service for work in the tabernacle of meeting— ⁴⁴those who were numbered by their

families were three thousand two hundred. ⁴⁵These *are* the ones who were numbered of the families of the sons of Merari, whom Moses and Aaron numbered according to the word of the LORD by the hand of Moses.

⁴⁶All who were numbered of the Levites, whom Moses, Aaron, and the leaders of Israel numbered, by their families and by their fathers' houses, ⁴⁷from thirty years old and above, even to fifty years old, everyone who came to do the work of service and the work of bearing burdens in the tabernacle of meeting— ⁴⁸those who were numbered were eight thousand five hundred and eighty.

⁴⁹According to the commandment of the LORD they were numbered by the hand of Moses, each according to his service and according to his task; thus were they numbered by him, as the LORD commanded Moses.

CHAPTER 5 LEPERS MUST LEAVE CAMP. And the

LORD spoke to Moses, saying: ²"Command the children of Israel that they put out of the camp every leper, everyone who has a discharge, and whoever becomes defiled by a corpse. ³You shall put out both male and female; you shall put them outside the camp, that they may not defile their camps in the midst of which I dwell." ⁴And the children of Israel did so, and put them outside the camp; as the LORD spoke to Moses, so the children of Israel did.

⁵Then the LORD spoke to Moses, saying, ⁶"Speak to the children of Israel: 'When a man or woman commits any sin that men commit in unfaithfulness against the LORD, and that person is guilty, ⁷then he shall confess the sin which he has committed. He shall make restitution for his trespass in full, plus one-fifth of it, and give *it* to the one he has wronged. ⁸But if the man has no relative to whom restitution may be made for the wrong, the restitution for the wrong *must go* to the LORD for the priest, in addition to the ram of the atonement with which atonement is made for him. ⁹Every offering of all the holy things of the children of Israel, which they bring to the priest, shall be his. ¹⁰And every man's holy things shall be his; whatever any man gives the priest shall be his.' "

¹¹And the LORD spoke to Moses, saying, ¹²"Speak to the children of Israel, and say to them: 'If any man's wife goes astray and behaves unfaithfully toward him, ¹³and a man lies with her carnally, and it is hidden from the eyes of her husband, and it is concealed that she has defiled herself, and *there was* no witness against her, nor was she caught— ¹⁴if the spirit of jealousy comes upon him and he becomes jealous of his wife, who has defiled herself; or if the spirit of jealousy comes upon him and he becomes jealous of his wife, although she has not defiled herself— ¹⁵then the man shall bring his wife to the priest. He shall bring the offering required for her, one-tenth of an ephah of barley meal; he shall pour no oil on it and put no frankincense on it, because it *is* a grain offering of jealousy, an offering for remembering, for bringing iniquity to remembrance.

¹⁶'And the priest shall bring her near, and set her before the LORD. ¹⁷The priest shall take holy water in an earthen vessel, and take some of the dust that is on the floor of the tabernacle and put *it* into the water. ¹⁸Then the priest shall stand the woman before the LORD, un-

cover the woman's head, and put the offering for remembering in her hands, which *is* the grain offering of jealousy. And the priest shall have in his hand the bitter water that brings a curse. ¹⁹And the priest shall put her under oath, and say to the woman, "If no man has lain with you, and if you have not gone astray to uncleanness *while* under your husband's *authority,* be free from this bitter water that brings a curse. ²⁰But if you have gone astray *while* under your husband's *authority,* and if you have defiled yourself and some man other than your husband has lain with you"— ²¹then the priest shall put the woman under the oath of the curse, and he shall say to the woman—"the LORD make you a curse and an oath among your people, when the LORD makes your thigh rot and your belly swell; ²²and may this water that causes the curse go into your stomach, and make *your* belly swell and *your* thigh rot."

'Then the woman shall say, "Amen, so be it."

²³'Then the priest shall write these curses in a book, and he shall scrape *them* off into the bitter water. ²⁴And he shall make the woman drink the bitter water that brings a curse, and the water that brings the curse shall enter her *to become* bitter. ²⁵Then the priest shall take the grain offering of jealousy from the woman's hand, shall wave the offering before the LORD, and bring it to the altar; ²⁶and the priest shall take a handful of the offering, as its memorial portion, burn *it* on the altar, and afterward make the woman drink the water. ²⁷When he has made her drink the water, then it shall be, if she has defiled herself and behaved unfaithfully toward her husband, that the water that brings a curse will enter her *and become* bitter, and her belly will swell, her thigh will rot, and the woman will become a curse among her people. ²⁸But if the woman has not defiled herself, and is clean, then she shall be free and may conceive children.

²⁹'This *is* the law of jealousy, when a wife, *while* under her husband's *authority,* goes astray and defiles herself, ³⁰or when the spirit of jealousy comes upon a man, and he becomes jealous of his wife; then he shall stand the woman before the LORD, and the priest shall execute all this law upon her. ³¹Then the man shall be free from iniquity, but that woman shall bear her guilt.' "

CHAPTER 6 THE NAZIRITE. Then the LORD spoke to Moses, saying, ²"Speak to the children of Israel, and say to them: 'When either a man or woman consecrates an offering to take the vow of a Nazirite, to separate himself to the LORD, ³he shall separate himself from wine and *similar* drink; he shall drink neither vinegar made from wine nor vinegar made from *similar* drink; neither shall he drink any grape juice, nor eat fresh grapes or raisins. All the days of his separation he shall eat nothing that is produced by the grapevine, from seed to skin.

⁵'All the days of the vow of his separation no razor shall come upon his head; until the days are fulfilled for which he separated himself to the LORD, he shall be holy. *Then* he shall let the locks of the hair of his head grow. ⁶All the days that he separates himself to the LORD he shall not go near a dead body. ⁷He shall not make himself unclean even for his father or his mother, for his brother or his sister, when they die, because his separation to God *is* on his head. ⁸All the days of his separation he shall be holy to the LORD.

⁹'And if anyone dies very suddenly beside him, and he defiles his consecrated head, then he shall shave his head on the day of his cleansing; on the seventh day he shall shave it. ¹⁰Then on the eighth day he shall bring two turtledoves or two young pigeons to the priest, to the door of the tabernacle of meeting; ¹¹and the priest shall offer one as a sin offering and *the* other as a burnt offering, and make atonement for him, because he sinned in regard to the corpse; and he shall sanctify his head that same day. ¹²He shall consecrate to the LORD the days of his separation, and bring a male lamb in its first year as a trespass offering; but the former days shall be lost, because his separation was defiled.

¹³'Now this *is* the law of the Nazirite: When the days of his separation are fulfilled, he shall be brought to the door of the tabernacle of meeting. ¹⁴And he shall present his offering to the LORD: one male lamb in its first year without blemish as a burnt offering, one ewe lamb in its first year without blemish as a sin offering, one ram without blemish as a peace offering, ¹⁵a basket of unleavened bread, cakes of fine flour mixed with oil, unleavened wafers anointed with oil, and their grain offering with their drink offerings.

¹⁶'Then the priest shall bring *them* before the LORD and offer his sin offering and his burnt offering; ¹⁷and he shall offer the ram as a sacrifice of a peace offering to the LORD, with the basket of unleavened bread; the priest shall also offer its grain offering and its drink offering. ¹⁸Then the Nazirite shall shave his consecrated head *at* the door of the tabernacle of meeting, and shall take the hair from his consecrated head and put *it* on the fire which is under the sacrifice of the peace offering.

¹⁹'And the priest shall take the boiled shoulder of the ram, one unleavened cake from the basket, and one unleavened wafer, and put *them* upon the hands of the Nazirite after he has shaved his consecrated *hair,* ²⁰and the priest shall wave them as a wave offering before the LORD; they *are* holy for the priest, together with the breast of the wave offering and the thigh of the heave offering. After that the Nazirite may drink wine.'

²¹"This is the law of the Nazirite who vows to the LORD the offering for his separation, and besides that, whatever else his hand is able to provide; according to the vow which he takes, so he must do according to the law of his separation."

²²And the LORD spoke to Moses, saying: ²³"Speak to Aaron and his sons, saying, 'This is the way you shall bless the children of Israel. Say to them:

²⁴ "The LORD bless you and keep you;
²⁵ The LORD make His face shine upon you,
And be gracious to you;
²⁶ The LORD lift up His countenance upon you,
And give you peace." '

²⁷"So they shall put My name on the children of Israel, and I will bless them."

CHAPTER **7** **GIFTS FOR THE TABERNACLE.** Now it came to pass, when Moses had finished setting up the tabernacle, that he anointed it and consecrated it and all its furnishings, and the altar and all its utensils; so he anointed them and consecrated them. [2]Then the leaders of Israel, the heads of their fathers' houses, who *were* the leaders of the tribes and over those who were numbered, made an offering. [3]And they brought their offering before the LORD, six covered carts and twelve oxen, a cart for *every* two of the leaders, and for each one an ox; and they presented them before the tabernacle.

[4]Then the LORD spoke to Moses, saying, [5]"Accept *these* from them, that they may be used in doing the work of the tabernacle of meeting; and you shall give them to the Levites, *to* every man according to his service." [6]So Moses took the carts and the oxen, and gave them to the Levites. [7]Two carts and four oxen he gave to the sons of Gershon, according to their service; [8]and four carts and eight oxen he gave to the sons of Merari, according to their service, under the authority of Ithamar the son of Aaron the priest. [9]But to the sons of Kohath he gave none, because theirs *was* the service of the holy things, *which* they carried on their shoulders.

[10]Now the leaders offered the dedication *offering* for the altar when it was anointed; so the leaders offered their offering before the altar. [11]For the LORD said to Moses, "They shall offer their offering, one leader each day, for the dedication of the altar."

[12]And the one who offered his offering on the first day *was* Nahshon the son of Amminadab, from the tribe of Judah. [13]His offering *was* one silver platter, the weight of which *was* one hundred and thirty *shekels*, and one silver bowl of seventy shekels, according to the shekel of the sanctuary, both of them full of fine flour mixed with oil as a grain offering; [14]one gold pan of ten *shekels*, full of incense; [15]one young bull, one ram, and one male lamb in its first year, as a burnt offering; [16]one kid of the goats as a sin offering; [17]and for the sacrifice of peace offerings: two oxen, five rams, five male goats, and five male lambs in their first year. This *was* the offering of Nahshon the son of Amminadab.

[18]On the second day Nethanel the son of Zuar, leader of Issachar, presented *an offering.* [19]*For* his offering he offered one silver platter, the weight of which *was* one hundred and thirty *shekels*, and one silver bowl of seventy shekels, according to the shekel of the sanctuary, both of them full of fine flour mixed with oil as a grain offering; [20]one gold pan of ten *shekels*, full of incense; [21]one young bull, one ram, and one male lamb in its first year, as a burnt offering; [22]one kid of the goats as a sin offering; [23]and as the sacrifice of peace offerings: two oxen, five rams, five male goats, and five male lambs in their first year. This *was* the offering of Nethanel the son of Zuar.

[24]On the third day Eliab the son of Helon, leader of the children of Zebulun, *presented an offering.* [25]His offering *was* one silver platter, the weight of which *was* one hundred and thirty *shekels*, and one silver bowl of seventy shekels, according to the shekel of the sanctuary, both of them full of fine flour mixed with oil as a grain offering; [26]one gold pan of ten *shekels*, full of incense; [27]one young

bull, one ram, and one male lamb in its first year, as a burnt offering; [28]one kid of the goats as a sin offering; [29]and for the sacrifice of peace offerings: two oxen, five rams, five male goats, and five male lambs in their first year. This *was* the offering of Eliab the son of Helon.

[30]On the fourth day Elizur the son of Shedeur, leader of the children of Reuben, *presented an offering.* [31]His offering *was* one silver platter, the weight of which *was* one hundred and thirty *shekels*, and one silver bowl of seventy shekels, according to the shekel of the sanctuary, both of them full of fine flour mixed with oil as a grain offering; [32]one gold pan of ten *shekels*, full of incense; [33]one young bull, one ram, and one male lamb in its first year, as a burnt offering; [34]one kid of the goats as a sin offering; [35]and as the sacrifice of peace offerings: two oxen, five rams, five male goats, and five male lambs in their first year. This *was* the offering of Elizur the son of Shedeur.

[36]On the fifth day Shelumiel the son of Zurishaddai, leader of the children of Simeon, *presented an offering.* [37]His offering *was* one silver platter, the weight of which *was* one hundred and thirty *shekels*, and one silver bowl of seventy shekels, according to the shekel of the sanctuary, both of them full of fine flour mixed with oil as a grain offering; [38]one gold pan of ten *shekels*, full of incense; [39]one young bull, one ram, and one male lamb in its first year, as a burnt offering; [40]one kid of the goats as a sin offering; [41]and as the sacrifice of peace offerings: two oxen, five rams, five male goats, and five male lambs in their first year. This *was* the offering of Shelumiel the son of Zurishaddai.

[42]On the sixth day Eliasaph the son of Deuel, leader of the children of Gad, *presented an offering.* [43]His offering *was* one silver platter, the weight of which *was* one hundred and thirty *shekels*, and one silver bowl of seventy shekels, according to the shekel of the sanctuary, both of them full of fine flour mixed with oil as a grain offering; [44]one gold pan of ten *shekels*, full of incense; [45]one young bull, one ram, and one male lamb in its first year, as a burnt offering; [46]one kid of the goats as a sin offering; [47]and as the sacrifice of peace offerings: two oxen, five rams, five male goats, and five male lambs in their first year. This *was* the offering of Eliasaph the son of Deuel.

[48]On the seventh day Elishama the son of Ammihud, leader of the children of Ephraim, *presented an offering.* [49]His offering *was* one silver platter, the weight of which *was* one hundred and thirty *shekels*, and one silver bowl of seventy shekels, according to the shekel of the sanctuary, both of them full of fine flour mixed with oil as a grain offering; [50]one gold pan of ten *shekels*, full of incense; [51]one young bull, one ram, and one male lamb in its first year, as a burnt offering; [52]one kid of the goats as a sin offering; [53]and as the sacrifice of peace offerings: two oxen, five rams, five male goats, and five male lambs in their first year. This *was* the offering of Elishama the son of Ammihud.

[54]On the eighth day Gamaliel the son of Pedahzur, leader of the children of Manasseh, *presented an offering.* [55]His offering *was* one silver platter, the weight of which *was* one hundred and thirty *shekels*, and one silver bowl of seventy shekels, according to the shekel of the sanctu-

ary, both of them full of fine flour mixed with oil as a grain offering; ⁵⁶one gold pan of ten *shekels,* full of incense; ⁵⁷one young bull, one ram, and one male lamb in its first year, as a burnt offering; ⁵⁸one kid of the goats as a sin offering; ⁵⁹and as the sacrifice of peace offerings: two oxen, five rams, five male goats, and five male lambs in their first year. This *was* the offering of Gamaliel the son of Pedahzur.

⁶⁰On the ninth day Abidan the son of Gideoni, leader of the children of Benjamin, *presented an offering.* ⁶¹His offering *was* one silver platter, the weight of which *was* one hundred and thirty *shekels,* and one silver bowl of seventy shekels, according to the shekel of the sanctuary, both of them full of fine flour mixed with oil as a grain offering; ⁶²one gold pan of ten *shekels,* full of incense; ⁶³one young bull, one ram, and one male lamb in its first year, as a burnt offering; ⁶⁴one kid of the goats as a sin offering; ⁶⁵and as the sacrifice of peace offerings: two oxen, five rams, five male goats, and five male lambs in their first year. This *was* the offering of Abidan the son of Gideoni.

⁶⁶On the tenth day Ahiezer the son of Ammishaddai, leader of the children of Dan, *presented an offering.* ⁶⁷His offering *was* one silver platter, the weight of which *was* one hundred and thirty *shekels,* and one silver bowl of seventy shekels, according to the shekel of the sanctuary, both of them full of fine flour mixed with oil as a grain offering; ⁶⁸one gold pan of ten *shekels,* full of incense; ⁶⁹one young bull, one ram, and one male lamb in its first year, as a burnt offering; ⁷⁰one kid of the goats as a sin offering; ⁷¹and as the sacrifice of peace offerings: two oxen, five rams, five male goats, and five male lambs in their first year. This *was* the offering of Ahiezer the son of Ammishaddai.

⁷²On the eleventh day Pagiel the son of Ocran, leader of the children of Asher, *presented an offering.* ⁷³His offering *was* one silver platter, the weight of which *was* one hundred and thirty *shekels,* and one silver bowl of seventy shekels, according to the shekel of the sanctuary, both of them full of fine flour mixed with oil as a grain offering; ⁷⁴one gold pan of ten *shekels,* full of incense; ⁷⁵one young bull, one ram, and one male lamb in its first year, as a burnt offering; ⁷⁶one kid of the goats as a sin offering; ⁷⁷and as the sacrifice of peace offerings: two oxen, five rams, five male goats, and five male lambs in their first year. This *was* the offering of Pagiel the son of Ocran.

⁷⁸On the twelfth day Ahira the son of Enan, leader of the children of Naphtali, *presented an offering.* ⁷⁹His offering *was* one silver platter, the weight of which *was* one hundred and thirty *shekels,* and one silver bowl of seventy shekels, according to the shekel of the sanctuary, both of them full of fine flour mixed with oil as a grain offering; ⁸⁰one gold pan of ten *shekels,* full of incense; ⁸¹one young bull, one ram, and one male lamb in its first year, as a burnt offering; ⁸²one kid of the goats as a sin offering; ⁸³and as the sacrifice of peace offerings: two oxen, five rams, five male goats, and five male lambs in their first year. This *was* the offering of Ahira the son of Enan.

⁸⁴This *was* the dedication *offering* for the altar from the leaders of Israel, when it was anointed: twelve silver platters, twelve silver bowls, and twelve gold pans. ⁸⁵Each silver platter *weighed* one hundred and thirty *shekels* and each bowl seventy *shekels.* All the silver of the vessels *weighed* two thousand four hundred *shekels,* according to the shekel of the sanctuary. ⁸⁶The twelve gold pans full of incense *weighed* ten *shekels* apiece, according to the shekel of the sanctuary; all the gold of the pans *weighed* one hundred and twenty *shekels.* ⁸⁷All the oxen for the burnt offering *were* twelve young bulls, the rams twelve, the male lambs in their first year twelve, with their grain offering, and the kids of the goats as a sin offering twelve. ⁸⁸And all the oxen for the sacrifice of peace offerings were twenty-four bulls, the rams sixty, the male goats sixty, and the lambs in their first year sixty. This *was* the dedication *offering* for the altar after it was anointed.

◣■AWESOME

7:89 Imagine hearing the very voice of God! Moses must have trembled at the sound. Yet we have God's words recorded for us in the Bible, and we should have no less reverence and awe for them. God sometimes spoke directly to his people to tell them the proper way to live. The Bible records these conversations to give us insights into God's character. How tragic when we take these very words of God lightly.

⁸⁹Now when Moses went into the tabernacle of meeting to speak with Him, he heard the voice of One speaking to him from above the mercy seat that *was* on the ark of the Testimony, from between the two cherubim; thus He spoke to him.

CHAPTER **8** SETTING UP THE LAMPS.

And the LORD spoke to Moses, saying: ²"Speak to Aaron, and say to him, 'When you arrange the lamps, the seven lamps shall give light in front of the lampstand.' " ³And Aaron did so; he arranged the lamps to face toward the front of the lampstand, as the LORD commanded Moses. ⁴Now this workmanship of the lampstand *was* hammered gold; from its shaft to its flowers it *was* hammered work. According to the pattern which the LORD had shown Moses, so he made the lampstand.

⁵Then the LORD spoke to Moses, saying: ⁶"Take the Levites from among the children of Israel and cleanse them *ceremonially.* ⁷Thus you shall do to them to cleanse them: Sprinkle water of purification on them, and let them shave all their body, and let them wash their clothes, and *so* make themselves clean. ⁸Then let them take a young bull with its grain offering of fine flour mixed with oil, and you shall take another young bull as a sin offering. ⁹And you shall bring the Levites before the tabernacle of meeting, and you shall gather together the whole congregation of the children of Israel. ¹⁰So you shall bring the Levites before the LORD, and the children of Israel shall lay their hands on the Levites; ¹¹and Aaron shall offer the Levites before the LORD *like* a wave offering from the children of Israel, that they may perform the work of the LORD. ¹²Then the Levites shall lay their hands on the heads of the young bulls, and you shall offer one as a sin offering and the other as a burnt offering to the LORD, to make atonement for the Levites.

[13]"And you shall stand the Levites before Aaron and his sons, and then offer them *like* a wave offering to the LORD. [14]Thus you shall separate the Levites from among the children of Israel, and the Levites shall be Mine. [15]After that the Levites shall go in to service the tabernacle of meeting. So you shall cleanse them and offer them *like* a wave offering. [16]For they *are* wholly given to Me from among the children of Israel; I have taken them for Myself instead of all who open the womb, the firstborn of all the children of Israel. [17]For all the firstborn among the children of Israel *are* Mine, *both* man and beast; on the day that I struck all the firstborn in the land of Egypt I sanctified them to Myself. [18]I have taken the Levites instead of all the firstborn of the children of Israel. [19]And I have given the Levites as a gift to Aaron and his sons from among the children of Israel, to do the work for the children of Israel in the tabernacle of meeting, and to make atonement for the children of Israel, that there be no plague among the children of Israel when the children of Israel come near the sanctuary."

[20]Thus Moses and Aaron and all the congregation of the children of Israel did to the Levites; according to all that the LORD commanded Moses concerning the Levites, so the children of Israel did to them. [21]And the Levites purified themselves and washed their clothes; then Aaron presented them *like* a wave offering before the LORD, and Aaron made atonement for them to cleanse them. [22]After that the Levites went in to do their work in the tabernacle of meeting before Aaron and his sons; as the LORD commanded Moses concerning the Levites, so they did to them.

[23]Then the LORD spoke to Moses, saying, [24]"This *is* what *pertains* to the Levites: From twenty-five years old and above one may enter to perform service in the work of the tabernacle of meeting; [25]and at the age of fifty years they must cease performing this work, and shall work no more. [26]They may minister with their brethren in the tabernacle of meeting, to attend to needs, but they *themselves* shall do no work. Thus you shall do to the Levites regarding their duties."

CHAPTER 9 PASSOVER IS CELEBRATED AGAIN.

Now the LORD spoke to Moses in the Wilderness of Sinai, in the first month of the second year after they had come out of the land of Egypt, saying: [2]"Let the children of Israel keep the Passover at its appointed time. [3]On the fourteenth day of this month, at twilight, you shall keep it at its appointed time. According to all its rites and ceremonies you shall keep it." [4]So Moses told the children of Israel that they should keep the Passover. [5]And they kept the Passover on the fourteenth day of the first month, at twilight, in the Wilderness of Sinai; according to all that the LORD commanded Moses, so the children of Israel did.

[6]Now there were *certain* men who were defiled by a human corpse, so that they could not keep the Passover on that day; and they came before Moses and Aaron that day. [7]And those men said to him, "We *became* defiled by a human corpse. Why are we kept from presenting the offering of the LORD at its appointed time among the children of Israel?"

[8]And Moses said to them, "Stand still, that I may hear what the LORD will command concerning you."

[9]Then the LORD spoke to Moses, saying, [10]"Speak to the children of Israel, saying: 'If anyone of you or your posterity is unclean because of a corpse, or *is* far away on a journey, he may still keep the LORD's Passover. [11]On the fourteenth day of the second month, at twilight, they may keep it. They shall eat it with unleavened bread and bitter herbs. [12]They shall leave none of it until morning, nor break one of its bones. According to all the ordinances of the Passover they shall keep it. [13]But the man who *is* clean and is not on a journey, and ceases to keep the Passover, that same person shall be cut off from among his people, because he did not bring the offering of the LORD at its appointed time; that man shall bear his sin.

EVERYONE

9:14 Sometimes we are tempted to excuse non-Christians from following God's guidelines for living. Christmas and Easter, for example, often have other meanings for them. We would not expect them to understand Lent. Yet foreigners at this time were expected to follow the same laws and ordinances as the Israelites. God did not have a separate set of standards for unbelievers, and he still does not today. The phrase "You shall have one ordinance" emphasizes that non-Israelites were subject to God's commands and promises. God singled out Israel for a special purpose—to be an example of how one nation could, and should, follow him. His aim, however, was to have all people obey and worship him.

[14]"And if a stranger dwells among you, and would keep the LORD's Passover, he must do so according to the rite of the Passover and according to its ceremony; you shall have one ordinance, both for the stranger and the native of the land.' "

[15]Now on the day that the tabernacle was raised up, the cloud covered the tabernacle, the tent of the Testimony; from evening until morning it was above the tabernacle like the appearance of fire. [16]So it was always: the cloud covered it *by day*, and the appearance of fire by night. [17]Whenever the cloud was taken up from above the tabernacle, after that the children of Israel would journey; and in the place where the cloud settled, there the children of Israel would pitch their tents. [18]At the command of the LORD the children of Israel would journey, and at the command of the LORD they would camp; as long as the cloud stayed above the tabernacle they remained encamped. [19]Even when the cloud continued long, many days above the tabernacle, the children of Israel kept the charge of the LORD and did not journey. [20]So it was, when the cloud was above the tabernacle a few days: according to the command of the LORD they would remain encamped, and according to the command of the LORD they would journey. [21]So it was, when the cloud remained only from evening until morning, when the cloud was taken up in the morning, then they would journey; whether by day or by night, whenever the cloud was taken up, they would journey. [22]Whether it was

two days, a month, or a year that the cloud remained above the tabernacle, the children of Israel would remain encamped and not journey; but when it was taken up, they would journey. ²³At the command of the LORD they remained encamped, and at the command of the LORD they journeyed; they kept the charge of the LORD, at the command of the LORD by the hand of Moses.

CHAPTER **10** THE SILVER TRUMPETS. And the LORD spoke to Moses, saying: ²"Make two silver trumpets for yourself; you shall make them of hammered work; you shall use them for calling the congregation and for directing the movement of the camps. ³When they blow both of them, all the congregation shall gather before you at the door of the tabernacle of meeting. ⁴But if they blow only one, then the leaders, the heads of the divisions of Israel, shall gather to you. ⁵When you sound the advance, the camps that lie on the east side shall then begin their journey. ⁶When you sound the advance the second time, then the camps that lie on the south side shall begin their journey; they shall sound the call for them to begin their journeys. ⁷And when the assembly is to be gathered together, you shall blow, but not sound the advance. ⁸The sons of Aaron, the priests, shall blow the trumpets; and these shall be to you as an ordinance forever throughout your generations.

⁹"When you go to war in your land against the enemy who oppresses you, then you shall sound an alarm with the trumpets, and you will be remembered before the LORD your God, and you will be saved from your enemies. ¹⁰Also in the day of your gladness, in your appointed feasts, and at the beginning of your months, you shall blow the trumpets over your burnt offerings and over the sacrifices of your peace offerings; and they shall be a memorial for you before your God: I am the LORD your God."

¹¹Now it came to pass on the twentieth day of the second month, in the second year, that the cloud was taken up from above the tabernacle of the Testimony. ¹²And the children of Israel set out from the Wilderness of Sinai on their journeys; then the cloud settled down in the Wilderness of Paran. ¹³So they started out for the first time according to the command of the LORD by the hand of Moses.

¹⁴The standard of the camp of the children of Judah set out first according to their armies; over their army was Nahshon the son of Amminadab. ¹⁵Over the army of the tribe of the children of Issachar was Nethanel the son of Zuar. ¹⁶And over the army of the tribe of the children of Zebulun was Eliab the son of Helon.

¹⁷Then the tabernacle was taken down; and the sons of Gershon and the sons of Merari set out, carrying the tabernacle.

¹⁸And the standard of the camp of Reuben set out according to their armies; over their army was Elizur the son of Shedeur. ¹⁹Over the army of the tribe of the children of Simeon was Shelumiel the son of Zurishaddai. ²⁰And over the army of the tribe of the children of Gad was Eliasaph the son of Deuel.

²¹Then the Kohathites set out, carrying the holy things. (The tabernacle would be prepared for their arrival.)

²²And the standard of the camp of the children of

Ephraim set out according to their armies; over their army was Elishama the son of Ammihud. ²³Over the army of the tribe of the children of Manasseh was Gamaliel the son of Pedahzur. ²⁴And over the army of the tribe of the children of Benjamin was Abidan the son of Gideoni.

²⁵Then the standard of the camp of the children of Dan (the rear guard of all the camps) set out according to their armies; over their army was Ahiezer the son of Ammishaddai. ²⁶Over the army of the tribe of the children of Asher was Pagiel the son of Ocran. ²⁷And over the army of the tribe of the children of Naphtali was Ahira the son of Enan.

²⁸Thus was the order of march of the children of Israel, according to their armies, when they began their journey.

WHERE YOU ARE

9:23 The Hebrews traveled and camped as God guided. When you follow God's guidance, you know you are where God wants you whether you're moving or staying in one place. You are physically somewhere right now. Instead of praying, "God, what do you want me to do next?" ask, "God, what do you want me to do while I'm right here?" Direction from God is not just for your next big move. He has a purpose in placing you where you are right now. Begin to understand God's purpose for your life by discovering what he wants you to do now!

²⁹Now Moses said to Hobab the son of Reuel the Midianite, Moses' father-in-law, "We are setting out for the place of which the LORD said, 'I will give it to you.' Come with us, and we will treat you well; for the LORD has promised good things to Israel."

³⁰And he said to him, "I will not go, but I will depart to my own land and to my relatives."

³¹So Moses said, "Please do not leave, inasmuch as you know how we are to camp in the wilderness, and you can be our eyes. ³²And it shall be, if you go with us—indeed it shall be—that whatever good the LORD will do to us, the same we will do to you."

³³So they departed from the mountain of the LORD on a journey of three days; and the ark of the covenant of the LORD went before them for the three days' journey, to search out a resting place for them. ³⁴And the cloud of the LORD was above them by day when they went out from the camp.

³⁵So it was, whenever the ark set out, that Moses said:

"Rise up, O LORD!
Let Your enemies be scattered,
And let those who hate You flee before You."

³⁶And when it rested, he said:

"Return, O LORD,
To the many thousands of Israel."

COMPLIMENTS

10:29-32 By complimenting Hobab's wilderness skills, Moses let him know he was needed. People cannot know you appreciate them if you do not tell them they are important to you. Complimenting those who deserve it builds lasting relationships and helps people know they are valued. Think about those who have helped you this month. What can you do to let them know how much you need and appreciate them?

CHAPTER 11 SOMEONE TO HELP MOSES. Now *when*

the people complained, it displeased the LORD; for the LORD heard *it*, and His anger was aroused. So the fire of the LORD burned among them, and consumed *some* in the outskirts of the camp. ²Then the people cried out to Moses, and when Moses prayed to the LORD, the fire was quenched. ³So he called the name of the place Taberah, because the fire of the LORD had burned among them.

⁴Now the mixed multitude who were among them yielded to intense craving; so the children of Israel also wept again and said: "Who will give us meat to eat? ⁵We remember the fish which we ate freely in Egypt, the cucumbers, the melons, the leeks, the onions, and the garlic; ⁶but now our whole being *is* dried up; *there is* nothing at all except this manna *before* our eyes!"

GRATITUDE

11:4-6 Dissatisfaction comes when our attention shifts from what we have to what we don't have. The people of Israel didn't seem to notice what God was doing for them—setting them free, making them a nation, giving them a new land—because they were so wrapped up in what God wasn't doing for them. They could think of nothing but the delicious Egyptian food they had left behind. Somehow they forgot that the brutal whip of Egyptian slavery was the cost of eating that food. Before we judge the Israelites too harshly, it's helpful to think about what occupies our attention most of the time. Are we grateful for what God has given us, or are we always thinking about what we would like to have? We should not allow our unfulfilled desires to cause us to forget God's gifts of life, food, health, work, and friends.

⁷Now the manna *was* like coriander seed, and its color like the color of bdellium. ⁸The people went about and gathered *it*, ground *it* on millstones or beat *it* in the mortar, cooked *it* in pans, and made cakes of it; and its taste was like the taste of pastry prepared with oil. ⁹And when the dew fell on the camp in the night, the manna fell on it.

¹⁰Then Moses heard the people weeping throughout their families, everyone at the door of his tent; and the anger of the LORD was greatly aroused; Moses also was displeased. ¹¹So Moses said to the LORD, "Why have You afflicted Your servant? And why have I not found favor in Your sight, that You have laid the burden of all these people on me? ¹²Did I conceive all these people? Did I beget them, that You should say to me, 'Carry them in your bosom, as a guardian carries a nursing child,' to the land which You swore to their fathers? ¹³Where am I to get meat to give to all these people? For they weep all over me, saying, 'Give us meat, that we may eat.' ¹⁴I am not able to bear all these people alone, because the burden *is* too heavy for me. ¹⁵If You treat me like this, please kill me here and now—if I have found favor in Your sight—and do not let me see my wretchedness!"

¹⁶So the LORD said to Moses: "Gather to Me seventy men of the elders of Israel, whom you know to be the elders of the people and officers over them; bring them to the tabernacle of meeting, that they may stand there with you. ¹⁷Then I will come down and talk with you there. I will take of the Spirit that *is* upon you and will put *the same* upon them; and they shall bear the burden of

the people with you, that you may not bear *it* yourself alone. ¹⁸Then you shall say to the people, 'Consecrate yourselves for tomorrow, and you shall eat meat; for you have wept in the hearing of the LORD, saying, "Who will give us meat to eat? For *it was* well with us in Egypt." Therefore the LORD will give you meat, and you shall eat. ¹⁹You shall eat, not one day, nor two days, nor five days nor ten days, nor twenty days, ²⁰but *for* a whole month until it comes out of your nostrils and becomes loathsome to you, because you have despised the LORD who is among you, and have wept before Him, saying, "Why did we ever come up out of Egypt?" ' "

²¹And Moses said, "The people whom I *am* among *are* six hundred thousand men on foot; yet You have said, ' will give them meat, that they may eat *for* a whole month.' ²²Shall flocks and herds be slaughtered for them to provide enough for them? Or shall all the fish of the sea be gathered together for them, to provide enough for them?"

²³And the LORD said to Moses, "Has the LORD's arm been shortened? Now you shall see whether what I say will happen to you or not."

²⁴So Moses went out and told the people the words of the LORD, and he gathered the seventy men of the elders of the people and placed them around the tabernacle. ²⁵Then the LORD came down in the cloud, and spoke to him, and took of the Spirit that *was* upon him, and placed *the same* upon the seventy elders; and it happened, when the Spirit rested upon them, that they prophesied, although they never did *so* again.

²⁶But two men had remained in the camp: the name of one *was* Eldad, and the name of the other Medad. And the Spirit rested upon them. Now they *were* among those listed, but who had not gone out to the tabernacle; yet they prophesied in the camp. ²⁷And a young man ran and told Moses, and said, "Eldad and Medad are prophesying in the camp."

²⁸So Joshua the son of Nun, Moses' assistant, *one* of his choice men, answered and said, "Moses my lord, forbid them!"

²⁹Then Moses said to him, "Are you zealous for my sake? Oh, that all the LORD's people were prophets *and* that the LORD would put His Spirit upon them!" ³⁰And Moses returned to the camp, he and the elders of Israel.

³¹Now a wind went out from the LORD, and it brought quail from the sea and left *them* fluttering near the camp, about a day's journey on this side and about a day's journey on the other side, all around the camp, and about two cubits above the surface of the ground. ³²And the people stayed up all that day, all night, and all the next day, and gathered the quail (he who gathered least gathered ten homers); and they spread *them* out for themselves all around the camp. ³³But while the meat *was* still between their teeth, before it was chewed, the wrath of the LORD was aroused against the people, and the LORD struck the people with a very great plague. ³⁴So he called the name of that place Kibroth Hattaavah, because there they buried the people who had yielded to craving.

³⁵From Kibroth Hattaavah the people moved to Hazeroth, and camped at Hazeroth.

ISRAEL'S COMPLAINING

Complaint	Sin	Result
11:1 About their misfortunes	Complained about their problems instead of praying to God	Thousands of people were destroyed when God sent a plague of fire to punish them
11:4 About the lack of meat	Lusted after things they didn't have	God sent quail; but as the people began to eat, God struck them with a plague that killed many
14:1-4 About being stuck in the wilderness, facing the giants of the Promised Land, and wishing to return to Egypt	Openly rebelled against God's leaders and failed to trust in his promises	All who complained were not allowed to enter the Promised Land, being doomed to wander in the wilderness until they died
16:3 About Moses' and Aaron's authority and leadership	Were greedy for more power and authority	The families, friends, and possessions of Korah, Dathan, and Abiram were swallowed up by the earth. Fire then burned up the 250 other men who rebelled
16:41 That Moses and Aaron caused the deaths of Korah and his conspirators	Blamed others for their own troubles	God began to destroy Israel with a plague. Moses and Aaron made atonement for the people, but 14,700 of them were killed
20:2-3 About the lack of water	Refused to believe that God would provide as he had promised	Moses sinned along with the people. For this he was barred from entering the Promised Land
21:5 That God and Moses brought them into the wilderness	Failed to recognize that their problems were brought on by their own disobedience	God sent poisonous serpents that killed many people and seriously injured many others

CHAPTER 12 MIRIAM GETS LEPROSY. Then Miriam and Aaron spoke against Moses because of the Ethiopian woman whom he had married; for he had married an Ethiopian woman. ²So they said, "Has the LORD indeed spoken only through Moses? Has He not spoken through us also?" And the LORD heard *it*. ³(Now the man Moses *was* very humble, more than all men who *were* on the face of the earth.)

⁴Suddenly the LORD said to Moses, Aaron, and Miriam, "Come out, you three, to the tabernacle of meeting!" So the three came out. ⁵Then the LORD came down in the pillar of cloud and stood *in* the door of the tabernacle, and called Aaron and Miriam. And they both went forward. ⁶Then He said,

"Hear now My words:
If there is a prophet among you,
I, the LORD, make Myself known to him in a vision;
I speak to him in a dream.
Not so with My servant Moses;
He *is* faithful in all My house.
I speak with him face to face,
Even plainly, and not in dark sayings;
And he sees the form of the LORD.
Why then were you not afraid
To speak against My servant Moses?"

⁹So the anger of the LORD was aroused against them, and He departed. ¹⁰And when the cloud departed from above the tabernacle, suddenly Miriam *became* leprous, as *white as* snow. Then Aaron turned toward Miriam, and there she was, a leper. ¹¹So Aaron said to Moses, "Oh, my lord! Please do not lay *this* sin on us, in which we have done foolishly and in which we have sinned. ¹²Please do not let her be as one dead, whose flesh is half consumed when he comes out of his mother's womb!"

¹³So Moses cried out to the LORD, saying, "Please heal her, O God, I pray!"

¹⁴Then the LORD said to Moses, "If her father had but spit in her face, would she not be shamed seven days? Let her be shut out of the camp seven days, and afterward she may be received *again*." ¹⁵So Miriam was shut out of the camp seven days, and the people did not journey till Miriam was brought in *again*. ¹⁶And afterward the people moved from Hazeroth and camped in the Wilderness of Paran.

CHAPTER **13** **THE TWELVE SPIES.** And the LORD spoke to Moses, saying, ²"Send men to spy out the land of Canaan, which I am giving to the children of Israel; from each tribe of their fathers you shall send a man, every one a leader among them."

³So Moses sent them from the Wilderness of Paran according to the command of the LORD, all of them men who *were* heads of the children of Israel. ⁴Now these *were* their names: from the tribe of Reuben, Shammua the son of Zaccur; ⁵from the tribe of Simeon, Shaphat the son of Hori; ⁶from the tribe of Judah, Caleb the son of Jephunneh; ⁷from the tribe of Issachar, Igal the son of Joseph; ⁸from the tribe of Ephraim, Hoshea the son of Nun; ⁹from the tribe of Benjamin, Palti the son of Raphu; ¹⁰from the tribe of Zebulun, Gaddiel the son of Sodi; ¹¹from the tribe of Joseph, *that is,* from the tribe of Manasseh, Gaddi the son of Susi; ¹²from the tribe of Dan, Ammiel the son of Gemalli; ¹³from the tribe of Asher, Sethur the son of Michael; ¹⁴from the tribe of Naphtali, Nahbi the son of Vophsi; ¹⁵from the tribe of Gad, Geuel the son of Machi. ¹⁶These *are* the names of the men whom Moses sent to spy out the land. And Moses called Hoshea the son of Nun, Joshua.

¹⁷Then Moses sent them to spy out the land of Canaan, and said to them, "Go up this *way* into the South, and go up to the mountains, ¹⁸and see what the land is like: whether the people who dwell in it *are* strong or weak, few or many; ¹⁹whether the land they dwell in *is* good or bad; whether the cities they inhabit *are* like camps or strongholds; ²⁰whether the land *is* rich or poor; and whether there are forests there or not. Be of good courage. And bring some of the fruit of the land." Now the time *was* the season of the first ripe grapes.

²¹So they went up and spied out the land from the Wilderness of Zin as far as Rehob, near the entrance of Hamath. ²²And they went up through the South and came to Hebron; Ahiman, Sheshai, and Talmai, the descendants of Anak, *were* there. (Now Hebron was built seven years before Zoan in Egypt.) ²³Then they came to the Valley of Eshcol, and there cut down a branch with one cluster of grapes; they carried it between two of them on a pole. *They* also *brought* some of the pomegranates and figs. ²⁴The place was called the Valley of Eshcol, because of the cluster which the men of Israel cut down there. ²⁵And they returned from spying out the land after forty days.

²⁶Now they departed and came back to Moses and Aaron and all the congregation of the children of Israel in the Wilderness of Paran, at Kadesh; they brought back word to them and to all the congregation, and showed them the fruit of the land. ²⁷Then they told him, and said: "We went to the land where you sent us. It truly flows

with milk and honey, and this *is* its fruit. ²⁸Nevertheles the people who dwell in the land *are* strong; the cities ar fortified *and* very large; moreover we saw the descen dants of Anak there. ²⁹The Amalekites dwell in the land o the South; the Hittites, the Jebusites, and the Amorite dwell in the mountains; and the Canaanites dwell by th sea and along the banks of the Jordan."

³⁰Then Caleb quieted the people before Moses, an said, "Let us go up at once and take possession, for we ar well able to overcome it."

³¹But the men who had gone up with him said, "We ar not able to go up against the people, for they *are* stronge than we." ³²And they gave the children of Israel a ba report of the land which they had spied out, saying, "Th land through which we have gone as spies *is* a land tha devours its inhabitants, and all the people whom we saw in it *are* men of *great* stature. ³³There we saw the giant (the descendants of Anak came from the giants); and w were like grasshoppers in our own sight, and so we wer in their sight."

CHAPTER **14** **FORTY YEARS IN THE WILDERNESS**
So all the congregation lifted up their voices and cried and the people wept that night. ²And all the children Israel complained against Moses and Aaron, and th whole congregation said to them, "If only we had died i the land of Egypt! Or if only we had died in this wilder ness! ³Why has the LORD brought us to this land to fall b the sword, that our wives and children should becom

THE LORD
delights in
US US US US US US US US US US US US US US US US US US US US US US US US US US US US US

HE
will
bring us
into
this land
and give it
to us.

ictims? Would it not be better for us to return to Egypt?" So they said to one another, "Let us select a leader and return to Egypt."

⁵Then Moses and Aaron fell on their faces before all the assembly of the congregation of the children of Israel. ⁶But Joshua the son of Nun and Caleb the son of Jephunneh, *who were* among those who had spied out the land, tore their clothes; ⁷and they spoke to all the congregation of the children of Israel, saying: "The land we passed through to spy out *is* an exceedingly good land. ⁸If the LORD delights in us, then He will bring us into this land and give it to us, 'a land which flows with milk and honey.' ⁹Only do not rebel against the LORD, nor fear the people of the land, for they *are* our bread; their protection has departed from them, and the LORD *is* with us. Do not fear them."

¹⁰And all the congregation said to stone them with stones. Now the glory of the LORD appeared in the tabernacle of meeting before all the children of Israel.

¹¹Then the LORD said to Moses: "How long will these people reject Me? And how long will they not believe Me, with all the signs which I have performed among them? ¹²I will strike them with the pestilence and disinherit them, and I will make of you a nation greater and mightier than they."

¹³And Moses said to the LORD: "Then the Egyptians will hear *it*, for by Your might You brought these people up from among them, ¹⁴and they will tell *it* to the inhabitants of this land. They have heard that You, LORD, *are* among these people; that You, LORD, are seen face to face and Your cloud stands above them, and You go before them in a pillar of cloud by day and in a pillar of fire by night. ¹⁵Now *if* You kill these people as one man, then the nations which have heard of Your fame will speak, saying, ¹⁶'Because the LORD was not able to bring this people to the land which He swore to give them, therefore He killed them in the wilderness.' ¹⁷And now, I pray, let the power of my Lord be great, just as You have spoken, saying, ¹⁸'The LORD is longsuffering and abundant in mercy, forgiving iniquity and transgression; but He by no means clears *the guilty*, visiting the iniquity of the fathers on the children to the third and fourth *generation*.' ¹⁹Pardon the iniquity of this people, I pray, according to the greatness of Your mercy, just as You have forgiven this people, from Egypt even until now."

²⁰Then the LORD said: "I have pardoned, according to your word; ²¹but truly, as I live, all the earth shall be filled with the glory of the LORD— ²²because all these men who have seen My glory and the signs which I did in Egypt and in the wilderness, and have put Me to the test now these ten times, and have not heeded My voice, ²³they certainly shall not see the land of which I swore to their fathers, nor shall any of those who rejected Me see it. ²⁴But My servant Caleb, because he has a different spirit in him and has followed Me fully, I will bring into the land where he went, and his descendants shall inherit it. ²⁵Now the Amalekites and the Canaanites dwell in the valley; tomorrow turn and move out into the wilderness by the Way of the Red Sea."

²⁶And the LORD spoke to Moses and Aaron, saying, ²⁷"How long *shall I bear with* this evil congregation who complain against Me? I have heard the complaints which the children of Israel make against Me. ²⁸Say to them, 'As I live,' says the LORD, 'just as you have spoken in My hearing, so I will do to you: ²⁹The carcasses of you who have complained against Me shall fall in this wilderness, all of you who were numbered, according to your entire number, from twenty years old and above. ³⁰Except for Caleb the son of Jephunneh and Joshua the son of Nun, you shall by no means enter the land which I swore I

◣ADVICE

14:6-10 Two wise men, Joshua and Caleb, encouraged the people to act on God's promise. The people rejected their advice and even talked of killing them. Don't be too quick to reject advice you don't like. Evaluate it carefully; weigh it against God's Word. What you are hearing may be God's message.

would make you dwell in. ³¹But your little ones, whom you said would be victims, I will bring in, and they shall know the land which you have despised. ³²But *as for* you, your carcasses shall fall in this wilderness. ³³And your sons shall be shepherds in the wilderness forty years, and bear the brunt of your infidelity, until your carcasses are consumed in the wilderness. ³⁴According to the number of the days in which you spied out the land, forty days, for each day you shall bear your guilt one year, *namely* forty years, and you shall know My rejection. ³⁵I the LORD have spoken this. I will surely do so to all this evil congregation who are gathered together against Me. In this wilderness they shall be consumed, and there they shall die.' "

³⁶Now the men whom Moses sent to spy out the land, who returned and made all the congregation complain against him by bringing a bad report of the land, ³⁷those very men who brought the evil report about the land, died by the plague before the LORD. ³⁸But Joshua the son of Nun and Caleb the son of Jephunneh remained alive, of the men who went to spy out the land.

³⁹Then Moses told these words to all the children of Israel, and the people mourned greatly. ⁴⁰And they rose early in the morning and went up to the top of the mountain, saying, "Here we are, and we will go up to the place which the LORD has promised, for we have sinned!"

⁴¹And Moses said, "Now why do you transgress the command of the LORD? For this will not succeed. ⁴²Do not go up, lest you be defeated by your enemies, for the LORD *is* not among you. ⁴³For the Amalekites and the Canaanites *are* there before you, and you shall fall by the sword; because you have turned away from the LORD, the LORD will not be with you."

⁴⁴But they presumed to go up to the mountaintop. Nevertheless, neither the ark of the covenant of the LORD nor Moses departed from the camp. ⁴⁵Then the Amalekites and the Canaanites who dwelt in that mountain came down and attacked them, and drove them back as far as Hormah.

CHAPTER **15** MORE RULES ABOUT OFFERINGS.

And the LORD spoke to Moses, saying, ²"Speak to the children of Israel, and say to them: 'When you have come into the land you are to inhabit, which I am giving to you,

³and you make an offering by fire to the LORD, a burnt offering or a sacrifice, to fulfill a vow or as a freewill offering or in your appointed feasts, to make a sweet aroma to the LORD, from the herd or the flock, ⁴then he who presents his offering to the LORD shall bring a grain offering of one-tenth *of an ephah* of fine flour mixed with one-fourth of a hin of oil; ⁵and one-fourth of a hin of wine as a drink offering you shall prepare with the burnt offering or the sacrifice, for each lamb. ⁶Or for a ram you shall prepare as a grain offering two-tenths *of an ephah* of fine flour mixed with one-third of a hin of oil; ⁷and as a drink offering you shall offer one-third of a hin of wine as a sweet aroma to the LORD. ⁸And when you prepare a young bull as a burnt offering, or as a sacrifice to fulfill a vow, or as a peace offering to the LORD, ⁹then shall be offered with the young bull a grain offering of three-tenths *of an ephah* of fine flour mixed with half a hin of oil; ¹⁰and you shall bring as the drink offering half a hin of wine as an offering made by fire, a sweet aroma to the LORD.

¹¹Thus it shall be done for each young bull, for each ram, or for each lamb or young goat. ¹²According to the number that you prepare, so you shall do with everyone according to their number. ¹³All who are native-born shall do these things in this manner, in presenting an offering made by fire, a sweet aroma to the LORD. ¹⁴And if a stranger dwells with you, or whoever *is* among you throughout your generations, and would present an offering made by fire, a sweet aroma to the LORD, just as you do, so shall he do. ¹⁵One ordinance *shall be* for you of the assembly and for the stranger who dwells *with you*, an ordinance forever throughout your generations; as you are, so shall the stranger be before the LORD. ¹⁶One law and one custom shall be for you and for the stranger who dwells with you.' "

¹⁷Again the LORD spoke to Moses, saying, ¹⁸"Speak to the children of Israel, and say to them: 'When you come into the land to which I bring you, ¹⁹then it will be, when you eat of the bread of the land, that you shall offer up a heave offering to the LORD. ²⁰You shall offer up a cake of the first of your ground meal *as* a heave offering; as a heave offering of the threshing floor, so shall you offer it up. ²¹Of the first of your ground meal you shall give to the LORD a heave offering throughout your generations.

²²'If you sin unintentionally, and do not observe all these commandments which the LORD has spoken to Moses— ²³all that the LORD has commanded you by the hand of Moses, from the day the LORD gave commandment and onward throughout your generations— ²⁴then it will be, if it is unintentionally committed, without the knowledge of the congregation, that the whole congregation shall offer one young bull as a burnt offering, as a sweet aroma to the LORD, with its grain offering and its drink offering, according to the ordinance, and one kid of the goats as a sin offering. ²⁵So the priest shall make atonement for the whole congregation of the children of Israel, and it shall be forgiven them, for it was unintentional; they shall bring their offering, an offering made by fire to the LORD, and their sin offering before the LORD, for their unintended sin. ²⁶It shall be forgiven the whole congregation of the children of Israel and the stranger who dwells among them, because all the people *did it* unintentionally.

²⁷'And if a person sins unintentionally, then he shall bring a female goat in its first year as a sin offering. ²⁸So the priest shall make atonement for the person who sins unintentionally, when he sins unintentionally before the LORD, to make atonement for him; and it shall be forgiven him. ²⁹You shall have one law for him who sins unintentionally, *for* him who is native-born among the children of Israel and for the stranger who dwells among them.

³⁰'But the person who does *anything* presumptuously, *whether he is* native-born or a stranger, that one brings reproach on the LORD, and he shall be cut off from among his people. ³¹Because he has despised the word of the LORD, and has broken His commandment, that person shall be completely cut off; his guilt *shall be* upon him.' "

³²Now while the children of Israel were in the wilderness, they found a man gathering sticks on the Sabbath day. ³³And those who found him gathering sticks brought him to Moses and Aaron, and to all the congregation. ³⁴They put him under guard, because it had not been explained what should be done to him.

³⁵Then the LORD said to Moses, "The man must surely be put to death; all the congregation shall stone him with stones outside the camp." ³⁶So, as the LORD commanded Moses, all the congregation brought him outside the camp and stoned him with stones, and he died.

GET FOCUSED

15:39 Idol worship is self-centered, focusing on what a person d from serving an idol. Good luck, prosperity, long life, and success battle were expected from the gods. So were power and prestige. worship of the true God is a striking contrast: believers are to be s rather than self-centered. Instead of expecting God to serve us, w serve him, expecting nothing in return. We serve God for who he for what we get out of him.

³⁷Again the LORD spoke to Moses, saying, ³⁸"Speak to the children of Israel: Tell them to make tassels on the corners of their garments throughout their generations, and to put a blue thread in the tassels of the corners ³⁹And you shall have the tassel, that you may look upon it and remember all the commandments of the LORD and do them, and that you *may* not follow the harlotry to which your own heart and your own eyes are inclined, ⁴⁰and that you may remember and do all My commandments, and be holy for your God. ⁴¹I *am* the LORD your God, who brought you out of the land of Egypt, to be your God: I *am* the LORD your God."

CHAPTER 16 KORAH REBELS.

Now Korah the son of Izhar, the son of Kohath, the son of Levi, with Dathan and Abiram the sons of Eliab, and On the son of Peleth sons of Reuben, took *men*; ²and they rose up before Moses with some of the children of Israel, two hundred and fifty leaders of the congregation, representatives of the congregation, men of renown. ³They gathered together against Moses and Aaron, and said to them, "*You take* too much upon yourselves, for all the congregation *is* holy every one of them, and the LORD *is* among them. Why then do you exalt yourselves above the assembly of the LORD?"

[4]So when Moses heard *it,* he fell on his face; [5]and he spoke to Korah and all his company, saying, "Tomorrow morning the LORD will show who *is* His and *who is* holy, and will cause *him* to come near to Him. That one whom He chooses He will cause to come near to Him. [6]Do this: Take censers, Korah and all your company; [7]put fire in them and put incense in them before the LORD tomorrow, and it shall be *that* the man whom the LORD chooses *is* the holy one. *You take* too much upon yourselves, you sons of Levi!"

[8]Then Moses said to Korah, "Hear now, you sons of Levi: [9]*Is it* a small thing to you that the God of Israel has separated you from the congregation of Israel, to bring you near to Himself, to do the work of the tabernacle of the LORD, and to stand before the congregation to serve them; [10]and that He has brought you near *to Himself,* you and all your brethren, the sons of Levi, with you? And are you seeking the priesthood also? [11]Therefore you and all your company *are* gathered together against the LORD. And what *is* Aaron that you complain against him?"

[12]And Moses sent to call Dathan and Abiram the sons of Eliab, but they said, "We will not come up! [13]*Is it* a small thing that you have brought us up out of a land flowing with milk and honey, to kill us in the wilderness, that you should keep acting like a prince over us? [14]Moreover you have not brought us into a land flowing with milk and honey, nor given us inheritance of fields and vineyards. Will you put out the eyes of these men? We will not come up!"

[15]Then Moses was very angry, and said to the LORD, "Do not respect their offering. I have not taken one donkey from them, nor have I hurt one of them."

[16]And Moses said to Korah, "Tomorrow, you and all your company be present before the LORD—you and they, as well as Aaron. [17]Let each take his censer and put incense in it, and each of you bring his censer before the LORD, two hundred and fifty censers; both you and Aaron, each *with* his censer." [18]So every man took his censer, put fire in it, laid incense on it, and stood at the door of the tabernacle of meeting with Moses and Aaron. [19]And Korah gathered all the congregation against them at the door of the tabernacle of meeting. Then the glory of the LORD appeared to all the congregation.

[20]And the LORD spoke to Moses and Aaron, saying, [21]"Separate yourselves from among this congregation, that I may consume them in a moment."

[22]Then they fell on their faces, and said, "O God, the God of the spirits of all flesh, shall one man sin, and You be angry with all the congregation?"

[23]So the LORD spoke to Moses, saying, [24]"Speak to the congregation, saying, 'Get away from the tents of Korah, Dathan, and Abiram.' "

[25]Then Moses rose and went to Dathan and Abiram, and the elders of Israel followed him. [26]And he spoke to the congregation, saying, "Depart now from the tents of these wicked men! Touch nothing of theirs, lest you be consumed in all their sins." [27]So they got away from around the tents of Korah, Dathan, and Abiram; and

Dathan and Abiram came out and stood at the door of their tents, with their wives, their sons, and their little children.

[28]And Moses said: "By this you shall know that the LORD has sent me to do all these works, for *I have* not *done them* of my own will. [29]If these men die naturally like all men, or if they are visited by the common fate of all men, *then* the LORD has not sent me. [30]But if the LORD creates a new thing, and the earth opens its mouth and swallows them up with all that belongs to them, and they go down alive into the pit, then you will understand that these men have rejected the LORD."

MOTIVATION

16:8-10 Korah wanted the special qualities God had given others, even though he had his own significant, worthwhile abilities and responsibilities. In the end, his ambition caused him to lose everything. Inappropriate ambition is greed in disguise.

[31]Now it came to pass, as he finished speaking all these words, that the ground split apart under them, [32]and the earth opened its mouth and swallowed them up, with their households and all the men with Korah, with all *their* goods. [33]So they and all those with them went down alive into the pit; the earth closed over them, and they perished from among the assembly. [34]Then all Israel who *were* around them fled at their cry, for they said, "Lest the earth swallow us up *also!*"

[35]And a fire came out from the LORD and consumed the two hundred and fifty men who were offering incense.

[36]Then the LORD spoke to Moses, saying: [37]"Tell Eleazar, the son of Aaron the priest, to pick up the censers out of the blaze, for they are holy, and scatter the fire some distance away. [38]The censers of these men who sinned against their own souls, let them be made into hammered plates as a covering for the altar. Because they presented them before the LORD, therefore they are holy; and they shall be a sign to the children of Israel." [39]So Eleazar the priest took the bronze censers, which those who were burned up had presented, and they were hammered out as a covering on the altar, [40]to be a memorial to the children of Israel that no outsider, who *is* not a descendant of Aaron, should come near to offer incense before the LORD, that he might not become like Korah and his companions, just as the LORD had said to him through Moses.

[41]On the next day all the congregation of the children of Israel complained against Moses and Aaron, saying, "You have killed the people of the LORD." [42]Now it happened, when the congregation had gathered against Moses and Aaron, that they turned toward the tabernacle of meeting; and suddenly the cloud covered it, and the

REVENGE

16:22-27 Moses and Aaron prayed for those with whom they were most angry and frustrated. Do you pray for those who hurt you? Or do you seek revenge? Only those who have a deep relationship with God can understand that he will settle the score with those who rebel. It is not our job to seek revenge against those who wrong us. God will make certain that, in the end, justice is done.

17:5,10 After witnessing spectacular miracles, seeing the Egyptians punished by the plagues, and experiencing the actual presence of God, the Israelites still complained and rebelled. We wonder how they could be so blind and ignorant, and yet we often repeat this same pattern. We have centuries of evidence, the Bible in many translations, and the convincing results of archaeological and historical studies to show us God is who he says he is. But people today continue to disobey God and go their own way. We can escape this pattern only by paying attention to all the signs of God's presence that we have been given. Has God guided and protected you? Has he answered your prayers? Do you know Bible stories about the way God has led his people? Focus your thoughts on these things, and rebellion will become unthinkable.

glory of the LORD appeared. 43Then Moses and Aaron came before the tabernacle of meeting.

44And the LORD spoke to Moses, saying, 45"Get away from among this congregation, that I may consume them in a moment."

And they fell on their faces.

46So Moses said to Aaron, "Take a censer and put fire in it from the altar, put incense *on it,* and take it quickly to the congregation and make atonement for them; for wrath has gone out from the LORD. The plague has begun." 47Then Aaron took *it* as Moses commanded, and ran into the midst of the assembly; and already the plague had begun among the people. So he put in the incense and made atonement for the people. 48And he stood between the dead and the living; so the plague was stopped. 49Now those who died in the plague were fourteen thousand seven hundred, besides those who died in the Korah incident. 50So Aaron returned to Moses at the door of the tabernacle of meeting, for the plague had stopped.

CHAPTER 17 A ROD LIKE A FRUIT TREE.

And the LORD spoke to Moses, saying: 2"Speak to the children of Israel, and get from them a rod from each father's house, all their leaders according to their fathers' houses—twelve rods. Write each man's name on his rod. 3And you shall write Aaron's name on the rod of Levi. For there shall be one rod for the head of *each* father's house. 4Then you shall place them in the tabernacle of meeting before the Testimony, where I meet with you. 5And it shall be *that* the rod of the man whom I choose will blossom; thus I will rid Myself of the complaints of the children of Israel, which they make against you."

6So Moses spoke to the children of Israel, and each of their leaders gave him a rod apiece, for each leader according to their fathers' houses, twelve rods; and the rod of Aaron *was* among their rods. 7And Moses placed the rods before the LORD in the tabernacle of witness.

8Now it came to pass on the next day that Moses went into the tabernacle of witness, and behold, the rod of Aaron, of the house of Levi, had sprouted and put forth buds, had produced blossoms and yielded ripe almonds. 9Then Moses brought out all the rods from before the LORD to all the children of Israel; and they looked, and each man took his rod.

10And the LORD said to Moses, "Bring Aaron's rod back before the Testimony, to be kept as a sign against the rebels, that you may put their complaints away from Me, lest they die." 11Thus did Moses; just as the LORD had commanded him, so he did.

12So the children of Israel spoke to Moses, saying, "Surely we die, we perish, we all perish! 13Whoever even comes near the tabernacle of the LORD must die. Shall we all utterly die?"

CHAPTER 18 THE PRIESTS' AND LEVITES' DUTIES.

Then the LORD said to Aaron: "You and your sons and your father's house with you shall bear the iniquity *related to* the sanctuary, and you and your sons with you shall bear the iniquity *associated with* your priesthood. 2Also bring with you your brethren of the tribe of Levi, the tribe of your father, that they may be joined with you and serve you while you and your sons *are* with you before the tabernacle of witness. 3They shall attend to your needs and all the needs of the tabernacle; but they shall not come near the articles of the sanctuary and the altar, lest they die—they and you also. 4They shall be joined with you and attend to the needs of the tabernacle of meeting, for all the work of the tabernacle; but an outsider shall not come near you. 5And you shall attend to the duties of the sanctuary and the duties of the altar, that there *may* be no more wrath on the children of Israel. 6Behold, I Myself have taken your brethren the Levites from among the children of Israel; *they are* a gift to you, given by the LORD, to do the work of the tabernacle of meeting. 7Therefore you and your sons with you shall attend to your priesthood for everything at the altar and behind the veil; and you shall serve. I give your priesthood *to you* as a gift for service, but the outsider who comes near shall be put to death."

8And the LORD spoke to Aaron: "Here, I Myself have also given you charge of My heave offerings, all the holy gifts of the children of Israel; I have given them as a portion to you and your sons, as an ordinance forever. 9This shall be yours of the most holy things *reserved* from the fire: every offering of theirs, every grain offering and every sin offering and every trespass offering which they render to Me, *shall be* most holy for you and your sons. 10In a most holy *place* you shall eat it; every male shall eat it. It shall be holy to you.

11"This also *is* yours: the heave offering of their gift, with all the wave offerings of the children of Israel; I have given them to you, and your sons and daughters with you, as an ordinance forever. Everyone who is clean in your house may eat it.

12"All the best of the oil, all the best of the new wine and the grain, their firstfruits which they offer to the LORD, I have given them to you. 13Whatever first ripe fruit is in their land, which they bring to the LORD, shall be yours. Everyone who is clean in your house may eat it.

14"Every devoted thing in Israel shall be yours. 15"Everything that first opens the womb of all flesh, which they bring to the LORD, whether man or beast, shall be yours; nevertheless the firstborn of man you shall surely redeem, and the firstborn of unclean animals you shall redeem. 16And those redeemed of the devoted things you shall redeem when one month old, according to your valuation, for five shekels of silver, according to the shekel of the sanctuary, which *is* twenty gerahs. ¹⁷But the firstborn of a cow, the firstborn of a sheep, or the firstborn of a goat you shall not redeem; they *are* holy. You shall sprinkle their blood on the altar, and burn their fat *as* an offering made by fire for a sweet aroma to the LORD. ¹⁸And their flesh shall be yours, just as the wave breast and the right thigh are yours.

¹⁹"All the heave offerings of the holy things, which the children of Israel offer to the LORD, I have given to you and your sons and daughters with you as an ordinance forever; it *is* a covenant of salt forever before the LORD with you and your descendants with you."

²⁰Then the LORD said to Aaron: "You shall have no inheritance in their land, nor shall you have any portion among them; I *am* your portion and your inheritance among the children of Israel.

²¹"Behold, I have given the children of Levi all the tithes in Israel as an inheritance in return for the work which they perform, the work of the tabernacle of meeting. ²²Hereafter the children of Israel shall not come near the tabernacle of meeting, lest they bear sin and die. ²³But the Levites shall perform the work of the tabernacle of meeting, and they shall bear their iniquity; *it shall be* a statute forever, throughout your generations, that among the children of Israel they shall have no inheritance. ²⁴For the tithes of the children of Israel, which they offer up *as* a heave offering to the LORD, I have given to the Levites as an inheritance; therefore I have said to them, 'Among the children of Israel they shall have no inheritance.' "

²⁵Then the LORD spoke to Moses, saying, ²⁶"Speak thus to the Levites, and say to them: 'When you take from the children of Israel the tithes which I have given you from them as your inheritance, then you shall offer up a heave offering of it to the LORD, a tenth of the tithe. ²⁷And your heave offering shall be reckoned to you as though *it were* the grain of the threshing floor and as the fullness of the winepress. ²⁸Thus you shall also offer a heave offering to the LORD from all your tithes which you receive from the children of Israel, and you shall give the LORD's heave offering from it to Aaron the priest. ²⁹Of all your gifts you shall offer up every heave offering due to the LORD, from all the best of them, the consecrated part of them.' ³⁰Therefore you shall say to them: 'When you have lifted up the best of it, then *the rest* shall be accounted to the Levites as the produce of the threshing floor and as the produce of the winepress. ³¹You may eat it in any place, you and your households, for it *is* your reward for your work in the tabernacle of meeting. ³²And you shall bear no sin because of it, when you have lifted up the best of it. But you shall not profane the holy gifts of the children of Israel, lest you die.' "

CHAPTER **19** **WHAT TO DO WHEN DEFILED.** Now the LORD spoke to Moses and Aaron, saying, ²"This *is* the ordinance of the law which the LORD has commanded, saying: 'Speak to the children of Israel, that they bring you a red heifer without blemish, in which there *is* no defect *and* on which a yoke has never come. ³You shall give it to Eleazar the priest, that he may take it outside the camp, and it shall be slaughtered before him; ⁴and Eleazar the priest shall take some of its blood with his finger, and sprinkle some of its blood seven times directly in front of the tabernacle of meeting. ⁵Then the heifer shall be burned in his sight: its hide, its flesh, its blood, and its offal shall be burned. ⁶And the priest shall take cedar wood and hyssop and scarlet, and cast *them* into the midst of the fire burning the heifer. ⁷Then the priest shall wash his clothes, he shall bathe in water, and afterward he shall come into the camp; the priest shall be unclean until evening. ⁸And the one who burns it shall wash his clothes in water, bathe in water, and shall be unclean until evening. ⁹Then a man *who is* clean shall gather up the ashes of the heifer, and store *them* outside the camp in a clean place; and they shall be kept for the congregation of the children of Israel for the water of purification; it *is* for purifying from sin. ¹⁰And the one who gathers the ashes of the heifer shall wash his clothes, and be unclean until evening. It shall be a statute forever to the children of Israel and to the stranger who dwells among them.

◣◢◣◢ **MEAL TICKET**

18:25-26 Even the Levites, who were ministers, had to tithe to support the work of the tabernacle. No one was exempt from returning to God a portion of what was received from him. Though the Levites owned no land and operated no great enterprises, they were to treat their income the same as everyone else by giving a portion to care for the needs of the other Levites and of the tabernacle. The tithing principle is still relevant today. God expects all his followers to supply the material needs of those who devote themselves to meeting the spiritual needs of the community of faith.

¹¹"He who touches the dead body of anyone shall be unclean seven days. ¹²He shall purify himself with the water on the third day and on the seventh day; *then* he will be clean. But if he does not purify himself on the third day and on the seventh day, he will not be clean. ¹³Whoever touches the body of anyone who has died, and does not purify himself, defiles the tabernacle of the LORD. That person shall be cut off from Israel. He shall be unclean, because the water of purification was not sprinkled on him; his uncleanness *is* still on him.

¹⁴"This *is* the law when a man dies in a tent: All who come into the tent and all who *are* in the tent shall be unclean seven days; ¹⁵and every open vessel, which has no cover fastened on it, *is* unclean. ¹⁶Whoever in the open field touches one who is slain by a sword or who has died, or a bone of a man, or a grave, shall be unclean seven days.

¹⁷"And for an unclean *person* they shall take some of the ashes of the heifer burnt for purification from sin, and running water shall be put on them in a vessel. ¹⁸A clean person shall take hyssop and dip *it* in the water, sprinkle *it* on the tent, on all the vessels, on the persons who were there, or on the one who touched a bone, the slain, the dead, or a grave. ¹⁹The clean *person* shall sprinkle the unclean on the third day and on the seventh day; and on the seventh day he shall purify himself, wash his clothes, and bathe in water; and at evening he shall be clean.

20'But the man who is unclean and does not purify himself, that person shall be cut off from among the assembly, because he has defiled the sanctuary of the LORD. The water of purification has not been sprinkled on him; he *is* unclean. 21It shall be a perpetual statute for them. He who sprinkles the water of purification shall wash his clothes; and he who touches the water of purification shall be unclean until evening. 22Whatever the unclean *person* touches shall be unclean; and the person who touches *it* shall be unclean until evening.' "

CHAPTER 20 MOSES DISOBEYS GOD.

Then the children of Israel, the whole congregation, came into the Wilderness of Zin in the first month, and the people stayed in Kadesh; and Miriam died there and was buried there.

2Now there was no water for the congregation; so they gathered together against Moses and Aaron. 3And the people contended with Moses and spoke, saying: "If only we had died when our brethren died before the LORD! 4Why have you brought up the assembly of the LORD into this wilderness, that we and our animals should die here? 5And why have you made us come up out of Egypt, to bring us to this evil place? It *is* not a place of grain or figs or vines or pomegranates; nor *is* there any water to drink." 6So Moses and Aaron went from the presence of the assembly to the door of the tabernacle of meeting, and they fell on their faces. And the glory of the LORD appeared to them.

7Then the LORD spoke to Moses, saying, 8"Take the rod; you and your brother Aaron gather the congregation together. Speak to the rock before their eyes, and it will yield its water; thus you shall bring water for them out of the rock, and give drink to the congregation and their

animals." 9So Moses took the rod from before the LORD as He commanded him.

10And Moses and Aaron gathered the assembly together before the rock; and he said to them, "Hear now you rebels! Must we bring water for you out of this rock?' 11Then Moses lifted his hand and struck the rock twice with his rod; and water came out abundantly, and the congregation and their animals drank.

12Then the LORD spoke to Moses and Aaron, "Because you did not believe Me, to hallow Me in the eyes of the children of Israel, therefore you shall not bring this assembly into the land which I have given them."

13This *was* the water of Meribah, because the children of Israel contended with the LORD, and He was hallowed among them.

14Now Moses sent messengers from Kadesh to the king of Edom. "Thus says your brother Israel: 'You know all the hardship that has befallen us, 15how our fathers went down to Egypt, and we dwelt in Egypt a long time, and the Egyptians afflicted us and our fathers. 16When we cried out to the LORD, He heard our voice and sent the Angel and brought us up out of Egypt; now here we are in Kadesh, a city on the edge of your border. 17Please let us pass through your country. We will not pass through fields or vineyards, nor will we drink water from wells; we will go along the King's Highway; we will not turn aside to the right hand or to the left until we have passed through your territory.' "

18Then Edom said to him, "You shall not pass through my *land,* lest I come out against you with the sword."

19So the children of Israel said to him, "We will go by the Highway, and if I or my livestock drink any of your water, then I will pay for it; let me only pass through on foot, nothing *more.*"

20Then he said, "You shall not pass through." So Edom came out against them with many men and with a strong hand. 21Thus Edom refused to give Israel passage through his territory; so Israel turned away from him.

22Now the children of Israel, the whole congregation, journeyed from Kadesh and came to Mount Hor. 23And the LORD spoke to Moses and Aaron in Mount Hor by the border of the land of Edom, saying: 24"Aaron shall be gathered to his people, for he shall not enter the land which I have given to the children of Israel, because you rebelled against My word at the water of Meribah. 25Take Aaron and Eleazar his son, and bring them up to Mount Hor; 26and strip Aaron of his garments and put them on Eleazar his son; for Aaron shall be gathered *to his people* and die there." 27So Moses did just as the LORD commanded, and they went up to Mount Hor in the sight of

CONFLICT

20:21 Moses negotiated and reasoned with the Edomite king. When nothing worked, he was left with two choices—force a conflict or avoid it. Moses knew there would be enough barriers in the days and months ahead. There was no point in adding another one unnecessarily. Sometimes conflict is unavoidable. Sometimes, however, it isn't worth the consequences. Open warfare may seem heroic, couragous, and even righteous, but it is not always the best choice. When we can find a way to solve our problems, even if it is harder for us to do, we should consider Moses' example.

all the congregation. [28]Moses stripped Aaron of his garments and put them on Eleazar his son; and Aaron died there on the top of the mountain. Then Moses and Eleazar came down from the mountain. [29]Now when all the congregation saw that Aaron was dead, all the house of Israel mourned for Aaron thirty days.

CHAPTER **21** ISRAELITES DEFEAT KING OF ARAD.

The king of Arad, the Canaanite, who dwelt in the South, heard that Israel was coming on the road to Atharim. Then he fought against Israel and took *some* of them prisoners. [2]So Israel made a vow to the LORD, and said, "If You will indeed deliver this people into my hand, then I will utterly destroy their cities." [3]And the LORD listened to the voice of Israel and delivered up the Canaanites, and they utterly destroyed them and their cities. So the name of that place was called Hormah.

[4]Then they journeyed from Mount Hor by the Way of the Red Sea, to go around the land of Edom; and the soul of the people became very discouraged on the way. [5]And the people spoke against God and against Moses: "Why have you brought us up out of Egypt to die in the wilderness? For *there is* no food and no water, and our soul loathes this worthless bread." [6]So the LORD sent fiery serpents among the people, and they bit the people; and many of the people of Israel died.

[7]Therefore the people came to Moses, and said, "We have sinned, for we have spoken against the LORD and against you; pray to the LORD that He take away the serpents from us." So Moses prayed for the people. [8]Then the LORD said to Moses, "Make a fiery *serpent*, and set it on a pole; and it shall be that everyone who is bitten, when he looks at it, shall live." [9]So Moses made a bronze serpent, and put it on a pole; and so it was, if a serpent had bitten anyone, when he looked at the bronze serpent, he lived.

[10]Now the children of Israel moved on and camped in Oboth. [11]And they journeyed from Oboth and camped at Ije Abarim, in the wilderness which *is* east of Moab, toward the sunrise. [12]From there they moved and camped in the Valley of Zered. [13]From there they moved and camped on the other side of the Arnon, which *is* in the wilderness that extends from the border of the Amorites; for the Arnon *is* the border of Moab, between Moab and the Amorites. [14]Therefore it is said in the Book of the Wars of the LORD:

> "Waheb in Suphah,
> The brooks of the Arnon,
> [15] And the slope of the brooks
> That reaches to the dwelling of Ar,
> And lies on the border of Moab."

[16]From there *they went* to Beer, which *is* the well where the LORD said to Moses, "Gather the people together, and I will give them water." [17]Then Israel sang this song:

> "Spring up, O well!
> All of you sing to it—
> [18] The well the leaders sank,
> Dug by the nation's nobles,
> By the lawgiver, with their staves."

> And from the wilderness *they went* to Mattanah, [19]from Mattanah to Nahaliel, from Nahaliel to Bamoth, [20]and from Bamoth, *in* the valley that *is* in the country of Moab, to the top of Pisgah which looks down on the wasteland.

[21]Then Israel sent messengers to Sihon king of the Amorites, saying, [22]"Let me pass through your land. We will not turn aside into fields or vineyards; we will not drink water from wells. We will go by the King's Highway until we have passed through your territory." [23]But Sihon would not allow Israel to pass through his territory. So Sihon gathered all his people together and went out against Israel in the wilderness, and he came to Jahaz and fought against Israel. [24]Then Israel defeated him with the edge of the sword, and took possession of his land from the Arnon to the Jabbok, as far as the people of Ammon; for the border of the people of Ammon *was* fortified. [25]So Israel took all these cities, and Israel dwelt in all the cities of the Amorites, in Heshbon and in all its villages. [26]For Heshbon *was* the city of Sihon king of the Amorites, who had fought against the former king of Moab, and had taken all his land from his hand as far as the Arnon. [27]Therefore those who speak in proverbs say:

◣▬▬▬▬▬▬COMPLAINTS

21:5 In Psalm 78, we learn the sources of Israel's complaining: (1) they forgot the miracles God did for them, (2) they demanded more than what God had given them, (3) their repentance was insincere, and (4) they were ungrateful for what God had done for them. Our complaining often has its roots in one of these thoughtless actions and attitudes. If we can cut off the source of complaining, it will not take hold and grow in our life.

> "Come to Heshbon, let it be built;
> Let the city of Sihon be repaired.
>
> [28] "For fire went out from Heshbon,
> A flame from the city of Sihon;
> It consumed Ar of Moab,
> The lords of the heights of the Arnon.
> [29] Woe to you, Moab!
> You have perished, O people of Chemosh!
> He has given his sons as fugitives,
> And his daughters into captivity,
> To Sihon king of the Amorites.
>
> [30] "But we have shot at them;
> Heshbon has perished as far as Dibon.
> Then we laid waste as far as Nophah,
> Which *reaches* to Medeba."

[31]Thus Israel dwelt in the land of the Amorites. [32]Then Moses sent to spy out Jazer; and they took its villages and drove out the Amorites who *were* there.

[33]And they turned and went up by the way to Bashan. So Og king of Bashan went out against them, he and all his people, to battle at Edrei. [34]Then the LORD said to Moses, "Do not fear him, for I have delivered him into your hand, with all his people and his land; and you shall do to him as you did to Sihon king of the Amorites, who

21:34 God assured Moses that Israel's enemy was conquered even before the battle began! God wants to give us victory over our enemies—which usually are the problems related to sin, rather than armed soldiers. First we must believe that he can help us. Second, we must trust him to help us. Third, we must take the steps he shows us.

dwelt at Heshbon." [35]So they defeated him, his sons, and all his people, until there was no survivor left him; and they took possession of his land.

CHAPTER 22 BALAK OFFERS MONEY TO BALAAM.

Then the children of Israel moved, and camped in the plains of Moab on the side of the Jordan *across from* Jericho.

[2]Now Balak the son of Zippor saw all that Israel had done to the Amorites. [3]And Moab was exceedingly afraid of the people because they *were* many, and Moab was sick with dread because of the children of Israel. [4]So Moab said to the elders of Midian, "Now this company will lick up everything around us, as an ox licks up the grass of the field." And Balak the son of Zippor *was* king of the Moabites at that time. [5]Then he sent messengers to Balaam the son of Beor at Pethor, which *is* near the River in the land of the sons of his people, to call him, saying: "Look, a people has come from Egypt. See, they cover the face of the earth, and are settling next to me! [6]Therefore please come at once, curse this people for me, for they *are* too mighty for me. Perhaps I shall be able to defeat them and drive them out of the land, for I know that he whom you bless *is* blessed, and he whom you curse is cursed."

[7]So the elders of Moab and the elders of Midian departed with the diviner's fee in their hand, and they came to Balaam and spoke to him the words of Balak. [8]And he said to them, "Lodge here tonight, and I will bring back word to you, as the LORD speaks to me." So the princes of Moab stayed with Balaam.

[9]Then God came to Balaam and said, "Who *are* these men with you?"

[10]So Balaam said to God, "Balak the son of Zippor, king of Moab, has sent to me, *saying,* [11]'Look, a people has come out of Egypt, and they cover the face of the earth. Come now, curse them for me; perhaps I shall be able to overpower them and drive them out.' "

[12]And God said to Balaam, "You shall not go with them; you shall not curse the people, for they *are* blessed."

[13]So Balaam rose in the morning and said to the princes of Balak, "Go back to your land, for the LORD has refused to give me permission to go with you."

[14]And the princes of Moab rose and went to Balak, and said, "Balaam refuses to come with us."

[15]Then Balak again sent princes, more numerous and more honorable than they. [16]And they came to Balaam and said to him, "Thus says Balak the son of Zippor: 'Please let nothing hinder you from coming to me; [17]for I will certainly honor you greatly, and I will do whatever you say to me. Therefore please come, curse this people for me.' "

[18]Then Balaam answered and said to the servants of Balak, "Though Balak were to give me his house full of silver and gold, I could not go beyond the word of the LORD my God, to do less or more. [19]Now therefore, please, you also stay here tonight, that I may know what more the LORD will say to me."

[20]And God came to Balaam at night and said to him, "If the men come to call you, rise *and* go with them; but only the word which I speak to you—that you shall do." [21]So Balaam rose in the morning, saddled his donkey, and went with the princes of Moab.

[22]Then God's anger was aroused because he went, and the Angel of the LORD took His stand in the way as an adversary against him. And he was riding on his donkey, and his two servants *were* with him. [23]Now the donkey saw the Angel of the LORD standing in the way with His drawn sword in His hand, and the donkey turned aside out of the way and went into the field. So Balaam struck the donkey to turn her back onto the road. [24]Then the Angel of the LORD stood in a narrow path between the vineyards, *with* a wall on this side and a wall on that side. [25]And when the donkey saw the Angel of the LORD, she pushed herself against the wall and crushed Balaam's foot against the wall; so he struck her again. [26]Then the Angel of the LORD went further, and stood in a narrow place where there *was* no way to turn either to the right hand or to the left. [27]And when the donkey saw the Angel of the LORD, she lay down under Balaam; so Balaam's anger was aroused, and he struck the donkey with his staff.

[28]Then the LORD opened the mouth of the donkey, and she said to Balaam, "What have I done to you, that you have struck me these three times?"

[29]And Balaam said to the donkey, "Because you have abused me. I wish there were a sword in my hand, for now I would kill you!"

[30]So the donkey said to Balaam, "*Am* I not your donkey on which you have ridden, ever since *I became* yours, to this day? Was I ever disposed to do this to you?"

And he said, "No."

[31]Then the LORD opened Balaam's eyes, and he saw the Angel of the LORD standing in the way with His drawn sword in His hand; and he bowed his head and fell flat on his face. [32]And the Angel of the LORD said to him, "Why have you struck your donkey these three times? Behold, I have come out to stand against you, because *your* way is perverse before Me. [33]The donkey saw Me and turned aside from Me these three times. If she had not turned aside from Me, surely I would also have killed you by now, and let her live."

[34]And Balaam said to the Angel of the LORD, "I have sinned, for I did not know You stood in the way against me. Now therefore, if it displeases You, I will turn back."

[35]Then the Angel of the LORD said to Balaam, "Go with

BLIND GREED

22:20-23 God let Balaam go with Balak's messengers, but he angry about Balaam's greedy attitude. Balaam claimed that he w go against God just for money, but his resolve was beginning to s greed for the wealth offered by the king blinded him so that he see how God was trying to stop him. Though we may know what wants us to do, we can become blinded by our greedy desire for possessions, or prestige. We can avoid Balaam's mistake by look the allure of fame or fortune to the long-range benefits of follow

the men, but only the word that I speak to you, that you shall speak." So Balaam went with the princes of Balak.

³⁶Now when Balak heard that Balaam was coming, he went out to meet him at the city of Moab, which *is* on the border at the Arnon, the boundary of the territory. ³⁷Then Balak said to Balaam, "Did I not earnestly send to you, calling for you? Why did you not come to me? Am I not able to honor you?"

³⁸And Balaam said to Balak, "Look, I have come to you! Now, have I any power at all to say anything? The word that God puts in my mouth, that I must speak." ³⁹So Balaam went with Balak, and they came to Kirjath Huzoth. ⁴⁰Then Balak offered oxen and sheep, and he sent *some* to Balaam and to the princes who *were* with him.

⁴¹So it was, the next day, that Balak took Balaam and brought him up to the high places of Baal, that from there he might observe the extent of the people.

CHAPTER 23 WHO WILL BALAAM OBEY? Then

Balaam said to Balak, "Build seven altars for me here, and prepare for me here seven bulls and seven rams."

²And Balak did just as Balaam had spoken, and Balak and Balaam offered a bull and a ram on *each* altar. ³Then Balaam said to Balak, "Stand by your burnt offering, and I will go; perhaps the LORD will come to meet me, and whatever He shows me I will tell you." So he went to a desolate height. ⁴And God met Balaam, and he said to Him, "I have prepared the seven altars, and I have offered on *each* altar a bull and a ram."

⁵Then the LORD put a word in Balaam's mouth, and said, "Return to Balak, and thus you shall speak." ⁶So he returned to him, and there he was, standing by his burnt offering, he and all the princes of Moab.

⁷And he took up his oracle and said:

"Balak the king of Moab has brought me from Aram,
  From the mountains of the east.
'Come, curse Jacob for me,
  And come, denounce Israel!'

⁸ "How shall I curse whom God has not cursed?
  And how shall I denounce *whom* the LORD has not
    denounced?
⁹ For from the top of the rocks I see him,
  And from the hills I behold him;
  There! A people dwelling alone,
  Not reckoning itself among the nations.

¹⁰ "Who can count the dust of Jacob,
  Or number one-fourth of Israel?
  Let me die the death of the righteous,
  And let my end be like his!"

¹¹Then Balak said to Balaam, "What have you done to me? I took you to curse my enemies, and look, you have blessed *them* bountifully!"

¹²So he answered and said, "Must I not take heed to speak what the LORD has put in my mouth?"

¹³Then Balak said to him, "Please come with me to another place from which you may see them; you shall see only the outer part of them, and shall not see them all; curse them for me from there." ¹⁴So he brought him to the field of Zophim, to the top of Pisgah, and built seven altars, and offered a bull and a ram on *each* altar.

¹⁵And he said to Balak, "Stand here by your burnt offering while I meet *the* LORD over there."

¹⁶Then the LORD met Balaam, and put a word in his mouth, and said, "Go back to Balak, and thus you shall speak." ¹⁷So he came to him, and there he was, standing by his burnt offering, and the princes of Moab were with him. And Balak said to him, "What has the LORD spoken?"

NEW VIEW

23:27 King Balak took Balaam to several places to entice him to curse the Israelites. He thought a change of scenery might help change Balaam's mind. But changing locations won't change God's will. We must learn to face the source of our problems, especially when it is within ourselves. To make a change in geography or a change in jobs may only cloud the need for a change in heart.

¹⁸Then he took up his oracle and said:

"Rise up, Balak, and hear!
  Listen to me, son of Zippor!

¹⁹ "God *is* not a man, that He should lie,
  Nor a son of man, that He should repent.
  Has He said, and will He not do?
  Or has He spoken, and will He not make it good?
²⁰ Behold, I have received *a command* to bless;
  He has blessed, and I cannot reverse it.

²¹ "He has not observed iniquity in Jacob,
  Nor has He seen wickedness in Israel.
  The LORD his God *is* with him,
  And the shout of a King *is* among them.
²² God brings them out of Egypt;
  He has strength like a wild ox.

²³ "For *there is* no sorcery against Jacob,
  Nor any divination against Israel.
  It now must be said of Jacob
  And of Israel, 'Oh, what God has done!'
²⁴ Look, a people rises like a lioness,
  And lifts itself up like a lion;
  It shall not lie down until it devours the prey,
  And drinks the blood of the slain."

²⁵Then Balak said to Balaam, "Neither curse them at all, nor bless them at all!"

²⁶So Balaam answered and said to Balak, "Did I not tell you, saying, 'All that the LORD speaks, that I must do'?"

²⁷Then Balak said to Balaam, "Please come, I will take you to another place; perhaps it will please God that you may curse them for me from there." ²⁸So Balak took Balaam to the top of Peor, that overlooks the wasteland. ²⁹Then Balaam said to Balak, "Build for me here seven altars, and prepare for me here seven bulls and seven rams." ³⁰And Balak did as Balaam had said, and offered a bull and a ram on *every* altar.

CHAPTER 24 Now when Balaam saw that it

pleased the LORD to bless Israel, he did not go as at other times, to seek to use sorcery, but he set his face toward the wilderness. ²And Balaam raised his eyes, and saw Israel encamped according to their tribes; and the Spirit of God came upon him.

³Then he took up his oracle and said:

"The utterance of Balaam the son of Beor,
The utterance of the man whose eyes are opened,
⁴ The utterance of him who hears the words of God,
Who sees the vision of the Almighty,
Who falls down, with eyes wide open:

⁵ "How lovely are your tents, O Jacob!
Your dwellings, O Israel!
⁶ Like valleys that stretch out,
Like gardens by the riverside,
Like aloes planted by the LORD,
Like cedars beside the waters.
⁷ He shall pour water from his buckets,
And his seed *shall be* in many waters.

"His king shall be higher than Agag,
And his kingdom shall be exalted.

⁸ "God brings him out of Egypt;
He has strength like a wild ox;
He shall consume the nations, his enemies;
He shall break their bones
And pierce *them* with his arrows.
⁹ 'He bows down, he lies down as a lion;
And as a lion, who shall rouse him?'

"Blessed *is* he who blesses you,
And cursed *is* he who curses you."

¹⁰Then Balak's anger was aroused against Balaam, and he struck his hands together; and Balak said to Balaam, "I called you to curse my enemies, and look, you have bountifully blessed *them* these three times! ¹¹Now therefore, flee to your place. I said I would greatly honor you, but in fact, the LORD has kept you back from honor."

¹²So Balaam said to Balak, "Did I not also speak to your messengers whom you sent to me, saying, ¹³'If Balak were to give me his house full of silver and gold, I could not go beyond the word of the LORD, to do good or bad of my own will. What the LORD says, that I must speak'? ¹⁴And now, indeed, I am going to my people. Come, I will advise you what this people will do to your people in the latter days."

¹⁵So he took up his oracle and said:

"The utterance of Balaam the son of Beor,
And the utterance of the man whose eyes are opened;
¹⁶ The utterance of him who hears the words of God,
And has the knowledge of the Most High,
Who sees the vision of the Almighty,
Who falls down, with eyes wide open:

¹⁷ "I see Him, but not now;
I behold Him, but not near;
A Star shall come out of Jacob;
A Scepter shall rise out of Israel,
And batter the brow of Moab,
And destroy all the sons of tumult.

¹⁸ "And Edom shall be a possession;
Seir also, his enemies, shall be a possession,
While Israel does valiantly.
¹⁹ Out of Jacob One shall have dominion,
And destroy the remains of the city."

²⁰Then he looked on Amalek, and he took up his oracle and said:

"Amalek *was* first among the nations,
But *shall be* last until he perishes."

²¹Then he looked on the Kenites, and he took up his oracle and said:

"Firm is your dwelling place,
And your nest is set in the rock;
²² Nevertheless Kain shall be burned.
How long until Asshur carries you away captive?"

²³Then he took up his oracle and said:

"Alas! Who shall live when God does this?
²⁴ But ships *shall come* from the coasts of Cyprus,
And they shall afflict Asshur and afflict Eber,
And so shall *Amalek*, until he perishes."

²⁵So Balaam rose and departed and returned to his place; Balak also went his way.

CHAPTER **25** THE ISRAELITES WORSHIP BAAL.

Now Israel remained in Acacia Grove, and the people began to commit harlotry with the women of Moab. ²They invited the people to the sacrifices of their gods, and the people ate and bowed down to their gods. ³So Israel was joined to Baal of Peor, and the anger of the LORD was aroused against Israel.

⁴Then the LORD said to Moses, "Take all the leaders of the people and hang the offenders before the LORD, out in the sun, that the fierce anger of the LORD may turn away from Israel."

⁵So Moses said to the judges of Israel, "Every one of you kill his men who were joined to Baal of Peor."

⁶And indeed, one of the children of Israel came and presented to his brethren a Midianite woman in the sight of Moses and in the sight of all the congregation of the children of Israel, who *were* weeping at the door of the tabernacle of meeting. ⁷Now when Phinehas the son of Eleazar, the son of Aaron the priest, saw *it*, he rose from among the congregation and took a javelin in his hand; ⁸and he went after the man of Israel into the tent and thrust both of them through, the man of Israel, and the

PARTY HEARTY

25:1-2 Attending a local party with the Moabite girls may have harmless enough. But for these young Israelite men, "fun" turn tragedy. At first, they didn't think about worshiping idols. They j wanted to go to the party and have a good time. Before long, the started attending local feasts and family celebrations that involv worship. Soon they were in over their heads, absorbed into the of the heathen culture. Their desire for fun and companionship them to loosen their spiritual commitment. Consider your favori recreations—do they help you grow in faith, or do they push y relax your standards?

oman through her body. So the plague was stopped mong the children of Israel. [9]And those who died in the lague were twenty-four thousand.

[10]Then the LORD spoke to Moses, saying: [11]"Phinehas e son of Eleazar, the son of Aaron the priest, has turned ack My wrath from the children of Israel, because he as zealous with My zeal among them, so that I did not onsume the children of Israel in My zeal. [12]Therefore say, ehold, I give to him My covenant of peace; [13]and it shall e to him and his descendants after him a covenant of an verlasting priesthood, because he was zealous for his od, and made atonement for the children of Israel.' "

[14]Now the name of the Israelite who was killed, who as killed with the Midianite woman, *was* Zimri the son f Salu, a leader of a father's house among the Simeon- es. [15]And the name of the Midianite woman who was illed *was* Cozbi the daughter of Zur; he *was* head of the eople of a father's house in Midian.

[16]Then the LORD spoke to Moses, saying: [17]"Harass the lidianites, and attack them; [18]for they harassed you with eir schemes by which they seduced you in the matter f Peor and in the matter of Cozbi, the daughter of a ader of Midian, their sister, who was killed in the day of e plague because of Peor."

CHAPTER **26** **PEOPLE COUNTED AGAIN.** And it ame to pass, after the plague, that the LORD spoke to Ioses and Eleazar the son of Aaron the priest, saying: Take a census of all the congregation of the children of rael from twenty years old and above, by their fathers' ouses, all who are able to go to war in Israel." [3]So Moses nd Eleazar the priest spoke with them in the plains of Ioab by the Jordan, *across from* Jericho, saying: [4]"*Take a ensus of the people* from twenty years old and above, just s the LORD commanded Moses and the children of Israel ho came out of the land of Egypt."

[5]Reuben *was* the firstborn of Israel. The children of euben *were: of* Hanoch, the family of the Hanochites; *of* allu, the family of the Palluites; [6]*of* Hezron, the family of ie Hezronites; *of* Carmi, the family of the Carmites. These *are* the families of the Reubenites: those who were umbered of them were forty-three thousand seven undred and thirty. [8]And the son of Pallu *was* Eliab. [9]The ons of Eliab *were* Nemuel, Dathan, and Abiram. These re the Dathan and Abiram, representatives of the con- regation, who contended against Moses and Aaron in ie company of Korah, when they contended against the ORD; [10]and the earth opened its mouth and swallowed iem up together with Korah when that company died, vhen the fire devoured two hundred and fifty men; and iey became a sign. [11]Nevertheless the children of Korah id not die.

[12]The sons of Simeon according to their families *were: f* Nemuel, the family of the Nemuelites; *of* Jamin, the imily of the Jaminites; *of* Jachin, the family of the Jachin- es; [13]*of* Zerah, the family of the Zarhites; *of* Shaul, the imily of the Shaulites. [14]These *are* the families of the imeonites: twenty-two thousand two hundred.

[15]The sons of Gad according to their families *were: of* ephon, the family of the Zephonites; *of* Haggi, the fam-

ily of the Haggites; *of* Shuni, the family of the Shunites; [16]*of* Ozni, the family of the Oznites; *of* Eri, the family of the Erites; [17]*of* Arod, the family of the Arodites; *of* Areli, the family of the Arelites. [18]These *are* the families of the sons of Gad according to those who were numbered of them: forty thousand five hundred.

▬▬**RIGHTEOUS ANGER**

25:10-11 It is clear from Phinehas's story that some anger is proper and justified. But how can we know when our anger is appropriate and when it should be restrained? Ask these questions when you become angry: (1) Why am I angry? (2) Whose rights are being violated (mine or another's)? (3) Is the truth (a principle of God) being violated? If only your rights are at stake, it may be wiser to keep angry feelings under control. But if the truth is at stake, anger is often justified, although violence and retaliation are usually the wrong way to express it (Phinehas's case was unique). If we are becoming more and more like God, we should be angered by sin.

[19]The sons of Judah *were* Er and Onan; and Er and Onan died in the land of Canaan. [20]And the sons of Judah according to their families were: *of* Shelah, the family of the Shelanites; *of* Perez, the family of the Parzites; *of* Zerah, the family of the Zarhites. [21]And the sons of Perez were: *of* Hezron, the family of the Hezronites; *of* Hamul, the family of the Hamulites. [22]These *are* the families of Judah according to those who were numbered of them: seventy-six thousand five hundred.

[23]The sons of Issachar according to their families *were: of* Tola, the family of the Tolaites; of Puah, the family of the Punites; [24]of Jashub, the family of the Jashubites; of Shimron, the family of the Shimronites. [25]These *are* the families of Issachar according to those who were num- bered of them: sixty-four thousand three hundred.

[26]The sons of Zebulun according to their families *were:* of Sered, the family of the Sardites; of Elon, the family of the Elonites; of Jahleel, the family of the Jahleelites. [27]These *are* the families of the Zebulunites according to those who were numbered of them: sixty thousand five hundred.

[28]The sons of Joseph according to their families, by Manasseh and Ephraim, *were:* [29]The sons of Manasseh: of Machir, the family of the Machirites; and Machir begot Gilead; of Gilead, the family of the Gileadites. [30]These *are* the sons of Gilead: of Jeezer, the family of the Jeezerites; of Helek, the family of the Helekites; [31]of Asriel, the family of the Asrielites; of Shechem, the family of the Shechem- ites; [32]of Shemida, the family of the Shemidaites; of He- pher, the family of the Hepherites. [33]Now Zelophehad the son of Hepher had no sons, but daughters; and the names of the daughters of Zelophehad *were* Mahlah, Noah, Hoglah, Milcah, and Tirzah. [34]These *are* the fami- lies of Manasseh; and those who were numbered of them *were* fifty-two thousand seven hundred.

[35]These *are* the sons of Ephraim according to their families: of Shuthelah, the family of the Shuthalhites; of Becher, the family of the Bachrites; of Tahan, the family of the Tahanites. [36]And these *are* the sons of Shuthelah: of Eran, the family of the Eranites. [37]These *are* the families

of the sons of Ephraim according to those who were numbered of them: thirty-two thousand five hundred.

These *are* the sons of Joseph according to their families.

³⁸The sons of Benjamin according to their families were: of Bela, the family of the Belaites; of Ashbel, the family of the Ashbelites; of Ahiram, the family of the Ahiramites; ³⁹of Shupham, the family of the Shuphamites; of Hupham, the family of the Huphamites. ⁴⁰And the sons of Bela were Ard and Naaman: *of Ard*, the family of the Ardites; of Naaman, the family of the Naamites. ⁴¹These *are* the sons of Benjamin according to their families; and those who were numbered of them *were* forty-five thousand six hundred.

⁴²These *are* the sons of Dan according to their families: of Shuham, the family of the Shuhamites. These *are* the families of Dan according to their families. ⁴³All the families of the Shuhamites, according to those who were numbered of them, *were* sixty-four thousand four hundred.

⁴⁴The sons of Asher according to their families *were:* of Jimna, the family of the Jimnites; of Jesui, the family of the Jesuites; of Beriah, the family of the Beriites. ⁴⁵Of the sons of Beriah: of Heber, the family of the Heberites; of Malchiel, the family of the Malchielites. ⁴⁶And the name of the daughter of Asher *was* Serah. ⁴⁷These *are* the families of the sons of Asher according to those who were numbered of them: fifty-three thousand four hundred.

⁴⁸The sons of Naphtali according to their families *were:* of Jahzeel, the family of the Jahzeelites; of Guni, the family of the Gunites; ⁴⁹of Jezer, the family of the Jezerites; of Shillem, the family of the Shillemites. ⁵⁰These *are* the families of Naphtali according to their families; and those who were numbered of them *were* forty-five thousand four hundred.

⁵¹These *are* those who were numbered of the children of Israel: six hundred and one thousand seven hundred and thirty.

⁵²Then the LORD spoke to Moses, saying: ⁵³"To these the land shall be divided as an inheritance, according to the number of names. ⁵⁴To a large *tribe* you shall give a larger inheritance, and to a small *tribe* you shall give a smaller inheritance. Each shall be given its inheritance according to those who were numbered of them. ⁵⁵But the land shall be divided by lot; they shall inherit according to the names of the tribes of their fathers. ⁵⁶According to the lot their inheritance shall be divided between the larger and the smaller."

⁵⁷And these *are* those who were numbered of the Levites according to their families: of Gershon, the family of the Gershonites; of Kohath, the family of the Kohathites; of Merari, the family of the Merarites. ⁵⁸These *are* the families of the Levites: the family of the Libnites, the family of the Hebronites, the family of the Mahlites, the family of the Mushites, and the family of the Korathites. And Kohath begot Amram. ⁵⁹The name of Amram's wife *was* Jochebed the daughter of Levi, who was born to Levi in Egypt; and to Amram she bore Aaron and Moses and their sister Miriam. ⁶⁰To Aaron were born Nadab and Abihu, Eleazar and Ithamar. ⁶¹And Nadab and Abihu died when they offered profane fire before the LORD.

⁶²Now those who were numbered of them wer[e] twenty-three thousand, every male from a month o[ld] and above; for they were not numbered among the othe[r] children of Israel, because there was no inheritanc[e] given to them among the children of Israel.

⁶³These *are* those who were numbered by Moses an[d] Eleazar the priest, who numbered the children of Isra[el] in the plains of Moab by the Jordan, *across from* Jerich[o].

◤◢◤◢ QUIET WORK

26:64 A new census for a new generation. Thirty-eight years h[ad] elapsed since the first great census in chapter one of Numbers. D[uring] that time, every Israelite man and woman over 20 years of age— Caleb, Joshua, and Moses—had died, and yet God's laws and th[e] spiritual character of the nation were still intact. Numbers record[s] dramatic miracles. This is a quiet but powerful miracle often ove[r,] a whole nation moves from one land to another, loses its entire [older] population, yet manages to maintain its spiritual direction. Some [people] wonder why God isn't working dramatic miracles in our life. The [fact is] that God often works in quiet ways to bring about his long-range purposes.

⁶⁴But among these there was not a man of those who wer[e] numbered by Moses and Aaron the priest when the[y] numbered the children of Israel in the Wilderness [of] Sinai. ⁶⁵For the LORD had said of them, "They shall sure[ly] die in the wilderness." So there was not left a man [of] them, except Caleb the son of Jephunneh and Joshua th[e] son of Nun.

CHAPTER **27** ZELOPHEHAD'S DAUGHTERS

Then came the daughters of Zelophehad the son of He[-] pher, the son of Gilead, the son of Machir, the son [of] Manasseh, from the families of Manasseh the son [of] Joseph; and these *were* the names of his daughters: Mah[-] lah, Noah, Hoglah, Milcah, and Tirzah. ²And they stoo[d] before Moses, before Eleazar the priest, and before th[e] leaders and all the congregation, *by* the doorway of th[e] tabernacle of meeting, saying: ³"Our father died in th[e] wilderness; but he was not in the company of those wh[o] gathered together against the LORD, in company wit[h] Korah, but he died in his own sin; and he had no son[s.] ⁴Why should the name of our father be removed fro[m] among his family because he had no son? Give u[s] possession among our father's brothers."

⁵So Moses brought their case before the LORD.

⁶And the LORD spoke to Moses, saying: ⁷"The daugh[-] ters of Zelophehad speak *what is* right; you shall surel[y] give them a possession of inheritance among thei[r] father's brothers, and cause the inheritance of thei[r] father to pass to them. ⁸And you shall speak to the chil[-] dren of Israel, saying: 'If a man dies and has no son, the[n] you shall cause his inheritance to pass to his daughter. ⁹[If] he has no daughter, then you shall give his inheritance t[o] his brothers. ¹⁰If he has no brothers, then you shall giv[e] his inheritance to his father's brothers. ¹¹And if his fathe[r] has no brothers, then you shall give his inheritance to th[e] relative closest to him in his family, and he shall posses[s] it.' " And it shall be to the children of Israel a statute o[f] judgment, just as the LORD commanded Moses.

¹²Now the LORD said to Moses: "Go up into this Mount ₁arim, and see the land which I have given to the chil-en of Israel. ¹³And when you have seen it, you also shall ₂ gathered to your people, as Aaron your brother was ₂thered. ¹⁴For in the Wilderness of Zin, during the strife ¹ the congregation, you rebelled against My command ₂ hallow Me at the waters before their eyes." (These *are* ₂ waters of Meribah, at Kadesh in the Wilderness of ₂.)

¹⁵Then Moses spoke to the LORD, saying: ¹⁶"Let the ₂RD, the God of the spirits of all flesh, set a man over the ₂ngregation, ¹⁷who may go out before them and go in ₂fore them, who may lead them out and bring them in, ₂at the congregation of the LORD may not be like sheep ₂hich have no shepherd."

¹⁸And the LORD said to Moses: "Take Joshua the son of ₂un with you, a man in whom *is* the Spirit, and lay your ₂nd on him; ¹⁹set him before Eleazar the priest and ₂fore all the congregation, and inaugurate him in their ₂ght. ²⁰And you shall give *some* of your authority to him, ₂at all the congregation of the children of Israel may be ₂edient. ²¹He shall stand before Eleazar the priest, who ₂all inquire before the LORD for him by the judgment of ₂e Urim. At his word they shall go out, and at his word ₂ey shall come in, he and all the children of Israel with ₂m—all the congregation."

²²So Moses did as the LORD commanded him. He took ₂shua and set him before Eleazar the priest and before ₂ the congregation. ²³And he laid his hands on him and ₂augurated him, just as the LORD commanded by the ₂nd of Moses.

HAPTER 28 DAILY OFFERINGS. Now the LORD ₂oke to Moses, saying, ²"Command the children of Is-₂el, and say to them, 'My offering, My food for My offer-₂gs made by fire as a sweet aroma to Me, you shall be ₂reful to offer to Me at their appointed time.'

³"And you shall say to them, 'This *is* the offering made ₂ fire which you shall offer to the LORD: two male lambs ₂ their first year without blemish, day by day, as a regular ₂rnt offering. ⁴The one lamb you shall offer in the ₂orning, the other lamb you shall offer in the evening, ₂nd one-tenth of an ephah of fine flour as a grain offer-₂g mixed with one-fourth of a hin of pressed oil. ⁶*It is a* ₂gular burnt offering which was ordained at Mount Si-₂i for a sweet aroma, an offering made by fire to the ₂RD. ⁷And its drink offering *shall be* one-fourth of a hin ₂r each lamb; in a holy *place* you shall pour out the drink ₂ the LORD as an offering. ⁸The other lamb you shall offer ₂ the evening; as the morning grain offering and its ₂rink offering, you shall offer *it* as an offering made by ₂re, a sweet aroma to the LORD.

⁹And on the Sabbath day two lambs in their first year, ₂ithout blemish, and two-tenths *of an ephah* of fine ₂our as a grain offering, mixed with oil, with its drink ₂ffering— ¹⁰*this is* the burnt offering for every Sabbath, ₂esides the regular burnt offering with its drink offering.

¹¹At the beginnings of your months you shall present ₂ burnt offering to the LORD: two young bulls, one ram, ₂d seven lambs in their first year, without blemish;

¹²three-tenths *of an ephah* of fine flour as a grain offering, mixed with oil, for each bull; two-tenths *of an ephah* of fine flour as a grain offering, mixed with oil, for the one ram; ¹³and one-tenth *of an ephah* of fine flour, mixed with oil, as a grain offering for each lamb, as a burnt offering of sweet aroma, an offering made by fire to the LORD. ¹⁴Their drink offering shall be half a hin of wine for a bull, one-third of a hin for a ram, and one-fourth of a hin for a lamb; this *is* the burnt offering for each month throughout the months of the year. ¹⁵Also one kid of the goats as a sin offering to the LORD shall be offered, besides the regular burnt offering and its drink offering.

LEADER

27:15-17 Moses asked God to appoint a leader who was both courageous (could lead in battle) and caring. The Lord responded by appointing Joshua. Many people want to be known as leaders. Some are very capable of leading in battle and reaching their goal. Others care deeply for the people in their charge. A good leader is both goal-oriented and people-oriented.

¹⁶'On the fourteenth day of the first month *is* the Passover of the LORD. ¹⁷And on the fifteenth day of this month *is* the feast; unleavened bread shall be eaten for seven days. ¹⁸On the first day *you shall have* a holy convocation. You shall do no customary work. ¹⁹And you shall present an offering made by fire as a burnt offering to the LORD: two young bulls, one ram, and seven lambs in their first year. Be sure they are without blemish. ²⁰Their grain offering shall be of fine flour mixed with oil: three-tenths *of an ephah* you shall offer for a bull, and two-tenths for a ram; ²¹you shall offer one-tenth *of an ephah* for each of the seven lambs; ²²also one goat *as* a sin offering, to make atonement for you. ²³You shall offer these besides the burnt offering of the morning, which *is* for a regular burnt offering. ²⁴In this manner you shall offer the food of the offering made by fire daily for seven days, as a sweet aroma to the LORD; it shall be offered besides the regular burnt offering and its drink offering. ²⁵And on the seventh day you shall have a holy convocation. You shall do no customary work.

GET READY

28:1-2 Offerings had to be brought regularly and carried out a certain way under the supervision of the priests. The people had to undergo a period of preparation to be sure their hearts were ready for worship. By spending this much time and preparation in worshiping God, they gave idolatry little time to influence their lives. God is pleased today when we allow nothing to come between him and us. He also is delighted by hearts that are prepared to receive his guidance.

²⁶'Also on the day of the firstfruits, when you bring a new grain offering to the LORD at your *Feast of* Weeks, you shall have a holy convocation. You shall do no customary work. ²⁷You shall present a burnt offering as a sweet aroma to the LORD: two young bulls, one ram, and seven lambs in their first year, ²⁸with their grain offering of fine flour mixed with oil: three-tenths *of an ephah* for each bull, two-tenths for the one ram, ²⁹and one-tenth for each of the seven lambs; ³⁰*also* one kid of the goats, to

make atonement for you. [31]Be sure they are without blemish. You shall present *them* with their drink offerings, besides the regular burnt offering with its grain offering.

CHAPTER 29 FEAST OF TRUMPETS. [1]And in the seventh month, on the first *day* of the month, you shall have a holy convocation. You shall do no customary work. For you it is a day of blowing the trumpets. [2]You shall offer a burnt offering as a sweet aroma to the LORD: one young bull, one ram, *and* seven lambs in their first year, without blemish. [3]Their grain offering *shall be* fine flour mixed with oil: three-tenths *of an ephah* for the bull, two-tenths for the ram, [4]and one-tenth for each of the seven lambs; [5]also one kid of the goats *as* a sin offering, to make atonement for you; [6]besides the burnt offering with its grain offering for the New Moon, the regular burnt offering with its grain offering, and their drink offerings, according to their ordinance, as a sweet aroma, an offering made by fire to the LORD.

◣◣◣◣◣◣◣◣◣◣◣ **WORSHIP TODAY**

29:1-2 The Feast of Trumpets demonstrated three important principles that we should follow in our worship today: (1) The people gathered together to celebrate and worship. There is something special about worshiping with other believers. (2) The normal daily routine was suspended and no hard work was done. It takes time to worship, and setting aside the time allows us to prepare our heart before and reflect afterward. (3) The people sacrificed animals as burnt offerings to God. We show our commitment to God when we give something of value to him. The best gift, of course, is ourself.

[7]On the tenth *day* of this seventh month you shall have a holy convocation. You shall afflict your souls; you shall not do any work. [8]You shall present a burnt offering to the LORD *as* a sweet aroma: one young bull, one ram, *and* seven lambs in their first year. Be sure they are without blemish. [9]Their grain offering *shall be of* fine flour mixed with oil: three-tenths *of an ephah* for the bull, two-tenths for the one ram, [10]and one-tenth for each of the seven lambs; [11]also one kid of the goats *as* a sin offering, besides the sin offering for atonement, the regular burnt offering with its grain offering, and their drink offerings.

[12]On the fifteenth day of the seventh month you shall have a holy convocation. You shall do no customary work, and you shall keep a feast to the LORD seven days. [13]You shall present a burnt offering, an offering made by fire as a sweet aroma to the LORD: thirteen young bulls, two rams, *and* fourteen lambs in their first year. They shall be without blemish. [14]Their grain offering *shall be of* fine flour mixed with oil: three-tenths *of an ephah* for each of the thirteen bulls, two-tenths for each of the two rams, [15]and one-tenth for each of the fourteen lambs; [16]also one kid of the goats *as* a sin offering, besides the regular burnt offering, its grain offering, and its drink offering.

[17]On the second day *present* twelve young bulls, two rams, fourteen lambs in their first year without blemish, [18]and their grain offering and their drink offerings for the

bulls, for the rams, and for the lambs, by their numb[er] according to the ordinance; [19]also one kid of the goats [as] a sin offering, besides the regular burnt offering with [its] grain offering, and their drink offerings.

[20]On the third day *present* eleven bulls, two ram[s,] fourteen lambs in their first year without blemish, [21]a[nd] their grain offering and their drink offerings for the bu[ll,] for the rams, and for the lambs, by their number, accor[d]ing to the ordinance; [22]also one goat *as* a sin offerin[g,] besides the regular burnt offering, its grain offering, a[nd] its drink offering.

[23]On the fourth day *present* ten bulls, two rams, *a[nd]* fourteen lambs in their first year, without blemish, [24]a[nd] their grain offering and their drink offerings for the bu[ll,] for the rams, and for the lambs, by their number, accor[d]ing to the ordinance; [25]also one kid of the goats *as* a s[in] offering, besides the regular burnt offering, its grain [of]fering, and its drink offering.

[26]On the fifth day *present* nine bulls, two rams, *a[nd]* fourteen lambs in their first year without blemish, [27]a[nd] their grain offering and their drink offerings for the bu[ll] for the rams, and for the lambs, by their number, acco[r]ing to the ordinance; [28]also one goat *as* a sin offerin[g] besides the regular burnt offering, its grain offering, a[nd] its drink offering.

[29]On the sixth day *present* eight bulls, two rams, *a[nd]* fourteen lambs in their first year without blemish, [30]a[nd] their grain offering and their drink offerings for the bu[ll] for the rams, and for the lambs, by their number, acco[r]ing to the ordinance; [31]also one goat *as* a sin offerin[g] besides the regular burnt offering, its grain offering, a[nd] its drink offering.

[32]On the seventh day *present* seven bulls, two ram[s] *and* fourteen lambs in their first year without blemi[sh] [33]and their grain offering and their drink offerings for t[he] bulls, for the rams, and for the lambs, by their numb[er] according to the ordinance; [34]also one goat *as* a sin off[er]ing, besides the regular burnt offering, its grain offeri[ng] and its drink offering.

[35]On the eighth day you shall have a sacred assemb[ly.] You shall do no customary work. [36]You shall present [a] burnt offering, an offering made by fire as a sweet aro[ma] to the LORD: one bull, one ram, seven lambs in their fi[rst] year without blemish, [37]and their grain offering and th[eir] drink offerings for the bull, for the ram, and for t[he] lambs, by their number, according to the ordinan[ce;] [38]also one goat *as* a sin offering, besides the regular bur[nt] offering, its grain offering, and its drink offering.

[39]These you shall present to the LORD at your a[p]pointed feasts (besides your vowed offerings and yo[ur] freewill offerings) as your burnt offerings and your gra[in] offerings, as your drink offerings and your peace off[er]ings.' "

[40]So Moses told the children of Israel everything, ju[st] as the LORD commanded Moses.

CHAPTER 30 RULES ABOUT VOWS. Then Mos[es] spoke to the heads of the tribes concerning the childr[en] of Israel, saying, "This *is* the thing which the LORD h[as] commanded: [2]If a man makes a vow to the LORD,

wears an oath to bind himself by some agreement, he hall not break his word; he shall do according to all that proceeds out of his mouth.

³"Or if a woman makes a vow to the LORD, and binds *herself* by some agreement while in her father's house in her youth, ⁴and her father hears her vow and the agreement by which she has bound herself, and her father holds his peace, then all her vows shall stand, and every agreement with which she has bound herself shall stand. But if her father overrules her on the day that he hears, then none of her vows nor her agreements by which she has bound herself shall stand; and the LORD will release her, because her father overruled her.

⁶"If indeed she takes a husband, while bound by her vows or by a rash utterance from her lips by which she bound herself, ⁷and her husband hears *it*, and makes no response to her on the day that he hears, then her vows shall stand, and her agreements by which she bound herself shall stand. ⁸But if her husband overrules her on the day that he hears *it*, he shall make void her vow which he took and what she uttered with her lips, by which she bound herself, and the LORD will release her.

⁹"Also any vow of a widow or a divorced woman, by which she has bound herself, shall stand against her.

¹⁰"If she vowed in her husband's house, or bound herself by an agreement with an oath, ¹¹and her husband heard *it*, and made no response to her *and* did not overrule her, then all her vows shall stand, and every agreement by which she bound herself shall stand. ¹²But if her husband truly made them void on the day he heard *them*, then whatever proceeded from her lips concerning her vows or concerning the agreement binding her, it shall not stand; her husband has made them void, and the LORD will release her. ¹³Every vow and every binding oath to afflict her soul, her husband may confirm it, or her husband may make it void. ¹⁴Now if her husband makes no response whatever to her from day to day, then he confirms all her vows or all the agreements that bind her; he confirms them, because he made no response to her on the day that he heard *them*. ¹⁵But if he does make them void after he has heard *them*, then he shall bear her guilt."

¹⁶These *are* the statutes which the LORD commanded Moses, between a man and his wife, and between a father and his daughter in her youth in her father's house.

CHAPTER **31** THE WAR AGAINST MIDIAN. And the LORD spoke to Moses, saying: ²"Take vengeance on the Midianites for the children of Israel. Afterward you shall be gathered to your people."

³So Moses spoke to the people, saying, "Arm some of yourselves for war, and let them go against the Midianites to take vengeance for the LORD on Midian. ⁴A thousand from each tribe of all the tribes of Israel you shall send to the war."

⁵So there were recruited from the divisions of Israel one thousand from *each* tribe, twelve thousand armed for war. ⁶Then Moses sent them to the war, one thousand from *each* tribe; he sent them to the war with Phinehas the son of Eleazar the priest, with the holy articles and the signal trumpets in his hand. ⁷And they warred against the Midianites, just as the LORD commanded Moses, and they killed all the males. ⁸They killed the kings of Midian with *the rest of* those who were killed—Evi, Rekem, Zur, Hur, and Reba, the five kings of Midian. Balaam the son of Beor they also killed with the sword.

PROMISES

30:1-2 Moses reminded the people that their promises to God and others must be kept. In ancient times, people did not sign written contracts. A person's word was as binding as a signature. To make a vow even more binding, an offering was given along with it. No one was forced by law to make a vow; but once made, vows had to be fulfilled. Breaking a vow meant a broken trust and a broken relationship. Trust is still the basis of our relationships with God and others. Thus a broken promise today is just as harmful as it was in Moses' day.

⁹And the children of Israel took the women of Midian captive, with their little ones, and took as spoil all their cattle, all their flocks, and all their goods. ¹⁰They also burned with fire all the cities where they dwelt, and all their forts. ¹¹And they took all the spoil and all the booty—of man and beast.

¹²Then they brought the captives, the booty, and the spoil to Moses, to Eleazar the priest, and to the congregation of the children of Israel, to the camp in the plains of Moab by the Jordan, *across from* Jericho. ¹³And Moses, Eleazar the priest, and all the leaders of the congregation, went to meet them outside the camp. ¹⁴But Moses was angry with the officers of the army, *with* the captains over thousands and captains over hundreds, who had come from the battle.

¹⁵And Moses said to them: "Have you kept all the women alive? ¹⁶Look, these *women* caused the children of Israel, through the counsel of Balaam, to trespass against the LORD in the incident of Peor, and there was a plague among the congregation of the LORD. ¹⁷Now therefore, kill every male among the little ones, and kill every woman who has known a man intimately. ¹⁸But keep alive for yourselves all the young girls who have not known a man intimately. ¹⁹And as for you, remain outside the camp seven days; whoever has killed any person, and whoever has touched any slain, purify yourselves and your captives on the third day and on the seventh day. ²⁰Purify every garment, everything made of leather, everything woven of goats' *hair*, and everything made of wood."

²¹Then Eleazar the priest said to the men of war who had gone to the battle, "This *is* the ordinance of the law which the LORD commanded Moses: ²²"Only the gold, the

PARENTS

30:3-8 Under Israelite law, parents could overrule their children's vows. This helped young people avoid making foolish promises or costly commitments. From this law comes an important principle for both parents and children. Young people still living at home should seek their parents' help when they make decisions. A parent's experience could save a child from a serious mistake. Parents, however, should exercise their authority with caution and grace. They should let children learn from their mistakes while protecting them from disaster.

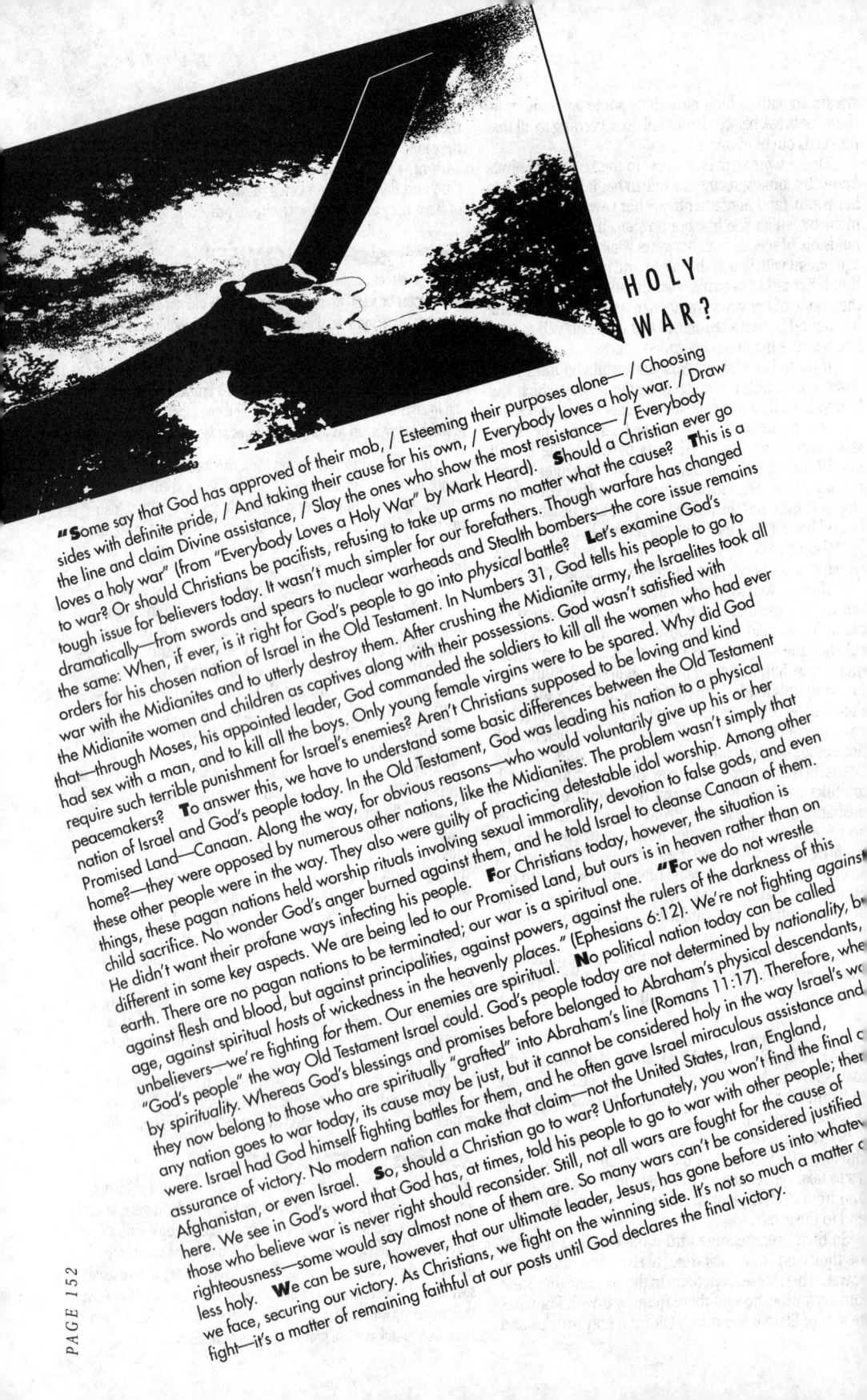

HOLY WAR?

"Some say that God has approved of their mob, / Esteeming their purposes alone— / Choosing sides with definite pride, / And taking their cause for his own, / Everybody loves a holy war. / Draw the line and claim Divine assistance, / Slay the ones who show the most resistance— / Everybody loves a holy war" (from "Everybody Loves a Holy War" by Mark Heard). **S**hould a Christian ever go to war? Or should Christians be pacifists, refusing to take up arms no matter what the cause? **T**his is a tough issue for believers today. It wasn't much simpler for our forefathers. Though warfare has changed dramatically—from swords and spears to nuclear warheads and Stealth bombers—the core issue remains the same: When, if ever, is it right for God's people to go into physical battle? **L**et's examine God's orders for his chosen nation of Israel in the Old Testament. In Numbers 31, God tells his people to go to war—through Moses, his appointed leader. Only young female virgins were to be spared. Why did God require such terrible punishment for Israel's enemies? Aren't Christians supposed to be loving and kind peacemakers? **T**o answer this, we have to understand some basic differences between the Old Testament nation of Israel and God's people today. In the Old Testament, God was leading his nation to a physical Promised Land—Canaan. Along the way, for obvious reasons, like the Midianites. God wasn't satisfied with these other people were in the way. They also were guilty of practicing detestable idol worship. Among other things, these pagan nations held worship rituals involving sexual immorality, devotion to false gods, and even child sacrifice. No wonder God's anger burned against them, and he told Israel to cleanse Canaan of them. He didn't want their profane ways infecting his people. For Christians today, however, the situation is different in some key aspects. We are being led to our Promised Land, but ours is in heaven rather than on earth. There are no pagan nations to be terminated; our war is a spiritual one. **"F**or we do not wrestle against flesh and blood, but against principalities, against powers, against the rulers of the darkness of this age, against spiritual hosts of wickedness in the heavenly places." (Ephesians 6:12). We're not fighting against unbelievers—we're fighting for them. Our enemies are spiritual. **N**o political nation today can be called "God's people" the way Old Testament Israel could. God's people today are not determined by nationality, but by spirituality. Whereas God's blessings and promises before belonged to Abraham's physical descendants, they now belong to those who are spiritually "grafted" into Abraham's line (Romans 11:17). Therefore, when any nation goes to war today, its cause may be just, but it cannot be considered holy in the way Israel's war were. Israel had God himself fighting battles for them, and he often gave Israel miraculous assistance and assurance of victory. No modern nation can make that claim—not the United States, Iran, England, Afghanistan, or even Israel. **S**o, should a Christian go to war? Unfortunately, you won't find the final a here. We see in God's word that God has, at times, told his people to go to war with other people; ther those who believe war is never right should reconsider. Still, not all wars are fought for the cause of righteousness—some would say almost none of them are. So many wars can't be considered justified less holy. **W**e can be sure, however, that our ultimate leader, Jesus, has gone before us into whatev we face, securing our victory. As Christians, we fight on the winning side. It's not so much a matter o fight—it's a matter of remaining faithful at our posts until God declares the final victory.

silver, the bronze, the iron, the tin, and the lead, ²³every-thing that can endure fire, you shall put through the fire, and it shall be clean; and it shall be purified with the water of purification. But all that cannot endure fire you shall put through water. ²⁴And you shall wash your clothes on the seventh day and be clean, and afterward you may come into the camp."

²⁵Now the LORD spoke to Moses, saying: ²⁶"Count up the plunder that was taken—of man and beast—you and Eleazar the priest and the chief fathers of the congregation; ²⁷and divide the plunder into two parts, between those who took part in the war, who went out to battle, and all the congregation. ²⁸And levy a tribute for the LORD on the men of war who went out to battle: one of every five hundred of the persons, the cattle, the donkeys, and the sheep; ²⁹take *it* from their half, and give *it* to Eleazar the priest as a heave offering to the LORD. ³⁰And from the children of Israel's half you shall take one of every fifty, drawn from the persons, the cattle, the donkeys, and the sheep, from all the livestock, and give them to the Levites who keep charge of the tabernacle of the LORD." ³¹So Moses and Eleazar the priest did as the LORD commanded Moses.

³²The booty remaining from the plunder, which the men of war had taken, was six hundred and seventy-five thousand sheep, ³³seventy-two thousand cattle, ³⁴sixty-one thousand donkeys, ³⁵and thirty-two thousand persons in all, of women who had not known a man intimately. ³⁶And the half, the portion for those who had gone out to war, was in number three hundred and thirty-seven thousand five hundred sheep; ³⁷and the LORD's tribute of the sheep was six hundred and seventy-five. ³⁸The cattle *were* thirty-six thousand, of which the LORD's tribute *was* seventy-two. ³⁹The donkeys *were* thirty thousand five hundred, of which the LORD's tribute *was* sixty-one. ⁴⁰The persons *were* sixteen thousand, of which the LORD's tribute *was* thirty-two persons. ⁴¹So Moses gave the tribute *which was* the LORD's heave offering to Eleazar the priest, as the LORD commanded Moses.

⁴²And from the children of Israel's half, which Moses separated from the men who fought— ⁴³now the half belonging to the congregation was three hundred and thirty-seven thousand five hundred sheep, ⁴⁴thirty-six thousand cattle, ⁴⁵thirty thousand five hundred donkeys, ⁴⁶and sixteen thousand persons— ⁴⁷and from the children of Israel's half Moses took one of every fifty, drawn from man and beast, and gave them to the Levites, who kept charge of the tabernacle of the LORD, as the LORD commanded Moses.

⁴⁸Then the officers who *were* over thousands of the army, the captains of thousands and captains of hundreds, came near to Moses; ⁴⁹and they said to Moses, "Your servants have taken a count of the men of war who *are* under our command, and not a man of us is missing. ⁵⁰Therefore we have brought an offering for the LORD, what every man found of ornaments of gold: armlets and bracelets and signet rings and earrings and necklaces, to make atonement for ourselves before the LORD." ⁵¹So Moses and Eleazar the priest received the gold from them, all the fashioned ornaments. ⁵²And all the gold of the offering that they offered to the LORD, from the cap-tains of thousands and captains of hundreds, was sixteen thousand seven hundred and fifty shekels. ⁵³(The men of war had taken spoil, every man for himself.) ⁵⁴And Moses and Eleazar the priest received the gold from the captains of thousands and of hundreds, and brought it into the tabernacle of meeting as a memorial for the children of Israel before the LORD.

CHAPTER **32** SOME TRIBES GET THEIR LAND.

Now the children of Reuben and the children of Gad had a very great multitude of livestock; and when they saw the land of Jazer and the land of Gilead, that indeed the region *was* a place for livestock, ²the children of Gad and the children of Reuben came and spoke to Moses, to Eleazar the priest, and to the leaders of the congregation, saying, ³"Ataroth, Dibon, Jazer, Nimrah, Heshbon, Ele-aleh, Shebam, Nebo, and Beon, ⁴the country which the LORD defeated before the congregation of Israel, *is* a land for livestock, and your servants have livestock." ⁵There-fore they said, "If we have found favor in your sight, let this land be given to your servants as a possession. Do not take us over the Jordan."

◣◥GENEROSITY

31:25-30 Moses told the Israelites to give a portion of the war booty to God. Another portion was to go to the people who remained behind. Similarly, the money we earn is not ours alone. Everything we possess comes directly or indirectly from God and ultimately belongs to him. We should return a portion to him (a "tribute") and also share a portion with those in need.

⁶And Moses said to the children of Gad and to the children of Reuben: "Shall your brethren go to war while you sit here? ⁷Now why will you discourage the heart of the children of Israel from going over into the land which the LORD has given them? ⁸Thus your fathers did when I sent them away from Kadesh Barnea to see the land. ⁹For when they went up to the Valley of Eshcol and saw the land, they discouraged the heart of the children of Israel, so that they did not go into the land which the LORD had given them. ¹⁰So the LORD's anger was aroused on that day, and He swore an oath, saying, ¹¹'Surely none of the men who came up from Egypt, from twenty years old and above, shall see the land of which I swore to Abraham, Isaac, and Jacob, because they have not wholly followed Me, ¹²except Caleb the son of Jephunneh, the Kenizzite, and Joshua the son of Nun, for they have wholly followed the LORD.' ¹³So the LORD's anger was aroused against Is-rael, and He made them wander in the wilderness forty

◣◥ASSUMING

32:1ff Three tribes (Reuben, Gad, and the half-tribe of Manasseh) wanted to live east of the Jordan River on land they had already conquered. Moses immediately assumed they had selfish motives and were trying to avoid helping the others fight for the land across the river. But Moses jumped to the wrong conclusion. In dealing with people, we must find out all the facts before making up our mind. We shouldn't automatically assume that their motives are wrong, even if their plans sound suspicious.

years, until all the generation that had done evil in the sight of the LORD was gone. ¹⁴And look! You have risen in your fathers' place, a brood of sinful men, to increase still more the fierce anger of the LORD against Israel. ¹⁵For if you turn away from following Him, He will once again leave them in the wilderness, and you will destroy all these people."

Be sure

NUMBERS 32:23

your sin WILL FIND YOU OUT YOU OUT YOU OUT WILL FIND YOU OUT YOU OUT WILL FIND YOU OUT

¹⁶Then they came near to him and said: "We will build sheepfolds here for our livestock, and cities for our little ones, ¹⁷but we ourselves will be armed, ready *to go* before the children of Israel until we have brought them to their place; and our little ones will dwell in the fortified cities because of the inhabitants of the land. ¹⁸We will not return to our homes until every one of the children of Israel has received his inheritance. ¹⁹For we will not inherit with them on the other side of the Jordan and beyond, because our inheritance has fallen to us on this eastern side of the Jordan."

²⁰Then Moses said to them: "If you do this thing, if you arm yourselves before the LORD for the war, ²¹and all your armed men cross over the Jordan before the LORD until He has driven out His enemies from before Him, ²²and the land is subdued before the LORD, then afterward you may return and be blameless before the LORD and before Israel; and this land shall be your possession before the LORD. ²³But if you do not do so, then take note, you have sinned against the LORD; and be sure your sin will find you out. ²⁴Build cities for your little ones and folds for your sheep, and do what has proceeded out of your mouth."

²⁵And the children of Gad and the children of Reuben spoke to Moses, saying: "Your servants will do as my lord commands. ²⁶Our little ones, our wives, our flocks, and all our livestock will be there in the cities of Gilead; ²⁷but your servants will cross over, every man armed for war, before the LORD to battle, just as my lord says."

²⁸So Moses gave command concerning them to Eleazar the priest, to Joshua the son of Nun, and to the chief fathers of the tribes of the children of Israel. ²⁹And Moses said to them: "If the children of Gad and the children of Reuben cross over the Jordan with you, every man armed for battle before the LORD, and the land is subdued before you, then you shall give them the land of Gilead as a possession. ³⁰But if they do not cross over armed with

you, they shall have possessions among you in the land of Canaan."

³¹Then the children of Gad and the children of Reuben answered, saying: "As the LORD has said to your servants, so we will do. ³²We will cross over armed before the LORD into the land of Canaan, but the possession of our inheritance *shall remain* with us on this side of the Jordan."

³³So Moses gave to the children of Gad, to the children of Reuben, and to half the tribe of Manasseh the son of Joseph, the kingdom of Sihon king of the Amorites and the kingdom of Og king of Bashan, the land with its cities within the borders, the cities of the surrounding country. ³⁴And the children of Gad built Dibon and Ataroth and Aroer, ³⁵Atroth and Shophan and Jazer and Jogbehah, ³⁶Beth Nimrah and Beth Haran, fortified cities, and folds for sheep. ³⁷And the children of Reuben built Heshbon and Elealeh and Kirjathaim, ³⁸Nebo and Baal Meon (*their* names being changed) and Shibmah; and they gave *other* names to the cities which they built.

³⁹And the children of Machir the son of Manasseh went to Gilead and took it, and dispossessed the Amorites who *were* in it. ⁴⁰So Moses gave Gilead to Machir the son of Manasseh, and he dwelt in it. ⁴¹Also Jair the son of Manasseh went and took its small towns, and called them Havoth Jair. ⁴²Then Nobah went and took Kenath and its villages, and he called it Nobah, after his own name.

CHAPTER **33** **THE PROMISED LAND.** These *are* the journeys of the children of Israel, who went out of the land of Egypt by their armies under the hand of Moses and Aaron. ²Now Moses wrote down the starting points of their journeys at the command of the LORD. And these *are* their journeys according to their starting points:

³They departed from Rameses in the first month, on the fifteenth day of the first month; on the day after the Passover the children of Israel went out with boldness in the sight of all the Egyptians. ⁴For the Egyptians were burying all *their* firstborn, whom the LORD had killed among them. Also on their gods the LORD had executed judgments.

⁵Then the children of Israel moved from Rameses and camped at Succoth. ⁶They departed from Succoth and camped at Etham, which *is* on the edge of the wilderness. ⁷They moved from Etham and turned back to Pi Hahiroth, which *is* east of Baal Zephon; and they camped near Migdol. ⁸They departed from before Hahiroth and passed through the midst of the sea into the wilderness, went three days' journey in the Wilderness of Etham, and camped at Marah. ⁹They moved from Marah and came to Elim. At Elim *were* twelve springs of water and seventy palm trees; so they camped there.

⟋⟋⟍ RECORD

33:2 Moses recorded the Israelites' journeys as God instructed, providing a record of their spiritual as well as geographic progress. Have you made spiritual progress lately? Recording your thoughts about and lessons you have learned over a period of time can be a valuable aid to spiritual growth. A record of your spiritual pilgrimage will let you up on your progress and avoid past mistakes.

¹⁰They moved from Elim and camped by the Red Sea. ¹¹They moved from the Red Sea and camped in the Wilderness of Sin. ¹²They journeyed from the Wilderness of Sin and camped at Dophkah. ¹³They departed from Dophkah and camped at Alush. ¹⁴They moved from Alush and camped at Rephidim, where there was no water for the people to drink.

¹⁵They departed from Rephidim and camped in the Wilderness of Sinai. ¹⁶They moved from the Wilderness of Sinai and camped at Kibroth Hattaavah. ¹⁷They departed from Kibroth Hattaavah and camped at Hazeroth. ¹⁸They departed from Hazeroth and camped at Rithmah. ¹⁹They departed from Rithmah and camped at Rimmon Perez. ²⁰They departed from Rimmon Perez and camped at Libnah. ²¹They moved from Libnah and camped at Rissah. ²²They journeyed from Rissah and camped at Kehelathah. ²³They went from Kehelathah and camped at Mount Shepher. ²⁴They moved from Mount Shepher and camped at Haradah. ²⁵They moved from Haradah and camped at Makheloth. ²⁶They moved from Makheloth and camped at Tahath. ²⁷They departed from Tahath and camped at Terah. ²⁸They moved from Terah and camped at Mithkah. ²⁹They went from Mithkah and camped at Hashmonah. ³⁰They departed from Hashmonah and camped at Moseroth. ³¹They departed from Moseroth and camped at Bene Jaakan. ³²They moved from Bene Jaakan and camped at Hor Hagidgad. ³³They went from Hor Hagidgad and camped at Jotbathah. ³⁴They moved from Jotbathah and camped at Abronah. ³⁵They departed from Abronah and camped at Ezion Geber. ³⁶They moved from Ezion Geber and camped in the Wilderness of Zin, which *is* Kadesh. ³⁷They moved from Kadesh and camped at Mount Hor, on the boundary of the land of Edom.

³⁸Then Aaron the priest went up to Mount Hor at the command of the LORD, and died there in the fortieth year after the children of Israel had come out of the land of Egypt, on the first *day* of the fifth month. ³⁹Aaron *was* one hundred and twenty-three years old when he died on Mount Hor.

⁴⁰Now the king of Arad, the Canaanite, who dwelt in the South in the land of Canaan, heard of the coming of the children of Israel.

⁴¹So they departed from Mount Hor and camped at Zalmonah. ⁴²They departed from Zalmonah and camped at Punon. ⁴³They departed from Punon and camped at Oboth. ⁴⁴They departed from Oboth and camped at Ije Abarim, at the border of Moab. ⁴⁵They departed from Ijim and camped at Dibon Gad. ⁴⁶They moved from Dibon Gad and camped at Almon Diblathaim. ⁴⁷They moved from Almon Diblathaim and camped in the mountains of Abarim, before Nebo. ⁴⁸They departed from the mountains of Abarim and camped in the plains of Moab by the Jordan, *across from* Jericho. ⁴⁹They camped by the Jordan, from Beth Jesimoth as far as the Abel Acacia Grove in the plains of Moab.

⁵⁰Now the LORD spoke to Moses in the plains of Moab by the Jordan, *across from* Jericho, saying, ⁵¹"Speak to the children of Israel, and say to them: 'When you have crossed the Jordan into the land of Canaan, ⁵²then you shall drive out all the inhabitants of the land from before you, destroy all their engraved stones, destroy all their molded images, and demolish all their high places; ⁵³you shall dispossess *the inhabitants of* the land and dwell in it, for I have given you the land to possess. ⁵⁴And you shall divide the land by lot as an inheritance among your families; to the larger you shall give a larger inheritance, and to the smaller you shall give a smaller inheritance; there everyone's *inheritance* shall be whatever falls to him by lot. You shall inherit according to the tribes of your fathers. ⁵⁵But if you do not drive out the inhabitants of the land from before you, then it shall be that those whom you let remain *shall be* irritants in your eyes and thorns in your sides, and they shall harass you in the land where you dwell. ⁵⁶Moreover it shall be *that* I will do to you as I thought to do to them.' "

CHAPTER **34** BORDERS OF THE NEW LAND.

Then the LORD spoke to Moses, saying, ²"Command the children of Israel, and say to them: 'When you come into the land of Canaan, this *is* the land that shall fall to you as an inheritance—the land of Canaan to its boundaries. ³Your southern border shall be from the Wilderness of Zin along the border of Edom; then your southern border shall extend eastward to the end of the Salt Sea; ⁴your border shall turn from the southern side of the Ascent of Akrabbim, continue to Zin, and be on the south of Kadesh Barnea; then it shall go on to Hazar Addar, and continue to Azmon; ⁵the border shall turn from Azmon to the Brook of Egypt, and it shall end at the Sea.

⁶'As for the western border, you shall have the Great Sea for a border; this shall be your western border.

⁷'And this shall be your northern border: From the Great Sea you shall mark out your *border* line to Mount Hor; ⁸from Mount Hor you shall mark out *your border* to the entrance of Hamath; then the direction of the border shall be toward Zedad; ⁹the border shall proceed to Ziphron, and it shall end at Hazar Enan. This shall be your northern border.

¹⁰'You shall mark out your eastern border from Hazar Enan to Shepham; ¹¹the border shall go down from Shepham to Riblah on the east side of Ain; the border shall go down and reach to the eastern side of the Sea of Chinnereth; ¹²the border shall go down along the Jordan, and it shall end at the Salt Sea. This shall be your land with its surrounding boundaries.' "

¹³Then Moses commanded the children of Israel, saying: "This *is* the land which you shall inherit by lot, which the LORD has commanded to give to the nine tribes and to the half-tribe. ¹⁴For the tribe of the children of Reuben according to the house of their fathers, and the tribe of the children of Gad according to the house of their fathers, have received *their inheritance;* and the half-tribe of Manasseh has received its inheritance. ¹⁵The two tribes and the half-tribe have received their inheritance on this side of the Jordan, *across from* Jericho eastward, toward the sunrise."

¹⁶And the LORD spoke to Moses, saying, ¹⁷"These *are* the names of the men who shall divide the land among you as an inheritance: Eleazar the priest and Joshua the son of Nun. ¹⁸And you shall take one leader of every tribe to divide the land for the inheritance. ¹⁹These *are* the

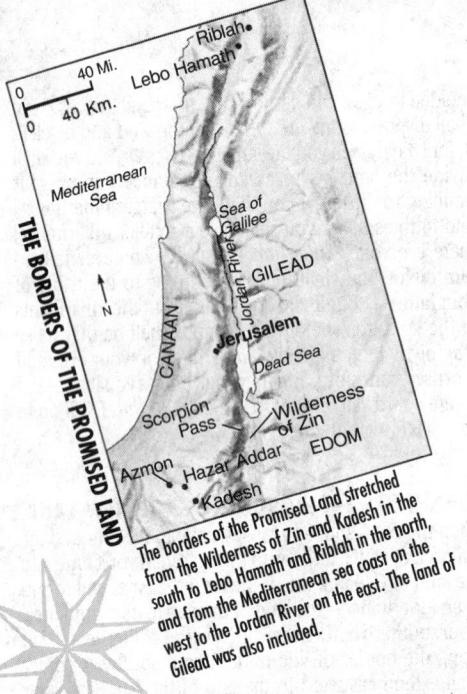

THE BORDERS OF THE PROMISED LAND

The borders of the Promised Land stretched from the Wilderness of Zin and Kadesh in the south to Lebo Hamath and Riblah in the north, and from the Mediterranean sea coast on the west to the Jordan River on the east. The land of Gilead was also included.

names of the men: from the tribe of Judah, Caleb the son of Jephunneh; [20]from the tribe of the children of Simeon, Shemuel the son of Ammihud; [21]from the tribe of Benjamin, Elidad the son of Chislon; [22]a leader from the tribe of the children of Dan, Bukki the son of Jogli; [23]from the sons of Joseph: a leader from the tribe of the children of Manasseh, Hanniel the son of Ephod, [24]and a leader from the tribe of the children of Ephraim, Kemuel the son of Shiphtan; [25]a leader from the tribe of the children of Zebulun, Elizaphan the son of Parnach; [26]a leader from the tribe of the children of Issachar, Paltiel the son of Azzan; [27]a leader from the tribe of the children of Asher, Ahihud the son of Shelomi; [28]and a leader from the tribe of the children of Naphtali, Pedahel the son of Ammihud."

[29]These *are* the ones the LORD commanded to divide the inheritance among the children of Israel in the land of Canaan.

CHAPTER 35 CITIES FOR THE LEVITES. And the LORD spoke to Moses in the plains of Moab by the Jordan *across from* Jericho, saying: [2]"Command the children of Israel that they give the Levites cities to dwell in from the inheritance of their possession, and you shall *also* give the Levites common-land around the cities. [3]They shall have the cities to dwell in; and their common-land shall be for their cattle, for their herds, and for all their animals. [4]The common-land of the cities which you will give the Levites *shall extend* from the wall of the city outward a thousand cubits all around. [5]And you shall measure outside the city on the east side two thousand cubits, on the south side two thousand cubits, on the west side two thousand cubits, and on the north side two thousand cubits. The city *shall be* in the middle. This shall belong to them as common-land for the cities.

[6]"Now among the cities which you will give to the Levites *you shall appoint* six cities of refuge, to which a manslayer may flee. And to these you shall add forty-two cities. [7]So all the cities you will give to the Levites *shall be* forty-eight; these *you shall give* with their common-land. [8]And the cities which you will give *shall be* from the possession of the children of Israel; from the larger *tribe* you shall give many, from the smaller you shall give few. Each shall give some of its cities to the Levites, in proportion to the inheritance that each receives."

▶ **DO YOUR JOB**

34:16-29 In God's plan for settling the land, he (1) explained wha[t] do, (2) communicated this clearly to Moses, and (3) assigned specific people to oversee the apportionment of the land. No plan is comple[te] until each job is assigned and everyone understands his or her responsibilities. When you have a job to do, determine what must be done, give clear instructions, and put specific people in charge of eac[h] part.

[9]Then the LORD spoke to Moses, saying, [10]"Speak to the children of Israel, and say to them: 'When you cross the Jordan into the land of Canaan, [11]then you shall appoint cities to be cities of refuge for you, that the manslayer who kills any person accidentally may flee there. [12]They shall be cities of refuge for you from the avenger, that the manslayer may not die until he stands before the congregation in judgment. [13]And of the cities which you give, you shall have six cities of refuge. [14]You shall appoint three cities on this side of the Jordan, and three cities you shall appoint in the land of Canaan, *which* will be cities of refuge. [15]These six cities shall be for refuge for the children of Israel, for the stranger, and for the sojourner among them, that anyone who kills a person accidentally may flee there.

[16]'But if he strikes him with an iron implement, so that he dies, he *is* a murderer; the murderer shall surely be put to death. [17]And if he strikes him with a stone in the hand, by which one could die, and he does die, he *is* a murderer; the murderer shall surely be put to death. [18]Or *if* he strikes him with a wooden hand weapon, by which one could die, and he does die, he *is* a murderer; the murderer shall surely be put to death. [19]The avenger of blood himself shall put the murderer to death; when he meets him, he shall put him to death. [20]If he pushes him out of hatred or, while lying in wait, hurls something at him so that he dies, [21]or in enmity he strikes him with his hand so that he dies, the one who struck *him* shall surely be put to death. He *is* a murderer. The avenger of blood shall put the murderer to death when he meets him.

▶ **JUSTICE**

35:11-28 If anyone died because of violence, murder was assu[med] but the murder suspect was not automatically assumed guilty. The[y] were to be intolerant of the sin, yet impartial to the accused so th[at] she could have a fair trial. The cities of refuge represented God's [plan] for justice in a culture that did not always protect the innocent. It [is] both to overlook wrongdoing and to jump to conclusions about gu[ilt.] When someone is accused of wrongdoing, stand up for justice, pr[otect] those not yet proven guilty, and listen carefully to all sides of the [story.]

²²'However, if he pushes him suddenly without enmity, or throws anything at him without lying in wait, ²³or uses a stone, by which a man could die, throwing *it* at him without seeing *him*, so that he dies, while he was not his enemy or seeking his harm, ²⁴then the congregation shall judge between the manslayer and the avenger of blood according to these judgments. ²⁵So the congregation shall deliver the manslayer from the hand of the avenger of blood, and the congregation shall return him to the city of refuge where he had fled, and he shall remain there until the death of the high priest who was anointed with the holy oil. ²⁶But if the manslayer at any time goes outside the limits of the city of refuge where he fled, ²⁷and the avenger of blood finds him outside the limits of his city of refuge, and the avenger of blood kills the manslayer, he shall not be guilty of blood, ²⁸because he should have remained in his city of refuge until the death of the high priest. But after the death of the high priest the manslayer may return to the land of his possession.

²⁹And these *things* shall be a statute of judgment to you throughout your generations in all your dwellings. ³⁰Whoever kills a person, the murderer shall be put to death on the testimony of witnesses; but one witness is not *sufficient* testimony against a person for the death *penalty.* ³¹Moreover you shall take no ransom for the life of a murderer who *is* guilty of death, but he shall surely be put to death. ³²And you shall take no ransom for him who has fled to his city of refuge, that he may return to dwell in the land before the death of the priest. ³³So you shall not pollute the land where you *are;* for blood defiles the land, and no atonement can be made for the land, for the blood that is shed on it, except by the blood of him who shed it. ³⁴Therefore do not defile the land which you inhabit, in the midst of which I dwell; for I the LORD dwell among the children of Israel.' "

CHAPTER 36 EACH TRIBE'S LAND TO REMAIN

SECURE. Now the chief fathers of the families of the children of Gilead the son of Machir, the son of Manasseh, of the families of the sons of Joseph, came near and spoke before Moses and before the leaders, the chief fathers of the children of Israel. ²And they said: "The LORD commanded my lord *Moses* to give the land as an inheritance by lot to the children of Israel, and my lord was commanded by the LORD to give the inheritance of our brother Zelophehad to his daughters. ³Now if they are married to any of the sons of the *other* tribes of the children of Israel, then their inheritance will be taken from the inheritance of our fathers, and it will be added to the inheritance of the tribe into which they marry; so it will be taken from the lot of our inheritance. ⁴And when the Jubilee of the children of Israel comes, then their inheritance will be added to the inheritance of the tribe into which they marry; so their inheritance will be taken away from the inheritance of the tribe of our fathers."

⁵Then Moses commanded the children of Israel according to the word of the LORD, saying: "What the tribe of the sons of Joseph speaks is right. ⁶This *is* what the

BITTERNESS

35:33 Murderers were to be executed because they corrupted the land. But Jesus startles us by saying that even becoming angry at someone for no reason is a sin like murder (Matthew 5:21-22). Murder and anger stem from the same root. While one seems a lesser sin, it often will lead to more sin. Unchecked bitterness and anger will ultimately destroy us. We need to deal with these unhealthy emotions before they fester and corrupt our life.

LORD commands concerning the daughters of Zelophehad, saying, 'Let them marry whom they think best, but they may marry only within the family of their father's tribe.' ⁷So the inheritance of the children of Israel shall not change hands from tribe to tribe, for every one of the children of Israel shall keep the inheritance of the tribe of his fathers. ⁸And every daughter who possesses an inheritance in any tribe of the children of Israel shall be the wife of one of the family of her father's tribe, so that the children of Israel each may possess the inheritance of his fathers. ⁹Thus no inheritance shall change hands from *one* tribe to another, but every tribe of the children of Israel shall keep its own inheritance."

¹⁰Just as the LORD commanded Moses, so did the daughters of Zelophehad; ¹¹for Mahlah, Tirzah, Hoglah, Milcah, and Noah, the daughters of Zelophehad, were married to the sons of their father's brothers. ¹²They were married into the families of the children of Manasseh the son of Joseph, and their inheritance remained in the tribe of their father's family.

¹³These *are* the commandments and the judgments which the LORD commanded the children of Israel by the hand of Moses in the plains of Moab by the Jordan, *across from* Jericho.

MEGA Themes

CENSUS Moses counted the Israelites twice. The first census organized the people into marching units for better defense. The second census prepared them to conquer the country east of the Jordan.

People have to be organized, trained, and led to be effective in making a difference in their world. Before beginning great tasks, it is always wise to count the cost that lies ahead. Preparation for being effective for God in this world also includes removing any barriers in our relationships with others so that we can work with his people to accomplish his will.

1. Musical groups are examples of how people work together to produce something greater than they could do as individuals. What other things require teamwork in order for people to reach their goals or produce the desired results?
2. In what ways is a church an example of teamwork?
3. Think of your church or perhaps your youth group. Consider these questions:
- What can you accomplish with God through working together that could not be done if you did not have teamwork?
- What actions or attitudes cause this group of people to fail to be a team?
- What are some of the actions or attitudes that contribute to this group of people being successful as a team?
- What are some specific ways you can contribute to the success of this group?
- Finish this sentence: I am important to this group because_____.

REBELLION At Kadesh 12 spies were sent out into the land of Canaan to see what the fortifications of the enemies looked like. When the spies returned, 10 said that they should give up and go back to Egypt. As a result, the people refused to go into the land. Thus, the people rebelled against the will of God. The decision to rebel was not a sudden change of attitude. It came after a long period of complaining about Moses and God.

Rebellion against God is always serious. It is not something to take lightly because God's punishment for sin is often very severe. Usually, rebellion is not an abrupt, radical departure from God as much as it is a result of a long-term drifting, often characterized by griping and criticizing.

1. What do your parents most often criticize or gripe about?

2. What do your friends most often criticize or gripe about?
3. When did you complain to God about something or someone? How did you feel before you complained? Afterwards?
4. Describe a time in your life when you felt unhappy with how life was going for you and wondered if God really was taking care of you. How did you work through your feelings?
5. What is an appropriate response when you are feeling frustrated or angry because you do not understand why God is allowing your life to be the way it is? Why is it important to avoid griping or criticizing God? How can you share your feelings without becoming rebellious?

WANDERING Because they rebelled, the Israelites wandered 40 years in the wilderness. This shows how strongly God feels about sinful rebellion. During this time, God trained a new generation to follow him while those who still had wrong attitudes died.

God judges sin not just because he does not like it, but because he is holy and cannot tolerate sinfulness. The Israelites serve as a negative example of how God punishes sin, and a positive example of how he raises up a younger generation of people who will obey him.

1. What happens in the lives of Christians who drift away from God?
2. If you saw a friend rebelling against God, what would you tell him or her as a warning about the consequences of rebellion? What if that friend replied, "It's OK. God will forgive me"?
3. What type of people do you think God is looking for in your generation? How can you prepare yourself to avoid drifting and, instead, become one of God's leaders?

CANAAN Canaan is the Promised Land. It was the land God promised to Abraham, Isaac, and Jacob—the land of the covenant. Canaan was to be the dwelling place of God's people, those set apart for true spiritual worship.

Because he is holy, God punishes sin severely. However, because he is Lord, God offers grace for forgiveness of sins. Just as God's holy law and loving grace led Israel into the Promised Land, God wants to lead us into his purpose and destiny for our life.

1. List some of the things you learned about God as he led his people into Canaan.

2. Based on this knowledge, describe the kind of relationship he wants to have with you as you live out your life.

3. What are some of your dreams for the future? How should God be a part of those dreams?

4. How would you complete these thoughts for your own life: (a) God's purpose in my life is _____. (b) I can trust God with this purpose because _____.

*D*o you have a "memories" drawer, a place where you keep various reminders from your past? Maybe you have a wall, or even a box filled with mementos of happy occasions. Some people save the petals off prom flowers. Others keep ticket stubs from movies, ball games, or concerts. Some store especially meaningful letters or old pictures. ■ If you are like most people, these treasures become even more meaningful when you are going through tough times: when you're sad or lonely or scared about the future. There is something comforting in remembering the good times you've had. Your keepsakes remind you that everything is going to be OK. ■ The book of Deuteronomy is a book of "memories." God had made a covenant, or promise, with the slaves who first came out of Egypt, pledging to take them into the Promised Land. But the Israelites refused to obey or trust God. So he left them to wander in the wilderness until they died. ■ But a new generation had grown up, so God, through Moses, reminded them of the convenant. Moses recounted to the people the mighty acts God had done for Israel. Then he let them know that, based on the past, they must trust, obey, and love God as they advanced on their new homeland. Only such an attitude would enable them to conquer the Promised Land. ■ As you read Deuteronomy, let God remind you of the ways he has helped you in the past. Then, when you are fearful, you will trust yourself to him.

STATS

PURPOSE: To remind the people of what God has done and encourage them to rededicate their lives to him

AUTHOR: Moses (except for the final summary which was probably written after Moses' death by Joshua)

TO WHOM WRITTEN: Israel (the new generation entering the Promised Land)

DATE WRITTEN: About 1407/6 B.C.

SETTING: The east side of the Jordan River, in view of the Promised Land

KEY PEOPLE: Moses, Joshua

KEY PLACE: The valley of Arabah in Moab, east of the Jordan River

Deuteronomy

CHAPTER 1 **MOSES TALKS TO THE PEOPLE.** These *are* the words which Moses spoke to all Israel on this side of the Jordan in the wilderness, in the plain opposite Suph, between Paran, Tophel, Laban, Hazeroth, and Dizahab. ²*It is* eleven days' *journey* from Horeb by way of Mount Seir to Kadesh Barnea. ³Now it came to pass in the fortieth year, in the eleventh month, on the first *day* of the month, *that* Moses spoke to the children of Israel according to all that the LORD had given him as commandments to them, ⁴after he had killed Sihon king of the Amorites, who dwelt in Heshbon, and Og king of Bashan, who dwelt at Ashtaroth in Edrei.

⁵On this side of the Jordan in the land of Moab, Moses began to explain this law, saying, ⁶"The LORD our God spoke to us in Horeb, saying: 'You have dwelt long enough at this mountain. ⁷Turn and take your journey, and go to the mountains of the Amorites, to all the neighboring *places* in the plain, in the mountains and in the lowland, in the South and on the seacoast, to the land of the Canaanites and to Lebanon, as far as the great river, the River Euphrates. ⁸See, I have set the land before you; go in and possess the land which the LORD swore to your fathers—to Abraham, Isaac, and Jacob—to give to them and their descendants after them.'

⁹"And I spoke to you at that time, saying: 'I alone am not able to bear you. ¹⁰The LORD your God has multiplied you, and here you *are* today, as the stars of heaven in multitude. ¹¹May the LORD God of your fathers make you a thousand times more numerous than you are, and bless you as He has promised you! ¹²How can I alone bear your problems and your burdens and your complaints?

¹³Choose wise, understanding, and knowledgeable men from among your tribes, and I will make them heads over you.' ¹⁴And you answered me and said, 'The thing which you have told *us* to do *is* good.' ¹⁵So I took the heads of your tribes, wise and knowledgeable men, and made them heads over you, leaders of thousands, leaders of hundreds, leaders of fifties, leaders of tens, and officers for your tribes.

LEADERSHIP

1:13-18 Moses identified some of the inner qualities of good leaders: (1) wisdom, (2) understanding, (3) impartiality, and (4) the ability to recognize their limitations. These characteristics differ greatly from the ones that often help elect leaders today: good looks, wealth, popularity, willingness to do anything to get to the top. The qualities Moses identified should be evident in our life as we lead, and we should look for them in the lives of those we elect to positions of leadership.

¹⁶"Then I commanded your judges at that time, saying, 'Hear *the cases* between your brethren, and judge righteously between a man and his brother or the stranger who is with him. ¹⁷You shall not show partiality in judgment; you shall hear the small as well as the great; you shall not be afraid in any man's presence, for the judgment *is* God's. The case that is too hard for you, bring to me, and I will hear it.' ¹⁸And I commanded you at that time all the things which you should do.

¹⁹"So we departed from Horeb, and went through all that great and terrible wilderness which you saw on the way to the mountains of the Amorites, as the LORD our God had commanded us. Then we came to Kadesh

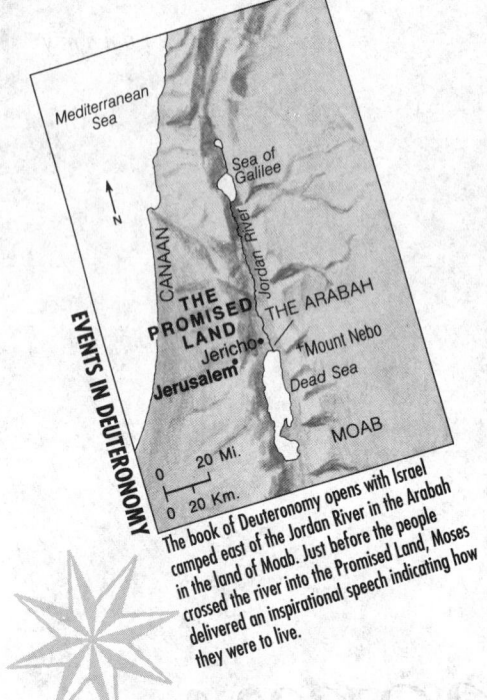

The book of Deuteronomy opens with Israel camped east of the Jordan River in the Arabah in the land of Moab. Just before the people crossed the river into the Promised Land, Moses delivered an inspirational speech indicating how they were to live.

Barnea. [20]And I said to you, 'You have come to the mountains of the Amorites, which the LORD our God is giving us. [21]Look, the LORD your God has set the land before you; go up *and* possess *it*, as the LORD God of your fathers has spoken to you; do not fear or be discouraged.'

[22]"And every one of you came near to me and said, 'Let us send men before us, and let them search out the land for us, and bring back word to us of the way by which we should go up, and of the cities into which we shall come.'

[23]"The plan pleased me well; so I took twelve of your men, one man from *each* tribe. [24]And they departed and went up into the mountains, and came to the Valley of Eshcol, and spied it out. [25]They also took *some* of the fruit of the land in their hands and brought *it* down to us; and they brought back word to us, saying, '*It is* a good land which the LORD our God is giving us.'

[26]"Nevertheless you would not go up, but rebelled against the command of the LORD your God; [27]and you complained in your tents, and said, 'Because the LORD hates us, He has brought us out of the land of Egypt to deliver us into the hand of the Amorites, to destroy us. [28]Where can we go up? Our brethren have discouraged our hearts, saying, "The people *are* greater and taller than we; the cities *are* great and fortified up to heaven; moreover we have seen the sons of the Anakim there." '

[29]"Then I said to you, 'Do not be terrified, or afraid of them. [30]The LORD your God, who goes before you, He will fight for you, according to all He did for you in Egypt before your eyes, [31]and in the wilderness where you saw how the LORD your God carried you, as a man carries his son, in all the way that you went until you came to this place.' [32]Yet, for all that, you did not believe the LORD your God, [33]who went in the way before you to search out a place for you to pitch your tents, to show you the way you should go, in the fire by night and in the cloud by day.

[34]"And the LORD heard the sound of your words, and was angry, and took an oath, saying, [35]'Surely not one of these men of this evil generation shall see that good land of which I swore to give to your fathers, [36]except Caleb the son of Jephunneh; he shall see it, and to him and his children I am giving the land on which he walked, because he wholly followed the LORD.' [37]The LORD was also angry with me for your sakes, saying, 'Even you shall not go in there. [38]Joshua the son of Nun, who stands before you, he shall go in there. Encourage him, for he shall cause Israel to inherit it.

[39]"Moreover your little ones and your children, who you say will be victims, who today have no knowledge of good and evil, they shall go in there; to them I will give it, and they shall possess it. [40]But *as for* you, turn and take your journey into the wilderness by the Way of the Red Sea.'

[41]"Then you answered and said to me, 'We have sinned against the LORD; we will go up and fight, just as the LORD our God commanded us.' And when everyone of you had girded on his weapons of war, you were ready to go up into the mountain.

[42]"And the LORD said to me, 'Tell them, "Do not go up nor fight, for I *am* not among you; lest you be defeated before your enemies." ' [43]So I spoke to you; yet you would not listen, but rebelled against the command of the LORD, and presumptuously went up into the mountain. [44]And the Amorites who dwelt in that mountain came out against you and chased you as bees do, and drove you back from Seir to Hormah. [45]Then you returned and wept before the LORD, but the LORD would not listen to your voice nor give ear to you.

[46]"So you remained in Kadesh many days, according to the days that you spent *there*.

CHAPTER **2** STUCK IN THE WILDERNESS. "Then we turned and journeyed into the wilderness of the Way of the Red Sea, as the LORD spoke to me, and we skirted Mount Seir for many days.

[2]"And the LORD spoke to me, saying: [3]'You have skirted this mountain long enough; turn northward. [4]And command the people, saying, "You *are about to* pass through the territory of your brethren, the descendants of Esau, who live in Seir; and they will be afraid of you. Therefore watch yourselves carefully. [5]Do not meddle with them, for I will not give you *any* of their land, no, not so much as one footstep, because I have given Mount Seir to Esau *as* a possession. [6]You shall buy food from them with money, that you may eat; and you shall also buy water from them with money, that you may drink.

[7]"For the LORD your God has blessed you in all the work of your hand. He knows your trudging through this great wilderness. These forty years the LORD your God *has been* with you; you have lacked nothing." '

[8]"And when we passed beyond our brethren, the descendants of Esau who dwell in Seir, away from the road of the plain, away from Elath and Ezion Geber, we turned and passed by way of the Wilderness of Moab. [9]Then the LORD said to me, 'Do not harass Moab, nor contend with them in battle, for I will not give you *any* of their land

possession, because I have given Ar to the descendants of Lot *as* a possession.' "

[10](The Emim had dwelt there in times past, a people as great and numerous and tall as the Anakim. [11]They were also regarded as giants, like the Anakim, but the Moabites call them Emim. [12]The Horites formerly dwelt in Seir, but the descendants of Esau dispossessed them and destroyed them from before them, and dwelt in their place, just as Israel did to the land of their possession which the LORD gave them.)

[13]" 'Now rise and cross over the Valley of the Zered.' So we crossed over the Valley of the Zered. [14]And the time we took to come from Kadesh Barnea until we crossed over the Valley of the Zered *was* thirty-eight years, until all the generation of the men of war was consumed from the midst of the camp, just as the LORD had sworn to them. For indeed the hand of the LORD was against them, to destroy them from the midst of the camp until they were consumed.

[16]"So it was, when all the men of war had finally perished from among the people, [17]that the LORD spoke to me, saying: [18]'This day you are to cross over at Ar, the boundary of Moab. [19]And *when* you come near the people of Ammon, do not harass them or meddle with them, for I will not give you *any* of the land of the people of Ammon *as* a possession, because I have given it to the descendants of Lot *as* a possession.' "

[20](That was also regarded as a land of giants; giants formerly dwelt there. But the Ammonites call them Zamzummim, [21]a people as great and numerous and tall as the Anakim. But the LORD destroyed them before them, and they dispossessed them and dwelt in their place, just as He had done for the descendants of Esau, who dwelt in Seir, when He destroyed the Horites from before them. They dispossessed them and dwelt in their place, even to this day. [23]And the Avim, who dwelt in villages as far as Gaza—the Caphtorim, who came from Caphtor, destroyed them and dwelt in their place.)

[24]" 'Rise, take your journey, and cross over the River Arnon. Look, I have given into your hand Sihon the Amorite, king of Heshbon, and his land. Begin to possess *it*, and engage him in battle. [25]This day I will begin to put the dread and fear of you upon the nations under the whole heaven, who shall hear the report of you, and shall tremble and be in anguish because of you.'

[26]"And I sent messengers from the Wilderness of Kedemoth to Sihon king of Heshbon, with words of peace, saying, [27]'Let me pass through your land; I will keep strictly to the road, and I will turn neither to the right nor to the left. [28]You shall sell me food for money, that I may eat, and give me water for money, that I may drink; only let me pass through on foot, [29]just as the descendants of Esau who dwell in Seir and the Moabites who dwell in Ar did for me, until I cross the Jordan to the land which the LORD our God is giving us.'

[30]"But Sihon king of Heshbon would not let us pass through, for the LORD your God hardened his spirit and made his heart obstinate, that He might deliver him into our hand, as *it is* this day.

[31]"And the LORD said to me, 'See, I have begun to give Sihon and his land over to you. Begin to possess *it*, that

you may inherit his land.' [32]Then Sihon and all his people came out against us to fight at Jahaz. [33]And the LORD our God delivered him over to us; so we defeated him, his sons, and all his people. [34]We took all his cities at that time, and we utterly destroyed the men, women, and little ones of every city; we left none remaining. [35]We took only the livestock as plunder for ourselves, with the spoil of the cities which we took. [36]From Aroer, which *is* on the bank of the River Arnon, and *from* the city that *is* in the ravine, as far as Gilead, there was not one city too strong for us; the LORD our God delivered all to us. [37]Only you did not go near the land of the people of Ammon—anywhere along the River Jabbok, or to the cities of the mountains, or wherever the LORD our God had forbidden us.

The Old Testament is long and sometimes boring. Why did God put it in the Bible?

I WONDER . . .

Have you ever asked one of your grandparents to tell you their whole life story? You would probably receive an all-day talk, full of wonderful stories. Though it would be fun for your grandparent, you would likely be bored because you would hear too many facts that would not relate to your life!

If, however, you asked him to relate the top ten experiences that shaped his personality and helped him make it through life, it would only take an hour, it would be fascinating, and you would learn a lot.

The Old Testament is not a detailed day-by-day account of history. Instead it is the story of the Jewish people. Their history points to Jesus Christ. Through this story, we see God's plan of sending his Son, Jesus, to die on the cross to pay the penalty for our sin.

Living in the twentieth century limits our appreciation of the fact that for 3000 years, the Old Testament has guided people from every walk of life. It was not just written for young people in the 1990s, but also for people who needed to hear from God in A.D. 320 Rome or A.D. 1540 Germany. What this means is that not every story will affect you the way it has others through the years. But as you read through the Old Testament, you will be surprised at how many stories relate to today. God's command to Moses and the Israelites to go into the Promised Land and possess it is the fulfillment of a promise to Abraham that God made long before Moses was even born. It shows that God has a plan for history and that he keeps his promises.

As a Christian, it is essential for you to realize that your heavenly Father keeps his promises! We are able to give him control of our life because for centuries he has proven himself trustworthy. (See Hebrews 11 for a brief recap of God's faithfulness.)

The Old Testament tells us about the real-life struggles people experienced when faced with the choice of trusting God or doing things their own way.

Instead of giving us all of history to read, God has condensed his story in one book. He has even pointed out the most important lessons we need to pay attention to in order to live life to the fullest as his children.

CHAPTER 3 DIVIDING THE LAND.

"Then we turned and went up the road to Bashan; and Og king of Bashan came out against us, he and all his people, to battle at Edrei. ²And the LORD said to me, 'Do not fear him, for I have delivered him and all his people and his land into your hand; you shall do to him as you did to Sihon king of the Amorites, who dwelt at Heshbon.'

OBSTACLES

3:1-3 The Israelites faced a big problem: the well-trained army of Og, king of Bashan. The Israelites hardly stood a chance. But they won because God fought for them. God can help his people regardless of the problems they face. No matter how insurmountable the obstacles may seem, remember that God is in control, and he will keep his promises.

³"So the LORD our God also delivered into our hands Og king of Bashan, with all his people, and we attacked him until he had no survivors remaining. ⁴And we took all his cities at that time; there was not a city which we did not take from them: sixty cities, all the region of Argob, the kingdom of Og in Bashan. ⁵All these cities *were* fortified with high walls, gates, and bars, besides a great many rural towns. ⁶And we utterly destroyed them, as we did to Sihon king of Heshbon, utterly destroying the men, women, and children of every city. ⁷But all the livestock and the spoil of the cities we took as booty for ourselves.

⁸"And at that time we took the land from the hand of the two kings of the Amorites who *were* on this side of the Jordan, from the River Arnon to Mount Hermon ⁹(the Sidonians call Hermon Sirion, and the Amorites call it Senir), ¹⁰all the cities of the plain, all Gilead, and all Bashan, as far as Salcah and Edrei, cities of the kingdom of Og in Bashan.

¹¹"For only Og king of Bashan remained of the remnant of the giants. Indeed his bedstead *was* an iron bedstead. (*Is* it not in Rabbah of the people of Ammon?) Nine cubits *is* its length and four cubits its width, according to the standard cubit.

¹²"And this land, *which* we possessed at that time, from Aroer, which *is* by the River Arnon, and half the mountains of Gilead and its cities, I gave to the Reubenites and the Gadites. ¹³The rest of Gilead, and all Bashan, the kingdom of Og, I gave to half the tribe of Manasseh. (All the region of Argob, with all Bashan, was called the land of the giants. ¹⁴Jair the son of Manasseh took all the region of Argob, as far as the border of the Geshurites and the Maachathites, and called Bashan after his own name, Havoth Jair, to this day.)

¹⁵"Also I gave Gilead to Machir. ¹⁶And to the Reubenites and the Gadites I gave from Gilead as far as the River Arnon, the middle of the river as *the* border, as far as the River Jabbok, the border of the people of Ammon; ¹⁷the plain also, with the Jordan as *the* border, from Chinnereth as far as the east side of the Sea of the Arabah (the Salt Sea), below the slopes of Pisgah.

¹⁸"Then I commanded you at that time, saying: 'The LORD your God has given you this land to possess. All you men of valor shall cross over armed before your brethren, the children of Israel. ¹⁹But your wives, your little ones, and your livestock (I know that you have much livestock) shall stay in your cities which I have given you, ²⁰until the LORD has given rest to your brethren as to you, and they also possess the land which the LORD your God is giving them beyond the Jordan. Then each of you may return to his possession which I have given you.'

²¹"And I commanded Joshua at that time, saying, 'Your eyes have seen all that the LORD your God has done to these two kings; so will the LORD do to all the kingdoms through which you pass. ²²You must not fear them, for the LORD your God Himself fights for you.'

²³"Then I pleaded with the LORD at that time, saying: ²⁴'O Lord GOD, You have begun to show Your servant Your greatness and Your mighty hand, for what god *is there* in heaven or on earth who can do *anything* like Your works and Your mighty *deeds*? ²⁵I pray, let me cross over and see the good land beyond the Jordan, those pleasant mountains, and Lebanon.'

BATTLES

3:21-22 "The LORD your God Himself fights for you." What encouraging news for Joshua, who was to lead his men against the persistent forces of evil in the Promised Land! Since God promised him win every battle, he had nothing to fear. Our battles may not against godless armies, but they are just as real as Joshua's. Whet are resisting temptation or battling fear, God has promised to figh and for us as we obey him.

²⁶"But the LORD was angry with me on your account, and would not listen to me. So the LORD said to me: 'Enough of that! Speak no more to Me of this matter. ²⁷Go up to the top of Pisgah, and lift your eyes toward the west, the north, the south, and the east; behold *it* with your eyes, for you shall not cross over this Jordan. ²⁸But command Joshua, and encourage him and strengthen him; for he shall go over before this people, and he shall cause them to inherit the land which you will see.'

²⁹"So we stayed in the valley opposite Beth Peor.

CHAPTER 4 OBEY GOD.

"Now, O Israel, listen to the statutes and the judgments which I teach you to observe, that you may live, and go in and possess the land which the LORD God of your fathers is giving you. ²You shall not add to the word which I command you, no take from it, that you may keep the commandments of the LORD your God which I command you. ³Your eye have seen what the LORD did at Baal Peor; for the LORD your God has destroyed from among you all the men who followed Baal of Peor. ⁴But you who held fast to the LORD your God *are* alive today, every one of you.

⁵"Surely I have taught you statutes and judgments, just as the LORD my God commanded me, that you should ac according to *them* in the land which you go to posses ⁶Therefore be careful to observe *them;* for this *is* you wisdom and your understanding in the sight of th peoples who will hear all these statutes, and say, 'Sure this great nation *is* a wise and understanding people.'

⁷"For what great nation *is there* that has God *so* near it, as the LORD our God *is* to us, for whatever *reason* v may call upon Him? ⁸And what great nation *is there* th has *such* statutes and righteous judgments as are in a

this law which I set before you this day? 9Only take heed
to yourself, and diligently keep yourself, lest you forget
the things your eyes have seen, and lest they depart from
your heart all the days of your life. And teach them to
your children and your grandchildren, 10*especially concerning* the day you stood before the LORD your God in
Horeb, when the LORD said to me, 'Gather the people to
Me, and I will let them hear My words, that they may
learn to fear Me all the days they live on the earth, and
that they may teach their children.'

11"Then you came near and stood at the foot of the
mountain, and the mountain burned with fire to the
midst of heaven, with darkness, cloud, and thick darkness. 12And the LORD spoke to you out of the midst of the
fire. You heard the sound of the words, but saw no form;
you only *heard* a voice. 13So He declared to you His covenant which He commanded you to perform, the Ten
Commandments; and He wrote them on two tablets of
stone. 14And the LORD commanded me at that time to
teach you statutes and judgments, that you might observe them in the land which you cross over to possess.

15"Take careful heed to yourselves, for you saw no form
when the LORD spoke to you at Horeb out of the midst of
the fire, 16lest you act corruptly and make for yourselves a
carved image in the form of any figure: the likeness of
male or female, 17the likeness of any animal that *is* on the
earth or the likeness of any winged bird that flies in the air,
18the likeness of anything that creeps on the ground or the
likeness of any fish that *is* in the water beneath the earth.
19And *take heed,* lest you lift your eyes to heaven, and *when*
you see the sun, the moon, and the stars, all the host of
heaven, you feel driven to worship them and serve them,
which the LORD your God has given to all the peoples
under the whole heaven as a heritage. 20But the LORD has
taken you and brought you out of the iron furnace, out of
Egypt, to be His people, an inheritance, as you are this day.
21Furthermore the LORD was angry with me for your sakes,
and swore that I would not cross over the Jordan, and that
I would not enter the good land which the LORD your God
is giving you as an inheritance. 22But I must die in this
land, I must not cross over the Jordan; but you shall cross
over and possess that good land. 23Take heed to yourselves, lest you forget the covenant of the LORD your God
which He made with you, and make for yourselves a
carved image in the form of anything which the LORD your
God has forbidden you. 24For the LORD your God *is* a consuming fire, a jealous God.

25"When you beget children and grandchildren and
have grown old in the land, and act corruptly and make
a carved image in the form of anything, and do evil in the
sight of the LORD your God to provoke Him to anger, 26I
call heaven and earth to witness against you this day, that
you will soon utterly perish from the land which you
cross over the Jordan to possess; you will not prolong
your days in it, but will be utterly destroyed. 27And the
LORD will scatter you among the peoples, and you will be
left few in number among the nations where the LORD
will drive you. 28And there you will serve gods, the work
of men's hands, wood and stone, which neither see nor
hear nor eat nor smell. 29But from there you will seek the
LORD your God, and you will find *Him* if you seek Him
with all your heart and with all your soul. 30When you are
in distress, and all these things come upon you in the
latter days, when you turn to the LORD your God and obey
His voice 31(for the LORD your God *is* a merciful God), He
will not forsake you nor destroy you, nor forget the covenant of your fathers which He swore to them.

32"For ask now concerning the days that are past,
which were before you, since the day that God created
man on the earth, and *ask* from one end of heaven to the
other, whether *any* great *thing* like this has happened, or
anything like it has been heard. 33Did *any* people *ever*
hear the voice of God speaking out of the midst of the
fire, as you have heard, and live? 34Or did God *ever* try to
go *and* take for Himself a nation from the midst of *another* nation, by trials, by signs, by wonders, by war, by a
mighty hand and an outstretched arm, and by great terrors, according to all that the LORD your God did for you
in Egypt before your eyes? 35To you it was shown, that you
might know that the LORD Himself *is* God; *there is* none
other besides Him. 36Out of heaven He let you hear His
voice, that He might instruct you; on earth He showed
you His great fire, and you heard His words out of the
midst of the fire. 37And because He loved your fathers,
therefore He chose their descendants after them; and He
brought you out of Egypt with His Presence, with His
mighty power, 38driving out from before you nations
greater and mightier than you, to bring you in, to give
you their land *as* an inheritance, as *it is* this day. 39There-
fore know this day, and consider *it* in your heart, that the
LORD Himself *is* God in heaven above and on the earth
beneath; *there is* no other. 40You shall therefore keep His
statutes and His commandments which I command you
today, that it may go well with you and with your children
after you, and that you may prolong *your* days in the land
which the LORD your God is giving you for all time."

41Then Moses set apart three cities on this side of the
Jordan, toward the rising of the sun, 42that the manslayer
might flee there, who kills his neighbor unintentionally,
without having hated him in time past, and that by fleeing to one of these cities he might live: 43Bezer in the
wilderness on the plateau for the Reubenites, Ramoth in
Gilead for the Gadites, and Golan in Bashan for the Manassites.

44Now this *is* the law which Moses set before the children of Israel. 45These *are* the testimonies, the statutes,
and the judgments which Moses spoke to the children
of Israel after they came out of Egypt, 46on this side of
the Jordan, in the valley opposite Beth Peor, in the land
of Sihon king of the Amorites, who dwelt at Heshbon,
whom Moses and the children of Israel defeated after
they came out of Egypt. 47And they took possession of

REMEMBER

4:9 Moses wanted to make sure that the people did not forget all they had seen God do, so he urged parents to tell their children about God's great miracles. This helped parents remember God's faithfulness, and it provided the way for passing on from one generation to the next the stories of God's great acts. It is easy to forget the wonderful ways God has worked in the lives of his people. But you can remember God's great acts of faithfulness by telling your friends what you have seen him do.

his land and the land of Og king of Bashan, two kings of the Amorites, who *were* on this side of the Jordan, toward the rising of the sun, ⁴⁸from Aroer, which *is* on the bank of the River Arnon, even to Mount Sion (that is, Hermon), ⁴⁹and all the plain on the east side of the Jordan as far as the Sea of the Arabah, below the slopes of Pisgah.

CHAPTER 5 THE TEN COMMANDMENTS.

And Moses called all Israel, and said to them: "Hear, O Israel, the statutes and judgments which I speak in your hearing today, that you may learn them and be careful to observe them. ²The LORD our God made a covenant with us in Horeb. ³The LORD did not make this covenant with our

ASTROLOGY

"What's that?" Kevin asks, pointing to a book in Kim's locker.

"Oh, that," Kim responds, picking up the skinny paperback. "That's a new book on astrology I got at the drugstore yesterday."

"Astrology?!" Kevin half screams. "Don't tell me you believe all that junk!"

"Laugh if you want," Kim responds matter-of-factly. "But I've seen it come true in my life so many times it's scary! Besides, lots of people in this country believe in astrology. So really, Kevin, if you don't read your horoscope, you're the one who's out of it."

Rhonda (the noisiest girl at school) walks up. "What are you guys looking at? Oh, I have that book. It's so good! What sign are you, Kevin? . . . Or aren't you into astrology?"

"Well, it's not like I don't ever read my horoscope. I'm a Leo. Sometimes it's pretty accurate, I guess."

Kim smiles. "Well, you're welcome to borrow my copy. My mom has another one at home."

Kevin coughs nervously, "I don't know—I, uh . . ."

"Kevin, it's completely harmless!" Rhonda urges. "Astrology is interesting . . . and a lot of fun. Take the book!"

Kim stands there offering the book. Kevin reluctantly takes it as the bell rings.

Is looking to the stars for guidance just an innocent diversion? See Deuteronomy 4:19 and 17:2-5.

fathers, but with us, those who *are* here today, all of us who *are* alive. ⁴The LORD talked with you face to face on the mountain from the midst of the fire. ⁵I stood between the LORD and you at that time, to declare to you the word of the LORD; for you were afraid because of the fire, and you did not go up the mountain. *He* said:

⁶ 'I *am* the LORD your God who brought you out of the land of Egypt, out of the house of bondage.

⁷ 'You shall have no other gods before Me.

⁸ 'You shall not make for yourself a carved image—any likeness *of anything* that *is* in heaven above, or that *is* in the earth beneath, or that *is* in the water under the earth; ⁹you shall not bow down to them nor serve them. For I, the LORD your God, *am* a jealous God, visiting the iniquity of the fathers upon the children to the third and fourth *generations* of those who hate Me, ¹⁰but showing mercy

to thousands, to those who love Me and keep My commandments.

¹¹ 'You shall not take the name of the LORD your God in vain, for the LORD will not hold *him* guiltless who takes His name in vain.

¹² 'Observe the Sabbath day, to keep it holy, as the LORD your God commanded you. ¹³Six days you shall labor and do all your work, ¹⁴but the seventh day *is* the Sabbath of the LORD your God. *In it* you shall do no work: you, nor your son, nor your daughter, nor your male servant, nor your female servant, nor your ox, nor your donkey, nor any of your cattle, nor your stranger who *is* within your gates, that your male servant and your female servant may rest as well as you. ¹⁵And remember that you were a slave in the land of Egypt, and the LORD your God brought you out from there by a mighty hand and by an outstretched arm; therefore the LORD your God commanded you to keep the Sabbath day.

¹⁶ 'Honor your father and your mother, as the LORD your God has commanded you, that your days may be long, and that it may be well with you in the land which the LORD your God is giving you.

¹⁷ 'You shall not murder.

¹⁸ 'You shall not commit adultery.

¹⁹ 'You shall not steal.

²⁰ 'You shall not bear false witness against your neighbor.

²¹ 'You shall not covet your neighbor's wife; and you shall not desire your neighbor's house, his field, his male servant, his female servant, his ox, his donkey, or anything that *is* your neighbor's.'

²²"These words the LORD spoke to all your assembly, in the mountain from the midst of the fire, the cloud, and the thick darkness, with a loud voice; and He added no more. And He wrote them on two tablets of stone and gave them to me.

²³"So it was, when you heard the voice from the midst of the darkness, while the mountain was burning with fire, that you came near to me, all the heads of your tribes and your elders. ²⁴And you said: 'Surely the LORD our God has shown us His glory and His greatness, and we have heard His voice from the midst of the fire. We have seen this day that God speaks with man; yet he *still* lives. ²⁵Now therefore, why should we die? For this great fire will consume us; if we hear the voice of the LORD our God anymore, then we shall die. ²⁶For who *is there* of all flesh who has heard the voice of the living God speaking from the midst of the fire, as we *have*, and lived? ²⁷You go near

COVENANT

5:1 The people had entered into a covenant with God, and Moses commanded them to hear, learn, and observe (or keep) his statute Christians also have entered into a covenant with God (through Je Christ) and should be sensitive to what God expects. Moses' threef command to the Israelites is excellent advice for all God's follower *Hearing* is absorbing and accepting information about God. *Learn* understanding its meaning and implications. *Observing* is putting action all we have learned and understood. All three parts are ess a growing relationship with God.

and hear all that the LORD our God may say, and tell us all that the LORD our God says to you, and we will hear and do it.'

28"Then the LORD heard the voice of your words when you spoke to me, and the LORD said to me: 'I have heard the voice of the words of this people which they have spoken to you. They are right *in* all that they have spoken. 29Oh, that they had such a heart in them that they would fear Me and always keep all My commandments, that it might be well with them and with their children forever! 30Go and say to them, "Return to your tents." 31But as for you, stand here by Me, and I will speak to you all the commandments, the statutes, and the judgments which you shall teach them, that they may observe *them* in the land which I am giving them to possess.'

32"Therefore you shall be careful to do as the LORD your God has commanded you; you shall not turn aside to the right hand or to the left. 33You shall walk in all the ways which the LORD your God has commanded you, that you may live and *that it may be* well with you, and *that* you may prolong *your* days in the land which you shall possess.

CHAPTER 6 LOVE GOD AND OBEY HIM. "Now this *is* the commandment, *and these are* the statutes and judgments which the LORD your God has commanded to teach you, that you may observe *them* in the land which you are crossing over to possess, 2that you may fear the LORD your God, to keep all His statutes and His commandments which I command you, you and your son and your grandson, all the days of your life, and that your days may be prolonged. 3Therefore hear, O Israel, and be careful to observe *it*, that it may be well with you, and that you may multiply greatly as the LORD God of your fathers has promised you—'a land flowing with milk and honey.'

4"Hear, O Israel: The LORD our God, the LORD *is* one! 5You shall love the LORD your God with all your heart, with all your soul, and with all your strength.

6"And these words which I command you today shall be in your heart. 7You shall teach them diligently to your children, and shall talk of them when you sit in your house, when you walk by the way, when you lie down, and when you rise up. 8You shall bind them as a sign on your hand, and they shall be as frontlets between your eyes. 9You shall write them on the doorposts of your house and on your gates.

10"So it shall be, when the LORD your God brings you into the land of which He swore to your fathers, to Abraham, Isaac, and Jacob, to give you large and beautiful cities which you did not build, 11houses full of all good things, which you did not fill, hewn-out wells which you did not dig, vineyards and olive trees which you did not plant—when you have eaten and are full— 12*then* beware, lest you forget the LORD who brought you out of the land of Egypt, from the house of bondage. 13You shall fear the LORD your God and serve Him, and shall take oaths in His name. 14You shall not go after other gods, the gods of the peoples who *are* all around you 15(for the LORD your God *is* a jealous God among you), lest the anger of the LORD your God be aroused against you and destroy you from the face of the earth.

"Here's what I did..."

My parents are Christians, and even though they are stricter than I'd like, I have to admit they're good parents. One day while reading the Bible, I came across the fifth commandment, the one about honoring your parents. The note in the margin pointed out that there is a promise attached to this commandment: If you follow it, you will lead a long and happy life.

What struck me is that my parents are always saying things like, "We're only saying this for your own good. We want you to be happy." It seemed like God was saying, "Your parents love you, they are trying to help you lead a happy life, so if you listen to them, your life will go better." It all made sense. For a while I felt guilty that I didn't listen to them as much as I should, but I determined to consult them more.

A few nights later I decided to talk to them about a relationship I was having trouble with. I was surprised to find that they really understood, and my mom even had some helpful advice about what she had done in a similar situation. I hadn't realized before how much wisdom my parents really have to give me.

Amy

AGE 15

16"You shall not tempt the LORD your God as you tempted *Him* in Massah. 17You shall diligently keep the commandments of the LORD your God, His testimonies, and His statutes which He has commanded you. 18And you shall do *what is* right and good in the sight of the

HOME SCHOOLS

6:4-9 This passage is often said to be the central theme of Deuteronomy. It sets a pattern that helps us relate the Word of God to our daily life. We are to love God, think constantly about his commandments, teach his commandments to our children, and live our daily life by the guidelines in his Word. God emphasized the importance of parents' teaching the Bible to their children. The church and Christian schools cannot be used to escape from this responsibility. The Bible provides so many opportunities for object lessons and practical teaching that it would be a shame to study it only one day a week. Eternal truths are most effectively learned in the loving environment of a God-fearing home.

LORD, that it may be well with you, and that you may go in and possess the good land of which the LORD swore to your fathers, [19]to cast out all your enemies from before you, as the LORD has spoken.

[20]"When your son asks you in time to come, saying, 'What *is the meaning of* the testimonies, the statutes, and the judgments which the LORD our God has commanded you?' [21]then you shall say to your son: 'We were slaves of Pharaoh in Egypt, and the LORD brought us out of Egypt with a mighty hand; [22]and the LORD showed signs and wonders before our eyes, great and severe, against Egypt, Pharaoh, and all his household. [23]Then He brought us out from there, that He might bring us in, to give us the land of which He swore to our fathers. [24]And the LORD commanded us to observe all these statutes, to fear the LORD our God, for our good always, that He might preserve us alive, as *it is* this day. [25]Then it will be righteousness for us, if we are careful to observe all these commandments before the LORD our God, as He has commanded us.'

CHAPTER **7** DEFEAT THE ENEMY NATIONS. "When the LORD your God brings you into the land which you go to possess, and has cast out many nations before you, the Hittites and the Girgashites and the Amorites and the Canaanites and the Perizzites and the Hivites and the Jebusites, seven nations greater and mightier than you, [2]and when the LORD your God delivers them over to you, you shall conquer them *and* utterly destroy them. You shall make no covenant with them nor show mercy

THE LORD YOUR GOD

KEEPS COVENANT

and mercy

FOR

A THOUSAND GENERATIONS GENERATIONS GENERATIONS

DEUTERONOMY 7:9

to them. [3]Nor shall you make marriages with them. You shall not give your daughter to their son, nor take their daughter for your son. [4]For they will turn your sons away from following Me, to serve other gods; so the anger of the LORD will be aroused against you and destroy you suddenly. [5]But thus you shall deal with them: you shall destroy their altars, and break down their *sacred* pillars, and cut down their wooden images, and burn their carved images with fire.

[6]"For you *are* a holy people to the LORD your God; the LORD your God has chosen you to be a people for Himself, a special treasure above all the peoples on the face of the earth. [7]The LORD did not set His love on you nor choose you because you were more in number than any other people, for you were the least of all peoples; [8]but because the LORD loves you, and because He would keep the oath which He swore to your fathers, the LORD has brought you out with a mighty hand, and redeemed you from the house of bondage, from the hand of Pharaoh king of Egypt.

[9]"Therefore know that the LORD your God, He *is* God, the faithful God who keeps covenant and mercy for a thousand generations with those who love Him and keep His commandments; [10]and He repays those who hate Him to their face, to destroy them. He will not be slack with him who hates Him; He will repay him to his face. [11]Therefore you shall keep the commandment, the statutes, and the judgments which I command you today, to observe them.

[12]"Then it shall come to pass, because you listen to these judgments, and keep and do them, that the LORD your God will keep with you the covenant and the mercy which He swore to your fathers. [13]And He will love you and bless you and multiply you; He will also bless the fruit of your womb and the fruit of your land, your grain and your new wine and your oil, the increase of your cattle and the offspring of your flock, in the land of which He swore to your fathers to give you. [14]You shall be blessed above all peoples; there shall not be a male or female barren among you or among your livestock. [15]And the LORD will take away from you all sickness, and will afflict you with none of the terrible diseases of Egypt which you have known, but will lay *them* on all those who hate you. [16]Also you shall destroy all the peoples whom the LORD your God delivers over to you; your eye shall have no pity on them; nor shall you serve their gods, for that *will be* a snare to you.

[17]"If you should say in your heart, 'These nations are

STEP-BY-STEP

7:21-24 Moses told the Israelites that God would destroy Israel enemies, but not all at once. God had the power to destroy those instantly, but he chose to do it in stages. In the same way and with same power, God could miraculously and instantaneously change life. Usually, however, he chooses to help you gradually, teaching lesson at a time. Rather than expect instant spiritual maturity an solutions to all your problems, slow down and work one step at a trusting God to make up the difference between where you shoul and where you are now. You'll soon look back and see that a mir transformation has occurred.

reater than I; how can I dispossess them?'— [18]you shall not be afraid of them, *but* you shall remember well what the LORD your God did to Pharaoh and to all Egypt: [19]the great trials which your eyes saw, the signs and the wonders, the mighty hand and the outstretched arm, by which the LORD your God brought you out. So shall the LORD your God do to all the peoples of whom you are afraid. [20]Moreover the LORD your God will send the hornet among them until those who are left, who hide themselves from you, are destroyed. [21]You shall not be terrified of them; for the LORD your God, the great and awesome God, *is* among you. [22]And the LORD your God will drive out those nations before you little by little; you will be unable to destroy them at once, lest the beasts of the field become *too* numerous for you. [23]But the LORD your God will deliver them over to you, and will inflict defeat upon them until they are destroyed. [24]And He will deliver their kings into your hand,

and you will destroy their name from under heaven; no one shall be able to stand against you until you have destroyed them. [25]You shall burn the carved images of their gods with fire; you shall not covet the silver or gold *that is* on them, nor take *it* for yourselves, lest you be snared by it; for it *is* an abomination to the LORD your God. [26]Nor shall you bring an abomination into your house, lest you be doomed to destruction like it. You shall utterly detest it and utterly abhor it, for it *is* an accursed thing.

CHAPTER **8** **DO NOT FORGET GOD.** "Every commandment which I command you today you must be careful to observe, that you may live and multiply, and go in and possess the land of which the LORD swore to your fathers. [2]And you shall remember that the LORD your God led you all the way these forty years in the wilderness, to

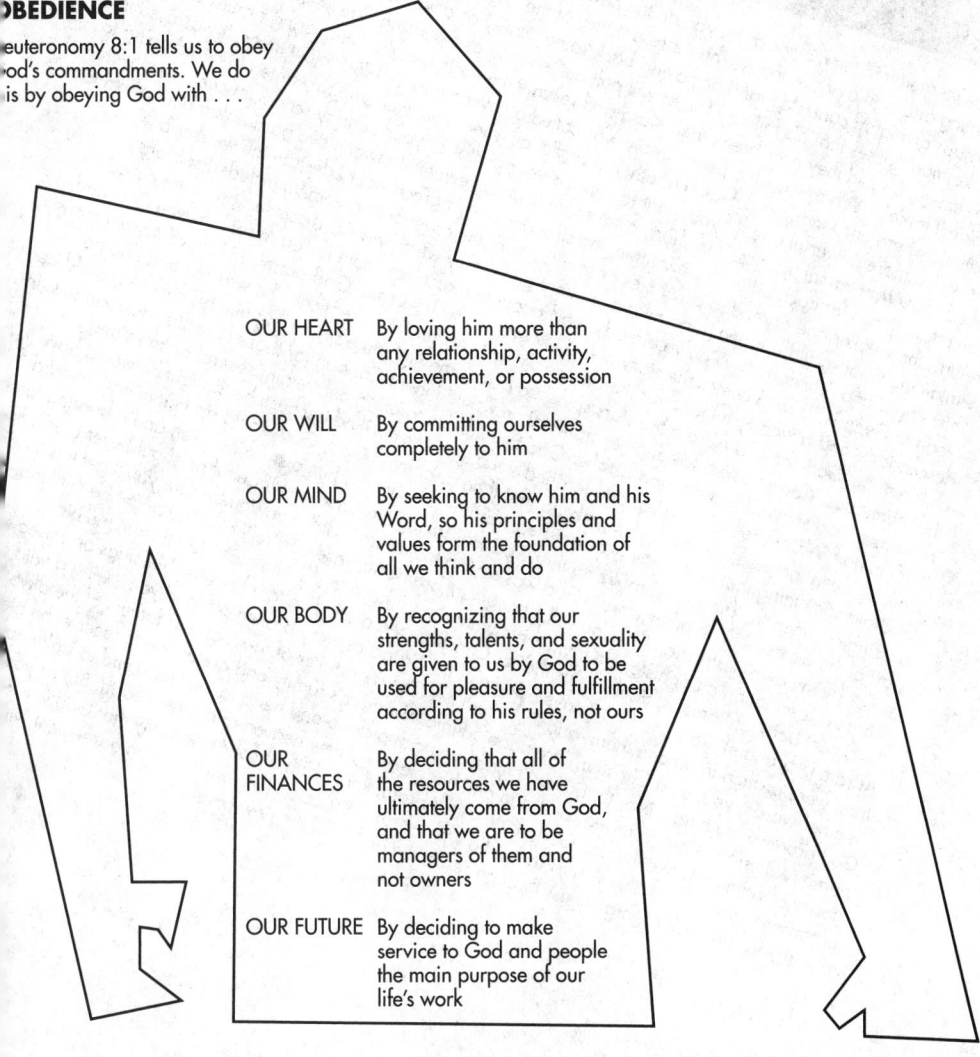

OBEDIENCE

Deuteronomy 8:1 tells us to obey God's commandments. We do this by obeying God with . . .

OUR HEART	By loving him more than any relationship, activity, achievement, or possession
OUR WILL	By committing ourselves completely to him
OUR MIND	By seeking to know him and his Word, so his principles and values form the foundation of all we think and do
OUR BODY	By recognizing that our strengths, talents, and sexuality are given to us by God to be used for pleasure and fulfillment according to his rules, not ours
OUR FINANCES	By deciding that all of the resources we have ultimately come from God, and that we are to be managers of them and not owners
OUR FUTURE	By deciding to make service to God and people the main purpose of our life's work

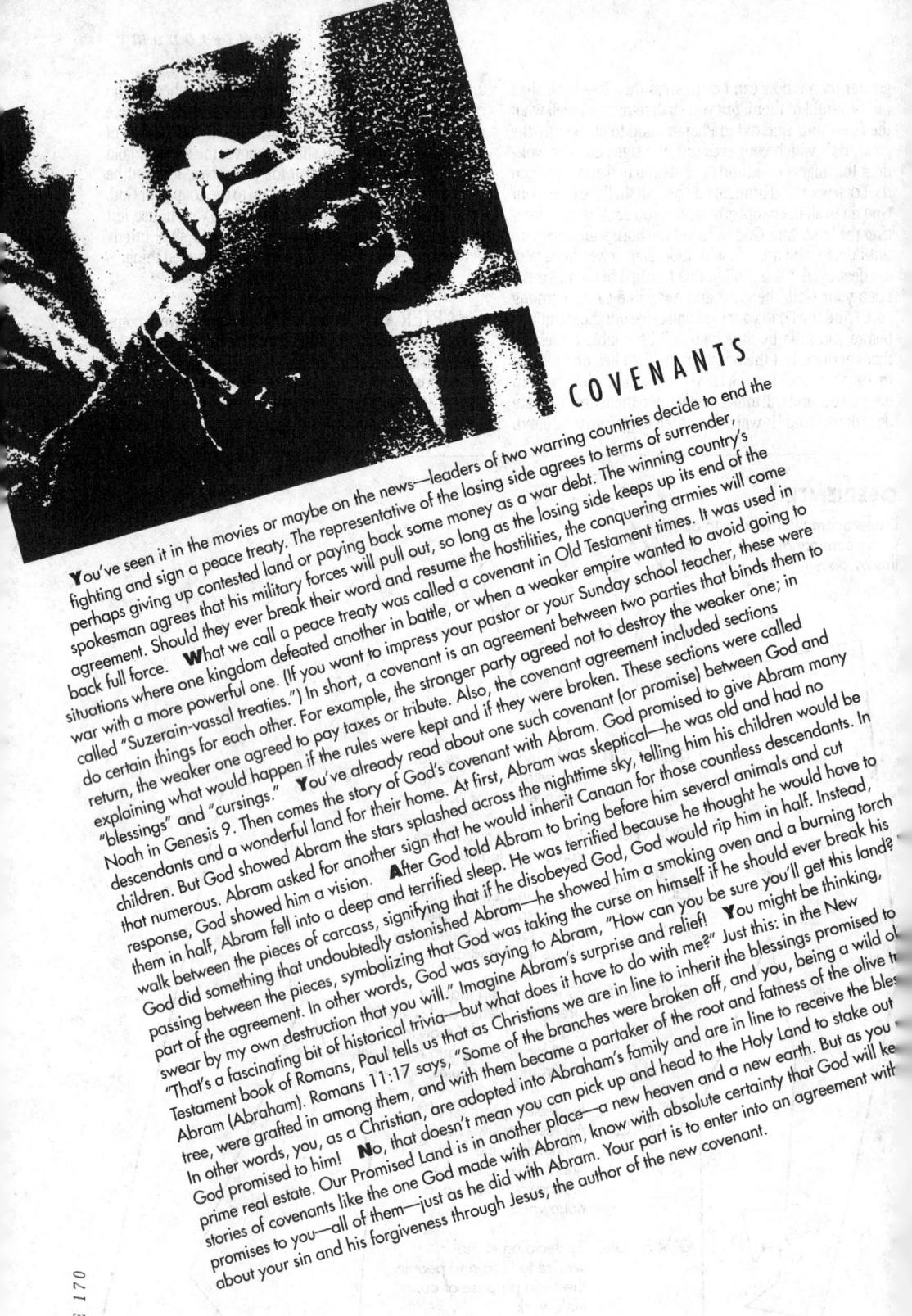

COVERNANTS

You've seen it in the movies or maybe on the news—leaders of two warring countries decide to end the fighting and sign a peace treaty. The representative of the losing side agrees to terms of surrender, perhaps giving up contested land or paying back some money as a war debt. The winning country's spokesman agrees that his military forces will pull out, so long as the losing side keeps up its end of the agreement. Should they ever break their word and resume the hostilities, the conquering armies will come back full force. **W**hat we call a peace treaty was called a covenant in Old Testament times. It was used in situations where one kingdom defeated another in battle, or when a weaker empire wanted to avoid going to war with a more powerful one. (If you want to impress your pastor or your Sunday school teacher, these were called "Suzerain-vassal treaties.") In short, a covenant is an agreement between two parties that binds them to do certain things for each other. For example, the weaker one agreed to pay taxes or tribute. Also, the covenant agreement included sections return, the stronger party agreed not to destroy the weaker one; in explaining what would happen if the rules were kept and if they were broken. These sections were called "blessings" and "cursings." **Y**ou've already read about one such covenant (or promise) between God and Noah in Genesis 9. Then comes the story of God's covenant with Abram. God promised to give Abram many descendants and a wonderful land for their home. At first, Abram was skeptical—he was old and had no children. But God showed Abram the stars splashed across the nighttime sky, telling him his children would be that numerous. Abram asked for another sign that he would inherit Canaan for those countless descendants. In response, God showed him a vision. **A**fter God told Abram to bring before him several animals and cut them in half, Abram fell into a deep and terrified sleep. He was terrified because he thought he would have to walk between the pieces of carcass, signifying that if he disobeyed God, God would rip him in half. Instead, God did something that undoubtedly astonished Abram—he showed him a smoking oven and a burning torch passing between the pieces, symbolizing that God was taking the curse on himself if he should ever break his part of the agreement. In other words, God was saying to Abram, "How can you be sure you'll get this land? swear by my own destruction that you will." Imagine Abram's surprise and relief! **Y**ou might be thinking, "That's a fascinating bit of historical trivia—but what does it have to do with me?" Just this: in the New Testament book of Romans, Paul tells us that as Christians we are in line to inherit the blessings promised to Abram (Abraham). Romans 11:17 says, "Some of the branches were broken off, and you, being a wild ol tree, were grafted in among them, and with them became a partaker of the root and fatness of the olive tr In other words, you, as a Christian, are adopted into Abraham's family and are in line to receive the bles God promised to him! **N**o, that doesn't mean you can pick up and head to the Holy Land to stake out prime real estate. Our Promised Land is in another place—a new heaven and a new earth. But as you stories of covenants like the one God made with Abram, know with absolute certainty that God will ke promises to you—all of them—just as he did with Abram. Your part is to enter into an agreement witl about your sin and his forgiveness through Jesus, the author of the new covenant.

humble you *and* test you, to know what *was* in your heart, whether you would keep His commandments or not. ³So He humbled you, allowed you to hunger, and fed you with manna which you did not know nor did your fathers know, that He might make you know that man shall not live by bread alone; but man lives by every *word* that proceeds from the mouth of the LORD. ⁴Your garments did not wear out on you, nor did your foot swell these forty years. ⁵You should know in your heart that as a man chastens his son, *so* the LORD your God chastens you.

⁶"Therefore you shall keep the commandments of the LORD your God, to walk in His ways and to fear Him. ⁷For the LORD your God is bringing you into a good land, a land of brooks of water, of fountains and springs, that flow out of valleys and hills; ⁸a land of wheat and barley, of vines and fig trees and pomegranates, a land of olive oil and honey; ⁹a land in which you will eat bread without scarcity, in which you will lack nothing; a land whose stones *are* iron and out of whose hills you can dig copper. ¹⁰When you have eaten and are full, then you shall bless the LORD your God for the good land which He has given you.

¹¹"Beware that you do not forget the LORD your God by not keeping His commandments, His judgments, and His statutes which I command you today, ¹²lest—*when* you have eaten and are full, and have built beautiful houses and dwell *in them;* ¹³and *when* your herds and your flocks multiply, and your silver and your gold are multiplied, and all that you have is multiplied; ¹⁴when your heart is lifted up, and you forget the LORD your God who brought you out of the land of Egypt, from the house of bondage; ¹⁵who led you through that great and terrible wilderness, *in which were* fiery serpents and scorpions and thirsty land where there was no water; who brought water for you out of the flinty rock; ¹⁶who fed you in the wilderness with manna, which your fathers did not know, that He might humble you and that He might test you, to do you good in the end— ¹⁷then you say in your heart, 'My power and the might of my hand have gained me this wealth.'

¹⁸"And you shall remember the LORD your God, for *it is* He who gives you power to get wealth, that He may establish His covenant which He swore to your fathers, as *it is* this day. ¹⁹Then it shall be, if you by any means forget the LORD your God, and follow other gods, and serve them and worship them, I testify against you this day that you shall surely perish. ²⁰As the nations which the LORD destroys before you, so you shall perish, because you would not be obedient to the voice of the LORD your God.

CHAPTER 9 DO NOT FORGET GOD'S MERCY.

Hear, O Israel: You *are* to cross over the Jordan today, and go in to dispossess nations greater and mightier than yourself, cities great and fortified up to heaven, ²a people great and tall, the descendants of the Anakim, whom you know, and *of whom* you heard *it said,* 'Who can stand before the descendants of Anak?' ³Therefore understand today that the LORD your God *is* He who goes over before

you *as* a consuming fire. He will destroy them and bring them down before you; so you shall drive them out and destroy them quickly, as the LORD has said to you.

⁴"Do not think in your heart, after the LORD your God has cast them out before you, saying, 'Because of my righteousness the LORD has brought me in to possess this land'; but *it is* because of the wickedness of these nations *that* the LORD is driving them out from before you. ⁵*It is* not because of your righteousness or the uprightness of your heart *that* you go in to possess their land, but because of the wickedness of these nations *that* the LORD your God drives them out from before you, and that He may fulfill the word which the LORD swore to your fathers, to Abraham, Isaac, and Jacob. ⁶Therefore understand that the LORD your God is not giving you this good land to possess because of your righteousness, for you *are* a stiff-necked people.

◤REMINDERS

8:10 The Israelites were to bless the Lord after eating their fill in the Promised Land. This verse is traditionally cited as the reason we say grace before or after meals. Its purpose, however, was not just to provide a time for prayer, but to warn the Israelites not to forget God when their needs and wants were satisfied. Let your table prayers serve as a constant reminder of God's goodness to you and your duty to those less fortunate.

⁷"Remember! Do not forget how you provoked the LORD your God to wrath in the wilderness. From the day that you departed from the land of Egypt until you came to this place, you have been rebellious against the LORD. ⁸Also in Horeb you provoked the LORD to wrath, so that the LORD was angry *enough* with you to have destroyed you. ⁹When I went up into the mountain to receive the tablets of stone, the tablets of the covenant which the LORD made with you, then I stayed on the mountain forty days and forty nights. I neither ate bread nor drank water. ¹⁰Then the LORD delivered to me two tablets of stone written with the finger of God, and on them *were* all the words which the LORD had spoken to you on the mountain from the midst of the fire in the day of the assembly. ¹¹And it came to pass, at the end of forty days and forty nights, *that* the LORD gave me the two tablets of stone, the tablets of the covenant.

¹²"Then the LORD said to me, 'Arise, go down quickly

◤MERCY

9:5-6 If the Israelites were so wicked and stubborn, why did God make such wonderful promises to them? There are two good reasons: (1) A bargain is a bargain. God and Israel had made a covenant (Genesis 15; 17; Exodus 19–20). God promised to be faithful to them and they promised to obey him. The agreement was irrevocable and eternal. Even though the Israelites rarely upheld their end of the bargain, God would always be faithful to his part. (Although he has punished them several times, he has always remained faithful.) (2) God's mercy is unconditional. No matter how many times the people turned from God, he was always there to restore them. It is comforting to know that despite our inconsistencies and sins, God loves us unconditionally. Eternal life is not achieved on the merit system, but on the mercy system. God loves us no matter who we are or what we have done.

10:12-13 Often we ask, "What does God expect of me?" Here Moses gives a summary that is simple in form and easy to remember. Here are the essentials: (1) Fear God (have reverence for him). (2) Walk in all his ways. (3) Love him. (4) Serve him with all your heart and soul. (5) Keep his commandments. How often we complicate faith with man-made rules, regulations, and requirements. Are you frustrated and burned out from trying hard to please God? Concentrate on his real requirements—to respect, follow, love, serve, and obey him—and find peace.

from here, for your people whom you brought out of Egypt have acted corruptly; they have quickly turned aside from the way which I commanded them; they have made themselves a molded image.'

¹³"Furthermore the LORD spoke to me, saying, 'I have seen this people, and indeed they are a stiff-necked people. ¹⁴Let Me alone, that I may destroy them and blot out their name from under heaven; and I will make of you a nation mightier and greater than they.'

¹⁵"So I turned and came down from the mountain, and the mountain burned with fire; and the two tablets of the covenant *were* in my two hands. ¹⁶And I looked, and behold, you had sinned against the LORD your God—had made for yourselves a molded calf! You had turned aside quickly from the way which the LORD had commanded you. ¹⁷Then I took the two tablets and threw them out of my two hands and broke them before your eyes. ¹⁸And I fell down before the LORD, as at the first, forty days and forty nights; I neither ate bread nor drank water, because of all your sin which you committed in doing wickedly in the sight of the LORD, to provoke Him to anger. ¹⁹For I was afraid of the anger and hot displeasure with which the LORD was angry with you, to destroy you. But the LORD listened to me at that time also. ²⁰And the LORD was very angry with Aaron *and* would have destroyed him; so I prayed for Aaron also at the same time. ²¹Then I took your sin, the calf which you had made, and burned it with fire and crushed it *and* ground *it* very small, until it was as fine as dust; and I threw its dust into the brook that descended from the mountain.

²²"Also at Taberah and Massah and Kibroth Hattaavah you provoked the LORD to wrath. ²³Likewise, when the LORD sent you from Kadesh Barnea, saying, 'Go up and possess the land which I have given you,' then you re-belled against the commandment of the LORD your God, and you did not believe Him nor obey His voice. ²⁴You have been rebellious against the LORD from the day that I knew you.

²⁵"Thus I prostrated myself before the LORD; forty days and forty nights I kept prostrating myself, because the LORD had said He would destroy you. ²⁶Therefore I prayed to the LORD, and said: 'O Lord GOD, do not destroy Your people and Your inheritance whom You have redeemed through Your greatness, whom You have brought out of Egypt with a mighty hand. ²⁷Remember Your servants, Abraham, Isaac, and Jacob; do not look on the stubbornness of this people, or on their wickedness or their sin, ²⁸lest the land from which You brought us should say, "Because the LORD was not able to bring them to the land which He promised them, and because He hated them, He has brought them out to kill them in the wilderness." ²⁹Yet they *are* Your people and Your inheritance, whom You brought out by Your mighty power and by Your outstretched arm.'

CHAPTER 10 TEN COMMANDMENTS REWRITTEN.

"At that time the LORD said to me, 'Hew for yourself two tablets of stone like the first, and come up to Me on the mountain and make yourself an ark of wood. ²And I will write on the tablets the words that were on the first tablets, which you broke; and you shall put them in the ark.'

³"So I made an ark of acacia wood, hewed two tablets of stone like the first, and went up the mountain, having the two tablets in my hand. ⁴And He wrote on the tablets according to the first writing, the Ten Commandments, which the LORD had spoken to you in the mountain from the midst of the fire in the day of the assembly; and the LORD gave them to me. ⁵Then I turned and came down from the mountain, and put the tablets in the ark which I had made; and there they are, just as the LORD commanded me."

⁶(Now the children of Israel journeyed from the wells of Bene Jaakan to Moserah, where Aaron died, and where he was buried; and Eleazar his son ministered as priest in his stead. ⁷From there they journeyed to Gudgodah, and from Gudgodah to Jotbathah, a land of rivers of water. ⁸At that time the LORD separated the tribe of Levi to bear the ark of the covenant of the LORD, to stand before the LORD to minister to Him and to bless in His name, to this day. ⁹Therefore Levi has no portion nor inheritance with his brethren; the LORD *is* his inheritance, just as the LORD your God promised him.)

¹⁰"As at the first time, I stayed in the mountain forty days and forty nights; the LORD also heard me at that time, *and* the LORD chose not to destroy you. ¹¹Then the LORD said to me, 'Arise, begin *your* journey before the people, that they may go in and possess the land which I swore to their fathers to give them.'

¹²"And now, Israel, what does the LORD your God require of you, but to fear the LORD your God, to walk in all His ways and to love Him, to serve the LORD your God with all your heart and with all your soul, ¹³and to keep the commandments of the LORD and His statutes which I command you today for your good? ¹⁴Indeed heaven and the highest heavens belong to the LORD your God, *also* the earth with all that *is* in it. ¹⁵The LORD delighted only in your fathers, to love them; and He chose their descendants after them, you above all peoples, as *it is* this day. ¹⁶Therefore circumcise the foreskin of your heart, and be stiff-necked no longer. ¹⁷For the LORD your God *is* God of gods and Lord of lords, the great God, mighty and awesome, who shows no partiality nor takes a bribe. ¹⁸He administers justice for the fatherless and the widow, and loves the stranger, giving him food and clothing. ¹⁹Therefore love the stranger, for you were strangers in the land of Egypt. ²⁰You shall fear the LORD your God; you shall serve Him, and to Him you shall hold fast, and take oaths in His name. ²¹He *is* your praise, and He *is* your God, who has done for you these great and awesome things which your eyes have seen. ²²Your fathers went down to Egypt with seventy persons, and now the LORD your God has made you as the stars of heaven in multitude.

CHAPTER 11 "Therefore you shall love the LORD your God, and keep His charge, His statutes, His judgments, and His commandments always. [2]Know today that *I do* not *speak* with your children, who have not known and who have not seen the chastening of the LORD your God, His greatness and His mighty hand and His outstretched arm— [3]His signs and His acts which He did in the midst of Egypt, to Pharaoh king of Egypt, and to all his land; what He did to the army of Egypt, to their horses and their chariots: how He made the waters of the Red Sea overflow them as they pursued you, and *how* the LORD has destroyed them to this day; [5]what He did for you in the wilderness until you came to this place; [6]and what He did to Dathan and Abiram the sons of Eliab, the son of Reuben: how the earth opened its mouth and swallowed them up, their households, their tents, and all the substance that *was* in their possession, in the midst of all Israel— [7]but your eyes have seen every great act of the LORD which He did.

[8]"Therefore you shall keep every commandment which I command you today, that you may be strong, and go in and possess the land which you cross over to possess, [9]and that you may prolong *your* days in the land which the LORD swore to give your fathers, to them and their descendants, 'a land flowing with milk and honey.' For the land which you go to possess *is* not like the land of Egypt from which you have come, where you sowed your seed and watered *it* by foot, as a vegetable garden; but the land which you cross over to possess *is* a land of hills and valleys, which drinks water from the rain of heaven, [12]a land for which the LORD your God cares; the eyes of the LORD your God *are* always on it, from the beginning of the year to the very end of the year.

[13]"And it shall be that if you earnestly obey My commandments which I command you today, to love the LORD your God and serve Him with all your heart and with all your soul, [14]then I will give *you* the rain for your land in its season, the early rain and the latter rain, that you may gather in your grain, your new wine, and your oil. [15]And I will send grass in your fields for your livestock, that you may eat and be filled.' [16]Take heed to yourselves, lest your heart be deceived, and you turn aside and serve other gods and worship them, [17]lest the LORD's anger be aroused against you, and He shut up the heavens so that there be no rain, and the land yield no produce, and you perish quickly from the good land which the LORD is giving you.

[18]"Therefore you shall lay up these words of mine in your heart and in your soul, and bind them as a sign on your hand, and they shall be as frontlets between your eyes. [19]You shall teach them to your children, speaking of them when you sit in your house, when you walk by the way, when you lie down, and when you rise up. [20]And you shall write them on the doorposts of your house and on your gates, [21]that your days and the days of your children may be multiplied in the land of which the LORD swore to your fathers to give them, like the days of the heavens above the earth.

[22]"For if you carefully keep all these commandments which I command you to do—to love the LORD your God, to walk in all His ways, and to hold fast to Him— [23]then the LORD will drive out all these nations from before you, and you will dispossess greater and mightier nations than yourselves. [24]Every place on which the sole of your foot treads shall be yours: from the wilderness and Lebanon, from the river, the River Euphrates, even to the Western Sea, shall be your territory. [25]No man shall be able to stand against you; the LORD your God will put the dread of you and the fear of you upon all the land where you tread, just as He has said to you.

[26]"Behold, I set before you today a blessing and a curse: [27]the blessing, if you obey the commandments of the LORD your God which I command you today; [28]and the curse, if you do not obey the commandments of the LORD your God, but turn aside from the way which I command you today, to go after other gods which you have not known. [29]Now it shall be, when the LORD your God has brought you into the land which you go to possess, that you shall put the blessing on Mount Gerizim and the curse on Mount Ebal. [30]*Are* they not on the other side of the Jordan, toward the setting sun, in the land of the Canaanites who dwell in the plain opposite Gilgal, beside the terebinth trees of Moreh? [31]For you will cross over the Jordan and go in to possess the land which the LORD your God is giving you, and you will possess it and dwell in it. [32]And you shall be careful to observe all the statutes and judgments which I set before you today.

CHAPTER 12 ONLY ONE ALTAR FOR SACRIFICES.

"These *are* the statutes and judgments which you shall be careful to observe in the land which the LORD God of your fathers is giving you to possess, all the days that you live on the earth. [2]You shall utterly destroy all the places where the nations which you shall dispossess served their gods, on the high mountains and on the hills and under every green tree. [3]And you shall destroy their altars, break their *sacred* pillars, and burn their wooden images with fire; you shall cut down the carved images of their gods and destroy their names from that place. [4]You shall not worship the LORD your God *with* such *things*.

[5]"But you shall seek the place where the LORD your God chooses, out of all your tribes, to put His name for His dwelling place; and there you shall go. [6]There you shall take your burnt offerings, your sacrifices, your tithes, the heave offerings of your hand, your vowed offerings, your freewill offerings, and the firstborn of your herds and flocks. [7]And there you shall eat before the LORD your God, and you shall rejoice in all to which you have put your hand, you and your households, in which the LORD your God has blessed you.

[8]"You shall not at all do as we are doing here today— every man doing whatever *is* right in his own eyes— [9]for as yet you have not come to the rest and the inheritance which the LORD your God is giving you. [10]But *when* you cross over the Jordan and dwell in the land which the LORD your God is giving you to inherit, and He gives you rest from all your enemies round about, so that you dwell in safety, [11]then there will be the place where the LORD your God chooses to make His name abide. There you shall bring all that I command you: your burnt offerings, your sacrifices, your tithes, the heave offerings of your

hand, and all your choice offerings which you vow to the LORD. ¹²And you shall rejoice before the LORD your God, you and your sons and your daughters, your male and female servants, and the Levite who *is* within your gates, since he has no portion nor inheritance with you. ¹³Take heed to yourself that you do not offer your burnt offerings in every place that you see; ¹⁴but in the place which the LORD chooses, in one of your tribes, there you shall offer your burnt offerings, and there you shall do all that I command you.

TOGETHERNESS

12:12,18 The Hebrews placed great emphasis on family worship. Whether offering a sacrifice or attending a great feast, the family was often together. This gave the children a healthy attitude toward worship, and it put extra meaning into it for the adults. Watching a family member confess his or her sin was just as important as celebrating a great holiday together. Although there are appropriate times to separate people by ages, some of the most meaningful worship can be experienced only when shared by old and young.

¹⁵"However, you may slaughter and eat meat within all your gates, whatever your heart desires, according to the blessing of the LORD your God which He has given you; the unclean and the clean may eat of it, of the gazelle and the deer alike. ¹⁶Only you shall not eat the blood; you shall pour it on the earth like water. ¹⁷You may not eat within your gates the tithe of your grain or your new wine or your oil, of the firstborn of your herd or your flock, of any of your offerings which you vow, of your freewill offerings, or of the heave offering of your hand. ¹⁸But you must eat them before the LORD your God in the place which the LORD your God chooses, you and your son and your daughter, your male servant and your female servant, and the Levite who *is* within your gates; and you shall rejoice before the LORD your God in all to which you put your hands. ¹⁹Take heed to yourself that you do not forsake the Levite as long as you live in your land.

²⁰"When the LORD your God enlarges your border as He has promised you, and you say, 'Let me eat meat,' because you long to eat meat, you may eat as much meat as your heart desires. ²¹If the place where the LORD your God chooses to put His name is too far from you, then you may slaughter from your herd and from your flock which the LORD has given you, just as I have commanded you, and you may eat within your gates as much as your heart desires. ²²Just as the gazelle and the deer are eaten, so you may eat them; the unclean and the clean alike may eat them. ²³Only be sure that you do not eat the blood, for the blood *is* the life; you may not eat the life with the meat. ²⁴You shall not eat it; you shall pour it on the earth like water. ²⁵You shall not eat it, that it may go well with you and your children after you, when you do *what is* right in the sight of the LORD. ²⁶Only the holy things which you have, and your vowed offerings, you shall take and go to the place which the LORD chooses. ²⁷And you shall offer your burnt offerings, the meat and the blood, on the altar of the LORD your God; and the blood of your sacrifices shall be poured out on the altar of the LORD your God, and you shall eat the meat. ²⁸Ob-

serve and obey all these words which I command yo[u] that it may go well with you and your children after y[ou] forever, when you do *what is* good and right in the sig[ht] of the LORD your God.

²⁹"When the LORD your God cuts off from before yo[u] the nations which you go to dispossess, and you di[s]place them and dwell in their land, ³⁰take heed to you[r]self that you are not ensnared to follow them, after th[ey] are destroyed from before you, and that you do n[ot] inquire after their gods, saying, 'How did these natio[ns] serve their gods? I also will do likewise.' ³¹You shall n[ot] worship the LORD your God in that way; for every abom[i]ination to the LORD which He hates they have done [to] their gods; for they burn even their sons and daughte[rs] in the fire to their gods.

³²"Whatever I command you, be careful to observe [it;] you shall not add to it nor take away from it.

CHAPTER 13 DON'T LISTEN TO FALSE PROPHET[S]

"If there arises among you a prophet or a dreamer [of] dreams, and he gives you a sign or a wonder, ²and t[he] sign or the wonder comes to pass, of which he spoke [to] you, saying, 'Let us go after other gods'—which you ha[ve] not known—'and let us serve them,' ³you shall not list[en] to the words of that prophet or that dreamer of dream[s,] for the LORD your God is testing you to know whether y[ou] love the LORD your God with all your heart and with [all] your soul. ⁴You shall walk after the LORD your God a[nd] fear Him, and keep His commandments and obey H[is] voice; you shall serve Him and hold fast to Him. ⁵But th[at] prophet or that dreamer of dreams shall be put to dea[th,] because he has spoken in order to turn *you* away fro[m] the LORD your God, who brought you out of the land [of] Egypt and redeemed you from the house of bondage, [to] entice you from the way in which the LORD your G[od] commanded you to walk. So you shall put away the e[vil] from your midst.

⁶"If your brother, the son of your mother, your son [or] your daughter, the wife of your bosom, or your frie[nd] who is as your own soul, secretly entices you, saying, 'L[et] us go and serve other gods,' which you have not know[n,] neither you nor your fathers, ⁷of the gods of the peop[le] which *are* all around you, near to you or far off from yo[u,] from *one* end of the earth to the *other* end of the eart[h,] ⁸you shall not consent to him or listen to him, nor sh[all] your eye pity him, nor shall you spare him or conce[al] him; ⁹but you shall surely kill him; your hand shall [be] first against him to put him to death, and afterward t[he] hand of all the people. ¹⁰And you shall stone him wi[th] stones until he dies, because he sought to entice y[ou]

WHISPERS

13:2-11 The Israelites were warned not to listen to false pro[phets] anyone else who tried to get them to worship other gods—eve[n if the] person was a close friend or family member. The temptation to [disobey] God's commands often sneaks up on us. It may come not with [a] shout, but in a whispering doubt. Whispers can be very persuas[ive,] especially if they come from loved ones. But love for relatives s[hould never] take precedence over devotion to God. We can overcome whisp[ering] temptations by pouring out our feelings to God in prayer and b[y reading] his Word.

way from the LORD your God, who brought you out of the land of Egypt, from the house of bondage. ¹¹So all Israel shall hear and fear, and not again do such wickedness as this among you.

¹²"If you hear someone in one of your cities, which the LORD your God gives you to dwell in, saying, ¹³'Corrupt men have gone out from among you and enticed the inhabitants of their city, saying, "Let us go and serve other gods" '—which you have not known— ¹⁴then you shall inquire, search out, and ask diligently. And *if it is* indeed true *and* certain *that* such an abomination was committed among you, ¹⁵you shall surely strike the inhabitants of that city with the edge of the sword, utterly destroying it, all that is in it and its livestock—with the edge of the sword. ¹⁶And you shall gather all its plunder into the middle of the street, and completely burn with fire the city and all its plunder, for the LORD your God. It shall be a heap forever; it shall not be built again. ¹⁷So none of the accursed things shall remain in your hand, that the LORD may turn from the fierceness of His anger and show you mercy, have compassion on you and multiply you, just as He swore to your fathers, ¹⁸because you have listened to the voice of the LORD your God, to keep all His commandments which I command you today, to do *what is* right in the eyes of the LORD your God.

CHAPTER 14 WHAT TO EAT AND NOT EAT. "You *are* the children of the LORD your God; you shall not cut yourselves nor shave the front of your head for the dead. ²For you *are* a holy people to the LORD your God, and the LORD has chosen you to be a people for Himself, a special treasure above all the peoples who *are* on the face of the earth.

³"You shall not eat any detestable thing. ⁴These *are* the animals which you may eat: the ox, the sheep, the goat, the deer, the gazelle, the roe deer, the wild goat, the mountain goat, the antelope, and the mountain sheep. ⁵And you may eat every animal with cloven hooves, having the hoof split into two parts, *and that* chews the cud, among the animals. ⁷Nevertheless, of those that chew the cud or have cloven hooves, you shall not eat, *such as* these: the camel, the hare, and the rock hyrax; for they chew the cud but do not have cloven hooves; they *are* unclean for you. ⁸Also the swine is unclean for you, because it has cloven hooves, yet *does* not *chew* the cud; you shall not eat their flesh or touch their dead carcasses.

⁹"These you may eat of all that *are* in the waters: you may eat all that have fins and scales. ¹⁰And whatever does not have fins and scales you shall not eat; it *is* unclean for you.

¹¹"All clean birds you may eat. ¹²But these you shall not eat: the eagle, the vulture, the buzzard, ¹³the red kite, the falcon, and the kite after their kinds; ¹⁴every raven after its kind; ¹⁵the ostrich, the short-eared owl, the sea gull, and the hawk after their kinds; ¹⁶the little owl, the screech owl, the white owl, ¹⁷the jackdaw, the carrion vulture, the fisher owl, ¹⁸the stork, the heron after its kind, and the hoopoe and the bat.

¹⁹"Also every creeping thing that flies is unclean for you; they shall not be eaten.

²⁰"You may eat all clean birds.

²¹"You shall not eat anything that dies *of itself;* you may give it to the alien who *is* within your gates, that he may eat it, or you may sell it to a foreigner; for you *are* a holy people to the LORD your God.

"You shall not boil a young goat in its mother's milk.

²²"You shall truly tithe all the increase of your grain that the field produces year by year. ²³And you shall eat before the LORD your God, in the place where He chooses to make His name abide, the tithe of your grain and your new wine and your oil, of the firstborn of your herds and your flocks, that you may learn to fear the LORD your God always. ²⁴But if the journey is too long for you, so that you are not able to carry *the tithe, or* if the place where the LORD your God chooses to put His name is too far from you, when the LORD your God has blessed you, ²⁵then you shall exchange *it* for money, take the money in your hand, and go to the place which the LORD your God chooses. ²⁶And you shall spend that money for whatever your heart desires: for oxen or sheep, for wine or similar drink, for whatever your heart desires; you shall eat there before the LORD your God, and you shall rejoice, you and your household. ²⁷You shall not forsake the Levite who *is* within your gates, for he has no part nor inheritance with you.

²⁸"At the end of *every* third year you shall bring out the tithe of your produce of that year and store *it* up within your gates. ²⁹And the Levite, because he has no portion nor inheritance with you, and the stranger and the fatherless and the widow who *are* within your gates, may come and eat and be satisfied, that the LORD your God may bless you in all the work of your hand which you do.

CHAPTER 15 LENDING MONEY. "At the end of *every* seven years you shall grant a release *of debts.* ²And this *is* the form of the release: Every creditor who has lent *anything* to his neighbor shall release *it;* he shall not require *it* of his neighbor or his brother, because it is called the LORD's release. ³Of a foreigner you may require *it;* but you shall give up your claim to what is owed by your brother, ⁴except when there may be no poor among you; for the LORD will greatly bless you in the land which the LORD your God is giving you to possess *as* an inheritance— ⁵only if you carefully obey the voice of the LORD your God, to observe with care all these commandments which I command you today. ⁶For the LORD your God will bless you just as He promised you; you shall lend to many nations, but you shall not borrow; you shall reign over many nations, but they shall not reign over you.

⁷"If there is among you a poor man of your brethren, within any of the gates in your land which the LORD your

POVERTY

15:7-11 God told the Israelites to help the poor among them when they arrived in the Promised Land. This was an important part of possessing the land. Many people conclude that people are poor through some fault of their own. This kind of reasoning makes it easy to close their hearts and hands against them. But we are not to invent reasons for ignoring the care of the poor. We are to respond to their needs no matter who or what was responsible for their condition. Who are the poor in your community? How could you help them?

God is giving you, you shall not harden your heart nor shut your hand from your poor brother, [8]but you shall open your hand wide to him and willingly lend him sufficient for his need, whatever he needs. [9]Beware lest there be a wicked thought in your heart, saying, 'The seventh year, the year of release, is at hand,' and your eye be evil against your poor brother and you give him nothing, and he cry out to the LORD against you, and it become sin among you. [10]You shall surely give to him, and your heart should not be grieved when you give to him, because for this thing the LORD your God will bless you in all your works and in all to which you put your hand. [11]For the poor will never cease from the land; therefore I command you, saying, 'You shall open your hand wide to your brother, to your poor and your needy, in your land.'

◀▬▬▬ PAY BACK

16:16-17 *Three times a year every male was to make a journey to the sanctuary located in the city designated as the religious capital of Israel. At these feasts, each participant was encouraged to give what he could in proportion to what God had given him. God does not expect us to give more than we can, but we are blessed when we are able to give cheerfully. For some of us, 10 percent may be a burden. For most of us, it is far too little. Look around at what you have, then give in proportion to what you have been given.*

[12]"If your brother, a Hebrew man, or a Hebrew woman, is sold to you and serves you six years, then in the seventh year you shall let him go free from you. [13]And when you send him away free from you, you shall not let him go away empty-handed; [14]you shall supply him liberally from your flock, from your threshing floor, and from your winepress. *From what* the LORD has blessed you with, you shall give to him. [15]You shall remember that you were a slave in the land of Egypt, and the LORD your God redeemed you; therefore I command you this thing today. [16]And if it happens that he says to you, 'I will not go away from you,' because he loves you and your house, since he prospers with you, [17]then you shall take an awl and thrust *it* through his ear to the door, and he shall be your servant forever. Also to your female servant you shall do likewise. [18]It shall not seem hard to you when you send him away free from you; for he has been worth a double hired servant in serving you six years. Then the LORD your God will bless you in all that you do.

[19]"All the firstborn males that come from your herd and your flock you shall sanctify to the LORD your God; you shall do no work with the firstborn of your herd, nor shear the firstborn of your flock. [20]You and your household shall eat *it* before the LORD your God year by year in the place which the LORD chooses. [21]But if there is a defect in it, *if it is* lame or blind *or has* any serious defect, you shall not sacrifice it to the LORD your God. [22]You may eat it within your gates; the unclean and the clean *person* alike *may eat it,* as *if it were* a gazelle or a deer. [23]Only you shall not eat its blood; you shall pour it on the ground like water.

CHAPTER **16** SPECIAL FEASTS. "Observe the month of Abib, and keep the Passover to the LORD your God, for

in the month of Abib the LORD your God brought you out of Egypt by night. [2]Therefore you shall sacrifice the Passover to the LORD your God, from the flock and the herd, in the place where the LORD chooses to put His name. [3]You shall eat no leavened bread with it; seven days you shall eat unleavened bread with it, *that is,* the bread of affliction (for you came out of the land of Egypt in haste), that you may remember the day in which you came out of the land of Egypt all the days of your life. [4]And no leaven shall be seen among you in all your territory for seven days, nor shall *any* of the meat which you sacrifice the first day at twilight remain overnight until morning.

[5]"You may not sacrifice the Passover within any of your gates which the LORD your God gives you; [6]but at the place where the LORD your God chooses to make His name abide, there you shall sacrifice the Passover at twilight, at the going down of the sun, at the time you came out of Egypt. [7]And you shall roast and eat *it* in the place which the LORD your God chooses, and in the morning you shall turn and go to your tents. [8]Six days you shall eat unleavened bread, and on the seventh day there *shall be* a sacred assembly to the LORD your God. You shall do no work *on it.*

[9]"You shall count seven weeks for yourself; begin to count the seven weeks from *the time* you begin *to put* the sickle to the grain. [10]Then you shall keep the Feast of Weeks to the LORD your God with the tribute of a freewill offering from your hand, which you shall give as the LORD your God blesses you. [11]You shall rejoice before the LORD your God, you and your son and your daughter, your male servant and your female servant, the Levite who *is* within your gates, the stranger and the fatherless and the widow who *are* among you, at the place where the LORD your God chooses to make His name abide. [12]And you shall remember that you were a slave in Egypt, and you shall be careful to observe these statutes.

[13]"You shall observe the Feast of Tabernacles seven days, when you have gathered from your threshing floor and from your winepress. [14]And you shall rejoice in your feast, you and your son and your daughter, your male servant and your female servant and the Levite, the stranger and the fatherless and the widow, who *are* within your gates. [15]Seven days you shall keep a sacred feast to the LORD your God in the place which the LORD chooses, because the LORD your God will bless you in all your produce and in all the work of your hands, so that you surely rejoice.

[16]"Three times a year all your males shall appear before the LORD your God in the place which He chooses: at the Feast of Unleavened Bread, at the Feast of Weeks, and at the Feast of Tabernacles; and they shall not appear before the LORD empty-handed. [17]Every man *shall give* as he is able, according to the blessing of the LORD your God which He has given you.

[18]"You shall appoint judges and officers in all your gates, which the LORD your God gives you, according to your tribes, and they shall judge the people with just judgment. [19]You shall not pervert justice; you shall not show partiality, nor take a bribe, for a bribe blinds the eyes of the wise and twists the words of the righteous. [20]You shall follow what is altogether just, that you may

ive and inherit the land which the LORD your God is giving you. ²¹"You shall not plant for yourself any tree, as a wooden image, near the altar which you build for yourself to the LORD your God. ²²You shall not set up a sacred pillar, which the LORD your God hates.

CHAPTER 17 "You shall not sacrifice to the LORD your God a bull or sheep which has any blemish *or* defect, for that *is* an abomination to the LORD your God.

²"If there is found among you, within any of your gates which the LORD your God gives you, a man or a woman who has been wicked in the sight of the LORD your God, in transgressing His covenant, ³who has gone and served other gods and worshiped them, either the sun or moon or any of the host of heaven, which I have not commanded, ⁴and it is told you, and you hear *of it,* then you shall inquire diligently. And if *it is* indeed true *and* certain that such an abomination has been committed in Israel, ⁵then you shall bring out to your gates that man or woman who has committed that wicked thing, and shall stone to death that man or woman with stones. ⁶Whoever is deserving of death shall be put to death on the testimony of two or three witnesses; he shall not be put to death on the testimony of one witness. ⁷The hands of the witnesses shall be the first against him to put him to death, and afterward the hands of all the people. So you shall put away the evil from among you.

⁸"If a matter arises which is too hard for you to judge, between degrees of guilt for bloodshed, between one judgment or another, or between one punishment or another, matters of controversy within your gates, then you shall arise and go up to the place which the LORD your God chooses. ⁹And you shall come to the priests, the Levites, and to the judge *there* in those days, and inquire *of them;* they shall pronounce upon you the sentence of judgment. ¹⁰You shall do according to the sentence which they pronounce upon you in that place which the LORD chooses. And you shall be careful to do according to all that they order you. ¹¹According to the sentence of the law in which they instruct you, according to the judgment which they tell you, you shall do; you shall not turn aside *to* the right hand or *to* the left from the sentence which they pronounce upon you. ¹²Now the man who acts presumptuously and will not heed the priest who stands to minister there before the LORD your God, or the judge, that man shall die. So you shall put away the evil from Israel. ¹³And all the people shall hear and fear, and no longer act presumptuously.

¹⁴"When you come to the land which the LORD your God is giving you, and possess it and dwell in it, and say, 'I will set a king over me like all the nations that *are* around me,' ¹⁵you shall surely set a king over you whom the LORD your God chooses; *one* from among your brethren you shall set as king over you; you may not set a foreigner over you, who *is* not your brother. ¹⁶But he shall not multiply horses for himself, nor cause the people to return to Egypt to multiply horses, for the LORD has said to you, 'You shall not return that way again.' ¹⁷Neither shall he multiply wives for himself, lest his heart turn away; nor shall he greatly multiply silver and gold for himself.

¹⁸"Also it shall be, when he sits on the throne of his kingdom, that he shall write for himself a copy of this law in a book, from *the one* before the priests, the Levites. ¹⁹And it shall be with him, and he shall read it all the days of his life, that he may learn to fear the LORD his God and be careful to observe all the words of this law and these statutes, ²⁰that his heart may not be lifted above his brethren, that he may not turn aside from the commandment *to* the right hand or *to* the left, and that he may prolong *his* days in his kingdom, he and his children in the midst of Israel.

CHAPTER 18 GIVING TO PRIESTS AND LEVITES.
"The priests, the Levites—all the tribe of Levi—shall have no part nor inheritance with Israel; they shall eat the offerings of the LORD made by fire, and His portion. ²Therefore they shall have no inheritance among their brethren; the LORD is their inheritance, as He said to them.

³"And this shall be the priest's due from the people, from those who offer a sacrifice, whether *it is* bull or sheep: they shall give to the priest the shoulder, the cheeks, and the stomach. ⁴The firstfruits of your grain and your new wine and your oil, and the first of the fleece of your sheep, you shall give him. ⁵For the LORD your God has chosen him out of all your tribes to stand to minister in the name of the LORD, him and his sons forever.

⁶"So if a Levite comes from any of your gates, from where he dwells among all Israel, and comes with all the desire of his mind to the place which the LORD chooses, ⁷then he may serve in the name of the LORD his God as all his brethren the Levites *do,* who stand there before the LORD. ⁸They shall have equal portions to eat, besides what comes from the sale of his inheritance.

⁹"When you come into the land which the LORD your God is giving you, you shall not learn to follow the abominations of those nations. ¹⁰There shall not be found among you *anyone* who makes his son or his daughter pass through the fire, *or one* who practices witchcraft, *or* a soothsayer, or one who interprets omens, or a sorcerer, ¹¹or one who conjures spells, or a medium, or a spiritist, or one who calls up the dead. ¹²For all who do these things *are* an abomination to the LORD, and because of these abominations the LORD your God drives them out

WITNESSES
17:6-7 A person was not put to death on the testimony of only one witness. On the witness of two or three, a person could be condemned and then sentenced to death by stoning. The condemned person was taken outside the city gates, and the witnesses were the first to throw heavy stones down on him or her. Bystanders would then pelt the dying person with stones. This system would "put away the evil" by putting the idolater to death. At the same time, it protected the rights of accused persons two ways. First, by requiring several witnesses, it prevented any angry individual from giving "false testimony." Second, by requiring the accusers to throw the first stones, it made them think twice about accusing unjustly. They were responsible to finish what they had started.

18:10-13 Just as most of us are naturally curious about a magician's trick, the Israelites were curious about the occult practices of the Canaanite religions. But Satan is behind the occult, and God flatly forbade Israel to have anything to do with it. People today are still fascinated by horoscopes, fortune-telling, witchcraft, and bizarre cults. Often their interest comes from a desire to know and control the future. But Satan is no less dangerous today than he was in Moses' time. In the Bible, God tells us all we need to know about what is going to happen. The information Satan offers is likely to be distorted or completely false. With the trustworthy guidance of the Holy Spirit through the Scriptures and the church, we don't need to turn to occult sources for information—especially since the information from such sources is faulty.

from before you. ¹³You shall be blameless before the LORD your God. ¹⁴For these nations which you will dispossess listened to soothsayers and diviners; but as for you, the LORD your God has not appointed such for you.

¹⁵"The LORD your God will raise up for you a Prophet like me from your midst, from your brethren. Him you shall hear, ¹⁶according to all you desired of the LORD your God in Horeb in the day of the assembly, saying, 'Let me not hear again the voice of the LORD my God, nor let me see this great fire anymore, lest I die.'

¹⁷"And the LORD said to me: 'What they have spoken is good. ¹⁸I will raise up for them a Prophet like you from among their brethren, and will put My words in His mouth, and He shall speak to them all that I command Him. ¹⁹And it shall be *that* whoever will not hear My words, which He speaks in My name, I will require *it* of him. ²⁰But the prophet who presumes to speak a word in My name, which I have not commanded him to speak, or who speaks in the name of other gods, that prophet shall die.' ²¹And if you say in your heart, 'How shall we know the word which the LORD has not spoken?'— ²²when a prophet speaks in the name of the LORD, if the thing does not happen or come to pass, that *is* the thing which the LORD has not spoken; the prophet has spoken it presumptuously; you shall not be afraid of him.

CHAPTER 19 CITIES OF REFUGE.

"When the LORD your God has cut off the nations whose land the LORD your God is giving you, and you dispossess them and dwell in their cities and in their houses, ²you shall separate three cities for yourself in the midst of your land which the LORD your God is giving you to possess. ³You shall prepare roads for yourself, and divide into three parts the territory of your land which the LORD your God is giving you to inherit, that any manslayer may flee there.

⁴"And this *is* the case of the manslayer who flees there, that he may live: Whoever kills his neighbor unintentionally, not having hated him in time past— ⁵as when *a man* goes to the woods with his neighbor to cut timber, and his hand swings a stroke with the ax to cut down the tree, and the head slips from the handle and strikes his neighbor so that he dies—he shall flee to one of these cities and live; ⁶lest the avenger of blood, while his anger is hot, pursue the manslayer and overtake him, because the way is long, and kill him, though he *was* not deserving of death, since he had not hated the victim in time past.

⁷Therefore I command you, saying, 'You shall separate three cities for yourself.'

⁸"Now if the LORD your God enlarges your territory, as He swore to your fathers, and gives you the land which He promised to give to your fathers, ⁹and if you keep all these commandments and do them, which I command you today, to love the LORD your God and to walk always in His ways, then you shall add three more cities for yourself besides these three, ¹⁰lest innocent blood be shed in the midst of your land which the LORD your God is giving you *as* an inheritance, and *thus* guilt of bloodshed be upon you.

¹¹"But if anyone hates his neighbor, lies in wait for him, rises against him and strikes him mortally, so that he dies, and he flees to one of these cities, ¹²then the elders of his city shall send and bring him from there, and deliver him over to the hand of the avenger of blood, that he may die. ¹³Your eye shall not pity him, but you shall put away *the guilt of* innocent blood from Israel, that it may go well with you.

¹⁴"You shall not remove your neighbor's landmark which the men of old have set, in your inheritance which you will inherit in the land that the LORD your God is giving you to possess.

¹⁵"One witness shall not rise against a man concerning any iniquity or any sin that he commits; by the mouth of two or three witnesses the matter shall be established. ¹⁶If a false witness rises against any man to testify against him of wrongdoing, ¹⁷then both men in the controversy shall stand before the LORD, before the priests and the judges who serve in those days. ¹⁸And the judges shall make careful inquiry, and indeed, *if* the witness *is* a false witness, who has testified falsely against his brother, ¹⁹then you shall do to him as he thought to have done to his brother; so you shall put away the evil from among you. ²⁰And those who remain shall hear and fear, and hereafter they shall not again commit such evil among you. ²¹Your eye shall not pity: life *shall be* for life, eye for eye, tooth for tooth, hand for hand, foot for foot.

CHAPTER 20 RULES ABOUT WAR.

"When you go out to battle against your enemies, and see horses and chariots *and* people more numerous than you, do not be afraid of them; for the LORD your God *is* with you, who brought you up from the land of Egypt. ²So it shall be, when you are on the verge of battle, that the priest shall approach and speak to the people. ³And he shall say to them, 'Hear, O Israel: Today you are on the verge of battle with your enemies. Do not let your heart faint, do not be afraid, and do not tremble or be terrified because of them; ⁴for the LORD your God *is* He who goes with you, to fight for you against your enemies, to save you.'

20:1 Just like the Israelites, we sometimes face overwhelming opposition. Whether at school, at work, or even at home, we can ▶ outnumbered and helpless. God bolstered the Israelites' confiden reminding them that he was always with them and that he had al saved them from the potential danger. We, too, can feel secure wh consider that God is able to overcome even the most difficult odds

⁵"Then the officers shall speak to the people, saying: 'What man *is there* who has built a new house and has not dedicated it? Let him go and return to his house, lest he die in the battle and another man dedicate it. ⁶Also what man *is there* who has planted a vineyard and has not eaten of it? Let him go and return to his house, lest he die in the battle and another man eat of it. ⁷And what man *is there* who is betrothed to a woman and has not married her? Let him go and return to his house, lest he die in the battle and another man marry her.'

⁸"The officers shall speak further to the people, and say, 'What man *is there who is* fearful and fainthearted? Let him go and return to his house, lest the heart of his brethren faint like his heart.' ⁹And so it shall be, when the officers have finished speaking to the people, that they shall make captains of the armies to lead the people.

¹⁰"When you go near a city to fight against it, then proclaim an offer of peace to it. ¹¹And it shall be that if they accept your offer of peace, and open to you, then all the people *who are* found in it shall be placed under tribute to you, and serve you. ¹²Now if *the city* will not make peace with you, but war against you, then you shall besiege it. ¹³And when the LORD your God delivers it into your hands, you shall strike every male in it with the edge of the sword. ¹⁴But the women, the little ones, the livestock, and all that is in the city, all its spoil, you shall plunder for yourself; and you shall eat the enemies' plunder which the LORD your God gives you. ¹⁵Thus you shall do to all the cities *which are* very far from you, which *are* not of the cities of these nations.

¹⁶"But of the cities of these peoples which the LORD your God gives you *as* an inheritance, you shall let nothing that breathes remain alive, ¹⁷but you shall utterly destroy them: the Hittite and the Amorite and the Canaanite and the Perizzite and the Hivite and the Jebusite, just as the LORD your God has commanded you, ¹⁸lest they teach you to do according to all their abominations which they have done for their gods, and you sin against the LORD your God.

¹⁹"When you besiege a city for a long time, while making war against it to take it, you shall not destroy its trees by wielding an ax against them; if you can eat of them, do not cut them down to use in the siege, for the tree of the field *is* man's *food.* ²⁰Only the trees which you know *are* not trees for food you may destroy and cut down, to build siegeworks against the city that makes war with you, until it is subdued.

CHAPTER **21** **AN UNSOLVED MURDER.** "If *anyone* is found slain, lying in the field in the land which the LORD your God is giving you to possess, *and* it is not known who killed him, ²then your elders and your judges shall go out and measure *the distance* from the slain man to the surrounding cities. ³And it shall be *that* the elders of the city nearest to the slain man will take a heifer which has not been worked *and* which has not pulled with a yoke. ⁴The elders of that city shall bring the heifer down to a valley with flowing water, which is neither plowed nor sown, and they shall break the heifer's neck there in the valley. ⁵Then the priests, the sons of Levi, shall come near, for the LORD your God has chosen them to minister to Him and to bless in the name of the LORD; by their word every controversy and every assault shall be *settled.* ⁶And all the elders of that city nearest to the slain *man* shall wash their hands over the heifer whose neck was broken in the valley. ⁷Then they shall answer and say, 'Our hands have not shed this blood, nor have our eyes seen *it.* ⁸Provide atonement, O LORD, for Your people Israel, whom You have redeemed, and do not lay innocent blood to the charge of Your people Israel.' And atonement shall be provided on their behalf for the blood. ⁹So you shall put away the *guilt of* innocent blood from among you when you do *what is* right in the sight of the LORD.

¹⁰"When you go out to war against your enemies, and the LORD your God delivers them into your hand, and you

---

"Here's what I did..."

It was strange how this one passage of Scripture—Ephesians 6:10-18, about putting on the whole armor of God—kept coming up again and again in one week. First it came up in my quiet time. Then we studied the same passage in the youth Bible study. Finally, my pastor preached a sermon on spiritual warfare.

Later that week my friend asked me if I would play the Ouija board with her. I felt uneasy about it, but it seemed like just a game, so I said yes. Some weird things happened; the piece that you put your fingers on really seemed to move of its own accord, and it spelled out some weird answers. I had a very creepy feeling that this was not of God. I told my friend I wanted to quit right now, that I didn't think God wanted us to do this. That night I called my youth pastor and told him about it. He pointed out that Deuteronomy 18:9-14 warns us against trying to seek the future from means other than God. He reminded me that Satan is always trying to find a way to sneak into our lives. And he reminded me of Ephesians 6 and the armor God gives us to fight the devil. I realized that God had been trying to prepare me for the temptation to use the Ouija board, but I wasn't paying close enough attention at the time.

I learned from my mistake. I will never touch or mess with a Ouija board or horoscopes or anything like that again.

Carolyn

AGE 16

take them captive, [11]and you see among the captives a beautiful woman, and desire her and would take her for your wife, [12]then you shall bring her home to your house, and she shall shave her head and trim her nails. [13]She shall put off the clothes of her captivity, remain in your house, and mourn her father and her mother a full month; after that you may go in to her and be her husband, and she shall be your wife. [14]And it shall be, if you have no delight in her, then you shall set her free, but you certainly shall not sell her for money; you shall not treat her brutally, because you have humbled her.

[15]"If a man has two wives, one loved and the other unloved, and they have borne him children, *both* the loved and the unloved, and *if* the firstborn son is of her who is unloved, [16]then it shall be, on the day he bequeaths his possessions to his sons, *that* he must not bestow firstborn status on the son of the loved wife in preference to the son of the unloved, the *true* firstborn? [17]But he shall acknowledge the son of the unloved wife *as* the firstborn by giving him a double portion of all that he has, for he *is* the beginning of his strength; the right of the firstborn *is* his.

[18]"If a man has a stubborn and rebellious son who will not obey the voice of his father or the voice of his mother, and *who*, when they have chastened him, will not heed them, [19]then his father and his mother shall take hold of him and bring him out to the elders of his city, to the gate of his city. [20]And they shall say to the elders of his city, 'This son of ours is stubborn and rebellious; he will not obey our voice; he is a glutton and a drunkard.' [21]Then all the men of his city shall stone him to death with stones; so you shall put away the evil from among you, and all Israel shall hear and fear.

[22]"If a man has committed a sin deserving of death, and he is put to death, and you hang him on a tree, [23]his body shall not remain overnight on the tree, but you shall surely bury him that day, so that you do not defile the land which the LORD your God is giving you *as* an inheritance; for he who is hanged *is* accursed of God.

CHAPTER **22** **HELPING NEIGHBORS.** "You shall not see your brother's ox or his sheep going astray, and hide yourself from them; you shall certainly bring them back to your brother. [2]And if your brother *is* not near you, or if you do not know him, then you shall bring it to your own house, and it shall remain with you until your brother seeks it; then you shall restore it to him. [3]You shall do the same with his donkey, and so shall you do with his garment; with any lost thing of your brother's, which he has lost and you have found, you shall do likewise; you must not hide yourself.

[4]"You shall not see your brother's donkey or his ox fall down along the road, and hide yourself from them; you shall surely help him lift *them* up again.

[5]"A woman shall not wear anything that pertains to a man, nor shall a man put on a woman's garment, for all who do so *are* an abomination to the LORD your God.

[6]"If a bird's nest happens to be before you along the way, in any tree or on the ground, with young ones or eggs, with the mother sitting on the young or on the eggs,

RETURNS

22:1-4 The Hebrews were to care for and return lost animals or possessions to their rightful owners. The way of the world, by contrast "Finders keepers, losers weepers." To go beyond the finders-keepers by protecting and returning the property of others keeps us from bei envious and greedy.

you shall not take the mother with the young; [7]you shall surely let the mother go, and take the young for yourself, that it may be well with you and *that* you may prolong *your* days.

[8]"When you build a new house, then you shall make a parapet for your roof, that you may not bring guilt of bloodshed on your household if anyone falls from it.

[9]"You shall not sow your vineyard with different kinds of seed, lest the yield of the seed which you have sown and the fruit of your vineyard be defiled.

[10]"You shall not plow with an ox and a donkey together.

[11]"You shall not wear a garment of different sorts, *such as* wool and linen mixed together.

[12]"You shall make tassels on the four corners of the clothing with which you cover *yourself*.

[13]"If any man takes a wife, and goes in to her, and detests her, [14]and charges her with shameful conduct, and brings a bad name on her, and says, 'I took this woman, and when I came to her I found she *was* not a virgin,' [15]then the father and mother of the young woman shall take and bring out *the evidence of* the young woman's virginity to the elders of the city at the gate. [16]And the young woman's father shall say to the elders, 'I gave my daughter to this man as wife, and he detests her. [17]Now he has charged her with shameful conduct, saying, "I found your daughter *was* not a virgin," and yet these *are the evidences of* my daughter's virginity.' And they shall spread the cloth before the elders of the city. [18]Then the elders of that city shall take that man and punish him; [19]and they shall fine him one hundred *shekels* of silver and give *them* to the father of the young woman, because he has brought a bad name on a virgin of Israel. And she shall be his wife; he cannot divorce her all his days.

[20]"But if the thing is true, *and evidences of* virginity are not found for the young woman, [21]then they shall bring out the young woman to the door of her father's house, and the men of her city shall stone her to death with stones, because she has done a disgraceful thing in Israel, to play the harlot in her father's house. So you shall put away the evil from among you.

[22]"If a man is found lying with a woman married to a husband, then both of them shall die—the man that lay with the woman, and the woman; so you shall put away the evil from Israel.

[23]"If a young woman *who is* a virgin is betrothed to a husband, and a man finds her in the city and lies with her, [24]then you shall bring them both out to the gate of

ROLES

22:5 This verse commands men and women not to reverse their roles. It is not a statement about clothing styles. Today role rejecti common—there are men who want to become women and wom want to become men. It's not the clothing style that offends God, using the style to act out a different sex role. God had a purpose making us uniquely male and female.

at city, and you shall stone them to death with stones,
e young woman because she did not cry out in the city,
d the man because he humbled his neighbor's wife; so
u shall put away the evil from among you.

25"But if a man finds a betrothed young woman in the
untryside, and the man forces her and lies with her,
en only the man who lay with her shall die. 26But you
all do nothing to the young woman; *there is* in the
ung woman no sin *deserving* of death, for just as when
man rises against his neighbor and kills him, even so *is*
is matter. 27For he found her in the countryside, *and* the
trothed young woman cried out, but *there was* no one
save her.

28"If a man finds a young woman *who is* a virgin, who
not betrothed, and he seizes her and lies with her, and
ey are found out, 29then the man who lay with her shall
ve to the young woman's father fifty *shekels* of silver,
d she shall be his wife because he has humbled her; he
all not be permitted to divorce her all his days.

30"A man shall not take his father's wife, nor uncover
s father's bed.

HAPTER 23 RULES ABOUT THE ASSEMBLY. "He
ho is emasculated by crushing or mutilation shall not
ter the assembly of the LORD.

2"One of illegitimate birth shall not enter the assembly
the LORD; even to the tenth generation none of his
escendants shall enter the assembly of the LORD.

3"An Ammonite or Moabite shall not enter the assem-
y of the LORD; even to the tenth generation none of his
escendants shall enter the assembly of the LORD forever,
ecause they did not meet you with bread and water on
e road when you came out of Egypt, and because they
red against you Balaam the son of Beor from Pethor of
esopotamia, to curse you. 5Nevertheless the LORD your
od would not listen to Balaam, but the LORD your God
rned the curse into a blessing for you, because the
RD your God loves you. 6You shall not seek their peace
r their prosperity all your days forever.

7"You shall not abhor an Edomite, for he *is* your
other. You shall not abhor an Egyptian, because you
ere an alien in his land. 8The children of the third gen-
ation born to them may enter the assembly of the
RD.

9"When the army goes out against your enemies, then
ep yourself from every wicked thing. 10If there is any
an among you who becomes unclean by some occur-
nce in the night, then he shall go outside the camp; he
all not come inside the camp. 11But it shall be, when
ening comes, that he shall wash with water; and when
e sun sets, he may come into the camp.

12"Also you shall have a place outside the camp, where
u may go out; 13and you shall have an implement
nong your equipment, and when you sit down outside,
u shall dig with it and turn and cover your refuse. 14For
e LORD your God walks in the midst of your camp, to
liver you and give your enemies over to you; therefore
ur camp shall be holy, that He may see no unclean
ing among you, and turn away from you.

15"You shall not give back to his master the slave who

has escaped from his master to you. 16He may dwell with
you in your midst, in the place which he chooses within
one of your gates, where it seems best to him; you shall
not oppress him.

17"There shall be no *ritual* harlot of the daughters of
Israel, or a perverted one of the sons of Israel. 18You shall
not bring the wages of a harlot or the price of a dog to the
house of the LORD your God for any vowed offering, for
both of these *are* an abomination to the LORD your God.

◣▬▬▬▬▬**SEX**

23:17-18 A harlot was a prostitute. Prostitution was strictly forbidden.
To forbid this practice may seem obvious to us, but it may not have been
so obvious to the Israelites. Almost every other religion known to them
included prostitution as an important part of its worship services.
Prostitution makes a mockery of God's original idea for sex. It treats sex
as an isolated physical act rather than an act of commitment to another
person. Outside of marriage, sex destroys relationships. Within marriage,
if approached with the right attitude, it can be a relationship builder. God
frequently had to warn the people against the practice of extramarital
sex. Today we still need to hear his warnings; young people need to be
reminded about premarital sex and adults need to be reminded about
sexual fidelity.

19"You shall not charge interest to your brother—interest on money *or* food *or* anything that is lent out at
interest. 20To a foreigner you may charge interest, but to
your brother you shall not charge interest, that the LORD
your God may bless you in all to which you set your hand
in the land which you are entering to possess.

21"When you make a vow to the LORD your God, you
shall not delay to pay it; for the LORD your God will surely
require it of you, and it would be sin to you. 22But if you
abstain from vowing, it shall not be sin to you. 23That
which has gone from your lips you shall keep and perform, for you voluntarily vowed to the LORD your God
what you have promised with your mouth.

24"When you come into your neighbor's vineyard, you
may eat your fill of grapes at your pleasure, but you shall
not put *any* in your container. 25When you come into
your neighbor's standing grain, you may pluck the heads
with your hand, but you shall not use a sickle on your
neighbor's standing grain.

CHAPTER 24 "When a man takes a wife and marries her, and it happens that she finds no favor in his eyes
because he has found some uncleanness in her, and he
writes her a certificate of divorce, puts *it* in her hand, and
sends her out of his house, 2when she has departed from
his house, and goes and becomes another man's *wife,* 3*if*
the latter husband detests her and writes her a certificate
of divorce, puts *it* in her hand, and sends her out of his
house, or if the latter husband dies who took her as his
wife, 4*then* her former husband who divorced her must
not take her back to be his wife after she has been defiled;
for that *is* an abomination before the LORD, and you shall
not bring sin on the land which the LORD your God is
giving you *as* an inheritance.

5"When a man has taken a new wife, he shall not go
out to war or be charged with any business; he shall be

free at home one year, and bring happiness to his wife whom he has taken.

[6]"No man shall take the lower or the upper millstone in pledge, for he takes one's living in pledge.

[7]"If a man is found kidnapping any of his brethren of the children of Israel, and mistreats him or sells him, then that kidnapper shall die; and you shall put away the evil from among you.

[8]"Take heed in an outbreak of leprosy, that you carefully observe and do according to all that the priests, the Levites, shall teach you; just as I commanded them, so you shall be careful to do. [9]Remember what the LORD your God did to Miriam on the way when you came out of Egypt!

◼ JUSTICE

24:10-22 God told his people to treat the poor with justice. The powerless and poverty-stricken are often looked upon as incompetent or lazy when, in fact, they may be victims of oppression and circumstance. God says we must do all we can to help these needy ones. His justice did not permit the Israelites to insist on profits or quick payment from those who were less fortunate. Instead, his laws gave the poor every opportunity to better their situation, while providing humane options for those who couldn't. We are called to treat the poor fairly and to see that their needs are met.

[10]"When you lend your brother anything, you shall not go into his house to get his pledge. [11]You shall stand outside, and the man to whom you lend shall bring the pledge out to you. [12]And if the man is poor, you shall not keep his pledge overnight. [13]You shall in any case return the pledge to him again when the sun goes down, that he may sleep in his own garment and bless you; and it shall be righteousness to you before the LORD your God.

[14]"You shall not oppress a hired servant who is poor and needy, whether one of your brethren or one of the aliens who is in your land within your gates. [15]Each day you shall give him his wages, and not let the sun go down on it, for he is poor and has set his heart on it; lest he cry out against you to the LORD, and it be sin to you.

[16]"Fathers shall not be put to death for their children, nor shall children be put to death for their fathers; a person shall be put to death for his own sin.

[17]"You shall not pervert justice due the stranger or the fatherless, nor take a widow's garment as a pledge. [18]But you shall remember that you were a slave in Egypt, and the LORD your God redeemed you from there; therefore I command you to do this thing.

[19]"When you reap your harvest in your field, and forget a sheaf in the field, you shall not go back to get it; it shall be for the stranger, the fatherless, and the widow, that the LORD your God may bless you in all the work of your hands. [20]When you beat your olive trees, you shall not go over the boughs again; it shall be for the stranger, the fatherless, and the widow. [21]When you gather the grapes of your vineyard, you shall not glean it afterward; it shall be for the stranger, the fatherless, and the widow. [22]And you shall remember that you were a slave in the land of Egypt; therefore I command you to do this thing.

CHAPTER 25

"If there is a dispute between me and they come to court, that the judges may judge them and they justify the righteous and condemn the wicke [2]then it shall be, if the wicked man deserves to be beate that the judge will cause him to lie down and be beate in his presence, according to his guilt, with a certa number of blows. [3]Forty blows he may give him and n more, lest he should exceed this and beat him with man blows above these, and your brother be humiliated your sight.

[4]"You shall not muzzle an ox while it treads out th grain.

[5]"If brothers dwell together, and one of them dies an has no son, the widow of the dead man shall not b married to a stranger outside the family; her husban brother shall go in to her, take her as his wife, and per form the duty of a husband's brother to her. [6]And it sha be that the firstborn son which she bears will succeed the name of his dead brother, that his name may not b blotted out of Israel. [7]But if the man does not want to tak his brother's wife, then let his brother's wife go up to th gate to the elders, and say, 'My husband's brother refuse to raise up a name to his brother in Israel; he will n perform the duty of my husband's brother.' [8]Then th elders of his city shall call him and speak to him. B if he stands firm and says, 'I do not want to take he [9]then his brother's wife shall come to him in the presen of the elders, remove his sandal from his foot, spit in h face, and answer and say, 'So shall it be done to the ma who will not build up his brother's house.' [10]And his nam shall be called in Israel, 'The house of him who had h sandal removed.'

[11]"If two men fight together, and the wife of one draw near to rescue her husband from the hand of the o attacking him, and puts out her hand and seizes him the genitals, [12]then you shall cut off her hand; your e shall not pity her.

[13]"You shall not have in your bag differing weights, heavy and a light. [14]You shall not have in your hou differing measures, a large and a small. [15]You shall have perfect and just weight, a perfect and just measure, th your days may be lengthened in the land which the Lo your God is giving you. [16]For all who do such things, who behave unrighteously, are an abomination to th LORD your God.

[17]"Remember what Amalek did to you on the way you were coming out of Egypt, [18]how he met you on th way and attacked your rear ranks, all the stragglers your rear, when you were tired and weary; and he did n fear God. [19]Therefore it shall be, when the LORD your Go has given you rest from your enemies all around, in th land which the LORD your God is giving you to possess an inheritance, that you will blot out the remembran of Amalek from under heaven. You shall not forget.

CHAPTER 26 GIVING GOD THE FIRST AND BES

"And it shall be, when you come into the land which th LORD your God is giving you as an inheritance, and yo possess it and dwell in it, [2]that you shall take some of t first of all the produce of the ground, which you sha

ring from your land that the LORD your God is giving
ou, and put *it* in a basket and go to the place where the
ORD your God chooses to make His name abide. ³And
ou shall go to the one who is priest in those days, and
ay to him, 'I declare today to the LORD your God that I
ave come to the country which the LORD swore to our
athers to give us.'

⁴"Then the priest shall take the basket out of your
and and set it down before the altar of the LORD your
od. ⁵And you shall answer and say before the LORD your
od: 'My father *was* a Syrian, about to perish, and he
vent down to Egypt and dwelt there, few in number; and
here he became a nation, great, mighty, and populous.
But the Egyptians mistreated us, afflicted us, and laid
ard bondage on us. ⁷Then we cried out to the LORD God
f our fathers, and the LORD heard our voice and looked
n our affliction and our labor and our oppression. ⁸So
he LORD brought us out of Egypt with a mighty hand and
vith an outstretched arm, with great terror and with
igns and wonders. ⁹He has brought us to this place and
as given us this land, "a land flowing with milk and
oney"; ¹⁰and now, behold, I have brought the firstfruits
f the land which you, O LORD, have given me.'

"Then you shall set it before the LORD your God, and
vorship before the LORD your God. ¹¹So you shall rejoice
n every good *thing* which the LORD your God has given
o you and your house, you and the Levite and the
tranger who *is* among you.

¹²"When you have finished laying aside all the tithe of
our increase in the third year—the year of tithing—and
ave given *it* to the Levite, the stranger, the fatherless,
nd the widow, so that they may eat within your gates
nd be filled, ¹³then you shall say before the LORD your
od: 'I have removed the holy *tithe* from *my* house, and
lso have given them to the Levite, the stranger, the fa-
herless, and the widow, according to all Your command-
nents which You have commanded me; I have not
ransgressed Your commandments, nor have I forgotten
hem. ¹⁴I have not eaten any of it when in mourning, nor
ave I removed *any* of it for an unclean *use,* nor given *any*
f it for the dead. I have obeyed the voice of the LORD my
od, and have done according to all that You have com-
nanded me. ¹⁵Look down from Your holy habitation,
om heaven, and bless Your people Israel and the land
vhich You have given us, just as You swore to our fathers,
a land flowing with milk and honey." '

¹⁶"This day the LORD your God commands you to ob-
erve these statutes and judgments; therefore you shall
e careful to observe them with all your heart and with
ll your soul. ¹⁷Today you have proclaimed the LORD to be
our God, and that you will walk in His ways and keep His
tatutes, His commandments, and His judgments, and
nat you will obey His voice. ¹⁸Also today the LORD has
roclaimed you to be His special people, just as He
romised you, that *you* should keep all His command-
nents, ¹⁹and that He will set you high above all nations
vhich He has made, in praise, in name, and in honor, and
nat you may be a holy people to the LORD your God, just
s He has spoken."

CHAPTER **27** THE ALTAR ON MOUNT EBAL. Now

Moses, with the elders of Israel, commanded the people,
saying: "Keep all the commandments which I command
you today. ²And it shall be, on the day when you cross
over the Jordan to the land which the LORD your God is
giving you, that you shall set up for yourselves large
stones, and whitewash them with lime. ³You shall write
on them all the words of this law, when you have crossed
over, that you may enter the land which the LORD your
God is giving you, 'a land flowing with milk and honey,'
just as the LORD God of your fathers promised you.
⁴Therefore it shall be, when you have crossed over the
Jordan, *that* on Mount Ebal you shall set up these stones,
which I command you today, and you shall whitewash
them with lime. ⁵And there you shall build an altar to the
LORD your God, an altar of stones; you shall not use an
iron *tool* on them. ⁶You shall build with whole stones the
altar of the LORD your God, and offer burnt offerings on
it to the LORD your God. ⁷You shall offer peace offerings,
and shall eat there, and rejoice before the LORD your God.
⁸And you shall write very plainly on the stones all the
words of this law."

◣━━━━━━━━━━▶ JOURNEY

26:5-10 In Israelite tradition, each person was required to recite the
history of God's dealings with his people. What is the history of your
relationship with God? Can you put into clear and concise words what God
has done for you? Find a friend with whom you can share your spiritual
journey. Take turns telling your stories. This will help you clearly
understand your personal spiritual history, as well as encourage and
inspire you both.

⁹Then Moses and the priests, the Levites, spoke to all
Israel, saying, "Take heed and listen, O Israel: This day
you have become the people of the LORD your God.
¹⁰Therefore you shall obey the voice of the LORD your
God, and observe His commandments and His statutes
which I command you today."

¹¹And Moses commanded the people on the same day,
saying, ¹²"These shall stand on Mount Gerizim to bless
the people, when you have crossed over the Jordan: Simeon, Levi, Judah, Issachar, Joseph, and Benjamin; ¹³and
these shall stand on Mount Ebal to curse: Reuben, Gad,
Asher, Zebulun, Dan, and Naphtali.

¹⁴"And the Levites shall speak with a loud voice and say
to all the men of Israel: ¹⁵'Cursed *is* the one who makes a
carved or molded image, an abomination to the LORD,
the work of the hands of the craftsman, and sets *it* up in
secret.'

"And all the people shall answer and say, 'Amen!'

¹⁶'Cursed *is* the one who treats his father or his mother
with contempt.'

"And all the people shall say, 'Amen!'

¹⁷'Cursed *is* the one who moves his neighbor's landmark.'

"And all the people shall say, 'Amen!'

¹⁸'Cursed *is* the one who makes the blind to wander off
the road.'

"And all the people shall say, 'Amen!'

¹⁹'Cursed *is* the one who perverts the justice due the
stranger, the fatherless, and widow.'

27:15-26 These curses were a series of oaths, spoken by the priests and affirmed by the people, by which the people promised to stay away from wrong actions. By saying *Amen,* "So be it," the people took responsibility for their actions. Sometimes looking at a list of curses like this gives us the idea that God has a bad temper and is out to crush anyone who steps out of line. But we need to see these restrictions not as threats, but as loving warnings about the plain facts of life. Just as we warn children to stay away from hot stoves and busy streets, God warns us to stay away from dangerous actions. But God does not leave us with only curses or consequences. Immediately following these curses, we discover the great blessings (positive consequences) that come from living for God (28:1-14). These give us extra incentive to obey God's laws. While all these blessings may not come in our lifetime on earth, those who obey God will experience the fullness of his blessing when he establishes the new heaven and the new earth.

"And all the people shall say, 'Amen!'

²⁰'Cursed *is* the one who lies with his father's wife, because he has uncovered his father's bed.'

"And all the people shall say, 'Amen!'

²¹'Cursed *is* the one who lies with any kind of animal.'

"And all the people shall say, 'Amen!'

²²'Cursed *is* the one who lies with his sister, the daughter of his father or the daughter of his mother.'

"And all the people shall say, 'Amen!'

²³'Cursed *is* the one who lies with his mother-in-law.'

"And all the people shall say, 'Amen!'

²⁴'Cursed *is* the one who attacks his neighbor secretly.'

"And all the people shall say, 'Amen!'

²⁵'Cursed *is* the one who takes a bribe to slay an innocent person.'

"And all the people shall say, 'Amen!'

²⁶'Cursed *is* the one who does not confirm *all* the words of this law.'

"And all the people shall say, 'Amen!' "

CHAPTER **28** OBEDIENCE BRINGS BLESSING.

"Now it shall come to pass, if you diligently obey the voice of the LORD your God, to observe carefully all His commandments which I command you today, that the LORD your God will set you high above all nations of the earth. ²And all these blessings shall come upon you and overtake you, because you obey the voice of the LORD your God:

³"Blessed *shall* you *be* in the city, and blessed *shall* you *be* in the country.

⁴"Blessed *shall be* the fruit of your body, the produce of your ground and the increase of your herds, the increase of your cattle and the offspring of your flocks.

⁵"Blessed *shall be* your basket and your kneading bowl.

⁶"Blessed *shall* you *be* when you come in, and blessed *shall* you *be* when you go out.

⁷"The LORD will cause your enemies who rise against you to be defeated before your face; they shall come out against you one way and flee before you seven ways.

⁸"The LORD will command the blessing on you in your storehouses and in all to which you set your hand, and He will bless you in the land which the LORD your God is giving you.

⁹"The LORD will establish you as a holy people to Himself, just as He has sworn to you, if you keep the commandments of the LORD your God and walk in His ways. ¹⁰Then all peoples of the earth shall see that you are called by the name of the LORD, and they shall be afraid of you. ¹¹And the LORD will grant you plenty of goods, in the fruit of your body, in the increase of your livestock, and in the produce of your ground, in the land of which the LORD swore to your fathers to give you. ¹²The LORD will open to you His good treasure, the heavens, to give the rain to your land in its season, and to bless all the work of your hand. You shall lend to many nations, but you shall not borrow. ¹³And the LORD will make you the head and not the tail; you shall be above only, and not be beneath, if you heed the commandments of the LORD your God, which I command you today, and are careful to observe *them.* ¹⁴So you shall not turn aside from any of the words which I command you this day, *to* the right or the left, to go after other gods to serve them.

¹⁵"But it shall come to pass, if you do not obey the voice of the LORD your God, to observe carefully all His commandments and His statutes which I command you today, that all these curses will come upon you and overtake you:

¹⁶"Cursed *shall* you *be* in the city, and cursed *shall* you *be* in the country.

¹⁷"Cursed *shall be* your basket and your kneading bowl.

¹⁸"Cursed *shall be* the fruit of your body and the produce of your land, the increase of your cattle and the offspring of your flocks.

¹⁹"Cursed *shall* you *be* when you come in, and cursed *shall* you *be* when you go out.

²⁰"The LORD will send on you cursing, confusion, and rebuke in all that you set your hand to do, until you are destroyed and until you perish quickly, because of the wickedness of your doings in which you have forsaken Me. ²¹The LORD will make the plague cling to you until He has consumed you from the land which you are going to possess. ²²The LORD will strike you with consumption, with fever, with inflammation, with severe burning fever, with the sword, with scorching, and with mildew; they shall pursue you until you perish. ²³And your heavens which *are* over your head shall be bronze, and the earth which is under you *shall be* iron. ²⁴The LORD will change the rain of your land to powder and dust; from the heaven it shall come down on you until you are destroyed.

²⁵"The LORD will cause you to be defeated before your enemies; you shall go out one way against them and flee seven ways before them; and you shall become troublesome to all the kingdoms of the earth. ²⁶Your carcasses shall be food for all the birds of the air and the beasts of the earth, and no one shall frighten *them* away. ²⁷The LORD will strike you with the boils of Egypt, with tumors, with the scab, and with the itch, from which you cannot be healed. ²⁸The LORD will strike you with madness and blindness and confusion of heart. ²⁹And you shall grope at noonday, as a blind man gropes in darkness; you shall not prosper in your ways; you shall be only oppressed and plundered continually, and no one shall save *you.*

³⁰"You shall betroth a wife, but another man shall lie with her; you shall build a house, but you shall not dwell in it; you shall plant a vineyard, but shall not gather its grapes. ³¹Your ox *shall be* slaughtered before your eyes, but you shall not eat of it; your donkey *shall be* violently taken away from before you, and shall not be restored to you; your sheep *shall be* given to your enemies, and you shall have no one to rescue *them*. ³²Your sons and your daughters *shall be* given to another people, and your eyes shall look and fail *with longing* for them all day long; and *there shall be* no strength in your hand. ³³A nation whom you have not known shall eat the fruit of your land and the produce of your labor, and you shall be only oppressed and crushed continually. ³⁴So you shall be driven mad because of the sight which your eyes see. ³⁵The LORD will strike you in the knees and on the legs with severe boils which cannot be healed, and from the sole of your foot to the top of your head.

³⁶"The LORD will bring you and the king whom you set over you to a nation which neither you nor your fathers have known, and there you shall serve other gods—wood and stone. ³⁷And you shall become an astonishment, a proverb, and a byword among all nations where the LORD will drive you.

³⁸"You shall carry much seed out to the field but gather little in, for the locust shall consume it. ³⁹You shall plant vineyards and tend *them*, but you shall neither drink *of* the wine nor gather the *grapes*; for the worms shall eat them. ⁴⁰You shall have olive trees throughout all your territory, but you shall not anoint *yourself* with the oil; for your olives shall drop off. ⁴¹You shall beget sons and daughters, but they shall not be yours; for they shall go into captivity. ⁴²Locusts shall consume all your trees and the produce of your land.

⁴³"The alien who *is* among you shall rise higher and higher above you, and you shall come down lower and lower. ⁴⁴He shall lend to you, but you shall not lend to him; he shall be the head, and you shall be the tail.

⁴⁵"Moreover all these curses shall come upon you and pursue and overtake you, until you are destroyed, because you did not obey the voice of the LORD your God, to keep His commandments and His statutes which He commanded you. ⁴⁶And they shall be upon you for a sign and a wonder, and on your descendants forever.

⁴⁷"Because you did not serve the LORD your God with joy and gladness of heart, for the abundance of everything, ⁴⁸therefore you shall serve your enemies, whom the LORD will send against you, in hunger, in thirst, in nakedness, and in need of everything; and He will put a yoke of iron on your neck until He has destroyed you. ⁴⁹The LORD will bring a nation against you from afar, from the end of the earth, *as swift* as the eagle flies, a nation whose language you will not understand, ⁵⁰a nation of fierce countenance, which does not respect the elderly nor show favor to the young. ⁵¹And they shall eat the increase of your livestock and the produce of your land, until you are destroyed; they shall not leave you grain or new wine or oil, *or* the increase of your cattle or the offspring of your flocks, until they have destroyed you. ⁵²They shall besiege you at all your gates until your high and fortified walls, in which you trust, come down throughout all your land; and they shall besiege you at all your gates throughout all your land which the LORD your God has given you. ⁵³You shall eat the fruit of your own body, the flesh of your sons and your daughters whom the LORD your God has given you, in the siege and desperate straits in which your enemy shall distress you. ⁵⁴The sensitive and very refined man among you will be hostile toward his brother, toward the wife of his bosom, and toward the rest of his children whom he leaves behind, ⁵⁵so that he will not give any of them the flesh of his children whom he will eat, because he has nothing left in the siege and desperate straits in which your enemy shall distress you at all your gates. ⁵⁶The tender and delicate woman among you, who would not venture to set the sole of her foot on the ground because of her delicateness and sensitivity, will refuse to the husband of her bosom, and to her son and her daughter, ⁵⁷her placenta which comes out from between her feet and her children whom she bears; for she will eat them secretly for lack of everything in the siege and desperate straits in which your enemy shall distress you at all your gates.

⁵⁸"If you do not carefully observe all the words of this law that are written in this book, that you may fear this glorious and awesome name, THE LORD YOUR GOD, ⁵⁹then the LORD will bring upon you and your descendants extraordinary plagues—great and prolonged plagues—and serious and prolonged sicknesses. ⁶⁰Moreover He will bring back on you all the diseases of Egypt, of which you were afraid, and they shall cling to you. ⁶¹Also every sickness and every plague, which *is* not written in this Book of the Law, will the LORD bring upon you until you are destroyed. ⁶²You shall be left few in number, whereas you were as the stars of heaven in multitude, because you would not obey the voice of the LORD your God. ⁶³And it shall be, *that* just as the LORD rejoiced over you to do you good and multiply you, so the LORD will rejoice over you to destroy you and bring you to nothing; and you shall be plucked from off the land which you go to possess.

⁶⁴"Then the LORD will scatter you among all peoples, from one end of the earth to the other, and there you shall serve other gods, which neither you nor your fathers have known—wood and stone. ⁶⁵And among those nations you shall find no rest, nor shall the sole of your foot have a resting place; but there the LORD will give you a trembling heart, failing eyes, and anguish of soul. ⁶⁶Your life shall hang in doubt before you; you shall fear day and night, and have no assurance of life. ⁶⁷In the morning you shall say, 'Oh, that it were evening!' And at evening you shall say, 'Oh, that it were morning!' because of the fear

◀▬▬▬▬ FLIPPED OUT

28:34 One of the curses for those who rejected God was that they would go mad from seeing all the tragedy around them. Do you ever feel that you will go crazy if you hear about one more rape, kidnapping, murder, or war? Much of the world's evil is a result of people's failure to acknowledge and serve God. When you hear bad news, don't groan helplessly as do unbelievers, who have no hope for the future. Remind yourself that in spite of it all, God has ultimate control and one day will come back to make everything right.

which terrifies your heart, and because of the sight which your eyes see.

⁶⁸"And the LORD will take you back to Egypt in ships, by the way of which I said to you, 'You shall never see it again.' And there you shall be offered for sale to your enemies as male and female slaves, but no one will buy *you*."

CHAPTER 29 GOD'S COVENANT REVIEWED.

These *are* the words of the covenant which the LORD commanded Moses to make with the children of Israel in the land of Moab, besides the covenant which He made with them in Horeb.

²Now Moses called all Israel and said to them: "You

◣◥ EVIL SEEDS

29:18 Moses cautioned that the day the Hebrews chose to turn from God, a root would be planted that would produce bitter fruit. When we decide to do what we know is wrong, we plant an evil seed that begins to grow out of control—eventually yielding a crop of sorrow and pain. But we can prevent those seeds of sin from taking root. If you have done something wrong, confess it to God and others immediately. If the seed never finds fertile soil, its bitter fruit will never ripen.

have seen all that the LORD did before your eyes in the land of Egypt, to Pharaoh and to all his servants and to all his land—³the great trials which your eyes have seen, the signs, and those great wonders. ⁴Yet the LORD has not given you a heart to perceive and eyes to see and ears to hear, to this *very* day. ⁵And I have led you forty years in the wilderness. Your clothes have not worn out on you, and your sandals have not worn out on your feet. ⁶You have not eaten bread, nor have you drunk wine or *similar* drink, that you may know that I *am* the LORD your God. ⁷And when you came to this place, Sihon king of Heshbon and Og king of Bashan came out against us to battle, and we conquered them. ⁸We took their land and gave it as an inheritance to the Reubenites, to the Gadites, and to half the tribe of Manasseh. ⁹Therefore keep the words of this covenant, and do them, that you may prosper in all that you do.

¹⁰"All of you stand today before the LORD your God: your leaders and your tribes and your elders and your officers, all the men of Israel, ¹¹your little ones and your wives—also the stranger who *is* in your camp, from the one who cuts your wood to the one who draws your water—¹²that you may enter into covenant with the LORD your God, and into His oath, which the LORD your God makes with you today, ¹³that He may establish you today as a people for Himself, and *that* He may be God to you, just as He has spoken to you, and just as He has sworn to your fathers, to Abraham, Isaac, and Jacob.

¹⁴"I make this covenant and this oath, not with you alone, ¹⁵but with *him* who stands here with us today before the LORD our God, as well as with *him* who *is* not here with us today ¹⁶(for you know that we dwelt in the land of Egypt and that we came through the nations which you passed by, ¹⁷and you saw their abominations and their idols which *were* among them—wood and stone and silver and gold); ¹⁸so that there may not be among you man or woman or family or tribe, whose

heart turns away today from the LORD our God, to go an serve the gods of these nations, and that there may no be among you a root bearing bitterness or wormwood ¹⁹and so it may not happen, when he hears the words o this curse, that he blesses himself in his heart, saying, ' shall have peace, even though I follow the dictates of m heart'—as though the drunkard could be included wit the sober.

²⁰"The LORD would not spare him; for then the ange of the LORD and His jealousy would burn against tha man, and every curse that is written in this book woul settle on him, and the LORD would blot out his nam from under heaven. ²¹And the LORD would separate hir from all the tribes of Israel for adversity, according to a the curses of the covenant that are written in this Book c the Law, ²²so that the coming generation of your childre who rise up after you, and the foreigner who comes fron a far land, would say, when they see the plagues of th land and the sicknesses which the LORD has laid on it:

²³'The whole land *is* brimstone, salt, and burning; it i not sown, nor does it bear, nor does any grass grow ther like the overthrow of Sodom and Gomorrah, Admah, an Zeboiim, which the LORD overthrew in His anger and H wrath.' ²⁴All nations would say, 'Why has the LORD don so to this land? What does the heat of this great ange mean?' ²⁵Then *people* would say: 'Because they have for saken the covenant of the LORD God of their father which He made with them when He brought them out c the land of Egypt; ²⁶for they went and served other god and worshiped them, gods that they did not know an that He had not given to them. ²⁷Then the anger of th LORD was aroused against this land, to bring on it ever curse that is written in this book. ²⁸And the LORD up rooted them from their land in anger, in wrath, and i great indignation, and cast them into another land, as *is* this day.'

²⁹"The secret *things belong* to the LORD our God, bu those *things which are* revealed *belong* to us and to ou children forever, that *we* may do all the words of this lav

CHAPTER 30 COMING BACK TO GOD. "Now shall come to pass, when all these things come upon you the blessing and the curse which I have set before yo and you call *them* to mind among all the nations whe the LORD your God drives you, ²and you return to th LORD your God and obey His voice, according to all that command you today, you and your children, with all you heart and with all your soul, ³that the LORD your God w bring you back from captivity, and have compassion o

◣◥ FRESH START

30:1-6 Moses told the Hebrews that when they were ready to God, he would be ready to receive them. God's mercy is unbelie goes far beyond what we can imagine. Even if the Jews delibera walked away from him and ruined their lives, God would still ta back. God wants to forgive us, too, and bring us back to himself. people will not learn this until their world has crashed in aroun Then the sorrow and pain seem to open their eyes to what God h saying all along. Are you separated from God by sin? No matter you have wandered, God promises a fresh start if only you will t him.

you, and gather you again from all the nations where the LORD your God has scattered you. [4]If *any* of you are driven out to the farthest *parts* under heaven, from there the LORD your God will gather you, and from there He will bring you. [5]Then the LORD your God will bring you to the land which your fathers possessed, and you shall possess it. He will prosper you and multiply you more than your fathers. [6]And the LORD your God will circumcise your heart and the heart of your descendants, to love the LORD your God with all your heart and with all your soul, that you may live.

[7]"Also the LORD your God will put all these curses on your enemies and on those who hate you, who persecuted you. [8]And you will again obey the voice of the LORD and do all His commandments which I command you today. [9]The LORD your God will make you abound in all the work of your hand, in the fruit of your body, in the increase of your livestock, and in the produce of your land for good. For the LORD will again rejoice over you for good as He rejoiced over your fathers, [10]if you obey the voice of the LORD your God, to keep His commandments and His statutes which are written in this Book of the Law, *and* if you turn to the LORD your God with all your heart and with all your soul.

[11]"For this commandment which I command you to-day *is* not *too* mysterious for you, nor *is* it far off. [12]It *is* not in heaven, that you should say, 'Who will ascend into heaven for us and bring it to us, that we may hear it and do it?' [13]Nor *is* it beyond the sea, that you should say, 'Who will go over the sea for us and bring it to us, that we may hear it and do it?' [14]But the word *is* very near you, in your mouth and in your heart, that you may do it.

[15]"See, I have set before you today life and good, death and evil, [16]in that I command you today to love the LORD your God, to walk in His ways, and to keep His commandments, His statutes, and His judgments, that you may live and multiply; and the LORD your God will bless you in the land which you go to possess. [17]But if your heart turns away so that you do not hear, and are drawn away, and worship other gods and serve them, [18]I announce to you today that you shall surely perish; you shall not prolong *your* days in the land which you cross over the Jordan to go in and possess. [19]I call heaven and earth as witnesses today against you, *that* I have set before you life and death, blessing and cursing; therefore choose life, that both you and your descendants may live; [20]that you may love the LORD your God, that you may obey His voice, and that you may cling to Him, for He *is* your life and the length of your days; and that you may dwell in the land which the LORD swore to your fathers, to Abraham, Isaac, and Jacob, to give them."

CHAPTER 31 JOSHUA APPOINTED LEADER. Then Moses went and spoke these words to all Israel. [2]And he said to them: "I *am* one hundred and twenty years old today. I can no longer go out and come in. Also the LORD has said to me, 'You shall not cross over this Jordan.' [3]The LORD your God Himself crosses over before you; He will destroy these nations from before you, and you shall dispossess them. Joshua himself crosses over before you,

just as the LORD has said. [4]And the LORD will do to them as He did to Sihon and Og, the kings of the Amorites and their land, when He destroyed them. [5]The LORD will give them over to you, that you may do to them according to every commandment which I have commanded you. [6]Be strong and of good courage, do not fear nor be afraid of them; for the LORD your God, He *is* the One who goes with you. He will not leave you nor forsake you."

[7]Then Moses called Joshua and said to him in the sight of all Israel, "Be strong and of good courage, for you must go with this people to the land which the LORD has sworn to their fathers to give them, and you shall cause them to inherit it. [8]And the LORD, He *is* the One who goes before you. He will be with you, He will not leave you nor forsake you; do not fear nor be dismayed."

[9]So Moses wrote this law and delivered it to the priests, the sons of Levi, who bore the ark of the covenant of the LORD, and to all the elders of Israel. [10]And Moses commanded them, saying: "At the end of *every* seven years, at the appointed time in the year of release, at the Feast of Tabernacles, [11]when all Israel comes to appear before the LORD your God in the place which He chooses, you shall read this law before all Israel in their hearing. [12]Gather the people together, men and women and little ones, and the stranger who *is* within your gates, that they may hear and that they may learn to fear the LORD your God and carefully observe all the words of this law, [13]and *that* their children, who have not known it, may hear and learn to fear the LORD your God as long as you live in the land which you cross the Jordan to possess."

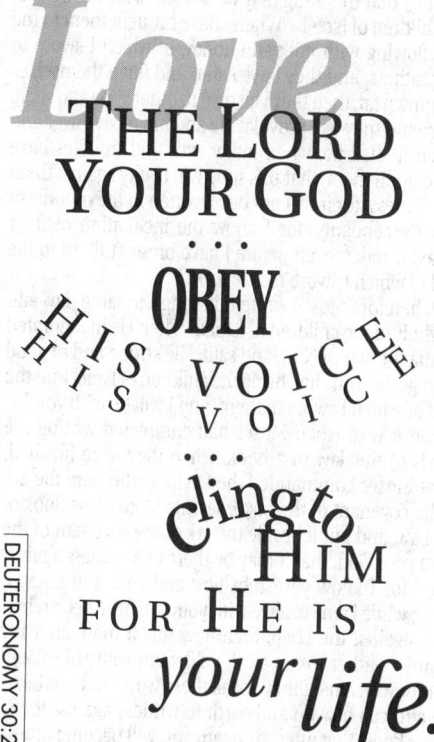

Love THE LORD YOUR GOD ... OBEY HIS VOICE ... cling to HIM FOR HE IS *your life.*

31:27-29 Moses knew that the Israelites, in spite of all they had seen of God's work, were rebellious at heart. They deserved God's punishment, although they often received his mercy instead. We, too, are stubborn and rebellious by nature. Throughout our lives we struggle with sin. Repentance once a month or once a week is not enough. We must constantly turn from our sins to God and let his mercy save us.

[14]Then the LORD said to Moses, "Behold, the days approach when you must die; call Joshua, and present yourselves in the tabernacle of meeting, that I may inaugurate him."

So Moses and Joshua went and presented themselves in the tabernacle of meeting. [15]Now the LORD appeared at the tabernacle in a pillar of cloud, and the pillar of cloud stood above the door of the tabernacle.

[16]And the LORD said to Moses: "Behold, you will rest with your fathers; and this people will rise and play the harlot with the gods of the foreigners of the land, where they go to be among them, and they will forsake Me and break My covenant which I have made with them. [17]Then My anger shall be aroused against them in that day, and I will forsake them, and I will hide My face from them, and they shall be devoured. And many evils and troubles shall befall them, so that they will say in that day, 'Have not these evils come upon us because our God is not among us?' [18]And I will surely hide My face in that day because of all the evil which they have done, in that they have turned to other gods.

[19]"Now therefore, write down this song for yourselves, and teach it to the children of Israel; put it in their mouths, that this song may be a witness for Me against the children of Israel. [20]When I have brought them to the land flowing with milk and honey, of which I swore to their fathers, and they have eaten and filled themselves and grown fat, then they will turn to other gods and serve them; and they will provoke Me and break My covenant. [21]Then it shall be, when many evils and troubles have come upon them, that this song will testify against them as a witness; for it will not be forgotten in the mouths of their descendants, for I know the inclination of their behavior today, even before I have brought them to the land of which I swore to give them."

[22]Therefore Moses wrote this song the same day, and taught it to the children of Israel. [23]Then He inaugurated Joshua the son of Nun, and said, "Be strong and of good courage; for you shall bring the children of Israel into the land of which I swore to them, and I will be with you."

[24]So it was, when Moses had completed writing the words of this law in a book, when they were finished, [25]that Moses commanded the Levites, who bore the ark of the covenant of the LORD, saying: [26]"Take this Book of the Law, and put it beside the ark of the covenant of the LORD your God, that it may be there as a witness against you; [27]for I know your rebellion and your stiff neck. If today, while I am yet alive with you, you have been rebellious against the LORD, then how much more after my death? [28]Gather to me all the elders of your tribes, and your officers, that I may speak these words in their hearing and call heaven and earth to witness against them. [29]For I know that after my death you will become utterly

corrupt, and turn aside from the way which I have commanded you. And evil will befall you in the latter days, because you will do evil in the sight of the LORD, to provoke Him to anger through the work of your hands."

[30]Then Moses spoke in the hearing of all the assembly of Israel the words of this song until they were ended:

CHAPTER 32 MOSES' SONG.

"Give ear, O heavens, and I will speak;
And hear, O earth, the words of my mouth.
[2] Let my teaching drop as the rain,
My speech distill as the dew,
As raindrops on the tender herb,
And as showers on the grass.
[3] For I proclaim the name of the LORD:
Ascribe greatness to our God.
[4] He is the Rock, His work is perfect;
For all His ways are justice,
A God of truth and without injustice;
Righteous and upright is He.

[5] "They have corrupted themselves;
They are not His children,
Because of their blemish:
A perverse and crooked generation.
[6] Do you thus deal with the LORD,
O foolish and unwise people?
Is He not your Father, who bought you?
Has He not made you and established you?

[7] "Remember the days of old,
Consider the years of many generations.
Ask your father, and he will show you;
Your elders, and they will tell you:
[8] When the Most High divided their inheritance to the nations,
When He separated the sons of Adam,
He set the boundaries of the peoples
According to the number of the children of Israel.
[9] For the LORD's portion is His people;
Jacob is the place of His inheritance.

[10] "He found him in a desert land
And in the wasteland, a howling wilderness;
He encircled him, He instructed him,
He kept him as the apple of His eye.
[11] As an eagle stirs up its nest,
Hovers over its young,
Spreading out its wings, taking them up,
Carrying them on its wings,
[12] So the LORD alone led him,
And there was no foreign god with him.

[13] "He made him ride in the heights of the earth,
That he might eat the produce of the fields;
He made him draw honey from the rock,
And oil from the flinty rock;
[14] Curds from the cattle, and milk of the flock,
With fat of lambs;
And rams of the breed of Bashan, and goats,
With the choicest wheat;
And you drank wine, the blood of the grapes.

"But Jeshurun grew fat and kicked;
You grew fat, you grew thick,
You are obese!
Then he forsook God *who* made him,
And scornfully esteemed the Rock of his salvation.
They provoked Him to jealousy with foreign *gods;*
With abominations they provoked Him to anger.
They sacrificed to demons, not to God,
To gods they did not know,
To new *gods,* new arrivals
That your fathers did not fear.
Of the Rock *who* begot you, you are unmindful,
And have forgotten the God who fathered you.

"And when the LORD saw *it,* He spurned *them,*
Because of the provocation of His sons and His
daughters.
And He said: 'I will hide My face from them,
I will see what their end *will be,*
For they *are* a perverse generation,
Children in whom *is* no faith.
They have provoked Me to jealousy by *what* is not
God;
They have moved Me to anger by their foolish idols.
But I will provoke them to jealousy by *those who are*
not a nation;
I will move them to anger by a foolish nation.
For a fire is kindled in My anger,
And shall burn to the lowest hell;
It shall consume the earth with her increase,
And set on fire the foundations of the mountains.

'I will heap disasters on them;
I will spend My arrows on them.
24 *They shall be* wasted with hunger,
Devoured by pestilence and bitter destruction;
I will also send against them the teeth of beasts,
With the poison of serpents of the dust.
25 The sword shall destroy outside;
There shall be terror within
For the young man and virgin,
The nursing child with the man of gray hairs.
26 I would have said, "I will dash them in pieces,
I will make the memory of them to cease from
among men,"
27 Had I not feared the wrath of the enemy,
Lest their adversaries should misunderstand,
Lest they should say, "Our hand *is* high;
And it is not the LORD who has done all this." '

28 "For they *are* a nation void of counsel,
Nor *is there any* understanding in them.
29 Oh, that they were wise, *that* they understood this,
That they would consider their latter end!
30 How could one chase a thousand,
And two put ten thousand to flight,
Unless their Rock had sold them,
And the LORD had surrendered them?
31 For their rock *is* not like our Rock,
Even our enemies themselves *being* judges.
32 For their vine *is* of the vine of Sodom
And of the fields of Gomorrah;
Their grapes *are* grapes of gall,
Their clusters *are* bitter.
33 Their wine *is* the poison of serpents,
And the cruel venom of cobras.

VARIETY IN WORSHIP

Israel's worship involved all of the senses. This reinforced the meaning of the ceremony and painted a dramatic picture that worship touches all areas of life.

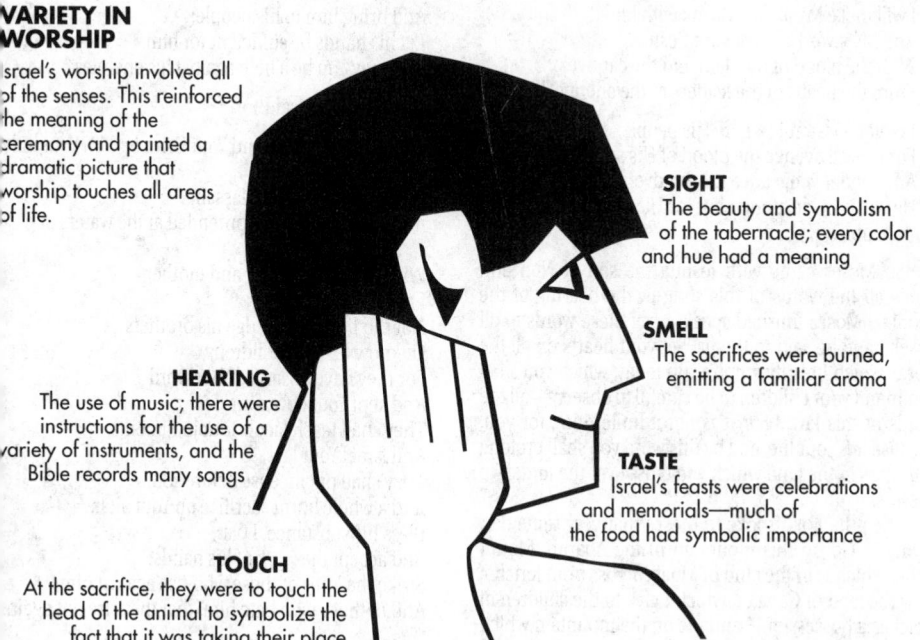

SIGHT
The beauty and symbolism of the tabernacle; every color and hue had a meaning

SMELL
The sacrifices were burned, emitting a familiar aroma

HEARING
The use of music; there were instructions for the use of a variety of instruments, and the Bible records many songs

TASTE
Israel's feasts were celebrations and memorials—much of the food had symbolic importance

TOUCH
At the sacrifice, they were to touch the head of the animal to symbolize the fact that it was taking their place

33:6-25 Note the difference in blessings God gave each tribe. To one he gave the best land, to another strength, to another safety. Too often we see someone with a particular blessing and think that God must love that person more than others. Think rather that God draws out in all people their unique talents. All these gifts are needed to complete his plan. Don't be envious of the gifts others have. Instead, look for the gifts God has given you, and do the tasks he has uniquely qualified you to do.

34 '*Is* this not laid up in store with Me,
Sealed up among My treasures?
35 Vengeance is Mine, and recompense;
Their foot shall slip in *due* time;
For the day of their calamity *is* at hand,
And the things to come hasten upon them.'

36 "For the LORD will judge His people
And have compassion on His servants,
When He sees that *their* power is gone,
And *there is* no one *remaining*, bond or free.
37 He will say: 'Where *are* their gods,
The rock in which they sought refuge?
38 Who ate the fat of their sacrifices,
And drank the wine of their drink offering?
Let them rise and help you,
And be your refuge.

39 'Now see that I, *even* I, *am* He,
And *there is* no God besides Me;
I kill and I make alive;
I wound and I heal;
Nor *is there any* who can deliver from My hand.
40 For I raise My hand to heaven,
And say, "*As* I live forever,
41 If I whet My glittering sword,
And My hand takes hold on judgment,
I will render vengeance to My enemies,
And repay those who hate Me.
42 I will make My arrows drunk with blood,
And My sword shall devour flesh,
With the blood of the slain and the captives,
From the heads of the leaders of the enemy." '

43 "Rejoice, O Gentiles, *with* His people;
For He will avenge the blood of His servants,
And render vengeance to His adversaries;
He will provide atonement for His land *and* His
people."

44So Moses came with Joshua the son of Nun and spoke all the words of this song in the hearing of the people. 45Moses finished speaking all these words to all Israel, 46and he said to them: "Set your hearts on all the words which I testify among you today, which you shall command your children to be careful to observe—all the words of this law. 47For it *is* not a futile thing for you, because it *is* your life, and by this word you shall prolong *your* days in the land which you cross over the Jordan to possess."

48Then the LORD spoke to Moses that very same day, saying: 49"Go up this mountain of the Abarim, Mount Nebo, which *is* in the land of Moab, across from Jericho; view the land of Canaan, which I give to the children of Israel as a possession; 50and die on the mountain which you ascend, and be gathered to your people, just as

Aaron your brother died on Mount Hor and was gathered to his people; 51because you trespassed against Me among the children of Israel at the waters of Meribah Kadesh, in the Wilderness of Zin, because you did not hallow Me in the midst of the children of Israel. 52Yet you shall see the land before *you*, though you shall not go there, into the land which I am giving to the children of Israel."

CHAPTER 33 MOSES BLESSES ALL THE PEOPLE

Now this *is* the blessing with which Moses the man of God blessed the children of Israel before his death. 2And he said:

"The LORD came from Sinai,
And dawned on them from Seir;
He shone forth from Mount Paran,
And He came with ten thousands of saints;
From His right hand
Came a fiery law for them.
3 Yes, He loves the people;
All His saints *are* in Your hand;
They sit down at Your feet;
Everyone receives Your words.
4 Moses commanded a law for us,
A heritage of the congregation of Jacob.
5 And He was King in Jeshurun,
When the leaders of the people were gathered,
All the tribes of Israel together.

6 "Let Reuben live, and not die,
Nor let his men be few."

7And this he said of Judah:

"Hear, LORD, the voice of Judah,
And bring him to his people;
Let his hands be sufficient for him,
And may You be a help against his enemies."

8And of Levi he said:

"*Let* Your Thummim and Your Urim *be* with Your holy
one,
Whom You tested at Massah,
And with whom You contended at the waters of
Meribah,
9 Who says of his father and mother,
'I have not seen them';
Nor did he acknowledge his brothers,
Or know his own children;
For they have observed Your word
And kept Your covenant.
10 They shall teach Jacob Your judgments,
And Israel Your law.
They shall put incense before You,
And a whole burnt sacrifice on Your altar.
11 Bless his substance, LORD,
And accept the work of his hands;
Strike the loins of those who rise against him,
And of those who hate him, that they rise not again.

12Of Benjamin he said:

"The beloved of the LORD shall dwell in safety by Him,
Who shelters him all the day long;
And he shall dwell between His shoulders."

¹³And of Joseph he said:

"Blessed of the LORD *is* his land,
With the precious things of heaven, with the dew,
And the deep lying beneath,
⁴ With the precious fruits of the sun,
With the precious produce of the months,
⁵ With the best things of the ancient mountains,
With the precious things of the everlasting hills,
⁶ With the precious things of the earth and its fullness,
And the favor of Him who dwelt in the bush.
Let *the blessing* come 'on the head of Joseph,
And on the crown of the head of him *who was*
      separate from his brothers.'
⁷ His glory *is like* a firstborn bull,
And his horns *like* the horns of the wild ox;
Together with them
He shall push the peoples
To the ends of the earth;
They *are* the ten thousands of Ephraim,
And they *are* the thousands of Manasseh."

¹⁸And of Zebulun he said:

"Rejoice, Zebulun, in your going out,
And Issachar in your tents!
⁹ They shall call the peoples *to* the mountain;
There they shall offer sacrifices of righteousness;
For they shall partake *of* the abundance of the seas
And *of* treasures hidden in the sand."

²⁰And of Gad he said:

"Blessed *is* he who enlarges Gad;
He dwells as a lion,
And tears the arm and the crown of his head.
He provided the first *part* for himself,
Because a lawgiver's portion was reserved there.
He came *with* the heads of the people;
He administered the justice of the LORD,
And His judgments with Israel."

²²And of Dan he said:

"Dan *is* a lion's whelp;
He shall leap from Bashan."

²³And of Naphtali he said:

"O Naphtali, satisfied with favor,
And full of the blessing of the LORD,
Possess the west and the south."

²⁴And of Asher he said:

"Asher *is* most blessed of sons;
Let him be favored by his brothers,
And let him dip his foot in oil.
Your sandals *shall be* iron and bronze;
As your days, *so shall* your strength *be*.

"*There is* no one like the God of Jeshurun,
Who rides the heavens to help you,
And in His excellency on the clouds.
²⁷ The eternal God *is your* refuge,
And underneath *are* the everlasting arms;
He will thrust out the enemy from before you,
And will say, 'Destroy!'
²⁸ Then Israel shall dwell in safety,
The fountain of Jacob alone,
In a land of grain and new wine;
His heavens shall also drop dew.
²⁹ Happy *are* you, O Israel!
Who *is* like you, a people saved by the LORD,
The shield of your help
And the sword of your majesty!
Your enemies shall submit to you,
And you shall tread down their high places."

CHAPTER **34** MOSES DIES. Then Moses went up from the plains of Moab to Mount Nebo, to the top of Pisgah, which is across from Jericho. And the LORD showed him all the land of Gilead as far as Dan, ²all Naphtali and the land of Ephraim and Manasseh, all the land of Judah as far as the Western Sea, ³the South, and the plain of the Valley of Jericho, the city of palm trees, as far as Zoar. ⁴Then the LORD said to him, "This *is* the land of which I swore to give Abraham, Isaac, and Jacob, saying, 'I will give it to your descendants.' I have caused you to see *it* with your eyes, but you shall not cross over there."

⁵So Moses the servant of the LORD died there in the land of Moab, according to the word of the LORD. ⁶And He buried him in a valley in the land of Moab, opposite Beth Peor; but no one knows his grave to this day. ⁷Moses *was* one hundred and twenty years old when he died. His eyes were not dim nor his natural vigor diminished. ⁸And the children of Israel wept for Moses in the plains of Moab thirty days. So the days of weeping *and* mourning for Moses ended.

⁹Now Joshua the son of Nun was full of the spirit of wisdom, for Moses had laid his hands on him; so the children of Israel heeded him, and did as the LORD had commanded Moses.

¹⁰But since then there has not arisen in Israel a prophet like Moses, whom the LORD knew face to face, ¹¹in all the signs and wonders which the LORD sent him to do in the land of Egypt, before Pharaoh, before all his servants, and in all his land, ¹²and by all that mighty power and all the great terror which Moses performed in the sight of all Israel.

SUCCESS

34:10-12 Moses, the man who did not want to be sent to Egypt because he was "slow of speech" (Exodus 4:10), delivered the three addresses to Israel that make up the book of Deuteronomy. God gave him the power to develop from a stuttering shepherd into a national leader and powerful orator. His courage, humility, and wisdom molded the Hebrew slaves into a nation. But Moses was one person who did not let success go to his head. In the end, God was still Moses' best friend. His love, respect, and awe for God had grown daily throughout his life. Moses knew that it was not any greatness in himself that made him successful; it was the greatness of the all-powerful God in whom he trusted.

MEGA Themes

HISTORY Moses reviews the mighty acts of God through which he set Israel free from slavery in Egypt.

By reviewing God's promises and mighty acts, we can learn about his character. We come to know God more intimately through understanding how he has acted in the past. We can learn to do his will and to avoid Israel's mistakes.

1. What do you learn about God from Moses' review of history?
2. How would this review prepare the people to live for God in the Promised Land?
3. Review your personal history with God. What have been the "high" points? The "low" points?
4. What do you learn about God from a review of your personal history?
5. How should this prepare you to live in the present and future for him?

LAWS God reviews his laws with the people. The legal contract between God and his people had to be renewed for the new generation entering the Promised Land.

Commitment to God and his truth cannot be taken for granted. Each generation and each person must respond anew to God's call.

1. What was God's purpose for giving his people the law? (Check the book of Exodus as well.)
2. Why did Moses review the law for the people?
3. Why is it important to read, study, and be reminded of God's commands in your life?
4. What difference does it seem to make in your life that you have the Bible available to you for making decisions about God's will?

LOVE God's faithful and patient love is portrayed more often than his punishment. God reveals his love in keeping his promises to people, even when they are disobedient. God seeks the love of his people displayed in their wholehearted devotion to his will, not just by a strict, legalistic following of the law.

God's love forms the foundation for our trust in him. We can be confident that the one who loves us perfectly can be trusted with our life. Therefore, we can trust that the commands he gives us are good and are designed to help us live fully in our relationships with him and others.

1. What are some of the words which best describe God's love (e.g., constant, merciful . . .)?
2. What are some specific ways this love from God has made you the person you are today?

3. Can you think of some friends who need to know more of God's love? What qualities of God's love do they most need to experience? (Check your responses to question one.)
4. What if one of those friends replied, "But I have sinned too much for God to still love me." Based on your study of God's love for the Israelites, how would you respond to such a statement? Based on how God's love has made a difference in your life, how would you respond?
5. Think of one or two friends from the list you made for question three. What are some specific ways you could show them God's love?

CHOICES God reminded his people that in order to enjoy the blessings of his will for them, they would have to continue in obedience. Personal choices to obey could bring benefits to their lives; rebellion would bring disaster.

Our choices make a difference. Choosing to follow God produces good results in our lives and in our relationships with others. Choosing to abandon God's ways brings harmful results to us and to others.

1. Respond to the following statement: "You always have a choice. It always makes a difference."
2. How do you feel when a friend makes a choice that leads to bad consequences in his or her life?
3. How do you feel when a friend makes a choice that is a bad one according to God's will, but it seems like he or she is not experiencing any negative consequences?
4. Is it possible for a person to make a choice against God's will and "get away with it"? Explain.
5. What are some of the choices facing you in the present or in the near future? Complete this statement: "I will choose to obey what I believe to be God's way in my life because _____."

TEACHING God commanded the Israelites to teach their children his ways. They were to use ritual, instruction, and memorization to make sure that their children understood God's principles and passed them on to the next generation.

God's truth must be passed on to future generations. It is not, however, just the traditions or commands that are to be passed on. Rather, we are to teach each new generation to know and love God personally.

1. Who are some of the people from the older generation who have passed on God's truth to you?

. How were those from the previous generation able to teach you about knowing and loving God?

. What are some of the most important things you have learned from older Christians?

. How would you take these things that you have learned and teach them to the children in your family? Your neighborhood? Your church?

5. Develop a plan of action for becoming an important older Christian in the life of someone younger than you (e.g., volunteer as a leader for Bible school, or become a Sunday school teacher for children, or spend time with a child in your community who needs a big brother or big sister). Now, follow your plan!

What characteristics are important in a leader? If you were chosen captain of the football team, head cheerleader, or student body president, what would you need to be like? Strong? Smart? Clever? Good with people? Good-looking? Enthusiastic? Devoted? ■ God called Joshua to be the leader of Israel as they were about to enter the Promised Land. Joshua was unsure about his own leadership capabilities. But God told him: "No man shall *be able to* stand before you all the days of your life; as I was with Moses, *so* I will be with you. I will not leave you nor forsake you" (1:5). Then God explained the qualities Joshua needed in order to be a good leader for his people. ■ The first quality was obedience to God's law: "Only be strong and very courageous, that you may observe to do according to all the law which Moses My servant commanded you; do not turn from it to the right hand or to the left. . . . For then you will make your way prosperous, and then you will have good success" (1:7-8). ■ The second was total dependence on God for the victory. God had taken care of Israel in the past. Joshua continued to depend on him. ■ Listen to the wisdom of this book. God does not demand that you be strong, clever, efficient, or even good-looking to be an effective leader. Instead, God wants you to obey his Word and depend on his power. Then, if God has called you, he will use you.

STATS

PURPOSE: To give the history of Israel's conquest of the Promised Land

AUTHOR: Joshua, except for the ending, which may have been written by the high priest Phinehas, an eyewitness to the events recounted there

SETTING: Canaan, also called the Promised Land, which occupied the same general geographical territory of modern-day Israel

KEY PEOPLE: Joshua, Rahab, Achan, Phinehas, Eleazar

KEY PLACES: Jericho, Ai, Mount Ebal, Mount Gerizim, Gibeon, Gilgal, Shiloh, Shechem

SPECIAL FEATURE: Out of over a million people, Joshua and Caleb were the only two who left Egypt and entered the Promised Land

Joshua

CHAPTER 1 **"BE BRAVE, JOSHUA!"** After the death of Moses the servant of the LORD, it came to pass that the LORD spoke to Joshua the son of Nun, Moses' assistant, saying: ²"Moses My servant is dead. Now therefore, arise, go over this Jordan, you and all this people, to the land which I am giving to them—the children of Israel. ³Every place that the sole of your foot will tread upon I have given you, as I said to Moses. ⁴From the wilderness and this Lebanon as far as the great river, the River Euphrates, all the land of the Hittites, and to the Great Sea toward the going down of the sun, shall be your territory. ⁵No man shall *be able to* stand before you all the days of your life; as I was with Moses, *so* I will be with you. I will not leave you nor forsake you. ⁶Be strong and of good courage, for to this people you shall divide as an inheritance the land which I swore to their fathers to give them. ⁷Only be strong and very courageous, that you may observe to do according to all the law which Moses My servant commanded you; do not turn from it to the right hand or to the left, that you may prosper wherever you go. ⁸This Book of the Law shall not depart from your mouth, but you shall meditate in it day and night, that you may observe to do according to all that is written in it. For then you will make your way prosperous, and then you will have good success. ⁹Have I not commanded you? Be strong and of good courage; do not be afraid, nor be dismayed, for the LORD your God *is* with you wherever you go."

¹⁰Then Joshua commanded the officers of the people, saying, ¹¹"Pass through the camp and command the people, saying, 'Prepare provisions for yourselves, for within three days you will cross over this Jordan, to go in to possess the land which the LORD your God is giving you to possess.' "

¹²And to the Reubenites, the Gadites, and half the tribe of Manasseh Joshua spoke, saying, ¹³"Remember the word which Moses the servant of the LORD commanded you, saying, 'The LORD your God is giving you rest and is giving you this land.' ¹⁴Your wives, your little ones, and your livestock shall remain in the land which Moses gave you on this side of the Jordan. But you shall pass before your brethren armed, all your mighty men of valor, and help them, ¹⁵until the LORD has given your brethren rest, as He *gave* you, and they also have taken possession of the land which the LORD your God is giving them. Then you shall return to the land of your possession and enjoy it, which Moses the LORD's servant gave you on this side of the Jordan toward the sunrise."

¹⁶So they answered Joshua, saying, "All that you command us we will do, and wherever you send us we will go. ¹⁷Just as we heeded Moses in all things, so we will heed you. Only the LORD your God be with you, as He was with Moses. ¹⁸Whoever rebels against your command and does not heed your words, in all that you command him, shall be put to death. Only be strong and of good courage."

CHALLENGE

1:5 Joshua's new job consisted of leading more than two million people into a strange new land and conquering it. What a challenge—even for a man of Joshua's caliber! Every new job is a challenge. Without God it can be frightening. With God it can be a great adventure. Just as God assured Joshua he would be with him, so he is with us as we face our new challenges. We may not conquer nations, but every day we face tough situations, difficult people, and temptations. However, God promises that he will never abandon us or fail to help us, regardless of how we feel. By asking God to direct us we can conquer many of life's challenges.

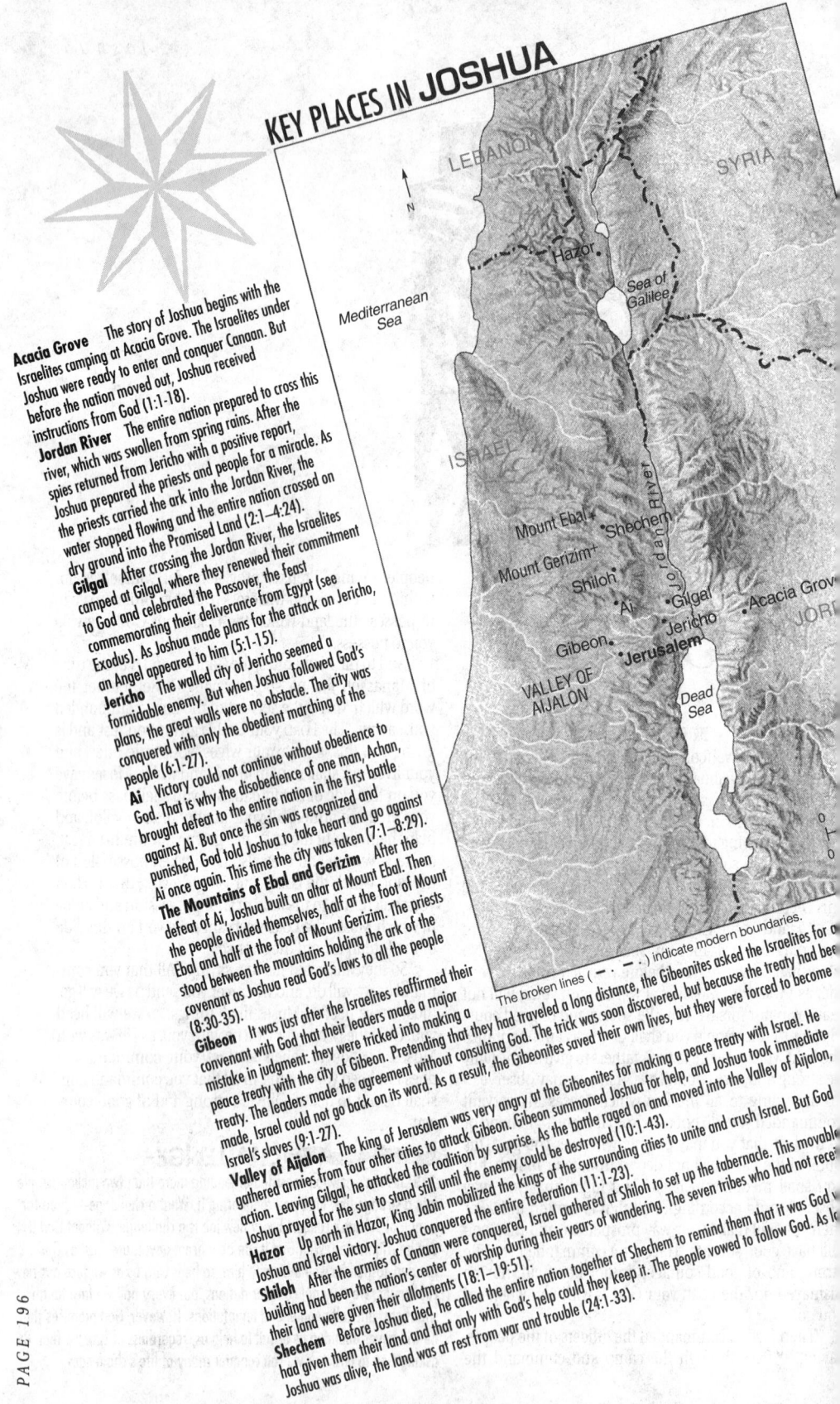

KEY PLACES IN JOSHUA

Acacia Grove The story of Joshua begins with the Israelites camping at Acacia Grove. The Israelites under Joshua were ready to enter and conquer Canaan. But before the nation moved out, Joshua received instructions from God (1:1-18).

Jordan River The entire nation prepared to cross this river, which was swollen from spring rains. After the spies returned from Jericho with a positive report, Joshua prepared the priests and people for a miracle. As the priests carried the ark into the Jordan River, the water stopped flowing and the entire nation crossed on dry ground into the Promised Land (2:1–4:24).

Gilgal After crossing the Jordan River, the Israelites camped at Gilgal, where they renewed their commitment to God and celebrated the Passover, the feast commemorating their deliverance from Egypt (see Exodus). As Joshua made plans for the attack on Jericho, an Angel appeared to him (5:1-15).

Jericho The walled city of Jericho seemed a formidable enemy. But when Joshua followed God's plans, the great walls were no obstacle. The city was conquered with only the obedient marching of the people (6:1-27).

Ai Victory could not continue without obedience to God. That is why the disobedience of one man, Achan, brought defeat to the entire nation in the first battle against Ai. But once the sin was recognized and punished, God told Joshua to take heart and go against Ai once again. This time the city was taken (7:1–8:29).

The Mountains of Ebal and Gerizim After the defeat of Ai, Joshua built an altar at Mount Ebal. Then the people divided themselves, half at the foot of Mount Ebal and half at the foot of Mount Gerizim. The priests stood between the mountains holding the ark of the covenant as Joshua read God's laws to all the people (8:30-35).

Gibeon It was just after the Israelites reaffirmed their covenant with God that their leaders made a major mistake in judgment: they were tricked into making a peace treaty with the city of Gibeon. Pretending that they had traveled a long distance, the Gibeonites asked the Israelites for a treaty. The leaders made the agreement without consulting God. The trick was soon discovered, but because the treaty had bee made, Israel could not go back on its word. As a result, the Gibeonites saved their own lives, but they were forced to become Israel's slaves (9:1-27).

Valley of Aijalon The king of Jerusalem was very angry at the Gibeonites for making a peace treaty with Israel. He gathered armies from four other cities to attack Gibeon. Gibeon summoned Joshua for help, and Joshua took immediate action. Leaving Gilgal, he attacked the coalition by surprise. As the battle raged on and moved into the Valley of Aijalon, Joshua prayed for the sun to stand still until the enemy could be destroyed (10:1-43).

Hazor Up north in Hazor, King Jabin mobilized the kings of the surrounding cities to unite and crush Israel. But God gave Joshua and Israel victory. Joshua conquered the entire federation (11:1-23).

Shiloh After the armies of Canaan were conquered, Israel gathered at Shiloh to set up the tabernacle. This movable building had been the nation's center of worship during their years of wandering. The seven tribes who had not recei their land were given their allotments (18:1–19:51).

Shechem Before Joshua died, he called the entire nation together at Shechem to remind them that it was God had given them their land and that only with God's help could they keep it. The people vowed to follow God. As lo Joshua was alive, the land was at rest from war and trouble (24:1-33).

The broken lines (– · – · –) indicate modern boundaries.

Map labels: LEBANON, SYRIA, Hazor, Sea of Galilee, Mediterranean Sea, ISRAEL, Jordan River, Mount Ebal, Shechem, Mount Gerizim, Shiloh, Ai, Gilgal, Acacia Grov, Gibeon, Jericho, Jerusalem, JOR, VALLEY OF AIJALON, Dead Sea, N

CHAPTER **2** **SPIES VISIT JERICHO.** Now Joshua the son of Nun sent out two men from Acacia Grove to spy secretly, saying, "Go, view the land, especially Jericho."

So they went, and came to the house of a harlot named Rahab, and lodged there. ²And it was told the king of Jericho, saying, "Behold, men have come here tonight from the children of Israel to search out the country."

³So the king of Jericho sent to Rahab, saying, "Bring out the men who have come to you, who have entered your house, for they have come to search out all the country."

⁴Then the woman took the two men and hid them. So she said, "Yes, the men came to me, but I did not know where they *were* from. ⁵And it happened as the gate was being shut, when it was dark, that the men went out. Where the men went I do not know; pursue them quickly, for you may overtake them." ⁶(But she had brought them up to the roof and hidden them with the stalks of flax, which she had laid in order on the roof.) ⁷Then the men pursued them by the road to the Jordan, to the fords. And as soon as those who pursued them had gone out, they shut the gate.

⁸Now before they lay down, she came up to them on the roof, ⁹and said to the men: "I know that the LORD has given you the land, that the terror of you has fallen on us, and that all the inhabitants of the land are fainthearted because of you. ¹⁰For we have heard how the LORD dried up the water of the Red Sea for you when you came out of Egypt, and what you did to the two kings of the Amorites who *were* on the other side of the Jordan, Sihon and Og, whom you utterly destroyed. ¹¹And as soon as we heard *these things,* our hearts melted; neither did there remain any more courage in anyone because of you, for the LORD your God, He *is* God in heaven above and on earth beneath. ¹²Now therefore, I beg you, swear to me by the LORD, since I have shown you kind-

ness, that you also will show kindness to my father's house, and give me a true token, ¹³and spare my father, my mother, my brothers, my sisters, and all that they have, and deliver our lives from death."

¹⁴So the men answered her, "Our lives for yours, if none of you tell this business of ours. And it shall be, when the LORD has given us the land, that we will deal kindly and truly with you."

THE PAST

2:1 Why would the spies stop at the house of Rahab the prostitute? Several reasons: (1) It was a good place to gather information and have no questions asked in return; (2) Rahab's house was in an ideal location for a quick escape because it was built into the city wall; (3) God directed the spies to Rahab's house because he knew her heart was open to him and that she would be instrumental in the Israelite victory over Jericho. God often uses people with simple faith to accomplish his great purposes, no matter what kind of past they have had or how insignificant they seem to be. Rahab didn't allow her past to keep her from the new role God had for her.

¹⁵Then she let them down by a rope through the window, for her house *was* on the city wall; she dwelt on the wall. ¹⁶And she said to them, "Get to the mountain, lest the pursuers meet you. Hide there three days, until the pursuers have returned. Afterward you may go your way."

¹⁷So the men said to her: "We *will be* blameless of this oath of yours which you have made us swear, ¹⁸unless, *when* we come into the land, you bind this line of scarlet cord in the window through which you let us down, and unless you bring your father, your mother, your brothers, and all your father's household to your own home. ¹⁹So it shall be *that* whoever goes outside the doors of your house into the street, his blood *shall be* on his own head, and we *will be* guiltless. And whoever is with you in the house, his blood *shall be* on our head if a hand is laid on him. ²⁰And if you tell this business of ours, then we will be free from your oath which you made us swear."

²¹Then she said, "According to your words, so *be* it." And she sent them away, and they departed. And she bound the scarlet cord in the window.

²²They departed and went to the mountain, and stayed there three days until the pursuers returned. The pursuers sought *them* all along the way, but did not find *them.* ²³So the two men returned, descended from the mountain, and crossed over; and they came to Joshua the son of Nun, and told him all that had befallen them. ²⁴And they said to Joshua, "Truly the LORD has delivered all the land into our hands, for indeed all the inhabitants of the country are fainthearted because of us."

CHAPTER **3** **CROSSING THE JORDAN RIVER.** Then Joshua rose early in the morning; and they set out from Acacia Grove and came to the Jordan, he and all the children of Israel, and lodged there before they crossed over. ²So it was, after three days, that the officers went through the camp; ³and they commanded the people, saying, "When you see the ark of the covenant of the LORD your God, and the priests, the Levites, bearing it, then you shall set out from your place and go after it. ⁴Yet

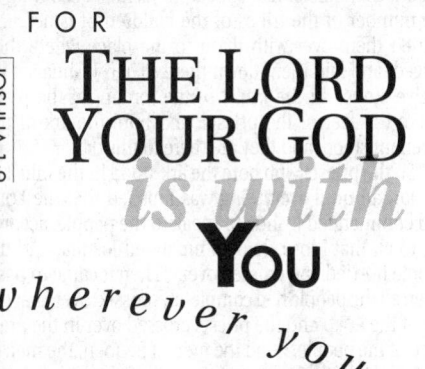

BE **STRONG** AND OF **GOOD COURAGE** FOR THE LORD YOUR GOD *is with* **YOU** *wherever you go.*

JOSHUA 1:9

there shall be a space between you and it, about two thousand cubits by measure. Do not come near it, that you may know the way by which you must go, for you have not passed *this* way before."

⁵And Joshua said to the people, "Sanctify yourselves, for tomorrow the LORD will do wonders among you." ⁶Then Joshua spoke to the priests, saying, "Take up the ark of the covenant and cross over before the people."

So they took up the ark of the covenant and went before the people.

⁷And the LORD said to Joshua, "This day I will begin to exalt you in the sight of all Israel, that they may know that, as I was with Moses, *so* I will be with you. ⁸You shall command the priests who bear the ark of the covenant,

RESPONSIBILITY

Marcy, a 16-year-old junior at Jefferson High, is popular and always smiling. She seems to have it all together . . . but appearances really can be deceiving. Let's listen as she describes her inner turmoil to a friend.

"Gwen, what am I going to do? Chris asked me to be the girls' ministry leader this year."

"What does that mean?"

"Well, I'd have to be involved in all the things going on on campus. You know—Bible studies, morning prayer group, outreaches—all that stuff. Ministry leaders are expected to talk a lot about their faith. . . . That's what's so weird—I mean, out of all the people Chris could have asked, he came to me! I've only been a Christian for three years."

"Sounds like an honor—"

"Yeah, I guess so."

"—and a lot of responsibility."

"That's what has me so scared and stressed out: having to plan everything and give everybody direction. I mean, I'd kind of like to do it, but what if I can't handle it? What if I do something stupid or let Chris down? What if I turn out to be a horrible leader and they fire me or something?"

"Oh, Marcy! You'll do great and you know it."

"I don't know. . . ."

Read Joshua 1:5-9. How can that passage provide comfort and encouragement to Marcy, or to anyone who is facing big responsibilities?

saying, 'When you have come to the edge of the water of the Jordan, you shall stand in the Jordan.' "

⁹So Joshua said to the children of Israel, "Come here, and hear the words of the LORD your God." ¹⁰And Joshua said, "By this you shall know that the living God *is* among you, and *that* He will without fail drive out from before you the Canaanites and the Hittites and the Hivites and the Perizzites and the Girgashites and the Amorites and the Jebusites: ¹¹Behold, the ark of the covenant of the Lord of all the earth is crossing over before you into the Jordan. ¹²Now therefore, take for yourselves twelve men from the tribes of Israel, one man from every tribe. ¹³And it shall come to pass, as soon as the soles of the feet of the priests who bear the ark of the LORD, the Lord of all the earth, shall rest in the waters of the Jordan, *that* the

waters of the Jordan shall be cut off, the waters that come down from upstream, and they shall stand as a heap."

¹⁴So it was, when the people set out from their camp to cross over the Jordan, with the priests bearing the ark of the covenant before the people, ¹⁵and as those who bore the ark came to the Jordan, and the feet of the priests who bore the ark dipped in the edge of the water (for the Jordan overflows all its banks during the whole time of harvest), ¹⁶that the waters which came down from upstream stood *still, and* rose in a heap very far away at Adam, the city that *is* beside Zaretan. So the waters that went down into the Sea of the Arabah, the Salt Sea, failed *and* were cut off; and the people crossed over opposite Jericho. ¹⁷Then the priests who bore the ark of the covenant of the LORD stood firm on dry ground in the midst of the Jordan; and all Israel crossed over on dry ground until all the people had crossed completely over the Jordan.

CHAPTER 4 And it came to pass, when all the people had completely crossed over the Jordan, that the LORD spoke to Joshua, saying: ²"Take for yourself twelve men from the people, one man from every tribe, ³and command them, saying, 'Take for yourselves twelve stones from here, out of the midst of the Jordan, from the place where the priests' feet stood firm. You shall carry them over with you and leave them in the lodging place where you lodge tonight.' "

⁴Then Joshua called the twelve men whom he had appointed from the children of Israel, one man from every tribe; ⁵and Joshua said to them: "Cross over before the ark of the LORD your God into the midst of the Jordan, and each one of you take up a stone on his shoulder, according to the number of the tribes of the children of Israel, ⁶that this may be a sign among you when your children ask in time to come, saying, 'What do these stones *mean* to you?' ⁷Then you shall answer them that the waters of the Jordan were cut off before the ark of the covenant of the LORD; when it crossed over the Jordan, the waters of the Jordan were cut off. And these stones shall be for a memorial to the children of Israel forever."

⁸And the children of Israel did so, just as Joshua commanded, and took up twelve stones from the midst of the Jordan, as the LORD had spoken to Joshua, according to the number of the tribes of the children of Israel, and carried them over with them to the place where they lodged, and laid them down there. ⁹Then Joshua set up twelve stones in the midst of the Jordan, in the place where the feet of the priests who bore the ark of the covenant stood; and they are there to this day.

¹⁰So the priests who bore the ark stood in the midst of the Jordan until everything was finished that the LORD had commanded Joshua to speak to the people, according to all that Moses had commanded Joshua; and the people hurried and crossed over. ¹¹Then it came to pass, when all the people had completely crossed over, that the ark of the LORD and the priests crossed over in the presence of the people. ¹²And the men of Reuben, the men of Gad, and half the tribe of Manasseh crossed over armed

before the children of Israel, as Moses had spoken to them. [13]About forty thousand prepared for war crossed over before the LORD for battle, to the plains of Jericho. [14]On that day the LORD exalted Joshua in the sight of all Israel; and they feared him, as they had feared Moses, all the days of his life.

[15]Then the LORD spoke to Joshua, saying, [16]"Command the priests who bear the ark of the Testimony to come up from the Jordan." [17]Joshua therefore commanded the priests, saying, "Come up from the Jordan." [18]And it came to pass, when the priests who bore the ark of the covenant of the LORD had come from the midst of the Jordan, *and* the soles of the priests' feet touched the dry land, that the waters of the Jordan returned to their place and overflowed all its banks as before.

[19]Now the people came up from the Jordan on the tenth *day* of the first month, and they camped in Gilgal on the east border of Jericho. [20]And those twelve stones which they took out of the Jordan, Joshua set up in Gilgal. [21]Then he spoke to the children of Israel, saying: "When your children ask their fathers in time to come, saying, 'What *are* these stones?' [22]then you shall let your children know, saying, 'Israel crossed over this Jordan on dry land'; [23]for the LORD your God dried up the waters of the Jordan before you until you had crossed over, as the LORD your God did to the Red Sea, which He dried up before us until we had crossed over, [24]that all the peoples of the earth may know the hand of the LORD, that it *is* mighty, that you may fear the LORD your God forever."

CHAPTER **5** JOSHUA CIRCUM-CISES THE MEN. So it was, when all the kings of the Amorites who *were* on the west side of the Jordan, and all the kings of the Canaanites who *were* by the sea, heard that the LORD had dried up the waters of the Jordan from before the children of Israel until we had crossed over, that their heart melted; and there was no spirit in them any longer because of the children of Israel.

[2]At that time the LORD said to Joshua, "Make flint knives for yourself, and circumcise the sons of Israel again the second time." [3]So Joshua made flint knives for himself, and circumcised the sons of Israel at the hill of the foreskins. [4]And this *is* the reason why Joshua circumcised them: All the people who came out of Egypt who *were* males, all the men of war, had died in the wilderness on the way, after they had come out of Egypt. [5]For all the people who came out had been circumcised, but all the people born in the wilderness, on the way as they came out of Egypt, had not been circumcised. [6]For the children of Israel walked forty years in the wilderness, till all the people *who were* men of war, who came

out of Egypt, were consumed, because they did not obey the voice of the LORD—to whom the LORD swore that He would not show them the land which the LORD had sworn to their fathers that He would give us, "a land flowing with milk and honey." [7]Then Joshua circumcised their sons *whom* He raised up in their place; for they were uncircumcised, because they had not been circumcised on the way.

[8]So it was, when they had finished circumcising all the people, that they stayed in their places in the camp till they were healed. [9]Then the LORD said to Joshua, "This day I have rolled away the reproach of Egypt from you." Therefore the name of the place is called Gilgal to this day.

[10]Now the children of Israel camped in Gilgal, and kept the Passover on the fourteenth day of the month at twilight on the plains of Jericho. [11]And they ate of the pro-

"Here's what I did..."

When I was in first grade, I memorized Joshua 1:9: "Be strong and of good courage; do not be afraid, nor be dismayed, for the LORD your God *is* with you wherever you go."

Recently I took part in a school play. I developed a bad case of stage fright before the performance. I didn't think I was going to make it through. I prayed, asking God to help me feel more comfortable with my part, and the verse came to mind again. I was concentrating on this encouragement, straight from God's Word, and it dispelled my fear. I remembered my lines and even did pretty well in the play, according to several people.

There have been many other times when I've recalled this verse and gained courage from it. Whenever I feel scared and alone, I remember this verse. It always comforts me.

Steve
AGE 15

duce of the land on the day after the Passover, unleavened bread and parched grain, on the very same day. [12]Then the manna ceased on the day after they had eaten the produce of the land; and the children of Israel no longer had manna, but they ate the food of the land of Canaan that year.

[13]And it came to pass, when Joshua was by Jericho, that he lifted his eyes and looked, and behold, a Man stood opposite him with His sword drawn in His hand. And Joshua went to Him and said to Him, "*Are* You for us or for our adversaries?"

[14]So He said, "No, but *as* Commander of the army of the LORD I have now come."

And Joshua fell on his face to the earth and worshiped, and said to Him, "What does my Lord say to His servant?"

[15]Then the Commander of the LORD's army said to Joshua, "Take your sandal off your foot, for the place where you stand *is* holy." And Joshua did so.

CHAPTER 6 THE BATTLE FOR JERICHO.

Now Jericho was securely shut up because of the children of Israel; none went out, and none came in. [2]And the LORD said to Joshua: "See! I have given Jericho into your hand, its king, *and* the mighty men of valor. [3]You shall march around the city, all *you* men of war; you shall go all around the city once. This you shall do six days. [4]And seven priests shall bear seven trumpets of rams' horns before the ark. But the seventh day you shall march around the city seven times, and the priests shall blow the trumpets. [5]It shall come to pass, when they make a long *blast* with the ram's horn, *and* when you hear the sound of the trumpet, that all the people shall shout with a great shout; then the wall of the city will fall down flat. And the people shall go up every man straight before him."

[6]Then Joshua the son of Nun called the priests and said to them, "Take up the ark of the covenant, and let seven priests bear seven trumpets of rams' horns before the ark of the LORD." [7]And he said to the people, "Proceed, and march around the city, and let him who is armed advance before the ark of the LORD."

ALREADY WON

6:2-5 God told Joshua that the enemy was already defeated! What confidence Joshua must have had as he went into battle! Christians also fight against a defeated enemy. Our enemy, Satan, has been defeated by Christ (Romans 8:37-39; Hebrews 2:14-15; 1 John 3:8). Although we still fight battles every day and sin runs rampant in the world, we have the assurance that the war has already been won. We do not have to be paralyzed by the power of a defeated enemy; we can overcome temptation through Christ's power.

[8]So it was, when Joshua had spoken to the people, that the seven priests bearing the seven trumpets of rams' horns before the LORD advanced and blew the trumpets, and the ark of the covenant of the LORD followed them. [9]The armed men went before the priests who blew the trumpets, and the rear guard came after the ark, while *the priests* continued blowing the trumpets. [10]Now Joshua had commanded the people, saying, "You shall not shout or make any noise with your voice, nor shall a word proceed out of your mouth, until the day I say to you, 'Shout!' Then you shall shout." [11]So he had the ark of the LORD circle the city, going around *it* once. Then they came into the camp and lodged in the camp.

[12]And Joshua rose early in the morning, and the priests took up the ark of the LORD. [13]Then seven priests bearing seven trumpets of rams' horns before the ark of the LORD went on continually and blew with the trumpets. And the armed men went before them. But the rear guard came after the ark of the LORD, while *the priests* continued blowing the trumpets. [14]And the second day they marched around the city once and returned to the camp. So they did six days.

[15]But it came to pass on the seventh day that they rose early, about the dawning of the day, and marched around the city seven times in the same manner. On that day only they marched around the city seven times. [16]And the seventh time it happened, when the priests blew the

LESSONS

7:7 When Joshua first went against Ai (7:3), he did not consult G[od]; relied on the strength of his army to defeat the small city. Only af[ter] Israel was defeated did they turn to God and ask, "What happene[d]? often we rely on our own skills and strength, especially when the [task] before us seems easy. We go to God only when the obstacles seem great. However, only God knows what lies ahead. Consulting him, [even] when we are on a winning streak, may save us from grave mistake[s or] misjudgments. God may want us to learn lessons, remove pride, o[r] consult others before he will work through us.

trumpets, that Joshua said to the people: "Shout, for the LORD has given you the city! [17]Now the city shall be doomed by the LORD to destruction, it and all who *are* in it. Only Rahab the harlot shall live, she and all who *are* with her in the house, because she hid the messengers that we sent. [18]And you, by all means abstain from the accursed things, lest you become accursed when you take of the accursed things, and make the camp of Israel a curse, and trouble it. [19]But all the silver and gold, and vessels of bronze and iron, *are* consecrated to the LORD; they shall come into the treasury of the LORD."

[20]So the people shouted when *the priests* blew the trumpets. And it happened when the people heard the sound of the trumpet, and the people shouted with a great shout, that the wall fell down flat. Then the people went up into the city, every man straight before him, and they took the city. [21]And they utterly destroyed all that *was* in the city, both man and woman, young and old, ox and sheep and donkey, with the edge of the sword.

[22]But Joshua had said to the two men who had spied out the country, "Go into the harlot's house, and from there bring out the woman and all that she has, as you swore to her." [23]And the young men who had been spies went in and brought out Rahab, her father, her mother, her brothers, and all that she had. So they brought out all her relatives and left them outside the camp of Israel. [24]But they burned the city and all that *was* in it with fire. Only the silver and gold, and the vessels of bronze and iron, they put into the treasury of the house of the LORD. [25]And Joshua spared Rahab the harlot, her father's household, and all that she had. So she dwells in Israel to this day, because she hid the messengers whom Joshua sen[t] to spy out Jericho.

[26]Then Joshua charged *them* at that time, saying, "Cursed *be* the man before the LORD who rises up and builds this city Jericho; he shall lay its foundation wit[h] his firstborn, and with his youngest he shall set up it[s] gates."

[27]So the LORD was with Joshua, and his fame spread throughout all the country.

CHAPTER 7 ACHAN DISOBEYS GOD.

But the chil[d]ren of Israel committed a trespass regarding the ac[-] cursed things, for Achan the son of Carmi, the son o[f] Zabdi, the son of Zerah, of the tribe of Judah, took of th[e] accursed things; so the anger of the LORD burned agains[t] the children of Israel.

[2]Now Joshua sent men from Jericho to Ai, which [is] beside Beth Aven, on the east side of Bethel, and spoke t[o] them, saying, "Go up and spy out the country." So th[e] men went up and spied out Ai. [3]And they returned t[o]

Joshua and said to him, "Do not let all the people go up, but let about two or three thousand men go up and attack Ai. Do not weary all the people there, for *the people of Ai are* few." ⁴So about three thousand men went up there from the people, but they fled before the men of Ai. ⁵And the men of Ai struck down about thirty-six men, for they chased them *from* before the gate as far as Shebarim, and struck them down on the descent; therefore the hearts of the people melted and became like water.

⁶Then Joshua tore his clothes, and fell to the earth on his face before the ark of the LORD until evening, he and the elders of Israel; and they put dust on their heads. ⁷And Joshua said, "Alas, Lord GOD, why have You brought this people over the Jordan at all—to deliver us into the hand of the Amorites, to destroy us? Oh, that we had been content, and dwelt on the other side of the Jordan! ⁸O Lord, what shall I say when Israel turns its back before its enemies? ⁹For the Canaanites and all the inhabitants of the land will hear *it*, and surround us, and cut off our name from the earth. Then what will You do for Your great name?"

¹⁰So the LORD said to Joshua: "Get up! Why do you lie thus on your face? ¹¹Israel has sinned, and they have also transgressed My covenant which I commanded them. For they have even taken some of the accursed things, and have both stolen and deceived; and they have also put *it* among their own stuff. ¹²Therefore the children of Israel could not stand before their enemies, *but* turned *their* backs before their enemies, because they have become doomed to destruction. Neither will I be with you anymore, unless you destroy the accursed from among you. ¹³Get up, sanctify the people, and say, 'Sanctify yourselves for tomorrow, because thus says the LORD God of Israel: "*There is* an accursed thing in your midst, O Israel; you cannot stand before your enemies until you take away the accursed thing from among you. ¹⁴In the morning therefore you shall be brought according to your tribes. And it shall be *that* the tribe which the LORD takes shall come according to families; and the family which the LORD takes shall come by households; and the household which the LORD takes shall come man by man. ¹⁵Then it shall be *that* he who is taken with the accursed thing shall be burned with fire, he and all that he has, because he has transgressed the covenant of the LORD, and because he has done a disgraceful thing in Israel.' "

¹⁶So Joshua rose early in the morning and brought Israel by their tribes, and the tribe of Judah was taken. ¹⁷He brought the clan of Judah, and he took the family of the Zarhites; and he brought the family of the Zarhites man by man, and Zabdi was taken. ¹⁸Then he brought his household man by man, and Achan the son of Carmi, the son of Zabdi, the son of Zerah, of the tribe of Judah, was taken.

¹⁹Now Joshua said to Achan, "My son, I beg you, give glory to the LORD God of Israel, and make confession to Him, and tell me now what you have done; do not hide *it* from me."

²⁰And Achan answered Joshua and said, "Indeed I have sinned against the LORD God of Israel, and this is what I have done: ²¹When I saw among the spoils a beautiful Babylonian garment, two hundred shekels of silver, and a wedge of gold weighing fifty shekels, I coveted them and took them. And there they are, hidden in the earth in the midst of my tent, with the silver under it."

²²So Joshua sent messengers, and they ran to the tent; and there it was, hidden in his tent, with the silver under it. ²³And they took them from the midst of the tent, brought them to Joshua and to all the children of Israel, and laid them out before the LORD. ²⁴Then Joshua, and all Israel with

RAHAB

Rahab was a surprise. She was one of those people we wouldn't expect God to use. But God looks at people differently than we do.

As a harlot, or prostitute, in the city of Jericho, Rahab lived on the edge of society. She was used in private, rejected in public. Her house, built right into the city wall, was a natural place for the Israelite spies to hide, since they would be mistaken for Rahab's customers.

Rumors about the coming Israelite invasion were all over the city, but having spies in her home convinced Rahab there would be war. Living on the city wall, everyone, but she alone turned to the Lord for her salvation. Her faith gave her the courage to hide the spies and lie to the authorities. All she knew of God was that the Israelites trusted and served him, but it was a start—and we all have to start knowing God someplace and sometime.

God works through people—like Rahab—whom we might reject. God remembers her because of her faith, not her profession! She was a sinner, but she didn't stay in her sin. And God rewarded her: she became one of God's people—in fact, she became a part of the lineage of Christ! If at times you feel like a failure, remember that Rahab overcame failure through her trust in God. You can do the same!

LESSONS: She did not let fear affect her faith in God's ability to deliver

KEY VERSE: "By faith the harlot Rahab did not perish with those who did not believe, when she had received the spies with peace" (Hebrews 11:31). Rahab's story is told in Joshua 2 and 6. She is also mentioned in Matthew 1:5; Hebrews 11:31; and James 2:25.

UPS:
• Relative of Boaz, and thus an ancestor of David and Jesus
• One of only two women listed in the Hall of Faith in Hebrews 11
• Resourceful, willing to help others at great cost to herself

DOWNS:
• She was a prostitute

STATS:
• Where: Jericho
• Occupation: Prostitute, innkeeper; later became a wife
• Relatives: Ancestor of David and Jesus (Matthew 1:5)
• Contemporaries: Joshua

7:24-25 Achan underestimated God and didn't take his commands seriously (6:18). It may have seemed a small thing to Achan, but the effects of his sin were felt by the entire nation, especially his family. Like Achan, our actions affect more people than just ourselves. Beware of the temptation to rationalize your sins by saying they are too small or too personal to hurt anyone but you.

him, took Achan the son of Zerah, the silver, the garment, the wedge of gold, his sons, his daughters, his oxen, his donkeys, his sheep, his tent, and all that he had, and they brought them to the Valley of Achor. ²⁵And Joshua said, "Why have you troubled us? The LORD will trouble you this day." So all Israel stoned him with stones; and they burned them with fire after they had stoned them with stones.

²⁶Then they raised over him a great heap of stones, still there to this day. So the LORD turned from the fierceness of His anger. Therefore the name of that place has been called the Valley of Achor to this day.

CHAPTER 8 **THE ISRAELITES ATTACK AI.** Now the LORD said to Joshua: "Do not be afraid, nor be dismayed; take all the people of war with you, and arise, go up to Ai. See, I have given into your hand the king of Ai, his people, his city, and his land. ²And you shall do to Ai and its king as you did to Jericho and its king. Only its spoil and its cattle you shall take as booty for yourselves. Lay an ambush for the city behind it."

³So Joshua arose, and all the people of war, to go up against Ai; and Joshua chose thirty thousand mighty men of valor and sent them away by night. ⁴And he commanded them, saying: "Behold, you shall lie in ambush against the city, behind the city. Do not go very far from the city, but all of you be ready. ⁵Then I and all the people who *are* with me will approach the city; and it will come about, when they come out against us as at the first, that we shall flee before them. ⁶For they will come out after us till we have drawn them from the city, for they will say, '*They are* fleeing before us as at the first.' Therefore we will flee before them. ⁷Then you shall rise from the ambush and seize the city, for the LORD your God will deliver it into your hand. ⁸And it will be, when you have taken the city, *that* you shall set the city on fire. According to the commandment of the LORD you shall do. See, I have commanded you."

⁹Joshua therefore sent them out; and they went to lie in ambush, and stayed between Bethel and Ai, on the west side of Ai; but Joshua lodged that night among the people. ¹⁰Then Joshua rose up early in the morning and mustered the people, and went up, he and the elders of Israel, before the people to Ai. ¹¹And all the people of war who *were* with him went up and drew near; and they came before the city and camped on the north side of Ai. Now a valley *lay* between them and Ai. ¹²So he took about five thousand men and set them in ambush between Bethel and Ai, on the west side of the city. ¹³And when they had set the people, all the army that *was* on the north of the city, and its rear guard on the west of the city, Joshua went that night into the midst of the valley. ¹⁴Now it happened, when the king of Ai saw *it*, that the men of the city hurried and rose early and went out against Israel to battle, he and all his people, at an ap-

pointed place before the plain. But he did not know that *there was* an ambush against him behind the city. ¹⁵And Joshua and all Israel made as if they were beaten before them, and fled by the way of the wilderness. ¹⁶So all the people who *were* in Ai were called together to pursue them. And they pursued Joshua and were drawn away from the city. ¹⁷There was not a man left in Ai or Bethel who did not go out after Israel. So they left the city open and pursued Israel.

¹⁸Then the LORD said to Joshua, "Stretch out the spear that *is* in your hand toward Ai, for I will give it into your hand." And Joshua stretched out the spear that *was* in his hand toward the city. ¹⁹So *those in* ambush arose quickly out of their place; they ran as soon as he had stretched out his hand, and they entered the city and took it, and hurried to set the city on fire. ²⁰And when the men of Ai looked behind them, they saw, and behold, the smoke of the city ascended to heaven. So they had no power to flee this way or that way, and the people who had fled to the wilderness turned back on the pursuers.

²¹Now when Joshua and all Israel saw that the ambush had taken the city and that the smoke of the city ascended, they turned back and struck down the men of Ai. ²²Then the others came out of the city against them; so they were *caught* in the midst of Israel, some on this side and some on that side. And they struck them down, so that they let none of them remain or escape. ²³But the king of Ai they took alive, and brought him to Joshua.

²⁴And it came to pass when Israel had made an end of slaying all the inhabitants of Ai in the field, in the wilderness where they pursued them, and when they all had fallen by the edge of the sword until they were consumed, that all the Israelites returned to Ai and struck it with the edge of the sword. ²⁵So it was *that* all who fell that day, both men and women, *were* twelve thousand— all the people of Ai. ²⁶For Joshua did not draw back his hand, with which he stretched out the spear, until he had utterly destroyed all the inhabitants of Ai. ²⁷Only the livestock and the spoil of that city Israel took as booty for themselves, according to the word of the LORD which He had commanded Joshua. ²⁸So Joshua burned Ai and made it a heap forever, a desolation to this day. ²⁹And the king of Ai he hanged on a tree until evening. And as soon as the sun was down, Joshua commanded that they should take his corpse down from the tree, cast it at the entrance of the gate of the city, and raise over it a great heap of stones *that remains* to this day.

³⁰Now Joshua built an altar to the LORD God of Israel in Mount Ebal, ³¹as Moses the servant of the LORD had commanded the children of Israel, as it is written in the Book of the Law of Moses: "an altar of whole stones over which no man has wielded an iron *tool.*" And they offered on it burnt offerings to the LORD, and sacrificed peace offerings. ³²And there, in the presence of the children of Israel, he wrote on the stones a copy of the law of Moses, which he had written. ³³Then all Israel, with their elders and officers and judges, stood on either side of the ark before the priests, the Levites, who bore the ark of the covenant of the LORD, the stranger as well as he who was born among them. Half of them *were* in front of Mount Gerizim and half of them in front of Mount Ebal, as Moses the

servant of the LORD had commanded before, that they should bless the people of Israel. ³⁴And afterward he read all the words of the law, the blessings and the cursings, according to all that is written in the Book of the Law. ³⁵There was not a word of all that Moses had commanded which Joshua did not read before all the assembly of Israel, with the women, the little ones, and the strangers who were living among them.

CHAPTER 9 GIBEONITES TRICK JOSHUA.

And it came to pass when all the kings who *were* on this side of the Jordan, in the hills and in the lowland and in all the coasts of the Great Sea toward Lebanon—the Hittite, the Amorite, the Canaanite, the Perizzite, the Hivite, the Jebusite—heard *about it,* ²that they gathered together to fight with Joshua and Israel with one accord.

³But when the inhabitants of Gibeon heard what Joshua had done to Jericho and Ai, ⁴they worked craftily, and went and pretended to be ambassadors. And they took old sacks on their donkeys, old wineskins torn and mended, ⁵old and patched sandals on their feet, and old garments on themselves; and all the bread of their provision was dry *and* moldy. ⁶And they went to Joshua, to the camp at Gilgal, and said to him and to the men of Israel, "We have come from a far country; now therefore, make a covenant with us."

⁷Then the men of Israel said to the Hivites, "Perhaps you dwell among us; so how can we make a covenant with you?"

⁸But they said to Joshua, "We *are* your servants."

And Joshua said to them, "Who *are* you, and where do you come from?"

⁹So they said to him: "From a very far country your servants have come, because of the name of the LORD your God; for we have heard of His fame, and all that He did in Egypt, ¹⁰and all that He did to the two kings of the Amorites who *were* beyond the Jordan—to Sihon king of Heshbon, and Og king of Bashan, who was at Ashtaroth. ¹¹Therefore our elders and all the inhabitants of our country spoke to us, saying, 'Take provisions with you for the journey, and go to meet them, and say to them, "We *are* your servants; now therefore, make a covenant with us."' ¹²This bread of ours we took hot *for* our provision from our houses on the day we departed to come to you. But now look, it is dry and moldy. ¹³And these wineskins which we filled *were* new, and see, they are torn; and these our garments and our sandals have become old because of the very long journey."

¹⁴Then the men of Israel took some of their provisions; but they did not ask counsel of the LORD. ¹⁵So Joshua made peace with them, and made a covenant with them to let them live; and the rulers of the congregation swore to them.

¹⁶And it happened at the end of three days, after they had made a covenant with them, that they heard that they *were* their neighbors who dwelt near them. ¹⁷Then the children of Israel journeyed and came to their cities on the third day. Now their cities *were* Gibeon, Chephirah, Beeroth, and Kirjath Jearim. ¹⁸But the children of Israel did not attack them, because the rulers of the con-

gregation had sworn to them by the LORD God of Israel. And all the congregation complained against the rulers.

¹⁹Then all the rulers said to all the congregation, "We have sworn to them by the LORD God of Israel; now therefore, we may not touch them. ²⁰This we will do to them: We will let them live, lest wrath be upon us because of the oath which we swore to them." ²¹And the rulers said to them, "Let them live, but let them be woodcutters and water carriers for all the congregation, as the rulers had promised them."

²²Then Joshua called for them, and he spoke to them, saying, "Why have you deceived us, saying, 'We *are* very far from you,' when you dwell near us? ²³Now therefore, you *are* cursed, and none of you shall be freed from being slaves—woodcutters and water carriers for the house of my God."

◥◥◥ REFRESHER COURSE

8:33,35 After Israel's military victory, Joshua obeyed God's command by gathering the people together and reminding them of God's laws (1:8). God knows how easily we forget. We, like the Israelites, constantly need to review what God says. We should not read the Bible as we do most other books—once through quickly. We should read it daily as a constant reminder of who God is and what we can become.

²⁴So they answered Joshua and said, "Because your servants were clearly told that the LORD your God commanded His servant Moses to give you all the land, and to destroy all the inhabitants of the land from before you; therefore we were very much afraid for our lives because of you, and have done this thing. ²⁵And now, here we are, in your hands; do with us as it seems good and right to do to us." ²⁶So he did to them, and delivered them out of the hand of the children of Israel, so that they did not kill them. ²⁷And that day Joshua made them woodcutters and water carriers for the congregation and for the altar of the LORD, in the place which He would choose, even to this day.

CHAPTER 10 THE SUN AND MOON STAND STILL.

Now it came to pass when Adoni-Zedek king of Jerusalem heard how Joshua had taken Ai and had utterly destroyed it—as he had done to Jericho and its king, so he had done to Ai and its king—and how the inhabitants of Gibeon had made peace with Israel and were among them, ²that they feared greatly, because Gibeon *was* a great city, like one of the royal cities, and because it *was* greater than Ai, and all its men *were* mighty. ³Therefore Adoni-Zedek king of Jerusalem sent to Hoham king of Hebron, Piram king of Jarmuth, Japhia king of Lachish, and Debir king of Eglon, saying, ⁴"Come up to me and help me, that we may attack Gibeon, for it has made peace with Joshua and with the children of Israel." ⁵Therefore the five kings of the Amorites, the king of Jerusalem, the king of Hebron, the king of Jarmuth, the king of Lachish, *and* the king of Eglon, gathered together and went up, they and all their armies, and camped before Gibeon and made war against it.

⁶And the men of Gibeon sent to Joshua at the camp at Gilgal, saying, "Do not forsake your servants; come up to us quickly, save us and help us, for all the kings of the

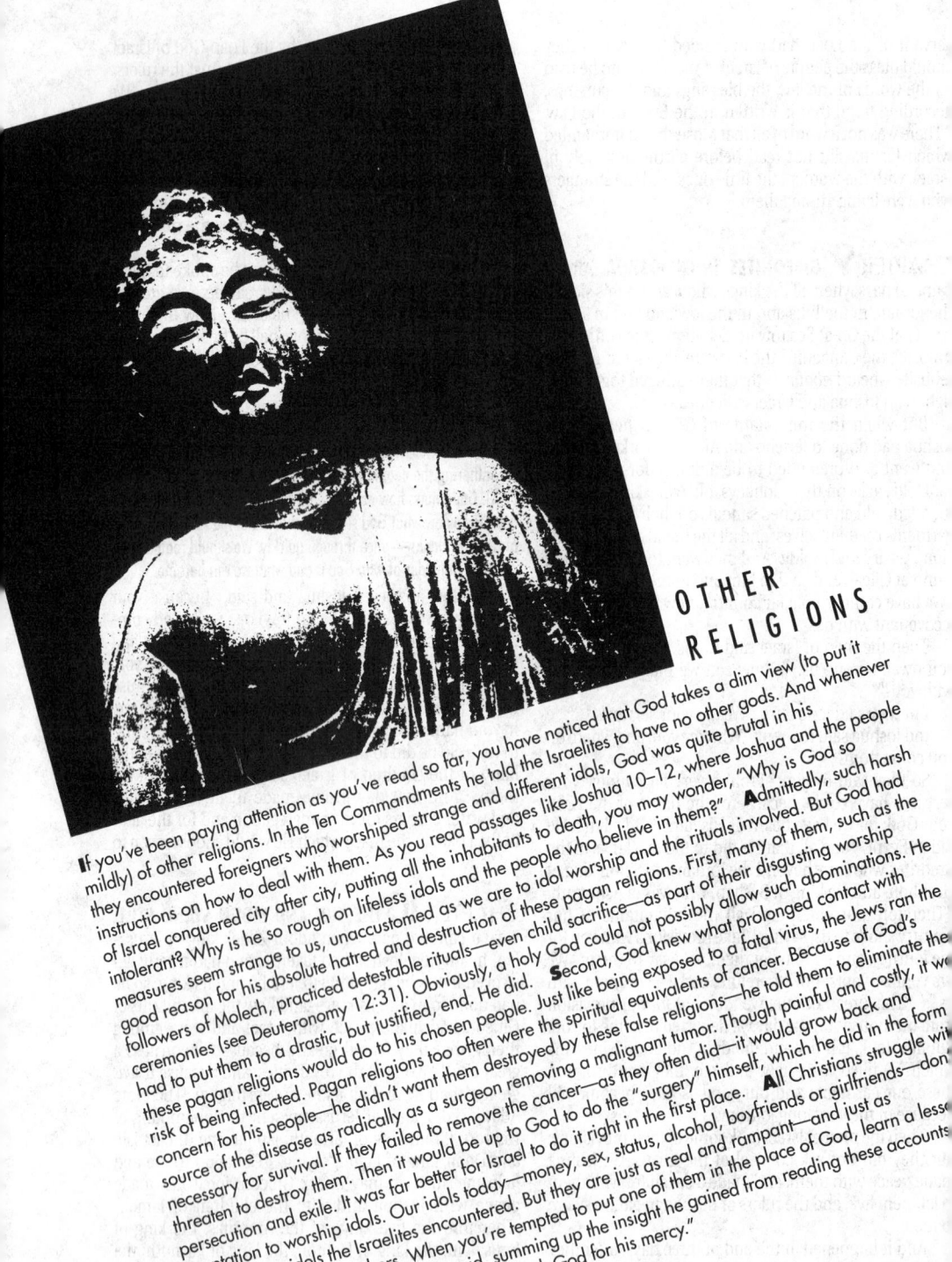

OTHER RELIGIONS

If you've been paying attention as you've read so far, you have noticed that God takes a dim view (to put it mildly) of other religions. In the Ten Commandments he told the Israelites to have no other gods. And whenever they encountered foreigners who worshiped strange and different idols, God was quite brutal in his instructions on how to deal with them. As you read passages like Joshua 10–12, where Joshua and the people of Israel conquered city after city, putting all the inhabitants to death, you may wonder, "Why is God so intolerant? Why is he so rough on lifeless idols and the people who believe in them?" **A**dmittedly, such harsh measures seem strange to us, unaccustomed as we are to idol worship and the rituals involved. But God had good reason for his absolute hatred and destruction of these pagan religions. First, many of them, such as the followers of Molech, practiced detestable rituals—even child sacrifice—as part of their disgusting worship ceremonies (see Deuteronomy 12:31). Obviously, a holy God could not possibly allow such abominations. He had to put them to a drastic, but justified, end. He did. **S**econd, God knew what prolonged contact with these pagan religions would do to his chosen people. Just like being exposed to a fatal virus, the Jews ran the risk of being infected. Pagan religions too often were the spiritual equivalents of cancer. Because of God's concern for his people—he didn't want them destroyed by these false religions—he told them to eliminate the source of the disease as radically as a surgeon removing a malignant tumor. Though painful and costly, it wa necessary for survival. If they failed to remove the cancer—as they often did—it would grow back and threaten to destroy them. Then it would be up to God to do the "surgery" himself, which he did in the form persecution and exile. It was far better for Israel to do it right in the first place. **A**ll Christians struggle wi temptation to worship idols. Our idols today—money, sex, status, alcohol, boyfriends or girlfriends—don much like the idols the Israelites encountered. But they are just as real and rampant—and just as dangerous—as those others. When you're tempted to put one of them in the place of God, learn a lesse the Old Testament. As one person said, summing up the insight he gained from reading these accounts **T**hen he added, "Thank God for his mercy."

mess with this God."

Amorites who dwell in the mountains have gathered together against us."

⁷So Joshua ascended from Gilgal, he and all the people of war with him, and all the mighty men of valor. ⁸And the LORD said to Joshua, "Do not fear them, for I have delivered them into your hand; not a man of them shall stand before you." ⁹Joshua therefore came upon them suddenly, having marched all night from Gilgal. ¹⁰So the LORD routed them before Israel, killed them with a great slaughter at Gibeon, chased them along the road that goes to Beth Horon, and struck them down as far as Azekah and Makkedah. ¹¹And it happened, as they fled before Israel *and* were on the descent of Beth Horon, that the LORD cast down large hailstones from heaven on them as far as Azekah, and they died. *There were* more who died from the hailstones than the children of Israel killed with the sword.

¹²Then Joshua spoke to the LORD in the day when the LORD delivered up the Amorites before the children of Israel, and he said in the sight of Israel:

"Sun, stand still over Gibeon;
And Moon, in the Valley of Aijalon."
¹³ So the sun stood still,
And the moon stopped,
Till the people had revenge
Upon their enemies.

Is this not written in the Book of Jasher? So the sun stood still in the midst of heaven, and did not hasten to go *down* for about a whole day. ¹⁴And there has been no day like that, before it or after it, that the LORD heeded the voice of a man; for the LORD fought for Israel.

¹⁵Then Joshua returned, and all Israel with him, to the camp at Gilgal.

¹⁶But these five kings had fled and hidden themselves in a cave at Makkedah. ¹⁷And it was told Joshua, saying, "The five kings have been found hidden in the cave at Makkedah."

¹⁸So Joshua said, "Roll large stones against the mouth of the cave, and set men by it to guard them. ¹⁹And do not stay *there* yourselves, *but* pursue your enemies, and attack their rear *guard*. Do not allow them to enter their cities, for the LORD your God has delivered them into your hand." ²⁰Then it happened, while Joshua and the children of Israel made an end of slaying them with a very great slaughter, till they had finished, that those who escaped entered fortified cities. ²¹And all the people returned to the camp, to Joshua at Makkedah, in peace. No one moved his tongue against any of the children of Israel.

²²Then Joshua said, "Open the mouth of the cave, and bring out those five kings to me from the cave." ²³And they did so, and brought out those five kings to him from the cave: the king of Jerusalem, the king of Hebron, the king of Jarmuth, the king of Lachish, *and* the king of Eglon.

²⁴So it was, when they brought out those kings to Joshua, that Joshua called for all the men of Israel, and said to the captains of the men of war who went with him, "Come near, put your feet on the necks of these kings." And they drew near and put their feet on their necks. ²⁵Then Joshua said to them, "Do not be afraid, nor be dismayed; be strong and of good courage, for thus the LORD will do to all your enemies against whom you fight." ²⁶And afterward Joshua struck them and killed them, and hanged them on five trees; and they were hanging on the trees until evening. ²⁷So it was at the time of the going down of the sun *that* Joshua commanded, and they took them down from the trees, cast them into the cave where they had been hidden, and laid large stones against the cave's mouth, *which remain* until this very day.

▶ HOPE

10:25 With God's help, Israel won the battle against five armies. Such a triumph was part of God's daily business as he worked with his people for victory. Joshua told his men never to be afraid, because God would give them similar victories over all their enemies. God has often protected us and won victories in our lives. The same God who empowered Joshua and who has led us in the past will help us with our present and future needs. Reminding ourselves of his help in the past will give us hope for the struggles that lie ahead.

²⁸On that day Joshua took Makkedah, and struck it and its king with the edge of the sword. He utterly destroyed them—all the people who *were* in it. He let none remain. He also did to the king of Makkedah as he had done to the king of Jericho.

²⁹Then Joshua passed from Makkedah, and all Israel with him, to Libnah; and they fought against Libnah. ³⁰And the LORD also delivered it and its king into the hand of Israel; he struck it and all the people who *were* in it with the edge of the sword. He let none remain in it, but did to its king as he had done to the king of Jericho.

³¹Then Joshua passed from Libnah, and all Israel with him, to Lachish; and they encamped against it and fought against it. ³²And the LORD delivered Lachish into the hand of Israel, who took it on the second day, and struck it and all the people who *were* in it with the edge of the sword, according to all that he had done to Libnah. ³³Then Horam king of Gezer came up to help Lachish; and Joshua struck him and his people, until he left him none remaining.

³⁴From Lachish Joshua passed to Eglon, and all Israel with him; and they encamped against it and fought against it. ³⁵They took it on that day and struck it with the edge of the sword; all the people who *were* in it he utterly destroyed that day, according to all that he had done to Lachish.

³⁶So Joshua went up from Eglon, and all Israel with him, to Hebron; and they fought against it. ³⁷And they took it and struck it with the edge of the sword—its king, all its cities, and all the people who *were* in it; he left none remaining, according to all that he had done to Eglon, but utterly destroyed it and all the people who *were* in it.

³⁸Then Joshua returned, and all Israel with him, to Debir; and they fought against it. ³⁹And he took it and its king and all its cities; they struck them with the edge of the sword and utterly destroyed all the people who *were* in it. He left none remaining; as he had done to Hebron, so he did to Debir and its king, as he had done also to Libnah and its king.

⁴⁰So Joshua conquered all the land: the mountain

10:40-43 God had commanded Joshua to take the leadership in ridding the land of sin so God's people could occupy it. Joshua did his part thoroughly—leading the united army to weaken the inhabitants. When God orders us to eliminate sin from our life, we must not pause to debate, consider the options, negotiate a compromise, or rationalize. Instead, like Joshua, our response must be swift and complete. We must be ruthless in removing sin from our life.

country and the South and the lowland and the wilderness slopes, and all their kings; he left none remaining, but utterly destroyed all that breathed, as the LORD God of Israel had commanded. 41And Joshua conquered them from Kadesh Barnea as far as Gaza, and all the country of Goshen, even as far as Gibeon. 42All these kings and their land Joshua took at one time, because the LORD God of Israel fought for Israel. 43Then Joshua returned, and all Israel with him, to the camp at Gilgal.

CHAPTER **11** THE SURPRISE ATTACK. And it came to pass, when Jabin king of Hazor heard *these things*, that he sent to Jobab king of Madon, to the king of Shimron, to the king of Achshaph, 2and to the kings who *were* from the north, in the mountains, in the plain south of Chinneroth,

11:15 Joshua carefully obeyed all the instructions given by God. This theme of obedience is repeated frequently in the book of Joshua, partly because obedience is one aspect of life the individual believer can control. We can't always control understanding because we may not have all the facts. We can't control what other people do or how they treat us. However, we can *choose* to obey God. Whatever new challenges we may face, the Bible contains relevant instructions that we can choose to ignore or choose to follow.

in the lowland, and in the heights of Dor on the west, 3to the Canaanites in the east and in the west, the Amorite, the Hittite, the Perizzite, the Jebusite in the mountains, and the Hivite below Hermon in the land of Mizpah. 4So they went out, they and all their armies with them, *as* many people *as* the sand that *is* on the seashore in multitude, with very many horses and chariots. 5And when all these kings had met together, they came and camped together at the waters of Merom to fight against Israel.

6But the LORD said to Joshua, "Do not be afraid because of them, for tomorrow about this time I will deliver all of them slain before Israel. You shall hamstring their horses and burn their chariots with fire." 7So Joshua and all the people of war with him came against them suddenly by the waters of Merom, and they attacked them. 8And the LORD delivered them into the hand of Israel, who defeated them and chased them to Greater Sidon, to the Brook Misrephoth, and to the Valley of Mizpah eastward; they attacked them until they left none of them remaining. 9So Joshua did to them as the LORD had told him: he hamstrung their horses and burned their chariots with fire.

10Joshua turned back at that time and took Hazor, and struck its king with the sword; for Hazor was formerly the head of all those kingdoms. 11And they struck all the people who *were* in it with the edge of the sword, utterly destroying *them*. There was none left breathing. Then he burned Hazor with fire.

12So all the cities of those kings, and all their kings, Joshua took and struck with the edge of the sword. He utterly destroyed them, as Moses the servant of the LORD had commanded. 13But *as for* the cities that stood on their mounds, Israel burned none of them, except Hazor only, *which* Joshua burned. 14And all the spoil of these cities and the livestock, the children of Israel took as booty for themselves; but they struck every man with the edge of the sword until they had destroyed them, and they left none breathing. 15As the LORD had commanded Moses his servant, so Moses commanded Joshua, and so Joshua did. He left nothing undone of all that the LORD had commanded Moses.

16Thus Joshua took all this land: the mountain country, all the South, all the land of Goshen, the lowland, and the Jordan plain—the mountains of Israel and its lowlands, 17from Mount Halak and the ascent to Seir, even as far as Baal Gad in the Valley of Lebanon below Mount Hermon. He captured all their kings, and struck them down and killed them. 18Joshua made war a long time with all those kings. 19There was not a city that made peace with the children of Israel, except the Hivites, inhabitants of Gibeon. All *the others* they took in battle. 20For it was of the LORD to harden their hearts, that they should come against Israel in battle, that He might utterly destroy them, *and* that they might receive no mercy, but that He might destroy them, as the LORD had commanded Moses.

21And at that time Joshua came and cut off the Anakim from the mountains: from Hebron, from Debir, from Anab, from all the mountains of Judah, and from all the mountains of Israel; Joshua utterly destroyed them with their cities. 22None of the Anakim were left in the land of the children of Israel; they remained only in Gaza, in Gath, and in Ashdod.

23So Joshua took the whole land, according to all that the LORD had said to Moses; and Joshua gave it as an inheritance to Israel according to their divisions by their tribes. Then the land rested from war.

CHAPTER **12** A LIST OF CONQUERED KINGS. These *are* the kings of the land whom the children of Israel defeated, and whose land they possessed on the other side of the Jordan toward the rising of the sun, from the River Arnon to Mount Hermon, and all the eastern Jordan plain: 2One king *was* Sihon king of the Amorites, who dwelt in Heshbon *and* ruled half of Gilead, from Aroer which is on the bank of the River Arnon, from the middle of that river, even as far as the River Jabbok, *which is* the border of the Ammonites, 3and the eastern Jordan plain from the Sea of Chinneroth as far as the Sea of the Ara

11:18 The conquest of much of the land of Canaan seems to h happened quickly (we can read about it in one sitting), but it act took seven years. We often expect quick changes in our lives and victories over sin. But our journey with God is a lifelong process, changes and victories may take time. It is easy to grow impatie God and feel like giving up hope because things are moving too When we are close to a situation, it is difficult to see progress. B we look back, we can see that God never stops working.

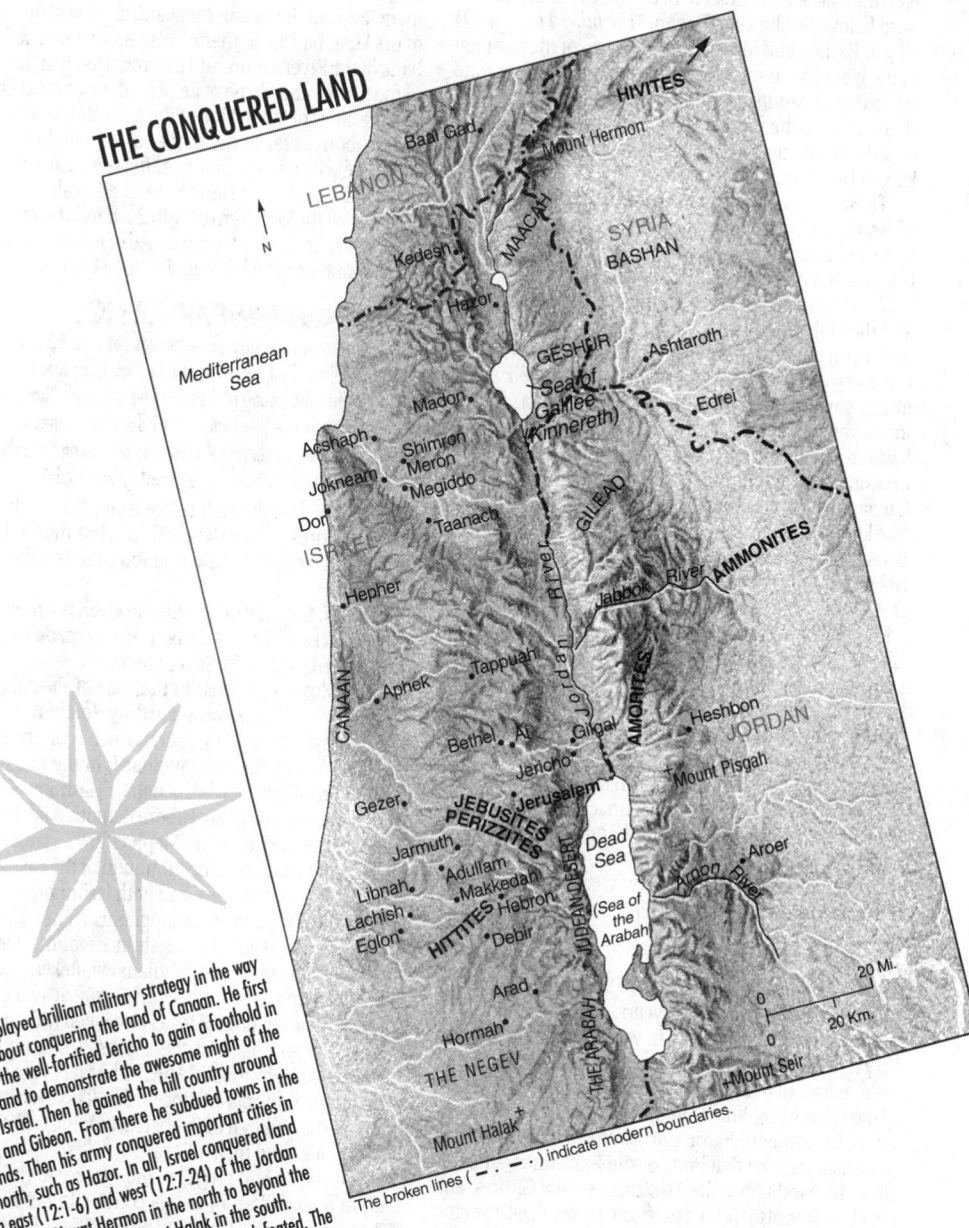

THE CONQUERED LAND

HIVITES

Baal Gad

Mount Hermon

LEBANON

Kedesh

MAACAH

SYRIA

BASHAN

Hazor

GESHUR

Ashtaroth

Mediterranean
Sea

Madon

Sea of
Galilee
(Kinnereth)

Edrei

Acshaph

Shimron

Meron

Jokneam

Megiddo

GILEAD

Taanach

AMMONITES

Dor

ISRAEL

Hepher

Jabbok River

Jordan River

Aphek

Tappuah

AMORITES

CANAAN

Heshbon

JORDAN

Bethel Ai

Gilgal

Jericho

Mount Pisgah

Gezer

Jerusalem

JEBUSITES

PERIZZITES

Jarmuth

Dead
Sea

Aroer

Adullam

Libnah

Makkedah

(Sea of
the
Arabah)

Lachish

Hebron

Arnon River

Eglon

HITTITES

Debir

JUDEAN DESERT

Arad

Hormah

THE NEGEV

THE ARABAH

Mount Seir

Mount Halak

0   20 Mi.

0   20 Km.

The broken lines (— · — ·) indicate modern boundaries.

shua displayed brilliant military strategy in the way
e went about conquering the land of Canaan. He first
captured the well-fortified Jericho to gain a foothold in
Canaan and to demonstrate the awesome might of the
God of Israel. Then he gained the hill country around
Bethel and Gibeon. From there he subdued towns in the
lowlands. Then his army conquered important cities in
the north, such as Hazor. In all, Israel conquered land
both east (12:1-6) and west (12:7-24) of the Jordan
River, from Mount Hermon in the north to beyond the
Negev ("the South") to Mount Halak in the south. The
Thirty-one kings and their cities had been defeated. The
Israelites had overpowered the Hittites, the Amorites, the
Canaanites, the Perizzites, the Hivites, and the Jebusites.
Other people living in Canaan were yet to be conquered.

bah (the Salt Sea), the road to Beth Jeshimoth, and southward below the slopes of Pisgah. [4] *The other king was* Og king of Bashan and his territory, *who was* of the remnant of the giants, who dwelt at Ashtaroth and at Edrei, [5] and reigned over Mount Hermon, over Salcah, over all Bashan, as far as the border of the Geshurites and the Maachathites, and over half of Gilead *to* the border of Sihon king of Heshbon.

[6] These Moses the servant of the LORD and the children of Israel had conquered; and Moses the servant of the LORD had given *as* a possession to the Reubenites, the Gadites, and half the tribe of Manasseh.

[7] And these *are* the kings of the country which Joshua and the children of Israel conquered on this side of the Jordan, on the west, from Baal Gad in the Valley of Lebanon as far as Mount Halak and the ascent to Seir, which Joshua gave to the tribes of Israel *as* a possession according to their divisions, [8] in the mountain country, in the lowlands, in the *Jordan* plain, in the slopes, in the wilderness, and in the South—the Hittites, the Amorites, the Canaanites, the Perizzites, the Hivites, and the Jebusites: [9] the king of Jericho, one; the king of Ai, which *is* beside Bethel, one; [10] the king of Jerusalem, one; the king of Hebron, one; [11] the king of Jarmuth, one; the king of Lachish, one; [12] the king of Eglon, one; the king of Gezer, one; [13] the king of Debir, one; the king of Geder, one; [14] the king of Hormah, one; the king of Arad, one; [15] the king of Libnah, one; the king of Adullam, one; [16] the king of Makkedah, one; the king of Bethel, one; [17] the king of Tappuah, one; the king of Hepher, one; [18] the king of Aphek, one; the king of Lasharon, one; [19] the king of Madon, one; the king of Hazor, one; [20] the king of Shimron Meron, one; the king of Achshaph, one; [21] the king of Taanach, one; the king of Megiddo, one; [22] the king of Kedesh, one; the king of Jokneam in Carmel, one; [23] the king of Dor in the heights of Dor, one; the king of the people of Gilgal, one; [24] the king of Tirzah, one—all the kings, thirty-one.

CHAPTER 13 JOSHUA DIVIDES UP THE LAND. Now Joshua was old, advanced in years. And the LORD said to him: "You are old, advanced in years, and there remains very much land yet to be possessed. [2] This is the land that yet remains: all the territory of the Philistines and all *that of* the Geshurites, [3] from Sihor, which *is* east of Egypt, as far as the border of Ekron northward (*which* is counted as Canaanite); the five lords of the Philistines—the Gazites, the Ashdodites, the Ashkelonites, the Gittites, and the Ekronites; also the Avites; [4] from the south, all the land of the Canaanites, and Mearah that belongs to the Sidonians as far as Aphek, to the border of the Amorites; [5] the land of the Gebalites, and all Lebanon, toward the sunrise, from Baal Gad below Mount Hermon as far as the entrance to Hamath; [6] all the inhabitants of the mountains from Lebanon as far as the Brook Misrephoth, *and* all the Sidonians—them I will drive out from before the children of Israel; only divide it by lot to Israel as an inheritance, as I have commanded you. [7] Now therefore, divide this land as an inheritance to the nine tribes and half the tribe of Manasseh."

[8] With the other half-tribe the Reubenites and the Gad-

ites received their inheritance, which Moses had give them, beyond the Jordan eastward, as Moses the servan of the LORD had given them: [9] from Aroer which *is* on th bank of the River Arnon, and the town that *is* in the mid of the ravine, and all the plain of Medeba as far as Dibo [10] all the cities of Sihon king of the Amorites, who reigne in Heshbon, as far as the border of the children of Am mon; [11] Gilead, and the border of the Geshurites and Ma achathites, all Mount Hermon, and all Bashan as far a Salcah; [12] all the kingdom of Og in Bashan, who reigned Ashtaroth and Edrei, who remained of the remnant of th giants; for Moses had defeated and cast out these.

EXPERIENCE

13:1 Joshua was getting old—he was between 85 and 100 y age at this time. God, however, still had work for him to do. Our often glorifies the young and strong and sets aside those who an Yet older people are filled with the wisdom that comes with expe They are capable of serving if given the chance and should be encouraged to do so. How do you treat older people?

[13] Nevertheless the children of Israel did not drive o the Geshurites or the Maachathites, but the Geshurite and the Maachathites dwell among the Israelites un this day.

[14] Only to the tribe of Levi he had given no inheritanc the sacrifices of the LORD God of Israel made by fire *a* their inheritance, as He said to them.

[15] And Moses had given to the tribe of the children Reuben *an inheritance* according to their familie [16] Their territory was from Aroer, which *is* on the bank the River Arnon, and the city that *is* in the midst of t ravine, and all the plain by Medeba; [17] Heshbon and all cities that *are* in the plain: Dibon, Bamoth Baal, Beth Ba Meon, [18] Jahaza, Kedemoth, Mephaath, [19] Kirjathaim, Si mah, Zereth Shahar on the mountain of the valley, [20] Be Peor, the slopes of Pisgah, and Beth Jeshimoth— [21] all th cities of the plain and all the kingdom of Sihon king of th Amorites, who reigned in Heshbon, whom Moses ha struck with the princes of Midian: Evi, Rekem, Zur, Hu and Reba, who *were* princes of Sihon dwelling in t country. [22] The children of Israel also killed with the swo Balaam the son of Beor, the soothsayer, among tho who were killed by them. [23] And the border of the childre of Reuben was the bank of the Jordan. This *was* the inhe itance of the children of Reuben according to their fam lies, the cities and their villages.

[24] Moses also had given *an inheritance* to the tribe Gad, to the children of Gad according to their familie [25] Their territory was Jazer, and all the cities of Gilead, an half the land of the Ammonites as far as Aroer, which before Rabbah, [26] and from Heshbon to Ramath Mizp. and Betonim, and from Mahanaim to the border of D bir, [27] and in the valley Beth Haram, Beth Nimrah, Su coth, and Zaphon, the rest of the kingdom of Sihon ki of Heshbon, with the Jordan as *its* border, as far as t edge of the Sea of Chinnereth, on the other side of t Jordan eastward. [28] This *is* the inheritance of the childr of Gad according to their families, the cities and th villages.

[29] Moses also had given *an inheritance* to half the tri

of Manasseh; it was for half the tribe of the children of Manasseh according to their families: ³⁰Their territory was from Mahanaim, all Bashan, all the kingdom of Og king of Bashan, and all the towns of Jair which are in Bashan, sixty cities; ³¹half of Gilead, and Ashtaroth and Edrei, cities of the kingdom of Og in Bashan, *were* for the children of Machir the son of Manasseh, for half of the children of Machir according to their families.

³²These *are the areas* which Moses had distributed as an inheritance in the plains of Moab on the other side of the Jordan, by Jericho eastward. ³³But to the tribe of Levi Moses had given no inheritance; the LORD God of Israel *was* their inheritance, as He had said to them.

CHAPTER **14** WEST OF THE JORDAN RIVER. These *are the areas* which the children of Israel inherited in the land of Canaan, which Eleazar the priest, Joshua the son of Nun, and the heads of the fathers of the tribes of the children of Israel distributed as an inheritance to them. ²Their inheritance *was* by lot, as the LORD had commanded by the hand of Moses, for the nine tribes and the half-tribe. ³For Moses had given the inheritance of the two tribes and the half-tribe on the other side of the Jordan; but to the Levites he had given no inheritance among them. ⁴For the children of Joseph were two tribes: Manasseh and Ephraim. And they gave no part to the Levites in the land, except cities to dwell *in,* with their common-lands for their livestock and their property. ⁵As the LORD had commanded Moses, so the children of Israel did; and they divided the land.

⁶Then the children of Judah came to Joshua in Gilgal. And Caleb the son of Jephunneh the Kenizzite said to him: "You know the word which the LORD said to Moses the man of God concerning you and me in Kadesh Barnea. ⁷I *was* forty years old when Moses the servant of the LORD sent me from Kadesh Barnea to spy out the land, and I brought back word to him as *it was* in my heart. ⁸Nevertheless my brethren who went up with me made the heart of the people melt, but I wholly followed the LORD my God. ⁹So Moses swore on that day, saying, 'Surely the land where your foot has trodden shall be your inheritance and your children's forever, because you have wholly followed the LORD my God.' ¹⁰And now, behold, the LORD has kept me alive, as He said, these forty-five years, ever since the LORD spoke this word to Moses while Israel wandered in the wilderness; and now, here I am this day, eighty-five years old. ¹¹As yet I *am as* strong this day as on the day that Moses sent me; just as my strength *was* then, so now *is* my strength for war, both for going out and for coming in. ¹²Now therefore, give me this mountain of which the LORD spoke in that day; for you heard in that day how the Anakim *were* there, and *that* the cities *were* great *and* fortified. It may be that the LORD *will be* with me, and I shall be able to drive them out as the LORD said."

¹³And Joshua blessed him, and gave Hebron to Caleb the son of Jephunneh as an inheritance. ¹⁴Hebron therefore became the inheritance of Caleb the son of Jephunneh the Kenizzite to this day, because he wholly followed the LORD God of Israel. ¹⁵And the name of Hebron formerly was Kirjath Arba (*Arba was* the greatest man among the Anakim).

Then the land had rest from war.

CHAPTER **15** LAND FOR JUDAH. So *this* was the lot of the tribe of the children of Judah according to their families:

The border of Edom at the Wilderness of Zin southward *was* the extreme southern boundary. ²And their southern border began at the shore of the Salt Sea, from the bay that faces southward. ³Then it went out to the southern side of the Ascent of Akrabbim, passed along to Zin, ascended on the south side of Kadesh Barnea, passed along to Hezron, went up to Adar, and went around to Karkaa. ⁴*From there* it passed toward Azmon and went out to the Brook of Egypt; and the border ended at the sea. This shall be your southern border.

⁵The east border *was* the Salt Sea as far as the mouth of the Jordan.

▶ PRECISELY

14:5 The land was divided exactly as God had instructed Moses years before. Joshua did not change a word. He followed God's commands precisely. Often we believe that "almost" is close enough, and this idea can carry over into our spiritual lives. For example, we may follow God's Word as long as we agree with it, but ignore it when the demands seem difficult. But God is looking for leaders who follow instructions thoroughly.

And the border on the northern quarter *began* at the bay of the sea at the mouth of the Jordan. ⁶The border went up to Beth Hoglah and passed north of Beth Arabah; and the border went up to the stone of Bohan the son of Reuben. ⁷Then the border went up toward Debir from the Valley of Achor, and it turned northward toward Gilgal, which *is* before the Ascent of Adummim, which *is* on the south side of the valley. The border continued toward the waters of En Shemesh and ended at En Rogel. ⁸And the border went up by the Valley of the Son of Hinnom to the southern slope of the Jebusite *city* (which *is* Jerusalem). The border went up to the top of the mountain that *lies* before the Valley of Hinnom westward, which *is* at the end of the Valley of Rephaim northward. ⁹Then the border went around from the top of the hill to the fountain of the water of Nephtoah, and extended to the cities of Mount Ephron. And the border went around to Baalah (which *is* Kirjath Jearim). ¹⁰Then the border turned westward from Baalah to Mount Seir, passed along to the side of Mount Jearim on the north (which *is* Chesalon), went down to Beth Shemesh, and passed on to Timnah. ¹¹And the border went out to the side of Ekron northward. Then the border went around to Shicron,

---

◀ INTEGRITY

14:6-12 When Joshua gave Caleb his land, he fulfilled a promise God had made to Caleb 45 years earlier. We expect such integrity and reliability from God, but do we expect the same from his followers? How about you? Is your word this reliable? Would you honor a 45-year-old promise? God would—and does. Even today he is honoring promises he made *thousands* of years ago. In fact, some of his greatest promises are yet to be fulfilled. This gives us much to look forward to. Let your faith grow as you realize how God keeps his word.

16:1 Though Joseph was one of Jacob's 12 sons, he did not have a tribe named after him. This was because Joseph, as the oldest son of Jacob's wife Rachel, received a double portion of the inheritance. This double portion was given to Joseph's two sons, Ephraim and Manasseh, whom Jacob considered as his own (Genesis 48:5). The largest territory and the greatest influence in the northern half of Israel belonged to the tribes of Ephraim and Manasseh.

passed along to Mount Baalah, and extended to Jabneel; and the border ended at the sea.

¹²The west border *was* the coastline of the Great Sea. This *is* the boundary of the children of Judah all around according to their families.

¹³Now to Caleb the son of Jephunneh he gave a share among the children of Judah, according to the commandment of the LORD to Joshua, *namely,* Kirjath Arba, which *is* Hebron (*Arba was* the father of Anak). ¹⁴Caleb drove out the three sons of Anak from there: Sheshai, Ahiman, and Talmai, the children of Anak. ¹⁵Then he went up from there to the inhabitants of Debir (formerly the name of Debir *was* Kirjath Sepher).

¹⁶And Caleb said, "He who attacks Kirjath Sepher and takes it, to him I will give Achsah my daughter as wife." ¹⁷So Othniel the son of Kenaz, the brother of Caleb, took it; and he gave him Achsah his daughter as wife. ¹⁸Now it was so, when she came *to him,* that she persuaded him to ask her father for a field. So she dismounted from *her* donkey, and Caleb said to her, "What do you wish?" ¹⁹She answered, "Give me a blessing; since you have given me land in the South, give me also springs of water." So he gave her the upper springs and the lower springs.

²⁰This *was* the inheritance of the tribe of the children of Judah according to their families:

²¹The cities at the limits of the tribe of the children of Judah, toward the border of Edom in the South, were Kabzeel, Eder, Jagur, ²²Kinah, Dimonah, Adadah, ²³Kedesh, Hazor, Ithnan, ²⁴Ziph, Telem, Bealoth, ²⁵Hazor, Hadattah, Kerioth, Hezron (which *is* Hazor), ²⁶Amam, Shema, Moladah, ²⁷Hazar Gaddah, Heshmon, Beth Pelet, ²⁸Hazar Shual, Beersheba, Bizjothjah, ²⁹Baalah, Ijim, Ezem, ³⁰Eltolad, Chesil, Hormah, ³¹Ziklag, Madmannah, Sansannah, ³²Lebaoth, Shilhim, Ain, and Rimmon: all the cities *are* twenty-nine, with their villages.

³³In the lowland: Eshtaol, Zorah, Ashnah, ³⁴Zanoah, En Gannim, Tappuah, Enam, ³⁵Jarmuth, Adullam, Socoh, Azekah, ³⁶Sharaim, Adithaim, Gederah, and Gederothaim: fourteen cities with their villages; ³⁷Zenan, Hadashah, Migdal Gad, ³⁸Dilean, Mizpah, Joktheel, ³⁹Lachish, Bozkath, Eglon, ⁴⁰Cabbon, Lahmas, Kithlish, ⁴¹Gederoth, Beth Dagon, Naamah, and Makkedah: sixteen cities with their villages; ⁴²Libnah, Ether, Ashan, ⁴³Jiphtah, Ashnah, Nezib, ⁴⁴Keilah, Achzib, and Mareshah: nine cities with their villages; ⁴⁵Ekron, with its towns and villages; ⁴⁶from Ekron to the sea, all that *lay* near Ashdod, with their villages; ⁴⁷Ashdod with its towns and villages, Gaza with its towns and villages—as far as the Brook of Egypt and the Great Sea with *its* coastline.

⁴⁸And in the mountain country: Shamir, Jattir, Sochoh, ⁴⁹Dannah, Kirjath Sannah (which *is* Debir), ⁵⁰Anab, Eshtemoh, Anim, ⁵¹Goshen, Holon, and Giloh: eleven cities with their villages; ⁵²Arab, Dumah, Eshean, ⁵³Janum, Beth Tappuah, Aphekah, ⁵⁴Humtah, Kirjath Arba (which *is* He-

bron), and Zior: nine cities with their villages; ⁵⁵Maon, Carmel, Ziph, Juttah, ⁵⁶Jezreel, Jokdeam, Zanoah, ⁵⁷Kain, Gibeah, and Timnah: ten cities with their villages; ⁵⁸Halhul, Beth Zur, Gedor, ⁵⁹Maarath, Beth Anoth, and Eltekon: six cities with their villages; ⁶⁰Kirjath Baal (which *is* Kirjath Jearim) and Rabbah: two cities with their villages.

⁶¹In the wilderness: Beth Arabah, Middin, Secacah, ⁶²Nibshan, the City of Salt, and En Gedi: six cities with their villages.

⁶³As for the Jebusites, the inhabitants of Jerusalem, the children of Judah could not drive them out; but the Jebusites dwell with the children of Judah at Jerusalem to this day.

CHAPTER 16 LAND FOR EPHRAIM. The lot fell to the children of Joseph from the Jordan, by Jericho, to the waters of Jericho on the east, to the wilderness that goes up from Jericho through the mountains to Bethel, ²then went out from Bethel to Luz, passed along to the border of the Archites at Ataroth, ³and went down westward to the boundary of the Japhletites, as far as the boundary of Lower Beth Horon to Gezer; and it ended at the sea.

⁴So the children of Joseph, Manasseh and Ephraim, took their inheritance.

⁵The border of the children of Ephraim, according to their families, was *thus:* The border of their inheritance on the east side was Ataroth Addar as far as Upper Beth Horon.

⁶And the border went out toward the sea on the north side of Michmethath; then the border went around eastward to Taanath Shiloh, and passed by it on the east of Janohah. ⁷Then it went down from Janohah to Ataroth and Naarah, reached to Jericho, and came out at the Jordan.

⁸The border went out from Tappuah westward to the Brook Kanah, and it ended at the sea. This *was* the inheritance of the tribe of the children of Ephraim according to their families. ⁹The separate cities for the children of Ephraim *were* among the inheritance of the children of Manasseh, all the cities with their villages.

¹⁰And they did not drive out the Canaanites who dwelt in Gezer; but the Canaanites dwell among the Ephraimites to this day and have become forced laborers.

CHAPTER 17 LAND FOR MANASSEH. There was also a lot for the tribe of Manasseh, for he *was* the firstborn of Joseph: *namely* for Machir the firstborn of Manasseh, the father of Gilead, because he was a man of war; therefore he was given Gilead and Bashan. ²An-

17:3-4 Although women did not traditionally receive property inheritance in Israelite society, Moses put justice ahead of tradition, gave these five women the land they deserved (see Numbers 27). In fact, God told Moses to add a law that would help other women in similar circumstances inherit property as well. Joshua was now carrying out this law. It is easy to refuse to honor a reasonable request because "things have never been done that way before." But it is best for us, like Moses and Joshua, to look carefully at the purpose of the law and the merits of each case before deciding, rather than basing our decision solely on tradition.

there was *a lot* for the rest of the children of Manasseh according to their families: for the children of Abiezer, the children of Helek, the children of Asriel, the children of Shechem, the children of Hepher, and the children of Shemida; these *were* the male children of Manasseh the son of Joseph according to their families.

³But Zelophehad the son of Hepher, the son of Gilead, the son of Machir, the son of Manasseh, had no sons, but only daughters. And these *are* the names of his daughters: Mahlah, Noah, Hoglah, Milcah, and Tirzah. ⁴And they came near before Eleazar the priest, before Joshua the son of Nun, and before the rulers, saying, "The LORD commanded Moses to give us an inheritance among our brothers." Therefore, according to the commandment of the LORD, he gave them an inheritance among their father's brothers. ⁵Ten shares fell to Manasseh, besides the land of Gilead and Bashan, which *were* on the other side of the Jordan, ⁶because the daughters of Manasseh received an inheritance among his sons; and the rest of Manasseh's sons had the land of Gilead.

⁷And the territory of Manasseh was from Asher to Michmethath, that *lies* east of Shechem; and the border went along south to the inhabitants of En Tappuah. ⁸Manasseh had the land of Tappuah, but Tappuah on the border of Manasseh *belonged* to the children of Ephraim. ⁹And the border descended to the Brook Kanah, southward to the brook. These cities of Ephraim *are* among the cities of Manasseh. The border of Manasseh *was* on the north side of the brook; and it ended at the sea. ¹⁰Southward *it was* Ephraim's, northward *it was* Manasseh's, and the sea was its border. Manasseh's territory was adjoining Asher on the north and Issachar on the east. ¹¹And in Issachar and in Asher, Manasseh had Beth Shean and its towns, Ibleam and its towns, the inhabitants of Dor and its towns, the inhabitants of En Dor and its towns, the inhabitants of Taanach and its towns, and the inhabitants of Megiddo and its towns—three hilly regions. ¹²Yet the children of Manasseh could not drive out *the inhabitants of* those cities, but the Canaanites were determined to dwell in that land. ¹³And it happened, when the children of Israel grew strong, that they put the Canaanites to forced labor, but did not utterly drive them out.

¹⁴Then the children of Joseph spoke to Joshua, saying, "Why have you given us *only* one lot and one share to inherit, since we *are* a great people, inasmuch as the LORD has blessed us until now?"

¹⁵So Joshua answered them, "If you *are* a great people, *then* go up to the forest *country* and clear a place for yourself there in the land of the Perizzites and the giants, since the mountains of Ephraim are too confined for you."

¹⁶But the children of Joseph said, "The mountain country is not enough for us; and all the Canaanites who dwell in the land of the valley have chariots of iron, *both* those who *are* of Beth Shean and its towns and those who *are* of the Valley of Jezreel."

¹⁷And Joshua spoke to the house of Joseph—to Ephraim and Manasseh—saying, "You *are* a great people and have great power; you shall not have *only* one lot, but the mountain country shall be yours. Although it *is*

wooded, you shall cut it down, and its farthest extent shall be yours; for you shall drive out the Canaanites, though they have iron chariots *and* are strong."

CHAPTER 18 JOSHUA ASSIGNS THE REST. Now the whole congregation of the children of Israel assembled together at Shiloh, and set up the tabernacle of meeting there. And the land was subdued before them. ²But there remained among the children of Israel seven tribes which had not yet received their inheritance.

◗ PUTTING OFF

18:3-6 Joshua asked why some of the tribes were putting off the job of possessing the land. Often we delay doing jobs that seem large, difficult, boring, or disagreeable. But to continue putting them off shows lack of discipline, poor stewardship of time, and—in some cases—disobedience to God. Jobs we don't enjoy require concentration, teamwork, twice as much time, lots of encouragement, and accountability. Remember this when you are tempted to procrastinate.

³Then Joshua said to the children of Israel: "How long will you neglect to go and possess the land which the LORD God of your fathers has given you? ⁴Pick out from among you three men for *each* tribe, and I will send them; they shall rise and go through the land, survey it according to their inheritance, and come *back* to me. ⁵And they shall divide it into seven parts. Judah shall remain in their territory on the south, and the house of Joseph shall remain in their territory on the north. ⁶You shall therefore survey the land in seven parts and bring *the survey* here to me, that I may cast lots for you here before the LORD our God. ⁷But the Levites have no part among you, for the priesthood of the LORD *is* their inheritance. And Gad, Reuben, and half the tribe of Manasseh have received their inheritance beyond the Jordan on the east, which Moses the servant of the LORD gave them."

⁸Then the men arose to go away; and Joshua charged those who went to survey the land, saying, "Go, walk through the land, survey it, and come back to me, that I may cast lots for you here before the LORD in Shiloh." ⁹So the men went, passed through the land, and wrote the survey in a book in seven parts by cities; and they came to Joshua at the camp in Shiloh. ¹⁰Then Joshua cast lots for them in Shiloh before the LORD, and there Joshua divided the land to the children of Israel according to their divisions.

¹¹Now the lot of the tribe of the children of Benjamin came up according to their families, and the territory of their lot came out between the children of Judah and the children of Joseph. ¹²Their border on the north side began at the Jordan, and the border went up to the side of Jericho on the north, and went up through the mountains westward; it ended at the Wilderness of Beth Aven. ¹³The border went over from there toward Luz, to the side of Luz (which *is* Bethel) southward; and the border descended to Ataroth Addar, near the hill that *lies* on the south side of Lower Beth Horon. ¹⁴Then the border extended around the west side to the south, from the hill that *lies* before Beth Horon southward; and it ended at Kirjath Baal (which *is* Kirjath

Jearim), a city of the children of Judah. This *was* the west side.

15The south side *began* at the end of Kirjath Jearim, and the border extended on the west and went out to the spring of the waters of Nephtoah. 16Then the border came down to the end of the mountain that *lies* before the Valley of the Son of Hinnom, which *is* in the Valley of the Rephaim on the north, descended to the Valley of Hinnom, to the side of the Jebusite *city* on the south, and descended to En Rogel. 17And it went around from the north, went out to En Shemesh, and extended toward Geliloth, which is before the Ascent of Adummim, and descended to the stone of Bohan the son of Reuben. 18Then it passed along toward the north side of Arabah, and went down to Arabah. 19And the border passed along to the north side of Beth Hoglah; then the border ended at the north bay at the Salt Sea, at the south end of the Jordan. This *was* the southern boundary.

20The Jordan was its border on the east side. This *was* the inheritance of the children of Benjamin, according to its boundaries all around, according to their families.

21Now the cities of the tribe of the children of Benjamin, according to their families, were Jericho, Beth Hoglah, Emek Keziz, 22Beth Arabah, Zemaraim, Bethel, 23Avim, Parah, Ophrah, 24Chephar Haammoni, Ophni, and Gaba: twelve cities with their villages; 25Gibeon, Ramah, Beeroth, 26Mizpah, Chephirah, Mozah, 27Rekem, Irpeel, Taralah, 28Zelah, Eleph, Jebus (which *is* Jerusalem), Gibeath, *and* Kirjath: fourteen cities with their villages. This was the inheritance of the children of Benjamin according to their families.

CHAPTER 19 LAND FOR SIMEON. The second lot came out for Simeon, for the tribe of the children of Simeon according to their families. And their inheritance was within the inheritance of the children of Judah. 2They had in their inheritance Beersheba (Sheba), Moladah, 3Hazar Shual, Balah, Ezem, 4Eltolad, Bethul, Hormah, 5Ziklag, Beth Marcaboth, Hazar Susah, 6Beth Lebaoth, and Sharuhen: thirteen cities and their villages; 7Ain, Rimmon, Ether, and Ashan: four cities and their villages; 8and all the villages that *were* all around these cities as far as Baalath Beer, Ramah of the South. This *was* the inheritance of the tribe of the children of Simeon according to their families.

9The inheritance of the children of Simeon *was included* in the share of the children of Judah, for the share of the children of Judah was too much for them. Therefore the children of Simeon had *their* inheritance within the inheritance of that people.

10The third lot came out for the children of Zebulun according to their families, and the border of their inheritance was as far as Sarid. 11Their border went toward the west and to Maralah, went to Dabbasheth, and extended along the brook that is east of Jokneam. 12Then from Sarid it went eastward toward the sunrise along the border of Chisloth Tabor, and went out toward Daberath, bypassing Japhia. 13And from there it passed along on the east of Gath Hepher, toward Eth Kazin, and extended to Rimmon, which borders on Neah. 14Then the border

went around it on the north side of Hannathon, and i ended in the Valley of Jiphthah El. 15Included were Ka tath, Nahallal, Shimron, Idalah, and Bethlehem: twelv cities with their villages. 16This *was* the inheritance of th children of Zebulun according to their families, thes cities with their villages.

17The fourth lot came out to Issachar, for the childre of Issachar according to their families. 18And their terri tory went to Jezreel, and *included* Chesulloth, Shunem 19Haphraim, Shion, Anaharath, 20Rabbith, Kishion, Abe 21Remeth, En Gannim, En Haddah, and Beth Pazze 22And the border reached to Tabor, Shahazimah, and Bet Shemesh; their border ended at the Jordan: sixteen citie with their villages. 23This *was* the inheritance of the trib of the children of Issachar according to their families, th cities and their villages.

24The fifth lot came out for the tribe of the children c Asher according to their families. 25And their territor included Helkath, Hali, Beten, Achshaph, 26Alammelec Amad, and Mishal; it reached to Mount Carmel west ward, along *the Brook* Shihor Libnath. 27It turned towar the sunrise to Beth Dagon; and it reached to Zebulun an to the Valley of Jiphthah El, then northward beyond Bet Emek and Neiel, bypassing Cabul *which was* on the lef 28including Ebron, Rehob, Hammon, and Kanah, as far a Greater Sidon. 29And the border turned to Ramah and t the fortified city of Tyre; then the border turned to Hosa and ended at the sea by the region of Achzib. 30Also Um mah, Aphek, and Rehob *were included:* twenty-two citie with their villages. 31This *was* the inheritance of the trib of the children of Asher according to their families, thes cities with their villages.

32The sixth lot came out to the children of Naphtali, f the children of Naphtali according to their families. 33An their border began at Heleph, enclosing the territor from the terebinth tree in Zaanannim, Adami Nekeb, an Jabneel, as far as Lakkum; it ended at the Jordan. 34Fro Heleph the border extended westward to Aznoth Tabc and went out from there toward Hukkok; it adjoine Zebulun on the south side and Asher on the west sid and ended at Judah by the Jordan toward the sunris 35And the fortified cities *are* Ziddim, Zer, Hammath, Ra kath, Chinnereth, 36Adamah, Ramah, Hazor, 37Kedes Edrei, En Hazor, 38Iron, Migdal El, Horem, Beth Anat and Beth Shemesh: nineteen cities with their village 39This *was* the inheritance of the tribe of the children Naphtali according to their families, the cities and the villages.

40The seventh lot came out for the tribe of the childre of Dan according to their families. 41And the territory their inheritance was Zorah, Eshtaol, Ir Shemesh, 42Sh alabbin, Aijalon, Jethlah, 43Elon, Timnah, Ekron, 44Elt keh, Gibbethon, Baalath, 45Jehud, Bene Berak, Ga Rimmon, 46Me Jarkon, and Rakkon, with the region ne Joppa. 47And the border of the children of Dan went b yond these, because the children of Dan went up to fig against Leshem and took it; and they struck it with th edge of the sword, took possession of it, and dwelt in They called Leshem, Dan, after the name of Dan the father. 48This *is* the inheritance of the tribe of the childre of Dan according to their families, these cities with their villages.

⁴⁹When they had made an end of dividing the land as an inheritance according to their borders, the children of Israel gave an inheritance among them to Joshua the son of Nun. ⁵⁰According to the word of the LORD they gave him the city which he asked for, Timnath Serah in the mountains of Ephraim; and he built the city and dwelt in it.

⁵¹These *were* the inheritances which Eleazar the priest, Joshua the son of Nun, and the heads of the fathers of the tribes of the children of Israel divided as an inheritance by lot in Shiloh before the LORD, at the door of the tabernacle of meeting. So they made an end of dividing the country.

CHAPTER 20 CITIES OF REFUGE.

The LORD also spoke to Joshua, saying, ²"Speak to the children of Israel, saying: 'Appoint for yourselves cities of refuge, of which I spoke to you through Moses, ³that the slayer who kills a person accidentally *or* unintentionally may flee there; and they shall be your refuge from the avenger of blood. ⁴And when he flees to one of those cities, and stands at the entrance of the gate of the city, and declares his case in the hearing of the elders of that city, they shall take him into the city as one of them, and give him a place, that he may dwell among them. ⁵Then if the avenger of blood pursues him, they shall not deliver the slayer into his hand, because he struck his neighbor unintentionally, but did not hate him beforehand. ⁶And he shall dwell in that city until he stands before the congregation for judgment, *and* until the death of the one who is high priest in those days. Then the slayer may return and come to his own city and his own house, to the city from which he fled.' "

⁷So they appointed Kedesh in Galilee, in the mountains of Naphtali, Shechem in the mountains of Ephraim, and Kirjath Arba (which *is* Hebron) in the mountains of Judah. ⁸And on the other side of the Jordan, by Jericho eastward, they assigned Bezer in the wilderness on the plain, from the tribe of Reuben, Ramoth in Gilead, from the tribe of Gad, and Golan in Bashan, from the tribe of Manasseh. ⁹These were the cities appointed for all the children of Israel and for the stranger who dwelt among them, that whoever killed a person accidentally might flee there, and not die by the hand of the avenger of blood until he stood before the congregation.

CHAPTER 21 TOWNS FOR THE LEVITES.

Then the heads of the fathers' *houses* of the Levites came near to Eleazar the priest, to Joshua the son of Nun, and to the heads of the fathers' *houses* of the tribes of the children of Israel. ²And they spoke to them at Shiloh in the land of Canaan, saying, "The LORD commanded through Moses to give us cities to dwell in, with their common-lands for our livestock." ³So the children of Israel gave to the Levites from their inheritance, at the commandment of the LORD, these cities and their common-lands:

⁴Now the lot came out for the families of the Kohathites. And the children of Aaron the priest, *who were* of the Levites, had thirteen cities by lot from the tribe of Judah, from the tribe of Simeon, and from the tribe of Benjamin. ⁵The rest of the children of Kohath had ten cities by lot from the families of the tribe of Ephraim, from the tribe of Dan, and from the half-tribe of Manasseh.

▬▬▬WEAK FAITH

19:47-48 The tribe of Dan thought that some of their land looked difficult to conquer, so they chose to migrate to Leshem where they knew victory would be easier. Anyone can trust God when the going is easy. It is when everything looks impossible that our faith and courage are put to the test. Have faith that God is great enough to tackle your most difficult situations.

⁶And the children of Gershon had thirteen cities by lot from the families of the tribe of Issachar, from the tribe of Asher, from the tribe of Naphtali, and from the half-tribe of Manasseh in Bashan.

⁷The children of Merari according to their families had twelve cities from the tribe of Reuben, from the tribe of Gad, and from the tribe of Zebulun.

⁸And the children of Israel gave these cities with their common-lands by lot to the Levites, as the LORD had commanded by the hand of Moses.

⁹So they gave from the tribe of the children of Judah and from the tribe of the children of Simeon these cities which are designated by name, ¹⁰which were for the children of Aaron, one of the families of the Kohathites, *who were* of the children of Levi; for the lot was theirs first. ¹¹And they gave them Kirjath Arba (*Arba was* the father of Anak), which *is* Hebron, in the mountains of Judah, with the common-land surrounding it. ¹²But the fields of the city and its villages they gave to Caleb the son of Jephunneh as his possession.

¹³Thus to the children of Aaron the priest they gave Hebron with its common-land (a city of refuge for the slayer), Libnah with its common-land, ¹⁴Jattir with its common-land, Eshtemoa with its common-land, ¹⁵Holon with its common-land, Debir with its common-land, ¹⁶Ain with its common-land, Juttah with its common-land, and Beth Shemesh with its common-land: nine cities from those two tribes; ¹⁷and from the tribe of Benjamin, Gibeon with its common-land, Geba with its common-land, ¹⁸Anathoth with its common-land, and Almon with its common-land: four cities. ¹⁹All the cities of the children of Aaron, the priests, *were* thirteen cities with their common-lands.

²⁰And the families of the children of Kohath, the Levites, the rest of the children of Kohath, even they had the cities of their lot from the tribe of Ephraim. ²¹For they gave them Shechem with its common-land in the mountains of Ephraim (a city of refuge for the slayer), Gezer with its common-land, ²²Kibzaim with its common-land, and Beth Horon with its common-land: four cities; ²³and from the tribe of Dan, Eltekeh with its common-land, Gibbethon with its common-land, ²⁴Aijalon with its common-land, *and* Gath Rimmon with its common-land: four cities; ²⁵and from the half-tribe of Manasseh, Tanach with its common-land and Gath Rimmon with its common-land: two cities. ²⁶All the ten cities with their com-

mon-lands were for the rest of the families of the children of Kohath.

²⁷Also to the children of Gershon, of the families of the Levites, from the *other* half-tribe of Manasseh, *they gave* Golan in Bashan with its common-land (a city of refuge for the slayer), and Be Eshterah with its common-land: two cities; ²⁸and from the tribe of Issachar, Kishion with its common-land, Daberath with its common-land, ²⁹Jarmuth with its common-land, *and* En Gannim with its common-land: four cities; ³⁰and from the tribe of Asher, Mishal with its common-land, Abdon with its common-land, ³¹Helkath with its common-land, and Rehob with its common-land: four cities; ³²and from the tribe of Naphtali, Kedesh in Galilee with its common-land (a city of refuge for the slayer), Hammoth Dor with its common-land, and Kartan with its common-land: three cities. ³³All the cities of the Gershonites according to their families *were* thirteen cities with their common-lands.

◤ FINISH THE JOB

22:2-4 Before the conquest had begun, these tribes were given land on the east side of the Jordan River. But before they could settle down they first had to promise to help the other tribes conquer the land on the west side (Numbers 32:20-22). They had patiently and diligently carried out their promised duties. Joshua now commended them for doing just that. At last they are permitted to return to their families and build their cities. Follow-through is vital in God's work. Beware of the temptation to quit early and leave God's work undone.

³⁴And to the families of the children of Merari, the rest of the Levites, from the tribe of Zebulun, Jokneam with its common-land, Kartah with its common-land, ³⁵Dimnah with its common-land, *and* Nahalal with its common-land: four cities; ³⁶and from the tribe of Reuben, Bezer with its common-land, Jahaz with its common-land, ³⁷Kedemoth with its common-land, and Mephaath with its common-land: four cities; ³⁸and from the tribe of Gad, Ramoth in Gilead with its common-land (a city of refuge for the slayer), Mahanaim with its common-land, ³⁹Heshbon with its common-land, *and* Jazer with its common-land: four cities in all. ⁴⁰So all the cities for the children of Merari according to their families, the rest of the families of the Levites, were *by* their lot twelve cities.

⁴¹All the cities of the Levites within the possession of the children of Israel *were* forty-eight cities with their common-lands. ⁴²Every one of these cities had its common-land surrounding it; thus *were* all these cities.

⁴³So the LORD gave to Israel all the land of which He had sworn to give to their fathers, and they took possession of it and dwelt in it. ⁴⁴The LORD gave them rest all around, according to all that He had sworn to their fathers. And not a man of all their enemies stood against them; the LORD delivered all their enemies into their hand. ⁴⁵Not a word failed of any good thing which the LORD had spoken to the house of Israel. All came to pass.

CHAPTER **22** THE EASTERN TRIBES SETTLE DOWN. Then Joshua called the Reubenites, the Gadites, and half the tribe of Manasseh, ²and said to them: "You have kept all that Moses the servant of the LORD com-

◤ REACTIONS

22:11-34 When the tribes of Reuben and Gad and the half-tribe Manasseh built an altar at the Jordan River, the rest of Israel feared these tribes were starting their own religion and rebelling against Go But before beginning an all-out war, Phinehas led a delegation to le the truth. He was prepared to negotiate rather than fight if a battle not necessary. When he learned that the altar was for a memorial ra than for heathen sacrifice, war was averted and unity restored.

We would benefit from a similar approach to resolving conflicts. Assuming the worst about the intentions of others only brings troubl Israel averted the threat of civil war by asking before assaulting. Be of reacting before you hear the whole story.

manded you, and have obeyed my voice in all that I commanded you. ³You have not left your brethren these many days, up to this day, but have kept the charge of the commandment of the LORD your God. ⁴And now the LORD your God has given rest to your brethren, as He promised them; now therefore, return and go to your tents *and* to the land of your possession, which Moses the servant of the LORD gave you on the other side of the Jordan. ⁵But take careful heed to do the commandment and the law which Moses the servant of the LORD commanded you, to love the LORD your God, to walk in all His ways, to keep His commandments, to hold fast to Him, and to serve Him with all your heart and with all your soul." ⁶So Joshua blessed them and sent them away, and they went to their tents.

⁷Now to half the tribe of Manasseh Moses had given a possession in Bashan, but to the *other* half of it Joshua gave *a possession* among their brethren on this side of the Jordan, westward. And indeed, when Joshua sent them away to their tents, he blessed them, ⁸and spoke to them, saying, "Return with much riches to your tents, with very much livestock, with silver, with gold, with bronze, with iron, and with very much clothing. Divide the spoil of your enemies with your brethren."

⁹So the children of Reuben, the children of Gad, and half the tribe of Manasseh returned, and departed from the children of Israel at Shiloh, which *is* in the land of Canaan, to go to the country of Gilead, to the land of their possession, which they had obtained according to the word of the LORD by the hand of Moses.

¹⁰And when they came to the region of the Jordan which *is* in the land of Canaan, the children of Reuben, the children of Gad, and half the tribe of Manasseh built an altar there by the Jordan—a great, impressive altar. ¹¹Now the children of Israel heard *someone* say, "Behold, the children of Reuben, the children of Gad, and half the tribe of Manasseh have built an altar on the frontier of the lan of Canaan, in the region of the Jordan—on the children o Israel's side." ¹²And when the children of Israel heard *of i* the whole congregation of the children of Israel gathere together at Shiloh to go to war against them.

¹³Then the children of Israel sent Phinehas the son o Eleazar the priest to the children of Reuben, to the chil dren of Gad, and to half the tribe of Manasseh, into the land of Gilead, ¹⁴and with him ten rulers, one ruler eac from the chief house of every tribe of Israel; and each on *was* the head of the house of his father among the div sions of Israel. ¹⁵Then they came to the children of Reu ben, to the children of Gad, and to half the tribe o Manasseh, to the land of Gilead, and they spoke wi

hem, saying, ¹⁶"Thus says the whole congregation of the LORD: 'What treachery *is* this that you have committed against the God of Israel, to turn away this day from following the LORD, in that you have built for yourselves n altar, that you might rebel this day against the LORD? *Is* the iniquity of Peor not enough for us, from which we re not cleansed till this day, although there was a plague n the congregation of the LORD, ¹⁸but that you must turn way this day from following the LORD? And it shall be, if ou rebel today against the LORD, that tomorrow He will e angry with the whole congregation of Israel. ¹⁹Nevertheless, if the land of your possession *is* unclean, *then* ross over to the land of the possession of the LORD, vhere the LORD's tabernacle stands, and take possession mong us; but do not rebel against the LORD, nor rebel gainst us, by building yourselves an altar besides the ltar of the LORD our God.

'Did not Achan the son of Zerah commit a trespass n the accursed hing, and wrath fell n all the congregaion of Israel? And hat man did not erish alone in his niquity.' "

²¹Then the children of Reuben, the children of Gad, and half the tribe of Manasseh answered and aid to the heads of the divisions of Israel: ²²"The LORD God of gods, the LORD God f gods, He knows, and let srael itself know—if *it is* in ebellion, or if in treachery gainst the LORD, do not save us his day. ²³If we have built ourelves an altar to turn from folowing the LORD, or if to offer on it urnt offerings or grain offerings, r if to offer peace offerings on it, let he LORD Himself require *an account.* But in fact we have done it for fear, or a reason, saying, 'In time to come our descendants may speak to our decendants, saying, "What have you to do vith the LORD God of Israel? ²⁵For the LORD has made the Jordan a border beween you and us, *you* children of Reuben nd children of Gad. You have no part in the LORD." So your descendants would make ur descendants cease fearing the LORD.' Therefore we said, 'Let us now prepare to uild ourselves an altar, not for burnt offering or for sacrifice, ²⁷but *that* it *may be* a witness etween you and us and our generations after us, nat we may perform the service of the LORD beore Him with our burnt offerings, with our sacrices, and with our peace offerings; that your decendants may not say to our descendants in time

to come, "You have no part in the LORD." ' ²⁸Therefore we said that it will be, when they say *this* to us or to our generations in time to come, that we may say, 'Here is the replica of the altar of the LORD which our fathers made, though not for burnt offerings nor for sacrifices; but it *is* a witness between you and us.' ²⁹Far be it from us that we should rebel against the LORD, and turn from following the LORD this day, to build an altar for burnt offerings, for grain offerings, or for sacrifices, besides the altar of the LORD our God which *is* before His tabernacle."

³⁰Now when Phinehas the priest and the rulers of the congregation, the heads of the divisions of Israel who *were* with him, heard the words that the children of Reuben, the children of Gad, and the children of Manasseh spoke, it pleased them. ³¹Then Phinehas the son

JOSHUA

Being a good leader means more than being in charge. The best leaders are those who help others learn to lead. This is true for two reasons: (1) Sometimes the job is too big for one person to do alone, so leadership has to be shared; and (2) some jobs take so long that they don't get done unless the first leader trains others to take over after he's gone. Joshua helped Moses with the huge job of leading the people of Israel. At the same time he was being trained as the new leader.

Moses made an excellent decision when he chose Joshua as his assistant. Later, God told Moses that Joshua would be the leader after he was gone. Joshua was an important part of the Exodus story. He led the army and he was the only person allowed to go with Moses partway up the mountain when Moses received the Ten Commandments. When 12 men were sent as spies into the Promised Land, only Joshua and Caleb were willing to tell the people that God could help them conquer the land. Joshua was always with Moses, like a shadow. His "basic training" was living with Moses, learning by watching everything his leader did and said.

Who is your Moses? Who is your Joshua? You are part of the unbroken chain of God's work in the world. Are you watching the lives of those who love God, learning from them? Can those who are watching you see how important God is in your life? Ask God to lead you to a Moses worth following. Ask him also to make you a good Joshua.

LESSONS: Effective leadership is often the product of good preparation and encouragement The person after whom we pattern ourselves will have a definite effect on us A person committed to God provides the best model for us

KEY VERSE: "Moses did as the LORD commanded him. He took Joshua and set him before Eleazar the priest and before all the congregation. And he laid his hands on him and inaugurated him, just as the LORD commanded by the hand of Moses" (Numbers 27:22-23).

Joshua is also mentioned in Exodus 17:24,32-33; Numbers 11:28; 13-14; 26:65; 27:18-22; 32:12,28; 34:17; Deuteronomy 1:38; 3:21,28; 31:3,14,23; 34:9; Joshua; Judges 2; 1 Kings 16:34; and Hebrews 4:8.

UPS:
- Moses' assistant and successor
- One of only two adults who experienced Egyptian slavery and lived to enter the Promised Land
- Led the Israelites into their God-given homeland
- Brilliant military strategist
- Faithful to ask God's direction in the challenges he faced

DOWNS:
- He was unable to complete the task of possessing all the land

STATS:
- Where: Joshua lived in Egypt, the Wilderness of Sinai, and Canaan (the Promised Land)
- Occupation: Special assistant to Moses; warrior, leader
- Relatives: Father: Nun
- Contemporaries: Moses, Caleb, Miriam, Aaron

23:12-16 This chilling prediction about the consequences of intermarriage with the Canaanite nations eventually became a reality. Numerous stories in the book of Judges show what Israel had to suffer because of failure to follow God wholeheartedly. God was supremely loving and patient with Israel, just as he is today with us. But we must not confuse his patience with approval. Beware of demanding your own way, because eventually you may get it—along with all its painful consequences.

of Eleazar the priest said to the children of Reuben, the children of Gad, and the children of Manasseh, "This day we perceive that the LORD *is* among us, because you have not committed this treachery against the LORD. Now you have delivered the children of Israel out of the hand of the LORD."

³²And Phinehas the son of Eleazar the priest, and the rulers, returned from the children of Reuben and the children of Gad, from the land of Gilead to the land of Canaan, to the children of Israel, and brought back word to them. ³³So the thing pleased the children of Israel, and the children of Israel blessed God; they spoke no more of going against them in battle, to destroy the land where the children of Reuben and Gad dwelt.

³⁴The children of Reuben and the children of Gad called the altar, *Witness*, "For *it is* a witness between us that the LORD *is* God."

CHAPTER 23 JOSHUA'S FINAL ORDERS. Now it came to pass, a long time after the LORD had given rest to Israel from all their enemies round about, that Joshua was old, advanced in age. ²And Joshua called for all Israel, for their elders, for their heads, for their judges, and for their officers, and said to them:

"I am old, advanced in age. ³You have seen all that the LORD your God has done to all these nations because of you, for the LORD your God *is* He who has fought for you. ⁴See, I have divided to you by lot these nations that remain, to be an inheritance for your tribes, from the Jordan, with all the nations that I have cut off, as far as the Great Sea westward. ⁵And the LORD your God will expel them from before you and drive them out of your sight. So you shall possess their land, as the LORD your God promised you. ⁶Therefore be very courageous to keep and to do all that is written in the Book of the Law of Moses, lest you turn aside from it to the right hand or to the left, ⁷ *and* lest you go among these nations, these who remain among you. You shall not make mention of the name of their gods, nor cause *anyone* to swear *by them;* you shall not serve them nor bow down to them, ⁸but you shall hold fast to the LORD your God, as you have done to this day. ⁹For the LORD has driven out from before you great and strong nations; but *as for* you, no one has been able to stand against you to this day. ¹⁰One man of you shall chase a thousand, for the LORD your God *is* He who fights for you, as He promised you. ¹¹Therefore take careful heed to yourselves, that you love the LORD your God. ¹²Or else, if indeed you do go back, and cling to the remnant of these nations—these that remain among you—and make marriages with them, and go in to them and they to you, ¹³know for certain that the LORD your God will no longer drive out these nations from before

you. But they shall be snares and traps to you, and scourges on your sides and thorns in your eyes, until you perish from this good land which the LORD your God has given you.

¹⁴"Behold, this day I *am* going the way of all the earth. And you know in all your hearts and in all your souls that not one thing has failed of all the good things which the LORD your God spoke concerning you. All have come to pass for you; not one word of them has failed. ¹⁵Therefore it shall come to pass, that as all the good things have come upon you which the LORD your God promised you, so the LORD will bring upon you all harmful things, until He has destroyed you from this good land which the LORD your God has given you. ¹⁶When you have transgressed the covenant of the LORD your God, which He commanded you, and have gone and served other gods, and bowed down to them, then the anger of the LORD will burn against you, and you shall perish quickly from the good land which He has given you."

CHAPTER 24 JOSHUA'S GOOD-BYE SPEECH. Then Joshua gathered all the tribes of Israel to Shechem and called for the elders of Israel, for their heads, for their judges, and for their officers; and they presented themselves before God. ²And Joshua said to all the people, "Thus says the LORD God of Israel: 'Your fathers, *including* Terah, the father of Abraham and the father of Nahor, dwelt on the other side of the River in old times; and they served other gods. ³Then I took your father Abraham from the other side of the River, led him throughout all the land of Canaan, and multiplied his descendants and gave him Isaac. ⁴To Isaac I gave Jacob and Esau. To Esau I gave the mountains of Seir to possess, but Jacob and his children went down to Egypt. ⁵Also I sent Moses and Aaron, and I plagued Egypt, according to what I did among them. Afterward I brought you out.

⁶"Then I brought your fathers out of Egypt, and you came to the sea; and the Egyptians pursued your fathers with chariots and horsemen to the Red Sea. ⁷So they cried out to the LORD; and He put darkness between you and the Egyptians, brought the sea upon them, and covered them. And your eyes saw what I did in Egypt. Then you dwelt in the wilderness a long time. ⁸And I brought you into the land of the Amorites, who dwelt on the other side of the Jordan, and they fought with you. But I gave them into your hand, that you might possess their land, and I destroyed them from before you. ⁹Then Balak the son of Zippor, king of Moab, arose to make war against Israel, and sent and called Balaam the son of Beor to curse you. ¹⁰But I would not listen to Balaam; therefore he continued to bless you. So I delivered you out of h

▬▬▬▬▬►YOUR CHOICE

24:15 The people had to decide whether they would obey the who had proven his trustworthiness, or obey the local gods, whi only man-made idols. It's easy to slip into a quiet rebellion—gc life in your own way. But the time comes when you have to cho or what will control you. The choice is yours. Will it be God, or y limited personality, or another imperfect substitute? Once you h chosen to be controlled by God's Spirit, reaffirm your choice eve

them, saying, [16]"Thus says the whole congregation of the LORD: 'What treachery *is* this that you have committed against the God of Israel, to turn away this day from following the LORD, in that you have built for yourselves an altar, that you might rebel this day against the LORD? [17]*Is* the iniquity of Peor not enough for us, from which we are not cleansed till this day, although there was a plague in the congregation of the LORD, [18]but that you must turn away this day from following the LORD? And it shall be, if you rebel today against the LORD, that tomorrow He will be angry with the whole congregation of Israel. [19]Nevertheless, if the land of your possession *is* unclean, *then* cross over to the land of the possession of the LORD, where the LORD's tabernacle stands, and take possession among us; but do not rebel against the LORD, nor rebel against us, by building yourselves an altar besides the altar of the LORD our God.

[20]Did not Achan the son of Zerah commit a trespass in the accursed thing, and wrath fell on all the congregation of Israel? And that man did not perish alone in his iniquity.' "

[21]Then the children of Reuben, the children of Gad, and half the tribe of Manasseh answered and said to the heads of the divisions of Israel: [22]"The LORD God of gods, the LORD God of gods, He knows, and let Israel itself know—if *it is* in rebellion, or if in treachery against the LORD, do not save us this day, [23]If we have built ourselves an altar to turn from following the LORD, or if to offer on it burnt offerings or grain offerings, or if to offer peace offerings on it, let the LORD Himself require *an account.* [24]But in fact we have done it for fear, for a reason, saying, 'In time to come your descendants may speak to our descendants, saying, "What have you to do with the LORD God of Israel? [25]For the LORD has made the Jordan a border between you and us, *you* children of Reuben and children of Gad. You have no part in the LORD." So your descendants would make our descendants cease fearing the LORD.' [26]Therefore we said, 'Let us now prepare to build ourselves an altar, not for burnt offering nor for sacrifice, [27]but that *it may be* a witness between you and us and our generations after us, that we may perform the service of the LORD before Him with our burnt offerings, with our sacrifices, and with our peace offerings; that your descendants may not say to our descendants in time

to come, "You have no part in the LORD." ' [28]Therefore we said that it will be, when they say *this* to us or to our generations in time to come, that we may say, 'Here is the replica of the altar of the LORD which our fathers made, though not for burnt offerings nor for sacrifices; but it *is* a witness between you and us.' [29]Far be it from us that we should rebel against the LORD, and turn from following the LORD this day, to build an altar for burnt offerings, for grain offerings, or for sacrifices, besides the altar of the LORD our God which *is* before His tabernacle."

[30]Now when Phinehas the priest and the rulers of the congregation, the heads of the divisions of Israel who *were* with him, heard the words that the children of Reuben, the children of Gad, and the children of Manasseh spoke, it pleased them. [31]Then Phinehas the son

JOSHUA

Being a good leader means more than being in charge. The best leaders are those who help others learn to lead. This is true for two reasons: (1) Sometimes the job is too big for one person to do alone, so leadership has to be shared; and (2) some jobs take so long that they don't get done unless the first leader trains others to take over after he's gone. Joshua helped Moses with the huge job of leading the people of Israel. At the same time he was being trained as the new leader.

Moses made an excellent decision when he chose Joshua as his assistant. Later, God told Moses that Joshua would be the leader after he was gone. Joshua was an important part of the Exodus story. He led the army and he was the only person allowed to go with Moses partway up the mountain when Moses received the Ten Commandments. When 12 men were sent as spies into the Promised Land, only Joshua and Caleb were willing to tell the people that God could help them conquer the land. Joshua was always with Moses, like a shadow. His "basic training" was living with Moses, learning by watching everything his leader did and said.

Who is your Moses? Who is your Joshua? You are part of the unbroken chain of God's work in the world. Are you watching the lives of those who love God, learning from them? Can those who are watching you see how important God is in your life? Ask God to lead you to a Moses worth following. Ask him also to make you a good Joshua.

LESSONS: Effective leadership is often the product of good preparation and encouragement

The person after whom we pattern ourselves will have a definite effect on us

A person committed to God provides the best model for us

KEY VERSE: "Moses did as the LORD commanded him. He took Joshua and set him before Eleazar the priest and before all the congregation. And he laid his hands on him and inaugurated him, just as the LORD commanded by the hand of Moses" (Numbers 27:22-23).

Joshua is also mentioned in Exodus 17;24;32–33; Numbers 11:28; 13–14; 26:65; 27:18-22; 32:12,28; 34:17; Deuteronomy 1:38; 3:21,28; 31:3,14,23; 34:9; Joshua; Judges 2; 1 Kings 16:34; and Hebrews 4:8.

UPS:
- Moses' assistant and successor
- One of only two adults who experienced Egyptian slavery and lived to enter the Promised Land
- Led the Israelites into their God-given homeland
- Brilliant military strategist
- Faithful to ask God's direction in the challenges he faced

DOWNS:
- He was unable to complete the task of possessing all the land

STATS:
- Where: Joshua lived in Egypt, the Wilderness of Sinai, and Canaan (the Promised Land)
- Occupation: Special assistant to Moses; warrior, leader
- Relatives: Father: Nun
- Contemporaries: Moses, Caleb, Miriam, Aaron

hand. [11]Then you went over the Jordan and came to Jericho. And the men of Jericho fought against you—*also* the Amorites, the Perizzites, the Canaanites, the Hittites, the Girgashites, the Hivites, and the Jebusites. But I delivered them into your hand. [12]I sent the hornet before you which drove them out from before you, *also* the two kings of the Amorites, *but* not with your sword or with your bow. [13]I have given you a land for which you did not labor, and cities which you did not build, and you dwell in them; you eat of the vineyards and olive groves which you did not plant.'

[14]"Now therefore, fear the LORD, serve Him in sincerity and in truth, and put away the gods which your fathers served on the other side of the River and in Egypt. Serve the LORD! [15]And if it seems evil to you to serve the LORD, choose for yourselves this day whom you will serve, whether the gods which your fathers served that *were* on the other side of the River, or the gods of the Amorites, in whose land you dwell. But as for me and my house, we will serve the LORD."

[16]So the people answered and said: "Far be it from us that we should forsake the LORD to serve other gods; [17]for the LORD our God *is* He who brought us and our fathers up out of the land of Egypt, from the house of bondage, who did those great signs in our sight, and preserved us in all the way that we went and among all the people through whom we passed. [18]And the LORD drove out from before us all the people, including the Amorites who dwelt in the land. We also will serve the LORD, for He *is* our God."

[19]But Joshua said to the people, "You cannot serve the LORD, for He *is* a holy God. He *is* a jealous God; He will not forgive your transgressions nor your sins. [20]If you forsake the LORD and serve foreign gods, then He will turn and do you harm and consume you, after He has done you good."

[21]And the people said to Joshua, "No, but we will serve the LORD!"

[22]So Joshua said to the people, "You *are* witnesses against yourselves that you have chosen the LORD for yourselves, to serve Him."

And they said, "*We are* witnesses!"

[23]"Now therefore," *he said*, "put away the foreign gods which *are* among you, and incline your heart to the LORD God of Israel."

[24]And the people said to Joshua, "The LORD our God we will serve, and His voice we will obey!"

[25]So Joshua made a covenant with the people that day, and made for them a statute and an ordinance in Shechem.

[26]Then Joshua wrote these words in the Book of the Law of God. And he took a large stone, and set it up there under the oak that *was* by the sanctuary of the LORD. [27]And Joshua said to all the people, "Behold, this stone shall be a witness to us, for it has heard all the words of the LORD which He spoke to us. It shall therefore be a witness to you, lest you deny your God." [28]So Joshua let the people depart, each to his own inheritance.

[29]Now it came to pass after these things that Joshua the son of Nun, the servant of the LORD, died, *being* one hundred and ten years old. [30]And they buried him within the border of his inheritance at Timnath Serah, which *is* in the mountains of Ephraim, on the north side of Mount Gaash.

[31]Israel served the LORD all the days of Joshua, and all the days of the elders who outlived Joshua, who had known all the works of the LORD which He had done for Israel.

[32]The bones of Joseph, which the children of Israel had brought up out of Egypt, they buried at Shechem, in the plot of ground which Jacob had bought from the sons of Hamor the father of Shechem for one hundred pieces of silver, and which had become an inheritance of the children of Joseph.

[33]And Eleazar the son of Aaron died. They buried him in a hill *belonging to* Phinehas his son, which was given to him in the mountains of Ephraim.

If Christ controls my life, where does my freedom of choice fit in?

One way that God demonstrated his love for us was by giving us the freedom of choice.

Someone once said, "There is a door to your heart that can only be opened from the inside."

You make the choice to open the door of your heart to Jesus Christ when you receive him as Savior and Lord. Although his Spirit is at work prompting you to respond to his love, the choice is yours.

Picture your life like a house. Jesus Christ knocks on the front door and you decide to let him in (Revelation 3:20). Where do you invite him next? Some Christians live their whole life with Christ still standing in the entryway! Obviously this is not a very good way to treat an invited guest.

During your entire life as a Christian, you use your God-given freedom of choice to invite him into the rest of your house (your life) or to leave him at the front door.

Although your life is much more complicated than a house, let's take the illustration one step further.

In your house you probably have rooms that need repair. The living room, for example, could represent your relationships at home. How does the room look? When problems occur in this room the solution is to ask the Master Carpenter, Jesus, for some renovation. Through his Word, other people, and the prodding of the Holy Spirit, God gently tells us how to make things right.

This passage in Joshua (24:14-15) tells of his challenge to the nation of Israel: "Put away the gods which your fathers served on the other side of the River and in Egypt. Serve the LORD!" The Israelites were faced with a choice of who they were going to serve. On this day, they chose to serve the living God instead of idols made by human hands.

Every day you will be faced with the choice of serving God or something else. God loves you too much to take that choice away from you.

He has given to you the privilege of having him come into every area of your life.

I WONDER . . .

MEGA *Themes*

SUCCESS God gave success to the Israelites when they obeyed his master plan, not when they followed their own desires. Victory came when they trusted in him rather than in their military power, money, muscle, or mental capacity.

God's work done in God's way will bring success. The standard for success, however, is not to be set by the society around us but by God's Word. We must adjust our mind to God's way of thinking in order to see his standard for success.

1. Think of an adult whom your parent(s) view as successful. What is it about that person that makes him or her a success in your parent's mind?
2. What type of people are considered successful in your school?
3. Based upon the majority of commercials you see on television or in magazines, what is the media's image of a successful person?
4. What seems to be God's definition of success for Joshua? (See chapter 1.)
5. In what ways was Joshua a success according to God's point of view? What qualities in Joshua's life most contributed to this success?
6. Write a list of what you think God wants for your life in terms of being successful. What can you do to develop some of the qualities that Joshua had so that you will indeed become successful?

FAITH The Israelites demonstrated their faith by trusting God daily to save and guide them. By noticing how God fulfilled his promises in the past, they developed strong confidence that he would be faithful in the future.

Our strength to do God's work comes from trusting him. His promises reassure us of his love. We can be confident that God will be there to guide us in the decisions and struggles we face.

1. What factors helped the Israelites' faith grow?
2. What is happening in your life now that is contributing to the growth of your faith?
3. What else needs to happen to help your faith grow? What does God want you to do to increase your faith?

GUIDANCE God gave instructions to Israel for every aspect of their lives. His law guided their daily living and his specific marching orders gave them victory in battle.

Guidance from God for daily living can be found in his Word. By staying in touch with God, we will have the wisdom needed to meet life's great challenges.

1. Describe a time in your life when you felt you needed God's guidance. (It may be right now!)
2. How did you seek God's guidance during that time? What were the results?
3. What makes it difficult at times for us to know God's will for specific areas of our lives?
4. The more you know of God, the more you will know of his will. What resources has God given you for knowing more about him and his will for you?
5. At times, all Christians need God's guidance. How can you specifically prepare for those times before they occur? What can you do to seek God's guidance when they do occur?

LEADERSHIP Joshua was an example of an excellent leader. He was confident in God's strength, courageous in the face of opposition, and willing to seek God's advice.

To be a strong leader like Joshua, we must be ready to listen and to move quickly when God speaks. Once we have his instructions, we must carry them out. Strong leaders are characterized by their commitment to follow God first.

1. What were Joshua's strengths as a leader?
2. What types of challenges did Joshua face as a leader of the people?
3. All Christians have opportunities to be leaders for Christ. You do not have to hold an office or title in order to be a leader. What type of challenges are facing you as you try to lead friends closer to Christ in your church? School? Neighborhood?
4. What are your strengths as God's leader? What qualities do you need to develop as you are becoming an adult so that, like Joshua, you will spend your life leading others closer to God?

CONQUEST God commanded his people to conquer the Canaanites and take all their land. Completing this mission would have fulfilled God's promise to Abraham and brought judgment on the evil people living there. Unfortunately, Israel never finished the job.

Israel was faithful in accomplishing the mission at first, but their commitment faltered. To love God means more than being enthusiastic about him. Discipleship is more than "spiritual highs." We must complete all the work he gives us and apply his instructions to every part of our lives.

1. What was the difference in the lives of the Israelites when they were being successful and victorious as opposed to when they failed?
2. What can you learn from the Israelites' examples of success and failure?
3. Christians should look at a life of faith as a long-term process in which the goal is to finish stronger than we were when we began. Based on this study of Joshua and the Israelites' entry into the Promised Land, how can you insure yourself of victory over the obstacles that lie ahead in your life?

*S*uperman, Batman, Wonder Woman, Spiderman. Superheroes. The world longs for them. Always arriving in the nick of time to ward off evil, beat up bad guys, prevent corruption, and promote truth and justice and goodness. Unfortunately, there are no superheroes. And, eventually, every human being will let us down. ■ The book of Judges is about heroes—12 men and women God used to deliver Israel from its enemies. No way were they superheroes. Some didn't want the job. One was even a murderer. But God used them to rescue Israel. ■ Judges also talks about the horrible results of sin, but also about God's mercy. The people of Israel had become evil. Judges describes them this way: "In those days *there was* no king in Israel; everyone did *what was* right in his own eyes" (17:6). They intermarried with wicked people and worshiped strange gods. When the stench of their actions became unbearable to God, he would raise up a neighboring nation to conquer them. Then the people would repent and turn back to God . . . and he would send a "judge" to rescue them. ■ Let the book of Judges remind you that God uses normal people to do his work; let it remind you of the effects of sin; and let it remind you that, above all, God is merciful to sinful children when they ask for forgiveness.

STATS

PURPOSE: To show that God's judgment against sin is certain, and his forgiveness of sin and restoration of fellowship is just as certain for those who repent

AUTHOR: Probably Samuel

SETTING: The land of Canaan, later called Israel. God had helped the Israelites conquer Canaan, which had been inhabited by a host of wicked nations. But they were in danger of losing this Promised Land because they compromised their convictions and disobeyed God

KEY PEOPLE: Othniel, Ehud, Deborah, Gideon, Abimelech, Jephthah, Samson, Delilah

SPECIAL FEATURE: Records Israel's first civil war

pursued him and caught him and cut off his thumbs and big toes. [7]And Adoni-Bezek said, "Seventy kings with their thumbs and big toes cut off used to gather *scraps* under my table; as I have done, so God has repaid me." Then they brought him to Jerusalem, and there he died.

[8]Now the children of Judah fought against Jerusalem and took it; they struck it with the edge of the sword and set the city on fire. [9]And afterward the children of Judah went down to fight against the Canaanites who dwelt in

COEXISTENCE

1:1 The Canaanites were all the people who lived in Canaan (the Promised Land). They lived in city-states where each city had its own government, army, and laws. One reason Canaan was so difficult to conquer was that each city had to be defeated individually. There was no single king who could surrender the entire country into the hands of the Israelites.

However, Canaan's greatest threat to Israel was not its military, but its religion. Canaanite religion idealized evil traits: cruelty in war, sexual immorality, selfish greed, and materialism. It was a "me first, anything goes" society. Obviously, the religions of Israel and Canaan could not coexist.

the mountains, in the South, and in the lowland. [10]Then Judah went against the Canaanites who dwelt in Hebron. (Now the name of Hebron *was* formerly Kirjath Arba.) And they killed Sheshai, Ahiman, and Talmai.

[11]From there they went against the inhabitants of Debir. (The name of Debir *was* formerly Kirjath Sepher.)

[12]Then Caleb said, "Whoever attacks Kirjath Sepher and takes it, to him I will give my daughter Achsah as wife." [13]And Othniel the son of Kenaz, Caleb's younger brother, took it; so he gave him his daughter Achsah as wife. [14]Now it happened, when she came *to him,* that she urged him to ask her father for a field. And she dismounted from *her* donkey, and Caleb said to her, "What do you wish?" [15]So she said to him, "Give me a blessing; since you have given me land in the South, give me also springs of water."

And Caleb gave her the upper springs and the lower springs.

[16]Now the children of the Kenite, Moses' father-in-law, went up from the City of Palms with the children of Judah into the Wilderness of Judah, which *lies* in the South *near* Arad; and they went and dwelt among the people. [17]And Judah went with his brother Simeon, and they attacked the Canaanites who inhabited Zephath, and utterly de-

CHAPTER 1 **GOD GIVES VICTORY.** Now after the death of Joshua it came to pass that the children of Israel asked the LORD, saying, "Who shall be first to go up for us against the Canaanites to fight against them?"

[2]And the LORD said, "Judah shall go up. Indeed I have delivered the land into his hand."

[3]So Judah said to Simeon his brother, "Come up with me to my allotted territory, that we may fight against the Canaanites; and I will likewise go with you to your allotted territory." And Simeon went with him. [4]Then Judah went up, and the LORD delivered the Canaanites and the Perizzites into their hand; and they killed ten thousand men at Bezek. [5]And they found Adoni-Bezek in Bezek, and fought against him; and they defeated the Canaanites and the Perizzites. [6]Then Adoni-Bezek fled, and they

KEY PLACES IN **JUDGES**

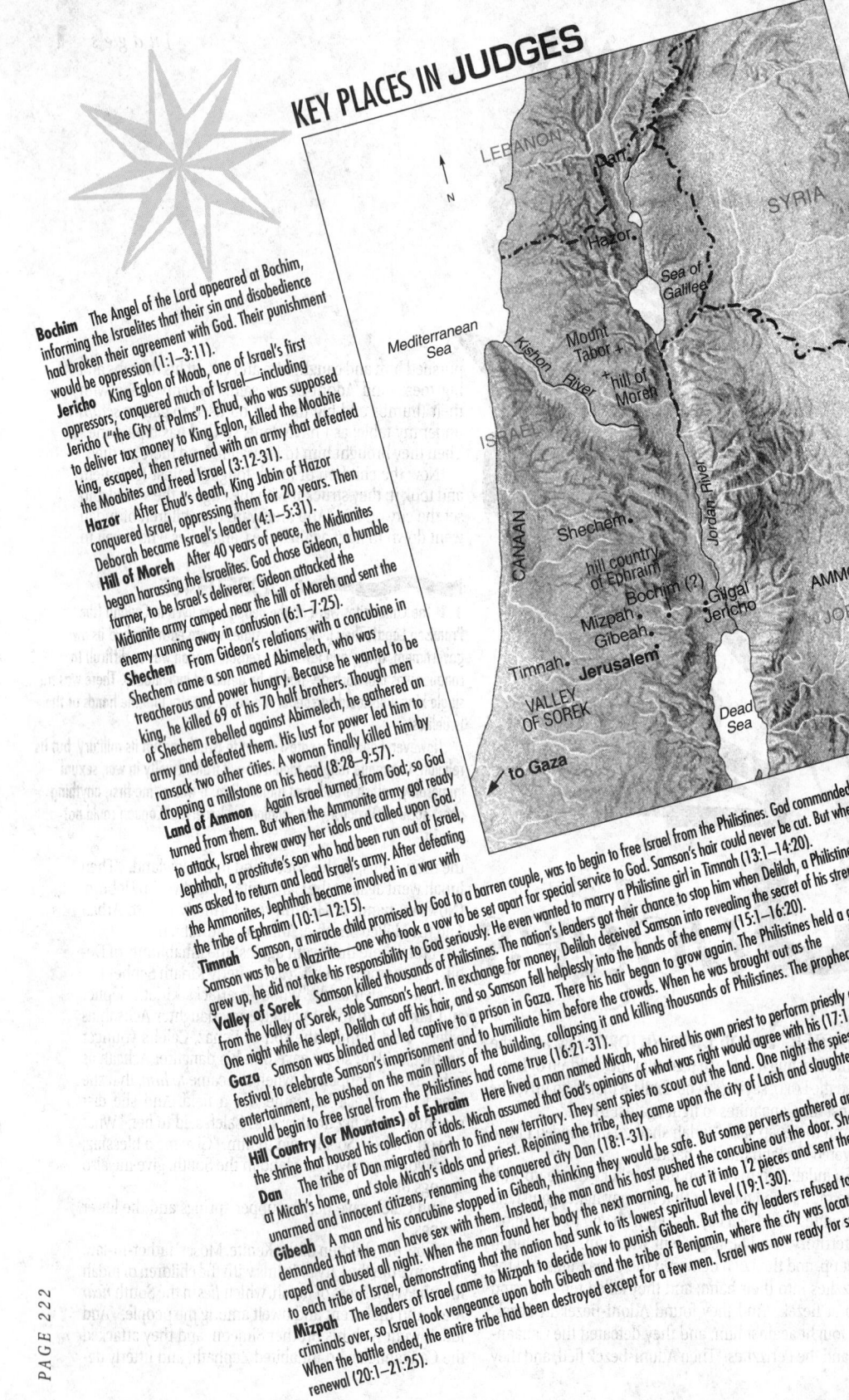

Bochim The Angel of the Lord appeared at Bochim, informing the Israelites that their sin and disobedience had broken their agreement with God. Their punishment would be oppression (1:1–3:11).

Jericho King Eglon of Moab, one of Israel's first oppressors, conquered much of Israel—including Jericho ("the City of Palms"). Ehud, who was supposed to deliver tax money to King Eglon, killed the Moabite king, escaped, then returned with an army that defeated the Moabites and freed Israel (3:12-31).

Hazor After Ehud's death, King Jabin of Hazor conquered Israel, oppressing them for 20 years. Then Deborah became Israel's leader (4:1–5:31).

Hill of Moreh After 40 years of peace, the Midianites began harassing the Israelites. God chose Gideon, a humble farmer, to be Israel's deliverer. Gideon attacked the Midianite army camped near the hill of Moreh and sent the enemy running away in confusion (6:1–7:25).

Shechem From Gideon's relations with a concubine in Shechem came a son named Abimelech, who was treacherous and power hungry. Because he wanted to be king, he killed 69 of his 70 half brothers. Though men of Shechem rebelled against Abimelech, he gathered an army and defeated them. His lust for power led him to ransack two other cities. A woman finally killed him by dropping a millstone on his head (8:28–9:57).

Land of Ammon Again Israel turned from God; so God turned from them. But when the Ammonite army got ready to attack, Israel threw away her idols and called upon God. Jephthah, a prostitute's son who had been run out of Israel, was asked to return and lead Israel's army. After defeating the Ammonites, Jephthah became involved in a war with the tribe of Ephraim (10:1–12:15).

Timnah Samson, a miracle child promised by God to a barren couple, was to begin to free Israel from the Philistines. God commanded Samson was to be a Nazirite—one who took a vow to be set apart for special service to God. Samson's hair could never be cut. But when he grew up, he did not take his responsibility to God seriously. He even wanted to marry a Philistine girl in Timnah (13:1–14:20).

Valley of Sorek Samson stole Samson's heart. In exchange for money, Delilah deceived Samson into revealing the secret of his stren... from the Valley of Sorek, Delilah cut off his hair, and so Samson fell helplessly into the hands of the enemy (15:1–16:20). One night while he slept, Delilah cut off his hair, and so Samson fell helplessly into the hands of the enemy. The Philistines held a g...

Gaza Samson was blinded and led captive to a prison in Gaza. There his hair began to grow again. The Philistines held a g... entertainment, he pushed on the main pillars of the building, collapsing it and killing thousands of Philistines. The prophecy... would begin to free Israel from the Philistines had come true (16:21-31).

Hill Country (or Mountains) of Ephraim Here lived a man named Micah, who hired his own priest to perform priestly d... the shrine that housed his collection of idols. Micah assumed that God's opinions of what was right would agree with his (17:1–...

Dan The tribe of Dan migrated north to find new territory. They sent spies to scout out the land. One night the spies... at Micah's home, and stole Micah's idols and priest. Rejoining the tribe, they came upon the city of Laish and slaughter... unarmed and innocent citizens, renaming the conquered city Dan (18:1-31).

Gibeah A man and his concubine stopped in Gibeah, thinking they would be safe. But some perverts gathered an... demanded that the man have sex with them. Instead, the man and his host pushed the concubine out the door. She... raped and abused all night. When the man found her body the next morning, he cut it into 12 pieces and sent the... to each tribe of Israel, demonstrating that the nation had sunk to its lowest spiritual level (19:1-30).

Mizpah The leaders of Israel came to Mizpah to decide how to punish Gibeah and the tribe of Benjamin, where the city was locate... criminals over, so Israel took vengeance upon both Gibeah and the tribe of Benjamin. The city leaders refused to... When the battle ended, the entire tribe had been destroyed except for a few men. Israel was now ready for sp... renewal (20:1–21:25).

troyed it. So the name of the city was called Hormah. ³Also Judah took Gaza with its territory, Ashkelon with its territory, and Ekron with its territory. ¹⁹So the LORD was with Judah. And they drove out the mountaineers, but they could not drive out the inhabitants of the lowland, because they had chariots of iron. ²⁰And they gave Hebron to Caleb, as Moses had said. Then he expelled from there the three sons of Anak. ²¹But the children of Benjamin did not drive out the Jebusites who inhabited Jerusalem; so the Jebusites dwell with the children of Benjamin in Jerusalem to this day.

²²And the house of Joseph also went up against Bethel, and the LORD *was* with them. ²³So the house of Joseph sent men to spy out Bethel. (The name of the city *was* formerly Luz.) ²⁴And when the spies saw a man coming out of the city, they said to him, "Please show us the entrance to the city, and we will show you mercy." ²⁵So he showed them the entrance to the city, and they struck the city with the edge of the sword; but they let the man and all his family go. ²⁶And the man went to the land of the Hittites, built a city, and called its name Luz, which *is* its name to this day.

²⁷However, Manasseh did not drive out *the inhabitants of* Beth Shean and its villages, or Taanach and its villages, or the inhabitants of Dor and its villages, or the inhabitants of Ibleam and its villages, or the inhabitants of Megiddo and its villages; for the Canaanites were determined to dwell in that land. ²⁸And it came to pass, when Israel was strong, that they put the Canaanites under tribute, but did not completely drive them out.

²⁹Nor did Ephraim drive out the Canaanites who dwelt in Gezer; so the Canaanites dwelt in Gezer among them.

³⁰Nor did Zebulun drive out the inhabitants of Kitron or the inhabitants of Nahalol; so the Canaanites dwelt among them, and were put under tribute.

³¹Nor did Asher drive out the inhabitants of Acco or the inhabitants of Sidon, or of Ahlab, Achzib, Helbah, Aphik, or Rehob. ³²So the Asherites dwelt among the Canaanites, the inhabitants of the land; for they did not drive them out.

³³Nor did Naphtali drive out the inhabitants of Beth Shemesh or the inhabitants of Beth Anath; but they dwelt among the Canaanites, the inhabitants of the land. Nevertheless the inhabitants of Beth Shemesh and Beth Anath were put under tribute to them.

³⁴And the Amorites forced the children of Dan into the mountains, for they would not allow them to come down to the valley; ³⁵and the Amorites were determined to dwell in Mount Heres, in Aijalon, and in Shaalbim; yet when the strength of the house of Joseph became greater, they were put under tribute.

³⁶Now the boundary of the Amorites *was* from the ascent of Akrabbim, from Sela, and upward.

CHAPTER **2** **COVENANT IS BROKEN.** Then the Angel of the LORD came up from Gilgal to Bochim, and said: "I led you up from Egypt and brought you to the land of which I swore to your fathers; and I said, 'I will never break My covenant with you. ²And you shall make no covenant with the inhabitants of this land; you shall tear

down their altars.' But you have not obeyed My voice. Why have you done this? ³Therefore I also said, 'I will not drive them out before you; but they shall be *thorns* in your side, and their gods shall be a snare to you.' " ⁴So it was, when the Angel of the LORD spoke these words to all the children of Israel, that the people lifted up their voices and wept.

PERSEVERE

1:21ff Why didn't God's people follow through and completely obey his command to destroy the evil Canaanites? (1) They had been fighting for a long time and were tired. (2) They were afraid the enemy was too strong. (3) Since Joshua's death, the tribes were no longer unified in purpose. (4) They thought they could handle the temptation and be more prosperous by doing business with the Canaanites. We, too, often fail to drive sin from our life. Often we know what to do but just don't follow through. This results in a gradual deterioration of our relationship with God. In our battles, we may grow tired and want rest, but we need to remember that victory comes only from obeying God and living according to his purpose.

⁵Then they called the name of that place Bochim; and they sacrificed there to the LORD. ⁶And when Joshua had dismissed the people, the children of Israel went each to his own inheritance to possess the land.

⁷So the people served the LORD all the days of Joshua, and all the days of the elders who outlived Joshua, who had seen all the great works of the LORD which He had done for Israel. ⁸Now Joshua the son of Nun, the servant of the LORD, died *when he was* one hundred and ten years old. ⁹And they buried him within the border of his inheritance at Timnath Heres, in the mountains of Ephraim, on the north side of Mount Gaash. ¹⁰When all that generation had been gathered to their fathers, another generation arose after them who did not know the LORD nor the work which He had done for Israel.

¹¹Then the children of Israel did evil in the sight of the LORD, and served the Baals; ¹²and they forsook the LORD God of their fathers, who had brought them out of the land of Egypt; and they followed other gods from *among* the gods of the people who *were* all around them, and they bowed down to them; and they provoked the LORD to anger. ¹³They forsook the LORD and served Baal and the Ashtoreths. ¹⁴And the anger of the LORD was hot against Israel. So He delivered them into the hands of plunderers who despoiled them; and He sold them into the hands of their enemies all around, so that they could no longer stand before their enemies. ¹⁵Wherever they went out, the hand of the LORD was against them for calamity, as the LORD had said, and as the LORD had sworn to them. And they were greatly distressed.

¹⁶Nevertheless, the LORD raised up judges who delivered them out of the hand of those who plundered them.

PEER PRESSURE

2:11-15 This generation of Israelites abandoned the faith of their parents and began worshiping the gods of their neighbors. Many things can tempt us to abandon what we know is right. The desire to be accepted by others can lead us into behavior that is unacceptable to God. Don't be pressured into disobedience.

WHY THE JEWS?

As you read the Old Testament, you may wonder, "Why the Jews? Why did God single them out for such favoritism?" That's a good question, and one that's not necessarily easy to answer. Hopefully, this will help you get some kind of handle on it. **First**, for reasons that are not entirely clear, God had singled out a man named Abram from the ancient city of Ur and promised to bless him and his descendants (Genesis 12:1-3). As the chapters following that account reveal, there was a condition attached: Abram had to obey God faithfully. Even though he had numerous lapses, Abram did remain faithful to his word, making Abram's descendants into the nation of home to a new land, Canaan. And God was true to his word, making Abram's descendants into the nation of Israel. This, then, is the primary reason God favored the Jews: He was keeping a promise made to his servant, Abram (who later became Abraham).

Second, God was setting the stage for his Son, the Messiah, to be ushered into the world many centuries later. Because God chose to have his Son born of a woman, he needed to provide an appropriate backdrop for the woman and her ancestry. This backdrop was the people of Israel, the descendants of Abraham. Guiding them throughout their history, God made sure that the scene was right for Mary, a virgin engaged to be married, to be available to be the mother of the child Jesus. At the right time, when God was ready to enter human space and time, he brought Mary and Joseph, descendants of Abraham, together to the stable in Bethlehem. His Son would be born a Jew. **Third**, it has been suggested that if God wanted to find an appropriate display case for his mercy and patient love, he could find no better one than the people of Israel—stubborn, rebellious, unfaithful—just like many believers today. As you continue reading the Old Testament, you will be impressed by God's protection and compassion for his people—and how quickly they forgot him time after time. No one would have blamed God for giving up on them and starting over with a new nation. But God kept his word to Abraham and never abandoned Abraham's descendants. He punished them, rebuked them, sent them into exile—but he never forgot them or his prom Many people today see the existence of the Jews as a powerful argument for the existence of God. In spi overwhelming opposition throughout history, they are still here, while most of their enemies (at least from Testament times) are long gone. How else could they have survived, except for the protection of a powe loving God who refused to give up on them? **In** the final analysis, we must remember that God does pleases. His reasons do not always make sense to us. While we cannot know with certainty why he ch make the Jews his special people, we know that he did. Now, all those who follow Christ are membe chosen nation. They don't become Jews, but they become God's covenant people—Christ's church. continue to read the unfolding drama we call the Old Testament, watch for ways God shows his lov people, and thank God for his kindness to them—and to you.

Yet they would not listen to their judges, but they played the harlot with other gods, and bowed down to them. They turned quickly from the way in which their fathers walked, in obeying the commandments of the LORD; they did not do so. ¹⁸And when the LORD raised up judges for them, the LORD was with the judge and delivered them out of the hand of their enemies all the days of the judge; for the LORD was moved to pity by their groaning because of those who oppressed them and harassed them. ¹⁹And it came to pass, when the judge was dead, that they reverted and behaved more corruptly than their fathers, by following other gods, to serve them and bow down to them. They did not cease from their own doings nor from their stubborn way.

²⁰Then the anger of the LORD was hot against Israel; and He said, "Because this nation has transgressed My covenant which I commanded their fathers, and has not heeded My voice, ²¹I also will no longer drive out before them any of the nations which Joshua left when he died, so that through them I may test Israel, whether they will keep the ways of the LORD, to walk in them as their fathers kept *them*, or not." ²³Therefore the LORD left those nations, without driving them out immediately; nor did He deliver them into the hand of Joshua.

CHAPTER 3 CANAANITES LEFT IN THE LAND. Now these *are* the nations which the LORD left, that He might test Israel by them, *that is*, all who had not known any of the wars in Canaan ²(*this was* only so that the generations of the children of Israel might be taught to know war, at least those who had not formerly known it), *namely*, five lords of the Philistines, all the Canaanites, the Sidonians, and the Hivites who dwelt in Mount Lebanon, from Mount Baal Hermon to the entrance of Hamath. ⁴And they were *left, that He might* test Israel by them, to know whether they would obey the commandments of the LORD, which He had commanded their fathers by the hand of Moses.

⁵Thus the children of Israel dwelt among the Canaanites, the Hittites, the Amorites, the Perizzites, the Hivites, and the Jebusites. ⁶And they took their daughters to be their wives, and gave their daughters to their sons; and they served their gods.

⁷So the children of Israel did evil in the sight of the LORD. They forgot the LORD their God, and served the Baals and Asherahs. ⁸Therefore the anger of the LORD was hot against Israel, and He sold them into the hand of Cushan-Rishathaim king of Mesopotamia; and the children of Israel served Cushan-Rishathaim eight years. ⁹When the children of Israel cried out to the LORD, the LORD raised up a deliverer for the children of Israel, who delivered them: Othniel the son of Kenaz, Caleb's younger brother. ¹⁰The Spirit of the LORD came upon him, and he judged Israel. He went out to war, and the LORD delivered Cushan-Rishathaim king of Mesopotamia into his hand; and his hand prevailed over Cushan-Rishathaim. So the land had rest for forty years. Then Othniel the son of Kenaz died.

¹²And the children of Israel again did evil in the sight of the LORD. So the LORD strengthened Eglon king of Moab against Israel, because they had done evil in the sight of the LORD. ¹³Then he gathered to himself the people of Ammon and Amalek, went and defeated Israel, and took possession of the City of Palms. ¹⁴So the children of Israel served Eglon king of Moab eighteen years.

¹⁵But when the children of Israel cried out to the LORD, the LORD raised up a deliverer for them: Ehud the son of Gera, the Benjamite, a left-handed man. By him the children of Israel sent tribute to Eglon king of Moab. ¹⁶Now Ehud made himself a dagger (it was double-edged and a cubit in length) and fastened it under his clothes on his right thigh. ¹⁷So he brought the tribute to Eglon king of Moab. (Now Eglon *was* a very fat man.) ¹⁸And when he had finished presenting the tribute, he sent away the people who had carried the tribute. ¹⁹But he himself turned back from the stone images that *were* at Gilgal, and said, "I have a secret message for you, O king."

He said, "Keep silence!" And all who attended him went out from him.

²⁰So Ehud came to him (now he was sitting upstairs in his cool private chamber). Then Ehud said, "I have a message from God for you." So he arose from *his* seat. ²¹Then Ehud reached with his left hand, took the dagger from his right thigh, and thrust it into his belly. ²²Even the hilt went in after the blade, and the fat closed over the blade, for he did not draw the dagger out of his belly; and his entrails came out. ²³Then Ehud went out through the porch and shut the doors of the upper room behind him and locked them.

²⁴When he had gone out, *Eglon's* servants came to look, and to *their* surprise, the doors of the upper room were locked. So they said, "He is probably attending to his needs in the cool chamber." ²⁵So they waited till they were embarrassed, and still he had not opened the doors of the upper room. Therefore they took the key and opened *them*. And there was their master, fallen dead on the floor.

²⁶But Ehud had escaped while they delayed, and passed beyond the stone images and escaped to Seirah. ²⁷And it happened, when he arrived, that he blew the trumpet in the mountains of Ephraim, and the children of Israel went down with him from the mountains; and he led them. ²⁸Then he said to them, "Follow *me*, for the LORD has delivered your enemies the Moabites into your hand." So they went down after him, seized the fords of the Jordan leading to Moab, and did not allow anyone to cross over. ²⁹And at that time they killed about ten thousand men of Moab, all stout men of valor; not a man escaped. ³⁰So Moab was subdued that day under the hand of Israel. And the land had rest for eighty years.

³¹After him was Shamgar the son of Anath, who killed six hundred men of the Philistines with an ox goad; and he also delivered Israel.

CHAPTER 4 DEBORAH AND BARAK. When Ehud was dead, the children of Israel again did evil in the sight of the LORD. ²So the LORD sold them into the hand of Jabin king of Canaan, who reigned in Hazor. The commander of his army *was* Sisera, who dwelt in Harosheth Hagoyim.

4:1 Israel's sin was also against the Lord. Our sins harm both ourselves and others, but all sin is ultimately against God because it disregards his commands and his authority over our lives. When confessing his sin, David prayed, "Against You, You only, have I sinned, and done *this* evil in Your sight" (Psalm 51:4). Recognizing the seriousness of sin is the first step toward removing it from our lives.

³And the children of Israel cried out to the LORD; for Jabin had nine hundred chariots of iron, and for twenty years he had harshly oppressed the children of Israel.

⁴Now Deborah, a prophetess, the wife of Lapidoth, was judging Israel at that time. ⁵And she would sit under the palm tree of Deborah between Ramah and Bethel in the mountains of Ephraim. And the children of Israel came up to her for judgment. ⁶Then she sent and called for Barak the son of Abinoam from Kedesh in Naphtali, and said to him, "Has not the LORD God of Israel commanded, 'Go and deploy *troops* at Mount Tabor; take with you ten thousand men of the sons of Naphtali and of the sons of Zebulun; ⁷and against you I will deploy Sisera, the commander of Jabin's army, with his chariots and his

multitude at the River Kishon; and I will deliver him into your hand'?"

⁸And Barak said to her, "If you will go with me, then I will go; but if you will not go with me, I will not go!"

⁹So she said, "I will surely go with you; nevertheless there will be no glory for you in the journey you are taking, for the LORD will sell Sisera into the hand of a woman." Then Deborah arose and went with Barak to Kedesh. ¹⁰And Barak called Zebulun and Naphtali to Kedesh; he went up with ten thousand men under his command, and Deborah went up with him.

A TRUE LEADER

4:9 How did Deborah command such respect? She was responsible leading the people into battle. But more than that, she influenced live for God after the battle was over. Her personality drew people together and commanded the respect of even Barak, a military g She was also a prophetess, whose main role was to encourage the to obey God. Those who lead must not forget about the spiritual of those being led. A true leader is concerned for people, not just

THE JUDGES OF ISRAEL

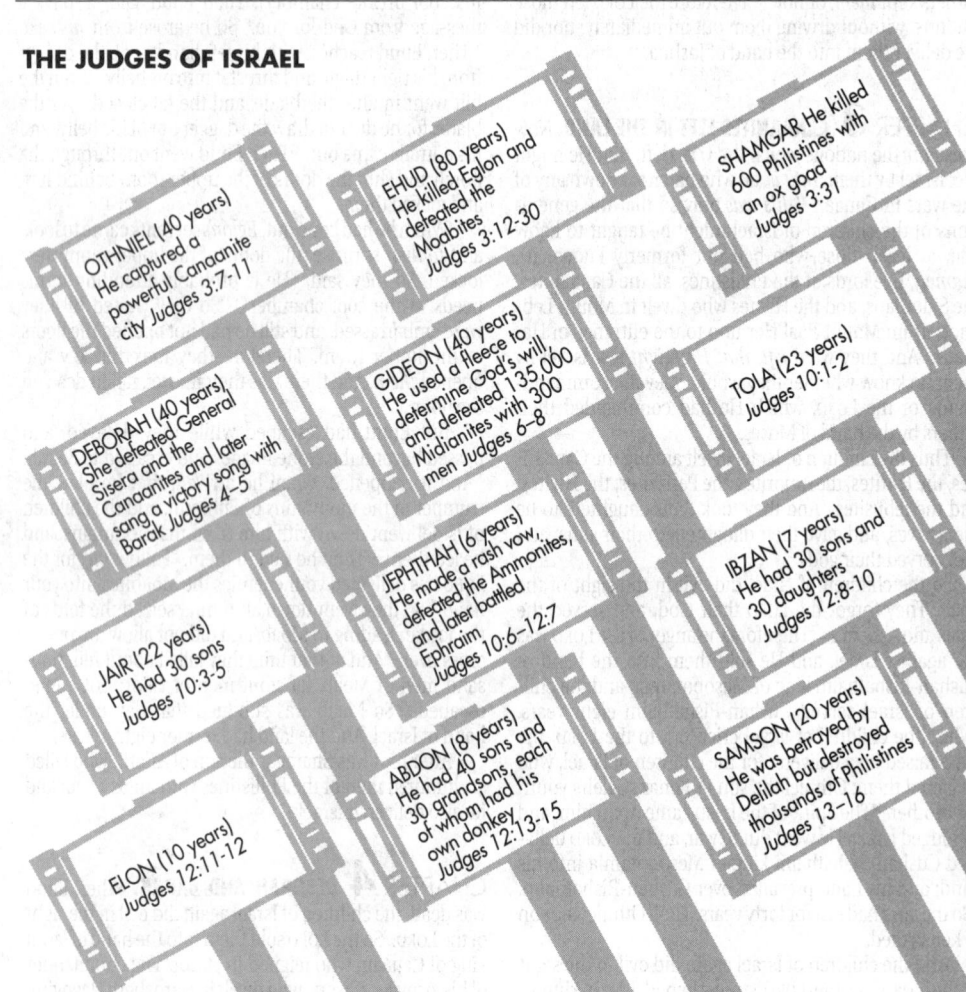

OTHNIEL (40 years)
He captured a powerful Canaanite city Judges 3:7-11

EHUD (80 years)
He killed Eglon and defeated the Moabites
Judges 3:12-30

SHAMGAR He killed 600 Philistines with an ox goad
Judges 3:31

DEBORAH (40 years)
She defeated General Sisera and the Canaanites and later sang a victory song with Barak Judges 4-5

GIDEON (40 years)
He used a fleece to determine God's will and defeated 135,000 Midianites with 300 men Judges 6-8

TOLA (23 years)
Judges 10:1-2

JAIR (22 years)
He had 30 sons
Judges 10:3-5

JEPHTHAH (6 years)
He made a rash vow, defeated the Ammonites, and later battled Ephraim
Judges 10:6-12:7

IBZAN (7 years)
He had 30 sons and 30 daughters
Judges 12:8-10

ELON (10 years)
Judges 12:11-12

ABDON (8 years)
He had 40 sons and 30 grandsons each of whom had his own donkey
Judges 12:13-15

SAMSON (20 years)
He was betrayed by Delilah but destroyed thousands of Philistines
Judges 13-16

¹¹Now Heber the Kenite, of the children of Hobab the father-in-law of Moses, had separated himself from the Kenites and pitched his tent near the terebinth tree at Zaanaim, which *is* beside Kedesh.

¹²And they reported to Sisera that Barak the son of Abinoam had gone up to Mount Tabor. ¹³So Sisera gathered together all his chariots, nine hundred chariots of iron, and all the people who *were* with him, from Harosheth Hagoyim to the River Kishon.

¹⁴Then Deborah said to Barak, "Up! For this *is* the day in which the LORD has delivered Sisera into your hand. Has not the LORD gone out before you?" So Barak went down from Mount Tabor with ten thousand men following him. ¹⁵And the LORD routed Sisera and all *his* chariots and all *his* army with the edge of the sword before Barak; and Sisera alighted from *his* chariot and fled away on foot. ¹⁶But Barak pursued the chariots and the army as far as Harosheth Hagoyim, and all the army of Sisera fell by the edge of the sword; not a man was left.

¹⁷However, Sisera had fled away on foot to the tent of Jael, the wife of Heber the Kenite; for *there was* peace between Jabin king of Hazor and the house of Heber the Kenite. ¹⁸And Jael went out to meet Sisera, and said to him, "Turn aside, my lord, turn aside to me; do not fear." And when he had turned aside with her into the tent, she covered him with a blanket.

¹⁹Then he said to her, "Please give me a little water to drink, for I am thirsty." So she opened a jug of milk, gave him a drink, and covered him. ²⁰And he said to her, "Stand at the door of the tent, and if any man comes and inquires of you, and says, 'Is there any man here?' you shall say, 'No.' "

²¹Then Jael, Heber's wife, took a tent peg and took a hammer in her hand, and went softly to him and drove the peg into his temple, and it went down into the ground; for he was fast asleep and weary. So he died. ²²And then, as Barak pursued Sisera, Jael came out to meet him, and said to him, "Come, I will show you the man whom you seek." And when he went into her *tent*, there lay Sisera, dead with the peg in his temple.

²³So on that day God subdued Jabin king of Canaan in the presence of the children of Israel. ²⁴And the hand of the children of Israel grew stronger and stronger against Jabin king of Canaan, until they had destroyed Jabin king of Canaan.

CHAPTER 5 **DEBORAH AND BARAK'S SONG.** Then Deborah and Barak the son of Abinoam sang on that day, saying:

² "When leaders lead in Israel,
When the people willingly offer themselves,
Bless the LORD!

³ "Hear, O kings! Give ear, O princes!
I, *even* I, will sing to the LORD;
I will sing praise to the LORD God of Israel.

⁴ "LORD, when You went out from Seir,
When You marched from the field of Edom,
The earth trembled and the heavens poured,
The clouds also poured water;

⁵ The mountains gushed before the LORD,
This Sinai, before the LORD God of Israel.

⁶ "In the days of Shamgar, son of Anath,
In the days of Jael,
The highways were deserted,
And the travelers walked along the byways.

⁷ Village life ceased, it ceased in Israel,
Until I, Deborah, arose,
Arose a mother in Israel.

SONGS

5:1ff In victory, Barak and Deborah sang praises to God. Songs of praise focus our attention on God, give us an outlet for spiritual celebration, and remind us of God's faithfulness and character. Whether you are in the middle of a great victory or a difficult problem, singing praises to God can have a positive effect on your attitude.

⁸ They chose new gods;
Then *there was* war in the gates;
Not a shield or spear was seen among forty
thousand in Israel.

⁹ My heart *is* with the rulers of Israel
Who offered themselves willingly with the people.
Bless the LORD!

¹⁰ "Speak, you who ride on white donkeys,
Who sit in judges' attire,
And who walk along the road.

¹¹ Far from the noise of the archers, among the
watering places,
There they shall recount the righteous acts of the
LORD,
The righteous acts *for* His villagers in Israel;
Then the people of the LORD shall go down to the
gates.

¹² "Awake, awake, Deborah!
Awake, awake, sing a song!
Arise, Barak, and lead your captives away,
O son of Abinoam!

¹³ "Then the survivors came down, the people against
the nobles;
The LORD came down for me against the mighty.

¹⁴ From Ephraim *were* those whose roots were in
Amalek.
After you, Benjamin, with your peoples,
From Machir rulers came down,
And from Zebulun those who bear the recruiter's
staff.

¹⁵ And the princes of Issachar *were* with Deborah;
As Issachar, so *was* Barak
Sent into the valley under his command;
Among the divisions of Reuben
There were great resolves of heart.

¹⁶ Why did you sit among the sheepfolds,
To hear the pipings for the flocks?
The divisions of Reuben have great searchings of
heart.

¹⁷ Gilead stayed beyond the Jordan,
And why did Dan remain on ships?

LAME EXCUSES

6:14-16 God promised to give Gideon the strength he needed to overcome the opposition. In spite of this clear promise for strength, Gideon made excuses. He saw only his limitations and weaknesses. He failed to see how God could work through him.

Like Gideon, we are called to serve God in specific ways. Although God promises us the tools and strength we need, we often make excuses, too. Reminding God of our limitations only implies that he does not know all about us or that he has made a mistake in evaluating our character. Don't spend time making excuses. Instead spend it doing what God wants.

> Asher continued at the seashore,
> And stayed by his inlets.
> 18 Zebulun *is* a people *who* jeopardized their lives to
>   the point of death,
> Naphtali also, on the heights of the battlefield.
>
> 19 "The kings came *and* fought,
> Then the kings of Canaan fought
> In Taanach, by the waters of Megiddo;
> They took no spoils of silver.
> 20 They fought from the heavens;
> The stars from their courses fought against Sisera.
> 21 The torrent of Kishon swept them away,
> That ancient torrent, the torrent of Kishon.
> O my soul, march on in strength!
> 22 Then the horses' hooves pounded,
> The galloping, galloping of his steeds.
> 23 'Curse Meroz,' said the angel of the LORD,
> 'Curse its inhabitants bitterly,
> Because they did not come to the help of the LORD,
> To the help of the LORD against the mighty.'
>
> 24 "Most blessed among women is Jael,
> The wife of Heber the Kenite;
> Blessed is she among women in tents.
> 25 He asked for water, she gave milk;
> She brought out cream in a lordly bowl.
> 26 She stretched her hand to the tent peg,
> Her right hand to the workmen's hammer;
> She pounded Sisera, she pierced his head,
> She split and struck through his temple.
> 27 At her feet he sank, he fell, he lay still;
> At her feet he sank, he fell;
> Where he sank, there he fell dead.
>
> 28 "The mother of Sisera looked through the window,
> And cried out through the lattice,
> 'Why is his chariot *so* long in coming?
> Why tarries the clatter of his chariots?'
> 29 Her wisest ladies answered her,
> Yes, she answered herself,
> 30 'Are they not finding and dividing the spoil:
> To every man a girl *or* two;
> For Sisera, plunder of dyed garments,
> Plunder of garments embroidered and dyed,
> Two pieces of dyed embroidery for the neck of the
>   looter?'
>
> 31 "Thus let all Your enemies perish, O LORD!
> But *let* those who love Him *be* like the sun
> When it comes out in full strength."

So the land had rest for forty years.

CHAPTER 6 GOD CALLS GIDEON TO LEAD ISRAEL

Then the children of Israel did evil in the sight of the LORD. So the LORD delivered them into the hand of Midian for seven years, ²and the hand of Midian prevailed against Israel. Because of the Midianites, the children of Israel made for themselves the dens, the caves, and the strongholds which *are* in the mountains. ³So it was, whenever Israel had sown, Midianites would come up; also Amalekites and the people of the East would come up against them. ⁴Then they would encamp against them and destroy the produce of the earth as far as Gaza, and leave no sustenance for Israel, neither sheep nor ox nor donkey. ⁵For they would come up with their livestock and their tents, coming in as numerous as locusts; both they and their camels were without number; and they would enter the land to destroy it. ⁶So Israel was greatly impoverished because of the Midianites, and the children of Israel cried out to the LORD.

⁷And it came to pass, when the children of Israel cried out to the LORD because of the Midianites, ⁸that the LORD sent a prophet to the children of Israel, who said to them, "Thus says the LORD God of Israel: 'I brought you up from Egypt and brought you out of the house of bondage; ⁹and I delivered you out of the hand of the Egyptians and out of the hand of all who oppressed you, and drove them out before you and gave you their land. ¹⁰Also I said to you, *I am* the LORD your God; do not fear the gods of the Amorites, in whose land you dwell." But you have not obeyed My voice.'"

¹¹Now the Angel of the LORD came and sat under the terebinth tree which *was* in Ophrah, which *belonged* to Joash the Abiezrite, while his son Gideon threshed wheat in the winepress, in order to hide *it* from the Midianites. ¹²And the Angel of the LORD appeared to him, and said to him, "The LORD *is* with you, you mighty man of valor!"

¹³Gideon said to Him, "O my lord, if the LORD is with us, why then has all this happened to us? And where *are* all His miracles which our fathers told us about, saying, 'Did not the LORD bring us up from Egypt?' But now the LORD has forsaken us and delivered us into the hands of the Midianites."

¹⁴Then the LORD turned to him and said, "Go in this might of yours, and you shall save Israel from the hand of the Midianites. Have I not sent you?"

GET GOING

6:37 Was Gideon really testing God or was he simply asking God for more encouragement? In either case, though his motive was right (obey God and defeat the enemy), his method was less than ideal. It seems to have known that his requests might displease God (6:39), yet he demanded two miracles (6:37,39) even after witnessing miraculous fire from the rock (6:21). It is true that to make good decisions we need facts. Gideon had all the facts, but still he hesitated, delayed his obedience because he wanted even more proof.

Demanding extra signs was an indication of Gideon's unbelief. God often makes us wait for more confirmation when we should be taking action. Visible signs are unnecessary if they only confirm what we know to be true. Today the greatest means of God's guidance is his Word. Unlike Gideon, we have God's complete, revealed Word. If you want to have more of God's guidance, don't ask for signs; study God's Word (2 Timothy 3:16-17).

¹⁵So he said to Him, "O my Lord, how can I save Israel? Indeed my clan *is* the weakest in Manasseh, and I *am* the least in my father's house."

¹⁶And the LORD said to him, "Surely I will be with you, and you shall defeat the Midianites as one man."

¹⁷Then he said to Him, "If now I have found favor in Your sight, then show me a sign that it is You who talk with me. ¹⁸Do not depart from here, I pray, until I come to You and bring out my offering and set *it* before You."

And He said, "I will wait until you come back."

¹⁹So Gideon went in and prepared a young goat, and unleavened bread from an ephah of flour. The meat he put in a basket, and he put the broth in a pot; and he brought *them* out to Him under the terebinth tree and presented *them*. ²⁰The Angel of God said to him, "Take the meat and the unleavened bread and lay *them* on this rock, and pour out the broth." And he did so.

²¹Then the Angel of the LORD put out the end of the staff that *was* in His hand, and touched the meat and the unleavened bread; and fire rose out of the rock and consumed the meat and the unleavened bread. And the Angel of the LORD departed out of his sight.

²²Now Gideon perceived that He *was* the Angel of the LORD. So Gideon said, "Alas, O Lord GOD! For I have seen the Angel of the LORD face to face."

²³Then the LORD said to him, "Peace *be* with you; do not fear, you shall not die." ²⁴So Gideon built an altar there to the LORD, and called it The-LORD-Is-Peace. To this day it *is* still in Ophrah of the Abiezrites.

²⁵Now it came to pass the same night that the LORD said to him, "Take your father's young bull, the second bull of seven years old, and tear down the altar of Baal that your father has, and cut down the wooden image that *is* beside it; ²⁶and build an altar to the LORD your God on top of this rock in the proper arrangement, and take the second bull and offer a burnt sacrifice with the wood of the image which you shall cut down." ²⁷So Gideon took ten men from among his servants and did as the LORD had said to him. But because he feared his father's household and the men of the city too much to do *it* by day, he did *it* by night.

²⁸And when the men of the city arose early in the morning, there was the altar of Baal, torn down; and the wooden image that *was* beside it was cut down, and the second bull was being offered on the altar *which had been* built. ²⁹So they said to one another, "Who has done this thing?" And when they had inquired and asked, they said, "Gideon the son of Joash has done this thing." ³⁰Then the men of the city said to Joash, "Bring out your son, that he may die, because he has torn down the altar of Baal, and because he has cut down the wooden image that *was* beside it."

³¹But Joash said to all who stood against him, "Would you plead for Baal? Would you

GIDEON

UPS:
- Israel's fifth judge
- A military strategist who was expert at surprise
- A member of the Hall of Faith in Hebrews
- Defeated the Midianite army
- Was offered the title of king by the men of Israel
- Though slow to be convinced, acted on his convictions

DOWNS:
- Feared that his own limitations would prevent God from working
- Collected Midianite gold and made a symbol which became an object of worship
- Through a sexual relationship outside marriage, fathered a son who would bring great grief and tragedy to both Gideon's family and the nation of Israel
- Failed to establish the nation in God's ways; after he died they all went back to idol worship

STATS:
- Where: Ophrah, Valley of Jezreel, well of Harod
- Occupation: Farmer, warrior, and judge
- Relatives: Father: Joash. Son: Abimelech.
- Contemporaries: King Zebah, King Zalmunna

Most of us want to know God's plan for our lives, but we're not always sure how to find it. It is easy to think that God's guidance is something hidden and that we might miss it if we are not watching. But if we're always looking around for God's next assignment, we will probably not do a very good job on what he has us doing now. If all you think about is tomorrow's test, you may miss the answers that are given in today's class. Fortunately, the Bible gives us and shows us a better way to understand God's guidance. In the Bible's descriptions of how God guided people, we can see that God usually showed them what he wanted next while they were completely involved in obeying him right where they were. A good example of this kind of guidance is seen in Gideon's life.

Times were hard. Gideon's job was to get food for his family. The Midianite invaders were determined to stop him. He was busy doing his duty when God's messenger arrived. If God's messenger showed up in your life today, would he find you doing what you are supposed to be doing? Gideon was surprised by God's orders. He found out God wanted to use him to help defeat the Midianites— but he had a few doubts. He still felt responsible for his family. He wasn't sure this was really God's command or if he was the right person for the task. Sometimes we ask questions about God's Word because we want to be sure. But sometimes we ask questions because we really don't want to obey. God was patient with Gideon's questions and doubts because he knew Gideon wanted to obey. Gideon made mistakes, but he was still God's servant. You can be sure that God will guide you as long as your desire is to serve and obey him wherever you are.

LESSONS: God expands and uses the abilities he has already built into us

God uses us in spite of our limitations and failures

Even those who make great spiritual progress can easily fall into sin if they don't consistently follow God

KEY VERSES: "So [Gideon] said to Him, 'O my Lord, how can I save Israel? Indeed my clan *is* the weakest in Manasseh, and I *am* the least in my father's house.' And the LORD said to him, 'Surely I will be with you, and you shall defeat the Midianites as one man.'" (Judges 6:15-16).

His story is told in Judges 6–8. He is also mentioned in Hebrews 11:32.

save him? Let the one who would plead for him be put to death by morning! If he *is* a god, let him plead for himself, because his altar has been torn down!" ³²Therefore on that day he called him Jerubbaal, saying, "Let Baal plead against him, because he has torn down his altar."

³³Then all the Midianites and Amalekites, the people of the East, gathered together; and they crossed over and encamped in the Valley of Jezreel. ³⁴But the Spirit of the LORD came upon Gideon; then he blew the trumpet, and the Abiezrites gathered behind him. ³⁵And he sent messengers throughout all Manasseh, who also gathered behind him. He also sent messengers to Asher, Zebulun, and Naphtali; and they came up to meet them.

³⁶So Gideon said to God, "If You will save Israel by my hand as You have said— ³⁷look, I shall put a fleece of wool on the threshing floor; if there is dew on the fleece only, and *it is* dry on all the ground, then I shall know that You will save Israel by my hand, as You have said." ³⁸And it was so. When he rose early the next morning and squeezed the fleece together, he wrung the dew out of the fleece, a bowlful of water. ³⁹Then Gideon said to God, "Do not be angry with me, but let me speak just once more: Let me test, I pray, just once more with the fleece; let it now be dry only on the fleece, but on all the ground let there be dew." ⁴⁰And God did so that night. It was dry on the fleece only, but there was dew on all the ground.

CHAPTER 7 GIDEON'S ARMY OF 300. Then

Jerubbaal (that *is*, Gideon) and all the people who *were* with him rose early and encamped beside the well of Harod, so that the camp of the Midianites was on the north side of them by the hill of Moreh in the valley.

²And the LORD said to Gideon, "The people who *are* with you *are* too many for Me to give the Midianites into their hands, lest Israel claim glory for itself against Me, saying, 'My own hand has saved me.' ³Now therefore, proclaim in the hearing of the people, saying, 'Whoever *is* fearful and afraid, let him turn and depart at once from Mount Gilead.'" And twenty-two thousand of the people returned, and ten thousand remained.

⁴But the LORD said to Gideon, "The people *are* still *too* many; bring them down to the water, and I will test them for you there. Then it will be, *that* of whom I say to you, 'This one shall go with you,' the same shall go with you; and of whomever I say to you, 'This one shall not go with you,' the same shall not go." ⁵So he brought the people down to the water. And the LORD said to Gideon, "Everyone who laps from the water with his tongue, as a dog laps, you shall set apart by himself; likewise everyone who gets down on his knees to drink." ⁶And the number of those who lapped, *putting* their hand to their mouth, was three hundred men; but all the rest of the people got down on their knees to drink water. ⁷Then the LORD said to Gideon, "By the three hundred men who lapped I will save you, and deliver the Midianites into your hand. Let all the *other* people go, every man to his place." ⁸So the people took provisions and their trumpets in their hands. And he sent away all *the rest of* Israel, every man to his tent, and retained those three hundred men. Now the camp of Midian was below him in the valley.

WORSHIP

7:15 Gideon stood just outside the enemy camp and worshiped motions, and loud praise would have announced his presence to enemy, so Gideon's worship must have been a silent attitude of j thanksgiving, and praise to God. Worship is not limited to a parti form or building. We can worship anywhere by changing our foc life's struggles to the God who cares. True worship begins with a worshipful attitude.

⁹It happened on the same night that the LORD said him, "Arise, go down against the camp, for I have deliv ered it into your hand. ¹⁰But if you are afraid to go dow go down to the camp with Purah your servant, ¹¹and yo shall hear what they say; and afterward your hands sha be strengthened to go down against the camp." Then h went down with Purah his servant to the outpost of th armed men who *were* in the camp. ¹²Now the Midianite and Amalekites, all the people of the East, were lying the valley as numerous as locusts; and their camels we without number, as the sand by the seashore in mult tude.

¹³And when Gideon had come, there was a man tellin a dream to his companion. He said, "I have had a drean *To my* surprise, a loaf of barley bread tumbled into th camp of Midian; it came to a tent and struck it so that fell and overturned, and the tent collapsed."

¹⁴Then his companion answered and said, "This nothing else but the sword of Gideon the son of Joash, man of Israel! Into his hand God has delivered Midia and the whole camp."

¹⁵And so it was, when Gideon heard the telling of th dream and its interpretation, that he worshiped. He r turned to the camp of Israel, and said, "Arise, for the LO has delivered the camp of Midian into your hand ¹⁶Then he divided the three hundred men *into* thre companies, and he put a trumpet into every man's han with empty pitchers, and torches inside the pitche ¹⁷And he said to them, "Look at me and do likewis watch, and when I come to the edge of the camp yo shall do as I do: ¹⁸When I blow the trumpet, I and all wh *are* with me, then you also blow the trumpets on ever side of the whole camp, and say, '*The sword of* the LOF and of Gideon!'"

¹⁹So Gideon and the hundred men who *were* with hi came to the outpost of the camp at the beginning of th middle watch, just as they had posted the watch; ar they blew the trumpets and broke the pitchers that *we* in their hands. ²⁰Then the three companies blew th trumpets and broke the pitchers—they held the torch in their left hands and the trumpets in their right han for blowing—and they cried, "The sword of the LORD an of Gideon!" ²¹And every man stood in his place all arour the camp; and the whole army ran and cried out and fle ²²When the three hundred blew the trumpets, the LO set every man's sword against his companion throughou the whole camp; and the army fled to Beth Acacia, t ward Zererah, as far as the border of Abel Meholah, Tabbath.

²³And the men of Israel gathered together from Nap tali, Asher, and all Manasseh, and pursued the Midia ites.

²⁴Then Gideon sent messengers throughout all the mountains of Ephraim, saying, "Come down against the Midianites, and seize from them the watering places as far as Beth Barah and the Jordan." Then all the men of Ephraim gathered together and seized the watering places as far as Beth Barah and the Jordan. ²⁵And they captured two princes of the Midianites, Oreb and Zeeb. They killed Oreb at the rock of Oreb, and Zeeb they killed at the winepress of Zeeb. They pursued Midian and brought the heads of Oreb and Zeeb to Gideon on the other side of the Jordan.

CHAPTER 8 GIDEON'S WISE ANSWER.

Now the men of Ephraim said to him, "Why have you done this to us by not calling us when you went to fight with the Midianites?" And they reprimanded him sharply.

²So he said to them, "What have I done now in comparison with you? *Is* not the gleaning *of the grapes* of Ephraim better than the vintage of Abiezer? ³God has delivered into your hands the princes of Midian, Oreb and Zeeb. And what was I able to do in comparison with you?" Then their anger toward him subsided when he said that.

⁴When Gideon came to the Jordan, he and the three hundred men who *were* with him crossed over, exhausted but still in pursuit. ⁵Then he said to the men of Succoth, "Please give loaves of bread to the people who follow me, for they are exhausted, and I am pursuing Zebah and Zalmunna, kings of Midian."

⁶And the leaders of Succoth said, "*Are* the hands of Zebah and Zalmunna now in your hand, that we should give bread to your army?"

⁷So Gideon said, "For this cause, when the LORD has delivered Zebah and Zalmunna into my hand, then I will tear your flesh with the thorns of the wilderness and with briers!" ⁸Then he went up from there to Penuel and spoke to them in the same way. And the men of Penuel answered him as the men of Succoth had answered. ⁹So he also spoke to the men of Penuel, saying, "When I come back in peace, I will tear down this tower!"

¹⁰Now Zebah and Zalmunna *were* at Karkor, and their armies with them, about fifteen thousand, all who were left of all the army of the people of the East; for one hundred and twenty thousand men who drew the sword had fallen. ¹¹Then Gideon went up by the road of those who dwell in tents on the east of Nobah and Jogbehah; and he attacked the army while the camp felt secure. ¹²When Zebah and Zalmunna fled, he pursued them; and he took the two kings of Midian, Zebah and Zalmunna, and routed the whole army.

¹³Then Gideon the son of Joash returned from battle, from the Ascent of Heres. ¹⁴And he caught a young man of the men of Succoth and interrogated him; and he wrote down for him the leaders of Succoth and its elders, seventy-seven men. ¹⁵Then he came to the men of Succoth and said, "Here are Zebah and Zalmunna, about whom you ridiculed me, saying, '*Are* the hands of Zebah and Zalmunna now in your hand, that we should give bread to your weary men?' " ¹⁶And he took the elders of the city, and thorns of the wilderness and briers, and with

them he taught the men of Succoth. ¹⁷Then he tore down the tower of Penuel and killed the men of the city.

¹⁸And he said to Zebah and Zalmunna, "What kind of men *were they* whom you killed at Tabor?"

So they answered, "As you *are*, so *were* they; each one resembled the son of a king."

¹⁹Then he said, "They *were* my brothers, the sons of my mother. *As* the LORD lives, if you had let them live, I would not kill you." ²⁰And he said to Jether his firstborn, "Rise, kill them!" But the youth would not draw his sword; for he was afraid, because he *was* still a youth.

²¹So Zebah and Zalmunna said, "Rise yourself, and kill us; for as a man *is, so is* his strength." So Gideon arose and killed Zebah and Zalmunna, and took the crescent ornaments that *were* on their camels' necks.

²²Then the men of Israel said to Gideon, "Rule over us, both you and your son, and your grandson also; for you have delivered us from the hand of Midian."

²³But Gideon said to them, "I will not rule over you, nor shall my son rule over you; the LORD shall rule over you." ²⁴Then Gideon said to them, "I would like to make a request of you, that each of you would give me the earrings from his plunder." For they had golden earrings, because they *were* Ishmaelites.

²⁵So they answered, "We will gladly give *them*." And they spread out a garment, and each man threw into it the earrings from his plunder. ²⁶Now the weight of the gold earrings that he requested was one thousand seven hundred *shekels* of gold, besides the crescent ornaments, pendants, and purple robes which *were* on the kings of Midian, and besides the chains that *were* around their camels' necks. ²⁷Then Gideon made it into an ephod and set it up in his city, Ophrah. And all Israel played the harlot with it there. It became a snare to Gideon and to his house.

²⁸Thus Midian was subdued before the children of Israel, so that they lifted their heads no more. And the country was quiet for forty years in the days of Gideon.

²⁹Then Jerubbaal the son of Joash went and dwelt in his own house. ³⁰Gideon had seventy sons who were his own offspring, for he had many wives. ³¹And his concubine who *was* in Shechem also bore him a son, whose name he called Abimelech. ³²Now Gideon the son of Joash died at a good old age, and was buried in the tomb of Joash his father, in Ophrah of the Abiezrites.

³³So it was, as soon as Gideon was dead, that the children of Israel again played the harlot with the Baals, and made Baal-Berith their god. ³⁴Thus the children of Israel did not remember the LORD their God, who had delivered them from the hands of all their enemies on every side;

◣ TEMPTATION

8:31 This relationship between Gideon and a concubine produced a son who tore apart Gideon's family and caused tragedy for the nation. Gideon's story illustrates the fact that heroes in battle are not always heroes in daily life. Gideon led the nation, but could not lead his family. No matter who you are, moral laxness will cause problems. Just because you have won a single battle with temptation does not mean you will automatically win the next. We need to be constantly watchful against temptation. Sometimes Satan's strongest attacks come after a victory.

³⁵nor did they show kindness to the house of Jerubbaal (Gideon) in accordance with the good he had done for Israel.

CHAPTER 9 ABIMELECH TRIES TO BECOME KING.

Then Abimelech the son of Jerubbaal went to Shechem, to his mother's brothers, and spoke with them and with all the family of the house of his mother's father, saying, ²"Please speak in the hearing of all the men of Shechem: 'Which is better for you, that all seventy of the sons of Jerubbaal reign over you, or that one reign over you?' Remember that I *am* your own flesh and bone."

³And his mother's brothers spoke all these words concerning him in the hearing of all the men of Shechem; and their heart was inclined to follow Abimelech, for they said, "He is our brother." ⁴So they gave him seventy *shekels* of silver from the temple of Baal-Berith, with which Abimelech hired worthless and reckless men; and they followed him. ⁵Then he went to his father's house at Ophrah and killed his brothers, the seventy sons of Jerubbaal, on one stone. But Jotham the youngest son of Jerubbaal was left, because he hid himself. ⁶And all the men of Shechem gathered together, all of Beth Millo, and they went and made Abimelech king beside the terebinth tree at the pillar that *was* in Shechem.

⁷Now when they told Jotham, he went and stood on top of Mount Gerizim, and lifted his voice and cried out. And he said to them:

"Listen to me, you men of Shechem,
That God may listen to you!

⁸ "The trees once went forth to anoint a king over them.
And they said to the olive tree,
'Reign over us!'
⁹ But the olive tree said to them,
'Should I cease giving my oil,
With which they honor God and men,
And go to sway over trees?'

¹⁰ "Then the trees said to the fig tree,
'You come *and* reign over us!'
¹¹ But the fig tree said to them,
'Should I cease my sweetness and my good fruit,
And go to sway over trees?'

¹² "Then the trees said to the vine,
'You come *and* reign over us!'
¹³ But the vine said to them,
'Should I cease my new wine,
Which cheers *both* God and men,
And go to sway over trees?'

¹⁴ "Then all the trees said to the bramble,
'You come *and* reign over us!'
¹⁵ And the bramble said to the trees,
'If in truth you anoint me as king over you,
Then come *and* take shelter in my shade;
But if not, let fire come out of the bramble
And devour the cedars of Lebanon!'

¹⁶"Now therefore, if you have acted in truth and sincerity in making Abimelech king, and if you have dealt well

with Jerubbaal and his house, and have done to him as he deserves— ¹⁷for my father fought for you, risked his life, and delivered you out of the hand of Midian; ¹⁸but you have risen up against my father's house this day, and killed his seventy sons on one stone, and made Abimelech, the son of his female servant, king over the men of Shechem, because he is your brother— ¹⁹if then you have acted in truth and sincerity with Jerubbaal and with his house this day, *then* rejoice in Abimelech, and let him also rejoice in you. ²⁰But if not, let fire come from Abimelech and devour the men of Shechem and Beth Millo; and let fire come from the men of Shechem and from Beth Millo and devour Abimelech!" ²¹And Jotham ran away and fled; and he went to Beer and dwelt there, for fear of Abimelech his brother.

²²After Abimelech had reigned over Israel three years, ²³God sent a spirit of ill will between Abimelech and the men of Shechem; and the men of Shechem dealt treacherously with Abimelech, ²⁴that the crime *done* to the seventy sons of Jerubbaal might be settled and their blood be laid on Abimelech their brother, who killed them, and on the men of Shechem, who aided him in the killing of his brothers. ²⁵And the men of Shechem set men in ambush against him on the tops of the mountains, and they robbed all who passed by them along that way; and it was told Abimelech.

²⁶Now Gaal the son of Ebed came with his brothers and went over to Shechem; and the men of Shechem put their confidence in him. ²⁷So they went out into the fields, and gathered *grapes* from their vineyards and trod *them,* and made merry. And they went into the house o their god, and ate and drank, and cursed Abimelech ²⁸Then Gaal the son of Ebed said, "Who *is* Abimelech, and who *is* Shechem, that we should serve him? *Is he* not the son of Jerubbaal, and *is not* Zebul his officer? Serve th men of Hamor the father of Shechem; but why should w serve him? ²⁹If only this people were under my authority Then I would remove Abimelech." So he said to Abime lech, "Increase your army and come out!"

³⁰When Zebul, the ruler of the city, heard the words c Gaal the son of Ebed, his anger was aroused. ³¹And h sent messengers to Abimelech secretly, saying, "Tak note! Gaal the son of Ebed and his brothers have come t Shechem; and here they are, fortifying the city again you. ³²Now therefore, get up by night, you and the peopl who *are* with you, and lie in wait in the field. ³³And it sha be, as soon as the sun is up in the morning, *that* you sha rise early and rush upon the city; and *when* he and th people who are with him come out against you, you ma then do to them as you find opportunity."

³⁴So Abimelech and all the people who *were* with hi rose by night, and lay in wait against Shechem in fo companies. ³⁵When Gaal the son of Ebed went out a

stood in the entrance to the city gate, Abimelech and the people who *were* with him rose from lying in wait. ³⁶And when Gaal saw the people, he said to Zebul, "Look, people are coming down from the tops of the mountains!"

But Zebul said to him, "You see the shadows of the mountains as *if they were* men."

³⁷So Gaal spoke again and said, "See, people are coming down from the center of the land, and another company is coming from the Diviners' Terebinth Tree."

³⁸Then Zebul said to him, "Where indeed *is* your mouth now, with which you said, 'Who is Abimelech, that we should serve him?' *Are* not these the people whom you despised? Go out, if you will, and fight with them now."

³⁹So Gaal went out, leading the men of Shechem, and fought with Abimelech. ⁴⁰And Abimelech chased him, and he fled from him; and many fell wounded, to the *very* entrance of the gate. ⁴¹Then Abimelech dwelt at Arumah, and Zebul drove out Gaal and his brothers, so that they would not dwell in Shechem.

⁴²And it came about on the next day that the people went out into the field, and they told Abimelech. ⁴³So he took his people, divided them into three companies, and lay in wait in the field. And he looked, and there were the people, coming out of the city; and he rose against them and attacked them. ⁴⁴Then Abimelech and the company that *was* with him rushed forward and stood at the entrance of the gate of the city; and the *other* two companies rushed upon all who *were* in the fields and killed them. ⁴⁵So Abimelech fought against the city all that day; he took the city and killed the people who *were* in it; and he demolished the city and sowed it with salt.

⁴⁶Now when all the men of the tower of Shechem had heard *that,* they entered the stronghold of the temple of the god Berith. ⁴⁷And it was told Abimelech that all the men of the tower of Shechem were gathered together. ⁴⁸Then Abimelech went up to Mount Zalmon, he and all the people who *were* with him. And Abimelech took an ax in his hand and cut down a bough from the trees, and took it and laid *it* on his shoulder; then he said to the people who were with him, "What you have seen me do, make haste *and* do as I *have* done." ⁴⁹So each of the people likewise cut down his own bough and followed Abimelech, put *them* against the stronghold, and set the stronghold on fire above them, so that all the people of the tower of Shechem died, about a thousand men and women.

⁵⁰Then Abimelech went to Thebez, and he encamped against Thebez and took it. ⁵¹But there was a strong tower in the city, and all the men and women—all the people of the city—fled there and shut themselves in; then they went up to the top of the tower. ⁵²So Abimelech came as far as the tower and fought against it; and he drew near the door of the tower to burn it with fire. ⁵³But a certain woman dropped an upper millstone on Abimelech's head and crushed his skull. ⁵⁴Then he called quickly to the young man, his armorbearer, and said to him, "Draw your sword and kill me, lest men say of me, 'A woman killed him.'" So his young man thrust him through, and he died. ⁵⁵And when the men of Israel saw that Abimelech was dead, they departed, every man to his place.

⁵⁶Thus God repaid the wickedness of Abimelech, which he had done to his father by killing his seventy brothers. ⁵⁷And all the evil of the men of Shechem God returned on their own heads, and on them came the curse of Jotham the son of Jerubbaal.

CHAPTER 10 TOLA AND JAIR. After Abimelech there arose to save Israel Tola the son of Puah, the son of Dodo, a man of Issachar; and he dwelt in Shamir in the mountains of Ephraim. ²He judged Israel twenty-three years; and he died and was buried in Shamir.

◣▬▬▬NOTEWORTHY

10:1-5 In five verses we read about two men who judged Israel for a total of 45 years. Yet all we know about them besides the length of their rules is that one had 30 sons who rode around on 30 donkeys. What are you doing for God that is worth noting? When your life is over, will people remember more than just what was in your bank account or the number of years you lived?

³After him arose Jair, a Gileadite; and he judged Israel twenty-two years. ⁴Now he had thirty sons who rode on thirty donkeys; they also had thirty towns, which are called "Havoth Jair" to this day, which *are* in the land of Gilead. ⁵And Jair died and was buried in Camon.

⁶Then the children of Israel again did evil in the sight of the LORD, and served the Baals and the Ashtoreths, the gods of Syria, the gods of Sidon, the gods of Moab, the gods of the people of Ammon, and the gods of the Philistines; and they forsook the LORD and did not serve Him. ⁷So the anger of the LORD was hot against Israel; and He sold them into the hands of the Philistines and into the hands of the people of Ammon. ⁸From that year they harassed and oppressed the children of Israel for eighteen years—all the children of Israel who *were* on the other side of the Jordan in the land of the Amorites, in Gilead. ⁹Moreover the people of Ammon crossed over the Jordan to fight against Judah also, against Benjamin, and against the house of Ephraim, so that Israel was severely distressed.

¹⁰And the children of Israel cried out to the LORD, saying, "We have sinned against You, because we have both forsaken our God and served the Baals!"

¹¹So the LORD said to the children of Israel, "*Did I* not *deliver you* from the Egyptians and from the Amorites and from the people of Ammon and from the Philistines? ¹²Also the Sidonians and Amalekites and Maonites oppressed you; and you cried out to Me, and I delivered you from their hand. ¹³Yet you have forsaken Me and served other gods. Therefore I will deliver you no more. ¹⁴Go and cry out to the gods which you have chosen; let them deliver you in your time of distress."

◣▬▬▬PUNISHMENT

10:7-10 God permitted the heathen nations to oppress the Israelites because of their sin (2:1-3). Because God is just, he will punish sin (Leviticus 26). God allows problems and pressures to enter our life in order to lovingly draw us back into relationship with him. When problems arise, before you ask, "Why me?" ask, "Is God trying to say something to me through this?"

¹⁵And the children of Israel said to the LORD, "We have sinned! Do to us whatever seems best to You; only deliver us this day, we pray." ¹⁶So they put away the foreign gods from among them and served the LORD. And His soul could no longer endure the misery of Israel.

¹⁷Then the people of Ammon gathered together and encamped in Gilead. And the children of Israel assembled together and encamped in Mizpah. ¹⁸And the people, the leaders of Gilead, said to one another, "Who is the man who will begin the fight against the people of Ammon? He shall be head over all the inhabitants of Gilead."

CHAPTER 11 JEPHTHAH'S FOOLISH VOW. Now
Jephthah the Gileadite was a mighty man of valor, but he *was* the son of a harlot; and Gilead begot Jephthah. ²Gilead's wife bore sons; and when his wife's sons grew up, they drove Jephthah out, and said to him, "You shall

▶ REJECTION
11:1-2 Jephthah, an illegitimate son of Gilead, was chased out of country by his half brothers. He suffered as a result of another pers decision and not for any wrong he had done. Yet in spite of his brot rejection, God used him. If you are suffering from unfair rejection, blame others and become discouraged. Remember how God used Jephthah despite his unjust circumstances, and realize that God is a use you even if you feel rejected by some.

have no inheritance in our father's house, for you *are* the son of another woman." ³Then Jephthah fled from his brothers and dwelt in the land of Tob; and worthless men banded together with Jephthah and went out *raiding* with him.

⁴It came to pass after a time that the people of Ammon made war against Israel. ⁵And so it was, when the people of Ammon made war against Israel, that the elders of Gilead went to get Jephthah from the land of Tob. ⁶Then

Person	Known as	Task	Reference
JACOB	A liar	To "father" the Israelite nation	Genesis 27
JOSEPH	A slave	To save his family	Genesis 39ff
MOSES	Shepherd in exile (and murderer)	To lead Israel out of bondage into the Promised Land	Exodus 3
GIDEON	A farmer	To deliver Israel from Midian	Judges 6:11
JEPHTHAH	Son of a prostitute	To deliver Israel from the Ammonites	Judges 11:1
HANNAH	A housewife	To be the mother of Samuel	1 Samuel 1
DAVID	A shepherd boy and youngest of the family	To be Israel's greatest king	1 Samuel 16
EZRA	A scribe	To lead the return to Judah and to write some of the Bible	Ezra, Nehemiah
ESTHER	A slave girl	To save her people from massacre	Esther
MARY	A peasant girl	To be the mother of Christ	Luke 1:27-38
MATTHEW	A tax collector	To be an apostle and Gospel writer	Matthew 9:9
LUKE	A Greek physician	To be a companion of Paul and a Gospel writer	Colossians 4:14
PETER	A fisherman	To be an apostle, a leader of the early church, and a writer of two New Testament letters	Matthew 4:18-20

GOD USES COMMON PEOPLE
God uses all sorts of people to do his work—people like you and me!

they said to Jephthah, "Come and be our commander, that we may fight against the people of Ammon."

[7]So Jephthah said to the elders of Gilead, "Did you not hate me, and expel me from my father's house? Why have you come to me now when you are in distress?"

[8]And the elders of Gilead said to Jephthah, "That is why we have turned again to you now, that you may go with us and fight against the people of Ammon, and be our head over all the inhabitants of Gilead."

[9]So Jephthah said to the elders of Gilead, "If you take me back home to fight against the people of Ammon, and the LORD delivers them to me, shall I be your head?"

[10]And the elders of Gilead said to Jephthah, "The LORD will be a witness between us, if we do not do according to your words." [11]Then Jephthah went with the elders of Gilead, and the people made him head and commander over them; and Jephthah spoke all his words before the LORD in Mizpah.

[12]Now Jephthah sent messengers to the king of the people of Ammon, saying, "What do you have against me, that you have come to fight against me in my land?"

[13]And the king of the people of Ammon answered the messengers of Jephthah, "Because Israel took away my land when they came up out of Egypt, from the Arnon as far as the Jabbok, and to the Jordan. Now therefore, restore those *lands* peaceably."

[14]So Jephthah again sent messengers to the king of the people of Ammon, [15]and said to him, "Thus says Jephthah: 'Israel did not take away the land of Moab, nor the land of the people of Ammon; [16]for when Israel came up from Egypt, they walked through the wilderness as far as the Red Sea and came to Kadesh. [17]Then Israel sent messengers to the king of Edom, saying, "Please let me pass through your land." But the king of Edom would not heed. And in like manner they sent to the king of Moab, but he would not *consent.* So Israel remained in Kadesh. [18]And they went along through the wilderness and bypassed the land of Edom and the land of Moab, came to the east side of the land of Moab, and encamped on the other side of the Arnon. But they did not enter the border of Moab, for the Arnon *was* the border of Moab. [19]Then Israel sent messengers to Sihon king of the Amorites, king of Heshbon; and Israel said to him, "Please let us pass through your land into our place." [20]But Sihon did not trust Israel to pass through his territory. So Sihon

gathered all his people together, encamped in Jahaz, and fought against Israel. [21]And the LORD God of Israel delivered Sihon and all his people into the hand of Israel, and they defeated them. Thus Israel gained possession of all the land of the Amorites, who inhabited that country. [22]They took possession of all the territory of the Amorites, from the Arnon to the Jabbok and from the wilderness to the Jordan.

[23]And now the LORD God of Israel has dispossessed the Amorites from before His people Israel; should you then possess it? [24]Will you not possess whatever Chemosh

◣◣◣◣◣ NO DEALS

11:34-35 Jephthah's rash vow brought him unspeakable grief. In the heat of emotion or personal turmoil it is easy to make foolish promises to God. These promises may sound very spiritual when we make them, but they may produce only guilt and frustration when we are forced to fulfill them. Making spiritual "deals" only brings disappointment. God does not want promises for the future, but obedience for today.

your god gives you to possess? So whatever the LORD our God takes possession of before us, we will possess. [25]And now, *are* you any better than Balak the son of Zippor, king of Moab? Did he ever strive against Israel? Did he ever fight against them? [26]While Israel dwelt in Heshbon and its villages, in Aroer and its villages, and in all the cities along the banks of the Arnon, for three hundred years, why did you not recover *them* within that time? [27]Therefore I have not sinned against you, but you wronged me by fighting against me. May the LORD, the Judge, render judgment this day between the children of Israel and the people of Ammon.' " [28]However, the king of the people of Ammon did not heed the words which Jephthah sent him.

[29]Then the Spirit of the LORD came upon Jephthah, and he passed through Gilead and Manasseh, and passed through Mizpah of Gilead; and from Mizpah of Gilead he advanced *toward* the people of Ammon. [30]And Jephthah made a vow to the LORD, and said, "If You will indeed deliver the people of Ammon into my hands, [31]then it will be that whatever comes out of the doors of my house to meet me, when I return in peace from the people of Ammon, shall surely be the LORD's, and I will offer it up as a burnt offering."

[32]So Jephthah advanced toward the people of Ammon to fight against them, and the LORD delivered them into his hands. [33]And he defeated them from Aroer as far as Minnith—twenty cities—and to Abel Keramim, with a very great slaughter. Thus the people of Ammon were subdued before the children of Israel.

[34]When Jephthah came to his house at Mizpah, there was his daughter, coming out to meet him with timbrels and dancing; and she *was his* only child. Besides her he had neither son nor daughter. [35]And it came to pass, when he saw her, that he tore his clothes, and said, "Alas, my daughter! You have brought me very low! You are among those who trouble me! For I have given my word to the LORD, and I cannot go back on it."

[36]So she said to him, "My father, *if* you have given your word to the LORD, do to me according to what has gone

I HAVE GIVEN MY WORD TO THE LORD
AND
I cannot go back on it.

out of your mouth, because the LORD has avenged you of your enemies, the people of Ammon." ³⁷Then she said to her father, "Let this thing be done for me: let me alone for two months, that I may go and wander on the mountains and bewail my virginity, my friends and I."

³⁸So he said, "Go." And he sent her away *for two* months; and she went with her friends, and bewailed her virginity on the mountains. ³⁹And it was so at the end of two months that she returned to her father, and he carried out his vow with her which he had vowed. She knew no man.

And it became a custom in Israel ⁴⁰*that* the daughters of Israel went four days each year to lament the daughter of Jephthah the Gileadite.

CHAPTER 12 JEPHTHAH ATTACKS EPHRAIM. Then

the men of Ephraim gathered together, crossed over toward Zaphon, and said to Jephthah, "Why did you cross over to fight against the people of Ammon, and did not call us to go with you? We will burn your house down on you with fire!"

▶▶▶ A JOB TO DO

13:5 Manoah's wife was told that her son would *begin* to rescue the Israelites from Philistine oppression. It wasn't until David's day that the Philistine opposition was completely crushed (2 Samuel 8:1). Samson's part in subduing the Philistines was just the beginning, but it was important nonetheless. It was the task God had given Samson to do. Be faithful in following God even if you don't see instant results, because you might be beginning an important job that others will finish.

²And Jephthah said to them, "My people and I were in a great struggle with the people of Ammon; and when I called you, you did not deliver me out of their hands. ³So when I saw that you would not deliver *me*, I took my life in my hands and crossed over against the people of Ammon; and the LORD delivered them into my hand. Why then have you come up to me this day to fight against me?" ⁴Now Jephthah gathered together all the men of Gilead and fought against Ephraim. And the men of Gilead defeated Ephraim, because they said, "You Gileadites *are* fugitives of Ephraim among the Ephraimites *and* among the Manassites." ⁵The Gileadites seized the fords of the Jordan before the Ephraimites *arrived.* And when *any* Ephraimite who escaped said, "Let me cross over," the men of Gilead would say to him, "*Are* you an Ephraimite?" If he said, "No," ⁶then they would say to him, "Then say, 'Shibboleth'!" And he would say, "Sibboleth," for he could not pronounce *it* right. Then they would take him and kill him at the fords of the Jordan. There fell at that time forty-two thousand Ephraimites.

⁷And Jephthah judged Israel six years. Then Jephthah the Gileadite died and was buried among the cities of Gilead.

⁸After him, Ibzan of Bethlehem judged Israel. ⁹He had thirty sons. And he gave away thirty daughters in marriage, and brought in thirty daughters from elsewhere for his sons. He judged Israel seven years. ¹⁰Then Ibzan died and was buried at Bethlehem.

¹¹After him, Elon the Zebulunite judged Israel. He judged Israel ten years. ¹²And Elon the Zebulunite died and was buried at Aijalon in the country of Zebulun.

¹³After him, Abdon the son of Hillel the Pirathonite judged Israel. ¹⁴He had forty sons and thirty grandsons, who rode on seventy young donkeys. He judged Israel eight years. ¹⁵Then Abdon the son of Hillel the Pirathonite died and was buried in Pirathon in the land of Ephraim, in the mountains of the Amalekites.

CHAPTER 13 SAMSON IS BORN. Again the children

of Israel did evil in the sight of the LORD, and the LORD delivered them into the hand of the Philistines for forty years.

²Now there was a certain man from Zorah, of the family of the Danites, whose name *was* Manoah; and his wife *was* barren and had no children. ³And the Angel of the LORD appeared to the woman and said to her, "Indeed now, you are barren and have borne no children, but you shall conceive and bear a son. ⁴Now therefore, please be careful not to drink wine or *similar* drink, and not to eat anything unclean. ⁵For behold, you shall conceive and bear a son. And no razor shall come upon his head, for the child shall be a Nazirite to God from the womb; and he shall begin to deliver Israel out of the hand of the Philistines."

⁶So the woman came and told her husband, saying, "A Man of God came to me, and His countenance *was* like the countenance of the Angel of God, very awesome; but I did not ask Him where He *was* from, and He did not tell me His name. ⁷And He said to me, 'Behold, you shall conceive and bear a son. Now drink no wine or *similar* drink, nor eat anything unclean, for the child shall be a Nazirite to God from the womb to the day of his death.' "

⁸Then Manoah prayed to the LORD, and said, "O my Lord, please let the Man of God whom You sent come to us again and teach us what we shall do for the child who will be born."

⁹And God listened to the voice of Manoah, and the Angel of God came to the woman again as she was sitting in the field; but Manoah her husband *was* not with her. ¹⁰Then the woman ran in haste and told her husband, and said to him, "Look, the Man who came to me the *other* day has just now appeared to me!"

▶▶▶ PREPARED

13:25 Samson's tribe, Dan, continued to wander in their inherit (18:1), which was yet unconquered (Joshua 19:47-48). Samson m have grown up with his warlike tribe's yearnings for a permanen settled territory. Thus his visits to the tribal army camp stirred his and God's Spirit began preparing him for his role as judge and le against the Philistines.

Perhaps there are things that excite you. These may indicate where God wants to use you. God uses a variety of means to dev prepare us: hereditary traits, environmental influences, and pers experiences. As with Samson, this preparation often begins long adulthood. Work at being sensitive to the Holy Spirit's leading an tasks God has prepared for you. Your past may be more useful than you imagine.

¹¹So Manoah arose and followed his wife. When he came to the Man, he said to Him, "Are You the Man who spoke to this woman?"

And He said, "I *am*."

¹²Manoah said, "Now let Your words come *to pass!* What will be the boy's rule of life, and his work?"

¹³So the Angel of the LORD said to Manoah, "Of all that I said to the woman let her be careful. ¹⁴She may not eat anything that comes from the vine, nor may she drink wine or *similar* drink, nor eat anything unclean. All that I commanded her let her observe."

¹⁵Then Manoah said to the Angel of the LORD, "Please let us detain You, and we will prepare a young goat for You."

¹⁶And the Angel of the LORD said to Manoah, "Though you detain Me, I will not eat your food. But if you offer a burnt offering, you must offer it to the LORD." (For Manoah did not know He *was* the Angel of the LORD.)

¹⁷Then Manoah said to the Angel of the LORD, "What *is* Your name, that when Your words come *to pass* we may honor You?"

¹⁸And the Angel of the LORD said to him, "Why do you ask My name, seeing it *is* wonderful?"

¹⁹So Manoah took the young goat with the grain offering, and offered it upon the rock to the LORD. And He did a wondrous thing while Manoah and his wife looked on— ²⁰it happened as the flame went up toward heaven from the altar—the Angel of the LORD ascended in the flame of the altar! When Manoah and his wife saw *this*, they fell on their faces to the ground. ²¹When the Angel of the LORD appeared no more to Manoah and his wife, then Manoah knew that He *was* the Angel of the LORD.

²²And Manoah said to his wife, "We shall surely die, because we have seen God!"

²³But his wife said to him, "If the LORD had desired to kill us, He would not have accepted a burnt offering and a grain offering from our hands, nor would He have shown us all these *things*, nor would He have told us *such things* as these at this time."

²⁴So the woman bore a son and called his name Samson; and the child grew, and the LORD blessed him. ²⁵And the Spirit of the LORD began to move upon him at Mahaneh Dan between Zorah and Eshtaol.

CHAPTER **14** **SAMSON GETS MARRIED.** Now Samson went down to Timnah, and saw a woman in Timnah of the daughters of the Philistines. ²So he went up and told his father and mother, saying, "I have seen a woman in Timnah of the daughters of the Philistines; now therefore, get her for me as a wife."

³Then his father and mother said to him, "*Is there* no woman among the daughters of your brethren, or among all my people, that you must go and get a wife from the uncircumcised Philistines?"

And Samson said to his father, "Get her for me, for she pleases me well."

⁴But his father and mother did not know that it was of the LORD—that He was seeking an occasion to move against the Philistines. For at that time the Philistines had dominion over Israel.

⁵So Samson went down to Timnah with his father and mother, and came to the vineyards of Timnah.

SAMSON

If it hasn't already happened, sooner or later someone is going to talk to you about your potential. "Potential" is what you could become compared to what you are right now. Samson had incredible potential! He had the potential to be a great servant of God. God planned to use him to lead the Israelites. To help him, God gave Samson enormous physical strength. (The special strength God has given you may not be physical, but he has built into you the potential to be a great servant of his.) Unfortunately, Samson became an example of what happens when we don't live up to God's plan for our life.

Samson's life included many opportunities to help his people. He wasted most of his chances. Yet, in spite of all his mistakes, God still used him. The last thing Samson did before he died was an act that started the work God had planned for him all along. Even if it is the last thing you do, you can start being obedient to God.

The New Testament does not mention Samson's failures or his great feats of strength. In Hebrews 11:32-33, he is simply called one who "through faith . . . worked righteousness." In the end, Samson recognized his dependence on God. When he died, God turned his failures and defeats into victory. Samson's story teaches us that it is never too late to start over. However badly we may have failed in the past, today is not too late for us to put our complete trust in God.

LESSONS: Great strength in one area of life does not make up for weaknesses in other areas

God's presence does not overwhelm a person's will

God can use people of faith in spite of their mistakes

KEY VERSES: "For behold, you shall conceive and bear a son. And no razor shall come upon his head, for the child shall be a Nazirite to God from the womb; and he shall begin to deliver Israel out of the hand of the Philistines" (Judges 13:5).

His story is told in Judges 13–16. He is also mentioned in Hebrews 11:32.

UPS:
• Dedicated to God from birth as a Nazirite
• Known for his feats of strength
• Listed in the Hall of Faith in Hebrews
• Began to free Israel from Philistine oppression

DOWNS:
• Violated his vow and God's laws on many occasions
• Was controlled by sensuality
• Confided in the wrong people
• Used his gifts and abilities unwisely

STATS:
• Where: Zorah, Timnah, Ashkelon, Gaza, Valley of Sorek
• Occupation: Judge
• Relatives: Father: Manoah
• Contemporaries: Delilah, Samuel (who might have been born while Samson was a judge)

BOOMERANG

15:1ff Samson's reply in 15:11 tells the story of this chapter: "As they did to me, so I have done to them." Revenge is an uncontrollable monster. Each act of retaliation brings another. It is a boomerang that cannot be thrown without cost to the thrower. The revenge cycle can be halted only by forgiveness.

Now *to his* surprise, a young lion *came* roaring against him. [6]And the Spirit of the LORD came mightily upon him, and he tore the lion apart as one would have torn apart a young goat, though *he had* nothing in his hand. But he did not tell his father or his mother what he had done.

[7]Then he went down and talked with the woman; and she pleased Samson well. [8]After some time, when he returned to get her, he turned aside to see the carcass of the lion. And behold, a swarm of bees and honey *were* in

SENSUALITY

It seems that Carrie and her boyfriend Dale have everything going for them:

- They are believers in Christ.
- They come from solid Christian homes.
- Friends constantly tease them by saying, "You guys are so good together. . . . You're just like an old married couple!"
- They are seniors at one of the best Christian schools in the country.
- They both have been accepted to a prestigious Christian college in the Midwest.
- They plan to marry in three years.
- They want to go to South America as missionaries.

Amazing, isn't it? The relationship seems perfect. Proud parents, teachers, and church leaders agree that Carrie and Dale each have been specially gifted by God, and so they predict great things. Says Coach Acker, "Those two will be mightily used by the Lord."

Well, if the scenario seems almost too good to be true, it is. In just about two weeks, this perfect couple will see their dream world collapse right before their eyes.

See, Carrie and Dale have let their physical relationship get out of hand. And now Carrie is pregnant.

Read another sad story about a young man with tremendous spiritual potential who let sexual passion ruin his life—Judges 16.

the carcass of the lion. [9]He took some of it in his hands and went along, eating. When he came to his father and mother, he gave *some* to them, and they also ate. But he did not tell them that he had taken the honey out of the carcass of the lion.

[10]So his father went down to the woman. And Samson gave a feast there, for young men used to do so. [11]And it happened, when they saw him, that they brought thirty companions to be with him.

[12]Then Samson said to them, "Let me pose a riddle to you. If you can correctly solve and explain it to me within the seven days of the feast, then I will give you thirty linen garments and thirty changes of clothing. [13]But if you cannot explain *it* to me, then you shall give me thirty linen garments and thirty changes of clothing."

And they said to him, "Pose your riddle, that we may hear it."

[14]So he said to them:

"Out of the eater came something to eat,
And out of the strong came something sweet."

Now for three days they could not explain the riddle.

[15]But it came to pass on the seventh day that they said to Samson's wife, "Entice your husband, that he may explain the riddle to us, or else we will burn you and your father's house with fire. Have you invited us in order to take what is ours? *Is that* not *so?*"

[16]Then Samson's wife wept on him, and said, "You only hate me! You do not love me! You have posed a riddle to the sons of my people, but you have not explained *it* to me."

And he said to her, "Look, I have not explained *it* to my father or my mother; so should I explain *it* to you?" [17]Now she had wept on him the seven days while their feast lasted. And it happened on the seventh day that he told her, because she pressed him so much. Then she explained the riddle to the sons of her people. [18]So the men of the city said to him on the seventh day before the sun went down:

"What *is* sweeter than honey?
And what *is* stronger than a lion?"

And he said to them:

"If you had not plowed with my heifer,
You would not have solved my riddle!"

[19]Then the Spirit of the LORD came upon him mightily, and he went down to Ashkelon and killed thirty of their men, took their apparel, and gave the changes *of clothing* to those who had explained the riddle. So his anger was aroused, and he went back up to his father's house. [20]And Samson's wife was *given* to his companion, who had been his best man.

CHAPTER 15 SAMSON KILLS MANY ENEMIES. After a while, in the time of wheat harvest, it happened that Samson visited his wife with a young goat. And he said, "Let me go in to my wife, into *her* room." But her father would not permit him to go in.

[2]Her father said, "I really thought that you thoroughly hated her; therefore I gave her to your companion. *Is* not her younger sister better than she? Please, take her instead."

[3]And Samson said to them, "This time I shall be blameless regarding the Philistines if I harm them!" [4]Then Samson went and caught three hundred foxes; and

EXHAUSTION

15:18 Samson was physically and emotionally exhausted. After personal victory, his attitude declined quickly into self-pity—"Sh of thirst?" Emotionally, we are most vulnerable after a great effo when faced with real physical needs. Depression often follows gre achievements, so don't be surprised if you feel drained after a pe victory.

During these times of vulnerability, avoid the temptation to th God owes you for your efforts. It was *his* strength that gave you Concentrate on keeping your attitudes, actions, and words focuse God instead of yourself.

he took torches, turned *the foxes* tail to tail, and put a torch between each pair of tails. [5]When he had set the torches on fire, he let *the foxes* go into the standing grain of the Philistines, and burned up both the shocks and the standing grain, as well as the vineyards *and* olive groves.

[6]Then the Philistines said, "Who has done this?"

And they answered, "Samson, the son-in-law of the Timnite, because he has taken his wife and given her to his companion." So the Philistines came up and burned her and her father with fire.

[7]Samson said to them, "Since you would do a thing like this, I will surely take revenge on you, and after that I will cease." [8]So he attacked them hip and thigh with a great slaughter; then he went down and dwelt in the cleft of the rock of Etam.

[9]Now the Philistines went up, encamped in Judah, and deployed themselves against Lehi. [10]And the men of Judah said, "Why have you come up against us?"

So they answered, "We have come up to arrest Samson, to do to him as he has done to us."

[11]Then three thousand men of Judah went down to the cleft of the rock of Etam, and said to Samson, "Do you not know that the Philistines rule over us? What *is* this you have done to us?"

And he said to them, "As they did to me, so I have done to them."

[12]But they said to him, "We have come down to arrest you, that we may deliver you into the hand of the Philistines."

Then Samson said to them, "Swear to me that you will not kill me yourselves."

[13]So they spoke to him, saying, "No, but we will tie you securely and deliver you into their hand; but we will surely not kill you." And they bound him with two new ropes and brought him up from the rock.

[14]When he came to Lehi, the Philistines came shouting against him. Then the Spirit of the LORD came mightily upon him; and the ropes that *were* on his arms became like flax that is burned with fire, and his bonds broke loose from his hands. [15]He found a fresh jawbone of a donkey, reached out his hand and took it, and killed a thousand men with it. [16]Then Samson said:

"With the jawbone of a donkey,
  Heaps upon heaps,
With the jawbone of a donkey
  I have slain a thousand men!"

[17]And so it was, when he had finished speaking, that he threw the jawbone from his hand, and called that place Ramath Lehi.

[18]Then he became very thirsty; so he cried out to the LORD and said, "You have given this great deliverance by the hand of Your servant; and now shall I die of thirst and fall into the hand of the uncircumcised?" [19]So God split the hollow place that *is* in Lehi, and water came out, and he drank; and his spirit returned, and he revived. Therefore he called its name En Hakkore, which is in Lehi to this day. [20]And he judged Israel twenty years in the days of the Philistines.

CHAPTER **16** SAMSON'S FOOLISH CHOICES. Now Samson went to Gaza and saw a harlot there, and went in to her. [2]*When* the Gazites *were* told, "Samson has come here!" they surrounded *the place* and lay in wait for him all night at the gate of the city. They were quiet all night, saying, "In the morning, when it is daylight, we will kill him." [3]And Samson lay *low* till midnight; then he arose at midnight, took hold of the doors of the gate of the city and the two gateposts, pulled them up, bar and all, put

---

A friend says that my new faith in Christ is too narrow. He doesn't think Christ is the only way to God. Why can't God allow different ideas by other religions?

I WONDER...

Suppose your history teacher told you that Columbus discovered America in 1492. Just then, four other people raised their hands and said, "I think he discovered America in 1454 [or 1678 or 1543 or 1733]. What makes you the authority on history anyway? We are going to believe what we think is right."

Do these kids have the freedom to believe what they think is right? Of course they do.

A wise teacher would respond, "You may believe any date you choose to believe, but there is only one right answer and I have told you what it is. If you put a different answer on the test at the end of the term, it will be checked wrong."

God has given people the freedom to choose what they want to believe about who he is and what his plan is for human beings. But when the test scores are graded at the end of the age, there will be only one right answer.

During this period in Jewish history they had no leader, so it says that "everyone did *what was* right in his own eyes" (Judges 17:6). What this means is that not only did people choose to disobey God as their leader, but their actions were evil as well! Throughout history people have behaved according to what they believe about God.

If people believe that God does not exist or that God does not care how we live and treat each other, they will likely act accordingly. Usually, this means that they treat themselves or others like there will be no final exam when they pass on to the next life!

Jesus said, "I am the way, the truth, and the life. No one comes to the Father except through Me" (John 14:6). This means that God grades on a pass/fail basis depending on what we have done with his Son, Jesus.

Many people would like to believe that God grades on a curve. In other words, if you do good things or go to church more than others or give more money than 60 percent of the rest of the world, you will get into heaven. Jesus makes it clear, however, that there is only one way to heaven.

God has given people the freedom to believe any religion they want. But the final authority is not their own beliefs. There is only one right answer. God's standard is faith in Jesus Christ, his death on the cross—so that our sin would not eternally separate us from God—and his resurrection.

them on his shoulders, and carried them to the top of the hill that faces Hebron.

⁴Afterward it happened that he loved a woman in the Valley of Sorek, whose name *was* Delilah. ⁵And the lords of the Philistines came up to her and said to her, "Entice him, and find out where his great strength *lies*, and by what *means* we may overpower him, that we may bind him to afflict him; and every one of us will give you eleven hundred *pieces* of silver."

⁶So Delilah said to Samson, "Please tell me where your great strength *lies*, and with what you may be bound to afflict you."

LOVE FOOL

16:15 Samson was deceived because he wanted to believe Delilah's lies. How can you keep your desire for love from deceiving you? 1) You must decide what type of person you will love before passion takes over. 2) Your companion's personality, temperament, and commitment to solve problems must be as gratifying as his or her kisses. 3) Be patient. The second look often reveals what is beneath the pleasant appearance and attentive touch.

⁷And Samson said to her, "If they bind me with seven fresh bowstrings, not yet dried, then I shall become weak, and be like any *other* man."

⁸So the lords of the Philistines brought up to her seven fresh bowstrings, not yet dried, and she bound him with them. ⁹Now *men were* lying in wait, staying with her in the room. And she said to him, "The Philistines *are* upon you, Samson!" But he broke the bowstrings as a strand of yarn breaks when it touches fire. So the secret of his strength was not known.

¹⁰Then Delilah said to Samson, "Look, you have mocked me and told me lies. Now, please tell me what you may be bound with."

¹¹So he said to her, "If they bind me securely with new ropes that have never been used, then I shall become weak, and be like any *other* man."

¹²Therefore Delilah took new ropes and bound him with them, and said to him, "The Philistines *are* upon you, Samson!" And *men were* lying in wait, staying in the room. But he broke them off his arms like a thread.

¹³Delilah said to Samson, "Until now you have mocked me and told me lies. Tell me what you may be bound with."

And he said to her, "If you weave the seven locks of my head into the web of the loom"—

¹⁴So she wove *it* tightly with the batten of the loom, and said to him, "The Philistines *are* upon you, Samson!" But he awoke from his sleep, and pulled out the batten and the web from the loom.

¹⁵Then she said to him, "How can you say, 'I love you,' when your heart *is* not with me? You have mocked me these three times, and have not told me where your great strength *lies*." ¹⁶And it came to pass, when she pestered him daily with her words and pressed him, *so* that his soul was vexed to death, ¹⁷that he told her all his heart, and said to her, "No razor has ever come upon my head, for I *have been* a Nazirite to God from my mother's womb.

NAGGING

16:16-17 Delilah kept asking Samson for the secret of his strength until he finally grew tired of hearing her nagging and gave in. What pitiful excuse for disobedience. Don't allow anyone, no matter how attractive or persuasive, to talk you into doing wrong.

If I am shaven, then my strength will leave me, and I shall become weak, and be like any *other* man."

¹⁸When Delilah saw that he had told her all his heart, she sent and called for the lords of the Philistines, saying, "Come up once more, for he has told me all his heart." So the lords of the Philistines came up to her and brought the money in their hand. ¹⁹Then she lulled him to sleep on her knees, and called for a man and had him shave off the seven locks of his head. Then she began to torment him, and his strength left him. ²⁰And she said, "The Philistines *are* upon you, Samson!" So he awoke from his sleep, and said, "I will go out as before, at other times, and shake myself free!" But he did not know that the LORD had departed from him.

²¹Then the Philistines took him and put out his eyes, and brought him down to Gaza. They bound him with bronze fetters, and he became a grinder in the prison. ²²However, the hair of his head began to grow again after it had been shaven.

²³Now the lords of the Philistines gathered together to offer a great sacrifice to Dagon their god, and to rejoice. And they said:

"Our god has delivered into our hands
   Samson our enemy!"

²⁴When the people saw him, they praised their god; for they said:

"Our god has delivered into our hands our enemy,
   The destroyer of our land,
   And the one who multiplied our dead."

²⁵So it happened, when their hearts were merry, that they said, "Call for Samson, that he may perform for us." So they called for Samson from the prison, and he performed for them. And they stationed him between the pillars. ²⁶Then Samson said to the lad who held him by the hand, "Let me feel the pillars which support the temple, so that I can lean on them." ²⁷Now the temple was full of men and women. All the lords of the Philistines *were* there—about three thousand men and women on the roof watching while Samson performed.

²⁸Then Samson called to the LORD, saying, "O Lord GOD, remember me, I pray! Strengthen me, I pray, just this once, O God, that I may with one *blow* take ven-

SALVAGED

16:28-30 In spite of Samson's past, God still answered his prayer destroyed the heathen temple and worshipers. God still loved Samson was willing to hear Samson's prayer of confession and repentance him this final time. One of the effects of sin in our life is that it keeps from feeling like praying. But perfect moral behavior is not a condition prayer. Don't let guilt feelings over sin keep you apart from God. matter how long you have been away from God, he is ready to hear you and restore you to a right relationship. Every situation can be if you are willing to turn again to him. If God could still work in Samson situation, he can certainly make something worthwhile out of you

geance on the Philistines for my two eyes!" ²⁹And Samson took hold of the two middle pillars which supported the temple, and he braced himself against them, one on his right and the other on his left. ³⁰Then Samson said, "Let me die with the Philistines!" And he pushed with *all his* might, and the temple fell on the lords and all the people who *were* in it. So the dead that he killed at his death were more than he had killed in his life.

³¹And his brothers and all his father's household came down and took him, and brought *him* up and buried him between Zorah and Eshtaol in the tomb of his father Manoah. He had judged Israel twenty years.

CHAPTER **17** MICAH'S IDOL COLLECTION. Now there was a man from the mountains of Ephraim, whose name *was* Micah. ²And he said to his mother, "The eleven hundred *shekels* of silver that were taken from you, and on which you put a curse, even saying it in my ears—here *is* the silver with me; I took it."

And his mother said, "*May you be* blessed by the LORD, my son!" ³So when he had returned the eleven hundred *shekels* of silver to his mother, his mother said, "I had wholly dedicated the silver from my hand to the LORD for my son, to make a carved image and a molded image; now therefore, I will return it to you." ⁴Thus he returned the silver to his mother. Then his mother took two hundred *shekels* of silver and gave them to the silversmith, and he made it into a carved image and a molded image; and they were in the house of Micah.

⁵The man Micah had a shrine, and made an ephod and household idols; and he consecrated one of his sons, who became his priest. ⁶In those days *there* was no king in Israel; everyone did *what was* right in his own eyes.

⁷Now there was a young man from Bethlehem in Judah, of the family of Judah; he *was* a Levite, and was staying there. ⁸The man departed from the city of Bethlehem in Judah to stay wherever he could find *a place*. Then he came to the mountains of Ephraim, to the house of Micah, as he journeyed. ⁹And Micah said to him, "Where do you come from?"

So he said to him, "I *am* a Levite from Bethlehem in Judah, and I am on my way to find *a place* to stay."

¹⁰Micah said to him, "Dwell with me, and be a father and a priest to me, and I will give you ten *shekels* of silver per year, a suit of clothes, and your sustenance." So the Levite went in. ¹¹Then the Levite was content to dwell with the man; and the young man became like one of his sons to him. ¹²So Micah consecrated the Levite, and the young man became his priest, and lived in the house of Micah. ¹³Then Micah said, "Now I know that the LORD will be good to me, since I have a Levite as priest!"

CHAPTER **18** THE DANITES STEAL MICAH'S IDOLS. In those days *there was* no king in Israel. And in those days the tribe of the Danites was seeking an inheritance for itself to dwell in; for until that day *their* inheritance among the tribes of Israel had not fallen to them. ²So the children of Dan sent five men of their family from their territory, men of valor from Zorah and Eshtaol, to spy out the land and search it. They said to them, "Go, search the

◥◣◢◤◥◣ MOTIVES

18:11-26 Through this entire incident, no one desired to worship God; instead they wanted to use God for selfish gain. Today some people go to church to feel better, be accepted, relieve guilt, and gain friends. Beware of following God for selfish gains rather than selfless service.

land." So they went to the mountains of Ephraim, to the house of Micah, and lodged there. ³While they *were* at the house of Micah, they recognized the voice of the young Levite. They turned aside and said to him, "Who brought you here? What are you doing in this *place?* What do you have here?"

⁴He said to them, "Thus and so Micah did for me. He has hired me, and I have become his priest."

⁵So they said to him, "Please inquire of God, that we may know whether the journey on which we go will be prosperous."

⁶And the priest said to them, "Go in peace. The presence of the LORD *be* with you on your way."

⁷So the five men departed and went to Laish. They saw the people who *were* there, how they dwelt safely, in the manner

DELILAH

There are two very different ways to get a reputation. One way is to help others do great things. Another is to keep others from doing great things. Delilah was only one person in Samson's life, but she almost completely ruined him. She persuaded him to go against what God wanted him to do. Because of what she thought she could get, Delilah used her persistence to wear Samson down. Others couldn't defeat his strength, but Delilah deceived him by pretending to love him, and he finally told her the secret of his strength. He found out too late that he couldn't trust her.

Delilah is never mentioned again in the Bible. But she is frequently remembered as an example of someone who betrayed a friend. That one relationship earned her a permanent reputation of the worst kind.

Are people helped by knowing you? Do they find that your friendship makes them want to be the best they can be? Even more important, does knowing you help their relationship with God?

LESSON: We need to be people who can be trusted

KEY VERSES: "She pestered him daily with her words and pressed him, so that his soul was vexed to death, that he told her all his heart" (Judges 16:16-17).

Her story is told in Judges 16.

UPS:
• Persistent when faced with obstacles

DOWNS:
• Valued money more than relationships
• Betrayed the man who trusted her

STATS:
• Where: Valley of Sorek
• Contemporary: Samson

of the Sidonians, quiet and secure. *There were* no rulers in the land who might put *them* to shame for anything. They *were* far from the Sidonians, and they had no ties with anyone.

[8]Then *the spies* came back to their brethren at Zorah and Eshtaol, and their brethren said to them, "What *is* your *report?*"

[9]So they said, "Arise, let us go up against them. For we have seen the land, and indeed it *is* very good. *Would* you *do* nothing? Do not hesitate to go, *and* enter to possess the land. [10]When you go, you will come to a secure people and a large land. For God has given it into your hands, a place where *there is* no lack of anything that *is* on the earth."

[11]And six hundred men of the family of the Danites went from there, from Zorah and Eshtaol, armed with weapons of war. [12]Then they went up and encamped in Kirjath Jearim in Judah. (Therefore they call that place Mahaneh Dan to this day. There *it is,* west of Kirjath Jearim.) [13]And they passed from there to the mountains of Ephraim, and came to the house of Micah.

[14]Then the five men who had gone to spy out the country of Laish answered and said to their brethren, "Do you know that there are in these houses an ephod, household idols, a carved image, and a molded image? Now therefore, consider what you should do." [15]So they turned aside there, and came to the house of the young Levite man—to the house of Micah—and greeted him. [16]The six hundred men armed with their weapons of war, who *were* of the children of Dan, stood by the entrance of the gate. [17]Then the five men who had gone to spy out the land went up. Entering there, they took the carved image, the ephod, the household idols, and the molded image. The priest stood at the entrance of the gate with the six hundred men *who were* armed with weapons of war.

[18]When these went into Micah's house and took the carved image, the ephod, the household idols, and the molded image, the priest said to them, "What are you doing?"

[19]And they said to him, "Be quiet, put your hand over your mouth, and come with us; be a father and a priest to us. *Is it* better for you to be a priest to the household of one man, or that you be a priest to a tribe and a family in Israel?" [20]So the priest's heart was glad; and he took the ephod, the household idols, and the carved image, and took his place among the people.

[21]Then they turned and departed, and put the little ones, the livestock, and the goods in front of them. [22]When they were a good way from the house of Micah, the men who *were* in the houses near Micah's house gathered together and overtook the children of Dan. [23]And they called out to the children of Dan. So they turned around and said to Micah, "What ails you, that you have gathered such a company?"

[24]So he said, "You have taken away my gods which I made, and the priest, and you have gone away. Now what more do I have? How can you say to me, 'What ails you?' "

[25]And the children of Dan said to him, "Do not let your voice be heard among us, lest angry men fall upon you, and you lose your life, with the lives of your household!"

[26]Then the children of Dan went their way. And whe[n] Micah saw that they *were* too strong for him, he turne[d] and went back to his house.

[27]So they took *the things* Micah had made, and th[e] priest who had belonged to him, and went to Laish, to people quiet and secure; and they struck them with th[e] edge of the sword and burned the city with fire. [28]*Ther[e] was* no deliverer, because it *was* far from Sidon, and the[y] had no ties with anyone. It was in the valley that belong[s] to Beth Rehob. So they rebuilt the city and dwelt there[.] [29]And they called the name of the city Dan, after the nam[e] of Dan their father, who was born to Israel. However, th[e] name of the city formerly *was* Laish.

[30]Then the children of Dan set up for themselves th[e] carved image; and Jonathan the son of Gershom, the so[n] of Manasseh, and his sons were priests to the tribe of Da[n] until the day of the captivity of the land. [31]So they set u[p] for themselves Micah's carved image which he made, a[ll] the time that the house of God was in Shiloh.

CHAPTER **19** **A HORRIBLE CRIME.** And it came [to] pass in those days, when *there was* no king in Israel, tha[t] there was a certain Levite staying in the remote moun[-] tains of Ephraim. He took for himself a concubine fro[m] Bethlehem in Judah. [2]But his concubine played the ha[r-] lot against him, and went away from him to her father['s] house at Bethlehem in Judah, and was there four who[le] months. [3]Then her husband arose and went after her, t[o] speak kindly to her *and* bring her back, having his se[r-] vant and a couple of donkeys with him. So she brough[t] him into her father's house; and when the father of th[e] young woman saw him, he was glad to meet him. [4]No[w] his father-in-law, the young woman's father, detaine[d] him; and he stayed with him three days. So they ate an[d] drank and lodged there.

[5]Then it came to pass on the fourth day that they aro[se] early in the morning, and he stood to depart; but th[e] young woman's father said to his son-in-law, "Refres[h] your heart with a morsel of bread, and afterward go yo[ur] way."

[6]So they sat down, and the two of them ate and dran[k] together. Then the young woman's father said to the ma[n,] "Please be content to stay all night, and let your heart b[e] merry." [7]And when the man stood to depart, his fathe[r-] in-law urged him; so he lodged there again. [8]Then [he] arose early in the morning on the fifth day to depart, b[ut] the young woman's father said, "Please refresh yo[ur] heart." So they delayed until afternoon; and both of the[m] ate.

[9]And when the man stood to depart—he and his co[n-] cubine and his servant—his father-in-law, the youn[g] woman's father, said to him, "Look, the day is now dra[w-] ing toward evening; please spend the night. See, the d[ay] is coming to an end; lodge here, that your heart may b[e] merry. Tomorrow go your way early, so that you may g[o] home."

[10]However, the man was not willing to spend th[e] night; so he rose and departed, and came opposite Jeb[us] (that *is,* Jerusalem). With him were the two saddled do[n-] keys; his concubine *was* also with him. [11]They *were* ne[ar]

Jebus, and the day was far spent; and the servant said to his master, "Come, please, and let us turn aside into this city of the Jebusites and lodge in it."

¹²But his master said to him, "We will not turn aside here into a city of foreigners, who *are* not of the children of Israel; we will go on to Gibeah." ¹³So he said to his servant, "Come, let us draw near to one of these places, and spend the night in Gibeah or in Ramah." ¹⁴And they passed by and went their way; and the sun went down on them near Gibeah, which belongs to Benjamin. ¹⁵They turned aside there to go in to lodge in Gibeah. And when he went in, he sat down in the open square of the city, for no one would take them into *his* house to spend the night.

¹⁶Just then an old man came in from his work in the field at evening, who also *was* from the mountains of Ephraim; he was staying in Gibeah, whereas the men of the place *were* Benjamites. ¹⁷And when he raised his eyes, he saw the traveler in the open square of the city; and the old man said, "Where are you going, and where do you come from?"

¹⁸So he said to him, "We *are* passing from Bethlehem in Judah toward the remote mountains of Ephraim; I *am* from there. I went to Bethlehem in Judah; *now* I am going to the house of the LORD. But there *is* no one who will take me into his house, ¹⁹although we have both straw and fodder for our donkeys, and bread and wine for myself, for your female servant, and for the young man *who is* with your servant; *there is* no lack of anything."

²⁰And the old man said, "Peace *be* with you! However, *let* all your needs *be* my responsibility; only do not spend the night in the open square." ²¹So he brought him into his house, and gave fodder to the donkeys. And they washed their feet, and ate and drank.

²²As they were enjoying themselves, suddenly certain men of the city, perverted men, surrounded the house *and* beat on the door. They spoke to the master of the house, the old man, saying, "Bring out the man who came to your house, that we may know him *carnally!*"

²³But the man, the master of the house, went out to them and said to them, "No, my brethren! I beg you, do not act *so* wickedly! Seeing this man has come into my house, do not commit this outrage. ²⁴Look, *here is* my virgin daughter and *the man's* concubine; let me bring them out now. Humble them, and do with them as you please; but to this man do not do such a vile thing!" ²⁵But the men would not heed him. So the man took his concubine and brought *her* out to them. And they knew her and abused her all night until morning; and when the day began to break, they let her go.

²⁶Then the woman came as the day was dawning, and fell down at the door of the man's house where her master *was*, till it was light.

²⁷When her master arose in the morning, and opened the doors of the house and went out to go his way, there was his concubine, fallen *at* the door of the house with her hands on the threshold. ²⁸And he said to her, "Get up and let us be going." But there was no answer. So the man lifted her onto the donkey; and the man got up and went to his place.

²⁹When he entered his house he took a knife, laid hold of his concubine, and divided her into twelve pieces, limb by limb, and sent her throughout all the territory of Israel. ³⁰And so it was that all who saw it said, "No such deed has been done or seen from the day that the children of Israel came up from the land of Egypt until this day. Consider it, confer, and speak up!"

CHAPTER **20** ISRAEL ATTACKS BENJAMIN. So all the children of Israel came out, from Dan to Beersheba, as well as from the land of Gilead, and the congregation gathered together as one man before the LORD at Mizpah. ²And the leaders of all the people, all the tribes of Israel, presented themselves in the assembly of the people of God, four hundred thousand foot soldiers who drew the sword. ³(Now the children of Benjamin heard that the children of Israel had gone up to Mizpah.)

Then the children of Israel said, "Tell *us*, how did this wicked deed happen?"

⁴So the Levite, the husband of the woman who was murdered, answered and said, "My concubine and I went into Gibeah, which belongs to Benjamin, to spend the night. ⁵And the men of Gibeah rose against me, and surrounded the house at night because of me. They intended to kill me, but instead they ravished my concubine so that she died. ⁶So I took hold of my concubine, cut her in pieces, and sent her throughout all the territory of the inheritance of Israel, because they committed lewdness and outrage in Israel. ⁷Look! All of you *are* children of Israel; give your advice and counsel here and now!"

⁸So all the people arose as one man, saying, "None *of us* will go to his tent, nor will any turn back to his house; ⁹but now this *is* the thing which we will do to Gibeah: *We will go up* against it by lot. ¹⁰We will take ten men out of *every* hundred throughout all the tribes of Israel, a hundred out of *every* thousand, and a thousand out of *every* ten thousand, to make provisions for the people, that when they come to Gibeah in Benjamin, they may repay all the vileness that they have done in Israel." ¹¹So all the men of Israel were gathered against the city, united together as one man.

¹²Then the tribes of Israel sent men through all the tribe of Benjamin, saying, "What *is* this wickedness that has occurred among you? ¹³Now therefore, deliver up the men, the perverted men who *are* in Gibeah, that we may put them to death and remove the evil from Israel!" But the children of Benjamin would not listen to the voice of

GOVERNMENT

19:30 The horrible crime described in this chapter wasn't Israel's worst offense. Even worse was the nation's failure to establish a government based upon God's moral principles, where the law of God was the law of the land. As a result, laws were usually unenforced and crime was ignored. Sexual perversion and lawlessness were a by-product of Israel's disobedience to God. The Israelites weren't willing to speak up until events had gone too far.

Whenever we get away from God and his Word, all sorts of evil can follow. Our drifting away from God may be slow and almost imperceptible, with the ultimate results affecting a future generation. We must continually call our nation back to God and tell people about Christ.

their brethren, the children of Israel. [14]Instead, the children of Benjamin gathered together from their cities to Gibeah, to go to battle against the children of Israel. [15]And from their cities at that time the children of Benjamin numbered twenty-six thousand men who drew the sword, besides the inhabitants of Gibeah, who numbered seven hundred select men. [16]Among all this people *were* seven hundred select men *who were* left-handed; every one could sling a stone at a hair's *breadth* and not miss. [17]Now besides Benjamin, the men of Israel numbered four hundred thousand men who drew the sword; all of these *were* men of war.

[18]Then the children of Israel arose and went up to the house of God to inquire of God. They said, "Which of us shall go up first to battle against the children of Benjamin?"

◣◤ QUICK ACTION

20:46-48 The effects of the horrible rape and murder should never have been felt outside the community where the crime happened. The local people should have brought the criminals to justice and corrected the laxness that originally permitted this crime. Instead, first the town and then the entire tribe defended this wickedness, even going to war over it. To prevent unresolved problems from turning into major conflicts, firm action must be taken quickly, wisely, and forcefully *before* the situation gets out of hand.

The LORD said, "Judah first!"

[19]So the children of Israel rose in the morning and encamped against Gibeah. [20]And the men of Israel went out to battle against Benjamin, and the men of Israel put themselves in battle array to fight against them at Gibeah. [21]Then the children of Benjamin came out of Gibeah, and on that day cut down to the ground twenty-two thousand men of the Israelites. [22]And the people, that is, the men of Israel, encouraged themselves and again formed the battle line at the place where they had put themselves in array on the first day. [23]Then the children of Israel went up and wept before the LORD until evening, and asked counsel of the LORD, saying, "Shall I again draw near for battle against the children of my brother Benjamin?"

And the LORD said, "Go up against him."

[24]So the children of Israel approached the children of Benjamin on the second day. [25]And Benjamin went out against them from Gibeah on the second day, and cut down to the ground eighteen thousand more of the children of Israel; all these drew the sword.

[26]Then all the children of Israel, that is, all the people, went up and came to the house of God and wept. They sat there before the LORD and fasted that day until evening; and they offered burnt offerings and peace offerings before the LORD. [27]So the children of Israel inquired of the LORD (the ark of the covenant of God *was* there in those days, [28]and Phinehas the son of Eleazar, the son of Aaron, stood before it in those days), saying, "Shall I yet again go out to battle against the children of my brother Benjamin, or shall I cease?"

And the LORD said, "Go up, for tomorrow I will deliver them into your hand."

[29]Then Israel set men in ambush all around Gibeah. [30]And the children of Israel went up against the children of Benjamin on the third day, and put themselves in battle array against Gibeah as at the other times. [31]So the children of Benjamin went out against the people, *and* were drawn away from the city. They began to strike down *and* kill some of the people, as at the other times, in the highways (one of which goes up to Bethel and the other to Gibeah) and in the field, about thirty men of Israel. [32]And the children of Benjamin said, "They *are* defeated before us, as at first."

But the children of Israel said, "Let us flee and draw them away from the city to the highways." [33]So all the men of Israel rose from their place and put themselves in battle array at Baal Tamar. Then Israel's men in ambush burst forth from their position in the plain of Geba. [34]And ten thousand select men from all Israel came against Gibeah, and the battle was fierce. But *the* Benjamites did not know that disaster *was* upon them. [35]The LORD defeated Benjamin before Israel. And the children of Israel destroyed that day twenty-five thousand one hundred Benjamites; all these drew the sword.

[36]So the children of Benjamin saw that they were defeated. The men of Israel had given ground to the Benjamites, because they relied on the men in ambush whom they had set against Gibeah. [37]And the men in ambush quickly rushed upon Gibeah; the men in ambush spread out and struck the whole city with the edge of the sword. [38]Now the appointed signal between the men of Israel and the men in ambush was that they would make a great cloud of smoke rise up from the city, [39]whereupon the men of Israel would turn in battle. Now Benjamin had begun to strike *and* kill about thirty of the men of Israel. For they said, "Surely they are defeated before us as *in* the first battle." [40]But when the cloud began to rise from the city in a column of smoke, the Benjamites looked behind them, and there was the whole city going up *in smoke* to heaven. [41]And when the men of Israel turned back, the men of Benjamin panicked, for they saw that disaster had come upon them. [42]Therefore they turned *their backs* before the men of Israel in the direction of the wilderness; but the battle overtook them, and whoever *came* out of the cities they destroyed in their midst. [43]They surrounded the Benjamites, chased them *and* easily trampled them down as far as the front of Gibeah toward the east. [44]And eighteen thousand men of Benjamin fell; all these *were* men of valor. [45]Then they turned and fled toward the wilderness to the rock of Rimmon; and they cut down five thousand of them on the highways. Then they pursued them relentlessly up to Gidom, and killed two thousand of them. [46]So all who fell of Benjamin that day were twenty-five thousand men who drew the sword; all these *were* men of valor.

[47]But six hundred men turned and fled toward the wilderness to the rock of Rimmon, and they stayed at the rock of Rimmon for four months. [48]And the men of Israel turned back against the children of Benjamin, and struck them down with the edge of the sword—from *every* city, men and beasts, all who were found. They also set fire to all the cities they came to.

CHAPTER 21 WIVES FOR THE MEN OF BENJAMIN.

Now the men of Israel had sworn an oath at Mizpah, saying, "None of us shall give his daughter to Benjamin as a wife." ²Then the people came to the house of God, and remained there before God till evening. They lifted up their voices and wept bitterly, ³and said, "O LORD God of Israel, why has this come to pass in Israel, that today there should be one tribe *missing* in Israel?"

⁴So it was, on the next morning, that the people rose early and built an altar there, and offered burnt offerings and peace offerings. ⁵The children of Israel said, "Who *is there* among all the tribes of Israel who did not come up with the assembly to the LORD?" For they had made a great oath concerning anyone who had not come up to the LORD at Mizpah, saying, "He shall surely be put to death." ⁶And the children of Israel grieved for Benjamin their brother, and said, "One tribe is cut off from Israel today. ⁷What shall we do for wives for those who remain, seeing we have sworn by the LORD that we will not give them our daughters as wives?"

⁸And they said, "What one *is there* from the tribes of Israel who did not come up to Mizpah to the LORD?" And, in fact, no one had come to the camp from Jabesh Gilead to the assembly. ⁹For when the people were counted, indeed, not one of the inhabitants of Jabesh Gilead *was* there. ¹⁰So the congregation sent out there twelve thousand of their most valiant men, and commanded them, saying, "Go and strike the inhabitants of Jabesh Gilead with the edge of the sword, including the women and children. ¹¹And this *is* the thing that you shall do: You shall utterly destroy every male, and every woman who has known a man intimately." ¹²So they found among the inhabitants of Jabesh Gilead four hundred young virgins who had not known a man intimately; and they brought them to the camp at Shiloh, which is in the land of Canaan.

¹³Then the whole congregation sent *word* to the children of Benjamin who *were* at the rock of Rimmon, and announced peace to them. ¹⁴So Benjamin came back at that time, and they gave them the women whom they had saved alive of the women of Jabesh Gilead; and yet they had not found enough for them.

¹⁵And the people grieved for Benjamin, because the LORD had made a void in the tribes of Israel. ¹⁶Then the elders of the congregation said, "What shall we do for wives for those who remain, since the women of Benjamin have been destroyed?" ¹⁷And they said, *There must be* an inheritance for the survivors of Benja-

min, that a tribe may not be destroyed from Israel. ¹⁸However, we cannot give them wives from our daughters, for the children of Israel have sworn an oath, saying, 'Cursed *be* the one who gives a wife to Benjamin.' " ¹⁹Then they said, "In fact, *there is* a yearly feast of the LORD in Shiloh, which *is* north of Bethel, on the east side of the highway that goes up from Bethel to Shechem, and south of Lebonah."

HEROES

21:25 During the time of the judges, the people of Israel experienced trouble because everyone became his own authority and acted on his own opinions of right and wrong. This produced horrendous results. Our world is similar. Individuals, groups, and societies have made themselves the final authorities without reference to God. When people selfishly try to satisfy their personal desires at all costs, everyone pays the price.

It is the ultimate heroic act to submit all our plans, desires, and motives to God. Men like Gideon, Jephthah, and Samson are known for their heroism in battle. But their personal lives were far from heroic.

To be truly heroic, we must go into battle each day in our home, school, church, and society to make God's kingdom a reality. Our weapons are the standards, morals, truths, and convictions we receive from God's Word. We will lose the battle if we gather the spoils of earthly treasures rather than seeking the treasures of heaven.

²⁰Therefore they instructed the children of Benjamin, saying, "Go, lie in wait in the vineyards, ²¹and watch; and just when the daughters of Shiloh come out to perform their dances, then come out from the vineyards, and every man catch a wife for himself from the daughters of Shiloh; then go to the land of Benjamin. ²²Then it shall be, when their fathers or their brothers come to us to complain, that we will say to them, 'Be kind to them for our sakes, because we did not take a wife for any of them in the war; for *it is* not *as though* you have given the *women* to them at this time, making yourselves guilty of your oath.' "

²³And the children of Benjamin did so; they took enough wives for their number from those who danced, whom they caught. Then they went and returned to their inheritance, and they rebuilt the cities and dwelt in them. ²⁴So the children of Israel departed from there at that time, every man to his tribe and family; they went out from there, every man to his inheritance.

²⁵In those days *there was* no king in Israel; everyone did *what was* right in his own eyes.

MEGA Themes

DECLINE/COMPROMISE The people faced decline and failure because they compromised their high spiritual purpose in many ways. They abandoned their mission to drive all the people out of the land, and they adopted the customs of the people living around them.

Society offers many rewards to those who compromise their faith: wealth, acceptance, recognition, power, and influence. But when God gives us a mission, it must not be polluted by a desire for approval from social groups.

1. List some of the ways you have seen people compromise their faith and values for wealth, pleasure, power, acceptance, etc.
2. Can you think of a time when you compromised your faith and/or values? At the time, how were you feeling? Why did you make the choice you made? How did you feel after you realized the price you had paid?
3. The Israelites began living entirely different life-styles following a few major compromises. Why does it get easier and easier to compromise after you have done it for a while?
4. Why does it get easier not to compromise if you continually make decisions based on your faith and values?
5. Consider the temptations that you face in school, at work, or with friends. Given the many opportunities you have to make choices that would compromise your faith and values, it takes a serious commitment not to compromise. Fill in the following statement of faith with some specific areas where you must choose not to compromise. I will not compromise my faith and values in the area of _____ because of my commitment to trust God with my life.

DECAY/APOSTASY Israel's moral downfall had its roots in the fierce independence that each tribe cherished. It led to everyone doing whatever seemed good in his own eyes. There was no unity in government or in worship. Law and order broke down. Finally idol worship and man-made religion led to the complete abandoning of faith in God.

We can expect things to fall apart when we value anything more highly than God. If we value our own independence more than God, we are putting an idol in our heart, and soon our life will become a temple to the god of self. We must constantly keep God first in our life and in all our desires.

1. The Israelites had difficulty giving up their idols.

What are the idols in our contemporary society? How do people worship these idols?
2. List the top three "idols" that you find among those your age. What is it about these "idols" that attracts people to them?
3. All idols are false representations of God's truth. How does knowing and obeying God's truth keep you from idols?
4. What is there in your life that you are tempted to put in God's place? What do you know about God that causes you to believe that you should have him first in your life? How can this be accomplished?

DEFEAT/OPPRESSION God used evil oppressors to punish the Israelites for their sin, to bring them to the point of repentance, and to test their allegiance to him.

Rebelling against God leads to disaster. God may use oppression to bring wandering hearts back to him. At times God's love is tough.

1. Why did God allow the Israelites' enemies to defeat them?
2. How did these defeats affect the people?
3. Why does it often take painful experiences to turn people from their rebellion against God? What does this teach you about human nature?
4. In what ways are you currently expressing your commitment to Christ? In what areas are you expressing rebellion? Besides the fact that this may result in painful experiences, why should you turn away from rebellion and turn toward God?

REPENTANCE Decline, decay, and defeat caused the people to cry out for help. They vowed to turn from idolatry and to turn to God for mercy and deliverance.

Idolatry gains a foothold in our heart when we make anything more important than God. We must identify modern idols in our heart, renounce them, and turn to God for his love and mercy.

1. Describe the feelings of the people when they repented of their sin and rebellion. What led to those feelings?
2. Is repentance an emotion or an action? Explain your response.
3. To repent means literally "turning from," that is, changing direction. Describe a time in your life when you turned from a sin or sinful attitude and redirected your life toward God. What did you do? What was the evidence of your repentance?

4. Looking back at question four under DEFEAT/OPPRESSION, perhaps you see the need to repent today. What are some new directions you can take that will lead you back toward the Lord who lovingly draws you?

DELIVERANCE/HEROES Because Israel repented, God raised up heroes to deliver his people from their path of sin and the oppression it brought. He used many kinds of people to accomplish this purpose.

God's love and mercy are available to all people. Anyone who is dedicated to God can be used for his service. Real heroes recognize the futility of human effort without God's leading.

1. What qualities did the judges possess that enabled them to make a difference for God?

2. What seem to be the differences between the superstars that our society idolizes and the people God uses as heroes?

3. What people have made the biggest positive impact in your life? In what ways could they be described as God's heroes?

4. What qualities would God's hero need in your school? At your church? In your community?

5. God wants to make a difference in you. He wants you to be a hero for his plan in the world. What qualities do you possess that he could use to make an impact in others' lives?

6. To make a difference in our world, we must begin by seeking a difference in our life. In what areas do you need to grow so that you will be better prepared to be God's hero?

"Mom, that food looks awful!" "Dad, you always make me take out the garbage." "She's the worst teacher ever!" "My allowance isn't enough." "I hate the way I look." Sound familiar? Everyone likes to complain. When things don't go exactly as we think they should, we are quick to let others know we feel cheated and angry. ■ In the book of Ruth, we read of Naomi's complaints. Her husband and two sons had recently died, and she decided to blame God. She figured that since God had caused her loved ones' deaths, he deserved her anger. ■ But God didn't deserve her anger. And Naomi learned that God wasn't to be blamed for her family members' deaths; he was to be thanked for his kindness. ■ We tend to complain against God. If something in life is wrong, we conclude that it must be his fault. The book of Ruth reminds us strongly and clearly that this is not the case. God is not to be blamed for our problems, but praised for his goodness. ■ Read the book of Ruth—a story of relationships, rescue, and romance— and thank God for his goodness in your life.

STATS

PURPOSE: To show how three people remained strong in character and true to God even when the society around them was collapsing

AUTHOR: Unknown. Some think it was Samuel, but internal evidence suggests that it was written after his death.

DATE WRITTEN: Sometime after the period of the judges (1375–1050 B.C.)

SETTING: A dark time in Israel's history when people lived to please themselves, not God (Judges 17:6)

KEY PEOPLE: Ruth, Naomi, Boaz

KEY PLACES: Moab, Bethlehem

CHAPTER 1 RUTH GOES HOME WITH NAOMI.

Now it came to pass, in the days when the judges ruled, that there was a famine in the land. And a certain man of Bethlehem, Judah, went to dwell in the country of Moab, he and his wife and his two sons. ²The name of the man *was* Elimelech, the name of his wife *was* Naomi, and the names of his two sons *were* Mahlon and Chilion—Ephrathites of Bethlehem, Judah. And they went to the country of Moab and remained there. ³Then Elimelech, Naomi's husband, died; and she was left, and her two sons. ⁴Now they took wives of the women of Moab: the name of the one *was* Orpah, and the name of the other Ruth. And they dwelt there about ten years. ⁵Then both Mahlon and Chilion also died; so the woman survived her two sons and her husband.

⁶Then she arose with her daughters-in-law that she might return from the country of Moab, for she had heard in the country of Moab that the LORD had visited His people by giving them bread. ⁷Therefore she went out from the place where she was, and her two daughters-in-law with her; and they went on the way to return to the land of Judah. ⁸And Naomi said to her two daughters-in-law, "Go, return each to her mother's house. The LORD deal kindly with you, as you have dealt with the dead and with me. ⁹The LORD grant that you may find rest, each in the house of her husband."

So she kissed them, and they lifted up their voices and wept. ¹⁰And they said to her, "Surely we will return with you to your people."

¹¹But Naomi said, "Turn back, my daughters; why will you go with me? *Are* there still sons in my womb, that they may be your husbands? ¹²Turn back, my daughters, go—for I am too old to have a husband. If I should say I have hope, *if* I should have a husband tonight and should also bear sons, ¹³would you wait for them till they were grown? Would you restrain yourselves from having husbands? No, my daughters; for it grieves me very much for your sakes that the hand of the LORD has gone out against me!"

¹⁴Then they lifted up their voices and wept again; and Orpah kissed her mother-in-law, but Ruth clung to her.

WIDOWS

1:8-9 There was almost nothing worse than being a widow in the ancient world. Widows were taken advantage of or ignored. They were almost always poverty-stricken. The law, therefore, provided that the nearest relative of the dead husband should care for the widow; but Naomi had no relatives in Moab, and she did not know if any of her relatives were alive in Israel.

In her desperate situation, Naomi had a very selfless attitude. Although she had decided to return to Israel, she encouraged Ruth and Orpah to stay in Moab and start their lives over, even though this would mean hardship for herself. Like Naomi, we must consider others' needs and not just our own. As Naomi discovered, when you reach out to others, they often respond by reaching out to you.

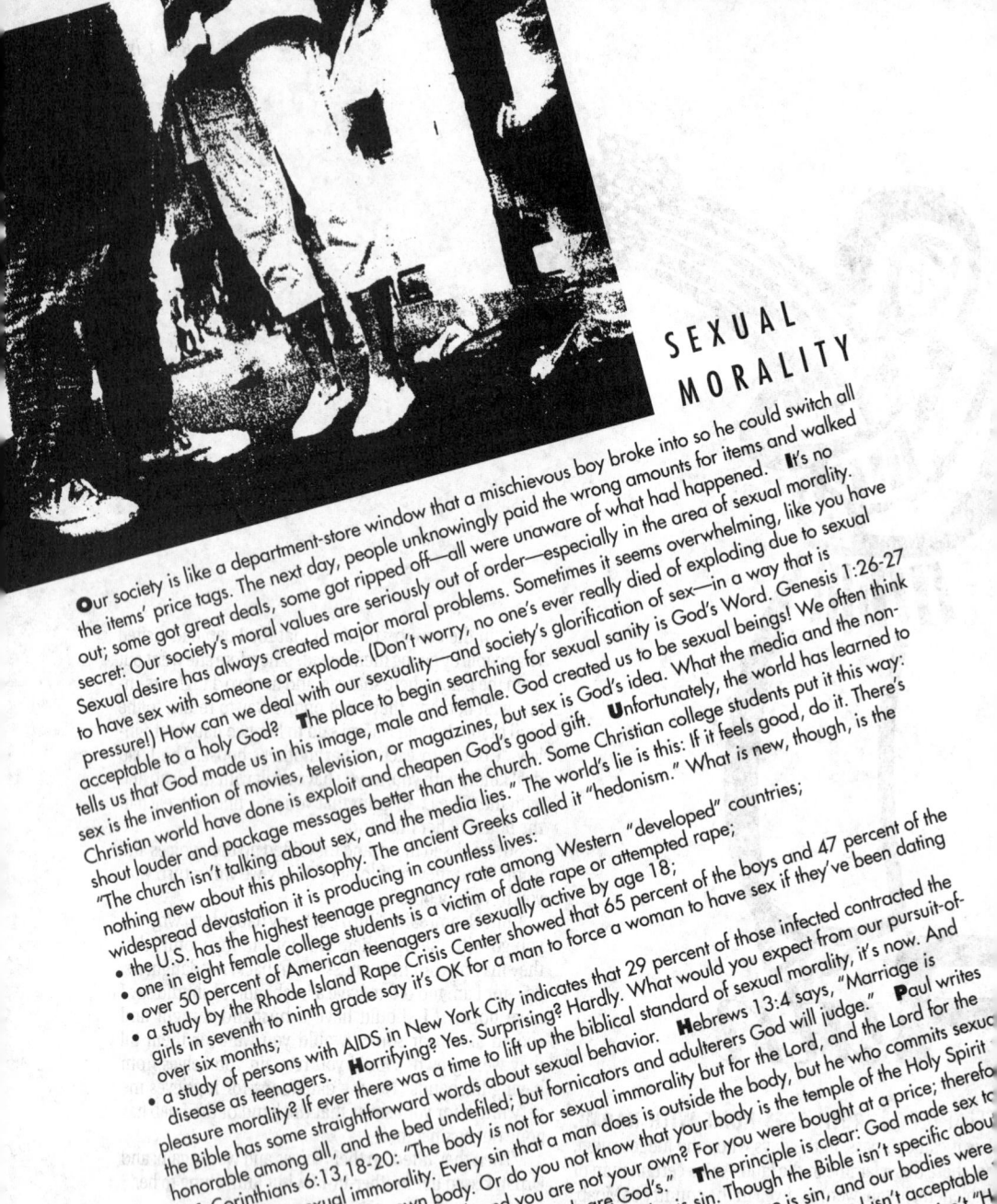

SEXUAL MORALITY

Our society is like a department-store window that a mischievous boy broke into so he could switch all the items' price tags. The next day, people unknowingly paid the wrong amounts for items and walked out; some got great deals, some got ripped off—all were unaware of what had happened. **I**t's no secret: Our society's moral values are seriously out of order—especially in the area of sexual morality. Sexual desire has always created major moral problems. Sometimes it seems overwhelming, like you have to have sex with someone or explode. (Don't worry, no one's ever really died of exploding due to sexual pressure!) How can we deal with our sexuality—and society's glorification of sex—in a way that is acceptable to a holy God? **T**he place to begin searching for sexual sanity is God's Word. Genesis 1:26-27 tells us that God made us in his image, male and female. God created us to be sexual beings! We often think sex is the invention of movies, television, or magazines, but sex is God's idea. What the media and the non-Christian world have done is exploit and cheapen God's good gift. **U**nfortunately, the world has learned to shout louder and package messages better than the church." The world's lie is this: If it feels good, do it. There's nothing new about this philosophy. The ancient Greeks called it "hedonism." What is new, though, is the widespread devastation it is producing in countless lives:

- the U.S. has the highest teenage pregnancy rate among Western "developed" countries;
- one in eight female college students is a victim of date rape or attempted rape;
- over 50 percent of American teenagers are sexually active by age 18;
- a study by the Rhode Island Rape Crisis Center showed that 65 percent of the boys and 47 percent of the girls in seventh to ninth grade say it's OK for a man to force a woman to have sex if they've been dating over six months;
- a study of persons with AIDS in New York City indicates that 29 percent of those infected contracted the disease as teenagers. **H**orrifying? Yes. Surprising? Hardly. What would you expect from our pursuit-of-pleasure morality? If ever there was a time to lift up the biblical standard of sexual morality, it's now. And

the Bible has some straightforward words about sexual behavior. **H**ebrews 13:4 says, "Marriage is honorable among all, and the bed undefiled; but fornicators and adulterers God will judge." **P**aul writes in 1 Corinthians 6:13,18-20: "The body is not for sexual immorality but for the Lord, and the Lord for the body. . . . Flee sexual immorality. Every sin that a man does is outside the body, but he who commits sexual immorality sins against his own body. Or do you not know that your body is the temple of the Holy Spirit is in you, whom you have from God, and you are not your own? For you were bought at a price; therefo glorify God in your body and in your spirit, which are God's." **T**he principle is clear: God made sex to part of the bond between a husband and wife. Anything else is sin. Though the Bible isn't specific abou ing activities, the main biblical instruction is plain: Sex outside of marriage is sin, and our bodies were meant for this kind of sin. **O**f course, this leaves a sizable gray area of what is and isn't acceptable God's eyes. Go to an older Christian for counsel in these matters, remembering that the issue isn't "H much can I do before I'm sinning?" If you want to please God, the question is, "What would God ho me do in my opposite-sex relationships? How can I best honor him and the other person?" **N**avig the waters of sexual morality is difficult, but with the Bible, prayer, and other Christians' input as y compass, you can do it without crashing on the rocks of sexual sin.

Entreat me *not* to le *a v e* *you*...

for wherever you go, I will go
and w h e r e v e r
you lodge,
I will lodge;

YOUR PEOPLE
shall be
MY PEOPLE
and ## YOUR GOD,
MY GOD.

CHAPTER 2 RUTH GLEANS IN THE FIELDS. There was a relative of Naomi's husband, a man of great wealth, of the family of Elimelech. His name *was* Boaz. ²So Ruth the Moabitess said to Naomi, "Please let me go to the field, and glean heads of grain after *him* in whose sight I may find favor."

And she said to her, "Go, my daughter."

³Then she left, and went and gleaned in the field after the reapers. And she happened to come to the part of the field *belonging* to Boaz, who *was* of the family of Elimelech.

⁴Now behold, Boaz came from Bethlehem, and said to the reapers, "The LORD *be* with you!"

And they answered him, "The LORD bless you!"

⁵Then Boaz said to his servant who was in charge of the reapers, "Whose young woman *is* this?"

⁶So the servant who was in charge of the reapers answered and said, "It *is* the young Moabite woman who came back with Naomi from the country of Moab. ⁷And she said, 'Please let me glean and gather after the reapers among the sheaves.' So she came and has continued from morning until now, though she rested a little in the house."

⁸Then Boaz said to Ruth, "You will listen, my daughter, will you not? Do not go to glean in another field, nor go from here, but stay close by my young women. ⁹*Let* your eyes *be* on the field which they reap, and go after them. Have I not commanded the young men not to touch you?

Who wrote the Bible, and how do I know if it really came from God?

I WONDER . . .

God gave the words that are in the Bible by working in the minds of his chosen writers. Then these men wrote down what he wanted.

The Bible contains 66 books written by 40 authors at various points in history. Many of the "books" are actually letters.

If you know a mathematician, ask him or her the probability of 66 separate documents, written over a period of 1,500 years by 40 different authors, not having any contradictions. He'd have to conclude what you've described is mathematically impossible. Yet that is what God did as he wrote and arranged the Bible.

The theme, the history, the way the Bible reveals God's character, and, especially, the way it describes God's way of bringing salvation to people, are consistent throughout.

More important than how we got the Bible is why. God gave the Bible to us to prepare us for anything, to help us do good to everyone.

God's Word also serves as our offensive weapon against all the problems we encounter. "For the word of God *is* living and powerful, and sharper than any two-edged sword, piercing even to the division of soul and spirit, . . . and is a discerner of the thoughts and intents of the heart" (Hebrews 4:12).

God is in the business of molding our character and strengthening us for future use. He's given us all of the resources for strength we'll ever need, in the Bible.

---

¹⁵And she said, "Look, your sister-in-law has gone back to her people and to her gods; return after your sister-in-law."

¹⁶But Ruth said:

"Entreat me not to leave you,
    Or to turn back from following after you;
    For wherever you go, I will go;
    And wherever you lodge, I will lodge;
    Your people *shall be* my people,
    And your God, my God.
⁷   Where you die, I will die,
    And there will I be buried.
    The LORD do so to me, and more also,
    If *anything but* death parts you and me."

⁸When she saw that she was determined to go with her, she stopped speaking to her.

¹⁹Now the two of them went until they came to Bethlehem. And it happened, when they had come to Bethlehem, that all the city was excited because of them; and the women said, "*Is* this Naomi?"

²⁰But she said to them, "Do not call me Naomi; call me Mara, for the Almighty has dealt very bitterly with me. ²¹I went out full, and the LORD has brought me home again empty. Why do you call me Naomi, since the LORD has testified against me, and the Almighty has afflicted me?"

²²So Naomi returned, and Ruth the Moabitess her daughter-in-law with her, who returned from the country of Moab. Now they came to Bethlehem at the beginning of barley harvest.

◤▶ADVICE

3:5 As a foreigner, Ruth may have thought that Naomi's advice was odd. But Ruth followed the advice because she knew Naomi was kind, trustworthy, and filled with moral integrity. Each of us knows a parent, older friend, or relative who is always looking out for our best interests. The experience and knowledge of such a person can be invaluable. Imagine what Ruth's life would have been like had she ignored her mother-in-law.

And when you are thirsty, go to the vessels and drink from what the young men have drawn."

¹⁰So she fell on her face, bowed down to the ground, and said to him, "Why have I found favor in your eyes, that you should take notice of me, since I *am* a foreigner?"

COMMITMENT

Wendy and Susan have been friends ever since the third grade. Girl Scouts, softball, Sunday school—they've done it all together.

As they've grown older, however, the girls have developed vastly different interests. In fact, now, as teenagers, they couldn't be more opposite.

Wendy is short and round. Extremely outgoing, she makes good grades and keeps everyone in the band in stitches. She's also very involved in the drama club. Susan is tall, pretty, and extremely shy. An average student, Susan dates quite a bit and works at an expensive dress shop in the mall.

Since the two girls have such contrasting personalities, nobody can quite understand why they're still friends. But they are. They're best friends.

Just how close are they? Well, get this: last week, Wendy and Susan made Saturday plans to go shopping. The very next day, Susan got a call from the cutest guy at school (a guy she's secretly liked all year). The call went like this:

"Susan? Hi, this is Brett. Listen, I was just wondering if you'd like to go horseback riding this Saturday?"

"This weekend?" Susan paused. "Um, Brett, I'd really like to, but I kind of already made plans. Can we do it some other time?"

Would you have been that loyal to a friend? Read about another woman who understood the meaning of commitment—Ruth 1:1-19.

¹¹And Boaz answered and said to her, "It has been fully reported to me, all that you have done for your mother-in-law since the death of your husband, and *how* you have left your father and your mother and the land of your birth, and have come to a people whom you did not know before. ¹²The LORD repay your work, and a full reward be given you by the LORD God of Israel, under whose wings you have come for refuge."

¹³Then she said, "Let me find favor in your sight, my lord; for you have comforted me, and have spoken kindly to your maidservant, though I am not like one of your maidservants."

¹⁴Now Boaz said to her at mealtime, "Come here, and eat of the bread, and dip your piece of bread in the vinegar." So she sat beside the reapers, and he passed parched *grain* to her; and she ate and was satisfied, and kept some back. ¹⁵And when she rose up to glean, Boaz commanded his young men, saying, "Let her glean even

among the sheaves, and do not reproach her. ¹⁶Also le *grain* from the bundles fall purposely for her; leave *it* tha she may glean, and do not rebuke her."

¹⁷So she gleaned in the field until evening, and bea out what she had gleaned, and it was about an ephah c barley. ¹⁸Then she took *it* up and went into the city, an her mother-in-law saw what she had gleaned. So sh brought out and gave to her what she had kept back afte she had been satisfied.

¹⁹And her mother-in-law said to her, "Where have yo gleaned today? And where did you work? Blessed be th one who took notice of you."

So she told her mother-in-law with whom she ha worked, and said, "The man's name with whom I worke today *is* Boaz."

²⁰Then Naomi said to her daughter-in-law, "Blessed *l* he of the LORD, who has not forsaken His kindness to th living and the dead!" And Naomi said to her, "This ma *is* a relation of ours, one of our close relatives."

²¹Ruth the Moabitess said, "He also said to me, 'Yo shall stay close by my young men until they have finishe all my harvest.'"

²²And Naomi said to Ruth her daughter-in-law, "*It* good, my daughter, that you go out with his youn women, and that people do not meet you in any othe field." ²³So she stayed close by the young women c Boaz, to glean until the end of barley harvest and whea harvest; and she dwelt with her mother-in-law.

CHAPTER 3 RUTH MARRIES BOAZ.

Then Naom her mother-in-law said to her, "My daughter, shall I nc seek security for you, that it may be well with you? ²Nov Boaz, whose young women you were with, *is he* not ou relative? In fact, he is winnowing barley tonight at th threshing floor. ³Therefore wash yourself and anoir yourself, put on your *best* garment and go down to th threshing floor; *but* do not make yourself known to th man until he has finished eating and drinking. ⁴Then shall be, when he lies down, that you shall notice th place where he lies; and you shall go in, uncover his fee and lie down; and he will tell you what you should do."

⁵And she said to her, "All that you say to me I will do.

⁶So she went down to the threshing floor and di according to all that her mother-in-law instructed he ⁷And after Boaz had eaten and drunk, and his heart wa cheerful, he went to lie down at the end of the heap c grain; and she came softly, uncovered his feet, and la down.

⁸Now it happened at midnight that the man was sta.

◤▶TOUGH TIMES

4:15 God brought great blessings out of Naomi's tragedy, eve blessings than "seven sons" (indicating the great blessing of an abundance of heirs). Throughout her tough times, Naomi continu trust God. And God, in his time, blessed her greatly. Even in our and calamity, God can bring great blessings. Be like Naomi, and turn your back on God when tragedy strikes. Don't ask, "How c allow this to happen to me?" Instead, trust him. He will be with in the hard times.

ed, and turned himself; and there, a woman was lying
at his feet. ⁹And he said, "Who *are* you?"

So she answered, "I *am* Ruth, your maidservant. Take
your maidservant under your wing, for you are a close
relative."

¹⁰Then he said, "Blessed *are* you of the Lᴏʀᴅ, my daughter! For you have shown more kindness at the end than at
the beginning, in that you did not go after young men,
whether poor or rich. ¹¹And now, my daughter, do not fear.
I will do for you all that you request, for all the people of
my town know that you *are* a virtuous woman. ¹²Now it is
true that I *am* a close relative; however, there is a relative
closer than I. ¹³Stay this night, and in the morning it shall
be *that* if he will perform the duty of a close relative for
you—good; let him do it. But if he does not want to perform the duty for you, then I will perform the duty for you,
as the Lᴏʀᴅ lives! Lie down until morning."

¹⁴So she lay at his feet until morning, and she arose
before one could recognize another. Then he said, "Do
not let it be known that the woman came to the threshing
floor." ¹⁵Also he said, "Bring the shawl that *is*
on you and hold it." And when she
held it, he measured six *ephahs*
of barley, and laid *it* on
her. Then she went
into the city.

¹⁶When she came to
her mother-in-law, she
said, "*Is* that you, my
daughter?"

Then she told her all
that the man had done for
her. ¹⁷And she said, "These
six *ephahs* of barley he gave
me; for he said to me, 'Do not
go empty-handed to your
mother-in-law.'"

¹⁸Then she said, "Sit still, my
daughter, until you know how the
matter will turn out; for the man
will not rest until he has concluded
the matter this day."

CHAPTER 4 Now Boaz went up
to the gate and sat down there; and
behold, the close relative of whom Boaz
had spoken came by. So Boaz said,
"Come aside, friend, sit down here." So
he came aside and sat down. ²And he
took ten men of the elders of the city, and
said, "Sit down here." So they sat down.
³Then he said to the close relative, "Naomi,
who has come back from the country of
Moab, sold the piece of land which *belonged*
to our brother Elimelech. ⁴And I thought to inform you, saying, 'Buy *it* back in the presence of
the inhabitants and the elders of my people. If you
will redeem *it*, redeem *it*; but if you will not redeem *it, then* tell me, that I may know; for *there is* no
one but you to redeem *it*, and I *am* next after you.'"

And he said, "I will redeem *it*."

⁵Then Boaz said, "On the day you buy the field from
the hand of Naomi, you must also buy *it* from Ruth the
Moabitess, the wife of the dead, to perpetuate the name
of the dead through his inheritance."

⁶And the close relative said, "I cannot redeem *it* for
myself, lest I ruin my own inheritance. You redeem my
right of redemption for yourself, for I cannot redeem *it*."

⁷Now this *was the custom* in former times in Israel
concerning redeeming and exchanging, to confirm anything: one man took off his sandal and gave *it* to the
other, and this *was* a confirmation in Israel.

⁸Therefore the close relative said to Boaz, "Buy *it* for
yourself." So he took off his sandal. ⁹And Boaz said to the
elders and all the people, "You *are* witnesses this day that
I have bought all that was Elimelech's, and all that *was*
Chilion's and Mahlon's, from the hand of Naomi. ¹⁰Moreover, Ruth the Moabitess, the widow of Mahlon, I have
acquired as my wife, to perpetuate the name of
the dead through his
inheritance,

RUTH & NAOMI

Real friends enjoy each other's company. Friendship weaves lives together. One of the greatest friendships described in the Bible was between Ruth and Naomi. In fact, we know more about their friendship than we know about them as individuals. In our world today we sometimes try too hard to make it on our own. Ruth and Naomi teach us how wonderful a good friendship can be.

Naomi and Ruth did not share many of the typical things that bring people together. They came from different cultures, families, and places. Naomi was older than Ruth. Ruth had been married to Naomi's son. But both women had lost their husbands. They were left with almost nothing but each other.

Yet there was real freedom in their friendship. Often in relationships people try to hold each other too tightly. Friendship can fade when there is no room to breathe. Naomi was willing to let Ruth return to her family. Ruth was willing to leave her homeland to go to Israel. Naomi even helped arrange Ruth's marriage to Boaz although she knew it would change their relationship.

God was always part of Naomi and Ruth's friendship. Ruth met God through Naomi as the older woman allowed Ruth to see, hear, and feel all the joy and sorrow of her relationship with God. How often do you feel that your thoughts, feelings, and questions about God should be kept from your best friends? If you are really getting to know God, he wants to be part of all your friendships.

LESSON: God's living presence in a relationship overcomes differences that might otherwise create division and disharmony

KEY VERSE: "But Ruth said: 'Entreat me not to leave you, or to turn back from following after you; for wherever you go, I will go; and wherever you lodge, I will lodge; your people shall be my people, and your God, my God'" (Ruth 1:16).

Their story is told in the book of Ruth. Ruth is also mentioned in Matthew 1:5.

UPS:
- A relationship where the greatest bond was their faith in God
- A relationship of strong mutual commitment
- A relationship in which each person tried to do what was best for the other

STATS:
- Where: Moab, Bethlehem
- Occupation: Wives, widows, gleaners
- Relatives: Elimelech, Mahlon, Chilion, Orpah, Boaz

Elimelech, Naomi, and their sons traveled from Bethlehem to the land of Moab because of a famine. After her husband and sons died, Naomi returned to Bethlehem with her daughter-in-law Ruth.

that the name of the dead may not be cut off from among his brethren and from his position at the gate. You *are* witnesses this day."

[11]And all the people who *were* at the gate, and the elders, said, "*We are* witnesses. The LORD make the woman who is coming to your house like Rachel and Leah, the two who built the house of Israel; and may you prosper in Ephrathah and be famous in Bethlehem. [12]May your house be like the house of Perez, whom Tamar bore to Judah, because of the offspring which the LORD will give you from this young woman."

[13]So Boaz took Ruth and she became his wife; and when he went in to her, the LORD gave her conception, and she bore a son. [14]Then the women said to Naomi, "Blessed *be* the LORD, who has not left you this day without a close relative; and may his name be famous in Israel! [15]And may he be to you a restorer of life and a nourisher of your old age; for your daughter-in-law, who loves you, who is better to you than seven sons, has borne him." [16]Then Naomi took the child and laid him on her bosom, and became a nurse to him. [17]Also the neighbor women gave him a name, saying, "There is a son born to Naomi." And they called his name Obed. He *is* the father of Jesse, the father of David.

[18]Now this *is* the genealogy of Perez: Perez begot Hezron; [19]Hezron begot Ram, and Ram begot Amminadab; [20]Amminadab begot Nahshon, and Nahshon begot Salmon; [21]Salmon begot Boaz, and Boaz begot Obed; [22]Obed begot Jesse, and Jesse begot David.

MEGA Themes

FAITHFULNESS Ruth's faithfulness to Naomi as a daughter-in-law and friend is a great example of love and loyalty. Ruth, Naomi, and Boaz were also faithful to God and his laws. Throughout the story we see how God is faithful in return.

Ruth's life was guided by faithfulness toward God, and it was exhibited in her loyalty to the people she knew. We should also imitate God's faithfulness by being loyal and loving in our relationships.

1. Describe the type of relationship Ruth had with Naomi.
2. How did this relationship reflect Ruth's relationship with God?
3. What have you learned through other people about God's love? When and how did you learn these things?
4. How does growing in your relationship with God enable you to have deeper relationships with the important people in your life?

5. Who are your important friends? What are some specific ways you could show them more of God's love?

KINDNESS Ruth showed great kindness to Naomi. And Boaz showed kindness to Ruth—a despised Moabite woman with no money. God showed his kindness to Ruth, Naomi, and Boaz by bringing them together for his purposes.

Just as Boaz showed his kindness by buying back land to guarantee Ruth and Naomi's inheritance, so Christ showed his kindness by purchasing us to guarantee our eternal life. God's kindness in providing a redeemer for our lives should motivate us to love and honor him.

1. What makes kindness such an important quality?
2. What do you learn about the kindness of God from the life of Ruth? From the life of Jesus?
3. What could a person learn about God's kindness

KEY PLACES IN 1 SAMUEL

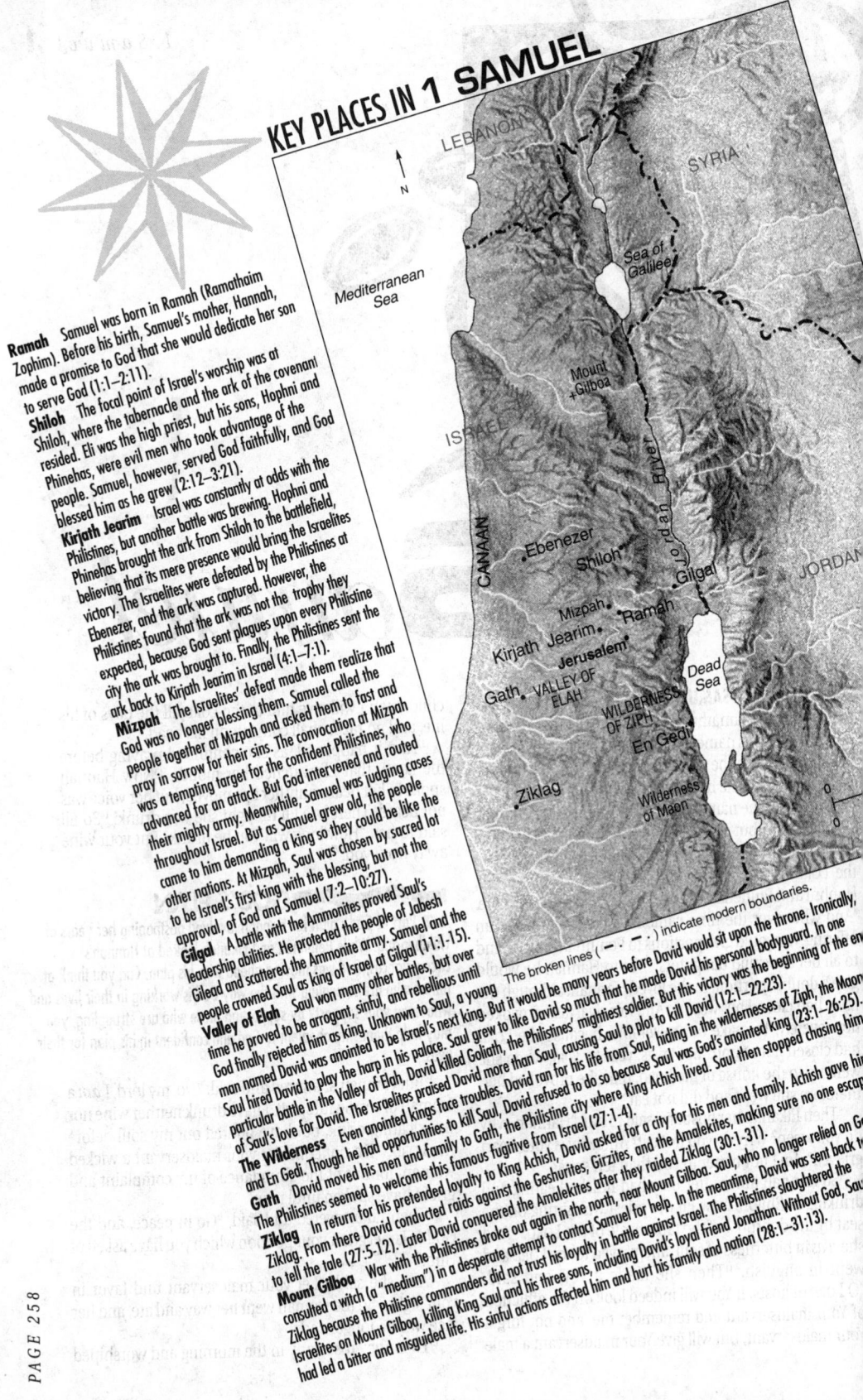

Ramah Samuel was born in Ramah (Ramathaim Zophim). Before his birth, Samuel's mother, Hannah, made a promise to God that she would dedicate her son to serve God (1:1–2:11).

Shiloh The focal point of Israel's worship was at Shiloh, where the tabernacle and the ark of the covenant resided. Eli was the high priest, but his sons, Hophni and Phinehas, were evil men who took advantage of the people. Samuel, however, served God faithfully, and God blessed him as he grew (2:12–3:21).

Kirjath Jearim Israel was constantly at odds with the Philistines, but another battle was brewing. Hophni and Phinehas brought the ark from Shiloh to the battlefield, believing that its mere presence would bring the Israelites victory. The Israelites were defeated by the Philistines at Ebenezer, and the ark was captured. However, the Philistines found that the ark was not the trophy they expected, because God sent plagues upon every Philistine city the ark was brought to. Finally, the Philistines sent the ark back to Kirjath Jearim in Israel (4:1–7:1).

Mizpah The Israelites' defeat made them realize that God was no longer blessing them. Samuel called the people together at Mizpah and asked them to fast and pray in sorrow for their sins. The convocation at Mizpah was a tempting target for the confident Philistines, who advanced for an attack. But God intervened and routed their mighty army. Meanwhile, Samuel was judging cases throughout Israel. But as Samuel grew old, the people came to him demanding a king so they could be like the other nations. At Mizpah, Saul was chosen by sacred lot to be Israel's first king with the blessing, but not the approval, of God and Samuel (7:2–10:27).

Gilgal A battle with the Ammonites proved Saul's leadership abilities. He protected the people of Jabesh Gilead and scattered the Ammonite army. Samuel and the people crowned Saul as king of Israel at Gilgal (11:1-15).

Valley of Elah Saul won many other battles, but over time he proved to be arrogant, sinful, and rebellious until God finally rejected him as king. Unknown to Saul, a young man named David was anointed to be Israel's next king. Saul hired David to play the harp in his palace. Saul grew to like David so much that he made David his personal bodyguard. In one particular battle in the Valley of Elah, David killed Goliath, the Philistines' mightiest soldier. But this victory was the beginning of the en... of Saul's love for David. The Israelites praised David more than Saul, causing Saul to plot to kill David (12:1–22:23).

The Wilderness Even anointed kings face troubles. David ran for his life from Saul, hiding in the wildernesses of Ziph, the Maon and En Gedi. Though he had opportunities to kill Saul, David refused to do so because Saul was God's anointed king (23:1–26:25).

Gath David moved with his men and family to Gath, the Philistine city where King Achish lived. Saul then stopped chasing him... The Philistines seemed to welcome this famous fugitive from Israel (27:1-4).

Ziklag In return for his pretended loyalty to King Achish, David asked for a city for his men and family. Achish gave him... Ziklag. From there David conducted raids against the Geshurites, Girzites, and the Amalekites, making sure no one escap... to tell the tale (27:5-12). Later David broke out again in the north, near Mount Gilboa. Saul, who no longer relied on G... War with the Philistines broke out again in a desperate attempt to contact Samuel for help. In the meantime, David was sent back t...

Mount Gilboa War with the Philistines led to trouble. David refused to trust his loyalty in battle against Israel. The Philistines slaughtered the... consulted a witch (a "medium") in a desperate attempt to contact the Amalekites after they raided Ziklag (30:1-31). Ziklag because the Philistine commanders did not trust his loyalty in battle against Israel. The Philistines slaughtered the Israelites on Mount Gilboa, killing King Saul and his three sons, including David's loyal friend Jonathan. Without God, Saul had led a bitter and misguided life. His sinful actions affected him and hurt his family and nation (28:1–31:13).

The broken lines (‒ ‒ ‒) indicate modern boundaries.

Map labels: LEBANON, SYRIA, Sea of Galilee, Mount Gilboa, ISRAEL, CANAAN, Jordan River, JORDAN, Ebenezer, Shiloh, Gilgal, Mizpah, Ramah, Kirjath Jearim, Jerusalem, Gath, VALLEY OF ELAH, Dead Sea, WILDERNESS OF ZIPH, En Gedi, Ziklag, Wilderness of Maon, Mediterranean Sea

1 Samuel

CHAPTER 1 **SAMUEL IS BORN.** Now there was a certain man of Ramathaim Zophim, of the mountains of Ephraim, and his name *was* Elkanah the son of Jeroham, the son of Elihu, the son of Tohu, the son of Zuph, an Ephraimite. ²And he had two wives: the name of one *was* Hannah, and the name of the other Peninnah. Peninnah had children, but Hannah had no children. ³This man went up from his city yearly to worship and sacrifice to the LORD of hosts in Shiloh. Also the two sons of Eli, Hophni and Phinehas, the priests of the LORD, *were* there. ⁴And whenever the time came for Elkanah to make an offering, he would give portions to Peninnah his wife and to all her sons and daughters. ⁵But to Hannah he would give a double portion, for he loved Hannah, although the LORD had closed her womb. ⁶And her rival also provoked her severely, to make her miserable, because the LORD had closed her womb. ⁷So it was, year by year, when she went up to the house of the LORD, that she provoked her; therefore she wept and did not eat.

⁸Then Elkanah her husband said to her, "Hannah, why do you weep? Why do you not eat? And why is your heart grieved? *Am* I not better to you than ten sons?"

⁹So Hannah arose after they had finished eating and drinking in Shiloh. Now Eli the priest was sitting on the seat by the doorpost of the tabernacle of the LORD. ¹⁰And she *was* in bitterness of soul, and prayed to the LORD and wept in anguish. ¹¹Then she made a vow and said, "O LORD of hosts, if You will indeed look on the affliction of Your maidservant and remember me, and not forget Your maidservant, but will give Your maidservant a male

child, then I will give him to the LORD all the days of his life, and no razor shall come upon his head."

¹²And it happened, as she continued praying before the LORD, that Eli watched her mouth. ¹³Now Hannah spoke in her heart; only her lips moved, but her voice was not heard. Therefore Eli thought she was drunk. ¹⁴So Eli said to her, "How long will you be drunk? Put your wine away from you!"

GOD'S PLAN

1:7 Part of God's plan for Hannah involved postponing her years of childbearing. While Peninnah and Elkanah looked at Hannah's circumstances, God was moving ahead with his plan. Can you think of others who are struggling with the way God is working in their lives and who need your support? By supporting those who are struggling, you may help them stay obedient to God and confident in his plan for their lives.

¹⁵But Hannah answered and said, "No, my lord, I *am* a woman of sorrowful spirit. I have drunk neither wine nor intoxicating drink, but have poured out my soul before the LORD. ¹⁶Do not consider your maidservant a wicked woman, for out of the abundance of my complaint and grief I have spoken until now."

¹⁷Then Eli answered and said, "Go in peace, and the God of Israel grant your petition which you have asked of Him."

¹⁸And she said, "Let your maidservant find favor in your sight." So the woman went her way and ate, and her face was no longer *sad*.

¹⁹Then they rose early in the morning and worshiped

Susan, is that you?" Susan had just answered her phone, expecting it to be Jill, her best friend. Instead, the voice was unfamiliar. ■ "Yeah," she replied. "Who is this?" ■ "Oh, my name is Eric. You don't know me, but I see you at school a lot." ■ Susan was popular—she had been voted class princess and had been dating the captain of the basketball team, Allen. ■ "Why did you call me?" she asked.

■ Eric said that he just wanted to talk. So they did, for an hour that night, and for several hours over the next few weeks—about everything they could think of. ■ Susan started looking forward to Eric's calls. She wanted to meet him, but he always refused. She wondered what he looked like. So far, she'd only dated popular guys: a football player, the class president, a guy with a new Porsche, and now Allen—about the cutest guy in school. ■ Soon, though, Susan realized Eric's popularity didn't really matter. He had become a good friend. She started to understand that though we often judge people by what we see on the outside, what really matters is what's on the inside. ■ First Samuel shows how looks can be deceiving. It tells about the first two kings of Israel: Saul and David. Saul was tall, handsome, and brave. He looked like a king. David, on the other hand, didn't look like a leader, much less a king. He was young and small. ■ Yet Saul, who looked like a king, proved he wasn't worthy to be one, while David, who wasn't so impressive, became a great king. ■ As you read 1 Samuel, watch the rise and fall of Saul and the rise of David. Remember that while people judge by outward appearances, God looks at thoughts and intentions (1 Samuel 16:7).

STATS

PURPOSE: To record the life of Samuel, Israel's last judge; the reign and decline of Saul, the first king; and the choice and preparation of David, Israel's greatest king

AUTHOR: Probably Samuel, but also includes writings from the prophets Nathan and Gad (1 Chronicles 29:29)

SETTING: The book begins in the days of the judges and describes Israel's transition from a theocracy (being led by God) to a monarchy (being led by a king)

KEY PEOPLE: Eli, Hannah, Samuel, Saul, Jonathan, David

from seeing your relationships with your friends? Your family?

4. In what ways could you display more of this kindness in your important relationships?

INTEGRITY Ruth showed high moral character by being loyal to Naomi, by her clean break from her former land and customs, and by her hard work in the field. Boaz showed integrity in his moral standards, his honesty, and by following through on his commitments.

When we have experienced God's faithfulness and kindness, we should respond by living a godly life. Just as Ruth's and Boaz's values contrasted with those of the culture portrayed in Judges, so should our life stand out from the world around us.

1. Give examples of people you know or know about who have integrity.
2. Give examples of people you know or know about who lack integrity.
3. What is the connection between being a witness for Jesus Christ and being a person of integrity?
4. List several specific areas where Christians might be tempted to compromise their integrity as followers of Christ.
5. What can you do to help maintain your integrity?

PROTECTION We see God's care and protection of Naomi and Ruth. His supreme control over circumstances brings them safety and security. God guides the minds and activities of people to fulfill his purpose.

No matter how devastating our present situation may be, we can hope in God. His resources are infinite. We must believe that he can work in any person's life, whether that person is a king or a stranger in a foreign land.

1. Think of a time when, as a child, you were frightened and an adult comforted you. What was it about that person that calmed your fears? How did you feel toward that person?
2. Every person has fears. What are some of the things that cause you to feel afraid or insecure?

3. What qualities do you find in God that tend to calm your fears and bring you a sense of security?
4. What fears do you have about the present? About the future?
5. To whom can you go to be reminded of God's secure love?
6. Do you know someone who is in a very difficult, possibly scary, time in his or her life? Based on your understanding of God and the way he uses us to communicate his protection, how can you help this person?

PROSPERITY/BLESSING Ruth and Naomi came to Bethlehem as poor widows, but they soon became prosperous through Ruth's marriage to Boaz. Ruth became a mother (and eventually the great-grandmother of King David). Yet the greatest blessing was not the money, the marriage, or the children: it was the quality of love and respect between Ruth, Boaz, and Naomi.

We tend to think of blessings in terms of prosperity rather than the high-quality relationships that God makes possible for us. No matter what our economic situation, we can love and respect the people God has brought into our life. In so doing, we give and receive blessings.

1. Define what the word *rich* means to you.
2. What is dangerous about always comparing what you have with what others have?
3. What should be your attitude about gaining riches?
4. Some Christians have large amounts of possessions, and others have very little. Is the person with more possessions more blessed by God? Explain.
5. Summarize what you think is God's will for you concerning gaining possessions and becoming rich.
6. What does it mean for you to be blessed by God?

before the LORD, and returned and came to their house at Ramah. And Elkanah knew Hannah his wife, and the LORD remembered her. ²⁰So it came to pass in the process of time that Hannah conceived and bore a son, and called his name Samuel, *saying*, "Because I have asked for him from the LORD."

²¹Now the man Elkanah and all his house went up to offer to the LORD the yearly sacrifice and his vow. ²²But Hannah did not go up, for she said to her husband, "*Not* until the child is weaned; then I will take him, that he may appear before the LORD and remain there forever."

²³So Elkanah her husband said to her, "Do what seems best to you; wait until you have weaned him. Only let the LORD establish His word." Then the woman stayed and nursed her son until she had weaned him.

²⁴Now when she had weaned him, she took him up with her, with three bulls, one ephah of flour, and a skin of wine, and brought him to the house of the LORD in Shiloh. And the child *was* young. ²⁵Then they slaughtered a bull, and brought the child to Eli. ²⁶And she said, "O my lord! As your soul lives, my lord, I *am* the woman who stood by you here, praying to the LORD. ²⁷For this child I prayed, and the LORD has granted me my petition which I asked of Him. ²⁸Therefore I also have lent him to the LORD; as long as he lives he shall be lent to the LORD." So they worshiped the LORD there.

CHAPTER 2 HANNAH'S PRAYER OF THANKS. And
Hannah prayed and said:

"My heart rejoices in the LORD;
   My horn is exalted in the LORD.
I smile at my enemies,
   Because I rejoice in Your salvation.

² "No one is holy like the LORD,
   For *there is* none besides You,
   Nor *is there* any rock like our God.

³ "Talk no more so very proudly;
   Let no arrogance come from your mouth,
For the LORD *is* the God of knowledge;
   And by Him actions are weighed.

⁴ "The bows of the mighty men *are* broken,
   And those who stumbled are girded with strength.
⁵ *Those who were* full have hired themselves out for
      bread,
   And the hungry have ceased *to hunger.*
Even the barren has borne seven,
   And she who has many children has become feeble.

⁶ "The LORD kills and makes alive;
   He brings down to the grave and brings up.
⁷ The LORD makes poor and makes rich;
   He brings low and lifts up.
⁸ He raises the poor from the dust
And lifts the beggar from the ash heap,
To set *them* among princes
   And make them inherit the throne of glory.

"For the pillars of the earth *are* the LORD's,
   And He has set the world upon them.

⁹ He will guard the feet of His saints,
   But the wicked shall be silent in darkness.

"For by strength no man shall prevail.
¹⁰ The adversaries of the LORD shall be broken in
      pieces;
   From heaven He will thunder against them.
The LORD will judge the ends of the earth.

"He will give strength to His king,
   And exalt the horn of His anointed."

HELP!
2:2 Hannah praised God for being a "rock"—firm, strong, and unchanging. In our fast-paced world, friends come and go and circumstances change. It's difficult to find a solid foundation that will not change. Those who devote their lives to people, causes, possessions, or other finite things are trusting things that will all pass away. But God is always present and ready to help, even when everything else seems to be falling apart.

¹¹Then Elkanah went to his house at Ramah. But the child ministered to the LORD before Eli the priest.

¹²Now the sons of Eli *were* corrupt; they did not know the LORD. ¹³And the priests' custom with the people *was that* when any man offered a sacrifice, the priest's servant would come with a three-pronged fleshhook in his hand while the meat was boiling. ¹⁴Then he would thrust *it* into the pan, or kettle, or caldron, or pot; and the priest would take for himself all that the fleshhook brought up. So they did in Shiloh to all the Israelites who came there. ¹⁵Also, before they burned the fat, the priest's servant would come and say to the man who sacrificed, "Give meat for roasting to the priest, for he will not take boiled meat from you, but raw."

¹⁶And *if* the man said to him, "They should really burn the fat first; *then* you may take *as much* as your heart desires," he would then answer him, "*No*, but you must give *it* now; and if not, I will take *it* by force."

¹⁷Therefore the sin of the young men was very great before the LORD, for men abhorred the offering of the LORD.

¹⁸But Samuel ministered before the LORD, *even as* a child, wearing a linen ephod. ¹⁹Moreover his mother used to make him a little robe, and bring *it* to him year by year when she came up with her husband to offer the yearly sacrifice. ²⁰And Eli would bless Elkanah and his wife, and say, "The LORD give you descendants from this woman for the loan that was given to the LORD." Then they would go to their own home.

²¹And the LORD visited Hannah, so that she conceived and bore three sons and two daughters. Meanwhile the child Samuel grew before the LORD.

²²Now Eli was very old; and he heard everything his sons did to all Israel, and how they lay with the women

OLD ENOUGH
2:18 Samuel was a young child, and yet he "ministered before the LORD." Often children can serve God just as effectively as adults. God will use anyone who is willing to learn from him and serve him. He has no age limits. Don't discount the faith of a child or let your age keep you from serving God.

who assembled at the door of the tabernacle of meeting. [23]So he said to them, "Why do you do such things? For I hear of your evil dealings from all the people. [24]No, my sons! For it is not a good report that I hear. You make the LORD's people transgress. [25]If one man sins against another, God will judge him. But if a man sins against the LORD, who will intercede for him?" Nevertheless they did not heed the voice of their father, because the LORD desired to kill them.

◗◗◗◗◗ LISTENING

3:1-5 Although this was the era when God still gave direct and audible messages to his people, such messages became rare in the days of Eli. Why? Look at the attitude of Eli's sons. They either refused to listen to God or allowed greed to get in the way of any communication with him.

Listening and responding are vital in a relationship with God. Although God may not use the sound of a human voice, he speaks just as clearly today through his Word. To receive his messages, we must be ready to listen and to act upon what he tells us. Like Samuel, be ready to say "Speak, for Your servant hears" (3:10) when God calls you to action.

[26]And the child Samuel grew in stature, and in favor both with the LORD and men.

[27]Then a man of God came to Eli and said to him, "Thus says the LORD: 'Did I not clearly reveal Myself to the house of your father when they were in Egypt in Pharaoh's house? [28]Did I not choose him out of all the tribes of Israel to be My priest, to offer upon My altar, to burn incense, and to wear an ephod before Me? And did I not give to the house of your father all the offerings of the children of Israel made by fire? [29]Why do you kick at My sacrifice and My offering which I have commanded in My dwelling place, and honor your sons more than Me, to make yourselves fat with the best of all the offerings of Israel My people?' [30]Therefore the LORD God of Israel says: 'I said indeed that your house and the house of your father would walk before Me forever.' But now the LORD says: 'Far be it from Me; for those who honor Me I will honor, and those who despise Me shall be lightly esteemed. [31]Behold, the days are coming that I will cut off your arm and the arm of your father's house, so that there will not be an old man in your house. [32]And you will see an enemy in My dwelling place, despite all the good which God does for Israel. And there shall not be an old man in your house forever. [33]But any of your men whom I do not cut off from My altar shall consume your eyes and grieve your heart. And all the descendants of your house shall die in the flower of their age. [34]Now this shall be a sign to you that will come upon your two sons, on Hophni and Phinehas: in one day they shall die, both of them. [35]Then I will raise up for Myself a faithful priest who shall do according to what is in My heart and in My mind. I will build him a sure house, and he shall walk before My anointed forever. [36]And it shall come to pass that everyone who is left in your house will come and bow down to him for a piece of silver and a morsel of bread, and say, "Please, put me in one of the priestly positions, that I may eat a piece of bread." ' "

CHAPTER **3** **GOD SPEAKS TO SAMUEL.** Now the boy Samuel ministered to the LORD before Eli. And the word of the LORD was rare in those days; there was no widespread revelation. [2]And it came to pass at that time, while Eli was lying down in his place, and when his eyes had begun to grow so dim that he could not see, [3]and before the lamp of God went out in the tabernacle of the LORD where the ark of God was, and while Samuel was lying down, [4]that the LORD called Samuel. And he answered, "Here I am!" [5]So he ran to Eli and said, "Here I am, for you called me."

And he said, "I did not call; lie down again." And he went and lay down.

[6]Then the LORD called yet again, "Samuel!"

So Samuel arose and went to Eli, and said, "Here I am, for you called me." He answered, "I did not call, my son; lie down again." [7](Now Samuel did not yet know the LORD, nor was the word of the LORD yet revealed to him.)

[8]And the LORD called Samuel again the third time. So he arose and went to Eli, and said, "Here I am, for you did call me."

Then Eli perceived that the LORD had called the boy. [9]Therefore Eli said to Samuel, "Go, lie down; and it shall be, if He calls you, that you must say, 'Speak, LORD, for Your servant hears.' " So Samuel went and lay down in his place.

[10]Now the LORD came and stood and called as at other times, "Samuel! Samuel!"

And Samuel answered, "Speak, for Your servant hears."

[11]Then the LORD said to Samuel: "Behold, I will do something in Israel at which both ears of everyone who hears it will tingle. [12]In that day I will perform against Eli all that I have spoken concerning his house, from beginning to end. [13]For I have told him that I will judge his house forever for the iniquity which he knows, because his sons made themselves vile, and he did not restrain them. [14]And therefore I have sworn to the house of Eli that the iniquity of Eli's house shall not be atoned for by sacrifice or offering forever."

[15]So Samuel lay down until morning, and opened the doors of the house of the LORD. And Samuel was afraid to tell Eli the vision. [16]Then Eli called Samuel and said, "Samuel, my son!"

He answered, "Here I am."

[17]And he said, "What is the word that the LORD spoke to you? Please do not hide it from me. God do so to you, and more also, if you hide anything from me of all the things that He said to you." [18]Then Samuel told him everything, and hid nothing from him. And he said, "It is the LORD. Let Him do what seems good to Him."

[19]So Samuel grew, and the LORD was with him and let none of his words fall to the ground. [20]And all Israel from Dan to Beersheba knew that Samuel had been established as a prophet of the LORD. [21]Then the LORD appeared again in Shiloh. For the LORD revealed Himself to Samuel in Shiloh by the word of the LORD.

before the LORD, and returned and came to their house at Ramah. And Elkanah knew Hannah his wife, and the LORD remembered her. ²⁰So it came to pass in the process of time that Hannah conceived and bore a son, and called his name Samuel, *saying*, "Because I have asked for him from the LORD."

²¹Now the man Elkanah and all his house went up to offer to the LORD the yearly sacrifice and his vow. ²²But Hannah did not go up, for she said to her husband, "*Not* until the child is weaned; then I will take him, that he may appear before the LORD and remain there forever."

²³So Elkanah her husband said to her, "Do what seems best to you; wait until you have weaned him. Only let the LORD establish His word." Then the woman stayed and nursed her son until she had weaned him.

²⁴Now when she had weaned him, she took him up with her, with three bulls, one ephah of flour, and a skin of wine, and brought him to the house of the LORD in Shiloh. And the child *was* young. ²⁵Then they slaughtered a bull, and brought the child to Eli. ²⁶And she said, "O my lord! As your soul lives, my lord, I *am* the woman who stood by you here, praying to the LORD. ²⁷For this child I prayed, and the LORD has granted me my petition which I asked of Him. ²⁸Therefore I also have lent him to the LORD; as long as he lives he shall be lent to the LORD." So they worshiped the LORD there.

CHAPTER 2 HANNAH'S PRAYER OF THANKS. And Hannah prayed and said:

"My heart rejoices in the LORD;
My horn is exalted in the LORD.
I smile at my enemies,
Because I rejoice in Your salvation.

² "No one is holy like the LORD,
For *there is* none besides You,
Nor *is there* any rock like our God.

³ "Talk no more so very proudly;
Let no arrogance come from your mouth,
For the LORD *is* the God of knowledge;
And by Him actions are weighed.

⁴ "The bows of the mighty men *are* broken,
And those who stumbled are girded with strength.

⁵ *Those who were* full have hired themselves out for bread,
And the hungry have ceased *to hunger*.
Even the barren has borne seven,
And she who has many children has become feeble.

⁶ "The LORD kills and makes alive;
He brings down to the grave and brings up.

⁷ The LORD makes poor and makes rich;
He brings low and lifts up.

⁸ He raises the poor from the dust
And lifts the beggar from the ash heap,
To set *them* among princes
And make them inherit the throne of glory.

"For the pillars of the earth *are* the LORD's,
And He has set the world upon them.

⁹ He will guard the feet of His saints,
But the wicked shall be silent in darkness.

"For by strength no man shall prevail.

¹⁰ The adversaries of the LORD shall be broken in pieces;
From heaven He will thunder against them.
The LORD will judge the ends of the earth.

"He will give strength to His king,
And exalt the horn of His anointed."

▰▰▰HELP!

2:2 Hannah praised God for being a "rock"—firm, strong, and unchanging. In our fast-paced world, friends come and go and circumstances change. It's difficult to find a solid foundation that will not change. Those who devote their lives to people, causes, possessions, or other finite things are trusting things that will all pass away. But God is always present and ready to help, even when everything else seems to be falling apart.

¹¹Then Elkanah went to his house at Ramah. But the child ministered to the LORD before Eli the priest.

¹²Now the sons of Eli *were* corrupt; they did not know the LORD. ¹³And the priests' custom with the people *was that* when any man offered a sacrifice, the priest's servant would come with a three-pronged fleshhook in his hand while the meat was boiling. ¹⁴Then he would thrust *it* into the pan, or kettle, or caldron, or pot; and the priest would take for himself all that the fleshhook brought up. So they did in Shiloh to all the Israelites who came there. ¹⁵Also, before they burned the fat, the priest's servant would come and say to the man who sacrificed, "Give meat for roasting to the priest, for he will not take boiled meat from you, but raw."

¹⁶And *if* the man said to him, "They should really burn the fat first; *then* you may take *as much* as your heart desires," he would then answer him, "*No*, but you must give *it* now; and if not, I will take *it* by force."

¹⁷Therefore the sin of the young men was very great before the LORD, for men abhorred the offering of the LORD.

¹⁸But Samuel ministered before the LORD, *even as* a child, wearing a linen ephod. ¹⁹Moreover his mother used to make him a little robe, and bring *it* to him year by year when she came up with her husband to offer the yearly sacrifice. ²⁰And Eli would bless Elkanah and his wife, and say, "The LORD give you descendants from this woman for the loan that was given to the LORD." Then they would go to their own home.

²¹And the LORD visited Hannah, so that she conceived and bore three sons and two daughters. Meanwhile the child Samuel grew before the LORD.

²²Now Eli was very old; and he heard everything his sons did to all Israel, and how they lay with the women

▰▰▰OLD ENOUGH

2:18 Samuel was a young child, and yet he "ministered before the LORD." Often children can serve God just as effectively as adults. God will use anyone who is willing to learn from him and serve him. He has no age limits. Don't discount the faith of a child or let your age keep you from serving God.

CHAPTER **4** **THE ARK IS STOLEN.** And the word of Samuel came to all Israel.

Now Israel went out to battle against the Philistines, and encamped beside Ebenezer; and the Philistines encamped in Aphek. ²Then the Philistines put themselves in battle array against Israel. And when they joined battle, Israel was defeated by the Philistines, who killed about four thousand men of the army in the field. ³And when the people had come into the camp, the elders of Israel said, "Why has the LORD defeated us today before the Philistines? Let us bring the ark of the covenant of the LORD from Shiloh to us, that when it comes among us it may save us from the hand of our enemies." ⁴So the people sent to Shiloh, that they might bring from there the ark of the covenant of the LORD of hosts, who dwells *between* the cherubim. And the two sons of Eli, Hophni and Phinehas, *were* there with the ark of the covenant of God.

⁵And when the ark of the covenant of the LORD came into the camp, all Israel shouted so loudly that the earth shook. ⁶Now when the Philistines heard the noise of the shout, they said, "What *does* the sound of this great shout in the camp of the Hebrews *mean?*" Then they understood that the ark of the LORD had come into the camp. So the Philistines were afraid, for they said, "God has come into the camp!" And they said, "Woe to us! For such a thing has never happened before. ⁸Woe to us! Who will deliver us from the hand of these mighty gods? These *are* the gods who struck the Egyptians with all the plagues in the wilderness. ⁹Be strong and conduct yourselves like men, you Philistines, that you do not become servants of the Hebrews, as they have been to you. Conduct yourselves like men, and fight!"

¹⁰So the Philistines fought, and Israel was defeated, and every man fled to his tent. There was a very great slaughter, and there fell of Israel thirty thousand foot soldiers. ¹¹Also the ark of God was captured; and the two sons of Eli, Hophni and Phinehas, died.

¹²Then a man of Benjamin ran from the battle line that day, and came to Shiloh with his clothes torn and dirt on his head. ¹³Now when he came, there was Eli, sitting on a seat by the wayside watching, for his heart trembled for the ark of God. And when the man came into the city and told *it*, all the city cried out. ¹⁴When Eli heard the noise of the outcry, he said, "What *does* the sound of this tumult *mean?*" And the man came quickly and told Eli. ¹⁵Eli was ninety-eight years old, and his eyes were so dim that he could not see.

¹⁶Then the man said to Eli, "I *am* he who came from the battle. And I fled today from the battle line."

And he said, "What happened, my son?"

¹⁷So the messenger answered and said, "Israel has fled before the Philistines, and there has been a great slaughter among the people. Also your two sons, Hophni and Phinehas, are dead; and the ark of God has been captured."

¹⁸Then it happened, when he made mention of the ark of God, that Eli fell off the seat backward by the side of the gate; and his neck was broken and he died, for the man was old and heavy. And he had judged Israel forty years.

¹⁹Now his daughter-in-law, Phinehas' wife, was with child, *due* to be delivered; and when she heard the news that the ark of God was captured, and that her father-in-law and her husband were dead, she bowed herself and gave birth, for her labor pains came upon her. ²⁰And about the time of her death the women who stood by her said to her, "Do not fear, for you have borne a son." But

NEW AND FRESH

4:5-8 The Philistines were frightened by stories of how God intervened for Israel when they left Egypt. But Israel had turned away from God and now clung only to a form of godliness.

People, churches, and organizations often try to live on the memories of God's blessings. Israel wrongly assumed that because God had given them victory in the past he would do it again, even though they had strayed far from him. Today, spiritual victories come by continually renewing our relationship with God. Don't live off the past. Keep your relationship with God new and fresh.

she did not answer, nor did she regard *it.* ²¹Then she named the child Ichabod, saying, "The glory has departed from Israel!" because the ark of God had been captured and because of her father-in-law and her husband. ²²And she said, "The glory has departed from Israel, for the ark of God has been captured."

CHAPTER **5** **PHILISTINES ARE PUNISHED.** Then the Philistines took the ark of God and brought it from Ebenezer to Ashdod. ²When the Philistines took the ark of God, they brought it into the house of Dagon and set it by Dagon. ³And when the people of Ashdod arose early in the morning, there was Dagon, fallen on its face to the earth before the ark of the LORD. So they took Dagon and set it in its place again. ⁴And when they arose early the next morning, there was Dagon, fallen on its face to the ground before the ark of the LORD. The head of Dagon and both the palms of its hands *were* broken off on the threshold; only Dagon's torso was left of it. ⁵Therefore neither the priests of Dagon nor any who come into Dagon's house tread on the threshold of Dagon in Ashdod to this day.

⁶But the hand of the LORD was heavy on the people of Ashdod, and He ravaged them and struck them with tumors, *both* Ashdod and its territory. ⁷And when the men of Ashdod saw how *it was,* they said, "The ark of the God of Israel must not remain with us, for His hand is harsh toward us and Dagon our god." ⁸Therefore they sent and gathered to themselves all the lords of the Philistines, and said, "What shall we do with the ark of the God of Israel?"

And they answered, "Let the ark of the God of Israel be carried away to Gath." So they carried the ark of the God of Israel away. ⁹So it was, after they had carried it away,

PAIN

5:6-7 Although the Philistines had just witnessed a great victory by Israel's God over their idol, Dagon, they didn't act upon that insight until they were personally afflicted with tumors (probably boils). Similarly, many people don't respond to biblical truth until they experience personal pain and suddenly feel they have no place else to turn. Are you willing to listen to God for truth's sake, or do you turn to him only when you are afflicted?

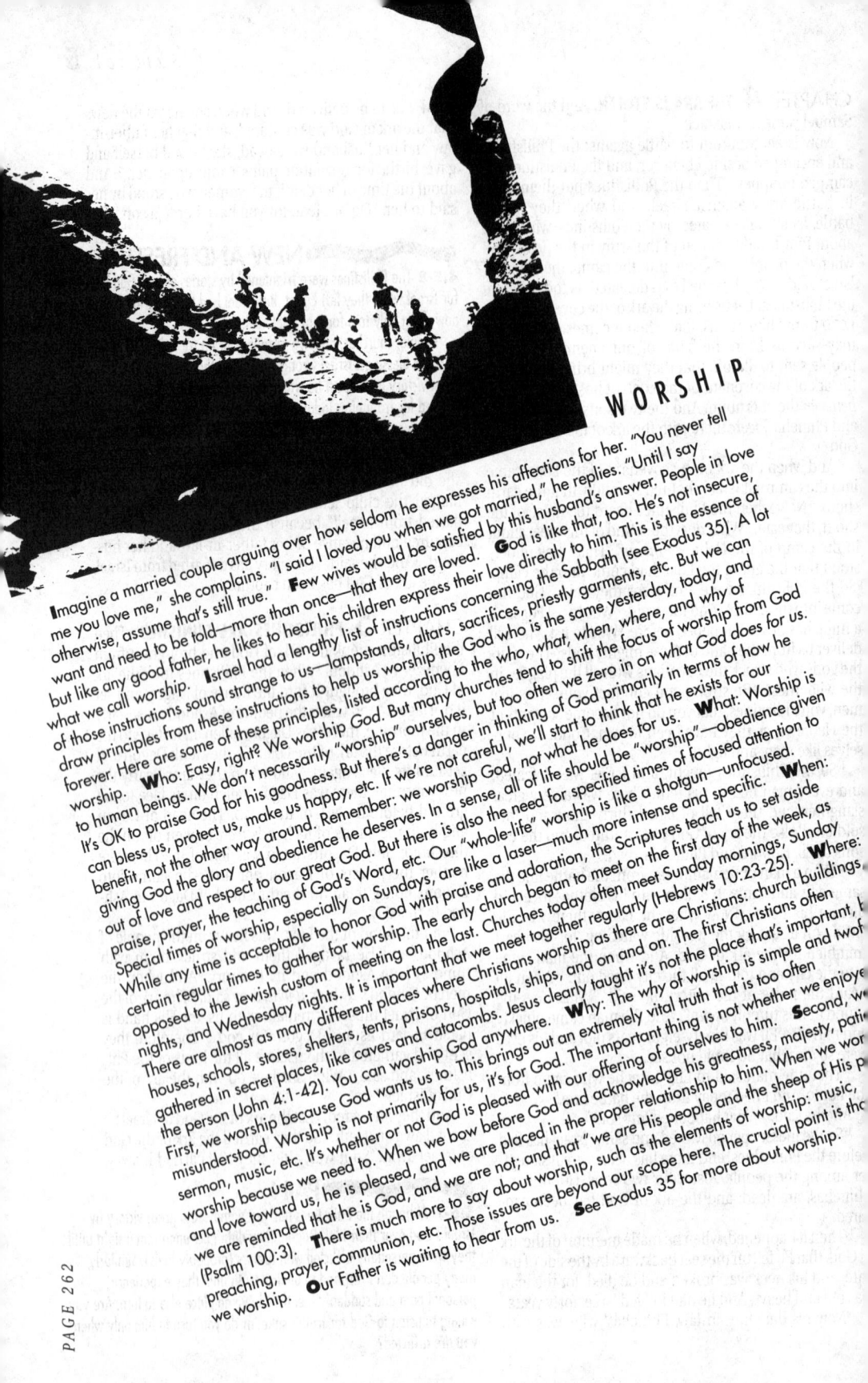

WORSHIP

Imagine a married couple arguing over how seldom he expresses his affections for her. "You never tell me you love me," she complains. "I said I loved you when we got married," he replies. "Until I say otherwise, assume that's still true." Few wives would be satisfied by this husband's answer. People in love want and need to be told—more than once—that they are loved. God is like that, too. He's not insecure, but like any good father, he likes to hear his children express their love directly to him. This is the essence of what we call worship. Israel had a lengthy list of instructions concerning the Sabbath (see Exodus 35). A lot of those instructions sound strange to us—lampstands, altars, sacrifices, priestly garments, etc. But we can draw principles from these instructions to help us worship the God who is the same yesterday, today, and forever. Here are some of these principles, listed according to the who, what, when, where, and why of worship.

Who: Easy, right? We worship God. But many churches tend to shift the focus of worship from God to human beings. We don't necessarily "worship" ourselves, but too often we zero in on what God does for us. It's OK to praise God for his goodness. But there's a danger in thinking of God primarily in terms of how he can bless us, protect us, make us happy, etc. If we're not careful, we'll start to think that he exists for our benefit, not the other way around. Remember: we worship God, not what he does for us. **What:** Worship is giving God the glory and obedience he deserves. In a sense, all of life should be "worship"—obedience given out of love and respect, the teaching of God's Word, etc. Our "whole-life" worship is like a shotgun—unfocused. But there is also the need for specified times of focused attention to praise, prayer, the teaching of God's Word, etc. Our "whole-life" worship is like a laser—much more intense and specific. **When:** Special times of worship, especially on Sundays, are like a laser—much more intense and specific. **When:** While any time is acceptable to honor God with praise and adoration, the Scriptures teach us to set aside certain regular times to gather for worship. The early church began to meet on the first day of the week, as opposed to the Jewish custom of meeting on the last. Churches today often meet Sunday mornings, Sunday nights, and Wednesday nights. It is important that we meet together regularly (Hebrews 10:23-25). **Where:** There are almost as many different places where Christians worship as there are Christians. The first Christians often gathered in secret places, like caves and catacombs. Jesus clearly taught it's not the place that's important, but the person (John 4:1-42). You can worship God anywhere. houses, schools, stores, shelters, tents, prisons, hospitals, ships, and on and on. The first Christians often First, we worship because God wants us to. This brings out an extremely vital truth that is too often misunderstood. Worship is not primarily for us, it's for God. The important thing is not whether we enjoy worship because we need to. When we bow before God and acknowledge his greatness, majesty, pati and love toward us, he is pleased, and we are placed in the proper relationship to him. When we wor we are reminded that he is God, and we are not; and that "we are His people and the sheep of His p (Psalm 100:3). There is much more to say about worship, such as the elements of worship: music, preaching, prayer, communion, etc. Those issues are beyond our scope here. The crucial point is tho we worship. Our Father is waiting to hear from us. See Exodus 35 for more about worship.

hat the hand of the LORD was against the city with a very reat destruction; and He struck the men of the city, both mall and great, and tumors broke out on them.

[10]Therefore they sent the ark of God to Ekron. So it was, s the ark of God came to Ekron, that the Ekronites cried ut, saying, "They have brought the ark of the God of srael to us, to kill us and our people!" [11]So they sent and athered together all the lords of the Philistines, and said, Send away the ark of the God of Israel, and let it go back ɔ its own place, so that it does not kill us and our eople." For there was a deadly destruction throughout ll the city; the hand of God was very heavy there. [12]And ɪe men who did not die were stricken with the tumors, ɪd the cry of the city went up to heaven.

CHAPTER **6** **THE ARK COMES BACK.** Now the ark of ɪe LORD was in the country of the Philistines seven ɪonths. [2]And the Philistines called for the priests and the iviners, saying, "What shall we do with the ark of the ɔRD? Tell us how we should send it to its place."

[3]So they said, "If you send away the ark of the God of srael, do not send it empty; but by all means return *it* to ʃim *with* a trespass offering. Then you will be healed, ɪd it will be known to you why His hand is not removed ɔm you."

[4]Then they said, "What *is* the trespass offering which ʃe shall return to Him?"

They answered, "Five golden tumors and five golden ɪts, *according to* the number of the lords of the Philis-ɪnes. For the same plague *was* on all of you and on your ɔrds. [5]Therefore you shall make images of your tumors ɪd images of your rats that ravage the land, and you ɪall give glory to the God of Israel; perhaps He will ʒhten His hand from you, from your gods, and from ɔur land. [6]Why then do you harden your hearts as the ʒyptians and Pharaoh hardened their hearts? When He ɪd mighty things among them, did they not let the eople go, that they might depart? [7]Now therefore, make new cart, take two milk cows which have never been ɔked, and hitch the cows to the cart; and take their ɪlves home, away from them. [8]Then take the ark of the ɔRD and set it on the cart; and put the articles of gold hich you are returning to Him *as* a trespass offering in chest by its side. Then send it away, and let it go. [9]And atch: if it goes up the road to its own territory, to Beth hemesh, *then* He has done us this great evil. But if not, ɪen we shall know that *it is* not His hand *that* struck s—it happened to us by chance."

[10]Then the men did so; they took two milk cows and ɪtched them to the cart, and shut up their calves at ɔme. [11]And they set the ark of the LORD on the cart, and ɪe chest with the gold rats and the images of their tu-ɪors. [12]Then the cows headed straight for the road to ɛth Shemesh, *and* went along the highway, lowing as ɪey went, and did not turn aside to the right hand or the ft. And the lords of the Philistines went after them to ɪe border of Beth Shemesh.

[13]Now *the people of* Beth Shemesh *were* reaping their ɪeat harvest in the valley; and they lifted their eyes and w the ark, and rejoiced to see *it*. [14]Then the cart came

into the field of Joshua of Beth Shemesh, and stood there; a large stone *was* there. So they split the wood of the cart and offered the cows as a burnt offering to the LORD. [15]The Levites took down the ark of the LORD and the chest that *was* with it, in which *were* the articles of gold, and put *them* on the large stone. Then the men of Beth Shemesh offered burnt offerings and made sacrifices the same day to the LORD. [16]So when the five lords of the Philistines had seen *it*, they returned to Ekron the same day.

◀━━━━━━ INGREDIENT

6:9 The Philistines acknowledged the existence of the Hebrew God, but only as one of many "gods" whose favor they sought. Thinking of God in this way made it easy for them to ignore God's demand that people worship him alone. Many people "worship" God this way. They see him as just one ingredient in a successful life. But God is not an ingredient—he is the source of life itself. Are you a "Philistine," seeing God's favor as just one ingredient in the good life?

[17]These *are* the golden tumors which the Philistines returned *as* a trespass offering to the LORD: one for Ash-dod, one for Gaza, one for Ashkelon, one for Gath, one for Ekron; [18]and the golden rats, *according to* the number of all the cities of the Philistines *belonging* to the five lords, *both* fortified cities and country villages, even as far as the large *stone of* Abel on which they set the ark of the LORD, *which stone remains* to this day in the field of Joshua of Beth Shemesh.

[19]Then He struck the men of Beth Shemesh, because they had looked into the ark of the LORD. He struck fifty thousand and seventy men of the people, and the people lamented because the LORD had struck the people with a great slaughter.

[20]And the men of Beth Shemesh said, "Who is able to stand before this holy LORD God? And to whom shall it go up from us?" [21]So they sent messengers to the inhab-itants of Kirjath Jearim, saying, "The Philistines have brought back the ark of the LORD; come down *and* take it up with you."

CHAPTER **7** **GOD SENDS THUNDER.** Then the men of Kirjath Jearim came and took the ark of the LORD, and brought it into the house of Abinadab on the hill, and consecrated Eleazar his son to keep the ark of the LORD.

[2]So it was that the ark remained in Kirjath Jearim a long time; it was there twenty years. And all the house of Israel lamented after the LORD.

[3]Then Samuel spoke to all the house of Israel, saying,

◀━━━━━ ON THE SHELF

7:2-3 Sorrow gripped Israel for 20 years. The ark was put away like an unwanted box in an attic, and it seemed as if the Lord had abandoned his people. Samuel, now a grown man, roused them to action by saying that if they were truly sorry, they should do something about it. How easy it is for us to complain about our problems, even to God, while we refuse to act, to change, and to do what he requires. We don't even take the advice he has already given us. Do you ever feel as if God has abandoned you? Check to see if there is anything he has already told you to do. You may not be able to receive new guidance until you have acted on his previous directions.

"If you return to the LORD with all your hearts, *then* put away the foreign gods and the Ashtoreths from among you, and prepare your hearts for the LORD, and serve Him only; and He will deliver you from the hand of the Philistines." ⁴So the children of Israel put away the Baals and the Ashtoreths, and served the LORD only.

⁵And Samuel said, "Gather all Israel to Mizpah, and I will pray to the LORD for you." ⁶So they gathered together at Mizpah, drew water, and poured *it* out before the LORD. And they fasted that day, and said there, "We have sinned against the LORD." And Samuel judged the children of Israel at Mizpah.

◣▬▬▬▬▬**BY DESIGN**

9:3ff Often we think that events just happen to us, but as we learn from this story about Saul, God often uses common occurrences to lead us where he wants. It is important to evaluate all situations as potential "divine appointments" designed to shape our life. Think of all the good and bad circumstances that have affected you lately. Can you see God's purpose in them? Perhaps he is building a certain quality in your life or leading you to serve him in a new area.

⁷Now when the Philistines heard that the children of Israel had gathered together at Mizpah, the lords of the Philistines went up against Israel. And when the children of Israel heard *of it*, they were afraid of the Philistines. ⁸So the children of Israel said to Samuel, "Do not cease to cry out to the LORD our God for us, that He may save us from the hand of the Philistines."

⁹And Samuel took a suckling lamb and offered *it as* a whole burnt offering to the LORD. Then Samuel cried out to the LORD for Israel, and the LORD answered him. ¹⁰Now as Samuel was offering up the burnt offering, the Philistines drew near to battle against Israel. But the LORD thundered with a loud thunder upon the Philistines that day, and so confused them that they were overcome before Israel. ¹¹And the men of Israel went out of Mizpah and pursued the Philistines, and drove them back as far as below Beth Car. ¹²Then Samuel took a stone and set *it* up between Mizpah and Shen, and called its name Ebenezer, saying, "Thus far the LORD has helped us."

¹³So the Philistines were subdued, and they did not come anymore into the territory of Israel. And the hand of the LORD was against the Philistines all the days of Samuel. ¹⁴Then the cities which the Philistines had taken from Israel were restored to Israel, from Ekron to Gath; and Israel recovered its territory from the hands of the Philistines. Also there was peace between Israel and the Amorites.

¹⁵And Samuel judged Israel all the days of his life. ¹⁶He went from year to year on a circuit to Bethel, Gilgal, and Mizpah, and judged Israel in all those places. ¹⁷But he always returned to Ramah, for his home *was* there. And he judged Israel, and there he built an altar to the LORD.

CHAPTER **8** ISRAEL DEMANDS A KING. Now it came to pass when Samuel was old that he made his sons judges over Israel. ²The name of his firstborn was Joel, and the name of his second, Abijah; *they were* judges in Beersheba. ³But his sons did not walk in his ways; they turned aside after dishonest gain, took bribes, and perverted justice.

⁴Then all the elders of Israel gathered together and came to Samuel at Ramah, ⁵and said to him, "Look, you are old, and your sons do not walk in your ways. Now make us a king to judge us like all the nations."

⁶But the thing displeased Samuel when they said, "Give us a king to judge us." So Samuel prayed to the LORD. ⁷And the LORD said to Samuel, "Heed the voice of the people in all that they say to you; for they have not rejected you, but they have rejected Me, that I should not reign over them. ⁸According to all the works which they have done since the day that I brought them up out of Egypt, even to this day—with which they have forsaken Me and served other gods—so they are doing to you also. ⁹Now therefore, heed their voice. However, you shall solemnly forewarn them, and show them the behavior of the king who will reign over them."

¹⁰So Samuel told all the words of the LORD to the people who asked him for a king. ¹¹And he said, "This will be the behavior of the king who will reign over you: He will take your sons and appoint *them* for his own chariots and *to be* his horsemen, and *some* will run before his chariots. ¹²He will appoint captains over his thousands and captains over his fifties, *will set some* to plow his ground and reap his harvest, and *some* to make his weapons of war and equipment for his chariots. ¹³He will take your daughters *to be* perfumers, cooks, and bakers. ¹⁴And he will take the best of your fields, your vineyards, and your olive groves, and give *them* to his servants. ¹⁵He will take a tenth of your grain and your vintage, and give it to his officers and servants. ¹⁶And he will take your male servants, your female servants, your finest young men, and your donkeys, and put *them* to his work. ¹⁷He will take a tenth of your sheep. And you will be his servants. ¹⁸And you will cry out in that day because of your king whom you have chosen for yourselves, and the LORD will not hear you in that day."

¹⁹Nevertheless the people refused to obey the voice of Samuel; and they said, "No, but we will have a king over us, ²⁰that we also may be like all the nations, and that our king may judge us and go out before us and fight our battles."

²¹And Samuel heard all the words of the people, and he repeated them in the hearing of the LORD. ²²So the LORD said to Samuel, "Heed their voice, and make them a king."

And Samuel said to the men of Israel, "Every man go to his city."

CHAPTER **9** SAUL BECOMES KING. There was a man of Benjamin whose name *was* Kish the son of Abiel, the son of Zeror, the son of Bechorath, the son of Aphiah, a Benjamite, a mighty man of power. ²And he had a choice and handsome son whose name *was* Saul. *There was* not a more handsome person than he among the children of Israel. From his shoulders upward *he was* taller than any of the people.

³Now the donkeys of Kish, Saul's father, were lost. And Kish said to his son Saul, "Please take one of the servants

with you, and arise, go and look for the donkeys." ⁴So he passed through the mountains of Ephraim and through the land of Shalisha, but they did not find *them.* Then they passed through the land of Shaalim, and *they were* not *there.* Then he passed through the land of the Benjamites, but they did not find *them.*

⁵When they had come to the land of Zuph, Saul said to his servant who *was* with him, "Come, let us return, lest my father cease *caring* about the donkeys and become worried about us."

⁶And he said to him, "Look now, *there is* in this city a man of God, and *he is* an honorable man; all that he says surely comes to pass. So let us go there; perhaps he can show us the way that we should go."

⁷Then Saul said to his servant, "But look, *if* we go, what shall we bring the man? For the bread in our vessels is all gone, and *there is* no present to bring to the man of God. What do we have?"

⁸And the servant answered Saul again and said, "Look, I have here at hand one-fourth of a shekel of silver. I will give *that* to the man of God, to tell us our way." ⁹(Formerly in Israel, when a man went to inquire of God, he spoke thus: "Come, let us go to the seer"; for *he who is* now *called* a prophet was formerly called a seer.)

¹⁰Then Saul said to his servant, "Well said; come, let us go." So they went to the city where the man of God *was.*

¹¹As they went up the hill to the city, they met some young women going out to draw water, and said to them, "Is the seer here?"

¹²And they answered them and said, "Yes, there he is, just ahead of you. Hurry now; for today he came to this city, because there is a sacrifice of the people today on the high place. ¹³As soon as you come into the city, you will surely find him before he goes up to the high place to eat. For the people will not eat until he comes, because he must bless the sacrifice; afterward those who are invited will eat. Now therefore, go up, for about this time you will find him." ¹⁴So they went up to the city. As they were coming into the city, there was Samuel, coming out toward them on his way up to the high place.

¹⁵Now the LORD had told Samuel in his ear the day before Saul came, saying, ¹⁶"Tomorrow about this time I will send you a man from the land of Benjamin, and you shall anoint him commander over My people Israel, that he may save My people from the hand of the Philistines; for I have looked upon My people, because their cry has come to Me."

¹⁷So when Samuel saw Saul, the LORD said to him, "There he is, the man of whom I spoke to you. This one shall reign over My people." ¹⁸Then Saul drew near to Samuel in the gate, and said, "Please tell me, where *is* the seer's house?"

¹⁹Samuel answered Saul and said, "I *am* the seer. Go up before me to the high place, for you shall eat with me today; and tomorrow I will let you go and will tell you all that *is* in your heart. ²⁰But as for your donkeys that were lost three days ago, do not be anxious about them, for they have been found. And on whom *is* all the desire of Israel? *Is it* not on you and on all your father's house?"

²¹And Saul answered and said, "*Am* I not a Benjamite, of the smallest of the tribes of Israel, and my family the least of all the families of the tribe of Benjamin? Why then do you speak like this to me?"

²²Now Samuel took Saul and his servant and brought them into the hall, and had them sit in the place of honor among those who were invited; there *were* about thirty persons. ²³And Samuel said to the cook, "Bring the portion which I gave you, of which I said to you, 'Set it apart.'" ²⁴So the cook took up the thigh with its upper part and set *it* before Saul. And *Samuel* said, "Here it is, what was kept back. *It* was set apart for you. Eat; for until this time it has been kept for you, since I said I invited the people." So Saul ate with Samuel that day.

²⁵When they had come down from the high place into the city, *Samuel* spoke with Saul on the top of the house. ²⁶They arose early; and it was about the dawning of the day that Samuel called to Saul on the top of the house, saying, "Get up, that I may send you on your way." And Saul arose, and both of them went outside, he and Samuel.

So many things try to crowd God out of my life. How much of me does God want?

I WONDER...

He wants all of you. God does not want to be just another addition to your life—he wants everything you do to revolve around him!

Bike tires are only as strong as the hub of the wheel. If a tire was made up only of rim and spokes, the wheel would soon collapse under the constant pounding and pressure.

The spokes in our life are those things that are important to us: family, friends, school, sports, entertainment, etc. If our life revolves around any one of these "spokes," eventually the constant pounding and pressures of our world will wear us down and possibly cause us to collapse!

God knows this and has provided the strong center that will hold us together. By ignoring God and trying to run our own life, we will be living as though we believe the spokes are strong enough to carry us.

For centuries the Jewish people complained to God and asked him for a king to rule over them. What they were actually saying was, "God, since we can't see you, we can't trust you to take care of us. Give us someone we can see who will rule over us." Eventually God gave in to their request. (See 1 Samuel 8:7.) The results, however, were devastating. Because they put their focus on what a man could do for them (a weak "spoke"!), their enemies soon overpowered the entire nation until all of the people of Israel were forced to live away from the Promised Land.

The Old Testament graphically describes what happened when God's people rejected him as their leader (the hub).

Jesus Christ should be the hub of our life. This means that we should consult him and his Word first.

When things begin to crowd out your relationship with God, try writing down all of your "priorities." Ask a trusted Christian friend if he or she thinks any one of these "spokes" is taking the place of God in your life.

27As they were going down to the outskirts of the city, Samuel said to Saul, "Tell the servant to go on ahead of us." And he went on. "But you stand here awhile, that I may announce to you the word of God."

CHAPTER 10 Then Samuel took a flask of oil and poured *it* on his head, and kissed him and said: "*Is it* not because the LORD has anointed you commander over His inheritance? 2When you have departed from me today, you will find two men by Rachel's tomb in the territory of Benjamin at Zelzah; and they will say to you, 'The donkeys which you went to look for have been found. And now your father has ceased caring about the donkeys and is worrying about you, saying, "What shall I do about my son?" ' 3Then you shall go on forward from there and come to the terebinth tree of Tabor. There three men going up to God at Bethel will meet you, one carrying three young goats, another carrying three loaves of bread, and another carrying a skin of wine. 4And they will greet you and give you two *loaves* of bread, which you

◄ HIDING

10:22 When the king was to be chosen, Saul already knew that he was the one (10:1). Instead of coming forward, however, he hid. Often we hide from important responsibilities because we are afraid of failure, afraid of what others will think, or perhaps unsure about how to proceed. Don't run from your responsibilities.

shall receive from their hands. 5After that you shall come to the hill of God where the Philistine garrison *is*. And it will happen, when you have come there to the city, that you will meet a group of prophets coming down from the high place with a stringed instrument, a tambourine, a flute, and a harp before them; and they will be prophesying. 6Then the Spirit of the LORD will come upon you, and you will prophesy with them and be turned into another man. 7And let it be, when these signs come to you, *that* you do as the occasion demands; for God *is* with you. 8You shall go down before me to Gilgal; and surely I will come down to you to offer burnt offerings *and* make sacrifices of peace offerings. Seven days you shall wait, till I come to you and show you what you should do."

9So it was, when he had turned his back to go from Samuel, that God gave him another heart; and all those signs came to pass that day. 10When they came there to the hill, there was a group of prophets to meet him; then the Spirit of God came upon him, and he prophesied among them. 11And it happened, when all who knew him formerly saw that he indeed prophesied among the prophets, that the people said to one another, "What *is* this *that* has come upon the son of Kish? *Is* Saul also among the prophets?" 12Then a man from there answered and said, "But who *is* their father?" Therefore it became a proverb: "*Is* Saul also among the prophets?" 13And when he had finished prophesying, he went to the high place.

14Then Saul's uncle said to him and his servant, "Where did you go?"

So he said, "To look for the donkeys. When we saw that *they were* nowhere *to be found*, we went to Samuel."

15And Saul's uncle said, "Tell me, please, what Samuel said to you."

16So Saul said to his uncle, "He told us plainly that the donkeys had been found." But about the matter of the kingdom, he did not tell him what Samuel had said.

17Then Samuel called the people together to the LORD at Mizpah, 18and said to the children of Israel, "Thus says the LORD God of Israel: 'I brought up Israel out of Egypt, and delivered you from the hand of the Egyptians *and* from the hand of all kingdoms and from those who oppressed you.' 19But you have today rejected your God, who Himself saved you from all your adversities and your tribulations; and you have said to Him, 'No, set a king over us!' Now therefore, present yourselves before the LORD by your tribes and by your clans."

20And when Samuel had caused all the tribes of Israel to come near, the tribe of Benjamin was chosen. 21When he had caused the tribe of Benjamin to come near by their families, the family of Matri was chosen. And Saul the son of Kish was chosen. But when they sought him, he could not be found. 22Therefore they inquired of the LORD further, "Has the man come here yet?"

And the LORD answered, "There he is, hidden among the equipment."

23So they ran and brought him from there; and when he stood among the people, he was taller than any of the people from his shoulders upward. 24And Samuel said to all the people, "Do you see him whom the LORD has chosen, that *there is* no one like him among all the people?"

So all the people shouted and said, "Long live the king!"

25Then Samuel explained to the people the behavior of royalty, and wrote *it* in a book and laid *it* up before the LORD. And Samuel sent all the people away, every man to his house. 26And Saul also went home to Gibeah; and valiant *men* went with him, whose hearts God had touched. 27But some rebels said, "How can this man save us?" So they despised him, and brought him no presents. But he held his peace.

CHAPTER 11 A SURPRISE ATTACK. Then Nahash the Ammonite came up and encamped against Jabesh Gilead; and all the men of Jabesh said to Nahash, "Make a covenant with us, and we will serve you."

2And Nahash the Ammonite answered them, "On this *condition* I will make *a covenant* with you, that I may put out all your right eyes, and bring reproach on all Israel."

3Then the elders of Jabesh said to him, "Hold off for seven days, that we may send messengers to all the territory of Israel. And then, if *there is* no one to save us, we will come out to you."

◄ ANGER

11:6 Anger is a powerful emotion. Often it is used wrongly to h others with words or physical violence. But anger directed at sin c mistreatment of others is not wrong. Saul was angered by the Ammonites' threat to humiliate and mistreat his fellow Israelites. used Saul's anger to bring justice and freedom. When injustice or makes you angry, ask God how you can channel that anger in constructive ways to help bring about a positive change.

⁴So the messengers came to Gibeah of Saul and told the news in the hearing of the people. And all the people lifted up their voices and wept. ⁵Now there was Saul, coming behind the herd from the field; and Saul said, "What *troubles* the people, that they weep?" And they told him the words of the men of Jabesh. ⁶Then the Spirit of God came upon Saul when he heard this news, and his anger was greatly aroused. ⁷So he took a yoke of oxen and cut them in pieces, and sent *them* throughout all the territory of Israel by the hands of messengers, saying, "Whoever does not go out with Saul and Samuel to battle, so it shall be done to his oxen."

And the fear of the LORD fell on the people, and they came out with one consent. ⁸When he numbered them in Bezek, the children of Israel were three hundred thousand, and the men of Judah thirty thousand. ⁹And they said to the messengers who came, "Thus you shall say to the men of Jabesh Gilead: 'Tomorrow, by *the time* the sun is hot, you shall have help.'" Then the messengers came and reported *it* to the men of Jabesh, and they were glad. ¹⁰Therefore the men of Jabesh said, "Tomorrow we will come out to you, and you may do with us whatever seems good to you."

¹¹So it was, on the next day, that Saul put the people in three companies; and they came into the midst of the camp in the morning watch, and killed Ammonites until the heat of the day. And it happened that those who survived were scattered, so that no two of them were left together. ¹²Then the people said to Samuel, "Who *is* he who said, 'Shall Saul reign over us?' Bring the men, that we may put them to death."

¹³But Saul said, "Not a man shall be put to death this day, for today the LORD has accomplished salvation in Israel."

¹⁴Then Samuel said to the people, "Come, let us go to Gilgal and renew the kingdom there." ¹⁵So all the people went to Gilgal, and there they made Saul king before the LORD in Gilgal. There they made sacrifices of peace offerings before the LORD, and there Saul and all the men of Israel rejoiced greatly.

CHAPTER 12 SAMUEL REMINDS THE PEOPLE. Now Samuel said to all Israel: "Indeed I have heeded your voice in all that you said to me, and have made a king over you. ²And now here is the king, walking before you; and I am old and grayheaded, and look, my sons *are* with you. I have walked before you from my childhood to this day. ³Here I am. Witness against me before the LORD and before His anointed: Whose ox have I taken, or whose donkey have I taken, or whom have I cheated? Whom have I oppressed, or from whose hand have I received *any* bribe with which to blind my eyes? I will restore *it* to you."

⁴And they said, "You have not cheated us or oppressed us, nor have you taken anything from any man's hand."

⁵Then he said to them, "The LORD *is* witness against you, and His anointed *is* witness this day, that you have not found anything in my hand."

And they answered, "*He is* witness."

⁶Then Samuel said to the people, "*It is* the LORD who raised up Moses and Aaron, and who brought your fathers up from the land of Egypt. ⁷Now therefore, stand still, that I may reason with you before the LORD concerning all the righteous acts of the LORD which He did to you and your fathers: ⁸When Jacob had gone into Egypt,

SAMUEL

We often wonder about the childhood of great people. We have little information in the Bible. One delightful exception is Samuel, who was born as a result of God's answer to Hannah's prayer for a child. (In fact, the name "Samuel" comes from the Hebrew expression, "asked of God.") God had plans for Samuel from the start. He used Samuel in many different and important ways. The reason God was able to use Samuel so much is because Samuel was willing to be one thing—God's servant. What would it take for God to use our lives as much?

Samuel's life teaches us that those who are faithful to God in small things will be trusted with greater things. Little jobs like helping the high priest may not have seemed very important, but God was using those jobs to train Samuel for bigger responsibilities. We can't tell what parts of today are preparations for tomorrow. But God knows! Samuel moved ahead because he was listening to God's directions. Too often we ask God to control our life without being willing to give up the goals we've chosen. We ask God to help us get where we want to go. The first step in correcting this tendency is to turn over both the control and destination of our life to him. The second step is to be obedient to what we already know God wants us to do. The third step is to watch for further direction from his Word—God's map for life.

LESSONS: The significance of what people accomplish in life is directly related to their relationship with God

The kind of person we are is more important than anything we might do

KEY VERSES: "So Samuel grew, and the LORD was with him and let none of his words fall to the ground. And all Israel from Dan to Beersheba knew that Samuel had been established as a prophet of the LORD" (1 Samuel 3:19–20).

His story is told in 1 Samuel 1–28. He is also mentioned in Psalm 99:6; Jeremiah 15:1; Acts 3:24; 13:20; Hebrews 11:32.

UPS:
- Used by God to assist Israel's transition from a loosely governed tribal people to a monarchy
- Anointed the first two kings of Israel
- The last and most effective of Israel's judges
- Listed in the Hall of Faith in Hebrews 11

DOWNS:
- Unable to instill in his sons the same relationship he had with God

STATS:
- Where: Ephraim
- Occupation: Judge, prophet, priest
- Relatives: Mother: Hannah. Father: Elkanah. Sons: Joel and Abijah.
- Contemporaries: Eli, Saul, David

SELF DESTRUCTING

12:25 If we continue sinning, we will not enjoy fellowship with God and we will end up destroying ourselves. Persisting in destructive habits, immoral thoughts, harbored resentments, and failing to heed God's Word are examples of "doing wickedly."

and your fathers cried out to the LORD, then the LORD sent Moses and Aaron, who brought your fathers out of Egypt and made them dwell in this place. ⁹And when they forgot the LORD their God, He sold them into the hand of Sisera, commander of the army of Hazor, into the hand of the Philistines, and into the hand of the king of Moab; and they fought against them. ¹⁰Then they cried out to the LORD, and said, 'We have sinned, because we have forsaken the LORD and served the Baals and Ashtoreths; but now deliver us from the hand of our enemies, and we will serve You.' ¹¹And the LORD sent Jerubbaal, Bedan, Jephthah, and Samuel, and delivered you out of the hand of your enemies on every side; and you dwelt in safety. ¹²And when you saw that Nahash king of the Ammonites came against you, you said to me, 'No, but a king shall reign over us,' when the LORD your God *was* your king.

EXCUSES

13:12-13 Saul had plenty of excuses for his disobedience. But Samuel zeroed in on the real issue: "You have not kept the commandment of the LORD your God." Like Saul, we often gloss over our mistakes and sins, trying to justify and spiritualize our actions because of our "special" circumstances. Our excuses, however, are nothing more than disobedience. God knows our true motives. He forgives, restores, and blesses only when we are honest about our sins. By trying to hide his sins behind excuses, Saul lost his kingship (13:14).

¹³"Now therefore, here is the king whom you have chosen *and* whom you have desired. And take note, the LORD has set a king over you. ¹⁴If you fear the LORD and serve Him and obey His voice, and do not rebel against the commandment of the LORD, then both you and the king who reigns over you will continue following the LORD your God. ¹⁵However, if you do not obey the voice of the LORD, but rebel against the commandment of the LORD, then the hand of the LORD will be against you, as *it was* against your fathers.

¹⁶"Now therefore, stand and see this great thing which the LORD will do before your eyes: ¹⁷*Is* today not the wheat harvest? I will call to the LORD, and He will send thunder and rain, that you may perceive and see that your wickedness *is* great, which you have done in the sight of the LORD, in asking a king for yourselves."

¹⁸So Samuel called to the LORD, and the LORD sent thunder and rain that day; and all the people greatly feared the LORD and Samuel.

¹⁹And all the people said to Samuel, "Pray for your servants to the LORD your God, that we may not die; for we have added to all our sins the evil of asking a king for ourselves."

²⁰Then Samuel said to the people, "Do not fear. You have done all this wickedness; yet do not turn aside from following the LORD, but serve the LORD with all your heart. ²¹And do not turn aside; for *then you would go* after empty things which cannot profit or deliver, for they *are* nothing. ²²For the LORD will not forsake His people, for His great name's sake, because it has pleased the LORD to make you His

people. ²³Moreover, as for me, far be it from me that I should sin against the LORD in ceasing to pray for you; but I will teach you the good and the right way. ²⁴Only fear the LORD, and serve Him in truth with all your heart; for consider what great things He has done for you. ²⁵But if you still do wickedly, you shall be swept away, both you and your king."

CHAPTER 13 SAUL'S MISTAKE.

Saul reigned one year; and when he had reigned two years over Israel, ²Saul chose for himself three thousand *men* of Israel. Two thousand were with Saul in Michmash and in the mountains of Bethel, and a thousand were with Jonathan in Gibeah of Benjamin. The rest of the people he sent away, every man to his tent.

³And Jonathan attacked the garrison of the Philistines that *was* in Geba, and the Philistines heard *of it*. Then Saul blew the trumpet throughout all the land, saying, "Let the Hebrews hear!" ⁴Now all Israel heard it said *that* Saul had attacked a garrison of the Philistines, and *that* Israel had also become an abomination to the Philistines. And the people were called together to Saul at Gilgal.

⁵Then the Philistines gathered together to fight with Israel, thirty thousand chariots and six thousand horsemen, and people as the sand which *is* on the seashore in multitude. And they came up and encamped in Michmash, to the east of Beth Aven. ⁶When the men of Israel saw that they were in danger (for the people were distressed), then the people hid in caves, in thickets, in rocks, in holes, and in pits. ⁷And *some of* the Hebrews crossed over the Jordan to the land of Gad and Gilead.

As for Saul, he *was* still in Gilgal, and all the people followed him trembling. ⁸Then he waited seven days, according to the time set by Samuel. But Samuel did not come to Gilgal; and the people were scattered from him. ⁹So Saul said, "Bring a burnt offering and peace offerings here to me." And he offered the burnt offering. ¹⁰Now it happened, as soon as he had finished presenting the burnt offering, that Samuel came; and Saul went out to meet him, that he might greet him.

¹¹And Samuel said, "What have you done?"

Saul said, "When I saw that the people were scattered from me, and *that* you did not come within the days appointed, and *that* the Philistines gathered together at Michmash, ¹²then I said, 'The Philistines will now come down on me at Gilgal, and I have not made supplication to the LORD.' Therefore I felt compelled, and offered a burnt offering."

¹³And Samuel said to Saul, "You have done foolishly

SURROUNDED

14:6 Jonathan and his armorbearer weren't much of a force to the huge Philistine army. But while everyone else was afraid, they trusted God, knowing that the size of the enemy army had no relationship to God's ability to help them. God honored the faith and brave action of these two men with a tremendous victory.

Have you ever felt surrounded by the "enemy" or faced overwhelming odds? God is never intimidated by the size of the or the complexity of a problem. With him, there always are enough resources to resist the pressures and win our battles. If God has you to action, then bravely commit what few resources you have and rely upon him to give you the victory.

You have not kept the commandment of the LORD your God, which He commanded you. For now the LORD would have established your kingdom over Israel forever. ¹⁴But now your kingdom shall not continue. The LORD has sought for Himself a man after His own heart, and the LORD has commanded him *to be* commander over His people, because you have not kept what the LORD commanded you."

¹⁵Then Samuel arose and went up from Gilgal to Gibeah of Benjamin. And Saul numbered the people present with him, about six hundred men.

¹⁶Saul, Jonathan his son, and the people present with them remained in Gibeah of Benjamin. But the Philistines encamped in Michmash. ¹⁷Then raiders came out of the camp of the Philistines in three companies. One company turned onto the road to Ophrah, to the land of Shual, ¹⁸another company turned to the road *to* Beth Horon, and another company turned *to* the road of the border that overlooks the Valley of Zeboim toward the wilderness.

¹⁹Now there was no blacksmith to be found throughout all the land of Israel, for the Philistines said, "Lest the Hebrews make swords or spears." ²⁰But all the Israelites would go down to the Philistines to sharpen each man's plowshare, his mattock, his ax, and his sickle; ²¹and the charge for a sharpening was a pim for the plowshares, the mattocks, the forks, and the axes, and to set the points of the goads. ²²So it came about, on the day of battle, that there was neither sword nor spear found in the hand of any of the people who *were* with Saul and Jonathan. But they were found with Saul and Jonathan his son. ²³And the garrison of the Philistines went out to the pass of Michmash.

CHAPTER 14 JONATHAN'S BRAVE FIGHT.

Now it happened one day that Jonathan the son of Saul said to the young man who bore his armor, "Come, let us go over to the Philistines' garrison that *is* on the other side." But he did not tell his father. ²And Saul was sitting in the outskirts of Gibeah under a pomegranate tree which *is* in Migron. The people who *were* with him *were* about six hundred men. ³Ahijah the son of Ahitub, Ichabod's brother, the son of Phinehas, the son of Eli, the LORD's priest in Shiloh, was wearing an ephod. But the people did not know that Jonathan had gone.

⁴Between the passes, by which Jonathan sought to go over to the Philistines' garrison, *there was* a sharp rock on one side and a sharp rock on the other side. And the name of one *was* Bozez, and the name of the other Seneh. ⁵The front of one faced northward opposite Michmash, and the other southward opposite Gibeah.

⁶Then Jonathan said to the young man who bore his armor, "Come, let us go over to the garrison of these uncircumcised; it may be that the LORD will work for us. For nothing restrains the LORD from saving by many or by few."

⁷So his armorbearer said to him, "Do all that is in your heart. Go then; here I am with you, according to your heart."

⁸Then Jonathan said, "Very well, let us cross over to *these* men, and we will show ourselves to them. ⁹If they say thus to us, 'Wait until we come to you,' then we will stand still in our place

SAUL

First impressions don't always turn out to be right. Sometimes a person who has a great image looks very different when we discover his or her abilities or qualities. Saul was one of those people. He looked like a king, but he lacked the traits that would have helped him be a good one. He often forgot or disobeyed God's directions. He was God's chosen leader, but God's choice did not mean that Saul was capable of being king on his own. He needed God's help. We do, too.

During his reign, Saul had his greatest successes when he obeyed God. His greatest failures resulted from acting on his own. Saul had the raw materials to be a good leader—appearance, courage, and action. Even his weaknesses could have been used by God if Saul had recognized them and left them in God's control. His own choices cut him off from God and eventually alienated him from his own people.

From Saul we learn that while our strengths and abilities make us useful, it is our weaknesses that make us usable. Our skills and talents make us tools, but our failures and shortcomings remind us that we need a craftsman in control of our life. Whatever we accomplish on our own is only a hint of what God could do through our life. Does he control your life?

LESSONS: God wants obedience from the heart, not mere acts of religious ritual
Obedience always involves sacrifice, but sacrifice is not always obedience
God wants to make use of our strengths and weaknesses
Our weaknesses should help us remember our need for God's guidance and help

KEY VERSES: "So Samuel said: 'Has the LORD as great delight in burnt offerings and sacrifices, as in obeying the voice of the LORD? Behold, to obey is better than sacrifice, and to heed than the fat of rams, for rebellion is as the sin of witchcraft, and stubbornness is as iniquity and idolatry. Because you have rejected the word of the LORD, He also has rejected you from being king'" (1 Samuel 15:22-23).

His story is told in 1 Samuel 9—31. He is also mentioned in Acts 13:21.

UPS:
- First God-appointed king of Israel
- Known for his personal courage and generosity
- Stood tall, with a striking appearance

DOWNS:
- Leadership abilities did not match the expectations created by his appearance
- Impulsive by nature, he tended to overstep his bounds
- Jealous of David, he tried to kill him
- Deliberately disobeyed God on several occasions

STATS:
- Where: The land of Benjamin
- Occupation: King of Israel
- Relatives: Father: Kish. Sons: Jonathan, Ishbosheth, Abinadab, and Malchishua. Wife: Ahinoam. Daughters: Merab and Michal.

and not go up to them. [10]But if they say thus, 'Come up to us,' then we will go up. For the LORD has delivered them into our hand, and this *will be* a sign to us."

[11]So both of them showed themselves to the garrison of the Philistines. And the Philistines said, "Look, the Hebrews are coming out of the holes where they have hidden." [12]Then the men of the garrison called to Jonathan and his armorbearer, and said, "Come up to us, and we will show you something."

Jonathan said to his armorbearer, "Come up after me, for the LORD has delivered them into the hand of Israel." [13]And Jonathan climbed up on his hands and knees with his armorbearer after him; and they fell before Jonathan. And as he came after him, his armorbearer killed them.

LYING

On her way out the door for a company party, Mrs. Richards addresses her sophomore daughter, whom she has just grounded. "Janel, remember—no visitors, and under no circumstances may you leave the house."

"Yes, ma'am," mumbles the hacked-off teen.

After her mom leaves, Janel grabs the phone. "Katherine, everything's cool."

Ten minutes later Katherine is there.

"How 'bout checking the mall to see if Greg's there?" Janel suggests.

"What if your mom calls?"

"Oh, I'll just tell her I was taking a bath."

The girls go to the mall. They eat ice cream and return home. Janel slides into bed, thinking, "My mom is so out of it . . . I could have stayed out till midnight."

The next morning, Mrs. Richards, obviously ticked, summons Janel into the living room.

"Care to tell me about last night?"

"Huh?" Janel asks.

"Where did you go?"

"What are you talking about?" (It's an Oscar-caliber performance.)

"Look, Janel," Mrs. Richards states, "I know what you did. On my way to the party, I got a run in my hose. I stopped at the mall to get another pair, and guess who I saw there?"

Janel sees her life flash before her eyes!

For a reminder of the high cost of dishonesty and disobedience, read 1 Samuel 15:1-23.

[14]That first slaughter which Jonathan and his armorbearer made was about twenty men within about half an acre of land.

[15]And there was trembling in the camp, in the field, and among all the people. The garrison and the raiders also trembled; and the earth quaked, so that it was a very great trembling. [16]Now the watchmen of Saul in Gibeah of Benjamin looked, and *there* was the multitude, melting away; and they went here and there. [17]Then Saul said to the people who *were* with him, "Now call the roll and see who has gone from us." And when they had called the roll, surprisingly, Jonathan and his armorbearer *were* not there. [18]And Saul said to Ahijah, "Bring the ark of God here" (for at that time the ark of God was with the children of Israel). [19]Now it happened, while Saul talked to the priest, that the noise which *was* in the camp of the

14:24-25 Saul made an oath without thinking through the implications. The results? (1) Saul's men were too tired to fight; (2) were so hungry they ate raw meat that still contained blood, which against God's law; (3) Saul almost killed his own son (14:42-44).

Saul's impulsive vow sounded heroic, but its disastrous side effe made it little more than "shooting off at the mouth." If you are in middle of a conflict, guard against impulsive statements that you n forced to honor.

Philistines continued to increase; so Saul said to the priest, "Withdraw your hand." [20]Then Saul and all the people who *were* with him assembled, and they went to the battle; and indeed every man's sword was against his neighbor, *and there was* very great confusion. [21]Moreover the Hebrews *who* were with the Philistines before that time, who went up with them into the camp *from the* surrounding *country,* they also joined the Israelites who *were* with Saul and Jonathan. [22]Likewise all the men of Israel who had hidden in the mountains of Ephraim, *when* they heard that the Philistines fled, they also followed hard after them in the battle. [23]So the LORD saved Israel that day, and the battle shifted to Beth Aven.

[24]And the men of Israel were distressed that day, for Saul had placed the people under oath, saying, "Cursed *is* the man who eats *any* food until evening, before I have taken vengeance on my enemies." So none of the people tasted food. [25]Now all *the people* of the land came to a forest; and there was honey on the ground. [26]And when the people had come into the woods, there was the honey, dripping; but no one put his hand to his mouth, for the people feared the oath. [27]But Jonathan had no heard his father charge the people with the oath; therefore he stretched out the end of the rod that *was* in his hand and dipped it in a honeycomb, and put his hand to his mouth; and his countenance brightened. [28]Then one of the people said, "Your father strictly charged the people with an oath, saying, 'Cursed *is* the man who eat food this day.'" And the people were faint.

[29]But Jonathan said, "My father has troubled the land Look now, how my countenance has brightened because I tasted a little of this honey. [30]How much better if the people had eaten freely today of the spoil of their enemies which they found! For now would there not have been a much greater slaughter among the Philistines?"

[31]Now they had driven back the Philistines that da from Michmash to Aijalon. So the people were very faint [32]And the people rushed on the spoil, and took sheep oxen, and calves, and slaughtered *them* on the ground and the people ate *them* with the blood. [33]Then they tol Saul, saying, "Look, the people are sinning against th LORD by eating with the blood!"

So he said, "You have dealt treacherously; roll a larg stone to me this day." [34]Then Saul said, "Disperse your selves among the people, and say to them, 'Bring me her every man's ox and every man's sheep, slaughter *the* here, and eat; and do not sin against the LORD by eatin with the blood.'" So every one of the people brought h ox with him that night, and slaughtered *it* there. [35]The Saul built an altar to the LORD. This was the first altar th he built to the LORD.

[36]Now Saul said, "Let us go down after the Philistine

by night, and plunder them until the morning light; and let us not leave a man of them."

And they said, "Do whatever seems good to you."

Then the priest said, "Let us draw near to God here." ³⁷So Saul asked counsel of God, "Shall I go down after the Philistines? Will You deliver them into the hand of Israel?" But He did not answer him that day. ³⁸And Saul said, "Come over here, all you chiefs of the people, and know and see what this sin was today. ³⁹For *as* the LORD lives, who saves Israel, though it be in Jonathan my son, he shall surely die." But not a man among all the people answered him. ⁴⁰Then he said to all Israel, "You be on one side, and my son Jonathan and I will be on the other side."

And the people said to Saul, "Do what seems good to you."

⁴¹Therefore Saul said to the LORD God of Israel, "Give a perfect *lot.*" So Saul and Jonathan were taken, but the people escaped. ⁴²And Saul said, "Cast *lots* between my son Jonathan and me." So Jonathan was taken. ⁴³Then Saul said to Jonathan, "Tell me what you have done."

And Jonathan told him, and said, "I only tasted a little honey with the end of the rod that *was* in my hand. So now I must die!"

⁴⁴Saul answered, "God do so and more also; for you shall surely die, Jonathan."

⁴⁵But the people said to Saul, "Shall Jonathan die, who has accomplished this great deliverance in Israel? Certainly not! *As* the LORD lives, not one hair of his head shall fall to the ground, for he has worked with God this day." So the people rescued Jonathan, and he did not die.

⁴⁶Then Saul returned from pursuing the Philistines, and the Philistines went to their own place.

⁴⁷So Saul established his sovereignty over Israel, and fought against all his enemies on every side, against Moab, against the people of Ammon, against Edom, against the kings of Zobah, and against the Philistines. Wherever he turned, he harassed *them.* ⁴⁸And he gathered an army and attacked the Amalekites, and delivered Israel from the hands of those who plundered them.

⁴⁹The sons of Saul were Jonathan, Jishui, and Malchishua. And the names of his two daughters *were these:* the name of the firstborn Merab, and the name of the younger Michal. ⁵⁰The name of Saul's wife *was* Ahinoam the daughter of Ahimaaz. And the name of the commander of his army *was* Abner the son of Ner, Saul's uncle. ⁵¹Kish *was* the father of Saul, and Ner the father of Abner *was* the son of Abiel.

⁵²Now there was fierce war with the Philistines all the days of Saul. And when Saul saw any strong man or any valiant man, he took him for himself.

CHAPTER **15** SAUL FAILS TO OBEY. Samuel also said to Saul, "The LORD sent me to anoint you king over His people, over Israel. Now therefore, heed the voice of the words of the LORD. ²Thus says the LORD of hosts: 'I will punish Amalek *for* what he did to Israel, how he ambushed him on the way when he came up from Egypt. Now go and attack Amalek, and utterly destroy all that they have, and do not spare them. But kill both man and

woman, infant and nursing child, ox and sheep, camel and donkey.'"

⁴So Saul gathered the people together and numbered them in Telaim, two hundred thousand foot soldiers and ten thousand men of Judah. ⁵And Saul came to a city of Amalek, and lay in wait in the valley.

► **FAILURE**

15:13-14 Saul thought he had won a great victory over the Amalekites, but God saw it as a great failure because Saul had disobeyed him and then had lied to Samuel about the results of the battle. Saul may have thought his lie wouldn't be detected, or that what he did was not wrong. Saul was mistaken.

Dishonest people soon begin to believe the lies they construct around themselves. Then they lose the ability to tell the difference between telling the truth and lying. By believing your own lies, you will move away from God. That is why honesty is so important in our relationships, both with God and with others.

⁶Then Saul said to the Kenites, "Go, depart, get down from among the Amalekites, lest I destroy you with them. For you showed kindness to all the children of Israel when they came up out of Egypt." So the Kenites departed from among the Amalekites. ⁷And Saul attacked the Amalekites, from Havilah all the way to Shur, which is east of Egypt. ⁸He also took Agag king of the Amalekites alive, and utterly destroyed all the people with the edge of the sword. ⁹But Saul and the people spared Agag and the best of the sheep, the oxen, the fatlings, the lambs, and all *that was* good, and were unwilling to utterly destroy them. But everything despised and worthless, that they utterly destroyed.

¹⁰Now the word of the LORD came to Samuel, saying, ¹¹"I greatly regret that I have set up Saul *as* king, for he has turned back from following Me, and has not performed My commandments." And it grieved Samuel, and he cried out to the LORD all night. ¹²So when Samuel rose early in the morning to meet Saul, it was told Samuel, saying, "Saul went to Carmel, and indeed, he set up a monument for himself; and he has gone on around, passed by, and gone down to Gilgal." ¹³Then Samuel went to Saul, and Saul said to him, "Blessed *are* you of the LORD! I have performed the commandment of the LORD."

¹⁴But Samuel said, "What then *is* this bleating of the sheep in my ears, and the lowing of the oxen which I hear?"

¹⁵And Saul said, "They have brought them from the Amalekites; for the people spared the best of the sheep and the oxen, to sacrifice to the LORD your God; and the rest we have utterly destroyed."

¹⁶Then Samuel said to Saul, "Be quiet! And I will tell you what the LORD said to me last night."

And he said to him, "Speak on."

¹⁷So Samuel said, "When you *were* little in your own eyes, *were* you not head of the tribes of Israel? And did not the LORD anoint you king over Israel? ¹⁸Now the LORD sent you on a mission, and said, 'Go, and utterly destroy the sinners, the Amalekites, and fight against them until they are consumed.' ¹⁹Why then did you not obey the

voice of the LORD? Why did you swoop down on the spoil, and do evil in the sight of the LORD?"

²⁰And Saul said to Samuel, "But I have obeyed the voice of the LORD, and gone on the mission on which the LORD sent me, and brought back Agag king of Amalek; I have utterly destroyed the Amalekites. ²¹But the people took of the plunder, sheep and oxen, the best of the things which should have been utterly destroyed, to sacrifice to the LORD your God in Gilgal."

²²So Samuel said:

"Has the LORD *as great* delight in burnt offerings and
    sacrifices,
As in obeying the voice of the LORD?
Behold, to obey is better than sacrifice,
And to heed than the fat of rams.
²³ For rebellion *is as* the sin of witchcraft,
And stubbornness *is as* iniquity and idolatry.
Because you have rejected the word of the LORD,
He also has rejected you from *being* king."

²⁴Then Saul said to Samuel, "I have sinned, for I have transgressed the commandment of the LORD and your words, because I feared the people and obeyed their voice. ²⁵Now therefore, please pardon my sin, and return with me, that I may worship the LORD."

◤▬▬▬ GOOD LOOKS

16:7 Saul was tall and handsome; he was an impressive-looking man. Samuel may have been trying to find someone who looked like Saul to be Israel's next king, but God warned him against judging by appearance alone. When people judge by outward appearance, they may overlook quality individuals who simply lack the particular physical qualities that society currently admires. But appearance doesn't reveal what people are really like or what their true value is.

Fortunately, God judges by character, not appearances. And because only God can see the inside, only he can accurately judge people. While we spend hours each week maintaining our outward appearance, we should do even more to develop our inner character. While everyone can see your face, only you and God know what your heart really looks like. Which is the more attractive part of you?

²⁶But Samuel said to Saul, "I will not return with you, for you have rejected the word of the LORD, and the LORD has rejected you from being king over Israel."

²⁷And as Samuel turned around to go away, *Saul* seized the edge of his robe, and it tore. ²⁸So Samuel said to him, "The LORD has torn the kingdom of Israel from you today, and has given it to a neighbor of yours, *who is* better than you. ²⁹And also the Strength of Israel will not lie nor relent. For He *is* not a man, that He should relent."

³⁰Then he said, "I have sinned; *yet* honor me now, please, before the elders of my people and before Israel, and return with me, that I may worship the LORD your God." ³¹So Samuel turned back after Saul, and Saul worshiped the LORD.

³²Then Samuel said, "Bring Agag king of the Amalekites here to me." So Agag came to him cautiously.
And Agag said, "Surely the bitterness of death is past."

³³But Samuel said, "As your sword has made women childless, so shall your mother be childless among

THE LORD
does not see
as man sees;

FOR MAN LOOKS AT
THE OUTWARD APPEARANCE
BUT
THE LORD
LOOKS AT THE HEART

1 SAMUEL 16:7

women." And Samuel hacked Agag in pieces before the LORD in Gilgal.

³⁴Then Samuel went to Ramah, and Saul went up to hi[s] house at Gibeah of Saul. ³⁵And Samuel went no more t[o] see Saul until the day of his death. Nevertheless Samue[l] mourned for Saul, and the LORD regretted that He ha[d] made Saul king over Israel.

CHAPTER **16** SAMUEL ANOINTS DAVID. Now th[e] LORD said to Samuel, "How long will you mourn for Sau[l,] seeing I have rejected him from reigning over Israel? Fi[ll] your horn with oil, and go; I am sending you to Jesse th[e] Bethlehemite. For I have provided Myself a king amon[g] his sons."

²And Samuel said, "How can I go? If Saul hears *it*, h[e] will kill me."

But the LORD said, "Take a heifer with you, and say, [']I have come to sacrifice to the LORD.' ³Then invite Jesse t[o] the sacrifice, and I will show you what you shall do; yo[u] shall anoint for Me the one I name to you."

⁴So Samuel did what the LORD said, and went to Beth[-] lehem. And the elders of the town trembled at his com[-] ing, and said, "Do you come peaceably?"

⁵And he said, "Peaceably; I have come to sacrifice t[o] the LORD. Sanctify yourselves, and come with me to th[e] sacrifice." Then he consecrated Jesse and his sons, an[d] invited them to the sacrifice.

◤▬▬▬ GROWTH

16:19-21 When Saul asked David to join his palace staff, he [
did not know that David had been secretly anointed king (16:12[
invitation presented an excellent opportunity for the young, futu[re
to gain firsthand information about leading a nation.

Sometimes our plans— even the ones we think God has app[roved
have to be put on hold indefinitely. Like David, we can use this w[aiting
time profitably. We can choose to learn and grow in our present
circumstances, whatever they may be.

⁶So it was, when they came, that he looked at Eliab and [s]aid, "Surely the LORD's anointed *is* before Him!"

⁷But the LORD said to Samuel, "Do not look at his [a]ppearance or at his physical stature, because I have [r]efused him. For *the* LORD does not *see* as man sees; for [m]an looks at the outward appearance, but the LORD [l]ooks at the heart."

⁸So Jesse called Abinadab, and made him pass before [S]amuel. And he said, "Neither has the LORD chosen this [o]ne." ⁹Then Jesse made Shammah pass by. And he said, "Neither has the LORD chosen this one." ¹⁰Thus Jesse [m]ade seven of his sons pass before Samuel. And Samuel [s]aid to Jesse, "The LORD has not chosen these." ¹¹And [S]amuel said to Jesse, "Are all the young men here?" [T]hen he said, "There remains yet [t]he youngest, and [t]here he is, keep-[in]g the sheep."

[And] Samuel [sa]id to Jesse, [S]end and bring [h]im. For we will [n]ot sit down till he [co]mes here." ¹²So he [s]ent and brought [h]im in. Now he *was* [r]uddy, with bright [ey]es, and good-looking. [A]nd the LORD said, [A]rise, anoint him; for this [is] the one!" ¹³Then Samuel [to]ok the horn of oil and [an]ointed him in the midst [of] his brothers; and the [Sp]irit of the LORD came upon [D]avid from that day forward. [So] Samuel arose and went to [R]amah.

¹⁴But the Spirit of the LORD de-[p]arted from Saul, and a distress-[in]g spirit from the LORD troubled [hi]m. ¹⁵And Saul's servants said to [hi]m, "Surely, a distressing spirit [fr]om God is troubling you. ¹⁶Let our [m]aster now command your servants, [w]ho *are* before you, to seek out a man [w]ho *is* a skillful player on the harp. And [it] shall be that he will play it with his [h]and when the distressing spirit from [G]od is upon you, and you shall be well."

¹⁷So Saul said to his servants, "Provide [m]e now a man who can play well, and bring [hi]m to me."

¹⁸Then one of the servants answered and [sa]id, "Look, I have seen a son of Jesse the [B]ethlehemite, *who is* skillful in playing, a [m]ighty man of valor, a man of war, prudent in [sp]eech, and a handsome person; and the LORD [is] with him."

¹⁹Therefore Saul sent messengers to Jesse, and [sa]id, "Send me your son David, who *is* with the sheep." ²⁰And Jesse took a donkey *loaded with* bread, a skin of wine, and a young goat, and sent *them* by his son David to Saul. ²¹So David came to Saul and stood before him. And he loved him greatly, and he became his armorbearer. ²²Then Saul sent to Jesse, saying, "Please let David stand before me, for he has found favor in my sight." ²³And so it was, whenever the spirit from God was upon Saul, that David would take a harp and play *it* with his hand. Then Saul would become refreshed and well, and the distressing spirit would depart from him.

DAVID

When we think of David, we think of a shepherd, poet, giant-killer, king, ancestor of Jesus—in short, we think of one of the greatest heroes in the Old Testament. But other words could also be used to describe David: betrayer, liar, adulterer, murderer. The first list includes qualities we all might like to have; the second, qualities that might be true of any one of us. What five or six words would summarize your life?

The Bible makes no effort to hide David's failures. Yet he is remembered and respected as a godly hero. Knowing how much more we are like David in his failures than in his successes, we should be curious to find out what made God refer to David as a man after God's heart.

David believed as deeply as he could that God was loving and forgiving. He was a man who lived with great energy and joy. He sinned many times, but he was quick to confess his sins. His confessions were from the heart and his repentance was real. David never took God's forgiveness lightly or his blessing for granted. In return, God never held back from David either his forgiveness or the consequences of his actions. David experienced the joy of forgiveness even when he had to suffer the conse-quences of his sins.

One big example David gives to us is that while he sinned greatly, he did not sin repeatedly. He didn't make the same mistakes over and over. Rather, he learned from his mistakes because he accepted the suffering they brought. Often we don't seem to learn from our mistakes or the consequences that come from those mistakes. The next time you make a mistake, think how you could be more like David.

LESSONS: Willingness to honestly admit our mis-takes is the first step in dealing with them

Forgiveness does not remove the consequences of sin

God greatly desires our complete trust and worship

KEY VERSES: "And now, O Lord GOD, You are God, and Your words are true, and You have promised this goodness to Your servant. Now therefore, let it please You to bless the house of Your servant, that it may continue before You forever; for You, O Lord GOD, have spoken it, and with Your blessing let the house of Your servant be blessed forever" (2 Samuel 7:28-29).

His story is told in 1 Samuel 16—1 Kings 2. He is also mentioned in Amos 6:5; Matthew 1:1, 6; Romans 1:3; 22:43-45; Luke 1:32; Hebrews 11:32.

UPS:
- Greatest king of Israel
- Ancestor of Jesus Christ
- Listed in the Hall of Faith in Hebrews 11
- Described by God as "a man after His own heart" (1 Samuel 13:14)

DOWNS:
- Committed adultery with Bathsheba
- Arranged the murder of Uriah, Bathsheba's husband
- Directly disobeyed God in taking a census of the people

STATS:
- Where: Bethlehem, Jerusalem
- Occupation: Shepherd, musician, poet, soldier, king
- Relatives: Father: Jesse. Wives included Michal, Ahinoam, Bathsheba, Abigail. Sons: Absalom, Amnon, Solomon, Adonijah. Daughter: Tamar. Seven brothers.
- Contemporaries: Saul, Jonathan, Samuel, Nathan

CHAPTER 17 DAVID FIGHTS GOLIATH.

Now the Philistines gathered their armies together to battle, and were gathered at Sochoh, which *belongs* to Judah; they encamped between Sochoh and Azekah, in Ephes Dammim. ²And Saul and the men of Israel were gathered together, and they encamped in the Valley of Elah, and drew up in battle array against the Philistines. ³The Philistines stood on a mountain on one side, and Israel stood on a mountain on the other side, with a valley between them.

⁴And a champion went out from the camp of the Philistines, named Goliath, from Gath, whose height *was* six cubits and a span. ⁵*He had* a bronze helmet on his head, and he *was* armed with a coat of mail, and the weight of the coat *was* five thousand shekels of bronze. ⁶And *he had* bronze armor on his legs and a bronze javelin between his shoulders. ⁷Now the staff of his spear *was* like a weaver's beam, and his iron spearhead *weighed* six hundred shekels; and a shield-bearer went before him. ⁸Then he stood and cried out to the armies of Israel, and said to them, "Why have you come out to line up for battle? *Am* I not a Philistine, and you the servants of Saul? Choose a man for yourselves, and let him come down to me. ⁹If he is able to fight with me and kill me, then we will be your servants. But if I prevail against him and kill him, then you shall be our servants and serve us." ¹⁰And the Philistine said, "I defy the armies of Israel this day; give me a man, that we may fight together." ¹¹When Saul and all Israel heard these words of the Philistine, they were dismayed and greatly afraid.

¹²Now David *was* the son of that Ephrathite of Bethlehem Judah, whose name *was* Jesse, and who had eight sons. And the man was old, advanced *in years*, in the days of Saul. ¹³The three oldest sons of Jesse had gone to follow Saul to the battle. The names of his three sons who went to the battle *were* Eliab the firstborn, next to him Abinadab, and the third Shammah. ¹⁴David *was* the youngest. And the three oldest followed Saul. ¹⁵But David occasionally went and returned from Saul to feed his father's sheep at Bethlehem.

¹⁶And the Philistine drew near and presented himself forty days, morning and evening.

Object	Reference	Who used it?	How was it used?
a rod	Exodus 4:2-4	Moses	To work miracles before Pharaoh
trumpets	Joshua 6:3-5	Joshua	To flatten the walls of Jericho
a fleece	Judges 6:36-40	Gideon	To confirm God's will
trumpets, pitchers, and torches	Judges 7:19-22	Gideon	To defeat the Midianites
jawbone	Judges 15:15	Samson	To kill 1,000 Philistines
small stone	1 Samuel 17:40	David	To kill Goliath
oil	2 Kings 4:1-7	Elisha	To demonstrate God's power to provide
a river	2 Kings 5:9-14	Elisha	To heal a man of leprosy
linen sash	Jeremiah 13:1-11	Jeremiah	As an object lesson of God's wrath
pottery	Jeremiah 19:1-13	Jeremiah	As an object lesson of God's wrath
iron plate, water, and food	Ezekiel 4:1-17	Ezekiel	As an object lesson of judgment
five loaves of bread and two fish	Mark 6:30-44	Jesus	To feed a crowd of over 5,000 people

SIMPLE OBJECTS God often uses simple, ordinary objects to accomplish his tasks in the world. It only needs to be dedicated to him for his use. What do you have that God can use? Anything and everything is a possible "instrument" for him.

¹⁷Then Jesse said to his son David, "Take now for your brothers an ephah of this dried *grain* and these ten loaves, and run to your brothers at the camp. ¹⁸And carry these ten cheeses to the captain of *their* thousand, and see how your brothers fare, and bring back news of them." ¹⁹Now Saul and they and all the men of Israel *were* in the Valley of Elah, fighting with the Philistines.

²⁰So David rose early in the morning, left the sheep with a keeper, and took *the things* and went as Jesse had commanded him. And he came to the camp as the army was going out to the fight and shouting for the battle. ²¹For Israel and the Philistines had drawn up in battle array, army against army. ²²And David left his supplies in the hand of the supply keeper, ran to the army, and came and greeted his brothers. ²³Then as he talked with them, there was the champion, the Philistine of Gath, Goliath by name, coming up from the armies of the Philistines; and he spoke according to the same words. So David heard *them*. ²⁴And all the men of Israel, when they saw the man, fled from him and were dreadfully afraid. ²⁵So the men of Israel said, "Have you seen this man who has come up? Surely he has come up to defy Israel; and it shall be *that* the man who kills him the king will enrich with great riches, will give him his daughter, and give his father's house exemption *from taxes* in Israel."

²⁶Then David spoke to the men who stood by him, saying, "What shall be done for the man who kills this Philistine and takes away the reproach from Israel? For who *is* this uncircumcised Philistine, that he should defy the armies of the living God?"

²⁷And the people answered him in this manner, saying, "So shall it be done for the man who kills him."

²⁸Now Eliab his oldest brother heard when he spoke to the men; and Eliab's anger was aroused against David, and he said, "Why did you come down here? And with whom have you left those few sheep in the wilderness? I know your pride and the insolence of your heart, for you have come down to see the battle."

²⁹And David said, "What have I done now? *Is there* not a cause?" ³⁰Then he turned from him toward another and said the same thing; and these people answered him as the first ones *did*.

³¹Now when the words which David spoke were heard, they reported *them* to Saul; and he sent for him. ³²Then David said to Saul, "Let no man's heart fail because of him; your servant will go and fight with this Philistine."

³³And Saul said to David, "You are not able to go against this Philistine to fight with him; for you *are* a youth, and he a man of war from his youth."

³⁴But David said to Saul, "Your servant used to keep his father's sheep, and when a lion or a bear came and took a lamb out of the flock, ³⁵I went out after it and struck it, and delivered *the lamb* from its mouth; and when it arose against me, I caught *it* by its beard, and struck and killed it. ³⁶Your servant has killed both lion and bear; and this uncircumcised Philistine will be like one of them, seeing he has defied the armies of the living God." ³⁷Moreover David said, "The LORD, who delivered me from the paw of the lion and from the paw of the bear, He will deliver me from the hand of this Philistine."

And Saul said to David, "Go, and the LORD be with you!"

³⁸So Saul clothed David with his armor, and he put a bronze helmet on his head; he also clothed him with a coat of mail. ³⁹David fastened his sword to his armor and tried to walk, for he had not tested *them*. And David said to Saul, "I cannot walk with these, for I have not tested *them*." So David took them off.

◣◣◣◣◣◣◣**OUTLOOK**

17:26 What a difference outlook or perspective can make! Saul saw only a giant and a young boy. David, however, saw a mortal man defying almighty God. He knew he would not be alone when he faced Goliath; God would fight with him. He looked at his situation from God's point of view. Viewing impossible situations from God's point of view helps us put giant problems in perspective.

⁴⁰Then he took his staff in his hand; and he chose for himself five smooth stones from the brook, and put them in a shepherd's bag, in a pouch which he had, and his sling was in his hand. And he drew near to the Philistine. ⁴¹So the Philistine came, and began drawing near to David, and the man who bore the shield *went* before him. ⁴²And when the Philistine looked about and saw David, he disdained him; for he was *only* a youth, ruddy and good-looking. ⁴³So the Philistine said to David, "*Am* I a dog, that you come to me with sticks?" And the Philistine cursed David by his gods. ⁴⁴And the Philistine said to David, "Come to me, and I will give your flesh to the birds of the air and the beasts of the field!"

⁴⁵Then David said to the Philistine, "You come to me with a sword, with a spear, and with a javelin. But I come to you in the name of the LORD of hosts, the God of the armies of Israel, whom you have defied. ⁴⁶This day the LORD will deliver you into my hand, and I will strike you and take your head from you. And this day I will give the carcasses of the camp of the Philistines to the birds of the air and the wild beasts of the earth, that all the earth may know that there is a God in Israel. ⁴⁷Then all this assembly shall know that the LORD does not save with sword and spear; for the battle *is* the LORD's, and He will give you into our hands."

⁴⁸So it was, when the Philistine arose and came and drew near to meet David, that David hurried and ran toward the army to meet the Philistine. ⁴⁹Then David put his hand in his bag and took out a stone; and he slung *it* and struck the Philistine in his forehead, so that the stone sank into his forehead, and he fell on his face to the earth. ⁵⁰So David prevailed over the Philistine with a sling and a stone, and struck the Philistine and killed him. But *there was* no sword in the hand of David. ⁵¹Therefore David ran and stood over the Philistine, took his sword and drew it out of its sheath and killed him, and cut off his head with it.

And when the Philistines saw that their champion was dead, they fled. ⁵²Now the men of Israel and Judah arose and shouted, and pursued the Philistines as far as the entrance of the valley and to the gates of Ekron. And the wounded of the Philistines fell along the road to Shaaraim, even as far as Gath and Ekron. ⁵³Then the children of Israel returned from chasing the Philistines, and they

18:1-4 When David and Jonathan met, they became close friends at once. Although Jonathan was probably somewhat older than David, their friendship is one of the deepest and closest recorded in the Bible because they (1) based their friendship on commitment to God, not just each other; (2) let nothing come between them, not even career or family problems; (3) drew closer together when their friendship was tested; and (4) were able to remain friends to the end.

Jonathan, the prince of Israel, later realized that David, and not he, would be king (23:17). But that did not weaken his love for David. Jonathan would much rather lose the throne of Israel than his closest friend.

plundered their tents. ⁵⁴And David took the head of the Philistine and brought it to Jerusalem, but he put his armor in his tent.

⁵⁵When Saul saw David going out against the Philistine, he said to Abner, the commander of the army, "Abner, whose son *is* this youth?"

And Abner said, "As your soul lives, O king, I do not know."

⁵⁶So the king said, "Inquire whose son this young man *is*."

⁵⁷Then, as David returned from the slaughter of the Philistine, Abner took him and brought him before Saul with the head of the Philistine in his hand. ⁵⁸And Saul said to him, "Whose son *are* you, young man?"

So David answered, "*I am* the son of your servant Jesse the Bethlehemite."

CHAPTER 18 DAVID AND JONATHAN.

Now when he had finished speaking to Saul, the soul of Jonathan was knit to the soul of David, and Jonathan loved him as his own soul. ²Saul took him that day, and would not let him go home to his father's house anymore. ³Then Jonathan and David made a covenant, because he loved him as his own soul. ⁴And Jonathan took off the robe that *was* on him and gave it to David, with his armor, even to his sword and his bow and his belt.

⁵So David went out wherever Saul sent him, *and* behaved wisely. And Saul set him over the men of war, and he was accepted in the sight of all the people and also in the sight of Saul's servants. ⁶Now it had happened as they were coming *home*, when David was returning from the slaughter of the Philistine, that the women had come out of all the cities of Israel, singing and dancing, to meet King Saul, with tambourines, with joy, and with musical instruments. ⁷So the women sang as they danced, and said:

> "Saul has slain his thousands,
> And David his ten thousands."

⁸Then Saul was very angry, and the saying displeased him; and he said, "They have ascribed to David ten thousands, and to me they have ascribed *only* thousands. Now *what* more can he have but the kingdom?" ⁹So Saul eyed David from that day forward.

¹⁰And it happened on the next day that the distressing spirit from God came upon Saul, and he prophesied inside the house. So David played *music* with his hand, as at other times; but *there was* a spear in Saul's hand. ¹¹And Saul cast the spear, for he said, "I will pin David to the wall!" But David escaped his presence twice.

¹²Now Saul was afraid of David, because the LORD was with him, but had departed from Saul. ¹³Therefore Saul removed him from his presence, and made him his captain over a thousand; and he went out and came in before the people. ¹⁴And David behaved wisely in all his ways, and the LORD *was* with him. ¹⁵Therefore, when Saul saw that he behaved very wisely, he was afraid of him. ¹⁶But all Israel and Judah loved David, because he went out and came in before them.

¹⁷Then Saul said to David, "Here is my older daughter Merab; I will give her to you as a wife. Only be valiant for me, and fight the LORD's battles." For Saul thought, "Let my hand not be against him, but let the hand of the Philistines be against him."

¹⁸So David said to Saul, "Who *am* I, and what *is* my life *or* my father's family in Israel, that I should be son-in-law to the king?" ¹⁹But it happened at the time when Merab, Saul's daughter, should have been given to David, that she was given to Adriel the Meholathite as a wife.

²⁰Now Michal, Saul's daughter, loved David. And they told Saul, and the thing pleased him. ²¹So Saul said, "I will give her to him, that she may be a snare to him, and that the hand of the Philistines may be against him." Therefore Saul said to David a second time, "You shall be my son-in-law today."

²²And Saul commanded his servants, "Communicate with David secretly, and say, 'Look, the king has delight in you, and all his servants love you. Now therefore, become the king's son-in-law.'"

²³So Saul's servants spoke those words in the hearing of David. And David said, "Does it seem to you *a* light *thing* to be a king's son-in-law, seeing I *am* a poor and lightly esteemed man?" ²⁴And the servants of Saul told him, saying, "In this manner David spoke."

²⁵Then Saul said, "Thus you shall say to David: 'The king does not desire any dowry but one hundred foreskins of the Philistines, to take vengeance on the king's enemies.'" But Saul thought to make David fall by the hand of the Philistines. ²⁶So when his servants told David these words, it pleased David well to become the king's son-in-law. Now the days had not expired; ²⁷therefore David arose and went, he and his men, and killed two hundred men of the Philistines. And David brought their foreskins, and they gave them in full count to the king that he might become the king's son-in-law. Then Saul gave him Michal his daughter as a wife.

²⁸Thus Saul saw and knew that the LORD *was* with David, and *that* Michal, Saul's daughter, loved him; ²⁹and Saul was still more afraid of David. So Saul became David's enemy continually. ³⁰Then the princes of the Philistines went out *to war*. And so it was, whenever they went out, *that* David behaved more wisely than all the servants of Saul, so that his name became highly esteemed.

18:15-18 While Saul's popularity made him proud and arrogant, David remained humble even when the entire nation praised him. Although David succeeded in almost everything he tried and became famous throughout the land, he refused to use his popular support to advantage against Saul. Don't allow popularity to twist your perception of your own importance. It's easy to be humble when you're not on center stage, but how will you react to praise and honor?

CHAPTER **19** SAUL TRIES TO KILL DAVID.

Now Saul spoke to Jonathan his son and to all his servants, that they should kill David; but Jonathan, Saul's son, delighted greatly in David. ²So Jonathan told David, saying, "My father Saul seeks to kill you. Therefore please be on your guard until morning, and stay in a secret *place* and hide. ³And I will go out and stand beside my father in the field where you *are*, and I will speak with my father about you. Then what I observe, I will tell you."

⁴Thus Jonathan spoke well of David to Saul his father, and said to him, "Let not the king sin against his servant, against David, because he has not sinned against you, and because his works *have been* very good toward you. ⁵For he took his life in his hands and killed the Philistine, and the LORD brought about a great deliverance for all Israel. You saw *it* and rejoiced. Why then will you sin against innocent blood, to kill David without a cause?"

⁶So Saul heeded the voice of Jonathan, and Saul swore, "*As* the LORD lives, he shall not be killed." ⁷Then Jonathan called David, and Jonathan told him all these things. So Jonathan brought David to Saul, and he was in his presence as in times past.

⁸And there was war again; and David went out and fought with the Philistines, and struck them with a mighty blow, and they fled from him.

⁹Now the distressing spirit from the LORD came upon Saul as he sat in his house with his spear in his hand. And David was playing *music* with *his* hand. ¹⁰Then Saul sought to pin David to the wall with the spear, but he slipped away from Saul's presence; and he drove the spear into the wall. So David fled and escaped that night.

¹¹Saul also sent messengers to David's house to watch him and to kill him in the morning. And Michal, David's wife, told him, saying, "If you do not save your life tonight, tomorrow you will be killed." ¹²So Michal let David down through a window. And he went and fled and escaped. ¹³And Michal took an image and laid *it* in the bed, put a cover of goats' *hair* for his head, and covered *it* with clothes. ¹⁴So when Saul sent messengers to take David, she said, "He *is* sick."

¹⁵Then Saul sent the messengers *back* to see David, saying, "Bring him up to me in the bed, that I may kill him." ¹⁶And when the messengers had come in, there was the image in the bed, with a cover of goats' *hair* for his head. ¹⁷Then Saul said to Michal, "Why have you deceived me like this, and sent my enemy away, so that he has escaped?"

And Michal answered Saul, "He said to me, 'Let me go! Why should I kill you?'"

¹⁸So David fled and escaped, and went to Samuel at Ramah, and told him all that Saul had done to him. And he and Samuel went and stayed in Naioth. ¹⁹Now it was told Saul, saying, "Take note, David *is* at Naioth in Ramah!" ²⁰Then Saul sent messengers to take David. And when they saw the group of prophets prophesying, and Samuel standing *as* leader over them, the Spirit of God came upon the messengers of Saul, and they also prophesied. ²¹And when Saul was told, he sent other messengers, and they prophesied likewise. Then Saul sent messengers again the third time, and they prophesied also. ²²Then he also went to Ramah, and came to the great well that *is* at Sechu. So he asked, and said, "Where *are* Samuel and David?"

JONATHAN

Loyalty is one of life's most costly qualities and is the most unselfish part of love. To be loyal, you cannot live only for yourself. Loyal people not only stand by their commitments, they are also willing to suffer for them. Jonathan is a shining example of loyalty. Sometimes he was forced to deal with a conflict between his loyalties to his father, Saul, and to his friend David. His solution to that conflict teaches us both how to be loyal and what must guide loyalty.

Jonathan, truth always guided loyalty. Jonathan found the source of truth in his relationship with God. He realized that no matter what, he must be loyal to him. It was this ultimate loyalty to God that gave Jonathan the wisdom to deal effectively with the complicated situations in his life. He was loyal to Saul because Saul was his father and the king. He was loyal to David because David was his friend. But his loyalty to God helped him see the limits of each of those other relationships.

The conflicting demands of our relationships can be real challenges to us as well. If we try to settle these conflicts only at the human level, we will be constantly dealing with a sense of betrayal. No other human can claim the loyalty we can only give to God. If we communicate to our friends that our number-one loyalty is to God and his truth, many of our choices will be much clearer. The truth in his word, the Bible, will bring wisdom to our decisions. Do those closest to you know who has your greatest loyalty?

LESSONS: Loyalty is one of the strongest aspects of courage
An allegiance to God puts all other relationships in perspective
Great friendships are costly

KEY VERSE: "I am distressed for you, my brother Jonathan; you have been very pleasant to me; your love to me was wonderful, surpassing the love of women" (2 Samuel 1:26).
His story is told in 1 Samuel 13–31. He is also mentioned in 2 Samuel 9.

UPS:
- Brave, loyal, and a natural leader
- Closest friend David ever had
- Did not put his personal well-being ahead of those he loved
- Depended on God

STATS:
- Occupation: Military leader
- Relatives: Father: Saul. Mother: Ahinoam. Brothers: Abinadab, Malchishua, and Ishbosheth. Sisters: Merab and Michal. Son: Mephibosheth.

19:23 Jonathan spoke up for David (19:4); Michal helped him escape (19:11-17); Samuel gave him a place to hide (19:18); and the Spirit of God interrupted Saul's manhunt (19:23). Each of these events protected David from harm or death. They were more than coincidence; God was at work. When you are spared from harm, recognize that God may be protecting you because he has a purpose for you.

And *someone* said, "Indeed *they are* at Naioth in Ramah." ²³So he went there to Naioth in Ramah. Then the Spirit of God was upon him also, and he went on and prophesied until he came to Naioth in Ramah. ²⁴And he also stripped off his clothes and prophesied before Samuel in like manner, and lay down naked all that day and all that night. Therefore they say, "*Is* Saul also among the prophets?"

CHAPTER **20** JONATHAN WARNS DAVID. Then David fled from Naioth in Ramah, and went and said to Jonathan, "What have I done? What *is* my iniquity, and what *is* my sin before your father, that he seeks my life?"

²So Jonathan said to him, "By no means! You shall not die! Indeed, my father will do nothing either great or small without first telling me. And why should my father hide this thing from me? It *is* not so!"

³Then David took an oath again, and said, "Your father certainly knows that I have found favor in your eyes, and he has said, 'Do not let Jonathan know this, lest he be grieved.' But truly, *as* the LORD lives and *as* your soul lives, *there is* but a step between me and death."

⁴So Jonathan said to David, "Whatever you yourself desire, I will do *it* for you."

⁵And David said to Jonathan, "Indeed tomorrow *is* the New Moon, and I should not fail to sit with the king to eat. But let me go, that I may hide in the field until the third *day* at evening. ⁶If your father misses me at all, then say, 'David earnestly asked *permission* of me that he might run over to Bethlehem, his city, for *there is* a yearly sacrifice there for all the family.' ⁷If he says thus: '*It is* well,' your servant will be safe. But if he is very angry, be sure that evil is determined by him. ⁸Therefore you shall deal kindly with your servant, for you have brought your servant into a covenant of the LORD with you. Nevertheless, if there is iniquity in me, kill me yourself, for why should you bring me to your father?"

⁹But Jonathan said, "Far be it from you! For if I knew certainly that evil was determined by my father to come upon you, then would I not tell you?"

¹⁰Then David said to Jonathan, "Who will tell me, or what *if* your father answers you roughly?"

¹¹And Jonathan said to David, "Come, let us go out into the field." So both of them went out into the field. ¹²Then Jonathan said to David: "The LORD God of Israel *is* witness! When I have sounded out my father sometime tomorrow, *or* the third *day*, and indeed *there is* good toward David, and I do not send to you and tell you, ¹³may the LORD do so and much more to Jonathan. But if it pleases my father *to do* you evil, then I will report it to you and send you away, that you may go in safety. And the LORD be with you as He has been with my father. ¹⁴And you shall not only show me the kindness of the LORD while I

still live, that I may not die; ¹⁵but you shall not cut off your kindness from my house forever, no, not when the LORD has cut off every one of the enemies of David from the face of the earth." ¹⁶So Jonathan made *a covenant* with the house of David, *saying*, "Let the LORD require *it* at the hand of David's enemies."

¹⁷Now Jonathan again caused David to vow, because he loved him; for he loved him as he loved his own soul. ¹⁸Then Jonathan said to David, "Tomorrow *is* the New Moon; and you will be missed, because your seat will be empty. ¹⁹And *when* you have stayed three days, go down quickly and come to the place where you hid on the day of the deed; and remain by the stone Ezel. ²⁰Then I will shoot three arrows to the side, as though I shot at a target; ²¹and there I will send a lad, *saying*, 'Go, find the arrows.' If I expressly say to the lad, 'Look, the arrows *are* on this side of you; get them and come'— then, as the LORD lives, *there is* safety for you and no harm. ²²But if I say thus to the young man, 'Look, the arrows *are* beyond you'—go your way, for the LORD has sent you away. ²³And as for the matter which you and I have spoken of, indeed the LORD *be* between you and me forever."

²⁴Then David hid in the field. And when the New Moon had come, the king sat down to eat the feast. ²⁵Now the king sat on his seat, as at other times, on a seat by the wall. And Jonathan arose, and Abner sat by Saul's side, but David's place was empty. ²⁶Nevertheless Saul did not say anything that day, for he thought, "Something has happened to him; he *is* unclean, surely he *is* unclean." ²⁷And it happened the next day, the second *day* of the month, that David's place was empty. And Saul said to Jonathan his son, "Why has the son of Jesse not come to eat, either yesterday or today?"

²⁸So Jonathan answered Saul, "David earnestly asked *permission* of me *to go* to Bethlehem. ²⁹And he said, 'Please let me go, for our family has a sacrifice in the city, and my brother has commanded me *to be there*. And now, if I have found favor in your eyes, please let me get away and see my brothers.' Therefore he has not come to the king's table."

³⁰Then Saul's anger was aroused against Jonathan, and he said to him, "You son of a perverse, rebellious *woman!* Do I not know that you have chosen the son of Jesse to your own shame and to the shame of your mother's nakedness? ³¹For as long as the son of Jesse lives on the earth, you shall not be established, nor your kingdom. Now therefore, send and bring him to me, for he shall surely die."

³²And Jonathan answered Saul his father, and said to him, "Why should he be killed? What has he done?" ³³Then Saul cast a spear at him to kill him, by which Jonathan knew that it was determined by his father to kill David.

³⁴So Jonathan arose from the table in fierce anger, and ate no food the second day of the month, for he was grieved for David, because his father had treated him shamefully.

³⁵And so it was, in the morning, that Jonathan went out into the field at the time appointed with David, and a little lad *was* with him. ³⁶Then he said to his lad, "No

run, find the arrows which I shoot." As the lad ran, he shot an arrow beyond him. [37]When the lad had come to the place where the arrow was which Jonathan had shot, Jonathan cried out after the lad and said, "*Is* not the arrow beyond you?" [38]And Jonathan cried out after the lad, "Make haste, hurry, do not delay!" So Jonathan's lad gathered up the arrows and came back to his master. [39]But the lad did not know anything. Only Jonathan and David knew of the matter. [40]Then Jonathan gave his weapons to his lad, and said to him, "Go, carry *them* to the city."

[41]As soon as the lad had gone, David arose from *a place* toward the south, fell on his face to the ground, and bowed down three times. And they kissed one another; and they wept together, but David more so. [42]Then Jonathan said to David, "Go in peace, since we have both sworn in the name of the LORD, saying, 'May the LORD be between you and me, and between your descendants and my descendants, forever.'" So he arose and departed, and Jonathan went into the city.

CHAPTER **21** DAVID EATS THE HOLY BREAD. Now

David came to Nob, to Ahimelech the priest. And Ahimelech was afraid when he met David, and said to him, "Why *are* you alone, and no one is with you?"

[2]So David said to Ahimelech the priest, "The king has ordered me on some business, and said to me, 'Do not let anyone know anything about the business on which I send you, or what I have commanded you.' And I have directed *my* young men to such and such a place. [3]Now therefore, what have you on hand? Give *me* five *loaves of* bread in my hand, or whatever can be found."

[4]And the priest answered David and said, "*There is* no common bread on hand; but there is holy bread, if the young men have at least kept themselves from women."

[5]Then David answered the priest, and said to him, "Truly, women *have been* kept from us about three days since I came out. And the vessels of the young men are holy, and *the bread is* in effect common, even though it was consecrated in the vessel this day."

[6]So the priest gave him holy *bread;* for there was no bread there but the showbread which had been taken from before the LORD, in order to put hot bread *in its* place on the day when it was taken away.

[7]Now a certain man of the servants of Saul *was* there that day, detained before the LORD. And his name *was* Doeg, an Edomite, the chief of the herdsmen who belonged to Saul.

[8]And David said to Ahimelech, "Is there not here on hand a spear or a sword? For I have brought neither my sword nor my weapons with me, because the king's business required haste."

[9]So the priest said, "The sword of Goliath the Philistine, whom you killed in the Valley of Elah, there it is, wrapped in a cloth behind the ephod. If you will take that, take *it.* For *there is* no other except that one here." And David said, "*There is* none like it; give it to me."

[10]Then David arose and fled that day from before Saul, and went to Achish the king of Gath. [11]And the servants of Achish said to him, "*Is* this not David the king of the land? Did they not sing of him to one another in dances, saying:

'Saul has slain his thousands,
And David his ten thousands'?"

[12]Now David took these words to heart, and was very much afraid of Achish the king of Gath. [13]So he changed his behavior before them, pretended madness in their hands, scratched on the doors of the gate, and let his saliva fall down on his beard. [14]Then Achish said to his servants, "Look, you see the man is insane. Why have you brought him to me? [15]Have I need of madmen, that you have brought this *fellow* to play the madman in my presence? Shall this *fellow* come into my house?"

CHAPTER **22** DAVID HIDES IN A CAVE. David

therefore departed from there and escaped to the cave of Adullam. So when his brothers and all his father's house heard *it,* they went down there to him. [2]And everyone *who was* in distress, everyone who *was* in debt, and everyone *who was* discontented gathered to him. So he became captain over them. And there were about four hundred men with him.

[3]Then David went from there to Mizpah of Moab; and he said to the king of Moab, "Please let my father and mother come here with you, till I know what God will do for me." [4]So he brought them before the king of Moab, and they dwelt with him all the time that David was in the stronghold.

⌇ LYING

21:2 David lied to protect himself from Saul (21:10). Some excuse this lie because a war was going on and it is the duty of a good soldier to deceive the enemy. But nowhere is David's lie condoned. In fact, the opposite is true because his lie led to the death of 85 priests (22:9-19). David's small lie seemed harmless enough, but it led to tragedy. The Bible makes it very clear that lying is wrong (Leviticus 19:11). Lying, like every other sin, is serious in God's sight and may lead to all sorts of harmful consequences. All sins must be avoided regardless of whether or not we can foresee their potential consequences.

[5]Now the prophet Gad said to David, "Do not stay in the stronghold; depart, and go to the land of Judah." So David departed and went into the forest of Hereth.

[6]When Saul heard that David and the men who *were* with him had been discovered—now Saul was staying in Gibeah under a tamarisk tree in Ramah, with his spear in his hand, and all his servants standing about him—[7]then Saul said to his servants who stood about him, "Hear now, you Benjamites! Will the son of Jesse give every one of you fields and vineyards, *and* make you all captains of thousands and captains of hundreds? [8]All of you have conspired against me, and *there is* no one who reveals to me that my son has made a covenant with the son of Jesse; and *there is* not one of you who is sorry for me or reveals to me that my son has stirred up my servant against me, to lie in wait, as *it is* this day."

[9]Then answered Doeg the Edomite, who was set over the servants of Saul, and said, "I saw the son of Jesse going to Nob, to Ahimelech the son of Ahitub. [10]And he

inquired of the LORD for him, gave him provisions, and gave him the sword of Goliath the Philistine."

11So the king sent to call Ahimelech the priest, the son of Ahitub, and all his father's house, the priests who *were* in Nob. And they all came to the king. 12And Saul said, "Hear now, son of Ahitub!"

He answered, "Here I am, my lord."

13Then Saul said to him, "Why have you conspired against me, you and the son of Jesse, in that you have given him bread and a sword, and have inquired of God for him, that he should rise against me, to lie in wait, as it is this day?"

14So Ahimelech answered the king and said, "And who among all your servants *is as* faithful as David, who is the king's son-in-law, who goes at your bidding, and is honorable in your house? 15Did I then begin to inquire of God for him? Far be it from me! Let not the king impute anything to his servant, *or* to any in the house of my father. For your servant knew nothing of all this, little or much."

◥◣ FAITHFULNESS

22:18-19 Why did God allow 85 innocent priests to be killed? Scripture does not give a specific answer to this question, but it gives some insight into the issue.

Serving God is not a ticket to guaranteed wealth, success, or health. While God does not promise that good people will never be touched by the evil in this world, we can find comfort in his promise that ultimately all evil will be abolished. Those who have remained faithful through their trials will experience untold blessings in the age to come (Matthew 5:11-12; Revelation 21:1-7; 22:1-21).

16And the king said, "You shall surely die, Ahimelech, you and all your father's house!" 17Then the king said to the guards who stood about him, "Turn and kill the priests of the LORD, because their hand also *is* with David, and because they knew when he fled and did not tell it to me." But the servants of the king would not lift their hands to strike the priests of the LORD. 18And the king said to Doeg, "You turn and kill the priests!" So Doeg the Edomite turned and struck the priests, and killed on that day eighty-five men who wore a linen ephod. 19Also Nob, the city of the priests, he struck with the edge of the sword, both men and women, children and nursing infants, oxen and donkeys and sheep—with the edge of the sword.

20Now one of the sons of Ahimelech the son of Ahitub, named Abiathar, escaped and fled after David. 21And Abiathar told David that Saul had killed the LORD's priests. 22So David said to Abiathar, "I knew that day, when Doeg the Edomite *was* there, that he would surely tell Saul. I have caused *the death* of all the persons of your father's house. 23Stay with me; do not fear. For he who seeks my life seeks your life, but with me you *shall be* safe."

CHAPTER **23** DAVID PROTECTS KEILAH. Then they told David, saying, "Look, the Philistines are fighting against Keilah, and they are robbing the threshing floors."

◥◣ DECISIONS

23:2 David sought the Lord's guidance *before* he took action, prob[ably] through the Urim and Thummim that Abiathar the priest had brough[t] (23:6). He listened to God's directions and then proceeded according[ly]. Rather than trying to find God's will *after* the fact or having to ask [to] undo the results of our hasty decisions, we should take time to disce[rn] God's will beforehand. We can hear him speak through the counsel [of] others, through his Word, and through the leading of his Spirit in ou[r] heart, as well as through circumstances.

2Therefore David inquired of the LORD, saying, "Shall I go and attack these Philistines?"

And the LORD said to David, "Go and attack the Philistines, and save Keilah."

3But David's men said to him, "Look, we are afraid here in Judah. How much more then if we go to Keilah against the armies of the Philistines?" 4Then David inquired of the LORD once again.

And the LORD answered him and said, "Arise, go down to Keilah. For I will deliver the Philistines into your hand." 5And David and his men went to Keilah and fought with the Philistines, struck them with a mighty blow, and took away their livestock. So David saved the inhabitants of Keilah.

6Now it happened, when Abiathar the son of Ahimelech fled to David at Keilah, *that* he went down *with* an ephod in his hand.

7And Saul was told that David had gone to Keilah. So Saul said, "God has delivered him into my hand, for he has shut himself in by entering a town that has gates and bars." 8Then Saul called all the people together for war, to go down to Keilah to besiege David and his men.

9When David knew that Saul plotted evil against him, he said to Abiathar the priest, "Bring the ephod here." 10Then David said, "O LORD God of Israel, Your servant has certainly heard that Saul seeks to come to Keilah to destroy the city for my sake. 11Will the men of Keilah deliver me into his hand? Will Saul come down, as Your servant has heard? O LORD God of Israel, I pray, tell Your servant."

And the LORD said, "He will come down."

12Then David said, "Will the men of Keilah deliver me and my men into the hand of Saul?"

And the LORD said, "They will deliver *you*."

13So David and his men, about six hundred, arose and departed from Keilah and went wherever they could go. Then it was told Saul that David had escaped from Keilah; so he halted the expedition.

14And David stayed in strongholds in the wilderness, and remained in the mountains in the Wilderness o[f] Ziph. Saul sought him every day, but God did not delive[r] him into his hand. 15So David saw that Saul had come ou[t]

◥◣ FRIENDS

23:16-18 This may have been the last time David and Jonath[an] together. As true friends they were more than just companions w[ho] enjoyed each other's company. They encouraged each other's fai[th] and trusted each other with their deepest thoughts and closest confidences. These are the marks of true friendship.

As Jonathan prepared to leave David, he not only promised t[o] David's friend to the end, but he also encouraged David to reme[mber] God's faithfulness. As a friend, remember that you have even m[ore to] offer than companionship.

to seek his life. And David *was* in the Wilderness of Ziph in a forest. ¹⁶Then Jonathan, Saul's son, arose and went to David in the woods and strengthened his hand in God. ¹⁷And he said to him, "Do not fear, for the hand of Saul my father shall not find you. You shall be king over Israel, and I shall be next to you. Even my father Saul knows that." ¹⁸So the two of them made a covenant before the LORD. And David stayed in the woods, and Jonathan went to his own house.

¹⁹Then the Ziphites came up to Saul at Gibeah, saying, "Is David not hiding with us in strongholds in the woods, in the hill of Hachilah, which *is* on the south of Jeshimon? ²⁰Now therefore, O king, come down according to all the desire of your soul to come down; and our part *shall be* to deliver him into the king's hand."

²¹And Saul said, "Blessed *are* you of the LORD, for you have compassion on me. ²²Please go and find out for sure, and see the place where his hideout is, *and* who has seen him there. For I am told he is very crafty. ²³See therefore, and take knowledge of all the lurking places where he hides; and come back to me with certainty, and I will go with you. And it shall be, if he is in the land, that I will search for him throughout all the clans of Judah."

²⁴So they arose and went to Ziph before Saul. But David and his men *were* in the Wilderness of Maon, in the plain on the south of Jeshimon. ²⁵When Saul and his men went to seek *him*, they told David. Therefore he went down to the rock, and stayed in the Wilderness of Maon. And when Saul heard *that*, he pursued David in the Wilderness of Maon. ²⁶Then Saul went on one side of the mountain, and David and his men on the other side of the mountain. So David made haste to get away from Saul, for Saul and his men were encircling David and his men to take them.

²⁷But a messenger came to Saul, saying, "Hurry and come, for the Philistines have invaded the land!" ²⁸Therefore Saul returned from pursuing David, and went against the Philistines; so they called that place the Rock of Escape. ²⁹Then David went up from there and dwelt in strongholds at En Gedi.

CHAPTER 24 **DAVID REFUSES TO GET EVEN.** Now it happened, when Saul had returned from following the Philistines, that it was told him, saying, "Take note! David *is* in the Wilderness of En Gedi." ²Then Saul took three thousand chosen men from all Israel, and went to seek David and his men on the Rocks of the Wild Goats. ³So he came to the sheepfolds by the road, where there *was* a cave; and Saul went in to attend to his needs. (David and his men were staying in the recesses of the cave.) ⁴Then the men of David said to him, "This is the day of which the LORD said to you, 'Behold, I will deliver your enemy into your hand, that you may do to him as it seems good to you.'" And David arose and secretly cut off a corner of Saul's robe. ⁵Now it happened afterward that David's heart troubled him because he had cut Saul's *robe*. ⁶And he said to his men, "The LORD forbid that I should do this thing to my master, the LORD's anointed, to stretch out my hand against him, seeing he *is* the anointed of the

LORD." ⁷So David restrained his servants with *these* words, and did not allow them to rise against Saul. And Saul got up from the cave and went on *his* way.

⁸David also arose afterward, went out of the cave, and called out to Saul, saying, "My lord the king!" And when Saul looked behind him, David stooped with his face to the earth, and bowed down. ⁹And David said to Saul: "Why do you listen to the words of men who say, 'Indeed David seeks your harm'? ¹⁰Look, this day your eyes have seen that the LORD delivered you today into my hand in

▶ RESPECT

24:5 David had great respect for Saul, even though Saul was trying to kill him. Although Saul was in a state of sin and rebellion against God, David still respected the position he held as God's anointed king. David knew he would one day be king—but he also knew it was not right to strike down the man God had placed on the throne. If David assassinated Saul, he would be setting a precedent for his own opponents to remove him some day.

Romans 13:1-7 teaches that God has placed the government and its leaders in power. We may not know why, but like David, we are to respect the positions and roles of those to whom God has given authority. There is one exception, however. Because God is our highest authority, we should not allow a leader to force us to violate God's law.

the cave, and *someone* urged *me* to kill you. But *my eye* spared you, and I said, 'I will not stretch out my hand against my lord, for he *is* the LORD's anointed.' ¹¹Moreover, my father, see! Yes, see the corner of your robe in my hand! For in that I cut off the corner of your robe, and did not kill you, know and see that *there is* neither evil nor rebellion in my hand, and I have not sinned against you. Yet you hunt my life to take it. ¹²Let the LORD judge between you and me, and let the LORD avenge me on you. But my hand shall not be against you. ¹³As the proverb of the ancients says, 'Wickedness proceeds from the wicked.' But my hand shall not be against you. ¹⁴After whom has the king of Israel come out? Whom do you pursue? A dead dog? A flea? ¹⁵Therefore let the LORD be judge, and judge between you and me, and see and plead my case, and deliver me out of your hand."

¹⁶So it was, when David had finished speaking these words to Saul, that Saul said, "*Is* this your voice, my son David?" And Saul lifted up his voice and wept. ¹⁷Then he said to David: "You *are* more righteous than I; for you have rewarded me with good, whereas I have rewarded you with evil. ¹⁸And you have shown this day how you have dealt well with me; for when the LORD delivered me into your hand, you did not kill me. ¹⁹For if a man finds his enemy, will he let him get away safely? Therefore may the LORD reward you with good for what you have done to me this day. ²⁰And now I know indeed that you shall surely be king, and that the kingdom of Israel shall be established in your hand. ²¹Therefore swear now to me by the LORD that you will not cut off my descendants after me, and that you will not destroy my name from my father's house."

²²So David swore to Saul. And Saul went home, but David and his men went up to the stronghold.

CHAPTER 25 ABIGAIL STOPS A FIGHT.

Then Samuel died; and the Israelites gathered together and lamented for him, and buried him at his home in Ramah. And David arose and went down to the Wilderness of Paran.

²Now *there was* a man in Maon whose business *was* in Carmel, and the man *was* very rich. He had three thousand sheep and a thousand goats. And he was shearing his sheep in Carmel. ³The name of the man *was* Nabal, and the name of his wife Abigail. And *she was* a woman of good understanding and beautiful appearance; but the man *was* harsh and evil in *his* doings. He *was of the house of* Caleb.

◄ LISTENING

25:24 David was in no mood to listen when he set out for Nabal's property (25:13,22). Nevertheless, he stopped to hear what Abigail had to say. If he had ignored her, he would have been guilty of taking vengeance into his own hands. No matter how right we think we are, we must always be careful to stop and listen to what others have to say. The extra time and effort can save us much pain and trouble in the long run.

⁴When David heard in the wilderness that Nabal was shearing his sheep, ⁵David sent ten young men; and David said to the young men, "Go up to Carmel, go to Nabal, and greet him in my name. ⁶And thus you shall say to him who lives *in prosperity:* 'Peace *be* to you, peace to your house, and peace to all that you have! ⁷Now I have heard that you have shearers. Your shepherds were with us, and we did not hurt them, nor was there anything missing from them all the while they were in Carmel. ⁸Ask your young men, and they will tell you. Therefore let *my* young men find favor in your eyes, for we come on a feast day. Please give whatever comes to your hand to your servants and to your son David.' "

⁹So when David's young men came, they spoke to Nabal according to all these words in the name of David, and waited.

¹⁰Then Nabal answered David's servants, and said, "Who *is* David, and who *is* the son of Jesse? There are many servants nowadays who break away each one from his master. ¹¹Shall I then take my bread and my water and my meat that I have killed for my shearers, and give *it* to men who I do not know where they *are* from?"

¹²So David's young men turned on their heels and went back; and they came and told him all these words. ¹³Then David said to his men, "Every man gird on his sword." So every man girded on his sword, and David also girded on his sword. And about four hundred men went with David, and two hundred stayed with the supplies.

¹⁴Now one of the young men told Abigail, Nabal's wife, saying, "Look, David sent messengers from the wilderness to greet our master; and he reviled them. ¹⁵But the men *were* very good to us, and we were not hurt, nor did we miss anything as long as we accompanied them, when we were in the fields. ¹⁶They were a wall to us both by night and day, all the time we were with them keeping the sheep. ¹⁷Now therefore, know and consider what you will do, for harm is determined against our master and against all his household. For he *is such* a scoundrel that *one* cannot speak to him."

¹⁸Then Abigail made haste and took two hundred *loaves* of bread, two skins of wine, five sheep already dressed, five seahs of roasted *grain*, one hundred clusters of raisins, and two hundred cakes of figs, and loaded *them* on donkeys. ¹⁹And she said to her servants, "Go on before me; see, I am coming after you." But she did not tell her husband Nabal.

²⁰So it was, *as* she rode on the donkey, that she went down under cover of the hill; and there were David and his men, coming down toward her, and she met them. ²¹Now David had said, "Surely in vain I have protected all that this *fellow* has in the wilderness, so that nothing was missed of all that *belongs* to him. And he has repaid me evil for good. ²²May God do so, and more also, to the enemies of David, if I leave one male of all who *belong* to him by morning light."

²³Now when Abigail saw David, she dismounted quickly from the donkey, fell on her face before David, and bowed down to the ground. ²⁴So she fell at his feet and said: "On me, my lord, *on* me *let* this iniquity *be!* And please let your maidservant speak in your ears, and hear the words of your maidservant. ²⁵Please, let not my lord regard this scoundrel Nabal. For as his name *is,* so *is* he: Nabal *is* his name, and folly *is* with him! But I, your maidservant, did not see the young men of my lord whom you sent. ²⁶Now therefore, my lord, *as* the LORD lives and *as* your soul lives, since the LORD has held you back from coming to bloodshed and from avenging yourself with your own hand, now then, let your enemies and those who seek harm for my lord be as Nabal. ²⁷And now this present which your maidservant has brought to my lord, let it be given to the young men who follow my lord. ²⁸Please forgive the trespass of your maidservant. For the LORD will certainly make for my lord an enduring house, because my lord fights the battles of the LORD, and evil is not found in you throughout your days. ²⁹Yet a man has risen to pursue you and seek your life, but the life of my lord shall be bound in the bundle of the living with the LORD your God; and the lives of your enemies He shall sling out, *as from* the pocket of a sling. ³⁰And it shall come to pass, when the LORD has done for my lord according to all the good that He has spoken concerning you, and has appointed you ruler over Israel, ³¹that this will be no grief to you, nor offense of heart to my lord, either that you have shed blood without cause, or that my lord has avenged himself. But when the LORD has dealt well with my lord, then remember your maidservant."

³²Then David said to Abigail: "Blessed *is* the LORD God of Israel, who sent you this day to meet me! ³³And blessed *is* your advice and blessed *are* you, because you have kept me this day from coming to bloodshed and from avenging myself with my own hand. ³⁴For indeed, *as* the LORD God of Israel lives, who has kept me back from hurting you, unless you had hurried and come to meet me, surely by morning light no males would have been left to Nabal!" ³⁵So David received from her hand what she had brought him, and said to her, "Go up in peace to your house. See, I have heeded your voice and respected your person."

³⁶Now Abigail went to Nabal, and there he was, holding a feast in his house, like the feast of a king. And Nabal's heart *was* merry within him, for he *was* very drunk; therefore she told him nothing, little or much, until morning light. ³⁷So it was, in the morning, when the wine had gone from Nabal, and his wife had told him these things, that his heart died within him, and he became *like* a stone. ³⁸Then it happened, *after* about ten days, that the LORD struck Nabal, and he died.

³⁹So when David heard that Nabal was dead, he said, "Blessed *be* the LORD, who has pleaded the cause of my reproach from the hand of Nabal, and has kept His servant from evil! For the LORD has returned the wickedness of Nabal on his own head."

And David sent and proposed to Abigail, to take her as his wife. ⁴⁰When the servants of David had come to Abigail at Carmel, they spoke to her saying, "David sent us to you, to ask you to become his wife."

⁴¹Then she arose, bowed her face to the earth, and said, "Here is your maidservant, a servant to wash the feet of the servants of my lord." ⁴²So Abigail rose in haste and rode on a donkey, attended by five of her maidens; and she followed the messengers of David, and became his wife. ⁴³David also took Ahinoam of Jezreel, and so both of them were his wives.

⁴⁴But Saul had given Michal his daughter, David's wife, to Palti the son of Laish, who *was* from Gallim.

CHAPTER 26 DAVID SNEAKS INTO CAMP.

Now the Ziphites came to Saul at Gibeah, saying, "Is David not hiding in the hill of Hachilah, opposite Jeshimon?" ²Then Saul arose and went down to the Wilderness of Ziph, having three thousand chosen men of Israel with him, to seek David in the Wilderness of Ziph. ³And Saul encamped in the hill of Hachilah, which *is* opposite Jeshimon, by the road. But David stayed in the wilderness, and he saw that Saul came after him into the wilderness. David therefore sent out spies, and understood that Saul had indeed come.

⁵So David arose and came to the place where Saul had encamped. And David saw the place where Saul lay, and Abner the son of Ner, the commander of his army. Now Saul lay within the camp, with the people encamped all around him. ⁶Then David answered, and said to Ahimelech the Hittite and to Abishai the son of Zeruiah, brother of Joab, saying, "Who will go down with me to Saul in the camp?"

And Abishai said, "I will go down with you."

⁷So David and Abishai came to the people by night; and there Saul lay sleeping within the camp, with his spear stuck in the ground by his head. And Abner and the people lay all around him. ⁸Then Abishai said to David, "God has delivered your enemy into your hand this day. Now therefore, please, let me strike him at once with the spear, right to the earth; and I will not *have to strike* him a second time!"

⁹But David said to Abishai, "Do not destroy him; for who can stretch out his hand against the LORD's anointed, and be guiltless?" ¹⁰David said furthermore, "As the LORD lives, the LORD shall strike him, or his day

shall come to die, or he shall go out to battle and perish. ¹¹The LORD forbid that I should stretch out my hand against the LORD's anointed. But please, take now the spear and the jug of water that *are* by his head, and let us go." ¹²So David took the spear and the jug of water *by* Saul's head, and they got away; and no man saw or knew *it* or awoke. For they *were* all asleep, because a deep sleep from the LORD had fallen on them.

▶ GOD FIRST

26:8ff The strongest moral decisions are the ones we make before temptation strikes. David was determined to follow God. This carried over into his decision not to murder God's chosen king, Saul, even when David's men and the circumstances seemed to make it possible. Whom would you have been like in such a situation—David or David's men? To be like David and follow God, we must realize that we can't do wrong in order to execute justice. Even when our closest friends counsel us to do a certain action that seems right, we must always put God's commands first.

¹³Now David went over to the other side, and stood on the top of a hill afar off, a great distance *being* between them. ¹⁴And David called out to the people and to Abner the son of Ner, saying, "Do you not answer, Abner?"

Then Abner answered and said, "Who *are* you, calling out to the king?"

¹⁵So David said to Abner, "*Are* you not a man? And who *is* like you in Israel? Why then have you not guarded your lord the king? For one of the people came in to destroy your lord the king. ¹⁶This thing that you have done *is* not good. *As* the LORD lives, you deserve to die, because you have not guarded your master, the LORD's anointed. And now see where the king's spear *is*, and the jug of water that *was* by his head."

¹⁷Then Saul knew David's voice, and said, "*Is* that your voice, my son David?"

David said, "*It is* my voice, my lord, O king." ¹⁸And he said, "Why does my lord thus pursue his servant? For what have I done, or what evil *is* in my hand? ¹⁹Now therefore, please, let my lord the king hear the words of his servant: If the LORD has stirred you up against me, let Him accept an offering. But if *it is* the children of men, *may* they *be* cursed before the LORD, for they have driven me out this day from sharing in the inheritance of the LORD, saying, 'Go, serve other gods.' ²⁰So now, do not let my blood fall to the earth before the face of the LORD. For the king of Israel has come out to seek a flea, as when one hunts a partridge in the mountains."

²¹Then Saul said, "I have sinned. Return, my son David. For I will harm you no more, because my life was precious in your eyes this day. Indeed I have played the fool and erred exceedingly."

²²And David answered and said, "Here is the king's

▶ CREATIVITY

26:15-16 David could have killed Saul and Abner and made a point, but he would have disobeyed God and set into motion unknown consequences. Instead, he took a water jug and a spear, showing that he had had the opportunity to do evil but had not done it. David made the point that he had great respect for both God and God's chosen king. When you need to make a point, look for creative, God-honoring ways to do so. It will have a more significant impact.

spear. Let one of the young men come over and get it. ²³May the LORD repay every man *for* his righteousness and his faithfulness; for the LORD delivered you into *my* hand today, but I would not stretch out my hand against the LORD's anointed. ²⁴And indeed, as your life was valued much this day in my eyes, so let my life be valued much in the eyes of the LORD, and let Him deliver me out of all tribulation."

²⁵Then Saul said to David, "*May* you *be* blessed, my son David! You shall both do great things and also still prevail."

So David went on his way, and Saul returned to his place.

CHAPTER **27** **DAVID AMONG THE PHILISTINES.** And David said in his heart, "Now I shall perish someday by the hand of Saul. *There is* nothing better for me than that I should speedily escape to the land of the Philistines; and Saul will despair of me, to seek me anymore in any part of Israel. So I shall escape out of his hand." ²Then David arose and went over with the six hundred men who *were* with him to Achish the son of Maoch, king of Gath. ³So David dwelt with Achish at Gath, he and his men, each man with his household, *and* David with his two wives, Ahinoam the Jezreelitess, and Abigail the Carmelitess, Nabal's widow. ⁴And it was told Saul that David had fled to Gath; so he sought him no more.

⁵Then David said to Achish, "If I have now found favor in your eyes, let them give me a place in some town in the country, that I may dwell there. For why should your servant dwell in the royal city with you?" ⁶So Achish gave him Ziklag that day. Therefore Ziklag has belonged to the kings of Judah to this day. ⁷Now the time that David dwelt in the country of the Philistines was one full year and four months.

⁸And David and his men went up and raided the Geshurites, the Girzites, and the Amalekites. For those nations were the inhabitants of the land from of old, as you go to Shur, even as far as the land of Egypt. ⁹Whenever David attacked the land, he left neither man nor woman alive, but took away the sheep, the oxen, the donkeys, the camels, and the apparel, and returned and came to Achish. ¹⁰Then Achish would say, "Where have you made a raid today?" And David would say, "Against the southern *area* of Judah, or against the southern *area* of the Jerahmeelites, or against the southern *area* of the Kenites." ¹¹David would save neither man nor woman alive, to bring *news* to Gath, saying, "Lest they should inform on us, saying, 'Thus David did.' " And thus *was* his behavior all the time he dwelt in the country of the Philistines. ¹²So Achish believed David, saying, "He has made his people Israel utterly abhor him; therefore he will be my servant forever."

CHAPTER **28** **SAUL VISITS A WITCH.** Now it happened in those days that the Philistines gathered their armies together for war, to fight with Israel. And Achish said to David, "You assuredly know that you will go out with me to battle, you and your men."

²So David said to Achish, "Surely you know what you servant can do."

And Achish said to David, "Therefore I will make you one of my chief guardians forever."

³Now Samuel had died, and all Israel had lamented for him and buried him in Ramah, in his own city. And Saul had put the mediums and the spiritists out of the land.

⁴Then the Philistines gathered together, and came and encamped at Shunem. So Saul gathered all Israel together, and they encamped at Gilboa. ⁵When Saul saw the army of the Philistines, he was afraid, and his heart trembled greatly. ⁶And when Saul inquired of the LORD, the LORD did not answer him, either by dreams or by Urim or by the prophets.

⁷Then Saul said to his servants, "Find me a woman who is a medium, that I may go to her and inquire of her."

And his servants said to him, "In fact, *there is* a woman who is a medium at En Dor."

⁸So Saul disguised himself and put on other clothes, and he went, and two men with him; and they came to the woman by night. And he said, "Please conduct a séance for me, and bring up for me the one I shall name to you."

⁹Then the woman said to him, "Look, you know what Saul has done, how he has cut off the mediums and the spiritists from the land. Why then do you lay a snare for my life, to cause me to die?"

¹⁰And Saul swore to her by the LORD, saying, "*As the* LORD lives, no punishment shall come upon you for this thing."

¹¹Then the woman said, "Whom shall I bring up for you?"

And he said, "Bring up Samuel for me."

¹²When the woman saw Samuel, she cried out with a loud voice. And the woman spoke to Saul, saying, "Why have you deceived me? For you *are* Saul!"

¹³And the king said to her, "Do not be afraid. What did you see?"

And the woman said to Saul, "I saw a spirit ascending out of the earth."

¹⁴So he said to her, "What *is* his form?"

And she said, "An old man is coming up, and he is covered with a mantle." And Saul perceived that it *was* Samuel, and he stooped with *his* face to the ground and bowed down.

¹⁵Now Samuel said to Saul, "Why have you disturbed me by bringing me up?"

And Saul answered, "I am deeply distressed; for the Philistines make war against me, and God has departed from me and does not answer me anymore, neither by prophets nor by dreams. Therefore I have called you, that you may reveal to me what I should do."

¹⁶Then Samuel said: "So why do you ask me, seeing the

OCCULT

28:3-8 It was Saul who had banned all mediums and spiritists Israel, but in desperation he turned to one for counsel. Although removed the sin of witchcraft from the land, he did not remove i his heart. We may make a great show of denouncing sin, but if w does not change, the sins will return. Knowing what is right and condemning what is wrong does not take the place of *doing* wha

LORD has departed from you and has become your enemy? [17]And the LORD has done for Himself as He spoke by me. For the LORD has torn the kingdom out of your hand and given it to your neighbor, David. [18]Because you did not obey the voice of the LORD nor execute His fierce wrath upon Amalek, therefore the LORD has done this thing to you this day. [19]Moreover the LORD will also deliver Israel with you into the hand of the Philistines. And tomorrow you and your sons *will be* with me. The LORD will also deliver the army of Israel into the hand of the Philistines."

[20]Immediately Saul fell full length on the ground, and was dreadfully afraid because of the words of Samuel. And there was no strength in him, for he had eaten no food all day or all night.

[21]And the woman came to Saul and saw that he was severely troubled, and said to him, "Look, your maidservant has obeyed your voice, and I have put my life in my hands and heeded the words which you spoke to me. [22]Now therefore, please, heed also the voice of your maidservant, and let me set a piece of bread before you; and eat, that you may have strength when you go on *your* way."

[23]But he refused and said, "I will not eat."

So his servants, together with the woman, urged him; and he heeded their voice. Then he arose from the ground and sat on the bed. [24]Now the woman had a fatted calf in the house, and she hastened to kill it. And she took flour and kneaded *it*, and baked unleavened bread from it. [25]So she brought *it* before Saul and his servants, and they ate. Then they rose and went away that night.

CHAPTER 29 DAVID LEAVES THE PHILISTINES.

Then the Philistines gathered together all their armies at Aphek, and the Israelites encamped by a fountain which *is* in Jezreel. [2]And the lords of the Philistines passed in review by hundreds and by thousands, but David and his men passed in review at the rear with Achish. [3]Then the princes of the Philistines said, "What *are* these Hebrews *doing here?*"

And Achish said to the princes of the Philistines, "*Is* this not David, the servant of Saul king of Israel, who has been with me these days, or these years? And to this day I have found no fault in him since he defected *to me.*"

[4]But the princes of the Philistines were angry with him; so the princes of the Philistines said to him, "Make this fellow return, that he may go back to the place which you have appointed for him, and do not let him go down with us to battle, lest in the battle he become our adversary. For with what could he reconcile himself to his master, if not with the heads of these men? [5]*Is* this not David, of whom they sang to one another in dances, saying:

'Saul has slain his thousands,
And David his ten thousands'?"

[6]Then Achish called David and said to him, "Surely, *as* the LORD lives, you have been upright, and your going out and your coming in with me in the army *is* good in my sight. For to this day I have not found evil in you since the day of your coming to me. Nevertheless the lords do not favor you. [7]Therefore return now, and go in peace, that you may not displease the lords of the Philistines."

[8]So David said to Achish, "But what have I done? And to this day what have you found in your servant as long as I have been with you, that I may not go and fight against the enemies of my lord the king?"

[9]Then Achish answered and said to David, "I know that you *are* as good in my sight as an angel of God; nevertheless the princes of the Philistines have said, 'He shall not go up with us to the battle.' [10]Now therefore, rise early in the morning with your master's servants who have come with you. And as soon as you are up early in the morning and have light, depart."

▰▰▰▰▰▰▰▰ DIRECTIONS

28:15 God did not answer Saul's appeals because Saul had not followed God's previous directions. Sometimes people wonder why their prayers are not answered. But if they don't fulfill the responsibilities God has already given them, they should not be surprised when he does not give further guidance.

[11]So David and his men rose early to depart in the morning, to return to the land of the Philistines. And the Philistines went up to Jezreel.

CHAPTER 30

Now it happened, when David and his men came to Ziklag, on the third day, that the Amalekites had invaded the South and Ziklag, attacked Ziklag and burned it with fire, [2]and had taken captive the women and those who *were* there, from small to great; they did not kill anyone, but carried *them* away and went their way. [3]So David and his men came to the city, and there it was, burned with fire; and their wives, their sons, and their daughters had been taken captive. [4]Then David and the people who *were* with him lifted up their voices and wept, until they had no more power to weep. [5]And David's two wives, Ahinoam the Jezreelitess, and Abigail the widow of Nabal the Carmelite, had been taken captive. [6]Now David was greatly distressed, for the people spoke of stoning him, because the soul of all the people was grieved, every man for his sons and his daughters. But David strengthened himself in the LORD his God.

[7]Then David said to Abiathar the priest, Ahimelech's son, "Please bring the ephod here to me." And Abiathar brought the ephod to David. [8]So David inquired of the LORD, saying, "Shall I pursue this troop? Shall I overtake them?"

And He answered him, "Pursue, for you shall surely overtake *them* and without fail recover *all.*"

[9]So David went, he and the six hundred men who *were* with him, and came to the Brook Besor, where those stayed who were left behind. [10]But David pursued, he and four hundred men; for two hundred stayed *behind*, who were so weary that they could not cross the Brook Besor.

[11]Then they found an Egyptian in the field, and brought him to David; and they gave him bread and he ate, and they let him drink water. [12]And they gave him a piece of a cake of figs and two clusters of raisins. So when he had eaten, his strength came back to him; for he had

▰▰▰ KINDNESS

30:11-15 The Amalekites cruelly left this servant to die, but God used him to help David. David and his men treated the young man kindly, and he returned the kindness by leading them to the enemy, the Amalekites. Treat those you meet with respect and dignity no matter how insignificant they may seem. You never know how God might use them to help you or haunt you, depending on your response to them.

eaten no bread nor drunk water for three days and three nights. [13]Then David said to him, "To whom do you *belong*, and where *are* you from?"

And he said, "I *am* a young man from Egypt, servant of an Amalekite; and my master left me behind, because three days ago I fell sick. [14]We made an invasion of the southern *area* of the Cherethites, in the *territory* which *belongs* to Judah, and of the southern *area* of Caleb; and we burned Ziklag with fire."

[15]And David said to him, "Can you take me down to this troop?"

So he said, "Swear to me by God that you will neither kill me nor deliver me into the hands of my master, and I will take you down to this troop."

[16]And when he had brought him down, there they were, spread out over all the land, eating and drinking and dancing, because of all the great spoil which they had taken from the land of the Philistines and from the land of Judah. [17]Then David attacked them from twilight until the evening of the next day. Not a man of them escaped, except four hundred young men who rode on camels and fled. [18]So David recovered all that the Ama-

▰▰▰ CHARACTER

31:3-4 Saul was tall, handsome, strong, rich, and powerful. But all of this was not enough to make him someone we should copy. He was tall physically, but he was small in God's eyes. He was handsome, but his sin made him ugly. He was strong, but his lack of faith made him weak. He was rich, but he was spiritually bankrupt. He could give orders to many, but he couldn't command their respect or allegiance. Saul looked good on the outside, but he was decaying on the inside. Godly character is much more valuable than good looks.

lekites had carried away, and David rescued his two wives. [19]And nothing of theirs was lacking, either small or great, sons or daughters, spoil or anything which they had taken from them; David recovered all. [20]Then David took all the flocks and herds they had driven before those *other* livestock, and said, "This *is* David's spoil."

[21]Now David came to the two hundred men who had been so weary that they could not follow David, whom they also had made to stay at the Brook Besor. So they went out to meet David and to meet the people who *were* with him. And when David came near the people, he greeted them. [22]Then all the wicked and worthless men of those who went with David answered and said, "Because they did not go with us, we will not give them *any* of the spoil that we have recovered, except for every man's wife and children, that they may lead *them* away and depart."

[23]But David said, "My brethren, you shall not do so with what the LORD has given us, who has preserved us and delivered into our hand the troop that came against

us. [24]For who will heed you in this matter? But as his part *is* who goes down to the battle, so *shall* his part *be* who stays by the supplies; they shall share alike." [25]So it was, from that day forward; he made it a statute and an ordinance for Israel to this day.

[26]Now when David came to Ziklag, he sent *some* of the spoil to the elders of Judah, to his friends, saying, "Here is a present for you from the spoil of the enemies of the LORD"— [27]to *those* who *were* in Bethel, *those* who *were* in Ramoth of the South, *those* who *were* in Jattir, [28]*those* who *were* in Aroer, *those* who *were* in Siphmoth, *those* who *were* in Eshtemoa, [29]*those* who *were* in Rachal, *those* who *were* in the cities of the Jerahmeelites, *those* who *were* in the cities of the Kenites, [30]*those* who *were* in Hormah, *those* who *were* in Chorashan, *those* who *were* in Athach, [31]*those* who *were* in Hebron, and to all the places where David himself and his men were accustomed to rove.

CHAPTER **31** SAUL DIES IN BATTLE. Now the Philistines fought against Israel; and the men of Israel fled from before the Philistines, and fell slain on Mount Gilboa. [2]Then the Philistines followed hard after Saul and his sons. And the Philistines killed Jonathan, Abinadab, and Malchishua, Saul's sons. [3]The battle became fierce against Saul. The archers hit him, and he was severely wounded by the archers.

[4]Then Saul said to his armorbearer, "Draw your sword, and thrust me through with it, lest these uncircumcised men come and thrust me through and abuse me."

But his armorbearer would not, for he was greatly afraid. Therefore Saul took a sword and fell on it. [5]And when his armorbearer saw that Saul was dead, he also fell on his sword, and died with him. [6]So Saul, his three sons, his armorbearer, and all his men died together that same day.

[7]And when the men of Israel who *were* on the other side of the valley, and *those* who *were* on the other side of the Jordan, saw that the men of Israel had fled and that Saul and his sons were dead, they forsook the cities and fled; and the Philistines came and dwelt in them. [8]So it happened the next day, when the Philistines came to strip the slain, that they found Saul and his three sons fallen on Mount Gilboa. [9]And they cut off his head and stripped off his armor, and sent *word* throughout the land of the Philistines, to proclaim *it in* the temple of their idols and among the people. [10]Then they put his armor in the temple of the Ashtoreths, and they fastened his body to the wall of Beth Shan.

[11]Now when the inhabitants of Jabesh Gilead heard what the Philistines had done to Saul, [12]all the valiant men arose and traveled all night, and took the body of Saul and the bodies of his sons from the wall of Beth Shan; and they came to Jabesh and burned them there. [13]Then they took their bones and buried *them* under the tamarisk tree at Jabesh, and fasted seven days.

MEGA Themes

KING Because Israel had corrupt priests and judges, the people wanted a king. They wanted to be organized like the surrounding nations. Although it was against his original purpose, God answered their request and gave them Saul.

Unfortunately, establishing a monarchy did not solve Israel's problems. God wants each person to give the genuine devotion of his or her mind and heart to him—not to some "king." No government or set of laws can substitute for the rule of God.

1. List a few reasons for describing God as the King.
2. What does it mean when you say Jesus Christ is Lord in a person's life?
3. How do you feel about having God as your King? If you consider Jesus to be Lord, what difference does it make in your daily life?

GOD'S CONTROL Israel prospered as long as the people regarded God as their true King. When the leaders strayed from God and his law, he intervened in their lives and overruled their actions. This way, God maintained ultimate control.

God is always at work in this world, even when we can't see what he is doing. No matter what kinds of pressures we must endure or how many changes we must face, ultimately God is in control. When we grow confident of God's sovereignty, we can face the difficult situations in our life with boldness.

1. As King, God is in control of the world. Has there been a time you felt God was not in control? How did you feel? What were you thinking? How did you choose to deal with the situation?
2. God is in control, even when you do not feel like he is. How can you be sure this is true?
3. What difference does it make for you that God is in control of the world?
4. In what areas of your life do you feel the need to know that he is in control? How will you deal with those times when it seems like he is not in control? How can you prepare yourself for those times?

LEADERSHIP God guided his people using different forms of leadership: judges, priests, prophets, and kings. Those chosen for these different offices, such as Eli, Samuel, Saul, and David, portrayed different styles of leadership. Yet the success of each leader depended on his devotion to God.

When Eli, Samuel, Saul, and David disobeyed God, they faced tragic consequences. Sin affected what they achieved for God, as well as how they raised their children. Being a true leader means letting God guide your activities, values, and goals—including your relationships in your family.

1. Evaluate the strengths and weaknesses of the following leaders:
   a. Eli   b. Samuel   c. Saul   d. David

2. Taking the best from each leader, what qualities characterize godly leadership?
3. Taking the worst from each leader, what qualities characterize leadership that's not godly?
4. What characteristics of godly leadership do you possess?
5. What characteristics do you see in yourself that you must always be giving over to God so that they do not trap you or lead you into sin?
6. Each of us has a chance to be a leader by leading others toward Christ. Describe the kind of leader you want to be for God.

OBEDIENCE To God, "to obey is better than sacrifice" (15:22). God wanted his people to obey, serve, and follow him with a whole heart, rather than maintaining a superficial commitment based on traditions or ceremonies.

Although we don't have to perform all the Jewish sacrifices, we may still rely on outward observances to substitute for inward commitment. God wants all our work and worship to be motivated by genuine, heartfelt devotion to him.

1. Rewrite 1 Samuel 15:22 in your own words.
2. In what ways can being "religious" interfere with a person's relationship with God?
3. What is the connection in your life between loving God and obeying God? What is the connection between obedience and sacrifice?

GOD'S FAITHFULNESS God faithfully kept the promises he made to Israel. He responded to his people with tender mercy and swift justice. In showing mercy, he faithfully acted in the best interest of his people. In showing justice, he was faithful to his word and perfect moral nature.

God's mercy is seen in the way he withholds the punishment for our sins. Because God is faithful, he can be counted on to show us mercy. Yet God is also just and will not tolerate rebellion. His faithfulness and unselfish love should inspire us to dedicate ourselves to him completely. We must never take this precious mercy for granted.

1. What do you learn about God's mercy from his relationships with the following people?
   a. Eli   b. Samuel   c. Saul
   d. David   e. The Hebrew nation
2. What do you learn about God's justice from those relationships?
3. How are both his loving mercy and holy justice examples of his faithfulness?
4. How should Christians respond to our faithful God? Why?
5. Complete these statements:
   a. Because God is faithful, I know:
   b. Because God is faithful, I will:

*G*enuine heroes are hard to find—those men and women who excel in their careers and in life. They are people we watch carefully and even copy. The problem is that whenever we put them on pedestals, they all seem to fall. Under the magnifying glass of public scrutiny, people's shortcomings and weaknesses become painfully obvious, and we become very disappointed. ■ That's the way it is with any human being. All of us sin and fall . . . all the time. But somehow we expect our heroes to be bigger than life, to be perfect. ■ David was the essence of a hero. Strong, brave, handsome, forceful, and committed. He had reached the top of the world. He was king, his enemies were defeated, and the people loved him. But David was human, too, and at the pinnacle of his success he fell, committing lust, adultery, and murder. ■ With modern heroes, that would be the end of the story—another one bites the dust. But with David, there was more. Recognizing his sin, he turned back to God and led the nation God's way. His comeback complete, he again became a "man after [God's] own heart." ■ Do you need a hero? David would be a good one. Not for his glory and accomplishments—and certainly not for his sin—but for his humble repentance and his determination to do things God's way.

STATS

PURPOSE: (1) To record the history of David's reign; (2) to demonstrate effective leadership under God; (3) to reveal that one person *can* make a difference; (4) to show the personal qualities that please God; (5) to depict David as an ideal leader of an imperfect kingdom, and to foreshadow Christ, who will be the ideal leader of a new and perfect kingdom (chapter 7)

AUTHOR: Unknown. Some have suggested that Nathan's son Zabud may have been the author (1 Kings 4:5). The book also includes the writings of Nathan and Gad (1 Chronicles 29:29).

DATE WRITTEN: 930 B.C.; written soon after David's reign, 1010–970 B.C.

SETTING: The land of Israel under David's rule

SPECIAL FEATURES: This book was named after the prophet who anointed David and guided him in godly living

2 Samuel

CHAPTER 1 Now it came to pass after the death of Saul, when David had returned from the slaughter of the Amalekites, and David had stayed two days in Ziklag, ²on the third day, behold, it happened that a man came from Saul's camp with his clothes torn and dust on his head. So it was, when he came to David, that he fell to the ground and prostrated himself.

³And David said to him, "Where have you come from?"

So he said to him, "I have escaped from the camp of Israel."

⁴Then David said to him, "How did the matter go? Please tell me."

And he answered, "The people have fled from the battle, many of the people are fallen and dead, and Saul and Jonathan his son are dead also."

⁵So David said to the young man who told him, "How do you know that Saul and Jonathan his son are dead?"

⁶Then the young man who told him said, "As I happened by chance *to be* on Mount Gilboa, there was Saul, leaning on his spear; and indeed the chariots and horsemen followed hard after him. ⁷Now when he looked behind him, he saw me and called to me. And I answered, 'Here I am.' ⁸And he said to me, 'Who *are* you?' So I answered him, 'I *am* an Amalekite.' ⁹He said to me again,

'Please stand over me and kill me, for anguish has come upon me, but my life still *remains* in me.' ¹⁰So I stood over him and killed him, because I was sure that he could not live after he had fallen. And I took the crown that *was* on his head and the bracelet that *was* on his arm, and have brought them here to my lord."

¹¹Therefore David took hold of his own clothes and tore them, and *so did* all the men who *were* with him. ¹²And they mourned and wept and fasted until evening for Saul and for Jonathan his son, for the people of the LORD and for the house of Israel, because they had fallen by the sword.

¹³Then David said to the young man who told him, "Where *are* you from?"

And he answered, "I *am* the son of an alien, an Amalekite."

¹⁴So David said to him, "How was it you were not afraid to put forth your hand to destroy the LORD's anointed?" ¹⁵Then David called one of the young men and said, "Go near, *and* execute him!" And he struck him so that he

◤GRIEF

1:1-12 David and his men were visibly shaken over Saul's death: "They mourned and wept and fasted until evening." This showed their genuine sorrow over the loss of their king, their friend Jonathan, and the other soldiers of Israel who died that day. They were not ashamed to grieve. Today, expressing our emotions is considered by some to be a sign of weakness. Those who wish to appear strong try to hide their grief. But mourning can help us deal with our intense sorrow when a loved one dies.

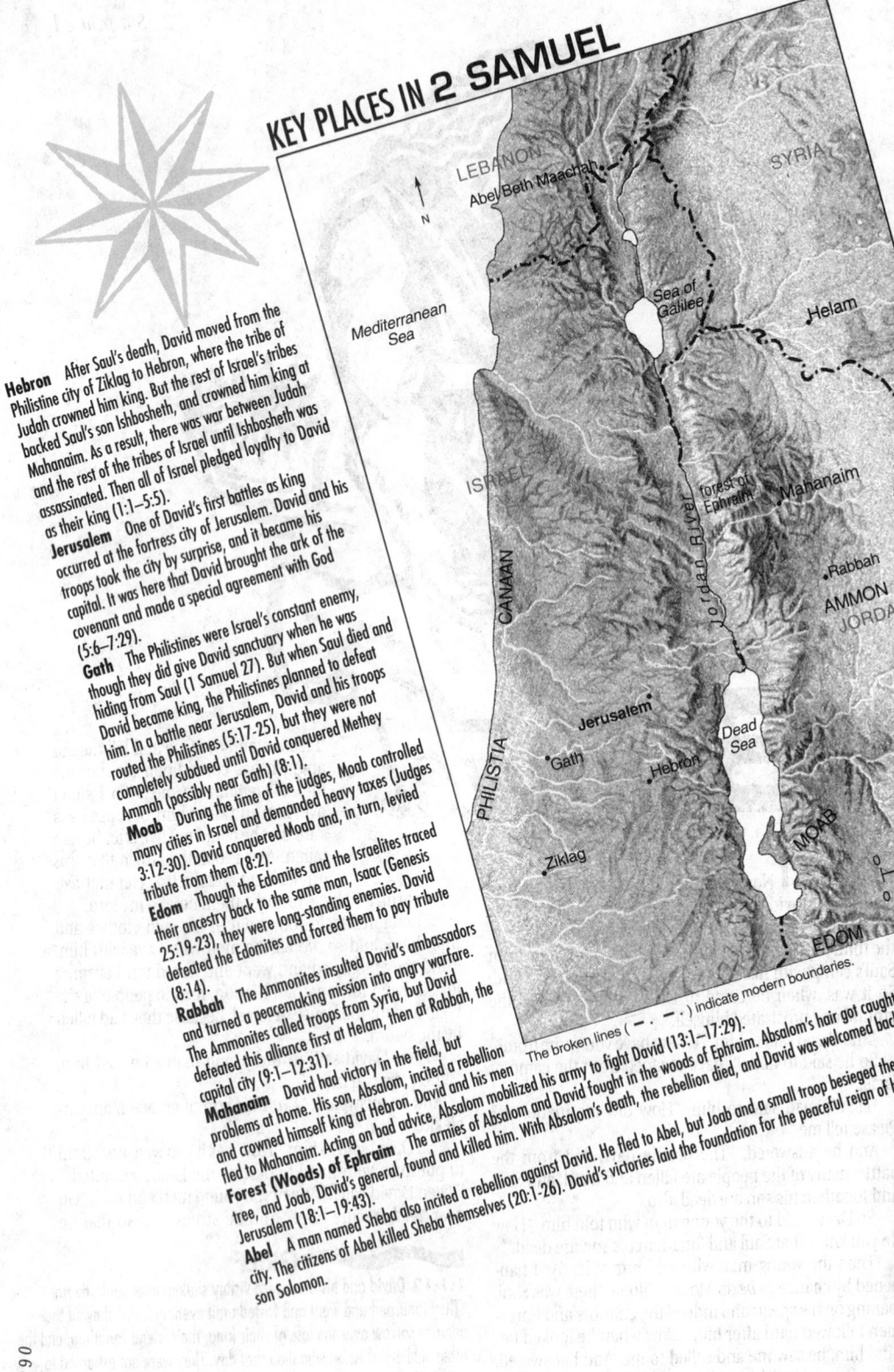

KEY PLACES IN 2 SAMUEL

Hebron After Saul's death, David moved from the Philistine city of Ziklag to Hebron, where the tribe of Judah crowned him king. But the rest of Israel's tribes backed Saul's son Ishbosheth, and crowned him king at Mahanaim. As a result, there was war between Ishbosheth and the rest of the tribes of Israel until Ishbosheth was assassinated. Then all of Israel pledged loyalty to David as their king (1:1–5:5).

Jerusalem One of David's first battles as king occurred at the fortress city of Jerusalem. David and his troops took the city by surprise, and it became his capital. It was here that David brought the ark of the covenant and made a special agreement with God (5:6–7:29).

Gath The Philistines were Israel's constant enemy, though they did give David sanctuary when he was hiding from Saul (1 Samuel 27). But when Saul died and David became king, the Philistines planned to defeat him. In a battle near Jerusalem, David and his troops routed the Philistines (5:17-25), but they were not completely subdued until David conquered Methey Ammah (possibly near Gath) (8:1).

Moab During the time of the judges, Moab controlled many cities in Israel and demanded heavy taxes (Judges 3:12-30). David conquered Moab and, in turn, levied tribute from them (8:2).

Edom Though the Edomites and the Israelites traced their ancestry back to the same man, Isaac (Genesis 25:19-23), they were long-standing enemies. David defeated the Edomites and forced them to pay tribute (8:14).

Rabbah The Ammonites insulted David's ambassadors and turned a peacemaking mission into angry warfare. The Ammonites called troops from Syria, but David defeated this alliance first at Helam, then at Rabbah, the capital city (9:1–12:31).

Mahanaim David had victory in the field, but problems at home. His son, Absalom, incited a rebellion and crowned himself king at Hebron. David and his men fled to Mahanaim. Acting on bad advice, Absalom mobilized his army to fight David (13:1–17:29).

Forest (Woods) of Ephraim The armies of Absalom and David fought in the woods of Ephraim. Absalom's hair got caught in a tree, and Joab, David's general, found and killed him. With Absalom's death, the rebellion died, and David was welcomed back to Jerusalem (18:1–19:43).

Abel A man named Sheba also incited a rebellion against David. He fled to Abel, but Joab and a small troop besieged the city. The citizens of Abel killed Sheba themselves (20:1-26). David's victories laid the foundation for the peaceful reign of his son Solomon.

The broken lines (– · –) indicate modern boundaries.

died. ¹⁶So David said to him, "Your blood *is* on your own head, for your own mouth has testified against you, saying, 'I have killed the LORD's anointed.'"

¹⁷Then David lamented with this lamentation over Saul and over Jonathan his son, ¹⁸and he told *them* to teach the children of Judah *the Song of* the Bow; indeed *it is* written in the Book of Jasher:

¹⁹ "The beauty of Israel is slain on your high places!
How the mighty have fallen!
²⁰ Tell *it* not in Gath,
Proclaim *it* not in the streets of Ashkelon—
Lest the daughters of the Philistines rejoice,
Lest the daughters of the uncircumcised triumph.

²¹ "O mountains of Gilboa,
Let there be no dew nor rain upon you,
Nor fields of offerings.
For the shield of the mighty is cast away there!
The shield of Saul, not anointed with oil.
²² From the blood of the slain,
From the fat of the mighty,
The bow of Jonathan did not turn back,
And the sword of Saul did not return empty.

²³ "Saul and Jonathan *were* beloved and pleasant in
their lives,
And in their death they were not divided;
They were swifter than eagles,
They were stronger than lions.

²⁴ "O daughters of Israel, weep over Saul,
Who clothed you in scarlet, with luxury;
Who put ornaments of gold on your apparel.

²⁵ "How the mighty have fallen in the midst of the battle!
Jonathan *was* slain in your high places.
²⁶ I am distressed for you, my brother Jonathan;
You have been very pleasant to me;
Your love to me was wonderful,
Surpassing the love of women.

²⁷ "How the mighty have fallen,
And the weapons of war perished!"

CHAPTER 2 **JUDAH CROWNS DAVID KING.** It happened after this that David inquired of the LORD, saying, "Shall I go up to any of the cities of Judah?"

And the LORD said to him, "Go up."

David said, "Where shall I go up?"

And He said, "To Hebron."

²So David went up there, and his two wives also, Ahinoam the Jezreelitess, and Abigail the widow of Nabal the Carmelite. ³And David brought up the men who *were* with him, every man with his household. So they dwelt in the cities of Hebron.

⁴Then the men of Judah came, and there they anointed David king over the house of Judah. And they told David, saying, "The men of Jabesh Gilead *were the ones* who buried Saul." ⁵So David sent messengers to the men of Jabesh Gilead, and said to them, "You *are* blessed of the LORD, for you have shown this kindness to your lord, to Saul, and have buried him. ⁶And now may the

LORD show kindness and truth to you. I also will repay you this kindness, because you have done this thing. ⁷Now therefore, let your hands be strengthened, and be valiant; for your master Saul is dead, and also the house of Judah has anointed me king over them."

⁸But Abner the son of Ner, commander of Saul's army, took Ishbosheth the son of Saul and brought him over to Mahanaim; ⁹and he made him king over Gilead, over the Ashurites, over Jezreel, over Ephraim, over Benjamin, and over all Israel. ¹⁰Ishbosheth, Saul's son, *was* forty years old when he began to reign over Israel, and he reigned two years. Only the house of Judah followed David. ¹¹And the time that David was king in Hebron over the house of Judah was seven years and six months.

◤◢ SEEING GOOD

1:17-27 Saul had caused much trouble for David, but when he died, David composed a lament, or poem, for the king and his son. David had every reason to hate Saul, yet he chose not to. He chose to look at the good Saul had done and to forget the times when Saul had attacked him. It takes courage to lay aside hatred and hurt in order to show respect for another person—especially an enemy.

¹²Now Abner the son of Ner, and the servants of Ishbosheth the son of Saul, went out from Mahanaim to Gibeon. ¹³And Joab the son of Zeruiah, and the servants of David, went out and met them by the pool of Gibeon. So they sat down, one on one side of the pool and the other on the other side of the pool. ¹⁴Then Abner said to Joab, "Let the young men now arise and compete before us."

And Joab said, "Let them arise."

¹⁵So they arose and went over by number, twelve from Benjamin, *followers* of Ishbosheth the son of Saul, and twelve from the servants of David. ¹⁶And each one grasped his opponent by the head and *thrust* his sword in his opponent's side; so they fell down together. Therefore that place was called the Field of Sharp Swords, which *is* in Gibeon. ¹⁷So there was a very fierce battle that day, and Abner and the men of Israel were beaten before the servants of David.

¹⁸Now the three sons of Zeruiah were there: Joab and Abishai and Asahel. And Asahel *was as* fleet of foot as a wild gazelle. ¹⁹So Asahel pursued Abner, and in going he did not turn to the right hand or to the left from following Abner.

²⁰Then Abner looked behind him and said, "*Are* you Asahel?"

He answered, "I *am*."

²¹And Abner said to him, "Turn aside to your right hand or to your left, and lay hold on one of the young men and take his armor for yourself." But Asahel would

◤◢ STUBBORN

2:21-23 Abner repeatedly warned Asahel to turn back or risk losing his life, but Asahel refused to turn from his self-imposed duty. Persistence is a good trait if it is for a worthy cause. But if the goal is only personal honor or gain, persistence may be no more than stubbornness. Asahel's stubbornness not only cost his life, but also spurred unfortunate disunity in David's army for years to come (3:26-27; 1 Kings 2:28-35). Before you decide to pursue a goal, make sure it is worthy of your devotion.

not turn aside from following him. ²²So Abner said again to Asahel, "Turn aside from following me. Why should I strike you to the ground? How then could I face your brother Joab?" ²³However, he refused to turn aside. Therefore Abner struck him in the stomach with the blunt end of the spear, so that the spear came out of his back; and he fell down there and died on the spot. So it was *that* as many as came to the place where Asahel fell down and died, stood still.

²⁴Joab and Abishai also pursued Abner. And the sun was going down when they came to the hill of Ammah, which *is* before Giah by the road to the Wilderness of Gibeon. ²⁵Now the children of Benjamin gathered together behind Abner and became a unit, and took their stand on top of a hill. ²⁶Then Abner called to Joab and said, "Shall the sword devour forever? Do you not know that it will be bitter in the latter end? How long will it be then until you tell the people to return from pursuing their brethren?"

²⁷And Joab said, "*As* God lives, unless you had spoken, surely then by morning all the people would have given up pursuing their brethren." ²⁸So Joab blew a trumpet; and all the people stood still and did not pursue Israel anymore, nor did they fight anymore. ²⁹Then Abner and his men went on all that night through the plain, crossed over the Jordan, and went through all Bithron; and they came to Mahanaim.

³⁰So Joab returned from pursuing Abner. And when he had gathered all the people together, there were missing of David's servants nineteen men and Asahel. ³¹But the servants of David had struck down, of Benjamin and Abner's men, three hundred and sixty men who died. ³²Then they took up Asahel and buried him in his father's tomb, which *was in* Bethlehem. And Joab and his men went all night, and they came to Hebron at daybreak.

CHAPTER 3 DAVID BECOMES STRONGER.

Now there was a long war between the house of Saul and the house of David. But David grew stronger and stronger, and the house of Saul grew weaker and weaker.

²Sons were born to David in Hebron: His firstborn was Amnon by Ahinoam the Jezreelitess; ³his second, Chileab, by Abigail the widow of Nabal the Carmelite; the third, Absalom the son of Maacah, the daughter of Talmai, king of Geshur; ⁴the fourth, Adonijah the son of Haggith; the fifth, Shephatiah the son of Abital; ⁵and the sixth, Ithream, by David's wife Eglah. These were born to David in Hebron.

⁶Now it was so, while there was war between the house of Saul and the house of David, that Abner was strengthening *his hold* on the house of Saul.

⁷And Saul had a concubine, whose name *was* Rizpah, the daughter of Aiah. So *Ishbosheth* said to Abner, "Why have you gone in to my father's concubine?"

⁸Then Abner became very angry at the words of Ishbosheth, and said, "*Am* I a dog's head that belongs to Judah? Today I show loyalty to the house of Saul your father, to his brothers, and to his friends, and have not delivered you into the hand of David; and you charge me today with a fault concerning this woman? ⁹May God do

3:7 Ishbosheth was right to speak out against Abner's behavior, bu didn't have the moral strength to maintain his authority (3:11). Lack moral backbone became the root of Israel's troubles over the next f centuries. Only four of the next forty kings of Israel were called "go It takes courage and strength to stand firm in your convictions and t confront wrongdoing in the face of opposition. When you believe something is wrong, do not let yourself be talked out of your positio Firmly attack the wrong and uphold the right.

so to Abner, and more also, if I do not do for David as the LORD has sworn to him— ¹⁰to transfer the kingdom from the house of Saul, and set up the throne of David over Israel and over Judah, from Dan to Beersheba." ¹¹And he could not answer Abner another word, because he feared him.

¹²Then Abner sent messengers on his behalf to David, saying, "Whose *is* the land?" saying *also*, "Make your covenant with me, and indeed my hand *shall be* with you to bring all Israel to you."

¹³And *David* said, "Good, I will make a covenant with you. But one thing I require of you: you shall not see my face unless you first bring Michal, Saul's daughter, when you come to see my face." ¹⁴So David sent messengers to Ishbosheth, Saul's son, saying, "Give *me* my wife Michal, whom I betrothed to myself for a hundred foreskins of the Philistines." ¹⁵And Ishbosheth sent and took her from *her* husband, from Paltiel the son of Laish. ¹⁶Then her husband went along with her to Bahurim, weeping behind her. So Abner said to him, "Go, return!" And he returned.

¹⁷Now Abner had communicated with the elders of Israel, saying, "In time past you were seeking for David *to be* king over you. ¹⁸Now then, do *it!* For the LORD has spoken of David, saying, 'By the hand of My servant David, I will save My people Israel from the hand of the Philistines and the hand of all their enemies.'" ¹⁹And Abner also spoke in the hearing of Benjamin. Then Abner also went to speak in the hearing of David in Hebron all that seemed good to Israel and the whole house of Benjamin.

²⁰So Abner and twenty men with him came to David at Hebron. And David made a feast for Abner and the men who *were* with him. ²¹Then Abner said to David, "I will arise and go, and gather all Israel to my lord the king, that they may make a covenant with you, and that you may reign over all that your heart desires." So David sent Abner away, and he went in peace.

²²At that moment the servants of David and Joab came from a raid and brought much spoil with them. But Abner *was* not with David in Hebron, for he had sent him away, and he had gone in peace. ²³When Joab and all the troops that *were* with him had come, they told Joab saying, "Abner the son of Ner came to the king, and he sent him away, and he has gone in peace." ²⁴Then Joab came to the king and said, "What have you done? Look Abner came to you; why *is* it *that* you sent him away, and he has already gone? ²⁵Surely you realize that Abner the son of Ner came to deceive you, to know your going ou and your coming in, and to know all that you are doing.

²⁶And when Joab had gone from David's presence, h sent messengers after Abner, who brought him bac

from the well of Sirah. But David did not know *it*. ²⁷Now when Abner had returned to Hebron, Joab took him aside in the gate to speak with him privately, and there stabbed him in the stomach, so that he died for the blood of Asahel his brother.

²⁸Afterward, when David heard *it*, he said, "My kingdom and I *are* guiltless before the LORD forever of the blood of Abner the son of Ner. ²⁹Let it rest on the head of Joab and on all his father's house; and let there never fail to be in the house of Joab one who has a discharge or is a leper, who leans on a staff or falls by the sword, or who lacks bread." ³⁰So Joab and Abishai his brother killed Abner, because he had killed their brother Asahel at Gibeon in the battle.

³¹Then David said to Joab and to all the people who were with him, "Tear your clothes, gird yourselves with sackcloth, and mourn for Abner." And King David followed the coffin. ³²So they buried Abner in Hebron; and the king lifted up his voice and wept at the grave of Abner, and all the people wept. ³³And the king sang *a lament* over Abner and said:

"Should Abner die as a fool dies?
³⁴ Your hands were not bound
    Nor your feet put into fetters;
    As a man falls before wicked men, *so* you fell."

Then all the people wept over him again.

³⁵And when all the people came to persuade David to eat food while it was still day, David took an oath, saying, "God do so to me, and more also, if I taste bread or anything else till the sun goes down!" ³⁶Now all the people took note *of it*, and it pleased them, since whatever the king did pleased all the people. ³⁷For all the people and all Israel understood that day that it had not been the king's *intent* to kill Abner the son of Ner. ³⁸Then the king said to his servants, "Do you not know that a prince and a great man has fallen this day in Israel? ³⁹And I *am* weak today, though anointed king; and these men, the sons of Zeruiah, *are* too harsh for me. The LORD shall repay the evildoer according to his wickedness."

CHAPTER 4 KING ISHBOSHETH IS MURDERED.

When Saul's son heard that Abner had died in Hebron, he lost heart, and all Israel was troubled. ²Now Saul's son *had* two men *who were* captains of troops. The name of one *was* Baanah and the name of the other Rechab, the sons of Rimmon the Beerothite, of the children of Benjamin. (For Beeroth also was *part* of Benjamin, ³because the Beerothites fled to Gittaim and have been sojourners there until this day.)

⁴Jonathan, Saul's son, had a son *who was* lame in *his* feet. He was five years old when the news about Saul and Jonathan came from Jezreel; and his nurse took him up and fled. And it happened, as she made haste to flee, that he fell and became lame. His name *was* Mephibosheth.

⁵Then the sons of Rimmon the Beerothite, Rechab and Baanah, set out and came at about the heat of the day to the house of Ishbosheth, who was lying on his bed at noon. ⁶And they came there, all the way into the house, *as though* to get wheat, and they stabbed him in the

stomach. Then Rechab and Baanah his brother escaped. ⁷For when they came into the house, he was lying on his bed in his bedroom; then they struck him and killed him, beheaded him and took his head, and were all night escaping through the plain. ⁸And they brought the head of Ishbosheth to David at Hebron, and said to the king, "Here is the head of Ishbosheth, the son of Saul your enemy, who sought your life; and the LORD has avenged my lord the king this day of Saul and his descendants."

～～～BE BOLD!

4:1 Ishbosheth was a man who took his courage from another man (Abner) rather than from God. When Abner died, Ishbosheth was left with nothing. In crisis and under pressure, he collapsed in fear. Fear can paralyze us, but faith and trust in God can overcome fear (2 Timothy 1:6-8; Hebrews 13:6). If we trust in God, we will be free to respond boldly to the events around us.

⁹But David answered Rechab and Baanah his brother, the sons of Rimmon the Beerothite, and said to them, "*As* the LORD lives, who has redeemed my life from all adversity, ¹⁰when someone told me, saying, 'Look, Saul is dead,' thinking to have brought good news, I arrested him and had him executed in Ziklag—the one who *thought* I would give him a reward for *his* news. ¹¹How much more, when wicked men have killed a righteous person in his own house on his bed? Therefore, shall I not now require his blood at your hand and remove you from the earth?" ¹²So David commanded his young men, and they executed them, cut off their hands and feet, and hanged *them* by the pool in Hebron. But they took the head of Ishbosheth and buried *it* in the tomb of Abner in Hebron.

CHAPTER 5 DAVID BECOMES KING.

Then all the tribes of Israel came to David at Hebron and spoke, saying, "Indeed we *are* your bone and your flesh. ²Also, in time past, when Saul was king over us, you were the one who led Israel out and brought them in; and the LORD said to you, 'You shall shepherd My people Israel, and be ruler over Israel.'" ³Therefore all the elders of Israel came to the king at Hebron, and King David made a covenant with them at Hebron before the LORD. And they anointed David king over Israel. ⁴David *was* thirty years old when he began to reign, *and* he reigned forty years. ⁵In Hebron he reigned over Judah seven years and six months, and in Jerusalem he reigned thirty-three years over all Israel and Judah.

⁶And the king and his men went to Jerusalem against the Jebusites, the inhabitants of the land, who spoke to David, saying, "You shall not come in here; but the blind and the lame will repel you," thinking, "David cannot come in here." ⁷Nevertheless David took the stronghold of Zion (that *is*, the City of David). ⁸Now David said on that day, "Whoever climbs up by way of the water shaft and defeats the Jebusites (the lame and the blind, *who are* hated by David's soul), *he shall be chief and captain*." Therefore they say, "The blind and the lame shall not come into the house."

⁹Then David dwelt in the stronghold, and called it the City of David. And David built all around from the Millo

PATIENCE

5:4-5 David did not become king of all Israel until he was 37 years old, although he had been promised the kingship many years earlier (1 Samuel 16:13). During those years, David had to wait patiently for the fulfillment of God's promise. If you feel pressured to achieve instant results and success, remember David's patience. Just as his time of waiting prepared him for his important task, a waiting period may help prepare you by strengthening your spiritual character.

and inward. ¹⁰So David went on and became great, and the LORD God of hosts *was* with him.

¹¹Then Hiram king of Tyre sent messengers to David, and cedar trees, and carpenters and masons. And they built David a house. ¹²So David knew that the LORD had established him as king over Israel, and that He had exalted His kingdom for the sake of His people Israel.

¹³And David took more concubines and wives from Jerusalem, after he had come from Hebron. Also more sons and daughters were born to David. ¹⁴Now these *are* the names of those who were born to him in Jerusalem: Shammua, Shobab, Nathan, Solomon, ¹⁵Ibhar, Elishua, Nepheg, Japhia, ¹⁶Elishama, Eliada, and Eliphelet.

¹⁷Now when the Philistines heard that they had anointed David king over Israel, all the Philistines went up to search for David. And David heard *of it* and went down to the stronghold. ¹⁸The Philistines also went and deployed themselves in the Valley of Rephaim. ¹⁹So David inquired of the LORD, saying, "Shall I go up against the Philistines? Will You deliver them into my hand?"

And the LORD said to David, "Go up, for I will doubtless deliver the Philistines into your hand."

BATTLES

5:19-25 David fought his battles the way God instructed him. In each instance he (1) asked if he should fight or not; (2) followed instructions carefully; and (3) gave God the glory. We can err in our "battles" by ignoring these steps and instead (1) doing what we want without considering God's will; (2) doing things our way and ignoring advice in the Bible or from other wise people; and (3) taking the glory ourselves or giving it to someone else without acknowledging the help we received from God. All of these responses are sinful.

²⁰So David went to Baal Perazim, and David defeated them there; and he said, "The LORD has broken through my enemies before me, like a breakthrough of water." Therefore he called the name of that place Baal Perazim. ²¹And they left their images there, and David and his men carried them away.

²²Then the Philistines went up once again and deployed themselves in the Valley of Rephaim. ²³Therefore David inquired of the LORD, and He said, "You shall not go up; circle around behind them, and come upon them in front of the mulberry trees. ²⁴And it shall be, when you hear the sound of marching in the tops of the mulberry trees, then you shall advance quickly. For then the LORD will go out before you to strike the camp of the Philistines." ²⁵And David did so, as the LORD commanded him; and he drove back the Philistines from Geba as far as Gezer.

CHAPTER 6 DAVID BRINGS THE ARK HOME.

Again David gathered all *the* choice *men* of Israel, thirty thousand. ²And David arose and went with all the people who *were* with him from Baale Judah to bring up from there the ark of God, whose name is called by the Name, the LORD of Hosts, who dwells *between* the cherubim. ³So they set the ark of God on a new cart, and brought it out of the house of Abinadab, which *was* on the hill; and Uzzah and Ahio, the sons of Abinadab, drove the new cart. ⁴And they brought it out of the house of Abinadab, which *was* on the hill, accompanying the ark of God; and Ahio went before the ark. ⁵Then David and all the house of Israel played *music* before the LORD on all kinds of *instruments of* fir wood, on harps, on stringed instruments, on tambourines, on sistrums, and on cymbals.

⁶And when they came to Nachon's threshing floor, Uzzah put out *his hand* to the ark of God and took hold of it, for the oxen stumbled. ⁷Then the anger of the LORD was aroused against Uzzah, and God struck him there for *his* error; and he died there by the ark of God. ⁸And David became angry because of the LORD's outbreak against Uzzah; and he called the name of the place Perez Uzzah to this day.

⁹David was afraid of the LORD that day; and he said "How can the ark of the LORD come to me?" ¹⁰So David would not move the ark of the LORD with him into the City of David; but David took it aside into the house of Obed-Edom the Gittite. ¹¹The ark of the LORD remained in the house of Obed-Edom the Gittite three months. And the LORD blessed Obed-Edom and all his household.

¹²Now it was told King David, saying, "The LORD has blessed the house of Obed-Edom and all that *belongs* to him, because of the ark of God." So David went and brought up the ark of God from the house of Obed-Edom to the City of David with gladness. ¹³And so it was, when those bearing the ark of the LORD had gone six paces, that he sacrificed oxen and fatted sheep. ¹⁴Then David danced before the LORD with all *his* might; and David *was* wearing a linen ephod. ¹⁵So David and all the house of Israel brought up the ark of the LORD with shouting and with the sound of the trumpet.

¹⁶Now as the ark of the LORD came into the City of David, Michal, Saul's daughter, looked through a window and saw King David leaping and whirling before the LORD; and she despised him in her heart. ¹⁷So they brought the ark of the LORD, and set it in its place in the midst of the tabernacle that David had erected for it. Then David offered burnt offerings and peace offerings before the LORD. ¹⁸And when David had finished offering burnt offerings and peace offerings, he blessed the people in the name of the LORD of hosts. ¹⁹Then he distributed among all the people, among the whole multitude of Israel, both the women and the men, to everyone a loaf of bread, a piece *of meat*, and a cake of raisins. So all the people departed, everyone to his house.

²⁰Then David returned to bless his household. And Michal the daughter of Saul came out to meet David, and said, "How glorious was the king of Israel today, uncovering himself today in the eyes of the maids of his servants, as one of the base fellows shamelessly uncovers himself!"

²¹So David said to Michal, "*It was* before the LORD, wh

chose me instead of your father and all his house, to appoint me ruler over the people of the LORD, over Israel. Therefore I will play *music* before the LORD. 22And I will be even more undignified than this, and will be humble in my own sight. But as for the maidservants of whom you have spoken, by them I will be held in honor."

23Therefore Michal the daughter of Saul had no children to the day of her death.

CHAPTER 7 Now it came to pass when the king was dwelling in his house, and the LORD had given him rest from all his enemies all around, 2that the king said to Nathan the prophet, "See now, I dwell in a house of cedar, but the ark of God dwells inside tent curtains."

3Then Nathan said to the king, "Go, do all that *is* in your heart, for the LORD *is* with you."

4But it happened that night that the word of the LORD came to Nathan, saying, 5"Go and tell My servant David, 'Thus says the LORD: "Would you build a house for Me to dwell in? 6For I have not dwelt in a house since the time that I brought the children of Israel up from Egypt, even to this day, but have moved about in a tent and in a tabernacle. 7Wherever I have moved about with all the children of Israel, have I ever spoken a word to anyone from the tribes of Israel, whom I commanded to shepherd My people Israel, saying, 'Why have you not built Me a house of cedar?' ' 8Now therefore, thus shall you say to My servant David, 'Thus says the LORD of hosts: "I took you from the sheepfold, from following the sheep, to be ruler over My people, over Israel. 9And I have been with you wherever you have gone, and have cut off all your enemies from before you, and have made you a great name, like the name of the great men who *are* on the earth. 10Moreover I will appoint a place for My people Israel, and will plant them, that they may dwell in a place of their own and move no more; nor shall the sons of wickedness oppress them anymore, as previously, 11since the time that I commanded judges *to be* over My people Israel, and have caused you to rest from all your enemies. Also the LORD tells you that He will make you a house.

12"When your days are fulfilled and you rest with your fathers, I will set up your seed after you, who will come from your body, and I will establish his kingdom. 13He shall build a house for My name, and I will establish the throne of his kingdom forever. 14I will be his Father, and he shall be My son. If he commits iniquity, I will chasten him with the rod of men and with the blows of the sons of men. 15But My mercy shall not depart from him, as I took *it* from Saul, whom I removed from before you. 16And your house and your kingdom shall be established forever before you. Your throne shall be established forever." ' "

MICHAL

Sometimes love is not enough—especially if that love is little more than the strong emotional attraction that grows between a hero and an admirer. To Michal, Saul's daughter, the courageous young David must have seemed like a dream come true. Her feelings for this hero gradually became obvious to others, and eventually her father heard about her love for David. Seeing this as an opportunity to get rid of his rival, Saul promised Michal's hand in marriage in exchange for David's success in the impossible mission of killing one hundred Philistines. But David was victorious. As a result, Saul lost a daughter, and David became even more popular with the people.

Michal's love for David did not have time to be tested by the realities of marriage. Instead, she became involved in saving his life. Her quick thinking helped him escape, but the price was Saul's anger and Michal's separation from David. Her father gave her to another man, Palti, although David eventually took her back.

Unlike her brother Jonathan, Michal did not have the kind of deep relationship with God that would have helped her come through the difficulties in her life. Instead, she became bitter. She could not share David's joyful worship of God, so she hated it. When the same faith in God is not shared by a couple, the One who can hold them together sometimes seems to come between them. Sadly, Michal never bore David any children.

Beyond feeling sorry for her, we need to see Michal as a person like us. How quickly and easily we become bitter when life takes unexpected turns. But bitterness cannot change the bad things that have happened. Often, bitterness only makes a bad situation worse. On the other hand, a willingness to turn to God gives him the opportunity to bring good out of our difficulties. That willingness has two parts: asking God for his guidance, and looking for that guidance in his Word.

LESSONS: We are not as responsible for what happens to us as we are for how we respond to our circumstances

Disobedience to God almost always harms us as well as others

KEY VERSE: "Now as the ark of the LORD came into the City of David, Michal, Saul's daughter, looked through a window and saw King David leaping and whirling before the LORD; and she despised him in her heart" (2 Samuel 6:16).

Michal's story is told in 1 Samuel 14—2 Samuel 6. She is also mentioned in 1 Chronicles 15:29.

UPS:
- Loved David and became his first wife
- Saved David's life
- Could think and act quickly when it was needed

DOWNS:
- Lied under pressure
- Allowed herself to become bitter over her circumstances
- In her unhappiness, hated David because of his love for God

STATS:
- Occupation: Daughter of one king (Saul) and wife of another (David)
- Relatives: Parents: Saul and Ahinoam. Brothers: Abinadab, Jonathan, Malchishua. Sister: Merab. Husbands: David and Palti.

7:8-16 David's request was good, but God said no. This does not mean that God rejected David. In fact, God was planning to do something even greater in David's life than allowing him the prestige of building the temple. Although God turned down David's request, he promised that David's descendants would rule the kingdom forever. David's earthly dynasty ended four centuries later, but Jesus Christ, a direct descendant of David, was the ultimate fulfillment of this promise (Acts 2:22-36). Christ will reign for eternity—first in his spiritual kingdom, and ultimately on earth in the New Jerusalem (Luke 1:30-33; Revelation 21). Have you prayed with good intentions, only to have God say no? Realize that this is not rejection, but God's way of fulfilling a greater purpose in your life.

[17]According to all these words and according to all this vision, so Nathan spoke to David.

[18]Then King David went in and sat before the LORD; and he said: "Who *am* I, O Lord GOD? And what is my house, that You have brought me this far? [19]And yet this was a small thing in Your sight, O Lord GOD; and You have also spoken of Your servant's house for a great while to come. *Is* this the manner of man, O Lord GOD? [20]Now what more can David say to You? For You, Lord GOD, know Your servant. [21]For Your word's sake, and according to Your own heart, You have done all these great things, to make Your servant know *them*. [22]Therefore You are great, O Lord GOD. For *there is* none like You, nor *is there any* God besides You, according to all that we have heard with our ears. [23]And who *is* like Your people, like Israel, the one nation on the earth whom God went to redeem for Himself as a people, to make for Himself a name—and to do for Yourself great and awesome deeds for Your land—before Your people whom You redeemed for Yourself from Egypt, the nations, and their gods? [24]For You have made Your people Israel Your very own people forever; and You, LORD, have become their God.

[25]"Now, O LORD God, the word which You have spoken concerning Your servant and concerning his house, establish *it* forever and do as You have said. [26]So let Your name be magnified forever, saying, 'The LORD of hosts *is* the God over Israel.' And let the house of Your servant David be established before You. [27]For You, O LORD of hosts, God of Israel, have revealed *this* to Your servant, saying, 'I will build you a house.' Therefore Your servant has found it in his heart to pray this prayer to You. [28]"And now, O Lord GOD, You are God, and Your words are true, and You have promised this goodness to Your servant. [29]Now therefore, let it please You to bless the house of Your servant, that it may continue before You forever; for You, O Lord GOD, have spoken *it*, and with Your blessing let the house of Your servant be blessed forever."

CHAPTER 8 DAVID STRENGTHENS HIS KINGDOM.

After this it came to pass that David attacked the Philistines and subdued them. And David took Metheg Ammah from the hand of the Philistines.

[2]Then he defeated Moab. Forcing them down to the ground, he measured them off with a line. With two lines he measured off those to be put to death, and with one full line those to be kept alive. So the Moabites became David's servants, *and* brought tribute.

[3]David also defeated Hadadezer the son of Rehob, king of Zobah, as he went to recover his territory at the River Euphrates. [4]David took from him one thousand *chariots*, seven hundred horsemen, and twenty thousand foot soldiers. Also David hamstrung all the chariot horses, except that he spared *enough* of them for one hundred chariots.

[5]When the Syrians of Damascus came to help Hadadezer king of Zobah, David killed twenty-two thousand of the Syrians. [6]Then David put garrisons in Syria of Damascus; and the Syrians became David's servants, *and* brought tribute. So the LORD preserved David wherever he went. [7]And David took the shields of gold that had belonged to the servants of Hadadezer, and brought them to Jerusalem. [8]Also from Betah and from Berothai, cities of Hadadezer, King David took a large amount of bronze.

THE PUBLIC EYE

8:15 Everything David did pleased the people (3:35-36), not because he tried to please them, but because he tried to please God. Often who try the hardest to become popular never make it. But the praise of people is not that important. Don't spend your time devising ways to please others so you will be accepted in the public eye. Instead, simply do what is right—and both God and people will respect your conduct.

[9]When Toi king of Hamath heard that David had defeated all the army of Hadadezer, [10]then Toi sent Joram his son to King David, to greet him and bless him, because he had fought against Hadadezer and defeated him (for Hadadezer had been at war with Toi); and *Joram* brought with him articles of silver, articles of gold, and articles of bronze. [11]King David also dedicated these to the LORD, along with the silver and gold that he had dedicated from all the nations which he had subdued—[12]from Syria, from Moab, from the people of Ammon, from the Philistines, from Amalek, and from the spoil of Hadadezer the son of Rehob, king of Zobah.

[13]And David made *himself* a name when he returned from killing eighteen thousand Syrians in the Valley of Salt. [14]He also put garrisons in Edom; throughout all Edom he put garrisons, and all the Edomites became David's servants. And the LORD preserved David wherever he went.

[15]So David reigned over all Israel; and David administered judgment and justice to all his people. [16]Joab the son of Zeruiah *was* over the army; Jehoshaphat the son of Ahilud *was* recorder; [17]Zadok the son of Ahitub and Ahimelech the son of Abiathar *were* the priests; Seraiah *was* the scribe; [18]Benaiah the son of Jehoiada *was over* both the Cherethites and the Pelethites; and David's sons were chief ministers.

CHAPTER 9 DAVID IS KIND TO MEPHIBOSHETH

Now David said, "Is there still anyone who is left of the house of Saul, that I may show him kindness for Jonathan's sake?"

[2]And *there was* a servant of the house of Saul whose name *was* Ziba. So when they had called him to David, the king said to him, "*Are* you Ziba?"

He said, "At your service!"

³Then the king said, "*Is* there not still someone of the house of Saul, to whom I may show the kindness of God?"

And Ziba said to the king, "There is still a son of Jonathan *who is* lame in *his* feet."

⁴So the king said to him, "Where *is* he?"

And Ziba said to the king, "Indeed he *is* in the house of Machir the son of Ammiel, in Lo Debar."

⁵Then King David sent and brought him out of the house of Machir the son of Ammiel, from Lo Debar.

⁶Now when Mephibosheth the son of Jonathan, the son of Saul, had come to David, he fell on his face and prostrated himself. Then David said, "Mephibosheth?"

And he answered, "Here is your servant!"

⁷So David said to him, "Do not fear, for I will surely show you kindness for Jonathan your father's sake, and will restore to you all the land of Saul your grandfather; and you shall eat bread at my table continually."

⁸Then he bowed himself, and said, "What *is* your servant, that you should look upon such a dead dog as I?"

⁹And the king called to Ziba, Saul's servant, and said to him, "I have given to your master's son all that belonged to Saul and to all his house. ¹⁰You therefore, and your sons and your servants, shall work the land for him, and you shall bring in *the harvest*, that your master's son may have food to eat. But Mephibosheth your master's son shall eat bread at my table always." Now Ziba had fifteen sons and twenty servants.

¹¹Then Ziba said to the king, "According to all that my lord the king has commanded his servant, so will your servant do."

"As for Mephibosheth," *said the king*, "he shall eat at my table like one of the king's sons." ¹²Mephibosheth had a young son whose name *was* Micha. And all who dwelt in the house of Ziba *were* servants of Mephibosheth. ¹³So Mephibosheth dwelt in Jerusalem, for he ate continually at the king's table. And he was lame in both his feet.

CHAPTER **10** A KING MOCKS DAVID'S MEN. It happened after this that the king of the people of Ammon died, and Hanun his son reigned in his place. ²Then David said, "I will show kindness to Hanun the son of Nahash, as his father showed kindness to me."

So David sent by the hand of his servants to comfort him concerning his father. And David's servants came into the land of the people of Ammon. ³And the princes of the people of Ammon said to Hanun their lord, "Do you think that David really honors your father because he has sent comforters to you? Has David not *rather* sent his servants to you to search the city, to spy it out, and to overthrow it?"

⁴Therefore Hanun took David's servants, shaved off half of their beards, cut off their garments in the middle, at their buttocks, and sent them away. ⁵When they told David, he sent to meet them, because the men were greatly ashamed. And the king said, "Wait at Jericho until your beards have grown, and *then* return."

⁶When the people of Ammon saw that they had made themselves repulsive to David, the people of Ammon

sent and hired the Syrians of Beth Rehob and the Syrians of Zoba, twenty thousand foot soldiers; and from the king of Maacah one thousand men, and from Ish-Tob twelve thousand men. ⁷Now when David heard *of it*, he sent Joab and all the army of the mighty men. ⁸Then the people of Ammon came out and put themselves in battle array at the entrance of the gate. And the Syrians of Zoba, Beth Rehob, Ish-Tob, and Maacah *were* by themselves in the field.

▬▬▬ BALANCE

10:12 There must be a balance between our actions and our faith in God. In this verse, David says, "Let us be strong." In other words, do what you can. Plan the battle strategy, use your mind to figure out the best techniques, and use your resources. But he also says, "May the LORD do what is good in His sight." He knew that the outcome was in God's hands. In the same way, we are to use our mind and our resources to obey God, while living by faith and trusting God for the outcome.

⁹When Joab saw that the battle line was against him before and behind, he chose some of Israel's best and put *them* in battle array against the Syrians. ¹⁰And the rest of the people he put under the command of Abishai his brother, that he might set *them* in battle array against the people of Ammon. ¹¹Then he said, "If the Syrians are too strong for me, then you shall help me; but if the people of Ammon are too strong for you, then I will come and help you. ¹²Be of good courage, and let us be strong for our people and for the cities of our God. And may the LORD do *what is* good in His sight."

¹³So Joab and the people who *were* with him drew near for the battle against the Syrians, and they fled before him. ¹⁴When the people of Ammon saw that the Syrians were fleeing, they also fled before Abishai, and entered the city. So Joab returned from the people of Ammon and went to Jerusalem.

¹⁵When the Syrians saw that they had been defeated by Israel, they gathered together. ¹⁶Then Hadadezer sent and brought out the Syrians who *were* beyond the River, and they came to Helam. And Shobach the commander of Hadadezer's army *went* before them. ¹⁷When it was told David, he gathered all Israel, crossed over the Jordan, and came to Helam. And the Syrians set themselves in battle array against David and fought with him. ¹⁸Then the Syrians fled before Israel; and David killed seven hundred charioteers and forty thousand horsemen of the Syrians, and struck Shobach the commander of their army, who died there. ¹⁹And when all the kings *who were* servants to Hadadezer saw that they were defeated by Israel, they made peace with Israel and served them. So the Syrians were afraid to help the people of Ammon anymore.

CHAPTER **11** DAVID AND BATHSHEBA. It happened in the spring of the year, at the time when kings go out *to battle*, that David sent Joab and his servants with him, and all Israel; and they destroyed the people of Ammon and besieged Rabbah. But David remained at Jerusalem.

²Then it happened one evening that David arose from his bed and walked on the roof of the king's house. And

from the roof he saw a woman bathing, and the woman *was* very beautiful to behold. ³So David sent and inquired about the woman. And *someone* said, "*Is* this not Bathsheba, the daughter of Eliam, the wife of Uriah the Hittite?" ⁴Then David sent messengers, and took her; and she came to him, and he lay with her, for she was cleansed from her impurity; and she returned to her house. ⁵And the woman conceived; so she sent and told David, and said, "I *am* with child."

⁶Then David sent to Joab, *saying*, "Send me Uriah the Hittite." And Joab sent Uriah to David. ⁷When Uriah had come to him, David asked how Joab was doing, and how the people were doing, and how the war prospered. ⁸And David said to Uriah, "Go down to your house and wash

^^^^^^^^^^^^^^^^^^^^^^^^^^^^^^^^

LIVING FOR THE MOMENT

All winter, 17-year-old Traci thought about only one thing—spring break.

"It's gonna be so great! I'm going with my three best friends and my older sister. I had to, like, beg my mom for a year to get her permission, but she finally said I could. Anyway, I cannot wait to leave behind all this crummy weather and get away from my mom. I'm serious. Anyway, in just a few weeks, I'll have it made—tons of rays, millions of guys, and no nosy mother!"

That was before. Now spring break is history, and it's not so much fun to get Traci talking about her trip. In fact, it's sad. See, the minute Traci hit the beach, she forgot everything she stands for. She let herself get sucked up into the "let-it-all-hang-out, party-till-you-puke, if-it-feels-good-do-it" mentality. And that attitude has left Traci with a lot of scars.

"Why didn't I listen? My friends and my sister kept telling me to mellow out. But I just blew them off and went out by myself. The third night I met these college guys at a poolside party and started hanging out with them. The next thing I remember, I was waking up in a motel room . . . in bed with some guy I'd never seen before. I don't even know what happened."

For another look at the consequences of living for the moment, read 2 Samuel 11–12.

^^^^^^^^^^^^^^^^^^^^^^^^^^^^^^^^

your feet." So Uriah departed from the king's house, and a gift *of food* from the king followed him. ⁹But Uriah slept at the door of the king's house with all the servants of his lord, and did not go down to his house. ¹⁰So when they told David, saying, "Uriah did not go down to his house," David said to Uriah, "Did you not come from a journey? Why did you not go down to your house?"

¹¹And Uriah said to David, "The ark and Israel and Judah are dwelling in tents, and my lord Joab and the servants of my lord are encamped in the open fields. Shall I then go to my house to eat and drink, and to lie with my wife? *As* you live, and *as* your soul lives, I will not do this thing."

¹²Then David said to Uriah, "Wait here today also, and tomorrow I will let you depart." So Uriah remained in Jerusalem that day and the next. ¹³Now when David called him, he ate and drank before him; and he made him drunk. And at evening he went out to lie on his bed with the servants of his lord, but he did not go down to his house.

TEMPTATION

11:3-4 As David gazed from his palace roof, he saw a beautif[ul] taking a bath, and lust filled his heart. He should have left the r[oof] fled from the temptation. Instead, he went farther by asking ab[out] Bathsheba. The results of letting temptation stay in his heart we[re] devastating.

To flee temptation: (1) Ask God in earnest prayer to help yo[u] away from people, places, and situations that offer temptation. (2) Memorize and meditate on portions of Scripture that combat specific weaknesses. At the root of most temptation is a real nee[d/] desire that God can fill. (3) Find another believer with whom yo[u] openly share your temptations and call this person for help whe[n] temptation strikes.

¹⁴In the morning it happened that David wrote a lette[r] to Joab and sent *it* by the hand of Uriah. ¹⁵And he wro[te] in the letter, saying, "Set Uriah in the forefront of th[e] hottest battle, and retreat from him, that he may b[e] struck down and die." ¹⁶So it was, while Joab besieged th[e] city, that he assigned Uriah to a place where he kne[w] there *were* valiant men. ¹⁷Then the men of the city cam[e] out and fought with Joab. And *some* of the people of th[e] servants of David fell; and Uriah the Hittite died also.

¹⁸Then Joab sent and told David all the things con[n]cerning the war, ¹⁹and charged the messenger, sayin[g,] "When you have finished telling the matters of the war t[o] the king, ²⁰if it happens that the king's wrath rises, and h[e] says to you: 'Why did you approach so near to the cit[y] when you fought? Did you not know that they woul[d] shoot from the wall? ²¹Who struck Abimelech the son o[f] Jerubbesheth? Was it not a woman who cast a piece of millstone on him from the wall, so that he died in The[-] bez? Why did you go near the wall?'—then you shall sa[y,] 'Your servant Uriah the Hittite is dead also.'"

²²So the messenger went, and came and told David a[ll] that Joab had sent by him. ²³And the messenger said t[o] David, "Surely the men prevailed against us and cam[e] out to us in the field; then we drove them back as far a[s] the entrance of the gate. ²⁴The archers shot from the wa[ll] at your servants; and *some* of the king's servants ar[e] dead, and your servant Uriah the Hittite is dead also."

²⁵Then David said to the messenger, "Thus you shall sa[y] to Joab: 'Do not let this thing displease you, for the swor[d] devours one as well as another. Strengthen your attac[k] against the city, and overthrow it.' So encourage him.[?]

²⁶When the wife of Uriah heard that Uriah her husban[d] was dead, she mourned for her husband. ²⁷And when he[r] mourning was over, David sent and brought her to h[is] house, and she became his wife and bore him a son. B[ut] the thing that David had done displeased the LORD.

CHAPTER 12 NATHAN SCOLDS DAVID. Then th[e] LORD sent Nathan to David. And he came to him, an[d] said to him: "There were two men in one city, one ric[h,] and the other poor. ²The rich *man* had exceedingly man[y]

CONFRONT

12:1ff As a prophet, Nathan was required to confront sin, eve[n] of a king. It took great courage, skill, and tact to speak to Davi[d] that would make him aware of his wrong actions. When you hav[e to] confront someone with unpleasant news, pray for courage, skill, [and] How you present your message may be as important as what yo[u]

locks and herds. ³But the poor *man* had nothing, except one little ewe lamb which he had bought and nourished; and it grew up together with him and with his children. t ate of his own food and drank from his own cup and lay in his bosom; and it was like a daughter to him. ⁴And a raveler came to the rich man, who refused to take from his own flock and from his own herd to prepare one for the wayfaring man who had come to him; but he took the poor man's lamb and prepared it for the man who had come to him."

⁵So David's anger was greatly aroused against the man, and he said to Nathan, "*As* the LORD lives, the man who has done this shall surely die! ⁶And he shall restore fourfold for the lamb, because he did this thing and because he had no pity."

⁷Then Nathan said to David, "You *are* the man! Thus says the LORD God of Israel: 'I anointed you king over Israel, and I delivered you from the hand of Saul. ⁸I gave you your master's house and your master's wives into your keeping, and gave you the house of Israel and Judah. And if *that had been* too little, I also would have given you much more! ⁹Why have you despised the commandment of the LORD, to do evil in His sight? You have killed Uriah the Hittite with the sword; you have taken his wife *to be* your wife, and have killed him with the sword of the people of Ammon. ¹⁰Now therefore, the sword shall never depart from your house, because you have despised Me, and have taken the wife of Uriah the Hittite to be your wife.' ¹¹Thus says the LORD: 'Behold, I will raise up adversity against you from your own house; and I will take your wives before your eyes and give *them* to your neighbor, and he shall lie with your wives in the sight of this sun. ¹²For you did *it* secretly, but I will do this thing before all Israel, before the sun.'"

¹³So David said to Nathan, "I have sinned against the LORD."

And Nathan said to David, "The LORD also has put away your sin; you shall not die. ¹⁴However, because by this deed you have given great occasion to the enemies of the LORD to blaspheme, the child also *who is* born to you shall surely die." ¹⁵Then Nathan departed to his house.

And the LORD struck the child that Uriah's wife bore to David, and it became ill. ¹⁶David therefore pleaded with God for the child, and David fasted and went in and lay all night on the ground. ¹⁷So the elders of his house arose and went to him, to raise him up from the ground. But he would not, nor did he eat food with them. ¹⁸Then on the seventh day it came to pass that the child died. And the servants of David were afraid to tell him that the child was dead. For they said, "Indeed, while the child was alive, we spoke to him, and he would not heed our voice. How can we tell him that the child is dead? He may do some harm!"

¹⁹When David saw that his servants were whispering, David perceived that the child was dead. Therefore David said to his servants, "Is the child dead?"

And they said, "He is dead."

²⁰So David arose from the ground, washed and anointed himself, and changed his clothes; and he went into the house of the LORD and worshiped. Then he went to his own house; and when he requested, they set food before him, and he ate. ²¹Then his servants said to him, "What *is* this that you have done? You fasted and wept for the child *while he was* alive, but when the child died, you arose and ate food."

²²And he said, "While the child was alive, I fasted and wept; for I said, 'Who can tell *whether* the LORD will be gracious to me, that the child may live?' ²³But now he is dead; why should I fast? Can I bring him back again? I shall go to him, but he shall not return to me."

²⁴Then David comforted Bathsheba his wife, and went in to her and lay with her. So she bore a son, and he called his name Solomon. Now the LORD loved him, ²⁵and He sent *word* by the hand of Nathan the prophet: So he called his name Jedidiah, because of the LORD.

²⁶Now Joab fought against Rabbah of the people of Ammon, and took the royal city. ²⁷And Joab sent messengers to David, and said, "I have fought against Rabbah, and I have taken the city's water *supply.* ²⁸Now therefore, gather the rest of the people together and encamp against the city and take it, lest I take the city and it be called after my name." ²⁹So David gathered all the people together and went to Rabbah, fought against it, and took it. ³⁰Then he took their king's crown from his head. Its weight *was* a talent of gold, with precious stones. And it was *set* on David's head. Also he brought out the spoil of the city in great abundance. ³¹And he brought out the people who *were* in it, and put *them to work* with saws and iron picks and iron axes, and made them cross over to the brick works. So he did to all the cities of the people of Ammon. Then David and all the people returned to Jerusalem.

CHAPTER **13** AMNON RAPES TAMAR. After this Absalom the son of David had a lovely sister, whose name *was* Tamar; and Amnon the son of David loved her. ²Amnon was so distressed over his sister Tamar that he became sick; for she *was* a virgin. And it was improper for Amnon to do anything to her. ³But Amnon had a friend whose name *was* Jonadab the son of Shimeah, David's brother. Now Jonadab *was* a very crafty man. ⁴And he said to him, "Why *are* you, the king's son, becoming thinner day after day? Will you not tell me?"

Amnon said to him, "I love Tamar, my brother Absalom's sister."

⁵So Jonadab said to him, "Lie down on your bed and pretend to be ill. And when your father comes to see you, say to him, 'Please let my sister Tamar come and give me food, and prepare the food in my sight, that I may see *it* and eat it from her hand.'" ⁶Then Amnon lay down and pretended to be ill; and when the king came to see him, Amnon said to the king, "Please let Tamar my sister come and make a couple of cakes for me in my sight, that I may eat from her hand."

⁷And David sent home to Tamar, saying, "Now go to your brother Amnon's house, and prepare food for him." ⁸So Tamar went to her brother Amnon's house; and he was lying down. Then she took flour and kneaded *it*, made cakes in his sight, and baked the cakes. ⁹And she took the pan and placed *them* out before him, but he

DATE RAPE

It's every woman's worst nightmare. It's one of the ugliest words we know. And it takes on even more nightmarish dimensions when the woman knows and trusts the rapist. Then it's called "date rape" or "acquaintance rape." Studies indicate the horrifying fact that as many as one out of every five women has been or will be raped. In America, a rape occurs every six minutes. One in eight female college students will experience rape or attempted rape, usually from a date or acquaintance. Even men are not immune: 16 percent of male college students admit to having been forced into having sex. (These figures do not include incest or other family-related sexual abuse.) Most experts agree that these frightening numbers may reflect only a fraction of the reality. As much as 90 percent of all rapes go unreported. We have a terrible plague on our hands—one we as Christians and churches must respond to. What should you do if you've been a rape victim? First, understand you are a victim. What happened was not your fault. If you said no, and a man, any man—boyfriend, stranger, father, acquaintance—forced himself on you, you were raped. The circumstances make no difference. If you said no and he ignored you, you were raped. It was not your fault. Second, realize you are not alone. There are, unfortunately, countless women who share your experience, who understand your pain. Find one of those women—a counselor at a rape treatment center, a hospital staff worker, or someone you know—and tell your story. Talking about it helps break the power the incident(s) has over you; not talking about it will keep you a victim forever. Third, understand that whatever guilt you experience—and many women experience intense guilt—is false guilt. Regardless of what your conscience—or he—may tell you, you did nothing to deserve this. You may have exercised poor judgment. Don't take responsibility for someone else's sin. If you have been a rape victim, seek help. And remember, the best source of help is God himself. He alone is able to heal your damaged body, emotions, and spirit. Turn to God and let him make you whole again. He can do it. If you are a guy who is trying to help a girl work through this shattering experience, consider this: never tell a rape victim she should "just get over it" or "get on with her life." Every woman who has been sexually violated wants to do just that, but it is impossible to "carry on" as though the rape never happened. Rape changes a woman's life. The inner anguish must be dealt with. There is no way to gauge when a woman will recover from this kind of devastation. Try to be patient, supportive, and loving. Not allowing her to deal with the pain, fear, and conflict encourages her to deny the problem. If you are a guy who has committed rape, or if you consider it OK to force a girl to do anything sexually agai her will, consider this: There is no excuse for rape or sexual abuse. NONE. The Bible has very harsh words people who commit sexual immorality and for those who victimize others. Consider Galatians 6:7: "Do no deceived, God is not mocked; for whatever a man sows, that he will also reap." Don't think you can mock God's laws and abuse his image—which is what you do when you abuse any person—and get away wit The thought of God's wrath waiting to be poured out on those who commit such sins should be enough t anyone in his tracks. And don't try to justify the act by saying, "She said no, but her body said yes," or wouldn't have gone out with me if she didn't want it, too." If a woman says no, she means no. Ignore you are legally guilty of rape—and you can go to jail. If you have committed this sin, cry out to Go mercy and forgiveness, and seek counseling. If you don't, not only are innocent women in danger; so soul. Don't test God's wrath. Confess, repent, and get help. God is waiting—and willing—to help yo

refused to eat. Then Amnon said, "Have everyone go out from me." And they all went out from him. ¹⁰Then Amnon said to Tamar, "Bring the food into the bedroom, that I may eat from your hand." And Tamar took the cakes which she had made, and brought *them* to Amnon her brother in the bedroom. ¹¹Now when she had brought *them* to him to eat, he took hold of her and said to her, "Come, lie with me, my sister."

¹²But she answered him, "No, my brother, do not force me, for no such thing should be done in Israel. Do not do this disgraceful thing! ¹³And I, where could I take my shame? And as for you, you would be like one of the fools in Israel. Now therefore, please speak to the king; for he will not withhold me from you." ¹⁴However, he would not heed her voice; and being stronger than she, he forced her and lay with her.

¹⁵Then Amnon hated her exceedingly, so that the hatred with which he hated her *was* greater than the love with which he had loved her. And Amnon said to her, "Arise, be gone!"

¹⁶So she said to him, "No, indeed! This evil of sending me away *is* worse than the other that you did to me."

But he would not listen to her. ¹⁷Then he called his servant who attended him, and said, "Here! Put this *woman* out, away from me, and bolt the door behind her." ¹⁸Now she had on a robe of many colors, for the king's virgin daughters wore such apparel. And his servant put her out and bolted the door behind her.

¹⁹Then Tamar put ashes on her head, and tore her robe of many colors that *was* on her, and laid her hand on her head and went away crying bitterly. ²⁰And Absalom her brother said to her, "Has Amnon your brother been with you? But now hold your peace, my sister. He *is* your brother; do not take this thing to heart." So Tamar remained desolate in her brother Absalom's house.

²¹But when King David heard of all these things, he was very angry. ²²And Absalom spoke to his brother Amnon neither good nor bad. For Absalom hated Amnon, because he had forced his sister Tamar.

²³And it came to pass, after two full years, that Absalom had sheepshearers in Baal Hazor, which *is* near Ephraim; so Absalom invited all the king's sons. ²⁴Then Absalom came to the king and said, "Kindly note, your servant has sheepshearers; please, let the king and his servants go with your servant."

²⁵But the king said to Absalom, "No, my son, let us not all go now, lest we be a burden to you." Then he urged him, but he would not go; and he blessed him.

²⁶Then Absalom said, "If not, please let my brother Amnon go with us."

And the king said to him, "Why should he go with you?" ²⁷But Absalom urged him; so he let Amnon and all the king's sons go with him.

²⁸Now Absalom had commanded his servants, saying, "Watch now, when Amnon's heart is merry with wine, and when I say to you, 'Strike Amnon!' then kill him. Do not be afraid. Have I not commanded you? Be courageous and valiant." ²⁹So the servants of Absalom did to Amnon as Absalom had commanded. Then all the king's sons arose, and each one got on his mule and fled.

³⁰And it came to pass, while they were on the way, that news came to David, saying, "Absalom has killed all the king's sons, and not one of them is left!" ³¹So the king arose and tore his garments and lay on the ground, and all his servants stood by with their clothes torn. ³²Then Jonadab the son of Shimeah, David's brother, answered and said, "Let not my lord suppose they have killed all the young men, the king's sons, for only Amnon is dead. For by the command of Absalom this has been determined from the day that he forced his sister Tamar. ³³Now therefore, let not my lord the king take the thing to his heart, to think that all the king's sons are dead. For only Amnon is dead."

◄══════LOVE VS. LUST

13:14-15 *Love and lust are very different. After Amnon raped his half-sister, his "love" turned to hate. Although he had claimed to be in love, he was actually overcome by lust. Love is patient; lust requires immediate sexual satisfaction. Love is kind; lust is harsh. Love does not demand its own way; lust does. You can read about the characteristics of real love in 1 Corinthians 13.*

³⁴Then Absalom fled. And the young man who was keeping watch lifted his eyes and looked, and there, many people were coming from the road on the hillside behind him. ³⁵And Jonadab said to the king, "Look, the king's sons are coming; as your servant said, so it is." ³⁶So it was, as soon as he had finished speaking, that the king's sons indeed came, and they lifted up their voice and wept. Also the king and all his servants wept very bitterly.

³⁷But Absalom fled and went to Talmai the son of Ammihud, king of Geshur. And *David* mourned for his son every day. ³⁸So Absalom fled and went to Geshur, and was there three years. ³⁹And King David longed to go to Absalom. For he had been comforted concerning Amnon, because he was dead.

CHAPTER **14** A WIDOW ASKS FOR HELP. So Joab the son of Zeruiah perceived that the king's heart *was* concerned about Absalom. ²And Joab sent to Tekoa and brought from there a wise woman, and said to her, "Please pretend to be a mourner, and put on mourning apparel; do not anoint yourself with oil, but act like a woman who has been mourning a long time for the dead. ³Go to the king and speak to him in this manner." So Joab put the words in her mouth.

⁴And when the woman of Tekoa spoke to the king, she fell on her face to the ground and prostrated herself, and said, "Help, O king!"

⁵Then the king said to her, "What troubles you?"

And she answered, "Indeed I *am* a widow, my husband is dead. ⁶Now your maidservant had two sons; and the two fought with each other in the field, and *there was* no one to part them, but the one struck the other and killed him. ⁷And now the whole family has risen up against your maidservant, and they said, 'Deliver him who struck his brother, that we may execute him for the life of his brother whom he killed; and we will destroy the heir also.' So they would extinguish my ember that is left, and leave to my husband *neither* name nor remnant on the earth."

⁸Then the king said to the woman, "Go to your house, and I will give orders concerning you."

⁹And the woman of Tekoa said to the king, "My lord, O king, *let* the iniquity *be* on me and on my father's house, and the king and his throne *be* guiltless."

¹⁰So the king said, "Whoever says *anything* to you, bring him to me, and he shall not touch you anymore."

¹¹Then she said, "Please let the king remember the LORD your God, and do not permit the avenger of blood to destroy anymore, lest they destroy my son."

And he said, "*As* the LORD lives, not one hair of your son shall fall to the ground."

¹²Therefore the woman said, "Please, let your maidervant speak *another* word to my lord the king."

And he said, "Say on."

¹³So the woman said: "Why then have you schemed such a thing against the people of God? For the king speaks this thing as one who is guilty, *in that* the king does not bring his banished one home again. ¹⁴For we will surely die and *become* like water spilled on the ground, which cannot be gathered up again. Yet God does not take away a life; but He devises means, so that His banished ones are not expelled from Him. ¹⁵Now therefore, I have come to speak of this thing to my lord the king because the people have made me afraid. And your maidservant said, 'I will now speak to the king; it may be that the king will perform the request of his maidservant. ¹⁶For the king will hear and deliver his maidservant from the hand of the man *who would* destroy me and my son together from the inheritance of God.' ¹⁷Your maidservant said, 'The word of my lord the king will now be comforting; for as the angel of God, so *is* my lord the king in discerning good and evil. And may the LORD your God be with you.'"

¹⁸Then the king answered and said to the woman, "Please do not hide from me anything that I ask you."

And the woman said, "Please, let my lord the king speak."

¹⁹So the king said, "*Is* the hand of Joab with you in all this?" And the woman answered and said, "*As* you live, my lord the king, no one can turn to the right hand or to the left from anything that my lord the king has spoken. For your servant Joab commanded me, and he put all these words in the mouth of your maidservant. ²⁰To bring about this change of affairs your servant Joab has done this thing; but my lord *is* wise, according to the wisdom of the angel of God, to know everything that *is* in the earth."

²¹And the king said to Joab, "All right, I have granted this thing. Go therefore, bring back the young man Absalom."

²²Then Joab fell to the ground on his face and bowed himself, and thanked the king. And Joab said, "Today your servant knows that I have found favor in your sight,

my lord, O king, in that the king has fulfilled the request of his servant." ²³So Joab arose and went to Geshur, and brought Absalom to Jerusalem. ²⁴And the king said, "Let him return to his own house, but do not let him see my face." So Absalom returned to his own house, but did not see the king's face.

²⁵Now in all Israel there was no one who was praised as much as Absalom for his good looks. From the sole of his foot to the crown of his head there was no blemish in him. ²⁶And when he cut the hair of his head—at the end of every year he cut *it* because it was heavy on him—when he cut it, he weighed the hair of his head at two hundred shekels according to the king's standard. ²⁷To Absalom were born three sons, and one daughter whose name *was* Tamar. She was a woman of beautiful appearance.

²⁸And Absalom dwelt two full years in Jerusalem, but did not see the king's face. ²⁹Therefore Absalom sent for Joab, to send him to the king, but he would not come to him. And when he sent again the second time, he would not come. ³⁰So he said to his servants, "See, Joab's field is near mine, and he has barley there; go and set it on fire." And Absalom's servants set the field on fire.

³¹Then Joab arose and came to Absalom's house, and said to him, "Why have your servants set my field on fire?"

³²And Absalom answered Joab, "Look, I sent to you, saying, 'Come here, so that I may send you to the king, to say, "Why have I come from Geshur? *It would be* better for me *to be* there still.' ' Now therefore, let me see the king's face; but if there is iniquity in me, let him execute me."

³³So Joab went to the king and told him. And when he had called for Absalom, he came to the king and bowed himself on his face to the ground before the king. Then the king kissed Absalom.

CHAPTER 15 ABSALOM REBELS. After this it happened that Absalom provided himself with chariots and horses, and fifty men to run before him. ²Now Absalom would rise early and stand beside the way to the gate. So it was, whenever anyone who had a lawsuit came to the king for a decision, that Absalom would call to him and say, "What city *are* you from?" And he would say, "Your servant *is* from such and such a tribe of Israel." ³Then Absalom would say to him, "Look, your case *is* good and right; but *there is* no deputy of the king to hear you." ⁴Moreover Absalom would say, "Oh, that I were made judge in the land, and everyone who has any suit or cause would come to me; then I would give him justice." ⁵And so it was, whenever anyone came near to bow down to him, that he would put out his hand and take him and

...iss him. [6]In this manner Absalom acted toward all Israel who came to the king for judgment. So Absalom stole the hearts of the men of Israel.

[7]Now it came to pass after forty years that Absalom said to the king, "Please, let me go to Hebron and pay the ...ow which I made to the LORD. [8]For your servant took a ...ow while I dwelt at Geshur in Syria, saying, 'If the LORD ...ndeed brings me back to Jerusalem, then I will serve the ...ORD.'"

[9]And the king said to him, "Go in peace." So he arose ...nd went to Hebron.

[10]Then Absalom sent spies throughout all the tribes of ...srael, saying, "As soon as you hear the sound of the ...rumpet, then you shall say, 'Absalom reigns in Hebron!'" And with Absalom went two hundred men invited from ...erusalem, and they went along innocently and did not ...now anything. [12]Then Absalom sent for Ahithophel the ...ilonite, David's counselor, from his city—from Giloh—...hile he offered sacrifices. And the conspiracy ...rew strong, for the people with ...bsalom continually ...ncreased in number.

[13]Now a messenger ...ame to David, say-...g, "The hearts of the ...en of Israel are with ...bsalom."

[14]So David said to all ...is servants who *were* ...ith him at Jerusalem, ...rise, and let us flee, or we ...hall not escape from Absa-...m. Make haste to depart, ...st he overtake us suddenly ...nd bring disaster upon us, ...nd strike the city with the edge ...f the sword."

[15]And the king's servants said ...o the king, "We *are* your servants, ...eady to do whatever my lord the ...ing commands." [16]Then the king ...ent out with all his household after ...im. But the king left ten women, ...oncubines, to keep the house. [17]And ...he king went out with all the people ...fter him, and stopped at the outskirts. ...Then all his servants passed before him; ...nd all the Cherethites, all the Pelethites, ...nd all the Gittites, six hundred men who ...ad followed him from Gath, passed before ...he king.

[19]Then the king said to Ittai the Gittite, ...Why are you also going with us? Return and ...emain with the king. For you *are* a foreigner ...nd also an exile from your own place. [20]In fact, ...ou came *only* yesterday. Should I make you ...ander up and down with us today, since I go I ...now not where? Return, and take your brethren ...ack. Mercy and truth *be* with you."

[21]But Ittai answered the king and said, "*As the* ...ORD lives, and *as* my lord the king lives, surely in

whatever place my lord the king shall be, whether in death or life, even there also your servant will be."

[22]So David said to Ittai, "Go, and cross over." Then Ittai the Gittite and all his men and all the little ones who *were* with him crossed over. [23]And all the country wept with a loud voice, and all the people crossed over. The king himself also crossed over the Brook Kidron, and all the people crossed over toward the way of the wilderness.

[24]There was Zadok also, and all the Levites with him, bearing the ark of the covenant of God. And they set down the ark of God, and Abiathar went up until all the people had finished crossing over from the city. [25]Then the king said to Zadok, "Carry the ark of God back into the city. If I find favor in the eyes of the LORD, He will bring me back and show me *both* it and His dwelling place. [26]But if He says thus: 'I have no delight in you,' here I am, let Him do to me as seems

ABSALOM

Sometimes parents make big mistakes that get passed on to their children. It's like a sad instant-replay. David saw his son Absalom make some of the same mistakes he had made. Even though God forgave David, his sins still hurt the rest of his family. Our sins sometimes also leave a lasting mark on our life, even after we've asked God to forgive us. Our sins hurt others, too.

Absalom was the kind of person who looks and talks great, but turns out to be bad on the inside. It seemed he would make the perfect king. The people loved him. But it takes a lot more than good looks to be a good leader. One of the biggest ways we disappoint others is by seeming to be one kind of person on the outside while on the inside, as people later discover, we are actually very different.

David's sins took him away from God; repentance brought him back. But Absalom sinned and kept on sinning. As you read his story you will see that he got a lot of advice from people, but he chose the wrong advice too often.

Maybe you are a lot like Absalom. You know your life is going the wrong way fast. Absalom's most basic problem was that he never admitted, "I was wrong. I need forgiveness." Forgiveness is exactly what God offers to us, but we can't experience it until we confess our sins to God. Absalom not only walked away from his father David's love, he also rejected God's love. Your life doesn't have to hold the same tragedy. God's love is waiting.

LESSONS: The sins of parents are often repeated and amplified in their children
A smart man gets a lot of advice; a wise man evaluates the advice he gets
Actions against God's plans will fail sooner or later

KEY VERSE: "Then Absalom sent spies throughout all the tribes of Israel, saying, 'As soon as you hear the sound of the trumpet, then you shall say, "Absalom reigns in Hebron!"'" (2 Samuel 15:10).

Absalom's story is told in 2 Samuel 3:3; 13–19.

DOWNS:
- Avenged the rape of his sister Tamar by killing his half brother Amnon
- Plotted against his father to take away the throne
- Consistently listened to the wrong advice

STATS:
- Where: Hebron
- Occupation: Prince
- Relatives: Father: David. Mother: Maacah. Brothers: Amnon, Chileab, Solomon, and others. Sister: Tamar
- Contemporaries: Nathan, Jonadab, Joab, Ahithophel, Hushai

good to Him." [27]The king also said to Zadok the priest, "Are you not a seer? Return to the city in peace, and your two sons with you, Ahimaaz your son, and Jonathan the son of Abiathar. [28]See, I will wait in the plains of the wilderness until word comes from you to inform me." [29]Therefore Zadok and Abiathar carried the ark of God back to Jerusalem. And they remained there.

[30]So David went up by the Ascent of the *Mount of* Olives, and wept as he went up; and he had his head covered and went barefoot. And all the people who *were* with him covered their heads and went up, weeping as they went up. [31]Then *someone* told David, saying, "Ahithophel *is* among the conspirators with Absalom." And David said, "O LORD, I pray, turn the counsel of Ahithophel into foolishness!"

[32]Now it happened when David had come to the top *of the mountain,* where he worshiped God—there was Hushai the Archite coming to meet him with his robe torn and dust on his head. [33]David said to him, "If you go on with me, then you will become a burden to me. [34]But if you return to the city, and say to Absalom, 'I will be your servant, O king; *as* I *was* your father's servant previously, so I *will* now also *be* your servant,' then you may defeat the counsel of Ahithophel for me. [35]And *do* you not *have* Zadok and Abiathar the priests with you there? Therefore it will be *that* whatever you hear from the king's house, you shall tell to Zadok and Abiathar the priests. [36]Indeed *they have* there with them their two sons, Ahimaaz, Zadok's *son,* and Jonathan, Abiathar's *son;* and by them you shall send me everything you hear."

[37]So Hushai, David's friend, went into the city. And Absalom came into Jerusalem.

CHAPTER 16 ZIBA JOINS DAVID.
When David was a little past the top *of the mountain,* there was Ziba the servant of Mephibosheth, who met him with a couple of saddled donkeys, and on them two hundred *loaves* of bread, one hundred clusters of raisins, one hundred summer fruits, and a skin of wine. [2]And the king said to Ziba, "What do you mean to do with these?"

So Ziba said, "The donkeys *are* for the king's household to ride on, the bread and summer fruit for the young men to eat, and the wine for those who are faint in the wilderness to drink."

[3]Then the king said, "And where *is* your master's son?"

And Ziba said to the king, "Indeed he is staying in Jerusalem, for he said, 'Today the house of Israel will restore the kingdom of my father to me.'"

[4]So the king said to Ziba, "Here, all that *belongs* to Mephibosheth *is* yours."

And Ziba said, "I humbly bow before you, *that* I may find favor in your sight, my lord, O king!"

[5]Now when King David came to Bahurim, there was a man from the family of the house of Saul, whose name *was* Shimei the son of Gera, coming from there. He came out, cursing continuously as he came. [6]And he threw stones at David and at all the servants of King David. And all the people and all the mighty men *were* on his right hand and on his left. [7]Also Shimei said thus when he cursed: "Come out! Come out! You bloodthirsty man, you rogue! [8]The LORD has brought upon you all the blood of the house of Saul, in whose place you have reigned; and the LORD has delivered the kingdom into the hand of Absalom your son. So now you *are caught* in your own evil, because you are a bloodthirsty man!"

[9]Then Abishai the son of Zeruiah said to the king, "Why should this dead dog curse my lord the king? Please, let me go over and take off his head!"

[10]But the king said, "What have I to do with you, you

CHECK IT OUT

16:4 David believed Ziba's charge against Mephibosheth without checking into it. Don't be hasty to accept someone's condemnation of another person, especially when the accuser may profit from the downfall. David should have been skeptical of Ziba's comments and checked them out for himself.

sons of Zeruiah? So let him curse, because the LORD has said to him, 'Curse David.' Who then shall say, 'Why have you done so?'"

[11]And David said to Abishai and all his servants, "See how my son who came from my own body seeks my life. How much more now *may this* Benjamite? Let him alone, and let him curse; for so the LORD has ordered him. [12]It may be that the LORD will look on my affliction, and that the LORD will repay me with good for his cursing this day." [13]And as David and his men went along the road, Shimei went along the hillside opposite him and cursed as he went, threw stones at him and kicked up dust. [14]Now the king and all the people who *were* with him became weary; so they refreshed themselves there.

[15]Meanwhile Absalom and all the people, the men of Israel, came to Jerusalem; and Ahithophel *was* with him. [16]And so it was, when Hushai the Archite, David's friend, came to Absalom, that Hushai said to Absalom, "Long live the king! *Long* live the king!"

[17]So Absalom said to Hushai, "*Is* this your loyalty to your friend? Why did you not go with your friend?"

[18]And Hushai said to Absalom, "No, but whom the LORD and this people and all the men of Israel choose, his I will be, and with him I will remain. [19]Furthermore, whom should I serve? *Should* I not *serve* in the presence of his son? As I have served in your father's presence, so will I be in your presence."

[20]Then Absalom said to Ahithophel, "Give advice as to what we should do."

[21]And Ahithophel said to Absalom, "Go in to your father's concubines, whom he has left to keep the house; and all Israel will hear that you are abhorred by your father. Then the hands of all who are with you will be strong." [22]So they pitched a tent for Absalom on the top of the house, and Absalom went in to his father's concubines in the sight of all Israel.

[23]Now the advice of Ahithophel, which he gave in those days, *was* as if one had inquired at the oracle of God. So *was* all the advice of Ahithophel both with David and with Absalom.

CHAPTER 17 ABSALOM FOLLOWS BAD ADVICE
Moreover Ahithophel said to Absalom, "Now let me choose twelve thousand men, and I will arise and pursue

David tonight. [2]I will come upon him while he *is* weary and weak, and make him afraid. And all the people who *are* with him will flee, and I will strike only the king. [3]Then I will bring back all the people to you. When all return except the man whom you seek, all the people will be at peace." [4]And the saying pleased Absalom and all the elders of Israel.

[5]Then Absalom said, "Now call Hushai the Archite also, and let us hear what he says too." [6]And when Hushai came to Absalom, Absalom spoke to him, saying, "Ahithophel has spoken in this manner. Shall we do as he says? If not, speak up."

[7]So Hushai said to Absalom: "The advice that Ahithophel has given *is* not good at this time. [8]For," said Hushai, "you know your father and his men, that they *are* mighty men, and they *are* enraged in their minds, like a bear robbed of her cubs in the field; and your father *is* a man of war, and will not camp with the people. [9]Surely by now he is hidden in some pit, or in some *other* place. And it will be, when some of them are overthrown at the first, that whoever hears *it* will say, 'There is a slaughter among the people who follow Absalom.' [10]And even he *who is* valiant, whose heart *is* like the heart of a lion, will melt completely. For all Israel knows that your father *is* a mighty man, and *those* who *are* with him *are* valiant men. [11]Therefore I advise that all Israel be fully gathered to you, from Dan to Beersheba, like the sand that *is* by the sea for multitude, and that you go to battle in person. [12]So we will come upon him in some place where he may be found, and we will fall on him as the dew falls on the ground. And of him and all the men who *are* with him there shall not be left so much as one. [13]Moreover, if he has withdrawn into a city, then all Israel shall bring ropes to that city; and we will pull it into the river, until there is not one small stone found there."

[14]So Absalom and all the men of Israel said, "The advice of Hushai the Archite *is* better than the advice of Ahithophel." For the LORD had purposed to defeat the good advice of Ahithophel, to the intent that the LORD might bring disaster on Absalom.

[15]Then Hushai said to Zadok and Abiathar the priests, "Thus and so Ahithophel advised Absalom and the elders of Israel, and thus and so I have advised. [16]Now therefore, send quickly and tell David, saying, 'Do not spend this night in the plains of the wilderness, but speedily cross over, lest the king and all the people who *are* with him be swallowed up.'" [17]Now Jonathan and Ahimaaz stayed at En Rogel, for they dared not be seen coming into the city; so a female servant would come and tell them, and they would go and tell King David. [18]Nevertheless a lad saw them, and told Absalom. But both of them went away quickly and came to a man's house in Bahurim, who had a well in his court; and they went down into it. [19]Then the woman took and spread a covering over the well's mouth, and spread ground grain on it; and the thing was not known. [20]And when Absalom's servants came to the woman at the house, they said, "Where *are* Ahimaaz and Jonathan?"

So the woman said to them, "They have gone over the water brook."

And when they had searched and could not find *them*, they returned to Jerusalem. [21]Now it came to pass, after they had departed, that they came up out of the well and went and told King David, and said to David, "Arise and cross over the water quickly. For thus has Ahithophel advised against you." [22]So David and all the people who *were* with him arose and crossed over the Jordan. By morning light not one of them was left who had not gone over the Jordan.

[23]Now when Ahithophel saw that his advice was not

VANITY

17:11 Hushai appealed to Absalom through flattery, and Absalom was trapped by his vanity. Hushai predicted great glory for Absalom if he personally led the entire army against David. "Pride [goes] before destruction" (Proverbs 16:18) is an appropriate comment on Absalom's ambitions.

followed, he saddled a donkey, and arose and went home to his house, to his city. Then he put his household in order, and hanged himself, and died; and he was buried in his father's tomb.

[24]Then David went to Mahanaim. And Absalom crossed over the Jordan, he and all the men of Israel with him. [25]And Absalom made Amasa captain of the army

My older brother is always making fun of my new faith. How do I get him to stop?

I WONDER . . .

People ridicule what they don't understand or what they wish they had themselves. It's really tough, though, when it comes from someone in your own family! (See 2 Samuel 15.)

Your best defense is a quiet offense: "Love as brothers . . . not returning evil for evil or reviling for reviling, but on the contrary blessing" (1 Peter 3:8-9).

When anyone makes fun of your faith, hold your tongue, pray for the person, be kind to him or her, and then wait for God's blessing. This verse ends with a promise directly from God. Though it doesn't say when or how God will bless you, it promises that he will bless you.

Here are some steps to take when facing opposition for your faith (see 1 Peter 3:13-15):

First, check your attitude. If you understand that God is allowing you to experience this for a reason, you'll be able to thank him for it. It means that he believes in you enough to allow you to be tested!

Second, quietly trust yourself to Christ. You trusted Christ to be Lord of your life; now allow him to be Lord over your circumstances. God is trying to develop your character.

Third, be real and be ready to explain your faith when the opportunities arise. Admit your faults, and don't act like you're superior or better than the other person. This may disarm him or her to the point where he or she will see that you're not a threat. Then you may be able to share about Christ.

Even doing all of this still may not relieve the tension. But, "*It is* better . . . to suffer for doing good than for doing evil" (1 Peter 3:17).

instead of Joab. This Amasa *was* the son of a man whose name *was* Jithra, an Israelite, who had gone in to Abigail the daughter of Nahash, sister of Zeruiah, Joab's mother. [26]So Israel and Absalom encamped in the land of Gilead.

[27]Now it happened, when David had come to Mahanaim, that Shobi the son of Nahash from Rabbah of the people of Ammon, Machir the son of Ammiel from Lo Debar, and Barzillai the Gileadite from Rogelim, [28]brought beds and basins, earthen vessels and wheat, barley and flour, parched *grain* and beans, lentils and parched *seeds,* [29]honey and curds, sheep and cheese of the herd, for David and the people who *were* with him to eat. For they said, "The people are hungry and weary and thirsty in the wilderness."

CHAPTER **18** ABSALOM IS DEFEATED. And David numbered the people who *were* with him, and set captains of thousands and captains of hundreds over them. [2]Then David sent out one third of the people under the hand of Joab, one third under the hand of Abishai the son of Zeruiah, Joab's brother, and one third under the hand of Ittai the Gittite. And the king said to the people, "I also will surely go out with you myself."

[3]But the people answered, "You shall not go out! For if we flee away, they will not care about us; nor if half of us die, will they care about us. But *you are* worth ten thousand of us now. For you are now more help to us in the city."

[4]Then the king said to them, "Whatever seems best to you I will do." So the king stood beside the gate, and all the people went out by hundreds and by thousands. [5]Now the king had commanded Joab, Abishai, and Ittai, saying, "*Deal* gently for my sake with the young man Absalom." And all the people heard when the king gave all the captains orders concerning Absalom.

[6]So the people went out into the field of battle against Israel. And the battle was in the woods of Ephraim. [7]The people of Israel were overthrown there before the servants of David, and a great slaughter of twenty thousand took place there that day. [8]For the battle there was scattered over the face of the whole countryside, and the woods devoured more people that day than the sword devoured.

[9]Then Absalom met the servants of David. Absalom rode on a mule. The mule went under the thick boughs of a great terebinth tree, and his head caught in the terebinth; so he was left hanging between heaven and earth. And the mule which *was* under him went on. [10]Now a certain man saw *it* and told Joab, and said, "I just saw Absalom hanging in a terebinth tree!"

[11]So Joab said to the man who told him, "You just saw *him!* And why did you not strike him there to the ground? I would have given you ten *shekels* of silver and a belt."

[12]But the man said to Joab, "Though I were to receive a thousand *shekels* of silver in my hand, I would not raise my hand against the king's son. For in our hearing the king commanded you and Abishai and Ittai, saying, 'Beware lest anyone *touch* the young man Absalom!' [13]Otherwise I would have dealt falsely against my own life. For there is nothing hidden from the king, and you yourself would have set yourself against *me.*"

[14]Then Joab said, "I cannot linger with you." And he took three spears in his hand and thrust them through Absalom's heart, while he was *still* alive in the midst of the terebinth tree. [15]And ten young men who bore Joab's armor surrounded Absalom, and struck and killed him.

[16]So Joab blew the trumpet, and the people returned from pursuing Israel. For Joab held back the people. [17]And they took Absalom and cast him into a large pit in the woods, and laid a very large heap of stones over him. Then all Israel fled, everyone to his tent.

[18]Now Absalom in his lifetime had taken and set up a pillar for himself, which *is* in the King's Valley. For he said, "I have no son to keep my name in remembrance." He called the pillar after his own name. And to this day it is called Absalom's Monument.

[19]Then Ahimaaz the son of Zadok said, "Let me run now and take the news to the king, how the LORD has avenged him of his enemies."

[20]And Joab said to him, "You shall not take the news

HIGHS AND LOWS OF DAVID'S LIFE

The Bible calls David a man after God's own heart (Acts 13:22), but that didn't mean his life was free of troubles. David's life was full of highs and lows. Some of David's troubles were a result of his sins; some were a result of the sins of others. We can't always control our ups and downs, but we can trust God every day. We can be certain that he will help us through our trials, just as he helped David. In the end, he will reward us for our consistent faith.

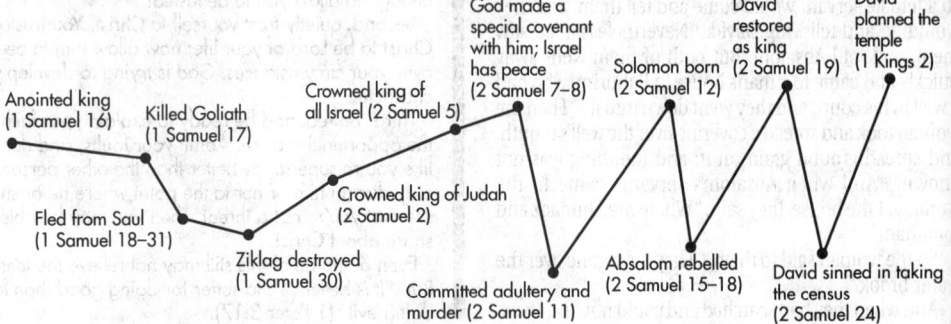

God made a special covenant with him; Israel has peace (2 Samuel 7–8)

Solomon born (2 Samuel 12)

David restored as king (2 Samuel 19)

David planned the temple (1 Kings 2)

Anointed king (1 Samuel 16)

Killed Goliath (1 Samuel 17)

Crowned king of all Israel (2 Samuel 5)

Crowned king of Judah (2 Samuel 2)

Fled from Saul (1 Samuel 18–31)

Ziklag destroyed (1 Samuel 30)

Committed adultery and murder (2 Samuel 11)

Absalom rebelled (2 Samuel 15–18)

David sinned in taking the census (2 Samuel 24)

his day, for you shall take the news another day. But today you shall take no news, because the king's son is dead." ²¹Then Joab said to the Cushite, "Go, tell the king what you have seen." So the Cushite bowed himself to Joab and ran.

²²And Ahimaaz the son of Zadok said again to Joab, But whatever happens, please let me also run after the Cushite."

So Joab said, "Why will you run, my son, since you have no news ready?"

²³"But whatever happens," *he said,* "let me run."

So he said to him, "Run." Then Ahimaaz ran by way of the plain, and outran the Cushite.

²⁴Now David was sitting between the two gates. And the watchman went up to the roof over the gate, to the wall, lifted his eyes and looked, and there was a man, running alone. ²⁵Then the watchman cried out and told the king. And the king said, "If he *is* alone, *there is* news in his mouth." And he came rapidly and drew near.

²⁶Then the watchman saw *another* man running, and the watchman called to the gatekeeper and said, "There is *another* man, running alone!"

And the king said, "He also brings news."

²⁷So the watchman said, "I think the running of the first is like the running of Ahimaaz the son of Zadok."

And the king said, "He *is* a good man, and comes with good news."

²⁸So Ahimaaz called out and said to the king, "All is well!" Then he bowed down with his face to the earth before the king, and said, "Blessed *be* the LORD your God, who has delivered up the men who raised their hand against my lord the king!"

²⁹The king said, "Is the young man Absalom safe?"

Ahimaaz answered, "When Joab sent the king's servant and *me* your servant, I saw a great tumult, but I did not know what *it was about.*"

³⁰And the king said, "Turn aside *and* stand here." So he turned aside and stood still.

³¹Just then the Cushite came, and the Cushite said, "There is good news, my lord the king! For the LORD has avenged you this day of all those who rose against you."

³²And the king said to the Cushite, "Is the young man Absalom safe?"

So the Cushite answered, "May the enemies of my lord the king, and all who rise against you to do harm, be like *that* young man!"

³³Then the king was deeply moved, and went up to the chamber over the gate, and wept. And as he went, he said thus: "O my son Absalom—my son, my son Absalom—if only I had died in your place! O Absalom my son, my son!"

CHAPTER **19** DAVID RETURNS TO JERUSALEM.

And Joab was told, "Behold, the king is weeping and mourning for Absalom." ²So the victory that day was turned into mourning for all the people. For the people heard it said that day, "The king is grieved for his son." ³And the people stole back into the city that day, as people who are ashamed steal away when they flee in battle. ⁴But the king covered his face, and the king cried

out with a loud voice, "O my son Absalom! O Absalom, my son, my son!"

⁵Then Joab came into the house to the king, and said, "Today you have disgraced all your servants who today have saved your life, the lives of your sons and daughters, the lives of your wives and the lives of your concubines, ⁶in that you love your enemies and hate your friends. For you have declared today that you regard neither princes nor servants; for today I perceive that if Absalom had lived and all of us had died today, then it would have pleased you well. ⁷Now therefore, arise, go out and speak comfort to your servants. For I swear by the LORD, if you do not go out, not one will stay with you this night. And that will be worse for you than all the evil that has befallen you from your youth until now." ⁸Then the king arose and sat in the gate. And they told all the people, saying, "There is the king, sitting in the gate." So all the people came before the king.

For everyone of Israel had fled to his tent.

� UNDESERVED

18:33 Why was David so upset over the death of his rebel son? (1) David realized that he, in part, was responsible for Absalom's death. Nathan, the prophet, had said that because David had killed Uriah, his own sons would rebel against him; (2) David was angry at Joab and his officers for killing Absalom against his wishes; (3) David truly loved his son. Absalom did nothing to deserve David's love. Just as God bestows undeserved grace upon us, David was gracious to Absalom.

⁹Now all the people were in a dispute throughout all the tribes of Israel, saying, "The king saved us from the hand of our enemies, he delivered us from the hand of the Philistines, and now he has fled from the land because of Absalom. ¹⁰But Absalom, whom we anointed over us, has died in battle. Now therefore, why do you say nothing about bringing back the king?"

¹¹So King David sent to Zadok and Abiathar the priests, saying, "Speak to the elders of Judah, saying, 'Why are you the last to bring the king back to his house, since the words of all Israel have come to the king, to his *very* house? ¹²You *are* my brethren, you *are* my bone and my flesh. Why then are you the last to bring back the king?' ¹³And say to Amasa, '*Are* you not my bone and my flesh? God do so to me, and more also, if you are not commander of the army before me continually in place of Joab.'" ¹⁴So he swayed the hearts of all the men of Judah, just as *the heart of* one man, so that they sent *this word* to the king: "Return, you and all your servants!"

¹⁵Then the king returned and came to the Jordan. And Judah came to Gilgal, to go to meet the king, to escort the king across the Jordan. ¹⁶And Shimei the son of Gera, a Benjamite, who *was* from Bahurim, hurried and came down with the men of Judah to meet King David. ¹⁷*There*

� THE CROWD

19:8-10 Just a few days before, Absalom had turned the hearts of Israel away from David. Here the people wanted David back as their king. Because crowds are known to be fickle, there must be a higher moral code to follow than the pleasure of the majority. Following the moral principles given in God's Word will help you avoid being swayed by the crowd.

were a thousand men of Benjamin with him, and Ziba the servant of the house of Saul, and his fifteen sons and his twenty servants with him; and they went over the Jordan before the king. [18]Then a ferryboat went across to carry over the king's household, and to do what he thought good.

Now Shimei the son of Gera fell down before the king when he had crossed the Jordan. [19]Then he said to the king, "Do not let my lord impute iniquity to me, or remember what wrong your servant did on the day that my lord the king left Jerusalem, that the king should take *it* to heart. [20]For I, your servant, know that I have sinned. Therefore here I am, the first to come today of all the house of Joseph to go down to meet my lord the king."

[21]But Abishai the son of Zeruiah answered and said, "Shall not Shimei be put to death for this, because he cursed the LORD's anointed?"

[22]And David said, "What have I to do with you, you sons of Zeruiah, that you should be adversaries to me today? Shall any man be put to death today in Israel? For do I not know that today I *am* king over Israel?" [23]Therefore the king said to Shimei, "You shall not die." And the king swore to him.

[24]Now Mephibosheth the son of Saul came down to

JUSTICE

20:7-10 Once again Joab's murderous treachery went unpunished, just as it did when he killed Abner (3:26-27). Eventually, however, justice caught up with him (1 Kings 2:28-35). It may seem that sin and treachery often go unpunished, but God's justice is not limited to this life's rewards. Even if Joab had died of old age, he would have to face the day of judgment.

meet the king. And he had not cared for his feet, nor trimmed his mustache, nor washed his clothes, from the day the king departed until the day he returned in peace. [25]So it was, when he had come to Jerusalem to meet the king, that the king said to him, "Why did you not go with me, Mephibosheth?"

[26]And he answered, "My lord, O king, my servant deceived me. For your servant said, 'I will saddle a donkey for myself, that I may ride on it and go to the king,' because your servant *is* lame. [27]And he has slandered your servant to my lord the king, but my lord the king *is* like the angel of God. Therefore do *what is* good in your eyes. [28]For all my father's house were but dead men before my lord the king. Yet you set your servant among those who eat at your own table. Therefore what right have I still to cry out anymore to the king?"

[29]So the king said to him, "Why do you speak anymore of your matters? I have said, 'You and Ziba divide the land.'"

[30]Then Mephibosheth said to the king, "Rather, let him take it all, inasmuch as my lord the king has come back in peace to his own house."

[31]And Barzillai the Gileadite came down from Rogelim and went across the Jordan with the king, to escort him across the Jordan. [32]Now Barzillai was a very aged man, eighty years old. And he had provided the king with supplies while he stayed at Mahanaim, for he *was* a very rich

man. [33]And the king said to Barzillai, "Come across with me, and I will provide for you while you are with me in Jerusalem."

[34]But Barzillai said to the king, "How long have I to live, that I should go up with the king to Jerusalem? [35]I *am* today eighty years old. Can I discern between the good and bad? Can your servant taste what I eat or what I drink? Can I hear any longer the voice of singing men and singing women? Why then should your servant be a further burden to my lord the king? [36]Your servant will go a little way across the Jordan with the king. And why should the king repay me *with* such a reward? [37]Please let your servant turn back again, that I may die in my own city, near the grave of my father and mother. But here is your servant Chimham; let him cross over with my lord the king, and do for him what seems good to you."

[38]And the king answered, "Chimham shall cross over with me, and I will do for him what seems good to you. Now whatever you request of me, I will do for you." [39]Then all the people went over the Jordan. And when the king had crossed over, the king kissed Barzillai and blessed him, and he returned to his own place.

[40]Now the king went on to Gilgal, and Chimham went on with him. And all the people of Judah escorted the king, and also half the people of Israel. [41]Just then all the men of Israel came to the king, and said to the king, "Why have our brethren, the men of Judah, stolen you away and brought the king, his household, and all David's men with him across the Jordan?"

[42]So all the men of Judah answered the men of Israel, "Because the king *is* a close relative of ours. Why then are you angry over this matter? Have we ever eaten at the king's *expense*? Or has he given us any gift?"

[43]And the men of Israel answered the men of Judah, and said, "We have ten shares in the king; therefore we also have more *right* to David than you. Why then do you despise us—were we not the first to advise bringing back our king?"

Yet the words of the men of Judah were fiercer than the words of the men of Israel.

CHAPTER 20 SHEBA REBELS AGAINST DAVID.

And there happened to be there a rebel, whose name *was* Sheba the son of Bichri, a Benjamite. And he blew a trumpet, and said:

"We have no share in David,
  Nor do we have inheritance in the son of Jesse;
  Every man to his tents, O Israel!"

[2]So every man of Israel deserted David, *and* followed Sheba the son of Bichri. But the men of Judah, from the Jordan as far as Jerusalem, remained loyal to their king.

[3]Now David came to his house at Jerusalem. And the king took the ten women, his concubines whom he had left to keep the house, and put them in seclusion and supported them, but did not go in to them. So they were shut up to the day of their death, living in widowhood.

[4]And the king said to Amasa, "Assemble the men of Judah for me within three days, and be present here yourself." [5]So Amasa went to assemble *the men of*

idah. But he delayed longer than the set time which David had appointed him. ⁶And David said to Abishai, Now Sheba the son of Bichri will do us more harm than bsalom. Take your lord's servants and pursue him, lest e find for himself fortified cities, and escape us." ⁷So ɔab's men, with the Cherethites, the Pelethites, and all ie mighty men, went out after him. And they went out f Jerusalem to pursue Sheba the son of Bichri. ⁸When iey *were* at the large stone which *is* in Gibeon, Amasa ame before them. Now Joab was dressed in battle ar-ior; on it was a belt *with* a sword fastened in its sheath t his hips; and as he was going forward, it fell out. ⁹Then ɔab said to Amasa, "*Are* you in health, my brother?" ind Joab took Amasa by the beard with his right hand ɔ kiss him. ¹⁰But Amasa did not notice the sword that *ias* in Joab's hand. And he struck him with it in the tomach, and his entrails poured out on the ground; ind he did not *strike* him again. Thus he died.

Then Joab and Abishai his brother pursued Sheba the on of Bichri. ¹¹Meanwhile one of Joab's men stood near masa, and said, "Whoever favors Joab and whoever *is* ɔr David—follow Joab!" ¹²But Amasa wallowed in *his* lood in the middle of the highway. And when the man aw that all the people stood still, he moved Amasa from ie highway to the field and threw a garment over him, ʰen he saw that everyone who came upon him halted. When he was removed from the highway, all the people ʲent on after Joab to pursue Sheba the son of Bichri.

¹⁴And he went through all the tribes of Israel to Abel ind Beth Maachah and all the Berites. So they were gath-red together and also went after *Sheba*. ¹⁵Then they ame and besieged him in Abel of Beth Maachah; and iey cast up a siege mound against the city, and it stood y the rampart. And all the people who *were* with Joab attered the wall to throw it down.

¹⁶Then a wise woman cried out from the city, "Hear, ear! Please say to Joab, 'Come nearby, that I may speak ʲith you.'" ¹⁷When he had come near to her, the woman aid, "*Are* you Joab?"

He answered, "I *am*."

Then she said to him, "Hear the words of your maid-ervant."

And he answered, "I am listening."

¹⁸So she spoke, saying, "They used to talk in former mes, saying, 'They shall surely seek *guidance* at Abel,' ind so they would end *disputes*. ¹⁹I *am among the* peace-ble *and* faithful in Israel. You seek to destroy a city and a iother in Israel. Why would you swallow up the inheri-ince of the LORD?"

²⁰And Joab answered and said, "Far be it, far be it from ie, that I should swallow up or destroy! ²¹That *is* not so. ut a man from the mountains of Ephraim, Sheba the on of Bichri by name, has raised his hand against the ing, against David. Deliver him only, and I will depart ʳom the city."

So the woman said to Joab, "Watch, his head will be irown to you over the wall." ²²Then the woman in her ʲisdom went to all the people. And they cut off the head f Sheba the son of Bichri, and threw *it* out to Joab. Then e blew a trumpet, and they withdrew from the city,

every man to his tent. So Joab returned to the king at Jerusalem.

²³And Joab *was* over all the army of Israel; Benaiah the son of Jehoiada *was* over the Cherethites and the Pele-thites; ²⁴Adoram *was* in charge of revenue; Jehosha-phat the son of Ahilud *was* recorder; ²⁵Sheva *was* scribe; Zadok and Abiathar *were* the priests; ²⁶and Ira the Jairite was a chief minister under David.

CHAPTER **21** SAUL'S SONS ARE EXECUTED. Now

there was a famine in the days of David for three years, year after year; and David inquired of the LORD. And the LORD answered, "*It is* because of Saul and *his* blood-thirsty house, because he killed the Gibeonites." ²So the king called the Gibeonites and spoke to them. Now the Gibeonites *were* not of the children of Israel, but of the remnant of the Amorites; the children of Israel had sworn protection to them, but Saul had sought to kill them in his zeal for the children of Israel and Judah.

³Therefore David said to the Gibeonites, "What shall I do for you? And with what shall I make atonement, that you may bless the inheritance of the LORD?"

⁴And the Gibeonites said to him, "We will have no silver or gold from Saul or from his house, nor shall you kill any man in Israel for us."

So he said, "Whatever you say, I will do for you."

⁵Then they answered the king, "As for the man who consumed us and plotted against us, *that* we should be destroyed from remaining in any of the territories of Israel, ⁶let seven men of his descendants be delivered to us, and we will hang them before the LORD in Gibeah of Saul, *whom* the LORD chose."

◀▬▬▬▬SPEAK UP

20:16ff Joab's men were attacking the city, and it looked as if it would be destroyed. Though women in that society were usually quiet in public, this woman spoke out. She stopped Joab's attack, not with weapons, but with wise words and a plan of action. Sometimes the courage to speak a few sensible words can prevent great disaster.

And the king said, "I will give *them*."

⁷But the king spared Mephibosheth the son of Jona-than, the son of Saul, because of the LORD's oath that *was* between them, between David and Jonathan the son of Saul. ⁸So the king took Armoni and Mephibosheth, the two sons of Rizpah the daughter of Aiah, whom she bore to Saul, and the five sons of Michal the daughter of Saul, whom she brought up for Adriel the son of Barzillai the Meholathite; ⁹and he delivered them into the hands of the Gibeonites, and they hanged them on the hill before the LORD. So they fell, *all* seven together, and were put to

◀▬▬▬▬RAIN

21:1 Farmers relied heavily on spring and fall rains for their crops. If the rains stopped or came at the wrong time, or if the plants became insect-infested, drastic food shortages could occur in the coming year. Agriculture at that time was completely dependent upon natural conditions. There were no irrigation methods, fertilizers, or pesticides. Even moderate variations in rainfall or insect activity could destroy an entire harvest.

22:22-24 David was not saying that he had never sinned. Psalm 51 shows his tremendous anguish over his sin against Uriah and Bathsheba. But David understood God's faithfulness and was writing this hymn from God's perspective. He knew that God had made him clean again—"whiter than snow," (Psalm 51:7) with a "clean heart" (Psalm 51:10). Through the death and resurrection of Jesus Christ, we also are made clean and perfect. Our sin is replaced with his purity and forgiveness; God no longer sees our sin.

death in the days of harvest, in the first *days*, in the beginning of barley harvest.

¹⁰Now Rizpah the daughter of Aiah took sackcloth and spread it for herself on the rock, from the beginning of harvest until the late rains poured on them from heaven. And she did not allow the birds of the air to rest on them by day nor the beasts of the field by night.

¹¹And David was told what Rizpah the daughter of Aiah, the concubine of Saul, had done. ¹²Then David went and took the bones of Saul, and the bones of Jonathan his son, from the men of Jabesh Gilead who had stolen them from the street of Beth Shan, where the Philistines had hung them up, after the Philistines had struck down Saul in Gilboa. ¹³So he brought up the bones of Saul and the bones of Jonathan his son from there; and they gathered the bones of those who had been hanged. ¹⁴They buried the bones of Saul and Jonathan his son in the country of Benjamin in Zelah, in the tomb of Kish his father. So they performed all that the king commanded. And after that God heeded the prayer for the land.

¹⁵When the Philistines were at war again with Israel, David and his servants with him went down and fought against the Philistines; and David grew faint. ¹⁶Then Ishbi-Benob, who *was* one of the sons of the giant, the weight of whose bronze spear *was* three hundred *shekels*, who was bearing a new *sword*, thought he could kill David. ¹⁷But Abishai the son of Zeruiah came to his aid, and struck the Philistine and killed him. Then the men of David swore to him, saying, "You shall go out no more with us to battle, lest you quench the lamp of Israel."

¹⁸Now it happened afterward that there was again a battle with the Philistines at Gob. Then Sibbechai the Hushathite killed Saph, who *was* one of the sons of the giant. ¹⁹Again there was war at Gob with the Philistines, where Elhanan the son of Jaare-Oregim the Bethlehemite killed *the brother of* Goliath the Gittite, the shaft of whose spear *was* like a weaver's beam.

²⁰Yet again there was war at Gath, where there was a man of *great* stature, who had six fingers on each hand and six toes on each foot, twenty-four in number; and he also was born to the giant. ²¹So when he defied Israel, Jonathan the son of Shimea, David's brother, killed him.

²²These four were born to the giant in Gath, and fell by the hand of David and by the hand of his servants.

CHAPTER **22** **DAVID'S SONG OF PRAISE.** Then David spoke to the LORD the words of this song, on the day when the LORD had delivered him from the hand of all his enemies, and from the hand of Saul. ²And he said:

"The LORD *is* my rock and my fortress and my
 deliverer;

³ The God of my strength, in whom I will trust;
 My shield and the horn of my salvation,
 My stronghold and my refuge;
 My Savior, You save me from violence.
⁴ I will call upon the LORD, *who is worthy* to be praised;
 So shall I be saved from my enemies.

⁵ "When the waves of death surrounded me,
 The floods of ungodliness made me afraid.
⁶ The sorrows of Sheol surrounded me;
 The snares of death confronted me.
⁷ In my distress I called upon the LORD,
 And cried out to my God;
 He heard my voice from His temple,
 And my cry *entered* His ears.

22:51 The book of 2 Samuel describes David's reign. Since the Israelites first entered the Promised Land under Joshua, they had struggling to unite the nation and drive out the wicked inhabitant time, after more than 400 years, Israel was finally at peace. Da accomplished what no leader before him, judge or king, had do administration was run on the principle of dedication to God and well being of the people. Yet David also sinned. Despite his sins, the Bible calls David a man after God's own heart (1 Samuel 13: 13:22), because when he sinned he recognized it and confessed God. David committed his life to God and remained loyal to God throughout his lifetime. Reading the Psalms gives an even deepe into David's love for God.

⁸ "Then the earth shook and trembled;
 The foundations of heaven quaked and were shaken,
 Because He was angry.
⁹ Smoke went up from His nostrils,
 And devouring fire from His mouth;
 Coals were kindled by it.
¹⁰ He bowed the heavens also, and came down
 With darkness under His feet.
¹¹ He rode upon a cherub, and flew;
 And He was seen upon the wings of the wind.
¹² He made darkness canopies around Him,
 Dark waters *and* thick clouds of the skies.
¹³ From the brightness before Him
 Coals of fire were kindled.

¹⁴ "The LORD thundered from heaven,
 And the Most High uttered His voice.
¹⁵ He sent out arrows and scattered them;
 Lightning bolts, and He vanquished them.
¹⁶ Then the channels of the sea were seen,
 The foundations of the world were uncovered,
 At the rebuke of the LORD,
 At the blast of the breath of His nostrils.

¹⁷ "He sent from above, He took me,
 He drew me out of many waters.
¹⁸ He delivered me from my strong enemy,
 From those who hated me;
 For they were too strong for me.
¹⁹ They confronted me in the day of my calamity,
 But the LORD was my support.

⁴⁰ He also brought me out into a broad place;
He delivered me because He delighted in me.

²¹ "The LORD rewarded me according to my
righteousness;
According to the cleanness of my hands
He has recompensed me.
²² For I have kept the ways of the LORD,
And have not wickedly departed from my God.
²³ For all His judgments *were* before me;
And *as for* His statutes, I did not depart from them.
²⁴ I was also blameless before Him,
And I kept myself from my iniquity.
²⁵ Therefore the LORD has recompensed me according
to my righteousness,
According to my cleanness in His eyes.

²⁶ "With the merciful You will show
Yourself merciful;
With a blameless man You will
show Yourself blameless;
²⁷ With the pure You will show
Yourself pure;
And with the devious You will
show Yourself shrewd.
²⁸ You will save the humble people;
But Your eyes *are* on the haughty,
that You may bring *them* down.

²⁹ "For You *are* my lamp, O LORD;
The LORD shall enlighten my
darkness.
³⁰ For by You I can run against a
troop;
By my God I can leap over a wall.
³¹ *As for* God, His way *is* perfect;
The word of the LORD *is* proven;
He *is* a shield to all who trust in
Him.

³² "For who *is* God, except the LORD?
And who *is* a rock, except our
God?
³³ God *is* my strength *and* power,
And He makes my way perfect.
³⁴ He makes my feet like the *feet* of
deer,
And sets me on my high places.
³⁵ He teaches my hands to make war,
So that my arms can bend a bow of bronze.

³⁶ "You have also given me the shield of Your salvation;
Your gentleness has made me great.
³⁷ You enlarged my path under me;
So my feet did not slip.

³⁸ "I have pursued my enemies and destroyed them;
Neither did I turn back again till they were
destroyed.
³⁹ And I have destroyed them and wounded them,
So that they could not rise;
They have fallen under my feet.
⁴⁰ For You have armed me with strength for the battle;

You have subdued under me those who rose against
me.
⁴¹ You have also given me the necks of my enemies,
So that I destroyed those who hated me.
⁴² They looked, but *there was* none to save;
Even to the LORD, but He did not answer them.
⁴³ Then I beat them as fine as the dust of the earth;
I trod them like dirt in the streets,
And I spread them out.

⁴⁴ "You have also delivered me from the strivings of my
people;
You have kept me as the head of the nations.
A people I have not known shall serve me.
⁴⁵ The foreigners submit to me;
As soon as they hear, they obey me.

"Here's what I did..."

I was at a summer camp in Florida. Our group wanted to go swimming in the Gulf of Mexico, but we couldn't because there was a hurricane off the coast at the time and the riptides and undertow were too strong.

After dinner I walked down to the beach to look for a hat I had lost. Another guy in my group noticed four boys about 100 feet out in the water. They started swimming in, but one couldn't make it. He kept drifting farther out. The other boy I was with ran into the water to save him. I stood on the shore for 10 seconds and then without thinking jumped in also.

When I was halfway to the boy the guy from my group passed me; he couldn't make it so he turned back. When I finally reached the boy, he was semiconscious. I grabbed him and tried to walk back to shore, but the water was over my head. I told the boy that every time there was a wave we would kick and try to ride it. I began to pray; I didn't know whether to just try to save my own life or hang onto the guy and keep trying to swim. I remembered 2 Samuel 22:17 and 2 Samuel 22:40a. I kept on swimming. After five minutes I stopped swimming; I was able to stand up. Before long we were on the shore. I believe the only reason I made it was because God was giving me the strength. I never saw the boy again.

mike AGE 16

⁴⁶ The foreigners fade away,
And come frightened from their hideouts.

⁴⁷ "The LORD lives!
Blessed *be* my Rock!
Let God be exalted,
The Rock of my salvation!
⁴⁸ *It is* God who avenges me,
And subdues the peoples under me;
⁴⁹ He delivers me from my enemies.
You also lift me up above those who rise against me;
You have delivered me from the violent man.
⁵⁰ Therefore I will give thanks to You, O LORD, among
the Gentiles,

23:16 David poured out the water as an offering to God because he was so moved by the sacrifice it represented. When Hebrews offered sacrifices, they never consumed the blood. It represented life, and they poured it out before God. David would not drink this water, which represented the lives of his soldiers. Instead, he offered it to God.

And sing praises to Your name.

51 " *He is* the tower of salvation to His king,
And shows mercy to His anointed,
To David and his descendants forevermore."

CHAPTER 23 DAVID'S LAST WORDS. Now these *are* the last words of David.

Thus says David the son of Jesse;
Thus says the man raised up on high,
The anointed of the God of Jacob,
And the sweet psalmist of Israel:

2 "The Spirit of the LORD spoke by me,
And His word *was* on my tongue.
3 The God of Israel said,
The Rock of Israel spoke to me:
'He who rules over men *must be* just,
Ruling in the fear of God.
4 And *he shall be* like the light of the morning *when*
the sun rises,
A morning without clouds,
Like the tender grass *springing* out of the earth,
By clear shining after rain.'

5 "Although my house *is* not so with God,
Yet He has made with me an everlasting covenant,
Ordered in all *things* and secure.
For *this is* all my salvation and all *my* desire;
Will He not make *it* increase?
6 But *the sons* of rebellion *shall* all *be* as thorns thrust
away,
Because they cannot be taken with hands.
7 But the man *who* touches them
Must be armed with iron and the shaft of a spear,
And they shall be utterly burned with fire in *their*
place."

8 These *are* the names of the mighty men whom David had: Josheb-Basshebeth the Tachmonite, chief among the captains. He was called Adino the Eznite, because he had killed eight hundred men at one time. 9 And after him *was* Eleazar the son of Dodo, the Ahohite, *one* of the three mighty men with David when they defied the Philistines *who* were gathered there for battle, and the men of Israel had retreated. 10 He arose and attacked the Philistines until his hand was weary, and his hand stuck to the sword. The LORD brought about a great victory that day; and the people returned after him only to plunder. 11 And after him *was* Shammah the son of Agee the Hararite. The Philistines had gathered together into a troop where there was a piece of ground full of lentils. So the people fled from the Philistines. 12 But he stationed himself in the middle of the field, defended it, and killed the Philistines. So the LORD brought about a great victory.

13 Then three of the thirty chief men went down at harvest time and came to David at the cave of Adullam. And the troop of Philistines encamped in the Valley of Rephaim. 14 David *was* then in the stronghold, and the garrison of the Philistines *was* then *in* Bethlehem. 15 And David said with longing, "Oh, that someone would give me a drink of the water from the well of Bethlehem which *is* by the gate!" 16 So the three mighty men broke through the camp of the Philistines, drew water from the well of Bethlehem that *was* by the gate, and took it and brought *it* to David. Nevertheless he would not drink it, but poured it out to the LORD. 17 And he said, "Far be it from me, O LORD, that I should do this! Is *this not* the blood of the men who went in *jeopardy of* their lives?" Therefore he would not drink it.

These things were done by the three mighty men.

18 Now Abishai the brother of Joab, the son of Zeruiah was chief of *another* three. He lifted his spear against three hundred *men*, killed *them*, and won a name among *these* three. 19 Was he not the most honored of three? Therefore he became their captain. However, he did not attain to the *first* three.

20 Benaiah *was* the son of Jehoiada, the son of a valiant man from Kabzeel, who had done many deeds. He had killed two lion-like heroes of Moab. He also had gone down and killed a lion in the midst of a pit on a snowy day. 21 And he killed an Egyptian, a spectacular man. The Egyptian *had* a spear in his hand; so he went down to him with a staff, wrested the spear out of the Egyptian's hand, and killed him with his own spear. 22 These *things* Benaiah the son of Jehoiada did, and won a name among three mighty men. 23 He was more honored than the thirty, but he did not attain to the *first* three. And David appointed him over his guard.

24 Asahel the brother of Joab *was* one of the thirty, Elhanan the son of Dodo of Bethlehem, 25 Shammah the Harodite, Elika the Harodite, 26 Helez the Paltite, Ira the son of Ikkesh the Tekoite, 27 Abiezer the Anathothite, Mebunnai the Hushathite, 28 Zalmon the Ahohite, Maharai the Netophathite, 29 Heleb the son of Baanah (the Netophathite), Ittai the son of Ribai from Gibeah of the children of Benjamin, 30 Benaiah a Pirathonite, Hiddai from the brooks of Gaash, 31 Abi-Albon the Arbathite, Azmaveth the Barhumite, 32 Eliahba the Shaalbonite (of the sons of Jashen), Jonathan, 33 Shammah the Hararite, Ahiam the son of Sharar the Hararite, 34 Eliphelet the son of Ahasbai, the son of the Maachathite, Eliam the son of Ahithophel the Gilonite, 35 Hezrai the Carmelite, Paarai the Arbite, 36 Igal the son of Nathan of Zobah, Bani the Gadite, 37 Zelek the Ammonite, Naharai the Beerothite (armorbearer of Joab the son of Zeruiah), 38 Ira the Ithrite, Gareb the Ithrite, 39 *and* Uriah the Hittite: thirty-seven in all.

CHAPTER 24 DAVID'S THRESHING FLOOR
Again the anger of the LORD was aroused against Israel, and He moved David against them to say, "Go, number Israel and Judah."

2 So the king said to Joab the commander of the army who *was* with him, "Now go throughout all the tribes of

Israel, from Dan to Beersheba, and count the people, that I may know the number of the people."

³And Joab said to the king, "Now may the LORD your God add to the people a hundred times more than there are, and may the eyes of my lord the king see *it*. But why does my lord the king desire this thing?" ⁴Nevertheless the king's word prevailed against Joab and against the captains of the army. Therefore Joab and the captains of the army went out from the presence of the king to count the people of Israel.

⁵And they crossed over the Jordan and camped in Aroer, on the right side of the town which *is* in the midst of the ravine of Gad, and toward Jazer. ⁶Then they came to Gilead and to the land of Tahtim Hodshi; they came to Dan Jaan and around to Sidon; ⁷and they came to the stronghold of Tyre and to all the cities of the Hivites and the Canaanites. Then they went out to South Judah *as far as* Beersheba. ⁸So when they had gone through all the land, they came to Jerusalem at the end of nine months and twenty days. ⁹Then Joab gave the sum of the number of the people to the king. And there were in Israel eight hundred thousand valiant men who drew the sword, and the men of Judah were five hundred thousand men.

¹⁰And David's heart condemned him after he had numbered the people. So David said to the LORD, "I have sinned greatly in what I have done; but now, I pray, O LORD, take away the iniquity of Your servant, for I have done very foolishly."

¹¹Now when David arose in the morning, the word of the LORD came to the prophet Gad, David's seer, saying, ¹²"Go and tell David, 'Thus says the LORD: "I offer you three *things*; choose one of them for yourself, that I may do *it* to you."' " ¹³So Gad came to David and told him; and he said to him, "Shall seven years of famine come to you in your land? Or shall you flee three months before your enemies, while they pursue you? Or shall there be three days' plague in your land? Now consider and see what answer I should take back to Him who sent me."

¹⁴And David said to Gad, "I am in great distress. Please let us fall into the hand of the LORD, for His mercies *are* great; but do not let me fall into the hand of man."

¹⁵So the LORD sent a plague upon Israel from the morning till the appointed time. From Dan to Beersheba seventy thousand men of the people died. ¹⁶And when the angel stretched out His hand over Jerusalem to destroy it, the LORD relented from the destruction, and said to the angel who was de-

stroying the people, "It is enough; now restrain your hand." And the angel of the LORD was by the threshing floor of Araunah the Jebusite.

¹⁷Then David spoke to the LORD when he saw the angel who was striking the people, and said, "Surely I have sinned, and I have done wickedly; but these sheep, what have they done? Let Your hand, I pray, be against me and against my father's house."

¹⁸And Gad came that day to David and said to him, "Go up, erect an altar to the LORD on the threshing floor of Araunah the Jebusite." ¹⁹So David, according to the word of Gad, went up as the LORD commanded. ²⁰Now Araunah looked, and saw the king and his servants coming toward him. So Araunah went out and bowed before the king with his face to the ground.

²¹Then Araunah said, "Why has my lord the king come to his servant?"

And David said, "To buy the threshing floor from you, to build an altar to

DAVID'S MIGHTY MEN

One way to understand David's success is to notice the kind of men who followed him. During the time he was being hunted by Saul, David gradually built a fighting force of several hundred men. Some were relatives, others were outcasts of society, many were in trouble with the law. They all had at least one trait in common—complete devotion to David. Their achievements made them famous. Among these men were elite military groups like "the thirty" and "the three." They were true heroes.

Scripture gives the impression that these men were motivated to greatness by the personal qualities of their leader. David inspired them to achieve beyond their goals and meet their true potential. Likewise, the leaders we follow and the causes to which we commit ourselves will affect our life. David's effectiveness was clearly connected with his awareness of God's leading. He was a good leader when he was following his Leader. Do you know whom the people you respect most are following? Your answer should help you decide whether or not they deserve your loyalty. Do you also recognize God's leading in your life? No one can lead you to excellence as your Creator can.

LESSONS: Greatness is often inspired by the quality and character of leadership. Even a small force of able and loyal men can accomplish great feats.

KEY VERSES: "David therefore departed from there and escaped to the cave of Adullam. So when his brothers and all his father's house heard it, they went down there to him. And everyone who was in distress, everyone who was in debt, and everyone who was discontented gathered to him. So he became captain over them. And there were about four hundred men with him" (1 Samuel 22:1-2).

Their stories are told in 1 Samuel 22—2 Samuel 23:39. They are also mentioned in 1 Chronicles 11–12.

UPS:
- Able
- Shared many special skills
- Though frequently outnumbered, were consistently victorious
- Loyal to David

STATS:
- Where: They came from all over Israel (primarily Judah and Benjamin), and from some of the other surrounding nations as well
- Occupations: Various backgrounds—almost all were fugitives

the LORD, that the plague may be withdrawn from the people."

²²Now Araunah said to David, "Let my lord the king take and offer up whatever *seems* good to him. Look, *here are* oxen for burnt sacrifice, and threshing implements and the yokes of the oxen for wood. ²³All these, O king, Araunah has given to the king."

And Araunah said to the king, "May the LORD your God accept you."

²⁴Then the king said to Araunah, "No, but I will surely buy *it* from you for a price; nor will I offer burnt offerings to the LORD my God with that which costs me nothing." So David bought the threshing floor and the oxen for fifty shekels of silver. ²⁵And David built there an altar to the LORD, and offered burnt offerings and peace offerings. S the LORD heeded the prayers for the land, and the plague was withdrawn from Israel.

MEGA Themes

KINGDOM GROWTH Under David's leadership, Israel grew rapidly. With the growth came many changes; from tribal independence to centralized government, from the leadership of judges to a monarchy, from decentralized worship to worship at Jerusalem.

No matter how much growth or how many changes we experience, God will meet our needs if we love him and highly regard his principles.

1. What do you think life was like in Israel during the high points of David's reign?
2. How did God supply his blessing through David?
3. What are some of the "high points" of your life? How did God bless you during those times?
4. Why do some people seem to forget God when things are going great?
5. List a couple of principles you can use to guide you when everything seems to be going great for you.

PERSONAL GREATNESS David's popularity and influence increased greatly. He realized that the Lord was behind his success because he wanted to pour out his kindness on Israel.

God graciously favors us because of what Christ has done. God does not regard personal greatness as something to be used selfishly, but as an instrument to carry out his work among his people. The greatness we should desire is to love others as God loves us. We should never use or take advantage of someone for our own benefit.

1. When God exalted David, how did he respond? How did others respond?
2. What attitude should we have toward those who are raised by God to be our leaders?

3. What qualities would be seen by God as qualities of greatness?
4. What would it take for you to achieve true greatness?

JUSTICE King David showed justice, mercy, and fairness to Saul's family, enemies, rebels, allies, and close friends alike. His just rule was grounded in his faith and knowledge of God.

Although David was the most just of all Israel's kings, he was still imperfect. His use of justice offered hope for a heavenly, ideal kingdom. This hope will never be satisfied in the hearts of human beings until Christ, the Son of David, comes to rule in perfect justice forever.

1. How is God's justice revealed in David's life?
2. What difference does it make whether or not you live according to God's will?
3. How should you respond when another Christian indicates concern about the justice of a decision you are making?
4. As an individual Christian, what can you do to work for justice in the world?

CONSEQUENCES OF SIN Because David sinned with Bathsheba, he experienced the consequences of his sin, which ruined both his family and the nation. David's prosperity and ease led him from triumph to temptation—to trouble.

Temptation quite often comes when a person's life has no direction. Sometimes we may think that sinful pleasures will bring us a sense of life and adventure; but sin creates a cycle of suffering that is not worth the fleeting pleasure or "rush" it offers.

1. What led to David's choosing to sin with Bathsheba?
2. List a few of the results of that choice and other sinful choices that followed.
3. What causes Christians to choose sin even though they know what is right?
4. Suppose you sinned against God knowingly and then nothing seemed to go wrong in your life. Could it then be said that you had "gotten away with it"? Explain.
5. Based on this study of 2 Samuel, what areas of your life need to be changed in order to avoid the type of mistakes that David made?

*H*ere's a quick quiz. What do you think of when you hear each of these names: Solomon . . . Elijah . . . Ahab . . . Jezebel . . . Nadab? ■ The usual response for Solomon would be "wisdom" or "the temple." For Elijah, you might answer, "prophet" or "defeated the Baal worshipers on the mountain." Ahab and Jezebel are most certainly associated with evil. And you may not even have heard of Nadab. ■ It's amazing what people remember about other people, even after they're gone. Whether good or evil, a person's reputation often remains long after his or her death. ■ First Kings tells the stories of many of the leaders of Israel. Some, like Solomon, take chapters to relate. Others, like Nadab, just take a line or two. No matter what the length, when we read these accounts we gain a snapshot of what these people were like—their character and their lives. As we read, we can learn what it takes to be someone who is remembered for good and not for evil, for following God and not self. ■ What would your friends and acquaintances say if given your name in a similar quiz? What kind of a reputation are you building?

STATS

PURPOSE: To contrast the lives of those who live for God with the lives of those who refuse to do so, using the history of the kings of Israel and Judah

AUTHOR: Unknown. Possibly Jeremiah or a group of prophets.

SETTING: The once great nation of Israel turns into a divided land, both physically and spiritually

KEY PEOPLE: David, Solomon, Rehoboam, Jeroboam, Elijah, Ahab, Jezebel

SPECIAL FEATURE: The books of 1 and 2 Kings were originally one book

1 Kings

CHAPTER 1 **SOLOMON BECOMES KING.** Now King David was old, advanced in years; and they put covers on him, but he could not get warm. ²Therefore his servants said to him, "Let a young woman, a virgin, be sought for our lord the king, and let her stand before the king, and let her care for him; and let her lie in your bosom, that our lord the king may be warm." ³So they sought for a lovely young woman throughout all the territory of Israel, and found Abishag the Shunammite, and brought her to the king. ⁴The young woman *was* very lovely; and she cared for the king, and served him; but the king did not know her.

⁵Then Adonijah the son of Haggith exalted himself, saying, "I will be king"; and he prepared for himself chariots and horsemen, and fifty men to run before him. ⁶(And his father had not rebuked him at any time by saying, "Why have you done so?" He *was* also very good-looking. *His mother* had borne him after Absalom.) ⁷Then he conferred with Joab the son of Zeruiah and with Abiathar the priest, and they followed and helped Adonijah. ⁸But Zadok the priest, Benaiah the son of Jehoiada, Nathan the prophet, Shimei, Rei, and the mighty men who *belonged* to David were not with Adonijah.

⁹And Adonijah sacrificed sheep and oxen and fattened cattle by the stone of Zoheleth, which *is* by En Rogel; he also invited all his brothers, the king's sons, and all the men of Judah, the king's servants. ¹⁰But he did not invite Nathan the prophet, Benaiah, the mighty men, or Solomon his brother.

¹¹So Nathan spoke to Bathsheba the mother of Solomon, saying, "Have you not heard that Adonijah the son of Haggith has become king, and David our lord does not know *it?* ¹²Come, please, let me now give you advice,

that you may save your own life and the life of your son Solomon. ¹³Go immediately to King David and say to him, 'Did you not, my lord, O king, swear to your maidservant, saying, "Assuredly your son Solomon shall reign after me, and he shall sit on my throne"? Why then has Adonijah become king?' ¹⁴Then, while you are still talking there with the king, I also will come in after you and confirm your words."

◣◣◣◣**ACTION**

1:5-14 When Nathan learned of Adonijah's conspiracy, he immediately tried to stop it. He was a man of both faith and action. Nathan knew the right course to take—that Solomon should be king—and he moved quickly when he saw someone trying to block what was right. We often know what is right, but don't act on it. Perhaps we don't want to get involved, or maybe we are lazy. Don't stop with prayer, good intentions, or angry feelings. Take the action needed to correct the situation.

¹⁵So Bathsheba went into the chamber to the king. (Now the king was very old, and Abishag the Shunammite was serving the king.) ¹⁶And Bathsheba bowed and did homage to the king. Then the king said, "What is your wish?"

¹⁷Then she said to him, "My lord, you swore by the LORD your God to your maidservant, *saying,* 'Assuredly Solomon your son shall reign after me, and he shall sit on my throne.' ¹⁸So now, look! Adonijah has become king; and now, my lord the king, you do not know about *it.* ¹⁹He has sacrificed oxen and fattened cattle and sheep in abundance, and has invited all the sons of the king, Abiathar the priest, and Joab the commander of the army; but Solomon your servant he has not invited. ²⁰And as for you, my lord, O king, the eyes of all Israel *are* on you, that

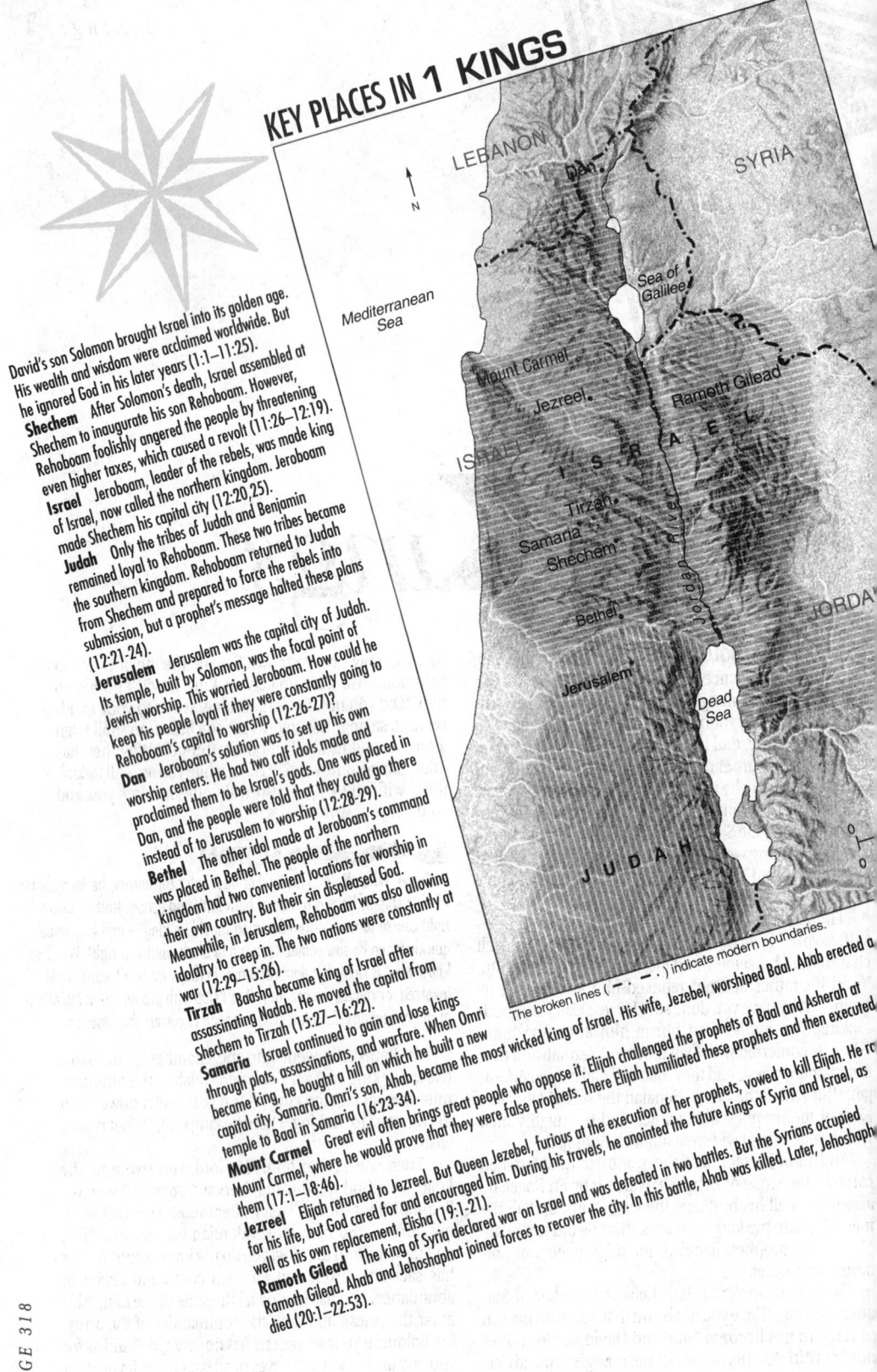

KEY PLACES IN 1 KINGS

David's son Solomon brought Israel into its golden age. His wealth and wisdom were acclaimed worldwide. But he ignored God in his later years (1:1–11:25).

Shechem   After Solomon's death, Israel assembled at Shechem to inaugurate his son Rehoboam. However, Rehoboam foolishly angered the people by threatening even higher taxes, which caused a revolt (11:26–12:19).

Israel   Jeroboam, leader of the rebels, was made king of Israel, now called the northern kingdom. Jeroboam made Shechem his capital city (12:20,25).

Judah   Only the tribes of Judah and Benjamin remained loyal to Rehoboam. These two tribes became the southern kingdom. Rehoboam returned to Judah from Shechem and prepared to force the rebels into submission, but a prophet's message halted these plans (12:21-24).

Jerusalem   Jerusalem was the capital city of Judah. Its temple, built by Solomon, was the focal point of Jewish worship. This worried Jeroboam. How could he keep his people loyal if they were constantly going to Rehoboam's capital to worship (12:26-27)?

Dan   Jeroboam's solution was to set up his own worship centers. He had two calf idols made and proclaimed them to be Israel's gods. One was placed in Dan, and the people were told that they could go there instead of to Jerusalem to worship (12:28-29).

Bethel   The other idol made at Jeroboam's command was placed in Bethel. The people of the northern kingdom had two convenient locations for worship in their own country. But their sin displeased God. Meanwhile, in Jerusalem, Rehoboam was also allowing idolatry to creep in. The two nations were constantly at war (12:29–15:26).

Tirzah   Baasha became king of Israel after assassinating Nadab. He moved the capital from Shechem to Tirzah (15:27–16:22).

Samaria   Israel continued to gain and lose kings through plots, assassinations, and warfare. When Omri became king, he bought a hill on which he built a new capital city, Samaria. Omri's son, Ahab, became the most wicked king of Israel. His wife, Jezebel, worshiped Baal. Ahab erected a temple to Baal in Samaria (16:23-34).

Mount Carmel   Great evil often brings great people who oppose it. Elijah challenged the prophets of Baal and Asherah at Mount Carmel, where he would prove that they were false prophets. There Elijah humiliated these prophets and then executed them (17:1–18:46).

Jezreel   Elijah returned to Jezreel. But Queen Jezebel, furious at the execution of her prophets, vowed to kill Elijah. He ran for his life, but God cared for and encouraged him. During his travels, he anointed the future kings of Syria and Israel, as well as his own replacement, Elisha (19:1-21).

Ramoth Gilead   The king of Syria declared war on Israel and was defeated in two battles. But the Syrians occupied Ramoth Gilead. Ahab and Jehoshaphat joined forces to recover the city. In this battle, Ahab was killed. Later, Jehoshaphat died (20:1–22:53).

The broken lines (— - — -) indicate modern boundaries.

you should tell them who will sit on the throne of my lord the king after him. ²¹Otherwise it will happen, when my lord the king rests with his fathers, that I and my son Solomon will be counted as offenders."

²²And just then, while she was still talking with the king, Nathan the prophet also came in. ²³So they told the king, saying, "Here is Nathan the prophet." And when he came in before the king, he bowed down before the king with his face to the ground. ²⁴And Nathan said, "My lord, O king, have you said, 'Adonijah shall reign after me, and he shall sit on my throne'? ²⁵For he has gone down today, and has sacrificed oxen and fattened cattle and sheep in abundance, and has invited all the king's sons, and the commanders of the army, and Abiathar the priest; and look! They are eating and drinking before him; and they say, '*Long* live King Adonijah!'

²⁶But he has not invited me—me your servant— nor Zadok the priest, nor Benaiah the son of Jehoiada, nor your servant Solomon. ²⁷Has this thing been done by my lord the king, and you have not told your servant who should sit on the throne of my lord the king after him?"

²⁸Then King David answered and said, "Call Bathsheba to me." So she came into the king's presence and stood before the king. ²⁹And the king took an oath and said, "*As* the LORD lives, who has redeemed my life from every distress, ³⁰just as I swore to you by the LORD God of Israel, saying, 'Assuredly Solomon your son shall be king after me, and he shall sit on my throne in my place,' so I certainly will do this day."

³¹Then Bathsheba bowed with *her* face to the earth, and paid homage to the king, and said, "Let my lord King David live forever!"

³²And King David said, "Call to me Zadok the priest, Nathan the prophet, and Benaiah the son of Jehoiada." So they came before the king. ³³The king also said to them, "Take with you the servants of your lord, and have Solomon my son ride on my own mule, and take him down to Gihon. ³⁴There let Zadok the priest and Nathan the prophet anoint him king over Israel; and blow the horn, and say, '*Long* live King Solomon!' ³⁵Then you shall come up after him, and he shall come and sit on my throne, and he shall be king

in my place. For I have appointed him to be ruler over Israel and Judah."

³⁶Benaiah the son of Jehoiada answered the king and said, "Amen! May the LORD God of my lord the king say so *too.* ³⁷As the LORD has been with my lord the king, even so may He be with Solomon, and make his throne greater than the throne of my lord King David."

³⁸So Zadok the priest, Nathan the prophet, Benaiah the son of Jehoiada, the Cherethites, and the Pelethites went down and had Solomon ride on King David's mule, and took him to Gihon. ³⁹Then Zadok the priest took a horn of oil from the tabernacle and anointed Solomon.

SOLOMON

Having wisdom doesn't help unless you use it. Early in his life, Solomon had the sense to realize his need for wisdom. But even when he asked God to give him wisdom to be a good king, he was already showing poor judgment as a man. He married a heathen woman as part of a political deal. She was the first of several hundred wives he married. In doing this, Solomon went against not only his father's last words, but also God's direct commands. His actions remind us how easy it is to know what is right and yet not do it.

God's gift of wisdom to Solomon did not mean that he couldn't make mistakes. He had been given great opportunities as the king of God's chosen people, but with those opportunities came great responsibilities. Solomon took advantage of the opportunities, building temples and palaces, but he became infamous as a king who charged high taxes and overworked his people.

Little is mentioned in the Bible about the last decade of Solomon's reign. Ecclesiastes probably records his final reflections on life. In that book, we observe a man proving through bitter experience that finding meaning in life apart from God doesn't work. Real security and contentment are only found in a personal relationship with God. The contentment we find in the opportunities and successes of this life is real, but temporary. The more we expect those feelings to last, the more quickly they are gone. Be sure to balance your pursuit of all the opportunities in life with keeping up with your responsibilities. Or, as Solomon put it, "Remember now your Creator in the days of your youth" (Ecclesiastes 12:1).

LESSONS: Effective leadership can be nullified by an ineffective personal life
Solomon failed to obey God and did not learn the lesson of repentance until late in life
Knowing what actions are required of us means little if we don't have the will to perform those actions

KEY VERSE: "Did not Solomon king of Israel sin by these things? Yet among many nations there was no king like him, who was beloved of his God; and God made him king over all Israel. Nevertheless pagan women caused even him to sin" (Nehemiah 13:26).

Solomon's story is told in 2 Samuel 12:24—1 Kings 11:43. He is also mentioned in 1 Chronicles 28–29; 2 Chronicles 1–9; Nehemiah 13:26; Psalm 72; and Matthew 6:29; 12:42.

UPS:
- Third king of Israel, David's chosen heir
- The wisest man who ever lived
- Author of Ecclesiastes and Song of Solomon, as well as many of the proverbs and some of the psalms
- Built God's temple in Jerusalem
- Diplomat, trader, collector, patron of the arts

DOWNS:
- Sealed many foreign agreements by marrying heathen women
- Allowed his wives to affect his loyalty to God
- Taxed his people excessively and drafted them into a labor force

STATS:
- Where: Jerusalem
- Occupation: King of Israel
- Relatives: Father: David. Mother: Bathsheba. Brothers: Absalom, Adonijah. Sister: Tamar. Son: Rehoboam.

1:49-50 Sometimes it takes getting caught before someone is willing to give up his scheme. When Adonijah learned that his plans had been exposed, he ran in panic to the sacred altar, the highest symbol of God's mercy and forgiveness. He went there, however, *after* his plans for treason were exposed. If Adonijah had first considered what God wanted, he might have avoided trouble. Don't wait until you have made a mess of things to run to God; it's much better to seek God's guidance *before* you act.

And they blew the horn, and all the people said, *"Long live King Solomon!"* ⁴⁰And all the people went up after him; and the people played the flutes and rejoiced with great joy, so that the earth *seemed to* split with their sound.

⁴¹Now Adonijah and all the guests who *were* with him heard *it* as they finished eating. And when Joab heard the sound of the horn, he said, "Why *is* the city in such a noisy uproar?" ⁴²While he was still speaking, there came Jonathan, the son of Abiathar the priest. And Adonijah said to him, "Come in, for you *are* a prominent man, and bring good news."

⁴³Then Jonathan answered and said to Adonijah, "No! Our lord King David has made Solomon king. ⁴⁴The king has sent with him Zadok the priest, Nathan the prophet, Benaiah the son of Jehoiada, the Cherethites, and the Pelethites; and they have made him ride on the king's mule. ⁴⁵So Zadok the priest and Nathan the prophet have anointed him king at Gihon; and they have gone up from there rejoicing, so that the city is in an uproar. This *is* the noise that you have heard. ⁴⁶Also Solomon sits on the throne of the kingdom. ⁴⁷And moreover the king's servants have gone to bless our lord King David, saying, 'May God make the name of Solomon better than your name, and may He make his throne greater than your throne.' Then the king bowed himself on the bed. ⁴⁸Also the king said thus, 'Blessed *be* the LORD God of Israel, who has given *one* to sit on my throne this day, while my eyes see *it!*'"

⁴⁹So all the guests who were with Adonijah were afraid, and arose, and each one went his way.

⁵⁰Now Adonijah was afraid of Solomon; so he arose, and went and took hold of the horns of the altar. ⁵¹And it was told Solomon, saying, "Indeed Adonijah is afraid of King Solomon; for look, he has taken hold of the horns of the altar, saying, 'Let King Solomon swear to me today that he will not put his servant to death with the sword.'"

⁵²Then Solomon said, "If he proves himself a worthy man, not one hair of him shall fall to the earth; but if wickedness is found in him, he shall die." ⁵³So King Solomon sent them to bring him down from the altar. And he came and fell down before King Solomon; and Solomon said to him, "Go to your house."

CHAPTER 2 INSTRUCTIONS FOR SOLOMON.

Now the days of David drew near that he should die, and he charged Solomon his son, saying: ²"I go the way of all the earth; be strong, therefore, and prove yourself a man. ³And keep the charge of the LORD your God: to walk in His ways, to keep His statutes, His commandments, His judgments, and His testimonies, as it is written in the Law of Moses, that you may prosper in all that you do and

wherever you turn; ⁴that the LORD may fulfill His word which He spoke concerning me, saying, 'If your sons take heed to their way, to walk before Me in truth with all their heart and with all their soul,' He said, 'you shall not lack a man on the throne of Israel.'

⁵"Moreover you know also what Joab the son of Zeruiah did to me, *and* what he did to the two commanders of the armies of Israel, to Abner the son of Ner and Amasa the son of Jether, whom he killed. And he shed the blood of war in peacetime, and put the blood of war on his belt that *was* around his waist, and on his sandals that *were* on his feet. ⁶Therefore do according to your wisdom, and do not let his gray hair go down to the grave in peace.

⁷"But show kindness to the sons of Barzillai the Gileadite, and let them be among those who eat at your table, for so they came to me when I fled from Absalom your brother.

⁸"And see, *you have* with you Shimei the son of Gera, a Benjamite from Bahurim, who cursed me with a malicious curse in the day when I went to Mahanaim. But he came down to meet me at the Jordan, and I swore to him by the LORD, saying, 'I will not put you to death with the sword.' ⁹Now therefore, do not hold him guiltless, for you *are* a wise man and know what you ought to do to him; but bring his gray hair down to the grave with blood."

¹⁰So David rested with his fathers, and was buried in the City of David. ¹¹The period that David reigned over Israel *was* forty years; seven years he reigned in Hebron, and in Jerusalem he reigned thirty-three years. ¹²Then Solomon sat on the throne of his father David; and his kingdom was firmly established.

¹³Now Adonijah the son of Haggith came to Bathsheba the mother of Solomon. So she said, "Do you come peaceably?"

And he said, "Peaceably." ¹⁴Moreover he said, "I have something *to say* to you."

And she said, "Say it."

¹⁵Then he said, "You know that the kingdom was mine, and all Israel had set their expectations on me, that I should reign. However, the kingdom has been turned over, and has become my brother's; for it was his from the LORD. ¹⁶Now I ask one petition of you; do not deny me."

And she said to him, "Say it."

¹⁷Then he said, "Please speak to King Solomon, for he will not refuse you, that he may give me Abishag the Shunammite as wife."

¹⁸So Bathsheba said, "Very well, I will speak for you to the king."

¹⁹Bathsheba therefore went to King Solomon, to speak to him for Adonijah. And the king rose up to meet her and bowed down to her, and sat down on his throne and had a throne set for the king's mother; so she sat at his right hand. ²⁰Then she said, "I desire one small petition of you; do not refuse me."

And the king said to her, "Ask it, my mother, for I will not refuse you."

²¹So she said, "Let Abishag the Shunammite be given to Adonijah your brother as wife."

²²And King Solomon answered and said to his mother, "Now why do you ask Abishag the Shunammite for Adonijah? Ask for him the kingdom also—for he *is* my older

brother—for him, and for Abiathar the priest, and for Joab the son of Zeruiah." ²³Then King Solomon swore by the Lord, saying, "May God do so to me, and more also, if Adonijah has not spoken this word against his own life! ²⁴Now therefore, *as* the Lord lives, who has confirmed me and set me on the throne of David my father, and who has established a house for me, as He promised, Adonijah shall be put to death today!"

²⁵So King Solomon sent by the hand of Benaiah the son of Jehoiada; and he struck him down, and he died.

²⁶And to Abiathar the priest the king said, "Go to Anathoth, to your own fields, for you *are* deserving of death; but I will not put you to death at this time, because you carried the ark of the Lord God before my father David, and because you were afflicted every time my father was afflicted." ²⁷So Solomon removed Abiathar from being priest to the Lord, that he might fulfill the word of the Lord which He spoke concerning the house of Eli at Shiloh.

²⁸Then news came to Joab, for Joab had defected to Adonijah, though he had not defected to Absalom. So Joab fled to the tabernacle of the Lord, and took hold of the horns of the altar. ²⁹And King Solomon was told, "Joab has fled to the tabernacle of the Lord; there *he is,* by the altar." Then Solomon sent Benaiah the son of Jehoiada, saying, "Go, strike him down." ³⁰So Benaiah went to the tabernacle of the Lord, and said to him, "Thus says the king, 'Come out!'"

And he said, "No, but I will die here." And Benaiah brought back word to the king, saying, "Thus said Joab, and thus he answered me."

³¹Then the king said to him, "Do as he has said, and strike him down and bury him, that you may take away from me and from the house of my father the innocent blood which Joab shed. ³²So the Lord will return his blood on his head, because he struck down two men more righteous and better than he, and killed them with the sword—Abner the son of Ner, the commander of the army of Israel, and Amasa the son of Jether, the commander of the army of Judah—though my father David did not know *it.* ³³Their blood shall therefore return upon the head of Joab and upon the head of his descendants forever. But upon David and his descendants, upon his house and his throne, there shall be peace forever from the Lord."

³⁴So Benaiah the son of Jehoiada went up and struck and killed him; and he was buried in his own house in the wilderness. ³⁵The king put Benaiah the son of Jehoiada in his place over the army, and the king put Zadok the priest in the place of Abiathar.

³⁶Then the king sent and called for Shimei, and said to him, "Build yourself a house in Jerusalem and dwell there, and do not go out from there anywhere. ³⁷For it shall be, on the day you go out and cross the Brook Kidron, know for certain you shall surely die; your blood shall be on your own head."

³⁸And Shimei said to the king, "The saying *is* good. As my lord the king has said, so your servant will do." So Shimei dwelt in Jerusalem many days.

³⁹Now it happened at the end of three years, that two slaves of Shimei ran away to Achish the son of Maachah, king of Gath. And they told Shimei, saying, "Look, your slaves *are* in Gath!" ⁴⁰So Shimei arose, saddled his donkey, and went to Achish at Gath to seek his slaves. And Shimei went and brought his slaves from Gath. ⁴¹And Solomon was told that Shimei had gone from Jerusalem to Gath and had come back. ⁴²Then the king sent and

◣◣◣MOTIVES

2:23-24 In this plot against Solomon, all the conspirators lost. Adonijah and Joab were killed, and the priest, Abiathar, lost his job. They all thought they would gain something by their alliance: influence, position, recognition, authority. But they had a poor leader and wrong motives. Consider your motives carefully before making alliances with others.

called for Shimei, and said to him, "Did I not make you swear by the Lord, and warn you, saying, 'Know for certain that on the day you go out and travel anywhere, you shall surely die'? And you said to me, 'The word I have heard *is* good.' ⁴³Why then have you not kept the oath of the Lord and the commandment that I gave you?" ⁴⁴The king said moreover to Shimei, "You know, as your heart acknowledges, all the wickedness that you did to my father David; therefore the Lord will return your wickedness on your own head. ⁴⁵But King Solomon *shall be* blessed, and the throne of David shall be established before the Lord forever."

⁴⁶So the king commanded Benaiah the son of Jehoiada; and he went out and struck him down, and he died. Thus the kingdom was established in the hand of Solomon.

CHAPTER **3** **SOLOMON ASKS FOR WISDOM.** Now Solomon made a treaty with Pharaoh king of Egypt, and married Pharaoh's daughter; then he brought her to the City of David until he had finished building his own house, and the house of the Lord, and the wall all around Jerusalem. ²Meanwhile the people sacrificed at the high places, because there was no house built for the name of the Lord until those days. ³And Solomon loved the Lord, walking in the statutes of his father David, except that he sacrificed and burned incense at the high places.

⁴Now the king went to Gibeon to sacrifice there, for that *was* the great high place: Solomon offered a thousand burnt offerings on that altar. ⁵At Gibeon the Lord appeared to Solomon in a dream by night; and God said, "Ask! What shall I give you?"

◣◣◣INROADS

3:1 Marriage between royal families was a common practice in the ancient Near East because it secured peace. Although Solomon's marital alliances built friendships with surrounding nations, they were also the beginning of his downfall. These relationships became inroads for heathen ideas and practices. Solomon's foreign wives brought their idols to Jerusalem and eventually lured him into idolatry (11:1-8).

It is easy to minimize religious differences in order to encourage the development of a friendship. But seemingly small differences can have an enormous impact upon a relationship. God gives us standards to follow for all our relationships, including marriage. If we follow God's will, we will not be lured away from our true focus.

3:6-9 When given a chance to have anything in the world, Solomon asked for wisdom so that he could lead well and make right decisions. We can ask God for this same wisdom (James 1:5). Notice that Solomon asked for wisdom to carry out his job. He did not ask God to do the job for him. We should not ask God to do *for* us what he wants to equip us to do ourselves. Instead we should ask God to give us the wisdom to know what to do and the courage to follow through on it.

⁶And Solomon said: "You have shown great mercy to Your servant David my father, because he walked before You in truth, in righteousness, and in uprightness of heart with You; You have continued this great kindness for him, and You have given him a son to sit on his throne, as *it is* this day. ⁷Now, O Lᴏʀᴅ my God, You have made Your servant king instead of my father David, but I *am* a little child; I do not know *how* to go out or come in. ⁸And Your servant *is* in the midst of Your people whom You have chosen, a great people, too numerous to be numbered or counted. ⁹Therefore give to Your servant an understanding heart to judge Your people, that I may discern between good and evil. For who is able to judge this great people of Yours?"

¹⁰The speech pleased the Lᴏʀᴅ, that Solomon had asked this thing. ¹¹Then God said to him: "Because you have asked this thing, and have not asked long life for yourself, nor have asked riches for yourself, nor have asked the life of your enemies, but have asked for yourself understanding to discern justice, ¹²behold, I have done according to your words; see, I have given you a wise and understanding heart, so that there has not been anyone like you before you, nor shall any like you arise after you. ¹³And I have also given you what you have not asked: both riches and honor, so that there shall not be anyone like you among the kings all your days. ¹⁴So if you walk in My ways, to keep My statutes and My commandments, as your father David walked, then I will lengthen your days."

¹⁵Then Solomon awoke; and indeed it had been a dream. And he came to Jerusalem and stood before the ark of the covenant of the Lᴏʀᴅ, offered up burnt offerings, offered peace offerings, and made a feast for all his servants.

¹⁶Now two women *who were* harlots came to the king, and stood before him. ¹⁷And one woman said, "O my lord, this woman and I dwell in the same house; and I gave birth while she *was* in the house. ¹⁸Then it happened, the third day after I had given birth, that this woman also gave birth. And we *were* together; no one *was* with us in the house, except the two of us in the house. ¹⁹And this woman's son died in the night, because she lay on him. ²⁰So she arose in the middle of the night and took my son from my side, while your maidservant slept, and laid him in her bosom, and laid her dead child in my bosom. ²¹And when I rose in the morning to nurse my son, there he was, dead. But when I had examined him in the morning, indeed, he was not my son whom I had borne."

²²Then the other woman said, "No! But the living one *is* my son, and the dead one *is* your son."

And the first woman said, "No! But the dead one *is* your son, and the living one *is* my son."

Thus they spoke before the king.

²³And the king said, "The one says, 'This *is* my son, who lives, and your son *is* the dead one'; and the other says, 'No! But your son *is* the dead one, and my son *is* the living one.' " ²⁴Then the king said, "Bring me a sword." So they brought a sword before the king. ²⁵And the king said, "Divide the living child in two, and give half to one, and half to the other."

²⁶Then the woman whose son *was* living spoke to the king, for she yearned with compassion for her son; and she said, "O my lord, give her the living child, and by no means kill him!"

But the other said, "Let him be neither mine nor yours, *but* divide *him.*"

²⁷So the king answered and said, "Give the first woman the living child, and by no means kill him; she *is* his mother."

²⁸And all Israel heard of the judgment which the king had rendered; and they feared the king, for they saw that the wisdom of God *was* in him to administer justice.

CHAPTER 4 SOLOMON'S CABINET MEMBERS. So

King Solomon was king over all Israel. ²And these *were* his officials: Azariah the son of Zadok, the priest; ³Elihoreph and Ahijah, the sons of Shisha, scribes; Jehoshaphat the son of Ahilud, the recorder; ⁴Benaiah the son of Jehoiada, over the army; Zadok and Abiathar, the priests; ⁵Azariah the son of Nathan, over the officers; Zabud the son of Nathan, a priest *and* the king's friend; ⁶Ahishar, over the household; and Adoniram the son of Abda, over the labor force.

4:20-25 Throughout most of his reign, Solomon applied his wisd... well because he sought after God. The fruits of this wisdom were p... security, and prosperity for the nation. Solomon's era is often look... upon as the ideal of what any nation can become when united in t... and obedience to God.

⁷And Solomon had twelve governors over all Israel, who provided food for the king and his household; each one made provision for one month of the year. ⁸These *are* their names: Ben-Hur, in the mountains of Ephraim; ⁹Ben-Deker, in Makaz, Shaalbim, Beth Shemesh, and Elon Beth Hanan; ¹⁰Ben-Hesed, in Arubboth; to him *belonged* Sochoh and all the land of Hepher; ¹¹Ben-Abinadab, *in* all the regions of Dor; he had Taphath the daughter of Solomon as wife; ¹²Baana the son of Ahilud, *in* Taanach, Megiddo, and all Beth Shean, which *is* beside Zaretan below Jezreel, from Beth Shean to Abel Meholah, as far as the other side of Jokneam; ¹³Ben-Geber, in Ramoth Gilead; to him *belonged* the towns of Jair the son of Manasseh, in Gilead; to him *also belonged* the region of Argob in Bashan—sixty large cities with walls and bronze gate-bars; ¹⁴Ahinadab the son of Iddo, *in* Mahanaim; ¹⁵Ahimaaz, in Naphtali; he also took Basemath the daughter of Solomon as wife; ¹⁶Baanah the son of Hushai in Asher and Aloth; ¹⁷Jehoshaphat the son of Paruah, in

Issachar; ¹⁸Shimei the son of Elah, in Benjamin; ¹⁹Geber the son of Uri, in the land of Gilead, *in* the country of Sihon king of the Amorites, and of Og king of Bashan. *He was* the only governor who *was* in the land.

²⁰Judah and Israel *were* as numerous as the sand by the sea in multitude, eating and drinking and rejoicing. ²¹So Solomon reigned over all kingdoms from the River *to* the land of the Philistines, as far as the border of Egypt. *They* brought tribute and served Solomon all the days of his life.

²²Now Solomon's provision for one day was thirty kors of fine flour, sixty kors of meal, ²³ten fatted oxen, twenty oxen from the pastures, and one hundred sheep, besides deer, gazelles, roebucks, and fatted fowl.

²⁴For he had dominion over all *the region* on this side of the River from Tiphsah even to Gaza, namely over all the kings on this side of the River; and he had peace on every side all around him. ²⁵And Judah and Israel dwelt safely, each man under his vine and his fig tree, from Dan as far as Beersheba, all the days of Solomon.

²⁶Solomon had forty thousand stalls of horses for his chariots, and twelve thousand horsemen. ²⁷And these governors, each man in his month, provided food for King Solomon and for all who came to King Solomon's table. There was no lack in their supply. ²⁸They also brought barley and straw to the proper place, for the horses and steeds, each man according to his charge.

²⁹And God gave Solomon wisdom and exceedingly great understanding, and largeness of heart like the sand on the seashore. ³⁰Thus Solomon's wisdom excelled the wisdom of all the men of the East and all the wisdom of Egypt. ³¹For he was wiser than all men—than Ethan the Ezrahite, and Heman, Chalcol, and Darda, the sons of Mahol; and his fame was in all the surrounding nations. ³²He spoke three thousand proverbs, and his songs were one thousand and five. ³³Also he spoke of trees, from the cedar tree of Lebanon even to the hyssop that springs out of the wall; he spoke also of animals, of birds, of creeping things, and of fish. ³⁴And men of all nations, from all the kings of the earth who had heard of his wisdom, came to hear the wisdom of Solomon.

CHAPTER **5** **SOLOMON BUILDS THE TEMPLE.** Now Hiram king of Tyre sent his servants to Solomon, because he heard that they had anointed him king in place of his father, for Hiram had always loved David. ²Then Solomon sent to Hiram, saying:

³ You know how my father David could not build a house for the name of the LORD his God because of the wars which were fought against him on every side, until the LORD put *his foes* under the soles of his feet.

⁴ But now the LORD my God has given me rest on every side; *there is* neither adversary nor evil occurrence.

⁵ And behold, I propose to build a house for the name of the LORD my God, as the LORD spoke to my father David, saying, "Your son, whom I will set on your throne in your place, he shall build the house for My name."

⁶ Now therefore, command that they cut down cedars for me from Lebanon; and my servants will be with your servants, and I will pay you wages for your servants according to whatever you say. For you know *there is* none among us who has skill to cut timber like the Sidonians.

⁷So it was, when Hiram heard the words of Solomon, that he rejoiced greatly and said,

With so many things out there that I want and so many things I know I need, how do I know what to pray for?

I WONDER . . .

Do you realize your mom or dad are faced with the same question every time they go to the grocery store? They know what you want to eat, but they buy what you need to eat. Their experience and wisdom keep you healthy!

God also wants you to be healthy. He knows exactly what to give you and when to give it to you. Jesus said:

"What man is there among you who, if his son asks for bread, will give him a stone? Or if he asks for a fish, will he give him a serpent? If you then, being evil, know how to give good gifts to your children, how much more will your Father who is in heaven give good things to those who ask Him!" (Matthew 7:9-11).

Your mother was probably very glad the day you asked for an apple for a snack instead of ice cream (has that day come?). It shows you are becoming aware of what it will take to keep yourself healthy. Though ice cream tastes better, apples are far better for you.

Our requests to God can sometimes be very selfish, centered only on what we want and not what we need. God the Father longs for the day when we ask him for what we really need or, better yet, what others need.

Solomon had the privilege of asking for anything he wanted from God. Of all of the choices available to him, Solomon made the one that was most pleasing to God—he asked for wisdom. God responded by giving Solomon more wisdom than any other man, and God gave him riches and honor as well, so that others could benefit from the wisdom God gave him. (See 1 Kings 3:3-14.)

Although a child whines for candy an hour before dinner, a wise parent will always say no. Likewise, selfish prayers are rarely answered yes by God because he loves us too much.

The best things to pray for are those that ultimately will help other people. Good examples of the right kinds of things to pray for are character qualities (like patience, self-control, gentleness) that will help you get along better with other people and will help point others toward Christ. Another example is praying for the health of someone who is sick (James 5:14-16).

When you have needs, however, you should never be afraid to ask God to meet them. He loves to answer the prayers of his children!

Blessed *be* the Lord this day, for He has given David a wise son over this great people!

[8]Then Hiram sent to Solomon, saying:

I have considered *the message* which you sent me, *and* I will do all you desire concerning the cedar and cypress logs.

[9] My servants shall bring *them* down from Lebanon to the sea; I will float them in rafts by sea to the place you indicate to me, and will have them broken apart there; then you can take *them* away. And you shall fulfill my desire by giving food for my household.

[10]Then Hiram gave Solomon cedar and cypress logs *according to* all his desire. [11]And Solomon gave Hiram twenty thousand kors of wheat *as* food for his household, and twenty kors of pressed oil. Thus Solomon gave to Hiram year by year.

FAMILY TIME

5:13-14 Solomon drafted three times the number of workers needed for the temple project and then arranged their schedules so they didn't have to be away from home for long periods of time. This showed his concern for the welfare of his workers and the importance he placed on family life. The strength of a nation is in direct proportion to the strength of its families. Solomon wisely recognized that family should always be a top priority. As you structure your own work or arrange the schedules of others, watch for the impact of your plans on your family.

[12]So the Lord gave Solomon wisdom, as He had promised him; and there was peace between Hiram and Solomon, and the two of them made a treaty together.

[13]Then King Solomon raised up a labor force out of all Israel; and the labor force was thirty thousand men. [14]And he sent them to Lebanon, ten thousand a month in shifts: they were one month in Lebanon *and* two months at home; Adoniram *was* in charge of the labor force. [15]Solomon had seventy thousand who carried burdens, and eighty thousand who quarried *stone* in the mountains, [16]besides three thousand three hundred from the chiefs of Solomon's deputies, who supervised the people who labored in the work. [17]And the king commanded them to quarry large stones, costly stones, *and* hewn stones, to lay the foundation of the temple. [18]So Solomon's builders, Hiram's builders, and the Gebalites quarried *them;* and they prepared timber and stones to build the temple.

CHAPTER 6 And it came to pass in the four hundred and eightieth year after the children of Israel had come out of the land of Egypt, in the fourth year of Solomon's reign over Israel, in the month of Ziv, which *is* the second month, that he began to build the house of the Lord. [2]Now the house which King Solomon built for the Lord, its length *was* sixty cubits, its width twenty, and its height thirty cubits. [3]The vestibule in front of the sanctuary of the house *was* twenty cubits long across the width of the house, *and* the width of *the vestibule ex-*

RESPECT

6:7 In honor of God, the temple in Jerusalem was built without the sound of a hammer or any tool at the building site. This meant cutting the stone miles away at the quarry. The people's honor and respect God extended to every aspect of constructing this building in which worship him. This detail is recorded not to teach us how to build a ch but to show us the importance of demonstrating care, concern, hono respect for God and his sanctuary. How do you, in your actions and attitude, treat the place in which you worship God?

tended ten cubits from the front of the house. [4]And he made for the house windows with beveled frames.

[5]Against the wall of the temple he built chambers all around, *against* the walls of the temple, all around the sanctuary and the inner sanctuary. Thus he made side chambers all around it. [6]The lowest chamber *was* five cubits wide, the middle *was* six cubits wide, and the third *was* seven cubits wide; for he made narrow ledges around the outside of the temple, so that *the support beams* would not be fastened into the walls of the temple. [7]And the temple, when it was being built, was built with stone finished at the quarry, so that no hammer or chisel *or* any iron tool was heard in the temple while it was being built. [8]The doorway for the middle story *was* on the right side of the temple. They went up by stairs to the middle *story,* and from the middle to the third.

[9]So he built the temple and finished it, and he paneled the temple with beams and boards of cedar. [10]And he built side chambers against the entire temple, each five cubits high; they were attached to the temple with cedar beams.

[11]Then the word of the Lord came to Solomon, saying: [12]"*Concerning* this temple which you are building, if you walk in My statutes, execute My judgments, keep all My commandments, and walk in them, then I will perform My word with you, which I spoke to your father David. [13]And I will dwell among the children of Israel, and will not forsake My people Israel."

[14]So Solomon built the temple and finished it. [15]And he built the inside walls of the temple with cedar boards; from the floor of the temple to the ceiling he paneled the inside with wood; and he covered the floor of the temple with planks of cypress. [16]Then he built the twenty-cubit room at the rear of the temple, from floor to ceiling, with cedar boards; he built *it* inside as the inner sanctuary, as the Most Holy *Place.* [17]And in front of it the temple sanctuary was forty cubits *long.* [18]The inside of the temple was cedar, carved with ornamental buds and open flowers. All *was* cedar; there was no stone *to be* seen.

[19]And he prepared the inner sanctuary inside the temple, to set the ark of the covenant of the Lord there. [20]The inner sanctuary *was* twenty cubits long, twenty cubits wide, and twenty cubits high. He overlaid it with pure gold, and overlaid the altar of cedar. [21]So Solomon overlaid the inside of the temple with pure gold. He stretched gold chains across the front of the inner sanc tuary, and overlaid it with gold. [22]The whole temple he overlaid with gold, until he had finished all the temple also he overlaid with gold the entire altar that *was* by the inner sanctuary.

[23]Inside the inner sanctuary he made two cherubim of olive wood, *each* ten cubits high. [24]One wing of the

cherub *was* five cubits, and the other wing of the cherub five cubits: ten cubits from the tip of one wing to the tip of the other. ²⁵And the other cherub *was* ten cubits; both cherubim *were* of the same size and shape. ²⁶The height of one cherub *was* ten cubits, and so *was* the other cherub. ²⁷Then he set the cherubim inside the inner room; and they stretched out the wings of the cherubim so that the wing of the one touched *one* wall, and the wing of the other cherub touched the other wall. And their wings touched each other in the middle of the room. ²⁸Also he overlaid the cherubim with gold.

²⁹Then he carved all the walls of the temple all around, both the inner and outer *sanctuaries,* with carved figures of cherubim, palm trees, and open flowers. ³⁰And the floor of the temple he overlaid with gold, both the inner and outer *sanctuaries.*

³¹For the entrance of the inner sanctuary he made doors *of* olive wood; the lintel *and* doorposts *were* one-fifth *of the wall.* ³²The two doors *were of* olive wood; and he carved on them figures of cherubim, palm trees, and open flowers, and overlaid *them* with gold; and he spread gold on the cherubim and on the palm trees. ³³So for the door of the sanctuary he also made doorposts *of* olive wood, one-fourth *of the wall.* ³⁴And the two doors *were of* cypress wood; two panels *comprised* one folding door, and two panels *comprised* the other folding door. ³⁵Then he carved cherubim, palm trees, and open flowers *on them,* and overlaid *them* with gold applied evenly on the carved work.

³⁶And he built the inner court with three rows of hewn stone and a row of cedar beams.

³⁷In the fourth year the foundation of the house of the LORD was laid, in the month of Ziv. ³⁸And in the eleventh year, in the month of Bul, which is the eighth month, the house was finished in all its details and according to all its plans. So he was seven years in building it.

CHAPTER **7** SOLOMON BUILDS HIS PALACE. But Solomon took thirteen years to build his own house; so he finished all his house.

²He also built the House of the Forest of Lebanon; its length *was* one hundred cubits, its width fifty cubits, and its height thirty cubits, with four rows of cedar pillars, and cedar beams on the pillars. ³And *it was* paneled with cedar above the beams that *were* on forty-five pillars, fifteen *to* a row. ⁴*There were* windows *with beveled frames in* three rows, and window *was* opposite window *in* three tiers. ⁵And all the doorways and doorposts *had* rectangular frames; and window *was* opposite window *in* three tiers.

⁶He also made the Hall of Pillars: its length *was* fifty cubits, and its width thirty cubits; and in front of them *was* a portico with pillars, and a canopy *was* in front of them.

⁷Then he made a hall for the throne, the Hall of Judgment, where he might judge; and *it was* paneled with cedar from floor to ceiling.

⁸And the house where he dwelt *had* another court inside the hall, of like workmanship. Solomon also made a house like this hall for Pharaoh's daughter, whom he had taken *as wife.*

⁹All these *were of* costly stones cut to size, trimmed with saws, inside and out, from the foundation to the eaves, and also on the outside to the great court. ¹⁰The foundation *was of* costly stones, large stones, some ten cubits and some eight cubits. ¹¹And above *were* costly stones, hewn to size, and cedar wood. ¹²The great court *was* enclosed with three rows of hewn stones and a row of cedar beams. So were the inner court of the house of the LORD and the vestibule of the temple.

¹³Now King Solomon sent and brought Huram from Tyre. ¹⁴He *was* the son of a widow from the tribe of Naphtali, and his father *was* a man of Tyre, a bronze worker; he was filled with wisdom and understanding and skill in working with all kinds of bronze work. So he came to King Solomon and did all his work.

¹⁵And he cast two pillars of bronze, each one eighteen cubits high, and a line of twelve cubits measured the circumference of each. ¹⁶Then he made two capitals *of* cast bronze, to set on the tops of the pillars. The height of one capital *was* five cubits, and the height of the other capital *was* five cubits. ¹⁷*He made* a lattice network, with wreaths of chainwork, for the capitals which *were* on top of the pillars: seven chains for one capital and seven for the other capital. ¹⁸So he made the pillars, and two rows of pomegranates above the network all around to cover the capitals that *were* on top; and thus he did for the other capital.

¹⁹The capitals which *were* on top of the pillars in the hall *were* in the shape of lilies, four cubits. ²⁰The capitals on the two pillars also *had pomegranates* above, by the convex surface which *was* next to the network; and there *were* two hundred such pomegranates in rows on each of the capitals all around.

²¹Then he set up the pillars by the vestibule of the temple; he set up the pillar on the right and called its name Jachin, and he set up the pillar on the left and called its name Boaz. ²²The tops of the pillars were in the shape of lilies. So the work of the pillars was finished.

²³And he made the Sea of cast bronze, ten cubits from one brim to the other; *it was* completely round. Its height *was* five cubits, and a line of thirty cubits measured its circumference.

²⁴Below its brim *were* ornamental buds encircling it all around, ten to a cubit, all the way around the Sea. The ornamental buds *were* cast in two rows when it was cast. ²⁵It stood on twelve oxen: three looking toward the north, three looking toward the west, three looking toward the south, and three looking toward the east; the Sea *was set* upon them, and all their back parts *pointed* inward. ²⁶It *was* a handbreadth thick; and its brim was shaped like the brim of a cup, *like* a lily blossom. It contained two thousand baths.

²⁷He also made ten carts of bronze; four cubits *was* the length of each cart, four cubits its width, and three cubits its height. ²⁸And this *was* the design of the carts: They had panels, and the panels *were* between frames; ²⁹on the panels that *were* between the frames *were* lions, oxen, and cherubim. And on the frames *was* a pedestal on top. Below the lions and oxen *were* wreaths of plaited work.

³⁰Every cart had four bronze wheels and axles of bronze, and its four feet had supports. Under the laver *were* supports of cast *bronze* beside each wreath. ³¹Its opening inside the crown at the top *was* one cubit in diameter; and the opening *was* round, shaped *like* a pedestal, one and a half cubits in outside diameter; and also on the opening *were* engravings, but the panels were square, not round. ³²Under the panels *were* the four wheels, and the axles of the wheels *were joined* to the cart. The height of a wheel *was* one and a half cubits. ³³The workmanship of the wheels *was* like the workmanship of a chariot wheel; their axle pins, their rims, their spokes, and their hubs *were* all of cast *bronze*. ³⁴And *there were* four supports at the four corners of each cart; its supports *were* part of the cart itself. ³⁵On the top of the cart, at the height of half a cubit, *it was* perfectly round. And on the top of the cart, its flanges and its panels *were* of the same casting. ³⁶On the plates of its flanges and on its panels he engraved cherubim, lions, and palm trees, wherever there was a clear space on each, with wreaths all around. ³⁷Thus he made the ten carts. All of them were of the same mold, one measure, *and* one shape.

◣◣◣◣◣◣ STAINED-GLASS

7:41-46 Huram's items of bronze would look strange in today's churches, but some Christians use other articles to enhance worship. Stained-glass windows, crosses, pulpits, hymn books, baptisteries, and communion tables serve as aids to worship. While the instruments of worship may change, the purpose—to give honor and praise to God—should never change.

³⁸Then he made ten lavers of bronze; each laver contained forty baths, *and* each laver *was* four cubits. On each of the ten carts *was* a laver. ³⁹And he put five carts on the right side of the house, and five on the left side of the house. He set the Sea on the right side of the house, toward the southeast.

⁴⁰Huram made the lavers and the shovels and the bowls. So Huram finished doing all the work that he was to do for King Solomon *for* the house of the LORD: ⁴¹the two pillars, the *two* bowl-shaped capitals that *were* on top of the two pillars; the two networks covering the two bowl-shaped capitals which *were* on top of the pillars; ⁴²four hundred pomegranates for the two networks (two rows of pomegranates for each network, to cover the two bowl-shaped capitals that *were* on top of the pillars); ⁴³the ten carts, and ten lavers on the carts; ⁴⁴one Sea, and twelve oxen under the Sea; ⁴⁵the pots, the shovels, and the bowls.

All these articles which Huram made for King Solomon *for* the house of the LORD *were of* burnished bronze. ⁴⁶In the plain of Jordan the king had them cast in clay molds, between Succoth and Zaretan. ⁴⁷And Solomon did not weigh all the articles, because *there were* so many; the weight of the bronze was not determined.

⁴⁸Thus Solomon had all the furnishings made for the house of the LORD: the altar of gold, and the table of gold on which *was* the showbread; ⁴⁹the lampstands of pure gold, five on the right *side* and five on the left in front of the inner sanctuary, with the flowers and the lamps and the wick-trimmers of gold; ⁵⁰the basins, the trimmers, the bowls, the ladles, and the censers of pure gold; and the hinges of gold, *both* for the doors of the inner room (the Most Holy *Place*) *and* for the doors of the main hall of the temple.

⁵¹So all the work that King Solomon had done for the house of the LORD was finished; and Solomon brought in the things which his father David had dedicated: the silver and the gold and the furnishings. He put them in the treasuries of the house of the LORD.

CHAPTER 8 THE ARK AND THE TEMPLE. Now

Solomon assembled the elders of Israel and all the heads of the tribes, the chief fathers of the children of Israel, to King Solomon in Jerusalem, that they might bring up the ark of the covenant of the LORD from the City of David, which *is* Zion. ²Therefore all the men of Israel assembled with King Solomon at the feast in the month of Ethanim, which *is* the seventh month. ³So all the elders of Israel came, and the priests took up the ark. ⁴Then they brought up the ark of the LORD, the tabernacle of meeting, and all the holy furnishings that *were* in the tabernacle. The priests and the Levites brought them up. ⁵Also King Solomon, and all the congregation of Israel who were assembled with him, *were* with him before the ark, sacrificing sheep and oxen that could not be counted or numbered for multitude. ⁶Then the priests brought in the ark of the covenant of the LORD to its place, into the inner sanctuary of the temple, to the Most Holy *Place*, under the wings of the cherubim. ⁷For the cherubim spread *their* two wings over the place of the ark, and the cherubim overshadowed the ark and its poles. ⁸The poles extended so that the ends of the poles could be seen from the holy *place*, in front of the inner sanctuary; but they could not be seen from outside. And they are there to this day. ⁹Nothing *was* in the ark except the two tablets of stone which Moses put there at Horeb, when the LORD made *a covenant* with the children of Israel, when they came out of the land of Egypt.

¹⁰And it came to pass, when the priests came out of the holy *place*, that the cloud filled the house of the LORD, ¹¹so that the priests could not continue ministering because of the cloud; for the glory of the LORD filled the house of the LORD.

¹²Then Solomon spoke:

"The LORD said He would dwell in the dark cloud.
¹³   I have surely built You an exalted house,
      And a place for You to dwell in forever."

¹⁴Then the king turned around and blessed the whole assembly of Israel, while all the assembly of Israel was standing. ¹⁵And he said: "Blessed *be* the LORD God of Israel, who spoke with His mouth to my father David, and with His hand has fulfilled *it*, saying, ¹⁶'Since the day that I brought My people Israel out of Egypt, I have chosen no city from any tribe of Israel *in which* to build a house, that My name might be there; but I chose David to be over My people Israel.' ¹⁷Now it was in the heart of my father David to build a temple for the name of the LORD God of Israel. ¹⁸But the LORD said to my father

David, 'Whereas it was in your heart to build a temple for My name, you did well that it was in your heart. [19]Nevertheless you shall not build the temple, but your son who will come from your body, he shall build the temple for My name.' [20]So the LORD has fulfilled His word which He spoke; and I have filled the position of my father David, and sit on the throne of Israel, as the LORD promised; and I have built a temple for the name of the LORD God of Israel. [21]And there I have made a place for the ark, in which *is* the covenant of the LORD which He made with our fathers, when He brought them out of the land of Egypt."

[22]Then Solomon stood before the altar of the LORD in the presence of all the assembly of Israel, and spread out his hands toward heaven; [23]and he said: "LORD God of Israel, *there is* no God in heaven above or on earth below like You, who keep *Your* covenant and mercy with Your servants who walk before You with all their hearts. [24]You have kept what You promised Your servant David my father; You have both spoken with Your mouth and fulfilled *it* with Your hand, as *it is* this day. [25]Therefore, LORD God of Israel, now keep what You promised Your servant David my father, saying, 'You shall not fail to have a man sit before Me on the throne of Israel, only if your sons take heed to their way, that they walk before Me as you have walked before Me.' [26]And now I pray, O God of Israel, let Your word come true, which You have spoken to Your servant David my father.

[27]"But will God indeed dwell on the earth? Behold, heaven and the heaven of heavens cannot contain You. How much less this temple which I have built! [28]Yet regard the prayer of Your servant and his supplication, O LORD my God, and listen to the cry and the prayer which Your servant is praying before You today: [29]that Your eyes may be open toward this temple night and day, toward the place of which You said, 'My name shall be there,' that You may hear the prayer which Your servant makes toward this place. [30]And may You hear the supplication of Your servant and of Your people Israel, when they pray toward this place. Hear in heaven Your dwelling place; and when You hear, forgive.

[31]"When anyone sins against his neighbor, and is forced to take an oath, and comes *and* takes an oath before Your altar in this temple, [32]then hear in heaven, and act, and judge Your servants, condemning the wicked, bringing his way on his head, and justifying the righteous by giving him according to his righteousness.

[33]"When Your people Israel are defeated before an enemy because they have sinned against You, and when they turn back to You and confess Your name, and pray and make supplication to You in this temple, [34]then hear in heaven, and forgive the sin of Your people Israel, and bring them back to the land which You gave to their fathers.

[35]"When the heavens are shut up and there is no rain because they have sinned against You, when they pray toward this place and confess Your name, and turn from their sin because You afflict them, [36]then hear in heaven, and forgive the sin of Your servants, Your people Israel, that You may teach them the good way in which they should walk; and send rain on Your land which You have given to Your people as an inheritance.

[37]"When there is famine in the land, pestilence *or* blight *or* mildew, locusts *or* grasshoppers; when their enemy besieges them in the land of their cities; whatever plague or whatever sickness *there is;* [38]whatever prayer, whatever supplication is made by anyone, *or* by all Your people Israel, when each one knows the plague of his own heart, and spreads out his hands toward this temple: [39]then hear in heaven Your dwelling place, and forgive, and act, and give to everyone according to all his ways, whose heart You know (for You alone know the hearts of all the sons of men), [40]that they may fear You all the days that they live in the land which You gave to our fathers.

GOD'S HOME

8:27 Solomon declared that even the highest heavens couldn't contain God. Isn't it amazing that, though the heavens can't contain him, he is willing to live in the hearts of those who love him? The God of the universe has taken up residence in the lives of his people—he lives in us! What are you doing to welcome him home?

[41]"Moreover, concerning a foreigner, who *is* not of Your people Israel, but has come from a far country for Your name's sake [42](for they will hear of Your great name and Your strong hand and Your outstretched arm), when he comes and prays toward this temple, [43]hear in heaven Your dwelling place, and do according to all for which the foreigner calls to You, that all peoples of the earth may know Your name and fear You, as *do* Your people Israel, and that they may know that this temple which I have built is called by Your name.

[44]"When Your people go out to battle against their enemy, wherever You send them, and when they pray to the LORD toward the city which You have chosen and the temple which I have built for Your name, [45]then hear in heaven their prayer and their supplication, and maintain their cause.

[46]"When they sin against You (for *there is* no one who does not sin), and You become angry with them and deliver them to the enemy, and they take them captive to the land of the enemy, far or near; [47]yet when they come to themselves in the land where they were carried captive, and repent, and make supplication to You in the land of those who took them captive, saying, 'We have sinned and done wrong, we have committed wickedness'; [48]and *when* they return to You with all their heart and with all their soul in the land of their enemies who led them away captive, and pray to You toward their land which You gave to their fathers, the city which You have chosen and the temple which I have built for Your name: [49]then hear in heaven Your dwelling place their prayer and their supplication, and maintain their cause, [50]and forgive Your people who have sinned against You, and all their transgressions which they have transgressed against You; and grant them compassion before those who took them captive, that they may have compassion on them [51](for they *are* Your people and Your inheritance, whom You brought out of Egypt, out of the iron furnace), [52]that Your eyes may be open to the sup-

plication of Your servant and the supplication of Your people Israel, to listen to them whenever they call to You. ⁵³For You separated them from among all the peoples of the earth *to be* Your inheritance, as You spoke by Your servant Moses, when You brought our fathers out of Egypt, O Lord GOD."

⁵⁴And so it was, when Solomon had finished praying all this prayer and supplication to the LORD, that he arose from before the altar of the LORD, from kneeling on his knees with his hands spread up to heaven. ⁵⁵Then he stood and blessed all the assembly of Israel with a loud voice, saying: ⁵⁶"Blessed *be* the LORD, who has given rest to His people Israel, according to all that He promised. There has not failed one word of all His good promise, which He promised through His servant Moses. ⁵⁷May the LORD our God be with us, as He was with our fathers. May He not leave us nor forsake us, ⁵⁸that He may incline our hearts to Himself, to walk in all His ways, and to keep His commandments and His statutes and His judgments, which He commanded our fathers. ⁵⁹And may these words of mine, with which I have made supplication before the LORD, be near the LORD our God day and night, that He may maintain the cause of His servant and the cause of His people Israel, as each day may require, ⁶⁰that all the peoples of the earth may know that the LORD *is* God; *there is* no other. ⁶¹Let your heart therefore be loyal to the LORD our God, to walk in His statutes and keep His commandments, as at this day."

PRAYER PATTERNS

8:56-61 Solomon blessed the people and prayed for them. His prayer can be a pattern for our prayers. He had five basic requests: (1) for God's presence (8:57); (2) for the desire to do God's will in everything (8:58); (3) for help with daily needs (8:59); (4) for the desire and ability to obey God's laws and commandments (8:58,61); (5) for the spread of God's kingdom to the entire world (8:60). These prayer requests are just as appropriate today as they were in Solomon's time.

⁶²Then the king and all Israel with him offered sacrifices before the LORD. ⁶³And Solomon offered a sacrifice of peace offerings, which he offered to the LORD, twenty-two thousand bulls and one hundred and twenty thousand sheep. So the king and all the children of Israel dedicated the house of the LORD. ⁶⁴On the same day the king consecrated the middle of the court that *was* in front of the house of the LORD; for there he offered burnt offerings, grain offerings, and the fat of the peace offerings, because the bronze altar that *was* before the LORD *was* too small to receive the burnt offerings, the grain offerings, and the fat of the peace offerings.

⁶⁵At that time Solomon held a feast, and all Israel with him, a great assembly from the entrance of Hamath to the Brook of Egypt, before the LORD our God, seven days and seven *more* days—fourteen days. ⁶⁶On the eighth day he sent the people away; and they blessed the king, and went to their tents joyful and glad of heart for all the good that the LORD had done for His servant David, and for Israel His people.

CHAPTER **9** **GOD'S WARNING TO SOLOMON.** And it came to pass, when Solomon had finished building the house of the LORD and the king's house, and all Solomon's desire which he wanted to do, ²that the LORD appeared to Solomon the second time, as He had appeared to him at Gibeon. ³And the LORD said to him: "I have heard your prayer and your supplication that you have made before Me; I have consecrated this house which you have built to put My name there forever, and My eyes and My heart will be there perpetually. ⁴Now if you walk before Me as your father David walked, in integrity of heart and in uprightness, to do according to all that I have commanded you, *and* if you keep My statutes and My judgments, ⁵then I will establish the throne of your kingdom over Israel forever, as I promised David your father, saying, 'You shall not fail to have a man on the throne of Israel.' ⁶*But* if you or your sons at all turn from following Me, and do not keep My commandments *and* My statutes which I have set before you, but go and serve other gods and worship them, ⁷then I will cut off Israel from the land which I have given them; and this house which I have consecrated for My name I will cast out of My sight. Israel will be a proverb and a byword among all peoples. ⁸And *as for* this house, *which* is exalted, everyone who passes by it will be astonished and will hiss, and say, 'Why has the LORD done thus to this land and to this house?' ⁹Then they will answer, 'Because they forsook the LORD their God, who brought their fathers out of the land of Egypt, and have embraced other gods, and worshiped them and served them; therefore the LORD has brought all this calamity on them.'"

¹⁰Now it happened at the end of twenty years, when Solomon had built the two houses, the house of the LORD and the king's house ¹¹(Hiram the king of Tyre had supplied Solomon with cedar and cypress and gold, as much as he desired), *that* King Solomon then gave Hiram twenty cities in the land of Galilee. ¹²Then Hiram went from Tyre to see the cities which Solomon had given him, but they did not please him. ¹³So he said, "What *kind of* cities *are* these which you have given me, my brother?" And he called them the land of Cabul, as they are to this day. ¹⁴Then Hiram sent the king one hundred and twenty talents of gold.

¹⁵And this *is* the reason for the labor force which King Solomon raised: to build the house of the LORD, his own house, the Millo, the wall of Jerusalem, Hazor, Megiddo, and Gezer. ¹⁶(Pharaoh king of Egypt had gone up and taken Gezer and burned it with fire, had killed the Canaanites who dwelt in the city, and had given it *as* dowry to his daughter, Solomon's wife.) ¹⁷And Solomon built Gezer, Lower Beth Horon, ¹⁸Baalath, and Tadmor in the wilderness, in the land *of Judah*, ¹⁹all the storage cities

ROYAL FAMILIES

9:16 At this time, Israel and Egypt were the world powers in the East. During Solomon's reign the Egyptian king captured Gezer. To peace, Solomon married one of Pharaoh's daughters. Intermarriage among royal families was common, but it was not endorsed by God (Deuteronomy 17:17). Because the princess's dowry included the Gezer, which the Egyptian king had conquered earlier, it was returned Israel.

that Solomon had, cities for his chariots and cities for his cavalry, and whatever Solomon desired to build in Jerusalem, in Lebanon, and in all the land of his dominion.

²⁰All the people *who were* left of the Amorites, Hittites, Perizzites, Hivites, and Jebusites, who *were* not of the children of Israel— ²¹that is, their descendants who were left in the land after them, whom the children of Israel had not been able to destroy completely—from these Solomon raised forced labor, as it is to this day. ²²But of the children of Israel Solomon made no forced laborers, because they *were* men of war and his servants: his officers, his captains, commanders of his chariots, and his cavalry.

²³Others *were* chiefs of the officials who *were* over Solomon's work: five hundred and fifty, who ruled over the people who did the work.

²⁴But Pharaoh's daughter came up from the City of David to her house which *Solomon* had built for her. Then he built the Millo.

²⁵Now three times a year Solomon offered burnt offerings and peace offerings on the altar which he had built for the LORD, and he burned incense with them *on the altar* that *was* before the LORD. So he finished the temple.

²⁶King Solomon also built a fleet of ships at Ezion Geber, which *is* near Elath on the shore of the Red Sea, in the land of Edom. ²⁷Then Hiram sent his servants with the fleet, seamen who knew the sea, to work with the servants of Solomon. ²⁸And they went to Ophir, and acquired four hundred and twenty talents of gold from there, and brought *it* to King Solomon.

CHAPTER **10** THE QUEEN OF SHEBA VISITS. Now when the queen of Sheba heard of the fame of Solomon concerning the name of the LORD, she came to test him with hard questions. ²She came to Jerusalem with a very great retinue, with camels that bore spices, very much gold, and precious stones; and when she came to Solomon, she spoke with him about all that was in her heart. ³So Solomon answered all her questions; there was nothing so difficult for the king that he could not explain *it* to her. ⁴And when the queen of Sheba had seen all the wisdom of Solomon, the house that he had built, ⁵the food on his table, the seating of his servants, the service of his waiters and their apparel, his cupbearers, and his entryway by which he went up to the house of the LORD, there was no more spirit in her. ⁶Then she said to the king: "It was a true report which I heard in my own land about your words and your wisdom. ⁷However I did not believe the words until I came and saw with my own eyes; and indeed the half was not told me. Your wisdom and prosperity exceed the fame of which I heard. ⁸Happy *are* your men and happy *are* these your servants, who stand continually before you *and* hear your wisdom! ⁹Blessed be the LORD your God, who delighted in you, setting you on the throne of Israel! Because the LORD has loved Israel forever, therefore He made you king, to do justice and righteousness."

¹⁰Then she gave the king one hundred and twenty talents of gold, spices in great quantity, and precious stones. There never again came such abundance of spices as the queen of Sheba gave to King Solomon. ¹¹Also, the ships of Hiram, which brought gold from Ophir, brought great *quantities* of almug wood and precious stones from Ophir. ¹²And the king made steps of the almug wood for the house of the LORD and for the king's house, also harps and stringed instruments for singers. There never again came such almug wood, nor has the like been seen to this day.

◣◣◣◣◣◣◣◣ SEEDS OF PEACE

10:8 Because of Solomon's wisdom, the people were happy and the palace servants content. Wisdom's quality is shown by how well it works. In James 3:17 we learn that wisdom helps plant the seeds of peace. Are you seeking the kind of wisdom that establishes peace in your relationships?

¹³Now King Solomon gave the queen of Sheba all she desired, whatever she asked, besides what Solomon had given her according to the royal generosity. So she turned and went to her own country, she and her servants.

¹⁴The weight of gold that came to Solomon yearly was six hundred and sixty-six talents of gold, ¹⁵besides *that* from the traveling merchants, from the income of traders, from all the kings of Arabia, and from the governors of the country.

¹⁶And King Solomon made two hundred large shields *of* hammered gold; six hundred *shekels* of gold went into each shield. ¹⁷He also *made* three hundred shields *of* hammered gold; three minas of gold went into each shield. The king put them in the House of the Forest of Lebanon.

¹⁸Moreover the king made a great throne of ivory, and overlaid it with pure gold. ¹⁹The throne had six steps, and the top of the throne *was* round at the back; *there were* armrests on either side of the place of the seat, and two lions stood beside the armrests. ²⁰Twelve lions stood there, one on each side of the six steps; nothing like *this* had been made for any *other* kingdom.

²¹All King Solomon's drinking vessels *were* gold, and all the vessels of the House of the Forest of Lebanon *were* pure gold. Not *one was* silver, for this was accounted as nothing in the days of Solomon. ²²For the king had merchant ships at sea with the fleet of Hiram. Once every three years the merchant ships came bringing gold, silver, ivory, apes, and monkeys. ²³So King Solomon surpassed all the kings of the earth in riches and wisdom.

²⁴Now all the earth sought the presence of Solomon to hear his wisdom, which God had put in his heart. ²⁵Each man brought his present: articles of silver and gold, garments, armor, spices, horses, and mules, at a set rate year by year.

²⁶And Solomon gathered chariots and horsemen; he had one thousand four hundred chariots and twelve thousand horsemen, whom he stationed in the chariot cities and with the king at Jerusalem. ²⁷The king made silver *as common* in Jerusalem as stones, and he made cedar trees as abundant as the sycamores which *are* in the lowland.

²⁸Also Solomon had horses imported from Egypt and Keveh; the king's merchants bought them in Keveh at the

current price. [29]Now a chariot that was imported from Egypt cost six hundred *shekels* of silver, and a horse one hundred and fifty; and thus, through their agents, they exported *them* to all the kings of the Hittites and the kings of Syria.

CHAPTER 11 SOLOMON TURNS FROM GOD.

But King Solomon loved many foreign women, as well as the daughter of Pharaoh: women of the Moabites, Ammonites, Edomites, Sidonians, *and* Hittites— [2]from the nations of whom the LORD had said to the children of Israel, "You shall not intermarry with them, nor they with you. Surely they will turn away your hearts after their gods." Solomon clung to these in love. [3]And he had seven hun-

---

DATING

Watch what happened when Lizza, a 15-year-old Christian, started dating Matt, an older non-Christian.

February—Lizza brought Matt to some youth group meetings and activities. He said her church friends were "OK," but he wanted her to do things with his friends, too.

March—Lizza asked Matt to the spring retreat. He snapped, "Lizza! If you want to date St. Peter, go for it. But that's not for me, OK?"

April—Lizza began going to parties and heavy metal concerts with Matt and his pals.

May—Lizza's church/youth group attendance dropped drastically. She quit youth choir.

June—Lizza had her first cigarette, beer, and sexual experience.

July—Lizza and her parents fought almost all month because she wouldn't "break up with that bum!"

August—Lizza has now gone 4 1/2 months without reading her Bible (she isn't even sure where it is).

"Wait a minute!" you say. "Do Christian/non-Christian relationships always turn out bad? Haven't Christians fallen in love with non-Christians and led them to the Lord?" Yes. But that is rare. It's a sad fact that healthy Christian/non-Christian dating situations are the exception. First Kings 11:1-13 shows how you can get burned through close relationships with those who don't share your spiritual beliefs and values.

---

dred wives, princesses, and three hundred concubines; and his wives turned away his heart. [4]For it was so, when Solomon was old, that his wives turned his heart after other gods; and his heart was not loyal to the LORD his God, as *was* the heart of his father David. [5]For Solomon went after Ashtoreth the goddess of the Sidonians, and after Milcom the abomination of the Ammonites. [6]Solomon did evil in the sight of the LORD, and did not fully follow the LORD, as *did* his father David. [7]Then Solomon built a high place for Chemosh the abomination of Moab, on the hill that *is* east of Jerusalem, and for Molech the abomination of the people of Ammon. [8]And he did likewise for all his foreign wives, who burned incense and sacrificed to their gods.

[9]So the LORD became angry with Solomon, because his heart had turned from the LORD God of Israel, who had appeared to him twice, [10]and had commanded him

concerning this thing, that he should not go after other gods; but he did not keep what the LORD had commanded. [11]Therefore the LORD said to Solomon, "Because you have done this, and have not kept My covenant and My statutes, which I have commanded you, I will surely tear the kingdom away from you and give it to your servant. [12]Nevertheless I will not do it in your days, for the sake of your father David; I will tear it out of the hand of your son. [13]However I will not tear away the whole kingdom; I will give one tribe to your son for the sake of my servant David, and for the sake of Jerusalem which I have chosen."

[14]Now the LORD raised up an adversary against Solomon, Hadad the Edomite; he *was* a descendant of the king in Edom. [15]For it happened, when David was in Edom, and Joab the commander of the army had gone up to bury the slain, after he had killed every male in Edom [16](because for six months Joab remained there with all Israel, until he had cut down every male in Edom), [17]that Hadad fled to go to Egypt, he and certain Edomites of his father's servants with him. Hadad *was* still a little child. [18]Then they arose from Midian and came to Paran; and they took men with them from Paran and came to Egypt, to Pharaoh king of Egypt, who gave him a house, apportioned food for him, and gave him land. [19]And Hadad found great favor in the sight of Pharaoh, so that he gave him as wife the sister of his own wife, that is, the sister of Queen Tahpenes. [20]Then the sister of Tahpenes bore him Genubath his son, whom Tahpenes weaned in Pharaoh's house. And Genubath was in Pharaoh's household among the sons of Pharaoh.

[21]So when Hadad heard in Egypt that David rested with his fathers, and that Joab the commander of the army was dead, Hadad said to Pharaoh, "Let me depart, that I may go to my own country."

[22]Then Pharaoh said to him, "But what have you lacked with me, that suddenly you seek to go to your own country?"

So he answered, "Nothing, but do let me go anyway."

[23]And God raised up *another* adversary against him Rezon the son of Eliadah, who had fled from his lord, Hadadezer king of Zobah. [24]So he gathered men to him and became captain over a band *of raiders*, when David killed those *of Zobah*. And they went to Damascus and dwelt there, and reigned in Damascus. [25]He was an adversary of Israel all the days of Solomon (besides the trouble that Hadad *caused*); and he abhorred Israel, and reigned over Syria.

[26]Then Solomon's servant, Jeroboam the son of Nebat

OBEDIENCE

11:2 Although Solomon had clear instructions from God *not* to m women from foreign nations, he chose to disregard God's comma married not one, but many heathen wives, who subsequently led away from God. God knows our human strengths and weaknesse his commands are always for our good. Some people ignore God' commands, but there are inevitable negative consequences result such action. It is not enough to know God's Word or even to belie must follow it and apply it to life's daily activities and decisions. T God's commands seriously. Like Solomon, the wisest man who ev we are not as strong as we may think.

an Ephraimite from Zereda, whose mother's name *was* Zeruah, a widow, also rebelled against the king.

²⁷And this *is* what caused him to rebel against the king: Solomon had built the Millo *and* repaired the damages to the City of David his father. ²⁸The man Jeroboam *was* a mighty man of valor; and Solomon, seeing that the young man was industrious, made him the officer over all the labor force of the house of Joseph.

²⁹Now it happened at that time, when Jeroboam went out of Jerusalem, that the prophet Ahijah the Shilonite met him on the way; and he had clothed himself with a new garment, and the two *were* alone in the field. ³⁰Then Ahijah took hold of the new garment that *was* on him, and tore it *into* twelve pieces. ³¹And he said to Jeroboam, "Take for yourself ten pieces, for thus says the LORD, the God of Israel: 'Behold, I will tear the kingdom out of the hand of Solomon and will give ten tribes to you ³²(but he shall have one tribe for the sake of My servant David, and for the sake of Jerusalem, the city which I have chosen out of all the tribes of Israel), ³³because they have forsaken Me, and worshiped Ashtoreth the goddess of the Sidonians, Chemosh the god of the Moabites, and Milcom the god of the people of Ammon, and have not walked in My ways to do *what is* right in My eyes and *keep* My statutes and My judgments, as *did* his father David. ³⁴However I will not take the whole kingdom out of his hand, because I have made him ruler all the days of his life for the sake of My servant David, whom I chose because he kept My commandments and My statutes. ³⁵But I will take the kingdom out of his son's hand and give it to you—ten tribes. ³⁶And to his son I will give one tribe, that My servant David may always have a lamp before Me in Jerusalem, the city which I have chosen for Myself, to put My name there. ³⁷So I will take you, and you shall reign over all your heart desires, and you shall be king over Israel. ³⁸Then it shall be, if you heed all that I command you, walk in My ways, and do *what is* right in My sight, to keep My statutes and My commandments, as My servant David did, then I will be with you and build for you an enduring house, as I built for David, and will give Israel to you. ³⁹And I will afflict the descendants of David because of this, but not forever.'"

⁴⁰Solomon therefore sought to kill Jeroboam. But Jeroboam arose and fled to Egypt, to Shishak king of Egypt, and was in Egypt until the death of Solomon.

⁴¹Now the rest of the acts of Solomon, all that he did, and his wisdom, *are* they not written in the book of the acts of Solomon? ⁴²And the period that Solomon reigned in Jerusalem over all Israel *was* forty years. ⁴³Then Solomon rested with his fathers, and was buried in the City of David his father. And Rehoboam his son reigned in his place.

CHAPTER 12 THE KINGDOM SPLITS IN TWO. And

Rehoboam went to Shechem, for all Israel had gone to Shechem to make him king. ²So it happened, when Jeroboam the son of Nebat heard *it* (he was still in Egypt, for he had fled from the presence of King Solomon and had been dwelling in Egypt), ³that they sent and called him. Then Jeroboam and the whole assembly of Israel came

and spoke to Rehoboam, saying, ⁴"Your father made our yoke heavy; now therefore, lighten the burdensome service of your father, and his heavy yoke which he put on us, and we will serve you."

⁵So he said to them, "Depart *for* three days, then come back to me." And the people departed.

PRESSURE

11:4 Solomon handled great pressures in running the government, but he could not handle the pressures from his wives who wanted him to worship their gods. In marriage and other close friendships, it is difficult to resist pressure to compromise. Our love leads us to identify with the desires of those we care about.

Faced with such pressure, Solomon at first *resisted* it, maintaining pure faith. Then he *tolerated* a more widespread practice of idolatry. Finally he himself became involved in idolatrous worship; he *rationalized* away the potential danger to himself and the kingdom. It is because we naturally wish to identify with those we love that God told Solomon (and us) not to marry those who do not share our commitment to him.

⁶Then King Rehoboam consulted the elders who stood before his father Solomon while he still lived, and he said, "How do you advise *me* to answer these people?"

⁷And they spoke to him, saying, "If you will be a servant to these people today, and serve them, and answer them, and speak good words to them, then they will be your servants forever."

GOOD ADVICE

12:6-8 Rehoboam asked for advice, but he didn't carefully evaluate that advice. If he had, he would have realized that the advice offered by the older men was wiser than that of his peers. To evaluate advice, ask if it is realistic, workable, and consistent with the Bible. Determine if the results of following the advice will be fair, make improvements, and give a positive solution or direction. Seek counsel from those more experienced and wiser. Advice is helpful only if we evaluate it with God's standards in mind.

⁸But he rejected the advice which the elders had given him, and consulted the young men who had grown up with him, who stood before him. ⁹And he said to them, "What advice do you give? How should we answer this people who have spoken to me, saying, 'Lighten the yoke which your father put on us'?"

¹⁰Then the young men who had grown up with him spoke to him, saying, "Thus you should speak to this people who have spoken to you, saying, 'Your father made our yoke heavy, but you make *it* lighter on us'—thus you shall say to them: 'My little *finger* shall be thicker than my father's waist! ¹¹And now, whereas my father put a heavy yoke on you, I will add to your yoke; my father chastised you with whips, but I will chastise you with scourges!'"

¹²So Jeroboam and all the people came to Rehoboam the third day, as the king had directed, saying, "Come back to me the third day." ¹³Then the king answered the people roughly, and rejected the advice which the elders had given him; ¹⁴and he spoke to them according to the advice of the young men, saying, "My father made your

yoke heavy, but I will add to your yoke; my father chastised you with whips, but I will chastise you with scourges!" [15]So the king did not listen to the people; for the turn *of events* was from the LORD, that He might fulfill His word, which the LORD had spoken by Ahijah the Shilonite to Jeroboam the son of Nebat.

[16]Now when all Israel saw that the king did not listen to them, the people answered the king, saying:

"What share have we in David?
We have no inheritance in the son of Jesse.
To your tents, O Israel!
Now, see to your own house, O David!"

So Israel departed to their tents. [17]But Rehoboam reigned over the children of Israel who dwelt in the cities of Judah.

◀▬▬▬▬▬DO RIGHT

12:28 All Jewish men were required to travel to the temple three times each year (Deuteronomy 16:16), but Jeroboam set up his own worship centers and told his people it was too much trouble to travel all the way to Jerusalem. Those who obeyed Jeroboam were disobeying God. Some ideas, although practical, may include suggestions that lead you away from God. Don't let anyone talk you out of doing what is right by telling you that your actions are not worth the effort. Do what God wants no matter what the cost in time, energy, reputation, or resources.

[18]Then King Rehoboam sent Adoram, who *was* in charge of the revenue; but all Israel stoned him with stones, and he died. Therefore King Rehoboam mounted his chariot in haste to flee to Jerusalem. [19]So Israel has been in rebellion against the house of David to this day.

[20]Now it came to pass when all Israel heard that Jeroboam had come back, they sent for him and called him to the congregation, and made him king over all Israel. There was none who followed the house of David, but the tribe of Judah only.

[21]And when Rehoboam came to Jerusalem, he assembled all the house of Judah with the tribe of Benjamin, one hundred and eighty thousand chosen *men* who were warriors, to fight against the house of Israel, that he might restore the kingdom to Rehoboam the son of Solomon. [22]But the word of God came to Shemaiah the man of God, saying, [23]"Speak to Rehoboam the son of Solomon, king of Judah, to all the house of Judah and Benjamin, and to the rest of the people, saying, [24]'Thus says the LORD: "You shall not go up nor fight against your brethren the children of Israel. Let every man return to his house, for this thing is from Me." ' " Therefore they obeyed the word of the LORD, and turned back, according to the word of the LORD.

[25]Then Jeroboam built Shechem in the mountains of Ephraim, and dwelt there. Also he went out from there and built Penuel. [26]And Jeroboam said in his heart, "Now the kingdom may return to the house of David: [27]If these people go up to offer sacrifices in the house of the LORD at Jerusalem, then the heart of this people will turn back to their lord, Rehoboam king of Judah, and they will kill me and go back to Rehoboam king of Judah."

[28]Therefore the king asked advice, made two calves of gold, and said to the people, "It is too much for you to go up to Jerusalem. Here are your gods, O Israel, which brought you up from the land of Egypt!" [29]And he set up one in Bethel, and the other he put in Dan. [30]Now this thing became a sin, for the people went *to worship* before the one as far as Dan. [31]He made shrines on the high places, and made priests from every class of people, who were not of the sons of Levi.

[32]Jeroboam ordained a feast on the fifteenth day of the eighth month, like the feast that *was* in Judah, and offered sacrifices on the altar. So he did at Bethel, sacrificing to the calves that he had made. And at Bethel he installed the priests of the high places which he had made. [33]So he made offerings on the altar which he had made at Bethel on the fifteenth day of the eighth month, in the month which he had devised in his own heart. And he ordained a feast for the children of Israel, and offered sacrifices on the altar and burned incense.

CHAPTER **13** JEROBOAM MAKES TWO GOLDEN

CALVES. And behold, a man of God went from Judah to Bethel by the word of the LORD, and Jeroboam stood by the altar to burn incense. [2]Then he cried out against the altar by the word of the LORD, and said, "O altar, altar! Thus says the LORD: 'Behold, a child, Josiah by name, shall be born to the house of David; and on you he shall sacrifice the priests of the high places who burn incense on you, and men's bones shall be burned on you.' " [3]And he gave a sign the same day, saying, "This *is* the sign which the LORD has spoken: Surely the altar shall split apart, and the ashes on it shall be poured out."

[4]So it came to pass when King Jeroboam heard the saying of the man of God, who cried out against the altar in Bethel, that he stretched out his hand from the altar, saying, "Arrest him!" Then his hand, which he stretched out toward him, withered, so that he could not pull it back to himself. [5]The altar also was split apart, and the ashes poured out from the altar, according to the sign which the man of God had given by the word of the LORD. [6]Then the king answered and said to the man of God, "Please entreat the favor of the LORD your God, and pray for me, that my hand may be restored to me."

So the man of God entreated the LORD, and the king's hand was restored to him, and became as before. [7]Then the king said to the man of God, "Come home with me and refresh yourself, and I will give you a reward."

[8]But the man of God said to the king, "If you were to give me half your house, I would not go in with you; nor would I eat bread nor drink water in this place. [9]For so it was commanded me by the word of the LORD, saying 'You shall not eat bread, nor drink water, nor return by the same way you came.' " [10]So he went another way and did not return by the way he came to Bethel.

[11]Now an old prophet dwelt in Bethel, and his sons came and told him all the works that the man of God had done that day in Bethel; they also told their father the words which he had spoken to the king. [12]And their father said to them, "Which way did he go?" For his sons had seen which way the man of God went who came from Judah. [13]Then he said to his sons, "Saddle the donkey for

me." So they saddled the donkey for him; and he rode on it, [14]and went after the man of God, and found him sitting under an oak. Then he said to him, "*Are* you the man of God who came from Judah?"

And he said, "I *am*."

[15]Then he said to him, "Come home with me and eat bread."

[16]And he said, "I cannot return with you nor go in with you; neither can I eat bread nor drink water with you in this place. [17]For I have been told by the word of the LORD, 'You shall not eat bread nor drink water there, nor return by going the way you came.'"

[18]He said to him, "I too *am* a prophet as you *are*, and an angel spoke to me by the word of the LORD, saying, 'Bring him back with you to your house, that he may eat bread and drink water.'" (He was lying to him.)

[19]So he went back with him, and ate bread in his house, and drank water.

[20]Now it happened, as they sat at the table, that the word of the LORD came to the prophet who had brought him back; [21]and he cried out to the man of God who came from Judah, saying, "Thus says the LORD: 'Because you have disobeyed the word of the LORD, and have not kept the commandment which the LORD your God commanded you, [22]but you came back, ate bread, and drank water in the place of which *the LORD* said to you, "Eat no bread and drink no water," your corpse shall not come to the tomb of your fathers.'"

[23]So it was, after he had eaten bread and after he had drunk, that he saddled the donkey for him, the prophet whom he had brought back. [24]When he was gone, a lion met him on the road and killed him. And his corpse was thrown on the road, and the donkey stood by it. The lion also stood by the corpse. [25]And there, men passed by and saw the corpse thrown on the road, and the lion standing by the corpse. Then they went and told *it* in the city where the old prophet dwelt.

[26]Now when the prophet who had brought him back from the way heard *it*, he said, "It *is* the man of God who was disobedient to the word of the LORD. Therefore the LORD has delivered him to the lion, which has torn him and killed him, according to the word of the LORD which He spoke to him." [27]And he spoke to his sons, saying, "Saddle the donkey for me." So they saddled *it*. [28]Then he went and found his corpse thrown on the road, and the donkey and the lion standing by the corpse. The lion had not eaten the corpse nor torn the donkey. [29]And the prophet took up the corpse of the man of God, laid it on the donkey, and brought it back. So the old prophet came to the city to mourn, and to bury him. [30]Then he laid the corpse in his own tomb; and they mourned over him, saying, "Alas, my brother!" [31]So it was, after he had buried him, that he spoke to his sons, saying, "When I am dead, then bury me in the tomb where the man of God *is* buried; lay my bones beside his bones. [32]For the saying which he cried out by the word of the LORD against the altar in Bethel, and against all the shrines on the high places which *are* in the cities of Samaria, will surely come to pass."

[33]After this event Jeroboam did not turn from his evil way, but again he made priests from every class of people for the high places; whoever wished, he consecrated him, and he became *one* of the priests of the high places. [34]And this thing was the sin of the house of Jeroboam, so as to exterminate and destroy *it* from the face of the earth.

CHAPTER **14** JEROBOAM'S SON DIES.

At that time Abijah the son of Jeroboam became sick. [2]And Jeroboam said to his wife, "Please arise, and disguise yourself, that they may not recognize you as the wife of Jeroboam, and go to Shiloh. Indeed, Ahijah the prophet *is* there, who told me that I *would be* king over this people. [3]Also take with you ten loaves, *some* cakes, and a jar of honey, and go to him; he will tell you what will become of the child." [4]And Jeroboam's wife did so; she arose and went to Shiloh, and came to the house of Ahijah. But Ahijah could not see, for his eyes were glazed by reason of his age.

━━━━━ HEARSAY

13:7-32 This prophet had been given strict orders from God not to eat or drink anything while on his mission (13:9). He died because he listened to a man who claimed to have a message from God, rather than to God himself. The prophet should have followed God's word instead of hearsay. Trust what Scripture says rather than what someone claims is true. And disregard what others claim to be messages from God if their words contradict the Bible.

[5]Now the LORD had said to Ahijah, "Here is the wife of Jeroboam, coming to ask you something about her son, for he *is* sick. Thus and thus you shall say to her; for it will be, when she comes in, that she will pretend *to be* another *woman*."

[6]And so it was, when Ahijah heard the sound of her footsteps as she came through the door, he said, "Come in, wife of Jeroboam. Why do you pretend *to be* another *person*? For I *have been* sent to you *with* bad *news*. [7]Go, tell Jeroboam, 'Thus says the LORD God of Israel: "Because I exalted you from among the people, and made you ruler over My people Israel, [8]and tore the kingdom away from the house of David, and gave it to you; and *yet* you have not been as My servant David, who kept My commandments and who followed Me with all his heart, to do only *what was* right in My eyes; [9]but you have done more evil than all who were before you, for you have gone and made for yourself other gods and molded images to provoke Me to anger, and have cast Me behind your back— [10]therefore behold! I will bring disaster on the house of Jeroboam, and will cut off from Jeroboam every male in Israel, bond and free; I will take away the remnant of the house of Jeroboam, as one takes away refuse until it is all gone. [11]The dogs shall eat whoever belongs to Jeroboam and dies in the city, and the birds of the air shall eat whoever dies in the field; for the LORD has spoken!" ' [12]Arise therefore, go to your own house. When your feet enter the city, the child shall die. [13]And all Israel shall mourn for him and bury him, for he is the only one of Jeroboam who shall come to the grave, because in him there is found something good toward the LORD God of Israel in the house of Jeroboam.

[14]"Moreover the LORD will raise up for Himself a king

14:25 Just five years after Solomon died, the temple and palace were ransacked by foreign invaders. How quickly the glory, power, and money disappeared! When the people became spiritually corrupt and immoral (14:24), it was just a short time until they lost everything. Their possessions and wealth had become more important to them than God. When we remove God from our life, everything else becomes useless, no matter how valuable it seems.

over Israel who shall cut off the house of Jeroboam; this is the day. What? Even now! [15]For the LORD will strike Israel, as a reed is shaken in the water. He will uproot Israel from this good land which He gave to their fathers, and will scatter them beyond the River, because they have made their wooden images, provoking the LORD to anger. [16]And He will give Israel up because of the sins of Jeroboam, who sinned and who made Israel sin."

[17]Then Jeroboam's wife arose and departed, and came to Tirzah. When she came to the threshold of the house, the child died. [18]And they buried him; and all Israel mourned for him, according to the word of the LORD which He spoke through His servant Ahijah the prophet.

[19]Now the rest of the acts of Jeroboam, how he made war and how he reigned, indeed they *are* written in the book of the chronicles of the kings of Israel. [20]The period that Jeroboam reigned *was* twenty-two years. So he rested with his fathers. Then Nadab his son reigned in his place.

[21]And Rehoboam the son of Solomon reigned in Judah. Rehoboam *was* forty-one years old when he became king. He reigned seventeen years in Jerusalem, the city which the LORD had chosen out of all the tribes of Israel, to put His name there. His mother's name *was* Naamah, an Ammonitess. [22]Now Judah did evil in the sight of the LORD, and they provoked Him to jealousy with their sins which they committed, more than all that their fathers had done. [23]For they also built for themselves high places, *sacred* pillars, and wooden images on every high hill and under every green tree. [24]And there were also perverted persons in the land. They did according to all the abominations of the nations which the LORD had cast out before the children of Israel.

The appeal of idols	POWER	PLEASURE	PASSION	PRAISE AND POPULARITY
	The people wanted freedom from the authority of both God and the priests. They wanted their religion to fit their life-style, not their life-style to fit their religion.	Idol worship exalted sensuality without responsibility or guilt. People acted out the vicious and sensuous personalities of the gods they worshiped, thus gaining approval for their degraded lives.	Mankind was reduced to little more than animals. The people did not have to be viewed as unique individuals, but could be exploited sexually, politically, and economically.	The high and holy nature of God was replaced by gods who were more a reflection of human nature, thus more culturally suitable to the people. These gods no longer required sacrifice, just a token of appeasement.
Modern parallel	People do not want to answer to a greater authority. Instead of having power over others, God wants us to have the Holy Spirit's power to help others.	People deify pleasure, seeking it at the expense of everything else. Instead of seeking pleasure that leads to long-range disaster, God calls us to seek the kind of pleasure that leads to long-range rewards.	Like animals, people let physical drives and passions rule them. Instead of seeking passion that exploits others, God calls us to redirect our passions to areas that build others up.	Sacrifice is seen as a self-inflicted punishment, making no sense. Success is to be sought at all costs. Instead of seeking praise for ourselves, God calls us to praise him and those who honor him.

THE APPEAL OF IDOLS On the surface, the lives of the kings don't make sense. How could they run to idolatry so fast when they had God's Word (at least some of it), the prophets, and the example of David? Above are some of the reasons for the enticement of idols. As societies change and evolve, they often throw out norms and values no longer considered necessary or acceptable. Believers must be careful not to follow society's example when it discards God's Word. When society does that, only godlessness and evil remain.

²⁵It happened in the fifth year of King Rehoboam *that* Shishak king of Egypt came up against Jerusalem. ²⁶And he took away the treasures of the house of the LORD and the treasures of the king's house; he took away everything. He also took away all the gold shields which Solomon had made. ²⁷Then King Rehoboam made bronze shields in their place, and committed *them* to the hands of the captains of the guard, who guarded the doorway of the king's house. ²⁸And whenever the king entered the house of the LORD, the guards carried them, then brought them back into the guardroom.

²⁹Now the rest of the acts of Rehoboam, and all that he did, *are* they not written in the book of the chronicles of the kings of Judah? ³⁰And there was war between Rehoboam and Jeroboam all *their* days. ³¹So Rehoboam rested with his fathers, and was buried with his fathers in the City of David. His mother's name *was* Naamah, an Ammonitess. Then Abijam his son reigned in his place.

CHAPTER **15** ABIJAM RULES JUDAH. In the eighteenth year of King Jeroboam the son of Nebat, Abijam became king over Judah. ²He reigned three years in Jerusalem. His mother's name *was* Maachah the granddaughter of Abishalom. ³And he walked in all the sins of his father, which he had done before him; his heart was not loyal to the LORD his God, as was the heart of his father David. ⁴Nevertheless for David's sake the LORD his God gave him a lamp in Jerusalem, by setting up his son after him and by establishing Jerusalem; ⁵because David did *what was* right in the eyes of the LORD, and had not turned aside from anything that He commanded him all the days of his life, except in the matter of Uriah the Hittite. ⁶And there was war between Rehoboam and Jeroboam all the days of his life. ⁷Now the rest of the acts of Abijam, and all that he did, *are* they not written in the book of the chronicles of the kings of Judah? And there was war between Abijam and Jeroboam.

⁸So Abijam rested with his fathers, and they buried him in the City of David. Then Asa his son reigned in his place.

⁹In the twentieth year of Jeroboam king of Israel, Asa became king over Judah. ¹⁰And he reigned forty-one years in Jerusalem. His grandmother's name *was* Maachah the granddaughter of Abishalom. ¹¹Asa did *what was* right in the eyes of the LORD, as *did* his father David. ¹²And he banished the perverted persons from the land, and removed all the idols that his fathers had made. ¹³Also he removed Maachah his grandmother from *being* queen mother, because she had made an obscene image of Asherah. And Asa cut down her obscene image and burned *it* by the Brook Kidron. ¹⁴But the high places were not removed. Nevertheless Asa's heart was loyal to the LORD all his days. ¹⁵He also brought into the house of the LORD the things which his father had dedicated, and the things which he himself had dedicated: silver and gold and utensils.

¹⁶Now there was war between Asa and Baasha king of Israel all their days. ¹⁷And Baasha king of Israel came up against Judah, and built Ramah, that he might let none go out or come in to Asa king of Judah. ¹⁸Then Asa took all the silver and gold *that was* left in the treasuries of the house of the LORD and the treasuries of the king's house, and delivered them into the hand of his servants. And King Asa sent them to Ben-Hadad the son of Tabrimmon, the son of Hezion, king of Syria, who dwelt in Damascus, saying, ¹⁹"*Let there be* a treaty between you and me, as there was between my father and your father. See, I have sent you a present of silver and gold. Come and break your treaty with Baasha king of Israel, so that he will withdraw from me."

²⁰So Ben-Hadad heeded King Asa, and sent the captains of his armies against the cities of Israel. He attacked Ijon, Dan, Abel Beth Maachah, and all Chinneroth, with all the land of Naphtali. ²¹Now it happened, when Baasha heard *it*, that he stopped building Ramah, and remained in Tirzah.

²²Then King Asa made a proclamation throughout all Judah; none *was* exempted. And they took away the stones and timber of Ramah, which Baasha had used for building; and with them King Asa built Geba of Benjamin, and Mizpah.

²³The rest of all the acts of Asa, all his might, all that he did, and the cities which he built, *are* they not written in the book of the chronicles of the kings of Judah? But in the time of his old age he was diseased in his feet. ²⁴So Asa rested with his fathers, and was buried with his fathers in the City of David his father. Then Jehoshaphat his son reigned in his place.

²⁵Now Nadab the son of Jeroboam became king over Israel in the second year of Asa king of Judah, and he reigned over Israel two years. ²⁶And he did evil in the sight of the LORD, and walked in the way of his father, and in his sin by which he had made Israel sin.

²⁷Then Baasha the son of Ahijah, of the house of Issachar, conspired against him. And Baasha killed him at Gibbethon, which *belonged* to the Philistines, while Nadab and all Israel laid siege to Gibbethon. ²⁸Baasha killed him in the third year of Asa king of Judah, and reigned in his place. ²⁹And it was so, when he became king, *that* he killed all the house of Jeroboam. He did not leave to Jeroboam anyone that breathed, until he had destroyed him, according to the word of the LORD which He had spoken by His servant Ahijah the Shilonite, ³⁰because of the sins of Jeroboam, which he had sinned and by which he had made Israel sin, because of his provocation with which he had provoked the LORD God of Israel to anger.

³¹Now the rest of the acts of Nadab, and all that he did, *are* they not written in the book of the chronicles of the kings of Israel? ³²And there was war between Asa and Baasha king of Israel all their days.

³³In the third year of Asa king of Judah, Baasha the son of Ahijah became king over all Israel in Tirzah, and *reigned* twenty-four years. ³⁴He did evil in the sight of the LORD, and walked in the way of Jeroboam, and in his sin by which he had made Israel sin.

CHAPTER **16** BAASHA RULES ISRAEL. Then the word of the LORD came to Jehu the son of Hanani, against Baasha, saying: ²"Inasmuch as I lifted you out of the dust and made you ruler over My people Israel, and you have walked in the way of Jeroboam, and have made My people Israel sin, to provoke Me to anger with their sins, ³surely I will take away the posterity of Baasha and the posterity of his house, and I will make your house like the house of Jeroboam the son of Nebat. ⁴The dogs shall eat whoever belongs to Baasha and dies in the city, and the birds of the air shall eat whoever dies in the fields."

MISTAKES

16:1-7 God destroyed Jeroboam's descendants for their flagrant sins, and yet King Baasha repeated the same mistakes. He did not learn from the example of those who went before him; he did not stop to think that his sin would be punished. Make sure you learn the lessons from your own past, the lives of others, and the lives of those whose stories are told in the Bible. Don't repeat their mistakes.

⁵Now the rest of the acts of Baasha, what he did, and his might, *are* they not written in the book of the chronicles of the kings of Israel? ⁶So Baasha rested with his fathers and was buried in Tirzah. Then Elah his son reigned in his place.

⁷And also the word of the LORD came by the prophet Jehu the son of Hanani against Baasha and his house, because of all the evil that he did in the sight of the LORD in provoking Him to anger with the work of his hands, in being like the house of Jeroboam, and because he killed them.

⁸In the twenty-sixth year of Asa king of Judah, Elah the son of Baasha became king over Israel, *and reigned* two years in Tirzah. ⁹Now his servant Zimri, commander of half *his* chariots, conspired against him as he was in Tirzah drinking himself drunk in the house of Arza, steward of *his* house in Tirzah. ¹⁰And Zimri went in and struck him and killed him in the twenty-seventh year of Asa king of Judah, and reigned in his place.

¹¹Then it came to pass, when he began to reign, as soon as he was seated on his throne, *that* he killed all the household of Baasha; he did not leave him one male, neither of his relatives nor of his friends. ¹²Thus Zimri destroyed all the household of Baasha, according to the word of the LORD, which He spoke against Baasha by Jehu the prophet, ¹³for all the sins of Baasha and the sins of Elah his son, by which they had sinned and by which they had made Israel sin, in provoking the LORD God of Israel to anger with their idols.

¹⁴Now the rest of the acts of Elah, and all that he did, *are* they not written in the book of the chronicles of the kings of Israel?

¹⁵In the twenty-seventh year of Asa king of Judah, Zimri had reigned in Tirzah seven days. And the people *were* encamped against Gibbethon, which *belonged* to the Philistines. ¹⁶Now the people *who were* encamped heard it said, "Zimri has conspired and also has killed the king." So all Israel made Omri, the commander of the army, king over Israel that day in the camp. ¹⁷Then Omri and all Israel with him went up from Gibbethon, and they besieged Tirzah. ¹⁸And it happened, when Zimri saw that the city was taken, that he went into the citadel of the king's house and burned the king's house down upon himself with fire, and died, ¹⁹because of the sins which he had committed in doing evil in the sight of the LORD, in walking in the way of Jeroboam, and in his sin which he had committed to make Israel sin.

²⁰Now the rest of the acts of Zimri, and the treason he committed, *are* they not written in the book of the chronicles of the kings of Israel?

²¹Then the people of Israel were divided into two parts: half of the people followed Tibni the son of Ginath, to make him king, and half followed Omri. ²²But the people who followed Omri prevailed over the people who followed Tibni the son of Ginath. So Tibni died and Omri reigned. ²³In the thirty-first year of Asa king of Judah, Omri became king over Israel, *and reigned* twelve years. Six years he reigned in Tirzah. ²⁴And he bought the hill of Samaria from Shemer for two talents of silver; then he built on the hill, and called the name of the city which he built, Samaria, after the name of Shemer, owner of the hill. ²⁵Omri did evil in the eyes of the LORD, and did worse than all who *were* before him. ²⁶For he walked in all the ways of Jeroboam the son of Nebat, and in his sin by which he had made Israel sin, provoking the LORD God of Israel to anger with their idols.

²⁷Now the rest of the acts of Omri which he did, and the might that he showed, *are* they not written in the book of the chronicles of the kings of Israel?

PROVIDENCE

17:1ff In a nation that was required by law to care for its poor, is ironic that God turned to ravens (unclean birds) and a widow (a foreigner from Jezebel's home territory) to care for Elijah. God h where we least expect it. He provides for us in ways that go beyo narrow definitions or expectations. No matter how bitter our trial seemingly hopeless our situation, we should look for God's hand We may find his providence in some strange places!

²⁸So Omri rested with his fathers and was buried in Samaria. Then Ahab his son reigned in his place.

²⁹In the thirty-eighth year of Asa king of Judah, Ahab the son of Omri became king over Israel; and Ahab the son of Omri reigned over Israel in Samaria twenty-two years. ³⁰Now Ahab the son of Omri did evil in the sight of the LORD, more than all who *were* before him. ³¹And it came to pass, as though it had been a trivial thing for him to walk in the sins of Jeroboam the son of Nebat, that he took as wife Jezebel the daughter of Ethbaal, king of the Sidonians; and he went and served Baal and worshiped him. ³²Then he set up an altar for Baal in the temple of Baal, which he had built in Samaria. ³³And Ahab made a wooden image. Ahab did more to provoke the LORD God of Israel to anger than all the kings of Israel who were before him. ³⁴In his days Hiel of Bethel built Jericho. He laid its foundation with Abiram his firstborn, and with his youngest *son* Segub he set up its gates, according to the word of the LORD, which He had spoken through Joshua the son of Nun.

TRIALS

17:17 Even when God has done a miracle in our life, our troub not be over. The famine was a terrible experience, but the worst to come. God's provision is never given in order to let us rest upa are to depend on him as each new trial faces us.

CHAPTER 17 RAVENS FEED ELIJAH. And Elijah the Tishbite, of the inhabitants of Gilead, said to Ahab, "As the LORD God of Israel lives, before whom I stand, there shall not be dew nor rain these years, except at my word."

²Then the word of the LORD came to him, saying, ³"Get away from here and turn eastward, and hide by the Brook Cherith, which flows into the Jordan. ⁴And it will be *that* you shall drink from the brook, and I have commanded the ravens to feed you there."

⁵So he went and did according to the word of the LORD, for he went and stayed by the Brook Cherith, which flows into the Jordan. ⁶The ravens brought him bread and meat in the morning, and bread and meat in the evening; and he drank from the brook. ⁷And it happened after a while that the brook dried up, because there had been no rain in the land.

⁸Then the word of the LORD came to him, saying, ⁹"Arise, go to Zarephath, which *belongs* to Sidon, and dwell there. See, I have commanded a widow there to provide for you." ¹⁰So he arose and went to Zarephath. And when he came to the gate of the city, indeed a widow *was* there gathering sticks. And he called to her and said, "Please bring me a little water in a cup, that I may drink." ¹¹And as she was going to get *it*, he called to her and said, "Please bring me a morsel of bread in your hand."

¹²So she said, "As the LORD your God lives, I do not have bread, only a handful of flour in a bin, and a little oil in a jar; and see, I *am* gathering a couple of sticks that I may go in and prepare it for myself and my son, that we may eat it, and die."

¹³And Elijah said to her, "Do not fear; go *and* do as you have said, but make me a small cake from it first, and bring *it* to me; and afterward make *some* for yourself and your son. ¹⁴For thus says the LORD God of Israel: 'The bin of flour shall not be used up, nor shall the jar of oil run dry, until the day the LORD sends rain on the earth.'"

¹⁵So she went away and did according to the word of Elijah; and she and he and her household ate for *many* days. ¹⁶The bin of flour was not used up, nor did the jar of oil run dry, according to the word of the LORD which He spoke by Elijah.

¹⁷Now it happened after these things *that* the son of the woman who owned the house became sick. And his sickness was so serious that there was no breath left in him. ¹⁸So she said to Elijah, "What have I to do with you, O man of God? Have you come to me to bring my sin to remembrance, and to kill my son?"

¹⁹And he said to her, "Give me your son." So he took him out of her arms and carried him to the upper room where he was staying, and laid him on his own bed. ²⁰Then he cried out to the LORD and said, "O LORD my God, have You also brought tragedy on the widow with whom I lodge, by killing her son?" ²¹And he

ELIJAH

Elijah's complete commitment to God shocks and challenges us. God made him a confronter rather than a comforter. He had to speak God's words to a king who often rejected his message. Elijah experienced real loneliness even though he was working for God.

It is interesting to read about the amazing miracles God accomplished through Elijah, but it is more helpful to think about the relationship they shared. All that happened in Elijah's life began with the step we can take—he responded to the miracle of being able to know God.

In Elijah's life we really see the thrills of victory and the agonies of defeat. God had to teach Elijah that many of his problems came from missing God's presence. He showed the depressed prophet a windstorm, an earthquake, and a fire—just the kind of awesome things we usually think prove God's power. But God told Elijah that we can know him even better in the quiet, when he comes like a whisper.

Elijah also had to learn another lesson. He was part of God's plan, and he knew about God's power and presence, but he was lonely sometimes because he didn't know that God also had other people in his plan. God had to remind Elijah there were 7,000 others in Israel who were faithful.

Even today, God speaks more often through the quiet and obvious than the spectacular and unusual. God has work for us to do even when we feel fear and failure. And God always has more plans and people than we know about. We may want to be heroes for God, but it all starts with a relationship with him. The real miracle in Elijah's life was his very personal relationship with God.

LESSONS: We are never as alone as we may feel; God is always there

God speaks more frequently in persistent whispers than in shouts

KEY VERSES: "And it came to pass, at the time of the offering of the evening sacrifice, that Elijah the prophet came near and said, 'LORD God of Abraham, Isaac, and Israel, let it be known this day that You are God in Israel and I am Your servant, and that I have done all these things at Your word. . . .' Then the fire of the LORD fell and consumed the burnt sacrifice, and the wood and the stones and the dust, and it licked up the water that was in the trench" (1 Kings 18:36,38).

Elijah's story is told in 1 Kings 17:1—2 Kings 2:11. He is also mentioned in 2 Chronicles 21:12-15; Malachi 4:5-6; Matthew 11:14; 16:14; 17:3-13; 27:47-49; Luke 1:17; 4:25-26; John 1:19-25; Romans 11:2-4; James 5:17-18.

UPS:
- The most famous and dramatic of Israel's prophets
- Predicted the beginning and end of a three-year drought
- Used by God to restore a dead child to his mother
- God's representative in a showdown with priests of Baal and Asherah
- Appeared with Moses and Jesus in the New Testament transfiguration scene

DOWNS:
- Chose to work alone and paid for it through isolation
- Fled in fear from Jezebel when she threatened his life

STATS:
- Where: Gilead
- Occupation: Prophet
- Contemporaries: Ahab, Jezebel, Ahaziah, Obadiah, Jehu, Hazael

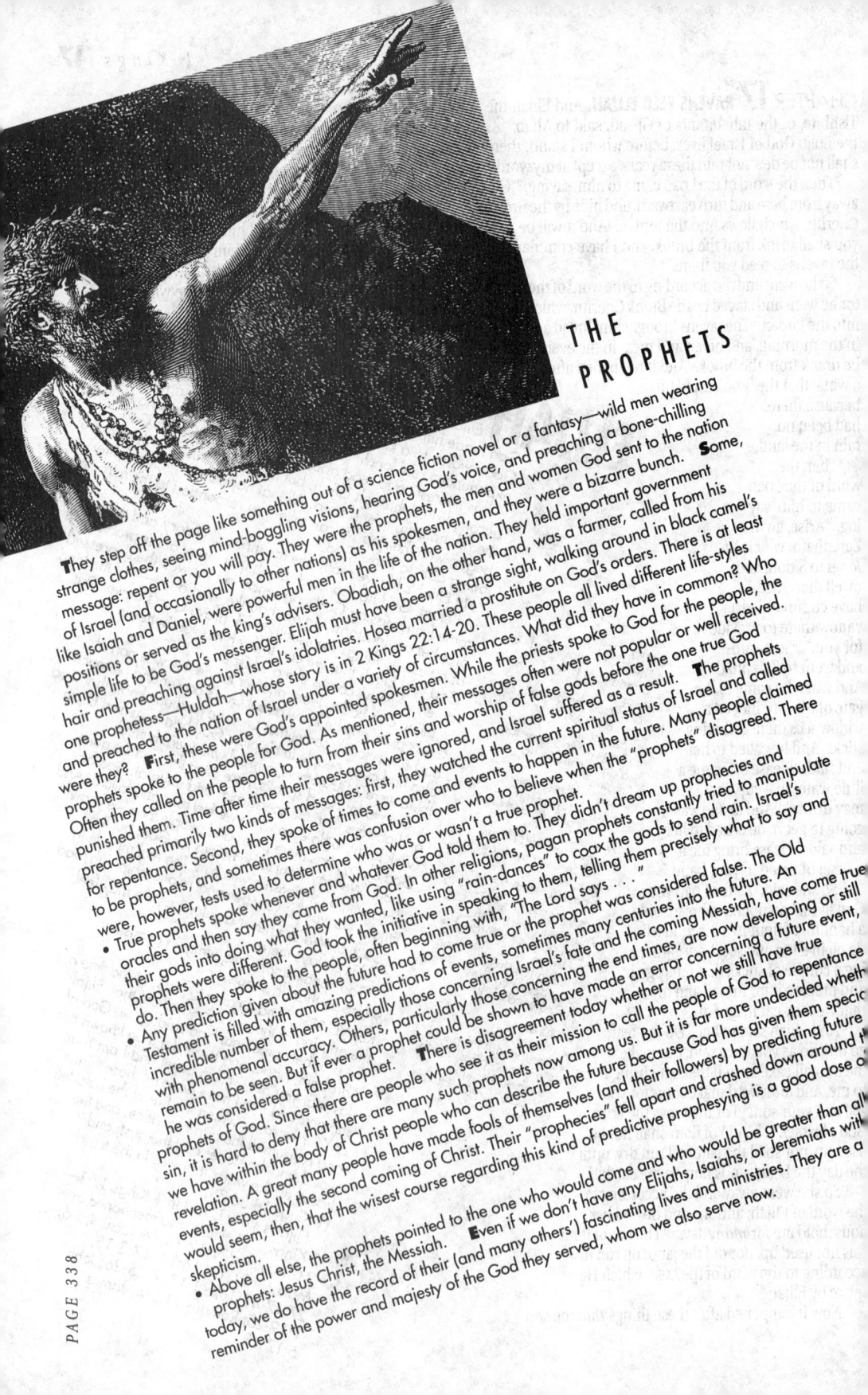

THE PROPHETS

They step off the page like something out of a science fiction novel or a fantasy—wild men wearing strange clothes, seeing mind-boggling visions, hearing God's voice, and preaching a bone-chilling message: repent or you will pay. They were the prophets, the men and women God sent to the nation of Israel (and occasionally to other nations) as his spokesmen, and they were a bizarre bunch. Some, like Isaiah and Daniel, were powerful men in the life of the nation. They held important government positions or served as the king's advisers. Obadiah, on the other hand, was a farmer, called from his simple life to be God's messenger. Elijah must have been a strange sight, walking around in black camel's hair and preaching against Israel's idolatries. Hosea married a prostitute on God's orders. There is at least one prophetess—Huldah—whose story is in 2 Kings 22:14-20. These people all lived different life-styles and preached to the nation of Israel under a variety of circumstances. What did they have in common? Who were they?

First, these were God's appointed spokesmen. While the priests spoke to God for the people, the prophets spoke to the people for God. As mentioned, their messages often were not popular or well received. Often they called on the people to turn from their sins and worship of false gods before the one true God punished them. Time after time their messages were ignored, and Israel suffered as a result. The prophets preached primarily two kinds of messages: first, they watched the current spiritual status of Israel and called for repentance. Second, they spoke of times to come and events to happen in the future. Many people claimed to be prophets, and sometimes there was confusion over who to believe when the "prophets" disagreed. There were, however, tests used to determine who was or wasn't a true prophet.

- True prophets spoke whenever and whatever God told them to. They didn't dream up prophecies and oracles and then say they came from God. In other religions, pagan prophets constantly tried to manipulate their gods into doing what they wanted, like using "rain-dances" to coax the gods to send rain. Israel's prophets were different. God took the initiative in speaking to them, telling them precisely what to say and do. Then they spoke to the people, often beginning with, "The Lord says . . ."

- Any prediction given about the future had to come true or the prophet was considered false. The Old Testament is filled with amazing predictions of events, sometimes many centuries into the future. An incredible number of them, especially those concerning Israel's fate and the coming Messiah, have come true with phenomenal accuracy. Others, particularly those concerning the end times, are now developing or still remain to be seen. But if ever a prophet could be shown to have made an error concerning a future event, he was considered a false prophet. There is disagreement today whether or not we still have true prophets of God. Since there are many such prophets now among us. But it is far more undecided whether we have within the body of Christ people who see it as their mission to call the people of God to repentance, it is hard to deny that there are people who can describe the future because God has given them specific revelation. A great many people have made fools of themselves (and their followers) by predicting future events, especially the second coming of Christ. Their "prophecies" fell apart and crashed down around their would seem, then, that the wisest course regarding this kind of predictive prophesying is a good dose of skepticism.

- Above all else, the prophets pointed to the one who would come and who would be greater than all prophets: Jesus Christ, the Messiah. Even if we don't have any Elijahs, Isaiahs, or Jeremiahs with today, we do have the record of their (and many others') fascinating lives and ministries. They are a reminder of the power and majesty of the God they served, whom we also serve now.

stretched himself out on the child three times, and cried out to the LORD and said, "O LORD my God, I pray, let this child's soul come back to him." ²²Then the LORD heard the voice of Elijah; and the soul of the child came back to him, and he revived.

²³And Elijah took the child and brought him down from the upper room into the house, and gave him to his mother. And Elijah said, "See, your son lives!"

²⁴Then the woman said to Elijah, "Now by this I know that you *are* a man of God, *and* that the word of the LORD in your mouth *is* the truth."

CHAPTER **18** ELIJAH DEFEATS BAAL'S PROPHETS.

And it came to pass *after* many days that the word of the LORD came to Elijah, in the third year, saying, "Go, present yourself to Ahab, and I will send rain on the earth."

²So Elijah went to present himself to Ahab; and *there was* a severe famine in Samaria. ³And Ahab had called Obadiah, who *was* in charge of *his* house. (Now Obadiah feared the LORD greatly. ⁴For so it was, while Jezebel massacred the prophets of the LORD, that Obadiah had taken one hundred prophets and hidden them, fifty to a cave, and had fed them with bread and water.) ⁵And Ahab had said to Obadiah, "Go into the land to all the springs of water and to all the brooks; perhaps we may find grass to keep the horses and mules alive, so that we will not have to kill any livestock." ⁶So they divided the land between them to explore it; Ahab went one way by himself, and Obadiah went another way by himself.

⁷Now as Obadiah was on his way, suddenly Elijah met him; and he recognized him, and fell on his face, and said, "*Is* that you, my lord Elijah?"

⁸And he answered him, "*It is* I. Go, tell your master, 'Elijah *is here.*'"

⁹So he said, "How have I sinned, that you are delivering your servant into the hand of Ahab, to kill me? ¹⁰*As the* LORD your God lives, there is no nation or kingdom where my master has not sent someone to hunt for you; and when they said, '*He is* not *here,*' he took an oath from the kingdom or nation that they could not find you. ¹¹And now you say, 'Go, tell your master, "Elijah *is here*" '! ¹²And it shall come to pass, *as soon as* I am gone from you, that the Spirit of the LORD will carry you to a place I do not know; so when I go and tell Ahab, and he cannot find you, he will kill me. But I your servant have feared the LORD from my youth. ¹³Was it not reported to my lord what I did when Jezebel killed the prophets of the LORD, how I hid one hundred men of the LORD's prophets, fifty to a cave, and fed them with bread and water? ¹⁴And now you say, 'Go, tell your master, "Elijah *is here.*" ' He will kill me!"

¹⁵Then Elijah said, "*As* the LORD of hosts lives, before whom I stand, I will surely present myself to him today."

¹⁶So Obadiah went to meet Ahab, and told him; and Ahab went to meet Elijah.

¹⁷Then it happened, when Ahab saw Elijah, that Ahab said to him, "*Is that* you, O troubler of Israel?"

¹⁸And he answered, "I have not troubled Israel, but you and your father's house *have,* in that you have forsaken the commandments of the LORD and have followed the Baals. ¹⁹Now therefore, send *and* gather all Israel to me on Mount Carmel, the four hundred and fifty prophets of Baal, and the four hundred prophets of Asherah, who eat at Jezebel's table."

²⁰So Ahab sent for all the children of Israel, and gathered the prophets together on Mount Carmel. ²¹And Elijah came to all the people, and said, "How long will you

◣ STAND FIRM

18:21 Elijah challenged the people to take a stand—to follow whoever was the true God. Why did so many people waver between the two choices? Perhaps some were not sure. Many, however, knew that the Lord was God, but they enjoyed the sinful pleasures and other benefits that came with following Ahab and his idolatrous worship. It is important to take a stand for the Lord. If we just drift along with whatever is pleasant and easy, we will someday discover that we have been worshiping a false god—ourselves.

falter between two opinions? If the LORD *is* God, follow Him; but if Baal, follow him." But the people answered him not a word. ²²Then Elijah said to the people, "I alone am left a prophet of the LORD; but Baal's prophets *are* four hundred and fifty men. ²³Therefore let them give us two bulls; and let them choose one bull for themselves, cut it in pieces, and lay *it* on the wood, but put no fire *under it;* and I will prepare the other bull, and lay *it* on the wood, but put no fire *under it.* ²⁴Then you call on the name of

PROPHETS—FALSE AND TRUE

The false prophets were an obstacle to bringing God's word to the people. They would bring "messages" that contradicted the words of the true prophets. They gave messages that appealed to the people's sinful natures and comforted their fears. False prophets told people what they wanted to hear; true prophets told God's truth.

False Prophets	True Prophets
Worked for political purposes to benefit themselves	Worked for spiritual purposes to serve God and the people
Held positions of great wealth	Owned little or nothing
Gave false messages	Spoke only true messages
Spoke only what the people wanted to hear	Spoke only what God told them to say—no matter how unpopular

18:36-38 Just as God flashed fire from heaven for Elijah, he will help us accomplish what he commands us to do. The proof may not be as dramatic in our life as in Elijah's, but God will make resources available to us in creative ways to accomplish his purposes. He will give us the wisdom to raise a family, the courage to take a stand for truth, or the means to provide help for someone in need. Like Elijah, we can have faith that, whatever God commands us to do, he will provide what we need to carry it through.

your gods, and I will call on the name of the LORD; and the God who answers by fire, He is God."

So all the people answered and said, "It is well spoken."

²⁵Now Elijah said to the prophets of Baal, "Choose one bull for yourselves and prepare *it* first, for you *are* many; and call on the name of your god, but put no fire *under it.*"

²⁶So they took the bull which was given them, and they prepared *it,* and called on the name of Baal from morning even till noon, saying, "O Baal, hear us!" But *there was* no voice; no one answered. Then they leaped about the altar which they had made.

²⁷And so it was, at noon, that Elijah mocked them and said, "Cry aloud, for he *is* a god; either he is meditating, or he is busy, or he is on a journey, *or* perhaps he is sleeping and must be awakened." ²⁸So they cried aloud, and cut themselves, as was their custom, with knives and lances, until the blood gushed out on them. ²⁹And when midday was past, they prophesied until the *time* of the offering of the *evening* sacrifice. But *there was* no voice; no one answered, no one paid attention.

³⁰Then Elijah said to all the people, "Come near to me." So all the people came near to him. And he repaired the altar of the LORD *that was* broken down. ³¹And Elijah took twelve stones, according to the number of the tribes of the sons of Jacob, to whom the word of the LORD had come, saying, "Israel shall be your name." ³²Then with the stones he built an altar in the name of the LORD; and he made a trench around the altar large enough to hold two seahs of seed. ³³And he put the wood in order, cut the bull in pieces, and laid *it* on the wood, and said, "Fill four waterpots with water, and pour *it* on the burnt sacrifice and on the wood." ³⁴Then he said, "Do *it* a second time," and they did *it* a second time; and he said, "Do *it* a third time," and they did *it* a third time. ³⁵So the water ran all around the altar; and he also filled the trench with water.

³⁶And it came to pass, at *the time of* the offering of the *evening* sacrifice, that Elijah the prophet came near and said, "LORD God of Abraham, Isaac, and Israel, let it be known this day that You *are* God in Israel and I *am* Your servant, and *that* I have done all these things at Your word. ³⁷Hear me, O LORD, hear me, that this people may know that You *are* the LORD God, and *that* You have turned their hearts back *to* You again."

³⁸Then the fire of the LORD fell and consumed the burnt sacrifice, and the wood and the stones and the dust, and it licked up the water that *was* in the trench. ³⁹Now when all the people saw *it,* they fell on their faces; and they said, "The LORD, He *is* God! The LORD, He *is* God!"

⁴⁰And Elijah said to them, "Seize the prophets of Baal!

Do not let one of them escape!" So they seized them; and Elijah brought them down to the Brook Kishon and executed them there.

⁴¹Then Elijah said to Ahab, "Go up, eat and drink; for *there is* the sound of abundance of rain." ⁴²So Ahab went up to eat and drink. And Elijah went up to the top of Carmel; then he bowed down on the ground, and put his face between his knees, ⁴³and said to his servant, "Go up now, look toward the sea."

So he went up and looked, and said, "*There is* nothing." And seven times he said, "Go again."

⁴⁴Then it came to pass the seventh *time,* that he said, "There is a cloud, as small as a man's hand, rising out of the sea!" So he said, "Go up, say to Ahab, 'Prepare *your chariot,* and go down before the rain stops you.'"

⁴⁵Now it happened in the meantime that the sky became black with clouds and wind, and there was a heavy rain. So Ahab rode away and went to Jezreel. ⁴⁶Then the hand of the LORD came upon Elijah; and he girded up his loins and ran ahead of Ahab to the entrance of Jezreel.

CHAPTER 19 GOD WHISPERS TO ELIJAH. And

Ahab told Jezebel all that Elijah had done, also how he had executed all the prophets with the sword. ²Then Jezebel sent a messenger to Elijah, saying, "So let the gods do *to me,* and more also, if I do not make your life as the life of one of them by tomorrow about this time." ³And when he saw *that,* he arose and ran for his life, and went to Beersheba, which *belongs* to Judah, and left his servant there.

⁴But he himself went a day's journey into the wilderness, and came and sat down under a broom tree. And he prayed that he might die, and said, "It is enough! Now, LORD, take my life, for I *am* no better than my fathers!"

⁵Then as he lay and slept under a broom tree, suddenly an angel touched him, and said to him, "Arise *and* eat." ⁶Then he looked, and there by his head *was* a cake baked on coals, and a jar of water. So he ate and drank, and lay down again. ⁷And the angel of the LORD came back the second time, and touched him, and said, "Arise *and* eat, because the journey *is* too great for you." ⁸So he arose, and ate and drank; and he went in the strength of that food forty days and forty nights as far as Horeb, the mountain of God.

⁹And there he went into a cave, and spent the night in that place; and behold, the word of the LORD *came* to him, and He said to him, "What are you doing here, Elijah?"

¹⁰So he said, "I have been very zealous for the LORD God of hosts; for the children of Israel have forsaken Your

19:3-4 Elijah experienced the depths of fatigue and discourage just after his two great spiritual victories: the defeat of the prophe Baal and the answered prayer for rain. Often discouragement set after great spiritual experiences, especially those requiring physi or producing emotional excitement. To lead him out of depression first let Elijah rest and eat. Then God confronted him with the nee return to his mission in life—to be God's prophet. Elijah's battles not over; there was still work for him to do. When you feel let do a great spiritual experience, remember that God's purpose for yo not over yet.

covenant, torn down Your altars, and killed Your prophets with the sword. I alone am left; and they seek to take my life."

[11]Then He said, "Go out, and stand on the mountain before the LORD." And behold, the LORD passed by, and a great and strong wind tore into the mountains and broke the rocks in pieces before the LORD, *but* the LORD *was* not in the wind; and after the wind an earthquake, *but* the LORD *was* not in the earthquake; [12]and after the earthquake a fire, *but* the LORD *was* not in the fire; and after the fire a still small voice.

[13]So it was, when Elijah heard *it*, that he wrapped his face in his mantle and went out and stood in the entrance of the cave. Suddenly a voice *came* to him, and said, "What are you doing here, Elijah?"

[14]And he said, "I have been very zealous for the LORD God of hosts; because the children of Israel have forsaken Your covenant, torn down Your altars, and killed Your prophets with the sword. I alone am left; and they seek to take my life."

[15]Then the LORD said to him: "Go, return on your way to the Wilderness of Damascus; and when you arrive, anoint Hazael *as* king over Syria. [16]Also you shall anoint Jehu the son of Nimshi *as* king over Israel. And Elisha the son of Shaphat of Abel Meholah you shall anoint *as* prophet in your place. [17]It shall be *that* whoever escapes the sword of Hazael, Jehu will kill; and whoever escapes the sword of Jehu, Elisha will kill. [18]Yet I have reserved seven thousand in Israel, all whose knees have not bowed to Baal, and every mouth that has not kissed him."

[19]So he departed from there, and found Elisha the son of Shaphat, who *was* plowing *with* twelve yoke *of oxen* before him, and he was with the twelfth. Then Elijah passed by him and threw his mantle on him. [20]And he left the oxen and ran after Elijah, and said, "Please let me kiss my father and my mother, and *then* I will follow you."

And he said to him, "Go back again, for what have I done to you?"

[21]So *Elisha* turned back from him, and took a yoke of oxen and slaughtered them and boiled their flesh, using the oxen's equipment, and gave it to the people, and they ate. Then he arose and followed Elijah, and became his servant.

CHAPTER **20** GOD GIVES ISRAEL VICTORY. Now Ben-Hadad the king of Syria gathered all his forces together; thirty-two kings *were* with him, with horses and chariots. And he went up and besieged Samaria, and made war against it. [2]Then he sent messengers into the city to Ahab king of Israel, and said to him, "Thus says Ben-Hadad: [3]'Your silver and your gold *are* mine; your loveliest wives and children are mine.'"

[4]And the king of Israel answered and said, "My lord, O king, just as you say, I and all that I have *are* yours."

[5]Then the messengers came back and said, "Thus speaks Ben-Hadad, saying, 'Indeed I have sent to you, saying, "You shall deliver to me your silver and your gold, your wives and your children"; [6]but I will send my servants to you tomorrow about this time, and they shall

search your house and the houses of your servants. And it shall be, *that* whatever is pleasant in your eyes, they will put *it* in their hands and take *it*.'"

[7]So the king of Israel called all the elders of the land, and said, "Notice, please, and see how this *man* seeks trouble, for he sent to me for my wives, my children, my silver, and my gold; and I did not deny him."

WHISPERS

19:11-13 Elijah knew that the still small voice belonged to God. He realized that God doesn't reveal himself only in powerful, miraculous ways. To look for God only in something big (camps, churches, conferences, visible leaders) may be to miss him, because he is often found gently whispering in the quietness of a humbled heart. Are you listening for God? Step back from the noise and activity of your busy life and listen humbly and quietly for his guidance. It may come when you least expect it.

[8]And all the elders and all the people said to him, "Do not listen or consent."

[9]Therefore he said to the messengers of Ben-Hadad, "Tell my lord the king, 'All that you sent for to your servant the first time I will do, but this thing I cannot do.'"

And the messengers departed and brought back word to him.

[10]Then Ben-Hadad sent to him and said, "The gods do so to me, and more also, if enough dust is left of Samaria for a handful for each of the people who follow me."

[11]So the king of Israel answered and said, "Tell *him*,

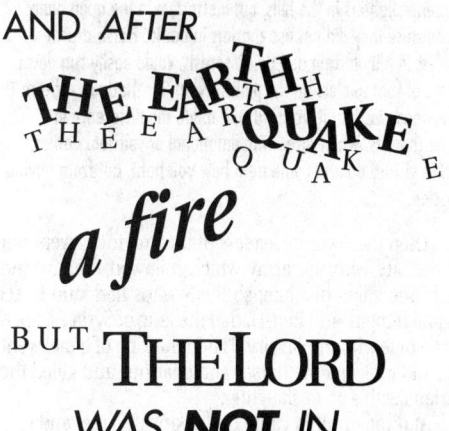

AND AFTER THE EARTHQUAKE THE EARTHQUAKE a fire BUT THE LORD WAS **NOT** IN the fire; AND AFTER the fire a still small voice a still small voice a still small voice

'Let not the one who puts on *his armor* boast like the one who takes *it off.*'"

[12]And it happened when *Ben-Hadad* heard this message, as he and the kings *were* drinking at the command post, that he said to his servants, "Get ready." And they got ready to attack the city.

[13]Suddenly a prophet approached Ahab king of Israel, saying, "Thus says the LORD: 'Have you seen all this great multitude? Behold, I will deliver it into your hand today, and you shall know that I *am* the LORD.'"

[14]So Ahab said, "By whom?"

And he said, "Thus says the LORD: 'By the young leaders of the provinces.'"

Then he said, "Who will set the battle in order?"

And he answered, "You."

[15]Then he mustered the young leaders of the provinces, and there were two hundred and thirty-two; and after them he mustered all the people, all the children of Israel—seven thousand.

[16]So they went out at noon. Meanwhile Ben-Hadad and the thirty-two kings helping him were getting drunk at the command post. [17]The young leaders of the provinces went out first. And Ben-Hadad sent out *a patrol,* and they told him, saying, "Men are coming out of Samaria!" [18]So he said, "If they have come out for peace, take them alive; and if they have come out for war, take them alive."

▶ BATTLE

20:23 Since the days of Joshua, Israel's soldiers had had a reputation for being superior fighters in the hills, but ineffective in the open plains and valleys because they did not use chariots in battle. Horse-drawn chariots, useless in hilly terrain and dense forests, could easily run down great numbers of foot soldiers on the plains. What Ben-Hadad's officers did not understand was that it was God who made the difference in battle, not the chariots. When faced with emotional or spiritual battles, remember that victory doesn't come from how you fight, but from having God at your side.

[19]Then these young leaders of the provinces went out of the city with the army which followed them. [20]And each one killed his man; so the Syrians fled, and Israel pursued them; and Ben-Hadad the king of Syria escaped on a horse with the cavalry. [21]Then the king of Israel went out and attacked the horses and chariots, and killed the Syrians with a great slaughter.

[22]And the prophet came to the king of Israel and said to him, "Go, strengthen yourself; take note, and see what you should do, for in the spring of the year the king of Syria will come up against you."

[23]Then the servants of the king of Syria said to him, "Their gods *are* gods of the hills. Therefore they were stronger than we; but if we fight against them in the plain, surely we will be stronger than they. [24]So do this thing: Dismiss the kings, each from his position, and put captains in their places; [25]and you shall muster an army like the army that you have lost, horse for horse and chariot for chariot. Then we will fight against them in the plain; surely we will be stronger than they."

And he listened to their voice and did so.

[26]So it was, in the spring of the year, that Ben-Hadad mustered the Syrians and went up to Aphek to fight against Israel. [27]And the children of Israel were mustered and given provisions, and they went against them. Now the children of Israel encamped before them like two little flocks of goats, while the Syrians filled the countryside.

[28]Then a man of God came and spoke to the king of Israel, and said, "Thus says the LORD: 'Because the Syrians have said, "The LORD *is* God of the hills, but He *is* not God of the valleys," therefore I will deliver all this great multitude into your hand, and you shall know that I *am* the LORD.'" [29]And they encamped opposite each other for seven days. So it was that on the seventh day the battle was joined; and the children of Israel killed one hundred thousand foot soldiers *of* the Syrians in one day. [30]But the rest fled to Aphek, into the city; then a wall fell on twenty-seven thousand of the men *who were* left.

And Ben-Hadad fled and went into the city, into an inner chamber.

[31]Then his servants said to him, "Look now, we have heard that the kings of the house of Israel *are* merciful kings. Please, let us put sackcloth around our waists and ropes around our heads, and go out to the king of Israel; perhaps he will spare your life." [32]So they wore sackcloth around their waists and *put* ropes around their heads, and came to the king of Israel and said, "Your servant Ben-Hadad says, 'Please let me live.'"

And he said, "*Is* he still alive? He *is* my brother."

[33]Now the men were watching closely to see whether *any sign of mercy would come* from him; and they quickly grasped *at this word* and said, "Your brother Ben-Hadad."

So he said, "Go, bring him." Then Ben-Hadad came out to him; and he had him come up into the chariot.

[34]So *Ben-Hadad* said to him, "The cities which my father took from your father I will restore; and you may set up marketplaces for yourself in Damascus, as my father did in Samaria."

Then *Ahab said,* "I will send you away with this treaty." So he made a treaty with him and sent him away.

[35]Now a certain man of the sons of the prophets said to his neighbor by the word of the LORD, "Strike me please." And the man refused to strike him. [36]Then he said to him, "Because you have not obeyed the voice of the LORD, surely, as soon as you depart from me, a lion shall kill you." And as soon as he left him, a lion found him and killed him.

[37]And he found another man, and said, "Strike me please." So the man struck him, inflicting a wound [38]Then the prophet departed and waited for the king by the road, and disguised himself with a bandage over his eyes. [39]Now as the king passed by, he cried out to the king and said, "Your servant went out into the midst of the battle; and there, a man came over and brought a man to me, and said, 'Guard this man; if by any means he is missing, your life shall be for his life, or else you shall pay a talent of silver.' [40]While your servant was busy here and there, he was gone."

Then the king of Israel said to him, "So *shall* your judgment *be;* you yourself have decided *it.*"

[41]And he hastened to take the bandage away from hi

eyes; and the king of Israel recognized him as one of the prophets. [42]Then he said to him, "Thus says the LORD: 'Because you have let slip out of *your* hand a man whom I appointed to utter destruction, therefore your life shall go for his life, and your people for his people.'"

[43]So the king of Israel went to his house sullen and displeased, and came to Samaria.

CHAPTER 21 AHAB STEALS A VINEYARD.

And it came to pass after these things *that* Naboth the Jezreelite had a vineyard which *was* in Jezreel, next to the palace of Ahab king of Samaria. [2]So Ahab spoke to Naboth, saying, "Give me your vineyard, that I may have it for a vegetable garden, because it *is* near, next to my house; and for it I will give you a vineyard better than it. *Or*, if it seems good to you, I will give you its worth in money."

[3]But Naboth said to Ahab, "The LORD forbid that I should give the inheritance of my fathers to you!"

[4]So Ahab went into his house sullen and displeased because of the word which Naboth the Jezreelite had spoken to him; for he had said, "I will not give you the inheritance of my fathers." And he lay down on his bed, and turned away his face, and would eat no food. [5]But Jezebel his wife came to him, and said to him, "Why is your spirit so sullen that you eat no food?"

[6]He said to her, "Because I spoke to Naboth the Jezreelite, and said to him, 'Give me your vineyard for money; or else, if it pleases you, I will give you *another* vineyard for it.' And he answered, 'I will not give you my vineyard.'"

[7]Then Jezebel his wife said to him, "You now exercise authority over Israel! Arise, eat food, and let your heart be cheerful; I will give you the vineyard of Naboth the Jezreelite."

[8]And she wrote letters in Ahab's name, sealed *them* with his seal, and sent the letters to the elders and the nobles who *were* dwelling in the city with Naboth. [9]She wrote in the letters, saying,

Proclaim a fast, and seat Naboth with high honor among the people; [10]and seat two men,

scoundrels, before him to bear witness against him, saying, You have blasphemed God and the king. *Then* take him out, and stone him, that he may die.

[11]So the men of his city, the elders and nobles who were inhabitants of his city, did as Jezebel had sent to them, as it *was* written in the letters which she had sent to them. [12]They proclaimed a fast, and seated Naboth with high honor among the people. [13]And two men, scoundrels, came in and sat before him; and the scoundrels witnessed against him, against Naboth, in

AHAB

The kings of Israel and Judah, both good and evil, had prophets sent by God to advise, confront, and aid them. King David had a faithful friend in God's prophet Nathan; Ahab could have had an equally faithful friend in Elijah. But Ahab saw Elijah as his enemy. Why? Because he blamed Elijah for bringing bad news to Ahab, and Ahab refused to acknowledge that it was his own disobedience and persistent idol worship, not Elijah's prophecies, that brought the evil on his nation.

Ahab was trapped by his own choices, and he was unwilling to take the right action. He took his evil wife's advice, listened only to the "prophets" who gave good news, and surrounded himself with people who encouraged him to do whatever he wanted. But the value of advice cannot be judged by the number of people for or against it. Ahab consistently chose to follow the majority opinion of his friends, and that led to his death.

It may seem nice to have someone encourage us to do whatever we want because advice that goes against our wishes is difficult to accept. However, our decisions must be based on the quality of the advice, not its attractiveness or what our friends think. God encourages us to get advice from wise counselors, but how can we test the advice we receive? Advice that agrees with the principles in God's Word is reliable. We must always separate advice from our own desires or whatever our friends say, and weigh it against God's commands. He will never lead us to do what he has forbidden in his Word. Unlike Ahab, we should trust godly counselors and have the courage to stand against those who want us to do otherwise.

LESSONS: The choice of a mate will have a significant effect on life—physically, spiritually, and emotionally

Selfishness, left unchecked, can lead to great evil

KEY VERSES: "Now Ahab the son of Omri did evil in the sight of the LORD. . . He took as wife Jezebel the daughter of Ethbaal, king of the Sidonians; and he went and served Baal and worshiped him. Then he set up an altar for Baal in the temple of Baal, which he had built in Samaria. And Ahab made a wooden image. Ahab did more to provoke the LORD God of Israel to anger than all the kings of Israel who were before him" (1 Kings 16:30-33).

Ahab's story is told in 1 Kings 16:28–22:40. He is also mentioned in 2 Chronicles 18–22; Micah 6:16.

UPS:
- Eighth king of Israel
- Capable leader and military strategist

DOWNS:
- Was the most evil king of Israel
- Married Jezebel, a heathen woman, and allowed her to promote Baal worship
- Brooded about not being able to get a piece of land, so his wife had its owner, Naboth, killed
- Was used to getting his own way, and got depressed when he didn't

STATS:
- Where: Northern kingdom of Israel
- Occupation: King
- Relatives: Wife: Jezebel. Father: Omri. Sons: Ahaziah, Jehoram.
- Contemporaries: Elijah, Naboth, Jehu, Ben-Hadad, Jehoshaphat

the presence of the people, saying, "Naboth has blasphemed God and the king!" Then they took him outside the city and stoned him with stones, so that he died. ¹⁴Then they sent to Jezebel, saying, "Naboth has been stoned and is dead."

BLINDNESS

21:20 Ahab still refused to admit his sin against God. Instead he accused Elijah of being his enemy. When we are blinded by envy and hatred, it is almost impossible to see our own sin.

¹⁵And it came to pass, when Jezebel heard that Naboth had been stoned and was dead, that Jezebel said to Ahab, "Arise, take possession of the vineyard of Naboth the Jezreelite, which he refused to give you for money; for Naboth is not alive, but dead." ¹⁶So it was, when Ahab heard that Naboth was dead, that Ahab got up and went down to take possession of the vineyard of Naboth the Jezreelite.

¹⁷Then the word of the LORD came to Elijah the Tishbite, saying, ¹⁸"Arise, go down to meet Ahab king of Israel, who *lives* in Samaria. There *he is*, in the vineyard of Naboth, where he has gone down to take possession of it. ¹⁹You shall speak to him, saying, 'Thus says the LORD: "Have you murdered and also taken possession?" ' And you shall speak to him, saying, 'Thus says the LORD: "In the place where dogs licked the blood of Naboth, dogs shall lick your blood, even yours." ' "

²⁰So Ahab said to Elijah, "Have you found me, O my enemy?"

NEVER TOO LATE

21:29 Ahab was more wicked than any other king of Israel (16:30; 21:25), but when he repented in deep humility, God took notice and reduced his punishment. The same Lord who was merciful to Ahab wants to be merciful to you. No matter how bad you've acted, it is never too late to humble yourself, turn to God, and ask for forgiveness.

And he answered, "I have found *you*, because you have sold yourself to do evil in the sight of the LORD: ²¹'Behold, I will bring calamity on you. I will take away your posterity, and will cut off from Ahab every male in Israel, both bond and free. ²²I will make your house like the house of Jeroboam the son of Nebat, and like the house of Baasha the son of Ahijah, because of the provocation with which you have provoked *Me* to anger, and made Israel sin.' ²³And concerning Jezebel the LORD also spoke, saying, 'The dogs shall eat Jezebel by the wall of Jezreel.' ²⁴The dogs shall eat whoever belongs to Ahab and dies in the city, and the birds of the air shall eat whoever dies in the field."

²⁵But there was no one like Ahab who sold himself to do wickedness in the sight of the LORD, because Jezebel his wife stirred him up. ²⁶And he behaved very abominably in following idols, according to all *that* the Amorites had done, whom the LORD had cast out before the children of Israel.

²⁷So it was, when Ahab heard those words, that he tore his clothes and put sackcloth on his body, and fasted and lay in sackcloth, and went about mourning.

²⁸And the word of the LORD came to Elijah the Tishbite, saying, ²⁹"See how Ahab has humbled himself before Me? Because he has humbled himself before Me, I will not bring the calamity in his days. In the days of his son I will bring the calamity on his house."

CHAPTER 22 AHAB DIES IN BATTLE.

Now three years passed without war between Syria and Israel. ²Then it came to pass, in the third year, that Jehoshaphat the king of Judah went down to *visit* the king of Israel. ³And the king of Israel said to his servants, "Do you know that Ramoth in Gilead *is* ours, but we hesitate to take it out of the hand of the king of Syria?" ⁴So he said to Jehoshaphat, "Will you go with me to fight at Ramoth Gilead?"

Jehoshaphat said to the king of Israel, "I *am* as you *are*, my people as your people, my horses as your horses." ⁵Also Jehoshaphat said to the king of Israel, "Please inquire for the word of the LORD today."

⁶Then the king of Israel gathered the prophets together, about four hundred men, and said to them, "Shall I go against Ramoth Gilead to fight, or shall I refrain?"

So they said, "Go up, for the Lord will deliver *it* into the hand of the king."

⁷And Jehoshaphat said, "*Is there* not still a prophet of the LORD here, that we may inquire of Him?"

⁸So the king of Israel said to Jehoshaphat, "*There is* still one man, Micaiah the son of Imlah, by whom we may inquire of the LORD; but I hate him, because he does not prophesy good concerning me, but evil."

And Jehoshaphat said, "Let not the king say such things!"

⁹Then the king of Israel called an officer and said, "Bring Micaiah the son of Imlah quickly!"

¹⁰The king of Israel and Jehoshaphat the king of Judah, having put on *their* robes, sat each on his throne, at a threshing floor at the entrance of the gate of Samaria; and all the prophets prophesied before them. ¹¹Now Zedekiah the son of Chenaanah had made horns of iron for himself; and he said, "Thus says the LORD: 'With these you shall gore the Syrians until they are destroyed.' " ¹²And all the prophets prophesied so, saying, "Go up to Ramoth Gilead and prosper, for the LORD will deliver *it* into the king's hand."

¹³Then the messenger who had gone to call Micaiah spoke to him, saying, "Now listen, the words of the prophets with one accord encourage the king. Please, let your word be like the word of one of them, and speak encouragement."

¹⁴And Micaiah said, "*As* the LORD lives, whatever the LORD says to me, that I will speak."

¹⁵Then he came to the king; and the king said to him, "Micaiah, shall we go to war against Ramoth Gilead, or shall we refrain?"

And he answered him, "Go and prosper, for the LORD will deliver *it* into the hand of the king!"

¹⁶So the king said to him, "How many times shall I make you swear that you tell me nothing but the truth in the name of the LORD?"

¹⁷Then he said, "I saw all Israel scattered on the moun-

tains, as sheep that have no shepherd. And the LORD said, 'These have no master. Let each return to his house in peace.'"

¹⁸And the king of Israel said to Jehoshaphat, "Did I not tell you he would not prophesy good concerning me, but evil?"

¹⁹Then *Micaiah* said, "Therefore hear the word of the LORD: I saw the LORD sitting on His throne, and all the host of heaven standing by, on His right hand and on His left. ²⁰And the LORD said, 'Who will persuade Ahab to go up, that he may fall at Ramoth Gilead?' So one spoke in this manner, and another spoke in that manner. ²¹Then a spirit came forward and stood before the LORD, and said, 'I will persuade him.' ²²The LORD said to him, 'In what way?' So he said, 'I will go out and be a lying spirit in the mouth of all his prophets.' And the LORD said, 'You shall persuade *him*, and also prevail. Go out and do so.' ²³Therefore look! The LORD has put a lying spirit in the mouth of all these prophets of yours, and the LORD has declared disaster against you."

²⁴Now Zedekiah the son of Chenaanah went near and struck Micaiah on the cheek, and said, "Which way did the spirit from the LORD go from me to speak to you?"

²⁵And Micaiah said, "Indeed, you shall see on that day when you go into an inner chamber to hide!"

²⁶So the king of Israel said, "Take Micaiah, and return him to Amon the governor of the city and to Joash the king's son; ²⁷and say, 'Thus says the king: "Put this *fellow* in prison, and feed him with bread of affliction and water of affliction, until I come in peace."'"

²⁸But Micaiah said, "If you ever return in peace, the LORD has not spoken by me." And he said, "Take heed, all you people!"

²⁹So the king of Israel and Jehoshaphat the king of Judah went up to Ramoth Gilead. ³⁰And the king of Israel said to Jehoshaphat, "I will disguise myself and go into battle; but you put on your robes." So the king of Israel disguised himself and went into battle.

³¹Now the king of Syria had commanded the thirty-two captains of his chariots, saying, "Fight with no one small or great, but only with the king of Israel." ³²So it was, when the captains of the chariots saw Jehoshaphat, that they said, "Surely it *is* the king of Israel!" Therefore they turned aside to fight against him, and Jehoshaphat cried out. ³³And it happened, when the captains of the chariots saw that it *was* not the king of Israel, that they turned back from pursuing him. ³⁴Now a *certain* man drew a bow at random, and struck the king of Israel between the joints of his armor. So he said to the driver of his chariot, "Turn around and take me out of the battle, for I am wounded."

³⁵The battle increased that day; and the king was propped up in his chariot, facing the Syrians, and died at evening. The blood ran out from the wound onto the floor of the chariot. ³⁶Then, as the sun was going down, a shout went throughout the army, saying, "Every man to his city, and every man to his own country!"

³⁷So the king died, and was brought to Samaria. And they buried the king in Samaria. ³⁸Then *someone* washed the chariot at a pool in Samaria, and the dogs licked up his blood while the harlots bathed, according to the word of the LORD which He had spoken.

³⁹Now the rest of the acts of Ahab, and all that he did,

◣ DISGUISED

22:34 Ahab could not escape God's judgment. Ben-Hadad sent 32 of his best chariot captains with the sole purpose of killing Ahab. Thinking he could escape, Ahab tried a disguise, but a random shot struck him while the chariots chased the wrong king, Jehoshaphat. It was foolish for Ahab to think he could escape with a disguise. Sometimes people today try to escape reality by disguising themselves: acting differently, changing schools, moving to a new town. Yet when God judges a person, attempted escape is futile.

the ivory house which he built and all the cities that he built, *are* they not written in the book of the chronicles of the kings of Israel? ⁴⁰So Ahab rested with his fathers. Then Ahaziah his son reigned in his place.

⁴¹Jehoshaphat the son of Asa had become king over Judah in the fourth year of Ahab king of Israel. ⁴²Jehoshaphat *was* thirty-five years old when he became king, and he reigned twenty-five years in Jerusalem. His mother's name *was* Azubah the daughter of Shilhi. ⁴³And he walked in all the ways of his father Asa. He did not turn aside from them, doing *what was* right in the eyes of the LORD. Nevertheless the high places were not taken away, *for* the people offered sacrifices and burned incense on the high places. ⁴⁴Also Jehoshaphat made peace with the king of Israel.

⁴⁵Now the rest of the acts of Jehoshaphat, the might that he showed, and how he made war, *are* they not written in the book of the chronicles of the kings of Judah? ⁴⁶And the rest of the perverted persons, who remained in the days of his father Asa, he banished from the land. ⁴⁷*There was* then no king in Edom, only a deputy of the king.

⁴⁸Jehoshaphat made merchant ships to go to Ophir for gold; but they never sailed, for the ships were wrecked at Ezion Geber. ⁴⁹Then Ahaziah the son of Ahab said to Jehoshaphat, "Let my servants go with your servants in the ships." But Jehoshaphat would not.

⁵⁰And Jehoshaphat rested with his fathers, and was buried with his fathers in the City of David his father. Then Jehoram his son reigned in his place.

⁵¹Ahaziah the son of Ahab became king over Israel in Samaria in the seventeenth year of Jehoshaphat king of Judah, and reigned two years over Israel. ⁵²He did evil in the sight of the LORD, and walked in the way of his father and in the way of his mother and in the way of Jeroboam the son of Nebat, who had made Israel sin; ⁵³for he served Baal and worshiped him, and provoked the LORD God of Israel to anger, according to all that his father had done.

MEGA Themes

THE KING Solomon's wisdom, power, and achievements brought honor to the Israelite nation and to God. All the kings of Israel and Judah were told to obey God and to govern according to his laws. But their tendency to abandon God's Word and to worship other gods led them to change the religion and government to meet their personal desires. This neglect of God's law led to their downfall.

Wisdom, power, and achievement do not ultimately come from any human source; they are from God. No matter how we lead or govern, we won't do well if we ignore God's guidelines. Whether or not we are in a position of leadership, we can be successful by listening to and obeying God's Word.

1. What qualities were characteristic of the kings whose reigns were successful? Of those who failed?
2. Which of these characteristics were evident in the life of Solomon?
3. How did each king's relationship with God affect the people?
4. What qualities will you look for in those whom you follow as Christian teachers, pastors, and disciplers?

THE TEMPLE Solomon's temple was a beautiful place of worship and prayer. This sanctuary was the center of Jewish religion. It was the place of God's special presence and housed the ark of the covenant containing the Ten Commandments.

A beautiful house of worship doesn't always indicate that the people gathered there are truly worshiping God. Providing opportunities for true worship doesn't guarantee that it will happen. God wants to live in our heart, not just meet us in a sanctuary. We need to worship God daily as individuals and once or twice a week with others.

1. Why was building the temple so important to Solomon?
2. Solomon was successful in building the temple, but in other ways he failed to glorify God. What do you learn about worshiping God as you read about Solomon's life and reign?
3. Many people believe that being a "good Christian" means going to church every week. Do you agree or disagree? Why?
4. List some specific ways you can "enter the temple"

to worship God, whether you are inside or outside of a church building. Commit yourself to personally worship God at least once a day during the coming week.

OTHER GODS Although the Israelites had God's law and had experienced his presence among them, they became attracted to other gods. When this happened, their hearts became cold to God's law, resulting in the ruin of families and government, and eventually leading to the destruction of the nation.

Through the years, the people took on the false qualities of the false gods they worshiped. They became cruel, power-hungry, and sexually perverse. We tend to become what we worship. Unless we serve the one true God, we will become slaves to whatever takes his place.

1. In what ways did the Israelites worship false gods? What were the results of this worship?
2. What are some of the false gods of our society?
3. What is the same and what is different between the results of the Israelites' false worship and the "worship" of false gods in modern culture?
4. Why do Christians still need to beware of the attraction of false gods?
5. What will you do to ensure that you never fall into the trap of false worship?

PROPHETIC MESSAGE The prophet's responsibility was to confront and correct any deviation from God's law. Elijah brought a bolt of judgment against Israel. His messages and miracles warned the evil and rebellious kings and people.

The Bible, sermons that teach the truth, and the wise counsel of believers are warnings to us. Anyone who points out how we may be moving away from God's Word is a blessing. Changing our life in order to obey God often takes painful discipline and hard work. We should seek people who will be honest with us about weaknesses in our life.

1. List several of the judgments that Elijah announced
2. What do you learn about God's will for his people from these judgments?
3. In what ways do these judgments apply to contemporary churches? To Christians today?
4. What is happening in your relationship with God that you know is in his will?

SIN/REPENTANCE Each king had God's Word, a priest or prophet, and the lessons of the past to draw him back to God. All the people had the same resources. Whenever they turned away from their sin and returned to God, God heard their prayers and forgave them.

God hears us when we pray. We have the assurance of forgiveness if we are willing to trust him and turn from sin. When God forgives us, he provides a fresh start and a new desire to live for him.

1. How did God respond to the kings who repented?
2. Contrast those kings' lives with the lives of those who chose to continue in their rebellion. How did God respond to those rebellious kings?
3. What does this study reveal to you about how you should deal with sin when God reveals it to you?
4. Spend a few moments reflecting on your life as it compares to God's will. Write a list of sins that you need to confess to God. Once you have written the list and prayed over each item, destroy the list as a symbol of the fresh start God provides his people when they turn from their sins and to him.

*H*e used to be such a nice guy. But since he became president, he thinks he owns the school!" ■ "We used to be friends. But she turned into a snob about a week after making cheerleader!" ■ Maybe you've heard, thought, or even spoken lines like that. It's amazing, isn't it, how some people change when they get a little power or an important position? Suddenly they're in the spotlight, and you're not good enough or popular enough or rich enough to be seen with them. ■ Someone else put it this way: "Power corrupts." ■ Of course, it doesn't always happen that way. Now and then someone who has made it to the top will remember who he or she is and the people who put him or her there. But with so many examples on the other side (politicians, businessmen, athletes, entertainment stars, etc.), it's clear that such people are the exceptions. ■ Second Kings tells about the leaders of the two nations of Israel and Judah. These kings could have used their power to help their people and lead them God's way. But of the 12 northern kings (in Israel) and the 16 southern kings (in Judah) whose stories are recorded in 2 Kings, only 2— Hezekiah and Josiah—are called "good." ■ As you read, learn from the negative examples of the kings and determine to be God's person—even if you win the race, get elected, or gain the prize.

STATS

PURPOSE: To demonstrate the fate that awaits all who refuse to make God their true leader

AUTHOR: Unknown. Possibly Jeremiah or a group of prophets.

SETTING: The once united nation of Israel has been divided into two kingdoms, Israel and Judah, for over a century

KEY PEOPLE: Elijah, Elisha, Shunammite woman, Naaman, Jezebel, Jehu, Joash, Hezekiah, Sennacherib, Isaiah, Manasseh, Josiah, Jehoiakim, Zedekiah, Nebuchadnezzar

SPECIAL FEATURE: The 17 prophetic books at the end of the Old Testament give great insights into the time period of 2 Kings

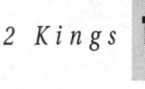

ℓ Kings

CHAPTER 1 KING AHAZIAH DIES FOR HIS SIN.
Moab rebelled against Israel after the death of Ahab.

²Now Ahaziah fell through the lattice of his upper room in Samaria, and was injured; so he sent messengers and said to them, "Go, inquire of Baal-Zebub, the god of Ekron, whether I shall recover from this injury." ³But the angel of the LORD said to Elijah the Tishbite, "Arise, go up to meet the messengers of the king of Samaria, and say to them, '*Is it* because *there is* no God in Israel *that* you are going to inquire of Baal-Zebub, the god of Ekron?' ⁴Now therefore, thus says the LORD: 'You shall not come down from the bed to which you have gone up, but you shall surely die.'" So Elijah departed.

⁵And when the messengers returned to him, he said to them, "Why have you come back?"

⁶So they said to him, "A man came up to meet us, and said to us, 'Go, return to the king who sent you, and say to him, "Thus says the LORD: '*Is it* because *there is* no God in Israel *that* you are sending to inquire of Baal-Zebub, the god of Ekron? Therefore you shall not come down

from the bed to which you have gone up, but you shall surely die.'"'"

⁷Then he said to them, "What kind of man *was it* who came up to meet you and told you these words?"

⁸So they answered him, "A hairy man wearing a leather belt around his waist."

And he said, "It *is* Elijah the Tishbite."

⁹Then the king sent to him a captain of fifty with his fifty men. So he went up to him; and there he was, sitting on the top of a hill. And he spoke to him: "Man of God, the king has said, 'Come down!'"

¹⁰So Elijah answered and said to the captain of fifty, "If I *am* a man of God, then let fire come down from heaven

◥ ATTITUDE

1:13-15 Notice how the third captain went to Elijah. Although the first two captains called Elijah "man of God," they were not being genuine. The third captain also called him "man of God," but he humbly begged for mercy. His attitude, which showed respect for God and his power, saved the lives of his men. Effective living begins with a right attitude toward God. Let respect characterize your attitude toward God and others.

KEY PLACES IN 2 KINGS

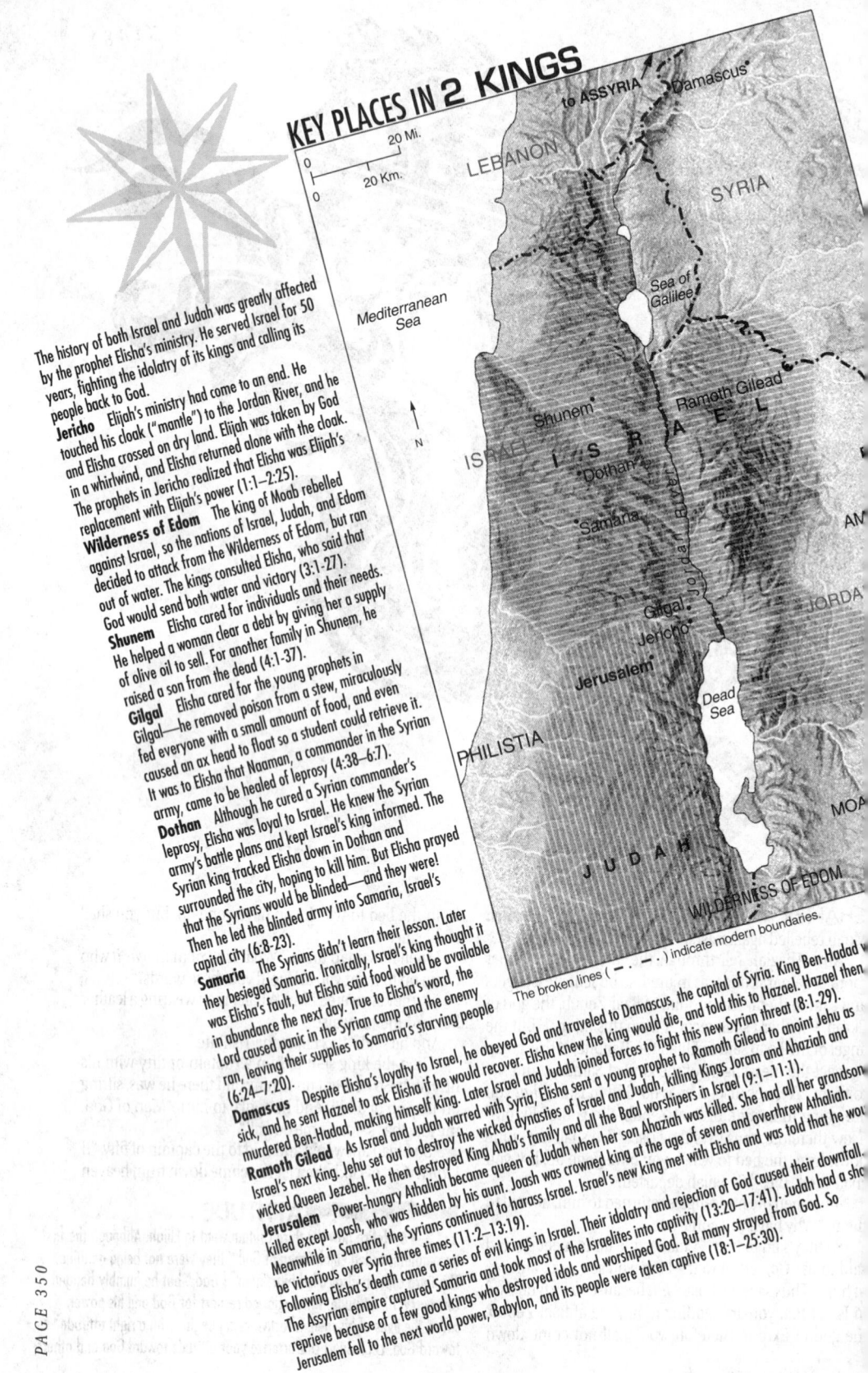

The broken lines (— · — · —) indicate modern boundaries.

The history of both Israel and Judah was greatly affected by the prophet Elisha's ministry. He served Israel for 50 years, fighting the idolatry of its kings and calling its people back to God.

Jericho   Elijah's ministry had come to an end. He touched his cloak ("mantle") to the Jordan River, and he and Elisha crossed on dry land. Elijah was taken by God in a whirlwind, and Elisha returned alone with the cloak. The prophets in Jericho realized that Elisha was Elijah's replacement with Elijah's power (1:1–2:25).

Wilderness of Edom   The king of Moab rebelled against Israel, so the nations of Israel, Judah, and Edom decided to attack from the Wilderness of Edom, but ran out of water. The kings consulted Elisha, who said that God would send both water and victory (3:1-27).

Shunem   Elisha cared for individuals and their needs. He helped a woman clear a debt by giving her a supply of olive oil to sell. For another family in Shunem, he raised a son from the dead (4:1-37).

Gilgal   Elisha cared for the young prophets in Gilgal—he removed poison from a stew, miraculously fed everyone with a small amount of food, and even caused an ax head to float so a student could retrieve it. It was to Elisha that Naaman, a commander in the Syrian army, came to be healed of leprosy (4:38–6:7).

Dothan   Although he cured a Syrian commander's leprosy, Elisha was loyal to Israel. He knew the Syrian army's battle plans and kept Israel's king informed. The Syrian king tracked Elisha down in Dothan and surrounded the city, hoping to kill him. But Elisha prayed that the Syrians would be blinded—and they were! Then he led the blinded army into Samaria, Israel's capital city (6:8-23).

Samaria   The Syrians didn't learn their lesson. Later they besieged Samaria. Ironically, Israel's king thought it was Elisha's fault, but Elisha said food would be available in abundance the next day. True to Elisha's word, the Lord caused panic in the Syrian camp and the enemy ran, leaving their supplies to Samaria's starving people (6:24–7:20).

Damascus   Despite Elisha's loyalty to Israel, he obeyed God and traveled to Damascus, the capital of Syria. King Ben-Hadad w sick, and he sent Hazael to ask Elisha if he would recover. Elisha knew the king would die, and told this to Hazael. Hazael then murdered Ben-Hadad, making himself king. Later Israel and Judah joined forces to fight this new Syrian threat (8:1-29).

Ramoth Gilead   As Israel and Judah warred with Syria, Elisha sent a young prophet to Ramoth Gilead to anoint Jehu as Israel's next king. Jehu set out to destroy King Ahab's family and all the Baal worshipers in Israel (9:1–11:1). He then destroyed King Ahab's family and Judah when her son Ahaziah was killed. She had all her grandson wicked Queen Jezebel. Power-hungry Athaliah became queen of Judah when her son Ahaziah was killed. She had all her grandson

Jerusalem   Power-hungry Athaliah became queen of Judah when her son Ahaziah was killed. She had all her grandson killed except Joash, who was hidden by his aunt. Joash was crowned king at the age of seven and overthrew Athaliah. Meanwhile in Samaria, the Syrians continued to harass Israel. Israel's new king met with Elisha and was told that he wou be victorious over Syria three times (11:2–13:19). Following Elisha's death came a series of evil kings in Israel. Their idolatry and rejection of God caused their downfall. The Assyrian empire captured Samaria and took most of the Israelites into captivity (13:20–17:41). Judah had a sho reprieve because of a few good kings who destroyed idols and worshiped God. But many strayed from God. So Jerusalem fell to the next world power, Babylon, and its people were taken captive (18:1–25:30).

arrow of deliverance from Syria; for you must strike the Syrians at Aphek till you have destroyed *them*." ¹⁸Then he said, "Take the arrows"; so he took *them*. And he said to the king of Israel, "Strike the ground"; so he struck three times, and stopped. ¹⁹And the man of God was angry with him, and said, "You should have struck five or six times; then you would have struck Syria till you had destroyed *it!* But now you will strike Syria *only* three times."

²⁰Then Elisha died, and they buried him. And the *raiding* bands from Moab invaded the land in the spring of the year. ²¹So it was, as they were burying a man, that suddenly they spied a band *of raiders;* and they put the man in the tomb of Elisha; and when the man was let down and touched the bones of Elisha, he revived and stood on his feet.

²²And Hazael king of Syria oppressed Israel all the days of Jehoahaz. ²³But the LORD was gracious to them, had compassion on them, and regarded them, because of His covenant with Abraham, Isaac, and Jacob, and would not yet destroy them or cast them from His presence.

²⁴Now Hazael king of Syria died. Then Ben-Hadad his son reigned in his place. ²⁵And Jehoash the son of Jehoahaz recaptured from the hand of Ben-Hadad, the son of Hazael, the cities which he had taken out of the hand of Jehoahaz his father by war. Three times Joash defeated him and recaptured the cities of Israel.

CHAPTER 14 AMAZIAH RULES JUDAH. In the second year of Joash the son of Jehoahaz, king of Israel, Amaziah the son of Joash, king of Judah, became king. ²He was twenty-five years old when he became king, and he reigned twenty-nine years in Jerusalem. His mother's name was Jehoaddan of Jerusalem. ³And he did *what was* right in the sight of the LORD, yet not like his father David; he did everything as his father Joash had done. ⁴However the high places were not taken away, and the people still sacrificed and burned incense on the high places.

⁵Now it happened, as soon as the kingdom was established in his hand, that he executed his servants who had murdered his father the king. ⁶But the children of the murderers he did not execute, according to what is written in the Book of the Law of Moses, in which the LORD commanded, saying, "Fathers shall not be put to death for their children, nor shall children be put to death for their fathers; but a person shall be put to death for his own sin."

⁷He killed ten thousand Edomites in the Valley of Salt, and took Sela by war, and called its name Joktheel to this day.

⁸Then Amaziah sent messengers to Jehoash the son of Jehoahaz, the son of Jehu, king of Israel, saying, "Come, let us face one another *in battle*." ⁹And Jehoash king of Israel sent to Amaziah king of Judah, saying, "The thistle that *was* in Lebanon sent to the cedar that *was* in Lebanon, saying, 'Give your daughter to my son as wife'; and a wild beast that *was* in Lebanon passed by and trampled the thistle. ¹⁰You have indeed defeated Edom, and your heart has lifted you up. Glory *in that*, and stay at home; for why should you meddle with trouble so that you fall—you and Judah with you?"

¹¹But Amaziah would not heed. Therefore Jehoash king of Israel went out; so he and Amaziah king of Judah faced one another at Beth Shemesh, which *belongs* to Judah. ¹²And Judah was defeated by Israel, and every man fled to his tent. ¹³Then Jehoash king of Israel captured Amaziah king of Judah, the son of Jehoash, the son of Ahaziah, at Beth Shemesh; and he went to Jerusalem, and broke down the wall of Jerusalem from the Gate of Ephraim to the Corner Gate—four hundred cubits. ¹⁴And he took all the gold and silver, all the articles that were found in the house of the LORD and in the treasuries of the king's house, and hostages, and returned to Samaria.

¹⁵Now the rest of the acts of Jehoash which he did—his might, and how he fought with Amaziah king of Judah— *are* they not written in the book of the chronicles of the kings of Israel? ¹⁶So Jehoash rested with his fathers, and was buried in Samaria with the kings of Israel. Then Jeroboam his son reigned in his place.

¹⁷Amaziah the son of Joash, king of Judah, lived fifteen years after the death of Jehoash the son of Jehoahaz, king of Israel. ¹⁸Now the rest of the acts of Amaziah, *are* they not written in the book of the chronicles of the kings of Judah? ¹⁹And they formed a conspiracy against him in Jerusalem, and he fled to Lachish; but they sent after him to Lachish and killed him there. ²⁰Then they brought him on horses, and he was buried at Jerusalem with his fathers in the City of David.

²¹And all the people of Judah took Azariah, who *was* sixteen years old, and made him king instead of his father Amaziah. ²²He built Elath and restored it to Judah, after the king rested with his fathers.

²³In the fifteenth year of Amaziah the son of Joash, king of Judah, Jeroboam the son of Joash, king of Israel, became king in Samaria, *and reigned* forty-one years. ²⁴And he did evil in the sight of the LORD; he did not depart from all the sins of Jeroboam the son of Nebat, who had made Israel sin. ²⁵He restored the territory of Israel from the entrance of Hamath to the Sea of the Arabah, according to the word of the LORD God of Israel, which He had spoken through His servant Jonah the son of Amittai, the prophet who *was* from Gath Hepher. ²⁶For the LORD saw *that* the affliction of Israel *was* very bitter; and whether bond or free, there was no helper for Israel. ²⁷And the LORD did not say that He would blot out the name of Israel from under heaven; but He saved them by the hand of Jeroboam the son of Joash.

²⁸Now the rest of the acts of Jeroboam, and all that he did—his might, how he made war, and how he recaptured for Israel, from Damascus and Hamath, *what had belonged* to Judah—*are* they not written in the book of

▶◀▬▬▬▬RICH

14:28 Jeroboam had no devotion to God, yet under his warlike policies and skillful administration Israel enjoyed power and prosperity. The prophets Amos and Hosea, however, tell us what was really happening within the kingdom (Hosea 13:4-8; Amos 6:11-13). Jeroboam's administration ignored policies of justice, so the rich became richer and the poor, poorer. The rich people grew self-centered; the poor grew discouraged. If you are experiencing prosperity, remember that God holds us accountable for how we attain success and how we use our wealth.

MODELS

15:4 Although Azariah accomplished a great deal, he failed to destroy the high places in Judah where the people worshiped idols, just as his father Amaziah and grandfather Joash had failed to do. Azariah imitated the kings he had heard stories about and watched while growing up. Although Azariah's father and grandfather were basically good kings, they were poor models in some important areas. To rise above the influence of poor models, we must find better ones. Christ provides a perfect model. No matter how you were raised or who influenced your life, you can move beyond those limitations by taking Christ as your example and consciously trying to live as he did.

the chronicles of the kings of Israel? ²⁹So Jeroboam rested with his fathers, the kings of Israel. Then Zechariah his son reigned in his place.

CHAPTER **15** **AZARIAH RULES JUDAH.** In the twenty-seventh year of Jeroboam king of Israel, Azariah the son of Amaziah, king of Judah, became king. ²He was sixteen years old when he became king, and he reigned fifty-two years in Jerusalem. His mother's name *was* Jecholiah of Jerusalem. ³And he did *what was* right in the sight of the LORD, according to all that his father Amaziah had done, ⁴except that the high places were not removed; the people still sacrificed and burned incense on the high places. ⁵Then the LORD struck the king, so that he was a leper until the day of his death; so he dwelt in an isolated house. And Jotham the king's son *was* over the *royal* house, judging the people of the land.

⁶Now the rest of the acts of Azariah, and all that he did, *are* they not written in the book of the chronicles of the kings of Judah? ⁷So Azariah rested with his fathers, and they buried him with his fathers in the City of David. Then Jotham his son reigned in his place.

⁸In the thirty-eighth year of Azariah king of Judah, Zechariah the son of Jeroboam reigned over Israel in Samaria six months. ⁹And he did evil in the sight of the LORD, as his fathers had done; he did not depart from the sins of Jeroboam the son of Nebat, who had made Israel sin. ¹⁰Then Shallum the son of Jabesh conspired against him, and struck and killed him in front of the people; and he reigned in his place.

¹¹Now the rest of the acts of Zechariah, indeed they *are* written in the book of the chronicles of the kings of Israel. ¹²This *was* the word of the LORD which He spoke to Jehu, saying, "Your sons shall sit on the throne of Israel to the fourth *generation*." And so it was.

¹³Shallum the son of Jabesh became king in the thirty-ninth year of Uzziah king of Judah; and he reigned a full month in Samaria. ¹⁴For Menahem the son of Gadi went up from Tirzah, came to Samaria, and struck Shallum the son of Jabesh in Samaria and killed him; and he reigned in his place.

¹⁵Now the rest of the acts of Shallum, and the conspiracy which he led, indeed they *are* written in the book of the chronicles of the kings of Israel. ¹⁶Then from Tirzah, Menahem attacked Tiphsah, all who *were* there, and its territory. Because they did not surrender, therefore he attacked *it*. All the women there who were with child he ripped open.

¹⁷In the thirty-ninth year of Azariah king of Judah, Menahem the son of Gadi became king over Israel, *and*

reigned ten years in Samaria. ¹⁸And he did evil in the sight of the LORD; he did not depart all his days from the sins of Jeroboam the son of Nebat, who had made Israel sin. ¹⁹Pul king of Assyria came against the land; and Menahem gave Pul a thousand talents of silver, that his hand might be with him to strengthen the kingdom under his control. ²⁰And Menahem exacted the money from Israel, from all the very wealthy, from each man fifty shekels of silver, to give to the king of Assyria. So the king of Assyria turned back, and did not stay there in the land.

²¹Now the rest of the acts of Menahem, and all that he did, *are* they not written in the book of the chronicles of the kings of Israel? ²²So Menahem rested with his fathers. Then Pekahiah his son reigned in his place.

²³In the fiftieth year of Azariah king of Judah, Pekahiah the son of Menahem became king over Israel in Samaria, *and reigned* two years. ²⁴And he did evil in the sight of the LORD; he did not depart from the sins of Jeroboam the son of Nebat, who had made Israel sin. ²⁵Then Pekah the son of Remaliah, an officer of his, conspired against him and killed him in Samaria, in the citadel of the king's house, along with Argob and Arieh; and with him were fifty men of Gilead. He killed him and reigned in his place.

INFLUENCE

15:8 Zechariah was an evil king because he encouraged Israel to worshiping idols. Sin in our own lives is serious, but even more te[rrible] than sinning ourselves is encouraging others to disobey God. We a[re] responsible for the way we influence others. Beware of double sin[s] that not only hurt us, but also hurt others by encouraging them to [sin].

²⁶Now the rest of the acts of Pekahiah, and all that he did, indeed they *are* written in the book of the chronicles of the kings of Israel.

²⁷In the fifty-second year of Azariah king of Judah, Pekah the son of Remaliah became king over Israel in Samaria, *and reigned* twenty years. ²⁸And he did evil in the sight of the LORD; he did not depart from the sins of Jeroboam the son of Nebat, who had made Israel sin. ²⁹In the days of Pekah king of Israel, Tiglath-Pileser king of Assyria came and took Ijon, Abel Beth Maachah, Janoah, Kedesh, Hazor, Gilead, and Galilee, all the land of Naphtali; and he carried them captive to Assyria. ³⁰Then Hoshea the son of Elah led a conspiracy against Pekah the son of Remaliah, and struck and killed him; so he reigned in his place in the twentieth year of Jotham the son of Uzziah.

³¹Now the rest of the acts of Pekah, and all that he did, indeed they *are* written in the book of the chronicles of the kings of Israel.

PRIORITY

15:34-35 Much good can be said of Jotham and his reign as k[ing of] Judah, but he failed in a most critical area: he didn't destroy the [high] places where the people worshiped idols, although leaving them [in place] violated the first commandment (Exodus 20:3). Like Jotham, we [can live] a basically good life and yet miss doing what is most important. [A] lifetime of doing good is not enough if we make the crucial mista[ke of] not following God with all our heart. A true follower of God puts [God] in all areas of life.

³²In the second year of Pekah the son of Remaliah, king of Israel, Jotham the son of Uzziah, king of Judah, began to reign. ³³He was twenty-five years old when he became king, and he reigned sixteen years in Jerusalem. His mother's name *was* Jerusha the daughter of Zadok. ³⁴And he did *what was* right in the sight of the LORD; he did according to all that his father Uzziah had done. ³⁵However the high places were not removed; the people still sacrificed and burned incense on the high places. He built the Upper Gate of the house of the LORD.

³⁶Now the rest of the acts of Jotham, and all that he did, *are* they not written in the book of the chronicles of the kings of Judah? ³⁷In those days the LORD began to send Rezin king of Syria and Pekah the son of Remaliah against Judah. ³⁸So Jotham rested with his fathers, and was buried with his fathers in the City of David his father. Then Ahaz his son reigned in his place.

CHAPTER **16** **AHAZ RULES JUDAH.** In the seventeenth year of Pekah the son of Remaliah, Ahaz the son of Jotham, king of Judah, began to reign. ²Ahaz *was* twenty years old when he became king, and he reigned sixteen years in Jerusalem; and he did not do *what was* right in the sight of the LORD his God, as his father David *had done*. ³But he walked in the way of the kings of Israel; indeed he made his son pass through the fire, according to the abominations of the nations whom the LORD had cast out from before the children of Israel. ⁴And he sacrificed and burned incense on the high places, on the hills, and under every green tree.

⁵Then Rezin king of Syria and Pekah the son of Remaliah, king of Israel, came up to Jerusalem to *make* war; and they besieged Ahaz but could not overcome *him*. ⁶At that time Rezin king of Syria captured Elath for Syria, and drove the men of Judah from Elath. Then the Edomites went to Elath, and dwell there to this day.

⁷So Ahaz sent messengers to Tiglath-Pileser king of Assyria, saying, "I *am* your servant and your son. Come up and save me from the hand of the king of Syria and from the hand of the king of Israel, who rise up against me." ⁸And Ahaz took the silver and gold that was found in the house of the LORD, and in the treasuries of the king's house, and sent *it as* a present to the king of Assyria. ⁹So the king of Assyria heeded him; for the king of Assyria went up against Damascus and took it, carried *its people* captive to Kir, and killed Rezin.

¹⁰Now King Ahaz went to Damascus to meet Tiglath-Pileser king of Assyria, and saw an altar that *was* at Damascus; and King Ahaz sent to Urijah the priest the design of the altar and its pattern, according to all its workmanship. ¹¹Then Urijah the priest built an altar according to all that King Ahaz had sent from Damascus. So Urijah the priest made *it* before King Ahaz came back from Damascus. ¹²And when the king came back from Damascus, the king saw the altar; and the king approached the altar and made offerings on it. ¹³So he burned his burnt offering and his grain offering; and he poured his drink offering and sprinkled the blood of his peace offerings on the altar. ¹⁴He also brought the bronze altar which *was* before the LORD, from the front of the temple—from between the *new* altar and the house of the LORD—and put it on the north side of the *new* altar. ¹⁵Then King Ahaz commanded Urijah the priest, saying, "On the great *new* altar burn the morning burnt offering, the evening grain offering, the king's burnt sacrifice, and

▰▰▰▰CALLOUS WORSHIP

16:10-16 Evil King Ahaz copied heathen religious customs, changed the temple services, and used the temple altar for his personal benefit. In so doing, he demonstrated a callous disregard for God's commands. We condemn Ahaz for his action, but we do the same thing if we try to mold God's message to fit our personal preferences. We must worship God for who he is, not what we would selfishly like him to be.

his grain offering, with the burnt offering of all the people of the land, their grain offering, and their drink offerings; and sprinkle on it all the blood of the burnt offering and all the blood of the sacrifice. And the bronze altar shall be for me to inquire *by*." ¹⁶Thus did Urijah the priest, according to all that King Ahaz commanded.

¹⁷And King Ahaz cut off the panels of the carts, and removed the lavers from them; and he took down the Sea from the bronze oxen that *were* under it, and put it on a pavement of stones. ¹⁸Also he removed the Sabbath pavilion which they had built in the temple, and he removed the king's outer entrance from the house of the LORD, on account of the king of Assyria.

¹⁹Now the rest of the acts of Ahaz which he did, *are* they not written in the book of the chronicles of the kings of Judah? ²⁰So Ahaz rested with his fathers, and was buried with his fathers in the City of David. Then Hezekiah his son reigned in his place.

CHAPTER **17** **ISRAEL IS TAKEN INTO CAPTIVITY.** In the twelfth year of Ahaz king of Judah, Hoshea the son of Elah became king of Israel in Samaria, *and he reigned* nine years. ²And he did evil in the sight of the LORD, but not as the kings of Israel who were before him. ³Shalmaneser king of Assyria came up against him; and Hoshea became his vassal, and paid him tribute money. ⁴And the king of Assyria uncovered a conspiracy by Hoshea; for he had sent messengers to So, king of Egypt, and brought no tribute to the king of Assyria, as *he had done* year by year. Therefore the king of Assyria shut him up, and bound him in prison.

⁵Now the king of Assyria went throughout all the land, and went up to Samaria and besieged it for three years. ⁶In the ninth year of Hoshea, the king of Assyria took

▰▰▰▰COPYING

17:7-17 The Lord judged the people of Israel because they copied the evil customs of the surrounding nations, worshiping false gods, accommodating heathen customs, and following their own desires. It is not safe to copy the world's customs, because godless people tend to live selfishly. And to live for yourself, as Israel learned, brings serious consequences from God. Sometimes it is difficult and painful to follow God, but consider the alternative. You can live for God, or die for yourself. Determine to be God's person and do what he says regardless of the cost. What God thinks of you is infinitely more important than what the world thinks. (See Romans 12:1-2; 1 John 2:15-17.)

Samaria and carried Israel away to Assyria, and placed them in Halah and by the Habor, the River of Gozan, and in the cities of the Medes.

[7]For so it was that the children of Israel had sinned against the LORD their God, who had brought them up out of the land of Egypt, from under the hand of Pharaoh king of Egypt; and they had feared other gods, [8]and had walked in the statutes of the nations whom the LORD had cast out from before the children of Israel, and of the kings of Israel, which they had made. [9]Also the children of Israel secretly did against the LORD their God things that *were* not right, and they built for themselves high places in all their cities, from watchtower to fortified city. [10]They set up for themselves *sacred* pillars and wooden images on every high hill and under every green tree. [11]There they burned incense on all the high places, like the nations whom the LORD had carried away before them; and they did wicked things to provoke the LORD to anger, [12]for they served idols, of which the LORD had said to them, "You shall not do this thing."

ISRAEL TAKEN CAPTIVE

Finally the sins of Israel's people caught up with them. God allowed Assyria to defeat and disperse the people. They were led into captivity, swallowed up by the mighty, evil Assyrian empire. Sin always brings discipline, and the consequences that sin are sometimes irreversible.

GOOD LUCK CHARMS

17:27-29 The new settlers in Israel worshiped God without giving up their heathen customs. They worshiped God to appease him rather than to please him, treating him as a good luck charm or just another idol to add to their collection. A similar attitude is common today. Many people claim to believe in God while refusing to give up attitudes and actions that God denounces. God cannot be added to the values we already have. He must come first, and his Word must shape all our actions and attitudes.

[13]Yet the LORD testified against Israel and against Judah, by all of His prophets, every seer, saying, "Turn from your evil ways, and keep My commandments *and* My statutes, according to all the law which I commanded your fathers, and which I sent to you by My servants the prophets." [14]Nevertheless they would not hear, but stiffened their necks, like the necks of their fathers, who did not believe in the LORD their God. [15]And they rejected His statutes and His covenant that He had made with their fathers, and His testimonies which He had testified against them; they followed idols, became idolaters, and *went* after the nations who *were* all around them, *concerning* whom the LORD had charged them that they should not do like them. [16]So they left all the commandments of the LORD their God, made for themselves a molded image *and* two calves, made a wooden image and worshiped all the host of heaven, and served Baal. [17]And they caused their sons and daughters to pass through the fire, practiced witchcraft and soothsaying, and sold themselves to do evil in the sight of the LORD, to provoke Him to anger. [18]Therefore the LORD was very angry with Israel, and removed them from His sight; there was none left but the tribe of Judah alone.

[19]Also Judah did not keep the commandments of the LORD their God, but walked in the statutes of Israel which they made. [20]And the LORD rejected all the descendants of Israel, afflicted them, and delivered them into the hand of plunderers, until He had cast them from His sight. [21]For He tore Israel from the house of David, and they made Jeroboam the son of Nebat king. Then Jeroboam

drove Israel from following the LORD, and made them commit a great sin. [22]For the children of Israel walked in all the sins of Jeroboam which he did; they did not depart from them, [23]until the LORD removed Israel out of His sight, as He had said by all His servants the prophets. So Israel was carried away from their own land to Assyria, *as it is* to this day.

[24]Then the king of Assyria brought *people* from Babylon, Cuthah, Ava, Hamath, and from Sepharvaim, and placed *them* in the cities of Samaria instead of the children of Israel; and they took possession of Samaria and dwelt in its cities. [25]And it was so, at the beginning of their dwelling there, *that* they did not fear the LORD; therefore the LORD sent lions among them, which killed *some* of them. [26]So they spoke to the king of Assyria, saying, "The nations whom you have removed and placed in the cities of Samaria do not know the rituals of the God of the land; therefore He has sent lions among them, and indeed, they are killing them because they do not know the rituals of the God of the land." [27]Then the king of Assyria commanded, saying, "Send there one of the priests whom you brought from there; let him go and dwell there, and let him teach them the rituals of the God of the land." [28]Then one of the priests whom they had carried away from Samaria came and dwelt in Bethel, and taught them how they should fear the LORD.

[29]However every nation continued to make gods of its own, and put *them* in the shrines of the high places which the Samaritans had made, *every* nation in the cities where they dwelt. [30]The men of Babylon made Succoth Benoth, the men of Cuth made Nergal, the men of Hamath made Ashima, [31]and the Avites made Nibhaz and Tartak; and the Sepharvites burned their children in fire to Adrammelech and Anammelech, the gods of Sepharvaim. [32]So they feared the LORD, and from every class they appointed for themselves priests of the high places, who sacrificed for them in the shrines of the high places. [33]They feared the LORD, yet served their own gods—according to the rituals of the nations from among whom they were carried away.

[34]To this day they continue practicing the former rituals; they do not fear the LORD, nor do they follow their

statutes or their ordinances, or the law and commandment which the LORD had commanded the children of Jacob, whom He named Israel, [35]with whom the LORD had made a covenant and charged them, saying: "You shall not fear other gods, nor bow down to them nor serve them nor sacrifice to them; [36]but the LORD, who brought you up from the land of Egypt with great power and an outstretched arm, Him you shall fear, Him you shall worship, and to Him you shall offer sacrifice. [37]And the statutes, the ordinances, the law, and the commandment which He wrote for you, you shall be careful to observe forever; you shall not fear other gods. [38]And the covenant that I have made with you, you shall not forget, nor shall you fear other gods. [39]But the LORD your God you shall fear; and He will deliver you from the hand of all your enemies." [40]However they did not obey, but they followed their former rituals. [41]So these nations feared the LORD, yet served their carved images; also their children and their children's children have continued doing as their fathers did, even to this day.

CHAPTER 18 HEZEKIAH RULES JUDAH. Now it came to pass in the third year of Hoshea the son of Elah, king of Israel, *that* Hezekiah the son of Ahaz, king of Judah, began to reign. [2]He was twenty-five years old when he became king, and he reigned twenty-nine years in Jerusalem. His mother's name *was* Abi the daughter of Zechariah. [3]And he did *what was* right in the sight of the LORD, according to all that his father David had done.

[4]He removed the high places and broke the *sacred* pillars, cut down the wooden image and broke in pieces the bronze serpent that Moses had made; for until those days the children of Israel burned incense to it, and called it Nehushtan. [5]He trusted in the LORD God of Israel, so that after him was none like him among all the kings of Judah, nor who were before him. [6]For he held fast to the LORD; he did not depart from following Him, but kept His commandments, which the LORD had commanded Moses. [7]The LORD was with him; he prospered wherever he went. And he rebelled against the king of Assyria and did not serve him. [8]He subdued the Philistines, as far as Gaza and its territory, from watchtower to fortified city.

[9]Now it came to pass in the fourth year of King Hezekiah, which *was* the seventh year of Hoshea the son of Elah, king of Israel, *that* Shalmaneser king of Assyria came up against Samaria and besieged it. [10]And at the end of three years they took it. In the sixth year of Hezekiah, that *is*, the ninth year of Hoshea king of Israel, Samaria was taken. [11]Then the king of Assyria carried Israel away captive to Assyria, and put them in Halah and by the Habor, the River of Gozan, and in the cities of the Medes, [12]because they did not obey the voice of the LORD their God, but transgressed His covenant *and* all that Moses the servant of the LORD had commanded; and they would neither hear nor do *them*.

[13]And in the fourteenth year of King Hezekiah, Sennacherib king of Assyria came up against all the fortified cities of Judah and took them. [14]Then Hezekiah king of Judah sent to the king of Assyria at Lachish, saying, "I have done wrong; turn away from me; whatever you impose on me I will pay." And the king of Assyria assessed Hezekiah king of Judah three hundred talents of silver and thirty talents of gold. [15]So Hezekiah gave *him* all the silver that was found in the house of the LORD and in the treasuries of the king's house. [16]At that time Hezekiah stripped *the gold from* the doors of the temple of the LORD, and *from* the pillars which Hezekiah king of Judah had overlaid, and gave it to the king of Assyria.

[17]Then the king of Assyria sent *the* Tartan, *the* Rabsaris, *and the* Rabshakeh from Lachish, with a great army against Jerusalem, to King Hezekiah. And they went up and came to Jerusalem. When they had come up, they went and stood by the aqueduct from the upper pool, which *was* on the highway to the Fuller's Field. [18]And when they had called to the king, Eliakim the son of Hilkiah, who *was* over the household, Shebna the scribe, and Joah the son of Asaph, the recorder, came out to them. [19]Then *the* Rabshakeh said to them, "Say now to Hezekiah, 'Thus says the great king, the king of Assyria: "What confidence *is* this in which you trust? [20]You speak of *having* plans and power for war; but *they are* mere words. And in whom do you trust, that you rebel against me? [21]Now look! You are trusting in the staff of this broken reed, Egypt, on which if a man leans, it will go into his hand and pierce it. So *is* Pharaoh king of Egypt to all who trust in him. [22]But if you say to me, 'We trust in the LORD our God,' *is* it not He whose high places and whose altars Hezekiah has taken away, and said to Judah and Jerusalem, 'You shall worship before this altar in Jerusalem'?" ' [23]Now therefore, I urge you, give a pledge to my master the king of Assyria, and I will give you two thousand horses—if you are able on your part to put riders on them! [24]How then will you repel one captain of the least of my master's servants, and put your trust in Egypt for chariots and horsemen? [25]Have I now come up without the LORD against this place to destroy it? The LORD said to me, 'Go up against this land, and destroy it.' "

[26]Then Eliakim the son of Hilkiah, Shebna, and Joah said to *the* Rabshakeh, "Please speak to your servants in Aramaic, for we understand *it;* and do not speak to us in Hebrew in the hearing of the people who *are* on the wall."

[27]But *the* Rabshakeh said to them, "Has my master sent me to your master and to you to speak these words, and not to the men who sit on the wall, who will eat and drink their own waste with you?"

[28]Then *the* Rabshakeh stood and called out with a loud voice in Hebrew, and spoke, saying, "Hear the word of the great king, the king of Assyria! [29]Thus says the king: 'Do not let Hezekiah deceive you, for he shall not be able to deliver you from his hand; [30]nor let Hezekiah make you trust in the LORD, saying, "The LORD will surely deliver us;

▬▬▬▬▬▬▬▬▬▬▬▬▬IDOL CURE

18:4 The bronze serpent had been made to cure the Israelites of a deadly plague (Numbers 21:4-9). It demonstrated God's presence and power and reminded the people of his mercy and forgiveness. But it had become an object of worship instead of a reminder of *whom* to worship, so Hezekiah was forced to destroy it. We must be careful that the things we use to aid our worship don't become objects of worship themselves. Most objects are not made to be idols—they become idols by the way people use them.

this city shall not be given into the hand of the king of Assyria." ' ³¹Do not listen to Hezekiah; for thus says the king of Assyria: 'Make *peace* with me by a present and come out to me; and every one of you eat from his own vine and every one from his own fig tree, and every one of you drink the waters of his own cistern; ³²until I come and take you away to a land like your own land, a land of grain and new wine, a land of bread and vineyards, a land of olive groves and honey, that you may live and not die. But do not listen to Hezekiah, lest he persuade you, saying, "The LORD will deliver us." ³³Has any of the gods of the nations at all delivered its land from the hand of the king of Assyria? ³⁴Where *are* the gods of Hamath and Arpad? Where *are* the gods of Sepharvaim and Hena and Ivah? Indeed, have they delivered Samaria from my hand? ³⁵Who among all the gods of the lands have delivered their countries from my hand, that the LORD should deliver Jerusalem from my hand?' "

³⁶But the people held their peace and answered him not a word; for the king's commandment was, "Do not answer him." ³⁷Then Eliakim the son of Hilkiah, who *was* over the household, Shebna the scribe, and Joah the son of Asaph, the recorder, came to Hezekiah with *their* clothes torn, and told him the words of *the* Rabshakeh.

CHAPTER 19 ISAIAH TELLS OF GOD'S PLAN. And

so it was, when King Hezekiah heard *it*, that he tore his clothes, covered himself with sackcloth, and went into the house of the LORD. ²Then he sent Eliakim, who *was* over the household, Shebna the scribe, and the elders of the priests, covered with sackcloth, to Isaiah the prophet, the son of Amoz. ³And they said to him, "Thus says Hezekiah: 'This day *is* a day of trouble, and rebuke, and blasphemy; for the children have come to birth, but *there is* no strength to bring them forth. ⁴It may be that the LORD your God will hear all the words of *the* Rabshakeh, whom his master the king of Assyria has sent to reproach the living God, and will rebuke the words which the LORD your God has heard. Therefore lift up *your* prayer for the remnant that is left.' "

⁵So the servants of King Hezekiah came to Isaiah. ⁶And Isaiah said to them, "Thus you shall say to your master, 'Thus says the LORD: "Do not be afraid of the words which you have heard, with which the servants of the king of Assyria have blasphemed Me. ⁷Surely I will send a spirit upon him, and he shall hear a rumor and return to his own land; and I will cause him to fall by the sword in his own land." ' "

⁸Then *the* Rabshakeh returned and found the king of Assyria warring against Libnah, for he heard that he had departed from Lachish. ⁹And the king heard concerning Tirhakah king of Ethiopia, "Look, he has come out to make war with you." So he again sent messengers to Hezekiah, saying, ¹⁰"Thus you shall speak to Hezekiah king of Judah, saying: 'Do not let your God in whom you trust deceive you, saying, "Jerusalem shall not be given into the hand of the king of Assyria." ¹¹Look! You have heard what the kings of Assyria have done to all lands by utterly destroying them; and shall you be delivered? ¹²Have the gods of the nations delivered those whom my

━━━━━PRAYER

19:1 Sennacherib, whose armies had captured all the fortified cit[ies] [of] Judah, sent a message to Hezekiah to surrender because resistance [was] futile. Realizing the situation was hopeless, Hezekiah went to the te[mple] and prayed. He knew that God specializes in impossible situations. [God] answered Hezekiah's prayer and delivered Judah by sending an a[rmy to] attack the Assyrian capital, forcing Sennacherib to leave at once. P[rayer] should be our first response in any crisis. Our problems are God's opportunities.

fathers have destroyed, Gozan and Haran and Rezeph, and the people of Eden who *were* in Telassar? ¹³Where *is* the king of Hamath, the king of Arpad, and the king of the city of Sepharvaim, Hena, and Ivah?' "

¹⁴And Hezekiah received the letter from the hand of the messengers, and read it; and Hezekiah went up to the house of the LORD, and spread it before the LORD. ¹⁵Then Hezekiah prayed before the LORD, and said: "O LORD God of Israel, *the One* who dwells *between* the cherubim, You are God, You alone, of all the kingdoms of the earth. You have made heaven and earth. ¹⁶Incline Your ear, O LORD, and hear; open Your eyes, O LORD, and see; and hear the words of Sennacherib, which he has sent to reproach the living God. ¹⁷Truly, LORD, the kings of Assyria have laid waste the nations and their lands, ¹⁸and have cast their gods into the fire; for they *were* not gods, but the work of men's hands—wood and stone. Therefore they destroyed them. ¹⁹Now therefore, O LORD our God, I pray, save us from his hand, that all the kingdoms of the earth may know that You *are* the LORD God, You alone."

²⁰Then Isaiah the son of Amoz sent to Hezekiah, saying, "Thus says the LORD God of Israel: 'Because you have prayed to Me against Sennacherib king of Assyria, I have heard.' ²¹This *is* the word which the LORD has spoken concerning him:

'The virgin, the daughter of Zion,
  Has despised you, laughed you to scorn;
  The daughter of Jerusalem
  Has shaken *her* head behind your back!

²² 'Whom have you reproached and blasphemed?
  Against whom have you raised *your* voice,
  And lifted up your eyes on high?
  Against the Holy *One* of Israel.

²³ By your messengers you have reproached the Lord,
  And said: "By the multitude of my chariots
  I have come up to the height of the mountains,
  To the limits of Lebanon;
  I will cut down its tall cedars
  And its choice cypress trees;
  I will enter the extremity of its borders,
  To its fruitful forest.

²⁴ I have dug and drunk strange water,
  And with the soles of my feet I have dried up

━━━━━NO FEAR

19:15-19 Although Hezekiah came boldly to God, he did not [take it] for granted or approach him flippantly. Instead, he acknowledge[d God's] sovereignty and Judah's total dependence upon him. Hezekiah's [prayer] provides a good model for us. We should not be afraid to appro[ach him] with our prayers, but we must come to him with respect for who [he is and] what he can do.

All the brooks of defense."

²⁵ 'Did you not hear long ago
How I made it,
From ancient times that I formed it?
Now I have brought it to pass,
That you should be
For crushing fortified cities *into* heaps of ruins.
²⁶ Therefore their inhabitants had little power;
They were dismayed and confounded;
They were *as* the grass of the field
And the green herb,
As the grass on the housetops
And *grain* blighted before it is grown.

²⁷ 'But I know your dwelling place,
Your going out and your coming in,
And your rage against Me.
²⁸ Because your rage against Me and your tumult
Have come up to My ears,
Therefore I will put My hook in your nose
And My bridle in your lips,
And I will turn you back
By the way which you came.

²⁹'This *shall be* a sign to you:

You shall eat this year such as grows of itself,
And in the second year what springs from the same;
Also in the third year sow and reap,
Plant vineyards and eat the fruit of them.
³⁰ And the remnant who have escaped of the house of
Judah
Shall again take root downward,
And bear fruit upward.
³¹ For out of Jerusalem shall go a remnant,
And those who escape from Mount Zion.
The zeal of the LORD of hosts will do this.'

³²"Therefore thus says the LORD concerning the king of
Assyria:

'He shall not come into this city,
Nor shoot an arrow there,
Nor come before it with shield,
Nor build a siege mound against it.
³³ By the way that he came,
By the same shall he return;
And he shall not come into this city,'
Says the LORD.
³⁴ 'For I will defend this city, to save it
For My own sake and for My servant David's sake.' "

³⁵And it came to pass on a certain night that the angel of the LORD went out, and killed in the camp of the Assyrians one hundred and eighty-five thousand; and when *people* arose early in the morning, there were the corpses—all dead. ³⁶So Sennacherib king of Assyria departed and went away, returned *home,* and remained at Nineveh. ³⁷Now it came to pass, as he was worshiping in the temple of Nisroch his god, that his sons Adrammelech and Sharezer struck him down with the sword; and they escaped into the land of Ararat. Then Esarhaddon his son reigned in his place.

CHAPTER **20** HEZEKIAH GETS SICK. In those days Hezekiah was sick and near death. And Isaiah the prophet, the son of Amoz, went to him and said to him, "Thus says the LORD: 'Set your house in order, for you shall die, and not live.' "

²Then he turned his face toward the wall, and prayed to the LORD, saying, ³"Remember now, O LORD, I pray, how I have walked before You in truth and with a loyal heart, and have done *what was* good in Your sight." And Hezekiah wept bitterly.

⁴And it happened, before Isaiah had gone out into the middle court, that the word of the LORD came to him, saying, ⁵"Return and tell Hezekiah the leader of My people, 'Thus says the LORD, the God of David your father: "I have heard your prayer, I have seen your tears; surely I will heal you. On the third day you shall go up to the house of the LORD. ⁶And I will add to your days fifteen years. I will deliver you and this city from the hand of the king of Assyria; and I will defend this city for My own sake, and for the sake of My servant David." ' "

◄■■■■ IN THE MINORITY

20:5-6 Over a 100-year period of Judah's history (732–640 B.C.), Hezekiah was the only faithful king; but what a difference he made! Because of Hezekiah's faith and prayer, God healed him and saved his city from the Assyrians. You can make a difference, too, even if your faith puts you in the minority. Faith and prayer, if they are sincere and directed toward the one true God, can bring about change in any situation.

⁷Then Isaiah said, "Take a lump of figs." So they took and laid *it* on the boil, and he recovered.

⁸And Hezekiah said to Isaiah, "What *is* the sign that the LORD will heal me, and that I shall go up to the house of the LORD the third day?"

⁹Then Isaiah said, "This is the sign to you from the LORD, that the LORD will do the thing which He has spoken: *shall* the shadow go forward ten degrees or go backward ten degrees?"

¹⁰And Hezekiah answered, "It is an easy thing for the shadow to go down ten degrees; no, but let the shadow go backward ten degrees."

¹¹So Isaiah the prophet cried out to the LORD, and He brought the shadow ten degrees backward, by which it had gone down on the sundial of Ahaz.

¹²At that time Berodach-Baladan the son of Baladan, king of Babylon, sent letters and a present to Hezekiah, for he heard that Hezekiah had been sick. ¹³And Hezekiah was attentive to them, and showed them all the house of his treasures—the silver and gold, the spices and precious ointment, and all his armory—all that was found among his treasures. There was nothing in his house or in all his dominion that Hezekiah did not show them.

¹⁴Then Isaiah the prophet went to King Hezekiah, and said to him, "What did these men say, and from where did they come to you?"

So Hezekiah said, "They came from a far country, from Babylon."

¹⁵And he said, "What have they seen in your house?"

So Hezekiah answered, "They have seen all that *is* in

21:6 Manasseh was an evil king, and he angered God with his sin. Listed among his sins are occult practices— soothsaying and witchcraft, and consulting spiritists and mediums. God has specific laws against the occult (Leviticus 19:31; Deuteronomy 18:9-13) because it demonstrates a lack of faith in him, involves sinful actions, and opens the door to demonic influences. Today, many books, television shows, and games emphasize fortune-telling, seances, and other occult practices. Don't let desire to know the future or the mistaken belief that superstition is harmless lead you into any occult practices. They are counterfeits of God's power and have as their root a system of beliefs totally opposed to God.

my house; there is nothing among my treasures that I have not shown them."

[16]Then Isaiah said to Hezekiah, "Hear the word of the LORD: [17]'Behold, the days are coming when all that is in your house, and what your fathers have accumulated until this day, shall be carried to Babylon; nothing shall be left,' says the LORD. [18]'And they shall take away some of your sons who will descend from you, whom you will beget; and they shall be eunuchs in the palace of the king of Babylon.' "

[19]So Hezekiah said to Isaiah, "The word of the LORD which you have spoken is good!" For he said, "Will there not be peace and truth at least in my days?"

[20]Now the rest of the acts of Hezekiah—all his might, and how he made a pool and a tunnel and brought water into the city—are they not written in the book of the chronicles of the kings of Judah? [21]So Hezekiah rested with his fathers. Then Manasseh his son reigned in his place.

CHAPTER 21 MANASSEH RULES JUDAH.

Manasseh was twelve years old when he became king, and he reigned fifty-five years in Jerusalem. His mother's name was Hephzibah. [2]And he did evil in the sight of the LORD, according to the abominations of the nations whom the LORD had cast out before the children of Israel. [3]For he rebuilt the high places which Hezekiah his father had destroyed; he raised up altars for Baal, and made a wooden image, as Ahab king of Israel had done; and he worshiped all the host of heaven and served them. [4]He also built altars in the house of the LORD, of which the LORD had said, "In Jerusalem I will put My name." [5]And he built altars for all the host of heaven in the two courts of the house of the LORD. [6]Also he made his son pass through the fire, practiced soothsaying, used witchcraft, and consulted spiritists and mediums. He did much evil in the sight of the LORD, to provoke Him to anger. [7]He even set a carved image of Asherah that he had made, in the house of which the LORD had said to David and to Solomon his son, "In this house and in Jerusalem, which I have chosen out of all the tribes of Israel, I will put My name forever; [8]and I will not make the feet of Israel wander anymore from the land which I gave their fathers— only if they are careful to do according to all that I have commanded them, and according to all the law that My servant Moses commanded them." [9]But they paid no attention, and Manasseh seduced them to do more evil than the nations whom the LORD had destroyed before the children of Israel.

[10]And the LORD spoke by His servants the prophets, saying, [11]"Because Manasseh king of Judah has done these abominations (he has acted more wickedly than all the Amorites who were before him, and has also made Judah sin with his idols), [12]therefore thus says the LORD God of Israel: 'Behold, I am bringing such calamity upon Jerusalem and Judah, that whoever hears of it, both his ears will tingle. [13]And I will stretch over Jerusalem the measuring line of Samaria and the plummet of the house of Ahab; I will wipe Jerusalem as one wipes a dish, wiping it and turning it upside down. [14]So I will forsake the remnant of My inheritance and deliver them into the hand of their enemies; and they shall become victims of plunder to all their enemies, [15]because they have done evil in My sight, and have provoked Me to anger since the day their fathers came out of Egypt, even to this day.' "

[16]Moreover Manasseh shed very much innocent blood, till he had filled Jerusalem from one end to another, besides his sin by which he made Judah sin, in doing evil in the sight of the LORD.

[17]Now the rest of the acts of Manasseh—all that he did, and the sin that he committed—are they not written in the book of the chronicles of the kings of Judah? [18]So Manasseh rested with his fathers, and was buried in the garden of his own house, in the garden of Uzza. Then his son Amon reigned in his place.

[19]Amon was twenty-two years old when he became king, and he reigned two years in Jerusalem. His mother's name was Meshullemeth the daughter of Haruz of Jotbah. [20]And he did evil in the sight of the LORD, as his father Manasseh had done. [21]So he walked in all the ways that his father had walked; and he served the idols that his father had served, and worshiped them. [22]He forsook the LORD God of his fathers, and did not walk in the way of the LORD.

[23]Then the servants of Amon conspired against him, and killed the king in his own house. [24]But the people of the land executed all those who had conspired against King Amon. Then the people of the land made his son Josiah king in his place.

[25]Now the rest of the acts of Amon which he did, are they not written in the book of the chronicles of the kings of Judah? [26]And he was buried in his tomb in the garden of Uzza. Then Josiah his son reigned in his place.

CHAPTER 22 JOSIAH BECOMES KING.

Josiah was eight years old when he became king, and he reigned thirty-one years in Jerusalem. His mother's name was Jedidah the daughter of Adaiah of Bozkath. [2]And he did what was right in the sight of the LORD, and walked in all

22:1-2 In reading the biblical lists of kings, it is rare to find one obeyed God completely. Josiah was such a person, and he was on years old when he began to reign. For 18 years he reigned obedi then, when he was 26, he began the reforms based on God's law Children are the future leaders of our churches and our world. A major work for God may have to wait until he is an adult, but no ever too young to take God seriously and obey him. Josiah's earl laid the base for his later task of reforming Judah.

this city shall not be given into the hand of the king of Assyria." ' ³¹Do not listen to Hezekiah; for thus says the king of Assyria: 'Make *peace* with me by a present and come out to me; and every one of you eat from his own vine and every one from his own fig tree, and every one of you drink the waters of his own cistern; ³²until I come and take you away to a land like your own land, a land of grain and new wine, a land of bread and vineyards, a land of olive groves and honey, that you may live and not die. But do not listen to Hezekiah, lest he persuade you, saying, "The LORD will deliver us." ³³Has any of the gods of the nations at all delivered its land from the hand of the king of Assyria? ³⁴Where *are* the gods of Hamath and Arpad? Where *are* the gods of Sepharvaim and Hena and Ivah? Indeed, have they delivered Samaria from my hand? ³⁵Who among all the gods of the lands have delivered their countries from my hand, that the LORD should deliver Jerusalem from my hand?'"

³⁶But the people held their peace and answered him not a word; for the king's commandment was, "Do not answer him." ³⁷Then Eliakim the son of Hilkiah, who *was* over the household, Shebna the scribe, and Joah the son of Asaph, the recorder, came to Hezekiah with *their* clothes torn, and told him the words of *the* Rabshakeh.

CHAPTER **19** ISAIAH TELLS OF GOD'S PLAN. And so it was, when King Hezekiah heard *it*, that he tore his clothes, covered himself with sackcloth, and went into the house of the LORD. ²Then he sent Eliakim, who *was* over the household, Shebna the scribe, and the elders of the priests, covered with sackcloth, to Isaiah the prophet, the son of Amoz. ³And they said to him, "Thus says Hezekiah: 'This day *is* a day of trouble, and rebuke, and blasphemy; for the children have come to birth, but *there is* no strength to bring them forth. ⁴It may be that the LORD your God will hear all the words of *the* Rabshakeh, whom his master the king of Assyria has sent to reproach the living God, and will rebuke the words which the LORD your God has heard. Therefore lift up *your* prayer for the remnant that is left.'"

⁵So the servants of King Hezekiah came to Isaiah. ⁶And Isaiah said to them, "Thus you shall say to your master, 'Thus says the LORD: "Do not be afraid of the words which you have heard, with which the servants of the king of Assyria have blasphemed Me. ⁷Surely I will send a spirit upon him, and he shall hear a rumor and return to his own land; and I will cause him to fall by the sword in his own land."'"

⁸Then *the* Rabshakeh returned and found the king of Assyria warring against Libnah, for he heard that he had departed from Lachish. ⁹And the king heard concerning Tirhakah king of Ethiopia, "Look, he has come out to make war with you." So he again sent messengers to Hezekiah, saying, ¹⁰"Thus you shall speak to Hezekiah king of Judah, saying: 'Do not let your God in whom you trust deceive you, saying, "Jerusalem shall not be given into the hand of the king of Assyria." ¹¹Look! You have heard what the kings of Assyria have done to all lands by utterly destroying them; and shall you be delivered? ¹²Have the gods of the nations delivered those whom my

fathers have destroyed, Gozan and Haran and Rezeph, and the people of Eden who *were* in Telassar? ¹³Where *is* the king of Hamath, the king of Arpad, and the king of the city of Sepharvaim, Hena, and Ivah?'"

¹⁴And Hezekiah received the letter from the hand of the messengers, and read it; and Hezekiah went up to the house of the LORD, and spread it before the LORD. ¹⁵Then Hezekiah prayed before the LORD, and said: "O LORD God of Israel, *the One* who dwells *between* the cherubim, You are God, You alone, of all the kingdoms of the earth. You have made heaven and earth. ¹⁶Incline Your ear, O LORD, and hear; open Your eyes, O LORD, and see; and hear the words of Sennacherib, which he has sent to reproach the living God. ¹⁷Truly, LORD, the kings of Assyria have laid waste the nations and their lands, ¹⁸and have cast their gods into the fire; for they *were* not gods, but the work of men's hands—wood and stone. Therefore they destroyed them. ¹⁹Now therefore, O LORD our God, I pray, save us from his hand, that all the kingdoms of the earth may know that You *are* the LORD God, You alone."

²⁰Then Isaiah the son of Amoz sent to Hezekiah, saying, "Thus says the LORD God of Israel: 'Because you have prayed to Me against Sennacherib king of Assyria, I have heard.' ²¹This *is* the word which the LORD has spoken concerning him:

'The virgin, the daughter of Zion,
  Has despised you, laughed you to scorn;
  The daughter of Jerusalem
  Has shaken *her* head behind your back!

²² 'Whom have you reproached and blasphemed?
  Against whom have you raised *your* voice,
  And lifted up your eyes on high?
  Against the Holy *One* of Israel.

²³ By your messengers you have reproached the Lord,
  And said: "By the multitude of my chariots
  I have come up to the height of the mountains,
  To the limits of Lebanon;
  I will cut down its tall cedars
  And its choice cypress trees;
  I will enter the extremity of its borders,
  To its fruitful forest.

²⁴ I have dug and drunk strange water,
  And with the soles of my feet I have dried up

statutes or their ordinances, or the law and commandment which the LORD had commanded the children of Jacob, whom He named Israel, ³⁵with whom the LORD had made a covenant and charged them, saying: "You shall not fear other gods, nor bow down to them nor serve them nor sacrifice to them; ³⁶but the LORD, who brought you up from the land of Egypt with great power and an outstretched arm, Him you shall fear, Him you shall worship, and to Him you shall offer sacrifice. ³⁷And the statutes, the ordinances, the law, and the commandment which He wrote for you, you shall be careful to observe forever; you shall not fear other gods, ³⁸And the covenant that I have made with you, you shall not forget, nor shall you fear other gods. ³⁹But the LORD your God you shall fear; and He will deliver you from the hand of all your enemies." ⁴⁰However they did not obey, but they followed their former rituals. ⁴¹So these nations feared the LORD, yet served their carved images; also their children and their children's children have continued doing as their fathers did, even to this day.

CHAPTER **18** HEZEKIAH RULES JUDAH. Now it
came to pass in the third year of Hoshea the son of Elah, king of Israel, *that* Hezekiah the son of Ahaz, king of Judah, began to reign. ²He was twenty-five years old when he became king, and he reigned twenty-nine years in Jerusalem. His mother's name *was* Abi the daughter of Zechariah. ³And he did *what was* right in the sight of the LORD, according to all that his father David had done.

⁴He removed the high places and broke the *sacred* pillars, cut down the wooden image and broke in pieces the bronze serpent that Moses had made; for until those days the children of Israel burned incense to it, and called it Nehushtan. ⁵He trusted in the LORD God of Israel, so that after him was none like him among all the kings of Judah, nor who were before him. ⁶For he held fast to the LORD; he did not depart from following Him, but kept His commandments, which the LORD had commanded Moses. ⁷The LORD was with him; he prospered wherever he went. And he rebelled against the king of Assyria and did not serve him. ⁸He subdued the Philistines, as far as Gaza and its territory, from watchtower to fortified city.

⁹Now it came to pass in the fourth year of King Hezekiah, which *was* the seventh year of Hoshea the son of Elah, king of Israel, *that* Shalmaneser king of Assyria came up against Samaria and besieged it. ¹⁰And at the end of three years they took it. In the sixth year of Hezekiah, that *is*, the ninth year of Hoshea king of Israel, Samaria was taken. ¹¹Then the king of Assyria carried Israel away captive to Assyria, and put them in Halah and by the Habor, the River of Gozan, and in the cities of the Medes, ¹²because they did not obey the voice of the LORD their God, but transgressed His covenant *and* all that Moses the servant of the LORD had commanded; and they would neither hear nor do *them*.

¹³And in the fourteenth year of King Hezekiah, Sennacherib king of Assyria came up against all the fortified cities of Judah and took them. ¹⁴Then Hezekiah king of Judah sent to the king of Assyria at Lachish, saying, "I have done wrong; turn away from me; whatever you

impose on me I will pay." And the king of Assyria assessed Hezekiah king of Judah three hundred talents of silver and thirty talents of gold. ¹⁵So Hezekiah gave *him* all the silver that was found in the house of the LORD and in the treasuries of the king's house. ¹⁶At that time Hezekiah stripped *the gold from* the doors of the temple of the LORD, and *from* the pillars which Hezekiah king of Judah had overlaid, and gave it to the king of Assyria.

¹⁷Then the king of Assyria sent *the* Tartan, *the* Rabsaris, *and the* Rabshakeh from Lachish, with a great army against Jerusalem, to King Hezekiah. And they went up and came to Jerusalem. When they had come up, they went and stood by the aqueduct from the upper pool, which *was* on the highway to the Fuller's Field. ¹⁸And when they had called to the king, Eliakim the son of Hilkiah, who *was* over the household, Shebna the scribe, and Joah the son of Asaph, the recorder, came out to them. ¹⁹Then *the* Rabshakeh said to them, "Say now to Hezekiah, 'Thus says the great king, the king of Assyria: "What confidence *is* this in which you trust? ²⁰You speak of *having* plans and power for war; but *they are* mere words. And in whom do you trust, that you rebel against me? ²¹Now look! You are trusting in the staff of this broken reed, Egypt, on which if a man leans, it will go into his hand and pierce it. So *is* Pharaoh king of Egypt to all who trust in him. ²²But if you say to me, 'We trust in the LORD our God,' *is* it not He whose high places and whose altars Hezekiah has taken away, and said to Judah and Jerusalem, 'You shall worship before this altar in Jerusalem'?" ' ²³Now therefore, I urge you, give a pledge to my master the king of Assyria, and I will give you two thousand horses—if you are able on your part to put riders on them! ²⁴How then will you repel one captain of the least of my master's servants, and put your trust in Egypt for chariots and horsemen? ²⁵Have I now come up without the LORD against this place to destroy it? The LORD said to me, 'Go up against this land, and destroy it.'"

²⁶Then Eliakim the son of Hilkiah, Shebna, and Joah said to *the* Rabshakeh, "Please speak to your servants in Aramaic, for we understand *it;* and do not speak to us in Hebrew in the hearing of the people who *are* on the wall." ²⁷But *the* Rabshakeh said to them, "Has my master sent me to your master and to you to speak these words, and not to the men who sit on the wall, who will eat and drink their own waste with you?"

²⁸Then *the* Rabshakeh stood and called out with a loud voice in Hebrew, and spoke, saying, "Hear the word of the great king, the king of Assyria! ²⁹Thus says the king: 'Do not let Hezekiah deceive you, for he shall not be able to deliver you from his hand; ³⁰nor let Hezekiah make you trust in the LORD, saying, "The LORD will surely deliver us;

◣▬▬▬▬▬▬▬▬▬█IDOL CURE

18:4 The bronze serpent had been made to cure the Israelites of a deadly plague (Numbers 21:4-9). It demonstrated God's presence and power and reminded the people of his mercy and forgiveness. But it had become an object of worship instead of a reminder of *whom* to worship, so Hezekiah was forced to destroy it. We must be careful that the things we use to aid our worship don't become objects of worship themselves. Most objects are not made to be idols—they become idols by the way people use them.

Samaria and carried Israel away to Assyria, and placed them in Halah and by the Habor, the River of Gozan, and in the cities of the Medes.

⁷For so it was that the children of Israel had sinned against the LORD their God, who had brought them up out of the land of Egypt, from under the hand of Pharaoh king of Egypt; and they had feared other gods, ⁸and had walked in the statutes of the nations whom the LORD had cast out from before the children of Israel, and of the kings of Israel, which they had made. ⁹Also the children of Israel secretly did against the LORD their God things that *were* not right, and they built for themselves high places in all their cities, from watchtower to fortified city. ¹⁰They set up for themselves *sacred* pillars and wooden images on every high hill and under every green tree. ¹¹There they burned incense on all the high places, like the nations whom the LORD had carried away before them; and they did wicked things to provoke the LORD to anger, ¹²for they served idols, of which the LORD had said to them, "You shall not do this thing."

GOOD LUCK CHARMS

17:27-29 The new settlers in Israel worshiped God without giving up their heathen customs. They worshiped God to appease him rather than to please him, treating him as a good luck charm or just another idol to add to their collection. A similar attitude is common today. Many people claim to believe in God while refusing to give up attitudes and actions that God denounces. God cannot be added to the values we already have. He must come first, and his Word must shape all our actions and attitudes.

¹³Yet the LORD testified against Israel and against Judah, by all of His prophets, every seer, saying, "Turn from your evil ways, and keep My commandments *and* My statutes, according to all the law which I commanded your fathers, and which I sent to you by My servants the prophets." ¹⁴Nevertheless they would not hear, but stiffened their necks, like the necks of their fathers, who did not believe in the LORD their God. ¹⁵And they rejected His statutes and His covenant that He had made with their fathers, and His testimonies which He had testified against them; they followed idols, became idolaters, and *went* after the nations who *were* all around them, *concerning* whom the LORD had charged them that they should not do like them. ¹⁶So they left all the commandments of the LORD their God, made for themselves a molded image *and* two calves, made a wooden image and worshiped all the host of heaven, and served Baal. ¹⁷And they caused their sons and daughters to pass through the fire, practiced witchcraft and soothsaying, and sold themselves to do evil in the sight of the LORD, to provoke Him to anger. ¹⁸Therefore the LORD was very angry with Israel, and removed them from His sight; there was none left but the tribe of Judah alone.

¹⁹Also Judah did not keep the commandments of the LORD their God, but walked in the statutes of Israel which they made. ²⁰And the LORD rejected all the descendants of Israel, afflicted them, and delivered them into the hand of plunderers, until He had cast them from His sight. ²¹For He tore Israel from the house of David, and they made Jeroboam the son of Nebat king. Then Jeroboam

drove Israel from following the LORD, and made them commit a great sin. ²²For the children of Israel walked in all the sins of Jeroboam which he did; they did not depart from them, ²³until the LORD removed Israel out of His sight, as He had said by all His servants the prophets. So Israel was carried away from their own land to Assyria, *as it is* to this day.

²⁴Then the king of Assyria brought *people* from Babylon, Cuthah, Ava, Hamath, and from Sepharvaim, and placed *them* in the cities of Samaria instead of the children of Israel; and they took possession of Samaria and dwelt in its cities. ²⁵And it was so, at the beginning of their dwelling there, *that* they did not fear the LORD; therefore the LORD sent lions among them, which killed *some* of them. ²⁶So they spoke to the king of Assyria, saying, "The nations whom you have removed and placed in the cities of Samaria do not know the rituals of the God of the land; therefore He has sent lions among them, and indeed, they are killing them because they do not know the rituals of the God of the land." ²⁷Then the king of Assyria commanded, saying, "Send there one of the priests whom you brought from there; let him go and dwell there, and let him teach them the rituals of the God of the land." ²⁸Then one of the priests whom they had carried away from Samaria came and dwelt in Bethel, and taught them how they should fear the LORD.

²⁹However every nation continued to make gods of its own, and put *them* in the shrines on the high places which the Samaritans had made, *every* nation in the cities where they dwelt. ³⁰The men of Babylon made Succoth Benoth, the men of Cuth made Nergal, the men of Hamath made Ashima, ³¹and the Avites made Nibhaz and Tartak; and the Sepharvites burned their children in fire to Adrammelech and Anammelech, the gods of Sepharvaim. ³²So they feared the LORD, and from every class they appointed for themselves priests of the high places, who sacrificed for them in the shrines of the high places. ³³They feared the LORD, yet served their own gods—according to the rituals of the nations from among whom they were carried away.

³⁴To this day they continue practicing the former rituals; they do not fear the LORD, nor do they follow their

³²In the second year of Pekah the son of Remaliah, king of Israel, Jotham the son of Uzziah, king of Judah, began to reign. ³³He was twenty-five years old when he became king, and he reigned sixteen years in Jerusalem. His mother's name *was* Jerusha the daughter of Zadok. ³⁴And he did *what was* right in the sight of the LORD; he did according to all that his father Uzziah had done. ³⁵However the high places were not removed; the people still sacrificed and burned incense on the high places. He built the Upper Gate of the house of the LORD.

³⁶Now the rest of the acts of Jotham, and all that he did, *are* they not written in the book of the chronicles of the kings of Judah? ³⁷In those days the LORD began to send Rezin king of Syria and Pekah the son of Remaliah against Judah. ³⁸So Jotham rested with his fathers, and was buried with his fathers in the City of David his father. Then Ahaz his son reigned in his place.

CHAPTER 16 AHAZ RULES JUDAH.

In the seventeenth year of Pekah the son of Remaliah, Ahaz the son of Jotham, king of Judah, began to reign. ²Ahaz *was* twenty years old when he became king, and he reigned sixteen years in Jerusalem; and he did not do *what was* right in the sight of the LORD his God, as his father David *had done*. ³But he walked in the way of the kings of Israel; indeed he made his son pass through the fire, according to the abominations of the nations whom the LORD had cast out from before the children of Israel. ⁴And he sacrificed and burned incense on the high places, on the hills, and under every green tree.

⁵Then Rezin king of Syria and Pekah the son of Remaliah, king of Israel, came up to Jerusalem to *make* war; and they besieged Ahaz but could not overcome *him*. ⁶At that time Rezin king of Syria captured Elath for Syria, and drove the men of Judah from Elath. Then the Edomites went to Elath, and dwell there to this day.

⁷So Ahaz sent messengers to Tiglath-Pileser king of Assyria, saying, "I *am* your servant and your son. Come up and save me from the hand of the king of Syria and from the hand of the king of Israel, who rise up against me." ⁸And Ahaz took the silver and gold that was found in the house of the LORD, and in the treasuries of the king's house, and sent *it as* a present to the king of Assyria. ⁹So the king of Assyria heeded him; for the king of Assyria went up against Damascus and took it, carried *its people* captive to Kir, and killed Rezin.

¹⁰Now King Ahaz went to Damascus to meet Tiglath-Pileser king of Assyria, and saw an altar that *was* at Damascus; and King Ahaz sent to Urijah the priest the design of the altar and its pattern, according to all its workmanship. ¹¹Then Urijah the priest built an altar according to all that King Ahaz had sent from Damascus. So Urijah the priest made *it* before King Ahaz came back from Damascus. ¹²And when the king came back from Damascus, the king saw the altar; and the king approached the altar and made offerings on it. ¹³So he burned his burnt offering and his grain offering; and he poured his drink offering and sprinkled the blood of his peace offerings on the altar. ¹⁴He also brought the bronze altar which *was* before the LORD, from the front of the

temple—from between the *new* altar and the house of the LORD—and put it on the north side of the *new* altar. ¹⁵Then King Ahaz commanded Urijah the priest, saying, "On the great *new* altar burn the morning burnt offering, the evening grain offering, the king's burnt sacrifice, and

CALLOUS WORSHIP

16:10-16 Evil King Ahaz copied heathen religious customs, changed the temple services, and used the temple altar for his personal benefit. In so doing, he demonstrated a callous disregard for God's commands. We condemn Ahaz for his action, but we do the same thing if we try to mold God's message to fit our personal preferences. We must worship God for who he is, not what we would selfishly like him to be.

his grain offering, with the burnt offering of all the people of the land, their grain offering, and their drink offerings; and sprinkle on it all the blood of the burnt offering and all the blood of the sacrifice. And the bronze altar shall be for me to inquire *by*." ¹⁶Thus did Urijah the priest, according to all that King Ahaz commanded.

¹⁷And King Ahaz cut off the panels of the carts, and removed the lavers from them; and he took down the Sea from the bronze oxen that *were* under it, and put it on a pavement of stones. ¹⁸Also he removed the Sabbath pavilion which they had built in the temple, and he removed the king's outer entrance from the house of the LORD, on account of the king of Assyria.

¹⁹Now the rest of the acts of Ahaz which he did, *are* they not written in the book of the chronicles of the kings of Judah? ²⁰So Ahaz rested with his fathers, and was buried with his fathers in the City of David. Then Hezekiah his son reigned in his place.

CHAPTER 17 ISRAEL IS TAKEN INTO CAPTIVITY.

In the twelfth year of Ahaz king of Judah, Hoshea the son of Elah became king of Israel in Samaria, *and he reigned* nine years. ²And he did evil in the sight of the LORD, but not as the kings of Israel who were before him. ³Shalmaneser king of Assyria came up against him; and Hoshea became his vassal, and paid him tribute money. ⁴And the king of Assyria uncovered a conspiracy by Hoshea; for he had sent messengers to So, king of Egypt, and brought no tribute to the king of Assyria, as *he had done* year by year. Therefore the king of Assyria shut him up, and bound him in prison.

⁵Now the king of Assyria went throughout all the land, and went up to Samaria and besieged it for three years. ⁶In the ninth year of Hoshea, the king of Assyria took

COPYING

17:7-17 The Lord judged the people of Israel because they copied the evil customs of the surrounding nations, worshiping false gods, accommodating heathen customs, and following their own desires. It is not safe to copy the world's customs, because godless people tend to live selfishly. And to live for yourself, as Israel learned, brings serious consequences from God. Sometimes it is difficult and painful to follow God, but consider the alternative. You can live for God, or die for yourself. Determine to be God's person and do what he says regardless of the cost. What God thinks of you is infinitely more important than what the world thinks. (See Romans 12:1-2; 1 John 2:15-17.)

15:4 Although Azariah accomplished a great deal, he failed to destroy the high places in Judah where the people worshiped idols, just as his father Amaziah and grandfather Joash had failed to do. Azariah imitated the kings he had heard stories about and watched while growing up. Although Azariah's father and grandfather were basically good kings, they were poor role models in some important areas. To rise above the influence of poor models, we must find better ones. Christ provides a perfect model. No matter how you were raised or who influenced your life, you can move beyond those limitations by taking Christ as your example and consciously trying to live as he did.

the chronicles of the kings of Israel? [29]So Jeroboam rested with his fathers, the kings of Israel. Then Zechariah his son reigned in his place.

CHAPTER 15 AZARIAH RULES JUDAH.

In the twenty-seventh year of Jeroboam king of Israel, Azariah the son of Amaziah, king of Judah, became king. [2]He was sixteen years old when he became king, and he reigned fifty-two years in Jerusalem. His mother's name *was* Jecholiah of Jerusalem. [3]And he did *what was* right in the sight of the LORD, according to all that his father Amaziah had done, [4]except that the high places were not removed; the people still sacrificed and burned incense on the high places. [5]Then the LORD struck the king, so that he was a leper until the day of his death; so he dwelt in an isolated house. And Jotham the king's son *was* over the *royal* house, judging the people of the land.

[6]Now the rest of the acts of Azariah, and all that he did, *are* they not written in the book of the chronicles of the kings of Judah? [7]So Azariah rested with his fathers, and they buried him with his fathers in the City of David. Then Jotham his son reigned in his place.

[8]In the thirty-eighth year of Azariah king of Judah, Zechariah the son of Jeroboam reigned over Israel in Samaria six months. [9]And he did evil in the sight of the LORD, as his fathers had done; he did not depart from the sins of Jeroboam the son of Nebat, who had made Israel sin. [10]Then Shallum the son of Jabesh conspired against him, and struck and killed him in front of the people; and he reigned in his place.

[11]Now the rest of the acts of Zechariah, indeed they *are* written in the book of the chronicles of the kings of Israel.

[12]This *was* the word of the LORD which He spoke to Jehu, saying, "Your sons shall sit on the throne of Israel to the fourth *generation.*" And so it was.

[13]Shallum the son of Jabesh became king in the thirty-ninth year of Uzziah king of Judah; and he reigned a full month in Samaria. [14]For Menahem the son of Gadi went up from Tirzah, came to Samaria, and struck Shallum the son of Jabesh in Samaria and killed him; and he reigned in his place.

[15]Now the rest of the acts of Shallum, and the conspiracy which he led, indeed they *are* written in the book of the chronicles of the kings of Israel. [16]Then from Tirzah, Menahem attacked Tiphsah, all who *were* there, and its territory. Because they did not surrender, therefore he attacked *it.* All the women there who were with child he ripped open.

[17]In the thirty-ninth year of Azariah king of Judah, Menahem the son of Gadi became king over Israel, *and* *reigned* ten years in Samaria. [18]And he did evil in the sight of the LORD; he did not depart all his days from the sins of Jeroboam the son of Nebat, who had made Israel sin. [19]Pul king of Assyria came against the land; and Menahem gave Pul a thousand talents of silver, that his hand might be with him to strengthen the kingdom under his control. [20]And Menahem exacted the money from Israel, from all the very wealthy, from each man fifty shekels of silver, to give to the king of Assyria. So the king of Assyria turned back, and did not stay there in the land.

[21]Now the rest of the acts of Menahem, and all that he did, *are* they not written in the book of the chronicles of the kings of Israel? [22]So Menahem rested with his fathers. Then Pekahiah his son reigned in his place.

[23]In the fiftieth year of Azariah king of Judah, Pekahiah the son of Menahem became king over Israel in Samaria, *and reigned* two years. [24]And he did evil in the sight of the LORD; he did not depart from the sins of Jeroboam the son of Nebat, who had made Israel sin. [25]Then Pekah the son of Remaliah, an officer of his, conspired against him and killed him in Samaria, in the citadel of the king's house, along with Argob and Arieh; and with him were fifty men of Gilead. He killed him and reigned in his place.

15:8 Zechariah was an evil king because he encouraged Israel to worshiping idols. Sin in our own lives is serious, but even more ter▮ than sinning ourselves is encouraging others to disobey God. We a▮ responsible for the way we influence others. Beware of double sin▮ that not only hurt us, but also hurt others by encouraging them to

[26]Now the rest of the acts of Pekahiah, and all that he did, indeed they *are* written in the book of the chronicles of the kings of Israel.

[27]In the fifty-second year of Azariah king of Judah, Pekah the son of Remaliah became king over Israel in Samaria, *and reigned* twenty years. [28]And he did evil in the sight of the LORD; he did not depart from the sins of Jeroboam the son of Nebat, who had made Israel sin. [29]In the days of Pekah king of Israel, Tiglath-Pileser king of Assyria came and took Ijon, Abel Beth Maachah, Janoah, Kedesh, Hazor, Gilead, and Galilee, all the land of Naphtali; and he carried them captive to Assyria. [30]Then Hoshea the son of Elah led a conspiracy against Pekah the son of Remaliah, and struck and killed him; so he reigned in his place in the twentieth year of Jotham the son of Uzziah.

[31]Now the rest of the acts of Pekah, and all that he did, indeed they *are* written in the book of the chronicles of the kings of Israel.

15:34-35 Much good can be said of Jotham and his reign as k▮ Judah, but he failed in a most critical area: he didn't destroy the places where the people worshiped idols, although leaving them ▮ violated the first commandment (Exodus 20:3). Like Jotham, we a basically good life and yet miss doing what is most important. ▮ lifetime of doing good is not enough if we make the crucial mista not following God with all our heart. A true follower of God puts in all areas of life.

arrow of deliverance from Syria; for you must strike the Syrians at Aphek till you have destroyed *them*." ¹⁸Then he said, "Take the arrows"; so he took *them*. And he said to the king of Israel, "Strike the ground"; so he struck three times, and stopped. ¹⁹And the man of God was angry with him, and said, "You should have struck five or six times; then you would have struck Syria till you had destroyed *it!* But now you will strike Syria *only* three times."

²⁰Then Elisha died, and they buried him. And the *raiding* bands from Moab invaded the land in the spring of the year. ²¹So it was, as they were burying a man, that suddenly they spied a band *of raiders;* and they put the man in the tomb of Elisha; and when the man was let down and touched the bones of Elisha, he revived and stood on his feet.

²²And Hazael king of Syria oppressed Israel all the days of Jehoahaz. ²³But the LORD was gracious to them, had compassion on them, and regarded them, because of His covenant with Abraham, Isaac, and Jacob, and would not yet destroy them or cast them from His presence.

²⁴Now Hazael king of Syria died. Then Ben-Hadad his son reigned in his place. ²⁵And Jehoash the son of Jehoahaz recaptured from the hand of Ben-Hadad, the son of Hazael, the cities which he had taken out of the hand of Jehoahaz his father by war. Three times Joash defeated him and recaptured the cities of Israel.

CHAPTER **14** **AMAZIAH RULES JUDAH.** In the second year of Joash the son of Jehoahaz, king of Israel, Amaziah the son of Joash, king of Judah, became king. ²He was twenty-five years old when he became king, and he reigned twenty-nine years in Jerusalem. His mother's name was Jehoaddan of Jerusalem. ³And he did *what was* right in the sight of the LORD, yet not like his father David; he did everything as his father Joash had done. ⁴However the high places were not taken away, and the people still sacrificed and burned incense on the high places.

⁵Now it happened, as soon as the kingdom was established in his hand, that he executed his servants who had murdered his father the king. ⁶But the children of the murderers he did not execute, according to what is written in the Book of the Law of Moses, in which the LORD commanded, saying, "Fathers shall not be put to death for their children, nor shall children be put to death for their fathers; but a person shall be put to death for his own sin."

⁷He killed ten thousand Edomites in the Valley of Salt, and took Sela by war, and called its name Joktheel to this day.

⁸Then Amaziah sent messengers to Jehoash the son of Jehoahaz, the son of Jehu, king of Israel, saying, "Come, let us face one another *in battle*." ⁹And Jehoash king of Israel sent to Amaziah king of Judah, saying, "The thistle that *was* in Lebanon sent to the cedar that *was* in Lebanon, saying, 'Give your daughter to my son as wife'; and a wild beast that *was* in Lebanon passed by and trampled the thistle. ¹⁰You have indeed defeated Edom, and your heart has lifted you up. Glory *in that*, and stay at home; for why should you meddle with trouble so that you fall—you and Judah with you?"

¹¹But Amaziah would not heed. Therefore Jehoash king of Israel went out; so he and Amaziah king of Judah faced one another at Beth Shemesh, which *belongs* to Judah. ¹²And Judah was defeated by Israel, and every man fled to his tent. ¹³Then Jehoash king of Israel captured Amaziah king of Judah, the son of Jehoash, the son of Ahaziah, at Beth Shemesh; and he went to Jerusalem, and broke down the wall of Jerusalem from the Gate of Ephraim to the Corner Gate—four hundred cubits. ¹⁴And he took all the gold and silver, all the articles that were found in the house of the LORD and in the treasuries of the king's house, and hostages, and returned to Samaria.

¹⁵Now the rest of the acts of Jehoash which he did—his might, and how he fought with Amaziah king of Judah—*are* they not written in the book of the chronicles of the kings of Israel? ¹⁶So Jehoash rested with his fathers, and was buried in Samaria with the kings of Israel. Then Jeroboam his son reigned in his place.

¹⁷Amaziah the son of Joash, king of Judah, lived fifteen years after the death of Jehoash the son of Jehoahaz, king of Israel. ¹⁸Now the rest of the acts of Amaziah, *are* they not written in the book of the chronicles of the kings of Judah? ¹⁹And they formed a conspiracy against him in Jerusalem, and he fled to Lachish; but they sent after him to Lachish and killed him there. ²⁰Then they brought him on horses, and he was buried at Jerusalem with his fathers in the City of David.

²¹And all the people of Judah took Azariah, who *was* sixteen years old, and made him king instead of his father Amaziah. ²²He built Elath and restored it to Judah, after the king rested with his fathers.

²³In the fifteenth year of Amaziah the son of Joash, king of Judah, Jeroboam the son of Joash, king of Israel, became king in Samaria, *and reigned* forty-one years. ²⁴And he did evil in the sight of the LORD; he did not depart from all the sins of Jeroboam the son of Nebat, who had made Israel sin. ²⁵He restored the territory of Israel from the entrance of Hamath to the Sea of the Arabah, according to the word of the LORD God of Israel, which He had spoken through His servant Jonah the son of Amittai, the prophet who *was* from Gath Hepher. ²⁶For the LORD saw *that* the affliction of Israel *was* very bitter; and whether bond or free, there was no helper for Israel. ²⁷And the LORD did not say that He would blot out the name of Israel from under heaven; but He saved them by the hand of Jeroboam the son of Joash.

²⁸Now the rest of the acts of Jeroboam, and all that he did—his might, how he made war, and how he recaptured for Israel, from Damascus and Hamath, *what had belonged* to Judah—*are* they not written in the book of

RICH

14:28 Jeroboam had no devotion to God, yet under his warlike policies and skillful administration Israel enjoyed power and prosperity. The prophets Amos and Hosea, however, tell us what was really happening within the kingdom (Hosea 13:4-8; Amos 6:11-13). Jeroboam's administration ignored policies of justice, so the rich became richer and the poor, poorer. The rich people grew self-centered; the poor grew discouraged. If you are experiencing prosperity, remember that God holds us accountable for how we attain success and how we use our wealth.

13:15-19 When Jehoash was told to strike the ground with the arrows, he did it only halfheartedly. As a result, Elisha told him that victory over Syria would not be complete. Receiving the full benefits God's plan for our life requires full receptiveness of and obedience t God's commands. If we don't follow God's complete instructions, we should not be surprised if his full benefits and blessings are not pres

²⁰And his servants arose and formed a conspiracy, and killed Joash in the house of the Millo, which goes down to Silla. ²¹For Jozachar the son of Shimeath and Jehozabad the son of Shomer, his servants, struck him. So he died, and they buried him with his fathers in the City of David. Then Amaziah his son reigned in his place.

CHAPTER **13** JEHOAHAZ RULES ISRAEL. In the twenty-third year of Joash the son of Ahaziah, king of Judah, Jehoahaz the son of Jehu became king over Israel in Samaria, *and reigned* seventeen years. ²And he did evil in the sight of the LORD, and followed the sins of Jeroboam the son of Nebat, who had made Israel sin. He did not depart from them.

YES!

13:4-6 The Lord heard Jehoahaz's prayer for help. God delayed his judgment on Israel when they turned to him for help, but they did not sustain their dependence on God for long. Although there were periodic breaks in their idol worship, there was rarely evidence of genuine faith. It is not enough to say no to sin; we must also say yes to a life of commitment to God.

³Then the anger of the LORD was aroused against Israel, and He delivered them into the hand of Hazael king of Syria, and into the hand of Ben-Hadad the son of Hazael, all *their* days. ⁴So Jehoahaz pleaded with the LORD, and the LORD listened to him; for He saw the oppression of Israel, because the king of Syria oppressed them. ⁵Then the LORD gave Israel a deliverer, so that they escaped from under the hand of the Syrians; and the children of Israel dwelt in their tents as before. ⁶Nevertheless they did not depart from the sins of the house of Jeroboam, who had made Israel sin, *but* walked in them; and the wooden image also remained in Samaria. ⁷For He left of the army of Jehoahaz only fifty horsemen, ten

chariots, and ten thousand foot soldiers; for the king of Syria had destroyed them and made them like the dust at threshing.

⁸Now the rest of the acts of Jehoahaz, all that he did, and his might, *are* they not written in the book of the chronicles of the kings of Israel? ⁹So Jehoahaz rested with his fathers, and they buried him in Samaria. Then Joash his son reigned in his place.

¹⁰In the thirty-seventh year of Joash king of Judah, Jehoash the son of Jehoahaz became king over Israel in Samaria, *and reigned* sixteen years. ¹¹And he did evil in the sight of the LORD. He did not depart from all the sins of Jeroboam the son of Nebat, who made Israel sin, *but* walked in them.

¹²Now the rest of the acts of Joash, all that he did, and his might with which he fought against Amaziah king of Judah, *are* they not written in the book of the chronicles of the kings of Israel? ¹³So Joash rested with his fathers. Then Jeroboam sat on his throne. And Joash was buried in Samaria with the kings of Israel.

¹⁴Elisha had become sick with the illness of which he would die. Then Joash the king of Israel came down to him, and wept over his face, and said, "O my father, my father, the chariots of Israel and their horsemen!"

¹⁵And Elisha said to him, "Take a bow and some arrows." So he took himself a bow and some arrows. ¹⁶Then he said to the king of Israel, "Put your hand on the bow." So he put his hand *on it*, and Elisha put his hands on the king's hands. ¹⁷And he said, "Open the east window"; and he opened *it*. Then Elisha said, "Shoot"; and he shot. And he said, "The arrow of the LORD's deliverance and the

GOD OR IDOLS
Why did people continually turn to idols instead of to God?

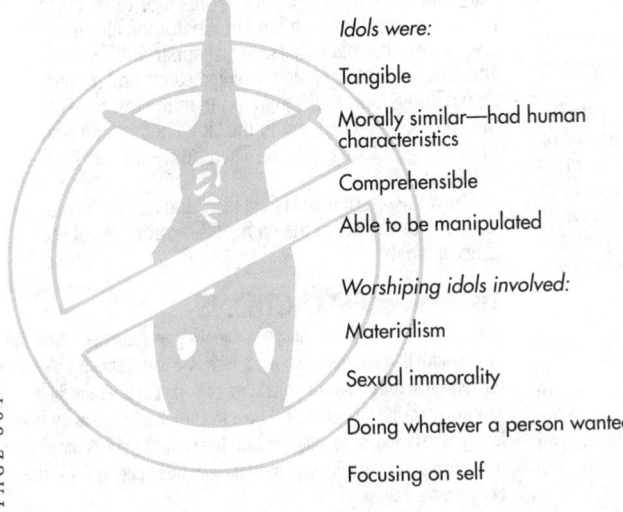

Idols were:	God is:
Tangible	Intangible—no physical form
Morally similar—had human characteristics	Morally dissimilar—has divine characteristics
Comprehensible	Incomprehensible
Able to be manipulated	Not able to be manipulated

Worshiping idols involved:	Worshiping God involves:
Materialism	Sacrifice
Sexual immorality	Purity and commitment
Doing whatever a person wanted	Doing what God wants
Focusing on self	Focusing on others

hand, all around the king, from the right side of the temple to the left side of the temple, by the altar and the house. [12]And he brought out the king's son, put the crown on him, and *gave him* the Testimony; they made him king and anointed him, and they clapped their hands and said, "Long live the king!"

[13]Now when Athaliah heard the noise of the escorts *and* the people, she came to the people *in* the temple of the LORD. [14]When she looked, there was the king standing by a pillar according to custom; and the leaders and the trumpeters were by the king. All the people of the land were rejoicing and blowing trumpets. So Athaliah tore her clothes and cried out, "Treason! Treason!"

[15]And Jehoiada the priest commanded the captains of the hundreds, the officers of the army, and said to them, "Take her outside under guard, and slay with the sword whoever follows her." For the priest had said, "Do not let her be killed in the house of the LORD." [16]So they seized her; and she went by way of the horses' entrance *into* the king's house, and there she was killed.

[17]Then Jehoiada made a covenant between the LORD, the king, and the people, that they should be the LORD's people, and *also* between the king and the people. [18]And all the people of the land went to the temple of Baal, and tore it down. They thoroughly broke in pieces its altars and images, and killed Mattan the priest of Baal before the altars. And the priest appointed officers over the house of the LORD. [19]Then he took the captains of hundreds, the bodyguards, the escorts, and all the people of the land; and they brought the king down from the house of the LORD, and went by way of the gate of the escorts to the king's house. Then he sat on the throne of the kings. [20]So all the people of the land rejoiced; and the city was quiet, for they had slain Athaliah with the sword *in* the king's house. [21]Jehoash *was* seven years old when he became king.

CHAPTER **12** JOASH RULES JUDAH.

In the seventh year of Jehu, Jehoash became king, and he reigned forty years in Jerusalem. His mother's name *was* Zibiah of Beersheba. [2]Jehoash did *what was* right in the sight of the LORD all the days in which Jehoiada the priest instructed him. [3]But the high places were not taken away; the people still sacrificed and burned incense on the high places.

[4]And Jehoash said to the priests, "All the money of the dedicated gifts that are brought into the house of the LORD—each man's census money, each man's assessment money—*and* all the money that a man purposes in his heart to bring into the house of the LORD, [5]let the priests take *it* themselves, each from his constituency; and let them repair the damages of the temple, wherever any dilapidation is found."

[6]Now it was so, by the twenty-third year of King Jehoash, *that* the priests had not repaired the damages of the temple. [7]So King Jehoash called Jehoiada the priest and the *other* priests, and said to them, "Why have you not repaired the damages of the temple? Now therefore, do not take *more* money from your constituency, but deliver *it* for repairing the damages of the temple." [8]And the priests agreed that they would neither receive *more* money from the people, nor repair the damages of the temple.

[9]Then Jehoiada the priest took a chest, bored a hole in its lid, and set it beside the altar, on the right side as one comes into the house of the LORD; and the priests who kept the door put there all the money brought into the house of the LORD. [10]So it was, whenever they saw that *there was* much money in the chest, that the king's scribe and the high priest came up and put it in bags, and counted the money that was found in the house of the LORD. [11]Then they gave the money, which had been ap-

◣◣INPUT

12:2 God's input yields good output. Joash had a good teacher in Jehoiada, the high priest. As long as he lived, Jehoiada's faith in God influenced Joash for good. Good intent must be fortified with good content. As long as Joash heeded Jehoiada's good instruction, he fulfilled God's plan for his life. All our plans and actions must be guided by God, and his counsel is made clear to us in his word. Our lives will be productive if we heed God's counsel.

portioned, into the hands of those who did the work, who had the oversight of the house of the LORD; and they paid it out to the carpenters and builders who worked on the house of the LORD, [12]and to masons and stonecutters, and for buying timber and hewn stone, to repair the damage of the house of the LORD, and for all that was paid out to repair the temple. [13]However there were not made for the house of the LORD basins of silver, trimmers, sprinkling-bowls, trumpets, any articles of gold or articles of silver, from the money brought into the house of the LORD. [14]But they gave that to the workmen, and they repaired the house of the LORD with it. [15]Moreover they did not require an account from the men into whose hand they delivered the money to be paid to workmen, for they dealt faithfully. [16]The money from the trespass offerings and the money from the sin offerings was not brought into the house of the LORD. It belonged to the priests.

[17]Hazael king of Syria went up and fought against Gath, and took it; then Hazael set his face to go up to Jerusalem. [18]And Jehoash king of Judah took all the sacred things that his fathers, Jehoshaphat and Jehoram and Ahaziah, kings of Judah, had dedicated, and his own sacred things, and all the gold found in the treasuries of the house of the LORD and in the king's house, and sent *them* to Hazael king of Syria. Then he went away from Jerusalem.

[19]Now the rest of the acts of Joash, and all that he did, *are* they not written in the book of the chronicles of the kings of Judah?

◣◣ACTIONS

12:3 Joash didn't go far enough in removing sin from the nation, but he did much that was good and right. When we aren't sure if we've gone far enough in correcting our actions, we can ask: (1) Does the Bible expressly prohibit this action? (2) Does this action take me away from loving, worshiping, or serving God? (3) Does it make me its slave? (4) Is it bringing out the best in me, consistent with God's purpose? (5) Does it benefit other believers?

the ways of his father David; he did not turn aside to the right hand or to the left.

³Now it came to pass, in the eighteenth year of King Josiah, *that* the king sent Shaphan the scribe, the son of Azaliah, the son of Meshullam, to the house of the LORD, saying: ⁴"Go up to Hilkiah the high priest, that he may count the money which has been brought into the house of the LORD, which the doorkeepers have gathered from the people. ⁵And let them deliver it into the hand of those doing the work, who are the overseers in the house of the LORD; let them give it to those who *are* in the house of the LORD doing the work, to repair the damages of the house— ⁶to carpenters and builders and masons—and to buy timber and hewn stone to repair the house. ⁷However there need be no accounting made with them of the money delivered into their hand, because they deal faithfully."

⁸Then Hilkiah the high priest said to Shaphan the scribe, "I have found the Book of the Law in the house of the LORD." And Hilkiah gave the book to Shaphan, and he read it. ⁹So Shaphan the scribe went to the king, bringing the king word, saying, "Your servants have gathered the money that was found in the house, and have delivered it into the hand of those who do the work, who oversee the house of the LORD." ¹⁰Then Shaphan the scribe showed the king, saying, "Hilkiah the priest has given me a book." And Shaphan read it before the king.

¹¹Now it happened, when the king heard the words of the Book of the Law, that he tore his clothes. ¹²Then the king commanded Hilkiah the priest, Ahikam the son of Shaphan, Achbor the son of Michaiah, Shaphan the scribe, and Asaiah a servant of the king, saying, ¹³"Go, inquire of the LORD for me, for the people and for all Judah, concerning the words of this book that has been found; for great *is* the wrath of the LORD that is aroused against us, because our fathers have not obeyed the words of this book, to do according to all that is written concerning us."

¹⁴So Hilkiah the priest, Ahikam, Achbor, Shaphan, and Asaiah went to Huldah the prophetess, the wife of Shallum the son of Tikvah, the son of Harhas, keeper of the wardrobe. (She dwelt in Jerusalem in the Second Quarter.) And they spoke

with her. ¹⁵Then she said to them, "Thus says the LORD God of Israel, 'Tell the man who sent you to Me, ¹⁶"Thus says the LORD: 'Behold, I will bring calamity on this place and on its inhabitants—all the words of the book which the king of Judah has read— ¹⁷because they have forsaken Me and burned incense to other gods, that they might provoke Me to anger with all the works of their hands. Therefore My wrath shall be aroused against this place and shall not be quenched.'"' ¹⁸But as for the king of Judah, who sent you to inquire of the LORD, in this manner you shall speak to him, 'Thus says the LORD God of Israel: "*Concerning* the words which you have heard—

HEZEKIAH

The people and kings of Judah had a rich past, filled with God's action, guidance, and commands. But with each passing generation, they forgot how God had cared for them. Hezekiah was one of the few kings of Judah who was constantly aware of God's acts in the past and his interest in the events of every day. He was a king who had a close relationship with God.

As a reformer, Hezekiah was most concerned with present obedience. Hezekiah destroyed heathen altars, idols, and temples. Even the bronze serpent Moses had made in the wilderness was not spared because it had become an idol. The temple in Jerusalem was cleaned and reopened. The Passover was reinstituted and there was revival in Judah.

Although he responded to present problems, Hezekiah wasn't concerned for the future. He took few actions to preserve the effects of his sweeping reforms. His unwise display of wealth to the Babylonian delegation got Judah included on Babylon's "Nations to Conquer" list. When Isaiah told Hezekiah of the foolishness of this, the king answered by saying he was thankful that any evil consequences would be delayed until after he died. And the lives of three kings who followed him—Manasseh, Amon, and Josiah—were deeply affected by both Hezekiah's accomplishments and his weaknesses.

The past affects your decisions and actions today, and these, in turn, affect the future. These are lessons to learn and errors to avoid repeating. Remember that part of the success of your past will be measured by what you do with it now and how well you use it to prepare for the future.

LESSONS: Sweeping reforms are short-lived when little action is taken to preserve them for the future
Past obedience to God does not remove the possibility of present disobedience
Complete dependence on God brings amazing results

KEY VERSES: "He [Hezekiah] trusted in the LORD God of Israel, so that after him was none like him among all the kings of Judah, nor who were before him. For he held fast to the LORD; he did not depart from following Him, but kept His commandments, which the LORD had commanded Moses." (2 Kings 18:5-6)

Hezekiah's story is told in 2 Kings 16:20—20:21; 2 Chronicles 28:27—32:33; Isaiah 36:1—39:8. He is also mentioned in Proverbs 25:1; Isaiah, 1:1; Jeremiah 15:4; 26:18-19; Hosea 1:1; Micah 1:1.

UPS:
- Was the king of Judah who instituted civil and religious reforms
- Had a personal, growing relationship with God
- Devoted to a powerful prayer life
- Noted as the patron of several chapters in the book of Proverbs (Proverbs 25:1)

DOWNS:
- Showed little interest or wisdom in planning for the future and protecting for others the spiritual heritage he enjoyed
- Rashly showed all his wealth to messengers from Babylon

STATS:
- Where: Jerusalem
- Occupation: 13th king of Judah, the southern kingdom
- Relatives: Father: Ahaz. Mother: Abi. Son: Manasseh.
- Contemporaries: Isaiah, Hoshea, Micah, Sennacherib

■ TURNAROUND

22:19 When Josiah realized how corrupt his nation had become, he tore his clothes and wept before God. Then God had mercy on him. Josiah used the customs of his day to show his repentance. When we repent today, we are unlikely to tear our clothing, but weeping, fasting, and making restitution or apologies (if our sin has involved others) are all acts of repentance that demonstrate our sincerity. The hardest part of repentance is changing the behavior that originally produced the sin.

¹⁹because your heart was tender, and you humbled yourself before the LORD when you heard what I spoke against this place and against its inhabitants, that they would become a desolation and a curse, and you tore your clothes and wept before Me, I also have heard *you*," says the LORD. ²⁰Surely, therefore, I will gather you to your fathers, and you shall be gathered to your grave in peace; and your eyes shall not see all the calamity which I will bring on this place." ' " So they brought back word to the king.

CHAPTER **23** JOSIAH OBEYS GOD'S LAW. Now the king sent them to gather all the elders of Judah and Jerusalem to him. ²The king went up to the house of the LORD with all the men of Judah, and with him all the inhabitants of Jerusalem—the priests and the prophets and all the people, both small and great. And he read in their hearing all the words of the Book of the Covenant which had been found in the house of the LORD.

■ JUST DO IT!

23:4-7 When Josiah realized the terrible state of Judah's religious life, he did something about it. It is not enough to say we believe what is right; we must respond with action, doing what faith requires. This is what James was emphasizing when he wrote, "faith without works is dead" (James 2:20). This will mean acting differently at home, school, work, or church.

³Then the king stood by a pillar and made a covenant before the LORD, to follow the LORD and to keep His commandments and His testimonies and His statutes, with all *his* heart and all *his* soul, to perform the words of this covenant that were written in this book. And all the people took a stand for the covenant. ⁴And the king commanded Hilkiah the high priest, the priests of the second order, and the doorkeepers, to bring out of the temple of the LORD all the articles that were made for Baal, for Asherah, and for all the host of heaven; and he burned them outside Jerusalem in the fields of Kidron, and carried their ashes to Bethel. ⁵Then he removed the idolatrous priests whom the kings of Judah had ordained to burn incense on the high places in the cities of Judah and in the places all around Jerusalem, and those who burned incense to Baal, to the sun, to the moon, to the constellations, and to all the host of heaven. ⁶And he brought out the wooden image from the house of the LORD, to the Brook Kidron outside Jerusalem, burned it at the Brook Kidron and ground *it* to ashes, and threw its ashes on the graves of the common people. ⁷Then he tore down the *ritual* booths of the perverted persons that *were* in the house of the LORD, where the women wove hangings for the wooden image. ⁸And he brought all the

priests from the cities of Judah, and defiled the high places where the priests had burned incense, from Geba to Beersheba; also he broke down the high places at the gates which *were* at the entrance of the Gate of Joshua the governor of the city, which *were* to the left of the city gate. ⁹Nevertheless the priests of the high places did not come up to the altar of the LORD in Jerusalem, but they ate unleavened bread among their brethren.

¹⁰And he defiled Topheth, which *is* in the Valley of the Son of Hinnom, that no man might make his son or his daughter pass through the fire to Molech. ¹¹Then he removed the horses that the kings of Judah had dedicated to the sun, at the entrance to the house of the LORD, by the chamber of Nathan-Melech, the officer who *was* in the court; and he burned the chariots of the sun with fire. ¹²The altars that *were* on the roof, the upper chamber of Ahaz, which the kings of Judah had made, and the altars which Manasseh had made in the two courts of the house of the LORD, the king broke down and pulverized there, and threw their dust into the Brook Kidron. ¹³Then the king defiled the high places that *were* east of Jerusalem, which *were* on the south of the Mount of Corruption, which Solomon king of Israel had built for Ashtoreth the abomination of the Sidonians, for Chemosh the abomination of the Moabites, and for Milcom the abomination of the people of Ammon. ¹⁴And he broke in pieces the *sacred* pillars and cut down the wooden images, and filled their places with the bones of men.

¹⁵Moreover the altar that *was* at Bethel, *and* the high place which Jeroboam the son of Nebat, who made Israel sin, had made, both that altar and the high place he broke down; and he burned the high place *and* crushed *it* to powder, and burned the wooden image. ¹⁶As Josiah turned, he saw the tombs that *were* there on the mountain. And he sent and took the bones out of the tombs and burned *them* on the altar, and defiled it according to the word of the LORD which the man of God proclaimed, who proclaimed these words. ¹⁷Then he said, "What gravestone *is* this that I see?"

So the men of the city told him, "*It is* the tomb of the man of God who came from Judah and proclaimed these things which you have done against the altar of Bethel."

¹⁸And he said, "Let him alone; let no one move his bones." So they let his bones alone, with the bones of the prophet who came from Samaria.

¹⁹Now Josiah also took away all the shrines of the high places that *were* in the cities of Samaria, which the kings of Israel had made to provoke the LORD to anger; and he

■ PARTY TIME!

23:21-23 When Josiah rediscovered the Passover in the *Book Covenant,* he ordered everyone to observe the ceremonies exactl prescribed. This Passover celebration was to have been a yearly celebrated in remembrance of the entire nation's deliverance fro slavery in Egypt (Exodus 12), but it had not been kept for many As a result, "such a Passover surely had never been held since th the judges." It is a common misconception that God is against cel wanting to take all the fun out of life. In reality, God wants to giv in its fullness (John 10:10), and those who love him have the mo celebrate.

did to them according to all the deeds he had done in Bethel. ²⁰He executed all the priests of the high places who *were* there, on the altars, and burned men's bones on them; and he returned to Jerusalem.

²¹Then the king commanded all the people, saying, "Keep the Passover to the LORD your God, as *it is* written in this Book of the Covenant." ²²Such a Passover surely had never been held since the days of the judges who judged Israel, nor in all the days of the kings of Israel and the kings of Judah. ²³But in the eighteenth year of King Josiah this Passover was held before the LORD in Jerusalem. ²⁴Moreover Josiah put away those who consulted mediums and spiritists, the household gods and idols, all the abominations that were seen in the land of Judah and in Jerusalem, that he might perform the words of the law which were written in the book that Hilkiah the priest found in the house of the LORD. ²⁵Now before him there was no king like him, who turned to the LORD with all his heart, with all his soul, and with all his might, according to all the Law of Moses; nor after him did *any* arise like him.

²⁶Nevertheless the LORD did not turn from the fierceness of His great wrath, with which His anger was aroused against Judah, because of all the provocations with which Manasseh had provoked Him. ²⁷And the LORD said, "I will also remove Judah from My sight, as I have removed Israel, and will cast off this city Jerusalem which I have chosen, and the house of which I said, 'My name shall be there.'"

²⁸Now the rest of the acts of Josiah, and all that he did, *are* they not written in the book of the chronicles of the kings of Judah? ²⁹In his days Pharaoh Necho king of Egypt went to the aid of the king of Assyria, to the River Euphrates; and King Josiah went against him. And *Pharaoh Necho* killed him at Megiddo when he confronted him. ³⁰Then his servants moved his body in a chariot from Megiddo, brought him to Jerusalem, and buried him in his own tomb. And the people of the land took Jehoahaz the son of Josiah, anointed him, and made him king in his father's place.

³¹Jehoahaz *was* twenty-three years old when he became king, and he reigned three months in Jerusalem. His mother's name *was* Hamutal the daughter

of Jeremiah of Libnah. ³²And he did evil in the sight of the LORD, according to all that his fathers had done. ³³Now Pharaoh Necho put him in prison at Riblah in the land of Hamath, that he might not reign in Jerusalem; and he imposed on the land a tribute of one hundred talents of silver and a talent of gold. ³⁴Then Pharaoh Necho made Eliakim the son of Josiah king in place of his father Josiah, and changed his name to Jehoiakim. And *Pharaoh* took Jehoahaz and went to Egypt, and he died there.

³⁵So Jehoiakim gave the silver and gold to Pharaoh; but he taxed the land to give money according to the command of Pharaoh; he exacted the silver and gold from the people of

JOSIAH

Most children have big dreams of what they want to be when they grow up. Few of them get the chance like Josiah had to become a king at age eight! Young King Josiah was different in other ways, too. He was not at all like his father or grandfather, who had both been very evil rulers. But he reminded many of his great-grandfather Hezekiah. They both had close, personal relationships with God.

At a young age, Josiah already understood that there was spiritual sickness in his land. In a sense, Josiah began his search for God by destroying and cleaning up whatever he found that didn't belong to the worship of the true God. Along the way, God's Word, the scrolls containing God's law, was rediscovered. For Josiah, it was better than finding a hidden treasure map. His reaction makes us realize how often we take God's Word for granted.

As the scroll of God's law was read to Josiah, he was shocked, frightened, and humbled. He realized that he and the nation had a long way to go to get right with God. He tried everything he could to help his people know God. Although he changed many things, he couldn't change hearts. On the outside, the people cooperated with Josiah, but there were few changes on the inside.

How would you describe your relationship with God? Would you have to admit that you usually just "go along" like the people of Judah? Or are you, like Josiah, deeply humbled by God's Word and anxious to do what he wants? Humble obedience pleases God. Outside changes aren't enough. You must allow God's Word to humble you and his Spirit to change your life, both inside and out.

LESSONS: God consistently responds to those who turn from their sins and who have a humble heart

Even sweeping outward reforms are of little lasting value if there are no changes in people's lives

KEY VERSES: " 'Shall you reign because you enclose yourself in cedar? Did not your father [Josiah] eat and drink, and do justice and righteousness? Then it was well with him. He judged the cause of the poor and needy; then it was well. Was not this knowing Me?' says the LORD" (Jeremiah 22:15-16).

Josiah's story is told in 2 Kings 21:24–23:30; 2 Chronicles 33:25–35:26. He is also mentioned in Jeremiah 1–3; 22:11-17.

UPS:
• King of Judah
• Wanted to know God and obey him
• A reformer like his great-grandfather, Hezekiah
• Cleaned out the temple and revived obedience to God's laws

DOWN:
• Became involved in a military conflict that he had been warned against

STATS:
• Where: Jerusalem
• Occupation: Eighteenth king of Judah, the southern kingdom
• Relatives: Father: Amon. Mother: Jedidah. Son: Jehoahaz.
• Contemporaries: Jeremiah, Huldah, Hilkiah, Zephaniah

the land, from every one according to his assessment, to give *it* to Pharaoh Necho. [36]Jehoiakim *was* twenty-five years old when he became king, and he reigned eleven years in Jerusalem. His mother's name *was* Zebudah the daughter of Pedaiah of Rumah. [37]And he did evil in the sight of the LORD, according to all that his fathers had done.

CHAPTER 24 JEHOIACHIN AND BABYLON. In his

days Nebuchadnezzar king of Babylon came up, and Jehoiakim became his vassal *for* three years. Then he turned and rebelled against him. [2]And the LORD sent against him *raiding* bands of Chaldeans, bands of Syrians, bands of Moabites, and bands of the people of Ammon; He sent them against Judah to destroy it, according to the word of the LORD which He had spoken by His servants the prophets. [3]Surely at the commandment of the LORD *this* came upon Judah, to remove *them* from His sight because of the sins of Manasseh, according to all that he had done, [4]and also because of the innocent blood that he had shed; for he had filled Jerusalem with innocent blood, which the LORD would not pardon.

[5]Now the rest of the acts of Jehoiakim, and all that he did, *are* they not written in the book of the chronicles of the kings of Judah? [6]So Jehoiakim rested with his fathers. Then Jehoiachin his son reigned in his place.

[7]And the king of Egypt did not come out of his land anymore, for the king of Babylon had taken all that belonged to the king of Egypt from the Brook of Egypt to the River Euphrates.

[8]Jehoiachin *was* eighteen years old when he became king, and he reigned in Jerusalem three months. His mother's name *was* Nehushta the daughter of Elnathan of Jerusalem. [9]And he did evil in the sight of the LORD, according to all that his father had done.

[10]At that time the servants of Nebuchadnezzar king of Babylon came up against Jerusalem, and the city was besieged. [11]And Nebuchadnezzar king of Babylon came against the city, as his servants were besieging it. [12]Then Jehoiachin king of Judah, his mother, his servants, his princes, and his officers went out to the king of Babylon; and the king of Babylon, in the eighth year of his reign, took him prisoner.

[13]And he carried out from there all the treasures of the house of the LORD and the treasures of the king's house, and he cut in pieces all the articles of gold which Solomon king of Israel had made in the temple of the LORD, as the LORD had said. [14]Also he carried into captivity all Jerusalem: all the captains and all the mighty men of valor, ten thousand captives, and all the craftsmen and smiths. None remained except the poorest people of the land. [15]And he carried Jehoiachin captive to Babylon. The king's mother, the king's wives, his officers, and the mighty of the land he carried into captivity from Jerusalem to Babylon. [16]All the valiant men, seven thousand, and craftsmen and smiths, one thousand, all *who were* strong *and* fit for war, these the king of Babylon brought captive to Babylon.

[17]Then the king of Babylon made Mattaniah, *Jehoia-*

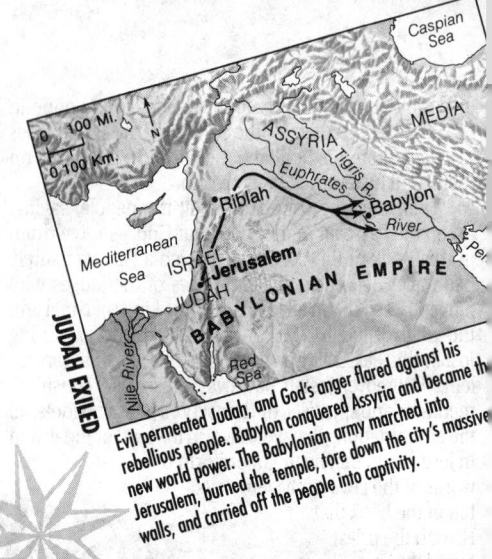

Evil permeated Judah, and God's anger flared against his rebellious people. Babylon conquered Assyria and became the new world power. The Babylonian army marched into Jerusalem, burned the temple, tore down the city's massive walls, and carried off the people into captivity.

chin's uncle, king in his place, and changed his name to Zedekiah.

[18]Zedekiah *was* twenty-one years old when he became king, and he reigned eleven years in Jerusalem. His mother's name *was* Hamutal the daughter of Jeremiah of Libnah. [19]He also did evil in the sight of the LORD, according to all that Jehoiakim had done. [20]For because of the anger of the LORD *this* happened in Jerusalem and Judah, that He finally cast them out from His presence. Then Zedekiah rebelled against the king of Babylon.

CHAPTER 25 JERUSALEM GETS DEMOLISHED.

Now it came to pass in the ninth year of his reign, in the tenth month, on the tenth *day* of the month, *that* Nebuchadnezzar king of Babylon and all his army came against Jerusalem and encamped against it; and they built a siege wall against it all around. [2]So the city was besieged until the eleventh year of King Zedekiah. [3]By the ninth *day* of the *fourth* month the famine had become so severe in the city that there was no food for the people of the land.

[4]Then the city wall was broken through, and all the men of war *fled* at night by way of the gate between two walls, which was by the king's garden, even though the Chaldeans *were* still encamped all around against the city. And *the king* went by way of the plain. [5]But the army of the Chaldeans pursued the king, and they overtook him in the plains of Jericho. All his army was scattered from him. [6]So they took the king and brought him up to the king of Babylon at Riblah, and they pronounced judgment on him. [7]Then they killed the sons of Zedekiah before his eyes, put out the eyes of Zedekiah, bound him with bronze fetters, and took him to Babylon.

[8]And in the fifth month, on the seventh *day* of the month (which *was* the nineteenth year of King Nebuchadnezzar king of Babylon), Nebuzaradan the captain of the guard, a servant of the king of Babylon, came to Jerusalem. [9]He burned the house of the LORD and the king's house; all the houses of Jerusalem, that is, all the houses of the great, he burned with fire. [10]And all the

army of the Chaldeans who *were with* the captain of the guard broke down the walls of Jerusalem all around.

[11]Then Nebuzaradan the captain of the guard carried away captive the rest of the people *who* remained in the city and the defectors who had deserted to the king of Babylon, with the rest of the multitude. [12]But the captain of the guard left *some* of the poor of the land as vinedressers and farmers. [13]The bronze pillars that *were* in the house of the LORD, and the carts and the bronze Sea that *were* in the house of the LORD, the Chaldeans broke in pieces, and carried their bronze to Babylon. [14]They also took away the pots, the shovels, the trimmers, the spoons, and all the bronze utensils with which the priests ministered. [15]The firepans and the basins, the things of solid gold and solid silver, the captain of the guard took away. [16]The two pillars, one Sea, and the carts, which Solomon had made for the house of the LORD, the bronze of all these articles was beyond measure. [17]The height of one pillar *was* eighteen cubits, and the capital on it *was* of bronze. The height of the capital was three cubits, and the network and pomegranates all around the capital were all of bronze. The second pillar was the same, with a network.

[18]And the captain of the guard took Seraiah the chief priest, Zephaniah the second priest, and the three doorkeepers. [19]He also took out of the city an officer who had charge of the men of war, five men of the king's close associates who were found in the city, the chief recruiting officer of the army, who mustered the people of the land, and sixty men of the people of the land *who were* found in the city. [20]So Nebuzaradan, captain of the guard, took these and brought them to the king of Babylon at Riblah. [21]Then the king of Babylon struck them and put them to death at Riblah in the land of Hamath. Thus Judah was carried away captive from its own land.

[22]Then he made Gedaliah the son of Ahikam, the son of Shaphan, governor over the people who remained in the land of Judah, whom Nebuchadnezzar king of Babylon had left. [23]Now when all the captains of the armies, they and *their* men, heard that the king of Babylon had made Gedaliah governor, they came to Gedaliah at Mizpah—Ishmael the son of Nethaniah, Johanan the son of Careah, Seraiah the son of Tanhumeth the Netophathite, and Jaazaniah the son of a Maachathite, they and their men. [24]And Gedaliah took an oath before them and their men, and said to them, "Do not be afraid of the servants of the Chaldeans. Dwell in the land and serve the king of Babylon, and it shall be well with you."

[25]But it happened in the seventh month that Ishmael the son of Nethaniah, the son of Elishama, of the royal family, came with ten men and struck and killed Gedaliah, the Jews, as well as the Chaldeans who were with him at Mizpah. [26]And all the people, small and great, and the captains of the armies, arose and went to Egypt; for they were afraid of the Chaldeans.

◣◣ EARLY WARNINGS

25:21 Judah, like Israel, was unfaithful to God. So God, as he had warned, allowed Judah to be destroyed and taken away (Deuteronomy 28). The book of Lamentations records the prophet Jeremiah's sorrow at seeing Jerusalem destroyed. God will fulfill his promises, and he will carry out his warnings. When he speaks words of warning to us, through his Word or through other believers, we need to heed what we are told. To continue in our sin is to invite destruction. Have you received any warnings in your life lately? How will you respond to them?

◣◣ STRAIGHTENED OUT

25:30 The book of 2 Kings opens with Elijah being carried to heaven—the destination awaiting those who follow God. But the book ends with the people of Judah being carried off to foreign lands as humiliated slaves—the result of failing to follow God.

Second Kings is an illustration of what happens when we make anything more important than God, when we make ruinous alliances, when our consciences become desensitized to right and wrong, and when we are no longer able to discern God's purpose for our life. We may fail, like the people of Judah and Israel, but God's promises do not. He is always there to help us straighten out our life and start over. And that is just what happens in the book of Ezra. When the people acknowledged their sins, God was ready and willing to help them return to their land and start again.

[27]Now it came to pass in the thirty-seventh year of the captivity of Jehoiachin king of Judah, in the twelfth month, on the twenty-seventh *day* of the month, *that* Evil-Merodach king of Babylon, in the year that he began to reign, released Jehoiachin king of Judah from prison. [28]He spoke kindly to him, and gave him a more prominent seat than those of the kings who *were* with him in Babylon. [29]So Jehoiachin changed from his prison garments, and he ate bread regularly before the king all the days of his life. [30]And as for his provisions, *there was* a regular ration given him by the king, a portion for each day, all the days of his life.

MEGA *Themes*

ELISHA The purpose of Elisha's ministry was to restore respect for God and his message. Elisha stood firmly against the evil kings of Israel. By faith, with courage and prayer, he revealed not only God's judgment on sin, but also his mercy, love, and tenderness toward faithful people.

Elisha's mighty miracles showed that God controls not only great armies, but also events in everyday life. God's care is not reserved for kings and leaders, but is for all who are willing to follow him. He can perform miracles in our life.

1. If you were writing a letter of reference for Elisha, how would you describe him?
2. What evidence do you find that Elisha had a heart willing to serve God?
3. Can you think of two people you know who have displayed evidence of hearts that were willing to serve God?
4. Who are the people in your life who need to see evidence of this willing heart in you? What can you do to be an example for them? What will you do to be God's living testimony of power to them?

IDOLATRY Every evil king in both Israel and Judah encouraged idolatry. These false gods represented war, cruelty, power, and sex; and the people began to take on their characteristics. Although they had God's law, priests, and prophets to guide them, the evil kings sought false priests and prophets whom they could control and manipulate to their own advantage.

An idol is any idea, ability, possession, or person that we regard more highly than God. We condemn Israel and Judah for foolishly worshiping idols, but we also worship other gods—power, money, physical attractiveness, and so on. Behind this "idol" worship is the desire to control our destiny, our pleasure, and other people. Even those who believe in God must resist the lure of these attractive idols.

1. Idols led to great destruction when the kings turned to them. What could have been so attractive about worshiping these idols? What did the kings hope to gain?
2. List just a few of the things in life that can only be supplied by the one true God.
3. With this knowledge in mind, what is it that you think attracts so many young people to idolatry,

to replacing the worship of God with the worship of power, pleasure, or possessions?
4. How could you specifically communicate to those around you (without just making an announcement or handing them a Bible) the truth about who God is and that he alone should be worshiped?

EVIL KINGS/GOOD KINGS The northern kingdom, Israel, had 19 evil kings and no good ones; the southern kingdom, Judah, had 12 evil kings and 8 good ones. Thus, only 20 percent of all the kings of both kingdoms followed God. The evil kings were shortsighted, thinking that they could control their nation's destiny by importing other religions with their idols, forming alliances with heathen nations and enriching themselves. The good kings had to spend most of their time undoing the evil done by their predecessors.

Although the evil kings led the people into sin, they were not the only ones responsible for the downfall of their nation. The priests, princes, heads of families, and military leaders all had to cooperate with the proposed evil plans and practices in order for them to be carried out. We cannot discharge our responsibility to obey God by blaming our leaders.

1. What qualities did the good kings have in common?
2. What qualities did the evil kings have in common?
3. Contrast the effect the good kings had on the people with the effect the evil kings had.
4. What leaders can you point out as ones who made or are making a good difference in the lives of their followers? What leaders made or are making an evil difference in the lives of their followers?
5. List several ways a Christian young person can choose to be a person of influence in the home, church, school, and community.
6. What choices have you decided to make that will affect people for God's glory?

GOD'S PATIENCE As recorded in Deuteronomy, God told his people that if they obeyed him they would live successfully; if they disobeyed, they would be judged and destroyed. God had been patient with the people for hundreds of years. He sent many prophets, including Elisha, to guide them, and he gave ample warning of coming destruction. But even God's patience has limits.

God is patient with us. In his mercy, he gives us many opportunities to hear his message, turn from sin, and believe in him. But his patience does not mean that he is indifferent to how we live, or that we are free to ignore his warnings. His patience should make us want to come to him now.

1. What does it mean to have patience?
2. Give several examples of God's patience with the Hebrews.
3. What evidence do you see of God's patience in your life?
4. A Christian friend seems to have the attitude that since God is so patient, we do not have to be so concerned about whether or not we sin. Based on 2 Kings, how would you correct the error in this friend's thinking?
5. In view of God's patience, how will you choose to live your life?

JUDGMENT Both kingdoms were destroyed as punishment for their sins. After King Solomon's reign, Israel lasted only 209 years before the Assyrians destroyed it; Judah lasted 345 years before the Babylonians conquered Jerusalem. After repeated warnings to his people, God used these evil nations as instruments for his justice.

When we reject God's commands and purpose for our life, the consequences are severe. He will not ignore unbelief or rebellion. To avoid the penalty for sin, we must believe in Christ and accept his sacrificial death on our behalf, or we will be judged. Having accepted Christ, we must still remain sensitive and responsive to God's will.

1. Would you describe God's discipline of his people as gentle, mild, serious, or severe? Explain.
2. What does this judgment reveal to you about God?
3. What does the death of Jesus on the cross reveal about the love of God? What does Jesus' death reveal about the holiness of God?
4. As a Christian who has been redeemed by Christ, how should you respond to the fact that God is a God of judgment?
5. What effect does God's holiness have on your daily choices? On the relationships you have with others? On the way you approach God?

1050 B.C.
Saul becomes king

1010
Saul dies; David becomes king of Judah

1003
David becomes king of all Israel

1000
David captures Jerusalem

997(?)
David captures Rabbah

980(?)
David's census

970
Solomon becomes king

930
The kingdom divides

I promise that we will demolish them tonight!" The coach's voice booms over the PA in the packed gymnasium. With those words the student body begins to clap and yell wildly. Somewhere in the back a few people start chanting, "Beat the Raiders! Beat the Raiders!" More people join in until soon everyone is screaming in unison. ■ Pep rallies can draw a school together. And for those few moments, all differences are forgotten as the crowd focuses on the one objective—winning the big game. ■ First Chronicles can be considered a written pep rally. Sent to the Jews who had returned to their homeland, the author attempts to form a sense of national conscience and awaken a sense of national pride and unity. ■ Beginning with Adam, 1 Chronicles relates the exciting history of Israel. By recalling the past, the author hopes to spur the Israelites on to a great future. But 1 Chronicles is more than a history lesson. It is a recounting of the spiritual strength of the nation. That, the author writes, is the hope for the greatness of the new Israel. Only as the nation unites in its worship of God can it regain the importance and vitality it once had. ■ We, too, have a great spiritual heritage—built by men and women who have contributed to any spiritual vitality we see today. As you read 1 Chronicles, learn to trace your heritage, and commit yourself to doing your part to pass on God's truth to the next generation.

STATS

PURPOSE: To unify God's people, to trace the Davidic line, and to teach that genuine worship ought to be the center of individual and national life

AUTHOR: Ezra, according to Jewish tradition

TO WHOM WRITTEN: All Israel

DATE WRITTEN: Approximately 430 B.C.; recording events which occurred about 1000–960 B.C.

SETTING: First Chronicles parallels 2 Samuel and serves as a commentary on it. Written after the exile from a priestly point of view, 1 Chronicles emphasizes the religious history of Judah and Israel.

KEY PLACES: Hebron, Jerusalem, the temple

Chronicles

CHAPTER 1 ADAM'S DESCENDANTS.

Adam, Seth, Enosh, ²Cainan, Mahalalel, Jared, ³Enoch, Methuselah, Lamech, ⁴Noah, Shem, Ham, and Japheth.

⁵The sons of Japheth *were* Gomer, Magog, Madai, Javan, Tubal, Meshech, and Tiras. ⁶The sons of Gomer *were* Ashkenaz, Diphath, and Togarmah. ⁷The sons of Javan *were* Elishah, Tarshishah, Kittim, and Rodanim.

⁸The sons of Ham *were* Cush, Mizraim, Put, and Canaan. ⁹The sons of Cush *were* Seba, Havilah, Sabta, Raama, and Sabtecha. The sons of Raama *were* Sheba and Dedan. ¹⁰Cush begot Nimrod; he began to be a mighty one on the earth. ¹¹Mizraim begot Ludim, Anamim, Lehabim, Naphtuhim, ¹²Pathrusim, Casluhim (from whom came the Philistines and the Caphtorim). ¹³Canaan begot Sidon, his firstborn, and Heth; ¹⁴the Jebusite, the Amorite, and the Girgashite; ¹⁵the Hivite, the Arkite, and the Sinite; ¹⁶the Arvadite, the Zemarite, and the Hamathite.

¹⁷The sons of Shem *were* Elam, Asshur, Arphaxad, Lud, Aram, Uz, Hul, Gether, and Meshech. ¹⁸Arphaxad begot Shelah, and Shelah begot Eber. ¹⁹To Eber were born two sons: the name of one *was* Peleg, for in his days the earth was divided; and his brother's name *was* Joktan. ²⁰Joktan begot Almodad, Sheleph, Hazarmaveth, Jerah, ²¹Hadoram, Uzal, Diklah, ²²Ebal, Abimael, Sheba, ²³Ophir, Havilah, and Jobab. All these *were* the sons of Joktan.

²⁴Shem, Arphaxad, Shelah, ²⁵Eber, Peleg, Reu, ²⁶Serug, Nahor, Terah, ²⁷and Abram, who *is* Abraham. ²⁸The sons of Abraham *were* Isaac and Ishmael.

²⁹These *are* their genealogies: The firstborn of Ishmael *was* Nebajoth; then Kedar, Adbeel, Mibsam, ³⁰Mishma, Dumah, Massa, Hadad, Tema, ³¹Jetur, Naphish, and Kedemah. These *were* the sons of Ishmael.

³²Now the sons born to Keturah, Abraham's concubine, *were* Zimran, Jokshan, Medan, Midian, Ishbak, and

SPECIAL

1:1 This record of names demonstrates that God is interested not only in nations, but also in individuals. Although billions of people have lived since Adam, God knows and remembers the face and name of each person. Each individual is more than a name on a list. He or she is a special person whom God knows and loves. As we recognize and accept God's love, we discover that we are unique as individuals and that we belong with the rest of his family.

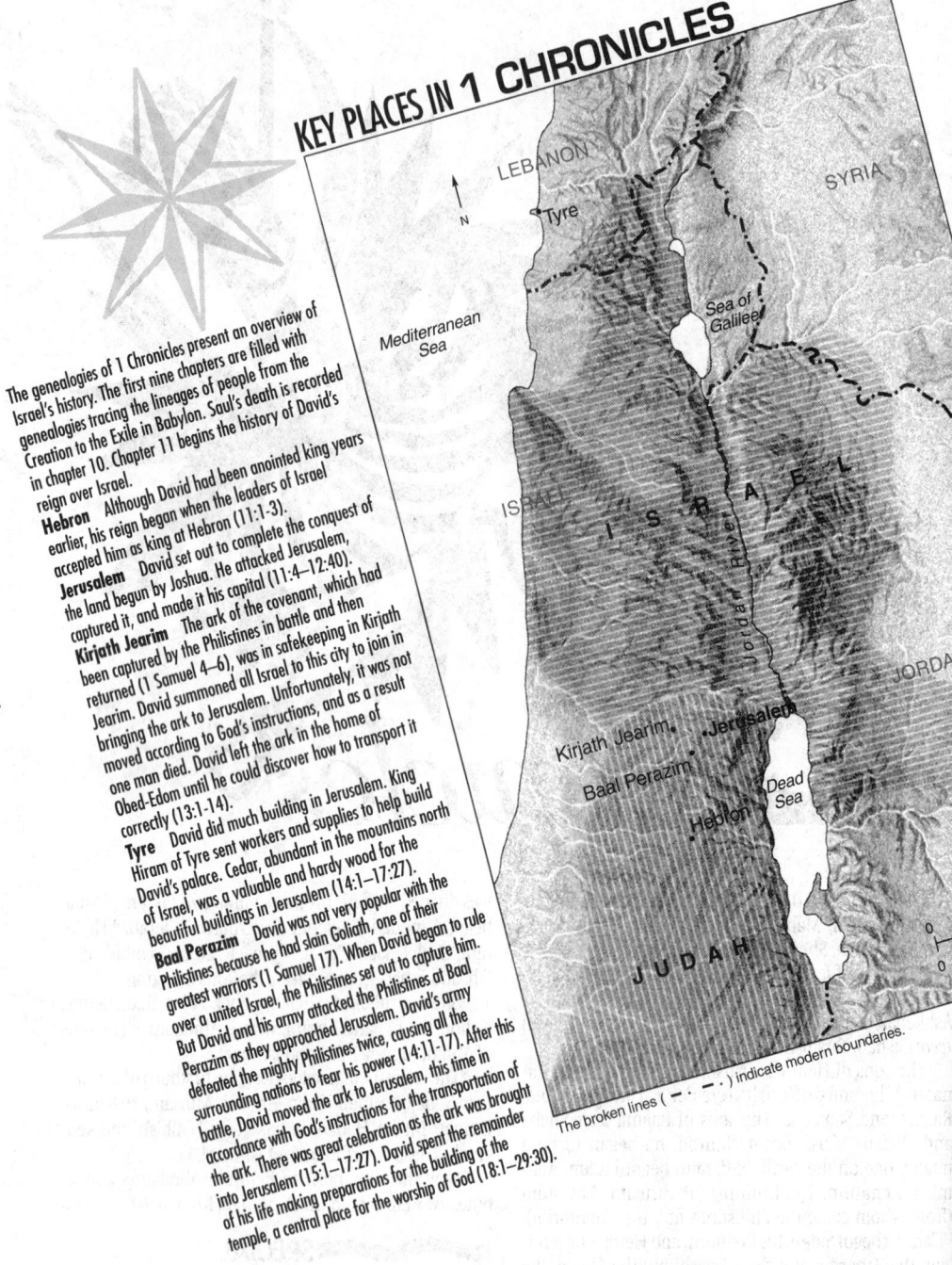

KEY PLACES IN 1 CHRONICLES

The genealogies of 1 Chronicles present an overview of Israel's history. The first nine chapters are filled with genealogies tracing the lineages of people from the Creation to the Exile in Babylon. Saul's death is recorded in chapter 10. Chapter 11 begins the history of David's reign over Israel.

Hebron   Although David had been anointed king years earlier, his reign began when the leaders of Israel accepted him as king at Hebron (11:1-3).

Jerusalem   David set out to complete the conquest of the land begun by Joshua. He attacked Jerusalem, captured it, and made it his capital (11:4–12:40).

Kirjath Jearim   The ark of the covenant, which had been captured by the Philistines in battle and then returned (1 Samuel 4–6), was in safekeeping in Kirjath Jearim. David summoned all Israel to this city to join in bringing the ark to Jerusalem. Unfortunately, it was not moved according to God's instructions, and as a result one man died. David left the ark in the home of Obed-Edom until he could discover how to transport it correctly (13:1-14).

Tyre   David did much building in Jerusalem. King Hiram of Tyre sent workers and supplies to help build David's palace. Cedar, abundant in the mountains north of Israel, was a valuable and hardy wood for the beautiful buildings in Jerusalem (14:1–17:27).

Baal Perazim   David was not very popular with the Philistines because he had slain Goliath, one of their greatest warriors (1 Samuel 17). When David began to rule over a united Israel, the Philistines set out to capture him. But David and his army attacked the Philistines at Baal Perazim as they approached Jerusalem. David's army defeated the mighty Philistines twice, causing all the surrounding nations to fear his power (14:11-17). After this battle, David moved the ark to Jerusalem, this time in accordance with God's instructions for the transportation of the ark. There was great celebration as the ark was brought into Jerusalem (15:1–17:27). David spent the remainder of his life making preparations for the building of the temple, a central place for the worship of God (18:1–29:30).

The broken lines (—·—·—) indicate modern boundaries.

Shuah. The sons of Jokshan *were* Sheba and Dedan. ³³The sons of Midian *were* Ephah, Epher, Hanoch, Abida, and Eldaah. All these were the children of Keturah.

³⁴And Abraham begot Isaac. The sons of Isaac *were* Esau and Israel. ³⁵The sons of Esau *were* Eliphaz, Reuel, Jeush, Jaalam, and Korah. ³⁶And the sons of Eliphaz *were* Teman, Omar, Zephi, Gatam, *and* Kenaz; and *by* Timna, Amalek. ³⁷The sons of Reuel *were* Nahath, Zerah, Shammah, and Mizzah.

³⁸The sons of Seir *were* Lotan, Shobal, Zibeon, Anah, Dishon, Ezer, and Dishan. ³⁹And the sons of Lotan *were* Hori and Homam; Lotan's sister *was* Timna. ⁴⁰The sons of Shobal *were* Alian, Manahath, Ebal, Shephi, and Onam. The sons of Zibeon *were* Ajah and Anah. ⁴¹The son of Anah *was* Dishon. The sons of Dishon *were* Hamran, Eshban, Ithran, and Cheran. ⁴²The sons of Ezer *were* Bilhan, Zaavan, *and* Jaakan. The sons of Dishan *were* Uz and Aran.

⁴³Now these *were* the kings who reigned in the land of Edom before a king reigned over the children of Israel: Bela the son of Beor, and the name of his city was Dinhabah. ⁴⁴And when Bela died, Jobab the son of Zerah of Bozrah reigned in his place. ⁴⁵When Jobab died, Husham of the land of the Temanites reigned in his place. ⁴⁶And when Husham died, Hadad the son of Bedad, who attacked Midian in the field of Moab, reigned in his place. The name of his city *was* Avith. ⁴⁷When Hadad died, Samlah of Masrekah reigned in his place. ⁴⁸And when Samlah died, Saul of Rehoboth-by-the-River reigned in his place. ⁴⁹When Saul died, Baal-Hanan the son of Achbor reigned in his place. ⁵⁰And when Baal-Hanan died, Hadad reigned in his place; and the name of his city was Pai. His wife's name was Mehetabel the daughter of Matred, the daughter of Mezahab. ⁵¹Hadad died also. And the chiefs of Edom were Chief Timnah, Chief Aliah, Chief Jetheth, ⁵²Chief Aholibamah, Chief Elah, Chief Pinon, ⁵³Chief Kenaz, Chief Teman, Chief Mibzar, ⁵⁴Chief Magdiel, and Chief Iram. These *were* the chiefs of Edom.

CHAPTER 2 JACOB'S DESCENDANTS.

These *were* the sons of Israel: Reuben, Simeon, Levi, Judah, Issachar, Zebulun, ²Dan, Joseph, Benjamin, Naphtali, Gad, and Asher.

³The sons of Judah *were* Er, Onan, and Shelah. *These* three were born to him by the daughter of Shua, the Canaanitess. Er, the firstborn of Judah, was wicked in the sight of the LORD; so He killed him. ⁴And Tamar, his daughter-in-law, bore him Perez and Zerah. All the sons of Judah *were* five.

⁵The sons of Perez *were* Hezron and Hamul. ⁶The sons of Zerah *were* Zimri, Ethan, Heman, Calcol, and Dara—five of them in all.

⁷The son of Carmi *was* Achar, the troubler of Israel, who transgressed in the accursed thing.

⁸The son of Ethan *was* Azariah.

⁹Also the sons of Hezron who were born to him *were* Jerahmeel, Ram, and Chelubai. ¹⁰Ram begot Amminadab, and Amminadab begot Nahshon, leader of the children of Judah; ¹¹Nahshon begot Salma, and Salma begot Boaz; ¹²Boaz begot Obed, and Obed begot Jesse; ¹³Jesse begot Eliab his firstborn, Abinadab the second, Shimea the third, ¹⁴Nethanel the fourth, Raddai the fifth, ¹⁵Ozem the sixth, *and* David the seventh.

¹⁶Now their sisters *were* Zeruiah and Abigail. And the sons of Zeruiah *were* Abishai, Joab, and Asahel—three. ¹⁷Abigail bore Amasa; and the father of Amasa *was* Jether the Ishmaelite.

▶ REPUTATION

2:3 This long genealogy not only lists names, but also gives us insights into some of the people. Here, almost as an epitaph, the genealogy states that Er "was wicked in the sight of the LORD; so He killed him." Now, centuries later, this is all we know of the man. Each of us is forging a reputation, developing personal qualities by which we will be remembered. How would God summarize your life up to now? Some defiantly claim that how they live is their own business, but Scripture teaches that the way you live today will determine how you will be remembered by others and how you will be judged by God. What you do now *does* matter.

¹⁸Caleb the son of Hezron had children by Azubah, *his* wife, and by Jerioth. Now these were her sons: Jesher, Shobab, and Ardon. ¹⁹When Azubah died, Caleb took Ephrath as his wife, who bore him Hur. ²⁰And Hur begot Uri, and Uri begot Bezalel.

²¹Now afterward Hezron went in to the daughter of Machir the father of Gilead, whom he married when he *was* sixty years old; and she bore him Segub. ²²Segub begot Jair, who had twenty-three cities in the land of Gilead. ²³(Geshur and Syria took from them the towns of Jair, with Kenath and its towns—sixty towns.) All these *belonged to* the sons of Machir the father of Gilead. ²⁴After Hezron died in Caleb Ephrathah, Hezron's wife Abijah bore him Ashhur the father of Tekoa.

²⁵The sons of Jerahmeel, the firstborn of Hezron, *were* Ram, the firstborn, and Bunah, Oren, Ozem, *and* Ahijah. ²⁶Jerahmeel had another wife, whose name was Atarah; she was the mother of Onam. ²⁷The sons of Ram, the firstborn of Jerahmeel, were Maaz, Jamin, and Eker. ²⁸The sons of Onam were Shammai and Jada. The sons of Shammai *were* Nadab and Abishur.

²⁹And the name of the wife of Abishur *was* Abihail, and she bore him Ahban and Molid. ³⁰The sons of Nadab *were* Seled and Appaim; Seled died without children. ³¹The son of Appaim *was* Ishi, the son of Ishi *was* Sheshan, and Sheshan's son *was* Ahlai. ³²The sons of Jada, the brother of Shammai, *were* Jether and Jonathan; Jether died without children. ³³The sons of Jonathan *were* Peleth and Zaza. These were the sons of Jerahmeel.

³⁴Now Sheshan had no sons, only daughters. And Sheshan had an Egyptian servant whose name *was* Jarha. ³⁵Sheshan gave his daughter to Jarha his servant as wife, and she bore him Attai. ³⁶Attai begot Nathan, and Nathan begot Zabad; ³⁷Zabad begot Ephlal, and Ephlal begot Obed; ³⁸Obed begot Jehu, and Jehu begot Azariah; ³⁹Azariah begot Helez, and Helez begot Eleasah; ⁴⁰Eleasah begot Sismai, and Sismai begot Shallum; ⁴¹Shallum begot Jekamiah, and Jekamiah begot Elishama.

⁴²The descendants of Caleb the brother of Jerahmeel *were* Mesha, his firstborn, who was the father of Ziph,

3:10-14 Many of King Solomon's descendants ruled the nation of Judah. For Rehoboam's story, see 2 Chronicles 10–12. For Jehoshaphat's story, see 2 Chronicles 17–20. For Azariah's (Uzziah's) story, see 2 Chronicles 26. For Hezekiah's story, see 2 Kings 18–20. For Josiah's story, see 2 Kings 22–23.

and the sons of Mareshah the father of Hebron. ⁴³The sons of Hebron *were* Korah, Tappuah, Rekem, and Shema. ⁴⁴Shema begot Raham the father of Jorkoam, and Rekem begot Shammai. ⁴⁵And the son of Shammai *was* Maon, and Maon *was* the father of Beth Zur.

⁴⁶Ephah, Caleb's concubine, bore Haran, Moza, and Gazez; and Haran begot Gazez. ⁴⁷And the sons of Jahdai *were* Regem, Jotham, Geshan, Pelet, Ephah, and Shaaph.

⁴⁸Maachah, Caleb's concubine, bore Sheber and Tirhanah. ⁴⁹She also bore Shaaph the father of Madmannah, Sheva the father of Machbenah and the father of Gibea. And the daughter of Caleb *was* Achsah.

⁵⁰These *were* the descendants of Caleb: The sons of Hur, the firstborn of Ephrathah, *were* Shobal the father of Kirjath Jearim, ⁵¹Salma the father of Bethlehem, *and* Hareph the father of Beth Gader.

⁵²And Shobal the father of Kirjath Jearim had descendants: Haroeh, *and* half of the *families of* Manuhoth. ⁵³The families of Kirjath Jearim *were* the Ithrites, the Puthites, the Shumathites, and the Mishraites. From these came the Zorathites and the Eshtaolites.

⁵⁴The sons of Salma *were* Bethlehem, the Netophathites, Atroth Beth Joab, half of the Manahethites, and the Zorites. ⁵⁵And the families of the scribes who dwelt at Jabez *were* the Tirathites, the Shimeathites, *and* the Suchathites. These *were* the Kenites who came from Hammath, the father of the house of Rechab.

CHAPTER 3 DAVID'S DESCENDANTS.

Now these were the sons of David who were born to him in Hebron: The firstborn *was* Amnon, by Ahinoam the Jezreelitess; the second, Daniel, by Abigail the Carmelitess; ²the third, Absalom the son of Maacah, the daughter of Talmai, king of Geshur; the fourth, Adonijah the son of Haggith; ³the fifth, Shephatiah, by Abital; the sixth, Ithream, by his wife Eglah.

⁴*These* six were born to him in Hebron. There he reigned seven years and six months, and in Jerusalem he reigned thirty-three years. ⁵And these were born to him in Jerusalem: Shimea, Shobab, Nathan, and Solomon—four by Bathshua the daughter of Ammiel. ⁶Also *there* were Ibhar, Elishama, Eliphelet, ⁷Nogah, Nepheg, Japhia, ⁸Elishama, Eliada, and Eliphelet—nine *in all*. ⁹*These were* all the sons of David, besides the sons of the concubines, and Tamar their sister.

¹⁰Solomon's son *was* Rehoboam; Abijah *was* his son, Asa his son, Jehoshaphat his son, ¹¹Joram his son, Ahaziah his son, Joash his son, ¹²Amaziah his son, Azariah his son, Jotham his son, ¹³Ahaz his son, Hezekiah his son, Manasseh his son, ¹⁴Amon his son, *and* Josiah his son. ¹⁵The sons of Josiah *were* Johanan the firstborn, the second Jehoiakim, the third Zedekiah, and the fourth Shallum. ¹⁶The sons of Jehoiakim *were* Jeconiah his son *and* Zedekiah his son.

¹⁷And the sons of Jeconiah *were* Assir, Shealtiel his son, ¹⁸*and* Malchiram, Pedaiah, Shenazzar, Jecamiah, Hoshama, and Nedabiah. ¹⁹The sons of Pedaiah *were* Zerubbabel and Shimei. The sons of Zerubbabel *were* Meshullam, Hananiah, Shelomith their sister, ²⁰and Hashubah, Ohel, Berechiah, Hasadiah, and Jushab-Hesed—five *in all*.

²¹The sons of Hananiah *were* Pelatiah and Jeshaiah, the sons of Rephaiah, the sons of Arnan, the sons of Obadiah, and the sons of Shechaniah. ²²The son of Shechaniah was Shemaiah. The sons of Shemaiah *were* Hattush, Igal, Bariah, Neariah, and Shaphat—six *in all*. ²³The sons of Neariah *were* Elioenai, Hezekiah, and Azrikam—three *in all*. ²⁴The sons of Elioenai *were* Hodaviah, Eliashib, Pelaiah, Akkub, Johanan, Delaiah, and Anani—seven *in all*.

CHAPTER 4 JUDAH'S DESCENDANTS.

The sons of Judah *were* Perez, Hezron, Carmi, Hur, and Shobal. ²And Reaiah the son of Shobal begot Jahath, and Jahath begot Ahumai and Lahad. These *were* the families of the Zorathites. ³These *were* the sons *of the father* of Etam: Jezreel, Ishma, and Idbash; and the name of their sister *was* Hazelelponi; ⁴and Penuel *was* the father of Gedor, and Ezer *was the* father of Hushah.

These *were* the sons of Hur, the firstborn of Ephrathah the father of Bethlehem.

⁵And Ashhur the father of Tekoa had two wives, Helah and Naarah. ⁶Naarah bore him Ahuzzam, Hepher, Temeni, and Haahashtari. These *were* the sons of Naarah. ⁷The sons of Helah *were* Zereth, Zohar, and Ethnan; ⁸and Koz begot Anub, Zobebah, and the families of Aharhel the son of Harum.

⁹Now Jabez was more honorable than his brothers, and his mother called his name Jabez, saying, "Because I bore *him* in pain." ¹⁰And Jabez called on the God of Israel saying, "Oh, that You would bless me indeed, and enlarge my territory, that Your hand would be with me, and that You would keep *me* from evil, that I may not cause pain!" So God granted him what he requested.

¹¹Chelub the brother of Shuhah begot Mehir, who *was* the father of Eshton. ¹²And Eshton begot Beth-Rapha, Paseah, and Tehinnah the father of Ir-Nahash. These *were* the men of Rechah.

¹³The sons of Kenaz *were* Othniel and Seraiah. The sons of Othniel *were* Hathath, ¹⁴and Meonothai *who* begot Ophrah. Seraiah begot Joab the father of Ge Harashim, for they were craftsmen. ¹⁵The sons of Caleb the son of Jephunneh *were* Iru, Elah, and Naam. The son of Elah *was* Kenaz. ¹⁶The sons of Jehallelel *were* Ziph, Ziphah, Tiria, and Asarel. ¹⁷The sons of Ezrah *were* Jether, Mered, Epher, and Jalon. And *Mered's wife bore* Miriam, Shammai, and Ishbah the father of Eshtemoa.

4:10 Jabez is remembered as the one who "called on the God of Israel." It is significant that he is remembered for a prayer rather heroic act. In his prayer, he asked God to (1) bless him, (2) help h his work, (3) be with him in all he did, and (4) keep him from evi disaster. Jabez acknowledged God as the true center of his work. V we pray for God's blessing, we should also pray that he will take h rightful position as Lord over all areas of our life. Then we, too, m remembered for more than just a heroic deed.

¹⁸(His wife Jehudijah bore Jered the father of Gedor, Heber the father of Sochoh, and Jekuthiel the father of Zanoah.) And these were the sons of Bithiah the daughter of Pharaoh, whom Mered took.

¹⁹The sons of Hodiah's wife, the sister of Naham, *were* the fathers of Keilah the Garmite and of Eshtemoa the Maachathite. ²⁰And the sons of Shimon *were* Amnon, Rinnah, Ben-Hanan, and Tilon. And the sons of Ishi *were* Zoheth and Ben-Zoheth.

²¹The sons of Shelah the son of Judah *were* Er the father of Lecah, Laadah the father of Mareshah, and the families of the house of the linen workers of the house of Ashbea; ²²also Jokim, the men of Chozeba, and Joash; Saraph, who ruled in Moab, and Jashubi-Lehem. Now the records are ancient. ²³These *were* the potters and those who dwell at Netaim and Gederah; there they dwelt with the king for his work.

²⁴The sons of Simeon *were* Nemuel, Jamin, Jarib, Zerah, *and* Shaul, ²⁵Shallum his son, Mibsam his son, and Mishma his son. ²⁶And the sons of Mishma *were* Hamuel his son, Zacchur his son, and Shimei his son. ²⁷Shimei had sixteen sons and six daughters; but his brothers did not have many children, nor did any of their families multiply as much as the children of Judah.

²⁸They dwelt at Beersheba, Moladah, Hazar Shual, ²⁹Bilhah, Ezem, Tolad, ³⁰Bethuel, Hormah, Ziklag, ³¹Beth Marcaboth, Hazar Susim, Beth Biri, and at Shaaraim. These *were* their cities until the reign of David. ³²And their villages *were* Etam, Ain, Rimmon, Tochen, and Ashan—five cities— ³³and all the villages that *were* around these cities as far as Baal. These *were* their dwelling places, and they maintained their genealogy: ³⁴Meshobab, Jamlech, and Joshah the son of Amaziah; ³⁵Joel, and Jehu the son of Joshibiah, the son of Seraiah, the son of Asiel; ³⁶Elioenai, Jaakobah, Jeshohaiah, Asaiah, Adiel, Jesimiel, and Benaiah; ³⁷Ziza the son of Shiphi, the son of Allon, the son of Jedaiah, the son of Shimri, the son of Shemaiah— ³⁸these mentioned by name *were* leaders in their families, and their father's house increased greatly.

³⁹So they went to the entrance of Gedor, as far as the east side of the valley, to seek pasture for their flocks. ⁴⁰And they found rich, good pasture, and the land *was* broad, quiet, and peaceful; for some Hamites formerly lived there.

⁴¹These recorded by name came in the days of Hezekiah king of Judah; and they attacked their tents and the Meunites who were found there, and utterly destroyed them, as it is to this day. So they dwelt in their place, because *there was* pasture for their flocks there. ⁴²Now *some* of them, five hundred men of the sons of Simeon, went to Mount Seir, having as their captains Pelatiah, Neariah, Rephaiah, and Uzziel, the sons of Ishi. ⁴³And they defeated the rest of the Amalekites who had escaped. They have dwelt there to this day.

CHAPTER **5** REUBEN'S DESCENDANTS. Now the sons of Reuben the firstborn of Israel—he *was* indeed the firstborn, but because he defiled his father's bed, his birthright was given to the sons of

ISHMAEL

Have you ever wondered whether you were born into the wrong family? That question must have haunted Ishmael at times. His life was trapped in a conflict between two jealous women. Ishmael's stepmother, Sarah, got impatient with God, so she decided to have a child through another woman. Since Hagar was a servant, she allowed herself to be used this way. But Hagar's pregnancy gave birth to strong feelings of superiority toward Sarah. Into this tense atmosphere Ishmael was born.

It is easy to think we can help God move faster. But we usually only create more problems. Much of what happened to Ishmael cannot be blamed on him. He was caught in a process much bigger than himself. But his actions showed that he chose to become part of the problem, not the solution. He chose to live in his circumstances instead of living above them.

The choice Ishmael had is one we all must make. There are circumstances over which we have no control (heredity, for instance), but there are others over which we do have control (our decisions). We all have inherited a sin-oriented nature. It can be partly controlled—but not overcome—by human effort. Ishmael's life is a picture of the mess we make when we don't try to change those things that we can change.

The God of the Bible has offered us a solution. His answer is not control, but a changed life freely given by God. To begin a changed life, trust in God to forgive your sinful past, and ask him to help you change your attitude toward him and others.

UPS:
• One of the first to experience the physical sign of God's covenant—circumcision
• Known for his ability as an archer and hunter
• Fathered 12 sons who became leaders of warrior tribes

DOWNS:
• Failed to recognize the place of his half brother, Isaac, and mocked him

STATS:
• Where: Canaan and Egypt
• Occupation: Archer, hunter, warrior
• Relatives: Parents: Hagar and Abraham. Half brother: Isaac.

LESSONS: God's plans even use people's mistakes

KEY VERSES: "The sons of Abraham were Isaac and Ishmael" (1 Chronicles 1:28). "What ails you, Hagar? Fear not, for God has heard the voice of the lad where he is. Arise, lift up the lad and hold him with your hand, for I will make him a great nation" (Genesis 21:17-18).

Ishmael's complete story is told in Genesis 16–17; 21; 25–28; 36. He is also mentioned in Galatians 4:28-29.

5:1 Reuben's sin of incest was recorded for all future generations to read. The purpose of this epitaph, however, was not to smear Reuben's name, but to show that painful memories aren't the only results of sin. The real consequences of sin are ruined lives. As the oldest son, Reuben was the rightful heir to both a double portion of his father's estate and the leadership of Abraham's descendants, who had grown into a large tribe. But his sin stripped away his rights and privileges and ruined his family. Before you give in to temptation, take a close look at the disastrous consequences that sin may have in your life and the lives of others.

Joseph, the son of Israel, so that the genealogy is not listed according to the birthright; ²yet Judah prevailed over his brothers, and from him *came* a ruler, although the birthright was Joseph's— ³the sons of Reuben the firstborn of Israel were Hanoch, Pallu, Hezron, and Carmi.

⁴The sons of Joel *were* Shemaiah his son, Gog his son, Shimei his son, ⁵Micah his son, Reaiah his son, Baal his son, ⁶and Beerah his son, whom Tiglath-Pileser king of Assyria carried into captivity. He *was* leader of the Reubenites. ⁷And his brethren by their families, when the genealogy of their generations was registered: the chief, Jeiel, and Zechariah, ⁸and Bela the son of Azaz, the son of Shema, the son of Joel, who dwelt in Aroer, as far as Nebo and Baal Meon. ⁹Eastward they settled as far as the entrance of the wilderness this side of the River Euphrates, because their cattle had multiplied in the land of Gilead.

¹⁰Now in the days of Saul they made war with the Hagrites, who fell by their hand; and they dwelt in their tents throughout the entire *area* east of Gilead.

¹¹And the children of Gad dwelt next to them in the land of Bashan as far as Salcah: ¹²Joel *was* the chief, Shapham the next, then Jaanai and Shaphat in Bashan, ¹³and their brethren of their father's house: Michael, Meshullam, Sheba, Jorai, Jachan, Zia, and Eber—seven *in all*. ¹⁴These *were* the children of Abihail the son of Huri, the son of Jaroah, the son of Gilead, the son of Michael, the son of Jeshishai, the son of Jahdo, the son of Buz; ¹⁵Ahi the son of Abdiel, the son of Guni, *was* chief of their father's house. ¹⁶And *the Gadites* dwelt in Gilead, in Bashan and in its villages, and in all the common-lands of Sharon within their borders. ¹⁷All these were registered by genealogies in the days of Jotham king of Judah, and in the days of Jeroboam king of Israel.

¹⁸The sons of Reuben, the Gadites, and half the tribe of Manasseh *had* forty-four thousand seven hundred and sixty valiant men, men able to bear shield and sword, to shoot with the bow, and skillful in war, who went to war. ¹⁹They made war with the Hagrites, Jetur, Naphish, and Nodab. ²⁰And they were helped against them, and the Hagrites were delivered into their hand, and all who *were* with them, for they cried out to God in the battle. He heeded their prayer, because they put their trust in Him. ²¹Then they took away their livestock—fifty thousand of their camels, two hundred and fifty thousand of their sheep, and two thousand of their donkeys—also one hundred thousand of their men; ²²for many fell dead, because the war *was* God's. And they dwelt in their place until the captivity.

²³So the children of the half-tribe of Manasseh dwelt in the land. Their *numbers* increased from Bashan to Baal Hermon, that is, to Senir, or Mount Hermon. ²⁴These *were* the heads of their fathers' houses: Epher, Ishi, Eliel, Azriel, Jeremiah, Hodaviah, and Jahdiel. They were mighty men of valor, famous men, *and* heads of their fathers' houses.

²⁵And they were unfaithful to the God of their fathers, and played the harlot after the gods of the peoples of the land, whom God had destroyed before them. ²⁶So the God of Israel stirred up the spirit of Pul king of Assyria, that is, Tiglath-Pileser king of Assyria. He carried the Reubenites, the Gadites, and the half-tribe of Manasseh into captivity. He took them to Halah, Habor, Hara, and the river of Gozan to this day.

CHAPTER **6** **LEVI'S DESCENDANTS.** The sons of Levi *were* Gershon, Kohath, and Merari. ²The sons of Kohath *were* Amram, Izhar, Hebron, and Uzziel. ³The children of Amram *were* Aaron, Moses, and Miriam. And the sons of Aaron *were* Nadab, Abihu, Eleazar, and Ithamar. ⁴Eleazar begot Phinehas, *and* Phinehas begot Abishua; ⁵Abishua begot Bukki, and Bukki begot Uzzi; ⁶Uzzi begot Zerahiah, and Zerahiah begot Meraioth; ⁷Meraioth begot Amariah, and Amariah begot Ahitub; ⁸Ahitub begot Zadok, and Zadok begot Ahimaaz; ⁹Ahimaaz begot Azariah, and Azariah begot Johanan; ¹⁰Johanan begot Azariah (it was he who ministered as priest in the temple that Solomon built in Jerusalem); ¹¹Azariah begot Amariah, and Amariah begot Ahitub; ¹²Ahitub begot Zadok, and Zadok begot Shallum; ¹³Shallum begot Hilkiah, and Hilkiah begot Azariah; ¹⁴Azariah begot Seraiah, and Seraiah begot Jehozadak. ¹⁵Jehozadak went *into captivity* when the LORD carried Judah and Jerusalem into captivity by the hand of Nebuchadnezzar.

¹⁶The sons of Levi *were* Gershon, Kohath, and Merari. ¹⁷These are the names of the sons of Gershon: Libni and Shimei. ¹⁸The sons of Kohath *were* Amram, Izhar, Hebron, and Uzziel. ¹⁹The sons of Merari *were* Mahli and Mushi. Now these *are* the families of the Levites according to their fathers: ²⁰Of Gershon *were* Libni his son, Jahath his son, Zimmah his son, ²¹Joah his son, Iddo his son, Zerah his son, *and* Jeatherai his son. ²²The sons of Kohath *were* Amminadab his son, Korah his son, Assir his son, ²³Elkanah his son, Ebiasaph his son, Assir his son, ²⁴Tahath his son, Uriel his son, Uzziah his son, and Shaul his son. ²⁵The sons of Elkanah *were* Amasai and Ahimoth. ²⁶*As for* Elkanah, the sons of Elkanah *were* Zophai his son, Nahath his son, ²⁷Eliab his son, Jeroham his son, *and* Elkanah his son. ²⁸The sons of Samuel *were* Joel the firstborn, and Abijah the second. ²⁹The sons of Merari *were* Mahli, Libni his son, Shimei his son, Uzzah his son, ³⁰Shimea his son, Haggiah his son, *and* Asaiah his son.

WARRIORS

5:24-25 As warriors and leaders, these men had established ex reputations for their great skill and leadership qualities. But in Go they failed in the most important quality— putting God first in th lives. If you try to measure up to society's standards for fame and success, you will be in danger of neglecting your true quest—to p and obey God. In the end, God alone examines our heart and det our standing.

[31]Now these are the men whom David appointed over the service of song in the house of the LORD, after the ark came to rest. [32]They were ministering with music before the dwelling place of the tabernacle of meeting, until Solomon had built the house of the LORD in Jerusalem, and they served in their office according to their order.

[33]And these *are* the ones who ministered with their sons: Of the sons of the Kohathites *were* Heman the singer, the son of Joel, the son of Samuel, [34]the son of Elkanah, the son of Jeroham, the son of Eliel, the son of Toah, [35]the son of Zuph, the son of Elkanah, the son of Mahath, the son of Amasai, [36]the son of Elkanah, the son of Joel, the son of Azariah, the son of Zephaniah, [37]the son of Tahath, the son of Assir, the son of Ebiasaph, the son of Korah, [38]the son of Izhar, the son of Kohath, the son of Levi, the son of Israel. [39]And his brother Asaph, who stood at his right hand, *was* Asaph the son of Berachiah, the son of Shimea, [40]the son of Michael, the son of Baaseiah, the son of Malchijah, [41]the son of Ethni, the son of Zerah, the son of Adaiah, [42]the son of Ethan, the son of Zimmah, the son of Shimei, [43]the son of Jahath, the son of Gershon, the son of Levi.

[44]Their brethren, the sons of Merari, on the left hand, *were* Ethan the son of Kishi, the son of Abdi, the son of Malluch, [45]the son of Hashabiah, the son of Amaziah, the son of Hilkiah, [46]the son of Amzi, the son of Bani, the son of Shamer, [47]the son of Mahli, the son of Mushi, the son of Merari, the son of Levi.

[48]And their brethren, the Levites, *were* appointed to every kind of service of the tabernacle of the house of God.

[49]But Aaron and his sons offered sacrifices on the altar of burnt offering and on the altar of incense, for all the work of the Most Holy *Place*, and to make atonement for Israel, according to all that Moses the servant of God had commanded. [50]Now these *are* the sons of Aaron: Eleazar his son, Phinehas his son, Abishua his son, [51]Bukki his son, Uzzi his son, Zerahiah his son, [52]Meraioth his son, Amariah his son, Ahitub his son, [53]Zadok his son, *and* Ahimaaz his son.

[54]Now these *are* their dwelling places throughout their settlements in their territory, for they were *given* by lot to the sons of Aaron, of the family of the Kohathites: [55]They gave them Hebron in the land of Judah, with its surrounding common-lands. [56]But the fields of the city and its villages they gave to Caleb the son of Jephunneh. [57]And to the sons of Aaron they gave *one of* the cities of refuge, Hebron; also Libnah with its common-lands, Jattir, Eshtemoa with its common-lands, [58]Hilen with its common-lands, Debir with its common-lands, [59]Ashan with its common-lands, and Beth Shemesh with its common-lands. [60]And from the tribe of Benjamin: Geba with its common-lands, Alemeth with its common-lands, and Anathoth with its common-lands. All their cities among their families *were* thirteen.

[61]To the rest of the family of the tribe of the Kohathites *they gave* by lot ten cities from half the tribe of Manasseh. [62]And to the sons of Gershon, throughout their families, *they gave* thirteen cities from the tribe of Issachar, from the tribe of Asher, from the tribe of Naphtali, and from the tribe of Manasseh in Bashan. [63]To the sons of Merari, throughout their families, *they gave* twelve cities from the tribe of Reuben, from the tribe of Gad, and from the tribe of Zebulun. [64]So the children of Israel gave *these* cities with their common-lands to the Levites. [65]And they gave by lot from the tribe of the children of Judah, from the tribe of the children of Simeon, and from the tribe of the children of Benjamin these cities which are called by *their* names.

TALENTS

6:31-32 The builders and craftsmen had completed the temple, and the priests and the Levites had been given their responsibilities for taking care of it. Now it was time for another group of people—the choirs—to exercise their talents for God. Some of the songleaders' names are recorded here, showing you don't have to be an ordained minister to serve God. Builders, craftsmen, worship assistants, choir members, and songleaders all had significant contributions to make. God has given you a unique combination of talents. Use them to serve him.

[66]Now some of the families of the sons of Kohath *were* given cities as their territory from the tribe of Ephraim. [67]And they gave them *one of* the cities of refuge, Shechem with its common-lands, in the mountains of Ephraim, also Gezer with its common-lands, [68]Jokmeam with its common-lands, Beth Horon with its common-lands, [69]Aijalon with its common-lands, and Gath Rimmon with its common-lands. [70]And from the half-tribe of Manasseh: Aner with its common-lands and Bileam with its common-lands, for the rest of the family of the sons of Kohath.

[71]From the family of the half-tribe of Manasseh the sons of Gershon *were given* Golan in Bashan with its common-lands and Ashtaroth with its common-lands. [72]And from the tribe of Issachar: Kedesh with its common-lands, Daberath with its common-lands, [73]Ramoth with its common-lands, and Anem with its common-lands. [74]And from the tribe of Asher: Mashal with its common-lands, Abdon with its common-lands, [75]Hukok with its common-lands, and Rehob with its common-lands. [76]And from the tribe of Naphtali: Kedesh in Galilee with its common-lands, Hammon with its common-lands, and Kirjathaim with its common-lands.

[77]From the tribe of Zebulun the rest of the children of Merari *were given* Rimmon with its common-lands and Tabor with its common-lands. [78]And on the other side of the Jordan, across from Jericho, on the east side of the Jordan, *they were given* from the tribe of Reuben: Bezer in the wilderness with its common-lands, Jahzah with its common-lands, [79]Kedemoth with its common-lands, and Mephaath with its common-lands. [80]And from the tribe of Gad: Ramoth in Gilead with its common-lands, Mahanaim with its common-lands, [81]Heshbon with its common-lands, and Jazer with its common-lands.

BY THE BOOK

6:49 Aaron and his descendants strictly followed the details of worship commanded by God through Moses. They did not choose only those commands they *wanted* to obey. Note what happened to Uzza when important details in handling the ark of the covenant were neglected (13:6-10). We should not obey God selectively, choosing which commands we will obey and which we will ignore. God's Word has authority over *every* aspect of our lives, not just over selected portions.

CHAPTER 7 — ISSACHAR'S DESCENDANTS.

The sons of Issachar *were* Tola, Puah, Jashub, and Shimron—four *in all.* [2]The sons of Tola *were* Uzzi, Rephaiah, Jeriel, Jahmai, Jibsam, and Shemuel, heads of their father's house. *The sons* of Tola *were* mighty men of valor in their generations; their number in the days of David *was* twenty-two thousand six hundred. [3]The son of Uzzi *was* Izrahiah, and the sons of Izrahiah *were* Michael, Obadiah, Joel, and Ishiah. All five of them *were* chief men. [4]And with them, by their generations, according to their fathers' houses, *were* thirty-six thousand troops ready for war; for they had many wives and sons.

[5]Now their brethren among all the families of Issachar *were* mighty men of valor, listed by their genealogies, eighty-seven thousand in all.

[6]*The sons* of Benjamin *were* Bela, Becher, and Jediael—three *in all.* [7]The sons of Bela were Ezbon, Uzzi, Uzziel, Jerimoth, and Iri—five *in all.* They *were* heads of *their* fathers' houses, and they were listed by their genealogies, twenty-two thousand and thirty-four mighty men of valor.

[8]The sons of Becher *were* Zemirah, Joash, Eliezer, Elioenai, Omri, Jerimoth, Abijah, Anathoth, and Alemeth. All these *are* the sons of Becher. [9]And they were recorded by genealogy according to their generations, heads of their fathers' houses, twenty thousand two hundred mighty men of valor. [10]The son of Jediael *was* Bilhan, and the sons of Bilhan *were* Jeush, Benjamin, Ehud, Chenaanah, Zethan, Tharshish, and Ahishahar.

[11]All these sons of Jediael *were* heads of their fathers' houses; *there were* seventeen thousand two hundred mighty men of valor fit to go out for war *and* battle. [12]Shuppim and Huppim *were* the sons of Ir, *and* Hushim *was* the son of Aher.

[13]The sons of Naphtali *were* Jahziel, Guni, Jezer, and Shallum, the sons of Bilhah.

[14]The descendants of Manasseh: his Syrian concubine bore him Machir the father of Gilead, the father of Asriel. [15]Machir took as his wife *the sister* of Huppim and Shuppim, whose name *was* Maachah. The name of *Gilead's* grandson *was* Zelophehad, but Zelophehad begot only daughters. [16](Maachah the wife of Machir bore a son, and she called his name Peresh. The name of his brother *was* Sheresh, and his sons *were* Ulam and Rakem. [17]The son of Ulam *was* Bedan.) These *were* the descendants of Gilead the son of Machir, the son of Manasseh.

[18]His sister Hammoleketh bore Ishhod, Abiezer, and Mahlah.

[19]And the sons of Shemida *were* Ahian, Shechem, Likhi, and Aniam.

[20]The sons of Ephraim *were* Shuthelah, Bered his son, Tahath his son, Eladah his son, Tahath his son, [21]Zabad his son, Shuthelah his son, and Ezer and Elead. The men of Gath who were born in *that* land killed *them* because they came down to take away their cattle. [22]Then Ephraim their father mourned many days, and his brethren came to comfort him.

[23]And when he went in to his wife, she conceived and bore a son; and he called his name Beriah, because tragedy had come upon his house. [24]Now his daughter *was* Sheerah, who built Lower and Upper Beth Horon and Uzzen Sheerah; [25]and Rephah *was* his son, *as well* as Resheph, and Telah his son, Tahan his son, [26]Laadan his son, Ammihud his son, Elishama his son, [27]Nun his son, and Joshua his son.

[28]Now their possessions and dwelling places *were* Bethel and its towns: to the east Naaran, to the west Gezer and its towns, and Shechem and its towns, as far as Ayyah and its towns; [29]and by the borders of the children of Manasseh *were* Beth Shean and its towns, Taanach and its towns, Megiddo and its towns, Dor and its towns. In these dwelt the children of Joseph, the son of Israel.

[30]The sons of Asher *were* Imnah, Ishvah, Ishvi, Beriah, and their sister Serah. [31]The sons of Beriah *were* Heber and Malchiel, who was the father of Birzaith. [32]And Heber begot Japhlet, Shomer, Hotham, and their sister Shua. [33]The sons of Japhlet *were* Pasach, Bimhal, and Ashvath. These *were* the children of Japhlet. [34]The sons of Shemer *were* Ahi, Rohgah, Jehubbah, and Aram. [35]And the sons of his brother Helem *were* Zophah, Imna, Shelesh, and Amal. [36]The sons of Zophah *were* Suah, Harnepher, Shual, Beri, Imrah, [37]Bezer, Hod, Shamma, Shilshah, Jithran, and Beera. [38]The sons of Jether *were* Jephunneh, Pispah, and Ara. [39]The sons of Ulla *were* Arah, Haniel, and Rizia.

[40]All these *were* the children of Asher, heads of *their* fathers' houses, choice men, mighty men of valor, chief leaders. And they were recorded by genealogies among the army fit for battle; their number *was* twenty-six thousand.

CHAPTER 8 — BENJAMIN'S DESCENDANTS.

Now Benjamin begot Bela his firstborn, Ashbel the second, Aharah the third, [2]Nohah the fourth, and Rapha the fifth. [3]The sons of Bela *were* Addar, Gera, Abihud, [4]Abishua, Naaman, Ahoah, [5]Gera, Shephuphan, and Huram.

[6]These *are* the sons of Ehud, who were the heads of the fathers' *houses* of the inhabitants of Geba, and who forced them to move to Manahath: [7]Naaman, Ahijah, and Gera who forced them to move. He begot Uzza and Ahihud.

[8]Also Shaharaim had children in the country of Moab, after he had sent away Hushim and Baara his wives. [9]By Hodesh his wife he begot Jobab, Zibia, Mesha, Malcam, [10]Jeuz, Sachiah, and Mirmah. These *were* his sons, heads of their fathers' *houses.*

[11]And by Hushim he begot Abitub and Elpaal. [12]The sons of Elpaal *were* Eber, Misham, and Shemed, who built Ono and Lod with its towns; [13]and Beriah and Shema, who *were* heads of their fathers' *houses* of the inhabitants of Aijalon, who drove out the inhabitants of

APPROVAL

8:8-10 Divorce and polygamy are sometimes recorded in the Ol Testament without critical comments. This does not mean that God them lightly. Malachi 2:15-16 says, "Let none deal treacherously v wife of his youth. 'For the LORD God of Israel says that He hates divorce.'" Jesus explained that although divorce was allowed, it w God's will: "Moses, because of the hardness of your hearts, permit to divorce your wives, but from the beginning it was not so" (Matt 19:8). Don't assume that God approves of something because it is vigorously condemned in every Scripture reference.

Gath. ¹⁴Ahio, Shashak, Jeremoth, ¹⁵Zebadiah, Arad, Eder, ¹⁶Michael, Ispah, and Joha *were* the sons of Beriah. ¹⁷Zebadiah, Meshullam, Hizki, Heber, ¹⁸Ishmerai, Jizliah, and Jobab *were* the sons of Elpaal. ¹⁹Jakim, Zichri, Zabdi, ²⁰Elienai, Zillethai, Eliel, ²¹Adaiah, Beraiah, and Shimrath *were* the sons of Shimei. ²²Ishpan, Eber, Eliel, ²³Abdon, Zichri, Hanan, ²⁴Hananiah, Elam, Antothijah, ²⁵Iphdeiah, and Penuel *were* the sons of Shashak. ²⁶Shamsherai, Shehariah, Athaliah, ²⁷Jaareshiah, Elijah, and Zichri *were* the sons of Jeroham.

²⁸These *were* heads of the fathers' *houses* by their generations, chief men. These dwelt in Jerusalem.

²⁹Now the father of Gibeon, whose wife's name *was* Maachah, dwelt at Gibeon. ³⁰And his firstborn son *was* Abdon, then Zur, Kish, Baal, Nadab, ³¹Gedor, Ahio, Zecher, ³²and Mikloth, *who* begot Shimeah. They also dwelt alongside their relatives in Jerusalem, with their brethren. ³³Ner begot Kish, Kish begot Saul, and Saul begot Jonathan, Malchishua, Abinadab, and Esh-Baal. ³⁴The son of Jonathan *was* Merib-Baal, and Merib-Baal begot Micah. ³⁵The sons of Micah *were* Pithon, Melech, Tarea, and Ahaz. ³⁶And Ahaz begot Jehoaddah; Jehoaddah begot Alemeth, Azmaveth, and Zimri; and Zimri begot Moza. ³⁷Moza begot Binea, Raphah his son, Eleasah his son, *and* Azel his son.

³⁸Azel had six sons whose names *were* these: Azrikam, Bocheru, Ishmael, Sheariah, Obadiah, and Hanan. All these *were* the sons of Azel. ³⁹And the sons of Eshek his brother *were* Ulam his firstborn, Jeush the second, and Eliphelet the third.

⁴⁰The sons of Ulam were mighty men of valor—archers. *They* had many sons and grandsons, one hundred and fifty *in all*. These *were* all sons of Benjamin.

CHAPTER 9 THE EXILED PEOPLE RETURN HOME.

So all Israel was recorded by genealogies, and indeed, they *were* inscribed in the book of the kings of Israel. But Judah was carried away captive to Babylon because of their unfaithfulness. ²And the first inhabitants who *dwelt* in their possessions in their cities *were* Israelites, priests, Levites, and the Nethinim.

³Now in Jerusalem the children of Judah dwelt, and some of the children of Benjamin, and of the children of Ephraim and Manasseh: ⁴Uthai the son of Ammihud, the son of Omri, the son of Imri, the son of Bani, of the descendants of Perez, the son of Judah. ⁵Of the Shilonites: Asaiah the firstborn and his sons. ⁶Of the sons of Zerah: Jeuel, and their brethren—six hundred and ninety. ⁷Of the sons of Benjamin: Sallu the son of Meshullam, the son of Hodaviah, the son of Hassenuah; ⁸Ibneiah the son of Jeroham; Elah the son of Uzzi, the son of Michri; Meshullam the son of Shephatiah, the son of Reuel, the son of Ibnijah; ⁹and their brethren, according to their generations—nine hundred and fifty-six. All these men *were* heads of a father's *house* in their fathers' houses.

¹⁰Of the priests: Jedaiah, Jehoiarib, and Jachin; ¹¹Azariah the son of Hilkiah, the son of Meshullam, the son of Zadok, the son of Meraioth, the son of Ahitub, the officer over the house of God; ¹²Adaiah the son of Jeroham, the son of Pashur, the son of Malchijah; Maasai the son of

Adiel, the son of Jahzerah, the son of Meshullam, the son of Meshillemith, the son of Immer; ¹³and their brethren, heads of their fathers' *houses*—one thousand seven hundred and sixty. *They were* very able men for the work of the service of the house of God.

¹⁴Of the Levites: Shemaiah the son of Hasshub, the son of Azrikam, the son of Hashabiah, of the sons of Merari; ¹⁵Bakbakkar, Heresh, Galal, and Mattaniah the son of Micah, the son of Zichri, the son of Asaph; ¹⁶Obadiah the son of Shemaiah, the son of Galal, the son of Jeduthun; and Berechiah the son of Asa, the son of Elkanah, who lived in the villages of the Netophathites.

▰▰▰ SPEAK OUT

9:1 The entire nation of Judah suffered the consequences of idol worship. Idol worship is not just bowing down to statues of wood or stone, it is making anything more important than God—popularity, possessions, money, or even a good friend. Although every person in Judah did not worship idols, the entire nation was carried away into captivity. Everyone was affected by the sin of some. Even if we don't participate in a certain widespread wrongdoing, we will still be affected by those who do. It is not enough to say, "I don't do it." We must speak out against the sins of our society.

¹⁷And the gatekeepers *were* Shallum, Akkub, Talmon, Ahiman, and their brethren. Shallum *was* the chief. ¹⁸Until then *they had been* gatekeepers for the camps of the children of Levi at the King's Gate on the east.

¹⁹Shallum the son of Kore, the son of Ebiasaph, the son of Korah, and his brethren, from his father's house, the Korahites, *were* in charge of the work of the service, gatekeepers of the tabernacle. Their fathers had been keepers of the entrance to the camp of the LORD. ²⁰And Phinehas the son of Eleazar had been the officer over them in time past; the LORD *was* with him. ²¹Zechariah the son of Meshelemiah *was* keeper of the door of the tabernacle of meeting.

²²All those chosen as gatekeepers *were* two hundred and twelve. They were recorded by their genealogy, in their villages. David and Samuel the seer had appointed them to their trusted office. ²³So they and their children *were* in charge of the gates of the house of the LORD, the house of the tabernacle, by assignment. ²⁴The gatekeepers were assigned to the four directions: the east, west, north, and south. ²⁵And their brethren in their villages *had* to come with them from time to time for seven

▰▰▰ BE PREPARED

9:22-32 The priests and Levites put a great deal of time and care into worship. Not only did they perform rather complicated tasks (described in Leviticus 1–9), they also took care of many pieces of equipment. Everything relating to worship was carefully prepared and maintained so both they and all the people could enter worship with their minds and hearts focused on God.

In our busy world, it is easy to rush into our one-hour-a-week worship service without thinking about worship beforehand. We reflect and worry about the week's problems; we pray about whatever comes into our mind; and we do not meditate on the words we are singing. But God wants our worship to be conducted "decently and in order" (1 Corinthians 14:40). Just as we would prepare to meet an important person or a guest, we should carefully prepare to meet and worship our King.

days. ²⁶For in this trusted office *were* four chief gatekeepers; they were Levites. And they had charge over the chambers and treasuries of the house of God. ²⁷And they lodged *all* around the house of God because they *had* the responsibility, and they *were* in charge of opening *it* every morning.

²⁸Now *some* of them were in charge of the serving vessels, for they brought them in and took them out by count. ²⁹*Some* of them *were* appointed over the furnishings and over all the implements of the sanctuary, and over the fine flour and the wine and the oil and the incense and the spices. ³⁰And *some* of the sons of the priests made the ointment of the spices.

³¹Mattithiah of the Levites, the firstborn of Shallum the Korahite, had the trusted office over the things that were baked in the pans. ³²And some of their brethren of the sons of the Kohathites *were* in charge of preparing the showbread for every Sabbath.

³³These are the singers, heads of the fathers' *houses* of the Levites, *who lodged* in the chambers, *and were* free *from other duties;* for they were employed in *that* work day and night. ³⁴These heads of the fathers' *houses* of the Levites *were* heads throughout their generations. They dwelt at Jerusalem.

³⁵Jeiel the father of Gibeon, whose wife's name *was* Maacah, dwelt at Gibeon. ³⁶His firstborn son *was* Abdon, then Zur, Kish, Baal, Ner, Nadab, ³⁷Gedor, Ahio, Zechariah, and Mikloth. ³⁸And Mikloth begot Shimeam. They also dwelt alongside their relatives in Jerusalem, with their brethren. ³⁹Ner begot Kish, Kish begot Saul, and Saul begot Jonathan, Malchishua, Abinadab, and Esh-Baal. ⁴⁰The son of Jonathan *was* Merib-Baal, and Merib-Baal begot Micah. ⁴¹The sons of Micah *were* Pithon, Melech, Tahrea, *and Ahaz.* ⁴²And Ahaz begot Jarah; Jarah begot Alemeth, Azmaveth, and Zimri; and Zimri begot Moza; ⁴³Moza begot Binea, Rephaiah his son, Eleasah his son, and Azel his son.

⁴⁴And Azel had six sons whose names *were* these: Azrikam, Bocheru, Ishmael, Sheariah, Obadiah, and Hanan; these *were* the sons of Azel.

CHAPTER 10 SAUL DIES; DAVID BECOMES KING.

Now the Philistines fought against Israel; and the men of Israel fled from before the Philistines, and fell slain on Mount Gilboa. ²Then the Philistines followed hard after Saul and his sons. And the Philistines killed Jonathan, Abinadab, and Malchishua, Saul's sons. ³The battle became fierce against Saul. The archers hit him, and he was wounded by the archers. ⁴Then Saul said to his armorbearer, "Draw your sword, and thrust me through with it, lest these uncircumcised men come and abuse me." But his armorbearer would not, for he was greatly afraid. Therefore Saul took a sword and fell on it. ⁵And when his armorbearer saw that Saul was dead, he also fell on his sword and died. ⁶So Saul and his three sons died, and all his house died together. ⁷And when all the men of Israel who *were* in the valley saw that they had fled and that Saul and his sons were dead, they forsook their cities and fled; then the Philistines came and dwelt in them. ⁸So it happened the next day, when the Philistines

came to strip the slain, that they found Saul and his sons fallen on Mount Gilboa. ⁹And they stripped him and took his head and his armor, and sent word *throughout* the land of the Philistines to proclaim the news *in the temple* of their idols and among the people. ¹⁰Then they put his armor in the temple of their gods, and fastened his head in the temple of Dagon.

¹¹And when all Jabesh Gilead heard all that the Philistines had done to Saul, ¹²all the valiant men arose and took the body of Saul and the bodies of his sons; and they brought them to Jabesh, and buried their bones under the tamarisk tree at Jabesh, and fasted seven days.

¹³So Saul died for his unfaithfulness which he had committed against the LORD, because he did not keep the word of the LORD, and also because he consulted a medium for guidance. ¹⁴But *he* did not inquire of the LORD; therefore He killed him, and turned the kingdom over to David the son of Jesse.

CHAPTER 11 DAVID CONQUERS JERUSALEM.

Then all Israel came together to David at Hebron, saying, "Indeed we *are* your bone and your flesh. ²Also, in time past, even when Saul was king, you *were* the one who led Israel out and brought them in; and the LORD your God said to you, 'You shall shepherd My people Israel, and be ruler over My people Israel.' " ³Therefore all the elders of Israel came to the king at Hebron, and David made a covenant with them at Hebron before the LORD. And they anointed David king over Israel, according to the word of the LORD by Samuel.

⁴And David and all Israel went to Jerusalem, which is Jebus, where the Jebusites *were*, the inhabitants of the land. ⁵But the inhabitants of Jebus said to David, "You shall not come in here!" Nevertheless David took the stronghold of Zion (that is, the City of David). ⁶Now David said, "Whoever attacks the Jebusites first shall be chief and captain." And Joab the son of Zeruiah went up first, and became chief. ⁷Then David dwelt in the stronghold; therefore they called it the City of David. ⁸And he built the city around it, from the Millo to the surrounding area. Joab repaired the rest of the city. ⁹So David went on and became great, and the LORD of hosts *was* with him.

¹⁰Now these *were* the heads of the mighty men whom David had, who strengthened themselves with him in his

kingdom, with all Israel, to make him king, according to the word of the LORD concerning Israel.

[11]And this *is* the number of the mighty men whom David had: Jashobeam the son of a Hachmonite, chief of the captains; he had lifted up his spear against three hundred, killed *by him* at one time.

[12]After him *was* Eleazar the son of Dodo, the Ahohite, who *was one* of the three mighty men. [13]He was with David at Pasdammim. Now there the Philistines were gathered for battle, and there was a piece of ground full of barley. So the people fled from the Philistines. [14]But they stationed themselves in the middle of *that* field, defended it, and killed the Philistines. So the LORD brought about a great victory.

[15]Now three of the thirty chief men went down to the rock to David, into the cave of Adullam; and the army of the Philistines encamped in the Valley of Rephaim. [16]David *was* then in the stronghold, and the garrison of the Philistines *was* then in Bethlehem. [17]And David said with longing, "Oh, that someone would give me a drink of water from the well of Bethlehem, which is by the gate!" [18]So the three broke through the camp of the Philistines, drew water from the well of Bethlehem that *was* by the gate, and took *it* and brought *it* to David. Nevertheless David would not drink it, but poured it out to the LORD. [19]And he said, "Far be it from me, O my God, that I should do this! Shall I drink the blood of these men *who have put* their lives *in jeopardy?* For at the risk of their lives they brought it." Therefore he would not drink it. These things were done by the three mighty men.

[20]Abishai the brother of Joab was chief of *another* three. He had lifted up his spear against three hundred *men,* killed *them,* and won a name among *these* three. [21]Of the three he was more honored than the other two men. Therefore he became their captain. However he did not attain to the *first* three.

[22]Benaiah was the son of Jehoiada, the son of a valiant man from Kabzeel, who had done many deeds. He had killed two lion-like heroes of Moab. He also had gone down and killed a lion in the midst of a pit on a snowy day. [23]And he killed an Egyptian, a man of *great* height, five cubits tall. In the Egyptian's hand *there was* a spear like a weaver's beam; and he went down to him with a staff, wrested the spear out of the Egyptian's hand, and killed him with his own spear. [24]These *things* Benaiah the son of Jehoiada did, and won a name among three mighty men. [25]Indeed he was more honored than the thirty, but he did not attain to the *first* three. And David appointed him over his guard.

[26]Also the mighty warriors *were* Asahel the brother of Joab, Elhanan the son of Dodo of Bethlehem, [27]Shammoth the Harorite, Helez the Pelonite, [28]Ira the son of Ikkesh the Tekoite, Abiezer the Anathothite, [29]Sibbechai the Hushathite, Ilai the Ahohite, [30]Maharai the Netophathite, Heled the son of Baanah the Netophathite, [31]Ithai the son of Ribai of Gibeah, of the sons of Benjamin, Benaiah the Pirathonite, [32]Hurai of the brooks of Gaash, [33]Azmaveth the Baharumite, Eliahba the Shaalbonite, [34]the sons of Hashem the Gizonite, Jonathan the son of Shageh the Hararite, [35]Ahiam the son of Sacar the Hararite, Eliphal the son of Ur,

[36]Hepher the Mecherathite, Ahijah the Pelonite, [37]Hezro the Carmelite, Naarai the son of Ezbai, [38]Joel the brother of Nathan, Mibhar the son of Hagri, [39]Zelek the Ammonite, Naharai the Berothite (the armorbearer of Joab the son of Zeruiah), [40]Ira the Ithrite, Gareb the Ithrite, [41]Uriah the Hittite, Zabad the son of Ahlai, [42]Adina the son of Shiza the Reubenite (a chief of the Reubenites) and thirty with him, [43]Hanan the son of Maachah, Joshaphat the Mithnite, [44]Uzzia the Ashterathite, Shama and Jeiel the sons of Hotham the Aroerite, [45]Jediael the son of Shimri, and Joha his brother, the Tizite, [46]Eliel the Mahavite, Jeribai and Joshaviah the sons of Elnaam, Ithmah the Moabite, [47]Eliel, Obed, and Jaasiel the Mezobaite.

CHAPTER **12** MORE WARRIORS JOIN DAVID. Now these *were* the men who came to David at Ziklag while he was still a fugitive from Saul the son of Kish; and they *were* among the mighty men, helpers in the war, [2]armed with bows, using both the right hand and the left in *hurling* stones and *shooting* arrows with the bow. *They were* of Benjamin, Saul's brethren.

[3]The chief *was* Ahiezer, then Joash, the sons of Shemaah the Gibeathite; Jeziel and Pelet the sons of Azmaveth; Berachah, and Jehu the Anathothite; [4]Ishmaiah the Gibeonite, a mighty man among the thirty, and over the thirty; Jeremiah, Jahaziel, Johanan, and Jozabad the Gederathite; [5]Eluzai, Jerimoth, Bealiah, Shemariah, and Shephatiah the Haruphite; [6]Elkanah, Jisshiah, Azarel, Joezer, and Jashobeam, the Korahites; [7]and Joelah and Zebadiah the sons of Jeroham of Gedor.

[8]*Some* Gadites joined David at the stronghold in the wilderness, mighty men of valor, men trained for battle, who could handle shield and spear, whose faces *were like* the faces of lions, and *were* as swift as gazelles on the mountains: [9]Ezer the first, Obadiah the second, Eliab the third, [10]Mishmannah the fourth, Jeremiah the fifth, [11]Attai the sixth, Eliel the seventh, [12]Johanan the eighth, Elzabad the ninth, [13]Jeremiah the tenth, and Machbanai the eleventh. [14]These *were* from the sons of Gad, captains of the army; the least was over a hundred, and the greatest was over a thousand. [15]These *are* the ones who crossed the Jordan in the first month, when it had overflowed all its banks; and they put to flight all *those* in the valleys, to the east and to the west.

[16]Then some of the sons of Benjamin and Judah came to David at the stronghold. [17]And David went out to meet them, and answered and said to them, "If you have come peaceably to me to help me, my heart will be united with you; but if to betray me to my enemies, since *there is* no wrong in my hands, may the God of our fathers look and bring judgment." [18]Then the Spirit came upon Amasai, chief of the captains, *and he said:*

" *We are* yours, O David;
We *are* on your side, O son of Jesse!
Peace, peace to you,
And peace to your helpers!
For your God helps you."

12:18 How did the Holy Spirit work in Old Testament times? When there was an important job to be done, God chose a person to do it, and the Spirit gave that person the needed power and ability. The Spirit gave Bezalel artistic ability (Exodus 31:1-5), Jephthah military prowess (Judges 11:29), David power to rule (1 Samuel 16:13), and Zechariah an authoritative word of prophecy (2 Chronicles 24:20). Here the Holy Spirit came upon David's warriors. The Spirit came upon individuals in order to accomplish specific goals. Beginning at Pentecost, however, the Spirit came upon all believers (Acts 2:14-21). That same Spirit is ready to equip you.

So David received them, and made them captains of the troop.

¹⁹And *some* from Manasseh defected to David when he was going with the Philistines to battle against Saul; but they did not help them, for the lords of the Philistines sent him away by agreement, saying, "He may defect to his master Saul *and endanger* our heads." ²⁰When he went to Ziklag, those of Manasseh who defected to him were Adnah, Jozabad, Jediael, Michael, Jozabad, Elihu, and Zillethai, captains of the thousands who *were* from Manasseh. ²¹And they helped David against the bands *of raiders,* for they *were* all mighty men of valor, and they were captains in the army. ²²For at *that* time they came to David day by day to help him, until *it was* a great army, like the army of God.

²³Now these *were* the numbers of the divisions *that were* equipped for war, *and* came to David at Hebron to turn *over* the kingdom of Saul to him, according to the word of the LORD: ²⁴of the sons of Judah bearing shield and spear, six thousand eight hundred armed for war; ²⁵of the sons of Simeon, mighty men of valor fit for war, seven thousand one hundred; ²⁶of the sons of Levi four thousand six hundred; ²⁷Jehoiada, the leader of the Aaronites, and with him three thousand seven hundred; ²⁸Zadok, a young man, a valiant warrior, and from his father's house twenty-two captains; ²⁹of the sons of Benjamin, relatives of Saul, three thousand (until then the greatest part of them had remained loyal to the house of Saul); ³⁰of the sons of Ephraim twenty thousand eight hundred, mighty men of valor, famous men throughout their father's house; ³¹of the half-tribe of Manasseh eighteen thousand, who were designated by name to come and make David king; ³²of the sons of Issachar who had understanding of the times, to know what Israel ought to do, their chiefs were two hundred; and all their brethren were at their command; ³³of Zebulun there were fifty thousand who went out to battle, expert in war with all weapons of war, stouthearted men who could keep ranks; ³⁴of Naphtali one thousand captains, and with them thirty-seven thousand with shield and spear; ³⁵of the Danites who could keep battle formation, twenty-eight thousand six hundred; ³⁶of Asher, those who could go out to war, able to keep battle formation, forty thousand; ³⁷of the Reubenites and the Gadites and the half-tribe of Manasseh, from the other side of the Jordan, one hundred and twenty thousand armed for battle with every *kind* of weapon of war.

³⁸All these men of war, who could keep ranks, came to Hebron with a loyal heart, to make David king over all Israel; and all the rest of Israel *were* of one mind to make David king. ³⁹And they were there with David three days, eating and drinking, for their brethren had prepared for them. ⁴⁰Moreover those who were near to them, from as far away as Issachar and Zebulun and Naphtali, were bringing food on donkeys and camels, on mules and oxen—provisions of flour and cakes of figs and cakes of raisins, wine and oil and oxen and sheep abundantly, for *there was* joy in Israel.

CHAPTER 13 DAVID CELEBRATES BUT UZZA DIES.

Then David consulted with the captains of thousands and hundreds, *and* with every leader. ²And David said to all the assembly of Israel, "If *it seems* good to you, and if it is of the LORD our God, let us send out to our brethren everywhere *who are* left in all the land of Israel, and with them to the priests and Levites *who are* in their cities *and* their common-lands, that they may gather together to us; ³and let us bring the ark of our God back to us, for we have not inquired at it since the days of Saul." ⁴Then all the assembly said that they would do so, for the thing was right in the eyes of all the people.

13:3 The ark of God is also called the ark of the covenant. It rest the Most Holy Place in the temple and was the most sacred artifact Hebrew faith. It was a large box containing the stone tablets on wh God had written the Ten Commandments (Exodus 25:10-22). Davi already made Jerusalem his political capital (11:4-9). At this time, brought the ark there in hopes of making it the nation's center for worship, too.

⁵So David gathered all Israel together, from Shihor in Egypt to as far as the entrance of Hamath, to bring the ark of God from Kirjath Jearim. ⁶And David and all Israel went up to Baalah, to Kirjath Jearim, which belonged to Judah, to bring up from there the ark of God the LORD, who dwells *between* the cherubim, where *His* name is proclaimed. ⁷So they carried the ark of God on a new cart from the house of Abinadab, and Uzza and Ahio drove the cart. ⁸Then David and all Israel played *music* before God with all *their* might, with singing, on harps, on stringed instruments, on tambourines, on cymbals, and with trumpets.

⁹And when they came to Chidon's threshing floor, Uzza put out his hand to hold the ark, for the oxen stumbled. ¹⁰Then the anger of the LORD was aroused against Uzza, and He struck him because he put his hand to the ark; and he died there before God. ¹¹And David became angry because of the LORD's outbreak against Uzza; therefore that place is called Perez Uzza to this day. ¹²David was afraid of God that day, saying, "How can bring the ark of God to me?"

¹³So David would not move the ark with him into the City of David, but took it aside into the house of Obed-Edom the Gittite. ¹⁴The ark of God remained with the family of Obed-Edom in his house three months. And the LORD blessed the house of Obed-Edom and all that he had.

CHAPTER **14** **GOD BLESSES DAVID.** Now Hiram king of Tyre sent messengers to David, and cedar trees, with masons and carpenters, to build him a house. ²So David knew that the LORD had established him as king over Israel, for his kingdom was highly exalted for the sake of His people Israel.

³Then David took more wives in Jerusalem, and David begot more sons and daughters. ⁴And these are the names of his children whom he had in Jerusalem: Shammua, Shobab, Nathan, Solomon, ⁵Ibhar, Elishua, Elpelet, ⁶Nogah, Nepheg, Japhia, ⁷Elishama, Beeliada, and Eliphelet.

⁸Now when the Philistines heard that David had been anointed king over all Israel, all the Philistines went up to search for David. And David heard *of it* and went out against them. ⁹Then the Philistines went and made a raid on the Valley of Rephaim. ¹⁰And David inquired of God, saying, "Shall I go up against the Philistines? Will You deliver them into my hand?"

The LORD said to him, "Go up, for I will deliver them into your hand."

¹¹So they went up to Baal Perazim, and David defeated them there. Then David said, "God has broken through my enemies by my hand like a breakthrough of water." Therefore they called the name of that place Baal Perazim. ¹²And when they left their gods there, David gave a commandment, and they were burned with fire.

¹³Then the Philistines once again made a raid on the valley. ¹⁴Therefore David inquired again of God, and God said to him, "You shall not go up after them; circle around them, and come upon them in front of the mulberry trees. ¹⁵And it shall be, when you hear a sound of marching in the tops of the mulberry trees, then you shall go out to battle, for God has gone out before you to strike the camp of the Philistines." ¹⁶So David did as God commanded him, and they drove back the army of the Philistines from Gibeon as far as Gezer. ¹⁷Then the fame of David went out into all lands, and the LORD brought the fear of him upon all nations.

CHAPTER **15** **THE ARK COMES BACK.** *David* built houses for himself in the City of David; and he prepared a place for the ark of God, and pitched a tent for it. ²Then David said, "No one may carry the ark of God but the Levites, for the LORD has chosen them to carry the ark of God and to minister before Him forever." ³And David gathered all Israel together at Jerusalem, to bring up the ark of the LORD to its place, which he had prepared for it. ⁴Then David assembled the children of Aaron and the Levites: ⁵of the sons of Kohath, Uriel the chief, and one hundred and twenty of his brethren; ⁶of the sons of Merari, Asaiah the chief, and two hundred and twenty of his brethren; ⁷of the sons of Gershom, Joel the chief, and one hundred and thirty of his brethren; ⁸of the sons of Elizaphan, Shemaiah the chief, and two hundred of his brethren; ⁹of the sons of Hebron, Eliel the chief, and eighty of his brethren; ¹⁰of the sons of Uzziel, Amminadab the chief, and one hundred and twelve of his brethren.

¹¹And David called for Zadok and Abiathar the priests,

and for the Levites: for Uriel, Asaiah, Joel, Shemaiah, Eliel, and Amminadab. ¹²He said to them, "You *are* the heads of the fathers' *houses* of the Levites; sanctify yourselves, you and your brethren, that you may bring up the ark of the LORD God of Israel to *the place* I have prepared for it. ¹³For because you *did* not *do it* the first *time*, the LORD our God broke out against us, because we did not consult Him about the proper order."

⟫⟫⟫ GOD FIRST

14:10 Before David went to battle, he talked to God, asking for his presence and guidance. Too often we wait until we are in the middle of trouble before turning to God. By then the consequences of our actions are already unfolding. When do you ask for God's help? Only as a desperate last resort? Instead, go to God first! Like David, you may receive incredible help and avoid serious trouble.

¹⁴So the priests and the Levites sanctified themselves to bring up the ark of the LORD God of Israel. ¹⁵And the children of the Levites bore the ark of God on their shoulders, by its poles, as Moses had commanded according to the word of the LORD.

¹⁶Then David spoke to the leaders of the Levites to appoint their brethren *to be* the singers accompanied by instruments of music, stringed instruments, harps, and cymbals, by raising the voice with resounding joy. ¹⁷So the Levites appointed Heman the son of Joel; and of his brethren, Asaph the son of Berechiah; and of their brethren, the sons of Merari, Ethan the son of Kushaiah; ¹⁸and with them their brethren of the second *rank:* Zechariah, Ben, Jaaziel, Shemiramoth, Jehiel, Unni, Eliab, Benaiah, Maaseiah, Mattithiah, Elipheleh, Mikneiah, Obed-Edom, and Jeiel, the gatekeepers; ¹⁹the singers, Heman, Asaph, and Ethan, *were* to sound the cymbals of bronze; ²⁰Zechariah, Aziel, Shemiramoth, Jehiel, Unni, Eliab, Maaseiah, and Benaiah, with strings according to Alamoth; ²¹Mattithiah, Elipheleh, Mikneiah, Obed-Edom, Jeiel, and Azaziah, to direct with harps on the Sheminith; ²²Chenaniah, leader of the Levites, was instructor *in charge of* the music, because he *was* skillful; ²³Berechiah and Elkanah *were* doorkeepers for the ark; ²⁴Shebaniah, Joshaphat, Nethanel, Amasai, Zechariah, Benaiah, and Eliezer, the priests, were to blow the trumpets before the ark of God; and Obed-Edom and Jehiah, doorkeepers for the ark.

²⁵So David, the elders of Israel, and the captains over thousands went to bring up the ark of the covenant of the LORD from the house of Obed-Edom with joy. ²⁶And so it

⟫⟫⟫ EXACTLY

15:13-15 When David's first attempt to move the ark failed (13:8-14), he learned an important lesson: when God gives specific instructions, it is wise to follow them precisely. This time David saw to it that the Levites carried the ark (Numbers 4:5-15). We may not fully understand the reasons behind God's instructions, but we can know that his wisdom is complete and his judgment infallible. The way to know God's instructions is to know his Word. But just as children do not understand the reasons for all their parents' instructions until they are adults, we will not understand all of God's instructions in this life. It is far better to obey God first, and then seek to know the reasons.

was, when God helped the Levites who bore the ark of the covenant of the LORD, that they offered seven bulls and seven rams. ²⁷David was clothed with a robe of fine linen, as were all the Levites who bore the ark, the singers, and Chenaniah the music master *with* the singers. David also wore a linen ephod. ²⁸Thus all Israel brought up the ark of the covenant of the LORD with shouting and with the sound of the horn, with trumpets and with cymbals, making music with stringed instruments and harps.

²⁹And it happened, *as* the ark of the covenant of the LORD came to the City of David, that Michal, Saul's daughter, looked through a window and saw King David whirling and playing music; and she despised him in her heart.

CHAPTER **16** DAVID PRAISES GOD. So they brought the ark of God, and set it in the midst of the tabernacle that David had erected for it. Then they offered burnt offerings and peace offerings before God. ²And when David had finished offering the burnt offerings and the peace offerings, he blessed the people in the name of the LORD. ³Then he distributed to everyone of Israel, both man and woman, to everyone a loaf of bread, a piece *of meat*, and a cake of raisins.

⁴And he appointed some of the Levites to minister before the ark of the LORD, to commemorate, to thank, and to praise the LORD God of Israel: ⁵Asaph the chief, and next to him Zechariah, *then* Jeiel, Shemiramoth, Je-

MUSIC IN BIBLE TIMES

Paul clearly puts forth the Christian's view that things are not good or bad in and of themselves (see Romans 14 and 1 Corinthians 14:7-8,26). The point always should be to worship the Lord or help others by means of the things of this world, including music. Music was created by God and can be returned to him in praise. Does the music you play or listen to have a negative or positive impact upon your relationship with God?

Highlights of musical use in Scripture	References
Jubal was father of all musicians	Genesis 4:21
Miriam and other women sang and danced to praise God	Exodus 15:1-21
The priest was to have bells on his robes	Exodus 28:34-35
Jericho fell to the sound of trumpets	Joshua 6:4-20
Saul experienced the soothing effect of music	1 Samuel 16:14-23
The king's coronation was accompanied by music	1 Kings 1:39-40
David organized the use of music for worship	1 Chronicles 16:4-7
The ark of the covenant was accompanied by trumpeters	1 Chronicles 16:6
There were musicians for the king's court	Ecclesiastes 2:8
Everything was to be used by everyone to praise the Lord	Psalm 150
Jesus and the disciples sang a hymn	Matthew 26:30
Paul and Silas sang in jail	Acts 16:25
We are to sing to the Lord with thankful hearts	Colossians 3:16

In the New Testament, worship continued in the synagogues until the Christians became unwelcome there, so there was a rich musical heritage already established. The fact that music is mentioned less often in the New Testament does not mean it was less important.

was, when God helped the Levites who bore the ark of the covenant of the LORD, that they offered seven bulls and seven rams. 27David was clothed with a robe of fine linen, as were all the Levites who bore the ark, the singers, and Chenaniah the music master *with* the singers. David also wore a linen ephod. 28Thus all Israel brought up the ark of the covenant of the LORD with shouting and with the sound of the horn, with trumpets and with cymbals, making music with stringed instruments and harps.

29And it happened, *as* the ark of the covenant of the LORD came to the City of David, that Michal, Saul's daughter, looked through a window and saw King David whirling and playing music; and she despised him in her heart.

CHAPTER **16** **DAVID PRAISES GOD.** So they brought the ark of God, and set it in the midst of the tabernacle that David had erected for it. Then they offered burnt offerings and peace offerings before God. 2And when David had finished offering the burnt offerings and the peace offerings, he blessed the people in the name of the LORD. 3Then he distributed to everyone of Israel, both man and woman, to everyone a loaf of bread, a piece *of meat*, and a cake of raisins.

4And he appointed some of the Levites to minister before the ark of the LORD, to commemorate, to thank, and to praise the LORD God of Israel: 5Asaph the chief, and next to him Zechariah, *then* Jeiel, Shemiramoth, Je-

MUSIC IN BIBLE TIMES

Paul clearly puts forth the Christian's view that things are not good or bad in and of themselves (see Romans 14 and 1 Corinthians 14:7-8,26). The point always should be to worship the Lord or help others by means of the things of this world, including music. Music was created by God and can be returned to him in praise. Does the music you play or listen to have a negative or positive impact upon your relationship with God?

Highlights of musical use in Scripture	References
Jubal was father of all musicians	Genesis 4:21
Miriam and other women sang and danced to praise God	Exodus 15:1-21
The priest was to have bells on his robes	Exodus 28:34-35
Jericho fell to the sound of trumpets	Joshua 6:4-20
Saul experienced the soothing effect of music	1 Samuel 16:14-23
The king's coronation was accompanied by music	1 Kings 1:39-40
David organized the use of music for worship	1 Chronicles 16:4-7
The ark of the covenant was accompanied by trumpeters	1 Chronicles 16:6
There were musicians for the king's court	Ecclesiastes 2:8
Everything was to be used by everyone to praise the Lord	Psalm 150
Jesus and the disciples sang a hymn	Matthew 26:30
Paul and Silas sang in jail	Acts 16:25
We are to sing to the Lord with thankful hearts	Colossians 3:16

In the New Testament, worship continued in the synagogues until the Christians became unwelcome there, so there was a rich musical heritage already established. The fact that music is mentioned less often in the New Testament does not mean it was less important.

CHAPTER **14** **GOD BLESSES DAVID.** Now Hiram king of Tyre sent messengers to David, and cedar trees, with masons and carpenters, to build him a house. [2]So David knew that the LORD had established him as king over Israel, for his kingdom was highly exalted for the sake of His people Israel.

[3]Then David took more wives in Jerusalem, and David begot more sons and daughters. [4]And these are the names of his children whom he had in Jerusalem: Shammua, Shobab, Nathan, Solomon, [5]Ibhar, Elishua, Elpelet, [6]Nogah, Nepheg, Japhia, [7]Elishama, Beeliada, and Eliphelet.

[8]Now when the Philistines heard that David had been anointed king over all Israel, all the Philistines went up to search for David. And David heard *of it* and went out against them. [9]Then the Philistines went and made a raid on the Valley of Rephaim. [10]And David inquired of God, saying, "Shall I go up against the Philistines? Will You deliver them into my hand?"

The LORD said to him, "Go up, for I will deliver them into your hand."

[11]So they went up to Baal Perazim, and David defeated them there. Then David said, "God has broken through my enemies by my hand like a breakthrough of water." Therefore they called the name of that place Baal Perazim. [12]And when they left their gods there, David gave a commandment, and they were burned with fire.

[13]Then the Philistines once again made a raid on the valley. [14]Therefore David inquired again of God, and God said to him, "You shall not go up after them; circle around them, and come upon them in front of the mulberry trees. [15]And it shall be, when you hear a sound of marching in the tops of the mulberry trees, then you shall go out to battle, for God has gone out before you to strike the camp of the Philistines." [16]So David did as God commanded him, and they drove back the army of the Philistines from Gibeon as far as Gezer. [17]Then the fame of David went out into all lands, and the LORD brought the fear of him upon all nations.

CHAPTER **15** **THE ARK COMES BACK.** *David* built houses for himself in the City of David; and he prepared a place for the ark of God, and pitched a tent for it. [2]Then David said, "No one may carry the ark of God but the Levites, for the LORD has chosen them to carry the ark of God and to minister before Him forever." [3]And David gathered all Israel together at Jerusalem, to bring up the ark of the LORD to its place, which he had prepared for it. [4]Then David assembled the children of Aaron and the Levites: [5]of the sons of Kohath, Uriel the chief, and one hundred and twenty of his brethren; [6]of the sons of Merari, Asaiah the chief, and two hundred and twenty of his brethren; [7]of the sons of Gershom, Joel the chief, and one hundred and thirty of his brethren; [8]of the sons of Elizaphan, Shemaiah the chief, and two hundred of his brethren; [9]of the sons of Hebron, Eliel the chief, and eighty of his brethren; [10]of the sons of Uzziel, Amminadab the chief, and one hundred and twelve of his brethren.

[11]And David called for Zadok and Abiathar the priests,

and for the Levites: for Uriel, Asaiah, Joel, Shemaiah, Eliel, and Amminadab. [12]He said to them, "You *are* the heads of the fathers' *houses* of the Levites; sanctify yourselves, you and your brethren, that you may bring up the ark of the LORD God of Israel to *the place* I have prepared for it. [13]For because you *did* not *do it* the first *time,* the LORD our God broke out against us, because we did not consult Him about the proper order."

GOD FIRST

14:10 Before David went to battle, he talked to God, asking for his presence and guidance. Too often we wait until we are in the middle of trouble before turning to God. By then the consequences of our actions are already unfolding. When do you ask for God's help? Only as a desperate last resort? Instead, go to God first! Like David, you may receive incredible help and avoid serious trouble.

[14]So the priests and the Levites sanctified themselves to bring up the ark of the LORD God of Israel. [15]And the children of the Levites bore the ark of God on their shoulders, by its poles, as Moses had commanded according to the word of the LORD.

[16]Then David spoke to the leaders of the Levites to appoint their brethren *to be* the singers accompanied by instruments of music, stringed instruments, harps, and cymbals, by raising the voice with resounding joy. [17]So the Levites appointed Heman the son of Joel; and of his brethren, Asaph the son of Berechiah; and of their brethren, the sons of Merari, Ethan the son of Kushaiah; [18]and with them their brethren of the second *rank:* Zechariah, Ben, Jaaziel, Shemiramoth, Jehiel, Unni, Eliab, Benaiah, Maaseiah, Mattithiah, Elipheleh, Mikneiah, Obed-Edom, and Jeiel, the gatekeepers; [19]the singers, Heman, Asaph, and Ethan, *were* to sound the cymbals of bronze; [20]Zechariah, Aziel, Shemiramoth, Jehiel, Unni, Eliab, Maaseiah, and Benaiah, with strings according to Alamoth; [21]Mattithiah, Elipheleh, Mikneiah, Obed-Edom, Jeiel, and Azaziah, to direct with harps on the Sheminith; [22]Chenaniah, leader of the Levites, was instructor *in charge of* the music, because he *was* skillful; [23]Berechiah and Elkanah *were* doorkeepers for the ark; [24]Shebaniah, Joshaphat, Nethanel, Amasai, Zechariah, Benaiah, and Eliezer, the priests, were to blow the trumpets before the ark of God; and Obed-Edom and Jehiah, doorkeepers for the ark.

[25]So David, the elders of Israel, and the captains over thousands went to bring up the ark of the covenant of the LORD from the house of Obed-Edom with joy. [26]And so it

EXACTLY

15:13-15 When David's first attempt to move the ark failed (13:8-14), he learned an important lesson: when God gives specific instructions, it is wise to follow them precisely. This time David saw to it that the Levites carried the ark (Numbers 4:5-15). We may not fully understand the reasons behind God's instructions, but we can know that his wisdom is complete and his judgment infallible. The way to know God's instructions is to know his Word. But just as children do not understand the reasons for all their parents' instructions until they are adults, we will not understand all of God's instructions in this life. It is far better to obey God first, and then seek to know the reasons.

hiel, Mattithiah, Eliab, Benaiah, and Obed-Edom: Jeiel with stringed instruments and harps, but Asaph made music with cymbals; ⁶Benaiah and Jahaziel the priests regularly *blew* the trumpets before the ark of the covenant of God.

⁷On that day David first delivered *this psalm* into the hand of Asaph and his brethren, to thank the Lord:

⁸ Oh, give thanks to the Lord!
Call upon His name;
Make known His deeds among the peoples!
⁹ Sing to Him, sing psalms to Him;
Talk of all His wondrous works!
¹⁰ Glory in His holy name;
Let the hearts of those rejoice who seek the Lord!
¹¹ Seek the Lord and His strength;
Seek His face evermore!
¹² Remember His marvelous works which He has done,
His wonders, and the judgments of His mouth,
¹³ O seed of Israel His servant,
You children of Jacob, His chosen ones!

¹⁴ He *is* the Lord our God;
His judgments *are* in all the earth.
¹⁵ Remember His covenant forever,
The word which He commanded, for a thousand generations,
¹⁶ *The covenant which* He made with Abraham,
And His oath to Isaac,
¹⁷ And confirmed it to Jacob for a statute,
To Israel *for* an everlasting covenant,
¹⁸ Saying, "To you I will give the land of Canaan
As the allotment of your inheritance,"
¹⁹ When you were few in number,
Indeed very few, and strangers in it.

²⁰ When they went from one nation to another,
And from *one* kingdom to another people,
²¹ He permitted no man to do them wrong;
Yes, He rebuked kings for their sakes,
²² *Saying*, "Do not touch My anointed ones,
And do My prophets no harm."

²³ Sing to the Lord, all the earth;
Proclaim the good news of His salvation from day to day.
²⁴ Declare His glory among the nations,
His wonders among all peoples.

²⁵ For the Lord *is* great and greatly to be praised;
He *is* also to be feared above all gods.
²⁶ For all the gods of the peoples *are* idols,
But the Lord made the heavens.
²⁷ Honor and majesty *are* before Him;
Strength and gladness are in His place.

²⁸ Give to the Lord, O families of the peoples,
Give to the Lord glory and strength.
²⁹ Give to the Lord the glory *due* His name;
Bring an offering, and come before Him.
Oh, worship the Lord in the beauty of holiness!
³⁰ Tremble before Him, all the earth.
The world also is firmly established,
It shall not be moved.

³¹ Let the heavens rejoice, and let the earth be glad;
And let them say among the nations, "The Lord reigns."
³² Let the sea roar, and all its fullness;
Let the field rejoice, and all that *is* in it.
³³ Then the trees of the woods shall rejoice before the Lord,

◄━━━━━━━━━━━━**THANK YOU**

16:7-36 Does it ever seem that a simple "thank you" to God is not enough to express your appreciation? Four elements of true thanksgiving are found in the following song: (1) *remembering* what God has done, (2) *telling* others about it, (3) *showing* God's glory to others, and (4) *offering* gifts of self, time, and resources. Get into the habit of fully expressing your thanks to God.

For He is coming to judge the earth.

³⁴ Oh, give thanks to the Lord, for *He is* good!
For His mercy *endures* forever.
³⁵ And say, "Save us, O God of our salvation;
Gather us together, and deliver us from the Gentiles,
To give thanks to Your holy name,
To triumph in Your praise."

³⁶ Blessed *be* the Lord God of Israel
From everlasting to everlasting!

And all the people said, "Amen!" and praised the Lord.
³⁷So he left Asaph and his brothers there before the ark of the covenant of the Lord to minister before the ark regularly, as every day's work required; ³⁸and Obed-Edom with his sixty-eight brethren, including Obed-Edom the son of Jeduthun, and Hosah, *to be* gatekeepers; ³⁹and Zadok the priest and his brethren the priests, before the tabernacle of the Lord at the high place that *was* at Gibeon, ⁴⁰to offer burnt offerings to the Lord on the altar of burnt offering regularly morning and evening, and *to do* according to all that is written in the Law of the Lord which He commanded Israel; ⁴¹and with them Heman and Jeduthun and the rest who were chosen, who were designated by name, to give thanks to the Lord, because His mercy *endures* forever; ⁴²and with them Heman and Jeduthun, to sound aloud with trumpets and cymbals and the musical instruments of God. Now the sons of Jeduthun *were* gatekeepers.

⁴³Then all the people departed, every man to his house; and David returned to bless his house.

CHAPTER 17 GOD MAKES A PROMISE TO DAVID.
Now it came to pass, when David was dwelling in his house, that David said to Nathan the prophet, "See now, I dwell in a house of cedar, but the ark of the covenant of the Lord *is* under tent curtains."

²Then Nathan said to David, "Do all that *is* in your heart, for God *is* with you."

³But it happened that night that the word of God came to Nathan, saying, ⁴"Go and tell My servant David, 'Thus says the Lord: "You shall not build Me a house to dwell in. ⁵For I have not dwelt in a house since the time

that I brought up Israel, even to this day, but have gone from tent to tent, and from *one* tabernacle *to another.* ⁶Wherever I have moved about with all Israel, have I ever spoken a word to any of the judges of Israel, whom I commanded to shepherd My people, saying, 'Why have you not built Me a house of cedar?' " ' ⁷Now therefore, thus shall you say to My servant David, 'Thus says the LORD of hosts: "I took you from the sheepfold, from following the sheep, to be ruler over My people Israel. ⁸And I have been with you wherever you have gone, and have cut off all your enemies from before you, and have made you a name like the name of the great men who *are* on the earth. ⁹Moreover I will appoint a place for My people Israel, and will plant them, that they may dwell in a place of their own and move no more; nor shall the sons of wickedness oppress them anymore, as previously, ¹⁰since the time that I commanded judges *to be* over My people Israel. Also I will subdue all your enemies. Furthermore I tell you that the LORD will build you a house. ¹¹And it shall be, when your days are fulfilled, when you must go *to be* with your fathers, that I will set up your seed after you, who will be of your sons; and I will establish his kingdom. ¹²He shall build Me a house, and I will establish his throne forever. ¹³I will be his Father, and he shall be My son; and I will not take My mercy away from him, as I took *it* from *him* who was before you. ¹⁴And I will establish him in My house and in My kingdom forever; and his throne shall be established forever." ' "

¹⁵According to all these words and according to all this vision, so Nathan spoke to David.

THE REAL KING

17:16-27 David responded to God's answer and promises with deep humility, not resentment. This king who had conquered his enemies and was loved by his people said, "Who *am* I . . . that You have brought me this far?" David recognized that God was the *true* King. God has done just as much for us, and he plans to do even more! Like David, we should humble ourselves and give glory to God, saying, "O LORD, *there is* none like You."

¹⁶Then King David went in and sat before the LORD; and he said: "Who *am* I, O LORD God? And what is my house, that You have brought me this far? ¹⁷And *yet* this was a small thing in Your sight, O God; and You have *also* spoken of Your servant's house for a great while to come, and have regarded me according to the rank of a man of high degree, O LORD God. ¹⁸What more can David *say* to You for the honor of Your servant? For You know Your servant. ¹⁹O LORD, for Your servant's sake, and according to Your own heart, You have done all this greatness, in making known all these great things. ²⁰O LORD, *there is* none like You, nor *is there any* God besides You, according to all that we have heard with our ears. ²¹And who *is* like Your people Israel, the one nation on the earth whom God went to redeem for Himself *as* a people—to make for Yourself a name by great and awesome deeds, by driving out nations from before Your people whom You redeemed from Egypt? ²²For You have made Your people

Israel Your very own people forever; and You, LORD, have become their God.

²³"And now, O LORD, the word which You have spoken concerning Your servant and concerning his house, *let it* be established forever, and do as You have said. ²⁴So let it be established, that Your name may be magnified forever, saying, 'The LORD of hosts, the God of Israel, *is* Israel's God.' And let the house of Your servant David be established before You. ²⁵For You, O my God, have revealed to Your servant that You will build him a house. Therefore Your servant has found it *in his heart* to pray before You. ²⁶And now, LORD, You are God, and have promised this goodness to Your servant. ²⁷Now You have been pleased to bless the house of Your servant, that it may continue before You forever; for You have blessed it, O LORD, and *it shall be* blessed forever."

CHAPTER **18** DAVID CONQUERS MANY ENEMIES.

After this it came to pass that David attacked the Philistines, subdued them, and took Gath and its towns from the hand of the Philistines. ²Then he defeated Moab, and the Moabites became David's servants, *and* brought tribute.

³And David defeated Hadadezer king of Zobah *as far as* Hamath, as he went to establish his power by the River Euphrates. ⁴David took from him one thousand chariots, seven thousand horsemen, and twenty thousand foot soldiers. Also David hamstrung all the chariot *horses,* except that he spared enough of them for one hundred chariots.

⁵When the Syrians of Damascus came to help Hadadezer king of Zobah, David killed twenty-two thousand of the Syrians. ⁶Then David put *garrisons* in Syria of Damascus; and the Syrians became David's servants, *and* brought tribute. So the LORD preserved David wherever he went. ⁷And David took the shields of gold that were on the servants of Hadadezer, and brought them to Jerusalem. ⁸Also from Tibhath and from Chun, cities of Hadadezer, David brought a large amount of bronze, with which Solomon made the bronze Sea, the pillars, and the articles of bronze.

⁹Now when Tou king of Hamath heard that David had defeated all the army of Hadadezer king of Zobah, ¹⁰he sent Hadoram his son to King David, to greet him and bless him, because he had fought against Hadadezer and defeated him (for Hadadezer had been at war with Tou); and *Hadoram brought with him* all kinds of articles of gold, silver, and bronze. ¹¹King David also dedicated these to the LORD, along with the silver and gold that he had brought from all *these* nations—from Edom, from Moab, from the people of Ammon, from the Philistines, and from Amalek.

GLORY

18:6,14 God gave David victory and David was a just ruler. Alt[...] we are not promised victory in every military battle, we see in Da[...] glowing success a hint of what Christ's reign will be like—comple[...] victory and just government. If David's glory was great, how muc[...] greater Christ's glory will be. Our confidence is that we can be rig[...] related to Jesus Christ through faith. One day we will share in his [...] we reign with him.

¹²Moreover Abishai the son of Zeruiah killed eighteen thousand Edomites in the Valley of Salt. ¹³He also put garrisons in Edom, and all the Edomites became David's servants. And the LORD preserved David wherever he went.

¹⁴So David reigned over all Israel, and administered judgment and justice to all his people. ¹⁵Joab the son of Zeruiah *was* over the army; Jehoshaphat the son of Ahilud *was* recorder; ¹⁶Zadok the son of Ahitub and Abimelech the son of Abiathar *were* the priests; Shavsha *was* the scribe; ¹⁷Benaiah the son of Jehoiada *was* over the Cherethites and the Pelethites; and David's sons *were* chief ministers at the king's side.

CHAPTER 19 DAVID DEFENDS HIS PEOPLE.

It happened after this that Nahash the king of the people of Ammon died, and his son reigned in his place. ²Then David said, "I will show kindness to Hanun the son of Nahash, because his father showed kindness to me." So David sent messengers to comfort him concerning his father. And David's servants came to Hanun in the land of the people of Ammon to comfort him.

³And the princes of the people of Ammon said to Hanun, "Do you think that David really honors your father because he has sent comforters to you? Did his servants not come to you to search and to overthrow and to spy out the land?"

⁴Therefore Hanun took David's servants, shaved them, and cut off their garments in the middle, at their buttocks, and sent them away. ⁵Then *some* went and told David about the men; and he sent to meet them, because the men were greatly ashamed. And the king said, "Wait at Jericho until your beards have grown, and *then* return."

⁶When the people of Ammon saw that they had made themselves repulsive to David, Hanun and the people of Ammon sent a thousand talents of silver to hire for themselves chariots and horsemen from Mesopotamia, from Syrian Maacah, and from Zobah. ⁷So they hired for themselves thirty-two thousand chariots, with the king of Maacah and his people, who came and encamped before Medeba. Also the people of Ammon gathered together from their cities, and came to battle.

⁸Now when David heard *of it,* he sent Joab and all the army of the mighty men. ⁹Then the people of Ammon came out and put themselves in battle array before the gate of the city, and the kings who had come *were* by themselves in the field.

¹⁰When Joab saw that the battle line was against him before and behind, he chose some of Israel's best, and put *them* in battle array against the Syrians. ¹¹And the rest of the people he put under the command of Abishai his brother, and they set *themselves* in battle array against the people of Ammon. ¹²Then he said, "If the Syrians are too strong for me, then you shall help me; but if the people of Ammon are too strong for you, then I will help you. ¹³Be of good courage, and let us be strong for our people and for the cities of our God. And may the LORD do *what is* good in His sight."

¹⁴So Joab and the people who *were* with him drew near

for the battle against the Syrians, and they fled before him. ¹⁵When the people of Ammon saw that the Syrians were fleeing, they also fled before Abishai his brother, and entered the city. So Joab went to Jerusalem.

¹⁶Now when the Syrians saw that they had been defeated by Israel, they sent messengers and brought the Syrians who were beyond the River, and Shophach the commander of Hadadezer's army *went* before them. ¹⁷When it was told David, he gathered all Israel, crossed over the Jordan and came upon them, and set up in battle array against them. So when David had set up in *battle* array against the Syrians, they fought with him. ¹⁸Then the Syrians fled before Israel; and David killed seven thousand charioteers and forty thousand foot soldiers of the Syrians, and killed Shophach the commander of the army. ¹⁹And when the servants of Hadadezer saw that they were defeated by Israel, they made peace with David and became his servants. So the Syrians were not willing to help the people of Ammon anymore.

CHAPTER 20 DAVID DEFEATS THE AMMONITES.

It happened in the spring of the year, at the time kings go out *to battle,* that Joab led out the armed forces and ravaged the country of the people of Ammon, and came and besieged Rabbah. But David stayed at Jerusalem. And Joab defeated Rabbah and overthrew it. ²Then David took their king's crown from his head, and found it to weigh a talent of gold, and *there were* precious stones in it. And it was set on David's head. Also he brought out the spoil of the city in great abundance. ³And he brought out the people who *were* in it, and put *them* to work with saws, with iron picks, and with axes. So David did to all the cities of the people of Ammon. Then David and all the people returned *to* Jerusalem.

⁴Now it happened afterward that war broke out at Gezer with the Philistines, at which time Sibbechai the Hushathite killed Sippai, *who was one* of the sons of the giant. And they were subdued.

⁵Again there was war with the Philistines, and Elhanan the son of Jair killed Lahmi the brother of Goliath the Gittite, the shaft of whose spear *was* like a weaver's beam.

⁶Yet again there was war at Gath, where there was a man of *great* stature, with twenty-four fingers and toes, six *on each hand* and six *on each foot;* and he also was born to the giant. ⁷So when he defied Israel, Jonathan the son of Shimea, David's brother, killed him.

⁸These were born to the giant in Gath, and they fell by the hand of David and by the hand of his servants.

CHAPTER 21 DAVID COUNTS THE PEOPLE.

Now Satan stood up against Israel, and moved David to number Israel. ²So David said to Joab and to the leaders of the

◤ SPRING INTO WAR

20:1 Why was spring the season when wars usually began? During the winter, opposing kings plotted and planned future conquests. Then, when the fair weather permitted it, their pent-up rage and energy broke forth into war. Look for the "springs" in your life, the times when you are most sensitive to the conflicts around you. Then determine to diffuse them by confessing your fear, bitterness, and anger to God, allowing him to heal.

21:8 When David realized his sin, he took full responsibility, admitted he was wrong, and asked God to forgive him. Many people want to add God and his blessings to their life without acknowledging their personal sin and guilt. But confession and repentance must come before receiving forgiveness. Like David, we must take full responsibility for our actions and confess them to God before we can expect him to forgive us and continue his work in our life.

people, "Go, number Israel from Beersheba to Dan, and bring the number of them to me that I may know *it*."

³And Joab answered, "May the LORD make His people a hundred times more than they are. But, my lord the king, *are* they not all my lord's servants? Why then does my lord require this thing? Why should he be a cause of guilt in Israel?"

⁴Nevertheless the king's word prevailed against Joab. Therefore Joab departed and went throughout all Israel and came to Jerusalem. ⁵Then Joab gave the sum of the number of the people to David. All Israel *had* one million one hundred thousand men who drew the sword, and Judah *had* four hundred and seventy thousand men who drew the sword. ⁶But he did not count Levi and Benjamin among them, for the king's word was abominable to Joab.

⁷And God was displeased with this thing; therefore He struck Israel. ⁸So David said to God, "I have sinned greatly, because I have done this thing; but now, I pray, take away the iniquity of Your servant, for I have done very foolishly."

⁹Then the LORD spoke to Gad, David's seer, saying, ¹⁰"Go and tell David, saying, 'Thus says the LORD: "I offer you three *things*; choose one of them for yourself, that I may do *it* to you." ' "

¹¹So Gad came to David and said to him, "Thus says the LORD: 'Choose for yourself, ¹²either three years of famine, or three months to be defeated by your foes with the sword of your enemies overtaking *you,* or else for three days the sword of the LORD—the plague in the land, with the angel of the LORD destroying throughout all the territory of Israel.' Now consider what answer I should take back to Him who sent me."

¹³And David said to Gad, "I am in great distress. Please let me fall into the hand of the LORD, for His mercies *are* very great; but do not let me fall into the hand of man."

¹⁴So the LORD sent a plague upon Israel, and seventy thousand men of Israel fell. ¹⁵And God sent an angel to Jerusalem to destroy it. As he was destroying, the LORD looked and relented of the disaster, and said to the angel who was destroying, "It is enough; now restrain your hand." And the angel of the LORD stood by the threshing floor of Ornan the Jebusite.

¹⁶Then David lifted his eyes and saw the angel of the LORD standing between earth and heaven, having in his hand a drawn sword stretched out over Jerusalem. So David and the elders, clothed in sackcloth, fell on their faces. ¹⁷And David said to God, "Was it not I who commanded the people to be numbered? I am the one who has sinned and done evil indeed; but these sheep, what have they done? Let Your hand, I pray, O LORD my God, be against me and my father's house, but not against Your people that they should be plagued."

¹⁸Therefore, the angel of the LORD commanded Gad to say to David that David should go and erect an altar to the LORD on the threshing floor of Ornan the Jebusite. ¹⁹So David went up at the word of Gad, which he had spoken in the name of the LORD. ²⁰Now Ornan turned and saw the angel; and his four sons *who were* with him hid themselves, but Ornan continued threshing wheat. ²¹So David came to Ornan, and Ornan looked and saw David. And he went out from the threshing floor, and bowed before David with *his* face to the ground. ²²Then David said to Ornan, "Grant me the place of *this* threshing floor, that I may build an altar on it to the LORD. You shall grant it to me at the full price, that the plague may be withdrawn from the people."

²³But Ornan said to David, "Take *it* to yourself, and let my lord the king do *what is* good in his eyes. Look, I *also* give *you* the oxen for burnt offerings, the threshing implements for wood, and the wheat for the grain offering; I give *it* all."

²⁴Then King David said to Ornan, "No, but I will surely buy *it* for the full price, for I will not take what is yours for the LORD, nor offer burnt offerings with *that which* costs *me* nothing." ²⁵So David gave Ornan six hundred shekels of gold by weight for the place. ²⁶And David built there an altar to the LORD, and offered burnt offerings and peace offerings, and called on the LORD; and He answered him from heaven by fire on the altar of burnt offering.

²⁷So the LORD commanded the angel, and he returned his sword to its sheath.

²⁸At that time, when David saw that the LORD had answered him on the threshing floor of Ornan the Jebusite, he sacrificed there. ²⁹For the tabernacle of the LORD and the altar of the burnt offering, which Moses had made in the wilderness, *were* at that time at the high place in Gibeon. ³⁰But David could not go before it to inquire of God, for he was afraid of the sword of the angel of the LORD.

CHAPTER 22 THE TEMPLE MATERIALS. Then David said, "This *is* the house of the LORD God, and this *is* the altar of burnt offering for Israel." ²So David commanded to gather the aliens who *were* in the land of Israel; and he appointed masons to cut hewn stones to build the house of God. ³And David prepared iron in abundance for the nails of the doors of the gates and for the joints, and bronze in abundance beyond measure, ⁴and cedar trees in abundance; for the Sidonians and those from Tyre brought much cedar wood to David.

⁵Now David said, "Solomon my son *is* young and inexperienced, and the house to be built for the LORD *must be* exceedingly magnificent, famous and glorious throughout all countries. I will now make preparation for it." So David made abundant preparations before his death.

⁶Then he called for his son Solomon, and charged him to build a house for the LORD God of Israel. ⁷And David said to Solomon: "My son, as for me, it was in my mind to build a house to the name of the LORD my God; ⁸but the word of the LORD came to me, saying, 'You have shed much blood and have made great wars; you shall not build a house for My name, because you have shed much

blood on the earth in My sight. ⁹Behold, a son shall be born to you, who shall be a man of rest; and I will give him rest from all his enemies all around. His name shall be Solomon, for I will give peace and quietness to Israel in his days. ¹⁰He shall build a house for My name, and he shall be My son, and I *will be* his Father; and I will establish the throne of his kingdom over Israel forever.' ¹¹Now, my son, may the LORD be with you; and may you prosper, and build the house of the LORD your God, as He has said to you. ¹²Only may the LORD give you wisdom and understanding, and give you charge concerning Israel, that you may keep the law of the LORD your God. ¹³Then you will prosper, if you take care to fulfill the statutes and judgments with which the LORD charged Moses concerning Israel. Be strong and of good courage; do not fear nor be dismayed. ¹⁴Indeed I have taken much trouble to prepare for the house of the LORD one hundred thousand talents of gold and one million talents of silver, and bronze and iron beyond measure, for it is so abundant. I have prepared timber and stone also, and you may add to them. ¹⁵Moreover *there are* workmen with you in abundance: woodsmen and stonecutters, and all types of skillful men for every kind of work. ¹⁶Of gold and silver and bronze and iron *there is* no limit. Arise and begin working, and the LORD be with you."

¹⁷David also commanded all the leaders of Israel to help Solomon his son, *saying,* ¹⁸"*Is* not the LORD your God with you? And has He *not* given you rest on every side? For He has given the inhabitants of the land into my hand, and the land is subdued before the LORD and before His people. ¹⁹Now set your heart and your soul to seek the LORD your God. Therefore arise and build the sanctuary of the LORD God, to bring the ark of the covenant of the LORD and the holy articles of God into the house that is to be built for the name of the LORD."

CHAPTER 23 DAVID GIVES THE LEVITES JOBS.

So when David was old and full of days, he made his son Solomon king over Israel.

²And he gathered together all the leaders of Israel, with the priests and the Levites. ³Now the Levites were numbered from the age of thirty years and above; and the number of individual males was thirty-eight thousand. ⁴Of these, twenty-four thousand *were* to look after the work of the house of the LORD, six thousand *were* officers and judges, ⁵four thousand *were* gatekeepers, and four thousand praised the LORD with *musical* instruments, "which I made," *said David,* "for giving praise."

⁶Also David separated them into divisions among the sons of Levi: Gershon, Kohath, and Merari.

⁷Of the Gershonites: Laadan and Shimei. ⁸The sons of Laadan: the first Jehiel, then Zetham and Joel—three *in all.* ⁹The sons of Shimei: Shelomith, Haziel, and Haran—three *in all.* These were the heads of the fathers' *houses* of Laadan. ¹⁰And the sons of Shimei: Jahath, Zina, Jeush, and Beriah. These *were* the four sons of Shimei. ¹¹Jahath was the first and Zizah the second. But Jeush and Beriah did not have many sons; therefore they were assigned as one father's house.

¹²The sons of Kohath: Amram, Izhar, Hebron, and Uz-

ziel—four *in all.* ¹³The sons of Amram: Aaron and Moses; and Aaron was set apart, he and his sons forever, that he should sanctify the most holy things, to burn incense before the LORD, to minister to Him, and to give the blessing in His name forever. ¹⁴Now the sons of Moses the man of God were reckoned to the tribe of Levi. ¹⁵The sons

◄ WHOLEHEARTEDLY

22:12-13 David learned that it takes *total* dedication to please God—obeying with heart and soul (22:19). This requires both right decisions (good judgment), and right attitudes (strength, courage, and enthusiasm). It isn't enough just to understand what God wants; your heart must be totally dedicated to him. Jesus said, "No one, having put his hand to the plow, and looking back, is fit for the kingdom of God" (Luke 9:62). Remove the distractions that pull you away from God, and serve him wholeheartedly.

of Moses *were* Gershon and Eliezer. ¹⁶Of the sons of Gershon, Shebuel *was* the first. ¹⁷Of the descendants of Eliezer, Rehabiah was the first. And Eliezer had no other sons, but the sons of Rehabiah were very many. ¹⁸Of the sons of Izhar, Shelomith *was* the first. ¹⁹Of the sons of Hebron, Jeriah *was* the first, Amariah the second, Jahaziel the third, and Jekameam the fourth. ²⁰Of the sons of Uzziel, Michah *was* the first and Jesshiah the second.

²¹The sons of Merari *were* Mahli and Mushi. The sons of Mahli *were* Eleazar and Kish. ²²And Eleazar died, and had no sons, but only daughters; and their brethren, the sons of Kish, took them *as wives.* ²³The sons of Mushi *were* Mahli, Eder, and Jeremoth—three *in all.*

²⁴These *were* the sons of Levi by their fathers' houses—the heads of the fathers' *houses* as they were counted individually by the number of their names, who did the work for the service of the house of the LORD, from the age of twenty years and above.

²⁵For David said, "The LORD God of Israel has given rest to His people, that they may dwell in Jerusalem forever"; ²⁶and also to the Levites, "They shall no longer carry the tabernacle, or any of the articles for its service." ²⁷For by the last words of David the Levites *were* numbered from twenty years old and above; ²⁸because their duty *was* to help the sons of Aaron in the service of the house of the LORD, in the courts and in the chambers, in the purifying of all holy things and the work of the service of the house of God, ²⁹both with the showbread and the fine flour for the grain offering, with the unleavened cakes and *what is baked in* the pan, with what is mixed and with all kinds of measures and sizes; ³⁰to stand every morning to thank and praise the LORD, and likewise at evening; ³¹and at

◄ TOGETHER

23:28-32 Priests and Levites had different temple jobs. Priests performed the sacrifices. Levites helped the priests, working as elders, deacons, custodians, assistants, musicians, and more. Both priests and Levites came from the tribe of Levi, but priests had to be descendants of Aaron, Israel's first high priest (Exodus 28:1-3). Temple worship could not have taken place without the combined efforts of the priests and Levites. Their responsibilities differed, but they were equally important to God's plan. No matter what place of service you have in the church, you are important to the healthy functioning of the congregation.

every presentation of a burnt offering to the LORD on the Sabbaths and on the New Moons and on the set feasts, by number according to the ordinance governing them, regularly before the LORD; [32]and that they should attend to the needs of the tabernacle of meeting, the needs of the holy *place*, and the needs of the sons of Aaron their brethren in the work of the house of the LORD.

CHAPTER 24 DAVID DIVIDES THE PRIESTS. Now *these are* the divisions of the sons of Aaron. The sons of Aaron *were* Nadab, Abihu, Eleazar, and Ithamar. [2]And Nadab and Abihu died before their father, and had no children; therefore Eleazar and Ithamar ministered as priests. [3]Then David with Zadok of the sons of Eleazar, and Ahimelech of the sons of Ithamar, divided them according to the schedule of their service.

[4]There were more leaders found of the sons of Eleazar than of the sons of Ithamar, and *thus* they were divided. Among the sons of Eleazar *were* sixteen heads of *their* fathers' houses, and eight heads of their fathers' houses among the sons of Ithamar. [5]Thus they were divided by lot, one group as another, for there were officials of the sanctuary and officials *of the house* of God, from the sons of Eleazar and from the sons of Ithamar. [6]And the scribe, Shemaiah the son of Nethanel, *one of* the Levites, wrote them down before the king, the leaders, Zadok the priest, Ahimelech the son of Abiathar, and the heads of the fathers' *houses* of the priests and Levites, one father's house taken for Eleazar and *one* for Ithamar.

[7]Now the first lot fell to Jehoiarib, the second to Jedaiah, [8]the third to Harim, the fourth to Seorim, [9]the fifth to Malchijah, the sixth to Mijamin, [10]the seventh to Hakkoz, the eighth to Abijah, [11]the ninth to Jeshua, the tenth to Shecaniah, [12]the eleventh to Eliashib, the twelfth to Jakim, [13]the thirteenth to Huppah, the fourteenth to Jeshebeab, [14]the fifteenth to Bilgah, the sixteenth to Immer, [15]the seventeenth to Hezir, the eighteenth to Happizzez, [16]the nineteenth to Pethahiah, the twentieth to Jehezekel, [17]the twenty-first to Jachin, the twenty-second to Gamul, [18]the twenty-third to Delaiah, the twenty-fourth to Maaziah.

[19]This *was* the schedule of their service for coming into the house of the LORD according to their ordinance by the hand of Aaron their father, as the LORD God of Israel had commanded him.

[20]And the rest of the sons of Levi: of the sons of Amram, Shubael; of the sons of Shubael, Jehdeiah. [21]Concerning Rehabiah, of the sons of Rehabiah, the first *was* Isshiah. [22]Of the Izharites, Shelomoth; of the sons of Shelomoth, Jahath. [23]Of the sons *of Hebron*, Jeriah *was the first*, Amariah the second, Jahaziel the third, *and* Jekameam the fourth. [24]*Of* the sons of Uzziel, Michah; of the sons of Michah, Shamir. [25]The brother of Michah, Isshiah; of the sons of Isshiah, Zechariah. [26]The sons of Merari *were* Mahli and Mushi; the son of Jaaziah, Beno. [27]The sons of Merari by Jaaziah *were* Beno, Shoham, Zaccur, and Ibri. [28]Of Mahli: Eleazar, who had no sons. [29]Of Kish: the son of Kish, Jerahmeel. [30]Also the sons of Mushi *were* Mahli, Eder, and Jerimoth. These *were* the sons of the Levites according to their fathers' houses.

[31]These also cast lots just as their brothers the sons of Aaron did, in the presence of King David, Zadok, Ahimelech, and the heads of the fathers' *houses* of the priests and Levites. The chief fathers *did* just as their younger brethren.

CHAPTER 25 THE MUSICIANS' DUTIES. Moreover David and the captains of the army separated for the service *some* of the sons of Asaph, of Heman, and of Jeduthun, who *should* prophesy with harps, stringed instruments, and cymbals. And the number of the skilled men performing their service was: [2]Of the sons of Asaph: Zaccur, Joseph, Nethaniah, and Asharelah; the sons of Asaph *were* under the direction of Asaph, who prophesied according to the order of the king. [3]Of Jeduthun, the sons of Jeduthun: Gedaliah, Zeri, Jeshaiah, Shimei, Hashabiah, and Mattithiah, six, under the direction of their father Jeduthun, who prophesied with a harp to give thanks and to praise the LORD. [4]Of Heman, the sons of Heman: Bukkiah, Mattaniah, Uzziel, Shebuel, Jerimoth, Hananiah, Hanani, Eliathah, Giddalti, Romamti-Ezer, Joshbekashah, Mallothi, Hothir, *and* Mahazioth. [5]All these *were* the sons of Heman the king's seer in the words

PITCH IN

25:1-7 There were many ways to contribute to the worship in the tabernacle. Some prophesied (25:1), some led in prayer (25:3), and others played instruments and sang (25:6-7). God wants all his peo[ple to] participate in worship. You may not be a master musician, a proph[et, or a] teacher, but God can use whatever you have to offer. Develop your special gifts to offer in service to God (Romans 12:3-8; 1 Corinthia[ns] 12:29-31).

of God, to exalt his horn. For God gave Heman fourteen sons and three daughters.

[6]All these *were* under the direction of their father for the music *in* the house of the LORD, with cymbals, stringed instruments, and harps, for the service of the house of God. Asaph, Jeduthun, and Heman *were* under the authority of the king. [7]So the number of them, with their brethren who were instructed in the songs of the LORD, all who were skillful, *was* two hundred and eighty-eight.

[8]And they cast lots for their duty, the small as well as the great, the teacher with the student.

[9]Now the first lot for Asaph came out for Joseph; the second for Gedaliah, him with his brethren and sons, twelve; [10]the third for Zaccur, his sons and his brethren, twelve; [11]the fourth for Jizri, his sons and his brethren, twelve; [12]the fifth for Nethaniah, his sons and his brethren, twelve; [13]the sixth for Bukkiah, his sons and his brethren, twelve; [14]the seventh for Jesharelah, his sons and his brethren, twelve; [15]the eighth for Jeshaiah his sons and his brethren, twelve; [16]the ninth for Mattaniah, his sons and his brethren, twelve; [17]the tenth for Shimei, his sons and his brethren, twelve; [18]the eleventh for Azarel, his sons and his brethren, twelve; [19]the twelfth for Hashabiah, his sons and his brethren, twelve

[20]the thirteenth for Shubael, his sons and his brethren, twelve; [21]the fourteenth for Mattithiah, his sons and his brethren, twelve; [22]the fifteenth for Jeremoth, his sons and his brethren, twelve; [23]the sixteenth for Hananiah, his sons and his brethren, twelve; [24]the seventeenth for Joshbekashah, his sons and his brethren, twelve; [25]the eighteenth for Hanani, his sons and his brethren, twelve; [26]the nineteenth for Mallothi, his sons and his brethren, twelve; [27]the twentieth for Eliathah, his sons and his brethren, twelve; [28]the twenty-first for Hothir, his sons and his brethren, twelve; [29]the twenty-second for Giddalti, his sons and his brethren, twelve; [30]the twenty-third for Mahazioth, his sons and his brethren, twelve; [31]the twenty-fourth for Romamti-Ezer, his sons and his brethren, twelve.

CHAPTER 26 THE TEMPLE GUARDS' DUTIES.

Concerning the divisions of the gatekeepers: of the Korahites, Meshelemiah the son of Kore, of the sons of Asaph. [2]And the sons of Meshelemiah *were* Zechariah the firstborn, Jediael the second, Zebadiah the third, Jathniel the fourth, [3]Elam the fifth, Jehohanan the sixth, Eliehoenai the seventh.

[4]Moreover the sons of Obed-Edom *were* Shemaiah the firstborn, Jehozabad the second, Joah the third, Sacar the fourth, Nethanel the fifth, [5]Ammiel the sixth, Issachar the seventh, Peulthai the eighth; for God blessed him.

[6]Also to Shemaiah his son were sons born who governed their fathers' houses, because they *were* men of great ability. [7]The sons of Shemaiah *were* Othni, Rephael, Obed, and Elzabad, whose brothers Elihu and Semachiah *were* able men.

[8]All these *were* of the sons of Obed-Edom, they and their sons and their brethren, able men with strength for the work: sixty-two of Obed-Edom.

[9]And Meshelemiah had sons and brethren, eighteen able men.

[10]Also Hosah, of the children of Merari, had sons: Shimri the first (for *though* he was not the firstborn, his father made him the first), [11]Hilkiah the second, Tebaliah the third, Zechariah the fourth; all the sons and brethren of Hosah *were* thirteen.

[12]Among these *were* the divisions of the gatekeepers, among the chief men, *having* duties just like their brethren, to serve in the house of the LORD. [13]And they cast lots for each gate, the small as well as the great, according to their father's house. [14]The lot for the East Gate fell to Shelemiah. Then they cast lots *for* his son Zechariah, a wise counselor, and his lot came out for the North Gate; [15]to Obed-Edom the South Gate, and to his sons the storehouse. [16]To Shuppim and Hosah *the lot came out* for the West Gate, with the Shallecheth Gate on the ascending highway—watchman opposite watchman. [17]On the east were *six* Levites, on the north four each day, on the south four each day, and for the storehouse two by two. [18]As for the Parbar on the west, *there were* four on the highway *and* two at the Parbar. [19]These were the divisions of the gatekeepers among the sons of Korah and among the sons of Merari.

[20]Of the Levites, Ahijah *was* over the treasuries of the house of God and over the treasuries of the dedicated things. [21]The sons of Laadan, the descendants of the Gershonites of Laadan, heads of their fathers' *houses*, of Laadan the Gershonite: Jehieli. [22]The sons of Jehieli, Zetham and Joel his brother, *were* over the treasuries of the house of the LORD. [23]Of the Amramites, the Izharites, the Hebronites, and the Uzzielites: [24]Shebuel the son of Gershom, the son of Moses, *was* overseer of the treasuries. [25]And his brethren by Eliezer *were* Rehabiah his son, Jeshaiah his son, Joram his son, Zichri his son, and Shelomith his son.

[26]This Shelomith and his brethren *were* over all the treasuries of the dedicated things which King David and the heads of fathers' *houses*, the captains over thousands and hundreds, and the captains of the army, had dedicated. [27]Some of the spoils won in battles they dedicated to maintain the house of the LORD. [28]And all that Samuel the seer, Saul the son of Kish, Abner the son of Ner, and Joab the son of Zeruiah had dedicated, every dedicated *thing*, was under the hand of Shelomith and his brethren.

[29]Of the Izharites, Chenaniah and his sons *performed*

LOOT

26:27 War spoils rightfully belonged to the victorious army. These soldiers, however, gave their portion of all the battle spoils to the temple to express their dedication to God. Like these soldiers, we should think of what we *can* give, rather than what we are obligated to give. Is your giving a matter of rejoicing rather than duty? Give as a response of joy and love for God and others.

duties as officials and judges over Israel outside Jerusalem.

[30]Of the Hebronites, Hashabiah and his brethren, one thousand seven hundred able men, had the oversight of Israel on the west side of the Jordan for all the business of the LORD, and in the service of the king. [31]Among the Hebronites, Jerijah *was* head of the Hebronites according to his genealogy of the fathers. In the fortieth year of the reign of David they were sought, and there were found among them capable men at Jazer of Gilead. [32]And his brethren *were* two thousand seven hundred able men, heads of fathers' *houses*, whom King David made officials over the Reubenites, the Gadites, and the half-tribe of Manasseh, for every matter pertaining to God and the affairs of the king.

CHAPTER 27 THE COMMANDERS OF THE ARMY.

And the children of Israel, according to their number, the heads of fathers' *houses*, the captains of thousands and hundreds and their officers, served the king in every matter of the *military* divisions. *These divisions* came in and went out month by month throughout all the months of the year, each division *having* twenty-four thousand.

[2]Over the first division for the first month *was* Jashobeam the son of Zabdiel, and in his division *were* twenty-four thousand; [3]he *was* of the children of Perez, and the chief of all the captains of the army for the first month. [4]Over the division of the second month *was* Dodai an Ahohite, and of his division Mikloth also *was* the leader;

PRINCIPLES TO LIVE BY

King David gave his son Solomon principles to guide him through life (see 1 Chronicles 28:9-10). These same ideas are ones that any Christian can learn and follow.

1	2	3	4	5	6
Get to know God personally.	Learn God's commands and discover what he wants you to do.	Worship God with a clean heart.	Serve God with a willing mind.	Be faithful.	Don't become discouraged.

in his division *were* twenty-four thousand. ⁵The third captain of the army for the third month *was* Benaiah, the son of Jehoiada the priest, who was chief; in his division *were* twenty-four thousand. ⁶This was the Benaiah *who was* mighty *among* the thirty, and was over the thirty; in his division *was* Ammizabad his son. ⁷The fourth *captain* for the fourth month *was* Asahel the brother of Joab, and Zebadiah his son after him; in his division *were* twenty-four thousand. ⁸The fifth *captain* for the fifth month *was* Shamhuth the Izrahite; in his division were twenty-four thousand. ⁹The sixth *captain* for the sixth month *was* Ira the son of Ikkesh the Tekoite; in his division *were* twenty-four thousand. ¹⁰The seventh *captain* for the seventh month *was* Helez the Pelonite, of the children of Ephraim; in his division *were* twenty-four thousand. ¹¹The eighth *captain* for the eighth month *was* Sibbechai the Hushathite, of the Zarhites; in his division *were* twenty-four thousand. ¹²The ninth *captain* for the ninth month *was* Abiezer the Anathothite, of the Benjamites; in his division *were* twenty-four thousand. ¹³The tenth *captain* for the tenth month *was* Maharai the Netophathite, of the Zarhites; in his division *were* twenty-four thousand. ¹⁴The eleventh *captain* for the eleventh month *was* Benaiah the Pirathonite, of the children of Ephraim; in his division *were* twenty-four thousand. ¹⁵The twelfth *captain* for the twelfth month *was* Heldai the Netophathite, of Othniel; in his division *were* twenty-four thousand.

¹⁶Furthermore, over the tribes of Israel: the officer over the Reubenites *was* Eliezer the son of Zichri; over the Simeonites, Shephatiah the son of Maachah; ¹⁷*over* the Levites, Hashabiah the son of Kemuel; over the Aaronites, Zadok; ¹⁸*over* Judah, Elihu, *one* of David's brothers; *over* Issachar, Omri the son of Michael; ¹⁹*over* Zebulun, Ishmaiah the son of Obadiah; *over* Naphtali, Jerimoth the son of Azriel; ²⁰*over* the children of Ephraim, Hoshea the son of Azaziah; *over* the half-tribe of Manasseh, Joel the son of Pedaiah; ²¹*over* the half-*tribe* of Manasseh in Gilead, Iddo the son of Zechariah; *over* Benjamin, Jaasiel the son of Abner; ²²*over* Dan, Azarel the son of Jeroham. These *were* the leaders of the tribes of Israel.

²³But David did not take the number of those twenty years old and under, because the LORD had said He would multiply Israel like the stars of the heavens. ²⁴Joab the son of Zeruiah began a census, but he did not finish, for

wrath came upon Israel because of this census; nor was the number recorded in the account of the chronicles of King David.

²⁵And Azmaveth the son of Adiel *was* over the king's treasuries; and Jehonathan the son of Uzziah was over the storehouses in the field, in the cities, in the villages, and in the fortresses. ²⁶Ezri the son of Chelub was over those who did the work of the field for tilling the ground ²⁷And Shimei the Ramathite *was* over the vineyards, and Zabdi the Shiphmite was over the produce of the vineyards for the supply of wine. ²⁸Baal-Hanan the Gederite was over the olive trees and the sycamore trees that *were* in the lowlands, and Joash *was* over the store of oil. ²⁹And Shitrai the Sharonite *was* over the herds that fed in Sharon, and Shaphat the son of Adlai was over the herds *that were* in the valleys. ³⁰Obil the Ishmaelite *was* over the camels, Jehdeiah the Meronothite *was* over the donkeys ³¹and Jaziz the Hagrite *was* over the flocks. All these *were* the officials over King David's property.

³²Also Jehonathan, David's uncle, *was* a counselor, a wise man, and a scribe; and Jehiel the son of Hachmon *was* with the king's sons. ³³Ahithophel *was* the king's counselor, and Hushai the Archite *was* the king's companion. ³⁴After Ahithophel *was* Jehoiada the son of Benaiah, then Abiathar. And the general of the king's army *was* Joab.

CHAPTER 28 PLANS FOR THE TEMPLE. Now

David assembled at Jerusalem all the leaders of Israel: the officers of the tribes and the captains of the divisions who served the king, the captains over thousands and captains over hundreds, and the stewards over all the substance and possessions of the king and of his sons

◥ DUTY-BOUND

28:8 David told Solomon to search out and follow every one of commands to ensure Israel's prosperity and the continuation of D descendants upon the throne. It was the solemn duty of the king and obey God's laws. The teachings of Scripture are the keys to so happiness, and justice, but you'll never discover them unless you God's Word. If God's will is ignored and his teaching neglected, a we attempt to build, even if it has God's name on it, is headed for collapse. Get to know God's commands through regular Bible stud obey them every day.

with the officials, the valiant men, and all the mighty men of valor. ²Then King David rose to his feet and said, "Hear me, my brethren and my people: I *had* it in my heart to build a house of rest for the ark of the covenant of the LORD, and for the footstool of our God, and had made preparations to build it. ³But God said to me, 'You shall not build a house for My name, because you *have been* a man of war and have shed blood.' ⁴However the LORD God of Israel chose me above all the house of my father to be king over Israel forever, for He has chosen Judah *to be* the ruler. And of the house of Judah, the house of my father, and among the sons of my father, He was pleased with me to make *me* king over all Israel. ⁵And of all my sons (for the LORD has given me many sons) He has chosen my son Solomon to sit on the throne of the kingdom of the LORD over Israel. ⁶Now He said to me, 'It is your son Solomon *who* shall build My house and My courts; for I have chosen him *to be* My son, and I will be his Father. ⁷Moreover I will establish his kingdom forever, if he is steadfast to observe My commandments and My judgments, as it is this day.' ⁸Now therefore, in the sight of all Israel, the assembly of the LORD, and in the hearing of our God, be careful to seek out all the commandments of the LORD your God, that you may possess this good land, and leave *it* as an inheritance for your children after you forever.

⁹"As for you, my son Solomon, know the God of your father, and serve Him with a loyal heart and with a willing mind; for the LORD searches all hearts and understands all the intent of the thoughts. If you seek Him, He will be found by you; but if you forsake Him, He will cast you off forever. ¹⁰Consider now, for the LORD has chosen you to build a house for the sanctuary; be strong, and do it."

¹¹Then David gave his son Solomon the plans for the vestibule, its houses, its treasuries, its upper chambers, its inner chambers, and the place of the mercy seat; ¹²and the plans for all that he had by the Spirit, of the courts of the house of the LORD, of all the chambers all around, of the treasuries of the house of God, and of the treasuries for the dedicated things; ¹³also for the division of the priests and the Levites, for all the work of the service of the house of the LORD, and for all the articles of service in the house of the LORD. ¹⁴*He gave* gold by weight for *things* of gold, for all articles used in every kind of service; also *silver* for all articles of silver by weight, for all articles used in every kind of service; ¹⁵the weight for the lampstands of gold, and their lamps of gold, by weight for each lampstand and its lamps; for the lampstands of silver by weight, for the lampstand and its lamps, according to the use of each lampstand. ¹⁶And by weight *he gave* gold for the tables of the showbread, for each table, and silver for the tables of silver; ¹⁷also pure gold for the forks, the basins, the pitchers of pure gold, and the golden bowls—*he gave gold* by weight for every bowl; and for the silver bowls, *silver* by weight for every bowl; ¹⁸and refined gold by weight for the altar of incense, and for the construction of the chariot, that is, the gold cherubim that spread *their wings* and overshadowed the ark of the covenant of the LORD. ¹⁹"All *this*," said David, "the LORD made me understand in writing, by *His* hand upon me, all the works of these plans."

²⁰And David said to his son Solomon, "Be strong and of good courage, and do *it;* do not fear nor be dismayed, for the LORD God—my God—*will be* with you. He will not leave you nor forsake you, until you have finished all the

ALL-KNOWING

28:9 Nothing can be hidden from God. He sees and understands everything in our heart. David found this out the hard way when God sent Nathan to expose David's sins of adultery and murder (2 Samuel 12). David told Solomon to be completely open with God and dedicated to him. It makes no sense to try to hide any thoughts or actions from an all-knowing God. This should cause you joy, not fear, because God knows even the worst things about you and loves you anyway.

work for the service of the house of the LORD. ²¹*Here are* the divisions of the priests and the Levites for all the service of the house of God; and every willing craftsman *will be* with you for all manner of workmanship, for every kind of service; also the leaders and all the people *will be* completely at your command."

Recently I realized that I have been living off of the faith of my parents. How do I make my faith my own?

I WONDER . . .

This may be the most significant realization of your life. Some young people never understand that God wants us to know him personally. Living off of someone else's faith is like borrowing something from a friend. No matter what you borrow—a bike, clothes, skateboard, tapes, or faith—it isn't yours and must be returned.

Solomon was challenged to get to know the "God of your father" (1 Chronicles 28:9). In other words, he wasn't to settle for hearing how someone else trusted God. He needed to find out for himself.

During these years, your faith will be tested. Friends who do not believe in Christ may see nothing wrong with doing things that would cause your conscience to start screaming in protest. That's when you will have to make a choice: will you go along with your friends or will you stand on what you believe? If your faith is strong (if it is yours and not your parents' or your youth leader's), no amount of pressure from friends will be able to blow you away (Matthew 7:21-29).

Consider taking these steps to help develop your faith. First, make sure you have asked Jesus Christ to forgive your sin and come into your life. This is the first step to a personal relationship with God. Second, begin to ask questions about the Bible. God wants you to understand it as well as believe and obey it. God is not afraid of honest questions asked with good motives. Third, look for other Christians who are excited about developing their faith in God—people who do not want to settle for second best. Being around growing Christians is contagious. What you learn from them will convince you that being a Christian is worth the work and is 100 percent right for you!

CHAPTER 29 THE PEOPLE BRING GIFTS. Furthermore King David said to all the assembly: "My son Solomon, whom alone God has chosen, *is* young and inexperienced; and the work *is* great, because the temple *is* not for man but for the LORD God. [2]Now for the house of my God I have prepared with all my might: gold for *things to be made of* gold, silver for *things of* silver, bronze for *things of* bronze, iron for *things of* iron, wood for *things of* wood, onyx stones, *stones* to be set, glistening stones of various colors, all kinds of precious stones, and marble slabs in abundance. [3]Moreover, because I have set my affection on the house of my God, I have given to the house of my God, over and above all that I have prepared for the holy house, my own special treasure of gold and

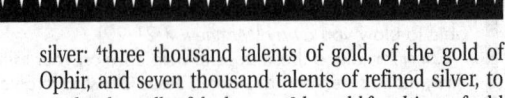

THE BOSS

"I just wish God would leave me alone. It's like I can't get away from him."

"What do you mean, Reed?"

"Well, my parents go to church all the time and they make *me* go—to everything."

"And you don't like that?"

"I'd rather do almost anything else—even homework. But with my parents, attendance isn't open for discussion."

"Your older brother is a missionary, isn't he?"

"Yeah."

"Do you stay in touch?"

"He sends me these thick letters every month—they're like handwritten sermons telling me to make Jesus the Lord of my life. I wish he'd let me live the way I want to live."

"How is that?"

"Well, I don't want to *totally* forget God, but I think it's extreme to think and talk about him all the time. I want to live my life without having to think about God every single day."

"Reed, are you a Christian? Have you ever really trusted Christ?"

"Yeah. When I was eleven."

"But now you're saying you want to live for God on *your* terms? Whenever you feel like it?"

"I guess so."

Like Reed, a lot of Christians don't want Christ to be their Master and Boss. They want to control their own lives. They believe they can do whatever they desire and still find fulfillment.

See 1 Chronicles 28:9 for the real secret to satisfaction in life.

silver: [4]three thousand talents of gold, of the gold of Ophir, and seven thousand talents of refined silver, to overlay the walls of the houses; [5]the gold for *things of* gold and the silver for *things of* silver, and for all kinds of work *to be done* by the hands of craftsmen. Who *then* is willing to consecrate himself this day to the LORD?"

[6]Then the leaders of the fathers' *houses,* leaders of the tribes of Israel, the captains of thousands and of hundreds, with the officers over the king's work, offered willingly. [7]They gave for the work of the house of God five thousand talents and ten thousand darics of gold, ten thousand talents of silver, eighteen thousand talents of

SECURITY

29:11-12 David acknowledged God's greatness. Our constantly changing world is controlled by a constant and unchanging God. A see life events come and go, objects fade, materials decay, and fri change, the only thing on which we can truly depend is God's cont love and purpose for us never change. Only when we understand we have real peace and security.

bronze, and one hundred thousand talents of iron. [8]And whoever had *precious* stones gave *them* to the treasury of the house of the LORD, into the hand of Jehiel the Gershonite. [9]Then the people rejoiced, for they had offered willingly, because with a loyal heart they had offered willingly to the LORD; and King David also rejoiced greatly.

[10]Therefore David blessed the LORD before all the assembly; and David said:

"Blessed are You, LORD God of Israel, our Father,
    forever and ever.
[11] Yours, O LORD, *is* the greatness,
The power and the glory,
The victory and the majesty;
For all *that is* in heaven and in earth *is Yours;*
Yours *is* the kingdom, O LORD,
And You are exalted as head over all.
[12] Both riches and honor *come* from You,
And You reign over all.
In Your hand *is* power and might;
In Your hand *it is* to make great
And to give strength to all.

[13] "Now therefore, our God,
We thank You
And praise Your glorious name.
[14] But who *am* I, and who *are* my people,
That we should be able to offer so willingly as this?
For all things *come* from You,
And of Your own we have given You.
[15] For we *are* aliens and pilgrims before You,
As *were* all our fathers;
Our days on earth *are* as a shadow,
And without hope.

[16]"O LORD our God, all this abundance that we have prepared to build You a house for Your holy name is from Your hand, and *is* all Your own. [17]I know also, my God, that You test the heart and have pleasure in uprightness. As for me, in the uprightness of my heart I have willingly offered all these *things;* and now with joy I have seen Your people, who are present here to offer willingly to You [18]O LORD God of Abraham, Isaac, and Israel, our fathers keep this forever in the intent of the thoughts of the heart of Your people, and fix their heart toward You. [19]And give my son Solomon a loyal heart to keep Your commandments and Your testimonies and Your statutes, to do all *these things,* and to build the temple for which I have made provision."

[20]Then David said to all the assembly, "Now bless the LORD your God." So all the assembly blessed the LORD God of their fathers, and bowed their heads and prostrated themselves before the LORD and the king.

²¹And they made sacrifices to the LORD and offered burnt offerings to the LORD on the next day: a thousand bulls, a thousand rams, a thousand lambs, with their drink offerings, and sacrifices in abundance for all Israel. ²²So they ate and drank before the LORD with great gladness on that day. And they made Solomon the son of David king the second time, and anointed *him* before the LORD *to be* the leader, and Zadok *to be* priest. ²³Then Solomon sat on the throne of the LORD as king instead of David his father, and prospered; and all Israel obeyed him. ²⁴All the leaders and the mighty men, and also all the sons of King David, submitted themselves to King Solomon. ²⁵So the LORD exalted Solomon exceedingly in the sight of all Israel, and bestowed on him *such* royal majesty as had not been on any king before him in Israel.

²⁶Thus David the son of Jesse reigned over all Israel. ²⁷And the period that he reigned over Israel *was* forty years; seven years he reigned in Hebron, and thirty-three *years* he reigned in Jerusalem. ²⁸So he died in a good old age, full of days and riches and honor; and Solomon his son reigned in his place. ²⁹Now the acts of King David, first and last, indeed they *are* written in the book of Samuel the seer, in the book of Nathan the prophet, and in the book of Gad the seer, ³⁰with all his reign and his might, and the events that happened to him, to Israel, and to all the kingdoms of the lands.

MEGA Themes

GOD'S PEOPLE By retelling Israel's history in the genealogies and the stories of the kings, the writer laid the true spiritual foundation for the nation. God kept his promises, and we are reminded of them in the historical record of his people, leaders, prophets, priests, and kings.

Israel's past formed a reliable basis for rebuilding the nation after the Exile. God's promises are written in the Bible—we can know God and trust him to keep his word. Like Israel, we can have no higher goal in life than serving God. Like Israel, we will find God to be trustworthy and faithful.

1. As you review Israel's history, what qualities of God are most evident? What do you learn about the people themselves?
2. There were definite differences in the lives of the people when they were submissive to God's will, as opposed to times when they ignored and/or rebelled against God. In what ways do you see a similar pattern developing in your life?
3. Think about the next 10 years of your life. How important is "doing God's will" in your future? Explain this importance.
4. Now think about the next generation. If God blesses you with children, what spiritual heritage do you want to give to them? How can you begin in the present to prepare that future heritage?

DAVID The story of David's life and his relationship with God showed that he was God's appointed leader. David's devotion to God, the law, the temple, true worship, the people, and justice sets the standard for what God's chosen king should have been.

Jesus Christ came to earth as a descendant of David. One day Christ will rule as King over all the earth. His strength and justice will fulfill God's ideal for the king. He is our hope.

1. Write out a review of David's life.
2. From looking at David's life, what do you learn about God? About living in God's will?
3. Do most people seek God's purposes in their lives or do they seem to live life based merely on what they want? Explain.
4. What do you think God wants to accomplish in your life? What can you do to see that God's purpose is accomplished in your life?

TRUE WORSHIP David brought the ark of the covenant to the tabernacle at Jerusalem to restore true worship to the people. God chose priests and Levites to guide the people in faithful worship. This worship was to be an important, central part of the Israelites' daily lives.

When we acknowledge and focus on God as the true King, we experience worship. This worship is to be the center of our life, with the rest of our thoughts and activities organized around God's kingship. Today we are all priests in the sense that each of us, in Christ, can personally enter into worship. Thus we also can encourage one another to deeper worship.

1. Describe the ways that the Israelites worshiped God.
2. Describe how you worship God.
3. In your worship, what is the importance of the church? Other Christians? The Bible?
4. In what ways can Christians be "priests" for one another? Picture your Christian friends. What can you do to be a "priest" for one of them?

Mom, I promise I'll never be late again! Please!" The mother desperately wanted to believe her daughter. But no matter how strong her promises to get in on time, she was always late. ■ "Honey," she began, "I'm sorry. But for the rest of the weekend you're grounded." The mother had been more than fair; now she had to mete out punishment. ■ Many times during Israel's history, God had sent messengers to the country's leaders threatening punishment for their disobedience. Each time, the leaders would beg for one more chance, but they never kept their promises. Finally God allowed them to be conquered and taken into captivity. ■ Second Chronicles was written after the return of some of the Jews from that captivity. The author reminded these people of their forefathers' sin and its results. Only by truly submitting to God could Israel regain its strength as a nation. "If My people who are called by My name will humble themselves, and pray and seek My face, and turn from their wicked ways, then I will hear from heaven, and will forgive their sin and heal their land" (7:14). ■ Second Chronicles was written for you, too. God punishes those who ignore him, but he blesses those who obey. Read this book and dedicate yourself to following after God.

STATS

PURPOSE: To unify the nation around true worship of Jehovah by showing his standard for judging kings. The righteous kings of Judah and the religious revivals under their rule are highlighted, and the sins of the evil kings are exposed.

AUTHOR: Ezra, according to Jewish tradition

TO WHOM WRITTEN: All Israel

DATE WRITTEN: Approximately 430 B.C.; recording events from the beginning of Solomon's reign (970 B.C.) to the beginning of the Babylonian captivity (586 B.C.)

SETTING: Second Chronicles parallels 1 and 2 Kings and serves as their commentary.

KEY PEOPLE: Solomon, the queen of Sheba, Rehoboam, Asa, Jehoshaphat, Jehoram, Joash, Uzziah, Ahaz, Hezekiah, Manasseh, Josiah

KEY PLACES: Jerusalem, the temple

SPECIAL FEATURES: Includes a detailed record of the temple's construction

2 *Chronicles*

CHAPTER 1   SOLOMON ASKS GOD FOR WISDOM.

Now Solomon the son of David was strengthened in his kingdom, and the LORD his God *was* with him and exalted him exceedingly.

²And Solomon spoke to all Israel, to the captains of thousands and of hundreds, to the judges, and to every leader in all Israel, the heads of the fathers' *houses.* ³Then Solomon, and all the assembly with him, went to the high place that *was* at Gibeon; for the tabernacle of meeting with God was there, which Moses the servant of the LORD had made in the wilderness. ⁴But David had brought up the ark of God from Kirjath Jearim to *the place* David had prepared for it, for he had pitched a tent for it at Jerusalem. ⁵Now the bronze altar that Bezalel the son of Uri, the son of Hur, had made, he put before the tabernacle of the LORD; Solomon and the assembly sought Him *there.* ⁶And Solomon went up there to the bronze altar before the LORD, which *was* at the tabernacle of meeting, and offered a thousand burnt offerings on it.

⁷On that night God appeared to Solomon, and said to him, "Ask! What shall I give you?"

⁸And Solomon said to God: "You have shown great mercy to David my father, and have made me king in his place. ⁹Now, O LORD God, let Your promise to David my father be established, for You have made me king over a people like the dust of the earth in multitude. ¹⁰Now give me wisdom and knowledge, that I may go out and come in before this people; for who can judge this great people of Yours?"

PRIORITIES

1:11-12 Solomon could have had anything, but he asked for wisdom to rule the nation. God approved of the way Solomon ordered his priorities, and he gave him the wisdom he asked for *and* riches, wealth, and honor. Jesus also spoke about priorities. He said that when we put God first, everything we really need will fall into place (Matthew 6:33). This does not guarantee that we will be wealthy and famous like Solomon. It means that when we wisely put God first, the wisdom he gives us will enable us to live a rich, rewarding life.

KEY PLACES IN 2 CHRONICLES

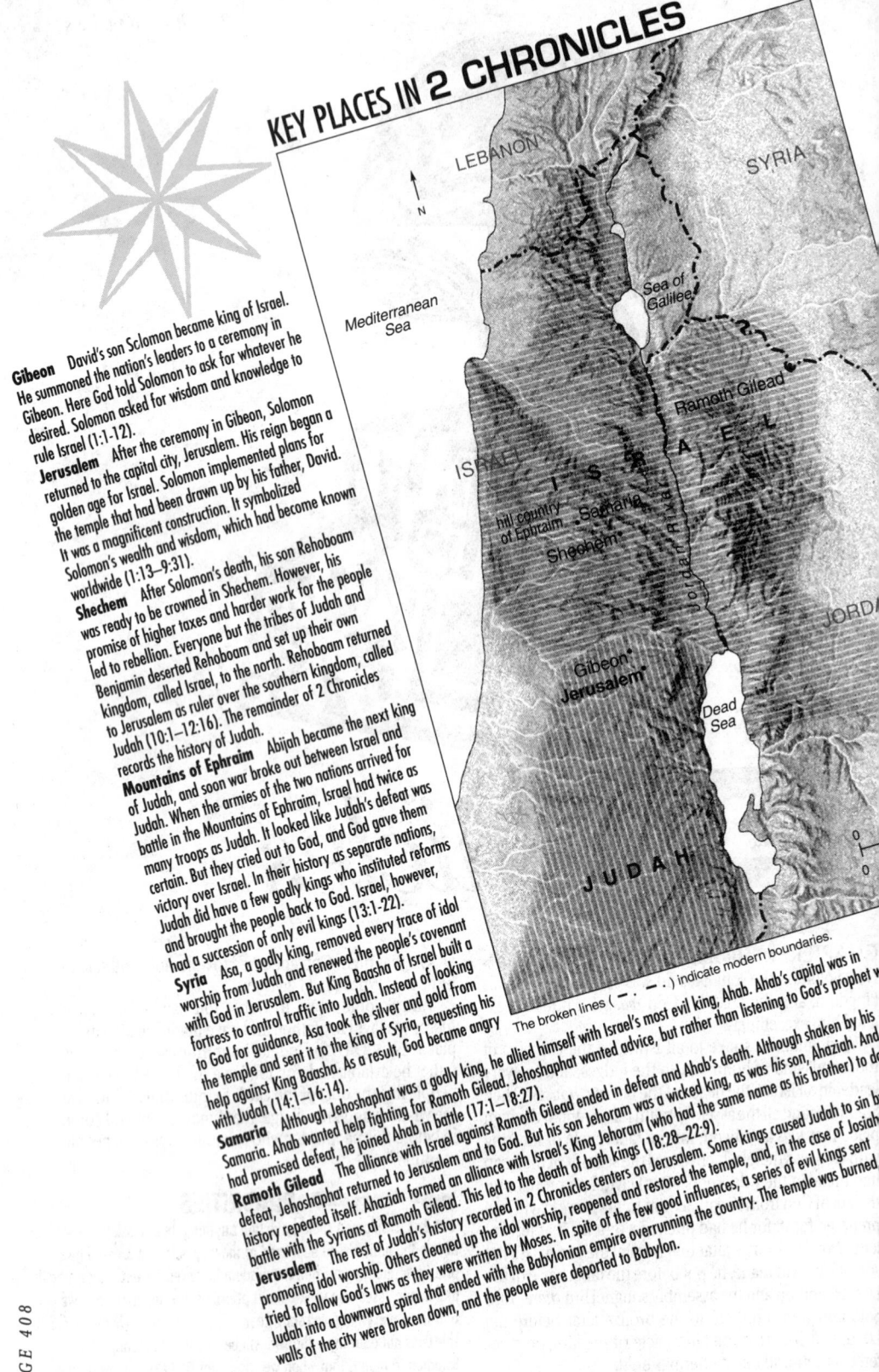

Gibeon David's son Solomon became king of Israel. He summoned the nation's leaders to a ceremony in Gibeon. Here God told Solomon to ask for whatever he desired. Solomon asked for wisdom and knowledge to rule Israel (1:1-12).

Jerusalem After the ceremony in Gibeon, Solomon returned to the capital city, Jerusalem. His reign began a golden age for Israel. Solomon implemented plans for the temple that had been drawn up by his father, David. It was a magnificent construction. It symbolized Solomon's wealth and wisdom, which had become known worldwide (1:13—9:31).

Shechem After Solomon's death, his son Rehoboam was ready to be crowned in Shechem. However, his promise of higher taxes and harder work for the people led to rebellion. Everyone but the tribes of Judah and Benjamin deserted Rehoboam and set up their own kingdom, called Israel, to the north. Rehoboam returned to Jerusalem as ruler over the southern kingdom, called Judah (10:1—12:16). The remainder of 2 Chronicles records the history of Judah.

Mountains of Ephraim Abijah became the next king of Judah, and soon war broke out between Israel and Judah. When the armies of the two nations arrived for battle in the Mountains of Ephraim, Israel had twice as many troops as Judah. It looked like Judah's defeat was certain. But they cried out to God, and God gave them victory over Israel. In their history as separate nations, Judah did have a few godly kings who instituted reforms and brought the people back to God. Israel, however, had a succession of only evil kings (13:1-22).

Syria Asa, a godly king, removed every trace of idol worship from Judah and renewed the people's covenant with God in Jerusalem. But King Baasha of Israel built a fortress to control traffic into Judah. Instead of looking to God for guidance, Asa took the silver and gold from the temple and sent it to the king of Syria, requesting his help against King Baasha. As a result, God became angry with Judah (14:1—16:14).

Samaria Although Jehoshaphat was a godly king, he allied himself with Israel's most evil king, Ahab. Ahab's capital was in Samaria. Ahab wanted help fighting for Ramoth Gilead. Jehoshaphat wanted advice, but rather than listening to God's prophet w had promised defeat, he joined Ahab in battle (17:1—18:27).

Ramoth Gilead The alliance with Israel against Ramoth Gilead ended in defeat and Ahab's death. Although shaken by his defeat, Jehoshaphat returned to Jerusalem and to God. But his son Jehoram was a wicked king, as was *his* son, Ahaziah. And history repeated itself. Ahaziah formed an alliance with Israel's King Jehoram (who had the same name as his brother) to d battle with the Syrians at Ramoth Gilead. This led to the death of both kings (18:28—22:9).

Jerusalem The rest of Judah's history recorded in 2 Chronicles centers on Jerusalem. Some kings caused Judah to sin b promoting idol worship. Others cleaned up the idol worship, reopened and restored the temple, and, in the case of Josiah tried to follow God's laws as they were written by Moses. In spite of the few good influences, a series of evil kings sent Judah into a downward spiral that ended with the Babylonian empire overrunning the country. The temple was burned walls of the city were broken down, and the people were deported to Babylon.

The broken lines (– · – ·) indicate modern boundaries.

¹¹Then God said to Solomon: "Because this was in your heart, and you have not asked riches or wealth or honor or the life of your enemies, nor have you asked long life—but have asked wisdom and knowledge for yourself, that you may judge My people over whom I have made you king— ¹²wisdom and knowledge *are* granted to you; and I will give you riches and wealth and honor, such as none of the kings have had who *were* before you, nor shall any after you have the like."

¹³So Solomon came to Jerusalem from the high place that *was* at Gibeon, from before the tabernacle of meeting, and reigned over Israel. ¹⁴And Solomon gathered chariots and horsemen; he had one thousand four hundred chariots and twelve thousand horsemen, whom he stationed in the chariot cities and with the king in Jerusalem. ¹⁵Also the king made silver and gold as common in Jerusalem as stones, and he made cedars as abundant as the sycamores which *are* in the lowland. ¹⁶And Solomon had horses imported from Egypt and Keveh; the king's merchants bought them in Keveh at the *current* price. ¹⁷They also acquired and imported from Egypt a chariot for six hundred *shekels* of silver, and a horse for one hundred and fifty; thus, through their agents, they exported them to all the kings of the Hittites and the kings of Syria.

CHAPTER **2** **SOLOMON MAKES PLANS.** Then Solomon determined to build a temple for the name of the LORD, and a royal house for himself. ²Solomon selected seventy thousand men to bear burdens, eighty thousand to quarry *stone* in the mountains, and three thousand six hundred to oversee them.

³Then Solomon sent to Hiram king of Tyre, saying:

As you have dealt with David my father, and sent him cedars to build himself a house to dwell in, *so deal with me.* ⁴Behold, I am building a temple for the name of the LORD my God, to dedicate *it* to Him, to burn before Him sweet incense, for the continual showbread, for the burnt offerings morning and evening, on the Sabbaths, on the New Moons, and on the set feasts of the LORD our God. This *is an ordinance* forever to Israel.

⁵ And the temple which I build *will be* great, for our God is greater than all gods. ⁶But who is able to build Him a temple, since heaven and the heaven of heavens cannot contain Him? Who *am* I then, that I should build Him a temple, except to burn sacrifice before Him?

⁷ Therefore send me at once a man skillful to work in gold and silver, in bronze and iron, in purple and crimson and blue, who has skill to engrave with the skillful men who are with me in Judah and Jerusalem, whom David my father provided. ⁸Also send me cedar and cypress and algum logs from Lebanon, for I know that your servants have skill to cut timber in Lebanon; and indeed my servants *will be* with your servants, ⁹to prepare timber for me in abundance, for the temple

which I am about to build *shall be* great and wonderful.

¹⁰ And indeed I will give to your servants, the woodsmen who cut timber, twenty thousand kors of ground wheat, twenty thousand kors of barley, twenty thousand baths of wine, and twenty thousand baths of oil.

◀━━━━━**CELEBRATE**

2:4 A celebration is an occasion of joy, and remembering God's goodness to his people was certainly a reason to be joyful. God wanted Israel to celebrate certain occasions regularly because the people were so forgetful, so quick to turn to other gods. In church we use celebrations to recall God's goodness. Because we have short memories, too, Christmas, Easter, and other special occasions are designed to help us remember what God has done for us.

¹¹Then Hiram king of Tyre answered in writing, which he sent to Solomon:

Because the LORD loves His people, He has made you king over them.

¹²Hiram also said:

Blessed *be* the LORD God of Israel, who made heaven and earth, for He has given King David a wise son, endowed with prudence and understanding, who will build a temple for the LORD and a royal house for himself!

¹³ And now I have sent a skillful man, endowed with understanding, Huram my master *craftsman* ¹⁴(the son of a woman of the daughters of Dan, and his father was a man of Tyre), skilled to work in gold and silver, bronze and iron, stone and wood, purple and blue, fine linen and crimson, and to make any engraving and to accomplish any plan which may be given to him, with your skillful men and with the skillful men of my lord David your father.

¹⁵ Now therefore, the wheat, the barley, the oil, and the wine which my lord has spoken of, let him send to his servants. ¹⁶And we will cut wood from Lebanon, as much as you need; we will bring it to you in rafts by sea to Joppa, and you will carry it up to Jerusalem.

¹⁷Then Solomon numbered all the aliens who *were* in the land of Israel, after the census in which David his father had numbered them; and there were found to be one hundred and fifty-three thousand six hundred. ¹⁸And he made seventy thousand of them bearers of burdens, eighty thousand stonecutters in the mountain, and three thousand six hundred overseers to make the people work.

CHAPTER **3** **THE CONSTRUCTION BEGINS.** Now Solomon began to build the house of the LORD at Jerusalem on Mount Moriah, where *the* LORD had appeared to his father David, at the place that David had prepared on the threshing floor of Ornan the Jebusite. ²And he began to build on the second *day* of the second month in the fourth year of his reign.

³This is the foundation which Solomon laid for building the house of God: The length *was* sixty cubits (by cubits according to the former measure) and the width twenty cubits. ⁴And the vestibule that *was* in front *of the sanctuary* was twenty cubits long across the width of the house, and the height *was* one hundred and twenty. He overlaid the inside with pure gold. ⁵The larger room he paneled with cypress which he overlaid with fine gold, and he carved palm trees and chainwork on it. ⁶And he decorated the house with precious stones for beauty, and the gold *was* gold from Parvaim. ⁷He also overlaid the house—the beams and doorposts, its walls and doors—with gold; and he carved cherubim on the walls.

⁸And he made the Most Holy Place. Its length was according to the width of the house, twenty cubits, and its width twenty cubits. He overlaid it with six hundred talents of fine gold. ⁹The weight of the nails *was* fifty shekels of gold; and he overlaid the upper area with gold. ¹⁰In the Most Holy Place he made two cherubim, fashioned by carving, and overlaid them with gold. ¹¹The wings of the cherubim *were* twenty cubits in *overall* length: one wing *of the one cherub was* five cubits, touching the wall of the room, and the other wing *was* five cubits, touching the wing of the other cherub; ¹²*one* wing of the other cherub *was* five cubits, touching the wall of the room, and the other wing *also was* five cubits, touching the wing of the other cherub. ¹³The wings of these cherubim spanned twenty cubits overall. They stood on their feet, and they faced inward. ¹⁴And he made the veil of blue, purple, crimson, and fine linen, and wove cherubim into it.

¹⁵Also he made in front of the temple two pillars thirty-five cubits high, and the capital that *was* on the top of each of *them* was five cubits. ¹⁶He made wreaths of chainwork, as in the inner sanctuary, and put *them* on top of the pillars; and he made one hundred pomegranates, and put *them* on the wreaths of chainwork. ¹⁷Then he set up the pillars before the temple, one on the right hand and the other on the left; he called the name of the one on the right hand Jachin, and the name of the one on the left Boaz.

CHAPTER 4 HURAM'S SKILLFUL WORK. Moreover

he made a bronze altar: twenty cubits was its length, twenty cubits its width, and ten cubits its height.

²Then he made the Sea of cast *bronze*, ten cubits from one brim to the other; *it was* completely round. Its height *was* five cubits, and a line of thirty cubits measured its circumference. ³And under it *was* the likeness of oxen encircling it all around, ten to a cubit, all the way around the Sea. The oxen *were* cast in two rows, when it was cast. ⁴It stood on twelve oxen: three looking toward the north, three looking toward the west, three looking toward the south, and three looking toward the east; the Sea *was set* upon them, and all their back parts *pointed* inward. ⁵It *was* a handbreadth thick; and its brim was shaped like

the brim of a cup, *like* a lily blossom. It contained three thousand baths.

⁶He also made ten lavers, and put five on the right side and five on the left, to wash in them; such things as they offered for the burnt offering they would wash in them, but the Sea *was* for the priests to wash in. ⁷And he made ten lampstands of gold according to their design, and set *them* in the temple, five on the right side and five on the left. ⁸He also made ten tables, and placed *them* in the temple, five on the right side and five on the left. And he made one hundred bowls of gold.

◣◣◣◣◣**WORSHIP TOOLS**

4:11-16 Pots, shovels, and bowls—these implements of worship not familiar to us. Although the articles we use to aid our worship h॰ changed, the purpose of worship remains the same: to give honor o॰ praise to God. We must never confuse our worship of God with the ▮ we use to help us worship him.

⁹Furthermore he made the court of the priests, and the great court and doors for the court; and he overlaid these doors with bronze. ¹⁰He set the Sea on the right side, toward the southeast. ¹¹Then Huram made the pots and the shovels and the bowls. So Huram finished doing the work that he was to do for King Solomon for the house of God: ¹²the two pillars and the bowl-shaped capitals *that were* on top of the two pillars; the two networks covering the two bowl-shaped capitals which *were* on top of the pillars; ¹³four hundred pomegranates for the two networks (two rows of pomegranates for each network, to cover the two bowl-shaped capitals that *were* on the pillars); ¹⁴he also made carts and the lavers on the carts; ¹⁵one Sea and twelve oxen under it; ¹⁶also the pots, the shovels, the forks—and all their articles Huram his master *craftsman* made of burnished bronze for King Solomon for the house of the LORD.

¹⁷In the plain of Jordan the king had them cast in clay molds, between Succoth and Zeredah. ¹⁸And Solomon had all these articles made in such great abundance that the weight of the bronze was not determined.

¹⁹Thus Solomon had all the furnishings made for the house of God: the altar of gold and the tables on which *was* the showbread; ²⁰the lampstands with their lamps of pure gold, to burn in the prescribed manner in front of the inner sanctuary, ²¹with the flowers and the lamps and the wick-trimmers of gold, of purest gold; ²²the trimmers, the bowls, the ladles, and the censers of pure gold. As for the entry of the sanctuary, its inner doors to the Most Holy *Place*, and the doors of the main hall of the temple, *were* gold.

CHAPTER 5 THE ARK AND THE TEMPLE. So all the

work that Solomon had done for the house of the LORD was finished; and Solomon brought in the things which his father David had dedicated: the silver and the gold and all the furnishings. And he put *them* in the treasuries of the house of God.

²Now Solomon assembled the elders of Israel and all the heads of the tribes, the chief fathers of the children of

Israel, in Jerusalem, that they might bring the ark of the covenant of the LORD up from the City of David, which *is* Zion. ³Therefore all the men of Israel assembled with the king at the feast, which *was* in the seventh month. ⁴So all the elders of Israel came, and the Levites took up the ark. ⁵Then they brought up the ark, the tabernacle of meeting, and all the holy furnishings that *were* in the tabernacle. The priests and the Levites brought them up. ⁶Also King Solomon, and all the congregation of Israel who were assembled with him before the ark, were sacrificing sheep and oxen that could not be counted or numbered for multitude. ⁷Then the priests brought in the ark of the covenant of the LORD to its place, into the inner sanctuary of the temple, to the Most Holy *Place*, under the wings of the cherubim. ⁸For the cherubim spread *their* wings over the place of the ark, and the cherubim overshadowed the ark and its poles. ⁹The poles extended so that the ends of the poles of the ark could be seen from *the holy place*, in front of the inner sanctuary; but they could not be seen from outside. And they are there to this day. ¹⁰Nothing was in the ark except the two tablets which Moses put *there* at Horeb, when the LORD made *a covenant* with the children of Israel, when they had come out of Egypt.

¹¹And it came to pass when the priests came out of the *Most Holy Place* (for all the priests who *were* present had sanctified themselves, without keeping to their divisions), ¹²and the Levites *who were* the singers, all those of Asaph and Heman and Jeduthun, with their sons and their brethren, stood at the east end of the altar, clothed in white linen, having cymbals, stringed instruments and harps, and with them one hundred and twenty priests sounding with trumpets— ¹³indeed it came to pass, when the trumpeters and singers *were* as one, to make one sound to be heard in praising and thanking the LORD, and when they lifted up their voice with the trumpets and cymbals and instruments of music, and praised the LORD, *saying:*

"*For He is* good,
For His mercy *endures* forever,"

that the house, the house of the LORD, was filled with a cloud, ¹⁴so that the priests could not continue ministering because of the cloud; for the glory of the LORD filled the house of God.

CHAPTER 6 SOLOMON BLESSES THE PEOPLE.

Then Solomon spoke:

"The LORD said
He would dwell in the dark cloud.
² I have surely built You an exalted house,
And a place for You to dwell in forever."

³Then the king turned around and blessed the whole assembly of Israel, while all the assembly of Israel was standing. ⁴And he said: "Blessed *be* the LORD God of Israel, who has fulfilled with His hands *what* He spoke with His mouth to my father David, saying, ⁵'Since the day that I brought My people out of the land of Egypt, I have chosen no city from any tribe of Israel *in which* to build

a house, that My name might be there, nor did I choose any man to be a ruler over My people Israel. ⁶Yet I have chosen Jerusalem, that My name may be there, and I have chosen David to be over My people Israel.' ⁷Now it was in the heart of my father David to build a temple for the name of the LORD God of Israel. ⁸But the LORD said to my father David, 'Whereas it was in your heart to build a temple for My name, you did well in that it was in your heart. ⁹Nevertheless you shall not build the temple, but your son who will come from your body, he shall build the temple for My name.' ¹⁰So the LORD has fulfilled His word which He spoke, and I have filled the position of my father David, and sit on the throne of Israel, as the LORD

◆◆◆◆◆◆◆◆◆◆ LIVING WORSHIP

5:13 The first service at the temple began with honoring God and acknowledging his presence and goodness. In the same way, our worship should begin with a recognition of God's love. Praise God first, and then you will be prepared to present your needs to him. Recalling God's love and mercy will bring daily worship to life. Psalm 107 is an example of how David recalled God's loving-kindness.

promised; and I have built the temple for the name of the LORD God of Israel. ¹¹And there I have put the ark, in which *is* the covenant of the LORD which He made with the children of Israel."

¹²Then *Solomon* stood before the altar of the LORD in the presence of all the assembly of Israel, and spread out his hands ¹³(for Solomon had made a bronze platform five cubits long, five cubits wide, and three cubits high, and had set it in the midst of the court; and he stood on it, knelt down on his knees before all the assembly of Israel, and spread out his hands toward heaven); ¹⁴and he said: "LORD God of Israel, *there is* no God in heaven or on earth like You, who keep *Your* covenant and mercy with Your servants who walk before You with all their hearts. ¹⁵You have kept what You promised Your servant David my father; You have both spoken with Your mouth and fulfilled *it* with Your hand, as *it is* this day. ¹⁶Therefore, LORD God of Israel, now keep what You promised Your servant David my father, saying, 'You shall not fail to have a man sit before Me on the throne of Israel, only if your sons take heed to their way, that they walk in My law as you have walked before Me.' ¹⁷And now, O LORD God of Israel, let Your word come true, which You have spoken to Your servant David.

¹⁸"But will God indeed dwell with men on the earth? Behold, heaven and the heaven of heavens cannot contain You. How much less this temple which I have built! ¹⁹Yet regard the prayer of Your servant and his supplication, O LORD my God, and listen to the cry and the prayer

◆◆◆◆◆◆◆◆◆◆ MARVEL

6:18 Solomon marveled that the temple could contain the power of God and that God would be willing to live on earth among sinful people. We marvel that God, through his Son, Jesus, dwelt among us in human form to reveal his eternal purposes to us. In doing so, God was reaching out to mankind in love. God wants us to reach back in return and get to know him. Only then will we come to love him with all our heart. Don't simply marvel at God's power, take the time to get to know him.

6:30 Have you ever felt far away from God—separated by personal problems and feelings of failure? In his prayer, Solomon underscores the fact that God stands ready to hear us, to forgive our sins, and to restore our relationship to him. God is waiting and listening for our confessions of guilt and our willingness to obey him. He is ready to forgive us and to restore us to fellowship with him. Don't wait to experience this loving forgiveness.

which Your servant is praying before You: [20]that Your eyes may be open toward this temple day and night, toward the place where *You* said *You would* put Your name, that You may hear the prayer which Your servant makes toward this place. [21]And may You hear the supplications of Your servant and of Your people Israel, when they pray toward this place. Hear from heaven Your dwelling place, and when You hear, forgive.

[22]"If anyone sins against his neighbor, and is forced to take an oath, and comes *and* takes an oath before Your altar in this temple, [23]then hear from heaven, and act, and judge Your servants, bringing retribution on the wicked by bringing his way on his own head, and justifying the righteous by giving him according to his righteousness.

IF MY PEOPLE will humble themselves AND *pray* AND *seek My face* AND TURN FROM *their wicked ways* THEN I WILL HEAR FROM HEAVEN AND *will forgive their sin* AND *heal their land.*

from 2 CHRONICLES 7:14

[24]"Or if Your people Israel are defeated before an enemy because they have sinned against You, and return and confess Your name, and pray and make supplication before You in this temple, [25]then hear from heaven and forgive the sin of Your people Israel, and bring them back to the land which You gave to them and their fathers.

[26]"When the heavens are shut up and there is no rain because they have sinned against You, when they pray toward this place and confess Your name, and turn from their sin because You afflict them, [27]then hear *in* heaven, and forgive the sin of Your servants, Your people Israel, that You may teach them the good way in which they should walk; and send rain on Your land which You have given to Your people as an inheritance.

[28]"When there is famine in the land, pestilence or blight or mildew, locusts or grasshoppers; when their enemies besiege them in the land of their cities; whatever plague or whatever sickness *there is;* [29]whatever prayer, whatever supplication is *made* by anyone, or by all Your people Israel, when each one knows his own burden and his own grief, and spreads out his hands to this temple: [30]then hear from heaven Your dwelling place, and forgive, and give to everyone according to all his ways, whose heart You know (for You alone know the hearts of the sons of men), [31]that they may fear You, to walk in Your ways as long as they live in the land which You gave to our fathers.

[32]"Moreover, concerning a foreigner, who is not of Your people Israel, but has come from a far country for the sake of Your great name and Your mighty hand and Your outstretched arm, when they come and pray in this temple; [33]then hear from heaven Your dwelling place, and do according to all for which the foreigner calls to You, that all peoples of the earth may know Your name and fear You, as *do* Your people Israel, and that they may know that this temple which I have built is called by Your name.

[34]"When Your people go out to battle against their enemies, wherever You send them, and when they pray to You toward this city which You have chosen and the temple which I have built for Your name, [35]then hear from heaven their prayer and their supplication, and maintain their cause.

[36]"When they sin against You (for *there is* no one who does not sin), and You become angry with them and deliver them to the enemy, and they take them captive to a land far or near; [37]yet when they come to themselves in the land where they were carried captive, and repent, and make supplication to You in the land of their captivity, saying, 'We have sinned, we have done wrong, and have committed wickedness'; [38]and *when* they return to You with all their heart and with all their soul in the land of their captivity, where they have been carried captive and pray toward their land which You gave to their fathers, the city which You have chosen, and toward the temple which I have built for Your name: [39]then hear from heaven Your dwelling place their prayer and their supplications, and maintain their cause, and forgive Your people who have sinned against You. [40]Now, my God, I pray, let Your eyes be open and *let* Your ears *be* attentive to the prayer *made* in this place.

41 "Now therefore,
Arise, O LORD God, to Your resting place,
You and the ark of Your strength.
Let Your priests, O LORD God, be clothed with salvation,
And let Your saints rejoice in goodness.

42 "O LORD God, do not turn away the face of Your Anointed;
Remember the mercies of Your servant David."

CHAPTER 7 GOD'S GLORY FILLS THE TEMPLE.

When Solomon had finished praying, fire came down
from heaven and consumed the burnt offering and the
sacrifices; and the glory of the LORD filled the temple.
2 And the priests could not enter the house of the LORD,
because the glory of the LORD had filled the LORD's house.
3 When all the children of Israel saw how the fire came
down, and the glory of the LORD on the temple, they
bowed their faces to the ground on the pavement, and
worshiped and praised the LORD, *saying*:

"For *He is* good,
For His mercy *endures* forever."

4 Then the king and all the people offered sacrifices
before the LORD. 5 King Solomon offered a sacrifice of
twenty-two thousand bulls and one hundred and twenty
thousand sheep. So the king and all the people dedicated
the house of God. 6 And the priests attended to their services; the Levites also with instruments of the music of
the LORD, which King David had made to praise the LORD,
saying, "For His mercy *endures* forever," whenever David
offered praise by their ministry. The priests sounded
trumpets opposite them, while all Israel stood.
7 Furthermore Solomon consecrated the middle of the
court that *was* in front of the house of the LORD; for there
he offered burnt offerings and the fat of the peace offerings, because the bronze altar which Solomon had made
was not able to receive the burnt offerings, the grain
offerings, and the fat.
8 At that time Solomon kept the feast seven days, and
all Israel with him, a very great assembly from the entrance of Hamath to the Brook of Egypt. 9 And on the
eighth day they held a sacred assembly, for they observed
the dedication of the altar seven days, and the feast seven
days. 10 On the twenty-third day of the seventh month he
sent the people away to their tents, joyful and glad of
heart for the good that the LORD had done for David, for
Solomon, and for His people Israel. 11 Thus Solomon finished the house of the LORD and the king's house; and
Solomon successfully accomplished all that came into
his heart to make in the house of the LORD and in his own
house.
12 Then the LORD appeared to Solomon by night, and
said to him: "I have heard your prayer, and have chosen
this place for Myself as a house of sacrifice. 13 When I shut
up heaven and there is no rain, or command the locusts
to devour the land, or send pestilence among My people,
14 if My people who are called by My name will humble
themselves, and pray and seek My face, and turn from
their wicked ways, then I will hear from heaven, and will
forgive their sin and heal their land. 15 Now My eyes will
be open and My ears attentive to prayer *made* in this
place. 16 For now I have chosen and sanctified this house,
that My name may be there forever; and My eyes and My
heart will be there perpetually. 17 As for you, if you walk
before Me as your father David walked, and do according
to all that I have commanded you, and if you keep My
statutes and My judgments, 18 then I will establish the
throne of your kingdom, as I covenanted with David your
father, saying, 'You shall not fail *to have* a man as ruler in
Israel.'
19 "But if you turn away and forsake My statutes and My
commandments which I have set before you, and go and
serve other gods, and worship them, 20 then I will uproot
them from My land which I have given them; and this
house which I have sanctified for My name I will cast out
of My sight, and will make it a proverb and a byword
among all peoples.
21 "And *as for* this house, which is exalted, everyone
who passes by it will be astonished and say, 'Why has the
LORD done thus to this land and this house?' 22 Then they
will answer, 'Because they forsook the LORD God of their
fathers, who brought them out of the land of Egypt, and
embraced other gods, and worshiped them and served
them; therefore He has brought all this calamity on
them.' "

FORGIVEN

7:14 **In chapter 6, Solomon asked God to make provisions for the people when they sinned. God answered with four conditions for forgiveness: (1) humble yourself by admitting your sins, (2) pray to God, asking for forgiveness, (3) search for God continually, and (4) turn from sinful habits. True repentance is more than talk—it is changed behavior. Whether we sin individually, as a group, or as a nation, following these steps will lead to forgiveness.**

CHAPTER 8 SOLOMON'S BUILDING ACTIVITIES.

It
came to pass at the end of twenty years, when Solomon
had built the house of the LORD and his own house, 2 that
the cities which Hiram had given to Solomon, Solomon
built them; and he settled the children of Israel there. 3 And
Solomon went to Hamath Zobah and seized it. 4 He also
built Tadmor in the wilderness, and all the storage cities
which he built in Hamath. 5 He built Upper Beth Horon
and Lower Beth Horon, fortified cities *with* walls, gates,
and bars, 6 also Baalath and all the storage cities that Solomon had, and all the chariot cities and the cities of the
cavalry, and all that Solomon desired to build in Jerusalem, in Lebanon, and in all the land of his dominion.
7 All the people *who were* left of the Hittites, Amorites,
Perizzites, Hivites, and Jebusites, who *were* not of Israel— 8 that is, their descendants who were left in the land
after them, whom the children of Israel did not destroy—
from these Solomon raised forced labor, as it is to this
day. 9 But Solomon did not make the children of Israel
servants for his work. Some *were* men of war, captains of
his officers, captains of his chariots, and his cavalry.
10 And others *were* chiefs of the officials of King Solomon:
two hundred and fifty, who ruled over the people.

¹¹Now Solomon brought the daughter of Pharaoh up from the City of David to the house he had built for her, for he said, "My wife shall not dwell in the house of David king of Israel, because *the places* to which the ark of the LORD has come are holy."

¹²Then Solomon offered burnt offerings to the LORD on the altar of the LORD which he had built before the vestibule, ¹³according to the daily rate, offering according to the commandment of Moses, for the Sabbaths, the New Moons, and the three appointed yearly feasts—the Feast of Unleavened Bread, the Feast of Weeks, and the Feast of Tabernacles. ¹⁴And, according to the order of David his father, he appointed the divisions of the priests for their service, the Levites for their duties (to praise and serve before the priests) as the duty of each day required, and the gatekeepers by their divisions at each gate; for so David the man of God had commanded. ¹⁵They did not depart from the command of the king to the priests and Levites concerning any matter or concerning the treasuries.

¹⁶Now all the work of Solomon was well-ordered from the day of the foundation of the house of the LORD until it was finished. So the house of the LORD was completed.

¹⁷Then Solomon went to Ezion Geber and Elath on the seacoast, in the land of Edom. ¹⁸And Hiram sent him ships by the hand of his servants, and servants who knew the sea. They went with the servants of Solomon to Ophir, and acquired four hundred and fifty talents of gold from there, and brought it to King Solomon.

CHAPTER **9** **THE QUEEN OF SHEBA VISITS.** Now when the queen of Sheba heard of the fame of Solomon, she came to Jerusalem to test Solomon with hard questions, *having* a very great retinue, camels that bore spices, gold in abundance, and precious stones; and when she came to Solomon, she spoke with him about all that was in her heart. ²So Solomon answered all her questions; there was nothing so difficult for Solomon that he could not explain it to her. ³And when the queen of Sheba had seen the wisdom of Solomon, the house that he had built, ⁴the food on his table, the seating of his servants, the service of his waiters and their apparel, his cupbearers and their apparel, and his entryway by which he went up to the house of the LORD, there was no more spirit in her.

⁵Then she said to the king: "*It was* a true report which I heard in my own land about your words and your wisdom. ⁶However I did not believe their words until I came and saw with my own eyes; and indeed the half of the greatness of your wisdom was not told me. You exceed the fame of which I heard. ⁷Happy *are* your men and happy *are* these your servants, who stand continually before you and hear your wisdom! ⁸Blessed be the LORD your God, who delighted in you, setting you on His throne *to be* king for the LORD your God! Because your God has loved Israel, to establish them forever, therefore He made you king over them, to do justice and righteousness."

⁹And she gave the king one hundred and twenty talents of gold, spices in great abundance, and precious

9:1-8 The queen of Sheba had heard about Solomon's wisdom, b was overwhelmed when she saw for herself the fruits of that wisdo Although Solomon had married Pharaoh's daughter, he was still sin trying to follow God at this stage in his life. When people get to kn and begin to ask hard questions, will your responses reflect God? Y life is your most powerful witness; let others see God at work in yo

stones; there never were any spices such as those the queen of Sheba gave to King Solomon.

¹⁰Also, the servants of Hiram and the servants of Solomon, who brought gold from Ophir, brought algum wood and precious stones. ¹¹And the king made walkways *of* the algum wood for the house of the LORD and for the king's house, also harps and stringed instruments for singers; and there were none such *as these* seen before in the land of Judah.

¹²Now King Solomon gave to the queen of Sheba all she desired, whatever she asked, *much more* than she had brought to the king. So she turned and went to her own country, she and her servants.

¹³The weight of gold that came to Solomon yearly was six hundred and sixty-six talents of gold, ¹⁴besides *what* the traveling merchants and traders brought. And all the kings of Arabia and governors of the country brought gold and silver to Solomon. ¹⁵And King Solomon made two hundred large shields of hammered gold; six hundred *shekels* of hammered gold went into each shield. ¹⁶*He* also *made* three hundred shields of hammered gold; three hundred *shekels* of gold went into each shield. The king put them in the House of the Forest of Lebanon.

¹⁷Moreover the king made a great throne of ivory, and overlaid it with pure gold. ¹⁸The throne *had* six steps, with a footstool of gold, *which were* fastened to the throne; there were armrests on either side of the place of the seat, and two lions stood beside the armrests. ¹⁹Twelve lions stood there, one on each side of the six steps; nothing like *this* had been made for any *other* kingdom.

²⁰All King Solomon's drinking vessels *were* gold, and all the vessels of the House of the Forest of Lebanon *were* pure gold. Not *one was* silver, for this was accounted as nothing in the days of Solomon. ²¹For the king's ships went to Tarshish with the servants of Hiram. Once every three years the merchant ships came, bringing gold, silver, ivory, apes, and monkeys.

²²So King Solomon surpassed all the kings of the earth in riches and wisdom. ²³And all the kings of the earth sought the presence of Solomon to hear his wisdom, which God had put in his heart. ²⁴Each man brought his present: articles of silver and gold, garments, armor, spices, horses, and mules, at a set rate year by year.

²⁵Solomon had four thousand stalls for horses and chariots, and twelve thousand horsemen whom he stationed in the chariot cities and with the king at Jerusalem.

²⁶So he reigned over all the kings from the River to the land of the Philistines, as far as the border of Egypt. ²⁷The king made silver *as common* in Jerusalem as stones, and he made cedar trees as abundant as the sycamores which *are* in the lowland. ²⁸And they brought horses to Solomon from Egypt and from all lands.

²⁹Now the rest of the acts of Solomon, first and last, *are*

they not written in the book of Nathan the prophet, in the prophecy of Ahijah the Shilonite, and in the visions of Iddo the seer concerning Jeroboam the son of Nebat? ³⁰Solomon reigned in Jerusalem over all Israel forty years. ³¹Then Solomon rested with his fathers, and was buried in the City of David his father. And Rehoboam his son reigned in his place.

CHAPTER 10 REHOBOAM TAKES BAD ADVICE. And

Rehoboam went to Shechem, for all Israel had gone to Shechem to make him king. ²So it happened, when Jeroboam the son of Nebat heard *it* (he was in Egypt, where he had fled from the presence of King Solomon), that Jeroboam returned from Egypt. ³Then they sent for him and called him. And Jeroboam and all Israel came and spoke to Rehoboam, saying, ⁴"Your father made our yoke heavy; now therefore, lighten the burdensome service of your father and his heavy yoke which he put on us, and we will serve you."

⁵So he said to them, "Come back to me after three days." And the people departed.

⁶Then King Rehoboam consulted the elders who stood before his father Solomon while he still lived, saying, "How do you advise *me* to answer these people?"

⁷And they spoke to him, saying, "If you are kind to these people, and please them, and speak good words to them, they will be your servants forever."

⁸But he rejected the advice which the elders had given him, and consulted the young men who had grown up with him, who stood before him. ⁹And he said to them, "What advice do you give? How should we answer this people who have spoken to me, saying, 'Lighten the yoke which your father put on us'?"

¹⁰Then the young men who had grown up with him spoke to him, saying, "Thus you should speak to the people who have spoken to you, saying, 'Your father made our yoke heavy, but you make *it* lighter on us'— thus you shall say to them: 'My little *finger* shall be thicker than my father's waist! ¹¹And now, whereas my father put a heavy yoke on you, I will add to your yoke; my father chastised you with whips, but I *will chastise you* with scourges!' "

¹²So Jeroboam and all the people came to Rehoboam on the third day, as the king had directed, saying, "Come back to me the third day." ¹³Then the king answered them roughly. King Rehoboam rejected the advice of the elders, ¹⁴and he spoke to them according to the advice of the young men, saying, "My father made your yoke heavy, but I will add to it; my father chastised you with whips, but I *will chastise you* with scourges!" ¹⁵So the king did not listen to the people; for the turn *of events* was from God, that the LORD might fulfill His word, which He had spoken by the hand of Ahijah the Shilonite to Jeroboam the son of Nebat.

¹⁶Now when all Israel *saw* that the king did not listen to them, the people answered the king, saying:

"What share have we in David?
We have no inheritance in the son of Jesse.
Every man to your tents, O Israel!
Now see to your own house, O David!"

So all Israel departed to their tents. ¹⁷But Rehoboam reigned over the children of Israel who dwelt in the cities of Judah.

¹⁸Then King Rehoboam sent Hadoram, who *was* in charge of revenue; but the children of Israel stoned him with stones, and he died. Therefore King Rehoboam mounted *his* chariot in haste to flee to Jerusalem. ¹⁹So Israel has been in rebellion against the house of David to this day.

CHAPTER 11 GOD SAYS NOT TO FIGHT. Now when

Rehoboam came to Jerusalem, he assembled from the house of Judah and Benjamin one hundred and eighty thousand chosen *men* who were warriors, to fight against Israel, that he might restore the kingdom to Rehoboam.

◣◢◣◢◣◢ PEERS

10:1-14 Following bad advice can cause disaster. Rehoboam lost the chance to rule a peaceful, united kingdom because he rejected the advice of Solomon's older counselors, preferring that of his peers. Rehoboam made two errors in seeking advice: (1) he did not give extra consideration to the suggestions of those who knew the situation better than he, and (2) he did not ask God for wisdom to discern which was the better option.

It is easy to follow the advice of our peers because they often feel as we do. But their view may be limited. It is important to listen carefully to those who have more experience than we do, those who can see the bigger picture.

²But the word of the LORD came to Shemaiah the man of God, saying, ³"Speak to Rehoboam the son of Solomon, king of Judah, and to all Israel in Judah and Benjamin, saying, ⁴'Thus says the LORD: "You shall not go up or fight against your brethren! Let every man return to his house, for this thing is from Me." ' " Therefore they obeyed the words of the LORD, and turned back from attacking Jeroboam.

⁵So Rehoboam dwelt in Jerusalem, and built cities for defense in Judah. ⁶And he built Bethlehem, Etam, Tekoa, ⁷Beth Zur, Sochoh, Adullam, ⁸Gath, Mareshah, Ziph, ⁹Adoraim, Lachish, Azekah, ¹⁰Zorah, Aijalon, and Hebron, which are in Judah and Benjamin, fortified cities. ¹¹And he fortified the strongholds, and put captains in them, and stores of food, oil, and wine. ¹²Also in every city *he put* shields and spears, and made them very strong, having Judah and Benjamin on his side.

¹³And from all their territories the priests and the Levites who *were* in all Israel took their stand with him. ¹⁴For the Levites left their common-lands and their possessions and came to Judah and Jerusalem, for Jeroboam

◣◢◣◢◣◢ GREEDY

10:16-19 In trying to have it all, Rehoboam lost almost everything. Motivated by greed and power, he pressed too hard and divided his kingdom. He didn't need more money or power because he had inherited the richest kingdom in the world. He didn't need more control because the land was at peace. His demands were based on selfishness rather than reason or spiritual discernment. Those who selfishly insist on having it all often wind up with little or nothing.

12:1 At the height of his popularity and power, Rehoboam abandoned the Lord. What happened? Often it is more difficult to be a believer in good times than in bad. Tough times push us toward God; but easy times can make us feel self-sufficient and self-satisfied. When everything is going right, guard your faith closely.

and his sons had rejected them from serving as priests to the LORD. ¹⁵Then he appointed for himself priests for the high places, for the demons, and the calf idols which he had made. ¹⁶And after *the Levites left,* those from all the tribes of Israel, such as set their heart to seek the LORD God of Israel, came to Jerusalem to sacrifice to the LORD God of their fathers. ¹⁷So they strengthened the kingdom of Judah, and made Rehoboam the son of Solomon strong for three years, because they walked in the way of David and Solomon for three years.

¹⁸Then Rehoboam took for himself as wife Mahalath the daughter of Jerimoth the son of David, *and of* Abihail the daughter of Eliah the son of Jesse. ¹⁹And she bore him children: Jeush, Shamariah, and Zaham. ²⁰After her he took Maachah the granddaughter of Absalom; and she bore him Abijah, Attai, Ziza, and Shelomith. ²¹Now Rehoboam loved Maachah the granddaughter of Absalom more than all his wives and his concubines; for he took eighteen wives and sixty concubines, and begot twenty-eight sons and sixty daughters. ²²And Rehoboam appointed Abijah the son of Maachah as chief, *to be* leader among his brothers; for he *intended* to make him king. ²³He dealt wisely, and dispersed some of his sons throughout all the territories of Judah and Benjamin, to every fortified city; and he gave them provisions in abundance. He also sought many wives *for them.*

CHAPTER 12 EGYPT CONQUERS JERUSALEM.

Now it came to pass, when Rehoboam had established the kingdom and had strengthened himself, that he forsook the law of the LORD, and all Israel along with him. ²And it happened in the fifth year of King Rehoboam *that* Shishak king of Egypt came up against Jerusalem, because they had transgressed against the LORD, ³with twelve hundred chariots, sixty thousand horsemen, and people without number who came with him out of Egypt—the Lubim and the Sukkiim and the Ethiopians. ⁴And he took the fortified cities of Judah and came to Jerusalem.

⁵Then Shemaiah the prophet came to Rehoboam and the leaders of Judah, who were gathered together in Jerusalem because of Shishak, and said to them, "Thus says the LORD: 'You have forsaken Me, and therefore I also have left you in the hand of Shishak.' "

⁶So the leaders of Israel and the king humbled themselves; and they said, "The LORD *is* righteous."

⁷Now when the LORD saw that they humbled themselves, the word of the LORD came to Shemaiah, saying, "They have humbled themselves; *therefore* I will not destroy them, but I will grant them some deliverance. My wrath shall not be poured out on Jerusalem by the hand of Shishak. ⁸Nevertheless they will be his servants, that they may distinguish My service from the service of the kingdoms of the nations."

⁹So Shishak king of Egypt came up against Jerusalem, and took away the treasures of the house of the LORD and the treasures of the king's house; he took everything. He also carried away the gold shields which Solomon had made. ¹⁰Then King Rehoboam made bronze shields in their place, and committed *them* to the hands of the captains of the guard, who guarded the doorway of the king's house. ¹¹And whenever the king entered the house of the LORD, the guard would go and bring them out; then they would take them back into the guardroom. ¹²When he humbled himself, the wrath of the LORD turned from him, so as not to destroy *him* completely; and things also went well in Judah.

¹³Thus King Rehoboam strengthened himself in Jerusalem and reigned. Now Rehoboam *was* forty-one years old when he became king; and he reigned seventeen years in Jerusalem, the city which the LORD had chosen out of all the tribes of Israel, to put His name there. His mother's name *was* Naamah, an Ammonitess. ¹⁴And he did evil, because he did not prepare his heart to seek the LORD.

¹⁵The acts of Rehoboam, first and last, *are* they not written in the book of Shemaiah the prophet, and of Iddo the seer concerning genealogies? And *there were* wars between Rehoboam and Jeroboam all their days. ¹⁶So Rehoboam rested with his fathers, and was buried in the City of David. Then Abijah his son reigned in his place.

CHAPTER 13 ABIJAH DEFEATS JEROBOAM.

In the eighteenth year of King Jeroboam, Abijah became king over Judah. ²He reigned three years in Jerusalem. His mother's name *was* Michaiah the daughter of Uriel of Gibeah.

And there was war between Abijah and Jeroboam. ³Abijah set the battle in order with an army of valiant warriors, four hundred thousand choice men. Jeroboam also drew up in battle formation against him with eight hundred thousand choice men, mighty men of valor.

⁴Then Abijah stood on Mount Zemaraim, which *is* in the mountains of Ephraim, and said, "Hear me, Jeroboam and all Israel: ⁵Should you not know that the LORD God of Israel gave the dominion over Israel to David forever, to him and his sons, by a covenant of salt? ⁶Yet Jeroboam the son of Nebat, the servant of Solomon the son of David, rose up and rebelled against his lord. ⁷Then worthless rogues gathered to him, and strengthened themselves against Rehoboam the son of Solomon, when Rehoboam was young and inexperienced and could not withstand them. ⁸And now you think to withstand the kingdom of the LORD, which is in the hand of the sons of David; and you *are* a great multitude, and with you are the gold calves which Jeroboam made for you as gods. ⁹Have you not cast out the priests of the LORD, the sons of Aaron, and the Levites, and made for yourselves priests, like the peoples of *other* lands, so that

GOLD CALVES

13:8 Jeroboam's army was cursed because of the gold calves the[y] carried with them. It was as though they had put sin into a physica[l] so they could haul it around. Consider carefully the things you che[rish?] you value anything more than God, it becomes your golden calf a[nd?] day will condemn you. Let go of anything that interferes with you[r] relationship with God.

whoever comes to consecrate himself with a young bull and seven rams may be a priest of *things that are* not gods? ¹⁰But as for us, the LORD *is* our God, and we have not forsaken Him; and the priests who minister to the LORD *are* the sons of Aaron, and the Levites *attend* to *their* duties. ¹¹And they burn to the LORD every morning and every evening burnt sacrifices and sweet incense; *they* also *set* the showbread *in order on* the pure *gold* table, and the lampstand of gold with its lamps to burn every evening; for we keep the command of the LORD our God, but you have forsaken Him. ¹²Now look, God Himself is with us as *our* head, and His priests with sounding trumpets to sound the alarm against you. O children of Israel, do not fight against the LORD God of your fathers, for you shall not prosper!"

¹³But Jeroboam caused an ambush to go around behind them; so they were in front of Judah, and the ambush *was* behind them. ¹⁴And when Judah looked around, to their surprise the battle line *was* at both front and rear; and they cried out to the LORD, and the priests sounded the trumpets. ¹⁵Then the men of Judah gave a shout; and as the men of Judah shouted, it happened that God struck Jeroboam and all Israel before Abijah and Judah. ¹⁶And the children of Israel fled before Judah, and God delivered them into their hand. ¹⁷Then Abijah and his people struck them with a great slaughter; so five hundred thousand choice men of Israel fell slain. ¹⁸Thus the children of Israel were subdued at that time; and the children of Judah prevailed, because they relied on the LORD God of their fathers.

¹⁹And Abijah pursued Jeroboam and took cities from him: Bethel with its villages, Jeshanah with its villages, and Ephrain with its villages. ²⁰So Jeroboam did not recover strength again in the days of Abijah; and the LORD struck him, and he died.

²¹But Abijah grew mighty, married fourteen wives, and begot twenty-two sons and sixteen daughters. ²²Now the rest of the acts of Abijah, his ways, and his sayings *are* written in the annals of the prophet Iddo.

CHAPTER **14** ASA RULES JUDAH. So Abijah rested with his fathers, and they buried him in the City of David. Then Asa his son reigned in his place. In his days the land was quiet for ten years.

²Asa did *what was* good and right in the eyes of the LORD his God, ³for he removed the altars of the foreign *gods* and the high places, and broke down the *sacred* pillars and cut down the wooden images. ⁴He commanded Judah to seek the LORD God of their fathers, and to observe the law and the commandment. ⁵He also removed the high places and the incense altars from all the cities of Judah, and the kingdom was quiet under him. ⁶And he built fortified cities in Judah, for the land had rest; he had no war in those years, because the LORD had given him rest. ⁷Therefore he said to Judah, "Let us build these cities and make walls around *them,* and towers, gates, and bars, *while* the land *is* yet before us, because we have sought the LORD our God; we have sought *Him,* and He has given us rest on every side." So they built and prospered. ⁸And Asa had an army of three hundred thousand from Judah who carried shields and spears, and from Benjamin two hundred and eighty thousand men who carried shields and drew bows; all these *were* mighty men of valor.

⁹Then Zerah the Ethiopian came out against them with an army of a million men and three hundred chariots, and he came to Mareshah. ¹⁰So Asa went out against him, and they set the troops in battle array in the Valley of Zephathah at Mareshah. ¹¹And Asa cried out to the LORD his God, and said, "LORD, *it is* nothing for You to help, whether with many or with those who have no power; help us, O LORD our God, for we rest on You, and in Your name we go against this multitude. O LORD, You *are* our God; do not let man prevail against You!"

~~~~~~~BE PREPARED

14:7 Times of peace are not just for resting. They allow us to prepare for times of trouble. King Asa recognized the period of peace as the right time to build his defenses. He knew that it would be too late to prepare defenses at the moment of attack. It also is difficult to withstand spiritual attack unless defenses are prepared beforehand. Decisions about what to do when temptations arise must be made with a cool head in the peace of untroubled moments, long before the heat of temptation is upon us. Build your defenses now, before temptation strikes.

¹²So the LORD struck the Ethiopians before Asa and Judah, and the Ethiopians fled. ¹³And Asa and the people who *were* with him pursued them to Gerar. So the Ethiopians were overthrown, and they could not recover, for they were broken before the LORD and His army. And they carried away very much spoil. ¹⁴Then they defeated all the cities around Gerar, for the fear of the LORD came upon them; and they plundered all the cities, for there was exceedingly much spoil in them. ¹⁵They also attacked the livestock enclosures, and carried off sheep and camels in abundance, and returned to Jerusalem.

CHAPTER **15** ASA REBUILDS THE ALTAR. Now the Spirit of God came upon Azariah the son of Oded. ²And he went out to meet Asa, and said to him: "Hear me, Asa, and all Judah and Benjamin. The LORD *is* with you while you are with Him. If you seek Him, He will be found by you; but if you forsake Him, He will forsake you. ³For a long time Israel *has been* without the true God, without a teaching priest, and without law; ⁴but when in their trouble they turned to the LORD God of Israel, and sought Him, He was found by them. ⁵And in those times *there was* no peace to the one who went out, nor to the one who came in, but great turmoil *was* on all the inhabitants of the lands. ⁶So nation was destroyed by nation, and city by city; for God troubled them with every adversity. ⁷But you, be strong and do not let your hands be weak, for your work shall be rewarded!"

⁸And when Asa heard these words and the prophecy of Oded the prophet, he took courage, and removed the abominable idols from all the land of Judah and Benjamin and from the cities which he had taken in the mountains of Ephraim; and he restored the altar of the LORD that *was* before the vestibule of the LORD. ⁹Then he gathered all Judah and Benjamin, and those who dwelt with

them from Ephraim, Manasseh, and Simeon, for they came over to him in great numbers from Israel when they saw that the LORD his God was with him.

¹⁰So they gathered together at Jerusalem in the third month, in the fifteenth year of the reign of Asa. ¹¹And they offered to the LORD at that time seven hundred bulls and seven thousand sheep from the spoil they had brought. ¹²Then they entered into a covenant to seek the LORD God of their fathers with all their heart and with all their soul; ¹³and whoever would not seek the LORD God of Israel was to be put to death, whether small or great, whether man or woman. ¹⁴Then they took an oath before the LORD with a loud voice, with shouting and trumpets and rams' horns. ¹⁵And all Judah rejoiced at the oath, for they had sworn with all their heart and sought Him with all their soul; and He was found by them, and the LORD gave them rest all around.

¹⁶Also he removed Maachah, the mother of Asa the king, from *being* queen mother, because she had made an obscene image of Asherah; and Asa cut down her obscene image, then crushed and burned *it* by the Brook Kidron. ¹⁷But the high places were not removed from Israel. Nevertheless the heart of Asa was loyal all his days.

¹⁸He also brought into the house of God the things that his father had dedicated and that he himself had dedicated: silver and gold and utensils. ¹⁹And there was no war until the thirty-fifth year of the reign of Asa.

CHAPTER **16** ASA FORGETS GOD. In the thirty-sixth year of the reign of Asa, Baasha king of Israel came up against Judah and built Ramah, that he might let none go out or come in to Asa king of Judah. ²Then Asa brought silver and gold from the treasuries of the house of the LORD and of the king's house, and sent to Ben-Hadad king of Syria, who dwelt in Damascus, saying, ³"*Let there be* a treaty between you and me, as there was between my father and your father. See, I have sent you silver and gold; come, break your treaty with Baasha king of Israel, so that he will withdraw from me."

⁴So Ben-Hadad heeded King Asa, and sent the captains of his armies against the cities of Israel. They attacked Ijon, Dan, Abel Maim, and all the storage cities of Naphtali. ⁵Now it happened, when Baasha heard *it*, that he stopped building Ramah and ceased his work. ⁶Then King Asa took all Judah, and they carried away the stones and timber of Ramah, which Baasha had used for building; and with them he built Geba and Mizpah.

⁷And at that time Hanani the seer came to Asa king of Judah, and said to him: "Because you have relied on the king of Syria, and have not relied on the LORD your God, therefore the army of the king of Syria has escaped from your hand. ⁸Were the Ethiopians and the Lubim not a huge army with very many chariots and horsemen? Yet, because you relied on the LORD, He delivered them into your hand. ⁹For the eyes of the LORD run to and fro throughout the whole earth, to show Himself strong on behalf of *those* whose heart *is* loyal to Him. In this you have done foolishly; therefore from now on you shall have wars." ¹⁰Then Asa was angry with the seer, and put

16:10 Asa was angry with Hanani's message, so he threw the pr[o] in jail. God's truth will not always be welcomed with open arms, especially when it reveals people's sins. But we must speak and liv[e] God's truth, regardless of the consequences.

him in prison, for *he was* enraged at him because of this. And Asa oppressed *some* of the people at that time.

¹¹Note that the acts of Asa, first and last, are indeed written in the book of the kings of Judah and Israel. ¹²And in the thirty-ninth year of his reign, Asa became diseased in his feet, and his malady was severe; yet in his disease he did not seek the LORD, but the physicians.

¹³So Asa rested with his fathers; he died in the forty-first year of his reign. ¹⁴They buried him in his own tomb, which he had made for himself in the City of David; and they laid him in the bed which was filled with spices and various ingredients prepared in a mixture of ointments. They made a very great burning for him.

CHAPTER **17** JEHOSHAPHAT RULES JUDAH. Then Jehoshaphat his son reigned in his place, and strengthened himself against Israel. ²And he placed troops in all the fortified cities of Judah, and set garrisons in the land of Judah and in the cities of Ephraim which Asa his father had taken. ³Now the LORD was with Jehoshaphat, because he walked in the former ways of his father David; he did not seek the Baals, ⁴but sought the God of his father, and walked in His commandments and not according to the acts of Israel. ⁵Therefore the LORD established the kingdom in his hand; and all Judah gave presents to Jehoshaphat, and he had riches and honor in abundance. ⁶And his heart took delight in the ways of the LORD; moreover he removed the high places and wooden images from Judah.

⁷Also in the third year of his reign he sent his leaders, Ben-Hail, Obadiah, Zechariah, Nethanel, and Michaiah, to teach in the cities of Judah. ⁸And with them *he sent* Levites: Shemaiah, Nethaniah, Zebadiah, Asahel, Shemiramoth, Jehonathan, Adonijah, Tobijah, and Tobadonijah—the Levites; and with them Elishama and Jehoram, the priests. ⁹So they taught in Judah, and *had* the Book of the Law of the LORD with them; they went throughout all the cities of Judah and taught the people.

¹⁰And the fear of the LORD fell on all the kingdoms of the lands that *were* around Judah, so that they did not make war against Jehoshaphat. ¹¹Also *some* of the Philistines brought Jehoshaphat presents and silver as tribute; and the Arabians brought him flocks, seven thousand seven hundred rams and seven thousand seven hundred male goats.

¹²So Jehoshaphat became increasingly powerful, and he built fortresses and storage cities in Judah. ¹³He ha[d] much property in the cities of Judah; and the men of war, mighty men of valor, *were* in Jerusalem.

¹⁴These *are* their numbers, according to their fathers houses. Of Judah, the captains of thousands: Adnah t[he] captain, and with him three hundred thousand might[y] men of valor; ¹⁵and next to him *was* Jehohanan the captain, and with him two hundred and eighty thousand ¹⁶and next to him *was* Amasiah the son of Zichri, wh[o] willingly offered himself to the LORD, and with him tw[o]

hundred thousand mighty men of valor. ¹⁷Of Benjamin: Eliada a mighty man of valor, and with him two hundred thousand men armed with bow and shield; ¹⁸and next to him *was* Jehozabad, and with him one hundred and eighty thousand prepared for war. ¹⁹These served the king, besides those the king put in the fortified cities throughout all Judah.

CHAPTER **18** JEHOSHAPHAT AND AHAB. Jehoshaphat had riches and honor in abundance; and by marriage he allied himself with Ahab. ²After some years he went down to *visit* Ahab in Samaria; and Ahab killed sheep and oxen in abundance for him and the people who were with him, and persuaded him to go up *with him* to Ramoth Gilead. ³So Ahab king of Israel said to Jehoshaphat king of Judah, "Will you go with me *against* Ramoth Gilead?"

And he answered him, "I *am* as you *are*, and my people as your people; *we will be* with you in the war."

⁴Also Jehoshaphat said to the king of Israel, "Please inquire for the word of the LORDtoday."

⁵Then the king of Israel gathered the prophets together, four hundred men, and said to them, "Shall we go to war against Ramoth Gilead, or shall I refrain?"

So they said, "Go up, for God will deliver it into the king's hand."

⁶But Jehoshaphat said, "*Is there* not still a prophet of the LORD here, that we may inquire of Him?"

⁷So the king of Israel said to Jehoshaphat, "*There is* still one man by whom we may inquire of the LORD; but I hate him, because he never prophesies good concerning me, but always evil. He is Micaiah the son of Imla."

And Jehoshaphat said, "Let not the king say such things!"

⁸Then the king of Israel called one *of his* officers and said, "Bring Micaiah the son of Imla quickly!"

⁹The king of Israel and Jehoshaphat king of Judah, clothed in *their* robes, sat each on his throne; and they sat at a threshing floor at the entrance of the gate of Samaria; and all the prophets prophesied before them. ¹⁰Now Zedekiah the son of Chenaanah had made horns of iron for himself; and he said, "Thus says the LORD: 'With these you shall gore the Syrians until they are destroyed.' "

¹¹And all the prophets prophesied so, saying, "Go up to Ramoth Gilead and prosper, for the LORD will deliver *it* into the king's hand."

¹²Then the messenger who had gone to call Micaiah spoke to him, saying, "Now listen, the words of the prophets with one accord encourage the king. Therefore please let your word be like *the word of* one of them, and speak encouragement."

¹³And Micaiah said, "*As* the LORD lives, whatever my God says, that I will speak."

¹⁴Then he came to the king; and the king said to him, "Micaiah, shall we go to war against Ramoth Gilead, or shall I refrain?"

And he said, "Go and prosper, and they shall be delivered into your hand!"

¹⁵So the king said to him, "How many times shall I make you swear that you tell me nothing but the truth in the name of the LORD?"

¹⁶Then he said, "I saw all Israel scattered on the mountains, as sheep that have no shepherd.

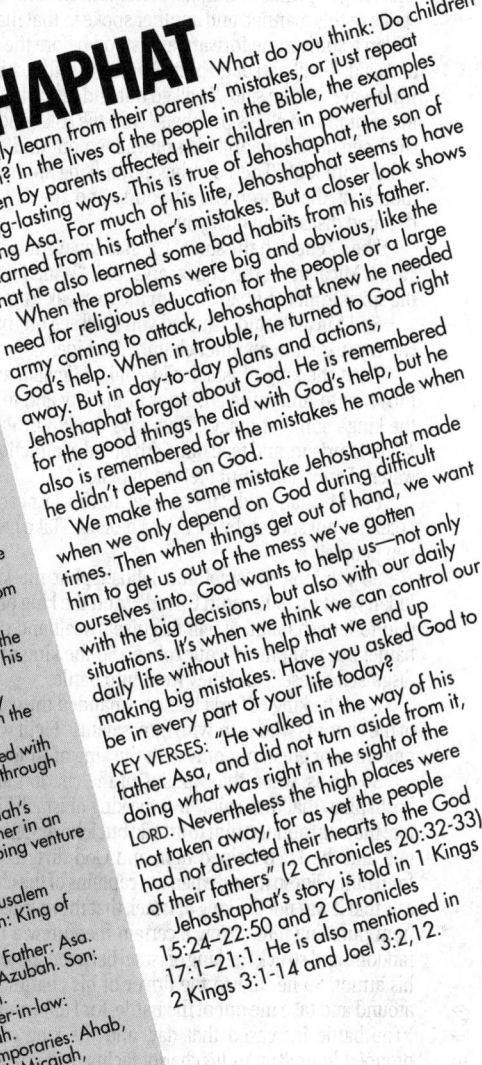

JEHOSHAPHAT

What do you think: Do children usually learn from their parents' mistakes, or just repeat them? In the lives of the people in the Bible, the examples given by parents affected their children in powerful and long-lasting ways. This is true of Jehoshaphat, the son of King Asa. For much of his life, Jehoshaphat seems to have learned from his father's mistakes. But a closer look shows that he also learned some bad habits from his father.

When the problems were big and obvious, like the need for religious education for the people or a large army coming to attack, Jehoshaphat knew he needed God's help. When in trouble, he turned to God right away. But in day-to-day plans and actions, Jehoshaphat forgot about God. He is remembered for the good things he did with God's help, but he also is remembered for the mistakes he made when he didn't depend on God.

We make the same mistake Jehoshaphat made when we only depend on God during difficult times. Then when things get out of hand, we want him to get us out of the mess we've gotten ourselves into. God wants to help us—not only with the big decisions, but also with our daily life. It's when we think that we can control our daily life without his help that we end up making big mistakes. Have you asked God to be in every part of your life today?

KEY VERSES: "He walked in the way of his father Asa, and did not turn aside from it, doing what was right in the sight of the LORD. Nevertheless the high places were not taken away, for as yet the people had not directed their hearts to the God of their fathers" (2 Chronicles 20:32-33). Jehoshaphat's story is told in 1 Kings 15:24–22:50 and 2 Chronicles 17:1–21:1. He is also mentioned in 2 Kings 3:1-14 and Joel 3:2,12.

UPS:
• A bold follower of God, he reminded the people of the early years with his father, Asa
• Carried out a national program of religious education
• Had many military victories
• Developed an extensive legal structure throughout the kingdom

DOWNS:
• Failed to recognize the long-term results of his decisions
• Did not completely destroy idolatry in the land
• Became entangled with evil King Ahab through alliances
• Became Ahaziah's business partner in an ill-fated shipping venture

STATS:
• Where: Jerusalem
• Occupation: King of Judah
• Relatives: Father: Asa. Mother: Azubah. Son: Jehoram. Daughter-in-law: Athaliah.
• Contemporaries: Ahab, Jezebel, Micaiah, Ahaziah, Jehu

DISGUISED

18:22 Micaiah prophesied death for King Ahab (18:16,27), so Ahab disguised himself to fool the enemy. Apparently the disguise worked, but that didn't change the prophecy. A random Syrian arrow found a crack in his armor and killed him. God's will is always fulfilled despite the defenses people try to erect. God can use anything, even an error, to bring his will to pass. This is good news for God's followers because we can trust him to work his plans and keep his promises, no matter what the circumstances.

And the LORD said, 'These have no master. Let each return to his house in peace.' "

¹⁷And the king of Israel said to Jehoshaphat, "Did I not tell you he would not prophesy good concerning me, but evil?"

¹⁸Then *Micaiah* said, "Therefore hear the word of the LORD: I saw the LORD sitting on His throne, and all the host of heaven standing on His right hand and His left. ¹⁹And the LORD said, 'Who will persuade Ahab king of Israel to go up, that he may fall at Ramoth Gilead?' So one spoke in this manner, and another spoke in that manner. ²⁰Then a spirit came forward and stood before the LORD, and said, 'I will persuade him.' The LORD said to him, 'In what way?' ²¹So he said, 'I will go out and be a lying spirit in the mouth of all his prophets.' And *the* LORD said, 'You shall persuade *him* and also prevail; go out and do so.' ²²Therefore look! The LORD has put a lying spirit in the mouth of these prophets of yours, and the LORD has declared disaster against you."

²³Then Zedekiah the son of Chenaanah went near and struck Micaiah on the cheek, and said, "Which way did the spirit from the LORD go from me to speak to you?"

²⁴And Micaiah said, "Indeed you shall see on that day when you go into an inner chamber to hide!"

²⁵Then the king of Israel said, "Take Micaiah, and return him to Amon the governor of the city and to Joash the king's son; ²⁶and say, 'Thus says the king: "Put this *fellow* in prison, and feed him with bread of affliction and water of affliction, until I return in peace." ' "

²⁷But Micaiah said, "If you ever return in peace, the LORD has not spoken by me." And he said, "Take heed, all you people!"

²⁸So the king of Israel and Jehoshaphat the king of Judah went up to Ramoth Gilead. ²⁹And the king of Israel said to Jehoshaphat, "I will disguise myself and go into battle; but you put on your robes." So the king of Israel disguised himself, and they went into battle.

³⁰Now the king of Syria had commanded the captains of the chariots who *were* with him, saying, "Fight with no one small or great, but only with the king of Israel."

³¹So it was, when the captains of the chariots saw Jehoshaphat, that they said, "It *is* the king of Israel!" Therefore they surrounded him to attack; but Jehoshaphat cried out, and the LORD helped him, and God diverted them from him. ³²For so it was, when the captains of the chariots saw that it was not the king of Israel, that they turned back from pursuing him. ³³Now a certain man drew a bow at random, and struck the king of Israel between the joints of his armor. So he said to the driver of his chariot, "Turn around and take me out of the battle, for I am wounded." ³⁴The battle increased that day, and the king of Israel propped *himself* up in *his* chariot facing the Syrians until evening; and about the time of sunset he died.

CHAPTER **19** A MESSAGE FOR JEHOSHAPHAT.

Then Jehoshaphat the king of Judah returned safely to his house in Jerusalem. ²And Jehu the son of Hanani the seer went out to meet him, and said to King Jehoshaphat, "Should you help the wicked and love those who hate the LORD? Therefore the wrath of the LORD *is* upon you. ³Nevertheless good things are found in you, in that you have removed the wooden images from the land, and have prepared your heart to seek God."

⁴So Jehoshaphat dwelt at Jerusalem; and he went out again among the people from Beersheba to the mountains of Ephraim, and brought them back to the LORD God of their fathers. ⁵Then he set judges in the land

ACCOUNTABLE

19:5-10 Jehoshaphat delegated some of the responsibilities for r and judging the people, but he warned his appointees that they wer accountable to God for the standards they used to judge others. Jehoshaphat's advice is helpful for all leaders: (1) allow God to help be just (19:6); (2) be impartial (19:7); (3) be honest (19:9); (4) ac out of fear of God, not men (19:9).

throughout all the fortified cities of Judah, city by city, ⁶and said to the judges, "Take heed to what you are doing, for you do not judge for man but for the LORD, who *is* with you in the judgment. ⁷Now therefore, let the fear of the LORD be upon you; take care and do *it*, for *there is* no iniquity with the LORD our God, no partiality, nor taking of bribes."

⁸Moreover in Jerusalem, for the judgment of the LORD and for controversies, Jehoshaphat appointed some of the Levites and priests, and some of the chief fathers of Israel, when they returned to Jerusalem. ⁹And he commanded them, saying, "Thus you shall act in the fear of the LORD, faithfully and with a loyal heart: ¹⁰Whatever case comes to you from your brethren who dwell in their cities, whether of bloodshed or offenses against law or commandment, against statutes or ordinances, you shall warn them, lest they trespass against the LORD and wrath come upon you and your brethren. Do this, and you will not be guilty. ¹¹And take notice: Amariah the chief priest *is* over you in all matters of the LORD; and Zebadiah the son of Ishmael, the ruler of the house of Judah, for all the king's matters; also the Levites *will be* officials before you. Behave courageously, and the LORD will be with the good."

BATTLES

20:15 As the enemy bore down on Judah, God spoke through Ja "Do not be afraid nor dismayed . . . for the battle *is* not yours, but God's." We may not fight an enemy army, but every day we battle temptation, pressure, and "rulers of the darkness of this age" (Eph 6:12) who want us to rebel against God. We must remember that, believers, we have God's Spirit in us. If we ask for God's help when face struggles, he will fight for us. And God always triumphs.

How do we let God fight for us? (1) By realizing the battle is n but God's; (2) by recognizing human limitations and allowing God strength and power to work through our fears and weaknesses; (3 making sure our battle is for God and not just our own selfish desi and (4) by asking God for help.

CHAPTER **20** **GOD GIVES A VICTORY.** It happened after this *that* the people of Moab with the people of Ammon, and *others* with them besides the Ammonites, came to battle against Jehoshaphat. ²Then some came and told Jehoshaphat, saying, "A great multitude is coming against you from beyond the sea, from Syria; and they are in Hazazon Tamar" (which *is* En Gedi). ³And Jehoshaphat feared, and set himself to seek the LORD, and proclaimed a fast throughout all Judah. ⁴So Judah gathered together to ask *help* from the LORD; and from all the cities of Judah they came to seek the LORD.

⁵Then Jehoshaphat stood in the assembly of Judah and Jerusalem, in the house of the LORD, before the new court, ⁶and said: "O LORD God of our fathers, *are* You not God in heaven, and do You *not* rule over all the kingdoms of the nations, and in Your hand *is there not* power and might, so that no one is able to withstand You? ⁷*Are* You not our God, *who* drove out the inhabitants of this land before Your people Israel, and gave it to the descendants of Abraham Your friend forever? ⁸And they dwell in it, and have built You a sanctuary in it for Your name, saying, ⁹'If disaster comes upon us—sword, judgment, pestilence, or famine—we will stand before this temple and in Your presence (for Your name *is* in this temple), and cry out to You in our affliction, and You will hear and save.' ¹⁰And now, here are the people of Ammon, Moab, and Mount Seir—whom You would not let Israel invade when they came out of the land of Egypt, but they turned from them and did not destroy them— ¹¹here they are, rewarding us by coming to throw us out of Your possession which You have given us to inherit. ¹²O our God, will You not judge them? For we have no power against this great multitude that is coming against us; nor do we know what to do, but our eyes *are* upon You."

¹³Now all Judah, with their little ones, their wives, and their children, stood before the LORD.

¹⁴Then the Spirit of the LORD came upon Jahaziel the son of Zechariah, the son of Benaiah, the son of Jeiel, the son of Mattaniah, a Levite of the sons of Asaph, in the midst of the assembly. ¹⁵And he said, "Listen, all you of Judah and you inhabitants of Jerusalem, and you, King Jehoshaphat! Thus says the LORD to you: 'Do not be afraid nor dismayed because of this great multitude, for the battle *is* not yours, but God's. ¹⁶Tomorrow go down against them. They will surely come up by the Ascent of Ziz, and you will find them at the end of the brook before the Wilderness of Jeruel. ¹⁷You will not *need* to fight in this *battle*. Position yourselves, stand still and see the salvation of the LORD, who is with you, O Judah and Jerusalem!' Do not fear or be dismayed; tomorrow go out against them, for the LORD *is* with you."

¹⁸And Jehoshaphat bowed his head with *his* face to the ground, and all Judah and the inhabitants of Jerusalem bowed before the LORD, worshiping the LORD. ¹⁹Then the Levites of the children of the Kohathites and of the children of the Korahites stood up to praise the LORD God of Israel with voices loud and high.

²⁰So they rose early in the morning and went out into the Wilderness of Tekoa; and as they went out, Jehoshaphat stood and said, "Hear me, O Judah and you inhabitants of Jerusalem: Believe in the LORD your God, and you shall be established; believe His prophets, and you shall prosper." ²¹And when he had consulted with the people, he appointed those who should sing to the LORD, and who should praise the beauty of holiness, as they went out before the army and were saying:

"Praise the LORD,
For His mercy *endures* forever."

I like the people in my church, but sometimes the worship service seems boring and confusing. Are all of the songs, readings, and rituals necessary?

A family decided to get a new refrigerator, and so they bought one that was the top of the line. Then they filled it with groceries. It was Friday, and they had a trip out of town planned, so they left. When they returned on Sunday, they opened the refrigerator door and were overwhelmed by a terrible odor. All of the food had spoiled!

There had been no power failure and the refrigerator wasn't broken. Instead, they had forgotten to plug it in! Their brand-new appliance, stuffed with food, was useless (and smelly) without being plugged into the power.

We need to be plugged in too, and worship is one way to do this. In worship we recognize God as the one who is in control and who has the power to change our circumstances and life. (See 2 Chronicles 20:20-22.)

Jehoshaphat discovered this fact very graphically as he sent the worshipers out with his army. As the worshipers were singing, God miraculously provided a victory!

Worship takes many forms. Most of the songs and readings come right from Scripture. If you concentrate on the meaning behind what is being sung or read, you will see that the words communicate very important facts about God.

When we sing a song many times, we will memorize it more easily. You can probably sing every word of your favorite popular songs. Music helps us remember.

Another purpose of worship is to encourage us to grow in our faith. With all of the negative influences around us, we need to be filled with courage to go out to face the world. This courage can help us live the Christian life when it seems that there is a war going on around us.

Worship is also the time for us to praise God for who he is and to thank him for all he has done. Being in church with our brothers and sisters in Christ is like a family reunion—worshiping together.

Ephesians 5:19 was written during a time when Christians were put in prison for their faith. It says that believers should always be "speaking to one another in psalms and hymns and spiritual songs, singing and making melody . . . to the Lord." By doing what this verse talks about, believers were able to encourage each other as they reminded themselves of the faithfulness, goodness, and strength of God.

²²Now when they began to sing and to praise, the LORD set ambushes against the people of Ammon, Moab, and Mount Seir, who had come against Judah; and they were defeated. ²³For the people of Ammon and Moab stood up against the inhabitants of Mount Seir to utterly kill and destroy *them*. And when they had made an end of the inhabitants of Seir, they helped to destroy one another.

²⁴So when Judah came to a place overlooking the wilderness, they looked toward the multitude; and there *were* their dead bodies, fallen on the earth. No one had escaped.

²⁵When Jehoshaphat and his people came to take away their spoil, they found among them an abundance of valuables on the dead bodies, and precious jewelry, which they stripped off for themselves, more than they could carry away; and they were three days gathering the spoil because there was so much. ²⁶And on the fourth day they assembled in the Valley of Berachah, for there they blessed the LORD; therefore the name of that place was called The Valley of Berachah until this day. ²⁷Then they returned, every man of Judah and Jerusalem, with Jehoshaphat in front of them, to go back to Jerusalem with joy, for the LORD had made them rejoice over their enemies. ²⁸So they came to Jerusalem, with stringed instruments and harps and trumpets, to the house of the LORD. ²⁹And the fear of God was on all the kingdoms of *those* countries when they heard that the LORD had fought against the enemies of Israel. ³⁰Then the realm of Jehoshaphat was quiet, for his God gave him rest all around.

³¹So Jehoshaphat was king over Judah. *He was* thirty-five years old when he became king, and he reigned twenty-five years in Jerusalem. His mother's name *was* Azubah the daughter of Shilhi. ³²And he walked in the way of his father Asa, and did not turn aside from it, doing *what was* right in the sight of the LORD. ³³Nevertheless the high places were not taken away, for as yet the people had not directed their hearts to the God of their fathers.

³⁴Now the rest of the acts of Jehoshaphat, first and last, indeed they *are* written in the book of Jehu the son of Hanani, which *is* mentioned in the book of the kings of Israel.

³⁵After this Jehoshaphat king of Judah allied himself with Ahaziah king of Israel, who acted very wickedly. ³⁶And he allied himself with him to make ships to go to Tarshish, and they made the ships in Ezion Geber. ³⁷But Eliezer the son of Dodavah of Mareshah prophesied against Jehoshaphat, saying, "Because you have allied yourself with Ahaziah, the LORD has destroyed your works." Then the ships were wrecked, so that they were not able to go to Tarshish.

CHAPTER 21 JEHORAM DISPLEASES GOD.

And Jehoshaphat rested with his fathers, and was buried with his fathers in the City of David. Then Jehoram his son reigned in his place. ²He had brothers, the sons of Jehoshaphat: Azariah, Jehiel, Zechariah, Azaryahu, Michael, and Shephatiah; all these *were* the sons of Jehoshaphat king of Israel. ³Their father gave them great gifts of silver and gold and precious things, with fortified cities in Judah; but he gave the kingdom to Jehoram, because he *was* the firstborn.

⁴Now when Jehoram was established over the kingdom of his father, he strengthened himself and killed all his brothers with the sword, and also *others* of the princes of Israel.

⁵Jehoram *was* thirty-two years old when he became king, and he reigned eight years in Jerusalem. ⁶And he walked in the way of the kings of Israel, just as the house of Ahab had done, for he had the daughter of Ahab as a wife; and he did evil in the sight of the LORD. ⁷Yet the LORD would not destroy the house of David, because of the covenant that He had made with David, and since He had promised to give a lamp to him and to his sons forever.

⁸In his days Edom revolted against Judah's authority, and made a king over themselves. ⁹So Jehoram went out with his officers, and all his chariots with him. And he rose by night and attacked the Edomites who had surrounded him and the captains of the chariots. ¹⁰Thus Edom has been in revolt against Judah's authority to this day. At that time Libnah revolted against his rule, because he had forsaken the LORD God of his fathers. ¹¹Moreover he made high places in the mountains of Judah, and caused the inhabitants of Jerusalem to commit harlotry, and led Judah astray.

MADE RIGHT

21:8-11 Jehoram's reign was marked by sin and cruelty. He ma[rried a] woman who worshiped idols; he killed his six brothers; he allowed [and] even promoted idol worship. Yet he was not killed in battle or by treachery—he died by a lingering and painful disease (21:18-19)[.] because punishment is not immediate or dramatic does not mean [God is] indifferent to our sin. We cannot ignore God's laws and think we a[re] immune from the consequences of our sin. There can be no healin[g or] deliverance for those who rebel against God until their relationship [with] God is made right.

¹²And a letter came to him from Elijah the prophet, saying,

> Thus says the LORD God of your father David: Because you have not walked in the ways of Jehoshaphat your father, or in the ways of Asa king of Judah, ¹³but have walked in the way of the kings of Israel, and have made Judah and the inhabitants of Jerusalem to play the harlot like the harlotry of the house of Ahab, and also have killed your brothers, those of your father's household, *who were* better than yourself, ¹⁴behold, the LORD will strike your people with a serious affliction—your children, your wives, and all your possessions; ¹⁵and you *will become* very sick with a disease of your intestines, until your intestines come out by reason of the sickness, day by day.

¹⁶Moreover the LORD stirred up against Jehoram the spirit of the Philistines and the Arabians who *were* nea[r] the Ethiopians. ¹⁷And they came up into Judah and invaded it, and carried away all the possessions that were

found in the king's house, and also his sons and his wives, so that there was not a son left to him except Jehoahaz, the youngest of his sons.

¹⁸After all this the LORD struck him in his intestines with an incurable disease. ¹⁹Then it happened in the course of time, after the end of two years, that his intestines came out because of his sickness; so he died in severe pain. And his people made no burning for him, like the burning for his fathers.

²⁰He was thirty-two years old when he became king. He reigned in Jerusalem eight years and, to no one's sorrow, departed. However they buried him in the City of David, but not in the tombs of the kings.

CHAPTER 22 AHAZIAH GETS EVIL ADVICE. Then

the inhabitants of Jerusalem made Ahaziah his youngest son king in his place, for the raiders who came with the Arabians into the camp had killed all the older *sons.* So Ahaziah the son of Jehoram, king of Judah, reigned. ²Ahaziah *was* forty-two years old when he became king, and he reigned one year in Jerusalem. His mother's name *was* Athaliah the granddaughter of Omri. ³He also walked in the ways of the house of Ahab, for his mother advised him to do wickedly. ⁴Therefore he did evil in the sight of the LORD, like the house of Ahab; for they were his counselors after the death of his father, to his destruction. ⁵He also followed their advice, and went with Jehoram the son of Ahab king of Israel to war against Hazael king of Syria at Ramoth Gilead; and the Syrians wounded Joram. ⁶Then he returned to Jezreel to recover from the wounds which he had received at Ramah, when he fought against Hazael king of Syria. And Azariah the son of Jehoram, king of Judah, went down to see Jehoram the son of Ahab in Jezreel, because he was sick.

⁷His going to Joram was God's occasion for Ahaziah's downfall; for when he arrived, he went out with Jehoram against Jehu the son of Nimshi, whom the LORD had anointed to cut off the house of Ahab. ⁸And it happened, when Jehu was executing judgment on the house of Ahab, and found the princes of Judah and the sons of Ahaziah's brothers who served Ahaziah, that he killed them. ⁹Then he searched for Ahaziah; and they caught him (he was hiding in Samaria), and brought him to Jehu. When they had killed him, they buried him, "because," they said, "he is the son of Jehoshaphat, who sought the LORD with all his heart."

So the house of Ahaziah had no one to assume power over the kingdom.

¹⁰Now when Athaliah the mother of Ahaziah saw that her son was dead, she arose and destroyed all the royal heirs of the house of Judah. ¹¹But Jehoshabeath, the daughter of the king, took Joash the son of Ahaziah, and stole him away from among the king's sons who were being murdered, and put him and his nurse in a bedroom. So Jehoshabeath, the daughter of King Jehoram, the wife of Jehoiada the priest (for she was the sister of Ahaziah), hid him from Athaliah so that she did not kill him. ¹²And he was hidden with them in the house of God for six years, while Athaliah reigned over the land.

CHAPTER 23 YOUNG JOASH BECOMES KING. In

the seventh year Jehoiada strengthened himself, *and made a* covenant with the captains of hundreds: Azariah the son of Jeroham, Ishmael the son of Jehohanan, Azariah the son of Obed, Maaseiah the son of Adaiah, and Elishaphat the son of Zichri. ²And they went throughout Judah and gathered the Levites from all the cities of Judah, and the chief fathers of Israel, and they came to Jerusalem.

³Then all the assembly made a covenant with the king in the house of God. And he said to them, "Behold, the king's son shall reign, as the LORD has said of the sons of David. ⁴This *is* what you shall do: One-third of you entering on the Sabbath, of the priests and the Levites, *shall be* keeping watch over the doors; ⁵one-third *shall be* at the king's house; and one-third at the Gate of the Foundation. All the people *shall be* in the courts of the house of the LORD. ⁶But let no one come into the house of the LORD

► EVALUATION

22:4-5 Although it is good to seek advice, we must also carefully weigh what is said. Ahaziah had advisers, but they were wicked and led him to ruin. When you seek advice, listen carefully and use God's Word to "test all things; hold fast what is good" (1 Thessalonians 5:21).

except the priests and those of the Levites who serve. They may go in, for they *are* holy; but all the people shall keep the watch of the LORD. ⁷And the Levites shall surround the king on all sides, every man with his weapons in his hand; and whoever comes into the house, let him be put to death. You are to be with the king when he comes in and when he goes out."

⁸So the Levites and all Judah did according to all that Jehoiada the priest commanded. And each man took his men who were to be on duty on the Sabbath, with those who were going *off duty* on the Sabbath; for Jehoiada the priest had not dismissed the divisions. ⁹And Jehoiada the priest gave to the captains of hundreds the spears and the large and small shields which *had belonged* to King David, that *were* in the temple of God. ¹⁰Then he set all the people, every man with his weapon in his hand, from the right side of the temple to the left side of the temple, along by the altar and by the temple, all around the king. ¹¹And they brought out the king's son, put the crown on him, *gave him* the Testimony, and made him king. Then Jehoiada and his sons anointed him, and said, "*Long* live the king!"

¹²Now when Athaliah heard the noise of the people running and praising the king, she came to the people *in* the temple of the LORD. ¹³*When* she looked, there was the king standing by his pillar at the entrance; and the leaders and the trumpeters *were* by the king. All the people of the land were rejoicing and blowing trumpets, also the

► COURAGE

23:1 Although it could have cost him his life, this priest gathered up his courage and did what was right, restoring the temple worship and anointing the new king. There are times when we must correct a wrong or speak out for what is right. When such a situation arises, gather up your courage and take action.

singers with musical instruments, and those who led in praise. So Athaliah tore her clothes and said, "Treason! Treason!"

14And Jehoiada the priest brought out the captains of hundreds who were set over the army, and said to them, "Take her outside under guard, and slay with the sword whoever follows her." For the priest had said, "Do not kill her in the house of the LORD."

15So they seized her; and she went by way of the entrance of the Horse Gate *into* the king's house, and they killed her there.

16Then Jehoiada made a covenant between himself, the people, and the king, that they should be the LORD's people. 17And all the people went to the temple of Baal, and tore it down. They broke in pieces its altars and images, and killed Mattan the priest of Baal before the altars. 18Also Jehoiada appointed the oversight of the house of the LORD to the hand of the priests, the Levites, whom David had assigned in the house of the LORD, to offer the burnt offerings of the LORD, as *it is* written in the Law of Moses, with rejoicing and with singing, *as it was established* by David. 19And he set the gatekeepers at the gates of the house of the LORD, so that no one *who was* in any way unclean should enter.

20Then he took the captains of hundreds, the nobles, the governors of the people, and all the people of the land, and brought the king down from the house of the LORD; and they went through the Upper Gate to the king's house, and set the king on the throne of the kingdom. 21So all the people of the land rejoiced; and the city was quiet, for they had slain Athaliah with the sword.

CHAPTER 24 JOASH REPAIRS THE TEMPLE. Joash *was* seven years old when he became king, and he reigned forty years in Jerusalem. His mother's name *was* Zibiah of Beersheba. 2Joash did *what was* right in the sight of the LORD all the days of Jehoiada the priest. 3And Jehoiada took two wives for him, and he had sons and daughters.

4Now it happened after this *that* Joash set his heart on repairing the house of the LORD. 5Then he gathered the priests and the Levites, and said to them, "Go out to the cities of Judah, and gather from all Israel money to repair the house of your God from year to year, and see that you do it quickly."

However the Levites did not do it quickly. 6So the king called Jehoiada the chief *priest,* and said to him, "Why have you not required the Levites to bring in from Judah and from Jerusalem the collection, *according to the commandment* of Moses the servant of the LORD and of the assembly of Israel, for the tabernacle of witness?" 7For the sons of Athaliah, that wicked woman, had broken into the house of God, and had also presented all the dedicated things of the house of the LORD to the Baals.

8Then at the king's command they made a chest, and set it outside at the gate of the house of the LORD. 9And they made a proclamation throughout Judah and Jerusalem to bring to the LORD the collection *that* Moses the servant of God *had imposed* on Israel in the wilderness. 10Then all the leaders and all the people rejoiced, brought

their contributions, and put *them* into the chest until all had given. 11So it was, at that time, when the chest was brought to the king's official by the hand of the Levites, and when they saw that *there was* much money, that the king's scribe and the high priest's officer came and emptied the chest, and took it and returned it to its place. Thus they did day by day, and gathered money in abundance.

12The king and Jehoiada gave it to those who did the work of the service of the house of the LORD; and they hired masons and carpenters to repair the house of the LORD, and also those who worked in iron and bronze to restore the house of the LORD. 13So the workmen labored, and the work was completed by them; they restored the house of God to its original condition and reinforced it. 14When they had finished, they brought the rest of the money before the king and Jehoiada; they made from it articles for the house of the LORD, articles for serving and offering, spoons and vessels of gold and silver. And they offered burnt offerings in the house of the LORD continually all the days of Jehoiada.

15But Jehoiada grew old and was full of days, and he died; *he was* one hundred and thirty years old when he died. 16And they buried him in the City of David among the kings, because he had done good in Israel, both toward God and His house.

17Now after the death of Jehoiada the leaders of Judah came and bowed down to the king. And the king listened to them. 18Therefore they left the house of the LORD God of their fathers, and served wooden images and idols; and wrath came upon Judah and Jerusalem because of their trespass. 19Yet He sent prophets to them, to bring them back to the LORD; and they testified against them, but they would not listen.

20Then the Spirit of God came upon Zechariah the son of Jehoiada the priest, who stood above the people, and said to them, "Thus says God: 'Why do you transgress the commandments of the LORD, so that you cannot prosper? Because you have forsaken the LORD, He also has forsaken you.' " 21So they conspired against him, and at the command of the king they stoned him with stones in the court of the house of the LORD. 22Thus Joash the king did not remember the kindness which Jehoiada his father had done to him, but killed his son; and as he died, he said, "The LORD look on *it,* and repay!"

²³So it happened in the spring of the year *that* the army of Syria came up against him; and they came to Judah and Jerusalem, and destroyed all the leaders of the people from among the people, and sent all their spoil to the king of Damascus. ²⁴For the army of the Syrians came with a small company of men; but the LORD delivered a very great army into their hand, because they had forsaken the LORD God of their fathers. So they executed judgment against Joash. ²⁵And when they had withdrawn from him (for they left him severely wounded), his own servants conspired against him because of the blood of the sons of Jehoiada the priest, and killed him on his bed. So he died. And they buried him in the City of David, but they did not bury him in the tombs of the kings.

²⁶These are the ones who conspired against him: Zabad the son of Shimeath the Ammonitess, and Jehozabad the son of Shimrith the Moabitess. ²⁷Now *concerning* his sons, and the many oracles about him, and the repairing of the house of God, indeed they *are* written in the annals of the book of the kings. Then Amaziah his son reigned in his place.

CHAPTER **25**

AMAZIAH DOES GOOD AND EVIL.

Amaziah *was* twenty-five years old *when* he became king, and he reigned twenty-nine years in Jerusalem. His mother's name *was* Jehoaddan of Jerusalem. ²And he did *what was* right in the sight of the LORD, but not with a loyal heart.

³Now it happened, as soon as the kingdom was established for him, that he executed his servants who had murdered his father the king. ⁴However he did not execute their children, but *did* as *it is* written in the Law in the Book of Moses, where the LORD commanded, saying, "The fathers shall not be put to death for their children, nor shall the children be put to death for their fathers; but a person shall die for his own sin."

⁵Moreover Amaziah gathered Judah together and set over them captains of thousands and captains of hundreds, according to *their* fathers' houses, throughout all Judah and Benjamin; and he numbered them from twenty years old and above, and found them to be three hundred thousand choice *men, able* to go to war, who could handle spear and shield. ⁶He also

hired one hundred thousand mighty men of valor from Israel for one hundred talents of silver. ⁷But a man of God came to him, saying, "O king, do not let the army of Israel go with you, for the LORD *is* not with Israel—*not with* any of the children of Ephraim. ⁸But if you go, be gone! Be strong in battle! *Even so,* God shall make you fall before the enemy; for God has power to help and to overthrow."

⁹Then Amaziah said to the man of God, "But what *shall we* do about the hundred talents which I have given to the troops of Israel?"

And the man of God answered, "The LORD is able to give you much more than this." ¹⁰So Amaziah discharged the troops that had come to him from Ephraim, to go back home. Therefore their anger was greatly aroused against Judah, and they returned home in great anger.

¹¹Then Amaziah strengthened himself, and leading his

JOASH

All parents want their children to make the right decisions. But to do this, children first must learn to make their own decisions. The bad choices we make on our own can be our best teachers in learning to make right choices. Children don't develop the skills for wise decision making if parents decide everything for them. King Joash had this problem, in an unusual way.

Joash wasn't raised by his parents—they had been killed. An aunt and uncle protected and raised the young prince. When Joash became king at age seven, his uncle Jehoiada made most of the decisions for him. Jehoiada was a good man, but he never taught Joash what he needed to know to be a good king. After Jehoiada died, it only took Joash a short time to make a mess of his life and his kingdom.

We prove how well we've learned the lessons we need to learn when we're on our own.

Even though Joash depended on Jehoiada, it seems he never learned to be dependent on Jehoiada's God. Like many children, Joash's knowledge of God was secondhand. He worshiped his uncle's God instead of having his own relationship with God. Is your relationship with God just part of your family tradition, or is there something real and important between you and him? God wants you to know him personally!

LESSONS: A good and hopeful start can be ruined by an evil end.

Even the best counsel is ineffective if it doesn't help us make wise decisions.

As helpful or hurtful as others may be, we are individually responsible for what we do.

KEY VERSES: "Now after the death of Jehoiada the leaders of Judah came and bowed down to the king. And the king listened to them. Therefore they left the house of the LORD God of their fathers, and served wooden images and idols; and wrath came upon Judah and Jerusalem because of their trespass" (2 Chronicles 24:17-18).

Joash's story is told in 2 Kings 11:1–14:23 and 2 Chronicles 22:11–25:25.

UPS:
• Carried out extensive repairs on the temple
• Was faithful to God as long as Jehoiada was alive

DOWNS:
• Allowed idolatry to continue among his people
• Used the temple treasures to bribe King Hazael of Syria
• Killed Jehoiada's son Zechariah
• Allowed his advisers to lead the people away from God

STATS:
• Where: Jerusalem
• Occupation: King of Judah
• Relatives: Father: Ahaziah. Mother: Zibiah. Grandmother: Athaliah. Aunt: Jehosheba. Uncle: Jehoiada. Son: Amaziah. Cousin: Zechariah.
• Contemporaries: Jehu, Hazael

25:14 After the victory, Amaziah returned and burned incense to idols. We are very susceptible to sin after great victories. It is then that we feel confident. We let our defenses down, and Satan attacks with all sorts of temptations. When you win, watch out. After the mountain peaks come the valleys.

people, he went to the Valley of Salt and killed ten thousand of the people of Seir. [12]Also the children of Judah took captive ten thousand alive, brought them to the top of the rock, and cast them down from the top of the rock, so that they all were dashed in pieces.

[13]But as for the soldiers of the army which Amaziah had

discharged, so that they would not go with him to battle, they raided the cities of Judah from Samaria to Beth Horon, killed three thousand in them, and took much spoil.

[14]Now it was so, after Amaziah came from the slaughter of the Edomites, that he brought the gods of the people of Seir, set them up *to be* his gods, and bowed down before them and burned incense to them. [15]Therefore the anger of the LORD was aroused against Amaziah, and He sent him a prophet who said to him, "Why have you sought the gods of the people, which could not rescue their own people from your hand?"

26:15-16 After God gave Uzziah great blessings and power, he became proud and corrupt. It is true that "pride *goes* before destruction" (Proverbs 16:18). If God has given you money, influence, popularity, and power, be thankful and careful. God hates pride. Check your attitudes and remember to give God the credit for what you have. Use your gifts in ways that please him.

[16]So it was, as he talked with him, that *the king* said to him, "Have we made you the king's counselor? Cease! Why should you be killed?"

Then the prophet ceased, and said, "I know that God has determined to destroy you, because you have done this and have not heeded my advice."

[17]Now Amaziah king of Judah asked advice and sent to Joash the son of Jehoahaz, the son of Jehu, king of Israel, saying, "Come, let us face one another *in battle*."

[18]And Joash king of Israel sent to Amaziah king of Judah, saying, "The thistle that *was* in Lebanon sent to the cedar that was in Lebanon, saying, 'Give your daughter to my son as wife'; and a wild beast that *was* in Lebanon passed by and trampled the thistle. [19]Indeed you say that you have defeated the Edomites, and your heart is lifted up to boast. Stay at home now; why should you meddle with trouble, that you should fall—you and Judah with you?"

[20]But Amaziah would not heed, for it *came* from God, that He might give them into the hand *of their enemies*, because they sought the gods of Edom. [21]So Joash king of Israel went out; and he and Amaziah king of Judah faced one another at Beth Shemesh, which *belongs* to Judah. [22]And Judah was defeated by Israel, and every man fled to his tent. [23]Then Joash the king of Israel captured Amaziah king of Judah, the son of Joash, the son of Jehoahaz, at Beth Shemesh; and he brought him to Jerusalem, and

broke down the wall of Jerusalem from the Gate of Ephraim to the Corner Gate—four hundred cubits. [24]And *he took* all the gold and silver, all the articles that were found in the house of God with Obed-Edom, the treasures of the king's house, and hostages, and returned to Samaria.

[25]Amaziah the son of Joash, king of Judah, lived fifteen years after the death of Joash the son of Jehoahaz, king of Israel. [26]Now the rest of the acts of Amaziah, from first to last, indeed *are* they not written in the book of the kings of Judah and Israel? [27]After the time that Amaziah turned away from following the LORD, they made a conspiracy against him in Jerusalem, and he fled to Lachish; but they sent after him to Lachish and killed him there. [28]Then they brought him on horses and buried him with his fathers in the City of Judah.

CHAPTER **26** **A KING TURNS INTO A LEPER.** Now all the people of Judah took Uzziah, who *was* sixteen years old, and made him king instead of his father Amaziah. [2]He built Elath and restored it to Judah, after the king rested with his fathers.

[3]Uzziah *was* sixteen years old when he became king, and he reigned fifty-two years in Jerusalem. His mother's name was Jecholiah of Jerusalem. [4]And he did *what was* right in the sight of the LORD, according to all that his father Amaziah had done. [5]He sought God in the days of Zechariah, who had understanding in the visions of God; and as long as he sought the LORD, God made him prosper.

[6]Now he went out and made war against the Philistines, and broke down the wall of Gath, the wall of Jabneh, and the wall of Ashdod; and he built cities *around* Ashdod and among the Philistines. [7]God helped him against the Philistines, against the Arabians who lived in Gur Baal, and against the Meunites. [8]Also the Ammonites brought tribute to Uzziah. His fame spread as far as the entrance of Egypt, for he became exceedingly strong.

[9]And Uzziah built towers in Jerusalem at the Corner Gate, at the Valley Gate, and at the corner buttress of the wall; then he fortified them. [10]Also he built towers in the desert. He dug many wells, for he had much livestock both in the lowlands and in the plains; *he also had* farmers and vinedressers in the mountains and in Carmel, for he loved the soil.

[11]Moreover Uzziah had an army of fighting men who went out to war by companies, according to the number on their roll as prepared by Jeiel the scribe and Maaseiah the officer, under the hand of Hananiah, *one* of the king's captains. [12]The total number of chief officers of the mighty men of valor *was* two thousand six hundred. [13]And under their authority *was* an army of three hundred and seven thousand five hundred, that made war with mighty power, to help the king against the enemy. [14]Then Uzziah prepared for them, for the entire army, shields, spears, helmets, body armor, bows, and slings *to* cast stones. [15]And he made devices in Jerusalem, invented by skillful men, to be on the towers and the corners, to shoot arrows and large stones. So his fame spread far and wide, for he was marvelously helped till he became strong.

[16]But when he was strong his heart was lifted up, to *his* destruction, for he transgressed against the LORD his God by entering the temple of the LORD to burn incense on the altar of incense. [17]So Azariah the priest went in after him, and with him were eighty priests of the LORD—valiant men. [18]And they withstood King Uzziah, and said to him, "*It is* not for you, Uzziah, to burn incense to the LORD, but for the priests, the sons of Aaron, who are consecrated to burn incense. Get out of the sanctuary, for you have trespassed! You *shall have* no honor from the LORD God."

[19]Then Uzziah became furious; and he *had* a censer in his hand to burn incense. And while he was angry with the priests, leprosy broke out on his forehead, before the priests in the house of the LORD, beside the incense altar. [20]And Azariah the chief priest and all the priests looked at him, and there, on his forehead, he *was* leprous; so they thrust him out of that place. Indeed he also hurried to get out, because the LORD had struck him. [21]King Uzziah was a leper until the day of his death. He dwelt in an isolated house, because he was a leper; for he was cut off from the house of the LORD. Then Jotham his son *was* over the king's house, judging the people of the land.

[22]Now the rest of the acts of Uzziah, from first to last, the prophet Isaiah the son of Amoz wrote. [23]So Uzziah rested with his fathers, and they buried him with his fathers in the field of burial which *belonged* to the kings, for they said, "He is a leper." Then Jotham his son reigned in his place.

CHAPTER 27 **KING JOTHAM FOLLOWS GOD.** Jotham *was* twenty-five years old when he became king, and he reigned sixteen years in Jerusalem. His mother's name *was* Jerushah the daughter of Zadok. [2]And he did *what was* right in the sight of the LORD, according to all that his father Uzziah had done (although he did not enter the temple of the LORD). But still the people acted corruptly.

[3]He built the Upper Gate of the house of the LORD, and he built extensively on the wall of Ophel. [4]Moreover he built cities in the mountains of Judah, and in the forests he built fortresses and towers. [5]He also fought with the king of the Ammonites and defeated them. And the people of Ammon gave him in that year one hundred talents of silver, ten thousand kors of wheat, and ten thousand of barley. The people of Ammon paid this to him in the second and third years also. [6]So Jotham be-

Who	God's instruction	Disobedience	Result
Adam and Eve	Don't eat fruit from the tree of the knowledge of good and evil (Genesis 2:16-17)	Satan tempted them and they ate (Genesis 3:1-6)	They were banished from the Garden of Eden; pain and death were inflicted on all mankind (Genesis 3:24; Romans 5:12)
Nadab and Abihu	Fire for the sacrifice must come from the proper source (Leviticus 6:12-13)	They used profane fire for their sacrifice (Leviticus 10:1)	They were struck dead (Leviticus 10:2)
Moses	"Speak to the rock before their eyes, and it will yield its water" (Numbers 20:8)	He spoke to the rock, but also struck it with his rod (Numbers 20:11)	He was not allowed to enter the Promised Land (Numbers 20:12)
Saul	Completely destroy the evil Amalekites (1 Samuel 15:3)	He spared the king and kept some of the plunder (1 Samuel 15:8-9)	God promised to end his reign (1 Samuel 15:16-26)
Uzza	Only a priest can touch the tabernacle's furnishings and articles (Numbers 4:15)	He touched the ark of the covenant (2 Samuel 6:6)	He died instantly (2 Samuel 6:7)
Uzziah	Only the priests can offer incense in the temple or tabernacle sanctuary (Numbers 16:39-40; 18:7)	He entered the holy place in the temple where only priests were allowed to go (2 Chronicles 26:16-18)	He became a leper (2 Chronicles 26:19)

CAREFUL OBEDIENCE

Solomon and his workers carefully followed God's instructions (4:7). As a result, the temple work was blessed by God and completed in every detail. Here are a few examples of (1) people in the Bible who did not carefully follow one of God's instructions and (2) the resulting consequences. It is not enough to obey God halfheartedly.

ABORTION

"Keep your laws off my body!" scream the words on one placard. A woman in an opposing group carries a sign with a picture of an aborted baby. The caption reads "Who imposed their morality on this little one?" The news programs run story after story, pro-life and pro-abortion forces hold endless debates, and courts and legislatures are all but paralyzed over this most heated social issue: Abortion. **O**bviously, this is not a simple, one-dimensional issue. Besides the central problem of whether or not it is ever right to take the life of an unborn person, there are the related issues of parental consent for girls under 18 who want to have an abortion; legalizing abortion up to a certain age of the fetus (e.g., three months); "harvesting" fetal tissues to help people with diseases like Parkinson's disease; and many more. While these concerns complicate the issue, there is one question that cuts across all of them: who can say what's right? **I**f a person (a judge, a doctor, or a legislator) or a human institution (the Supreme Court or the Senate) makes a decision in this matter, there is always the potential for another person or institution to overturn that decision later on. It has happened countless times. What is needed, it would seem, is a judgment or a ruling from someone or something higher than human opinion. **F**or 2,000 years, Christians have turned to the Bible for just such input. Believing the Bible to be God's own words on matters such as this, Jesus' followers have historically looked to the Scriptures for answers to life's most important—and most difficult—questions. **U**nfortunately, there is no verse of Scripture that says, "Thus saith the Lord: abortion is wrong [or right]." If there was, it would be an open-and-shut case for believers. There are, however, passages that give principles that apply to this difficult topic. In Psalm 139, David praises God for overseeing his life, starting before he was born. David thanks God first for the fantastic way the human body is designed and constructed and then for the fact that every day of his life is "scheduled" and "recorded in [God's] book." **I**f indeed God is the Creator and Designer of human life, it is a logical conclusion that no one should tamper with or destroy that life lightly. If we are God's workmanship, who has the right to tamper with or destroy that workmanship? (Another verse, 2 Chronicles 28:3, shows how evil one king was by saying that he even sacrificed his own children to idols.) Yet, tragically that is what has happened in contemporary society. Abortion has become simply a means of birth control, removing an unwanted complication. For those who take seriously the sanctity of life as an expression of G handiwork, this can be seen only as an abomination, a sin of the most serious kind. As such, we as a society desperately need to cry out to God in repentance and ask his forgiveness for what we have allowed to be done to millions of his little ones. **T**here are a number of related topics (being made in th image of God, sexual morality, etc.) and Scripture passages (e.g., Exodus 21:22-25; Leviticus 24:17-2 Jeremiah 1:4-5) that are closely related to the abortion issue. Concerned Christians should think throu their stand on the rights of the unborn in relation to these other issues and in light of the whole counse of God, not just one passage. (One principle which should always be kept in mind when considering abortion or any other moral problem is forgiveness.) Psalm 139 is a good place to start.

came mighty, because he prepared his ways before the LORD his God.

⁷Now the rest of the acts of Jotham, and all his wars and his ways, indeed they *are* written in the book of the kings of Israel and Judah. ⁸He was twenty-five years old when he became king, and he reigned sixteen years in Jerusalem. ⁹So Jotham rested with his fathers, and they buried him in the City of David. Then Ahaz his son reigned in his place.

CHAPTER 28 AHAZ ANGERS GOD.

Ahaz *was* twenty years old when he became king, and he reigned sixteen years in Jerusalem; and he did not do *what was* right in the sight of the LORD, as his father David *had done*. ²For he walked in the ways of the kings of Israel, and made molded images for the Baals. ³He burned incense in the Valley of the Son of Hinnom, and burned his children in the fire, according to the abominations of the nations whom the LORD had cast out before the children of Israel. ⁴And he sacrificed and burned incense on the high places, on the hills, and under every green tree.

⁵Therefore the LORD his God delivered him into the hand of the king of Syria. They defeated him, and carried away a great multitude of them as captives, and brought *them* to Damascus. Then he was also delivered into the hand of the king of Israel, who defeated him with a great slaughter. ⁶For Pekah the son of Remaliah killed one hundred and twenty thousand in Judah in one day, all valiant men, because they had forsaken the LORD God of their fathers. ⁷Zichri, a mighty man of Ephraim, killed Maaseiah the king's son, Azrikam the officer over the house, and Elkanah *who was* second to the king. ⁸And the children of Israel carried away captive of their brethren two hundred thousand women, sons, and daughters; and they also took away much spoil from them, and brought the spoil to Samaria.

⁹But a prophet of the LORD was there, whose name *was* Oded; and he went out before the army that came to Samaria, and said to them: "Look, because the LORD God of your fathers was angry with Judah, He has delivered them into your hand; but you have killed them in a rage *that* reaches up to heaven. ¹⁰And now you propose to force the children of Judah and Jerusalem to be your male and female slaves; *but are* you not also guilty before the LORD your God? ¹¹Now hear me, therefore, and return the captives, whom you have taken captive from your brethren, for the fierce wrath of the LORD *is* upon you."

¹²Then some of the heads of the children of Ephraim, Azariah the son of Johanan, Berechiah the son of Meshillemoth, Jehizkiah the son of Shallum, and Amasa the son of Hadlai, stood up against those who came from the war, ¹³and said to them, "You shall not bring the captives here, for we *already* have offended the LORD. You intend to add to our sins and to our guilt; for our guilt is great, and *there is* fierce wrath against Israel." ¹⁴So the armed men left the captives and the spoil before the leaders and all the assembly. ¹⁵Then the men who were designated by name rose up and took the captives, and from the spoil they clothed all who were naked among them, dressed them and gave them sandals, gave them food and drink, and

anointed them; and they let all the feeble ones ride on donkeys. So they brought them to their brethren at Jericho, the city of palm trees. Then they returned to Samaria.

¹⁶At the same time King Ahaz sent to the kings of Assyria to help him. ¹⁷For again the Edomites had come, attacked Judah, and carried away captives. ¹⁸The Philistines also had invaded the cities of the lowland and of the South of Judah, and had taken Beth Shemesh, Aijalon, Gederoth, Sochoh with its villages, Timnah with its villages, and Gimzo with its villages; and they dwelt there. ¹⁹For the LORD brought Judah low because of Ahaz king of Israel, for he had encouraged moral decline in Judah and had been continually unfaithful to the LORD. ²⁰Also Tiglath-Pileser king of Assyria came to him and distressed him, and did not assist him. ²¹For Ahaz took part *of the treasures* from the house of the LORD, from the house of the king, and from the leaders, and he gave *it* to the king of Assyria; but he did not help him.

²²Now in the time of his distress King Ahaz became increasingly unfaithful to the LORD. This *is that* King Ahaz. ²³For he sacrificed to the gods of Damascus which had defeated him, saying, "Because the gods of the kings of Syria help them, I will sacrifice to them that they may help me." But they were the ruin of him and of all Israel. ²⁴So Ahaz gathered the articles of the house of God, cut in pieces the articles of the house of God, shut up the doors of the house of the LORD, and made for himself altars in every corner of Jerusalem. ²⁵And in every single city of Judah he made high places to burn incense to other gods, and provoked to anger the LORD God of his fathers.

²⁶Now the rest of his acts and all his ways, from first to last, indeed they *are* written in the book of the kings of Judah and Israel. ²⁷So Ahaz rested with his fathers, and they buried him in the city, in Jerusalem; but they did not bring him into the tombs of the kings of Israel. Then Hezekiah his son reigned in his place.

CHAPTER 29 HEZEKIAH OPENS GOD'S HOUSE.

Hezekiah became king *when he was* twenty-five years old, and he reigned twenty-nine years in Jerusalem. His mother's name *was* Abijah the daughter of Zechariah. ²And he did *what was* right in the sight of the LORD, according to all that his father David had done.

³In the first year of his reign, in the first month, he opened the doors of the house of the LORD and repaired them. ⁴Then he brought in the priests and the Levites, and gathered them in the East Square, ⁵and said to them: "Hear me, Levites! Now sanctify yourselves, sanctify the house of the LORD God of your fathers, and carry out the rubbish from the holy *place*. ⁶For our fathers have trespassed and done evil in the eyes of the LORD our God; they have forsaken Him, have turned their faces away from the dwelling place of the LORD, and turned *their* backs *on Him*. ⁷They have also shut up the doors of the vestibule, put out the lamps, and have not burned incense or offered burnt offerings in the holy *place* to the God of Israel. ⁸Therefore the wrath of the LORD fell upon Judah and Jerusalem, and He has given them up to trouble, to desolation, and to jeering, as you see with

your eyes. ⁹For indeed, because of this our fathers have fallen by the sword; and our sons, our daughters, and our wives *are* in captivity.

¹⁰"Now *it is* in my heart to make a covenant with the LORD God of Israel, that His fierce wrath may turn away from us. ¹¹My sons, do not be negligent now, for the LORD has chosen you to stand before Him, to serve Him, and that you should minister to Him and burn incense."

REACTIVATE

29:11 The Levites, chosen by God to serve in the temple, had been kept from their duties by Ahaz's wickedness (28:24). But Hezekiah called them back into service, reminding them that the Lord had chosen them to minister.

We may not have to face a wicked king, but pressures or responsibilities can render us inactive and ineffective. When you have been given the responsibility to minister, don't neglect your duty. If your Christian service has been rendered inactive, whether by choice or by force, look for the opportunities (and listen to the "Hezekiahs") God will send your way to help you resume your responsibilities. Then, like the Levites, be ready for action (29:12-15).

¹²Then these Levites arose: Mahath the son of Amasai and Joel the son of Azariah, of the sons of the Kohathites; of the sons of Merari, Kish the son of Abdi and Azariah the son of Jehallelel; of the Gershonites, Joah the son of Zimmah and Eden the son of Joah; ¹³of the sons of Elizaphan, Shimri and Jeiel; of the sons of Asaph, Zechariah and Mattaniah; ¹⁴of the sons of Heman, Jehiel and Shimei; and of the sons of Jeduthun, Shemaiah and Uzziel.

¹⁵And they gathered their brethren, sanctified themselves, and went according to the commandment of the king, at the words of the LORD, to cleanse the house of the LORD. ¹⁶Then the priests went into the inner part of the house of the LORD to cleanse *it*, and brought out all the debris that they found in the temple of the LORD to the court of the house of the LORD. And the Levites took *it* out and carried *it* to the Brook Kidron.

¹⁷Now they began to sanctify on the first *day* of the first month, and on the eighth day of the month they came to the vestibule of the LORD. So they sanctified the house of the LORD in eight days, and on the sixteenth day of the first month they finished.

¹⁸Then they went in to King Hezekiah and said, "We have cleansed all the house of the LORD, the altar of burnt offerings with all its articles, and the table of the showbread with all its articles. ¹⁹Moreover all the articles which King Ahaz in his reign had cast aside in his transgression we have prepared and sanctified; and there they *are*, before the altar of the LORD."

²⁰Then King Hezekiah rose early, gathered the rulers of the city, and went up to the house of the LORD. ²¹And they brought seven bulls, seven rams, seven lambs, and seven male goats for a sin offering for the kingdom, for the sanctuary, and for Judah. Then he commanded the priests, the sons of Aaron, to offer *them* on the altar of the LORD. ²²So they killed the bulls, and the priests received the blood and sprinkled *it* on the altar. Likewise they killed the rams and sprinkled the blood on the altar. They also killed the lambs and sprinkled the blood on the altar. ²³Then they brought out the male goats *for* the sin offering before the king and the assembly, and they laid their hands on them. ²⁴And the priests killed them; and they presented their blood on the altar as a sin offering to make an atonement for all Israel, for the king commanded *that* the burnt offering and the sin offering *be made* for all Israel.

²⁵And he stationed the Levites in the house of the LORD with cymbals, with stringed instruments, and with harps, according to the commandment of David, of Gad the king's seer, and of Nathan the prophet; for thus *was* the commandment of the LORD by his prophets. ²⁶The Levites stood with the instruments of David, and the priests with the trumpets. ²⁷Then Hezekiah commanded *them* to offer the burnt offering on the altar. And when the burnt offering began, the song of the LORD *also* began, with the trumpets and with the instruments of David king of Israel. ²⁸So all the assembly worshiped, the singers sang, and the trumpeters sounded; all *this continued* until the burnt offering was finished. ²⁹And when they had finished offering, the king and all who were present with him bowed and worshiped. ³⁰Moreover King Hezekiah and the leaders commanded the Levites to sing praise to the LORD with the words of David and of Asaph the seer. So they sang praises with gladness, and they bowed their heads and worshiped.

³¹Then Hezekiah answered and said, "Now *that* you have consecrated yourselves to the LORD, come near, and bring sacrifices and thank offerings into the house of the LORD." So the assembly brought in sacrifices and thank offerings, and as many as were of a willing heart *brought* burnt offerings. ³²And the number of the burnt offerings which the assembly brought was seventy bulls, one hundred rams, *and* two hundred lambs; all these *were* for a burnt offering to the LORD. ³³The consecrated things *were* six hundred bulls and three thousand sheep. ³⁴But the priests were too few, so that they could not skin all the burnt offerings; therefore their brethren the Levites helped them until the work was ended and until the *other* priests had sanctified themselves, for the Levites were more diligent in sanctifying themselves than the priests. ³⁵Also the burnt offerings *were* in abundance, with the fat of the peace offerings and *with* the drink offerings for *every* burnt offering.

So the service of the house of the LORD was set in order. ³⁶Then Hezekiah and all the people rejoiced that God had prepared the people, since the events took place so suddenly.

CHAPTER **30** PASSOVER—HAPPY AGAIN. And Hezekiah sent to all Israel and Judah, and also wrote letters to Ephraim and Manasseh, that they should come

FIRST PLACE

30:6-9 Hezekiah was a king dedicated to God and to the spiritu of the nation. He sent letters throughout Judah and Israel urging everyone to return to God. He told them not to be stubborn, but t themselves to the Lord. We, too, must temper our stubborn selfish putting God first in our life, acknowledging that he knows what is us, and living his way.

to the house of the LORD at Jerusalem, to keep the Passover to the LORD God of Israel. [2]For the king and his leaders and all the assembly in Jerusalem had agreed to keep the Passover in the second month. [3]For they could not keep it at the regular time, because a sufficient number of priests had not consecrated themselves, nor had the people gathered together at Jerusalem. [4]And the matter pleased the king and all the assembly. [5]So they resolved to make a proclamation throughout all Israel, from Beersheba to Dan, that they should come to keep the Passover to the LORD God of Israel at Jerusalem, since they had not done *it* for a long *time* in the *prescribed* manner.

[6]Then the runners went throughout all Israel and Judah with the letters from the king and his leaders, and spoke according to the command of the king: "Children of Israel, return to the LORD God of Abraham, Isaac, and Israel; then He will return to the remnant of you who have escaped from the hand of the kings of Assyria. [7]And do not be like your fathers and your brethren, who trespassed against the LORD God of their fathers, so that He gave them up to desolation, as you see. [8]Now do not be stiff-necked, as your fathers *were, but* yield yourselves to the LORD; and enter His sanctuary, which He has sanctified forever, and serve the LORD your God, that the fierceness of His wrath may turn away from you. [9]For if you return to the LORD, your brethren and your children *will be treated* with compassion by those who lead them captive, so that they may come back to this land; for the LORD your God *is* gracious and merciful, and will not turn *His* face from you if you return to Him."

[10]So the runners passed from city to city through the country of Ephraim and Manasseh, as far as Zebulun; but they laughed at them and mocked them. [11]Nevertheless some from Asher, Manasseh, and Zebulun humbled themselves and came to Jerusalem. [12]Also the hand of God was on Judah to give them singleness of heart to obey the command of the king and the leaders, at the word of the LORD.

[13]Now many people, a very great assembly, gathered at Jerusalem to keep the Feast of Unleavened Bread in the second month. [14]They arose and took away the altars that *were* in Jerusalem, and they took away all the incense altars and cast *them* into the Brook Kidron. [15]Then they slaughtered the Passover *lambs* on the fourteenth *day* of the second month. The priests and the Levites were ashamed, and sanctified themselves, and brought the burnt offerings to the house of the LORD. [16]They stood in their place according to their custom, according to the Law of Moses the man of God; the priests sprinkled the blood *received* from the hand of the Levites. [17]For *there were* many in the assembly who had not sanctified themselves; therefore the Levites had charge of the slaughter of the Passover *lambs* for everyone *who was* not clean, to sanctify *them* to the LORD. [18]For a multitude of the people, many from Ephraim, Manasseh, Issachar, and Zebulun, had not cleansed themselves, yet they ate the Passover contrary to what was written. But Hezekiah prayed for them, saying, "May the good LORD provide atonement for everyone [19]*who* prepares his heart to seek God, the LORD God of his fathers, though *he is* not *cleansed* according to

the purification of the sanctuary." [20]And the LORD listened to Hezekiah and healed the people.

[21]So the children of Israel who were present at Jerusalem kept the Feast of Unleavened Bread seven days with great gladness; and the Levites and the priests praised the LORD day by day, *singing* to the LORD, accompanied by loud instruments. [22]And Hezekiah gave encouragement to all the Levites who taught the good knowledge of the LORD; and they ate throughout the feast seven days, offering peace offerings and making confession to the LORD God of their fathers.

[23]Then the whole assembly agreed to keep *the feast* another seven days, and they kept it *another* seven days with gladness. [24]For Hezekiah king of Judah gave to the assembly a thousand bulls and seven thousand sheep, and the leaders gave to the assembly a thousand bulls and ten thousand sheep; and a great number of priests sanctified themselves. [25]The whole assembly of Judah rejoiced, also the priests and Levites, all the assembly that came from Israel, the sojourners who came from the land of Israel, and those who dwelt in Judah. [26]So there was great joy in Jerusalem, for since the time of Solomon the son of David, king of Israel, *there had* been nothing like this in Jerusalem. [27]Then the priests, the Levites, arose and blessed the people, and their voice was heard; and their prayer came *up* to His holy dwelling place, to heaven.

CHAPTER **31** **THE PEOPLE WORSHIP AGAIN.** Now when all this was finished, all Israel who were present went out to the cities of Judah and broke the sacred pillars in pieces, cut down the wooden images, and threw down the high places and the altars—from all Judah, Benjamin, Ephraim, and Manasseh—until they had utterly destroyed them all. Then all the children of Israel returned to their own cities, every man to his possession.

[2]And Hezekiah appointed the divisions of the priests and the Levites according to their divisions, each man according to his service, the priests and Levites for burnt offerings and peace offerings, to serve, to give thanks, and to praise in the gates of the camp of the LORD. [3]The king also *appointed* a portion of his possessions for the burnt offerings: for the morning and evening burnt offerings, the burnt offerings for the Sabbaths and the New Moons and the set feasts, as *it is* written in the Law of the LORD.

[4]Moreover he commanded the people who dwelt in Jerusalem to contribute support for the priests and the Levites, that they might devote themselves to the Law of the LORD.

◣◥◤**OFF THE TOP**

31:4-6 Hezekiah reinstated the practice of tithing— giving the first portion of one's income to the priests and Levites so they could be free to serve God and minister to the people. The people responded immediately and generously with their first crops. God's work needs the support of his people. Does God receive the first portion of your income? Generosity makes our giving delightful to God (2 Corinthians 8–9). How different the church would be today if all believers consistently followed this pattern.

⁵As soon as the commandment was circulated, the children of Israel brought in abundance the firstfruits of grain and wine, oil and honey, and of all the produce of the field; and they brought in abundantly the tithe of everything. ⁶And the children of Israel and Judah, who dwelt in the cities of Judah, brought the tithe of oxen and sheep; also the tithe of holy things which were consecrated to the LORD their God they laid in heaps.

⁷In the third month they began laying them in heaps, and they finished in the seventh month. ⁸And when Hezekiah and the leaders came and saw the heaps, they blessed the LORD and His people Israel. ⁹Then Hezekiah questioned the priests and the Levites concerning the heaps. ¹⁰And Azariah the chief priest, from the house of Zadok, answered him and said, "Since *the people* began to bring the offerings into the house of the LORD, we have had enough to eat and have plenty left, for the LORD has blessed His people; and what is left *is* this great abundance."

¹¹Now Hezekiah commanded *them* to prepare rooms in the house of the LORD, and they prepared them. ¹²Then they faithfully brought in the offerings, the tithes, and the dedicated things; Cononiah the Levite had charge of them, and Shimei his brother *was* the next. ¹³Jehiel, Azaziah, Nahath, Asahel, Jerimoth, Jozabad, Eliel, Ismachiah, Mahath, and Benaiah *were* overseers under the hand of Cononiah and Shimei his brother, at the commandment of Hezekiah the king and Azariah the ruler of the house of God. ¹⁴Kore the son of Imnah the Levite, the keeper of the East Gate, *was* over the freewill offerings to God, to distribute the offerings of the LORD and the most holy things. ¹⁵And under him *were* Eden, Miniamin, Jeshua, Shemaiah, Amariah, and Shecaniah, *his* faithful assistants in the cities of the priests, to distribute allotments to their brethren by divisions, to the great as well as the small.

¹⁶Besides those males from three years old and up who were written in the genealogy, they distributed to everyone who entered the house of the LORD his daily portion for the work of his service, by his division, ¹⁷and to the priests who were written in the genealogy according to their father's house, and to the Levites from twenty years old and up according to their work, by their divisions, ¹⁸and to all who were written in the genealogy—their little ones and their wives, their sons and daughters, the whole company of them—for in their faithfulness they sanctified themselves in holiness.

¹⁹Also for the sons of Aaron the priests, *who were* in the fields of the common-lands of their cities, in every single city, *there were* men who were designated by name to distribute portions to all the males among the priests and to all who were listed by genealogies among the Levites.

²⁰Thus Hezekiah did throughout all Judah, and he did what *was* good and right and true before the LORD his God. ²¹And in every work that he began in the service of the house of God, in the law and in the commandment, to seek his God, he did *it* with all his heart. So he prospered.

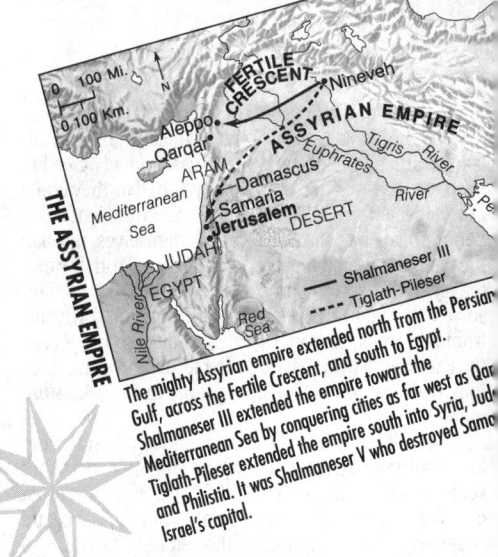

The mighty Assyrian empire extended north from the Persian Gulf, across the Fertile Crescent, and south to Egypt. Shalmaneser III extended the empire toward the Mediterranean Sea by conquering cities as far west as Qarqar and Philistia. It was Shalmaneser V who destroyed Samaria, Israel's capital.

CHAPTER **32** AN ANGEL FIGHTS FOR JUDAH. After these deeds of faithfulness, Sennacherib king of Assyria came and entered Judah; he encamped against the fortified cities, thinking to win them over to himself. ²And when Hezekiah saw that Sennacherib had come, and that his purpose *was* to make war against Jerusalem, ³he consulted with his leaders and commanders to stop the water from the springs which *were* outside the city; and they helped him. ⁴Thus many people gathered together who stopped all the springs and the brook that ran through the land, saying, "Why should the kings of Assyria come and find much water?" ⁵And he strengthened himself, built up all the wall that was broken, raised *it* up to the towers, and *built* another wall outside; also he repaired the Millo *in* the City of David, and made weapons and shields in abundance. ⁶Then he set military captains over the people, gathered them together to him in the open square of the city gate, and gave them encouragement, saying, ⁷"Be strong and courageous; do not be afraid nor dismayed before the king of Assyria, nor before all the multitude that *is* with him; for *there are* more with us than with him. ⁸With him *is* an arm of flesh; but with us *is* the LORD our God, to help us and to fight our battles." And the people were strengthened by the words of Hezekiah king of Judah.

⁹After this Sennacherib king of Assyria sent his servants to Jerusalem (but he and all the forces with him *laid siege* against Lachish), to Hezekiah king of Judah, and to all Judah who *were* in Jerusalem, saying, ¹⁰"Thus says Sennacherib king of Assyria: 'In what do you trust, that you remain under siege in Jerusalem? ¹¹Does not Hezekiah persuade you to give yourselves over to die by famine and by thirst, saying, "The LORD our God will

FRIGHTENING

32:1ff When King Hezekiah was confronted with the frightening prospect of an Assyrian invasion, he made two important decisions: did everything he could to deal with the situation, and he trusted the outcome. That is exactly what we must do when faced with frightening situations. Do everything you possibly can to solve the problem or improve the situation. As you do this, commit it to God prayer and trust him for the solution.

deliver us from the hand of the king of Assyria"? [12]Has not the same Hezekiah taken away His high places and His altars, and commanded Judah and Jerusalem, saying, "You shall worship before one altar and burn incense on it"? [13]Do you not know what I and my fathers have done to all the peoples of *other* lands? Were the gods of the nations of those lands in any way able to deliver their lands out of my hand? [14]Who *was there* among all the gods of those nations that my fathers utterly destroyed that could deliver his people from my hand, that your God should be able to deliver you from my hand? [15]Now therefore, do not let Hezekiah deceive you or persuade you like this, and do not believe him; for no god of any nation or kingdom was able to deliver his people from my hand or the hand of my fathers. How much less will your God deliver you from my hand?' "

[16]Furthermore, his servants spoke against the LORD God and against His servant Hezekiah.

[17]He also wrote letters to revile the LORD God of Israel, and to speak against Him, saying, "As the gods of the nations of *other* lands have not delivered their people from my hand, so the God of Hezekiah will not deliver His people from my hand." [18]Then they called out with a loud voice in Hebrew to the people of Jerusalem who *were* on the wall, to frighten them and trouble them, that they might take the city. [19]And they spoke against the God of Jerusalem, as against the gods of the people of the earth—the work of men's hands.

[20]Now because of this King Hezekiah and the prophet Isaiah, the son of Amoz, prayed and cried out to heaven. [21]Then the LORD sent an angel who cut down every mighty man of valor, leader, and captain in the camp of the king of Assyria. So he returned shamefaced to his own land. And when he had gone into the temple of his god, some of his own offspring struck him down with the sword there.

[22]Thus the LORD saved Hezekiah and the inhabitants of Jerusalem from the hand of Sennacherib the king of Assyria, and from the hand of all *others*, and guided them on every side. [23]And many brought gifts to the LORD at Jerusalem, and presents to Hezekiah king of Judah, so that he was exalted in the sight of all nations thereafter.

[24]In those days Hezekiah was sick and near death, and he prayed to the LORD; and He spoke to him and gave him a sign. [25]But Hezekiah did not repay according to the favor *shown* him, for his heart was lifted up; therefore wrath was looming over him and over Judah and Jerusalem. [26]Then Hezekiah humbled himself for the pride of his heart, he and the inhabitants of Jerusalem, so that the wrath of the LORD did not come upon them in the days of Hezekiah.

[27]Hezekiah had very great riches and honor. And he made himself treasuries for silver, for gold, for precious stones, for spices, for shields, and for all kinds of desirable items; [28]storehouses for the harvest of grain, wine, and oil; and stalls for all kinds of livestock, and folds for flocks. [29]Moreover he provided cities for himself, and possessions of flocks and herds in abundance; for God had given him very much property. [30]This same Hezekiah also stopped the water outlet of Upper Gihon, and brought the water by tunnel to the west side of the City of David. Hezekiah prospered in all his works.

[31]However, *regarding* the ambassadors of the princes of Babylon, whom they sent to him to inquire about the wonder that was *done* in the land, God withdrew from him, in order to test him, that He might know all *that was* in his heart.

[32]Now the rest of the acts of Hezekiah, and his goodness, indeed they *are* written in the vision of Isaiah the

MANASSEH

Even a brief outline of King Manasseh's evil sickens us, and we wonder how God could have ever forgiven him. Not only did he intentionally offend God by desecrating Solomon's temple with idols, but he also worshiped heathen gods and even sacrificed his children to them! Child sacrifice is a vile act of heathen idolatry, an act against both God and people. Such blatant sins require severe correction.

God showed justice to Manasseh in warning and punishing him. He showed mercy in responding to Manasseh's heartfelt repentance by forgiving and restoring him. Given the nature of Manasseh's rebellion, we are not surprised by God's punishment—defeat and exile at the hands of the Assyrians. But Manasseh's repentance and God's forgiveness are unexpected. Manasseh's life was changed. He was given a new start.

How far has God gone to get your attention? Have you ever, like Manasseh, come to your senses and cried out to God for help? Only your repentance and a prayer for a new attitude stand between you and God's complete forgiveness.

LESSONS: God will go a long way to get someone's attention. Forgiveness is limited not by the amount of sin, but by our willingness to repent.

KEY VERSES: "Now when he [Manasseh] was in affliction, he implored the LORD his God, and humbled himself greatly before the God of his fathers, and prayed to Him; and He received his entreaty, heard his supplication, and brought him back to Jerusalem into his kingdom. Then Manasseh knew that the LORD was God" (2 Chronicles 33:12-13).

Manasseh's story is told in 2 Kings 21:1-18 and 2 Chronicles 32:33–33:20. He is also mentioned in Jeremiah 15:4.

UPS:
- Despite the bitter consequences of his sins, he learned from them
- Humbly repented of his sins before God

DOWNS:
- Challenged God's authority and was defeated
- Reversed many of his positive effects of his father Hezekiah's rule
- Sacrificed his children to idols

STATS:
- Where: Jerusalem
- Occupation: King of Judah
- Relatives: Father: Hezekiah. Mother: Hephzibah. Son: Amon.

prophet, the son of Amoz, *and* in the book of the kings of Judah and Israel. ³³So Hezekiah rested with his fathers, and they buried him in the upper tombs of the sons of David; and all Judah and the inhabitants of Jerusalem honored him at his death. Then Manasseh his son reigned in his place.

CHAPTER 33 MANASSEH'S HEART IS CHANGED.

Manasseh *was* twelve years old when he became king, and he reigned fifty-five years in Jerusalem. ²But he did evil in the sight of the LORD, according to the abominations of the nations whom the LORD had cast out before the children of Israel. ³For he rebuilt the high places which Hezekiah his father had broken down; he raised

STONE AGE

Chuck normally uses anthropology class to snooze or do algebra homework. Not today. Mr. Roper spent the hour talking about the religious beliefs of certain Stone Age tribes. The discussion of human sacrifices and strange rituals had Chuck paying extra special attention.

After school, he continued to rattle on about what he had heard. "Annie, how in the world can those people actually bow down to a piece of wood or stone? Don't you think that's weird?"

"Well, it is pretty strange. But we do almost the same thing in this country."

"What are you talking about?"

"Idolatry."

"Aw, come on! Nobody worships totem poles around here."

"Well, no. We don't come right out and bow down in front of a statue. We're too sophisticated for that. But think about it. Think about the people who build their lives around people, possessions, or jobs. Or the people who devote their time and energy to cars, or sports, or getting good grades, or—"

"Hey! What's wrong with sports?"

"Nothing! . . . unless it becomes your whole life. Chuck, anything that becomes more important than God is an idol."

Annie's right. The Bible repeatedly warns us not to let things or people replace God in our life. See the story of King Josiah in 2 Chronicles 34.

up altars for the Baals, and made wooden images; and he worshiped all the host of heaven and served them. ⁴He also built altars in the house of the LORD, of which the LORD had said, "In Jerusalem shall My name be forever." ⁵And he built altars for all the host of heaven in the two courts of the house of the LORD. ⁶Also he caused his sons to pass through the fire in the Valley of the Son of Hinnom; he practiced soothsaying, used witchcraft and sorcery, and consulted mediums and spiritists. He did much evil in the sight of the LORD, to provoke Him to anger. ⁷He even set a carved image, the idol which he had made, in the house of God, of which God had said to David and to Solomon his son, "In this house and in Jerusalem, which I have chosen out of all the tribes of Israel, I will put My name forever; ⁸and I will not again remove the foot of Israel from the land which I have appointed for your fathers—only if they are careful to do all that I have commanded them, according to the whole law and the statutes and the ordinances by the hand of Moses." ⁹So

BEYOND FORGIVENES

33:12-13 In a list of corrupt kings, Manasseh would rank near th top. His life is a catalog of evil deeds including idol worship, sacrifici own children, and temple desecration. Eventually, however, he realiz his sins and cried out to God for forgiveness. And God listened. If Gc forgive Manasseh, surely he can forgive anyone. Are you burdened overpowering guilt? Do you doubt that anyone could forgive what y have done? Take heart—until death, no one is beyond God's forgiv

Manasseh seduced Judah and the inhabitants of Jerusalem to do more evil than the nations whom the LORD had destroyed before the children of Israel.

¹⁰And the LORD spoke to Manasseh and his people, but they would not listen. ¹¹Therefore the LORD brought upon them the captains of the army of the king of Assyria, who took Manasseh with hooks, bound him with bronze *fetters*, and carried him off to Babylon. ¹²Now when he was in affliction, he implored the LORD his God, and humbled himself greatly before the God of his fathers, ¹³and prayed to Him; and He received his entreaty, heard his supplication, and brought him back to Jerusalem into his kingdom. Then Manasseh knew that the LORD *was* God.

¹⁴After this he built a wall outside the City of David on the west side of Gihon, in the valley, as far as the entrance of the Fish Gate; and *it* enclosed Ophel, and he raised it to a very great height. Then he put military captains in all the fortified cities of Judah. ¹⁵He took away the foreign gods and the idol from the house of the LORD, and all the altars that he had built in the mount of the house of the LORD and in Jerusalem; and he cast *them* out of the city. ¹⁶He also repaired the altar of the LORD, sacrificed peace offerings and thank offerings on it, and commanded Judah to serve the LORD God of Israel. ¹⁷Nevertheless the people still sacrificed on the high places, *but* only to the LORD their God.

¹⁸Now the rest of the acts of Manasseh, his prayer to his God, and the words of the seers who spoke to him in the name of the LORD God of Israel, indeed they *are written* in the book of the kings of Israel. ¹⁹Also his prayer and *how God* received his entreaty, and all his sin and trespass, and the sites where he built high places and set up wooden images and carved images, before he was humbled, indeed they *are* written among the sayings of Hozai. ²⁰So Manasseh rested with his fathers, and they buried him in his own house. Then his son Amon reigned in his place.

²¹Amon *was* twenty-two years old when he became king, and he reigned two years in Jerusalem. ²²But he did evil in the sight of the LORD, as his father Manasseh had done; for Amon sacrificed to all the carved images which his father Manasseh had made, and served them. ²³And he did not humble himself before the LORD, as his father Manasseh had humbled himself; but Amon trespassed more and more.

²⁴Then his servants conspired against him, and killed him in his own house. ²⁵But the people of the land executed all those who had conspired against King Amon. Then the people of the land made his son Josiah king in his place.

CHAPTER 34 THE BOOK OF THE LAW IS FOUND.

Josiah *was* eight years old when he became king, and he reigned thirty-one years in Jerusalem. ²And he did *what was* right in the sight of the LORD, and walked in the ways of his father David; *he* did *not* turn aside to the right hand or to the left.

³For in the eighth year of his reign, while he was still young, he began to seek the God of his father David; and in the twelfth year he began to purge Judah and Jerusalem of the high places, the wooden images, the carved images, and the molded images. ⁴They broke down the altars of the Baals in his presence, and the incense altars which *were* above them he cut down; and the wooden images, the carved images, and the molded images he broke in pieces, and made dust of them and scattered *it* on the graves of those who had sacrificed to them. ⁵He also burned the bones of the priests on their altars, and cleansed Judah and Jerusalem. ⁶And *so he did* in the cities of Manasseh, Ephraim, and Simeon, as far as Naphtali and all around, with axes. ⁷When he had broken down the altars and the wooden images, had beaten the carved images into powder, and cut down all the incense altars throughout all the land of Israel, he returned to Jerusalem.

⁸In the eighteenth year of his reign, when he had purged the land and the temple, he sent Shaphan the son of Azaliah, Maaseiah the governor of the city, and Joah the son of Joahaz the recorder, to repair the house of the LORD his God. ⁹When they came to Hilkiah the high priest, they delivered the money that was brought into the house of God, which the Levites who kept the doors had gathered from the hand of Manasseh and Ephraim, from all the remnant of Israel, from all Judah and Benjamin, and *which* they had brought back to Jerusalem. ¹⁰Then they put *it* in the hand of the foremen who had the oversight of the house of the LORD; and they gave it to the workmen who worked in the house of the LORD, to repair and restore the house. ¹¹They gave *it* to the craftsmen and builders to buy hewn stone and timber for beams, and to floor the houses which the kings of Judah had destroyed. ¹²And the men did the work faithfully. Their overseers *were* Jahath and Obadiah the Levites, of the sons of Merari, and Zechariah and Meshullam, of the sons of the Kohathites, to supervise. *Others of* the Levites, all of whom were skillful with instruments of music, ¹³*were* over the burden bearers and *were* overseers of all who did work in any kind of service. And *some* of the Levites *were* scribes, officers, and gatekeepers.

¹⁴Now when they brought out the money that was brought into the house of the LORD, Hilkiah the priest found the Book of the Law of the LORD *given* by Moses. ¹⁵Then Hilkiah answered and said to Shaphan the scribe, "I have found the Book of the Law in the house of the LORD." And Hilkiah gave the book to Shaphan. ¹⁶So Shaphan carried the book to the king, bringing the king word, saying, "All that was committed to your servants they are doing. ¹⁷And they have gathered the money that was found in the house of the LORD, and have delivered it into the hand of the overseers and the workmen." ¹⁸Then Shaphan the scribe told the king, saying, "Hilkiah the priest has given me a book." And Shaphan read it before the king.

¹⁹Thus it happened, when the king heard the words of the Law, that he tore his clothes. ²⁰Then the king commanded Hilkiah, Ahikam the son of Shaphan, Abdon the son of Micah, Shaphan the scribe, and Asaiah a servant of the king, saying, ²¹"Go, inquire of the LORD for me, and for those who are left in Israel and Judah, concerning the words of the book that is found; for great *is* the wrath of the LORD that is poured out on us, because our fathers have not kept the word of the LORD, to do according to all that is written in this book."

◣〰️〰️〰️ YOUNG BUT WISE

34:3 In Josiah's day, boys were considered men at age 12. By 16, Josiah understood the responsibility of his office. Even at this young age, he showed greater wisdom than many of the older kings who came before him because he decided to seek the Lord God and his wisdom. Clearly, wisdom from God is not the exclusive possession of the old. Young people may also be wise enough to fill spiritual leadership positions. Paul counseled Timothy, "Let no one despise your youth" (1 Timothy 4:12). If God has given you wisdom and spiritual insight, use it in his service regardless of your age.

²²So Hilkiah and those the king *had appointed* went to Huldah the prophetess, the wife of Shallum the son of Tokhath, the son of Hasrah, keeper of the wardrobe. (She dwelt in Jerusalem in the Second Quarter.) And they spoke to her to that *effect*.

²³Then she answered them, "Thus says the LORD God of Israel, 'Tell the man who sent you to Me, ²⁴"Thus says the LORD: 'Behold, I will bring calamity on this place and on its inhabitants, all the curses that are written in the book which they have read before the king of Judah, ²⁵because they have forsaken Me and burned incense to other gods, that they might provoke Me to anger with all the works of their hands. Therefore My wrath will be poured out on this place, and not be quenched.' " ' ²⁶But as for the king of Judah, who sent you to inquire of the LORD, in this manner you shall speak to him, 'Thus says the LORD God of Israel: "*Concerning* the words which you have heard— ²⁷because your heart was tender, and you humbled yourself before God when you heard His words against this place and against its inhabitants, and you humbled yourself before Me, and you tore your clothes and wept before Me, I also have heard *you*," says the LORD. ²⁸"Surely I will gather you to your fathers, and you shall be gathered to your grave in peace; and your eyes shall not see all the calamity which I will bring on this place and its inhabitants." ' " So they brought back word to the king.

²⁹Then the king sent and gathered all the elders of Judah and Jerusalem. ³⁰The king went up to the house of

◣〰️〰️〰️ UNREAD

34:31 When Josiah read the book that Hilkiah discovered (34:14), he responded with repentance and humility and promised to follow God's commandments as written in the book. The Bible is God's Word to us, "living and powerful" (Hebrews 4:12), but we cannot know what God wants us to do if we do not read it. And even reading God's Word is not enough; we must be willing to do what it says. There is not much difference between the book hidden in the temple and the Bible hidden on the bookshelf. An unread Bible is just as useless as a lost one.

the LORD, with all the men of Judah and the inhabitants of Jerusalem—the priests and the Levites, and all the people, great and small. And he read in their hearing all the words of the Book of the Covenant which had been found in the house of the LORD. [31]Then the king stood in his place and made a covenant before the LORD, to follow the LORD, and to keep His commandments and His testimonies and His statutes with all his heart and all his soul, to perform the words of the covenant that were written in this book. [32]And he made all who were present in Jerusalem and Benjamin take a stand. So the inhabitants of Jerusalem did according to the covenant of God, the God of their fathers. [33]Thus Josiah removed all the abominations from all the country that *belonged* to the children of Israel, and made all who were present in Israel diligently serve the LORD their God. All his days they did not depart from following the LORD God of their fathers.

EXILE TO BABYLON

Caspian Sea

Despite Judah's few good kings and timely reforms, the people never truly changed. Their evil continued, and finally God used the Babylonian empire under Nebuchadnezzar to conquer Judah, destroy Jerusalem, and take the people captive to Babylon.

CHAPTER 35 JOSIAH CELEBRATES PASSOVER.

Now Josiah kept a Passover to the LORD in Jerusalem, and they slaughtered the Passover *lambs* on the fourteenth *day* of the first month. [2]And he set the priests in their duties and encouraged them for the service of the house of the LORD. [3]Then he said to the Levites who taught all Israel, who were holy to the LORD: "Put the holy ark in the house which Solomon the son of David, king of Israel, built. *It shall* no longer *be* a burden on *your* shoulders. Now serve the LORD your God and His people Israel. [4]Prepare *yourselves* according to your fathers' houses, according to your divisions, following the written instruction of David king of Israel and the written instruction of Solomon his son. [5]And stand in the holy *place* according to the divisions of the fathers' houses of your brethren the *lay* people, and *according to* the division of the father's house of the Levites. [6]So slaughter the Passover *offerings*, consecrate yourselves, and prepare *them* for your brethren, that *they* may do according to the word of the LORD by the hand of Moses."

[7]Then Josiah gave the *lay* people lambs and young goats from the flock, all for Passover *offerings* for all who were present, to the number of thirty thousand, as well as three thousand cattle; these *were* from the king's possessions. [8]And his leaders gave willingly to the people, to the priests, and to the Levites. Hilkiah, Zechariah, and Jehiel, rulers of the house of God, gave to the priests for the Passover *offerings* two thousand six hundred *from the flock*, and three hundred cattle. [9]Also Conaniah, his brothers Shemaiah and Nethanel, and Hashabiah and Jeiel and Jozabad, chief of the Levites, gave to the Levites for Passover *offerings* five thousand *from the flock* and five hundred cattle.

[10]So the service was prepared, and the priests stood in their places, and the Levites in their divisions, according to the king's command. [11]And they slaughtered the Passover *offerings;* and the priests sprinkled *the blood* with their hands, while the Levites skinned *the animals*. [12]Then they removed the burnt offerings that *they* might give them to the divisions of the fathers' houses of the *lay* people, to offer to the LORD, as *it is* written in the Book of Moses. And so *they did* with the cattle. [13]Also they roasted the Passover *offerings* with fire according to the ordinance; but the *other* holy *offerings* they boiled in pots, in caldrons, and in pans, and divided *them* quickly among all the *lay* people. [14]Then afterward they prepared portions for themselves and for the priests, because the priests, the sons of Aaron, *were busy* in offering burnt offerings and fat until night; therefore the Levites prepared portions for themselves and for the priests, the sons of Aaron. [15]And the singers, the sons of Asaph, *were* in their places, according to the command of David, Asaph, Heman, and Jeduthun the king's seer. Also the gatekeepers were at each gate; they did not have to leave their position, because their brethren the Levites prepared portions for them.

[16]So all the service of the LORD was prepared the same day, to keep the Passover and to offer burnt offerings on the altar of the LORD, according to the command of King Josiah. [17]And the children of Israel who were present kept the Passover at that time, and the Feast of Unleavened Bread for seven days. [18]There had been no Passover kept in Israel like that since the days of Samuel the prophet; and none of the kings of Israel had kept such a Passover as Josiah kept, with the priests and the Levites, all Judah and Israel who were present, and the inhabitants of Jerusalem. [19]In the eighteenth year of the reign of Josiah this Passover was kept.

[20]After all this, when Josiah had prepared the temple, Necho king of Egypt came up to fight against Carchemish by the Euphrates; and Josiah went out against him. [21]But he sent messengers to him, saying, "What have I to do with you, king of Judah? *I have* not *come* against you this day, but against the house with which I have war; for God commanded me to make haste. Refrain *from meddling with* God, who *is* with me, lest He destroy you." [22]Nevertheless Josiah would not turn his face from him, but

▶ MESSAGE

35:21-24 Josiah ignored Necho's message because of who Necho was—the king of a heathen nation. The mistaken assumption that Necho could not be part of God's larger plan cost Josiah his life. A message from God may come in unexpected ways. Don't let prejudice or false assumptions blind you to God's message.

disguised himself so that he might fight with him, and did not heed the words of Necho from the mouth of God. So he came to fight in the Valley of Megiddo.

²³And the archers shot King Josiah; and the king said to his servants, "Take me away, for I am severely wounded." ²⁴His servants therefore took him out of that chariot and put him in the second chariot that he had, and they brought him to Jerusalem. So he died, and was buried in *one of* the tombs of his fathers. And all Judah and Jerusalem mourned for Josiah.

²⁵Jeremiah also lamented for Josiah. And to this day all the singing men and the singing women speak of Josiah in their lamentations. They made it a custom in Israel; and indeed they *are* written in the Laments.

²⁶Now the rest of the acts of Josiah and his goodness, according to *what was* written in the Law of the LORD, ²⁷and his deeds from first to last, indeed they *are* written in the book of the kings of Israel and Judah.

CHAPTER 36 JERUSALEM IS DESTROYED.

Then the people of the land took Jehoahaz the son of Josiah, and made him king in his father's place in Jerusalem. ²Jehoahaz *was* twenty-three years old when he became king, and he reigned three months in Jerusalem. ³Now the king of Egypt deposed him at Jerusalem; and he imposed on the land a tribute of one hundred talents of silver and a talent of gold. ⁴Then the king of Egypt made *Jehoahaz's* brother Eliakim king over Judah and Jerusalem, and changed his name to Jehoiakim. And Necho took Jehoahaz his brother and carried him off to Egypt.

⁵Jehoiakim *was* twenty-five years old when he became king, and he reigned eleven years in Jerusalem. And he did evil in the sight of the LORD his God. ⁶Nebuchadnezzar king of Babylon came up against him, and bound him in bronze *fetters* to carry him off to Babylon. ⁷Nebuchadnezzar also carried off *some* of the articles from the house of the LORD to Babylon, and put them in his temple at Babylon. ⁸Now the rest of the acts of Jehoiakim, the abominations which he did, and what was found against him, indeed they *are* written in the book of the kings of Israel and Judah. Then Jehoiachin his son reigned in his place.

⁹Jehoiachin *was* eight years old when he became king, and he reigned in Jerusalem three months and ten days. And he did evil in the sight of the LORD. ¹⁰At the turn of the year King Nebuchadnezzar summoned *him* and took him to Babylon, with the costly articles from the house of the LORD, and made Zedekiah, *Jehoiakim's* brother, king over Judah and Jerusalem.

¹¹Zedekiah *was* twenty-one years old when he became king, and he reigned eleven years in Jerusalem. ¹²He did evil in the sight of the LORD his God, *and* did not humble himself before Jeremiah the prophet, *who spoke* from the mouth of the LORD. ¹³And he also rebelled against King Nebuchadnezzar, who had made him swear *an oath* by God; but he stiffened his neck and hardened his heart against turning to the LORD God of Israel. ¹⁴Moreover all the leaders of the priests and the people transgressed more and more, *according* to all the abominations of the nations, and defiled the house of the LORD which He had consecrated in Jerusalem.

¹⁵And the LORD God of their fathers sent *warnings* to them by His messengers, rising up early and sending *them*, because He had compassion on His people and on His dwelling place. ¹⁶But they mocked the messengers of God, despised His words, and scoffed at His prophets, until the wrath of the LORD arose against His people, till *there was* no remedy.

¹⁷Therefore He brought against them the king of the Chaldeans, who killed their young men with the sword in the house of their sanctuary, and had no compassion on young man or virgin, on the aged or the weak; He gave *them* all into his hand. ¹⁸And all the articles from the house of God, great and small, the treasures of the house of the LORD, and the treasures of the king and of his leaders, all *these* he took to Babylon. ¹⁹Then they burned the house of God, broke down the wall of Jerusalem, burned all its palaces with fire, and destroyed all its precious possessions. ²⁰And those who escaped from the sword he carried away to Babylon, where they became servants to him and his sons until the rule of the kingdom of Persia, ²¹to fulfill the word of the LORD by the mouth of Jeremiah, until the land had enjoyed her Sabbaths. As long as she lay desolate she kept Sabbath, to fulfill seventy years.

▰▰▰ STRIPPED

36:22-23 Second Chronicles focuses on the rise and fall of the worship of God as symbolized by the Jerusalem temple. David planned the temple; Solomon built it and then put on the greatest dedication service the world had ever seen. Worship in the temple was superbly organized. But several evil kings defiled the temple and degraded worship so that the people revered idols more highly than God. Finally, King Nebuchadnezzar of Babylon destroyed the temple (36:19). The kings were gone, the temple was destroyed, and the people were removed. The nation was stripped to its very foundation. But fortunately there was a greater foundation—God himself. When everything in life seems stripped away from us, we too still have God—his Word, his presence, and his promises.

²²Now in the first year of Cyrus king of Persia, that the word of the LORD by the mouth of Jeremiah might be fulfilled, the LORD stirred up the spirit of Cyrus king of Persia, so that he made a proclamation throughout all his kingdom, and also *put it* in writing, saying,

²³   Thus says Cyrus king of Persia:

All the kingdoms of the earth the LORD God of heaven has given me. And He has commanded me to build Him a house at Jerusalem which is in Judah. Who *is* among you of all His people? May the LORD his God *be* with him, and let him go up!

MEGA Themes

TEMPLE The temple was the symbol of God's presence and the place set aside for worship and prayer. Built by Solomon from the plans God gave to David, the temple was the nation's spiritual center.

As Christians meet together to worship God, they experience the presence of God in a way that no individual believer can. We need to experience the fullness of worship by regularly joining with other Christians to worship God.

1. How did the people feel about the temple? What caused them to feel this way?
2. What did the temple provide for the nation?
3. Because Christians are the temple of God, what attitude should they have toward each other?
4. What attitudes keep the body of Christ from fulfilling its intended role as the temple?
5. Is there a Christian toward whom you have a negative attitude? How could you improve your attitude and restore that relationship?

PEACE Solomon and his descendants were faithful to God. They experienced victory in battle, success in government, and peace with other nations. Peace was, and is, the result of loyalty to God and his law.

Only God can bring true peace, and he is greater than any enemy, army, or national alliance. Israel's peace and survival as a nation depended on its faithfulness to God. Our obedience to God as individuals and as a nation is also vital to our individual and national peace today.

1. What causes nations to go to war? Families to break apart? Friends to fight?
2. What do the above causes have in common?
3. What was the source of Israel's peace?
4. What does it mean to you to "be at peace"?
5. Jesus said, "Blessed *are* the peacemakers" (Matthew 5:9). What does it mean to be a peacemaker?
6. What can you do to be a peacemaker?

PRAYER After Solomon died, the kingdom divided. When a king led the Israelites into idolatry, the nation suffered. When the king and his people prayed to God for deliverance and they turned from their sinful ways, God delivered them.

God still answers prayer. We have God's promise that if we humble ourselves, seek him, turn from our sin, and pray, God will hear, heal, and forgive us.

When we pray, we should be seeking to know and experience God's will for our lives.

1. Describe the attitudes of the king and the people as they went to God in prayer.
2. How did the people put their prayers into action?
3. What attitudes do you think are most important for you to have when you pray?
4. What are five important prayer requests in your life today? What can you expect from God when you share these with him?
5. Take ten minutes to bring your requests and your life before God. Approach your prayers not as a time to share your "shopping list" with God, but as a time to understand more of your Father's love, provision, and grace for you.

REFORM Although idolatry and injustice were common, some kings led the people back to God and reformed their society. This involved destroying idols, obeying the law, and restoring the priesthood.

We must constantly commit ourselves to obeying God. We can't rely on what others have done. Each generation of believers must rededicate themselves to the task of doing God's will in their own lives, as well as in society.

1. Changes in the society began with people coming back to God. What caused the people to return to God? What did they do next?
2. What changes need to take place in the world? In your community? In your school?
3. Christian young people can be agents of change in the world, but to do so they must have a desire for a relationship with God and a commitment to obey him. What changes would happen if a group of committed Christian friends were to begin to work together in your school? In your community?
4. Seek God's will in your own life and in the lives of your Christian friends. Share your vision with them of how, with God's help, you could join together to create positive change.

COLLAPSE In 586 B.C. the Babylonians completely destroyed Solomon's beautiful temple. The Israelites had abandoned God. As a result, God brought judgment upon his people, and they were carried off into captivity.

Although our disobedience may not be as obvious

as Israel's, quite often our commitment to God is casual, or even phony. When we forget that all our power, wisdom, and wealth come from God and not from ourselves, we are in danger of suffering the same spiritual and moral collapse that Israel experienced.

1. What decisions led to the collapse of Judah?

2. What causes men and women in leadership positions, who claim to be serving God, to turn away from God and be immoral?

3. In what specific ways can you prevent such failure in your life? How can you be a person who changes your world, rather than someone who is changed by it?

When a celebrity commits suicide, we can't believe it. *After all, we think, he had everything: millions of fans, talent, good looks, a beautiful wife, fame, and fortune. What more could he want?* From all surface appearances, the person's life seemed perfect. Inside, though—where it really counts—it was full of loneliness, depression, and turmoil. ■ Ezra, a devoted priest and scribe, knew what was important. He was concerned for the Jews living in Jerusalem. Years earlier, under Zerubbabel's leadership, a group of Jews had been given permission to leave Babylon and return to build the temple. Though the returnees had met with some opposition, eventually they were successful. The temple was completed and dedicated. Everything looked good on the outside. ■ But when Ezra reached Jerusalem, he wept. The people *looked* obedient because they had rebuilt the temple, but their personal and spiritual lives were in shambles. The inside had fallen apart. Ezra realized that if this went unchanged, the new nation of Israel would commit spiritual suicide. ■ How does your "inside life" match with your outside? Read Ezra and decide to be a person who follows God in every area.

STATS

PURPOSE: To show God's faithfulness and the way he kept his promise to restore his people to their land

AUTHOR: Not stated, but probably Ezra

DATE WRITTEN: Around 450 B.C., recording events from about 538–450 B.C. (omitting 516–458 B.C.). Possibly begun earlier in Babylon and finished in Jerusalem.

SETTING: Ezra follows 2 Chronicles as a history of the Jews, recording their return to the Promised Land after their captivity

KEY PEOPLE: Cyrus, Zerubbabel, Haggai, Zechariah, Darius, Artaxerxes I, Ezra

KEY PLACES: Babylon, Jerusalem

SPECIAL FEATURES: Ezra and Nehemiah originally were one book in the Hebrew Bible and, with Esther, comprise the post-captivity historical books. The post-captivity prophetic books are Haggai, Zechariah, and Malachi. Haggai and Zechariah should be studied with Ezra since they prophesied during the period of the reconstruction.

Ezra

CHAPTER 1 THE ISRAELITES RETURN HOME.

Now in the first year of Cyrus king of Persia, that the word of the LORD by the mouth of Jeremiah might be fulfilled, the LORD stirred up the spirit of Cyrus king of Persia, so that he made a proclamation throughout all his kingdom, and also *put it* in writing, saying,

2   Thus says Cyrus king of Persia:
All the kingdoms of the earth the LORD God of heaven has given me. And He has commanded me to build Him a house at Jerusalem which *is* in Judah. ³Who *is* among you of all His people? May his God be with him, and let him go up to Jerusalem which *is* in Judah, and build the house of the LORD God of Israel (He *is* God), which *is* in Jerusalem. ⁴And whoever is left in any place where he dwells, let the men of his place help him with silver and gold, with goods and livestock, besides the freewill offerings for the house of God which *is* in Jerusalem.

⁵Then the heads of the fathers' *houses* of Judah and Benjamin, and the priests and the Levites, with all whose spirits God had moved, arose to go up and build the house of the LORD which *is* in Jerusalem. ⁶And all those who *were* around them encouraged them with articles of silver and gold, with goods and livestock, and with precious things, besides all *that* was willingly offered.

⁷King Cyrus also brought out the articles of the house of the LORD, which Nebuchadnezzar had taken from Jerusalem and put in the temple of his gods; ⁸and Cyrus king of Persia brought them out by the hand of Mithredath the treasurer, and counted them out to Sheshbazzar the prince of Judah. ⁹This *is* the number of them: thirty gold platters, one thousand silver platters, twenty-nine knives, ¹⁰thirty gold basins, four hundred and ten silver basins of a similar *kind, and* one thousand other articles. ¹¹All the articles of gold and silver *were* five thousand four hundred. All *these* Sheshbazzar took with the captives who were brought from Babylon to Jerusalem.

CHAPTER 2

Now these *are* the people of the province who came back from the captivity, of those who had been carried away, whom Nebuchadnezzar the king of Babylon had carried away to Babylon, and who returned to Jerusalem and Judah, everyone to his *own* city.

²*Those* who came with Zerubbabel *were* Jeshua, Nehemiah, Seraiah, Reelaiah, Mordecai, Bilshan, Mispar, Bigvai, Rehum, *and* Baanah. The number of the men of the people of Israel: ³the people of Parosh, two thousand one

CAPTIVES

1:1 The book of Ezra opens in 538 B.C., 48 years after Nebuchadnezzar destroyed Jerusalem, defeated the southern kingdom of Judah, and carried the Jews away to Babylon as captives (2 Kings 25; 2 Chronicles 36). Nebuchadnezzar died in 562, and because his successor was not strong, Babylon was overthrown by Persia in 539, just prior to the events recorded in this book. Both the Babylonians and the Persians had a relaxed policy toward their captives, allowing them to own land and homes and to take ordinary jobs. Many of the Jews, like Daniel, Mordecai, and Esther, rose to prominent positions within the nation. King Cyrus of Persia went a step further: he allowed many groups of exiles, including the Jews, to return to their homeland. By doing this, he hoped to win their loyalty and thus provide buffer zones around the borders of his empire.

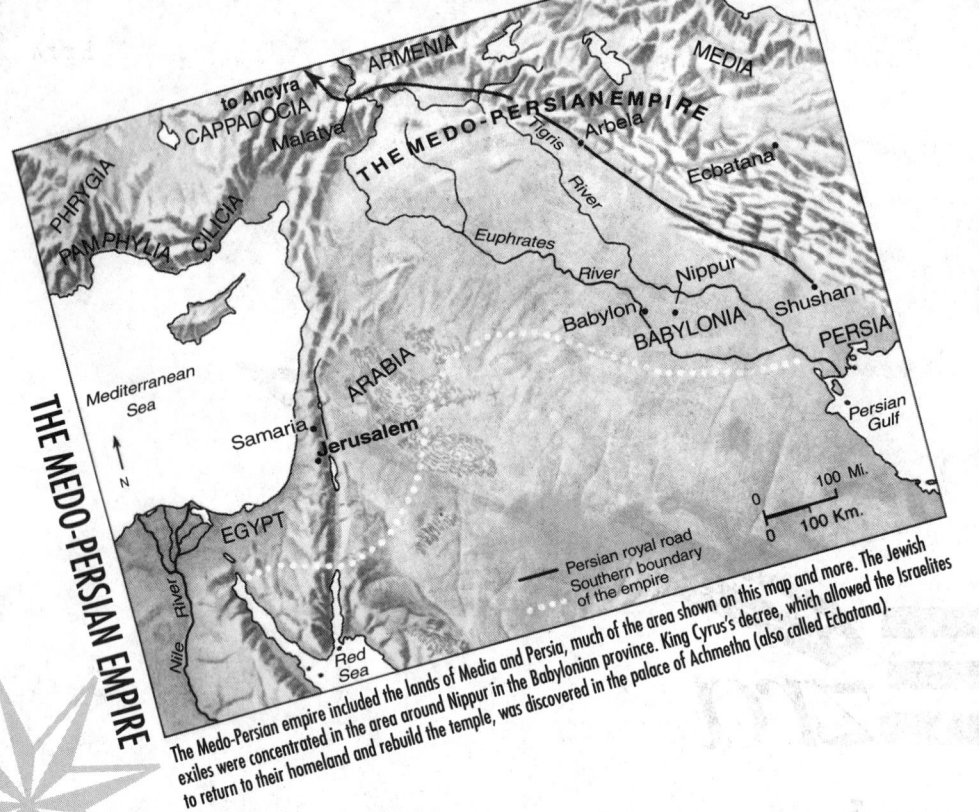

THE MEDO-PERSIAN EMPIRE

The Medo-Persian empire included the lands of Media and Persia, much of the area shown on this map and more. The Jewish exiles were concentrated in the area around Nippur in the Babylonian province. King Cyrus's decree, which allowed the Israelites to return to their homeland and rebuild the temple, was discovered in the palace of Achmetha (also called Ecbatana).

— Persian royal road
····· Southern boundary of the empire

hundred and seventy-two; ⁴the people of Shephatiah, three hundred and seventy-two; ⁵the people of Arah, seven hundred and seventy-five; ⁶the people of Pahath-Moab, of the people of Jeshua *and* Joab, two thousand eight hundred and twelve; ⁷the people of Elam, one thousand two hundred and fifty-four; ⁸the people of Zattu, nine hundred and forty-five; ⁹the people of Zaccai, seven hundred and sixty; ¹⁰the people of Bani, six hundred and forty-two; ¹¹the people of Bebai, six hundred and twenty-three; ¹²the people of Azgad, one thousand two hundred and twenty-two; ¹³the people of Adonikam, six hundred and sixty-six; ¹⁴the people of Bigvai, two thousand and fifty-six; ¹⁵the people of Adin, four hundred and fifty-four; ¹⁶the people of Ater of Hezekiah, ninety-eight; ¹⁷the people of Bezai, three hundred and twenty-three; ¹⁸the people of Jorah, one hundred and twelve; ¹⁹the people of Hashum, two hundred and twenty-three; ²⁰the people of Gibbar, ninety-five; ²¹the people of Bethlehem, one hundred and twenty-three; ²²the men of Netophah, fifty-six; ²³the men of Anathoth, one hundred and twenty-eight; ²⁴the people of Azmaveth, forty-two; ²⁵the people of Kirjath Arim, Chephirah, and Beeroth, seven hundred and forty-three; ²⁶the people of Ramah and Geba, six hundred and twenty-one; ²⁷the men of Michmas, one hundred and twenty-two; ²⁸the men of Bethel and Ai, two hundred and twenty-three; ²⁹the people of Nebo, fifty-two; ³⁰the people of Magbish, one hundred and fifty-six; ³¹the people of the other Elam, one thousand two hundred and fifty-four; ³²the people of Harim, three hundred and twenty; ³³the people of Lod, Hadid, and Ono, seven hundred and twenty-five; ³⁴the people of Jericho, three hun-

dred and forty-five; ³⁵the people of Senaah, three thousand six hundred and thirty.

³⁶The priests: the sons of Jedaiah, of the house of Jeshua, nine hundred and seventy-three; ³⁷the sons of Immer, one thousand and fifty-two; ³⁸the sons of Pashhur, one thousand two hundred and forty-seven; ³⁹the sons of Harim, one thousand and seventeen.

⁴⁰The Levites: the sons of Jeshua and Kadmiel, of the sons of Hodaviah, seventy-four.

⁴¹The singers: the sons of Asaph, one hundred and twenty-eight.

⁴²The sons of the gatekeepers: the sons of Shallum, the sons of Ater, the sons of Talmon, the sons of Akkub, the sons of Hatita, and the sons of Shobai, one hundred and thirty-nine *in* all.

⁴³The Nethinim: the sons of Ziha, the sons of Hasupha, the sons of Tabbaoth, ⁴⁴the sons of Keros, the sons of Siaha, the sons of Padon, ⁴⁵the sons of Lebanah, the sons of Hagabah, the sons of Akkub, ⁴⁶the sons of Hagab, the sons of Shalmai, the sons of Hanan, ⁴⁷the sons of Giddel, the sons of Gahar, the sons of Reaiah, ⁴⁸the sons of Rezin, the sons of Nekoda, the sons of Gazzam, ⁴⁹the sons of Uzza, the sons of Paseah, the sons of Besai, ⁵⁰the sons of Asnah, the sons of Meunim, the sons of Nephusim, ⁵¹the sons of Bakbuk, the sons of Hakupha, the sons of Harhur, ⁵²the sons of Bazluth, the sons of Mehida, the sons of Harsha, ⁵³the sons of Barkos, the sons of Sisera, the sons of Tamah, ⁵⁴the sons of Neziah, and the sons of Hatipha.

⁵⁵The sons of Solomon's servants: the sons of Sotai, the sons of Sophereth, the sons of Peruda, ⁵⁶the sons of Jaala, the sons of Darkon, the sons of Giddel, ⁵⁷the sons of Shephatiah, the sons of Hattil, the sons of Pochereth of

Zebaim, and the sons of Ami. [58]All the Nethinim and the children of Solomon's servants were three hundred and ninety-two.

[59]And these *were* the ones who came up from Tel Melah, Tel Harsha, Cherub, Addan, and Immer; but they could not identify their father's house or their genealogy, whether they *were* of Israel: [60]the sons of Delaiah, the sons of Tobiah, and the sons of Nekoda, six hundred and fifty-two; [61]and of the sons of the priests: the sons of Habaiah, the sons of Koz, and the sons of Barzillai, who took a wife of the daughters of Barzillai the Gileadite, and was called by their name. [62]These sought their listing *among* those who were registered by genealogy, but they were not found; therefore they *were excluded* from the priesthood as defiled. [63]And the governor said to them that they should not eat of the most holy things till a priest could consult with the Urim and Thummim.

[64]The whole assembly together *was* forty-two thousand three hundred *and* sixty, [65]besides their male and female servants, of whom *there were* seven thousand three hundred and thirty-seven; and they had two hundred men and women singers. [66]Their horses *were* seven hundred and thirty-six, their mules two hundred and forty-five, [67]their camels four hundred and thirty-five, and *their* donkeys six thousand seven hundred and twenty.

[68]*Some* of the heads of the fathers' *houses,* when they came to the house of the LORD which *is* in Jerusalem, offered freely for the house of God, to erect it in its place: [69]According to their ability, they gave to the treasury for the work sixty-one thousand gold drachmas, five thousand minas of silver, and one hundred priestly garments.

[70]So the priests and the Levites, *some* of the people, the singers, the gatekeepers, and the Nethinim, dwelt in their cities, and all Israel in their cities.

CHAPTER **3** **THE NEW TEMPLE.** And when the seventh month had come, and the children of Israel *were* in the cities, the people gathered together as one man to Jerusalem. [2]Then Jeshua the son of Jozadak and his brethren the priests, and Zerubbabel the son of Shealtiel and his brethren, arose and built the altar of the God of Israel, to offer burnt offerings on it, as *it is* written in the Law of Moses the man of God. [3]Though fear *had come* upon them because of the people of those countries, they set the altar on its bases; and they offered burnt offerings on it to the LORD, *both* the morning and evening burnt offerings. [4]They also kept the Feast of Tabernacles, as *it is* written, and *offered* the daily burnt offerings in the number required by ordinance for each day. [5]Afterwards *they offered* the regular burnt offering, and *those* for New Moons and for all the appointed feasts of the LORD that were consecrated, and *those* of everyone who willingly offered a freewill offering to the LORD. [6]From the first day of the seventh month they began to offer burnt offerings to the LORD, although the foundation of the temple of the LORD had not been laid. [7]They also gave money to the masons and the carpenters, and food, drink, and oil to the people of Sidon and Tyre to bring cedar logs from Lebanon to the sea, to Joppa, according to the permission which they had from Cyrus king of Persia.

[8]Now in the second month of the second year of their coming to the house of God at Jerusalem, Zerubbabel the son of Shealtiel, Jeshua the son of Jozadak, and the rest of their brethren the priests and the Levites, and all those who had come out of the captivity to Jerusalem, began *work* and appointed the Levites from twenty years old and above to oversee the work of the house of the LORD. [9]Then Jeshua *with* his sons and brothers, Kadmiel *with* his sons, and the sons of Judah, arose as one to oversee those working on the house of God: the sons of Henadad *with* their sons and their brethren the Levites.

▶ PREPARE

3:8 It took from September to June just to *prepare* to build the temple. During this time, the altar was built, materials were ordered and collected, and workers were hired. The exiles took some time to make plans because the project was important to them. Preparation may not feel heroic or spiritual, but it is vital to any project meant to be done well.

[10]When the builders laid the foundation of the temple of the LORD, the priests stood in their apparel with trumpets, and the Levites, the sons of Asaph, with cymbals, to praise the LORD, according to the ordinance of David king of Israel. [11]And they sang responsively, praising and giving thanks to the LORD:

"For *He is* good,
For His mercy *endures* forever toward Israel."

Then all the people shouted with a great shout, when they praised the LORD, because the foundation of the house of the LORD was laid.

[12]But many of the priests and Levites and heads of the fathers' *houses,* old men who had seen the first temple, wept with a loud voice when the foundation of this temple was laid before their eyes. Yet many shouted aloud for joy, [13]so that the people could not discern the noise of the shout of joy from the noise of the weeping of the people, for the people shouted with a loud shout, and the sound was heard afar off.

CHAPTER **4** **ENEMIES TRY TO STOP THE TEMPLE.** Now when the adversaries of Judah and Benjamin heard that the descendants of the captivity were building the temple of the LORD God of Israel, [2]they came to Zerubbabel and the heads of the fathers' *houses,* and said to them, "Let us build with you, for we seek your God as you *do;* and we have sacrificed to Him since the days of Esarhaddon king of Assyria, who brought us here." [3]But Zerubbabel and Jeshua and the rest of the heads of the

▶ OBSTACLES

4:1-6 Believers can expect opposition as they do God's work (2 Timothy 3:12). Unbelievers and evil spiritual forces are always working against God and his people. The opposition may involve offers of alliance (4:2), attempts to discourage and intimidate (4:4-5), or unjust accusations (4:6). If you learn to expect this opposition, you won't be halted by it. Move ahead with the work God has planned for you, and trust him to show you the way to overcome the obstacles.

fathers' *houses* of Israel said to them, "You may do nothing with us to build a house for our God; but we alone will build to the LORD God of Israel, as King Cyrus the king of Persia has commanded us." ⁴Then the people of the land tried to discourage the people of Judah. They troubled them in building, ⁵and hired counselors against them to frustrate their purpose all the days of Cyrus king of Persia, even until the reign of Darius king of Persia.

⁶In the reign of Ahasuerus, in the beginning of his reign, they wrote an accusation against the inhabitants of Judah and Jerusalem.

⁷In the days of Artaxerxes also, Bishlam, Mithredath, Tabel, and the rest of their companions wrote to Artaxerxes king of Persia; and the letter *was* written in Aramaic script, and translated into the Aramaic language. ⁸Rehum the commander and Shimshai the scribe wrote a letter against Jerusalem to King Artaxerxes in this fashion:

⁹ From Rehum the commander, Shimshai the scribe, and the rest of their companions— representatives of the Dinaites, the Apharsathchites, the Tarpelites, the people of Persia and Erech and Babylon and Shushan, the Dehavites, the Elamites, ¹⁰and the rest of the nations whom the great and noble Osnapper took captive and settled in the cities of Samaria and the remainder beyond the River—and so forth.

¹¹(This *is* a copy of the letter that they sent him)

To King Artaxerxes from your servants, the men *of the region* beyond the River, and so forth:

¹² Let it be known to the king that the Jews who came up from you have come to us at Jerusalem, and are building the rebellious and evil city, and are finishing *its* walls and repairing the foundations. ¹³Let it now be known to the king that, if this city is built and the walls completed, they will not pay tax, tribute, or custom, and the king's treasury will be diminished. ¹⁴Now because we receive support from the palace, it was not proper for us to see the king's dishonor; therefore we have sent and informed the king, ¹⁵that search may be made in the book of the records of your fathers. And you will find in the book of the records and know that this city *is* a rebellious city, harmful to kings and provinces, and that they have incited sedition within the city in former times, for which cause this city was destroyed.

¹⁶ We inform the king that if this city is rebuilt and its walls are completed, the result will be that you will have no dominion beyond the River.

¹⁷The king sent an answer:

To Rehum the commander, *to* Shimshai the scribe, *to* the rest of their companions who dwell in Samaria, and *to* the remainder beyond the River:

Peace, and so forth.

¹⁸ The letter which you sent to us has been clearly read before me. ¹⁹And I gave the command, and a search has been made, and it was found that this city in former times has revolted against kings, and rebellion and sedition have been fostered in it. ²⁰There have also been mighty kings over Jerusalem, who have ruled over all *the region* beyond the River; and tax, tribute, and custom were paid to them. ²¹Now give the command to make these men cease, that this city may not be built until the command is given by me.

²² Take heed now that you do not fail to do this. Why should damage increase to the hurt of the kings?

²³Now when the copy of King Artaxerxes' letter *was* read before Rehum, Shimshai the scribe, and their companions, they went up in haste to Jerusalem against the Jews, and by force of arms made them cease. ²⁴Thus the work of the house of God which *is* at Jerusalem ceased, and it was discontinued until the second year of the reign of Darius king of Persia.

CHAPTER 5 THE REBUILDING CONTINUES. Then

the prophet Haggai and Zechariah the son of Iddo, prophets, prophesied to the Jews who *were* in Judah and Jerusalem, in the name of the God of Israel, *who was* over them. ²So Zerubbabel the son of Shealtiel and Jeshua the son of Jozadak rose up and began to build the house of God which *is* in Jerusalem; and the prophets of God *were* with them, helping them.

³At the same time Tattenai the governor of *the region* beyond the River and Shethar-Boznai and their companions came to them and spoke thus to them: "Who has commanded you to build this temple and finish this wall?" ⁴Then, accordingly, we told them the names of the men who were constructing this building. ⁵But the eye of their God was upon the elders of the Jews, so that they could not make them cease till a report could go to Darius. Then a written answer was returned concerning this *matter.* ⁶This is a copy of the letter that Tattenai sent:

The governor of *the region* beyond the River, and Shethar-Boznai, and his companions, the Persians who *were in the region* beyond the River, to Darius the king.

⁷(They sent a letter to him, in which was written thus)

To Darius the king:

All peace.

⁸ Let it be known to the king that we went into the province of Judea, to the temple of the great God, which is being built with heavy stones, and timber is being laid in the walls; and this work goes on diligently and prospers in their hands.

⁹ Then we asked those elders, *and* spoke thus to them: "Who commanded you to build this temple and to finish these walls?" ¹⁰We also asked them their names to inform you, that we might write

the names of the men who *were* chief among them.

11 And thus they returned us an answer, saying: "We are the servants of the God of heaven and earth, and we are rebuilding the temple that was built many years ago, which a great king of Israel built and completed. ¹²But because our fathers provoked the God of heaven to wrath, He gave them into the hand of Nebuchadnezzar king of Babylon, the Chaldean, *who* destroyed this temple and carried the people away to Babylon. ¹³However, in the first year of Cyrus king of Babylon, King Cyrus issued a decree to build this house of God. ¹⁴Also, the gold and silver articles of the house of God, which Nebuchadnezzar had taken from the temple that *was* in Jerusalem and carried into the temple of Babylon—those King Cyrus took from the temple of Babylon, and they were given to one named Sheshbazzar, whom he had made governor. ¹⁵And he said to him, 'Take these articles; go, carry them to the temple *site* that *is* in Jerusalem, and let the house of God be rebuilt on its former site.' ¹⁶Then the same Sheshbazzar came *and* laid the foundation of the house of God which *is* in Jerusalem; but from that time even until now it has been under construction, and it is not finished."

17 Now therefore, if *it seems* good to the king, let a search be made in the king's treasure house, which *is* there in Babylon, whether it is *so* that a decree was issued by King Cyrus to build this house of God at Jerusalem, and let the king send us his pleasure concerning this *matter.*

CHAPTER **6** KING DARIUS APPROVES. Then King Darius issued a decree, and a search was made in the archives, where the treasures were stored in Babylon. ²And at Achmetha, in the palace that *is* in the province of Media, a scroll was found, and in it a record *was* written thus:

3 In the first year of King Cyrus, King Cyrus issued a decree *concerning* the house of God at Jerusalem: "Let the house be rebuilt, the place where they offered sacrifices; and let the foundations of it be firmly laid, its height sixty cubits *and* its width sixty cubits, ⁴*with* three rows of heavy stones and one row of new timber. Let the expenses be paid from the king's treasury. ⁵Also let the gold and silver articles of the house of God, which Nebuchadnezzar took from the temple which *is* in Jerusalem and brought to Babylon, be restored and taken back to the temple which *is* in Jerusalem, *each* to its place; and deposit *them* in the house of God"—

6 Now *therefore,* Tattenai, governor of *the region* beyond the River, and Shethar-Boznai, and your companions the Persians who *are* beyond the River, keep yourselves far from there. ⁷Let the work of this house of God alone; let the governor

of the Jews and the elders of the Jews build this house of God on its site.

◀━━━━━━━▶**BOLD**

5:11 While rebuilding the temple, the workers were confronted by the Persia-appointed governor demanding to know who gave permission for their construction project (5:3). This could have been intimidating, but, as we learn from the letter, they boldly replied, "We are the servants of the God of heaven and earth."

It is not always easy to speak up for our faith in an unbelieving world, but we must. The way to deal with pressure and intimidation is to recognize that we are workers for God. Our allegiance is to him first, people second. When we contemplate the reactions and criticisms of hostile people, we can become paralyzed with fear. If we make a policy of offending no one or pleasing everyone, our effectiveness will be stopped. God is our leader, and his rewards are most important. So don't be intimidated. Let others know by your actions and words whom you serve first.

8 Moreover I issue a decree *as to* what you shall do for the elders of these Jews, for the building of this house of God: Let the cost be paid at the king's expense from taxes *on the region* beyond the River; this is to be given immediately to these men, so that they are not hindered. ⁹And whatever they need—young bulls, rams, and lambs for the burnt offerings of the God of heaven, wheat, salt, wine, and oil, according to the request of the priests who *are* in Jerusalem—let it be given them day by day without fail, ¹⁰that they may offer sacrifices of sweet aroma to the God of heaven, and pray for the life of the king and his sons.

11 Also I issue a decree that whoever alters this edict, let a timber be pulled from his house and erected, and let him be hanged on it; and let his house be made a refuse heap because of this. ¹²And may the God who causes His name to dwell there destroy any king or people who put their hand to alter it, or to destroy this house of God which is in Jerusalem. I Darius issue a decree; let it be done diligently.

¹³Then Tattenai, governor of *the region* beyond the River, Shethar-Boznai, and their companions diligently did according to what King Darius had sent. ¹⁴So the elders of the Jews built, and they prospered through the prophesying of Haggai the prophet and Zechariah the son of Iddo. And they built and finished *it,* according to the commandment of the God of Israel, and according to the command of Cyrus, Darius, and Artaxerxes king of Persia. ¹⁵Now the temple was finished on the third day of the month of Adar, which was in the sixth year of the reign of King Darius. ¹⁶Then the children of Israel, the priests and the Levites and the rest of the descendants of the captivity, celebrated the dedication of this house of God with joy. ¹⁷And they offered sacrifices at the dedication of this house of God, one hundred bulls, two hundred rams, four hundred lambs, and as a sin offering for all Israel twelve male goats, according to the number of

the tribes of Israel. [18]They assigned the priests to their divisions and the Levites to their divisions, over the service of God in Jerusalem, as it is written in the Book of Moses.

[19]And the descendants of the captivity kept the Passover on the fourteenth *day* of the first month. [20]For the priests and the Levites had purified themselves; all of them *were ritually* clean. And they slaughtered the Passover *lambs* for all the descendants of the captivity, for their brethren the priests, and for themselves. [21]Then the children of Israel who had returned from the captivity ate together with all who had separated themselves from the filth of the nations of the land in order to seek the LORD God of Israel. [22]And they kept the Feast of Unleavened

VALUES

See Sylvia, the brown-haired girl sitting on the bench in front of the gym? Watch her for a few minutes.

Though she seems pretty happy on the outside, on the inside she's seriously confused!

It all started two weeks ago when she attended an after-school debate on this resolution: "Resolved: Absolute standards for human behavior do not exist."

What Sylvia first saw as an easy opportunity for some quick extra credit in speech class has turned into a long and difficult struggle of the soul. She's not sure what she thinks about anything . . . or even *how* to think about anything.

"The team that was to argue in favor of the resolution just about had me convinced," Sylvia says, "but then the other team raised a lot of troubling questions in my mind.

"Even though the crowd ended up voting for the resolution, I'm not so sure. I mean, if there aren't any hard and fast rules about anything, then nothing makes sense. 'Right' and 'wrong' don't have meaning.

"There must be some values that hold true for everyone. But once you get beyond murder and child abuse, I'm not sure what they are."

If you are looking for some help concerning how you should live and what values to base your actions upon, take a lesson from an Old Testament scribe named Ezra. Read Ezra 7:10 to find out the best standard for right and wrong.

Bread seven days with joy; for the LORD made them joyful, and turned the heart of the king of Assyria toward them, to strengthen their hands in the work of the house of God, the God of Israel.

CHAPTER 7 EZRA COMES TO TEACH.

Now after these things, in the reign of Artaxerxes king of Persia, Ezra the son of Seraiah, the son of Azariah, the son of Hilkiah, [2]the son of Shallum, the son of Zadok, the son of Ahitub, [3]the son of Amariah, the son of Azariah, the son of Meraioth, [4]the son of Zerahiah, the son of Uzzi, the son of Bukki, [5]the son of Abishua, the son of Phinehas, the son of Eleazar, the son of Aaron the chief priest— [6]this Ezra came up from Babylon; and he *was* a skilled scribe in the Law of Moses, which the LORD God of Israel had given. The king granted him all his request, according to the hand of the LORD his God upon him. [7]*Some* of the children of Israel, the priests, the Levites, the singers, the gatekeepers, and the Nethinim came up to Jerusalem in

TIMING

6:16-22 Feasting and celebration were in order at the great ten dedication. But the priests and Levites were organized into groups order to do "the service of God . . . as it is written in the Book of M There is a time to celebrate, but there also is a time to work. Both, their time, are proper and necessary when worshiping and serving and God is evident in both.

the seventh year of King Artaxerxes. [8]And Ezra came to Jerusalem in the fifth month, which *was* in the seventh year of the king. [9]On the first *day* of the first month he began *his* journey from Babylon, and on the first *day* of the fifth month he came to Jerusalem, according to the good hand of his God upon him. [10]For Ezra had prepared his heart to seek the Law of the LORD, and to do *it*, and to teach statutes and ordinances in Israel.

[11]This *is* a copy of the letter that King Artaxerxes gave Ezra the priest, the scribe, expert in the words of the commandments of the LORD, and of His statutes to Israel:

[12] Artaxerxes, king of kings,

To Ezra the priest, a scribe of the Law of the God of heaven:

Perfect *peace*, and so forth.

[13] I issue a decree that all those of the people of Israel and the priests and Levites in my realm, who volunteer to go up to Jerusalem, may go with you. [14]And whereas you are being sent by the king and his seven counselors to inquire concerning Judah and Jerusalem, with regard to the Law of your God which *is* in your hand; [15]and *whereas you are* to carry the silver and gold which the king and his counselors have freely offered to the God of Israel, whose dwelling *is* in Jerusalem; [16]and *whereas* all the silver and gold that you may find in all the province of Babylon, along with the freewill offering of the people and the priests, *are to be* freely offered for the house of their God in Jerusalem— [17]now therefore, be careful to buy with this money bulls, rams, and lambs, with their grain offerings and their drink offerings, and offer them on the altar of the house of your God in Jerusalem.

[18] And whatever seems good to you and your brethren to do with the rest of the silver and the gold, do it according to the will of your God. [19]Also the articles that are given to you for the service of the house of your God, deliver in full before the God of Jerusalem. [20]And whatever more may be needed for the house of your God, which you may have occasion to provide, pay *for it* from the king's treasury.

[21] And I, *even* I, Artaxerxes the king, issue a decree to all the treasurers who *are in the region* beyond the River, that whatever Ezra the priest, the scribe of the Law of the God of heaven, may require of you, let it be done diligently, [22]up to one hundred talents of silver, one hundred kors of wheat, one hundred baths of wine, one hundred baths of oil, and salt without prescribed limit. [23]Whatever is

commanded by the God of heaven, let it diligently be done for the house of the God of heaven. For why should there be wrath against the realm of the king and his sons?

24 Also we inform you that it shall not be lawful to impose tax, tribute, or custom *on* any of the priests, Levites, singers, gatekeepers, Nethinim, or servants of this house of God. 25And you, Ezra, according to your God-given wisdom, set magistrates and judges who may judge all the people who *are in the region* beyond the River, all such as know the laws of your God; and teach those who do not know *them.* 26Whoever will not observe the law of your God and the law of the king, let judgment be executed speedily on him, whether *it be* death, or banishment, or confiscation of goods, or imprisonment.

27Blessed *be* the LORD God of our fathers, who has put *such a thing* as this in the king's heart, to beautify the house of the LORD which *is* in Jerusalem, 28and has extended mercy to me before the king and his counselors, and before all the king's mighty princes.

So I was encouraged, as the hand of the LORD my God *was* upon me; and I gathered leading men of Israel to go up with me.

CHAPTER 8 THE EXILES WHO RETURNED. These *are* the heads of their fathers' *houses,* and *this is* the genealogy of those who went up with me from Babylon, in the reign of King Artaxerxes: 2of the sons of Phinehas, Gershom; of the sons of Ithamar, Daniel; of the sons of David, Hattush; 3of the sons of Shecaniah, of the sons of Parosh, Zechariah; and registered with him *were* one hundred and fifty males; 4of the sons of Pahath-Moab, Eliehoenai the son of Zerahiah, and with him two hundred males; 5of the sons of Shechaniah, Ben-Jahaziel, and with him three hundred males; 6of the sons of Adin, Ebed the son of Jonathan, and with him fifty males; 7of the sons of Elam, Jeshaiah the son of Athaliah, and with him seventy males; 8of the sons of Shephatiah, Zebadiah the son of Michael, and with him eighty males; 9of the sons of Joab, Obadiah the son of Jehiel, and with him two hundred and eighteen males; 10of the sons of Shelomith, Ben-Josiphiah, and with him one hundred and sixty males; 11of the sons of Bebai, Zechariah the son of Bebai, and with him twenty-eight males; 12of the sons of Azgad, Johanan the son of Hakkatan, and with him one hundred and ten males; 13of the last sons of Adonikam, whose names *are* these—Eliphelet, Jeiel, and Shemaiah—and with them sixty males; 14also of the sons of Bigvai, Uthai and Zabbud, and with them seventy males.

15Now I gathered them by the river that flows to Ahava, and we camped there three days. And I looked among the people and the priests, and found none of the sons of Levi there. 16Then I sent for Eliezer, Ariel, Shemaiah, Elnathan, Jarib, Elnathan, Nathan, Zechariah, and Meshullam, leaders; also for Joiarib and Elnathan, men of understanding. 17And I gave them a command for Iddo the chief man at the place Casiphia, and I told them what they should say to Iddo *and* his brethren the Nethinim at the place Casiphia—that they should bring us servants for the house of our God. 18Then, by the good hand of our God upon us, they brought us a man of understanding, of the sons of Mahli the son of Levi, the son of Israel, namely Sherebiah, with his sons and brothers, eighteen men; 19and Hashabiah, and with him Jeshaiah of the sons of Merari, his brothers and their sons, twenty men; 20also of the Nethinim, whom David and the leaders had appointed for the service of the Levites, two hundred and twenty Nethinim. All of them were designated by name.

CREDIT

7:27-28 Ezra praised God for all he had done for him and through him. Ezra had honored God throughout his life, and God chose to honor him. Ezra could have assumed that his own greatness and charisma had won over the king and his princes, but he gave the credit to God. We, too, should be grateful when things work out well for us, refusing to let our pride make us think we did it in our own power.

21Then I proclaimed a fast there at the river of Ahava, that we might humble ourselves before our God, to seek from Him the right way for us and our little ones and all our possessions. 22For I was ashamed to request of the king an escort of soldiers and horsemen to help us against the enemy on the road, because we had spoken to the king, saying, "The hand of our God *is* upon all those for good who seek Him, but His power and His wrath *are* against all those who forsake Him." 23So we fasted and entreated our God for this, and He answered our prayer.

24And I separated twelve of the leaders of the priests—Sherebiah, Hashabiah, and ten of their brethren with them— 25and weighed out to them the silver, the gold, and the articles, the offering for the house of our God which the king and his counselors and his princes, and all Israel *who were* present, had offered. 26I weighed into their hand six hundred and fifty talents of silver, silver articles *weighing* one hundred talents, one hundred talents of gold, 27twenty gold basins *worth* a thousand drachmas, and two vessels of fine polished bronze, precious as gold. 28And I said to them, "You *are* holy to the LORD; the articles *are* holy also; and the silver and the gold *are* a freewill offering to the LORD God of your fathers. 29Watch and keep *them* until you weigh *them* before the leaders of the priests and the Levites and heads of the fathers' *houses* of Israel in Jerusalem, *in* the chambers of the house of the LORD." 30So the priests and the Levites received the silver and the gold and the articles by weight, to bring *them* to Jerusalem to the house of our God.

31Then we departed from the river of Ahava on the

JOURNEY

8:21 Ezra and the people traveled approximately nine hundred miles on foot. The trip took them through dangerous and difficult territory and lasted about four months. They prayed that God would protect them and give them a good journey. Our journeys today may not be as difficult and dangerous as Ezra's, but we should feel free to ask God for guidance and protection.

twelfth *day* of the first month, to go to Jerusalem. And the hand of our God was upon us, and He delivered us from the hand of the enemy and from ambush along the road. [32]So we came to Jerusalem, and stayed there three days.

[33]Now on the fourth day the silver and the gold and the articles were weighed in the house of our God by the hand of Meremoth the son of Uriah the priest, and with him *was* Eleazar the son of Phinehas; with them *were* the Levites, Jozabad the son of Jeshua and Noadiah the son of Binnui, [34]with the number *and* weight of everything. All the weight was written down at that time.

[35]The children of those who had been carried away captive, who had come from the captivity, offered burnt offerings to the God of Israel: twelve bulls for all Israel, ninety-six rams, seventy-seven lambs, and twelve male goats *as* a sin offering. All *this was* a burnt offering to the LORD.

[36]And they delivered the king's orders to the king's satraps and the governors *in the region* beyond the River. So they gave support to the people and the house of God.

CHAPTER 9 EZRA CONFESSES HIS PEOPLE'S SIN.

When these things were done, the leaders came to me, saying, "The people of Israel and the priests and the Levites have not separated themselves from the peoples of the lands, with respect to the abominations of the Canaanites, the Hittites, the Perizzites, the Jebusites, the Ammonites, the Moabites, the Egyptians, and the Amorites. [2]For they have taken some of their daughters *as wives* for themselves and their sons, so that the holy seed is mixed with the peoples of *those* lands. Indeed, the hand of the leaders and rulers has been foremost in this trespass." [3]So when I heard this thing, I tore my garment and my robe, and plucked out some of the hair of my head and beard, and sat down astonished. [4]Then everyone who trembled at the words of the God of Israel assembled to me, because of the transgression of those who had been carried away captive, and I sat astonished until the evening sacrifice.

[5]At the evening sacrifice I arose from my fasting; and having torn my garment and my robe, I fell on my knees and spread out my hands to the LORD my God. [6]And I said: "O my God, I am too ashamed and humiliated to lift up my face to You, my God; for our iniquities have risen higher than *our* heads, and our guilt has grown up to the heavens. [7]Since the days of our fathers to this day we *have been* very guilty, and for our iniquities we, our kings, *and* our priests have been delivered into the hand of the kings of the lands, to the sword, to captivity, to plunder, and to humiliation, as *it is* this day. [8]And now for a little while grace has been *shown* from the LORD our God, to leave us a remnant to escape, and to give us a peg in His holy place, that our God may enlighten our eyes and give us a measure of revival in our bondage. [9]For we *were* slaves. Yet our God did not forsake us in our bondage; but He extended mercy to us in the sight of the kings of Persia, to revive us, to repair the house of our God, to rebuild its ruins, and to give us a wall in Judah and Jerusalem. [10]And now, O our God, what shall we say after this? For we have forsaken Your commandments, [11]which You commanded

MARRIAGE

9:2 Some Israelites had married heathen spouses and had lost trac God's purpose for them. The New Testament says that believers shou not marry unbelievers (2 Corinthians 6:14). Such marriages cannot unity in the most important issue in life—commitment and obedien God. Because marriage involves two people becoming one, faith ma become an issue. One spouse may have to compromise beliefs for th sake of unity. Don't allow emotion or passion to blind you to the ulti importance of marrying someone with whom you can truly be unite

by Your servants the prophets, saying, 'The land which you are entering to possess is an unclean land, with the uncleanness of the peoples of the lands, with their abominations which have filled it from one end to another with their impurity. [12]Now therefore, do not give your daughters as wives for their sons, nor take their daughters to your sons; and never seek their peace or prosperity, that you may be strong and eat the good of the land, and leave *it* as an inheritance to your children forever.' [13]And after all that has come upon us for our evil deeds and for our great guilt, since You our God have punished us less than our iniquities *deserve*, and have given us *such* deliverance as this, [14]should we again break Your commandments, and join in marriage with the people *committing* these abominations? Would You not be angry with us until You had consumed *us*, so that *there would be* no remnant or survivor? [15]O LORD God of Israel, You *are* righteous, for we are left as a remnant, as *it is* this day. Here we *are* before You, in our guilt, though no one can stand before You because of this!"

CHAPTER 10 THE PEOPLE CONFESS THEIR SIN.

Now while Ezra was praying, and while he was confessing, weeping, and bowing down before the house of God, a very large assembly of men, women, and children gathered to him from Israel; for the people wept very bitterly. [2]And Shechaniah the son of Jehiel, *one* of the sons of Elam, spoke up and said to Ezra, "We have trespassed against our God, and have taken pagan wives from the peoples of the land; yet now there is hope in Israel in spite of this. [3]Now therefore, let us make a covenant with our God to put away all these wives and those who have been born to them, according to the advice of my master and of those who tremble at the commandment of our God; and let it be done according to the law. [4]Arise, for *this* matter *is* your *responsibility*. We also *are* with you. Be of good courage, and do *it*."

[5]Then Ezra arose, and made the leaders of the priests, the Levites, and all Israel swear an oath that they would do according to this word. So they swore an oath. [6]Then Ezra rose up from before the house of God, and went into the chamber of Jehohanan the son of Eliashib; and *when*

ON HIS KNEES

9:5-15 After learning about the sins of the people, Ezra fell to hi knees in prayer. His heartfelt prayer provides a good perspective o He recognized (1) that sin is serious (9:6); (2) that no one sins with affecting others (9:7); (3) that he was not sinless, although he didn have a heathen wife (9:10ff); and (4) that God's love and mercy h spared the nation when they did nothing to deserve it (9:8-9,15). easy to view sin lightly in a world that sees sin as inconsequential, should view sin as seriously as Ezra did.

he came there, he ate no bread and drank no water, for he mourned because of the guilt of those from the captivity.

⁷And they issued a proclamation throughout Judah and Jerusalem to all the descendants of the captivity, that they must gather at Jerusalem, ⁸and that whoever would not come within three days, according to the instructions of the leaders and elders, all his property would be confiscated, and he himself would be separated from the assembly of those from the captivity.

⁹So all the men of Judah and Benjamin gathered at Jerusalem within three days. It *was* the ninth month, on the twentieth of the month; and all the people sat in the open square of the house of God, trembling because of *this* matter and because of heavy rain. ¹⁰Then Ezra the priest stood up and said to them, "You have transgressed and have taken pagan wives, adding to the guilt of Israel. ¹¹Now therefore, make confession to the LORD God of your fathers, and do His will; separate yourselves from the peoples of the land, and from the pagan wives."

¹²Then all the assembly answered and said with a loud voice, "Yes! As you have said, so we must do. ¹³But *there are* many people; *it is* the season for heavy rain, and we are not able to stand outside. Nor *is this* the work of one or two days, for *there are* many of us who have transgressed in this matter. ¹⁴Please, let the leaders of our entire assembly stand; and let all those in our cities who have taken pagan wives come at appointed times, together with the elders and judges of their cities, until the fierce wrath of our God is turned away from us in this matter." ¹⁵Only Jonathan the son of Asahel and Jahaziah the son of Tikvah opposed this, and Meshullam and Shabbethai the Levite gave them support.

¹⁶Then the descendants of the captivity did so. And Ezra the priest, *with* certain heads of the fathers' *households*, were set apart by the fathers' *households*, each of them by name; and they sat down on the first day of the tenth month to examine the matter. ¹⁷By the first day of the first month they finished *questioning* all the men who had taken pagan wives.

¹⁸And among the sons of the priests who had taken pagan wives *the following* were found of the sons of Jeshua the son of Jozadak, and his brothers: Maaseiah, Eliezer, Jarib, and Gedaliah. ¹⁹And they gave their promise that they would put away their wives; and *being* guilty, *they presented* a ram of the flock as their trespass offering.

²⁰Also of the sons of Immer: Hanani and Zebadiah; ²¹of the sons of Harim: Maaseiah, Elijah, Shemaiah, Jehiel, and Uzziah; ²²of the sons of Pashhur: Elioenai, Maaseiah, Ishmael, Nethanel, Jozabad, and Elasah.

²³Also of the Levites: Jozabad, Shimei, Kelaiah (the same *is* Kelita), Pethahiah, Judah, and Eliezer. ²⁴Also of the singers: Eliashib; and of the gatekeepers: Shallum, Telem, and Uri.

²⁵And others of Israel: of the sons of Parosh: Ramiah, Jeziah, Malchiah, Mijamin, Eleazar, Malchijah, and Benaiah; ²⁶of the sons of Elam: Mattaniah, Zechariah, Jehiel, Abdi, Jeremoth, and Eliah; ²⁷of the sons of Zattu: Elioenai, Eliashib, Mattaniah, Jeremoth, Zabad, and Aziza; ²⁸of the

CHANGED

10:3-4, 11 Following Ezra's earnest prayer, the people admitted their sin to God. Then they asked for direction in restoring their relationship with God. True repentance does not end when we speak words of confession—that would be mere lip service. It must lead to corrected behavior and changed attitudes. When you sin and are truly sorry, confess this to God, ask his forgiveness, and accept his grace and mercy. Then, as an act of thankfulness for your forgiveness, change your ways.

sons of Bebai: Jehohanan, Hananiah, Zabbai, *and* Athlai; ²⁹of the sons of Bani: Meshullam, Malluch, Adaiah, Jashub, Sheal, *and* Ramoth; ³⁰of the sons of Pahath-Moab: Adna, Chelal, Benaiah, Maaseiah, Mattaniah, Bezalel, Binnui, and Manasseh; ³¹*of* the sons of Harim: Eliezer, Ishijah, Malchijah, Shemaiah, Shimeon, ³²Benjamin, Malluch, *and* Shemariah; ³³of the sons of Hashum: Mattenai, Mattattah, Zabad, Eliphelet, Jeremai, Manasseh, *and* Shimei; ³⁴of the sons of Bani: Maadai, Amram, Uel, ³⁵Benaiah, Bedeiah, Cheluh, ³⁶Vaniah, Meremoth, Eliashib, ³⁷Mattaniah, Mattenai, Jaasai, ³⁸Bani, Binnui,

REBUILT

10:44 The book of Ezra opens with God's temple in ruins and the people of Judah captive in Babylon. Ezra tells of the return of God's people, the rebuilding of the temple, and the restoration of the sacrificial worship system. Similarly, God is able to restore and rebuild the lives of people today. No one is so far away from God that he or she cannot be restored. Repentance is all that is required. No matter how far we have strayed, or how long it has been since we have worshiped God, he is able to restore our relationship to him and rebuild our life.

Shimei, ³⁹Shelemiah, Nathan, Adaiah, ⁴⁰Machnadebai, Shashai, Sharai, ⁴¹Azarel, Shelemiah, Shemariah, ⁴²Shallum, Amariah, *and* Joseph; ⁴³of the sons of Nebo: Jeiel, Mattithiah, Zabad, Zebina, Jaddai, Joel, *and* Benaiah.

⁴⁴All these had taken pagan wives, and *some* of them had wives *by whom* they had children.

MEGA *Themes*

JEWS RETURN By returning to the land of Israel from Babylon, the Jews showed their faith in God's promise to restore them as people. They returned not only to their homeland, but also to the place where their forefathers had promised to follow God.

God shows his mercy to every generation. He compassionately restores his people. No matter how difficult our present "captivity," we are never far from his love and mercy. He restores us when we return to him.

1. Imagine that you are one of those who returned to the homeland after being released from captivity. How do you feel? What are you thinking about as you return to your home?
2. Undoubtedly this generation of Jews had heard about the sins that had led their forefathers into captivity. What type of commitment to God do you think they carried with them as they returned to Jerusalem? How do you think they would use their new freedom to worship?
3. In what sense were you a slave to sin until you received Christ's forgiveness? How are you using your freedom in Christ to worship God?
4. Identify creative ways (1) to worship God in your freedom and (2) to communicate this freedom to those still enslaved by sin.

OPPOSITION Opposition came soon after the altar was built and the temple foundation was laid. For more than six years, the enemies of the Jews used deceit to hinder the building. Finally, there was a decree to stop construction altogether. This opposition severely tested the Jews' wavering faith.

There always will be people who oppose God's work. The life of faith is never easy, but God can overrule all opposition. We must not falter or withdraw from our enemies; we need to stay active and patient. God is with us in every circumstance.

1. Why and how did some people try to keep the Jews from building the temple?
2. Why do some people strongly oppose Christianity and Christians? Give some examples of how they do this.
3. When have you thought about giving up your Christian witness because you felt alone or opposed? How did you work through those feelings so that you did not give up?
4. If a Christian friend was facing tough opposition from kids at school who were making fun of him and trying to discourage his faith, what would you do to encourage him to remain true to Christ?
5. Do you know someone who needs encouragement because of obstacles and/or opposition he or she is facing? List specific ways you can encourage that person. How will you do this in the next week?
6. If you were (or are) facing opposition, to whom could you go for encouragement?

GOD'S WORD When the people returned to the Promised Land, they were also returning to the influence of God's Word. The prophets Haggai and Zechariah helped encourage them, while Ezra's preaching of Scripture built them up. God's Word gave them what they needed to do God's work.

We also need the encouragement and direction of God's Word. We must never waver in our commitment to hear and obey his Word and to keep the Word in our life daily.

1. What was the main message God gave through Haggai? Through Zechariah? Through Ezra?
2. What difference did it make whether or not the people obeyed the prophets' messages?
3. What are some of the most important lessons you have learned through reading and studying God's Word?
4. What difference has obeying (or not obeying) God's Word made in your life?
5. Based on this study, what would you tell a new Christian about the importance of the Bible in the Christian life?

FAITH/ACTION The urging of Israel's leaders motivated the people to complete the temple. But over the years, many of them had intermarried with idol worshipers and adopted their heathen practices. It wasn't until their faith was tested and strengthened that they removed these sins from their lives.

Faith led God's people to complete the temple and to remove sin from their society. As we trust God with our heart and mind, we also must put our faith into action.

1. In this book, how did the Jews put their faith into action?
2. In the last year, what decisions did you make as a result of your faith in God? The last month? The last week?
3. What decisions are you facing right now that will give you the opportunity to act on your faith?
4. The people supported each other in their commit-ment to put their faith into action. To whom can you turn for support in the decisions you listed in number three?

Are you a leader? Most people think they are leaders, but real leadership is proven in adversity, in working through tough problems and painful situations. When tough times come, many would-be leaders find they fall apart. ■ Nehemiah was a proven leader. He left a secure position in the government of Persia to return to his homeland and rebuild the walls of Jerusalem. He succeeded, too, despite incredible obstacles and opposition. The book of Nehemiah tells his story. ■ We often dream of the glory and the praise of leadership, but we tend to forget about the turmoil and difficulty leadership can carry. God uses men and women who show the same tenacity that Nehemiah had. Unfortunately, not many people are like Nehemiah. Read the book to see true leadership in action. And ask God to help you become a leader like Nehemiah.

STATS

PURPOSE: Nehemiah is the last of the Old Testament historical books. It records the history of the third return to Jerusalem after captivity, telling how the walls were rebuilt and how the people were renewed in their faith.

AUTHOR: Much of the book is written in the first person, suggesting Nehemiah as the author. Nehemiah probably wrote the book, with Ezra serving as editor.

DATE WRITTEN: Approximately 445–432 B.C.

SETTING: Zerubbabel led the first return to Jerusalem in 537 B.C. In 458, Ezra led the second return. Finally, in 445, Nehemiah returned with the third group of exiles to rebuild the city walls.

KEY PEOPLE: Nehemiah, Ezra, Sanballat, Tobiah

KEY PLACE: Jerusalem

SPECIAL FEATURE: The book shows the fulfillment of the prophecies of Zechariah and Daniel concerning the rebuilding of Jerusalem's walls

Nehemiah

CHAPTER 1 **NEHEMIAH BEGS TO GO HOME.** The words of Nehemiah the son of Hachaliah.

It came to pass in the month of Chislev, *in* the twentieth year, as I was in Shushan the citadel, ²that Hanani one of my brethren came with men from Judah; and I asked them concerning the Jews who had escaped, who had survived the captivity, and concerning Jerusalem. ³And they said to me, "The survivors who are left from the captivity in the province *are* there in great distress and reproach. The wall of Jerusalem *is* also broken down, and its gates *are* burned with fire."

⁴So it was, when I heard these words, that I sat down and wept, and mourned *for many* days; I was fasting and praying before the God of heaven.

⁵And I said: "I pray, LORD God of heaven, O great and awesome God, *You* who keep *Your* covenant and mercy with those who love You and observe Your commandments, ⁶please let Your ear be attentive and Your eyes open, that You may hear the prayer of Your servant which I pray before You now, day and night, for the children of Israel Your servants, and confess the sins of the children of Israel which we have sinned against You. Both my father's house and I have sinned. ⁷We have acted very corruptly against You, and have not kept the commandments, the statutes, nor the ordinances which You commanded Your servant Moses. ⁸Remember, I pray, the word that You commanded Your servant Moses, saying, '*If* you are unfaithful, I will scatter you among the nations; ⁹but *if* you return to Me, and keep My commandments and do them, though some of you were cast out to

the farthest part of the heavens, *yet* I will gather them from there, and bring them to the place which I have chosen as a dwelling for My name.' ¹⁰Now these *are* Your servants and Your people, whom You have redeemed by Your great power, and by Your strong hand. ¹¹O Lord, I pray, please let Your ear be attentive to the prayer of Your servant, and to the prayer of Your servants who desire to fear Your name; and let Your servant prosper this day, I pray, and grant him mercy in the sight of this man."

For I was the king's cupbearer.

CHAPTER 2 And it came to pass in the month of Nisan, in the twentieth year of King Artaxerxes, *when* wine *was* before him, that I took the wine and gave it to the king. Now I had never been sad in his presence before. ²Therefore the king said to me, "Why *is* your face sad, since you *are* not sick? This *is* nothing but sorrow of heart."

So I became dreadfully afraid, ³and said to the king, "May the king live forever! Why should my face not be

TAKE ACTION

1:4 Nehemiah was deeply grieved about the condition of Jerusalem, but he didn't just brood about it. After his initial grief, he poured his heart out to God (1:5-11) and looked for ways to improve the situation. He put all his resources of knowledge, experience, and organization into determining what should be done. When tragic news comes to you, first pray. Then seek ways to move beyond grief to specific action that offers help to those who need it.

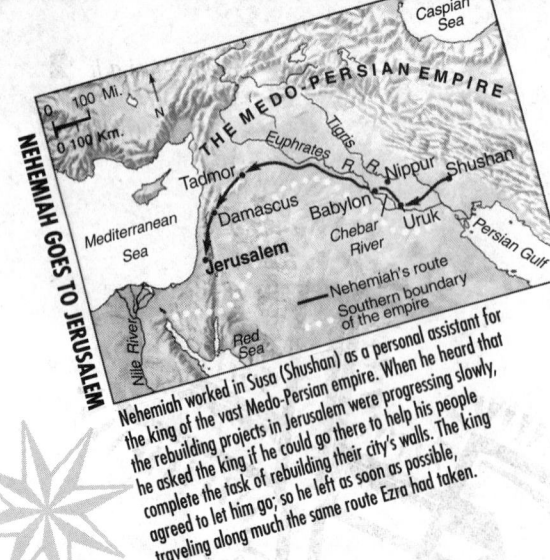

Nehemiah worked in Susa (Shushan) as a personal assistant for the king of the vast Medo-Persian empire. When he heard that the rebuilding projects in Jerusalem were progressing slowly, he asked the king if he could go there to help his people complete the task of rebuilding their city's walls. The king agreed to let him go; so he left as soon as possible, traveling along much the same route Ezra had taken.

sad, when the city, the place of my fathers' tombs, *lies* waste, and its gates are burned with fire?"

⁴Then the king said to me, "What do you request?"

So I prayed to the God of heaven. ⁵And I said to the king, "If it pleases the king, and if your servant has found favor in your sight, I ask that you send me to Judah, to the city of my fathers' tombs, that I may rebuild it."

⁶Then the king said to me (the queen also sitting beside him), "How long will your journey be? And when will you return?" So it pleased the king to send me; and I set him a time.

◤◤◤◤◤ HAVE NO FEAR

2:3 Nehemiah wasn't ashamed to admit his fear, but he refused to allow fear to stop him from doing what God had called him to do. When we allow our fears to rule our life, we make them more powerful than God. Is there something God wants you to do, but fear is holding you back? God is greater than all our fears. Recognizing your fear is the first step in committing it to God. If God has called you to a task, he will help you accomplish it.

⁷Furthermore I said to the king, "If it pleases the king, let letters be given to me for the governors *of the region* beyond the River, that they must permit me to pass through till I come to Judah, ⁸and a letter to Asaph the keeper of the king's forest, that he must give me timber to make beams for the gates of the citadel which *pertains* to the temple, for the city wall, and for the house that I will occupy." And the king granted *them* to me according to the good hand of my God upon me.

⁹Then I went to the governors *in the region* beyond the River, and gave them the king's letters. Now the king had sent captains of the army and horsemen with me. ¹⁰When Sanballat the Horonite and Tobiah the Ammonite official heard *of it*, they were deeply disturbed that a man had come to seek the well-being of the children of Israel.

¹¹So I came to Jerusalem and was there three days. ¹²Then I arose in the night, I and a few men with me; I told no one what my God had put in my heart to do at Jerusalem; nor was there any animal with me, except the one on which I rode. ¹³And I went out by night through the

◣◣◣◣◣ VISION

2:17-18 Spiritual renewal often begins with one person's vision. Nehemiah had a vision, and he shared it with enthusiasm, inspiring Jerusalem's leaders to rebuild the walls.

We frequently underestimate people and don't challenge them our dreams for God's work in the world. When God plants an idea i mind to accomplish something for him, share it with others and tru Holy Spirit to impress them with similar thoughts. Don't see yourse the only one through whom God is working. Often God uses one pe to express the vision and others to turn it into reality. When you encourage and inspire others, you put teamwork into action to accomplish God's goals.

Valley Gate to the Serpent Well and the Refuse Gate, and viewed the walls of Jerusalem which were broken down and its gates which were burned with fire. ¹⁴Then I went on to the Fountain Gate and to the King's Pool, but *there was* no room for the animal under me to pass. ¹⁵So I went up in the night by the valley, and viewed the wall; then I turned back and entered by the Valley Gate, and so returned. ¹⁶And the officials did not know where I had gone or what I had done; I had not yet told the Jews, the priests, the nobles, the officials, or the others who did the work.

¹⁷Then I said to them, "You see the distress that we *are* in, how Jerusalem *lies* waste, and its gates are burned with fire. Come and let us build the wall of Jerusalem, that we may no longer be a reproach." ¹⁸And I told them of the hand of my God which had been good upon me, and also of the king's words that he had spoken to me.

So they said, "Let us rise up and build." Then they set their hands to *this* good *work*.

¹⁹But when Sanballat the Horonite, Tobiah the Ammonite official, and Geshem the Arab heard *of it*, they laughed at us and despised us, and said, "What *is* this thing that you are doing? Will you rebel against the king?"

²⁰So I answered them, and said to them, "The God of heaven Himself will prosper us; therefore we His servants will arise and build, but you have no heritage or right or memorial in Jerusalem."

CHAPTER **3** THE BUILDERS OF THE CITY WALL.

Then Eliashib the high priest rose up with his brethren the priests and built the Sheep Gate; they consecrated it and hung its doors. They built as far as the Tower of the Hundred, *and* consecrated it, then as far as the Tower of Hananel. ²Next to *Eliashib* the men of Jericho built. And next to them Zaccur the son of Imri built.

³Also the sons of Hassenaah built the Fish Gate; they laid its beams and hung its doors with its bolts and bars. ⁴And next to them Meremoth the son of Urijah, the son of Koz, made repairs. Next to them Meshullam the son of Berechiah, the son of Meshezabel, made repairs. Next to them Zadok the son of Baana made repairs. ⁵Next to them the Tekoites made repairs; but their nobles did not put their shoulders to the work of their Lord.

⁶Moreover Jehoiada the son of Paseah and Meshullam the son of Besodeiah repaired the Old Gate; they laid its beams and hung its doors, with its bolts and bars. ⁷And next to them Melatiah the Gibeonite, Jadon the Meronothite, the men of Gibeon and Mizpah, repaired the residence of the governor *of the region* beyond the River. ⁸Next to him Uzziel the son of Harhaiah, one of the gold-

smiths, made repairs. Also next to him Hananiah, one of the perfumers, made repairs; and they fortified Jerusalem as far as the Broad Wall. ⁹And next to them Rephaiah the son of Hur, leader of half the district of Jerusalem, made repairs. ¹⁰Next to them Jedaiah the son of Harumaph made repairs in front of his house. And next to him Hattush the son of Hashabniah made repairs.

¹¹Malchijah the son of Harim and Hashub the son of Pahath-Moab repaired another section, as well as the Tower of the Ovens. ¹²And next to him was Shallum the son of Hallohesh, leader of half the district of Jerusalem; he and his daughters made repairs.

¹³Hanun and the inhabitants of Zanoah repaired the Valley Gate. They built it, hung its doors with its bolts and bars, and *repaired* a thousand cubits of the wall as far as the Refuse Gate.

¹⁴Malchijah the son of Rechab, leader of the district of Beth Haccerem, repaired the Refuse Gate; he built it and hung its doors with its bolts and bars.

¹⁵Shallun the son of Col-Hozeh, leader of the district of Mizpah, repaired the Fountain Gate; he built it, covered it, hung its doors with its bolts and bars, and repaired the wall of the Pool of Shelah by the King's Garden, as far as the stairs that go down from the City of David. ¹⁶After him Nehemiah the son of Azbuk, leader of half the district of Beth Zur, made repairs as far as *the place* in front of the tombs of David, to the man-made pool, and as far as the House of the Mighty.

¹⁷After him the Levites, *under* Rehum the son of Bani, made repairs. Next to him Hashabiah, leader of half the district of Keilah, made repairs for his district. ¹⁸After him their brethren, *under* Bavai the son of Henadad, leader of the *other* half of the district of Keilah, made repairs. ¹⁹And next to him Ezer the son of Jeshua, the leader of Mizpah, repaired another section in front of the Ascent to the Armory at the buttress. ²⁰After him Baruch the son of Zabbai carefully repaired the other section, from the buttress to the door of the house of Eliashib the high priest. ²¹After him Meremoth the son of Urijah, the son of Koz, repaired another section, from the door of the house of Eliashib to the end of the house of Eliashib.

²²And after him the priests, the men of the plain, made repairs. ²³After him Benjamin and Hasshub made repairs opposite their house. After them Azariah the son of Maaseiah, the son of Ananiah, made repairs by his house. ²⁴After him Binnui the son of Henadad repaired another section, from the house of Azariah to the buttress, even as far as the corner. ²⁵Palal the son of Uzai *made repairs* opposite the buttress, and on the tower which projects from the king's upper house that *was* by the court of the prison. After him Pedaiah the son of Parosh *made repairs.*

²⁶Moreover the Nethinim who dwelt in Ophel *made repairs* as far as *the place* in front of the Water Gate toward the east, and on the projecting tower. ²⁷After them the Tekoites repaired another section, next to the great projecting tower, and as far as the wall of Ophel.

²⁸Beyond the Horse Gate the priests made repairs, each in front of his *own* house. ²⁹After them Zadok the son of Immer made repairs in front of his *own* house. After him Shemaiah the son of Shechaniah, the keeper of the East Gate, made repairs. ³⁰After him Hananiah the son of Shelemiah, and Hanun, the sixth son of Zalaph, repaired another section. After him Meshullam the son of Berechiah made repairs in front of his dwelling. ³¹After him Malchijah, one of the goldsmiths, made repairs as far as the house of the Nethinim and of the merchants, in front of the Miphkad Gate, and as far as the upper room at the corner. ³²And between the upper room at the corner, as far as the Sheep Gate, the goldsmiths and the merchants made repairs.

CHAPTER **4** NEHEMIAH BUILDS THE WALLS. But it so happened, when Sanballat heard that we were rebuilding the wall, that he was furious and very indignant, and mocked the Jews. ²And he spoke before his brethren and the army of Samaria, and said, "What are these feeble Jews doing? Will they fortify themselves? Will they offer sacrifices? Will they complete it in a day? Will they revive the stones from the heaps of rubbish—*stones* that are burned?"

³Now Tobiah the Ammonite *was* beside him, and he said, "Whatever they build, if even a fox goes up *on it*, he will break down their stone wall."

⁴Hear, O our God, for we are despised; turn their reproach on their own heads, and give them as plunder to a land of captivity! ⁵Do not cover their iniquity, and do not let their sin be blotted out from before You; for they have provoked *You* to anger before the builders.

⁶So we built the wall, and the entire wall was joined together up to half its *height,* for the people had a mind to work.

⁷Now it happened, when Sanballat, Tobiah, the Arabs, the Ammonites, and the Ashdodites heard that the walls of Jerusalem were being restored and the gaps were beginning to be closed, that they became very angry, ⁸and all of them conspired together to come *and* attack Jerusalem and create confusion. ⁹Nevertheless we made our prayer to our God, and because of them we set a watch against them day and night.

¹⁰Then Judah said, "The strength of the laborers is failing, and *there is* so much rubbish that we are not able to build the wall."

¹¹And our adversaries said, "They will neither know nor see anything, till we come into their midst and kill them and cause the work to cease."

¹²So it was, when the Jews who dwelt near them came, that they told us ten times, "From whatever place you turn, *they will be* upon us."

¹³Therefore I positioned *men* behind the lower parts of the wall, at the openings; and I set the people according to their families, with their swords, their spears, and their

▰▰▰▰▰▰ **TIRED**

4:10-14 Accomplishing any large task is tiring. There are always pressures that bring discouragement—the task seems impossible, it can never be finished, or too many things are working against you. The only cure for fatigue and discouragement is focusing on God's purposes. Nehemiah reminded the workers of their calling, of their goal, and of God's protection. If you are overwhelmed by an assignment, feeling tired and discouraged, remember God's purpose for your life and the special purpose of the project.

bows. ¹⁴And I looked, and arose and said to the nobles, to the leaders, and to the rest of the people, "Do not be afraid of them. Remember the Lord, great and awesome, and fight for your brethren, your sons, your daughters, your wives, and your houses."

¹⁵And it happened, when our enemies heard that it was known to us, and *that* God had brought their plot to nothing, that all of us returned to the wall, everyone to his work. ¹⁶So it was, from that time on, *that* half of my servants worked at construction, while the other half held the spears, the shields, the bows, and *wore* armor; and the leaders *were* behind all the house of Judah. ¹⁷Those who built on the wall, and those who carried burdens, loaded themselves so that with one hand they

OPPOSITION

At a church camp this summer, Billy was challenged to "try to start a Bible study at your school when classes start again in the fall."

That's an awesome idea! Billy thought. So he started praying about it and, in time, he became convinced that this was something God wanted him to do. Billy decided to go for it. He never dreamed such a simple plan would become such a big deal.

From the beginning, he's encountered opposition.

- The principal doesn't want to give him a room (even though Billy keeps assuring him that the Bible study will not take place during school hours).
- No faculty members will agree to sponsor the group.
- A few Christian friends are urging him to forget it.
- A lot of Billy's classmates are calling him "the Pope" and "Brother Billy."
- One big guy (who's very anti-Christian) has been trying to pick a fight during P.E. class.

With all these obstacles, Billy is wondering whether it's worth it after all. "I don't have to start a Bible study to be a good Christian. Besides, I can do without all this grief."

Is Billy right in dumping his plan? Would you like to learn how to remain calm in the face of opposition? Are you interested in discovering the secret to hanging in there when people mock your faith? Read Nehemiah 4.

worked at construction, and with the other held a weapon. ¹⁸Every one of the builders had his sword girded at his side as he built. And the one who sounded the trumpet *was* beside me.

¹⁹Then I said to the nobles, the rulers, and the rest of the people, "The work *is* great and extensive, and we are separated far from one another on the wall. ²⁰Wherever you hear the sound of the trumpet, rally to us there. Our God will fight for us."

²¹So we labored in the work, and half of *the men* held the spears from daybreak until the stars appeared. ²²At the same time I also said to the people, "Let each man and his servant stay at night in Jerusalem, that they may be our guard by night and a working party by day." ²³So neither I, my brethren, my servants, nor the men of the guard who followed me took off our clothes, *except* that everyone took them off for washing.

CHAPTER **5** NEHEMIAH DEFENDS THE POOR. And there was a great outcry of the people and their wives against their Jewish brethren. ²For there were those who said, "We, our sons, and our daughters *are* many; therefore let us get grain, that we may eat and live."

³There were also *some* who said, "We have mortgaged our lands and vineyards and houses, that we might buy grain because of the famine."

⁴There were also those who said, "We have borrowed money for the king's tax *on* our lands and vineyards. ⁵Yet now our flesh *is* as the flesh of our brethren, our children as their children; and indeed we are forcing our sons and our daughters to be slaves, and *some* of our daughters have been brought into slavery. *It is* not in our power *to redeem them,* for other men have our lands and vineyards."

⁶And I became very angry when I heard their outcry and these words. ⁷After serious thought, I rebuked the nobles and rulers, and said to them, "Each of you is exacting usury from his brother." So I called a great assembly against them. ⁸And I said to them, "According to our ability we have redeemed our Jewish brethren who were sold to the nations. Now indeed, will you even sell your brethren? Or should they be sold to us?"

Then they were silenced and found nothing *to say.* ⁹Then I said, "What you are doing *is* not good. Should you not walk in the fear of our God because of the reproach of the nations, our enemies? ¹⁰I also, *with* my brethren and my servants, am lending them money and grain. Please, let us stop this usury! ¹¹Restore now to them, this day, their lands, their vineyards, their olive groves, and their houses, also a hundredth of the money and the grain, the new wine and the oil, that you have charged them."

¹²So they said, "We will restore *it,* and will require nothing from them; we will do as you say."

Then I called the priests, and required an oath from them that they would do according to this promise. ¹³Then I shook out the fold of my garment and said, "So may God shake out each man from his house, and from his property, who does not perform this promise. Even thus may he be shaken out and emptied."

And all the assembly said, "Amen!" and praised the LORD. Then the people did according to this promise.

¹⁴Moreover, from the time that I was appointed to be their governor in the land of Judah, from the twentieth year until the thirty-second year of King Artaxerxes, twelve years, neither I nor my brothers ate the governor's provisions. ¹⁵But the former governors who *were* before me laid burdens on the people, and took from them bread and wine, besides forty shekels of silver. Yes, even their servants bore rule over the people, but I did not do so, because of the fear of God. ¹⁶Indeed, I also continued the work on this wall, and we did not buy any land. All my servants *were* gathered there for the work.

¹⁷And at my table *were* one hundred and fifty Jews and rulers, besides those who came to us from the nations around us. ¹⁸Now *that* which was prepared daily *was* one ox *and* six choice sheep. Also fowl were prepared for me, and once every ten days an abundance of all kinds of wine. Yet in spite of this I did not demand the governor's

provisions, because the bondage was heavy on this people.

¹⁹Remember me, my God, for good, *according to* all that I have done for this people.

CHAPTER **6** NEHEMIAH FINISHES THE WALLS.

Now it happened when Sanballat, Tobiah, Geshem the Arab, and the rest of our enemies heard that I had rebuilt the wall, and *that* there were no breaks left in it (though at that time I had not hung the doors in the gates), ²that Sanballat and Geshem sent to me, saying, "Come, let us meet together among the villages in the plain of Ono." But they thought to do me harm.

³So I sent messengers to them, saying, "I *am* doing a great work, so that I cannot come down. Why should the work cease while I leave it and go down to you?"

⁴But they sent me this message four times, and I answered them in the same manner.

⁵Then Sanballat sent his servant to me as before, the fifth time, with an open letter in his hand. ⁶In it *was* written:

It is reported among the nations, and Geshem says, *that* you and the Jews plan to rebel; therefore, according to these rumors, you are rebuilding the wall, that you may be their king. ⁷And you have also appointed prophets to proclaim concerning you at Jerusalem, saying, "*There is* a king in Judah!" Now these matters will be reported to the king. So come, therefore, and let us consult together.

⁸Then I sent to him, saying, "No such things as you say are being done, but you invent them in your own heart."

⁹For they all *were trying to* make us afraid, saying, "Their hands will be weakened in the work, and it will not be done."

Now therefore, *O God,* strengthen my hands.

¹⁰Afterward I came to the house of Shemaiah the son of Delaiah, the son of Mehetabel, who *was* a secret informer; and he said, "Let us meet together in the house of God, within the temple, and let us close the doors of the temple, for they are coming to kill you; indeed, at night they will come to kill you."

¹¹And I said, "Should such a man as I flee? And who *is there* such as I who would go into the temple to save his life? I will not go in!" ¹²Then I perceived that God had not sent him at all, but that he pronounced *this* prophecy against me because Tobiah and Sanballat had hired him. ¹³For this reason he *was* hired, that I should be afraid and act that way and sin, so *that* they might have *cause* for an evil report, that they might reproach me.

¹⁴My God, remember Tobiah and Sanballat, according to these their works, and the prophetess Noadiah and the rest of the prophets who would have made me afraid.

¹⁵So the wall was finished on the twenty-fifth *day* of Elul, in fifty-two days. ¹⁶And it happened, when all our enemies heard *of it,* and all the nations around us saw *these things,* that they were very disheartened in their own eyes; for they perceived that this work was done by our God.

¹⁷Also in those days the nobles of Judah sent many letters to Tobiah, and *the letters of* Tobiah came to them. ¹⁸For many in Judah were pledged to him, because he was the son-in-law of Shechaniah the son of Arah, and his son Jehohanan had married the daughter of Meshullam the son of Berechiah. ¹⁹Also they reported his good deeds before me, and reported my words to him. Tobiah sent letters to frighten me.

CHAPTER **7** Then it was, when the wall was built and I had hung the doors, when the gatekeepers, the singers, and the Levites had been appointed, ²that I gave the charge of Jerusalem to my brother Hanani, and Hananiah the leader of the citadel, for he *was* a faithful man and feared God more than many.

³And I said to them, "Do not let the gates of Jerusalem

◤◤◤◣ COURAGE

6:10-13 When Nehemiah was attacked personally, he refused to give in to fear and flee to the temple. According to God's law, it would have been wrong for Nehemiah to go into the temple to hide because he wasn't a priest (Numbers 18:22). If he had run for his life, he would have undermined the courage he was trying to instill in the people. Leaders are targets for attacks. Make it a practice to pray for those in authority (1 Timothy 2:2). Pray that they will stand against personal attacks and temptation. They need God-given courage to overcome fear.

be opened until the sun is hot; and while they stand *guard,* let them shut and bar the doors; and appoint guards from among the inhabitants of Jerusalem, one at his watch station and another in front of his own house."

⁴Now the city *was* large and spacious, but the people in it *were* few, and the houses *were* not rebuilt. ⁵Then my God put it into my heart to gather the nobles, the rulers, and the people, that they might be registered by genealogy. And I found a register of the genealogy of those who had come up in the first *return,* and found written in it:

⁶ These *are* the people of the province who came back from the captivity, of those who had been carried away, whom Nebuchadnezzar the king of Babylon had carried away, and who returned to Jerusalem and Judah, everyone to his city.

⁷ Those who came with Zerubbabel *were* Jeshua, Nehemiah, Azariah, Raamiah, Nahamani, Mordecai, Bilshan, Mispereth, Bigvai, Nehum, and Baanah.

The number of the men of the people of Israel: ⁸the sons of Parosh, two thousand one hundred and seventy-two;

◤◤◤◣ FOLLOW-UP

7:3-4 The wall was complete, but the work was not finished. Nehemiah assigned each family the task of protecting the section of wall next to their home. It is tempting to relax our guard and rest on past accomplishments after we have completed a large task. But we must continue to serve and to take care of all that God has entrusted to us. Following through after a project is completed is as vital as doing the project itself.

⁹the sons of Shephatiah, three hundred and seventy-two;

¹⁰the sons of Arah, six hundred and fifty-two;

¹¹the sons of Pahath-Moab, of the sons of Jeshua and Joab, two thousand eight hundred and eighteen;

¹²the sons of Elam, one thousand two hundred and fifty-four;

¹³the sons of Zattu, eight hundred and forty-five;

¹⁴the sons of Zaccai, seven hundred and sixty;

¹⁵the sons of Binnui, six hundred and forty-eight;

¹⁶the sons of Bebai, six hundred and twenty-eight;

¹⁷the sons of Azgad, two thousand three hundred and twenty-two;

¹⁸the sons of Adonikam, six hundred and sixty-seven;

¹⁹the sons of Bigvai, two thousand and sixty-seven;

²⁰the sons of Adin, six hundred and fifty-five;

²¹the sons of Ater of Hezekiah, ninety-eight;

²²the sons of Hashum, three hundred and twenty-eight;

²³the sons of Bezai, three hundred and twenty-four;

²⁴the sons of Hariph, one hundred and twelve;

²⁵the sons of Gibeon, ninety-five;

²⁶the men of Bethlehem and Netophah, one hundred and eighty-eight;

²⁷the men of Anathoth, one hundred and twenty-eight;

²⁸the men of Beth Azmaveth, forty-two;

²⁹the men of Kirjath Jearim, Chephirah, and Beeroth, seven hundred and forty-three;

³⁰the men of Ramah and Geba, six hundred and twenty-one;

³¹the men of Michmas, one hundred and twenty-two;

³²the men of Bethel and Ai, one hundred and twenty-three;

³³the men of the other Nebo, fifty-two;

³⁴the sons of the other Elam, one thousand two hundred and fifty-four;

³⁵the sons of Harim, three hundred and twenty;

³⁶the sons of Jericho, three hundred and forty-five;

³⁷the sons of Lod, Hadid, and Ono, seven hundred and twenty-one;

³⁸the sons of Senaah, three thousand nine hundred and thirty.

³⁹ The priests: the sons of Jedaiah, of the house of Jeshua, nine hundred and seventy-three;

⁴⁰the sons of Immer, one thousand and fifty-two;

⁴¹the sons of Pashhur, one thousand two hundred and forty-seven;

⁴²the sons of Harim, one thousand and seventeen.

⁴³ The Levites: the sons of Jeshua, of Kadmiel, *and* of the sons of Hodevah, seventy-four.

⁴⁴ The singers: the sons of Asaph, one hundred and forty-eight.

⁴⁵ The gatekeepers: the sons of Shallum,

the sons of Ater,
the sons of Talmon,
the sons of Akkub,
the sons of Hatita,
the sons of Shobai, one hundred and thirty-eight.

⁴⁶ The Nethinim: the sons of Ziha,
the sons of Hasupha,
the sons of Tabbaoth,
⁴⁷the sons of Keros,
the sons of Sia,
the sons of Padon,
⁴⁸the sons of Lebana,
the sons of Hagaba,
the sons of Salmai,
⁴⁹the sons of Hanan,
the sons of Giddel,
the sons of Gahar,
⁵⁰the sons of Reaiah,
the sons of Rezin,
the sons of Nekoda,
⁵¹the sons of Gazzam,
the sons of Uzza,
the sons of Paseah,
⁵²the sons of Besai,
the sons of Meunim,
the sons of Nephishesim,
⁵³the sons of Bakbuk,
the sons of Hakupha,
the sons of Harhur,
⁵⁴the sons of Bazlith,
the sons of Mehida,
the sons of Harsha,
⁵⁵the sons of Barkos,
the sons of Sisera,
the sons of Tamah,
⁵⁶the sons of Neziah,
and the sons of Hatipha.

⁵⁷ The sons of Solomon's servants: the sons of Sotai,
the sons of Sophereth,
the sons of Perida,
⁵⁸the sons of Jaala,
the sons of Darkon,
the sons of Giddel,
⁵⁹the sons of Shephatiah,
the sons of Hattil,
the sons of Pochereth of Zebaim,
and the children of Amon.
⁶⁰All the Nethinim, and the sons of Solomon's servants, *were* three hundred and ninety-two.

⁶¹ And these *were* the ones who came up from Tel Melah, Tel Harsha, Cherub, Addon, and Immer, but they could not identify their father's house nor their lineage, whether they *were* of Israel:
⁶²the sons of Delaiah,
the sons of Tobiah,
the sons of Nekoda, six hundred and forty-two;
⁶³and of the priests: the sons of Habaiah,
the sons of Koz,
the sons of Barzillai, who took a wife of the

daughters of Barzillai the Gileadite, and was called by their name. [64]These sought their listing *among* those who were registered by genealogy, but it was not found; therefore they were excluded from the priesthood as defiled. [65]And the governor said to them that they should not eat of the most holy things till a priest could consult with the Urim and Thummim.

[66] Altogether the whole assembly *was* forty-two thousand three hundred and sixty, [67]besides their male and female servants, of whom *there were* seven thousand three hundred and thirty-seven; and they had two hundred and forty-five men and women singers. [68]Their horses were seven hundred and thirty-six, their mules two hundred and forty-five, [69]*their* camels four hundred and thirty-five, *and* donkeys six thousand seven hundred and twenty.

[70] And some of the heads of the fathers' houses gave to the work. The governor gave to the treasury one thousand gold drachmas, fifty basins, and five hundred and thirty priestly garments. [71]Some of the heads of the fathers' *houses* gave to the treasury of the work twenty thousand gold drachmas, and two thousand two hundred silver minas. [72]And that which the rest of the people gave *was* twenty thousand gold drachmas, two thousand silver minas, and sixty-seven priestly garments.

[73]So the priests, the Levites, the gatekeepers, the singers, *some* of the people, the Nethinim, and all Israel dwelt in their cities.

When the seventh month came, the children of Israel *were* in their cities.

CHAPTER 8 EZRA READS THE LAW.

Now all the people gathered together as one man in the open square that *was* in front of the Water Gate; and they told Ezra the scribe to bring the Book of the Law of Moses, which the LORD had commanded Israel. [2]So Ezra the priest brought the Law before the assembly of men and women and all who *could* hear with understanding on the first day of the seventh month. [3]Then he read from it in the open square that *was* in front of the Water Gate from morning until midday, before the men and women and those who could understand; and the ears of all the people *were* attentive to the Book of the Law.

[4]So Ezra the scribe stood on a platform of wood which they had made for the purpose; and beside him, at his right hand, stood Mattithiah, Shema, Anaiah, Urijah, Hilkiah, and Maaseiah; and at his left hand Pedaiah, Mishael, Malchijah, Hashum, Hashbadana, Zechariah, *and* Meshullam. [5]And Ezra opened the book in the sight of all the people, for he was *standing* above all the people; and when he opened it, all the people stood up. [6]And Ezra blessed the LORD, the great God.

Then all the people answered, "Amen, Amen!" while lifting up their hands. And they bowed their heads and worshiped the LORD with *their* faces to the ground.

[7]Also Jeshua, Bani, Sherebiah, Jamin, Akkub, Shabbethai, Hodijah, Maaseiah, Kelita, Azariah, Jozabad, Hanan, Pelaiah, and the Levites, helped the people to understand the Law; and the people *stood* in their place. [8]So they read distinctly from the book, in the Law of God; and they gave the sense, and helped *them* to understand the reading.

[9]And Nehemiah, who *was* the governor, Ezra the priest *and* scribe, and the Levites who taught the people said to all the people, "This day *is* holy to the LORD your God; do not mourn nor weep." For all the people wept, when they heard the words of the Law.

APPLY IT

8:1-5 The people paid close attention to Ezra as he read God's Word, and their lives were changed. Because we hear the Bible so often, we can become dulled to its words and immune to its teachings. Instead, we should *listen* carefully to every verse and ask the Holy Spirit to help us answer the question, "How does this apply to *my* life?"

[10]Then he said to them, "Go your way, eat the fat, drink the sweet, and send portions to those for whom nothing is prepared; for *this* day *is* holy to our Lord. Do not sorrow, for the joy of the LORD is your strength."

[11]So the Levites quieted all the people, saying, "Be still, for the day *is* holy; do not be grieved." [12]And all the people went their way to eat and drink, to send portions and rejoice greatly, because they understood the words that were declared to them.

[13]Now on the second day the heads of the fathers' *houses* of all the people, with the priests and Levites, were gathered to Ezra the scribe, in order to understand the words of the Law. [14]And they found written in the Law, which the LORD had commanded by Moses, that the children of Israel should dwell in booths during the feast of the seventh month, [15]and that they should announce and proclaim in all their cities and in Jerusalem, saying, "Go out to the mountain, and bring olive branches, branches of oil trees, myrtle branches, palm branches, and branches of leafy trees, to make booths, as *it is* written."

[16]Then the people went out and brought *them* and made themselves booths, each one on the roof of his house, or in their courtyards or the courts of the house of God, and in the open square of the Water Gate and in the open square of the Gate of Ephraim. [17]So the whole assembly of those who had returned from the captivity made booths and sat under the booths; for since the days of Joshua the son of Nun until that day the children of Israel had not done so. And there was very great gladness. [18]Also day by day, from the first day until the last day, he read from the Book of the Law of God. And they kept the feast seven days; and on the eighth day *there was* a sacred assembly, according to the *prescribed* manner.

ACT ON IT!

8:13ff After Ezra read God's laws to the people, they studied them further and then acted upon them. A careful reading of Scripture always calls for a response to these questions: "What should I *do* with this knowledge?" "How should my life change?" We must *do* something about what we have learned if it is to have real significance for our life.

CHAPTER 9 EZRA LEADS IN CONFESSION.

Now on the twenty-fourth day of this month the children of Israel were assembled with fasting, in sackcloth, and with dust on their heads. ²Then those of Israelite lineage separated themselves from all foreigners; and they stood and confessed their sins and the iniquities of their fathers. ³And they stood up in their place and read from the Book of the Law of the LORD their God *for one*-fourth of the day; and *for another* fourth they confessed and worshiped the LORD their God.

◄ I CONFESS!

9:2-3 The Hebrews practiced open confession, admitting their sins to one another. Reading and studying God's Word should precede confession (see 8:18) because God can show us where we are sinning. Honest confession should precede worship, because we cannot have a right relationship with God if we hold on to certain sins.

⁴Then Jeshua, Bani, Kadmiel, Shebaniah, Bunni, Sherebiah, Bani, *and* Chenani stood on the stairs of the Levites and cried out with a loud voice to the LORD their God. ⁵And the Levites, Jeshua, Kadmiel, Bani, Hashabniah, Sherebiah, Hodijah, Shebaniah, *and* Pethahiah, said:

"Stand up *and* bless the LORD your God
Forever and ever!

"Blessed be Your glorious name,
Which is exalted above all blessing and praise!
⁶ You alone *are* the LORD;
You have made heaven,
The heaven of heavens, with all their host,
The earth and everything on it,
The seas and all that is in them,
And You preserve them all.
The host of heaven worships You.

⁷ "You *are* the LORD God,
Who chose Abram,
And brought him out of Ur of the Chaldeans,
And gave him the name Abraham;
⁸ You found his heart faithful before You,
And made a covenant with him
To give the land of the Canaanites,
The Hittites, the Amorites,
The Perizzites, the Jebusites,
And the Girgashites—
To give *it* to his descendants.
You have performed Your words,
For You *are* righteous.

⁹ "You saw the affliction of our fathers in Egypt,
And heard their cry by the Red Sea.
¹⁰ You showed signs and wonders against Pharaoh,
Against all his servants,
And against all the people of his land.
For You knew that they acted proudly against them.
So You made a name for Yourself, as *it is* this day.
¹¹ And You divided the sea before them,
So that they went through the midst of the sea on the dry land;

And their persecutors You threw into the deep,
As a stone into the mighty waters.
¹² Moreover You led them by day with a cloudy pillar,
And by night with a pillar of fire,
To give them light on the road
Which they should travel.

¹³ "You came down also on Mount Sinai,
And spoke with them from heaven,
And gave them just ordinances and true laws,
Good statutes and commandments.
¹⁴ You made known to them Your holy Sabbath,
And commanded them precepts, statutes and laws,
By the hand of Moses Your servant.
¹⁵ You gave them bread from heaven for their hunger,
And brought them water out of the rock for their thirst,
And told them to go in to possess the land
Which You had sworn to give them.

¹⁶ "But they and our fathers acted proudly,
Hardened their necks,
And did not heed Your commandments.
¹⁷ They refused to obey,
And they were not mindful of Your wonders
That You did among them.
But they hardened their necks,
And in their rebellion
They appointed a leader
To return to their bondage.
But You *are* God,
Ready to pardon,
Gracious and merciful,
Slow to anger,
Abundant in kindness,
And did not forsake them.

◄ AMAZING PATIENCE

9:16-21 Seeing how God continued to be with his people shows ʰ his patience is amazing! In spite of our repeated failings, pride, anᵈ stubbornness, he is always ready to pardon (9:17), and his Spirit isˢ always ready to instruct (9:20). Realizing the extent of God's forgiʲ helps us forgive those who fail us, even "seventy times seven" timeˢ necessary (Matthew 18:21-22).

¹⁸ "Even when they made a molded calf for themselves,
And said, 'This *is* your god
That brought you up out of Egypt,'
And worked great provocations,
¹⁹ Yet in Your manifold mercies
You did not forsake them in the wilderness.
The pillar of the cloud did not depart from them by day,
To lead them on the road;
Nor the pillar of fire by night,
To show them light,
And the way they should go.
²⁰ You also gave Your good Spirit to instruct them,
And did not withhold Your manna from their mouth,
And gave them water for their thirst.
²¹ Forty years You sustained them in the wilderness;

They lacked nothing;
Their clothes did not wear out
And their feet did not swell.

22 "Moreover You gave them kingdoms and nations,
And divided them into districts.
So they took possession of the land of Sihon,
The land of the king of Heshbon,
And the land of Og king of Bashan.
23 You also multiplied their children as the stars of
heaven,
And brought them into the land
Which You had told their fathers
To go in and possess.
24 So the people went in
And possessed the land;
You subdued before them the inhabitants of the
land,
The Canaanites,
And gave them into their hands,
With their kings
And the people of the land,
That they might do with them as they wished.
25 And they took strong cities and a rich land,
And possessed houses full of all goods,
Cisterns *already* dug, vineyards, olive groves,
And fruit trees in abundance.
So they ate and were filled and grew fat,
And delighted themselves in Your great goodness.

26 "Nevertheless they were disobedient
And rebelled against You,
Cast Your law behind their backs
And killed Your prophets, who testified against them
To turn them to Yourself;
And they worked great provocations.
27 Therefore You delivered them into the hand of their
enemies,
Who oppressed them;
And in the time of their trouble,
When they cried to You,
You heard from heaven;
And according to Your abundant mercies
You gave them deliverers who saved them
From the hand of their enemies.

28 "But after they had rest,
They again did evil before You.
Therefore You left them in the hand of their enemies,
So that they had dominion over them;
Yet when they returned and cried out to You,
You heard from heaven;
And many times You delivered them according to
Your mercies,
29 And testified against them,
That You might bring them back to Your law.
Yet they acted proudly,
And did not heed Your commandments,
But sinned against Your judgments,
'Which if a man does, he shall live by them.'
And they shrugged their shoulders,
Stiffened their necks,

And would not hear.
30 Yet for many years You had patience with them,
And testified against them by Your Spirit in Your
prophets.
Yet they would not listen;
Therefore You gave them into the hand of the
peoples of the lands.
31 Nevertheless in Your great mercy
You did not utterly consume them nor forsake them;
For You *are* God, gracious and merciful.

32 "Now therefore, our God,
The great, the mighty, and awesome God,
Who keeps covenant and mercy:
Do not let all the trouble seem small before You
That has come upon us,
Our kings and our princes,
Our priests and our prophets,
Our fathers and on all Your people,
From the days of the kings of Assyria until this day.
33 However You *are* just in all that has befallen us;
For You have dealt faithfully,
But we have done wickedly.
34 Neither our kings nor our princes,
Our priests nor our fathers,
Have kept Your law,
Nor heeded Your commandments and Your
testimonies,
With which You testified against them.
35 For they have not served You in their kingdom,
Or in the many good *things* that You gave them,
Or in the large and rich land which You set before
them;
Nor did they turn from their wicked works.

36 "Here we *are*, servants today!
And the land that You gave to our fathers,
To eat its fruit and its bounty,
Here we *are*, servants in it!
37 And it yields much increase to the kings
You have set over us,
Because of our sins;
Also they have dominion over our bodies and our
cattle
At their pleasure;
And we *are* in great distress.

38 "And because of all this,
We make a sure *covenant* and write *it*;
Our leaders, our Levites, *and* our priests seal *it*."

CHAPTER **10** **THE PEOPLE AGREE TO OBEY.** Now
those who placed *their* seal on *the document* were:
Nehemiah the governor, the son of Hacaliah, and Zedekiah, ²Seraiah, Azariah, Jeremiah, ³Pashhur, Amariah,

◣▬▬▬▬▬▬▬▬▬▬▬▬**SHOWERED**

9:35-36 Sometimes the very blessings God has showered on us make
us forget him. We often are tempted to rely on money for security rather
than on God. As you see what happened to the Israelites, look at your
own life. Do your blessings make you thankful to God and draw you
closer to him, or do they make you feel independent and forgetful of
God?

COMMITTED

10:28ff The wall was completed, and the covenant God made with his people in the days of Moses was restored (Deuteronomy 8). This covenant includes principles that are important for us today. Our relationship with God goes far beyond church attendance and regular devotions. It should affect our relationships (10:30), our time (10:31), and our material resources (10:32-40). When you chose to follow God, you promised to serve him. The Israelites had fallen away from the original commitment they had made to follow God. We must be careful not to do the same.

Malchijah, ⁴Hattush, Shebaniah, Malluch, ⁵Harim, Meremoth, Obadiah, ⁶Daniel, Ginnethon, Baruch, ⁷Meshullam, Abijah, Mijamin, ⁸Maaziah, Bilgai, *and* Shemaiah. These *were* the priests.

⁹The Levites: Jeshua the son of Azaniah, Binnui of the sons of Henadad, *and* Kadmiel.

¹⁰Their brethren: Shebaniah, Hodijah, Kelita, Pelaiah, Hanan, ¹¹Micha, Rehob, Hashabiah, ¹²Zaccur, Sherebiah, Shebaniah, ¹³Hodijah, Bani, *and* Beninu.

¹⁴The leaders of the people: Parosh, Pahath-Moab, Elam, Zattu, Bani, ¹⁵Bunni, Azgad, Bebai, ¹⁶Adonijah, Bigvai, Adin, ¹⁷Ater, Hezekiah, Azzur, ¹⁸Hodijah, Hashum, Bezai, ¹⁹Hariph, Anathoth, Nebai, ²⁰Magpiash, Meshullam, Hezir, ²¹Meshezabel, Zadok, Jaddua, ²²Pelatiah, Hanan, Anaiah, ²³Hoshea, Hananiah, Hasshub, ²⁴Hallohesh, Pilha, Shobek, ²⁵Rehum, Hashabnah, Maaseiah, ²⁶Ahijah, Hanan, Anan, ²⁷Malluch, Harim, *and* Baanah.

²⁸Now the rest of the people—the priests, the Levites, the gatekeepers, the singers, the Nethinim, and all those who had separated themselves from the peoples of the lands to the Law of God, their wives, their sons, and their daughters, everyone who had knowledge and understanding— ²⁹these joined with their brethren, their nobles, and entered into a curse and an oath to walk in God's Law, which was given by Moses the servant of God, and to observe and do all the commandments of the LORD our Lord, and His ordinances and His statutes: ³⁰We would not give our daughters as wives to the peoples of the land, nor take their daughters for our sons; ³¹*if* the peoples of the land brought wares or any grain to sell on the Sabbath day, we would not buy it from them on the

LURED AWAY

10:31 God recognized that the lure of money would conflict with the need for a day of rest, so trade was forbidden inside the city on the Sabbath. By deciding to honor God first, the Israelites would be refusing to make money their god. Our culture often makes us choose between convenience and profit on the one hand, and setting God first on the other. Look at your work and worship habits: is God really first?

Sabbath, or on a holy day; and we would forego the seventh year's *produce* and the exacting of every debt.

³²Also we made ordinances for ourselves, to exact from ourselves yearly one-third of a shekel for the service of the house of our God: ³³for the showbread, for the regular grain offering, for the regular burnt offering of the Sabbaths, the New Moons, and the set feasts; for the holy things, for the sin offerings to make atonement for Israel, and all the work of the house of our God. ³⁴We cast lots among the priests, the Levites, and the people, for bring-

ing the wood offering into the house of our God, according to our fathers' houses, at the appointed times year by year, to burn on the altar of the LORD our God as *it is* written in the Law.

³⁵And *we made ordinances* to bring the firstfruits of our ground and the firstfruits of all fruit of all trees, year by year, to the house of the LORD; ³⁶to bring the firstborn of our sons and our cattle, as *it is* written in the Law, and the firstborn of our herds and our flocks, to the house of our God, to the priests who minister in the house of our God; ³⁷to bring the firstfruits of our dough, our offerings, the fruit from all kinds of trees, *the* new wine and oil, to the priests, to the storerooms of the house of our God; and to bring the tithes of our land to the Levites, for the Levites should receive the tithes in all our farming communities. ³⁸And the priest, the descendant of Aaron, shall be with the Levites when the Levites receive tithes; and the Levites shall bring up a tenth of the tithes to the house of our God, to the rooms of the storehouse.

GIFTS

10:36 This practice was instituted at the time of the exodus from ▮ The people needed to relearn the importance of dedicating the first▮ of their yield to God. Nehemiah was simply reinstating this practice the early days of the nation (Exodus 13:1-2; Numbers 3:40-51).

We, too, need to remember that everything that we have—possessions, talents, money, friends, etc.—is from God. We should dedicate all that we have to his use. Don't withhold anything from G Instead, ask him to show you how to honor him with your time, tale relationships, and possessions.

³⁹For the children of Israel and the children of Levi shall bring the offering of the grain, of the new wine and the oil, to the storerooms where the articles of the sanctuary *are, where* the priests who minister and the gatekeepers and the singers *are*; and we will not neglect the house of our God.

CHAPTER **11** THE MOVE INTO THE NEW CITY. Now the leaders of the people dwelt at Jerusalem; the rest of the people cast lots to bring one out of ten to dwell in Jerusalem, the holy city, and nine-tenths *were to dwell* in *other* cities. ²And the people blessed all the men who willingly offered themselves to dwell at Jerusalem.

³These *are* the heads of the province who dwelt in Jerusalem. (But in the cities of Judah everyone dwelt in

VOLUNTEER

11:1 The exiles who returned were few in number compared to Jerusalem's population in the days of the kings. Because the walls ▮ been rebuilt on their original foundations, the city seemed sparsely populated. Nehemiah asked one-tenth of the people from the outly areas to move inside the city walls to keep large areas of the city f▮ being vacant. Apparently these people did not want to move into th Only a few volunteered. Finally, Nehemiah cast lots to determine w among the remaining people would have to move.

How do you respond when God calls you into action? Do you re grumble about what you are being asked to do? Or are you a willi▮ volunteer? Ask God to help you become someone who is willing to God's call, no matter where it may lead.

his own possession in their cities—Israelites, priests, Levites, Nethinim, and descendants of Solomon's servants.) ⁴Also in Jerusalem dwelt *some* of the children of Judah and of the children of Benjamin.

The children of Judah: Athaiah the son of Uzziah, the son of Zechariah, the son of Amariah, the son of Shephatiah, the son of Mahalalel, of the children of Perez; ⁵and Maaseiah the son of Baruch, the son of Col-Hozeh, the son of Hazaiah, the son of Adaiah, the son of Joiarib, the son of Zechariah, the son of Shiloni. ⁶All the sons of Perez who dwelt at Jerusalem *were* four hundred and sixty-eight valiant men.

⁷And these are the sons of Benjamin: Sallu the son of Meshullam, the son of Joed, the son of Pedaiah, the son of Kolaiah, the son of Maaseiah, the son of Ithiel, the son of Jeshaiah; ⁸and after him Gabbai *and* Sallai, nine hundred and twenty-eight. ⁹Joel the son of Zichri *was* their overseer, and Judah the son of Senuah *was* second over the city.

¹⁰Of the priests: Jedaiah the son of Joiarib, and Jachin; ¹¹Seraiah the son of Hilkiah, the son of Meshullam, the son of Zadok, the son of Meraioth, the son of Ahitub, *was* the leader of the house of God. ¹²Their brethren who did the work of the house *were* eight hundred and twenty-two; and Adaiah the son of Jeroham, the son of Pelaliah, the son of Amzi, the son of Zechariah, the son of Pashhur, the son of Malchijah, ¹³and his brethren, heads of the fathers' *houses*, *were* two hundred and forty-two; and Amashai the son of Azarel, the son of Ahzai, the son of Meshillemoth, the son of Immer, ¹⁴and their brethren, mighty men of valor, *were* one hundred and twenty-eight. Their overseer *was* Zabdiel the son of *one of* the great men.

¹⁵Also of the Levites: Shemaiah the son of Hasshub, the son of Azrikam, the son of Hashabiah, the son of Bunni; ¹⁶Shabbethai and Jozabad, of the heads of the Levites, *had* the oversight of the business outside of the house of God; ¹⁷Mattaniah the son of Micha, the son of Zabdi, the son of Asaph, the leader *who* began the thanksgiving with prayer; Bakbukiah, the second among his brethren; and Abda the son of Shammua, the son of Galal, the son of Jeduthun. ¹⁸All the Levites in the holy city *were* two hundred and eighty-four.

¹⁹Moreover the gatekeepers, Akkub, Talmon, and their brethren who kept the gates, *were* one hundred and seventy-two.

²⁰And the rest of Israel, of the priests *and* Levites, *were* in all the cities of Judah, everyone in his inheritance. ²¹But the Nethinim dwelt in Ophel. And Ziha and Gishpa *were* over the Nethinim.

²²Also the overseer of the Levites at Jerusalem *was* Uzzi the son of Bani, the son of Hashabiah, the son of Mattaniah, the son of Micha, of the sons of Asaph, the singers in charge of the service of the house of God. ²³For *it was* the king's command concerning them that a certain portion should be for the singers, a quota day by day. ²⁴Pethahiah the son of Meshezabel, of the children of Zerah the son of Judah, *was* the king's deputy in all matters concerning the people.

²⁵And as for the villages with their fields, *some* of the children of Judah dwelt in Kirjath Arba and its villages,

Dibon and its villages, Jekabzeel and its villages; ²⁶in Jeshua, Moladah, Beth Pelet, ²⁷Hazar Shual, and Beersheba and its villages; ²⁸in Ziklag and Meconah and its villages; ²⁹in En Rimmon, Zorah, Jarmuth, ³⁰Zanoah, Adullam, and their villages; in Lachish and its fields; in Azekah and its villages. They dwelt from Beersheba to the Valley of Hinnom.

³¹Also the children of Benjamin from Geba *dwelt* in Michmash, Aija, and Bethel, and their villages; ³²in Anathoth, Nob, Ananiah; ³³in Hazor, Ramah, Gittaim; ³⁴in Hadid, Zeboim, Neballat; ³⁵in Lod, Ono, *and* the Valley of Craftsmen. ³⁶Some of the Judean divisions of Levites *were* in Benjamin.

CHAPTER 12 THE PRIESTS AND LEVITES. Now these *are* the priests and the Levites who came up with Zerubbabel the son of Shealtiel, and Jeshua: Seraiah, Jeremiah, Ezra, ²Amariah, Malluch, Hattush, ³Shechaniah, Rehum, Meremoth, ⁴Iddo, Ginnethoi, Abijah, ⁵Mijamin, Maadiah, Bilgah, ⁶Shemaiah, Joiarib, Jedaiah, ⁷Sallu, Amok, Hilkiah, *and* Jedaiah.

These *were* the heads of the priests and their brethren in the days of Jeshua.

⁸Moreover the Levites *were* Jeshua, Binnui, Kadmiel, Sherebiah, Judah, *and* Mattaniah *who led* the thanksgiving *psalms*, he and his brethren. ⁹Also Bakbukiah and Unni, their brethren, *stood* across from them in *their* duties.

¹⁰Jeshua begot Joiakim, Joiakim begot Eliashib, Eliashib begot Joiada, ¹¹Joiada begot Jonathan, and Jonathan begot Jaddua.

¹²Now in the days of Joiakim, the priests, the heads of the fathers' *houses were:* of Seraiah, Meraiah; of Jeremiah, Hananiah; ¹³of Ezra, Meshullam; of Amariah, Jehohanan; ¹⁴of Melichu, Jonathan; of Shebaniah, Joseph; ¹⁵of Harim, Adna; of Meraioth, Helkai; ¹⁶of Iddo, Zechariah; of Ginnethon, Meshullam; ¹⁷of Abijah, Zichri; *the son* of Minjamin; of Moadiah, Piltai; ¹⁸of Bilgah, Shammua; of Shemaiah, Jehonathan; ¹⁹of Joiarib, Mattenai; of Jedaiah, Uzzi; ²⁰of Sallai, Kallai; of Amok, Eber; ²¹of Hilkiah, Hashabiah; *and* of Jedaiah, Nethanel.

²²During the reign of Darius the Persian, a record *was also kept* of the Levites and priests *who had been* heads of their fathers' *houses* in the days of Eliashib, Joiada, Johanan, and Jaddua. ²³The sons of Levi, the heads of the fathers' *houses* until the days of Johanan the son of Eliashib, *were* written in the book of the chronicles.

²⁴And the heads of the Levites *were* Hashabiah, Sherebiah, and Jeshua the son of Kadmiel, with their brothers across from them, to praise *and* give thanks, group alternating with group, according to the command of David the man of God. ²⁵Mattaniah, Bakbukiah, Obadiah, Meshullam, Talmon, and Akkub *were* gatekeepers keeping the watch at the storerooms of the gates. ²⁶These *lived* in the days of Joiakim the son of Jeshua, the son of Jozadak, and in the days of Nehemiah the governor, and of Ezra the priest, the scribe.

²⁷Now at the dedication of the wall of Jerusalem they sought out the Levites in all their places, to bring them to Jerusalem to celebrate the dedication with gladness,

both with thanksgivings and singing, *with* cymbals and stringed instruments and harps. [28]And the sons of the singers gathered together from the countryside around Jerusalem, from the villages of the Netophathites, [29]from the house of Gilgal, and from the fields of Geba and Azmaveth; for the singers had built themselves villages all around Jerusalem. [30]Then the priests and Levites purified themselves, and purified the people, the gates, and the wall.

[31]So I brought the leaders of Judah up on the wall, and appointed two large thanksgiving choirs. *One* went to the right hand on the wall toward the Refuse Gate. [32]After them went Hoshaiah and half of the leaders of Judah, [33]and Azariah, Ezra, Meshullam, [34]Judah, Benjamin, Shemaiah, Jeremiah, [35]and some of the priests' sons with trumpets—Zechariah the son of Jonathan, the son of Shemaiah, the son of Mattaniah, the son of Michaiah, the son of Zaccur, the son of Asaph, [36]and his brethren, Shemaiah, Azarel, Milalai, Gilalai, Maai, Nethanel, Judah, *and* Hanani, with the musical instruments of David the man of God. And Ezra the scribe *went* before them. [37]By the Fountain Gate, in front of them, they went up the stairs of the City of David, on the stairway of the wall, beyond the house of David, as far as the Water Gate eastward.

MUSIC

12:35-36 How could the priests have used King David's original musical instruments? David had instituted music into worship in the temple, and so his instruments had probably been stored there. Although Nebuchadnezzar destroyed the temple, he took many temple items back to Babylon with him (2 Chronicles 36:18). These most likely were preserved in Babylon and given back to the Israelites by Cyrus when they returned to their land (Ezra 1:7-11).

Music was an important part of the dedication of the city wall. It still is an important part of worship today. We delight God when we sing our praises to him. What is there in your life that you can sing praises to God about? Take some time to sing your own praise song to him today. He is a willing and appreciative audience.

[38]The other thanksgiving choir went the opposite *way*, and I *was* behind them with half of the people on the wall, going past the Tower of the Ovens as far as the Broad Wall, [39]and above the Gate of Ephraim, above the Old Gate, above the Fish Gate, the Tower of Hananel, the Tower of the Hundred, as far as the Sheep Gate; and they stopped by the Gate of the Prison.

[40]So the two thanksgiving choirs stood in the house of God, likewise I and the half of the rulers with me; [41]and the priests, Eliakim, Maaseiah, Minjamin, Michaiah, Elioenai, Zechariah, *and* Hananiah, with trumpets; [42]also Maaseiah, Shemaiah, Eleazar, Uzzi, Jehohanan, Malchijah, Elam, and Ezer. The singers sang loudly with Jezrahiah the director.

[43]Also that day they offered great sacrifices, and rejoiced, for God had made them rejoice with great joy; the women and the children also rejoiced, so that the joy of Jerusalem was heard afar off.

[44]And at the same time some were appointed over the rooms of the storehouse for the offerings, the firstfruits,

INFLUENCE

13:3 "The mixed multitude" refers to the Moabites and Ammonit‑ nations who were bitter enemies of Israel (13:1). God's law clearly that these two peoples should never be allowed in the temple (Deuteronomy 23:3-5). This had nothing to do with racial prejudice because God loves all people. Rather, the relationships between Jev the heathen had caused their captivity in the first place. While God all people to come to him (2 Pet. 3:9), he warns believers to stay a from those intent on evil (Proverbs 24:1). We need to be careful ab the people we spent time with, because, like Israel, we may find th unbelievers are more of an influence on us than we are on them.

and the tithes, to gather into them from the fields of the cities the portions specified by the Law for the priests and Levites; for Judah rejoiced over the priests and Levites who ministered. [45]Both the singers and the gatekeepers kept the charge of their God and the charge of the purification, according to the command of David *and* Solomon his son. [46]For in the days of David and Asaph of old *there were* chiefs of the singers, and songs of praise and thanksgiving to God. [47]In the days of Zerubbabel and in the days of Nehemiah all Israel gave the portions for the singers and the gatekeepers, a portion for each day. They also consecrated *holy things* for the Levites, and the Levites consecrated *them* for the children of Aaron.

CHAPTER **13** FOREIGNERS ARE SENT AWAY. On that day they read from the Book of Moses in the hearing of the people, and in it was found written that no Ammonite or Moabite should ever come into the assembly of God, [2]because they had not met the children of Israel with bread and water, but hired Balaam against them to curse them. However, our God turned the curse into a blessing. [3]So it was, when they had heard the Law, that they separated all the mixed multitude from Israel.

[4]Now before this, Eliashib the priest, having authority over the storerooms of the house of our God, *was* allied with Tobiah. [5]And he had prepared for him a large room, where previously they had stored the grain offerings, the frankincense, the articles, the tithes of grain, the new wine and oil, which were commanded *to be given* to the Levites and singers and gatekeepers, and the offerings for the priests. [6]But during all this I was not in Jerusalem, for in the thirty-second year of Artaxerxes king of Babylon I had returned to the king. Then after certain days I obtained leave from the king, [7]and I came to Jerusalem and discovered the evil that Eliashib had done for Tobiah, in preparing a room for him in the courts of the house of God. [8]And it grieved me bitterly; therefore I threw all the

DEDICATION

12:44-47 The dedication of the city wall was characterized by j praise, and singing (12:24,27-29,35-36,40-42). Nehemiah repea mentioned King David, who began the custom of using choirs in w In David's day, Israel was a vigorous, God-fearing nation. These e: who had returned wanted their rebuilt Jerusalem to be the hub of renewed nation that was strengthened by God. Therefore, they de themselves and their city to God.

household goods of Tobiah out of the room. ⁹Then I commanded them to cleanse the rooms; and I brought back into them the articles of the house of God, with the grain offering and the frankincense.

¹⁰I also realized that the portions for the Levites had not been given *them;* for each of the Levites and the singers who did the work had gone back to his field. ¹¹So I contended with the rulers, and said, "Why is the house of God forsaken?" And I gathered them together and set them in their place. ¹²Then all Judah brought the tithe of the grain and the new wine and the oil to the storehouse. ¹³And I appointed as treasurers over the storehouse Shelemiah the priest and Zadok the scribe, and of the Levites, Pedaiah; and next to them *was* Hanan the son of Zaccur, the son of Mattaniah; for they were considered faithful, and their task *was* to distribute to their brethren.

¹⁴Remember me, O my God, concerning this, and do not wipe out my good deeds that I have done for the house of my God, and for its services!

¹⁵In those days I saw *people* in Judah treading wine presses on the Sabbath, and bringing in sheaves, and loading donkeys with wine, grapes, figs, and all *kinds of* burdens, which they brought into Jerusalem on the Sabbath day. And I warned *them* about the day on which they were selling provisions. ¹⁶Men of Tyre dwelt there also, who brought in fish and all kinds of goods, and sold *them* on the Sabbath to the children of Judah, and in Jerusalem.

¹⁷Then I contended with the nobles of Judah, and said to them, "What evil thing *is* this that you do, by which you profane the Sabbath day? ¹⁸Did not your fathers do thus, and did not our God bring all this disaster on us and on this city? Yet you bring added wrath on Israel by profaning the Sabbath."

¹⁹So it was, at the gates of Jerusalem, as it began to be dark before the Sabbath, that I commanded the gates to be shut, and charged that they must not be opened till after the Sabbath. Then I posted *some* of my servants at the gates, *so that* no burdens would be brought in on the Sabbath day. ²⁰Now the merchants and sellers of all kinds of wares lodged outside Jerusalem once or twice. ²¹Then I warned them, and said to them, "Why do you spend the night around the wall? If you do *so* again, I will lay hands on you!" From that time on they came no *more* on the Sabbath. ²²And I commanded the Levites that they should cleanse themselves, and that they should go and guard the gates, to sanctify the Sabbath day.

Remember me, O my God, *concerning* this also, and spare me according to the greatness of Your mercy!

²³In those days I also saw Jews *who* had married women of Ashdod, Ammon, *and* Moab. ²⁴And half of their children spoke the language of Ashdod, and could not speak the language of Judah, but spoke according to the language of one or the other people.

²⁵So I contended with them and cursed them, struck some of them and pulled out their hair, and made them swear by God, *saying,* "You shall not give your daughters as wives to their sons, nor take their daughters for your sons or yourselves. ²⁶Did not Solomon king of Israel sin by these things? Yet among many nations there was no king like him, who was beloved of his God; and God made him king over all Israel. Nevertheless pagan women caused even him to sin. ²⁷Should we then hear of your doing all this great evil, transgressing against our God by marrying pagan women?"

◢▬▬▬▬TO LEAD

13:31 Nehemiah's life story provides many principles of effective leadership that are still valid today. (1) *Have a clear purpose;* and keep evaluating it in light of God's will. Nothing prevented Nehemiah from staying on track. (2) *Be straightforward and honest.* Everyone knew exactly what Nehemiah needed, and he spoke the truth even when it made his goal harder to achieve. (3) *Live above reproach.* The accusations against Nehemiah were empty and false. (4) *Be a person of constant prayer,* deriving power and wisdom from your contact with God. Everything Nehemiah did glorified God.

Leadership appears glamorous at times, but it often is lonely, thankless, and filled with pressures to compromise values and standards. Nehemiah was able to accomplish a huge task against incredible odds because he learned that there is no success without risk of failure, no reward without hard work, no opportunity without criticism, and no true leadership without trust in God.

²⁸And *one* of the sons of Joiada, the son of Eliashib the high priest, *was* a son-in-law of Sanballat the Horonite; therefore I drove him from me.

²⁹Remember them, O my God, because they have defiled the priesthood and the covenant of the priesthood and the Levites.

³⁰Thus I cleansed them of everything pagan. I also assigned duties to the priests and the Levites, each to his service, ³¹and *to bringing* the wood offering and the first-fruits at appointed times.

Remember me, O my God, for good!

MEGA Themes

VISION Although the Jews completed the temple in 516 B.C., the city walls remained in shambles for the next 70 years. The walls represented power, protection, and beauty. The walls also were needed to protect the temple from attack. God put the desire to rebuild the walls in Nehemiah's heart, giving him a vision for the work.

Does God have a vision for us? Are there "walls" that need to be built today? God still wants his people to be united and trained to do his work. As we recognize deep needs in our world, God can give us the vision and desire to "build." Look for construction projects that you can complete for God.

1. Nehemiah's vision for doing what God wanted began with his relationship with God. Based on the first chapter, how would you describe that relationship?
2. What qualities can you find in Nehemiah that could serve as your example of what it means to be God's visionary?
3. How can you prepare yourself now to be a person who not only has a vision for God's will, but who also is used by God to fulfill that vision?
4. You may not be ready for a task as large as Nehemiah's, but what small tasks are available to you that would be "building" for God's people? How will you begin your "construction project" in the coming days?

PRAYER Both Nehemiah and Ezra responded to problems with prayer. When Nehemiah began his work he recognized the problem, prayed right away, and then acted on the problem.

Prayer still is God's way to solve problems. Prayer and action go hand-in-hand. Through prayer, God guides our preparation, teamwork, and efforts to carry out his will. Without prayer, we are limited to our own finite resources.

1. How did prayer enter into Nehemiah's preparation for doing God's work?
2. Describe the importance of both attitude and action in terms of Nehemiah's prayer life.
3. Complete this sentence: I can prepare myself to be God's builder by beginning with prayer that includes _____.

4. Write out a prayer to God based on the "construction project" you listed above under VISION.

LEADERSHIP Nehemiah was an excellent leader. He was spiritually ready to heed God's call. He used careful planning, teamwork, problem solving, and courage to get the work done. Although he had tremendous faith, he never avoided the extra work necessary for good leadership.

Being God's leader is not just getting recognition, holding a position, or being the boss. It requires planning, hard work, courage, and perseverance. And there is no substitute for doing the difficult work. In order to lead others, you need to follow God's direction in your own life.

1. What are a few specific examples of Nehemiah's excellent leadership?
2. Based upon your study of Nehemiah and your experience with leaders you have known personally, make a list of the qualities that make a strong leader.
3. Evaluate yourself based on your list from number two. Which qualities are your strengths? Which are your weaknesses?
4. Describe ways in which you could use your strengths to influence others for Christ. Also, how can you develop those strengths and overcome your weaknesses?

PROBLEMS After the work began, Nehemiah faced scorn, slander, and threats from enemies, as well as fear, conflict, and discouragement from his own workers. Although these problems were difficult, they did not stop Nehemiah from finishing the work.

When difficulties come, it is easy to get discouraged. But remember, there are no triumphs without troubles. When problems arise, we must face them squarely and press on to complete God's work. We do not have to retreat—our God is a God of absolute victory.

1. How would you have felt had you been Nehemiah when he faced all of his problems? What would you have wanted to do when you were threatened and slandered?

2. Nehemiah overcame these problems. What seems to have been the key to his not giving in or giving up?

3. Choose one problem you have faced in the past or are now facing in your attempts to obey God. Based on Nehemiah's example, what will you do to be an overcomer rather than being a person who is overcome?

REPENTANCE Although God had enabled them to build the wall, the work wasn't complete until the people rebuilt their lives spiritually. Ezra taught the people God's Word. As they listened, they recognized the sin in their lives, admitted it, and took steps to remove it.

Recognizing and admitting sin is not enough. Being serious about God must result in a changed life, or it is merely enthusiasm. God does not want halfhearted measures. We must not only remove sin from our life, but also ask God to move into the center of all we do.

1. Based on Nehemiah, do you think the following statement is true or false: "God is not just concerned that we take care of big tasks, he wants our entire life surrendered to him." Explain your answer based only on the book of Nehemiah.

2. What are examples of "little things" in your life that are important to God, although no one else may ever notice them?

3. The people in Jerusalem responded to the new wall with a recommitment to God in all of life. After reading chapters 10 and 11, write out some statements of your own recommitment to live all of your life, from the heart, for God.

O verflowing with fans, the gymnasium rocks with excitement. It's the crucial moment—the one anticipated all season—but joy mixes with fear and tension. Only one point behind, the team could find its season ending abruptly. But two seconds remain in the game, and *their* player is at the free throw line. Cheers erupt as the ball swishes through the hoop. But then silence engulfs the stands as the player approaches the line for the second shot. Everything seems to be on the line—the play-offs, the dreams, the season. But the shooter's training pays off. The basket is made, the game is won, and a hero is made. He came through when it counted. ■ In Persia, Esther similarly faced a crucial moment—but the stakes were the lives of thousands. All the Jews in Persia were to be killed, and Esther, the queen and a Jew, was the only one who could save them. She could make the difference. She could have pled "not me," or looked for an easy out. But Esther knew God had placed her in an influential position "for *such* a time as this" (4:14). She seized the moment and took action, regardless of the consequences (4:16). Because of Esther, lives were spared, the victory won. ■ Read Esther and commit yourself to act for God when he gives you the opportunity. Remember, he places you where you can make a difference "for *such* a time as this."

STATS

PURPOSE: To demonstrate God's sovereignty and his loving care for his people

AUTHOR: Unknown. Possibly Mordecai (9:29). Some have suggested Ezra or Nehemiah because of the similarity of the writing style.

DATE WRITTEN: Approximately 483–471 B.C. (Esther became queen in 479)

SETTING: Although Esther follows Nehemiah in the Bible, the events are about 30 years prior to those recorded in Nehemiah. The story is set in the Persian empire, and most of the action takes place in the king's palace in Shushan (Susa), the Persian capital.

KEY PEOPLE: Esther, Mordecai, King Ahasuerus, Haman

KEY PLACE: The king's palace in Shushan (Susa), Persia

SPECIAL FEATURES: Esther is one of only two books named for women (Ruth is the other). The book is unusual in that, in the original version, God's name doesn't appear in it. This caused some early church leaders to question its inclusion in the Bible. But God's presence is clear throughout the book.

present in Shushan the citadel, from great to small, in the court of the garden of the king's palace. ⁶*There were* white and blue linen *curtains* fastened with cords of fine linen and purple on silver rods and marble pillars; *and the* couches *were* of gold and silver on a *mosaic* pavement of alabaster, turquoise, and white and black marble. ⁷And they served drinks in golden vessels, each vessel being different from the other, with royal wine in abundance, according to the generosity of the king. ⁸In accordance with the law, the drinking was not compulsory; for so the king had ordered all the officers of his household, that they should do according to each man's pleasure.

DECISIONS

1:10-11 Ahasuerus made a rash, half-drunk decision, based purely on feelings. His self-restraint and practical wisdom were weakened by too much wine, and he later regretted his decision (2:1). Poor decisions are made when clear thinking is not involved. Base your decisions on careful thinking, not on the spur of the moment.

⁹Queen Vashti also made a feast for the women *in* the royal palace which *belonged* to King Ahasuerus.

¹⁰On the seventh day, when the heart of the king was merry with wine, he commanded Mehuman, Biztha, Harbona, Bigtha, Abagtha, Zethar, and Carcas, seven eunuchs who served in the presence of King Ahasuerus, ¹¹to bring Queen Vashti before the king, *wearing* her royal crown, in order to show her beauty to the people and the officials, for she *was* beautiful to behold. ¹²But Queen Vashti refused to come at the king's command *brought* by *his* eunuchs; therefore the king was furious, and his anger burned within him.

¹³Then the king said to the wise men who understood the times (for this *was* the king's manner toward all who knew law and justice, ¹⁴those closest to him *being* Carshena, Shethar, Admatha, Tarshish, Meres, Marsena, and Memucan, the seven princes of Persia and Media, who had access to the king's presence, *and* who ranked highest in the kingdom): ¹⁵"What *shall we* do to Queen Vashti, according to law, because she did not obey the command of King Ahasuerus *brought to her* by the eunuchs?"

¹⁶And Memucan answered before the king and the princes: "Queen Vashti has not only wronged the king, but also all the princes, and all the people who *are* in all

ᴇsther

CHAPTER 1 TROUBLE IN THE PALACE. Now it came to pass in the days of Ahasuerus (this *was* the Ahasuerus who reigned over one hundred and twenty-seven provinces, from India to Ethiopia), ²in those days when King Ahasuerus sat on the throne of his kingdom, which *was* in Shushan the citadel, ³*that* in the third year of his reign he made a feast for all his officials and servants—the powers of Persia and Media, the nobles, and the princes of the provinces *being* before him— ⁴when he showed the riches of his glorious kingdom and the splendor of his excellent majesty for many days, one hundred and eighty days *in all.*

⁵And when these days were completed, the king made a feast lasting seven days for all the people who were

Esther lived in the capital of the vast Medo-Persian empire, which incorporated the provinces of Media and Persia, as well as the previous empires of Assyria and Babylon. Esther, a Jewess, was chosen by King Ahasuerus to be his queen. The story of how she saved her people takes place in the palace in Susa (Shushan).

the provinces of King Ahasuerus. ¹⁷For the queen's behavior will become known to all women, so that they will despise their husbands in their eyes, when they report, 'King Ahasuerus commanded Queen Vashti to be brought in before him, but she did not come.' ¹⁸This very day the *noble* ladies of Persia and Media will say to all the king's officials that they have heard of the behavior of the queen. Thus *there will be* excessive contempt and wrath.

◗◗◗◗◗◗ RESPECT AND LOVE

1:20-21 One way to rule is to issue edicts that force people to comply. King Ahasuerus and his advisers responded this way. But in Matthew 20:25-26, Jesus states that this is how the heathen act, lording it over everyone. As believers, we are to act differently. God offers his free gift of salvation to all (Titus 2:11), and he tells us to treat each other with respect and love (1 Corinthians 13).

¹⁹If it pleases the king, let a royal decree go out from him, and let it be recorded in the laws of the Persians and the Medes, so that it will not be altered, that Vashti shall come no more before King Ahasuerus; and let the king give her royal position to another who is better than she. ²⁰When the king's decree which he will make is proclaimed throughout all his empire (for it is great), all wives will honor their husbands, both great and small."

²¹And the reply pleased the king and the princes, and the king did according to the word of Memucan. ²²Then he sent letters to all the king's provinces, to each province in its own script, and to every people in their own language, that each man should be master in his own house, and speak in the language of his own people.

CHAPTER **2** **ESTHER BECOMES QUEEN.** After these things, when the wrath of King Ahasuerus subsided, he remembered Vashti, what she had done, and what had been decreed against her. ²Then the king's servants who attended him said: "Let beautiful young virgins be sought for the king; ³and let the king appoint officers in all the provinces of his kingdom, that they may gather all the beautiful young virgins to Shushan the citadel, into the women's quarters, under the custody of Hegai the king's eunuch, custodian of the women. And let beauty preparations be given *them*. ⁴Then let the young woman who pleases the king be queen instead of Vashti."

This thing pleased the king, and he did so.

⁵In Shushan the citadel there was a certain Jew whose name *was* Mordecai the son of Jair, the son of Shimei, the son of Kish, a Benjamite. ⁶*Kish* had been carried away from Jerusalem with the captives who had been captured with Jeconiah king of Judah, whom Nebuchadnezzar the king of Babylon had carried away. ⁷And *Mordecai* had brought up Hadassah, that *is*, Esther, his uncle's daughter, for she had neither father nor mother. The young woman *was* lovely and beautiful. When her father and mother died, Mordecai took her as his own daughter.

⁸So it was, when the king's command and decree were heard, and when many young women were gathered at Shushan the citadel, *under* the custody of Hegai, that Esther also was taken to the king's palace, into the care of Hegai the custodian of the women. ⁹Now the young woman pleased him, and she obtained his favor; so he readily gave beauty preparations to her, besides her allowance. Then seven choice maidservants were provided for her from the king's palace, and he moved her and her

maidservants to the best *place* in the house of the women.

¹⁰Esther had not revealed her people or family, for Mordecai had charged her not to reveal *it.* ¹¹And every day Mordecai paced in front of the court of the women's quarters, to learn of Esther's welfare and what was happening to her.

¹²Each young woman's turn came to go in to King Ahasuerus after she had completed twelve months' preparation, according to the regulations for the women, for thus were the days of their preparation apportioned: six months with oil of myrrh, and six months with perfumes and preparations for beautifying women. ¹³Thus *prepared, each* young woman went to the king, and she was given whatever she desired to take with her from the women's quarters to the king's palace. ¹⁴In the evening she went, and in the morning she returned to the second house of the women, to the custody of Shaashgaz, the king's eunuch who kept the concubines. She would not go in to the king again unless the king delighted in her and called for her by name.

¹⁵Now when the turn came for Esther the daughter of Abihail the uncle of Mordecai, who had taken her as his daughter, to go in to the king, she requested nothing but what Hegai the king's eunuch, the custodian of the women, advised. And Esther obtained favor in the sight of all who saw her. ¹⁶So Esther was taken to King Ahasuerus, into his royal palace, in the tenth month, which *is* the month of Tebeth, in the seventh year of his reign. ¹⁷The king loved Esther more than all the *other* women, and she obtained grace and favor in his sight more than all the virgins; so he set the royal crown upon her head and made her queen instead of Vashti. ¹⁸Then the king made a great feast, the Feast of Esther, for all his officials and servants; and he proclaimed a holiday in the provinces and gave gifts according to the generosity of a king.

¹⁹When virgins were gathered together a second time, Mordecai sat within the king's gate. ²⁰*Now* Esther had not revealed her family and her people, just as Mordecai had charged her, for Esther obeyed the command of Mordecai as when she was brought up by him.

²¹In those days, while Mordecai sat within the king's gate, two of the king's eunuchs, Bigthan and Teresh, doorkeepers, became furious and sought to lay hands on King Ahasuerus. ²²So the matter became known to Mordecai, who told Queen Esther, and Esther informed the king in Mordecai's name. ²³And when an inquiry was made into the matter, it was confirmed, and both were hanged on a gallows; and it was written in the book of the chronicles in the presence of the king.

CHAPTER **3** **HAMAN TRICKS THE KING.** After these things King Ahasuerus promoted Haman, the son of Hammedatha the Agagite, and advanced him and set his seat above all the princes who *were* with him. ²And all the king's servants who *were* within the king's gate bowed and paid homage to Haman, for so the king had commanded

ESTHER

Most of us really want to feel secure, even though we know that security in this life carries no guarantees—possessions can be destroyed or lost, beauty fades, relationships can be broken, and death is always waiting. So what we hope will bring security doesn't last. Real security has to be found in something or Someone else. Only when our security depends on God's unchanging love for us can we face the challenges that life is sure to bring our way.

In Esther's day, kings could have any and as many wives as they wished, but Esther became King Ahasuerus's queen. God placed her in a special position to represent her people, the Jews, who were in danger. She had to risk her own security to help others. Have you noticed how often we don't help people because we are afraid of what might happen to us?

Esther made her plans carefully. She got help. Knowing she needed God's help, too, Esther had all her people fasting and praying. Realizing God is with us is the best medicine for the feeling that we're all alone. As you read her story, you will be amazed how God and Esther worked together. God was behind the scenes, but he made things happen! The way Esther acted showed how much she depended on God for her security.

How much of your security lies in what you have, who you are, or what others think of you? God has a definite plan in placing you where you are right now. He put you there to serve him. As in Esther's case, this may involve risking your security. Are you willing to let God be your ultimate security?

LESSONS: Serving God often demands that we risk our own security

God has a purpose for the situations in which he places us

Courage, while often vital, does not replace careful planning

KEY VERSE: "Go, gather all the Jews who are present in Shushan, and fast for me; neither eat nor drink for three days, night or day. My maids and I will fast likewise. And so I will go to the king, which *is* against the law; and if I perish, I perish!" (Esther 4:16).

Esther's story is told in the book of Esther.

UPS:
• Her beauty and character won the heart of Persia's king
• Combined courage with careful planning
• Open to advice and willing to act
• More concerned for others than for her own security

STATS:
• Where: Persian empire
• Occupation: Ahasuerus's wife, queen of Persia
• Relatives: Cousin: Mordecai. Husband: Ahasuerus. Father: Abihail.

concerning him. But Mordecai would not bow or pay homage. ³Then the king's servants who *were* within the king's gate said to Mordecai, "Why do you transgress the king's command?" ⁴Now it happened, when they spoke to him daily and he would not listen to them, that they told *it* to Haman, to see whether Mordecai's words would stand; for *Mordecai* had told them that he *was* a Jew. ⁵When Haman saw that Mordecai did not bow or pay him homage, Haman was filled with wrath. ⁶But he disdained to lay hands on Mordecai alone, for they had told him of the people of Mordecai. Instead, Haman sought to destroy all the Jews who *were* throughout the whole kingdom of Ahasuerus—the people of Mordecai.

TAKING A STAND

You wouldn't want to be in Ryan's shoes. He's in the middle of a sticky situation and none of his options are very appealing.

See, in just a few minutes, Ryan and K.D. will be face to face with one of Mrs. Seal's infamous geometry exams. But K.D. just announced, "Hey, Ryan! You've got to help me out, dude. I didn't have time to study last night. I don't know any of the formulas. So look, just write big and when I tap you on the shoulder, lean to your left, OK?"

Lunch is almost over. The bell will be ringing any minute. Ryan's mind is racing: "Do I let K.D. copy off me just this once? But what if I get accused of cheating? I probably should tell him no now—before class starts. But then he'll tell everyone I wouldn't help him out, and I'll never hear the end of it. Sheesh, what am I going to do?

"It ticks me off the way he uses people. . . . It's not my fault if he fails. He shouldn't be so lazy. Still, I don't want everybody thinking I'm a geek. Maybe I should—"

BBBBRRRIIIINNNNNGGGGG!!!

What would you do in Ryan's shoes?

Chapters 3 and 4 of the exciting book of Esther are about taking a stand for what is right, no matter what. Read about the young queen who made tough decisions when the stakes were—literally—life and death.

⁷In the first month, which is the month of Nisan, in the twelfth year of King Ahasuerus, they cast Pur (that *is,* the lot), before Haman to determine the day and the month, until *it fell on the* twelfth *month,* which *is* the month of Adar.

⁸Then Haman said to King Ahasuerus, "There is a certain people scattered and dispersed among the people in all the provinces of your kingdom; their laws *are* different from all *other* people's, and they do not keep the king's laws. Therefore it *is* not fitting for the king to let them remain. ⁹If it pleases the king, let *a decree* be written that they be destroyed, and I will pay ten thousand talents of silver into the hands of those who do the work, to bring *it* into the king's treasuries."

¹⁰So the king took his signet ring from his hand and gave it to Haman, the son of Hammedatha the Agagite, the enemy of the Jews. ¹¹And the king said to Haman,

PAGE 472

CONVICTION

3:2 Mordecai's faith was based on conviction. He did not first tak[e] to determine the safest or most popular course of action; he had th[e] courage to stand alone. Doing what is right is not always popular. [Those] who do right often will be in the minority. But to obey God is more [] important than to obey people (Acts 5:29).

"The money and the people *are* given to you, to do with them as seems good to you."

¹²Then the king's scribes were called on the thirteenth day of the first month, and *a decree* was written according to all that Haman commanded—to the king's satraps, to the governors who *were* over each province, to the officials of all people, to every province according to its script, and to every people in their language. In the name of King Ahasuerus it was written, and sealed with the king's signet ring. ¹³And the letters were sent by couriers into all the king's provinces, to destroy, to kill, and to annihilate all the Jews, both young and old, little children and women, in one day, on the thirteenth *day* of the twelfth *month,* which *is* the month of Adar, and to plunder their possessions. ¹⁴A copy of the document was to be issued as law in every province, being published for all people, that they should be ready for that day. ¹⁵The couriers went out, hastened by the king's command; and the decree was proclaimed in Shushan the citadel. So the king and Haman sat down to drink, but the city of Shushan was perplexed.

CHAPTER 4

When Mordecai learned all that had happened, he tore his clothes and put on sackcloth and ashes, and went out into the midst of the city. He cried out with a loud and bitter cry. ²He went as far as the front of the king's gate, for no one *might* enter the king's gate clothed with sackcloth. ³And in every province where the king's command and decree arrived, *there was* great mourning among the Jews, with fasting, weeping, and wailing; and many lay in sackcloth and ashes.

⁴So Esther's maids and eunuchs came and told her, and the queen was deeply distressed. Then she sent garments to clothe Mordecai and take his sackcloth away from him, but he would not accept *them.* ⁵Then Esther called Hathach, *one* of the king's eunuchs whom he had appointed to attend her, and she gave him a command concerning Mordecai, to learn what and why this *was.* ⁶So Hathach went out to Mordecai in the city square that *was* in front of the king's gate. ⁷And Mordecai told him all that had happened to him, and the sum of money that Haman had promised to pay into the king's treasuries to destroy the Jews. ⁸He also gave him a copy of the written decree for their destruction, which was given at Shushan, that he might show it to Esther and explain it to her, and that he might command her to go in to the king to make supplication to him and plead before him for her people. ⁹So Hathach returned and told Esther the words of Mordecai.

¹⁰Then Esther spoke to Hathach, and gave him a command for Mordecai: ¹¹"All the king's servants and the people of the king's provinces know that any man or

woman who goes into the inner court to the king, who has not been called, *he has* but one law: put *all* to death, except the one to whom the king holds out the golden scepter, that he may live. Yet I myself have not been called to go in to the king these thirty days." ¹²So they told Mordecai Esther's words.

¹³And Mordecai told *them* to answer Esther: "Do not think in your heart that you will escape in the king's palace any more than all the other Jews. ¹⁴For if you remain completely silent at this time, relief and deliverance will arise for the Jews from another place, but you and your father's house will perish. Yet who knows whether you have come to the kingdom for *such* a time as this?"

¹⁵Then Esther told *them* to reply to Mordecai: ¹⁶"Go, gather all the Jews who are present in Shushan, and fast for me; neither eat nor drink for three days, night or day. My maids and I will fast likewise. And so I will go to the king, which *is* against the law; and if I perish, I perish!"

¹⁷So Mordecai went his way and did according to all that Esther commanded him.

CHAPTER 5   QUEEN ESTHER DEFEATS HAMAN.

Now it happened on the third day that Esther put on *her* royal *robes* and stood in the inner court of the king's palace, across from the king's house, while the king sat on his royal throne in the royal house, facing the entrance of the house. ²So it was, when the king saw Queen Esther standing in the court, *that* she found favor in his sight, and the king held out to Esther the golden scepter that *was* in his hand. Then Esther went near and touched the top of the scepter.

³And the king said to her, "What do you wish, Queen Esther? What *is* your request? It shall be given to you—up to half the kingdom!"

⁴So Esther answered, "If it pleases the king, let the king

and Haman come today to the banquet that I have prepared for him."

⁵Then the king said, "Bring Haman quickly, that he may do as Esther has said." So the king and Haman went to the banquet that Esther had prepared.

⁶At the banquet of wine the king said to Esther, "What *is* your petition? It shall be granted you. What *is* your request, up to half the kingdom? It shall be done!"

⁷Then Esther answered and said, "My petition and request *is this:* ⁸If I have found favor in the sight of the king, and if it pleases the king to grant my petition and fulfill my request, then let the king and Haman come to the banquet which I will prepare for them, and tomorrow I will do as the king has said."

⁹So Haman went out that day joyful and with a glad heart; but when Haman saw Mordecai in the king's gate, and that he did not stand or tremble before him, he was filled with indignation against Mordecai. ¹⁰Nevertheless Haman restrained himself and went home, and he sent and called for his friends and his wife Zeresh. ¹¹Then Haman told them of his great riches, the multitude of his children, everything in which the king had promoted him, and how he had advanced him above the officials and servants of the king.

¹²Moreover Haman said, "Besides, Queen Esther invited no one but me to come in with the king to the banquet that she prepared; and tomorrow I am again invited by her, along with the king. ¹³Yet all this avails me nothing, so long as I see Mordecai the Jew sitting at the king's gate."

¹⁴Then his wife Zeresh and all his friends said to him, "Let a gallows be made, fifty cubits high, and in the morning suggest to the king that Mordecai be hanged on it; then go merrily with the king to the banquet."

And the thing pleased Haman; so he had the gallows made.

CHAPTER 6   That night the king could not sleep. So

one was commanded to bring the book of the records of the chronicles; and they were read before the king. ²And it was found written that Mordecai had told of Bigthana and Teresh, two of the king's eunuchs, the doorkeepers who had sought to lay hands on King Ahasuerus. ³Then the king said, "What honor or dignity has been bestowed on Mordecai for this?"

And the king's servants who attended him said, "Nothing has been done for him."

⁴So the king said, "Who *is* in the court?" Now Haman had *just* entered the outer court of the king's palace to suggest that the king hang Mordecai on the gallows that he had prepared for him.

⁵The king's servants said to him, "Haman is there, standing in the court."

And the king said, "Let him come in."

⁶So Haman came in, and the king asked him, "What shall be done for the man whom the king delights to honor?"

Now Haman thought in his heart, "Whom would the king delight to honor more than me?" ⁷And Haman answered the king, "*For* the man whom the king delights to

WHO KNOWS
WHO KNOWS
WHO KNOWS
whether
you have come
to the
KINGDOM
*for such
a time
as this?*

6:12 Just the night before (5:9-14), Haman had bragged about his position and the honor he was about to receive. Now he was humiliated and soon to be marked for death (7:8-10). How quickly the course of life can change! Because we cannot predict what will happen, it is best to avoid bragging (James 4:13-16). God is displeased with this kind of self-confidence and self-reliance.

honor, [8]let a royal robe be brought which the king has worn, and a horse on which the king has ridden, which has a royal crest placed on its head. [9]Then let this robe and horse be delivered to the hand of one of the king's most noble princes, that he may array the man whom the king delights to honor. Then parade him on horseback through the city square, and proclaim before him: 'Thus shall it be done to the man whom the king delights to honor!' "

[10]Then the king said to Haman, "Hurry, take the robe and the horse, as you have suggested, and do so for Mordecai the Jew who sits within the king's gate! Leave nothing undone of all that you have spoken."

[11]So Haman took the robe and the horse, arrayed Mordecai and led him on horseback through the city square, and proclaimed before him, "Thus shall it be done to the man whom the king delights to honor!"

[12]Afterward Mordecai went back to the king's gate. But Haman hurried to his house, mourning and with his head covered. [13]When Haman told his wife Zeresh and all his friends everything that had happened to him, his wise men and his wife Zeresh said to him, "If Mordecai, before whom you have begun to fall, is of Jewish descent, you will not prevail against him but will surely fall before him."

[14]While they *were* still talking with him, the king's eunuchs came, and hastened to bring Haman to the banquet which Esther had prepared.

CHAPTER 7 So the king and Haman went to dine with Queen Esther. [2]And on the second day, at the banquet of wine, the king again said to Esther, "What *is* your petition, Queen Esther? It shall be granted you. And what *is* your request, up to half the kingdom? It shall be done!"

[3]Then Queen Esther answered and said, "If I have found favor in your sight, O king, and if it pleases the king, let my life be given me at my petition, and my people at my request. [4]For we have been sold, my people and I, to be destroyed, to be killed, and to be annihilated. Had we been sold as male and female slaves, I would have held my tongue, although the enemy could never compensate for the king's loss."

[5]So King Ahasuerus answered and said to Queen Esther, "Who is he, and where is he, who would dare presume in his heart to do such a thing?"

[6]And Esther said, "The adversary and enemy *is* this wicked Haman!"

So Haman was terrified before the king and queen.

[7]Then the king arose in his wrath from the banquet of wine *and went* into the palace garden; but Haman stood before Queen Esther, pleading for his life, for he saw that evil was determined against him by the king. [8]When the king returned from the palace garden to the place of the banquet of wine, Haman had fallen across the couch

where Esther *was*. Then the king said, "Will he also assault the queen while I *am* in the house?"

As the word left the king's mouth, they covered Haman's face. [9]Now Harbonah, one of the eunuchs, said to the king, "Look! The gallows, fifty cubits high, which Haman made for Mordecai, who spoke good on the king's behalf, is standing at the house of Haman."

Then the king said, "Hang him on it!"

[10]So they hanged Haman on the gallows that he had prepared for Mordecai. Then the king's wrath subsided.

CHAPTER 8 A NEW LAW TO PROTECT THE JEWS. On that day King Ahasuerus gave Queen Esther the house of Haman, the enemy of the Jews. And Mordecai came before the king, for Esther had told how he *was related* to her. [2]So the king took off his signet ring, which he had taken from Haman, and gave it to Mordecai; and Esther appointed Mordecai over the house of Haman.

[3]Now Esther spoke again to the king, fell down at his feet, and implored him with tears to counteract the evil of Haman the Agagite, and the scheme which he had devised against the Jews. [4]And the king held out the golden scepter toward Esther. So Esther arose and stood before the king, [5]and said, "If it pleases the king, and if I have found favor in his sight, and the thing *seems* right to the king and I am pleasing in his eyes, let it be written to revoke the letters devised by Haman, the son of Hammedatha the Agagite, which he wrote to annihilate the Jews who *are* in all the king's provinces. [6]For how can I endure to see the evil that will come to my people? Or how can I endure to see the destruction of my countrymen?"

[7]Then King Ahasuerus said to Queen Esther and Mordecai the Jew, "Indeed, I have given Esther the house of Haman, and they have hanged him on the gallows because he *tried to* lay his hand on the Jews. [8]You yourselves write *a decree* concerning the Jews, as you please, in the king's name, and seal *it* with the king's signet ring; for whatever is written in the king's name and sealed with the king's signet ring no one can revoke."

[9]So the king's scribes were called at that time, in the third month, which *is* the month of Sivan, on the twenty-third *day;* and it was written, according to all that Mordecai commanded, to the Jews, the satraps, the governors, and the princes of the provinces from India to Ethiopia, one hundred and twenty-seven provinces *in all,* to every province in its own script, to every people in their own language, and to the Jews in their own script and language. [10]And he wrote in the name of King Ahasuerus, sealed *it* with the king's signet ring, and sent letters by couriers on horseback, riding on royal horses bred from swift steeds.

[11]By these letters the king permitted the Jews who *were* in every city to gather together and protect their lives—to destroy, kill, and annihilate all the forces of any people or

■PAY THE PRICE

8:15-17 Everyone wants to be a hero and receive praise, honor, wealth. But few are willing to pay the price. Mordecai served the government faithfully for years, bore Haman's hatred and oppres~ and risked his life for his people. The price to be paid by God's her long-term commitment. Are you ready and willing to pay the price

HOW GOD WORKS IN THE WORLD

God's will . . . What God wants done—He works through . . .

God's action	◆ Natural order ◆ God set into action through creation a normal working of his universe. He also revealed his expectations of people through his Word and people's consciences.	◆ Miracles ◆ God breaks into the natural order to respond to the expressed needs of people.	◆ Providence ◆ God overrules the natural order to accomplish an act that people may or may not have requested.
Examples from Esther	◆ God gave Esther natural beauty. ▲ Esther planned a way to save her people.	◆ God allowed Esther to speak to the king. ▲ The people prayed and fasted.	◆ God allowed Mordecai to overhear a plot. ▲ Mordecai trusted God to accomplish what was impossible in human terms.

Our will . . . What we want done—We either . . .

Action we can take	▲ Plan ▲ Can make plans based on the order and dependability of God's creation. Know and obey his words. or . . .	▲ Pray ▲ Can ask God to intervene in certain affairs while realizing that our knowledge and perspective are limited.	▲ Trust & Obey ▲ Can trust that God is in control even when the circumstances may not seem to indicate that he is.
Mistakes we can make	◆ Disobey ◆ Can violate the natural order, disobey God's commands.	◆ Demand ◆ Can assume that we understand what is needed and expect God to agree and answer our prayers that way.	◆ Despair ◆ Can assume God doesn't answer prayer or respond to our needs and live as though there is nothing but the natural order.

province that would assault them, *both* little children and women, and to plunder their possessions, [12]on one day in all the provinces of King Ahasuerus, on the thirteenth *day* of the twelfth month, which *is* the month of Adar. [13]A copy of the document was to be issued as a decree in every province and published for all people, so that the Jews would be ready on that day to avenge themselves on their enemies. [14]The couriers who rode on royal horses went out, hastened and pressed on by the king's command. And the decree was issued in Shushan the citadel.

[15]So Mordecai went out from the presence of the king in royal apparel of blue and white, with a great crown of gold and a garment of fine linen and purple; and the city of Shushan rejoiced and was glad. [16]The Jews had light and gladness, joy and honor. [17]And in every province and city, wherever the king's command and decree came, the Jews had joy and gladness, a feast and a holiday. Then many of the people of the land became Jews, because fear of the Jews fell upon them.

CHAPTER 9 THE JEWS DEFEAT THEIR ENEMIES.

Now in the twelfth month, that *is,* the month of Adar, on the thirteenth day, *the time* came for the king's command and his decree to be executed. On the day that the enemies of the Jews had hoped to overpower them, the op-

posite occurred, in that the Jews themselves overpowered those who hated them. [2]The Jews gathered together in their cities throughout all the provinces of King Ahasuerus to lay hands on those who sought their harm. And no one could withstand them, because fear of them fell upon all people. [3]And all the officials of the provinces, the satraps, the governors, and all those doing the king's work, helped the Jews, because the fear of Mordecai fell upon them. [4]For Mordecai *was* great in the king's palace, and his fame spread throughout all the provinces; for this man Mordecai became increasingly prominent. [5]Thus the Jews defeated all their enemies with the stroke of the sword, with slaughter and destruction, and did what they pleased with those who hated them.

[6]And in Shushan the citadel the Jews killed and destroyed five hundred men. [7]Also Parshandatha, Dalphon, Aspatha, [8]Poratha, Adalia, Aridatha, [9]Parmashta, Arisai, Aridai, and Vajezatha— [10]the ten sons of Haman the son of Hammedatha, the enemy of the Jews—they killed; but they did not lay a hand on the plunder.

[11]On that day the number of those who were killed in Shushan the citadel was brought to the king. [12]And the king said to Queen Esther, "The Jews have killed and destroyed five hundred men in Shushan the citadel, and the ten sons of Haman. What have they done in the rest of the king's provinces? Now what *is* your petition? It shall

WOMEN OF THE BIBLE

Depending on your point of view, you may be thrilled, irritated, intrigued, or just surprised to see a book of the Bible—two, even—named for a woman. The Bible is, admittedly, a male-dominated work. But, as the books of Ruth and Esther point out, women are very important in the story of God's redemption of humanity. In

Ruth is the story of a young widow who, out of loyalty, follows her mother-in-law back to Jerusalem to live. In the midst of tough times for the two of them, Ruth shows she is a hard worker and a woman of integrity and high moral character. God rewards her faithfulness by providing her a new husband, Boaz, a good man who had attained some measure of wealth and could therefore provide for both women. In addition, Ruth and Boaz become the great-grandparents of David, the king of Israel, and ancestors of Jesus, the Jewish Messiah.

Ruth is an excellent role model for young believers today, female or male. **E**sther is the story of another faithful woman in radically different circumstances. A young Jewish girl in exile in Babylon, Esther, by virtue of her good looks, catches the eye of King Ahasuerus and is made queen. Even as queen, however, she has to watch her step, being careful not to displease her husband and risk being banished or even killed. There comes a point, though, where she must risk the king's displeasure to save her people, the Jews, from mass destruction. Although afraid at first to stick her neck out, she finally decides to risk it, saying, "I will go to the king, which is against the law; and if I perish, I perish" (Esther 4:16). That's gutsy, courageous faith, the kind that Christian women—and men—today would do well to imitate. **A**lthough these are the only two books named for women, there are lots of other stories of important women in Scripture; some good, some bad. If you're interested, look at the accounts of Rahab (Joshua 2; 6); Mary and Martha (Luke 10); and, of course, Mary, Jesus' mother (Luke 1—2; (1 Kings 16—2 Kings 9); Deborah (Judges 4–5); Jezebel 19, etc.). **F**or a number of reasons, cultural and otherwise, most of the prominent characters in the Bible are men. But women play a vital role in the unfolding drama of both the Old and New Testaments, just as they do in God's work in the world today.

be granted to you. Or what *is* your further request? It shall be done."

¹³Then Esther said, "If it pleases the king, let it be granted to the Jews who *are* in Shushan to do again tomorrow according to today's decree, and let Haman's ten sons be hanged on the gallows."

¹⁴So the king commanded this to be done; the decree was issued in Shushan, and they hanged Haman's ten sons.

¹⁵And the Jews who *were* in Shushan gathered together again on the fourteenth day of the month of Adar and killed three hundred men at Shushan; but they did not lay a hand on the plunder.

¹⁶The remainder of the Jews in the king's provinces gathered together and protected their lives, had rest from their enemies, and killed seventy-five thousand of their enemies; but they did not lay a hand on the plunder. ¹⁷*This was* on the thirteenth day of the month of Adar. And on the fourteenth of *the month* they rested and made it a day of feasting and gladness.

¹⁸But the Jews who *were* at Shushan assembled together on the thirteenth *day*, as well as on the fourteenth; and on the fifteenth of *the month* they rested, and made it a day of feasting and gladness. ¹⁹Therefore the Jews of the villages who dwelt in the unwalled towns celebrated the fourteenth day of the month of Adar *with* gladness and feasting, as a holiday, and for sending presents to one another.

²⁰And Mordecai wrote these things and sent letters to all the Jews, near and far, who *were* in all the provinces of King Ahasuerus, ²¹to establish among them that they should celebrate yearly the fourteenth and fifteenth days of the month of Adar, ²²as the days on which the Jews had rest from their enemies, as the month which was turned from sorrow to joy for them, and from mourning to a holiday; that they should make them days of feasting and joy, of sending presents to one another and gifts to the poor. ²³So the Jews accepted the custom which they had begun, as Mordecai had written to them, ²⁴because Haman, the son of Hammedatha the Agagite, the enemy of all the Jews, had plotted against the Jews to annihilate them, and had cast Pur (that *is*, the lot), to consume them and destroy them; ²⁵but when *Esther* came before the king, he commanded by letter that this wicked plot which *Haman* had devised against the Jews should return on his own head, and that he and his sons should be hanged on the gallows.

²⁶So they called these days Purim, after the name Pur. Therefore, because of all the words of this letter, what they had seen concerning this matter, and what had happened to them, ²⁷the Jews established and imposed it upon themselves and their descendants and all who would join them, that without fail they should celebrate these two days every year, according to the written *in-structions* and according to the *prescribed* time, ²⁸*that* these days *should be* remembered and kept throughout every generation, every family, every province, and every city, that these days of Purim should not fail *to be observed* among the Jews, and *that* the memory of them should not perish among their descendants.

AVAILABLE

9:29-31 Among Jews, women were expected to be quiet, to serve in the home, and to stay on the fringe of religious and political life. But Esther was a Jewish woman who broke through the cultural norms, stepping outside her expected role to risk her life to help God's people. Whatever your place in life, God can use you. Be open, available, and ready—God may use you to do what others are afraid even to consider.

²⁹Then Queen Esther, the daughter of Abihail, with Mordecai the Jew, wrote with full authority to confirm this second letter about Purim. ³⁰And *Mordecai* sent letters to all the Jews, to the one hundred and twenty-seven provinces of the kingdom of Ahasuerus, *with* words of peace and truth, ³¹to confirm these days of Purim at their *appointed* time, as Mordecai the Jew and Queen Esther had prescribed for them, and as they had decreed for themselves and their descendants concerning matters of their fasting and lamenting. ³²So the decree of Esther confirmed these matters of Purim, and it was written in the book.

CHAPTER 10 GOD REWARDS MORDECAI. And King Ahasuerus imposed tribute on the land and *on* the islands of the sea. ²Now all the acts of his power and his might, and the account of the greatness of Mordecai, to which the king advanced him, *are* they not written in the book of the chronicles of the kings of Media and Persia? ³For Mordecai the Jew *was* second to King Ahasuerus, and was great among the Jews and well received by the multitude of his brethren, seeking the good of his people and speaking peace to all his countrymen.

IN CONTROL

10:3 In the book of Esther, we clearly see God at work in the lives of individuals and in the affairs of a nation. Even when it looks as if the world is in the hands of evil people, God is still in control, protecting those who belong to him. Although we may not understand everything happening around us, we must trust in God's protection and retain our integrity by doing what we know is right. Esther, who risked her life appearing before the king, became a heroine. Mordecai, who was on "death row" (so to speak), rose to become the second highest ranking official in the nation. No matter how hopeless our condition, or how much we would like to give up, we need not despair. God is in control of our world.

MEGA Themes

IN CONTROL The book of Esther tells of the circumstances that were essential for the survival of God's people in Persia. The "circumstances" were not the result of chance, but of God's grand design. God is in control of every area of life.

With God in charge, we can take courage. He can guide us through the circumstances we face in our life. We should expect God to display his power in carrying out his will.

1. Esther showed great courage in the face of frightening circumstances. How would you have felt if you were Esther, risking your life for your people?
2. How do Esther's choices reflect a trust in God's control of her life?
3. Think of a time when things worked out just the opposite of what you had wanted and expected. How did you feel toward God?
4. What choices in your life show that you believe that God is in control?
5. In what areas of your life do you want to learn to trust God's control more? How can you begin to do this today?

RACISM The Jews in Persia had been a minority since their deportation from Judea 100 years earlier. Haman was a descendant of King Agag, an enemy of the Jews. Lust for power and pride drove Haman to hate Mordecai, Esther's cousin. Haman convinced the king to kill all the Jews.

Racial hatred is always sinful. We must never condone it in any form. Every person on earth has intrinsic worth because God created human beings in his image. Therefore, God's people must stand against racism whenever and wherever it occurs. We must learn to see others with God's "eyes," rather than through the often cloudy lenses of our own cultural "glasses."

1. What results did racial hatred have in the book of Esther?

2. What are some results of racial hatred we have seen in history? In the present world?
3. Are there people in your school and/or community who suffer because of racial hatred? Who are they?
4. What could Christians in your school and/or community do to show how God's love overcomes racial hatred?

DELIVERANCE On February 28, the Jews celebrate the Feast of Purim, which symbolizes God's deliverance. "Purim" means dice, such as those used by Haman to set the date for the extermination of all Jews from Persia. But God overruled, using Queen Esther to intercede on behalf of the Jews.

Because God is in control of history, he is never frustrated by any turn of events or by any human action. He is able to save us from the evil in this world and deliver us from sin and death. Because we trust God, we should not fear what people may do to us; instead, we should be confident in God's control.

1. Haman planned the destruction of the Jews. What did he learn about God when he tried to carry out his plan?
2. Where else in the Bible did God deliver his people?
3. What are specific instances where you know that God intervened to deliver you?
4. What does this study of deliverance teach you about placing your confidence in God? What difference can this confidence make in your life?

ACTION Faced with death, Esther and Mordecai set aside their own fear and took action. Mordecai took great risks to talk with Esther about the situation; Esther risked her life by asking King Ahasuerus to save the Jews. They were not paralyzed by fear.

When outnumbered and powerless, it is natural to feel helpless. Instead, Esther and Mordecai resisted and acted with courage. It is not enough to know that God is in control, we must courageously follow God's guidance.

1. Complete this sentence: Esther showed herself to be a woman of action when _____.
2. From what you've read in this book, describe Esther's view of God.
3. Why can you tell a person's view of God more by how he or she acts than what he or she says?
4. How would you describe your view of God based on your actions this past week? What strengths do you see? Weaknesses?

WISDOM The Jews were a minority in a world hostile to them. It took great wisdom for Mordecai to survive. Serving as a faithful official of the king, Mordecai took steps to understand and work with the Persian law. Yet he did not compromise his integrity.

It takes great wisdom to survive in a nonbelieving world. In a setting that is for the most part hostile to Christianity, we can demonstrate wisdom by giving respect to what is true and good and by standing against what is wrong. An important step in becoming mature is learning to distinguish good from evil. God will help us in that process through his Word, his Spirit, and the body of Christ, the church.

1. How does Mordecai provide an example of godly wisdom in an ungodly environment?
2. In what ways does God want believers to be active in non-Christian environments? What makes this difficult?
3. What situations or relationships do you face where you need godly wisdom in order to not compromise your faith?
4. What sources does God give you for getting the godly wisdom you need?
5. What specific wisdom will you seek from God through his Word, through prayer, and through godly advice in order to be a more effective witness for Christ?

Why me, God?" Have you ever thought, whispered, or screamed that question? Have you ever thought that God was against you personally? At one time or another, everyone does . . . even people in the Bible. That is not surprising. What *is* surprising is God's answer to their questions. ■ Job loved God, and everything was going great in his life. He had money, land, possessions, and a large, wonderful family. But one day his world fell apart. He lost everything . . . except his life, a bitter wife, and accusing "friends." As you might imagine, Job asked why. Why him? Why now? The book of Job tells this story, and it gives God's reply. And after God spoke, Job was silent. ■ Job is a book about success, tragedy, friends, and faith. As you read Job, allow God to begin changing your ideas about suffering. Learn to trust God even when you don't understand.

STATS

PURPOSE: To demonstrate God's sovereignty and the meaning of true faith. It addresses the question "Why do the righteous suffer?"

AUTHOR: Possibly Job. Some have suggested Moses, Solomon, or Elihu.

DATE WRITTEN: Unknown. Records events that probably occurred during the time of the patriarchs, approximately 2000–1800 B.C.

SETTING: The land of Uz, probably located northeast of Palestine, near desert land between Damascus and the Euphrates River

KEY PEOPLE: Job, Eliphaz the Temanite, Bildad the Shuhite, Zophar the Naamathite, Elihu the Buzite

SPECIAL FEATURES: Job is the first of the poetic books in the Hebrew Bible. Many believe this to be the oldest book in the Bible. The book gives us insights into the work of Satan. Ezekiel 14:14,20 and James 5:11 mention Job as a historical character.

Job

CHAPTER 1 JOB LOSES EVERYTHING. There was a man in the land of Uz, whose name *was* Job; and that man was blameless and upright, and one who feared God and shunned evil. ²And seven sons and three daughters were born to him. ³Also, his possessions were seven thousand sheep, three thousand camels, five hundred yoke of oxen, five hundred female donkeys, and a very large household, so that this man was the greatest of all the people of the East.

⁴And his sons would go and feast *in their* houses, each on his *appointed* day, and would send and invite their three sisters to eat and drink with them. ⁵So it was, when the days of feasting had run their course, that Job would send and sanctify them, and he would rise early in the morning and offer burnt offerings *according to* the number of them all. For Job said, "It may be that my sons have sinned and cursed God in their hearts." Thus Job did regularly.

⁶Now there was a day when the sons of God came to present themselves before the LORD, and Satan also came among them. ⁷And the LORD said to Satan, "From where do you come?"

So Satan answered the LORD and said, "From going to and fro on the earth, and from walking back and forth on it."

⁸Then the LORD said to Satan, "Have you considered My servant Job, that *there is* none like him on the earth, a blameless and upright man, one who fears God and shuns evil?"

⁹So Satan answered the LORD and said, "Does Job fear God for nothing? ¹⁰Have You not made a hedge around him, around his household, and around all that he has on every side? You have blessed the work of his hands, and his possessions have increased in the land. ¹¹But now, stretch out Your hand and touch all that he has, and he will surely curse You to Your face!"

WHY ME?

1:1 When reading the book of Job, we have information that the characters of the story do not. Job, the main character of the book, lost all he had through no fault of his own. As he struggled to understand why all this was happening to him, it became clear that he was not meant to know the reasons. He would have to face life with the answers and explanations held back. Only then would his faith fully develop.

We must experience life as Job did—one day at a time and without complete answers to all of life's questions. Will we, like Job, trust God no matter what? Or will we give in to the temptation to say that God doesn't really care?

¹²And the LORD said to Satan, "Behold, all that he has *is* in your power; only do not lay a hand on his *person.*"

So Satan went out from the presence of the LORD.

¹³Now there was a day when his sons and daughters *were* eating and drinking wine in their oldest brother's house; ¹⁴and a messenger came to Job and said, "The oxen were plowing and the donkeys feeding beside them, ¹⁵when the Sabeans raided *them* and took them away— indeed they have killed the servants with the edge of the sword; and I alone have escaped to tell you!"

¹⁶While he *was* still speaking, another also came and

said, "The fire of God fell from heaven and burned up the sheep and the servants, and consumed them; and I alone have escaped to tell you!"

¹⁷While he *was* still speaking, another also came and said, "The Chaldeans formed three bands, raided the camels and took them away, yes, and killed the servants with the edge of the sword; and I alone have escaped to tell you!"

¹⁸While he *was* still speaking, another also came and said, "Your sons and daughters *were* eating and drinking wine in their oldest brother's house, ¹⁹and suddenly a great wind came from across the wilderness and struck the four corners of the house, and it fell on the young people, and they are dead; and I alone have escaped to tell you!"

◣▬▬ HEARTBREAK

1:20-22 Job did not hide his overwhelming grief. This emotional display did not mean he had lost his faith in God; instead, it showed that he was human and that he loved his family. God created our emotions, and it is not sinful to express them as Job did. If you have experienced deep loss, disappointment, or heartbreak, admit your feelings to yourself and others, and grieve.

²⁰Then Job arose, tore his robe, and shaved his head; and he fell to the ground and worshiped. ²¹And he said:
"Naked I came from my mother's womb,
And naked shall I return there.
The LORD gave, and the LORD has taken away;
Blessed be the name of the LORD."

²²In all this Job did not sin nor charge God with wrong.

CHAPTER 2

Again there was a day when the sons of God came to present themselves before the LORD, and Satan came also among them to present himself before the LORD. ²And the LORD said to Satan, "From where do you come?"

Satan answered the LORD and said, "From going to and fro on the earth, and from walking back and forth on it."

³Then the LORD said to Satan, "Have you considered My servant Job, that *there is* none like him on the earth, a blameless and upright man, one who fears God and shuns evil? And still he holds fast to his integrity, although you incited Me against him, to destroy him without cause."

⁴So Satan answered the LORD and said, "Skin for skin! Yes, all that a man has he will give for his life. ⁵But stretch out Your hand now, and touch his bone and his flesh, and he will surely curse You to Your face!"

⁶And the LORD said to Satan, "Behold, he *is* in your hand, but spare his life."

⁷So Satan went out from the presence of the LORD, and struck Job with painful boils from the sole of his foot to the crown of his head. ⁸And he took for himself a potsherd with which to scrape himself while he sat in the midst of the ashes.

⁹Then his wife said to him, "Do you still hold fast to your integrity? Curse God and die!"

¹⁰But he said to her, "You speak as one of the foolish

◣▬▬ SILENT COMFORT

2:13 Why did Job's friends arrive and then just sit quietly? Accord[ing to] Jewish tradition, people who come to comfort someone in mourning [are] not to speak until the mourner speaks. Often the best response to another person's suffering is silence. Job's friends realized that his p[ain] was too deep to be healed with mere words, so they said nothing. (I[f only] they had *continued* to just sit quietly!) Often, we feel we must say something spiritual and insightful to a hurting friend. Perhaps what she needs most is just our presence, showing that we care. Pat answ[ers] and trite quotations say much less than caring silence and loving companionship.

women speaks. Shall we indeed accept good from God, and shall we not accept adversity?" In all this Job did not sin with his lips.

¹¹Now when Job's three friends heard of all this adversity that had come upon him, each one came from his own place—Eliphaz the Temanite, Bildad the Shuhite, and Zophar the Naamathite. For they had made an appointment together to come and mourn with him, and to comfort him. ¹²And when they raised their eyes from afar, and did not recognize him, they lifted their voices and wept; and each one tore his robe and sprinkled dust on his head toward heaven. ¹³So they sat down with him on the ground seven days and seven nights, and no one spoke a word to him, for they saw that *his* grief was very great.

CHAPTER 3 JOB: I WISH I HAD DIED AT BIRTH.

After this Job opened his mouth and cursed the day of his *birth.* ²And Job spoke, and said:

³ "May the day perish on which I was born,
And the night *in which* it was said,
'A male child is conceived.'
⁴ May that day be darkness;
May God above not seek it,
Nor the light shine upon it.
⁵ May darkness and the shadow of death claim it;
May a cloud settle on it;
May the blackness of the day terrify it.
⁶ *As for* that night, may darkness seize it;
May it not rejoice among the days of the year,
May it not come into the number of the months.
⁷ Oh, may that night be barren!
May no joyful shout come into it!
⁸ May those curse it who curse the day,
Those who are ready to arouse Leviathan.
⁹ May the stars of its morning be dark;
May it look for light, but *have* none,
And not see the dawning of the day;
¹⁰ Because it did not shut up the doors of my *mother's* womb,
Nor hide sorrow from my eyes.

¹¹ "Why did I not die at birth?
Why did I *not* perish when I came from the womb?
¹² Why did the knees receive me?
Or why the breasts, that I should nurse?
¹³ For now I would have lain still and been quiet,
I would have been asleep;
Then I would have been at rest

14 With kings and counselors of the earth,
Who built ruins for themselves,

15 Or with princes who had gold,
Who filled their houses *with* silver;

16 Or *why* was I not hidden like a stillborn child,
Like infants who never saw light?

17 There the wicked cease *from* troubling,
And there the weary are at rest.

18 *There* the prisoners rest together;
They do not hear the voice of the oppressor.

19 The small and great are there,
And the servant *is* free from his master.

20 "Why is light given to him who is in misery,
And life to the bitter of soul,

21 Who long for death, but it does not *come*,
And search for it more than hidden treasures;

22 Who rejoice exceedingly,
And are glad when they
can find the grave?

23 *Why is light given*
to a man
whose way is
hidden,
And whom God
has hedged in?

24 For my sighing
comes before I
eat,
And my groanings
pour out like
water.

25 For the thing I greatly
feared has come
upon me,
And what I dreaded has
happened to me.

26 I am not at ease, nor am I
quiet;
I have no rest, for trouble
comes."

CHAPTER 4 ELIPHAZ:
WORDS. Then Eliphaz the Temanite answered and said:

2 " *If* one attempts a word with you,
will you become weary?
But who can withhold himself from
speaking?

3 Surely you have instructed many,
And you have strengthened weak hands.

4 Your words have upheld him who was
stumbling,
And you have strengthened the feeble
knees;

5 But now it comes upon you, and you are
weary;
It touches you, and you are troubled.

6 *Is* not your reverence your confidence?
And the integrity of your ways your hope?

7 "Remember now, who *ever* perished being innocent?
Or where were the upright *ever* cut off?

8 Even as I have seen,
Those who plow iniquity
And sow trouble reap the same.

9 By the blast of God they perish,
And by the breath of His anger they are consumed.

10 The roaring of the lion,
The voice of the fierce lion,
And the teeth of the young lions are broken.

11 The old lion perishes for lack of prey,
And the cubs of the lioness are scattered.

12 "Now a word was secretly brought to me,
And my ear received
a whisper of it.

JOB

UPS:
- A man of faith, patience, and endurance
- Known as a generous and caring person
- Very wealthy

DOWN:
- Allowed his suffering to overwhelm him and make him question God

STATS:
- Where: Land of Uz
- Occupation: Wealthy land and livestock owner
- Relatives: Wife and first ten children not named. Daughters from the second set of children: Jemimah, Keziah, Keren- Happuch.
- Contemporaries: Eliphaz, Bildad, Zophar, Elihu

The first question most children learn to ask is why. It doesn't take long for kids to notice that things don't just happen. There's a system. The system is called cause and effect. When kids ask why, they are trying to figure out the system.

Sometimes, though, we don't know why. We think that good things should happen to people who do good things, and that bad things should happen to people who do bad things. It often works out that way—but not always. Job was a man who did many good things and had many terrible things happen to him. His life can teach us what God wants us to do when we don't understand what is happening to us.

When the question why becomes important, we can use the letters of that word to remind us of Job's lessons. We need to wait, hope, and yield.

Waiting is hard. Our "instant" age has taught us to expect answers and help fast. Job wanted to know why. When God finally spoke, he didn't offer Job an answer. He showed Job that it is better to know God than to know answers.

That's why hope is important. When we remember that God loves us, that he has good plans for us, and that he is more powerful than any situation we might encounter, we have hope. Hope means we trust God even if we never find out why something happened.

Yielding means wanting to do whatever God wants. It means praying like this: "God, I'm willing to wait and hope, because you are my God." Are there some areas in your life that need this prayer?

LESSONS: Knowing God is better than knowing answers
   God is not arbitrary or uncaring
   Pain is not always punishment

KEY VERSES: "My brethren, take the prophets, who spoke in the name of the Lord, as an example of suffering and patience. Indeed we count them blessed who endure. You have heard of the perseverance of Job and seen the end intended by the Lord—that the Lord is very compassionate and merciful" (James 5:10-11).
   Job's story is told in the book of Job. He is also referred to in Ezekiel 14:14,20.

GOOD ADVICE

5:17 Eliphaz was correct—it is a blessing to be disciplined by God when we do wrong. His advice, however, did not apply to Job. As we know from the beginning of the book, Job's suffering was not a result of some great sin. We sometimes give people excellent advice only to learn that it does not apply to them and is therefore not very helpful. All those who offer counsel from God's Word should take care to thoroughly understand a person's situation *before* giving advice.

13 In disquieting thoughts from the visions of the night,
When deep sleep falls on men,
14 Fear came upon me, and trembling,
Which made all my bones shake.
15 Then a spirit passed before my face;
The hair on my body stood up.
16 It stood still,
But I could not discern its appearance.
A form *was* before my eyes;
There was silence;
Then I heard a voice *saying:*
17 'Can a mortal be more righteous than God?
Can a man be more pure than his Maker?
18 If He puts no trust in His servants,
If He charges His angels with error,
19 How much more those who dwell in houses of clay,
Whose foundation is in the dust,
Who are crushed before a moth?
20 They are broken in pieces from morning till evening;
They perish forever, with no one regarding.
21 Does not their own excellence go away?
They die, even without wisdom.'

CHAPTER 5

"Call out now;
Is there anyone who will answer you?
And to which of the holy ones will you turn?
2 For wrath kills a foolish man,
And envy slays a simple one.
3 I have seen the foolish taking root,
But suddenly I cursed his dwelling place.
4 His sons are far from safety,
They are crushed in the gate,
And *there is* no deliverer.
5 Because the hungry eat up his harvest,
Taking it even from the thorns,
And a snare snatches their substance.
6 For affliction does not come from the dust,
Nor does trouble spring from the ground;
7 Yet man is born to trouble,
As the sparks fly upward.

8 "But as for me, I would seek God,
And to God I would commit my cause—
9 Who does great things, and unsearchable,
Marvelous things without number.
10 He gives rain on the earth,
And sends waters on the fields.
11 He sets on high those who are lowly,
And those who mourn are lifted to safety.
12 He frustrates the devices of the crafty,
So that their hands cannot carry out their plans.
13 He catches the wise in their own craftiness,
And the counsel of the cunning comes quickly upon them.
14 They meet with darkness in the daytime,
And grope at noontime as in the night.
15 But He saves the needy from the sword,
From the mouth of the mighty,
And from their hand.
16 So the poor have hope,
And injustice shuts her mouth.

17 "Behold, happy *is* the man whom God corrects;
Therefore do not despise the chastening of the Almighty.
18 For He bruises, but He binds up;
He wounds, but His hands make whole.
19 He shall deliver you in six troubles,
Yes, in seven no evil shall touch you.
20 In famine He shall redeem you from death,
And in war from the power of the sword.
21 You shall be hidden from the scourge of the tongue,
And you shall not be afraid of destruction when it comes.
22 You shall laugh at destruction and famine,
And you shall not be afraid of the beasts of the earth.
23 For you shall have a covenant with the stones of the field,
And the beasts of the field shall be at peace with you.
24 You shall know that your tent *is* in peace;
You shall visit your dwelling and find nothing amiss.
25 You shall also know that your descendants *shall be* many,
And your offspring like the grass of the earth.
26 You shall come to the grave at a full age,
As a sheaf of grain ripens in its season.
27 Behold, this we have searched out;
It *is* true.
Hear it, and know for yourself."

CHAPTER 6 JOB: WHY AM I SUFFERING? Then Job answered and said:

2 "Oh, that my grief were fully weighed,
And my calamity laid with it on the scales!
3 For then it would be heavier than the sand of the sea—
Therefore my words have been rash.
4 For the arrows of the Almighty *are* within me;
My spirit drinks in their poison;
The terrors of God are arrayed against me.
5 Does the wild donkey bray when it has grass,
Or does the ox low over its fodder?
6 Can flavorless food be eaten without salt?
Or is there *any* taste in the white of an egg?
7 My soul refuses to touch them;
They *are* as loathsome food to me.

8 "Oh, that I might have my request,
That God would grant *me* the thing that I long for!
9 That it would please God to crush me,
That He would loose His hand and cut me off!
10 Then I would still have comfort;
Though in anguish I would exult,

He will not spare;
For I have not concealed the words of the Holy One.

11 "What strength do I have, that I should hope?
And what *is* my end, that I should prolong my life?
12 *Is* my strength the strength of stones?
Or is my flesh bronze?
13 *Is* my help not within me?
And is success driven from me?

14 "To him who is afflicted, kindness *should be shown* by his friend,
Even though he forsakes the fear of the Almighty.
15 My brothers have dealt deceitfully like a brook,
Like the streams of the brooks that pass away,
16 Which are dark because of the ice,
And into which the snow vanishes.
17 When it is warm, they cease to flow;
When it is hot, they vanish from their place.
18 The paths of their way turn aside,
They go nowhere and perish.
19 The caravans of Tema look,
The travelers of Sheba hope for them.
20 They are disappointed because they were confident;
They come there and are confused.
21 For now you are nothing,
You see terror and are afraid.
22 Did I ever say, 'Bring *something* to me'?
Or, 'Offer a bribe for me from your wealth'?
23 Or, 'Deliver me from the enemy's hand'?
Or, 'Redeem me from the hand of oppressors'?

24 "Teach me, and I will hold my tongue;
Cause me to understand wherein I have erred.
25 How forceful are right words!
But what does your arguing prove?
26 Do you intend to rebuke *my* words,
And the speeches of a desperate one, *which are* as wind?
27 Yes, you overwhelm the fatherless,
And you undermine your friend.
28 Now therefore, be pleased to look at me;
For I would never lie to your face.
29 Yield now, let there be no injustice!
Yes, concede, my righteousness still stands!
30 Is there injustice on my tongue?
Cannot my taste discern the unsavory?

CHAPTER 7

" *Is there* not a time of hard service for man on earth?
Are not his days also like the days of a hired man?
2 Like a servant who earnestly desires the shade,
And like a hired man who eagerly looks for his wages,
3 So I have been allotted months of futility,
And wearisome nights have been appointed to me.
4 When I lie down, I say, 'When shall I arise,
And the night be ended?'
For I have had my fill of tossing till dawn.
5 My flesh is caked with worms and dust,
My skin is cracked and breaks out afresh.

6 "My days are swifter than a weaver's shuttle,
And are spent without hope.
7 Oh, remember that my life *is* a breath!
My eye will never again see good.
8 The eye of him who sees me will see me no *more;*
While your *eyes* are upon me, I shall no longer *be.*
9 *As* the cloud disappears and vanishes away,
So he who goes down to the grave does not come up.
10 He shall never return to his house,
Nor shall his place know him anymore.

STRUGGLES

6:8-9 In his grief, Job wanted to give in, to be freed from his discomfort, and to die. But God did not grant Job's request. He had a greater plan for him. Our tendency, like Job's, is to want to give up and get out when the going gets tough. To trust God in the good times is commendable, but to trust him during the difficult times tests us to our limits and exercises our faith. In your struggles, large or small, trust that God is in control (Romans 8:28).

11 "Therefore I will not restrain my mouth;
I will speak in the anguish of my spirit;
I will complain in the bitterness of my soul.
12 *Am* I a sea, or a sea serpent,
That You set a guard over me?
13 When I say, 'My bed will comfort me,
My couch will ease my complaint,'
14 Then You scare me with dreams
And terrify me with visions,
15 So that my soul chooses strangling
And death rather than my body.
16 I loathe *my life;*
I would not live forever.
Let me alone,
For my days *are but* a breath.

17 "What *is* man, that You should exalt him,
That You should set Your heart on him,
18 That You should visit him every morning,
And test him every moment?
19 How long?
Will You not look away from me,
And let me alone till I swallow my saliva?
20 Have I sinned?
What have I done to You, O watcher of men?
Why have You set me as Your target,
So that I am a burden to myself?
21 Why then do You not pardon my transgression,
And take away my iniquity?
For now I will lie down in the dust,
And You will seek me diligently,
But I *will* no longer *be.*"

CHAPTER 8 BILDAD: IF YOU WERE PURE. Then

Bildad the Shuhite answered and said:

2 "How long will you speak these *things,*
And the words of your mouth *be like* a strong wind?
3 Does God subvert judgment?
Or does the Almighty pervert justice?
4 If your sons have sinned against Him,
He has cast them away for their transgression.

5 If you would earnestly seek God
   And make your supplication to the Almighty,
6 If you *were* pure and upright,
   Surely now He would awake for you,
   And prosper your rightful dwelling place.
7 Though your beginning was small,
   Yet your latter end would increase abundantly.

8 "For inquire, please, of the former age,
   And consider the things discovered by their fathers;
9 For we *were born* yesterday, and know nothing,
   Because our days on earth *are* a shadow.
10 Will they not teach you and tell you,
   And utter words from their heart?

11 "Can the papyrus grow up without a marsh?
   Can the reeds flourish without water?
12 While it *is* yet green *and* not cut down,
   It withers before any *other* plant.
13 So *are* the paths of all who forget God;
   And the hope of the hypocrite shall perish,

◣ FEELING SECURE

8:14-15 Bildad wrongly assumed that Job was trusting in something other than God for security, so he pointed out that such supports will collapse. One of man's basic needs is security, and people will do almost anything to feel secure. Eventually, however, our money, possessions, knowledge, and relationships will fail or be gone. Only God can give lasting security. What have you trusted for your security? How lasting is it? If you have a secure foundation with God, then feelings of insecurity cannot uproot you.

14 Whose confidence shall be cut off,
   And whose trust *is* a spider's web.
15 He leans on his house, but it does not stand.
   He holds it fast, but it does not endure.
16 He grows green in the sun,
   And his branches spread out in his garden.
17 His roots wrap around the rock heap,
   And look for a place in the stones.
18 If he is destroyed from his place,
   Then *it* will deny him, *saying,* 'I have not seen you.'

19 "Behold, this is the joy of His way,
   And out of the earth others will grow.
20 Behold, God will not cast away the blameless,
   Nor will He uphold the evildoers.
21 He will yet fill your mouth with laughing,
   And your lips with rejoicing.
22 Those who hate you will be clothed with shame,
   And the dwelling place of the wicked will come to
   nothing."

CHAPTER 9 JOB HAS MORE QUESTIONS. Then Job answered and said:

2 "Truly I know *it is* so,
   But how can a man be righteous before God?
3 If one wished to contend with Him,
   He could not answer Him one time out of a
   thousand.
4 *God is* wise in heart and mighty in strength.

Who has hardened *himself* against Him and
   prospered?
5 He removes the mountains, and they do not know
   When He overturns them in His anger;
6 He shakes the earth out of its place,
   And its pillars tremble;
7 He commands the sun, and it does not rise;
   He seals off the stars;
8 He alone spreads out the heavens,
   And treads on the waves of the sea;
9 He made the Bear, Orion, and the Pleiades,
   And the chambers of the south;
10 He does great things past finding out,
   Yes, wonders without number.
11 If He goes by me, I do not see *Him;*
   If He moves past, I do not perceive Him;
12 If He takes away, who can hinder Him?
   Who can say to Him, 'What are You doing?'
13 God will not withdraw His anger,
   The allies of the proud lie prostrate beneath Him.

14 "How then can I answer Him,
   And choose my words *to reason* with Him?
15 For though I were righteous, I could not answer Him;
   I would beg mercy of my Judge.
16 If I called and He answered me,
   I would not believe that He was listening to my voice.
17 For He crushes me with a tempest,
   And multiplies my wounds without cause.
18 He will not allow me to catch my breath,
   But fills me with bitterness.
19 If *it is a matter* of strength, indeed *He is* strong;
   And if of justice, who will appoint my day *in court?*
20 Though I were righteous, my own mouth would
   condemn me;
   Though I *were* blameless, it would prove me perverse.

21 "I am blameless, yet I do not know myself;
   I despise my life.
22 It *is* all one *thing;*
   Therefore I say, 'He destroys the blameless and the
   wicked.'
23 If the scourge slays suddenly,
   He laughs at the plight of the innocent.
24 The earth is given into the hand of the wicked.
   He covers the faces of its judges.
   If it is not *He,* who else could it be?

25 "Now my days are swifter than a runner;
   They flee away, they see no good.
26 They pass by like swift ships,
   Like an eagle swooping on its prey.
27 If I say, 'I will forget my complaint,
   I will put off my sad face and wear a smile,'
28 I am afraid of all my sufferings;
   I know that You will not hold me innocent.
29 *If* I am condemned,
   Why then do I labor in vain?
30 If I wash myself with snow water,
   And cleanse my hands with soap,
31 Yet You will plunge me into the pit,
   And my own clothes will abhor me.

³² "For *He is* not a man, as I *am*,
That I may answer Him,
And that we should go to court together.
³³ Nor is there any mediator between us,
Who may lay his hand on us both.
³⁴ Let Him take His rod away from me,
And do not let dread of Him terrify me.
³⁵ *Then* I would speak and not fear Him,
But it is not so with me.

CHAPTER 10

"My soul loathes my life;
I will give free course to my complaint,
I will speak in the bitterness of my soul.
² I will say to God, 'Do not condemn me;
Show me why You contend with me.
³ *Does it* seem good to You that You should oppress,
That You should despise the work of Your hands,
And smile on the counsel of the wicked?
⁴ Do You have eyes of flesh?
Or do You see as man sees?
⁵ *Are* Your days like the days of a mortal man?
Are Your years like the days of a mighty man,
⁶ That You should seek for my iniquity
And search out my sin,
⁷ Although You know that I am not wicked,
And *there is* no one who can deliver from Your hand?

⁸ 'Your hands have made me and fashioned me,
An intricate unity;
Yet You would destroy me.
⁹ Remember, I pray, that You have made me like clay.
And will You turn me into dust again?
¹⁰ Did You not pour me out like milk,
And curdle me like cheese,
¹¹ Clothe me with skin and flesh,
And knit me together with bones and sinews?
¹² You have granted me life and favor,
And Your care has preserved my spirit.

¹³ 'And these *things* You have hidden in Your heart;
I know that this *was* with You:
¹⁴ If I sin, then You mark me,
And will not acquit me of my iniquity.
¹⁵ If I am wicked, woe to me;
Even *if* I am righteous, I cannot lift up my head.
I am full of disgrace;
See my misery!
¹⁶ If *my head* is exalted,
You hunt me like a fierce lion,
And again You show Yourself awesome against me.
¹⁷ You renew Your witnesses against me,
And increase Your indignation toward me;
Changes and war are *ever* with me.

¹⁸ 'Why then have You brought me out of the womb?
Oh, that I had perished and no eye had seen me!
¹⁹ I would have been as though I had not been.
I would have been carried from the womb to the grave.
²⁰ Are not my days few?

Cease! Leave me alone, that I may take a little comfort,
²¹ Before I go *to the place from which* I shall not return,
To the land of darkness and the shadow of death,
²² A land as dark as darkness *itself*,
As the shadow of death, without any order,
Where even the light *is* like darkness.' "

CHAPTER 11 ZOPHAR: SEE YOURSELF. Then Zophar the Naamathite answered and said:

² "Should not the multitude of words be answered?
And should a man full of talk be vindicated?
³ Should your empty talk make men hold their peace?
And when you mock, should no one rebuke you?
⁴ For you have said,
'My doctrine *is* pure,
And I am clean in your eyes.'
⁵ But oh, that God would speak,
And open His lips against you,
⁶ That He would show you the secrets of wisdom!
For *they would* double *your* prudence.
Know therefore that God exacts from you
Less than your iniquity *deserves*.

HOW UNFAIR!

10:1 When we face baffling affliction, a natural response is to feel sorry for ourselves. Pain pushes us toward self-pity. At this point we are only one step from self-righteousness, where we keep track of life's injustices and say, "Look what happened to me; how unfair it is!" This comes close to saying that God is unfair. Remember that life's trials, whether allowed by God or sent by God, can help us grow and mature. When facing difficult situations, ask, "What can I learn and how can I grow?" rather than "Who did this to me and how can I get out of it?"

⁷ "Can you search out the deep things of God?
Can you find out the limits of the Almighty?
⁸ *They are* higher than heaven—what can you do?
Deeper than Sheol—what can you know?
⁹ Their measure *is* longer than the earth
And broader than the sea.

¹⁰ "If He passes by, imprisons, and gathers *to judgment*,
Then who can hinder Him?
¹¹ For He knows deceitful men;
He sees wickedness also.
Will He not then consider *it*?
¹² For an empty-headed man will be wise,
When a wild donkey's colt is born a man.

¹³ "If you would prepare your heart,

NO HIDING FROM GOD

11:11 By calling Job "deceitful," Zophar incorrectly assumed that Job was hiding secret faults and sins. Although his assumption was wrong, he explained quite accurately that God knows and sees everything. We are often tempted by the thought, *No one will ever know!* Perhaps we can hide some sin from others, but we can do *nothing* without God knowing about it. Our very thoughts are known to God, so of course he will notice our sins. Job understood this as well as Zophar did, but it didn't apply to his current dilemma.

And stretch out your hands toward Him;

14 If iniquity *were* in your hand, *and you* put it far away,
And would not let wickedness dwell in your tents;

15 Then surely you could lift up your face without spot;
Yes, you could be steadfast, and not fear;

16 Because you would forget *your* misery,
And remember *it* as waters *that have* passed away,

◀ GUIDANCE

12:24-25 Job affirms that no leader has any real wisdom apart from God. No research or report can outweigh God's opinion. When we look for guidance for our lives, we must recognize that God's wisdom is superior to any the world has to offer.

17 And *your* life would be brighter than noonday.
Though you were dark, you would be like the morning.

18 And you would be secure, because there is hope;
Yes, you would dig *around you, and* take your rest in safety.

19 You would also lie down, and no one would make *you* afraid;
Yes, many would court your favor.

20 But the eyes of the wicked will fail,
And they shall not escape,
And their hope—loss of life!"

CHAPTER 12   JOB: I LONG TO SPEAK TO GOD.

Then Job answered and said:

2 "No doubt you *are* the people,
And wisdom will die with you!

3 But I have understanding as well as you;
I *am* not inferior to you.
Indeed, who does not *know* such things as these?

4 "I am one mocked by his friends,
Who called on God, and He answered him,
The just and blameless *who is* ridiculed.

5 A lamp is despised in the thought of one who is at ease;
It is made ready for those whose feet slip.

6 The tents of robbers prosper,
And those who provoke God are secure—
In what God provides by His hand.

7 "But now ask the beasts, and they will teach you;
And the birds of the air, and they will tell you;

8 Or speak to the earth, and it will teach you;
And the fish of the sea will explain to you.

9 Who among all these does not know
That the hand of the LORD has done this,

10 In whose hand *is* the life of every living thing,
And the breath of all mankind?

11 Does not the ear test words
And the mouth taste its food?

12 Wisdom *is* with aged men,
And with length of days, understanding.

13 "With Him *are* wisdom and strength,
He has counsel and understanding.

14 If He breaks *a thing* down, it cannot be rebuilt;

If He imprisons a man, there can be no release.

15 If He withholds the waters, they dry up;
If He sends them out, they overwhelm the earth.

16 With Him *are* strength and prudence.
The deceived and the deceiver *are* His.

17 He leads counselors away plundered,
And makes fools of the judges.

18 He loosens the bonds of kings,
And binds their waist with a belt.

19 He leads princes away plundered,
And overthrows the mighty.

20 He deprives the trusted ones of speech,
And takes away the discernment of the elders.

21 He pours contempt on princes,
And disarms the mighty.

22 He uncovers deep things out of darkness,
And brings the shadow of death to light.

23 He makes nations great, and destroys them;
He enlarges nations, and guides them.

24 He takes away the understanding of the chiefs of the people of the earth,
And makes them wander in a pathless wilderness.

25 They grope in the dark without light,
And He makes them stagger like a drunken *man.*

CHAPTER 13

"Behold, my eye has seen all *this,*
My ear has heard and understood it.

2 What you know, I also know;
I *am* not inferior to you.

3 But I would speak to the Almighty,
And I desire to reason with God.

4 But you forgers of lies,
You *are* all worthless physicians.

5 Oh, that you would be silent,
And it would be your wisdom!

6 Now hear my reasoning,
And heed the pleadings of my lips.

7 Will you speak wickedly for God,
And talk deceitfully for Him?

8 Will you show partiality for Him?
Will you contend for God?

9 Will it be well when He searches you out?
Or can you mock Him as one mocks a man?

10 He will surely rebuke you
If you secretly show partiality.

11 Will not His excellence make you afraid,
And the dread of Him fall upon you?

12 Your platitudes *are* proverbs of ashes,
Your defenses are defenses of clay.

13 "Hold your peace with me, and let me speak,
Then let come on me what *may!*

14 Why do I take my flesh in my teeth,
And put my life in my hands?

15 Though He slay me, yet will I trust Him.
Even so, I will defend my own ways before Him.

16 He also *shall* be my salvation,
For a hypocrite could not come before Him.

17 Listen carefully to my speech,
And to my declaration with your ears.

18   See now, I have prepared *my* case,
    I know that I shall be vindicated.

19   Who *is* he *who* will contend with me?
    If now I hold my tongue, I perish.

20   "Only two *things* do not do to me,
    Then I will not hide myself from You:

21   Withdraw Your hand far from me,
    And let not the dread of You make me afraid.

22   Then call, and I will answer;
    Or let me speak, then You respond to me.

23   How many *are* my iniquities and sins?
    Make me know my transgression and my sin.

24   Why do You hide Your face,
    And regard me as Your enemy?

25   Will You frighten a leaf driven to and fro?
    And will You pursue dry stubble?

26   For You write bitter things against me,
    And make me inherit the iniquities of my youth.

27   You put my feet in the stocks,
    And watch closely all my paths.
    You set a limit for the soles of my feet.

28   "*Man* decays like a rotten thing,
    Like a garment that is moth-eaten.

CHAPTER 14

  "Man *who is* born of woman
    Is of few days and full of trouble.

2   He comes forth like a flower and fades away;
    He flees like a shadow and does not continue.

3   And do You open Your eyes on such a one,
    And bring me to judgment with Yourself?

4   Who can bring a clean *thing* out of an unclean?
    No one!

5   Since his days *are* determined,
    The number of his months *is* with You;
    You have appointed his limits, so that he cannot
       pass.

6   Look away from him that he may rest,
    Till like a hired man he finishes his day.

7   "For there is hope for a tree,
    If it is cut down, that it will sprout again,
    And that its tender shoots will not cease.

8   Though its root may grow old in the earth,
    And its stump may die in the ground,

9   *Yet* at the scent of water it will bud
    And bring forth branches like a plant.

10   But man dies and is laid away;
    Indeed he breathes his last
    And where *is* he?

11   *As* water disappears from the sea,
    And a river becomes parched and dries up,

12   So man lies down and does not rise.
    Till the heavens *are* no more,
    They will not awake
    Nor be roused from their sleep.

13   "Oh, that You would hide me in the grave,
    That You would conceal me until Your wrath is past,
    That You would appoint me a set time, and
       remember me!

14   If a man dies, shall he live *again*?
    All the days of my hard service I will wait,
    Till my change comes.

15   You shall call, and I will answer You;
    You shall desire the work of Your hands.

GUARANTEED LIFE

14:1ff Life is brief and full of trouble, Job lamented in his closing remarks. Sickness, loneliness, disappointment, and the deaths of others caused him to say that life is not fair. Still, Job held on to the one truth that also gives hope to us: resurrection (14:14-15). God's solution to an unfair world is to guarantee life with him forever. No matter how unfair your present world seems, God offers the hope of being in his presence eternally.

16   For now You number my steps,
    But do not watch over my sin.

17   My transgression *is* sealed up in a bag,
    And You cover my iniquity.

18   "But *as* a mountain falls *and* crumbles away,
    And *as* a rock is moved from its place;

19   *As* water wears away stones,
    And as torrents wash away the soil of the earth;
    So You destroy the hope of man.

20   You prevail forever against him, and he passes on;
    You change his countenance and send him away.

21   His sons come to honor, and he does not know *it*;
    They are brought low, and he does not perceive *it*.

22   But his flesh will be in pain over it,
    And his soul will mourn over it."

CHAPTER 15 ELIPHAZ: HAVE YOU NO FEAR? Then

Eliphaz the Temanite answered and said:

2   "Should a wise man answer with empty knowledge,
    And fill himself with the east wind?

3   Should he reason with unprofitable talk,
    Or by speeches with which he can do no good?

4   Yes, you cast off fear,
    And restrain prayer before God.

5   For your iniquity teaches your mouth,
    And you choose the tongue of the crafty.

6   Your own mouth condemns you, and not I;
    Yes, your own lips testify against you.

7   "*Are* you the first man *who* was born?
    Or were you made before the hills?

8   Have you heard the counsel of God?
    Do you limit wisdom to yourself?

9   What do you know that we do not know?
    What do you understand that *is* not in us?

10   Both the gray-haired and the aged *are* among us,
    Much older than your father.

11   *Are* the consolations of God too small for you,
    And the word *spoken* gently with you?

12   Why does your heart carry you away,
    And what do your eyes wink at,

13   That you turn your spirit against God,
    And let *such* words go out of your mouth?

SUFFERING
AND
EVIL

Sooner or later, every Christian faces this question: Why does God allow suffering and evil? Why do horrible things happen to good people? Theologians and philosophers express it like this: "If God is good, he must not be all-powerful, otherwise he wouldn't allow evil. If he *is* all-powerful, he must not be good." **D**oes God see what's going on here? Does he care? If so, why doesn't he intervene? **T**he book of Job addresses this question more than any portion of Scripture. For reasons unknown to Job, a series of crushing catastrophes hit him, leaving him to ask, "Why me, God?" And God responds (chapters 38–41) with his longest unbroken speech in the Bible—but he never tells Job why. He basically tells Job that as God he can do whatever he wants, and that's all the answer Job needs. **B**ig help, right? **I**t's like the story about the guy who goes home from work one day to find his wife gone, the kids moved out, and his house empty. Then the dog bites him. He lifts his hands toward heaven and cries out, "Why me, God?" From the skies there comes a rumbling voice saying: "Frankly, Sam, there's just something about you that ticks me off." **T**he fact that God doesn't answer Job's question is somewhat disturbing. But the following perspectives may help when you are faced with suffering and evil. **F**irst, remember that though God never answered Job directly, he didn't condemn Job for asking. He just reminded Job who he was talking to. It seems that why is a question we are free to ask, but God is not bound to answer. Sometimes he will; sometimes he won't. **S**econd, remember that we live in a broken world of sinful people. It is a planet in rebellion against its Creator; it should hardly surprise us that believers are caught in the crossfire. When you are tempted to blame God for your suffering, think of it like this. It's like giving a fragile, priceless family heirloom to a child. He looks it over and then smashes it to the floor. As he stands there in the midst of the shattered pieces of what you gave him, he shakes his clenched fist in your face and says, "Look what you've done! Look at this piece of junk you gave me!" The child is wrong; you gave him a wonderful, treasured possession and he ruined it. God gave us a perfect world; we've turned it into the chaos it is today. **T**hird, remember that being a Christian—or a "good person"—does not exempt you from pain and suffering. Jesus even guaranteed us (in John 16:33) that we will experience trials and heartache. But the test is how we respond when the storm washes over us. And if you're serious about following Jesus, brace yourself: storms will come. **F**ourth, contrary to what a lot of Christians believe, God does not promise his children happiness. He's much more concerned with our holiness, and th involves pain and sacrifice. Worthwhile things seldom, if ever, come without great cost. Following Jesus is to serve God when life is sunny; the test is how we respond when the storm washes over us. And if you're exception. Of course, God isn't a cosmic killjoy, getting his kicks out of watching us squirm. He just wants imitate his Son—even when it isn't all fun and games. **F**inally, when nothing else helps, remember this: you or someone you love suffers, no one hurts more than God. He's a good Father, and it pains him dee see his children hurt. He feels with us so genuinely that he got personally involved in our struggle—he a man and suffered and died for us. So when you hurt, remember: You never cry alone. God knows, sees, and God cares.

14 "What *is* man, that he could be pure?
And *he who is* born of a woman, that he could be righteous?

15 If *God* puts no trust in His saints,
And the heavens are not pure in His sight,

16 How much less man, *who is* abominable and filthy,
Who drinks iniquity like water!

17 "I will tell you, hear me;
What I have seen I will declare,

18 What wise men have told,
Not hiding *anything received* from their fathers,

19 To whom alone the land was given,
And no alien passed among them:

20 The wicked man writhes with pain all *his* days,
And the number of years is hidden from the oppressor.

21 Dreadful sounds *are* in his ears;
In prosperity the destroyer comes upon him.

22 He does not believe that he will return from darkness,
For a sword is waiting for him.

23 He wanders about for bread, *saying,* 'Where *is it?*'
He knows that a day of darkness is ready at his hand.

24 Trouble and anguish make him afraid;
They overpower him, like a king ready for battle.

25 For he stretches out his hand against God,
And acts defiantly against the Almighty,

26 Running stubbornly against Him
With his strong, embossed shield.

27 "Though he has covered his face with his fatness,
And made *his* waist heavy with fat,

28 He dwells in desolate cities,
In houses which no one inhabits,
Which are destined to become ruins.

29 He will not be rich,
Nor will his wealth continue,
Nor will his possessions overspread the earth.

30 He will not depart from darkness;
The flame will dry out his branches,
And by the breath of His mouth he will go away.

31 Let him not trust in futile *things,* deceiving himself,
For futility will be his reward.

32 It will be accomplished before his time,
And his branch will not be green.

33 He will shake off his unripe grape like a vine,
And cast off his blossom like an olive tree.

34 For the company of hypocrites *will be* barren,
And fire will consume the tents of bribery.

35 They conceive trouble and bring forth futility;
Their womb prepares deceit."

CHAPTER 16 JOB: YOU ARE NO HELP. Then Job answered and said:

2 "I have heard many such things;
Miserable comforters *are* you all!

3 Shall words of wind have an end?
Or what provokes you that you answer?

4 I also could speak as you *do,*
If your soul were in my soul's place.

I could heap up words against you,
And shake my head at you;

5 *But* I would strengthen you with my mouth,
And the comfort of my lips would relieve *your grief.*

6 "Though I speak, my grief is not relieved;
And *if* I remain silent, how am I eased?

7 But now He has worn me out;
You have made desolate all my company.

8 You have shriveled me up,
And it is a witness *against me;*
My leanness rises up against me
And bears witness to my face.

◀〜〜〜〜〜〜 PAT ANSWERS

16:1ff Job's friends were supposed to be comforting him in his grief. Instead they condemned him for causing his own suffering. Job began his reply to Eliphaz by calling him and his friends "miserable comforters." Job's words reveal several ways to become a better comforter to those in pain: (1) don't talk just for the sake of talking; (2) don't sermonize by giving pat answers; (3) don't criticize; (4) put yourself in the other person's place; and (5) offer sincere help and encouragement. Try Job's suggestions, knowing that they are given by a person who needed great comfort. The best comforters are those who know something about personal suffering.

9 He tears *me* in His wrath, and hates me;
He gnashes at me with His teeth;
My adversary sharpens His gaze on me.

10 They gape at me with their mouth,
They strike me reproachfully on the cheek,
They gather together against me.

11 God has delivered me to the ungodly,
And turned me over to the hands of the wicked.

12 I was at ease, but He has shattered me;
He also has taken *me* by my neck, and shaken me to pieces;
He has set me up for His target,

13 His archers surround me.
He pierces my heart and does not pity;
He pours out my gall on the ground.

14 He breaks me with wound upon wound;
He runs at me like a warrior.

15 "I have sewn sackcloth over my skin,
And laid my head in the dust.

16 My face is flushed from weeping,
And on my eyelids *is* the shadow of death;

17 Although no violence *is* in my hands,
And my prayer *is* pure.

18 "O earth, do not cover my blood,
And let my cry have no *resting* place!

19 Surely even now my witness *is* in heaven,
And my evidence *is* on high.

20 My friends scorn me;
My eyes pour out *tears* to God.

21 Oh, that one might plead for a man with God,
As a man *pleads* for his neighbor!

22 For when a few years are finished,
I shall go the way of no return.

CHAPTER 17

"My spirit is broken,
My days are extinguished,
The grave *is ready* for me.
2 *Are* not mockers with me?
And does not my eye dwell on their provocation?

3 "Now put down a pledge for me with Yourself.
Who *is* he *who* will shake hands with me?
4 For You have hidden their heart from understanding;
Therefore You will not exalt *them*.
5 He who speaks flattery to *his* friends,
Even the eyes of his children will fail.

6 "But He has made me a byword of the people,
And I have become one in whose face men spit.
7 My eye has also grown dim because of sorrow,
And all my members *are* like shadows.
8 Upright *men* are astonished at this,
And the innocent stirs himself up against the
hypocrite.

◣◥◣◥ NEVER-ENDING HOPE

17:15 Job gave up hope of any future restoration of wealth and family, and he wrapped himself in thoughts of death and the rest from grief and pain it promised. The rewards Job's friends mentioned all were related to this present life. They were silent about the possibility of life after death. We must be careful to avoid viewing life only in terms of this present world, because God promises the faithful a never-ending future.

9 Yet the righteous will hold to his way,
And he who has clean hands will be stronger and
stronger.

10 "But please, come back again, all of you,
For I shall not find *one* wise *man* among you.
11 My days are past,
My purposes are broken off,
Even the thoughts of my heart.
12 They change the night into day;
'The light *is* near,' *they say,* in the face of darkness.
13 If I wait *for* the grave *as* my house,
If I make my bed in the darkness,
14 If I say to corruption, 'You *are* my father,'
And to the worm, 'You *are* my mother and my sister,'
15 Where then *is* my hope?
As for my hope, who can see it?
16 *Will* they go down to the gates of Sheol?
Shall *we have* rest together in the dust?"

CHAPTER 18 BILDAD: YOU ARE WICKED. Then Bildad the Shuhite answered and said:

2 "How long *till* you put an end to words?
Gain understanding, and afterward we will speak.
3 Why are we counted as beasts,
And regarded as stupid in your sight?
4 You who tear yourself in anger,
Shall the earth be forsaken for you?
Or shall the rock be removed from its place?

5 "The light of the wicked indeed goes out,
And the flame of his fire does not shine.

6 The light is dark in his tent,
And his lamp beside him is put out.
7 The steps of his strength are shortened,
And his own counsel casts him down.
8 For he is cast into a net by his own feet,
And he walks into a snare.
9 The net takes *him* by the heel,
And a snare lays hold of him.
10 A noose *is* hidden for him on the ground,
And a trap for him in the road.
11 Terrors frighten him on every side,
And drive him to his feet.
12 His strength is starved,
And destruction *is* ready at his side.
13 It devours patches of his skin;
The firstborn of death devours his limbs.
14 He is uprooted from the shelter of his tent,
And they parade him before the king of terrors.
15 They dwell in his tent *who are* none of his;
Brimstone is scattered on his dwelling.
16 His roots are dried out below,
And his branch withers above.
17 The memory of him perishes from the earth,
And he has no name among the renowned.
18 He is driven from light into darkness,
And chased out of the world.
19 He has neither son nor posterity among his people,
Nor any remaining in his dwellings.
20 Those in the west are astonished at his day,
As those in the east are frightened.
21 Surely such *are* the dwellings of the wicked,
And this *is* the place *of him who* does not know God."

CHAPTER 19 JOB: IMPATIENT BUT TRUSTING GOD.

Then Job answered and said:

2 "How long will you torment my soul,
And break me in pieces with words?
3 These ten times you have reproached me;
You are not ashamed *that* you have wronged me.
4 And if indeed I have erred,
My error remains with me.
5 If indeed you exalt *yourselves* against me,
And plead my disgrace against me,
6 Know then that God has wronged me,
And has surrounded me with His net.

7 "If I cry out concerning wrong, I am not heard.
If I cry aloud, *there is* no justice.
8 He has fenced up my way, so that I cannot pass;
And He has set darkness in my paths.
9 He has stripped me of my glory,
And taken the crown *from* my head.
10 He breaks me down on every side,
And I am gone;
My hope He has uprooted like a tree.
11 He has also kindled His wrath against me,
And He counts me as *one of* His enemies.
12 His troops come together
And build up their road against me;
They encamp all around my tent.

13 "He has removed my brothers far from me,
   And my acquaintances are completely estranged
      from me.
14 My relatives have failed,
   And my close friends have forgotten me.
15 Those who dwell in my house, and my maidservants,
   Count me as a stranger;
   I am an alien in their sight.
16 I call my servant, but he gives no answer;
   I beg him with my mouth.
17 My breath is offensive to my wife,
   And I am repulsive to the children of my own body.
18 Even young children despise me;
   I arise, and they speak against me.
19 All my close friends abhor me,
   And those whom I love have turned against me.
20 My bone clings to my skin and to my flesh,
   And I have escaped by the skin of my teeth.

21 "Have pity on me, have pity on me, O you my friends,
   For the hand of God has struck me!
22 Why do you persecute me as God *does,*
   And are not satisfied with my flesh?

23 "Oh, that my words were written!
   Oh, that they were inscribed in a book!
24 That they were engraved on a rock
   With an iron pen and lead, forever!
25 For I know *that* my Redeemer lives,
   And He shall stand at last on the earth;
26 And after my skin is destroyed, this *I know,*
   That in my flesh I shall see God,
27 Whom I shall see for myself,
   And my eyes shall behold, and not another.
   How my heart yearns within me!
28 If you should say, 'How shall we persecute him?'—
   Since the root of the matter is found in me,
29 Be afraid of the sword for yourselves;
   For wrath *brings* the punishment of the sword,
   That you may know *there is* a judgment."

CHAPTER 20 ZOPHAR: I HAVE THE ANSWER.
Then Zophar the Naamathite answered and said:

2 "Therefore my anxious thoughts make me answer,
   Because of the turmoil within me.
3 I have heard the rebuke that reproaches me,
   And the spirit of my understanding causes me to
      answer.

4 "Do you *not* know this of old,
   Since man was placed on earth,
5 That the triumphing of the wicked is short,
   And the joy of the hypocrite is *but* for a moment?
6 Though his haughtiness mounts up to the heavens,
   And his head reaches to the clouds,
7 *Yet* he will perish forever like his own refuse;
   Those who have seen him will say, 'Where is he?'
8 He will fly away like a dream, and not be found;
   Yes, he will be chased away like a vision of the night.
9 The eye *that* saw him will *see him* no more,
   Nor will his place behold him anymore.

10 His children will seek the favor of the poor,
   And his hands will restore his wealth.
11 His bones are full of his youthful vigor,
   But it will lie down with him in the dust.

12 "Though evil is sweet in his mouth,
   And he hides it under his tongue,
13 *Though* he spares it and does not forsake it,
   But still keeps it in his mouth,
14 *Yet* his food in his stomach turns sour;
   It becomes cobra venom within him.
15 He swallows down riches
   And vomits them up again;
   God casts them out of his belly.
16 He will suck the poison of cobras;
   The viper's tongue will slay him.
17 He will not see the streams,
   The rivers flowing with honey and cream.
18 He will restore that for which he labored,
   And will not swallow *it* down;
   From the proceeds of business
   He will get no enjoyment.
19 For he has oppressed *and* forsaken the poor,
   He has violently seized a house which he did not
      build.

20 "Because he knows no quietness in his heart,
   He will not save anything he desires.
21 Nothing is left for him to eat;
   Therefore his well-being will not last.
22 In his self-sufficiency he will be in distress;
   Every hand of misery will come against him.
23 *When* he is about to fill his stomach,
   God will cast on him the fury of His wrath,
   And will rain *it* on him while he is eating.
24 He will flee from the iron weapon;
   A bronze bow will pierce him through.
25 It is drawn, and comes out of the body;
   Yes, the glittering *point comes* out of his gall.
   Terrors *come* upon him;
26 Total darkness *is* reserved for his treasures.
   An unfanned fire will consume him;
   It shall go ill with him who is left in his tent.
27 The heavens will reveal his iniquity,
   And the earth will rise up against him.
28 The increase of his house will depart,
   And his goods will flow away in the day of His wrath.
29 This *is* the portion from God for a wicked man,
   The heritage appointed to him by God."

◆ PAYBACK

20:6-7 Although Zophar was wrong in directing this tirade against Job, he was correct in talking about the final end of evil people. At first, sin seems enjoyable and attractive. Lying, stealing, or oppressing others often brings temporary gain to those who practice these sins. Some even live a long time with ill-gotten gain. But in the end, God's justice will prevail. What Zophar missed is that judgment for these sins may not come in the lifetime of the sinner. Punishment may be deferred until the last judgment, when sinners will be eternally cut off from God. We should not be impressed with the success and power of evil people. God's judgment on them is certain.

CHAPTER 21 JOB: YOU DO NOT UNDERSTAND.

Then Job answered and said:

2 "Listen carefully to my speech,
And let this be your consolation.
3 Bear with me that I may speak,
And after I have spoken, keep mocking.

SUCCESS

21:1ff Job refuted Zophar's idea that evil people never experience wealth and happiness, pointing out that in the real world the wicked do indeed prosper. God does what he wants to individuals (21:22-25), and people should not use their circumstances to measure their own goodness or God's—prosperity and goodness are not necessarily related. To Job's friends, success was based on outward performance; to God, however, success is based on a person's heart.

4 "As for me, is my complaint against man?
And if it were, why should I not be impatient?
5 Look at me and be astonished;
Put your hand over your mouth.
6 Even when I remember I am terrified,
And trembling takes hold of my flesh.
7 Why do the wicked live and become old,
Yes, become mighty in power?
8 Their descendants are established with them in their
sight,
And their offspring before their eyes.
9 Their houses are safe from fear,
Neither is the rod of God upon them.
10 Their bull breeds without failure;
Their cow calves without miscarriage.
11 They send forth their little ones like a flock,
And their children dance.
12 They sing to the tambourine and harp,
And rejoice to the sound of the flute.
13 They spend their days in wealth,
And in a moment go down to the grave.
14 Yet they say to God, 'Depart from us,
For we do not desire the knowledge of Your ways.

ABOUT YOUR ATTITUDE

21:22 In the middle of Job's confusion about his suffering, he asked, "Can anyone teach God knowledge, since He judges those on high?" Even if your personal struggles seem as great and difficult as Job's, your response will indicate your current attitude toward God. Rather than becoming angry with God, continue to trust him, no matter what your circumstances may be. Although it is sometimes difficult to see, God is in control.

15 Who is the Almighty, that we should serve Him?
And what profit do we have if we pray to Him?'
16 Indeed their prosperity is not in their hand;
The counsel of the wicked is far from me.

17 "How often is the lamp of the wicked put out?
How often does their destruction come upon them,
The sorrows God distributes in His anger?
18 They are like straw before the wind,
And like chaff that a storm carries away.
19 They say, 'God lays up one's iniquity for his children';

Let Him recompense him, that he may know it.
20 Let his eyes see his destruction,
And let him drink of the wrath of the Almighty.
21 For what does he care about his household after him,
When the number of his months is cut in half?

22 "Can anyone teach God knowledge,
Since He judges those on high?
23 One dies in his full strength,
Being wholly at ease and secure;
24 His pails are full of milk,
And the marrow of his bones is moist.
25 Another man dies in the bitterness of his soul,
Never having eaten with pleasure.
26 They lie down alike in the dust,
And worms cover them.

27 "Look, I know your thoughts,
And the schemes with which you would wrong me.
28 For you say,
'Where is the house of the prince?
And where is the tent,
The dwelling place of the wicked?'
29 Have you not asked those who travel the road?
And do you not know their signs?
30 For the wicked are reserved for the day of doom;
They shall be brought out on the day of wrath.
31 Who condemns his way to his face?
And who repays him for what he has done?
32 Yet he shall be brought to the grave,
And a vigil kept over the tomb.
33 The clods of the valley shall be sweet to him;
Everyone shall follow him,
As countless have gone before him.
34 How then can you comfort me with empty words,
Since falsehood remains in your answers?"

CHAPTER 22 ELIPHAZ: YOU MUST GIVE IN.

Then Eliphaz the Temanite answered and said:

2 "Can a man be profitable to God,
Though he who is wise may be profitable to himself?
3 Is it any pleasure to the Almighty that you are
righteous?
Or is it gain to Him that you make your ways
blameless?

4 "Is it because of your fear of Him that He corrects you,
And enters into judgment with you?
5 Is not your wickedness great,
And your iniquity without end?
6 For you have taken pledges from your brother for no
reason,
And stripped the naked of their clothing.
7 You have not given the weary water to drink,
And you have withheld bread from the hungry.
8 But the mighty man possessed the land,
And the honorable man dwelt in it.
9 You have sent widows away empty,
And the strength of the fatherless was crushed.
10 Therefore snares are all around you,
And sudden fear troubles you,

11 Or darkness *so that* you cannot see;
And an abundance of water covers you.

12 "Is not God in the height of heaven?
And see the highest stars, how lofty they are!

13 And you say, 'What does God know?
Can He judge through the deep darkness?

14 Thick clouds cover Him, so that He cannot see,
And He walks above the circle of heaven.'

15 Will you keep to the old way
Which wicked men have trod,

16 Who were cut down before their time,
Whose foundations were swept away by a flood?

17 They said to God, 'Depart from us!
What can the Almighty do to them?'

18 Yet He filled their houses with good *things;*
But the counsel of the wicked is far from me.

19 "The righteous see *it* and are glad,
And the innocent laugh at them:

20 'Surely our adversaries are cut down,
And the fire consumes their remnant.'

21 "Now acquaint yourself with Him, and be at peace;
Thereby good will come to you.

22 Receive, please, instruction from His mouth,
And lay up His words in your heart.

23 If you return to the Almighty, you will be built up;
You will remove iniquity far from your tents.

24 Then you will lay your gold in the dust,
And the *gold* of Ophir among the stones of the brooks.

25 Yes, the Almighty will be your gold
And your precious silver;

26 For then you will have your delight in the Almighty,
And lift up your face to God.

27 You will make your prayer to Him,
He will hear you,
And you will pay your vows.

28 You will also declare a thing,
And it will be established for you;
So light will shine on your ways.

29 When they cast *you* down, and you say, 'Exaltation
will come!
Then He will save the humble *person.*

30 He will *even* deliver one who is not innocent;
Yes, he will be delivered by the purity of your hands."

CHAPTER **23** JOB: I WANT TO FIND GOD. Then
Job answered and said:

2 "Even today my complaint is bitter;
My hand is listless because of my groaning.

3 Oh, that I knew where I might find Him,
That I might come to His seat!

4 I would present *my* case before Him,
And fill my mouth with arguments.

5 I would know the words *which* He would answer me,
And understand what He would say to me.

6 Would He contend with me in His great power?
No! But He would take *note* of me.

7 There the upright could reason with Him,
And I would be delivered forever from my Judge.

8 "Look, I go forward, but He is not *there,*
And backward, but I cannot perceive Him;

9 When He works on the left hand, I cannot behold *Him;*
When He turns to the right hand, I cannot see *Him.*

10 But He knows the way that I take;
When He has tested me, I shall come forth as gold.

11 My foot has held fast to His steps;
I have kept His way and not turned aside.

12 I have not departed from the commandment of His
lips;
I have treasured the words of His mouth
More than my necessary *food.*

13 "But He *is* unique, and who can make Him change?
And *whatever* His soul desires, *that* He does.

14 For He performs *what is* appointed for me,
And many such *things are* with Him.

DEEP PURPOSES

23:14 Job wavered back and forth, first proclaiming loyalty to God and then calling God his enemy. His friends' words and his own suspicions were undermining his confidence in God. When affliction comes, it is natural to blame God and to think that our suffering must be divine punishment. But we must not assume that God is being hostile toward us. His purposes go deeper than our ability to grasp all that is really happening. While this sounds like a pat answer, it is the same answer God gave Job in chapters 38—41. We shouldn't demand to know why certain calamities hit us. Often we cannot know, or are not meant to know, until later.

15 Therefore I am terrified at His presence;
When I consider *this,* I am afraid of Him.

16 For God made my heart weak,
And the Almighty terrifies me;

17 Because I was not cut off from the presence of
darkness,
And He did *not* hide deep darkness from my face.

CHAPTER **24**

"*Since* times are not hidden from the Almighty,
Why do those who know Him see not His days?

2 "*Some* remove landmarks;
They seize flocks violently and feed *on them;*

3 They drive away the donkey of the fatherless;
They take the widow's ox as a pledge.

4 They push the needy off the road;
All the poor of the land are forced to hide.

5 Indeed, *like* wild donkeys in the desert,
They go out to their work, searching for food.
The wilderness *yields* food for them *and* for *their*
children.

6 They gather their fodder in the field
And glean in the vineyard of the wicked.

7 They spend the night naked, without clothing,
And have no covering in the cold.

8 They are wet with the showers of the mountains,
And huddle around the rock for want of shelter.

9 "*Some* snatch the fatherless from the breast,
And take a pledge from the poor.

GREATER RESULTS

26:2-4 With great sarcasm, Job attacked his friends' comments. Their theological explanations failed to bring any relief because they were unable to turn their knowledge into helpful counsel. When dealing with people, it is more important to love and understand them than to analyze them or give advice. Compassion produces greater results than criticism or blame.

10 They cause *the poor* to go naked, without clothing;
And they take away the sheaves from the hungry.
11 They press out oil within their walls,
And tread winepresses, yet suffer thirst.
12 The dying groan in the city,
And the souls of the wounded cry out;
Yet God does not charge *them* with wrong.

13 "There are those who rebel against the light;
They do not know its ways
Nor abide in its paths.
14 The murderer rises with the light;
He kills the poor and needy;
And in the night he is like a thief.
15 The eye of the adulterer waits for the twilight,
Saying, 'No eye will see me';
And he disguises *his* face.
16 In the dark they break into houses
Which they marked for themselves in the daytime;
They do not know the light.
17 For the morning is the same to them as the shadow of death;
If *someone* recognizes *them,*
They are in the terrors of the shadow of death.

18 "They *should be* swift on the face of the waters,
Their portion *should be* cursed in the earth,
So that no *one would* turn into the way of their vineyards.
19 As drought and heat consume the snow waters,
So the grave *consumes those who* have sinned.
20 The womb *should* forget him,
The worm *should* feed sweetly on him;
He *should* be remembered no more,
And wickedness *should* be broken like a tree.
21 For he preys on the barren *who* do not bear,
And does no good for the widow.

22 "But *God* draws the mighty away with His power;
He rises up, but no *man* is sure of life.
23 He gives them security, and they rely *on it;*
Yet His eyes *are* on their ways.
24 They are exalted for a little while,
Then they are gone.
They are brought low;
They are taken out of the way like all *others;*
They dry out like the heads of grain.

25 "Now if *it is* not *so,* who will prove me a liar,
And make my speech worth nothing?"

CHAPTER 25 BILDAD: WHO STANDS BEFORE GOD? Then Bildad the Shuhite answered and said:

2 "Dominion and fear *belong* to Him;
He makes peace in His high places.
3 Is there any number to His armies?

Upon whom does His light not rise?
4 How then can man be righteous before God?
Or how can he be pure *who is* born of a woman?
5 If even the moon does not shine,
And the stars are not pure in His sight,
6 How much less man, *who is* a maggot,
And a son of man, *who is* a worm?"

CHAPTER 26 JOB: I WILL NEVER AGREE. But Job answered and said:

2 "How have you helped *him who is* without power?
How have you saved the arm *that has* no strength?
3 How have you counseled *one who has* no wisdom?
And *how* have you declared sound advice to many?
4 To whom have you uttered words?
And whose spirit came from you?

5 "The dead tremble,
Those under the waters and those inhabiting them.
6 Sheol *is* naked before Him,
And Destruction has no covering.
7 He stretches out the north over empty space;
He hangs the earth on nothing.

CLEAR CONSCIENCE

27:6 To all the accusations, Job was able to declare that his consc was clear. Only right living before God can bring a clear conscience how important Job's record became as he was being accused! Like we can't claim sinless lives, but we *can* claim forgiven lives. When v confess our sins to God, we are forgiven and can live our lives with consciences (1 John 1:9).

8 He binds up the water in His thick clouds,
Yet the clouds are not broken under it.
9 He covers the face of *His* throne,
And spreads His cloud over it.
10 He drew a circular horizon on the face of the waters,
At the boundary of light and darkness.
11 The pillars of heaven tremble,
And are astonished at His rebuke.
12 He stirs up the sea with His power,
And by His understanding He breaks up the storm.
13 By His Spirit He adorned the heavens;
His hand pierced the fleeing serpent.
14 Indeed these *are* the mere edges of His ways,
And how small a whisper we hear of Him!
But the thunder of His power who can understand?"

CHAPTER 27 JOB: FEAR THE LORD. Moreover Job continued his discourse, and said:

2 "*As* God lives, *who* has taken away my justice,
And the Almighty, *who* has made my soul bitter,
3 As long as my breath *is* in me,
And the breath of God in my nostrils,
4 My lips will not speak wickedness,
Nor my tongue utter deceit.
5 Far be it from me
That I should say you are right;
Till I die I will not put away my integrity from me.

⁶ My righteousness I hold fast, and will not let it go;
 My heart shall not reproach *me* as long as I live.

⁷ "May my enemy be like the wicked,
 And he who rises up against me like the unrighteous.
⁸ For what is the hope of the hypocrite,
 Though he may gain *much*,
 If God takes away his life?
⁹ Will God hear his cry
 When trouble comes upon him?
¹⁰ Will he delight himself in the Almighty?
 Will he always call on God?

¹¹ "I will teach you about the hand of God;
 What *is* with the Almighty I will not conceal.
¹² Surely all of you have seen *it*;
 Why then do you behave with complete nonsense?

¹³ "This is the portion of a wicked man with God,
 And the heritage of oppressors, received from the Almighty:
¹⁴ If his children are multiplied, *it is* for the sword;
 And his offspring shall not be satisfied with bread.
¹⁵ Those who survive him shall be buried in death,
 And their widows shall not weep,
¹⁶ Though he heaps up silver like dust,
 And piles up clothing like clay—
¹⁷ He may pile *it* up, but the just will wear *it*,
 And the innocent will divide the silver.
¹⁸ He builds his house like a moth,
 Like a booth *which* a watchman makes.
¹⁹ The rich man will lie down,
 But not be gathered *up*;
 He opens his eyes,
 And he *is* no more.
²⁰ Terrors overtake him like a flood;
 A tempest steals him away in the night.
²¹ The east wind carries him away, and he is gone;
 It sweeps him out of his place.
²² It hurls against him and does not spare;
 He flees desperately from its power.
²³ *Men* shall clap their hands at him,
 And shall hiss him out of his place.

CHAPTER 28

"Surely there is a mine for silver,
 And a place *where* gold is refined.
² Iron is taken from the earth,
 And copper *is* smelted *from* ore.
³ *Man* puts an end to darkness,
 And searches every recess
 For ore in the darkness and the shadow of death.
⁴ He breaks open a shaft away from people;
 In places forgotten by feet
 They hang far away from men;
 They swing to and fro.
⁵ *As for* the earth, from it comes bread,
 But underneath it is turned up as by fire;
⁶ Its stones *are* the source of sapphires,
 And it contains gold dust.
⁷ *That* path no bird knows,
 Nor has the falcon's eye seen it.

⁸ The proud lions have not trodden it,
 Nor has the fierce lion passed over it.
⁹ He puts his hand on the flint;
 He overturns the mountains at the roots.
¹⁰ He cuts out channels in the rocks,
 And his eye sees every precious thing.
¹¹ He dams up the streams from trickling;
 What is hidden he brings forth to light.

◄━━━━━━ WISE WITHOUT GOD?

28:12 People can perform all kinds of technological wonders. They can find stars invisible to the eye, they can visit space, they can store volumes of information on a microchip. But even the greatest scientists, on their own, are at a loss to discover wisdom for their daily lives. Only God can show them where to look to find wisdom because he is the source of wisdom (28:27). True wisdom is having God's perspective on life. As the Creator of life, only he knows what is best for his creation. It is fruitless for us to try to become wise merely through our own observations and efforts because God alone sees the greater purpose for his world.

¹² "But where can wisdom be found?
 And where *is* the place of understanding?
¹³ Man does not know its value,
 Nor is it found in the land of the living.
¹⁴ The deep says, '*It is* not in me';
 And the sea says, '*It is* not with me.'
¹⁵ It cannot be purchased for gold,
 Nor can silver be weighed *for* its price.
¹⁶ It cannot be valued in the gold of Ophir,
 In precious onyx or sapphire.
¹⁷ Neither gold nor crystal can equal it,
 Nor can it be exchanged for jewelry of fine gold.
¹⁸ No mention shall be made of coral or quartz,
 For the price of wisdom *is* above rubies.
¹⁹ The topaz of Ethiopia cannot equal it,
 Nor can it be valued in pure gold.

²⁰ "From where then does wisdom come?
 And where *is* the place of understanding?
²¹ It is hidden from the eyes of all living,
 And concealed from the birds of the air.
²² Destruction and Death say,
 'We have heard a report about it with our ears.'
²³ God understands its way,
 And He knows its place.
²⁴ For He looks to the ends of the earth,
 And sees under the whole heavens,
²⁵ To establish a weight for the wind,
 And apportion the waters by measure.
²⁶ When He made a law for the rain,
 And a path for the thunderbolt,
²⁷ Then He saw *wisdom* and declared it;
 He prepared it, indeed, He searched it out.
²⁸ And to man He said,
 'Behold, the fear of the Lord, that *is* wisdom,
 And to depart from evil *is* understanding.' "

CHAPTER 29 JOB: GOD'S CARE FOR ME. Job further continued his discourse, and said:

2 "Oh, that I were as *in* months past,
As *in* the days *when* God watched over me;
3 When His lamp shone upon my head,
And when by His light I walked *through* darkness;
4 Just as I was in the days of my prime,
When the friendly counsel of God *was* over my tent;
5 When the Almighty *was* yet with me,
When my children *were* around me;
6 When my steps were bathed with cream,
And the rock poured out rivers of oil for me!

7 "When I went out to the gate by the city,
When I took my seat in the open square,

PORNOGRAPHY

Cary's problem started three years ago when he and some friends found an abandoned trailer in the woods behind their neighborhood. Cary was 12.

Inside the trailer were several pornographic magazines. The guys quickly wore a path to their new hideout, and Cary made himself the guardian of the group's "erotic treasures."

One winter night, the ramshackle trailer—including the nasty pictures—mysteriously went up in smoke. The other boys moved on to other things. But Cary was hooked. He couldn't seem to see enough naked bodies. Whether it was through explicit videos, graphic novels, or trashy movies on cable, Cary was almost totally controlled by his desire to see some skin.

Not only did Cary's obsession bring him great frustration (because pornography is such a lie), but it also caused him unbelievable guilt. He couldn't even glance at a woman without mentally undressing her. And no matter how hard he tried, he couldn't get all the dirty images out of his mind. Christ's warning about lust (Matthew 5:28) haunted him.

Thank the Lord that Cary finally had enough sense to talk to Bill, his youth leader. Bill got Cary into a good Bible study, and he now prays with him and checks up on him regularly.

Cary's gonna make it.

See one of the verses Cary and Bill studied: Job 31:1. It is a great example to follow for those who struggle with lust!

8 The young men saw me and hid,
And the aged arose *and* stood;
9 The princes refrained from talking,
And put *their* hand on their mouth;
10 The voice of nobles was hushed,
And their tongue stuck to the roof of their mouth.
11 When the ear heard, then it blessed me,
And when the eye saw, then it approved me;
12 Because I delivered the poor who cried out,
The fatherless and *the one who* had no helper.
13 The blessing of a perishing *man* came upon me,
And I caused the widow's heart to sing for joy.
14 I put on righteousness, and it clothed me;
My justice *was* like a robe and a turban.
15 I *was* eyes to the blind,
And I *was* feet to the lame.
16 I *was* a father to the poor,
And I searched out the case *that* I did not know.

17 I broke the fangs of the wicked,
And plucked the victim from his teeth.

18 "Then I said, 'I shall die in my nest,
And multiply *my* days as the sand.
19 My root *is* spread out to the waters,
And the dew lies all night on my branch.
20 My glory *is* fresh within me,
And my bow is renewed in my hand.'

21 " *Men* listened to me and waited,
And kept silence for my counsel.
22 After my words they did not speak again,
And my speech settled on them *as dew.*
23 They waited for me *as* for the rain,
And they opened their mouth wide *as* for the spring rain.
24 *If* I mocked at them, they did not believe *it,*
And the light of my countenance they did not cast down.
25 I chose the way for them, and sat as chief;
So I dwelt as a king in the army,
As one *who* comforts mourners.

CHAPTER 30

"But now they mock at me, *men* younger than I,
Whose fathers I disdained to put with the dogs of my flock.
2 Indeed, what *profit* is the strength of their hands to me?
Their vigor has perished.
3 *They are* gaunt from want and famine,
Fleeing late to the wilderness, desolate and waste,
4 Who pluck mallow by the bushes,
And broom tree roots *for* their food.
5 They were driven out from among *men,*
They shouted at them as *at* a thief.
6 *They had* to live in the clefts of the valleys,
In caves of the earth and the rocks.
7 Among the bushes they brayed,
Under the nettles they nestled.
8 *They were* sons of fools,
Yes, sons of vile men;
They were scourged from the land.

9 "And now I am their taunting song;
Yes, I am their byword.
10 They abhor me, they keep far from me;
They do not hesitate to spit in my face.
11 Because He has loosed my bowstring and afflicted me,
They have cast off restraint before me.
12 At *my* right *hand* the rabble arises;
They push away my feet,
And they raise against me their ways of destruction.
13 They break up my path,
They promote my calamity;
They have no helper.
14 They come as broad breakers;
Under the ruinous storm they roll along.
15 Terrors are turned upon me;
They pursue my honor as the wind,
And my prosperity has passed like a cloud.

16 "And now my soul is poured out because of my *plight;*
   The days of affliction take hold of me.
17 My bones are pierced in me at night,
   And my gnawing pains take no rest.
18 By great force my garment is disfigured;
   It binds me about as the collar of my coat.
19 He has cast me into the mire,
   And I have become like dust and ashes.

20 "I cry out to You, but You do not answer me;
   I stand up, and You regard me.
21 *But* You have become cruel to me;
   With the strength of Your hand You oppose me.
22 You lift me up to the wind and cause me to ride *on it;*
   You spoil my success.
23 For I know *that* You will bring me *to* death,
   And *to* the house appointed for all living.

24 "Surely He would not stretch out *His* hand against a
      heap of ruins,
   If they cry out when He destroys *it.*
25 Have I not wept for him who was in trouble?
   Has *not* my soul grieved for the poor?
26 But when I looked for good, evil came *to me;*
   And when I waited for light, then came darkness.
27 My heart is in turmoil and cannot rest;
   Days of affliction confront me.
28 I go about mourning, but not in the sun;
   I stand up in the assembly *and* cry out for help.
29 I am a brother of jackals,
   And a companion of ostriches.
30 My skin grows black and falls from me;
   My bones burn with fever.
31 My harp is *turned* to mourning,
   And my flute to the voice of those who weep.

CHAPTER **31**

1 "I have made a covenant with my eyes;
   Why then should I look upon a young woman?
2 For what *is* the allotment of God from above,
   And the inheritance of the Almighty from on high?
3 *Is* it not destruction for the wicked,
   And disaster for the workers of iniquity?
4 Does He not see my ways,
   And count all my steps?

5 "If I have walked with falsehood,
   Or if my foot has hastened to deceit,
6 Let me be weighed on honest scales,
   That God may know my integrity.
7 If my step has turned from the way,
   Or my heart walked after my eyes,
   Or if any spot adheres to my hands,
8 *Then* let me sow, and another eat;
   Yes, let my harvest be rooted out.

9 "If my heart has been enticed by a woman,
   Or *if* I have lurked at my neighbor's door,
10 *Then* let my wife grind for another,
   And let others bow down over her.
11 For that *would be* wickedness;
   Yes, it *would be* iniquity *deserving of* judgment.

12 For that *would be* a fire *that* consumes to
      destruction,
   And would root out all my increase.

13 "If I have despised the cause of my male or female
      servant
   When they complained against me,
14 What then shall I do when God rises up?
   When He punishes, how shall I answer Him?
15 Did not He who made me in the womb make them?
   Did not the same One fashion us in the womb?

16 "If I have kept the poor from *their* desire,
   Or caused the eyes of the widow to fail,
17 Or eaten my morsel by myself,
   So that the fatherless could not eat of it
18 (But from my youth I reared him as a father,
   And from my mother's womb I guided *the widow*);
19 If I have seen anyone perish for lack of clothing,
   Or any poor *man* without covering;
20 If his heart has not blessed me,
   And *if* he was *not* warmed with the fleece of my
      sheep;
21 If I have raised my hand against the fatherless,
   When I saw I had help in the gate;
22 *Then* let my arm fall from my shoulder,
   Let my arm be torn from the socket.
23 For destruction *from* God *is* a terror to me,
   And because of His magnificence I cannot endure.

24 "If I have made gold my hope,
   Or said to fine gold, '*You are* my confidence';
25 If I have rejoiced because my wealth *was* great,
   And because my hand had gained much;
26 If I have observed the sun when it shines,
   Or the moon moving *in* brightness,
27 So that my heart has been secretly enticed,
   And my mouth has kissed my hand;
28 This also *would be* an iniquity *deserving of* judgment,
   For I would have denied God *who is* above.

29 "If I have rejoiced at the destruction of him who
      hated me,
   Or lifted myself up when evil found him
30 (Indeed I have not allowed my mouth to sin
   By asking for a curse on his soul);
31 If the men of my tent have not said,
   'Who is there that has not been satisfied with his
      meat?'
32 (*But* no sojourner had to lodge in the street,
   For I have opened my doors to the traveler);
33 If I have covered my transgressions as Adam,
   By hiding my iniquity in my bosom,

◣◣◣◣▶ COVER-UP

31:33-34 Job declared that he did not try to hide his sin as Adam did (Genesis 3). Adam did not have a crowd watching him, but he tried to hide from God. The fear that our sins will be discovered leads us to patterns of deception. We cover up with lies so that we will appear good to others. But we cannot hide from God. Do you try to keep people from seeing the real you? Acknowledge your sins and free yourself to receive forgiveness and a new life.

32:7-9 It is not enough to recognize a great truth; the truth must be lived out in our lives. Elihu recognized the truth that God was the only source of real wisdom, but he did not use God's wisdom to help Job. While he recognized where wisdom came from, he did not seek to acquire it. Becoming wise is an ongoing, lifelong pursuit. Don't be content just to know about wisdom; make it part of your life.

34 Because I feared the great multitude,
And dreaded the contempt of families,
So that I kept silence
And did not go out of the door—
35 Oh, that I had one to hear me!
Here is my mark.
Oh, that the Almighty would answer me,
That my Prosecutor had written a book!
36 Surely I would carry it on my shoulder,
And bind it on me *like* a crown;
37 I would declare to Him the number of my steps;
Like a prince I would approach Him.

38 "If my land cries out against me,
And its furrows weep together;
39 If I have eaten its fruit without money,
Or caused its owners to lose their lives;
40 *Then* let thistles grow instead of wheat,
And weeds instead of barley."

The words of Job are ended.

CHAPTER **32** ELIHU: I AM FULL OF WORDS. So these three men ceased answering Job, because he *was* righteous in his own eyes. ²Then the wrath of Elihu, the son of Barachel the Buzite, of the family of Ram, was aroused against Job; his wrath was aroused because he justified himself rather than God. ³Also against his three friends his wrath was aroused, because they had found no answer, and *yet* had condemned Job.

⁴Now because they *were* years older than he, Elihu had waited to speak to Job. ⁵When Elihu saw that *there was* no answer in the mouth of these three men, his wrath was aroused.

⁶So Elihu, the son of Barachel the Buzite, answered and said:

"I *am* young in years, and you *are* very old;
Therefore I was afraid,
And dared not declare my opinion to you.
7 I said, 'Age should speak,
And multitude of years should teach wisdom.'
8 But *there is* a spirit in man,
And the breath of the Almighty gives him
understanding.
9 Great men are not *always* wise,
Nor do the aged *always* understand justice.

10 "Therefore I say, 'Listen to me,
I also will declare my opinion.'
11 Indeed I waited for your words,
I listened to your reasonings, while you searched out
what to say.
12 I paid close attention to you;
And surely not one of you convinced Job,

Or answered his words—
13 Lest you say,
'We have found wisdom';
God will vanquish him, not man.
14 Now he has not directed *his* words against me;
So I will not answer him with your words.

15 "They are dismayed and answer no more;
Words escape them.
16 And I have waited, because they did not speak,
Because they stood still *and* answered no more.
17 I also will answer my part,
I too will declare my opinion.
18 For I am full of words;
The spirit within me compels me.
19 Indeed my belly *is* like wine *that* has no vent;
It is ready to burst like new wineskins.
20 I will speak, that I may find relief;
I must open my lips and answer.
21 Let me not, I pray, show partiality to anyone;
Nor let me flatter any man.
22 For I do not know how to flatter,
Else my Maker would soon take me away.

CHAPTER **33**
"But please, Job, hear my speech,
And listen to all my words.
2 Now, I open my mouth;
My tongue speaks in my mouth.
3 My words *come* from my upright heart;
My lips utter pure knowledge.
4 The Spirit of God has made me,
And the breath of the Almighty gives me life.
5 If you can answer me,
Set *your words* in order before me;
Take your stand.
6 Truly I *am* as your spokesman before God;
I also have been formed out of clay.
7 Surely no fear of me will terrify you,
Nor will my hand be heavy on you.

8 "Surely you have spoken in my hearing,
And I have heard the sound of *your* words, *saying,*
9 'I *am* pure, without transgression;
I *am* innocent, and *there is* no iniquity in me.
10 Yet He finds occasions against me,
He counts me as His enemy;
11 He puts my feet in the stocks,
He watches all my paths.'

12 "Look, *in* this you are not righteous.
I will answer you,
For God is greater than man.
13 Why do you contend with Him?
For He does not give an accounting of any of His
words.
14 For God may speak in one way, or in another,
Yet man does not perceive it.
15 In a dream, in a vision of the night,
When deep sleep falls upon men,
While slumbering on their beds,
16 Then He opens the ears of men,

WISDOM LIVED OUT

16 "And now my soul is poured out because of my *plight;*
 The days of affliction take hold of me.
17 My bones are pierced in me at night,
 And my gnawing pains take no rest.
18 By great force my garment is disfigured;
 It binds me about as the collar of my coat.
19 He has cast me into the mire,
 And I have become like dust and ashes.

20 "I cry out to You, but You do not answer me;
 I stand up, and You regard me.
21 *But* You have become cruel to me;
 With the strength of Your hand You oppose me.
22 You lift me up to the wind and cause me to ride *on it;*
 You spoil my success.
23 For I know *that* You will bring me *to* death,
 And *to* the house appointed for all living.

24 "Surely He would not stretch out *His* hand against a
 heap of ruins,
 If they cry out when He destroys *it.*
25 Have I not wept for him who was in trouble?
 Has *not* my soul grieved for the poor?
26 But when I looked for good, evil came *to me;*
 And when I waited for light, then came darkness.
27 My heart is in turmoil and cannot rest;
 Days of affliction confront me.
28 I go about mourning, but not in the sun;
 I stand up in the assembly *and* cry out for help.
29 I am a brother of jackals,
 And a companion of ostriches.
30 My skin grows black and falls from me;
 My bones burn with fever.
31 My harp is *turned* to mourning,
 And my flute to the voice of those who weep.

CHAPTER **31**

"I have made a covenant with my eyes;
 Why then should I look upon a young woman?
2 For what *is* the allotment of God from above,
 And the inheritance of the Almighty from on high?
3 *Is* it not destruction for the wicked,
 And disaster for the workers of iniquity?
4 Does He not see my ways,
 And count all my steps?

5 "If I have walked with falsehood,
 Or if my foot has hastened to deceit,
6 Let me be weighed on honest scales,
 That God may know my integrity.
7 If my step has turned from the way,
 Or my heart walked after my eyes,
 Or if any spot adheres to my hands,
8 *Then* let me sow, and another eat;
 Yes, let my harvest be rooted out.

9 "If my heart has been enticed by a woman,
 Or *if* I have lurked at my neighbor's door,
10 *Then* let my wife grind for another,
 And let others bow down over her.
11 For that *would be* wickedness;
 Yes, it *would be* iniquity *deserving of* judgment.

12 For that *would be* a fire *that* consumes to
 destruction,
 And would root out all my increase.

13 "If I have despised the cause of my male or female
 servant
 When they complained against me,
14 What then shall I do when God rises up?
 When He punishes, how shall I answer Him?
15 Did not He who made me in the womb make them?
 Did not the same One fashion us in the womb?

16 "If I have kept the poor from *their* desire,
 Or caused the eyes of the widow to fail,
17 Or eaten my morsel by myself,
 So that the fatherless could not eat of it
18 (But from my youth I reared him as a father,
 And from my mother's womb I guided *the widow*);
19 If I have seen anyone perish for lack of clothing,
 Or any poor *man* without covering;
20 If his heart has not blessed me,
 And *if* he was *not* warmed with the fleece of my
 sheep;
21 If I have raised my hand against the fatherless,
 When I saw I had help in the gate;
22 *Then* let my arm fall from my shoulder,
 Let my arm be torn from the socket.
23 For destruction *from* God *is* a terror to me,
 And because of His magnificence I cannot endure.

24 "If I have made gold my hope,
 Or said to fine gold, '*You are* my confidence';
25 If I have rejoiced because my wealth *was* great,
 And because my hand had gained much;
26 If I have observed the sun when it shines,
 Or the moon moving *in* brightness,
27 So that my heart has been secretly enticed,
 And my mouth has kissed my hand;
28 This also *would be* an iniquity *deserving of* judgment,
 For I would have denied God *who is* above.

29 "If I have rejoiced at the destruction of him who
 hated me,
 Or lifted myself up when evil found him
30 (Indeed I have not allowed my mouth to sin
 By asking for a curse on his soul);
31 If the men of my tent have not said,
 'Who is there that has not been satisfied with his
 meat?'
32 (*But* no sojourner had to lodge in the street,
 For I have opened my doors to the traveler);
33 If I have covered my transgressions as Adam,
 By hiding my iniquity in my bosom,

◆◆◆ COVER-UP

31:33-34 Job declared that he did not try to hide his sin as Adam did (Genesis 3). Adam did not have a crowd watching him, but he tried to hide from God. The fear that our sins will be discovered leads us to patterns of deception. We cover up with lies so that we will appear good to others. But we cannot hide from God. Do you try to keep people from seeing the real you? Acknowledge your sins and free yourself to receive forgiveness and a new life.

And seals their instruction.
¹⁷ In order to turn man *from his* deed,
And conceal pride from man,
¹⁸ He keeps back his soul from the Pit,
And his life from perishing by the sword.

¹⁹ "*Man* is also chastened with pain on his bed,
And with strong *pain* in many of his bones,
²⁰ So that his life abhors bread,
And his soul succulent food.
²¹ His flesh wastes away from sight,
And his bones stick out *which once* were not seen.
²² Yes, his soul draws near the Pit,
And his life to the executioners.

²³ "If there is a messenger for him,
A mediator, one among a thousand,
To show man His uprightness,
²⁴ Then He is gracious to him, and says,
'Deliver him from going down to the Pit;
I have found a ransom';
²⁵ His flesh shall be young like a child's,
He shall return to the days of his youth.
²⁶ He shall pray to God, and He will delight in him,
He shall see His face with joy,
For He restores to man His righteousness.
²⁷ Then he looks at men and says,
'I have sinned, and perverted *what was* right,
And it did not profit me.'
²⁸ He will redeem his soul from going down to the Pit,
And his life shall see the light.

²⁹ "Behold, God works all these *things*,
Twice, *in fact*, three *times* with a man,
³⁰ To bring back his soul from the Pit,
That he may be enlightened with the light of life.

³¹ "Give ear, Job, listen to me;
Hold your peace, and I will speak.
³² If you have anything to say, answer me;
Speak, for I desire to justify you.
³³ If not, listen to me;
Hold your peace, and I will teach you wisdom."

CHAPTER 34 ELIHU: LISTEN TO ME. Elihu further answered and said:

² "Hear my words, you wise *men;*
Give ear to me, you who have knowledge.
³ For the ear tests words
As the palate tastes food.
⁴ Let us choose justice for ourselves;
Let us know among ourselves what *is* good.

⁵ "For Job has said, 'I am righteous,
But God has taken away my justice;
⁶ Should I lie concerning my right?
My wound *is* incurable, *though I am* without
transgression.'
⁷ What man *is* like Job,
Who drinks scorn like water,
⁸ Who goes in company with the workers of iniquity,
And walks with wicked men?

⁹ For he has said, 'It profits a man nothing
That he should delight in God.'

¹⁰ "Therefore listen to me, you men of understanding:
Far be it from God *to do* wickedness,
And *from* the Almighty to *commit* iniquity.
¹¹ For He repays man *according to* his work,
And makes man to find a reward according to *his*
way.
¹² Surely God will never do wickedly,
Nor will the Almighty pervert justice.
¹³ Who gave Him charge over the earth?
Or who appointed *Him over* the whole world?
¹⁴ If He should set His heart on it,
If He should gather to Himself His Spirit and His
breath,
¹⁵ All flesh would perish together,
And man would return to dust.

¹⁶ "If *you have* understanding, hear this;
Listen to the sound of my words:
¹⁷ Should one who hates justice govern?
Will you condemn *Him who is* most just?
¹⁸ *Is it fitting* to say to a king, '*You are* worthless,'
And to nobles, '*You are* wicked'?
¹⁹ Yet He is not partial to princes,
Nor does He regard the rich more than the poor;
For they *are* all the work of His hands.
²⁰ In a moment they die, in the middle of the night;
The people are shaken and pass away;
The mighty are taken away without a hand.

²¹ "For His eyes *are* on the ways of man,
And He sees all his steps.
²² There is no darkness nor shadow of death
the workers of iniquity may hide themselves.
²³ For He need not further consider a man,
That he should go before God in judgment.
²⁴ He breaks in pieces mighty men without inquiry,
And sets others in their place.
²⁵ Therefore He knows their works;
He overthrows *them* in the night,
And they are crushed.
²⁶ He strikes them as wicked *men*
In the open sight of others,
²⁷ Because they turned back from Him,
And would not consider any of His ways,
²⁸ So that they caused the cry of the poor to come to
Him;
For He hears the cry of the afflicted.
²⁹ When He gives quietness, who then can make
trouble?
And when He hides *His* face, who then can see Him,
Whether *it is* against a nation or a man alone?—
³⁰ That the hypocrite should not reign,
Lest the people be ensnared.

³¹ "For has *anyone* said to God,
'I have borne *chastening;*
I will offend no more;
³² Teach me *what* I do not see;
If I have done iniquity, I will do no more'?

33 Should He repay *it* according to your *terms,*
Just because you disavow it?
You must choose, and not I;
Therefore speak what you know.

34 "Men of understanding say to me,
Wise men who listen to me:
35 'Job speaks without knowledge,
His words *are* without wisdom.'
36 Oh, that Job were tried to the utmost,
Because *his* answers *are like* those of wicked men!
37 For he adds rebellion to his sin;
He claps *his hands* among us,
And multiplies his words against God."

CHAPTER **35** Moreover Elihu answered and said:

2 "Do you think this is right?
Do you say,
'My righteousness is more than God's'?
3 For you say,
'What advantage will it be to You?
What profit shall I have, more than *if* I had sinned?'

4 "I will answer you,
And your companions with you.
5 Look to the heavens and see;
And behold the clouds—
They are higher than you.
6 If you sin, what do you accomplish against Him?
Or, *if* your transgressions are multiplied, what do
you do to Him?
7 If you are righteous, what do you give Him?
Or what does He receive from your hand?
8 Your wickedness affects a man such as you,
And your righteousness a son of man.

9 "Because of the multitude of oppressions they cry out;
They cry out for help because of the arm of the
mighty.
10 But no one says, 'Where *is* God my Maker,

Who gives songs in the night,
11 Who teaches us more than the beasts of the earth,
And makes us wiser than the birds of heaven?'
12 There they cry out, but He does not answer,
Because of the pride of evil men.
13 Surely God will not listen to empty *talk,*
Nor will the Almighty regard it.
14 Although you say you do not see Him,
Yet justice *is* before Him, and you must wait for Him.
15 And now, because He has not punished in His anger,
Nor taken much notice of folly,
16 Therefore Job opens his mouth in vain;
He multiplies words without knowledge."

CHAPTER **36**   ELIHU: I AM DEFENDING GOD.
Elihu also proceeded and said:

2 "Bear with me a little, and I will show you
That *there are* yet words to speak on God's behalf.
3 I will fetch my knowledge from afar;
I will ascribe righteousness to my Maker.
4 For truly my words *are* not false;
One who is perfect in knowledge *is* with you.

5 "Behold, God *is* mighty, but despises *no one;*
He *is* mighty in strength of understanding.
6 He does not preserve the life of the wicked,
But gives justice to the oppressed.
7 He does not withdraw His eyes from the righteous;
But *they are* on the throne with kings,
For He has seated them forever,
And they are exalted.
8 And if *they are* bound in fetters,
Held in the cords of affliction,
9 Then He tells them their work and their
transgressions—
That they have acted defiantly.
10 He also opens their ear to instruction,
And commands that they turn from iniquity.
11 If they obey and serve *Him,*

**HOW SUFFERING
AFFECTS US**

Suffering is helpful when:	Suffering is harmful when:
We turn to God for understanding, endurance, and deliverance	We become hardened and reject God
We ask important questions we might not take time to think about in our normal routine	We refuse to ask any questions and miss any lessons that might be good for us
We let it prepare us to identify with and comfort others who suffer	We allow it to make us self-centered and selfish
We are open to being helped by others who are obeying God	We withdraw from the help others can give
We realize we can identify with what Christ suffered on the cross for us	We accuse God of being unjust and perhaps lead others to reject him
We are sensitized to the amount of suffering in the world	We refuse to be open to any changes in our lives

They shall spend their days in prosperity,
And their years in pleasures.
¹² But if they do not obey,
They shall perish by the sword,
And they shall die without knowledge.

¹³ "But the hypocrites in heart store up wrath;
They do not cry for help when He binds them.
¹⁴ They die in youth,
And their life *ends* among the perverted persons.
¹⁵ He delivers the poor in their affliction,
And opens their ears in oppression.

¹⁶ "Indeed He would have brought you out of dire
distress,
Into a broad place where *there is* no restraint;
And what is set on your table *would be* full of richness.
¹⁷ But you are filled with the judgment due the wicked;
Judgment and justice take hold *of you*.
¹⁸ Because *there is* wrath, *beware* lest He take you away
with *one* blow;
For a large ransom would not help you avoid *it*.
¹⁹ Will your riches,
Or all the mighty forces,
Keep you from distress?
²⁰ Do not desire the night,
When people are cut off in their place.
²¹ Take heed, do not turn to iniquity,
For you have chosen this rather than affliction.

²² "Behold, God is exalted by His power;
Who teaches like Him?
²³ Who has assigned Him His way,
Or who has said, 'You have done wrong'?

²⁴ "Remember to magnify His work,
Of which men have sung.
²⁵ Everyone has seen it;
Man looks on *it* from afar.

²⁶ "Behold, God *is* great, and we do not know *Him*;
Nor can the number of His years *be* discovered.
²⁷ For He draws up drops of water,
Which distill as rain from the mist,
²⁸ Which the clouds drop down
And pour abundantly on man.
²⁹ Indeed, can *anyone* understand the spreading of
clouds,
The thunder from His canopy?
³⁰ Look, He scatters His light upon it,
And covers the depths of the sea.
³¹ For by these He judges the peoples;
He gives food in abundance.
³² He covers *His* hands with lightning,
And commands it to strike.
³³ His thunder declares it,
The cattle also, concerning the rising *storm*.

CHAPTER 37

"At this also my heart trembles,
And leaps from its place.
² Hear attentively the thunder of His voice,
And the rumbling *that* comes from His mouth.

³ He sends it forth under the whole heaven,
His lightning to the ends of the earth.
⁴ After it a voice roars;
He thunders with His majestic voice,
And He does not restrain them when His voice is
heard.
⁵ God thunders marvelously with His voice;
He does great things which we cannot comprehend.
⁶ For He says to the snow, 'Fall *on* the earth';
Likewise to the gentle rain and the heavy rain of His
strength.
⁷ He seals the hand of every man,
That all men may know His work.
⁸ The beasts go into dens,
And remain in their lairs.
⁹ From the chamber *of the south* comes the whirlwind,
And cold from the scattering winds *of the north*.

GOD'S DIMENSIONS

36:26 One theme in the poetic literature of the Bible is that we cannot know God completely. This does not mean that we cannot have any knowledge about God, because the Bible is full of details about who God is, how we can know him, and how we can have an eternal relationship with him. What it means is that we can never know enough to answer all of life's questions (Ecclesiastes 3:11), to predict our own future, or to manipulate God for our own ends. Life always has more questions than answers, and we must constantly go to God for fresh insights into life's dilemmas. (See 37:19-24.)

¹⁰ By the breath of God ice is given,
And the broad waters are frozen.
¹¹ Also with moisture He saturates the thick clouds;
He scatters His bright clouds.
¹² And they swirl about, being turned by His guidance,
That they may do whatever He commands them
On the face of the whole earth.
¹³ He causes it to come,
Whether for correction,
Or for His land,
Or for mercy.

¹⁴ "Listen to this, O Job;
Stand still and consider the wondrous works of God.
¹⁵ Do you know when God dispatches them,
And causes the light of His cloud to shine?
¹⁶ Do you know how the clouds are balanced,
Those wondrous works of Him who is perfect in
knowledge?
¹⁷ Why *are* your garments hot,
When He quiets the earth by the south *wind*?
¹⁸ With Him, have you spread out the skies,
Strong as a cast metal mirror?

¹⁹ "Teach us what we should say to Him,
For we can prepare nothing because of the darkness.
²⁰ Should He be told that I *wish to* speak?
If a man were to speak, surely he would be
swallowed up.
²¹ Even now *men* cannot look at the light *when it is*
bright in the skies,
When the wind has passed and cleared them.

²² He comes from the north *as* golden *splendor;*
With God *is* awesome majesty.
²³ *As for* the Almighty, we cannot find Him;
He is excellent in power,
In judgment and abundant justice;
He does not oppress.
²⁴ Therefore men fear Him;
He shows no partiality to any *who are* wise of heart."

CHAPTER 38 THE LORD SPEAKS TO JOB. Then
the Lord answered Job out of the whirlwind, and said:

² "Who *is* this who darkens counsel
By words without knowledge?
³ Now prepare yourself like a man;
I will question you, and you shall answer Me.

⁴ "Where were you when I laid the foundations of the
earth?
Tell *Me,* if you have understanding.
⁵ Who determined its measurements?
Surely you know!
Or who stretched the line upon it?
⁶ To what were its foundations fastened?
Or who laid its cornerstone,
⁷ When the morning stars sang together,
And all the sons of God shouted for joy?

⁸ "Or *who* shut in the sea with doors,
When it burst forth *and* issued from the womb;
⁹ When I made the clouds its garment,
And thick darkness its swaddling band;
¹⁰ When I fixed My limit for it,
And set bars and doors;
¹¹ When I said,
'This far you may come, but no farther,
And here your proud waves must stop!'

¹² "Have you commanded the morning since your days
began,
And caused the dawn to know its place,
¹³ That it might take hold of the ends of the earth,
And the wicked be shaken out of it?
¹⁴ It takes on form like clay *under* a seal,
And stands out like a garment.
¹⁵ From the wicked their light is withheld,
And the upraised arm is broken.

¹⁶ "Have you entered the springs of the sea?
Or have you walked in search of the depths?
¹⁷ Have the gates of death been revealed to you?
Or have you seen the doors of the shadow of death?
¹⁸ Have you comprehended the breadth of the earth?
Tell *Me,* if you know all this.

¹⁹ "Where *is* the way *to* the dwelling of light?
And darkness, where *is* its place,
²⁰ That you may take it to its territory,
That you may know the paths *to* its home?
²¹ Do you know *it,* because you were born then,
Or *because* the number of your days *is* great?

²² "Have you entered the treasury of snow,
Or have you seen the treasury of hail,

²³ Which I have reserved for the time of trouble,
For the day of battle and war?
²⁴ By what way is light diffused,
Or the east wind scattered over the earth?

²⁵ "Who has divided a channel for the overflowing *water,*
Or a path for the thunderbolt,
²⁶ To cause it to rain on a land *where there is* no one,
A wilderness in which *there is* no man;
²⁷ To satisfy the desolate waste,
And cause to spring forth the growth of tender
grass?
²⁸ Has the rain a father?
Or who has begotten the drops of dew?
²⁹ From whose womb comes the ice?
And the frost of heaven, who gives it birth?
³⁰ The waters harden like stone,
And the surface of the deep is frozen.

³¹ "Can you bind the cluster of the Pleiades,
Or loose the belt of Orion?
³² Can you bring out Mazzaroth in its season?
Or can you guide the Great Bear with its cubs?
³³ Do you know the ordinances of the heavens?
Can you set their dominion over the earth?

³⁴ "Can you lift up your voice to the clouds,
That an abundance of water may cover you?
³⁵ Can you send out lightnings, that they may go,
And say to you, 'Here we *are!*'?
³⁶ Who has put wisdom in the mind?
Or who has given understanding to the heart?
³⁷ Who can number the clouds by wisdom?
Or who can pour out the bottles of heaven,
³⁸ When the dust hardens in clumps,
And the clods cling together?

³⁹ "Can you hunt the prey for the lion,
Or satisfy the appetite of the young lions,
⁴⁰ When they crouch in *their* dens,
Or lurk in their lairs to lie in wait?
⁴¹ Who provides food for the raven,
When its young ones cry to God,
And wander about for lack of food?

CHAPTER 39
"Do you know the time when the wild mountain goats
bear young?
Or can you mark when the deer gives birth?
² Can you number the months *that* they fulfill?
Or do you know the time when they bear young?
³ They bow down,
They bring forth their young,
They deliver their offspring.
⁴ Their young ones are healthy,

▰▰▰ LIMITED KNOWLEDGE

39:1ff God asked Job several questions about the animal kingd◌
order to demonstrate how limited Job's knowledge really was. Go◌
not seeking answers from Job. Instead, he was getting Job to reco◌
and submit to God's power and sovereignty. Only then would he b◌
to hear what God was really saying to him.

They grow strong with grain;
They depart and do not return to them.

5 "Who set the wild donkey free?
Who loosed the bonds of the onager,
6 Whose home I have made the wilderness,
And the barren land his dwelling?
7 He scorns the tumult of the city;
He does not heed the shouts of the driver.
8 The range of the mountains *is* his pasture,
And he searches after every green thing.

9 "Will the wild ox be willing to serve you?
Will he bed by your manger?
10 Can you bind the wild ox in the furrow with ropes?
Or will he plow the valleys behind you?
11 Will you trust him because his strength *is* great?
Or will you leave your labor to him?
12 Will you trust him to bring home your grain,
And gather it to your threshing floor?

13 "The wings of the ostrich wave proudly,
But are her wings and pinions *like the* kindly stork's?
14 For she leaves her eggs on the ground,
And warms them in the dust;
15 She forgets that a foot may crush them,
Or that a wild beast may break them.
16 She treats her young harshly, as though *they were* not hers;
Her labor is in vain, without concern,
17 Because God deprived her of wisdom,
And did not endow her with understanding.
18 When she lifts herself on high,
She scorns the horse and its rider.

19 "Have you given the horse strength?
Have you clothed his neck with thunder?
20 Can you frighten him like a locust?
His majestic snorting strikes terror.
21 He paws in the valley, and rejoices in *his* strength;
He gallops into the clash of arms.
22 He mocks at fear, and is not frightened;
Nor does he turn back from the sword.
23 The quiver rattles against him,
The glittering spear and javelin.
24 He devours the distance with fierceness and rage;
Nor does he come to a halt because the trumpet *has* sounded.
25 At *the blast of* the trumpet he says, 'Aha!'
He smells the battle from afar,
The thunder of captains and shouting.

26 "Does the hawk fly by your wisdom,
And spread its wings toward the south?
27 Does the eagle mount up at your command,
And make its nest on high?
28 On the rock it dwells and resides,
On the crag of the rock and the stronghold.
29 From there it spies out the prey;
Its eyes observe from afar.
30 Its young ones suck up blood;
And where the slain *are*, there it *is*."

CHAPTER 40 JOB: I AM NOTHING. Moreover the LORD answered Job, and said:

2 "Shall the one who contends with the Almighty correct *Him*?
He who rebukes God, let him answer it."

3 Then Job answered the LORD and said:

4 "Behold, I am vile;
What shall I answer You?
I lay my hand over my mouth.
5 Once I have spoken, but I will not answer;
Yes, twice, but I will proceed no further."

6 Then the LORD answered Job out of the whirlwind, and said:

7 "Now prepare yourself like a man;
I will question you, and you shall answer Me:

8 "Would you indeed annul My judgment?
Would you condemn Me that you may be justified?
9 Have you an arm like God?
Or can you thunder with a voice like His?
10 Then adorn yourself *with* majesty and splendor,
And array yourself with glory and beauty.
11 Disperse the rage of your wrath;
Look on everyone *who is* proud, and humble him.
12 Look on everyone *who is* proud, *and* bring him low;
Tread down the wicked in their place.
13 Hide them in the dust together,
Bind their faces in hidden *darkness*.
14 Then I will also confess to you
That your own right hand can save you.

15 "Look now at the behemoth, which I made *along* with you;
He eats grass like an ox.
16 See now, his strength *is* in his hips,
And his power *is* in his stomach muscles.
17 He moves his tail like a cedar;
The sinews of his thighs are tightly knit.
18 His bones *are like* beams of bronze,
His ribs like bars of iron.
19 He *is* the first of the ways of God;
Only He who made him can bring near His sword.
20 Surely the mountains yield food for him,
And all the beasts of the field play there.
21 He lies under the lotus trees,
In a covert of reeds and marsh.
22 The lotus trees cover him *with* their shade;
The willows by the brook surround him.
23 Indeed the river may rage,
Yet he is not disturbed;
He is confident, though the Jordan gushes into his mouth,
24 *Though* he takes it in his eyes,
Or one pierces *his* nose with a snare.

CHAPTER 41

"Can you draw out Leviathan with a hook,
Or *snare* his tongue with a line *which* you lower?
2 Can you put a reed through his nose,

FRIENDS AGAIN

42:8-10 After receiving much criticism, Job was still able to pray for his three friends. It is difficult to forgive someone who has accused you of wrongdoing, but Job did. Are you praying for those who have wronged you? Can you forgive them? Follow the actions of Job, whom God called a good man, and pray for those who wrong you.

Or pierce his jaw with a hook?
3 Will he make many supplications to you?
Will he speak softly to you?
4 Will he make a covenant with you?
Will you take him as a servant forever?
5 Will you play with him as *with* a bird,
Or will you leash him for your maidens?
6 Will *your* companions make a banquet of him?
Will they apportion him among the merchants?
7 Can you fill his skin with harpoons,
Or his head with fishing spears?
8 Lay your hand on him;
Remember the battle—
Never do it again!
9 Indeed, *any* hope of *overcoming* him is false;
Shall *one not* be overwhelmed at the sight of him?
10 No one *is so* fierce that he would dare stir him up.
Who then is able to stand against Me?
11 Who has preceded Me, that I should pay *him?*
Everything under heaven is Mine.

12 "I will not conceal his limbs,
His mighty power, or his graceful proportions.
13 Who can remove his outer coat?
Who can approach *him* with a double bridle?
14 Who can open the doors of his face,
With his terrible teeth all around?
15 *His* rows of scales are *his* pride,
Shut up tightly *as with* a seal;
16 One is so near another
That no air can come between them;
17 They are joined one to another,
They stick together and cannot be parted.
18 His sneezings flash forth light,
And his eyes *are* like the eyelids of the morning.
19 Out of his mouth go burning lights;
Sparks of fire shoot out.
20 Smoke goes out of his nostrils,
As *from* a boiling pot and burning rushes.
21 His breath kindles coals,
And a flame goes out of his mouth.
22 Strength dwells in his neck,
And sorrow dances before him.
23 The folds of his flesh are joined together;
They are firm on him and cannot be moved.
24 His heart is as hard as stone,
Even as hard as the lower *millstone.*
25 When he raises himself up, the mighty are afraid;
Because of his crashings they are beside themselves.
26 *Though* the sword reaches him, it cannot avail;
Nor does spear, dart, or javelin.
27 He regards iron as straw,
And bronze as rotten wood.
28 The arrow cannot make him flee;
Slingstones become like stubble to him.
29 Darts are regarded as straw;
He laughs at the threat of javelins.

30 His undersides *are* like sharp potsherds;
He spreads pointed *marks* in the mire.
31 He makes the deep boil like a pot;
He makes the sea like a pot of ointment.
32 He leaves a shining wake behind him;
One would think the deep had white hair.
33 On earth there is nothing like him,
Which is made without fear.
34 He beholds every high *thing;*
He *is* king over all the children of pride."

CHAPTER 42 GOD GIVES JOB GOOD GIFTS. Then Job answered the LORD and said:

2 "I know that You can do everything,
And that no purpose *ofYours* can be withheld from You.
3 *You asked,* 'Who *is* this who hides counsel without knowledge?'
Therefore I have uttered what I did not understand,
Things too wonderful for me, which I did not know.
4 Listen, please, and let me speak;
You said, 'I will question you, and you shall answer Me.'

5 "I have heard of You by the hearing of the ear,
But now my eye sees You.
6 Therefore I abhor *myself,*
And repent in dust and ashes."

7 And so it was, after the LORD had spoken these words to Job, that the LORD said to Eliphaz the Temanite, "My wrath is aroused against you and your two friends, for you have not spoken of Me *what is* right, as My servant Job *has.* 8 Now therefore, take for yourselves seven bulls and seven rams, go to My servant Job, and offer up for yourselves a burnt offering; and My servant Job shall pray for you. For I will accept him, lest I deal with you *according to your* folly; because you have not spoken of Me *what is* right, as My servant Job *has.*"

9 So Eliphaz the Temanite and Bildad the Shuhite *and* Zophar the Naamathite went and did as the LORD commanded them; for the LORD had accepted Job. 10 And the LORD restored Job's losses when he prayed for his friends. Indeed the LORD gave Job twice as much as he had before. 11 Then all his brothers, all his sisters, and all those who had been his acquaintances before, came to him and ate food with him in his house; and they consoled him and comforted him for all the adversity that the LORD had brought upon him. Each one gave him a piece of silver and each a ring of gold.

12 Now the LORD blessed the latter *days* of Job more than his beginning; for he had fourteen thousand sheep, six thousand camels, one thousand yoke of oxen, and one thousand female donkeys. 13 He also had seven sons and three daughters. 14 And he called the name of the first Jemimah, the name of the second Keziah, and the name of the third Keren-Happuch. 15 In all the land were found no women *so* beautiful as the daughters of Job; and their father gave them an inheritance among their brothers.

16 After this Job lived one hundred and forty years, and saw his children and grandchildren *for* four generations. 17 So Job died, old and full of days.

MEGA Themes

SUFFERING Through no fault of his own, Job lost his wealth, children, and health. Even his friends were convinced that Job had brought this suffering upon himself. For Job, the greatest trial was not the pain or loss; it was not being able to understand why God was allowing him to suffer.

Suffering can be, but is not always, a penalty for sin. In the same way, prosperity is not always a reward for being good. Those who love God are not exempt from trouble. Although we may not be able to understand fully the pain we experience, it can lead us to rediscover God. He is always present, even in suffering.

1. If you were in Job's position, what would you have been thinking about yourself? About God?
2. Describe Job's attitude toward God throughout his suffering. In light of his personal pain, what does this tell you about Job's relationship with God?
3. Have you ever known someone who maintained a strong faith in God even when he or she was suffering? If so, explain what you observed in his or her life.
4. How does Job's example give you hope as you live in a world that often includes suffering, even for God's children?

SATAN'S ATTACKS Satan tried to drive a wedge between Job and God by getting Job to believe that God's governing of the world was not just and good. Satan had to ask God for permission to take Job's wealth, children, and health away. Satan was limited to what God allowed.

We must learn to recognize Satan's attacks, but we should not fear them. Satan cannot exceed the limits that God sets. Don't let any experience separate you from God. Although you can't control how or when Satan may attack, you can always choose how you will respond when it happens.

1. What did you learn about Satan from the book of Job?
2. Many people think of God and Satan as opposing equals, sort of like the "force," which had a powerful good side and an equally powerful dark side. What do you read in Job that shows you the error of this point of view?
3. What does this book teach you about how Christians should respond to the reality of Satan's power?
4. What examples do you see of Satan's work in the world? How should you respond to these situations?

TRUSTING GOD'S GOODNESS God is all-wise and all-powerful. His will is perfect, yet he doesn't always act in ways we understand. Job's suffering didn't make sense because everyone believed that good people were supposed to prosper. When Job was at the point of despair, God spoke, revealing his great power and wisdom.

Although God is present everywhere, at times he may seem far away. This may cause us to feel alone and to doubt his care for us. We should serve God for who he is, not for what we feel. He is never insensitive to our suffering. Because God is sufficient, we must hold on to him. This fact is greater than any feeling we might have that he has abandoned us.

1. What do you think it means to trust God with your circumstances? How did Job show this trust in God?
2. How did God reveal to Job that he (God) was worthy of that trust?
3. What circumstances or problems in the world cause people to question God's goodness?
4. What can you do to build your trust in God, even when it feels like his goodness is not present (e.g., in your pain and suffering)?

PRIDE Job's friends were sure that they were correct in their judgment of him. God rebuked them for their pride and arrogance. Man's wisdom is always partial and temporary.

We must be careful not to judge others who are suffering, because we may be demonstrating the sin of pride. And we should be cautious in declaring how sure we are about why God treats us the way he does. When we congratulate ourselves for being right, we become proud. We should always be willing to listen and to learn.

1. How did each of Job's friends display pride?
2. Why is pride so dangerous? Give an example of how a person's pride (someone you have known or read about) led to disaster.
3. How does God view pride? Why does he see it that way?
4. Give an example of a time when you struggled with pride in your attitude toward another person. How were you feeling about the person? About yourself?
5. What specific actions can you take to keep yourself from falling into this sin in the future?

*E*motions. We experience countless feelings every day, ranging from exuberant joy to deep grief. We feel pain when someone we love dies. We feel anger when things go wrong. We feel confusion when we don't understand. And we feel joy when something good happens. Emotions add spice and color to life. ■ The book of Psalms is about emotions. The pages are filled with them: anger, confusion, joy, pain, humility, bewilderment, contentment—all directed toward God. God created us with emotions, and he knows they will be part of our dealings with him. ■ Many people read the book of Psalms because of its honesty. Rather than ignoring the "negative" emotions or condemning them as sinful, the writers faced their feelings and continued to talk with God. ■ Psalms also is loved because of the clear picture of God it presents. Our emotions change constantly, but God is constant. While we fret, worry, and shout about injustice, God remains calm. When we fall on our face before him because of our awful sin, he isn't surprised—he is gentle and ready to forgive. Psalms reminds us that God is exalted, the Creator and Ruler of the world, and worthy of worship. He alone is God. ■ How are you feeling today? Angry? Afraid? Frustrated? Or are you joyful, happy, and excited? Read Psalms and express yourself honestly to God.

STATS

PURPOSE: To provide poetry for the expression of praise, worship, and confession to God

AUTHORS: David wrote 73 psalms; Asaph wrote 12; the sons of Korah wrote 9; Solomon wrote 2; Heman (with the sons of Korah), Ethan, and Moses each wrote 1; and 51 psalms are anonymous, though the New Testament ascribes two of the anonymous psalms—Psalms 2 and 95—to David (See Acts 4:25; Hebrews 4:7)

DATE WRITTEN: Between the time of Moses (around 1440 B.C.) and the Babylonian captivity (586 B.C.)

SETTING: For the most part, the psalms were not intended to be narrations of historical events. However, they often parallel events in history, such as David's flight from Saul and his sin with Bathsheba.

KEY PERSON: David

KEY PLACE: God's holy temple

SPECIAL FEATURES: Psalms has a unified plan, but each psalm can be read and understood alone. Psalms is probably the most widely read book of the Bible, because it is easy to relate to the writers' emotions.

Psalms

PSALM 1 PLEASING GOD.

1 Blessed *is* the man
  Who walks not in the counsel of the ungodly,
  Nor stands in the path of sinners,
  Nor sits in the seat of the scornful;
2 But his delight *is* in the law of the LORD,
  And in His law he meditates day and night.
3 He shall be like a tree
  Planted by the rivers of water,
  That brings forth its fruit in its season,
  Whose leaf also shall not wither;
And whatever he does shall prosper.

4 The ungodly *are* not so,
  But *are* like the chaff which the wind drives away.
5 Therefore the ungodly shall not stand in the
    judgment,
  Nor sinners in the congregation of the righteous.

6 For the LORD knows the way of the righteous,
  But the way of the ungodly shall perish.

PSALM 2 GREAT GOD.

1 Why do the nations rage,
  And the people plot a vain thing?
2 The kings of the earth set themselves,
  And the rulers take counsel together,
  Against the LORD and against His Anointed, *saying,*
3 "Let us break Their bonds in pieces
  And cast away Their cords from us."

4 He who sits in the heavens shall laugh;
  The LORD shall hold them in derision.
5 Then He shall speak to them in His wrath,
  And distress them in His deep displeasure:
6 "Yet I have set My King
  On My holy hill of Zion."

7 "I will declare the decree:
  The LORD has said to Me,
  'You *are* My Son,
  Today I have begotten You.
8 Ask of Me, and I will give *You*
  The nations *for* Your inheritance,
  And the ends of the earth *for* Your possession.
9 You shall break them with a rod of iron;
  You shall dash them to pieces like a potter's vessel.'"

10 Now therefore, be wise, O kings;
   Be instructed, you judges of the earth.
11 Serve the LORD with fear,
   And rejoice with trembling.
12 Kiss the Son, lest He be angry,

◣◣◣◣◣◣ FREEDOM

2:3 People often think they will be free if they can get away from God. Yet we all inevitably serve somebody or something, whether a human king, the wishes of friends, or our own selfish desires. Just as a fish is not free when it leaves the water and a tree is not free when it leaves the soil, we are not free when we leave the Lord. The one sure route to freedom is wholeheartedly serving God the Creator. He can set you free to be who he created you to be.

And you perish *in* the way,
When His wrath is kindled but a little.
Blessed *are* all those who put their trust in Him.

PSALM 3 MY HOPE. *A Psalm of David when he fled from Absalom his son.*

¹ LORD, how they have increased who trouble me!
Many *are* they who rise up against me.
² Many *are* they who say of me,
"*There is* no help for him in God."   Selah

³ But You, O LORD, *are* a shield for me,
My glory and the One who lifts up my head.

FRIENDSHIP

Last year Rhonda moved from a small Midwest town to Chicago. She didn't want to leave her hometown, but her dad got a job offer he'd been wanting to get for years. Rhonda left behind close friends, a great youth group, a good school, and 14 years' worth of memories.

Chicago was a brand-new world. In Baxter everybody knew everybody else (not to mention everybody else's business). In Chicago Rhonda felt invisible. The first month, she cried almost every night.

Even when Rhonda's family found a church with a big youth group, things didn't improve. Nobody in the group really reached out. They were so into their own little circle of friends, they barely noticed Rhonda.

At about that same time, however, a group of kids at school began reaching out to "the new girl." One guy called himself an agnostic. Two of the girls claimed to have had abortions. Another guy had a police record. None of the them went to church.

When Rhonda's parents expressed concern about her choice of friends, Rhonda retorted, "Well, they may be a little bit on the wild side, but at least they treat me like a person. I'd rather hang out with them than with those fakes at the church!"

What would you do in Rhonda's situation? Do friends really affect the direction of our life? Read Psalm 1, noting especially the first verse.

⁴ I cried to the LORD with my voice,
And He heard me from His holy hill.   Selah

⁵ I lay down and slept;
I awoke, for the LORD sustained me.
⁶ I will not be afraid of ten thousands of people
Who have set *themselves* against me all around.

⁷ Arise, O LORD;
Save me, O my God!
For You have struck all my enemies on the cheekbone;
You have broken the teeth of the ungodly.
⁸ Salvation *belongs* to the LORD.
Your blessing *is* upon Your people.   Selah

PSALM 4 WHO CAN KEEP US SAFE? *To the Chief Musician. With stringed instruments. A Psalm of David.*

¹ Hear me when I call, O God of my righteousness!
You have relieved me in *my* distress;
Have mercy on me, and hear my prayer.

OFF THE CEILING

4:3 David knew God heard his prayers and would answer him. We can know that God listens and answers when we call on him. Some we think God will not hear us because we have fallen short of his standards for holy living. But God listens to us because we have b forgiven. When you feel that your prayers are bouncing off the c remember that as a believer you have been set apart by God, an loves you. He hears and answers (although his answers may not we expect). Look at your problems in the light of God's power ins looking at God in the light of your problems.

² How long, O you sons of men,
Will you turn my glory to shame?
How long will you love worthlessness
And seek falsehood?   Selah
³ But know that the LORD has set apart for Himself him who is godly;
The LORD will hear when I call to Him.

⁴ Be angry, and do not sin.
Meditate within your heart on your bed, and be still.   Selah
⁵ Offer the sacrifices of righteousness,
And put your trust in the LORD.

⁶ *There are* many who say,
"Who will show us *any* good?"
LORD, lift up the light of Your countenance upon us.
⁷ You have put gladness in my heart,
More than in the season that their grain and wine increased.
⁸ I will both lie down in peace, and sleep;
For You alone, O LORD, make me dwell in safety.

PSALM 5 GOD HATES LIES. *To the Chief Musician. With flutes. A Psalm of David.*

¹ Give ear to my words, O LORD,
Consider my meditation.
² Give heed to the voice of my cry,
My King and my God,
For to You I will pray.
³ My voice You shall hear in the morning, O LORD;
In the morning I will direct *it* to You,
And I will look up.

⁴ For You *are* not a God who takes pleasure in wickedness,
Nor shall evil dwell with You.
⁵ The boastful shall not stand in Your sight;
You hate all workers of iniquity.
⁶ You shall destroy those who speak falsehood;
The LORD abhors the bloodthirsty and deceitful man.

⁷ But as for me, I will come into Your house in the multitude of Your mercy;
In fear of You I will worship toward Your holy temple.
⁸ Lead me, O LORD, in Your righteousness because of my enemies;
Make Your way straight before my face.

⁹ For *there is* no faithfulness in their mouth;
Their inward part *is* destruction;
Their throat *is* an open tomb;
They flatter with their tongue.

10 Pronounce them guilty, O God!
   Let them fall by their own counsels;
   Cast them out in the multitude of their
      transgressions,
   For they have rebelled against You.

11 But let all those rejoice who put their trust in You;
   Let them ever shout for joy, because You defend
      them;
   Let those also who love Your name
   Be joyful in You.

12 For You, O LORD, will bless the righteous;
   With favor You will surround him as *with* a shield.

PSALM **6** GOD HEARS MY PRAYERS. *To the Chief Musician. With stringed instruments. On an eight-stringed harp. A Psalm of David.*

1 O LORD, do not rebuke me in Your anger,
   Nor chasten me in Your hot displeasure.

2 Have mercy on me, O LORD, for I *am* weak;
   O LORD, heal me, for my bones are troubled.

3 My soul also is greatly troubled;
   But You, O LORD—how long?

4 Return, O LORD, deliver me!
   Oh, save me for Your mercies'
      sake!

5 For in death *there is* no
      remembrance of You;
   In the grave who will give You
      thanks?

6 I am weary with my groaning;
   All night I make my bed swim;
   I drench my couch with my tears.

7 My eye wastes away because of
      grief;
   It grows old because of all my
      enemies.

8 Depart from me, all you workers
      of iniquity;
   For the LORD has heard the voice
      of my weeping.

9 The LORD has heard my
      supplication;
   The LORD will receive my prayer.

10 Let all my enemies be ashamed
      and greatly troubled;
   Let them turn back *and* be
      ashamed suddenly.

PSALM **7** THE PERFECT JUDGE. *A Meditation of David, which he sang to the LORD concerning the words of Cush, a Benjamite.*

1 O LORD my God, in You I put my trust;
   Save me from all those who persecute me;
   And deliver me,

2 Lest they tear me like a lion,
   Rending *me* in pieces, while *there is* none to deliver.

3 O LORD my God, if I have done this:
   If there is iniquity in my hands,

4 If I have repaid evil to him who was at peace with
      me,

REVENGE

7:1-6 Have you ever been falsely accused or badly hurt and wanted revenge? David wrote this psalm in response to the slanderous accusations of those who claimed he was trying to kill King Saul and seize the throne (1 Samuel 24:9-11). Instead of seeking revenge, David cried out to God for justice. The proper response to slander is prayer, not revenge. God says, "Vengeance is Mine, I will repay" (Romans 12:19; Deuteronomy 32:35-36). Instead of striking back, ask God to take your case, bring justice, and restore your reputation.

      Or have plundered my enemy without cause,
5 Let the enemy pursue me and overtake *me;*
   Yes, let him trample my life to the earth,
   And lay my honor in the dust.   Selah

"Here's what I did..."

There was a time a couple of years ago when I was really down on myself, depressed and very confused. I couldn't do anything to make myself feel better. I prayed about it and one night I opened my Bible looking for consolation. I leafed through the Psalms, remembering that a Christian friend had once told me that whenever he felt bad, it helped to read the Psalms.

What caught my eye that night was the heading for Psalm 6: "A prayer for deliverance in time of distress. God is able to deliver us." That's what I felt—distressed; and what I needed was deliverance. I read and reread that psalm. It spoke straight to my heart, and it showed me that God was there for me, as always. Do I ever love him!

Now whenever I'm in doubt about God's love and care, I turn to that psalm. It reminds me that God is always there and that he will lead me through any dark time I experience, just as he did that one night when I first read Psalm 6.

Jenna   AGE 17

6 Arise, O LORD, in Your anger;
   Lift Yourself up because of the rage of my enemies;
   Rise up for me *to* the judgment You have
      commanded!

7 So the congregation of the peoples shall surround
      You;
   For their sakes, therefore, return on high.

8 The LORD shall judge the peoples;
   Judge me, O LORD, according to my righteousness,
   And according to my integrity within me.

9 Oh, let the wickedness of the wicked come to an end,

MADE
IN THE
IMAGE
OF GOD

"Van Gogh's Irises sells for $53.9 million." Art sales don't usually make headlines, but occasionally you'll see a front-page story about a particular painting being sold for an astronomical sum. To the untrained eye, even such an extremely expensive work may seem to be only a few lines splashed across the canvas, holding no meaning or appeal. What makes such a picture worth so much? **T**he answer is found tucked away, almost unnoticeably, in the lower right-hand corner—the artist's signature. Even if the image on the canvas seems rather ordinary or commonplace, the name Van Gogh or Gauguin or Rembrandt scrawled somewhere on it makes the piece priceless. The reason the artwork is worth so much is simple: it came from the hands of a master. **T**he same is true of humanity. Some people think that human beings are valuable because we have somehow acquired dignity in a meaningless universe. Others think our value comes from being the most highly evolved creatures on this planet. But Psalm 8 teaches that what makes us worthwhile is the fact that we are made in the image of God. In spite of our sinfulness, in spite of the fact that we have broken God's laws and warped his creation, we still bear the image of the One who made us. **I**t's easy to believe this of kind, attractive, thoughtful people. We're not God's image-bearers because we're good, but because he created us. We're like a airports. We're not God's image-bearers because we're good, but because he created us. We're like a masterpiece that has had mud and filth splattered on it. Underneath the dirt, we still have the Master's signature on us. That should help guide how we treat each other—even the people we don't like. **W**he are confronted by people who seem to exist only to criticize and put down, the teacher who takes pleasure being obnoxious, the parent who seems only to criticize and put down, the teacher who takes pleasure putting red marks on your papers—remember: that person bears the signature of the Master Artist. S you. Regardless of our sinfulness, that fact makes each of us the most priceless object in the universe

But establish the just;
For the righteous God tests the hearts and minds.
¹⁰ My defense *is* of God,
Who saves the upright in heart.

¹¹ God *is* a just judge,
And God is angry *with the wicked* every day.
¹² If he does not turn back,
He will sharpen His sword;
He bends His bow and makes it ready.
¹³ He also prepares for Himself instruments of death;
He makes His arrows into fiery shafts.

¹⁴ Behold, *the wicked* brings forth iniquity;
Yes, he conceives trouble and brings forth falsehood.
¹⁵ He made a pit and dug it out,
And has fallen into the ditch *which* he made.
¹⁶ His trouble shall return upon his own head,
And his violent dealing shall come down on his own crown.

¹⁷ I will praise the LORD according to His righteousness,
And will sing praise to the name of the LORD Most High.

PSALM **8** WHY GOD MADE US. *To the Chief Musician. On the instrument of Gath. A Psalm of David.*
¹ O LORD, our Lord,
How excellent *is* Your name in all the earth,
Who have set Your glory above the heavens!

² Out of the mouth of babes and nursing infants

You have ordained strength,
Because of Your enemies,
That You may silence the enemy and the avenger.

³ When I consider Your heavens, the work of Your fingers,
The moon and the stars, which You have ordained,
⁴ What is man that You are mindful of him,
And the son of man that You visit him?
⁵ For You have made him a little lower than the angels,
And You have crowned him with glory and honor.

⁶ You have made him to have dominion over the works of Your hands;
You have put all *things* under his feet,
⁷ All sheep and oxen—
Even the beasts of the field,
⁸ The birds of the air,
And the fish of the sea
That pass through the paths of the seas.

⁹ O LORD, our Lord,
How excellent *is* Your name in all the earth!

PSALM **9** GOD HEARS US. *To the Chief Musician. To the tune of "Death of the Son." A Psalm of David.*
¹ I will praise *You*, O LORD, with my whole heart;
I will tell of all Your marvelous works.
² I will be glad and rejoice in You;
I will sing praise to Your name, O Most High.

³ When my enemies turn back,

REASONS TO READ PSALMS

to find comfort
PSALM 23

to learn a new prayer
PSALM 136

to understand yourself more clearly
PSALM 8

to be forgiven for your sins
PSALM 51

to meet God intimately
PSALM 103

to learn a new song
PSALM 92

to know how to come to God each day
PSALM 5

to feel worthwhile
PSALM 139

to understand why you should read the Bible
PSALM 119

to know that God is in control
PSALM 146

to give thanks to God
PSALM 136

to know why you should worship God
PSALM 104

to please God
PSALM 15

to give praise to God PSALM 145

God's Word was written to be studied, understood, and applied, and the book of Psalms lends itself most directly to application. We may turn to Psalms looking for something, but sooner or later we will meet Someone. As we read and memorize the Psalms, we will discover how much they are already part of us. They put our deepest hurts, longings, thoughts, and prayers into words. They gently push us toward being what God designed us to be—people who love and live for him.

9:1-2 One of the natural results of praising God is witnessing. When we know God is wonderful, we naturally want to tell others and have them praise God with us.

They shall fall and perish at Your presence.
4 For You have maintained my right and my cause;
You sat on the throne judging in righteousness.
5 You have rebuked the nations,
You have destroyed the wicked;
You have blotted out their name forever and ever.

6 O enemy, destructions are finished forever!
And you have destroyed cities;
Even their memory has perished.
7 But the LORD shall endure forever;
He has prepared His throne for judgment.
8 He shall judge the world in righteousness,
And He shall administer judgment for the peoples in uprightness.

9 The LORD also will be a refuge for the oppressed,
A refuge in times of trouble.
10 And those who know Your name will put their trust in You;
For You, LORD, have not forsaken those who seek You.

11 Sing praises to the LORD, who dwells in Zion!
Declare His deeds among the people.
12 When He avenges blood, He remembers them;
He does not forget the cry of the humble.

13 Have mercy on me, O LORD!
Consider my trouble from those who hate me,
You who lift me up from the gates of death,
14 That I may tell of all Your praise
In the gates of the daughter of Zion.
I will rejoice in Your salvation.

15 The nations have sunk down in the pit *which* they made;
In the net which they hid, their own foot is caught.
16 The LORD is known *by* the judgment He executes;
The wicked is snared in the work of his own hands.
Meditation.   Selah

17 The wicked shall be turned into hell,
And all the nations that forget God.
18 For the needy shall not always be forgotten;
The expectation of the poor shall *not* perish forever.

19 Arise, O LORD,
Do not let man prevail;
Let the nations be judged in Your sight.
20 Put them in fear, O LORD,
That the nations may know themselves *to be but* men.   Selah

PSALM 10 WILL THE WICKED SUCCEED?

1 Why do You stand afar off, O LORD?
Why do You hide in times of trouble?
2 The wicked in *his* pride persecutes the poor;
Let them be caught in the plots which they have devised.

3 For the wicked boasts of his heart's desire;
He blesses the greedy *and* renounces the LORD.

4 The wicked in his proud countenance does not seek *God;*
God *is* in none of his thoughts.
5 His ways are always prospering;
Your judgments *are* far above, out of his sight;
As for all his enemies, he sneers at them.
6 He has said in his heart, "I shall not be moved;
I shall never be in adversity."
7 His mouth is full of cursing and deceit and oppression;
Under his tongue *is* trouble and iniquity.

8 He sits in the lurking places of the villages;

10:1 To the psalmist, God seemed far away. "*Why* do You hide in ti of trouble?" he asked God. But though he had honest doubts, he did stop praying or assume that God no longer cared. He was not complaining but was asking God to hurry to his aid. It is during thos times when we feel most alone or oppressed that we need to keep praying, telling God about our troubles.

In the secret places he murders the innocent;
His eyes are secretly fixed on the helpless.
9 He lies in wait secretly, as a lion in his den;
He lies in wait to catch the poor;
He catches the poor when he draws him into his net.
10 So he crouches, he lies low,
That the helpless may fall by his strength.
11 He has said in his heart,
"God has forgotten;
He hides His face;
He will never see."

12 Arise, O LORD!
O God, lift up Your hand!
Do not forget the humble.
13 Why do the wicked renounce God?
He has said in his heart,
"You will not require *an account.*"

14 But You have seen, for You observe trouble and grief,
To repay *it* by Your hand.
The helpless commits himself to You;
You are the helper of the fatherless.
15 Break the arm of the wicked and the evil *man;*
Seek out his wickedness *until* You find none.

16 The LORD *is* King forever and ever;
The nations have perished out of His land.
17 LORD, You have heard the desire of the humble;
You will prepare their heart;
You will cause Your ear to hear,
18 To do justice to the fatherless and the oppressed,
That the man of the earth may oppress no more.

PSALM 11 GOD SEES IT ALL. *To the Chief Musician. A Psalm of David.*

1 In the LORD I put my trust;
How can you say to my soul,

"Flee *as* a bird to your mountain"?
2 For look! The wicked bend *their* bow,
They make ready their arrow on the string,
That they may shoot secretly at the upright in heart.
3 If the foundations are destroyed,
What can the righteous do?

4 The LORD *is* in His holy temple,
The LORD's throne *is* in heaven;
His eyes behold,
His eyelids test the sons of men.
5 The LORD tests the righteous,
But the wicked and the one who loves violence His
soul hates.
6 Upon the wicked He will rain coals;
Fire and brimstone and a burning wind
Shall be the portion of their cup.

7 For the LORD *is* righteous,
He loves righteousness;
His countenance beholds the upright.

PSALM 12 CAN I TRUST GOD? *To the Chief Musician. On an eight-stringed harp. A Psalm of David.*
1 Help, LORD, for the godly man ceases!
For the faithful disappear from among the sons of
men.
2 They speak idly everyone with his neighbor;
With flattering lips *and* a double heart they speak.

3 May the LORD cut off all flattering lips,
And the tongue that speaks proud things,
4 Who have said,
"With our tongue we will prevail;
Our lips *are* our own;
Who *is* lord over us?"

5 "For the oppression of the poor,
for the sighing of the needy,
Now I will arise," says the LORD;
"I will set *him* in the safety for
which he yearns."

6 The words of the LORD *are* pure
words,
Like silver tried in a furnace of
earth,
Purified seven times.
7 You shall keep them, O LORD,
You shall preserve them from this
generation forever.

8 The wicked prowl on every side,
When vileness is exalted among
the sons of men.

PSALM 13 I NEED HELP. *To the Chief Musician. A Psalm of David.*
1 How long, O LORD? Will You forget
me forever?
How long will You hide Your face
from me?

2 How long shall I take counsel in my soul,
Having sorrow in my heart daily?
How long will my enemy be exalted over me?

3 Consider *and* hear me, O LORD my God;
Enlighten my eyes,

◄◄◄ LYING LIPS
12:2-4 We may be tempted to believe that lies are relatively harmless, even useful at times. But deceit, flattery, boasting, and lies are not overlooked by God. Each of these sins originates from a bad attitude that eventually is expressed in our speech. The tongue can be our greatest enemy because, though small, it can do great damage (James 3:5). Be careful how you use yours.

Lest I sleep the *sleep of* death;
4 Lest my enemy say,
"I have prevailed against him";
Lest those who trouble me rejoice when I am moved.

5 But I have trusted in Your mercy;
My heart shall rejoice in Your salvation.
6 I will sing to the LORD,
Because He has dealt bountifully with me.

PSALM 14 FOOLISH OR WISE? *To the Chief Musician. A Psalm of David.*
1 The fool has said in his heart,
"*There is* no God."
They are corrupt,
They have done abominable works,
There is none who does good.

"Here's what I did..."

I couldn't get out of my mind what my friend had told me. She said that when she was eight years old, her oldest brother raped her—more than once.

I felt angry, mainly at God. I just couldn't understand it. How could God let such a terrible thing happen to such a wonderful person? Why hadn't he done anything to stop it—like have the phone ring, or someone come to the door, or someone come home? Anything!

This really bothered me for a long time. Then I was reading in the Psalms, and I came across Psalm 13. I saw that the psalmist was angry at God, too—he was actually complaining to God! That gave me freedom to spill out my heart to God. I told God all my bitter and confused thoughts concerning what happened to my friend. I cried. I even lashed out at God. And the result of telling God what was on my mind and my heart was an incredible peace. Psalm 13 showed me that God always wants to hear what's on my mind, even when I'm angry with him. In the end, I found that God is there for me—even if I don't always understand all his ways.

Eric AGE 16

² The LORD looks down from heaven upon the
    children of men,
To see if there are any who understand, who seek
    God.
³ They have all turned aside,
They have together become corrupt;
There is none who does good,
No, not one.

⁴ Have all the workers of iniquity no knowledge,
Who eat up my people *as* they eat bread,
And do not call on the LORD?
⁵ There they are in great fear,
For God *is* with the generation of the righteous.
⁶ You shame the counsel of the poor,
But the LORD *is* his refuge.

⁷ Oh, that the salvation of Israel *would come* out of
    Zion!
When the LORD brings back the captivity of His
    people,
Let Jacob rejoice *and* Israel be glad.

PSALM 15 WHAT MAKES SOMEONE GOOD?
A Psalm of David.
¹ LORD, who may abide in Your tabernacle?
Who may dwell in Your holy hill?

² He who walks uprightly,
    And works righteousness,
    And speaks the truth in his heart;
³ He *who* does not backbite with his tongue,
    Nor does evil to his neighbor,
    Nor does he take up a reproach against his friend;
⁴ In whose eyes a vile person is despised,
    But he honors those who fear the LORD;
    He *who* swears to his own hurt and does not change;
⁵ He *who* does not put out his money at usury,
    Nor does he take a bribe against the innocent.

He who does these *things* shall never be moved.

PSALM 16 GOD'S FRIEND. *A Michtam of David.*
¹ Preserve me, O God, for in You I put my trust.

² *O my soul,* you have said to the LORD,
"You *are* my Lord,
My goodness is nothing apart from You."
³ As for the saints who *are* on the earth,
"They are the excellent ones, in whom is all my
    delight."

⁴ Their sorrows shall be multiplied who hasten *after*
    another *god;*
Their drink offerings of blood I will not offer,
Nor take up their names on my lips.

⁵ O LORD, *You are* the portion of my inheritance and
    my cup;
You maintain my lot.
⁶ The lines have fallen to me in pleasant *places;*
Yes, I have a good inheritance.

⁷ I will bless the LORD who has given me counsel;

My heart also instructs me in the night seasons.
⁸ I have set the LORD always before me;
Because *He is* at my right hand I shall not be moved.

⁹ Therefore my heart is glad, and my glory rejoices;
My flesh also will rest in hope.
¹⁰ For You will not leave my soul in Sheol,
Nor will You allow Your Holy One to see corruption.
¹¹ You will show me the path of life;
In Your presence *is* fullness of joy;
At Your right hand *are* pleasures forevermore.

PSALM 17 SEEING GOD FACE TO FACE. *A Prayer of David.*
¹ Hear a just cause, O LORD,
Attend to my cry;
Give ear to my prayer *which is* not from deceitful
    lips.
² Let my vindication come from Your presence;
Let Your eyes look on the things that are upright.

³ You have tested my heart;
You have visited *me* in the night;
You have tried me and have found nothing;
I have purposed that my mouth shall not transgress.
⁴ Concerning the works of men,
By the word of Your lips,
I have kept away from the paths of the destroyer.
⁵ Uphold my steps in Your paths,
That my footsteps may not slip.

⁶ I have called upon You, for You will hear me, O God;
Incline Your ear to me, *and* hear my speech.
⁷ Show Your marvelous lovingkindness by Your right
    hand,
O You who save those who trust *in You*
From those who rise up *against them.*
⁸ Keep me as the apple of Your eye;
Hide me under the shadow of Your wings,
⁹ From the wicked who oppress me,
From my deadly enemies who surround me.

¹⁰ They have closed up their fat *hearts;*
With their mouths they speak proudly.
¹¹ They have now surrounded us in our steps;
They have set their eyes, crouching down to the
    earth,
¹² As a lion is eager to tear his prey,
And like a young lion lurking in secret places.

¹³ Arise, O LORD,
Confront him, cast him down;
Deliver my life from the wicked with Your sword,
¹⁴ With Your hand from men, O LORD,

SHIELD
18:30 Many say belief in God is a crutch for weak people who c⟨
make it on their own. God is indeed a shield to protect us when we⟨
too weak to face certain trials by ourselves. He strengthens, prote⟨
guides us in order to send us back into an evil world to fight for hi⟨
David was not a coward; he was a mighty warrior who, with all his⟨
and weapons, knew that only God could ultimately protect and sa⟨

From men of the world *who have* their portion in
    this life,
And whose belly You fill with Your hidden treasure.
They are satisfied with children,
And leave the rest of their *possession* for their babes.

¹⁵ As for me, I will see Your face in righteousness;
I shall be satisfied when I awake in Your likeness.

PSALM **18** GOD CARES FOR US.

To the Chief Musician. A Psalm of David the servant of the LORD, who spoke to the LORD the words of this song on the day that the LORD delivered him from the hand of all his enemies and from the hand of Saul. And he said:

¹ I will love You, O LORD, my strength.
² The LORD is my rock and my fortress and my
    deliverer;
My God, my strength, in whom I will trust;
My shield and the horn of my salvation, my
    stronghold.
³ I will call upon the LORD, *who is worthy* to be praised;
So shall I be saved from my enemies.

⁴ The pangs of death surrounded me,
And the floods of ungodliness made me afraid.
⁵ The sorrows of Sheol surrounded me;
The snares of death confronted me.
⁶ In my distress I called upon the LORD,
And cried out to my God;
He heard my voice from His temple,
And my cry came before Him, *even* to His ears.

⁷ Then the earth shook and trembled;
The foundations of the hills also quaked and were
    shaken,
Because He was angry.
⁸ Smoke went up from His nostrils,
And devouring fire from His mouth;
Coals were kindled by it.
⁹ He bowed the heavens also, and came down
With darkness under His feet.
¹⁰ And He rode upon a cherub, and flew;
He flew upon the wings of the wind.
¹¹ He made darkness His secret place;
His canopy around Him *was* dark waters
And thick clouds of the skies.
¹² From the brightness before Him,
His thick clouds passed with hailstones and coals of
    fire.

¹³ The LORD thundered from heaven,
And the Most High uttered His voice,
Hailstones and coals of fire.
¹⁴ He sent out His arrows and scattered the foe,
Lightnings in abundance, and He vanquished them.
¹⁵ Then the channels of the sea were seen,
The foundations of the world were uncovered
At Your rebuke, O LORD,
At the blast of the breath of Your nostrils.

¹⁶ He sent from above, He took me;
He drew me out of many waters.
¹⁷ He delivered me from my strong enemy,

From those who hated me,
For they were too strong for me.
¹⁸ They confronted me in the day of my calamity,
But the LORD was my support.
¹⁹ He also brought me out into a broad place;
He delivered me because He delighted in me.

²⁰ The LORD rewarded me according to my
    righteousness;
According to the cleanness of my hands
He has recompensed me.
²¹ For I have kept the ways of the LORD,
And have not wickedly departed from my God.
²² For all His judgments *were* before me,
And I did not put away His statutes from me.
²³ I was also blameless before Him,

A friend of mine is convinced that being good will get him into heaven. I'm starting to agree with him. God won't send people who live good lives to hell, will he?

I WONDER...

Teachers have developed two systems for grading their students' performance. First, there is the "curve." Put simply, in a particular class 50 percent of the students will score above the average, 50 percent will score below. Often those who score below the average still have a chance to pass. That's why students seem to like this system best.

Then there is the "set" scale. With this system, a certain percentage determines your grade. If you get below a 75 percent grade, for example, you fail.

Most people would like to believe that God grades on a curve. In other words, if they're better than others, it will be all right with God. All they have to do to pass is not steal or kill anyone, mind their own business, and wait for heaven.

Unfortunately, God doesn't grade that way.

Psalm 14:1-3 is clear. There isn't anyone who is good. Not one! All of us have strayed away. This doesn't mean we're all murderers, it means our heart is stained with the sin of Adam—the desire to be god of our life and run it ourself. No one has a pure heart. (See Luke 18:18-26 for a great illustration.)

God has *one* method of salvation. In his wisdom, he gave everyone the opportunity to go to heaven by faith, not by works. All a person has to do to be saved is believe that Christ paid the penalty for sin and rose again from the dead: "For by grace you have been saved through faith, and that not of yourselves; *it is* the gift of God, not of works, lest anyone should boast" (Ephesians 2:8-9).

Most people say this is too simple. But that's the whole idea! God isn't trying to make it tough on us. He wants us to be with him forever!

Throughout your life you will run into people who believe that simply living a good life means heaven awaits. A good life is important to point people to a holy God, but it will not buy you a ticket to heaven. That ticket has already been paid for by Jesus Christ! But you must come to him to get it.

And I kept myself from my iniquity.

²⁴ Therefore the Lord has recompensed me according
to my righteousness,
According to the cleanness of my hands in His sight.

GREATNESS

18:35 David offers an interesting twist to the concept of greatness,
saying that God's gentleness made him great. Our society believes that
greatness is attained through a combination of opportunity, talent, and
aggressiveness. But true greatness comes from living according to God's
laws and standards and recognizing that all we have comes from the
gentleness of God's mercy.

²⁵ With the merciful You will show Yourself merciful;
With a blameless man You will show Yourself
blameless;

²⁶ With the pure You will show Yourself pure;
And with the devious You will show Yourself shrewd.

²⁷ For You will save the humble people,
But will bring down haughty looks.

²⁸ For You will light my lamp;
The Lord my God will enlighten my darkness.

²⁹ For by You I can run against a troop,
By my God I can leap over a wall.

³⁰ *As for* God, His way *is* perfect;
The word of the Lord is proven;
He *is* a shield to all who trust in Him.

³¹ For who *is* God, except the Lord?
And who *is* a rock, except our God?

³² *It is* God who arms me with strength,
And makes my way perfect.

³³ He makes my feet like the *feet of* deer,
And sets me on my high places.

³⁴ He teaches my hands to make war,
So that my arms can bend a bow of bronze.

³⁵ You have also given me the shield of Your salvation;
Your right hand has held me up,
Your gentleness has made me great.

³⁶ You enlarged my path under me,
So my feet did not slip.

³⁷ I have pursued my enemies and overtaken them;
Neither did I turn back again till they were destroyed.

³⁸ I have wounded them,
So that they could not rise;
They have fallen under my feet.

³⁹ For You have armed me with strength for the battle;
You have subdued under me those who rose up
against me.

⁴⁰ You have also given me the necks of my enemies,
So that I destroyed those who hated me.

⁴¹ They cried out, but *there was* none to save;
Even to the Lord, but He did not answer them.

⁴² Then I beat them as fine as the dust before the wind;
I cast them out like dirt in the streets.

⁴³ You have delivered me from the strivings of the
people;
You have made me the head of the nations;

A people I have not known shall serve me.

⁴⁴ As soon as they hear of me they obey me;
The foreigners submit to me.

⁴⁵ The foreigners fade away,
And come frightened from their hideouts.

⁴⁶ The Lord lives!
Blessed *be* my Rock!
Let the God of my salvation be exalted.

⁴⁷ *It is* God who avenges me,
And subdues the peoples under me;

⁴⁸ He delivers me from my enemies.
You also lift me up above those who rise against me;
You have delivered me from the violent man.

⁴⁹ Therefore I will give thanks to You, O Lord, among
the Gentiles,
And sing praises to Your name.

⁵⁰ Great deliverance He gives to His king,
And shows mercy to His anointed,
To David and his descendants forevermore.

PSALM 19 MORE VALUABLE THAN GOLD. *To the
Chief Musician. A Psalm of David.*

¹ The heavens declare the glory of God;
And the firmament shows His handiwork.

² Day unto day utters speech,
And night unto night reveals knowledge.

³ *There is* no speech nor language
Where their voice is not heard.

⁴ Their line has gone out through all the earth,
And their words to the end of the world.

The heavens heavens heavens heavens DECLARE THE GLORY OF GOD THE GLORY OF GOD THE GLORY OF GOD AND THE FIRMAMENT SHOWS HIS HANDIWORK

In them He has set a tabernacle for the sun,
5 Which *is* like a bridegroom coming out of his
     chamber,
And rejoices like a strong man to run its race.
6 Its rising *is* from one end of heaven,
     And its circuit to the other end;
     And there is nothing hidden from its heat.

7 The law of the LORD *is* perfect, converting the soul;
     The testimony of the LORD *is* sure, making wise the
       simple;
8 The statutes of the LORD *are* right, rejoicing the heart;
     The commandment of the LORD *is* pure,
       enlightening the eyes;
9 The fear of the LORD *is* clean, enduring forever;
     The judgments of the LORD *are* true *and* righteous
       altogether.
10 More to be desired *are they* than gold,
     Yea, than much fine gold;
     Sweeter also than honey and the honeycomb.
11 Moreover by them Your servant is warned,
     And in keeping them *there is* great reward.

12 Who can understand his errors?
     Cleanse me from secret *faults.*
13 Keep back Your servant also from presumptuous *sins;*
     Let them not have dominion over me.
     Then I shall be blameless,
     And I shall be innocent of great transgression.

14 Let the words of my mouth and the meditation of
     my heart
     Be acceptable in Your sight,
     O LORD, my strength and my Redeemer.

PSALM **20** GOD IS WITH US. *To the Chief Musician. A Psalm of David.*

1 May the LORD answer you in the day of trouble;
     May the name of the God of Jacob defend you;
2 May He send you help from the sanctuary,
     And strengthen you out of Zion;
3 May He remember all your offerings,
     And accept your burnt sacrifice.   Selah

4 May He grant you according to your heart's *desire,*
     And fulfill all your purpose.
5 We will rejoice in your salvation,
     And in the name of our God we will set up *our*
       banners!
     May the LORD fulfill all your petitions.

6 Now I know that the LORD saves His anointed;
     He will answer him from His holy heaven
     With the saving strength of His right hand.

7 Some *trust* in chariots, and some in horses;
     But we will remember the name of the LORD our God.
8 They have bowed down and fallen;
     But we have risen and stand upright.

9 Save, LORD!
     May the King answer us when we call.

PSALM **21** THANKING GOD FOR HIS ANSWERS.
To the Chief Musician. A Psalm of David.
1 The king shall have joy in Your strength, O LORD;
     And in Your salvation how greatly shall he rejoice!
2 You have given him his heart's desire,
     And have not withheld the request of his lips.   Selah

3 For You meet him with the blessings of goodness;
     You set a crown of pure gold upon his head.
4 He asked life from You, *and* You gave *it* to him—
     Length of days forever and ever.
5 His glory *is* great in Your salvation;
     Honor and majesty You have placed upon him.
6 For You have made him most blessed forever;
     You have made him exceedingly glad with Your
       presence.
7 For the king trusts in the LORD,

◤ LEADERS

21:7 A good leader trusts God and depends upon his steadfast love. Too often our leaders trust in their own cleverness and strength, or in the "god" of military power. But God is above all these gods. If you want to be a leader, keep the Lord God at the center of your life and depend on him.

     And through the mercy of the Most High he shall not
       be moved.

8 Your hand will find all Your enemies;
     Your right hand will find those who hate You.
9 You shall make them as a fiery oven in the time of
     Your anger;
     The LORD shall swallow them up in His wrath,
     And the fire shall devour them.
10 Their offspring You shall destroy from the earth,
     And their descendants from among the sons of men.
11 For they intended evil against You;
     They devised a plot *which* they are not able *to
       perform.*
12 Therefore You will make them turn their back;
     You will make ready *Your arrows* on Your string
       toward their faces.

13 Be exalted, O LORD, in Your own strength!
     We will sing and praise Your power.

PSALM **22** EVERYONE HATES ME—DOES GOD?
*To the Chief Musician. Set to "The Deer of the Dawn."
A Psalm of David.*
1 My God, My God, why have You forsaken Me?
     Why are You so far from helping Me,
     And from the words of My groaning?
2 O My God, I cry in the daytime, but You do not hear;
     And in the night season, and am not silent.

3 But You *are* holy,
     Enthroned in the praises of Israel.
4 Our fathers trusted in You;
     They trusted, and You delivered them.
5 They cried to You, and were delivered;
     They trusted in You, and were not ashamed.

■BEST INTERESTS

23:2-3 When we allow God our Shepherd to guide us, we have contentment. When we choose to sin, however, we are choosing to go our own way and we cannot blame God for the environment in which we find ourself. Our Shepherd knows the "green pastures" and "still waters" that will restore us. We will reach these places only by following him obediently. Rebelling against the Shepherd's leading is actually rebelling against our own best interests for the future. We must remember this the next time we are tempted to go our way rather than the Shepherd's way.

6 But I *am* a worm, and no man;
   A reproach of men, and despised by the people.
7 All those who see Me ridicule Me;
   They shoot out the lip, they shake the head, *saying,*
8 "He trusted in the LORD, let Him rescue Him;
   Let Him deliver Him, since He delights in Him!"

9 But You *are* He who took Me out of the womb;
   You made Me trust *while* on My mother's breasts.
10 I was cast upon You from birth.
   From My mother's womb
   You *have been* My God.
11 Be not far from Me,
   For trouble *is* near;
   For *there is* none to help.

12 Many bulls have surrounded Me;
   Strong *bulls* of Bashan have encircled Me.
13 They gape at Me *with* their mouths,
   Like a raging and roaring lion.

14 I am poured out like water,
   And all My bones are out of joint;
   My heart is like wax;
   It has melted within Me.
15 My strength is dried up like a potsherd,
   And My tongue clings to My jaws;
   You have brought Me to the dust of death.

16 For dogs have surrounded Me;
   The congregation of the wicked has enclosed Me.
   They pierced My hands and My feet;
17 I can count all My bones.
   They look *and* stare at Me.
18 They divide My garments among them,
   And for My clothing they cast lots.

19 But You, O LORD, do not be far from Me;
   O My Strength, hasten to help Me!
20 Deliver Me from the sword,
   My precious *life* from the power of the dog.
21 Save Me from the lion's mouth
   And from the horns of the wild oxen!

   You have answered Me.

22 I will declare Your name to My brethren;
   In the midst of the assembly I will praise You.
23 You who fear the LORD, praise Him!
   All you descendants of Jacob, glorify Him,
   And fear Him, all you offspring of Israel!
24 For He has not despised nor abhorred the affliction
      of the afflicted;
   Nor has He hidden His face from Him;
   But when He cried to Him, He heard.

25 My praise *shall be* of You in the great assembly;
   I will pay My vows before those who fear Him.
26 The poor shall eat and be satisfied;
   Those who seek Him will praise the LORD.
   Let your heart live forever!

27 All the ends of the world
   Shall remember and turn to the LORD,
   And all the families of the nations
   Shall worship before You.
28 For the kingdom *is* the LORD's,
   And He rules over the nations.

29 All the prosperous of the earth
   Shall eat and worship;
   All those who go down to the dust
   Shall bow before Him,
   Even he who cannot keep himself alive.

30 A posterity shall serve Him.
   It will be recounted of the Lord to the *next*
      generation,
31 They will come and declare His righteousness to a
      people who will be born,
   That He has done *this.*

PSALM **23** THE GOOD SHEPHERD. *A Psalm of David.*

1 The LORD *is* my shepherd;
   I shall not want.
2 He makes me to lie down in green pastures;
   He leads me beside the still waters.
3 He restores my soul;
   He leads me in the paths of righteousness
   For His name's sake.

THE LORD
is
MY SHEPHERD
I SHALL NOT WANT
I shall not want
I SHALL NOT WANT
I shall not want
I shall not want
I SHALL NOT WANT
I shall not want
I shall not want

PSALM 23:1

4 Yea, though I walk through the valley of the shadow
of death,
I will fear no evil;
For You *are* with me;
Your rod and Your staff, they comfort me.

5 You prepare a table before me in the presence of my
enemies;
You anoint my head with oil;
My cup runs over.
6 Surely goodness and mercy shall follow me
All the days of my life;
And I will dwell in the house of the LORD
Forever.

PSALM **24** WHO OWNS THE WORLD? *A Psalm of David.*

1 The earth *is* the LORD's, and all its fullness,
The world and those who dwell therein.
2 For He has founded it upon the seas,
And established it upon the waters.

3 Who may ascend into the hill of the LORD?
Or who may stand in His holy place?
4 He who has clean hands and a pure heart,
Who has not lifted up his soul to an idol,
Nor sworn deceitfully.
5 He shall receive blessing from the LORD,
And righteousness from the God of his salvation.
6 This *is* Jacob, the generation of those who seek Him,
Who seek Your face. Selah

7 Lift up your heads, O you gates!
And be lifted up, you everlasting doors!
And the King of glory shall come in.
8 Who *is* this King of glory?
The LORD strong and mighty,
The LORD mighty in battle.
9 Lift up your heads, O you gates!
Lift up, you everlasting doors!
And the King of glory shall come in.
10 Who is this King of glory?
The LORD of hosts,
He *is* the King of glory. Selah

PSALM **25** GOD WILL BE MY GUIDE. *A Psalm of David.*

1 To You, O LORD, I lift up my soul.
2 O my God, I trust in You;
Let me not be ashamed;
Let not my enemies triumph over me.
3 Indeed, let no one who waits on You be ashamed;
Let those be ashamed who deal treacherously
without cause.

4 Show me Your ways, O LORD;
Teach me Your paths.
5 Lead me in Your truth and teach me,
For You *are* the God of my salvation;
On You I wait all the day.

6 Remember, O LORD, Your tender mercies and Your
lovingkindnesses,
For they *are* from of old.
7 Do not remember the sins of my youth, nor my
transgressions;
According to Your mercy remember me,
For Your goodness' sake, O LORD.

◥◢◤ ENEMIES

25:2 Seventy-two psalms— almost half the book—speak about enemies. Enemies are those who not only oppose us, but also oppose God's way of living. Enemies can also be temptations—money, success, prestige, lust. And our greatest enemy is Satan. David asked God to keep his enemies from overcoming him because they opposed what God stood for. If his enemies succeeded, David feared that many would think that living for God was futile. David did not question his own faith—he knew that God would triumph. But he didn't want his enemies' success to be an obstacle to the faith of others.

8 Good and upright *is* the LORD;
Therefore He teaches sinners in the way.
9 The humble He guides in justice,
And the humble He teaches His way.
10 All the paths of the LORD *are* mercy and truth,
To such as keep His covenant and His testimonies.
11 For Your name's sake, O LORD,
Pardon my iniquity, for it *is* great.

12 Who *is* the man that fears the LORD?
Him shall He teach in the way He chooses.
13 He himself shall dwell in prosperity,
And his descendants shall inherit the earth.
14 The secret of the LORD *is* with those who fear Him,
And He will show them His covenant.
15 My eyes *are* ever toward the LORD,
For He shall pluck my feet out of the net.

16 Turn Yourself to me, and have mercy on me,
For I *am* desolate and afflicted.
17 The troubles of my heart have enlarged;
Bring me out of my distresses!
18 Look on my affliction and my pain,
And forgive all my sins.
19 Consider my enemies, for they are many;
And they hate me with cruel hatred.
20 Keep my soul, and deliver me;
Let me not be ashamed, for I put my trust in You.
21 Let integrity and uprightness preserve me,
For I wait for You.

22 Redeem Israel, O God,
Out of all their troubles!

PSALM **26** ON GOD'S SIDE. *A Psalm of David.*

1 Vindicate me, O LORD,
For I have walked in my integrity.
I have also trusted in the LORD;
I shall not slip.
2 Examine me, O LORD, and prove me;
Try my mind and my heart.
3 For Your lovingkindness *is* before my eyes,

And I have walked in Your truth.
4 I have not sat with idolatrous mortals,
Nor will I go in with hypocrites.
5 I have hated the assembly of evildoers,
And will not sit with the wicked.

6 I will wash my hands in innocence;
So I will go about Your altar, O LORD,
7 That I may proclaim with the voice of thanksgiving,
And tell of all Your wondrous works.
8 LORD, I have loved the habitation of Your house,
And the place where Your glory dwells.

27:5 We often run to God when we are experiencing difficulties. But David sought God's guiding presence *every day.* When troubles came his way, he was already in God's presence and prepared to handle any test. Believers can call to God for help at any time. How shortsighted it is to call on God only after trouble has come! Many of our problems could be avoided or handled far more easily by constantly relying on God's help and direction.

9 Do not gather my soul with sinners,
Nor my life with bloodthirsty men,
10 In whose hands *is* a sinister scheme,
And whose right hand is full of bribes.

11 But as for me, I will walk in my integrity;
Redeem me and be merciful to me.
12 My foot stands in an even place;
In the congregations I will bless the LORD.

PSALM 27 WHY SHOULD I BE AFRAID? *A Psalm of David.*

1 The LORD *is* my light and my salvation;
Whom shall I fear?
The LORD *is* the strength of my life;
Of whom shall I be afraid?
2 When the wicked came against me
To eat up my flesh,
My enemies and foes,
They stumbled and fell.
3 Though an army may encamp against me,
My heart shall not fear;
Though war may rise against me,
In this I *will be* confident.

4 One *thing* I have desired of the LORD,
That will I seek:
That I may dwell in the house of the LORD
All the days of my life,
To behold the beauty of the LORD,
And to inquire in His temple.
5 For in the time of trouble
He shall hide me in His pavilion;
In the secret place of His tabernacle
He shall hide me;
He shall set me high upon a rock.

6 And now my head shall be lifted up above my
enemies all around me;

Therefore I will offer sacrifices of joy in His
tabernacle;
I will sing, yes, I will sing praises to the LORD.

7 Hear, O LORD, *when* I cry with my voice!
Have mercy also upon me, and answer me.
8 *When You said,* "Seek My face,"
My heart said to You, "Your face, LORD, I will seek."
9 Do not hide Your face from me;
Do not turn Your servant away in anger;
You have been my help;
Do not leave me nor forsake me,
O God of my salvation.
10 When my father and my mother forsake me,
Then the LORD will take care of me.

11 Teach me Your way, O LORD,
And lead me in a smooth path, because of my
enemies.
12 Do not deliver me to the will of my adversaries;
For false witnesses have risen against me,
And such as breathe out violence.
13 *I would have lost heart,* unless I had believed
That I would see the goodness of the LORD
In the land of the living.

14 Wait on the LORD;
Be of good courage,
And He shall strengthen your heart;
Wait, I say, on the LORD!

PSALM 28 PRAYER IS POWERFUL. *A Psalm of David.*

1 To You I will cry, O LORD my Rock:
Do not be silent to me,
Lest, if You *are* silent to me,
I become like those who go down to the pit.
2 Hear the voice of my supplications
When I cry to You,
When I lift up my hands toward Your holy sanctuary.

3 Do not take me away with the wicked
And with the workers of iniquity,
Who speak peace to their neighbors,
But evil *is* in their hearts.
4 Give them according to their deeds,
And according to the wickedness of their endeavors;
Give them according to the work of their hands;
Render to them what they deserve.
5 Because they do not regard the works of the LORD,
Nor the operation of His hands,
He shall destroy them
And not build them up.

6 Blessed *be* the LORD,

28:3-5 It's easy to pretend friendship. Wicked people often masquerade in goodness, pretending kindness or friendship to gain own ends. David, in his royal position, may have met many who pretended friendship for selfish reasons. David knew God would pu them accordingly, but he prayed that their punishment would come swiftly. True believers live honest lives before God and others.

Because He has heard the voice of my supplications!
7 The Lord *is* my strength and my shield;
My heart trusted in Him, and I am helped;
Therefore my heart greatly rejoices,
And with my song I will praise Him.

8 The Lord *is* their strength,
And He *is* the saving refuge of His anointed.
9 Save Your people,
And bless Your inheritance;
Shepherd them also,
And bear them up forever.

PSALM **29** NATURE SPEAKS OF GOD. *A Psalm of David.*

1 Give unto the Lord, O you mighty ones,
Give unto the Lord glory and strength.
2 Give unto the Lord the glory due to His name;
Worship the Lord in the beauty of holiness.

3 The voice of the Lord *is* over the waters;
The God of glory thunders;
The Lord *is* over many waters.
4 The voice of the Lord *is* powerful;
The voice of the Lord *is* full of majesty.

5 The voice of the Lord breaks the cedars,
Yes, the Lord splinters the cedars of Lebanon.
6 He makes them also skip like a calf,
Lebanon and Sirion like a young wild ox.
7 The voice of the Lord divides the flames of fire.

8 The voice of the Lord shakes the wilderness;
The Lord shakes the Wilderness of Kadesh.
9 The voice of the Lord makes the deer give birth,
And strips the forests bare;
And in His temple everyone says, "Glory!"

10 The Lord sat *enthroned* at the Flood,
And the Lord sits as King forever.
11 The Lord will give strength to His people;
The Lord will bless His people with peace.

PSALM **30** SAVED FROM THE GRAVE. *A Psalm. A Song at the dedication of the house of David.*

1 I will extol You, O Lord, for You have lifted me up,
And have not let my foes rejoice over me.
2 O Lord my God, I cried out to You,
And You healed me.
3 O Lord, You brought my soul up from the grave;
You have kept me alive, that I should not go down to the pit.

4 Sing praise to the Lord, you saints of His,
And give thanks at the remembrance of His holy name.
5 For His anger *is but for* a moment,
His favor *is for* life;
Weeping may endure for a night,
But joy *comes* in the morning.

6 Now in my prosperity I said,
"I shall never be moved."

7 Lord, by Your favor You have made my mountain stand strong;
You hid Your face, *and* I was troubled.

8 I cried out to You, O Lord;
And to the Lord I made supplication:

9 "What profit *is there* in my blood,
When I go down to the pit?
Will the dust praise You?
Will it declare Your truth?
10 Hear, O Lord, and have mercy on me;
Lord, be my helper!"

11 You have turned for me my mourning into dancing;
You have put off my sackcloth and clothed me with gladness,

SECURITY

30:6-7 Prosperity had made David feel invincible. Although he knew his riches and power had come from God, they had gone to his head, making him proud. Wealth, power, and fame have an intoxicating effect on people, making them feel self-reliant, self-secure, and independent of God. But this is a false security that is shattered easily. Don't be trapped by the false security of prosperity. Depend on God for your security and you won't be shaken when worldly possessions disappear.

12 To the end that *my* glory may sing praise to You and not be silent.
O Lord my God, I will give thanks to You forever.

PSALM **31** BELIEVE, NO MATTER WHAT. *To the Chief Musician. A Psalm of David.*

1 In You, O Lord, I put my trust;
Let me never be ashamed;
Deliver me in Your righteousness.
2 Bow down Your ear to me,
Deliver me speedily;
Be my rock of refuge,
A fortress of defense to save me.

3 For You *are* my rock and my fortress;
Therefore, for Your name's sake,
Lead me and guide me.
4 Pull me out of the net which they have secretly laid for me,
For You *are* my strength.
5 Into Your hand I commit my spirit;
You have redeemed me, O Lord God of truth.

6 I have hated those who regard useless idols;
But I trust in the Lord.
7 I will be glad and rejoice in Your mercy,
For You have considered my trouble;
You have known my soul in adversities,
8 And have not shut me up into the hand of the enemy;
You have set my feet in a wide place.

9 Have mercy on me, O Lord, for I am in trouble;
My eye wastes away with grief,
Yes, my soul and my body!
10 For my life is spent with grief,

And my years with sighing;
My strength fails because of my iniquity,
And my bones waste away.
11 I am a reproach among all my enemies,
But especially among my neighbors,
And *am* repulsive to my acquaintances;
Those who see me outside flee from me.
12 I am forgotten like a dead man, out of mind;
I am like a broken vessel.
13 For I hear the slander of many;
Fear *is* on every side;
While they take counsel together against me,
They scheme to take away my life.

◣▬▬BELIEVING

33:4 A person's words are measured by the quality of his or her character. If your friends trust what you say, it is because they trust you. If you trust what God says, it is because you trust him to be the God he claims to be. If you doubt his words, you doubt the integrity of God himself. If you believe that God is truly God, then believe what he says!

14 But as for me, I trust in You, O LORD;
I say, "You *are* my God."
15 My times *are* in Your hand;
Deliver me from the hand of my enemies,
And from those who persecute me.
16 Make Your face shine upon Your servant;
Save me for Your mercies' sake.
17 Do not let me be ashamed, O LORD, for I have called upon You;
Let the wicked be ashamed;
Let them be silent in the grave.
18 Let the lying lips be put to silence,
Which speak insolent things proudly and
contemptuously against the righteous.

19 Oh, how great *is* Your goodness,
Which You have laid up for those who fear You,
Which You have prepared for those who trust in You
In the presence of the sons of men!
20 You shall hide them in the secret place of Your
presence
From the plots of man;
You shall keep them secretly in a pavilion
From the strife of tongues.

21 Blessed *be* the LORD,
For He has shown me His marvelous kindness in a
strong city!
22 For I said in my haste,
"I am cut off from before Your eyes";
Nevertheless You heard the voice of my supplications
When I cried out to You.

23 Oh, love the LORD, all you His saints!
For the LORD preserves the faithful,
And fully repays the proud person.
24 Be of good courage,
And He shall strengthen your heart,
All you who hope in the LORD.

PSALM **32** GOD FORGIVES. *A Psalm of David.*
A Contemplation.

1 Blessed *is he whose* transgression *is* forgiven,
Whose sin *is* covered.
2 Blessed *is* the man to whom the LORD does not
impute iniquity,
And in whose spirit *there is* no deceit.

3 When I kept silent, my bones grew old
Through my groaning all the day long.
4 For day and night Your hand was heavy upon me;
My vitality was turned into the drought of summer.
Selah

5 I acknowledged my sin to You,
And my iniquity I have not hidden.
I said, "I will confess my transgressions to the LORD,"
And You forgave the iniquity of my sin. Selah

6 For this cause everyone who is godly shall pray to
You
In a time when You may be found;
Surely in a flood of great waters
They shall not come near him.
7 You *are* my hiding place;
You shall preserve me from trouble;
You shall surround me with songs of deliverance.
Selah

8 I will instruct you and teach you in the way you
should go;
I will guide you with My eye.
9 Do not be like the horse *or* like the mule,
Which have no understanding,
Which must be harnessed with bit and bridle,
Else they will not come near you.

10 Many sorrows *shall be* to the wicked;
But he who trusts in the LORD, mercy shall surround
him.
11 Be glad in the LORD and rejoice, you righteous;
And shout for joy, all *you* upright in heart!

PSALM **33** WHO IS IN CHARGE?

1 Rejoice in the LORD, O you righteous!
For praise from the upright is beautiful.
2 Praise the LORD with the harp;
Make melody to Him with an instrument of ten
strings.
3 Sing to Him a new song;
Play skillfully with a shout of joy.

4 For the word of the LORD *is* right,
And all His work *is done* in truth.
5 He loves righteousness and justice;
The earth is full of the goodness of the LORD.

6 By the word of the LORD the heavens were made,
And all the host of them by the breath of His mouth.
7 He gathers the waters of the sea together as a heap;
He lays up the deep in storehouses.

8 Let all the earth fear the LORD;
Let all the inhabitants of the world stand in awe of
Him.

9 For He spoke, and it was *done;*
He commanded, and it stood fast.

10 The LORD brings the counsel of the nations to
nothing;
He makes the plans of the peoples of no effect.

11 The counsel of the LORD stands forever,
The plans of His heart to all generations.

12 Blessed *is* the nation whose God *is* the LORD,
The people He has chosen as His own inheritance.

13 The LORD looks from heaven;
He sees all the sons of men.

14 From the place of His dwelling He looks
On all the inhabitants of the earth;

15 He fashions their hearts individually;
He considers all their works.

16 No king *is* saved by the multitude of an army;
A mighty man is not delivered by great strength.

17 A horse *is* a vain hope for safety;
Neither shall it deliver *any* by its great strength.

18 Behold, the eye of the LORD *is* on those who fear Him,
On those who hope in His mercy,

19 To deliver their soul from death,
And to keep them alive in famine.

20 Our soul waits for the LORD;
He *is* our help and our shield.

21 For our heart shall rejoice in Him,
Because we have trusted in His holy name.

22 Let Your mercy, O LORD, be upon us,
Just as we hope in You.

PSALM **34** HOW TO TRUST GOD. *A Psalm of David when he pretended madness before Abimelech, who drove him away, and he departed.*

1 I will bless the LORD at all times;
His praise *shall* continually *be* in
my mouth.

2 My soul shall make its boast in
the LORD;
The humble shall hear *of it* and
be glad.

3 Oh, magnify the LORD with me,
And let us exalt His name
together.

4 I sought the LORD, and He heard
me,
And delivered me from all my
fears.

5 They looked to Him and were
radiant,
And their faces were not ashamed.

6 This poor man cried out, and the
LORD heard *him,*
And saved him out of all his
troubles.

7 The angel of the LORD encamps
all around those who fear Him,
And delivers them.

8 Oh, taste and see that the LORD *is* good;
Blessed *is* the man *who* trusts in Him!

9 Oh, fear the LORD, you His saints!
There is no want to those who fear Him.

10 The young lions lack and suffer hunger;
But those who seek the LORD shall not lack any good
thing.

11 Come, you children, listen to me;
I will teach you the fear of the LORD.

12 Who *is* the man *who* desires life,

ENOUGH

34:9-10 "Those who seek the LORD shall not lack any good *thing.*" This is not a blanket promise that all Christians will be rich. It is David's observation of God's goodness—all those who call upon God will be answered, sometimes in unexpected ways. Remember, our deepest needs are spiritual. Many Christians face unbearable poverty and hardship. David was saying that to have God is to have all that a person needs. God is enough. If you feel you don't have everything you need, ask yourself: (1) Is this really a need? (2) Is this really good for me? (3) Is this the best time for me to have what I desire? Even if you answer yes to all three questions, God may allow you to go without to help you grow more dependent on him. We may need to learn that we need *him* more than those things.

And loves *many* days, that he may see good?

13 Keep your tongue from evil,
And your lips from speaking deceit.

14 Depart from evil and do good;
Seek peace and pursue it.

15 The eyes of the LORD *are* on the righteous,
And His ears *are* open to their cry.

"Here's what I did..."

There are two Scriptures that sustain me daily. Because I have a disease called Epstein–Barr, I am always fatigued and often in pain. Psalm 34 reminds me that I can rely on God constantly for every ounce of strength I need, and it reminds me that God does hear the cry of those who are trusting him. I rely on these verses constantly for the "now" of every day.

Jeremiah 29:11 is my source of hope for the future. It reminds me that my constant worry about college and about ever getting over my illness is totally unnecessary; everything that happens is part of God's plan for my life. His plan is for good, not evil, and he intends to give me a future and a hope. He truly will take care of everything as I trust him.

I have memorized these passages, and I remind myself of the words whenever I need to—which is almost every day! They are a great source of comfort to me.

Anita AGE 17

16 The face of the LORD *is* against those who do evil,
To cut off the remembrance of them from the earth.
17 *The righteous* cry out, and the LORD hears,
And delivers them out of all their troubles.
18 The LORD *is* near to those who have a broken heart,
And saves such as have a contrite spirit.
19 Many *are* the afflictions of the righteous,
But the LORD delivers him out of them all.
20 He guards all his bones;
Not one of them is broken.
21 Evil shall slay the wicked,
And those who hate the righteous shall be
condemned.
22 The LORD redeems the soul of His servants,
And none of those who trust in Him shall be
condemned.

PSALM 35 WHEN PEOPLE AREN'T FAIR. *A Psalm of David.*

1 Plead *my cause,* O LORD, with those who strive with
me;
Fight against those who fight against me.
2 Take hold of shield and buckler,
And stand up for my help.
3 Also draw out the spear,
And stop those who pursue me.
Say to my soul,
"I *am* your salvation."

4 Let those be put to shame and brought to dishonor
Who seek after my life;
Let those be turned back and brought to confusion
Who plot my hurt.
5 Let them be like chaff before the wind,
And let the angel of the LORD chase *them.*
6 Let their way be dark and slippery,
And let the angel of the LORD pursue them.
7 For without cause they have hidden their net for me
in a pit,
Which they have dug without cause for my life.
8 Let destruction come upon him unexpectedly,
And let his net that he has hidden catch himself;
Into that very destruction let him fall.

9 And my soul shall be joyful in the LORD;
It shall rejoice in His salvation.
10 All my bones shall say,
"LORD, who *is* like You,
Delivering the poor from him who is too strong for
him,
Yes, the poor and the needy from him who plunders
him?"

11 Fierce witnesses rise up;
They ask me *things* that I do not know.
12 They reward me evil for good,
To the sorrow of my soul.
13 But as for me, when they were sick,
My clothing *was* sackcloth;
I humbled myself with fasting;
And my prayer would return to my own heart.

14 I paced about as though *he were* my friend *or*
brother;
I bowed down heavily, as one who mourns *for his*
mother.
15 But in my adversity they rejoiced
And gathered together;
Attackers gathered against me,
And I did not know *it;*
They tore *at me* and did not cease;
16 With ungodly mockers at feasts
They gnashed at me with their teeth.

17 Lord, how long will You look on?
Rescue me from their destructions,
My precious *life* from the lions.
18 I will give You thanks in the great assembly;
I will praise You among many people.

19 Let them not rejoice over me who are wrongfully my
enemies;
Nor let them wink with the eye who hate me without
a cause.
20 For they do not speak peace,
But they devise deceitful matters
Against *the* quiet ones in the land.
21 They also opened their mouth wide against me,
And said, "Aha, aha!
Our eyes have seen *it.*"

22 *This* You have seen, O LORD;
Do not keep silence.
O Lord, do not be far from me.
23 Stir up Yourself, and awake to my vindication,
To my cause, my God and my Lord.
24 Vindicate me, O LORD my God, according to Your
righteousness;
And let them not rejoice over me.
25 Let them not say in their hearts, "Ah, so we would
have it!"
Let them not say, "We have swallowed him up."

26 Let them be ashamed and brought to mutual confusion
Who rejoice at my hurt;
Let them be clothed with shame and dishonor
Who exalt themselves against me.

27 Let them shout for joy and be glad,
Who favor my righteous cause;
And let them say continually,
"Let the LORD be magnified,
Who has pleasure in the prosperity of His servant."
28 And my tongue shall speak of Your righteousness
And of Your praise all the day long.

PSALM 36 GOD'S GOODNESS IS GREAT. *To the Chief Musician. A Psalm of David the servant of the LORD.*

1 An oracle within my heart concerning the
transgression of the wicked:
There is no fear of God before his eyes.
2 For he flatters himself in his own eyes,
When he finds out his iniquity *and* when he hates.
3 The words of his mouth *are* wickedness and deceit;

He has ceased to be wise *and* to do good.
4 He devises wickedness on his bed;
He sets himself in a way *that is* not good;
He does not abhor evil.

5 Your mercy, O LORD, *is* in the heavens;
Your faithfulness *reaches* to the clouds.
6 Your righteousness *is* like the great mountains;
Your judgments *are* a great deep;
O LORD, You preserve man and beast.

7 How precious *is* Your lovingkindness, O God!
Therefore the children of men put their trust under
the shadow of Your wings.
8 They are abundantly satisfied with the fullness of
Your house,
And You give them drink from the river of Your
pleasures.
9 For with You *is* the fountain of life;
In Your light we see light.

10 Oh, continue Your lovingkindness to those who
know You,
And Your righteousness to the upright in heart.
11 Let not the foot of pride come against me,
And let not the hand of the wicked drive me away.
12 There the workers of iniquity have fallen;
They have been cast down and are not able to rise.

PSALM **37** KEEP DOING GOOD. *A Psalm of David.*

1 Do not fret because of evildoers,
Nor be envious of the workers of iniquity.
2 For they shall soon be cut down like the grass,
And wither as the green herb.

3 Trust in the LORD, and do good;
Dwell in the land, and feed on His faithfulness.
4 Delight yourself also in the LORD,
And He shall give you the desires of your heart.

5 Commit your way to the LORD,
Trust also in Him,
And He shall bring *it* to pass.
6 He shall bring forth your righteousness as the light,
And your justice as the noonday.

7 Rest in the LORD, and wait patiently for Him;
Do not fret because of him who prospers in his way,
Because of the man who brings wicked schemes to
pass.
8 Cease from anger, and forsake wrath;
Do not fret—*it* only *causes* harm.

9 For evildoers shall be cut off;
But those who wait on the LORD,
They shall inherit the earth.
10 For yet a little while and the wicked *shall be* no *more;*
Indeed, you will look carefully for his place,
But it *shall be* no *more.*
11 But the meek shall inherit the earth,
And shall delight themselves in the abundance of
peace.

12 The wicked plots against the just,

And gnashes at him with his teeth.
13 The Lord laughs at him,
For He sees that his day is coming.
14 The wicked have drawn the sword
And have bent their bow,
To cast down the poor and needy,
To slay those who are of upright conduct.
15 Their sword shall enter their own heart,
And their bows shall be broken.

16 A little that a righteous man has
Is better than the riches of many wicked.
17 For the arms of the wicked shall be broken,
But the LORD upholds the righteous.

18 The LORD knows the days of the upright,
And their inheritance shall be forever.
19 They shall not be ashamed in the evil time,

◀━━━━━━━━━━**TREASURE**

37:1 We should never envy the popularity or wealth of the wicked. No matter how much they have, it will fade and vanish like grass that withers and dies. Those who follow God live in a different manner than the wicked. And in the end, the godly will have far greater treasures in heaven. What the unbeliever gets lasts a lifetime, if he is lucky. What you get from following God lasts an eternity.

And in the days of famine they shall be satisfied.
20 But the wicked shall perish;
And the enemies of the LORD,
Like the splendor of the meadows, shall vanish.
Into smoke they shall vanish away.

21 The wicked borrows and does not repay,
But the righteous shows mercy and gives.
22 For *those* blessed by Him shall inherit the earth,
But *those* cursed by Him shall be cut off.

23 The steps of a *good* man are ordered by the LORD,
And He delights in his way.
24 Though he fall, he shall not be utterly cast down;
For the LORD upholds *him with* His hand.

25 I have been young, and *now* am old;
Yet I have not seen the righteous forsaken,
Nor his descendants begging bread.
26 *He is* ever merciful, and lends;
And his descendants *are* blessed.

27 Depart from evil, and do good;
And dwell forevermore.
28 For the LORD loves justice,
And does not forsake His saints;
They are preserved forever,
But the descendants of the wicked shall be cut off.
29 The righteous shall inherit the land,
And dwell in it forever.

30 The mouth of the righteous speaks wisdom,
And his tongue talks of justice.
31 The law of his God *is* in his heart;
None of his steps shall slide.

32 The wicked watches the righteous,

And seeks to slay him.
33 The LORD will not leave him in his hand,
Nor condemn him when he is judged.

34 Wait on the LORD,
And keep His way,
And He shall exalt you to inherit the land;
When the wicked are cut off, you shall see *it*.
35 I have seen the wicked in great power,
And spreading himself like a native green tree.
36 Yet he passed away, and behold, he *was* no *more*;
Indeed I sought him, but he could not be found.
37 Mark the blameless *man*, and observe the upright;
For the future of *that* man *is* peace.
38 But the transgressors shall be destroyed together;
The future of the wicked shall be cut off.

ON THE EDGE

38:17 In David's confession of sin, he acknowledged that he was *constantly* on the verge of sin. No matter how hard we try to follow God, we are sinners by nature and we often sin. It is difficult to escape situations in which we are tempted. We stand on the verge of sin as if we are walking along the edge of a cliff and could fall at any moment. Those who think they are beyond sin are sure to fall. Therefore, the first step toward avoiding sin is to acknowledge our tendency to sin. Only then will we be ready to say no.

39 But the salvation of the righteous *is* from the LORD;
He is their strength in the time of trouble.
40 And the LORD shall help them and deliver them;
He shall deliver them from the wicked,
And save them,
Because they trust in Him.

PSALM 38 CONFESSING OUR SIN. *A Psalm of David. To bring to remembrance.*

1 O LORD, do not rebuke me in Your wrath,
Nor chasten me in Your hot displeasure!
2 For Your arrows pierce me deeply,
And Your hand presses me down.

3 *There is* no soundness in my flesh
Because of Your anger,
Nor *any* health in my bones
Because of my sin.
4 For my iniquities have gone over my head;
Like a heavy burden they are too heavy for me.
5 My wounds are foul *and* festering
Because of my foolishness.

6 I am troubled, I am bowed down greatly;
I go mourning all the day long.
7 For my loins are full of inflammation,
And *there is* no soundness in my flesh.
8 I am feeble and severely broken;
I groan because of the turmoil of my heart.

9 Lord, all my desire *is* before You;
And my sighing is not hidden from You.
10 My heart pants, my strength fails me;
As for the light of my eyes, it also has gone from me.

11 My loved ones and my friends stand aloof from my
plague,
And my relatives stand afar off.
12 Those also who seek my life lay snares *for me*;
Those who seek my hurt speak of destruction,
And plan deception all the day long.

13 But I, like a deaf *man*, do not hear;
And *I am* like a mute *who* does not open his mouth.
14 Thus I am like a man who does not hear,
And in whose mouth *is* no response.

15 For in You, O LORD, I hope;
You will hear, O Lord my God.
16 For I said, *"Hear me,* lest they rejoice over me,
Lest, when my foot slips, they exalt *themselves*
against me."

17 For I *am* ready to fall,
And my sorrow *is* continually before me.
18 For I will declare my iniquity;
I will be in anguish over my sin.
19 But my enemies *are* vigorous, *and* they are strong;
And those who hate me wrongfully have multiplied.
20 Those also who render evil for good,
They are my adversaries, because I follow *what is*
good.

21 Do not forsake me, O LORD;
O my God, be not far from me!
22 Make haste to help me,
O Lord, my salvation!

PSALM 39 SO WHAT'S IMPORTANT? *To the Chief Musician. To Jeduthun. A Psalm of David.*

1 I said, "I will guard my ways,
Lest I sin with my tongue;
I will restrain my mouth with a muzzle,
While the wicked are before me."
2 I was mute with silence,
I held my peace *even* from good;
And my sorrow was stirred up.
3 My heart was hot within me;
While I was musing, the fire burned.
Then I spoke with my tongue:

4 "LORD, make me to know my end,
And what *is* the measure of my days,
That I may know how frail I *am*.
5 Indeed, You have made my days *as* handbreadths,
And my age *is* as nothing before You;
Certainly every man at his best state *is* but vapor.
Selah

6 Surely every man walks about like a shadow;

LIFE

39:4 Life is short no matter how long we live. If there is something important we want to do, we must not put it off for a better day. Ask yourself, "If I had only six months to live, what would I do?" Tell someone that you love him or her? Deal with an undisciplined area of your life? Tell someone about Jesus? Life is short—don't neglect what truly important.

Surely they busy themselves in vain;
He heaps up *riches,*
And does not know who will gather them.
7 "And now, Lord, what do I wait for?
My hope *is* in You.
8 Deliver me from all my transgressions;
Do not make me the reproach of the foolish.
9 I was mute, I did not open my mouth,
Because it was You who did *it.*
10 Remove Your plague from me;
I am consumed by the blow of Your hand.
11 When with rebukes You correct man for iniquity,
You make his beauty melt away like a moth;
Surely every man *is* vapor.   Selah

12 "Hear my prayer, O LORD,
And give ear to my cry;
Do not be silent at my tears;
For I *am* a stranger with You,
A sojourner, as all my fathers *were.*
13 Remove Your gaze from me, that I may regain
strength,
Before I go away and am no more."

PSALM **40** OBEYING BY WAITING. *To the Chief Musician. A Psalm of David.*

1 I waited patiently for the LORD;
And He inclined to me,
And heard my cry.
2 He also brought me up out of a horrible pit,
Out of the miry clay,
And set my feet upon a rock,
And established my steps.
3 He has put a new song in my mouth—
Praise to our God;
Many will see *it* and fear,
And will trust in the LORD.

4 Blessed *is* that man who makes the LORD his trust,
And does not respect the proud, nor such as turn
aside to lies.
5 Many, O LORD my God, *are* Your wonderful works
Which You have done;
And Your thoughts toward us
Cannot be recounted to You in order;
If I would declare and speak *of them,*
They are more than can be numbered.

6 Sacrifice and offering You did not desire;
My ears You have opened.
Burnt offering and sin offering You did not require.
7 Then I said, "Behold, I come;
In the scroll of the book *it is* written of me.
8 I delight to do Your will, O my God,
And Your law *is* within my heart."

9 I have proclaimed the good news of righteousness
In the great assembly;
Indeed, I do not restrain my lips,
O LORD, You Yourself know.
10 I have not hidden Your righteousness within my
heart;

I have declared Your faithfulness and Your salvation;
I have not concealed Your lovingkindness and Your
truth
From the great assembly.
11 Do not withhold Your tender mercies from me,
O LORD;
Let Your lovingkindness and Your truth continually
preserve me.
12 For innumerable evils have surrounded me;
My iniquities have overtaken me, so that I am not
able to look up;
They are more than the hairs of my head;
Therefore my heart fails me.
13 Be pleased, O LORD, to deliver me;
O LORD, make haste to help me!
14 Let them be ashamed and brought to mutual
confusion
Who seek to destroy my life;
Let them be driven backward and brought to
dishonor
Who wish me evil.
15 Let them be confounded because of their shame,
Who say to me, "Aha, aha!"
16 Let all those who seek You rejoice and be glad in You;
Let such as love Your salvation say continually,
"The LORD be magnified!"
17 But I *am* poor and needy;
Yet the LORD thinks upon me.
You *are* my help and my deliverer;
Do not delay, O my God.

PSALM **41** GOD: THE ONLY TRUE FRIEND. *To the Chief Musician. A Psalm of David.*

1 Blessed *is* he who considers the poor;
The LORD will deliver him in time of trouble.
2 The LORD will preserve him and keep him alive,
And he will be blessed on the earth;
You will not deliver him to the will of his enemies.
3 The LORD will strengthen him on his bed of illness;
You will sustain him on his sickbed.

4 I said, "LORD, be merciful to me;
Heal my soul, for I have sinned against You."
5 My enemies speak evil of me:
"When will he die, and his name perish?"
6 And if he comes to see *me,* he speaks lies;
His heart gathers iniquity to itself;
When he goes out, he tells *it.*
7 All who hate me whisper together against me;
Against me they devise my hurt.
8 "An evil disease," *they say,* "clings to him.
And *now* that he lies down, he will rise up no more."
9 Even my own familiar friend in whom I trusted,
Who ate my bread,
Has lifted up *his* heel against me.

10 But You, O LORD, be merciful to me, and raise me up,
That I may repay them.
11 By this I know that You are well pleased with me,

Because my enemy does not triumph over me.
12 As for me, You uphold me in my integrity,
And set me before Your face forever.

13 Blessed *be* the LORD God of Israel
From everlasting to everlasting!
Amen and Amen.

BOOK TWO: Psalms 42–72

PSALM 42 WHY AM I SO SAD? *To the Chief Musician. A Contemplation of the sons of Korah.*

1 As the deer pants for the water brooks,
So pants my soul for You, O God.
2 My soul thirsts for God, for the living God.
When shall I come and appear before God?
3 My tears have been my food day and night,
While they continually say to me,
"Where *is* your God?"

4 When I remember these *things,*
I pour out my soul within me.
For I used to go with the multitude;
I went with them to the house of God,
With the voice of joy and praise,
With a multitude that kept a pilgrim feast.

5 Why are you cast down, O my soul?
And *why* are you disquieted within me?
Hope in God, for I shall yet praise Him
For the help of His countenance.

6 O my God, my soul is cast down within me;
Therefore I will remember You from the land of the
Jordan,
And from the heights of Hermon,
From the Hill Mizar.
7 Deep calls unto deep at the noise of Your waterfalls;
All Your waves and billows have gone over me.
8 The LORD will command His lovingkindness in the
daytime,
And in the night His song *shall be* with me—
A prayer to the God of my life.

9 I will say to God my Rock,
"Why have You forgotten me?
Why do I go mourning because of the oppression of
the enemy?"
10 *As* with a breaking of my bones,
My enemies reproach me,
While they say to me all day long,
"Where *is* your God?"

11 Why are you cast down, O my soul?
And why are you disquieted within me?
Hope in God;
For I shall yet praise Him,
The help of my countenance and my God.

PSALM 43 GOD MAKES ME SMILE AGAIN.

1 Vindicate me, O God,
And plead my cause against an ungodly nation;
Oh, deliver me from the deceitful and unjust man!

2 For You *are* the God of my strength;
Why do You cast me off?
Why do I go mourning because of the oppression of
the enemy?

3 Oh, send out Your light and Your truth!
Let them lead me;
Let them bring me to Your holy hill
And to Your tabernacle.
4 Then I will go to the altar of God,
To God my exceeding joy;
And on the harp I will praise You,
O God, my God.

◀~~~~ DEPRESSION

42:6 Depression is one of the most common emotional ailments.
cure for depression is to meditate on the record of God's goodness
people. This will take your mind off the present situation and give
that it will improve. It will focus your thoughts on God's ability to h
you rather than on your inability to help yourself. When you feel
depressed, take advantage of this psalm's antidepressant. Read the
Bible's accounts of God's goodness and meditate on them.

5 Why are you cast down, O my soul?
And why are you disquieted within me?
Hope in God;
For I shall yet praise Him,
The help of my countenance and my God.

PSALM 44 GOD ALONE CAN SAVE US. *To the Chief Musician. A Contemplation of the sons of Korah.*

1 We have heard with our ears, O God,
Our fathers have told us,
The deeds You did in their days,
In days of old:
2 You drove out the nations with Your hand,
But them You planted;
You afflicted the peoples, and cast them out.
3 For they did not gain possession of the land by their
own sword,
Nor did their own arm save them;
But it was Your right hand, Your arm, and the light of
Your countenance,
Because You favored them.

4 You are my King, O God;
Command victories for Jacob.
5 Through You we will push down our enemies;
Through Your name we will trample those who rise
up against us.
6 For I will not trust in my bow,
Nor shall my sword save me.
7 But You have saved us from our enemies,
And have put to shame those who hated us.
8 In God we boast all day long,
And praise Your name forever.   Selah

9 But You have cast *us* off and put us to shame,
And You do not go out with our armies.
10 You make us turn back from the enemy,

And those who hate us have taken spoil for
themselves.
11 You have given us up like sheep *intended* for food,
And have scattered us among the nations.
12 You sell Your people for *next to* nothing,
And are not enriched by selling them.

13 You make us a reproach to our neighbors,
A scorn and a derision to those all around us.
14 You make us a byword among the nations,
A shaking of the head among the peoples.
15 My dishonor *is* continually before me,
And the shame of my face has covered me,
16 Because of the voice of him who reproaches and
reviles,
Because of the enemy and the
avenger.

17 All this has come upon us;
But we have not forgotten You,
Nor have we dealt falsely with
Your covenant.
18 Our heart has not turned back,
Nor have our steps departed from
Your way;
19 But You have severely broken us
in the place of jackals,
And covered us with the shadow
of death.

20 If we had forgotten the name of
our God,
Or stretched out our hands to a
foreign god,
21 Would not God search this out?
For He knows the secrets of the
heart.
22 Yet for Your sake we are killed all
day long;
We are accounted as sheep for the
slaughter.

23 Awake! Why do You sleep, O Lord?
Arise! Do not cast *us* off forever.
24 Why do You hide Your face,
And forget our affliction and our
oppression?
25 For our soul is bowed down to the
dust;
Our body clings to the ground.
26 Arise for our help,
And redeem us for Your mercies' sake.

PSALM **45** THE KING'S WEDDING. *To the Chief Musician. Set to "The Lilies." A Contemplation of the sons of Korah. A Song of Love.*

1 My heart is overflowing with a good theme;
I recite my composition concerning the King;
My tongue *is* the pen of a ready writer.

2 You are fairer than the sons of men;
Grace is poured upon Your lips;
Therefore God has blessed You forever.

3 Gird Your sword upon *Your* thigh, O Mighty One,
With Your glory and Your majesty.
4 And in Your majesty ride prosperously because of
truth, humility, *and* righteousness;
And Your right hand shall teach You awesome things.
5 Your arrows *are* sharp in the heart of the King's
enemies;
The peoples fall under You.

6 Your throne, O God, *is* forever and ever;
A scepter of righteousness *is* the scepter of Your
kingdom.
7 You love righteousness and hate wickedness;
Therefore God, Your God, has anointed You
With the oil of gladness more than Your companions.

"Here's what I did..."

Everything was going wrong in my life. My parents were getting a divorce. My boyfriend broke up with me. I couldn't concentrate in school, so my grades started going down.

It began to affect my faith. I couldn't understand why God was letting all this happen to me. When I prayed, I felt like I was talking to myself. I guess I was mad at God, blaming him in my heart for the things that were happening.

I tried to read the Bible anyway, even though I was struggling spiritually. One day I read Psalm 46. Verse 10 really made me stop and think. This verse seemed to say, "Stop looking at your problems and look at me. Look at who I am." I realized God was in charge—he knew exactly what he was doing and had a purpose in mind for what I was going through. I just needed to accept it and believe he is a loving God who would never do a thing to hurt me.

That changed my perspective. Instead of blaming God, I asked him to help me through my struggles. And he has. Things are still rough sometimes, but now I know that God is for me, and he will work things out for good. As Romans 8:31 says, "If God *is* for us, who *can be* against us?"

Jodi AGE 17

8 All Your garments are scented with myrrh and aloes
and cassia,
Out of the ivory palaces, by which they have made
You glad.
9 Kings' daughters *are* among Your honorable women;
At Your right hand stands the queen in gold from
Ophir.

DELIVERED

44:22-26 The writer cried to God to save his people by his constant love—they "are accounted as sheep for the slaughter." Nothing can separate us from God's love, not even death (Romans 8:36-39). When you fear for your life, ask God for deliverance and remember that even physical death cannot separate you from him.

¹⁰ Listen, O daughter,
Consider and incline your ear;
Forget your own people also, and your father's house;
¹¹ So the King will greatly desire your beauty;
Because He *is* your Lord, worship Him.
¹² And the daughter of Tyre *will come* with a gift;
The rich among the people will seek your favor.

¹³ The royal daughter *is* all glorious within *the palace;*
Her clothing *is* woven with gold.
¹⁴ She shall be brought to the King in robes of many colors;
The virgins, her companions who follow her, shall be brought to You.
¹⁵ With gladness and rejoicing they shall be brought;
They shall enter the King's palace.

¹⁶ Instead of Your fathers shall be Your sons,
Whom You shall make princes in all the earth.
¹⁷ I will make Your name to be remembered in all generations;
Therefore the people shall praise You forever and ever.

PSALM 46 GOD IS ON OUR SIDE. *To the Chief Musician. A Psalm of the sons of Korah. A Song for Alamoth.*

¹ God *is* our refuge and strength,
A very present help in trouble.

◢◣◢◣ CONFIDENCE

46:1-3 The fear of mountains or cities suddenly crumbling into the sea by a nuclear blast haunts many people today. But the psalmist says that even if the world ends, "We will not fear." Even in the face of utter destruction, he expressed a quiet confidence in God's ability to save him. It seems impossible to face the end of the world without fear, but the Bible is clear: God is our eternal refuge, even in the face of total destruction.

² Therefore we will not fear,
Even though the earth be removed,
And though the mountains be carried into the midst of the sea;
³ *Though* its waters roar *and* be troubled,
Though the mountains shake with its swelling. Selah

⁴ *There is* a river whose streams shall make glad the city of God,
The holy *place* of the tabernacle of the Most High.
⁵ God *is* in the midst of her, she shall not be moved;
God shall help her, just at the break of dawn.
⁶ The nations raged, the kingdoms were moved;
He uttered His voice, the earth melted.

⁷ The LORD of hosts *is* with us;
The God of Jacob *is* our refuge. Selah

⁸ Come, behold the works of the LORD,
Who has made desolations in the earth.
⁹ He makes wars cease to the end of the earth;
He breaks the bow and cuts the spear in two;

He burns the chariot in the fire.

¹⁰ Be still, and know that I *am* God;
I will be exalted among the nations,
I will be exalted in the earth!

¹¹ The LORD of hosts *is* with us;
The God of Jacob *is* our refuge. Selah

PSALM 47 GOD IS THE GREAT KING. *To the Chief Musician. A Psalm of the sons of Korah.*

¹ Oh, clap your hands, all you peoples!
Shout to God with the voice of triumph!
² For the LORD Most High *is* awesome;
He is a great King over all the earth.
³ He will subdue the peoples under us,
And the nations under our feet.
⁴ He will choose our inheritance for us,
The excellence of Jacob whom He loves. Selah

⁵ God has gone up with a shout,
The LORD with the sound of a trumpet.
⁶ Sing praises to God, sing praises!
Sing praises to our King, sing praises!
⁷ For God *is* the King of all the earth;
Sing praises with understanding.

⁸ God reigns over the nations;
God sits on His holy throne.
⁹ The princes of the people have gathered together,
The people of the God of Abraham.
For the shields of the earth *belong* to God;
He is greatly exalted.

PSALM 48 GOD PROTECTS JERUSALEM. *A Song. A Psalm of the sons of Korah.*

¹ Great *is* the LORD, and greatly to be praised
In the city of our God,
In His holy mountain.
² Beautiful in elevation,
The joy of the whole earth,
Is Mount Zion *on* the sides of the north,
The city of the great King.
³ God *is* in her palaces;
He is known as her refuge.

⁴ For behold, the kings assembled,
They passed by together.
⁵ They saw *it, and* so they marveled;
They were troubled, they hastened away.
⁶ Fear took hold of them there,
And pain, as of a woman in birth pangs,
⁷ *As when* You break the ships of Tarshish
With an east wind.

⁸ As we have heard,
So we have seen
In the city of the LORD of hosts,
In the city of our God:
God will establish it forever. Selah

⁹ We have thought, O God, on Your lovingkindness,
In the midst of Your temple.

¹⁰ According to Your name, O God,
So *is* Your praise to the ends of the earth;
Your right hand is full of righteousness.
¹¹ Let Mount Zion rejoice,
Let the daughters of Judah be glad,
Because of Your judgments.

¹² Walk about Zion,
And go all around her.
Count her towers;
¹³ Mark well her bulwarks;
Consider her palaces;
That you may tell *it* to the generation following.
¹⁴ For this *is* God,
Our God forever and ever;
He will be our guide
Even to death.

PSALM **49** MONEY CAN'T SAVE YOU. *To the Chief Musician. A Psalm of the sons of Korah.*
¹ Hear this, all peoples;
Give ear, all inhabitants of the world,
² Both low and high,
Rich and poor together.
³ My mouth shall speak wisdom,
And the meditation of my heart *shall give* understanding.
⁴ I will incline my ear to a proverb;
I will disclose my dark saying on the harp.

⁵ Why should I fear in the days of evil,
When the iniquity at my heels surrounds me?
⁶ Those who trust in their wealth
And boast in the multitude of their riches,
⁷ None *of them* can by any means redeem *his* brother,
Nor give to God a ransom for him—
⁸ For the redemption of their souls *is* costly,
And it shall cease forever—
⁹ That he should continue to live eternally,
And not see the Pit.

¹⁰ For he sees wise men die;
Likewise the fool and the senseless person perish,
And leave their wealth to others.
¹¹ Their inner thought *is that* their houses *will last* forever,
Their dwelling places to all generations;
They call *their* lands after their own names.
¹² Nevertheless man, *though* in honor, does not remain;
He is like the beasts *that* perish.

¹³ This is the way of those who *are* foolish,
And of their posterity who approve their sayings. *Selah*
¹⁴ Like sheep they are laid in the grave;
Death shall feed on them;
The upright shall have dominion over them in the morning;
And their beauty shall be consumed in the grave, far from their dwelling.

¹⁵ But God will redeem my soul from the power of the grave,
For He shall receive me. *Selah*

¹⁶ Do not be afraid when one becomes rich,
When the glory of his house is increased;
¹⁷ For when he dies he shall carry nothing away;
His glory shall not descend after him.

THE MAP

48:14 We often pray for God's guidance as we struggle with decisions. What we need is both guidance and a guide—a map that gives us landmarks and directions and a constant companion who has an intimate knowledge of the way and will make sure we interpret the map correctly. The Bible is just such a map, and God is our constant companion and guide. Lean upon both the map and the Guide.

¹⁸ Though while he lives he blesses himself
(For *men* will praise you when you do well for yourself),
¹⁹ He shall go to the generation of his fathers;
They shall never see light.
²⁰ A man *who is* in honor, yet does not understand,
Is like the beasts *that* perish.

PSALM **50** GOD WANTS OUR TRUE THANKS. *A Psalm of Asaph.*
¹ The Mighty One, God the LORD,
Has spoken and called the earth
From the rising of the sun to its going down.
² Out of Zion, the perfection of beauty,
God will shine forth.
³ Our God shall come, and shall not keep silent;
A fire shall devour before Him,
And it shall be very tempestuous all around Him.

⁴ He shall call to the heavens from above,
And to the earth, that He may judge His people:
⁵ "Gather My saints together to Me,
Those who have made a covenant with Me by sacrifice."
⁶ Let the heavens declare His righteousness,
For God Himself *is* Judge. *Selah*

⁷ "Hear, O My people, and I will speak,
O Israel, and I will testify against you;
I *am* God, your God!
⁸ I will not rebuke you for your sacrifices
Or your burnt offerings,
Which are continually before Me.
⁹ I will not take a bull from your house,
Nor goats out of your folds.
¹⁰ For every beast of the forest *is* Mine,
And the cattle on a thousand hills.
¹¹ I know all the birds of the mountains,
And the wild beasts of the field *are* Mine.

¹² "If I were hungry, I would not tell you;
For the world *is* Mine, and all its fullness.
¹³ Will I eat the flesh of bulls,
Or drink the blood of goats?

¹⁴ Offer to God thanksgiving,
And pay your vows to the Most High.
¹⁵ Call upon Me in the day of trouble;
I will deliver you, and you shall glorify Me."

¹⁶ But to the wicked God says:
"What *right* have you to declare My statutes,
Or take My covenant in your mouth,

▰▰▰▰▰ VICTIMS

51:4 Although David sinned with Bathsheba, he said he had sinned against God. When someone steals, murders, or slanders, it is against someone else—a victim. According to the world's standards, sex between two "consenting adults" is acceptable because nobody "gets hurt." But people *do* get hurt—in David's case, a man was murdered and a baby died. All sin hurts us and others, and ultimately it offends God because sin in any form is a rebellion against his way of living. When tempted to do wrong, remember that you will be sinning against God. That may help you stay on the right track.

¹⁷ Seeing you hate instruction
And cast My words behind you?
¹⁸ When you saw a thief, you consented with him,
And have been a partaker with adulterers.
¹⁹ You give your mouth to evil,
And your tongue frames deceit.
²⁰ You sit *and* speak against your brother;
You slander your own mother's son.
²¹ These *things* you have done, and I kept silent;
You thought that I was altogether like you;
But I will rebuke you,
And set *them* in order before your eyes.

²² "Now consider this, you who forget God,
Lest I tear *you* in pieces,
And *there be* none to deliver:
²³ Whoever offers praise glorifies Me;
And to him who orders *his* conduct *aright*
I will show the salvation of God."

PSALM 51 A PRAYER OF FORGIVENESS. *To the Chief Musician. A Psalm of David when Nathan the prophet went to him, after he had gone in to Bathsheba.*

¹ Have mercy upon me, O God,
According to Your lovingkindness;
According to the multitude of Your tender mercies,
Blot out my transgressions.
² Wash me thoroughly from my iniquity,
And cleanse me from my sin.

³ For I acknowledge my transgressions,
And my sin *is* always before me.
⁴ Against You, You only, have I sinned,
And done *this* evil in Your sight—
That You may be found just when You speak,
And blameless when You judge.

⁵ Behold, I was brought forth in iniquity,
And in sin my mother conceived me.
⁶ Behold, You desire truth in the inward parts,

And in the hidden *part* You will make me to know wisdom.

⁷ Purge me with hyssop, and I shall be clean;
Wash me, and I shall be whiter than snow.
⁸ Make me hear joy and gladness,
That the bones You have broken may rejoice.
⁹ Hide Your face from my sins,
And blot out all my iniquities.

¹⁰ Create in me a clean heart, O God,
And renew a steadfast spirit within me.
¹¹ Do not cast me away from Your presence,
And do not take Your Holy Spirit from me.

¹² Restore to me the joy of Your salvation,
And uphold me *by Your* generous Spirit.
¹³ *Then* I will teach transgressors Your ways,
And sinners shall be converted to You.

¹⁴ Deliver me from the guilt of bloodshed, O God,
The God of my salvation,
And my tongue shall sing aloud of Your righteousness.
¹⁵ O Lord, open my lips,
And my mouth shall show forth Your praise.

▰▰▰▰▰ FOOLS

53:1 Echoing the message of Psalm 14, David proclaimed that "t͏ has said in his heart, '*There is* no God'" (see also Romans 3:10). Pe͏ may say there is no God in order to cover their sin, to have an exc͏u continue in sin, and/or to ignore the Judge so they can avoid the judgment. A "fool" is not necessarily lacking intelligence; many at͏h and unbelievers are highly learned. Fools are people who reject Go͏ only one who can save them.

¹⁶ For You do not desire sacrifice, or else I would give *it*;
You do not delight in burnt offering.
¹⁷ The sacrifices of God *are* a broken spirit,
A broken and a contrite heart—
These, O God, You will not despise.

¹⁸ Do good in Your good pleasure to Zion;
Build the walls of Jerusalem.
¹⁹ Then You shall be pleased with the sacrifices of righteousness,
With burnt offering and whole burnt offering;
Then they shall offer bulls on Your altar.

PSALM 52 GOD PUNISHES THE WICKED. *To the Chief Musician. A Contemplation of David when Doeg the Edomite went and told Saul, and said to him, "David has gone to the house of Ahimelech."*

¹ Why do you boast in evil, O mighty man?
The goodness of God *endures* continually.
² Your tongue devises destruction,
Like a sharp razor, working deceitfully.
³ You love evil more than good,
Lying rather than speaking righteousness.   Selah
⁴ You love all devouring words,
You deceitful tongue.

⁵ God shall likewise destroy you forever;

He shall take you away, and pluck you out of *your* dwelling place,
And uproot you from the land of the living.   Selah
6 The righteous also shall see and fear,
And shall laugh at him, *saying,*
7 "Here is the man *who* did not make God his strength,
But trusted in the abundance of his riches,
And strengthened himself in his wickedness."

8 But I *am* like a green olive tree in the house of God;
I trust in the mercy of God forever and ever.
9 I will praise You forever,
Because You have done *it;*
And in the presence of Your saints
I will wait on Your name, for *it is* good.

PSALM **53**   SIN KEEPS US FROM GOD. *To the Chief Musician. Set to "Mahalath." A Contemplation of David.*

1 The fool has said in his heart,
" *There is* no God."
They are corrupt, and have done abominable iniquity;
There is none who does good.

2 God looks down from heaven upon the children of men,
To see if there are *any* who understand, who seek God.
3 Every one of them has turned aside;
They have together become corrupt;
There is none who does good,
No, not one.

4 Have the workers of iniquity no knowledge,
Who eat up my people *as* they eat bread,
And do not call upon God?
5 There they are in great fear
Where no fear was,
For God has scattered the bones of him who encamps against you;
You have put *them* to shame,
Because God has despised them.

6 Oh, that the salvation of Israel would come out of Zion!
When God brings back the captivity of His people,
Let Jacob rejoice *and* Israel be glad.

PSALM **54**   MY KEEPER. *To the Chief Musician. With stringed instruments. A Contemplation of David when the Ziphites went and said to Saul, "Is David not hiding with us?"*

1 Save me, O God, by Your name,
And vindicate me by Your strength.
2 Hear my prayer, O God;
Give ear to the words of my mouth.
3 For strangers have risen up against me,
And oppressors have sought after my life;
They have not set God before them.   Selah

4 Behold, God *is* my helper;

The Lord *is* with those who uphold my life.
5 He will repay my enemies for their evil.
Cut them off in Your truth.

6 I will freely sacrifice to You;
I will praise Your name, O LORD, for *it is* good.
7 For He has delivered me out of all trouble;
And my eye has seen *its desire* upon my enemies.

PSALM **55**   WHEN FRIENDS HURT US. *To the Chief Musician. With stringed instruments. A Contemplation of David.*

1 Give ear to my prayer, O God,
And do not hide Yourself from my supplication.
2 Attend to me, and hear me;
I am restless in my complaint, and moan noisily,
3 Because of the voice of the enemy,
Because of the oppression of the wicked;
For they bring down trouble upon me,

I heard something about a sin that God cannot forgive. What is it?

What you are referring to is sinning against the Holy Spirit. "Every sin and blasphemy will be forgiven men, but the blasphemy *against* the Spirit will not be forgiven men.

. . . whoever speaks against the Holy Spirit, it will not be forgiven him, either in this age or in the *age* to come" (Matthew 12:31-32).

As you read in Psalm 51, everyone is born a sinner (verse 5). Left to ourselves we certainly would die, because our sinful nature separates us from God and from life (Romans 3:23; 6:23).

The good news is God did not leave us on our own. He sent Jesus to pay the penalty for us and to die in our place. This way he killed sin forever. All who receive Christ into their life and accept his gift of forgiveness are forgiven—period (John 1:12).

The only sin that cannot be forgiven is when someone refuses to receive Christ, ignoring or rejecting the Holy Spirit's work in his or her life.

The incident that caused King David to pray the prayer in Psalm 51 is found in 2 Samuel 12:1-23. David not only committed adultery, but he had the woman's husband murdered so he could marry her! That's pretty bad behavior for anyone, let alone a king.

When confronted with his sin a year after those events, David repented. He asked God to forgive him and to renew their relationship once again.

Though David's sins were great, God forgave him. God is always willing to forgive those who admit their mistakes and who genuinely try not to repeat them.

It has been said that "the only sin God cannot forgive is the one we have not confessed."

By daily coming to God in humility, trust, and dependence, we show him that we mean business in keeping our relationship with him clean and growing.

David's prayer is the perfect example of a humble heart seeking after the only thing in life that really matters: a close relationship with God.

I WONDER . . .

And in wrath they hate me.
4 My heart is severely pained within me,
  And the terrors of death have fallen upon me.
5 Fearfulness and trembling have come upon me,
  And horror has overwhelmed me.
6 So I said, "Oh, that I had wings like a dove!
  I would fly away and be at rest.
7 Indeed, I would wander far off,
  And remain in the wilderness.   Selah
8 I would hasten my escape
  From the windy storm *and* tempest."

9 Destroy, O Lord, *and* divide their tongues,
  For I have seen violence and strife in the city.
10 Day and night they go around it on its walls;
  Iniquity and trouble *are* also in the midst of it.
11 Destruction *is* in its midst;
  Oppression and deceit do not depart from its streets.

12 For *it is* not an enemy *who* reproaches me;
  Then I could bear *it.*

◤ REAL FRIENDS

55:12-14 Nothing hurts as much as a wound from a "friend." Real friends, however, stick by you in times of trouble and bring healing, love, acceptance, and understanding. There will be times when friends lovingly confront us, but their motives will be to help. What kind of friend are you? Faithful or fickle? Don't betray those you love.

  Nor *is it* one *who* hates me who has exalted *himself*
    against me;
  Then I could hide from him.
13 But *it was* you, a man my equal,
  My companion and my acquaintance.
14 We took sweet counsel together,
  And walked to the house of God in the throng.

15 Let death seize them;
  Let them go down alive into hell,
  For wickedness *is* in their dwellings *and* among
    them.

16 As for me, I will call upon God,
  And the LORD shall save me.
17 Evening and morning and at noon
  I will pray, and cry aloud,
  And He shall hear my voice.
18 He has redeemed my soul in peace from the battle
    that was against me,
  For there were many against me.
19 God will hear, and afflict them,
  Even He who abides from of old.   Selah
  Because they do not change,
  Therefore they do not fear God.

20 He has put forth his hands against those who were
    at peace with him;
  He has broken his covenant.
21 *The words* of his mouth were smoother than butter,
  But war *was* in his heart;
  His words were softer than oil,
  Yet they *were* drawn swords.

22 Cast your burden on the LORD,
  And He shall sustain you;
  He shall never permit the righteous to be moved.
23 But You, O God, shall bring them down to the pit of
    destruction;
  Bloodthirsty and deceitful men shall not live out half
    their days;
  But I will trust in You.

PSALM 56   GOD IS ON MY SIDE. *To the Chief Musician. Set to "The Silent Dove in Distant Lands." A Michtam of David when the Philistines captured him in Gath.*

1 Be merciful to me, O God, for man would swallow
    me up;
  Fighting all day he oppresses me.
2 My enemies would hound *me* all day,
  For *there are* many who fight against me,
    O Most High.

3 Whenever I am afraid,
  I will trust in You.
4 In God (I will praise His word),
  In God I have put my trust;
  I will not fear.
  What can flesh do to me?

5 All day they twist my words;
  All their thoughts *are* against me for evil.
6 They gather together,
  They hide, they mark my steps,
  When they lie in wait for my life.
7 Shall they escape by iniquity?
  In anger cast down the peoples, O God!

8 You number my wanderings;
  Put my tears into Your bottle;
  Are they not in Your book?
9 When I cry out *to You,*
  Then my enemies will turn back;
  This I know, because God *is* for me.
10 In God (I will praise *His* word),
  In the LORD (I will praise *His* word),
11 In God I have put my trust;
  I will not be afraid.
  What can man do to me?

12 Vows *made* to You *are binding* upon me, O God;
  I will render praises to You,
13 For You have delivered my soul from death.
  Have You not *kept* my feet from falling,
  That I may walk before God
  In the light of the living?

PSALM 57   GREATER THAN HEAVEN. *To the Chief Musician. Set to "Do Not Destroy." A Michtam of David when he fled from Saul into the cave.*

1 Be merciful to me, O God, be merciful to me!
  For my soul trusts in You;
  And in the shadow of Your wings I will make my
    refuge,

Until *these* calamities have passed by.

2 I will cry out to God Most High,
 To God who performs *all things* for me.
3 He shall send from heaven and save me;
 He reproaches the one who would swallow me up.
 Selah

God shall send forth His mercy and His truth.

4 My soul *is* among lions;
 I lie *among* the sons of men
 Who are set on fire,
 Whose teeth *are* spears and arrows,
 And their tongue a sharp sword.
5 Be exalted, O God, above the
 heavens;
 Let Your glory *be* above all the
 earth.

6 They have prepared a net for my
 steps;
 My soul is bowed down;
 They have dug a pit before me;
 Into the midst of it they
 themselves have fallen.
 Selah

7 My heart is steadfast, O God, my
 heart is steadfast;
 I will sing and give praise.
8 Awake, my glory!
 Awake, lute and harp!
 I will awaken the dawn.

9 I will praise You, O Lord, among
 the peoples;
 I will sing to You among the
 nations.
10 For Your mercy reaches unto the
 heavens,
 And Your truth unto the clouds.

11 Be exalted, O God, above the
 heavens;
 Let Your glory *be* above all the
 earth.

PSALM **58** GOD CARES. *To the Chief Musician. Set to "Do Not Destroy." A Michtam of David.*

1 Do you indeed speak righteousness, you silent ones?
 Do you judge uprightly, you sons of men?
2 No, in heart you work wickedness;
 You weigh out the violence of your hands in the
 earth.

3 The wicked are estranged from the womb;
 They go astray as soon as they are born, speaking lies.
4 Their poison *is* like the poison of a serpent;
 They are like the deaf cobra *that* stops its ear,
5 Which will not heed the voice of charmers,
 Charming ever so skillfully.

6 Break their teeth in their mouth, O God!

Break out the fangs of the young lions, O LORD!
7 Let them flow away as waters *which* run continually;
 When he bends *his bow,*
 Let his arrows be as if cut in pieces.
8 *Let them be* like a snail which melts away as it goes,
 Like a stillborn child of a woman, that they may not
 see the sun.

9 Before your pots can feel *the burning* thorns,
 He shall take them away as with a whirlwind,
 As in His living and burning wrath.
10 The righteous shall rejoice when he sees the
 vengeance;

"Here's what I did..."

I'll never forget the day my father collapsed and was rushed to the hospital. The doctor told my mother and me that he'd suffered a severe heart attack and was now teetering between life and death; it could go either way. Standing with my mother by his bed, I prayed harder than I'd ever prayed before. I thought about how my father always reached out to others for Jesus, and I couldn't believe that God would be done with him yet. It almost seemed that God was reassuring me of this, but I asked him for a promise from his Word. I didn't want to go just on feelings. The verse he brought to mind is Psalm 57:1: "Be merciful to me, O God. . . . For my soul trust in You; and in the shadow of Your wings I will make my refuge, until *these* calamities have passed by."

I felt God was saying through this verse that if I took refuge in him and trusted him completely to be in control of the doctors and everything involved in my father's care, he would answer my prayer and make my father well. I was not to worry and not to try to make anything happen; hands off. I was to leave everything absolutely in God's hands and trust him for the outcome.

That's what I did. And I discovered that God is so faithful: my father did recover. God has continued to use Dad in marvelous ways to bring others to trust in Christ. And I learned something invaluable about trusting God and leaving everything in his hands when I'm facing life's storms.

David

AGE 17

He shall wash his feet in the blood of the wicked,
11 So that men will say,
 "Surely *there is* a reward for the righteous;
 Surely He is God who judges in the earth."

PSALM **59** SAFETY IN A WICKED WORLD. *To the Chief Musician. Set to "Do Not Destroy." A Michtam of David when Saul sent men, and they watched the house in order to kill him.*

1 Deliver me from my enemies, O my God;
 Defend me from those who rise up against me.
2 Deliver me from the workers of iniquity,
 And save me from bloodthirsty men.

3 For look, they lie in wait for my life;

The mighty gather against me,
Not *for* my transgression nor *for* my sin, O LORD.
4 They run and prepare themselves through no fault *of mine.*

Awake to help me, and behold!
5 You therefore, O LORD God of hosts, the God of Israel,
Awake to punish all the nations;
Do not be merciful to any wicked transgressors. *Selah*

6 At evening they return,
They growl like a dog,
And go all around the city.
7 Indeed, they belch with their mouth;
Swords *are* in their lips;
For *they say,* "Who hears?"

8 But You, O LORD, shall laugh at them;
You shall have all the nations in derision.
9 I will wait for You, O You his Strength;
For God *is* my defense.

CHANGELESS

59:10 David was hunted by those whose love had turned to jealousy, which was driving them to want to murder him. Trusted friends and his own son had turned against him. What changeable love these people had! But David knew that God's love for him was *changeless.* God's love for everyone who trusts him is changeless. When the love of others fails or disappoints us, we can rest in God's changeless love.

10 My God of mercy shall come to meet me;
God shall let me see *my desire* on my enemies.

11 Do not slay them, lest my people forget;
Scatter them by Your power,
And bring them down,
O Lord our shield.
12 *For* the sin of their mouth *and* the words of their lips,
Let them even be taken in their pride,
And for the cursing and lying *which* they speak.
13 Consume *them* in wrath, consume *them,*
That they *may* not *be;*
And let them know that God rules in Jacob
To the ends of the earth. *Selah*

14 And at evening they return,
They growl like a dog,
And go all around the city.
15 They wander up and down for food,
And howl if they are not satisfied.

16 But I will sing of Your power;
Yes, I will sing aloud of Your mercy in the morning;
For You have been my defense
And refuge in the day of my trouble.
17 To You, O my Strength, I will sing praises;
For God *is* my defense,
My God of mercy.

PSALM 60 REAL HELP COMES FROM GOD. *To the Chief Musician. Set to "Lily of the Testimony." A Michtam of David. For teaching. When he fought against Meso-*

potamia and Syria of Zobah, and Joab returned and killed twelve thousand Edomites in the Valley of Salt.
1 O God, You have cast us off;
You have broken us down;
You have been displeased;
Oh, restore us again!

EVERY DAY

61:5 David continually praised God through both the good and d times of his life. His commitment to praise God every day showed reverence for God. Do you find something to praise God for each d you do, you will find your heart elevated from daily distractions to confidence.

2 You have made the earth tremble;
You have broken it;
Heal its breaches, for it is shaking.
3 You have shown Your people hard things;
You have made us drink the wine of confusion.

4 You have given a banner to those who fear You,
That it may be displayed because of the truth. *Selah*

5 That Your beloved may be delivered,
Save *with* Your right hand, and hear me.

6 God has spoken in His holiness:
"I will rejoice;
I will divide Shechem
And measure out the Valley of Succoth.
7 Gilead *is* Mine, and Manasseh *is* Mine;
Ephraim also *is* the helmet for My head;
Judah *is* My lawgiver.
8 Moab *is* My washpot;
Over Edom I will cast My shoe;
Philistia, shout in triumph because of Me."

9 Who will bring me *to* the strong city?
Who will lead me to Edom?
10 *Is it* not You, O God, *who* cast us off?
And You, O God, *who* did not go out with our armies?
11 Give us help from trouble,
For the help of man *is* useless.
12 Through God we will do valiantly,
For *it is* He *who* shall tread down our enemies.

PSALM 61 GOD ALWAYS HEARS US. *To the Chief Musician. On a stringed instrument. A Psalm of David.*
1 Hear my cry, O God;
Attend to my prayer.
2 From the end of the earth I will cry to You,
When my heart is overwhelmed;
Lead me to the rock that is higher than I.

3 For You have been a shelter for me,
A strong tower from the enemy.
4 I will abide in Your tabernacle forever;
I will trust in the shelter of Your wings. *Selah*

5 For You, O God, have heard my vows;
You have given *me* the heritage of those who fear
Your name.

⁶ You will prolong the king's life,
His years as many generations.
⁷ He shall abide before God forever.
Oh, prepare mercy and truth, *which* may preserve
him!

⁸ So I will sing praise to Your name forever,
That I may daily perform my vows.

PSALM 62 GOD'S CONTROL. *To the Chief Musician. To Jeduthun. A Psalm of David.*

¹ Truly my soul silently *waits* for God;
From Him *comes* my salvation.
² He only *is* my rock and my salvation;
He is my defense;
I shall not be greatly moved.

³ How long will you attack a man?
You shall be slain, all of you,
Like a leaning wall and a tottering fence.
⁴ They only consult to cast *him* down from his high
position;
They delight in lies;
They bless with their mouth,
But they curse inwardly. Selah

⁵ My soul, wait silently for God alone,
For my expectation *is* from Him.
⁶ He only *is* my rock and my salvation;
He is my defense;
I shall not be moved.
⁷ In God *is* my salvation and my glory;
The rock of my strength,
And my refuge, *is* in God.

⁸ Trust in Him at all times, you people;
Pour out your heart before Him;
God *is* a refuge for us. Selah

⁹ Surely men of low degree *are* a vapor,
Men of high degree *are* a lie;
If they are weighed on the scales,
They *are* altogether *lighter* than vapor.
¹⁰ Do not trust in oppression,
Nor vainly hope in robbery;
If riches increase,
Do not set *your* heart *on them.*

¹¹ God has spoken once,
Twice I have heard this:
That power *belongs* to God.
¹² Also to You, O Lord, *belongs* mercy;
For You render to each one according to his work.

PSALM 63 I WANT TO BE NEAR GOD. *A Psalm of David when he was in the wilderness of Judah.*

¹ O God, You *are* my God;
Early will I seek You;
My soul thirsts for You;
My flesh longs for You
In a dry and thirsty land
Where there is no water.
² So I have looked for You in the sanctuary,

To see Your power and Your glory.
³ Because Your lovingkindness *is* better than life,
My lips shall praise You.
⁴ Thus I will bless You while I live;
I will lift up my hands in Your name.
⁵ My soul shall be satisfied as with marrow and
fatness,
And my mouth shall praise You with joyful lips.

⁶ When I remember You on my bed,
I meditate on You in the *night* watches.
⁷ Because You have been my help,
Therefore in the shadow of Your wings I will rejoice.
⁸ My soul follows close behind You;
Your right hand upholds me.

⁹ But those *who* seek my life, to destroy *it,*
Shall go into the lower parts of the earth.
¹⁰ They shall fall by the sword;
They shall be a portion for jackals.

¹¹ But the king shall rejoice in God;
Everyone who swears by Him shall glory;
But the mouth of those who speak lies shall be
stopped.

PSALM 64 WHEN PEOPLE MAKE TRAPS. *To the Chief Musician. A Psalm of David.*

¹ Hear my voice, O God, in my meditation;
Preserve my life from fear of the enemy.
² Hide me from the secret plots of the wicked,
From the rebellion of the workers of iniquity,
³ Who sharpen their tongue like a sword,
And bend *their bows to shoot* their arrows—bitter
words,
⁴ That they may shoot in secret at the blameless;
Suddenly they shoot at him and do not fear.

⁵ They encourage themselves *in* an evil matter;
They talk of laying snares secretly;
They say, "Who will see them?"
⁶ They devise iniquities:
"We have perfected a shrewd scheme."
Both the inward thought and the heart of man are
deep.

⁷ But God shall shoot at them *with* an arrow;
Suddenly they shall be wounded.
⁸ So He will make them stumble over their own
tongue;
All who see them shall flee away.
⁹ All men shall fear,
And shall declare the work of God;
For they shall wisely consider His doing.

¹⁰ The righteous shall be glad in the LORD, and trust in
Him.
And all the upright in heart shall glory.

PSALM 65 GIVING THANKS TO GOD. *To the Chief Musician. A Psalm of David. A Song.*

¹ Praise is awaiting You, O God, in Zion;

And to You the vow shall be performed.
2 O You who hear prayer,
To You all flesh will come.
3 Iniquities prevail against me;
As for our transgressions,
You will provide atonement for them.

4 Blessed *is the man* You choose,
And cause to approach *You,*
That he may dwell in Your courts.
We shall be satisfied with the goodness of Your house,
Of Your holy temple.

◼︎ FORGIVEN

65:3 Although sins fill our heart, God will forgive them all if we ask sincerely. Do you feel as though God could never forgive you, that your sins are too many, or that some of them are too great? Don't worry! God can and will forgive them all. Nobody is beyond redemption, and nobody is so full of sin that he cannot be made clean.

5 *By* awesome deeds in righteousness You will answer us,
O God of our salvation,
You who are the confidence of all the ends of the earth,
And of the far-off seas;
6 Who established the mountains by His strength,
Being clothed with power;
7 You who still the noise of the seas,
The noise of their waves,
And the tumult of the peoples.
8 They also who dwell in the farthest parts are afraid of Your signs;
You make the outgoings of the morning and evening rejoice.

9 You visit the earth and water it,
You greatly enrich it;
The river of God is full of water;
You provide their grain,
For so You have prepared it.
10 You water its ridges abundantly,
You settle its furrows;
You make it soft with showers,
You bless its growth.
11 You crown the year with Your goodness,
And Your paths drip *with* abundance.
12 They drop *on* the pastures of the wilderness,
And the little hills rejoice on every side.
13 The pastures are clothed with flocks;
The valleys also are covered with grain;
They shout for joy, they also sing.

PSALM 66 WE ARE IN GOD'S HAND. *To the Chief Musician. A Song. A Psalm.*
1 Make a joyful shout to God, all the earth!
2 Sing out the honor of His name;
Make His praise glorious.
3 Say to God,

"How awesome are Your works!
Through the greatness of Your power
Your enemies shall submit themselves to You.
4 All the earth shall worship You
And sing praises to You;
They shall sing praises *to* Your name."   Selah

5 Come and see the works of God;
He is awesome *in His* doing toward the sons of men.
6 He turned the sea into dry *land;*
They went through the river on foot.
There we will rejoice in Him.
7 He rules by His power forever;
His eyes observe the nations;
Do not let the rebellious exalt themselves.   Selah

8 Oh, bless our God, you peoples!
And make the voice of His praise to be heard,
9 Who keeps our soul among the living,
And does not allow our feet to be moved.
10 For You, O God, have tested us;
You have refined us as silver is refined.
11 You brought us into the net;
You laid affliction on our backs.
12 You have caused men to ride over our heads;
We went through fire and through water;
But You brought us out to rich *fulfillment.*
13 I will go into Your house with burnt offerings;
I will pay You my vows,
14 Which my lips have uttered
And my mouth has spoken when I was in trouble.
15 I will offer You burnt sacrifices of fat animals,

◼︎ PROMISES

66:14-15 People sometimes make bargains with God, saying, " heal me (or get me out of this mess), I'll obey you for the rest of m life." Soon after they recover, however, the vow is often forgotten the old life-style resumes. This writer had made a promise to God, remembered the promise and paid his vow. God always keeps his promises, and he wants us to follow his example. Be careful to foll through on whatever you promise to do.

With the sweet aroma of rams;
I will offer bulls with goats.   Selah

16 Come *and* hear, all you who fear God,
And I will declare what He has done for my soul.
17 I cried to Him with my mouth,
And He was extolled with my tongue.
18 If I regard iniquity in my heart,
The Lord will not hear.
19 *But* certainly God has heard *me;*
He has attended to the voice of my prayer.

20 Blessed *be* God,
Who has not turned away my prayer,
Nor His mercy from me!

PSALM 67 A MISSIONARY PSALM. *To the Chief Musician. On stringed instruments. A Psalm. A Song.*
1 God be merciful to us and bless us,

And cause His face to shine upon us,   Selah
2 That Your way may be known on earth,
Your salvation among all nations.

3 Let the peoples praise You, O God;
Let all the peoples praise You.
4 Oh, let the nations be glad and sing for joy!
For You shall judge the people righteously,
And govern the nations on earth.   Selah

5 Let the peoples praise You, O God;
Let all the peoples praise You.
6 *Then* the earth shall yield her increase;
God, our own God, shall bless us.
7 God shall bless us,
And all the ends of the earth shall fear Him.

PSALM **68**   THE GREAT PROVIDER. *To the Chief Musician. A Psalm of David. A Song.*

1 Let God arise,
Let His enemies be scattered;
Let those also who hate Him flee before Him.
2 As smoke is driven away,
So drive *them* away;
As wax melts before the fire,
So let the wicked perish at the presence of God.
3 But let the righteous be glad;
Let them rejoice before God;
Yes, let them rejoice exceedingly.

4 Sing to God, sing praises to His name;
Extol Him who rides on the clouds,
By His name YAH,
And rejoice before Him.

5 A father of the fatherless, a defender of widows,
Is God in His holy habitation.
6 God sets the solitary in families;
He brings out those who are bound into prosperity;
But the rebellious dwell in a dry *land.*

7 O God, when You went out before Your people,
When You marched through the wilderness,   Selah
8 The earth shook;
The heavens also dropped *rain* at the presence of
God;
Sinai itself *was moved* at the presence of God, the
God of Israel.
9 You, O God, sent a plentiful rain,
Whereby You confirmed Your inheritance,
When it was weary.
10 Your congregation dwelt in it;
You, O God, provided from Your goodness for the
poor.

11 The Lord gave the word;
Great *was* the company of those who proclaimed *it:*
12 "Kings of armies flee, they flee,
And she who remains at home divides the spoil.
13 Though you lie down among the sheepfolds,
You will be like the wings of a dove covered with
silver,
And her feathers with yellow gold."

14 When the Almighty scattered kings in it,
It was *white* as snow in Zalmon.

15 A mountain of God *is* the mountain of Bashan;
A mountain *of many* peaks *is* the mountain of
Bashan.
16 Why do you fume with envy, you mountains of
many peaks?
This is the mountain *which* God desires to dwell in;
Yes, the LORD will dwell *in it* forever.

17 The chariots of God *are* twenty thousand,
Even thousands of thousands;
The Lord is among them *as in* Sinai, in the Holy
Place.
18 You have ascended on high,
You have led captivity captive;
You have received gifts among men,
Even *from* the rebellious,
That the LORD God might dwell *there.*

19 Blessed *be* the Lord,
Who daily loads us *with benefits,*
The God of our salvation!   Selah
20 Our God *is* the God of salvation;
And to GOD the Lord *belong* escapes from death.

21 But God will wound the head of His enemies,
The hairy scalp of the one who still goes on in his
trespasses.
22 The Lord said, "I will bring back from Bashan,
I will bring *them* back from the depths of the sea,
23 That your foot may crush *them* in blood,
And the tongues of your dogs *may have* their portion
from *your* enemies."

24 They have seen Your procession, O God,
The procession of my God, my King, into the
sanctuary.
25 The singers went before, the players on instruments
followed after;
Among *them were* the maidens playing timbrels.
26 Bless God in the congregations,
The Lord, from the fountain of Israel.
27 There *is* little Benjamin, their leader,
The princes of Judah *and* their company,
The princes of Zebulun *and* the princes of Naphtali.

28 Your God has commanded your strength;
Strengthen, O God, what You have done for us.
29 Because of Your temple at Jerusalem,
Kings will bring presents to You.
30 Rebuke the beasts of the reeds,
The herd of bulls with the calves of the peoples,
Till everyone submits himself with pieces of silver.
Scatter the peoples *who* delight in war.
31 Envoys will come out of Egypt;
Ethiopia will quickly stretch out her hands to God.

32 Sing to God, you kingdoms of the earth;
Oh, sing praises to the Lord,   Selah
33 To Him who rides on the heaven of heavens, *which*
were of old!
Indeed, He sends out His voice, a mighty voice.

34 Ascribe strength to God;
His excellence *is* over Israel,
And His strength *is* in the clouds.

～～～BREATHLESS

68:34-35 We should feel an overwhelming sense of awe as we kneel before the Lord in his sanctuary. Surrounding us are countless signs of his wonderful power; shining down upon us are countless signs of his majesty. Unlimited power and unspeakable majesty leave us breathless in his presence. When you catch your breath, praise the Lord!

35 O God, *You are* more awesome than Your holy places.
The God of Israel *is* He who gives strength and
power to *His* people.

Blessed *be* God!

PSALM 69 A SEA OF TROUBLE. *To the Chief Musician. Set to "The Lilies." A Psalm of David.*

1 Save me, O God!
For the waters have come up to *my* neck.
2 I sink in deep mire,
Where *there is* no standing;
I have come into deep waters,
Where the floods overflow me.
3 I am weary with my crying;
My throat is dry;
My eyes fail while I wait for my God.

4 Those who hate me without a cause
Are more than the hairs of my head;
They are mighty who would destroy me,
Being my enemies wrongfully;
Though I have stolen nothing,
I *still* must restore *it.*
5 O God, You know my foolishness;
And my sins are not hidden from You.
6 Let not those who wait for You, O Lord GOD of hosts,
be ashamed because of me;
Let not those who seek You be confounded because
of me, O God of Israel.
7 Because for Your sake I have borne reproach;
Shame has covered my face.
8 I have become a stranger to my brothers,
And an alien to my mother's children;
9 Because zeal for Your house has eaten me up,
And the reproaches of those who reproach You have
fallen on me.
10 When I wept *and chastened* my soul with fasting,
That became my reproach.
11 I also made sackcloth my garment;
I became a byword to them.
12 Those who sit in the gate speak against me,
And I *am* the song of the drunkards.

13 But as for me, my prayer *is* to You,
O LORD, *in* the acceptable time;
O God, in the multitude of Your mercy,
Hear me in the truth of Your salvation.
14 Deliver me out of the mire,
And let me not sink;

Let me be delivered from those who hate me,
And out of the deep waters.
15 Let not the floodwater overflow me,
Nor let the deep swallow me up;
And let not the pit shut its mouth on me.

16 Hear me, O LORD, for Your lovingkindness *is* good;
Turn to me according to the multitude of Your
tender mercies.
17 And do not hide Your face from Your servant,
For I am in trouble;
Hear me speedily.
18 Draw near to my soul, *and* redeem it;
Deliver me because of my enemies.

19 You know my reproach, my shame, and my dishonor;
My adversaries *are* all before You.
20 Reproach has broken my heart,
And I am full of heaviness;
I looked *for someone* to take pity, but *there was* none;
And for comforters, but I found none.
21 They also gave me gall for my food,
And for my thirst they gave me vinegar to drink.

22 Let their table become a snare before them,
And their well-being a trap.
23 Let their eyes be darkened, so that they do not see;
And make their loins shake continually.
24 Pour out Your indignation upon them,
And let Your wrathful anger take hold of them.
25 Let their dwelling place be desolate;
Let no one live in their tents.
26 For they persecute the *ones* You have struck,
And talk of the grief of those You have wounded.
27 Add iniquity to their iniquity,
And let them not come into Your righteousness.
28 Let them be blotted out of the book of the living,
And not be written with the righteous.

29 But I *am* poor and sorrowful;
Let Your salvation, O God, set me up on high.
30 I will praise the name of God with a song,
And will magnify Him with thanksgiving.
31 *This* also shall please the LORD better than an ox *or* bull,
Which has horns and hooves.
32 The humble shall see *this and* be glad;
And you who seek God, your hearts shall live.
33 For the LORD hears the poor,
And does not despise His prisoners.

34 Let heaven and earth praise Him,
The seas and everything that moves in them.
35 For God will save Zion
And build the cities of Judah,
That they may dwell there and possess it.
36 Also, the descendants of His servants shall inherit it,
And those who love His name shall dwell in it.

PSALM 70 A SHORT PRAYER FOR HELP. *To the Chief Musician. A Psalm of David. To bring to remembrance.*

1 *Make haste,* O God, to deliver me!

Make haste to help me, O LORD!

2 Let them be ashamed and confounded
Who seek my life;
Let them be turned back and confused
Who desire my hurt.

3 Let them be turned back because of their shame,
Who say, "Aha, aha!"

4 Let all those who seek You rejoice and be glad in You;
And let those who love Your salvation say continually,
"Let God be magnified!"

5 But I *am* poor and needy;
Make haste to me, O God!
You *are* my help and my deliverer;
O LORD, do not delay.

PSALM 71   YOUNG OR OLD—GOD HELPS.

1 In You, O LORD, I put my trust;
Let me never be put to shame.

2 Deliver me in Your righteousness, and cause me to
escape;
Incline Your ear to me, and save me.

3 Be my strong refuge,
To which I may resort continually;
You have given the commandment to save me,
For You *are* my rock and my fortress.

4 Deliver me, O my God, out of the hand of the wicked,
Out of the hand of the unrighteous and cruel man.

5 For You are my hope, O Lord GOD;
You are my trust from my youth.

6 By You I have been upheld from birth;
You are He who took me out of my mother's womb.
My praise *shall be* continually of You.

7 I have become as a wonder to many,
But You *are* my strong refuge.

8 Let my mouth be filled *with* Your praise
And with Your glory all the day.

9 Do not cast me off in the time of old age;
Do not forsake me when my strength fails.

10 For my enemies speak against me;
And those who lie in wait for my life take counsel
together,

11 Saying, "God has forsaken him;
Pursue and take him, for *there is* none to deliver
him."

12 O God, do not be far from me;
O my God, make haste to help me!

13 Let them be confounded *and* consumed
Who are adversaries of my life;
Let them be covered *with* reproach and dishonor
Who seek my hurt.

14 But I will hope continually,
And will praise You yet more and more.

15 My mouth shall tell of Your righteousness
And Your salvation all the day,
For I do not know *their* limits.

16 I will go in the strength of the Lord GOD;

I will make mention of Your righteousness, of Yours
only.

17 O God, You have taught me from my youth;
And to this *day* I declare Your wondrous works.

18 Now also when *I am* old and grayheaded,
O God, do not forsake me,

◣━━━━━━━━━▶ **PANIC**

70:4 This short psalm was David's plea for God to rush to his aid. Yet even in this moment of panic, praise was not forgotten. Praise is important because it helps us remember who God is. Often our prayers are filled with requests for ourself and others; we forget to thank God for what he has done and to worship him for who he is. Don't take God for granted or treat him as a vending machine. Even in the midst of his fear, David praised God.

Until I declare Your strength to *this* generation,
Your power to everyone *who* is to come.

19 Also Your righteousness, O God, *is* very high,
You who have done great things;
O God, who *is* like You?

20 *You,* who have shown me great and severe troubles,
Shall revive me again,
And bring me up again from the depths of the earth.

21 You shall increase my greatness,
And comfort me on every side.

22 Also with the lute I will praise You—
And Your faithfulness, O my God!
To You I will sing with the harp,
O Holy One of Israel.

23 My lips shall greatly rejoice when I sing to You,
And my soul, which You have redeemed.

24 My tongue also shall talk of Your righteousness all
the day long;
For they are confounded,
For they are brought to shame
Who seek my hurt.

PSALM 72   THE PERFECT KING. *A Psalm of Solomon.*

1 Give the king Your judgments, O God,
And Your righteousness to the king's Son.

2 He will judge Your people with righteousness,
And Your poor with justice.

3 The mountains will bring peace to the people,
And the little hills, by righteousness.

4 He will bring justice to the poor of the people;
He will save the children of the needy,
And will break in pieces the oppressor.

5 They shall fear You
As long as the sun and moon endure,
Throughout all generations.

6 He shall come down like rain upon the grass before
mowing,
Like showers *that* water the earth.

7 In His days the righteous shall flourish,
And abundance of peace,

DOWN IN THE DUMPS

In the movie *The Accidental Tourist*, the main characters are a husband and wife named Macon and Sarah Leary. Their son Ethan has died tragically, leaving them in despair, struggling to pull their lives back together. In one particularly touching scene, Sarah says to her husband: **"I should have agreed to teach summer school or something. I open my eyes in the morning and I think, Why bother getting up? Why bother eating? Why bother breathing?"** This isn't just a scene from a movie—it's an experience common to people everywhere. Life can be terribly unfair, terribly tragic. When we're in the depths of despair, we feel like Sarah Leary: Why bother going on at all? **T**here are those who feel that Christians are—or should be—immune to depression. "After all," they say, "what have you got to be depressed about? You have a relationship with God, a family of brothers and sisters who love you, and a guaranteed ticket to heaven." When the person carrying the weight of gloom hears this, he is not only depressed, he feels guilty as well because it's "unspiritual" to be down in the dumps. **F**or those who struggle with feelings of depression, there is good news and bad news. **T**he bad news is that such feelings are a fact of life in this broken world. Man's fall into sin in the Garden of Eden affected every area of human existence. Look at it this way: when you inhabit a planet in open rebellion against its Creator, it's not surprising that sometimes you get caught in the cross fire. Depression is just one of the ways that we can be wounded. **N**ow the good news: you are not alone. As Psalm 73 (and many other passages) clearly shows, even God's chosen people experience anxiety, despair, and darkness in their soul. (If Psalm 73 doesn't convince you, check out the accounts of Jesus' experience in Gethsemane. Matthew 26 speaks of Jesus' soul being "exceedingly sorrowful, even to death." Don't be surprised when you face grief.) Feeling down—really down—seems to be an occasional fact of life. Obviou[s]ly, depression that is too deep or lasts too long indicates a need for counseling; but there is nothing unusual o[r] unspiritual about "walking through the dark valley" from time to time. **S**o when you are caught in one o[f] those unpleasant times, don't add guilt to your load. There's nothing wrong with you. When sailing thro[ugh] stormy seas, expect a little motion discomfort. And know for certain that the Captain is not asleep on the bridge. He'll guide you safely through.

Until the moon is no more.

8 He shall have dominion also from sea to sea,
And from the River to the ends of the earth.
9 Those who dwell in the wilderness will bow before Him,
And His enemies will lick the dust.
10 The kings of Tarshish and of the isles
Will bring presents;
The kings of Sheba and Seba
Will offer gifts.
11 Yes, all kings shall fall down before Him;
All nations shall serve Him.

12 For He will deliver the needy when he cries,
The poor also, and *him* who has no helper.
13 He will spare the poor and needy,
And will save the souls of the needy.
14 He will redeem their life from oppression and violence;
And precious shall be their blood in His sight.

15 And He shall live;
And the gold of Sheba will be given to Him;
Prayer also will be made for Him continually,
And daily He shall be praised.
16 There will be an abundance of grain in the earth,
On the top of the mountains;
Its fruit shall wave like Lebanon;
And *those* of the city shall flourish like grass of the earth.

17 His name shall endure forever;
His name shall continue as long as the sun.
And *men* shall be blessed in Him;
All nations shall call Him blessed.

18 Blessed *be* the LORD God, the God of Israel,
Who only does wondrous things!
19 And blessed *be* His glorious name forever!
And let the whole earth be filled *with* His glory.
Amen and Amen.

20 The prayers of David the son of Jesse are ended.

BOOK THREE: Psalms 73–89

PSALM **73** WHY ARE WICKED PEOPLE RICH?
A Psalm of Asaph.
1 Truly God *is* good to Israel,
To such as are pure in heart.
2 But as for me, my feet had almost stumbled;
My steps had nearly slipped.
3 For I *was* envious of the boastful,
When I saw the prosperity of the wicked.
4 For *there are* no pangs in their death,
But their strength *is* firm.
5 They *are* not in trouble *as other* men,
Nor are they plagued like *other* men.
6 Therefore pride serves as their necklace;
Violence covers them *like* a garment.
7 Their eyes bulge with abundance;

They have more than heart could wish.
8 They scoff and speak wickedly *concerning* oppression;
They speak loftily.
9 They set their mouth against the heavens,
And their tongue walks through the earth.
10 Therefore his people return here,
And waters of a full *cup* are drained by them.
11 And they say, "How does God know?
And is there knowledge in the Most High?"
12 Behold, these *are* the ungodly,
Who are always at ease;
They increase *in* riches.
13 Surely I have cleansed my heart *in* vain,
And washed my hands in innocence.

◤━━━━━━━━━HELPLESS

72:12-14 God cares for the needy and the poor because they are precious to him. If God feels so strongly about the poor and loves them so deeply, how can we ignore their plight? Examine what you are doing to reach out with God's love to the poor, weak, and needy in the world. Are you ignoring them?

14 For all day long I have been plagued,
And chastened every morning.
15 If I had said, "I will speak thus,"
Behold, I would have been untrue to the generation of Your children.
16 When I thought *how* to understand this,
It *was* too painful for me—
17 Until I went into the sanctuary of God;
Then I understood their end.
18 Surely You set them in slippery places;
You cast them down to destruction.
19 Oh, how they are *brought* to desolation, as in a moment!
They are utterly consumed with terrors.
20 As a dream when *one* awakes,
So, Lord, when You awake,
You shall despise their image.
21 Thus my heart was grieved,
And I was vexed in my mind.
22 I *was* so foolish and ignorant;
I was *like* a beast before You.
23 Nevertheless I *am* continually with You;
You hold *me* by my right hand.
24 You will guide me with Your counsel,
And afterward receive me *to* glory.
25 Whom have I in heaven *but You?*
And *there is* none upon earth *that* I desire besides You.
26 My flesh and my heart fail;
But God *is* the strength of my heart and my portion forever.
27 For indeed, those who are far from You shall perish;
You have destroyed all those who desert You for harlotry.

28 But *it is* good for me to draw near to God;
I have put my trust in the Lord GOD,
That I may declare all Your works.

PSALM 74 RECALL YOUR PROMISES, O LORD.

A Contemplation of Asaph.

1 O God, why have You cast *us* off forever?
Why does Your anger smoke against the sheep of
Your pasture?
2 Remember Your congregation, *which* You have
purchased of old,
The tribe of Your inheritance, *which* You have
redeemed—

*I*NJUSTICE "It isn't fair!" Joyce sobs. "I try really hard to live for
the Lord. I go to church, read my Bible, pray every day, try to be a witness to
my friends—everything! But does it do any good? No way! My life is still the
worst. My family is awful, my fat body is a wreck, I never get asked out, I have
only two friends, and I can't even pass geometry! You'd think God would at least
reward me a little bit.

"On the other hand, Amy has it made! She's tan and beautiful. She has dates
every weekend. She makes straight A's without even trying. Her family is rich—I
mean, how many other kids get their own Miata convertible? She never has any
problems. Her life is totally perfect . . . and here's the big rip-off: she's not even a
Christian! In fact, she couldn't care less about God. She's wild!

"It doesn't make any sense. Why do I get shot down for doing what's right, and
she gets rewarded for being 'Miss Party'?

"Doesn't God see what's going on? Doesn't he care? I'm serious . . . there is
absolutely no justice in this world. I might as well live like a heathen for all the
good it does me."

Ever feel like Joyce? Ever wonder why some non-Christians seem to have
perfect lives, while so many of God's people struggle and have lives full of pain? A
follower of God named Asaph once asked some of the very same questions. Psalm
73 describes the answers he found.

This Mount Zion where You have dwelt.
3 Lift up Your feet to the perpetual desolations.
The enemy has damaged everything in the
sanctuary.
4 Your enemies roar in the midst of Your meeting
place;
They set up their banners *for* signs.
5 They seem like men who lift up
Axes among the thick trees.
6 And now they break down its carved work, all at
once,
With axes and hammers.
7 They have set fire to Your sanctuary;
They have defiled the dwelling place of Your name to
the ground.
8 They said in their hearts,
"Let us destroy them altogether."
They have burned up all the meeting places of God
in the land.

9 We do not see our signs;
There is no longer any prophet;
Nor *is there* any among us who knows how long.
10 O God, how long will the adversary reproach?
Will the enemy blaspheme Your name forever?
11 Why do You withdraw Your hand, even Your right
hand?

HATE

74:8 When enemy armies defeated Israel, they sacked Jerusalem
trying to wipe out every trace of God. This has often been the respo[nse]
of people who hate God. Today many are trying to erase all traces [of]
God from traditions in our society and subjects taught in our schoo[l.]
what you can to help maintain a Christian influence, but don't beco[me]
discouraged when others appear to make great strides in eliminat[ing]
traces of God. They cannot eliminate his presence in the lives of
believers.

Take it out of Your bosom and destroy *them.*
12 For God *is* my King from of old,
Working salvation in the midst of the earth.
13 You divided the sea by Your strength;
You broke the heads of the sea serpents in the waters.
14 You broke the heads of Leviathan in pieces,
And gave him *as* food to the people inhabiting the
wilderness.
15 You broke open the fountain and the flood;
You dried up mighty rivers.
16 The day *is* Yours, the night also *is* Yours;
You have prepared the light and the sun.
17 You have set all the borders of the earth;
You have made summer and winter.

18 Remember this, *that* the enemy has reproached,
O LORD,
And *that* a foolish people has blasphemed Your
name.
19 Oh, do not deliver the life of Your turtledove to the
wild beast!
Do not forget the life of Your poor forever.
20 Have respect to the covenant;
For the dark places of the earth are full of the haunts
of cruelty.
21 Oh, do not let the oppressed return ashamed!
Let the poor and needy praise Your name.

22 Arise, O God, plead Your own cause;
Remember how the foolish man reproaches You
daily.
23 Do not forget the voice of Your enemies;
The tumult of those who rise up against You
increases continually.

PSALM 75 WICKED PEOPLE WILL BE JUDGED.

*To the Chief Musician. Set to "Do Not Destroy." A Psalm
of Asaph. A Song.*

1 We give thanks to You, O God, we give thanks!
For Your wondrous works declare *that* Your name is
near.

² "When I choose the proper time,
  I will judge uprightly.
³ The earth and all its inhabitants are dissolved;
  I set up its pillars firmly.   Selah

⁴ "I said to the boastful, 'Do not deal boastfully,'
  And to the wicked, 'Do not lift up the horn.
⁵ Do not lift up your horn on high;
  Do *not* speak with a stiff neck.'"

⁶ For exaltation *comes* neither from the east
  Nor from the west nor from the south.
⁷ But God *is* the Judge:
  He puts down one,
  And exalts another.
⁸ For in the hand of the LORD *there is* a cup,
  And the wine is red;
  It is fully mixed, and He pours it out;
  Surely its dregs shall all the wicked of the earth
  Drain *and* drink down.

⁹ But I will declare forever,
  I will sing praises to the God of Jacob.

¹⁰ "All the horns of the wicked I will also cut off,
  But the horns of the righteous shall be exalted."

PSALM **76** GOD IS GREAT. *To the Chief Musician. On stringed instruments. A Psalm of Asaph. A Song.*

¹ In Judah God *is* known;
  His name *is* great in Israel.
² In Salem also is His tabernacle,
  And His dwelling place in Zion.
³ There He broke the arrows of the bow,
  The shield and sword of battle.   Selah

⁴ You *are* more glorious and excellent
  Than the mountains of prey.
⁵ The stouthearted were plundered;
  They have sunk into their sleep;
  And none of the mighty men have found the use of
    their hands.
⁶ At Your rebuke, O God of Jacob,
  Both the chariot and horse were cast into a dead sleep.

⁷ You, Yourself, *are* to be feared;
  And who may stand in Your presence
  When once You are angry?
⁸ You caused judgment to be heard from heaven;
  The earth feared and was still,
⁹ When God arose to judgment,
  To deliver all the oppressed of the earth.   Selah

¹⁰ Surely the wrath of man shall praise You;
  With the remainder of wrath You shall gird Yourself.

¹¹ Make vows to the LORD your God, and pay *them*;
  Let all who are around Him bring presents to Him
    who ought to be feared.
¹² He shall cut off the spirit of princes;
  He is awesome to the kings of the earth.

PSALM **77** GOD HELPS IN HARD TIMES. *To the Chief Musician. To Jeduthun. A Psalm of Asaph.*

¹ I cried out to God with my voice—
  To God with my voice;
  And He gave ear to me.
² In the day of my trouble I sought the Lord;
  My hand was stretched out in the night without
    ceasing;
  My soul refused to be comforted.
³ I remembered God, and was troubled;
  I complained, and my spirit was overwhelmed.
                                                 Selah

◆───────────TIMING

75:2 Children have difficulty grasping the concept of time. "It's not time yet" is not a reason they easily understand. They only comprehend the present. As limited human beings, we can't comprehend God's perspective on time. We want everything now, not recognizing that God's timing is better for us. When God is ready, he will do what needs to be done, not what we would like him to do. We may be impatient as children, but it is clear that God's timing is perfect, so we should accept it.

⁴ You hold my eyelids *open*;
  I am so troubled that I cannot speak.
⁵ I have considered the days of old,
  The years of ancient times.
⁶ I call to remembrance my song in the night;
  I meditate within my heart,
  And my spirit makes diligent search.

⁷ Will the Lord cast off forever?
  And will He be favorable no more?
⁸ Has His mercy ceased forever?
  Has *His* promise failed forevermore?
⁹ Has God forgotten to be gracious?
  Has He in anger shut up His tender mercies?   Selah

¹⁰ And I said, "This *is* my anguish;
  But I will remember the years of the right hand of the
    Most High."
¹¹ I will remember the works of the LORD;
  Surely I will remember Your wonders of old.
¹² I will also meditate on all Your work,
  And talk of Your deeds.
¹³ Your way, O God, *is* in the sanctuary;
  Who *is* so great a God as *our* God?
¹⁴ You *are* the God who does wonders;
  You have declared Your strength among the peoples.
¹⁵ You have with *Your* arm redeemed Your people,
  The sons of Jacob and Joseph.   Selah

¹⁶ The waters saw You, O God;
  The waters saw You, they were afraid;
  The depths also trembled.
¹⁷ The clouds poured out water;
  The skies sent out a sound;
  Your arrows also flashed about.
¹⁸ The voice of Your thunder *was* in the whirlwind;
  The lightnings lit up the world;
  The earth trembled and shook.
¹⁹ Your way *was* in the sea,
  Your path in the great waters,

And Your footsteps were not known.
20 You led Your people like a flock
  By the hand of Moses and Aaron.

PSALM 78 HISTORY TEACHES US. *A Contemplation of Asaph.*

1 Give ear, O my people, *to* my law;
  Incline your ears to the words of my mouth.
2 I will open my mouth in a parable;
  I will utter dark sayings of old,
3 Which we have heard and known,
  And our fathers have told us.
4 We will not hide *them* from their children,
  Telling to the generation to come the praises of the
    LORD,
  And His strength and His wonderful works that He
    has done.

5 For He established a testimony in Jacob,
  And appointed a law in Israel,
  Which He commanded our fathers,
  That they should make them known to their
    children;
6 That the generation to come might know *them*,
  The children *who* would be born,
  That they may arise and declare *them* to their
    children,

ALL TALK

78:36-37 Over and over the children of Israel said they would follow God, but then they turned away from him. The problem was that they followed God with words and not with their hearts, thus their repentance was empty. Talk is cheap. God wants our life to back up our spiritual claims and promises—he wants us to be true believers.

7 That they may set their hope in God,
  And not forget the works of God,
  But keep His commandments;
8 And may not be like their fathers,
  A stubborn and rebellious generation,
  A generation *that* did not set its heart aright,
  And whose spirit was not faithful to God.

9 The children of Ephraim, *being* armed *and* carrying
    bows,
  Turned back in the day of battle.
10 They did not keep the covenant of God;
  They refused to walk in His law,
11 And forgot His works
  And His wonders that He had shown them.

12 Marvelous things He did in the sight of their fathers,
  In the land of Egypt, *in* the field of Zoan.
13 He divided the sea and caused them to pass through;
  And He made the waters stand up like a heap.
14 In the daytime also He led them with the cloud,
  And all the night with a light of fire.
15 He split the rocks in the wilderness,
  And gave *them* drink in abundance like the depths.
16 He also brought streams out of the rock,
  And caused waters to run down like rivers.

17 But they sinned even more against Him
  By rebelling against the Most High in the wilderness.
18 And they tested God in their heart
  By asking for the food of their fancy.
19 Yes, they spoke against God:
  They said, "Can God prepare a table in the
    wilderness?
20 Behold, He struck the rock,
  So that the waters gushed out,
  And the streams overflowed.
  Can He give bread also?
  Can He provide meat for His people?"

21 Therefore the LORD heard *this* and was furious;
  So a fire was kindled against Jacob,
  And anger also came up against Israel,
22 Because they did not believe in God,
  And did not trust in His salvation.
23 Yet He had commanded the clouds above,
  And opened the doors of heaven,
24 Had rained down manna on them to eat,
  And given them of the bread of heaven.
25 Men ate angels' food;
  He sent them food to the full.

26 He caused an east wind to blow in the heavens;
  And by His power He brought in the south wind.
27 He also rained meat on them like the dust,
  Feathered fowl like the sand of the seas;
28 And He let *them* fall in the midst of their camp,
  All around their dwellings.
29 So they ate and were well filled,
  For He gave them their own desire.
30 They were not deprived of their craving;
  But while their food *was* still in their mouths,
31 The wrath of God came against them,
  And slew the stoutest of them,
  And struck down the choice *men* of Israel.

32 In spite of this they still sinned,
  And did not believe in His wondrous works.
33 Therefore their days He consumed in futility,
  And their years in fear.

34 When He slew them, then they sought Him;
  And they returned and sought earnestly for God.
35 Then they remembered that God *was* their rock,
  And the Most High God their Redeemer.
36 Nevertheless they flattered Him with their mouth,
  And they lied to Him with their tongue;
37 For their heart was not steadfast with Him,
  Nor were they faithful in His covenant.
38 But He, *being* full of compassion, forgave *their*
    iniquity,
  And did not destroy *them*.
  Yes, many a time He turned His anger away,
  And did not stir up all His wrath;
39 For He remembered that they *were but* flesh,
  A breath that passes away and does not come again.

40 How often they provoked Him in the wilderness,
  And grieved Him in the desert!
41 Yes, again and again they tempted God,

And limited the Holy One of Israel.
42 They did not remember His power:
The day when He redeemed them from the enemy,
43 When He worked His signs in Egypt,
And His wonders in the field of Zoan;
44 Turned their rivers into blood,
And their streams, that they could not drink.
45 He sent swarms of flies among them, which
devoured them,
And frogs, which destroyed them.
46 He also gave their crops to the caterpillar,
And their labor to the locust.
47 He destroyed their vines with hail,
And their sycamore trees with frost.
48 He also gave up their cattle to the hail,
And their flocks to fiery lightning.
49 He cast on them the fierceness of His anger,
Wrath, indignation, and trouble,
By sending angels of destruction *among them.*
50 He made a path for His anger;
He did not spare their soul from death,
But gave their life over to the plague,
51 And destroyed all the firstborn in Egypt,
The first of *their* strength in the tents of Ham.
52 But He made His own people go forth like sheep,
And guided them in the wilderness like a flock;
53 And He led them on safely, so that they did not fear;
But the sea overwhelmed their enemies.
54 And He brought them to His holy border,
This mountain *which* His right hand had acquired.
55 He also drove out the nations before them,
Allotted them an inheritance by survey,
And made the tribes of Israel dwell in their tents.

56 Yet they tested and provoked the Most High God,
And did not keep His testimonies,
57 But turned back and acted unfaithfully like their
fathers;
They were turned aside like a deceitful bow.
58 For they provoked Him to anger with their high
places,
And moved Him to jealousy with their carved
images.
59 When God heard *this,* He was furious,
And greatly abhorred Israel,
60 So that He forsook the tabernacle of Shiloh,
The tent He had placed among men,
61 And delivered His strength into captivity,
And His glory into the enemy's hand.
62 He also gave His people over to the sword,
And was furious with His inheritance.
63 The fire consumed their young men,
And their maidens were not given in marriage.
64 Their priests fell by the sword,
And their widows made no lamentation.

65 Then the Lord awoke as *from* sleep,
Like a mighty man who shouts because of wine.
66 And He beat back His enemies;
He put them to a perpetual reproach.

67 Moreover He rejected the tent of Joseph,

And did not choose the tribe of Ephraim,
68 But chose the tribe of Judah,
Mount Zion which He loved.
69 And He built His sanctuary like the heights,
Like the earth which He has established forever.
70 He also chose David His servant,
And took him from the sheepfolds;
71 From following the ewes that had young He brought
him,

BASIC TRAINING

78:71-72 Although David had been on the throne when this psalm was written, he is called a shepherd and not a king. Shepherding, a common profession in biblical times, was a highly responsible job. The flocks were completely dependent upon shepherds for guidance, provision, and protection. David had spent his early years as a shepherd (1 Samuel 16:10-11). This was a training ground for the future responsibilities God had in store for him. When he was ready, God took him from caring for sheep to caring for Israel, God's people. Don't treat your present situation lightly or irresponsibly; it may be God's training ground for your future.

To shepherd Jacob His people,
And Israel His inheritance.
72 So he shepherded them according to the integrity of
his heart,
And guided them by the skillfulness of his hands.

PSALM 79   LIFE IS NOT FAIR, BUT GOD IS.

A Psalm of Asaph.
1 O God, the nations have come into Your inheritance;
Your holy temple they have defiled;
They have laid Jerusalem in heaps.
2 The dead bodies of Your servants
They have given *as* food for the birds of the heavens,
The flesh of Your saints to the beasts of the earth.
3 Their blood they have shed like water all around
Jerusalem,
And *there was* no one to bury *them.*
4 We have become a reproach to our neighbors,
A scorn and derision to those who are around us.

5 How long, LORD?
Will You be angry forever?
Will Your jealousy burn like fire?
6 Pour out Your wrath on the nations that do not know
You,
And on the kingdoms that do not call on Your name.
7 For they have devoured Jacob,
And laid waste his dwelling place.

8 Oh, do not remember former iniquities against us!
Let Your tender mercies come speedily to meet us,
For we have been brought very low.
9 Help us, O God of our salvation,
For the glory of Your name;
And deliver us, and provide atonement for our sins,
For Your name's sake!
10 Why should the nations say,
"Where *is* their God?"

Let there be known among the nations in our sight
The avenging of the blood of Your servants *which
has been* shed.

11 Let the groaning of the prisoner come before You;
According to the greatness of Your power
Preserve those who are appointed to die;

◣ BE PREPARED

79:10 Can we expect God to care for us so others won't scoff at our beliefs? In the end, God will bring himself glory (76:10), but in the meantime, we must endure suffering with patience and allow God to purify us through it. For reasons that we do not know, the heathen are allowed to scoff at believers. We should be prepared for criticism, jokes, and unkind remarks because God does not place us beyond the attacks of scoffers.

12 And return to our neighbors sevenfold into their bosom
Their reproach with which they have reproached You, O Lord.

13 So we, Your people and sheep of Your pasture,
Will give You thanks forever;
We will show forth Your praise to all generations.

PSALM 80 GOD WILL HELP US TRUST HIM.

To the Chief Musician. Set to "The Lilies." A Testimony of Asaph. A Psalm.

1 Give ear, O Shepherd of Israel,
You who lead Joseph like a flock;
You who dwell *between* the cherubim, shine forth!

2 Before Ephraim, Benjamin, and Manasseh,
Stir up Your strength,
And come *and* save us!

3 Restore us, O God;
Cause Your face to shine,
And we shall be saved!

4 O LORD God of hosts,
How long will You be angry
Against the prayer of Your people?

5 You have fed them with the bread of tears,
And given them tears to drink in great measure.

6 You have made us a strife to our neighbors,
And our enemies laugh among themselves.

7 Restore us, O God of hosts;
Cause Your face to shine,
And we shall be saved!

8 You have brought a vine out of Egypt;
You have cast out the nations, and planted it.

9 You prepared *room* for it,
And caused it to take deep root,
And it filled the land.

10 The hills were covered with its shadow,
And the mighty cedars with its boughs.

11 She sent out her boughs to the Sea,
And her branches to the River.

12 Why have You broken down her hedges,

So that all who pass by the way pluck her *fruit?*

13 The boar out of the woods uproots it,
And the wild beast of the field devours it.

14 Return, we beseech You, O God of hosts;
Look down from heaven and see,
And visit this vine

15 And the vineyard which Your right hand has planted,
And the branch *that* You made strong for Yourself.

16 *It is* burned with fire, *it is* cut down;
They perish at the rebuke of Your countenance.

17 Let Your hand be upon the man of Your right hand,
Upon the son of man *whom* You made strong for Yourself.

18 Then we will not turn back from You;
Revive us, and we will call upon Your name.

19 Restore us, O LORD God of hosts;
Cause Your face to shine,
And we shall be saved!

PSALM 81 A PSALM FOR SPECIAL TIMES. *To the Chief Musician. On an instrument of Gath. A Psalm of Asaph.*

1 Sing aloud to God our strength;
Make a joyful shout to the God of Jacob.

2 Raise a song and strike the timbrel,
The pleasant harp with the lute.

3 Blow the trumpet at the time of the New Moon,
At the full moon, on our solemn feast day.

4 For this *is* a statute for Israel,
A law of the God of Jacob.

◣ HOLIDAYS

81:4-5 Israel's holidays reminded the nation of God's great mir̶ was a time of rejoicing and a time to renew one's strength for life̶ struggles. At Christmas, do most of your thoughts revolve around presents? Is Easter only a warm anticipation of spring, and Thanks only a good meal? Remember the spiritual origins of these specia̶ and use them as opportunities to worship God for his goodness to your family, and your nation.

5 This He established in Joseph *as* a testimony,
When He went throughout the land of Egypt,
Where I heard a language I did not understand.

6 "I removed his shoulder from the burden;
His hands were freed from the baskets.

7 You called in trouble, and I delivered you;
I answered you in the secret place of thunder;
I tested you at the waters of Meribah. Selah

8 "Hear, O My people, and I will admonish you!
O Israel, if you will listen to Me!

9 There shall be no foreign god among you;
Nor shall you worship any foreign god.

10 I *am* the LORD your God,
Who brought you out of the land of Egypt;
Open your mouth wide, and I will fill it.

11 "But My people would not heed My voice,
And Israel would *have* none of Me.

¹² So I gave them over to their own stubborn heart,
To walk in their own counsels.

¹³ "Oh, that My people would listen to Me,
That Israel would walk in My ways!

¹⁴ I would soon subdue their enemies,
And turn My hand against their adversaries.

¹⁵ The haters of the LORD would pretend submission to
Him,
But their fate would endure forever.

¹⁶ He would have fed them also with the finest of
wheat;
And with honey from the rock I would have satisfied
you."

PSALM 82 GOD WILL JUDGE. *A Psalm of Asaph.*

¹ God stands in the congregation of the mighty;
He judges among the gods.

² How long will you judge unjustly,
And show partiality to the wicked?   Selah

³ Defend the poor and fatherless;
Do justice to the afflicted and needy.

⁴ Deliver the poor and needy;
Free *them* from the hand of the wicked.

⁵ They do not know, nor do they understand;
They walk about in darkness;
All the foundations of the earth are unstable.

⁶ I said, "You *are* gods,
And all of you *are* children of the Most High.

⁷ But you shall die like men,
And fall like one of the princes."

⁸ Arise, O God, judge the earth;
For You shall inherit all nations.

PSALM 83 TELL THE WORLD GOD IS GOOD.
A Song. A Psalm of Asaph.

¹ Do not keep silent, O God!
Do not hold Your peace,
And do not be still, O God!

² For behold, Your enemies make a tumult;
And those who hate You have lifted up their head.

³ They have taken crafty counsel against Your people,
And consulted together against Your sheltered ones.

⁴ They have said, "Come, and let us cut them off from
being a nation,
That the name of Israel may be remembered no
more."

⁵ For they have consulted together with one consent;
They form a confederacy against You:

⁶ The tents of Edom and the Ishmaelites;
Moab and the Hagrites;

⁷ Gebal, Ammon, and Amalek;
Philistia with the inhabitants of Tyre;

⁸ Assyria also has joined with them;
They have helped the children of Lot.   Selah

⁹ Deal with them as *with* Midian,
As *with* Sisera,
As *with* Jabin at the Brook Kishon,

¹⁰ Who perished at En Dor,
Who became *as* refuse on the earth.

¹¹ Make their nobles like Oreb and like Zeeb,
Yes, all their princes like Zebah and Zalmunna,

¹² Who said, "Let us take for ourselves
The pastures of God for a possession."

¹³ O my God, make them like the whirling dust,
Like the chaff before the wind!

◢ BLOWN AWAY

83:13-18 The rulers of the nations exercise great power, changing the course of history and its peoples. Surrounding Judah were heathen nations that sought its downfall. Asaph prayed that God would blow these nations away like chaff before the wind until, in their defeat, they recognized that the Lord is above all rulers of the earth. Sometimes we must be dragged in the dust before we will look up and see the Lord; we must be defeated before we can have the ultimate victory. Wouldn't it be better to seek the Lord in times of prosperity than to wait until his judgment is upon us?

¹⁴ As the fire burns the woods,
And as the flame sets the mountains on fire,

¹⁵ So pursue them with Your tempest,
And frighten them with Your storm.

¹⁶ Fill their faces with shame,
That they may seek Your name, O LORD.

¹⁷ Let them be confounded and dismayed forever;
Yes, let them be put to shame and perish,

¹⁸ That they may know that You, whose name alone *is*
the LORD,
Are the Most High over all the earth.

PSALM 84 OUR TRUST DELIGHTS GOD. *To the Chief Musician. On an instrument of Gath. A Psalm of the sons of Korah.*

¹ How lovely *is* Your tabernacle,
O LORD of hosts!

² My soul longs, yes, even faints
For the courts of the LORD;
My heart and my flesh cry out for the living God.

³ Even the sparrow has found a home,
And the swallow a nest for herself,
Where she may lay her young—
Even Your altars, O LORD of hosts,
My King and my God.

⁴ Blessed *are* those who dwell in Your house;
They will still be praising You.   Selah

⁵ Blessed *is* the man whose strength *is* in You,
Whose heart *is* set on pilgrimage.

⁶ *As they* pass through the Valley of Baca,
They make it a spring;
The rain also covers it with pools.

⁷ They go from strength to strength;
Each one appears before God in Zion.

⁸ O LORD God of hosts, hear my prayer;
Give ear, O God of Jacob!   Selah

⁹ O God, behold our shield,

And look upon the face of Your anointed.

10 For a day in Your courts *is* better than a thousand.
I would rather be a doorkeeper in the house of my
God
Than dwell in the tents of wickedness.

11 For the LORD God *is* a sun and shield;
The LORD will give grace and glory;
No good *thing* will He withhold
From those who walk uprightly.

12 O LORD of hosts,
Blessed *is* the man who trusts in You!

PSALM 85   FOLLOW GOD: FIND PEACE. *To the
Chief Musician. A Psalm of the sons of Korah.*

1 LORD, You have been favorable to Your land;
You have brought back the captivity of Jacob.

2 You have forgiven the iniquity of Your people;
You have covered all their sin.   Selah

3 You have taken away all Your wrath;
You have turned from the fierceness of Your anger.

4 Restore us, O God of our salvation,
And cause Your anger toward us to cease.

5 Will You be angry with us forever?
Will You prolong Your anger to all generations?

6 Will You not revive us again,
That Your people may rejoice in You?

7 Show us Your mercy, LORD,
And grant us Your salvation.

8 I will hear what God the LORD will speak,
For He will speak peace
To His people and to His saints;
But let them not turn back to folly.

9 Surely His salvation *is* near to those who fear Him,
That glory may dwell in our land.

10 Mercy and truth have met together;
Righteousness and peace have kissed.

11 Truth shall spring out of the earth,
And righteousness shall look down from heaven.

12 Yes, the LORD will give *what is* good;
And our land will yield its increase.

13 Righteousness will go before Him,
And shall make His footsteps *our* pathway.

PSALM 86   THERE IS ONLY ONE TRUE GOD.
A Prayer of David.

1 Bow down Your ear, O LORD, hear me;
For I *am* poor and needy.

2 Preserve my life, for I *am* holy;
You are my God;
Save Your servant who trusts in You!

3 Be merciful to me, O Lord,
For I cry to You all day long.

4 Rejoice the soul of Your servant,
For to You, O Lord, I lift up my soul.

5 For You, Lord, *are* good, and ready to forgive,
And abundant in mercy to all those who call upon
You.

6 Give ear, O LORD, to my prayer;
And attend to the voice of my supplications.

7 In the day of my trouble I will call upon You,
For You will answer me.

8 Among the gods *there is* none like You, O Lord;
Nor *are there any works* like Your works.

9 All nations whom You have made
Shall come and worship before You, O Lord,
And shall glorify Your name.

10 For You *are* great, and do wondrous things;
You alone *are* God.

11 Teach me Your way, O LORD;
I will walk in Your truth;
Unite my heart to fear Your name.

WHOLEHEARTED

86:11-12 Wholehearted reverence means appreciating God and
honoring him in all areas of life. We need to show our loyalty to him
every part of our life, not just in going to church. If we reverence G
with our whole heart, then our work, relationships, use of money, a
desires will be in keeping with his will.

12 I will praise You, O Lord my God, with all my heart,
And I will glorify Your name forevermore.

13 For great *is* Your mercy toward me,
And You have delivered my soul from the depths of
Sheol.

14 O God, the proud have risen against me,
And a mob of violent *men* have sought my life,
And have not set You before them.

15 But You, O Lord, *are* a God full of compassion, and
gracious,
Longsuffering and abundant in mercy and truth.

16 Oh, turn to me, and have mercy on me!
Give Your strength to Your servant,
And save the son of Your maidservant.

17 Show me a sign for good,
That those who hate me may see *it* and be ashamed,
Because You, LORD, have helped me and comforted
me.

PSALM 87   JERUSALEM: A CITY GOD LOVES.
A Psalm of the sons of Korah. A Song.

1 His foundation *is* in the holy mountains.

2 The LORD loves the gates of Zion
More than all the dwellings of Jacob.

3 Glorious things are spoken of you,
O city of God!   Selah

4 "I will make mention of Rahab and Babylon to those
who know Me;
Behold, O Philistia and Tyre, with Ethiopia:
'This *one* was born there.'"

5 And of Zion it will be said,
"This *one* and that *one* were born in her;
And the Most High Himself shall establish her."

6 The LORD will record,

When He registers the peoples:
"This *one* was born there."   Selah

Both the singers and the players on instruments *say*,
"All my springs *are* in you."

PSALM **88**   GOD UNDERSTANDS YOUR HURTS.

A Song. A Psalm of the sons of Korah. To the Chief Musician. Set to "Mahalath Leannoth." A Contemplation of Heman the Ezrahite.

O LORD, God of my salvation,
I have cried out day and night before You.
2 Let my prayer come before You;
Incline Your ear to my cry.

3 For my soul is full of troubles,
And my life draws near to the grave.
4 I am counted with those who go down to the pit;
I am like a man *who has* no strength,
5 Adrift among the dead,
Like the slain who lie in the grave,
Whom You remember no more,
And who are cut off from Your hand.

6 You have laid me in the lowest pit,
In darkness, in the depths.
7 Your wrath lies heavy upon me,
And You have afflicted *me* with all Your waves.   Selah
8 You have put away my acquaintances far from me;
You have made me an abomination to them;
I am shut up, and I cannot get out;
9 My eye wastes away because of affliction.

LORD, I have called daily upon You;
I have stretched out my hands to You.
10 Will You work wonders for the dead?
Shall the dead arise *and* praise You?   Selah
11 Shall Your lovingkindness be declared in the grave?
Or Your faithfulness in the place of destruction?
12 Shall Your wonders be known in the dark?
And Your righteousness in the land of forgetfulness?

13 But to You I have cried out, O LORD,
And in the morning my prayer comes before You.
14 LORD, why do You cast off my soul?
Why do You hide Your face from me?
15 *I have been* afflicted and ready to die from *my* youth;
I suffer Your terrors;
I am distraught.
16 Your fierce wrath has gone over me;
Your terrors have cut me off.
17 They came around me all day long like water;
They engulfed me altogether.
18 Loved one and friend You have put far from me,
And my acquaintances into darkness.

PSALM **89**   GOD KEEPS PROMISES FOREVER.

A Contemplation of Ethan the Ezrahite.

1 I will sing of the mercies of the LORD forever;
With my mouth will I make known Your faithfulness
to all generations.
2 For I have said, "Mercy shall be built up forever;

Your faithfulness You shall establish in the very
heavens."

3 "I have made a covenant with My chosen,
I have sworn to My servant David:
4 'Your seed I will establish forever,
And build up your throne to all generations.'"   Selah

5 And the heavens will praise Your wonders, O LORD;
Your faithfulness also in the assembly of the saints.
6 For who in the heavens can be compared to the LORD?
Who among the sons of the mighty can be likened to
the LORD?

Does God get tired of hearing about our troubles? I get frustrated when I struggle with the same problems over and over.

I WONDER . . .

Do you know someone who complains a lot? Perhaps you have a little brother or sister, a friend, or an acquaintance at school who is always complaining. Complainers aren't much fun to be around.

Complaining means that we aren't happy with what is going on around us and we think that by telling others we want something to change, it will happen. It also means we want attention. Complaining shines the spotlight on us for a while, and people give us attention. Sometimes, that's all we really wanted in the first place!

If you have been reading through Psalms, you can see that the psalmist seems to complain a lot! He is always in some sort of trouble, and he always wants God to get him out of it (see Psalm 88). Sound familiar?

The motivation behind our complaining is the key issue. When surrounded by enemies, David cried to God for protection. He had nowhere else to turn. Although this may seem like complaining, it actually is a very honest way to pray. God never gets tired of hearing us and coming to our rescue if we need his help.

But sometimes we complain or ask God for help because we have made wrong choices that have gotten us into trouble. Our natural response is to ask God to get us out of it. Although God always listens to us, he knows that the solution is not found in his coming to the rescue.

Instead, we must ask for forgiveness and then change the behavior that caused the problem in the first place. Some troubles are best solved by being humble and admitting we are wrong.

But if trouble comes from people or situations that are beyond our control, God is not only quick to hear, but also quick to answer. Either he will provide the internal resources necessary to handle the problem (peace "which surpasses all understanding" [Philippians 4:7]) or he will provide the way of escape. Remember, "No temptation has overtaken you except such as is common to man; but God *is* faithful, who will not allow you to be tempted beyond what you are able, but with the temptation will also make the way of escape, that you may be able to bear *it*" (1 Corinthians 10:13).

⁷ God is greatly to be feared in the assembly of the
saints,
And to be held in reverence by all *those* around Him.
⁸ O LORD God of hosts,
Who *is* mighty like You, O LORD?
Your faithfulness also surrounds You.
⁹ You rule the raging of the sea;
When its waves rise, You still them.
¹⁰ You have broken Rahab in pieces, as one who is
slain;
You have scattered Your enemies with Your mighty
arm.
¹¹ The heavens *are* Yours, the earth also *is* Yours;
The world and all its fullness, You have founded
them.
¹² The north and the south, You have created them;
Tabor and Hermon rejoice in Your name.
¹³ You have a mighty arm;
Strong is Your hand, *and* high is Your right hand.

◣ AMBASSADOR

89:14-15 God's throne is pictured with a foundation of righteousness
and justice, and he is attended by mercy and truth. These describe
fundamental aspects of the way God deals with people. As God's
ambassadors, we should deal with people similarly. Make sure your
actions flow out of righteousness, justice, mercy, and truth because any
unfair, unloving, or dishonest action cannot come from God.

¹⁴ Righteousness and justice *are* the foundation of Your
throne;
Mercy and truth go before Your face.
¹⁵ Blessed *are* the people who know the joyful sound!
They walk, O LORD, in the light of Your countenance.
¹⁶ In Your name they rejoice all day long,
And in Your righteousness they are exalted.
¹⁷ For You *are* the glory of their strength,
And in Your favor our horn is exalted.
¹⁸ For our shield *belongs* to the LORD,
And our king to the Holy One of Israel.

¹⁹ Then You spoke in a vision to Your holy one,
And said: "I have given help to *one who is* mighty;
I have exalted one chosen from the people.
²⁰ I have found My servant David;
With My holy oil I have anointed him,
²¹ With whom My hand shall be established;
Also My arm shall strengthen him.
²² The enemy shall not outwit him,
Nor the son of wickedness afflict him.
²³ I will beat down his foes before his face,
And plague those who hate him.

²⁴ "But My faithfulness and My mercy *shall be* with him,
And in My name his horn shall be exalted.
²⁵ Also I will set his hand over the sea,
And his right hand over the rivers.
²⁶ He shall cry to Me, 'You *are* my Father,
My God, and the rock of my salvation.'
²⁷ Also I will make him *My* firstborn,
The highest of the kings of the earth.

²⁸ My mercy I will keep for him forever,
And My covenant shall stand firm with him.
²⁹ His seed also I will make *to endure* forever,
And his throne as the days of heaven.

³⁰ "If his sons forsake My law
And do not walk in My judgments,
³¹ If they break My statutes
And do not keep My commandments,
³² Then I will punish their transgression with the rod,
And their iniquity with stripes.
³³ Nevertheless My lovingkindness I will not utterly
take from him,
Nor allow My faithfulness to fail.
³⁴ My covenant I will not break,
Nor alter the word that has gone out of My lips.
³⁵ Once I have sworn by My holiness;
I will not lie to David:
³⁶ His seed shall endure forever,
And his throne as the sun before Me;
³⁷ It shall be established forever like the moon,
Even *like* the faithful witness in the sky."   Selah

³⁸ But You have cast off and abhorred,
You have been furious with Your anointed.
³⁹ You have renounced the covenant of Your servant;
You have profaned his crown *by casting it* to the
ground.
⁴⁰ You have broken down all his hedges;
You have brought his strongholds to ruin.
⁴¹ All who pass by the way plunder him;
He is a reproach to his neighbors.
⁴² You have exalted the right hand of his adversaries;
You have made all his enemies rejoice.
⁴³ You have also turned back the edge of his sword,
And have not sustained him in the battle.
⁴⁴ You have made his glory cease,
And cast his throne down to the ground.
⁴⁵ The days of his youth You have shortened;
You have covered him with shame.   Selah

⁴⁶ How long, LORD?
Will You hide Yourself forever?
Will Your wrath burn like fire?
⁴⁷ Remember how short my time is;
For what futility have You created all the children of
men?
⁴⁸ What man can live and not see death?
Can he deliver his life from the power of the grave?
Selah

⁴⁹ Lord, where *are* Your former lovingkindnesses,
Which You swore to David in Your truth?
⁵⁰ Remember, Lord, the reproach of Your servants—
How I bear in my bosom *the reproach of* all the many
peoples,
⁵¹ With which Your enemies have reproached, O LORD,
With which they have reproached the footsteps of
Your anointed.

⁵² Blessed *be* the LORD forevermore!
Amen and Amen.

BOOK FOUR: Psalms 90-106

PSALM 90 GOD'S ETERNAL KINGDOM.

A Prayer of Moses the man of God.

1 LORD, You have been our dwelling place in all
   generations.
2 Before the mountains were brought forth,
   Or ever You had formed the earth and the world,
   Even from everlasting to everlasting, You *are* God.

3 You turn man to destruction,
   And say, "Return, O children of men."
4 For a thousand years in Your sight
   Are like yesterday when it is past,
   And *like* a watch in the night.
5 You carry them away *like* a flood;
   They are like a sleep.
   In the morning they are like grass *which* grows up:
6 In the morning it flourishes and grows up;
   In the evening it is cut down and withers.

7 For we have been consumed by Your anger,
   And by Your wrath we are terrified.
8 You have set our iniquities before You,
   Our secret *sins* in the light of Your countenance.
9 For all our days have passed away in Your wrath;
   We finish our years like a sigh.
10 The days of our lives *are* seventy years;
   And if by reason of strength *they are* eighty years,
   Yet their boast *is* only labor and sorrow;
   For it is soon cut off, and we fly away.
11 Who knows the power of Your anger?
   For as the fear of You, *so is* Your wrath.
12 So teach *us* to number our days,
   That we may gain a heart of wisdom.

13 Return, O LORD!
   How long?
   And have compassion on Your servants.
14 Oh, satisfy us early with Your mercy,
   That we may rejoice and be glad all our days!
15 Make us glad according to the days *in which* You
   have afflicted us,
   The years *in which* we have seen evil.
16 Let Your work appear to Your servants,
   And Your glory to their children.
17 And let the beauty of the LORD our God be upon us,
   And establish the work of our hands for us;
   Yes, establish the work of our hands.

PSALM 91 SAFE FROM DANGER.

1 He who dwells in the secret place of the Most High
   Shall abide under the shadow of the Almighty.
2 I will say of the LORD, "*He is* my refuge and my
   fortress;
   My God, in Him I will trust."

3 Surely He shall deliver you from the snare of the
   fowler
   And from the perilous pestilence.
4 He shall cover you with His feathers,
   And under His wings you shall take refuge;

His truth *shall be your* shield and buckler.
5 You shall not be afraid of the terror by night,
   Nor of the arrow *that* flies by day,
6 *Nor* of the pestilence *that* walks in darkness,
   Nor of the destruction *that* lays waste at noonday.

7 A thousand may fall at your side,
   And ten thousand at your right hand;
   But it shall not come near you.

THE PROTECTOR

91:5-6 God is a refuge, a shelter when we are afraid. The writer's faith in God as Protector would carry him through all the dangers and fears of life. This should be a picture of our trust—trading all our fears for faith in him, no matter what kind of fear it may be.

8 Only with your eyes shall you look,
   And see the reward of the wicked.

9 Because you have made the LORD, *who is* my refuge,
   Even the Most High, your dwelling place,
10 No evil shall befall you,
   Nor shall any plague come near your dwelling;
11 For He shall give His angels charge over you,
   To keep you in all your ways.
12 In *their* hands they shall bear you up,
   Lest you dash your foot against a stone.
13 You shall tread upon the lion and the cobra,
   The young lion and the serpent you shall trample
   underfoot.

14 "Because he has set his love upon Me, therefore I will
   deliver him;
   I will set him on high, because he has known My
   name.
15 He shall call upon Me, and I will answer him;
   I *will be* with him in trouble;
   I will deliver him and honor him.
16 With long life I will satisfy him,
   And show him My salvation."

PSALM 92 A SONG FOR THE LORD'S DAY.

A Psalm. A Song for the Sabbath day.

1 *It is* good to give thanks to the LORD,
   And to sing praises to Your name, O Most High;
2 To declare Your lovingkindness in the morning,
   And Your faithfulness every night,
3 On an instrument of ten strings,
   On the lute,
   And on the harp,
   With harmonious sound.
4 For You, LORD, have made me glad through Your
   work;
   I will triumph in the works of Your hands.

5 O LORD, how great are Your works!
   Your thoughts are very deep.
6 A senseless man does not know,
   Nor does a fool understand this.
7 When the wicked spring up like grass,
   And when all the workers of iniquity flourish,
   It is that they may be destroyed forever.

8 But You, LORD, *are* on high forevermore.
9 For behold, Your enemies, O LORD,
   For behold, Your enemies shall perish;
   All the workers of iniquity shall be scattered.

10 But my horn You have exalted like a wild ox;
   I have been anointed with fresh oil.
11 My eye also has seen *my desire* on my enemies;
   My ears hear *my desire* on the wicked
   Who rise up against me.

12 The righteous shall flourish like a palm tree,
   He shall grow like a cedar in Lebanon.
13 Those who are planted in the house of the LORD
   Shall flourish in the courts of our God.

◣▬▬▬ELDERLY

92:14 Honoring God is not limited to young people who are still blessed with physical strength and vitality. Even in old age, devoted believers can produce spiritual fruit. There are many faithful older people who have much to share and teach from a lifetime of living with God. Seek out an elderly friend or relative to tell you about life experiences with the Lord and challenge you to new heights of spiritual living.

14 They shall still bear fruit in old age;
   They shall be fresh and flourishing,
15 To declare that the LORD is upright;
   He is my rock, and *there is* no unrighteousness in
   Him.

PSALM 93 OUR ALMIGHTY GOD.

1 The LORD reigns, He is clothed with majesty;
   The LORD is clothed,
   He has girded Himself with strength.
   Surely the world is established, so that it cannot be
      moved.
2 Your throne *is* established from of old;
   You *are* from everlasting.

3 The floods have lifted up, O LORD,
   The floods have lifted up their voice;
   The floods lift up their waves.
4 The LORD on high *is* mightier
   Than the noise of many waters,
   Than the mighty waves of the sea.

5 Your testimonies are very sure;
   Holiness adorns Your house,
   O LORD, forever.

PSALM 94 GOD WILL DEAL WITH THE WICKED.

1 O LORD God, to whom vengeance belongs—
   O God, to whom vengeance belongs, shine forth!
2 Rise up, O Judge of the earth;
   Render punishment to the proud.
3 LORD, how long will the wicked,
   How long will the wicked triumph?

4 They utter speech, *and* speak insolent things;
   All the workers of iniquity boast in themselves.
5 They break in pieces Your people, O LORD,
   And afflict Your heritage.

6 They slay the widow and the stranger,
   And murder the fatherless.
7 Yet they say, "The LORD does not see,
   Nor does the God of Jacob understand."

8 Understand, you senseless among the people;
   And *you* fools, when will you be wise?
9 He who planted the ear, shall He not hear?
   He who formed the eye, shall He not see?
10 He who instructs the nations, shall He not correct,
   He who teaches man knowledge?
11 The LORD knows the thoughts of man,
   That they *are* futile.

12 Blessed *is* the man whom You instruct, O LORD,
   And teach out of Your law,
13 That You may give him rest from the days of
      adversity,
   Until the pit is dug for the wicked.
14 For the LORD will not cast off His people,
   Nor will He forsake His inheritance.
15 But judgment will return to righteousness,
   And all the upright in heart will follow it.

16 Who will rise up for me against the evildoers?
   Who will stand up for me against the workers of
      iniquity?
17 Unless the LORD *had been* my help,
   My soul would soon have settled in silence.
18 If I say, "My foot slips,"
   Your mercy, O LORD, will hold me up.
19 In the multitude of my anxieties within me,
   Your comforts delight my soul.

20 Shall the throne of iniquity, which devises evil by law,
   Have fellowship with You?
21 They gather together against the life of the righteous,
   And condemn innocent blood.
22 But the LORD has been my defense,
   And my God the rock of my refuge.
23 He has brought on them their own iniquity,
   And shall cut them off in their own wickedness;
   The LORD our God shall cut them off.

PSALM 95 LET'S WORSHIP GOD.

1 Oh come, let us sing to the LORD!
   Let us shout joyfully to the Rock of our salvation.
2 Let us come before His presence with thanksgiving;
   Let us shout joyfully to Him with psalms.
3 For the LORD *is* the great God,
   And the great King above all gods.
4 In His hand *are* the deep places of the earth;
   The heights of the hills *are* His also.
5 The sea *is* His, for He made it;
   And His hands formed the dry *land.*

6 Oh come, let us worship and bow down;
   Let us kneel before the LORD our Maker.
7 For He *is* our God,
   And we *are* the people of His pasture,
   And the sheep of His hand.

Today, if you will hear His voice:

8 "Do not harden your hearts, as in the rebellion,
As *in* the day of trial in the wilderness,
9 When your fathers tested Me;
They tried Me, though they saw My work.
10 For forty years I was grieved with *that* generation,
And said, 'It *is* a people who go astray in their hearts,
And they do not know My ways.'
11 So I swore in My wrath,
'They shall not enter My rest.'"

PSALM 96 HOW CAN I PRAISE GOD?

1 Oh, sing to the LORD a new song!
Sing to the LORD, all the earth.
2 Sing to the LORD, bless His name;
Proclaim the good news of His salvation from day to day.
3 Declare His glory among the nations,
His wonders among all peoples.

4 For the LORD *is* great and greatly to be praised;
He *is* to be feared above all gods.
5 For all the gods of the peoples *are* idols,
But the LORD made the heavens.
6 Honor and majesty *are* before Him;
Strength and beauty *are* in His sanctuary.

7 Give to the LORD, O families of the peoples,
Give to the LORD glory and strength.
8 Give to the LORD the glory *due* His name;
Bring an offering, and come into His courts.
9 Oh, worship the LORD in the beauty of holiness!
Tremble before Him, all the earth.

10 Say among the nations, "The LORD reigns;
The world also is firmly established,
It shall not be moved;
He shall judge the peoples righteously."

11 Let the heavens rejoice, and let the earth be glad;
Let the sea roar, and all its fullness;
12 Let the field be joyful, and all that *is* in it.
Then all the trees of the woods will rejoice before the LORD.
13 For He is coming, for He is coming to judge the earth.
He shall judge the world with righteousness,
And the peoples with His truth.

PSALM 97 GOD IS AWESOME AND JUST.

1 The LORD reigns;
Let the earth rejoice;
Let the multitude of isles be glad!

2 Clouds and darkness surround Him;
Righteousness and justice *are* the foundation of His throne.
3 A fire goes before Him,
And burns up His enemies round about.
4 His lightnings light the world;
The earth sees and trembles.
5 The mountains melt like wax at the presence of the LORD,

At the presence of the Lord of the whole earth.
6 The heavens declare His righteousness,
And all the peoples see His glory.

7 Let all be put to shame who serve carved images,
Who boast of idols.
Worship Him, all *you* gods.
8 Zion hears and is glad,
And the daughters of Judah rejoice
Because of Your judgments, O LORD.
9 For You, LORD, *are* most high above all the earth;
You are exalted far above all gods.

10 You who love the LORD, hate evil!
He preserves the souls of His saints;

▬▬▬▬HATE EVIL

97:10 A sincere desire to please God will result in an alignment of your desires with God's desires. You will love what God loves and hate what God hates. Here we read that God loves those who hate evil. If you do not despise the actions of people who take advantage of others, if you admire people who look out only for themselves, or if you envy those who get ahead using any means to accomplish their ends, then your primary desire in life is not to please God. Learn to love God's ways and hate evil in every form— not only the obvious sins, but the socially acceptable ones as well.

He delivers them out of the hand of the wicked.
11 Light is sown for the righteous,
And gladness for the upright in heart.
12 Rejoice in the LORD, you righteous,
And give thanks at the remembrance of His holy name.

PSALM 98 A SONG OF JOY AND VICTORY.

A Psalm.
1 Oh, sing to the LORD a new song!
For He has done marvelous things;
His right hand and His holy arm have gained Him the victory.
2 The LORD has made known His salvation;
His righteousness He has revealed in the sight of the nations.
3 He has remembered His mercy and His faithfulness to the house of Israel;
All the ends of the earth have seen the salvation of our God.

4 Shout joyfully to the LORD, all the earth;
Break forth in song, rejoice, and sing praises.
5 Sing to the LORD with the harp,
With the harp and the sound of a psalm,
6 With trumpets and the sound of a horn;
Shout joyfully before the LORD, the King.

7 Let the sea roar, and all its fullness,
The world and those who dwell in it;
8 Let the rivers clap *their* hands;
Let the hills be joyful together before the LORD,
9 For He is coming to judge the earth.
With righteousness He shall judge the world,
And the peoples with equity.

PSALM 99 GOD IS FAIR AND HOLY.

1 The LORD reigns;
Let the peoples tremble!
He dwells *between* the cherubim;
Let the earth be moved!
2 The LORD *is* great in Zion,
And He *is* high above all the peoples.
3 Let them praise Your great and awesome name—
He *is* holy.

FAMILY NAME

99:3 Everyone, even kings and rulers, should reverence God's great and holy name because his name symbolizes his nature, his personage, and his reputation. But the name of God is used so often in vulgar conversation that we have lost sight of its holiness. How easy it is to treat God lightly in everyday life! If you claim him as your father, live in a way that is worthy of the family name. Reverence God's name by both your *words* and your *life*.

4 The King's strength also loves justice;
You have established equity;
You have executed justice and righteousness in
Jacob.
5 Exalt the LORD our God,
And worship at His footstool—
He *is* holy.

6 Moses and Aaron were among His priests,
And Samuel was among those who called upon His
name;
They called upon the LORD, and He answered them.
7 He spoke to them in the cloudy pillar;
They kept His testimonies and the ordinance He
gave them.

8 You answered them, O LORD our God;
You were to them God-Who-Forgives,
Though You took vengeance on their deeds.
9 Exalt the LORD our God,
And worship at His holy hill;
For the LORD our God *is* holy.

PSALM 100 COME BEFORE GOD WITH PRAISE.

A Psalm of Thanksgiving.
1 Make a joyful shout to the LORD, all you lands!
2 Serve the LORD with gladness;
Come before His presence with singing.
3 Know that the LORD, He *is* God;
It is He *who* has made us, and not we ourselves;
We are His people and the sheep of His pasture.

4 Enter into His gates with thanksgiving,
And into His courts with praise.
Be thankful to Him, *and* bless His name.
5 For the LORD *is* good;
His mercy *is* everlasting,
And His truth *endures* to all generations.

PSALM 101 LIVING A CLEAN LIFE FOR GOD.

A Psalm of David.
1 I will sing of mercy and justice;

To You, O LORD, I will sing praises.
2 I will behave wisely in a perfect way.
Oh, when will You come to me?
I will walk within my house with a perfect heart.

3 I will set nothing wicked before my eyes;
I hate the work of those who fall away;
It shall not cling to me.
4 A perverse heart shall depart from me;
I will not know wickedness.

5 Whoever secretly slanders his neighbor,
Him I will destroy;
The one who has a haughty look and a proud heart,
Him I will not endure.

6 My eyes *shall be* on the faithful of the land,
That they may dwell with me;
He who walks in a perfect way,
He shall serve me.

HEROES

101:6 David set different standards for heroes than most. He said he would make the "faithful of the land" his heroes. Our heroes, the we set up in our minds as models to copy, have a great influence on life. Choose your heroes with care.

7 He who works deceit shall not dwell within my
house;
He who tells lies shall not continue in my presence.
8 Early I will destroy all the wicked of the land,
That I may cut off all the evildoers from the city of
the LORD.

PSALM 102 WHEN WE NEED HELP. *A Prayer of the afflicted, when he is overwhelmed and pours out his complaint before the LORD.*

1 Hear my prayer, O LORD,
And let my cry come to You.
2 Do not hide Your face from me in the day of my
trouble;
Incline Your ear to me;
In the day that I call, answer me speedily.

3 For my days are consumed like smoke,
And my bones are burned like a hearth.
4 My heart is stricken and withered like grass,
So that I forget to eat my bread.
5 Because of the sound of my groaning
My bones cling to my skin.
6 I am like a pelican of the wilderness;
I am like an owl of the desert.
7 I lie awake,
And am like a sparrow alone on the housetop.

8 My enemies reproach me all day long;
Those who deride me swear an oath against me.
9 For I have eaten ashes like bread,
And mingled my drink with weeping,
10 Because of Your indignation and Your wrath;
For You have lifted me up and cast me away.

11 My days *are* like a shadow that lengthens,
And I wither away like grass.

12 But You, O Lord, shall endure forever,
And the remembrance of Your name to all
generations.

13 You will arise *and* have mercy on Zion;
For the time to favor her,
Yes, the set time, has come.

14 For Your servants take pleasure in her stones,
And show favor to her dust.

15 So the nations shall fear the name of the Lord,
And all the kings of the earth Your glory.

16 For the Lord shall build up Zion;
He shall appear in His glory.

17 He shall regard the prayer of the destitute,
And shall not despise their prayer.

18 This will be written for the generation to come,
That a people yet to be created may praise the Lord.

19 For He looked down from the height of His
sanctuary;
From heaven the Lord viewed the earth,

20 To hear the groaning of the prisoner,
To release those appointed to death,

21 To declare the name of the Lord in Zion,
And His praise in Jerusalem,

22 When the peoples are gathered together,
And the kingdoms, to serve the Lord.

23 He weakened my strength in the way;
He shortened my days.

24 I said, "O my God,
Do not take me away in the midst of my days;
Your years *are* throughout all generations.

25 Of old You laid the foundation of the earth,
And the heavens *are* the work of Your hands.

26 They will perish, but You will endure;
Yes, they will all grow old like a garment;
Like a cloak You will change them,
And they will be changed.

27 But You *are* the same,
And Your years will have no end.

28 The children of Your servants will continue,
And their descendants will be established before
You."

PSALM **103** GOD'S GREAT LOVE FOR US.

A Psalm *of David.*

1 Bless the Lord, O my soul;
And all that is within me, *bless* His holy name!

2 Bless the Lord, O my soul,
And forget not all His benefits:

3 Who forgives all your iniquities,
Who heals all your diseases,

4 Who redeems your life from destruction,
Who crowns you with lovingkindness and tender
mercies,

5 Who satisfies your mouth with good *things,*
So *that* your youth is renewed like the eagle's.

6 The Lord executes righteousness

And justice for all who are oppressed.

7 He made known His ways to Moses,
His acts to the children of Israel.

8 The Lord *is* merciful and gracious,
Slow to anger, and abounding in mercy.

PLENTY

103:1ff David's praise focused on God's glorious acts. It is easy to complain about life, but David's list gives us plenty for which to praise God—his love, forgiveness, salvation, kindness, mercy, justice, patience, tenderness—we receive all of these without deserving any of them. No matter how difficult your life's journey, you can always count your blessings—past, present, and future. When you feel as though you have nothing for which to praise God, read David's list.

9 He will not always strive *with us,*
Nor will He keep *His anger* forever.

10 He has not dealt with us according to our sins,
Nor punished us according to our iniquities.

11 For as the heavens are high above the earth,
So great is His mercy toward those who fear Him;

12 As far as the east is from the west,
So far has He removed our transgressions from us.

ENTER
INTO HIS
GATES
WITH
thanksgiving
thanksgiving
AND
INTO HIS
COURTS
WITH
PRAISE
PRAISE
PRAISE

PSALM 100:4

Be thankful to HIM
AND *bless*
HIS NAME.

104:24 Creation is filled with stunning variety, revealing the rich creativity, goodness, and wisdom of our loving God. As you observe your natural surroundings, thank God for his creativity. Take a fresh look at people, seeing each one as his unique creation, each with his or her own special talents, abilities, and gifts.

13 As a father pities *his* children,
   So the LORD pities those who fear Him.
14 For He knows our frame;
   He remembers that we *are* dust.

15 *As for* man, his days *are* like grass;
   As a flower of the field, so he flourishes.
16 For the wind passes over it, and it is gone,
   And its place remembers it no more.
17 But the mercy of the LORD *is* from everlasting to
      everlasting
   On those who fear Him,
   And His righteousness to children's children,
18 To such as keep His covenant,
   And to those who remember His commandments to
      do them.

19 The LORD has established His throne in heaven,
   And His kingdom rules over all.

20 Bless the LORD, you His angels,
   Who excel in strength, who do His word,
   Heeding the voice of His word.
21 Bless the LORD, all *you* His hosts,
   You ministers of His, who do His pleasure.
22 Bless the LORD, all His works,
   In all places of His dominion.

   Bless the LORD, O my soul!

PSALM **104** GOD TAKES CARE OF HIS WORLD.

1 Bless the LORD, O my soul!

   O LORD my God, You are very great:
   You are clothed with honor and majesty,
2 Who cover *Yourself* with light as *with* a garment,
   Who stretch out the heavens like a curtain.

3 He lays the beams of His upper chambers in the
      waters,
   Who makes the clouds His chariot,
   Who walks on the wings of the wind,
4 Who makes His angels spirits,
   His ministers a flame of fire.

5 *You who* laid the foundations of the earth,
   So *that* it should not be moved forever,
6 You covered it with the deep as *with* a garment;
   The waters stood above the mountains.
7 At Your rebuke they fled;
   At the voice of Your thunder they hastened away.
8 They went up over the mountains;
   They went down into the valleys,
   To the place which You founded for them.
9 You have set a boundary that they may not pass over,
   That they may not return to cover the earth.

10 He sends the springs into the valleys;
   They flow among the hills.
11 They give drink to every beast of the field;

The wild donkeys quench their thirst.
12 By them the birds of the heavens have their home;
   They sing among the branches.
13 He waters the hills from His upper chambers;
   The earth is satisfied with the fruit of Your works.

14 He causes the grass to grow for the cattle,
   And vegetation for the service of man,
   That he may bring forth food from the earth,
15 And wine *that* makes glad the heart of man,
   Oil to make *his* face shine,
   And bread *which* strengthens man's heart.
16 The trees of the LORD are full *of sap*,
   The cedars of Lebanon which He planted,
17 Where the birds make their nests;
   The stork has her home in the fir trees.
18 The high hills *are* for the wild goats;
   The cliffs are a refuge for the rock badgers.

19 He appointed the moon for seasons;
   The sun knows its going down.
20 You make darkness, and it is night,
   In which all the beasts of the forest creep about.
21 The young lions roar after their prey,
   And seek their food from God.
22 *When* the sun rises, they gather together
   And lie down in their dens.
23 Man goes out to his work
   And to his labor until the evening.

24 O LORD, how manifold are Your works!
   In wisdom You have made them all.
   The earth is full of Your possessions—
25 This great and wide sea,
   In which *are* innumerable teeming things,
   Living things both small and great.
26 There the ships sail about;
   There is that Leviathan
   Which You have made to play there.

27 These all wait for You,
   That You may give *them* their food in due season.
28 *What* You give them they gather in;
   You open Your hand, they are filled with good.
29 You hide Your face, they are troubled;
   You take away their breath, they die and return to
      their dust.
30 You send forth Your Spirit, they are created;
   And You renew the face of the earth.

31 May the glory of the LORD endure forever;
   May the LORD rejoice in His works.
32 He looks on the earth, and it trembles;
   He touches the hills, and they smoke.

33 I will sing to the LORD as long as I live;
   I will sing praise to my God while I have my being.
34 May my meditation be sweet to Him;
   I will be glad in the LORD.
35 May sinners be consumed from the earth,
   And the wicked be no more.

   Bless the LORD, O my soul!
   Praise the LORD!

PSALM **105** REMEMBER GOD'S MIRACLES.

1 Oh, give thanks to the LORD!
   Call upon His name;
   Make known His deeds among the peoples!
2 Sing to Him, sing psalms to Him;
   Talk of all His wondrous works!
3 Glory in His holy name;
   Let the hearts of those rejoice who seek the LORD!
4 Seek the LORD and His strength;
   Seek His face evermore!
5 Remember His marvelous works which He has done,
   His wonders, and the judgments of His mouth,
6 O seed of Abraham His servant,
   You children of Jacob, His chosen ones!

7 He *is* the LORD our God;
   His judgments *are* in all the earth.
8 He remembers His covenant forever,
   The word *which* He commanded, for a thousand
        generations,
9 *The covenant* which He made with Abraham,
   And His oath to Isaac,
10 And confirmed it to Jacob for a statute,
   To Israel *as* an everlasting covenant,
11 Saying, "To you I will give the land of Canaan
   As the allotment of your inheritance,"
12 When they were few in number,
   Indeed very few, and strangers in it.

13 When they went from one nation to another,
   From *one* kingdom to another people,
14 He permitted no one to do them wrong;
   Yes, He rebuked kings for their sakes,
15 *Saying,* "Do not touch My anointed ones,
   And do My prophets no harm."

16 Moreover He called for a famine in the land;
   He destroyed all the provision of bread.
17 He sent a man before them—
   Joseph—*who* was sold as a slave.
18 They hurt his feet with fetters,
   He was laid in irons.
19 Until the time that his word came to pass,
   The word of the LORD tested him.
20 The king sent and released him,
   The ruler of the people let him go free.
21 He made him lord of his house,
   And ruler of all his possessions,
22 To bind his princes at his pleasure,
   And teach his elders wisdom.

23 Israel also came into Egypt,
   And Jacob dwelt in the land of Ham.
24 He increased His people greatly,
   And made them stronger than their enemies.
25 He turned their heart to hate His people,
   To deal craftily with His servants.

26 He sent Moses His servant,
   And Aaron whom He had chosen.
27 They performed His signs among them,
   And wonders in the land of Ham.
28 He sent darkness, and made *it* dark;

And they did not rebel against His word.
29 He turned their waters into blood,
   And killed their fish.
30 Their land abounded with frogs,
   Even in the chambers of their kings.
31 He spoke, and there came swarms of flies,
   And lice in all their territory.
32 He gave them hail for rain,
   And flaming fire in their land.
33 He struck their vines also, and their fig trees,
   And splintered the trees of their territory.
34 He spoke, and locusts came,
   Young locusts without number,
35 And ate up all the vegetation in their land,
   And devoured the fruit of their ground.
36 He also destroyed all the firstborn in their land,
   The first of all their strength.

HE IS THERE

105:4 If God seems far away, keep searching for him. God rewards those who sincerely look for him (Hebrews 11:6). Jesus promised, "seek, and you will find" (Matthew 7:7). David suggested a valuable way to search out God— become familiar with the way he has helped his people in the past. The Bible records the history of God's people. In searching its pages we will discover a loving God who is waiting for us to find him.

37 He also brought them out with silver and gold,
   And *there was* none feeble among His tribes.
38 Egypt was glad when they departed,
   For the fear of them had fallen upon them.
39 He spread a cloud for a covering,
   And fire to give light in the night.
40 *The people* asked, and He brought quail,
   And satisfied them with the bread of heaven.
41 He opened the rock, and water gushed out;
   It ran in the dry places *like* a river.

42 For He remembered His holy promise,
   And Abraham His servant.
43 He brought out His people with joy,
   His chosen ones with gladness.
44 He gave them the lands of the Gentiles,
   And they inherited the labor of the nations,
45 That they might observe His statutes
   And keep His laws.

   Praise the LORD!

PSALM **106** GOD ALWAYS FORGIVES.
1 Praise the LORD!

   Oh, give thanks to the LORD, for *He is* good!
   For His mercy *endures* forever.

2 Who can utter the mighty acts of the LORD?
   Who can declare all His praise?
3 Blessed *are* those who keep justice,
   And he who does righteousness at all times!

4 Remember me, O LORD, with the favor *You have
   toward* Your people.

Oh, visit me with Your salvation,
5 That I may see the benefit of Your chosen ones,
That I may rejoice in the gladness of Your nation,
That I may glory with Your inheritance.

6 We have sinned with our fathers,
We have committed iniquity,
We have done wickedly.
7 Our fathers in Egypt did not understand Your
wonders;
They did not remember the multitude of Your
mercies,
But rebelled by the sea—the Red Sea.

8 Nevertheless He saved them for His name's sake,
That He might make His mighty power known.
9 He rebuked the Red Sea also, and it dried up;
So He led them through the depths,
As through the wilderness.
10 He saved them from the hand of him who hated
them,
And redeemed them from the hand of the enemy.
11 The waters covered their enemies;
There was not one of them left.
12 Then they believed His words;
They sang His praise.

13 They soon forgot His works;
They did not wait for His counsel,
14 But lusted exceedingly in the wilderness,
And tested God in the desert.
15 And He gave them their request,
But sent leanness into their soul.

◣◣◣ TROUBLES

106:40-42 God allowed trouble to come to the Israelites to help them. Our troubles can be helpful because they (1) humble us, (2) pull us from the allurements of the world and drive us back to God, (3) quicken our prayers, (4) allow us to experience more of God's faithfulness, (5) make us more dependent upon God, (6) encourage us to submit to God's purpose for our life, and (7) make us more compassionate to others in trouble.

16 When they envied Moses in the camp,
And Aaron the saint of the LORD,
17 The earth opened up and swallowed Dathan,
And covered the faction of Abiram.
18 A fire was kindled in their company;
The flame burned up the wicked.

19 They made a calf in Horeb,
And worshiped the molded image.
20 Thus they changed their glory
Into the image of an ox that eats grass.
21 They forgot God their Savior,
Who had done great things in Egypt,
22 Wondrous works in the land of Ham,
Awesome things by the Red Sea.
23 Therefore He said that He would destroy them,
Had not Moses His chosen one stood before Him in
the breach,
To turn away His wrath, lest He destroy them.

24 Then they despised the pleasant land;
They did not believe His word,
25 But complained in their tents,
And did not heed the voice of the LORD.
26 Therefore He raised His hand in an oath against
them,
To overthrow them in the wilderness,
27 To overthrow their descendants among the nations,
And to scatter them in the lands.

28 They joined themselves also to Baal of Peor,
And ate sacrifices made to the dead.
29 Thus they provoked Him to anger with their deeds,
And the plague broke out among them.
30 Then Phinehas stood up and intervened,
And the plague was stopped.
31 And that was accounted to him for righteousness
To all generations forevermore.

32 They angered Him also at the waters of strife,
So that it went ill with Moses on account of them;
33 Because they rebelled against His Spirit,
So that he spoke rashly with his lips.

34 They did not destroy the peoples,
Concerning whom the LORD had commanded them,
35 But they mingled with the Gentiles
And learned their works;
36 They served their idols,
Which became a snare to them.
37 They even sacrificed their sons
And their daughters to demons,
38 And shed innocent blood,
The blood of their sons and daughters,
Whom they sacrificed to the idols of Canaan;
And the land was polluted with blood.
39 Thus they were defiled by their own works,
And played the harlot by their own deeds.

40 Therefore the wrath of the LORD was kindled against
His people,
So that He abhorred His own inheritance.
41 And He gave them into the hand of the Gentiles,
And those who hated them ruled over them.
42 Their enemies also oppressed them,
And they were brought into subjection under their
hand.
43 Many times He delivered them;
But they rebelled in their counsel,
And were brought low for their iniquity.
44 Nevertheless He regarded their affliction,
When He heard their cry;
45 And for their sake He remembered His covenant,
And relented according to the multitude of His
mercies.
46 He also made them to be pitied
By all those who carried them away captive.

47 Save us, O LORD our God,
And gather us from among the Gentiles,
To give thanks to Your holy name,
To triumph in Your praise.

48 Blessed *be* the LORD God of Israel
From everlasting to everlasting!
And let all the people say, "Amen!"

Praise the LORD!

BOOK FIVE: Psalms 107–150

PSALM 107 GIVE THANKS ALWAYS.

1 Oh, give thanks to the LORD, for *He is* good!
For His mercy *endures* forever.
2 Let the redeemed of the LORD say *so,*
Whom He has redeemed from the hand of the
enemy,
3 And gathered out of the lands,
From the east and from the west,
From the north and from the south.

4 They wandered in the wilderness in a desolate way;
They found no city to dwell in.
5 Hungry and thirsty,
Their soul fainted in them.
6 Then they cried out to the LORD in their trouble,
And He delivered them out of their distresses.
7 And He led them forth by the right way,
That they might go to a city for a dwelling place.
8 Oh, that *men* would give thanks to the LORD *for* His
goodness,
And *for* His wonderful works to the children of men!
9 For He satisfies the longing soul,
And fills the hungry soul with goodness.

10 Those who sat in darkness and in the shadow of
death,
Bound in affliction and irons—
11 Because they rebelled against the words of God,
And despised the counsel of the Most High,
12 Therefore He brought down their heart with labor;
They fell down, and *there was* none to help.
13 Then they cried out to the LORD in their trouble,
And He saved them out of their distresses.
14 He brought them out of darkness and the shadow of
death,
And broke their chains in pieces.
15 Oh, that *men* would give thanks to the LORD *for* His
goodness,
And *for* His wonderful works to the children of men!
16 For He has broken the gates of bronze,
And cut the bars of iron in two.

17 Fools, because of their transgression,
And because of their iniquities, were afflicted.
18 Their soul abhorred all manner of food,
And they drew near to the gates of death.
19 Then they cried out to the LORD in their trouble,
And He saved them out of their distresses.
20 He sent His word and healed them,
And delivered *them* from their destructions.
21 Oh, that *men* would give thanks to the LORD *for* His
goodness,
And *for* His wonderful works to the children of men!
22 Let them sacrifice the sacrifices of thanksgiving,

And declare His works with rejoicing.

23 Those who go down to the sea in ships,
Who do business on great waters,
24 They see the works of the LORD,
And His wonders in the deep.
25 For He commands and raises the stormy wind,
Which lifts up the waves of the sea.
26 They mount up to the heavens,
They go down again to the depths;
Their soul melts because of trouble.
27 They reel to and fro, and stagger like a drunken man,
And are at their wits' end.
28 Then they cry out to the LORD in their trouble,
And He brings them out of their distresses.
29 He calms the storm,
So that its waves are still.
30 Then they are glad because they are quiet;
So He guides them to their desired haven.
31 Oh, that *men* would give thanks to the LORD *for* His
goodness,
And *for* His wonderful works to the children of men!
32 Let them exalt Him also in the assembly of the
people,
And praise Him in the company of the elders.

33 He turns rivers into a wilderness,
And the watersprings into dry ground;
34 A fruitful land into barrenness,
For the wickedness of those who dwell in it.
35 He turns a wilderness into pools of water,
And dry land into watersprings.
36 There He makes the hungry dwell,
That they may establish a city for a dwelling place,
37 And sow fields and plant vineyards,
That they may yield a fruitful harvest.
38 He also blesses them, and they multiply greatly;
And He does not let their cattle decrease.

39 When they are diminished and brought low
Through oppression, affliction and sorrow,
40 He pours contempt on princes,
And causes them to wander in the wilderness *where
there is* no way;
41 Yet He sets the poor on high, far from affliction,
And makes *their* families like a flock.
42 The righteous see *it* and rejoice,
And all iniquity stops its mouth.

43 Whoever *is* wise will observe these *things,*
And they will understand the lovingkindness of the
LORD.

PSALM 108 WITH GOD, WE CAN. *A Song.*
A Psalm of David.
1 O God, my heart is steadfast;
I will sing and give praise, even with my glory.

◣◥━━ STRENGTH

107:28-32 Sometimes we feel as though all is hopeless. But trouble can lead us to depend on God as we cry to him for help. When he saves us, we will praise him for the good he has done. Then we understand that God can bring good out of troubles because our afflictions strengthen our faith.

2 Awake, lute and harp!
I will awaken the dawn.
3 I will praise You, O LORD, among the peoples,
And I will sing praises to You among the nations.
4 For Your mercy *is* great above the heavens,
And Your truth *reaches* to the clouds.

5 Be exalted, O God, above the heavens,
And Your glory above all the earth;
6 That Your beloved may be delivered,
Save *with* Your right hand, and hear me.

7 God has spoken in His holiness:
"I will rejoice;
I will divide Shechem
And measure out the Valley of Succoth.
8 Gilead *is* Mine; Manasseh *is* Mine;
Ephraim also *is* the helmet for My head;
Judah *is* My lawgiver.
9 Moab *is* My washpot;
Over Edom I will cast My shoe;
Over Philistia I will triumph."

◼STAKE A CLAIM

108:13 Do our prayers end with requests just to make it through stressful situations? David prayed not just for rescue, but for victory. With God's help we can claim more than just survival, we can claim victory! Look for ways God can use your distress as an opportunity to show his mighty power.

10 Who will bring me *into* the strong city?
Who will lead me to Edom?
11 *Is it* not *You,* O God, *who* cast us off?
And *You,* O God, *who* did not go out with our armies?
12 Give us help from trouble,
For the help of man is useless.
13 Through God we will do valiantly,
For *it is* He *who* shall tread down our enemies.

PSALM 109 HELP ME, O LORD! *To the Chief Musician. A Psalm of David.*

1 Do not keep silent,
O God of my praise!
2 For the mouth of the wicked and the mouth of the deceitful
Have opened against me;
They have spoken against me with a lying tongue.
3 They have also surrounded me with words of hatred,
And fought against me without a cause.
4 In return for my love they are my accusers,
But I *give myself to* prayer.
5 Thus they have rewarded me evil for good,
And hatred for my love.

6 Set a wicked man over him,
And let an accuser stand at his right hand.
7 When he is judged, let him be found guilty,
And let his prayer become sin.
8 Let his days be few,
And let another take his office.
9 Let his children be fatherless,
And his wife a widow.
10 Let his children continually be vagabonds, and beg;
Let them seek *their bread* also from their desolate places.
11 Let the creditor seize all that he has,
And let strangers plunder his labor.
12 Let there be none to extend mercy to him,
Nor let there be any to favor his fatherless children.
13 Let his posterity be cut off,
And in the generation following let their name be blotted out.
14 Let the iniquity of his fathers be remembered before the LORD,
And let not the sin of his mother be blotted out.
15 Let them be continually before the LORD,
That He may cut off the memory of them from the earth;
16 Because he did not remember to show mercy,
But persecuted the poor and needy man,
That he might even slay the broken in heart.
17 As he loved cursing, so let it come to him;
As he did not delight in blessing, so let it be far from him.
18 As he clothed himself with cursing as with his garment,
So let it enter his body like water,
And like oil into his bones.
19 Let it be to him like the garment which covers him,
And for a belt with which he girds himself continually.
20 *Let* this *be* the LORD's reward to my accusers,
And to those who speak evil against my person.

21 But You, O GOD the Lord,
Deal with me for Your name's sake;
Because Your mercy *is* good, deliver me.
22 For I *am* poor and needy,
And my heart is wounded within me.
23 I am gone like a shadow when it lengthens;
I am shaken off like a locust.
24 My knees are weak through fasting,
And my flesh is feeble from lack of fatness.
25 I also have become a reproach to them;
When they look at me, they shake their heads.

26 Help me, O LORD my God!
Oh, save me according to Your mercy,
27 That they may know that this *is* Your hand—
That You, LORD, have done it!
28 Let them curse, but You bless;
When they arise, let them be ashamed,
But let Your servant rejoice.
29 Let my accusers be clothed with shame,
And let them cover themselves with their own disgrace as with a mantle.

30 I will greatly praise the LORD with my mouth;
Yes, I will praise Him among the multitude.
31 For He shall stand at the right hand of the poor,
To save *him* from those who condemn him.

PSALM **110** JESUS CHRIST, THE MESSIAH.
A Psalm of David.

1 The LORD said to my Lord,
"Sit at My right hand,
Till I make Your enemies Your footstool."
2 The LORD shall send the rod of Your strength out of
Zion.
Rule in the midst of Your enemies!

3 Your people *shall be* volunteers
In the day of Your power;
In the beauties of holiness, from the womb of the
morning,
You have the dew of Your youth.
4 The LORD has sworn
And will not relent,
"You *are* a priest forever
According to the order of Melchizedek."

5 The Lord *is* at Your right hand;
He shall execute kings in the day of His wrath.
6 He shall judge among the nations,
He shall fill *the places* with dead bodies,
He shall execute the heads of many countries.
7 He shall drink of the brook by the wayside;
Therefore He shall lift up the head.

PSALM **111** ALL GOD DOES IS GOOD.
1 Praise the LORD!

I will praise the LORD with *my* whole heart,
In the assembly of the upright and *in* the
congregation.

2 The works of the LORD *are* great,
Studied by all who have pleasure in them.
3 His work *is* honorable and glorious,
And His righteousness endures forever.
4 He has made His wonderful works to be
remembered;
The LORD *is* gracious and full of compassion.
5 He has given food to those who fear Him;
He will ever be mindful of His covenant.
6 He has declared to His people the power of His
works,
In giving them the heritage of the nations.

7 The works of His hands *are* verity and justice;
All His precepts *are* sure.
8 They stand fast forever and ever,
And are done in truth and uprightness.
9 He has sent redemption to His people;
He has commanded His covenant forever:
Holy and awesome *is* His name.

10 The fear of the LORD *is* the beginning of wisdom;
A good understanding have all those who do *His*
commandments.
His praise endures forever.

PSALM **112** HAPPY ARE THOSE WHO OBEY.
1 Praise the LORD!

Blessed *is* the man *who* fears the LORD,
Who delights greatly in His commandments.
2 His descendants will be mighty on earth;
The generation of the upright will be blessed.
3 Wealth and riches *will be* in his house,
And his righteousness endures forever.
4 Unto the upright there arises light in the darkness;
He is gracious, and full of compassion, and
righteous.

ON THE FENCE?
110:1-7 Many people have a vague belief in God, but refuse to accept Jesus as anything more than a great human teacher. But the Bible does not allow that option. Both the Old and New Testaments proclaim the deity of the One who came to save and to reign. This psalm shows God's promise of sending the Messiah. The New Testament clearly shows that Jesus is God's Son, the Messiah. You can't straddle the fence, calling Jesus "just a good teacher," because the Bible clearly calls him the Messiah.

5 A good man deals graciously and lends;
He will guide his affairs with discretion.
6 Surely he will never be shaken;
The righteous will be in everlasting remembrance.
7 He will not be afraid of evil tidings;
His heart is steadfast, trusting in the LORD.
8 His heart *is* established;
He will not be afraid,
Until he sees *his desire* upon his enemies.

9 He has dispersed abroad,
He has given to the poor;
His righteousness endures forever;
His horn will be exalted with honor.
10 The wicked will see *it* and be grieved;
He will gnash his teeth and melt away;
The desire of the wicked shall perish.

PSALM **113** GOD CARES ABOUT EVERYONE.
1 Praise the LORD!

Praise, O servants of the LORD,
Praise the name of the LORD!
2 Blessed be the name of the LORD
From this time forth and forevermore!
3 From the rising of the sun to its going down
The LORD's name *is* to be praised.

4 The LORD *is* high above all nations,
His glory above the heavens.
5 Who *is* like the LORD our God,
Who dwells on high,
6 Who humbles Himself to behold
The things that are in the heavens and in the earth?

FEARLESS
112:7-8 We all want to live without fear; our heroes are fearless people who face dangers and overcome them. The psalmist teaches us that *fear* of God can lead to a *fearless* life. To fear God means to respect and reverence him as the almighty Lord. When we trust God completely to take care of us, we will find that our other fears—even of death itself—will subside.

7 He raises the poor out of the dust,
  And lifts the needy out of the ash heap,
8 That He may seat *him* with princes—
  With the princes of His people.
9 He grants the barren woman a home,
  Like a joyful mother of children.

  Praise the LORD!

PSALM 114 CELEBRATE GOD'S GREAT WORKS.

1 When Israel went out of Egypt,
  The house of Jacob from a people of strange
    language,
2 Judah became His sanctuary,
  And Israel His dominion.

3 The sea saw *it* and fled;
  Jordan turned back.
4 The mountains skipped like rams,
  The little hills like lambs.
5 What ails you, O sea, that you fled?
  O Jordan, *that* you turned back?
6 O mountains, *that* you skipped like rams?
  O little hills, like lambs?

7 Tremble, O earth, at the presence of the Lord,
  At the presence of the God of Jacob,
8 Who turned the rock *into* a pool of water,
  The flint into a fountain of waters.

PSALM 115 GOD LIVES.

1 Not unto us, O LORD, not unto us,
  But to Your name give glory,
  Because of Your mercy,
  Because of Your truth.
2 Why should the Gentiles say,
  "So where *is* their God?"

3 But our God *is* in heaven;
  He does whatever He pleases.
4 Their idols *are* silver and gold,
  The work of men's hands.
5 They have mouths, but they do not speak;
  Eyes they have, but they do not see;
6 They have ears, but they do not hear;
  Noses they have, but they do not smell;
7 They have hands, but they do not handle;
  Feet they have, but they do not walk;
  Nor do they mutter through their throat.
8 Those who make them are like them;
  So is everyone who trusts in them.

9 O Israel, trust in the LORD;
  He *is* their help and their shield.
10 O house of Aaron, trust in the LORD;
  He *is* their help and their shield.
11 You who fear the LORD, trust in the LORD;
  He *is* their help and their shield.

12 The LORD has been mindful of *us*;
  He will bless us;
  He will bless the house of Israel;
  He will bless the house of Aaron.

▬▬▬▬▬THINKING OF YOU

115:12 "The LORD has been mindful of *us*," says the psalm writer. What a fantastic truth! There are many times when we feel isolated, alone, and abandoned, even by God. In reality, he sees, understand is thinking about us. When depressed or struggling, be encouraged God keeps you in his thoughts. If he thinks about you, surely his he near.

13 He will bless those who fear the LORD,
  Both small and great.

14 May the LORD give you increase more and more,
  You and your children.
15 *May* you *be* blessed by the LORD,
  Who made heaven and earth.

16 The heaven, *even* the heavens, *are* the LORD's;
  But the earth He has given to the children of men.
17 The dead do not praise the LORD,
  Nor any who go down into silence.
18 But we will bless the LORD
  From this time forth and forevermore.

  Praise the LORD!

PSALM 116 GOD SAVES US; LET'S WORSHIP HIM.

1 I love the LORD, because He has heard
  My voice *and* my supplications.
2 Because He has inclined His ear to me,
  Therefore I will call *upon Him* as long as I live.

3 The pains of death surrounded me,
  And the pangs of Sheol laid hold of me;
  I found trouble and sorrow.
4 Then I called upon the name of the LORD:
  "O LORD, I implore You, deliver my soul!"

5 Gracious *is* the LORD, and righteous;
  Yes, our God *is* merciful.
6 The LORD preserves the simple;
  I was brought low, and He saved me.
7 Return to your rest, O my soul,
  For the LORD has dealt bountifully with you.

8 For You have delivered my soul from death,
  My eyes from tears,
  And my feet from falling.
9 I will walk before the LORD
  In the land of the living.
10 I believed, therefore I spoke,
  "I am greatly afflicted."
11 I said in my haste,
  "All men *are* liars."

12 What shall I render to the LORD
  For all His benefits toward me?
13 I will take up the cup of salvation,
  And call upon the name of the LORD.
14 I will pay my vows to the LORD
  Now in the presence of all His people.

15 Precious in the sight of the LORD
  Is the death of His saints.

16 O LORD, truly I *am* Your servant;
  I *am* Your servant, the son of Your maidservant;

You have loosed my bonds.
¹⁷ I will offer to You the sacrifice of thanksgiving,
And will call upon the name of the LORD.

¹⁸ I will pay my vows to the LORD
Now in the presence of all His people,
¹⁹ In the courts of the LORD's house,
In the midst of you, O Jerusalem.

Praise the LORD!

PSALM **117** PRAISE GOD FOR HIS LOVE.

¹ Praise the LORD, all you Gentiles!
Laud Him, all you peoples!
² For His merciful kindness is great toward us,
And the truth of the LORD *endures* forever.

Praise the LORD!

PSALM **118** GOD'S LOVE NEVER FAILS.

¹ Oh, give thanks to the LORD, for *He is* good!
For His mercy *endures* forever.

² Let Israel now say,
"His mercy *endures* forever."
³ Let the house of Aaron now say,
"His mercy *endures* forever."
⁴ Let those who fear the LORD now say,
"His mercy *endures* forever."

⁵ I called on the LORD in distress;
The LORD answered me *and set me* in a broad place.
⁶ The LORD *is* on my side;
I will not fear.
What can man do to me?
⁷ The LORD is for me among those who help me;
Therefore I shall see *my desire* on those who hate me.
⁸ *It is* better to trust in the LORD
Than to put confidence in man.
⁹ *It is* better to trust in the LORD
Than to put confidence in princes.

¹⁰ All nations surrounded me,
But in the name of the LORD I will destroy them.
¹¹ They surrounded me,
Yes, they surrounded me;
But in the name of the LORD I will destroy them.
¹² They surrounded me like bees;
They were quenched like a fire of thorns;
For in the name of the LORD I will destroy them.
¹³ You pushed me violently, that I might fall,
But the LORD helped me.
¹⁴ The LORD *is* my strength and song,
And He has become my salvation.

¹⁵ The voice of rejoicing and salvation
Is in the tents of the righteous;
The right hand of the LORD does valiantly.
¹⁶ The right hand of the LORD is exalted;
The right hand of the LORD does valiantly.
¹⁷ I shall not die, but live,
And declare the works of the LORD.
¹⁸ The LORD has chastened me severely,

But He has not given me over to death.

¹⁹ Open to me the gates of righteousness;
I will go through them,
And I will praise the LORD.
²⁰ This is the gate of the LORD,
Through which the righteous shall enter.

²¹ I will praise You,
For You have answered me,
And have become my salvation.

²² The stone *which* the builders rejected
Has become the chief cornerstone.
²³ This was the LORD's doing;
It *is* marvelous in our eyes.
²⁴ This *is* the day the LORD has made;
We will rejoice and be glad in it.

²⁵ Save now, I pray, O LORD;
O LORD, I pray, send now prosperity.
²⁶ Blessed *is* he who comes in the name of the LORD!
We have blessed you from the house of the LORD.
²⁷ God *is* the LORD,
And He has given us light;
Bind the sacrifice with cords to the horns of the altar.
²⁸ You *are* my God, and I will praise You;
You are my God, I will exalt You.

²⁹ Oh, give thanks to the LORD, for *He is* good!
For His mercy *endures* forever.

PSALM **119** HAPPINESS IS OBEYING GOD.

א ALEPH
¹ Blessed *are* the undefiled in the way,
Who walk in the law of the LORD!
² Blessed *are* those who keep His testimonies,
Who seek Him with the whole heart!
³ They also do no iniquity;
They walk in His ways.
⁴ You have commanded *us*
To keep Your precepts diligently.
⁵ Oh, that my ways were directed
To keep Your statutes!
⁶ Then I would not be ashamed,
When I look into all Your commandments.
⁷ I will praise You with uprightness of heart,
When I learn Your righteous judgments.
⁸ I will keep Your statutes;
Oh, do not forsake me utterly!

ב BETH
⁹ How can a young man cleanse his way?
By taking heed according to Your word.
¹⁰ With my whole heart I have sought You;
Oh, let me not wander from Your commandments!
¹¹ Your word I have hidden in my heart,

DETERRENT

119:11 Hiding (Keeping) God's Word in our heart and mind is a deterrent to sin. This alone should inspire us to want to memorize Scripture. But memorization alone will not keep us from sin; we must also put God's Word to work in our life, making it a vital guide to everything we do.

RULES

119:12-18 Most of us don't like rules because we think they keep us from doing what we want. So it may seem strange to hear the psalmist talk of rejoicing in God's laws more than in riches (119:14). But God's laws were given to free us to be all he wants us to be. They restrict us from doing those things that will cripple us and keep us from being our best. God's laws are guidelines to help us follow in his path and not wander onto paths that would lead to destruction.

That I might not sin against You.

12 Blessed *are* You, O LORD!
Teach me Your statutes.

13 With my lips I have declared
All the judgments of Your mouth.

14 I have rejoiced in the way of Your testimonies,
As *much as* in all riches.

15 I will meditate on Your precepts,
And contemplate Your ways.

16 I will delight myself in Your statutes;
I will not forget Your word.

ג GIMEL

17 Deal bountifully with Your servant,
That I may live and keep Your word.

18 Open my eyes, that I may see
Wondrous things from Your law.

19 I *am* a stranger in the earth;
Do not hide Your commandments from me.

20 My soul breaks with longing
For Your judgments at all times.

21 You rebuke the proud—the cursed,
Who stray from Your commandments.

22 Remove from me reproach and contempt,
For I have kept Your testimonies.

23 Princes also sit *and* speak against me,
But Your servant meditates on Your statutes.

24 Your testimonies also *are* my delight
And my counselors.

ד DALETH

25 My soul clings to the dust;
Revive me according to Your word.

26 I have declared my ways, and You answered me;
Teach me Your statutes.

27 Make me understand the way of Your precepts;
So shall I meditate on Your wonderful works.

28 My soul melts from heaviness;
Strengthen me according to Your word.

29 Remove from me the way of lying,
And grant me Your law graciously.

30 I have chosen the way of truth;
Your judgments I have laid *before me.*

31 I cling to Your testimonies;
O LORD, do not put me to shame!

32 I will run the course of Your commandments,
For You shall enlarge my heart.

ה HE

33 Teach me, O LORD, the way of Your statutes,
And I shall keep it *to* the end.

34 Give me understanding, and I shall keep Your law;
Indeed, I shall observe it with *my* whole heart.

35 Make me walk in the path of Your commandments,
For I delight in it.

36 Incline my heart to Your testimonies,
And not to covetousness.

37 Turn away my eyes from looking at worthless things,
And revive me in Your way.

38 Establish Your word to Your servant,
Who *is devoted* to fearing You.

39 Turn away my reproach which I dread,
For Your judgments *are* good.

40 Behold, I long for Your precepts;
Revive me in Your righteousness.

ו WAH

41 Let Your mercies come also to me, O LORD—
Your salvation according to Your word.

42 So shall I have an answer for him who reproaches me,
For I trust in Your word.

43 And take not the word of truth utterly out of my mouth,
For I have hoped in Your ordinances.

44 So shall I keep Your law continually,
Forever and ever.

45 And I will walk at liberty,
For I seek Your precepts.

46 I will speak of Your testimonies also before kings,
And will not be ashamed.

47 And I will delight myself in Your commandments,
Which I love.

48 My hands also I will lift up to Your commandments,
Which I love,
And I will meditate on Your statutes.

ז ZAYIN

49 Remember the word to Your servant,
Upon which You have caused me to hope.

50 This *is* my comfort in my affliction,
For Your word has given me life.

51 The proud have me in great derision,
Yet I do not turn aside from Your law.

52 I remembered Your judgments of old, O LORD,
And have comforted myself.

53 Indignation has taken hold of me
Because of the wicked, who forsake Your law.

54 Your statutes have been my songs
In the house of my pilgrimage.

55 I remember Your name in the night, O LORD,
And I keep Your law.

56 This has become mine,
Because I kept Your precepts.

ח HETH

57 *You are* my portion, O LORD;
I have said that I would keep Your words.

58 I entreated Your favor with *my* whole heart;
Be merciful to me according to Your word.

59 I thought about my ways,
And turned my feet to Your testimonies.

60 I made haste, and did not delay
To keep Your commandments.

61 The cords of the wicked have bound me,
But I have not forgotten Your law.

62 At midnight I will rise to give thanks to You,
Because of Your righteous judgments.
63 I *am* a companion of all who fear You,
And of those who keep Your precepts.
64 The earth, O LORD, is full of Your mercy;
Teach me Your statutes.

ט TETH

65 You have dealt well with Your servant,
O LORD, according to Your word.
66 Teach me good judgment and knowledge,
For I believe Your commandments.
67 Before I was afflicted I went astray,
But now I keep Your word.
68 You *are* good, and do good;
Teach me Your statutes.
69 The proud have forged a lie against me,
But I will keep Your precepts with *my* whole heart.
70 Their heart is as fat as grease,
But I delight in Your law.
71 *It is* good for me that I have been afflicted,
That I may learn Your statutes.
72 The law of Your mouth *is* better to me
Than thousands of *coins of* gold and silver.

י YOD

73 Your hands have made me and fashioned me;
Give me understanding, that I may learn Your
    commandments.
74 Those who fear You will be glad when they see me,
Because I have hoped in Your word.
75 I know, O LORD, that Your judgments *are* right,
And *that* in faithfulness You have afflicted me.
76 Let, I pray, Your merciful kindness be for my comfort,
According to Your word to Your servant.
77 Let Your tender mercies come to me, that I may live;
For Your law *is* my delight.
78 Let the proud be ashamed,
For they treated me wrongfully with falsehood;
But I will meditate on Your precepts.
79 Let those who fear You turn to me,
Those who know Your testimonies.
80 Let my heart be blameless regarding Your statutes,
That I may not be ashamed.

כ KAPH

81 My soul faints for Your salvation,
But I hope in Your word.
82 My eyes fail *from searching* Your word,
Saying, "When will You comfort me?"
83 For I have become like a wineskin in smoke,
Yet I do not forget Your statutes.
84 How many *are* the days of Your servant?
When will You execute judgment on those who
    persecute me?
85 The proud have dug pits for me,
Which *is* not according to Your law.
86 All Your commandments *are* faithful;
They persecute me wrongfully;
Help me!
87 They almost made an end of me on earth,
But I did not forsake Your precepts.

88 Revive me according to Your lovingkindness,
So that I may keep the testimony of Your mouth.

ל LAMED

89 Forever, O LORD,
Your word is settled in heaven.
90 Your faithfulness *endures* to all generations;
You established the earth, and it abides.
91 They continue this day according to Your ordinances,
For all *are* Your servants.
92 Unless Your law *had been* my delight,
I would then have perished in my affliction.
93 I will never forget Your precepts,
For by them You have given me life.
94 I *am* Yours, save me;
For I have sought Your precepts.
95 The wicked wait for me to destroy me,
But I will consider Your testimonies.
96 I have seen the consummation of all perfection,
But Your commandment *is* exceedingly broad.

מ MEM

97 Oh, how I love Your law!
It *is* my meditation all the day.
98 You, through Your commandments, make me wiser
    than my enemies;
For they *are* ever with me.

▬▬▬ WISER

119:97-104 God's Word makes us wise—wiser than our enemies, wiser than any teachers who ignore it. True wisdom is not amassing knowledge, but *applying* knowledge in a life-changing way. Intelligent or experienced people are not necessarily wise. Wisdom comes from allowing what God teaches to make a difference in our life.

99 I have more understanding than all my teachers,
For Your testimonies *are* my meditation.
100 I understand more than the ancients,
Because I keep Your precepts.
101 I have restrained my feet from every evil way,
That I may keep Your word.
102 I have not departed from Your judgments,
For You Yourself have taught me.
103 How sweet are Your words to my taste,
Sweeter than honey to my mouth!
104 Through Your precepts I get understanding;
Therefore I hate every false way.

נ NUN

105 Your word *is* a lamp to my feet
And a light to my path.
106 I have sworn and confirmed
That I will keep Your righteous judgments.
107 I am afflicted very much;
Revive me, O LORD, according to Your word.
108 Accept, I pray, the freewill offerings of my mouth,
    O LORD,
And teach me Your judgments.
109 My life *is* continually in my hand,
Yet I do not forget Your law.
110 The wicked have laid a snare for me,
Yet I have not strayed from Your precepts.

111 Your testimonies I have taken as a heritage forever,
For they *are* the rejoicing of my heart.
112 I have inclined my heart to perform Your statutes
Forever, to the very end.

ס SAMEK

113 I hate the double-minded,
But I love Your law.
114 You *are* my hiding place and my shield;
I hope in Your word.
115 Depart from me, you evildoers,
For I will keep the commandments of my God!
116 Uphold me according to Your word, that I may live;
And do not let me be ashamed of my hope.
117 Hold me up, and I shall be safe,
And I shall observe Your statutes continually.
118 You reject all those who stray from Your statutes,
For their deceit *is* falsehood.
119 You put away all the wicked of the earth *like* dross;
Therefore I love Your testimonies.
120 My flesh trembles for fear of You,
And I am afraid of Your judgments.

ע AYIN

121 I have done justice and righteousness;
Do not leave me to my oppressors.
122 Be surety for Your servant for good;
Do not let the proud oppress me.
123 My eyes fail *from seeking* Your salvation
And Your righteous word.
124 Deal with Your servant according to Your mercy,
And teach me Your statutes.
125 I *am* Your servant;
Give me understanding,
That I may know Your testimonies.
126 *It is* time for *You* to act, O LORD,
For they have regarded Your law as void.
127 Therefore I love Your commandments
More than gold, yes, than fine gold!
128 Therefore all *Your* precepts *concerning* all *things*
I consider *to be* right;
I hate every false way.

פ PE

129 Your testimonies are wonderful;
Therefore my soul keeps them.
130 The entrance of Your words gives light;
It gives understanding to the simple.
131 I opened my mouth and panted,
For I longed for Your commandments.
132 Look upon me and be merciful to me,
As Your custom *is* toward those who love Your name.
133 Direct my steps by Your word,
And let no iniquity have dominion over me.
134 Redeem me from the oppression of man,
That I may keep Your precepts.
135 Make Your face shine upon Your servant,
And teach me Your statutes.
136 Rivers of water run down from my eyes,
Because *men* do not keep Your law.

צ TSADDE

137 Righteous *are* You, O LORD,

And upright *are* Your judgments.
138 Your testimonies, *which* You have commanded,
Are righteous and very faithful.
139 My zeal has consumed me,
Because my enemies have forgotten Your words.
140 Your word *is* very pure;
Therefore Your servant loves it.
141 I *am* small and despised,
Yet I do not forget Your precepts.
142 Your righteousness *is* an everlasting righteousness,
And Your law *is* truth.
143 Trouble and anguish have overtaken me,
Yet Your commandments *are* my delights.
144 The righteousness of Your testimonies *is* everlasting;
Give me understanding, and I shall live.

ק QOPH

145 I cry out with *my* whole heart;
Hear me, O LORD!
I will keep Your statutes.
146 I cry out to You;
Save me, and I will keep Your testimonies.
147 I rise before the dawning of the morning,
And cry for help;
I hope in Your word.
148 My eyes are awake through the *night* watches,
That I may meditate on Your word.
149 Hear my voice according to Your lovingkindness;
O LORD, revive me according to Your justice.
150 They draw near who follow after wickedness;
They are far from Your law.
151 You *are* near, O LORD,
And all Your commandments *are* truth.
152 Concerning Your testimonies,
I have known of old that You have founded them
forever.

ר RESH

153 Consider my affliction and deliver me,
For I do not forget Your law.
154 Plead my cause and redeem me;
Revive me according to Your word.
155 Salvation *is* far from the wicked,
For they do not seek Your statutes.
156 Great *are* Your tender mercies, O LORD;
Revive me according to Your judgments.
157 Many *are* my persecutors and my enemies,
Yet I do not turn from Your testimonies.
158 I see the treacherous, and am disgusted,
Because they do not keep Your word.
159 Consider how I love Your precepts;
Revive me, O LORD, according to Your lovingkindness.
160 The entirety of Your word *is* truth,

MEDICINE

119:125 Faith comes alive at the points where we apply Scriptu[re to]
our life. Like the psalmist, we need the common sense and the desi[re to]
apply Scripture where we need help. The Bible is similar to medicin[e; it]
goes to work only when you put it on the infected areas. As you re[ad the]
Bible, be on the alert for lessons, commands, or examples that you [can]
apply to situations in your life.

And every one of Your righteous judgments *endures*
forever.

ש SHIN

161 Princes persecute me without a cause,
But my heart stands in awe of Your word.
162 I rejoice at Your word
As one who finds great treasure.
163 I hate and abhor lying,
But I love Your law.
164 Seven times a day I praise You,
Because of Your righteous judgments.
165 Great peace have those who love Your law,
And nothing causes them to stumble.
166 LORD, I hope for Your salvation,
And I do Your commandments.
167 My soul keeps Your testimonies,
And I love them exceedingly.
168 I keep Your precepts and Your testimonies,
For all my ways *are* before You.

ת TAU

169 Let my cry come before You, O LORD;
Give me understanding according to Your word.
170 Let my supplication come before You;
Deliver me according to Your word.
171 My lips shall utter praise,
For You teach me Your statutes.
172 My tongue shall speak of Your word,
For all Your commandments *are* righteousness.

173 Let Your hand become my help,
For I have chosen Your precepts.
174 I long for Your salvation, O LORD,
And Your law *is* my delight.
175 Let my soul live, and it shall praise You;
And let Your judgments help me.
176 I have gone astray like a lost sheep;
Seek Your servant,
For I do not forget Your commandments.

PSALM 120 GOD WILL HELP. *A Song of Ascents.*
1 In my distress I cried to the LORD,
And He heard me.
2 Deliver my soul, O LORD, from lying lips
And from a deceitful tongue.

PEACEMAKER

120:7 Peacemaking is not very popular because it is more human to
"fight for what is right." The glory of battle is the hope of winning, but
someone must be a loser. The glory of peacemaking is that it may
actually produce two winners. Peacemaking is God's way, so we should
carefully and prayerfully attempt to be peacemakers.

3 What shall be given to you,
Or what shall be done to you,
You false tongue?
4 Sharp arrows of the warrior,
With coals of the broom tree!

5 Woe is me, that I dwell in Meshech,
That I dwell among the tents of Kedar!
6 My soul has dwelt too long
With one who hates peace.
7 I *am for* peace;
But when I speak, they *are* for war.

PSALM 121 GOD GUARDS US. *A Song of Ascents.*
1 I will lift up my eyes to the hills—
From whence comes my help?
2 My help *comes* from the LORD,
Who made heaven and earth.

3 He will not allow your foot to be moved;
He who keeps you will not slumber.
4 Behold, He who keeps Israel
Shall neither slumber nor sleep.

5 The LORD *is* your keeper;
The LORD *is* your shade at your right hand.
6 The sun shall not strike you by day,
Nor the moon by night.

7 The LORD shall preserve you from all evil;
He shall preserve your soul.
8 The LORD shall preserve your going out and your
coming in
From this time forth, and even forevermore.

PSALM 122 WORSHIPING. *A Song of Ascents.*
Of David.
1 I was glad when they said to me,

I will lift up my eyes to the hills—
from whence comes my help?

MY HELP
COMES FROM
THE LORD
WHO MADE
HEAVEN
AND
earth.

FOR OTHERS

122:6-9 The psalmist was not praying for his own peace and prosperity, but for his fellow citizens of Jerusalem. This is intercessory prayer, prayer on the behalf of others. Such prayer is unselfish. Too often we pray for our own needs and desires when we should be interceding for others. Will you pray for someone in need today?

"Let us go into the house of the LORD."
2 Our feet have been standing
Within your gates, O Jerusalem!

3 Jerusalem is built
As a city that is compact together,
4 Where the tribes go up,
The tribes of the LORD,
To the Testimony of Israel,
To give thanks to the name of the LORD.
5 For thrones are set there for judgment,
The thrones of the house of David.

6 Pray for the peace of Jerusalem:
"May they prosper who love you.
7 Peace be within your walls,
Prosperity within your palaces."
8 For the sake of my brethren and companions,
I will now say, "Peace be within you."
9 Because of the house of the LORD our God
I will seek your good.

PSALM 123 GOD IS MERCIFUL. *A Song of Ascents.*

1 Unto You I lift up my eyes,
O You who dwell in the heavens.
2 Behold, as the eyes of servants *look* to the hand of their masters,
As the eyes of a maid to the hand of her mistress,
So our eyes *look* to the LORD our God,
Until He has mercy on us.

3 Have mercy on us, O LORD, have mercy on us!
For we are exceedingly filled with contempt.
4 Our soul is exceedingly filled
With the scorn of those who are at ease,
With the contempt of the proud.

PSALM 124 GOD IS ON OUR SIDE. *A Song of Ascents. Of David.*

1 "If it had not been the LORD who was on our side,"
Let Israel now say—
2 "If it had not been the LORD who was on our side,
When men rose up against us,
3 Then they would have swallowed us alive,
When their wrath was kindled against us;
4 Then the waters would have overwhelmed us,
The stream would have gone over our soul;
5 Then the swollen waters
Would have gone over our soul."

6 Blessed *be* the LORD,
Who has not given us *as* prey to their teeth.
7 Our soul has escaped as a bird from the snare of the fowlers;

The snare is broken, and we have escaped.
8 Our help *is* in the name of the LORD,
Who made heaven and earth.

PSALM 125 GOD IS OUR PROTECTOR. *A Song of Ascents.*

1 Those who trust in the LORD
Are like Mount Zion,
Which cannot be moved, *but* abides forever.
2 As the mountains surround Jerusalem,
So the LORD surrounds His people
From this time forth and forever.

3 For the scepter of wickedness shall not rest
On the land allotted to the righteous,
Lest the righteous reach out their hands to iniquity.

4 Do good, O LORD, to *those who are* good,
And to *those who are* upright in their hearts.

5 As for such as turn aside to their crooked ways,
The LORD shall lead them away
With the workers of iniquity.

Peace *be* upon Israel!

PSALM 126 TEARS TURN TO JOY. *A Song of Ascents.*

1 When the LORD brought back the captivity of Zion,
We were like those who dream.
2 Then our mouth was filled with laughter,
And our tongue with singing.
Then they said among the nations,
"The LORD has done great things for them."
3 The LORD has done great things for us,
And we are glad.

4 Bring back our captivity, O LORD,
As the streams in the South.

5 Those who sow in tears
Shall reap in joy.
6 He who continually goes forth weeping,
Bearing seed for sowing,
Shall doubtless come again with rejoicing,
Bringing his sheaves *with him.*

PSALM 127 GOD MAKES LIFE WORTHWHILE. *A Song of Ascents. Of Solomon.*

1 Unless the LORD builds the house,
They labor in vain who build it;
Unless the LORD guards the city,
The watchman stays awake in vain.
2 *It is* vain for you to rise up early,
To sit up late,

NUMBER ONE

127:1 Families establish homes, and watchmen guard cities, but of these activities are futile unless God is with them. A family witho can never experience the spiritual bond God brings to relationships without God will crumble from evil and corruption on the inside. D make the mistake of leaving God out of your life—if you do, it w lived in vain. Make God your highest priority and let him do the be

To eat the bread of sorrows;
For so He gives His beloved sleep.

3 Behold, children *are* a heritage from the LORD,
The fruit of the womb *is* a reward.
4 Like arrows in the hand of a warrior,
So *are* the children of one's youth.
5 Happy *is* the man who has his quiver full of them;
They shall not be ashamed,
But shall speak with their enemies in the gate.

PSALM **128** A FAMILY BLESSING. *A Song of Ascents.*

1 Blessed *is* every one who fears the LORD,
Who walks in His ways.

2 When you eat the labor of your hands,
You *shall be* happy, and *it shall be* well with you.
3 Your wife *shall be* like a fruitful vine
In the very heart of your house,
Your children like olive plants
All around your table.
4 Behold, thus shall the man be blessed
Who fears the LORD.

5 The LORD bless you out of Zion,
And may you see the good of Jerusalem
All the days of your life.
6 Yes, may you see your children's children.

Peace *be* upon Israel!

PSALM **129** LEAVE YOUR ENEMIES TO GOD. *A Song of Ascents.*

1 "Many a time they have afflicted me from my youth,"
Let Israel now say—
2 "Many a time they have afflicted me from my youth;
Yet they have not prevailed against me.
3 The plowers plowed on my back;
They made their furrows long."
4 The LORD *is* righteous;
He has cut in pieces the cords of the wicked.

5 Let all those who hate Zion
Be put to shame and turned back.
6 Let them be as the grass *on* the housetops,
Which withers before it grows up,
7 With which the reaper does not fill his hand,
Nor he who binds sheaves, his arms.
8 Neither let those who pass by them say,
"The blessing of the LORD *be* upon you;
We bless you in the name of the LORD!"

PSALM **130** GOD FORGIVES. *A Song of Ascents.*

1 Out of the depths I have cried to You, O LORD;
2 Lord, hear my voice!
Let Your ears be attentive
To the voice of my supplications.

3 If You, LORD, should mark iniquities,
O Lord, who could stand?
4 But *there is* forgiveness with You,
That You may be feared.

5 I wait for the LORD, my soul waits,
And in His word I do hope.
6 My soul *waits* for the Lord
More than those who watch for the morning—
Yes, more than those who watch for the morning.

7 O Israel, hope in the LORD;
For with the LORD *there is* mercy,
And with Him *is* abundant redemption.
8 And He shall redeem Israel
From all his iniquities.

PSALM **131** A PSALM OF CONTENTMENT. *A Song of Ascents. Of David.*

1 LORD, my heart is not haughty,
Nor my eyes lofty.
Neither do I concern myself with great matters,
Nor with things too profound for me.

2 Surely I have calmed and quieted my soul,
Like a weaned child with his mother;
Like a weaned child *is* my soul within me.

3 O Israel, hope in the LORD
From this time forth and forever.

PSALM **132** HONOR GOD. *A Song of Ascents.*

1 LORD, remember David
And all his afflictions;
2 How he swore to the LORD,
And vowed to the Mighty One of Jacob:
3 "Surely I will not go into the chamber of my house,
Or go up to the comfort of my bed;
4 I will not give sleep to my eyes
Or slumber to my eyelids,
5 Until I find a place for the LORD,
A dwelling place for the Mighty One of Jacob."

6 Behold, we heard of it in Ephrathah;
We found it in the fields of the woods.
7 Let us go into His tabernacle;
Let us worship at His footstool.
8 Arise, O LORD, to Your resting place,
You and the ark of Your strength.
9 Let Your priests be clothed with righteousness,
And let Your saints shout for joy.

10 For Your servant David's sake,
Do not turn away the face of Your Anointed.

11 The LORD has sworn *in* truth to David;
He will not turn from it:
"I will set upon your throne the fruit of your body.
12 If your sons will keep My covenant
And My testimony which I shall teach them,
Their sons also shall sit upon your throne
forevermore."

13 For the LORD has chosen Zion;
He has desired *it* for His dwelling place:
14 "This *is* My resting place forever;
Here I will dwell, for I have desired it.
15 I will abundantly bless her provision;

I will satisfy her poor with bread.
¹⁶ I will also clothe her priests with salvation,
And her saints shall shout aloud for joy.
¹⁷ There I will make the horn of David grow;
I will prepare a lamp for My Anointed.
¹⁸ His enemies I will clothe with shame,
But upon Himself His crown shall flourish."

PSALM 133 LIVING TOGETHER IN PEACE.
A Song of Ascents. Of David.
¹ Behold, how good and how pleasant *it is*
For brethren to dwell together in unity!

² *It is* like the precious oil upon the head,
Running down on the beard,
The beard of Aaron,
Running down on the edge of his garments.
³ *It is* like the dew of Hermon,
Descending upon the mountains of Zion;
For there the Lord commanded the blessing—
Life forevermore.

PSALM 134 WORSHIP THE LORD. *A Song of Ascents.*
¹ Behold, bless the Lord,
All *you* servants of the Lord,
Who by night stand in the house of the Lord!
² Lift up your hands *in* the sanctuary,
And bless the Lord.

³ The Lord who made heaven and earth
Bless you from Zion!

PSALM 135 OUR GOD IS REAL.
¹ Praise the Lord!

Praise the name of the Lord;
Praise *Him*, O you servants of the Lord!
² You who stand in the house of the Lord,
In the courts of the house of our God,
³ Praise the Lord, for the Lord *is* good;
Sing praises to His name, for *it is* pleasant.
⁴ For the Lord has chosen Jacob for Himself,
Israel for His special treasure.

⁵ For I know that the Lord *is* great,
And our Lord *is* above all gods.
⁶ Whatever the Lord pleases He does,
In heaven and in earth,
In the seas and in all deep places.
⁷ He causes the vapors to ascend from the ends of the
earth;
He makes lightning for the rain;
He brings the wind out of His treasuries.

⁸ He destroyed the firstborn of Egypt,
Both of man and beast.
⁹ He sent signs and wonders into the midst of you,
O Egypt,
Upon Pharaoh and all his servants.
¹⁰ He defeated many nations
And slew mighty kings—

135:18 In subtle, imperceptible ways we become like the "gods"
worship. So if the true God is your God, you will become more like
you worship him. What are your gods? What takes priority in your
Choose carefully, because you will take on the characteristics of wh▶
you worship.

¹¹ Sihon king of the Amorites,
Og king of Bashan,
And all the kingdoms of Canaan—
¹² And gave their land *as* a heritage,
A heritage to Israel His people.

¹³ Your name, O Lord, *endures* forever,
Your fame, O Lord, throughout all generations.
¹⁴ For the Lord will judge His people,
And He will have compassion on His servants.

¹⁵ The idols of the nations *are* silver and gold,
The work of men's hands.
¹⁶ They have mouths, but they do not speak;
Eyes they have, but they do not see;
¹⁷ They have ears, but they do not hear;
Nor is there *any* breath in their mouths.
¹⁸ Those who make them are like them;
So is everyone who trusts in them.

¹⁹ Bless the Lord, O house of Israel!
Bless the Lord, O house of Aaron!
²⁰ Bless the Lord, O house of Levi!
You who fear the Lord, bless the Lord!
²¹ Blessed be the Lord out of Zion,
Who dwells in Jerusalem!

Praise the Lord!

PSALM 136 NEVER-ENDING LOVE.
¹ Oh, give thanks to the Lord, for *He is* good!
For His mercy *endures* forever.
² Oh, give thanks to the God of gods!
For His mercy *endures* forever.
³ Oh, give thanks to the Lord of lords!
For His mercy *endures* forever:

⁴ To Him who alone does great wonders,
For His mercy *endures* forever;
⁵ To Him who by wisdom made the heavens,
For His mercy *endures* forever;
⁶ To Him who laid out the earth above the waters,
For His mercy *endures* forever;
⁷ To Him who made great lights,
For His mercy *endures* forever—
⁸ The sun to rule by day,
For His mercy *endures* forever;
⁹ The moon and stars to rule by night,
For His mercy *endures* forever.

¹⁰ To Him who struck Egypt in their firstborn,
For His mercy *endures* forever;
¹¹ And brought out Israel from among them,
For His mercy *endures* forever;
¹² With a strong hand, and with an outstretched arm,
For His mercy *endures* forever;
¹³ To Him who divided the Red Sea in two,
For His mercy *endures* forever;

14 And made Israel pass through the midst of it,
For His mercy *endures* forever;
15 But overthrew Pharaoh and his army in the Red Sea,
For His mercy *endures* forever;
16 To Him who led His people through the wilderness,
For His mercy *endures* forever;
17 To Him who struck down great kings,
For His mercy *endures* forever;
18 And slew famous kings,
For His mercy *endures* forever—
19 Sihon king of the Amorites,
For His mercy *endures* forever;
20 And Og king of Bashan,
For His mercy *endures* forever—
21 And gave their land as a heritage,
For His mercy *endures* forever;
22 A heritage to Israel His servant,
For His mercy *endures* forever.

23 Who remembered us in our lowly state,
For His mercy *endures* forever;
24 And rescued us from our enemies,
For His mercy *endures* forever;
25 Who gives food to all flesh,
For His mercy *endures* forever.

26 Oh, give thanks to the God of heaven!
For His mercy *endures* forever.

PSALM **137** SONG OF THE CAPTIVES.

1 By the rivers of Babylon,
There we sat down, yea, we wept
When we remembered Zion.
2 We hung our harps
Upon the willows in the midst of it.
3 For there those who carried us away captive asked of
us a song,
And those who plundered us *requested* mirth,
Saying, "Sing us *one* of the songs of Zion!"

4 How shall we sing the LORD's song
In a foreign land?
5 If I forget you, O Jerusalem,
Let my right hand forget *its skill!*
6 If I do not remember you,
Let my tongue cling to the roof of my mouth—
If I do not exalt Jerusalem
Above my chief joy.

7 Remember, O LORD, against the sons of Edom
The day of Jerusalem,
Who said, "Raze *it,* raze *it,*
To its very foundation!"

8 O daughter of Babylon, who are to be destroyed,
Happy the one who repays you as you have served
us!
9 Happy the one who takes and dashes
Your little ones against the rock!

PSALM **138** GOD HEARS AND ANSWERS US.
A Psalm *of David.*

1 I will praise You with my whole heart;
Before the gods I will sing praises to You.
2 I will worship toward Your holy temple,
And praise Your name
For Your lovingkindness and Your truth;
For You have magnified Your word above all Your
name.
3 In the day when I cried out, You answered me,
And made me bold *with* strength in my soul.

4 All the kings of the earth shall praise You, O LORD,
When they hear the words of Your mouth.
5 Yes, they shall sing of the ways of the LORD,
For great *is* the glory of the LORD.
6 Though the LORD *is* on high,
Yet He regards the lowly;
But the proud He knows from afar.

7 Though I walk in the midst of trouble, You will revive
me;
You will stretch out Your hand
Against the wrath of my enemies,
And Your right hand will save me.
8 The LORD will perfect *that which* concerns me;
Your mercy, O LORD, *endures* forever;
Do not forsake the works of Your hands.

PSALM **139** GOD KNOWS ALL ABOUT YOU. *For the Chief Musician. A Psalm of David.*

1 O LORD, You have searched me and known *me.*
2 You know my sitting down and my rising up;
You understand my thought afar off.
3 You comprehend my path and my lying down,
And are acquainted with all my ways.
4 For *there is* not a word on my tongue,
But behold, O LORD, You know it altogether.
5 You have hedged me behind and before,
And laid Your hand upon me.
6 *Such* knowledge *is* too wonderful for me;
It is high, I cannot *attain* it.

7 Where can I go from Your Spirit?
Or where can I flee from Your presence?
8 If I ascend into heaven, You *are* there;
If I make my bed in hell, behold, You *are there.*
9 *If* I take the wings of the morning,
And dwell in the uttermost parts of the sea,
10 Even there Your hand shall lead me,
And Your right hand shall hold me.
11 If I say, "Surely the darkness shall fall on me,"
Even the night shall be light about me;
12 Indeed, the darkness shall not hide from You,
But the night shines as the day;
The darkness and the light *are* both alike *to You.*

13 For You formed my inward parts;

PLANS

138:8 Each of us makes plans for our future. We work hard to see those dreams come true. But to truly make the most of life, we must include God's plans in our plans. He alone knows what is best for us. As you make plans and dream dreams, talk with God about them.

You covered me in my mother's womb.
14 I will praise You, for I am fearfully *and* wonderfully
made;
Marvelous are Your works,
And *that* my soul knows very well.
15 My frame was not hidden from You,
When I was made in secret,
And skillfully wrought in the lowest parts of the
earth.
16 Your eyes saw my substance, being yet unformed.
And in Your book they all were written,
The days fashioned for me,
When *as yet there were* none of them.

ABORTION

"Maybe you made a mistake—or maybe the test is wrong."

"I don't think so. . . . Oh, Kris, what am I gonna do?" The tears begin to roll down Sarah's face. "I'm pregnant!"

Kris hugs her friend. "Look, don't panic. Everything's gonna work out. My sister will help us. She knows about this clinic. The doctors are good, and nobody else has to find out."

Sarah is shocked. "You mean an abortion?"

"Well, do you have any better ideas? C'mon, Sarah, you're only 17. What are you gonna do with a kid? And what would you tell your mom?"

"I don't know . . . I'm so confused." Sarah sighs, wiping her eyes on her sleeve. "What would you do? I mean, could you kill your own baby?"

"What do you mean, 'kill'? It's just a bunch of cells! It's not a person yet. If you were six or seven months pregnant, I'd tell you not to do it. But you're probably only about five weeks along. I don't see what else you can do."

"You really think it's right?"

"Well, let's just say I don't think it's wrong."

Sarah is obviously in deep thought. "Well, how soon can you call your sister?" Kris picks up the phone. "I bet she's at her dorm right now."

Is Sarah making the right decision? Is Kris right about when life begins? See Psalm 139:13-18.

17 How precious also are Your thoughts to me, O God!
How great is the sum of them!
18 *If* I should count them, they would be more in
number than the sand;
When I awake, I am still with You.

19 Oh, that You would slay the wicked, O God!
Depart from me, therefore, you bloodthirsty men.
20 For they speak against You wickedly;
Your enemies take *Your name* in vain.
21 Do I not hate them, O LORD, who hate You?
And do I not loathe those who rise up against You?
22 I hate them with perfect hatred;
I count them my enemies.

23 Search me, O God, and know my heart;
Try me, and know my anxieties;
24 And see if *there is any* wicked way in me,
And lead me in the way everlasting.

PSALM 140 PRAYER FOR PROTECTION. *To the Chief Musician. A Psalm of David.*

1 Deliver me, O LORD, from evil men;
Preserve me from violent men,
2 Who plan evil things in *their* hearts;
They continually gather together *for* war.
3 They sharpen their tongues like a serpent;
The poison of asps *is* under their lips.   Selah

4 Keep me, O LORD, from the hands of the wicked;
Preserve me from violent men,
Who have purposed to make my steps stumble.
5 The proud have hidden a snare for me, and cords;
They have spread a net by the wayside;
They have set traps for me.   Selah

6 I said to the LORD: "You *are* my God;

RESPECT

139:13-15 God's character goes into the creation of every perso[n] When you feel worthless or even begin to hate yourself, remember God's Spirit is ready and willing to work within you to make your character all God meant it to be. God thinks of you constantly (139:17-18). We should have as much respect for ourselves as our [God] has for us.

Hear the voice of my supplications, O LORD.
7 O GOD the Lord, the strength of my salvation,
You have covered my head in the day of battle.
8 Do not grant, O LORD, the desires of the wicked;
Do not further his *wicked* scheme,
Lest they be exalted.   Selah

9 "*As for* the head of those who surround me,
Let the evil of their lips cover them;
10 Let burning coals fall upon them;
Let them be cast into the fire,
Into deep pits, that they rise not up again.
11 Let not a slanderer be established in the earth;
Let evil hunt the violent man to overthrow *him*."

12 I know that the LORD will maintain
The cause of the afflicted,
And justice for the poor.
13 Surely the righteous shall give thanks to Your name;
The upright shall dwell in Your presence.

PSALM 141 WHEN TEMPTED AND CRITICIZED. *A Psalm of David.*

1 LORD, I cry out to You;
Make haste to me!

THE TONGUE

141:3 James wrote that "the tongue is a little member and boast[s] great things" (James 3:5). On the average, a person opens his mou[th] approximately 700 times a day to speak. David wisely asked God t[o] him keep his mouth shut—sometimes even as he underwent persecution. Jesus himself was silent before his accusers (Matthew 26:63). Knowing the power of the tongue, we would do well to ask [God] to guard what we say so that our words will bring honor to his nam[e]

Give ear to my voice when I cry out to You.
2 Let my prayer be set before You *as* incense,
The lifting up of my hands *as* the evening sacrifice.

3 Set a guard, O LORD, over my mouth;
Keep watch over the door of my lips.
4 Do not incline my heart to any evil thing,
To practice wicked works
With men who work iniquity;
And do not let me eat of their delicacies.

5 Let the righteous strike me;
It shall be a kindness.
And let him rebuke me;
It shall be as excellent oil;
Let my head not refuse it.

For still my prayer *is* against the
deeds of the wicked.
6 Their judges are overthrown by
the sides of the cliff,
And they hear my words, for they
are sweet.
7 Our bones are scattered at the
mouth of the grave,
As when one plows and breaks up
the earth.

8 But my eyes *are* upon You, O GOD
the Lord;
In You I take refuge;
Do not leave my soul destitute.
9 Keep me from the snares they
have laid for me,
And from the traps of the workers
of iniquity.
10 Let the wicked fall into their own
nets,
While I escape safely.

PSALM **142** WHEN YOU FEEL
TRAPPED. *A Contemplation of
David. A Prayer when he was in the
cave.*

1 I cry out to the LORD with my
voice;
With my voice to the LORD I make
my supplication.
2 I pour out my complaint before Him;
I declare before Him my trouble.

3 When my spirit was overwhelmed within me,
Then You knew my path.
In the way in which I walk
They have secretly set a snare for me.
4 Look on *my* right hand and see,
For *there is* no one who acknowledges me;
Refuge has failed me;
No one cares for my soul.

5 I cried out to You, O LORD:
I said, "You *are* my refuge,
My portion in the land of the living.

6 Attend to my cry,
For I am brought very low;
Deliver me from my persecutors,
For they are stronger than I.
7 Bring my soul out of prison,
That I may praise Your name;
The righteous shall surround me,
For You shall deal bountifully with me."

PSALM **143** WHEN WEAK AND SCARED.
A Psalm of David.
1 Hear my prayer, O LORD,
Give ear to my supplications!
In Your faithfulness answer me,
And in Your righteousness.

"Here's what I did..."

I had an unusual, frightening experience at the beginning of tenth grade: I ate an apple that some disturbed person had tampered with. It wasn't poisonous—not like it would have killed me—but it did make me pretty sick. Most of all, the experience scared me. For about a year and a half, I wouldn't eat anything unless I shared it with someone, or someone else tried a bite first and was OK.

Finally the fear got to me. I talked to my youth worker about it. She encouraged me to read Psalm 140, and to realize that God was there to help and protect me—no matter what! Then she pointed out that God didn't want me to give in to a spirit of fear, and she showed me 2 Timothy 1:7. That verse became very meaningful to me. I memorized it and reminded myself of it over and over, until eventually I began to believe that most people could be trusted, that most people weren't out to hurt me. I have been learning that "God has not given us a spirit of fear, but of power and of love and of a sound mind." I'm very thankful for this verse; God is using it to deliver me from my fear.

Melinda AGE 18

2 Do not enter into judgment with Your servant,
For in Your sight no one living is righteous.

3 For the enemy has persecuted my soul;
He has crushed my life to the ground;
He has made me dwell in darkness,
Like those who have long been dead.
4 Therefore my spirit is overwhelmed within me;
My heart within me is distressed.

5 I remember the days of old;
I meditate on all Your works;
I muse on the work of Your hands.
6 I spread out my hands to You;
My soul *longs* for You like a thirsty land.   Selah

7 Answer me speedily, O LORD;

My spirit fails!
Do not hide Your face from me,
Lest I be like those who go down into the pit.
⁸ Cause me to hear Your lovingkindness in the
morning,
For in You do I trust;
Cause me to know the way in which I should walk,
For I lift up my soul to You.

⁹ Deliver me, O LORD, from my enemies;
In You I take shelter.
¹⁰ Teach me to do Your will,
For You *are* my God;
Your Spirit *is* good.
Lead me in the land of uprightness.

¹¹ Revive me, O LORD, for Your name's sake!
For Your righteousness' sake bring my soul out of
trouble.
¹² In Your mercy cut off my enemies,
And destroy all those who afflict my soul;
For I *am* Your servant.

PSALM **144** REJOICE IN GOD'S CARE. *A Psalm
of David.*
¹ Blessed *be* the LORD my Rock,
Who trains my hands for war,
And my fingers for battle—
² My lovingkindness and my fortress,
My high tower and my deliverer,
My shield and *the One* in whom I take refuge,
Who subdues my people under me.

³ LORD, what *is* man, that You take knowledge of him?
Or the son of man, that You are mindful of him?
⁴ Man is like a breath;
His days *are* like a passing shadow.

⁵ Bow down Your heavens, O LORD, and come down;
Touch the mountains, and they shall smoke.
⁶ Flash forth lightning and scatter them;
Shoot out Your arrows and destroy them.
⁷ Stretch out Your hand from above;
Rescue me and deliver me out of great waters,
From the hand of foreigners,
⁸ Whose mouth speaks lying words,
And whose right hand *is* a right hand of falsehood.

⁹ I will sing a new song to You, O God;
On a harp of ten strings I will sing praises to You,
¹⁰ *The One* who gives salvation to kings,
Who delivers David His servant
From the deadly sword.

¹¹ Rescue me and deliver me from the hand of
foreigners,
Whose mouth speaks lying words,
And whose right hand *is* a right hand of falsehood—
¹² That our sons *may be* as plants grown up in their
youth;
That our daughters *may be* as pillars,
Sculptured in palace style;
¹³ *That* our barns *may be* full,

Supplying all kinds of produce;
That our sheep may bring forth thousands
And ten thousands in our fields;
¹⁴ *That* our oxen *may be* well laden;
That there be no breaking in or going out;
That there be no outcry in our streets.
¹⁵ Happy *are* the people who are in such a state;
Happy *are* the people whose God *is* the LORD!

PSALM **145** A MAGNIFICENT GOD. *A Praise of
David.*
¹ I will extol You, my God, O King;
And I will bless Your name forever and ever.
² Every day I will bless You,
And I will praise Your name forever and ever.
³ Great *is* the LORD, and greatly to be praised;
And His greatness *is* unsearchable.

⁴ One generation shall praise Your works to another,
And shall declare Your mighty acts.
⁵ I will meditate on the glorious splendor of Your
majesty,
And on Your wondrous works.
⁶ *Men* shall speak of the might of Your awesome acts,
And I will declare Your greatness.
⁷ They shall utter the memory of Your great goodness,
And shall sing of Your righteousness.

⁸ The LORD *is* gracious and full of compassion,
Slow to anger and great in mercy.
⁹ The LORD *is* good to all,
And His tender mercies *are* over all His works.

¹⁰ All Your works shall praise You, O LORD,
And Your saints shall bless You.
¹¹ They shall speak of the glory of Your kingdom,
And talk of Your power,
¹² To make known to the sons of men His mighty acts,
And the glorious majesty of His kingdom.
¹³ Your kingdom *is* an everlasting kingdom,
And Your dominion *endures* throughout all
generations.

¹⁴ The LORD upholds all who fall,
And raises up all *who are* bowed down.
¹⁵ The eyes of all look expectantly to You,
And You give them their food in due season.
¹⁶ You open Your hand
And satisfy the desire of every living thing.

¹⁷ The LORD *is* righteous in all His ways,
Gracious in all His works.
¹⁸ The LORD *is* near to all who call upon Him,
To all who call upon Him in truth.
¹⁹ He will fulfill the desire of those who fear Him;
He also will hear their cry and save them.
²⁰ The LORD preserves all who love Him,
But all the wicked He will destroy.
²¹ My mouth shall speak the praise of the LORD,
And all flesh shall bless His holy name
Forever and ever.

PSALM **146** GOD'S HELP IS ALL YOU NEED.

1 Praise the LORD!

Praise the LORD, O my soul!
2 While I live I will praise the LORD;
I will sing praises to my God while I have my being.

3 Do not put your trust in princes,
Nor in a son of man, in whom *there is* no help.
4 His spirit departs, he returns to his earth;
In that very day his plans perish.

5 Happy *is he* who *has* the God of Jacob for his help,
Whose hope *is* in the LORD his God,
6 Who made heaven and earth,
The sea, and all that *is* in them;
Who keeps truth forever,
7 Who executes justice for the oppressed,
Who gives food to the hungry.
The LORD gives freedom to the prisoners.

8 The LORD opens *the eyes of* the blind;
The LORD raises those who are bowed down;
The LORD loves the righteous.
9 The LORD watches over the strangers;
He relieves the fatherless and widow;
But the way of the wicked He turns upside down.

10 The LORD shall reign forever—
Your God, O Zion, to all generations.

Praise the LORD!

PSALM **147** YES, PRAISE THE LORD!

1 Praise the LORD!
For *it is* good to sing praises to our God;
For *it is* pleasant, *and* praise is beautiful.

2 The LORD builds up Jerusalem;
He gathers together the outcasts of Israel.
3 He heals the brokenhearted
And binds up their wounds.
4 He counts the number of the stars;
He calls them all by name.
5 Great *is* our Lord, and mighty in power;
His understanding *is* infinite.
6 The LORD lifts up the humble;
He casts the wicked down to the ground.

7 Sing to the LORD with thanksgiving;
Sing praises on the harp to our God,
8 Who covers the heavens with clouds,
Who prepares rain for the earth,
Who makes grass to grow on the mountains.
9 He gives to the beast its food,
And to the young ravens that cry.

10 He does not delight in the strength of the horse;
He takes no pleasure in the legs of a man.
11 The LORD takes pleasure in those who fear Him,
In those who hope in His mercy.

12 Praise the LORD, O Jerusalem!
Praise your God, O Zion!
13 For He has strengthened the bars of your gates;

He has blessed your children within you.
14 He makes peace *in* your borders,
And fills you with the finest wheat.

15 He sends out His command *to the* earth;
His word runs very swiftly.
16 He gives snow like wool;
He scatters the frost like ashes;
17 He casts out His hail like morsels;
Who can stand before His cold?
18 He sends out His word and melts them;
He causes His wind to blow, *and* the waters flow.

▬▬▬▬▬▬▬UNLIMITED

147:5 Sometimes we feel as though we don't understand ourself—what we want, how we feel, what's wrong with us, or what we should do about it. But God's understanding is unlimited and therefore he understands us fully. If you feel troubled and don't understand yourself, remember that God understands you perfectly. Take your mind off yourself and focus it on God. Strive to become more and more like him. The more you learn about God and his ways, the better you will understand yourself.

19 He declares His word to Jacob,
His statutes and His judgments to Israel.
20 He has not dealt thus with any nation;
And *as for His* judgments, they have not known
them.

Praise the LORD!

PSALM **148** LET ALL CREATION GIVE PRAISE.

1 Praise the LORD!

Praise the LORD from the heavens;
Praise Him in the heights!
2 Praise Him, all His angels;
Praise Him, all His hosts!
3 Praise Him, sun and moon;
Praise Him, all you stars of light!
4 Praise Him, you heavens of heavens,
And you waters above the heavens!

5 Let them praise the name of the LORD,
For He commanded and they were created.
6 He also established them forever and ever;
He made a decree which shall not pass away.

7 Praise the LORD from the earth,
You great sea creatures and all the depths;
8 Fire and hail, snow and clouds;
Stormy wind, fulfilling His word;
9 Mountains and all hills;
Fruitful trees and all cedars;
10 Beasts and all cattle;
Creeping things and flying fowl;
11 Kings of the earth and all peoples;
Princes and all judges of the earth;
12 Both young men and maidens;
Old men and children.

13 Let them praise the name of the LORD,
For His name alone is exalted;

His glory *is* above the earth and heaven.
14 And He has exalted the horn of His people,
The praise of all His saints—
Of the children of Israel,
A people near to Him.

Praise the LORD!

PSALM 149 GOD ENJOYS US.
1 Praise the LORD!

Sing to the LORD a new song,
And His praise in the assembly of saints.

2 Let Israel rejoice in their Maker;
Let the children of Zion be joyful in their King.
3 Let them praise His name with the dance;
Let them sing praises to Him with the timbrel and
harp.

YOUR MUSIC

149:3-5 Although the Bible invites us to praise God, we often aren'
sure how to go about it. Here, several ways are suggested—with yo
voice, in music, in your actions. God enjoys his people. We should enj
praising him as well.

4 For the LORD takes pleasure in His people;
He will beautify the humble with salvation.

5 Let the saints be joyful in glory;
Let them sing aloud on their beds.
6 *Let* the high praises of God *be* in their mouth,
And a two-edged sword in their hand,
7 To execute vengeance on the nations,
And punishments on the peoples;
8 To bind their kings with chains,
And their nobles with fetters of iron;
9 To execute on them the written judgment—
This honor have all His saints.

Praise the LORD!

WHERE TO GET HELP
IN THE BOOK OF PSALMS

When you feel . . .

Afraid 3, 4, 27, 46, 49,
  56, 91, 118
Alone 9, 10, 12, 13, 27,
  40, 43
"Burned Out" 6, 63
Cheated 41
Confused 10, 12, 73
Depressed 27, 34, 42, 43,
  88, 143
Distressed 13, 25, 31, 40, 107
Elated 19, 96
Guilty 19, 32, 38, 51
Hateful 11
Impatient 13, 27, 37, 40
Insecure 3, 5, 12, 91
Insulted 41, 70
Jealous 37
Like Quitting 29, 43, 145
Lost 23, 139
Overwhelmed 25, 69, 142
Penitent/Sorry 32, 51, 66
Proud 14, 30, 49
Purposeless 14, 25, 39, 49, 90
Sad 13
Self-confident 24
Tense 4
Thankful 118, 136, 138
Threatened 3, 11, 17
Tired/Weak 6, 13, 18,
  28, 29, 40, 86
Trapped 7, 17, 42, 88, 142
Unimportant 8, 90, 139
Vengeful 3, 7, 109
Worried 37
Worshipful 8, 19, 27, 29, 150

When you're facing . . .

Atheists 10, 14, 19, 52,
  53, 115
Competition 133
Criticism 35, 56, 120
Danger 11
Death 6, 71, 90
Decisions 1, 119
Discrimination 54
Doubts 34, 37, 94
Evil people 10, 35, 36, 49,
  52, 109, 140
Enemies 3, 25, 35, 41, 56, 59
Handicap/Illness 6, 139
Heresy 14
Hypocrisy 26, 28, 40, 50
Lies 5, 12, 120
Old Age 71, 92
Persecution 1, 3, 7, 56
Poverty 9, 10, 12
Punishment 6, 38, 39
Slander/Insults 7, 15, 35,
  43, 120
Slaughter 6, 46, 83
Sorrow 23, 34
Success 18, 112, 127, 128
Temptation 38, 141
Troubles 34, 55, 86, 102,
  142, 145
Verbal Cruelty 35, 120

When you want . . .

Acceptance 139
Answers 4, 17
Confidence 46, 71
Courage 11, 42
Fellowship with God 5, 16,
  25, 27, 37, 133
Forgiveness 32, 38, 40, 51,
  69, 86, 103, 130
Friendship 16
Godliness 15, 25
Guidance 1, 5, 15, 19,
  25, 32, 48
Healing 6, 41
Hope 16, 17, 18, 23, 27
Humility 19, 147
Illumination 19
Integrity 24, 25
Joy 9, 16, 28, 126
Justice 2, 7, 14, 26, 37,
  49, 58, 82
Knowledge 2, 8, 18, 19,
  25, 29, 97, 103
Leadership 72
Miracles 60, 111
Money 15, 16, 17, 49
Peace 3, 4
Perspective 2, 11
Prayer 5, 17, 27, 61
Protection 3, 4, 7, 16, 17, 18,
  23, 27, 31, 91, 121, 125
Provision 23
Rest 23, 27
Salvation 26, 37, 49, 126
Stability 11, 33, 46
Vindication 9, 14, 28, 35, 109
Wisdom 1, 16, 19, 64, 111

PSALM **150** PRAISE THE LORD, ONE AND ALL.

¹ Praise the LORD!

Praise God in His sanctuary;
Praise Him in His mighty firmament!

² Praise Him for His mighty acts;
Praise Him according to His excellent greatness!

³ Praise Him with the sound of the trumpet;

Praise Him with the lute and harp!
⁴ Praise Him with the timbrel and dance;
Praise Him with stringed instruments and flutes!
⁵ Praise Him with loud cymbals;
Praise Him with clashing cymbals!

⁶ Let everything that has breath praise the LORD.

Praise the LORD!

MEGA Themes

PRAISE Psalms are songs of praise to God as our Creator, Sustainer, and Redeemer. Praise is recognizing, appreciating, and expressing God's greatness.

When we think about God, we want to praise him. The more we know of him, the more we will appreciate what he has done. We should focus on his specific, unique attributes as we worship him.
1. Read Psalm 145. How do you think the psalmist was feeling toward God when he wrote these verses? How do you feel when you read them?
2. What specific characteristics of God are praised?
3. Does praise always begin with feeling positive toward God? Explain your response.
4. How can praising God lead to a change of attitude, thoughts, and feelings?
5. List the ways you can live a life of praise to God. In other words, how can you become a living psalm?

GOD'S POWER God is all-powerful, and he always acts at the right time. He is in control of every situation. God's power is shown as he reveals himself in creation, history, and the Bible.

When we feel powerless, God can help us. His strength can overcome the despair of any pain or trial. We can always pray that he will deliver, protect, and sustain. And he will answer.
1. How is God's power revealed in the following psalms: 19; 21; 78?
2. How have you seen God's power in your life?
3. In what ways do you need God's power at the present time? How do you think you may need him in the future?
4. What do you learn from Psalms about relying on God's power during these times of need?

FORGIVENESS Many psalms are intense prayers asking God for forgiveness. God forgives us when we confess our sin and turn from it.

Because God forgives us, we can pray to him honestly and directly. When we receive God's forgiveness, we move from being separated from him to being close to him, from feeling guilty to feeling loved.
1. Psalm 51 is David's prayer after his sin with Bathsheba. Read this prayer with the following questions in mind: How was David feeling about himself? How was David feeling toward God?
2. What are David's specific prayer requests?
3. When you are facing a sin that you need to confess and repent of, how do you feel about yourself? About God?
4. Take a few moments to seek God's forgiveness in areas in which you have sinned.

THANKFULNESS We should be grateful to God for his personal concern, help, and mercy. He protects, guides, and forgives us, and he provides everything we need.

When we realize how much we benefit from knowing God, we can fully express our thanks to him. By thanking him often, we will develop spontaneity in our prayer life.
1. Read Psalms 100 and 136.
2. Make your own "Thanksgiving" list using the following statements:
I thank God that he is _____.
I thank God for showing me his love by _____.
I thank God for the people I love, including _____.
I thank God for providing me with _____.
I thank God for helping me _____.
I thank God that I am _____.
3. Write a prayer of thanksgiving to help you remember that God is your source of all that is good and eternal.

TRUST God is faithful and just. When we put our trust in him, he calms our heart. Because he has been faithful throughout history, we can trust him now.

People can be unfair and friends may desert us, but we can trust in God. Knowing God intimately drives away doubt, fear, and loneliness. We should remember that he is God, even when our feelings seem to be saying something else.
1. Psalm 23 is a psalm of trust in God. Complete this sentence: Psalm 23 shows that David trusts God because God _____.
2. Psalm 91 also expresses trust in God. Describe the psalmist's relationship with God.
3. What is the basis of your trust in God?
4. In what area of your life do you find it the most difficult to trust God? What truth do you find in Psalms that can build your trust in God?

*T*homas has a problem. He worked all summer to earn the money he now holds in his hands. It isn't a lot, a few hundred dollars, but it represents two months of long hours doing odd jobs. Thomas wonders what he should do with the money. Mom and Dad want him to put it into the bank. But his friends urge him to spend it. ("After all," they say, "it's *his* money.") Thomas isn't sure what to do. He wishes he were wiser about such things. ■ There are lots of areas where most of us would like to have more wisdom, the ability to make good (wise) decisions. Lots of people are smart (book knowledge), but only a few are wise. ■ Proverbs was written by Solomon, the wisest man who ever lived. In this book he shares his wisdom on such varied topics as money, marriage, family life, discipline, friends, laziness, speech, relationships, temptation, and leadership. Solomon's purpose was "to teach his people how to live—how to act in every circumstance." ■ Proverbs is a book of answers—answers to our questions about everyday life. As you read, ask God to make the wisdom of Solomon your wisdom too. And ask God to help you begin your steps toward wisdom by trusting him.

STATS

PURPOSE: To teach people how to be understanding, just, and fair in everything they do; to make the simple-minded wise; to warn young men about some problems they will face; and to help the wise become good leaders (see 1:2-6). In short, to help people apply divine wisdom to daily life and to provide them with moral instruction.

AUTHOR: Solomon wrote most of this book; Agur and Lemuel contributed some of the later sections

DATE WRITTEN: Solomon wrote and compiled most of these proverbs early in his reign

SETTING: This is a book of wise sayings, a textbook for teaching people how to live a godly life through the repetition of wise thought

SPECIAL FEATURES: The book uses varied *literary forms*: poems, brief parables, pointed questions, and couplets. Other *literary devices* include antithesis, comparison, and personification.

Proverbs

CHAPTER **1** **THE REASON FOR PROVERBS.** The proverbs of Solomon the son of David, king of Israel:

2 To know wisdom and instruction,
To perceive the words of understanding,
3 To receive the instruction of wisdom,
Justice, judgment, and equity;
4 To give prudence to the simple,
To the young man knowledge and discretion—
5 A wise *man* will hear and increase learning,
And a man of understanding will attain wise counsel,
6 To understand a proverb and an enigma,
The words of the wise and their riddles.

7 The fear of the LORD *is* the beginning of knowledge,
But fools despise wisdom and instruction.

8 My son, hear the instruction of your father,
And do not forsake the law of your mother;
9 For they *will be* a graceful ornament on your head,
And chains about your neck.

10 My son, if sinners entice you,
Do not consent.
11 If they say, "Come with us,
Let us lie in wait to *shed* blood;
Let us lurk secretly for the innocent without cause;
12 Let us swallow them alive like Sheol,
And whole, like those who go down to the Pit;
13 We shall find all *kinds* of precious possessions,
We shall fill our houses with spoil;
14 Cast in your lot among us,
Let us all have one purse"—
15 My son, do not walk in the way with them,
Keep your foot from their path;
16 For their feet run to evil,
And they make haste to shed blood.

17 Surely, in vain the net is spread
In the sight of any bird;
18 But they lie in wait for their *own* blood,
They lurk secretly for their *own* lives.
19 So *are* the ways of everyone who is greedy for gain;
It takes away the life of its owners.

20 Wisdom calls aloud outside;
She raises her voice in the open squares.
21 She cries out in the chief concourses,
At the openings of the gates in the city
She speaks her words:

TURN AND RUN

1:10-19 Sin is attractive because it offers a quick route to prosperity and makes us feel like "one of the crowd." When we go along with others and refuse to listen to the truth, our own appetites become our masters. We'll do anything to satisfy them. But sin is deadly. We must learn to make choices not on the basis of flashy appeal or short-range pleasure, but in view of the long-range effects. Sometimes this means steering clear of people who want to draw us into activities we know are wrong. We can't be friendly with sin and expect our life to remain unaffected. Turn and run—this is not cowardly; it is both brave and smart.

22 "How long, you simple ones, will you love simplicity?
For scorners delight in their scorning,
And fools hate knowledge.
23 Turn at my rebuke;
Surely I will pour out my spirit on you;
I will make my words known to you.
24 Because I have called and you refused,
I have stretched out my hand and no one regarded,
25 Because you disdained all my counsel,
And would have none of my rebuke,
26 I also will laugh at your calamity;

<head>

◣━━◤ CHOICES

2:9-10 Wisdom comes through a constant process of growth. First, we must trust and honor God. Second, we must realize that the Bible reveals God's wisdom to us. Third, we must learn to make right choices. Fourth, when we make sinful or mistaken choices, we must learn from our errors. People don't develop all aspects of wisdom at once. For example, some people have more insight than discretion; others have more knowledge than common sense. But we can pray for all the aspects of wisdom and seek to develop them in our life.

I will mock when your terror comes,
27 When your terror comes like a storm,
And your destruction comes like a whirlwind,
When distress and anguish come upon you.

28 "Then they will call on me, but I will not answer;
They will seek me diligently, but they will not find me.
29 Because they hated knowledge
And did not choose the fear of the LORD,
30 They would have none of my counsel
And despised my every rebuke.
31 Therefore they shall eat the fruit of their own way,
And be filled to the full with their own fancies.
32 For the turning away of the simple will slay them,
And the complacency of fools will destroy them;
33 But whoever listens to me will dwell safely,
And will be secure, without fear of evil."

CHAPTER 2 WISDOM COMES FROM GOD.

My son, if you receive my words,
And treasure my commands within you,
2 So that you incline your ear to wisdom,
And apply your heart to understanding;
3 Yes, if you cry out for discernment,
And lift up your voice for understanding,
4 If you seek her as silver,
And search for her as *for* hidden treasures;
5 Then you will understand the fear of the LORD,
And find the knowledge of God.
6 For the LORD gives wisdom;
From His mouth *come* knowledge and understanding;
7 He stores up sound wisdom for the upright;
He is a shield to those who walk uprightly;
8 He guards the paths of justice,
And preserves the way of His saints.
9 Then you will understand righteousness and justice,
Equity *and* every good path.

10 When wisdom enters your heart,
And knowledge is pleasant to your soul,
11 Discretion will preserve you;
Understanding will keep you,
12 To deliver you from the way of evil,
From the man who speaks perverse things,
13 From those who leave the paths of uprightness
To walk in the ways of darkness;
14 Who rejoice in doing evil,
And delight in the perversity of the wicked;
15 Whose ways *are* crooked,
And *who are* devious in their paths;
16 To deliver you from the immoral woman,

From the seductress *who* flatters with her words,
17 Who forsakes the companion of her youth,
And forgets the covenant of her God.
18 For her house leads down to death,
And her paths to the dead;
19 None who go to her return,
Nor do they regain the paths of life—
20 So you may walk in the way of goodness,
And keep *to* the paths of righteousness.
21 For the upright will dwell in the land,
And the blameless will remain in it;
22 But the wicked will be cut off from the earth,
And the unfaithful will be uprooted from it.

CHAPTER 3 WISDOM IS PRICELESS.

My son, do not forget my law,
But let your heart keep my commands;
2 For length of days and long life
And peace they will add to you.

3 Let not mercy and truth forsake you;
Bind them around your neck,
Write them on the tablet of your heart,
4 *And* so find favor and high esteem
In the sight of God and man.

5 Trust in the LORD with all your heart,

Trust in the LORD
with all your heart
and lean not
on your own
understanding

IN

ALL YOUR WAYS

ACKNOWLEDGE

HIM

AND

He shall direct your paths.

And lean not on your own understanding;
6 In all your ways acknowledge Him,
And He shall direct your paths.

7 Do not be wise in your own eyes;
Fear the LORD and depart from evil.
8 It will be health to your flesh,
And strength to your bones.

9 Honor the LORD with your possessions,
And with the firstfruits of all your increase;
10 So your barns will be filled with plenty,
And your vats will overflow with new wine.

11 My son, do not despise the chastening of the LORD,
Nor detest His correction;
12 For whom the LORD loves He corrects,
Just as a father the son *in whom* he delights.

13 Happy *is* the man *who* finds wisdom,
And the man *who* gains understanding;
14 For her proceeds *are* better than the profits of silver,
And her gain than fine gold.
15 She *is* more precious than rubies,
And all the things you may desire cannot compare
with her.
16 Length of days *is* in her right hand,
In her left hand riches and honor.
17 Her ways *are* ways of pleasantness,
And all her paths *are* peace.
18 She *is* a tree of life to those who take hold of her,
And happy *are all* who retain her.

19 The LORD by wisdom founded the earth;
By understanding He established the heavens;
20 By His knowledge the depths were broken up,
And clouds drop down the dew.

21 My son, let them not depart from your eyes—
Keep sound wisdom and discretion;
22 So they will be life to your soul
And grace to your neck.
23 Then you will walk safely in your way,
And your foot will not stumble.
24 When you lie down, you will not be afraid;
Yes, you will lie down and your sleep will be sweet.
25 Do not be afraid of sudden terror,
Nor of trouble from the wicked when it comes;
26 For the LORD will be your confidence,
And will keep your foot from being caught.

27 Do not withhold good from those to whom it is due,
When it is in the power of your hand to do *so.*
28 Do not say to your neighbor,
"Go, and come back,
And tomorrow I will give *it,*"
When *you have* it with you.
29 Do not devise evil against your neighbor,
For he dwells by you for safety's sake.
30 Do not strive with a man without cause,
If he has done you no harm.

31 Do not envy the oppressor,
And choose none of his ways;

32 For the perverse *person is* an abomination to the
LORD,
But His secret counsel *is* with the upright.
33 The curse of the LORD *is* on the house of the wicked,
But He blesses the home of the just.
34 Surely He scorns the scornful,
But gives grace to the humble.
35 The wise shall inherit glory,
But shame shall be the legacy of fools.

CHAPTER **4** YOU CAN LEARN WISDOM.
Hear, *my* children, the instruction of a father,
And give attention to know understanding;

**I'm always giving in to my friends. Lots
of times this goes against
what I think a Christian
should do. How do I
withstand the
pressure?**

I WONDER . . .

If every young person
had a dollar for every
time friends asked him
or her to "come along," most could pay for four years of
college!

Being included feels great, and everyone needs
friends. But friends don't always have our welfare at
heart. In fact, sometimes they only want us to join them
so they can feel better about doing whatever it is they
want to do.

But is this really pressure?

When someone invites you to go along with a
questionable (or bad) situation and you give in, you
haven't succumbed to peer pressure. You have chosen to
do something wrong and have concealed your true
identity.

Too often we hide our real character, hoping to be
liked by a group or person. We want to be accepted.
Unfortunately, this often works. If it didn't, people
wouldn't do it!

Everyone is tempted to bend their rules or beliefs in
order for someone to like them. During the teenage
years, this kind of pressure can be intense, and it can
generate a hungry urge to do what others are doing in
order to fit in.

But God wants to provide the inner muscle you'll need
to combat the outer pressure you feel. Ask him to give
you the courage and strength to say no.

He also wants to teach you what to do. Remember
when Mom or Dad taught you to do something like bake
cookies or start a lawnmower? They didn't just tell you to
do it, they showed you how.

God shows us how to act through the teachings and
stories in the Bible.

Commands like "Do not be conformed to this world,
but be transformed by the renewing of your mind"
(Romans 12:2) need to be read to understand God's
heart. But examples from throughout the Bible can help.

Consider these: Joseph ran from temptation (Genesis
39:12), and Daniel prayed his way through it (Daniel
6:10). And like the counsel in Proverbs 1:10, sometimes
we just have to realize that the consequences are not
worth the risk.

▬▬▬ AFFECTIONS

4:23-27 Our heart—our feelings of love and desire— dictates to a great extent how we live because we always find time to do what we enjoy. Solomon tells us to guard our heart, making sure we concentrate on those desires that will keep us on the right path. Make sure your affections are pushing you in the right direction. Put boundaries on your desires; don't go after everything you see. Look straight ahead, keeping your eyes fixed on your goal. Don't get sidetracked; watch out for detours that lead to temptation.

2 For I give you good doctrine:
Do not forsake my law.

3 When I was my father's son,
Tender and the only one in the sight of my mother,

4 He also taught me, and said to me:
"Let your heart retain my words;
Keep my commands, and live.

5 Get wisdom! Get understanding!
Do not forget, nor turn away from the words of my mouth.

6 Do not forsake her, and she will preserve you;
Love her, and she will keep you.

7 Wisdom *is* the principal thing;
Therefore get wisdom.
And in all your getting, get understanding.

8 Exalt her, and she will promote you;
She will bring you honor, when you embrace her.

9 She will place on your head an ornament of grace;
A crown of glory she will deliver to you."

10 Hear, my son, and receive my sayings,
And the years of your life will be many.

11 I have taught you in the way of wisdom;
I have led you in right paths.

12 When you walk, your steps will not be hindered,
And when you run, you will not stumble.

13 Take firm hold of instruction, do not let go;
Keep her, for she *is* your life.

14 Do not enter the path of the wicked,
And do not walk in the way of evil.

15 Avoid it, do not travel on it;
Turn away from it and pass on.

16 For they do not sleep unless they have done evil;
And their sleep is taken away unless they make *someone* fall.

17 For they eat the bread of wickedness,
And drink the wine of violence.

18 But the path of the just *is* like the shining sun,
That shines ever brighter unto the perfect day.

19 The way of the wicked *is* like darkness;
They do not know what makes them stumble.

20 My son, give attention to my words;
Incline your ear to my sayings.

21 Do not let them depart from your eyes;
Keep them in the midst of your heart;

22 For they *are* life to those who find them,
And health to all their flesh.

23 Keep your heart with all diligence,
For out of it *spring* the issues of life.

24 Put away from you a deceitful mouth,
And put perverse lips far from you.

25 Let your eyes look straight ahead,

And your eyelids look right before you.

26 Ponder the path of your feet,
And let all your ways be established.

27 Do not turn to the right or the left;
Remove your foot from evil.

CHAPTER 5 RUN FROM SIN.

My son, pay attention to my wisdom;
Lend your ear to my understanding,

2 That you may preserve discretion,
And your lips may keep knowledge.

3 For the lips of an immoral woman drip honey,
And her mouth *is* smoother than oil;

4 But in the end she is bitter as wormwood,
Sharp as a two-edged sword.

5 Her feet go down to death,
Her steps lay hold of hell.

6 Lest you ponder *her* path of life—
Her ways are unstable;
You do not know *them.*

7 Therefore hear me now, *my* children,
And do not depart from the words of my mouth.

8 Remove your way far from her,
And do not go near the door of her house,

9 Lest you give your honor to others,
And your years to the cruel *one;*

10 Lest aliens be filled with your wealth,
And your labors *go* to the house of a foreigner;

11 And you mourn at last,
When your flesh and your body are consumed,

12 And say:
"How I have hated instruction,
And my heart despised correction!

13 I have not obeyed the voice of my teachers,
Nor inclined my ear to those who instructed me!

14 I was on the verge of total ruin,
In the midst of the assembly and congregation."

15 Drink water from your own cistern,
And running water from your own well.

16 Should your fountains be dispersed abroad,
Streams of water in the streets?

17 Let them be only your own,
And not for strangers with you.

18 Let your fountain be blessed,
And rejoice with the wife of your youth.

19 *As a* loving deer and a graceful doe,
Let her breasts satisfy you at all times;
And always be enraptured with her love.

20 For why should you, my son, be enraptured by an immoral woman,
And be embraced in the arms of a seductress?

21 For the ways of man *are* before the eyes of the LORD,
And He ponders all his paths.

22 His own iniquities entrap the wicked *man,*
And he is caught in the cords of his sin.

23 He shall die for lack of instruction,
And in the greatness of his folly he shall go astray.

CHAPTER 6 RUN FROM FOOLISHNESS.

My son, if you become surety for your friend,
If you have shaken hands in pledge for a stranger,
2 You are snared by the words of your mouth;
You are taken by the words of your mouth.
3 So do this, my son, and deliver yourself;
For you have come into the hand of your friend:
Go and humble yourself;
Plead with your friend.
4 Give no sleep to your eyes,
Nor slumber to your eyelids.
5 Deliver yourself like a gazelle from the hand *of the hunter*,
And like a bird from the hand of the fowler.

6 Go to the ant, you sluggard!
Consider her ways and be wise,
7 Which, having no captain,
Overseer or ruler,
8 Provides her supplies in the summer,
And gathers her food in the harvest.
9 How long will you slumber, O sluggard?
When will you rise from your sleep?
10 A little sleep, a little slumber,
A little folding of the hands to sleep—
11 So shall your poverty come on you like a prowler,
And your need like an armed man.

12 A worthless person, a wicked man,
Walks with a perverse mouth;
13 He winks with his eyes,
He shuffles his feet,
He points with his fingers;
14 Perversity *is* in his heart,
He devises evil continually,
He sows discord.
15 Therefore his calamity shall come suddenly;
Suddenly he shall be broken without remedy.

16 These six *things* the LORD hates,
Yes, seven *are* an abomination to Him:
17 A proud look,
A lying tongue,
Hands that shed innocent blood,
18 A heart that devises wicked plans,
Feet that are swift in running to evil,
19 A false witness *who* speaks lies,
And one who sows discord among brethren.

20 My son, keep your father's command,
And do not forsake the law of your mother.
21 Bind them continually upon your heart;
Tie them around your neck.
22 When you roam, they will lead you;
When you sleep, they will keep you;
And *when* you awake, they will speak with you.
23 For the commandment *is* a lamp,
And the law a light;
Reproofs of instruction *are* the way of life,
24 To keep you from the evil woman,
From the flattering tongue of a seductress.

EXPERIENCE

6:20-24 It is natural and good for children as they grow toward adulthood to strive to become independent of their parents. Young adults, however, should take care not to turn a deaf ear to their parents—to reject their advice just when they may need it most. If you are struggling with a decision or looking for insight, check with your parents or other older adults who know you well. Their extra years of experience may have given them the wisdom you seek.

25 Do not lust after her beauty in your heart,
Nor let her allure you with her eyelids.
26 For by means of a harlot
A man is reduced to a crust of bread;
And an adulteress will prey upon his precious life.
27 Can a man take fire to his bosom,

"Here's what I did..."

Sometimes reading Scripture is like getting a good swift kick in the pants! That's what happened to me, anyway.

I've had this problem with procrastination and laziness. Basically I just don't make an effort with things that bore me (like school or chores my parents want me to do). One day I was reading along in Proverbs 6:6-11, which describes what a lazy person is like—and I knew that it was talking about me! Those verses taught me that putting things off isn't just a bad habit, it's a sin that can lead to some pretty bad consequences. This passage helped motivate me to quit sitting around, to take some action even if I don't feel like it.

John

AGE 14

And his clothes not be burned?
28 Can one walk on hot coals,
And his feet not be seared?
29 So *is* he who goes in to his neighbor's wife;
Whoever touches her shall not be innocent.

30 *People* do not despise a thief
If he steals to satisfy himself when he is starving.
31 Yet *when* he is found, he must restore sevenfold;
He may have to give up all the substance of his house.
32 Whoever commits adultery with a woman lacks understanding;
He *who* does so destroys his own soul.
33 Wounds and dishonor he will get,

And his reproach will not be wiped away.
34 For jealousy *is* a husband's fury;
Therefore he will not spare in the day of vengeance.
35 He will accept no recompense,
Nor will he be appeased though you give many gifts.

CHAPTER 7 KEEP YOURSELF PURE.

My son, keep my words,
And treasure my commands within you.
2 Keep my commands and live,
And my law as the apple of your eye.
3 Bind them on your fingers;
Write them on the tablet of your heart.
4 Say to wisdom, "You *are* my sister,"
And call understanding *your* nearest kin,
5 That they may keep you from the immoral woman,
From the seductress *who* flatters with her words.

6 For at the window of my house
I looked through my lattice,
7 And saw among the simple,
I perceived among the youths,
A young man devoid of understanding,
8 Passing along the street near her corner;
And he took the path to her house
9 In the twilight, in the evening,
In the black and dark night.

10 And there a woman met him,
With the attire of a harlot, and a crafty heart.
11 She *was* loud and rebellious,
Her feet would not stay at home.
12 At times *she was* outside, at times in the open square,
Lurking at every corner.
13 So she caught him and kissed him;
With an impudent face she said to him:
14 "*I have* peace offerings with me;
Today I have paid my vows.
15 So I came out to meet you,
Diligently to seek your face,
And I have found you.
16 I have spread my bed with tapestry,
Colored coverings of Egyptian linen.
17 I have perfumed my bed
With myrrh, aloes, and cinnamon.
18 Come, let us take our fill of love until morning;
Let us delight ourselves with love.

19 For my husband *is* not at home;
He has gone on a long journey;
20 He has taken a bag of money with him,
And will come home on the appointed day."
21 With her enticing speech she caused him to yield,
With her flattering lips she seduced him.
22 Immediately he went after her, as an ox goes to the slaughter,
Or as a fool to the correction of the stocks,
23 Till an arrow struck his liver.
As a bird hastens to the snare,
He did not know it *would cost* his life.

24 Now therefore, listen to me, *my* children;
Pay attention to the words of my mouth:
25 Do not let your heart turn aside to her ways,
Do not stray into her paths;
26 For she has cast down many wounded,
And all who were slain by her were strong *men*.
27 Her house *is* the way to hell,
Descending to the chambers of death.

CHAPTER 8 WISDOM GIVES GOOD ADVICE.

Does not wisdom cry out,
And understanding lift up her voice?
2 She takes her stand on the top of the high hill,
Beside the way, where the paths meet.
3 She cries out by the gates, at the entry of the city,
At the entrance of the doors:
4 "To you, O men, I call,
And my voice *is* to the sons of men.
5 O you simple ones, understand prudence,
And you fools, be of an understanding heart.
6 Listen, for I will speak of excellent things,
And from the opening of my lips *will come* right things;
7 For my mouth will speak truth;
Wickedness *is* an abomination to my lips.
8 All the words of my mouth *are* with righteousness;
Nothing crooked or perverse *is* in them.
9 They *are* all plain to him who understands,
And right to those who find knowledge.
10 Receive my instruction, and not silver,
And knowledge rather than choice gold;
11 For wisdom *is* better than rubies,

STRATEGY FOR EFFECTIVE LIVING

Begins with
GOD'S WISDOM
Respecting and appreciating who God is. Reverence and awe in recognizing the almighty God.

Requires
MORAL APPLICATION
Trusting in God and his Word. Allowing his Word to speak to us personally. Being willing to obey.

Requires
PRACTICAL APPLICATION
Acting on God's direction in daily devotions.

Results in
EFFECTIVE LIVING
Experiencing what God does with our obedience.

And all the things one may desire cannot be
  compared with her.
12 "I, wisdom, dwell with prudence,
  And find out knowledge *and* discretion.
13 The fear of the LORD *is* to hate evil;
  Pride and arrogance and the evil way
  And the perverse mouth I hate.
14 Counsel *is* mine, and sound wisdom;
  I *am* understanding, I have strength.
15 By me kings reign,
  And rulers decree justice.
16 By me princes rule, and nobles,
  All the judges of the earth.
17 I love those who love me,
  And those who seek me diligently will find me.
18 Riches and honor *are* with me,
  Enduring riches and righteousness.
19 My fruit *is* better than gold, yes, than fine gold,
  And my revenue than choice silver.
20 I traverse the way of righteousness,
  In the midst of the paths of justice,
21 That I may cause those who love me to inherit
    wealth,
  That I may fill their treasuries.

22 "The LORD possessed me at the beginning of His way,
  Before His works of old.
23 I have been established from everlasting,
  From the beginning, before there was ever an earth.
24 When *there were* no depths I was brought forth,
  When *there were* no fountains abounding with water.
25 Before the mountains were settled,
  Before the hills, I was brought forth;
26 While as yet He had not made the earth or the fields,
  Or the primal dust of the world.
27 When He prepared the heavens, I *was* there,
  When He drew a circle on the face of the deep,
28 When He established the clouds above,
  When He strengthened the fountains of the deep,
29 When He assigned to the sea its limit,
  So that the waters would not transgress His
    command,
  When He marked out the foundations of the earth,
30 Then I was beside Him *as* a master craftsman;
  And I was daily *His* delight,
  Rejoicing always before Him,
31 Rejoicing in His inhabited world,
  And my delight *was* with the sons of men.

32 "Now therefore, listen to me, *my* children,
  For blessed *are those who* keep my ways.
33 Hear instruction and be wise,
  And do not disdain *it.*
34 Blessed is the man who listens to me,
  Watching daily at my gates,
  Waiting at the posts of my doors.
35 For whoever finds me finds life,
  And obtains favor from the LORD;
36 But he who sins against me wrongs his own soul;
  All those who hate me love death."

CHAPTER **9** KNOWING GOD RESULTS IN WISDOM.
  Wisdom has built her house,
  She has hewn out her seven pillars;
2 She has slaughtered her meat,
  She has mixed her wine,
  She has also furnished her table.
3 She has sent out her maidens,
  She cries out from the highest places of the city,
4 "Whoever *is* simple, let him turn in here!"
  As for him who lacks understanding, she says to him,
5 "Come, eat of my bread
  And drink of the wine I have mixed.
6 Forsake foolishness and live,
  And go in the way of understanding.

7 "He who corrects a scoffer gets shame for himself,
  And he who rebukes a wicked *man only* harms himself.
8 Do not correct a scoffer, lest he hate you;
  Rebuke a wise *man,* and he will love you.
9 Give *instruction* to a wise *man,* and he will be still
    wiser;
  Teach a just *man,* and he will increase in learning.

10 "The fear of the LORD *is* the beginning of wisdom,
  And the knowledge of the Holy One *is* understanding.
11 For by me your days will be multiplied,
  And years of life will be added to you.
12 If you are wise, you are wise for yourself,
  And *if* you scoff, you will bear *it* alone."

13 A foolish woman is clamorous;
  She is simple, and knows nothing.
14 For she sits at the door of her house,
  On a seat *by* the highest places of the city,
15 To call to those who pass by,
  Who go straight on their way:
16 "Whoever *is* simple, let him turn in here";
  And *as for* him who lacks understanding, she says to
    him,
17 "Stolen water is sweet,
  And bread *eaten* in secret is pleasant."
18 But he does not know that the dead *are* there,
  That her guests *are* in the depths of hell.

CHAPTER **10** GOD'S WISDOM IS FOR EVERYONE.
  The proverbs of Solomon:

  A wise son makes a glad father,
  But a foolish son *is* the grief of his mother.

2 Treasures of wickedness profit nothing,
  But righteousness delivers from death.
3 The LORD will not allow the righteous soul to famish,
  But He casts away the desire of the wicked.

━━━━━━━━━━━━━ HYPNOTIZED

9:17 There is something hypnotic and intoxicating about wickedness.
One sin leads us to want more; sinful behavior seems more exciting than
the "boring" Christian life. That is why many people put aside all thought
of wisdom's sumptuous banquet (9:1-6) in order to eat the stolen food of
foolishness, the harlot. Don't be deceived— sin is dangerous. Before
reaching for forbidden fruit, take a long look at what happens to those
who eat it.

4 He who has a slack hand becomes poor,
   But the hand of the diligent makes rich.
5 He who gathers in summer *is* a wise son;
   He who sleeps in harvest *is* a son who causes shame.

6 Blessings *are* on the head of the righteous,
   But violence covers the mouth of the wicked.
7 The memory of the righteous *is* blessed,
   But the name of the wicked will rot.

8 The wise in heart will receive commands,
   But a prating fool will fall.

9 He who walks with integrity walks securely,
   But he who perverts his ways will become known.

CHEATING

If Tucker spent half as much time actually studying as he does trying to invent new ways to avoid doing his schoolwork, he probably could make straight A's.
Just look at some of his schemes:

- He knows of a company that sells term papers. For a few bucks and an hour's worth of editing, he can turn in a top-notch report on almost any subject.
- He gets his friends to divide the daily algebra assignments. In study hall they each spend about 15 minutes doing a part of the homework (instead of an hour or more doing the whole thing by themselves). Tucker takes the pages to his dad's office on the way home from school, makes photocopies for everyone, and passes them out first thing in the morning.
- Tucker has never read an assigned literary work for English class. Between videos and Cliffs Notes, he can always fake it.
- Two of his teachers use the exact same tests from last year. Tucker bought old copies from two college freshmen.
- He has a programmable watch that can store up to 100 facts and dates. On exam days, the watch gets a mean workout!

Tucker laughs at how stupid his teachers are and at how many people get away with cheating.
See Proverbs 11:1 for a look at how God views Tucker's life-style.

10 He who winks with the eye causes trouble,
   But a prating fool will fall.

11 The mouth of the righteous *is* a well of life,
   But violence covers the mouth of the wicked.

12 Hatred stirs up strife,
   But love covers all sins.

13 Wisdom is found on the lips of him who has understanding,
   But a rod *is* for the back of him who is devoid of understanding.

14 Wise *people* store up knowledge,
   But the mouth of the foolish *is* near destruction.

15 The rich man's wealth *is* his strong city;
   The destruction of the poor *is* their poverty.

16 The labor of the righteous *leads* to life,

WASTED TIME

10:4-5 Every day has 24 hours filled with opportunities to grow, se and be productive. It is so easy to waste time, letting life slip from ou grasp. Instead, refuse to be a lazy person, sleeping or squandering th hours meant for productive work. See time as God's gift, and seize th opportunities to live for him.

The wages of the wicked to sin.

17 He who keeps instruction *is in* the way of life,
   But he who refuses correction goes astray.

18 Whoever hides hatred *has* lying lips,
   And whoever spreads slander *is* a fool.

19 In the multitude of words sin is not lacking,
   But he who restrains his lips *is* wise.
20 The tongue of the righteous *is* choice silver;
   The heart of the wicked *is worth* little.
21 The lips of the righteous feed many,
   But fools die for lack of wisdom.

22 The blessing of the LORD makes *one* rich,
   And He adds no sorrow with it.

23 To do evil *is* like sport to a fool,
   But a man of understanding has wisdom.
24 The fear of the wicked will come upon him,
   And the desire of the righteous will be granted.
25 When the whirlwind passes by, the wicked *is* no more,
   But the righteous *has* an everlasting foundation.

26 As vinegar to the teeth and smoke to the eyes,
   So *is* the lazy *man* to those who send him.

27 The fear of the LORD prolongs days,
   But the years of the wicked will be shortened.
28 The hope of the righteous *will be* gladness,
   But the expectation of the wicked will perish.
29 The way of the LORD *is* strength for the upright,
   But destruction *will come* to the workers of iniquity.

30 The righteous will never be removed,
   But the wicked will not inhabit the earth.
31 The mouth of the righteous brings forth wisdom,
   But the perverse tongue will be cut out.
32 The lips of the righteous know what is acceptable,
   But the mouth of the wicked *what is* perverse.

CHAPTER 11 GOD HATES DISHONESTY.

Dishonest scales *are* an abomination to the LORD,
   But a just weight *is* His delight.

2 When pride comes, then comes shame;
   But with the humble *is* wisdom.

3 The integrity of the upright will guide them,
   But the perversity of the unfaithful will destroy them.
4 Riches do not profit in the day of wrath,
   But righteousness delivers from death.
5 The righteousness of the blameless will direct his way aright,
   But the wicked will fall by his own wickedness.
6 The righteousness of the upright will deliver them,
   But the unfaithful will be caught by *their* lust.

7 When a wicked man dies, *his* expectation will perish,
And the hope of the unjust perishes.

8 The righteous is delivered from trouble,
And it comes to the wicked instead.

9 The hypocrite with *his* mouth destroys his neighbor,
But through knowledge the righteous will be delivered.

10 When it goes well with the righteous, the city rejoices;
And when the wicked perish, *there is* jubilation.

11 By the blessing of the upright the city is exalted,
But it is overthrown by the mouth of the wicked.

12 He who is devoid of wisdom despises his neighbor,
But a man of understanding holds his peace.

13 A talebearer reveals secrets,
But he who is of a faithful spirit conceals a matter.

14 Where *there is* no counsel, the people fall;
But in the multitude of counselors *there is* safety.

15 He who is surety for a stranger will suffer,
But one who hates being surety is secure.

16 A gracious woman retains honor,
But ruthless *men* retain riches.

17 The merciful man does good for his own soul,
But *he who is* cruel troubles his own flesh.

18 The wicked *man* does deceptive work,
But he who sows righteousness *will have* a sure reward.

19 As righteousness *leads* to life,
So he who pursues evil *pursues it* to his own death.

20 Those who are of a perverse heart *are* an abomination to the LORD,
But *the* blameless in their ways *are* His delight.

21 *Though they join* forces, the wicked will not go unpunished;
But the posterity of the righteous will be delivered.

22 *As* a ring of gold in a swine's snout,
So is a lovely woman who lacks discretion.

23 The desire of the righteous *is* only good,
But the expectation of the wicked *is* wrath.

24 There is *one* who scatters, yet increases more;
And there is *one* who withholds more than is right,
But it *leads* to poverty.

25 The generous soul will be made rich,
And he who waters will also be watered himself.

26 The people will curse him who withholds grain,
But blessing *will be* on the head of him who sells *it.*

27 He who earnestly seeks good finds favor,
But trouble will come to him who seeks *evil.*

28 He who trusts in his riches will fall,
But the righteous will flourish like foliage.

29 He who troubles his own house will inherit the wind,
And the fool *will be* servant to the wise of heart.

30 The fruit of the righteous *is a* tree of life,
And he who wins souls *is* wise.

31 If the righteous will be recompensed on the earth,
How much more the ungodly and the sinner.

CHAPTER **12** GAIN WISDOM: AVOID MISTAKES.

Whoever loves instruction loves knowledge,
But he who hates correction *is* stupid.

2 A good *man* obtains favor from the LORD,
But a man of wicked intentions He will condemn.

3 A man is not established by wickedness,
But the root of the righteous cannot be moved.

4 An excellent wife *is* the crown of her husband,
But she who causes shame *is* like rottenness in his bones.

◣▬▬▬▬▬CAUGHT

11:31 Contrary to popular opinion, no one sins and gets away with it. Ultimately, the faithful are rewarded for their faith and the wicked are punished for their sins. Don't think for a moment that "it won't matter" or "nobody will know" or "we won't get caught." (See also 1 Peter 4:18.)

5 The thoughts of the righteous *are* right,
But the counsels of the wicked *are* deceitful.

6 The words of the wicked *are,* "Lie in wait for blood,"
But the mouth of the upright will deliver them.

7 The wicked are overthrown and *are* no more,
But the house of the righteous will stand.

8 A man will be commended according to his wisdom,
But he who is of a perverse heart will be despised.

9 Better *is the one* who is slighted but has a servant,
Than he who honors himself but lacks bread.

10 A righteous *man* regards the life of his animal,
But the tender mercies of the wicked *are* cruel.

11 He who tills his land will be satisfied with bread,
But he who follows frivolity *is* devoid of understanding.

12 The wicked covet the catch of evil *men,*
But the root of the righteous yields *fruit.*

13 The wicked is ensnared by the transgression of *his* lips,
But the righteous will come through trouble.

14 A man will be satisfied with good by the fruit of *his* mouth,
And the recompense of a man's hands will be rendered to him.

15 The way of a fool *is* right in his own eyes,
But he who heeds counsel *is* wise.

16 A fool's wrath is known at once,
But a prudent *man* covers shame.

◣▬▬▬▬▬COOL

12:16 When someone insults you, it is natural to insult in return. But this solves nothing and only encourages trouble. Instead, "keep your cool" and answer slowly and quietly. Your positive response will achieve positive results.

17 He *who* speaks truth declares righteousness,
But a false witness, deceit.

18 There is one who speaks like the piercings of a
sword,
But the tongue of the wise *promotes* health.

19 The truthful lip shall be established forever,
But a lying tongue *is* but for a moment.

20 Deceit is in the heart of those who devise evil,
But counselors of peace have joy.

21 No grave trouble will overtake the righteous,
But the wicked shall be filled with evil.

22 Lying lips *are* an abomination to the Lord,
But those who deal truthfully *are* His delight.

23 A prudent man conceals knowledge,
But the heart of fools proclaims foolishness.

24 The hand of the diligent will rule,
But the lazy *man* will be put to forced labor.

25 Anxiety in the heart of man causes depression,
But a good word makes it glad.

26 The righteous should choose his friends carefully,
For the way of the wicked leads them astray.

27 The lazy *man* does not roast what he took in
hunting,
But diligence *is* man's precious possession.

28 In the way of righteousness *is* life,
And in *its* pathway *there is* no death.

CHAPTER **13** THE WAY TO SUCCESS.
A wise son *heeds* his father's instruction,
But a scoffer does not listen to rebuke.

2 A man shall eat well by the fruit of *his* mouth,
But the soul of the unfaithful feeds on violence.

3 He who guards his mouth preserves his life,
But he who opens wide his lips shall have
destruction.

4 The soul of a lazy *man* desires, and *has* nothing;
But the soul of the diligent shall be made rich.

5 A righteous *man* hates lying,
But a wicked *man* is loathsome and comes to shame.

6 Righteousness guards *him whose* way is blameless,
But wickedness overthrows the sinner.

7 There is one who makes himself rich, yet *has*
nothing;
And one who makes himself poor, yet *has* great
riches.

8 The ransom of a man's life *is* his riches,
But the poor does not hear rebuke.

9 The light of the righteous rejoices,
But the lamp of the wicked will be put out.

10 By pride comes nothing but strife,
But with the well-advised *is* wisdom.

11 Wealth *gained by* dishonesty will be diminished,
But he who gathers by labor will increase.

12 Hope deferred makes the heart sick,
But *when* the desire comes, *it is* a tree of life.

13 He who despises the word will be destroyed,
But he who fears the commandment will be
rewarded.

14 The law of the wise *is* a fountain of life,
To turn *one* away from the snares of death.

15 Good understanding gains favor,
But the way of the unfaithful *is* hard.

16 Every prudent *man* acts with knowledge,
But a fool lays open *his* folly.

17 A wicked messenger falls into trouble,
But a faithful ambassador *brings* health.

18 Poverty and shame *will come* to him who disdains
correction,
But he who regards a rebuke will be honored.

19 A desire accomplished is sweet to the soul,
But *it is* an abomination to fools to depart from evil.

20 He who walks with wise *men* will be wise,
But the companion of fools will be destroyed.

21 Evil pursues sinners,
But to the righteous, good shall be repaid.

22 A good *man* leaves an inheritance to his children's
children,
But the wealth of the sinner is stored up for the
righteous.

23 Much food *is in* the fallow *ground* of the poor,
And for lack of justice there is waste.

24 He who spares his rod hates his son,
But he who loves him disciplines him promptly.

25 The righteous eats to the satisfying of his soul,
But the stomach of the wicked shall be in want.

CHAPTER **14** ANGER CAUSES MISTAKES.
The wise woman builds her house,
But the foolish pulls it down with her hands.

2 He who walks in his uprightness fears the Lord,
But *he who is* perverse in his ways despises Him.

3 In the mouth of a fool *is* a rod of pride,
But the lips of the wise will preserve them.

4 Where no oxen *are*, the trough *is* clean;
But much increase *comes* by the strength of an ox.

5 A faithful witness does not lie,
But a false witness will utter lies.

6 A scoffer seeks wisdom and does not *find it*,
But knowledge *is* easy to him who understands.

7 Go from the presence of a foolish man,
When you do not perceive *in him* the lips of
knowledge.

8 The wisdom of the prudent *is* to understand his way,
But the folly of fools *is* deceit.

⁹ Fools mock at sin,
But among the upright *there is* favor.

¹⁰ The heart knows its own bitterness,
And a stranger does not share its joy.

¹¹ The house of the wicked will be overthrown,
But the tent of the upright will flourish.

¹² There is a way *that seems* right to a man,
But its end *is* the way of death.

¹³ Even in laughter the heart may sorrow,
And the end of mirth *may be* grief.

¹⁴ The backslider in heart will be filled with his own
ways,
But a good man *will be satisfied* from above.

¹⁵ The simple believes every word,
But the prudent considers well his steps.

¹⁶ A wise *man* fears and departs from evil,
But a fool rages and is self-confident.

¹⁷ A quick-tempered *man* acts foolishly,
And a man of wicked intentions is hated.

¹⁸ The simple inherit folly,
But the prudent are crowned with knowledge.

¹⁹ The evil will bow before the good,
And the wicked at the gates of the righteous.

²⁰ The poor *man* is hated even by his own neighbor,
But the rich *has* many friends.

²¹ He who despises his neighbor sins;
But he who has mercy on the poor, happy *is* he.

²² Do they not go astray who devise evil?
But mercy and truth *belong* to those who devise
good.

²³ In all labor there is profit,
But idle chatter *leads* only to poverty.

²⁴ The crown of the wise is their riches,
But the foolishness of fools *is* folly.

²⁵ A true witness delivers souls,
But a deceitful *witness* speaks lies.

²⁶ In the fear of the LORD *there is* strong confidence,

GOODWILL

14:9 How rarely we find favor—goodwill—around us today! Angry drivers scowl at each other. People fight to be first in line. Disgruntled employers and employees demand their rights. But the common bond of God's people should be goodwill. Those with goodwill think the best of others and assume that others have good motives and intend to do what is right. When someone crosses you and your blood pressure starts to rise, ask yourself, "How can I show favor to this person?"

And His children will have a place of refuge.
²⁷ The fear of the LORD *is* a fountain of life,
To turn *one* away from the snares of death.

²⁸ In a multitude of people *is* a king's honor,
But in the lack of people *is* the downfall of a prince.

²⁹ *He who is* slow to wrath has great understanding,
But *he who is* impulsive exalts folly.

³⁰ A sound heart *is* life to the body,
But envy *is* rottenness to the bones.

³¹ He who oppresses the poor reproaches his Maker,
But he who honors Him has mercy on the needy.

QUIET

15:1 Have you ever tried to argue in a whisper? It is hard to argue with someone who insists on answering softly. On the other hand, a rising voice almost always triggers an angry response. If the most important goal is to win the argument, then you had better warm up your vocal cords. But if your goal is to seek peace, then a consistently quiet response is your best choice.

³² The wicked is banished in his wickedness,
But the righteous has a refuge in his death.

³³ Wisdom rests in the heart of him who has
understanding,
But *what is* in the heart of fools is made known.

³⁴ Righteousness exalts a nation,
But sin *is* a reproach to *any* people.

³⁵ The king's favor *is* toward a wise servant,
But his wrath *is against* him who causes shame.

CHAPTER **15** GOD DELIGHTS IN OUR PRAYERS.

A soft answer turns away wrath,
But a harsh word stirs up anger.
² The tongue of the wise uses knowledge rightly,
But the mouth of fools pours forth foolishness.

³ The eyes of the LORD *are* in every place,
Keeping watch on the evil and the good.

⁴ A wholesome tongue *is* a tree of life,
But perverseness in it breaks the spirit.

A soft answer turns away wrath
BUT
A HARSH WORD STIRS UP ANGER

15:22 Those with tunnel vision, people who are locked into one way of thinking, are likely to miss the right road because they have closed their mind to any new options. We need the help of those who can enlarge our vision and broaden our perspective. Seek out the advice of those who know you and have a wealth of experience. Build a network of counselors. Then be willing to weigh their suggestions carefully. Your plans will be strengthened, your chances for success increased.

5 A fool despises his father's instruction,
But he who receives correction is prudent.

6 *In* the house of the righteous *there is* much treasure,
But in the revenue of the wicked is trouble.

7 The lips of the wise disperse knowledge,
But the heart of the fool *does* not *do* so.

8 The sacrifice of the wicked *is* an abomination to the LORD,
But the prayer of the upright *is* His delight.

9 The way of the wicked *is* an abomination to the LORD,
But He loves him who follows righteousness.

10 Harsh discipline *is* for him who forsakes the way,
And he who hates correction will die.

11 Hell and Destruction *are* before the LORD;
So how much more the hearts of the sons of men.

12 A scoffer does not love one who corrects him,
Nor will he go to the wise.

13 A merry heart makes a cheerful countenance,
But by sorrow of the heart the spirit is broken.

14 The heart of him who has understanding seeks knowledge,
But the mouth of fools feeds on foolishness.

15 All the days of the afflicted *are* evil,
But he who is of a merry heart *has* a continual feast.

16 Better *is* a little with the fear of the LORD,
Than great treasure with trouble.

17 Better *is* a dinner of herbs where love is,
Than a fatted calf with hatred.

18 A wrathful man stirs up strife,
But *he who is* slow to anger allays contention.

19 The way of the lazy *man is* like a hedge of thorns,
But the way of the upright *is* a highway.

20 A wise son makes a father glad,
But a foolish man despises his mother.

21 Folly *is* joy *to him who is* destitute of discernment,
But a man of understanding walks uprightly.

22 Without counsel, plans go awry,
But in the multitude of counselors they are established.

23 A man has joy by the answer of his mouth,
And a word *spoken* in due season, how good *it is!*

24 The way of life *winds* upward for the wise,
That he may turn away from hell below.

25 The LORD will destroy the house of the proud,
But He will establish the boundary of the widow.

26 The thoughts of the wicked *are* an abomination to the LORD,
But *the words* of the pure *are* pleasant.

27 He who is greedy for gain troubles his own house,
But he who hates bribes will live.

28 The heart of the righteous studies how to answer,
But the mouth of the wicked pours forth evil.

29 The LORD *is* far from the wicked,
But He hears the prayer of the righteous.

30 The light of the eyes rejoices the heart,
And a good report makes the bones healthy.

31 The ear that hears the rebukes of life
Will abide among the wise.

32 He who disdains instruction despises his own soul,
But he who heeds rebuke gets understanding.

33 The fear of the LORD *is* the instruction of wisdom,
And before honor *is* humility.

CHAPTER 16 PRIDE LEADS TO TROUBLE.

The preparations of the heart *belong* to man,
But the answer of the tongue *is* from the LORD.

2 All the ways of a man *are* pure in his own eyes,
But the LORD weighs the spirits.

3 Commit your works to the LORD,
And your thoughts will be established.

4 The LORD has made all for Himself,
Yes, even the wicked for the day of doom.

5 Everyone proud in heart *is* an abomination to the LORD;
Though they join forces, none will go unpunished.

6 In mercy and truth
Atonement is provided for iniquity;
And by the fear of the LORD *one* departs from evil.

7 When a man's ways please the LORD,
He makes even his enemies to be at peace with him.

8 Better *is* a little with righteousness,
Than vast revenues without justice.

9 A man's heart plans his way,
But the LORD directs his steps.

10 Divination *is* on the lips of the king;
His mouth must not transgress in judgment.

11 Honest weights and scales *are* the LORD's;

17:5 Few acts are as cruel as making fun of those who are less fortunate, but many people do it because it makes them feel good better off or more successful than someone else. Mocking the poor mocking the God who made them. We also mock God when we moc weak, or those who are different, or anyone who is an easy target. you catch yourself putting down others just for fun, stop. If you don you will drag yourself down and anger God.

All the weights in the bag *are* His work.

12 *It is* an abomination for kings to commit wickedness,
For a throne is established by righteousness.

13 Righteous lips *are* the delight of kings,
And they love him who speaks *what is* right.

14 As messengers of death *is* the king's wrath,
But a wise man will appease it.

15 In the light of the king's face *is* life,
And his favor *is* like a cloud of the latter rain.

16 How much better to get wisdom than gold!
And to get understanding is to be chosen rather
than silver.

17 The highway of the upright *is* to depart from evil;
He who keeps his way preserves his soul.

18 Pride *goes* before destruction,
And a haughty spirit before a fall.

19 Better *to be* of a humble spirit with the lowly,
Than to divide the spoil with the proud.

20 He who heeds the word wisely will find good,
And whoever trusts in the LORD, happy *is* he.

21 The wise in heart will be called prudent,
And sweetness of the lips increases learning.

22 Understanding *is* a wellspring of life to him who
has it.
But the correction of fools *is* folly.

23 The heart of the wise teaches his mouth,
And adds learning to his lips.

24 Pleasant words *are like* a honeycomb,
Sweetness to the soul and health to the bones.

25 There is a way *that seems* right to a man,
But its end *is* the way of death.

26 The person who labors, labors for himself,
For his *hungry* mouth drives him *on.*

27 An ungodly man digs up evil,
And *it is* on his lips like a burning fire.

28 A perverse man sows strife,
And a whisperer separates the best of friends.

29 A violent man entices his neighbor,
And leads him in a way *that is* not good.

30 He winks his eye to devise perverse things;
He purses his lips *and* brings about evil.

31 The silver-haired head *is* a crown of glory,
If it is found in the way of righteousness.

32 *He who is* slow to anger *is* better than the mighty,
And he who rules his spirit than he who takes a city.

33 The lot is cast into the lap,
But its every decision *is* from the LORD.

CHAPTER **17** TRUE FRIENDS ARE LOYAL.
Better *is* a dry morsel with quietness,
Than a house full of feasting *with* strife.

2 A wise servant will rule over a son who causes
shame,
And will share an inheritance among the brothers.

3 The refining pot *is* for silver and the furnace for gold,
But the LORD tests the hearts.

4 An evildoer gives heed to false lips;
A liar listens eagerly to a spiteful tongue.

5 He who mocks the poor reproaches his Maker;
He who is glad at calamity will not go unpunished.

6 Children's children *are* the crown of old men,

I hear Christians talk a lot about God's will. Has God planned out everything I'll ever do?

I WONDER . . .

Follow these instructions: Put your right hand straight up in the air. Next place your index finger in your left ear (come on, your left ear). Now clap your hands.

Who controlled your hand and fingers?

Tough question. Especially if you were silly enough to do what we asked. But we know from experience that when people give us instructions, we choose whether or not we obey.

The question, however, is who has ultimate control—you or God. This question has been debated for centuries, and the discussion can get quite complicated. For now, let's keep it as simple as possible.

We each have a will, a part within our brains that is the "chooser." Because we are human, the things we do sometimes don't match up with what God wants us to do. It isn't God's will for us to sin.

Of course, God is strong enough to force his will on us. But because he loves us, he allows us to have choices. What loving, earthly father would force his child to say, "I love you, Daddy"? There would be no satisfaction at all in forced expressions of love.

God does not force us to follow him. And it is obvious that many use their will to reject Christ. In essence, they choose to go to hell!

Putting all of these facts together points to the conclusion that God has allowed us to use our will to sometimes go against his will. One of the highest acts of love you can give someone is the opportunity to reject you. This is exactly what God has done.

So what *is* God's will for us? First, it is to know him. Second, it is to help others. "For we are His workmanship, created in Christ Jesus for good works, which God prepared beforehand that we should walk in them" (Ephesians 2:10).

Third, it is to be filled with the Holy Spirit. "See then that you walk circumspectly, not as fools but as wise, redeeming the time, because the days are evil. Therefore do not be unwise, but understand what the will of the Lord is. And do not be drunk with wine, in which is dissipation, but be filled with the Spirit" (Ephesians 5:15-18).

By allowing God to fill you, you are really saying, "God, take my will and help me do what you want." You are following the good advice of Proverbs 16:9.

And the glory of children *is* their father.

7 Excellent speech is not becoming to a fool,
Much less lying lips to a prince.

8 A present *is* a precious stone in the eyes of its possessor;
Wherever he turns, he prospers.

9 He who covers a transgression seeks love,
But he who repeats a matter separates friends.

10 Rebuke is more effective for a wise *man*
Than a hundred blows on a fool.

11 An evil *man* seeks only rebellion;
Therefore a cruel messenger will be sent against him.

12 Let a man meet a bear robbed of her cubs,
Rather than a fool in his folly.

13 Whoever rewards evil for good,
Evil will not depart from his house.

14 The beginning of strife *is like* releasing water;
Therefore stop contention before a quarrel starts.

15 He who justifies the wicked, and he who condemns the just,
Both of them alike *are* an abomination to the LORD.

16 Why *is there* in the hand of a fool the purchase price of wisdom,
Since *he has* no heart *for it?*

17 A friend loves at all times,
And a brother is born for adversity.

18 A man devoid of understanding shakes hands in a pledge,
And becomes surety for his friend.

19 He who loves transgression loves strife,
And he who exalts his gate seeks destruction.

20 He who has a deceitful heart finds no good,
And he who has a perverse tongue falls into evil.

21 He who begets a scoffer *does so* to his sorrow,
And the father of a fool has no joy.

22 A merry heart does good, *like* medicine,
But a broken spirit dries the bones.

23 A wicked *man* accepts a bribe behind the back
To pervert the ways of justice.

24 Wisdom *is* in the sight of him who has understanding,
But the eyes of a fool *are* on the ends of the earth.

25 A foolish son *is* a grief to his father,
And bitterness to her who bore him.

26 Also, to punish the righteous *is* not good,
Nor to strike princes for *their* uprightness.

27 He who has knowledge spares his words,
And a man of understanding is of a calm spirit.

28 Even a fool is counted wise when he holds his peace;
When he shuts his lips, *he is considered* perceptive.

CHAPTER 18 GET THE FACTS BEFORE DECIDING.

A man who isolates himself seeks his own desire;
He rages against all wise judgment.

2 A fool has no delight in understanding,
But in expressing his own heart.

3 When the wicked comes, contempt comes also;
And with dishonor *comes* reproach.

4 The words of a man's mouth *are* deep waters;
The wellspring of wisdom *is* a flowing brook.

5 *It is* not good to show partiality to the wicked,
Or to overthrow the righteous in judgment.

6 A fool's lips enter into contention,
And his mouth calls for blows.

7 A fool's mouth *is* his destruction,
And his lips *are* the snare of his soul.

8 The words of a talebearer *are* like tasty trifles,
And they go down into the inmost body.

9 He who is slothful in his work
Is a brother to him who is a great destroyer.

10 The name of the LORD *is* a strong tower;
The righteous run to it and are safe.

11 The rich man's wealth *is* his strong city,
And like a high wall in his own esteem.

12 Before destruction the heart of a man is haughty,
And before honor *is* humility.

13 He who answers a matter before he hears *it,*
It *is* folly and shame to him.

14 The spirit of a man will sustain him in sickness,
But who can bear a broken spirit?

15 The heart of the prudent acquires knowledge,
And the ear of the wise seeks knowledge.

16 A man's gift makes room for him,
And brings him before great men.

17 The first *one* to plead his cause *seems* right,
Until his neighbor comes and examines him.

18 Casting lots causes contentions to cease,
And keeps the mighty apart.

19 A brother offended *is harder to win* than a strong city,
And contentions *are* like the bars of a castle.

20 A man's stomach shall be satisfied from the fruit of his mouth;
From the produce of his lips he shall be filled.

21 Death and life *are* in the power of the tongue,
And those who love it will eat its fruit.

22 *He who* finds a wife finds a good *thing,*
And obtains favor from the LORD.

23 The poor *man* uses entreaties,
But the rich answers roughly.

24 A man *who has* friends must himself be friendly,
But there is a friend *who* sticks closer than a brother.

CHAPTER **19** A LAZY MAN GOES HUNGRY.

Better *is* the poor who walks in his integrity
Than *one who is* perverse in his lips, and is a fool.

2 Also it is not good *for* a soul *to be* without knowledge,
And he sins who hastens with *his* feet.

3 The foolishness of a man twists his way,
And his heart frets against the LORD.

4 Wealth makes many friends,
But the poor is separated from his friend.

5 A false witness will not go unpunished,
And *he who* speaks lies will not escape.

6 Many entreat the favor of the nobility,
And every man *is* a friend to one who gives gifts.

7 All the brothers of the poor hate him;
How much more do his friends go far from him!
He may pursue *them with* words, *yet* they abandon
him.

8 He who gets wisdom loves his own soul;
He who keeps understanding will find good.

9 A false witness will not go unpunished,
And *he who* speaks lies shall perish.

10 Luxury is not fitting for a fool,
Much less for a servant to rule over princes.

11 The discretion of a man makes him slow to anger,
And his glory *is* to overlook a transgression.

12 The king's wrath *is* like the roaring of a lion,
But his favor *is* like dew on the grass.

13 A foolish son *is* the ruin of his father,
And the contentions of a wife *are* a continual
dripping.

14 Houses and riches *are* an inheritance from fathers,
But a prudent wife *is* from the LORD.

15 Laziness casts *one* into a deep sleep,
And an idle person will suffer hunger.

16 He who keeps the commandment keeps his soul,
But he who is careless of his ways will die.

17 He who has pity on the poor lends to the LORD,
And He will pay back what he has given.

18 Chasten your son while there is hope,
And do not set your heart on his destruction.

19 *A man of* great wrath will suffer punishment;
For if you rescue *him,* you will have to do it again.

20 Listen to counsel and receive instruction,
That you may be wise in your latter days.

21 There are many plans in a man's heart,
Nevertheless the LORD's counsel—that will stand.

22 What is desired in a man is kindness,
And a poor man is better than a liar.

23 The fear of the LORD *leads* to life,
And *he who has it* will abide in satisfaction;

He will not be visited with evil.

24 A lazy *man* buries his hand in the bowl,
And will not so much as bring it to his mouth again.

25 Strike a scoffer, and the simple will become wary;
Rebuke one who has understanding, *and* he will
discern knowledge.

TRUE FRIEND

18:24 Many people today feel cut off and alienated from others. Being in a crowd just makes people more aware of their isolation. Lonely people don't need to hear "Have a nice day." They need friends who will stick close, listen, care, and offer help when it is needed—in good and bad times. It is better to have one such friend than dozens of superficial acquaintances. Instead of wishing you could find a true friend, seek to become one yourself. There are people who need your friendship. Ask God to reveal them to you, and then take on the challenge of being a true friend.

26 He who mistreats *his* father *and* chases away *his*
mother
Is a son who causes shame and brings reproach.

27 Cease listening to instruction, my son,
And you will stray from the words of knowledge.

28 A disreputable witness scorns justice,
And the mouth of the wicked devours iniquity.

29 Judgments are prepared for scoffers,
And beatings for the backs of fools.

CHAPTER **20** YOUR ACTIONS TELL ABOUT YOU.

Wine *is* a mocker,
Strong drink *is* a brawler,
And whoever is led astray by it is not wise.

2 The wrath of a king *is* like the roaring of a lion;
Whoever provokes him to anger sins *against* his own
life.

3 *It is* honorable for a man to stop striving,
Since any fool can start a quarrel.

4 The lazy *man* will not plow because of winter;
He will beg during harvest and *have* nothing.

5 Counsel in the heart of man *is like* deep water,
But a man of understanding will draw it out.

6 Most men will proclaim each his own goodness,
But who can find a faithful man?

7 The righteous *man* walks in his integrity;
His children *are* blessed after him.

8 A king who sits on the throne of judgment
Scatters all evil with his eyes.

LOOKS

19:22 You can't do much about the body with which you were born. However, you can do a lot about what is on the inside. Inwardly, you can be as attractive as you want to be. You can have kindness, for example, in any amount you choose. You can control your most important asset: the attractiveness of your character.

◣◣◣◣◣ MOTIVES

21:2 People can find an excuse for doing almost anything, but God looks behind the excuse to the motives. We often have to make difficult choices in areas of life where the right action is hard to discern. We can help ourself make such decisions by trying to identify our motives first, and then asking, "Would God be pleased with my real reasons for doing this?" God is not pleased when we do good deeds only to receive something back.

9 Who can say, "I have made my heart clean,
   I am pure from my sin"?

10 Diverse weights *and* diverse measures,
   They *are* both alike, an abomination to the LORD.

11 Even a child is known by his deeds,
   Whether what he does *is* pure and right.

12 The hearing ear and the seeing eye,
   The LORD has made them both.

13 Do not love sleep, lest you come to poverty;
   Open your eyes, *and* you will be satisfied with bread.

14 "*It is* good for nothing," cries the buyer;
   But when he has gone his way, then he boasts.

15 There is gold and a multitude of rubies,
   But the lips of knowledge *are* a precious jewel.

16 Take the garment of one who is surety *for* a stranger,
   And hold it as a pledge *when it* is for a seductress.

17 Bread gained by deceit *is* sweet to a man,
   But afterward his mouth will be filled with gravel.

18 Plans are established by counsel;
   By wise counsel wage war.

19 He who goes about *as* a talebearer reveals secrets;
   Therefore do not associate with one who flatters with his lips.

20 Whoever curses his father or his mother,
   His lamp will be put out in deep darkness.

21 An inheritance gained hastily at the beginning
   Will not be blessed at the end.

22 Do not say, "I will recompense evil";
   Wait for the LORD, and He will save you.

23 Diverse weights *are* an abomination to the LORD,
   And dishonest scales *are* not good.

24 A man's steps *are* of the LORD;
   How then can a man understand his own way?

25 *It is* a snare for a man to devote rashly *something as* holy,
   And afterward to reconsider *his* vows.

26 A wise king sifts out the wicked,
   And brings the threshing wheel over them.

27 The spirit of a man *is* the lamp of the LORD,
   Searching all the inner depths of his heart.

28 Mercy and truth preserve the king,
   And by lovingkindness he upholds his throne.

29 The glory of young men *is* their strength,

And the splendor of old men *is* their gray head.

30 Blows that hurt cleanse away evil,
   As *do* stripes the inner depths of the heart.

CHAPTER 21 LEARN BY LISTENING.

The king's heart *is* in the hand of the LORD,
Like the rivers of water; He turns it wherever He wishes.

2 Every way of a man *is* right in his own eyes,
   But the LORD weighs the hearts.

3 To do righteousness and justice
   Is more acceptable to the LORD than sacrifice.

4 A haughty look, a proud heart,
   And the plowing of the wicked *are* sin.

5 The plans of the diligent *lead* surely to plenty,
   But *those of* everyone *who is* hasty, surely to poverty.

6 Getting treasures by a lying tongue
   Is the fleeting fantasy of those who seek death.

7 The violence of the wicked will destroy them,
   Because they refuse to do justice.

8 The way of a guilty man *is* perverse;
   But *as for* the pure, his work *is* right.

9 Better to dwell in a corner of a housetop,
   Than in a house shared with a contentious woman.

10 The soul of the wicked desires evil;
   His neighbor finds no favor in his eyes.

11 When the scoffer is punished, the simple is made wise;
   But when the wise is instructed, he receives knowledge.

12 The righteous *God* wisely considers the house of the wicked,
   Overthrowing the wicked for *their* wickedness.

13 Whoever shuts his ears to the cry of the poor
   Will also cry himself and not be heard.

14 A gift in secret pacifies anger,
   And a bribe behind the back, strong wrath.

15 *It is* a joy for the just to do justice,
   But destruction *will come* to the workers of iniquity.

16 A man who wanders from the way of understanding
   Will rest in the assembly of the dead.

17 He who loves pleasure *will be* a poor man;
   He who loves wine and oil will not be rich.

18 The wicked *shall be* a ransom for the righteous,
   And the unfaithful for the upright.

19 Better to dwell in the wilderness,
   Than with a contentious and angry woman.

20 *There is* desirable treasure,
   And oil in the dwelling of the wise,
   But a foolish man squanders it.

²¹ He who follows righteousness and mercy
Finds life, righteousness and honor.

²² A wise *man* scales the city of the mighty,
And brings down the trusted stronghold.

²³ Whoever guards his mouth and tongue
Keeps his soul from troubles.

²⁴ A proud *and* haughty *man*—"Scoffer" *is* his name;
He acts with arrogant pride.

²⁵ The desire of the lazy *man* kills him,
For his hands refuse to labor.

²⁶ He covets greedily all day long,
But the righteous gives and does not spare.

²⁷ The sacrifice of the wicked *is* an abomination;
How much more *when* he brings it with wicked
intent!

²⁸ A false witness shall perish,
But the man who hears *him* will speak endlessly.

²⁹ A wicked man hardens his face,
But *as for* the upright, he establishes his way.

³⁰ *There is* no wisdom or understanding
Or counsel against the LORD.

³¹ The horse *is* prepared for the day of battle,
But deliverance *is* of the LORD.

CHAPTER 22 GIVING CAN MAKE YOU HAPPY.

A *good* name is to be chosen rather than great riches,
Loving favor rather than silver and gold.

² The rich and the poor have this in common,
The LORD *is* the maker of them all.

³ A prudent *man* foresees evil and hides himself,
But the simple pass on and are punished.

⁴ By humility *and* the fear of the LORD
Are riches and honor and life.

⁵ Thorns *and* snares *are* in the way of the perverse;
He who guards his soul will be far from them.

⁶ Train up a child in the way he should go,
And when he is old he will not depart from it.

⁷ The rich rules over the poor,
And the borrower *is* servant to the lender.

⁸ He who sows iniquity will reap sorrow,
And the rod of his anger will fail.

⁹ He who has a generous eye will be blessed,
For he gives of his bread to the poor.

¹⁰ Cast out the scoffer, and contention will leave;
Yes, strife and reproach will cease.

¹¹ He who loves purity of heart
And has grace on his lips,
The king *will be* his friend.

¹² The eyes of the LORD preserve knowledge,
But He overthrows the words of the faithless.

¹³ The lazy *man* says, "*There is* a lion outside!
I shall be slain in the streets!"

¹⁴ The mouth of an immoral woman *is* a deep pit;
He who is abhorred by the LORD will fall there.

¹⁵ Foolishness *is* bound up in the heart of a child;
The rod of correction will drive it far from him.

¹⁶ He who oppresses the poor to increase his *riches,*
And he who gives to the rich, *will* surely *come* to
poverty.

¹⁷ Incline your ear and hear the words of the wise,
And apply your heart to my knowledge;

¹⁸ For *it is* a pleasant thing if you keep them within you;
Let them all be fixed upon your lips,

¹⁹ So that your trust may be in the LORD;
I have instructed you today, even you.

◢◣◤ COMPANIONS

22:24-25 People tend to become like those around them. Even the
negative characteristics sometimes rub off. The Bible exhorts us to be
cautious in our choice of companions. Choose companions who have the
characteristics you would like to develop in your own life.

²⁰ Have I not written to you excellent things
Of counsels and knowledge,

²¹ That I may make you know the certainty of the
words of truth,
That you may answer words of truth
To those who send to you?

²² Do not rob the poor because he *is* poor,
Nor oppress the afflicted at the gate;

²³ For the LORD will plead their cause,
And plunder the soul of those who plunder them.

²⁴ Make no friendship with an angry man,
And with a furious man do not go,

²⁵ Lest you learn his ways
And set a snare for your soul.

²⁶ Do not be one of those who shakes hands in a
pledge,
One of those who is surety for debts;

²⁷ If you have nothing *with which* to pay,
Why should he take away your bed from under you?

²⁸ Do not remove the ancient landmark
Which your fathers have set.

²⁹ Do you see a man *who* excels in his work?
He will stand before kings;
He will not stand before unknown *men.*

CHAPTER 23 CRITICISM CAN HELP YOU.

When you sit down to eat with a ruler,
Consider carefully what *is* before you;

² And put a knife to your throat
If you *are* a man given to appetite.

³ Do not desire his delicacies,
For they *are* deceptive food.

⁴ Do not overwork to be rich;

Because of your own understanding, cease!
5 Will you set your eyes on that which is not?
  For *riches* certainly make themselves wings;
  They fly away like an eagle *toward* heaven.

6 Do not eat the bread of a miser,
  Nor desire his delicacies;
7 For as he thinks in his heart, so *is* he.
  "Eat and drink!" he says to you,
  But his heart is not with you.
8 The morsel you have eaten, you will vomit up,
  And waste your pleasant words.

9 Do not speak in the hearing of a fool,

^^^^^^^^^^^^^^^^^^^^^^^^^^^^^^

DRINKING

The first time 13-year-old Paul drank with his friends, Mario and Cleve, it was kind of exciting. With the help of a college student, the three guys managed to get a six-pack—two beers each. It wasn't enough to get smashed, but it was enough to get a slight buzz. Sipping slowly as they sat around a campfire, the boys laughed for several hours. The next day Mario suggested, "We should do this more often!"

So each weekend they played the game, always coming up with a new scheme to acquire alcohol. Once they stumbled upon a block party where there were three "unguarded" kegs just sitting there. Another time they swiped a bottle of vodka from a neighbor's liquor cabinet. Another time a high school senior bought them some tequila and showed them how to shoot it.

Every now and then one of the guys would overdo it and end up with a mean hangover. But they never got caught. It didn't affect their grades at school since they only did it on weekends. Everything was cool . . . until Paul went on a church retreat one weekend.

Now Paul won't go with Mario and Cleve anymore. He thinks they're headed for trouble. And they think he's turned into a religious fanatic.

See one of the passages that changed Paul's mind about drinking. Read Proverbs 23:29-35.

^^^^^^^^^^^^^^^^^^^^^^^^^^^^^^

For he will despise the wisdom of your words.

10 Do not remove the ancient landmark,
   Nor enter the fields of the fatherless;
11 For their Redeemer *is* mighty;
   He will plead their cause against you.

12 Apply your heart to instruction,
   And your ears to words of knowledge.

13 Do not withhold correction from a child,
   For *if* you beat him with a rod, he will not die.
14 You shall beat him with a rod,
   And deliver his soul from hell.

15 My son, if your heart is wise,
   My heart will rejoice—indeed, I myself;
16 Yes, my inmost being will rejoice
   When your lips speak right things.

17 Do not let your heart envy sinners,
   But *be zealous* for the fear of the LORD all the day;

23:29-30 The soothing comfort of alcohol is only temporary. Re comes from dealing with the cause of anguish and sorrow, and turni God for peace. Don't lose yourself in alcohol; find yourself in God.

18 For surely there is a hereafter,
   And your hope will not be cut off.

19 Hear, my son, and be wise;
   And guide your heart in the way.
20 Do not mix with winebibbers,
   Or with gluttonous eaters of meat;
21 For the drunkard and the glutton will come to
      poverty,
   And drowsiness will clothe *a man* with rags.

22 Listen to your father who begot you,
   And do not despise your mother when she is old.

23 Buy the truth, and do not sell *it*,
   Also wisdom and instruction and understanding.

24 The father of the righteous will greatly rejoice,
   And he who begets a wise *child* will delight in him.
25 Let your father and your mother be glad,
   And let her who bore you rejoice.

26 My son, give me your heart,
   And let your eyes observe my ways.
27 For a harlot *is* a deep pit,
   And a seductress *is* a narrow well.
28 She also lies in wait as *for* a victim,
   And increases the unfaithful among men.

29 Who has woe?
   Who has sorrow?
   Who has contentions?
   Who has complaints?
   Who has wounds without cause?
   Who has redness of eyes?
30 Those who linger long at the wine,
   Those who go in search of mixed wine.
31 Do not look on the wine when it is red,
   When it sparkles in the cup,
   When it swirls around smoothly;
32 At the last it bites like a serpent,
   And stings like a viper.
33 Your eyes will see strange things,
   And your heart will utter perverse things.
34 Yes, you will be like one who lies down in the midst
      of the sea,
   Or like one who lies at the top of the mast, *saying:*
35 "They have struck me, *but* I was not hurt;
   They have beaten me, but I did not feel *it.*
   When shall I awake, that I may seek another *drink?*"

CHAPTER 24 PLANS ARE AS BAD AS ACTIONS.
Do not be envious of evil men,
Nor desire to be with them;
2 For their heart devises violence,
  And their lips talk of troublemaking.

3 Through wisdom a house is built,
  And by understanding it is established;
4 By knowledge the rooms are filled
  With all precious and pleasant riches.

5 A wise man *is* strong,
　Yes, a man of knowledge increases strength;
6 For by wise counsel you will wage your own war,
　And in a multitude of counselors *there is* safety.

7 Wisdom *is* too lofty for a fool;
　He does not open his mouth in the gate.

8 He who plots to do evil
　Will be called a schemer.
9 The devising of foolishness *is* sin,
　And the scoffer *is* an abomination to men.

10 *If* you faint in the day of adversity,
　Your strength *is* small.

11 Deliver *those who* are drawn toward death,
　And hold back *those* stumbling to the slaughter.
12 If you say, "Surely we did not know this,"
　Does not He who weighs the hearts consider *it?*
　He who keeps your soul, does He *not* know *it?*
　And will He *not* render to *each* man according to his
　　deeds?

13 My son, eat honey because *it is* good,
　And the honeycomb *which is* sweet to your taste;
14 So *shall* the knowledge of wisdom *be* to your soul;
　If you have found *it,* there is a prospect,
　And your hope will not be cut off.

15 Do not lie in wait, O wicked *man,* against the
　　dwelling of the righteous;
　Do not plunder his resting place;
16 For a righteous *man* may fall seven times
　And rise again,
　But the wicked shall fall by calamity.

17 Do not rejoice when your enemy falls,
　And do not let your heart be glad when he stumbles;
18 Lest the LORD see *it,* and it displease Him,
　And He turn away His wrath from him.

19 Do not fret because of evildoers,
　Nor be envious of the wicked;
20 For there will be no prospect for the evil *man;*
　The lamp of the wicked will be put out.

21 My son, fear the LORD and the king;
　Do not associate with those given to change;
22 For their calamity will rise suddenly,
　And who knows the ruin those two can bring?

23These *things* also *belong* to the wise:

　It is not good to show partiality in judgment.
24 He who says to the wicked, "You *are* righteous,"
　Him the people will curse;
　Nations will abhor him.
25 But those who rebuke *the wicked* will have delight,
　And a good blessing will come upon them.

26 He who gives a right answer kisses the lips.

27 Prepare your outside work,
　Make it fit for yourself in the field;
　And afterward build your house.

28 Do not be a witness against your neighbor without
　　cause,
　For would you deceive with your lips?
29 Do not say, "I will do to him just as he has done to
　　me;
　I will render to the man according to his work."

30 I went by the field of the lazy *man,*
　And by the vineyard of the man devoid of
　　understanding;
31 And there it was, all overgrown with thorns;
　Its surface was covered with nettles;
　Its stone wall was broken down.
32 When I saw *it,* I considered *it* well;
　I looked on *it and* received instruction:
33 A little sleep, a little slumber,
　A little folding of the hands to rest;
34 So shall your poverty come *like* a prowler,
　And your need like an armed man.

CHAPTER **25** **KEEP YOUR PROMISES.** These also
are proverbs of Solomon which the men of Hezekiah
king of Judah copied:

2 *It is* the glory of God to conceal a matter,
　But the glory of kings *is* to search out a matter.

3 *As* the heavens for height and the earth for depth,
　So the heart of kings *is* unsearchable.

4 Take away the dross from silver,
　And it will go to the silversmith *for* jewelry.
5 Take away the wicked from before the king,
　And his throne will be established in righteousness.

6 Do not exalt yourself in the presence of the king,
　And do not stand in the place of the great;
7 For *it is* better that he say to you,
　"Come up here,"
　Than that you should be put lower in the presence of
　　the prince,
　Whom your eyes have seen.

8 Do not go hastily to court;
　For what will you do in the end,
　When your neighbor has put you to shame?
9 Debate your case with your neighbor,
　And do not disclose the secret to another;
10 Lest he who hears *it* expose your shame,
　And your reputation be ruined.

11 A word fitly spoken *is like* apples of gold
　In settings of silver.
12 *Like* an earring of gold and an ornament of fine gold
　Is a wise rebuker to an obedient ear.

13 Like the cold of snow in time of harvest
　Is a faithful messenger to those who send him,
　For he refreshes the soul of his masters.

14 Whoever falsely boasts of giving
　Is like clouds and wind without rain.

15 By long forbearance a ruler is persuaded,
　And a gentle tongue breaks a bone.

16 Have you found honey?
Eat only as much as you need,
Lest you be filled with it and vomit.

17 Seldom set foot in your neighbor's house,
Lest he become weary of you and hate you.

LYING

25:18 Lying ("false witness") is vicious. Its effects can be as permanent as those of a stab wound. The next time you are tempted to pass on a bit of gossip, imagine yourself striking the victim of your remarks with a sword. This image may shock you into silence.

18 A man who bears false witness against his neighbor
Is like a club, a sword, and a sharp arrow.

19 Confidence in an unfaithful *man* in time of trouble
Is like a bad tooth and a foot out of joint.

20 *Like* one who takes away a garment in cold weather,
And like vinegar on soda,
Is one who sings songs to a heavy heart.

21 If your enemy is hungry, give him bread to eat;
And if he is thirsty, give him water to drink;

22 For *so* you will heap coals of fire on his head,
And the LORD will reward you.

23 The north wind brings forth rain,
And a backbiting tongue an angry countenance.

24 *It is* better to dwell in a corner of a housetop,
Than in a house shared with a contentious woman.

25 *As* cold water to a weary soul,
So *is* good news from a far country.

26 A righteous *man* who falters before the wicked
Is like a murky spring and a polluted well.

27 *It is* not good to eat much honey;
So to seek one's own glory *is not* glory.

28 Whoever *has* no rule over his own spirit
Is like a city broken down, without walls.

CHAPTER 26 REBELS ARE IMPOSSIBLE.

As snow in summer and rain in harvest,
So honor is not fitting for a fool.

2 Like a flitting sparrow, like a flying swallow,
So a curse without cause shall not alight.

3 A whip for the horse,
A bridle for the donkey,
And a rod for the fool's back.

4 Do not answer a fool according to his folly,
Lest you also be like him.

5 Answer a fool according to his folly,
Lest he be wise in his own eyes.

6 He who sends a message by the hand of a fool
Cuts off *his own* feet *and* drinks violence.

7 *Like* the legs of the lame that hang limp
Is a proverb in the mouth of fools.

8 Like one who binds a stone in a sling
Is he who gives honor to a fool.

9 *Like* a thorn *that* goes into the hand of a drunkard
Is a proverb in the mouth of fools.

10 The great *God* who formed everything
Gives the fool *his* hire and the transgressor *his* wages.

11 As a dog returns to his own vomit,
So a fool repeats his folly.

12 Do you see a man wise in his own eyes?
There is more hope for a fool than for him.

13 The lazy *man* says, "*There is* a lion in the road!
A fierce lion *is* in the streets!"

14 *As* a door turns on its hinges,
So *does* the lazy *man* on his bed.

15 The lazy *man* buries his hand in the bowl;
It wearies him to bring it back to his mouth.

16 The lazy *man is* wiser in his own eyes
Than seven men who can answer sensibly.

LAZINESS

26:13-16 If a person is not willing to work, he can find endless excuses to avoid it. But laziness is more dangerous than a fierce lio[n] less you do, the less you want to do, and the more useless you beco[me] To overcome laziness, take a few small steps toward change. Set a concrete, realistic goal. Figure out the steps needed to reach it. Pra[y] strength and persistence. And follow those steps. To keep your excu[ses] from making you useless, stop making useless excuses.

17 He who passes by *and* meddles in a quarrel not his own
Is like one who takes a dog by the ears.

18 Like a madman who throws firebrands, arrows, and death,

19 *Is* the man *who* deceives his neighbor,
And says, "I was only joking!"

20 Where *there is* no wood, the fire goes out;
And where *there is* no talebearer, strife ceases.

21 *As* charcoal *is* to burning coals, and wood to fire,
So *is* a contentious man to kindle strife.

22 The words of a talebearer *are* like tasty trifles,
And they go down into the inmost body.

23 Fervent lips with a wicked heart
Are like earthenware covered with silver dross.

24 He who hates, disguises *it* with his lips,
And lays up deceit within himself;

25 When he speaks kindly, do not believe him,
For *there are* seven abominations in his heart;

26 *Though his* hatred is covered by deceit,
His wickedness will be revealed before the assembly.

27 Whoever digs a pit will fall into it,
And he who rolls a stone will have it roll back on him.

28 A lying tongue hates *those who are* crushed by it,
And a flattering mouth works ruin.

CHAPTER 27 JEALOUSY IS DANGEROUS.

Do not boast about tomorrow,
For you do not know what a day may bring forth.

² Let another man praise you, and not your own mouth;
A stranger, and not your own lips.

³ A stone *is* heavy and sand *is* weighty,
But a fool's wrath *is* heavier than both of them.

⁴ Wrath *is* cruel and anger a torrent,
But who *is* able to stand before jealousy?

⁵ Open rebuke *is* better
Than love carefully concealed.

⁶ Faithful *are* the wounds of a friend,
But the kisses of an enemy *are* deceitful.

⁷ A satisfied soul loathes the honeycomb,
But to a hungry soul every bitter thing *is* sweet.

⁸ Like a bird that wanders from its nest
Is a man who wanders from his place.

⁹ Ointment and perfume delight the heart,
And the sweetness of a man's friend *gives delight* by hearty counsel.

¹⁰ Do not forsake your own friend or your father's friend,
Nor go to your brother's house in the day of your calamity;
Better *is* a neighbor nearby than a brother far away.

¹¹ My son, be wise, and make my heart glad,
That I may answer him who reproaches me.

¹² A prudent *man* foresees evil *and* hides himself;
The simple pass on *and* are punished.

¹³ Take the garment of him who is surety for a stranger,
And hold it in pledge *when* he is surety for a seductress.

¹⁴ He who blesses his friend with a loud voice, rising early in the morning,
It will be counted a curse to him.

¹⁵ A continual dripping on a very rainy day
And a contentious woman are alike;

¹⁶ Whoever restrains her restrains the wind,
And grasps oil with his right hand.

¹⁷ *As* iron sharpens iron,
So a man sharpens the countenance of his friend.

¹⁸ Whoever keeps the fig tree will eat its fruit;
So he who waits on his master will be honored.

¹⁹ As in water face *reflects* face,
So a man's heart *reveals* the man.

²⁰ Hell and Destruction are never full;
So the eyes of man are never satisfied.

²¹ The refining pot *is* for silver and the furnace for gold,
And a man *is valued* by what others say of him.

²² Though you grind a fool in a mortar with a pestle along with crushed grain,
Yet his foolishness will not depart from him.

²³ Be diligent to know the state of your flocks,
And attend to your herds;

²⁴ For riches *are* not forever,
Nor does a crown *endure* to all generations.

²⁵ *When* the hay is removed, and the tender grass shows itself,

◀▬▬▬▬▬NAGGING

27:15-16 Nagging, a steady stream of unwanted advice, is a form of torture. People nag because they think they're not getting through, but nagging hinders communication more than it helps. When tempted to engage in this destructive habit, stop and examine your motives. Are you more concerned about yourself— about getting your way or being right—than about the person you are pretending to help? If you truly are concerned about other people, is there a more effective way to get through to them? Surprise them with words of love and patience, and see what happens.

And the herbs of the mountains are gathered in,
²⁶ The lambs *will provide* your clothing,
And the goats the price of a field;
²⁷ *You shall have* enough goats' milk for your food,
For the food of your household,
And the nourishment of your maidservants.

CHAPTER **28** ADMIT YOUR MISTAKES.
The wicked flee when no one pursues,
But the righteous are bold as a lion.

² Because of the transgression of a land, many *are* its princes;
But by a man of understanding *and* knowledge
Right will be prolonged.

³ A poor man who oppresses the poor
Is like a driving rain which leaves no food.

⁴ Those who forsake the law praise the wicked,
But such as keep the law contend with them.

⁵ Evil men do not understand justice,
But those who seek the LORD understand all.

⁶ Better *is* the poor who walks in his integrity
Than one perverse *in his* ways, though he *be* rich.

⁷ Whoever keeps the law *is* a discerning son,
But a companion of gluttons shames his father.

⁸ One who increases his possessions by usury and extortion
Gathers it for him who will pity the poor.

⁹ One who turns away his ear from hearing the law,
Even his prayer *is* an abomination.

◀▬▬▬▬▬INTENTIONS

28:9 God does not listen to our prayers if we intend to go back to our sin as soon as we get off our knees. If we want to forsake our sin and follow him, however, he willingly listens—no matter how bad our sin has been. What closes his ears is not the depth of our sin, but the shallowness of our "repentance."

¹⁰ Whoever causes the upright to go astray in an evil way,
He himself will fall into his own pit;
But the blameless will inherit good.

¹¹ The rich man *is* wise in his own eyes,
But the poor who has understanding searches him out.

¹² When the righteous rejoice, *there is* great glory;
But when the wicked arise, men hide themselves.

¹³ He who covers his sins will not prosper,
But whoever confesses and forsakes *them* will have mercy.

¹⁴ Happy *is* the man who is always reverent,
But he who hardens his heart will fall into calamity.

¹⁵ *Like* a roaring lion and a charging bear
Is a wicked ruler over poor people.

¹⁶ A ruler who lacks understanding *is* a great oppressor,
But he who hates covetousness will prolong *his* days.

¹⁷ A man burdened with bloodshed will flee into a pit;
Let no one help him.

¹⁸ Whoever walks blamelessly will be saved,
But *he who is* perverse *in his* ways will suddenly fall.

¹⁹ He who tills his land will have plenty of bread,
But he who follows frivolity will have poverty enough!

²⁰ A faithful man will abound with blessings,
But he who hastens to be rich will not go unpunished.

²¹ To show partiality *is* not good,
Because for a piece of bread a man will transgress.

²² A man with an evil eye hastens after riches,
And does not consider that poverty will come upon him.

²³ He who rebukes a man will find more favor afterward
Than he who flatters with the tongue.

²⁴ Whoever robs his father or his mother,
And says, "*It is* no transgression,"
The same *is* companion to a destroyer.

²⁵ He who is of a proud heart stirs up strife,
But he who trusts in the LORD will be prospered.

²⁶ He who trusts in his own heart is a fool,
But whoever walks wisely will be delivered.

²⁷ He who gives to the poor will not lack,
But he who hides his eyes will have many curses.

²⁸ When the wicked arise, men hide themselves;
But when they perish, the righteous increase.

CHAPTER 29 GOD REWARDS FAIRNESS.
He who is often rebuked, *and* hardens *his* neck,
Will suddenly be destroyed, and that without remedy.

² When the righteous are in authority, the people rejoice;
But when a wicked *man* rules, the people groan.

³ Whoever loves wisdom makes his father rejoice,
But a companion of harlots wastes *his* wealth.

⁴ The king establishes the land by justice,
But he who receives bribes overthrows it.

⁵ A man who flatters his neighbor
Spreads a net for his feet.

⁶ By transgression an evil man is snared,
But the righteous sings and rejoices.

⁷ The righteous considers the cause of the poor,
But the wicked does not understand *such* knowledge.

⁸ Scoffers set a city aflame,
But wise *men* turn away wrath.

⁹ *If* a wise man contends with a foolish man,
Whether *the fool* rages or laughs, *there is* no peace.

¹⁰ The bloodthirsty hate the blameless,
But the upright seek his well-being.

¹¹ A fool vents all his feelings,
But a wise *man* holds them back.

¹² If a ruler pays attention to lies,
All his servants *become* wicked.

¹³ The poor *man* and the oppressor have this in common:
The LORD gives light to the eyes of both.

¹⁴ The king who judges the poor with truth,
His throne will be established forever.

¹⁵ The rod and rebuke give wisdom,
But a child left *to himself* brings shame to his mother.

¹⁶ When the wicked are multiplied, transgression increases;
But the righteous will see their fall.

¹⁷ Correct your son, and he will give you rest;
Yes, he will give delight to your soul.

¹⁸ Where *there is* no revelation, the people cast off restraint;
But happy *is* he who keeps the law.

¹⁹ A servant will not be corrected by mere words;
For though he understands, he will not respond.

²⁰ Do you see a man hasty in his words?
There is more hope for a fool than for him.

²¹ He who pampers his servant from childhood
Will have him as a son in the end.

²² An angry man stirs up strife,
And a furious man abounds in transgression.

²³ A man's pride will bring him low,
But the humble in spirit will retain honor.

²⁴ Whoever is a partner with a thief hates his own life;

He swears to tell the truth, but reveals nothing.

25 The fear of man brings a snare,
But whoever trusts in the LORD shall be safe.

26 Many seek the ruler's favor,
But justice for man *comes* from the LORD.

27 An unjust man *is* an abomination to the righteous,
And *he who is* upright in the way *is* an abomination to the wicked.

CHAPTER 30 WONDERFUL THINGS.

The words of Agur the son of Jakeh, *his* utterance. This man declared to Ithiel—to Ithiel and Ucal:

2 Surely I *am* more stupid than *any* man,
And do not have the
understanding of a man.

3 I neither learned wisdom
Nor have knowledge of the Holy
One.

4 Who has ascended into heaven,
or descended?
Who has gathered the wind in His
fists?
Who has bound the waters in a
garment?
Who has established all the ends
of the earth?
What *is* His name, and what *is* His
Son's name,
If you know?

5 Every word of God *is* pure;
He *is* a shield to those who put
their trust in Him.

6 Do not add to His words,
Lest He rebuke you, and you be
found a liar.

7 Two *things* I request of You
(Deprive me not before I die):

8 Remove falsehood and lies far
from me;
Give me neither poverty nor
riches—
Feed me with the food allotted to me;

9 Lest I be full and deny *You,*
And say, "Who *is* the LORD?"
Or lest I be poor and steal,
And profane the name of my God.

10 Do not malign a servant to his master,
Lest he curse you, and you be found guilty.

11 *There is* a generation *that* curses its father,
And does not bless its mother.

12 *There is* a generation *that is* pure in its own eyes,
Yet is not washed from its filthiness.

13 *There is* a generation— oh, how lofty are their eyes!
And their eyelids are lifted up.

14 *There is* a generation whose teeth *are like* swords,
And whose fangs *are like* knives,

To devour the poor from off the earth,
And the needy from *among* men.

15 The leech has two daughters—
Give *and* Give!

There are three *things that* are never satisfied,
Four never say, "Enough!":

16 The grave,
The barren womb,
The earth *that* is not satisfied with water—
And the fire never says, "Enough!"

17 The eye *that* mocks *his* father,
And scorns obedience to *his* mother,
The ravens of the valley will pick it out,
And the young eagles will eat it.

"Here's what I did..."

I went to England with a missions group to do street evangelism right after I graduated from high school. Once I got out on the street, supposedly ready to talk to someone, I froze. I was struck with fear and couldn't say a word.

It really bothered me. That evening I looked up "fear" in a concordance, and read through several Scriptures. The verse that helped me most was Proverbs 29:25: "The fear of man brings a snare, but whoever trusts in the LORD shall be safe." I realized that I had fallen into Satan's trap because I was afraid of people—what they would think of me, even what they might do to me, if I tried to share the gospel. I vowed that I would trust in God.

The next day I was still nervous, but I asked God to keep me from falling into the trap of fear and to help me know what to say. Things went much better. As I trusted God to help and protect me during that missions trip, I grew more and more bold in sharing my faith. I actually came to enjoy it! But I might have stayed stuck in fear if I hadn't found that verse and really applied it to my situation.

Kristen

AGE 19

18 There are three *things which* are too wonderful for
me,
Yes, four *which* I do not understand:

19 The way of an eagle in the air,
The way of a serpent on a rock,
The way of a ship in the midst of the sea,
And the way of a man with a virgin.

20 This *is* the way of an adulterous woman:
She eats and wipes her mouth,
And says, "I have done no wickedness."

21 For three *things* the earth is perturbed,
Yes, for four it cannot bear up:

22 For a servant when he reigns,
A fool when he is filled with food,

23 A hateful *woman* when she is married,
And a maidservant who succeeds her mistress.

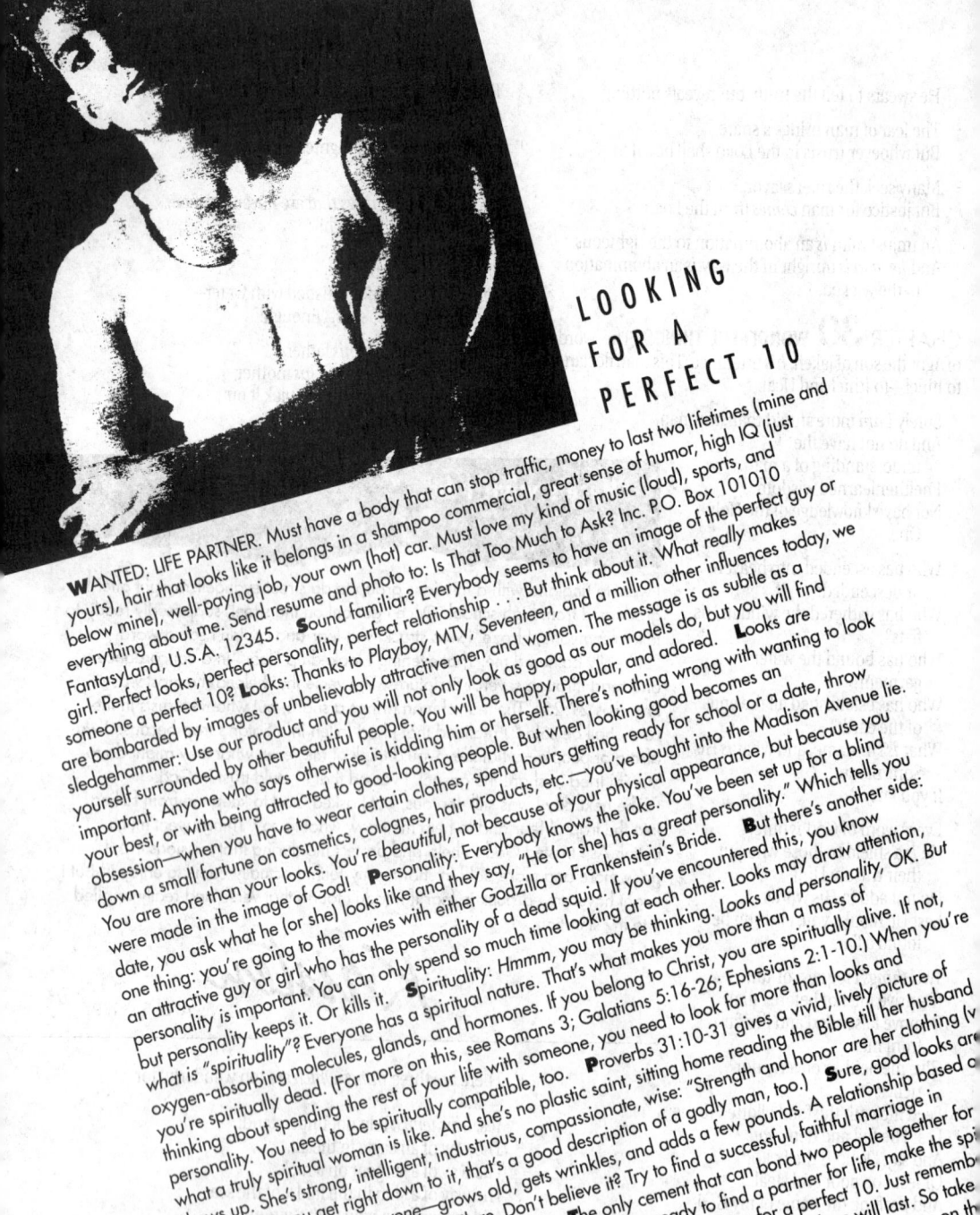

LOOKING FOR A PERFECT 10

WANTED: LIFE PARTNER. Must have a body that can stop traffic, money to last two lifetimes (mine and yours), hair that looks like it belongs in a shampoo commercial, great sense of humor, high IQ (just below mine), well-paying job, your own (hot) car. Must love my kind of music (loud), sports, and everything about me. Send resume and photo to: Is That Too Much to Ask? Inc. P.O. Box 101010 FantasyLand, U.S.A. 12345. **Sound familiar?** Everybody seems to have an image of the perfect guy or girl. Perfect looks, perfect personality, perfect relationship . . . But think about it. What really makes someone a perfect 10? **Looks:** Thanks to Playboy, MTV, Seventeen, and a million other influences today, we are bombarded by images of unbelievably attractive men and women. The message is as subtle as a sledgehammer: Use our product and you will not only look as good as our models do, but you will find yourself surrounded by other beautiful people. You will be happy, popular, and adored. **Looks are important.** Anyone who says otherwise is kidding him or herself. There's nothing wrong with wanting to look your best, or with being attracted to good-looking people. But when looking good becomes an obsession—when you have to wear certain clothes, spend hours getting ready for school or a date, throw down a small fortune on cosmetics, colognes, hair products, etc.—you've bought into the Madison Avenue lie. You are more than your looks. You're beautiful, not because of your physical appearance, but because you were made in the image of God! **Personality:** Everybody knows the joke. You've been set up for a blind date, you ask what he (or she) looks like and they say, "He (or she) has a great personality." Which tells you one thing: you're going to the movies with either Godzilla or Frankenstein's Bride. **But** there's another side: an attractive guy or girl who has the personality of a dead squid. If you've encountered this, you know personality *is* important. You can only spend so much time looking at each other. Looks may draw attention, but personality keeps it. Or kills it. **Spirituality:** Hmmm, you may be thinking. *Looks and personality, OK. But what is "spirituality"?* Everyone has a spiritual nature. That's what makes you more than a mass of oxygen-absorbing molecules, glands, and hormones. If you belong to Christ, you are spiritually alive. If not, you're spiritually dead. (For more on this, see Romans 3; Galatians 5:16-26; Ephesians 2:1-10.) When you're thinking about spending the rest of your life with someone, you need to look for more than looks and personality. You need to be spiritually compatible, too. **Proverbs 31:10-31** gives a vivid, lively picture of what a truly spiritual woman is like. And she's no plastic saint, sitting home reading the Bible till her husband shows up. She's strong, intelligent, industrious, compassionate, wise: "Strength and honor are her clothing [v 25]." (When you get right down to it, that's a good description of a godly man, too.) **Sure,** good looks are great. But everyone—everyone—grows old, gets wrinkles, and adds a few pounds. A relationship based on looks or personality is doomed to failure. Don't believe it? Try to find a successful, faithful marriage in Hollywood, Body Beautiful capital of the world. **The** only cement that can bond two people together for mutual commitment to God and to each other. There's nothing wrong with looking for a perfect 10. Just remember dimension your primary requirement. When you're ready to find a partner for life, make the spi takes more than beauty or a pleasant temperament to add up to someone whose love will last. So take at Proverbs 31. It's a great snapshot image of a person who has that something more. (For more on th of marriage itself, see the Ultimate Issue on marriage in Ephesians.)

²⁴ There are four *things which* are little on the earth,
But they *are* exceedingly wise:
²⁵ The ants *are* a people not strong,
Yet they prepare their food in the summer;
²⁶ The rock badgers are a feeble folk,
Yet they make their homes in the crags;
²⁷ The locusts have no king,
Yet they all advance in ranks;
²⁸ The spider skillfully grasps with its hands,
And it is in kings' palaces.

²⁹ There are three *things which* are majestic in pace,
Yes, four *which* are stately in walk:
³⁰ A lion, *which is* mighty among beasts
And does not turn away from any;
³¹ A greyhound,
A male goat also,
And a king *whose* troops *are* with him.

³² If you have been foolish in exalting yourself,
Or if you have devised evil, *put your* hand on *your*
mouth.
³³ For *as* the churning of milk produces butter,
And wringing the nose produces blood,
So the forcing of wrath produces strife.

CHAPTER **31** The words of King Lemuel, the utterance which his mother taught him:

² What, my son?
And what, son of my womb?
And what, son of my vows?
³ Do not give your strength to women,
Nor your ways to that which destroys kings.

⁴ *It is* not for kings, O Lemuel,
It is not for kings to drink wine,
Nor for princes intoxicating drink;
⁵ Lest they drink and forget the law,
And pervert the justice of all the afflicted.
⁶ Give strong drink to him who is perishing,
And wine to those who are bitter of heart.
⁷ Let him drink and forget his poverty,
And remember his misery no more.

⁸ Open your mouth for the speechless,
In the cause of all *who are* appointed to die.
⁹ Open your mouth, judge righteously,
And plead the cause of the poor and needy.
¹⁰ Who can find a virtuous wife?
For her worth *is* far above rubies.

HOW GOD IS DESCRIBED IN PROVERBS

Proverbs is a book about wise living. It often focuses on a person's response and attitude toward God, who is the source of wisdom. And a number of proverbs point out aspects of God's character. Knowing God helps us on the way to wisdom.

GOD . . .
is aware of all that happens 15:3
knows all people 15:11; 16:2; 21:2
is the maker of all things 16:4
controls all things 16:33; 21:30
is a strong tower 18:10
rescues good people from danger 11:8,21
rewards the godly 11:31
blesses good people, condemns the wicked 12:2
delights in our prayers 15:8,29
loves those who obey him 11:27; 15:9-10; 16:20; 22:12
cares for poor, sick, and widows 15:25; 22:22-23
purifies hearts 17:3
hates evil 17:5; 21:27; 28:9

OUR RESPONSE SHOULD BE . . .
to reverence God 10:27; 14:26-27; 15:16; 16:6; 19:23; 28:14
to obey God's Word 13:13; 19:16
to please God 16:7; 20:12; 21:3
to trust God 22:17-19; 29:25

◆IDEAL WOMAN

31:10-31 Proverbs has a lot to say about women. How fitting that the book ends with a picture of a woman of strong character, great wisdom, many skills, and great compassion.

Some people have the mistaken idea that the ideal woman in the Bible is retiring, servile, and entirely domestic. Not so! This woman is an excellent wife and mother. She also is a manufacturer, importer, manager, realtor, farmer, seamstress, upholsterer, and merchant. Her strength and dignity do not come from her amazing achievements, however. They are a result of her reverence for God. In our society where physical appearance counts for so much, it may surprise us to realize that her appearance is never mentioned. Her attractiveness comes entirely from her character.

The woman described in this chapter has outstanding abilities. Her family's social position is high. In fact, she may not be one woman at all—she may be a composite portrait of ideal womanhood. Do not see her as a model to imitate in every detail; your days are not long enough to do everything she does! See her instead as an inspiration to be all you can be. We can't be just like her, but we can learn from her industry, integrity, and resourcefulness.

11 The heart of her husband safely trusts her;
   So he will have no lack of gain.
12 She does him good and not evil
   All the days of her life.
13 She seeks wool and flax,
   And willingly works with her hands.
14 She is like the merchant ships,
   She brings her food from afar.
15 She also rises while it is yet night,
   And provides food for her household,
   And a portion for her maidservants.
16 She considers a field and buys it;

From her profits she plants a vineyard.
17 She girds herself with strength,
   And strengthens her arms.
18 She perceives that her merchandise *is* good,
   And her lamp does not go out by night.
19 She stretches out her hands to the distaff,
   And her hand holds the spindle.
20 She extends her hand to the poor,
   Yes, she reaches out her hands to the needy.
21 She is not afraid of snow for her household,
   For all her household *is* clothed with scarlet.
22 She makes tapestry for herself;
   Her clothing *is* fine linen and purple.
23 Her husband is known in the gates,
   When he sits among the elders of the land.
24 She makes linen garments and sells *them*,
   And supplies sashes for the merchants.
25 Strength and honor *are* her clothing;
   She shall rejoice in time to come.
26 She opens her mouth with wisdom,
   And on her tongue *is* the law of kindness.
27 She watches over the ways of her household,
   And does not eat the bread of idleness.
28 Her children rise up and call her blessed;
   Her husband *also*, and he praises her:
29 "Many daughters have done well,
   But you excel them all."
30 Charm *is* deceitful and beauty *is* passing,
   But a woman *who* fears the LORD, she shall be
   praised.
31 Give her of the fruit of her hands,
   And let her own works praise her in the gates.

MEGA *Themes*

WISDOM God wants his people to be wise. Two kinds of people portray two contrasting paths of life: The fool is the wicked, stubborn person who hates or ignores God; the wise person seeks to know and love God.

When we choose God's way, he grants us wisdom. His Word, the Bible, leads us to live right, have right relationships, and make right decisions.

1. Read 1:7 and 9:10. What did Solomon teach was the key to being wise?
2. What will be the results of wisdom in a person's life? (Check 3:13-26.)

3. How has knowing God and learning about his Word increased your personal wisdom?
4. In what areas of your life would you like to have more wisdom? Based on your study of Proverbs, how will you find that wisdom?

RELATIONSHIPS Proverbs gives us advice for developing our personal relationships with others, including friends, family members, and coworkers. In every relationship, we must show love, dedication, and high moral standards.

To relate to people, we need consistency, sensitivity, and discipline to use the wisdom God gives us. If we don't treat others according to the wisdom God gives, our relationships will suffer.

1. What type of relationships does Proverbs encourage? Discourage?
2. Why does the writer devote so much attention to avoiding sexual immorality? What wisdom is given regarding sex outside of marriage?
3. What seem to be the qualities that make relationships, including friendships and marriages, deeper and stronger? What ruins such relationships?
4. List three important relationships in your life. From what you've read in Proverbs, what should you change in those relationships?

SPEECH What we say shows our real attitude toward others. How we talk reveals what we're really like. Our speech is a test of how wise we've become.

To be wise in our speech we need to use self-control. Our words should be honest and well chosen. We need to remember that what we say affects others.

1. When is it hardest to control what you say?
2. What circumstances can cause you to lose control of your words? How do you feel after you blow it? How does this usually affect others?
3. Proverbs encourages speaking honestly, but with self-control. When have you been hurt by someone who did not speak with wisdom? How did it affect your relationship with that person?
4. List some specific actions you could take to develop honesty and self-control in your speech.

WORK God controls the final outcome of all we do. However, we must carry out our work with diligence and discipline, not laziness.

Because God evaluates how we live, we should work purposefully. We must never be lazy or self-satisfied. We don't always have to be the best in comparison to others, but we should always do our best with what God has given us.

1. What does Proverbs teach about the person who is lazy and unwilling to work?
2. What does Proverbs teach about the person who is diligent and self-disciplined?
3. How does being disciplined help you as a student?
4. How does being disciplined help you in your Christian life?
5. What is one area where you need to develop this discipline? Write out a specific plan for this development. (Be diligent in carrying it out!)

SUCCESS Although people work very hard for money and fame, God considers a good reputation, moral character, and spiritual devotion to obey him to be the true measures of success.

A successful relationship with God counts for eternity. Everything else is only temporary. All our resources, time, and talents come from God. We should do our best to use them wisely.

1. According to Proverbs, what is the value of riches? How important is wealth to most people who want to be successful?
2. How do your friends measure success? How do you think they will measure success when they are adults?
3. Do you agree or disagree with your friends' values? Explain.
4. How do you think God measures success?

*P*arty hearty! Do what feels good. Don't worry about tomorrow because we're all going to die soon anyway." You've probably heard expressions like that, or even know people who live that way. It's a very popular philosophy—but it's not a new one. In fact, essentially the same message appears in the Bible. Centuries ago, King Solomon wrote "every man should eat and drink and enjoy the good of all his labor—it *is* the gift of God" (Ecclesiastes 3:13). Solomon knew what he was talking about. As a very intelligent and wealthy king, he had spent a lifetime experiencing and analyzing everything the world had to offer. Wine, women, song . . . Solomon had done it all. His conclusion? Life is short, boring, and empty, so enjoy pleasure while you can! ■ "Wait a minute," you might interrupt. "You mean one of the Bible writers says that life is meaningless, so we should live it up?" ■ That's right. But there's a punch line. Solomon's last word is that to really enjoy life, we need to keep God right at the center of everything. Without God, people merely exist, moving quickly from the excitement of youth to the bitterness of old age. But with God, we can enjoy each moment, relationship, and experience along the way. ■ Read Ecclesiastes, Solomon's analysis of life, . . . and then have a real party!

STATS

PURPOSE: To spare future generations the bitterness of learning through their own experience that life is meaningless apart from God

AUTHOR: Solomon, although no passages mention him by name

TO WHOM WRITTEN: Solomon's subjects in particular, and all people in general

DATE WRITTEN: Probably around 935 B.C., late in Solomon's life

SETTING: Solomon looks back on his life, much of which was lived apart from God

Ecclesiastes

CHAPTER 1 **IS LIFE WORTH LIVING?** The words of the Preacher, the son of David, king in Jerusalem.

2 "Vanity of vanities," says the Preacher;
  "Vanity of vanities, all *is* vanity."

3 What profit has a man from all his labor
  In which he toils under the sun?
4 *One* generation passes away, and *another* generation comes;
  But the earth abides forever.
5 The sun also rises, and the sun goes down,
  And hastens to the place where it arose.
6 The wind goes toward the south,
  And turns around to the north;
  The wind whirls about continually,
  And comes again on its circuit.
7 All the rivers run into the sea,
  Yet the sea *is* not full;
  To the place from which the rivers come,
  There they return again.
8 All things *are* full of labor;
  Man cannot express *it.*
  The eye is not satisfied with seeing,
  Nor the ear filled with hearing.

9 That which has been *is* what will be,
  That which *is* done is what will be done,
  And *there is* nothing new under the sun.
10 Is there anything of which it may be said,
  "See, this *is* new"?
  It has already been in ancient times before us.
11 *There is* no remembrance of former *things,*

Nor will there be any remembrance of *things* that are
  to come
By *those* who will come after.

12 I, the Preacher, was king over Israel in Jerusalem. 13 And I set my heart to seek and search out by wisdom concerning all that is done under heaven; this burdensome task God has given to the sons of man, by which they may be exercised. 14 I have seen all the works that are done under the sun; and indeed, all *is* vanity and grasping for the wind.

15 *What is* crooked cannot be made straight,
  And what is lacking cannot be numbered.

16 I communed with my heart, saying, "Look, I have attained greatness, and have gained more wisdom than all who were before me in Jerusalem. My heart has understood great wisdom and knowledge." 17 And I set my heart to know wisdom and to know madness and folly. I perceived that this also is grasping for the wind.

18 For in much wisdom *is* much grief,
  And he who increases knowledge increases sorrow.

MEANING

1:8-11 Many people feel restless and dissatisfied. They wonder, (1) "If I am in God's will, why am I so dissatisfied?" (2) "What is the meaning of life?" (3) "When I look back on it all, will I be happy with my accomplishments?" (4) "Why do I feel burned out, disillusioned, dry?" (5) "What will become of me?" In this book, Solomon tests our faith, challenging us to find true and lasting meaning in God alone. If you take a hard look at your life, as Solomon did his, you will see how important serving God is over all other options. Perhaps God is asking you to rethink your purpose and direction in life.

IS THERE MEANING TO LIFE?

We've gotten pretty "shockproof" about what we read and hear in the news today. But every now and then a story cuts through our indifference and jolts even the most cynical of us. Like this one: WHITEFISH, MONTANA: Police today reported finding the bodies of 16-year-old "John Doe" and a 10-year-old friend. Doe apparently shot the younger boy to death and then turned the gun on himself. He left behind a note saying he was "bored with life" (AP News Service). Sixteen years old . . . and "bored with life." Literally bored to death. What a statement about our world! Unfortunately, it's not an isolated statement. The sad fact is that suicide is the second leading cause of death among American teenagers today. Many people, including young people, struggle to find meaning and purpose in life. If you are struggling with this, the book of Ecclesiastes was written for you. The message of Ecclesiastes is brutally straightforward. The writer, Solomon, tells us that he has tried everything life has to offer—wine, women, and song (the ancient equivalent of sex, drugs, and rock 'n' roll). His conclusion is this: "Fear God and keep His commandments, for this is man's all" (12:13). In other words, the book of Ecclesiastes tells us (and it needs to be read as a whole if we are to understand it properly): God gives meaning to our lives. No God, no meaning. Think of it this way: without God, you are just a bunch of molecules thrown together by chance. If there is no God, you came from—and are headed toward—impersonal nothingness. Any attempt at finding purpose is utterly ridiculous, doomed to failure. You might just as well be a lizard, or a rock, or nothing at all . . . if there is no God. Sounds pretty bleak, doesn't it? It is bleak, if we subtract God from the equation. This belief that there is no God and therefore no meaning is what has driven many, including some of the greatest minds in history, to despair, alcoholism, and even suicide. The noted historian Will Durant put it this way: "The greatest question of our time is not communism versus individualism, not Europe versus America, not even the East versus the West; it is whether men can live without God." Trina Paulus examines this question from another, wonderfully creative angle in her book Hope for the Flowers. The book tells the story of a caterpillar named Stripe and his quest for meaning. One day Stripe sees a giant column made of caterpillars standing on top of other caterpillars. All of them are trying to climb over the others to get to the top. So Stripe begins to climb, too, until he gets near the top—where he finds he can go no higher. Then someone says that to get any farther, they'd have to get rid of some of the other caterpillars. The column begins to shake, and Stripe sees caterpillars fall and hears them scream. Then—silence. Frustration surges through Stripe at the thought that this was the only way up. Then he hears a tiny whisper from the top: "There's nothing here at all!" It's answered by another: "Quiet, fool! They'll hear you down the pillar. We're where they want to get. That's what's here!" Stripe feels frozen. The top isn't so high after all! It only looks good from the bottom. There's another whisper: "Look over there—another pillar—and there, too—everywhere!" Angry and frustrated, S moans, "My pillar, only one of thousands. Millions of caterpillars climbing nowhere. We don't have to run pointless but . . . what else is there?" The good news is: there is something more. There is a personal C after illusions like a slightly more sophisticated version of a hamster on a treadmill. He gives purp who created you, knows you by name, loves you, and wants you to know him intimately. There is a personal and meaning to life as he calls us to follow him in his grand adventure. If you're searching for meani follow the writer of Ecclesiastes to its source: a lifelong personal encounter with God.

CHAPTER **2** **A GOOD TIME ISN'T EVERYTHING.** I said in my heart, "Come now, I will test you with mirth; therefore enjoy pleasure"; but surely, this also *was* vanity. ²I said of laughter—"Madness!"; and of mirth, "What does it accomplish?" ³I searched in my heart *how* to gratify my flesh with wine, while guiding my heart with wisdom, and how to lay hold on folly, till I might see what *was* good for the sons of men to do under heaven all the days of their lives.

⁴I made my works great, I built myself houses, and planted myself vineyards. ⁵I made myself gardens and orchards, and I planted all *kinds* of fruit trees in them. ⁶I made myself water pools from which to water the growing trees of the grove. ⁷I acquired male and female servants, and had servants born in my house. Yes, I had greater possessions of herds and flocks than all who were in Jerusalem before me. ⁸I also gathered for myself silver and gold and the special treasures of kings and of the provinces. I acquired male and female singers, the delights of the sons of men, *and* musical instruments of all kinds.

⁹So I became great and excelled more than all who were before me in Jerusalem. Also my wisdom remained with me.

¹⁰ Whatever my eyes desired I did
     not keep from them.
  I did not withhold my heart from
     any pleasure,
  For my heart rejoiced in all my
     labor;
  And this was my reward from all
     my labor.
¹¹ Then I looked on all the works
     that my hands had done
  And on the labor in which I had
     toiled;
  And indeed all *was* vanity and
     grasping for the wind.
  There was no profit under the sun.

¹² Then I turned myself to consider wisdom and
     madness and folly;
  For what *can* the man *do* who succeeds the king?—
  Only what he has already done.
¹³ Then I saw that wisdom excels folly
  As light excels darkness.
¹⁴ The wise man's eyes *are* in his head,
  But the fool walks in darkness.
  Yet I myself perceived
  That the same event happens to them all.

¹⁵ So I said in my heart,
  "As it happens to the fool,
  It also happens to me,
  And why was I then more wise?"

Then I said in my heart,
  "This also *is* vanity."
¹⁶ For *there is* no more remembrance of the wise than
     of the fool forever,
  Since all that now *is* will be forgotten in the days to
     come.
  And how does a wise *man* die?
  As the fool!

¹⁷Therefore I hated life because the work that was done

"Here's what I did..."

When I graduated from junior high school, I was popular and successful academically. I had everything going for me. During the summer before senior high school, though, I realized things would be different. Most of the friends I knew wouldn't be going to the same high school with me. I'd have to start over.

That summer I decided to live it up. I went to party after party with my friends and had a lot of fun. But in between these times I felt depressed. I was living for the moment, and somehow that felt lonely.

One day I was flipping through the Bible, and I decided to read the book of Ecclesiastes. The whole book really spoke to me. Here was a guy I could identify with. He too seemed to be living for the moment, and he found it just as empty as I did! One verse especially expressed my feelings: "Then I looked on all the works that my hands had done . . . and indeed all *was* vanity and grasping for the wind" (2:11). My whole summer to that point had been consumed with chasing pleasure—grasping for the wind. That verse may sound depressing, but it actually made me feel better. Here was someone who knew how I was feeling, and expressed it perfectly.

After reading Ecclesiastes, I realized how futile it is to strive after material possessions, money, fame, and even popularity. They are all fleeting. Once they've gone, so has happiness. But if you follow God's ways, there's nothing to take your happiness away.

Rick

AGE 16

under the sun *was* distressing to me, for all *is* vanity and grasping for the wind.

¹⁸Then I hated all my labor in which I had toiled under the sun, because I must leave it to the man who will come after me. ¹⁹And who knows whether he will be wise or a fool? Yet he will rule over all my labor in which I toiled and in which I have shown myself wise under the sun. This also *is* vanity. ²⁰Therefore I turned my heart and despaired of all the labor in which I had toiled under the sun. ²¹For there is a man whose labor *is* with wisdom, knowledge, and skill; yet he must leave his heritage to a man who has not labored for it. This also *is* vanity and a great evil. ²²For what has man for all his labor, and for the striving of his heart with which he has toiled under the sun? ²³For all his days *are* sorrowful, and his work burdensome; even in the night his heart takes no rest. This also is vanity.

²⁴Nothing *is* better for a man *than* that he should eat

2:24-26 Is Solomon recommending we make life a big, wild party? No, he is encouraging us to take pleasure in what we're doing now and to enjoy life because it comes from God's hand. True enjoyment in life comes only as we follow God's guidelines for living. Those who really know how to enjoy life are the ones who take life each day as a gift from God, thanking him for it and serving him in it.

and drink, and *that* his soul should enjoy good in his labor. This also, I saw, was from the hand of God. 25For who can eat, or who can have enjoyment, more than I? 26For *God* gives wisdom and knowledge and joy to a man who *is* good in His sight; but to the sinner He gives the work of gathering and collecting, that he may give to *him who is* good before God. This also *is* vanity and grasping for the wind.

CHAPTER 3 THERE'S A RIGHT TIME FOR EVERYTHING.

To everything *there is* a season,
A time for every purpose under heaven:

2 A time to be born,
    And a time to die;
   A time to plant,
    And a time to pluck *what is* planted;
3 A time to kill,
    And a time to heal;
   A time to break down,
    And a time to build up;
4 A time to weep,
    And a time to laugh;
   A time to mourn,
    And a time to dance;
5 A time to cast away stones,
    And a time to gather stones;
   A time to embrace,
    And a time to refrain from embracing;
6 A time to gain,
    And a time to lose;
   A time to keep,
    And a time to throw away;
7 A time to tear,
    And a time to sew;
   A time to keep silence,
    And a time to speak;
8 A time to love,
    And a time to hate;
   A time of war,
    And a time of peace.

9What profit has the worker from that in which he labors? 10I have seen the God-given task with which the sons of men are to be occupied. 11He has made everything beautiful in its time. Also He has put eternity in their hearts, except that no one can find out the work that God does from beginning to end.

12I know that nothing *is* better for them than to rejoice, and to do good in their lives, 13and also that every man should eat and drink and enjoy the good of all his labor—it *is* the gift of God.

14 I know that whatever God does,
     It shall be forever.

Nothing can be added to it,
And nothing taken from it.
God does *it*, that men should fear before Him.
15 That which is has already been,
     And what is to be has already been;
     And God requires an account of what is past.

16Moreover I saw under the sun:

In the place of judgment,
Wickedness *was* there;
And *in* the place of righteousness,
Iniquity *was* there.

17I said in my heart,

"God shall judge the righteous and the wicked,
For *there is* a time there for every purpose and for
    every work."

18I said in my heart, "Concerning the condition of the sons of men, God tests them, that they may see that they themselves are *like* animals." 19For what happens to the sons of men also happens to animals; one thing befalls them: as one dies, so dies the other. Surely, they all have one breath; man has no advantage over animals, for all *is* vanity. 20All go to one place: all are from the dust, and all return to dust. 21Who knows the spirit of the sons of men, which goes upward, and the spirit of the animal, which goes down to the earth? 22So I perceived that nothing *is* better than that a man should rejoice in his own works, for that *is* his heritage. For who can bring him to see what will happen after him?

CHAPTER 4 I WOULD RATHER BE DEAD.

Then I returned and considered all the oppression that is done under the sun:

And look! The tears of the oppressed,
But they have no comforter—
On the side of their oppressors *there is* power,
But they have no comforter.
2 Therefore I praised the dead who were already dead,
   More than the living who are still alive.
3 Yet, better than both *is he* who has never existed,
   Who has not seen the evil work that is done under
       the sun.

4Again, I saw that for all toil and every skillful work a man is envied by his neighbor. This also *is* vanity and grasping for the wind.

5 The fool folds his hands
   And consumes his own flesh.
6 Better a handful *with* quietness
   Than both hands full, *together with* toil and grasping
       for the wind.

7Then I returned, and I saw vanity under the sun:

8 There is one alone, without companion:
   He has neither son nor brother.
   Yet *there is* no end to all his labors,
   Nor is his eye satisfied with riches.
   But he never asks,

"For whom do I toil and deprive myself of good?"
This also *is* vanity and a grave misfortune.

9 Two *are* better than one,
Because they have a good reward for their labor.

10 For if they fall, one will lift up his companion.
But woe to him *who is* alone when he falls,
For *he has* no one to help him up.

11 Again, if two lie down together, they will keep warm;
But how can one be warm *alone*?

12 Though one may be overpowered
by another, two can withstand
him.
And a threefold cord is not
quickly broken.

13 Better a poor and wise youth
Than an old and foolish king who
will be admonished no more.

14 For he comes out of prison to be
king,
Although he was born poor in his
kingdom.

15 I saw all the living who walk
under the sun;
They were with the second youth
who stands in his place.

16 *There was* no end of all the people
over whom he was made king;
Yet those who come afterward
will not rejoice in him.
Surely this also *is* vanity and
grasping for the wind.

**CHAPTER 5 HAVE RESPECT FOR
GOD.** Walk prudently when you go to
the house of God; and draw near to
hear rather than to give the sacrifice
of fools, for they do not know that
they do evil.

2 Do not be rash with your mouth,
And let not your heart utter anything hastily before
God.
For God *is* in heaven, and you on earth;
Therefore let your words be few.

3 For a dream comes through much activity,
And a fool's voice *is known* by *his* many words.

4 When you make a vow to God, do not delay to pay it;
For *He has* no pleasure in fools.
Pay what you have vowed—

5 Better not to vow than to vow and not pay.

6 Do not let your mouth cause your flesh to sin, nor say
before the messenger *of God* that it *was* an error. Why
should God be angry at your excuse and destroy the work
of your hands? 7 For in the multitude of dreams and many
words *there is* also vanity. But fear God.

8 If you see the oppression of the poor, and the violent
perversion of justice and righteousness in a province, do
not marvel at the matter; for high official watches over
high official, and higher officials are over them.

9 Moreover the profit of the land is for all; *even* the king
is served from the field.

10 He who loves silver will not be satisfied with silver;
Nor he who loves abundance, with increase.
This also *is* vanity.

11 When goods increase,
They increase who eat them;
So what profit have the owners

"Here's what I did..."

I really wanted to grow in my walk with God, so I vowed that I would have
a quiet time every night. For a while everything went very well. I felt I
understood what I read, and as I tried to apply the Bible to my daily life,
I began to see changes in myself. That excited me.

But then I went through a period of time when I didn't seem to be getting
anything out of the Bible. For some reason, one night I started reading
Ecclesiastes. I felt stressed, in a rush to get to my homework so I could get to
bed at a decent hour. When I came across the passage in chapter 5, verses
1-7, I suddenly woke up! I remembered that I had vowed to spend time with
God every day and that it was *God* I was treating so rudely by rushing
through my time with him. My attitude was all wrong. Having a quiet time
wasn't like some chore I had to do; it was a privilege to meet with the
awesome God of the universe! I asked God to forgive me for my attitude and
thanked him for speaking to me through his Word.

Tammy AGE 16

Except to see *them* with their eyes?

12 The sleep of a laboring man *is* sweet,
Whether he eats little or much;
But the abundance of the rich will not permit him to
sleep.

13 There is a severe evil *which* I have seen under the
sun:
Riches kept for their owner to his hurt.

14 But those riches perish through misfortune;
When he begets a son, *there is* nothing in his hand.

15 As he came from his mother's womb, naked shall he
return,
To go as he came;
And he shall take nothing from his labor
Which he may carry away in his hand.

16 And this also *is* a severe evil—
Just exactly as he came, so shall he go.
And what profit has he who has labored for the
wind?

17 All his days he also eats in darkness,
And *he has* much sorrow and sickness and anger.

7:5-6 Have you ever been paid a compliment when you knew it was inappropriate or merely an attempt to flatter you? Some people would rather feel good than know the truth. Too often, pleasant compliments are valued above helpful information (Proverbs 27:6). Solomon reminds us that it is far better to face honest criticism than to wallow in the compliments of fools.

¹⁸Here is what I have seen: *It is* good and fitting *for one* to eat and drink, and to enjoy the good of all his labor in which he toils under the sun all the days of his life which God gives him; for it *is* his heritage. ¹⁹As for every man to whom God has given riches and wealth, and given him power to eat of it, to receive his heritage and rejoice in his labor—this *is* the gift of God. ²⁰For he will not dwell unduly on the days of his life, because God keeps *him* busy with the joy of his heart.

CHAPTER **6** IS LIFE REALLY WORTH LIVING?

There is an evil which I have seen under the sun, and it *is* common among men: ²A man to whom God has given riches and wealth and honor, so that he lacks nothing for himself of all he desires; yet God does not give him power to eat of it, but a foreigner consumes it. This *is* vanity, and it *is* an evil affliction.

³If a man begets a hundred *children* and lives many years, so that the days of his years are many, but his soul is not satisfied with goodness, or indeed he has no burial, I say *that* a stillborn child *is* better than he— ⁴for it comes in vanity and departs in darkness, and its name is covered with darkness. ⁵Though it has not seen the sun or known *anything*, this has more rest than that man, ⁶even if he lives a thousand years twice—but has not seen goodness. Do not all go to one place?

7   All the labor of man *is* for his mouth,
    And yet the soul is not satisfied.
8   For what more has the wise *man* than the fool?
    What does the poor man have,
    Who knows *how* to walk before the living?
9   Better *is* the sight of the eyes than the wandering of
        desire.
    This also *is* vanity and grasping for the wind.

10 Whatever one is, he has been named already,
    For it is known that he *is* man;
    And he cannot contend with Him who is mightier
        than he.
11 Since there are many things that increase vanity,
    How *is* man the better?

¹²For who knows what *is* good for man in life, all the days of his vain life which he passes like a shadow? Who can tell a man what will happen after him under the sun?

CHAPTER **7** SOME TIPS FOR A MEANINGFUL LIFE.

    A good name *is* better than precious ointment,
    And the day of death than the day of one's birth;
2   Better to go to the house of mourning
    Than to go to the house of feasting,
    For that *is* the end of all men;
    And the living will take *it* to heart.
3   Sorrow *is* better than laughter,

    For by a sad countenance the heart is made better.
4   The heart of the wise *is* in the house of mourning,
    But the heart of fools *is* in the house of mirth.
5   *It is* better to hear the rebuke of the wise
    Than for a man to hear the song of fools.
6   For like the crackling of thorns under a pot,
    So *is* the laughter of the fool.
    This also is vanity.
7   Surely oppression destroys a wise *man's* reason,
    And a bribe debases the heart.

8   The end of a thing *is* better than its beginning;
    The patient in spirit *is* better than the proud in spirit.
9   Do not hasten in your spirit to be angry,
    For anger rests in the bosom of fools.
10 Do not say,
    "Why were the former days better than these?"
    For you do not inquire wisely concerning this.

11 Wisdom *is* good with an inheritance,
    And profitable to those who see the sun.
12 For wisdom *is* a defense *as* money *is* a defense,
    But the excellence of knowledge *is that* wisdom
        gives life to those who have it.

13 Consider the work of God;
    For who can make straight what He has made
        crooked?
14 In the day of prosperity be joyful,
    But in the day of adversity consider:
    Surely God has appointed the one as well as the
        other,
    So that man can find out nothing *that will come*
        after him.

¹⁵I have seen everything in my days of vanity:

    There is a just *man* who perishes in his
        righteousness,
    And there is a wicked *man* who prolongs *life* in his
        wickedness.

16 Do not be overly righteous,
    Nor be overly wise:
    Why should you destroy yourself?
17 Do not be overly wicked,
    Nor be foolish:
    Why should you die before your time?
18 *It is* good that you grasp this,
    And also not remove your hand from the other;
    For he who fears God will escape them all.

19 Wisdom strengthens the wise
    More than ten rulers of the city.

20 For *there is* not a just man on earth who does good
    And does not sin.

21 Also do not take to heart everything people say,
    Lest you hear your servant cursing you.
22 For many times, also, your own heart has known
    That even you have cursed others.

23 All this I have proved by wisdom.
    I said, "I will be wise";

But it *was* far from me.
24 As for that which is far off and exceedingly deep,
Who can find it out?
25 I applied my heart to know,
To search and seek out wisdom and the reason *of things,*
To know the wickedness of folly,
Even of foolishness *and* madness.
26 And I find more bitter than death
The woman whose heart *is* snares and nets,
Whose hands *are* fetters.
He who pleases God shall escape from her,
But the sinner shall be trapped by her.
27 "Here is what I have found," says the Preacher,
"*Adding* one thing to the other to find out the reason,
28 Which my soul still seeks but I cannot find:
One man among a thousand I have found,
But a woman among all these I have not found.
29 Truly, this only I have found:
That God made man upright,
But they have sought out many schemes."

CHAPTER **8** OBEY THE LAW.

Who *is* like a wise *man?*
And who knows the interpretation of a thing?
A man's wisdom makes his face shine,
And the sternness of his face is changed.

2 I *say,* "Keep the king's command-ment for the sake of your oath to God. 3Do not be hasty to go from his presence. Do not take your stand for an evil thing, for he does whatever pleases him."

4 Where the word of a king *is, there is* power;
And who may say to him, "What are you doing?"
5 He who keeps his command will experience nothing harmful;
And a wise man's heart discerns both time and judgment,
6 Because for every matter there is a time and judgment,
Though the misery of man increases greatly.
7 For he does not know what will happen;
So who can tell him when it will occur?
8 No one has power over the spirit to retain the spirit,
And no one has power in the day of death.
There is no release from that war,
And wickedness will not deliver those who are given to it.

9 All this I have seen, and applied my heart to every work that is done under the sun: *There is* a time in which one man rules over another to his own hurt. 10Then I saw the wicked buried, who had come and gone from the place of holiness, and they were forgotten in the city where they had so done. This also *is* vanity. 11Because the sentence against an evil work is not exe-cuted speedily, therefore the heart of the sons of men is fully set in them to do evil. 12Though a sinner does evil a

hundred *times,* and his *days* are prolonged, yet I surely know that it will be well with those who fear God, who fear before Him. 13But it will not be well with the wicked; nor will he prolong *his* days, *which are* as a shadow, because he does not fear before God.

14There is a vanity which occurs on earth, that there are just *men* to whom it happens according to the work of the wicked; again, there are wicked *men* to whom it happens according to the work of the righteous. I said that this also *is* vanity.

CONSEQUENCES

8:11 We should never assume that God doesn't care if we have sinned, or that sin has no consequences, simply because he hasn't punished us immediately. Unfortunately, it is easier to sin when we don't feel immediate consequences. When a young child does something wrong without being discovered, it will be much easier for him to do the wrong again. But God knows every wrong we commit, and one day we *will* have to answer for everything we have done (12:14).

¹⁵So I commended enjoyment, because a man has nothing better under the sun than to eat, drink, and be merry; for this will remain with him in his labor *all* the days of his life which God gives him under the sun.

¹⁶When I applied my heart to know wisdom and to see the business that is done on earth, even though one sees no sleep day or night, ¹⁷then I saw all the work of God, that a man cannot find out the work that is done under the sun. For though a man labors to discover *it*, yet he will not find *it*; moreover, though a wise *man* attempts to know *it*, he will not be able to find *it*.

PLEASURE
At a youth rally, the speaker is pleading with the students—begging them not to make the mistakes he made.

"Please hear what I'm saying. When I was your age, I was empty inside. I came from a broken home. I hated myself and everybody else. I tried everything to fill the hole inside: drugs, alcohol, sleeping around, partying.

"I tried to convince myself I was having a good time. And those things did feel good . . . for a while. But the feeling was only temporary. No matter what I did, I couldn't shake that inner loneliness and hurt.

"Everything I did to try to ease my pain only made my hurt increase. Listen to me: You will never find what you're really looking for until you accept the love of Jesus Christ. Coming to know him—the Lord of life—will bring you the peace you so desperately need. There is life nowhere else."

As the speaker concludes, Lorraine thinks, "Yeah, he says all this after he's had all his fun. Maybe I'll just have a good time now . . . and get serious about God later."

The book of Ecclesiastes describes King Solomon's frantic search for satisfaction. Chapters 1 and 2 relate all the different ways he tried to find fulfillment apart from God. His conclusion is in 12:13-14.

Will you listen to the voices of experience and save yourself a lot of heartache? Or will you be stubborn and learn the hard way?

CHAPTER 9 LIFE IS WORTH LIVING: DO IT WELL.

For I considered all this in my heart, so that I could declare it all: that the righteous and the wise and their works *are* in the hand of God. People know neither love nor hatred *by* anything *they see* before them. ²All things *come* alike to all:

One event *happens* to the righteous and the wicked;
To the good, the clean, and the unclean;
To him who sacrifices and him who does not sacrifice.
As is the good, so *is* the sinner;
He who takes an oath as *he* who fears an oath.

³This *is* an evil in all that is done under the sun: that one thing *happens* to all. Truly the hearts of the sons of men are full of evil; madness *is* in their hearts while they live, and after that *they go* to the dead. ⁴But for him who is joined to all the living there is hope, for a living dog is better than a dead lion.

⁵ For the living know that they will die;
But the dead know nothing,

PAGE 618

POPULARITY

9:15-18 Our society honors wealth, attractiveness, and success a wisdom. It is sad to see people trying hard to look important in mankind's eyes while ruining their relationship with God.

And they have no more reward,
For the memory of them is forgotten.
⁶ Also their love, their hatred, and their envy have now perished;
Nevermore will they have a share
In anything done under the sun.

⁷ Go, eat your bread with joy,
And drink your wine with a merry heart;
For God has already accepted your works.
⁸ Let your garments always be white,
And let your head lack no oil.

⁹Live joyfully with the wife whom you love all the days of your vain life which He has given you under the sun, all your days of vanity; for that *is* your portion in life, and in the labor which you perform under the sun.

¹⁰Whatever your hand finds to do, do *it* with your might; for *there is* no work or device or knowledge or wisdom in the grave where you are going.

¹¹I returned and saw under the sun that—

The race *is* not to the swift,
Nor the battle to the strong,
Nor bread to the wise,
Nor riches to men of understanding,
Nor favor to men of skill;
But time and chance happen to them all.
¹² For man also does not know his time:
Like fish taken in a cruel net,
Like birds caught in a snare,
So the sons of men *are* snared in an evil time,
When it falls suddenly upon them.

¹³This wisdom I have also seen under the sun, and it *seemed* great to me: ¹⁴*There was* a little city with few men in it; and a great king came against it, besieged it, and built great snares around it. ¹⁵Now there was found in it a poor wise man, and he by his wisdom delivered the city. Yet no one remembered that same poor man.

¹⁶Then I said:

"Wisdom *is* better than strength.
Nevertheless the poor man's wisdom *is* despised,

MONEY

10:19 Government leaders, businesses, families, and even chur get trapped into thinking money is the answer to every problem. B as the effects of liquor are only temporary, the soothing effect of t purchase soon wears off, and we have to buy more. Scripture reco that money is necessary for survival, but it warns against the love money (see Matthew 6:24; 1 Timothy 6:10; Hebrews 13:5). Money be dangerous; we use it to deceive ourselves, thinking that wealth easiest way to get everything we want. The love of money is sinful because we trust it, rather than God, to solve our problems. Those pursue money's empty promises will discover one day that they ha nothing because they are spiritually bankrupt.

And his words are not heard.

17 Words of the wise, *spoken* quietly, *should be* heard
Rather than the shout of a ruler of fools.

18 Wisdom *is* better than weapons of war;
But one sinner destroys much good."

CHAPTER 10 BEHAVE WISELY.

Dead flies putrefy the perfumer's ointment,
And cause it to give off a foul odor;
So does a little folly to one respected for wisdom *and*
honor.

2 A wise man's heart *is* at his right hand,
But a fool's heart at his left.

3 Even when a fool walks along the way,
He lacks wisdom,
And he shows everyone *that* he *is* a fool.

4 If the spirit of the ruler rises against you,
Do not leave your post;
For conciliation pacifies great offenses.

5 There is an evil I have seen under the sun,
As an error proceeding from the ruler:

6 Folly is set in great dignity,
While the rich sit in a lowly place.

7 I have seen servants on horses,
While princes walk on the ground like servants.

8 He who digs a pit will fall into it,
And whoever breaks through a wall will be bitten by
a serpent.

9 He who quarries stones may be hurt by them,
And he who splits wood may be endangered by it.

10 If the ax is dull,
And one does not sharpen the edge,
Then he must use more strength;
But wisdom brings success.

11 A serpent may bite when *it is* not charmed;
The babbler is no different.

12 The words of a wise man's mouth *are* gracious,
But the lips of a fool shall swallow him up;

13 The words of his mouth begin with foolishness,
And the end of his talk *is* raving madness.

14 A fool also multiplies words.
No man knows what is to be;
Who can tell him what will be after him?

15 The labor of fools wearies them,
For they do not even know how to go to the city!

16 Woe to you, O land, when your king *is* a child,
And your princes feast in the morning!

17 Blessed *are* you, O land, when your king *is* the son of
nobles,
And your princes feast at the proper time—
For strength and not for drunkenness!

18 Because of laziness the building decays,
And through idleness of hands the house leaks.

19 A feast is made for laughter,
And wine makes merry;
But money answers everything.

20 Do not curse the king, even in your thought;
Do not curse the rich, even in your bedroom;
For a bird of the air may carry your voice,
And a bird in flight may tell the matter.

CHAPTER 11 KEEP IT UP: GOD WILL HONOR YOU.

Cast your bread upon the waters,
For you will find it after many days.

2 Give a serving to seven, and also to eight,
For you do not know what evil will be on the earth.

3 If the clouds are full of rain,
They empty *themselves* upon the earth;
And if a tree falls to the south or the north,
In the place where the tree falls, there it shall lie.

4 He who observes the wind will not sow,
And he who regards the clouds will not reap.

**I recently became a Christian, but I'm
having second thoughts.
I'm afraid I'll miss out
on a lot of fun during
my teenage years.
Can't I wait until
later to live for
Christ?**

I WONDER . . .

A speaker once
related a dream he'd had. The location was hell, and the
demons were trying to think of ways to stop people from
accepting Christ.

Each demon brought an idea to Satan and was told to
try it. The ideas included the typical ones people think
are responsible for turning others away: drugs, sexual
temptations, intellectualism, money, fame, status, etc.

All of these strategies were tried, but they weren't very
effective.

Finally, one demon suggested a plan that surprised
everyone. "Let's tell people that believing the Bible and
following Christ are the right things to do; and tell them
that being a committed believer is the only way to live
life. But," he concluded, "tell them to do it—*tomorrow!*"

That has become Satan's strategy—and for many
people tomorrow never comes!

This delaying tactic works like Novocain. It numbs
people and keeps them from turning to the truth when
they hear it.

We are creatures of habit. We've learned almost
everything—reading, writing, math, speech—by doing
the same thing over and over. Our thoughts about God
are the same way. Believing we can play now and get
committed later fulfills Satan's strategy.

Thought patterns become habits; habits become
beliefs; beliefs become actions; and actions determine
our eternity!

You may be afraid you'll miss out on the fun, but those
"good times" don't last. Most of what the world pursues
is shallow and meaningless (though sometimes "fun" for
a while).

Ecclesiastes 11:9–12:18 makes it clear that to live life
to the fullest, we must follow God—not in fear that he
wants to take away our fun, but in faith that he wants to
make our life into something wonderful.

Life begins the moment we realize that the world
doesn't revolve around us, but around God who made
the world and all that is in it.

⁵ As you do not know what *is* the way of the wind,
  Or how the bones *grow* in the womb of her who is
    with child,
  So you do not know the works of God who makes
    everything.
⁶ In the morning sow your seed,
  And in the evening do not withhold your hand;
  For you do not know which will prosper,
  Either this or that,
  Or whether both alike *will be* good.

⁷ Truly the light is sweet,
  And *it is* pleasant for the eyes to behold the sun;
⁸ But if a man lives many years
  And rejoices in them all,
  Yet let him remember the days of darkness,
  For they will be many.
  All that is coming *is* vanity.

CHOICES

11:10 Often people say, "It doesn't matter." But many of our choices will be irreversible—they will stay with us for a lifetime. What you do when you're young *does* matter. Enjoy life now, but don't do anything—physically, morally, or spiritually—that will prevent you from enjoying life when you are old.

⁹ Rejoice, O young man, in your youth,
  And let your heart cheer you in the days of your
    youth;
  Walk in the ways of your heart,
  And in the sight of your eyes;
  But know that for all these
  God will bring you into judgment.
¹⁰ Therefore remove sorrow from your heart,
  And put away evil from your flesh,
  For childhood and youth *are* vanity.

CHAPTER 12 HONOR GOD.

  Remember now your Creator in the days of your
    youth,
  Before the difficult days come,
  And the years draw near when you say,
  "I have no pleasure in them":
² While the sun and the light,
  The moon and the stars,
  Are not darkened,
  And the clouds do not return after the rain;
³ In the day when the keepers of the house tremble,
  And the strong men bow down;
  When the grinders cease because they are few,
  And those that look through the windows grow dim;
⁴ When the doors are shut in the streets,
  And the sound of grinding is low;
  When one rises up at the sound of a bird,
  And all the daughters of music are brought low.
⁵ Also they are afraid of height,
  And of terrors in the way;
  When the almond tree blossoms,
  The grasshopper is a burden,
  And desire fails.
  For man goes to his eternal home,

And the mourners go about the streets.
⁶ *Remember your Creator* before the silver cord is
    loosed,
  Or the golden bowl is broken,
  Or the pitcher shattered at the fountain,
  Or the wheel broken at the well.
⁷ Then the dust will return to the earth as it was,
  And the spirit will return to God who gave it.

⁸ "Vanity of vanities," says the Preacher,
  "All *is* vanity."

⁹And moreover, because the Preacher was wise, he still taught the people knowledge; yes, he pondered and sought out *and* set in order many proverbs. ¹⁰The Preacher sought to find acceptable words; and *what was* written *was* upright—words of truth. ¹¹The words of the wise are like goads, and the words of scholars are like well-driven nails, given by one Shepherd. ¹²And further, my son, be admonished by these. Of making many books *there is* no end, and much study *is* wearisome to the flesh.

¹³Let us hear the conclusion of the whole matter:

  Fear God and keep His commandments,
  For this is man's all.
¹⁴ For God will bring every work into judgment,
  Including every secret thing,
  Whether good or evil.

LET US HEAR THE CONCLUSION **FEAR GOD** A N D **KEEP HIS COMMANDMENTS** FOR THIS IS **MAN'S ALL.** FOR **GOD** WILL BRING **EVERY WORK INTO JUDGMENT** INCLUDING *every secret thing.*

ECCLESIASTES 12:13-14

MEGA Themes

SEARCHING Solomon searched for satisfaction almost as though it was a scientific experiment. In his search he discovered that life without God was meaningless. True happiness does not come from accumulating or attaining honors—we always want more than we can have, and there are circumstances beyond our control that can snatch away all our possessions and achievements.

People are still searching for meaning, enjoyment, fulfillment, and satisfaction. Yet the more they try to get, the more they realize how little they really have. No lasting pleasure or happiness is possible without God. Above all else, we should strive to know and love God, trusting him for true joy in life.
1. List all the ways in which Solomon searched for happiness and satisfaction.
2. In what ways do people today search for happiness and satisfaction?
3. How do most of your peers at school hope to find satisfaction in the present? In the future, as adults?
4. If you were to give a personal testimony of the satisfaction found in Christ, what would you say? To whom would you want to say this?
5. How can you share this testimony by example and word with those in your school, and/or with your friends at church, who are searching in the wrong places for satisfaction and happiness?

EMPTINESS Solomon shows how empty it is to pursue life's pleasures in place of a relationship with the eternal God. The search for pleasure, wealth, and success ultimately is disappointing. Nothing in the world can satisfy our longing, restless heart.

The cure for emptiness is to focus on God. Develop a fear or reverence for God throughout your life, and fill your life with serving God and others rather than selfishly chasing after pleasures.
1. Perhaps you have heard someone say, "He had everything, but he was empty inside." What do you think it means to be "empty" inside?
2. Who are some stars, athletes, or prominent people who seem to have all they could want, yet live seemingly empty lives (filled with drugs, broken relationships, sexual immorality, etc.)?
3. According to the book of Ecclesiastes, the answer to the emptiness of life is _____. How does this answer fill the emptiness?
4. What choices are you making now that will ensure that your life will continue to increase in fulfillment rather than becoming an empty shell? What difference does it make whether you do this when you are young?

WORK Solomon tried to shake people's confidence in their own efforts, abilities, and wisdom. He did

this to direct them to faith in God as the only sound basis for living. Without God, there is no lasting reward or benefit in hard work.

Work done with the wrong attitude leaves us empty. Work accepted as an assignment from God can be seen as a gift. Examine what you expect from your efforts at school and/or on the job. God gives you abilities and opportunities to work and to make a contribution with your life.
1. What seems to be the attitude most people have toward working?
2. How do you feel about the work you have to do, including school work and responsibilities at home? Describe your attitude.
3. What does the book of Ecclesiastes present as the proper attitude toward work?
4. Describe the attitude that will be most effective in enabling people to do their work for God. How can you develop this attitude, beginning with the work you have to do this week?

DEATH The certainty of death makes all human achievements futile. God has a plan for human destiny that goes beyond life and death. The reality of aging and dying reminds us of the end to come, when God will judge each person's life.

Life does not seem to be short when a person is young, yet the years pass all too quickly. Because life is so short, we need wisdom greater than this world can offer. We need the words of God. If we listen to him, his wisdom will spare us the bitterness of ending life without having fulfilled a worthwhile purpose.
1. To a person who does not know God through Christ, death could be described as _____.
2. To a person who is a Christian, death could be described as _____.
3. How do you feel about your own death?
4. Explain how your faith in Christ affects your thoughts and feelings regarding your death.
5. How does the knowledge of life after death influence the way you live life before death?

WISDOM Human wisdom doesn't have all the answers. Knowledge and education have their limits. To understand life, we need the wisdom that can be found only in God's Word to us—the Bible.

When we realize that God will evaluate all we do, we should learn to live wisely, remembering that God is with us at each moment. We can have God's wisdom only when we obey him.
1. What limits of human wisdom frustrated Solomon?
2. How can you tap into God's wisdom when your human knowledge and understanding fail you?
3. Since God has revealed himself, what can you do to get beyond the limits of human reasoning?

*C*heck out the words to the top 40 songs, and you'll probably find a sensuous mix of I-got-to-have-you-now lyrics. Check out the supermarket tabloids, and you'll find stories of adultery, divorce, and affairs by an assortment of entertainment figures. The message comes through loud and clear: lust is in, love is out; independence is in, marriage is out. In fact, it seems that commitment has become a dirty word. ■ That's not what God had in mind when he created sex and love, or when he began marriage. Sex is meant to be an exciting, fulfilling physical union of a man and a woman who are protected by the commitment of marriage—not an act of self-gratification. Love is meant to be a self-giving action, not a self-centered emotion.

■ Nowhere are the true meanings of love and sex more beautifully portrayed than in the Song of Solomon. Here we get an intimate glimpse into the personal relationship between the king (Solomon) and his bride. Love, sex, and marriage are celebrated in the context of living the way God designed us to live. ■ Don't fall for cultural lies and myths about love. Read Song of Solomon and commit yourself to living God's way. Believe me, the payoff is terrific!

STATS

PURPOSE: To tell of the love between a bridegroom (King Solomon) and his bride, to affirm the sanctity of marriage, and to picture God's love for his people

AUTHOR: Solomon

DATE WRITTEN: Probably early in Solomon's reign

SETTING: Israel—the Shulamite woman's garden and the king's palace

KEY PEOPLE: King Solomon, the Shulamite woman, and the daughters of Jerusalem

Check out the words to the top 40 songs, and you'll probably find a sensuous mix of I-got-to-have-you-now lyrics. Check out the supermarket tabloids, and you'll find stories of adultery, divorce, and affairs by an assortment of entertainment figures. The message comes through loud and clear: lust is in, love is out; independence is in, marriage is out. In fact, it seems that commitment has become a dirty word. ■ That's not what God had in mind when he created sex and love, or when he began marriage. Sex is meant to be an exciting, fulfilling physical union of a man and a woman who are protected by the commitment of marriage—not an act of self-gratification. Love is meant to be a self-giving action, not a self-centered emotion. ■ Nowhere are the true meanings of love and sex more beautifully portrayed than in the Song of Solomon. Here we get an intimate glimpse into the personal relationship between the king (Solomon) and his bride. Love, sex, and marriage are celebrated in the context of living the way God designed us to live. ■ Don't fall for cultural lies and myths about love. Read Song of Solomon and commit yourself to living God's way. Believe me, the payoff is terrific!

STATS

PURPOSE: To tell of the love between a bridegroom (King Solomon) and his bride, to affirm the sanctity of marriage, and to picture God's love for his people

AUTHOR: Solomon

DATE WRITTEN: Probably early in Solomon's reign

SETTING: Israel—the Shulamite woman's garden and the king's palace

KEY PEOPLE: King Solomon, the Shulamite woman, and the daughters of Jerusalem

MEGA *Themes*

SEARCHING Solomon searched for satisfaction almost as though it was a scientific experiment. In his search he discovered that life without God was meaningless. True happiness does not come from accumulating or attaining honors—we always want more than we can have, and there are circumstances beyond our control that can snatch away all our possessions and achievements.

People are still searching for meaning, enjoyment, fulfillment, and satisfaction. Yet the more they try to get, the more they realize how little they really have. No lasting pleasure or happiness is possible without God. Above all else, we should strive to know and love God, trusting him for true joy in life.

1. List all the ways in which Solomon searched for happiness and satisfaction.
2. In what ways do people today search for happiness and satisfaction?
3. How do most of your peers at school hope to find satisfaction in the present? In the future, as adults?
4. If you were to give a personal testimony of the satisfaction found in Christ, what would you say? To whom would you want to say this?
5. How can you share this testimony by example and word with those in your school, and/or with your friends at church, who are searching in the wrong places for satisfaction and happiness?

EMPTINESS Solomon shows how empty it is to pursue life's pleasures in place of a relationship with the eternal God. The search for pleasure, wealth, and success ultimately is disappointing. Nothing in the world can satisfy our longing, restless heart.

The cure for emptiness is to focus on God. Develop a fear or reverence for God throughout your life, and fill your life with serving God and others rather than selfishly chasing after pleasures.

1. Perhaps you have heard someone say, "He had everything, but he was empty inside." What do you think it means to be "empty" inside?
2. Who are some stars, athletes, or prominent people who seem to have all they could want, yet live seemingly empty lives (filled with drugs, broken relationships, sexual immorality, etc.)?
3. According to the book of Ecclesiastes, the answer to the emptiness of life is _____. How does this answer fill the emptiness?
4. What choices are you making now that will ensure that your life will continue to increase in fulfillment rather than becoming an empty shell? What difference does it make whether you do this when you are young?

WORK Solomon tried to shake people's confidence in their own efforts, abilities, and wisdom. He did this to direct them to faith in God as the only sound basis for living. Without God, there is no lasting reward or benefit in hard work.

Work done with the wrong attitude leaves us empty. Work accepted as an assignment from God can be seen as a gift. Examine what you expect from your efforts at school and/or on the job. God gives you abilities and opportunities to work and to make a contribution with your life.

1. What seems to be the attitude most people have toward working?
2. How do you feel about the work you have to do, including school work and responsibilities at home? Describe your attitude.
3. What does the book of Ecclesiastes present as the proper attitude toward work?
4. Describe the attitude that will be most effective in enabling people to do their work for God. How can you develop this attitude, beginning with the work you have to do this week?

DEATH The certainty of death makes all human achievements futile. God has a plan for human destiny that goes beyond life and death. The reality of aging and dying reminds us of the end to come, when God will judge each person's life.

Life does not seem to be short when a person is young, yet the years pass all too quickly. Because life is so short, we need wisdom greater than this world can offer. We need the words of God. If we listen to him, his wisdom will spare us the bitterness of ending life without having fulfilled a worthwhile purpose.

1. To a person who does not know God through Christ, death could be described as _____.
2. To a person who is a Christian, death could be described as _____.
3. How do you feel about your own death?
4. Explain how your faith in Christ affects your thoughts and feelings regarding your death.
5. How does the knowledge of life after death influence the way you live life before death?

WISDOM Human wisdom doesn't have all the answers. Knowledge and education have their limits. To understand life, we need the wisdom that can be found only in God's Word to us—the Bible.

When we realize that God will evaluate all we do, we should learn to live wisely, remembering that God is with us at each moment. We can have God's wisdom only when we obey him.

1. What limits of human wisdom frustrated Solomon?
2. How can you tap into God's wisdom when your human knowledge and understanding fail you?
3. Since God has revealed himself, what can you do to get beyond the limits of human reasoning?

Song of Solomon

CHAPTER 1 THE WEDDING DAY. The song of songs, which *is* Solomon's.

THE SHULAMITE
2 Let him kiss me with the kisses of his mouth—
    For your love *is* better than wine.
3 Because of the fragrance of your good ointments,
    Your name *is* ointment poured forth;
    Therefore the virgins love you.
4 Draw me away!

THE DAUGHTERS OF JERUSALEM
    We will run after you.

THE SHULAMITE
    The king has brought me into his chambers.

THE DAUGHTERS OF JERUSALEM
    We will be glad and rejoice in you.

    We will remember your love more than wine.

THE SHULAMITE
    Rightly do they love you.

5 I *am* dark, but lovely,
    O daughters of Jerusalem,
    Like the tents of Kedar,
    Like the curtains of Solomon.
6 Do not look upon me, because I *am* dark,
    Because the sun has tanned me.
    My mother's sons were angry with me;
    They made me the keeper of the vineyards,
    But my own vineyard I have not kept.

(TO HER BELOVED)
7 Tell me, O you whom I love,
    Where you feed *your flock*,
    Where you make *it* rest at noon.
    For why should I be as one who veils herself
    By the flocks of your companions?

THE BELOVED
8 If you do not know, O fairest among women,
    Follow in the footsteps of the flock,
    And feed your little goats
    Beside the shepherds' tents.

A TREAT

1:1-4 This vivid description of a love relationship begins with a picture of love itself. Love is "better than wine." We can enjoy love. God created it as a gift to us and a treat for all our senses.

⁹ I have compared you, my love,
  To my filly among Pharaoh's chariots.
¹⁰ Your cheeks are lovely with ornaments,
  Your neck with chains *of gold.*

THE DAUGHTERS OF JERUSALEM
¹¹ We will make you ornaments of gold
  With studs of silver.

THE SHULAMITE
¹² While the king *is* at his table,
  My spikenard sends forth its fragrance.
¹³ A bundle of myrrh *is* my beloved to me,
  That lies all night between my breasts.
¹⁴ My beloved *is* to me a cluster of henna *blooms*
  In the vineyards of En Gedi.

VIRGINITY

Cassie's 16th birthday tomorrow promises to be awesome. She'll finally get her driver's license, and she finally can officially date!

She and her boyfriend, Paul, will be able to leave . . . in a car . . . by themselves . . . for a whole evening! No more brothers barging into the living room. No more being dropped off at parties. Privacy at last!

Today Cassie got a package from her older sister Beth, who got married last month. Enclosed was a long letter—one of those that you keep forever. It said a lot of things, but maybe the best part was this advice: "Cass, I know how much you love Paul, and I know it will be hard for you two to stay pure now that you're officially dating. Take it from someone who waited: Sex is best when you save it for marriage! I promise you—virgins get the last (and the loudest and longest) laugh.

"Most of my friends—even my Christian friends—didn't wait. They traded short-term pleasure for long-term pain. Don't make that mistake! Make the commitment to God that you won't let your physical relationship get out of control!

"Give Paul a hug from me. And know that Mike and I pray for you two every single day. I love you, Cass.

"Beth"

What a great letter! Read another beautiful description of a virgin bride on her wedding night in Song of Solomon 4. Note especially verse 12.

THE BELOVED
¹⁵ Behold, you *are* fair, my love!
  Behold, you *are* fair!
  You *have* dove's eyes.

THE SHULAMITE
¹⁶ Behold, you *are* handsome, my beloved!
  Yes, pleasant!
  Also our bed *is* green.
¹⁷ The beams of our houses *are* cedar,
  And our rafters of fir.

CHAPTER 2 MEMORIES OF COURTSHIP.

  I *am* the rose of Sharon,
  And the lily of the valleys.

THE BELOVED
² Like a lily among thorns,
  So is my love among the daughters.

◄◄OVERPOWERED

2:7 Feelings of love can create intimacy that overpowers reason. ⟩ people too often are in a hurry to develop an intimate relationship on their strong feelings. But feelings aren't enough to support a last relationship. This verse encourages us not to force romance lest the feelings of love grow faster than the commitment needed to make ⟩ last. Patiently wait for feelings of love and commitment to develop together.

THE SHULAMITE
³ Like an apple tree among the trees of the woods,
  So *is* my beloved among the sons.
  I sat down in his shade with great delight,
  And his fruit *was* sweet to my taste.

THE SHULAMITE TO THE DAUGHTERS OF JERUSALEM
⁴ He brought me to the banqueting house,
  And his banner over me *was* love.
⁵ Sustain me with cakes of raisins,
  Refresh me with apples,
  For I *am* lovesick.

⁶ His left hand *is* under my head,
  And his right hand embraces me.
⁷ I charge you, O daughters of Jerusalem,
  By the gazelles or by the does of the field,
  Do not stir up nor awaken love
  Until it pleases.

THE SHULAMITE
⁸ The voice of my beloved!
  Behold, he comes
  Leaping upon the mountains,
  Skipping upon the hills.
⁹ My beloved is like a gazelle or a young stag.
  Behold, he stands behind our wall;
  He is looking through the windows,
  Gazing through the lattice.

¹⁰ My beloved spoke, and said to me:
  "Rise up, my love, my fair one,
  And come away.
¹¹ For lo, the winter is past,
  The rain is over *and* gone.
¹² The flowers appear on the earth;
  The time of singing has come,
  And the voice of the turtledove
  Is heard in our land.
¹³ The fig tree puts forth her green figs,
  And the vines *with* the tender grapes
  Give a good smell.
  Rise up, my love, my fair one,
  And come away!

¹⁴ "O my dove, in the clefts of the rock,
  In the secret *places* of the cliff,
  Let me see your face,
  Let me hear your voice;
  For your voice *is* sweet,
  And your face *is* lovely."

HER BROTHERS
¹⁵ Catch us the foxes,
  The little foxes that spoil the vines,
  For our vines *have* tender grapes.

THE SHULAMITE
16 My beloved *is* mine, and I *am* his.
   He feeds *his flock* among the lilies.

(TO HER BELOVED)
17 Until the day breaks
   And the shadows flee away,
   Turn, my beloved,
   And be like a gazelle
   Or a young stag
   Upon the mountains of Bether.

CHAPTER **3** MEMORIES OF ENGAGEMENT.

THE SHULAMITE
   By night on my bed I sought the one I love;
   I sought him, but I did not find him.
2 "I will rise now," *I said,*
   "And go about the city;
   In the streets and in the squares
   I will seek the one I love."
   I sought him, but I did not find him.
3 The watchmen who go about the city found me;
   I said,
   "Have you seen the one I love?"

4 Scarcely had I passed by them,
   When I found the one I love.
   I held him and would not let him go,
   Until I had brought him to the house of my mother,
   And into the chamber of her who conceived me.

5 I charge you, O daughters of Jerusalem,
   By the gazelles or by the does of the field,
   Do not stir up nor awaken love
   Until it pleases.

THE SHULAMITE
6 Who *is* this coming out of the wilderness
   Like pillars of smoke,
   Perfumed with myrrh and frankincense,
   With all the merchant's fragrant powders?
7 Behold, it *is* Solomon's couch,
   With sixty valiant men around it,
   Of the valiant of Israel.
8 They all hold swords,
   Being expert in war.
   Every man *has* his sword on his thigh
   Because of fear in the night.

9 Of the wood of Lebanon
   Solomon the King
   Made himself a palanquin:
10 He made its pillars *of* silver,
   Its support *of* gold,
   Its seat *of* purple,
   Its interior paved *with* love
   By the daughters of Jerusalem.
11 Go forth, O daughters of Zion,
   And see King Solomon with the crown
   With which his mother crowned him
   On the day of his wedding,
   The day of the gladness of his heart.

CHAPTER **4**

THE BELOVED
   Behold, you *are* fair, my love!
   Behold, you *are* fair!
   You *have* dove's eyes behind your veil.
   Your hair *is* like a flock of goats,
   Going down from Mount Gilead.
2 Your teeth *are* like a flock of shorn *sheep*
   Which have come up from the washing,
   Every one of which bears twins,
   And none *is* barren among them.
3 Your lips *are* like a strand of scarlet,
   And your mouth is lovely.
   Your temples behind your veil
   Are like a piece of pomegranate.
4 Your neck *is* like the tower of David,
   Built for an armory,
   On which hang a thousand bucklers,
   All shields of mighty men.
5 Your two breasts *are* like two fawns,
   Twins of a gazelle,
   Which feed among the lilies.

6 Until the day breaks
   And the shadows flee away,
   I will go my way to the mountain of myrrh
   And to the hill of frankincense.

7 You *are* all fair, my love,
   And *there is* no spot in you.
8 Come with me from Lebanon, *my* spouse,
   With me from Lebanon.
   Look from the top of Amana,
   From the top of Senir and Hermon,
   From the lions' dens,
   From the mountains of the leopards.

9 You have ravished my heart,
   My sister, *my* spouse;
   You have ravished my heart
   With one *look* of your eyes,
   With one link of your necklace.
10 How fair is your love,
   My sister, *my* spouse!
   How much better than wine is your love,
   And the scent of your perfumes
   Than all spices!
11 Your lips, O *my* spouse,
   Drip as the honeycomb;
   Honey and milk *are* under your tongue;
   And the fragrance of your garments
   Is like the fragrance of Lebanon.

12 A garden enclosed
   Is my sister, *my* spouse,

VIRGINITY

4:12 In comparing his bride to an enclosed garden, Solomon was praising her virginity. Virginity, considered old-fashioned by many people today, has always been God's plan for unmarried people—and with good reason. Sex without marriage is cheap. It cannot compare with the joy of giving yourself completely to the one who is totally committed to you.

A spring shut up,
A fountain sealed.
¹³ Your plants *are* an orchard of pomegranates
With pleasant fruits,
Fragrant henna with spikenard,
¹⁴ Spikenard and saffron,
Calamus and cinnamon,
With all trees of frankincense,
Myrrh and aloes,
With all the chief spices—
¹⁵ A fountain of gardens,
A well of living waters,
And streams from Lebanon.

THE SHULAMITE
¹⁶ Awake, O north *wind,*
And come, O south!
Blow upon my garden,
That its spices may flow out.
Let my beloved come to his garden
And eat its pleasant fruits.

CHAPTER 5 A DISTURBING DREAM.

THE BELOVED
I have come to my garden, my sister, *my* spouse;
I have gathered my myrrh with my spice;
I have eaten my honeycomb with my honey;
I have drunk my wine with my milk.

(TO HIS FRIENDS)
Eat, O friends!
Drink, yes, drink deeply,
O beloved ones!

THE SHULAMITE
² I sleep, but my heart is awake;
It is the voice of my beloved!
He knocks, *saying,*
"Open for me, my sister, my love,
My dove, my perfect one;
For my head is covered with dew,
My locks with the drops of the night."

³ I have taken off my robe;
How can I put it on *again?*
I have washed my feet;
How can I defile them?
⁴ My beloved put his hand
By the latch *of the door,*
And my heart yearned for him.
⁵ I arose to open for my beloved,
And my hands dripped *with* myrrh,
My fingers with liquid myrrh,
On the handles of the lock.

⁶ I opened for my beloved,
But my beloved had turned away *and* was gone.
My heart leaped up when he spoke.
I sought him, but I could not find him;
I called him, but he gave me no answer.
⁷ The watchmen who went about the city found me.
They struck me, they wounded me;
The keepers of the walls

I AM
My Beloved's
A N D
My Beloved
IS **M**INE.

Took my veil away from me.
⁸ I charge you, O daughters of Jerusalem,
If you find my beloved,
That you tell him I *am* lovesick!

THE DAUGHTERS OF JERUSALEM
⁹ What *is* your beloved
More than *another* beloved,
O fairest among women?
What *is* your beloved
More than *another* beloved,
That you so charge us?

THE SHULAMITE
¹⁰ My beloved *is* white and ruddy,
Chief among ten thousand.
¹¹ His head *is like* the finest gold;
His locks *are* wavy,
And black as a raven.
¹² His eyes *are* like doves
By the rivers of waters,
Washed with milk,
And fitly set.
¹³ His cheeks *are* like a bed of spices,
Banks of scented herbs.
His lips *are* lilies,
Dripping liquid myrrh.

¹⁴ His hands *are* rods of gold
Set with beryl.
His body *is* carved ivory
Inlaid *with* sapphires.
¹⁵ His legs *are* pillars of marble
Set on bases of fine gold.
His countenance *is* like Lebanon,
Excellent as the cedars.
¹⁶ His mouth *is* most sweet,
Yes, he *is* altogether lovely.
This *is* my beloved,
And this *is* my friend,
O daughters of Jerusalem!

CHAPTER 6 WOW! WHAT A BEAUTIFUL BRIDE.

THE DAUGHTERS OF JERUSALEM
Where has your beloved gone,
O fairest among women?
Where has your beloved turned aside,
That we may seek him with you?

THE SHULAMITE

2 My beloved has gone to his garden,
To the beds of spices,
To feed *his flock* in the gardens,
And to gather lilies.

3 I *am* my beloved's,
And my beloved *is* mine.
He feeds *his flock* among the lilies.

THE BELOVED

4 O my love, you *are as* beautiful as Tirzah,
Lovely as Jerusalem,
Awesome as *an army* with banners!

5 Turn your eyes away from me,
For they have overcome me.
Your hair *is* like a flock of goats
Going down from Gilead.

6 Your teeth *are* like a flock of sheep
Which have come up from the washing;
Every one bears twins,
And none *is* barren among them.

7 Like a piece of pomegranate
Are your temples behind your veil.

8 There are sixty queens
And eighty concubines,
And virgins without number.

9 My dove, my perfect one,
Is the only one,
The only one of her mother,
The favorite of the one who bore her.
The daughters saw her
And called her blessed,
The queens and the concubines,
And they praised her.

10 Who is she who looks forth as the morning,
Fair as the moon,
Clear as the sun,
Awesome as *an army* with banners?

THE SHULAMITE

11 I went down to the garden of nuts
To see the verdure of the valley,
To see whether the vine had budded
And the pomegranates had bloomed.

12 Before I was even aware,
My soul had made me
As the chariots of my noble people.

THE BELOVED AND HIS FRIENDS

13 Return, return, O Shulamite;
Return, return, that we may look upon you!

THE SHULAMITE

What would you see in the Shulamite—
As it were, the dance of the two camps?

CHAPTER 7 THE BRIDE TELLS OF HER LOVE.

THE BELOVED

How beautiful are your feet in sandals,
O prince's daughter!
The curves of your thighs *are* like jewels,

The work of the hands of a skillful workman.

2 Your navel *is* a rounded goblet;
It lacks no blended beverage.
Your waist *is* a heap of wheat
Set about with lilies.

3 Your two breasts *are* like two fawns,
Twins of a gazelle.

4 Your neck *is* like an ivory tower,
Your eyes *like* the pools in Heshbon
By the gate of Bath Rabbim.
Your nose *is* like the tower of Lebanon
Which looks toward Damascus.

5 Your head *crowns* you like *Mount* Carmel,
And the hair of your head *is* like purple;
A king *is* held captive by *your* tresses.

6 How fair and how pleasant you are,
O love, with your delights!

7 This stature of yours is like a palm tree,
And your breasts *like* its clusters.

8 I said, "I will go up to the palm tree,
I will take hold of its branches."
Let now your breasts be like clusters of the vine,
The fragrance of your breath like apples,

9 And the roof of your mouth like the best wine.

THE SHULAMITE

The wine goes *down* smoothly for my beloved,
Moving gently the lips of sleepers.

10 I *am* my beloved's,
And his desire *is* toward me.

11 Come, my beloved,
Let us go forth to the field;
Let us lodge in the villages.

12 Let us get up early to the vineyards;
Let us see if the vine has budded,
Whether the grape blossoms are open,
And the pomegranates are in bloom.
There I will give you my love.

13 The mandrakes give off a fragrance,
And at our gates *are* pleasant *fruits*,
All manner, new and old,
Which I have laid up for you, my beloved.

CHAPTER 8 THE POWER OF LOVE.

Oh, that you were like my brother,
Who nursed at my mother's breasts!
If I should find you outside,
I would kiss you;
I would not be despised.

◣▬▬▬▬▬◗ MORE LOVE

7:1-13 As a marriage matures, there should be more love and freedom between marriage partners. It is good and healthy for a married couple to enjoy and appreciate each other's body. When marriage partners are secure in their love and relationship, they find the freedom to initiate and enjoy acts of love. As you grow in your relationships to the opposite sex, remember that God knows what he is doing where love and sex are concerned. Don't accept anything less than the kind of love he wants for you: the secure, freeing, wonderful love that you will find only in marriage.

PRICELESS

8:6-7 In this final description of their love, the girl includes some of its significant characteristics (see also 1 Corinthians 13). Love is as strong as death; it cannot be killed by time or disaster; and it cannot be bought for any price because it is freely given. Love is priceless, and even the richest king cannot buy it. It must be accepted as a gift from God and then shared within the guidelines God provides.

2 I would lead you *and* bring you
Into the house of my mother,
She *who* used to instruct me.
I would cause you to drink of spiced wine,
Of the juice of my pomegranate.

(TO THE DAUGHTERS OF JERUSALEM)
3 His left hand *is* under my head,
And his right hand embraces me.
4 I charge you, O daughters of Jerusalem,
Do not stir up nor awaken love
Until it pleases.

A RELATIVE
5 Who *is* this coming up from the wilderness,
Leaning upon her beloved?

I awakened you under the apple tree.
There your mother brought you forth;
There she *who* bore you brought *you* forth.

THE SHULAMITE TO HER BELOVED
6 Set me as a seal upon your heart,
As a seal upon your arm;
For love *is as* strong as death,
Jealousy *as* cruel as the grave;
Its flames *are* flames of fire,
A most vehement flame.

7 Many waters cannot quench love,
Nor can the floods drown it.
If a man would give for love

All the wealth of his house,
It would be utterly despised.

THE SHULAMITE'S BROTHERS
8 We have a little sister,
And she has no breasts.
What shall we do for our sister
In the day when she is spoken for?
9 If she *is* a wall,
We will build upon her
A battlement of silver;
And if she *is* a door,
We will enclose her
With boards of cedar.

THE SHULAMITE
10 I *am* a wall,
And my breasts like towers;
Then I became in his eyes
As one who found peace.
11 Solomon had a vineyard at Baal Hamon;
He leased the vineyard to keepers;
Everyone was to bring for its fruit
A thousand silver coins.

(TO SOLOMON)
12 My own vineyard *is* before me.
You, O Solomon, *may have* a thousand,
And those who tend its fruit two hundred.

THE BELOVED
13 You who dwell in the gardens,
The companions listen for your voice—
Let me hear it!

THE SHULAMITE
14 Make haste, my beloved,
And be like a gazelle
Or a young stag
On the mountains of spices.

MEGA Themes

LOVE As the beauty and wonder of romance unfolded between Solomon and his bride, the intense power of love affected the two lovers' hearts, minds, and bodies.

Love is a powerful expression of feeling and commitment between two people; it is not to be regarded casually. We should not try to manipulate others into loving us, and love should not be pushed in a relationship.

1. The love in Song of Solomon is a very intense human love. List several words that could be used to describe this love.

2. When you think of marriage, what qualities do you want to be present in the love you will share with your spouse? Describe the qualities you want your spouse to have as an individual.

3. Explain God's role in the love between a man and a woman.
4. What implications does this study have for dating?
5. What impact does this study have on the way you view marriage? How could you apply this in the future?

SEX Sex is God's gift to his creatures. God endorses sex, but because sex is given as an ultimate gift for life, God says its expression should be limited to those who are committed to each other in marriage.

God wants sex to be motivated by love and commitment, not lust. God is glorified by sex within a godly marriage—sex that is for mutual pleasure, not selfish enjoyment.

1. What is different about Song of Solomon's description of sex and sexual desire and the way sex is presented on TV and in the movies?
2. How does Solomon feel about his bride? How does she feel about him?
3. Is the primary attraction between the couple in this book a physical attraction? Explain.
4. What do you learn about God's design of sexuality for you in reading the Song of Solomon? List several principles that can serve as your guidelines for sexual decision making.

COMMITMENT The power of love requires more than feelings to protect it. Sexual expression is such an integral part of our selfhood that we need the boundary of marriage to safeguard our love. Marriage is the celebration of daily commitment to each other.

Romance keeps a marriage interesting, and commitment keeps romance from dwindling away. The decision to commit yourself to your spouse alone *begins* at the marriage altar. It must be maintained day by day. In a world filled with divorce and brokenness, God calls us to learn to live according to commitment.

1. What words in Song of Solomon represent commitment?
2. Would this commitment best be described as a one-time commitment, a daily commitment, neither, or a combination of both? Explain.
3. What impact does a marriage with strong commitment have on the children in that family? What impact does weak commitment have on them?
4. List the things that strengthen commitment in a marriage. List the things that weaken commitment.

5. How can you make choices now, in friendship and dating, that will prepare you for a future marriage with a strong commitment? What role does God play in that preparation?

BEAUTY The two lovers praise the beauty they see in each other. The language they use shows the spontaneity and mystery of love. Our praise should not be limited to physical beauty. Beautiful personality and moral purity also should be praised.

The love one feels for a husband or wife reveals that person's inner beauty, and those inner qualities keep love alive. Don't look for just physical attractiveness in a spouse. Look for the qualities that don't fade with time—spiritual commitment, integrity, sensitivity, and sincerity. Character lasts much longer than good looks.

1. When you think of beauty, what comes to your mind first?
2. Describe the difference between a person's physical beauty and a person's inner beauty.
3. Give an example of a person you know who has true inner beauty. What makes this person so beautiful?
4. If you were looking for a husband or wife, what inner qualities would you most want him or her to have? Why are these important to you?
5. What inner qualities do you want to bring to a marriage someday? In what ways can you deepen those qualities in your present relationships?

PROBLEMS Over time, feelings of loneliness, indifference, and isolation came between Solomon and his bride. During those times, love grew cold and barriers arose.

Through careful communication, lovers can be reconciled, commitment can be renewed, and romance can be refreshed. Don't let walls come between you two. Take care of problems while they are still small.

1. Why do all human relationships include conflict?
2. What principles do you find in Song of Solomon that can be applied to working through difficult problems in relationships?
3. Where are your areas of interpersonal conflict? What are you doing in response to the problems you are facing now?
4. What can you do to apply the principles of Song of Solomon to the conflicts you are facing in relationships now?

Slowly, on shaky legs, Matt walked to the front of the room, the fluttering in his stomach growing with every step. As he turned to face the class he was sure everyone could hear the relentless pounding of his heart. Wiping his sweat-moistened palms on his pants, he pulled out his note cards and began to speak. ■ Stage fright. We know it all too well. According to many studies, the greatest fear most people have is doing what Matt did . . . giving a speech. You're in front of everyone, exposed and vulnerable—and the pressure can be incredible. ■ Now, if you think that's tough, imagine being a prophet. Not only would you have to speak in public, but usually the messages you would have to give would *not* be what people want to hear. As a prophet, you would have to speak of sin, judgment, and changes that had to be made. And often you would have to confront kings, men who could pronounce the death sentence on a whim. Sometimes, to really make a point, you would have to act out your messages. That wouldn't be too much fun either, but true prophets spoke out for God, regardless of how they felt. ■ Isaiah was one of the greatest prophets who ever lived, and the book of Isaiah contains his messages. In this book, you'll see Isaiah in action as he stays close to God and speaks to the people. That takes courage! As you read, listen to God's word for you, and determine to be a person of courage, too, faithfully taking God's message wherever he sends you.

STATS

PURPOSE: To call the nation of Judah back to God and to tell of God's salvation through the Messiah

AUTHOR: The prophet Isaiah, son of Amoz

DATE WRITTEN: The events of chapters 1–39 occurred during Isaiah's ministry, so they were probably written about 700 B.C. Chapters 40–66, however, may have been written near the end of his life, about 681 B.C.

SETTING: Isaiah is speaking and writing mainly in Jerusalem

KEY PEOPLE: Isaiah, his two sons Shear-Jashub and Maher-Shalal-Hash-Baz

SPECIAL FEATURES: The book of Isaiah contains both prose and poetry and uses personification (attributing personal qualities to divine beings or inanimate objects). Also, many of the prophecies in Isaiah contain predictions that foretell both a soon-to-occur event and a distant, future event at the same time.

Isaiah

CHAPTER 1 GOD'S MESSAGE TO HIS PEOPLE. The vision of Isaiah the son of Amoz, which he saw concerning Judah and Jerusalem in the days of Uzziah, Jotham, Ahaz, *and* Hezekiah, kings of Judah.

2 Hear, O heavens, and give ear, O earth!
    For the LORD has spoken:
    "I have nourished and brought up children,
    And they have rebelled against Me;
3 The ox knows its owner
    And the donkey its master's crib;
    But Israel does not know,
    My people do not consider."

4 Alas, sinful nation,
    A people laden with iniquity,
    A brood of evildoers,
    Children who are corrupters!
    They have forsaken the LORD,
    They have provoked to anger
    The Holy One of Israel,
    They have turned away backward.

5 Why should you be stricken again?
    You will revolt more and more.

The whole head is sick,
    And the whole heart faints.
6 From the sole of the foot even to the head,
    There is no soundness in it,
    But wounds and bruises and putrefying sores;
    They have not been closed or bound up,
    Or soothed with ointment.

7 Your country *is* desolate,
    Your cities *are* burned with fire;
    Strangers devour your land in your presence;
    And *it is* desolate, as overthrown by strangers.
8 So the daughter of Zion is left as a booth in a
        vineyard,
    As a hut in a garden of cucumbers,
    As a besieged city.
9 Unless the LORD of hosts
    Had left to us a very small remnant,
    We would have become like Sodom,
    We would have been made like Gomorrah.

10 Hear the word of the LORD,
    You rulers of Sodom;
    Give ear to the law of our God,
    You people of Gomorrah:
11 "To what purpose *is* the multitude of your sacrifices
        to Me?"

CUT OFF

1:4-9 As long as the people of Judah continued to sin, they cut themselves off from God's help. Has sin ever made you feel lonely and separated from God? Remember, God does not abandon you—it is your sin that cuts you off from him. The only sure cure for this kind of loneliness is to restore a meaningful relationship with God by confessing your sin, obeying his instructions, and communicating regularly with him (see Psalm 140:13; Isaiah 1:16-19; 1 John 1:9).

Says the LORD.
    "I have had enough of burnt offerings of rams
    And the fat of fed cattle.
    I do not delight in the blood of bulls,
    Or of lambs or goats.
12 "When you come to appear before Me,
    Who has required this from your hand,
    To trample My courts?
13 Bring no more futile sacrifices;

Incense is an abomination to Me.
The New Moons, the Sabbaths, and the calling of
    assemblies—
I cannot endure iniquity and the sacred meeting.
¹⁴ Your New Moons and your appointed feasts
My soul hates;
They are a trouble to Me,
I am weary of bearing *them*.
¹⁵ When you spread out your hands,
I will hide My eyes from you;
Even though you make many prayers,
I will not hear.
Your hands are full of blood.

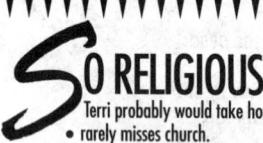

So RELIGIOUS

If there were a contest for being religious, Terri probably would take home first prize. Just look: She:
- rarely misses church.
- sings in the choir. (And sometimes even does solos!)
- is an officer in her youth group.
- puts 10 percent of all she earns in the offering plate.
- reads two chapters in her Bible every night.
- says a blessing before every meal she eats.

Yes, you would assume that Terri is a deeply spiritual person. Anyone involved in all those religious activities must be a great Christian, right?

Well, look again. If Terri is so close to God, then why does she use the language she uses? And why does she rip her classmates to shreds the way she does? And how come she's so mean to her little brothers and to her grandmother?

If Terri's so together spiritually, why does she talk back to her parents almost every day? If she is such an example of a mature child of God, why does she go to some of the parties she goes to? (And how in the world does she justify doing what she does at those parties?)

"Religious" people can brag about their religious activities all they want—God isn't impressed. In fact, he says that when our life is full of sin, our religious activities aren't worth a hill of beans. To please him, our life must be consistent in every way. See Isaiah 1:10-17.

¹⁶ "Wash yourselves, make yourselves clean;
Put away the evil of your doings from before My eyes.
Cease to do evil,
¹⁷ Learn to do good;
Seek justice,
Rebuke the oppressor;
Defend the fatherless,
Plead for the widow.
¹⁸ "Come now, and let us reason together,"
Says the LORD,
"Though your sins are like scarlet,
They shall be as white as snow;
Though they are red like crimson,
They shall be as wool.
¹⁹ If you are willing and obedient,
You shall eat the good of the land;
²⁰ But if you refuse and rebel,
You shall be devoured by the sword";
For the mouth of the LORD has spoken.

▬STAINS

1:18 A deep stain is virtually impossible to remove from clothing; stain of sin seems equally permanent. But God can remove the stai of sin from our lives just as he promised to do for the Israelites. We do have to go through life permanently soiled. Through prayer we can assured that Christ has forgiven our worst sins and removed our mo indelible stains (Psalm 51:1-7).

²¹ How the faithful city has become a harlot!
It was full of justice;
Righteousness lodged in it,
But now murderers.
²² Your silver has become dross,
Your wine mixed with water.
²³ Your princes *are* rebellious,
And companions of thieves;
Everyone loves bribes,
And follows after rewards.
They do not defend the fatherless,
Nor does the cause of the widow come before them.
²⁴ Therefore the Lord says,
The LORD of hosts, the Mighty One of Israel,
"Ah, I will rid Myself of My adversaries,
And take vengeance on My enemies.
²⁵ I will turn My hand against you,
And thoroughly purge away your dross,
And take away all your alloy.
²⁶ I will restore your judges as at the first,
And your counselors as at the beginning.
Afterward you shall be called the city of
    righteousness, the faithful city."
²⁷ Zion shall be redeemed with justice,
And her penitents with righteousness.
²⁸ The destruction of transgressors and of sinners *shall
be* together,
And those who forsake the LORD shall be consumed.
²⁹ For they shall be ashamed of the terebinth trees
Which you have desired;
And you shall be embarrassed because of the
    gardens
Which you have chosen.
³⁰ For you shall be as a terebinth whose leaf fades,
And as a garden that has no water.
³¹ The strong shall be as tinder,
And the work of it as a spark;
Both will burn together,
And no one shall quench *them*.

CHAPTER 2 WALK IN GOD'S LIGHT.

The word that Isaiah the son of Amoz saw concerning Judah and Jerusalem.

² Now it shall come to pass in the latter days
That the mountain of the LORD's house
Shall be established on the top of the mountains,
And shall be exalted above the hills;
And all nations shall flow to it.
³ Many people shall come and say,
"Come, and let us go up to the mountain of the LORD,
To the house of the God of Jacob;
He will teach us His ways,
And we shall walk in His paths."

For out of Zion shall go forth the law,
And the word of the LORD from Jerusalem.
⁴ He shall judge between the nations,
And rebuke many people;
They shall beat their swords into plowshares,
And their spears into pruning hooks;
Nation shall not lift up sword against nation,
Neither shall they learn war anymore.

⁵ O house of Jacob, come and let us walk
In the light of the LORD.

⁶ For You have forsaken Your people, the house of
Jacob,
Because they are filled with eastern ways;
They *are* soothsayers like the Philistines,
And they are pleased with the children of foreigners.
⁷ Their land is also full of silver and gold,
And there is no end to their treasures;
Their land is also full of horses,
And there is no end to their chariots.
⁸ Their land is also full of idols;
They worship the work of their own hands,
That which their own fingers have made.
⁹ People bow down,
And each man humbles himself;
Therefore do not forgive them.

¹⁰ Enter into the rock, and hide in the dust,
From the terror of the LORD
And the glory of His majesty.
¹¹ The lofty looks of man shall be humbled,
The haughtiness of men shall be bowed down,
And the LORD alone shall be exalted in that day.

¹² For the day of the LORD of hosts

Shall come upon everything proud and lofty,
Upon everything lifted up—
And it shall be brought low—
¹³ Upon all the cedars of Lebanon *that are* high and
lifted up,

◗RELIABLE

2:22 People are "nothing" compared to God. They are undependable, sinful, and mortal. Often we trust human beings with our life and our future instead of trusting the all-knowing God. Beware of people who want you to trust them instead of God. Remember that only God is completely reliable, because only God loves us with an eternal love (Psalm 100:5).

And upon all the oaks of Bashan;
¹⁴ Upon all the high mountains,
And upon all the hills *that are* lifted up;
¹⁵ Upon every high tower,
And upon every fortified wall;
¹⁶ Upon all the ships of Tarshish,
And upon all the beautiful sloops.
¹⁷ The loftiness of man shall be bowed down,
And the haughtiness of men shall be brought low;
The LORD alone will be exalted in that day,
¹⁸ But the idols He shall utterly abolish.

¹⁹ They shall go into the holes of the rocks,
And into the caves of the earth,
From the terror of the LORD
And the glory of His majesty,
When He arises to shake the earth mightily.

²⁰ In that day a man will cast away his idols of silver
And his idols of gold,
Which they made, *each* for himself to worship,

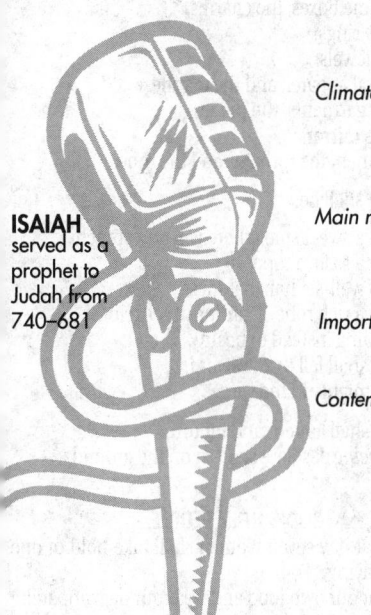

ISAIAH
served as a
prophet to
Judah from
740–681

Climate of the times	Society was in a great upheaval. Under King Ahaz and King Manasseh the people reverted to idolatry, and there was even child sacrifice.
Main message	Although judgment from other nations was inevitable, the people could still have a special relationship with God.
Importance of message	Sometimes we must suffer judgment and discipline before we are restored to God.
Contemporary prophets	Hosea (753–715) Micah (742–687)

To the moles and bats,
21 To go into the clefts of the rocks,
And into the crags of the rugged rocks,
From the terror of the LORD
And the glory of His majesty,
When He arises to shake the earth mightily.

22 Sever yourselves from such a man,
Whose breath *is* in his nostrils;
For of what account is he?

CHAPTER 3 A WELL-EARNED PUNISHMENT.

For behold, the Lord, the LORD of hosts,
Takes away from Jerusalem and from Judah
The stock and the store,
The whole supply of bread and the whole supply of
water;
2 The mighty man and the man of war,
The judge and the prophet,
And the diviner and the elder;
3 The captain of fifty and the honorable man,
The counselor and the skillful artisan,
And the expert enchanter.

4 "I will give children *to be* their princes,
And babes shall rule over them.
5 The people will be oppressed,
Every one by another and every one by his neighbor;
The child will be insolent toward the elder,
And the base toward the honorable."

6 When a man takes hold of his brother
In the house of his father, *saying,*
"You have clothing;
You be our ruler,
And *let* these ruins *be* under your power,"
7 In that day he will protest, saying,
"I cannot cure *your* ills,
For in my house *is* neither food nor clothing;
Do not make me a ruler of the people."

8 For Jerusalem stumbled,
And Judah is fallen,
Because their tongue and their doings
Are against the LORD,
To provoke the eyes of His glory.
9 The look on their countenance witnesses against
them,
And they declare their sin as Sodom;
They do not hide *it.*
Woe to their soul!
For they have brought evil upon themselves.

10 "Say to the righteous that *it shall be* well *with them,*
For they shall eat the fruit of their doings.
11 Woe to the wicked! *It shall be* ill *with him,*
For the reward of his hands shall be given him.
12 *As for* My people, children *are* their oppressors,
And women rule over them.
O My people! Those who lead you cause *you* to err,
And destroy the way of your paths."

13 The LORD stands up to plead,

And stands to judge the people.
14 The LORD will enter into judgment
With the elders of His people
And His princes:
"For you have eaten up the vineyard;
The plunder of the poor *is* in your houses.
15 What do you mean by crushing My people
And grinding the faces of the poor?"
Says the Lord GOD of hosts.

16Moreover the LORD says:

"Because the daughters of Zion are haughty,
And walk with outstretched necks
And wanton eyes,
Walking and mincing *as* they go,
Making a jingling with their feet,
17 Therefore the Lord will strike with a scab
The crown of the head of the daughters of Zion,
And the LORD will uncover their secret parts."

◀▬▬▬▬▬▬▬▬ FASHION

3:16-26 The women of Judah had placed their emphasis on cloth
and jewelry rather than on God. They dressed to be noticed, to gai
approval, and to be fashionable. Instead of being concerned about
oppression around them (3:14-15), they were self-serving and
self-centered. Those who misuse their possessions will end up with
nothing. These verses are not an indictment against clothing and je
but a judgment on those who use them lavishly while blind to the r
of others. When God blesses you, don't flaunt your wealth. Use wh
have to help others.

18 In that day the Lord will take away the finery:
The jingling anklets, the scarves, and the crescents;
19 The pendants, the bracelets, and the veils;
20 The headdresses, the leg ornaments, and the
headbands;
The perfume boxes, the charms,
21 and the rings;
The nose jewels,
22 the festal apparel, and the mantles;
The outer garments, the purses,
23 and the mirrors;
The fine linen, the turbans, and the robes.

24And so it shall be:

Instead of a sweet smell there will be a stench;
Instead of a sash, a rope;
Instead of well-set hair, baldness;
Instead of a rich robe, a girding of sackcloth;
And branding instead of beauty.
25 Your men shall fall by the sword,
And your mighty in the war.

26 Her gates shall lament and mourn,
And she *being* desolate shall sit on the ground.

CHAPTER 4 GOD'S HOLY PEOPLE.

And in that day seven women shall take hold of one
man, saying,
"We will eat our own food and wear our own apparel;

Only let us be called by your name,
To take away our reproach."

2 In that day the Branch of the LORD shall be beautiful and glorious;
And the fruit of the earth *shall be* excellent and appealing
For those of Israel who have escaped.

3And it shall come to pass that *he who is* left in Zion and remains in Jerusalem will be called holy—everyone who is recorded among the living in Jerusalem. 4When the Lord has washed away the filth of the daughters of Zion, and purged the blood of Jerusalem from her midst, by the spirit of judgment and by the spirit of burning, 5then the LORD will create above every dwelling place of Mount Zion, and above her assemblies, a cloud and smoke by day and the shining of a flaming fire by night. For over all the glory there *will be* a covering. 6And there will be a tabernacle for shade in the daytime from the heat, for a place of refuge, and for a shelter from storm and rain.

CHAPTER 5 WILD GRAPES IN GOD'S GARDEN.

Now let me sing to my Well-beloved
A song of my Beloved regarding His vineyard:

My Well-beloved has a vineyard
On a very fruitful hill.
2 He dug it up and cleared out its stones,
And planted it with the choicest vine.
He built a tower in its midst,
And also made a winepress in it;
So He expected *it* to bring forth *good* grapes,
But it brought forth wild grapes.

3 "And now, O inhabitants of Jerusalem and men of Judah,
Judge, please, between Me and My vineyard.
4 What more could have been done to My vineyard
That I have not done in it?
Why then, when I expected *it* to bring forth *good* grapes,
Did it bring forth wild grapes?
5 And now, please let Me tell you what I will do to My vineyard:
I will take away its hedge, and it shall be burned;
And break down its wall, and it shall be trampled down.
6 I will lay it waste;
It shall not be pruned or dug,
But there shall come up briers and thorns.
I will also command the clouds
That they rain no rain on it."

7 For the vineyard of the LORD of hosts *is* the house of Israel,
And the men of Judah are His pleasant plant.
He looked for justice, but behold, oppression;
For righteousness, but behold, a cry *for help*.

8 Woe to those who join house to house;
They add field to field,

Till *there is* no place
Where they may dwell alone in the midst of the land!
9 In my hearing the LORD of hosts *said*,
"Truly, many houses shall be desolate,
Great and beautiful ones, without inhabitant.
10 For ten acres of vineyard shall yield one bath,
And a homer of seed shall yield one ephah."

11 Woe to those who rise early in the morning,
That they may follow intoxicating drink;
Who continue until night, *till* wine inflames them!
12 The harp and the strings,
The tambourine and flute,
And wine are in their feasts;
But they do not regard the work of the LORD,
Nor consider the operation of His hands.

◥◥◥ HEROES

5:13 The nation's heroes—the great and honored men—would suffer the same humiliation as the common people. Why? Because they lived by their own values rather than God's. Many of today's heroes in TV, movies, and books are idolized because of their ability to live as they please. Are your heroes those who defy God, or those who defy the world in order to serve God?

13 Therefore my people have gone into captivity,
Because *they have* no knowledge;
Their honorable men *are* famished,
And their multitude dried up with thirst.
14 Therefore Sheol has enlarged itself
And opened its mouth beyond measure;
Their glory and their multitude and their pomp,
And he who is jubilant, shall descend into it.
15 People shall be brought down,
Each man shall be humbled,
And the eyes of the lofty shall be humbled.
16 But the LORD of hosts shall be exalted in judgment,
And God who is holy shall be hallowed in righteousness.
17 Then the lambs shall feed in their pasture,
And in the waste places of the fat ones strangers shall eat.

18 Woe to those who draw iniquity with cords of vanity,
And sin as if with a cart rope;
19 That say, "Let Him make speed *and* hasten His work,
That we may see *it;*
And let the counsel of the Holy One of Israel draw near and come,
That we may know *it.*"

20 Woe to those who call evil good, and good evil;
Who put darkness for light, and light for darkness;
Who put bitter for sweet, and sweet for bitter!

21 Woe to *those who are* wise in their own eyes,
And prudent in their own sight!

22 Woe to men mighty at drinking wine,
Woe to men valiant for mixing intoxicating drink,
23 Who justify the wicked for a bribe,
And take away justice from the righteous man!

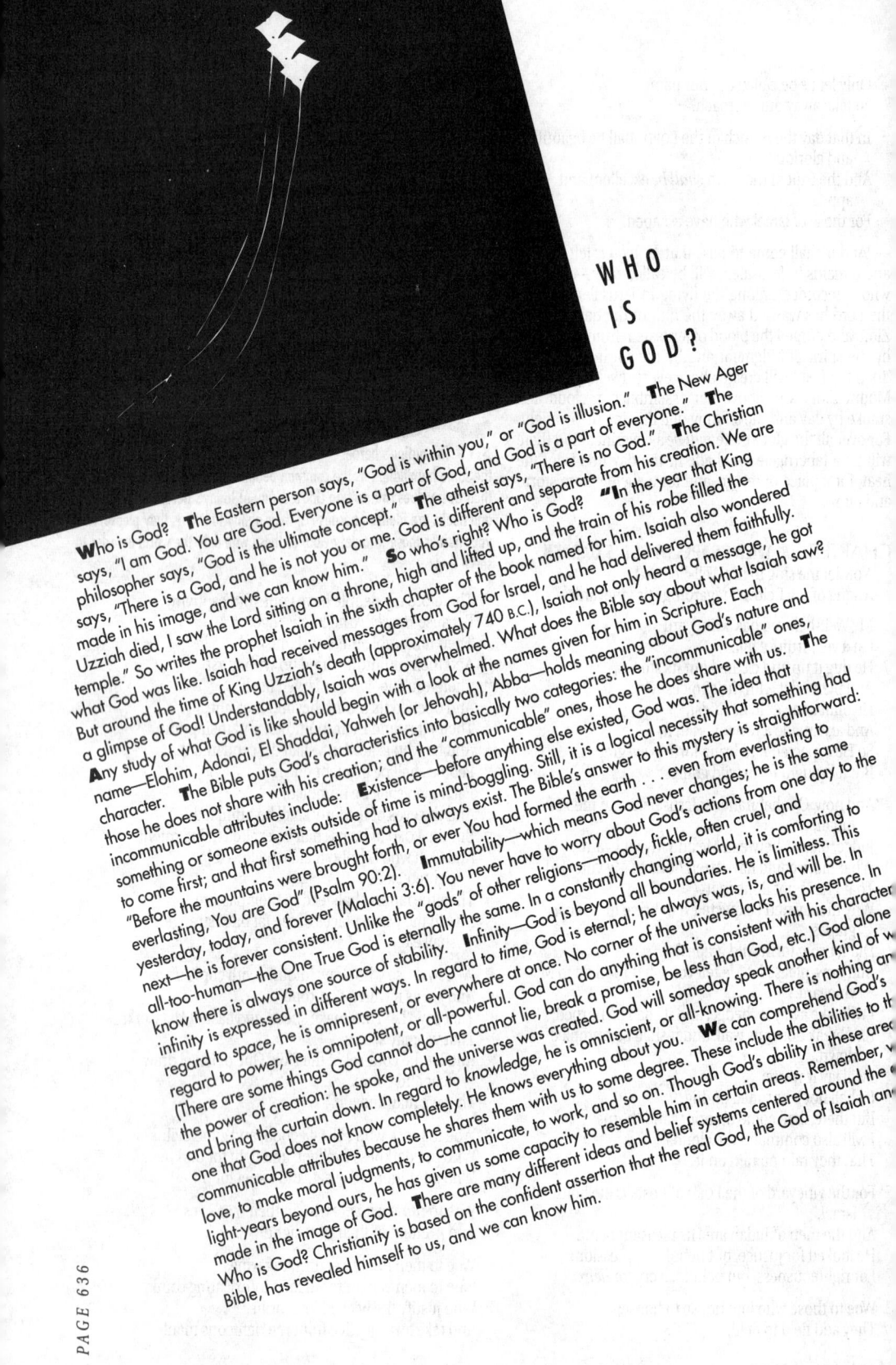

WHO IS GOD?

Who is God? **T**he Eastern person says, "God is within you," or "God is illusion." **T**he New Ager says, "I am God. You are God. Everyone is a part of God, and God is a part of everyone." **T**he philosopher says, "God is the ultimate concept." **T**he atheist says, "There is no God." **T**he Christian says, "There is a God, and he is not you or me. God is different and separate from his creation. We are made in his image, and we can know him." **S**o who's right? Who is God? **"I**n the year that King Uzziah died, I saw the Lord sitting on a throne, high and lifted up, and the train of his robe filled the temple." So writes the prophet Isaiah in the sixth chapter of the book named for him. Isaiah also wondered what God was like. Isaiah had received messages from God for Israel, and he had delivered them faithfully. But around the time of King Uzziah's death (approximately 740 B.C.), Isaiah not only heard a message, he got a glimpse of God! Understandably, Isaiah was overwhelmed. What does the Bible say about what Isaiah saw?

Any study of what God is like should begin with a look at the names given for him in Scripture. Each name—Elohim, Adonai, Yahweh (or Jehovah), Abba—holds meaning about God's nature and character. **T**he Bible puts God's characteristics into basically two categories: the "incommunicable" ones, those he does not share with his creation; and the "communicable" ones, those he does share with us. **T**he incommunicable attributes include: **E**xistence—before anything else existed, God was. The idea that something or someone exists outside of time is mind-boggling. Still, it is a logical necessity that something had to come first; and that first something had to always exist. The Bible's answer to this mystery is straightforward: "Before the mountains were brought forth, or ever You had formed the earth . . . even from everlasting to everlasting, You are God" (Psalm 90:2). **I**mmutability—which means God never changes; he is the same yesterday, today, and forever consistent. Unlike the "gods" of other religions—moody, fickle, often cruel, and all-too-human—the One True God is eternally the same. In a constantly changing world, it is comforting to know there is always one source of stability. **I**nfinity—God is eternal; he always was, is, and will be. He is limitless. This infinity is expressed in different ways. In regard to space, he is beyond all boundaries. No corner of the universe lacks his presence. In regard to power, he is omnipotent, or all-powerful. God can do anything that is consistent with his character (There are some things God cannot do—he cannot lie, break a promise, be less than God, etc.) God alone has the power of creation: he spoke, and the universe was created. God will someday speak another kind of word and bring the curtain down. In regard to knowledge, he is omniscient, or all-knowing. There is nothing an one that God does not know completely. He knows everything about you. **W**e can comprehend God's communicable attributes because he shares them with us to some degree. These include the abilities to th love, to make moral judgments, to communicate, to work, and so on. Though God's ability in these area light-years beyond ours, he has given us some capacity to resemble him in certain areas. Remember, v made in the image of God. **T**here are many different ideas and belief systems centered around the Who is God? Christianity is based on the confident assertion that the real God, the God of Isaiah an Bible, has revealed himself to us, and we can know him.

²⁴ Therefore, as the fire devours the stubble,
And the flame consumes the chaff,
So their root will be as rottenness,
And their blossom will ascend like dust;
Because they have rejected the law of the LORD of
hosts,
And despised the word of the Holy One of Israel.
²⁵ Therefore the anger of the LORD is aroused against
His people;
He has stretched out His hand against them
And stricken them,
And the hills trembled.
Their carcasses *were* as refuse in the midst of the
streets.

For all this His anger is not turned away,
But His hand *is* stretched out still.

²⁶ He will lift up a banner to the nations from afar,
And will whistle to them from the end of the earth;
Surely they shall come with speed, swiftly.
²⁷ No one will be weary or stumble among them,
No one will slumber or sleep;
Nor will the belt on their loins be loosed,
Nor the strap of their sandals be broken;
²⁸ Whose arrows *are* sharp,
And all their bows bent;
Their horses' hooves will seem like flint,
And their wheels like a whirlwind.
²⁹ Their roaring *will be* like a lion,
They will roar like young lions;
Yes, they will roar
And lay hold of the prey;
They will carry *it* away safely,
And no one will deliver.
³⁰ In that day they will roar against them
Like the roaring of the sea.
And if *one* looks to the land,
Behold, darkness *and* sorrow;
And the light is darkened by the clouds.

CHAPTER 6 GOD CALLS ISAIAH.

In the year that King Uzziah died, I saw the Lord sitting on a throne, high and lifted up, and the train of His *robe* filled the temple. ²Above it stood seraphim; each one had six wings: with two he covered his face, with two he covered his feet, and with two he flew. ³And one cried to another and said:

"Holy, holy, holy *is* the LORD of hosts;
The whole earth *is* full of His glory!"

⁴And the posts of the door were shaken by the voice of him who cried out, and the house was filled with smoke. ⁵So I said:

"Woe *is* me, for I am undone!
Because I *am* a man of unclean lips,
And I dwell in the midst of a people of unclean lips;
For my eyes have seen the King,
The LORD of hosts."

⁶Then one of the seraphim flew to me, having in his hand a live coal *which* he had taken with the tongs from the altar. ⁷And he touched my mouth *with it*, and said:

"Behold, this has touched your lips;
Your iniquity is taken away,
And your sin purged."

⁸Also I heard the voice of the Lord, saying:

"Whom shall I send,
And who will go for Us?"

Then I said, "Here *am* I! Send me."
⁹And He said, "Go, and tell this people:

'Keep on hearing, but do not understand;
Keep on seeing, but do not perceive.'

¹⁰ "Make the heart of this people dull,
And their ears heavy,
And shut their eyes;
Lest they see with their eyes,
And hear with their ears,
And understand with their heart,
And return and be healed."

¹¹Then I said, "Lord, how long?"
And He answered:

"Until the cities are laid waste and without inhabitant,
The houses are without a man,
The land is utterly desolate,
¹² The LORD has removed men far away,
And the forsaken places *are* many in the midst of the
land.
¹³ But yet a tenth *will be* in it,
And will return and be for consuming,
As a terebinth tree or as an oak,
Whose stump *remains* when it is cut down.
So the holy seed *shall be* its stump."

CHAPTER 7 IMMANUEL—GOD IS WITH US.

Now it came to pass in the days of Ahaz the son of Jotham, the son of Uzziah, king of Judah, *that* Rezin king of Syria and Pekah the son of Remaliah, king of Israel, went up to Jerusalem to *make* war against it, but could not prevail against it. ²And it was told to the house of David, saying, "Syria's forces are deployed in Ephraim." So his heart and the heart of his people were moved as the trees of the woods are moved with the wind.

³Then the LORD said to Isaiah, "Go out now to meet Ahaz, you and Shear-Jashub your son, at the end of the aqueduct from the upper pool, on the highway to the Fuller's Field, ⁴and say to him: 'Take heed, and be quiet; do not fear or be fainthearted for these two stubs of smoking firebrands, for the fierce anger of Rezin and

GREATNESS

6:1ff Isaiah's lofty view of God in 6:1-4 gives us a sense of God's greatness, mystery, and power. Isaiah's recognition of his sinfulness before God encourages us to confess our sin. His picture of forgiveness reminds us that we, too, are forgiven. When we recognize how great our God is, how sinful we are, and the extent of his forgiveness, we will be energized to do his work. How does your concept of the greatness of God measure up to Isaiah's?

NAMES FOR MESSIAH

Isaiah uses five names to describe the Messiah. These names have special meaning to us.

WONDERFUL
He is exceptional, distinguished, and without peers.

COUNSELOR
He gives the right advice.

THE MIGHTY GOD
He is God himself

Syria, and the son of Remaliah. ⁵Because Syria, Ephraim, and the son of Remaliah have plotted evil against you, saying, ⁶"Let us go up against Judah and trouble it, and let us make a gap in its wall for ourselves, and set a king over them, the son of Tabel"— ⁷thus says the Lord GOD:

"It shall not stand,
Nor shall it come to pass.
⁸ For the head of Syria *is* Damascus,
And the head of Damascus *is* Rezin.
Within sixty-five years Ephraim will be broken,
So that it will not *be* a people.
⁹ The head of Ephraim *is* Samaria,
And the head of Samaria *is* Remaliah's son.
If you will not believe,
Surely you shall not be established." ' "

¹⁰Moreover the LORD spoke again to Ahaz, saying, ¹¹"Ask a sign for yourself from the LORD your God; ask it either in the depth or in the height above."

¹²But Ahaz said, "I will not ask, nor will I test the LORD!"

¹³Then he said, "Hear now, O house of David! *Is it* a small thing for you to weary men, but will you weary my God also? ¹⁴Therefore the Lord Himself will give you a sign: Behold, the virgin shall conceive and bear a Son, and shall call His name Immanuel. ¹⁵Curds and honey He shall eat, that He may know to refuse the evil and choose

CHOICES

8:6,14-15 Because the people of Judah rejected God's gentle care, choosing instead to seek help from other nations, God would punish them. Here we see two distinct attributes of God—his love and his wrath. Ignoring God's love and guidance results in sin and invites his wrath. We must recognize the consequences of our choices. God seeks to protect us from bad choices, but he still gives us the freedom to make them.

the good. ¹⁶For before the Child shall know to refuse the evil and choose the good, the land that you dread will be forsaken by both her kings. ¹⁷The LORD will bring the king of Assyria upon you and your people and your father's house—days that have not come since the day that Ephraim departed from Judah."

¹⁸ And it shall come to pass in that day
That the LORD will whistle for the fly
That *is* in the farthest part of the rivers of Egypt,
And for the bee that *is* in the land of Assyria.
¹⁹ They will come, and all of them will rest
In the desolate valleys and in the clefts of the rocks,
And on all thorns and in all pastures.

²⁰ In the same day the Lord will shave with a hired razor,
With those from beyond the River, with the king of Assyria,
The head and the hair of the legs,
And will also remove the beard.

²¹ It shall be in that day
That a man will keep alive a young cow and two sheep;
²² So it shall be, from the abundance of milk they give,
That he will eat curds;
For curds and honey everyone will eat who is left in the land.

²³ It shall happen in that day,
That wherever there could be a thousand vines
Worth a thousand *shekels* of silver,
It will be for briers and thorns.
²⁴ With arrows and bows men will come there,
Because all the land will become briers and thorns.
²⁵ And to any hill which could be dug with the hoe,
You will not go there for fear of briers and thorns;
But it will become a range for oxen
And a place for sheep to roam.

CHAPTER 8 ISAIAH PREDICTS AN INVASION.

Moreover the LORD said to me, "Take a large scroll, and write on it with a man's pen concerning Maher-Shalal-Hash-Baz. ²And I will take for Myself faithful witnesses to record, Uriah the priest and Zechariah the son of Jeberechiah."

³Then I went to the prophetess, and she conceived and bore a son. Then the LORD said to me, "Call his name Maher-Shalal-Hash-Baz; ⁴for before the child shall have knowledge to cry 'My father' and 'My mother,' the riches of Damascus and the spoil of Samaria will be taken away before the king of Assyria."

⁵The LORD also spoke to me again, saying:

⁶ "Inasmuch as these people refused
The waters of Shiloah that flow softly,
And rejoice in Rezin and in Remaliah's son;
⁷ Now therefore, behold, the Lord brings up over them

BLAME

8:21 After rejecting God's plan for their lives, the people of Juda blamed God for their trials. People continually blame God for their self-induced problems. How do you respond to the unpleasant resu your sin? Where do you fix the blame? Instead of blaming God, lo ways to grow through your failures.

THE
EVERLASTING
FATHER He is timeless;
he is God our Father.

THE
PRINCE OF
PEACE
His government is
one of justice and peace.

The waters of the River, strong and mighty—
The king of Assyria and all his glory;
He will go up over all his channels
And go over all his banks.
8 He will pass through Judah,
He will overflow and pass over,
He will reach up to the neck;
And the stretching out of his wings
Will fill the breadth of Your land, O Immanuel.

9 "Be shattered, O you peoples, and be broken in pieces!
Give ear, all you from far countries.
Gird yourselves, but be broken in pieces;
Gird yourselves, but be broken in
pieces.
10 Take counsel together, but it will
come to nothing;
Speak the word, but it will not
stand,
For God *is* with us."

11For the LORD spoke thus to me
with a strong hand, and instructed
me that I should not walk in the way
of this people, saying:

12 "Do not say, 'A conspiracy,'
Concerning all that this people
call a conspiracy,
Nor be afraid of their threats, nor
be troubled.
13 The LORD of hosts, Him you shall
hallow;
Let Him *be* your fear,
And *let* Him *be* your dread.
14 He will be as a sanctuary,
But a stone of stumbling and a
rock of offense
To both the houses of Israel,
As a trap and a snare to the
inhabitants of Jerusalem.
15 And many among them shall
stumble;
They shall fall and be broken,
Be snared and taken."

16 Bind up the testimony,
Seal the law among my disciples.
17 And I will wait on the LORD,
Who hides His face from the
house of Jacob;
And I will hope in Him.

18 Here am I and the children whom the
LORD has given me!
We are for signs and wonders in Israel
From the LORD of hosts,
Who dwells in Mount Zion.

19And when they say to you, "Seek those
who are mediums and wizards, who whisper and mutter," should not a people seek
their God? *Should they seek* the dead on be-
half of the living? 20To the law and to the testimony! If they
do not speak according to this word, *it is* because *there is*
no light in them.

21They will pass through it hard-pressed and hungry;
and it shall happen, when they are hungry, that they will
be enraged and curse their king and their God, and look
upward. 22Then they will look to the earth, and see
trouble and darkness, gloom of anguish; and *they will be*
driven into darkness.

CHAPTER **9** **THE COMING MESSIAH.**
Nevertheless the gloom *will* not *be* upon her who *is*
distressed,

"Here's what I did..."

I always had trouble with peer pressure. I became a Christian in seventh
grade, but had trouble really living like one. I was good at wisecracks and
putting people down, for one thing. And I swore a lot. But probably the
biggest weakness I had was partying. When someone asked me to go to a
party, it was like I couldn't say no. Then when I got there, if there was
drinking, I couldn't resist. I tried a couple of times, but people would ask why I
wasn't having a beer. Once I even tried to tell them it was because I was a
Christian. I shouldn't have said that. They joked about my being too "holy" for
them, and I felt so bad I gave in and even drank too much that night. After
that, I was afraid to say anything about my faith because I thought it would be
worse if I said something and then didn't act at all like a Christian.
    Still, I read my Bible. And I started going to youth group in our church. That
helped me change some, but I continued to feel like a hypocrite.
    One day I was reading in Isaiah, and for some reason Isaiah 7:9 leaped
out at me. It said, "If you will not believe, surely you shall not be established."
I had been praying that God would make me a stronger Christian. This verse
seemed to be saying to me that I hadn't really believed that God could change
me, or that he could help me do what's right rather than give in to pressure.
    Reading that verse was a turning point for me. I decided that I had to learn
more about my faith and God's promises, and more about how God's Holy
Spirit worked in my life. I spent more time with my church friends and less with
my school friends. At first that was difficult, but it turned out to be easier than I
thought. The youth group often had things planned for the weekend, so when
someone invited me to a party, I could honestly say I had other plans. I'm still
struggling with peer pressure, but it's less of a struggle now. The more I learn
about God, the more I see how he works in me through his Holy Spirit, and
the more I believe God, the more he really does protect me.

Jason
AGE 16

As when at first He lightly esteemed
The land of Zebulun and the land of Naphtali,
And afterward more heavily oppressed *her,*
By the way of the sea, beyond the Jordan,
In Galilee of the Gentiles.

2 The people who walked in darkness
Have seen a great light;
Those who dwelt in the land of the shadow of death,
Upon them a light has shined.

3 You have multiplied the nation
And increased its joy;
They rejoice before You
According to the joy of harvest,
As *men* rejoice when they divide the spoil.

4 For You have broken the yoke of his burden
And the staff of his shoulder,
The rod of his oppressor,
As in the day of Midian.

5 For every warrior's sandal from the noisy battle,
And garments rolled in blood,
Will be used for burning *and* fuel of fire.

6 For unto us a Child is born,
Unto us a Son is given;
And the government will be upon His shoulder.
And His name will be called
Wonderful, Counselor, Mighty God,
Everlasting Father, Prince of Peace.

7 Of the increase of *His* government and peace
There will be no end,
Upon the throne of David and over His kingdom,
To order it and establish it with judgment and justice
From that time forward, even forever.
The zeal of the LORD of hosts will perform this.

8 The Lord sent a word against Jacob,
And it has fallen on Israel.

9 All the people will know—
Ephraim and the inhabitant of Samaria—
Who say in pride and arrogance of heart:

10 "The bricks have fallen down,
But we will rebuild with hewn stones;
The sycamores are cut down,
But we will replace *them* with cedars."

11 Therefore the LORD shall set up
The adversaries of Rezin against him,
And spur his enemies on,

12 The Syrians before and the Philistines behind;
And they shall devour Israel with an open mouth.

For all this His anger is not turned away,
But His hand *is* stretched out still.

13 For the people do not turn to Him who strikes them,
Nor do they seek the LORD of hosts.

14 Therefore the LORD will cut off head and tail from
Israel,
Palm branch and bulrush in one day.

15 The elder and honorable, he *is* the head;
The prophet who teaches lies, he *is* the tail.

16 For the leaders of this people cause *them* to err,
And *those who are* led by them are destroyed.

▶ ARROGANCE

9:8-10 Israel was called proud and arrogant for saying, in essence
"We've faced a temporary setback, but by our own strength we will
rebuild our city." Though God made Israel a nation and gave them the
land they occupied, the people put their trust in themselves rather than
him. Too often we take pride in our accomplishments, forgetting that God
has given us every ability we have. We even become proud of our own
status as Christians. God is not pleased with *any* pride or trust in
ourselves because it cuts off our contact with him.

17 Therefore the Lord will have no joy in their young
men,
Nor have mercy on their fatherless and widows;
For everyone *is* a hypocrite and an evildoer,
And every mouth speaks folly.

For all this His anger is not turned away,
But His hand *is* stretched out still.

18 For wickedness burns as the fire;
It shall devour the briers and thorns,
And kindle in the thickets of the forest;
They shall mount up *like* rising smoke.

19 Through the wrath of the LORD of hosts
The land is burned up,
And the people shall be as fuel for the fire;
No man shall spare his brother.

20 And he shall snatch on the right hand
And be hungry;
He shall devour on the left hand
And not be satisfied;
Every man shall eat the flesh of his own arm.

21 Manasseh *shall devour* Ephraim, and Ephraim
Manasseh;
Together they *shall be* against Judah.

For all this His anger is not turned away,
But His hand *is* stretched out still.

CHAPTER **10** GOD WILL PROTECT HIS PEOPLE.

"Woe to those who decree unrighteous decrees,
Who write misfortune,
Which they have prescribed

2 To rob the needy of justice,
And to take what is right from the poor of My people,
That widows may be their prey,
And *that* they may rob the fatherless.

3 What will you do in the day of punishment,
And in the desolation *which* will come from afar?
To whom will you flee for help?
And where will you leave your glory?

4 Without Me they shall bow down among the prisoners,
And they shall fall among the slain."

For all this His anger is not turned away,
But His hand *is* stretched out still.

5 "Woe to Assyria, the rod of My anger
And the staff in whose hand is My indignation.

6 I will send him against an ungodly nation,
And against the people of My wrath
I will give him charge,
To seize the spoil, to take the prey,
And to tread them down like the mire of the streets.

7 Yet he does not mean so,
  Nor does his heart think so;
  But *it is* in his heart to destroy,
  And cut off not a few nations.
8 For he says,
  'Are not my princes altogether kings?
9 *Is* not Calno like Carchemish?
  Is not Hamath like Arpad?
  Is not Samaria like Damascus?
10 As my hand has found the kingdoms of the idols,
  Whose carved images excelled those of Jerusalem
      and Samaria,
11 As I have done to Samaria and her idols,
  Shall I not do also to Jerusalem and her idols?' "

12Therefore it shall come to pass, when the Lord has performed all His work on Mount Zion and on Jerusalem, *that He will say,* "I will punish the fruit of the arrogant heart of the king of Assyria, and the glory of his haughty looks."

13For he says:

"By the strength of my hand I have done *it,*
  And by my wisdom, for I am prudent;
  Also I have removed the boundaries of the people,
  And have robbed their treasuries;
  So I have put down the inhabitants like a valiant
      man.
14 My hand has found like a nest the riches of the
      people,
  And as one gathers eggs *that are* left,
  I have gathered all the earth;
  And there was no one who moved *his* wing,
  Nor opened *his* mouth with even a peep."

15 Shall the ax boast itself against him who chops with
      it?
  Or shall the saw exalt itself against him who saws
      with it?
  As if a rod could wield *itself* against those who lift it
      up,
  Or as if a staff could lift up, *as if it were* not wood!
16 Therefore the Lord, the Lord of hosts,
  Will send leanness among his fat ones;
  And under his glory
  He will kindle a burning
  Like the burning of a fire.
17 So the Light of Israel will be for a fire,
  And his Holy One for a flame;
  It will burn and devour
  His thorns and his briers in one day.
18 And it will consume the glory of his forest and of his
      fruitful field,
  Both soul and body;
  And they will be as when a sick man wastes away.
19 Then the rest of the trees of his forest
  Will be so few in number
  That a child may write them.

20 And it shall come to pass in that day
  That the remnant of Israel,
  And such as have escaped of the house of Jacob,

Will never again depend on him who defeated them,
  But will depend on the LORD, the Holy One of Israel,
      in truth.
21 The remnant will return, the remnant of Jacob,
  To the Mighty God.

◣ THE REMNANT

10:20-21 Those who remained faithful to God despite the horrors of the invasion were called the remnant. The key to being a part of the remnant was *faith.* Being a descendant of Abraham, living in the Promised Land, having trusted God at one time— none of these characteristics were good enough. Are you relying on your Christian heritage, the rituals of worship, or past experiences to put you in a right relationship with God? The key to being set apart by God is faith in him.

22 For though your people, O Israel, be as the sand of
      the sea,
  A remnant of them will return;
  The destruction decreed shall overflow with
      righteousness.
23 For the Lord GOD of hosts
  Will make a determined end
  In the midst of all the land.

24Therefore thus says the Lord GOD of hosts: "O My people, who dwell in Zion, do not be afraid of the Assyrian. He shall strike you with a rod and lift up his staff against you, in the manner of Egypt. 25For yet a very little while and the indignation will cease, as will My anger in their destruction." 26And the LORD of hosts will stir up a scourge for him like the slaughter of Midian at the rock of Oreb; *as* His rod was on the sea, so will He lift it up in the manner of Egypt.

27 It shall come to pass in that day
  That his burden will be taken away from your
      shoulder,
  And his yoke from your neck,
  And the yoke will be destroyed because of the
      anointing oil.

28 He has come to Aiath,
  He has passed Migron;
  At Michmash he has attended to his equipment.
29 They have gone along the ridge,
  They have taken up lodging at Geba.
  Ramah is afraid,
  Gibeah of Saul has fled.
30 Lift up your voice,
  O daughter of Gallim!
  Cause it to be heard as far as Laish—
  O poor Anathoth!
31 Madmenah has fled,
  The inhabitants of Gebim seek refuge.
32 As yet he will remain at Nob that day;
  He will shake his fist at the mount of the daughter of
      Zion,
  The hill of Jerusalem.

33 Behold, the Lord,
  The LORD of hosts,
  Will lop off the bough with terror;

Those of high stature *will be* hewn down,
And the haughty will be humbled.
34 He will cut down the thickets of the forest with iron,
And Lebanon will fall by the Mighty One.

CHAPTER 11 GOD PROMISES A PERFECT LEADER.

There shall come forth a Rod from the stem of Jesse,
And a Branch shall grow out of his roots.
2 The Spirit of the LORD shall rest upon Him,
The Spirit of wisdom and understanding,
The Spirit of counsel and might,
The Spirit of knowledge and of the fear of the LORD.

FAIR TREATMENT

11:3-5 We all long for fair treatment from others, but do we give it?
We hate those who base their judgments on appearance, false evidence,
or hearsay. But we can be quick to judge others using those same criteria.
Only Christ can be the perfectly fair judge. And only as Christ governs our
heart can we learn to be as fair in our treatment of others as we expect
them to be with us.

3 His delight *is* in the fear of the LORD,
And He shall not judge by the sight of His eyes,
Nor decide by the hearing of His ears;
4 But with righteousness He shall judge the poor,
And decide with equity for the meek of the earth;
He shall strike the earth with the rod of His mouth,
And with the breath of His lips He shall slay the
wicked.
5 Righteousness shall be the belt of His loins,
And faithfulness the belt of His waist.

6 "The wolf also shall dwell with the lamb,
The leopard shall lie down with the young goat,
The calf and the young lion and the fatling together;
And a little child shall lead them.
7 The cow and the bear shall graze;
Their young ones shall lie down together;
And the lion shall eat straw like the ox.
8 The nursing child shall play by the cobra's hole,
And the weaned child shall put his hand in the
viper's den.
9 They shall not hurt nor destroy in all My holy
mountain,
For the earth shall be full of the knowledge of the
LORD
As the waters cover the sea.

10 "And in that day there shall be a Root of Jesse,
Who shall stand as a banner to the people;
For the Gentiles shall seek Him,
And His resting place shall be glorious."

11 It shall come to pass in that day
That the Lord shall set His hand again the second
time
To recover the remnant of His people who are left,
From Assyria and Egypt,
From Pathros and Cush,
From Elam and Shinar,
From Hamath and the islands of the sea.

12 He will set up a banner for the nations,
And will assemble the outcasts of Israel,
And gather together the dispersed of Judah
From the four corners of the earth.
13 Also the envy of Ephraim shall depart,
And the adversaries of Judah shall be cut off;
Ephraim shall not envy Judah,
And Judah shall not harass Ephraim.
14 But they shall fly down upon the shoulder of the
Philistines toward the west;
Together they shall plunder the people of the East;
They shall lay their hand on Edom and Moab;
And the people of Ammon shall obey them.
15 The LORD will utterly destroy the tongue of the Sea of
Egypt;
With His mighty wind He will shake His fist over the
River,
And strike it in the seven streams,
And make *men* cross over dryshod.
16 There will be a highway for the remnant of His
people
Who will be left from Assyria,
As it was for Israel
In the day that he came up from the land of Egypt.

CHAPTER 12 SINGING GOD'S PRAISE. And in that
day you will say:

"O LORD, I will praise You;
Though You were angry with me,
Your anger is turned away, and You comfort me.
2 Behold, God *is* my salvation,
I will trust and not be afraid;
'For YAH, the LORD, *is* my strength and song;
He also has become my salvation.'"

3 Therefore with joy you will draw water
From the wells of salvation.

4 And in that day you will say:

"Praise the LORD, call upon His name;
Declare His deeds among the peoples,
Make mention that His name is exalted.
5 Sing to the LORD,
For He has done excellent things;
This *is* known in all the earth.
6 Cry out and shout, O inhabitant of Zion,
For great *is* the Holy One of Israel in your midst!"

CHAPTER 13 BABYLON WILL BE DESTROYED. The
burden against Babylon which Isaiah the son of Amoz
saw.

2 "Lift up a banner on the high mountain,
Raise your voice to them;
Wave your hand, that they may enter the gates of the
nobles.
3 I have commanded My sanctified ones;
I have also called My mighty ones for My anger—
Those who rejoice in My exaltation."

4 The noise of a multitude in the mountains,

Like that of many people!
A tumultuous noise of the kingdoms of nations
　　gathered together!
The Lord of hosts musters
The army for battle.

5 They come from a far country,
From the end of heaven—
The Lord and His weapons of indignation,
To destroy the whole land.

6 Wail, for the day of the Lord *is* at hand!
It will come as destruction from the Almighty.
7 Therefore all hands will be limp,
Every man's heart will melt,
8 And they will be afraid.
Pangs and sorrows will take hold of *them;*
They will be in pain as a woman in childbirth;
They will be amazed at one another;
Their faces *will be like* flames.

9 Behold, the day of the Lord comes,
Cruel, with both wrath and fierce anger,
To lay the land desolate;
And He will destroy its sinners from it.
10 For the stars of heaven and their constellations
Will not give their light;
The sun will be darkened in its going forth,
And the moon will not cause its light to shine.

11 "I will punish the world for *its* evil,
And the wicked for their iniquity;
I will halt the arrogance of the proud,
And will lay low the haughtiness of the terrible.
12 I will make a mortal more rare than fine gold,
A man more than the golden wedge of Ophir.
13 Therefore I will shake the heavens,
And the earth will move out of her place,
In the wrath of the Lord of hosts
And in the day of His fierce anger.
14 It shall be as the hunted gazelle,
And as a sheep that no man takes up;
Every man will turn to his own people,
And everyone will flee to his own land.
15 Everyone who is found will be thrust through,
And everyone who is captured will fall by the sword.
16 Their children also will be dashed to pieces before
　　their eyes;
Their houses will be plundered
And their wives ravished.

17 "Behold, I will stir up the Medes against them,
Who will not regard silver;
And *as for* gold, they will not delight in it.
18 Also *their* bows will dash the young men to pieces,
And they will have no pity on the fruit of the womb;
Their eye will not spare children.
19 And Babylon, the glory of kingdoms,
The beauty of the Chaldeans' pride,
Will be as when God overthrew Sodom and
　　Gomorrah.
20 It will never be inhabited,
Nor will it be settled from generation to generation;

Nor will the Arabian pitch tents there,
Nor will the shepherds make their sheepfolds there.
21 But wild beasts of the desert will lie there,
And their houses will be full of owls;
Ostriches will dwell there,

◣▬▬▬▬▬▬UTTER RUIN

13:20 Even before Babylon became a world power, Isaiah prophesied that its destruction would be so complete that the land would never again be inhabited. The city was conquered in 539 B.C. by Cyrus. The details of Isaiah's prophecy may not be fulfilled until the end times.

And wild goats will caper there.
22 The hyenas will howl in their citadels,
And jackals in their pleasant palaces.
Her time *is* near to come,
And her days will not be prolonged."

CHAPTER **14** GOD PROMISES TO LOVE HIS

PEOPLE. For the Lord will have mercy on Jacob, and will still choose Israel, and settle them in their own land. The strangers will be joined with them, and they will cling to the house of Jacob. ²Then people will take them and bring them to their place, and the house of Israel will possess them for servants and maids in the land of the Lord; they will take them captive whose captives they were, and rule over their oppressors.

³It shall come to pass in the day the Lord gives you rest from your sorrow, and from your fear and the hard bondage in which you were made to serve, ⁴that you will take up this proverb against the king of Babylon, and say:

"How the oppressor has ceased,
The golden city ceased!

◣▬▬▬▬▬▬POWER FAILURE

14:5-6 Power is temporary. God permitted Babylon to have power for a purpose—to chastise his wayward people. When the purpose ended, so did the power. Beware of placing confidence in human power—one day it will fade, no matter how secure it appears.

5 The Lord has broken the staff of the wicked,
The scepter of the rulers;
6 He who struck the people in wrath with a continual
　　stroke,
He who ruled the nations in anger,
Is persecuted *and* no one hinders.
7 The whole earth is at rest *and* quiet;
They break forth into singing.
8 Indeed the cypress trees rejoice over you,
And the cedars of Lebanon,
Saying, 'Since you were cut down,
No woodsman has come up against us.'

9 "Hell from beneath is excited about you,
To meet *you* at your coming;
It stirs up the dead for you,
All the chief ones of the earth;
It has raised up from their thrones
All the kings of the nations.
10 They all shall speak and say to you:

'Have you also become as weak as we?
Have you become like us?

11 Your pomp is brought down to Sheol,
And the sound of your stringed instruments;
The maggot is spread under you,
And worms cover you.'

12 "How you are fallen from heaven,
O Lucifer, son of the morning!
How you are cut down to the ground,
You who weakened the nations!

13 For you have said in your heart:
'I will ascend into heaven,
I will exalt my throne above the stars of God;
I will also sit on the mount of the congregation
On the farthest sides of the north;

14 I will ascend above the heights of the clouds,
I will be like the Most High.'

15 Yet you shall be brought down to Sheol,
To the lowest depths of the Pit.

16 "Those who see you will gaze at you,
And consider you, *saying:*
'*Is* this the man who made the earth tremble,
Who shook kingdoms,

17 Who made the world as a wilderness
And destroyed its cities,
Who did not open the house of his prisoners?'

18 "All the kings of the nations,
All of them, sleep in glory,
Everyone in his own house;

19 But you are cast out of your grave
Like an abominable branch,
Like the garment of those who are slain,
Thrust through with a sword,
Who go down to the stones of the pit,
Like a corpse trodden underfoot.

20 You will not be joined with them in burial,
Because you have destroyed your land
And slain your people.
The brood of evildoers shall never be named.

21 Prepare slaughter for his children
Because of the iniquity of their fathers,
Lest they rise up and possess the land,
And fill the face of the world with cities."

22 "For I will rise up against them," says the LORD of
hosts,
"And cut off from Babylon the name and remnant,
And offspring and posterity," says the LORD.

23 "I will also make it a possession for the porcupine,
And marshes of muddy water;
I will sweep it with the broom of destruction," says
the LORD of hosts.

24 The LORD of hosts has sworn, saying,
"Surely, as I have thought, so it shall come to pass,
And as I have purposed, *so* it shall stand:

25 That I will break the Assyrian in My land,
And on My mountains tread him underfoot.
Then his yoke shall be removed from them,
And his burden removed from their shoulders.

■THE ENEMY
15:1 Moab was east of the Dead Sea. The Moabites were descendan
of Lot through his incestuous relationship with his older daughter
(Genesis 19:31-38). Moab had always been Israel's enemy. They
oppressed Israel and invaded their land (Judges 3:12-14), fought aga
Saul (1 Samuel 14:47), and fought against David (2 Samuel 8:2,11-
Moab would be punished for its harsh treatment of Israel.

26 This *is* the purpose that is purposed against the
whole earth,
And this *is* the hand that is stretched out over all the
nations.

27 For the LORD of hosts has purposed,
And who will annul *it?*
His hand *is* stretched out,
And who will turn it back?"

28This is the burden which came in the year that King
Ahaz died.

29 "Do not rejoice, all you of Philistia,
Because the rod that struck you is broken;
For out of the serpent's roots will come forth a viper,
And its offspring *will be* a fiery flying serpent.

30 The firstborn of the poor will feed,
And the needy will lie down in safety;
I will kill your roots with famine,
And it will slay your remnant.

31 Wail, O gate! Cry, O city!
All you of Philistia *are* dissolved;
For smoke will come from the north,
And no one *will be* alone in his appointed times."

32 What will they answer the messengers of the nation?
That the LORD has founded Zion,
And the poor of His people shall take refuge in it.

CHAPTER **15** **WHAT GOD WILL DO TO MOAB.** The
burden against Moab.

Because in the night Ar of Moab is laid waste
And destroyed,
Because in the night Kir of Moab is laid waste
And destroyed,

2 He has gone up to the temple and Dibon,
To the high places to weep.
Moab will wail over Nebo and over Medeba;
On all their heads *will be* baldness,
And every beard cut off.

3 In their streets they will clothe themselves with
sackcloth;
On the tops of their houses
And in their streets
Everyone will wail, weeping bitterly.

4 Heshbon and Elealeh will cry out,
Their voice shall be heard as far as Jahaz;
Therefore the armed soldiers of Moab will cry out;
His life will be burdensome to him.

5 "My heart will cry out for Moab;
His fugitives *shall flee* to Zoar,
Like a three-year-old heifer.
For by the Ascent of Luhith
They will go up with weeping;
For in the way of Horonaim

They will raise up a cry of destruction,
6 For the waters of Nimrim will be desolate,
For the green grass has withered away;
The grass fails, there is nothing green.
7 Therefore the abundance they have gained,
And what they have laid up,
They will carry away to the Brook of the Willows.
8 For the cry has gone all around the borders of Moab,
Its wailing to Eglaim
And its wailing to Beer Elim.
9 For the waters of Dimon will be full of blood;
Because I will bring more upon Dimon,
Lions upon him who escapes from Moab,
And on the remnant of the land."

CHAPTER **16**

Send the lamb to the ruler of the land,
From Sela to the wilderness,
To the mount of the daughter of Zion.
2 For it shall be as a wandering bird thrown out of the nest;
So shall be the daughters of Moab at the fords of the Arnon.

3 "Take counsel, execute judgment;
Make your shadow like the night in the middle of the day;
Hide the outcasts,
Do not betray him who escapes.
4 Let My outcasts dwell with you, O Moab;
Be a shelter to them from the face of the spoiler.
For the extortioner is at an end,
Devastation ceases,
The oppressors are consumed out of the land.
5 In mercy the throne will be established;
And One will sit on it in truth, in the tabernacle of David,
Judging and seeking justice and hastening righteousness."

6 We have heard of the pride of Moab—
He is very proud—
Of his haughtiness and his pride and his wrath;
But his lies *shall* not *be* so.
7 Therefore Moab shall wail for Moab;
Everyone shall wail.
For the foundations of Kir Hareseth you shall mourn;
Surely *they are* stricken.

8 For the fields of Heshbon languish,
And the vine of Sibmah;
The lords of the nations have broken down its choice plants,
Which have reached to Jazer
And wandered through the wilderness.
Her branches are stretched out,
They are gone over the sea.
9 Therefore I will bewail the vine of Sibmah,
With the weeping of Jazer;
I will drench you with my tears,
O Heshbon and Elealeh;
For battle cries have fallen

Over your summer fruits and your harvest.

10 Gladness is taken away,
And joy from the plentiful field;
In the vineyards there will be no singing,
Nor will there be shouting;
No treaders will tread out wine in the presses;
I have made their shouting cease.
11 Therefore my heart shall resound like a harp for Moab,
And my inner being for Kir Heres.

12 And it shall come to pass,
When it is seen that Moab is weary on the high place,
That he will come to his sanctuary to pray;
But he will not prevail.

13This *is* the word which the LORD has spoken concerning Moab since that time. 14But now the LORD has spoken, saying, "Within three years, as the years of a hired man, the glory of Moab will be despised with all that great multitude, and the remnant *will be* very small *and* feeble."

CHAPTER **17** WHAT GOD WILL DO TO SYRIA. The burden against Damascus.

"Behold, Damascus will cease from *being* a city,
And it will be a ruinous heap.
2 The cities of Aroer *are* forsaken;
They will be for flocks
Which lie down, and no one will make *them* afraid.
3 The fortress also will cease from Ephraim,
The kingdom from Damascus,
And the remnant of Syria;
They will be as the glory of the children of Israel,"
Says the LORD of hosts.

4 "In that day it shall come to pass
That the glory of Jacob will wane,
And the fatness of his flesh grow lean.
5 It shall be as when the harvester gathers the grain,
And reaps the heads with his arm;
It shall be as he who gathers heads of grain
In the Valley of Rephaim.
6 Yet gleaning grapes will be left in it,
Like the shaking of an olive tree,
Two *or* three olives at the top of the uppermost bough,
Four *or* five in its most fruitful branches,"
Says the LORD God of Israel.

7 In that day a man will look to his Maker,

▰▰▰ DEPENDENCE

17:7-11 God's message to Damascus is one of complete destruction. The Assyrians had turned from the God who could save them and depended instead on their idols and their own strength. No matter how successful they were, God's judgment was sure. Often we depend on the trappings of success (e.g., expensive cars, clothes, homes) to give us fulfillment. But God says we will reap grief and pain if we depend on things of this world to give us security. If we don't want the same treatment Damascus received, we must turn from these false allurements and trust in God.

ALLIANCES TODAY

GOVERNMENT
We rely on government legislation to protect the moral decisions we want made, but legislation cannot change people's hearts.

SCIENCE
We enjoy the benefits of science and technology. We look to scientific predictions and analysis before we look to the Bible.

MEDICAL CARE
We regard medicine as the way to prolong life and preserve its quality—quite apart from faith and moral living.

Isaiah warned Judah not to ally with Egypt. He knew that trust in any nation or military might was futile. Judah's only hope was to trust in God. Although we don't consciously put our hope for deliverance in political alliances in quite the same way, we often put our hope in other forces.

EDUCATION
We act as though education and degrees can guarantee our future and success without considering what God plans for our future.

FINANCIAL SYSTEMS
We place our faith in financial "security," making as much money as we can for ourselves and forgetting that, while being wise with our money, we must trust God for our needs.

And his eyes will have respect for the Holy One of Israel.
8 He will not look to the altars,
The work of his hands;
He will not respect what his fingers have made,
Nor the wooden images nor the incense altars.

9 In that day his strong cities will be as a forsaken bough
And an uppermost branch,
Which they left because of the children of Israel;
And there will be desolation.

10 Because you have forgotten the God of your salvation,
And have not been mindful of the Rock of your stronghold,
Therefore you will plant pleasant plants
And set out foreign seedlings;
11 In the day you will make your plant to grow,
And in the morning you will make your seed to flourish;
But the harvest *will be* a heap of ruins
In the day of grief and desperate sorrow.

12 Woe to the multitude of many people
Who make a noise like the roar of the seas,
And to the rushing of nations
That make a rushing like the rushing of mighty waters!
13 The nations will rush like the rushing of many waters;

But *God* will rebuke them and they will flee far away,
And be chased like the chaff of the mountains before the wind,
Like a rolling thing before the whirlwind.
14 Then behold, at eventide, trouble!
And before the morning, he *is* no more.
This *is* the portion of those who plunder us,
And the lot of those who rob us.

CHAPTER 18 WHAT GOD WILL DO TO ETHIOPIA.

Woe to the land shadowed with buzzing wings,
Which *is* beyond the rivers of Ethiopia,
2 Which sends ambassadors by sea,
Even in vessels of reed on the waters, *saying,*
"Go, swift messengers, to a nation tall and smooth *of skin,*
To a people terrible from their beginning onward,
A nation powerful and treading down,
Whose land the rivers divide."

3 All inhabitants of the world and dwellers on the earth:
When he lifts up a banner on the mountains, you see *it;*
And when he blows a trumpet, you hear *it.*
4 For so the LORD said to me,
"I will take My rest,
And I will look from My dwelling place
Like clear heat in sunshine,
Like a cloud of dew in the heat of harvest."

5 For before the harvest, when the bud is perfect
And the sour grape is ripening in the flower,
He will both cut off the sprigs with pruning hooks
And take away *and* cut down the branches.
6 They will be left together for the mountain birds of prey
And for the beasts of the earth;
The birds of prey will summer on them,
And all the beasts of the earth will winter on them.

7 In that time a present will be brought to the LORD of hosts
From a people tall and smooth *of skin,*
And from a people terrible from their beginning onward,
A nation powerful and treading down,
Whose land the rivers divide—
To the place of the name of the LORD of hosts,
To Mount Zion.

CHAPTER 19 WHAT GOD WILL DO TO EGYPT. The burden against Egypt.

Behold, the LORD rides on a swift cloud,
And will come into Egypt;
The idols of Egypt will totter at His presence,
And the heart of Egypt will melt in its midst.

2 "I will set Egyptians against Egyptians;
Everyone will fight against his brother,
And everyone against his neighbor,
City against city, kingdom against kingdom.
3 The spirit of Egypt will fail in its midst;
I will destroy their counsel,
And they will consult the idols and the charmers,
The mediums and the sorcerers.
4 And the Egyptians I will give
Into the hand of a cruel master,
And a fierce king will rule over them,"
Says the Lord, the LORD of hosts.

5 The waters will fail from the sea,
And the river will be wasted and dried up.
6 The rivers will turn foul;
The brooks of defense will be emptied and dried up;
The reeds and rushes will wither.
7 The papyrus reeds by the River, by the mouth of the River,
And everything sown by the River,
Will wither, be driven away, and be no more.
8 The fishermen also will mourn;
All those will lament who cast hooks into the River,
And they will languish who spread nets on the waters.
9 Moreover those who work in fine flax
And those who weave fine fabric will be ashamed;
10 And its foundations will be broken.
All who make wages *will be* troubled of soul.

11 Surely the princes of Zoan *are* fools;
Pharaoh's wise counselors give foolish counsel.
How do you say to Pharaoh, "I *am* the son of the wise,
The son of ancient kings?"
12 Where *are* they?
Where are your wise men?
Let them tell you now,
And let them know what the LORD of hosts has purposed against Egypt.
13 The princes of Zoan have become fools;
The princes of Noph are deceived;
They have also deluded Egypt,
Those who are the mainstay of its tribes.
14 The LORD has mingled a perverse spirit in her midst;
And they have caused Egypt to err in all her work,
As a drunken man staggers in his vomit.
15 Neither will there be *any* work for Egypt,
Which the head or tail,
Palm branch or bulrush, may do.

16In that day Egypt will be like women, and will be afraid and fear because of the waving of the hand of the LORD of hosts, which He waves over it. 17And the land of Judah will be a terror to Egypt; everyone who makes mention of it will be afraid in himself, because of the counsel of the LORD of hosts which He has determined against it.

18In that day five cities in the land of Egypt will speak the language of Canaan and swear by the LORD of hosts; one will be called the City of Destruction.

19In that day there will be an altar to the LORD in the midst of the land of Egypt, and a pillar to the LORD at its border. 20And it will be for a sign and for a witness to the LORD of hosts in the land of Egypt; for they will cry to the LORD because of the oppressors, and He will send them a Savior and a Mighty One, and He will deliver them. 21Then the LORD will be known to Egypt, and the Egyptians will know the LORD in that day, and will make sacrifice and offering; yes, they will make a vow to the LORD and perform *it.* 22And the LORD will strike Egypt, He will strike and heal *it;* they will return to the LORD, and He will be entreated by them and heal them.

23In that day there will be a highway from Egypt to Assyria, and the Assyrian will come into Egypt and the Egyptian into Assyria, and the Egyptians will serve with the Assyrians.

UNITY

19:23-25 In Jesus Christ, former enemies may unite in love. In Christ, people and nations who are poles apart politically will bow at his feet as brothers and sisters; Christ breaks down every barrier that threatens relationships.

24In that day Israel will be one of three with Egypt and Assyria—a blessing in the midst of the land, 25whom the LORD of hosts shall bless, saying, "Blessed *is* Egypt My people, and Assyria the work of My hands, and Israel My inheritance."

CHAPTER 20 ISAIAH GOES BAREFOOT. In the year that Tartan came to Ashdod, when Sargon the king of Assyria sent him, and he fought against Ashdod and took it, 2at the same time the LORD spoke by Isaiah the son of Amoz, saying, "Go, and remove the sackcloth from

your body, and take your sandals off your feet." And he did so, walking naked and barefoot.

³Then the LORD said, "Just as My servant Isaiah has walked naked and barefoot three years *for* a sign and a wonder against Egypt and Ethiopia, ⁴so shall the king of Assyria lead away the Egyptians as prisoners and the Ethiopians as captives, young and old, naked and barefoot, with their buttocks uncovered, to the shame of Egypt. ⁵Then they shall be afraid and ashamed of Ethiopia their expectation and Egypt their glory. ⁶And the inhabitant of this territory will say in that day, 'Surely such *is* our expectation, wherever we flee for help to be delivered from the king of Assyria; and how shall we escape?'"

CHAPTER 21 WHAT GOD WILL DO TO BABYLON.

The burden against the Wilderness of the Sea.

As whirlwinds in the South pass through,
So it comes from the desert, from a terrible land.
² A distressing vision is declared to me;
The treacherous dealer deals treacherously,
And the plunderer plunders.
Go up, O Elam!
Besiege, O Media!
All its sighing I have made to cease.

³ Therefore my loins are filled with pain;
Pangs have taken hold of me, like the pangs of a
woman in labor.
I was distressed when *I* heard *it;*
I was dismayed when *I* saw *it.*
⁴ My heart wavered, fearfulness frightened me;
The night for which I longed He turned into fear for
me.
⁵ Prepare the table,
Set a watchman in the tower,
Eat and drink.
Arise, you princes,
Anoint the shield!

⁶ For thus has the Lord said to me:
"Go, set a watchman,
Let him declare what he sees."
⁷ And he saw a chariot *with* a pair of horsemen,
A chariot of donkeys, *and* a chariot of camels,
And he listened earnestly with great care.
⁸ Then he cried, "A lion, my Lord!
I stand continually on the watchtower in the
daytime;
I have sat at my post every night.
⁹ And look, here comes a chariot of men *with* a pair of
horsemen!"
Then he answered and said,
"Babylon is fallen, is fallen!
And all the carved images of her gods
He has broken to the ground."

¹⁰ Oh, my threshing and the grain of my floor!
That which I have heard from the LORD of hosts,
The God of Israel,
I have declared to you.

▶▬▬▬ THE NEWS

21:11-12 Everyone wants to hear the good news that all trouble is over and prosperity lies ahead. The watchman tells how to get that g news—turn to God, and seek him with all your heart. Without God, news of world events and the world's future is anything but good. Without God, our personal future is bad news.

¹¹The burden against Dumah.

He calls to me out of Seir,
"Watchman, what of the night?
Watchman, what of the night?"
¹² The watchman said,
"The morning comes, and also the night.
If you will inquire, inquire;
Return! Come back!"

¹³The burden against Arabia.

In the forest in Arabia you will lodge,
O you traveling companies of Dedanites.
¹⁴ O inhabitants of the land of Tema,
Bring water to him who is thirsty;
With their bread they met him who fled.
¹⁵ For they fled from the swords, from the drawn sword,
From the bent bow, and from the distress of war.

¹⁶For thus the LORD has said to me: "Within a year, according to the year of a hired man, all the glory of Kedar will fail; ¹⁷and the remainder of the number of archers, the mighty men of the people of Kedar, will be diminished; for the LORD God of Israel has spoken *it.*"

CHAPTER 22 WHAT GOD WILL DO TO JERUSALEM.

The burden against the Valley of Vision.

What ails you now, that you have all gone up to the
housetops,
² You who are full of noise,
A tumultuous city, a joyous city?
Your slain *men are* not slain with the sword,
Nor dead in battle.
³ All your rulers have fled together;
They are captured by the archers.
All who are found in you are bound together;
They have fled from afar.
⁴ Therefore I said, "Look away from me,
I will weep bitterly;
Do not labor to comfort me
Because of the plundering of the daughter of my
people."

⁵ For *it is* a day of trouble and treading down and
perplexity
By the Lord GOD of hosts
In the Valley of Vision—
Breaking down the walls

▶▬▬▬ CONSEQUENCES

22:4 Isaiah had warned his people, but they did not repent—so t experienced God's judgment. Because Isaiah cared for the people, h hurt by their punishment and he mourned deeply for them. Someti people we care for ignore our attempts to help them, and then they suffer the consequences of actions we tried to stop. We grieve at tho times because of our concern. God expects us to be involved with others—this may cause us to suffer with them.

And of crying to the mountain.
⁶ Elam bore the quiver
  With chariots of men *and* horsemen,
  And Kir uncovered the shield.
⁷ It shall come to pass *that* your choicest valleys
  Shall be full of chariots,
  And the horsemen shall set themselves in array at
    the gate.

⁸ He removed the protection of Judah.
  You looked in that day to the armor of the House of
    the Forest;
⁹ You also saw the damage to the city of David,
  That it was great;
  And you gathered together the waters of the lower
    pool.
¹⁰ You numbered the houses of Jerusalem,
  And the houses you broke down
  To fortify the wall.
¹¹ You also made a reservoir between the two walls
  For the water of the old pool.
  But you did not look to its Maker,
  Nor did you have respect for Him who fashioned it
    long ago.

¹² And in that day the Lord GOD of hosts
  Called for weeping and for mourning,
  For baldness and for girding with sackcloth.
¹³ But instead, joy and gladness,
  Slaying oxen and killing sheep,
  Eating meat and drinking wine:
  "Let us eat and drink, for tomorrow we die!"

¹⁴ Then it was revealed in my hearing by the LORD of
    hosts,
  "Surely for this iniquity there will be no atonement
    for you,
  Even to your death," says the Lord GOD of hosts.

¹⁵Thus says the Lord GOD of hosts:

"Go, proceed to this steward,
  To Shebna, who *is* over the house, *and say:*
¹⁶ 'What have you here, and whom have you here,
  That you have hewn a sepulcher here,
  As he who hews himself a sepulcher on high,
  Who carves a tomb for himself in a rock?
¹⁷ Indeed, the LORD will throw you away violently,
  O mighty man,
  And will surely seize you.
¹⁸ He will surely turn violently and toss you like a ball
  Into a large country;
  There you shall die, and there your glorious chariots
  Shall be the shame of your master's house.
¹⁹ So I will drive you out of your office,
  And from your position he will pull you down.

²⁰ 'Then it shall be in that day,
  That I will call My servant Eliakim the son of Hilkiah;
²¹ I will clothe him with your robe
  And strengthen him with your belt;
  I will commit your responsibility into his hand.
  He shall be a father to the inhabitants of Jerusalem

And to the house of Judah.
²² The key of the house of David
  I will lay on his shoulder;
  So he shall open, and no one shall shut;
  And he shall shut, and no one shall open.
²³ I will fasten him *as* a peg in a secure place,
  And he will become a glorious throne to his father's
    house.

▶━━━━━━━━━**HOPE**

22:13-14 The people said, "Let us eat and drink" because they had
given up hope. Today, we see people giving up hope as well. There are
two common responses to hopelessness: despair and self-indulgence. But
this life is not all there is, so we should not act as if we have no hope. The
proper response is to turn to God and trust in his promise of a perfect and
just future in the new world he will create.

²⁴"They will hang on him all the glory of his father's
house, the offspring and the posterity, all vessels of small
quantity, from the cups to all the pitchers. ²⁵In that day,'
says the LORD of hosts, 'the peg that is fastened in the
secure place will be removed and be cut down and fall,
and the burden that *was* on it will be cut off; for the LORD
has spoken.'"

CHAPTER **23** **WHAT GOD WILL DO TO TYRE.** The
burden against Tyre.

Wail, you ships of Tarshish!
  For it is laid waste,
  So that there is no house, no harbor;
  From the land of Cyprus it is revealed to them.

² Be still, you inhabitants of the coastland,
  You merchants of Sidon,
  Whom those who cross the sea have filled.
³ And on great waters the grain of Shihor,
  The harvest of the River, *is* her revenue;
  And she is a marketplace for the nations.

⁴ Be ashamed, O Sidon;
  For the sea has spoken,
  The strength of the sea, saying,
  "I do not labor, nor bring forth children;
  Neither do I rear young men,
  Nor bring up virgins."
⁵ When the report *reaches* Egypt,
  They also will be in agony at the report of Tyre.

⁶ Cross over to Tarshish;
  Wail, you inhabitants of the coastland!
⁷ *Is* this your joyous *city*,
  Whose antiquity *is* from ancient days,
  Whose feet carried her far off to dwell?
⁸ Who has taken this counsel against Tyre, the
    crowning *city*,
  Whose merchants *are* princes,
  Whose traders *are* the honorable of the earth?
⁹ The LORD of hosts has purposed it,
  To bring to dishonor the pride of all glory,
  To bring into contempt all the honorable of the
    earth.

¹⁰ Overflow through your land like the River,
O daughter of Tarshish;
There is no more strength.
¹¹ He stretched out His hand over the sea,
He shook the kingdoms;
The LORD has given a commandment against
Canaan
To destroy its strongholds.
¹² And He said, "You will rejoice no more,
O you oppressed virgin daughter of Sidon.
Arise, cross over to Cyprus;
There also you will have no rest."

¹³ Behold, the land of the Chaldeans,
This people *which* was not;
Assyria founded it for wild beasts of the desert.
They set up its towers,
They raised up its palaces,
And brought it to ruin.

¹⁴ Wail, you ships of Tarshish!
For your strength is laid waste.

¹⁵Now it shall come to pass in that day that Tyre will be forgotten seventy years, according to the days of one king. At the end of seventy years it will happen to Tyre as *in* the song of the harlot:

¹⁶ "Take a harp, go about the city,
You forgotten harlot;
Make sweet melody, sing many songs,
That you may be remembered."

¹⁷And it shall be, at the end of seventy years, that the LORD will deal with Tyre. She will return to her hire, and commit fornication with all the kingdoms of the world on the face of the earth. ¹⁸Her gain and her pay will be set apart for the LORD; it will not be treasured nor laid up, for her gain will be for those who dwell before the LORD, to eat sufficiently, and for fine clothing.

CHAPTER **24** TROUBLE IS COMING!

Behold, the LORD makes the earth empty and makes it
waste,
Distorts its surface
And scatters abroad its inhabitants.
² And it shall be:
As with the people, so with the priest;
As with the servant, so with his master;
As with the maid, so with her mistress;
As with the buyer, so with the seller;
As with the lender, so with the borrower;
As with the creditor, so with the debtor.
³ The land shall be entirely emptied and utterly
plundered,
For the LORD has spoken this word.

⁴ The earth mourns *and* fades away,
The world languishes *and* fades away;
The haughty people of the earth languish.
⁵ The earth is also defiled under its inhabitants,
Because they have transgressed the laws,
Changed the ordinance,

STOP SIN

24:4-5 Not only the people suffered from their sins; even the land suffered with bad crops and crime. Today we see the results of sin in own land—pollution, crime, poverty, and more. Sin affects every a of society so extensively that even those faithful to God suffer. We c blame God for these conditions because human sin has brought them about. The more we who are believers renounce sin and share God's Word with others, the more we slow our society's deterioration. We not give up: sin is rampant, but we can make a difference.

Broken the everlasting covenant.
⁶ Therefore the curse has devoured the earth,
And those who dwell in it are desolate.
Therefore the inhabitants of the earth are burned,
And few men *are* left.

⁷ The new wine fails, the vine languishes,
All the merry-hearted sigh.
⁸ The mirth of the tambourine ceases,
The noise of the jubilant ends,
The joy of the harp ceases.
⁹ They shall not drink wine with a song;
Strong drink is bitter to those who drink it.
¹⁰ The city of confusion is broken down;
Every house is shut up, so that none may go in.
¹¹ *There is* a cry for wine in the streets,
All joy is darkened,
The mirth of the land is gone.
¹² In the city desolation is left,
And the gate is stricken with destruction.
¹³ When it shall be thus in the midst of the land among
the people,
It shall be like the shaking of an olive tree,
Like the gleaning of grapes when the vintage is done.

¹⁴ They shall lift up their voice, they shall sing;
For the majesty of the LORD
They shall cry aloud from the sea.
¹⁵ Therefore glorify the LORD in the dawning light,
The name of the LORD God of Israel in the coastlands
of the sea.
¹⁶ From the ends of the earth we have heard songs:
"Glory to the righteous!"
But I said, "I am ruined, ruined!
Woe to me!
The treacherous dealers have dealt treacherously,
Indeed, the treacherous dealers have dealt very
treacherously."

¹⁷ Fear and the pit and the snare
Are upon you, O inhabitant of the earth.
¹⁸ And it shall be
That he who flees from the noise of the fear
Shall fall into the pit,
And he who comes up from the midst of the pit
Shall be caught in the snare;
For the windows from on high are open,
And the foundations of the earth are shaken.

¹⁹ The earth is violently broken,
The earth is split open,
The earth is shaken exceedingly.
²⁰ The earth shall reel to and fro like a drunkard,
And shall totter like a hut;

Its transgression shall be heavy upon it,
And it will fall, and not rise again.

21 It shall come to pass in that day
That the LORD will punish on high the host of exalted ones,
And on the earth the kings of the earth.
22 They will be gathered together,
As prisoners are gathered in the pit,
And will be shut up in the prison;
After many days they will be punished.
23 Then the moon will be disgraced
And the sun ashamed;
For the LORD of hosts will reign
On Mount Zion and in Jerusalem
And before His elders, gloriously.

CHAPTER 25 A DAY OF REJOICING.

O LORD, You *are* my God.
I will exalt You,
I will praise Your name,
For You have done wonderful *things;*
Your counsels of old *are* faithfulness *and* truth.
2 For You have made a city a ruin,
A fortified city a ruin,
A palace of foreigners to be a city no more;
It will never be rebuilt.
3 Therefore the strong people will glorify You;
The city of the terrible nations will fear You.
4 For You have been a strength to the poor,
A strength to the needy in his distress,
A refuge from the storm,
A shade from the heat;
For the blast of the terrible ones *is* as a storm *against* the wall.
5 You will reduce the noise of aliens,
As heat in a dry place;
As heat in the shadow of a cloud,
The song of the terrible ones will be diminished.

6 And in this mountain
The LORD of hosts will make for all people
A feast of choice pieces,
A feast of wines on the lees,
Of fat things full of marrow,
Of well-refined wines on the lees.
7 And He will destroy on this mountain
The surface of the covering cast over all people,
And the veil that is spread over all nations.
8 He will swallow up death forever,
And the Lord GOD will wipe away tears from all faces;
The rebuke of His people
He will take away from all the earth;
For the LORD has spoken.

9 And it will be said in that day:
"Behold, this *is* our God;
We have waited for Him, and He will save us.
This *is* the LORD;
We have waited for Him;
We will be glad and rejoice in His salvation."

10 For on this mountain the hand of the LORD will rest,
And Moab shall be trampled down under Him,
As straw is trampled down for the refuse heap.
11 And He will spread out His hands in their midst
As a swimmer reaches out to swim,
And He will bring down their pride
Together with the trickery of their hands.
12 The fortress of the high fort of your walls
He will bring down, lay low,
And bring to the ground, down to the dust.

CHAPTER 26 THE PEOPLE SING. In that day this song will be sung in the land of Judah:

"We have a strong city;
God will appoint salvation *for* walls and bulwarks.
2 Open the gates,
That the righteous nation which keeps the truth may enter in.
3 You will keep *him* in perfect peace,
Whose mind *is* stayed *on* You,
Because he trusts in You.
4 Trust in the LORD forever,
For in YAH, the LORD, *is* everlasting strength.
5 For He brings down those who dwell on high,
The lofty city;
He lays it low,
He lays it low to the ground,
He brings it down to the dust.
6 The foot shall tread it down—
The feet of the poor
And the steps of the needy."

7 The way of the just *is* uprightness;
O Most Upright,
You weigh the path of the just.
8 Yes, in the way of Your judgments,

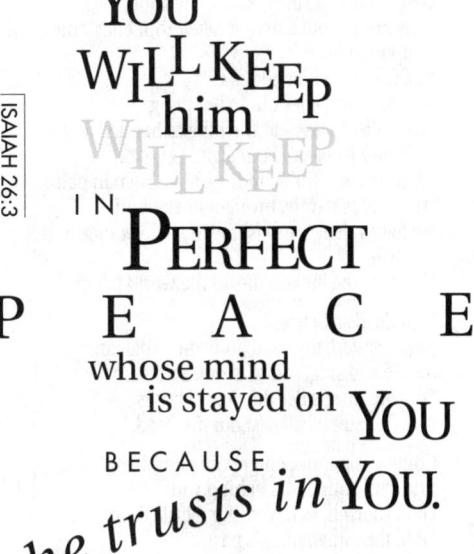

ISAIAH 26:3

YOU WILL KEEP him
WILL KEEP
IN PERFECT
P E A C E
whose mind is stayed on YOU
BECAUSE
he trusts in YOU.

O LORD, we have waited for You;
The desire of *our* soul *is* for Your name
And for the remembrance of You.
⁹ With my soul I have desired You in the night,
Yes, by my spirit within me I will seek You early;
For when Your judgments *are* in the earth,
The inhabitants of the world will learn
righteousness.

¹⁰ Let grace be shown to the wicked,
Yet he will not learn righteousness;
In the land of uprightness he will deal unjustly,
And will not behold the majesty of the LORD.
¹¹ LORD, *when* Your hand is lifted up, they will not see.
But they will see and be ashamed
For *their* envy of people;
Yes, the fire of Your enemies shall devour them.

◄◄◄► SECRET PLOTS

26:21 When God comes to judge the earth, the guilty will find no place to hide. Jesus said that secret plots will become public information because his truth, like a light shining in a dark corner, will reveal them (Matthew 10:26). Instead of trying to hide your shameful thoughts and actions from God, confess them to him and receive his forgiveness.

¹² LORD, You will establish peace for us,
For You have also done all our works in us.
¹³ O LORD our God, masters besides You
Have had dominion over us;
But by You only we make mention of Your name.
¹⁴ *They are* dead, they will not live;
They are deceased, they will not rise.
Therefore You have punished and destroyed them,
And made all their memory to perish.
¹⁵ You have increased the nation, O LORD,
You have increased the nation;
You are glorified;
You have expanded all the borders of the land.

¹⁶ LORD, in trouble they have visited You,
They poured out a prayer *when* Your chastening *was*
upon them.
¹⁷ As a woman with child
Is in pain and cries out in her pangs,
When she draws near the time of her delivery,
So have we been in Your sight, O LORD.
¹⁸ We have been with child, we have been in pain;
We have, as it were, brought forth wind;
We have not accomplished any deliverance in the
earth,
Nor have the inhabitants of the world fallen.

¹⁹ Your dead shall live;
Together with my dead body they shall arise.
Awake and sing, you who dwell in dust;
For your dew *is like* the dew of herbs,
And the earth shall cast out the dead.

²⁰ Come, my people, enter your chambers,
And shut your doors behind you;
Hide yourself, as it were, for a little moment,
Until the indignation is past.

²¹ For behold, the LORD comes out of His place
To punish the inhabitants of the earth for their
iniquity;
The earth will also disclose her blood,
And will no more cover her slain.

CHAPTER 27 GOD STOPS FEELING ANGRY.

In that day the LORD with His severe sword, great and
strong,
Will punish Leviathan the fleeing serpent,
Leviathan that twisted serpent;
And He will slay the reptile that *is* in the sea.

² In that day sing to her,
"A vineyard of red wine!
³ I, the LORD, keep it,
I water it every moment;
Lest any hurt it,
I keep it night and day.
⁴ Fury *is* not in Me.
Who would set briers *and* thorns
Against Me in battle?
I would go through them,
I would burn them together.
⁵ Or let him take hold of My strength,
That he may make peace with Me;
And he shall make peace with Me."

⁶ Those who come He shall cause to take root in Jacob;
Israel shall blossom and bud,
And fill the face of the world with fruit.

⁷ Has He struck Israel as He struck those who struck
him?
Or has He been slain according to the slaughter of
those who were slain by Him?
⁸ In measure, by sending it away,
You contended with it.
He removes *it* by His rough wind
In the day of the east wind.
⁹ Therefore by this the iniquity of Jacob will be
covered;
And this *is* all the fruit of taking away his sin:
When he makes all the stones of the altar
Like chalkstones that are beaten to dust,
Wooden images and incense altars shall not stand.

¹⁰ Yet the fortified city *will be* desolate,
The habitation forsaken and left like a wilderness;
There the calf will feed, and there it will lie down
And consume its branches.
¹¹ When its boughs are withered, they will be broken
off;
The women come *and* set them on fire.
For it *is* a people of no understanding;
Therefore He who made them will not have mercy
on them,
And He who formed them will show them no favor.

¹² And it shall come to pass in that day
That the LORD will thresh,
From the channel of the River to the Brook of Egypt;
And you will be gathered one by one,

O you children of Israel.

13 So it shall be in that day:
The great trumpet will be blown;
They will come, who are about to perish in the land
of Assyria,
And they who are outcasts in the land of Egypt,
And shall worship the LORD in the holy mount at
Jerusalem.

CHAPTER 28 A WONDERFUL TEACHER.

Woe to the crown of pride, to the drunkards of
Ephraim,
Whose glorious beauty *is* a fading flower
Which *is* at the head of the verdant valleys,
To those who are overcome with wine!
2 Behold, the Lord has a mighty and strong one,
Like a tempest of hail and a destroying storm,
Like a flood of mighty waters overflowing,
Who will bring *them* down to the earth with *His*
hand.
3 The crown of pride, the drunkards of Ephraim,
Will be trampled underfoot;
4 And the glorious beauty is a fading flower
Which *is* at the head of the verdant valley,
Like the first fruit before the summer,
Which an observer sees;
He eats it up while it is still in his hand.

5 In that day the LORD of hosts will be
For a crown of glory and a diadem of beauty
To the remnant of His people,
6 For a spirit of justice to him who sits in judgment,
And for strength to those who turn back the battle at
the gate.

7 But they also have erred through wine,
And through intoxicating drink are out of the way;
The priest and the prophet have erred through
intoxicating drink,
They are swallowed up by wine,
They are out of the way through intoxicating drink;
They err in vision, they stumble *in* judgment.
8 For all tables are full of vomit *and* filth;
No place *is clean.*

9 "Whom will he teach knowledge?
And whom will he make to understand the message?
Those *just* weaned from milk?
Those *just* drawn from the breasts?
10 For precept *must be* upon precept, precept upon
precept,
Line upon line, line upon line,
Here a little, there a little."

11 For with stammering lips and another tongue
He will speak to this people,
12 To whom He said, "This *is* the rest *with which*
You may cause the weary to rest,"
And, "This *is* the refreshing";
Yet they would not hear.
13 But the word of the LORD was to them,
"Precept upon precept, precept upon precept,

Line upon line, line upon line,
Here a little, there a little,"
That they might go and fall backward, and be broken
And snared and caught.

14 Therefore hear the word of the LORD, you scornful
men,
Who rule this people who *are* in Jerusalem,
15 Because you have said, "We have made a covenant
with death,
And with Sheol we are in agreement.
When the overflowing scourge passes through,
It will not come to us,
For we have made lies our refuge,
And under falsehood we have hidden ourselves."

◣ SIMPLICITY

28:13 God used repetition and simple words to get his messages through to the people. Do you find that God has to teach you the same lessons over and over? The simplicity of God's message can be a stumbling block for some (28:9-10), leading them to think it must have little value. We must not be too proud to heed God's simple message.

16 Therefore thus says the Lord GOD:

"Behold, I lay in Zion a stone for a foundation,
A tried stone, a precious cornerstone, a sure
foundation;
Whoever believes will not act hastily.
17 Also I will make justice the measuring line,
And righteousness the plummet;
The hail will sweep away the refuge of lies,
And the waters will overflow the hiding place.
18 Your covenant with death will be annulled,
And your agreement with Sheol will not stand;
When the overflowing scourge passes through,
Then you will be trampled down by it.
19 As often as it goes out it will take you;
For morning by morning it will pass over,
And by day and by night;
It will be a terror just to understand the report."

20 For the bed is too short to stretch out *on,*
And the covering so narrow that one cannot wrap
himself *in it.*
21 For the LORD will rise up as *at* Mount Perazim,
He will be angry as in the Valley of Gibeon—
That He may do His work, His awesome work,
And bring to pass His act, His unusual act.
22 Now therefore, do not be mockers,
Lest your bonds be made strong;
For I have heard from the Lord GOD of hosts,
A destruction determined even upon the whole
earth.

23 Give ear and hear my voice,
Listen and hear my speech.
24 Does the plowman keep plowing all day to sow?
Does he keep turning his soil and breaking the clods?
25 When he has leveled its surface,
Does he not sow the black cummin
And scatter the cummin,

Plant the wheat in rows,
The barley in the appointed place,
And the spelt in its place?
²⁶ For He instructs him in right judgment,
His God teaches him.

²⁷ For the black cummin is not threshed with a
threshing sledge,
Nor is a cartwheel rolled over the cummin;
But the black cummin is beaten out with a stick,
And the cummin with a rod.
²⁸ Bread *flour* must be ground;
Therefore he does not thresh it forever,
Break *it with* his cartwheel,
Or crush *it with* his horsemen.
²⁹ This also comes from the LORD of hosts,
Who is wonderful in counsel *and* excellent in
guidance.

CHAPTER 29 NO ONE CAN HIDE FROM GOD.

"Woe to Ariel, to Ariel, the city *where* David dwelt!
Add year to year;
Let feasts come around.
² Yet I will distress Ariel;
There shall be heaviness and sorrow,
And it shall be to Me as Ariel.
³ I will encamp against you all around,
I will lay siege against you with a mound,
And I will raise siegeworks against you.
⁴ You shall be brought down,
You shall speak out of the ground;
Your speech shall be low, out of the dust;
Your voice shall be like a medium's, out of the
ground;
And your speech shall whisper out of the dust.

⁵ "Moreover the multitude of your foes
Shall be like fine dust,
And the multitude of the terrible ones
Like chaff that passes away;
Yes, it shall be in an instant, suddenly.
⁶ You will be punished by the LORD of hosts
With thunder and earthquake and great noise,
With storm and tempest
And the flame of devouring fire.
⁷ The multitude of all the nations who fight against
Ariel,
Even all who fight against her and her fortress,
And distress her,
Shall be as a dream of a night vision.
⁸ It shall even be as when a hungry man dreams,
And look—he eats;
But he awakes, and his soul is still empty;
Or as when a thirsty man dreams,
And look—he drinks;
But he awakes, and indeed *he is* faint,
And his soul still craves:
So the multitude of all the nations shall be,
Who fight against Mount Zion."

⁹ Pause and wonder!
Blind yourselves and be blind!

They are drunk, but not with wine;
They stagger, but not with intoxicating drink.
¹⁰ For the LORD has poured out on you
The spirit of deep sleep,
And has closed your eyes, namely, the prophets;
And He has covered your heads, *namely,* the seers.

¹¹The whole vision has become to you like the words
of a book that is sealed, which *men* deliver to one who is
literate, saying, "Read this, please."
And he says, "I cannot, for it *is* sealed."
¹²Then the book is delivered to one who is illiterate,
saying, "Read this, please."
And he says, "I am not literate."
¹³Therefore the Lord said:

"Inasmuch as these people draw near with their
mouths
And honor Me with their lips,
But have removed their hearts far from Me,
And their fear toward Me is taught by the
commandment of men,
¹⁴ Therefore, behold, I will again do a marvelous work
Among this people,
A marvelous work and a wonder;
For the wisdom of their wise *men* shall perish,
And the understanding of their prudent *men* shall
be hidden."

◤▬▬▬▬▬ HYPOCRISY

29:13-14 The people claimed to belong to God, but because they
disobedient and merely went through the motions, God punished the
Religion had become routine instead of real. Isaiah condemned the
people for being hypocrites. Jesus quoted this verse (Matthew 15:8; ◗
7:6-7) when he spoke to the Pharisees, the religious leaders of his d◗
We all are capable of hypocrisy. Often we slip into routine forms of
worship that mean nothing to us. If we want to be called God's peopl◗
must be obedient and worship him honestly and sincerely.

¹⁵ Woe to those who seek deep to hide their counsel far
from the LORD,
And their works are in the dark;
They say, "Who sees us?" and, "Who knows us?"
¹⁶ Surely you have things turned around!
Shall the potter be esteemed as the clay;
For shall the thing made say of him who made it,
"He did not make me"?
Or shall the thing formed say of him who formed it,
"He has no understanding"?

¹⁷ *Is* it not yet a very little while
Till Lebanon shall be turned into a fruitful field,
And the fruitful field be esteemed as a forest?

◤▬▬▬▬▬ HIDING

29:15-16 The people of Jerusalem tried to hide their plans from ◗
They thought God couldn't see them and didn't know what was
happening. It's strange that so many people think they can hide fro◗
God. In Psalm 139 we learn that God has examined us and knows
everything about us. Would you be embarrassed if your best friends
knew your personal thoughts? Remember that God knows all of the◗

18 In that day the deaf shall hear the words of the book,
   And the eyes of the blind shall see out of obscurity
      and out of darkness.
19 The humble also shall increase *their* joy in the LORD,
   And the poor among men shall rejoice
      In the Holy One of Israel.
20 For the terrible one is brought to nothing,
   The scornful one is consumed,
   And all who watch for iniquity are cut off—
21 Who make a man an offender by a word,
   And lay a snare for him who reproves in the gate,
   And turn aside the just by empty words.

22Therefore thus says the LORD, who redeemed Abraham, concerning the house of Jacob:

   "Jacob shall not now be ashamed,
      Nor shall his face now grow pale;
23 But when he sees his children,
   The work of My hands, in his midst,
   They will hallow My name,
   And hallow the Holy One of Jacob,
   And fear the God of Israel.
24 These also who erred in spirit will come to
      understanding,
   And those who complained will learn doctrine."

CHAPTER **30** GOD IS WAITING.

   "Woe to the rebellious children," says the LORD,
   "Who take counsel, but not of Me,
   And who devise plans, but not of My Spirit,
   That they may add sin to sin;
2 Who walk to go down to Egypt,
   And have not asked My advice,
   To strengthen themselves in the strength of Pharaoh,
   And to trust in the shadow of Egypt!
3 Therefore the strength of Pharaoh
   Shall be your shame,
   And trust in the shadow of Egypt
   Shall be *your* humiliation.
4 For his princes were at Zoan,
   And his ambassadors came to Hanes.
5 They were all ashamed of a people *who* could not
      benefit them,
   Or be help or benefit,
   But a shame and also a reproach."

6The burden against the beasts of the South.

   Through a land of trouble and anguish,
   From which *came* the lioness and lion,
   The viper and fiery flying serpent,
   They will carry their riches on the backs of young
      donkeys,
   And their treasures on the humps of camels,
   To a people *who* shall not profit;
7 For the Egyptians shall help in vain and to no
      purpose.
   Therefore I have called her
   Rahab-Hem-Shebeth.

8 Now go, write it before them on a tablet,
   And note it on a scroll,
   That it may be for time to come,
   Forever and ever:
9 That this *is* a rebellious people,
   Lying children,
   Children *who* will not hear the law of the LORD;
10 Who say to the seers, "Do not see,"
   And to the prophets, "Do not prophesy to us right
      things;
   Speak to us smooth things, prophesy deceits.
11 Get out of the way,
   Turn aside from the path,
   Cause the Holy One of Israel
   To cease from before us."

12Therefore thus says the Holy One of Israel:

It seems like every other month my dad is complaining about hearing of another TV preacher getting into trouble or a local pastor who molested someone. What do I say to people who point to the hypocrites in this world as their reason for giving God the cold shoulder?

I WONDER . . .

Unfortunately, even some of God's children act shamefully. In fact, there probably is not a Christian alive who, at one time or another, hasn't betrayed God by his or her actions.

The word "hypocrite" means "play act," to claim to be a certain type of person while acting like someone else. God is pretty upset at hypocrites, those who claim to be his followers but really aren't.

Jesus said, "Beware of the leaven of the Pharisees, which is hypocrisy. For there is nothing covered that will not be revealed, nor hidden that will not be known. Therefore whatever you have spoken in the dark will be heard in the light, and what you have spoken in the ear in inner rooms will be proclaimed on the housetops" (Luke 12:1-3).

When our world's final act draws to a close, some of the first to receive God's wrath will be those who have been playacting with God (see Isaiah 29:13-14). He is not amused or impressed; they will be judged.

Unfortunately, there is nothing you can do to prevent strangers from misrepresenting Christ. The only person you can prevent being a hypocrite is you. Here are some ways to keep from becoming a hypocrite:

First, watch your own actions closely. Though God reads your heart, other people see your actions first (see 2 Corinthians 13:5). If what you say doesn't match what you say you believe, get ready to be called a hypocrite.

Second, don't come down on other people too hard. Remember, the only difference between you and those who aren't Christians is that you've received the gift of forgiveness.

Third, be quick to admit when you make a mistake. True humility is rare in our culture. For some reason, people are drawn to those who can readily admit their mistakes. It's called being genuine.

"Because you despise this word,
And trust in oppression and perversity,
And rely on them,

13 Therefore this iniquity shall be to you
Like a breach ready to fall,
A bulge in a high wall,
Whose breaking comes suddenly, in an instant.

14 And He shall break it like the breaking of the potter's
vessel,
Which is broken in pieces;
He shall not spare.
So there shall not be found among its fragments
A shard to take fire from the hearth,
Or to take water from the cistern."

15For thus says the Lord GOD, the Holy One of Israel:

"In returning and rest you shall be saved;
In quietness and confidence shall be your strength."
But you would not,

16 And you said, "No, for we will flee on horses"—
Therefore you shall flee!
And, "We will ride on swift *horses*"—
Therefore those who pursue you shall be swift!

17 One thousand *shall flee* at the threat of one,
At the threat of five you shall flee,
Till you are left as a pole on top of a mountain
And as a banner on a hill.

18 Therefore the LORD will wait, that He may be
gracious to you;
And therefore He will be exalted, that He may have
mercy on you.
For the LORD *is* a God of justice;
Blessed *are* all those who wait for Him.

19 For the people shall dwell in Zion at Jerusalem;
You shall weep no more.
He will be very gracious to you at the sound of your
cry;
When He hears it, He will answer you.

20 And *though* the Lord gives you
The bread of adversity and the water of affliction,
Yet your teachers will not be moved into a corner
anymore,
But your eyes shall see your teachers.

21 Your ears shall hear a word behind you, saying,
"This *is* the way, walk in it,"
Whenever you turn to the right hand
Or whenever you turn to the left.

22 You will also defile the covering of your images of
silver,
And the ornament of your molded images of gold.
You will throw them away as an unclean thing;
You will say to them, "Get away!"

23 Then He will give the rain for your seed
With which you sow the ground,
And bread of the increase of the earth;
It will be fat and plentiful.
In that day your cattle will feed
In large pastures.

24 Likewise the oxen and the young donkeys that work
the ground
Will eat cured fodder,
Which has been winnowed with the shovel and fan.

25 There will be on every high mountain
And on every high hill
Rivers *and* streams of waters,
In the day of the great slaughter,
When the towers fall.

26 Moreover the light of the moon will be as the light of
the sun,
And the light of the sun will be sevenfold,
As the light of seven days,
In the day that the LORD binds up the bruise of His
people
And heals the stroke of their wound.

27 Behold, the name of the LORD comes from afar,
Burning *with* His anger,
And *His* burden *is* heavy;
His lips are full of indignation,
And His tongue like a devouring fire.

28 His breath is like an overflowing stream,
Which reaches up to the neck,
To sift the nations with the sieve of futility;
And *there shall be* a bridle in the jaws of the people,
Causing *them* to err.

29 You shall have a song
As in the night *when* a holy festival is kept,
And gladness of heart as when one goes with a flute,
To come into the mountain of the LORD,
To the Mighty One of Israel.

30 The LORD will cause His glorious voice to be heard,
And show the descent of His arm,
With the indignation of *His* anger
And the flame of a devouring fire,
With scattering, tempest, and hailstones.

31 For through the voice of the LORD
Assyria will be beaten down,
As He strikes with the rod.

32 And *in* every place where the staff of punishment
passes,
Which the LORD lays on him,
It will be with tambourines and harps;
And in battles of brandishing He will fight with it.

33 For Tophet *was* established of old,
Yes, for the king it is prepared.
He has made *it* deep and large;
Its pyre *is* fire with much wood;
The breath of the LORD, like a stream of brimstone,
Kindles it.

CHAPTER **31** THE SWORD OF GOD.

Woe to those who go down to Egypt for help,
And rely on horses,
Who trust in chariots because *they are* many,
And in horsemen because they are very strong,
But who do not look to the Holy One of Israel,
Nor seek the LORD!

2 Yet He also *is* wise and will bring disaster,

And will not call back His words,
But will arise against the house of evildoers,
And against the help of those who work iniquity.
³ Now the Egyptians *are* men, and not God;
And their horses are flesh, and not spirit.
When the LORD stretches out His hand,
Both he who helps will fall,
And he who is helped will fall down;
They all will perish together.

⁴For thus the LORD has spoken to me:

"As a lion roars,
And a young lion over his prey
(When a multitude of shepherds is summoned
   against him,
He will not be afraid of their voice
Nor be disturbed by their noise),
So the LORD of hosts will come down
To fight for Mount Zion and for its hill.
⁵ Like birds flying about,
So will the LORD of hosts defend Jerusalem.
Defending, He will also deliver *it*;
Passing over, He will preserve *it*."

⁶Return *to Him* against whom the children of Israel have deeply revolted. ⁷For in that day every man shall throw away his idols of silver and his idols of gold—sin, which your own hands have made for yourselves.

⁸ "Then Assyria shall fall by a sword not of man,
And a sword not of mankind shall devour him.
But he shall flee from the sword,
And his young men shall become forced labor.
⁹ He shall cross over to his stronghold for fear,
And his princes shall be afraid of the banner,"
Says the LORD,
Whose fire *is* in Zion
And whose furnace *is* in Jerusalem.

CHAPTER **32** A PROMISE OF PEACE.
Behold, a king will reign in righteousness,
And princes will rule with justice.
² A man will be as a hiding place from the wind,
And a cover from the tempest,
As rivers of water in a dry place,
As the shadow of a great rock in a weary land.
³ The eyes of those who see will not be dim,
And the ears of those who hear will listen.
⁴ Also the heart of the rash will understand knowledge,
And the tongue of the stammerers will be ready to
   speak plainly.

⁵ The foolish person will no longer be called generous,
Nor the miser said *to be* bountiful;
⁶ For the foolish person will speak foolishness,
And his heart will work iniquity:
To practice ungodliness,
To utter error against the LORD,
To keep the hungry unsatisfied,
And he will cause the drink of the thirsty to fail.
⁷ Also the schemes of the schemer *are* evil;
He devises wicked plans

To destroy the poor with lying words,
Even when the needy speaks justice.
⁸ But a generous man devises generous things,
And by generosity he shall stand.

⁹ Rise up, you women who are at ease,
Hear my voice;
You complacent daughters,
Give ear to my speech.
¹⁰ In a year and *some* days
You will be troubled, you complacent women;
For the vintage will fail,
The gathering will not come.
¹¹ Tremble, you *women* who are at ease;
Be troubled, you complacent ones;
Strip yourselves, make yourselves bare,
And gird *sackcloth* on *your* waists.

IDOLS
31:7 Someday these people would throw their idols away, recognizing that the idols were nothing but wood or stone. Idols such as money, fame, or success are seductive. Instead of contributing to our spiritual development, they rob us of our thoughts, time, energy, and devotion to God. At first they seem exciting and promise to take us places, but in the end we will find that we have become their slaves. We need to recognize their worthlessness now, before they rob us of our freedom.

¹² People shall mourn upon their breasts
For the pleasant fields, for the fruitful vine.
¹³ On the land of my people will come up thorns *and*
   briers,
Yes, on all the happy homes *in* the joyous city;
¹⁴ Because the palaces will be forsaken,
The bustling city will be deserted.
The forts and towers will become lairs forever,
A joy of wild donkeys, a pasture of flocks—
¹⁵ Until the Spirit is poured upon us from on high,
And the wilderness becomes a fruitful field,
And the fruitful field is counted as a forest.

¹⁶ Then justice will dwell in the wilderness,
And righteousness remain in the fruitful field.
¹⁷ The work of righteousness will be peace,
And the effect of righteousness, quietness and
   assurance forever.
¹⁸ My people will dwell in a peaceful habitation,
In secure dwellings, and in quiet resting places,
¹⁹ Though hail comes down on the forest,
And the city is brought low in humiliation.

²⁰ Blessed *are* you who sow beside all waters,
Who send out freely the feet of the ox and the
   donkey.

AT EASE
32:9-13 The people turned their backs on God and concentrated on their own best interests. This warning is not just to the women of Israel, but to all who sit back in their thoughtless ease, enjoying crops, clothes, land, and cities while an enemy approaches. Wealth and luxury bring false security, lulling us into thinking all is well when disaster is around the corner. By abandoning God's purpose for our life, we also abandon his help.

CHAPTER 33 GOD'S GREAT FORGIVENESS.

Woe to you who plunder, though you *have* not *been*
    plundered;
And you who deal treacherously, though they have
    not dealt treacherously with you!
When you cease plundering,
    You will be plundered;
When you make an end of dealing treacherously,
    They will deal treacherously with you.

2 O LORD, be gracious to us;
    We have waited for You.
Be their arm every morning,
    Our salvation also in the time of trouble.
3 At the noise of the tumult the people shall flee;
    When You lift Yourself up, the nations shall be
      scattered;
4 And Your plunder shall be gathered
    Like the gathering of the caterpillar;
As the running to and fro of locusts,
    He shall run upon them.

5 The LORD is exalted, for He dwells on high;
    He has filled Zion with justice and righteousness.
6 Wisdom and knowledge will be the stability of your
      times,
    And the strength of salvation;
The fear of the LORD *is* His treasure.

7 Surely their valiant ones shall cry outside,
    The ambassadors of peace shall weep bitterly.
8 The highways lie waste,
    The traveling man ceases.
He has broken the covenant,
    He has despised the cities,
He regards no man.
9 The earth mourns *and* languishes,
    Lebanon is shamed *and* shriveled;
Sharon is like a wilderness,
    And Bashan and Carmel shake off *their fruits.*

10 "Now I will rise," says the LORD;
    "Now I will be exalted,
Now I will lift Myself up.
11 You shall conceive chaff,
    You shall bring forth stubble;
Your breath, *as* fire, shall devour you.
12 And the people shall be *like* the burnings of lime;
    Like thorns cut up they shall be burned in the fire.
13 Hear, you *who are* afar off, what I have done;
    And you *who are* near, acknowledge My might."

14 The sinners in Zion are afraid;
    Fearfulness has seized the hypocrites:
"Who among us shall dwell with the devouring fire?
    Who among us shall dwell with everlasting
      burnings?"
15 He who walks righteously and speaks uprightly,
    He who despises the gain of oppressions,
Who gestures with his hands, refusing bribes,
    Who stops his ears from hearing of bloodshed,
And shuts his eyes from seeing evil:
16 He will dwell on high;

33:1 The Assyrians continually broke their promises but demanded
others keep theirs. It is easy to put ourselves in the same selfish po
demanding our rights while violating the rights of others. Broken
promises shatter trust and destroy relationships. Determine to mak
promises you can't keep; and, equally important, ask forgiveness
promises you have broken. Exercise the same fairness with others
you demand for yourself.

His place of defense *will be* the fortress of rocks;
    Bread will be given him,
His water *will be* sure.

17 Your eyes will see the King in His beauty;
    They will see the land that is very far off.
18 Your heart will meditate on terror:
    "Where *is* the scribe?
Where *is* he who weighs?
    Where *is* he who counts the towers?"
19 You will not see a fierce people,
    A people of obscure speech, beyond perception,
Of a stammering tongue *that you* cannot
      understand.

20 Look upon Zion, the city of our appointed feasts;
    Your eyes will see Jerusalem, a quiet home,
A tabernacle *that* will not be taken down;
    Not one of its stakes will ever be removed,
Nor will any of its cords be broken.
21 But there the majestic LORD *will be* for us
    A place of broad rivers *and* streams,
In which no galley with oars will sail,
    Nor majestic ships pass by
22 (For the LORD *is* our Judge,
    The LORD *is* our Lawgiver,
The LORD *is* our King;
    He will save us);
23 Your tackle is loosed,
    They could not strengthen their mast,
They could not spread the sail.
    Then the prey of great plunder is divided;
The lame take the prey.
24 And the inhabitant will not say, "I am sick";
    The people who dwell in it *will be* forgiven *their*
      iniquity.

CHAPTER 34 COME AND LISTEN!

Come near, you nations, to hear;
    And heed, you people!
Let the earth hear, and all that is in it,
    The world and all things that come forth from it.
2 For the indignation of the LORD *is* against all nations,
    And *His* fury against all their armies;
He has utterly destroyed them,
    He has given them over to the slaughter.
3 Also their slain shall be thrown out;
    Their stench shall rise from their corpses,
And the mountains shall be melted with their blood.
4 All the host of heaven shall be dissolved,
    And the heavens shall be rolled up like a scroll;
All their host shall fall down
    As the leaf falls from the vine,
And as *fruit* falling from a fig tree.

5 "For My sword shall be bathed in heaven;
  Indeed it shall come down on Edom,
  And on the people of My curse, for judgment.
6 The sword of the LORD is filled with blood,
  It is made overflowing with fatness,
  With the blood of lambs and goats,
  With the fat of the kidneys of rams.
  For the LORD has a sacrifice in Bozrah,
  And a great slaughter in the land of Edom.
7 The wild oxen shall come down with them,
  And the young bulls with the mighty bulls;
  Their land shall be soaked with blood,
  And their dust saturated with fatness."

8 For *it is* the day of the LORD's vengeance,
  The year of recompense for the cause of Zion.
9 Its streams shall be turned into pitch,
  And its dust into brimstone;
  Its land shall become burning pitch.
10 It shall not be quenched night or day;
  Its smoke shall ascend forever.
  From generation to generation it shall lie waste;
  No one shall pass through it forever and ever.
11 But the pelican and the porcupine shall possess it,
  Also the owl and the raven shall dwell in it.
  And He shall stretch out over it
  The line of confusion and the stones of emptiness.
12 They shall call its nobles to the kingdom,
  But none *shall be* there, and all its princes shall be
    nothing.

13 And thorns shall come up in its palaces,
  Nettles and brambles in its fortresses;
  It shall be a habitation of jackals,
  A courtyard for ostriches.
14 The wild beasts of the desert shall also meet with the
    jackals,
  And the wild goat shall bleat to its companion;
  Also the night creature shall rest there,
  And find for herself a place of rest.
15 There the arrow snake shall make her nest and lay
    eggs
  And hatch, and gather *them* under her shadow;
  There also shall the hawks be gathered,
  Every one with her mate.

16 "Search from the book of the LORD, and read:
  Not one of these shall fail;
  Not one shall lack her mate.
  For My mouth has commanded it, and His Spirit has
    gathered them.
17 He has cast the lot for them,
  And His hand has divided it among them with a
    measuring line.
  They shall possess it forever;
  From generation to generation they shall dwell in it."

CHAPTER 35 STREAMS IN THE DESERT.

The wilderness and the wasteland shall be glad for
  them,
And the desert shall rejoice and blossom as the rose;
2 It shall blossom abundantly and rejoice,

Even with joy and singing.
The glory of Lebanon shall be given to it,
The excellence of Carmel and Sharon.
They shall see the glory of the LORD,
The excellency of our God.

3 Strengthen the weak hands,
  And make firm the feeble knees.
4 Say to those *who are* fearful-hearted,
  "Be strong, do not fear!
  Behold, your God will come *with* vengeance,
  With the recompense of God;
  He will come and save you."

VISIONS

35:1ff In chapters 1–34, Isaiah delivered a message of judgment on all nations, including Israel and Judah, for rejecting God. Although there were glimpses of relief and restoration for the remnant of faithful believers, the climate of wrath, fury, judgment, and destruction prevailed. Now Isaiah breaks through with a vision of beauty and encouragement. God is just as complete in his mercy as he is severe in his judgment. God's complete moral perfection is revealed by his hatred of all sin, and this leads to judgment. This same moral perfection is revealed in his love for all he has created. This leads to mercy for those who have been less than perfect but who have sincerely loved and obeyed him.

5 Then the eyes of the blind shall be opened,
  And the ears of the deaf shall be unstopped.
6 Then the lame shall leap like a deer,
  And the tongue of the dumb sing.
  For waters shall burst forth in the wilderness,
  And streams in the desert.
7 The parched ground shall become a pool,
  And the thirsty land springs of water;
  In the habitation of jackals, where each lay,
  There shall be grass with reeds and rushes.

8 A highway shall be there, and a road,
  And it shall be called the Highway of Holiness.
  The unclean shall not pass over it,
  But it *shall be* for others.
  Whoever walks the road, although a fool,
  Shall not go astray.
9 No lion shall be there,
  Nor shall *any* ravenous beast go up on it;
  It shall not be found there.
  But the redeemed shall walk *there*,
10 And the ransomed of the LORD shall return,
  And come to Zion with singing,
  With everlasting joy on their heads.
  They shall obtain joy and gladness,
  And sorrow and sighing shall flee away.

CHAPTER 36 AN ANGEL DESTROYS AN ARMY.

Now it came to pass in the fourteenth year of King Hezekiah *that* Sennacherib king of Assyria came up against all the fortified cities of Judah and took them. ²Then the king of Assyria sent *the* Rabshakeh with a great army from Lachish to King Hezekiah at Jerusalem. And he stood by the aqueduct from the upper pool, on the highway to the Fuller's Field. ³And Eliakim the son of Hilkiah, who was over the household, Shebna the scribe, and Joah the son of Asaph, the recorder, came out to him.

⁴Then *the* Rabshakeh said to them, "Say now to Hezekiah, 'Thus says the great king, the king of Assyria: "What confidence is this in which you trust? ⁵I say you speak of having plans and power for war; but *they are* mere words. Now in whom do you trust, that you rebel against me? ⁶Look! You are trusting in the staff of this broken reed, Egypt, on which if a man leans, it will go into his hand and pierce it. So *is* Pharaoh king of Egypt to all who trust in him.

⁷"But if you say to me, 'We trust in the LORD our God,' *is it* not He whose high places and whose altars Hezekiah has taken away, and said to Judah and Jerusalem, 'You shall worship before this altar'?" ' ⁸Now therefore, I urge you, give a pledge to my master the king of Assyria, and I will give you two thousand horses—if you are able on your part to put riders on them! ⁹How then will you repel one captain of the least of my master's servants, and put your trust in Egypt for chariots and horsemen? ¹⁰Have I now come up without the LORD against this land to destroy it? The LORD said to me, 'Go up against this land, and destroy it.' "

▰▰▰ DECEIT

36:7 The field commander (Rabshakeh) from Assyria claimed that Hezekiah insulted God by tearing down his altars in the hills and making the people worship in Jerusalem. But Hezekiah's reform sought to eliminate idol worship (which occurred mainly in the hills) so that the people worshiped only the true God. Either the Assyrians didn't know about the religion of the true God, or they wanted to deceive the people into thinking they had angered a powerful god. In the same way, Satan tries to confuse or deceive us. People don't necessarily need to be sinful to be ineffective for God; they need only be confused about what God wants. To avoid Satan's deceit, study God's Word carefully and regularly. When you know what God says, you will not fall for Satan's lies.

¹¹Then Eliakim, Shebna, and Joah said to *the* Rabshakeh, "Please speak to your servants in Aramaic, for we understand *it;* and do not speak to us in Hebrew in the hearing of the people who *are* on the wall."

¹²But *the* Rabshakeh said, "Has my master sent me to your master and to you to speak these words, and not to the men who sit on the wall, who will eat and drink their own waste with you?"

¹³Then *the* Rabshakeh stood and called out with a loud voice in Hebrew, and said, "Hear the words of the great king, the king of Assyria! ¹⁴Thus says the king: 'Do not let Hezekiah deceive you, for he will not be able to deliver you; ¹⁵nor let Hezekiah make you trust in the LORD, saying, "The LORD will surely deliver us; this city will not be given into the hand of the king of Assyria." ' ¹⁶Do not listen to Hezekiah; for thus says the king of Assyria: 'Make *peace* with me *by a* present and come out to me; and every one of you eat from his own vine and every one from his own fig tree, and every one of you drink the waters of his own cistern; ¹⁷until I come and take you away to a land like your own land, a land of grain and new wine, a land of bread and vineyards. ¹⁸Beware lest Hezekiah persuade you, saying, "The LORD will deliver us."

Has any one of the gods of the nations delivered its land from the hand of the king of Assyria? ¹⁹Where *are* the gods of Hamath and Arpad? Where *are* the gods of Sepharvaim? Indeed, have they delivered Samaria from my hand? ²⁰Who among all the gods of these lands have delivered their countries from my hand, that the LORD should deliver Jerusalem from my hand?' "

²¹But they held their peace and answered him not a word; for the king's commandment was, "Do not answer him." ²²Then Eliakim the son of Hilkiah, who *was* over the household, Shebna the scribe, and Joah the son of Asaph, the recorder, came to Hezekiah with *their* clothes torn, and told him the words of *the* Rabshakeh.

CHAPTER **37** And so it was, when King Hezekiah heard *it,* that he tore his clothes, covered himself with sackcloth, and went into the house of the LORD. ²Then he sent Eliakim, who *was* over the household, Shebna the scribe, and the elders of the priests, covered with sackcloth, to Isaiah the prophet, the son of Amoz. ³And they said to him, "Thus says Hezekiah: 'This day *is* a day of trouble and rebuke and blasphemy; for the children have come to birth, but *there is* no strength to bring them forth. ⁴It may be that the LORD your God will hear the words of *the* Rabshakeh, whom his master the king of Assyria has sent to reproach the living God, and will rebuke the words which the LORD your God has heard. Therefore lift up *your* prayer for the remnant that is left.' "

⁵So the servants of King Hezekiah came to Isaiah. ⁶And Isaiah said to them, "Thus you shall say to your master, 'Thus says the LORD: "Do not be afraid of the words which you have heard, with which the servants of the king of Assyria have blasphemed Me. ⁷Surely I will send a spirit upon him, and he shall hear a rumor and return to his own land; and I will cause him to fall by the sword in his own land." ' "

⁸Then *the* Rabshakeh returned, and found the king of Assyria warring against Libnah, for he heard that he had departed from Lachish. ⁹And the king heard concerning Tirhakah king of Ethiopia, "He has come out to make war with you." So when he heard *it,* he sent messengers to Hezekiah, saying, ¹⁰"Thus you shall speak to Hezekiah king of Judah, saying: 'Do not let your God in whom you trust deceive you, saying, "Jerusalem shall not be given into the hand of the king of Assyria." ¹¹Look! You have heard what the kings of Assyria have done to all lands by utterly destroying them; and shall you be delivered? ¹²Have the gods of the nations delivered those whom my fathers have destroyed, Gozan and Haran and Rezeph, and the people of Eden who *were* in Telassar? ¹³Where *is* the king of Hamath, the king of Arpad, and the king of the city of Sepharvaim, Hena, and Ivah?' "

¹⁴And Hezekiah received the letter from the hand of the messengers, and read it; and Hezekiah went up to the

▰▰▰ THE ANSWER

37:8-10 Although the answer to Hezekiah's prayer was already [in] motion because Tirhakah was poised to attack, Hezekiah did not k[now?]. He persisted in prayer and faith even though he could not see the [answer?] coming. When we pray, we must have faith that God has already prepared the best answer. Our task is to ask in faith and wait.

house of the LORD, and spread it before the LORD. ¹⁵Then Hezekiah prayed to the LORD, saying: ¹⁶"O LORD of hosts, God of Israel, *the One* who dwells *between* the cherubim, You *are* God, You alone, of all the kingdoms of the earth. You have made heaven and earth. ¹⁷Incline Your ear, O LORD, and hear; open Your eyes, O LORD, and see; and hear all the words of Sennacherib, which he has sent to reproach the living God. ¹⁸Truly, LORD, the kings of Assyria have laid waste all the nations and their lands, ¹⁹and have cast their gods into the fire; for they *were* not gods, but the work of men's hands—wood and stone. Therefore they destroyed them. ²⁰Now therefore, O LORD our God, save us from his hand, that all the kingdoms of the earth may know that You *are* the LORD, You alone."

²¹Then Isaiah the son of Amoz sent to Hezekiah, saying, "Thus says the LORD God of Israel, 'Because you have prayed to Me against Sennacherib king of Assyria, ²²this *is* the word which the LORD has spoken concerning him:

"The virgin, the daughter of Zion,
  Has despised you, laughed you to scorn;
  The daughter of Jerusalem
  Has shaken *her* head behind your back!

²³ "Whom have you reproached and blasphemed?
  Against whom have you raised *your* voice,
  And lifted up your eyes on high?
  Against the Holy One of Israel.

²⁴ By your servants you have reproached the Lord,
  And said, 'By the multitude of my chariots
  I have come up to the height of the mountains,
  To the limits of Lebanon;
  I will cut down its tall cedars
  And its choice cypress trees;
  I will enter its farthest height,
  To its fruitful forest.

²⁵ I have dug and drunk water,
  And with the soles of my feet I have dried up
  All the brooks of defense.'

²⁶ "Did you not hear long ago
  How I made it,
  From ancient times that I formed it?
  Now I have brought it to pass,
  That you should be
  For crushing fortified cities *into* heaps of ruins.

²⁷ Therefore their inhabitants *had* little power;
  They were dismayed and confounded;
  They were *as* the grass of the field
  And the green herb,
  As the grass on the housetops
  And grain blighted before it is grown.

²⁸ "But I know your dwelling place,
  Your going out and your coming in,
  And your rage against Me.

²⁹ Because your rage against Me and your tumult
  Have come up to My ears,
  Therefore I will put My hook in your nose
  And My bridle in your lips,
  And I will turn you back
  By the way which you came." '

³⁰"This *shall be* a sign to you:

You shall eat this year such as grows of itself,
  And the second year what springs from the same;
  Also in the third year sow and reap,
  Plant vineyards and eat the fruit of them.

³¹ And the remnant who have escaped of the house of
      Judah
  Shall again take root downward,
  And bear fruit upward.

³² For out of Jerusalem shall go a remnant,
  And those who escape from Mount Zion.
  The zeal of the LORD of hosts will do this.

³³"Therefore thus says the LORD concerning the king of Assyria:

'He shall not come into this city,
  Nor shoot an arrow there,
  Nor come before it with shield,
  Nor build a siege mound against it.

³⁴ By the way that he came,
  By the same shall he return;
  And he shall not come into this city,'
  Says the LORD.

³⁵ 'For I will defend this city, to save it
  For My own sake and for My servant David's sake.' "

³⁶Then the angel of the LORD went out, and killed in the camp of the Assyrians one hundred and eighty-five thousand; and when *people* arose early in the morning, there were the corpses—all dead. ³⁷So Sennacherib king of Assyria departed and went away, returned *home*, and remained at Nineveh. ³⁸Now it came to pass, as he was worshiping in the house of Nisroch his god, that his sons Adrammelech and Sharezer struck him down with the sword; and they escaped into the land of Ararat. Then Esarhaddon his son reigned in his place.

CHAPTER **38** A KING ASKS FOR A MIRACLE.

In those days Hezekiah was sick and near death. And Isaiah the prophet, the son of Amoz, went to him and said to him, "Thus says the LORD: 'Set your house in order, for you shall die and not live.' "

²Then Hezekiah turned his face toward the wall, and prayed to the LORD, ³and said, "Remember now, O LORD, I pray, how I have walked before You in truth and with a loyal heart, and have done *what is* good in Your sight." And Hezekiah wept bitterly.

⁴And the word of the LORD came to Isaiah, saying, ⁵"Go and tell Hezekiah, 'Thus says the LORD, the God of David your father: "I have heard your prayer, I have seen your tears; surely I will add to your days fifteen years. ⁶I will deliver you and this city from the hand of the king of Assyria, and I will defend this city." ' ⁷And this *is* the sign to you from the LORD, that the LORD will do this thing

RADICAL CHANGE

38:1-5 When Isaiah told Hezekiah of his impending death, Hezekiah immediately turned to God. God responded to Hezekiah's prayer, allowing him to live another 15 years. In response to fervent prayer, God may change the course of our life, too. Never hesitate to ask God for radical changes if you will honor him with those changes.

which He has spoken: [8]Behold, I will bring the shadow on the sundial, which has gone down with the sun on the sundial of Ahaz, ten degrees backward." So the sun returned ten degrees on the dial by which it had gone down.

[9]This is the writing of Hezekiah king of Judah, when he had been sick and had recovered from his sickness:

[10] I said,
"In the prime of my life
I shall go to the gates of Sheol;
I am deprived of the remainder of my years."
[11] I said,
"I shall not see YAH,
The LORD in the land of the living;
I shall observe man no more among the inhabitants
of the world.
[12] My life span is gone,
Taken from me like a shepherd's tent;
I have cut off my life like a weaver.
He cuts me off from the loom;
From day until night You make an end of me.
[13] I have considered until morning—
Like a lion,
So He breaks all my bones;
From day until night You make an end of me.
[14] Like a crane *or* a swallow, so I chattered;
I mourned like a dove;
My eyes fail *from looking* upward.
O LORD, I am oppressed;
Undertake for me!

◥◤◥◣ UNDERCURRENT

39:8 Hezekiah, one of Judah's most faithful kings, worked hard throughout his reign to stamp out idol worship and to purify the worship of the true God at the Jerusalem temple. Nevertheless, he knew his kingdom was not pure. Powerful undercurrents of evil invited destruction, and only God's miraculous interventions preserved Judah from its enemies. Here Hezekiah expressed gratefulness that God was preserving peace during his reign. As soon as Hezekiah died, evil burst forth under the leadership of Manasseh, Hezekiah's son, who actually rebuilt the centers of idolatry his father had destroyed.

[15] "What shall I say?
He has both spoken to me,
And He Himself has done *it.*
I shall walk carefully all my years
In the bitterness of my soul.
[16] O Lord, by these *things men* live;
And in all these *things is* the life of my spirit;
So You will restore me and make me live.
[17] Indeed *it was* for *my own* peace
That I had great bitterness;
But You have lovingly *delivered* my soul from the pit
of corruption,
For You have cast all my sins behind Your back.
[18] For Sheol cannot thank You,
Death cannot praise You;
Those who go down to the pit cannot hope for Your
truth.
[19] The living, the living man, he shall praise You,
As I *do* this day;

The father shall make known Your truth to the children.

[20] "The LORD *was ready* to save me;
Therefore we will sing my songs with stringed
instruments
All the days of our life, in the house of the LORD."

[21]Now Isaiah had said, "Let them take a lump of figs, and apply *it* as a poultice on the boil, and he shall recover."

[22]And Hezekiah had said, "What *is* the sign that I shall go up to the house of the LORD?"

CHAPTER 39 MESSENGERS FROM BABYLON. At

that time Merodach-Baladan the son of Baladan, king of Babylon, sent letters and a present to Hezekiah, for he heard that he had been sick and had recovered. [2]And Hezekiah was pleased with them, and showed them the house of his treasures—the silver and gold, the spices and precious ointment, and all his armory—all that was found among his treasures. There was nothing in his house or in all his dominion that Hezekiah did not show them.

[3]Then Isaiah the prophet went to King Hezekiah, and said to him, "What did these men say, and from where did they come to you?"

So Hezekiah said, "They came to me from a far country, from Babylon."

[4]And he said, "What have they seen in your house?"

So Hezekiah answered, "They have seen all that *is* in my house; there is nothing among my treasures that I have not shown them."

[5]Then Isaiah said to Hezekiah, "Hear the word of the LORD of hosts: [6]'Behold, the days are coming when all that *is* in your house, and what your fathers have accumulated until this day, shall be carried to Babylon; nothing shall be left,' says the LORD. [7]'And they shall take away *some* of your sons who will descend from you, whom you will beget; and they shall be eunuchs in the palace of the king of Babylon.'"

[8]So Hezekiah said to Isaiah, "The word of the LORD which you have spoken *is* good!" For he said, "At least there will be peace and truth in my days."

CHAPTER 40 GOD WILL FEED HIS FLOCK.

"Comfort, yes, comfort My people!"
Says your God.
[2] "Speak comfort to Jerusalem, and cry out to her,
That her warfare is ended,
That her iniquity is pardoned;

◥◤◥◣ COMFORT

40:1 God's people still had 100 years of trouble before Jerusalem would fall, then 70 years of exile. So God told Isaiah to speak tender and to comfort Jerusalem.

When your life seems to be falling apart, ask God to comfort you may not escape hard times, but you can find God's comfort during Sometimes, however, the only comfort we have is in the knowledge someday we will be with God. Appreciate the comfort and encourage found in God's Word, his presence, and his people.

For she has received from the LORD's hand
  Double for all her sins."

3 The voice of one crying in the wilderness:
  "Prepare the way of the LORD;
  Make straight in the desert
  A highway for our God.
4 Every valley shall be exalted
  And every mountain and hill brought low;
  The crooked places shall be made straight
  And the rough places smooth;
5 The glory of the LORD shall be revealed,
  And all flesh shall see *it* together;
  For the mouth of the LORD has spoken."

6 The voice said, "Cry out!"
  And he said, "What shall I cry?"

"All flesh *is* grass,
  And all its loveliness *is* like the flower of the field.
7 The grass withers, the flower fades,
  Because the breath of the LORD blows upon it;
  Surely the people *are* grass.
8 The grass withers, the flower fades,
  But the word of our God stands forever."

9 O Zion,
  You who bring good tidings,
  Get up into the high mountain;
  O Jerusalem,
  You who bring good tidings,
  Lift up your voice with strength,
  Lift *it* up, be not afraid;
  Say to the cities of Judah, "Behold your God!"

10 Behold, the Lord GOD shall come with a strong *hand*,
  And His arm shall rule for Him;
  Behold, His reward *is* with Him,
  And His work before Him.
11 He will feed His flock like a shepherd;
  He will gather the lambs with His arm,
  And carry *them* in His bosom,
  And gently lead those who are with young.

12 Who has measured the waters in the hollow of His
    hand,
  Measured heaven with a span
  And calculated the dust of the earth in a measure?
  Weighed the mountains in scales
  And the hills in a balance?
13 Who has directed the Spirit of the LORD,
  Or *as* His counselor has taught Him?
14 With whom did He take counsel, and *who* instructed
    Him,
  And taught Him in the path of justice?
  Who taught Him knowledge,
  And showed Him the way of understanding?

15 Behold, the nations *are* as a drop in a bucket,
  And are counted as the small dust on the scales;
  Look, He lifts up the isles as a very little thing.
16 And Lebanon *is* not sufficient to burn,
  Nor its beasts sufficient for a burnt offering.
17 All nations before Him *are* as nothing,

And they are counted by Him less than nothing and
    worthless.

18 To whom then will you liken God?
  Or what likeness will you compare to Him?
19 The workman molds an image,
  The goldsmith overspreads it with gold,
  And the silversmith casts silver chains.
20 Whoever *is* too impoverished for *such* a contribution
  Chooses a tree *that* will not rot;
  He seeks for himself a skillful workman
  To prepare a carved image *that* will not totter.

21 Have you not known?
  Have you not heard?
  Has it not been told you from the beginning?
  Have you not understood from the foundations of
    the earth?
22 *It is* He who sits above the circle of the earth,
  And its inhabitants *are* like grasshoppers,
  Who stretches out the heavens like a curtain,
  And spreads them out like a tent to dwell in.
23 He brings the princes to nothing;
  He makes the judges of the earth useless.

24 Scarcely shall they be planted,
  Scarcely shall they be sown,
  Scarcely shall their stock take root in the earth,
  When He will also blow on them,
  And they will wither,
  And the whirlwind will take them away like stubble.

25 "To whom then will you liken Me,
  Or *to whom* shall I be equal?" says the Holy One.
26 Lift up your eyes on high,
  And see who has created these *things*,
  Who brings out their host by number;
  He calls them all by name,
  By the greatness of His might
  And the strength of *His* power;
  Not one is missing.

27 Why do you say, O Jacob,
  And speak, O Israel:
  "My way is hidden from the LORD,
  And my just claim is passed over by my God"?
28 Have you not known?
  Have you not heard?
  The everlasting God, the LORD,
  The Creator of the ends of the earth,
  Neither faints nor is weary.
  His understanding is unsearchable.
29 He gives power to the weak,
  And to *those who have* no might He increases
    strength.
30 Even the youths shall faint and be weary,
  And the young men shall utterly fall,

STRENGTH

40:29-31 Even the strongest people get tired at times, but God's power and strength never diminish. He is never too tired or too busy to help and listen. His strength is our source of strength. When you feel all of life crushing you and you cannot go another step, remember that you can ask God to renew your strength.

31 But those who wait on the LORD
  Shall renew *their* strength;
  They shall mount up with wings like eagles,
  They shall run and not be weary,
  They shall walk and not faint.

CHAPTER 41 DON'T BE AFRAID, ISRAEL!

  "Keep silence before Me, O coastlands,
  And let the people renew *their* strength!
  Let them come near, then let them speak;
  Let us come near together for judgment.

2 "Who raised up one from the east?
  Who in righteousness called him to His feet?
  Who gave the nations before him,
  And made *him* rule over kings?
  Who gave *them* as the dust *to* his sword,
  As driven stubble to his bow?
3 Who pursued them, *and* passed safely
  By the way *that* he had not gone with his feet?
4 Who has performed and done *it*,

THE FUTURE

41:4 Each generation gets caught up in its own problems, but God's plan embraces all generations. When your great-grandparents lived, God worked personally in the lives of his people. When your great-grandchildren live, God will still work personally in the lives of his people. He is the only One who sees as clearly a hundred years from now as he saw a hundred years ago. When you are concerned about the future, talk with God—he knows the generations of the future as well as he knows the generations of the past.

  Calling the generations from the beginning?
  'I, the LORD, am the first;
  And with the last I *am* He.'"

5 The coastlands saw *it* and feared,
  The ends of the earth were afraid;
  They drew near and came.
6 Everyone helped his neighbor,
  And said to his brother,
  "Be of good courage!"
7 So the craftsman encouraged the goldsmith;
  He who smooths *with* the hammer *inspired* him
    who strikes the anvil,
  Saying, "It *is* ready for the soldering";
  Then he fastened it with pegs,
  That it might not totter.

8 "But you, Israel, *are* My servant,
  Jacob whom I have chosen,
  The descendants of Abraham My friend.
9 *You* whom I have taken from the ends of the earth,
  And called from its farthest regions,
  And said to you,
  'You *are* My servant,
  I have chosen you and have not cast you away:
10 Fear not, for I *am* with you;
  Be not dismayed, for I *am* your God.
  I will strengthen you,
  Yes, I will help you,

I will uphold you with My righteous right hand.'

11 "Behold, all those who were incensed against you
  Shall be ashamed and disgraced;
  They shall be as nothing,
  And those who strive with you shall perish.
12 You shall seek them and not find them—
  Those who contended with you.
  Those who war against you
  Shall be as nothing,
  As a nonexistent thing.
13 For I, the LORD your God, will hold your right hand,
  Saying to you, 'Fear not, I will help you.'

14 "Fear not, you worm Jacob,
  You men of Israel!
  I will help you," says the LORD
  And your Redeemer, the Holy One of Israel.
15 "Behold, I will make you into a new threshing sledge
    with sharp teeth;
  You shall thresh the mountains and beat *them* small,
  And make the hills like chaff.
16 You shall winnow them, the wind shall carry them
    away,
  And the whirlwind shall scatter them;
  You shall rejoice in the LORD,
  And glory in the Holy One of Israel.

17 "The poor and needy seek water, but *there is* none,
  Their tongues fail for thirst.
  I, the LORD, will hear them;
  I, the God of Israel, will not forsake them.
18 I will open rivers in desolate heights,
  And fountains in the midst of the valleys;
  I will make the wilderness a pool of water,
  And the dry land springs of water.
19 I will plant in the wilderness the cedar and the
    acacia tree,
  The myrtle and the oil tree;
  I will set in the desert the cypress tree *and* the pine
  And the box tree together,
20 That they may see and know,
  And consider and understand together,
  That the hand of the LORD has done this,
  And the Holy One of Israel has created it.

21 "Present your case," says the LORD.
  "Bring forth your strong *reasons*," says the King of
    Jacob.
22 "Let them bring forth and show us what will happen;
  Let them show the former things, what they *were*,
  That we may consider them,
  And know the latter end of them;
  Or declare to us things to come.
23 Show the things that are to come hereafter,
  That we may know that you *are* gods;
  Yes, do good or do evil,
  That we may be dismayed and see *it* together.
24 Indeed you *are* nothing,
  And your work *is* nothing;
  He who chooses you *is* an abomination.

25 "I have raised up one from the north,

And he shall come;
From the rising of the sun he shall call on My name;
And he shall come against princes as *though* mortar,
As the potter treads clay.

26 Who has declared from the beginning, that we may know?
And former times, that we may say, 'He is righteous'?
Surely *there is* no one who shows,
Surely *there is* no one who declares,
Surely *there is* no one who hears your words.

27 The first time *I said* to Zion,
'Look, there they are!'
And I will give to Jerusalem one who brings good tidings.

28 For I looked, and *there was* no man;
I looked among them, but *there was* no counselor,
Who, when I asked of them, could answer a word.

29 Indeed they *are* all worthless;
Their works *are* nothing;
Their molded images *are* wind and confusion.

CHAPTER **42** GOD'S CHOSEN ONE.

"Behold! My Servant whom I uphold,
My Elect One *in whom* My soul delights!
I have put My Spirit upon Him;
He will bring forth justice to the Gentiles.

2 He will not cry out, nor raise *His voice*,
Nor cause His voice to be heard in the street.

3 A bruised reed He will not break,
And smoking flax He will not quench;
He will bring forth justice for truth.

4 He will not fail nor be discouraged,
Till He has established justice in the earth;
And the coastlands shall wait for His law."

5 Thus says God the LORD,
Who created the heavens and stretched them out,
Who spread forth the earth and that which comes from it,
Who gives breath to the people on it,
And spirit to those who walk on it:

6 "I, the LORD, have called You in righteousness,
And will hold Your hand;
I will keep You and give You as a covenant to the people,
As a light to the Gentiles,

7 To open blind eyes,
To bring out prisoners from the prison,
Those who sit in darkness from the prison house.

8 I *am* the LORD, that *is* My name;
And My glory I will not give to another,
Nor My praise to carved images.

9 Behold, the former things have come to pass,

And new things I declare;
Before they spring forth I tell you of them."

10 Sing to the LORD a new song,
And His praise from the ends of the earth,
You who go down to the sea, and all that is in it,
You coastlands and you inhabitants of them!

11 Let the wilderness and its cities lift up *their voice*,
The villages *that* Kedar inhabits.
Let the inhabitants of Sela sing,
Let them shout from the top of the mountains.

12 Let them give glory to the LORD,
And declare His praise in the coastlands.

13 The LORD shall go forth like a mighty man;
He shall stir up *His* zeal like a man of war.
He shall cry out, yes, shout aloud;
He shall prevail against His enemies.

14 "I have held My peace a long time,
I have been still and restrained Myself.
Now I will cry like a woman in labor,
I will pant and gasp at once.

15 I will lay waste the mountains and hills,
And dry up all their vegetation;
I will make the rivers coastlands,
And I will dry up the pools.

16 I will bring the blind by a way they did not know;
I will lead them in paths they have not known.
I will make darkness light before them,
And crooked places straight.
These things I will do for them,
And not forsake them.

17 They shall be turned back,
They shall be greatly ashamed,
Who trust in carved images,
Who say to the molded images,
'You *are* our gods.'

18 "Hear, you deaf;
And look, you blind, that you may see.

"Here's what I did..."

I recently switched schools. In my old school, I knew everyone. In this new, much larger school, I knew no one. The situation forced me to depend on God. I knew that I really needed God's help and guidance to make it through those first few months.

During this time, I memorized Isaiah 41:10 and Philippians 4:13. Whenever I felt unnoticed or afraid to talk to someone, I would repeat these verses to myself. I remembered that God was with me, he will strengthen me, and that he has already won the victory for me. These two verses became a lifeline to me. They helped me make the adjustments so that now I do have friends and I feel pretty comfortable at my new school.

Amy
AGE 15

¹⁹ Who *is* blind but My servant,
Or deaf as My messenger *whom* I send?
Who *is* blind as *he who is* perfect,
And blind as the LORD's servant?
²⁰ Seeing many things, but you do not observe;
Opening the ears, but he does not hear."

²¹ The LORD is well pleased for His righteousness'
sake;
He will exalt the law and make *it* honorable.
²² But this *is* a people robbed and plundered;
All of them are snared in holes,
And they are hidden in prison houses;
They are for prey, and no one delivers;
For plunder, and no one says, "Restore!"

²³ Who among you will give ear to this?
Who will listen and hear for the time to come?
²⁴ Who gave Jacob for plunder, and Israel to the
robbers?
Was it not the LORD,
He against whom we have sinned?
For they would not walk in His ways,
Nor were they obedient to His law.
²⁵ Therefore He has poured on him the fury of His
anger
And the strength of battle;
It has set him on fire all around,
Yet he did not know;
And it burned him,
Yet he did not take *it* to heart.

CHAPTER **43** NO OTHER SAVIOR.

But now, thus says the LORD, who created you,
O Jacob,
And He who formed you, O Israel:
"Fear not, for I have redeemed you;
I have called *you* by your name;
You *are* Mine.
² When you pass through the waters, I *will be* with
you;
And through the rivers, they shall not overflow
you.
When you walk through the fire, you shall not be
burned,
Nor shall the flame scorch you.
³ For I *am* the LORD your God,
The Holy One of Israel, your Savior;
I gave Egypt for your ransom,
Ethiopia and Seba in your place.
⁴ Since you were precious in My sight,
You have been honored,
And I have loved you;
Therefore I will give men for you,
And people for your life.
⁵ Fear not, for I *am* with you;
I will bring your descendants from the east,
And gather you from the west;
⁶ I will say to the north, 'Give them up!'
And to the south, 'Do not keep them back!'
Bring My sons from afar,

And My daughters from the ends of the earth—
⁷ Everyone who is called by My name,
Whom I have created for My glory;
I have formed him, yes, I have made him."

⁸ Bring out the blind people who have eyes,
And the deaf who have ears.
⁹ Let all the nations be gathered together,
And let the people be assembled.
Who among them can declare this,
And show us former things?
Let them bring out their witnesses, that they may be
justified;
Or let them hear and say, "*It is* truth."
¹⁰ "You *are* My witnesses," says the LORD,
"And My servant whom I have chosen,
That you may know and believe Me,
And understand that I *am* He.
Before Me there was no God formed,
Nor shall there be after Me.

◄▬▬▬▬▬▬**WITNESS**

43:10-11 Israel's task was to be a witness, telling the world who
is and what he has done. Believers today share the responsibility o
God's witnesses. Do people know what God is like through your wo
and example? They cannot see God directly, but they can see him
reflected in you.

¹¹ I, *even* I, *am* the LORD,
And besides Me *there is* no savior.
¹² I have declared and saved,
I have proclaimed,
And *there was* no foreign *god* among you;
Therefore you *are* My witnesses,"
Says the LORD, "that I *am* God.
¹³ Indeed before the day *was*, I *am* He;
And *there is* no one who can deliver out of My hand;
I work, and who will reverse it?"

¹⁴ Thus says the LORD, your Redeemer,
The Holy One of Israel:
"For your sake I will send to Babylon,
And bring them all down as fugitives—
The Chaldeans, who rejoice in their ships.
¹⁵ I *am* the LORD, your Holy One,
The Creator of Israel, your King."

¹⁶ Thus says the LORD, who makes a way in the sea
And a path through the mighty waters,
¹⁷ Who brings forth the chariot and horse,
The army and the power
(They shall lie down together, they shall not rise;
They are extinguished, they are quenched like a wick):
¹⁸ "Do not remember the former things,
Nor consider the things of old.
¹⁹ Behold, I will do a new thing,
Now it shall spring forth;
Shall you not know it?
I will even make a road in the wilderness
And rivers in the desert.
²⁰ The beast of the field will honor Me,
The jackals and the ostriches,

Because I give waters in the wilderness
And rivers in the desert,
To give drink to My people, My chosen.
²¹ This people I have formed for Myself;
They shall declare My praise.

²² "But you have not called upon Me, O Jacob;
And you have been weary of Me, O Israel.
²³ You have not brought Me the sheep for your burnt
offerings,
Nor have you honored Me with your sacrifices.
I have not caused you to serve with grain offerings,
Nor wearied you with incense.
²⁴ You have bought Me no sweet cane with money,
Nor have you satisfied Me with the fat of your
sacrifices;
But you have burdened Me with your sins,
You have wearied Me with your iniquities.

²⁵ "I, *even* I, *am* He who blots out your transgressions
for My own sake;
And I will not remember your sins.
²⁶ Put Me in remembrance;
Let us contend together;
State your *case*, that you may be acquitted.
²⁷ Your first father sinned,
And your mediators have transgressed against Me.
²⁸ Therefore I will profane the princes of the sanctuary;
I will give Jacob to the curse,
And Israel to reproaches.

CHAPTER 44 IDOLS ARE FALSE GODS.

"Yet hear me now, O Jacob My servant,
And Israel whom I have chosen.
² Thus says the LORD who made you
And formed you from the womb, *who* will help you:
'Fear not, O Jacob My servant;
And you, Jeshurun, whom I have chosen.
³ For I will pour water on him who is thirsty,
And floods on the dry ground;
I will pour My Spirit on your descendants,
And My blessing on your offspring;
⁴ They will spring up among the grass
Like willows by the watercourses.'
⁵ One will say, 'I *am* the LORD's';
Another will call *himself* by the name of Jacob;
Another will write *with* his hand, 'The LORD's,'
And name *himself* by the name of Israel.

⁶ "Thus says the LORD, the King of Israel,
And his Redeemer, the LORD of hosts:
'I *am* the First and I *am* the Last;
Besides Me *there is* no God.
⁷ And who can proclaim as I do?
Then let him declare it and set it in order for Me,
Since I appointed the ancient people.
And the things that are coming and shall come,
Let them show these to them.
⁸ Do not fear, nor be afraid;
Have I not told you from that time, and declared *it*?
You *are* My witnesses.

TODAY'S IDOLATRY

God asks, "Who would form a
god or mold an image that profits
him nothing?" (44:10). We think of
idols as statues of wood or stone,
but in reality an idol is anything
natural that is given sacred
value and power. If your
answer to any of the following
questions is anything or anyone other
than God, you may need to check out
who or what you are ultimately
worshiping.

Who created me?

Whom do I ultimately trust?

To whom do I look for security and happiness?

To whom do I look for ultimate truth?

Who is in charge of my future?

Is there a God besides Me?
Indeed *there is* no other Rock;
I know not *one.*'"

9 Those who make an image, all of them *are* useless,
And their precious things shall not profit;
They *are* their own witnesses;
They neither see nor know, that they may be
ashamed.
10 Who would form a god or mold an image
That profits him nothing?
11 Surely all his companions would be ashamed;
And the workmen, they *are* mere men.
Let them all be gathered together,
Let them stand up;
Yet they shall fear,
They shall be ashamed together.

12 The blacksmith with the tongs works one in the
coals,
Fashions it with hammers,
And works it with the strength of his arms.
Even so, he is hungry, and his strength fails;
He drinks no water and is faint.
13 The craftsman stretches out *his* rule,
He marks one out with chalk;
He fashions it with a plane,
He marks it out with the compass,
And makes it like the figure of a man,
According to the beauty of a man, that it may remain
in the house.
14 He cuts down cedars for himself,
And takes the cypress and the oak;
He secures *it* for himself among the trees of the
forest.
He plants a pine, and the rain nourishes *it.*
15 Then it shall be for a man to burn,
For he will take some of it and warm himself;
Yes, he kindles *it* and bakes bread;
Indeed he makes a god and worships *it;*
He makes it a carved image, and falls down to it.
16 He burns half of it in the fire;
With this half he eats meat;
He roasts a roast, and is satisfied.
He even warms *himself* and says,
"Ah! I am warm,
I have seen the fire."
17 And the rest of it he makes into a god,
His carved image.
He falls down before it and worships *it,*
Prays to it and says,
"Deliver me, for you *are* my god!"

18 They do not know nor understand;
For He has shut their eyes, so that they cannot see,
And their hearts, so that they cannot understand.
19 And no one considers in his heart,
Nor *is there* knowledge nor understanding to say,
"I have burned half of it in the fire,
Yes, I have also baked bread on its coals;
I have roasted meat and eaten *it;*

And shall I make the rest of it an abomination?
Shall I fall down before a block of wood?"
20 He feeds on ashes;
A deceived heart has turned him aside;
And he cannot deliver his soul,
Nor say, "*Is there* not a lie in my right hand?"

21 "Remember these, O Jacob,
And Israel, for you *are* My servant;
I have formed you, you *are* My servant;
O Israel, you will not be forgotten by Me!
22 I have blotted out, like a thick cloud, your
transgressions,
And like a cloud, your sins.
Return to Me, for I have redeemed you."

23 Sing, O heavens, for the LORD has done *it!*
Shout, you lower parts of the earth;
Break forth into singing, you mountains,
O forest, and every tree in it!
For the LORD has redeemed Jacob,
And glorified Himself in Israel.

24 Thus says the LORD, your Redeemer,
And He who formed you from the womb:
"I *am* the LORD, who makes all *things,*
Who stretches out the heavens all alone,
Who spreads abroad the earth by Myself;
25 Who frustrates the signs of the babblers,
And drives diviners mad;
Who turns wise men backward,
And makes their knowledge foolishness;
26 Who confirms the word of His servant,
And performs the counsel of His messengers;
Who says to Jerusalem, 'You shall be inhabited,'
To the cities of Judah, 'You shall be built,'
And I will raise up her waste places;
27 Who says to the deep, 'Be dry!
And I will dry up your rivers';

PROPHECIES

44:28 Isaiah, who lived from about 740–681 B.C., called Cyrus by
name almost 150 years before he ruled (559–530 B.C.)! Later history
said that Cyrus read this prophecy and was so moved that he carried
out. Isaiah also had predicted the fall of Jerusalem more than 100
before it happened (586 B.C.), and the rebuilding of the temple abo
200 years before it happened. Obviously these prophecies came fr
God who knows the future.

28 Who says of Cyrus, '*He is* My shepherd,
And he shall perform all My pleasure,
Saying to Jerusalem, "You shall be built,"
And to the temple, "Your foundation shall be laid." '

CHAPTER **45** THE ONE, TRUE GOD.

"Thus says the LORD to His anointed,
To Cyrus, whose right hand I have held—
To subdue nations before him
And loose the armor of kings,
To open before him the double doors,
So that the gates will not be shut:

2 'I will go before you
And make the crooked places straight;
I will break in pieces the gates of bronze
And cut the bars of iron.
3 I will give you the treasures of darkness
And hidden riches of secret places,
That you may know that I, the LORD,
Who call *you* by your name,
Am the God of Israel.
4 For Jacob My servant's sake,
And Israel My elect,
I have even called you by your name;
I have named you, though you have not known Me.
5 I *am* the LORD, and *there is* no other;
There is no God besides Me.
I will gird you, though you have not known Me,
6 That they may know from the rising of the sun to its setting
That *there is* none besides Me.
I *am* the LORD, and *there is* no other;
7 I form the light and create darkness,
I make peace and create calamity;
I, the LORD, do all these *things*.'

8 "Rain down, you heavens, from above,
And let the skies pour down righteousness;
Let the earth open, let them bring forth salvation,
And let righteousness spring up together.
I, the LORD, have created it.

9 "Woe to him who strives with his Maker!
Let the potsherd *strive* with the potsherds of the earth!
Shall the clay say to him who forms it, 'What are you making?'
Or shall your handiwork *say,* 'He has no hands'?
10 Woe to him who says to *his* father, 'What are you begetting?'
Or to the woman, 'What have you brought forth?'"

11 Thus says the LORD,
The Holy One of Israel, and his Maker:
"Ask Me of things to come concerning My sons;
And concerning the work of My hands, you command Me.
12 I have made the earth,
And created man on it.
I—My hands—stretched out the heavens,
And all their host I have commanded.
13 I have raised him up in righteousness,
And I will direct all his ways;
He shall build My city

And let My exiles go free,
Not for price nor reward,"
Says the LORD of hosts.

14 Thus says the LORD:

▶ BAD TIMES

45:7 God tells us that he sends the good times and the bad. Our life is sprinkled with both types of experiences, and both are needed for us to grow spiritually. When good times come, thank God and use your prosperity for him. When bad times come, don't resent them, but ask what you can learn from this refining experience to make you a better servant of God.

"The labor of Egypt and merchandise of Cush
And of the Sabeans, men of stature,
Shall come over to you, and they shall be yours;
They shall walk behind you,
They shall come over in chains;
And they shall bow down to you.

"Here's what I did..."

When my family moved from Mexico to the United States, everything familiar to me was gone. I had to learn a new language, adjust to totally different ways of doing things, and make friends with people who seemed to have grown up on a different planet rather than in a different country. I was very, very lonely for a long time.

I turned often to the Bible. So many verses were meaningful to me. But Isaiah 46:4 especially helped because it spoke of God's tender care and how he would be with me always, even when I'm old. I would imagine God right there with me in this strange school, and I'd talk to him in my heart, telling him how I felt. It was a great comfort to know that he was right there with me and that he cared. I knew he heard my prayers and understood—and I could speak to him in Spanish! This experience has brought me closer to God as I depend on him every day for the understanding and help I need to make this adjustment.

Julio
AGE 16

They will make supplication to you, *saying,* 'Surely God *is* in you,
And *there is* no other;
There is no other God.'"

15 Truly You *are* God, who hide Yourself,
O God of Israel, the Savior!
16 They shall be ashamed
And also disgraced, all of them;
They shall go in confusion together,
Who are makers of idols.
17 *But* Israel shall be saved by the LORD

With an everlasting salvation;
You shall not be ashamed or disgraced
Forever and ever.

18 For thus says the LORD,
Who created the heavens,
Who is God,
Who formed the earth and made it,
Who has established it,
Who did not create it in vain,
Who formed it to be inhabited:
"I *am* the LORD, and *there is* no other.
19 I have not spoken in secret,
In a dark place of the earth;
I did not say to the seed of Jacob,
'Seek Me in vain';
I, the LORD, speak righteousness,
I declare things that are right.

20 "Assemble yourselves and come;
Draw near together,
You *who have* escaped from the nations.
They have no knowledge,
Who carry the wood of their carved image,
And pray to a god *that* cannot save.
21 Tell and bring forth *your case;*
Yes, let them take counsel together.
Who has declared this from ancient time?
Who has told it from that time?
Have not I, the LORD?
And *there is* no other God besides Me,
A just God and a Savior;
There is none besides Me.

22 "Look to Me, and be saved,
All you ends of the earth!
For I *am* God, and *there is* no other.
23 I have sworn by Myself;
The word has gone out of My mouth *in*
righteousness,
And shall not return,
That to Me every knee shall bow,
Every tongue shall take an oath.
24 He shall say,
'Surely in the LORD I have righteousness and strength.
To Him *men* shall come,
And all shall be ashamed
Who are incensed against Him.
25 In the LORD all the descendants of Israel
Shall be justified, and shall glory.' "

CHAPTER 46 WHO CAN COMPARE TO GOD?

Bel bows down, Nebo stoops;
Their idols were on the beasts and on the cattle.
Your carriages *were* heavily loaded,
A burden to the weary *beast.*
2 They stoop, they bow down together;
They could not deliver the burden,
But have themselves gone into captivity.

3 "Listen to Me, O house of Jacob,
And all the remnant of the house of Israel,

Who have been upheld *by Me* from birth,
Who have been carried from the womb:
4 Even to *your* old age, I *am* He,
And *even* to gray hairs I will carry *you!*
I have made, and I will bear;
Even I will carry, and will deliver *you.*

5 "To whom will you liken Me, and make *Me* equal
And compare Me, that we should be alike?
6 They lavish gold out of the bag,
And weigh silver on the scales;
They hire a goldsmith, and he makes it a god;
They prostrate themselves, yes, they worship.
7 They bear it on the shoulder, they carry it
And set it in its place, and it stands;
From its place it shall not move.
Though *one* cries out to it, yet it cannot answer
Nor save him out of his trouble.

8 "Remember this, and show yourselves men;
Recall to mind, O you transgressors.
9 Remember the former things of old,
For I *am* God, and *there is* no other;
I am God, and *there is* none like Me,
10 Declaring the end from the beginning,
And from ancient times *things* that are not *yet*
done,
Saying, 'My counsel shall stand,
And I will do all My pleasure,'
11 Calling a bird of prey from the east,
The man who executes My counsel, from a far
country.
Indeed I have spoken *it;*
I will also bring it to pass.
I have purposed *it;*
I will also do it.

12 "Listen to Me, you stubborn-hearted,
Who *are* far from righteousness:
13 I bring My righteousness near, it shall not be far off;
My salvation shall not linger.
And I will place salvation in Zion,
For Israel My glory.

CHAPTER 47 GOD'S REVENGE.

"Come down and sit in the dust,
O virgin daughter of Babylon;
Sit on the ground without a throne,
O daughter of the Chaldeans!
For you shall no more be called
Tender and delicate.
2 Take the millstones and grind meal.
Remove your veil,
Take off the skirt,
Uncover the thigh,
Pass through the rivers.
3 Your nakedness shall be uncovered,
Yes, your shame will be seen;
I will take vengeance,
And I will not arbitrate with a man."

4 *As for* our Redeemer, the LORD of hosts *is* His name,

The Holy One of Israel.

5 "Sit in silence, and go into darkness,
O daughter of the Chaldeans;
For you shall no longer be called
The Lady of Kingdoms.

6 I was angry with My people;
I have profaned My inheritance,
And given them into your hand.
You showed them no mercy;
On the elderly you laid your yoke very heavily.

7 And you said, 'I shall be a lady forever,'
So that you did not take these *things* to heart,
Nor remember the latter end of them.

8 "Therefore hear this now, *you who are* given to
pleasures,
Who dwell securely,
Who say in your heart, 'I *am*, and *there is* no one else
besides me;
I shall not sit *as* a widow,
Nor shall I know the loss of children';

9 But these two *things* shall come to you
In a moment, in one day:
The loss of children, and widowhood.
They shall come upon you in their fullness
Because of the multitude of your sorceries,
For the great abundance of your enchantments.

10 "For you have trusted in your wickedness;
You have said, 'No one sees me';
Your wisdom and your knowledge have warped you;
And you have said in your heart,
'I *am*, and *there is* no one else besides me.'

11 Therefore evil shall come upon you;
You shall not know from where it arises.
And trouble shall fall upon you;
You will not be able to put it off.
And desolation shall come upon you suddenly,
Which you shall not know.

12 "Stand now with your enchantments
And the multitude of your sorceries,
In which you have labored from your youth—
Perhaps you will be able to profit,
Perhaps you will prevail.

13 You are wearied in the multitude of your counsels;
Let now the astrologers, the stargazers,
And the monthly prognosticators
Stand up and save you
From what shall come upon you.

14 Behold, they shall be as stubble,
The fire shall burn them;
They shall not deliver themselves
From the power of the flame;
It shall not *be* a coal to be warmed by,
Nor a fire to sit before!

15 Thus shall they be to you
With whom you have labored,
Your merchants from your youth;
They shall wander each one to his quarter.
No one shall save you.

CHAPTER **48** NO PEACE FOR THE WICKED.

"Hear this, O house of Jacob,
Who are called by the name of Israel,
And have come forth from the wellsprings of Judah;
Who swear by the name of the LORD,

◢◣◥◤ POWER

47:8-9 Caught up in the pursuit of power and pleasure, Babylon believed in its own greatness and claimed to be the *only* power on earth. Babylon felt completely secure. Nebuchadnezzar, its king, called himself "god," but the true God taught him a powerful lesson by taking everything away from him (Daniel 4:27-37). Our society is addicted to pleasure and power, but these can pass away quickly. Look at your own life and ask yourself how you can be more responsible with the talents and possessions God has given you. How can you use your life to honor God rather than yourself?

And make mention of the God of Israel,
But not in truth or in righteousness;
2 For they call themselves after the holy city,
And lean on the God of Israel;

I used to look up my horoscope every day in the paper before a friend told me it was satanic. Do Christians believe in astrology?

I WONDER . . .

There are many "windows" that may lead people into satanic influence.

When Saul was king of Israel and in trouble, he consulted a medium (a witch) to gain knowledge of the future (see 1 Samuel 28). Isaiah 47:12-15 shows how effective such foretellers of the future really are. Many other passages deal with astrology, divination, wizards, sorcery, and soothsayers (see Deuteronomy 18:10-11; 2 Chronicles 33:6; Daniel 2:1-2; Acts 8:9-11; 16:16).

If Satan can get people to take in evil small doses at a time, eventually they may become desensitized and not recognize that they are being fed something that will dull their interest in God.

It's like the boy who tried to boil a frog. He filled up a beaker with water, put it on the Bunsen burner until it was boiling, and then put the frog in. Immediately the frog jumped out of the water. Had the boy put the frog in cold water and then slowly turned up the heat, the frog would have gotten used to its surroundings and put up with the increasing heat, unaware it was boiling to death.

Satan would never get anyone to follow him if he revealed all his evil. Instead, he slowly gives us small doses of evil until we're so desensitized to it that it seems a normal part of life.

This is the strategy: to capture our mind through one small compromise into darkness after another.

Our best defense is to know the truth of the Word of God, so we can discern when we are being tempted by evil. God knows it is real. And Jesus came to destroy the works of the devil. Remember, "He who is in you [Jesus Christ] is greater than he who is in the world [Satan]" (1 John 4:4).

The Lord of hosts *is* His name:

³ "I have declared the former things from the
beginning;
They went forth from My mouth, and I caused them
to hear it.
Suddenly I did *them*, and they came to pass.
⁴ Because I knew that you *were* obstinate,
And your neck *was* an iron sinew,
And your brow bronze,
⁵ Even from the beginning I have declared *it* to you;
Before it came to pass I proclaimed *it* to you,
Lest you should say, 'My idol has done them,
And my carved image and my molded image
Have commanded them.'

⁶ "You have heard;
See all this.
And will you not declare *it*?
I have made you hear new things from this time,
Even hidden things, and you did not know them.
⁷ They are created now and not from the beginning;
And before this day you have not heard them,
Lest you should say, 'Of course I knew them.'
⁸ Surely you did not hear,
Surely you did not know;
Surely from long ago your ear was not opened.
For I knew that you would deal very treacherously,
And were called a transgressor from the womb.

⁹ "For My name's sake I will defer My anger,
And *for* My praise I will restrain it from you,
So that I do not cut you off.
¹⁰ Behold, I have refined you, but not as silver;
I have tested you in the furnace of affliction.
¹¹ For My own sake, for My own sake, I will do *it*;
For how should *My name* be profaned?
And I will not give My glory to another.

¹² "Listen to Me, O Jacob,
And Israel, My called:
I *am* He, I *am* the First,
I *am* also the Last.
¹³ Indeed My hand has laid the foundation of the earth,
And My right hand has stretched out the heavens;
When I call to them,
They stand up together.

¹⁴ "All of you, assemble yourselves, and hear!
Who among them has declared these *things*?
The Lord loves him;
He shall do His pleasure on Babylon,
And His arm *shall be against* the Chaldeans.
¹⁵ I, *even* I, have spoken;
Yes, I have called him,
I have brought him, and his way will prosper.

¹⁶ "Come near to Me, hear this:
I have not spoken in secret from the beginning;
From the time that it was, I *was* there.
And now the Lord God and His Spirit
Have sent Me."

¹⁷ Thus says the Lord, your Redeemer,

48:16 God's message has been told plainly and clearly, not in secr
We have a tendency to complicate God's message. When God talks
through his messenger, whomever he has chosen, our job is to listen
closer we come to God, the better we can listen to what he says.

The Holy One of Israel:
"I *am* the Lord your God,
Who teaches you to profit,
Who leads you by the way you should go.
¹⁸ Oh, that you had heeded My commandments!
Then your peace would have been like a river,
And your righteousness like the waves of the sea.
¹⁹ Your descendants also would have been like the sand,
And the offspring of your body like the grains of sand;
His name would not have been cut off
Nor destroyed from before Me."

²⁰ Go forth from Babylon!
Flee from the Chaldeans!
With a voice of singing,
Declare, proclaim this,
Utter it to the end of the earth;
Say, "The Lord has redeemed
His servant Jacob!"
²¹ And they did not thirst
When He led them through the deserts;
He caused the waters to flow from the rock for them;
He also split the rock, and the waters gushed out.

²² "*There is* no peace," says the Lord, "for the wicked."

CHAPTER 49 A LIGHT FOR THE WORLD.

"Listen, O coastlands, to Me,
And take heed, you peoples from afar!
The Lord has called Me from the womb;
From the matrix of My mother He has made
mention of My name.
² And He has made My mouth like a sharp sword;
In the shadow of His hand He has hidden Me,
And made Me a polished shaft;
In His quiver He has hidden Me."

³ "And He said to me,
'You *are* My servant, O Israel,
In whom I will be glorified.'
⁴ Then I said, 'I have labored in vain,
I have spent my strength for nothing and in vain;
Yet surely my just reward *is* with the Lord,
And my work with my God.'"

⁵ "And now the Lord says,
Who formed Me from the womb *to be* His Servant,
To bring Jacob back to Him,
So that Israel is gathered to Him
(For I shall be glorious in the eyes of the Lord,
And My God shall be My strength),
⁶ Indeed He says,
'It is too small a thing that You should be My Servant
To raise up the tribes of Jacob,
And to restore the preserved ones of Israel;
I will also give You as a light to the Gentiles,
That You should be My salvation to the ends of the
earth.'"

⁷ Thus says the LORD,
The Redeemer of Israel, their Holy One,
To Him whom man despises,
To Him whom the nation abhors,
To the Servant of rulers:
"Kings shall see and arise,
Princes also shall worship,
Because of the LORD who is faithful,
The Holy One of Israel;
And He has chosen You."

⁸Thus says the LORD:

"In an acceptable time I have heard You,
And in the day of salvation I have helped You;
I will preserve You and give You
As a covenant to the people,
To restore the earth,
To cause them to inherit the desolate heritages;
⁹ That You may say to the prisoners, 'Go forth,'
To those who *are* in darkness, 'Show yourselves.'

"They shall feed along the roads,
And their pastures *shall be* on all desolate heights.
¹⁰ They shall neither hunger nor thirst,
Neither heat nor sun shall strike them;
For He who has mercy on them will lead them,
Even by the springs of water He will guide them.
¹¹ I will make each of My mountains a road,
And My highways shall be elevated.
¹² Surely these shall come from afar;
Look! Those from the north and the west,
And these from the land of Sinim."

¹³ Sing, O heavens!
Be joyful, O earth!
And break out in singing, O mountains!
For the LORD has comforted His people,
And will have mercy on His afflicted.

¹⁴ But Zion said, "The LORD has forsaken me,
And my Lord has forgotten me."

¹⁵ "Can a woman forget her nursing child,
And not have compassion on the son of her womb?
Surely they may forget,
Yet I will not forget you.
¹⁶ See, I have inscribed you on the palms *of My hands;*
Your walls *are* continually before Me.
¹⁷ Your sons shall make haste;
Your destroyers and those who laid you waste
Shall go away from you.
¹⁸ Lift up your eyes, look around and see;
All these gather together *and* come to you.
As I live," says the LORD,
"You shall surely clothe yourselves with them all as an
ornament,
And bind them *on you* as a bride *does.*

¹⁹ "For your waste and desolate places,
And the land of your destruction,
Will even now be too small for the inhabitants;
And those who swallowed you up will be far away.
²⁰ The children you will have,

After you have lost the others,
Will say again in your ears,
'The place *is* too small for me;
Give me a place where I may dwell.'
²¹ Then you will say in your heart,
'Who has begotten these for me,
Since I have lost my children and am desolate,
A captive, and wandering to and fro?
And who has brought these up?
There I was, left alone;
But these, where *were* they?' "

◀▬▬▬▬▬▬▬▬**DESERTED**

49:14-15 The people of Israel felt that God had deserted them in Babylon, but Isaiah points out that God would never leave them, as a mother would not leave her little child. When we feel that God has deserted us, we must ask if we have deserted God.

²²Thus says the Lord GOD:

"Behold, I will lift My hand in an oath to the nations,
And set up My standard for the peoples;
They shall bring your sons in *their* arms,
And your daughters shall be carried on *their*
shoulders;
²³ Kings shall be your foster fathers,
And their queens your nursing mothers;
They shall bow down to you with *their* faces to the
earth,
And lick up the dust of your feet.
Then you will know that I *am* the LORD,
For they shall not be ashamed who wait for Me."

²⁴ Shall the prey be taken from the mighty,
Or the captives of the righteous be delivered?

²⁵But thus says the LORD:

"Even the captives of the mighty shall be taken away,
And the prey of the terrible be delivered;
For I will contend with him who contends with you,
And I will save your children.
²⁶ I will feed those who oppress you with their own flesh,
And they shall be drunk with their own blood as
with sweet wine.
All flesh shall know
That I, the LORD, *am* your Savior,
And your Redeemer, the Mighty One of Jacob."

CHAPTER **50** **GOD'S SERVANT OBEYS.** Thus says
the LORD:

"Where *is* the certificate of your mother's divorce,
Whom I have put away?
Or which of My creditors *is it* to whom I have sold
you?
For your iniquities you have sold yourselves,
And for your transgressions your mother has been
put away.
² Why, when I came, *was there* no man?
Why, when I called, *was there* none to answer?
Is My hand shortened at all that it cannot redeem?

Or have I no power to deliver?
Indeed with My rebuke I dry up the sea,
I make the rivers a wilderness;
Their fish stink because *there is* no water,
And die of thirst.
3 I clothe the heavens with blackness,
And I make sackcloth their covering."

4 "The Lord GOD has given Me
The tongue of the learned,
That I should know how to speak
A word in season to *him who is* weary.
He awakens Me morning by morning,
He awakens My ear
To hear as the learned.
5 The Lord GOD has opened My ear;
And I was not rebellious,
Nor did I turn away.
6 I gave My back to those who struck *Me,*
And My cheeks to those who plucked out the beard;
I did not hide My face from shame and spitting.

7 "For the Lord GOD will help Me;
Therefore I will not be disgraced;
Therefore I have set My face like a flint,
And I know that I will not be ashamed.
8 *He is* near who justifies Me;
Who will contend with Me?
Let us stand together.
Who *is* My adversary?
Let him come near Me.
9 Surely the Lord GOD will help Me;
Who *is* he *who* will condemn Me?
Indeed they will all grow old like a garment;
The moth will eat them up.

10 "Who among you fears the LORD?
Who obeys the voice of His Servant?
Who walks in darkness
And has no light?
Let him trust in the name of the LORD
And rely upon his God.
11 Look, all you who kindle a fire,
Who encircle *yourselves* with sparks:
Walk in the light of your fire and in the sparks you
    have kindled—
This you shall have from My hand:
You shall lie down in torment.

CHAPTER 51 THE PEOPLE MUST FEAR GOD.

"Listen to Me, you who follow after righteousness,
You who seek the LORD:
Look to the rock *from which* you were hewn,
And to the hole of the pit *from which* you were dug.
2 Look to Abraham your father,
And to Sarah *who* bore you;
For I called him alone,
And blessed him and increased him."

3 For the LORD will comfort Zion,
He will comfort all her waste places;
He will make her wilderness like Eden,

51:7 Isaiah encouraged those who served God to discern right fro[m]
wrong and to follow God's laws. He also gave them hope when they[...]
people's scorn or slander because of their faith. We need not fear w[...]
people ridicule us for our faith because God is with us and truth will[...]
prevail. If people make fun of you or dislike you because you believ[e]
God, remember that they are not against you personally, but again[st]
God. He will deal with them; you should concentrate on loving and
obeying him.

And her desert like the garden of the LORD;
Joy and gladness will be found in it,
Thanksgiving and the voice of melody.

4 "Listen to Me, My people;
And give ear to Me, O My nation:
For law will proceed from Me,
And I will make My justice rest
As a light of the peoples.
5 My righteousness *is* near,
My salvation has gone forth,
And My arms will judge the peoples;
The coastlands will wait upon Me,
And on My arm they will trust.
6 Lift up your eyes to the heavens,
And look on the earth beneath.
For the heavens will vanish away like smoke,
The earth will grow old like a garment,
And those who dwell in it will die in like manner;
But My salvation will be forever,
And My righteousness will not be abolished.

7 "Listen to Me, you who know righteousness,
You people in whose heart *is* My law:
Do not fear the reproach of men,
Nor be afraid of their insults.
8 For the moth will eat them up like a garment,
And the worm will eat them like wool;
But My righteousness will be forever,
And My salvation from generation to generation."

9 Awake, awake, put on strength,
O arm of the LORD!
Awake as in the ancient days,
In the generations of old.
Are You not *the arm* that cut Rahab apart,
And wounded the serpent?

10 *Are* You not *the One* who dried up the sea,
The waters of the great deep;
That made the depths of the sea a road
For the redeemed to cross over?
11 So the ransomed of the LORD shall return,
And come to Zion with singing,
With everlasting joy on their heads.
They shall obtain joy and gladness;
Sorrow and sighing shall flee away.

12 "I, *even* I, *am* He who comforts you.
Who *are* you that you should be afraid
Of a man *who* will die,
And of the son of a man *who* will be made like grass?
13 And you forget the LORD your Maker,
Who stretched out the heavens
And laid the foundations of the earth;

You have feared continually every day
Because of the fury of the oppressor,
When *he has* prepared to destroy.
And where *is* the fury of the oppressor?
14 The captive exile hastens, that he may be loosed,
That he should not die in the pit,
And that his bread should not fail.
15 But I *am* the LORD your God,
Who divided the sea whose waves roared—
The LORD of hosts *is* His name.
16 And I have put My words in your mouth;
I have covered you with the shadow of My hand,
That I may plant the heavens,
Lay the foundations of the earth,
And say to Zion, 'You *are* My people.'"

17 Awake, awake!
Stand up, O Jerusalem,
You who have drunk at the hand of the LORD
The cup of His fury;
You have drunk the dregs of the cup of trembling,
And drained *it* out.
18 *There is* no one to guide her
Among all the sons she has brought forth;
Nor *is there any* who takes her by the hand
Among all the sons she has brought up.
19 These two *things* have come to you;
Who will be sorry for you?—
Desolation and destruction, famine and sword—
By whom will I comfort you?
20 Your sons have fainted,
They lie at the head of all the streets,
Like an antelope in a net;
They are full of the fury of the LORD,
The rebuke of your God.

21 Therefore please hear this, you afflicted,
And drunk but not with wine.
22 Thus says your Lord,
The LORD and your God,
Who pleads the cause of His people:
"See, I have taken out of your hand
The cup of trembling,
The dregs of the cup of My fury;
You shall no longer drink it.
23 But I will put it into the hand of those who afflict
you,
Who have said to you,
'Lie down, that we may walk over you.'
And you have laid your body like the ground,
And as the street, for those who walk over."

CHAPTER **52** GOD BRINGS HIS PEOPLE HOME.

Awake, awake!
Put on your strength, O Zion;
Put on your beautiful garments,
O Jerusalem, the holy city!
For the uncircumcised and the unclean
Shall no longer come to you.
2 Shake yourself from the dust, arise;
Sit down, O Jerusalem!

Loose yourself from the bonds of your neck,
O captive daughter of Zion!

3 For thus says the LORD:

"You have sold yourselves for nothing,
And you shall be redeemed without money."

4 For thus says the Lord GOD:

"My people went down at first
Into Egypt to dwell there;
Then the Assyrian oppressed them without cause.
5 Now therefore, what have I here," says the LORD,
"That My people are taken away for nothing?
Those who rule over them
Make them wail," says the LORD,
"And My name *is* blasphemed continually every day.
6 Therefore My people shall know My name;
Therefore *they shall know* in that day
That I *am* He who speaks:
'Behold, *it is* I.'"

7 How beautiful upon the mountains
Are the feet of him who brings good news,
Who proclaims peace,
Who brings glad tidings of good *things,*
Who proclaims salvation,
Who says to Zion,
"Your God reigns!"
8 Your watchmen shall lift up *their* voices,
With their voices they shall sing together;
For they shall see eye to eye
When the LORD brings back Zion.
9 Break forth into joy, sing together,
You waste places of Jerusalem!
For the LORD has comforted His people,
He has redeemed Jerusalem.
10 The LORD has made bare His holy arm
In the eyes of all the nations;
And all the ends of the earth shall see
The salvation of our God.

11 Depart! Depart! Go out from there,
Touch no unclean *thing;*
Go out from the midst of her,
Be clean,
You who bear the vessels of the LORD.
12 For you shall not go out with haste,
Nor go by flight;
For the LORD will go before you,
And the God of Israel *will be* your rear guard.

13 Behold, My Servant shall deal prudently;
He shall be exalted and extolled and be very high.
14 Just as many were astonished at you,
So His visage was marred more than any man,
And His form more than the sons of men;
15 So shall He sprinkle many nations.
Kings shall shut their mouths at Him;

MESSIAH

52:13 The Servant of the Lord, as the term is used here, is the Messiah,
our Lord Jesus. He would be highly exalted because of his sacrifice,
described in chapter 53.

For what had not been told them they shall see,
And what they had not heard they shall consider.

CHAPTER 53

Who has believed our report?
And to whom has the arm of the LORD been revealed?
2 For He shall grow up before Him as a tender plant,
And as a root out of dry ground.
He has no form or comeliness;
And when we see Him,
There is no beauty that we should desire Him.
3 He is despised and rejected by men,
A Man of sorrows and acquainted with grief.
And we hid, as it were, *our* faces from Him;
He was despised, and we did not esteem Him.

4 Surely He has borne our griefs
And carried our sorrows;
Yet we esteemed Him stricken,
Smitten by God, and afflicted.
5 But He *was* wounded for our transgressions,
He was bruised for our iniquities;
The chastisement for our peace *was* upon Him,
And by His stripes we are healed.
6 All we like sheep have gone astray;
We have turned, every one, to his own way;
And the LORD has laid on Him the iniquity of us all.

7 He was oppressed and He was afflicted,
Yet He opened not His mouth;
He was led as a lamb to the slaughter,
And as a sheep before its shearers is silent,
So He opened not His mouth.
8 He was taken from prison and from judgment,
And who will declare His generation?
For He was cut off from the land of the living;
For the transgressions of My people He was stricken.
9 And they made His grave with the wicked—
But with the rich at His death,
Because He had done no violence,
Nor *was any* deceit in His mouth.

10 Yet it pleased the LORD to bruise Him;
He has put *Him* to grief.
When You make His soul an offering for sin,
He shall see *His* seed, He shall prolong *His* days,
And the pleasure of the LORD shall prosper in His
hand.
11 He shall see the labor of His soul, *and* be satisfied.
By His knowledge My righteous Servant shall justify
many,
For He shall bear their iniquities.
12 Therefore I will divide Him a portion with the great,
And He shall divide the spoil with the strong,
Because He poured out His soul unto death,
And He was numbered with the transgressors,
And He bore the sin of many,
And made intercession for the transgressors.

CHAPTER 54   EVERLASTING LOVE.
"Sing, O barren,

You *who* have not borne!
Break forth into singing, and cry aloud,
You *who* have not labored with child!
For more *are* the children of the desolate
Than the children of the married woman," says the
LORD.
2 "Enlarge the place of your tent,
And let them stretch out the curtains of your
dwellings;
Do not spare;
Lengthen your cords,
And strengthen your stakes.
3 For you shall expand to the right and to the left,
And your descendants will inherit the nations,
And make the desolate cities inhabited.

4 "Do not fear, for you will not be ashamed;
Neither be disgraced, for you will not be put to
shame;
For you will forget the shame of your youth,
And will not remember the reproach of your
widowhood anymore.
5 For your Maker *is* your husband,

HE was wounded
FOR
our transgressions
HE was bruised
FOR
our iniquities
THE CHASTISEMENT
FOR
OUR PEACE
was upon
HIM
AND BY
His stripes
stripes
stripes
we are healed.

ISAIAH 53:5

The LORD of hosts *is* His name;
And your Redeemer *is* the Holy One of Israel;
He is called the God of the whole earth.

6 For the LORD has called you
Like a woman forsaken and grieved in spirit,
Like a youthful wife when you were refused,"
Says your God.

7 "For a mere moment I have forsaken you,
But with great mercies I will gather you.

8 With a little wrath I hid My face from you for a
moment;
But with everlasting kindness I will have mercy on
you,"
Says the LORD, your Redeemer.

9 "For this *is* like the waters of Noah to Me;
For as I have sworn
That the waters of Noah would no longer cover the
earth,
So have I sworn
That I would not be angry with you, nor rebuke you.

10 For the mountains shall depart
And the hills be removed,
But My kindness shall not depart from you,
Nor shall My covenant of peace be removed,"
Says the LORD, who has mercy on you.

11 "O you afflicted one,
Tossed with tempest, *and* not comforted,
Behold, I will lay your stones with colorful gems,
And lay your foundations with sapphires.

12 I will make your pinnacles of rubies,
Your gates of crystal,
And all your walls of precious stones.

13 All your children *shall be* taught by the LORD,
And great *shall be* the peace of your children.

14 In righteousness you shall be established;
You shall be far from oppression, for you shall not
fear;
And from terror, for it shall not come near you.

15 Indeed they shall surely assemble, *but* not because
of Me.
Whoever assembles against you shall fall for your
sake.

16 "Behold, I have created the blacksmith
Who blows the coals in the fire,
Who brings forth an instrument for his work;
And I have created the spoiler to destroy.

17 No weapon formed against you shall prosper,
And every tongue *which* rises against you in
judgment
You shall condemn.
This *is* the heritage of the servants of the LORD,
And their righteousness *is* from Me,"
Says the LORD.

CHAPTER 55 A PROMISE OF JOY AND PEACE.

"Ho! Everyone who thirsts,
Come to the waters;
And you who have no money,
Come, buy and eat.

Yes, come, buy wine and milk
Without money and without price.

2 Why do you spend money for *what is* not bread,
And your wages for *what* does not satisfy?
Listen carefully to Me, and eat *what is* good,
And let your soul delight itself in abundance.

3 Incline your ear, and come to Me.
Hear, and your soul shall live;
And I will make an everlasting covenant with you—
The sure mercies of David.

◥ REUNION

54:6-8 God says that he has abandoned Israel for a brief time, so she is like a young wife abandoned by her husband. But he still calls Israel his own. The God we serve is holy, and he cannot tolerate sin. When Israel blatantly sinned, God in his anger chose to punish her. Sin separates us from God and brings us pain and suffering. But if we confess our sin and repent, God forgives us. Have you ever been separated from a loved one and then experienced joy when that person returned? You can experience the same joy when you repent and return to God.

4 Indeed I have given him *as* a witness to the people,
A leader and commander for the people.

5 Surely you shall call a nation you do not know,
And nations *who* do not know you shall run to you,
Because of the LORD your God,
And the Holy One of Israel;
For He has glorified you."

◥ CALL NOW

55:6 Isaiah tells us to call upon the Lord while he is near. God is not planning to move away from us, but we often move far from God or erect a barrier between ourself and him. Don't wait until you have drifted away from God to seek him. Turning to God may be far more difficult later in life. Or God may come to judge the earth before you decide to seek him. Do it now while you can, before it is too late.

6 Seek the LORD while He may be found,
Call upon Him while He is near.

7 Let the wicked forsake his way,
And the unrighteous man his thoughts;
Let him return to the LORD,
And He will have mercy on him;
And to our God,
For He will abundantly pardon.

8 "For My thoughts *are* not your thoughts,
Nor *are* your ways My ways," says the LORD.

9 "For *as* the heavens are higher than the earth,
So are My ways higher than your ways,
And My thoughts than your thoughts.

10 "For as the rain comes down, and the snow from
heaven,
And do not return there,
But water the earth,
And make it bring forth and bud,
That it may give seed to the sower
And bread to the eater,

11 So shall My word be that goes forth from My mouth;

It shall not return to Me void,
But it shall accomplish what I please,
And it shall prosper *in the thing* for which I sent it.

12 "For you shall go out with joy,
And be led out with peace;
The mountains and the hills
Shall break forth into singing before you,
And all the trees of the field shall clap *their* hands.
13 Instead of the thorn shall come up the cypress tree,
And instead of the brier shall come up the myrtle
tree;
And it shall be to the LORD for a name,
For an everlasting sign *that* shall not be cut off."

CHAPTER 56 GOD WILL COME TO THE RESCUE.

Thus says the LORD:

"Keep justice, and do righteousness,
For My salvation *is* about to come,
And My righteousness to be revealed.
2 Blessed *is* the man *who* does this,
And the son of man *who* lays hold on it;
Who keeps from defiling the Sabbath,
And keeps his hand from doing any evil."

3 Do not let the son of the foreigner
Who has joined himself to the LORD
Speak, saying,
"The LORD has utterly separated me from His people";
Nor let the eunuch say,
"Here I am, a dry tree."
4 For thus says the LORD:
"To the eunuchs who keep My Sabbaths,
And choose what pleases Me,
And hold fast My covenant,
5 Even to them I will give in My house
And within My walls a place and a name
Better than that of sons and daughters;
I will give them an everlasting name
That shall not be cut off.

6 "Also the sons of the foreigner
Who join themselves to the LORD, to serve Him,
And to love the name of the LORD, to be His
servants—
Everyone who keeps from defiling the Sabbath,
And holds fast My covenant—
7 Even them I will bring to My holy mountain,
And make them joyful in My house of prayer.
Their burnt offerings and their sacrifices
Will be accepted on My altar;
For My house shall be called a house of prayer for all
nations."
8 The Lord GOD, who gathers the outcasts of Israel,
says,
"Yet I will gather to him
Others besides those who are gathered to him."

9 All you beasts of the field, come to devour,
All you beasts in the forest.
10 His watchmen *are* blind,
They are all ignorant;

They *are* all dumb dogs,
They cannot bark;
Sleeping, lying down, loving to slumber.
11 Yes, *they are* greedy dogs
Which never have enough.
And they *are* shepherds
Who cannot understand;
They all look to their own way,
Every one for his own gain,
From his *own* territory.
12 "Come," *one says,* "I will bring wine,
And we will fill ourselves with intoxicating drink;
Tomorrow will be as today,
And much more abundant."

CHAPTER 57 A REWARD FOR LOVING GOD.

The righteous perishes,
And no man takes *it* to heart;
Merciful men *are* taken away,
While no one considers
That the righteous is taken away from evil.
2 He shall enter into peace;
They shall rest in their beds,
Each one walking *in* his uprightness.

3 "But come here,
You sons of the sorceress,
You offspring of the adulterer and the harlot!
4 Whom do you ridicule?
Against whom do you make a wide mouth
And stick out the tongue?
Are you not children of transgression,
Offspring of falsehood,
5 Inflaming yourselves with gods under every green
tree,
Slaying the children in the valleys,
Under the clefts of the rocks?
6 Among the smooth *stones* of the stream
Is your portion;
They, they, *are* your lot!
Even to them you have poured a drink offering,
You have offered a grain offering.
Should I receive comfort in these?

7 "On a lofty and high mountain
You have set your bed;
Even there you went up
To offer sacrifice.
8 Also behind the doors and their posts
You have set up your remembrance;
For you have uncovered yourself *to those other* than
Me,
And have gone up to them;
You have enlarged your bed
And made *a covenant* with them;
You have loved their bed,
Where you saw *their* nudity.
9 You went to the king with ointment,
And increased your perfumes;
You sent your messengers far off,
And *even* descended to Sheol.

¹⁰ You are wearied in the length of your way;
    Yet you did not say, 'There is no hope.'
    You have found the life of your hand;
    Therefore you were not grieved.

¹¹ "And of whom have you been afraid, or feared,
    That you have lied
    And not remembered Me,
    Nor taken *it* to your heart?
    Is it not because I have held My peace from of old
    That you do not fear Me?
¹² I will declare your righteousness
    And your works,
    For they will not profit you.
¹³ When you cry out,
    Let your collection *of idols* deliver you.
    But the wind will carry them all away,
    A breath will take *them*.
    But he who puts his trust in Me shall possess the land,
    And shall inherit My holy mountain."

¹⁴ And one shall say,
    "Heap it up! Heap it up!
    Prepare the way,
    Take the stumbling block out of the way of My people."

¹⁵ For thus says the High and Lofty One
    Who inhabits eternity, whose name *is* Holy:
    "I dwell in the high and holy *place*,
    With him *who* has a contrite and humble spirit,
    To revive the spirit of the humble,
    And to revive the heart of the contrite ones.
¹⁶ For I will not contend forever,
    Nor will I always be angry;
    For the spirit would fail before Me,
    And the souls *which* I have made.
¹⁷ For the iniquity of his covetousness
    I was angry and struck him;
    I hid and was angry,
    And he went on backsliding in the way of his heart.
¹⁸ I have seen his ways, and will heal him;
    I will also lead him,
    And restore comforts to him
    And to his mourners.

¹⁹ "I create the fruit of the lips:
    Peace, peace to *him who is* far off and to *him who is* near,"
    Says the LORD,
    "And I will heal him."
²⁰ But the wicked *are* like the troubled sea,
    When it cannot rest,
    Whose waters cast up mire and dirt.

²¹ "*There is* no peace,"
    Says my God, "for the wicked."

CHAPTER 58   GOD TELLS THE PEOPLE TO SHARE.

"Cry aloud, spare not;
    Lift up your voice like a trumpet;
    Tell My people their transgression,

    And the house of Jacob their sins.
² Yet they seek Me daily,
    And delight to know My ways,
    As a nation that did righteousness,
    And did not forsake the ordinance of their God.
    They ask of Me the ordinances of justice;
    They take delight in approaching God.
³ 'Why have we fasted,' *they say,* 'and You have not seen?
    Why have we afflicted our souls, and You take no notice?'

◤◥ GOOD WORKS

57:12 Isaiah warned these people that their righteousness and good works would not save them any more than their weak, worthless idols. We cannot gain our salvation through good works because our best works are not good enough to outweigh our sins. Salvation is a gift from God.

"In fact, in the day of your fast you find pleasure,
    And exploit all your laborers.
⁴ Indeed you fast for strife and debate,
    And to strike with the fist of wickedness.
    You will not fast as *you do* this day,
    To make your voice heard on high.
⁵ Is it a fast that I have chosen,
    A day for a man to afflict his soul?
    Is it to bow down his head like a bulrush,
    And to spread out sackcloth and ashes?
    Would you call this a fast,
    And an acceptable day to the LORD?

⁶ "*Is* this not the fast that I have chosen:
    To loose the bonds of wickedness,
    To undo the heavy burdens,
    To let the oppressed go free,
    And that you break every yoke?
⁷ *Is it* not to share your bread with the hungry,
    And that you bring to your house the poor who are cast out;
    When you see the naked, that you cover him,
    And not hide yourself from your own flesh?
⁸ Then your light shall break forth like the morning,
    Your healing shall spring forth speedily,
    And your righteousness shall go before you;
    The glory of the LORD shall be your rear guard.
⁹ Then you shall call, and the LORD will answer;
    You shall cry, and He will say, 'Here I *am*.'

"If you take away the yoke from your midst,
    The pointing of the finger, and speaking wickedness,
¹⁰ *If* you extend your soul to the hungry
    And satisfy the afflicted soul,
    Then your light shall dawn in the darkness,

◤◥ TRUE WORSHIP

58:1ff True worship was more than religious ritual, going to the temple every day, and listening to Scripture readings. These people missed the point of a living, vital relationship with God. He doesn't want us fasting or acting pious when we have unforgiven sin in our heart and perform sinful practices with our hands. Even more important than correct worship and doctrine is genuine compassion for the poor, the helpless, and the oppressed.

And your darkness shall *be* as the noonday.
11 The LORD will guide you continually,
And satisfy your soul in drought,
And strengthen your bones;
You shall be like a watered garden,
And like a spring of water, whose waters do not fail.
12 Those from among you
Shall build the old waste places;
You shall raise up the foundations of many
    generations;
And you shall be called the Repairer of the Breach,
The Restorer of Streets to Dwell In.

13 "If you turn away your foot from the Sabbath,
From doing your pleasure on My holy day,
And call the Sabbath a delight,
The holy *day* of the LORD honorable,
And shall honor Him, not doing your own ways,
Nor finding your own pleasure,
Nor speaking *your own* words,
14 Then you shall delight yourself in the LORD;
And I will cause you to ride on the high hills of the
    earth,
And feed you with the heritage of Jacob your father.
The mouth of the LORD has spoken."

CHAPTER 59 GOD TELLS HIS PEOPLE TO OBEY.

Behold, the LORD's hand is not shortened,
That it cannot save;
Nor His ear heavy,
That it cannot hear.

WALL

59:1-12 Sin offends our holy God. Because God is holy, he cannot
ignore, excuse, or tolerate sin as though it doesn't matter. Sin cuts people
off from him, forming a wall to isolate God from the people he loves. No
wonder this long list of sins makes God angry and forces him to look the
other way. People who die with their sin unforgiven separate themselves
eternally from God. God wants them to live with him forever, but he
cannot take them into his holy presence unless their sin is removed.

2 But your iniquities have separated you from your
    God;
And your sins have hidden *His* face from you,
So that He will not hear.
3 For your hands are defiled with blood,
And your fingers with iniquity;
Your lips have spoken lies,
Your tongue has muttered perversity.

4 No one calls for justice,
Nor does *any* plead for truth.
They trust in empty words and speak lies;
They conceive evil and bring forth iniquity.
5 They hatch vipers' eggs and weave the spider's web;
He who eats of their eggs dies,
And *from* that which is crushed a viper breaks out.

6 Their webs will not become garments,
Nor will they cover themselves with their works;
Their works *are* works of iniquity,

And the act of violence *is* in their hands.
7 Their feet run to evil,
And they make haste to shed innocent blood;
Their thoughts *are* thoughts of iniquity;
Wasting and destruction *are* in their paths.
8 The way of peace they have not known,
And *there is* no justice in their ways;
They have made themselves crooked paths;
Whoever takes that way shall not know peace.

9 Therefore justice is far from us,
Nor does righteousness overtake us;
We look for light, but there is darkness!
For brightness, *but* we walk in blackness!
10 We grope for the wall like the blind,
And we grope as if *we had* no eyes;
We stumble at noonday as at twilight;
We are as dead *men* in desolate places.
11 We all growl like bears,
And moan sadly like doves;
We look for justice, but *there is* none;
For salvation, *but* it is far from us.
12 For our transgressions are multiplied before You,
And our sins testify against us;
For our transgressions *are* with us,
And *as for* our iniquities, we know them:
13 In transgressing and lying against the LORD,
And departing from our God,
Speaking oppression and revolt,
Conceiving and uttering from the heart words of
    falsehood.
14 Justice is turned back,
And righteousness stands afar off;
For truth is fallen in the street,
And equity cannot enter.
15 So truth fails,
And he *who* departs from evil makes himself a prey.

Then the LORD saw *it*, and it displeased Him
That *there was* no justice.
16 He saw that *there was* no man,
And wondered that *there was* no intercessor;
Therefore His own arm brought salvation for Him;
And His own righteousness, it sustained Him.
17 For He put on righteousness as a breastplate,
And a helmet of salvation on His head;
He put on the garments of vengeance for clothing,
And was clad with zeal as a cloak.
18 According to *their* deeds, accordingly He will repay,
Fury to His adversaries,
Recompense to His enemies;
The coastlands He will fully repay.
19 So shall they fear
The name of the LORD from the west,
And His glory from the rising of the sun;
When the enemy comes in like a flood,
The Spirit of the LORD will lift up a standard against
    him.

20 "The Redeemer will come to Zion,
And to those who turn from transgression in Jacob,"
Says the LORD.

²¹"As for Me," says the LORD, "this *is* My covenant with them: My Spirit who *is* upon you, and My words which I have put in your mouth, shall not depart from your mouth, nor from the mouth of your descendants, nor from the mouth of your descendants' descendants," says the LORD, "from this time and forevermore."

CHAPTER 60 THE GLORY OF THE LORD.

Arise, shine;
For your light has come!
And the glory of the LORD is risen upon you.
2 For behold, the darkness shall cover the earth,
And deep darkness the people;
But the LORD will arise over you,
And His glory will be seen upon you.
3 The Gentiles shall come to your light,
And kings to the brightness of your rising.

4 "Lift up your eyes all around, and see:
They all gather together, they come to you;
Your sons shall come from afar,
And your daughters shall be nursed at *your* side.
5 Then you shall see and become radiant,
And your heart shall swell with joy;
Because the abundance of the sea shall be turned to
you,
The wealth of the Gentiles shall come to you.
6 The multitude of camels shall cover your *land*,
The dromedaries of Midian and Ephah;
All those from Sheba shall come;
They shall bring gold and incense,
And they shall proclaim the praises of the LORD.
7 All the flocks of Kedar shall be gathered together to
you,
The rams of Nebaioth shall minister to you;
They shall ascend with acceptance on My altar,
And I will glorify the house of My glory.

8 "Who *are* these *who* fly like a cloud,
And like doves to their roosts?
9 Surely the coastlands shall wait for Me;
And the ships of Tarshish *will come* first,
To bring your sons from afar,
Their silver and their gold with them,
To the name of the LORD your God,
And to the Holy One of Israel,
Because He has glorified you.

10 "The sons of foreigners shall build up your walls,
And their kings shall minister to you;
For in My wrath I struck you,
But in My favor I have had mercy on you.
11 Therefore your gates shall be open continually;
They shall not be shut day or night,
That *men* may bring to you the wealth of the Gentiles,
And their kings in procession.
12 For the nation and kingdom which will not serve
you shall perish,
And *those* nations shall be utterly ruined.

13 "The glory of Lebanon shall come to you,
The cypress, the pine, and the box tree together,
To beautify the place of My sanctuary;
And I will make the place of My feet glorious.
14 Also the sons of those who afflicted you
Shall come bowing to you,
And all those who despised you shall fall prostrate at
the soles of your feet;
And they shall call you The City of the LORD,
Zion of the Holy One of Israel.

15 "Whereas you have been forsaken and hated,
So that no one went through *you,*
I will make you an eternal excellence,
A joy of many generations.
16 You shall drink the milk of the Gentiles,
And milk the breast of kings;
You shall know that I, the LORD, *am* your Savior
And your Redeemer, the Mighty One of Jacob.

PATIENCE

60:1ff As we read these promises, we long for their fulfillment. But we must patiently wait for God's timing. God is in control of history, and he weaves all our lives together into his plan.

17 "Instead of bronze I will bring gold,
Instead of iron I will bring silver,
Instead of wood, bronze,
And instead of stones, iron.
I will also make your officers peace,
And your magistrates righteousness.
18 Violence shall no longer be heard in your land,
Neither wasting nor destruction within your borders;
But you shall call your walls Salvation,
And your gates Praise.

19 "The sun shall no longer be your light by day,
Nor for brightness shall the moon give light to you;
But the LORD will be to you an everlasting light,
And your God your glory.
20 Your sun shall no longer go down,
Nor shall your moon withdraw itself;
For the LORD will be your everlasting light,
And the days of your mourning shall be ended.
21 Also your people *shall* all *be* righteous;
They shall inherit the land forever,
The branch of My planting,
The work of My hands,
That I may be glorified.
22 A little one shall become a thousand,
And a small one a strong nation.
I, the LORD, will hasten it in its time."

CHAPTER 61 GOOD NEWS.

"The Spirit of the Lord GOD *is* upon Me,
Because the LORD has anointed Me
To preach good tidings to the poor;
He has sent Me to heal the brokenhearted,
To proclaim liberty to the captives,
And the opening of the prison to *those who are*
bound;
2 To proclaim the acceptable year of the LORD,
And the day of vengeance of our God;

To comfort all who mourn,
3 To console those who mourn in Zion,
To give them beauty for ashes,
The oil of joy for mourning,
The garment of praise for the spirit of heaviness;
That they may be called trees of righteousness,
The planting of the LORD, that He may be glorified."

4 And they shall rebuild the old ruins,
They shall raise up the former desolations,
And they shall repair the ruined cities,
The desolations of many generations.
5 Strangers shall stand and feed your flocks,
And the sons of the foreigner
Shall be your plowmen and your vinedressers.
6 But you shall be named the priests of the LORD,
They shall call you the servants of our God.
You shall eat the riches of the Gentiles,
And in their glory you shall boast.
7 Instead of your shame *you shall have* double *honor,*
And *instead of* confusion they shall rejoice in their
portion.
Therefore in their land they shall possess double;
Everlasting joy shall be theirs.

8 "For I, the LORD, love justice;
I hate robbery for burnt offering;
I will direct their work in truth,
And will make with them an everlasting covenant.
9 Their descendants shall be known among the
Gentiles,
And their offspring among the people.

■INJUSTICE

61:8 We suffer for many reasons—our own mistakes, someone else's mistakes, injustice. When we suffer for our own mistakes, we get what we deserve. When we suffer because of others or injustice, God is angry. God in his mercy says that his people have suffered enough. God will reward those who suffer because of injustice. He will settle all accounts.

All who see them shall acknowledge them,
That they *are* the posterity *whom* the LORD has
blessed."

10 I will greatly rejoice in the LORD,
My soul shall be joyful in my God;
For He has clothed me with the garments of
salvation,
He has covered me with the robe of righteousness,
As a bridegroom decks *himself* with ornaments,
And as a bride adorns *herself* with her jewels.
11 For as the earth brings forth its bud,
As the garden causes the things that are sown in it to
spring forth,
So the Lord GOD will cause righteousness and praise
to spring forth before all the nations.

CHAPTER **62** ISAIAH'S PRAYER.

For Zion's sake I will not hold My peace,
And for Jerusalem's sake I will not rest,
Until her righteousness goes forth as brightness,

■DETERMINATION

62:1-7 Isaiah's zeal for his country and his desire to see the work salvation completed caused him to pray continually, hoping that Isra would be saved. We should have Isaiah's determination to see God's done. This is what we mean when we pray, "Your kingdom come. Yo will be done on earth as *it is* in heaven (Matthew 6:10)." It is good t keep praying for others.

And her salvation as a lamp *that* burns.
2 The Gentiles shall see your righteousness,
And all kings your glory.
You shall be called by a new name,
Which the mouth of the LORD will name.
3 You shall also be a crown of glory
In the hand of the LORD,
And a royal diadem
In the hand of your God.
4 You shall no longer be termed Forsaken,
Nor shall your land any more be termed Desolate;
But you shall be called Hephzibah, and your land
Beulah;
For the LORD delights in you,
And your land shall be married.
5 For *as* a young man marries a virgin,
So shall your sons marry you;
And *as* the bridegroom rejoices over the bride,
So shall your God rejoice over you.

6 I have set watchmen on your walls, O Jerusalem;
They shall never hold their peace day or night.
You who make mention of the LORD, do not keep
silent,
7 And give Him no rest till He establishes
And till He makes Jerusalem a praise in the earth.

8 The LORD has sworn by His right hand
And by the arm of His strength:
"Surely I will no longer give your grain
As food for your enemies;
And the sons of the foreigner shall not drink your
new wine,
For which you have labored.
9 But those who have gathered it shall eat it,
And praise the LORD;
Those who have brought it together shall drink it in
My holy courts."

10 Go through,
Go through the gates!
Prepare the way for the people;
Build up,
Build up the highway!
Take out the stones,
Lift up a banner for the peoples!

11 Indeed the LORD has proclaimed
To the end of the world:
"Say to the daughter of Zion,
'Surely your salvation is coming;
Behold, His reward *is* with Him,
And His work before Him.'"
12 And they shall call them The Holy People,
The Redeemed of the LORD;
And you shall be called Sought Out,
A City Not Forsaken.

CHAPTER **63** GOD IS LOVING AND KIND.

Who *is* this who comes from Edom,
With dyed garments from Bozrah,
This *One who is* glorious in His apparel,
Traveling in the greatness of His strength?—

"I who speak in righteousness, mighty to save."

² Why *is* Your apparel red,
And Your garments like one who treads in the
winepress?

³ "I have trodden the winepress alone,
And from the peoples no one *was* with Me.
For I have trodden them in My anger,
And trampled them in My fury;
Their blood is sprinkled upon My garments,
And I have stained all My robes.

⁴ For the day of vengeance *is* in My heart,
And the year of My redeemed has come.

⁵ I looked, but *there was* no one to help,
And I wondered
That *there was* no one to uphold;
Therefore My own arm brought salvation for Me;
And My own fury, it sustained Me.

⁶ I have trodden down the peoples in My anger,
Made them drunk in My fury,
And brought down their strength to the earth."

⁷ I will mention the lovingkindnesses of the LORD
And the praises of the LORD,
According to all that the LORD has bestowed on us,
And the great goodness toward the house of Israel,
Which He has bestowed on them according to His
mercies,
According to the multitude of His lovingkindnesses.

⁸ For He said, "Surely they *are* My people,
Children *who* will not lie."
So He became their Savior.

⁹ In all their affliction He was afflicted,
And the Angel of His Presence saved them;
In His love and in His pity He redeemed them;
And He bore them and carried them
All the days of old.

¹⁰ But they rebelled and grieved His Holy Spirit;
So He turned Himself against them as an enemy,
And He fought against them.

¹¹ Then he remembered the days of old,
Moses *and* his people, *saying:*
"Where *is* He who brought them up out of the sea
With the shepherd of His flock?
Where *is* He who put His Holy Spirit within them,

¹² Who led *them* by the right hand of Moses,
With His glorious arm,
Dividing the water before them
To make for Himself an everlasting name,

¹³ Who led them through the deep,
As a horse in the wilderness,
That they might not stumble?"

¹⁴ As a beast goes down into the valley,
And the Spirit of the LORD causes him to rest,

So You lead Your people,
To make Yourself a glorious name.

¹⁵ Look down from heaven,
And see from Your habitation, holy and glorious.
Where *are* Your zeal and Your strength,
The yearning of Your heart and Your mercies toward
me?
Are they restrained?

¹⁶ Doubtless You *are* our Father,
Though Abraham was ignorant of us,
And Israel does not acknowledge us.
You, O LORD, *are* our Father;
Our Redeemer from Everlasting *is* Your name.

¹⁷ O LORD, why have You made us stray from Your ways,
And hardened our heart from Your fear?
Return for Your servants' sake,
The tribes of Your inheritance.

¹⁸ Your holy people have possessed *it* but a little while;
Our adversaries have trodden down Your sanctuary.

¹⁹ We have become *like* those of old, over whom You
never ruled,
Those who were never called by Your name.

CHAPTER **64** GOD IS LIKE A POTTER.

Oh, that You would rend the heavens!
That You would come down!
That the mountains might shake at Your presence—

² As fire burns brushwood,
As fire causes water to boil—
To make Your name known to Your adversaries,
That the nations may tremble at Your presence!

³ When You did awesome things *for which* we did not
look,
You came down,
The mountains shook at Your presence.

⁴ For since the beginning of the world
Men have not heard nor perceived by the ear,
Nor has the eye seen any God besides You,
Who acts for the one who waits for Him.

⁵ You meet him who rejoices and does righteousness,
Who remembers You in Your ways.
You are indeed angry, for we have sinned—
In these ways we continue;
And we need to be saved.

⁶ But we are all like an unclean *thing,*
And all our righteousnesses *are* like filthy rags;
We all fade as a leaf,
And our iniquities, like the wind,
Have taken us away.

⁷ And *there is* no one who calls on Your name,
Who stirs himself up to take hold of You;
For You have hidden Your face from us,
And have consumed us because of our iniquities.

⁸ But now, O LORD,
You *are* our Father;
We *are* the clay, and You our potter;
And all we *are* the work of Your hand.

⁹ Do not be furious, O LORD,
Nor remember iniquity forever;

Indeed, please look—we all *are* Your people!

¹⁰ Your holy cities are a wilderness,
Zion is a wilderness,
Jerusalem a desolation.

¹¹ Our holy and beautiful temple,
Where our fathers praised You,
Is burned up with fire;
And all our pleasant things are laid waste.

¹² Will You restrain Yourself because of these *things,*
O LORD?
Will You hold Your peace, and afflict us very severely?

CHAPTER 65 NEW HEAVENS AND NEW EARTH.

"I was sought by *those who* did not ask *for Me;*
I was found by *those who* did not seek Me.
I said, 'Here I am, here I am,'
To a nation *that* was not called by My name.

² I have stretched out My hands all day long to a
rebellious people,
Who walk in a way *that is* not good,
According to their own thoughts;

³ A people who provoke Me to anger continually to
My face;
Who sacrifice in gardens,
And burn incense on altars of brick;

⁴ Who sit among the graves,
And spend the night in the tombs;
Who eat swine's flesh,
And the broth of abominable things is *in* their
vessels;

⁵ Who say, 'Keep to yourself,
Do not come near me,
For I am holier than you!'
These *are* smoke in My nostrils,
A fire that burns all the day.

REPAY

65:6 God said he would repay the people for their sins. Judgment is not our job but his, because he alone is just. Who else knows our heart and mind? Who else knows what is a completely fair reward or punishment?

⁶ "Behold, *it is* written before Me:
I will not keep silence, but will repay—
Even repay into their bosom—

⁷ Your iniquities and the iniquities of your fathers
together,"
Says the LORD,
"Who have burned incense on the mountains
And blasphemed Me on the hills;
Therefore I will measure their former work into their
bosom."

⁸Thus says the LORD:

"As the new wine is found in the cluster,
And *one* says, 'Do not destroy it,
For a blessing *is* in it,'
So will I do for My servants' sake,
That I may not destroy them all.

⁹ I will bring forth descendants from Jacob,
And from Judah an heir of My mountains;

My elect shall inherit it,
And My servants shall dwell there.

¹⁰ Sharon shall be a fold of flocks,
And the Valley of Achor a place for herds to lie down,
For My people who have sought Me.

¹¹ "But you *are* those who forsake the LORD,
Who forget My holy mountain,
Who prepare a table for Gad,
And who furnish a drink offering for Meni.

¹² Therefore I will number you for the sword,
And you shall all bow down to the slaughter;
Because, when I called, you did not answer;
When I spoke, you did not hear,
But did evil before My eyes,
And chose *that* in which I do not delight."

¹³Therefore thus says the Lord GOD:

"Behold, My servants shall eat,
But you shall be hungry;
Behold, My servants shall drink,
But you shall be thirsty;
Behold, My servants shall rejoice,
But you shall be ashamed;

¹⁴ Behold, My servants shall sing for joy of heart,
But you shall cry for sorrow of heart,
And wail for grief of spirit.

¹⁵ You shall leave your name as a curse to My chosen;
For the Lord GOD will slay you,
And call His servants by another name;

¹⁶ So that he who blesses himself in the earth
Shall bless himself in the God of truth;
And he who swears in the earth
Shall swear by the God of truth;
Because the former troubles are forgotten,
And because they are hidden from My eyes.

¹⁷ "For behold, I create new heavens and a new earth;
And the former shall not be remembered or come to
mind.

¹⁸ But be glad and rejoice forever in what I create;
For behold, I create Jerusalem *as* a rejoicing,
And her people a joy.

¹⁹ I will rejoice in Jerusalem,
And joy in My people;
The voice of weeping shall no longer be heard in her,
Nor the voice of crying.

²⁰ "No more shall an infant from there *live but a few*
days,
Nor an old man who has not fulfilled his days;
For the child shall die one hundred years old,
But the sinner *being* one hundred years old shall be
accursed.

²¹ They shall build houses and inhabit *them;*
They shall plant vineyards and eat their fruit.

²² They shall not build and another inhabit;
They shall not plant and another eat;
For as the days of a tree, *so shall be* the days of My
people,
And My elect shall long enjoy the work of their
hands.

²³ They shall not labor in vain,
Nor bring forth children for trouble;
For they *shall be* the descendants of the blessed of
the LORD,
And their offspring with them.
²⁴ "It shall come to pass
That before they call, I will answer;
And while they are still speaking, I will hear.
²⁵ The wolf and the lamb shall feed together,
The lion shall eat straw like the ox,
And dust *shall be* the serpent's food.
They shall not hurt nor destroy in all My holy
mountain,"
Says the LORD.

CHAPTER **66** THE WORLD WILL SEE. Thus says
the LORD:

"Heaven *is* My throne,
And earth *is* My footstool.
Where *is* the house that you will build Me?
And where *is* the place of My rest?
² For all those *things* My hand has made,
And all those *things* exist,"
Says the LORD.
"But on this *one* will I look:
On *him who is* poor and of a contrite spirit,
And who trembles at My word.

³ "He who kills a bull *is as if* he slays a man;
He who sacrifices a lamb, *as if* he breaks a dog's neck;
He who offers a grain offering, *as if he offers* swine's
blood;
He who burns incense, *as if* he blesses an idol.
Just as they have chosen their own ways,
And their soul delights in their abominations,
⁴ So will I choose their delusions,
And bring their fears on them;
Because, when I called, no one answered,
When I spoke they did not hear;
But they did evil before My eyes,
And chose *that* in which I do not delight."

⁵ Hear the word of the LORD,
You who tremble at His word:
"Your brethren who hated you,
Who cast you out for My name's sake, said,
'Let the LORD be glorified,
That we may see your joy.'
But they shall be ashamed."

⁶ The sound of noise from the city!
A voice from the temple!
The voice of the LORD,
Who fully repays His enemies!

⁷ "Before she was in labor, she gave birth;
Before her pain came,
She delivered a male child.
⁸ Who has heard such a thing?
Who has seen such things?
Shall the earth be made to give birth in one day?

Or shall a nation be born at once?
For as soon as Zion was in labor,
She gave birth to her children.
⁹ Shall I bring to the time of birth, and not cause
delivery?" says the LORD.
"Shall I who cause delivery shut up *the womb?*" says
your God.
¹⁰ "Rejoice with Jerusalem,
And be glad with her, all you who love her;
Rejoice for joy with her, all you who mourn for her;
¹¹ That you may feed and be satisfied
With the consolation of her bosom,
That you may drink deeply and be delighted
With the abundance of her glory."

¹²For thus says the LORD:

"Behold, I will extend peace to her like a river,
And the glory of the Gentiles like a flowing stream.
Then you shall feed;
On *her* sides shall you be carried,
And be dandled on *her* knees.
¹³ As one whom his mother comforts,
So I will comfort you;
And you shall be comforted in Jerusalem."

¹⁴ When you see *this,* your heart shall rejoice,
And your bones shall flourish like grass;
The hand of the LORD shall be known to His servants,
And *His* indignation to His enemies.
¹⁵ For behold, the LORD will come with fire
And with His chariots, like a whirlwind,
To render His anger with fury,
And His rebuke with flames of fire.
¹⁶ For by fire and by His sword
The LORD will judge all flesh;
And the slain of the LORD shall be many.

¹⁷ "Those who sanctify themselves and purify
themselves,
To go to the gardens
After an *idol* in the midst,
Eating swine's flesh and the abomination and the
mouse,
Shall be consumed together," says the LORD.

¹⁸"For I *know* their works and their thoughts. It shall be
that I will gather all nations and tongues; and they shall
come and see My glory. ¹⁹I will set a sign among them;
and those among them who escape I will send to the
nations: *to* Tarshish and Pul and Lud, who draw the bow,
and Tubal and Javan, *to* the coastlands afar off who have
not heard My fame nor seen My glory. And they shall
declare My glory among the Gentiles. ²⁰Then they shall
bring all your brethren for an offering to the LORD out of
all nations, on horses and in chariots and in litters, on
mules and on camels, to My holy mountain Jerusalem,"
says the LORD, "as the children of Israel bring an offering
in a clean vessel into the house of the LORD. ²¹And I will
also take some of them for priests *and* Levites," says the
LORD.

²² "For as the new heavens and the new earth

◣▶DRAMA

66:22-24 Isaiah brings his book to a close with great drama. For the faithless, there is a sobering portrayal of judgment. For the faithful, there is a glorious picture of rich reward—"as the new heavens and the new earth which I will make shall remain before Me . . .so shall your descendants and your name remain." The contrast is so striking that it would seem that everyone would want to follow God. But often we are just as foolish and reluctant to change as the Israelites. We are just as negligent in feeding the poor, working for justice, and obeying God's Word. Make sure you are among those who will be richly blessed.

Which I will make shall remain before Me," says the
LORD,
"So shall your descendants and your name remain.

23 And it shall come to pass
That from one New Moon to another,
And from one Sabbath to another,
All flesh shall come to worship before Me," says the
LORD.

24 "And they shall go forth and look
Upon the corpses of the men
Who have transgressed against Me.
For their worm does not die,
And their fire is not quenched.
They shall be an abhorrence to all flesh."

MEGA Themes

HOLINESS God is highly exalted above all his creatures. His moral perfection stands in contrast to evil people and nations. God is perfect and sinless, so he is in perfect control of his power, judgment, love, and mercy. His holy nature is our yardstick for morality.

Because God alone is without sin, he alone can help us with our sin. It is only right that we regard him as supreme in power and moral perfection. We must never treat God as common or ordinary. He—and only he—deserves our devotion.

1. God's holiness reveals how much he is beyond human beings. How do you feel when you consider his holiness?
2. How did Isaiah respond to God's holiness in 6:1-8?
3. What did God do for Isaiah because of his reaction?
4. What do you learn about God when you consider both his holiness and his personal love for you? How do you feel? How will you respond? (Check how Isaiah responded.)

PUNISHMENT Because God is holy, he requires his people to treat others justly. He promised to punish Israel, Judah, and other nations for faithless immorality and idolatry. Their true faith had degenerated into national pride and empty religious rituals.

We must trust in God alone and obey his commands. We cannot ignore his call to justice nor give in to selfishness. If we harden our heart against his message, we surely will be punished.

1. Whom does God punish?
2. If God forgives us, can we avoid all the consequences of our sins? Explain your answer, giving biblical support.

3. If a Christian friend were to say, "What difference does it make whether or not I sin?" how would you respond?
4. God does not want you to obey him just to avoid punishment. What is the heart motivation God wants you to have as you obey his will? Give yourself a heart check-up. How are you doing?

SALVATION/MESSIAH God promised to send a Savior—he knew that without one we would all stand condemned by his judgment. Christ's perfect sacrifice, his servant life, and his coming kingdom all are foretold by Isaiah. Through Christ, the promise of redemption and restoration are fulfilled.

Christ died to save us from sin. Salvation is in him alone. Trust Christ fully and experience the forgiveness and the wholeness he brings as your Prince of Peace.

1. Read Isaiah 9:6 and chapter 53. These describe Christ, our Savior and Messiah. What do these two contrasting descriptions reveal about Christ?
2. The Messiah was sent by God to save those who trusted him for their deliverance. Describe how you came to know and trust Christ. (If you have never trusted him, prayerfully seek him through his Word, through talking with people you trust who are Christians, and in prayer.)
3. What difference do you think it makes in your daily life that Christ is your Savior?
4. What areas of your life need recommitting to Christ? Open yourself up to him in trust. Christ came to deliver you and will not reject you if you seek him as Lord.

HOPE God promises comfort, deliverance, and restoration in his future kingdom. The Messiah will rule over his faithful followers in the age to come. Hope is possible because Christ is coming.

We can be hopeful because God has compassion for those who repent. No matter how bleak our current situation, or how evil the world becomes, we must continue to be God's faithful people who hope for his return.

1. In the latter part of the book, Isaiah begins to focus on the future when Christ will reign in his full glory. What seems to be Isaiah's attitude about this future? How did it affect his present?

2. Has there been a time when you had almost lost hope? How did you feel? What enabled you not to give up?

3. What can we expect God to provide in the future? How does this help you keep going, even when everything feels hopeless?

4. How would you live differently if there were no hope?

Y ou big crybaby. Stop your blubbering!" ■ Tears can seem embarrassing and awkward—even a sign of weakness. When we were young, tears came easily over a broken toy, a skinned knee, and other assorted real or imagined hurts. As we grew older, we learned to hide our feelings, especially our sadness. We tried to look tough or put on a happy face. That's a shame, really, because tears are important. In fact, tears can tell us a lot about people, letting us see what affects them deeply, what they care about . . . what breaks their heart. ■ Jeremiah is called the weeping prophet. In his books (Jeremiah and Lamentations), it seems as though all he does is cry. But Jeremiah's tears did not stem from immaturity, self-centeredness, or weakness. Jeremiah wept because he loved deeply, and because he knew the truth: that his beloved nation was in trouble and that God would punish them. He tried to tell the people, but they wouldn't listen. So he cried. ■ What brings tears to your eyes? What do you cry about? Most of us need to be more like Jeremiah, filled with compassion and concern. We need to cry out to God and minister to others with a broken and loving heart.

STATS

PURPOSE: To urge God's people to turn from their sins and to turn back to God

AUTHOR: Jeremiah

TO WHOM WRITTEN: Judah (the southern kingdom) and its capital city, Jerusalem

DATE WRITTEN: During Jeremiah's ministry, approximately 627–586 B.C.

SETTING: Jeremiah ministered during the reigns of Judah's last five kings—Josiah, Jehoahaz, Jehoiakim, Jehoiachin (Coniah), and Zedekiah. The nation was sliding quickly toward destruction and was eventually conquered by Babylon in 586 B.C. (see 2 Kings 21–25). The prophet Zephaniah preceded Jeremiah; Habakkuk was his contemporary.

KEY PEOPLE: Judah's kings (listed above), Baruch, Ebed-Melech, King Nebuchadnezzar, the Rechabites

KEY PLACES: Anathoth, Jerusalem, Ramah, Egypt

SPECIAL FEATURES: The book of Jeremiah is a combination of history, poetry, and biography. Jeremiah often used symbolism to communicate his message.

"Ah, Lord GOD!
Behold, I cannot speak, for I *am* a youth."

7But the LORD said to me:

"Do not say, 'I *am* a youth,'
For you shall go to all to whom I send you,
And whatever I command you, you shall speak.
8 Do not be afraid of their faces,
For I *am* with you to deliver you," says the LORD.

9 Then the LORD put forth His hand and touched my mouth, and the LORD said to me:

"Behold, I have put My words in your mouth.
10 See, I have this day set you over the nations
and over the kingdoms,
To root out and to pull down,
To destroy and to throw down,
To build and to plant."

11Moreover the word of the LORD came to me, saying, "Jeremiah, what do you see?"
And I said, "I see a branch of an almond tree."
12Then the LORD said to me, "You have seen well, for I am ready to perform My word."
13And the word of the LORD came to me the second time, saying, "What do you see?"
And I said, "I see a boiling pot, and it is facing away from the north."
14Then the LORD said to me:

"Out of the north calamity shall break forth
On all the inhabitants of the land.
15For behold, I am calling
All the families of the kingdoms of the north," says the LORD;
"They shall come and each one set his throne
At the entrance of the gates of Jerusalem,
Against all its walls all around,
And against all the cities of Judah.
16 I will utter My judgments
Against them concerning all their wickedness,
Because they have forsaken Me,
Burned incense to other gods,

JEREMIAH

CHAPTER 1 GOD CALLS JEREMIAH. The words of Jeremiah the son of Hilkiah, of the priests who *were* in Anathoth in the land of Benjamin, 2to whom the word of the LORD came in the days of Josiah the son of Amon, king of Judah, in the thirteenth year of his reign. 3It came also in the days of Jehoiakim the son of Josiah, king of Judah, until the end of the eleventh year of Zedekiah the son of Josiah, king of Judah, until the carrying away of Jerusalem captive in the fifth month.

4Then the word of the LORD came to me, saying:

5 "Before I formed you in the womb I knew you;
Before you were born I sanctified you;
I ordained you a prophet to the nations."

6Then said I:

TODAY

1:2-3 God spoke many times to Jeremiah over many years, but Jeremiah's job was to determine what God wanted him to do each day. So it is with us. God has given us his Word, with many messages. But as we search the Scriptures, we must keep asking, "What do you want me to do for you *today?*"

And worshiped the works of their own hands.

¹⁷ "Therefore prepare yourself and arise,
And speak to them all that I command you.
Do not be dismayed before their faces,
Lest I dismay you before them.
¹⁸ For behold, I have made you this day
A fortified city and an iron pillar,
And bronze walls against the whole land—
Against the kings of Judah,
Against its princes,
Against its priests,
And against the people of the land.
¹⁹ They will fight against you,
But they shall not prevail against you.
For I *am* with you," says the LORD, "to deliver you."

CHAPTER 2 GOD'S REBELLIOUS PEOPLE. Moreover the word of the LORD came to me, saying, ²"Go and cry in the hearing of Jerusalem, saying, 'Thus says the LORD:

"I remember you,
The kindness of your youth,
The love of your betrothal,
When you went after Me in the wilderness,
In a land not sown.

STAY TRUE

2:2 We appreciate a friend who remains true to his or her commitments, and we are disappointed with someone who fails to keep a promise. God was pleased when his people obeyed initially, but he became angry with them when they refused to keep their commitment. Temptations distract us from our original commitment to God. Think about your promise to obey God, and ask yourself if you are remaining true.

³ Israel *was* holiness to the LORD,
The firstfruits of His increase.
All that devour him will offend;
Disaster will come upon them," says the LORD.'"

⁴Hear the word of the LORD, O house of Jacob and all the families of the house of Israel. ⁵Thus says the LORD:

"What injustice have your fathers found in Me,
That they have gone far from Me,
Have followed idols,
And have become idolaters?
⁶ Neither did they say, 'Where *is* the LORD,
Who brought us up out of the land of Egypt,
Who led us through the wilderness,
Through a land of deserts and pits,
Through a land of drought and the shadow of death,
Through a land that no one crossed
And where no one dwelt?'
⁷ I brought you into a bountiful country,
To eat its fruit and its goodness.
But when you entered, you defiled My land
And made My heritage an abomination.
⁸ The priests did not say, 'Where *is* the LORD?'
And those who handle the law did not know Me;
The rulers also transgressed against Me;

SPARKLING WATER

2:13 Who would set aside a sparkling fountain of water for a cistern pit that collected rain water? God told the Israelites that that was what they were doing when they turned from him, the fountain of living water, to idols. Not only that, the cisterns they chose were broken and empty. The people had built religious systems to store truth in, but they were worthless. Why should we cling to the broken promises of unstable "cisterns" (money, power, religious systems, or whatever) when God promises to constantly refresh us with himself, the living water (John

The prophets prophesied by Baal,
And walked after *things that* do not profit.

⁹ "Therefore I will yet bring charges against you," says the LORD,
"And against your children's children I will bring charges.
¹⁰ For pass beyond the coasts of Cyprus and see,
Send to Kedar and consider diligently,
And see if there has been such *a thing*.
¹¹ Has a nation changed *its* gods,
Which *are* not gods?
But My people have changed their Glory
For *what* does not profit.
¹² Be astonished, O heavens, at this,
And be horribly afraid;
Be very desolate," says the LORD.
¹³ "For My people have committed two evils:
They have forsaken Me, the fountain of living waters,
And hewn themselves cisterns—broken cisterns that
can hold no water.

Your own wickedness WILL CORRECT YOU AND your backslidings WILL REBUKE YOU... IT IS an evil and bitter thing THAT you have forsaken THE LORD YOUR GOD.

JEREMIAH 2:19

14 " *Is* Israel a servant?
    Is he a homeborn *slave?*
    Why is he plundered?
15 The young lions roared at him, *and* growled;
    They made his land waste;
    His cities are burned, without inhabitant.
16 Also the people of Noph and Tahpanhes
    Have broken the crown of your head.
17 Have you not brought this on yourself,
    In that you have forsaken the LORD your God
    When He led you in the way?
18 And now why take the road to Egypt,
    To drink the waters of Sihor?
    Or why take the road to Assyria,
    To drink the waters of the River?
19 Your own wickedness will correct you,
    And your backslidings will rebuke you.
    Know therefore and see that *it is*
        an evil and bitter *thing*
    That you have forsaken the LORD
        your God,
    And the fear of Me *is* not in you,"
    Says the Lord GOD of hosts.

20 "For of old I have broken your
        yoke *and* burst your bonds;
    And you said, 'I will not
        transgress,'
    When on every high hill and
        under every green tree
    You lay down, playing the harlot.
21 Yet I had planted you a noble
        vine, a seed of highest quality.
    How then have you turned before
        Me
    Into the degenerate plant of an
        alien vine?
22 For though you wash yourself
        with lye, and use much soap,
    Yet your iniquity is marked before
        Me," says the Lord GOD.
23 "How can you say, 'I am not
        polluted,
    I have not gone after the Baals'?
    See your way in the valley;
    Know what you have done:
    You are a swift dromedary
        breaking loose in her ways,
24 A wild donkey used to the
        wilderness,
    That sniffs at the wind in her
        desire;
    In her time of mating, who can
        turn her away?
    All those who seek her will not
        weary themselves;
    In her month they will find her.
25 Withhold your foot from being
        unshod, and your throat from
        thirst.
    But you said, 'There is no hope.

No! For I have loved aliens, and after them I will go.'

26 "As the thief is ashamed when he is found out,
    So is the house of Israel ashamed;
    They and their kings and their princes, and their
        priests and their prophets,
27 Saying to a tree, 'You *are* my father,'
    And to a stone, 'You gave birth to me.'
    For they have turned *their* back to Me, and not *their*
        face.
    But in the time of their trouble
    They will say, 'Arise and save us.'
28 But where *are* your gods that you have made for
        yourselves?
    Let them arise,
    If they can save you in the time of your trouble;
    For *according to* the number of your cities

"Here's what I did..."

The topic of abortion comes up often in school, among friends and elsewhere. I had thought through my position in theory, but when my best friend told me she was pregnant and was going to get an abortion, it wasn't theoretical anymore.

When Lee called me on the phone one night and asked me to come talk, I knew something was wrong. As soon as we were alone, she blurted out: "I'm pregnant. And I have an appointment at an abortion clinic tomorrow."

I couldn't believe my ears. Lee was a Christian. We had discussed abortion often and had agreed on our stance: It was wrong. Now Lee was telling me she was going to have one tomorrow!

Trying to keep calm, I told her I realized it was her decision. Then I said, "You know I don't believe in abortion. You always said you didn't, either. It doesn't make it any more right now that you're pregnant. It's still a baby we're talking about.

"This is your decision. But as your friend, I want to make sure you've thought this through. Can we read a few passages of Scripture and pray together? Then I promise, I'll stick by you, whatever you decide."

We read Jeremiah 1:4-5 and Psalm 139. I told her, "Whenever I read these passages, they say to me that God knows us from the very beginning, and that he has a plan for each person. That's why I think you should have this baby, Lee. God will take care of your baby because he already loves the baby. And he'll take care of you, too."

We cried together, but I really believed what I said. I asked Lee if I could pray for the baby. She nodded, crying. So I prayed that God would give Lee the courage to make the right choice, and that he would take care of her baby.

Lee didn't promise she wouldn't have the abortion. I prayed hard all the next day. That evening, she called and said she hadn't gone through with it. I told her I was very happy and thought she made the right choice.

Lee will tell you that she believes she made the right choice, too. She had a beautiful girl that she placed for adoption with a loving Christian couple. It hurts her to think about the baby, but she knows she did the right thing.

Lori
AGE 17

◣▬▬ FORGETTING

2:31-32 Forgetting can be dangerous, whether it is intentional or an oversight. Israel forgot God by focusing its affections on the allurements of the world. The more we focus on the world's pleasures, the easier it becomes to forget God's care, love, dependability, guidance, and most of all, God himself. What pleases you most? Have you been forgetting God lately?

Are your gods, O Judah.

29 "Why will you plead with Me?
    You all have transgressed against Me," says the LORD.
30 "In vain I have chastened your children;
    They received no correction.
    Your sword has devoured your prophets
    Like a destroying lion.
31 "O generation, see the word of the LORD!
    Have I been a wilderness to Israel,
    Or a land of darkness?
    Why do My people say, 'We are lords;
    We will come no more to You'?
32 Can a virgin forget her ornaments,
    Or a bride her attire?
    Yet My people have forgotten Me days without
        number.
33 "Why do you beautify your way to seek love?
    Therefore you have also taught
    The wicked women your ways.
34 Also on your skirts is found
    The blood of the lives of the poor innocents.
    I have not found it by secret search,
    But plainly on all these things.
35 Yet you say, 'Because I am innocent,
    Surely His anger shall turn from me.'
    Behold, I will plead My case against you,
    Because you say, 'I have not sinned.'
36 Why do you gad about so much to change your way?
    Also you shall be ashamed of Egypt as you were
        ashamed of Assyria.
37 Indeed you will go forth from him
    With your hands on your head;
    For the LORD has rejected your trusted allies,
    And you will not prosper by them.

CHAPTER 3   THE PEOPLE GIVE UP GOD FOR IDOLS.

  "They say, 'If a man divorces his wife,
    And she goes from him
    And becomes another man's,
    May he return to her again?'
    Would not that land be greatly polluted?
    But you have played the harlot with many lovers;
    Yet return to Me," says the LORD.
2 "Lift up your eyes to the desolate heights and see:
    Where have you not lain *with men?*
    By the road you have sat for them
    Like an Arabian in the wilderness;
    And you have polluted the land
    With your harlotries and your wickedness.
3 Therefore the showers have been withheld,
    And there has been no latter rain.
    You have had a harlot's forehead;
    You refuse to be ashamed.

◣▬▬ MINIMIZED

3:4-5 Notice how the people of Israel tried to make their sin seem small. When we know we've done something wrong, we want to downplay the error by saying "It wasn't that bad!" thereby relieving some of the guilt we feel. As we minimize our sinfulness, we natural shy away from making changes, and so we keep on sinning. But if view every wrong attitude and action as a serious offense to God, w begin to understand what living for God is all about. Is there sin in y life that you've written off as too small to worry about? God says w must confess every sin, and in confessing it, turn from it.

4 Will you not from this time cry to Me,
  'My Father, You *are* the guide of my youth?
5 Will He remain angry forever?
  Will He keep it to the end?'
  Behold, you have spoken and done evil things,
  As you were able."

6 The LORD said also to me in the days of Josiah the king: "Have you seen what backsliding Israel has done? She has gone up on every high mountain and under every green tree, and there played the harlot. 7 And I said, after she had done all these *things,* 'Return to Me.' But she

---

Climate of the times	• Society was deteriorating economically, politically, spiritually. • Wars and captivity. • God's Word was outlawed.
Main message	Repentance from sin would postpone Judah's coming judgment at the hands of Babylon.
Importance of message.	Repentance is one of the greatest needs in our immoral world. God's promises to the faithful shine brightly by bringing hope for tomorrow and strength for today.
Contemporary prophets	Habakkuk (612–589) Zephaniah (640–621)

JEREMIAH
served as a prophet to Judah from 627 B.C. until the exile in 586 B.C.

did not return. And her treacherous sister Judah saw it. [8]Then I saw that for all the causes for which backsliding Israel had committed adultery, I had put her away and given her a certificate of divorce; yet her treacherous sister Judah did not fear, but went and played the harlot also. [9]So it came to pass, through her casual harlotry, that she defiled the land and committed adultery with stones and trees. [10]And yet for all this her treacherous sister Judah has not turned to Me with her whole heart, but in pretense," says the LORD.

[11]Then the LORD said to me, "Backsliding Israel has shown herself more righteous than treacherous Judah. [12]Go and proclaim these words toward the north, and say:

'Return, backsliding Israel,' says the LORD;
'I will not cause My anger to fall on you.
For I *am* merciful,' says the LORD;
'I will not remain angry forever.
[13] Only acknowledge your iniquity,
    That you have transgressed against the LORD your
        God,
And have scattered your charms
    To alien deities under every green tree,
And you have not obeyed My voice,' says the LORD.

[14]"Return, O backsliding children," says the LORD; "for I am married to you. I will take you, one from a city and two from a family, and I will bring you to Zion. [15]And I will give you shepherds according to My heart, who will feed you with knowledge and understanding.

[16]"Then it shall come to pass, when you are multiplied and increased in the land in those days," says the LORD, "that they will say no more, 'The ark of the covenant of the LORD.' It shall not come to mind, nor shall they remember it, nor shall they visit *it,* nor shall it be made anymore.

[17]"At that time Jerusalem shall be called The Throne of the LORD, and all the nations shall be gathered to it, to the name of the LORD, to Jerusalem. No more shall they follow the dictates of their evil hearts.

[18]"In those days the house of Judah shall walk with the house of Israel, and they shall come together out of the land of the north to the land that I have given as an inheritance to your fathers.

[19]"But I said:

'How can I put you among the children
    And give you a pleasant land,
A beautiful heritage of the hosts of nations?'

"And I said:

'You shall call Me, "My Father,"
    And not turn away from Me.'
[20] Surely, *as* a wife treacherously departs from her
        husband,
So have you dealt treacherously with Me,
    O house of Israel," says the LORD.

[21] A voice was heard on the desolate heights,
    Weeping *and* supplications of the children of Israel.
For they have perverted their way;
    They have forgotten the LORD their God.

[22] "Return, you backsliding children,
    And I will heal your backslidings."

"Indeed we do come to You,
    For You are the LORD our God.
[23] Truly, in vain *is salvation hoped for* from the hills,
    And from the multitude of mountains;
Truly, in the LORD our God
    Is the salvation of Israel.
[24] For shame has devoured

My mom used to go to church a lot, but she doesn't anymore. What can I do to get her to give God more attention?

Going from a close relationship with Christ to total neglect is like going from a two-wheel bike to one with training wheels. It seems safer, but it's not half the fun.

You may see many people who start out strong in their walk with God, but for some reason they begin to fade and eventually drop off.

Remember, the Christian life is not a sprint—it's a long-distance race, a marathon! How you start is not nearly as important as how you finish.

In a long race, many people get weary of waiting for the prize and decide to drop out. Your mother may be an example of that. She seems to have turned her attention elsewhere, forgetting about the race altogether.

As Jeremiah 2:13 says, when people reject God, they need other things to hold life together. But those other things are just "broken cisterns" that don't hold anything of value.

And like the person who goes back to the bike with training wheels because it's safer, some people allow distractions to push God aside.

Some people believe that the Christian life means having their problems solved immediately, always being treated right by people, never having doubts about the future, always having prayers answered right away, and always feeling good about church. Those people are pursuing the wrong goals! They will be disappointed, grow tired, and tend to drop out.

Our goal should be to get to know the God who created us and loved us enough to die on a cross to save us from sin—then we'll never get tired of the faith. There's always something new to discover about the richness and depth of God's love for us. If we work to let God change our selfish characters into selfless characters, the race will never seem too long.

Don't try to change your mom. She'll likely not appreciate it, no matter how good your motives are. Instead, give God permission to change you! Focus on how well *you* are doing, and let God take care of your mom.

Become more diligent in doing your chores and homework. Begin to treat your brothers and sisters better than you have. Pray for your mom to see these changes. Then give God time to work. Remember, he wants her to have a right relationship with him even more than you do!

The labor of our fathers from our youth—
Their flocks and their herds,
Their sons and their daughters.
25 We lie down in our shame,
And our reproach covers us.
For we have sinned against the LORD our God,
We and our fathers,
From our youth even to this day,
And have not obeyed the voice of the LORD our God."

CHAPTER 4 GOD ASKS HIS PEOPLE TO OBEY.

"If you will return, O Israel," says the LORD,
"Return to Me;
And if you will put away your abominations out of
My sight,
Then you shall not be moved.
2 And you shall swear, 'The LORD lives,'
In truth, in judgment, and in righteousness;
The nations shall bless themselves in Him,
And in Him they shall glory."

3For thus says the LORD to the men of Judah and Jerusalem:

"Break up your fallow ground,
And do not sow among thorns.
4 Circumcise yourselves to the LORD,
And take away the foreskins of your hearts,
You men of Judah and inhabitants of Jerusalem,
Lest My fury come forth like fire,
And burn so that no one can quench it,
Because of the evil of your doings."

5Declare in Judah and proclaim in Jerusalem, and say:

"Blow the trumpet in the land;
Cry, 'Gather together,'
And say, 'Assemble yourselves,
And let us go into the fortified cities.'
6 Set up the standard toward Zion.
Take refuge! Do not delay!
For I will bring disaster from the north,
And great destruction."

7 The lion has come up from his thicket,
And the destroyer of nations is on his way.
He has gone forth from his place
To make your land desolate.
Your cities will be laid waste,
Without inhabitant.
8 For this, clothe yourself with sackcloth,
Lament and wail.
For the fierce anger of the LORD
Has not turned back from us.

9 "And it shall come to pass in that day," says the LORD,
"That the heart of the king shall perish,
And the heart of the princes;
The priests shall be astonished,
And the prophets shall wonder."

10 Then I said, "Ah, Lord GOD!
Surely You have greatly deceived this people and
Jerusalem,

Saying, 'You shall have peace,'
Whereas the sword reaches to the heart."

11 At that time it will be said
To this people and to Jerusalem,
"A dry wind of the desolate heights blows in the
wilderness
Toward the daughter of My people—
Not to fan or to cleanse—
12 A wind too strong for these will come for Me;
Now I will also speak judgment against them."

13 "Behold, he shall come up like clouds,
And his chariots like a whirlwind.
His horses are swifter than eagles.
Woe to us, for we are plundered!"

14 O Jerusalem, wash your heart from wickedness,
That you may be saved.
How long shall your evil thoughts lodge within you?
15 For a voice declares from Dan
And proclaims affliction from Mount Ephraim:
16 "Make mention to the nations,
Yes, proclaim against Jerusalem,
That watchers come from a far country
And raise their voice against the cities of Judah.
17 Like keepers of a field they are against her all around,
Because she has been rebellious against Me," says
the LORD.
18 "Your ways and your doings
Have procured these things for you.
This is your wickedness,
Because it is bitter,
Because it reaches to your heart."

19 O my soul, my soul!
I am pained in my very heart!
My heart makes a noise in me;
I cannot hold my peace,
Because you have heard, O my soul,
The sound of the trumpet,
The alarm of war.
20 Destruction upon destruction is cried,
For the whole land is plundered.
Suddenly my tents are plundered,
And my curtains in a moment.
21 How long will I see the standard,
And hear the sound of the trumpet?

22 "For My people are foolish,
They have not known Me.
They are silly children,
And they have no understanding.
They are wise to do evil,
But to do good they have no knowledge."

23 I beheld the earth, and indeed it was without form,
and void;
And the heavens, they had no light.
24 I beheld the mountains, and indeed they trembled,
And all the hills moved back and forth.
25 I beheld, and indeed there was no man,
And all the birds of the heavens had fled.

²⁶ I beheld, and indeed the fruitful land *was* a
　　wilderness,
And all its cities were broken down
At the presence of the LORD,
By His fierce anger.

²⁷For thus says the LORD:

"The whole land shall be desolate;
Yet I will not make a full end.
²⁸ For this shall the earth mourn,
And the heavens above be black,
Because I have spoken.
I have purposed and will not relent,
Nor will I turn back from it.
²⁹ The whole city shall flee from the noise of the
　　horsemen and bowmen.
They shall go into thickets and climb up on the
　　rocks.
Every city *shall be* forsaken,
And not a man shall dwell in it.

³⁰ "And *when* you *are* plundered,
What will you do?
Though you clothe yourself with crimson,
Though you adorn *yourself* with ornaments of gold,
Though you enlarge your eyes with paint,
In vain you will make yourself fair;
Your lovers will despise you;
They will seek your life.

³¹ "For I have heard a voice as of a woman in labor,
The anguish as of her who brings forth her first child,
The voice of the daughter of Zion bewailing herself;
She spreads her hands, *saying,*
'Woe *is* me now, for my soul is weary
Because of murderers!'

CHAPTER **5** NO RESPECT FOR GOD.

"Run to and fro through the streets of Jerusalem;
See now and know;
And seek in her open places
If you can find a man,
If there is *anyone* who executes judgment,
Who seeks the truth,
And I will pardon her.
² Though they say, '*As* the LORD lives,'
Surely they swear falsely."

³ O LORD, *are* not Your eyes on the truth?
You have stricken them,
But they have not grieved;
You have consumed them,
But they have refused to receive correction.
They have made their faces harder than rock;
They have refused to return.

⁴ Therefore I said, "Surely these *are* poor.
They are foolish;
For they do not know the way of the LORD,
The judgment of their God.
⁵ I will go to the great men and speak to them,
For they have known the way of the LORD,
The judgment of their God."

But these have altogether broken the yoke
And burst the bonds.
⁶ Therefore a lion from the forest shall slay them,
A wolf of the deserts shall destroy them;
A leopard will watch over their cities.
Everyone who goes out from there shall be torn in
　　pieces,
Because their transgressions are many;

▰▰▰FAITHFUL

4:27 God warned that destruction was certain, but he promised that a remnant would remain faithful to him and would be spared, even though the nation would be wiped out. God is committed to preserving those who are faithful to him.

Their backslidings have increased.

⁷ "How shall I pardon you for this?
Your children have forsaken Me
And sworn by *those that are* not gods.
When I had fed them to the full,
Then they committed adultery
And assembled themselves by troops in the harlots'
　　houses.
⁸ They were *like* well-fed lusty stallions;
Every one neighed after his neighbor's wife.
⁹ Shall I not punish *them* for these *things?*" says the
　　LORD.
"And shall I not avenge Myself on such a nation as
　　this?

¹⁰ "Go up on her walls and destroy,
But do not make a complete end.
Take away her branches,
For they *are* not the LORD's.
¹¹ For the house of Israel and the house of Judah
Have dealt very treacherously with Me," says the
　　LORD.

¹² They have lied about the LORD,
And said, "*It is* not He.
Neither will evil come upon us,
Nor shall we see sword or famine.
¹³ And the prophets become wind,
For the word *is* not in them.
Thus shall it be done to them."

¹⁴Therefore thus says the LORD God of hosts:

"Because you speak this word,
Behold, I will make My words in your mouth fire,
And this people wood,
And it shall devour them.
¹⁵ Behold, I will bring a nation against you from afar,
O house of Israel," says the LORD.
"It *is* a mighty nation,
It *is* an ancient nation,
A nation whose language you do not know,
Nor can you understand what they say.
¹⁶ Their quiver *is* like an open tomb;
They *are* all mighty men.

¹⁷ And they shall eat up your harvest and your bread,
Which your sons and daughters should eat.
They shall eat up your flocks and your herds;
They shall eat up your vines and your fig trees;
They shall destroy your fortified cities,
In which you trust, with the sword.

¹⁸"Nevertheless in those days," says the LORD, "I will not make a complete end of you. ¹⁹And it will be when you say, 'Why does the LORD our God do all these *things* to us?' then you shall answer them, 'Just as you have forsaken Me and served foreign gods in your land, so you shall serve aliens in a land *that is* not yours.'

²⁰ "Declare this in the house of Jacob
And proclaim it in Judah, saying,
²¹ 'Hear this now, O foolish people,
Without understanding,
Who have eyes and see not,

▰▰▰ STRIPPED

5:22-24 What is your attitude when you come into God's presence? We should come with fear and trembling (awe and respect), for God sets the boundaries of the roaring seas and establishes the rains and harvests. God had to strip away all the things that Israel had grown to respect more than him. Without them, the people could once again reverence God. Don't wait until God removes the objects of your reverence and respect before you think of him as you should.

And who have ears and hear not:
²² Do you not fear Me?' says the LORD.
'Will you not tremble at My presence,
Who have placed the sand as the bound of the sea,
By a perpetual decree, that it cannot pass beyond it?
And though its waves toss to and fro,
Yet they cannot prevail;
Though they roar, yet they cannot pass over it.
²³ But this people has a defiant and rebellious heart;
They have revolted and departed.
²⁴ They do not say in their heart,
"Let us now fear the LORD our God,
Who gives rain, both the former and the latter, in its season.
He reserves for us the appointed weeks of the harvest."
²⁵ Your iniquities have turned these *things* away,
And your sins have withheld good from you.
²⁶ 'For among My people are found wicked *men;*
They lie in wait as one who sets snares;
They set a trap;
They catch men.
²⁷ As a cage is full of birds,
So their houses *are* full of deceit.
Therefore they have become great and grown rich.
²⁸ They have grown fat, they are sleek;
Yes, they surpass the deeds of the wicked;
They do not plead the cause,
The cause of the fatherless;
Yet they prosper,
And the right of the needy they do not defend.

²⁹ Shall I not punish *them* for these *things?* says the LORD.
'Shall I not avenge Myself on such a nation as this?'

³⁰ "An astonishing and horrible thing
Has been committed in the land:
³¹ The prophets prophesy falsely,
And the priests rule by their *own* power;
And My people love *to have it* so.
But what will you do in the end?

CHAPTER **6** ONE LAST WARNING.

"O you children of Benjamin,
Gather yourselves to flee from the midst of Jerusalem!
Blow the trumpet in Tekoa,
And set up a signal-fire in Beth Haccerem;
For disaster appears out of the north,
And great destruction.
² I have likened the daughter of Zion
To a lovely and delicate woman.
³ The shepherds with their flocks shall come to her.
They shall pitch *their* tents against her all around.
Each one shall pasture in his own place."

⁴ "Prepare war against her;
Arise, and let us go up at noon.
Woe to us, for the day goes away,
For the shadows of the evening are lengthening.
⁵ Arise, and let us go by night,
And let us destroy her palaces."

⁶For thus has the LORD of hosts said:

"Cut down trees,
And build a mound against Jerusalem.
This *is* the city to be punished.
She *is* full of oppression in her midst.
⁷ As a fountain wells up with water,
So she wells up with her wickedness.
Violence and plundering are heard in her.
Before Me continually *are* grief and wounds.
⁸ Be instructed, O Jerusalem,
Lest My soul depart from you;
Lest I make you desolate,
A land not inhabited."

⁹Thus says the LORD of hosts:

"They shall thoroughly glean as a vine the remnant of Israel;
As a grape-gatherer, put your hand back into the branches."

¹⁰ To whom shall I speak and give warning,
That they may hear?

▰▰▰ OUR RESPONSIBILITY

6:10 The people became angry and wanted no part of God's comm Living for God did not appear very exciting. There are people today, who dislike God's demand for disciplined living. As unsettling as peo responses might be, we must continue to share God's Word. Our responsibility is to present God's Word—their responsibility is to acc We must not let what people want to hear determine what we say.

Indeed their ear *is* uncircumcised,
And they cannot give heed.
Behold, the word of the LORD is a reproach to them;
They have no delight in it.
¹¹ Therefore I am full of the fury of the LORD.
I am weary of holding *it* in.
"I will pour it out on the children outside,
And on the assembly of young men together;
For even the husband shall be taken with the wife,
The aged with *him who is* full of days.
¹² And their houses shall be turned over to others,
Fields and wives together;
For I will stretch out My hand
Against the inhabitants of the land," says the LORD.
¹³ "Because from the least of them even to the greatest
of them,
Everyone *is* given to covetousness;
And from the prophet even to the priest,
Everyone deals falsely.
¹⁴ They have also healed the hurt of My people slightly,
Saying, 'Peace, peace!'
When *there is* no peace.
¹⁵ Were they ashamed when they had committed
abomination?
No! They were not at all ashamed;
Nor did they know how to blush.
Therefore they shall fall among those who fall;
At the time I punish them,
They shall be cast down," says the LORD.

¹⁶Thus says the LORD:

"Stand in the ways and see,
And ask for the old paths, where the good way *is,*
And walk in it;
Then you will find rest for your souls.
But they said, 'We will not walk *in it.*'
¹⁷ Also, I set watchmen over you, *saying,*
'Listen to the sound of the trumpet!'
But they said, 'We will not listen.'
¹⁸ Therefore hear, you nations,
And know, O congregation, what *is* among them.
¹⁹ Hear, O earth!
Behold, I will certainly bring calamity on this
people—
The fruit of their thoughts,
Because they have not heeded My words
Nor My law, but rejected it.
²⁰ For what purpose to Me
Comes frankincense from Sheba,
And sweet cane from a far country?
Your burnt offerings *are* not acceptable,
Nor your sacrifices sweet to Me."

²¹Therefore thus says the LORD:

"Behold, I will lay stumbling blocks before this
people,
And the fathers and the sons together shall fall on
them.
The neighbor and his friend shall perish."

²²Thus says the LORD:

"Behold, a people comes from the north country,
And a great nation will be raised from the farthest
parts of the earth.
²³ They will lay hold on bow and spear;
They *are* cruel and have no mercy;
Their voice roars like the sea;
And they ride on horses,
As men of war set in array against you, O daughter of
Zion."

²⁴ We have heard the report of it;
Our hands grow feeble.
Anguish has taken hold of us,
Pain as of a woman in labor.
²⁵ Do not go out into the field,
Nor walk by the way.
Because of the sword of the enemy,
Fear *is* on every side.
²⁶ O daughter of my people,
Dress in sackcloth
And roll about in ashes!
Make mourning *as for* an only son, most bitter
lamentation;
For the plunderer will suddenly come upon us.

²⁷ "I have set you *as* an assayer *and* a fortress among My
people,
That you may know and test their way.
²⁸ They *are* all stubborn rebels, walking as slanderers.
They are bronze and iron,
They *are* all corrupters;
²⁹ The bellows blow fiercely,
The lead is consumed by the fire;
The smelter refines in vain,
For the wicked are not drawn off.
³⁰ *People* will call them rejected silver,
Because the LORD has rejected them."

CHAPTER 7 FALSE WORSHIP. The word that came
to Jeremiah from the LORD, saying, ²"Stand in the gate of
the LORD's house, and proclaim there this word, and say,
'Hear the word of the LORD, all *you of* Judah who enter in
at these gates to worship the LORD!'" ³Thus says the LORD
of hosts, the God of Israel: "Amend your ways and your
doings, and I will cause you to dwell in this place. ⁴Do not
trust in these lying words, saying, 'The temple of the
LORD, the temple of the LORD, the temple of the LORD *are*
these.'
⁵"For if you thoroughly amend your ways and your
doings, if you thoroughly execute judgment between a
man and his neighbor, ⁶*if* you do not oppress the
stranger, the fatherless, and the widow, and do not shed
innocent blood in this place, or walk after other gods to
your hurt, ⁷then I will cause you to dwell in this place, in
the land that I gave to your fathers forever and ever.

RITUALS

7:8 The people followed a worship ritual but maintained a sinful
life-style. It was religion without personal commitment to God. We can
fall easily into this trap. Attending church, taking communion, teaching
Sunday school, singing in the choir—all are empty exercises unless we
are doing them for God.

⁸"Behold, you trust in lying words that cannot profit. ⁹Will you steal, murder, commit adultery, swear falsely, burn incense to Baal, and walk after other gods whom you do not know, ¹⁰and *then* come and stand before Me in this house which is called by My name, and say, 'We are delivered to do all these abominations'? ¹¹Has this house, which is called by My name, become a den of thieves in your eyes? Behold, I, even I, have seen *it*," says the LORD.

¹²"But go now to My place which *was* in Shiloh, where I set My name at the first, and see what I did to it because of the wickedness of My people Israel. ¹³And now, because you have done all these works," says the LORD, "and I spoke to you, rising up early and speaking, but you did not hear, and I called you, but you did not answer, ¹⁴therefore I will do to the house which is called by My name, in which you trust, and to this place which I gave to you and your fathers, as I have done to Shiloh. ¹⁵And I will cast you out of My sight, as I have cast out all your brethren—the whole posterity of Ephraim.

¹⁶"Therefore do not pray for this people, nor lift up a cry or prayer for them, nor make intercession to Me; for I will not hear you. ¹⁷Do you not see what they do in the cities of Judah and in the streets of Jerusalem? ¹⁸The children gather wood, the fathers kindle the fire, and the women knead dough, to make cakes for the queen of heaven; and *they* pour out drink offerings to other gods, that they may provoke Me to anger. ¹⁹Do they provoke Me to anger?" says the LORD. "*Do they* not *provoke* themselves, to the shame of their own faces?"

▬▬▬ HURT

7:19 This verse answers the question, "Who gets hurt when we turn away from God?" We do! Separating oneself from God is like keeping a green plant away from sunlight or water, or cutting off its food supply. God is our only source of spiritual strength. Cut yourself off from that source, and you cut off life itself.

²⁰Therefore thus says the Lord GOD: "Behold, My anger and My fury will be poured out on this place—on man and on beast, on the trees of the field and on the fruit of the ground. And it will burn and not be quenched."

²¹Thus says the LORD of hosts, the God of Israel: "Add your burnt offerings to your sacrifices and eat meat. ²²For I did not speak to your fathers, or command them in the day that I brought them out of the land of Egypt, concerning burnt offerings or sacrifices. ²³But this is what I commanded them, saying, 'Obey My voice, and I will be your God, and you shall be My people. And walk in all the ways that I have commanded you, that it may be well with you.' ²⁴Yet they did not obey or incline their ear, but followed the counsels *and* the dictates of their evil hearts, and went backward and not forward. ²⁵Since the day that your fathers came out of the land of Egypt until this day, I have even sent to you all My servants the prophets, daily rising up early and sending *them*. ²⁶Yet they did not obey Me or incline their ear, but stiffened their neck. They did worse than their fathers. ²⁷"Therefore you shall speak all these words to them, but they will not obey you. You shall also call to them, but they will not answer you.

²⁸"So you shall say to them, 'This *is* a nation that does not obey the voice of the LORD their God nor receive correction. Truth has perished and has been cut off from their mouth. ²⁹Cut off your hair and cast *it* away, and take up a lamentation on the desolate heights; for the LORD has rejected and forsaken the generation of His wrath.' ³⁰For the children of Judah have done evil in My sight," says the LORD. "They have set their abominations in the house which is called by My name, to pollute it. ³¹And they have built the high places of Tophet, which *is* in the Valley of the Son of Hinnom, to burn their sons and their daughters in the fire, which I did not command, nor did it come into My heart.

³²"Therefore behold, the days are coming," says the LORD, "when it will no more be called Tophet, or the Valley of the Son of Hinnom, but the Valley of Slaughter; for they will bury in Tophet until there is no room. ³³The corpses of this people will be food for the birds of the heaven and for the beasts of the earth. And no one will frighten *them away.* ³⁴Then I will cause to cease from the cities of Judah and from the streets of Jerusalem the voice of mirth and the voice of gladness, the voice of the bridegroom and the voice of the bride. For the land shall be desolate.

CHAPTER **8** **THE PEOPLE BELIEVE LIES.** "At that time," says the LORD, "they shall bring out the bones of the kings of Judah, and the bones of its princes, and the bones of the priests, and the bones of the prophets, and the bones of the inhabitants of Jerusalem, out of their graves. ²They shall spread them before the sun and the moon and all the host of heaven, which they have loved and which they have served and after which they have walked, which they have sought and which they have worshiped. They shall not be gathered nor buried; they shall be like refuse on the face of the earth. ³Then death shall be chosen rather than life by all the residue of those who remain of this evil family, who remain in all the places where I have driven them," says the LORD of hosts.

⁴"Moreover you shall say to them, 'Thus says the LORD:

"Will they fall and not rise?
Will one turn away and not return?
⁵ Why has this people slidden back,
Jerusalem, in a perpetual backsliding?
They hold fast to deceit,
They refuse to return.
⁶ I listened and heard,
But they do not speak aright.
No man repented of his wickedness,
Saying, 'What have I done?'
Everyone turned to his own course,
As the horse rushes into the battle.

⁷ "Even the stork in the heavens
Knows her appointed times;
And the turtledove, the swift, and the swallow
Observe the time of their coming.
But My people do not know the judgment of the
LORD.

⁸ "How can you say, 'We *are* wise,

And the law of the Lord *is* with us'?
Look, the false pen of the scribe certainly works
    falsehood.
9 The wise men are ashamed,
They are dismayed and taken.
Behold, they have rejected the word of the Lord;
So what wisdom do they have?
10 Therefore I will give their wives to others,
And their fields to those who will inherit *them;*
Because from the least even to the greatest
Everyone is given to covetousness;
From the prophet even to the priest
Everyone deals falsely.
11 For they have healed the hurt of the daughter of My
    people slightly,
Saying, 'Peace, peace!'
When *there is* no peace.
12 Were they ashamed when they had committed
    abomination?
No! They were not at all ashamed,
Nor did they know how to blush.
Therefore they shall fall among those who fall;
In the time of their punishment
They shall be cast down," says the Lord.

13 "I will surely consume them," says the Lord.
"No grapes *shall be* on the vine,
Nor figs on the fig tree,
And the leaf shall fade;
And *the things* I have given them shall pass away
    from them."' "

14 "Why do we sit still?
Assemble yourselves,
And let us enter the fortified cities,
And let us be silent there.
For the Lord our God has put us to silence
And given us water of gall to drink,
Because we have sinned against the Lord.
15 "*We* looked for peace, but no good *came;*
And for a time of health, and there was trouble!
16 The snorting of His horses was heard from Dan.
The whole land trembled at the sound of the
    neighing of His strong ones;
For they have come and devoured the land and all
    that is in it,
The city and those who dwell in it."

17 "For behold, I will send serpents among you,
Vipers which cannot be charmed,
And they shall bite you," says the Lord.

18 I would comfort myself in sorrow;
My heart *is* faint in me.
19 Listen! The voice,
The cry of the daughter of my people
From a far country:
"*Is* not the Lord in Zion?
Is not her King in her?"

"Why have they provoked Me to anger
With their carved images—

With foreign idols?"
20 "The harvest is past,
The summer is ended,
And we are not saved!"

21 For the hurt of the daughter of my people I am hurt.
I am mourning;

BEWARE

8:11 The prophets and priests were giving false assurances rather than correction. How can we correct a fault or turn from a sin if our leaders tell us all is well? Beware of people who are always agreeable. At best, they give you no help; at worst, they may be trying to manipulate you.

Astonishment has taken hold of me.
22 *Is there* no balm in Gilead,
Is there no physician there?
Why then is there no recovery
For the health of the daughter of my people?

CHAPTER 9 JEREMIAH CRIES.

Oh, that my head were waters,
And my eyes a fountain of tears,
That I might weep day and night
For the slain of the daughter of my people!
2 Oh, that I had in the wilderness
A lodging place for travelers;
That I might leave my people,
And go from them!
For they *are* all adulterers,
An assembly of treacherous men.

3 "And *like* their bow they have bent their tongues *for*
    lies.
They are not valiant for the truth on the earth.
For they proceed from evil to evil,
And they do not know Me," says the Lord.
4 "Everyone take heed to his neighbor,
And do not trust any brother;
For every brother will utterly supplant,
And every neighbor will walk with slanderers.
5 Everyone will deceive his neighbor,
And will not speak the truth;
They have taught their tongue to speak lies;
They weary themselves to commit iniquity.
6 Your dwelling place *is* in the midst of deceit;
Through deceit they refuse to know Me," says the
    Lord.

7Therefore thus says the Lord of hosts:

"Behold, I will refine them and try them;
For how shall I deal with the daughter of My people?

BROKEN

8:20-22 These verses provide a vivid picture of Jeremiah's emotions as he watched his people reject God. He responded with anguish to a world dying in sin. We watch that same world still dying in sin, still rejecting God. But how often is our heart broken for our lost friends and neighbors, our lost world? Only when we have Jeremiah's kind of concern will we be moved to help. We must begin by asking God to break our heart for the world he loves.

8 Their tongue *is* an arrow shot out;
It speaks deceit;
One speaks peaceably to his neighbor with his
mouth,
But in his heart he lies in wait.
9 Shall I not punish them for these *things?*" says the
LORD.
"Shall I not avenge Myself on such a nation as this?"

10 I will take up a weeping and wailing for the
mountains,
And for the dwelling places of the wilderness a
lamentation,
Because they are burned up,

PRIORITIES

In August, some guys from Adams High are sitting around discussing their summers:

Brandon: "Get this—my Dad is paying me $8 an hour to make deliveries! Counting that and my afternoon lawn business, I'm gonna clear $3,000 easy!"

Jim: "That's great, but money ain't gonna help you block on the football field. I've been in the gym every day. So far, I've increased my bench press from 200 to 250 pounds! I'll be all-district this year."

Glenn: "Too bad you didn't work out your brain muscle! I've had the best of all possible summers. I'm in shape, I earned a little money, I had a great social life, and I just got back from computer camp—"

All (laughing): "Computer camp?! You're kidding!"

Glenn: "Hey, laugh all you want. We'll see who's laughing next spring when I get a scholarship to Princeton or Harvard, and you guys are dinking around at some junior college."

Jim: "What about you, Rick? Didn't you just go on some church trip?"

Rick's kind of embarrassed. He did just return from a mission trip to Mexico. It was incredible, but compared to making tons of money, turning into Arnold Schwarzenegger, or getting a scholarship, it doesn't seem like much.

Can you relate to Rick's feelings? What does this scene show us about priorities? See Jeremiah 9:23-24 for a clear look at what really matters.

So that no one can pass through;
Nor can *men* hear the voice of the cattle.
Both the birds of the heavens and the beasts have
fled;
They are gone.

11 "I will make Jerusalem a heap of ruins, a den of
jackals.
I will make the cities of Judah desolate, without an
inhabitant."

12 Who *is* the wise man who may understand this? And *who is he* to whom the mouth of the LORD has spoken, that he may declare it? Why does the land perish *and* burn up like a wilderness, so that no one can pass through?
13 And the LORD said, "Because they have forsaken My law which I set before them, and have not obeyed My voice, nor walked according to it, 14 but they have walked according to the dictates of their own hearts and after the Baals, which their fathers taught them," 15 therefore thus says the LORD of hosts, the God of Israel: "Behold, I will feed them, this people, with wormwood, and give them water of gall to drink. 16 I will scatter them also among the Gentiles, whom neither they nor their fathers have known. And I will send a sword after them until I have consumed them."

17 Thus says the LORD of hosts:

"Consider and call for the mourning women,
That they may come;
And send for skillful wailing women,
That they may come.
18 Let them make haste
And take up a wailing for us,
That our eyes may run with tears,
And our eyelids gush with water.
19 For a voice of wailing is heard from Zion:
'How we are plundered!
We are greatly ashamed,
Because we have forsaken the land,
Because we have been cast out of our dwellings.'"

20 Yet hear the word of the LORD, O women,
And let your ear receive the word of His mouth;
Teach your daughters wailing,
And everyone her neighbor a lamentation.
21 For death has come through our windows,
Has entered our palaces,
To kill off the children—*no longer to be* outside!
And the young men—*no longer* on the streets!

22 Speak, "Thus says the LORD:

'Even the carcasses of men shall fall as refuse on the
open field,
Like cuttings after the harvester,
And no one shall gather *them.*'"

23 Thus says the LORD:

"Let not the wise *man* glory in his wisdom,
Let not the mighty *man* glory in his might,
Nor let the rich *man* glory in his riches;
24 But let him who glories glory in this,
That he understands and knows Me,
That I *am* the LORD, exercising lovingkindness,
judgment, and righteousness in the earth.
For in these I delight," says the LORD.

25 "Behold, the days are coming," says the LORD, "that I will punish all *who are* circumcised with the uncircumcised— 26 Egypt, Judah, Edom, the people of Ammon, Moab, and all *who are* in the farthest corners, who dwell in the wilderness. For all *these* nations *are* uncircumcised, and all the house of Israel *are* uncircumcised in the heart."

CHAPTER **10** THE GOD OF CREATION. Hear the word which the LORD speaks to you, O house of Israel.
2 Thus says the LORD:

"Do not learn the way of the Gentiles;

Do not be dismayed at the signs of heaven,
For the Gentiles are dismayed at them.
3 For the customs of the peoples *are* futile;
For *one* cuts a tree from the forest,
The work of the hands of the workman, with the ax.
4 They decorate it with silver and gold;
They fasten it with nails and hammers
So that it will not topple.
5 They *are* upright, like a palm tree,
And they cannot speak;
They must be carried,
Because they cannot go *by themselves.*
Do not be afraid of them,
For they cannot do evil,
Nor can they do any good."

6 Inasmuch as *there is* none like You, O LORD
(You *are* great, and Your name *is* great in might),
7 Who would not fear You, O King of the nations?
For this is Your rightful due.
For among all the wise *men* of the nations,
And in all their kingdoms,
There is none like You.
8 But they are altogether dull-hearted and foolish;
A wooden idol *is* a worthless doctrine.
9 Silver is beaten into plates;
It is brought from Tarshish,
And gold from Uphaz,
The work of the craftsman
And of the hands of the metalsmith;
Blue and purple *are* their clothing;
They *are* all the work of skillful *men.*
10 But the LORD *is* the true God;
He *is* the living God and the everlasting King.
At His wrath the earth will tremble,
And the nations will not be able to endure His
indignation.

11 Thus you shall say to them: "The gods that have not
made the heavens and the earth shall perish from the
earth and from under these heavens."

12 He has made the earth by His power,
He has established the world by His wisdom,
And has stretched out the heavens at His discretion.
13 When He utters His voice,
There is a multitude of waters in the heavens:
"And He causes the vapors to ascend from the ends
of the earth.
He makes lightning for the rain,
He brings the wind out of His treasuries."

14 Everyone is dull-hearted, without knowledge;
Every metalsmith is put to shame by an image;
For his molded image *is* falsehood,
And *there is* no breath in them.
15 They *are* futile, a work of errors;
In the time of their punishment they shall perish.
16 The Portion of Jacob *is* not like them,
For He *is* the Maker of all *things,*
And Israel *is* the tribe of His inheritance;
The LORD of hosts *is* His name.

17 Gather up your wares from the land,
O inhabitant of the fortress!

18 For thus says the LORD:

"Behold, I will throw out at this time
The inhabitants of the land,
And will distress them,
That they may find *it so.*"

STAR CHARTS

10:2-3 Everyone would like to know the future. Decisions would be
easier, failures avoided, and success assured. The people of Judah wanted
to know the future, too, and they tried to discern by reading signs in the
sky (like horoscopes). Jeremiah's response applies today: God made the
stars that people consult. No one will discover the future in made-up
charts of God's stars. God, who promises to guide you, knows your future
and will be with you all the way. He may not reveal your future to you,
but he will walk with you as the future unfolds. Don't trust the stars; trust
the One who made the stars.

19 Woe is me for my hurt!
My wound is severe.
But I say, "Truly this *is* an infirmity,
And I must bear it."
20 My tent is plundered,
And all my cords are broken;
My children have gone from me,
And they *are* no more.
There is no one to pitch my tent anymore,
Or set up my curtains.

21 For the shepherds have become dull-hearted,
And have not sought the LORD;
Therefore they shall not prosper,
And all their flocks shall be scattered.
22 Behold, the noise of the report has come,
And a great commotion out of the north country,
To make the cities of Judah desolate, a den of jackals.
23 O LORD, I know the way of man *is* not in himself;
It is not in man who walks to direct his own steps.
24 O LORD, correct me, but with justice;
Not in Your anger, lest You bring me to nothing.
25 Pour out Your fury on the Gentiles, who do not know
You,
And on the families who do not call on Your name;
For they have eaten up Jacob,
Devoured him and consumed him,
And made his dwelling place desolate.

CHAPTER **11** **REMEMBER GOD'S PROMISE.** The
word that came to Jeremiah from the LORD, saying,
2 "Hear the words of this covenant, and speak to the men
of Judah and to the inhabitants of Jerusalem; 3 and say to
them, 'Thus says the LORD God of Israel: "Cursed *is* the
man who does not obey the words of this covenant
4 which I commanded your fathers in the day I brought
them out of the land of Egypt, from the iron furnace,
saying, 'Obey My voice, and do according to all that I
command you; so shall you be My people, and I will be
your God,' 5 that I may establish the oath which I have

IDOLATRY

A drunken orgy around a golden calf . . . the latest sports car . . . offering sacrifices to Baal . . . teenagers screaming approval at a rock 'n' roll concert . . . **W**hat do these scenes have in common? They all represent forms of idol worship. **"W**ait a minute," you say. "The golden calf and Baal worship, OK; but what in the world does this have to do with fast cars and rock 'n' roll?" **J**ust this: an idol doesn't have to be a "religious" object. An idol is anything we desire above God and his will for our lives. Ouch! **W**e can see the evil in what Israel did, and we're sure we would never commit that sin. But for us, idolatry comes in more subtle forms. Instead of a golden calf, we're enticed by a "golden" credit card. Instead of Baal, we "worship" ball players, imitating them from their hairstyles to their shoes. Instead of temple prostitutes, we're seduced by the glossy covers of skin magazines peering from behind magazine racks and the explicit sex cable TV brings into our homes. So are credit cards, sports, or sex wrong? Of course not. All those things may have a place in the lives of God's people. The problem comes in using them the wrong way, or in loving things (or people) more than we love God. That's when it becomes idolatry. **W**hy is idolatry so bad? Why does God hate it so much? **F**irst, worshiping a false god (anything that comes before the real God is a false god) degrades us. It makes us less than what we are intended to be. We are made in the image of God, with the opportunity through Christ to know him and, in some ways, to be like him. When we worship an idol—a lesser god—we aim much lower and, all too often, hit our target. We become like the phony instead of the genuine article. Psalm 115:8 says, "Those who make [idols] are like them." In other words, you come to resemble what you worship. **W**e should think seriously before giving our undying allegiance to someone. Is the person you admire a worthy role model? Is he or she a Christian? Does his or her life-style reflect Christlike values? Too often, our "heroes" are a photographic negative of Christ—blasphemous, obscene, self-centered heathens. Be careful—you become like what you worship. **S**econd, idolatry often is subtle and hard to detect. Think about a boyfriend or girlfriend you have or used to have. (OK—one you wish you had.) Usually, the relationship starts out fine: physically, you're under control; emotionally, you make each other feel more positive; spiritually, you build each other up. But as time passes, it gets more and more difficult to keep your sexual relationship in check . . . you begin to depend on each other to an unhealthy degree . . . and your spiritual growth slows to zero miles per hour. Why? While there can be lots of reasons, often the problem is that you have (maybe unintentionally) committed idolatry together. You put each other before God, which is disastrous for your relationship with each other and with him. Confession and repentance can make right; but often the relationship is so warped that you have to end it. Idolatry has a way of creeping in and destroying parts of your life, just as cancer destroys parts of your body. We must guard against idolatry's creeping poison. **F**inally, idol worship steals from God. Nobody with functional brain cells would knowingly do that. When we love someone or something else more than God, we rob him of the worship and loyalty that rightly belong only to him. In Exodus 20:4-5, God says: "You shall not make for yourself a carved image. . . . For I, the LORD your God, am a jealous God." He alone is worthy of our love and trust. **H**istory is crowded with people who would be gods, but there's only one God who would be man. Don't commit idolatry. Give your devotion to the God who loved you enough to die for you; worship only him.

sworn to your fathers, to give them 'a land flowing with milk and honey,' as *it is* this day."'"

And I answered and said, "So be it, LORD."

⁶Then the LORD said to me, "Proclaim all these words in the cities of Judah and in the streets of Jerusalem, saying: 'Hear the words of this covenant and do them. ⁷For I earnestly exhorted your fathers in the day I brought them up out of the land of Egypt, until this day, rising early and exhorting, saying, "Obey My voice." ⁸Yet they did not obey or incline their ear, but everyone followed the dictates of his evil heart; therefore I will bring upon them all the words of this covenant, which I commanded *them* to do, but *which* they have not done.'"

⁹And the LORD said to me, "A conspiracy has been found among the men of Judah and among the inhabitants of Jerusalem. ¹⁰They have turned back to the iniquities of their forefathers who refused to hear My words, and they have gone after other gods to serve them; the house of Israel and the house of Judah have broken My covenant which I made with their fathers."

¹¹Therefore thus says the LORD: "Behold, I will surely bring calamity on them which they will not be able to escape; and though they cry out to Me, I will not listen to them. ¹²Then the cities of Judah and the inhabitants of Jerusalem will go and cry out to the gods to whom they offer incense, but they will not save them at all in the time of their trouble. ¹³For *according to* the number of your cities were your gods, O Judah; and *according to* the number of the streets of Jerusalem you have set up altars to *that* shameful thing, altars to burn incense to Baal.

¹⁴"So do not pray for this people, or lift up a cry or prayer for them; for I will not hear *them* in the time that they cry out to Me because of their trouble.

¹⁵ "What has My beloved to do in My house,
Having done lewd deeds with many?
And the holy flesh has passed from you.
When you do evil, then you rejoice.
¹⁶ The LORD called your name,
Green Olive Tree, Lovely *and* of Good Fruit.
With the noise of a great tumult
He has kindled fire on it,
And its branches are broken.

¹⁷"For the LORD of hosts, who planted you, has pronounced doom against you for the evil of the house of Israel and of the house of Judah, which they have done against themselves to provoke Me to anger in offering incense to Baal."

¹⁸Now the LORD gave me knowledge *of it,* and I know *it;* for You showed me their doings. ¹⁹But I *was* like a docile lamb brought to the slaughter; and I did not know that they had devised schemes against me, *saying,* "Let us destroy the tree with its fruit, and let us cut him off from the land of the living, that his name may be remembered no more."

²⁰ But, O LORD of hosts,
You who judge righteously,
Testing the mind and the heart,
Let me see Your vengeance on them,
For to You I have revealed my cause.

²¹"Therefore thus says the LORD concerning the men of Anathoth who seek your life, saying, 'Do not prophesy in the name of the LORD, lest you die by our hand'— ²²therefore thus says the LORD of hosts: 'Behold, I will punish them. The young men shall die by the sword, their sons and their daughters shall die by famine; ²³and there shall be no remnant of them, for I will bring catastrophe on the men of Anathoth, *even* the year of their punishment.'"

CHAPTER **12** JEREMIAH COMPLAINS TO GOD.

Righteous *are* You, O LORD, when I plead with You;
Yet let me talk with You about *Your* judgments.
Why does the way of the wicked prosper?
Why are those happy who deal so treacherously?
² You have planted them, yes, they have taken root;
They grow, yes, they bear fruit.
You *are* near in their mouth
But far from their mind.

³ But You, O LORD, know me;
You have seen me,
And You have tested my heart toward You.
Pull them out like sheep for the slaughter,
And prepare them for the day of slaughter.
⁴ How long will the land mourn,
And the herbs of every field wither?
The beasts and birds are consumed,
For the wickedness of those who dwell there,
Because they said, "He will not see our final end."

◢TOUGH TIMES

12:5-6 Life was difficult for Jeremiah despite his love for and obedience to God. When he asked God for relief, God's reply in effect was, "If you think this is bad, how are you going to cope when it gets really tough?"

Not all of God's answers to prayer are nice or easy to accept. Any Christian who has experienced war, grief, or a serious illness knows this. But we are to be committed to God even when the going gets tough, and when he doesn't answer our prayers with immediate relief.

⁵ "If you have run with the footmen, and they have
wearied you,
Then how can you contend with horses?
And *if* in the land of peace,
In which you trusted, *they wearied you,*
Then how will you do in the floodplain of the Jordan?
⁶ For even your brothers, the house of your father,
Even they have dealt treacherously with you;
Yes, they have called a multitude after you.
Do not believe them,
Even though they speak smooth words to you.

⁷ "I have forsaken My house, I have left My heritage;
I have given the dearly beloved of My soul into the
hand of her enemies.
⁸ My heritage is to Me like a lion in the forest;
It cries out against Me;
Therefore I have hated it.
⁹ My heritage *is* to Me *like* a speckled vulture;

The vultures all around *are* against her.
Come, assemble all the beasts of the field,
Bring them to devour!

10 "Many rulers have destroyed My vineyard,
They have trodden My portion underfoot;
They have made My pleasant portion a desolate
wilderness.
11 They have made it desolate;
Desolate, it mourns to Me;
The whole land is made desolate,
Because no one takes *it* to heart.
12 The plunderers have come
On all the desolate heights in the wilderness,
For the sword of the LORD shall devour
From *one* end of the land to the *other* end of the
land;
No flesh shall have peace.
13 They have sown wheat but reaped thorns;
They have put themselves to pain *but* do not profit.
But be ashamed of your harvest
Because of the fierce anger of the LORD."

14Thus says the LORD: "Against all My evil neighbors who touch the inheritance which I have caused My people Israel to inherit—behold, I will pluck them out of their land and pluck out the house of Judah from among them. 15Then it shall be, after I have plucked them out, that I will return and have compassion on them and bring them back, everyone to his heritage and everyone to his land. 16And it shall be, if they will learn carefully the ways of My people, to swear by My name, 'As the LORD lives,' as they taught My people to swear by Baal, then they shall be established in the midst of My people. 17But if they do not obey, I will utterly pluck up and destroy that nation," says the LORD.

CHAPTER **13** **GOOD FOR NOTHING.** Thus the LORD said to me: "Go and get yourself a linen sash, and put it around your waist, but do not put it in water." 2So I got a sash according to the word of the LORD, and put *it* around my waist.

3And the word of the LORD came to me the second time, saying, 4"Take the sash that you acquired, which *is* around your waist, and arise, go to the Euphrates, and hide it there in a hole in the rock." 5So I went and hid it by the Euphrates, as the LORD commanded me.

6Now it came to pass after many days that the LORD said to me, "Arise, go to the Euphrates, and take from there the sash which I commanded you to hide there." 7Then I went to the Euphrates and dug, and I took the sash from the place where I had hidden it; and there was the sash, ruined. It was profitable for nothing.

8Then the word of the LORD came to me, saying, 9"Thus says the LORD: 'In this manner I will ruin the pride of Judah and the great pride of Jerusalem. 10This evil people, who refuse to hear My words, who follow the dictates of their hearts, and walk after other gods to serve them and worship them, shall be just like this sash which is profitable for nothing. 11For as the sash clings to the waist of a man, so I have caused the whole house of Israel and the

USELESS

13:1-11 Actions speak louder than words. Jeremiah often used v object lessons to arouse the people's curiosity and get his point acro This lesson of the linen sash illustrated Judah's destiny. Although the people had once been close to God, their pride had made them use A proud person may look important, but God says his pride makes him good for nothing. Pride rots our heart until we lose our usefuln to God.

whole house of Judah to cling to Me,' says the LORD, 'that they may become My people, for renown, for praise, and for glory; but they would not hear.'

12"Therefore you shall speak to them this word: 'Thus says the LORD God of Israel: "Every bottle shall be filled with wine." '

"And they will say to you, 'Do we not certainly know that every bottle will be filled with wine?'

13"Then you shall say to them, 'Thus says the LORD: "Behold, I will fill all the inhabitants of this land—even the kings who sit on David's throne, the priests, the prophets, and all the inhabitants of Jerusalem—with drunkenness! 14And I will dash them one against another, even the fathers and the sons together," says the LORD. "I will not pity nor spare nor have mercy, but will destroy them." '"

15 Hear and give ear:
Do not be proud,
For the LORD has spoken.
16 Give glory to the LORD your God
Before He causes darkness,
And before your feet stumble
On the dark mountains,
And while you are looking for light,
He turns it into the shadow of death
And makes *it* dense darkness.
17 But if you will not hear it,
My soul will weep in secret for *your* pride;
My eyes will weep bitterly
And run down with tears,
Because the LORD's flock has been taken captive.

18 Say to the king and to the queen mother,
"Humble yourselves;
Sit down,
For your rule shall collapse, the crown of your glory."
19 The cities of the South shall be shut up,
And no one shall open *them;*
Judah shall be carried away captive, all of it;
It shall be wholly carried away captive.

20 Lift up your eyes and see
Those who come from the north.
Where *is* the flock *that* was given to you,
Your beautiful sheep?
21 What will you say when He punishes you?

DANGER

13:15 While it is good to respect our country and our church, our loyalties always carry a hidden danger—pride. When is pride harr When it causes us to (1) to look down on others; (2) to be selfish with resources; (3) to force our solutions on others' problems; (4) to thir is blessing us because of our own merits; (5) to be content with our rather than seeking God's plans.

For you have taught them
To be chieftains, to be head over you.
Will not pangs seize you,
Like a woman in labor?
²² And if you say in your heart,
  "Why have these things come upon me?"
For the greatness of your iniquity
Your skirts have been uncovered,
Your heels made bare.
²³ Can the Ethiopian change his skin or the leopard its
    spots?
  Then may you also do good who are accustomed to
    do evil.

²⁴ "Therefore I will scatter them like stubble
That passes away by the wind of the wilderness.
²⁵ This is your lot,
The portion of your measures from Me," says the
  LORD,
  "Because you have forgotten Me
And trusted in falsehood.
²⁶ Therefore I will uncover your skirts over your face,
That your shame may appear.
²⁷ I have seen your adulteries
And your *lustful* neighings,
The lewdness of your harlotry,
Your abominations on the hills in the fields.
Woe to you, O Jerusalem!
Will you still not be made clean?"

CHAPTER **14** GOD LOSES HIS PATIENCE. The word
of the LORD that came to Jeremiah concerning the
droughts.

² "Judah mourns,
And her gates languish;
They mourn for the land,
And the cry of Jerusalem has gone up.
³ Their nobles have sent their lads for water;
They went to the cisterns *and* found no water.
They returned with their vessels empty;
They were ashamed and confounded
And covered their heads.
⁴ Because the ground is parched,
For there was no rain in the land,
The plowmen were ashamed;
They covered their heads.
⁵ Yes, the deer also gave birth in the field,
But left because there was no grass.
⁶ And the wild donkeys stood in the desolate heights;
They sniffed at the wind like jackals;
Their eyes failed because *there was* no grass."

⁷ O LORD, though our iniquities testify against us,
Do it for Your name's sake;
For our backslidings are many,
We have sinned against You.
⁸ O the Hope of Israel, his Savior in time of trouble,
Why should You be like a stranger in the land,
And like a traveler *who* turns aside to tarry for a
    night?
⁹ Why should You be like a man astonished,

Like a mighty one *who* cannot save?
Yet You, O LORD, *are* in our midst,
And we are called by Your name;
Do not leave us!

¹⁰Thus says the LORD to this people:

"Thus they have loved to wander;
They have not restrained their feet.
Therefore the LORD does not accept them;
He will remember their iniquity now,
And punish their sins."

▶︎◀︎ TOO LATE

14:11-12 The people of Judah had stretched God's patience. Their
false repentance and empty rituals had continued long enough, and so
God turned deaf ears to their cries. For a third time, God told Jeremiah
not to pray for the people. Why should people pray to God, when he was
less important to them than handmade idols of wood or stone? Why not
let the idols answer their prayers? If you are putting something ahead of
God when all is going well, will you be content to trust in this false god
when you are in trouble?

¹¹Then the LORD said to me, "Do not pray for this
people, for *their* good. ¹²When they fast, I will not hear
their cry; and when they offer burnt offering and grain
offering, I will not accept them. But I will consume them
by the sword, by the famine, and by the pestilence."
¹³Then I said, "Ah, Lord GOD! Behold, the prophets say
to them, 'You shall not see the sword, nor shall you have
famine, but I will give you assured peace in this place.'"
¹⁴And the LORD said to me, "The prophets prophesy
lies in My name. I have not sent them, commanded
them, nor spoken to them; they prophesy to you a false
vision, divination, a worthless thing, and the deceit of
their heart. ¹⁵Therefore thus says the LORD concerning
the prophets who prophesy in My name, whom I did not
send, and who say, 'Sword and famine shall not be in this
land'—'By sword and famine those prophets shall be
consumed! ¹⁶And the people to whom they prophesy
shall be cast out in the streets of Jerusalem because of the
famine and the sword; they will have no one to bury
them—them nor their wives, their sons nor their daughters—for I will pour their wickedness on them.'
¹⁷"Therefore you shall say this word to them:

'Let my eyes flow with tears night and day,
And let them not cease;
For the virgin daughter of my people
Has been broken with a mighty stroke, with a very
    severe blow.
¹⁸ If I go out to the field,
Then behold, those slain with the sword!
And if I enter the city,
Then behold, those sick from famine!
Yes, both prophet and priest go about in a land they
    do not know.'"

¹⁹ Have You utterly rejected Judah?
Has Your soul loathed Zion?
Why have You stricken us so that *there is* no healing
    for us?

We looked for peace, but *there was* no good;
And for the time of healing, and there was trouble.
20 We acknowledge, O LORD, our wickedness
And the iniquity of our fathers,
For we have sinned against You.
21 Do not abhor *us,* for Your name's sake;
Do not disgrace the throne of Your glory.
Remember, do not break Your covenant with us.
22 Are there any among the idols of the nations that
can cause rain?
Or can the heavens give showers?
Are You not He, O LORD our God?
Therefore we will wait for You,
Since You have made all these.

CHAPTER 15 JERUSALEM, A CITY IN TROUBLE.

Then the LORD said to me, "*Even* if Moses and Samuel
stood before Me, My mind *would* not *be* favorable toward
this people. Cast *them* out of My sight, and let them go
forth. ²And it shall be, if they say to you, 'Where should we
go?' then you shall tell them, 'Thus says the LORD:

"Such as *are* for death, to death;
And such as *are* for the sword, to the sword;
And such as *are* for the famine, to the famine;
And such as *are* for the captivity, to the captivity." '

◣▬▬▬▬▬▬ INFLUENCE

15:17-21 Jeremiah accused God of not helping him when he really
needed it. Jeremiah had taken his eyes off God's purposes and was
feeling sorry for himself. He was angry, hurt, and afraid. In response,
God didn't get angry at Jeremiah; he answered by reminding Jeremiah
of his promise—"You shall be as My mouth." There are three important
lessons in this passage: (1) in prayer we can reveal our deepest thoughts
to God; (2) God expects us to trust no matter what; and (3) we are here
to influence others for God.

³"And I will appoint over them four forms *of destruction,*" says the LORD: "the sword to slay, the dogs to drag,
the birds of the heavens and the beasts of the earth to
devour and destroy. ⁴I will hand them over to trouble, to
all kingdoms of the earth, because of Manasseh the son
of Hezekiah, king of Judah, for what he did in Jerusalem.

5 "For who will have pity on you, O Jerusalem?
Or who will bemoan you?
Or who will turn aside to ask how you are doing?
6 You have forsaken Me," says the LORD,
"You have gone backward.
Therefore I will stretch out My hand against you and
destroy you;
I am weary of relenting!
7 And I will winnow them with a winnowing fan in the
gates of the land;
I will bereave *them* of children;
I will destroy My people,
Since they do not return from their ways.
8 Their widows will be increased to Me more than the
sand of the seas;
I will bring against them,

Against the mother of the young men,
A plunderer at noonday;
I will cause anguish and terror to fall on them
suddenly.

9 "She languishes who has borne seven;
She has breathed her last;
Her sun has gone down
While *it was* yet day;
She has been ashamed and confounded.
And the remnant of them I will deliver to the sword
Before their enemies," says the LORD.

10 Woe is me, my mother,
That you have borne me,
A man of strife and a man of contention to the
whole earth!
I have neither lent for interest,
Nor have men lent to me for interest.
Every one of them curses me.

11The LORD said:

"Surely it will be well with your remnant;
Surely I will cause the enemy to intercede with you
In the time of adversity and in the time of affliction.
12 Can anyone break iron,
The northern iron and the bronze?
13 Your wealth and your treasures
I will give as plunder without price,
Because of all your sins,
Throughout your territories.
14 And I will make *you* cross over with your enemies
Into a land *which* you do not know;
For a fire is kindled in My anger,
Which shall burn upon you."

15 O LORD, You know;
Remember me and visit me,
And take vengeance for me on my persecutors.
In Your enduring patience, do not take me away.
Know that for Your sake I have suffered rebuke.
16 Your words were found, and I ate them,
And Your word was to me the joy and rejoicing of my
heart;
For I am called by Your name,
O LORD God of hosts.
17 I did not sit in the assembly of the mockers,
Nor did I rejoice;
I sat alone because of Your hand,
For You have filled me with indignation.
18 Why is my pain perpetual
And my wound incurable,
Which refuses to be healed?
Will You surely be to me like an unreliable stream,
As waters *that* fail?

19Therefore thus says the LORD:

"If you return,
Then I will bring you back;
You shall stand before Me;
If you take out the precious from the vile,
You shall be as My mouth.

Let them return to you,
But you must not return to them.
20 And I will make you to this people a fortified bronze
wall;
And they will fight against you,
But they shall not prevail against you;
For I *am* with you to save you
And deliver you," says the LORD.
21 "I will deliver you from the hand of the wicked,
And I will redeem you from the grip of the terrible."

CHAPTER 16 A PEOPLE TRY TO RUN FROM GOD.

The word of the LORD also came to me, saying, 2"You shall not take a wife, nor shall you have sons or daughters in this place." 3For thus says the LORD concerning the sons and daughters who are born in this place, and concerning their mothers who bore them and their fathers who begot them in this land: 4"They shall die gruesome deaths; they shall not be lamented nor shall they be buried, *but* they shall be like refuse on the face of the earth. They shall be consumed by the sword and by famine, and their corpses shall be meat for the birds of heaven and for the beasts of the earth."

5For thus says the LORD: "Do not enter the house of mourning, nor go to lament or bemoan them; for I have taken away My peace from this people," says the LORD, "lovingkindness and mercies. 6Both the great and the small shall die in this land. They shall not be buried; neither shall men lament for them, cut themselves, nor make themselves bald for them. 7Nor shall *men* break *bread* in mourning for them, to comfort them for the dead; nor shall *men* give them the cup of consolation to drink for their father or their mother. 8Also you shall not go into the house of feasting to sit with them, to eat and drink."

9For thus says the LORD of hosts, the God of Israel: "Behold, I will cause to cease from this place, before your eyes and in your days, the voice of mirth and the voice of gladness, the voice of the bridegroom and the voice of the bride.

10"And it shall be, when you show this people all these words, and they say to you, 'Why has the LORD pronounced all this great disaster against us? Or what *is* our iniquity? Or what *is* our sin that we have committed against the LORD our God?' 11then you shall say to them, 'Because your fathers have forsaken Me,' says the LORD; 'they have walked after other gods and have served them and worshiped them, and have forsaken Me and not kept My law. 12And you have done worse than your fathers, for behold, each one follows the dictates of his own evil heart, so that no one listens to Me. 13Therefore I will cast you out of this land into a land that you do not know, neither you nor your fathers; and there you shall serve other gods day and night, where I will not show you favor.'

14"Therefore behold, the days are coming," says the LORD, "that it shall no more be said, 'The LORD lives who brought up the children of Israel from the land of Egypt,' 15but, 'The LORD lives who brought up the children of Israel from the land of the north and from all the lands

where He had driven them.' For I will bring them back into their land which I gave to their fathers.

16"Behold, I will send for many fishermen," says the LORD, "and they shall fish them; and afterward I will send for many hunters, and they shall hunt them from every mountain and every hill, and out of the holes of the rocks. 17For My eyes *are* on all their ways; they are not hidden from My face, nor is their iniquity hidden from My eyes. 18And first I will repay double for their iniquity and their sin, because they have defiled My land; they have filled My inheritance with the carcasses of their detestable and abominable idols."

19 O LORD, my strength and my fortress,
My refuge in the day of affliction,
The Gentiles shall come to You
From the ends of the earth and say,
"Surely our fathers have inherited lies,
Worthlessness and unprofitable *things*."
20 Will a man make gods for himself,
Which *are* not gods?

◄━━━━━ HE KNOWS

16:17 Small children think that if they can't see you, then you can't see them. The people may have wished that hiding from God was as simple as closing their eyes. Although they closed their eyes to their sinful ways, their sins certainly weren't hidden from God. He who sees all cannot be deceived. Do you have a sinful attitude or action that you hope God won't notice? He knows about it. The first step to repentance is to acknowledge that God knows about our sins.

21 "Therefore behold, I will this once cause them to
know,
I will cause them to know
My hand and My might;
And they shall know that My name *is* the LORD.

CHAPTER 17 A GREEN AND GROWING TREE.

"The sin of Judah *is* written with a pen of iron;
With the point of a diamond *it is* engraved
On the tablet of their heart,
And on the horns of your altars,
2 While their children remember
Their altars and their wooden images
By the green trees on the high hills.
3 O My mountain in the field,
I will give as plunder your wealth, all your treasures,
And your high places of sin within all your borders.
4 And you, even yourself,
Shall let go of your heritage which I gave you;
And I will cause you to serve your enemies
In the land which you do not know;
For you have kindled a fire in My anger *which* shall
burn forever."

5Thus says the LORD:

"Cursed *is* the man who trusts in man
And makes flesh his strength,
Whose heart departs from the LORD.
6 For he shall be like a shrub in the desert,

And shall not see when good comes,
But shall inhabit the parched places in the
    wilderness,
In a salt land *which is* not inhabited.

7 "Blessed *is* the man who trusts in the LORD,
And whose hope is the LORD.
8 For he shall be like a tree planted by the waters,
Which spreads out its roots by the river,
And will not fear when heat comes;
But its leaf will be green,
And will not be anxious in the year of drought,
Nor will cease from yielding fruit.

9 "The heart *is* deceitful above all *things,*
And desperately wicked;
Who can know it?
10 I, the LORD, search the heart,
I test the mind,
Even to give every man according to his ways,
According to the fruit of his doings.

11 "*As* a partridge that broods but does not hatch,
So is he who gets riches, but not by right;
It will leave him in the midst of his days,
And at his end he will be a fool."

12 A glorious high throne from the beginning
Is the place of our sanctuary.
13 O LORD, the hope of Israel,
All who forsake You shall be ashamed.

"Those who depart from Me
Shall be written in the earth,
Because they have forsaken the LORD,
The fountain of living waters."

14 Heal me, O LORD, and I shall be healed;
Save me, and I shall be saved,
For You *are* my praise.
15 Indeed they say to me,
"Where *is* the word of the LORD?
Let it come now!"
16 As for me, I have not hurried away from *being* a
    shepherd *who* follows You,
Nor have I desired the woeful day;
You know what came out of my lips;
It was right there before You.
17 Do not be a terror to me;
You *are* my hope in the day of doom.
18 Let them be ashamed who persecute me,
But do not let me be put to shame;
Let them be dismayed,
But do not let me be dismayed.
Bring on them the day of doom,
And destroy them with double destruction!

19 Thus the LORD said to me: "Go and stand in the gate of the children of the people, by which the kings of Judah come in and by which they go out, and in all the gates of Jerusalem; 20 and say to them, 'Hear the word of the LORD, you kings of Judah, and all Judah, and all the inhabitants of Jerusalem, who enter by these gates. 21 Thus says the LORD: "Take heed to yourselves, and bear no burden on

18:18 Jeremiah's words and actions challenged the people's social moral behavior. He wasn't afraid to give unpopular criticism. The pe[ople] could either obey Jeremiah or silence him. They chose the latter. Th[ey did] not think they needed Jeremiah; their false prophets told them wh[at they] wanted to hear.

the Sabbath day, nor bring *it* in by the gates of Jerusalem; 22 nor carry a burden out of your houses on the Sabbath day, nor do any work, but hallow the Sabbath day, as I commanded your fathers. 23 But they did not obey nor incline their ear, but made their neck stiff, that they might not hear nor receive instruction.

24 "And it shall be, if you heed Me carefully," says the LORD, "to bring no burden through the gates of this city on the Sabbath day, but hallow the Sabbath day, to do no work in it, 25 then shall enter the gates of this city kings and princes sitting on the throne of David, riding in chariots and on horses, they and their princes, accompanied by the men of Judah and the inhabitants of Jerusalem; and this city shall remain forever. 26 And they shall come from the cities of Judah and from the places around Jerusalem, from the land of Benjamin and from the lowland, from the mountains and from the South, bringing burnt offerings and sacrifices, grain offerings and incense, bringing sacrifices of praise to the house of the LORD.

27 "But if you will not heed Me to hallow the Sabbath day, such as not carrying a burden when entering the gates of Jerusalem on the Sabbath day, then I will kindle a fire in its gates, and it shall devour the palaces of Jerusalem, and it shall not be quenched." ' "

CHAPTER 18 NO ONE LISTENS TO JEREMIAH.

The word which came to Jeremiah from the LORD, saying: 2 "Arise and go down to the potter's house, and there I will cause you to hear My words." 3 Then I went down to the potter's house, and there he was, making something at the wheel. 4 And the vessel that he made of clay was marred in the hand of the potter; so he made it again into another vessel, as it seemed good to the potter to make.

5 Then the word of the LORD came to me, saying: 6 "O house of Israel, can I not do with you as this potter?" says the LORD. "Look, as the clay *is* in the potter's hand, so *are* you in My hand, O house of Israel! 7 The instant I speak concerning a nation and concerning a kingdom, to pluck up, to pull down, and to destroy *it,* 8 if that nation against whom I have spoken turns from its evil, I will relent of the disaster that I thought to bring upon it. 9 And the instant I speak concerning a nation and concerning a kingdom, to build and to plant *it,* 10 if it does evil in My sight so that it does not obey My voice, then I will relent concerning the good with which I said I would benefit it.

11 "Now therefore, speak to the men of Judah and to the inhabitants of Jerusalem, saying, 'Thus says the LORD: "Behold, I am fashioning a disaster and devising a plan against you. Return now every one from his evil way, and make your ways and your doings good." ' "

12 And they said, "That is hopeless! So we will walk according to our own plans, and we will every one obey the dictates of his evil heart."

13 Therefore thus says the LORD:

"Ask now among the Gentiles,
Who has heard such things?
The virgin of Israel has done a very horrible thing.
¹⁴ Will *a man* leave the snow water of Lebanon,
Which comes from the rock of the field?
Will the cold flowing waters be forsaken for strange waters?

¹⁵ "Because My people have forgotten Me,
They have burned incense to worthless idols.
And they have caused themselves to stumble in their ways,
From the ancient paths,
To walk in pathways and not on a highway,
¹⁶ To make their land desolate *and* a perpetual hissing;
Everyone who passes by it will be astonished
And shake his head.
¹⁷ I will scatter them as with an east wind before the enemy;
I will show them the back and not the face
In the day of their calamity."

¹⁸Then they said, "Come and let us devise plans against Jeremiah; for the law shall not perish from the priest, nor counsel from the wise, nor the word from the prophet. Come and let us attack him with the tongue, and let us not give heed to any of his words."

¹⁹ Give heed to me, O LORD,
And listen to the voice of those who contend with me!
²⁰ Shall evil be repaid for good?
For they have dug a pit for my life.
Remember that I stood before You
To speak good for them,
To turn away Your wrath from them.
²¹ Therefore deliver up their children to the famine,
And pour out their *blood*
By the force of the sword;
Let their wives *become* widows
And bereaved of their children.
Let their men be put to death,
Their young men *be* slain
By the sword in battle.
²² Let a cry be heard from their houses,
When You bring a troop suddenly upon them;
For they have dug a pit to take me,
And hidden snares for my feet.
²³ Yet, LORD, You know all their counsel
Which is against me, to slay *me.*
Provide no atonement for their iniquity,
Nor blot out their sin from Your sight;
But let them be overthrown before You.
Deal *thus* with them
In the time of Your anger.

CHAPTER **19** JERUSALEM WILL BE DESTROYED.

Thus says the LORD: "Go and get a potter's earthen flask, and *take* some of the elders of the people and some of the elders of the priests. ²And go out to the Valley of the Son of Hinnom, which *is* by the entry of the Potsherd Gate; and proclaim there the words that I will tell you, ³and say,

'Hear the word of the LORD, O kings of Judah and inhabitants of Jerusalem. Thus says the LORD of hosts, the God of Israel: "Behold, I will bring such a catastrophe on this place, that whoever hears of it, his ears will tingle.

GARBAGE

19:1-6 This valley was the garbage dump of Jerusalem and the place where children were sacrificed to the god Molech. It is also mentioned in 7:31-32.

⁴"Because they have forsaken Me and made this an alien place, because they have burned incense in it to other gods whom neither they, their fathers, nor the kings of Judah have known, and have filled this place with the blood of the innocents ⁵(they have also built the high places of Baal, to burn their sons with fire *for* burnt offerings to Baal, which I did not command or speak, nor did it come into My mind), ⁶therefore behold, the days are coming," says the LORD, "that this place shall no more

I have done some pretty awful things in my life—things that other kids never even think about doing. How could God forgive me for what I've done?

I WONDER . . .

Recognizing that you've done wrong is 90 percent of the battle.

Usually people who build up years of wrong actions also have built a shell around their hearts. This shell protects them from feeling guilty about the wrong they have done. As the shell gets harder and thicker, they continue a downward spiral, doing more and more things that are wrong.

Jeremiah, a prophet of God, looked at the human tendency to sin and came to this conclusion: "The heart *is* deceitful above all *things,* and desperately wicked; who can know it? I, the LORD, search the heart, I test the mind, even to give every man according to his ways, according to the fruit of his doings" (Jeremiah 17:9-10).

As you'll notice, this verse doesn't say that some people's hearts are more wicked than others. All of us have the potential for actions that destroy ourselves and others.

Thankfully, God has chosen not to leave us this way. We all would be without hope if it weren't for God's grace. God says in Isaiah 43:25, "I, *even* I, *am* He who blots out your transgressions for My own sake; and I will not remember your sins."

Whatever you have done, God is not surprised and will forgive you if you let him. Your own recognition of wrong is the first step. God has opened up your heart so you can take a look at its ugliness. Now you must decide whether you want to leave it that way, or allow him to come in and clean it up.

"'Come now, and let us reason together,' says the LORD, 'though your sins are like scarlet, they shall be as white as snow; though they are red like crimson, they shall be as wool'" (Isaiah 1:18).

Don't give up—give in . . . to God. Ask him to forgive you and help you start over.

SUICIDE

"Cursed be the day in which I was born! . . . Why did I come forth from the womb to see labor and sorrow, that my days should be consumed with shame?" This doesn't sound like one of God's greatest prophets. Yet it is! It's Jeremiah, pouring his heart out to God, wishing he'd never been born. Everyone has felt that way at one time or another. Most of us have wished we could just check out of this life. For some, though, that desire gets so intense that they act on it. Suicide is the third leading cause of death among American teenagers. Teenage suicides have tripled in the last 25 years. Why do so many young people decide life isn't worth it? What does God say about suicide? What can we do to guard against suicide? There are many reasons people take their lives. Everyone occasionally faces despair, but why does one person struggle through while another ends his life? The critical factor is loss of hope. A suicidal person looks at his or her problems and says, "It's dark outside, and I am powerless to change things. Unfortunately, the Bible does not give a simple here's-what-God-says-about-the-issue answer. But it does give us some helpful principles. First, man isn't the author of life, God is. There are no "self-made" men or women. You're here because God made you in his image; because he loves you, he wants to know you, and he wants you to know him. When someone commits suicide, he or she is saying, "Look, God, you goofed when you let me slip into this world. So I'm going to correct your mistake." But life—and death—are God's territory. To trespass on that holy ground means you've decided to play God. All sin is playing God—choosing to do what you want instead of what God wants—and suicide is a sin. But suicide is playing God in a major way, and God does not look on it lightly. However, suicide is not an unforgivable sin. Jesus said there is only one of those, and it isn't suicide. No, the person who takes his own life cannot ask forgiveness, but we are not forgiven because of our unerring faithfulness in asking forgiveness. We're forgiven because of God's mercy and Jesus' death on the cross. That is bigger and more reliable than any of our efforts. Thank God! This doesn't mean suicide is OK. Actually, suicide is one of the most selfish, cowardly, and hateful acts anyone can commit. Those who have ever had to deal with someone's suicide know: the emotional devastation for those left behind is unbelievable. Suicide doesn't solve problems. It dumps them on someone else, multiplied many times over. Don't believe the lie that "everyone will be better off without me." They won't. You'll just cause overwhelming pain and heartbreak. So what do you do when you—or someone you care about—decide you simply want to end it all? First, don't lose hope. Things can get better. Sometimes all you need is time. Mitch Anthony, founder of the National Suicide Help Center, puts it like this: "Suicide is a permanent solution to a temporary problem. It's like cutting off your leg because your little toe hurts." Third, know the danger signals that indicate someone might be considering suicide: going through a family crisis; being the victim of abuse or neglect; drug abuse (yours or a family member's); death of a frien or family member; approaching the anniversary date of a significant loss or death; previous suicide attem family history of suicide; preoccupation with death and/or talk of suicide. If you or a friend are experienc one or more of these signals, talk to someone you can trust—someone trained to help you with your prob Counseling is extremely important. Finally, remember, even if it seems no one else cares about you an your pain, God cares. He cares deeply. Pour your troubles out to him. He understands because he, too, experienced the depths of human experience. When you are tempted to give up, to take the coward way out and end it all, remember what Winston Churchill once said: "Success is never final; failure is nev fatal; it is courage that counts." And Jesus says, "Be of good cheer, I have overcome the world."

be called Tophet or the Valley of the Son of Hinnom, but the Valley of Slaughter. ⁷And I will make void the counsel of Judah and Jerusalem in this place, and I will cause them to fall by the sword before their enemies and by the hands of those who seek their lives; their corpses I will give as meat for the birds of the heaven and for the beasts of the earth. ⁸I will make this city desolate and a hissing; everyone who passes by it will be astonished and hiss because of all its plagues. ⁹And I will cause them to eat the flesh of their sons and the flesh of their daughters, and everyone shall eat the flesh of his friend in the siege and in the desperation with which their enemies and those who seek their lives shall drive them to despair." '

¹⁰"Then you shall break the flask in the sight of the men who go with you, ¹¹and say to them, 'Thus says the LORD of hosts: "Even so I will break this people and this city, as *one* breaks a potter's vessel, which cannot be made whole again; and they shall bury *them* in Tophet till *there is* no place to bury. ¹²Thus I will do to this place," says the LORD, "and to its inhabitants, and make this city like Tophet. ¹³And the houses of Jerusalem and the houses of the kings of Judah shall be defiled like the place of Tophet, because of all the houses on whose roofs they have burned incense to all the host of heaven, and poured out drink offerings to other gods." ' "

¹⁴Then Jeremiah came from Tophet, where the LORD had sent him to prophesy; and he stood in the court of the Lord's house and said to all the people, ¹⁵"Thus says the LORD of hosts, the God of Israel: 'Behold, I will bring on this city and on all her towns all the doom that I have pronounced against it, because they have stiffened their necks that they might not hear My words.' "

CHAPTER 20 JEREMIAH IS ARRESTED. Now Pashhur the son of Immer, the priest who *was* also chief governor in the house of the LORD, heard that Jeremiah prophesied these things. ²Then Pashhur struck Jeremiah the prophet, and put him in the stocks that *were* in the high gate of Benjamin, which *was* by the house of the LORD.

³And it happened on the next day that Pashhur brought Jeremiah out of the stocks. Then Jeremiah said to him, "The LORD has not called your name Pashhur, but Magor-Missabib. ⁴For thus says the LORD: 'Behold, I will make you a terror to yourself and to all your friends; and they shall fall by the sword of their enemies, and your eyes shall see *it*. I will give all Judah into the hand of the king of Babylon, and he shall carry them captive to Babylon and slay them with the sword. ⁵Moreover I will deliver all the wealth of this city, all its produce, and all its precious things; all the treasures of the kings of Judah I will give into the hand of their enemies, who will plunder them, seize them, and carry them to Babylon. ⁶And you, Pashhur, and all who dwell in your house, shall go into captivity. You shall go to Babylon, and there you shall die, and be buried there, you and all your friends, to whom you have prophesied lies.' "

⁷ O LORD, You induced me, and I was persuaded;
You are stronger than I, and have prevailed.
I am in derision daily;

Everyone mocks me.
⁸ For when I spoke, I cried out;
I shouted, "Violence and plunder!"
Because the word of the LORD was made to me
A reproach and a derision daily.
⁹ Then I said, "I will not make mention of Him,
Nor speak anymore in His name."
But *His word* was in my heart like a burning fire
Shut up in my bones;
I was weary of holding *it* back,
And I could not.
¹⁰ For I heard many mocking:
"Fear on every side!"
"Report," *they say,* "and we will report it!"
All my acquaintances watched for my stumbling,
saying,
"Perhaps he can be induced;
Then we will prevail against him,
And we will take our revenge on him."

¹¹ But the LORD *is* with me as a mighty, awesome One.
Therefore my persecutors will stumble, and will not
prevail.
They will be greatly ashamed, for they will not
prosper.
Their everlasting confusion will never be forgotten.
¹² But, O LORD of hosts,
You who test the righteous,
And see the mind and heart,
Let me see Your vengeance on them;
For I have pleaded my cause before You.

¹³ Sing to the LORD! Praise the LORD!
For He has delivered the life of the poor
From the hand of evildoers.

¹⁴ Cursed *be* the day in which I was born!
Let the day not be blessed in which my mother bore
me!
¹⁵ Let the man *be* cursed
Who brought news to my father, saying,
"A male child has been born to you!"
Making him very glad.
¹⁶ And let that man be like the cities
Which the LORD overthrew, and did not relent;
Let him hear the cry in the morning
And the shouting at noon,
¹⁷ Because he did not kill me from the womb,
That my mother might have been my grave,
And her womb always enlarged *with me.*
¹⁸ Why did I come forth from the womb to see labor
and sorrow,
That my days should be consumed with shame?

◀▬▬▬ STUNG!

20:1-3 Pashhur heard Jeremiah's words and, because of his guilt, locked Jeremiah up instead of taking his message to heart and acting on it. The truth sometimes stings, but our reaction to the truth shows what we are made of. We can deny the changes and destroy the evidence of our misdeeds, or we can take the truth humbly to heart and let it change us. Pashhur may have thought he was a strong leader, but he was really a coward.

CHAPTER 21 GOD'S ANSWER TO THE KING IS NO.

The word which came to Jeremiah from the LORD when King Zedekiah sent to him Pashhur the son of Melchiah, and Zephaniah the son of Maaseiah, the priest, saying, ²"Please inquire of the LORD for us, for Nebuchadnezzar king of Babylon makes war against us. Perhaps the LORD will deal with us according to all His wonderful works, that *the king* may go away from us."

³Then Jeremiah said to them, "Thus you shall say to Zedekiah, ⁴'Thus says the LORD God of Israel: "Behold, I will turn back the weapons of war that *are* in your hands, with which you fight against the king of Babylon and the Chaldeans who besiege you outside the walls; and I will assemble them in the midst of this city. ⁵I Myself will fight against you with an outstretched hand and with a strong arm, even in anger and fury and great wrath. ⁶I will strike the inhabitants of this city, both man and beast; they shall die of a great pestilence. ⁷And afterward," says the LORD, "I will deliver Zedekiah king of Judah, his servants and the people, and such as are left in this city from the pestilence and the sword and the famine, into the hand of Nebuchadnezzar king of Babylon, into the hand of their enemies, and into the hand of those who seek their life; and he shall strike them with the edge of the sword. He shall not spare them, or have pity or mercy." '

⁸"Now you shall say to this people, 'Thus says the LORD: "Behold, I set before you the way of life and the way of death. ⁹He who remains in this city shall die by the sword, by famine, and by pestilence; but he who goes out and defects to the Chaldeans who besiege you, he shall live, and his life shall be as a prize to him. ¹⁰For I have set My face against this city for adversity and not for good," says the LORD. "It shall be given into the hand of the king of Babylon, and he shall burn it with fire." '

¹¹"And concerning the house of the king of Judah, *say,* 'Hear the word of the LORD, ¹²O house of David! Thus says the LORD:

"Execute judgment in the morning;
    And deliver *him who is* plundered
    Out of the hand of the oppressor,
    Lest My fury go forth like fire
    And burn so that no one can quench *it,*
    Because of the evil of your doings.

¹³ "Behold, I *am* against you, O inhabitant of the valley,
    And rock of the plain," says the LORD,
"Who say, 'Who shall come down against us?
    Or who shall enter our dwellings?'
¹⁴ But I will punish you according to the fruit of your
        doings," says the LORD;
"I will kindle a fire in its forest,
    And it shall devour all things around it." ' "

CHAPTER 22 EVIL KINGS WILL BE JUDGED. Thus

says the LORD: "Go down to the house of the king of Judah, and there speak this word, ²and say, 'Hear the word of the LORD, O king of Judah, you who sit on the throne of David, you and your servants and your people who enter these gates! ³Thus says the LORD: "Execute judgment and righteousness, and deliver the plundered

out of the hand of the oppressor. Do no wrong and do no violence to the stranger, the fatherless, or the widow, nor shed innocent blood in this place. ⁴For if you indeed do this thing, then shall enter the gates of this house, riding on horses and in chariots, accompanied by servants and people, kings who sit on the throne of David. ⁵But if you will not hear these words, I swear by Myself," says the LORD, "that this house shall become a desolation." ' "

⁶For thus says the LORD to the house of the king of Judah:

"You *are* Gilead to Me,
    The head of Lebanon;
    Yet I surely will make you a wilderness,
    Cities *which* are not inhabited.
⁷ I will prepare destroyers against you,
    Everyone with his weapons;
    They shall cut down your choice cedars
    And cast *them* into the fire.

⁸And many nations will pass by this city; and everyone will say to his neighbor, 'Why has the LORD done so to this great city?' ⁹Then they will answer, 'Because they have forsaken the covenant of the LORD their God, and worshiped other gods and served them.' "

¹⁰ Weep not for the dead, nor bemoan him;
    Weep bitterly for him who goes away,
    For he shall return no more,
    Nor see his native country.

¹¹For thus says the LORD concerning Shallum the son of Josiah, king of Judah, who reigned instead of Josiah his father, who went from this place: "He shall not return here anymore, ¹²but he shall die in the place where they have led him captive, and shall see this land no more.

¹³ "Woe to him who builds his house by
        unrighteousness
    And his chambers by injustice,
    Who uses his neighbor's service without wages
    And gives him nothing for his work,
¹⁴ Who says, 'I will build myself a wide house with
        spacious chambers,
    And cut out windows for it,
    Paneling *it* with cedar
    And painting *it* with vermilion.'
¹⁵ "Shall you reign because you enclose *yourself* in
        cedar?
    Did not your father eat and drink,
    And do justice and righteousness?

◣▬▬▬▬▬▬▬▬▬ INHERITED

22:15-16 God passed judgment on King Jehoiakim. His father, Jo[siah] had been one of Judah's great kings, but Jehoiakim was evil. Josiah [had] been faithful with his responsibility to teach his son and to model rig[ht] living, but Jehoiakim had been unfaithful with his responsibility to imitate his father. God's judgment was on unfaithful Jehoiakim. He c[ould] not claim his father's blessings when he had not followed his father's [ways.] We may inherit our parents' money, but we cannot inherit their faith [or] blessings. A great heritage, a good education, or a beautiful home doesn't guarantee a strong character. We must choose and build our relationship with God.

Then *it was* well with him.

16 He judged the cause of the poor and needy;
Then *it was* well.
Was not this knowing Me?" says the LORD.

17 "Yet your eyes and your heart *are* for nothing but your
covetousness,
For shedding innocent blood,
And practicing oppression and violence."

18Therefore thus says the LORD concerning Jehoiakim
the son of Josiah, king of Judah:

"They shall not lament for him,
Saying, 'Alas, my brother!' or 'Alas, my sister!'
They shall not lament for him,
Saying, 'Alas, master!' or 'Alas, his glory!'

19 He shall be buried with the burial of a donkey,
Dragged and cast out beyond the gates of Jerusalem.

20 "Go up to Lebanon, and cry out,
And lift up your voice in Bashan;
Cry from Abarim,
For all your lovers are destroyed.

21 I spoke to you in your prosperity,
But you said, 'I will not hear.'
This *has been* your manner from your youth,
That you did not obey My voice.

22 The wind shall eat up all your rulers,
And your lovers shall go into captivity;
Surely then you will be ashamed and humiliated
For all your wickedness.

23 O inhabitant of Lebanon,
Making your nest in the cedars,
How gracious will you be when pangs come upon
you,
Like the pain of a woman in labor?

24"*As* I live," says the LORD, "though Coniah the son of
Jehoiakim, king of Judah, were the signet on My right
hand, yet I would pluck you off; 25and I will give you into
the hand of those who seek your life, and into the hand
of those whose face you fear—the hand of Nebuchadnezzar king of Babylon and the hand of the Chaldeans. 26So I
will cast you out, and your mother who bore you, into
another country where you were not born; and there you
shall die. 27But to the land to which they desire to return,
there they shall not return.

28 "Is this man Coniah a despised, broken idol—
A vessel in which *is* no pleasure?
Why are they cast out, he and his descendants,
And cast into a land which they do not know?

29 O earth, earth, earth,
Hear the word of the LORD!

30 Thus says the LORD:
'Write this man down as childless,
A man *who* shall not prosper in his days;
For none of his descendants shall prosper,
Sitting on the throne of David,
And ruling anymore in Judah.'"

CHAPTER 23 **A PERFECT KING WILL COME.** "Woe
to the shepherds who destroy and scatter the sheep of My
pasture!" says the LORD. 2Therefore thus says the LORD
God of Israel against the shepherds who feed My people:
"You have scattered My flock, driven them away, and not
attended to them. Behold, I will attend to you for the evil
of your doings," says the LORD. 3"But I will gather the
remnant of My flock out of all countries where I have
driven them, and bring them back to their folds; and they
shall be fruitful and increase. 4I will set up shepherds over
them who will feed them; and they shall fear no more,
nor be dismayed, nor shall they be lacking," says the
LORD.

5 "Behold, *the* days are coming," says the LORD,
"That I will raise to David a Branch of righteousness;
A King shall reign and prosper,
And execute judgment and righteousness in the
earth.

6 In His days Judah will be saved,
And Israel will dwell safely;
Now this *is* His name by which He will be called:

THE LORD OUR RIGHTEOUSNESS.

7"Therefore, behold, *the* days are coming," says the
LORD, "that they shall no longer say, 'As the LORD lives who
brought up the children of Israel from the land of Egypt,'
8but, 'As the LORD lives who brought up and led the descendants of the house of Israel from the north country
and from all the countries where I had driven them.' And
they shall dwell in their own land."

◤◣◢◥ **CORRUPTION**

23:9-14 How did the nation become so corrupt? A major factor was
false prophecy. The false prophets had a large, enthusiastic audience and
were very popular because they made the people believe that all was
well. By contrast, Jeremiah's message from God was unpopular because it
showed the people how bad they were. There are four warning signs of
false prophets— characteristics we need to watch for even today:
(1) They may appear to live according to religious principles, but they do
not speak God's message; (2) They water down God's message to make it
more acceptable; (3) They encourage their listeners, often subtly, to
disobey God; (4) They tend to be arrogant and self-serving, appealing to
the desires of their audience instead of being true to God's Word.

9 My heart within me is broken
Because of the prophets;
All my bones shake.
I am like a drunken man,
And like a man whom wine has overcome,
Because of the LORD,
And because of His holy words.

10 For the land is full of adulterers;
For because of a curse the land mourns.
The pleasant places of the wilderness are dried up.
Their course of life is evil,
And their might *is* not right.

11 "For both prophet and priest are profane;
Yes, in My house I have found their wickedness,"
says the LORD.

12 "Therefore their way shall be to them

Like slippery *ways;*
In the darkness they shall be driven on
And fall in them;
For I will bring disaster on them,
The year of their punishment," says the LORD.
¹³"And I have seen folly in the prophets of Samaria:
They prophesied by Baal
And caused My people Israel to err.
¹⁴ Also I have seen a horrible thing in the prophets of
Jerusalem:
They commit adultery and walk in lies;
They also strengthen the hands of evildoers,
So that no one turns back from his wickedness.
All of them are like Sodom to Me,
And her inhabitants like Gomorrah.

¹⁵"Therefore thus says the LORD of hosts concerning
the prophets:

'Behold, I will feed them with wormwood,
And make them drink the water of gall;
For from the prophets of Jerusalem
Profaneness has gone out into all the land.'"

¹⁶Thus says the LORD of hosts:

"Do not listen to the words of the prophets who
prophesy to you.
They make you worthless;
They speak a vision of their own heart,
Not from the mouth of the LORD.
¹⁷ They continually say to those who despise Me,
'The LORD has said, "You shall have peace" ';
And *to* everyone who walks according to the dictates
of his own heart, they say,
'No evil shall come upon you.'"

¹⁸ For who has stood in the counsel of the LORD,
And has perceived and heard His word?
Who has marked His word and heard *it?*
¹⁹ Behold, a whirlwind of the LORD has gone forth in
fury—
A violent whirlwind!
It will fall violently on the head of the wicked.
²⁰ The anger of the LORD will not turn back
Until He has executed and performed the thoughts
of His heart.
In the latter days you will understand it perfectly.

²¹ "I have not sent these prophets, yet they ran.
I have not spoken to them, yet they prophesied.
²² But if they had stood in My counsel,
And had caused My people to hear My words,
Then they would have turned them from their evil
way
And from the evil of their doings.

²³ "*Am* I a God near at hand," says the LORD,
"And not a God afar off?
²⁴ Can anyone hide himself in secret places,
So I shall not see him?" says the LORD;
"Do I not fill heaven and earth?" says the LORD.

²⁵"I have heard what the prophets have said who

LIVE IT!

23:28 True prophets and false prophets are as different as chaff o wheat. Worthless chaff blows away with the wind, while wheat rema nourish many. To share God's Word is a great responsibility because way we present it and live it will encourage people either to accept i reject it. Whether we speak from a pulpit, teach in a class, or share v friends, our responsibility is to accurately communicate and live out Word. As you share God's Word with friends and neighbors, they wil for its effectiveness in your life. Unless it has changed you, why sho they let it change them? If you don't live it, don't preach it!

---

prophesy lies in My name, saying, 'I have dreamed, I have dreamed!' ²⁶How long will *this* be in the heart of the prophets who prophesy lies? Indeed *they are* prophets of the deceit of their own heart, ²⁷who try to make My people forget My name by their dreams which everyone tells his neighbor, as their fathers forgot My name for Baal.

²⁸ "The prophet who has a dream, let him tell a dream;
And he who has My word, let him speak My word
faithfully.
What *is* the chaff to the wheat?" says the LORD.
²⁹ "*Is* not My word like a fire?" says the LORD,
"And like a hammer *that* breaks the rock in pieces?

³⁰"Therefore behold, I *am* against the prophets," says the LORD, "who steal My words every one from his neighbor. ³¹Behold, I *am* against the prophets," says the LORD, "who use their tongues and say, 'He says.' ³²Behold, I *am* against those who prophesy false dreams," says the LORD, "and tell them, and cause My people to err by their lies and by their recklessness. Yet I did not send them or command them; therefore they shall not profit this people at all," says the LORD.

³³"So when these people or the prophet or the priest ask you, saying, 'What is the oracle of the LORD?' you shall then say to them, 'What oracle?' I will even forsake you," says the LORD. ³⁴"And *as for* the prophet and the priest and the people who say, 'The oracle of the LORD!' I will even punish that man and his house. ³⁵Thus every one of you shall say to his neighbor, and every one to his brother, 'What has the LORD answered?' and, 'What has the LORD spoken?' ³⁶And the oracle of the LORD you shall mention no more. For every man's word will be his oracle, for you have perverted the words of the living God, the LORD of hosts, our God. ³⁷Thus you shall say to the prophet, 'What has the LORD answered you?' and, 'What has the LORD spoken?' ³⁸But since you say, 'The oracle of the LORD!' therefore thus says the LORD: 'Because you say this word, "The oracle of the LORD!" and I have sent to you, saying, "Do not say, 'The oracle of the LORD!'" ³⁹therefore behold, I, even I, will utterly forget you and forsake you, and the city that I gave you and your fathers, and *will cast you* out of My presence. ⁴⁰And I will bring an everlasting reproach upon you, and a perpetual shame, which shall not be forgotten.'"

CHAPTER **24** **GOOD FIGS, BAD FIGS.** The LORD showed me, and there were two baskets of figs set before the temple of the LORD, after Nebuchadnezzar king of Babylon had carried away captive Jeconiah the son of Jehoiakim, king of Judah, and the princes of Judah with the craftsmen and smiths, from Jerusalem, and had brought them to Babylon. ²One basket *had* very good figs, like the figs *that are* first ripe; and the other basket *had* very bad figs which could not be eaten, they were so bad. ³Then the LORD said to me, "What do you see, Jeremiah?"

And I said, "Figs, the good figs, very good; and the bad, very bad, which cannot be eaten, they are so bad."

⁴Again the word of the LORD came to me, saying, ⁵"Thus says the LORD, the God of Israel: 'Like these good figs, so will I acknowledge those who are carried away captive from Judah, whom I have sent out of this place for *their own* good, into the land of the Chaldeans. ⁶For I will set My eyes on them for good, and I will bring them back to this land; I will build them and not pull *them* down, and I will plant them and not pluck *them* up. ⁷Then I will give them a heart to know Me, that I *am* the LORD; and they shall be My people, and I will be their God, for they shall return to Me with their whole heart.

⁸'And as the bad figs which cannot be eaten, they are so bad'—surely thus says the LORD—'so will I give up Zedekiah the king of Judah, his princes, the residue of Jerusalem who remain in this land, and those who dwell in the land of Egypt. ⁹I will deliver them to trouble into all the kingdoms of the earth, for *their* harm, *to be* a reproach and a byword, a taunt and a curse, in all places where I shall drive them. ¹⁰And I will send the sword, the famine, and the pestilence among them, till they are consumed from the land that I gave to them and their fathers.'"

CHAPTER **25** **DISASTER AHEAD.** The word that came to Jeremiah concerning all the people of Judah, in the fourth year of Jehoiakim the son of Josiah, king of Judah (which *was* the first year of Nebuchadnezzar king of Babylon), ²which Jeremiah the prophet spoke to all the people of Judah and to all the inhabitants of Jerusalem, saying: ³"From the thirteenth year of Josiah the son of Amon, king of Judah, even to this day, this *is* the twenty-third year in which the word of the LORD has come to me; and I have spoken to you, rising early and speaking, but you have not listened. ⁴And the LORD has sent to you all His servants the prophets, rising early and sending *them*, but you have not listened nor inclined your ear to hear. ⁵They said, 'Repent now everyone of his evil way and his evil doings, and dwell in the land that the LORD has given to you and your fathers forever and ever. ⁶Do not go after other gods to serve them and worship them, and do not provoke Me to anger with the works of your hands; and I will not harm you.' ⁷Yet you have not listened to Me," says the LORD, "that you might provoke Me to anger with the works of your hands to your own hurt.

⁸"Therefore thus says the LORD of hosts: 'Because you have not heard My words, ⁹behold, I will send and take all the families of the north,' says the LORD, 'and Nebuchadnezzar the king of Babylon, My servant, and will bring them against this land, against its inhabitants, and against these nations all around, and will utterly destroy them, and make them an astonishment, a hissing, and perpetual desolations. ¹⁰Moreover I will take from them the voice of mirth and the voice of gladness, the voice of the bride-

groom and the voice of the bride, the sound of the millstones and the light of the lamp. ¹¹And this whole land shall be a desolation *and* an astonishment, and these nations shall serve the king of Babylon seventy years.

◄▬▬▬▬▬▬**FIGS**

24:2-10 The good figs represented the exiles to Babylon—not because they were good, but because their hearts would respond to God. So he would preserve them and bring them back to the land. The bad figs represented those who remained in Judah or ran away to Egypt. The people believed they would be blessed if they remained in the land, but the opposite was true because God would use the captivity to refine the exiles. We may believe we are blessed when life goes well and cursed when it does not. But trouble is a blessing when it makes us stronger, and prosperity is a curse if it entices us away from God. If you are facing trouble, ask God to help you grow stronger for him. If things are going your way, ask God to help you use your prosperity faithfully for him.

¹²"Then it will come to pass, when seventy years are completed, *that* I will punish the king of Babylon and that nation, the land of the Chaldeans, for their iniquity,' says the LORD; 'and I will make it a perpetual desolation. ¹³So I will bring on that land all My words which I have pronounced against it, all that is written in this book, which Jeremiah has prophesied concerning all the nations. ¹⁴(For many nations and great kings shall be served by them also; and I will repay them according to their deeds and according to the works of their own hands.)'"

¹⁵For thus says the LORD God of Israel to me: "Take this wine cup of fury from My hand, and cause all the nations, to whom I send you, to drink it. ¹⁶And they will drink and stagger and go mad because of the sword that I will send among them."

¹⁷Then I took the cup from the LORD's hand, and made all the nations drink, to whom the LORD had sent me: ¹⁸Jerusalem and the cities of Judah, its kings and its princes, to make them a desolation, an astonishment, a hissing, and a curse, as *it is* this day; ¹⁹Pharaoh king of Egypt, his servants, his princes, and all his people; ²⁰all the mixed multitude, all the kings of the land of Uz, all the kings of the land of the Philistines (namely, Ashkelon, Gaza, Ekron, and the remnant of Ashdod); ²¹Edom, Moab, and the people of Ammon; ²²all the kings of Tyre, all the kings of Sidon, and the kings of the coastlands which *are* across the sea; ²³Dedan, Tema, Buz, and all *who are* in the farthest corners; ²⁴all the kings of Arabia and all the kings of the mixed multitude who dwell in the desert; ²⁵all the kings of Zimri, all the kings of Elam, and all the kings of

◄▬▬▬▬▬▬**DON'T QUIT!**

25:2-6 Imagine preaching the same message for 23 years and continually being rejected! Jeremiah faced this, but because he had committed his life to God he continued to proclaim the message "Repent now everyone of his evil way and his evil doings." Regardless of the people's response, Jeremiah did not give up. God never stops loving us, even when we reject him. We can thank God that he won't give up on us, and, like Jeremiah, we can commit ourselves to never giving God up. No matter how people respond when you tell them about God, remain faithful to his high call and continue to witness for him.

26:16-17,24 Jeremiah's life was in serious danger, but God used officials and wise men to protect him. God spared Jeremiah because his work was not done. Believers, even some of God's prophets, sometimes die painful deaths. God does not promise to keep every follower from suffering. But he promises to be with us in the middle of trials.

the Medes; 26all the kings of the north, far and near, one with another; and all the kingdoms of the world which *are* on the face of the earth. Also the king of Sheshach shall drink after them.

27"Therefore you shall say to them, 'Thus says the LORD of hosts, the God of Israel: "Drink, be drunk, and vomit! Fall and rise no more, because of the sword which I will send among you." ' 28And it shall be, if they refuse to take the cup from your hand to drink, then you shall say to them, 'Thus says the LORD of hosts: "You shall certainly drink! 29For behold, I begin to bring calamity on the city which is called by My name, and should you be utterly unpunished? You shall not be unpunished, for I will call for a sword on all the inhabitants of the earth," says the LORD of hosts.'

30"Therefore prophesy against them all these words, and say to them:

'The LORD will roar from on high,
And utter His voice from His holy habitation;
He will roar mightily against His fold.
He will give a shout, as those who tread *the grapes,*
Against all the inhabitants of the earth.
31 A noise will come to the ends of the earth—
For the LORD has a controversy with the nations;
He will plead His case with all flesh.
He will give those *who are* wicked to the sword,' says
   the LORD."

32Thus says the LORD of hosts:

"Behold, disaster shall go forth
From nation to nation,
And a great whirlwind shall be raised up
From the farthest parts of the earth.

33"And at that day the slain of the LORD shall be from *one* end of the earth even to the *other* end of the earth. They shall not be lamented, or gathered, or buried; they shall become refuse on the ground.

34 "Wail, shepherds, and cry!
Roll about *in the ashes,*
You leaders of the flock!
For the days of your slaughter and your dispersions
   are fulfilled;
You shall fall like a precious vessel.
35 And the shepherds will have no way to flee,
Nor the leaders of the flock to escape.
36 A voice of the cry of the shepherds,
And a wailing of the leaders to the flock *will be heard.*
For the LORD has plundered their pasture,
37 And the peaceful dwellings are cut down
Because of the fierce anger of the LORD.
38 He has left His lair like the lion;
For their land is desolate
Because of the fierceness of the Oppressor,
And because of His fierce anger."

CHAPTER 26 JEREMIAH ALMOST DIES. In the beginning of the reign of Jehoiakim the son of Josiah, king of Judah, this word came from the LORD, saying, 2"Thus says the LORD: 'Stand in the court of the LORD's house, and speak to all the cities of Judah, which come to worship *in* the LORD's house, all the words that I command you to speak to them. Do not diminish a word. 3Perhaps everyone will listen and turn from his evil way, that I may relent concerning the calamity which I purpose to bring on them because of the evil of their doings.' 4And you shall say to them, 'Thus says the LORD: "If you will not listen to Me, to walk in My law which I have set before you, 5to heed the words of My servants the prophets whom I sent to you, both rising up early and sending *them* (but you have not heeded), 6then I will make this house like Shiloh, and will make this city a curse to all the nations of the earth."'"

7So the priests and the prophets and all the people heard Jeremiah speaking these words in the house of the LORD. 8Now it happened, when Jeremiah had made an end of speaking all that the LORD had commanded *him* to speak to all the people, that the priests and the prophets and all the people seized him, saying, "You will surely die! 9Why have you prophesied in the name of the LORD, saying, 'This house shall be like Shiloh, and this city shall be desolate, without an inhabitant'?" And all the people were gathered against Jeremiah in the house of the LORD.

10When the princes of Judah heard these things, they came up from the king's house to the house of the LORD and sat down in the entry of the New Gate of the LORD's *house.* 11And the priests and the prophets spoke to the princes and all the people, saying, "This man deserves to die! For he has prophesied against this city, as you have heard with your ears."

12Then Jeremiah spoke to all the princes and all the people, saying: "The LORD sent me to prophesy against this house and against this city with all the words that you have heard. 13Now therefore, amend your ways and your doings, and obey the voice of the LORD your God; then the LORD will relent concerning the doom that He has pronounced against you. 14As for me, here I am, in your hand; do with me as seems good and proper to you. 15But know for certain that if you put me to death, you will surely bring innocent blood on yourselves, on this city, and on its inhabitants; for truly the LORD has sent me to you to speak all these words in your hearing."

16So the princes and all the people said to the priests and the prophets, "This man does not deserve to die. For he has spoken to us in the name of the LORD our God."

17Then certain of the elders of the land rose up and spoke to all the assembly of the people, saying: 18"Micah of Moresheth prophesied in the days of Hezekiah king of Judah, and spoke to all the people of Judah, saying, 'Thus says the LORD of hosts:

"Zion shall be plowed *like* a field,
Jerusalem shall become heaps of ruins,
And the mountain of the temple
Like the bare hills of the forest." '

19Did Hezekiah king of Judah and all Judah ever put him to death? Did he not fear the LORD and seek the LORD's favor? And the LORD relented concerning the doom which He had pronounced against them. But we are doing great evil against ourselves."

²⁰Now there was also a man who prophesied in the name of the LORD, Urijah the son of Shemaiah of Kirjath Jearim, who prophesied against this city and against this land according to all the words of Jeremiah. ²¹And when Jehoiakim the king, with all his mighty men and all the princes, heard his words, the king sought to put him to death; but when Urijah heard *it*, he was afraid and fled, and went to Egypt. ²²Then Jehoiakim the king sent men to Egypt: Elnathan the son of Achbor, and *other* men *who went* with him to Egypt. ²³And they brought Urijah from Egypt and brought him to Jehoiakim the king, who killed him with the sword and cast his dead body into the graves of the common people.

²⁴Nevertheless the hand of Ahikam the son of Shaphan was with Jeremiah, so that they should not give him into the hand of the people to put him to death.

CHAPTER 27 THE PEOPLE WILL BE SLAVES. In the beginning of the reign of Jehoiakim the son of Josiah, king of Judah, this word came to Jeremiah from the LORD, saying, ²"Thus says the LORD to me: 'Make for yourselves bonds and yokes, and put them on your neck, ³and send them to the king of Edom, the king of Moab, the king of the Ammonites, the king of Tyre, and the king of Sidon, by the hand of the messengers who come to Jerusalem to Zedekiah king of Judah. ⁴And command them to say to their masters, "Thus says the LORD of hosts, the God of Israel—thus you shall say to your masters: ⁵'I have made the earth, the man and the beast that *are* on the ground, by My great power and by My outstretched arm, and have given it to whom it seemed proper to Me. ⁶And now I have given all these lands into the hand of Nebuchadnezzar the king of Babylon, My servant; and the beasts of the field I have also given him to serve him. ⁷So all nations shall serve him and his son and his son's son, until the time of his land comes; and then many nations and great kings shall make him serve them. ⁸And it shall be, *that* the nation and kingdom which will not serve Nebuchadnezzar the king of Babylon, and which will not put its neck under the yoke of the king of Babylon, that nation I will punish,' says the LORD, 'with the sword, the famine, and the pestilence, until I have consumed them by his hand. ⁹Therefore do not listen to your prophets, your diviners, your dreamers, your soothsayers, or your sorcerers, who speak to you, saying, "You shall not serve the king of Babylon." ¹⁰For they prophesy a lie to you, to remove you far from your land; and I will drive you out, and you will perish. ¹¹But the nations that bring their necks under the yoke of the king of Babylon and serve him, I will let them remain in their own land,' says the LORD, 'and they shall till it and dwell in it.' " ' "

¹²I also spoke to Zedekiah king of Judah according to all these words, saying, "Bring your necks under the yoke of the king of Babylon, and serve him and his people, and live! ¹³Why will you die, you and your people, by the sword, by the famine, and by the pestilence, as the LORD has spoken against the nation that will not serve the king

of Babylon? ¹⁴Therefore do not listen to the words of the prophets who speak to you, saying, 'You shall not serve the king of Babylon,' for they prophesy a lie to you; ¹⁵for I have not sent them," says the LORD, "yet they prophesy a lie in My name, that I may drive you out, and that you may perish, you and the prophets who prophesy to you."

◀▬▬▬▬▬TRUE FRIEND

27:9-11 The false prophets told the people what they wanted to hear, even though these "prophets" knew the message was not true. The people in Jeremiah's day needed a true friend like Jeremiah, who brought God's painful, corrective word. A true friend speaks the truth no matter how much it hurts to hear. Seek friends who speak truthfully, even though their correction is painful. Someone who flatters you by telling you lies is not a true friend.

¹⁶Also I spoke to the priests and to all this people, saying, "Thus says the LORD: 'Do not listen to the words of your prophets who prophesy to you, saying, "Behold, the vessels of the LORD's house will now shortly be brought back from Babylon"; for they prophesy a lie to you. ¹⁷Do not listen to them; serve the king of Babylon, and live! Why should this city be laid waste? ¹⁸But if they *are* prophets, and if the word of the LORD is with them, let them now make intercession to the LORD of hosts, that the vessels which are left in the house of the LORD, *in* the house of the king of Judah, and at Jerusalem, do not go to Babylon.'

¹⁹"For thus says the LORD of hosts concerning the pillars, concerning the Sea, concerning the carts, and concerning the remainder of the vessels that remain in this city, ²⁰which Nebuchadnezzar king of Babylon did not take, when he carried away captive Jeconiah the son of Jehoiakim, king of Judah, from Jerusalem to Babylon, and all the nobles of Judah and Jerusalem— ²¹yes, thus says the LORD of hosts, the God of Israel, concerning the vessels that remain in the house of the LORD, and in the house of the king of Judah and of Jerusalem: ²²'They shall be carried to Babylon, and there they shall be until the day that I visit them,' says the LORD. 'Then I will bring them up and restore them to this place.'"

CHAPTER 28 A FALSE PROPHET. And it happened in the same year, at the beginning of the reign of Zedekiah king of Judah, in the fourth year *and* in the fifth month, *that* Hananiah the son of Azur the prophet, who *was* from Gibeon, spoke to me in the house of the LORD in the presence of the priests and of all the people, saying, ²"Thus speaks the LORD of hosts, the God of Israel, saying: 'I have broken the yoke of the king of Babylon. ³Within two full years I will bring back to this place all the vessels of the LORD's house, that Nebuchadnezzar king of Babylon took away from this place and carried to Babylon. ⁴And I will bring back to this place Jeconiah the son of Jehoiakim, king of Judah, with all the captives of Judah who went to Babylon,' says the LORD, 'for I will break the yoke of the king of Babylon.'"

⁵Then the prophet Jeremiah spoke to the prophet Hananiah in the presence of the priests and in the presence of all the people who stood in the house of the LORD, ⁶and

28:8-17 Jeremiah spoke the truth, but it was unpopular; Hananiah spoke lies, but his deceitful words brought false hope and comfort to the people. God had already outlined the marks of a true prophet: a true prophet's predictions always come true and his words never contradict previous revelation (Deuteronomy 13; 18:9-22). Jeremiah's predictions were already coming true, from Hananiah's death to the Babylonian invasions. But the people still preferred to listen to comforting lies rather than painful truth. Do your best to be open to God's words to you, even if you don't particularly like what he has to say. As painful as it may sometimes be, the truth is always best.

the prophet Jeremiah said, "Amen! The LORD do so; the LORD perform your words which you have prophesied, to bring back the vessels of the LORD's house and all who were carried away captive, from Babylon to this place. ⁷Nevertheless hear now this word that I speak in your hearing and in the hearing of all the people: ⁸The prophets who have been before me and before you of old prophesied against many countries and great kingdoms—of war and disaster and pestilence. ⁹As for the prophet who prophesies of peace, when the word of the prophet comes to pass, the prophet will be known *as* one whom the LORD has truly sent."

¹⁰Then Hananiah the prophet took the yoke off the prophet Jeremiah's neck and broke it. ¹¹And Hananiah spoke in the presence of all the people, saying, "Thus says the LORD: 'Even so I will break the yoke of Nebuchadnezzar king of Babylon from the neck of all nations within the space of two full years.'" And the prophet Jeremiah went his way.

¹²Now the word of the LORD came to Jeremiah, after Hananiah the prophet had broken the yoke from the neck of the prophet Jeremiah, saying, ¹³"Go and tell Hananiah, saying, 'Thus says the LORD: "You have broken the yokes of wood, but you have made in their place yokes of iron." ¹⁴For thus says the LORD of hosts, the God of Israel: "I have put a yoke of iron on the neck of all these nations, that they may serve Nebuchadnezzar king of Babylon; and they shall serve him. I have given him the beasts of the field also."'"

¹⁵Then the prophet Jeremiah said to Hananiah the prophet, "Hear now, Hananiah, the LORD has not sent you, but you make this people trust in a lie. ¹⁶Therefore thus says the LORD: 'Behold, I will cast you from the face of the earth. This year you shall die, because you have taught rebellion against the LORD.'"

¹⁷So Hananiah the prophet died the same year in the seventh month.

CHAPTER 29 MORE WARNINGS. Now these *are* the words of the letter that Jeremiah the prophet sent from Jerusalem to the remainder of the elders who were carried away captive—to the priests, the prophets, and all the people whom Nebuchadnezzar had carried away captive from Jerusalem to Babylon. ²(This happened after Jeconiah the king, the queen mother, the eunuchs, the princes of Judah and Jerusalem, the craftsmen, and the smiths had departed from Jerusalem.) ³*The letter was sent* by the hand of Elasah the son of Shaphan, and Gemariah the son of Hilkiah, whom Zedekiah king of Judah

sent to Babylon, to Nebuchadnezzar king of Babylon, saying,

⁴ Thus says the LORD of hosts, the God of Israel, to all who were carried away captive, whom I have caused to be carried away from Jerusalem to Babylon:

⁵ Build houses and dwell *in them;* plant gardens and eat their fruit. ⁶Take wives and beget sons and daughters; and take wives for your sons and give your daughters to husbands, so that they may bear sons and daughters—that you may be increased there, and not diminished. ⁷And seek the peace of the city where I have caused you to be carried away captive, and pray to the LORD for it; for in its peace you will have peace. ⁸For thus says the LORD of hosts, the God of Israel: Do not let your prophets and your diviners who are in your midst deceive you, nor listen to your dreams which you cause to be dreamed. ⁹For they prophesy falsely to you in My name; I have not sent them, says the LORD.

¹⁰ For thus says the LORD: After seventy years are completed at Babylon, I will visit you and perform My good word toward you, and cause you to return to this place. ¹¹For I know the thoughts that I think toward you, says the LORD, thoughts of peace and not of evil, to give you a future and a hope. ¹²Then you will call upon Me and go and pray to Me, and I will listen to you. ¹³And you will seek Me and find *Me,* when you search for Me with all your heart. ¹⁴I will be found

FOR I KNOW the thoughts that I think toward YOU SAYS THE LORD thoughts of peace AND not of evil to give you A FUTURE AND A HOPE

by you, says the LORD, and I will bring you back from your captivity; I will gather you from all the nations and from all the places where I have driven you, says the LORD, and I will bring you to the place from which I cause you to be carried away captive.

15 Because you have said, "The LORD has raised up prophets for us in Babylon"— 16therefore thus says the LORD concerning the king who sits on the throne of David, concerning all the people who dwell in this city, and concerning your brethren who have not gone out with you into captivity— 17thus says the LORD of hosts: Behold, I will send on them the sword, the famine, and the pestilence, and will make them like rotten figs that cannot be eaten, they are so bad. 18And I will pursue them with the sword, with famine, and with pestilence; and I will deliver them to trouble among all the kingdoms of the earth—to be a curse, an astonishment, a hissing, and a reproach among all the nations where I have driven them, 19because they have not heeded My words, says the LORD, which I sent to them by My servants the prophets, rising up early and sending *them;* neither would you heed, says the LORD. 20Therefore hear the word of the LORD, all you of the captivity, whom I have sent from Jerusalem to Babylon.

21 Thus says the LORD of hosts, the God of Israel, concerning Ahab the son of Kolaiah, and Zedekiah the son of Maaseiah, who prophesy a lie to you in My name: Behold, I will deliver them into the hand of Nebuchadnezzar king of Babylon, and he shall slay them before your eyes. 22And because of them a curse shall be taken up by all the captivity of Judah who *are* in Babylon, saying, "The LORD make you like Zedekiah and Ahab, whom the king of Babylon roasted in the fire"; 23because they have done disgraceful things in Israel, have committed adultery with their neighbors' wives, and have spoken lying words in My name, which I have not commanded them. Indeed I know, and *am* a witness, says the LORD.

24 You shall also speak to Shemaiah the Nehelamite, saying, 25Thus speaks the LORD of hosts, the God of Israel, saying: You have sent letters in your name to all the people who *are* at Jerusalem, to Zephaniah the son of Maaseiah the priest, and to all the priests, saying, 26"The LORD has made you priest instead of Jehoiada the priest, so that there should be officers *in* the house of the LORD over every man *who* is demented and considers himself a prophet, that you should put him in prison and in the stocks. 27Now therefore, why have you not rebuked Jeremiah of Anathoth who makes himself a prophet to you? 28For he has sent to us *in* Babylon, saying, 'This *captivity is* long; build houses and dwell *in them,* and plant gardens and eat their fruit.'"

29 Now Zephaniah the priest read this letter in the hearing of Jeremiah the prophet. 30Then the word of the LORD came to Jeremiah, saying: 31Send to all those in captivity, saying, Thus says the LORD concerning Shemaiah the Nehelamite: Because Shemaiah has prophesied to you, and I have not sent him, and he has caused you to trust in a lie— 32therefore thus says the LORD: Behold, I will punish Shemaiah the Nehelamite and his family:

I'm afraid to give my whole life to God. I'm afraid he's going to ask me to do things later on, like be a missionary in another country. I really don't want to do that. What happens if I hold back part of my life from God? Imagine going out for basketball and telling the coach that you only want to practice, not play in the games. Or that you only want to play in the first half of each game. How would your coach react? What would your teammates say?

Undoubtedly they would be a little put off by your selfish attitude. After all, if you're going to be on the team, you should play in the games. And if you play, you shouldn't avoid the last half when your team might need you the most. Playing the game is a lot better than practice, and the second half is when the game is on the line!

Unfortunately, many Christians, by their attitudes and their actions, tell the Coach (God) two things: they don't really want the benefits and the fun of playing on the team (except heaven, of course); and they don't want to contribute during the times when other people might need them the most!

God wants your whole life, so he can make something extraordinary out of it. Jesus told his followers, "The thief does not come except to steal, and to kill, and to destroy. I have come that they may have life, and that they may have *it* more abundantly" (John 10:10). That's a level of trust you haven't reached yet.

The Christian life was never meant to be done halfway. You're either sold out to God or sold out to the world. For God to give you "abundant life," you must give your life in full to God. Jesus said, "He who finds his life will lose it, and he who loses his life for My sake will find it" (Matthew 10:39).

And don't worry about what God will ask of you. If he asks you to be a missionary, in effect he is saying; "I know you better than anyone else does. I made you, and I love you more than you'll ever know. Because I put you together, I know what it will take to make you the happiest and most fulfilled in life. If you choose any other direction, you'll be settling for second best. Please don't."

God's goal isn't to make his kids miserable. Just take a look at Jeremiah 29:11-13. You'll see that God wants to lead us in a direction that will cause us to say, "The game wasn't easy God, especially the last quarter. But thanks for believing in me enough to put me in—I really had fun."

he shall not have anyone to dwell among this people, nor shall he see the good that I will do for My people, says the LORD, because he has taught rebellion against the LORD.

CHAPTER **30** BRINGING BACK THE PEOPLE. The word that came to Jeremiah from the LORD, saying, ²"Thus speaks the LORD God of Israel, saying: 'Write in a book for yourself all the words that I have spoken to you. ³For behold, the days are coming,' says the LORD, 'that I will bring back from captivity My people Israel and Judah,' says the LORD. 'And I will cause them to return to the land that I gave to their fathers, and they shall possess it.'"

⁴Now these *are* the words that the LORD spoke concerning Israel and Judah.

⁵"For thus says the LORD:

'We have heard a voice of trembling,
Of fear, and not of peace.
⁶ Ask now, and see,
Whether a man is ever in labor with child?
So why do I see every man *with* his hands on his loins
Like a woman in labor,
And all faces turned pale?
⁷ Alas! For that day *is* great,
So that none *is* like it;
And it *is* the time of Jacob's trouble,
But he shall be saved out of it.

⁸ 'For it shall come to pass in that day,'
Says the LORD of hosts,
'*That* I will break his yoke from your neck,
And will burst your bonds;
Foreigners shall no more enslave them.
⁹ But they shall serve the LORD their God,
And David their king,
Whom I will raise up for them.

¹⁰ 'Therefore do not fear, O My servant Jacob,' says the LORD,
'Nor be dismayed, O Israel;
For behold, I will save you from afar,
And your seed from the land of their captivity.
Jacob shall return, have rest and be quiet,
And no one shall make *him* afraid.
¹¹ For I *am* with you,' says the LORD, 'to save you;
Though I make a full end of all nations where I have scattered you,
Yet I will not make a complete end of you.
But I will correct you in justice,
And will not let you go altogether unpunished.'

¹²"For thus says the LORD:

'Your affliction *is* incurable,
Your wound *is* severe.
¹³ *There is* no one to plead your cause,
That you may be bound up;
You have no healing medicines.
¹⁴ All your lovers have forgotten you;
They do not seek you;

For I have wounded you with the wound of an enemy,
With the chastisement of a cruel one,
For the multitude of your iniquities,
Because your sins have increased.
¹⁵ Why do you cry about your affliction?
Your sorrow *is* incurable.
Because of the multitude of your iniquities,
Because your sins have increased,
I have done these things to you.

¹⁶ 'Therefore all those who devour you shall be devoured;
And all your adversaries, every one of them, shall go into captivity;
Those who plunder you shall become plunder,
And all who prey upon you I will make a prey.
¹⁷ For I will restore health to you
And heal you of your wounds,' says the LORD,
'Because they called you an outcast *saying:*
"This *is* Zion;
No one seeks her." '

¹⁸"Thus says the LORD:

'Behold, I will bring back the captivity of Jacob's tents,
And have mercy on his dwelling places;
The city shall be built upon its own mound,
And the palace shall remain according to its own plan.
¹⁹ Then out of them shall proceed thanksgiving
And the voice of those who make merry;
I will multiply them, and they shall not diminish;
I will also glorify them, and they shall not be small.
²⁰ Their children also shall be as before,
And their congregation shall be established before Me;
And I will punish all who oppress them.
²¹ Their nobles shall be from among them,
And their governor shall come from their midst;
Then I will cause him to draw near,
And he shall approach Me;
For who *is* this who pledged his heart to approach Me?' says the LORD.
²² 'You shall be My people,
And I will be your God.' "

²³ Behold, the whirlwind of the LORD
Goes forth with fury,
A continuing whirlwind;
It will fall violently on the head of the wicked.
²⁴ The fierce anger of the LORD will not return until He has done it,
And until He has performed the intents of His heart.

In the latter days you will consider it.

CHAPTER **31** GOD STILL LOVES THE PEOPLE. "At the same time," says the LORD, "I will be the God of all the families of Israel, and they shall be My people."

²Thus says the LORD:

"The people who survived the sword
Found grace in the wilderness—
Israel, when I went to give him rest."

³ The LORD has appeared of old to me, *saying:*
"Yes, I have loved you with an everlasting love;
Therefore with lovingkindness I have drawn you.
⁴ Again I will build you, and you shall be rebuilt,
O virgin of Israel!
You shall again be adorned with your tambourines,
And shall go forth in the dances of those who rejoice.
⁵ You shall yet plant vines on the mountains of Samaria;
The planters shall plant and eat *them* as ordinary food.
⁶ For there shall be a day
When the watchmen will cry on Mount Ephraim,
'Arise, and let us go up *to* Zion,
To the LORD our God.'"

⁷For thus says the LORD:

"Sing with gladness for Jacob,
And shout among the chief of the nations;
Proclaim, give praise, and say,
'O LORD, save Your people,
The remnant of Israel!'
⁸ Behold, I will bring them from the north country,
And gather them from the ends of the earth,
Among them the blind and the lame,
The woman with child
And the one who labors with child, together;
A great throng shall return there.
⁹ They shall come with weeping,
And with supplications I will lead them.
I will cause them to walk by the rivers of waters,
In a straight way in which they shall not stumble;
For I am a Father to Israel,
And Ephraim *is* My firstborn.

¹⁰ "Hear the word of the LORD, O nations,
And declare *it* in the isles afar off, and say,
'He who scattered Israel will gather him,
And keep him as a shepherd *does* his flock.'
¹¹ For the LORD has redeemed Jacob,
And ransomed him from the hand of one stronger than he.
¹² Therefore they shall come and sing in the height of Zion,
Streaming to the goodness of the LORD—
For wheat and new wine and oil,
For the young of the flock and the herd;
Their souls shall be like a well-watered garden,
And they shall sorrow no more at all.

¹³ "Then shall the virgin rejoice in the dance,
And the young men and the old, together;
For I will turn their mourning to joy,

Will comfort them,
And make them rejoice rather than sorrow.
¹⁴ I will satiate the soul of the priests with abundance,
And My people shall be satisfied with My goodness, says the LORD."

¹⁵Thus says the LORD:

"A voice was heard in Ramah,
Lamentation *and* bitter weeping,
Rachel weeping for her children,

━━ **MAGNIFICENT LOVE**

31:3 God reaches toward his people with kindness motivated by deep and everlasting love. God is eager to do the best for his people if they will only let him. After many words of warning about sin, this reminder of God's magnificent love is refreshing. We may often think of God with dread or fear; but if we look carefully, we can see him lovingly drawing us toward himself.

Refusing to be comforted for her children,
Because they *are* no more."

¹⁶Thus says the LORD:

"Refrain your voice from weeping,
And your eyes from tears;
For your work shall be rewarded, says the LORD,
And they shall come back from the land of the enemy.
¹⁷ There is hope in your future, says the LORD,
That *your* children shall come back to their own border.

¹⁸ "I have surely heard Ephraim bemoaning himself:
'You have chastised me, and I was chastised,
Like an untrained bull;
Restore me, and I will return,
For You *are* the LORD my God.
¹⁹ Surely, after my turning, I repented;
And after I was instructed, I struck myself on the thigh;
I was ashamed, yes, even humiliated,
Because I bore the reproach of my youth.'
²⁰ *Is* Ephraim My dear son?
Is he a pleasant child?
For though I spoke against him,
I earnestly remember him still;
Therefore My heart yearns for him;
I will surely have mercy on him, says the LORD.

²¹ "Set up signposts,
Make landmarks;
Set your heart toward the highway,
The way in *which* you went.

━━ **RETURN**

31:18-20 These verses describe grief and mourning. Ephraim was one of the major tribes of the northern kingdom (Israel). Although the northern kingdom had sunk into the most degrading sins, God still loved the people. A remnant would turn to God, repenting of their sins, and God would forgive. God still loves you, despite what you have done. He will forgive you if you will return to him.

Turn back, O virgin of Israel,
Turn back to these your cities.
²² How long will you gad about,
O you backsliding daughter?
For the LORD has created a new thing in the earth—
A woman shall encompass a man."

²³Thus says the LORD of hosts, the God of Israel: "They shall again use this speech in the land of Judah and in its cities, when I bring back their captivity: 'The LORD bless you, O home of justice, *and* mountain of holiness!' ²⁴And there shall dwell in Judah itself, and in all its cities together, farmers and those going out with flocks. ²⁵For I have satiated the weary soul, and I have replenished every sorrowful soul."

²⁶After this I awoke and looked around, and my sleep was sweet to me.

²⁷"Behold, the days are coming, says the LORD, that I will sow the house of Israel and the house of Judah with the seed of man and the seed of beast. ²⁸And it shall come to pass, *that* as I have watched over them to pluck up, to break down, to throw down, to destroy, and to afflict, so I will watch over them to build and to plant, says the LORD. ²⁹In those days they shall say no more:

'The fathers have eaten sour grapes,
And the children's teeth are set on edge.'

³⁰But every one shall die for his own iniquity; every man who eats the sour grapes, his teeth shall be set on edge. ³¹"Behold, the days are coming, says the LORD, when I will make a new covenant with the house of Israel and with the house of Judah— ³²not according to the covenant that I made with their fathers in the day *that* I took them by the hand to lead them out of the land of Egypt, My covenant which they broke, though I was a husband to them, says the LORD. ³³But this *is* the covenant that I will make with the house of Israel after those days, says the LORD: I will put My law in their minds, and write it on their hearts; and I will be their God, and they shall be My people. ³⁴No more shall every man teach his neighbor, and every man his brother, saying, 'Know the LORD,' for they all shall know Me, from the least of them to the greatest of them, says the LORD. For I will forgive their iniquity, and their sin I will remember no more."

³⁵ Thus says the LORD,
Who gives the sun for a light by day,
The ordinances of the moon and the stars for a light
by night,
Who disturbs the sea,
And its waves roar
(The LORD of hosts *is* His name):

³⁶ "If those ordinances depart
From before Me, says the LORD,
Then the seed of Israel shall also cease
From being a nation before Me forever."

³⁷Thus says the LORD:

"If heaven above can be measured,
And the foundations of the earth searched out
beneath,

31:33 The old covenant, broken by the people, would be replaced new covenant. The foundation of this new covenant is Christ (Hebre 8:6). It is revolutionary, involving not only Israel and Judah, but als Gentiles. It offers a unique personal relationship with God himself, w his laws inscribed on heart instead of on stone. Jeremiah looked for to the day when Jesus would come to establish this covenant. For us today, this covenant is here. We have the wonderful opportunity to a fresh start and establish a permanent, personal relationship with G

I will also cast off all the seed of Israel
For all that they have done, says the LORD.

³⁸"Behold, the days are coming, says the LORD, that the city shall be built for the LORD from the Tower of Hananel to the Corner Gate. ³⁹The surveyor's line shall again extend straight forward over the hill Gareb; then it shall turn toward Goath. ⁴⁰And the whole valley of the dead bodies and of the ashes, and all the fields as far as the Brook Kidron, to the corner of the Horse Gate toward the east, *shall be* holy to the LORD. It shall not be plucked up or thrown down anymore forever."

CHAPTER 32 JEREMIAH BUYS A FIELD. The word that came to Jeremiah from the LORD in the tenth year of Zedekiah king of Judah, which was the eighteenth year of Nebuchadnezzar. ²For then the king of Babylon's army besieged Jerusalem, and Jeremiah the prophet was shut up in the court of the prison, which *was in* the king of Judah's house. ³For Zedekiah king of Judah had shut him up, saying, "Why do you prophesy and say, 'Thus says the LORD: "Behold, I will give this city into the hand of the king of Babylon, and he shall take it; ⁴and Zedekiah king of Judah shall not escape from the hand of the Chaldeans, but shall surely be delivered into the hand of the king of Babylon, and shall speak with him face to face, and see him eye to eye; ⁵then he shall lead Zedekiah to Babylon, and there he shall be until I visit him," says the LORD; "though you fight with the Chaldeans, you shall not succeed" '?"

⁶And Jeremiah said, "The word of the LORD came to me, saying, ⁷'Behold, Hanamel the son of Shallum your uncle will come to you, saying, "Buy my field which *is* in Anathoth, for the right of redemption *is* yours to buy *it.*" ' ⁸Then Hanamel my uncle's son came to me in the court of the prison according to the word of the LORD, and said to me, 'Please buy my field that *is* in Anathoth, which *is* in the country of Benjamin; for the right of inheritance *is* yours, and the redemption yours; buy *it* for yourself.' Then I knew that this was the word of the LORD. ⁹So I

32:6-12 Trust doesn't come easy. It wasn't easy for Jeremiah to publicly buy land already captured by the enemy. But he trusted Go wasn't easy for David to think that he would become king, even afte was anointed. But he trusted God (1 Samuel 16–31). It wasn't easy Moses to believe that he and his people would escape Egypt, even a God spoke to him from a burning bush. But he trusted God (Exodus 3:1–4:20). It isn't easy for us to believe that God can transform our when we see the mess we've made. But we must trust God. He who worked in the lives of biblical heroes is the same God who offers to in our life, if we will let him.

bought the field from Hanamel, the son of my uncle who *was* in Anathoth, and weighed *out to* him the money—seventeen shekels of silver. ¹⁰And I signed the deed and sealed *it*, took witnesses, and weighed the money on the scales. ¹¹So I took the purchase deed, *both* that which was sealed *according* to the law and custom, and that which was open; ¹²and I gave the purchase deed to Baruch the son of Neriah, son of Mahseiah, in the presence of Hanamel my uncle's *son*, and in the presence of the witnesses who signed the purchase deed, before all the Jews who sat in the court of the prison.

¹³"Then I charged Baruch before them, saying, ¹⁴"Thus says the LORD of hosts, the God of Israel: "Take these deeds, both this purchase deed which is sealed and this deed which is open, and put them in an earthen vessel, that they may last many days." ¹⁵For thus says the LORD of hosts, the God of Israel: "Houses and fields and vineyards shall be possessed again in this land." '

¹⁶"Now when I had delivered the purchase deed to Baruch the son of Neriah, I prayed to the LORD, saying: ¹⁷'Ah, Lord GOD! Behold, You have made the heavens and the earth by Your great power and outstretched arm. There is nothing too hard for You. ¹⁸*You* show lovingkindness to thousands, and repay the iniquity of the fathers into the bosom of their children after them—the Great, the Mighty God, whose name *is* the LORD of hosts. ¹⁹*You are* great in counsel and mighty in work, for your eyes *are* open to all the ways of the sons of men, to give everyone according to his ways and according to the fruit of his doings. ²⁰You have set signs and wonders in the land of Egypt, to this day, and in Israel and among *other* men; and You have made Yourself a name, as it is this day. ²¹You have brought Your people Israel out of the land of Egypt with signs and wonders, with a strong hand and an outstretched arm, and with great terror; ²²You have given them this land, of which You swore to their fathers to give them—"a land flowing with milk and honey." ²³And they came in and took possession of it, but they have not obeyed Your voice or walked in Your law. They have done nothing of all that You commanded them to do; therefore You have caused all this calamity to come upon them.

²⁴'Look, the siege mounds! They have come to the city to take it; and the city has been given into the hand of the Chaldeans who fight against it, because of the sword and famine and pestilence. What You have spoken has happened; there You see *it!* ²⁵And You have said to me, O Lord GOD, "Buy the field for money, and take witnesses"!—yet the city has been given into the hand of the Chaldeans.' "

²⁶Then the word of the LORD came to Jeremiah, saying, ²⁷"Behold, I *am* the LORD, the God of all flesh. Is there anything too hard for Me? ²⁸Therefore thus says the LORD: 'Behold, I will give this city into the hand of the Chaldeans, into the hand of Nebuchadnezzar king of Babylon, and he shall take it. ²⁹And the Chaldeans who fight against this city shall come and set fire to this city and burn it, with the houses on whose roofs they have offered incense to Baal and poured out drink offerings to other gods, to provoke Me to anger; ³⁰because the children of Israel and the children of Judah have done only evil before Me from their youth. For the children of Israel have provoked Me only to anger with the work of their hands,'

says the LORD. ³¹'For this city has been to Me *a provocation of* My anger and My fury from the day that they built it, even to this day; so I will remove it from before My face ³²because of all the evil of the children of Israel and the children of Judah, which they have done to provoke Me to anger—they, their kings, their princes, their priests, their prophets, the men of Judah, and the inhabitants of Jerusalem. ³³And they have turned to Me the back, and not the face; though I taught them, rising up early and teaching *them*, yet they have not listened to receive instruction. ³⁴But they set their abominations in the house which is called by My name, to defile it. ³⁵And they built the high places of Baal which *are* in the Valley of the Son of Hinnom, to cause their sons and their daughters to pass through *the fire* to Molech, which I did not command them, nor did it come into My mind that they should do this abomination, to cause Judah to sin.'

³⁶"Now therefore, thus says the LORD, the God of Israel, concerning this city of which you say, 'It shall be delivered into the hand of the king of Babylon by the sword, by the famine, and by the pestilence: ³⁷Behold, I will gather them out of all countries where I have driven them in My anger, in My fury, and in great wrath; I will bring them back to this place, and I will cause them to dwell safely. ³⁸They shall be My people, and I will be their God; ³⁹then I will give them one heart and one way, that they may fear Me forever, for the good of them and their children after them. ⁴⁰And I will make an everlasting covenant with them, that I will not turn away from doing them good; but I will put My fear in their hearts so that they will not depart from Me. ⁴¹Yes, I will rejoice over them to do them good, and I will assuredly plant them in this land, with all My heart and with all My soul.'

⁴²"For thus says the LORD: 'Just as I have brought all this great calamity on this people, so I will bring on them all the good that I have promised them. ⁴³And fields will be bought in this land of which you say, "*It is* desolate, without man or beast; it has been given into the hand of the Chaldeans." ⁴⁴Men will buy fields for money, sign deeds and seal *them*, and take witnesses, in the land of Benjamin, in the places around Jerusalem, in the cities of Judah, in the cities of the mountains, in the cities of the lowland, and in the cities of the South; for I will cause their captives to return,' says the LORD."

CHAPTER **33** A WONDERFUL PROMISE.

Moreover the word of the LORD came to Jeremiah a second time, while he was still shut up in the court of the prison, saying, ²"Thus says the LORD who made it, the LORD who formed it to establish it (the LORD *is* His name): ³'Call to Me, and I will answer you, and show you great and mighty things, which you do not know.'

⁴"For thus says the LORD, the God of Israel, concerning the houses of this city and the houses of the kings of Judah, which have been pulled down *to fortify* against the siege mounds and the sword: ⁵'They come to fight with the Chaldeans, but *only* to fill their places with the dead bodies of men whom I will slay in My anger and My fury, all for whose wickedness I have hidden My face from this city. ⁶Behold, I will bring it health and healing;

I will heal them and reveal to them the abundance of peace and truth. ⁷And I will cause the captives of Judah and the captives of Israel to return, and will rebuild those places as at the first. ⁸I will cleanse them from all their iniquity by which they have sinned against Me, and I will pardon all their iniquities by which they have sinned and by which they have transgressed against Me. ⁹Then it shall be to Me a name of joy, a praise, and an honor before all nations of the earth, who shall hear all the good that I do to them; they shall fear and tremble for all the goodness and all the prosperity that I provide for it.'

¹⁰"Thus says the LORD: 'Again there shall be heard in this place—of which you say, "It *is* desolate, without man and without beast"—in the cities of Judah, in the streets of Jerusalem that are desolate, without man and without inhabitant and without beast, ¹¹the voice of joy and the voice of gladness, the voice of the bridegroom and the voice of the bride, the voice of those who will say:

"Praise the LORD of hosts,
For the LORD *is* good,
For His mercy *endures* forever"—

and of those *who will* bring the sacrifice of praise into the house of the LORD. For I will cause the captives of the land to return as at the first,' says the LORD.

¹²"Thus says the LORD of hosts: 'In this place which is desolate, without man and without beast, and in all its cities, there shall again be a dwelling place of shepherds causing *their* flocks to lie down. ¹³In the cities of the mountains, in the cities of the lowland, in the cities of the South, in the land of Benjamin, in the places around Jerusalem, and in the cities of Judah, the flocks shall again pass under the hands of him who counts *them*,' says the LORD.

¹⁴'Behold, the days are coming,' says the LORD, 'that I will perform that good thing which I have promised to the house of Israel and to the house of Judah:

¹⁵ 'In those days and at that time
I will cause to grow up to David
A Branch of righteousness;
He shall execute judgment and righteousness in the earth.
¹⁶ In those days Judah will be saved,
And Jerusalem will dwell safely.
And this *is the name* by which she will be called:

THE LORD OUR RIGHTEOUSNESS.'

¹⁷"For thus says the LORD: 'David shall never lack a man to sit on the throne of the house of Israel; ¹⁸nor shall the priests, the Levites, lack a man to offer burnt offerings before Me, to kindle grain offerings, and to sacrifice continually.'"

¹⁹And the word of the LORD came to Jeremiah, saying, ²⁰"Thus says the LORD: 'If you can break My covenant with the day and My covenant with the night, so that there will not be day and night in their season, ²¹then My covenant may also be broken with David My servant, so that he shall not have a son to reign on his throne, and with the Levites, the priests, My ministers. ²²As the host of heaven cannot be numbered, nor the sand of the sea measured,

so will I multiply the descendants of David My servant and the Levites who minister to Me.'"

²³Moreover the word of the LORD came to Jeremiah, saying, ²⁴"Have you not considered what these people have spoken, saying, 'The two families which the LORD has chosen, He has also cast them off'? Thus they have despised My people, as if they should no more be a nation before them.

²⁵"Thus says the LORD: 'If My covenant *is* not with day and night, *and if* I have not appointed the ordinances of heaven and earth, ²⁶then I will cast away the descendants of Jacob and David My servant, *so* that I will not take *any* of his descendants *to be* rulers over the descendants of Abraham, Isaac, and Jacob. For I will cause their captives to return, and will have mercy on them.'"

CHAPTER **34** KING ZEDEKIAH WILL BE CAPTURED.

The word which came to Jeremiah from the LORD, when Nebuchadnezzar king of Babylon and all his army, all the kingdoms of the earth under his dominion, and all the people, fought against Jerusalem and all its cities, saying, ²"Thus says the LORD, the God of Israel: 'Go and speak to Zedekiah king of Judah and tell him, "Thus says the LORD: 'Behold, I will give this city into the hand of the king of Babylon, and he shall burn it with fire. ³And you shall not escape from his hand, but shall surely be taken and delivered into his hand; your eyes shall see the eyes of the king of Babylon, he shall speak with you face to face, and you shall go to Babylon.'"' ⁴Yet hear the word of the LORD, O Zedekiah king of Judah! Thus says the LORD concerning you: 'You shall not die by the sword. ⁵You shall die in peace; as in the ceremonies of your fathers, the former kings who were before you, so they shall burn incense for you and lament for you, *saying*, "Alas, lord!" For I have pronounced the word, says the LORD.'"

⁶Then Jeremiah the prophet spoke all these words to Zedekiah king of Judah in Jerusalem, ⁷when the king of Babylon's army fought against Jerusalem and all the cities of Judah that were left, against Lachish and Azekah; for *only* these fortified cities remained of the cities of Judah.

⁸*This is* the word that came to Jeremiah from the LORD, after King Zedekiah had made a covenant with all the people who *were* at Jerusalem to proclaim liberty to them: ⁹that every man should set free his male and female slave—a Hebrew man or woman—that no one should keep a Jewish brother in bondage. ¹⁰Now when all the princes and all the people, who had entered into the covenant, heard that everyone should set free his male and female slaves, that no one should keep them in bondage anymore, they obeyed and let *them* go. ¹¹But afterward they changed their minds and made the male and female slaves return, whom they had set free, and brought them into subjection as male and female slaves.

¹²Therefore the word of the LORD came to Jeremiah from the LORD, saying, ¹³"Thus says the LORD, the God of Israel: 'I made a covenant with your fathers in the day that I brought them out of the land of Egypt, out of the house of bondage, saying, ¹⁴"At the end of seven years let every man set free his Hebrew brother, who has been sold to him; and when he has served you six years, you shall let him go free from you." But your fathers did not obey Me nor incline their ear. ¹⁵Then you recently turned and did what was right in My sight—every man proclaiming liberty to his neighbor; and you made a covenant before Me in the house which is called by My name. ¹⁶Then you turned around and profaned My name, and every one of you brought back his male and female slaves, whom he had set at liberty, at their pleasure, and brought them back into subjection, to be your male and female slaves.'

¹⁷"Therefore thus says the LORD: 'You have not obeyed Me in proclaiming liberty, every one to his brother and every one to his neighbor. Behold, I proclaim liberty to you,' says the LORD—'to the sword, to pestilence, and to famine! And I will deliver you to trouble among all the kingdoms of the earth. ¹⁸And I will give the men who have transgressed My covenant, who have not performed the words of the covenant which they made before Me, when they cut the calf in two and passed between the parts of it— ¹⁹the princes of Judah, the princes of Jerusalem, the eunuchs, the priests, and all the people of the land who passed between the parts of the calf— ²⁰I will give them into the hand of their enemies and into the hand of those who seek their life. Their dead bodies shall be for meat for the birds of the heaven and the beasts of the earth. ²¹And I will give Zedekiah king of Judah and his princes into the hand of their enemies, into the hand of those who seek their life, and into the hand of the king of Babylon's army which has gone back from you. ²²Behold, I will command,' says the LORD, 'and cause them to return to this city. They will fight against it and take it and burn it with fire; and I will make the cities of Judah a desolation without inhabitant.'"

CHAPTER **35** SOME OBEY, SOME DISOBEY. The word which came to Jeremiah from the LORD in the days of Jehoiakim the son of Josiah, king of Judah, saying, ²"Go to the house of the Rechabites, speak to them, and bring them into the house of the LORD, into one of the chambers, and give them wine to drink."

³Then I took Jaazaniah the son of Jeremiah, the son of Habazziniah, his brothers and all his sons, and the whole house of the Rechabites, ⁴and I brought them into the house of the LORD, into the chamber of the sons of Hanan the son of Igdaliah, a man of God, which *was* by the chamber of the princes, above the chamber of Maaseiah the son of Shallum, the keeper of the door. ⁵Then I set before the sons of the house of the Rechabites bowls full of wine, and cups; and I said to them, "Drink wine."

⁶But they said, "We will drink no wine, for Jonadab the son of Rechab, our father, commanded us, saying, 'You shall drink no wine, you nor your sons, forever. ⁷You shall not build a house, sow seed, plant a vineyard, nor have *any of these;* but all your days you shall dwell in tents, that

you may live many days in the land where you are sojourners.' ⁸Thus we have obeyed the voice of Jonadab the son of Rechab, our father, in all that he charged us, to drink no wine all our days, we, our wives, our sons, or our daughters, ⁹nor to build ourselves houses to dwell in; nor do we have vineyard, field, or seed. ¹⁰But we have dwelt in tents, and have obeyed and done according to all that Jonadab our father commanded us. ¹¹But it came to pass, when Nebuchadnezzar king of Babylon came up into the land, that we said, 'Come, let us go to Jerusalem for fear of the army of the Chaldeans and for fear of the army of the Syrians.' So we dwell at Jerusalem."

PROMISES

34:15-16 The people of Israel had a hard time keeping their promises to God. In the temple, they would solemnly promise to obey God, but back in their homes and at work they wouldn't do it. God expressed his great displeasure. If you want to please God, make sure you keep your promises. God wants promises lived out, not just piously made.

¹²Then came the word of the LORD to Jeremiah, saying, ¹³"Thus says the LORD of hosts, the God of Israel: 'Go and tell the men of Judah and the inhabitants of Jerusalem, "Will you not receive instruction to obey My words?" says the LORD. ¹⁴"The words of Jonadab the son of Rechab, which he commanded his sons, not to drink wine, are performed; for to this day they drink none, and obey their father's commandment. But although I have spoken to you, rising early and speaking, you did not obey Me. ¹⁵I have also sent to you all My servants the prophets, rising up early and sending *them,* saying, 'Turn now everyone from his evil way, amend your doings, and do not go after other gods to serve them; then you will dwell in the land which I have given you and your fathers.' But you have not inclined your ear, nor obeyed Me. ¹⁶Surely the sons of Jonadab the son of Rechab have performed the commandment of their father, which he commanded them, but this people has not obeyed Me." '

¹⁷"Therefore thus says the LORD God of hosts, the God of Israel: 'Behold, I will bring on Judah and on all the inhabitants of Jerusalem all the doom that I have pronounced against them; because I have spoken to them but they have not heard, and I have called to them but they have not answered.'"

¹⁸And Jeremiah said to the house of the Rechabites, "Thus says the LORD of hosts, the God of Israel: 'Because you have obeyed the commandment of Jonadab your father, and kept all his precepts and done according to all

WHY OBEY?

35:13-17 Consider the contrast between the Rechabites and the other Israelites: (1) The Rechabites kept their vows to a fallible human leader; Israel broke their covenant with their infallible divine Leader.
(2) Jonadab told his family once not to drink and they didn't; God continually commanded Israel to turn from sin and they refused. (3) The Rechabites obeyed laws dealing with temporal issues; Israel disobeyed God's laws dealing with eternal issues. (4) The Rechabites would be rewarded; Israel would be punished. Often we observe customs because they are tradition. Shouldn't we be even more willing to obey God's Word because it is eternal?

that he commanded you, [19]therefore thus says the LORD of hosts, the God of Israel: "Jonadab the son of Rechab shall not lack a man to stand before Me forever." ' "

CHAPTER 36   JEREMIAH'S SCROLL BURNED.

Now it came to pass in the fourth year of Jehoiakim the son of Josiah, king of Judah, *that* this word came to Jeremiah from the LORD, saying: [2]"Take a scroll of a book and write on it all the words that I have spoken to you against Israel, against Judah, and against all the nations, from the day I spoke to you, from the days of Josiah even to this day. [3]It may be that the house of Judah will hear all the adversities which I purpose to bring upon them, that everyone may turn from his evil way, that I may forgive their iniquity and their sin."

[4]Then Jeremiah called Baruch the son of Neriah; and Baruch wrote on a scroll of a book, at the instruction of Jeremiah, all the words of the LORD which He had spoken to him. [5]And Jeremiah commanded Baruch, saying, "I *am* confined, I cannot go into the house of the LORD. [6]You go, therefore, and read from the scroll which you have written at my instruction, the words of the LORD, in the hearing of the people in the LORD's house on the day of fasting. And you shall also read them in the hearing of all Judah who come from their cities. [7]It may be that they will present their supplication before the LORD, and everyone will turn from his evil way. For great *is* the anger and the fury that the LORD has pronounced against this people." [8]And Baruch the son of Neriah did according to all that Jeremiah the prophet commanded him, reading from the book the words of the LORD in the LORD's house.

[9]Now it came to pass in the fifth year of Jehoiakim the son of Josiah, king of Judah, in the ninth month, *that* they proclaimed a fast before the LORD to all the people in Jerusalem, and to all the people who came from the cities of Judah to Jerusalem. [10]Then Baruch read from the book the words of Jeremiah in the house of the LORD, in the chamber of Gemariah the son of Shaphan the scribe, in the upper court at the entry of the New Gate of the LORD's house, in the hearing of all the people.

[11]When Michaiah the son of Gemariah, the son of Shaphan, heard all the words of the LORD from the book, [12]he then went down to the king's house, into the scribe's chamber; and there all the princes were sitting—Elishama the scribe, Delaiah the son of Shemaiah, Elnathan the son of Achbor, Gemariah the son of Shaphan, Zedekiah the son of Hananiah, and all the princes. [13]Then Michaiah declared to them all the words that he had heard when Baruch read the book in the hearing of the people. [14]Therefore all the princes sent Jehudi the son of Nethaniah, the son of Shelemiah, the son of Cushi, to Baruch, saying, "Take in your hand the scroll from which you have read in the hearing of the people, and come." So Baruch the son of Neriah took the scroll in his hand and came to them. [15]And they said to him, "Sit down now, and read it in our hearing." So Baruch read *it* in their hearing.

[16]Now it happened, when they had heard all the words, that they looked in fear from one to another, and said to Baruch, "We will surely tell the king of all these words."

CONCENTRATE

36:9 Days of fasting often were called at times of national emer[gency.] At such times, the people abstained from eating food and concentr[ated] their energies on showing their humility and repentance. When fac[ed] with a spiritual emergency or emotional upheaval, don't let yourse[lf] entangled or caught up in the situation. Instead, try drawing away [from] distractions and concentrating on God. Seek his guidance and, if necessary, his forgiveness.

[17]And they asked Baruch, saying, "Tell us now, how did you write all these words—at his instruction?"

[18]So Baruch answered them, "He proclaimed with his mouth all these words to me, and I wrote *them* with ink in the book."

[19]Then the princes said to Baruch, "Go and hide, you and Jeremiah; and let no one know where you are."

[20]And they went to the king, into the court; but they stored the scroll in the chamber of Elishama the scribe, and told all the words in the hearing of the king. [21]So the king sent Jehudi to bring the scroll, and he took it from Elishama the scribe's chamber. And Jehudi read it in the hearing of the king and in the hearing of all the princes who stood beside the king. [22]Now the king was sitting in the winter house in the ninth month, with *a fire* burning on the hearth before him. [23]And it happened, when Jehudi had read three or four columns, *that the king* cut it with the scribe's knife and cast *it* into the fire that *was* on the hearth, until all the scroll was consumed in the fire that *was* on the hearth. [24]Yet they were not afraid, nor did they tear their garments, the king nor any of his servants who heard all these words. [25]Nevertheless Elnathan, Delaiah, and Gemariah implored the king not to burn the scroll; but he would not listen to them. [26]And the king commanded Jerahmeel the king's son, Seraiah the son of Azriel, and Shelemiah the son of Abdeel, to seize Baruch the scribe and Jeremiah the prophet, but the LORD hid them.

[27]Now after the king had burned the scroll with the words which Baruch had written at the instruction of Jeremiah, the word of the LORD came to Jeremiah, saying: [28]"Take yet another scroll, and write on it all the former words that were in the first scroll which Jehoiakim the king of Judah has burned. [29]And you shall say to Jehoiakim king of Judah, 'Thus says the LORD: "You have burned this scroll, saying, 'Why have you written in it that the king of Babylon will certainly come and destroy this land, and cause man and beast to cease from here?' " [30]Therefore thus says the LORD concerning Jehoiakim king of Judah: "He shall have no one to sit on the throne of David, and his dead body shall be cast out to the heat of the day and the frost of the night. [31]I will punish him, his

GOD'S WORD

36:27-32 God told Jeremiah to write his words on a scroll. Bec[ause he] was not allowed to go to the temple, Jeremiah asked his scribe, B[aruch,] to whom he had dictated the message, to read the scroll to the pe[ople] gathered there. Baruch then read it to the officials, and finally Jeh[udi] read it to the king himself. Although the king burned the scroll, h[e could] not destroy God's Word. Today many people try to put God's Word [down] or say that it contains errors and cannot be trusted. People may re[ject] God's Word, but they cannot destroy it. God's Word will stand fore[ver] (Psalm 119:89).

family, and his servants for their iniquity; and I will bring on them, on the inhabitants of Jerusalem, and on the men of Judah all the doom that I have pronounced against them; but they did not heed."'"

³²Then Jeremiah took another scroll and gave it to Baruch the scribe, the son of Neriah, who wrote on it at the instruction of Jeremiah all the words of the book which Jehoiakim king of Judah had burned in the fire. And besides, there were added to them many similar words.

CHAPTER 37 EBED-MELECH RESCUES JEREMIAH.

Now King Zedekiah the son of Josiah reigned instead of Coniah the son of Jehoiakim, whom Nebuchadnezzar king of Babylon made king in the land of Judah. ²But neither he nor his servants nor the people of the land gave heed to the words of the LORD which He spoke by the prophet Jeremiah.

³And Zedekiah the king sent Jehucal the son of Shelemiah, and Zephaniah the son of Maaseiah, the priest, to the prophet Jeremiah, saying, "Pray now to the LORD our God for us." ⁴Now Jeremiah was coming and going among the people, for they had not *yet* put him in prison. ⁵Then Pharaoh's army came up from Egypt; and when the Chaldeans who were besieging Jerusalem heard news of them, they departed from Jerusalem.

⁶Then the word of the LORD came to the prophet Jeremiah, saying, ⁷"Thus says the LORD, the God of Israel, 'Thus you shall say to the king of Judah, who sent you to Me to inquire of Me: "Behold, Pharaoh's army which has come up to help you will return to Egypt, to their own land. ⁸And the Chaldeans shall come back and fight against this city, and take it and burn it with fire." ' ⁹Thus says the LORD: 'Do not deceive yourselves, saying, "The Chaldeans will surely depart from us," for they will not depart. ¹⁰For though you had defeated the whole army of the Chaldeans who fight against you, and there remained *only* wounded men among them, they would rise up, every man in his tent, and burn the city with fire.'"

¹¹And it happened, when the army of the Chaldeans left *the siege* of Jerusalem for fear of Pharaoh's army, ¹²that Jeremiah went out of Jerusalem to go into the land of Benjamin to claim his property there among the people. ¹³And when he was in the Gate of Benjamin, a captain of the guard *was* there whose name *was* Irijah the son of Shelemiah, the son of Hananiah; and he seized Jeremiah the prophet, saying, "You are defecting to the Chaldeans!"

¹⁴Then Jeremiah said, "False! I am not defecting to the Chaldeans." But he did not listen to him.

So Irijah seized Jeremiah and brought him to the princes. ¹⁵Therefore the princes were angry with Jeremiah, and they struck him and put him in prison in the house of Jonathan the scribe. For they had made that the prison.

¹⁶When Jeremiah entered the dungeon and the cells, and Jeremiah had remained there many days, ¹⁷then Zedekiah the king sent and took him *out*. The king asked him secretly in his house, and said, "Is there *any* word from the LORD?"

And Jeremiah said, "There is." Then he said, "You shall be delivered into the hand of the king of Babylon!"

¹⁸Moreover Jeremiah said to King Zedekiah, "What offense have I committed against you, against your servants, or against this people, that you have put me in prison? ¹⁹Where now *are* your prophets who prophesied to you, saying, 'The king of Babylon will not come against you or against this land?' ²⁰Therefore please hear now, O my lord the king. Please, let my petition be accepted before you, and do not make me return to the house of Jonathan the scribe, lest I die there."

²¹Then Zedekiah the king commanded that they should commit Jeremiah to the court of the prison, and that they should give him daily a piece of bread from the bakers' street, until all the bread in the city was gone. Thus Jeremiah remained in the court of the prison.

CHAPTER 38 Now Shephatiah the son of Mattan,

Gedaliah the son of Pashhur, Jucal the son of Shelemiah, and Pashhur the son of Malchiah heard the words that Jeremiah had spoken to all the people, saying, ²"Thus says the LORD: 'He who remains in this city shall die by the sword, by famine, and by pestilence; but he who goes over to the Chaldeans shall live; his life shall be as a prize to him, and he shall live.' ³Thus says the LORD: 'This city shall surely be given into the hand of the king of Babylon's army, which shall take it.'"

▶ REWARDS

38:6 Judah's leaders persecuted Jeremiah repeatedly for faithfully proclaiming God's messages. For 40 years of faithful ministry, he received no acclaim, no love, no popular following. He was beaten, jailed, threatened, and even forced to leave his homeland. Only the heathen Babylonians showed him any respect. God does not guarantee that even his faithful servants will escape persecution. But he does promise that he will be with them and will give them strength to endure (2 Corinthians 1:3-7). As you minister to others, recognize that your service is for God and not just for human approval. God's rewards often don't come in this life.

⁴Therefore the princes said to the king, "Please, let this man be put to death, for thus he weakens the hands of the men of war who remain in this city, and the hands of all the people, by speaking such words to them. For this man does not seek the welfare of this people, but their harm."

⁵Then Zedekiah the king said, "Look, he *is* in your hand. For the king can *do* nothing against you." ⁶So they took Jeremiah and cast him into the dungeon of Malchiah the king's son, which *was* in the court of the prison, and they let Jeremiah down with ropes. And in the dungeon *there was* no water, but mire. So Jeremiah sank in the mire.

⁷Now Ebed-Melech the Ethiopian, one of the eunuchs, who was in the king's house, heard that they had put Jeremiah in the dungeon. When the king was sitting at the Gate of Benjamin, ⁸Ebed-Melech went out of the king's house and spoke to the king, saying: ⁹"My lord the king, these men have done evil in all that they have done

to Jeremiah the prophet, whom they have cast into the dungeon, and he is likely to die from hunger in the place where he is. For *there is* no more bread in the city." [10]Then the king commanded Ebed-Melech the Ethiopian, saying, "Take from here thirty men with you, and lift Jeremiah the prophet out of the dungeon before he dies." [11]So Ebed-Melech took the men with him and went into the house of the king under the treasury, and took from there old clothes and old rags, and let them down by ropes into the dungeon to Jeremiah. [12]Then Ebed-Melech the Ethiopian said to Jeremiah, "Please put these old clothes and rags under your armpits, under the ropes." And Jeremiah did so. [13]So they pulled Jeremiah up with ropes and lifted him out of the dungeon. And Jeremiah remained in the court of the prison.

[14]Then Zedekiah the king sent and had Jeremiah the prophet brought to him at the third entrance of the house of the LORD. And the king said to Jeremiah, "I will ask you something. Hide nothing from me."

[15]Jeremiah said to Zedekiah, "If I declare *it* to you, will you not surely put me to death? And if I give you advice, you will not listen to me."

[16]So Zedekiah the king swore secretly to Jeremiah, saying, "*As* the LORD lives, who made our very souls, I will not put you to death, nor will I give you into the hand of these men who seek your life."

[17]Then Jeremiah said to Zedekiah, "Thus says the LORD, the God of hosts, the God of Israel: 'If you surely surrender to the king of Babylon's princes, then your soul shall live; this city shall not be burned with fire, and you and your house shall live. [18]But if you do not surrender to the king of Babylon's princes, then this city shall be given into the hand of the Chaldeans; they shall burn it with fire, and you shall not escape from their hand.'"

[19]And Zedekiah the king said to Jeremiah, "I am afraid of the Jews who have defected to the Chaldeans, lest they deliver me into their hand, and they abuse me."

[20]But Jeremiah said, "They shall not deliver *you.* Please, obey the voice of the LORD which I speak to you. So it shall be well with you, and your soul shall live. [21]But if you refuse to surrender, this *is* the word that the LORD has shown me: [22]Now behold, all the women who are left in the king of Judah's house *shall be* surrendered to the king of Babylon's princes, and those *women* shall say:

"Your close friends have set upon you
And prevailed against you;
Your feet have sunk in the mire,
And they have turned away again.'

[23]'So they shall surrender all your wives and children to the Chaldeans. You shall not escape from their hand, but shall be taken by the hand of the king of Babylon. And you shall cause this city to be burned with fire.'"

[24]Then Zedekiah said to Jeremiah, "Let no one know of these words, and you shall not die. [25]But if the princes hear that I have talked with you, and they come to you and say to you, 'Declare to us now what you have said to the king, and also what the king said to you; do not hide *it* from us, and we will not put you to death,' [26]then you shall say to them, 'I presented my request before the king,

that he would not make me return to Jonathan's house to die there.'"

[27]Then all the princes came to Jeremiah and asked him. And he told them according to all these words that the king had commanded. So they stopped speaking with him, for the conversation had not been heard. [28]Now Jeremiah remained in the court of the prison until the day that Jerusalem was taken. And he was *there* when Jerusalem was taken.

CHAPTER **39** **JERUSALEM IS CAPTURED.** In the ninth year of Zedekiah king of Judah, in the tenth month, Nebuchadnezzar king of Babylon and all his army came against Jerusalem, and besieged it. [2]In the eleventh year of Zedekiah, in the fourth month, on the ninth *day* of the month, the city was penetrated.

[3]Then all the princes of the king of Babylon came in and sat in the Middle Gate: Nergal-Sharezer, Samgar-Nebo, Sarsechim, Rabsaris, Nergal-Sarezer, Rabmag, with the rest of the princes of the king of Babylon.

[4]So it was, when Zedekiah the king of Judah and all the men of war saw them, that they fled and went out of the city by night, by way of the king's garden, by the gate between the two walls. And he went out by way of the plain. [5]But the Chaldean army pursued them and overtook Zedekiah in the plains of Jericho. And when they had captured him, they brought him up to Nebuchadnezzar king of Babylon, to Riblah in the land of Hamath, where he pronounced judgment on him. [6]Then the king of Babylon killed the sons of Zedekiah before his eyes in Riblah; the king of Babylon also killed all the nobles of Judah. [7]Moreover he put out Zedekiah's eyes, and bound him with bronze fetters to carry him off to Babylon. [8]And the Chaldeans burned the king's house and the houses of the people with fire, and broke down the walls of Jerusalem. [9]Then Nebuzaradan the captain of the guard carried away captive to Babylon the remnant of the people who remained in the city and those who defected to him, with the rest of the people who remained. [10]But Nebuzaradan the captain of the guard left in the land of Judah the poor people, who had nothing, and gave them vineyards and fields at the same time.

[11]Now Nebuchadnezzar king of Babylon gave charge concerning Jeremiah to Nebuzaradan the captain of the guard, saying, [12]"Take him and look after him, and do him no harm; but do to him just as he says to you." [13]So Nebuzaradan the captain of the guard sent Nebushasban, Rabsaris, Nergal-Sharezer, Rabmag, and all the king of Babylon's chief officers; [14]then they sent *someone* to take Jeremiah from the court of the prison, and commit-

▰▰▰ **COURAGE**

38:9-13 Ebed-Melech feared God more than man. He alone am the palace officials stood up against the murder plot. His obedienc have cost him his life. Because he obeyed, however, he was sparec Jerusalem fell (39:15-18). You can either go along with the crowd speak up for God. When someone is treated unkindly or unjustly, ▰ example, reach out to that person with God's love. You may be the one who does. And, when you're being treated unkindly yourself, to thank God when he sends an "Ebed-Melech" your way.

ted him to Gedaliah the son of Ahikam, the son of Shaphan, that he should take him home. So he dwelt among the people.

¹⁵Meanwhile the word of the LORD had come to Jeremiah while he was shut up in the court of the prison, saying, ¹⁶"Go and speak to Ebed-Melech the Ethiopian, saying, 'Thus says the LORD of hosts, the God of Israel: "Behold, I will bring My words upon this city for adversity and not for good, and they shall be *performed* in that day before you. ¹⁷But I will deliver you in that day," says the LORD, "and you shall not be given into the hand of the men of whom you *are* afraid. ¹⁸For I will surely deliver you, and you shall not fall by the sword; but your life shall be as a prize to you, because you have put your trust in Me," says the LORD.'"

CHAPTER **40** JEREMIAH IS SET FREE. The word that came to Jeremiah from the LORD after Nebuzaradan the captain of the guard had let him go from Ramah, when he had taken him bound in chains among all who were carried away captive from Jerusalem and Judah, who were carried away captive to Babylon.

²And the captain of the guard took Jeremiah and said to him: "The LORD your God has pronounced this doom on this place. ³Now the LORD has brought *it*, and has done just as He said. Because you *people* have sinned against the LORD, and not obeyed His voice, therefore this thing has come upon you. ⁴And now look, I free you this day from the chains that *were* on your hand. If it seems good to you to come with me to Babylon, come, and I will look after you. But if it seems wrong for you to come with me to Babylon, remain here. See, all the land *is* before you; wherever it seems good and convenient for you to go, go there."

⁵Now while Jeremiah had not yet gone back, *Nebuzaradan said*, "Go back to Gedaliah the son of Ahikam, the son of Shaphan, whom the king of Babylon has made governor over the cities of Judah, and dwell with him among the people. Or go wherever it seems convenient for you to go." So the captain of the guard gave him rations and a gift and let him go. ⁶Then Jeremiah went to Gedaliah the son of Ahikam, to Mizpah, and dwelt with him among the people who were left in the land.

⁷And when all the captains of the armies who *were* in the fields, they and their men, heard that the king of Babylon had made Gedaliah the son of Ahikam governor in the land, and had committed to him men, women, children, and the poorest of the land who had not been carried away captive to Babylon, ⁸then they came to Gedaliah at Mizpah—Ishmael the son of Nethaniah, Johanan and Jonathan the sons of Kareah, Seraiah the son of Tanhumeth, the sons of Ephai the Netophathite, and Jezaniah the son of a Maachathite, they and their men. ⁹And Gedaliah the son of Ahikam, the son of Shaphan, took an oath before them and their men, saying, "Do not be afraid to serve the Chaldeans. Dwell in the land and serve the king of Babylon, and it shall be well with you. ¹⁰As for me, I will indeed dwell at Mizpah and serve the Chaldeans who come to us. But you, gather wine and summer fruit and oil, put *them* in your vessels, and dwell

in your cities that you have taken." ¹¹Likewise, when all the Jews who *were* in Moab, among the Ammonites, in Edom, and who *were* in all the countries, heard that the king of Babylon had left a remnant of Judah, and that he had set over them Gedaliah the son of Ahikam, the son of Shaphan, ¹²then all the Jews returned out of all places where they had been driven, and came to the land of Judah, to Gedaliah at Mizpah, and gathered wine and summer fruit in abundance.

◄■■■A GOOD TURN

39:17-18 Ebed-Melech risked his life to save God's prophet, Jeremiah. When Babylon conquered Jerusalem, God protected Ebed-Melech from the Babylonians. God has special rewards for his faithful people.

¹³Moreover Johanan the son of Kareah and all the captains of the forces that *were* in the fields came to Gedaliah at Mizpah, ¹⁴and said to him, "Do you certainly know that Baalis the king of the Ammonites has sent Ishmael the son of Nethaniah to murder you?" But Gedaliah the son of Ahikam did not believe them.

¹⁵Then Johanan the son of Kareah spoke secretly to Gedaliah in Mizpah, saying, "Let me go, please, and I will kill Ishmael the son of Nethaniah, and no one will know *it.* Why should he murder you, so that all the Jews who are gathered to you would be scattered, and the remnant in Judah perish?"

¹⁶But Gedaliah the son of Ahikam said to Johanan the son of Kareah, "You shall not do this thing, for you speak falsely concerning Ishmael."

CHAPTER **41** THE GOVERNOR DIES. Now it came to pass in the seventh month *that* Ishmael the son of Nethaniah, the son of Elishama, of the royal family and of the officers of the king, came with ten men to Gedaliah the son of Ahikam, at Mizpah. And there they ate bread together in Mizpah. ²Then Ishmael the son of Nethaniah, and the ten men who were with him, arose and struck Gedaliah the son of Ahikam, the son of Shaphan, with the sword, and killed him whom the king of Babylon had made governor over the land. ³Ishmael also struck down all the Jews who were with him, *that is,* with Gedaliah at Mizpah, and the Chaldeans who were found there, the men of war.

⁴And it happened, on the second day after he had killed Gedaliah, when as yet no one knew *it,* ⁵that certain men came from Shechem, from Shiloh, and from Samaria, eighty men with their beards shaved and their clothes torn, having cut themselves, with offerings and incense in their hand, to bring *them* to the house of the LORD. ⁶Now Ishmael the son of Nethaniah went out from Mizpah to meet them, weeping as he went along; and it happened as he met them that he said to them, "Come to

◄■■■KNOW HIM

40:2-3 The Babylonian captain, who did not know God, acknowledged that God had given the Babylonians victory. It is strange when people recognize that God exists and does miracles, but still they do not personally accept him. Knowing God is more than knowing about him. Be sure you know him personally.

41:4-9 The 80 men came from three cities of the northern kingdom to worship in Jerusalem. Ishmael probably killed them for the money and food they were carrying. Without a king, with no law, and no loyalty to God, Judah was subjected to complete anarchy, or lawlessness. We need God's law to keep us from destroying each other.

Gedaliah the son of Ahikam!" [7]So it was, when they came into the midst of the city, that Ishmael the son of Nethaniah killed them *and cast them* into the midst of a pit, he and the men who were with him. [8]But ten men were found among them who said to Ishmael, "Do not kill us, for we have treasures of wheat, barley, oil, and honey in the field." So he desisted and did not kill them among their brethren. [9]Now the pit into which Ishmael had cast all the dead bodies of the men whom he had slain, because of Gedaliah, *was* the same one Asa the king had made for fear of Baasha king of Israel. Ishmael the son of Nethaniah filled it with *the* slain. [10]Then Ishmael carried away captive all the rest of the people who *were* in Mizpah, the king's daughters and all the people who remained in Mizpah, whom Nebuzaradan the captain of the guard had committed to Gedaliah the son of Ahikam. And Ishmael the son of Nethaniah carried them away captive and departed to go over to the Ammonites.

[11]But when Johanan the son of Kareah and all the captains of the forces that *were* with him heard of all the evil that Ishmael the son of Nethaniah had done, [12]they took all the men and went to fight with Ishmael the son of Nethaniah; and they found him by the great pool that *is* in Gibeon. [13]So it was, when all the people who *were* with Ishmael saw Johanan the son of Kareah, and all the captains of the forces who *were* with him, that they were glad. [14]Then all the people whom Ishmael had carried away captive from Mizpah turned around and came back, and went to Johanan the son of Kareah. [15]But Ishmael the son of Nethaniah escaped from Johanan with eight men and went to the Ammonites.

[16]Then Johanan the son of Kareah, and all the captains of the forces that were with him, took from Mizpah all the rest of the people whom he had recovered from Ishmael the son of Nethaniah after he had murdered Gedaliah the son of Ahikam—the mighty men of war and the women and the children and the eunuchs, whom he had brought back from Gibeon. [17]And they departed and dwelt in the habitation of Chimham, which is near Bethlehem, as they went on their way to Egypt, [18]because of the Chaldeans; for they were afraid of them, because Ishmael the son of Nethaniah had murdered Gedaliah the son of Ahikam, whom the king of Babylon had made governor in the land.

CHAPTER 42 DON'T GO TO EGYPT! Now all the captains of the forces, Johanan the son of Kareah, Jezaniah the son of Hoshaiah, and all the people, from the least to the greatest, came near [2]and said to Jeremiah the prophet, "Please, let our petition be acceptable to you, and pray for us to the LORD your God, for all this remnant (since we are left *but* a few of many, as you can see), [3]that the LORD your God may show us the way in which we should walk and the thing we should do."

[4]Then Jeremiah the prophet said to them, "I have heard. Indeed, I will pray to the LORD your God according to your words, and it shall be, *that* whatever the LORD answers you, I will declare *it* to you. I will keep nothing back from you."

[5]So they said to Jeremiah, "Let the LORD be a true and faithful witness between us, if we do not do according to everything which the LORD your God sends us by you. [6]Whether *it is* pleasing or displeasing, we will obey the voice of the LORD our God to whom we send you, that it may be well with us when we obey the voice of the LORD our God."

42:5-6 Johanan and his associates spoke their own curse; Jeremiah merely elaborated on it. It was a tragic mistake to ask for God's guidance with no intention of following it. Be sure never to ask God for something if you know in your heart that you do not want it. It is better not to than to pray deceptively. God cannot be deceived.

[7]And it happened after ten days that the word of the LORD came to Jeremiah. [8]Then he called Johanan the son of Kareah, all the captains of the forces which *were* with him, and all the people from the least even to the greatest, [9]and said to them, "Thus says the LORD, the God of Israel, to whom you sent me to present your petition before Him: [10]'If you will still remain in this land, then I will build you and not pull *you* down, and I will plant you and not pluck *you* up. For I relent concerning the disaster that I have brought upon you. [11]Do not be afraid of the king of Babylon, of whom you are afraid; do not be afraid of him,' says the LORD, 'for I *am* with you, to save you and deliver you from his hand. [12]And I will show you mercy, that he may have mercy on you and cause you to return to your own land.'

[13]"But if you say, 'We will not dwell in this land,' disobeying the voice of the LORD your God, [14]saying, 'No, we will go to the land of Egypt where we shall see no war, nor hear the sound of the trumpet, nor be hungry for bread, and there we will dwell'— [15]Then hear now the word of the LORD, O remnant of Judah! Thus says the LORD of hosts, the God of Israel: 'If you wholly set your faces to enter Egypt, and go to dwell there, [16]then it shall be *that* the sword which you feared shall overtake you there in the land of Egypt; the famine of which you were afraid shall follow close after you there *in* Egypt; and there you shall die. [17]So shall it be with all the men who set their faces to go to Egypt to dwell there. They shall die by the sword, by famine, and by pestilence. And none of them shall remain or escape from the disaster that I will bring upon them.'

[18]"For thus says the LORD of hosts, the God of Israel: 'As My anger and My fury have been poured out on the inhabitants of Jerusalem, so will My fury be poured out on you when you enter Egypt. And you shall be an oath, an astonishment, a curse, and a reproach; and you shall see this place no more.'

[19]"The LORD has said concerning you, O remnant of Judah, 'Do not go to Egypt!' Know certainly that I have admonished you this day. [20]For you were hypocrites in your hearts when you sent me to the LORD your God,

saying, 'Pray for us to the LORD our God, and according to all that the LORD your God says, so declare to us and we will do *it.*' ²¹And I have this day declared *it* to you, but you have not obeyed the voice of the LORD your God, or anything which He has sent you by me. ²²Now therefore, know certainly that you shall die by the sword, by famine, and by pestilence in the place where you desire to go to dwell."

CHAPTER **43** THE PEOPLE WON'T BELIEVE. Now it happened, when Jeremiah had stopped speaking to all the people all the words of the LORD their God, for which the LORD their God had sent him to them, all these words, ²that Azariah the son of Hoshaiah, Johanan the son of Kareah, and all the proud men spoke, saying to Jeremiah, "You speak falsely! The LORD our God has not sent you to say, 'Do not go to Egypt to dwell there.' ³But Baruch the son of Neriah has set you against us, to deliver us into the hand of the Chaldeans, that they may put us to death or carry us away captive to Babylon." ⁴So Johanan the son of Kareah, all the captains of the forces, and all the people would not obey the voice of the LORD, to remain in the land of Judah. ⁵But Johanan the son of Kareah and all the captains of the forces took all the remnant of Judah who had returned to dwell in the land of Judah, from all nations where they had been driven— ⁶men, women, children, the king's daughters, and every person whom Nebuzaradan the captain of the guard had left with Gedaliah the son of Ahikam, the son of Shaphan, and Jeremiah the prophet and Baruch the son of Neriah. ⁷So they went to the land of Egypt, for they did not obey the voice of the LORD. And they went as far as Tahpanhes.

⁸Then the word of the LORD came to Jeremiah in Tahpanhes, saying, ⁹"Take large stones in your hand, and hide them in the sight of the men of Judah, in the clay in the brick courtyard which *is* at the entrance to Pharaoh's house in Tahpanhes; ¹⁰and say to them, 'Thus says the LORD of hosts, the God of Israel: "Behold, I will send and bring Nebuchadnezzar the king of Babylon, My servant, and will set his throne above these stones that I have hidden. And he will spread his royal pavilion over them. ¹¹When he comes, he shall strike the land of Egypt *and* deliver to death *those appointed* for death, and to captivity *those appointed* for captivity, and to the sword *those appointed* for the sword. ¹²I will kindle a fire in the houses of the gods of Egypt, and he shall burn them and carry them away captive. And he shall array himself with the land of Egypt, as a shepherd puts on his garment, and he shall go out from there in peace. ¹³He shall also break the sacred pillars of Beth Shemesh that *are* in the land of Egypt; and the houses of the gods of the Egyptians he shall burn with fire."'"

CHAPTER **44** GOD GETS ANGRY. The word that came to Jeremiah concerning all the Jews who dwell in the land of Egypt, who dwell at Migdol, at Tahpanhes, at Noph, and in the country of Pathros, saying, ²"Thus says the LORD of hosts, the God of Israel: 'You have seen all the calamity that I have brought on Jerusalem and on all the cities of Judah; and behold, this day they *are* a deso-

lation, and no one dwells in them, ³because of their wickedness which they have committed to provoke Me to anger, in that they went to burn incense *and* to serve other gods whom they did not know, they nor you nor your fathers. ⁴However I have sent to you all My servants the prophets, rising early and sending *them,* saying, "Oh, do not do this abominable thing that I hate!" ⁵But they did not listen or incline their ear to turn from their wickedness, to burn no incense to other gods. ⁶So My fury and My anger were poured out and kindled in the cities of Judah and in the streets of Jerusalem; and they are wasted *and* desolate, as it is this day.'

⁷"Now therefore, thus says the LORD, the God of hosts, the God of Israel: 'Why do you commit *this* great evil against yourselves, to cut off from you man and woman, child and infant, out of Judah, leaving none to remain, ⁸in that you provoke Me to wrath with the works of your hands, burning incense to other gods in the land of Egypt where you have gone to dwell, that you may cut yourselves off and be a curse and a reproach among all the nations of the earth? ⁹Have you forgotten the wickedness of your fathers, the wickedness of the kings of Judah, the wickedness of their wives, your own wickedness, and the wickedness of your wives, which they committed in the land of Judah and in the streets of Jerusalem? ¹⁰They have not been humbled, to this day, nor have they feared; they have not walked in My law or in My statutes that I set before you and your fathers.'

▶ **REPEATING**

44:9-10 When we forget a lesson or refuse to learn it, we risk repeating our mistakes. The people of Judah struggled with this same matter; to forget their former sins was to repeat them. To fail to learn from failure is to assure future failure. Your past is your school of experience. Let your past mistakes point you to God's way.

¹¹"Therefore thus says the LORD of hosts, the God of Israel: 'Behold, I will set My face against you for catastrophe and for cutting off all Judah. ¹²And I will take the remnant of Judah who have set their faces to go into the land of Egypt to dwell there, and they shall all be consumed *and* fall in the land of Egypt. They shall be consumed by the sword *and* by famine. They shall die, from the least to the greatest, by the sword and by famine; and they shall be an oath, an astonishment, a curse and a reproach! ¹³For I will punish those who dwell in the land of Egypt, as I have punished Jerusalem, by the sword, by famine, and by pestilence, ¹⁴so that none of the remnant of Judah who have gone into the land of Egypt to dwell there shall escape or survive, lest they return to the land of Judah, to which they desire to return and dwell. For none shall return except those who escape.'"

¹⁵Then all the men who knew that their wives had burned incense to other gods, with all the women who stood by, a great multitude, and all the people who dwelt in the land of Egypt, in Pathros, answered Jeremiah, saying: ¹⁶"*As for* the word that you have spoken to us in the name of the LORD, we will not listen to you! ¹⁷But we will certainly do whatever has gone out of our own mouth, to burn incense to the queen of heaven and pour out drink

offerings to her, as we have done, we and our fathers, our kings and our princes, in the cities of Judah and in the streets of Jerusalem. For *then* we had plenty of food, were well-off, and saw no trouble. [18]But since we stopped burning incense to the queen of heaven and pouring out drink offerings to her, we have lacked everything and have been consumed by the sword and by famine."

▰▰▰▰ ESCAPE

44:14 Only those who repented of going to Egypt and returned to their own land would escape judgment. God wanted both a change of attitude and some action. God always offers a way of escape—even when we get in so deep it doesn't look like there is any way out. And the steps always are the same: (1) admitting we have rebelled against God, (2) forsaking our sinful direction, and (3) seeking to live as God instructs in his Word.

[19]*The women also said,* "And when we burned incense to the queen of heaven and poured out drink offerings to her, did we make cakes for her, to worship her, and pour out drink offerings to her without our husbands' *permission?*"

[20]Then Jeremiah spoke to all the people—the men, the women, and all the people who had given him *that* answer—saying: [21]"The incense that you burned in the cities of Judah and in the streets of Jerusalem, you and your fathers, your kings and your princes, and the people of the land, did not the LORD remember them, and did it *not* come into His mind? [22]So the LORD could no longer bear *it,* because of the evil of your doings *and* because of the abominations which you committed. Therefore your land is a desolation, an astonishment, a curse, and without an inhabitant, as *it is* this day. [23]Because you have burned incense and because you have sinned against the LORD, and have not obeyed the voice of the LORD or walked in His law, in His statutes or in His testimonies, therefore this calamity has happened to you, as *at* this day."

[24]Moreover Jeremiah said to all the people and to all the women, "Hear the word of the LORD, all Judah who *are* in the land of Egypt! [25]Thus says the LORD of hosts, the God of Israel, saying: 'You and your wives have spoken with your mouths and fulfilled with your hands, saying, "We will surely keep our vows that we have made, to burn incense to the queen of heaven and pour out drink offerings to her." You will surely keep your vows and perform your vows!' [26]Therefore hear the word of the LORD, all Judah who dwell in the land of Egypt: 'Behold, I have sworn by My great name,' says the LORD, 'that My name shall no more be named in the mouth of any man of Judah in all the land of Egypt, saying, "The Lord GOD lives." [27]Behold, I will watch over them for adversity and not for good. And all the men of Judah who *are* in the land of Egypt shall be consumed by the sword and by famine, until there is an end to them. [28]Yet a small number who escape the sword shall return from the land of Egypt to the land of Judah; and all the remnant of Judah, who have gone to the land of Egypt to dwell there, shall know whose words will stand, Mine or theirs. [29]And this *shall be* a sign to you,' says the LORD, 'that I will punish you in this place, that you may know that My words will surely stand against you for adversity.'

[30]"Thus says the LORD: 'Behold, I will give Pharaoh Hophra king of Egypt into the hand of his enemies and into the hand of those who seek his life, as I gave Zedekiah king of Judah into the hand of Nebuchadnezzar king of Babylon, his enemy who sought his life.'"

CHAPTER **45** The word that Jeremiah the prophet spoke to Baruch the son of Neriah, when he had written these words in a book at the instruction of Jeremiah, in the fourth year of Jehoiakim the son of Josiah, king of Judah, saying, [2]"Thus says the LORD, the God of Israel, to you, O Baruch: [3]'You said, "Woe is me now! For the LORD has added grief to my sorrow. I fainted in my sighing, and I find no rest." '

[4]"Thus you shall say to him, 'Thus says the LORD: "Behold, what I have built I will break down, and what I have planted I will pluck up, that is, this whole land. [5]And do you seek great things for yourself? Do not seek *them;* for behold, I will bring adversity on all flesh," says the LORD. "But I will give your life to you as a prize in all places, wherever you go." ' "

CHAPTER **46** A MESSAGE TO THE EGYPTIANS. The word of the LORD which came to Jeremiah the prophet against the nations. [2]Against Egypt.

▰▰▰▰ INSIGHTS

46:1 In this chapter, we gain several insights about God and his p[.] this world. (1) Although God chose Israel for a special purpose, he [.] all people and wants them to come to him. (2) God is holy and will [.] tolerate sin. (3) God's judgments are not based on prejudice and a [.] for revenge, but on fairness and justice. (4) God does not delight in [.] judgment, but in salvation. (5) God is impartial—he judges every[.] the same standard.

Concerning the army of Pharaoh Necho, king of Egypt, which was by the River Euphrates in Carchemish, and which Nebuchadnezzar king of Babylon defeated in the fourth year of Jehoiakim the son of Josiah, king of Judah:

[3] "Order the buckler and shield,
And draw near to battle!
[4] Harness the horses,
And mount up, you horsemen!
Stand forth with *your* helmets,
Polish the spears,
Put on the armor!
[5] Why have I seen them dismayed *and* turned back?
Their mighty ones are beaten down;
They have speedily fled,
And did not look back,
For fear *was* all around," says the LORD.
[6] "Do not let the swift flee away,
Nor the mighty man escape;
They will stumble and fall
Toward the north, by the River Euphrates.
[7] "Who *is* this coming up like a flood,

Whose waters move like the rivers?
8 Egypt rises up like a flood,
And *its* waters move like the rivers;
And he says, 'I will go up *and* cover the earth,
I will destroy the city and its inhabitants.'
9 Come up, O horses, and rage, O chariots!
And let the mighty men come forth:
The Ethiopians and the Libyans who handle the
 shield,
And the Lydians who handle *and* bend the bow.
10 For this *is* the day of the Lord GOD of hosts,
A day of vengeance,
That He may avenge Himself on His adversaries.
The sword shall devour;
It shall be satiated and made drunk with their blood;
For the Lord GOD of hosts has a sacrifice
In the north country by the River Euphrates.

11 "Go up to Gilead and take balm,
O virgin, the daughter of Egypt;
In vain you will use many medicines;
You shall not be cured.
12 The nations have heard of your shame,
And your cry has filled the land;
For the mighty man has stumbled against the
 mighty;
They both have fallen together."

13 The word that the LORD spoke to Jeremiah the prophet, how Nebuchadnezzar king of Babylon would come *and* strike the land of Egypt.

14 "Declare in Egypt, and proclaim in Migdol;
Proclaim in Noph and in Tahpanhes;
Say, 'Stand fast and prepare yourselves,
For the sword devours all around you.'
15 Why are your valiant *men* swept away?
They did not stand
Because the LORD drove them away.
16 He made many fall;
Yes, one fell upon another.
And they said, 'Arise!
Let us go back to our own people
And to the land of our nativity
From the oppressing sword.'
17 They cried there,
'Pharaoh, king of Egypt, *is but* a noise.
He has passed by the appointed time!'
18 "*As* I live," says the King,
Whose name *is* the LORD of hosts,
"Surely as Tabor *is* among the mountains
And as Carmel by the sea, *so* he shall come.
19 O you daughter dwelling in Egypt,
Prepare yourself to go into captivity!
For Noph shall be waste and desolate, without
 inhabitant.

20 "Egypt *is* a very pretty heifer,
But destruction comes, it comes from the north.
21 Also her mercenaries are in her midst like fat bulls,
For they also are turned back,
They have fled away together.

They did not stand,
For the day of their calamity had come upon them,
The time of their punishment.
22 Her noise shall go like a serpent,
For they shall march with an army
And come against her with axes,
Like those who chop wood.

23 "They shall cut down her forest," says the LORD,
"Though it cannot be searched,
Because they *are* innumerable,
And more numerous than grasshoppers.
24 The daughter of Egypt shall be ashamed;
She shall be delivered into the hand
Of the people of the north."

25 The LORD of hosts, the God of Israel, says: "Behold, I will bring punishment on Amon of No, and Pharaoh and Egypt, with their gods and their kings—Pharaoh and those who trust in him. 26 And I will deliver them into the hand of those who seek their lives, into the hand of Nebuchadnezzar king of Babylon and the hand of his servants. Afterward it shall be inhabited as in the days of old," says the LORD.

27 "But do not fear, O My servant Jacob,
And do not be dismayed, O Israel!
For behold, I will save you from afar,
And your offspring from the land of their captivity;
Jacob shall return, have rest and be at ease;
No one shall make *him* afraid.
28 Do not fear, O Jacob My servant," says the LORD,
"For I *am* with you;
For I will make a complete end of all the nations
To which I have driven you,
But I will not make a complete end of you.
I will rightly correct you,
For I will not leave you wholly unpunished."

CHAPTER **47** **A MESSAGE TO THE PHILISTINES.**
The word of the LORD that came to Jeremiah the prophet against the Philistines, before Pharaoh attacked Gaza.
2 Thus says the LORD:

"Behold, waters rise out of the north,
And shall be an overflowing flood;
They shall overflow the land and all that is in it,
The city and those who dwell within;
Then the men shall cry,
And all the inhabitants of the land shall wail.
3 At the noise of the stamping hooves of his strong
 horses,
At the rushing of his chariots,
At the rumbling of his wheels,
The fathers will not look back for *their* children,
Lacking courage,
4 Because of the day that comes to plunder all the
 Philistines,
To cut off from Tyre and Sidon every helper who
 remains;
For the LORD shall plunder the Philistines,
The remnant of the country of Caphtor.

SEXUAL ABUSE

Seventeen-year-old Shelly sat on the couch in her youth pastor's office, sobbing quietly. "I've never told anyone this," she choked out. "I feel so dirty. . . . When I was younger, my father made me have sex with him . . . lots of times . . . over several years. He said if I ever told anyone, I'd regret it. He said it was 'our little secret.' Besides, he's an elder in the church—who would believe me?" Unfortunately, this is not an isolated incident. Sexual abuse may be defined as any contact or interaction (visual, verbal, psychological, or physical) between a child or adolescent and an adult when the younger person is being used for the sexual gratification of the older person (or anyone else).* A recent survey indicates that 38 percent of the women in this country have been sexually abused by age 18. The actual percentage may be even higher. The percentage of sexually abused males, though lower, is still shockingly high. Sexual abuse is like some huge, silent tidal wave that has reached unbelievable proportions, threatening to destroy countless lives. Surprisingly enough, victims of sexual abuse don't always know they've been abused. Some victims believe it wasn't abuse because the perpetrator was a family member or a friend, not a total stranger. Others believe they must somehow have invited the offense. With still others, the abuse was more subtle—perhaps an older person introduced the younger person to pornography. Regardless of the relationship or the form the abuse takes, it still is abuse and it is wrong. Common results of sexual abuse include feelings of betrayal, fear, anger, powerlessness, shame, depression, and, later on, difficulty in having healthy relationships, especially with the opposite sex. Having been betrayed so devastatingly, many victims have an overwhelming fear of letting anyone get close enough to hurt them again. They become little more than empty shells who spend their time trying to keep anyone from breaking through their protective front. It is a miserable way to live. So what should a person do who has been, or is now being, sexually abused? First, remember you are not alone. A staggering number of people, male and female, have been sexually abused. Sometimes the violation is obvious, like incest or date rape; sometimes it is more subtle, like lewd comments or "accidentally" walking in on someone in the shower. Regardless of the form of abuse, there are people who understand and can help you. Second, talk to someone about what has happened or about what you are going through. The abuser's greatest weapon over you is your silence. Regardless of what you've been told, you must share your pain with someone else. If possible, talk with your youth pastor, Campus Life or Young Life director, school counselor, or a psychologist or psychiatrist you trust. If that person is unable or unwilling to help, don't give up. Find someone who will listen and understand. There may be a "hotline" or agency in your area designed specifically to help victims of sexual abuse. Third, remember that if you have been sexually abused in any way, it is not your fault. You are not responsible for what happened to you. You are a victim. Do not give feelings that you somehow "asked for it" or brought the abuse on yourself. Seek counsel from someone who can help you understand this and can help you work through your pain. Finally, remember that you are made in the image of God. Sexual abuse is a serious crime against that image, and God will deal with those who inflict such damage on others. But there is great comfort in knowing that the same God who judges sin was once a victim of sin himself. Christ knows, he cares, and he understands.

*This definition is based on one given by Dr. Dan Allender in his excellent book, The Wounded Heart (NavPress, 1990), p. 30.

5 Baldness has come upon Gaza,
Ashkelon is cut off
With the remnant of their valley.
How long will you cut yourself?
6 "O you sword of the LORD,
How long until you are quiet?
Put yourself up into your scabbard,
Rest and be still!
7 How can it be quiet,
Seeing the LORD has given it a charge
Against Ashkelon and against the seashore?
There He has appointed it."

CHAPTER **48** THE PROUD MOABITES ARE DOOMED. Against Moab.

Thus says the LORD of hosts, the God of Israel:

"Woe to Nebo!
For it is plundered,
Kirjathaim is shamed *and* taken;
The high stronghold is shamed and dismayed—
2 No more praise of Moab.
In Heshbon they have devised evil against her:
'Come, and let us cut her off as a nation.'
You also shall be cut down, O Madmen!
The sword shall pursue you;
3 A voice of crying *shall be* from Horonaim:
'Plundering and great destruction!'

4 "Moab is destroyed;
Her little ones have caused a cry to be heard;
5 For in the Ascent of Luhith they ascend with
continual weeping;
For in the descent of Horonaim the enemies have
heard a cry of destruction.

6 "Flee, save your lives!
And be like the juniper in the wilderness.
7 For because you have trusted in your works and
your treasures,
You also shall be taken.
And Chemosh shall go forth into captivity,
His priests and his princes together.
8 And the plunderer shall come against every city;
No one shall escape.
The valley also shall perish,
And the plain shall be destroyed,
As the LORD has spoken.

9 "Give wings to Moab,
That she may flee and get away;
For her cities shall be desolate,
Without any to dwell in them.
10 Cursed *is* he who does the work of the LORD
deceitfully,
And cursed *is* he who keeps back his sword from
blood.

11 "Moab has been at ease from his youth;
He has settled on his dregs,
And has not been emptied from vessel to vessel,
Nor has he gone into captivity.

Therefore his taste remained in him,
And his scent has not changed.

12 "Therefore behold, the days are coming," says the
LORD,
"That I shall send him wine-workers
Who will tip him over
And empty his vessels
And break the bottles.
13 Moab shall be ashamed of Chemosh,
As the house of Israel was ashamed of Bethel, their
confidence.

14 "How can you say, 'We *are* mighty
And strong men for the war'?
15 Moab is plundered and gone up *from* her cities;
Her chosen young men have gone down to the
slaughter," says the King,
Whose name *is* the LORD of hosts.

16 "The calamity of Moab *is* near at hand,
And his affliction comes quickly.
17 Bemoan him, all you who are around him;
And all you who know his name,
Say, 'How the strong staff is broken,
The beautiful rod!'

18 "O daughter inhabiting Dibon,
Come down from *your* glory,
And sit in thirst;
For the plunderer of Moab has come against you,
He has destroyed your strongholds.
19 O inhabitant of Aroer,
Stand by the way and watch;
Ask him who flees
And her who escapes;
Say, 'What has happened?'
20 Moab is shamed, for he is broken down.
Wail and cry!
Tell it in Arnon, that Moab is plundered.

21 "And judgment has come on the plain country:
On Holon and Jahzah and Mephaath,
22 On Dibon and Nebo and Beth Diblathaim,
23 On Kirjathaim and Beth Gamul and Beth Meon,
24 On Kerioth and Bozrah,
On all the cities of the land of Moab,
Far or near.
25 The horn of Moab is cut off,
And his arm is broken," says the LORD.

26 "Make him drunk,
Because he exalted *himself* against the LORD.
Moab shall wallow in his vomit,
And he shall also be in derision.
27 For was not Israel a derision to you?
Was he found among thieves?
For whenever you speak of him,
You shake *your head in scorn.*
28 You who dwell in Moab,
Leave the cities and dwell in the rock,
And be like the dove *which* makes her nest
In the sides of the cave's mouth.

29 "We have heard the pride of Moab
(He *is* exceedingly proud),
Of his loftiness and arrogance and pride,
And of the haughtiness of his heart."

30 "I know his wrath," says the LORD,
"But it *is* not right;
His lies have made nothing right.
31 Therefore I will wail for Moab,
And I will cry out for all Moab;
I will mourn for the men of Kir Heres.
32 O vine of Sibmah! I will weep for you with the
weeping of Jazer.
Your plants have gone over the sea,
They reach to the sea of Jazer.
The plunderer has fallen on your summer fruit and
your vintage.
33 Joy and gladness are taken
From the plentiful field
And from the land of Moab;
I have caused wine to fail from the winepresses;
No one will tread with joyous shouting—
Not joyous shouting!

34 "From the cry of Heshbon to Elealeh and to Jahaz
They have uttered their voice,
From Zoar to Horonaim,
Like a three-year-old heifer;
For the waters of Nimrim also shall be desolate.

35 "Moreover," says the LORD,
"I will cause to cease in Moab
The one who offers *sacrifices* in the high places
And burns incense to his gods.
36 Therefore My heart shall wail like flutes for Moab,
And like flutes My heart shall wail
For the men of Kir Heres.
Therefore the riches they have acquired have
perished.

37 "For every head *shall be* bald, and every beard
clipped;
On all the hands *shall be* cuts, and on the loins
sackcloth—
38 A general lamentation
On all the housetops of Moab,
And in its streets;
For I have broken Moab like a vessel in which *is* no
pleasure," says the LORD.
39 "They shall wail:
'How she is broken down!
How Moab has turned her back with shame!'
So Moab shall be a derision
And a dismay to all those about her."

40 For thus says the LORD:

"Behold, one shall fly like an eagle,
And spread his wings over Moab.
41 Kerioth is taken,
And the strongholds are surprised;
The mighty men's hearts in Moab on that day shall be
Like the heart of a woman in birth pangs.

42 And Moab shall be destroyed as a people,
Because he exalted *himself* against the LORD.
43 Fear and the pit and the snare *shall be* upon you,
O inhabitant of Moab," says the LORD.
44 "He who flees from the fear shall fall into the pit,
And he who gets out of the pit shall be caught in the
snare.
For upon Moab, upon it I will bring
The year of their punishment," says the LORD.

45 "Those who fled stood under the shadow of Heshbon
Because of exhaustion.
But a fire shall come out of Heshbon,
A flame from the midst of Sihon,
And shall devour the brow of Moab,
The crown of the head of the sons of tumult.
46 Woe to you, O Moab!
The people of Chemosh perish;
For your sons have been taken captive,
And your daughters captive.

47 "Yet I will bring back the captives of Moab
In the latter days," says the LORD.

Thus far *is* the judgment of Moab.

CHAPTER 49 A MESSAGE TO THE AMMONITES.

Against the Ammonites.
Thus says the LORD:

"Has Israel no sons?
Has he no heir?
Why *then* does Milcom inherit Gad,
And his people dwell in its cities?
2 Therefore behold, the days are coming," says the
LORD,
"That I will cause to be heard an alarm of war
In Rabbah of the Ammonites;
It shall be a desolate mound,
And her villages shall be burned with fire.
Then Israel shall take possession of his inheritance,"
says the LORD.

3 "Wail, O Heshbon, for Ai is plundered!
Cry, you daughters of Rabbah,
Gird yourselves with sackcloth!
Lament and run to and fro by the walls;
For Milcom shall go into captivity
With his priests and his princes together.
4 Why do you boast in the valleys,
Your flowing valley, O backsliding daughter?

DON'T PUSH IT

49:4,7 God is loving, merciful, and kind. But he is also just. Eventu[a]
he will judge and punish those who do wrong. Listen to God's words
prophecies of Jeremiah as he speaks to the Moabites who trusted in
military might (48:14), the Ammonites who trusted in their wealth
(49:4), the Edomites who trusted in their wisdom (49:7) and secure
location (49:16), and others. For a while it may seem as though we
get away with disobeying and defying God. But that's because he is
giving us time to repent, to change our ways. What are you doing th[at]
you know is wrong? Is there a habit, a hatred, a hassle? Don't push
luck—turn to God and live his way now!

Who trusted in her treasures, *saying,*
'Who will come against me?'
5 Behold, I will bring fear upon you,"
Says the Lord GOD of hosts,
"From all those who are around you;
You shall be driven out, everyone headlong,
And no one will gather those who wander off.
6 But afterward I will bring back
The captives of the people of Ammon," says the
LORD.

7Against Edom.
Thus says the LORD of hosts:

"*Is* wisdom no more in Teman?
Has counsel perished from the prudent?
Has their wisdom vanished?
8 Flee, turn back, dwell in the depths, O inhabitants of
Dedan!
For I will bring the calamity of Esau upon him,
The time *that* I will punish him.
9 If grape-gatherers came to you,
Would they not leave *some* gleaning grapes?
If thieves by night,
Would they not destroy until they have enough?
10 But I have made Esau bare;
I have uncovered his secret places,
And he shall not be able to hide himself.
His descendants are plundered,
His brethren and his neighbors,
And he *is* no more.
11 Leave your fatherless children,
I will preserve *them* alive;
And let your widows trust in Me."

12For thus says the LORD: "Behold, those whose judgment *was* not to drink of the cup have assuredly drunk. And *are* you the one who will altogether go unpunished? You shall not go unpunished, but you shall surely drink of it. 13For I have sworn by Myself," says the LORD, "that Bozrah shall become a desolation, a reproach, a waste, and a curse. And all its cities shall be perpetual wastes."

14 I have heard a message from the LORD,
And an ambassador has been sent to the nations:
"Gather together, come against her,
And rise up to battle!

15 "For indeed, I will make you small among nations,
Despised among men.
16 Your fierceness has deceived you,
The pride of your heart,
O you who dwell in the clefts of the rock,
Who hold the height of the hill!
Though you make your nest as high as the eagle,
I will bring you down from there," says the LORD.

17 "Edom also shall be an astonishment;
Everyone who goes by it will be astonished
And will hiss at all its plagues.
18 As in the overthrow of Sodom and Gomorrah
And their neighbors," says the LORD,
"No one shall remain there,

Nor shall a son of man dwell in it.

19 "Behold, he shall come up like a lion from the
floodplain of the Jordan
Against the dwelling place of the strong;
But I will suddenly make him run away from her.
And who *is* a chosen *man that* I may appoint over
her?
For who *is* like Me?
Who will arraign Me?
And who *is* that shepherd
Who will withstand Me?"

◀━━━━ SELF-CENTERED

49:16 Edom was destroyed because of its pride. Pride destroys individuals as well as nations. It makes us think we can take care of ourself without God's help. Even serving God and others can lead us into pride. Take inventory of your life and service for God, asking God to point out and remove any self-centeredness.

20 Therefore hear the counsel of the LORD that He has
taken against Edom,
And His purposes that He has proposed against the
inhabitants of Teman:
Surely the least of the flock shall draw them out;
Surely He shall make their dwelling places desolate
with them.
21 The earth shakes at the noise of their fall;
At the cry its noise is heard at the Red Sea.
22 Behold, He shall come up and fly like the eagle,
And spread His wings over Bozrah;
The heart of the mighty men of Edom in that day
shall be
Like the heart of a woman in birth pangs.

23Against Damascus.

"Hamath and Arpad are shamed,
For they have heard bad news.
They are fainthearted;
There is trouble on the sea;
It cannot be quiet.
24 Damascus has grown feeble;
She turns to flee,
And fear has seized *her.*
Anguish and sorrows have taken her like a woman in
labor.
25 Why is the city of praise not deserted, the city of My
joy?
26 Therefore her young men shall fall in her streets,
And all the men of war shall be cut off in that day,"
says the LORD of hosts.
27 "I will kindle a fire in the wall of Damascus,
And it shall consume the palaces of Ben-Hadad."

28Against Kedar and against the kingdoms of Hazor, which Nebuchadnezzar king of Babylon shall strike. Thus says the LORD:

"Arise, go up to Kedar,
And devastate the men of the East!
29 Their tents and their flocks they shall take away.

They shall take for themselves their curtains,
All their vessels and their camels;
And they shall cry out to them,
'Fear *is* on every side!'

30 "Flee, get far away! Dwell in the depths,
O inhabitants of Hazor!" says the LORD.
"For Nebuchadnezzar king of Babylon has taken
counsel against you,
And has conceived a plan against you.

31 "Arise, go up to the wealthy nation that dwells
securely," says the LORD,
"Which has neither gates nor bars,
Dwelling alone.

32 Their camels shall be for booty,
And the multitude of their cattle for plunder.
I will scatter to all winds those in the farthest
corners,
And I will bring their calamity from all its sides,"
says the LORD.

33 "Hazor shall be a dwelling for jackals, a desolation
forever;
No one shall reside there,
Nor son of man dwell in it."

34The word of the LORD that came to Jeremiah the
prophet against Elam, in the beginning of the reign of
Zedekiah king of Judah, saying, 35"Thus says the LORD of
hosts:

'Behold, I will break the bow of Elam,
The foremost of their might.

36 Against Elam I will bring the four winds
From the four quarters of heaven,
And scatter them toward all those winds;
There shall be no nations where the outcasts of Elam
will not go.

37 For I will cause Elam to be dismayed before their
enemies
And before those who seek their life.
I will bring disaster upon them,
My fierce anger,' says the LORD;
'And I will send the sword after them
Until I have consumed them.

38 I will set My throne in Elam,
And will destroy from there the king and the
princes,' says the LORD.

39 'But it shall come to pass in the latter days:
I will bring back the captives of Elam,' says the
LORD."

CHAPTER **50** A MESSAGE TO BABYLON. The
word that the LORD spoke against Babylon *and* against
the land of the Chaldeans by Jeremiah the prophet.

2 "Declare among the nations,
Proclaim, and set up a standard;
Proclaim—do not conceal *it*—
Say, 'Babylon is taken, Bel is shamed.
Merodach is broken in pieces;
Her idols are humiliated,

PAGE 738

▰▰▰▰▰WIPED OUT

50:1ff Babylon is another name for the nation of the Chaldeans
height of its power, this empire seemed immovable. But when Bab
had finished serving God's purpose of punishing Judah for her sins
would be punished and crushed for its own. Babylon was destroye
539 B.C. by the Medo-Persians (Daniel 5:30-31). Babylon is also us
Scripture as a symbol of all evil. This message can thus apply to th
times when God wipes out all evil, once and for all.

Her images are broken in pieces.'
3 For out of the north a nation comes up against her,
Which shall make her land desolate,
And no one shall dwell therein.
They shall move, they shall depart,
Both man and beast.

4 "In those days and in that time," says the LORD,
"The children of Israel shall come,
They and the children of Judah together;
With continual weeping they shall come,
And seek the LORD their God.

5 They shall ask the way to Zion,
With their faces toward it, *saying*,
'Come and let us join ourselves to the LORD
In a perpetual covenant
That will not be forgotten.'

6 "My people have been lost sheep.
Their shepherds have led them astray;
They have turned them away *on* the mountains.
They have gone from mountain to hill;
They have forgotten their resting place.

7 All who found them have devoured them;
And their adversaries said, 'We have not offended,
Because they have sinned against the LORD, the
habitation of justice,
The LORD, the hope of their fathers.'

8 "Move from the midst of Babylon,
Go out of the land of the Chaldeans;
And be like the rams before the flocks.

9 For behold, I will raise and cause to come up against
Babylon
An assembly of great nations from the north country,
And they shall array themselves against her;
From there she shall be captured.
Their arrows *shall be* like *those* of an expert warrior;
None shall return in vain.

10 And Chaldea shall become plunder;
All who plunder her shall be satisfied," says the LORD

11 "Because you were glad, because you rejoiced,
You destroyers of My heritage,
Because you have grown fat like a heifer threshing
grain,
And you bellow like bulls,

12 Your mother shall be deeply ashamed;
She who bore you shall be ashamed.
Behold, the least of the nations *shall be* a wilderness,
A dry land and a desert.

13 Because of the wrath of the LORD
She shall not be inhabited,
But she shall be wholly desolate.
Everyone who goes by Babylon shall be horrified

And hiss at all her plagues.

14 "Put yourselves in array against Babylon all around,
All you who bend the bow;
Shoot at her, spare no arrows,
For she has sinned against the LORD.
15 Shout against her all around;
She has given her hand,
Her foundations have fallen,
Her walls are thrown down;
For it *is* the vengeance of the LORD.
Take vengeance on her.
As she has done, so do to her.
16 Cut off the sower from Babylon,
And him who handles the sickle at harvest time.
For fear of the oppressing sword
Everyone shall turn to his own people,
And everyone shall flee to his own land.

17 "Israel *is* like scattered sheep;
The lions have driven *him* away.
First the king of Assyria devoured him;
Now at last this Nebuchadnezzar king of Babylon
has broken his bones."

18 Therefore thus says the LORD of hosts, the God of Israel:

"Behold, I will punish the king of Babylon and his
land,
As I have punished the king of Assyria.
19 But I will bring back Israel to his home,
And he shall feed on Carmel and Bashan;
His soul shall be satisfied on Mount Ephraim and
Gilead.
20 In those days and in that time," says the LORD,
"The iniquity of Israel shall be sought, but *there shall
be* none;
And the sins of Judah, but they shall not be found;
For I will pardon those whom I preserve.

21 "Go up against the land of Merathaim, against it,
And against the inhabitants of Pekod.
Waste and utterly destroy them," says the LORD,
"And do according to all that I have commanded you.
22 A sound of battle *is* in the land,
And of great destruction.
23 How the hammer of the whole earth has been cut
apart and broken!
How Babylon has become a desolation among the
nations!
I have laid a snare for you;
24 You have indeed been trapped, O Babylon,
And you were not aware;
You have been found and also caught,
Because you have contended against the LORD.
25 The LORD has opened His armory,
And has brought out the weapons of His indignation;
For this *is* the work of the Lord GOD of hosts
In the land of the Chaldeans.
26 Come against her from the farthest border;
Open her storehouses;
Cast her up as heaps of ruins,

And destroy her utterly;
Let nothing of her be left.
27 Slay all her bulls,
Let them go down to the slaughter.
Woe to them!
For their day has come, the time of their
punishment.
28 The voice of those who flee and escape from the
land of Babylon
Declares in Zion the vengeance of the LORD our God,
The vengeance of His temple.

29 "Call together the archers against Babylon.
All you who bend the bow, encamp against it all
around;
Let none of them escape.
Repay her according to her work;
According to all she has done, do to her;
For she has been proud against the LORD,
Against the Holy One of Israel.
30 Therefore her young men shall fall in the streets,
And all her men of war shall be cut off in that day,"
says the LORD.
31 "Behold, I *am* against you,
O most haughty one!" says the Lord GOD of hosts;
"For your day has come,
The time *that* I will punish you.
32 The most proud shall stumble and fall,
And no one will raise him up;
I will kindle a fire in his cities,
And it will devour all around him."

33 Thus says the LORD of hosts:

"The children of Israel *were* oppressed,
Along with the children of Judah;
All who took them captive have held them fast;
They have refused to let them go.
34 Their Redeemer *is* strong;
The LORD of hosts *is* His name.
He will thoroughly plead their case,
That He may give rest to the land,
And disquiet the inhabitants of Babylon.

35 "A sword *is* against the Chaldeans," says the LORD,
"Against the inhabitants of Babylon,
And against her princes and her wise men.
36 A sword *is* against the soothsayers, and they will be
fools.
A sword *is* against her mighty men, and they will be
dismayed.
37 A sword *is* against their horses,
Against their chariots,
And against all the mixed peoples who *are* in her
midst;
And they will become like women.
A sword *is* against her treasures, and they will be
robbed.
38 A drought *is* against her waters, and they will be
dried up.
For it *is* the land of carved images,
And they are insane with *their* idols.

³⁹ "Therefore the wild desert beasts shall dwell *there*
with the jackals,
And the ostriches shall dwell in it.
It shall be inhabited no more forever,
Nor shall it be dwelt in from generation to
generation.
⁴⁰ As God overthrew Sodom and Gomorrah
And their neighbors," says the LORD,
"*So* no one shall reside there,
Nor son of man dwell in it.

⁴¹ "Behold, a people shall come from the north,
And a great nation and many kings
Shall be raised up from the ends of the earth.
⁴² They shall hold the bow and the lance;
They *are* cruel and shall not show mercy.
Their voice shall roar like the sea;
They shall ride on horses,
Set in array, like a man for the battle,
Against you, O daughter of Babylon.

⁴³ "The king of Babylon has heard the report about
them,
And his hands grow feeble;
Anguish has taken hold of him,
Pangs as of a woman in childbirth.

⁴⁴ "Behold, he shall come up like a lion from the
floodplain of the Jordan
Against the dwelling place of the strong;
But I will make them suddenly run away from her.
And who *is* a chosen *man that* I may appoint over
her?
For who *is* like Me?
Who will arraign Me?
And who *is* that shepherd
Who will withstand Me?"

⁴⁵ Therefore hear the counsel of the LORD that He has
taken against Babylon,
And His purposes that He has proposed against the
land of the Chaldeans:
Surely the least of the flock shall draw them out;
Surely He will make their dwelling place desolate
with them.
⁴⁶ At the noise of the taking of Babylon
The earth trembles,
And the cry is heard among the nations.

CHAPTER 51 OUR GREAT AND MIGHTY GOD.

Thus says the LORD:

"Behold, I will raise up against Babylon,
Against those who dwell in Leb Kamai,
A destroying wind.
² And I will send winnowers to Babylon,
Who shall winnow her and empty her land.
For in the day of doom
They shall be against her all around.
³ Against *her* let the archer bend his bow,
And lift himself up against *her* in his armor.
Do not spare her young men;
Utterly destroy all her army.

51:2 Winnowers worked to separate the wheat from the chaff. W
they threw the mixture into the air, the wind blew away the worthle
chaff while the wheat settled to the ground. Babylon would be blow
away like chaff in the wind. (See also Matthew 3:12 where John th
Baptist says Jesus will separate the wheat from the chaff.) Is there
in your life?

⁴ Thus the slain shall fall in the land of the Chaldeans,
And *those* thrust through in her streets.
⁵ For Israel is not forsaken, nor Judah,
By his God, the LORD of hosts,
Though their land was filled with sin against the
Holy One of Israel."

⁶ Flee from the midst of Babylon,
And every one save his life!
Do not be cut off in her iniquity,
For this *is* the time of the LORD's vengeance;
He shall recompense her.
⁷ Babylon *was* a golden cup in the LORD's hand,
That made all the earth drunk.
The nations drank her wine;
Therefore the nations are deranged.
⁸ Babylon has suddenly fallen and been destroyed.
Wail for her!
Take balm for her pain;
Perhaps she may be healed.

⁹ We would have healed Babylon,
But she is not healed.
Forsake her, and let us go everyone to his own
country;
For her judgment reaches to heaven and is lifted up
to the skies.
¹⁰ The LORD has revealed our righteousness.
Come and let us declare in Zion the work of the
LORD our God.

¹¹ Make the arrows bright!
Gather the shields!
The LORD has raised up the spirit of the kings of the
Medes.
For His plan *is* against Babylon to destroy it,
Because it *is* the vengeance of the LORD,
The vengeance for His temple.
¹² Set up the standard on the walls of Babylon;
Make the guard strong,
Set up the watchmen,
Prepare the ambushes.
For the LORD has both devised and done
What He spoke against the inhabitants of Babylon.
¹³ O you who dwell by many waters,
Abundant in treasures,
Your end has come,
The measure of your covetousness.
¹⁴ The LORD of hosts has sworn by Himself:
"Surely I will fill you with men, as with locusts,
And they shall lift up a shout against you."

¹⁵ He has made the earth by His power;
He has established the world by His wisdom,
And stretched out the heaven by His understanding.
¹⁶ When He utters *His* voice—
There is a multitude of waters in the heavens:

"He causes the vapors to ascend from the ends of the
    earth;
He makes lightnings for the rain;
He brings the wind out of His treasuries."

17 Everyone is dull-hearted, without knowledge;
Every metalsmith is put to shame by the carved
    image;
For his molded image *is* falsehood,
And *there is* no breath in them.
18 They *are* futile, a work of errors;
In the time of their punishment they shall perish.
19 The Portion of Jacob *is* not like them,
For He *is* the Maker of all things;
And *Israel is* the tribe of His inheritance.
The LORD of hosts *is* His name.

20 "You *are* My battle-ax *and* weapons of war:
For with you I will break the nation in pieces;
With you I will destroy kingdoms;
21 With you I will break in pieces the horse and its rider;
With you I will break in pieces the chariot and its
    rider;
22 With you also I will break in pieces man and woman;
With you I will break in pieces old and young;
With you I will break in pieces the young man and
    the maiden;
23 With you also I will break in pieces the shepherd and
    his flock;
With you I will break in pieces the farmer and his
    yoke of oxen;
And with you I will break in pieces governors and
    rulers.

24 "And I will repay Babylon
And all the inhabitants of Chaldea
For all the evil they have done
In Zion in your sight," says the LORD.

25 "Behold, I *am* against you, O destroying mountain,
Who destroys all the earth," says the LORD.
"And I will stretch out My hand against you,
Roll you down from the rocks,
And make you a burnt mountain.
26 They shall not take from you a stone for a corner
Nor a stone for a foundation,
But you shall be desolate forever," says the LORD.

27 Set up a banner in the land,
Blow the trumpet among the nations!
Prepare the nations against her,
Call the kingdoms together against her:
Ararat, Minni, and Ashkenaz.
Appoint a general against her;
Cause the horses to come up like the bristling
    locusts.
28 Prepare against her the nations,
With the kings of the Medes,
Its governors and all its rulers,
All the land of his dominion.
29 And the land will tremble and sorrow;
For every purpose of the LORD shall be performed
    against Babylon,

To make the land of Babylon a desolation without
    inhabitant.
30 The mighty men of Babylon have ceased fighting,
They have remained in their strongholds;
Their might has failed,
They became *like* women;
They have burned her dwelling places,
The bars of her *gate* are broken.
31 One runner will run to meet another,
And one messenger to meet another,
To show the king of Babylon that his city is taken on
    all sides;
32 The passages are blocked,
The reeds they have burned with fire,
And the men of war are terrified.

33For thus says the LORD of hosts, the God of Israel:

"The daughter of Babylon *is* like a threshing floor
When it is time to thresh her;
Yet a little while
And the time of her harvest will come."

34 "Nebuchadnezzar the king of Babylon
Has devoured me, he has crushed me;
He has made me an empty vessel,
He has swallowed me up like a monster;
He has filled his stomach with my delicacies,
He has spit me out.
35 Let the violence *done* to me and my flesh *be* upon
    Babylon,"
The inhabitant of Zion will say;
"And my blood be upon the inhabitants of Chaldea!"
Jerusalem will say.

36Therefore thus says the LORD:

"Behold, I will plead your case and take vengeance
    for you.
I will dry up her sea and make her springs dry.
37 Babylon shall become a heap,
A dwelling place for jackals,
An astonishment and a hissing,
Without an inhabitant.
38 They shall roar together like lions,
They shall growl like lions' whelps.
39 In their excitement I will prepare their feasts;
I will make them drunk,
That they may rejoice,
And sleep a perpetual sleep
And not awake," says the LORD.
40 "I will bring them down
Like lambs to the slaughter,
Like rams with male goats.

41 "Oh, how Sheshach is taken!
Oh, how the praise of the whole earth is seized!

◣◢◣◢ SECURITY

51:17-19 It is foolish to trust in man-made images rather than God. It
is easy to think that the things we see and touch will bring us more
security than God. But things rust, rot, and decay. God is eternal. Why put
your trust in something that will disappear within a few years?

How Babylon has become desolate among the
    nations!
42 The sea has come up over Babylon;
    She is covered with the multitude of its waves.
43 Her cities are a desolation,
    A dry land and a wilderness,
    A land where no one dwells,
    Through which no son of man passes.
44 I will punish Bel in Babylon,
    And I will bring out of his mouth what he has
      swallowed;
    And the nations shall not stream to him anymore.
    Yes, the wall of Babylon shall fall.

45 "My people, go out of the midst of her!
    And let everyone deliver himself from the fierce
      anger of the LORD.
46 And lest your heart faint,
    And you fear for the rumor that *will be* heard in the
      land
    (A rumor will come *one* year,
    And after that, in *another* year
    A rumor *will come,*
    And violence in the land,
    Ruler against ruler),
47 Therefore behold, the days are coming
    That I will bring judgment on the carved images of
      Babylon;
    Her whole land shall be ashamed,
    And all her slain shall fall in her midst.
48 Then the heavens and the earth and all that *is* in
      them
    Shall sing joyously over Babylon;
    For the plunderers shall come to her from the
      north," says the LORD.

49 As Babylon *has caused* the slain of Israel to fall,
    So at Babylon the slain of all the earth shall fall.
50 You who have escaped the sword,
    Get away! Do not stand still!
    Remember the LORD afar off,
    And let Jerusalem come to your mind.

51 We are ashamed because we have heard reproach.
    Shame has covered our faces,
    For strangers have come into the sanctuaries of the
      LORD's house.

52 "Therefore behold, the days are coming," says the
      LORD,
    "That I will bring judgment on her carved images,
    And throughout all her land the wounded shall
      groan.
53 Though Babylon were to mount up to heaven,
    And though she were to fortify the height of her
      strength,
    Yet from Me plunderers would come to her," says the
      LORD.

54 The sound of a cry *comes* from Babylon,
    And great destruction from the land of the
      Chaldeans,
55 Because the LORD is plundering Babylon

    And silencing her loud voice,
    Though her waves roar like great waters,
    And the noise of their voice is uttered,
56 Because the plunderer comes against her, against
      Babylon,
    And her mighty men are taken.
    Every one of their bows is broken;
    For the LORD *is* the God of recompense,
    He will surely repay.

57 "And I will make drunk
    Her princes and wise men,
    Her governors, her deputies, and her mighty men.
    And they shall sleep a perpetual sleep
    And not awake," says the King,
    Whose name *is* the LORD of hosts.

58 Thus says the LORD of hosts:

"The broad walls of Babylon shall be utterly broken,
    And her high gates shall be burned with fire;
    The people will labor in vain,
    And the nations, because of the fire;
    And they shall be weary."

◣▬▬▬▬▬ JUDGMENT

51:60-64 In this the last of Jeremiah's messages, we find again the
twin themes of God's sovereignty and his judgment. Babylon had been
allowed to oppress the people of Israel, but here Babylon itself will be
judged. Although God brings good out of evil, he does not allow evil to
remain unpunished. The wicked may succeed for a while, but they will
not last. Resist the temptation to follow them or you may share in their
judgment.

59 The word which Jeremiah the prophet commanded
Seraiah the son of Neriah, the son of Mahseiah, when he
went with Zedekiah the king of Judah to Babylon in the
fourth year of his reign. And Seraiah *was* the quarter-
master. 60 So Jeremiah wrote in a book all the evil that
would come upon Babylon, all these words that are written against Babylon. 61 And Jeremiah said to Seraiah,
"When you arrive in Babylon and see it, and read all these
words, 62 then you shall say, 'O LORD, You have spoken
against this place to cut it off, so that none shall remain
in it, neither man nor beast, but it shall be desolate
forever.' 63 Now it shall be, when you have finished reading this book, *that* you shall tie a stone to it and throw it
out into the Euphrates. 64 Then you shall say, 'Thus Babylon shall sink and not rise from the catastrophe that I will
bring upon her. And they shall be weary.' "

Thus far *are* the words of Jeremiah.

CHAPTER 52

Zedekiah *was* twenty-one years old
when he became king, and he reigned eleven years in
Jerusalem. His mother's name *was* Hamutal the daughter
of Jeremiah of Libnah. 2 He also did evil in the sight of the
LORD, according to all that Jehoiakim had done. 3 For because of the anger of the LORD *this* happened in Jerusalem and Judah, till He finally cast them out from His
presence. Then Zedekiah rebelled against the king of
Babylon.

4Now it came to pass in the ninth year of his reign, in the tenth month, on the tenth *day* of the month, *that* Nebuchadnezzar king of Babylon and all his army came against Jerusalem and encamped against it; and *they* built a siege wall against it all around. 5So the city was besieged until the eleventh year of King Zedekiah. 6By the fourth month, on the ninth day of the month, the famine had become so severe in the city that there was no food for the people of the land. 7Then the city wall was broken through, and all the men of war fled and went out of the city at night by way of the gate between the two walls, which *was* by the king's garden, even though the Chaldeans *were* near the city all around. And they went by way of the plain.

8But the army of the Chaldeans pursued the king, and they overtook Zedekiah in the plains of Jericho. All his army was scattered from him. 9So they took the king and brought him up to the king of Babylon at Riblah in the land of Hamath, and he pronounced judgment on him. 10Then the king of Babylon killed the sons of Zedekiah before his eyes. And he killed all the princes of Judah in Riblah. 11He also put out the eyes of Zedekiah; and the king of Babylon bound him in bronze fetters, took him to Babylon, and put him in prison till the day of his death.

12Now in the fifth month, on the tenth *day* of the month (which *was* the nineteenth year of King Nebuchadnezzar king of Babylon), Nebuzaradan, the captain of the guard, *who* served the king of Babylon, came to Jerusalem. 13He burned the house of the LORD and the king's house; all the houses of Jerusalem, that is, all the houses of the great, he burned with fire. 14And all the army of the Chaldeans who *were* with the captain of the guard broke down all the walls of Jerusalem all around. 15Then Nebuzaradan the captain of the guard carried away captive *some* of the poor people, the rest of the people who remained in the city, the defectors who had deserted to the king of Babylon, and the rest of the craftsmen. 16But Nebuzaradan the captain of the guard left *some* of the poor of the land as vinedressers and farmers.

17The bronze pillars that *were* in the house of the LORD, and the carts and the bronze Sea that *were* in the house of the LORD, the Chaldeans broke in pieces, and carried all their bronze to Babylon. 18They also took away the pots, the shovels, the trimmers, the bowls, the spoons, and all the bronze utensils with which the priests ministered. 19The basins, the firepans, the bowls, the pots, the lampstands, the spoons, and the cups, whatever *was* solid gold and whatever *was* solid silver, the captain of the guard took away. 20The two pillars, one Sea, the twelve bronze bulls which *were* under *it, and* the carts, which King Solomon had made for the house of the LORD—the bronze of all these articles was beyond measure. 21Now *concerning* the pillars: the height of one pillar *was* eighteen cubits, a measuring line of twelve cubits could measure its circumference, and its thickness *was* four fingers;

it was hollow. 22A capital of bronze *was* on it; and the height of one capital *was* five cubits, with a network and pomegranates all around the capital, all of bronze. The second pillar, with pomegranates was the same. 23There were ninety-six pomegranates on the sides; all the pomegranates, all around on the network, *were* one hundred.

24The captain of the guard took Seraiah the chief priest, Zephaniah the second priest, and the three doorkeepers. 25He also took out of the city an officer who had charge of the men of war, seven men of the king's close associates who were found in the city, the principal scribe of the army who mustered the people of the land, and sixty men of the people of the land who were found

IN GOD'S EYES

52:34 In the world's eyes, Jeremiah looked totally unsuccessful. He had no money, family, or friends. He prophesied the destruction of the nation, the capital city, and the temple, but the political and religious leaders would not accept or follow his advice. No one liked him or listened to him. Yet we can see that he successfully completed the work God gave him to do. Success must never be measured by prosperity, fame, or fortune—they don't last. King Zedekiah lost everything. God measures our success with the yardsticks of obedience, faithfulness, and righteousness. If you are faithfully doing the work God gives you, you are successful in his eyes.

in the midst of the city. 26And Nebuzaradan the captain of the guard took these and brought them to the king of Babylon at Riblah. 27Then the king of Babylon struck them and put them to death at Riblah in the land of Hamath. Thus Judah was carried away captive from its own land.

28These *are* the people whom Nebuchadnezzar carried away captive: in the seventh year, three thousand and twenty-three Jews; 29in the eighteenth year of Nebuchadnezzar he carried away captive from Jerusalem eight hundred and thirty-two persons; 30in the twenty-third year of Nebuchadnezzar, Nebuzaradan the captain of the guard carried away captive of the Jews seven hundred and forty-five persons. All the persons *were* four thousand six hundred.

31Now it came to pass in the thirty-seventh year of the captivity of Jehoiachin king of Judah, in the twelfth month, on the twenty-fifth *day* of the month, *that* Evil-Merodach king of Babylon, in the first *year* of his reign, lifted up the head of Jehoiachin king of Judah and brought him out of prison. 32And he spoke kindly to him and gave him a more prominent seat than those of the kings who *were* with him in Babylon. 33So Jehoiachin changed from his prison garments, and he ate bread regularly before the king all the days of his life. 34And as for his provisions, there was a regular ration given him by the king of Babylon, a portion for each day until the day of his death, all the days of his life.

MEGA Themes

SIN King Josiah's reformation failed because the people's repentance was shallow. They continued in their sin. All the leaders rejected God's law and will for the people. Jeremiah lists all their sins, predicts God's judgment, and begs for repentance.

Judah's deterioration and disaster came from the nation's callous disregard and disobedience of God. When we ignore our sin and refuse to listen to God's warnings, we invite disaster. Our heart must remain "tuned in" to his will for us.

1. Describe the people's sins during the reign of King Josiah (3:6-25). You may want to read 2 Kings 22:1–23:30 in order to review Josiah's reign.
2. How does God expect you to respond when you discover a sin in your life?
3. What difference does it make in your life whether or not you respond by dealing with your sin?
4. In what areas of your life do you think God wants you to make changes to avoid sin or to stop sinning? Based on this study, what will you do to respond to his will in these areas?

PUNISHMENT Because of sin, Jerusalem was destroyed, the temple was ruined, and the people were carried off to Babylon. The people were responsible for their destruction and captivity because they refused to listen to God's message.

Unconfessed sin brings God's full punishment. It is useless to blame anyone else for our sin. We must answer to God for how we live.

1. How did God punish Israel and Judah?
2. Describe how you feel about these punishments. Do they seem harsh or lenient to you? Explain.
3. What provision does God supply so that you can be forgiven of your sins?
4. God holds each of us responsible for our own sin, and yet God forgives us. What difference does it make whether or not you sin?
5. Based on Jeremiah, list principles from Jeremiah

that you can use as reasons for why you should not sin against God.

LORD OF ALL God is the righteous Creator. He is accountable to no one. He wisely and lovingly directs all creation to fulfill his plans, and he brings events to pass according to his timetable. He is Lord over all the world.

Because of God's majestic power and love, our only duty is to submit to his authority. By following his plans, we can enjoy a loving relationship with God and serve him with our whole heart.

1. What evidence do you see in chapters 46–52 that God is indeed the Lord of all?
2. What type of attitudes and actions in your life currently reflect God's lordship over you? What attitudes and actions do you need to change or adjust to comply with his lordship?
3. Write two ways you will respond to his lordship in the next two weeks. Be specific and hold yourself accountable for applying his lordship in the ways you have listed.

NEW HEARTS Jeremiah predicted that after the destruction of the nation, God would send a new Shepherd, the Messiah. The Messiah would lead them into a new future, a new covenant, and a new day of hope. He would accomplish this by changing their sinful hearts into hearts that loved God.

God still restores his people by renewing their hearts. His love can transform the problems created by sin. We can have hope for a new heart by loving God, trusting Christ to save us, and repenting. Rejoice in the new heart that is God's gift in Christ.

1. What do you think the text means when it speaks of providing a new heart?
2. How does a person receive a new heart when he or she becomes a disciple of Christ?
3. How does becoming a Christian involve a change of behavior? In the motivation for behavior? In one's view of God?

4. In what ways are you living out your new heart? In what ways can this be improved?

FAITHFUL SERVICE Jeremiah served God faithfully for 40 years. During that time the people ignored, rejected, and persecuted him. Jeremiah's preaching was unsuccessful by human standards, yet he did not fail. He remained faithful to God.

People's acceptance or rejection of us is not the measure of our success. God's approval alone should be our standard for service. We must bring God's message to others even when we are rejected. We must do God's work even if it means suffering. As Jeremiah shows, being faithful is not always easy.

1. Describe some of the feelings Jeremiah must have experienced as he brought these judgments to the people. (Begin with how he felt about God's calling him in chapter 1.)

2. What do you think kept Jeremiah going through all of his difficult experiences and encounters with people who opposed him?

3. When does it seem difficult for you to continue to serve God faithfully (i.e., when others reject you, when it feels like God is distant, etc.)?

4. How could 1:4-8 provide you with confidence that God can use you even when you feel useless? When you face rejection? When it seems too difficult to keep going?

5. What can you do to be sure that you will not let go of this confidence? How can you help young Christian friends develop this same confidence?

*A*fter Susan broke up with Brad, depression filled his sad eyes for weeks. ■ Tears streamed down Pam's face as she gave a last hug to her best friend. She stood waving good-bye as the moving van pulled out of the drive. ■ The night Chris lost the election, he cried himself to sleep. ■ As the final seconds of the state tournament ticked away, the cheerleaders wept uncontrollably. ■ What breaks your heart? Losing? Saying good-bye? Being dumped or ignored? These are emotional experiences, and worthy of tears. But there are other situations that should tug at our feelings, too: injustice, poverty, war, and famine, to name just a few. And what about the fact that people who don't know Christ are lost and bound for destruction? ■ The things that make a person cry say a lot about that person. They show whether he or she is self-centered or God-centered. The book of Lamentations shows us what made Jeremiah sorrowful. As a prophet and one of God's choice servants, he stands alone in the depths of his emotions, his care for the people, his love for the nation, and his devotion to God. ■ Read Lamentations and discover what it was that broke Jeremiah's—and God's—heart. As you do so, begin to see your world in a new light, through tears. Then determine to do something about it—for God.

STATS

PURPOSE: To teach people that to disobey God is to invite disaster and to show that God suffers when his people suffer

AUTHOR: Jeremiah

TO WHOM WRITTEN: The nation of Judah and believers everywhere

DATE WRITTEN: Soon after the fall of Jerusalem in 586 B.C.

SETTING: Jerusalem had been destroyed by Babylon and her people killed, tortured, or taken captive

KEY PEOPLE: Jeremiah, the people of Jerusalem

KEY PLACE: Jerusalem

SPECIAL FEATURES: Three strands of Hebrew thought meet in Lamentations—prophecy, ritual, and wisdom. Lamentations is written in the rhythm and style of ancient Jewish funeral songs or chants. It contains five poems corresponding to the five chapters.

Lamentations

CHAPTER **1** **JEREMIAH'S GREAT SADNESS.**

How lonely sits the city
That was full of people!
How like a widow is she,
Who *was* great among the nations!
The princess among the provinces
Has become a slave!

2 She weeps bitterly in the night,
Her tears *are* on her cheeks;
Among all her lovers
She has none to comfort *her.*
All her friends have dealt treacherously with her;
They have become her enemies.

3 Judah has gone into captivity,
Under affliction and hard servitude;
She dwells among the nations,
She finds no rest;
All her persecutors overtake her in dire straits.

4 The roads to Zion mourn
Because no one comes to the set feasts.
All her gates are desolate;
Her priests sigh,
Her virgins are afflicted,
And she *is* in bitterness.

5 Her adversaries have become the master,
Her enemies prosper;
For the LORD has afflicted her
Because of the multitude of her transgressions.
Her children have gone into captivity before the
     enemy.

6 And from the daughter of Zion
All her splendor has departed.
Her princes have become like deer
That find no pasture,
That flee without strength
Before the pursuer.

7 In the days of her affliction and roaming,
Jerusalem remembers all her pleasant things
That she had in the days of old.
When her people fell into the hand of the enemy,

FALSE FREEDOM

1:1-14 At first, sin seems to offer freedom. But the liberty to do anything we want gradually becomes a desire to do everything. Then we become captive to sin. Freedom from sin's captivity comes only from God. He gives us the freedom, not to do anything we want, but to do what he knows is best for us. Strange as it may seem, true freedom comes in obeying God—following his guidance so that we can receive his best.

With no one to help her,
The adversaries saw her
And mocked at her downfall.

8 Jerusalem has sinned gravely,
Therefore she has become vile.
All who honored her despise her
Because they have seen her nakedness;
Yes, she sighs and turns away.

9 Her uncleanness *is* in her skirts;
She did not consider her destiny;
Therefore her collapse was awesome;
She had no comforter.
"O LORD, behold my affliction,
For *the* enemy is exalted!"

10 The adversary has spread his hand
Over all her pleasant things;
For she has seen the nations enter her sanctuary,
Those whom You commanded
Not to enter Your assembly.

11 All her people sigh,
They seek bread;
They have given their valuables for food to restore
life.
"See, O LORD, and consider,
For I am scorned."

12 "*Is it* nothing to you, all you who pass by?
Behold and see
If there is any sorrow like my sorrow,
Which has been brought on me,
Which the LORD has inflicted
In the day of His fierce anger.

13 "From above He has sent fire into my bones,
And it overpowered them;
He has spread a net for my feet
And turned me back;
He has made me desolate
And faint all the day.

14 "The yoke of my transgressions was bound;
They were woven together by His hands,
And thrust upon my neck.
He made my strength fail;
The Lord delivered me into the hands of *those whom*
I am not able to withstand.

15 "The Lord has trampled underfoot all my mighty *men*
in my midst;
He has called an assembly against me
To crush my young men;
The Lord trampled *as* in a winepress
The virgin daughter of Judah.

16 "For these *things* I weep;
My eye, my eye overflows with water;
Because the comforter, who should restore my life,
Is far from me.
My children are desolate
Because the enemy prevailed."

WEAK ALLIES

1:19 Jerusalem's allies could not come to her aid because, like
Jerusalem, they failed to seek God. Though these allies appeared st
they were actually weak because God was not with them. Dependal
assistance can come only from an ally whose power is from God. Wr
you seek wise counsel, go to Christians who get their wisdom from tr
all-knowing God.

17 Zion spreads out her hands,
But no one comforts her;
The LORD has commanded concerning Jacob
That those around him *become* his adversaries;
Jerusalem has become an unclean thing among
them.

18 "The LORD is righteous,
For I rebelled against His commandment.
Hear now, all peoples,
And behold my sorrow;
My virgins and my young men
Have gone into captivity.

19 "I called for my lovers,
But they deceived me;
My priests and my elders
Breathed their last in the city,
While they sought food
To restore their life.

20 "See, O LORD, that I *am* in distress;
My soul is troubled;
My heart is overturned within me,
For I have been very rebellious.
Outside the sword bereaves,
At home *it is* like death.

21 "They have heard that I sigh,
But no one comforts me.
All my enemies have heard of my trouble;
They are glad that You have done *it*.
Bring on the day You have announced,
That they may become like me.

22 "Let all their wickedness come before You,
And do to them as You have done to me
For all my transgressions;
For my sighs *are* many,
And my heart *is* faint."

CHAPTER 2 GOD HATES SIN.

How the Lord has covered the daughter of Zion
With a cloud in His anger!
He cast down from heaven to the earth
The beauty of Israel,
And did not remember His footstool
In the day of His anger.

2 The Lord has swallowed up and has not pitied
All the dwelling places of Jacob.
He has thrown down in His wrath
The strongholds of the daughter of Judah;
He has brought *them* down to the ground;
He has profaned the kingdom and its princes.

3 He has cut off in fierce anger

Every horn of Israel;
He has drawn back His right hand
From before the enemy.
He has blazed against Jacob like a flaming fire
Devouring all around.

⁴ Standing like an enemy, He has bent His bow;
With His right hand, like an adversary,
He has slain all *who were* pleasing to His eye;
On the tent of the daughter of Zion,
He has poured out His fury like fire.

⁵ The Lord was like an enemy.
He has swallowed up Israel,
He has swallowed up all her palaces;
He has destroyed her strongholds,
And has increased mourning and lamentation
In the daughter of Judah.

⁶ He has done violence to His tabernacle,
As if it were a garden;
He has destroyed His place of assembly;
The LORD has caused
The appointed feasts and Sabbaths to be forgotten
 in Zion.
In His burning indignation He has spurned the king
 and the priest.

⁷ The Lord has spurned His altar,
He has abandoned His sanctuary;
He has given up the walls of her palaces
Into the hand of the enemy.
They have made a noise in the house of the LORD
As on the day of a set feast.

⁸ The LORD has purposed to destroy
The wall of the daughter of Zion.
He has stretched out a line;
He has not withdrawn His hand from destroying;
Therefore He has caused the rampart and wall to
 lament;
They languished together.

⁹ Her gates have sunk into the ground;
He has destroyed and broken her bars.
Her king and her princes *are* among the nations;
The Law *is* no *more*,
And her prophets find no vision from the LORD.

¹⁰ The elders of the daughter of Zion
Sit on the ground *and* keep silence;
They throw dust on their heads
And gird themselves with sackcloth.
The virgins of Jerusalem
Bow their heads to the ground.

¹¹ My eyes fail with tears,
My heart is troubled;
My bile is poured on the ground
Because of the destruction of the daughter of my
 people,
Because the children and the infants
Faint in the streets of the city.

¹² They say to their mothers,

"Where *is* grain and wine?"
As they swoon like the wounded
In the streets of the city,
As their life is poured out
In their mothers' bosom.

¹³ How shall I console you?
To what shall I liken you,
O daughter of Jerusalem?
What shall I compare with you, that I may comfort
 you,
O virgin daughter of Zion?
For your ruin *is* spread wide as the sea;
Who can heal you?

◣ CATCH THE VISION

2:7 Where we worship is not so important to God as how we worship. A church may be beautiful, but if its people don't sincerely follow God, it decays from within. The people of Judah had a beautiful temple, but had rejected in their lives what they proclaimed in their worship, thus making their worship a mocking lie. When you worship, do you mean the words you say? Do you believe the help you pray for will come? Do you really have the love you express for God? Seek God and catch a fresh vision of his love and care. Then worship him wholeheartedly.

¹⁴ Your prophets have seen for you
False and deceptive visions;
They have not uncovered your iniquity,
To bring back your captives,
But have envisioned for you false prophecies and
 delusions.

¹⁵ All who pass by clap *their* hands at you;
They hiss and shake their heads
At the daughter of Jerusalem:
"*Is* this the city that is called
'The perfection of beauty,
The joy of the whole earth'?"

¹⁶ All your enemies have opened their mouth against
 you;
They hiss and gnash *their* teeth.
They say, "We have swallowed *her* up!
Surely this *is* the day we have waited for;
We have found *it*, we have seen *it!*"

¹⁷ The LORD has done what He purposed;
He has fulfilled His word
Which He commanded in days of old.
He has thrown down and has not pitied,
And He has caused an enemy to rejoice over you;
He has exalted the horn of your adversaries.

¹⁸ Their heart cried out to the Lord,
"O wall of the daughter of Zion,
Let tears run down like a river day and night;
Give yourself no relief;
Give your eyes no rest.

¹⁹ "Arise, cry out in the night,
At the beginning of the watches;
Pour out your heart like water before the face of the
 Lord.

Lift your hands toward Him
For the life of your young children,
Who faint from hunger at the head of every street."

20 "See, O LORD, and consider!
To whom have You done this?
Should the women eat their offspring,
The children they have cuddled?
Should the priest and prophet be slain
In the sanctuary of the Lord?

DOWNHILL

Sitting on an uncomfortable bench in the visitor's area at a large juvenile correctional facility, Dwight is somber and subdued. He claws unconsciously at the handcuffs that bite into his bony wrists.

Who would imagine that this tiny 14-year-old is a convicted felon—with a rap sheet that includes car theft and armed robbery? How could a young life go so wrong?

"I knew better," Dwight mutters. "My grandmother was always on me to straighten up and do right. I did for a while. I even sang in the church choir. But when it came down to it, I picked my homeboys over church. I chose the wrong thing, and from there it was all downhill. I kept making bad decisions. I let my friends tell me what to do. And, well, here I am.

"I ask the Lord to forgive me every day, but I don't know if it does any good. I just don't know. . . ."

The conversation continues for another twenty minutes. At last the guards come in and usher Dwight away. *Clang!*—just like that, the steel doors slam shut and the little guy disappears from view.

Jeremiah's diary—the book of Lamentations—is a similarly sad account of what happens when people neglect and/or reject the Lord. Yet, despite the book's generally depressing tone, there is a wonderful note of hope in 3:19-26.

The message? Sin always has horrible consequences, but God's love is greater than any sin!

21 "Young and old lie
On the ground in the streets;
My virgins and my young men
Have fallen by the sword;
You have slain *them* in the day of Your anger,
You have slaughtered *and* not pitied.

22 "You have invited as to a feast day
The terrors that surround me.
In the day of the LORD's anger
There was no refugee or survivor.
Those whom I have borne and brought up
My enemies have destroyed."

CHAPTER 3 I HAVE HOPE.

I *am* the man *who* has seen affliction by the rod of His wrath.
2 He has led me and made *me* walk
In darkness and not *in* light.
3 Surely He has turned His hand against me
Time and time again throughout the day.

NEVER ENDING

3:21 Jeremiah saw one ray of hope in all the sin and sorrow surrounding him: *God's compassion never ends.* Compassion is love in action. God willingly responds with help when we ask. Perhaps there is some sin in your life that you thought God would not forgive. God's compassion is greater than any sin, and he promises forgiveness.

4 He has aged my flesh and my skin,
And broken my bones.
5 He has besieged me
And surrounded *me* with bitterness and woe.
6 He has set me in dark places
Like the dead of long ago.

7 He has hedged me in so that I cannot get out;
He has made my chain heavy.
8 Even when I cry and shout,
He shuts out my prayer.
9 He has blocked my ways with hewn stone;
He has made my paths crooked.

10 He *has been* to me a bear lying in wait,
Like a lion in ambush.
11 He has turned aside my ways and torn me in pieces;
He has made me desolate.
12 He has bent His bow
And set me up as a target for the arrow.

13 He has caused the arrows of His quiver
To pierce my loins.
14 I have become the ridicule of all my people—
Their taunting song all the day.
15 He has filled me with bitterness,
He has made me drink wormwood.

16 He has also broken my teeth with gravel,
And covered me with ashes.
17 You have moved my soul far from peace;
I have forgotten prosperity.
18 And I said, "My strength and my hope
Have perished from the LORD."

19 Remember my affliction and roaming,
The wormwood and the gall.
20 My soul still remembers

THE LORD IS GOOD to those who wait for HIM, to the soul who seeks HIM.

And sinks within me.
21 This I recall to my mind,
Therefore I have hope.

22 *Through* the LORD's mercies we are not consumed,
Because His compassions fail not.
23 *They are* new every morning;
Great *is* Your faithfulness.
24 "The LORD *is* my portion," says my soul,
"Therefore I hope in Him!"

25 The LORD *is* good to those who wait for Him,
To the soul *who* seeks Him.
26 *It is* good that *one* should hope and wait quietly
For the salvation of the LORD.
27 *It is* good for a man to bear
The yoke in his youth.

28 Let him sit alone and keep silent,
Because *God* has laid *it* on him;
29 Let him put his mouth in the dust—
There may yet be hope.
30 Let him give *his* cheek to the one who strikes him,
And be full of reproach.

31 For the Lord will not cast off
forever.
32 Though He causes grief,
Yet He will show compassion
According to the multitude of His
mercies.
33 For He does not afflict willingly,
Nor grieve the children of men.

34 To crush under one's feet
All the prisoners of the earth,
35 To turn aside the justice *due* a
man
Before the face of the Most High,
36 Or subvert a man in his cause—
The Lord does not approve.

37 Who *is* he *who* speaks and it
comes to pass,
When the Lord has not
commanded *it?*
38 *Is it* not from the mouth of the
Most High
That woe and well-being proceed?
39 Why should a living man
complain,
A man for the punishment of his
sins?

40 Let us search out and examine
our ways,
And turn back to the LORD;
41 Let us lift our hearts and hands
To God in heaven.
42 We have transgressed and
rebelled;
You have not pardoned.

43 You have covered *Yourself* with anger
And pursued us;
You have slain *and* not pitied.
44 You have covered Yourself with a cloud,
That prayer should not pass through.

◣〰 HOMEWORK

3:27-33 To "bear the yoke" means to willingly come under God's discipline and learn what he wants to teach. True learning involves several important factors: (1) reflective silence on what God wants, (2) repentant humility, (3) self-control in the face of adversity, and (4) confident patience, depending on the Teacher to bring about the loving lesson in our life. God has several long-term and short-term lessons for you right now. Are you doing your homework?

45 You have made us an offscouring and refuse
In the midst of the peoples.

46 All our enemies
Have opened their mouths against us.
47 Fear and a snare have come upon us,

"Here's what I did..."

I had blown it again—my parents and I had another major disagreement. I ran to my room, slammed the door, and threw myself on the bed. Then I burst into tears. It wasn't fair! They weren't being fair! And there seemed to be nothing I could do about it.

After I had cried for a while, I thought about our fight. I still thought my parents were wrong, but I also had to admit that I'd said some pretty ugly things. The more I thought about it, the more I realized I would have to apologize.

It took me a couple of hours. Finally I came out and apologized for some of the hurtful things I had said. My mother's response was, "You think it's that easy? Just say you're sorry, and everything's OK? Well, it doesn't work that way."

I just turned and went back to my room. I cried some more. I had said I was sorry, and I was. Couldn't they forgive me? It seemed like they didn't really know much about forgiveness.

The next morning, still feeling bad, I picked up my Bible. I remembered reading a verse one time that I wanted to look up. Something about God's mercies being new. Something from a strange book in the Old Testament . . . Lamentations. Chapter 3, verses 21-23. "I have hope. . . . His compassions fail not. *They are* new every morning."

His love for me is being replenished every day. This was a new day; God has forgiven me, his love and mercy are fresh for this day. I don't have to carry my burdens by myself. Even if my parents didn't forgive me, God did. He knew I was sincere, and would help me do better today. And even if I didn't, he'd love me. His compassion would be there for me tomorrow, just like the sun coming up to warm me.

Kara
AGE 19

Desolation and destruction.
48 My eyes overflow with rivers of water
For the destruction of the daughter of my people.

49 My eyes flow and do not cease,
Without interruption,
50 Till the LORD from heaven
Looks down and sees.
51 My eyes bring suffering to my soul
Because of all the daughters of my city.

52 My enemies without cause
Hunted me down like a bird.
53 They silenced my life in the pit
And threw stones at me.
54 The waters flowed over my head;
I said, "I am cut off!"

55 I called on Your name, O LORD,
From the lowest pit.
56 You have heard my voice:
"Do not hide Your ear
From my sighing, from my cry for help."
57 You drew near on the day I called on You,
And said, "Do not fear!"

58 O Lord, You have pleaded the case for my soul;
You have redeemed my life.
59 O LORD, You have seen *how* I am wronged;
Judge my case.
60 You have seen all their vengeance,
All their schemes against me.

61 You have heard their reproach, O LORD,
All their schemes against me,
62 The lips of my enemies
And their whispering against me all the day.
63 Look at their sitting down and their rising up;
I *am* their taunting song.

64 Repay them, O LORD,
According to the work of their hands.
65 Give them a veiled heart;
Your curse *be* upon them!
66 In Your anger,
Pursue and destroy them
From under the heavens of the LORD.

CHAPTER 4 GOD IS NO LONGER ANGRY.

How the gold has become dim!
How changed the fine gold!
The stones of the sanctuary are scattered
At the head of every street.

2 The precious sons of Zion,
Valuable as fine gold,
How they are regarded as clay pots,
The work of the hands of the potter!

3 Even the jackals present their breasts
To nurse their young;
But the daughter of my people *is* cruel,
Like ostriches in the wilderness.

4 The tongue of the infant clings

4:1ff This chapter contrasts the situation before the siege of Jeru
with the situation after the siege. The sights and sounds of prosperit
were gone because of the people's sin. This chapter warns us not to
assume that when life is going well, it will always stay that way. We
be careful not to glory in our prosperity and fall into spiritual bank

To the roof of its mouth for thirst;
The young children ask for bread,
But no one breaks *it* for them.

5 Those who ate delicacies
Are desolate in the streets;
Those who were brought up in scarlet
Embrace ash heaps.

6 The punishment of the iniquity of the daughter of
my people
Is greater than the punishment of the sin of Sodom,
Which was overthrown in a moment,
With no hand to help her!

7 Her Nazirites were brighter than snow
And whiter than milk;
They were more ruddy in body than rubies,
Like sapphire in their appearance.

8 *Now* their appearance is blacker than soot;
They go unrecognized in the streets;
Their skin clings to their bones,
It has become as dry as wood.

9 *Those* slain by the sword are better off
Than *those* who die of hunger;
For these pine away,
Stricken *for lack* of the fruits of the field.

10 The hands of the compassionate women
Have cooked their own children;
They became food for them
In the destruction of the daughter of my people.

11 The LORD has fulfilled His fury,
He has poured out His fierce anger.
He kindled a fire in Zion,
And it has devoured its foundations.

12 The kings of the earth,
And all inhabitants of the world,
Would not have believed
That the adversary and the enemy
Could enter the gates of Jerusalem—

13 Because of the sins of her prophets
And the iniquities of her priests,
Who shed in her midst
The blood of the just.

14 They wandered blind in the streets;
They have defiled themselves with blood,
So that no one would touch their garments.

15 They cried out to them,
"Go away, unclean!
Go away, go away,
Do not touch us!"
When they fled and wandered,

Those among the nations said,
"They shall no longer dwell *here*."

¹⁶ The face of the LORD scattered them;
He no longer regards them.
The people do not respect the priests
Nor show favor to the elders.

¹⁷ Still our eyes failed us,
Watching vainly for our help;
In our watching we watched
For a nation *that* could not save *us*.

¹⁸ They tracked our steps
So that we could not walk in our streets.
Our end was near;
Our days were over,
For our end had come.

¹⁹ Our pursuers were swifter
Than the eagles of the heavens.
They pursued us on the mountains
And lay in wait for us in the wilderness.

²⁰ The breath of our nostrils, the anointed of the LORD,
Was caught in their pits,
Of whom we said, "Under his shadow
We shall live among the nations."

²¹ Rejoice and be glad, O daughter of Edom,
You who dwell in the land of Uz!
The cup shall also pass over to you
And you shall become drunk and make yourself
naked.

²² *The punishment of* your iniquity is accomplished,
O daughter of Zion;
He will no longer send you into captivity.
He will punish your iniquity,
O daughter of Edom;
He will uncover your sins!

CHAPTER **5** JEREMIAH PRAYS.

Remember, O LORD, what has come upon us;
Look, and behold our reproach!
² Our inheritance has been turned over to aliens,
And our houses to foreigners.
³ We have become orphans and waifs,
Our mothers *are* like widows.

⁴ We pay for the water we drink,
And our wood comes at a price.
⁵ *They* pursue at our heels;

We labor *and* have no rest.
⁶ We have given our hand *to* the Egyptians
And the Assyrians, to be satisfied with bread.

⁷ Our fathers sinned *and are* no more,
But we bear their iniquities.
⁸ Servants rule over us;
There is none to deliver *us* from their hand.
⁹ We get our bread *at the risk* of our lives,
Because of the sword in the wilderness.

¹⁰ Our skin is hot as an oven,
Because of the fever of famine.
¹¹ They ravished the women in Zion,
The maidens in the cities of Judah.
¹² Princes were hung up by their hands,
And elders were not respected.

◣ TURN ABOUT

5:22 A high calling flouted by low living results in deep suffering. Lamentations gives us a portrait of the bitter suffering the people of Jerusalem experienced when sin caught up with them and God turned his back on them. Every material goal they had lived for disappeared. Even though God turned away from them because of their sin, he did not abandon them—that was their great hope. Despite their sinful past, God would restore them if they returned to him. There is no hope except in the Lord. Thus, our grief should turn us toward him, not away from him.

¹³ Young men ground at the millstones;
Boys staggered under *loads of* wood.
¹⁴ The elders have ceased *gathering at* the gate,
And the young men from their music.

¹⁵ The joy of our heart has ceased;
Our dance has turned into mourning.
¹⁶ The crown has fallen *from* our head.
Woe to us, for we have sinned!
¹⁷ Because of this our heart is faint;
Because of these *things* our eyes grow dim;
¹⁸ Because of Mount Zion which is desolate,
With foxes walking about on it.

¹⁹ You, O LORD, remain forever;
Your throne from generation to generation.
²⁰ Why do You forget us forever,
And forsake us for so long a time?
²¹ Turn us back to You, O LORD, and we will be restored;
Renew our days as of old,
²² Unless You have utterly rejected us,
And are very angry with us!

MEGA Themes

DESTRUCTION OF JERUSALEM Lamentations is a sad funeral song for Jerusalem, the great capital city of the Jews. The temple had been destroyed, the king was gone, and the people were in exile. God had warned the nation that he would destroy them if they abandoned him. Afterward, the people realized their condition and confessed their sin.

God's warnings will be fulfilled. He will do what he promises. His punishment for sin is certain. Only if we confess and renounce our sin will he deliver us. How much better to do so before his warnings are fulfilled.

1. What feelings does Jeremiah express over the devastation of Jerusalem and the Jews?
2. Jeremiah had predicted this destruction and the exile. So why would seeing his prophecy fulfilled be especially painful?
3. What results of sin in your world cause you to feel sad?
4. What can you do in your world to help others see the destruction that comes from sin? How can you help them avoid these results?

SIN'S CONSEQUENCES God was angry at the prolonged rebellion by his people. Sin was the cause of their misery, and destruction was the result of their sin. The destruction of the nation shows the emptiness of human glory and pride.

To continue to rebel against God invites disaster. We should never trust our own leadership, resources, intelligence, or power more than God. If we do, we will suffer painful consequences.

1. What were the specific sins of the people that led

to their exile? What had they put in place of God as most important in their lives?
2. Are there things or relationships that might possibly replace God as most important in your life?
3. Have you ever placed something or someone before the Lord? What were the consequences? What did you learn from that experience?
4. What are you doing right now to make sure that God remains first in your life?

GOD'S MERCY God's loving compassion was at work even when the Israelites were suffering under their Babylonian conquerors. Although the people had been unfaithful, God was faithful to them. He used their suffering to bring them back to him.

God will always be faithful to his people. His mercy is evident even during suffering. At those times, we must pray for forgiveness and then turn to God for deliverance. He always hears our cries of repentance.

1. What evidence do you find that God had not abandoned the Jews, even in their slavery?
2. Describe the attitude you should have toward God when you find yourself suffering the consequences of a sinful choice.
3. How have you needed God's mercy in your life? In what ways has he proven faithful?
4. How does God want you to respond to his mercy?

HOPE God's mercy in sparing some of the people offers hope for better days. Eventually they will be restored to a close relationship with God.

Only God can deliver us from sin. Without him there is no comfort or hope for the future. Christ's death for us and his promise to return give us bright hope for tomorrow.

1. God provided hope during punishment. What do you learn about God's character from his sparing the faithful group?

2. How would you encourage a suffering friend to find hope in God?

3. What could you tell a non-Christian friend about his/her need to place ultimate hope in Christ? What would it mean for him or her to do so?

4. What difference does it make in your life that you can place your hope in God? How will that affect your future choices? The choices you make this week?

*D*on't worry," Danny chided his friends. "I can get away with anything. I'm my father's favorite." Danny's dad had gone out of town, leaving his new sports car in the garage. Danny could drive the family station wagon, but not the sports car. "Come on you guys," he continued, "Dad will never even know." ■ The drive to the movie was great. Girls honked and guys stared. "See," Danny said. "No problem. It sure beats the old wagon!" His friends had to agree. ■ After the movie, they headed to the car. It was late, and the parking lot was no longer full. "Danny! Danny!" one of his friends suddenly yelled when he reached the car. "It's gone!" Wires dangled where the stereo used to be. ■ "What are we going to do?" another friend asked. "Your father will kill us!" ■ Danny smiled weakly. "Hey, I'm my dad's favorite. No sweat!" ■ Israel reacted like Danny. They thought they could get away with anything. The book of Ezekiel was written to Jews who were captives in Babylon. They were "God's favorites." Surely Jerusalem (their capital) would not be harmed, and they would return home very soon. Ezekiel corrected their thinking: they were captives in Babylon because they had disobeyed God. Though they were his chosen people, God could not overlook sin. ■ Ezekiel reminds us that no one can sin without punishment. Just as God loves us, he also loves justice. ■ As you read Ezekiel, stand in awe at the God who judges all sin. Then thank him for providing a way (through Jesus) to escape the judgment that we all deserve for our sins.

STATS

PURPOSE: To announce God's judgment; to foretell the salvation of God's people

AUTHOR: Ezekiel—the son of Buzi, a Zadokite priest

TO WHOM WRITTEN: The Jews in captivity in Babylon and God's people everywhere

DATE WRITTEN: Approximately 571 B.C.

SETTING: While Jeremiah ministered to the people still in Judah, Ezekiel prophesied to those already exiled in Babylon after the defeat of Jehoiachin. He was among the captives taken there in 597 B.C.

KEY PEOPLE: Ezekiel, Israel's leaders, Ezekiel's wife, Nebuchadnezzar, the "prince"

KEY PLACES: Jerusalem, Babylon, and Egypt

Ezekiel

CHAPTER 1 A FIERY CLOUD. Now it came to pass in the thirtieth year, in the fourth *month,* on the fifth *day* of the month, as I *was* among the captives by the River Chebar, *that* the heavens were opened and I saw visions of God. ²On the fifth *day* of the month, which *was* in the fifth year of King Jehoiachin's captivity, ³the word of the LORD came expressly to Ezekiel the priest, the son of Buzi, in the land of the Chaldeans by the River Chebar; and the hand of the LORD was upon him there.

⁴Then I looked, and behold, a whirlwind was coming out of the north, a great cloud with raging fire engulfing itself; and brightness *was* all around it and radiating out of its midst like the color of amber, out of the midst of the fire. ⁵Also from within it *came* the likeness of four living creatures. And this *was* their appearance: they had the likeness of a man. ⁶Each one had four faces, and each one had four wings. ⁷Their legs *were* straight, and the soles of their feet *were* like the soles of calves' feet. They sparkled like the color of burnished bronze. ⁸The hands of a man *were* under their wings on their four sides; and each of the four had faces and wings. ⁹Their wings touched one another. *The creatures* did not turn when they went, but each one went straight forward.

¹⁰As for the likeness of their faces, *each* had the face of a man; each of the four had the face of a lion on the right side, each of the four had the face of an ox on the left side, and each of the four had the face of an eagle. ¹¹Thus *were* their faces. Their wings stretched upward; two *wings* of each one touched one another, and two covered their bodies. ¹²And each one went straight forward; they went wherever the spirit wanted to go, and they did not turn when they went.

¹³As for the likeness of the living creatures, their appearance *was* like burning coals of fire, like the appearance of torches going back and forth among the living creatures. The fire was bright, and out of the fire went lightning. ¹⁴And the living creatures ran back and forth, in appearance like a flash of lightning.

¹⁵Now as I looked at the living creatures, behold, a wheel *was* on the earth beside each living creature with its four faces. ¹⁶The appearance of the wheels and their workings *was* like the color of beryl, and all four had the same likeness. The appearance of their workings *was,* as it were, a wheel in the middle of a wheel. ¹⁷When they moved, they went toward any one of four directions; they did not turn aside when they went. ¹⁸As for their rims, they were so high they were awesome; and their rims *were* full of eyes, all around the four of them. ¹⁹When the living creatures went, the wheels went beside them; and when the living creatures were lifted up from the earth, the wheels were lifted up. ²⁰Wherever the spirit wanted to go, they went, *because* there the spirit went; and the wheels were lifted together with them, for the spirit of the living creatures *was* in the wheels. ²¹When those went, *these* went; when those stood, *these* stood; and when those were lifted up from the earth, the wheels were lifted up together with them, for the spirit of the living creatures *was* in the wheels.

²²The likeness of the firmament above the heads of the living creatures *was* like the color of an awesome crystal, stretched out over their heads. ²³And under the firmament their wings *spread out* straight, one toward an-

◆ BLAZING GLORY

1:13-28 A bright light, a dazzling fire—that is what the glory of the Lord looked like to Ezekiel. He fell to the ground, overwhelmed by the holiness of God and his own sinfulness and insignificance. Eventually every person will kneel before God, either out of reverence and awe for his mercy or out of fear of his judgment. Based on the way you are living today, how will you respond?

other. Each one had two which covered one side, and each one had two which covered the other side of the body. ²⁴When they went, I heard the noise of their wings, like the noise of many waters, like the voice of the Almighty, a tumult like the noise of an army; and when they stood still, they let down their wings. ²⁵A voice came from above the firmament that *was* over their heads; whenever they stood, they let down their wings.

²⁶And above the firmament over their heads *was* the likeness of a throne, in appearance like a sapphire stone; on the likeness of the throne *was* a likeness with the appearance of a man high above it. ²⁷Also from the appearance of His waist and upward I saw, as it were, the color of amber with the appearance of fire all around

ᴄONFRONT

Chad's been hearing little rumors about his friend Eric for a couple of weeks now. Rumors like:
"Did you hear about Eric's and Brandon's latest drinking binge?"
"You should have seen Eric at Rebecca's party last weekend!"
"Man, Eric sure has changed!"

Tonight Chad's worst fears were confirmed. Driving through the school parking lot after a game, Chad happened to see Eric and Brandon sitting in the back of a pick-up truck, drinking tequila. Chad didn't stop, so Eric doesn't know his friend saw him.

Chad is concerned, but also confused. Here's his childhood friend starting to run with a pretty wild crowd. It seems Eric is headed for major-league trouble. Chad ponders what to do: "Should I talk to Eric or just keep my mouth shut? Should I tell my parents what's going on and get their advice? I mean, I want to do what's right, but I'm afraid if I speak up, Eric will just laugh at me. Besides, who am I to tell him how to live?"

When friends start heading for trouble, we have a God-given responsibility to pull them aside and help them get back on track. The question isn't how they may or may not respond—that's irrelevant. The real question is whether or not we love them enough to do what's right and confront them. See Ezekiel 2:3-7.

within it; and from the appearance of His waist and downward I saw, as it were, the appearance of fire with brightness all around. ²⁸Like the appearance of a rainbow in a cloud on a rainy day, so *was* the appearance of the brightness all around it. This *was* the appearance of the likeness of the glory of the Lᴏʀᴅ.

So when I saw *it*, I fell on my face, and I heard a voice of One speaking.

CHAPTER 2 GOD CALLS EZEKIEL.

And He said to me, "Son of man, stand on your feet, and I will speak to you." ²Then the Spirit entered me when He spoke to me, and set me on my feet; and I heard Him who spoke to me. ³And He said to me: "Son of man, I am sending you to the children of Israel, to a rebellious nation that has rebelled against Me; they and their fathers have transgressed against Me to this very day. ⁴For *they are* impudent and stubborn children. I am sending you to them, and you shall say to them, 'Thus says the Lord Gᴏᴅ.' ⁵As for them, whether they hear or whether they refuse—for they *are* a

TOUGH TALK

2:6-8 Ezekiel was given the difficult responsibility of presenting ⌐ message to the ungrateful and abusive. Sometimes we are also cal⌐ be an example or share our faith with people who may be unkind⌐ Just as the Lord told Ezekiel not to give up, he tells us not give up⌐ join the rebels, but rather to tell the Good News whether it's conve⌐ or not (2 Timothy 4:2).

rebellious house—yet they will know that a prophet has been among them.

⁶"And you, son of man, do not be afraid of them nor be afraid of their words, though briers and thorns *are* with you and you dwell among scorpions; do not be afraid of their words or dismayed by their looks, though they *are* a rebellious house. ⁷You shall speak My words to them, whether they hear or whether they refuse, for they *are* rebellious. ⁸But you, son of man, hear what I say to you. Do not be rebellious like that rebellious house; open your mouth and eat what I give you."

⁹Now when I looked, there was a hand stretched out to me; and behold, a scroll of a book *was* in it. ¹⁰Then He spread it before me; and *there was* writing on the inside and on the outside, and written on it *were* lamentations and mourning and woe.

CHAPTER 3 GOD MAKES EZEKIEL HIS WATCHMAN.

Moreover He said to me, "Son of man, eat what you find; eat this scroll, and go, speak to the house of Israel." ²So I opened my mouth, and He caused me to eat that scroll.

³And He said to me, "Son of man, feed your belly, and fill your stomach with this scroll that I give you." So I ate, and it was in my mouth like honey in sweetness.

⁴Then He said to me: "Son of man, go to the house of Israel and speak with My words to them. ⁵For you *are* not sent to a people of unfamiliar speech and of hard language, *but* to the house of Israel, ⁶not to many people of unfamiliar speech and of hard language, whose words you cannot understand. Surely, had I sent you to them, they would have listened to you. ⁷But the house of Israel will not listen to you, because they will not listen to Me; for all the house of Israel *are* impudent and hardhearted. ⁸Behold, I have made your face strong against their faces, and your forehead strong against their foreheads. ⁹Like adamant stone, harder than flint, I have made your forehead; do not be afraid of them, nor be dismayed at their looks, though they *are* a rebellious house."

¹⁰Moreover He said to me: "Son of man, receive into your heart all My words that I speak to you, and hear with your ears. ¹¹And go, get to the captives, to the children of your people, and speak to them and tell them, 'Thus says the Lord Gᴏᴅ,' whether they hear, or whether they refuse."

¹²Then the Spirit lifted me up, and I heard behind me a great thunderous voice: "Blessed *is* the glory of the Lᴏʀᴅ from His place!" ¹³*I* also *heard* the noise of the wings of the living creatures that touched one another, and the noise of the wheels beside them, and a great thunderous noise. ¹⁴So the Spirit lifted me up and took me away, and I went in bitterness, in the heat of my spirit; but the hand of the Lᴏʀᴅ was strong upon me. ¹⁵Then I came to the captives at Tel Abib, who dwelt by the River Chebar; and

EZEKIEL
served as a prophet to the
exiles in Babylon from
593–571 B.C.

*Climate of
the times*
• Ezekiel and
his people
are taken to
Babylon as
captives.

• The Jews
become
foreigners in
a strange
land ruled
by an
authoritarian
government.

Main message
God allowed the
nation of Judah
to be destroyed
because of the
people's sins,
but there was
still hope —
God promised
to restore the
land to those
who remained
faithful to him.

*Importance
of message*
God never
forgets those
who faithfully
seek to obey him.
They have a
glorious future
ahead.

*Contemporary
prophets*
Daniel (605–536)
Habakkuk (612–588)
Jeremiah (627–586)

I sat where they sat, and remained there astonished among them seven days.

¹⁶Now it came to pass at the end of seven days that the word of the LORD came to me, saying, ¹⁷"Son of man, I have made you a watchman for the house of Israel; therefore hear a word from My mouth, and give them warning from Me: ¹⁸When I say to the wicked, 'You shall surely die,' and you give him no warning, nor speak to warn the wicked from his wicked way, to save his life, that same wicked *man* shall die in his iniquity; but his blood I will require at your hand. ¹⁹Yet, if you warn the wicked, and he does not turn from his wickedness, nor from his wicked way, he shall die in his iniquity; but you have delivered your soul.

²⁰"Again, when a righteous *man* turns from his righteousness and commits iniquity, and I lay a stumbling block before him, he shall die; because you did not give him warning, he shall die in his sin, and his righteousness which he has done shall not be remembered; but his blood I will require at your hand. ²¹Nevertheless if you warn the righteous *man* that the righteous should not sin, and he does not sin, he shall surely live because he took warning; also you will have delivered your soul."

²²Then the hand of the LORD was upon me there, and He said to me, "Arise, go out into the plain, and there I shall talk with you."

²³So I arose and went out into the plain, and behold, the glory of the LORD stood there, like the glory which I saw by the River Chebar; and I fell on my face. ²⁴Then the Spirit entered me and set me on my feet, and spoke with me and said to me: "Go, shut yourself inside your house. ²⁵And you, O son of man, surely they will put ropes on you and bind you with them, so that you cannot go out among them. ²⁶I will make your tongue cling to the roof of your mouth, so that you shall be mute and not be one

to rebuke them, for they *are* a rebellious house. ²⁷But when I speak with you, I will open your mouth, and you shall say to them, 'Thus says the Lord GOD.' He who hears, let him hear; and he who refuses, let him refuse; for they *are* a rebellious house.

CHAPTER 4 EZEKIEL DRAWS A PICTURE. "You also, son of man, take a clay tablet and lay it before you, and portray on it a city, Jerusalem. ²Lay siege against it, build a siege wall against it, and heap up a mound against it; set camps against it also, and place battering rams against it all around. ³Moreover take for yourself an iron plate, and set it *as* an iron wall between you and the city. Set your face against it, and it shall be besieged, and you shall lay siege against it. This *will be* a sign to the house of Israel.

⁴"Lie also on your left side, and lay the iniquity of the house of Israel upon it. *According* to the number of the days that you lie on it, you shall bear their iniquity. ⁵For I have laid on you the years of their iniquity, according to the number of the days, three hundred and ninety days; so you shall bear the iniquity of the house of Israel. ⁶And when you have completed them, lie again on your right side; then you shall bear the iniquity of the house of Judah forty days. I have laid on you a day for each year.

⁷"Therefore you shall set your face toward the siege of Jerusalem; your arm *shall be* uncovered, and you shall

DETAILS

4:1ff Ezekiel enacted the coming siege and fall of Jerusalem before it actually happened. God gave Ezekiel specific instructions about what to say and how to say it. Each detail had a special meaning. Often we ignore or disregard the smaller details of God's Word, thinking he probably doesn't care. Like Ezekiel, we should want to obey God completely, even in the details.

prophesy against it. [8]And surely I will restrain you so that you cannot turn from one side to another till you have ended the days of your siege.

[9]"Also take for yourself wheat, barley, beans, lentils, millet, and spelt; put them into one vessel, and make bread of them for yourself. *During* the number of days that you lie on your side, three hundred and ninety days, you shall eat it. [10]And your food which you eat *shall be* by weight, twenty shekels a day; from time to time you shall eat it. [11]You shall also drink water by measure, one-sixth of a hin; from time to time you shall drink. [12]And you shall eat it *as* barley cakes; and bake it using fuel of human waste in their sight."

[13]Then the LORD said, "So shall the children of Israel eat their defiled bread among the Gentiles, where I will drive them."

[14]So I said, "Ah, Lord GOD! Indeed I have never defiled myself from my youth till now; I have never eaten what died of itself or was torn by beasts, nor has abominable flesh ever come into my mouth."

[15]Then He said to me, "See, I am giving you cow dung instead of human waste, and you shall prepare your bread over it."

[16]Moreover He said to me, "Son of man, surely I will cut off the supply of bread in Jerusalem; they shall eat bread by weight and with anxiety, and shall drink water by measure and with dread, [17]that they may lack bread and water, and be dismayed with one another, and waste away because of their iniquity.

CHAPTER 5 A CRAZY HAIRCUT. "And you, son of man, take a sharp sword, take it as a barber's razor, and pass *it* over your head and your beard; then take scales to weigh and divide the hair. [2]You shall burn with fire one-third in the midst of the city, when the days of the siege are finished; then you shall take one-third and strike around *it* with the sword, and one-third you shall scatter in the wind: I will draw out a sword after them. [3]You shall also take a small number of them and bind them in the edge of your *garment*. [4]Then take some of them again and throw them into the midst of the fire, and burn them in the fire. From there a fire will go out into all the house of Israel.

[5]"Thus says the Lord GOD: 'This *is* Jerusalem; I have set her in the midst of the nations and the countries all around her. [6]She has rebelled against My judgments by doing wickedness more than the nations, and against My statutes more than the countries that *are* all around her; for they have refused My judgments, and they have not walked in My statutes.' [7]Therefore thus says the Lord GOD: 'Because you have multiplied *disobedience* more than the nations that *are* all around you, have not walked in My statutes nor kept My judgments, nor even done according to the judgments of the nations that *are* all around you'— [8]therefore thus says the Lord GOD: 'Indeed I, even I, *am* against you and will execute judgments in your midst in the sight of the nations. [9]And I will do among you what I have never done, and the like of which I will never do again, because of all your abominations. [10]Therefore fathers shall eat *their* sons in your midst, and

5:13 Have you ever seen a parent try to discipline a child by sayi~~ng~~ you do that one more time . . ."? If the parent doesn't follow throu~~gh~~ the child learns not to listen. Empty threats backfire. God was going ~~to~~ punish the Israelites for their blatant sins, and he wanted them to k~~now~~ that he would do what he said. The people learned the hard way th~~at God~~ always follows through on his word. Too many people ignore God's warnings that he will punish sin. But what God threatens, he does. ~~Don't~~ make the mistake of thinking that God doesn't really mean what h~~e says.~~

sons shall eat their fathers; and I will execute judgments among you, and all of you who remain I will scatter to all the winds.

[11]"Therefore, *as* I live,' says the Lord GOD, 'surely, because you have defiled My sanctuary with all your detestable things and with all your abominations, therefore I will also diminish *you;* My eye will not spare, nor will I have any pity. [12]One-third of you shall die of the pestilence, and be consumed with famine in your midst; and one-third shall fall by the sword all around you; and I will scatter another third to all the winds, and I will draw out a sword after them.

[13]"Thus shall My anger be spent, and I will cause My fury to rest upon them, and I will be avenged; and they shall know that I, the LORD, have spoken *it* in My zeal, when I have spent My fury upon them. [14]Moreover I will make you a waste and a reproach among the nations that *are* all around you, in the sight of all who pass by.

[15]"So it shall be a reproach, a taunt, a lesson, and an astonishment to the nations that *are* all around you, when I execute judgments among you in anger and in fury and in furious rebukes. I, the LORD, have spoken. [16]When I send against them the terrible arrows of famine which shall be for destruction, which I will send to destroy you, I will increase the famine upon you and cut off your supply of bread. [17]So I will send against you famine and wild beasts, and they will bereave you. Pestilence and blood shall pass through you, and I will bring the sword against you. I, the LORD, have spoken.'"

CHAPTER 6 EZEKIEL TALKS TO THE MOUNTAINS. Now the word of the LORD came to me, saying: [2]"Son of man, set your face toward the mountains of Israel, and prophesy against them, [3]and say, 'O mountains of Israel, hear the word of the Lord GOD! Thus says the Lord GOD to the mountains, to the hills, to the ravines, and to the valleys: "Indeed I, *even* I, will bring a sword against you, and I will destroy your high places. [4]Then your altars shall be desolate, your incense altars shall be broken, and I will cast down your slain *men* before your idols. [5]And I will lay the corpses of the children of Israel before their idols, and I will scatter your bones all around your altars. [6]In all your dwelling places the cities shall be laid waste, and the high places shall be desolate, so that your altars may be laid waste and made desolate, your idols may be broken and made to cease, your incense altars may be cut down, and your works may be abolished. [7]The slain shall fall in your midst, and you shall know that I *am* the LORD.

[8]"Yet I will leave a remnant, so that you may have *some* who escape the sword among the nations, when you are scattered through the countries. [9]Then those of you who escape will remember Me among the nations where they

EZEKIEL

served as a prophet to the exiles in Babylon from 593–571 B.C.

Climate of the times
- Ezekiel and his people are taken to Babylon as captives.
- The Jews become foreigners in a strange land ruled by an authoritarian government.

Main message
God allowed the nation of Judah to be destroyed because of the people's sins, but there was still hope — God promised to restore the land to those who remained faithful to him.

Importance of message
God never forgets those who faithfully seek to obey him. They have a glorious future ahead.

Contemporary prophets
Daniel (605–536)
Habakkuk (612–588)
Jeremiah (627–586)

I sat where they sat, and remained there astonished among them seven days.

¹⁶Now it came to pass at the end of seven days that the word of the LORD came to me, saying, ¹⁷"Son of man, I have made you a watchman for the house of Israel; therefore hear a word from My mouth, and give them warning from Me: ¹⁸When I say to the wicked, 'You shall surely die,' and you give him no warning, nor speak to warn the wicked from his wicked way, to save his life, that same wicked *man* shall die in his iniquity; but his blood I will require at your hand. ¹⁹Yet, if you warn the wicked, and he does not turn from his wickedness, nor from his wicked way, he shall die in his iniquity; but you have delivered your soul.

²⁰"Again, when a righteous *man* turns from his righteousness and commits iniquity, and I lay a stumbling block before him, he shall die; because you did not give him warning, he shall die in his sin, and his righteousness which he has done shall not be remembered; but his blood I will require at your hand. ²¹Nevertheless if you warn the righteous *man* that the righteous should not sin, and he does not sin, he shall surely live because he took warning; also you will have delivered your soul."

²²Then the hand of the LORD was upon me there, and He said to me, "Arise, go out into the plain, and there I shall talk with you."

²³So I arose and went out into the plain, and behold, the glory of the LORD stood there, like the glory which I saw by the River Chebar; and I fell on my face. ²⁴Then the Spirit entered me and set me on my feet, and spoke with me and said to me: "Go, shut yourself inside your house. ²⁵And you, O son of man, surely they will put ropes on you and bind you with them, so that you cannot go out among them. ²⁶I will make your tongue cling to the roof of your mouth, so that you shall be mute and not be one to rebuke them, for they *are* a rebellious house. ²⁷But when I speak with you, I will open your mouth, and you shall say to them, 'Thus says the Lord GOD.' He who hears, let him hear; and he who refuses, let him refuse; for they *are* a rebellious house.

CHAPTER **4** **EZEKIEL DRAWS A PICTURE.** "You also, son of man, take a clay tablet and lay it before you, and portray on it a city, Jerusalem. ²Lay siege against it, build a siege wall against it, and heap up a mound against it; set camps against it also, and place battering rams against it all around. ³Moreover take for yourself an iron plate, and set it *as* an iron wall between you and the city. Set your face against it, and it shall be besieged, and you shall lay siege against it. This *will be* a sign to the house of Israel.

⁴"Lie also on your left side, and lay the iniquity of the house of Israel upon it. *According* to the number of the days that you lie on it, you shall bear their iniquity. ⁵For I have laid on you the years of their iniquity, according to the number of the days, three hundred and ninety days; so you shall bear the iniquity of the house of Israel. ⁶And when you have completed them, lie again on your right side; then you shall bear the iniquity of the house of Judah forty days. I have laid on you a day for each year.

⁷"Therefore you shall set your face toward the siege of Jerusalem; your arm *shall be* uncovered, and you shall

DETAILS

4:1ff Ezekiel enacted the coming siege and fall of Jerusalem before it actually happened. God gave Ezekiel specific instructions about what to say and how to say it. Each detail had a special meaning. Often we ignore or disregard the smaller details of God's Word, thinking he probably doesn't care. Like Ezekiel, we should want to obey God completely, even in the details.

are carried captive, because I was crushed by their adulterous heart which has departed from Me, and by their eyes which play the harlot after their idols; they will loathe themselves for the evils which they committed in all their abominations. [10]And they shall know that I *am* the LORD; I have not said in vain that I would bring this calamity upon them."

[11]Thus says the Lord GOD: "Pound your fists and stamp your feet, and say, 'Alas, for all the evil abominations of the house of Israel! For they shall fall by the sword, by famine, and by pestilence. [12]He who is far off shall die by the pestilence, he who is near shall fall by the sword, and he who remains and is besieged shall die by the famine. Thus will I spend My fury upon them. [13]Then you shall know that I *am* the LORD, when their slain are among their idols all around their altars, on every high hill, on all the mountaintops, under every green tree, and under every thick oak, wherever they offered sweet incense to all their idols. [14]So I will stretch out My hand against them and make the land desolate, yes, more desolate than the wilderness toward Diblah, in all their dwelling places. Then they shall know that I *am* the LORD.' """

CHAPTER 7 JERUSALEM WILL BE PUNISHED.

Moreover the word of the LORD came to me, saying, [2]"And you, son of man, thus says the Lord GOD to the land of Israel:

'An end! The end has come upon the four corners of
the land.
[3] Now the end *has come* upon you,
And I will send My anger against you;
I will judge you according to your ways,
And I will repay you for all your abominations.
[4] My eye will not spare you,
Nor will I have pity;
But I will repay your ways,
And your abominations will be in your midst;
Then you shall know that I *am* the LORD!'

[5]"Thus says the Lord GOD:

'A disaster, a singular disaster;
Behold, it has come!
[6] An end has come,
The end has come;
It has dawned for you;
Behold, it has come!
[7] Doom has come to you, you who dwell in the land;
The time has come,
A day of trouble *is* near,
And not of rejoicing in the mountains.
[8] Now upon you I will soon pour out My fury,
And spend My anger upon you;
I will judge you according to your ways,
And I will repay you for all your abominations.

[9] 'My eye will not spare,
Nor will I have pity;
I will repay you according to your ways,
And your abominations will be in your midst.

Then you shall know that I *am* the LORD who strikes.

[10] 'Behold, the day!
Behold, it has come!
Doom has gone out;
The rod has blossomed,
Pride has budded.

ONE AND ONLY

6:14 The phrase "then they shall know that I *am* the LORD" (or a variation on this phrase) occurs 70 times in the book of Ezekiel. The purpose of God's punishment was not revenge, but to impress upon the people the truth that the Lord is the only true and living God. Many people in Ezekiel's day were worshiping man-made idols and calling them gods. Today, money, sex, and power have become idols for many. Punishment will come upon all who put other things ahead of God. It is easy in our secular world to forget that the Lord alone is God, the supreme authority and the only source of eternal love and life. Remember that God may be using the difficulties of your life to remind you that he alone is God.

[11] Violence has risen up into a rod of wickedness;
None of them *shall remain*,
None of their multitude,
None of them;
Nor *shall there be* wailing for them.
[12] The time has come,
The day draws near.

'Let not the buyer rejoice,
Nor the seller mourn,
For wrath *is* on their whole multitude.
[13] For the seller shall not return to what has been sold,
Though he may still be alive;
For the vision concerns the whole multitude,
And it shall not turn back;
No one will strengthen himself
Who lives in iniquity.

[14] 'They have blown the trumpet and made everyone
ready,
But no one goes to battle;
For My wrath *is* on all their multitude.
[15] The sword *is* outside,
And the pestilence and famine within.
Whoever *is* in the field
Will die by the sword;
And whoever *is* in the city,
Famine and pestilence will devour him.
[16] 'Those who survive will escape and be on the
mountains
Like doves of the valleys,
All of them mourning,
Each for his iniquity.
[17] Every hand will be feeble,
And every knee will be *as* weak *as* water.
[18] They will also be girded with sackcloth;
Horror will cover them;
Shame *will be* on every face,
Baldness on all their heads.

7:19 Money too often seems to lead people into sin. Paul said the love of money is the first step to sin (1 Timothy 6:10). How ironic that we use wealth—a gift of God—to buy things that separate us from him. How tragic it is that we spend so much time looking for ways to satisfy ourselves with money and so little time looking for God, the true source of satisfaction.

19 'They will throw their silver into the streets,
And their gold will be like refuse;
Their silver and their gold will not be able to deliver
them
In the day of the wrath of the LORD;
They will not satisfy their souls,
Nor fill their stomachs,
Because it became their stumbling block of iniquity.

20 'As for the beauty of his ornaments,
He set it in majesty;
But they made from it
The images of their abominations—
Their detestable things;
Therefore I have made it
Like refuse to them.
21 I will give it as plunder
Into the hands of strangers,
And to the wicked of the earth as spoil;
And they shall defile it.
22 I will turn My face from them,
And they will defile My secret place;
For robbers shall enter it and defile it.

23 'Make a chain,
For the land is filled with crimes of blood,
And the city is full of violence.
24 Therefore I will bring the worst of the Gentiles,
And they will possess their houses;
I will cause the pomp of the strong to cease,
And their holy places shall be defiled.
25 Destruction comes;
They will seek peace, but *there shall be* none.
26 Disaster will come upon disaster,
And rumor will be upon rumor.
Then they will seek a vision from a prophet;
But the law will perish from the priest,
And counsel from the elders.

27 'The king will mourn,
The prince will be clothed with desolation,
And the hands of the common people will tremble.
I will do to them according to their way,
And according to what they deserve I will judge
them;
Then they shall know that I *am* the LORD!'"

CHAPTER 8 THE SINS OF THE PEOPLE.

And it came to pass in the sixth year, in the sixth *month*, on the fifth *day* of the month, as I sat in my house with the elders of Judah sitting before me, that the hand of the Lord GOD fell upon me there. 2Then I looked, and there was a likeness, like the appearance of fire—from the appearance of His waist and downward, fire; and from His waist and upward, like the appearance of brightness, like the color of amber. 3He stretched out the form of a hand, and took me by a lock of my hair; and the Spirit lifted me up between earth and heaven, and brought me in visions of God to Jerusalem, to the door of the north gate of the inner *court*, where the seat of the image of jealousy *was*, which provokes to jealousy. 4And behold, the glory of the God of Israel *was* there, like the vision that I saw in the plain.

5Then He said to me, "Son of man, lift your eyes now toward the north." So I lifted my eyes toward the north, and there, north of the altar gate, was this image of jealousy in the entrance.

6Furthermore He said to me, "Son of man, do you see what they are doing, the great abominations that the house of Israel commits here, to make Me go far away from My sanctuary? Now turn again, you will see greater abominations." 7So He brought me to the door of the court; and when I looked, there was a hole in the wall. 8Then He said to me, "Son of man, dig into the wall"; and when I dug into the wall, there was a door.

9And He said to me, "Go in, and see the wicked abominations which they are doing there." 10So I went in and saw, and there—every sort of creeping thing, abominable beasts, and all the idols of the house of Israel, portrayed all around on the walls. 11And there stood before them seventy men of the elders of the house of Israel, and in their midst stood Jaazaniah the son of Shaphan. Each man had a censer in his hand, and a thick cloud of incense went up. 12Then He said to me, "Son of man, have you seen what the elders of the house of Israel do in the dark, every man in the room of his idols? For they say, 'The LORD does not see us, the LORD has forsaken the land.'"

13And He said to me, "Turn again, *and* you will see greater abominations that they are doing." 14So He brought me to the door of the north gate of the LORD's house; and to my dismay, women were sitting there weeping for Tammuz.

15Then He said to me, "Have you seen *this*, O son of man? Turn again, you will see greater abominations than these." 16So He brought me into the inner court of the LORD's house; and there, at the door of the temple of the LORD, between the porch and the altar, *were* about twenty-five men with their backs toward the temple of the LORD and their faces toward the east, and they were worshiping the sun toward the east.

17And He said to me, "Have you seen *this*, O son of man? Is it a trivial thing to the house of Judah to commit the abominations which they commit here? For they have filled the land with violence; then they have returned to provoke Me to anger. Indeed they put the branch to their nose. 18Therefore I also will act in fury. My eye will not spare nor will I have pity; and though they cry in My ears with a loud voice, I will not hear them."

◣◥◤ OPEN HOUSE

8:6ff In scene after scene, God revealed to Ezekiel the extent that the people had embraced idolatry and wickedness. God's Spirit works with us in a similar way, revealing sin that lurks in our life. How comfortable would you feel if God held an open house in your life?

CHAPTER 9 SOME WICKED PEOPLE DIE.

Then He called out in my hearing with a loud voice, saying, "Let those who have charge over the city draw near, each *with* a deadly weapon in his hand." ²And suddenly six men came from the direction of the upper gate, which faces north, each with his battle-ax in his hand. One man among them *was* clothed with linen and had a writer's inkhorn at his side. They went in and stood beside the bronze altar.

³Now the glory of the God of Israel had gone up from the cherub, where it had been, to the threshold of the temple. And He called to the man clothed with linen, who *had* the writer's inkhorn at his side; ⁴and the LORD said to him, "Go through the midst of the city, through the midst of Jerusalem, and put a mark on the foreheads of the men who sigh and cry over all the abominations that are done within it."

⁵To the others He said in my hearing, "Go after him through the city and kill; do not let your eye spare, nor have any pity. ⁶Utterly slay old *and* young men, maidens and little children and women; but do not come near anyone on whom *is* the mark; and begin at My sanctuary." So they began with the elders who *were* before the temple. ⁷Then He said to them, "Defile the temple, and fill the courts with the slain. Go out!" And they went out and killed in the city.

⁸So it was, that while they were killing them, I was left *alone*; and I fell on my face and cried out, and said, "Ah, Lord GOD! Will You destroy all the remnant of Israel in pouring out Your fury on Jerusalem?"

⁹Then He said to me, "The iniquity of the house of Israel and Judah *is* exceedingly great, and the land is full of bloodshed, and the city full of perversity; for they say, 'The LORD has forsaken the land, and the LORD does not see!' ¹⁰And as for Me also, My eye will neither spare, nor will I have pity, *but* I will recompense their deeds on their own head."

¹¹Just then, the man clothed with linen, who *had* the inkhorn at his side, reported back and said, "I have done as You commanded me."

CHAPTER 10 BURNING COALS.

And I looked, and there in the firmament that was above the head of the cherubim, there appeared something like a sapphire stone, having the appearance of the likeness of a throne. ²Then He spoke to the man clothed with linen, and said, "Go in among the wheels, under the cherub, fill your hands with coals of fire from among the cherubim, and scatter *them* over the city." And he went in as I watched.

³Now the cherubim were standing on the south side of the temple when the man went in, and the cloud filled the inner court. ⁴Then the glory of the LORD went up from the cherub, *and paused* over the threshold of the temple; and the house was filled with the cloud, and the court was full of the brightness of the LORD's glory. ⁵And the sound of the wings of the cherubim was heard *even* in the outer court, like the voice of Almighty God when He speaks.

⁶Then it happened, when He commanded the man clothed in linen, saying, "Take fire from among the wheels, from among the cherubim," that he went in and stood beside the wheels. ⁷And the cherub stretched out his hand from among the cherubim to the fire that *was* among the cherubim, and took *some of it* and put *it* into the hands of the *man* clothed with linen, who took *it* and went out. ⁸The cherubim appeared to have the form of a man's hand under their wings.

⁹And when I looked, there were four wheels by the cherubim, one wheel by one cherub and another wheel by each other cherub; the wheels appeared *to have* the color of a beryl stone. ¹⁰*As for* their appearance, all four looked alike—as it were, a wheel in the middle of a wheel. ¹¹When they went, they went toward *any of* their four directions; they did not turn aside when they went, but followed in the direction the head was facing. They did not turn aside when they went. ¹²And their whole body, with their back, their hands, their wings, and the wheels that the four had, *were* full of eyes all around. ¹³As for the wheels, they were called in my hearing, "Wheel."

◥◣◢ NO EXCUSE

9:9-10 The people said that God had gone away and wouldn't see their sin. People have many convenient explanations to make it easier to sin: "It doesn't matter." "Everybody's doing it." Or, "Nobody will ever know." Do you find yourself making excuses for sin? Rationalizing makes it easier to commit sin, but it does not influence God's promise to punish sin.

¹⁴Each one had four faces: the first face *was* the face of a cherub, the second face the face of a man, the third the face of a lion, and the fourth the face of an eagle. ¹⁵And the cherubim were lifted up. This *was* the living creature I saw by the River Chebar. ¹⁶When the cherubim went, the wheels went beside them; and when the cherubim lifted their wings to mount up from the earth, the same wheels also did not turn from beside them. ¹⁷When *the cherubim* stood still, *the wheels* stood still, and when *one* was lifted up, *the other* lifted itself up, for the spirit of the living creature *was* in them.

¹⁸Then the glory of the LORD departed from the threshold of the temple and stood over the cherubim. ¹⁹And the cherubim lifted their wings and mounted up from the earth in my sight. When they went out, the wheels *were* beside them; and they stood at the door of the east gate of the LORD's house, and the glory of the God of Israel *was* above them.

²⁰This *is* the living creature I saw under the God of Israel by the River Chebar, and I knew they *were* cherubim. ²¹Each one had four faces and each one four wings, and the likeness of the hands of a man *was* under their wings. ²²And the likeness of their faces *was* the same *as* the faces which I had seen by the River Chebar, their appearance and their persons. They each went straight forward.

CHAPTER 11 GOD WILL BRING HIS PEOPLE BACK.

Then the Spirit lifted me up and brought me to the East Gate of the LORD's house, which faces eastward; and there at the door of the gate were twenty-five men, among whom I saw Jaazaniah the son of Azzur, and Pelatiah the

11:12 From the time they entered the Promised Land, the Israelites were warned not to copy the customs and religious practices of other nations. Disobeying this command and following heathen customs instead of God's laws always got them into trouble. Today, believers are still tempted to copy the ways of the world. But we must get our standards of right and wrong from God, not from the popular trends of society.

son of Benaiah, princes of the people. ²And He said to me: "Son of man, these *are* the men who devise iniquity and give wicked counsel in this city, ³who say, '*The time is* not near to build houses; this *city is* the caldron, and we *are* the meat.' ⁴Therefore prophesy against them, prophesy, O son of man!"

⁵Then the Spirit of the LORD fell upon me, and said to me, "Speak! 'Thus says the LORD: "Thus you have said, O house of Israel; for I know the things that come into your mind. ⁶You have multiplied your slain in this city, and you have filled its streets with the slain." ⁷Therefore thus says the Lord GOD: "Your slain whom you have laid in its midst, they *are* the meat, and this *city is* the caldron; but I shall bring you out of the midst of it. ⁸You have feared the sword; and I will bring a sword upon you," says the Lord GOD. ⁹"And I will bring you out of its midst, and deliver you into the hands of strangers, and execute judgments on you. ¹⁰You shall fall by the sword. I will judge you at the border of Israel. Then you shall know that I *am* the LORD. ¹¹This *city* shall not be your caldron, nor shall you be the meat in its midst. I will judge you at the border of Israel. ¹²And you shall know that I *am* the LORD; for you have not walked in My statutes nor executed My judgments, but have done according to the customs of the Gentiles which *are* all around you." ' "

¹³Now it happened, while I was prophesying, that Pelatiah the son of Benaiah died. Then I fell on my face and cried with a loud voice, and said, "Ah, Lord GOD! Will You make a complete end of the remnant of Israel?"

¹⁴Again the word of the LORD came to me, saying, ¹⁵"Son of man, your brethren, your relatives, your countrymen, and all the house of Israel in its entirety, *are* those about whom the inhabitants of Jerusalem have said, 'Get far away from the LORD; this land has been given to us as a possession.' ¹⁶Therefore say, 'Thus says the Lord GOD: "Although I have cast them far off among the Gentiles, and although I have scattered them among the countries, yet I shall be a little sanctuary for them in the countries where they have gone." ' ¹⁷Therefore say, 'Thus says the Lord GOD: "I will gather you from the peoples, assemble you from the countries where you have been scattered, and I will give you the land of Israel." ' ¹⁸And they will go there, and they will take away all its detestable things and all its abominations from there. ¹⁹Then I will give them one heart, and I will put a new spirit within them, and take the stony heart out of their flesh, and give them a heart of flesh, ²⁰that they may walk in My statutes and keep My judgments and do them; and they shall be My people, and I will be their God. ²¹But *as for those* whose hearts follow the desire for their detestable things and their abominations, I will recompense their deeds on their own heads," says the Lord GOD.

²²So the cherubim lifted up their wings, with the wheels beside them, and the glory of the God of Israel *was* high above them. ²³And the glory of the LORD went up from the midst of the city and stood on the mountain, which *is* on the east side of the city.

²⁴Then the Spirit took me up and brought me in a vision by the Spirit of God into Chaldea, to those in captivity. And the vision that I had seen went up from me. ²⁵So I spoke to those in captivity of all the things the LORD had shown me.

CHAPTER 12 EZEKIEL DIGS THROUGH A WALL.

Now the word of the LORD came to me, saying: ²"Son of man, you dwell in the midst of a rebellious house, which has eyes to see but does not see, and ears to hear but does not hear; for they *are* a rebellious house.

³"Therefore, son of man, prepare your belongings for captivity, and go into captivity by day in their sight. You shall go from your place into captivity to another place in their sight. It may be that they will consider, though they *are* a rebellious house. ⁴By day you shall bring out your belongings in their sight, as though going into captivity; and at evening you shall go in their sight, like those who go into captivity. ⁵Dig through the wall in their sight, and carry your belongings out through it. ⁶In their sight you shall bear *them* on *your* shoulders *and* carry *them* out at twilight; you shall cover your face, so that you cannot see the ground, for I have made you a sign to the house of Israel."

⁷So I did as I was commanded. I brought out my belongings by day, as though going into captivity, and at evening I dug through the wall with my hand. I brought *them* out at twilight, *and* I bore *them* on *my* shoulder in their sight.

⁸And in the morning the word of the LORD came to me, saying, ⁹"Son of man, has not the house of Israel, the rebellious house, said to you, 'What are you doing?' ¹⁰Say to them, 'Thus says the Lord GOD: "This burden *concerns* the prince in Jerusalem and all the house of Israel who are among them." ' ¹¹Say, 'I *am* a sign to you. As I have done, so shall it be done to them; they shall be carried away into captivity.' ¹²And the prince who *is* among them shall bear *his belongings* on *his* shoulder at twilight and go out. They shall dig through the wall to carry *them* out through it. He shall cover his face, so that he cannot see the ground with *his* eyes. ¹³I will also spread My net over him, and he shall be caught in My snare. I will bring him to Babylon, *to* the land of the Chaldeans; yet he shall not see it, though he shall die there. ¹⁴I will scatter to every wind all who *are* around him to help him, and all his troops; and I will draw out the sword after them.

¹⁵"Then they shall know that I *am* the LORD, when I scatter them among the nations and disperse them throughout the countries. ¹⁶But I will spare a few of their men from the sword, from famine, and from pestilence, that they may declare all their abominations among the Gentiles wherever they go. Then they shall know that I *am* the LORD."

¹⁷Moreover the word of the LORD came to me, saying, ¹⁸"Son of man, eat your bread with quaking, and drink your water with trembling and anxiety. ¹⁹And say to the people of the land, 'Thus says the Lord GOD to the inhab-

itants of Jerusalem *and* to the land of Israel: "They shall eat their bread with anxiety, and drink their water with dread, so that her land may be emptied of all who are in it, because of the violence of all those who dwell in it. ²⁰Then the cities that are inhabited shall be laid waste, and the land shall become desolate; and you shall know that I *am* the LORD." ' "

²¹And the word of the LORD came to me, saying, ²²"Son of man, what *is* this proverb *that* you *people* have about the land of Israel, which says, 'The days are prolonged, and every vision fails'? ²³Tell them therefore, 'Thus says the Lord GOD: "I will lay this proverb to rest, and they shall no more use it as a proverb in Israel." But say to them, "The days are at hand, and the fulfillment of every vision. ²⁴For no more shall there be any false vision or flattering divination within the house of Israel. ²⁵For I *am* the LORD. I speak, and the word which I speak will come to pass; it will no more be postponed; for in your days, O rebellious house, I will say the word and perform it," says the Lord GOD.' "

²⁶Again the word of the LORD came to me, saying, ²⁷"Son of man, look, the house of Israel is saying, 'The vision that he sees *is* for many days *from now,* and he prophesies of times far off.' ²⁸Therefore say to them, 'Thus says the Lord GOD: "None of My words will be postponed any more, but the word which I speak will be done," says the Lord GOD.' "

CHAPTER **13** FALSE TEACHERS GET IN TROUBLE.

And the word of the LORD came to me, saying, ²"Son of man, prophesy against the prophets of Israel who prophesy, and say to those who prophesy out of their own heart, 'Hear the word of the LORD!' "

³Thus says the Lord GOD: "Woe to the foolish prophets, who follow their own spirit and have seen nothing! ⁴O Israel, your prophets are like foxes in the deserts. ⁵You have not gone up into the gaps to build a wall for the house of Israel to stand in battle on the day of the LORD. ⁶They have envisioned futility and false divination, saying, 'Thus says the LORD!' But the LORD has not sent them; yet they hope that the word may be confirmed. ⁷Have you not seen a futile vision, and have you not spoken false divination? You say, 'The LORD says,' but I have not spoken."

⁸Therefore thus says the Lord GOD: "Because you have spoken nonsense and envisioned lies, therefore I *am* indeed against you," says the Lord GOD. ⁹"My hand will be against the prophets who envision futility and who divine lies; they shall not be in the assembly of My people, nor be written in the record of the house of Israel, nor shall they enter into the land of Israel. Then you shall know that I *am* the Lord GOD.

¹⁰"Because, indeed, because they have seduced My people, saying, 'Peace!' when *there is* no peace—and one builds a wall, and they plaster it with untempered *mortar*— ¹¹say to those who plaster *it* with untempered *mortar,* that it will fall. There will be flooding rain, and you, O great hailstones, shall fall; and a stormy wind shall tear *it* down. ¹²Surely, when the wall has fallen, will it not be said to you, 'Where *is* the mortar with which you plastered *it?* "

¹³Therefore thus says the Lord GOD: "I will cause a stormy wind to break forth in My fury; and there shall be a flooding rain in My anger, and great hailstones in fury to consume *it.* ¹⁴So I will break down the wall you have plastered with untempered *mortar,* and bring it down to the ground, so that its foundation will be uncovered; it will fall, and you shall be consumed in the midst of it. Then you shall know that I *am* the LORD.

▬▬▬▬OUT OF TIME

12:21-28 These two short messages were warnings that God's words would come true—*soon!* Less than six years later, Jerusalem was destroyed. Judgment comes swiftly. No one—not you or anyone you know—should dare to assume there is plenty of time to get right with God.

¹⁵"Thus will I accomplish My wrath on the wall and on those who have plastered it with untempered *mortar;* and I will say to you, 'The wall *is* no *more,* nor those who plastered it, ¹⁶*that is,* the prophets of Israel who prophesy concerning Jerusalem, and who see visions of peace for her when *there is* no peace,' " says the Lord GOD.

¹⁷"Likewise, son of man, set your face against the daughters of your people, who prophesy out of their own heart; prophesy against them, ¹⁸and say, 'Thus says the Lord GOD: "Woe to the *women* who sew *magic* charms on their sleeves and make veils for the heads of people of every height to hunt souls! Will you hunt the souls of My people, and keep yourselves alive? ¹⁹And will you profane Me among My people for handfuls of barley and for pieces of bread, killing people who should not die, and keeping people alive who should not live, by your lying to My people who listen to lies?"

²⁰Therefore thus says the Lord GOD: "Behold, I *am* against your *magic* charms by which you hunt souls there like birds. I will tear them from your arms, and let the souls go, the souls you hunt like birds. ²¹I will also tear off your veils and deliver My people out of your hand, and they shall no longer be as prey in your hand. Then you shall know that I *am* the LORD.

²²"Because with lies you have made the heart of the righteous sad, whom I have not made sad; and you have strengthened the hands of the wicked, so that he does not turn from his wicked way to save his life. ²³Therefore you shall no longer envision futility nor practice divination; for I will deliver My people out of your hand, and you shall know that I *am* the LORD." ' "

CHAPTER **14** GOD HATES IDOLS. Now some of the

elders of Israel came to me and sat before me. ²And the

▬▬▬▬▬LIES

13:2-3 The false prophets had a large following because they comforted the people and approved of their actions even while they were sinning. Lies often are attractive, and liars may have large followings. Today, for example, some leaders assure us that God wants everyone to have health and material success. This is comforting, but is it true? God's own Son did not have an easy life on earth—he didn't even have a place to lay his head (Matthew 8:20). Make sure the messages you believe are consistent with what God teaches in his Word.

word of the LORD came to me, saying, [3]"Son of man, these men have set up their idols in their hearts, and put before them that which causes them to stumble into iniquity. Should I let Myself be inquired of at all by them? [4]"Therefore speak to them, and say to them, 'Thus says the Lord GOD: "Everyone of the house of Israel who sets up his idols in his heart, and puts before him what causes him to stumble into iniquity, and then comes to the prophet, I the LORD will answer him who comes, according to the multitude of his idols, [5]that I may seize the house of Israel by their heart, because they are all estranged from Me by their idols." '

[6]"Therefore say to the house of Israel, 'Thus says the Lord GOD: "Repent, turn away from your idols, and turn your faces away from all your abominations. [7]For anyone of the house of Israel, or of the strangers who dwell in Israel, who separates himself from Me and sets up his idols in his heart and puts before him what causes him to stumble into iniquity, then comes to a prophet to inquire of him concerning Me, I the LORD will answer him by Myself. [8]I will set My face against that man and make him a sign and a proverb, and I will cut him off from the midst of My people. Then you shall know that I *am* the LORD.

[9]"And if the prophet is induced to speak anything, I the LORD have induced that prophet, and I will stretch out My hand against him and destroy him from among My people Israel. [10]And they shall bear their iniquity; the punishment of the prophet shall be the same as the punishment of the one who inquired, [11]that the house of Israel may no longer stray from Me, nor be profaned anymore with all their transgressions, but that they may be My people and I may be their God," says the Lord GOD.' "

[12]The word of the LORD came again to me, saying: [13]"Son of man, when a land sins against Me by persistent unfaithfulness, I will stretch out My hand against it; I will cut off its supply of bread, send famine on it, and cut off man and beast from it. [14]Even *if* these three men, Noah, Daniel, and Job, were in it, they would deliver *only* themselves by their righteousness," says the Lord GOD.

[15]"If I cause wild beasts to pass through the land, and they empty it, and make it so desolate that no man may pass through because of the beasts, [16]*even though* these three men *were* in it, *as* I live," says the Lord GOD, "they would deliver neither sons nor daughters; only they would be delivered, and the land would be desolate.

[17]"Or *if* I bring a sword on that land, and say, 'Sword, go through the land,' and I cut off man and beast from it, [18]even *though* these three men *were* in it, *as* I live," says the Lord GOD, "they would deliver neither sons nor daughters, but only they themselves would be delivered. [19]"Or *if* I send a pestilence into that land and pour out My fury on it in blood, and cut off from it man and beast,

[20]even *though* Noah, Daniel, and Job *were* in it, *as* I live," says the Lord GOD, "they would deliver neither son nor daughter; they would deliver *only* themselves by their righteousness."

[21]For thus says the Lord GOD: "How much more it shall be when I send My four severe judgments on Jerusalem—the sword and famine and wild beasts and pestilence—to cut off man and beast from it? [22]Yet behold, there shall be left in it a remnant who will be brought out, *both* sons and daughters; surely they will come out to you, and you will see their ways and their doings. Then you will be comforted concerning the disaster that I have brought upon Jerusalem, all that I have brought upon it. [23]And they shall comfort you, when you see their ways and their doings; and you shall know that I have done nothing without cause that I have done in it," says the Lord GOD.

CHAPTER 15 A USELESS VINE.

Then the word of the LORD came to me, saying: [2]"Son of man, how is the wood of the vine *better* than any other wood, the vine branch which is among the trees of the forest? [3]Is wood taken from it to make any object? Or can *men* make a peg

from it to hang any vessel on? [4]Instead, it is thrown into the fire for fuel; the fire devours both ends of it, and its middle is burned. Is it useful for *any* work? [5]Indeed, when it was whole, no object could be made from it. How much less will it be useful for *any* work when the fire has devoured it, and it is burned?

[6]"Therefore thus says the Lord GOD: 'Like the wood of the vine among the trees of the forest, which I have given to the fire for fuel, so I will give up the inhabitants of Jerusalem; [7]and I will set My face against them. They will go out from *one* fire, but *another* fire shall devour them. Then you shall know that I *am* the LORD, when I set My face against them. [8]Thus I will make the land desolate, because they have persisted in unfaithfulness,' says the Lord GOD."

CHAPTER 16 TERRIBLE SINS.

Again the word of the LORD came to me, saying, [2]"Son of man, cause Jerusalem to know her abominations, [3]and say, 'Thus says the Lord GOD to Jerusalem: "Your birth and your nativity *are* from the land of Canaan; your father *was* an Amorite and your mother a Hittite. [4]*As for* your nativity, on the day you were born your navel cord was not cut, nor were you washed in water to cleanse *you;* you were not rubbed with salt nor wrapped in swaddling cloths. [5]No eye pitied you, to do any of these things for you, to have compassion on you; but you were thrown out into the open field, when you yourself were loathed on the day you were born.

[6]"And when I passed by you and saw you struggling in your own blood, I said to you in your blood, 'Live!' Yes, I said to you in your blood, 'Live!' [7]I made you thrive like a plant in the field; and you grew, matured, and became very beautiful. *Your* breasts were formed, your hair grew, but you *were* naked and bare.

[8]"When I passed by you again and looked upon you, indeed your time *was* the time of love; so I spread My wing over you and covered your nakedness. Yes, I swore an oath to you and entered into a covenant with you, and you became Mine," says the Lord GOD.

[9]"Then I washed you in water; yes, I thoroughly washed off your blood, and I anointed you with oil. [10]I clothed you in embroidered cloth and gave you sandals of badger skin; I clothed you with fine linen and covered you with silk. [11]I adorned you with ornaments, put bracelets on your wrists, and a chain on your neck. [12]And I put a jewel in your nose, earrings in your ears, and a beautiful crown on your head. [13]Thus you were adorned with gold and silver, and your clothing *was of* fine linen, silk, and embroidered cloth. You ate *pastry of* fine flour, honey, and oil. You were exceedingly beautiful, and succeeded to royalty. [14]Your fame went out among the nations because of your beauty, for it *was* perfect through My splendor which I had bestowed on you," says the Lord GOD.

[15]"But you trusted in your own beauty, played the harlot because of your fame, and poured out your harlotry on everyone passing by who *would have* it. [16]You took some of your garments and adorned multicolored high places for yourself, and played the harlot on them. *Such* things should not happen, nor be. [17]You have also taken your beautiful jewelry from My gold and My silver, which I had given you, and made for yourself male images and played the harlot with them. [18]You took your embroidered garments and covered them, and you set My oil and My incense before them. [19]Also My food which I gave you—the pastry of fine flour, oil, and honey *which* I fed you—you set it before them as sweet incense; and *so* it was," says the Lord GOD.

[20]"Moreover you took your sons and your daughters, whom you bore to Me, and these you sacrificed to them to be devoured. *Were* your *acts* of harlotry a small matter, [21]that you have slain My children and offered them up to them by causing them to pass through *the fire?* [22]And in all your abominations and acts of harlotry you did not remember the days of your youth, when you were naked and bare, struggling in your blood.

[23]"Then it was so, after all your wickedness—'Woe, woe to you!' says the Lord GOD— [24]*that* you also built for yourself a shrine, and made a high place for yourself in every street. [25]You built your high places at the head of every road, and made your beauty to be abhorred. You offered yourself to everyone who passed by, and multiplied your acts of harlotry. [26]You also committed harlotry with the Egyptians, your very fleshly neighbors, and increased your acts of harlotry to provoke Me to anger.

[27]"Behold, therefore, I stretched out My hand against you, diminished your allotment, and gave you up to the will of those who hate you, the daughters of the Philistines, who were ashamed of your lewd behavior. [28]You also played the harlot with the Assyrians, because you were insatiable; indeed you played the harlot with them

SPECIAL PRIVILEGES

16:8-14 God chose Israel to be the channel through whom he would communicate his message of salvation to the entire world. God gave Israel special privileges and trained Israel to do his work. But these resources and advantages became Israel's source of pride and vanity. We must remember that God made us what we are. To use our gifts and opportunities only for our own selfish pursuits is both dangerous and foolish.

and still were not satisfied. [29]Moreover you multiplied your acts of harlotry as far as the land of the trader, Chaldea; and even then you were not satisfied.

It doesn't seem like I'm making too much progress as a Christian. It even seems like I'm going backward. What can I do to reverse my reversal?

I WONDER...

Until about age 25, we grow physically.

After that, we start to die. Fortunately, it usually takes another 40 to 50 years to complete the dying process!

Our spiritual life often goes through a living and dying process, too. It's either living and growing, or it's in the process of dying. There is no such thing as leveling out or "plateauing."

You've hit the first stage of beginning to grow spiritually again: you recognize that you've been dying.

The second stage is discovering what caused the dying process. God confronted his people continually about this. Speaking through Ezekiel, he showed them that idols had replaced God in their hearts (see Ezekiel 14:1-5).

Has something been pushing God out of your life—television, a friendship, sports, a boyfriend or girlfriend, music, fun? Any of these can become idols. If they do, they must be removed from the center of your life. When you recognize that something has drawn your heart away from God, turn around! Confess the problem to God and turn it over to him (see 1 John 1:9).

The third stage is the one that many Christians forget—finding someone to hold us accountable. You need someone to encourage you, to ask tough questions, to kick you in the pants when you need it, and to pray for you.

This could be a friend your own age who has a real desire to grow spiritually. It could be a Christian adult whom you like and respect—or anyone who is genuinely concerned for you, who won't get down on you, who will always pull for you.

Ask God to send you such a person. This may be scary, but Christians who are growing have learned the secret of asking others to help them stay on track. Always seek out someone who will walk with you. It will help keep you from falling and provide you with close, lifelong friends.

³⁰"How degenerate is your heart!" says the Lord God, "seeing you do all these *things,* the deeds of a brazen harlot.

³¹"You erected your shrine at the head of every road, and built your high place in every street. Yet you were not like a harlot, because you scorned payment. ³² *You are* an adulterous wife, *who* takes strangers instead of her husband. ³³Men make payment to all harlots, but you made your payments to all your lovers, and hired them to come to you from all around for your harlotry. ³⁴You are the opposite of *other* women in your harlotry, because no one solicited you to be a harlot. In that you gave payment but no payment was given you, therefore you are the opposite."

³⁵'Now then, O harlot, hear the word of the LORD! ³⁶Thus says the Lord God: "Because your filthiness was poured out and your nakedness uncovered in your harlotry with your lovers, and with all your abominable idols, and because of the blood of your children which you gave to them, ³⁷surely, therefore, I will gather all your lovers with whom you took pleasure, all those you loved, *and* all those you hated; I will gather them from all around against you and will uncover your nakedness to them, that they may see all your nakedness. ³⁸And I will judge you as women who break wedlock or shed blood are judged; I will bring blood upon you in fury and jealousy. ³⁹I will also give you into their hand, and they shall throw down your shrines and break down your high places. They shall also strip you of your clothes, take your beautiful jewelry, and leave you naked and bare.

⁴⁰"They shall also bring up an assembly against you, and they shall stone you with stones and thrust you through with their swords. ⁴¹They shall burn your houses with fire, and execute judgments on you in the sight of many women; and I will make you cease playing the harlot, and you shall no longer hire lovers. ⁴²So I will lay to rest My fury toward you, and My jealousy shall depart from you. I will be quiet, and be angry no more. ⁴³Because you did not remember the days of your youth, but agitated Me with all these *things,* surely I will also recompense your deeds on *your own* head," says the Lord God. "And you shall not commit lewdness in addition to all your abominations.

⁴⁴"Indeed everyone who quotes proverbs will use *this* proverb against you: 'Like mother, like daughter!' ⁴⁵You *are* your mother's daughter, loathing husband and children; and you *are* the sister of your sisters, who loathed their husbands and children; your mother *was* a Hittite and your father an Amorite.

⁴⁶"Your elder sister *is* Samaria, who dwells with her daughters to the north of you; and your younger sister, who dwells to the south of you, *is* Sodom and her daughters. ⁴⁷You did not walk in their ways nor act according to their abominations; but, as *if that were* too little, you became more corrupt than they in all your ways.

⁴⁸"*As* I live," says the Lord God, "neither your sister Sodom nor her daughters have done as you and your daughters have done. ⁴⁹Look, this was the iniquity of your sister Sodom: She and her daughter had pride, fullness of food, and abundance of idleness; neither did she strengthen the hand of the poor and needy. ⁵⁰And they

were haughty and committed abomination before Me; therefore I took them away as I saw *fit.*

⁵¹"Samaria did not commit half of your sins; but you have multiplied your abominations more than they, and have justified your sisters by all the abominations which you have done. ⁵²You who judged your sisters, bear your own shame also, because the sins which you committed were more abominable than theirs; they are more righteous than you. Yes, be disgraced also, and bear your own shame, because you justified your sisters.

⁵³"When I bring back their captives, the captives of Sodom and her daughters, and the captives of Samaria and her daughters, then *I will also bring back* the captives of your captivity among them, ⁵⁴that you may bear your own shame and be disgraced by all that you did when you comforted them. ⁵⁵When your sisters, Sodom and her daughters, return to their former state, and Samaria and her daughters return to their former state, then you and your daughters will return to your former state. ⁵⁶For your sister Sodom was not a byword in your mouth in the days of your pride, ⁵⁷before your wickedness was uncovered. It was like the time of the reproach of the daughters of Syria and all *those* around her, and of the daughters of the Philistines, who despise you everywhere. ⁵⁸You have paid for your lewdness and your abominations," says the LORD. ⁵⁹For thus says the Lord God: "I will deal with you as you have done, who despised the oath by breaking the covenant.

⁶⁰"Nevertheless I will remember My covenant with you in the days of your youth, and I will establish an everlasting covenant with you. ⁶¹Then you will remember your ways and be ashamed, when you receive your older and your younger sisters; for I will give them to you for daughters, but not because of My covenant with you. ⁶²And I will establish My covenant with you. Then you shall know that I *am* the LORD, ⁶³that you may remember and be ashamed, and never open your mouth anymore because of your shame, when I provide you an atonement for all you have done," says the Lord God.'"

CHAPTER **17** THE GREAT EAGLE. And the word of the LORD came to me, saying, ²"Son of man, pose a riddle, and speak a parable to the house of Israel, ³and say, 'Thus says the Lord God:

17:1 The first eagle in this chapter represents King Nebuchadnez█ Babylon (see 17:12), who appointed, or "planted," Zedekiah as ki█ Jerusalem. Zedekiah rebelled against this arrangement and tried █ with Egypt, the second eagle, to battle Babylon. Miles away in Bab█ Ezekiel was describing these events. Jeremiah, a prophet in Judah, was warning Zedekiah not to form this alliance (Jeremiah 2:36-37█ Though miles apart, the prophets had the same message because █ spoke for God. God still directs his chosen spokespeople to speak h█ all around the world.

"A great eagle with large wings and long pinions,
Full of feathers of various colors,
Came to Lebanon
And took from the cedar the highest branch.
4 He cropped off its topmost young twig
And carried it to a land of trade;
He set it in a city of merchants.
5 Then he took some of the seed of the land
And planted it in a fertile field;
He placed *it* by abundant waters
And set it like a willow tree.
6 And it grew and became a spreading vine of low
stature;
Its branches turned toward him,
But its roots were under it.
So it became a vine,
Brought forth branches,
And put forth shoots.

7 "But there was another great eagle with large wings
and many feathers;
And behold, this vine bent its roots toward him,
And stretched its branches toward him,
From the garden terrace where it had been planted,
That he might water it.
8 It was planted in good soil by many waters,
To bring forth branches, bear fruit,
And become a majestic vine." '

9"Say, 'Thus says the Lord GOD:

"Will it thrive?
Will he not pull up its roots,
Cut off its fruit,
And leave it to wither?
All of its spring leaves will wither,
And no great power or many people
Will be needed to pluck it up by its roots.
10 Behold, *it is* planted,
Will it thrive?
Will it not utterly wither when the east wind touches
it?
It will wither in the garden terrace where it grew." ' "

11Moreover the word of the LORD came to me, saying,
12"Say now to the rebellious house: 'Do you not know
what these *things* mean?' Tell *them,* 'Indeed the king of
Babylon went to Jerusalem and took its king and princes,
and led them with him to Babylon. 13And he took the
king's offspring, made a covenant with him, and put him
under oath. He also took away the mighty of the land,
14that the kingdom might be brought low and not lift
itself up, *but* that by keeping his covenant it might stand.
15But he rebelled against him by sending his ambassadors to Egypt, that they might give him horses and many
people. Will he prosper? Will he who does such *things*
escape? Can he break a covenant and still be delivered?
16"*As* I live,' says the Lord GOD, 'surely in the place
where the king *dwells* who made him king, whose oath he
despised and whose covenant he broke—with him in the
midst of Babylon he shall die. 17Nor will Pharaoh with *his*
mighty army and great company do anything in the war,
when they heap up a siege mound and build a wall to cut
off many persons. 18Since he despised the oath by breaking the covenant, and in fact gave his hand and still did
all these *things,* he shall not escape.' "

19Therefore thus says the Lord GOD: "*As* I live, surely My
oath which he despised, and My covenant which he
broke, I will recompense on his own head. 20I will spread
My net over him, and he shall be taken in My snare. I will
bring him to Babylon and try him there for the treason
which he committed against Me. 21All his fugitives with
all his troops shall fall by the sword, and those who remain shall be scattered to every wind; and you shall
know that I, the LORD, have spoken."

22Thus says the Lord GOD: "I will take also *one* of the
highest branches of the high cedar and set *it* out. I will
crop off from the topmost of its young twigs a tender one,
and will plant *it* on a high and prominent mountain. 23On
the mountain height of Israel I will plant it; and it will
bring forth boughs, and bear fruit, and be a majestic
cedar. Under it will dwell birds of every sort; in the
shadow of its branches they will dwell. 24And all the trees
of the field shall know that I, the LORD, have brought
down the high tree and exalted the low tree, dried up the
green tree and made the dry tree flourish; I, the LORD,
have spoken and have done *it.*"

CHAPTER **18** TURN AND LIVE! The word of the
LORD came to me again, saying, 2"What do you mean
when you use this proverb concerning the land of Israel,
saying:

'The fathers have eaten sour grapes,
And the children's teeth are set on edge'?

3"*As* I live," says the Lord GOD, "you shall no longer use
this proverb in Israel.

4 "Behold, all souls are Mine;
The soul of the father
As well as the soul of the son is Mine;
The soul who sins shall die.
5 But if a man is just
And does what is lawful and right;
6 If he has not eaten on the mountains,
Nor lifted up his eyes to the idols of the house of
Israel,
Nor defiled his neighbor's wife,
Nor approached a woman during her impurity;
7 If he has not oppressed anyone,
But has restored to the debtor his pledge;
Has robbed no one by violence,
But has given his bread to the hungry
And covered the naked with clothing;
8 If he has not exacted usury
Nor taken any increase,
But has withdrawn his hand from iniquity
And executed true judgment between man and man;
9 *If* he has walked in My statutes
And kept My judgments faithfully—
He *is* just;
He shall surely live!"
Says the Lord GOD.

¹⁰ "If he begets a son *who is* a robber
    Or a shedder of blood,
    Who does any of these *things*
¹¹ And does none of those *duties,*
    But has eaten on the mountains
    Or defiled his neighbor's wife;
¹² If he has oppressed the poor and needy,
    Robbed by violence,
    Not restored the pledge,
    Lifted his eyes to the idols,
    Or committed abomination;
¹³ If he has exacted usury
    Or taken increase—
    Shall he then live?
    He shall not live!
    If he has done any of these abominations,
    He shall surely die;
    His blood shall be upon him.

◣◣◣ FAMILY TRADITION

18:14-18 Family traditions were very important to the Jews, but God made it clear that people should not follow a tradition of sin. Although your family is a powerful influence in your life, your actions are not determined by them. You can choose not to follow a pattern of sin. Even if you come from a sinful family, you can follow God. It is far better to begin a new spiritual heritage than to hold on to traditions of sin.

¹⁴ " *If,* however, he begets a son
    Who sees all the sins which his father has done,
    And considers but does not do likewise;
¹⁵ *Who* has not eaten on the mountains,
    Nor lifted his eyes to the idols of the house of Israel,
    Nor defiled his neighbor's wife;
¹⁶ Has not oppressed anyone,
    Nor withheld a pledge,
    Nor robbed by violence,
    But has given his bread to the hungry
    And covered the naked with clothing;
¹⁷ *Who* has withdrawn his hand from the poor
    And not received usury or increase,
    But has executed My judgments
    And walked in My statutes—
    He shall not die for the iniquity of his father;
    He shall surely live!
¹⁸ " *As for* his father,
    Because he cruelly oppressed,
    Robbed his brother by violence,
    And did what *is* not good among his people,
    Behold, he shall die for his iniquity.

¹⁹"Yet you say, 'Why should the son not bear the guilt of the father?' Because the son has done what is lawful and right, and has kept all My statutes and observed them, he shall surely live. ²⁰The soul who sins shall die. The son shall not bear the guilt of the father, nor the father bear the guilt of the son. The righteousness of the righteous shall be upon himself, and the wickedness of the wicked shall be upon himself.

²¹"But if a wicked man turns from all his sins which he has committed, keeps all My statutes, and does what is

◣◣◣ NO FAIR

18:25 A typical childish response to punishment is to say, "That is◼ fair!" In reality, God is fair, but *we* have broken the rules. It is not G◼ who must live up to our ideas of fairness; instead, we must live up t◼ Don't spend your time looking for the loopholes in God's law; decide◼ instead to work toward living up to God's standards.

lawful and right, he shall surely live; he shall not die. ²²None of the transgressions which he has committed shall be remembered against him; because of the righteousness which he has done, he shall live. ²³Do I have any pleasure at all that the wicked should die?" says the Lord God, "*and* not that he should turn from his ways and live?

²⁴"But when a righteous man turns away from his righteousness and commits iniquity, and does according to all the abominations that the wicked *man* does, shall he live? All the righteousness which he has done shall not be remembered; because of the unfaithfulness of which he is guilty and the sin which he has committed, because of them he shall die.

²⁵"Yet you say, 'The way of the Lord is not fair.' Hear now, O house of Israel, is it not My way which is fair, and your ways which are not fair? ²⁶When a righteous *man* turns away from his righteousness, commits iniquity, and dies in it, it is because of the iniquity which he has done that he dies. ²⁷Again, when a wicked *man* turns away from the wickedness which he committed, and does what is lawful and right, he preserves himself alive. ²⁸Because he considers and turns away from all the transgressions which he committed, he shall surely live; he shall not die. ²⁹Yet the house of Israel says, 'The way of the Lord is not fair.' O house of Israel, is it not My ways which are fair, and your ways which are not fair?

³⁰"Therefore I will judge you, O house of Israel, every one according to his ways," says the Lord God. "Repent, and turn from all your transgressions, so that iniquity will not be your ruin. ³¹Cast away from you all the transgressions which you have committed, and get yourselves a new heart and a new spirit. For why should you die, O house of Israel? ³²For I have no pleasure in the death of one who dies," says the Lord God. "Therefore turn and live!"

CHAPTER **19** **A DEATH SONG.** "Moreover take up a lamentation for the princes of Israel, ²and say:

'What *is* your mother? A lioness:
    She lay down among the lions;
    Among the young lions she nourished her cubs.
³ She brought up one of her cubs,
    And he became a young lion;
    He learned to catch prey,
    And he devoured men.
⁴ The nations also heard of him;
    He was trapped in their pit,
    And they brought him with chains to the land of
    Egypt.
⁵ 'When she saw that she waited, *that* her hope was
    lost,
    She took another of her cubs *and* made him a young
    lion.

⁶ He roved among the lions,
  And became a young lion;
  He learned to catch prey;
  He devoured men.
⁷ He knew their desolate places,
  And laid waste their cities;
  The land with its fullness was desolated
  By the noise of his roaring.
⁸ Then the nations set against him from the provinces
      on every side,
  And spread their net over him;
  He was trapped in their pit.
⁹ They put him in a cage with chains,
  And brought him to the king of Babylon;
  They brought him in nets,
  That his voice should no longer be heard on the
      mountains of Israel.

¹⁰ 'Your mother *was* like a vine in your bloodline,
  Planted by the waters,
  Fruitful and full of branches
  Because of many waters.
¹¹ She had strong branches for scepters of rulers.
  She towered in stature above the thick branches,
  And was seen in her height amid the dense foliage.
¹² But she was plucked up in fury,
  She was cast down to the ground,
  And the east wind dried her fruit.
  Her strong branches were broken and withered;
  The fire consumed them.
¹³ And now she *is* planted in the wilderness,
  In a dry and thirsty land.
¹⁴ Fire has come out from a rod of her branches
  And devoured her fruit,
  So that she has no strong branch— a scepter for
      ruling.'"

This *is* a lamentation, and has become a lamentation.

CHAPTER **20** GOD SAYS "REMEMBER!" It came

to pass in the seventh year, in the fifth *month*, on the tenth *day* of the month, *that* certain of the elders of Israel came to inquire of the LORD, and sat before me. ²Then the word of the LORD came to me, saying, ³"Son of man, speak to the elders of Israel, and say to them, 'Thus says the Lord GOD: "Have you come to inquire of Me? *As* I live," says the Lord GOD, "I will not be inquired of by you." ' ⁴Will you judge them, son of man, will you judge *them?* Then make known to them the abominations of their fathers.
  ⁵"Say to them, 'Thus says the Lord GOD: "On the day when I chose Israel and raised My hand in an oath to the descendants of the house of Jacob, and made Myself known to them in the land of Egypt, I raised My hand in an oath to them, saying, 'I *am* the LORD your God.' ⁶On that day I raised My hand in an oath to them, to bring them out of the land of Egypt into a land that I had searched out for them, 'flowing with milk and honey,' the glory of all lands. ⁷Then I said to them, 'Each of you, throw away the abominations which are before his eyes, and do not defile yourselves with the idols of Egypt. I *am* the

LORD your God.' ⁸But they rebelled against Me and would not obey Me. They did not all cast away the abominations which were before their eyes, nor did they forsake the idols of Egypt. Then I said, 'I will pour out My fury on them and fulfill My anger against them in the midst of the land of Egypt.' ⁹But I acted for My name's sake, that it should not be profaned before the Gentiles among whom they *were*, in whose sight I had made Myself known to them, to bring them out of the land of Egypt.

▶ POWER

19:11-12 Not even the political and military might of Judah's kings could save the nation. Like branches of a vine, they would be cut off and uprooted by "the east wind"—the Babylonian army. Don't ever make the mistake of thinking your strength, whether physical or spiritual, can stand against the true power—or judgment—of almighty God.

¹⁰"Therefore I made them go out of the land of Egypt and brought them into the wilderness. ¹¹And I gave them My statutes and showed them My judgments, 'which, *if* a man does, he shall live by them.' ¹²Moreover I also gave them My Sabbaths, to be a sign between them and Me, that they might know that I *am* the LORD who sanctifies them. ¹³Yet the house of Israel rebelled against Me in the wilderness; they did not walk in My statutes; they despised My judgments, 'which, *if* a man does, he shall live by them'; and they greatly defiled My Sabbaths. Then I said I would pour out My fury on them in the wilderness, to consume them. ¹⁴But I acted for My name's sake, that it should not be profaned before the Gentiles, in whose sight I had brought them out. ¹⁵So I also raised My hand in an oath to them in the wilderness, that I would not bring them into the land which I had given *them*, 'flowing with milk and honey,' the glory of all lands, ¹⁶because they despised My judgments and did not walk in My statutes, but profaned My Sabbaths; for their heart went after their idols. ¹⁷Nevertheless My eye spared them from destruction. I did not make an end of them in the wilderness.
  ¹⁸"But I said to their children in the wilderness, 'Do not walk in the statutes of your fathers, nor observe their judgments, nor defile yourselves with their idols. ¹⁹I *am* the LORD your God: Walk in My statutes, keep My judgments, and do them; ²⁰hallow My Sabbaths, and they will be a sign between Me and you, that you may know that I *am* the LORD your God.'
  ²¹"Notwithstanding, the children rebelled against Me; they did not walk in My statutes, and were not careful to observe My judgments, 'which, *if* a man does, he shall live by them'; but they profaned My Sabbaths. Then I said I would pour out My fury on them and fulfill My anger against them in the wilderness. ²²Nevertheless I withdrew My hand and acted for My name's sake, that it should not be profaned in the sight of the Gentiles, in whose sight I had brought them out. ²³Also I raised My hand in an oath to those in the wilderness, that I would scatter them among the Gentiles and disperse them throughout the countries, ²⁴because they had not executed My judgments, but had despised My statutes, pro-

20:30 Water containing contaminants is defiled or polluted. Likewise, our life is polluted when we accept the contaminants—immoral values—of this world. If we love money, we become greedy. If we lust, we become sexually immoral. Remaining pure in a polluted world is difficult, to say the least. But a heart filled with God's Holy Spirit leaves little room for pollution (see Titus 1:15-16).

faned My Sabbaths, and their eyes were fixed on their fathers' idols.

[25]"Therefore I also gave them up to statutes *that were* not good, and judgments by which they could not live; [26]and I pronounced them unclean because of their ritual gifts, in that they caused all their firstborn to pass through *the fire*, that I might make them desolate and that they might know that I am the LORD." '

[27]"Therefore, son of man, speak to the house of Israel, and say to them, 'Thus says the Lord GOD: "In this too your fathers have blasphemed Me, by being unfaithful to Me. [28]When I brought them into the land *concerning* which I had raised My hand in an oath to give them, and they saw all the high hills and all the thick trees, there they offered their sacrifices and provoked Me with their offerings. There they also sent up their sweet aroma and poured out their drink offerings. [29]Then I said to them, 'What *is* this high place to which you go?' So its name is called Bamah to this day." ' [30]Therefore say to the house of Israel, 'Thus says the Lord GOD: "Are you defiling yourselves in the manner of your fathers, and committing harlotry according to their abominations? [31]For when you offer your gifts and make your sons pass through the fire, you defile yourselves with all your idols, even to this day. So shall I be inquired of by you, O house of Israel? *As* I live," says the Lord GOD, "I will not be inquired of by you. [32]What you have in your mind shall never be, when you say, 'We will be like the Gentiles, like the families in other countries, serving wood and stone.'

[33]"*As* I live," says the Lord GOD, "surely with a mighty hand, with an outstretched arm, and with fury poured out, I will rule over you. [34]I will bring you out from the peoples and gather you out of the countries where you are scattered, with a mighty hand, with an outstretched arm, and with fury poured out. [35]And I will bring you into the wilderness of the peoples, and there I will plead My case with you face to face. [36]Just as I pleaded My case with your fathers in the wilderness of the land of Egypt, so I will plead My case with you," says the Lord GOD. [37]"I will make you pass under the rod, and I will bring you into the bond of the covenant; [38]I will purge the rebels from among you, and those who transgress against Me; I will bring them out of the country where they dwell, but they shall not enter the land of Israel. Then you will know that I *am* the LORD.

[39]"As for you, O house of Israel," thus says the Lord GOD: "Go, serve every one of you his idols—and hereafter—if you will not obey Me; but profane My holy name no more with your gifts and your idols. [40]For on My holy mountain, on the mountain height of Israel," says the Lord GOD, "there all the house of Israel, all of them in the land, shall serve Me; there I will accept them, and there I will require your offerings and the firstfruits of your sacrifices, together with all your holy things. [41]I will accept

you as a sweet aroma when I bring you out from the peoples and gather you out of the countries where you have been scattered; and I will be hallowed in you before the Gentiles. [42]Then you shall know that I *am* the LORD, when I bring you into the land of Israel, into the country *for* which I raised My hand in an oath to give to your fathers. [43]And there you shall remember your ways and all your doings with which you were defiled; and you shall loathe yourselves in your own sight because of all the evils that you have committed. [44]Then you shall know that I *am* the LORD, when I have dealt with you for My name's sake, not according to your wicked ways nor according to your corrupt doings, O house of Israel," says the Lord GOD.' "

20:39 The Israelites were worshiping idols and sacrificing to God same time! Often we think that some religion is better than none a While persisting in a life of sin, we may think, *Well, at least I go to church. God will be pleased with this effort.* But God wants all of ou not just part of it. No amount of religious ritual or personal sacrific make up for continuing sinful practices.

[45]Furthermore the word of the LORD came to me, saying, [46]"Son of man, set your face toward the south; preach against the south and prophesy against the forest land, the South, [47]and say to the forest of the South, 'Hear the word of the LORD! Thus says the Lord GOD: "Behold, I will kindle a fire in you, and it shall devour every green tree and every dry tree in you; the blazing flame shall not be quenched, and all faces from the south to the north shall be scorched by it. [48]All flesh shall see that I, the LORD, have kindled it; it shall not be quenched." ' "

[49]Then I said, "Ah, Lord GOD! They say of me, 'Does he not speak parables?' "

CHAPTER 21 EZEKIEL'S GLITTERING SWORD. And the word of the LORD came to me, saying, [2]"Son of man, set your face toward Jerusalem, preach against the holy places, and prophesy against the land of Israel; [3]and say to the land of Israel, 'Thus says the LORD: "Behold, I *am* against you, and I will draw My sword out of its sheath and cut off both righteous and wicked from you. [4]Because I will cut off both righteous and wicked from you, therefore My sword shall go out of its sheath against all flesh from south *to* north, [5]that all flesh may know that I, the LORD, have drawn My sword out of its sheath; it shall not return anymore." ' [6]Sigh therefore, son of man, with a breaking heart, and sigh with bitterness before their eyes. [7]And it shall be when they say to you, 'Why are you sighing?' that you shall answer, 'Because of the news;

21:1ff The short message in 20:45-48 introduces the four messo chapter 21 about the judgments that would come upon Jerusalem. city would be destroyed because it was defiled. According to Jewish defiled objects were to be passed through fire in order to purify th (see Numbers 31:22-23; Psalm 66:10-12; Proverbs 17:3). God's judgment is designed to purify; destruction often is a necessary pa that process.

when it comes, every heart will melt, all hands will be feeble, every spirit will faint, and all knees will be weak *as* water. Behold, it is coming and shall be brought to pass,' says the Lord GOD."

⁸Again the word of the LORD came to me, saying, ⁹"Son of man, prophesy and say, 'Thus says the LORD!' Say:

'A sword, a sword is sharpened
And also polished!
¹⁰ Sharpened to make a dreadful slaughter,
Polished to flash like lightning!
Should we then make mirth?
It despises the scepter of My son,
As it does all wood.
¹¹ And He has given it to be polished,
That it may be handled;
This sword is sharpened, and it is polished
To be given into the hand of the slayer.'

¹² "Cry and wail, son of man;
For it will be against My people,
Against all the princes of Israel.
Terrors including the sword will be against My
    people;
Therefore strike *your* thigh.

¹³ "Because *it is* a testing,
And what if *the sword* despises even the scepter?
The scepter shall be no *more*,"

says the Lord GOD.

¹⁴ "You therefore, son of man, prophesy,
And strike *your* hands together.
The third time let the sword do double *damage.*
It *is* the sword *that* slays,
The sword that slays the great *men,*
That enters their private chambers.
¹⁵ I have set the point of the sword against all their
    gates,
That the heart may melt and many may stumble.
Ah! *It is* made bright;
It is grasped for slaughter:

¹⁶ "Swords at the ready!
Thrust right!
Set your blade!
Thrust left—
Wherever your edge is ordered!

¹⁷ "I also will beat My fists together,
And I will cause My fury to rest;
I, the LORD, have spoken."

¹⁸The word of the LORD came to me again, saying: ¹⁹"And son of man, appoint for yourself two ways for the sword of the king of Babylon to go; both of them shall go from the same land. Make a sign; put *it* at the head of the road to the city. ²⁰Appoint a road for the sword to go to Rabbah of the Ammonites, and to Judah, into fortified Jerusalem. ²¹For the king of Babylon stands at the parting of the road, at the fork of the two roads, to use divination: he shakes the arrows, he consults the images, he looks at the liver. ²²In his right hand is the divination for Jerusa-

lem: to set up battering rams, to call for a slaughter, to lift the voice with shouting, to set battering rams against the gates, to heap up a *siege* mound, and to build a wall. ²³And it will be to them like a false divination in the eyes of those who have sworn oaths with them; but he will bring their iniquity to remembrance, that they may be taken.

²⁴"Therefore thus says the Lord GOD: 'Because you have made your iniquity to be remembered, in that your transgressions are uncovered, so that in all your doings your sins appear—because you have come to remembrance, you shall be taken in hand.

²⁵'Now to you, O profane, wicked prince of Israel, whose day has come, whose iniquity *shall* end, ²⁶thus says the Lord GOD:

"Remove the turban, and take off the crown;
Nothing *shall remain* the same.
Exalt the humble, and humble the exalted.
²⁷ Overthrown, overthrown,
I will make it overthrown!
It shall be no *longer,*
Until He comes whose right it is,
And I will give it *to Him.*" '

²⁸"And you, son of man, prophesy and say, 'Thus says the Lord GOD concerning the Ammonites and concerning their reproach,' and say:

'A sword, a sword *is* drawn,
Polished for slaughter,
For consuming, for flashing—
²⁹ While they see false visions for you,
While they divine a lie to you,
To bring you on the necks of the wicked, the slain
Whose day has come,
Whose iniquity *shall* end.

³⁰ 'Return *it* to its sheath.
I will judge you
In the place where you were created,
In the land of your nativity.
³¹ I will pour out My indignation on you;
I will blow against you with the fire of My wrath,
And deliver you into the hands of brutal men *who
    are* skillful to destroy.
³² You shall be fuel for the fire;
Your blood shall be in the midst of the land.
You shall not be remembered,
For I the LORD have spoken.' "

CHAPTER **22** GOD LISTS THE PEOPLE'S SINS.
Moreover the word of the LORD came to me, saying, ²"Now, son of man, will you judge, will you judge the bloody city? Yes, show her all her abominations! ³Then say, 'Thus says the Lord GOD: "The city sheds blood in her own midst, that her time may come; and she makes idols within herself to defile herself. ⁴You have become guilty by the blood which you have shed, and have defiled yourself with the idols which you have made. You have caused your days to draw near, and have come to *the end of* your years; therefore I have made you a reproach to the

nations, and a mockery to all countries. ⁵*Those* near and *those* far from you will mock you as infamous *and* full of tumult.

⁶"Look, the princes of Israel: each one has used his power to shed blood in you. ⁷In you they have made light of father and mother; in your midst they have oppressed the stranger; in you they have mistreated the fatherless and the widow. ⁸You have despised My holy things and profaned My Sabbaths. ⁹In you are men who slander to cause bloodshed; in you are those who eat on the mountains; in your midst they commit lewdness. ¹⁰In you men uncover their fathers' nakedness; in you they violate women who are set apart during their impurity. ¹¹One commits abomination with his neighbor's wife; another lewdly defiles his daughter-in-law; and another in you violates his sister, his father's daughter. ¹²In you they take bribes to shed blood; you take usury and increase; you have made profit from your neighbors by extortion, and have forgotten Me," says the Lord GOD.

◣▬▬▬LEADERS

22:6-13 The leaders were especially responsible for the moral climate of the nation because they had been chosen by God to lead. The same is true today (see James 3:1-2). Unfortunately, many of the sins mentioned here have been committed in recent years by Christian leaders. We are living in a time of unprecedented attacks by Satan. It is vital that we uphold our leaders in prayer, and it is vital for leaders to seek accountability and help in their walk with God.

¹³"Behold, therefore, I beat My fists at the dishonest profit which you have made, and at the bloodshed which has been in your midst. ¹⁴Can your heart endure, or can your hands remain strong, in the days when I shall deal with you? I, the LORD, have spoken, and will do *it.* ¹⁵I will scatter you among the nations, disperse you throughout the countries, and remove your filthiness completely from you. ¹⁶You shall defile yourself in the sight of the nations; then you shall know that I *am* the LORD.'"'"

¹⁷The word of the LORD came to me, saying, ¹⁸"Son of man, the house of Israel has become dross to Me; they *are* all bronze, tin, iron, and lead, in the midst of a furnace; they have become dross from silver. ¹⁹Therefore thus says the Lord GOD: 'Because you have all become dross, therefore behold, I will gather you into the midst of Jerusalem. ²⁰*As men* gather silver, bronze, iron, lead, and tin into the midst of a furnace, to blow fire on it, to melt *it;* so I will gather *you* in My anger and in My fury, and I will leave *you there* and melt you. ²¹Yes, I will gather you and blow on you with the fire of My wrath, and you shall be melted in its midst. ²²As silver is melted in the midst of a furnace, so shall you be melted in its midst; then you shall know that I, the LORD, have poured out My fury on you.'"

²³And the word of the LORD came to me, saying, ²⁴"Son of man, say to her: 'You *are* a land that is not cleansed or rained on in the day of indignation.' ²⁵The conspiracy of her prophets in her midst is like a roaring lion tearing the prey; they have devoured people; they have taken treasure and precious things; they have made many widows in her midst. ²⁶Her priests have violated My law and profaned My holy things; they have not distinguished between the holy and unholy, nor have they made known *the difference* between the unclean and the clean; and they have hidden their eyes from My Sabbaths, so that I am profaned among them. ²⁷Her princes in her midst *are* like wolves tearing the prey, to shed blood, to destroy people, and to get dishonest gain. ²⁸Her prophets plastered them with untempered *mortar,* seeing false visions, and divining lies for them, saying, 'Thus says the Lord GOD,' when the LORD had not spoken. ²⁹The people of the land have used oppressions, committed robbery, and mistreated the poor and needy; and they wrongfully oppress the stranger. ³⁰So I sought for a man among them who would make a wall, and stand in the gap before Me on behalf of the land, that I should not destroy it; but I found no one. ³¹Therefore I have poured out My indignation on them; I have consumed them with the fire of My wrath; and I have recompensed their deeds on their own heads," says the Lord GOD.

CHAPTER **23** **TWO SISTERS.** The word of the LORD came again to me, saying:

² "Son of man, there were two women,
   The daughters of one mother.
³   They committed harlotry in Egypt,
   They committed harlotry in their youth;
   Their breasts were there embraced,
   Their virgin bosom was there pressed.
⁴   Their names: Oholah the elder and Oholibah her
      sister;
   They were Mine,
   And they bore sons and daughters.
   As for their names,
   Samaria *is* Oholah, and Jerusalem *is* Oholibah.

⁵ "Oholah played the harlot even though she was Mine;
   And she lusted for her lovers, the neighboring
      Assyrians,
⁶   *Who were* clothed in purple,
   Captains and rulers,
   All of them desirable young men,
   Horsemen riding on horses.
⁷   Thus she committed her harlotry with them,
   All of them choice men of Assyria;
   And with all for whom she lusted,
   With all their idols, she defiled herself.
⁸   She has never given up her harlotry *brought* from
      Egypt,
   For in her youth they had lain with her,
   Pressed her virgin bosom,
   And poured out their immorality upon her.

⁹ "Therefore I have delivered her
   Into the hand of her lovers,
   Into the hand of the Assyrians,
   For whom she lusted.
¹⁰   They uncovered her nakedness,
   Took away her sons and daughters,
   And slew her with the sword;
   She became a byword among women,
   For they had executed judgment on her.

¹¹"Now although her sister Oholibah saw *this,* she became more corrupt in her lust than she, and in her harlotry more corrupt than her sister's harlotry.

¹² "She lusted for the neighboring Assyrians,
Captains and rulers,
Clothed most gorgeously,
Horsemen riding on horses,
All of them desirable young men.
¹³ Then I saw that she was defiled;
Both *took* the same way.
¹⁴ But she increased her harlotry;
She looked at men portrayed on the wall,
Images of Chaldeans portrayed in vermilion,
¹⁵ Girded with belts around their waists,
Flowing turbans on their heads,
All of them looking like captains,
In the manner of the Babylonians of Chaldea,
The land of their nativity.
¹⁶ As soon as her eyes saw them,
She lusted for them
And sent messengers to them in Chaldea.

¹⁷ "Then the Babylonians came to her, into the bed of
love,
And they defiled her with their immorality;
So she was defiled by them, and alienated herself
from them.
¹⁸ She revealed her harlotry and uncovered her
nakedness.
Then I alienated Myself from her,
As I had alienated Myself from her sister.

¹⁹ "Yet she multiplied her harlotry
In calling to remembrance the days of her youth,
When she had played the harlot in the land of Egypt.
²⁰ For she lusted for her paramours,
Whose flesh *is like* the flesh of donkeys,
And whose issue *is like* the issue of horses.
²¹ Thus you called to remembrance the lewdness of
your youth,
When the Egyptians pressed your bosom
Because of your youthful breasts.

²²"Therefore, Oholibah, thus says the Lord GOD:

'Behold, I will stir up your lovers against you,
From whom you have alienated yourself,
And I will bring them against you from every side:
²³ The Babylonians,
All the Chaldeans,
Pekod, Shoa, Koa,
All the Assyrians with them,
All of them desirable young men,
Governors and rulers,
Captains and men of renown,
All of them riding on horses.
²⁴ And they shall come against you
With chariots, wagons, and war-horses,
With a horde of people.
They shall array against you
Buckler, shield, and helmet all around.

'I will delegate judgment to them,
And they shall judge you according to their
judgments.
²⁵ I will set My jealousy against you,
And they shall deal furiously with you;
They shall remove your nose and your ears,
And your remnant shall fall by the sword;
They shall take your sons and your daughters,
And your remnant shall be devoured by fire.
²⁶ They shall also strip you of your clothes
And take away your beautiful jewelry.

²⁷ 'Thus I will make you cease your lewdness and your
harlotry
Brought from the land of Egypt,
So that you will not lift your eyes to them,
Nor remember Egypt anymore.'

²⁸"For thus says the Lord GOD: 'Surely I will deliver you into the hand of those you hate, into the hand *of those* from whom you alienated yourself. ²⁹They will deal hatefully with you, take away all you have worked for, and leave you naked and bare. The nakedness of your harlotry shall be uncovered, both your lewdness and your harlotry. ³⁰I will do these *things* to you because you have gone as a harlot after the Gentiles, because you have become defiled by their idols. ³¹You have walked in the way of your sister; therefore I will put her cup in your hand.'

³²"Thus says the Lord GOD:

'You shall drink of your sister's cup,
The deep and wide one;
You shall be laughed to scorn
And held in derision;
It contains much.
³³ You will be filled with drunkenness and sorrow,
The cup of horror and desolation,
The cup of your sister Samaria.
³⁴ You shall drink and drain it,
You shall break its shards,
And tear at your own breasts;
For I have spoken,'
Says the Lord GOD.

³⁵"Therefore thus says the Lord GOD:

'Because you have forgotten Me and cast Me behind
your back,
Therefore you shall bear the *penalty*
Of your lewdness and your harlotry.' "

³⁶The LORD also said to me: "Son of man, will you judge Oholah and Oholibah? Then declare to them their abominations. ³⁷For they have committed adultery, and blood *is* on their hands. They have committed adultery with

◣◥▬▬▬▬▬NO WAY!

23:39 The Israelites went so far as to sacrifice their own children to idols and then sacrifice to the Lord the same day. This made a mockery of worship. We cannot praise God and willfully sin at the same time! That would be like agreeing to go steady with one person, then going on a date with someone else. You have to do more than just say the words; you must show what you really believe and value by your actions.

their idols, and even sacrificed their sons whom they bore to Me, passing them through *the fire,* to devour *them.* ³⁸Moreover they have done this to Me: They have defiled My sanctuary on the same day and profaned My Sabbaths. ³⁹For after they had slain their children for their idols, on the same day they came into My sanctuary to profane it; and indeed thus they have done in the midst of My house.

⁴⁰"Furthermore you sent for men to come from afar, to whom a messenger *was* sent; and there they came. And you washed yourself for them, painted your eyes, and adorned yourself with ornaments. ⁴¹You sat on a stately couch, with a table prepared before it, on which you had set My incense and My oil. ⁴²The sound of a carefree multitude *was* with her, and Sabeans *were* brought from the wilderness with men of the common sort, who put bracelets on their wrists and beautiful crowns on their heads. ⁴³Then I said concerning *her who had grown* old in adulteries, 'Will they commit harlotry with her now, and she *with them?*' ⁴⁴Yet they went in to her, as men go in to a woman who plays the harlot; thus they went in to Oholah and Oholibah, the lewd women. ⁴⁵But righteous men will judge them after the manner of adulteresses, and after the manner of women who shed blood, because they *are* adulteresses, and blood *is* on their hands.

⁴⁶"For thus says the Lord GOD: 'Bring up an assembly against them, give them up to trouble and plunder. ⁴⁷The assembly shall stone them with stones and execute them with their swords; they shall slay their sons and their daughters, and burn their houses with fire. ⁴⁸Thus I will cause lewdness to cease from the land, that all women may be taught not to practice your lewdness. ⁴⁹They shall repay you for your lewdness, and you shall pay for your idolatrous sins. Then you shall know that I *am* the Lord GOD.'"

CHAPTER 24 A COOKING POT. Again, in the ninth year, in the tenth month, on the tenth *day* of the month, the word of the LORD came to me, saying, ²"Son of man, write down the name of the day, this very day— the king of Babylon started his siege against Jerusalem this very day. ³And utter a parable to the rebellious house, and say to them, 'Thus says the Lord GOD:

"Put on a pot, set *it* on,
And also pour water into it.
⁴ Gather pieces *of meat* in it,
Every good piece,
The thigh and the shoulder.
Fill *it* with choice cuts;
⁵ Take the choice of the flock.
Also pile *fuel* bones under it,
Make it boil well,
And let the cuts simmer in it."

⁶'Therefore thus says the Lord GOD:

"Woe to the bloody city,
To the pot whose scum *is* in it,
And whose scum is not gone from it!
Bring it out piece by piece,
On which no lot has fallen.

◀▶ BURNED

24:6-13 The city of Jerusalem was like a pot that was so encrusted with the filth of sin that it would not come clean, even in the hottest fire. God wanted to cleanse those who lived in Jerusalem, and he wants to cleanse people today. Sometimes he tries to purify us through difficult and troublesome circumstances. When you face tough times, let sin be burned from your life. Look at your problems as an opportunity for faith to grow. Above all, do not allow sin to dominate your life (see 1 Corinthians 11:29-30).

⁷ For her blood is in her midst;
She set it on top of a rock;
She did not pour it on the ground,
To cover it with dust.
⁸ That it may raise up fury and take vengeance,
I have set her blood on top of a rock,
That it may not be covered."

⁹Therefore thus says the Lord GOD:

"Woe to the bloody city!
I too will make the pyre great.
¹⁰ Heap on the wood,
Kindle the fire;
Cook the meat well,
Mix in the spices,
And let the cuts be burned up.

¹¹ "Then set the pot empty on the coals,
That it may become hot and its bronze may burn,
That its filthiness may be melted in it,
That its scum may be consumed.
¹² She has grown weary with lies,
And her great scum has not gone from her.
Let her scum *be* in the fire!
¹³ In your filthiness *is* lewdness.
Because I have cleansed you, and you were not cleansed,
You will not be cleansed of your filthiness anymore,
Till I have caused My fury to rest upon you.
¹⁴ I, the LORD, have spoken *it;*
It shall come to pass, and I will do *it;*
I will not hold back,
Nor will I spare,
Nor will I relent;
According to your ways
And according to your deeds
They will judge you,"
Says the Lord GOD.'"

¹⁵Also the word of the LORD came to me, saying, ¹⁶"Son of man, behold, I take away from you the desire of your eyes with one stroke; yet you shall neither mourn nor weep, nor shall your tears run down. ¹⁷Sigh in silence, make no mourning for the dead; bind your turban on your head, and put your sandals on your feet; do not cover *your* lips, and do not eat man's bread *of sorrow.*"

¹⁸So I spoke to the people in the morning, and at evening my wife died; and the next morning I did as I was commanded.

¹⁹And the people said to me, "Will you not tell us what these *things signify* to us, that you behave so?"

²⁰Then I answered them, "The word of the LORD came to me, saying, ²¹'Speak to the house of Israel, "Thus says the Lord GOD: 'Behold, I will profane My sanctuary, your

arrogant boast, the desire of your eyes, the delight of your soul; and your sons and daughters whom you left behind shall fall by the sword. ²²And you shall do as I have done; you shall not cover *your* lips nor eat man's bread *of sorrow.* ²³Your turbans shall be on your heads and your sandals on your feet; you shall neither mourn nor weep, but you shall pine away in your iniquities and mourn with one another. ²⁴Thus Ezekiel is a sign to you; according to all that he has done you shall do; and when this comes, you shall know that I *am* the Lord GOD.'"

²⁵'And you, son of man—*will it* not *be* in the day when I take from them their stronghold, their joy and their glory, the desire of their eyes, and that on which they set their minds, their sons and their daughters: ²⁶on that day one who escapes will come to you to let *you* hear *it* with *your* ears; ²⁷on that day your mouth will be opened to him who has escaped; you shall speak and no longer be mute. Thus you will be a sign to them, and they shall know that I *am* the LORD.'"

CHAPTER 25 THIEVES FROM THE EAST. The word of the LORD came to me, saying, ²"Son of man, set your face against the Ammonites, and prophesy against them. ³Say to the Ammonites, 'Hear the word of the Lord GOD! Thus says the Lord GOD: "Because you said, 'Aha!' against My sanctuary when it was profaned, and against the land of Israel when it was desolate, and against the house of Judah when they went into captivity, ⁴indeed, therefore, I will deliver you as a possession to the men of the East, and they shall set their encampments among you and make their dwellings among you; they shall eat your fruit, and they shall drink your milk. ⁵And I will make Rabbah a stable for camels and Ammon a resting place for flocks. Then you shall know that I *am* the LORD."

⁶'For thus says the Lord GOD: "Because you clapped *your* hands, stamped your feet, and rejoiced in heart with all your disdain for the land of Israel, ⁷indeed, therefore, I will stretch out My hand against you, and give you as plunder to the nations; I will cut you off from the peoples, and I will cause you to perish from the countries; I will destroy you, and you shall know that I *am* the LORD."

⁸'Thus says the Lord GOD: "Because Moab and Seir say, 'Look! The house of Judah *is* like all the nations,' ⁹therefore, behold, I will clear the territory of Moab of cities, of the cities on its frontier, the glory of the country, Beth Jeshimoth, Baal Meon, and Kirjathaim. ¹⁰To the men of the East I will give it as a possession, together with the Ammonites, that the Ammonites may not be remembered among the nations. ¹¹And I will execute judgments upon Moab, and they shall know that I *am* the LORD."

¹²'Thus says the Lord GOD: "Because of what Edom did against the house of Judah by taking vengeance, and has greatly offended by avenging itself on them," ¹³therefore thus says the Lord GOD: "I will also stretch out My hand against Edom, cut off man and beast from it, and make it desolate from Teman; Dedan shall fall by the sword. ¹⁴I will lay My vengeance on Edom by the hand of My people Israel, that they may do in Edom according to My anger and according to My fury; and they shall know My vengeance," says the Lord GOD.

¹⁵'Thus says the Lord GOD: "Because the Philistines dealt vengefully and took vengeance with a spiteful heart, to destroy because of the old hatred," ¹⁶therefore thus says the Lord GOD: "I will stretch out My hand against the Philistines, and I will cut off the Cherethites and destroy the remnant of the seacoast. ¹⁷I will execute great vengeance on them with furious rebukes; and they shall know that I *am* the LORD, when I lay My vengeance upon them."'"

CHAPTER 26 A CITY WILL BE RUINED. And it came to pass in the eleventh year, on the first *day* of the month, *that* the word of the LORD came to me, saying, ²"Son of man, because Tyre has said against Jerusalem, 'Aha! She is broken who *was* the gateway of the peoples; now she is turned over to me; I shall be filled; she is laid waste.'

³"Therefore thus says the Lord GOD: 'Behold, I *am* against you, O Tyre, and will cause many nations to come up against you, as the sea causes its waves to come up. ⁴And they shall destroy the walls of Tyre and break down her towers; I will also scrape her dust from her, and make her like the top of a rock. ⁵It shall be *a place for* spreading nets in the midst of the sea, for I have spoken,' says the Lord GOD; 'it shall become plunder for the nations. ⁶Also her daughter *villages* which *are* in the fields shall be slain by the sword. Then they shall know that I am the LORD.'

⁷"For thus says the Lord GOD: 'Behold, I will bring against Tyre from the north Nebuchadnezzar king of Babylon, king of kings, with horses, with chariots, and with horsemen, and an army with many people. ⁸He will slay with the sword your daughter *villages* in the fields; he will heap up a siege mound against you, build a wall against you, and raise a defense against you. ⁹He will direct his battering rams against your walls, and with his axes he will break down your towers. ¹⁰Because of the abundance of his horses, their dust will cover you; your walls will shake at the noise of the horsemen, the wagons, and the chariots, when he enters your gates, as men enter a city that has been breached. ¹¹With the hooves of his horses he will trample all your streets; he will slay your people by the sword, and your strong pillars will fall to the ground. ¹²They will plunder your riches and pillage your merchandise; they will break down your walls and destroy your pleasant houses; they will lay your stones, your timber, and your soil in the midst of the water. ¹³I will put an end to the sound of your songs, and the sound of your harps shall be heard no more. ¹⁴I will make you like the top of a rock; you shall be *a place for* spreading nets, and you shall never be rebuilt, for I the LORD have spoken,' says the Lord GOD.

ROCK PILE

26:14 After a 15-year siege, Nebuchadnezzar could not conquer the part of Tyre located on the island; thus certain aspects of the description in 26:12,14 actually go beyond the damage done to Tyre by Nebuchadnezzar and predict what would happen to the island settlement later during the conquests of Alexander the Great. Alexander threw the rubble of the mainland city into the sea until it made a bridge to the island. Today, the island city is still a pile of rubble, a testimony to God's judgment.

¹⁵"Thus says the Lord GOD to Tyre: 'Will the coastlands not shake at the sound of your fall, when the wounded cry, when slaughter is made in the midst of you? ¹⁶Then all the princes of the sea will come down from their thrones, lay aside their robes, and take off their embroidered garments; they will clothe themselves with trembling; they will sit on the ground, tremble *every* moment, and be astonished at you. ¹⁷And they will take up a lamentation for you, and say to you:

"How you have perished,
 O one inhabited by seafaring men,
 O renowned city,
 Who was strong at sea,
 She and her inhabitants,
 Who caused their terror *to be* on all her inhabitants!
¹⁸ Now the coastlands tremble on the day of your fall;
 Yes, the coastlands by the sea are troubled at your
  departure." '

¹⁹"For thus says the Lord GOD: 'When I make you a desolate city, like cities that are not inhabited, when I bring the deep upon you, and great waters cover you, ²⁰then I will bring you down with those who descend into the Pit, to the people of old, and I will make you dwell in the lowest part of the earth, in places desolate from antiquity, with those who go down to the Pit, so that you may never be inhabited; and I shall establish glory in the land of the living. ²¹I will make you a terror, and you *shall be* no *more;* though you are sought for, you will never be found again,' says the Lord GOD."

CHAPTER 27 A GREAT SEAPORT CITY.

The word of the LORD came again to me, saying, ²"Now, son of man, take up a lamentation for Tyre, ³and say to Tyre, 'You who are situated at the entrance of the sea, merchant of the peoples on many coastlands, thus says the Lord GOD:

▶ DANGER SIGNAL

27:3-4 The beauty of Tyre was the source of its pride, and Tyre's pride guaranteed its judgment. Pride in our own accomplishments should be a danger signal to us (see James 4:13-17). We must maintain a humble dependence upon God.

"O Tyre, you have said,
 'I *am* perfect in beauty.'
⁴ Your borders *are* in the midst of the seas.
 Your builders have perfected your beauty.
⁵ They made all *your* planks of fir trees from Senir;
 They took a cedar from Lebanon to make you a mast.
⁶ *Of* oaks from Bashan they made your oars;
 The company of Ashurites have inlaid your planks
 With ivory from the coasts of Cyprus.
⁷ Fine embroidered linen from Egypt was what you
  spread for your sail;
 Blue and purple from the coasts of Elishah was what
  covered you.

⁸ "Inhabitants of Sidon and Arvad were your oarsmen;
 Your wise men, O Tyre, were in you;
 They became your pilots.

⁹ Elders of Gebal and its wise men
 Were in you to caulk your seams;
 All the ships of the sea
 And their oarsmen were in you
 To market your merchandise.

¹⁰ "Those from Persia, Lydia, and Libya
 Were in your army as men of war;
 They hung shield and helmet in you;
 They gave splendor to you.
¹¹ Men of Arvad with your army *were* on your walls *all*
  around,
 And the men of Gammad were in your towers;
 They hung their shields on your walls *all* around;
 They made your beauty perfect.

¹²"Tarshish *was* your merchant because of your many luxury goods. They gave you silver, iron, tin, and lead for your goods. ¹³Javan, Tubal, and Meshech *were* your traders. They bartered human lives and vessels of bronze for your merchandise. ¹⁴Those from the house of Togarmah traded for your wares with horses, steeds, and mules. ¹⁵The men of Dedan *were* your traders; many isles *were* the market of your hand. They brought you ivory tusks and ebony as payment. ¹⁶Syria *was* your merchant because of the abundance of goods you made. They gave you for your wares emeralds, purple, embroidery, fine linen, corals, and rubies. ¹⁷Judah and the land of Israel *were* your traders. They traded for your merchandise wheat of Minnith, millet, honey, oil, and balm. ¹⁸Damascus *was* your merchant because of the abundance of goods you made, because of your many luxury items, with the wine of Helbon and with white wool. ¹⁹Dan and Javan paid for your wares, traversing back and forth. Wrought iron, cassia, and cane were among your merchandise. ²⁰Dedan *was* your merchant in saddlecloths for riding. ²¹Arabia and all the princes of Kedar *were* your regular merchants. They traded with you in lambs, rams, and goats. ²²The merchants of Sheba and Raamah *were* your merchants. They traded for your wares the choicest spices, all kinds of precious stones, and gold. ²³Haran, Canneh, Eden, the merchants of Sheba, Assyria, *and* Chilmad *were* your merchants. ²⁴These *were* your merchants in choice items—in purple clothes, in embroidered garments, in chests of multicolored apparel, in sturdy woven cords, which were in your marketplace.

²⁵ "The ships of Tarshish were carriers of your
  merchandise.
 You were filled and very glorious in the midst of the
  seas.
²⁶ Your oarsmen brought you into many waters,
 But the east wind broke you in the midst of the seas.

²⁷ "Your riches, wares, and merchandise,
 Your mariners and pilots,
 Your caulkers and merchandisers,
 All your men of war who *are* in you,
 And the entire company which *is* in your midst,
 Will fall into the midst of the seas on the day of your
  ruin.

28 The common-land will shake at the sound of the cry
of your pilots.

29 "All who handle the oar,
The mariners,
All the pilots of the sea
Will come down from their ships *and* stand on the
shore.

30 They will make their voice heard because of you;
They will cry bitterly and cast dust on their heads;
They will roll about in ashes;

31 They will shave themselves completely bald because
of you,
Gird themselves with sackcloth,
And weep for you
With bitterness of heart *and* bitter wailing.

32 In their wailing for you
They will take up a lamentation,
And lament for you:
'What *city is* like Tyre,
Destroyed in the midst of the sea?

33 'When your wares went out by sea,
You satisfied many people;
You enriched the kings of the earth
With your many luxury goods and your merchandise.

34 But you are broken by the seas in the depths of the
waters;
Your merchandise and the entire company will fall
in your midst.

35 All the inhabitants of the isles will be astonished at
you;
Their kings will be greatly afraid,
And *their* countenance will be troubled.

36 The merchants among the peoples will hiss at you;
You will become a horror, and *be* no more
forever.'"'"

CHAPTER 28 A PROUD KING WILL FALL. The
word of the LORD came to me again, saying, 2"Son of man,
say to the prince of Tyre, 'Thus says the Lord GOD:

"Because your heart *is* lifted up,
And you say, 'I *am* a god,
I sit *in* the seat of gods,
In the midst of the seas,'
Yet you *are* a man, and not a god,
Though you set your heart as the heart of a god

3 (Behold, you *are* wiser than Daniel!
There is no secret that can be hidden from you!

4 With your wisdom and your understanding
You have gained riches for yourself,
And gathered gold and silver into your treasuries;

5 By your great wisdom in trade you have increased
your riches,
And your heart is lifted up because of your riches),"

6"Therefore thus says the Lord GOD:

"Because you have set your heart as the heart of a
god,

7 Behold, therefore, I will bring strangers against you,
The most terrible of the nations;

And they shall draw their swords against the beauty
of your wisdom,
And defile your splendor.

8 They shall throw you down into the Pit,
And you shall die the death of the slain
In the midst of the seas.

9 "Will you still say before him who slays you,
'I *am* a god'?
But you *shall be* a man, and not a god,
In the hand of him who slays you.

10 You shall die the death of the uncircumcised
By the hand of aliens;
For I have spoken," says the Lord GOD.'"

11Moreover the word of the LORD came to me, saying,
12"Son of man, take up a lamentation for the king of Tyre,
and say to him, 'Thus says the Lord GOD:

"You *were* the seal of perfection,
Full of wisdom and perfect in beauty.

13 You were in Eden, the garden of God;
Every precious stone *was* your covering:
The sardius, topaz, and diamond,
Beryl, onyx, and jasper,
Sapphire, turquoise, and emerald with gold.
The workmanship of your timbrels and pipes
Was prepared for you on the day you were created.

14 "You *were* the anointed cherub who covers;
I established you;
You were on the holy mountain of God;
You walked back and forth in the midst of fiery
stones.

15 You *were* perfect in your ways from the day you were
created,
Till iniquity was found in you.

16 "By the abundance of your trading
You became filled with violence within,
And you sinned;
Therefore I cast you as a profane thing
Out of the mountain of God;
And I destroyed you, O covering cherub,
From the midst of the fiery stones.

17 "Your heart was lifted up because of your beauty;
You corrupted your wisdom for the sake of your
splendor;
I cast you to the ground,
I laid you before kings,
That they might gaze at you.

18 "You defiled your sanctuaries
By the multitude of your iniquities,
By the iniquity of your trading;
Therefore I brought fire from your midst;
It devoured you,
And I turned you to ashes upon the earth
In the sight of all who saw you.

19 All who knew you among the peoples are astonished
at you;
You have become a horror,
And *shall be* no more forever."'"

28:24-26 The promise that God's people will live in complete safety has yet to be fulfilled. Although many Jews were allowed to return from exile under Zerubbabel, Ezra, and Nehemiah, and the political nation is restored today, the inhabitants do not yet live in complete safety (28:26). Therefore, this promise will have its ultimate fulfillment when Christ sets up his eternal kingdom. Then all people who have been faithful to God will dwell together in harmony and safety. Never doubt God's promises. They will come true—if not now, then in eternity!

²⁰Then the word of the LORD came to me, saying, ²¹"Son of man, set your face toward Sidon, and prophesy against her, ²²and say, 'Thus says the Lord GOD:

"Behold, I *am* against you, O Sidon;
I will be glorified in your midst;
And they shall know that I *am* the LORD,
When I execute judgments in her and am hallowed
    in her.
²³ For I will send pestilence upon her,
And blood in her streets;
The wounded shall be judged in her midst
By the sword against her on every side;
Then they shall know that I *am* the LORD.

²⁴"And there shall no longer be a pricking brier or a painful thorn for the house of Israel from among all *who are* around them, who despise them. Then they shall know that I *am* the Lord GOD."

²⁵'Thus says the Lord GOD: "When I have gathered the house of Israel from the peoples among whom they are scattered, and am hallowed in them in the sight of the Gentiles, then they will dwell in their own land which I gave to My servant Jacob. ²⁶And they will dwell safely there, build houses, and plant vineyards; yes, they will dwell securely, when I execute judgments on all those around them who despise them. Then they shall know that I *am* the LORD their God."'"

CHAPTER 29 A PROUD KING.

In the tenth year, in the tenth *month,* on the twelfth *day* of the month, the word of the LORD came to me, saying, ²"Son of man, set your face against Pharaoh king of Egypt, and prophesy against him, and against all Egypt. ³Speak, and say, 'Thus says the Lord GOD:

"Behold, I *am* against you,
O Pharaoh king of Egypt,
O great monster who lies in the midst of his rivers,
Who has said, 'My River *is* my own;
I have made *it* for myself.'
⁴ But I will put hooks in your jaws,
And cause the fish of your rivers to stick to your
    scales;
I will bring you up out of the midst of your rivers,
And all the fish in your rivers will stick to your scales.
⁵ I will leave you in the wilderness,
You and all the fish of your rivers;
You shall fall on the open field;
You shall not be picked up or gathered.
I have given you as food
To the beasts of the field
And to the birds of the heavens.

⁶ "Then all the inhabitants of Egypt
Shall know that I *am* the LORD,
Because they have been a staff of reed to the house
    of Israel.
⁷ When they took hold of you with the hand,
You broke and tore all their shoulders;
When they leaned on you,
You broke and made all their backs quiver."

⁸'Therefore thus says the Lord GOD: "Surely I will bring a sword upon you and cut off from you man and beast. ⁹And the land of Egypt shall become desolate and waste; then they will know that I *am* the LORD, because he said, 'The River *is* mine, and I have made *it.*' ¹⁰Indeed, there-

29:9 "The River" refers to the Nile, Egypt's pride and joy, a life-giv river cutting through the middle of the desert. Rather than thanking however, Egypt declared, "The Nile is mine!" We do the same when say, "This house is mine." Or, "I have brought myself to where I am today." Or, "I did it by myself." These statements reveal our pride. W sometimes take for granted what God has given us, thinking we hav made it ourselves. Of course, we have put forth a lot of hard effort, God supplied us with the resources, abilities, and opportunities to m happen. Don't claim your own greatness, as the Egyptians did—pro God's greatness and give him the credit.

fore, I *am* against you and against your rivers, and I will make the land of Egypt utterly waste and desolate, from Migdol *to* Syene, as far as the border of Ethiopia. ¹¹Neither foot of man shall pass through it nor foot of beast pass through it, and it shall be uninhabited forty years. ¹²I will make the land of Egypt desolate in the midst of the countries *that are* desolate; and among the cities *that are* laid waste, her cities shall be desolate forty years; and I will scatter the Egyptians among the nations and disperse them throughout the countries."

¹³'Yet, thus says the Lord GOD: "At the end of forty years I will gather the Egyptians from the peoples among whom they were scattered. ¹⁴I will bring back the captives of Egypt and cause them to return to the land of Pathros, to the land of their origin, and there they shall be a lowly kingdom. ¹⁵It shall be the lowliest of kingdoms; it shall never again exalt itself above the nations, for I will diminish them so that they will not rule over the nations anymore. ¹⁶No longer shall it be the confidence of the house of Israel, but will remind them of *their* iniquity when they turned to follow them. Then they shall know that I *am* the Lord GOD."'"

¹⁷And it came to pass in the twenty-seventh year, in the first *month,* on the first *day* of the month, *that* the word of the LORD came to me, saying, ¹⁸"Son of man, Nebuchadnezzar king of Babylon caused his army to labor strenuously against Tyre; every head *was* made bald, and every shoulder rubbed raw; yet neither he nor his army received wages from Tyre, for the labor which they expended on it. ¹⁹Therefore thus says the Lord GOD: 'Surely I will give the land of Egypt to Nebuchadnezzar king of Babylon; he shall take away her wealth, carry off her spoil, and remove her pillage; and that will be the wages

for his army. ²⁰I have given him the land of Egypt *for* his labor, because they worked for Me,' says the Lord GOD.

²¹'In that day I will cause the horn of the house of Israel to spring forth, and I will open your mouth to speak in their midst. Then they shall know that I *am* the LORD.' "

CHAPTER 30 A DAY OF CLOUDS.
The word of the LORD came to me again, saying, ²"Son of man, prophesy and say, 'Thus says the Lord GOD:

"Wail, 'Woe to the day!'
³ For the day *is* near,
 Even the day of the LORD *is* near;
 It will be a day of clouds, the time of the Gentiles.
⁴ The sword shall come upon Egypt,
 And great anguish shall be in Ethiopia,
 When the slain fall in Egypt,
 And they take away her wealth,
 And her foundations are broken down.

⁵"Ethiopia, Libya, Lydia, all the mingled people, Chub, and the men of the lands who are allied, shall fall with them by the sword."
⁶'Thus says the LORD:

"Those who uphold Egypt shall fall,
 And the pride of her power shall come down.
 From Migdol *to* Syene
 Those within her shall fall by the sword,"
 Says the Lord GOD.

⁷ "They shall be desolate in the midst of the desolate countries,
 And her cities shall be in the midst of the cities *that are* laid waste.
⁸ Then they will know that I *am* the LORD,
 When I have set a fire in Egypt
 And all her helpers are destroyed.
⁹ On that day messengers shall go forth from Me in ships
 To make the careless Ethiopians afraid,
 And great anguish shall come upon them,
 As on the day of Egypt;
 For indeed it is coming!"

¹⁰'Thus says the Lord GOD:

"I will also make a multitude of Egypt to cease
 By the hand of Nebuchadnezzar king of Babylon.
¹¹ He and his people with him, the most terrible of the nations,
 Shall be brought to destroy the land;
 They shall draw their swords against Egypt,
 And fill the land with the slain.
¹² I will make the rivers dry,
 And sell the land into the hand of the wicked;
 I will make the land waste, and all that is in it,
 By the hand of aliens.
 I, the LORD, have spoken."

¹³'Thus says the Lord GOD:

"I will also destroy the idols,
 And cause the images to cease from Noph;

There shall no longer be princes from the land of Egypt;
 I will put fear in the land of Egypt.
¹⁴ I will make Pathros desolate,
 Set fire to Zoan,
 And execute judgments in No.
¹⁵ I will pour My fury on Sin, the strength of Egypt;
 I will cut off the multitude of No,
¹⁶ And set a fire in Egypt;
 Sin shall have great pain,
 No shall be split open,
 And Noph *shall be in* distress daily.
¹⁷ The young men of Aven and Pi Beseth shall fall by the sword,
 And these *cities* shall go into captivity.
¹⁸ At Tehaphnehes the day shall also be darkened,
 When I break the yokes of Egypt there.
 And her arrogant strength shall cease in her;
 As for her, a cloud shall cover her,
 And her daughters shall go into captivity.
¹⁹ Thus I will execute judgments on Egypt,
 Then they shall know that I *am* the LORD." ' "

▶ ARMIES
30:21-26 This prophecy was given to Ezekiel in 587 B.C. God destroyed Egypt's military superiority and gave it to Babylon. God allows nations to rise to power to accomplish a particular purpose, often beyond our immediate understanding. When you read about armies and wars, don't despair. Remember that God is sovereign and in charge of everything, even military might. Besides praying for your military and government leaders, pray that God's greater purposes be carried out and that his will be done "on earth as *it is* in heaven" (see Matthew 6:10).

²⁰And it came to pass in the eleventh year, in the first *month*, on the seventh *day* of the month, *that* the word of the LORD came to me, saying, ²¹"Son of man, I have broken the arm of Pharaoh king of Egypt; and see, it has not been bandaged for healing, nor a splint put on to bind it, to make it strong enough to hold a sword. ²²Therefore thus says the Lord GOD: 'Surely I *am* against Pharaoh king of Egypt, and will break his arms, both the strong one and the one that was broken; and I will make the sword fall out of his hand. ²³I will scatter the Egyptians among the nations, and disperse them throughout the countries. ²⁴I will strengthen the arms of the king of Babylon and put My sword in his hand; but I will break Pharaoh's arms, and he will groan before him with the groanings of a mortally wounded *man*. ²⁵Thus I will strengthen the arms of the king of Babylon, but the arms of Pharaoh shall fall down; they shall know that I *am* the LORD, when I put My sword into the hand of the king of Babylon and he stretches it out against the land of Egypt. ²⁶I will scatter the Egyptians among the nations and disperse them throughout the countries. Then they shall know that I *am* the LORD.' "

CHAPTER 31 A MAGNIFICENT TREE CUT DOWN.
Now it came to pass in the eleventh year, in the third *month*, on the first *day* of the month, *that* the word of the

GOD'S SOVEREIGNTY OR MAN'S RESPONSIBILITY?

"I do not believe in predestination. In fact, if I ever became convinced that God predestines some people to go to heaven and some to hell, I'd quit serving him."—Actual comment from a teenage male. Have you ever felt the way that young man did? The idea that God decides our eternal destiny goes against our American notions of fairness and individual choice. And yet, we draw strength and comfort from the belief that God is running the universe. (That's what "sovereignty" means.) Which is right? Is God truly sovereign—is he calling the shots—or are we free and ultimately responsible for making our own decisions, even those that have eternal consequences? This question has perplexed people for thousands of years. It raises itself here, in the account of Pharaoh in Ezekiel 32. It raised itself about another Pharaoh, too, in the Exodus account of the Pharaoh who held the Israelites captive. Did God know even before he put Pharaoh on the earth that he would sin? Did he allow it—or cause it? Or did God simply roll the dice, placing this man in authority without knowing whether or not he would obey his command to let his people go? If so, does that mean that since creation, God has been a spectator in human events, allowing us total freedom and responsibility? Either conclusion leads to some awesome implications. If God is truly and completely sovereign, then I have no real freedom and I'm little better than a puppet. But if I'm truly free to do whatever I want, then God isn't really in control of the universe. Help! The greatest minds of history have wrestled with this issue and, quite frankly, it remains as impenetrable today as ever. So if you were hoping this article would resolve it, you're going to be disappointed. But it is possible to consider it from a slightly different angle. Contemporary theologian J. I. Packer, one of the greatest minds of our time, was once asked, "If God is truly sovereign, in what sense is man responsible? And if man is truly responsible, in what sense is God sovereign?" Packer replied, "I think that it could understand, free will . . . and that there's not much getting behind that. . . . The really surprising thing would be if we real a 'mystery,' and if man is truly responsible, then he wouldn't be any bigger than we are." Sovereignty, responsibility, predestination, free will . . . and mystery. The Bible teaches them all. The modern American mind balks at accepting two truths that seem to be contradictory. But when you think about it, it makes sense that God is bigger than our minds—big enough to encompass what seems to us to be paradoxical. One thinker said he thought of the twin truths of predestination and free will as parallel lines—he didn't know how to brin together, and no one could make them cross, either. If someone asks you whether you believe in God sovereignty or people's freedom, the best answer is yes.

LORD came to me, saying, ²"Son of man, say to Pharaoh king of Egypt and to his multitude:

'Whom are you like in your greatness?
³ Indeed Assyria *was* a cedar in Lebanon,
   With fine branches that shaded the forest,
   And of high stature;
   And its top was among the thick boughs.
⁴ The waters made it grow;
   Underground waters gave it height,
   With their rivers running around the place where it
      was planted,
   And sent out rivulets to all the trees of the field.

⁵ 'Therefore its height was exalted above all the trees of
      the field;
   Its boughs were multiplied,
   And its branches became long because of the
      abundance of water,
   As it sent them out.
⁶ All the birds of the heavens made their nests in its
      boughs;
   Under its branches all the beasts of the field brought
      forth their young;
   And in its shadow all great nations made their home.

⁷ 'Thus it was beautiful in greatness and in the length
      of its branches,
   Because its roots reached to abundant waters.
⁸ The cedars in the garden of God could not hide it;
   The fir trees were not like its boughs,
   And the chestnut trees were not like its branches;
   No tree in the garden of God was like it in beauty.
⁹ I made it beautiful with a multitude of branches,
   So that all the trees of Eden envied it,
   That *were* in the garden of God.'

¹⁰"Therefore thus says the Lord GOD: 'Because you have increased in height, and it set its top among the thick boughs, and its heart was lifted up in its height, ¹¹therefore I will deliver it into the hand of the mighty one of the nations, and he shall surely deal with it; I have driven it out for its wickedness. ¹²And aliens, the most terrible of the nations, have cut it down and left it; its branches have fallen on the mountains and in all the valleys; its boughs lie broken by all the rivers of the land; and all the peoples of the earth have gone from under its shadow and left it.

¹³ 'On its ruin will remain all the birds of the heavens,
   And all the beasts of the field will come to its
      branches—

¹⁴"So that no trees by the waters may ever again exalt themselves for their height, nor set their tops among the thick boughs, that no tree which drinks water may ever be high enough to reach up to them.

'For they have all been delivered to death,
   To the depths of the earth,
   Among the children of men who go down to the Pit.'

¹⁵"Thus says the Lord GOD: 'In the day when it went down to hell, I caused mourning. I covered the deep because of it. I restrained its rivers, and the great waters were held back. I caused Lebanon to mourn for it, and all the trees of the field wilted because of it. ¹⁶I made the nations shake at the sound of its fall, when I cast it down to hell together with those who descend into the Pit; and

◄━━━━━━━━━━━━▶ **THE CRASH**

31:1ff This message was given in 587 B.C. Ezekiel compared Egypt to Assyria, calling Assyria a great cedar tree that had crashed to the ground. The fall of the mighty nation of Assyria was to be an example to the Egyptians of what would happen to them. Just like Assyria, Egypt took pride in her strength and beauty; just like Assyria, Egypt would come crashing down. Nothing can last apart from God—not even a great society with magnificent culture and military power. Always remember where your strength and survival lie: in the hands of the almighty, all-loving God.

all the trees of Eden, the choice and best of Lebanon, all that drink water, were comforted in the depths of the earth. ¹⁷They also went down to hell with it, with those *slain* by the sword; and *those who were* its *strong* arm dwelt in its shadows among the nations.

¹⁸"To which of the trees in Eden will you then be likened in glory and greatness? Yet you shall be brought down with the trees of Eden to the depths of the earth; you shall lie in the midst of the uncircumcised, with *those* slain by the sword. This *is* Pharaoh and all his multitude,' says the Lord GOD."

CHAPTER 32 LION OR MONSTER? And it came to pass in the twelfth year, in the twelfth *month,* on the first *day* of the month, *that* the word of the LORD came to me, saying, ²"Son of man, take up a lamentation for Pharaoh king of Egypt, and say to him:

'You are like a young lion among the nations,
   And you *are* like a monster in the seas,
   Bursting forth in your rivers,
   Troubling the waters with your feet,
   And fouling their rivers.'

³"Thus says the Lord GOD:

'I will therefore spread My net over you with a
      company of many people,
   And they will draw you up in My net.
⁴ Then I will leave you on the land;
   I will cast you out on the open fields,
   And cause to settle on you all the birds of the
      heavens.
   And with you I will fill the beasts of the whole earth.
⁵ I will lay your flesh on the mountains,
   And fill the valleys with your carcass.

⁶ 'I will also water the land with the flow of your blood,
   Even to the mountains;
   And the riverbeds will be full of you.
⁷ When *I* put out your light,
   I will cover the heavens, and make its stars dark;
   I will cover the sun with a cloud,
   And the moon shall not give her light.

8 All the bright lights of the heavens I will make dark
   over you,
And bring darkness upon your land,'
Says the Lord GOD.

9 'I will also trouble the hearts of many peoples, when I bring your destruction among the nations, into the countries which you have not known. 10 Yes, I will make many peoples astonished at you, and their kings shall be horribly afraid of you when I brandish My sword before them; and they shall tremble *every* moment, every man for his own life, in the day of your fall.'

11 "For thus says the Lord GOD: 'The sword of the king of Babylon shall come upon you. 12 By the swords of the mighty warriors, all of them the most terrible of the nations, I will cause your multitude to fall.

'They shall plunder the pomp of Egypt,
And all its multitude shall be destroyed.
13 Also I will destroy all its animals
From beside its great waters;
The foot of man shall muddy them no more,
Nor shall the hooves of animals muddy them.
14 Then I will make their waters clear,
And make their rivers run like oil,'
Says the Lord GOD.

◣▬▬▬▬ FUTURE

32:18 The Hebrews believed in an existence beyond the grave for all people, good and bad. Ezekiel's message assumed that the evil nations had already been sent there and that Egypt would soon follow. The Egyptians had a preoccupation with the afterlife (the pyramids were built solely to ensure the pharaohs' comfort in the next life). This message should remind us that such human attempts are foolish. God alone controls the future and life after death.

15 'When I make the land of Egypt desolate,
   And the country is destitute of all that once filled it,
   When I strike all who dwell in it,
   Then they shall know that I *am* the LORD.

16 'This *is* the lamentation
   With which they shall lament her;
   The daughters of the nations shall lament her;
   They shall lament for her, for Egypt,
   And for all her multitude,'
   Says the Lord GOD."

17 It came to pass also in the twelfth year, on the fifteenth *day* of the month, *that* the word of the LORD came to me, saying:

18 "Son of man, wail over the multitude of Egypt,
   And cast them down to the depths of the earth,
   Her and the daughters of the famous nations,
   With those who go down to the Pit:
19 'Whom do you surpass in beauty?
   Go down, be placed with the uncircumcised.'

20 "They shall fall in the midst of *those* slain by the
      sword;
   She is delivered to the sword,

Drawing her and all her multitudes.
21 The strong among the mighty
   Shall speak to him out of the midst of hell
   With those who help him:
   'They have gone down,
   They lie with the uncircumcised, slain by the sword.'

22 "Assyria *is* there, and all her company,
   With their graves all around her,
   All of them slain, fallen by the sword.
23 Her graves are set in the recesses of the Pit,
   And her company is all around her grave,
   All of them slain, fallen by the sword,
   Who caused terror in the land of the living.

24 "There *is* Elam and all her multitude,
   All around her grave,
   All of them slain, fallen by the sword,
   Who have gone down uncircumcised to the lower
      parts of the earth,
   Who caused their terror in the land of the living;
   Now they bear their shame with those who go down
      to the Pit.
25 They have set her bed in the midst of the slain,
   With all her multitude,
   With her graves all around it,
   All of them uncircumcised, slain by the sword;
   Though their terror was caused
   In the land of the living,
   Yet they bear their shame
   With those who go down to the Pit;
   It was put in the midst of the slain.

26 "There *are* Meshech and Tubal and all their
      multitudes,
   With all their graves around it,
   All of them uncircumcised, slain by the sword,
   Though they caused their terror in the land of the
      living.
27 They do not lie with the mighty
   Who are fallen of the uncircumcised,
   Who have gone down to hell with their weapons of
      war;
   They have laid their swords under their heads,
   But their iniquities will be on their bones,
   Because of the terror of the mighty in the land of the
      living.
28 Yes, you shall be broken in the midst of the
      uncircumcised,
   And lie with *those* slain by the sword.

29 "There *is* Edom,
   Her kings and all her princes,
   Who despite their might
   Are laid beside *those* slain by the sword;
   They shall lie with the uncircumcised,
   And with those who go down to the Pit.
30 There *are* the princes of the north,
   All of them, and all the Sidonians,
   Who have gone down with the slain
   In shame at the terror which they caused by their
      might;

They lie uncircumcised with *those* slain by the sword,
And bear their shame with those who go down to the Pit.

³¹ "Pharaoh will see them
And be comforted over all his multitude,
Pharaoh and all his army,
Slain by the sword,"
Says the Lord GOD.

³² "For I have caused My terror in the land of the living;
And he shall be placed in the midst of the uncircumcised
With *those* slain by the sword,
Pharaoh and all his multitude,"
Says the Lord GOD.

CHAPTER **33** **GOD WILL BE THE JUDGE.** Again the word of the LORD came to me, saying, ²"Son of man, speak to the children of your people, and say to them: 'When I bring the sword upon a land, and the people of the land take a man from their territory and make him their watchman, ³when he sees the sword coming upon the land, if he blows the trumpet and warns the people, ⁴then whoever hears the sound of the trumpet and does not take warning, if the sword comes and takes him away, his blood shall be on his *own* head. ⁵He heard the sound of the trumpet, but did not take warning; his blood shall be upon himself. But he who takes warning will save his life. ⁶But if the watchman sees the sword coming and does not blow the trumpet, and the people are not warned, and the sword comes and takes *any* person from among them, he is taken away in his iniquity; but his blood I will require at the watchman's hand.'

⁷"So you, son of man: I have made you a watchman for the house of Israel; therefore you shall hear a word from My mouth and warn them for Me. ⁸When I say to the wicked, 'O wicked *man*, you shall surely die!' and you do not speak to warn the wicked from his way, that wicked *man* shall die in his iniquity; but his blood I will require at your hand. ⁹Nevertheless if you warn the wicked to turn from his way, and he does not turn from his way, he shall die in his iniquity; but you have delivered your soul.

¹⁰"Therefore you, O son of man, say to the house of Israel: 'Thus you say, "If our transgressions and our sins *lie* upon us, and we pine away in them, how can we then live?" ' ¹¹Say to them: '*As* I live,' says the Lord GOD, 'I have no pleasure in the death of the wicked, but that the wicked turn from his way and live. Turn, turn from your evil ways! For why should you die, O house of Israel?'

¹²"Therefore you, O son of man, say to the children of your people: 'The righteousness of the righteous man shall not deliver him in the day of his transgression; as for the wickedness of the wicked, he shall not fall because of it in the day that he turns from his wickedness; nor shall the righteous be able to live because of *his righteousness* in the day that he sins.' ¹³When I say to the righteous *that* he shall surely live, but he trusts in his own righteousness and commits iniquity, none of his righteous works shall be remembered; but because of the iniquity that he has committed, he shall die. ¹⁴Again, when I say to the wicked, 'You shall surely die,' if he turns from his sin and does what is lawful and right, ¹⁵if the wicked restores the pledge, gives back what he has stolen, and walks in the statutes of life without committing iniquity, he shall surely live; he shall not die. ¹⁶None of his sins which he has committed shall be remembered against him; he has done what is lawful and right; he shall surely live.

¹⁷"Yet the children of your people say, 'The way of the LORD is not fair.' But it is their way which is not fair! ¹⁸When the righteous turns from his righteousness and commits iniquity, he shall die because of it. ¹⁹But when the wicked turns from his wickedness and does what is lawful and right, he shall live because of it. ²⁰Yet you say, 'The way of the LORD is not fair.' O house of Israel, I will judge every one of you according to his own ways."

²¹And it came to pass in the twelfth year of our captivity, in the tenth *month*, on the fifth *day* of the month, *that* one who had escaped from Jerusalem came to me and said, "The city has been captured!"

²²Now the hand of the LORD had been upon me the evening before the man came who had escaped. And He had opened my mouth; so when he came to me in the morning, my mouth was opened, and I was no longer mute.

▶ FAITHFUL

33:1ff This chapter shows a new direction for Ezekiel's prophecies. Up to this point, he had pronounced judgment on Judah (chapters 1–24) and the surrounding evil nations (25–32). After Jerusalem fell, his messages of doom turned to messages of comfort, hope, and restoration for God's people (33–48). Previously God appointed Ezekiel to be a watchman, warning the nation of coming judgment (see 3:17-21). Here God appointed him to be a watchman again, to preach a message of hope. There are still warnings (33:23–34:10; 36:1-7), but these are part of the larger picture of hope. God would not forsake his promise to restore his blessings to the faithful. We must pay attention to both aspects of Ezekiel's message: warning and promise. The hope is given only to the righteous "remnant" in our churches who remain true to God.

²³Then the word of the LORD came to me, saying: ²⁴"Son of man, they who inhabit those ruins in the land of Israel are saying, 'Abraham was only one, and he inherited the land. But we *are* many; the land has been given to us as a possession.' ²⁵"Therefore say to them, 'Thus says the Lord GOD: "You eat *meat* with blood, you lift up your eyes toward your idols, and shed blood. Should you then possess the land? ²⁶You rely on your sword, you commit abominations, and you defile one another's wives. Should you then possess the land?" '

▶ FACE IT

33:10-12 The exiles were discouraged by their past sins. They felt heavy guilt for living in rebellion against God for so many years. This was an important turning point—elsewhere in Ezekiel the people had refused to face their sins. But, God assured them of forgiveness if they repented. God *wants* everyone to turn to him. He looks at what we are and will become, not what we have been. God gives every person the opportunity to turn to him, so take it. Sincerely try to follow him, and ask him to forgive you when you fail.

²⁷"Say thus to them, 'Thus says the Lord GOD: "*As* I live, surely those who *are* in the ruins shall fall by the sword, and the one who *is* in the open field I will give to the beasts to be devoured, and those who *are* in the strongholds and caves shall die of the pestilence. ²⁸For I will make the land most desolate, her arrogant strength shall cease, and the mountains of Israel shall be so desolate that no one will pass through. ²⁹Then they shall know that I *am* the LORD, when I have made the land most desolate because of all their abominations which they have committed." '

IGNORED

33:30-32 The people ignored Ezekiel's message. When people mock your witness for Christ or fail to take your advice, don't give up. You are not witnessing for their sakes alone, but out of faithfulness to God. You cannot make others accept your message; you can only be faithful in delivering it.

³⁰"As for you, son of man, the children of your people are talking about you beside the walls and in the doors of the houses; and they speak to one another, everyone saying to his brother, 'Please come and hear what the word is that comes from the LORD.' ³¹So they come to you as people do, they sit before you *as* My people, and they hear your words, but they do not do them; for with their mouth they show much love, *but* their hearts pursue

PLAY CHURCH

33:32 Many people think of church as entertainment. They enjoy the music, the people, and the activities, but they don't take the messages to heart. Have you reduced church services to the level of entertainment, or does your worship truly have an impact on your life?

their *own* gain. ³²Indeed you *are* to them as a very lovely song of one who has a pleasant voice and can play well on an instrument; for they hear your words, but they do not do them. ³³And when this comes to pass—surely it will come—then they will know that a prophet has been among them."

CHAPTER **34** GOD'S FLOCK. And the word of the LORD came to me, saying, ²"Son of man, prophesy against the shepherds of Israel, prophesy and say to them, 'Thus says the Lord GOD to the shepherds: "Woe to the shepherds of Israel who feed themselves! Should not the shepherds feed the flocks? ³You eat the fat and clothe yourselves with the wool; you slaughter the fatlings, *but* you do not feed the flock. ⁴The weak you have not strengthened, nor have you healed those who were sick, nor bound up the broken, nor brought back what was driven away, nor sought what was lost; but with force and cruelty you have ruled them. ⁵So they were scattered because *there was* no shepherd; and they became food for all the beasts of the field when they were scattered. ⁶My sheep wandered through all the mountains, and on every high hill; yes, My flock was scattered over the whole face of the earth, and no one was seeking or searching *for* them."

⁷'Therefore, you shepherds, hear the word of the LORD:

⁸"*As* I live," says the Lord GOD, "surely because My flock became a prey, and My flock became food for every beast of the field, because *there was* no shepherd, nor did My shepherds search for My flock, but the shepherds fed themselves and did not feed My flock"— ⁹therefore, O shepherds, hear the word of the LORD! ¹⁰Thus says the Lord GOD: "Behold, I *am* against the shepherds, and I will require My flock at their hand; I will cause them to cease feeding the sheep, and the shepherds shall feed themselves no more; for I will deliver My flock from their mouths, that they may no longer be food for them."

¹¹'For thus says the Lord GOD: "Indeed I Myself will search for My sheep and seek them out. ¹²As a shepherd seeks out his flock on the day he is among his scattered sheep, so will I seek out My sheep and deliver them from all the places where they were scattered on a cloudy and dark day. ¹³And I will bring them out from the peoples and gather them from the countries, and will bring them to their own land; I will feed them on the mountains of Israel, in the valleys and in all the inhabited places of the country. ¹⁴I will feed them in good pasture, and their fold shall be on the high mountains of Israel. There they shall lie down in a good fold and feed in rich pasture on the mountains of Israel. ¹⁵I will feed My flock, and I will make them lie down," says the Lord GOD. ¹⁶"I will seek what was lost and bring back what was driven away, bind up the broken and strengthen what was sick; but I will destroy the fat and the strong, and feed them in judgment."

¹⁷'And *as for* you, O My flock, thus says the Lord GOD: "Behold, I shall judge between sheep and sheep, between rams and goats. ¹⁸*Is it* too little for you to have eaten up the good pasture, that you must tread down with your feet the residue of your pasture—and to have drunk of the clear waters, that you must foul the residue with your feet? ¹⁹And *as for* My flock, they eat what you have trampled with your feet, and they drink what you have fouled with your feet."

²⁰'Therefore thus says the Lord GOD to them: "Behold, I Myself will judge between the fat and the lean sheep. ²¹Because you have pushed with side and shoulder, butted all the weak ones with your horns, and scattered them abroad, ²²therefore I will save My flock, and they shall no longer be a prey; and I will judge between sheep and sheep. ²³I will establish one shepherd over them, and he shall feed them—My servant David. He shall feed them and be their shepherd. ²⁴And I, the LORD, will be their God, and My servant David a prince among them; I, the LORD, have spoken.

²⁵"I will make a covenant of peace with them, and cause wild beasts to cease from the land; and they will dwell safely in the wilderness and sleep in the woods. ²⁶I will make them and the places all around My hill a blessing; and I will cause showers to come down in their season; there shall be showers of blessing. ²⁷Then the trees of the field shall yield their fruit, and the earth shall

SHEPHERD

34:18-20 A bad shepherd is not only selfish, but also destructive. A minister who confuses people by raising unnecessary doubts, teaching false ideas, and acting sinfully is destroying his flock's spiritual nourishment.

yield her increase. They shall be safe in their land; and they shall know that I *am* the LORD, when I have broken the bands of their yoke and delivered them from the hand of those who enslaved them. ²⁸And they shall no longer be a prey for the nations, nor shall beasts of the land devour them; but they shall dwell safely, and no one shall make *them* afraid. ²⁹I will raise up for them a garden of renown, and they shall no longer be consumed with hunger in the land, nor bear the shame of the Gentiles anymore. ³⁰Thus they shall know that I, the LORD their God, *am* with them, and they, the house of Israel, *are* My people," says the Lord GOD.'"

³¹"You are My flock, the flock of My pasture; you *are* men, *and* I *am* your God," says the Lord GOD.

CHAPTER **35** **EDOM WILL BE RUINED.** Moreover the word of the LORD came to me, saying, ²"Son of man, set your face against Mount Seir and prophesy against it, ³and say to it, 'Thus says the Lord GOD:

"Behold, O Mount Seir, I *am* against you;
I will stretch out My hand against you,
And make you most desolate;
⁴ I shall lay your cities waste,
And you shall be desolate.
Then you shall know that I *am* the LORD.

⁵"Because you have had an ancient hatred, and have shed *the blood of* the children of Israel by the power of the sword at the time of their calamity, *when* their iniquity *came to an* end, ⁶therefore, *as* I live," says the Lord GOD, "I will prepare you for blood, and blood shall pursue you; since you have not hated blood, therefore blood shall pursue you. ⁷Thus I will make Mount Seir most desolate, and cut off from it the one who leaves and the one who returns. ⁸And I will fill its mountains with the slain; on your hills and in your valleys and in all your ravines those who are slain by the sword shall fall. ⁹I will make you perpetually desolate, and your cities shall be uninhabited; then you shall know that I *am* the LORD.

¹⁰"Because you have said, 'These two nations and these two countries shall be mine, and we will possess them,' although the LORD was there, ¹¹therefore, *as* I live," says the Lord GOD, "I will do according to your anger and according to the envy which you showed in your hatred against them; and I will make Myself known among them when I judge you. ¹²Then you shall know that I *am* the LORD. I have heard all your blasphemies which you have spoken against the mountains of Israel, saying, 'They are desolate; they are given to us to consume.' ¹³Thus with your mouth you have boasted against Me and multiplied your words against Me; I have heard *them*."

¹⁴Thus says the Lord GOD: "The whole earth will rejoice when I make you desolate. ¹⁵As you rejoiced because the inheritance of the house of Israel was desolate, so I will do to you; you shall be desolate, O Mount Seir, as well as all of Edom—all of it! Then they shall know that I *am* the LORD."'

CHAPTER **36** **A PROMISE OF GOOD TIMES.** "And you, son of man, prophesy to the mountains of Israel, and say, 'O mountains of Israel, hear the word of the LORD! ²Thus says the Lord GOD: "Because the enemy has said of you, 'Aha! The ancient heights have become our possession,'"' ³therefore prophesy, and say, 'Thus says the Lord GOD: "Because they made *you* desolate and swallowed you up on every side, so that you became the possession of the rest of the nations, and you are taken up by the lips of talkers and slandered by the people"— ⁴therefore, O mountains of Israel, hear the word of the Lord GOD! Thus says the Lord GOD to the mountains, the hills, the rivers, the valleys, the desolate wastes, and the cities that have been forsaken, which became plunder and mockery to the rest of the nations all around— ⁵therefore thus says the Lord GOD: "Surely I have spoken in My burning jealousy against the rest of the nations and against all Edom, who gave My land to themselves as a possession, with wholehearted joy *and* spiteful minds, in order to plunder its open country." '

◤〰️◥WRATH

35:8 Ezekiel prophesied not only against the people of Edom, but also against their mountains and land. Mountains, symbols of strength and power, represent the pride of these people who thought they could get away with evil. Does such worldly pride typify the nation in which you live? If so, it is in danger of divine wrath similar to that experienced by Edom.

⁶"Therefore prophesy concerning the land of Israel, and say to the mountains, the hills, the rivers, and the valleys, 'Thus says the Lord GOD: "Behold, I have spoken in My jealousy and My fury, because you have borne the shame of the nations." ⁷Therefore thus says the Lord GOD: "I have raised My hand in an oath that surely the nations that *are* around you shall bear their own shame. ⁸But you, O mountains of Israel, you shall shoot forth your branches and yield your fruit to My people Israel, for they are about to come. ⁹For indeed I *am* for you, and I will turn to you, and you shall be tilled and sown. ¹⁰I will multiply men upon you, all the house of Israel, all of it; and the cities shall be inhabited and the ruins rebuilt. ¹¹I will multiply upon you man and beast; and they shall increase and bear young; I will make you inhabited as in former times, and do better *for you* than at your beginnings. Then you shall know that I *am* the LORD. ¹²Yes, I will cause men to walk on you, My people Israel; they shall take possession of you, and you shall be their inheritance; no more shall you bereave them *of children*."

¹³Thus says the Lord GOD: "Because they say to you, 'You devour men and bereave your nation *of children,*' ¹⁴therefore you shall devour men no more, nor bereave your nation anymore," says the Lord GOD. ¹⁵Nor will I let you hear the taunts of the nations anymore, nor bear the reproach of the peoples anymore, nor shall you cause your nation to stumble anymore," says the Lord GOD.' "

¹⁶Moreover the word of the LORD came to me, saying: ¹⁷"Son of man, when the house of Israel dwelt in their own land, they defiled it by their own ways and deeds; to Me their way was like the uncleanness of a woman in her customary impurity. ¹⁸Therefore I poured out My fury on them for the blood they had shed on the land, and for

their idols *with which* they had defiled it. ¹⁹So I scattered them among the nations, and they were dispersed throughout the countries; I judged them according to their ways and their deeds. ²⁰When they came to the nations, wherever they went, they profaned My holy name—when they said of them, 'These *are* the people of the LORD, *and* yet they have gone out of His land.' ²¹But I had concern for My holy name, which the house of Israel had profaned among the nations wherever they went.

²²"Therefore say to the house of Israel, 'Thus says the Lord GOD: "I do not do *this* for your sake, O house of Israel, but for My holy name's sake, which you have profaned among the nations wherever you went. ²³And I will sanctify My great name, which has been profaned among the nations, which you have profaned in their midst; and the nations shall know that I *am* the LORD," says the Lord GOD, "when I am hallowed in you before their eyes. ²⁴For I will take you from among the nations, gather you out of all countries, and bring you into your own land. ²⁵Then I will sprinkle clean water on you, and you shall be clean; I will cleanse you from all your filthiness and from all your idols. ²⁶I will give you a new heart and put a new spirit within you; I will take the heart of stone out of your flesh and give you a heart of flesh. ²⁷I will put My Spirit within you and cause you to walk in My statutes, and you will keep My judgments and do *them*. ²⁸Then you shall dwell in the land that I gave to your fathers; you shall be My people, and I will be your God. ²⁹I will deliver you from all your uncleannesses. I will call for the grain and multiply it, and bring no famine upon you. ³⁰And I will multiply the fruit of

◤▬▬▬▬▬WATCHING

36:21 Why did God want to protect his holy name—his reputation? God was concerned about the salvation not only of his people, but also of the whole world. To allow his people to remain in sin and be destroyed by their enemies would lead other nations to believe their heathen gods were victorious (Isaiah 48:11). God will not share his glory with false gods—he alone is true. The people had the responsibility to represent God properly to the rest of the world. Believers today have that same responsibility. What do people think about God from watching you?

your trees and the increase of your fields, so that you need never again bear the reproach of famine among the nations. ³¹Then you will remember your evil ways and your deeds that *were* not good; and you will loathe yourselves in your own sight, for your iniquities and your abominations. ³²Not for your sake do I do *this*," says the Lord GOD, "let it be known to you. Be ashamed and confounded for your own ways, O house of Israel!"

³³'Thus says the Lord GOD: "On the day that I cleanse you from all your iniquities, I will also enable *you* to dwell in the cities, and the ruins shall be rebuilt. ³⁴The desolate land shall be tilled instead of lying desolate in the sight of all who pass by. ³⁵So they will say, 'This land that was desolate has become like the garden of Eden; and the wasted, desolate, and ruined cities *are now* fortified *and* inhabited.' ³⁶Then the nations which are left all around you shall know that I, the LORD, have rebuilt the ruined places *and* planted what was desolate. I, the LORD, have spoken *it*, and I will do *it*."

I will give you a new heart and put a new spirit within you... and cause you to WALK IN MY STATUTES.

EZEKIEL 36:26-27

³⁷'Thus says the Lord GOD: "I will also let the house of Israel inquire of Me to do this for them: I will increase their men like a flock. ³⁸Like a flock *offered as* holy *sacrifices*, like the flock at Jerusalem on its feast days, so shall the ruined cities be filled with flocks of men. Then they shall know that I *am* the LORD."'"

CHAPTER **37** **DRIED BONES.** The hand of the LORD came upon me and brought me out in the Spirit of the LORD, and set me down in the midst of the valley; and it *was* full of bones. ²Then He caused me to pass by them all around, and behold, *there were* very many in the open valley; and indeed *they were* very dry. ³And He said to me, "Son of man, can these bones live?"

So I answered, "O Lord GOD, You know."

⁴Again He said to me, "Prophesy to these bones, and say to them, 'O dry bones, hear the word of the LORD! ⁵Thus says the Lord GOD to these bones: "Surely I will cause breath to enter into you, and you shall live. ⁶I will put sinews on you and bring flesh upon you, cover you with skin and put breath in you; and you shall live. Then you shall know that I *am* the LORD."'"

⁷So I prophesied as I was commanded; and as I prophesied, there was a noise, and suddenly a rattling; and the bones came together, bone to bone. ⁸Indeed, as I looked, the sinews and the flesh came upon them, and the skin covered them over; but *there was* no breath in them.

⁹Also He said to me, "Prophesy to the breath, prophesy, son of man, and say to the breath, 'Thus says the Lord

◤▬▬▬▬▬DRIED UP

37:5 The dry bones represented the people's spiritually dead cond◖ Your church may seem like a heap of dried-up bones to you, spiritu◖ dead with no hope of vitality. But just as God promised to restore hi◖ nation, he can restore any church, no matter how dry or dead it ma◖ Rather than give up, pray for renewal, for God can restore it to life◖ hope and prayer of every church should be that God will put his Spi◖ into it (37:14). In fact, God is at work calling his people back to him◖ bringing new life into dead churches.

GOD: "Come from the four winds, O breath, and breathe on these slain, that they may live." ' " [10]So I prophesied as He commanded me, and breath came into them, and they lived, and stood upon their feet, an exceedingly great army.

[11]Then He said to me, "Son of man, these bones are the whole house of Israel. They indeed say, 'Our bones are dry, our hope is lost, and we ourselves are cut off!' [12]Therefore prophesy and say to them, 'Thus says the Lord GOD: "Behold, O My people, I will open your graves and cause you to come up from your graves, and bring you into the land of Israel. [13]Then you shall know that I *am* the LORD, when I have opened your graves, O My people, and brought you up from your graves. [14]I will put My Spirit in you, and you shall live, and I will place you in your own land. Then you shall know that I, the LORD, have spoken *it* and performed *it*," says the LORD.' "

[15]Again the word of the LORD came to me, saying, [16]"As for you, son of man, take a stick for yourself and write on it: 'For Judah and for the children of Israel, his companions.' Then take another stick and write on it, 'For Joseph, the stick of Ephraim, and *for* all the house of Israel, his companions.' [17]Then join them one to another for yourself into one stick, and they will become one in your hand.

[18]"And when the children of your people speak to you, saying, 'Will you not show us what you *mean* by these?'— [19]say to them, 'Thus says the Lord GOD: "Surely I will take the stick of Joseph, which *is* in the hand of Ephraim, and the tribes of Israel, his companions; and I will join them with it, with the stick of Judah, and make them one stick, and they will be one in My hand." ' [20]And the sticks on which you write will be in your hand before their eyes.

[21]"Then say to them, 'Thus says the Lord GOD: "Surely I will take the children of Israel from among the nations, wherever they have gone, and will gather them from every side and bring them into their own land; [22]and I will make them one nation in the land, on the mountains of Israel; and one king shall be king over them all; they shall no longer be two nations, nor shall they ever be divided into two kingdoms again. [23]They shall not defile themselves anymore with their idols, nor with their detestable things, nor with any of their transgressions; but I will deliver them from all their dwelling places in which they have sinned, and will cleanse them. Then they shall be My people, and I will be their God.

[24]"David My servant *shall be* king over them, and they shall all have one shepherd; they shall also walk in My judgments and observe My statutes, and do them. [25]Then they shall dwell in the land that I have given to Jacob My servant, where your fathers dwelt; and they shall dwell there, they, their children, and their children's children, forever; and My servant David *shall be* their prince forever. [26]Moreover I will make a covenant of peace with them, and it shall be an everlasting covenant with them; I will establish them and multiply them, and I will set My sanctuary in their midst forevermore. [27]My tabernacle also shall be with them; indeed I will be their God, and they shall be My people. [28]The nations also will know that I, the LORD, sanctify Israel, when My sanctuary is in their midst forevermore." ' "

CHAPTER **38** EZEKIEL'S MESSAGE TO GOG.

Now the word of the LORD came to me, saying, [2]"Son of man, set your face against Gog, of the land of Magog, the prince of Rosh, Meshech, and Tubal, and prophesy against him, [3]and say, 'Thus says the Lord GOD: "Behold, I *am* against you, O Gog, the prince of Rosh, Meshech, and Tubal. [4]I will turn you around, put hooks into your jaws, and lead you out, with all your army, horses, and horsemen, all splendidly clothed, a great company *with* bucklers and shields, all of them handling swords. [5]Persia, Ethiopia, and Libya are with them, all of them *with* shield and helmet; [6]Gomer and all its troops; the house of Togarmah *from* the far north and all its troops—many people *are* with you.

[7]"Prepare yourself and be ready, you and all your companies that are gathered about you; and be a guard for them. [8]After many days you will be visited. In the latter years you will come into the land of those brought back from the sword *and* gathered from many people on the mountains of Israel, which had long been desolate; they were brought out of the nations, and now all of them dwell safely. [9]You will ascend, coming like a storm, covering the land like a cloud, you and all your troops and many peoples with you."

OLD AND NEW COVENANTS

OLD COVENANT	NEW COVENANT
Placed upon stone	Placed upon people's hearts
Based on the law	Based on desire to love and serve God
Must be taught	Known by all
Legal relationship with God	Personal relationship with God

¹⁰"Thus says the Lord GOD: "On that day it shall come to pass *that* thoughts will arise in your mind, and you will make an evil plan: ¹¹You will say, 'I will go up against a land of unwalled villages; I will go to a peaceful people, who dwell safely, all of them dwelling without walls, and having neither bars nor gates'— ¹²to take plunder and to take booty, to stretch out your hand against the waste places *that are again* inhabited, and against a people gathered from the nations, who have acquired livestock and goods, who dwell in the midst of the land. ¹³Sheba, Dedan, the merchants of Tarshish, and all their young lions will say to you, 'Have you come to take plunder? Have you gathered your army to take booty, to carry away silver and gold, to take away livestock and goods, to take great plunder?'"'

¹⁴"Therefore, son of man, prophesy and say to Gog, 'Thus says the Lord GOD: "On that day when My people Israel dwell safely, will you not know *it?* ¹⁵Then you will come from your place out of the far north, you and many peoples with you, all of them riding on horses, a great company and a mighty army. ¹⁶You will come up against My people Israel like a cloud, to cover the land. It will be in the latter days that I will bring you against My land, so that the nations may know Me, when I am hallowed in you, O Gog, before their eyes." ¹⁷Thus says the Lord GOD: "Are *you* he of whom I have spoken in former days by My servants the prophets of Israel, who prophesied for years in those days that I would bring you against them?

¹⁸"And it will come to pass at the same time, when Gog comes against the land of Israel," says the Lord GOD, "*that* My fury will show in My face. ¹⁹For in My jealousy *and* in the fire of My wrath I have spoken: 'Surely in that day there shall be a great earthquake in the land of Israel, ²⁰so that the fish of the sea, the birds of the heavens, the beasts of the field, all creeping things that creep on the earth, and all men who *are* on the face of the earth shall shake at My presence. The mountains shall be thrown down, the steep places shall fall, and every wall shall fall to the ground.' ²¹I will call for a sword against Gog throughout all My mountains," says the Lord GOD. "Every man's sword will be against his brother. ²²And I will bring him to judgment with pestilence and bloodshed; I will rain down on him, on his troops, and on the many peoples who *are* with him, flooding rain, great hailstones, fire, and brimstone. ²³Thus I will magnify Myself and sanctify Myself, and I will be known in the eyes of many nations. Then they shall know that I *am* the LORD."'

CHAPTER **39** GOD'S HOLINESS. "And you, son of man, prophesy against Gog, and say, 'Thus says the Lord GOD: "Behold, I *am* against you, O Gog, the prince of Rosh, Meshech, and Tubal; ²and I will turn you around and lead you on, bringing you up from the far north, and bring you against the mountains of Israel. ³Then I will knock the bow out of your left hand, and cause the arrows to fall out of your right hand. ⁴You shall fall upon the mountains of Israel, you and all your troops and the peoples who *are* with you; I will give you to birds of prey of every sort and *to* the beasts of the field to be devoured.

⁵You shall fall on the open field; for I have spoken," says the Lord GOD. ⁶"And I will send fire on Magog and on those who live in security in the coastlands. Then they shall know that I *am* the LORD. ⁷So I will make My holy name known in the midst of My people Israel, and I will not *let them* profane My holy name anymore. Then the nations shall know that I *am* the LORD, the Holy One in Israel. ⁸Surely it is coming, and it shall be done," says the Lord GOD. "This *is* the day of which I have spoken.

⁹"Then those who dwell in the cities of Israel will go out and set on fire and burn the weapons, both the shields and bucklers, the bows and arrows, the javelins and spears; and they will make fires with them for seven years. ¹⁰They will not take wood from the field nor cut down *any* from the forests, because they will make fires with the weapons; and they will plunder those who plundered them, and pillage those who pillaged them," says the Lord GOD.

¹¹"It will come to pass in that day *that* I will give Gog a burial place there in Israel, the valley of those who pass by east of the sea; and it will obstruct travelers, because there they will bury Gog and all his multitude. Therefore they will call *it* the Valley of Hamon Gog. ¹²For seven months the house of Israel will be burying them, in order to cleanse the land. ¹³Indeed all the people of the land will be burying, and they will gain renown for it on the day that I am glorified," says the Lord GOD. ¹⁴"They will set apart men regularly employed, with the help of a search party, to pass through the land and bury those bodies remaining on the ground, in order to cleanse it. At the end of seven months they will make a search. ¹⁵The search party will pass through the land; and *when anyone* sees a man's bone, he shall set up a marker by it, till the buriers have buried it in the Valley of Hamon Gog. ¹⁶*The* name of *the* city *will* also *be* Hamonah. Thus they shall cleanse the land." '

¹⁷"And as for you, son of man, thus says the Lord GOD, 'Speak to every sort of bird and to every beast of the field:

"Assemble yourselves and come;
  Gather together from all sides to My sacrificial meal
  Which I am sacrificing for you,
  A great sacrificial meal on the mountains of Israel,
  That you may eat flesh and drink blood.
¹⁸ You shall eat the flesh of the mighty,
  Drink the blood of the princes of the earth,
  Of rams and lambs,
  Of goats and bulls,
  All of them fatlings of Bashan.
¹⁹ You shall eat fat till you are full,
  And drink blood till you are drunk,
  At My sacrificial meal

▰▰▰▰▰▰▰▰▰▰▰ **A SURE WIN**

39:12-16 Two themes are intertwined: God's total victory over his enemies and the need to purify the land to make it holy. After the fi... battle, teams will give proper burial to the bodies of the dead enemie... that the land may be cleansed. Yet there will be so many bodies that scavenger birds will be called to help dispose of the corpses (39:17-2... The message for us is an exciting one: with God on our side, we are assured of ultimate victory over any foe, for God will fight on our be... (see also Zephaniah 3:14-17; Romans 8:38-39).

Which I am sacrificing for you.
20 You shall be filled at My table
With horses and riders,
With mighty men
And with all the men of war," says the Lord GOD.

21"I will set My glory among the nations; all the nations shall see My judgment which I have executed, and My hand which I have laid on them. 22So the house of Israel shall know that I *am* the LORD their God from that day forward. 23The Gentiles shall know that the house of Israel went into captivity for their iniquity; because they were unfaithful to Me, therefore I hid My face from them. I gave them into the hand of their enemies, and they all fell by the sword. 24According to their uncleanness and according to their transgressions I have dealt with them, and hidden My face from them." '

25"Therefore thus says the Lord GOD: 'Now I will bring back the captives of Jacob, and have mercy on the whole house of Israel; and I will be jealous for My holy name— 26after they have borne their shame, and all their unfaithfulness in which they were unfaithful to Me, when they dwelt safely in their *own* land and no one made *them* afraid. 27When I have brought them back from the peoples and gathered them out of their enemies' lands, and I am hallowed in them in the sight of many nations, 28then they shall know that I *am* the LORD their God, who sent them into captivity among the nations, but also brought them back to their land, and left none of them captive any longer. 29And I will not hide My face from them anymore; for I shall have poured out My Spirit on the house of Israel,' says the Lord GOD."

CHAPTER **40** THE NEW TEMPLE. In the twenty-fifth year of our captivity, at the beginning of the year, on the tenth *day* of the month, in the fourteenth year after the city was captured, on the very same day the hand of the LORD was upon me; and He took me there. 2In the visions of God He took me into the land of Israel and set me on a very high mountain; on it toward the south *was* something like the structure of a city. 3He took me there, and behold, *there was* a man whose appearance *was* like the appearance of bronze. He had a line of flax and a measuring rod in his hand, and he stood in the gateway.

4And the man said to me, "Son of man, look with your eyes and hear with your ears, and fix your mind on everything I show you; for you *were* brought here so that I might show *them* to you. Declare to the house of Israel everything you see." 5Now there was a wall all around the outside of the temple. In the man's hand was a measuring rod six cubits *long, each being a* cubit and a handbreadth; and he measured the width of the wall structure, one rod; and the height, one rod.

6Then he went to the gateway which faced east; and he went up its stairs and measured the threshold of the gateway, *which was* one rod wide, and the other threshold *was* one rod wide. 7Each gate chamber *was* one rod long and one rod wide; between the gate chambers *was a space of* five cubits; and the threshold of the gateway by the vestibule of the inside gate *was* one rod. 8He also measured the vestibule of the inside gate, one rod. 9Then

he measured the vestibule of the gateway, eight cubits; and the gateposts, two cubits. The vestibule of the gate *was* on the inside. 10In the eastern gateway *were* three gate chambers on one side and three on the other; the three *were* all the same size; also the gateposts were of the same size on this side and that side.

PLANS

40:1ff Ezekiel explained God's dwelling place in words and images that the people could understand. God wanted them to see the great splendor he had planned for those who were faithful and would live with him forever. The temple is a symbol of the perfect sacrifice of Jesus Christ; it was never built, but it was a vision intended to typify God's perfect plans for his people. Don't let the details obscure the point of this vision—one day all those who have been faithful to God will enjoy eternal life with him. Let the majesty of this vision lift you and teach you about the God you worship and serve.

11He measured the width of the entrance to the gateway, ten cubits; *and* the length of the gate, thirteen cubits. 12*There was* a space in front of the gate chambers, one cubit *on this side* and one cubit on that side; the gate chambers *were* six cubits on this side and six cubits on that side. 13Then he measured the gateway from the roof of *one* gate chamber to the roof of the other; the width *was* twenty-five cubits, as door faces door. 14He measured the gateposts, sixty cubits high, and the court all around the gateway *extended* to the gatepost. 15*From* the front of the entrance gate to the front of the vestibule of the inner gate *was* fifty cubits. 16*There were* beveled window *frames* in the gate chambers and in their intervening archways on the inside of the gateway all around, and likewise in the vestibules. *There were* windows all around on the inside. And on each gatepost *were* palm trees.

17Then he brought me into the outer court; and *there were* chambers and a pavement made all around the court; thirty chambers faced the pavement. 18The pavement was by the side of the gateways, corresponding to the length of the gateways; *this was* the lower pavement. 19Then he measured the width from the front of the lower gateway to the front of the inner court exterior, one hundred cubits toward the east and the north.

20On the outer court was also a gateway facing north, and he measured its length and its width. 21Its gate chambers, three on this side and three on that side, its gateposts and its archways, had the same measurements as the first gate; its length *was* fifty cubits and its width twenty-five cubits. 22Its windows and those of its archways, and also its palm trees, *had* the same measurements as the gateway facing east; it was ascended by seven steps, and its archway *was* in front of it. 23A gate of the inner court was opposite the northern gateway, just as the eastern *gateway;* and he measured from gateway to gateway, one hundred cubits.

24After that he brought me toward the south, and there a gateway was facing south; and he measured its gateposts and archways according to these same measurements. 25*There were* windows in it and in its archways all around like those windows; its length *was* fifty cubits and its width twenty-five cubits. 26Seven steps led up to it, and its archway *was* in front of them; and it had palm trees on its gateposts, one on this side and one on that side. [27]*There was* also a gateway on the inner court, facing south; and he measured from gateway to gateway toward the south, one hundred cubits.

[28]Then he brought me to the inner court through the southern gateway; he measured the southern gateway according to these same measurements. [29]Also its gate chambers, its gateposts, and its archways *were* according to these same measurements; *there were* windows in it and in its archways all around; *it was* fifty cubits long and twenty-five cubits wide. [30]*There were* archways all around, twenty-five cubits long and five cubits wide. [31]Its archways faced the outer court, palm trees *were* on its gateposts, and going up to it *were* eight steps.

CLEANED UP

40:38-39 The washing of the sacrifices was done according to the standards of preparation established in Leviticus 1:6-9. This washing was part of the process of presenting an acceptable sacrifice to God. What is there in your life that you would like to present as a sacrifice to God?

[32]And he brought me into the inner court facing east; he measured the gateway according to these same measurements. [33]Also its gate chambers, its gateposts, and its archways *were* according to these same measurements; and *there were* windows in it and in its archways all around; *it was* fifty cubits long and twenty-five cubits wide. [34]Its archways faced the outer court, and palm trees *were* on its gateposts on this side and on that side; and going up to it *were* eight steps.

[35]Then he brought me to the north gateway and measured *it* according to these same measurements— [36]also its gate chambers, its gateposts, and its archways. It had windows all around; its length *was* fifty cubits and its width twenty-five cubits. [37]Its gateposts faced the outer court, palm trees *were* on its gateposts on this side and on that side, and going up to it *were* eight steps.

[38]*There was* a chamber and its entrance by the gateposts of the gateway, where they washed the burnt offering. [39]In the vestibule of the gateway *were* two tables on this side and two tables on that side, on which to slay the burnt offering, the sin offering, and the trespass offering. [40]At the outer side of the vestibule, as one goes up to the entrance of the northern gateway, *were* two tables; and on the other side of the vestibule of the gateway *were* two tables. [41]Four tables *were* on this side and four tables on that side, by the side of the gateway, eight tables on which they slaughtered *the sacrifices.* [42]*There were* also four tables of hewn stone for the burnt offering, one cubit and a half long, one cubit and a half wide, and one cubit high; on these they laid the instruments with which they slaughtered the burnt offering and the sacrifice. [43]Inside *were* hooks, a handbreadth wide, fastened all around; and the flesh of the sacrifices *was* on the tables.

[44]Outside the inner gate *were* the chambers for the singers in the inner court, one facing south at the side of the northern gateway, and the other facing north at the side of the southern gateway. [45]Then he said to me, "This chamber which faces south *is* for the priests who have charge of the temple. [46]The chamber which faces north *is* for the priests who have charge of the altar; these *are* the sons of Zadok, from the sons of Levi, who come near the LORD to minister to Him."

[47]And he measured the court, one hundred cubits long and one hundred cubits wide, foursquare. The altar *was* in front of the temple. [48]Then he brought me to the vestibule of the temple and measured the doorposts of the vestibule, five cubits on this side and five cubits on that side; and the width of the gateway was three cubits on this side and three cubits on that side. [49]The length of the vestibule *was* twenty cubits, and the width eleven cubits; and by the steps which led up to it *there were* pillars by the doorposts, one on this side and another on that side.

CHAPTER 41 THE MOST HOLY PLACE.

Then he brought me into the sanctuary and measured the doorposts, six cubits wide on one side and six cubits wide on the other side—the width of the tabernacle. [2]The width of the entryway *was* ten cubits, and the side walls of the entrance *were* five cubits on this side and five cubits on the other side; and he measured its length, forty cubits, and its width, twenty cubits.

[3]Also he went inside and measured the doorposts, two cubits; and the entrance, six cubits *high;* and the width of the entrance, seven cubits. [4]He measured the length, twenty cubits; and the width, twenty cubits, beyond the sanctuary; and he said to me, "This *is* the Most Holy *Place.*"

INNER SANCTUM

41:4 The Most Holy Place was the innermost room in the temple (Exodus 26:33-34). This was where the ark of the covenant was ke▪ where God's glory was said to dwell. It was entered only once a ye▪ the high priest, who performed a ceremony to atone for the nation▪ God's holiness is a central theme throughout both the Old and New Testaments.

[5]Next, he measured the wall of the temple, six cubits. The width of each side chamber all around the temple *was* four cubits on every side. [6]The side chambers *were* in three stories, one above the other, thirty chambers in each story; they rested on ledges which *were* for the side chambers all around, that they might be supported, but not fastened to the wall of the temple. [7]As one went up from story to story, the side chambers became wider all around, because their supporting ledges in the wall of the temple ascended like steps; therefore the width of the structure increased as one went up *from* the lowest *story* to the highest by way of the middle one. [8]I also saw an elevation all around the temple; it was the foundation of the side chambers, a full rod, *that is,* six cubits *high.* [9]The thickness of the outer wall of the side chambers *was* five cubits, and so also the remaining terrace by the place of the side chambers of the temple. [10]And between *it and* the *wall* chambers was a width of twenty cubits all around the temple on every side. [11]The doors of the side chambers opened on the terrace, one door toward the

north and another toward the south; and the width of the terrace *was* five cubits all around.

¹²The building that faced the separating courtyard at its western end *was* seventy cubits wide; the wall of the building *was* five cubits thick all around, and its length ninety cubits.

¹³So he measured the temple, one hundred cubits long; and the separating courtyard with the building and its walls *was* one hundred cubits long; ¹⁴also the width of the eastern face of the temple, including the separating courtyard, *was* one hundred cubits. ¹⁵He measured the length of the building behind it, facing the separating courtyard, with its galleries on the one side and on the other side, one hundred cubits, as well as the inner temple and the porches of the court, ¹⁶their doorposts and the beveled window frames. And the galleries all around their three stories opposite the threshold were paneled with wood from the ground to the windows—the windows were covered— ¹⁷from the space above the door, even to the inner room, as well as outside, and on every wall all around, inside and outside, by measure.

¹⁸And *it was* made with cherubim and palm trees, a palm tree between cherub and cherub. *Each* cherub had two faces, ¹⁹so that the face of a man *was* toward a palm tree on one side, and the face of a young lion toward a palm tree on the other side; thus *it was* made throughout the temple all around. ²⁰From the floor to the space above the door, and on the wall of the sanctuary, cherubim and palm trees *were* carved.

²¹The doorposts of the temple *were* square, *as was* the front of the sanctuary; their appearance was similar. ²²The altar *was* of wood, three cubits high, and its length two cubits. Its corners, its length, and its sides *were* of wood; and he said to me, "This *is* the table that *is* before the LORD."

²³The temple and the sanctuary had two doors. ²⁴The doors had two panels *apiece*, two folding panels: two *panels* for one door and two panels for the other *door.* ²⁵Cherubim and palm trees *were* carved on the doors of the temple just as they *were* carved on the walls. A wooden canopy *was* on the front of the vestibule outside. ²⁶*There were* beveled window *frames* and palm trees on one side and on the other, on the sides of the vestibule—also on the side chambers of the temple and on the canopies.

CHAPTER **42** **THE PRIESTS' ROOMS.** Then he brought me out into the outer court, by the way toward the north; and he brought me into the chamber which *was* opposite the separating courtyard, and which *was* opposite the building toward the north. ²Facing the length, *which was* one hundred cubits (the width was fifty cubits), was the north door. ³Opposite the inner court of twenty *cubits*, and opposite the pavement of the outer court, *was* gallery against gallery in three *stories.* ⁴In front of the chambers, toward the inside, *was* a walk ten cubits wide, at a distance of one cubit; and their doors faced north. ⁵Now the upper chambers *were* shorter, because the galleries took away *space* from them more than from the lower and middle stories of the building. ⁶For

they *were* in three *stories* and did not have pillars like the pillars of the courts; therefore *the upper level* was shortened more than the lower and middle levels from the ground up. ⁷And a wall which *was* outside ran parallel to the chambers, at the front of the chambers, toward the outer court; its length *was* fifty cubits. ⁸The length of the chambers toward the outer court *was* fifty cubits, whereas that facing the temple *was* one hundred cubits. ⁹At the lower chambers *was* the entrance on the east side, as one goes into them from the outer court.

¹⁰Also *there were* chambers in the thickness of the wall of the court toward the east, opposite the separating courtyard and opposite the building. ¹¹*There was* a walk in front of them also, and their appearance *was* like the chambers which *were* toward the north; they *were* as long and as wide as the others, and all their exits and entrances *were* according to plan. ¹²And corresponding to the doors of the chambers that *were* facing south, as one enters them, *there was* a door in front of the walk, the way directly in front of the wall toward the east.

¹³Then he said to me, "The north chambers *and* the south chambers, which *are* opposite the separating courtyard, *are* the holy chambers where the priests who approach the LORD shall eat the most holy offerings. There they shall lay the most holy offerings—the grain offering, the sin offering, and the trespass offering—for the place *is* holy. ¹⁴When the priests enter them, they shall not go out of the holy *chamber* into the outer court; but there they shall leave their garments in which they minister, for they *are* holy. They shall put on other garments; then they may approach *that* which *is* for the people."

![HARMONY banner] **HARMONY**

42:16-20 The perfect symmetry of the temple may represent the order and harmony in God's kingdom.

¹⁵Now when he had finished measuring the inner temple, he brought me out through the gateway that faces toward the east, and measured it all around. ¹⁶He measured the east side with the measuring rod, five hundred rods by the measuring rod all around. ¹⁷He measured the north side, five hundred rods by the measuring rod all around. ¹⁸He measured the south side, five hundred rods by the measuring rod. ¹⁹He came around to the west side *and* measured five hundred rods by the measuring rod. ²⁰He measured it on the four sides; it had a wall all around, five hundred *cubits* long and five hundred wide, to separate the holy areas from the common.

CHAPTER **43** **EZEKIEL RECORDS SOME RULES.** Afterward he brought me to the gate, the gate that faces toward the east. ²And behold, the glory of the God of Israel came from the way of the east. His voice *was* like the sound of many waters; and the earth shone with His glory. ³*It was* like the appearance of the vision which I saw—like the vision which I saw when I came to destroy the city. The visions *were* like the vision which I saw by the River Chebar; and I fell on my face. ⁴And the glory of the LORD came into the temple by way of the gate which faces toward the east. ⁵The Spirit lifted me up and

43:1ff This is the culmination of chapters 40—42, for God's glory returns to the temple. It reverses the negative cast of the book and concludes all the passages dealing with the blessings reserved for the restored remnant. All true believers should long for that moment when God's name will finally be glorified once and for all.

brought me into the inner court; and behold, the glory of the LORD filled the temple.

⁶Then I heard *Him* speaking to me from the temple, while a man stood beside me. ⁷And He said to me, "Son of man, *this is* the place of My throne and the place of the soles of My feet, where I will dwell in the midst of the children of Israel forever. No more shall the house of Israel defile My holy name, they nor their kings, by their harlotry or with the carcasses of their kings on their high places. ⁸When they set their threshold by My threshold, and their doorpost by My doorpost, with a wall between them and Me, they defiled My holy name by the abominations which they committed; therefore I have consumed them in My anger. ⁹Now let them put their harlotry and the carcasses of their kings far away from Me, and I will dwell in their midst forever.

¹⁰"Son of man, describe the temple to the house of Israel, that they may be ashamed of their iniquities; and let them measure the pattern. ¹¹And if they are ashamed of all that they have done, make known to them the design of the temple and its arrangement, its exits and its entrances, its entire design and all its ordinances, all its forms and all its laws. Write *it* down in their sight, so that they may keep its whole design and all its ordinances, and perform them. ¹²This *is* the law of the temple: The whole area surrounding the mountaintop *is* most holy. Behold, this *is* the law of the temple.

¹³"These *are* the measurements of the altar in cubits (the *cubit is* one cubit and a handbreadth): the base one cubit high and one cubit wide, with a rim all around its edge of one span. This *is* the height of the altar: ¹⁴from the base on the ground to the lower ledge, two cubits; the width of the ledge, one cubit; from the smaller ledge to the larger ledge, four cubits; and the width of the ledge, *one* cubit. ¹⁵The altar hearth *is* four cubits high, with four horns extending upward from the hearth. ¹⁶The altar hearth *is* twelve cubits long, twelve wide, square at its four corners; ¹⁷the ledge, fourteen *cubits* long and fourteen wide on its four sides, with a rim of half a cubit around it; its base, one cubit all around; and its steps face toward the east."

¹⁸And He said to me, "Son of man, thus says the Lord GOD: 'These *are* the ordinances for the altar on the day when it is made, for sacrificing burnt offerings on it, and for sprinkling blood on it. ¹⁹You shall give a young bull for a sin offering to the priests, the Levites, who are of the seed of Zadok, who approach Me to minister to Me,' says the Lord GOD. ²⁰You shall take some of its blood and put *it* on the four horns of the altar, on the four corners of the ledge, and on the rim around it; thus you shall cleanse it and make atonement for it. ²¹Then you shall also take the bull of the sin offering, and burn it in the appointed place of the temple, outside the sanctuary. ²²On the second day you shall offer a kid of the goats without blemish for a sin offering; and they shall cleanse the altar, as they cleansed

it with the bull. ²³When you have finished cleansing *it*, you shall offer a young bull without blemish, and a ram from the flock without blemish. ²⁴When you offer them before the LORD, the priests shall throw salt on them, and they will offer them up *as* a burnt offering to the LORD. ²⁵Every day for seven days you shall prepare a goat *for* a sin offering; they shall also prepare a young bull and a ram from the flock, both without blemish. ²⁶Seven days they shall make atonement for the altar and purify it, and so consecrate *it*. ²⁷When these days are over it shall be, on the eighth day and thereafter, that the priests shall offer your burnt offerings and your peace offerings on the altar; and I will accept you,' says the Lord GOD."

CHAPTER 44 WHAT THE PRIESTS SHOULD DO.

Then He brought me back to the outer gate of the sanctuary which faces toward the east, but it *was* shut. ²And the LORD said to me, "This gate shall be shut; it shall not be opened, and no man shall enter by it, because the LORD God of Israel has entered by it; therefore it shall be shut. ³*As* for the prince, *because* he *is* the prince, he may sit in it to eat bread before the LORD; he shall enter by way of the vestibule of the gateway, and go out the same way."

⁴Also He brought me by way of the north gate to the front of the temple; so I looked, and behold, the glory of the LORD filled the house of the LORD; and I fell on my face. ⁵And the LORD said to me, "Son of man, mark well, see with your eyes and hear with your ears, all that I say to you concerning all the ordinances of the house of the LORD and all its laws. Mark well who may enter the house and all who go out from the sanctuary.

⁶"Now say to the rebellious, to the house of Israel, 'Thus says the Lord GOD: "O house of Israel, let Us have no more of all your abominations. ⁷When you brought in foreigners, uncircumcised in heart and uncircumcised in flesh, to be in My sanctuary to defile it—My house—and when you offered My food, the fat and the blood, then they broke My covenant because of all your abominations. ⁸And you have not kept charge of My holy things, but you have set *others* to keep charge of My sanctuary for you." ⁹Thus says the Lord GOD: "No foreigner, uncircumcised in heart or uncircumcised in flesh, shall enter My sanctuary, including any foreigner who *is* among the children of Israel.

¹⁰"And the Levites who went far from Me, when Israel went astray, who strayed away from Me after their idols, they shall bear their iniquity. ¹¹Yet they shall be ministers in My sanctuary, *as* gatekeepers of the house and ministers of the house; they shall slay the burnt offering and the sacrifice for the people, and they shall stand before them to minister to them. ¹²Because they ministered to them before their idols and caused the house of Israel to fall into iniquity, therefore I have raised My hand in an oath against them," says the Lord GOD, "that they shall bear their iniquity. ¹³And they shall not come near Me to minister to Me as priest, nor come near any of My holy things, nor into the Most Holy *Place;* but they shall bear their shame and their abominations which they have committed. ¹⁴Nevertheless I will make them keep charge

of the temple, for all its work, and for all that has to be done in it.

15"But the priests, the Levites, the sons of Zadok, who kept charge of My sanctuary when the children of Israel went astray from Me, they shall come near Me to minister to Me; and they shall stand before Me to offer to Me the fat and the blood," says the Lord GOD. 16"They shall enter My sanctuary, and they shall come near My table to minister to Me, and they shall keep My charge. 17And it shall be, whenever they enter the gates of the inner court, that they shall put on linen garments; no wool shall come upon them while they minister within the gates of the inner court or within the house. 18They shall have linen turbans on their heads and linen trousers on their bodies; they shall not clothe themselves with *anything that causes* sweat. 19When they go out to the outer court, to the *outer* court to the people, they shall take off their garments in which they have ministered, leave them in the holy chambers, and put on other garments; and in their holy garments they shall not sanctify the people.

20"They shall neither shave their heads, nor let their hair grow long, but they shall keep their hair well trimmed. 21No priest shall drink wine when he enters the inner court. 22They shall not take as wife a widow or a divorced woman, but take virgins of the descendants of the house of Israel, or widows of priests.

23"And they shall teach My people *the difference* between the holy and the unholy, and cause them to discern between the unclean and the clean. 24In controversy they shall stand as judges, *and* judge it according to My judgments. They shall keep My laws and My statutes in all My appointed meetings, and they shall hallow My Sabbaths.

25"They shall not defile *themselves* by coming near a dead person. Only for father or mother, for son or daughter, for brother or unmarried sister may they defile themselves. 26After he is cleansed, they shall count seven days for him. 27And on the day that he goes to the sanctuary to minister in the sanctuary, he must offer his sin offering in the inner court," says the Lord GOD.

28"It shall be, in regard to their inheritance, *that* I *am* their inheritance. You shall give them no possession in Israel, for I *am* their possession. 29They shall eat the grain offering, the sin offering, and the trespass offering; every dedicated thing in Israel shall be theirs. 30The best of all firstfruits of any kind, and every sacrifice of any kind from all your sacrifices, shall be the priest's; also you shall give to the priest the first of your ground meal, to cause a blessing to rest on your house. 31The priests shall not eat anything, bird or beast, that died naturally or was torn *by wild beasts.*

CHAPTER 45 SOME LAND FOR THE LORD.

"Moreover, when you divide the land by lot into inheritance, you shall set apart a district for the LORD, a holy section of the land; its length *shall be* twenty-five thousand *cubits*, and the width ten thousand. It *shall be* holy throughout its territory all around. 2Of this there shall be a square plot for the sanctuary, five hundred by five hundred *rods*, with fifty cubits around it for an open space.

3So this is the district you shall measure: twenty-five thousand *cubits* long and ten thousand wide; in it shall be the sanctuary, the Most Holy *Place*. 4It shall be a holy *section* of the land, belonging to the priests, the ministers of the sanctuary, who come near to minister to the LORD; it shall be a place for their houses and a holy place for the sanctuary. 5An *area* twenty-five thousand *cubits* long and ten thousand wide shall belong to the Levites, the ministers of the temple; they shall have twenty chambers as a possession.

◄ SPEAK OUT

44:23 Teaching people the difference between right and wrong is one of the responsibilities of ministers (see also Leviticus 10:8-11; Philippians 1:10). Ministers are God's representatives and spokesmen. Encourage your minister to speak out on moral issues.

6"You shall appoint as the property of the city *an area* five thousand *cubits* wide and twenty-five thousand long, adjacent to the district of the holy *section;* it shall belong to the whole house of Israel.

7"The prince shall have *a section* on one side and the other of the holy district and the city's property; and bordering on the holy district and the city's property, extending westward on the west side and eastward on the east side, the length *shall be* side by side with one of the *tribal* portions, from the west border to the east border. 8The land shall be his possession in Israel; and My princes shall no more oppress My people, but they shall give *the rest of* the land to the house of Israel, according to their tribes."

9Thus says the Lord GOD: "Enough, O princes of Israel! Remove violence and plundering, execute justice and righteousness, and stop dispossessing My people," says the Lord GOD. 10"You shall have honest scales, an honest ephah, and an honest bath. 11The ephah and the bath shall be of the same measure, so that the bath contains one-tenth of a homer, and the ephah one-tenth of a homer; their measure shall be according to the homer. 12The shekel *shall be* twenty gerahs; twenty shekels, twenty-five shekels, *and* fifteen shekels shall be your mina.

13"This *is* the offering which you shall offer: you shall give one-sixth of an ephah from a homer of wheat, and one-sixth of an ephah from a homer of barley. 14The ordinance concerning oil, the bath of oil, *is* one-tenth of a bath from a kor. A kor *is* a homer or ten baths, for ten baths *are* a homer. 15And one lamb shall be given from a flock of two hundred, from the rich pastures of Israel.

◄ HONESTY

45:9-12 Greed and extortion were two of the major social sins of the nation during this time (see Amos 5:7-13). In the new economy there would be plenty of land for the "princes" (45:7-8) and no longer any basis for greed. Therefore, the princes and the people were commanded to be fair and honest, especially when they did business. Consider the ways you measure goods, money, or services. If you are paid for an hour of work, be sure you work for a full hour. If you sell a bushel of apples, make sure it is a full bushel. God is completely trustworthy, and his followers should be too.

46:1-15 Ezekiel continues to describe various aspects of daily worship. While allowing for diversity in worship, God has prescribed order and continuity. This gave a healthy rhythm to the spiritual life of his people.

These shall be for grain offerings, burnt offerings, and peace offerings, to make atonement for them," says the Lord GOD. [16]"All the people of the land shall give this offering for the prince in Israel. [17]Then it shall be the prince's part *to give* burnt offerings, grain offerings, and drink offerings, at the feasts, the New Moons, the Sabbaths, and at all the appointed seasons of the house of Israel. He shall prepare the sin offering, the grain offering, the burnt offering, and the peace offerings to make atonement for the house of Israel."

[18]"Thus says the Lord GOD: "In the first *month,* on the first *day* of the month, you shall take a young bull without blemish and cleanse the sanctuary. [19]The priest shall take some of the blood of the sin offering and put *it* on the doorposts of the temple, on the four corners of the ledge of the altar, and on the gateposts of the gate of the inner court. [20]And so you shall do on the seventh *day* of the month for everyone who has sinned unintentionally or in ignorance. Thus you shall make atonement for the temple.

[21]"In the first *month,* on the fourteenth day of the month, you shall observe the Passover, a feast of seven days; unleavened bread shall be eaten. [22]And on that day the prince shall prepare for himself and for all the people of the land a bull *for* a sin offering. [23]On the seven days of the feast he shall prepare a burnt offering to the LORD, seven bulls and seven rams without blemish, daily for seven days, and a kid of the goats daily *for* a sin offering. [24]And he shall prepare a grain offering of one ephah for each bull and one ephah for each ram, together with a hin of oil for each ephah.

[25]"In the seventh *month,* on the fifteenth day of the month, at the feast, he shall do likewise for seven days, according to the sin offering, the burnt offering, the grain offering, and the oil.""

CHAPTER 46 SPECIAL OFFERINGS.

[1]'Thus says the Lord GOD: "The gateway of the inner court that faces toward the east shall be shut the six working days; but on the Sabbath it shall be opened, and on the day of the New Moon it shall be opened. [2]The prince shall enter by way of the vestibule of the gateway from the outside, and stand by the gatepost. The priests shall prepare his burnt offering and his peace offerings. He shall worship at the threshold of the gate. Then he shall go out, but the gate shall not be shut until evening. [3]Likewise the people of the land shall worship at the entrance to this gateway before the LORD on the Sabbaths and the New Moons. [4]The burnt offering that the prince offers to the LORD on the Sabbath day *shall be* six lambs without blemish, and a ram without blemish; [5]and the grain offering *shall be* one ephah for a ram, and the grain offering for the lambs, as much as he wants to give, as well as a hin of oil with every ephah. [6]On the day of the New Moon *it shall be* a young bull without blemish, six lambs, and a ram; they shall be without blemish. [7]He shall prepare a grain offering of an ephah for a bull, an ephah for a ram, as much as

he wants to give for the lambs, and a hin of oil with every ephah. [8]When the prince enters, he shall go in by way of the vestibule of the gateway, and go out the same way.

[9]"But when the people of the land come before the LORD on the appointed feast days, whoever enters by way of the north gate to worship shall go out by way of the south gate; and whoever enters by way of the south gate shall go out by way of the north gate. He shall not return by way of the gate through which he came, but shall go out through the opposite gate. [10]The prince shall then be in their midst. When they go in, he shall go in; and when they go out, he shall go out. [11]At the festivals and the appointed feast days the grain offering shall be an ephah for a bull, an ephah for a ram, as much as he wants to give for the lambs, and a hin of oil with every ephah.

[12]"Now when the prince makes a voluntary burnt offering or voluntary peace offering to the LORD, the gate that faces toward the east shall then be opened for him; and he shall prepare his burnt offering and his peace offerings as he did on the Sabbath day. Then he shall go out, and after he goes out the gate shall be shut.

[13]"You shall daily make a burnt offering to the LORD *of* a lamb of the first year without blemish; you shall prepare it every morning. [14]And you shall prepare a grain offering with it every morning, a sixth of an ephah, and a third of a hin of oil to moisten the fine flour. This grain offering is a perpetual ordinance, to be made regularly to the LORD. [15]Thus they shall prepare the lamb, the grain offering, and the oil, *as* a regular burnt offering every morning."

[16]"Thus says the Lord GOD: "If the prince gives a gift *of some* of his inheritance to any of his sons, it shall belong to his sons; it is their possession by inheritance. [17]But if he gives a gift of some of his inheritance to one of his servants, it shall be his until the year of liberty, after which it shall return to the prince. But his inheritance shall belong to his sons; it shall become theirs. [18]Moreover the prince shall not take any of the people's inheritance by evicting them from their property; he shall provide an inheritance for his sons from his own property, so that none of My people may be scattered from his property.""

[19]Now he brought me through the entrance, which *was* at the side of the gate, into the holy chambers of the priests which face toward the north; and there a place *was* situated at their extreme western end. [20]And he said to me, "This *is* the place where the priests shall boil the trespass offering and the sin offering, *and* where they shall bake the grain offering, so that they do not bring *them* out into the outer court to sanctify the people."

[21]Then he brought me out into the outer court and caused me to pass by the four corners of the court; and in fact, in every corner of the court *there was another* court. [22]In the four corners of the court *were* enclosed courts, forty *cubits* long and thirty wide; all four corners *were* the same size. [23]*There was* a row *of building stones* all around in them, all around the four of them; and cooking hearths were made under the rows of stones all around. [24]And he said to me, "These *are* the kitchens where the ministers of the temple shall boil the sacrifices of the people."

CHAPTER **47** **THE RIVER OF HEALING.** Then he brought me back to the door of the temple; and there was water, flowing from under the threshold of the temple toward the east, for the front of the temple faced east; the water was flowing from under the right side of the temple, south of the altar. [2]He brought me out by way of the north gate, and led me around on the outside to the outer gateway that faces east; and there was water, running out on the right side.

[3]And when the man went out to the east with the line in his hand, he measured one thousand cubits, and he brought me through the waters; the water *came up to my* ankles. [4]Again he measured one thousand and brought me through the waters; the water *came up to my* knees. Again he measured one thousand and brought me through; the water *came up to my* waist. [5]Again he measured one thousand, *and it was* a river that I could not cross; for the water was too deep, water in which one must swim, a river that could not be crossed. [6]He said to me, "Son of man, have you seen *this*?" Then he brought me and returned me to the bank of the river.

[7]When I returned, there, along the bank of the river, *were* very many trees on one side and the other. [8]Then he said to me: "This water flows toward the eastern region, goes down into the valley, and enters the sea. *When it* reaches the sea, *its* waters are healed. [9]And it shall be *that* every living thing that moves, wherever the rivers go, will live. There will be a very great multitude of fish, because these waters go there; for they will be healed, and everything will live wherever the river goes. [10]It shall be *that* fishermen will stand by it from En Gedi to En Eglaim; they will be *places* for spreading their nets. Their fish will be of the same kinds as the fish of the Great Sea, exceedingly many. [11]But its swamps and marshes will not be healed; they will be given over to salt. [12]Along the bank of the river, on this side and that, will grow all *kinds of* trees used for food; their leaves will not wither, and their fruit will not fail. They will bear fruit every month, because their water flows from the sanctuary. Their fruit will be for food, and their leaves for medicine."

[13]Thus says the Lord GOD: "These *are* the borders by which you shall divide the land as an inheritance among the twelve tribes of Israel. Joseph *shall have two* portions. [14]You shall inherit it equally with one another; for I raised My hand in an oath to give it to your fathers, and this land shall fall to you as your inheritance.

[15]"This *shall be* the border of the land on the north: from the Great Sea, *by* the road to Hethlon, as one goes to Zedad, [16]Hamath, Berothah, Sibraim (which *is* between the border of Damascus and the border of Hamath), to Hazar Hatticon (which *is* on the border of Hauran). [17]Thus the boundary shall be from the Sea to Hazar Enan, the border of Damascus; and as for the north, northward, it is the border of Hamath. *This is* the north side.

[18]"On the east side you shall mark out the border from between Hauran and Damascus, and between Gilead and the land of Israel, along the Jordan, and along the eastern side of the sea. *This is* the east side.

[19]"The south side, toward the South, *shall be* from Tamar to the waters of Meribah by Kadesh, along the brook to the Great Sea. *This is* the south side, toward the South.

[20]"The west side *shall be* the Great Sea, from the *southern* boundary until one comes to a point opposite Hamath. This *is* the west side.

SAFE RIVER

47:1-12 This river (or stream) is similar to the river mentioned in Revelation 22:1-2, both of which are associated with the river in the Garden of Eden (see Genesis 2:10). The river symbolizes life from God and the blessings that flow from his throne. It is a gentle, safe, deep river that expands as it flows.

[21]"Thus you shall divide this land among yourselves according to the tribes of Israel. [22]It shall be that you will divide it by lot as an inheritance for yourselves, and for the strangers who dwell among you and who bear children among you. They shall be to you as native-born among the children of Israel; they shall have an inheritance with you among the tribes of Israel. [23]And it shall be *that* in whatever tribe the stranger dwells, there you shall give *him* his inheritance," says the Lord GOD.

CHAPTER **48** **THE LAND IS DIVIDED.** "Now these *are* the names of the tribes: From the northern border along the road to Hethlon at the entrance of Hamath, to Hazar Enan, the border of Damascus northward, in the direction of Hamath, *there shall be* one *section for* Dan from its east to its west side; [2]by the border of Dan, from the east side to the west, one *section for* Asher; [3]by the border of Asher, from the east side to the west, one *section for* Naphtali; [4]by the border of Naphtali, from the east side to the west, one *section for* Manasseh; [5]by the border of Manasseh, from the east side to the west, one *section for* Ephraim; [6]by the border of Ephraim, from the east side to the west, one *section for* Reuben; [7]by the border of Reuben, from the east side to the west, one *section for* Judah; [8]by the border of Judah, from the east side to the west, shall be the district which you shall set apart, twenty-five thousand *cubits* in width, and *in* length the same as one of the *other* portions, from the east side to the west, with the sanctuary in the center.

[9]"The district that you shall set apart for the LORD *shall be* twenty-five thousand *cubits* in length and ten thousand in width. [10]To these—to the priests—the holy district shall belong: on the north twenty-five thousand *cubits in length*, on the west ten thousand in width, on

THE PRESENCE

48:1-35 The book of Ezekiel begins by describing the holiness of God, which Israel had despised and ignored. As a result, God's presence had departed from the temple, the city, and the people. The book ends with a detailed vision of the new temple, the new city, and the new people—all demonstrating God's holiness. The pressures of everyday life can persuade us to focus on the here and now and thus forget God. That is why worship is so important; it takes our eyes off our current worries, gives us a glimpse of God's holiness, and allows us to look toward his future kingdom. God's presence makes everything glorious, and worship brings us into his presence.

the east ten thousand in width, and on the south twenty-five thousand in length. The sanctuary of the LORD shall be in the center. [11]*It shall be* for the priests of the sons of Zadok, who are sanctified, who have kept My charge, who did not go astray when the children of Israel went astray, as the Levites went astray. [12]And *this* district of land that is set apart shall be to them a thing most holy by the border of the Levites.

[13]"Opposite the border of the priests, the Levites *shall have an area* twenty-five thousand *cubits* in length and ten thousand in width; its entire length *shall be* twenty-five thousand and its width ten thousand. [14]And they shall not sell or exchange any of it; they may not alienate this best *part* of the land, for *it is* holy to the LORD.

[15]"The five thousand *cubits* in width that remain, along the edge of the twenty-five thousand, shall be for general use by the city, for dwellings and common-land; and the city shall be in the center. [16]These *shall be* its measurements: the north side four thousand five hundred *cubits*, the south side four thousand five hundred, the east side four thousand five hundred, and the west side four thousand five hundred. [17]The common-land of the city shall be: to the north two hundred and fifty *cubits*, to the south two hundred and fifty, to the east two hundred and fifty, and to the west two hundred and fifty. [18]The rest of the length, alongside the district of the holy *section, shall be* ten thousand *cubits* to the east and ten thousand to the west. It shall be adjacent to the district of the holy *section*, and its produce shall be food for the workers of the city. [19]The workers of the city, from all the tribes of Israel, shall cultivate it. [20]The entire district *shall be* twenty-five thousand *cubits* by twenty-five thousand *cubits*, foursquare. You shall set apart the holy district with the property of the city.

[21]"The rest *shall belong* to the prince, on one side and on the other of the holy district and of the city's property, next to the twenty-five thousand *cubits* of the *holy* district as far as the eastern border, and westward next to the twenty-five thousand as far as the western border, adjacent to the *tribal* portions; *it shall belong* to the prince. It shall be the holy district, and the sanctuary of the temple *shall be* in the center. [22]Moreover, apart from the possession of the Levites and the possession of the city *which are* in the midst of what *belongs* to the prince, *the area* between the border of Judah and the border of Benjamin shall belong to the prince.

[23]"As for the rest of the tribes, from the east side to the west, Benjamin *shall have* one *section;* [24]by the border of Benjamin, from the east side to the west, Simeon *shall have* one *section;* [25]by the border of Simeon, from the east side to the west, Issachar *shall have* one *section;* [26]by the border of Issachar, from the east side to the west, Zebulun *shall have* one *section;* [27]by the border of Zebulun, from the east side to the west, Gad *shall have* one *section;* [28]by the border of Gad, on the south side, toward the South, the border shall be from Tamar *to* the waters of Meribah *by* Kadesh, along the brook to the Great Sea. [29]This *is* the land which you shall divide by lot as an inheritance among the tribes of Israel, and these *are* their portions," says the Lord GOD.

[30]"These *are* the exits of the city. On the north side, measuring four thousand five hundred *cubits* [31](the gates of the city *shall be* named after the tribes of Israel), the three gates northward: one gate for Reuben, one gate for Judah, and one gate for Levi; [32]on the east side, four thousand five hundred *cubits*, three gates: one gate for Joseph, one gate for Benjamin, and one gate for Dan; [33]on the south side, measuring four thousand five hundred *cubits*, three gates: one gate for Simeon, one gate for Issachar, and one gate for Zebulun; [34]on the west side, four thousand five hundred *cubits* with their three gates: one gate for Gad, one gate for Asher, and one gate for Naphtali. [35]All the way around *shall be* eighteen thousand *cubits;* and the name of the city from *that* day *shall be:* THE LORD *IS* THERE."

MEGA Themes

GOD'S HOLINESS Ezekiel wrote of his vision revealing God's moral perfection. God was spiritually and morally superior to Israel's corrupt and compromising society. Ezekiel also wrote to let the people know that God was present with them in Babylon, not just in Jerusalem.

Because God is morally perfect, he can help us live above our tendency to compromise. He can give us the power to overcome sin and to reflect his holiness. Moral purity is an important part of Christian discipleship.

1. List some of the key visions God gave to Ezekiel. How did Ezekiel respond to these visions?
2. What did these visions have to say about God?

3. Why were the messages of these visions so important for the people during their captivity?

4. Why is moral purity important for any person who wants to glorify God?

SIN Israel sinned, so God punished them. The fall of Jerusalem and the Babylonian exile were used by God to correct the rebels and draw them back from their sinful way of life. Ezekiel warned them that not only was the nation responsible for sin, but each individual was also accountable to God.

We cannot excuse ourselves from our responsibilities before God. We are accountable to him. Rather than avoid God, we must recognize sin for what it is—rebellion against God—and choose to follow him instead.

1. What sins had the people committed?

2. What do you think was God's purpose for punishing the people like he did?

3. How did God want individuals to respond to his warnings and punishments? How did he want the nation to respond?

4. How has God specifically dealt with sin in your life? How have you responded?

RESTORATION Ezekiel consoled the people by telling them that the day would come when God would restore those who turn away from sin. God would be their King and Shepherd. He would give his people a new heart to worship him and establish a new government and a new temple.

Knowing that they will eventually be rescued and restored should encourage believers during difficult times. But we must be faithful to God because we love him, not for what he can do for us. Our faith must be in *him*, not in possible future benefits.

1. What qualities of God do you see revealed in his promise of restoration?

2. Suppose you had a friend who was a Christian yet had chosen to be deeply involved in a continuous habit of sin. What would you tell this friend about God's restoration as an encouragement to turn from sin and to God?

3. In what ways can you continue to seek and experience God's restoration on a daily basis?

LEADERS Ezekiel condemned the unfaithful priests and leaders ("shepherds") who led the people astray. By contrast, Ezekiel was a caring shepherd and a watchful sentry as he warned the people about their sin.

Jesus is our perfect leader. If we truly want him to lead us, our devotion must be more than talk. If we are given the responsibility of leading others, we must take care of them even if it means sacrificing personal pleasure, happiness, time, or money. We are responsible to God for witnessing to and teaching those we lead.

1. Contrast Ezekiel as a man of God and leader of the people with the Hebrews' priests and leaders who led them away from God.

2. What qualities does Jesus have that make him the greatest of all leaders? Which of these qualities did Ezekiel have?

3. Based on this study, what are the most important qualities of a godly leader? Why?

4. Like Ezekiel, we are to reflect godly qualities. We have Jesus' perfect example as well as the example of people like Ezekiel. If someone were to examine your life, what would that person see that reflects the qualities of Jesus?

5. Complete this sentence: "In order to be the most effective I can be in leading others to God, I want to grow more like Jesus in the area of _____." Commit to God the choice you intend to make in order to develop in this area.

WORSHIP An angel gave Ezekiel a detailed vision of the temple. God's holy presence had left Israel and the temple because of sin. This ideal temple pictures the return of God's presence when God will cleanse his people and restore true worship.

All of God's promises will be fulfilled under the rule of the Messiah. The faithful followers will be brought back to perfect fellowship with God and with one another. To prepare for this, we must focus on God through regular worship, learning about God's holiness, and making needed changes in our life.

1. What was the role of the temple in the Hebrew worship during Ezekiel's lifetime?

2. Describe your worship of God in the past week (where, how, attitudes, thoughts, feelings, individual or with others, etc.).

3. Evaluate your worship of God in the past week (value, importance, strengths and weaknesses, of things you would change).

Courage is . . . risking injury to help a friend . . . doing what is right against all odds . . . standing for the truth despite the consequences . . . living for God, no matter what. ■ Daniel had courage. Living in a foreign land, he stood for what he believed and did what was right, in spite of incredible pressure, from society, from peers, and from the government. And courage was Daniel's trademark throughout his life and through the reigns of four kings. He boldly interpreted dreams, rejected royal food and drink, and publicly lived his faith. Daniel was a man of great courage and faith in God. ■ God still needs men and women of courage and faith. What kinds of risks do you face? What kinds of pressures do you feel to conform or to turn away from God? ■ As you read the book of Daniel, marvel at the man who refused to give in or give up. Ask God to give you the courage to live out your faith, like Daniel did, as you develop a stronger relationship with "the God of gods" (2:47).

STATS

PURPOSE: To give a historical account of the faithful Jews who lived in captivity and to show how God is in control of heaven and earth, directing the forces of nature, the destiny of nations, and the care of his people

AUTHOR: Daniel

TO WHOM WRITTEN: The other captives in Babylon and God's people everywhere

DATE WRITTEN: Approximately 535 B.C., recording events that occurred from about 605–535 B.C.

SETTING: Daniel had been taken captive and deported to Babylon by Nebuchadnezzar in 605 B.C. There he served in the government for about 60 years during the reigns of Nebuchadnezzar, Belshazzar, Darius, and Cyrus.

KEY PEOPLE: Daniel, Nebuchadnezzar, Shadrach, Meshach, Abed-Nego, Belshazzar, Darius

KEY PLACES: Nebuchadnezzar's palace, the fiery furnace, Belshazzar's banquet, the den of lions

SPECIAL FEATURES: Daniel's apocalyptic visions (chapters 8–12) give a glimpse of God's plan for the ages, including a direct prediction of the Messiah

Daniel

CHAPTER 1   DANIEL WON'T EAT THE KING'S FOOD.

In the third year of the reign of Jehoiakim king of Judah, Nebuchadnezzar king of Babylon came to Jerusalem and besieged it. ²And the Lord gave Jehoiakim king of Judah into his hand, with some of the articles of the house of God, which he carried into the land of Shinar to the house of his god; and he brought the articles into the treasure house of his god.

³Then the king instructed Ashpenaz, the master of his eunuchs, to bring some of the children of Israel and some of the king's descendants and some of the nobles, ⁴young men in whom *there was* no blemish, but good-looking, gifted in all wisdom, possessing knowledge and quick to understand, who *had* ability to serve in the king's palace, and whom they might teach the language and literature of the Chaldeans. ⁵And the king appointed for them a daily provision of the king's delicacies and of the wine which he drank, and three years of training for them, so that at the end of *that time* they might serve before the king. ⁶Now from among those of the sons of Judah were Daniel, Hananiah, Mishael, and Azariah. ⁷To them the chief of the eunuchs gave names: he gave Daniel *the name* Belteshazzar; to Hananiah, Shadrach; to Mishael, Meshach; and to Azariah, Abed-Nego.

⁸But Daniel purposed in his heart that he would not defile himself with the portion of the king's delicacies, nor with the wine which he drank; therefore he requested of the chief of the eunuchs that he might not defile himself. ⁹Now God had brought Daniel into the favor and goodwill of the chief of the eunuchs. ¹⁰And the chief of the eunuchs said to Daniel, "I fear my lord the king, who has appointed your food and drink. For why should he see your faces looking worse than the young men who *are* your age? Then you would endanger my head before the king."

¹¹So Daniel said to the steward whom the chief of the eunuchs had set over Daniel, Hananiah, Mishael, and Azariah, ¹²"Please test your servants for ten days, and let

◼ TEMPTATION

1:8 It is easier to resist temptation if you have thought through your convictions well before the temptation arises. Daniel and his friends made their decision to be faithful to the laws of their religion before they were faced with the king's delicacies, so they did not hesitate to stick with their convictions. Sometimes we get into trouble because we have not previously decided where to draw the line. Before such situations arise, decide on your commitments. Then, when temptation comes, you will be ready.

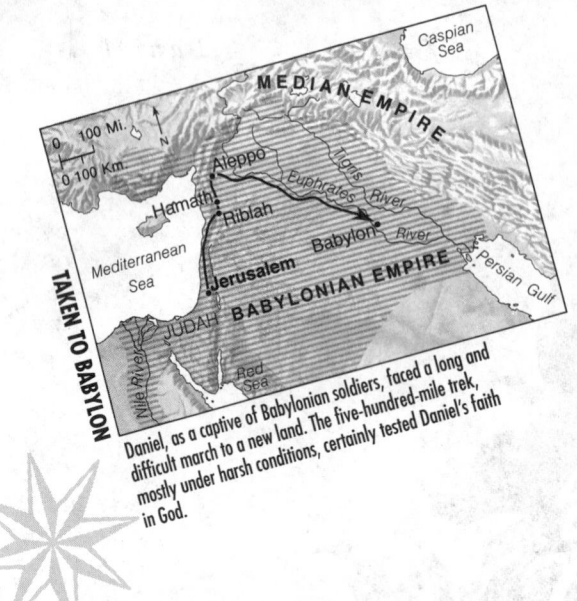

TAKEN TO BABYLON

Daniel, as a captive of Babylonian soldiers, faced a long and difficult march to a new land. The five-hundred-mile trek, mostly under harsh conditions, certainly tested Daniel's faith in God.

them give us vegetables to eat and water to drink. ¹³Then let our appearance be examined before you, and the appearance of the young men who eat the portion of the king's delicacies; and as you see fit, *so* deal with your servants." ¹⁴So he consented with them in this matter, and tested them ten days.

¹⁵And at the end of ten days their features appeared better and fatter in flesh than all the young men who ate the portion of the king's delicacies. ¹⁶Thus the steward took away their portion of delicacies and the wine that they were to drink, and gave them vegetables.

¹⁷As for these four young men, God gave them knowledge and skill in all literature and wisdom; and Daniel had understanding in all visions and dreams.

¹⁸Now at the end of the days, when the king had said that they should be brought in, the chief of the eunuchs

◣◣◣◣ ALLEGIANCE

1:17 Daniel and his friends learned all they could about their new culture so they could do their work with excellence. But while they learned, they maintained steadfast allegiance to God. Culture need ▸ be God's enemy. If it does not violate his commands, it can aid in accomplishing his purpose. We who follow God are free to be leader our culture, but we must put our allegiance to God first.

brought them in before Nebuchadnezzar. ¹⁹Then the king interviewed them, and among them all none was found like Daniel, Hananiah, Mishael, and Azariah; therefore they served before the king. ²⁰And in all matters of wisdom *and* understanding about which the king examined them, he found them ten times better than all the magicians *and* astrologers who *were* in all his realm. ²¹Thus Daniel continued until the first year of King Cyrus.

CHAPTER **2** **DANIEL DESCRIBES THE KING'S DREAM.** Now in the second year of Nebuchadnezzar's reign, Nebuchadnezzar had dreams; and his spirit was *so* troubled that his sleep left him. ²Then the king gave the command to call the magicians, the astrologers, the sorcerers, and the Chaldeans to tell the king his dreams. So they came and stood before the king. ³And the king said to them, "I have had a dream, and my spirit is anxious to know the dream."

◣◣◣◣ IMPOSSIBLE

2:11 The Chaldeans told the king that no one could know the drea of another person. But Daniel was able to give the answer because ◖ was working through him. In daily life, we face many apparently impossible situations that would be hopeless if we had to handle the with limited human strength alone. But God specializes in the impos▸

⁴Then the Chaldeans spoke to the king in Aramaic, "O king, live forever! Tell your servants the dream, and we will give the interpretation."

⁵The king answered and said to the Chaldeans, "My

DANIEL

served as a prophet to the exiles in Babylon from 605–536 B.C.

Climate of the times
The people of Judah were captives in a strange land, feeling hopeless.

Main message
God is sovereign over all of human history, past, present, and future.

Importance of message
We should spend less time wondering when future events will happen and more time learning how we should live now.

Contemporary prophets
Jeremiah (627–586)
Habakkuk (612–589)
Ezekiel (593–571)

decision is firm: if you do not make known the dream to me, and its interpretation, you shall be cut in pieces, and your houses shall be made an ash heap. 6However, if you tell the dream and its interpretation, you shall receive from me gifts, rewards, and great honor. Therefore tell me the dream and its interpretation."

7They answered again and said, "Let the king tell his servants the dream, and we will give its interpretation."

8The king answered and said, "I know for certain that you would gain time, because you see that my decision is firm: 9if you do not make known the dream to me, *there is only* one decree for you! For you have agreed to speak lying and corrupt words before me till the time has changed. Therefore tell me the dream, and I shall know that you can give me its interpretation."

10The Chaldeans answered the king, and said, "There is not a man on earth who can tell the king's matter; therefore no king, lord, or ruler has *ever* asked such things of any magician, astrologer, or Chaldean. 11*It is* a difficult thing that the king requests, and there is no other who can tell it to the king except the gods, whose dwelling is not with flesh."

12For this reason the king was angry and very furious, and gave the command to destroy all the wise *men* of Babylon. 13So the decree went out, and they began killing the wise *men;* and they sought Daniel and his companions, to kill *them.*

14Then with counsel and wisdom Daniel answered Arioch, the captain of the king's guard, who had gone out to kill the wise *men* of Babylon; 15he answered and said to Arioch the king's captain, "Why is the decree from the king so urgent?" Then Arioch made the decision known to Daniel.

16So Daniel went in and asked the king to give him time, that he might tell the king the interpretation. 17Then Daniel went to his house, and made the decision known to Hananiah, Mishael, and Azariah, his companions, 18that they might seek mercies from the God of heaven concerning this secret, so that Daniel and his companions might not perish with the rest of the wise *men* of Babylon. 19Then the secret was revealed to Daniel in a night vision. So Daniel blessed the God of heaven.

20Daniel answered and said:

"Blessed be the name of God forever and ever,
For wisdom and might are His.

21 And He changes the times and the seasons;
He removes kings and raises up kings;
He gives wisdom to the wise
And knowledge to those who have understanding.

22 He reveals deep and secret things;
He knows what *is* in the darkness,
And light dwells with Him.

23 "I thank You and praise You,
O God of my fathers;
You have given me wisdom and might,
And have now made known to me what we asked of You,
For You have made known to us the king's demand."

24Therefore Daniel went to Arioch, whom the king had appointed to destroy the wise *men* of Babylon.

DANIEL

Daniel's early life shows us there is more to being young than making mistakes. Adults can't help being impressed whenever a young person speaks and acts wisely. Those were Daniel's strongest personal traits—wise words and actions. He spoke the truth and did the right thing, even when it looked like he was the only one doing it. Have you ever noticed how often life's biggest mistakes begin with this thought: *I can do this because everybody else is doing it?*

One example of Daniel's wisdom is the way he held on to his convictions. He didn't give in to pressure. His habits and convictions came from God's Word, and pleasing God was more important to Daniel than pleasing anyone else.

Where do your habits come from? What happens to your convictions when the pressure is on?

Daniel's convictions weren't just beliefs; they created positive actions in his life. For instance, he ate carefully and lived prayerfully. His position gave him all-you-can-eat privileges at the king's table, but Daniel chose a simpler menu and proved it was a healthy choice. Our eating habits are a good measure of how well we are doing at controlling all our appetites.

While Daniel cut back on food, he cut loose on prayer. He felt comfortable talking to God because he did it all the time. Even lions couldn't come between him and his habit of prayer. Notice, though, that prayer doesn't necessarily keep us from "lions' dens." Rather, prayer keeps us in touch with God even in the middle of "lions' dens"! Make prayer a daily action in your life.

LESSONS: Wise words and actions often earn long-term respect
Don't wait until you are in a tough situation to learn about prayer
God can use people wherever they are

KEY VERSE: "Inasmuch as an excellent spirit, knowledge, understanding, interpreting dreams, solving riddles, and explaining enigmas were found in this Daniel, whom the king named Belteshazzar, now let Daniel be called, and he will give the interpretation" (5:12).
Daniel's story is told in the book of Daniel. He is also mentioned in Matthew 24:15.

UPS
- Although taken from his home at an early age; he remained true to his faith
- Served as a counselor to two Babylonian kings and two Medo-Persian kings
- Was a man of prayer and a statesman with the gift of prophecy
- Survived the lions' den

STATS
- Where: Judah and the courts of Babylon and Persia
- Occupation: A captive of Israel who became a counselor of kings
- Contemporaries: Hananiah, Mishael, Azariah, Nebuchadnezzar, Belshazzar, Darius, Cyrus

He went and said thus to him: "Do not destroy the wise *men* of Babylon; take me before the king, and I will tell the king the interpretation."

[25]Then Arioch quickly brought Daniel before the king, and said thus to him, "I have found a man of the captives of Judah, who will make known to the king the interpretation."

[26]The king answered and said to Daniel, whose name *was* Belteshazzar, "Are you able to make known to me the dream which I have seen, and its interpretation?"

[27]Daniel answered in the presence of the king, and said, "The secret which the king has demanded, the wise *men*, the astrologers, the magicians, and the soothsayers cannot declare to the king. [28]But there is a God in heaven

FRIENDSHIP

Sarah, Rebecca, and Melanie are inseparable. Find one and you'll find the other two.

Besides a lot of laughs and six years' worth of great memories, the three-way friendship has helped keep the girls on track with God all through high school. Whenever one of the girls has faltered in her faith, the other two have been there to pick her up. For instance:

- When Rebecca began dating a non-Christian, the other two girls confronted her and convinced her that she was making a mistake.
- When Melanie's parents split up one winter and Melanie was wondering if God really cared, Sarah and Rebecca showered their hurting friend with love and concern.
- When Sarah got so involved in extracurricular school activities one semester that she quit coming to Bible study, the other girls practically dragged her back into the fold!
- When the girls didn't get asked to the prom because of their stand against alcohol, they all dressed up and went to dinner instead.

Without such a strong Christ-centered friendship, the girls might have wandered away from God when the pressure got too intense. However, because they had a friendship like this to lean on, they all were able to have a huge impact for Christ!

Do you have close Christian friends who constantly challenge you to grow in Christ? Read in Daniel 3 about three godly guys who braved some serious heat together.

who reveals secrets, and He has made known to King Nebuchadnezzar what will be in the latter days. Your dream, and the visions of your head upon your bed, are these: [29]As for you, O king, thoughts came *to* your *mind while* on your bed, *about* what would come to pass after this; and He who reveals secrets has made known to you what will be. [30]But as for me, this secret has not been revealed to me because I have more wisdom than anyone living, but for *our* sakes who make known the interpretation to the king, and that you may know the thoughts of your heart.

[31]"You, O king, were watching; and behold, a great image! This great image, whose splendor *was* excellent, stood before you; and its form *was* awesome. [32]This image's head *was* of fine gold, its chest and arms of silver, its belly and thighs of bronze, [33]its legs of iron, its feet partly of iron and partly of clay. [34]You watched while a stone was

cut out without hands, which struck the image on its feet of iron and clay, and broke them in pieces. [35]Then the iron, the clay, the bronze, the silver, and the gold were crushed together, and became like chaff from the summer threshing floors; the wind carried them away so that no trace of them was found. And the stone that struck the image became a great mountain and filled the whole earth.

[36]"This *is* the dream. Now we will tell the interpretation of it before the king. [37]You, O king, *are* a king of kings. For the God of heaven has given you a kingdom, power, strength, and glory; [38]and wherever the children of men dwell, or the beasts of the field and the birds of the heaven, He has given *them* into your hand, and has made you ruler over them all—you *are* this head of gold. [39]But after you shall arise another kingdom inferior to yours; then another, a third kingdom of bronze, which shall rule over all the earth. [40]And the fourth kingdom shall be as strong as iron, inasmuch as iron breaks in pieces and shatters everything; and like iron that crushes, *that kingdom* will break in pieces and crush all the others. [41]Whereas you saw the feet and toes, partly of potter's clay and partly of iron, the kingdom shall be divided; yet the strength of the iron shall be in it, just as you saw the iron mixed with ceramic clay. [42]And *as* the toes of the feet *were* partly of iron and partly of clay, *so* the kingdom shall be partly strong and partly fragile. [43]As you saw iron mixed with ceramic clay, they will mingle with the seed of men; but they will not adhere to one another, just as iron does not mix with clay. [44]And in the days of these kings the God of heaven will set up a kingdom which shall never be destroyed; and the kingdom shall not be left to other people; it shall break in pieces and consume all these kingdoms, and it shall stand forever. [45]Inasmuch as you saw that the stone was cut out of the mountain without hands, and that it broke in pieces the iron, the bronze, the clay, the silver, and the gold—the great God has made known to the king what will come to pass after this. The dream is certain, and its interpretation is sure."

[46]Then King Nebuchadnezzar fell on his face, prostrate before Daniel, and commanded that they should present an offering and incense to him. [47]The king answered Daniel, and said, "Truly your God *is* the God of gods, the Lord of kings, and a revealer of secrets, since you could reveal this secret." [48]Then the king promoted

Daniel and gave him many great gifts; and he made him ruler over the whole province of Babylon, and chief administrator over all the wise *men* of Babylon. ⁴⁹Also Daniel petitioned the king, and he set Shadrach, Meshach, and Abed-Nego over the affairs of the province of Babylon; but Daniel *sat* in the gate of the king.

CHAPTER **3** **THE FIERY FURNACE.** Nebuchadnezzar the king made an image of gold, whose height *was* sixty cubits *and* its width six cubits. He set it up in the plain of Dura, in the province of Babylon. ²And King Nebuchadnezzar sent *word* to gather together the satraps, the administrators, the governors, the counselors, the treasurers, the judges, the magistrates, and all the officials of the provinces, to come to the dedication of the image which King Nebuchadnezzar had set up. ³So the satraps, the administrators, the governors, the counselors, the treasurers, the judges, the magistrates, and all the officials of the provinces gathered together for the dedication of the image that King Nebuchadnezzar had set up; and they stood before the image that Nebuchadnezzar had set up. ⁴Then a herald cried aloud: "To you it is commanded, O peoples, nations, and languages, ⁵*that* at the time you hear the sound of the horn, flute, harp, lyre, *and* psaltery, in symphony with all kinds of music, you shall fall down and worship the gold image that King Nebuchadnezzar has set up; ⁶and whoever does not fall down and worship shall be cast immediately into the midst of a burning fiery furnace."

⁷So at that time, when all the people heard the sound of the horn, flute, harp, *and* lyre, in symphony with all kinds of music, all the people, nations, and languages fell down *and* worshiped the gold image which King Nebuchadnezzar had set up.

⁸Therefore at that time certain Chaldeans came forward and accused the Jews. ⁹They spoke and said to King Nebuchadnezzar, "O king, live forever! ¹⁰You, O king, have made a decree that everyone who hears the sound of the horn, flute, harp, lyre, *and* psaltery, in symphony with all kinds of music, shall fall down and worship the gold image; ¹¹and whoever does not fall down and worship shall be cast into the midst of a burning fiery furnace. ¹²There are certain Jews whom you have set over the affairs of the province of Babylon: Shadrach, Meshach, and Abed-Nego; these men, O king, have not paid due regard to you. They do not serve your gods or worship the gold image which you have set up."

¹³Then Nebuchadnezzar, in rage and fury, gave the command to bring Shadrach, Meshach, and Abed-Nego. So they brought these men before the king.

SHADRACH, MESHACH, & ABED-NEGO

Have you ever gotten too close to a fire that suddenly sent out flames, catching you off guard and sending you hurrying away? If so, you know how powerful and frightening fire can be. Now, imagine willingly walking into a blast furnace rather than denying God . . . and you begin to understand the courageous, tenacious faith of Daniel's friends Shadrach, Meshach, and Abed-Nego.

Along with Daniel and the other people of Jerusalem, these three young Jewish men were taken into captivity by the Babylonians in 605 B.C. Their way of life was totally uprooted, and they were forced to serve in the court of the heathen King Nebuchadnezzar. Although the king obviously respected and admired his young Hebrew servants, he just as clearly did not understand the depth of their relationship with the One True God.

Nebuchadnezzar built a huge golden idol and ordered all his officials to worship it. Whoever refused would be burned alive. Of course, with a choice like that, almost everyone obeyed . . . but not Shadrach, Meshach, and Abed-Nego. Angrily, the king ordered them to worship the idol or be thrown into the fire. Shadrach, Meshach, and Abed-Nego refused, preferring instead to face the fire. That's putting your faith on the line!

Furious, Nebuchadnezzar ordered the fire stoked up seven times hotter than usual. It was so hot, the soldiers assigned to carry out the execution died as they threw the three men in! The men fell in, no doubt expecting to be incinerated. Instead, the ropes which held them fell away, and they miraculously walked around in the midst of the flames unharmed . . . escorted by a fourth person who looked "like the Son of God" (3:25). You never know how God will meet you when you put your faith on the line. But you can be sure he will.

LESSONS: There is great strength in real friendship with others with whom we share convictions. It is important to stand God can be trusted even when we can't predict the outcome.

KEY VERSES: "O Nebuchadnezzar, we have no need to answer you in this matter. If that is the case, our God whom we serve is able to deliver us from the burning fiery furnace, and He will deliver us from your hand, O king. But if not, let it be known to you, O king, that we do not serve your gods, nor will we worship the gold image which you have set up" (3:16-18).

The story of Shadrach (Hananiah), Meshach (Mishael), and Abed-Nego (Azariah) is told in the book of Daniel.

UPS:
- Stood with Daniel against eating food from the king's table
- Shared a friendship that stood the tests of hardship, success, wealth, and possible death
- Would not compromise their convictions even in the face of death
- Survived the fiery furnace

STATS:
- Where: Babylon
- Occupations: King's servants and counselors
- Contemporaries: Daniel, Nebuchadnezzar

¹⁴Nebuchadnezzar spoke, saying to them, "*Is it* true, Shadrach, Meshach, and Abed-Nego, *that* you do not serve my gods or worship the gold image which I have set up? ¹⁵Now if you are ready at the time you hear the sound of the horn, flute, harp, lyre, *and* psaltery, in symphony with all kinds of music, and you fall down and worship the image which I have made, *good!* But if you do not worship, you shall be cast immediately into the midst of a burning fiery furnace. And who *is* the god who will deliver you from my hands?"

¹⁶Shadrach, Meshach, and Abed-Nego answered and said to the king, "O Nebuchadnezzar, we have no need to answer you in this matter. ¹⁷If that *is the case,* our God whom we serve is able to deliver us from the burning fiery furnace, and He will deliver *us* from your hand, O king. ¹⁸But if not, let it be known to you, O king, that we do not serve your gods, nor will we worship the gold image which you have set up."

¹⁹Then Nebuchadnezzar was full of fury, and the expression on his face changed toward Shadrach, Meshach, and Abed-Nego. He spoke and commanded that they heat the furnace seven times more than it was usually heated. ²⁰And he commanded certain mighty men of valor who *were* in his army to bind Shadrach, Meshach, and Abed-Nego, *and* cast *them* into the burning fiery furnace. ²¹Then these men were bound in their coats, their trousers, their turbans, and their *other* garments, and were cast into the midst of the burning fiery furnace. ²²Therefore, because the king's command was urgent, and the furnace exceedingly hot, the flame of the fire killed those men who took up Shadrach, Meshach, and Abed-Nego. ²³And these three men, Shadrach, Meshach, and Abed-Nego, fell down bound into the midst of the burning fiery furnace.

²⁴Then King Nebuchadnezzar was astonished; and he rose in haste *and* spoke, saying to his counselors, "Did we not cast three men bound into the midst of the fire?"

They answered and said to the king, "True, O king."

²⁵"Look!" he answered, "I see four men loose, walking in the midst of the fire; and they are not hurt, and the form of the fourth is like the Son of God."

²⁶Then Nebuchadnezzar went near the mouth of the burning fiery furnace *and* spoke, saying, "Shadrach, Meshach, and Abed-Nego, servants of the Most High God, come out, and come *here.*" Then Shadrach, Meshach, and Abed-Nego came from the midst of the fire. ²⁷And the satraps, administrators, governors, and the king's counselors gathered together, and they saw these men on whose bodies the fire had no power; the hair of their head was not singed nor were their garments affected, and the smell of fire was not on them.

²⁸Nebuchadnezzar spoke, saying, "Blessed be the God of Shadrach, Meshach, and Abed-Nego, who sent His Angel and delivered His servants who trusted in Him, and they have frustrated the king's word, and yielded their bodies, that they should not serve nor worship any god except their own God! ²⁹Therefore I make a decree that any people, nation, or language which speaks anything amiss against the God of Shadrach, Meshach, and Abed-Nego shall be cut in pieces, and their houses shall be made an ash heap; because there is no other God who can deliver like this."

³⁰Then the king promoted Shadrach, Meshach, and Abed-Nego in the province of Babylon.

CHAPTER 4 THE KING DREAMS ABOUT A TREE.

Nebuchadnezzar the king,

To all peoples, nations, and languages that dwell in all the earth:

Peace be multiplied to you.

² I thought it good to declare the signs and wonders that the Most High God has worked for me.

³ How great *are* His signs,
And how mighty His wonders!
His kingdom *is* an everlasting kingdom,
And His dominion *is* from generation to generation.

⁴ I, Nebuchadnezzar, was at rest in my house, and flourishing in my palace. ⁵I saw a dream which made me afraid, and the thoughts on my bed and the visions of my head troubled me. ⁶Therefore I issued a decree to bring in all the wise *men* of Babylon before me, that they might make known to me the interpretation of the dream. ⁷Then the magicians, the astrologers, the Chaldeans, and the soothsayers came in, and I told them the dream; but they did not make known to me its interpretation. ⁸But at last Daniel came before me (his name *is* Belteshazzar, according to the name of my god; in him *is* the Spirit of the Holy God), and I told the dream before him, *saying:* ⁹"Belteshazzar, chief of the magicians, because I know that the Spirit of the Holy God *is* in you, and no secret troubles you, explain to me the visions of my dream that I have seen, and its interpretation.

¹⁰ "These *were* the visions of my head *while* on my bed:

I was looking, and behold,
A tree in the midst of the earth,
And its height was great.
¹¹ The tree grew and became strong;
Its height reached to the heavens,
And it could be seen to the ends of all the earth.
¹² Its leaves *were* lovely,
Its fruit abundant,
And in it *was* food for all.
The beasts of the field found shade under it,
The birds of the heavens dwelt in its branches,
And all flesh was fed from it.

¹³ "I saw in the visions of my head *while* on my bed,
and there was a watcher, a holy one, coming
down from heaven. ¹⁴He cried aloud and said thus:

'Chop down the tree and cut off its branches,
Strip off its leaves and scatter its fruit.
Let the beasts get out from under it,
And the birds from its branches.
¹⁵ Nevertheless leave the stump and roots in the earth,
Bound with a band of iron and bronze,
In the tender grass of the field.
Let it be wet with the dew of heaven,
And *let* him graze with the beasts
On the grass of the earth.

16 Let his heart be changed from *that of* a man,
Let him be given the heart of a beast,
And let seven times pass over him.

17 'This decision *is* by the decree of the watchers,
And the sentence by the word of the holy ones,
In order that the living may know
That the Most High rules in the kingdom of men,
Gives it to whomever He will,
And sets over it the lowest of men.'

18 "This dream I, King Nebuchadnezzar, have seen. Now you, Belteshazzar, declare its interpretation, since all the wise *men* of my kingdom are not able to make known to me the interpretation; but you *are* able, for the Spirit of the Holy God *is* in you."

19 Then Daniel, whose name was Belteshazzar, was astonished for a time, and his thoughts troubled him. *So* the king spoke, and said, "Belteshazzar, do not let the dream or its interpretation trouble you."

Belteshazzar answered and said, "My lord, *may* the dream concern those who hate you, and its interpretation concern your enemies!

20 "The tree that you saw, which grew and became strong, whose height reached to the heavens and which *could be seen* by all the earth, 21whose leaves *were* lovely and its fruit abundant, in which *was* food for all, under which the beasts of the field dwelt, and in whose branches the birds of the heaven had their home— 22it *is* you, O king, who have grown and become strong; for your greatness has grown and reaches to the heavens, and your dominion to the end of the earth.

23 "And inasmuch as the king saw a watcher, a holy one, coming down from heaven and saying, 'Chop down the tree and destroy it, but leave its stump and roots in the earth, *bound* with a band of iron and bronze in the tender grass of the field; let it be wet with the dew of heaven, and let him graze with the beasts of the field, till seven times pass over him'; 24this is the interpretation, O king, and this is the decree of the Most High, which has come upon my lord the king: 25They shall drive you from men, your dwelling shall be with the beasts of the field, and they shall make you eat grass like oxen. They shall wet you with the dew of heaven, and seven times shall pass over you, till you know that the Most High rules in the kingdom of men, and gives it to whomever He chooses.

26 "And inasmuch as they gave the command to leave the stump *and* roots of the tree, your kingdom shall be assured to you, after you come to know that Heaven rules. 27Therefore, O king, let my advice be acceptable to you; break off your sins by *being* righteous, and your iniquities by showing mercy to *the* poor. Perhaps there may be a lengthening of your prosperity."

28 All *this* came upon King Nebuchadnezzar. 29At the end of the twelve months he was walking about the royal palace of Babylon. 30The king spoke, saying, "Is not this great Babylon, that I have built for a royal dwelling by my mighty power and for the honor of my majesty?"

HARD TO FORGIVE

4:19 When Daniel understood Nebuchadnezzar's dream, he was stunned. How could he be so deeply grieved at the fate of Nebuchadnezzar—the king who was responsible for the destruction of his home and nation? Daniel had forgiven the king, and so God was able to use Daniel. Often when we have been wronged by someone, we find it difficult to forget the past. We may even be glad if that person suffers. Forgiving people means putting the past behind us. Can you love someone who has hurt you? Ask God to help you forgive, forget, and love. God may use you in an extraordinary way in that person's life!

31 While the word *was still* in the king's mouth, a voice fell from heaven: "King Nebuchadnezzar, to you it is spoken: the kingdom has departed from you! 32And they shall drive you from men, and your dwelling *shall be* with the beasts of the field. They shall make you eat grass like oxen; and seven times shall pass over you, until you know that the Most High rules in the kingdom of men, and gives it to whomever He chooses."

33 That very hour the word was fulfilled concerning Nebuchadnezzar; he was driven from men and ate grass like oxen; his body was wet with the dew of heaven till his hair had grown like eagles' *feathers* and his nails like birds' *claws*.

34 And at the end of the time I, Nebuchadnezzar, lifted my eyes to heaven, and my understanding returned to me; and I blessed the Most High and praised and honored Him who lives forever:

For His dominion *is* an everlasting dominion,

ACKNOWLEDGE

4:34 Nebuchadnezzar's pilgrimage with God is one of the themes of this book. In 2:47, he acknowledged that God revealed dreams to Daniel. In 3:28-29, he praised the God who delivered the three Hebrews. Despite Nebuchadnezzar's recognition that God exists and works great miracles, in 4:30 we see that he still did not acknowledge God as his own ruler. We may recognize that God exists and does wonderful miracles, but God is not going to shape our life until we acknowledge him as Lord.

And His kingdom *is* from generation to generation.
35 All the inhabitants of the earth *are* reputed as nothing;
He does according to His will in the army of heaven
And *among* the inhabitants of the earth.
No one can restrain His hand
Or say to Him, "What have You done?"

36 At the same time my reason returned to me, and for the glory of my kingdom, my honor and splendor returned to me. My counselors and nobles resorted to me, I was restored to my kingdom, and

excellent majesty was added to me. [37]Now I, Nebuchadnezzar, praise and extol and honor the King of heaven, all of whose works *are* truth, and His ways justice. And those who walk in pride He is able to put down.

CHAPTER 5 STRANGE WRITING ON THE WALL.

Belshazzar the king made a great feast for a thousand of his lords, and drank wine in the presence of the thousand. [2]While he tasted the wine, Belshazzar gave the command to bring the gold and silver vessels which his father Nebuchadnezzar had taken from the temple which *had been* in Jerusalem, that the king and his lords, his wives, and his concubines might drink from them. [3]Then they brought the gold vessels that had been taken from the temple of the house of God which *had been* in Jerusalem; and the king and his lords, his wives, and his concubines drank from them. [4]They drank wine, and praised the gods of gold and silver, bronze and iron, wood and stone.

UNBIASED

5:17 The king offered Daniel beautiful gifts and great power if he would explain the writing, but Daniel turned them down. He knew they would be short-lived and he wanted to show that he was giving an unbiased interpretation to the king. Like Daniel, we need to avoid letting others influence our response to God's call or urgings in our life.

[5]In the same hour the fingers of a man's hand appeared and wrote opposite the lampstand on the plaster of the wall of the king's palace; and the king saw the part of the hand that wrote. [6]Then the king's countenance changed, and his thoughts troubled him, so that the joints of his hips were loosened and his knees knocked against each other. [7]The king cried aloud to bring in the astrologers, the Chaldeans, and the soothsayers. The king spoke, saying to the wise *men* of Babylon, "Whoever reads this writing, and tells me its interpretation, shall be clothed with purple and *have* a chain of gold around his neck; and he shall be the third ruler in the kingdom." [8]Now all the king's wise *men* came, but they could not read the writing, or make known to the king its interpretation. [9]Then King Belshazzar was greatly troubled, his countenance was changed, and his lords were astonished.

[10]The queen, because of the words of the king and his lords, came to the banquet hall. The queen spoke, saying, "O king, live forever! Do not let your thoughts trouble you, nor let your countenance change. [11]There is a man in your kingdom in whom *is* the Spirit of the Holy God. And in the days of your father, light and understanding and wisdom, like the wisdom of the gods, were found in him; and King Nebuchadnezzar your father—your father the king—made him chief of the magicians, astrologers, Chaldeans, *and* soothsayers. [12]Inasmuch as an excellent spirit, knowledge, understanding, interpreting dreams, solving riddles, and explaining enigmas were found in this Daniel, whom the king named Belteshazzar, now let Daniel be called, and he will give the interpretation."

[13]Then Daniel was brought in before the king. The king

5:27 The handwriting on the wall was for Belshazzar. Although he power and wealth, his kingdom was totally corrupt and he could no withstand the judgment of God. God's time of judgment comes for people. If there is sin in your life, turn away from it now. Ask God t forgive you, and begin to live by his standards of justice.

spoke, and said to Daniel, "*Are* you that Daniel who is one of the captives from Judah, whom my father the king brought from Judah? [14]I have heard of you, that the Spirit of God *is* in you, and *that* light and understanding and excellent wisdom are found in you. [15]Now the wise *men*, the astrologers, have been brought in before me, that they should read this writing and make known to me its interpretation, but they could not give the interpretation of the thing. [16]And I have heard of you, that you can give interpretations and explain enigmas. Now if you can read the writing and make known to me its interpretation, you shall be clothed with purple and *have* a chain of gold around your neck, and shall be the third ruler in the kingdom."

[17]Then Daniel answered, and said before the king, "Let your gifts be for yourself, and give your rewards to another; yet I will read the writing to the king, and make known to him the interpretation. [18]O king, the Most High God gave Nebuchadnezzar your father a kingdom and majesty, glory and honor. [19]And because of the majesty that He gave him, all peoples, nations, and languages trembled and feared before him. Whomever he wished, he executed; whomever he wished, he kept alive; whomever he wished, he set up; and whomever he wished, he put down. [20]But when his heart was lifted up, and his spirit was hardened in pride, he was deposed from his kingly throne, and they took his glory from him. [21]Then he was driven from the sons of men, his heart was made like the beasts, and his dwelling *was* with the wild donkeys. They fed him with grass like oxen, and his body was wet with the dew of heaven, till he knew that the Most High God rules in the kingdom of men, and appoints over it whomever He chooses.

[22]"But you his son, Belshazzar, have not humbled your heart, although you knew all this. [23]And you have lifted yourself up against the Lord of heaven. They have brought the vessels of His house before you, and you and your lords, your wives and your concubines, have drunk wine from them. And you have praised the gods of silver and gold, bronze and iron, wood and stone, which do not see or hear or know; and the God who *holds* your breath in His hand and owns all your ways, you have not glorified. [24]Then the fingers of the hand were sent from Him, and this writing was written.

[25]"And this is the inscription that was written:

MENE, MENE, TEKEL, UPHARSIN.

[26]This *is* the interpretation of *each* word. MENE: God has

RESPECT

6:1-3 At this time, Daniel was in his eighties and one of Darius's three administrators. He was working with those who did not belie his God, but he worked more efficiently and capably than all the Thus, Daniel attracted the attention of the heathen king and earne place of respect. One of the best ways to influence non-Christian employers is to work hard. How do you represent God to your em

numbered your kingdom, and finished it; ²⁷TEKEL: You have been weighed in the balances, and found wanting; ²⁸PERES: Your kingdom has been divided, and given to the Medes and Persians." ²⁹Then Belshazzar gave the command, and they clothed Daniel with purple and *put a* chain of gold around his neck, and made a proclamation concerning him that he should be the third ruler in the kingdom.

³⁰That very night Belshazzar, king of the Chaldeans, was slain. ³¹And Darius the Mede received the kingdom, *being* about sixty-two years old.

CHAPTER 6 DANIEL IN THE LIONS' DEN.

It pleased Darius to set over the kingdom one hundred and twenty satraps, to be over the whole kingdom; ²and over these, three governors, of whom Daniel *was* one, that the satraps might give account to them, so that the king would suffer no loss. ³Then this Daniel distinguished himself above the governors and satraps, because an excellent spirit *was* in him; and the king gave thought to setting him over the whole realm. ⁴So the governors and satraps sought to find *some* charge against Daniel concerning the kingdom; but they could find no charge or fault, because he *was* faithful; nor was there any error or fault found in him. ⁵Then these men said, "We shall not find any charge against this Daniel unless we find *it* against him concerning the law of his God."

⁶So these governors and satraps thronged before the king, and said thus to him: "King Darius, live forever! ⁷All the governors of the kingdom, the administrators and satraps, the counselors and advisors, have consulted together to establish a royal statute and to make a firm decree, that whoever petitions any god or man for thirty days, except you, O king, shall be cast into the den of lions. ⁸Now, O king, establish the decree and sign the writing, so that it cannot be changed, according to the law of the Medes and Persians, which does not alter." ⁹Therefore King Darius signed the written decree.

¹⁰Now when Daniel knew that the writing was signed, he went home. And in his upper room, with his windows open toward Jerusalem, he knelt down on his knees three times that day, and prayed and gave thanks before his God, as was his custom since early days.

¹¹Then these men assembled and found Daniel praying and making supplication before his God. ¹²And they went before the king, and spoke concerning the king's decree: "Have you not signed a decree that every man who petitions any god or man within thirty days, except you, O king, shall be cast into the den of lions?"

The king answered and said, "The thing *is* true, according to the law of the Medes and Persians, which does not alter."

¹³So they answered and said before the king, "That Daniel, who is one of the captives from Judah, does not show due regard for you, O king, or for the decree that you have signed, but makes his petition three times a day."

¹⁴And the king, when he heard *these* words, was greatly displeased with himself, and set *his* heart on Daniel to deliver him; and he labored till the going down of the sun

to deliver him. ¹⁵Then these men approached the king, and said to the king, "Know, O king, that *it is* the law of the Medes and Persians that no decree or statute which the king establishes may be changed."

CRITICS

6:4-5 The jealous officials couldn't find anything about Daniel's life to criticize, so they attacked his religion. If you face jealous critics because of your faith, be glad they're criticizing that part of your life—perhaps they had to focus on your religion as a last resort! Respond by continuing to believe and live as you should. Then remember that God is in control, fighting this battle for you.

¹⁶So the king gave the command, and they brought Daniel and cast *him* into the den of lions. *But* the king spoke, saying to Daniel, "Your God, whom you serve continually, He will deliver you." ¹⁷Then a stone was brought and laid on the mouth of the den, and the king sealed it with his own signet ring and with the signets of his lords, that the purpose concerning Daniel might not be changed.

¹⁸Now the king went to his palace and spent the night fasting; and no musicians were brought before him. Also his sleep went from him. ¹⁹Then the king arose very early in the morning and went in haste to the den of lions. ²⁰And when he came to the den, he cried out with a

I'm involved in so many activities at school and church lately that I haven't had any time to spend with God. How do I keep from getting too busy for him?
God knows you live in a busy world, but being busy is no excuse for ignoring him. The pressures and demands on you will increase as you grow older, so you must decide now to do what's important and make your relationship with God your number-one priority.

Busyness is a hard habit to break. People have a tendency to think God wants them rushing from one thing to the next. But busyness, even with "Christian" things, can be unhealthy. It can end up pulling us away from God and spiritual nourishment.

Daniel understood that. He risked death to spend time with God! (Check out Daniel 6:10-15). It's tough for many Christians to risk missing TV shows, friends, phone calls, and magazines to spend time with him! Our priorities are mixed up, and unless they're brought back in line with what's really best for us—spending time alone with Christ—we'll always be running around, confused about what's really important.

Learn this lesson early in your Christian life: The joy you can have just spending time with Christ is far greater than any positive strokes you may get from being busy. Listen to this plea from Jesus.

"Do not labor for the food which perishes, but for the food which endures to everlasting life, which the Son of Man will give you, because God the Father has set His seal on Him" (John 6:27).

6:25-27 Nebuchadnezzar had believed in God because of the faithfulness of Daniel and his friends. Here Darius was also convinced of God's power because Daniel was faithful and God delivered him. Although Daniel was captive in a strange land, his devotion to God was a testimony to powerful rulers. If you find yourself in new surroundings, take the opportunity to testify about God's power in your life. Be faithful to God so he can use you to reach others.

lamenting voice to Daniel. The king spoke, saying to Daniel, "Daniel, servant of the living God, has your God, whom you serve continually, been able to deliver you from the lions?"

²¹Then Daniel said to the king, "O king, live forever! ²²My God sent His angel and shut the lions' mouths, so that they have not hurt me, because I was found innocent before Him; and also, O king, I have done no wrong before you."

²³Now the king was exceedingly glad for him, and commanded that they should take Daniel up out of the den. So Daniel was taken up out of the den, and no injury whatever was found on him, because he believed in his God.

²⁴And the king gave the command, and they brought those men who had accused Daniel, and they cast *them* into the den of lions—them, their children, and their wives; and the lions overpowered them, and broke all their bones in pieces before they ever came to the bottom of the den.

²⁵Then King Darius wrote:

To all peoples, nations, and languages that dwell in all the earth:

Peace be multiplied to you.

²⁶ I make a decree that in every dominion of my kingdom *men must* tremble and fear before the God of Daniel.

For He *is* the living God,
And steadfast forever;
His kingdom *is the one* which shall not be destroyed,
And His dominion *shall endure* to the end.

²⁷ He delivers and rescues,
And He works signs and wonders
In heaven and on earth,
Who has delivered Daniel from the power of the lions.

²⁸So this Daniel prospered in the reign of Darius and in the reign of Cyrus the Persian.

CHAPTER 7 DANIEL DREAMS ABOUT FOUR BEASTS. In the first year of Belshazzar king of Babylon, Daniel had a dream and visions of his head *while* on his bed. Then he wrote down the dream, telling the main facts.

²Daniel spoke, saying, "I saw in my vision by night, and behold, the four winds of heaven were stirring up the Great Sea. ³And four great beasts came up from the sea, each different from the other. ⁴The first *was* like a lion, and had eagle's wings. I watched till its wings were plucked off; and it was lifted up from the earth and made

to stand on two feet like a man, and a man's heart was given to it.

⁵"And suddenly another beast, a second, like a bear. It was raised up on one side, and *had* three ribs in its mouth between its teeth. And they said thus to it: 'Arise, devour much flesh!'

⁶"After this I looked, and there was another, like a leopard, which had on its back four wings of a bird. The beast also had four heads, and dominion was given to it.

⁷"After this I saw in the night visions, and behold, a fourth beast, dreadful and terrible, exceedingly strong. It had huge iron teeth; it was devouring, breaking in pieces, and trampling the residue with its feet. It *was* different from all the beasts that *were* before it, and it had ten horns. ⁸I was considering the horns, and there was another horn, a little one, coming up among them, before whom three of the first horns were plucked out by the roots. And there, in this horn, *were* eyes like the eyes of a man, and a mouth speaking pompous words.

⁹ "I watched till thrones were put in place,
And the Ancient of Days was seated;
His garment *was* white as snow,
And the hair of His head *was* like pure wool.
His throne *was* a fiery flame,
Its wheels a burning fire;
¹⁰ A fiery stream issued
And came forth from before Him.
A thousand thousands ministered to Him;
Ten thousand times ten thousand stood before Him.
The court was seated,
And the books were opened.

¹¹"I watched then because of the sound of the pompous words which the horn was speaking; I watched till the beast was slain, and its body destroyed and given to the burning flame. ¹²As for the rest of the beasts, they had their dominion taken away, yet their lives were prolonged for a season and a time.

¹³ "I was watching in the night visions,
And behold, *One* like the Son of Man,
Coming with the clouds of heaven!
He came to the Ancient of Days,
And they brought Him near before Him.
¹⁴ Then to Him was given dominion and glory and a kingdom,
That all peoples, nations, and languages should serve Him.
His dominion *is* an everlasting dominion,
Which shall not pass away,
And His kingdom *the one*
Which shall not be destroyed.

JUDGMENT

7:10 Daniel saw God judging millions of people as they stood befo him. We all must stand before almighty God and give an account of life. If your life were to be judged by God today, what would he say about it? How would he measure it against his Word? As we look tow God's judgment, we should ask what we would like him to see at tha time. Then we should live that way today!

¹⁵"I, Daniel, was grieved in my spirit within *my* body, and the visions of my head troubled me. ¹⁶I came near to one of those who stood by, and asked him the truth of all this. So he told me and made known to me the interpretation of these things: ¹⁷'Those great beasts, which are four, *are* four kings *which* arise out of the earth. ¹⁸But the saints of the Most High shall receive the kingdom, and possess the kingdom forever, even forever and ever.'

¹⁹"Then I wished to know the truth about the fourth beast, which was different from all the others, exceedingly dreadful, *with* its teeth of iron and its nails of bronze, *which* devoured, broke in pieces, and trampled the residue with its feet; ²⁰and the ten horns that *were* on its head, and the other *horn* which came up, before which three fell, namely, that horn which had eyes and a mouth which spoke pompous words, whose appearance *was* greater than his fellows.

²¹"I was watching; and the same horn was making war against the saints, and prevailing against them, ²²until the Ancient of Days came, and a judgment was made *in favor* of the saints of the Most High, and the time came for the saints to possess the kingdom.

²³"Thus he said:

'The fourth beast shall be
A fourth kingdom on earth,
Which shall be different from all *other* kingdoms,
And shall devour the whole earth,
Trample it and break it in pieces.
²⁴ The ten horns *are* ten kings
Who shall arise from this kingdom.
And another shall rise after them;
He shall be different from the first *ones*,
And shall subdue three kings.
²⁵ He shall speak *pompous* words against the Most
     High,
Shall persecute the saints of the Most High,
And shall intend to change times and law.
Then *the saints* shall be given into his hand
For a time and times and half a time.

²⁶ 'But the court shall be seated,
And they shall take away his dominion,
To consume and destroy *it* forever.
²⁷ Then the kingdom and dominion,
And the greatness of the kingdoms under the whole
     heaven,
Shall be given to the people, the saints of the Most
     High.
His kingdom *is* an everlasting kingdom,
And all dominions shall serve and obey Him.'

²⁸"This *is* the end of the account. As for me, Daniel, my thoughts greatly troubled me, and my countenance changed; but I kept the matter in my heart."

CHAPTER **8**   **A RAM AND A GOAT.** In the third year of the reign of King Belshazzar a vision appeared *to* me— to me, Daniel—after the one that appeared to me the first time. ²I saw in the vision, and it so happened while I was looking, that I *was* in Shushan, the citadel, which *is* in the province of Elam; and I saw in the vision that I was by the River Ulai. ³Then I lifted my eyes and saw, and there, standing beside the river, was a ram which had two horns, and the two horns *were* high; but one *was* higher than the other, and the higher *one* came up last. ⁴I saw the ram pushing westward, northward, and southward, so that no animal could withstand him; nor *was there any* that could deliver from his hand, but he did according to his will and became great.

〜〜〜CONFUSED

7:15 If you feel as Daniel did about these prophecies— disturbed and confused— recognize with him that their full meaning has not been revealed. The full implications of these prophecies will not be known until God reveals them to his people.

⁵And as I was considering, suddenly a male goat came from the west, across the surface of the whole earth, without touching the ground; and the goat *had* a notable horn between his eyes. ⁶Then he came to the ram that had two horns, which I had seen standing beside the river, and ran at him with furious power. ⁷And I saw him confronting the ram; he was moved with rage against him, attacked the ram, and broke his two horns. There was no power in the ram to withstand him, but he cast him down to the ground and trampled him; and there was no one that could deliver the ram from his hand.

〜〜〜HORNS

8:3 The two horns were the kings of Media and Persia (8:20). The higher horn represented the growing dominance of Persia in the Medo-Persian empire.

⁸Therefore the male goat grew very great; but when he became strong, the large horn was broken, and in place of it four notable ones came up toward the four winds of heaven. ⁹And out of one of them came a little horn which grew exceedingly great toward the south, toward the east, and toward the Glorious *Land*. ¹⁰And it grew up to the host of heaven; and it cast down *some* of the host and *some* of the stars to the ground, and trampled them. ¹¹He even exalted *himself* as high as the Prince of the host; and by him the daily *sacrifices* were taken away, and the place of His sanctuary was cast down. ¹²Because of transgression, an army was given over *to the horn* to oppose the daily *sacrifices;* and he cast truth down to the ground. He did *all this* and prospered.

¹³Then I heard a holy one speaking; and *another* holy one said to that certain *one* who was speaking, "How long *will* the vision *be, concerning* the daily *sacrifices* and the transgression of desolation, the giving of both the sanctuary and the host to be trampled underfoot?"

¹⁴And he said to me, "For two thousand three hundred days; then the sanctuary shall be cleansed."

¹⁵Then it happened, when I, Daniel, had seen the vision and was seeking the meaning, that suddenly there stood before me one having the appearance of a man. ¹⁶And I heard a man's voice between *the banks of* the Ulai, who called, and said, "Gabriel, make this *man* understand the vision." ¹⁷So he came near where I stood, and

when he came I was afraid and fell on my face; but he said to me, "Understand, son of man, that the vision *refers* to the time of the end."

[18]Now, as he was speaking with me, I was in a deep sleep with my face to the ground; but he touched me, and stood me upright. [19]And he said, "Look, I am making known to you what shall happen in the latter time of the indignation; for at the appointed time the end *shall be.* [20]The ram which you saw, having the two horns—*they are* the kings of Media and Persia. [21]And the male goat *is* the kingdom of Greece. The large horn that *is* between its eyes *is* the first king. [22]As for the broken *horn* and the four that stood up in its place, four kingdoms shall arise out of that nation, but not with its power.

[23] "And in the latter time of their kingdom,
　　When the transgressors have reached their fullness,
　　A king shall arise,
　　Having fierce features,
　　Who understands sinister schemes.
[24] His power shall be mighty, but not by his own power;
　　He shall destroy fearfully,
　　And shall prosper and thrive;
　　He shall destroy the mighty, and *also* the holy people.

INVINCIBLE

8:25 This Prince of princes is God himself. No human power could defeat the king whom Daniel saw in his vision, but God would bring him down. There is only one king who will never be defeated—God almighty.

[25] "Through his cunning
　　He shall cause deceit to prosper under his rule;
　　And he shall exalt *himself* in his heart.
　　He shall destroy many in *their* prosperity.
　　He shall even rise against the Prince of princes;
　　But he shall be broken without *human* means.

[26] "And the vision of the evenings and mornings
　　Which was told is true;
　　Therefore seal up the vision,
　　For *it refers* to many days *in the future.*"

[27]And I, Daniel, fainted and was sick for days; afterward I arose and went about the king's business. I was astonished by the vision, but no one understood it.

CHAPTER 9 DANIEL PRAYS FOR HIS PEOPLE.
In the first year of Darius the son of Ahasuerus, of the lineage of the Medes, who was made king over the realm of the Chaldeans— [2]in the first year of his reign I, Daniel, understood by the books the number of the years *specified* by the word of the LORD through Jeremiah the prophet, that He would accomplish seventy years in the desolations of Jerusalem.

[3]Then I set my face toward the Lord God to make request by prayer and supplications, with fasting, sackcloth, and ashes. [4]And I prayed to the LORD my God, and made confession, and said, "O Lord, great and awesome God, who keeps His covenant and mercy with those who love Him, and with those who keep His commandments, [5]we have sinned and committed iniquity, we have done

VULNERABLE

9:3-19 Daniel knew how to pray. He had read God's words and believed them. As he prayed, he fasted, confessed his sins, and ple⬛ that God would reveal his will. He prayed with complete surrender ⬛ and with complete openness to what God was saying to him. When ⬛ pray, do you speak openly to God? Examine your attitude. Talk to ⬛ with openness, vulnerability, and honesty.

wickedly and rebelled, even by departing from Your precepts and Your judgments. [6]Neither have we heeded Your servants the prophets, who spoke in Your name to our kings and our princes, to our fathers and all the people of the land. [7]O Lord, righteousness *belongs* to You, but to us shame of face, as *it is* this day—to the men of Judah, to the inhabitants of Jerusalem and all Israel, those near and those far off in all the countries to which You have driven them, because of the unfaithfulness which they have committed against You.

[8]"O Lord, to us *belongs* shame of face, to our kings, our princes, and our fathers, because we have sinned against You. [9]To the Lord our God *belong* mercy and forgiveness, though we have rebelled against Him. [10]We have not obeyed the voice of the LORD our God, to walk in His laws, which He set before us by His servants the prophets. [11]Yes, all Israel has transgressed Your law, and has departed so as not to obey Your voice; therefore the curse and the oath written in the Law of Moses the servant of God have been poured out on us, because we have sinned against Him. [12]And He has confirmed His words, which He spoke against us and against our judges who judged us, by bringing upon us a great disaster; for under the whole heaven such has never been done as what has been done to Jerusalem.

[13]"As *it is* written in the Law of Moses, all this disaster has come upon us; yet we have not made our prayer before the LORD our God, that we might turn from our iniquities and understand Your truth. [14]Therefore the LORD has kept the disaster in mind, and brought it upon us; for the LORD our God *is* righteous in all the works which He does, though we have not obeyed His voice. [15]And now, O Lord our God, who brought Your people out of the land of Egypt with a mighty hand, and made Yourself a name, as *it is* this day—we have sinned, we have done wickedly!

[16]"O Lord, according to all Your righteousness, I pray, let Your anger and Your fury be turned away from Your city Jerusalem, Your holy mountain; because for our sins, and for the iniquities of our fathers, Jerusalem and Your people *are* a reproach to all *those* around us. [17]Now therefore, our God, hear the prayer of Your servant, and his supplications, and for the Lord's sake cause Your face to shine on Your sanctuary, which is desolate. [18]O my God, incline Your ear and hear; open Your eyes and see our

TRUTH HURTS

9:6 God had sent many prophets to speak to his people through th⬛ years, but their messages had been ignored. The truth was too pain⬛ hear. God still speaks infallibly and authoritatively through the Bible⬛ he also speaks through preachers, teachers, and concerned friends. Sometimes the truth hurts, and we would rather accept soothing falsehoods. Don't settle for a soothing lie that will bring harsh judgm⬛ Accept and obey God's truth.

desolations, and the city which is called by Your name; for we do not present our supplications before You because of our righteous deeds, but because of Your great mercies. ¹⁹O Lord, hear! O Lord, forgive! O Lord, listen and act! Do not delay for Your own sake, my God, for Your city and Your people are called by Your name."

²⁰Now while I *was* speaking, praying, and confessing my sin and the sin of my people Israel, and presenting my supplication before the LORD my God for the holy mountain of my God, ²¹yes, while I *was* speaking in prayer, the man Gabriel, whom I had seen in the vision at the beginning, being caused to fly swiftly, reached me about the time of the evening offering. ²²And he informed *me*, and talked with me, and said, "O Daniel, I have now come forth to give you skill to understand. ²³At the beginning of your supplications the command went out, and I have come to tell *you*, for you *are* greatly beloved; therefore consider the matter, and understand the vision:

²⁴ "Seventy weeks are determined
  For your people and for your holy city,
  To finish the transgression,
  To make an end of sins,
  To make reconciliation for iniquity,
  To bring in everlasting righteousness,
  To seal up vision and prophecy,
  And to anoint the Most Holy.

²⁵ "Know therefore and understand,
  That from the going forth of the command
  To restore and build Jerusalem
  Until Messiah the Prince,
  There shall be seven weeks and sixty-two weeks;
  The street shall be built again, and the wall,
  Even in troublesome times.

²⁶ "And after the sixty-two weeks
  Messiah shall be cut off, but not for Himself;
  And the people of the prince who is to come
  Shall destroy the city and the sanctuary.
  The end of it *shall be* with a flood,
  And till the end of the war desolations are
    determined.

²⁷ Then he shall confirm a covenant with many for one
    week;
  But in the middle of the week
  He shall bring an end to sacrifice and offering.
  And on the wing of abominations shall be one who
    makes desolate,
  Even until the consummation, which is determined,
  Is poured out on the desolate."

CHAPTER **10** A HEAVENLY MESSENGER. In the third year of Cyrus king of Persia a message was revealed to Daniel, whose name was called Belteshazzar. The message *was* true, but the appointed time *was* long; and he understood the message, and had understanding of the vision. ²In those days I, Daniel, was mourning three full weeks. ³I ate no pleasant food, no meat or wine came into my mouth, nor did I anoint myself at all, till three whole weeks were fulfilled.

⁴Now on the twenty-fourth day of the first month, as I was by the side of the great river, that *is*, the Tigris, ⁵I lifted my eyes and looked, and behold, a certain man clothed in linen, whose waist *was* girded with gold of Uphaz! ⁶His body *was* like beryl, his face like the appearance of lightning, his eyes like torches of fire, his arms and feet like burnished bronze in color, and the sound of his words like the voice of a multitude.

⁷And I, Daniel, alone saw the vision, for the men who were with me did not see the vision; but a great terror fell upon them, so that they fled to hide themselves. ⁸Therefore I was left alone when I saw this great vision, and no strength remained in me; for my vigor was turned to frailty in me, and I retained no strength. ⁹Yet I heard the sound of his words; and while I heard the sound of his words I was in a deep sleep on my face, with my face to the ground.

¹⁰Suddenly, a hand touched me, which made me tremble on my knees and *on* the palms of my hands. ¹¹And he said to me, "O Daniel, man greatly beloved, understand the words that I speak to you, and stand upright, for I have now been sent to you." While he was speaking this word to me, I stood trembling. ¹²Then he said to me, "Do not fear, Daniel, for from the first day that you set your heart to understand, and to humble yourself before your God, your words were heard; and I have come because of your words. ¹³But the prince of the kingdom of Persia withstood me twenty-one days; and behold, Michael, one of the chief princes, came to help me, for I had been left alone there with the kings of Persia. ¹⁴Now I have come to make you understand what will happen to your people in the latter days, for the vision *refers* to *many* days yet *to come*."

¹⁵When he had spoken such words to me, I turned my face toward the ground and became speechless. ¹⁶And suddenly, *one* having the likeness of the sons of men touched my lips; then I opened my mouth and spoke, saying to him who stood before me, "My lord, because of the vision my sorrows have overwhelmed me, and I have retained no strength. ¹⁷For how can this servant of my lord talk with you, my lord? As for me, no strength remains in me now, nor is any breath left in me."

¹⁸Then again, *the one* having the likeness of a man touched me and strengthened me. ¹⁹And he said, "O man greatly beloved, fear not! Peace *be* to you; be strong, yes, be strong!"

So when he spoke to me I was strengthened, and said, "Let my lord speak, for you have strengthened me."

²⁰Then he said, "Do you know why I have come to you? And now I must return to fight with the prince of Persia; and when I have gone forth, indeed the prince of Greece will come. ²¹But I will tell you what is noted in the Scripture of Truth. (No one upholds me against these, except Michael your prince.

▰▰▰▰▰▰▰**THE TOUCH**

10:10-18 Daniel was frightened by this vision, but the messenger's hand calmed his fears; Daniel lost his speech, but the messenger's touch restored it; Daniel felt weak, but the messenger's words strengthened him. God can bring us healing when we are hurt, peace when we are troubled, and strength when we are weak. Ask God to minister to you as he did to Daniel.

CHAPTER 11 THE MESSENGER PREDICTS THE FUTURE.

"Also in the first year of Darius the Mede, I, *even* I, stood up to confirm and strengthen him.) ²And now I will tell you the truth: Behold, three more kings will arise in Persia, and the fourth shall be far richer than *them* all; by his strength, through his riches, he shall stir up all against the realm of Greece. ³Then a mighty king shall arise, who shall rule with great dominion, and do according to his will. ⁴And when he has arisen, his kingdom shall be broken up and divided toward the four winds of heaven, but not among his posterity nor according to his dominion with which he ruled; for his kingdom shall be uprooted, even for others besides these.

◗━━━━UNSHAKABLE

11:1ff The angelic messenger was revealing Israel's future (see 10:20-21). Only God can reveal future events so clearly. God's work not only deals with the sweeping panorama of history, but also focuses on the intricate details of people's lives. And his plans—whether for nations or for individuals—are unshakable.

⁵"Also the king of the South shall become strong, as well as *one* of his princes; and he shall gain power over him and have dominion. His dominion *shall be* a great dominion. ⁶And at the end of *some* years they shall join forces, for the daughter of the king of the South shall go to the king of the North to make an agreement; but she shall not retain the power of her authority, and neither he nor his authority shall stand; but she shall be given up, with those who brought her, and with him who begot her, and with him who strengthened her in *those* times. ⁷But from a branch of her roots *one* shall arise in his place, who shall come with an army, enter the fortress of the king of the North, and deal with them and prevail. ⁸And he shall also carry their gods captive to Egypt, with their princes *and* their precious articles of silver and gold; and he shall continue *more* years than the king of the North.

⁹"Also *the king of the North* shall come to the kingdom of the king of the South, but shall return to his own land. ¹⁰However his sons shall stir up strife, and assemble a multitude of great forces; and *one* shall certainly come and overwhelm and pass through; then he shall return to his fortress and stir up strife.

¹¹"And the king of the South shall be moved with rage, and go out and fight with him, with the king of the North, who shall muster a great multitude; but the multitude shall be given into the hand of his *enemy*. ¹²When he has taken away the multitude, his heart will be lifted up; and he will cast down tens of thousands, but he will not prevail. ¹³For the king of the North will return and muster a multitude greater than the former, and shall certainly come at the end of some years with a great army and much equipment.

¹⁴"Now in those times many shall rise up against the king of the South. Also, violent men of your people shall exalt themselves in fulfillment of the vision, but they shall fall. ¹⁵So the king of the North shall come and build a siege mound, and take a fortified city; and the forces of the South shall not withstand *him*. Even his choice troops *shall have* no strength to resist. ¹⁶But he who

comes against him shall do according to his own will, and no one shall stand against him. He shall stand in the Glorious Land with destruction in his power.

¹⁷"He shall also set his face to enter with the strength of his whole kingdom, and upright ones with him; thus shall he do. And he shall give him the daughter of women to destroy it; but she shall not stand *with him*, or be for him. ¹⁸After this he shall turn his face to the coastlands, and shall take many. But a ruler shall bring the reproach against them to an end; and with the reproach removed, he shall turn back on him. ¹⁹Then he shall turn his face toward the fortress of his own land; but he shall stumble and fall, and not be found.

²⁰"There shall arise in his place one who imposes taxes *on* the glorious kingdom; but within a few days he shall be destroyed, but not in anger or in battle. ²¹And in his place shall arise a vile person, to whom they will not give the honor of royalty; but he shall come in peaceably, and seize the kingdom by intrigue. ²²With the force of a flood they shall be swept away from before him and be broken, and also the prince of the covenant. ²³And after the league *is made* with him he shall act deceitfully, for he shall come up and become strong with a small *number of* people. ²⁴He shall enter peaceably, even into the richest places of the province; and he shall do *what* his fathers have not done, nor his forefathers: he shall disperse among them the plunder, spoil, and riches; and he shall devise his plans against the strongholds, but *only* for a time.

²⁵"He shall stir up his power and his courage against the king of the South with a great army. And the king of the South shall be stirred up to battle with a very great and mighty army; but he shall not stand, for they shall devise plans against him. ²⁶Yes, those who eat of the portion of his delicacies shall destroy him; his army shall be swept away, and many shall fall down slain. ²⁷Both these kings' hearts *shall be* bent on evil, and they shall speak lies at the same table; but it shall not prosper, for the end *will* still *be* at the appointed time. ²⁸While returning to his land with great riches, his heart shall be *moved* against the holy covenant; so he shall do *damage* and return to his own land.

²⁹"At the appointed time he shall return and go toward the south; but it shall not be like the former or the latter. ³⁰For ships from Cyprus shall come against him; therefore he shall be grieved, and return in rage against the holy covenant, and do *damage*.

"So he shall return and show regard for those who forsake the holy covenant. ³¹And forces shall be mustered by him, and they shall defile the sanctuary fortress; then they shall take away the daily *sacrifices*, and place *there* the abomination of desolation. ³²Those who do wickedly against the covenant he shall corrupt with flattery; but

◗━━━━GET READY

11:33 Trying times remind us of our weaknesses and inability to We reach out for answers, for leadership, for clear direction. God's begins to interest even those who, in better times, would never lool We who are believers should prepare ourselves to meet opportuniti share God's Word in needy times. We must also prepare ourselves persecution and rejection as we teach God's Word.

the people who know their God shall be strong, and carry out *great exploits.* [33]And those of the people who understand shall instruct many; yet *for many* days they shall fall by sword and flame, by captivity and plundering. [34]Now when they fall, they shall be aided with a little help; but many shall join with them by intrigue. [35]And *some* of those of understanding shall fall, to refine them, purify *them,* and make *them* white, *until* the time of the end; because *it is* still for the appointed time.

[36]"Then the king shall do according to his own will: he shall exalt and magnify himself above every god, shall speak blasphemies against the God of gods, and shall prosper till the wrath has been accomplished; for what has been determined shall be done. [37]He shall regard neither the God of his fathers nor the desire of women, nor regard any god; for he shall exalt himself above *them* all. [38]But in their place he shall honor a god of fortresses; and a god which his fathers did not know he shall honor with gold and silver, with precious stones and pleasant things. [39]Thus he shall act against the strongest fortresses with a foreign god, which he shall acknowledge, *and* advance *its* glory; and he shall cause them to rule over many, and divide the land for gain.

[40]"At the time of the end the king of the South shall attack him; and the king of the North shall come against him like a whirlwind, with chariots, horsemen, and with many ships; and he shall enter the countries, overwhelm *them,* and pass through. [41]He shall also enter the Glorious Land, and many *countries* shall be overthrown; but these shall escape from his hand: Edom, Moab, and the prominent people of Ammon. [42]He shall stretch out his hand against the countries, and the land of Egypt shall not escape. [43]He shall have power over the treasures of gold and silver, and over all the precious things of Egypt; also the Libyans and Ethiopians *shall follow* at his heels. [44]But news from the east and the north shall trouble him; therefore he shall go out with great fury to destroy and annihilate many. [45]And he shall plant the tents of his palace between the seas and the glorious holy mountain; yet he shall come to his end, and no one will help him.

CHAPTER 12 THE END OF TIME.

" At that time Michael shall stand up,
The great prince who stands *watch* over the sons of
   your people;
And there shall be a time of trouble,
Such as never was since there was a nation,
Even to that time.
And at that time your people shall be delivered,
Every one who is found written in the book.
[2] And many of those who sleep in the dust of the earth
    shall awake,
Some to everlasting life,
Some to shame *and* everlasting contempt.

STARS

12:3 Many people strive to be "stars" in the temporary world of entertainment, only to find that their stardom quickly fades. God tells us how we can be eternal "stars"—by turning many to *God's* righteousness. If we share our Lord with others, we can be true stars— radiantly beautiful in God's sight!

[3] Those who are wise shall shine
   Like the brightness of the firmament,
   And those who turn many to righteousness
   Like the stars forever and ever.

[4]"But you, Daniel, shut up the words, and seal the book until the time of the end; many shall run to and fro, and knowledge shall increase."

[5]Then I, Daniel, looked; and there stood two others, one on this riverbank and the other on that riverbank. [6]And *one* said to the man clothed in linen, who *was* above the waters of the river, "How long shall the fulfillment of these wonders *be?*"

BE OPEN

12:10 Daniel was told that to understand what is happening, people have to be open to instruction. Trials and persecutions, when we are in the middle of them, make very little sense. But they can purify us if we are willing to learn from them. After you survive a difficult time, seek to learn from it so that it can help you in the future.

[7]Then I heard the man clothed in linen, who *was* above the waters of the river, when he held up his right hand and his left hand to heaven, and swore by Him who lives forever, that *it shall be* for a time, times, and half *a time;* and when the power of the holy people has been completely shattered, all these *things* shall be finished.

THOSE WHO ARE WISE SHALL SHINE LIKE THE BRIGHTNESS OF THE FIRMAMENT and THOSE who turn many to RIGHTEOUSNESS like the stars forever and ever forever and ever ever

◗◖◗◖◗◖ REWARD

12:13 Daniel stands tall in the gallery of God's remarkable servants. Born of royal heritage, yet taken into captivity when young, Daniel remained faithful to God in the land of his captivity and advised his captors with unusual wisdom. God chose Daniel to record events of the captivity and significant events concerning the future. As an old man, having always been faithful to God, Daniel was assured by God that he would be resurrected from the dead and receive his portion in God's eternal kingdom. Faithfulness to God has a rich reward, not necessarily in this life, but most certainly in the life to come.

⁸Although I heard, I did not understand. Then I said, "My lord, what *shall be* the end of these *things?*"

⁹And he said, "Go *your way*, Daniel, for the words *are* closed up and sealed till the time of the end. ¹⁰Many shall be purified, made white, and refined; but the wicked shall do wickedly; and none of the wicked shall understand, but the wise shall understand.

¹¹"And from the time *that* the daily *sacrifice* is taken away, and the abomination of desolation is set up, *there shall be* one thousand two hundred and ninety days. ¹²Blessed *is* he who waits, and comes to the one thousand three hundred and thirty-five days.

¹³"But you, go *your way* till the end; for you shall rest, and will arise to your inheritance at the end of the days."

MEGA *Themes*

GOD'S CONTROL God is all-knowing, and he is in charge of world events. God overrules and removes rebellious leaders who defy him. God will overcome evil; no one will escape. He will, however, deliver the faithful who follow him.

Although nations compete for world control now, one day Christ will rule. Our faith is sure because our future is secure in him. We must have courage and put our faith in God, who controls everything. Our role is to be faithful to Christ.

1. Compare the way Nebuchadnezzar responded to God's sovereign control and the way Daniel, Shadrach, Meshach, and Abed-Nego responded.
2. Contrast the difference in the lives of kids who submit to God's control and of those who refuse to acknowledge him.
3. What will be the final results in the lives of those who refuse to submit to God's control?
4. Why do you think so many people choose not to submit to God?
5. Identify one specific area that you need to submit to God's control. Develop a plan for submitting this area to him daily.

PURPOSE IN LIFE Daniel and his three friends are examples of dedication and commitment. These three young men, still in their teens at the time of captivity, determined to serve God regardless of the consequences. They did not give in to pressures from an ungodly society because they had a clear purpose in life: to glorify God.

Trusting and obeying God should be our true purpose in life. This will give us direction and peace in any situation. And we should disobey anyone who asks us to disobey God. Young people who make this type of commitment can have a tremendous impact on their world.

1. If you could interview Daniel, how do you think he would respond to this question: "What is your purpose in life?"
2. How do you think most of the kids in your school answer that same question?
3. If someone were to spend a week with you, following you around, listening to your conversations, and observing your behavior, what would that person identify as your priorities in life? Your purpose?
4. Considering your response to question 3, what adjustments should you make based on the purpose you want to have for your life?
5. Write a short statement of your life's purpose. Keep this in a place where it will remind you as you make your daily choices.

PERSEVERANCE Daniel served for 70 years in a foreign land that was hostile to God, yet he did not compromise his faith in God. He was truthful, persistent in prayer, and humble.

In order to fulfill your life's purpose, you need staying power. Don't let your Christian values and commitments slip away just because you are surrounded by kids who are not Christ's followers. Be relentless in your prayers, stay firm in your integrity, and be content to serve God wherever he puts you.

1. What do you think Daniel might have been feeling in each of these situations: when he chose not to eat the king's food; when he interpreted the king's dreams; when he was thrown into the lions' den?
2. What kept Daniel from giving in or giving up?
3. When do you find it most difficult to obey and to keep your commitment to Christ strong?

4. What keeps you from giving up?

GOD'S FAITHFULNESS God was faithful in Daniel's life, delivering him from prison, from a den of lions, and from enemies. God cares for his people and deals patiently with them.

We can trust God to take us through any trial because he promises to be with us. Because he has been faithful to us, we should remain faithful to him.

1. Identify a time in your life when you experienced God's faithfulness. How did this affect your relationship with God?

2. In what ways can thinking about God's faithfulness to you strengthen your faith?

3. Complete this sentence with as many statements as you can from your understanding of God in Scripture, especially in Daniel:
"I can be confident of God's faithfulness in my life because _____."

Oh," she whispered. "I love you, too!" Together the reunited lovers rode off into the sunset. ■ Isn't love wonderful? We've grown up believing love is a cure-all; someday we'll meet "Mr. Right" or "Miss Perfect." He will be gorgeous (big muscles and beautiful eyes), or she will be lovely (long hair and a stunning smile). The rest of the world will then lose its meaning as the two of you enter your own private paradise, a totally honest relationship where neither of you ever hurts the other. Now, *that* would be wonderful. ■ Hosea is a book about love, but with an unusual twist. Hosea was a prophet, and he married Gomer (believe it or not, that was her name). But far from "Miss Perfect," Gomer was a prostitute. In fact, after they were married, she remained a prostitute. But God told Hosea to marry her anyway. ■ The book of Hosea is a love story—but it's not just about Hosea and Gomer—it's about God's love for his people, who, incidentally, acted a lot like Gomer. ■ As you read this story, you'll learn a lot about God and what he expects of his followers. But look for yourself in the story, too. Are you like Hosea? Gomer? Israel? Then decide to have a true love relationship with God.

STATS

PURPOSE: To illustrate God's love for his sinful people

AUTHOR: Hosea, son of Beeri ("Hosea" means "salvation")

TO WHOM WRITTEN: Israel (the northern kingdom) and God's people everywhere

DATE WRITTEN: Approximately 715 B.C., recording events from about 753–715 B.C.

SETTING: Hosea began his ministry during the end of the prosperous but morally declining reign of Jeroboam II of Israel (the upper classes were doing well, but they were oppressing the poor). He prophesied until shortly after the fall of Samaria in 722 B.C.

KEY PEOPLE: Hosea, Gomer, their children

KEY PLACES: The northern kingdom (Israel), Samaria, Ephraim

SPECIAL FEATURES: Hosea employs many images from daily life—God is depicted as husband, father, lion, leopard, she-bear, dew, rain, moth, and others; Israel is pictured as wife, sick person, grapevine, grapes, early fig, olive tree, woman in labor, oven, morning mist, chaff, and smoke, to name a few

osea

CHAPTER **1** HOSEA'S WIFE AND CHILDREN. The word of the LORD that came to Hosea the son of Beeri, in the days of Uzziah, Jotham, Ahaz, *and* Hezekiah, kings of Judah, and in the days of Jeroboam the son of Joash, king of Israel.

²When the LORD began to speak by Hosea, the LORD said to Hosea:

"Go, take yourself a wife of harlotry
 And children of harlotry,
 For the land has committed great harlotry
 By departing from the LORD."

³So he went and took Gomer the daughter of Diblaim, and she conceived and bore him a son. ⁴Then the LORD said to him:

"Call his name Jezreel,
 For in a little *while*
 I will avenge the bloodshed of Jezreel on the house
  of Jehu,
 And bring an end to the kingdom of the house of
  Israel.
⁵ It shall come to pass in that day
 That I will break the bow of Israel in the Valley of
  Jezreel."

⁶And she conceived again and bore a daughter. Then *God* said to him:

"Call her name Lo-Ruhamah,

For I will no longer have mercy on the house of
  Israel,
 But I will utterly take them away.!
⁷ Yet I will have mercy on the house of Judah,
 Will save them by the LORD their God,
 And will not save them by bow,
 Nor by sword or battle,
 By horses or horsemen."

⁸Now when she had weaned Lo-Ruhamah, she conceived and bore a son. ⁹Then *God* said:

"Call his name Lo-Ammi,
 For you *are* not My people,
 And I will not be your *God.*

¹⁰ "Yet the number of the children of Israel
 Shall be as the sand of the sea,
 Which cannot be measured or numbered.
 And it shall come to pass
 In the place where it was said to them,

EXTRAORDINARY

1:2 It is hard to imagine Hosea's feelings when God told him to marry a woman who would be unfaithful to him. He may not have wanted to do this, but he obeyed. God often asked extraordinary obedience from his prophets who were facing extraordinary times. He may ask you to do something difficult and extraordinary, too. If he does, how will you respond? Will you obey him, trusting that he who knows everything has a special purpose for his request? Will you be satisfied with the knowledge that the pain involved in obedience may benefit those you serve, and not you personally?

'You *are* not My people,'
 There it shall be said to them,
 '*You are* sons of the living God.'
¹¹ Then the children of Judah and the children of Israel
 Shall be gathered together,
 And appoint for themselves one head;
 And they shall come up out of the land,
 For great *will be* the day of Jezreel!

CHAPTER **2** PUNISHMENT AND FORGIVENESS.
 Say to your brethren, 'My people,'
 And to your sisters, 'Mercy *is shown.*'

² "Bring charges against your mother, bring charges;
  For she *is* not My wife, nor *am* I her Husband!
  Let her put away her harlotries from her sight,
  And her adulteries from between her breasts;
³ Lest I strip her naked
  And expose her, as in the day she was born,
  And make her like a wilderness,
  And set her like a dry land,
  And slay her with thirst.

⁴ "I will not have mercy on her children,
  For they *are* the children of harlotry.
⁵ For their mother has played the harlot;
  She who conceived them has behaved shamefully.

ADULTERY People are numb. They've heard about things like this; they've read about them happening in big-city churches . . . but not here! It's the biggest scandal ever in the sleepy little town of Crystal Cove: Why would Reverend Johnson leave his wife and kids and run off with his secretary?

Two members of the youth group are discussing the shocking events.

"I still don't believe it. I think there must be some mistake."

"Aw, c'mon, Jan! It's true. Everybody knows it. You've just got to face up to it. My dad found out that Johnson's been cheating on his wife for years!"

"Well, it's just awful. And imagine how Mrs. Johnson must feel. I mean, wouldn't you just die if you married someone and then found out he was messing around with other people behind your back?"

"Oh, I know. That would be like getting a knife right through your heart."

Jan is right—adultery is awful. But how many Christians are guilty of spiritual adultery? We claim to belong to God while we flirt with the world and spend most of our time in other pursuits. Imagine how rejected God must feel!

Don't just imagine it. Read the startling book of Hosea for an intimate look at how our unfaithfulness hurts God's heart. Chapter 2 is especially expressive as it depicts God as a wounded lover who wants desperately for his people to come back.

  For she said, 'I will go after my lovers,
  Who give *me* my bread and my water,
  My wool and my linen,
  My oil and my drink.'

⁶ "Therefore, behold,
  I will hedge up your way with thorns,
  And wall her in,
  So that she cannot find her paths.
⁷ She will chase her lovers,
  But not overtake them;
  Yes, she will seek them, but not find *them*.
  Then she will say,
  'I will go and return to my first husband,
  For then *it was* better for me than now.'
⁸ For she did not know
  That I gave her grain, new wine, and oil,
  And multiplied her silver and gold—
  Which they prepared for Baal.

⁹ "Therefore I will return and take away
  My grain in its time
  And My new wine in its season,
  And will take back My wool and My linen,
  Given to cover her nakedness.
¹⁰ Now I will uncover her lewdness in the sight of her lovers,
  And no one shall deliver her from My hand.
¹¹ I will also cause all her mirth to cease,
  Her feast days,
  Her New Moons,
  Her Sabbaths—
  All her appointed feasts.

¹² "And I will destroy her vines and her fig trees,
  Of which she has said,
  'These *are* my wages that my lovers have given me.'
  So I will make them a forest,
  And the beasts of the field shall eat them.
¹³ I will punish her
  For the days of the Baals to which she burned incense.
  She decked herself with her earrings and jewelry,
  And went after her lovers;
  But Me she forgot," says the LORD.

¹⁴ "Therefore, behold, I will allure her,
  Will bring her into the wilderness,
  And speak comfort to her.
¹⁵ I will give her her vineyards from there,
  And the Valley of Achor as a door of hope;
  She shall sing there,
  As in the days of her youth,
  As in the day when she came up from the land of Egypt.

¹⁶ "And it shall be, in that day,"
  Says the LORD,
  "*That* you will call Me 'My Husband,'
  And no longer call Me 'My Master,'
¹⁷ For I will take from her mouth the names of the Baals,
  And they shall be remembered by their name no more.
¹⁸ In that day I will make a covenant for them
  With the beasts of the field,
  With the birds of the air,
  And *with* the creeping things of the ground.
  Bow and sword of battle I will shatter from the earth,
  To make them lie down safely.

¹⁹ "I will betroth you to Me forever;
  Yes, I will betroth you to Me
  In righteousness and justice,
  In lovingkindness and mercy;

POSSESSIONS

2:8 Material possessions are success symbols in most societies. Is[rael] was a wealthy nation at this time, and Gomer may have accumula[ted] silver and gold. But Gomer didn't realize that Hosea had given he[r all she] owned, just as Israel did not recognize God as the Giver of blessing[s.] Gomer and Israel used their possessions irresponsibly as they ran [after] other lovers and other gods. How do you use your possessions? Us[e what] God has given you to honor him.

20 I will betroth you to Me in faithfulness,
   And you shall know the LORD.

21 "It shall come to pass in that day
    That I will answer," says the LORD;
   "I will answer the heavens,
   And they shall answer the earth.
22 The earth shall answer
   With grain,
   With new wine,
   And with oil;
   They shall answer Jezreel.
23 Then I will sow her for Myself in the earth,
   And I will have mercy on *her who had* not obtained
      mercy;
   Then I will say to *those who were* not My people,
   'You *are* My people!'
   And they shall say, '*You are* my God!'"

CHAPTER 3 HOSEA BRINGS GOMER BACK HOME.

Then the LORD said to me, "Go again, love a woman *who is* loved by a lover and is committing adultery, just like the love of the LORD for the children of Israel, who look to other gods and love *the* raisin cakes *of the pagans.*"

2So I bought her for myself for fifteen *shekels* of silver, and one and one-half homers of barley. 3And I said to her, "You shall stay with me many days; you shall not play the harlot, nor shall you have a man—so, too, *will* I *be* toward you."

4For the children of Israel shall abide many days without king or prince, without sacrifice or sacred pillar, without ephod or teraphim. 5Afterward the children of Israel shall return and seek the LORD their God and David their king. They shall fear the LORD and His goodness in the latter days.

CHAPTER 4 GOD'S CASE AGAINST ISRAEL.

Hear the word of the LORD,
You children of Israel,
For the LORD *brings* a charge against the inhabitants
   of the land:

"There is no truth or mercy
   Or knowledge of God in the land.
2 *By* swearing and lying,
   Killing and stealing and committing adultery,
   They break all restraint,
   With bloodshed upon bloodshed.

NO HOPE

3:3 After this, Gomer is no longer mentioned by Hosea. This is explained in 3:4. Gomer's absence and isolation show how God will deal with the constantly rebellious northern kingdom (5:6,15). It is dangerous to rebel against God. If he were ever to withdraw his love and mercy, we would be without hope.

3 Therefore the land will mourn;
   And everyone who dwells there will waste away
   With the beasts of the field
   And the birds of the air;
   Even the fish of the sea will be taken away.

4 "Now let no man contend, or rebuke another;
   For your people *are* like those who contend with the
      priest.
5 Therefore you shall stumble in the day;
   The prophet also shall stumble with you in the night;
   And I will destroy your mother.
6 My people are destroyed for lack of knowledge.
   Because you have rejected knowledge,
   I also will reject you from being priest for Me;
   Because you have forgotten the law of your God,
   I also will forget your children.

7 "The more they increased,
   The more they sinned against Me;
   I will change their glory into shame.
8 They eat up the sin of My people;

HOSEA
served as a prophet
to Israel
(the northern kingdom)
from 753–715 B.C.

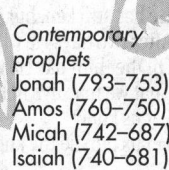

*Contemporary
prophets*
Jonah (793–753)
Amos (760–750)
Micah (742–687)
Isaiah (740–681)

Climate of the times
Israel's last six kings were especially wicked; they promoted heavy taxes, oppression of the poor, idol worship, and total disregard for God. Israel was subjected to Assyria and was forced to pay tribute, which robbed its few remaining resources.

Main message
The people of Israel had sinned against God as an adulterous woman sins against her husband. They were sure to be judged for living in total disregard for God and fellow humans. Hosea saw the nation fall to Assyria in 722 B.C.

Importance of message
When we sin, we sever our relationship with God, which breaks our commitment to him. While all must answer to God for their sins, those who seek God's forgiveness are spared eternal judgment.

They set their heart on their iniquity.

9 And it shall be: like people, like priest.
So I will punish them for their ways,
And reward them for their deeds.

10 For they shall eat, but not have enough;
They shall commit harlotry, but not increase;
Because they have ceased obeying the LORD.

11 "Harlotry, wine, and new wine enslave the heart.

12 My people ask counsel from their wooden *idols*,
And their staff informs them.
For the spirit of harlotry has caused *them* to stray,
And they have played the harlot against their God.

13 They offer sacrifices on the mountaintops,
And burn incense on the hills,
Under oaks, poplars, and terebinths,
Because their shade *is* good.
Therefore your daughters commit harlotry,
And your brides commit adultery.

14 "I will not punish your daughters when they commit harlotry,
Nor your brides when they commit adultery;
For *the men* themselves go apart with harlots,
And offer sacrifices with a ritual harlot.
Therefore people *who* do not understand will be trampled.

15 "Though you, Israel, play the harlot,
Let not Judah offend.
Do not come up to Gilgal,
Nor go up to Beth Aven,
Nor swear an oath, *saying,* 'As the LORD lives'—

16 "For Israel is stubborn
Like a stubborn calf;
Now the LORD will let them forage
Like a lamb in open country.

17 "Ephraim *is* joined to idols,
Let him alone.

18 Their drink is rebellion,
They commit harlotry continually.
Her rulers dearly love dishonor.

19 The wind has wrapped her up in its wings,
And they shall be ashamed because of their sacrifices.

CHAPTER 5 THE VERDICT IS IN: GUILTY.

"Hear this, O priests!
Take heed, O house of Israel!
Give ear, O house of the king!
For yours *is* the judgment,
Because you have been a snare to Mizpah
And a net spread on Tabor.

2 The revolters are deeply involved in slaughter,
Though I rebuke them all.

3 I know Ephraim,
And Israel is not hidden from Me;
For now, O Ephraim, you commit harlotry;
Israel is defiled.

4 "They do not direct their deeds

◄▬▬▬▬▬ STEER AWAY

5:4 Persistent sin hardens a person's heart and makes it difficult repent. Deliberately choosing to disobey God can sear the conscien each sin makes the next one easier to commit. Don't allow sin to w you down, building a hard path deep within you. Steer as far away sinful practices as possible.

Toward turning to their God,
For the spirit of harlotry is in their midst,
And they do not know the LORD.

5 The pride of Israel testifies to his face;
Therefore Israel and Ephraim stumble in their iniquity;
Judah also stumbles with them.

6 "With their flocks and herds
They shall go to seek the LORD,
But they will not find *Him;*
He has withdrawn Himself from them.

7 They have dealt treacherously with the LORD,
For they have begotten pagan children.
Now a New Moon shall devour them and their heritage.

8 "Blow the ram's horn in Gibeah,
The trumpet in Ramah!
Cry aloud *at* Beth Aven,
'*Look* behind you, O Benjamin!'

9 Ephraim shall be desolate in the day of rebuke;
Among the tribes of Israel I make known what is sure.

10 "The princes of Judah are like those who remove a landmark;
I will pour out my wrath on them like water.

11 Ephraim is oppressed *and* broken in judgment,
Because he willingly walked by *human* precept.

12 Therefore I *will be* to Ephraim like a moth,
And to the house of Judah like rottenness.

13 "When Ephraim saw his sickness,
And Judah *saw* his wound,
Then Ephraim went to Assyria
And sent to King Jareb;
Yet he cannot cure you,
Nor heal you of your wound.

14 For I *will be* like a lion to Ephraim,
And like a young lion to the house of Judah.
I, *even* I, will tear *them* and go away;
I will take *them* away, and no one shall rescue.

15 I will return again to My place
Till they acknowledge their offense.
Then they will seek My face;
In their affliction they will earnestly seek Me."

CHAPTER 6 GOD WANTS ISRAEL'S LOVE.

Come, and let us return to the LORD;
For He has torn, but He will heal us;
He has stricken, but He will bind us up.

2 After two days He will revive us;
On the third day He will raise us up,
That we may live in His sight.

3 Let us know,
Let us pursue the knowledge of the LORD.

His going forth is established as the morning;
He will come to us like the rain,
Like the latter *and* former rain to the earth.

4 "O Ephraim, what shall I do to you?
O Judah, what shall I do to you?
For your faithfulness is like a morning cloud,
And like the early dew it goes away.
5 Therefore I have hewn *them* by the prophets,
I have slain them by the words of My mouth;
And your judgments *are like* light *that* goes forth.
6 For I desire mercy and not sacrifice,
And the knowledge of God more than burnt
offerings.

7 "But like men they transgressed the covenant;
There they dealt treacherously with Me.
8 Gilead *is* a city of evildoers
And defiled with blood.
9 As bands of robbers lie in wait for a man,
So the company of priests murder on the way to
Shechem;
Surely they commit lewdness.
10 I have seen a horrible thing in the house of Israel:
There *is* the harlotry of Ephraim;
Israel is defiled.
11 Also, O Judah, a harvest is appointed for you,
When I return the captives of My people.

CHAPTER 7 ISRAEL: A TREACHEROUS BOW.
"When I would have healed Israel,
Then the iniquity of Ephraim was uncovered,
And the wickedness of Samaria.
For they have committed fraud;
A thief comes in;
A band of robbers takes spoil outside.

LET US KNOW
LET US PURSUE THE
KNOWLEDGE OF THE LORD
HIS GOING FORTH IS ESTABLISHED
AS THE MORNING
He will come
to us like
the rain

2 They do not consider in their hearts
That I remember all their wickedness;
Now their own deeds have surrounded them;
They are before My face.
3 They make a king glad with their wickedness,
And princes with their lies.

◀▬▬▬▬CHANGES

6:1-3 This is far from genuine repentance. The people did not understand the depth of their sins. They did not turn from idols, pledge to change, or regret their sins. They thought God's wrath would last only a few days; little did they know that their nation would soon be taken into exile. Israel was interested in God only for the material benefits he provided; they did not value the eternal benefits of worshiping him. Before judging these people, however, consider *your* attitude. What do you hope to gain from your religion? Do you "repent" easily, without seriously considering what you need to change? Don't treat your relationship with God carelessly.

4 "They *are* all adulterers.
Like an oven heated by a baker—
He ceases stirring *the fire* after kneading the dough,
Until it is leavened.
5 In the day of our king
Princes have made *him* sick, inflamed with wine;
He stretched out his hand with scoffers.
6 They prepare their heart like an oven,
While they lie in wait;
Their baker sleeps all night;
In the morning it burns like a flaming fire.
7 They are all hot, like an oven,
And have devoured their judges;
All their kings have fallen.
None among them calls upon Me.

8 "Ephraim has mixed himself among the peoples;
Ephraim is a cake unturned.
9 Aliens have devoured his strength,
But he does not know *it*;
Yes, gray hairs are here and there on him,
Yet he does not know *it*.
10 And the pride of Israel testifies to his face,
But they do not return to the LORD their God,
Nor seek Him for all this.

11 "Ephraim also is like a silly dove, without sense—
They call to Egypt,
They go to Assyria.
12 Wherever they go, I will spread My net on them;
I will bring them down like birds of the air;
I will chastise them
According to what their congregation has heard.

13 "Woe to them, for they have fled from Me!
Destruction to them,
Because they have transgressed against Me!
Though I redeemed them,
Yet they have spoken lies against Me.
14 They did not cry out to Me with their heart
When they wailed upon their beds.

"They assemble together for grain and new wine,
They rebel against Me;
15 Though I disciplined *and* strengthened their arms,
Yet they devise evil against Me;
16 They return, *but* not to the Most High;
They are like a treacherous bow.
Their princes shall fall by the sword
For the cursings of their tongue.
This *shall be* their derision in the land of Egypt.

CHAPTER 8 A PREDICTION OF CAPTIVITY.

"*Set* the trumpet to your mouth!
He *shall come* like an eagle against the house of the
LORD,
Because they have transgressed My covenant
And rebelled against My law.
2 Israel will cry to Me,
'My God, we know You!'
3 Israel has rejected the good;
The enemy will pursue him.

4 "They set up kings, but not by Me;
They made princes, but I did not acknowledge *them.*
From their silver and gold
They made idols for themselves—
That they might be cut off.
5 Your calf is rejected, O Samaria!
My anger is aroused against them—
How long until they attain to innocence?
6 For from Israel *is* even this:
A workman made it, and it *is* not God;
But the calf of Samaria shall be broken to pieces.

7 "They sow the wind,
And reap the whirlwind.
The stalk has no bud;
It shall never produce meal.
If it should produce,
Aliens would swallow it up.
8 Israel is swallowed up;
Now they are among the Gentiles
Like a vessel in which *is* no pleasure.
9 For they have gone up to Assyria,
Like a wild donkey alone by itself;
Ephraim has hired lovers.
10 Yes, though they have hired among the nations,
Now I will gather them;
And they shall sorrow a little,
Because of the burden of the king of princes.

11 "Because Ephraim has made many altars for sin,
They have become for him altars for sinning.
12 I have written for him the great things of My law,
But they were considered a strange thing.
13 *For* the sacrifices of My offerings they sacrifice flesh
and eat *it,*
But the LORD does not accept them.
Now He will remember their iniquity and punish
their sins.
They shall return to Egypt.

14 "For Israel has forgotten his Maker,

8:12 It is easy to listen to a sermon and think of all the people w
know who should be listening, or to read the Bible and think of tho
who should do what the passage teaches. The Israelites did this
constantly, applying God's laws to others but not to themselves. Thi
just another way to deflect God's Word and avoid making needed
changes. As you think of others who need to apply what you are he
or reading, check to see if the same application could fit you. And k
mind that often our own faults are the very ones we see in others.

And has built temples;
Judah also has multiplied fortified cities;
But I will send fire upon his cities,
And it shall devour his palaces."

CHAPTER 9 WANDERING WITHOUT GOD.

Do not rejoice, O Israel, with joy like *other* peoples,
For you have played the harlot against your God.
You have made love *for* hire on every threshing floor.
2 The threshing floor and the winepress
Shall not feed them,
And the new wine shall fail in her.

3 They shall not dwell in the LORD's land,
But Ephraim shall return to Egypt,
And shall eat unclean *things* in Assyria.
4 They shall not offer wine *offerings* to the LORD,
Nor shall their sacrifices be pleasing to Him.
It shall be like bread of mourners to them;
All who eat it shall be defiled.
For their bread *shall be* for their *own* life;
It shall not come into the house of the LORD.

5 What will you do in the appointed day,
And in the day of the feast of the LORD?
6 For indeed they are gone because of destruction.
Egypt shall gather them up;
Memphis shall bury them.
Nettles shall possess their valuables of silver;
Thorns *shall be* in their tents.

7 The days of punishment have come;
The days of recompense have come.
Israel knows!
The prophet *is* a fool,
The spiritual man *is* insane,
Because of the greatness of your iniquity and great
enmity.
8 The watchman of Ephraim *is* with my God;
But the prophet *is* a fowler's snare in all his ways—
Enmity in the house of his God.
9 They are deeply corrupted,
As in the days of Gibeah.
He will remember their iniquity;
He will punish their sins.

10 "I found Israel
Like grapes in the wilderness;
I saw your fathers
As the firstfruits on the fig tree in its first season.
But they went to Baal Peor,
And separated themselves *to that* shame;

They became an abomination like the thing they
    loved.

11 *As for* Ephraim, their glory shall fly away like a bird—
    No birth, no pregnancy, and no conception!

12 Though they bring up their children,
    Yet I will bereave them to the last man.
    Yes, woe to them when I depart from them!

13 Just as I saw Ephraim like Tyre, planted in a pleasant
    place,
    So Ephraim will bring out his children to the
    murderer."

14 Give them, O LORD—
    What will You give?
    Give them a miscarrying womb
    And dry breasts!

15 "All their wickedness *is* in Gilgal,
    For there I hated them.
    Because of the evil of their deeds
    I will drive them from My house;
    I will love them no more.
    All their princes *are* rebellious.

16 Ephraim is stricken,
    Their root is dried up;
    They shall bear no fruit.
    Yes, were they to bear children,
    I would kill the darlings of their womb."

17 My God will cast them away,
    Because they did not obey Him;
    And they shall be wanderers among the nations.

CHAPTER **10** A VINE FULL OF SIN.

Israel empties *his* vine;
    He brings forth fruit for himself.
    According to the multitude of his fruit
    He has increased the altars;
    According to the bounty of his land
    They have embellished *his* sacred pillars.

2 Their heart is divided;
    Now they are held guilty.
    He will break down their altars;
    He will ruin their sacred pillars.

3 For now they say,
    "We have no king,
    Because we did not fear the LORD.
    And as for a king, what would he do for us?"

4 They have spoken words,
    Swearing falsely in making a covenant.
    Thus judgment springs up like hemlock in the
    furrows of the field.

5 The inhabitants of Samaria fear
    Because of the calf of Beth Aven.
    For its people mourn for it,
    And its priests shriek for it—
    Because its glory has departed from it.

6 *The idol* also shall be carried to Assyria
    As a present for King Jareb.
    Ephraim shall receive shame,
    And Israel shall be ashamed of his own counsel.

7 *As for* Samaria, her king is cut off
    Like a twig on the water.

8 Also the high places of Aven, the sin of Israel,
    Shall be destroyed.
    The thorn and thistle shall grow on their altars;
    They shall say to the mountains, "Cover us!"
    And to the hills, "Fall on us!"

LOOK-ALIKES

9:10 Baal Peor was the god of Peor, a mountain in Moab. In Numbers 23, Balaam, a prophet, was hired by King Balak of Moab to curse the Israelites. The Moabites enticed the Israelites into sexual sin and Baal worship. Before long, they became as corrupt as the gods they worshiped. People can take on the characteristics of what or whom they love or worship. What do you worship? Are you becoming more like God, or are you becoming more like someone or something else?

9 "O Israel, you have sinned from the days of Gibeah;
    There they stood.
    The battle in Gibeah against the children of iniquity
    Did not overtake them.

10 When *it is* My desire, I will chasten them.
    Peoples shall be gathered against them
    When I bind them for their two transgressions.

11 Ephraim *is* a trained heifer
    That loves to thresh *grain;*
    But I harnessed her fair neck,
    I will make Ephraim pull *a plow.*
    Judah shall plow;
    Jacob shall break his clods."

12 Sow for yourselves righteousness;
    Reap in mercy;
    Break up your fallow ground,
    For *it is* time to seek the LORD,
    Till He comes and rains righteousness on you.

13 You have plowed wickedness;
    You have reaped iniquity.
    You have eaten the fruit of lies,
    Because you trusted in your own way,
    In the multitude of your mighty men.

14 Therefore tumult shall arise among your people,
    And all your fortresses shall be plundered
    As Shalman plundered Beth Arbel in the day of
    battle—
    A mother dashed in pieces upon *her* children.

15 Thus it shall be done to you, O Bethel,
    Because of your great wickedness.
    At dawn the king of Israel
    Shall be cut off utterly.

SPENDING

10:1 Israel prospered under Jeroboam II, gaining military and economic strength. But the more prosperous the nation became, the more it spent on idols. It seems as if the more God gives, the more we spend. We want bigger houses, better cars, finer clothes, and more expensive education. But the finest things the world offers may line the pathway to destruction. As you prosper, consider where your money is going. Is it being used for God's purposes, or are you spending it all on yourself?

CHAPTER 11 GOD STILL LOVES ISRAEL.

"When Israel *was* a child, I loved him,
And out of Egypt I called My son.
2 *As* they called them,
So they went from them;
They sacrificed to the Baals,
And burned incense to carved images.

3 "I taught Ephraim to walk,
Taking them by their arms;
But they did not know that I healed them.
4 I drew them with gentle cords,
With bands of love,
And I was to them as those who take the yoke from
their neck.
I stooped *and* fed them.

5 "He shall not return to the land of Egypt;
But the Assyrian shall be his king,
Because they refused to repent.
6 And the sword shall slash in his cities,
Devour his districts,
And consume *them*,
Because of their own counsels.
7 My people are bent on backsliding from Me.
Though they call to the Most High,
None at all exalt *Him*.

8 "How can I give you up, Ephraim?
How can I hand you over, Israel?
How can I make you like Admah?
How can I set you like Zeboiim?
My heart churns within Me;
My sympathy is stirred.
9 I will not execute the fierceness of My anger;
I will not again destroy Ephraim.
For I *am* God, and not man,
The Holy One in your midst;
And I will not come with terror.

10 "They shall walk after the LORD.
He will roar like a lion.
When He roars,
Then *His* sons shall come trembling from the west;
11 They shall come trembling like a bird from Egypt,
Like a dove from the land of Assyria.
And I will let them dwell in their houses,"
Says the LORD.

12 "Ephraim has encircled Me with lies,
And the house of Israel with deceit;
But Judah still walks with God,
Even with the Holy One *who is* faithful.

CHAPTER 12 GOD WANTS HIS PEOPLE BACK.

"Ephraim feeds on the wind,
And pursues the east wind;
He daily increases lies and desolation.
Also they make a covenant with the Assyrians,
And oil is carried to Egypt.

2 "The LORD also *brings* a charge against Judah,
And will punish Jacob according to his ways;
According to his deeds He will recompense him.
3 He took his brother by the heel in the womb,
And in his strength he struggled with God.
4 Yes, he struggled with the Angel and prevailed;
He wept, and sought favor from Him.
He found Him *in* Bethel,
And there He spoke to us—
5 That is, the LORD God of hosts.
The LORD *is* His memorable name.
6 So you, by *the help of* your God, return;
Observe mercy and justice,
And wait on your God continually.

7 "A cunning Canaanite!
Deceitful scales *are* in his hand;
He loves to oppress.

◀◀◀ REMEMBER

12:8 Rich people and nations often claim that their material succe
due to their own hard work, initiative, and intelligence. Because the
have all they want, they don't feel the need for God. They believe th
riches are their own, and they feel they have the right to use them o
way they please. If you find yourself feeling proud of your
accomplishments, remember that all your opportunities, abilities, an
resources come from God—and that you hold them in sacred trust
him.

8 And Ephraim said,
'Surely I have become rich,
I have found wealth for myself;
In all my labors
They shall find in me no iniquity that *is* sin.'

9 "But I *am* the LORD your God,
Ever since the land of Egypt;
I will again make you dwell in tents,
As in the days of the appointed feast.
10 I have also spoken by the prophets,
And have multiplied visions;
I have given symbols through the witness of the
prophets."

11 Though Gilead *has* idols—
Surely they are vanity—
Though they sacrifice bulls in Gilgal,
Indeed their altars *shall be* heaps in the furrows of
the field.

12 Jacob fled to the country of Syria;
Israel served for a spouse,
And for a wife he tended *sheep*.
13 By a prophet the LORD brought Israel out of Egypt,
And by a prophet he was preserved.
14 Ephraim provoked *Him* to anger most bitterly;
Therefore his Lord will leave the guilt of his
bloodshed upon him,
And return his reproach upon him.

CHAPTER 13 GOD IS ANGRY.

When Ephraim spoke, trembling,
He exalted *himself* in Israel;

But when he offended through Baal *worship*, he
died.
2 Now they sin more and more,
And have made for themselves molded images,
Idols of their silver, according to their skill;
All of it *is* the work of craftsmen.
They say of them,
"Let the men who sacrifice kiss the calves!"
3 Therefore they shall be like the morning cloud
And like the early dew that passes away,
Like chaff blown off from a threshing floor
And like smoke from a chimney.

4 "Yet I *am* the LORD your God
Ever since the land of Egypt,
And you shall know no God but Me;
For *there is* no savior besides Me.
5 I knew you in the wilderness,
In the land of great drought.
6 When they had pasture, they were filled;
They were filled and their heart was exalted;
Therefore they forgot Me.

7 "So I will be to them like a lion;
Like a leopard by the road I will lurk;
8 I will meet them like a bear deprived *of her cubs;*
I will tear open their rib cage,
And there I will devour them like a lion.
The wild beast shall tear them.

9 "O Israel, you are destroyed,
But your help *is* from Me.
10 I will be your King;
Where *is any other,*
That he may save you in all your cities?
And your judges to whom you said,
'Give me a king and princes'?
11 I gave you a king in My anger,
And took *him* away in My wrath.

12 "The iniquity of Ephraim *is* bound up;
His sin *is* stored up.
13 The sorrows of a woman in childbirth shall come
upon him.
He *is* an unwise son,
For he should not stay long where children are born.

14 "I will ransom them from the power of the grave;
I will redeem them from death.
O Death, I will be your plagues!
O Grave, I will be your destruction!
Pity is hidden from My eyes."

15 Though he is fruitful among *his* brethren,
An east wind shall come;
The wind of the LORD shall come up from the
wilderness.
Then his spring shall become dry,
And his fountain shall be dried up.
He shall plunder the treasury of every desirable prize.
16 Samaria is held guilty,
For she has rebelled against her God.
They shall fall by the sword,

Their infants shall be dashed in pieces,
And their women with child ripped open.

CHAPTER 14 GOD OFFERS FORGIVENESS.

O Israel, return to the LORD your God,
For you have stumbled because of your iniquity;
2 Take words with you,
And return to the LORD.
Say to Him,
"Take away all iniquity;
Receive *us* graciously,
For we will offer the sacrifices of our lips.
3 Assyria shall not save us,
We will not ride on horses,

People around me don't act like they need God. How can I share my faith in Christ with them if they don't feel a need to know him?

I WONDER...

Rarely will people want a relationship with someone whom they feel they don't need. The Bible is filled with stories of people who have actively rejected God, who felt no need for him because their lives were going so well. In Hosea 13:6, he confronted the people of Israel—his chosen people—for doing that very thing.

It's funny, though, that when things are rough, people quickly pin the blame on God. This makes as much sense as a six-year-old child hitting himself on the thumb with a hammer and then blaming his dad.

"I saw you use your hammer once, Dad. I know you told me not to use it, but I did it anyway. You should have made sure I never hurt myself with it! So it's your fault I hurt myself!"

People do the same with God: "I'm going to take my life and run it the way I want to, God—but if things go wrong, it's your fault!"

You can't make someone need God, but here are some things you can do:

First, be ready to help your friends when they do have needs. Keep the friendship bridges strong so they will come to you for help. Then you can point them to Christ. Seek the help of a mature Christian friend for advice on how to do this best.

Second, look for people who are hurt already and share the Good News with them. Be sensitive when you do this. Don't make it sound as though you have all the answers, or as if having a relationship with God means you'll never go through bad times. Simply share how God has helped you, and what he means in your life.

Third, watch out for your own heart. The Bible warns us that some things can distract us from God: "He who trusts in his riches will fall, but the righteous will flourish like foliage" (Proverbs 11:28), and "There is a way *that seems* right to a man, but its end *is* the way of death" (Proverbs 14:12).

Satan wants us to live the "easy" life, apart from (and even numb to) God. Hey, the stakes are high. Being separated from God now affects where we spend eternity.

RESTORED

14:1-2 The people could return to God by asking him to take away their sins. The same is true for us: we can pray Hosea's prayer and know our sins are forgiven because Christ paid the penalty for them on the cross (John 3:16).

Forgiveness begins when we see the destructiveness of sin and the futility of life without God. Then we admit we cannot save ourself; our only hope is in God's mercy. Though you do not deserve forgiveness and therefore cannot demand it, you can—and must—appeal for God's love and mercy. And you can be confident you will receive God's forgiveness because he is gracious and loving and wants to restore you to himself, just as he wanted to restore Israel.

> Nor will we say anymore to the work of our hands,
>   '*You are* our gods.'
> For in You the fatherless finds mercy."

4 "I will heal their backsliding,
  I will love them freely,
  For My anger has turned away from him.
5 I will be like the dew to Israel;
  He shall grow like the lily,
  And lengthen his roots like Lebanon.
6 His branches shall spread;
  His beauty shall be like an olive tree,
  And his fragrance like Lebanon.
7 Those who dwell under his shadow shall return;
  They shall be revived *like* grain,

And grow like a vine.
  Their scent *shall be* like the wine of Lebanon.

8 "Ephraim *shall say,* 'What have I to do anymore with
    idols?'
I have heard and observed him.
I *am* like a green cypress tree;
Your fruit is found in Me."

9 Who *is* wise?
  Let him understand these things.
  Who is prudent?
  Let him know them.
  For the ways of the LORD *are* right;
  The righteous walk in them,
  But transgressors stumble in them.

NEVER-FAILING

14:8 When our will is weak, when our reason is confused, when o[ur] conscience is burdened with a load of guilt, we must remember that mercies never fail. When friends and family desert us or don't understand us, when we are tired of being good, God's mercies nev[er] When we can't see the way or hear God's voice, when we lack coura[ge] go on, when our shortcomings or an awareness of our sins overwhe[lm] us, God's mercies never fail. Regardless of how things seem or even [how] you feel, rely on this truth: God's mercies *never* fail.

MEGA Themes

NATION'S SIN Just as Hosea's wife, Gomer, was unfaithful to him, so the nation of Israel had been unfaithful to God. Israel's idolatry was like adultery. They sought "illicit" relationships with Assyria and Egypt to give Israel military might, and they mixed Baal worship with the worship of God.

Like Gomer, we can chase after other loves—power, popularity, pleasure, or money. The temptations in this world can be very seductive. Are you loyal to God, remaining completely faithful, or have other loves taken his rightful place?

1. In what ways did Gomer represent the nation of Israel?

2. In today's world, what sins tempt God's people to stray from him?

3. How can you, as a Christian young person, live close to God in a world filled with opportunities to be unfaithful to him?

GOD'S JUDGMENT Hosea was solemnly warning Judah not to follow Israel's example.

Because Judah broke the covenant, turned away from God, and forgot her maker, she experienced a devastating invasion and exile. Sin has terrible consequences.

Disaster follows rebellion and ingratitude toward God. The Lord is our only true refuge. We will find no safety or security anywhere else. No one who rebels against God will escape his judgment.

1. What happened to Israel as a result of her disobedience?

2. Describe the qualities of God you see revealed both in his promise to judge and his warning to not fall into judgment.

3. When you consider the reality of God's judgment, how do you feel about him? How does that affect the way you relate to God? The way you live your life daily?

GOD'S LOVE Just as Hosea went after his unfaithful wife to bring her back, so the Lord pursues us with his love. His love is tender, loyal, unchanging, and undying. No matter what, God still loves us.

Have you forgotten God and become disloyal to him? Don't let prosperity diminish your love for him or success blind you to your need for his love.

1. God used Hosea's relationship with Gomer to illustrate God's relationship with his people. What do you learn about God from this illustration?

2. In what ways could Gomer's failure to remain faithful to Hosea lead her to miss out on love?

3. Gomer's life was sad and empty. How is this like people who know God but fail to respond to his love?

4. What in your life threatens to keep you from fully experiencing God's love for you? Remove this obstacle before it robs you of the best love you will ever know.

RESTORATION God said he would discipline his people for sin, but he encouraged and restored those who repented. True repentance opens the way to a new beginning. God forgives and restores those who return to his love.

There is hope for all who turn back to God. Nothing compares to loving him. Turn to the Lord while the offer is still good. No matter how far you have strayed, God is willing to bring you back because his love never fails.

1. After surveying chapters 11 and 14, describe what you discover about God.

2. Through Hosea we see that God wants to rebuild the relationship with the person who has sinned. What does he expect from the sinner for this to happen?

3. Think of an area in your life that has been or is being affected by sin. How did God bring you back to himself?

4. What about this study of restoration can be used to bring hope to those who feel guilty and think God could never love them? What about your experience with God could you share with a person who was feeling and thinking that way?

OK, students, your final papers are due. Students who do not hand in a paper will receive a zero for 25 percent of this quarter's grade. Don't look startled—we discussed the penalty for late papers when I gave you this assignment." ■ Mr. Donley was a good teacher, but he was tough. Tina expected to get an A or a B in his class, but her paper wasn't ready. She'd meant to write it last weekend but didn't get around to it. Maybe if she talked to him. . . . ■ Tina walked up to Mr. Donley's desk. "Mr. Donley," she began, "I know what you said about the paper being due, but I've been really busy. Can I hand it in next week?" ■ Mr. Donley frowned and answered, "Tina, you're one of my better students, but two months ago I told the class there would be only a few acceptable reasons for a late paper. Not having time isn't good enough. I can't extend the deadline for you. I'm sorry." Sadly, Tina left the room. ■ Deadlines and penalties are a part of life. The book of Joel also is about a deadline . . . for Judah to turn back to God. Joel called this deadline "the day of the LORD," when God would judge people for their actions. The people of Judah had forgotten about God and were living evil, rebellious lives. Joel reminded them that those who ignored God would one day face God's wrath. ■ Joel forces us to remember that God judges sin. As you read this book, ask God to make you aware of the areas in your life where you need to repent. Remember, there is a deadline.

STATS

PURPOSE: To warn Judah of God's impending judgment because of their sins and to urge them to turn back to God

AUTHOR: Joel, son of Pethuel

TO WHOM WRITTEN: The people of Judah, the southern kingdom, and God's people everywhere

DATE WRITTEN: Probably during the time Joel prophesied, from about 835 to 796 B.C.

SETTING: The people of Judah had become prosperous and complacent. Taking God for granted, they had turned to self-centeredness, idolatry, and sin. Joel warned them that this kind of life-style will inevitably bring down God's judgment.

KEY PEOPLE: Joel, the people of Judah

KEY PLACE: Jerusalem

Joel

CHAPTER 1 **A PLAGUE OF LOCUSTS.** The word of the LORD that came to Joel the son of Pethuel.

2 Hear this, you elders,
  And give ear, all you inhabitants of the land!
  Has *anything like* this happened in your days,
  Or even in the days of your fathers?
3 Tell your children about it,
  Let your children *tell* their children,
  And their children another generation.

4 What the chewing locust left, the swarming locust
    has eaten;
  What the swarming locust left, the crawling locust
    has eaten;
  And what the crawling locust left, the consuming
    locust has eaten.

5 Awake, you drunkards, and weep;
  And wail, all you drinkers of wine,
  Because of the new wine,
  For it has been cut off from your mouth.
6 For a nation has come up against My land,
  Strong, and without number;
  His teeth *are* the teeth of a lion,
  And he has the fangs of a fierce lion.
7 He has laid waste My vine,
  And ruined My fig tree;
  He has stripped it bare and thrown *it* away;
  Its branches are made white.

8 Lament like a virgin girded with sackcloth
  For the husband of her youth.

9 The grain offering and the drink offering
  Have been cut off from the house of the LORD;
  The priests mourn, who minister to the LORD.
10 The field is wasted,
  The land mourns;
  For the grain is ruined,
  The new wine is dried up,
  The oil fails.

11 Be ashamed, you farmers,
    Wail, you vinedressers,
  For the wheat and the barley;
  Because the harvest of the field has perished.
12 The vine has dried up,
  And the fig tree has withered;
  The pomegranate tree,
  The palm tree also,
  And the apple tree—
  All the trees of the field are withered;
  Surely joy has withered away from the sons of men.

13 Gird yourselves and lament, you priests;
  Wail, you who minister before the altar;
  Come, lie all night in sackcloth,
  You who minister to my God;
  For the grain offering and the drink offering
  Are withheld from the house of your God.
14 Consecrate a fast,
  Call a sacred assembly;
  Gather the elders
  And all the inhabitants of the land
  Into the house of the LORD your God,
  And cry out to the LORD.

LULLED ASLEEP

1:5 The people's moral senses were dulled, making them oblivious to sin. Joel called them to awaken from their complacency and admit their sins before it was too late. Otherwise, everything would be destroyed, even the grapes and wine that caused their drunkenness. Our times of peace and prosperity can lull us to sleep. We must never let material abundance be a substitute for spiritual readiness.

15 Alas for the day!
  For the day of the LORD *is* at hand;
  It shall come as destruction from the Almighty.
16 Is not the food cut off before our eyes,
  Joy and gladness from the house of our God?
17 The seed shrivels under the clods,
  Storehouses are in shambles;
  Barns are broken down,
  For the grain has withered.
18 How the animals groan!

The herds of cattle are restless,
Because they have no pasture;
Even the flocks of sheep suffer punishment.

19 O LORD, to You I cry out;
For fire has devoured the open pastures,
And a flame has burned all the trees of the field.
20 The beasts of the field also cry out to You,
For the water brooks are dried up,
And fire has devoured the open pastures.

FORGIVENESS

After praying together, volunteers from The Shelter, an inner-city mission to troubled youth, hit the streets. The theater district will soon be teeming with teens—runaways, pimps, prostitutes (both male and female), dealers, you name it. These are kids on the edge; their goal is to make it through another night.

Making his rounds, Tom notices a strange face—a young boy who's new to the streets. When the minister approaches the youngster, the kid begins to sob. His name is Sean, and he hasn't eaten in three days. Tom takes Sean to The Shelter, gives him some food, and listens.

Sean tells of an abusive father, an unstable mother, and a history of personal failure. He describes his decision to run away a month ago, and the horrible things he's done to survive on the streets.

Tom nods knowingly and begins to tell Sean about the love of Christ and the unconditional forgiveness he offers. Sean can't believe it. "That's too good to be true," he says. "Nobody could ever love me—not after what I've done."

Maybe you can relate to Sean's feelings. Perhaps you feel hopelessly guilty due to your decisions and choices. Don't despair!

Consider the message of Joel 2:12-13: When people genuinely turn to God—no matter what kind of mess they've gotten into—he responds with love and forgiveness.

No matter what.

CHAPTER 2 JUDGMENT WILL COME.
Blow the trumpet in Zion,
And sound an alarm in My holy mountain!
Let all the inhabitants of the land tremble;
For the day of the LORD is coming,
For it is at hand:
2 A day of darkness and gloominess,
A day of clouds and thick darkness,
Like the morning *clouds* spread over the mountains.
A people *come*, great and strong,
The like of whom has never been;
Nor will there ever be any *such* after them,
Even for many successive generations.

3 A fire devours before them,
And behind them a flame burns;
The land *is* like the Garden of Eden before them,
And behind them a desolate wilderness;
Surely nothing shall escape them.
4 Their appearance *is* like the appearance of horses;
And like swift steeds, so they run.
5 With a noise like chariots

Over mountaintops they leap,
Like the noise of a flaming fire that devours the stubble,
Like a strong people set in battle array.

6 Before them the people writhe in pain;
All faces are drained of color.
7 They run like mighty men,
They climb the wall like men of war;
Every one marches in formation,
And they do not break ranks.
8 They do not push one another;
Every one marches in his own column.
Though they lunge between the weapons,
They are not cut down.
9 They run to and fro in the city,
They run on the wall;
They climb into the houses,
They enter at the windows like a thief.

10 The earth quakes before them,
The heavens tremble;
The sun and moon grow dark,
And the stars diminish their brightness.
11 The LORD gives voice before His army,
For His camp is very great;
For strong *is the One* who executes His word.

I will pour out My Spirit on all flesh all flesh all flesh

Your sons and your daughters SHALL PROPHESY

YOUR OLD MEN shall dream dreams

YOUR YOUNG MEN SHALL SEE VISIONS SHALL SEE VISIONS SHALL SEE VISIONS

JOEL 2:28

For the day of the LORD *is* great and very terrible;
Who can endure it?

12 "Now, therefore," says the LORD,
"Turn to Me with all your heart,
With fasting, with weeping, and with mourning."
13 So rend your heart, and not your garments;
Return to the LORD your God,
For He *is* gracious and merciful,
Slow to anger, and of great kindness;
And He relents from doing harm.
14 Who knows *if* He will turn and relent,
And leave a blessing behind Him—
A grain offering and a drink offering
For the LORD your God?

15 Blow the trumpet in Zion,
Consecrate a fast,
Call a sacred assembly;
16 Gather the people,
Sanctify the congregation,
Assemble the elders,
Gather the children and nursing babes;
Let the bridegroom go out from his chamber,
And the bride from her dressing room.
17 Let the priests, who minister to the LORD,
Weep between the porch and the altar;
Let them say, "Spare Your people, O LORD,
And do not give Your heritage to reproach,
That the nations should rule over them.
Why should they say among the peoples,
'Where *is* their God?'"

18 Then the LORD will be zealous for His land,
And pity His people.
19 The LORD will answer and say to His people,
"Behold, I will send you grain and new wine and oil,
And you will be satisfied by them;
I will no longer make you a reproach among the
nations.

20 "But I will remove far from you the northern *army*,
And will drive him away into a barren and desolate
land,
With his face toward the eastern sea
And his back toward the western sea;
His stench will come up,
And his foul odor will rise,
Because he has done monstrous things."

21 Fear not, O land;
Be glad and rejoice,
For the LORD has done marvelous things!
22 Do not be afraid, you beasts of the field;
For the open pastures are springing up,
And the tree bears its fruit;
The fig tree and the vine yield their strength.
23 Be glad then, you children of Zion,
And rejoice in the LORD your God;
For He has given you the former rain faithfully,
And He will cause the rain to come down for you—
The former rain,
And the latter rain in the first *month*.

24 The threshing floors shall be full of wheat,
And the vats shall overflow with new wine and oil.

25 "So I will restore to you the years that the swarming
locust has eaten,
The crawling locust,
The consuming locust,
And the chewing locust,
My great army which I sent among you.
26 You shall eat in plenty and be satisfied,
And praise the name of the LORD your God,
Who has dealt wondrously with you;
And My people shall never be put to shame.
27 Then you shall know that I *am* in the midst of Israel:
I *am* the LORD your God
And there is no other.
My people shall never be put to shame.

28 "And it shall come to pass afterward
That I will pour out My Spirit on all flesh;
Your sons and your daughters shall prophesy,
Your old men shall dream dreams,
Your young men shall see visions.

I wish God would do more "miracle" type of things in my life. Why don't amazing things happen more often?

I WONDER . . .

Miracles and "amazing things" are great, but the best miracle God could ever perform is the miracle of salvation.

The fact that God actually chose to forgive our sin and live inside us is an incredible miracle. We should thank him for that every day. But often we forget.

Some teachers of the law once came to Jesus and said, "We want to see a sign" (Matthew 12:38). He answered that they wouldn't see any greater miracle than him being dead, buried in the ground three days, and then coming back to life! But they weren't satisfied.

The real question is, What kind of miracles do you want God to do in your life?

Do you want him to give you A's in subjects you haven't studied for? Let you score the winning touchdown? Perform some healing to "prove" he's there? If so, you'll be disappointed. He doesn't do anything just to prove he exists—beyond, of course, what he's already done through Christ.

But if you want to see him do miracles in your life and in the lives of those around you, stand back. That's the kind he specializes in.

God promised his followers that he would perform wonderful things through them (see Joel 2:28-32). And you'll find that the most exciting miracles are when God uses you to lead someone else to him. Those miracles are better; they lead to something eternal!

The longer you follow Christ, the more you'll see things happen. When someone's eternal destiny is changed, and God used *you* to make it happen, you'll experience a "high" like you've never known.

So ask God to use you to perform the greatest miracle of all—to lead someone to Christ.

3:14 Joel described multitudes waiting in the "valley of decision" (the Valley of Jehoshaphat of verses 2 and 12). Billions of people have lived on earth, and every one of them— dead, living, and yet to be born—will face judgment. Look around you. See your friends, those with whom you work and live? Have they received God's forgiveness? Have they been warned about sin's consequences? If we understand the

29 And also on *My* menservants and on *My* maidservants
I will pour out My Spirit in those days.

30 "And I will show wonders in the heavens and in the earth:
Blood and fire and pillars of smoke.

31 The sun shall be turned into darkness,
And the moon into blood,
Before the coming of the great and awesome day of the LORD.

32 And it shall come to pass
That whoever calls on the name of the LORD
Shall be saved.
For in Mount Zion and in Jerusalem there shall be deliverance,
As the LORD has said,
Among the remnant whom the LORD calls.

CHAPTER 3 BAD NEWS FOR ISRAEL'S ENEMIES.

"For behold, in those days and at that time,
When I bring back the captives of Judah and Jerusalem,

2 I will also gather all nations,
And bring them down to the Valley of Jehoshaphat;
And I will enter into judgment with them there
On account of My people, My heritage Israel,
Whom they have scattered among the nations;
They have also divided up My land.

3 They have cast lots for My people,
Have given a boy *as payment* for a harlot,
And sold a girl for wine, that they may drink.

4 "Indeed, what have you to do with Me,

O Tyre and Sidon, and all the coasts of Philistia?
Will you retaliate against Me?
But if you retaliate against Me,
Swiftly and speedily I will return your retaliation upon your own head;

5 Because you have taken My silver and My gold,
And have carried into your temples My prized possessions.

6 Also the people of Judah and the people of Jerusalem
You have sold to the Greeks,
That you may remove them far from their borders.

7 "Behold, I will raise them
Out of the place to which you have sold them,
And will return your retaliation upon your own head.

8 I will sell your sons and your daughters
Into the hand of the people of Judah,
And they will sell them to the Sabeans,
To a people far off;
For the LORD has spoken."

9 Proclaim this among the nations:
"Prepare for war!
Wake up the mighty men,
Let all the men of war draw near,
Let them come up.

10 Beat your plowshares into swords
And your pruning hooks into spears;
Let the weak say, 'I *am* strong.'"

11 Assemble and come, all you nations,
And gather together all around.
Cause Your mighty ones to go down there, O LORD.

12 "Let the nations be wakened, and come up to the Valley of Jehoshaphat;
For there I will sit to judge all the surrounding nations.

13 Put in the sickle, for the harvest is ripe.
Come, go down;
For the winepress is full,
The vats overflow—
For their wickedness *is* great."

JOEL

served as a prophet to Judah from 835–796 B.C.

Climate of the times
Wicked Queen Athaliah seized power in a bloody coup but was overthrown after a few years. Joash was crowned king, but he was only seven years old and in great need of spiritual guidance. Joash followed God in his early years, then turned away from him.

Main message
A plague of locusts had come to discipline the nation. Joel called the people to turn back to God before an even greater judgment occurred.

Importance of message
God judges all people for their sins but is merciful and offers eternal salvation to those who turn to him in repentance.

Contemporary prophets
Elisha (848–797)
Jonah (793–753)

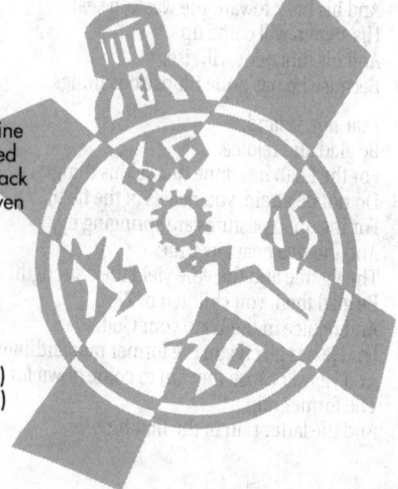

¹⁴ Multitudes, multitudes in the valley of decision!
  For the day of the LORD *is* near in the valley of
    decision.
¹⁵ The sun and moon will grow dark,
  And the stars will diminish their brightness.
¹⁶ The LORD also will roar from Zion,
  And utter His voice from Jerusalem;
  The heavens and earth will shake;
  But the LORD will be a shelter for His people,
  And the strength of the children of Israel.

¹⁷ "So you shall know that I *am* the LORD your God,
  Dwelling in Zion My holy mountain.
  Then Jerusalem shall be holy,
  And no aliens shall ever pass through her
    again."

¹⁸ And it will come to pass in that day
  That the mountains shall drip with new wine,
  The hills shall flow with milk,
  And all the brooks of Judah shall be flooded with water;
  A fountain shall flow from the house of the LORD
  And water the Valley of Acacias.

¹⁹ "Egypt shall be a desolation,
  And Edom a desolate wilderness,
  Because of violence *against* the people of Judah,
  For they have shed innocent blood in their land.
²⁰ But Judah shall abide forever,
  And Jerusalem from generation to generation.
²¹ For I will acquit them of the guilt of bloodshed,
    whom I had not acquitted;
  For the LORD dwells in Zion."

MEGA Themes

PUNISHMENT Like a destroying army of locusts, God's punishment for sin is overwhelming, dreadful, and unavoidable. When it comes, there will be no food, no water, no protection, and no escape. The day for settling accounts with God for how we have lived is fast approaching.

All of us must be accountable to God—not to nature, the economy, rulers of nations, or an invading army. We can't ignore or offend God forever. We must pay attention to his message now or face the consequences of his anger later.

1. In what ways were the locusts an accurate illustration of God's judgment and punishment?
2. God's holiness leads him to punish sin severely. What does this teach you about the holiness of God? The danger of sin?
3. Our need for salvation is often illustrated by a large gap between us and God. This gap is caused by our sin. Why does sin cause such a gap?
4. Based on this study of sin and punishment, what do you learn about the importance of the sinless Christ bridging that gap?

FORGIVENESS God was ready to forgive and restore all those who would come to him and turn away from sin. God wanted to shower his people with his love and restore them to a proper relationship with him.

Forgiveness comes by turning from sin and turning toward God. As long as we are alive, it is never too late to receive God's forgiveness. God's greatest desire is for you to enjoy his love and forgiveness.

1. What promise is found in 2:32? How is that promise available to sinners today?
2. The sinless Christ bridged the gap caused by our sin. What specifically has Christ done for you in relationship to God's holiness?
3. What specific ways could you and your Christian friends communicate this message of forgiveness and restoration to non-Christians in your school and community?
4. Develop a plan for sharing this hope of forgiveness with a non-Christian.

PROMISE OF THE HOLY SPIRIT Joel predicted the time when God would pour out his Holy Spirit on all people. It would be the beginning of new and fresh worship of God by those who believe in him, but also the beginning of judgment on those who reject him.

God is in control. Justice and restoration are in his hands. The Holy Spirit confirms God's love for us just as he did for the first Christians (Acts 2). We must be faithful to God and place our life under the guidance and power of his Holy Spirit.

1. What does Joel teach you about the work of the Holy Spirit?
2. Why is the Holy Spirit a significant part of God's provision for his people?
3. John 14, Acts 2, and Ephesians 1 are New Testament passages that give more insight on the role of the Holy Spirit. Look at these passages with the following question in mind: As a Christian, how should I respond to the presence of the Holy Spirit in my life?

*S*it down, right here!" Mr. Evans, the principal, demanded to the four boys he marched into his office. On the couch were Bobby Thomas, Eric Hardin, and Sheldon Milroy: the most feared trio in school. Near Mr. Evans' desk sat Robert Bledsoe—the bullies' skinny, smart, pimply-faced target. ■ "You boys," began Mr. Evans, pointing at the terrible trio, "had better quit. I won't stand for you harassing Robert. Such behavior is totally unacceptable." ■ Mr. Evans wanted to be calm, but his face was turning red and his volume was increasing. "If I ever, *ever* catch you three bothering *anyone* in the schoolyard again, I will make sure you are expelled. Understand?" All three nodded. ■ Robert listened and smiled smugly. The bullies deserved what they were getting. ■ "And you, Mr. Bledsoe." Mr. Evans turned to a startled Robert. "You are not without blame. These boys were wrong, but . . . I might have done the same thing if you had treated me like you treated them. You teased these boys, saying they are stupid and probably headed for lives as bums." Mr. Evans was yelling again. "Mr. Bledsoe, you have been the victim here, but you are just as guilty. Now, all of you, get out." ■ Amos wasn't a professional prophet, but as God's spokesman he gave a similar message to the "bullying" nations and to Israel, the victim. And Amos has lessons for us today. He reminds us to be careful in pointing judgmental fingers at others, since they could end up pointed back at us. If God asked to have a talk with you, in what areas would he find you lacking?

STATS

PURPOSE: To show God's judgment on Israel, the northern kingdom, for their idolatry and oppression of the poor

AUTHOR: Amos

TO WHOM WRITTEN: Israel, the northern kingdom, and God's people everywhere

DATE WRITTEN: Probably during the reigns of Jeroboam II of Israel and Uzziah of Judah (about 760–750 B.C)

SETTING: The wealthy people of Israel were happy, but at the cost of the poor! Soon, however, Israel would be conquered by Assyria, and the rich would themselves be made slaves.

KEY PEOPLE: Amos, Amaziah, Jeroboam II

KEY PLACES: Bethel, Samaria

Amos

CHAPTER 1 GOD PUNISHES ISRAEL'S NEIGH-
BORS. The words of Amos, who was among the sheepbreeders of Tekoa, which he saw concerning Israel in the days of Uzziah king of Judah, and in the days of Jeroboam the son of Joash, king of Israel, two years before the earthquake.

²And he said:

"The LORD roars from Zion,
And utters His voice from Jerusalem;
The pastures of the shepherds mourn,
And the top of Carmel withers."

³Thus says the LORD:

"For three transgressions of Damascus, and for four,
I will not turn away its *punishment*,
Because they have threshed Gilead with implements
of iron.
⁴ But I will send a fire into the house of Hazael,
Which shall devour the palaces of Ben-Hadad.
⁵ I will also break the *gate* bar of Damascus,
And cut off the inhabitant from the Valley of Aven,
And the one who holds the scepter from Beth Eden.
The people of Syria shall go captive to Kir,"
Says the LORD.

⁶Thus says the LORD:

"For three transgressions of Gaza, and for four,
I will not turn away its *punishment*,
Because they took captive the whole captivity
To deliver *them* up to Edom.
⁷ But I will send a fire upon the wall of Gaza,

Which shall devour its palaces.
⁸ I will cut off the inhabitant from Ashdod,
And the one who holds the scepter from
Ashkelon;
I will turn My hand against Ekron,
And the remnant of the Philistines shall
perish,"
Says the Lord GOD.

⁹Thus says the LORD:

"For three transgressions of Tyre, and
for four,
I will not turn away its *punishment*,
Because they delivered up the whole
captivity to Edom,
And did not remember the covenant of
brotherhood.
¹⁰ But I will send a fire upon the wall of Tyre,
Which shall devour its palaces."

¹¹Thus says the LORD:

"For three transgressions of Edom, and for four,
I will not turn away its *punishment*,
Because he pursued his brother with the sword,

◣◣◣◣◣◣WORK

1:1 All day long Amos took care of sheep—not a particularly "spiritual" job—yet he became a channel of God's message to others. Your job may not cause you to feel spiritual or successful, but it is a vital work if you are in the place God wants you to be. God can work through you to do extraordinary things, no matter how ordinary your occupation.

And cast off all pity;
His anger tore perpetually,
And he kept his wrath forever.
¹² But I will send a fire upon Teman,
Which shall devour the palaces of Bozrah."

¹³Thus says the LORD:

"For three transgressions of the people of Ammon,
and for four,
I will not turn away its *punishment*,
Because they ripped open the women with child in
Gilead,
That they might enlarge their territory.
¹⁴ But I will kindle a fire in the wall of Rabbah,
And it shall devour its palaces,

◣◣◣◣◣ POOR PEOPLE

2:6-7 Amos spoke to the upper class. There was no middle class in the country—only the very rich and the very poor. The rich kept religious rituals. They gave extra tithes, went to places of worship, and offered sacrifices. But they were greedy and unjust, and they took advantage of the helpless. Be sure that you do not neglect the needs of the poor while you faithfully attend church and fulfill religious rituals. God expects us to live out our faith, and this means responding to those in need.

> Amid shouting in the day of battle,
> And a tempest in the day of the whirlwind.
> ¹⁵ Their king shall go into captivity,
> He and his princes together,"
> Says the LORD.

CHAPTER **2** GOD PUNISHES ISRAEL, TOO. Thus says the LORD:

> "For three transgressions of Moab, and for four,
> I will not turn away its *punishment*,
> Because he burned the bones of the king of Edom to lime.
> ² But I will send a fire upon Moab,
> And it shall devour the palaces of Kerioth;
> Moab shall die with tumult,
> With shouting *and* trumpet sound.
> ³ And I will cut off the judge from its midst,
> And slay all its princes with him,"
> Says the LORD.

> ⁴Thus says the LORD:

> "For three transgressions of Judah, and for four,
> I will not turn away its *punishment*,
> Because they have despised the law of the LORD,
> And have not kept His commandments.
> Their lies lead them astray,
> *Lies* which their fathers followed.
> ⁵ But I will send a fire upon Judah,
> And it shall devour the palaces of Jerusalem."

> ⁶Thus says the LORD:

> "For three transgressions of Israel, and for four,

> I will not turn away its *punishment*,
> Because they sell the righteous for silver,
> And the poor for a pair of sandals.
> ⁷ They pant after the dust of the earth *which is* on the head of the poor,
> And pervert the way of the humble.
> A man and his father go in to the *same* girl,
> To defile My holy name.
> ⁸ They lie down by every altar on clothes taken in pledge,
> And drink the wine of the condemned *in* the house of their god.

> ⁹ "Yet *it was* I *who* destroyed the Amorite before them,
> Whose height *was* like the height of the cedars,
> And he *was as* strong as the oaks;
> Yet I destroyed his fruit above
> And his roots beneath.
> ¹⁰ Also *it was* I *who* brought you up from the land of Egypt,
> And led you forty years through the wilderness,
> To possess the land of the Amorite.
> ¹¹ I raised up some of your sons as prophets,
> And some of your young men as Nazirites.
> *Is it* not so, O you children of Israel?"
> Says the LORD.
> ¹² "But you gave the Nazirites wine to drink,
> And commanded the prophets saying,
> 'Do not prophesy!'

> ¹³ "Behold, I am weighed down by you,
> As a cart full of sheaves is weighed down.
> ¹⁴ Therefore flight shall perish from the swift,
> The strong shall not strengthen his power,
> Nor shall the mighty deliver himself;
> ¹⁵ He shall not stand who handles the bow,
> The swift of foot shall not escape,
> Nor shall he who rides a horse deliver himself.
> ¹⁶ The most courageous men of might
> Shall flee naked in that day,"
> Says the LORD.

AMOS

served as a prophet to Israel (the northern kingdom) from 760–750 B.C.

Climate of the times
Israel was enjoying economic prosperity and peace. But this had caused her to become a selfish, materialistic society. Those who were well off ignored the needs of those less fortunate. The people were self-centered and indifferent toward God.

Main message
Amos spoke against those who exploited or ignored the needy.

Importance of message
Believing in God is more than a personal matter. God calls all believers to work against injustices in society and to aid those less fortunate.

Contemporary prophets
Jonah (793–753)
Hosea (753–715)

CHAPTER 3 THEY CANNOT WALK WITH GOD.

Hear this word that the LORD has spoken against you,
O children of Israel, against the whole family which I
brought up from the land of Egypt, saying:

2 "You only have I known of all the families of the earth;
  Therefore I will punish you for all your iniquities."

3 Can two walk together, unless they are agreed?
4 Will a lion roar in the forest, when he has no prey?
  Will a young lion cry out of his den, if he has caught
  nothing?
5 Will a bird fall into a snare on the earth, where there
  is no trap for it?
  Will a snare spring up from the earth, if it has caught
  nothing at all?
6 If a trumpet is blown in a city, will not the people be
  afraid?
  If there is calamity in a city, will not the LORD have
  done *it*?

7 Surely the Lord GOD does nothing,
  Unless He reveals His secret to His servants the
  prophets.
8 A lion has roared!
  Who will not fear?
  The Lord GOD has spoken!
  Who can but prophesy?

9 "Proclaim in the palaces at Ashdod,
  And in the palaces in the land of Egypt, and say:
  'Assemble on the mountains of Samaria;
  See great tumults in her midst,
  And the oppressed within her.
10 For they do not know to do right,'
  Says the LORD,
  'Who store up violence and robbery in their
  palaces.'"

11Therefore thus says the Lord GOD:

"An adversary *shall be* all around the land;
  He shall sap your strength from you,
  And your palaces shall be plundered."

12Thus says the LORD:

"As a shepherd takes from the mouth of a lion
  Two legs or a piece of an ear,
  So shall the children of Israel be taken out
  Who dwell in Samaria—
  In the corner of a bed and on the edge of a couch!
13 Hear and testify against the house of Jacob,"
  Says the Lord GOD, the God of hosts,
14 "That in the day I punish Israel for their
  transgressions,
  I will also visit *destruction* on the altars of Bethel;
  And the horns of the altar shall be cut off
  And fall to the ground.
15 I will destroy the winter house along with the
  summer house;
  The houses of ivory shall perish,
  And the great houses shall have an end,"
  Says the LORD.

CHAPTER 4 THE PEOPLE CONTINUE TO SIN.

Hear this word, you cows of Bashan, who *are* on the
  mountain of Samaria,
Who oppress the poor,
Who crush the needy,

COW GIRLS

4:1 Israel's wealthy women were compared to the cows of
Bashan—pampered, sleek, and well fed (see Psalm 22:12). These women
selfishly pushed their husbands to oppress the helpless in order to supply
their lavish life-style. Be careful not to desire material possessions so much
that you are willing to oppress others and displease God to get them.

Who say to your husbands, "Bring *wine*, let us drink!"
2 The Lord GOD has sworn by His holiness:
  "Behold, the days shall come upon you
  When He will take you away with fishhooks,
  And your posterity with fishhooks.
3 You will go out *through* broken *walls*,
  Each one straight ahead of her,

**My friends do things that my conscience
won't let me get away
with—yet they never
seem to get caught.
Why do a lot of
people who do
wrong never
seem to get
punished?**

At the dentist, Novocain deadens the nerves in our
mouth so we won't feel the drill. Repeated sin deadens
the conscience, so the person no longer feels guilty
about wrong behavior. But whether a person feels guilty
or not, sin *does* have consequences. Some are
immediate, like when the teacher catches you cheating
on a test and gives you an F. Other consequences are
short-term and delayed, such as with people who cheat
on their income-tax return and seem to get away with it.
Then they are audited and receive a hefty fine or even a
prison sentence from the IRS.

Without a doubt, the Bible is clear about what will
eventually happen to those who act contrary to God's
plan: "Do not be deceived, God is not mocked; for
whatever a man sows, that he will also reap. For he who
sows to his flesh will of the flesh reap corruption, but he
who sows to the Spirit will of the Spirit reap everlasting
life" (Galatians 6:7-8).

If we "sow" bad actions, we'll reap that kind of fruit. If
we sow good things and genuinely try to follow God's
instructions, God will use us, and we'll reap a wonderful
harvest.

It can get tiring, however, always trying to be good.
Especially when there's so much bad around us. That's
when we have to remember God's promise of the
eventual harvest: "And let us not grow weary while
doing good, for in due season we shall reap if we do
not lose heart" (Galatians 6:9).

The prophet Amos told the people of Israel what would
happen if they didn't shape up (see Amos 2:6-16).
Though his predictions didn't immediately come true, he
did prove to be right after many years. The Israelites
were conquered by the Assyrians and were made
slaves, receiving exactly what they had given out.

I WONDER . . .

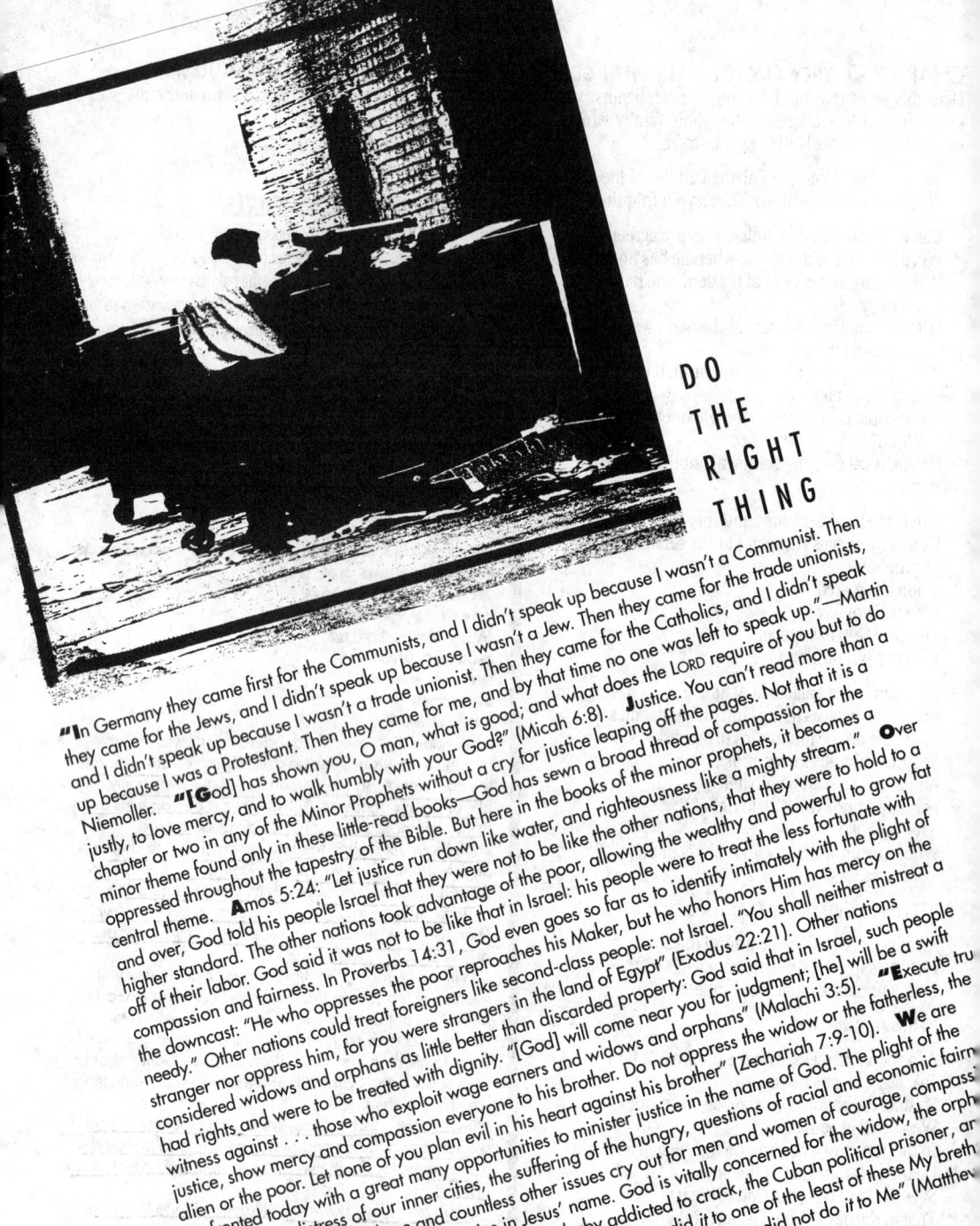

DO
THE
RIGHT
THING

"In Germany they came first for the Communists, and I didn't speak up because I wasn't a Communist. Then they came for the Jews, and I didn't speak up because I wasn't a Jew. Then they came for the trade unionists, and I didn't speak up because I wasn't a trade unionist. Then they came for the Catholics, and I didn't speak up because I was a Protestant. Then they came for me, and by that time no one was left to speak up."—Martin Niemoller. **"[G**od] has shown you, O man, what is good; and what does the LORD require of you but to do justly, to love mercy, and to walk humbly with your God?" (Micah 6:8). **J**ustice. You can't read more than a chapter or two in any of the Minor Prophets without a cry for justice leaping off the pages. Not that it is a minor theme found only in these little-read books—God has sewn a broad thread of compassion for the oppressed throughout the tapestry of the Bible. But here in the books of the minor prophets, it becomes a central theme. **A**mos 5:24: "Let justice run down like water, and righteousness like a mighty stream." **O**ver and over, God told his people Israel that they were not to be like the other nations, that they were to hold to a higher standard. God said it was not to be like that in Israel: his people were to treat the less fortunate with compassion and fairness. In Proverbs 14:31, God even goes so far as to identify intimately with the plight of the downcast: "He who oppresses the poor reproaches his Maker, but he who honors Him has mercy on the needy." Other nations could treat foreigners like second-class people: not Israel. "You shall neither mistreat a stranger nor oppress him, for you were strangers in the land of Egypt" (Exodus 22:21). Other nations considered widows and orphans as little better than discarded property: God said that in Israel, such people had rights and were to be treated with dignity. "[God] will come near you for judgment; [he] will be a swift witness against . . . those who exploit wage earners and widows and orphans" (Malachi 3:5). **"E**xecute true justice, show mercy and compassion everyone to his brother. Do not oppress the widow or the fatherless, the alien or the poor. Let none of you plan evil in his heart against his brother" (Zechariah 7:9-10). **W**e are confronted today with a great many opportunities to minister justice in the name of God. The plight of the homeless, the distress of our inner cities, the suffering of the hungry, questions of racial and economic fairne the struggle for peace—these and countless other issues cry out for men and women of courage, compassi and conviction to stand strong for justice in Jesus' name. God is vitally concerned for the widow, the orph the Cambodian refugee, the Ethiopian child, the baby addicted to crack, the Cuban political prisoner, ar everyone who suffers and needs help. **A**re you? **"A**s you did it to one of the least of these My breth you did it to Me. . . . As you did not do it to one of the least of these, you did not do it to Me" (Matthew 25:40,45).

And you will be cast into Harmon,"
Says the LORD.

4 "Come to Bethel and transgress,
At Gilgal multiply transgression;
Bring your sacrifices every morning,
Your tithes every three days.

5 Offer a sacrifice of thanksgiving with leaven,
Proclaim *and* announce the freewill offerings;
For this you love,
You children of Israel!"
Says the Lord GOD.

6 "Also I gave you cleanness of teeth in all your cities.
And lack of bread in all your places;
Yet you have not returned to Me,"
Says the LORD.

7 "I also withheld rain from you,
When *there were* still three months to the harvest.
I made it rain on one city,
I withheld rain from another city.
One part was rained upon,
And where it did not rain the part withered.

8 So two *or* three cities wandered to another city to
drink water,
But they were not satisfied;
Yet you have not returned to Me,"
Says the LORD.

9 "I blasted you with blight and mildew.
When your gardens increased,
Your vineyards,
Your fig trees,
And your olive trees,
The locust devoured *them;*
Yet you have not returned to Me,"
Says the LORD.

10 "I sent among you a plague after the manner of Egypt;
Your young men I killed with a sword,
Along with your captive horses;
I made the stench of your camps come up into your
nostrils;
Yet you have not returned to Me,"
Says the LORD.

11 "I overthrew *some* of you,
As God overthrew Sodom and Gomorrah,
And you were like a firebrand plucked from the
burning;
Yet you have not returned to Me,"
Says the LORD.

12 "Therefore thus will I do to you, O Israel;
Because I will do this to you,
Prepare to meet your God, O Israel!"

13 For behold,
He who forms mountains,
And creates the wind,
Who declares to man what his thought *is,*
And makes the morning darkness,
Who treads the high places of the earth—
The LORD God of hosts *is* His name.

CHAPTER 5 A SAD SONG OF GRIEF. Hear this word

which I take up against you, a lamentation, O house of
Israel:

2 The virgin of Israel has fallen;
She will rise no more.
She lies forsaken on her land;
There is no one to raise her up.

3 For thus says the Lord GOD:

"The city that goes out by a thousand
Shall have a hundred left,
And that which goes out by a hundred
Shall have ten left to the house of Israel."

4 For thus says the LORD to the house of Israel:

"Seek Me and live;
5 But do not seek Bethel,
Nor enter Gilgal,
Nor pass over to Beersheba;
For Gilgal shall surely go into captivity,
And Bethel shall come to nothing.

6 Seek the LORD and live,
Lest He break out like fire *in* the house of Joseph,
And devour *it,*
With no one to quench *it* in Bethel—

7 You who turn justice to wormwood,
And lay righteousness to rest in the earth!"

8 He made the Pleiades and Orion;
He turns the shadow of death into morning
And makes the day dark as night;
He calls for the waters of the sea
And pours them out on the face of the earth;
The LORD *is* His name.

9 He rains ruin upon the strong,
So that fury comes upon the fortress.

10 They hate the one who rebukes in the gate,
And they abhor the one who speaks uprightly.

11 Therefore, because you tread down the poor
And take grain taxes from him,
Though you have built houses of hewn stone,
Yet you shall not dwell in them;
You have planted pleasant vineyards,
But you shall not drink wine from them.

12 For I know your manifold transgressions
And your mighty sins:
Afflicting the just *and* taking bribes;
Diverting the poor *from justice* at the gate.

13 Therefore the prudent keep silent at that time,
For it *is* an evil time.

14 Seek good and not evil,
That you may live;
So the LORD God of hosts will be with you,

◤▬▬▬▬NO GAIN

5:12 Why does God put so much emphasis on the way we treat the poor? How we treat the rich or those of equal station too often reflects what we hope to get from them. But since the poor can give us nothing, how we treat them reflects our true character. Do we, like Christ, give without thought of gain? We should treat the poor as we would like God to treat us.

As you have spoken.
15 Hate evil, love good;
Establish justice in the gate.
It may be that the LORD God of hosts
Will be gracious to the remnant of Joseph.

16Therefore the LORD God of hosts, the Lord, says this:

"*There shall be* wailing in all streets,
And they shall say in all the highways,
'Alas! Alas!'
They shall call the farmer to mourning,
And skillful lamenters to wailing.
17 In all vineyards *there shall be* wailing,

For I will pass through you,"
Says the LORD.

18 Woe to you who desire the day of the LORD!
For what good *is* the day of the LORD to you?
It *will be* darkness, and not light.
19 It *will be* as though a man fled from a lion,
And a bear met him!
Or *as though* he went into the house,
Leaned his hand on the wall,
And a serpent bit him!
20 *Is* not the day of the LORD darkness, and not light?
Is it not very dark, with no brightness in it?

21 "I hate, I despise your feast days,
And I do not savor your sacred assemblies.
22 Though you offer Me burnt offerings and your grain
offerings,
I will not accept *them*,
Nor will I regard your fattened peace offerings.
23 Take away from Me the noise of your songs,

For I will not hear the melody of your stringed
instruments.
24 But let justice run down like water,
And righteousness like a mighty stream.

25 "Did you offer Me sacrifices and offerings
In the wilderness forty years, O house of Israel?
26 You also carried Sikkuth your king
And Chiun, your idols,
The star of your gods,
Which you made for yourselves.
27 Therefore I will send you into captivity beyond
Damascus,"
Says the LORD, whose name *is* the God of hosts.

CHAPTER 6 GOD HATES ISRAEL'S PRIDE.

Woe to you *who are* at ease in Zion,
And trust in Mount Samaria,
Notable persons in the chief nation,
To whom the house of Israel comes!
2 Go over to Calneh and see;
And from there go to Hamath the great;
Then go down to Gath of the Philistines.
Are you better than these kingdoms?
Or is their territory greater than your territory?

3 *Woe to* you who put far off the day of doom,
Who cause the seat of violence to come near;
4 Who lie on beds of ivory,
Stretch out on your couches,
Eat lambs from the flock
And calves from the midst of the stall;
5 Who sing idly to the sound of stringed instruments,
And invent for yourselves musical instruments like
David;
6 Who drink wine from bowls,
And anoint yourselves with the best ointments,
But are not grieved for the affliction of Joseph.
7 Therefore they shall now go captive as the first of the
captives,
And those who recline at banquets shall be removed.

8 The Lord GOD has sworn by Himself,
The LORD God of hosts says:
"I abhor the pride of Jacob,
And hate his palaces;
Therefore I will deliver up *the* city
And all that is in it."

9Then it shall come to pass, that if ten men remain in one house, they shall die. 10And when a relative *of the dead*, with one who will burn *the bodies*, picks up the bodies to take them out of the house, he will say to one inside the house, "*Are there* any more with you?"
Then someone will say, "None."
And he will say, "Hold your tongue! For we dare not mention the name of the LORD."

11 For behold, the LORD gives a command:
He will break the great house into bits,
And the little house into pieces.

12 Do horses run on rocks?

Does *one* plow *there* with oxen?
Yet you have turned justice into gall,
And the fruit of righteousness into wormwood,
13 You who rejoice over Lo Debar,
Who say, "Have we not taken Karnaim for ourselves
By our own strength?"

14 "But, behold, I will raise up a nation against you,
O house of Israel,"
Says the LORD God of hosts;
"And they will afflict you from the entrance of
Hamath
To the Valley of the Arabah."

CHAPTER 7 LOCUSTS, FIRE, AND A PLUMB LINE.

Thus the Lord GOD showed me: Behold, He formed locust swarms at the beginning of the late crop; indeed *it was* the late crop after the king's mowings. ²And so it was, when they had finished eating the grass of the land, that I said:

"O Lord GOD, forgive, I pray!
Oh, that Jacob may stand,
For he *is* small!"

3 *So* the LORD relented concerning this.
"It shall not be," said the LORD.

⁴Thus the Lord GOD showed me: Behold, the Lord GOD called for conflict by fire, and it consumed the great deep and devoured the territory. ⁵Then I said:

"O Lord GOD, cease, I pray!
Oh, that Jacob may stand,
For he *is* small!"

6 *So* the LORD relented concerning this.
"This also shall not be," said the Lord GOD.

⁷Thus He showed me: Behold, the Lord stood on a wall *made* with a plumb line, with a plumb line in His hand. ⁸And the LORD said to me, "Amos, what do you see?"
And I said, "A plumb line."
Then the Lord said:

"Behold, I am setting a plumb line
In the midst of My people Israel;
I will not pass by them anymore.
9 The high places of Isaac shall be desolate,
And the sanctuaries of Israel shall be laid waste.
I will rise with the sword against the house of
Jeroboam."

¹⁰Then Amaziah the priest of Bethel sent to Jeroboam king of Israel, saying, "Amos has conspired against you in the midst of the house of Israel. The land is not able to bear all his words. ¹¹For thus Amos has said:

'Jeroboam shall die by the sword,
And Israel shall surely be led away captive
From their own land.'"

¹²Then Amaziah said to Amos:

"Go, you seer!
Flee to the land of Judah.
There eat bread,

And there prophesy.
13 But never again prophesy at Bethel,
For it *is* the king's sanctuary,
And it *is* the royal residence."

PRAYER POWER

7:1-9 Twice Amos was shown a vision of Israel's impending punishment, and his immediate response was to pray that God would spare Israel. Prayer is a powerful privilege. Amos's prayers should remind us to pray for our nation.

¹⁴Then Amos answered, and said to Amaziah:

"I *was* no prophet,
Nor *was* I a son of a prophet,
But I *was* a sheepbreeder
And a tender of sycamore fruit.
15 Then the LORD took me as I followed the flock,
And the LORD said to me,
'Go, prophesy to My people Israel.'
16 Now therefore, hear the word of the LORD:
You say, 'Do not prophesy against Israel,
And do not spout against the house of Isaac.'

¹⁷"Therefore thus says the LORD:

'Your wife shall be a harlot in the city;
Your sons and daughters shall fall by the sword;
Your land shall be divided by *survey* line;
You shall die in a defiled land;
And Israel shall surely be led away captive
From his own land.'"

CHAPTER 8 AMOS SEES A BASKET OF FRUIT.

Thus the Lord GOD showed me: Behold, a basket of summer fruit. ²And He said, "Amos, what do you see?"
So I said, "A basket of summer fruit."
Then the LORD said to me:

"The end has come upon My people Israel;
I will not pass by them anymore.
3 And the songs of the temple
Shall be wailing in that day,"
Says the Lord GOD—
"Many dead bodies everywhere,
They shall be thrown out in silence."

4 Hear this, you who swallow up the needy,
And make the poor of the land fail,

⁵Saying:

"When will the New Moon be past,
That we may sell grain?
And the Sabbath,
That we may trade wheat?
Making the ephah small and the shekel large,
Falsifying the scales by deceit,
6 That we may buy the poor for silver,
And the needy for a pair of sandals—
Even sell the bad wheat?"

7 The LORD has sworn by the pride of Jacob:
"Surely I will never forget any of their works.

8 Shall the land not tremble for this,
And everyone mourn who dwells in it?
All of it shall swell like the River,
Heave and subside
Like the River of Egypt.

9 "And it shall come to pass in that day," says the Lord GOD,
"That I will make the sun go down at noon,
And I will darken the earth in broad daylight;
10 I will turn your feasts into mourning,
And all your songs into lamentation;
I will bring sackcloth on every waist,
And baldness on every head;
I will make it like mourning for an only *son*,
And its end like a bitter day.

11 "Behold, the days are coming," says the Lord GOD,
"That I will send a famine on the land,
Not a famine of bread,
Nor a thirst for water,
But of hearing the words of the LORD.
12 They shall wander from sea to sea,
And from north to east;
They shall run to and fro, seeking the word of the LORD,
But shall not find *it*.

13 "In that day the fair virgins
And strong young men
Shall faint from thirst.
14 Those who swear by the sin of Samaria,
Who say,
'As your god lives, O Dan!'
And, 'As the way of Beersheba lives!'
They shall fall and never rise again."

CHAPTER **9** **ISRAEL WILL BE DESTROYED.** I saw
the Lord standing by the altar, and He said:

"Strike the doorposts, that the thresholds may shake,
And break them on the heads of them all.
I will slay the last of them with the sword.
He who flees from them shall not get away,
And he who escapes from them shall not be delivered.

2 "Though they dig into hell,
From there My hand shall take them;
Though they climb up to heaven,
From there I will bring them down;
3 And though they hide themselves on top of Carmel,
From there I will search and take them;
Though they hide from My sight at the bottom of the sea,
From there I will command the serpent, and it shall bite them;
4 Though they go into captivity before their enemies,
From there I will command the sword,
And it shall slay them.
I will set My eyes on them for harm and not for good."

■THE ANSWER

8:11-13 The people had no appetite for God's word when proph
like Amos brought it. Because of their apathy, God said he would to
away even the opportunity to hear his word. We have God's Word,
Bible, but many people still look everywhere for answers to life's
problems *except* in Scripture. You can help them by directing them
Bible, showing them the parts that speak to their special needs and
questions. God's Word is available to us. Let us help people know it
before a time comes when they cannot find it.

5 The Lord GOD of hosts,
He who touches the earth and it melts,
And all who dwell there mourn;
All of it shall swell like the River,
And subside like the River of Egypt.
6 He who builds His layers in the sky,
And has founded His strata in the earth;
Who calls for the waters of the sea,
And pours them out on the face of the earth—
The LORD *is* His name.

7 "*Are* you not like the people of Ethiopia to Me,
O children of Israel?" says the LORD.
"Did I not bring up Israel from the land of Egypt,
The Philistines from Caphtor,
And the Syrians from Kir?

8 "Behold, the eyes of the Lord GOD *are* on the sinful kingdom,
And I will destroy it from the face of the earth;
Yet I will not utterly destroy the house of Jacob,"
Says the LORD.

9 "For surely I will command,
And will sift the house of Israel among all nations,
As *grain* is sifted in a sieve;
Yet not the smallest grain shall fall to the ground.
10 All the sinners of My people shall die by the sword,
Who say, 'The calamity shall not overtake nor confront us.'

11 "On that day I will raise up
The tabernacle of David, which has fallen down,
And repair its damages;
I will raise up its ruins,
And rebuild it as in the days of old;
12 That they may possess the remnant of Edom,
And all the Gentiles who are called by My name,"
Says the LORD who does this thing.

13 "Behold, the days are coming," says the LORD,
"When the plowman shall overtake the reaper,
And the treader of grapes him who sows seed;
The mountains shall drip with sweet wine,
And all the hills shall flow *with it*.
14 I will bring back the captives of My people Israel;
They shall build the waste cities and inhabit *them*;

■SIGN OF LOVE

9:8 Amos assured the Israelites that God would not "utterly destroy
Israel—in other words, the punishment would not be permanent or
total." God wants to redeem, not punish. But when punishment is
necessary, he doesn't withhold it. Like a loving father, God disciplines
those he loves in order to correct them. If he disciplines you, accept it
sign of his love.

They shall plant vineyards and drink wine from
  them;
They shall also make gardens and eat fruit from
  them.

¹⁵ I will plant them in their land,
  And no longer shall they be pulled up
  From the land I have given them,"
  Says the LORD your God.

MEGA Themes

EVERYONE ANSWERS TO GOD Amos
pronounced judgment from God on all the
surrounding nations. Then he included Judah and
Israel. God is in supreme control of the nations.
Everyone is accountable to him.

All people will have to account for their sin. When
those who reject God seem to be living the good life,
don't be jealous of their prosperity or feel sorry for
yourself. Remember that we all must answer to God.

1. At times it seems that terrorists and evil leaders are
   able to avoid punishment for their violent, terrible
   actions. What does Amos say that contradicts
   this apparent injustice?
2. How does this truth apply in general to men and
   women who feel they don't have to be
   responsible for the way they behave?
3. How would you respond to the following statement
   from a non-Christian: "Everybody has to decide
   what is right for himself or herself as an individual.
   Nobody can say what is and is not a sin."
4. How does the fact that you must answer to God
   affect your relationship with Christ? How you live?

COMPLACENCY Everyone was optimistic,
business was booming, people were happy (except
for the poor and oppressed). With all the comfort
and luxury came self-sufficiency and a false sense of
security. But prosperity brought corruption and
destruction.

A complacent present can lead to a disastrous
future. Don't congratulate yourself for the blessings
and benefits you enjoy. They are from God. If you
are more satisfied with yourself than with God,
remember that everything is meaningless without
him. A self-sufficient attitude may be your downfall.

1. What are some things that cause Christians to
   become complacent about God or to take God
   for granted?
2. Describe a time in your life when you took God's
   relationship with you for granted. How did you
   feel about God during this time? About yourself?
   What shook you out of it?
3. What have you learned about being complacent in
   your relationship with God from the book of
   Amos?
4. What can you do to avoid becoming complacent
   in your relationship with Christ?

OPPRESSION The wealthy and powerful people
of Samaria, the capital of Israel, had become
prosperous, greedy, and unfair. Illegal and immoral
slavery had come as the result of overtaxation and
land grabbing. There also was cruelty and
indifference toward the poor. God grows weary and
angry with greed and will not tolerate injustice.

God made everyone, so ignoring the poor is
ignoring those whom God loves and whom Christ
came to save. We must go beyond feeling bad for the
poor and oppressed. We must act compassionately
to stop injustice and to help care for those in need.

1. In what ways were the wealthy taking advantage
   of the poor? What seems to have been their
   attitude about the poor?
2. How does God view the poor? The rich who
   oppress the poor?
3. Who are the poor in your community? In what
   ways could they be described as oppressed?
4. Who are the outcasts in your school? In what ways
   could they be described as oppressed?
5. Give specific examples of how you could stand
   against oppression in your school and community.

SUPERFICIAL RELIGION Although many
people had abandoned real faith in God, they still
pretended to be religious. They "performed" as
religious people, just going through the motions
instead of having spiritual integrity and practicing
heartfelt obedience toward God.

Merely participating in ceremony or ritual falls
short of true faith. This leads to religion without
relationship. God wants trust in him, not a show.
Don't settle for impressing others when God wants
sincere obedience and commitment.

1. Give examples of what you think would qualify as
   superficial religion.
2. Describe a time in your own life when you were
   just "going through the motions." How do you
   feel about this type of living?
3. Many people identify a "good Christian" as a
   person who goes to church and behaves morally.
   Based on Scripture, what does it mean to be a
   true disciple of Christ? How is this different from
   going through the motions?
4. What will you do in the coming week to deepen
   your relationship with God? What will you do to
   avoid getting caught in superficial religion?

*L*et me tell you a joke!" Five-year-old Alice bubbled with excitement as she spoke. "Which do you want first, the bad news or the bad news?" ■ "You dummy," her brother Al retorted, "don't you know anything? Those jokes are supposed to have *good* news and bad news, not just bad news." ■ "Not this one," answered Alice. ■ Like those jokes, most of life includes both good news and bad news. Positive things almost always seem to have a downside. More important, negative things often have some "silver lining" to give us hope. ■ The books in the Bible written by the prophets (Isaiah—Malachi) are like that. The bad news was that Israel was going to be punished for their sins by becoming prisoners to their enemies. The good news is that God would someday bring his people back from captivity and restore Israel's glory. ■ But one prophetical book is unique: it has no good news. That book is Obadiah. Written about Edom (a nearby nation), the prophet graphically describes the utter ruin that was about to come. Why? Because Edom had rejoiced when Israel was taken captive and had taken advantage of Israel's plight. ■ God loves his children. He will protect his children and will deal harshly with those who attempt to hurt them. ■ If you are God's child, God loves you just as he loved Israel. He will guard and protect you and react angrily against any who might attempt to harm you. ■ As you read Obadiah ask God to help you be more aware that he indeed is watching over you.

STATS

PURPOSE: To show that God judges those who have harmed his people

AUTHOR: Obadiah. Little is known about him. His name means "servant of the Lord" or "worshiper of Jehovah."

TO WHOM WRITTEN: The Edomites, the Jews in Judah, and God's people everywhere

DATE WRITTEN: Possibly during the reign of Jehoram in Judah, 853–841 B.C.

SETTING: Historically, Edom had constantly harassed the Jews. Prior to the time this book was written, they had participated in attacks against Judah. Given the dates above, this prophecy comes after the division of Israel into the northern and southern kingdoms and before the conquering of Judah by Nebuchadnezzar in 586 B.C.

KEY PEOPLE: The Edomites

KEY PLACES: Edom, Jerusalem

badiah

CHAPTER 1 EDOM WILL BE DESTROYED. The vision of Obadiah.

Thus says the Lord GOD concerning Edom
(We have heard a report from the LORD,
And a messenger has been sent among the nations,
    saying,
  "Arise, and let us rise up against her for battle"):

2 "Behold, I will make you small among the nations;
You shall be greatly despised.
3 The pride of your heart has deceived you,
You who dwell in the clefts of the rock,
Whose habitation is high;
You who say in your heart, 'Who will bring me down
    to the ground?'

4 Though you ascend *as* high as the eagle,
And though you set your nest among the stars,
From there I will bring you down," says the LORD.

5 "If thieves had come to you,
If robbers by night—
Oh, how you will be cut off!—

▰▰▰ VANISHING ACT

3 The Edomites felt secure, and they were proud of their self-sufficiency. But they were fooling themselves because there is no lasting security apart from God. Is your security in objects or people? Ask yourself how much lasting security they really offer. Possessions and people can disappear in a moment, but God does not change. Only he can supply true security.

Would they not have stolen till they had enough?
If grape gatherers had come to you,
Would they not have left *some* gleanings?

6 "Oh, how Esau shall be searched out!
 How his hidden treasures shall be sought after!
7 All the men in your confederacy
 Shall force you to the border;
 The men at peace with you
 Shall deceive you *and* prevail against you.
 Those who eat your bread shall lay a trap for you.
 No one is aware of it.

8 "Will I not in that day," says the LORD,

13 You should not have entered the gate of My people
 In the day of their calamity.
 Indeed, you should not have gazed on their affliction
 In the day of their calamity,
 Nor laid *hands* on their substance
 In the day of their calamity.
14 You should not have stood at the crossroads
 To cut off those among them who escaped;
 Nor should you have delivered up those among
  them who remained
 In the day of distress.

15 "For the day of the LORD upon all the nations *is* near;
 As you have done, it shall be done to you;
 Your reprisal shall return upon your own head.
16 For as you drank on My holy mountain,
 So shall all the nations drink continually;
 Yes, they shall drink, and swallow,
 And they shall be as though they had never been.

17 "But on Mount Zion there shall be deliverance,
 And there shall be holiness;

COCKINESS

Henderson Heights is a basketball community. Between the two high schools there are at least a dozen good basketball players. Then there is Kyle. Kyle is something special. He'll be able to play collegiate ball just about wherever he wants. Some people think that if he works hard enough, Kyle has the skills to one day play in the NBA.

Kyle's 21 points-per-game scoring average is the good news. The bad news is his hot-dog personality. Kyle talks a steady stream of trash out on the court. Not only does he like to run up the score on his opponents, but he often goes out of his way to humiliate whoever happens to be guarding him. Even his own teammates sometimes get embarrassed by Kyle's showboat antics.

Last night Kyle came crashing back to reality. His team lost a game they were supposed to win easily. Kyle was ejected late in the game for questioning a referee's call. He scored a grand total of seven points. And there were three college scouts in the stands.

See what happened when a whole nation (Edom) had an arrogant, cocky attitude. Read Obadiah 2-10.

OBADIAH
served as a prophet
to Judah around
853 B.C.

"Even destroy the wise *men* from Edom,
 And understanding from the mountains of Esau?
9 Then your mighty men, O Teman, shall be dismayed,
 To the end that everyone from the mountains of Esau
 May be cut off by slaughter.

10 "For violence against your brother Jacob,
 Shame shall cover you,
 And you shall be cut off forever.
11 In the day that you stood on the other side—
 In the day that strangers carried captive his forces,
 When foreigners entered his gates
 And cast lots for Jerusalem—
 Even you *were* as one of them.
12 "But you should not have gazed on the day of your
  brother
 In the day of his captivity;
 Nor should you have rejoiced over the children of
  Judah
 In the day of their destruction;
 Nor should you have spoken proudly
 In the day of distress.

Climate of the times
Edom was a constant thorn in Judah's side. They often participated in attacks initiated by other enemies.

Main message
God will judge Edom for its evil actions toward God's people.

Importance of message
Just as Edom was destroyed and disappeared as a nation, so God will destroy proud and wicked people.

Contemporary prophets
Elijah (875–848)
Micaiah (865–853)
Jehu (855–840?)

The house of Jacob shall possess their possessions.

18 The house of Jacob shall be a fire,
And the house of Joseph a flame;
But the house of Esau *shall be* stubble;
They shall kindle them and devour them,
And no survivor shall *remain* of the house of Esau,"
For the LORD has spoken.

19 The South shall possess the mountains of Esau,
And the Lowland shall possess Philistia.
They shall possess the fields of Ephraim
And the fields of Samaria.
Benjamin *shall possess* Gilead.

20 And the captives of this host of the children of Israel
Shall possess the land of the Canaanites
As far as Zarephath.
The captives of Jerusalem who are in Sepharad
Shall possess the cities of the South.

21 Then saviors shall come to Mount Zion
To judge the mountains of Esau,
And the kingdom shall be the LORD's.

MEGA Themes

JUSTICE Obadiah predicted that God would destroy Edom as punishment for helping Babylon invade Judah. Because of their treachery, Edom's land would be given to Judah in the day when God rights the wrongs against his people.

God will judge and fiercely punish all who harm his people. We can be confident in God's final victory. He is our champion, and we can trust him to bring about true justice.

1. What sin of the Edomites violated God's holy will?
2. What have you learned about God's qualities as a father to his people?
3. What is meant by the statement "God is a just God"?
4. What hope does this provide for the person who is being persecuted for being a believer?

PRIDE Because of their seemingly invincible rock fortress, the Edomites were proud and self-confident.

But God humbled them, and their nation disappeared from the face of the earth.

All those who defy God will meet their doom, as Edom did. Any nation that trusts in power, wealth, technology, or wisdom more than in God will be brought down. All who are proud will one day be shocked to discover that no one can escape God's justice.

1. Edom had an attitude of self-reliance and pride. How did their pride lead to their destruction?
2. How does knowing, experiencing, and responding to God as Lord eliminate the roots of pride?
3. In what situations do you tend to be self-reliant and prideful?
4. What knowledge and experience of God leads you to depend on him? What can you do to depend more on God?

*D*on't get mad, get even." We've all heard or said that. Movies reflect the "get even" idea. We watch, cheering and yelling as the victim evens the score and the bad guys get what they deserve. We often live that way, too, sometimes without even knowing it. We do or say things to get back at those whom we think have offended us. ■ Jonah was like that. He's famous for being swallowed by a "great fish," but he ended up in that fish because of his "get even" attitude. ■ God told Jonah to go to Assyria (Israel's greatest enemy) and warn the people of Nineveh (the capital) to repent from their evil life-style or God would destroy them. But Jonah thought Assyria should be destroyed (and he was afraid to go there), so he ran the other direction—straight into the fish. Finally, when Jonah cried out to God and was rescued, he obeyed and preached in Nineveh. ■ "Don't get mad, get even." Fortunately, God doesn't work that way. Instead, God is "a gracious and merciful God, slow to anger and abundant in lovingkindness." That's what our attitude should be, too. As you read Jonah, give your attitude to God, and ask him to replace it with his attitude.

STATS

PURPOSE: To show the extent of God's grace—the message of salvation is for *all* people

AUTHOR: Jonah, son of Amittai

TO WHOM WRITTEN: Israel and God's people everywhere

DATE WRITTEN: Approximately 785–760 B.C.

SETTING: Jonah preceded Amos and ministered under Jeroboam II, Israel's most powerful king (793–753 B.C., see 2 Kings 14:23-25). Assyria was Israel's greatest enemy; Israel was conquered by them in 722 B.C. Nineveh's repentance must have been short-lived.

KEY PEOPLE: Jonah, the ship's captain and crew

KEY PLACES: Joppa, Nineveh

SPECIAL FEATURES: This book is different from the other prophetic books because it centers on the prophet, not his prophecies. Only one verse summarizes Jonah's message to Nineveh (3:4). Jonah is a historical narrative. It also is mentioned by Jesus as a picture of his death and resurrection (Matthew 12:38-42).

onah

CHAPTER 1 A BIG FISH SWALLOWS JONAH. Now the word of the LORD came to Jonah the son of Amittai, saying, ²"Arise, go to Nineveh, that great city, and cry out against it; for their wickedness has come up before Me." ³But Jonah arose to flee to Tarshish from the presence of the LORD. He went down to Joppa, and found a ship going to Tarshish; so he paid the fare, and went down into it, to go with them to Tarshish from the presence of the LORD.

⁴But the LORD sent out a great wind on the sea, and there was a mighty tempest on the sea, so that the ship was about to be broken up.

⁵Then the mariners were afraid; and every man cried out to his god, and threw the cargo that *was* in the ship into the sea, to lighten the load. But Jonah had gone down into the lowest parts of the ship, had lain down, and was fast asleep.

⁶So the captain came to him, and said to him, "What do you mean, sleeper? Arise, call on your God; perhaps your God will consider us, so that we may not perish."

⁷And they said to one another, "Come, let us cast lots,

RUNNING AWAY

1:3 Jonah was afraid. He knew that God had a specific job for him, but he didn't want to do it. When God gives us directions through his Word, sometimes we run in fear, claiming that God is asking too much. Fear made Jonah run. But running got him into worse trouble. In the end, Jonah knew that it was best to do what God had asked in the first place. But by then he had paid a costly price for running. It is far better to obey from the start.

CHAPTER 2

Then Jonah prayed to the LORD his God from the fish's belly. ²And he said:

"I cried out to the LORD because of my affliction,
And He answered me.

"Out of the belly of Sheol I cried,
And You heard my voice.
3   For You cast me into the deep,
Into the heart of the seas,
And the floods surrounded me;
All Your billows and Your waves passed over me.
4   Then I said, 'I have been cast out of Your sight;
Yet I will look again toward Your holy temple.'
5   The waters surrounded me, *even* to my soul;
The deep closed around me;
Weeds were wrapped around my head.
6   I went down to the moorings of the mountains;
The earth with its bars *closed* behind me forever;
Yet You have brought up my life from the pit,
O LORD, my God.

7 "When my soul fainted within me,
I remembered the LORD;
And my prayer went *up* to You,
Into Your holy temple.

8 "Those who regard worthless idols
Forsake their own Mercy.
9   But I will sacrifice to You
With the voice of thanksgiving;
I will pay what I have vowed.
Salvation *is* of the LORD."

¹⁰So the LORD spoke to the fish, and it vomited Jonah onto dry *land.*

CHAPTER **3** **JONAH PREACHES AT NINEVEH.** Now the word of the LORD came to Jonah the second time, saying, ²"Arise, go to Nineveh, that great city, and preach to it the message that I tell you." ³So Jonah arose and went to Nineveh, according to the word of the LORD. Now Nineveh was an exceedingly great city, a three-day journey *in extent.* ⁴And Jonah began to enter the city on the

---

ATTITUDES   Sharon's favorite TV show is a hot new drama, "Manhattan Nights." It's really not new—just a shameless rip-off of the afternoon soaps and programs like "Dallas," "Dynasty," and "L.A. Law." The only difference is that this show is set in New York, and all the characters work on Wall Street.

Tonight Sharon is dying to find out if Heather is pregnant with Dade's child. But just as the show gets underway, the local TV station breaks in with a special report about a natural gas explosion in a nearby community.

"At least 12 people are known dead, another 17 are en route to area hospitals, at least 9 are still missing," the shaken reporter explains as fires rage out of control behind him.

"Great!" Sharon yells. "Because of this *stupid* fire, I'm gonna miss my show! Why can't they wait until the regular newscast to report all this junk? How stupid can you get?"

Sharon picks up the phone and dials her friend Ashley. "Can you *believe* they're doing this?" she says.

Sharon has a major attitude problem. She's more concerned about some fictional characters on TV than she is about her real-life neighbors. As a child of God, she should know better.

Read about a prophet of God who also had some misplaced priorities—Jonah 3–4.

---

that we may know for whose cause this trouble *has come* upon us." So they cast lots, and the lot fell on Jonah. ⁸Then they said to him, "Please tell us! For whose cause *is* this trouble upon us? What is your occupation? And where do you come from? What is your country? And of what people are you?"

⁹So he said to them, "I *am* a Hebrew; and I fear the LORD, the God of heaven, who made the sea and the dry *land.*"

¹⁰Then the men were exceedingly afraid, and said to him, "Why have you done this?" For the men knew that he fled from the presence of the LORD, because he had told them. ¹¹Then they said to him, "What shall we do to you that the sea may be calm for us?"—for the sea was growing more tempestuous.

¹²And he said to them, "Pick me up and throw me into the sea; then the sea will become calm for you. For I know that this great tempest *is* because of me."

¹³Nevertheless the men rowed hard to return to land, but they could not, for the sea continued to grow more tempestuous against them. ¹⁴Therefore they cried out to the LORD and said, "We pray, O LORD, please do not let us perish for this man's life, and do not charge us with innocent blood; for You, O LORD, have done as it pleased You." ¹⁵So they picked up Jonah and threw him into the sea, and the sea ceased from its raging. ¹⁶Then the men feared the LORD exceedingly, and offered a sacrifice to the LORD and took vows.

¹⁷Now the LORD had prepared a great fish to swallow Jonah. And Jonah was in the belly of the fish three days and three nights.

When my soul fainted within me

I REMEMBERED THE LORD

and my prayer went up to YOU

first day's walk. Then he cried out and said, "Yet forty days, and Nineveh shall be overthrown!"

⁵So the people of Nineveh believed God, proclaimed a fast, and put on sackcloth, from the greatest to the least of them. ⁶Then word came to the king of Nineveh; and he arose from his throne and laid aside his robe, covered *himself* with sackcloth and sat in ashes. ⁷And he caused *it* to be proclaimed and published throughout Nineveh by the decree of the king and his nobles, saying,

Let neither man nor beast, herd nor flock, taste anything; do not let them eat, or drink water. ⁸But let man and beast be covered with sackcloth, and cry mightily to God; yes, let every one turn from his evil way and from the violence that is in his hands. ⁹Who can tell *if* God will turn and relent, and turn away from His fierce anger, so that we may not perish?

¹⁰Then God saw their works, that they turned from their evil way; and God relented from the disaster that He had said He would bring upon them, and He did not do it.

CHAPTER **4** But it displeased Jonah exceedingly, and he became angry. ²So he prayed to the LORD, and said, "Ah, LORD, was not this what I said when I was still in my country? Therefore I fled previously to Tarshish; for I know that You *are* a gracious and merciful God, slow to anger and abundant in lovingkindness, One who relents from doing harm. ³Therefore now, O LORD, please take my life from me, for *it is* better for me to die than to live!"

⁴Then the LORD said, "*Is it* right for you to be angry?"

⁵So Jonah went out of the city and sat on the east side of the city. There he made himself a shelter and sat under it in the shade, till he might see what would become of the city. ⁶And the LORD God prepared a plant and made it come up over Jonah, that it might be shade for his head to deliver him from his misery. So Jonah was very grateful for the plant. ⁷But as morning dawned the next day God prepared a worm, and it *so* damaged the plant that it withered. ⁸And it happened, when the sun arose, that God prepared a vehement east wind; and the sun beat on Jonah's head, so that he grew faint. Then he wished death for himself, and said, "*It is* better for me to die than to live."

BROAD VIEW

4:1-2 Jonah revealed the reason for his reluctance to go to Nineveh (1:3): he wanted the Ninevites destroyed, not forgiven. Jonah didn't understand that the God of Israel is also the God of the world. Are you surprised when some unexpected person turns to God? Maybe your view is as narrow as Jonah's. Don't forget that, in reality, none of us deserve to be forgiven by God.

⁹Then God said to Jonah, "*Is it* right for you to be angry about the plant?"

And he said, "*It is* right for me to be angry, even to death!"

SENSITIVE

4:9 Jonah was angry at the death of the plant, but not over what could have happened to Nineveh. Most of us have cried at the death of a pet or when an object with sentimental value is broken—but have we cried over a friend who does not know God? It is much easier to be more sensitive to our own interests than to the spiritual needs of people around us. What are you sensitive to?

¹⁰But the LORD said, "You have had pity on the plant for which you have not labored, nor made it grow, which came up in a night and perished in a night. ¹¹And should I not pity Nineveh, that great city, in which are more than one hundred and twenty thousand persons who cannot discern between their right hand and their left—and much livestock?"

JONAH
served as a prophet to Israel and Assyria from 793–753 B.C.

Climate of the times
While Nineveh was the most important city in Assyria and would soon become the capital of the huge Assyrian empire, it also was very wicked city.

Main message
Jonah, who hated the powerful and wicked Assyrians, was called by God to warn the Assyrians that they would receive judgment if they did not repent.

Importance of message
Jonah didn't want to go to Nineveh, so he tried to run from God. But God has ways of teaching us to obey and follow him. When Jonah finally did preach, the people repented and God withheld his judgment. Even the most wicked will be saved if they truly repent of their sins and turn to God.

Contemporary prophets
Joel (853–796?)
Amos (760–750)

MIRACLES IN THE BOOK OF JONAH

God caused a great storm 1:4

God arranged for a great fish to swallow Jonah 1:17

God ordered the fish to spit up Jonah 2:10

God made a plant to shade Jonah 4:6

God prepared a worm to eat the vine 4:7

God ordered a scorching wind to blow on Jonah 4:8

MEGA Themes

GOD'S SOVEREIGNTY Although the prophet Jonah tried to run away from God, God was in control. By controlling the stormy seas and a great fish, God displayed his absolute, yet loving guidance.

Rather than running from God, trust him with your past, present, and future. Saying no to God quickly leads to disaster. Saying yes brings new understanding of God and his purpose in the world. Just say yes to God and his will for you.

1. What do you think Jonah was thinking and feeling in these situations: when he ran from God's command to go to Nineveh; when he was on the ship in the storm; when he was in the belly of the great fish?
2. What did Jonah learn about God's sovereignty through these experiences?
3. Have you felt the way Jonah did when he ran from God? What made it difficult for you to obey God at that time?
4. In what ways has God revealed his control in your life even when you were not aware of it or were

in rebellion against his will? What does this teach you about God's sovereignty?

MISSIONARY MESSAGE God had given Jonah a purpose—to preach to the great Assyrian city of Nineveh. Jonah hated Nineveh, and so he responded with anger and indifference. Jonah had yet to learn that God loves all people. Through Jonah, God reminded Israel of their missionary purpose.

God wants his people to proclaim his love in words and actions to the whole world. He wants us to be his missionaries wherever we are and wherever he sends us.

1. Why was Jonah so opposed to preaching to Nineveh?
2. Jonah seemed to understand and accept part of God's message, yet he missed a key ingredient. What was it that he failed to understand or accept? Why do you think this happened?

3. Put God's message for the Ninevites into your own words.
4. What message do you think God might want to send to your school? How do you think most of the kids would respond to that message?
5. What opportunities do you have to communicate God's message through your own life?

REPENTANCE When the reluctant preacher went to Nineveh, there was a great response. People turned from their sins and turned to God. This was a powerful rebuke to Israel who thought they were better than nations like Nineveh, and yet refused to respond to God's message of forgiveness for repentance of sin.

God doesn't honor those who fake it. He wants the sincere devotion of each person. It is not enough to share the privileges of Christianity; we must ask God to forgive us and to remove our sin. Refusing to repent is the same as loving our sin—it keeps us from God.

1. What were the people of Nineveh like before Jonah's message? Afterward?
2. Why was repentance (turning away from sin) so necessary for the Ninevites?
3. Why is repentance necessary for those who do not know God today? For those who already are Christians?
4. List any areas in your life where you need to repent in order to be living fully in God's will.

GOD'S COMPASSION God's message of love and forgiveness was not just for the Jews. God loves all the people of the world. The Assyrians didn't deserve it, but God spared them when they repented. In his mercy, God did not reject Jonah for aborting his mission. God had great love, patience, and forgiveness.

God loves each of us even when we fail him. He also loves all other people, including those outside our social group, cultural background, race, or denomination. When we accept his love, we must also learn to accept all those he loves. We will find it much easier to love others when we receive and return God's love.

1. Contrast God's view of the Ninevites with Jonah's view.
2. What does it mean to have a godly attitude toward people who are not Christians? Toward those who are racially or culturally different?
3. Who are the people in your world who need to experience God's love through you? How will you demonstrate love and compassion?

Yesterday, at 2 A.M., our country officially surrendered. Realizing our situation was hopeless, generals from both sides agreed to end the bloodshed provided we hand over all guns and ammunition. Morale is low. The most perplexing question yet unanswered is, How could we have been overrun?" ■ Imagine reading that in your newspaper. What a terrible thought! Yet history proves it's possible. It happened to both Israel (the northern 10 tribes) and Judah (the southern 2 tribes). They couldn't understand how they could have been defeated: they were God's chosen people; God had a special love for them; he'd rescued them out of slavery in Egypt; he'd destroyed mighty forces to give them their homeland; and he'd protected them. ■ God had been faithful—but neither Israel nor Judah had. Micah wrote, "All this is for the transgression of Jacob . . . and for the sins of the house of Israel!" (1:5). Israel and Judah were being judged for their sins. Instead of worshiping the true God, the people were worshiping idols they had made. Many were using the religious ceremonies God had prescribed to make money. Those who were rich and influential were harassing the poor. God was going to punish them all because none of them were without guilt. ■ There are lessons in Micah we need to learn. God punishes sin—even in those in whom he has shown special favor—by sometimes humbling whole nations. ■ As you read Micah, remember that we as individuals and as a nation are responsible before God to serve him. Ask God to give you the strength to be faithful to him.

STATS

PURPOSE: To warn God's people that judgment is coming and to offer pardon to all who repent

AUTHOR: Micah, a native of Moresheth, near Gath, about 20 miles southwest of Jerusalem

TO WHOM WRITTEN: The people of Israel (the northern kingdom) and of Judah (the southern kingdom)

DATE WRITTEN: Possibly during the reigns of Jotham, Ahaz, and Hezekiah (742–687 B.C.)

SETTING: The political situation is described in 2 Kings 15–20 and 2 Chronicles 26–30. Micah was a contemporary of Isaiah and Hosea.

KEY PLACES: Samaria, Jerusalem, Bethlehem

Micah

CHAPTER 1 DARK DAYS FOR ISRAEL AND JUDAH.
The word of the LORD that came to Micah of Moresheth in the days of Jotham, Ahaz, *and* Hezekiah, kings of Judah, which he saw concerning Samaria and Jerusalem.

2 Hear, all you peoples!
Listen, O earth, and all that is in it!
Let the Lord GOD be a witness against you,
The Lord from His holy temple.

3 For behold, the LORD is coming out of His place;
He will come down
And tread on the high places of the earth.

4 The mountains will melt under Him,
And the valleys will split
Like wax before the fire,
Like waters poured down a steep place.

5 All this is for the transgression of Jacob

And for the sins of the house of Israel.
What *is* the transgression of Jacob?
Is it not Samaria?
And what *are* the high places of Judah?
Are they not Jerusalem?

6 "Therefore I will make Samaria a heap of
ruins in the field,
Places for planting a vineyard;
I will pour down her stones into the valley,
And I will uncover her foundations.

7 All her carved images shall be beaten to
pieces,
And all her pay as a harlot shall be burned with the
fire;
All her idols I will lay desolate,
For she gathered *it* from the pay of a harlot,
And they shall return to the pay of a harlot."

8 Therefore I will wail and howl,
I will go stripped and naked;
I will make a wailing like the jackals
And a mourning like the ostriches,

9 For her wounds *are* incurable.
For it has come to Judah;
It has come to the gate of My people—
To Jerusalem.

10 Tell *it* not in Gath,
Weep not at all;
In Beth Aphrah

FOLLOW ME

1:13 The people of Lachish influenced many to follow their evil example. We often do the same when we sin. Regardless of whether or not you consider yourself a leader, your actions and words are observed by others more than you suspect—and they may choose to follow your example, whether you know it or not.

MICAH

served as a prophet to Judah from 742–687 B.C.

Climate of the times
King Ahaz set up heathen idols in the temple and finally nailed the temple door shut. Four different nations harassed Judah. When Hezekiah became king, the nation began a slow road to recovery and economic strength. Hezekiah probably heeded much of Micah's advice.

Main message
Predicted the fall of both the northern kingdom of Israel and the southern kingdom of Judah. Through his disciplining the people, God was actually showing how much he cared for them. Hezekiah's good reign helped postpone Judah's punishment.

Importance of message
Choosing to live a life apart from God is making a commitment to sin. Sin leads to judgment and death. God alone shows us the way to eternal peace. His discipline often keeps us on the right path.

Contemporary prophets
Hosea (753–715)
Isaiah (740–681)

Roll yourself in the dust.
11 Pass by in naked shame, you inhabitant of Shaphir;
The inhabitant of Zaanan does not go out.
Beth Ezel mourns;
Its place to stand is taken away from you.

12 For the inhabitant of Maroth pined for good,
But disaster came down from the LORD
To the gate of Jerusalem.
13 O inhabitant of Lachish,
Harness the chariot to the swift steeds
(She *was* the beginning of sin to the daughter of Zion),
For the transgressions of Israel were found in you.

14 Therefore you shall give presents to Moresheth Gath;
The houses of Achzib *shall be* a lie to the kings of Israel.
15 I will yet bring an heir to you, O inhabitant of Mareshah;

The glory of Israel shall come to Adullam.
16 Make yourself bald and cut off your hair,
Because of your precious children;
Enlarge your baldness like an eagle,
For they shall go from you into captivity.

CHAPTER 2 GOD PUNISHES INJUSTICE.

Woe to those who devise iniquity,
And work out evil on their beds!

IN YOUR DREAMS

2:1-2 Micah spoke out against those who planned evil deeds at ni
and rose at dawn to carry them out. A person's thoughts reflect his
character. What do you think about as you lie down to sleep? Do yo
desires involve greed or stepping on others to achieve your goals? I
thoughts lead to evil deeds as surely as morning follows night.

At morning light they practice it,
Because it is in the power of their hand.
2 They covet fields and take *them* by violence,
Also houses, and seize *them*.
So they oppress a man and his house,
A man and his inheritance.

3 Therefore thus says the LORD:

"Behold, against this family I am devising disaster,
From which you cannot remove your necks;
Nor shall you walk haughtily,
For this *is* an evil time.
4 In that day *one* shall take up a proverb against you,
And lament with a bitter lamentation, saying:
'We are utterly destroyed!
He has changed the heritage of my people;
How He has removed *it* from me!
To a turncoat He has divided our fields.'"

5 Therefore you will have no one to determine boundaries by lot
In the assembly of the LORD.

6 "Do not prattle," *you say to those* who prophesy.
So they shall not prophesy to you;
They shall not return insult for insult.
7 *You who are* named the house of Jacob:
"Is the Spirit of the LORD restricted?
Are these His doings?
Do not My words do good
To him who walks uprightly?

8 "Lately My people have risen up as an enemy—
You pull off the robe with the garment
From those who trust *you,* as they pass by,
Like men returned from war.
9 The women of My people you cast out
From their pleasant houses;
From their children
You have taken away My glory forever.

10 "Arise and depart,
For this *is* not *your* rest;
Because it is defiled, it shall destroy,
Yes, with utter destruction.

11 If a man should walk in a false spirit
   And speak a lie, *saying,*
   'I will prophesy to you of wine and drink,'
   Even he would be the prattler of this people.

12 "I will surely assemble all of you, O Jacob,
   I will surely gather the remnant of Israel;
   I will put them together like sheep of the fold,
   Like a flock in the midst of their pasture;
   They shall make a loud noise because of *so many* people.

13 The one who breaks open will come up before them;
   They will break out,
   Pass through the gate,
   And go out by it;
   Their king will pass before them,
   With the LORD at their head."

CHAPTER 3 GOD PUNISHES THE LEADERS. And I said:

   "Hear now, O heads of Jacob,
   And you rulers of the house of Israel:
   Is it not for you to know justice?

2 You who hate good and love evil;
   Who strip the skin from My people,
   And the flesh from their bones;

3 Who also eat the flesh of My people,
   Flay their skin from them,
   Break their bones,
   And chop *them* in pieces
   Like *meat* for the pot,
   Like flesh in the caldron."

4 Then they will cry to the LORD,
   But He will not hear them;
   He will even hide His face from
      them at that time,
   Because they have been evil in
      their deeds.

5 Thus says the LORD concerning
      the prophets
   Who make my people stray;
   Who chant "Peace"
   While they chew with their teeth,
   But who prepare war against him
   Who puts nothing into their
      mouths:

6 "Therefore you shall have night
      without vision,
   And you shall have darkness
      without divination;
   The sun shall go down on the
      prophets,
   And the day shall be dark for them.

7 So the seers shall be ashamed,
   And the diviners abashed;
   Indeed they shall all cover their lips;
   For *there is* no answer from God."

8 But truly I am full of power by the
      Spirit of the LORD,
   And of justice and might,
   To declare to Jacob his transgression
   And to Israel his sin.

9 Now hear this,
   You heads of the house of Jacob
   And rulers of the house of Israel,

SPIRIT POWER

3:8 Micah attributed the power of his ministry to the spirit of the Lord. Our power comes from the same source. Jesus told his followers they would receive power to witness about him when the Holy Spirit came to them (Acts 1:8). You can't witness effectively by relying on your own strength because fear will keep you from speaking out for God. Only by relying on the power of the Holy Spirit can you live and witness for Jesus.

   Who abhor justice
   And pervert all equity,

10 Who build up Zion with bloodshed
   And Jerusalem with iniquity:

11 Her heads judge for a bribe,
   Her priests teach for pay,
   And her prophets divine for money.
   Yet they lean on the LORD, and say,
   "Is not the LORD among us?
   No harm can come upon us."

12 Therefore because of you
   Zion shall be plowed *like* a field,
   Jerusalem shall become heaps of ruins,
   And the mountain of the temple
   Like the bare hills of the forest.

"Here's what I did..."

It wasn't easy being a Christian in my junior high and high schools. One time, several of the more popular girls were putting down another girl, Nicole, for being a Christian. I didn't think it was right to remain silent, so I said, "So what if she's a Christian? I am, too. Why does that bother you?"

"Because it's weird," one of them said. "I mean, you don't party, you don't fool around with guys, you don't drink—you must lead a pretty boring life." They all laughed.

"Why don't you try it yourself and see how boring it is," I said. They just laughed and made fun of me.

A few days later, I was walking down the hall and one of the girls from that group called out, "What are you going to do for fun today, Christine? Gonna pray on your knees for a couple of hours?" They all laughed. Other people heard and looked at me curiously. I was beginning to feel like a social outcast.

One day, Nicole told me to read Micah 4:6-13. I did, and it helped me a lot. It reminded me that even though these kids who rejected me were considered "cool" by the school, they weren't cool in God's eyes. In the end, God will punish those who disobey him and reward those who seek to obey him. This passage helped take away the pain of being rejected because I stood up for someone else and for my beliefs.

Christine AGE 15

CHAPTER 4   SOMEDAY THE LORD WILL BE KING.

Now it shall come to pass in the latter days
That the mountain of the LORD's house
Shall be established on the top of the mountains,
And shall be exalted above the hills;
And peoples shall flow to it.
2   Many nations shall come and say,
"Come, and let us go up to the mountain of the LORD,
To the house of the God of Jacob;
He will teach us His ways,
And we shall walk in His paths."
For out of Zion the law shall go forth,
And the word of the LORD from Jerusalem.
3   He shall judge between many peoples,
And rebuke strong nations afar off;
They shall beat their swords into plowshares,
And their spears into pruning hooks;
Nation shall not lift up sword against nation,
Neither shall they learn war anymore.

4   But everyone shall sit under his vine and under his
    fig tree,
And no one shall make *them* afraid;
For the mouth of the LORD of hosts has spoken.
5   For all people walk each in the name of his god,
But we will walk in the name of the LORD our God
Forever and ever.

6 "In that day," says the LORD,
"I will assemble the lame,
I will gather the outcast
And those whom I have afflicted;
7   I will make the lame a remnant,
And the outcast a strong nation;
So the LORD will reign over them in Mount Zion
From now on, even forever.
8   And you, O tower of the flock,
The stronghold of the daughter of Zion,
To you shall it come,
Even the former dominion shall come,
The kingdom of the daughter of Jerusalem."

9   Now why do you cry aloud?
Is there no king in your midst?
Has your counselor perished?
For pangs have seized you like a woman in labor.
10   Be in pain, and labor to bring forth,
O daughter of Zion,
Like a woman in birth pangs.
For now you shall go forth from the city,
You shall dwell in the field,
And to Babylon you shall go.
There you shall be delivered;
There the LORD will redeem you
From the hand of your enemies.

11   Now also many nations have gathered against you,
Who say, "Let her be defiled,
And let our eye look upon Zion."
12   But they do not know the thoughts of the LORD,
Nor do they understand His counsel;

For He will gather them like sheaves to the threshing
  floor.

13 "Arise and thresh, O daughter of Zion;
For I will make your horn iron,
And I will make your hooves bronze;
You shall beat in pieces many peoples;
I will consecrate their gain to the LORD,
And their substance to the Lord of the whole earth."

CHAPTER 5   A RULER WILL COME FROM BETHLEHEM.

Now gather yourself in troops,
O daughter of troops;
He has laid siege against us;
They will strike the judge of Israel with a rod on the
  cheek.

CHRISTMAS

5:2 This Ruler is Jesus, the Messiah. Micah accurately predicted C
birthplace hundreds of years before Jesus was born. The promised
eternal King in David's line, who would come to live as a man, had
alive forever—"from of old, from everlasting." Although eternal,
entered human history as the man Jesus of Nazareth.

2 "But you, Bethlehem Ephrathah,
Though you are little among the thousands of Judah,
Yet out of you shall come forth to Me
The One to be Ruler in Israel,
Whose goings forth *are* from of old,
From everlasting."

3   Therefore He shall give them up,
Until the time *that* she who is in labor has given
  birth;
Then the remnant of His brethren
Shall return to the children of Israel.
4   And He shall stand and feed *His flock*
In the strength of the LORD,
In the majesty of the name of the LORD His God;
And they shall abide,
For now He shall be great
To the ends of the earth;
5   And this *One* shall be peace.

When the Assyrian comes into our land,
And when he treads in our palaces,
Then we will raise against him
Seven shepherds and eight princely men.
6   They shall waste with the sword the land of Assyria,
And the land of Nimrod at its entrances;
Thus He shall deliver *us* from the Assyrian,
When he comes into our land
And when he treads within our borders.

7   Then the remnant of Jacob
Shall be in the midst of many peoples,
Like dew from the LORD,
Like showers on the grass,
That tarry for no man
Nor wait for the sons of men.
8   And the remnant of Jacob
Shall be among the Gentiles,

In the midst of many peoples,
Like a lion among the beasts of the forest,
Like a young lion among flocks of sheep,
Who, if he passes through,
Both treads down and tears in pieces,
And none can deliver.
9 Your hand shall be lifted against your adversaries,
And all your enemies shall be cut off.

10 "And it shall be in that day," says the LORD,
"That I will cut off your horses from your midst
And destroy your chariots.
11 I will cut off the cities of your land
And throw down all your strongholds.
12 I will cut off sorceries from your hand,
And you shall have no soothsayers.
13 Your carved images I will also cut off,
And your sacred pillars from your midst;
You shall no more worship the work of your
hands;
14 I will pluck your wooden images from your midst;
Thus I will destroy your cities.
15 And I will execute vengeance in anger and fury
On the nations that have not heard."

CHAPTER **6** GOD'S CASE AGAINST HIS PEOPLE.

Hear now what the LORD says:

"Arise, plead your case before the mountains,
And let the hills hear your voice.
2 Hear, O you mountains, the LORD's complaint,
And you strong foundations of the earth;
For the LORD has a complaint against His people,
And He will contend with Israel.

3 "O My people, what have I done to you?
And how have I wearied you?
Testify against Me.
4 For I brought you up from the land of Egypt,
I redeemed you from the house of bondage;
And I sent before you Moses, Aaron, and Miriam.
5 O My people, remember now
What Balak king of Moab counseled,
And what Balaam the son of Beor answered him,
From Acacia Grove to Gilgal,
That you may know the righteousness of the LORD."

6 With what shall I come before the LORD,
And bow myself before the High God?
Shall I come before Him with burnt offerings,
With calves a year old?
7 Will the LORD be pleased with thousands of rams,
Ten thousand rivers of oil?
Shall I give my firstborn *for* my transgression,
The fruit of my body *for* the sin of my soul?

8 He has shown you, O man, what *is* good;
And what does the LORD require of you
But to do justly,
To love mercy,
And to walk humbly with your God?

9 The LORD's voice cries to the city—

Wisdom shall see Your name:
"Hear the rod!
Who has appointed it?
10 Are there yet the treasures of wickedness
In the house of the wicked,
And the short measure *that is* an abomination?
11 Shall I count pure *those* with the wicked scales,
And with the bag of deceitful weights?
12 For her rich men are full of violence,
Her inhabitants have spoken lies,
And their tongue is deceitful in their mouth.

13 "Therefore I will also make *you* sick by striking you,
By making *you* desolate because of your sins.
14 You shall eat, but not be satisfied;
Hunger *shall be* in your midst.
You may carry *some* away, but shall not save *them;*
And what you do rescue I will give over to the
sword.
15 "You shall sow, but not reap;
You shall tread the olives, but not anoint yourselves
with oil;
And *make* sweet wine, but not drink wine.
16 For the statutes of Omri are kept;
All the works of Ahab's house *are done;*
And you walk in their counsels,
That I may make you a desolation,
And your inhabitants a hissing.
Therefore you shall bear the reproach of My people."

CHAPTER **7** HARD TIMES FOR EVERYONE.

Woe is me!
For I am like those who gather summer fruits,
Like those who glean vintage grapes;
There is no cluster to eat

What does the LORD require of you

BUT

TO DO JUSTLY

to love mercy

AND

to walk humbly

with

YOUR GOD

MICAH 6:8

Of the first-ripe fruit *which* my soul desires.
² The faithful *man* has perished from the earth,
And *there is* no one upright among men.
They all lie in wait for blood;
Every man hunts his brother with a net.

³ That they may successfully do evil with both
hands—
The prince asks *for gifts,*
The judge *seeks* a bribe,
And the great *man* utters his evil desire;
So they scheme together.
⁴ The best of them *is* like a brier;

HONESTY

Terrance needs some new basketball shoes. He's got the perfect pair all picked out—an air-cushioned, super-grip, lightweight model with reinforced ankle supports. The exact shoe all the best dunkers in the NBA wear. Problem is, the shoe costs well over $100.

A few other guys in the neighborhood already have the shoes. One guy who deals drugs has three pairs. Another kid stole some from a locker at school. A third teenager shoplifted his pair. Terrance really wants these new basketball shoes, but he would never do something illegal or dishonest to get them . . . or would he?

This afternoon, a young guy from the neighborhood, who is the assistant manager of a downtown shoe store, came up with a foolproof plan. By marking certain shoes defective, he can cut the price, then cover it all up by juggling some figures.

"It's cool," a friend tells Terrance. "The store makes money, you get your shoes cheap, and you're not stealing."

Terrance thinks long and hard, then decides it's wrong. "It's hard to walk away from such a good deal," Terrance says, "but those shoes aren't worth doing something dishonest."

Meanwhile all his friends are taking advantage of the store's "defective" merchandise.

Read Micah 7:1-4. Do you think Terrance might be feeling the way the prophet Micah felt? How would you have handled his situation?

The most upright *is sharper* than a thorn hedge;
The day of your watchman and your punishment
comes;
Now shall be their perplexity.

⁵ Do not trust in a friend;
Do not put your confidence in a companion;
Guard the doors of your mouth
From her who lies in your bosom.
⁶ For son dishonors father,
Daughter rises against her mother,
Daughter-in-law against her mother-in-law;
A man's enemies *are* the men of his own household.

⁷ Therefore I will look to the LORD;
I will wait for the God of my salvation;
My God will hear me.

⁸ Do not rejoice over me, my enemy;

NOT OK

7:1-4 Micah could not find an upright person anywhere. Upright (honesty, integrity) is hard to find. Society rationalizes sin; Christi sometimes compromise what is right in order to do what they war often we convince ourselves it's OK, especially when "everyone els doing it." But the standards for honesty come from God, not socie is truth, and we are to be like him.

When I fall, I will arise;
When I sit in darkness,
The LORD *will be* a light to me.
⁹ I will bear the indignation of the LORD,
Because I have sinned against Him,
Until He pleads my case
And executes justice for me.
He will bring me forth to the light;
I will see His righteousness.
¹⁰ Then *she who is* my enemy will see,
And shame will cover her who said to me,
"Where is the LORD your God?"
My eyes will see her;
Now she will be trampled down
Like mud in the streets.

¹¹ *In* the day when your walls are to be built,
In that day the decree shall go far and wide.
¹² *In* that day they shall come to you
From Assyria and the fortified cities,
From the fortress to the River,
From sea to sea,
And mountain *to* mountain.
¹³ Yet the land shall be desolate
Because of those who dwell in it,
And for the fruit of their deeds.

¹⁴ Shepherd Your people with Your staff,
The flock of Your heritage,
Who dwell solitarily *in* a woodland,
In the midst of Carmel;
Let them feed *in* Bashan and Gilead,
As in days of old.

¹⁵ "As in the days when you came out of the land of
Egypt,
I will show them wonders."

¹⁶ The nations shall see and be ashamed of all their
might;
They shall put *their* hand over *their* mouth;
Their ears shall be deaf.
¹⁷ They shall lick the dust like a serpent;
They shall crawl from their holes like snakes of the
earth.
They shall be afraid of the LORD our God,
And shall fear because of You.

MERCY

7:18 God delights in showing mercy! He does not forgive grudg but is glad when we repent. He offers forgiveness to all who come back to him. Today you can confess your sins and receive his lovin forgiveness. Don't be too proud to accept God's mercy.

18 Who *is* a God like You,
Pardoning iniquity
And passing over the transgression of the remnant
   of His heritage?

He does not retain His anger forever,
Because He delights *in* mercy.
19 He will again have compassion on us,

And will subdue our iniquities.

You will cast all our sins
Into the depths of the sea.
20 You will give truth to Jacob
And mercy to Abraham,
Which You have sworn to our fathers
From days of old.

MEGA Themes

PERVERTING FAITH God said that he would judge the false prophets, dishonest leaders, and selfish priests in Israel and Judah. While they publicly carried out religious ceremonies, they privately were seeking to gain money and influence. Mixing selfish motives with an empty display of religion perverts faith.

Don't mix your selfish desires with true faith in God. One day God will reveal how foolish it is to substitute anything for loyalty to him. Coming up with your own private blend of religion will pervert your faith.

1. What were the specific sins of the religious leaders? Why were they so offensive to God?
2. What does it mean for someone to pervert the faith today?
3. What can you do to keep your faith pure rather than having it be ruined by self-centered choices?

OPPRESSION Micah predicted ruin for all nations and leaders who were oppressing others. The upper classes oppressed and exploited the poor. Yet no one was speaking against them or doing anything to stop them. God will not put up with such injustice.

We dare not ask God to help us while we ignore those who are needy and oppressed, or silently condone the actions of those who oppress them. Sharing God's love includes meeting the needs of those who are rejected and neglected by society.

1. What types of oppression were present in Micah's day?
2. What types of oppression are found in today's world?
3. What are Christians doing to bring about God's justice for the poor and oppressed people in your community?
4. What could you do to help people become more aware of the poor in your community and God's concern for them?
5. What can you do to help those who are poor and/or oppressed?

PLEASING GOD Micah preached that God's greatest desire was not the offering of sacrifices at the temple. God delights in faith that produces fairness, love to others, and obedience to him.

True faith in God generates kindness, compassion, justice, mercy, and humility. We can please God by seeking these results in our school, family, church, and neighborhood.

1. In Micah, what false ideas did the people have about pleasing God?
2. What false ideas do you see in the world about what it means to please God?
3. List a few examples of individuals you have seen who are truly pleasing God.
4. What ways in your own life do you find to please God?
5. Commit yourself to specific ways that you can be pleasing to God in the next week at school, home, church, and/or work.

Oh no, thought Bobby, *we're going to lose again. 'Supe' is on their side.* "Supe" was Robert Owens, the best athlete in the school. Whichever team got "Supe" always won. Bobby's phys ed class was beginning to play football, and he loved it—except when "Supe" was on the other team. Bobby was good, but "Supe" was great. He could outrun, outthrow, outcatch, out*everything* anyone. ■ Nineveh, the Assyrian capital, was like "Supe." No one had been able to stand against the Assyrians. They had overthrown Israel, and now their sights were on Judah. The people of Judah were afraid; how could they withstand such a terrible enemy? ■ Through Nahum God brought words of comfort to Judah and words of doom to Assyria. He said, "God *is* jealous. . . . He reserves *wrath* for his enemies" (1:2). To Judah God declared, "For now I will break off his yoke from you, and burst your bonds apart" (1:13). To Assyria God announced, "'I *am* against you,' says the LORD of hosts, 'I will burn your chariots . . . and the voice of your messengers shall be heard no more'" (2:13). ■ Such is the end of those who oppose the Lord and hurt his people. God loves his children and will protect them, at all costs. ■ Let Nahum remind you of the futility of fighting against God; let his words encourage you. God protects those whom he loves.

STATS

PURPOSE: To pronounce God's judgment on Assyria and to comfort Judah with this truth

AUTHOR: Nahum

TO WHOM WRITTEN: The people of Nineveh and Judah

DATE WRITTEN: Sometime during Nahum's prophetic ministry (probably between 663 and 612 B.C.)

SETTING: This particular prophecy takes place after the fall of Thebes (No) in 663 B.C. (see 3:8-10)

KEY PLACE: Nineveh, the capital of Assyria

Nahum

8 But with an overflowing flood
   He will make an utter end of its place,
   And darkness will pursue His enemies.

9 What do you conspire against the LORD?
   He will make an utter end *of it.*
   Affliction will not rise up a second time.

10 For while tangled *like* thorns,
   And while drunken *like* drunkards,
   They shall be devoured like stubble fully dried.

11 From you comes forth *one*
   Who plots evil against the LORD,
   A wicked counselor.

12 Thus says the LORD:

   " Though *they are* safe, and likewise
        many,
        Yet in this manner they will be cut down
   When he passes through.
   Though I have afflicted you,
   I will afflict you no more;

13 For now I will break off his yoke from you,
   And burst your bonds apart."

14 The LORD has given a command concerning you:
   "Your name shall be perpetuated no longer.
   Out of the house of your gods

CHAPTER 1 GOD IS PATIENT AND POWERFUL.

The burden against Nineveh. The book of the vision of
Nahum the Elkoshite.

2 God *is* jealous, and the LORD avenges;
   The LORD avenges and *is* furious.
   The LORD will take vengeance on His adversaries,
   And He reserves *wrath* for His enemies;

3 The LORD *is* slow to anger and great in power,
   And will not at all acquit *the wicked.*

   The LORD has His way
   In the whirlwind and in the storm,
   And the clouds *are* the dust of His feet.

4 He rebukes the sea and makes it dry,
   And dries up all the rivers.
   Bashan and Carmel wither,
   And the flower of Lebanon wilts.

5 The mountains quake before Him,
   The hills melt,
   And the earth heaves at His presence,
   Yes, the world and all who dwell in it.

6 Who can stand before His indignation?
   And who can endure the fierceness of His anger?
   His fury is poured out like fire,
   And the rocks are thrown down by Him.

7 The LORD *is* good,
   A stronghold in the day of trouble;
   And He knows those who trust in Him.

▶ TIME'S UP

1:3 God is slow to get angry, but when he is ready to punish, even the
earth trembles. Often people avoid God because they see evildoers in the
world and hypocrites in the church. They don't realize that because God is
slow to anger, he gives his true followers time to share his love and truth
with evildoers. But judgment *will* come; God will not allow sin to go
unchecked forever. When people wonder why God doesn't punish evil
immediately, remind them that if he did, none of us would be here. We
can all be thankful that God gives people time to turn to him.

   I will cut off the carved image and the molded image.
   I will dig your grave,
   For you are vile."

15 Behold, on the mountains
   The feet of him who brings good tidings,
   Who proclaims peace!
   O Judah, keep your appointed feasts,
   Perform your vows.
   For the wicked one shall no more pass through you;
   He is utterly cut off.

CHAPTER 2 NINEVEH WILL FALL.

He who scatters has come up before your face. Man
   the fort!
Watch the road!

Strengthen *your* flanks!
Fortify *your* power mightily.

2 For the LORD will restore the excellence of Jacob
Like the excellence of Israel,
For the emptiers have emptied them out
And ruined their vine branches.

3 The shields of his mighty men *are* made red,
The valiant men *are* in scarlet.

VENGEANCE

Whit is one angry guy. And rightly so. Yesterday before practice he confided in teammates Don and David about his secret attraction to Carolyn, and how he wished he could get up the nerve to ask her to the winter formal.

Not only did Whit's confidants take that information, twist it, and spread embarrassing rumors all over the locker room, but Don went home last night, called Carolyn himself, and asked her to the dance!

All day Whit has wanted to punch Don out, or at the very least, knock his head off in practice this afternoon. He's been daydreaming of ways to get even. Mixed in with his rage is also a measure of hurt. "I thought those guys were my friends."

But at football practice, Whit doesn't react at all. He doesn't yell or scream, he doesn't throw any punches, he even passes up several prime opportunities to hit Don and David with cheap shots and blindsides.

"Just because they were jerks doesn't mean I have to be one, too," he tells a surprised friend later.

When people wrong us, it's natural to want to take revenge. But, like Whit, we need to resist that powerful urge to get even!

The fact is, it's best to leave vengeance in God's hands. He's the One who knows how to handle it the best. See Nahum 1:2-8.

The chariots *come* with flaming torches
In the day of his preparation,
And the spears are brandished.
4 The chariots rage in the streets,
They jostle one another in the broad roads;
They seem like torches,
They run like lightning.

5 He remembers his nobles;
They stumble in their walk;
They make haste to her walls,
And the defense is prepared.
6 The gates of the rivers are opened,
And the palace is dissolved.
7 It is decreed:
She shall be led away captive,
She shall be brought up;
And her maidservants shall lead *her* as with the
voice of doves,
Beating their breasts.
8 Though Nineveh of old *was* like a pool of water,
Now they flee away.
"Halt! Halt!" *they cry;*
But no one turns back.

ANGRY GOD

2:12–3:1 The major source of the Assyrians' wealth was what they stole from other nations. The Assyrians took the food of innocent people to maintain their own luxurious standard of living. They deprived others to supply their excesses. Depriving innocent people to support the luxury of a few is a sin that angers God. Do you ever find yourself willing to take from someone so that you can benefit or have more? As Christians we must stand firm against this common but evil practice.

9 Take spoil of silver!
Take spoil of gold!
There is no end of treasure,
Or wealth of every desirable prize.
10 She is empty, desolate, and waste!
The heart melts, and the knees shake;
Much pain *is* in every side,
And all their faces are drained of color.

11 Where *is* the dwelling of the lions,
And the feeding place of the young lions,
Where the lion walked, the lioness *and* lion's cub,
And no one made *them* afraid?
12 The lion tore in pieces enough for his cubs,
Killed for his lionesses,
Filled his caves with prey,
And his dens with flesh.

13 "Behold, I *am* against you," says the LORD of hosts, "I will burn your chariots in smoke, and the sword shall devour your young lions; I will cut off your prey from the earth, and the voice of your messengers shall be heard no more."

CHAPTER 3 DESTRUCTION.

Woe to the bloody city!
It *is* all full of lies *and* robbery.
Its victim never departs.
2 The noise of a whip
And the noise of rattling wheels,
Of galloping horses,
Of clattering chariots!
3 Horsemen charge with bright sword and glittering
spear.
There is a multitude of slain,
A great number of bodies,
Countless corpses—
They stumble over the corpses—
4 Because of the multitude of harlotries of the
seductive harlot,
The mistress of sorceries,
Who sells nations through her harlotries,
And families through her sorceries.

5 "Behold, I *am* against you," says the LORD of hosts;
"I will lift your skirts over your face,
I will show the nations your nakedness,
And the kingdoms your shame.
6 I will cast abominable filth upon you,
Make you vile,
And make you a spectacle.
7 It shall come to pass *that* all who look upon you
Will flee from you, and say,

'Nineveh is laid waste!
Who will bemoan her?'
Where shall I seek comforters for you?"

8 Are you better than No Amon
That was situated by the River,
That had the waters around her,
Whose rampart *was* the sea,
Whose wall *was* the sea?
9 Ethiopia and Egypt *were* her strength,
And *it was* boundless;
Put and Lubim were your helpers.
10 Yet she *was* carried away,
She went into captivity;
Her young children also were dashed to pieces
At the head of every street;
They cast lots for her honorable men,
And all her great men were bound in chains.
11 You also will be drunk;
You will be hidden;
You also will seek refuge from the enemy.

12 All your strongholds *are* fig trees with ripened figs:
If they are shaken,
They fall into the mouth of the eater.
13 Surely, your people in your midst *are* women!
The gates of your land are wide open for your
enemies;
Fire shall devour the bars of your *gates.*

14 Draw your water for the siege!
Fortify your strongholds!
Go into the clay and tread the mortar!
Make strong the brick kiln!
15 There the fire will devour you,
The sword will cut you off;
It will eat you up like a locust.

Make yourself many—like the locust!
Make yourself many— like the *swarming* locusts!
16 You have multiplied your merchants more than the
stars of heaven.
The locust plunders and flies away.
17 Your commanders *are* like *swarming* locusts,
And your generals like great grasshoppers,
Which camp in the hedges on a cold day;
When the sun rises they flee away,
And the place where they *are* is not known.

18 Your shepherds slumber, O king of Assyria;
Your nobles rest *in the dust.*
Your people are scattered on the mountains,
And no one gathers them.
19 Your injury *has* no healing,
Your wound is severe.
All who hear news of you
Will clap *their* hands over you,
For upon whom has not your wickedness passed
continually?

MEGA Themes

GOD JUDGES God would judge the city of Nineveh for its idolatry, arrogance, and oppression. Although Assyria was the leading military power in the world, God would completely destroy this "invincible" nation. God allows no person or power to assume or scoff at his authority.

Anyone who remains arrogant and resists God's authority will face his anger. No ruler or nation will get away with rejecting him. No individual will be able to hide from his judgment. But those who keep trusting God will be kept safe forever.

1. What sins were leading to Nineveh's punishment?
2. In your world, what things do you see that God will certainly judge in the future?
3. What would you say to a person who lived an ungodly life-style with the attitude, "I can do what I please"?
4. Describe your hope in light of the holiness of God's judgment.

GOD RULES God rules over all the earth, even over those who don't acknowledge him. God is all-powerful, and no one can thwart his plans. God will overcome any who attempt to defy him. Human power is futile against God.

If you are impressed by or afraid of any weapons, armies, or powerful people, remember that God alone can truly rescue you from fear or oppression. We must place our confidence in God because he alone is all powerful.

1. List the most powerful forces that exist in the world today.
2. Which of the forces do you think are the most feared? Why?
3. What does Nahum teach you about God's ability and power to control the awesome forces that so many people fear?
4. How does knowing about God's power make you feel? What difference does it make in how you live?

*I*t was Sunday, and Julie had some questions she wanted answered. She sat in Sunday school listening intently. Each week they had discussed questions that seemed to have no easy answers: Is there a God? If God is so good, why is there suffering in the world? How do we know that people can't get to heaven except by Jesus? ■ But Julie had her own question to ask. Finally, as the room settled down, Julie awkwardly raised her hand. She began, "Why does it seem like those who are trying to live the way Jesus would want them to are so often abused by those who don't care how they live? Doesn't God care? It doesn't seem fair!" ■ Many centuries ago, Habakkuk posed a similar question. He looked over his own country, Judah, and saw that wherever he looked there was "strife, and contention . . . the wicked surround the righteous" (1:3-4). He questioned God's care for those trying to live righteous lives; it seemed the wicked always got the upper hand. ■ God answered Habakkuk. He answered him well enough that Habakkuk replied, "O LORD, I have heard your speech *and* was afraid; O LORD, revive Your work . . . make *it* known; in wrath remember mercy" (3:2). ■ As you read this book, take note of God's answer. It may surprise you. And then, like Habakkuk, resolve to trust God to care for you.

STATS

PURPOSE: To show that God is still in control of the world despite the apparent triumph of evil

AUTHOR: Habakkuk

TO WHOM WRITTEN: Judah (the southern kingdom) and God's people everywhere

DATE WRITTEN: Between 612 and 588 B.C.

SETTING: Babylon was becoming the dominant world power and Judah would soon feel Babylon's destructive force

KEY PEOPLE: Habakkuk, the Chaldeans (Babylonians)

KEY PLACE: Judah

*H*abakkuk

CHAPTER **1** HABAKKUK HAS QUESTIONS FOR GOD.

The burden which the prophet Habakkuk saw.

2 O LORD, how long shall I cry,
   And You will not hear?
   Even cry out to You, "Violence!"
   And You will not save.
3 Why do You show me iniquity,
   And cause *me* to see trouble?
   For plundering and violence *are* before me;
   There is strife, and contention arises.
4 Therefore the law is powerless,
   And justice never goes forth.
   For the wicked surround the righteous;
   Therefore perverse judgment proceeds.

5 "Look among the nations and watch—
   Be utterly astounded!
   For *I will* work a work in your days

Which you would not believe, though it were told
   you.
6 For indeed I am raising up the Chaldeans,
   A bitter and hasty nation
   Which marches through the breadth of the earth,
   To possess dwelling places *that are* not theirs.
7 They are terrible and dreadful;
   Their judgment and their dignity proceed from
      themselves.
8 Their horses also are swifter than leopards,
   And more fierce than evening wolves.
   Their chargers charge ahead;
   Their cavalry comes from afar;

◥▬▬ FORGOTTEN

1:2-4 When circumstances around us become almost unbearable, we
wonder if God has forgotten us. But remember, he is in control. God has a
plan and will judge evildoers in *his* time. If we are truly humble, we will
be willing to accept God's answers and await his timing.

They fly as the eagle *that* hastens to eat.

⁹ "They all come for violence;
   Their faces are set *like* the east wind.
   They gather captives like sand.
¹⁰ They scoff at kings,
   And princes are scorned by them.
   They deride every stronghold,
   For they heap up earthen *mounds* and seize it.
¹¹ Then *his* mind changes, and he transgresses;
   He commits offense,
   Ascribing this power to his god."

¹² Are You not from everlasting,

HARD TIMES

When people drive past the Hunter house, they almost always shake their heads and say: "I just don't understand why one family has had to undergo so much grief." "I know—it's been one crisis after another." "How does Mrs. Hunter keep going? Facing the heartache she's encountered would kill me."

Exaggerations? Not at all.

- Randy, the youngest son, committed suicide two years ago.
- Mr. Hunter had hepatitis, strokes, serious back problems—and finally died last spring.
- The family has faced serious financial problems.
- Nancy, the 18-year-old daughter, has been rebellious and promiscuous. She just moved in with an older, married man.

How *does* Mrs. Hunter keep going? She relies on her faith in God. She keeps clinging to the promise that somehow, some way, God is in control. And in the dark and lonely nights of her ordeals, she keeps hoping that God will one day bring some restoration to her shattered family.

Habakkuk tackles the tough issue of "Where is God when my world is falling apart?" The situation facing the ancient Hebrew prophet was very different from Mrs. Hunter's problems—and probably from yours—but the words of 3:17-19 give hope to all who hurt.

O LORD my God, my Holy One?
We shall not die.
O LORD, You have appointed them for judgment;
O Rock, You have marked them for correction.
¹³ *You are* of purer eyes than to behold evil,
   And cannot look on wickedness.
   Why do You look on those who deal treacherously,
   And hold Your tongue when the wicked devours
   A *person* more righteous than he?
¹⁴ *Why* do You make men like fish of the sea,
   Like creeping things *that have* no ruler over them?

¹⁵ They take up all of them with a hook,
   They catch them in their net,
   And gather them in their dragnet.
   Therefore they rejoice and are glad.
¹⁶ Therefore they sacrifice to their net,
   And burn incense to their dragnet;

WAIT FOR IT

2:3 Evil seems to have the upper hand in the world. Like Habakk Christians often feel angry and discouraged as they see what goes Habakkuk complained vigorously to God about it. God's answer to the same answer he would give us, "Be patient! God will work out plans." It isn't easy to be patient, but it helps to remember that Go hates sin even more than we do. It is certain—sin will be punished God told Habakkuk, "Wait for it." Trusting God fully means trustin even when we don't understand why events occur as they do.

Because by them their share *is* sumptuous
   And their food plentiful.
¹⁷ Shall they therefore empty their net,
   And continue to slay nations without pity?

CHAPTER 2 GOD EXPLAINS HIS WAYS.

I will stand my watch
And set myself on the rampart,
And watch to see what He will say to me,
And what I will answer when I am corrected.

²Then the LORD answered me and said:

"Write the vision
And make *it* plain on tablets,
That he may run who reads it.
³ For the vision *is* yet for an appointed time;
   But at the end it will speak, and it will not lie.
   Though it tarries, wait for it;
   Because it will surely come,
   It will not tarry.

⁴ "Behold the proud,
   His soul is not upright in him;
   But the just shall live by his faith.

⁵ "Indeed, because he transgresses by wine,
   He is a proud man,
   And he does not stay at home.
   Because he enlarges his desire as hell,
   And he *is* like death, and cannot be satisfied,
   He gathers to himself all nations
   And heaps up for himself all peoples.

⁶ "Will not all these take up a proverb against him,

FAMOUS FAITH

2:4 The just (righteous) live by their faith and trust in God. This has inspired countless Christians. Paul refers to it in Romans 1:17 quotes it in Galatians 3:11. The writer of Hebrews quotes it in 10: before the famous chapter on faith. And it is helpful to all Christia must live through difficult times without seeing the outcome. Chri can trust that God is directing all things according to his purposes.

And a taunting riddle against him, and say,
   'Woe to him who increases
   What is not his—how long?
   And to him who loads himself with many pledges'?
⁷ Will not your creditors rise up suddenly?
   Will they not awaken who oppress you?
   And you will become their booty.
⁸ Because you have plundered many nations,

All the remnant of the people shall plunder you,
Because of men's blood
And the violence of the land *and* the city,
And of all who dwell in it.

9 "Woe to him who covets evil gain for his house,
That he may set his nest on high,
That he may be delivered from the power of disaster!
10 You give shameful counsel to your house,
Cutting off many peoples,
And sin *against* your soul.
11 For the stone will cry out from the wall,
And the beam from the timbers will answer it.

12 "Woe to him who builds a town with bloodshed,
Who establishes a city by iniquity!
13 Behold, *is it* not of the LORD of hosts
That the peoples labor to feed the fire,
And nations weary themselves in vain?
14 For the earth will be filled
With the knowledge of the glory of the LORD,
As the waters cover the sea.

15 "Woe to him who gives drink to his neighbor,
Pressing *him to* your bottle,
Even to make *him* drunk,
That you may look on his nakedness!
16 You are filled with shame instead of glory.
You also—drink!
And be exposed as uncircumcised!
The cup of the LORD's right hand *will be* turned
    against you,
And utter shame will be on your glory.
17 For the violence *done to* Lebanon will cover you,
And the plunder of beasts *which* made them afraid,
Because of men's blood
And the violence of the land *and* the city,
And of all who dwell in it.

18 "What profit is the image, that its maker should carve
    it,
The molded image, a teacher of lies,
That the maker of its mold should trust in it,
To make mute idols?
19 Woe to him who says to wood, 'Awake!'
To silent stone, 'Arise! It shall teach!'
Behold, it is overlaid with gold and silver,
Yet in it there is no breath at all.

20 "But the LORD is in His holy temple.
Let all the earth keep silence before Him."

CHAPTER 3 HABAKKUK'S PRAYER. A prayer of Habakkuk the prophet, on Shigionoth.

2 O LORD, I have heard Your speech *and* was afraid;
O LORD, revive Your work in the midst of the years!
In the midst of the years make *it* known;
In wrath remember mercy.

3 God came from Teman,
The Holy One from Mount Paran.   Selah

His glory covered the heavens,

And the earth was full of His praise.
4 *His* brightness was like the light;
He had rays *flashing* from His hand,
And there His power *was* hidden.
5 Before Him went pestilence,
And fever followed at His feet.

6 He stood and measured the earth;
He looked and startled the nations.
And the everlasting mountains were scattered,
The perpetual hills bowed.
His ways *are* everlasting.
7 I saw the tents of Cushan in affliction;
The curtains of the land of Midian trembled.

8 O LORD, were *You* displeased with the rivers,
Was Your anger against the rivers,
Was Your wrath against the sea,
That You rode on Your horses,
Your chariots of salvation?
9 Your bow was made quite ready;
Oaths were sworn over *Your* arrows.   Selah

You divided the earth with rivers.
10 The mountains saw You *and* trembled;
The overflowing of the water passed by.
The deep uttered its voice,
And lifted its hands on high.
11 The sun and moon stood still in their habitation;
At the light of Your arrows they went,
At the shining of Your glittering spear.

12 You marched through the land in indignation;
You trampled the nations in anger.

THE LORD GOD IS MY STRENGTH
HE WILL MAKE MY FEET LIKE DEER'S FEET
AND
He will make me walk on my high hills.

HABAKKUK served as a prophet to Judah from 612–588 B.C.

Climate of the times
Judah's last four kings were wicked men who rejected God and oppressed their own people. Babylon invaded Judah twice before finally destroying it in 586. It was a time of fear, oppression, persecution, lawlessness, and immorality.

Main message
Habakkuk couldn't understand why God seemed to do nothing about the wickedness in society. Then he realized that faith in God alone would supply the answers to his questions.

Importance of message
Instead of questioning the ways of God, we should realize that he is totally just, and we should have faith that he is in control and that one day evil will be utterly destroyed.

Contemporary prophets
Jeremiah (627–586)
Daniel (605–536)
Ezekiel (593–571)

---

¹³ You went forth for the salvation of Your people,
  For salvation with Your Anointed.
  You struck the head from the house of the wicked,
  By laying bare from foundation to neck.　　　Selah

¹⁴ You thrust through with his own arrows
  The head of his villages.

◣AMAZING STRENGTH

3:17-19 Crop failure and the death of animals would devastate Judah. But Habakkuk affirmed that even in the midst of starvation, he would still rejoice in the Lord. Habakkuk's feelings were not controlled by the events around him, but by faith in God's ability to give him strength. When nothing seems to make sense, and when troubles seem more than you can handle, remember that God gives strength. Take your eyes off of your difficulties and look to God.

  They came out like a whirlwind to scatter me;
  Their rejoicing was like feasting on the poor in
      secret.
¹⁵ You walked through the sea with Your horses,
  Through the heap of great waters.

¹⁶ When I heard, my body trembled;
  My lips quivered at *the* voice;
  Rottenness entered my bones;
  And I trembled in myself,

  That I might rest in the day of trouble.
  When he comes up to the people,
  He will invade them with his troops.

¹⁷ Though the fig tree may not blossom,
  Nor fruit be on the vines;
  Though the labor of the olive may fail,
  And the fields yield no food;
  Though the flock may be cut off from the fold,
  And there be no herd in the stalls—

¹⁸ Yet I will rejoice in the LORD,
  I will joy in the God of my salvation.

¹⁹ The LORD God is my strength;
  He will make my feet like deer's *feet*,
  And He will make me walk on my high hills.

  To the Chief Musician. With my stringed instruments.

◣CONFIDENCE

3:19 Habakkuk had asked God why evil people prosper while the righteous suffer. God's answer: they don't, not in the long run. Haba saw his own limitations in contrast to God's unlimited control of all th world's events. God is alive and in control of the world and its events cannot see all that God is doing, and we cannot see all that God will But we can be assured that he is God and will do what is right. Know this brings us confidence and hope in the midst of a confusing world.

MEGA Themes

STRUGGLE AND DOUBT Habakkuk asked God why the people of Judah were not being punished for their sin. He couldn't understand why a just God would allow such evil to exist. God promised to use the Babylonians to punish Judah. When Habakkuk cried out for answers in his time of struggle, God answered him with words of hope.

God wants us to come to him with our struggles and doubts. But his answers may not be what we expect. God sustains us by revealing himself to us. Trusting in him leads to quiet hope, not bitterness, because we do not see the immediate results we want.

1. In chapter 1, how did Habakkuk feel about God?
2. When have you felt that way? How did you deal with your emotions and thoughts during that time?
3. What did Habakkuk do with his emotions and thoughts? How did God respond?
4. Describe Habakkuk's feelings toward God in chapter 3. What had made the difference?
5. When in doubt, a Christian must rely on God's revealed truth, even though it temporarily does not feel as though it is true. How can you build your confidence for those times of doubt and struggle?

GOD'S SOVEREIGNTY Habakkuk asked God why he would use the wicked Babylonians to punish his people. God said that he would also punish the Babylonians after they had fulfilled his purpose.

God is still in control of this world, despite the apparent triumph of evil; God doesn't overlook sin. One day he will rule the whole earth with perfect justice.

1. How did God use Babylon? What made this so difficult for Habakkuk to accept?
2. When is it most difficult for you to understand God's sovereignty?
3. What confuses you about God and his control? What questions would you ask if you could have a direct conversation with him?
4. For now, how does knowing that God is sovereign help you deal with your questions?

HOPE God, the Creator, is all-powerful. God has a plan that he will carry out. God will punish sin. He is our strength and our place of safety. We can have confidence that he will love us and guard our relationship with him forever.

Hope means going beyond our unpleasant daily experiences to the job of knowing God. We live by trusting in him, not in the benefits, happiness, or success we may experience in this life.

1. What can you learn from Habakkuk about hope?
2. How can you build your confidence in God and his love and control in your life?
3. How can you get to really know God?
4. What things do you base your hope on? Do you need to redirect the focus of your hope to God? How can you do that?

*I*t was the day for report cards and parent/teacher meetings—probably the most dreaded day on the school calendar. No classes were held, but appointments were set between student, parents, homeroom teacher, and the most recent report card. What a deadly mix! ■ Most students hated the idea of such a grand gathering, especially those who were not doing well in school. It was one thing to get bad grades, but quite another to sit in a room with three adults and talk about those grades. Parents were known to scream or cry or both. One never knew. At times, the teachers would get emotional, too. Even students who were doing well in school sometimes got reprimanded— they could be doing better. Not many students slept too well the night before meeting day. ■ When the school paper wrote an article about this day (affectionately termed "death day"), the reactions were varied—but most of the student body agreed with one student who was quoted as saying, "I don't think Judgment Day could be any worse!" ■ Well, that student was wrong. Judgment Day will be much worse! God's prophet, Zephaniah, tells us about it in his book. Like "death day," it will be a day of reckoning. Judgment Day will be a time of terrible wrath and punishment—and it will be a time of mercy. ■ As you read Zephaniah, tremble at the awesomeness of God on the day of judgment—and be thankful that he is merciful to those who are faithful to him.

STATS

PURPOSE: To shake the people of Judah out of their complacency and urge them to return to God

AUTHOR: Zephaniah

TO WHOM WRITTEN: Judah and all nations

DATE WRITTEN: Probably near the end of Zephaniah's ministry (640–621 B.C.), when King Josiah's great reforms began

SETTING: King Josiah of Judah was attempting to reverse the evil trends set by the two previous kings—Manasseh and Amon. Josiah extended his influence because there wasn't a strong superpower dominating the world at that time (Assyria was declining rapidly). Zephaniah's prophecy may have been the motivating factor in Josiah's reform. Zephaniah was a contemporary of Jeremiah.

KEY PLACE: Jerusalem

Zephaniah

CHAPTER 1 A GRIM PREDICTION FOR JUDAH.

The word of the LORD which came to Zephaniah the son of Cushi, the son of Gedaliah, the son of Amariah, the son of Hezekiah, in the days of Josiah the son of Amon, king of Judah.

2 "I will utterly consume everything
  From the face of the land,"
  Says the LORD;
3 "I will consume man and beast;
  I will consume the birds of the heavens,
  The fish of the sea,
  And the stumbling blocks along with the wicked.
  I will cut off man from the face of the land,"
  Says the LORD.

4 "I will stretch out My hand against Judah,
  And against all the inhabitants of Jerusalem.
  I will cut off every trace of Baal from this place,
  The names of the idolatrous priests with the *pagan*
    priests—

5 Those who worship the host of heaven on the
    housetops;
  Those who worship and swear *oaths* by the LORD,
  But who *also* swear by Milcom;
6 Those who have turned back from *following* the
    LORD,
  And have not sought the LORD, nor inquired of Him."

7 Be silent in the presence of the Lord GOD;
  For the day of the LORD *is* at hand,
  For the LORD has prepared a sacrifice;
  He has invited His guests.

SHORTSIGHTED

1:2ff The people of Judah were clearly warned by the highest authority of all—God. But they refused to listen, either because they doubted God's prophet and thus did not believe the message was from God, or because they doubted God himself and thus did not believe he would do what he said. If we refuse to listen to God's Word, the Bible, we are as shortsighted as the people of Judah.

8 "And it shall be,
   In the day of the LORD's sacrifice,
   That I will punish the princes and the king's children,
   And all such as are clothed with foreign apparel.
9 In the same day I will punish
   All those who leap over the threshold,
   Who fill their masters' houses with violence and
      deceit.

10 "And there shall be on that day," says the LORD,
   "The sound of a mournful cry from the Fish Gate,
   A wailing from the Second Quarter,
   And a loud crashing from the hills.
11 Wail, you inhabitants of Maktesh!

JUDGMENT

The people of First Church sit in shocked silence as the guest preacher delivers his thundering message of moral decay and imminent judgment.

Point by point, he describes in gripping detail how "our nation has turned its back on God." He cites court decisions, humanistic trends, disturbing statistics, and alarming examples of Christians in this country who are being persecuted by the government.

Afterwards Joey, Skip, and Traci are discussing the evening service over a large pepperoni pizza.

"Do you think that what that preacher said is true?"

"Pretty much."

"So you think this nation is going to be judged by God?"

"Probably so."

"But can't we do anything?"

"I guess if there was a nationwide revival or something like that, maybe God would hold back."

"What are the odds of a revival?"

"I don't know. Who knows what might happen if all the Christians in this town would really get right with God? Just think, if we all started praying and living right and loving people, maybe it would spread. Maybe then things would turn around."

Around 635 B.C. Zephaniah prophesied judgment on the nation of Judah. Read about the only alternative to national (as well as personal) disaster in 1:14—2:3.

For all the merchant people are cut down;
   All those who handle money are cut off.

12 "And it shall come to pass at that time
   That I will search Jerusalem with lamps,
   And punish the men
   Who are settled in complacency,
   Who say in their heart,
   'The LORD will not do good,
   Nor will He do evil.'
13 Therefore their goods shall become booty,
   And their houses a desolation;
   They shall build houses, but not inhabit them;
   They shall plant vineyards, but not drink their wine."

14 The great day of the LORD is near;
   It is near and hastens quickly.

The noise of the day of the LORD is bitter;
   There the mighty men shall cry out.
15 That day is a day of wrath,
   A day of trouble and distress,
   A day of devastation and desolation,
   A day of darkness and gloominess,
   A day of clouds and thick darkness,
16 A day of trumpet and alarm
   Against the fortified cities
   And against the high towers.

17 "I will bring distress upon men,
   And they shall walk like blind men,
   Because they have sinned against the LORD;
   Their blood shall be poured out like dust,
   And their flesh like refuse."

18 Neither their silver nor their gold
   Shall be able to deliver them
   In the day of the LORD's wrath;
   But the whole land shall be devoured
   By the fire of His jealousy,
   For He will make speedy riddance
   Of all those who dwell in the land.

CHAPTER 2 CHANGE AND GOD MAY SAVE YOU.

Gather yourselves together, yes, gather together,
   O undesirable nation,
2 Before the decree is issued,
   Or the day passes like chaff,
   Before the LORD's fierce anger comes upon you,
   Before the day of the LORD's anger comes upon you!
3 Seek the LORD, all you meek of the earth,
   Who have upheld His justice.
   Seek righteousness, seek humility.
   It may be that you will be hidden
   In the day of the LORD's anger.

4 For Gaza shall be forsaken,
   And Ashkelon desolate;
   They shall drive out Ashdod at noonday,
   And Ekron shall be uprooted.
5 Woe to the inhabitants of the seacoast,
   The nation of the Cherethites!
   The word of the LORD is against you,
   O Canaan, land of the Philistines:
   "I will destroy you;
   So there shall be no inhabitant."

6 The seacoast shall be pastures,
   With shelters for shepherds and folds for flocks.
7 The coast shall be for the remnant of the house of
      Judah;
   They shall feed their flocks there;

DAD KNOWS

2:7 Though God said he would destroy Judah, he also promised to a remnant, thus keeping his original covenant to preserve Abraham descendants (Genesis 17:4-8). God is holy and can't allow sin to co but he also is faithful to his promises. He cannot stay angry with Is with you if you are his child. Like a good parent, he loves his childr always seeks their good.

In the houses of Ashkelon they shall lie down at
  evening.
For the LORD their God will intervene for them,
And return their captives.

8 "I have heard the reproach of Moab,
  And the insults of the people of Ammon,
  With which they have reproached My people,
  And made arrogant threats against their borders."
9 Therefore, as I live,"
  Says the LORD of hosts, the God of Israel,
  "Surely Moab shall be like Sodom,
  And the people of Ammon like Gomorrah—
  Overrun with weeds and saltpits,
  And a perpetual desolation.
  The residue of My people shall plunder them,
  And the remnant of My people shall possess them."

10 This they shall have for their pride,
  Because they have reproached and made arrogant
    threats
  Against the people of the LORD of hosts.
11 The LORD *will be* awesome to them,
  For He will reduce to nothing all the gods of the
    earth;
  People shall worship Him,
  Each one from his place,
  Indeed all the shores of the nations.

12 "You Ethiopians also,
  You shall be slain by My sword."

13 And He will stretch out His hand against the north,
  Destroy Assyria,
  And make Nineveh a desolation,
  As dry as the wilderness.
14 The herds shall lie down in her midst,
  Every beast of the nation.
  Both the pelican and the bittern
  Shall lodge on the capitals *of* her *pillars;*
  Their voice shall sing in the windows;
  Desolation *shall be* at the threshold;
  For He will lay bare the cedar work.
15 This is the rejoicing city
  That dwelt securely,
  That said in her heart,
  "I *am it,* and *there is* none besides me."
  How has she become a desolation,
  A place for beasts to lie down!
  Everyone who passes by her
  Shall hiss and shake his fist.

CHAPTER **3** JUDGMENT FOR JERUSALEM.
Woe to her who is rebellious and polluted,
  To the oppressing city!
2 She has not obeyed *His* voice,
  She has not received correction;
  She has not trusted in the LORD,
  She has not drawn near to her God.

3 Her princes in her midst *are* roaring lions;
  Her judges *are* evening wolves
  That leave not a bone till morning.

4 Her prophets are insolent, treacherous people;
  Her priests have polluted the sanctuary,
  They have done violence to the law.
5 The LORD *is* righteous in her midst,
  He will do no unrighteousness.
  Every morning He brings His justice to light;
  He never fails,
  But the unjust knows no shame.

CLOSED EARS

3:2 Do you know people who refuse to listen when someone disagrees with their opinions? Those who are proud often refuse to listen to anything that contradicts their inflated self-esteem, and God's people had become so proud that they would not hear or accept God's correction. Do you find it difficult to listen to the spiritual counsel of others or God's words from the Bible? You will be more willing to listen when you consider how weak and sinful you really are.

6 "I have cut off nations,
  Their fortresses are devastated;
  I have made their streets desolate,
  With none passing by.
  Their cities are destroyed;
  There is no one, no inhabitant.
7 I said, 'Surely you will fear Me,
  You will receive instruction'—
  So that her dwelling would not be cut off,
  Despite everything for which I punished her.
  But they rose early and corrupted all their deeds.

8 "Therefore wait for Me," says the LORD,
  "Until the day I rise up for plunder;
  My determination *is* to gather the nations
  To My assembly of kingdoms,
  To pour on them My indignation,
  All My fierce anger;
  All the earth shall be devoured
  With the fire of My jealousy.

9 "For then I will restore to the peoples a pure language,
  That they all may call on the name of the LORD,
  To serve Him with one accord.
10 From beyond the rivers of Ethiopia
  My worshipers,
  The daughter of My dispersed ones,
  Shall bring My offering.
11 In that day you shall not be shamed for any of your
    deeds
  In which you transgress against Me;
  For then I will take away from your midst
  Those who rejoice in your pride,
  And you shall no longer be haughty
  In My holy mountain.
12 I will leave in your midst
  A meek and humble people,

BE BLESSED

3:12 God is opposed to the proud and haughty of every generation. But the meek and humble, both physically and spiritually, will be blessed because they trust in God. Self-reliance and arrogance have no place among God's people or in his kingdom.

ZEPHANIAH

served as a prophet to Judah
from 640–621 B.C.

Climate of the times
Josiah was the last good king in Judah. His bold
attempts to reform the nation and turn it back to God
were probably influenced by Zephaniah.

Main message
A day will come when God, as Judge, will
severely punish all nations. But after judgment,
he will show mercy to all who have been
faithful to him.

Importance of message
We all will be judged for our disobedience to
God—but if we remain faithful to him, he will show
us mercy.

**Contemporary
prophet**
Jeremiah (627–586)

And they shall trust in the name of the LORD.
13 The remnant of Israel shall do no unrighteousness
And speak no lies,
Nor shall a deceitful tongue be found in their mouth;
For they shall feed *their* flocks and lie down,
And no one shall make *them* afraid."

14 Sing, O daughter of Zion!
Shout, O Israel!
Be glad and rejoice with all *your* heart,
O daughter of Jerusalem!
15 The LORD has taken away your judgments,
He has cast out your enemy.
The King of Israel, the LORD, *is* in your midst;
You shall see disaster no more.

16 In that day it shall be said to Jerusalem:
"Do not fear;
Zion, let not your hands be weak.
17 The LORD your God in your midst,
The Mighty One, will save;
He will rejoice over you with gladness,
He will quiet *you* with His love,
He will rejoice over you with singing."

18 "I will gather those who sorrow over the appointed
assembly,
Who are among you,
To whom its reproach *is* a burden.
19 Behold, at that time
I will deal with all who afflict you;
I will save the lame,
And gather those who were driven out;
I will appoint them for praise and fame
In every land where they were put to shame.
20 At that time I will bring you back,
Even at the time I gather you;
For I will give you fame and praise
Among all the peoples of the earth,
When I return your captives before your eyes,"
Says the LORD.

Do not fear...
**THE LORD
YOUR GOD**
IN YOUR MIDST
THE MIGHTY ONE
will save
He will rejoice over you
with gladness
He will quiet you
with His love

ZEPHANIAH 3:16-17

MEGA Themes

DAY OF JUDGMENT Destruction was coming because Judah had forsaken the Lord. The people worshiped Baal, Milcom (Molech), and nature. Even the priests mixed heathen practices with faith in God. God's punishment for sin was on the way.

To escape God's judgment we must listen to him, accept his correction, trust him, and seek his guidance. If we accept God as our Lord, we will escape his condemnation.

1. What is God's attitude toward worshiping idols? Why do you think he has such an intense response to this false worship?
2. In what ways do people worship false idols in today's world?
3. Based upon this study, how can worshipers of false idols expect God to respond?
4. What are the consequences for Christians who replace God with contemporary idols? What can you do to prevent this from happening in your life?

INDIFFERENCE TO GOD Although there had been occasional attempts at renewal, Judah had no sorrow for her sins. The people were prosperous and no longer cared about God. God's demands for righteous living seemed irrelevant to the people of Judah, whose security and wealth made them complacent.

Don't let material comfort be a barrier to your commitment to God. Prosperity can produce an attitude of proud self-sufficiency. The only answer is to admit that money won't save us and that we cannot save ourselves. Only God can save us and cure our indifference to spiritual matters.

1. How did prosperity hinder the people's repentance?
2. Do you agree or disagree with this statement: "Prosperity is a false sense of security"? Explain.
3. What tempts you to become indifferent to God?
4. Do you need to sell all your possessions and give up everything you enjoy in order to avoid becoming indifferent to God? Explain.

DAY OF JOY The day of judgment will also be a day of joy. God will judge all those who mistreat his people. He will purify his people, purging all sin and evil. God will restore his people and give them hope.

When people are purged of sin, there is great relief and hope. No matter how difficult our experience now, we can look forward to the day of celebration when God will completely restore us.

1. Condemnation is not inevitable because of God's gift of Jesus. How does Jesus provide hope for a day of great joy?
2. When you think about the hope you have in Jesus and the destiny that would be yours without Jesus, how do you feel about God?
3. What difference does this hope make in your daily life as a Christian?

*H*al and Jimmy were camping. Actually, they were in Jimmy's backyard, but it was a big backyard. You could barely see the lights in the house from their tent. On "camping nights" Hal and Jimmy would talk. Their conversations sometimes went on and on. Of course, the topic often was girls, but sometimes they discussed other things. ■ "Jimmy," Hal asked, "if you had to give up everything but one thing in your life, what would you keep?" Hal was not very serious most of the time, but he was that night. ■ "I'd have to give up everything?" Jimmy responded. ■ "All but one thing. What's the most important thing to you?" Hal really was being serious. ■ Jimmy thought and answered, "I can narrow it down to three. I would keep my family, Becky (the girl he just started liking), and my TV." ■ "What about God?" Hal questioned. "You would give him up for Becky?" ■ "Oh," laughed Jimmy, "I didn't even think about God." ■ The Jews, who had returned from captivity, were like Jimmy—they'd forgotten about God. They had let him slip from their life. So God sent Haggai, a prophet, to remind them of what is really important in life. ■ God refuses to be forgotten. He demanded priority in the Jews' life, and he demands priority in our life. As you read the book of Haggai, notice how God blesses those who make him number one. Then ask God to help you live with him in first place.

STATS

PURPOSE: To call the people to complete the rebuilding of the temple

AUTHOR: Haggai

TO WHOM WRITTEN: The people living in Jerusalem and those who had returned from exile

DATE WRITTEN: 520 B.C.

SETTING: The temple in Jerusalem had been destroyed in 586 B.C. Cyrus allowed the Jews to return to their homeland and rebuild their temple in 538 B.C. They began the work but were unable to complete it. During the ministry of Haggai and Zechariah, the temple was completed (520–515 B.C.).

KEY PEOPLE: Haggai, Zerubbabel, Joshua

KEY PLACE: Jerusalem

SPECIAL FEATURES: Haggai was the first of the postexilic prophets. The other two were Zechariah and Malachi. The literary style of this book is simple and direct.

Haggai

CHAPTER 1 LET'S REBUILD THE TEMPLE. In the second year of King Darius, in the sixth month, on the first day of the month, the word of the LORD came by Haggai the prophet to Zerubbabel the son of Shealtiel, governor of Judah, and to Joshua the son of Jehozadak, the high priest, saying, ²"Thus speaks the LORD of hosts, saying: 'This people says, "The time has not come, the time that the LORD's house should be built."'"

³Then the word of the LORD came by Haggai the prophet, saying, ⁴"*Is it* time for you yourselves to dwell in your paneled houses, and this temple *to lie* in ruins?" ⁵Now therefore, thus says the LORD of hosts: "Consider your ways!

⁶ "You have sown much, and bring in little;
  You eat, but do not have enough;
  You drink, but you are not filled with drink;
  You clothe yourselves, but no one is warm;
  And he who earns wages,
  Earns wages *to put* into a bag with holes."

⁷Thus says the LORD of hosts: "Consider your ways! ⁸Go up to the mountains and bring wood and build the temple, that I may take pleasure in it and be glorified," says the LORD. ⁹"*You* looked for much, but indeed *it came to* little; and when you brought it home, I blew it away. Why?" says the LORD of hosts. "Because of My house that *is in* ruins, while every one of you runs to his own house. ¹⁰Therefore the heavens above you withhold the dew, and the earth withholds its fruit. ¹¹For I called for a drought on the land and the mountains, on the grain and the new wine and the oil, on whatever the ground brings forth, on men and livestock, and on all the labor of *your* hands."

¹²Then Zerubbabel the son of Shealtiel, and Joshua the son of Jehozadak, the high priest, with all the remnant of the people, obeyed the voice of the LORD their God, and the words of Haggai the prophet, as the LORD their God had sent him; and the people feared the presence of the LORD. ¹³Then Haggai, the LORD's messenger, spoke the LORD's message to the people, saying, "I *am* with you,

▶PRIORITIES

1:9 Judah's problem was confused priorities. Like Judah, our priorities relating to work, family, and God's work often are mixed up. Friends, possessions, and fun may rank higher on our list of importance than God. What is most important to you? Where does God rank?

says the LORD." ¹⁴So the LORD stirred up the spirit of Zerubbabel the son of Shealtiel, governor of Judah, and the spirit of Joshua the son of Jehozadak, the high priest, and the spirit of all the remnant of the people; and they came and worked on the house of the LORD of hosts, their God, ¹⁵on the twenty-fourth day of the sixth month, in the second year of King Darius.

CHAPTER 2 PROMISES TO BLESS GOD'S PEOPLE. In the seventh *month*, on the twenty-first of the month, the word of the LORD came by Haggai the prophet, saying: ²"Speak now to Zerubbabel the son of Shealtiel, governor of Judah, and to Joshua the son of Jehozadak, the high priest, and to the remnant of the people, saying: ³'Who is left among you who saw this temple in its former glory? And how do you see it now? In comparison with it, *is this* not in your eyes as nothing? ⁴Yet now be strong, Zerubbabel,' says the LORD; 'and be strong, Joshua, son of Jehozadak, the high priest; and be strong, all you people of the land,' says the LORD, 'and work; for I *am* with you,' says

SATISFACTION

With nothing more demanding to do than catch rays at the Fairfield Swim Club in early August, 15-year-old Melissa is bored silly. She'd been looking forward to summer ever since the first winter storm (and since her first day in algebra). She'd had big plans to relax and sleep late and have fun—to enjoy three months of doing whatever she wanted.

Now here she sits, frustrated and unsatisfied. She's done a ton of things in the last two months, but summer hasn't been nearly as exciting as she'd imagined it would be. *Something's missing,* she thinks as she sips her diet cola and watches the clouds form shapes against the crystal blue sky.

Two thousand miles away, 14-year-old Greg is drenched in sweat. Along with 19 other teens from his youth group, he's helping to build a church in a poor village near the Texas-Mexico border. It's backbreaking work, the living conditions are brutal, the food is . . . well, not exactly gourmet fare.

Yet Greg and his friends are having the time of their life serving God and serving the Mexican people.

What a paradox! When we chase after satisfaction, we inevitably find frustration. When we stop trying to find personal fulfillment and give our life away in service to God, we find indescribable joy. See Haggai 1 for another example of this truth.

---

the LORD of hosts. ⁵*According to* the word that I covenanted with you when you came out of Egypt, so My Spirit remains among you; do not fear!'

⁶"For thus says the LORD of hosts: 'Once more (it *is* a little while) I will shake heaven and earth, the sea and dry land; ⁷and I will shake all nations, and they shall come to the Desire of All Nations, and I will fill this temple with glory,' says the LORD of hosts. ⁸'The silver *is* Mine, and the gold *is* Mine,' says the LORD of hosts. ⁹'The glory of this latter temple shall be greater than the former,' says the LORD of hosts. 'And in this place I will give peace,' says the LORD of hosts."

---

¹⁰On the twenty-fourth *day* of the ninth *month,* in the second year of Darius, the word of the LORD came by Haggai the prophet, saying, ¹¹"Thus says the LORD of hosts: 'Now, ask the priests *concerning the* law, saying,

TOXIC

2:10-19 The example given in this message (delivered in Decer 520 B.C.) makes it clear that holiness will not rub off on others, but contamination will. Now that the people were beginning to obey G promised to bless them. But they needed to understand that activi the temple would not clean up their sin; only repentance and obed could do that. If we insist on harboring wrong or "toxic" attitudes sins, or on maintaining close relationships with sinful people, we w contaminated. Holy living will come only when we are empowered God's Holy Spirit. How toxic are you?

¹²"If one carries holy meat in the fold of his garment, and with the edge he touches bread or stew, wine or oil, or any food, will it become holy?" '"

Then the priests answered and said, "No."

¹³And Haggai said, "If *one who is* unclean *because* of a dead body touches any of these, will it be unclean?"

So the priests answered and said, "It shall be unclean."

¹⁴Then Haggai answered and said, " 'So is this people, and so is this nation before Me,' says the LORD, 'and so is every work of their hands; and what they offer there is unclean.

¹⁵And now, carefully consider from this day forward:

CHOSEN

2:23 God closes his message to Zerubbabel with this tremendous affirmation: "I have chosen you." Such a proclamation is ours as well—each of us has been chosen b God (Ephesians 1:4). This truth should make us see our valu God's eyes and motivate us to work for him. When you feel down, remind yourself, "God has chosen me!"

HAGGAI
served as a prophet to Judah about 520 B.C. after the return from exile.

Climate of the times
The people of Judah had been exiled to Babylon in 586 B.C. and Jerusalem and the temple had been destroyed. Under Cyrus, king of Persia, the Jews were allowed to return to Judah and rebuild their temple.

Main message
The people had returned to Jerusalem to begin rebuilding the temple, but they stopped. Haggai's message encouraged the people to finish rebuilding God's temple.

Importance of message
The temple lay half-finished while the people lived in beautiful homes. Haggai warned them against putting their possessions and jobs ahead of God. We must put God first in our life.

Contemporary prophet
Zechariah (520–480)

from before stone was laid upon stone in the temple of the LORD— ¹⁶since those *days,* when *one* came to a heap of twenty ephahs, there were *but* ten; when *one* came to the wine vat to draw out fifty baths from the press, there were *but* twenty. ¹⁷I struck you with blight and mildew and hail in all the labors of your hands; yet you did not *turn* to Me,' says the LORD. ¹⁸Consider now from this day forward, from the twenty-fourth day of the ninth month, from the day that the foundation of the LORD's temple was laid—consider it: ¹⁹Is the seed still in the barn? As yet the vine, the fig tree, the pomegranate, and the olive tree have not yielded *fruit. But* from this day I will bless *you.'* "

²⁰And again the word of the LORD came to Haggai on the twenty-fourth day of the month, saying, ²¹"Speak to Zerubbabel, governor of Judah, saying:

'I will shake heaven and earth.
²² I will overthrow the throne of kingdoms;
I will destroy the strength of the Gentile kingdoms.
I will overthrow the chariots
And those who ride in them;
The horses and their riders shall come down,
Every one by the sword of his brother.

²³'In that day,' says the LORD of hosts, 'I will take you, Zerubbabel My servant, the son of Shealtiel,' says the LORD, 'and will make you like a signet *ring;* for I have chosen you,' says the LORD of hosts."

MEGA Themes

RIGHT PRIORITIES God had given the Jews the assignment to finish the temple in Jerusalem when they returned from captivity. But after 15 years, they still had not completed it. They were more concerned about building their own homes than about finishing God's work. Haggai told them to get their priorities straight.

It is easy to make other activities more important than doing God's work. But God wants us to build his kingdom. Don't stop and don't make excuses. Set your heart on what is right and do it. Get your priorities straight by centering them on Christ.

1. How had the people begun to live in Jerusalem (their life-style)? Contrast this life-style with the way they lived when they first returned from captivity.
2. What had happened in the past 15 years that changed their priorities?
3. What are your priorities?
4. How have your priorities changed in the past five years? The past year?
5. As you think about the next five years, what do you think will be God's challenge to you about right priorities?

GOD'S ENCOURAGEMENT Haggai encouraged the people as they worked, assuring them of the presence of the Holy Spirit, of final victory, and the future reign of the Messiah.

If God gives you a task, don't be afraid to get started. His resources are infinite. God will help you complete it by giving you encouragement from others along the way.

1. What do you find in 2:14-19 that served as an encouragement to the people?
2. How would you expect such encouragement to affect them?
3. Think of two instances in which someone's encouragement made a real difference in your life. What did he or she do or say? Why was this so important to you at the time?
4. Think of two people who could use encouragement, especially in their relationship with God. Develop a plan for being God's encourager to them.

Look into my eyes. I see a shadow . . . the future doesn't look good. But now the shadow is passing. Ah yes, now it looks much better. . . ." ■ Almost everyone wants to know the future. Some people fear the future, wondering what evils lurk around the corner; others consult fortune-tellers, astrologers, and other future-telling charlatans who make a living providing personal prophecies. ■ But tomorrow's story is known only by God and by those special messengers, the prophets, to whom he has revealed a chapter or two. A prophet's job was to proclaim the word of the Lord, point out sin, explain its consequences, and point men and women to God. ■ Nestled here, among what are known as the Minor Prophets, is the book of Zechariah. As one of God's spokesmen, Zechariah ministered to the small group of Jews who had returned to Judah to rebuild the temple and the nation. Zechariah encouraged them, but his message went far beyond. Zechariah gave a spectacular and graphic telling of the Messiah, the one whom God would send to rescue his people and reign over the earth. ■ Zechariah is an important prophetic book because it gives detailed messianic references that were clearly fulfilled in Jesus. Jesus *is* the Messiah, the promised great deliverer of Israel, and the only hope for humankind. ■ God knows and controls the future. We may never see a moment ahead, but we can be secure if we trust in him. Read Zechariah and strengthen your faith in God—he alone is your hope and security.

STATS

PURPOSE: To give hope to God's people by revealing God's future deliverance through the Messiah

AUTHOR: Zechariah

TO WHOM WRITTEN: The Jews in Jerusalem who had returned from their captivity in Babylon and to God's people everywhere

DATE WRITTEN: Chapters 1–8 were written about 520–518 B.C. Chapters 9–14 were written around 480 B.C.

SETTING: The exiles had returned from Babylon to rebuild the temple, but the work had been thwarted and stalled. Haggai and Zechariah confronted the people with their task and encouraged them to complete it.

KEY PEOPLE: Zerubbabel, Joshua

KEY PLACE: Jerusalem

SPECIAL FEATURES: This book is the most apocalyptic and messianic of all the Minor Prophets.

Zechariah

CHAPTER 1 RETURN TO THE LORD. In the eighth month of the second year of Darius, the word of the LORD came to Zechariah the son of Berechiah, the son of Iddo the prophet, saying, ²"The LORD has been very angry with your fathers. ³Therefore say to them, 'Thus says the LORD of hosts: "Return to Me," says the LORD of hosts, "and I will return to you," says the LORD of hosts. ⁴"Do not be like your fathers, to whom the former prophets preached, saying, 'Thus says the LORD of hosts: "Turn now from your evil ways and your evil deeds." ' But they did not hear nor heed Me," says the LORD.

⁵ "Your fathers, where *are* they?
And the prophets, do they live forever?
⁶ Yet surely My words and My statutes,
Which I commanded My servants the prophets,
Did they not overtake your fathers?

"So they returned and said:

'Just as the LORD of hosts determined to do to us,
According to our ways and according to our deeds,
So He has dealt with us.' "

⁷On the twenty-fourth day of the eleventh month, which is the month Shebat, in the second year of Darius, the word of the LORD came to Zechariah the son of Berechiah, the son of Iddo the prophet: ⁸I saw by night, and behold, a man riding on a red horse, and it stood among the myrtle trees in the hollow; and behind him *were* horses: red, sorrel, and white. ⁹Then I said, "My lord, what *are* these?" So the angel who talked with me said to me, "I will show you what they *are*."

¹⁰And the man who stood among the myrtle trees answered and said, "These *are the ones* whom the LORD has sent to walk to and fro throughout the earth."

HEREDITY

1:2-3 The familiar phrase "Like father, like son" implies that children turn out like their parents. But God warned Israel *not* to be like their fathers who disobeyed him and reaped the consequences—his judgment. We are responsible before God for our actions. We aren't trapped by our heredity or environment, and we can't use these as excuses for our sins. We can choose, and we must individually return to God and follow him.

1:13 God's people had lived under his judgment for 70 years during their captivity in Babylon. But here God spoke words of comfort and assurance. God promises that when we return to him, he will heal us (Hosea 6:1). If you feel wounded and torn by the events of your life, turn to God so he can heal and comfort you.

[11]So they answered the Angel of the LORD, who stood among the myrtle trees, and said, "We have walked to and fro throughout the earth, and behold, all the earth is resting quietly." [12]Then the Angel of the LORD answered and said, "O LORD of hosts, how long will You not have mercy on Jerusalem and on the cities of Judah, against which You were angry these seventy years?" [13]And the LORD answered the angel who talked to me, *with* good *and* comforting words. [14]So the angel who

---

ZECHARIAH
served as a prophet to Judah about 520 B.C., after the return from exile.

Climate of the times
The exiles had returned from captivity to rebuild their temple. But work on the temple had stalled, and the people were neglecting their service to God.

Main message
Zechariah, like Haggai, encouraged the people to finish rebuilding the temple. His visions gave the people hope. He told the people of a future king who one day would establish an eternal kingdom.

Importance of message
Even in times of discouragement and despair, God is working out his plan. God protects and guides us; we must trust and follow him.

Contemporary prophet Haggai (about 520 B.C.)

spoke with me said to me, "Proclaim, saying, 'Thus says the LORD of hosts:

"I am zealous for Jerusalem
  And for Zion with great zeal.
[15] I am exceedingly angry with the nations at ease;
  For I was a little angry,
  And they helped—*but* with evil *intent*."

[16]"Therefore thus says the LORD:

"I am returning to Jerusalem with mercy;
  My house shall be built in it," says the LORD of hosts,
"And a *surveyor's* line shall be stretched out over
  Jerusalem." '

[17]"Again proclaim, saying, 'Thus says the LORD of hosts:

"My cities shall again spread out through prosperity;
  The LORD will again comfort Zion,
  And will again choose Jerusalem." ' "

[18]Then I raised my eyes and looked, and there *were* four horns. [19]And I said to the angel who talked with me, "What *are* these?"

So he answered me, "These *are* the horns that have scattered Judah, Israel, and Jerusalem."

[20]Then the LORD showed me four craftsmen. [21]And I said, "What are these coming to do?"

So he said, "These *are* the horns that scattered Judah, so that no one could lift up his head; but the craftsmen are coming to terrify them, to cast out the horns of the nations that lifted up *their* horn against the land of Judah to scatter it."

CHAPTER **2** A MAN WITH A MEASURING LINE.
Then I raised my eyes and looked, and behold, a man with a measuring line in his hand. [2]So I said, "Where are you going?"

And he said to me, "To measure Jerusalem, to see what *is* its width and what *is* its length."

[3]And there *was* the angel who talked with me, going out; and another angel was coming out to meet him, [4]who said to him, "Run, speak to this young man, saying: 'Jerusalem shall be inhabited *as* towns without walls, because of the multitude of men and livestock in it. [5]For I,' says the LORD, 'will be a wall of fire all around her, and I will be the glory in her midst.' "

[6]"Up, up! Flee from the land of the north," says the LORD; "for I have spread you abroad like the four winds of heaven," says the LORD. [7]Up, Zion! Escape, you who dwell with the daughter of Babylon.

[8]For thus says the LORD of hosts: "He sent Me after glory, to the nations which plunder you; for he who

━━━━━**HELPING GOD**

2:8 Believers are precious to God (Psalm 116:15); they are his very own children (Psalm 103:13). Treating any believer unkindly is the sc as treating God that way. As Jesus told his disciples, when we help oth we are helping him; when we neglect them we are neglecting him (Matthew 25:34-46). Be careful, therefore, how you treat fellow believers—that is the way you are treating God.

touches you touches the apple of His eye. ⁹For surely I will shake My hand against them, and they shall become spoil for their servants. Then you will know that the LORD of hosts has sent Me.

¹⁰"Sing and rejoice, O daughter of Zion! For behold, I am coming and I will dwell in your midst," says the LORD. ¹¹"Many nations shall be joined to the LORD in that day, and they shall become My people. And I will dwell in your midst. Then you will know that the LORD of hosts has sent Me to you. ¹²And the LORD will take possession of Judah as His inheritance in the Holy Land, and will again choose Jerusalem. ¹³Be silent, all flesh, before the LORD, for He is aroused from His holy habitation!"

CHAPTER 3 ZECHARIAH SEES THE HIGH PRIEST.

Then he showed me Joshua the high priest standing before the Angel of the LORD, and Satan standing at his right hand to oppose him. ²And the LORD said to Satan, "The LORD rebuke you, Satan! The LORD who has chosen Jerusalem rebuke you! *Is* this not a brand plucked from the fire?"

³Now Joshua was clothed with filthy garments, and was standing before the Angel.

⁴Then He answered and spoke to those who stood before Him, saying, "Take away the filthy garments from him." And to him He said, "See, I have removed your iniquity from you, and I will clothe you with rich robes."

⁵And I said, "Let them put a clean turban on his head."

So they put a clean turban on his head, and they put the clothes on him. And the Angel of the LORD stood by.

⁶Then the Angel of the LORD admonished Joshua, saying, ⁷"Thus says the LORD of hosts:

'If you will walk in My ways,

And if you will keep My command,
Then you shall also judge My house,
And likewise have charge of My courts;
I will give you places to walk
Among these who stand here.

⁸ 'Hear, O Joshua, the high priest,
You and your companions who sit before you,
For they are a wondrous sign;
For behold, I am bringing forth My Servant the
      BRANCH.
⁹ For behold, the stone
That I have laid before Joshua:
Upon the stone *are* seven eyes.
Behold, I will engrave its inscription,'
Says the LORD of hosts,
'And I will remove the iniquity of that land in one day.
¹⁰ In that day,' says the LORD of hosts,
'Everyone will invite his neighbor
Under his vine and under his fig tree.'"

CHAPTER 4 THE GOLDEN LAMPSTAND.

Now the angel who talked with me came back and wakened me, as a man who is wakened out of his sleep. ²And he said to me, "What do you see?"

So I said, "I am looking, and there *is* a lampstand of solid gold with a bowl on top of it, and on the *stand* seven

THE KEY

4:6 Many people believe that to survive in this world a person must be tough, strong, unbending, and harsh. But God says, "Not by might nor by power, but by My Spirit." The key words are "by My Spirit." It is *only* through God's Spirit that anything of lasting value is accomplished. The returned exiles were indeed weak—harassed by their enemies, tired, discouraged, and poor. But they had God on their side! As you live for God, determine not to trust in your own strength or abilities. Instead, depend on God and work in the power of his Spirit!

lamps with seven pipes to the seven lamps. ³Two olive trees *are* by it, one at the right of the bowl and the other at its left." ⁴So I answered and spoke to the angel who talked with me, saying, "What *are* these, my lord?"

⁵Then the angel who talked with me answered and said to me, "Do you not know what these are?"

And I said, "No, my lord."

⁶So he answered and said to me:

"This *is* the word of the LORD to Zerubbabel:
'Not by might nor by power, but by My Spirit,'
Says the LORD of hosts.

⁷ 'Who *are* you, O great mountain?
Before Zerubbabel *you shall become* a plain!
And he shall bring forth the capstone
With shouts of "Grace, grace to it!"'"

⁸Moreover the word of the LORD came to me, saying:

⁹ "The hands of Zerubbabel
Have laid the foundation of this temple;
His hands shall also finish *it*.
Then you will know

NOT BY MIGHT NOR BY POWER
BUT
by My *Spirit*
SAYS THE LORD
OF HOSTS

That the LORD of hosts has sent Me to you.

¹⁰ For who has despised the day of small things?
For these seven rejoice to see
The plumb line in the hand of Zerubbabel.
They are the eyes of the LORD,
Which scan to and fro throughout the whole earth."

¹¹Then I answered and said to him, "What *are* these two olive trees—at the right of the lampstand and at its left?" ¹²And I further answered and said to him, "What *are these* two olive branches that *drip* into the receptacles of the two gold pipes from which the golden *oil* drains?"

JUSTICE

Christopher has a twisted sense of humor:

- When a convenience store clerk gave him change for $20 instead of $10 (it was her first day on the job and she was nervous), he never said a word. He eagerly pocketed the extra bucks. "She shouldn't have been so stupid," he laughed.
- When he baby-sat his little brother last weekend, he locked the kid in a closet for about an hour.
- While keeping score for an intramural basketball game, Christopher gave his favorite team three extra points.

But you can bet Chris was not amused today when he was treated wrongly. He was docked an hour's pay just for being a measly five minutes late for work because of a wreck on the expressway!

"That's not fair!" he whined.

Like Christopher, we're quick to complain whenever we feel as though we've been treated unfairly. But Zechariah 7:8-14 tells us to watch out for others as well. It insists that we not mistreat and take advantage of those who are weak.

Are you a just and fair person?

¹³Then he answered me and said, "Do you not know what these *are*?"

And I said, "No, my lord."

¹⁴So he said, "These *are* the two anointed ones, who stand beside the Lord of the whole earth."

CHAPTER 5 ZECHARIAH SEES A FLYING SCROLL.

Then I turned and raised my eyes, and saw there a flying scroll.

²And he said to me, "What do you see?"

So I answered, "I see a flying scroll. Its length *is* twenty cubits and its width ten cubits."

³Then he said to me, "This *is* the curse that goes out over the face of the whole earth: 'Every thief shall be expelled,' according *to* this side of *the scroll;* and, 'Every perjurer shall be expelled,' according *to* that side of it."

⁴ "I will send out *the curse*," says the LORD of hosts; "It shall enter the house of the thief

WIPED OUT

5:9-11 Wickedness and sin (as represented by the woman) were away from Israel. One day, when Christ reigns, all sin will be eliminated and people will live in safety and security. When Christ died, he rem sin's power and penalty. When we trust him to forgive us, he removes sin's penalty and gives us the power to overcome sin in our life. Wh returns, he will remove sin's presence from the earth.

And the house of the one who swears falsely by My name.
It shall remain in the midst of his house
And consume it, with its timber and stones."

⁵Then the angel who talked with me came out and said to me, "Lift your eyes now, and see what this *is* that goes forth."

⁶So I asked, "What *is* it?" And he said, "It *is* a basket that is going forth."

He also said, "This *is* their resemblance throughout the earth: ⁷Here *is* a lead disc lifted up, and this *is* a woman sitting inside the basket"; ⁸then he said, "This *is* Wickedness!" And he thrust her down into the basket, and threw the lead cover over its mouth. ⁹Then I raised my eyes and looked, and there *were* two women, coming with the wind in their wings; for they had wings like the wings of a stork, and they lifted up the basket between earth and heaven.

¹⁰So I said to the angel who talked with me, "Where are they carrying the basket?"

¹¹And he said to me, "To build a house for it in the land of Shinar; when it is ready, *the basket* will be set there on its base."

CHAPTER 6 ZECHARIAH SEES FOUR CHARIOTS.

Then I turned and raised my eyes and looked, and behold, four chariots *were* coming from between two mountains, and the mountains *were* mountains of bronze. ²With the first chariot *were* red horses, with the second chariot black horses, ³with the third chariot white horses, and with the fourth chariot dappled horses—strong *steeds.* ⁴Then I answered and said to the angel who talked with me, "What *are* these, my lord?"

⁵And the angel answered and said to me, "These *are* four spirits of heaven, who go out from *their* station before the Lord of all the earth. ⁶The one with the black horses is going to the north country, the white are going after them, and the dappled are going toward the south country." ⁷Then the strong *steeds* went out, eager to go, that they might walk to and fro throughout the earth. And He said, "Go, walk to and fro throughout the earth." So they walked to and fro throughout the earth. ⁸And He called to me, and spoke to me, saying, "See, those who go toward the north country have given rest to My Spirit in the north country."

⁹Then the word of the LORD came to me, saying: ¹⁰"Receive *the gift* from the captives—from Heldai, Tobijah, and Jedaiah, who have come from Babylon—and go the same day and enter the house of Josiah the son of Zephaniah. ¹¹Take the silver and gold, make an elaborate crown, and set *it* on the head of Joshua the son of

Jehozadak, the high priest. ¹²Then speak to him, saying, 'Thus says the LORD of hosts, saying:

"Behold, the Man whose name *is* the BRANCH!
From His place He shall branch out,
And He shall build the temple of the LORD;
¹³ Yes, He shall build the temple of the LORD.
He shall bear the glory,
And shall sit and rule on His throne;
So He shall be a priest on His throne,
And the counsel of peace shall be between them
both." '

¹⁴"Now the elaborate crown shall be for a memorial in the temple of the LORD for Helem, Tobijah, Jedaiah, and Hen the son of Zephaniah. ¹⁵Even those from afar shall come and build the temple of the LORD. Then you shall know that the LORD of hosts has sent Me to you. And *this* shall come to pass if you diligently obey the voice of the LORD your God."

CHAPTER 7 BE JUST AND KIND. Now in the fourth year of King Darius it came to pass *that* the word of the LORD came to Zechariah, on the fourth day of the ninth month, Chislev, ²when *the people* sent Sherezer, with Regem-Melech and his men, *to* the house of God, to pray before the LORD, ³*and* to ask the priests who *were* in the house of the LORD of hosts, and the prophets, saying, "Should I weep in the fifth month and fast as I have done for so many years?"

⁴Then the word of the LORD of hosts came to me, saying, ⁵"Say to all the people of the land, and to the priests: 'When you fasted and mourned in the fifth and seventh *months* during those seventy years, did you really fast for Me—for Me? ⁶When you eat and when you drink, do you not eat and drink *for yourselves?* ⁷*Should you* not *have obeyed* the words which the LORD proclaimed through the former prophets when Jerusalem and the cities around it were inhabited and prosperous, and the South and the Lowland were inhabited?' "

⁸Then the word of the LORD came to Zechariah, saying, ⁹"Thus says the LORD of hosts:

'Execute true justice,
Show mercy and compassion
Everyone to his brother.
¹⁰ Do not oppress the widow or the fatherless,
The alien or the poor.
Let none of you plan evil in his heart
Against his brother.'

¹¹But they refused to heed, shrugged their shoulders, and stopped their ears so that they could not hear. ¹²Yes, they made their hearts like flint, refusing to hear the law and the words which the LORD of hosts had sent by His Spirit through the former prophets. Thus great wrath came from the LORD of hosts. ¹³Therefore it happened, *that* just as He proclaimed and they would not hear, so they called out and I would not listen," says the LORD of hosts. ¹⁴"But I scattered them with a whirlwind among all the nations which they had not known. Thus the land

became desolate after them, so that no one passed through or returned; for they made the pleasant land desolate."

CHAPTER 8 JUDAH WILL BE BLESSED. Again the word of the LORD of hosts came, saying, ²"Thus says the LORD of hosts:

'I am zealous for Zion with great zeal;
With great fervor I am zealous for her.'

³"Thus says the LORD:

'I will return to Zion,
And dwell in the midst of Jerusalem.
Jerusalem shall be called the City of Truth,
The Mountain of the LORD of hosts,
The Holy Mountain.'

⁴"Thus says the LORD of hosts:

'Old men and old women shall again sit
In the streets of Jerusalem,
Each one with his staff in his hand
Because of great age.
⁵ The streets of the city
Shall be full of boys and girls
Playing in its streets.'

GET GOING!

8:9 God had to give the temple workers a push. He as much as said, "Get going and finish the job! You've listened long enough!" Listen to what God says, but once he has shown you a course of action, get going and finish the job.

⁶"Thus says the LORD of hosts:

'If it is marvelous in the eyes of the remnant of this
people in these days,
Will it also be marvelous in My eyes?'
Says the LORD of hosts.

⁷"Thus says the LORD of hosts:

'Behold, I will save My people from the land of the
east
And from the land of the west;
⁸ I will bring them *back*,
And they shall dwell in the midst of Jerusalem.
They shall be My people
And I will be their God,
In truth and righteousness.'

⁹"Thus says the LORD of hosts:

'Let your hands be strong,
You who have been hearing in these days
These words by the mouth of the prophets,
Who *spoke* in the day the foundation was laid
For the house of the LORD of hosts,
That the temple might be built.
¹⁰ For before these days
There were no wages for man nor any hire for beast;

There was no peace from the enemy for whoever
    went out or came in;
    For I set all men, everyone, against his neighbor.

11 But now I *will* not *treat* the remnant of this people as in the former days,' says the LORD of hosts.

12 'For the seed *shall be* prosperous,
    The vine shall give its fruit,
    The ground shall give her increase,
    And the heavens shall give their dew—
    I will cause the remnant of this people
    To possess all these.
13 And it shall come to pass
    That just as you were a curse among the nations,
    O house of Judah and house of Israel,
    So I will save you, and you shall be a blessing.
    Do not fear,
    Let your hands be strong.'

14 "For thus says the LORD of hosts:

'Just as I determined to punish you
    When your fathers provoked Me to wrath,'
    Says the LORD of hosts,
    'And I would not relent,
15 So again in these days
    I am determined to do good
    To Jerusalem and to the house of Judah.
    Do not fear.
16 These *are* the things you shall do:
    Speak each man the truth to his neighbor;
    Give judgment in your gates for truth, justice, and
      peace;
17 Let none of you think evil in your heart against your
      neighbor;
    And do not love a false oath.
    For all these *are things* that I hate,'
    Says the LORD."

18 Then the word of the LORD of hosts came to me, saying, 19 "Thus says the LORD of hosts:

'The fast of the fourth *month,*
    The fast of the fifth,
    The fast of the seventh,
    And the fast of the tenth,
    Shall be joy and gladness and cheerful feasts
    For the house of Judah.
    Therefore love truth and peace.'

20 "Thus says the LORD of hosts:

'Peoples shall yet come,
    Inhabitants of many cities;
21 The inhabitants of one *city* shall go to another,
    saying,
"Let us continue to go and pray before the LORD,
    And seek the LORD of hosts.
    I myself will go also."
22 Yes, many peoples and strong nations
    Shall come to seek the LORD of hosts in Jerusalem,
    And to pray before the LORD.'

23 "Thus says the LORD of hosts: 'In those days ten men

from every language of the nations shall grasp the sleeve of a Jewish man, saying, "Let us go with you, for we have heard *that* God *is* with you." ' "

CHAPTER 9   ISRAEL'S ENEMIES WILL BE PUNISHED.

The burden of the word of the LORD
    Against the land of Hadrach,
    And Damascus its resting place
    (For the eyes of men
    And all the tribes of Israel
    Are on the LORD);
2 Also *against* Hamath, *which* borders on it,
    And *against* Tyre and Sidon, though they are very
      wise.

3 For Tyre built herself a tower,
    Heaped up silver like the dust,
    And gold like the mire of the streets.
4 Behold, the LORD will cast her out;
    He will destroy her power in the sea,
    And she will be devoured by fire.

5 Ashkelon shall see *it* and fear;
    Gaza also shall be very sorrowful;
    And Ekron, for He dried up her expectation.
    The king shall perish from Gaza,
    And Ashkelon shall not be inhabited.

6 "A mixed race shall settle in Ashdod,
    And I will cut off the pride of the Philistines.
7 I will take away the blood from his mouth,
    And the abominations from between his teeth.
    But he who remains, even he *shall be* for our God,
    And shall be like a leader in Judah,
    And Ekron like a Jebusite.
8 I will camp around My house
    Because of the army,
    Because of him who passes by and him who returns.
    No more shall an oppressor pass through them,
    For now I have seen with My eyes.

9 "Rejoice greatly, O daughter of Zion!
    Shout, O daughter of Jerusalem!
    Behold, your King is coming to you;
    He *is* just and having salvation,

◣ PREDICTIONS

9:9 The triumphal entry of Jesus riding into Jerusalem (Matthew 21:1-11) is predicted here, more than 500 years before it happened. Just as this prophecy was fulfilled when Jesus came to earth, so the prophecies of his second coming are certain to come true. We should ready for his return because he is coming!

    Lowly and riding on a donkey,
    A colt, the foal of a donkey.
10 I will cut off the chariot from Ephraim
    And the horse from Jerusalem;
    The battle bow shall be cut off.
    He shall speak peace to the nations;
    His dominion *shall be* 'from sea to sea,
    And from the River to the ends of the earth.'

¹¹ "As for you also,
  Because of the blood of your covenant,
  I will set your prisoners free from the waterless pit.
¹² Return to the stronghold,
  You prisoners of hope.
  Even today I declare
  That I will restore double to you.
¹³ For I have bent Judah, My *bow,*
  Fitted the bow with Ephraim,
  And raised up your sons, O Zion,
  Against your sons, O Greece,
  And made you like the sword of a mighty man."

¹⁴ Then the LORD will be seen over them,
  And His arrow will go forth like lightning.
  The Lord GOD will blow the trumpet,
  And go with whirlwinds from the south.
¹⁵ The LORD of hosts will defend them;
  They shall devour and subdue with slingstones.
  They shall drink *and* roar as if with wine;
  They shall be filled *with blood* like basins,
  Like the corners of the altar.
¹⁶ The LORD their God will save them in that day,
  As the flock of His people.
  For they *shall be like* the jewels of a crown,
  Lifted like a banner over His land—
¹⁷ For how great is its goodness
  And how great its beauty!
  Grain shall make the young men thrive,
  And new wine the young women.

CHAPTER **10** PROMISES FOR ISRAEL AND JUDAH.

  Ask the LORD for rain
  In the time of the latter rain.
  The LORD will make flashing clouds;
  He will give them showers of rain,
  Grass in the field for everyone.

² For the idols speak delusion;
  The diviners envision lies,
  And tell false dreams;
  They comfort in vain.
  Therefore *the people* wend their way like sheep;
  They are in trouble because *there is* no shepherd.

³ "My anger is kindled against the shepherds,
  And I will punish the goatherds.
  For the LORD of hosts will visit His flock,
  The house of Judah,
  And will make them as His royal horse in the battle.
⁴ From him comes the cornerstone,
  From him the tent peg,
  From him the battle bow,
  From him every ruler together.
⁵ They shall be like mighty men,
  Who tread down *their enemies*
  In the mire of the streets in the battle.
  They shall fight because the LORD is with them,
  And the riders on horses shall be put to shame.

⁶ "I will strengthen the house of Judah,
  And I will save the house of Joseph.

I will bring them back,
  Because I have mercy on them.
  They shall be as though I had not cast them aside;
  For I *am* the LORD their God,
  And I will hear them.
⁷ *Those of* Ephraim shall be like a mighty man,

▬▬▬▬▬▬ FOOLISH TRUST

10:2 How often we create idols of popularity, power, fame, or money, and then expect them to give us happiness and security. But these idols can't supply what we need any more than a stone image can make it rain. How foolish it is to trust in idols. Instead, trust God's promises for your future.

And their heart shall rejoice as if with wine.
  Yes, their children shall see *it* and be glad;
  Their heart shall rejoice in the LORD.
⁸ I will whistle for them and gather them,
  For I will redeem them;
  And they shall increase as they once increased.

⁹ "I will sow them among the peoples,
  And they shall remember Me in far countries;
  They shall live, together with their children,
  And they shall return.
¹⁰ I will also bring them back from the land of Egypt,
  And gather them from Assyria.
  I will bring them into the land of Gilead and
      Lebanon,
  Until no *more room* is found for them.
¹¹ He shall pass through the sea with affliction,
  And strike the waves of the sea:
  All the depths of the River shall dry up.
  Then the pride of Assyria shall be brought down,
  And the scepter of Egypt shall depart.

¹² "So I will strengthen them in the LORD,
  And they shall walk up and down in His name,"
  Says the LORD.

CHAPTER **11** THE TWO SHEPHERDS.

  Open your doors, O Lebanon,
  That fire may devour your cedars.
² Wail, O cypress, for the cedar has fallen,
  Because the mighty *trees* are ruined.
  Wail, O oaks of Bashan,
  For the thick forest has come down.
³ *There is* the sound of wailing shepherds!
  For their glory is in ruins.
  There is the sound of roaring lions!
  For the pride of the Jordan is in ruins.

⁴Thus says the LORD my God, "Feed the flock for slaughter, ⁵whose owners slaughter them and feel no guilt; those who sell them say, 'Blessed be the LORD, for I am rich'; and their shepherds do not pity them. ⁶For I will no longer pity the inhabitants of the land," says the LORD. "But indeed I will give everyone into his neighbor's hand and into the hand of his king. They shall attack the land, and I will not deliver *them* from their hand."

⁷So I fed the flock for slaughter, in particular the poor

of the flock. I took for myself two staffs: the one I called Beauty, and the other I called Bonds; and I fed the flock. [8]I dismissed the three shepherds in one month. My soul loathed them, and their soul also abhorred me. [9]Then I said, "I will not feed you. Let what is dying die, and what is perishing perish. Let those that are left eat each other's flesh." [10]And I took my staff, Beauty, and cut it in two, that I might break the covenant which I had made with all the peoples. [11]So it was broken on that day. Thus the poor of the flock, who were watching me, knew that it *was* the word of the LORD. [12]Then I said to them, "If it is agreeable to you, give *me* my wages; and if not, refrain." So they weighed out for my wages thirty *pieces* of silver.

[13]And the LORD said to me, "Throw it to the potter"—that princely price they set on me. So I took the thirty *pieces* of silver and threw them into the house of the LORD for the potter. [14]Then I cut in two my other staff, Bonds, that I might break the brotherhood between Judah and Israel.

◀▬▬▬ TOUGH JOB

11:17 It is a great tragedy for God's people when their leaders fail to care for them adequately. God holds leaders particularly accountable for the condition of his people. The New Testament tells church leaders, "Let not many of you become teachers, knowing that we shall receive a stricter judgment" (James 3:1). If God puts you in a position of leadership, remember that it is also a place of great responsibility.

[15]And the LORD said to me, "Next, take for yourself the implements of a foolish shepherd. [16]For indeed I will raise up a shepherd in the land *who* will not care for those who are cut off, nor seek the young, nor heal those that are broken, nor feed those that still stand. But he will eat the flesh of the fat and tear their hooves in pieces.

[17] "Woe to the worthless shepherd,
Who leaves the flock!
A sword *shall be* against his arm
And against his right eye;
His arm shall completely wither,
And his right eye shall be totally blinded."

CHAPTER **12** GOD DEFENDS HIS PEOPLE.

The burden of the word of the LORD against Israel. Thus says the LORD, who stretches out the heavens, lays the foundation of the earth, and forms the spirit of man within him: [2]"Behold, I will make Jerusalem a cup of drunkenness to all the surrounding peoples, when they lay siege against Judah and Jerusalem. [3]And it shall happen in that day that I will make Jerusalem a very heavy stone for all peoples; all who would heave it away will surely be cut in pieces, though all nations of the earth are gathered against it. [4]In that day," says the LORD, "I will strike every horse with confusion, and its rider with madness; I will open My eyes on the house of Judah, and will strike every horse of the peoples with blindness. [5]And the governors of Judah shall say in their heart, 'The inhabitants of Jerusalem *are* my strength in the LORD of hosts, their God.' [6]In that day I will make the governors

of Judah like a firepan in the woodpile, and like a fiery torch in the sheaves; they shall devour all the surrounding peoples on the right hand and on the left, but Jerusalem shall be inhabited again in her own place—Jerusalem.

◀▬▬▬ A GREAT DAY!

12:3-4 This speaks of a great future battle against Jerusalem. So say it is Armaggedon, the last great battle on earth. Those who go ● God's people will not prevail forever. Evil, pain, and oppression one ● will be abolished once and for all. What a great day that will be for people!

[7]"The LORD will save the tents of Judah first, so that the glory of the house of David and the glory of the inhabitants of Jerusalem shall not become greater than that of Judah. [8]In that day the LORD will defend the inhabitants of Jerusalem; the one who is feeble among them in that day shall be like David, and the house of David *shall be* like God, like the Angel of the LORD before them. [9]It shall be in that day *that* I will seek to destroy all the nations that come against Jerusalem.

[10]"And I will pour on the house of David and on the inhabitants of Jerusalem the Spirit of grace and supplication; then they will look on Me whom they pierced. Yes, they will mourn for Him as one mourns for *his* only *son*, and grieve for Him as one grieves for a firstborn. [11]In that day there shall be a great mourning in Jerusalem, like the mourning at Hadad Rimmon in the plain of Megiddo. [12]And the land shall mourn, every family by itself: the family of the house of David by itself, and their wives by themselves; the family of the house of Nathan by itself, and their wives by themselves; [13]the family of the house of Levi by itself, and their wives by themselves; the family of Shimei by itself, and their wives by themselves; [14]all the families that remain, every family by itself, and their wives by themselves.

CHAPTER **13** GOD'S FOUNTAIN OF FORGIVENESS.

"In that day a fountain shall be opened for the house of David and for the inhabitants of Jerusalem, for sin and for uncleanness.

[2]"It shall be in that day," says the LORD of hosts, "*that* I will cut off the names of the idols from the land, and they shall no longer be remembered. I will also cause the prophets and the unclean spirit to depart from the land. [3]It shall come to pass *that* if anyone still prophesies, then his father and mother who begot him will say to him, 'You shall not live, because you have spoken lies in the name of the LORD.' And his father and mother who begot him shall thrust him through when he prophesies.

[4]"And it shall be in that day *that* every prophet will be ashamed of his vision when he prophesies; they will not wear a robe of coarse hair to deceive. [5]But he will say, 'I *am* no prophet, I *am* a farmer; for a man taught me to keep cattle from my youth.' [6]And *one* will say to him, 'What are these wounds between your arms?' Then he

will answer, '*Those* with which I was wounded in the house of my friends.'

7 "Awake, O sword, against My Shepherd,
    Against the Man who is My Companion,"
    Says the LORD of hosts.
  "Strike the Shepherd,
    And the sheep will be scattered;
    Then I will turn My hand against the little ones.
8 And it shall come to pass in all the land,"
    Says the LORD,
  "*That* two-thirds in it shall be cut off *and* die,
    But *one*-third shall be left in it:
9 I will bring the *one*-third through the fire,
    Will refine them as silver is refined,
    And test them as gold is tested.
    They will call on My name,
    And I will answer them.
    I will say, 'This *is* My people';
    And each one will say, 'The LORD *is* my God.'"

CHAPTER **14** GOD'S RULE OVER ALL THE EARTH.

  Behold, the day of the LORD is coming,
    And your spoil will be divided in your midst.
2 For I will gather all the nations to battle against
      Jerusalem;
    The city shall be taken,
    The houses rifled,
    And the women ravished.
    Half of the city shall go into captivity,
    But the remnant of the people shall not be cut off
      from the city.
3 Then the LORD will go forth
    And fight against those nations,
    As He fights in the day of battle.
4 And in that day His feet will stand on the Mount of
      Olives,
    Which faces Jerusalem on the east.
    And the Mount of Olives shall be split in two,
    From east to west,
    Making a very large valley;
    Half of the mountain shall move toward the north
    And half of it toward the south.
5 Then you shall flee *through* My mountain valley,
    For the mountain valley shall reach to Azal.
    Yes, you shall flee
    As you fled from the earthquake
    In the days of Uzziah king of Judah.

  Thus the LORD my God will come,
    And all the saints with You.

6 It shall come to pass in that day
    That there will be no light;
    The lights will diminish.
7 It shall be one day
    Which is known to the LORD—
    Neither day nor night.
    But at evening time it shall happen
    That it will be light.

8 And in that day it shall be
    That living waters shall flow from Jerusalem,
    Half of them toward the eastern sea
    And half of them toward the western sea;
    In both summer and winter it shall occur.

REMNANT

13:9 This "one-third" was a remnant, a small part of the whole. Throughout the history of Israel, whenever the whole nation seemed to turn against God, God said that a righteous remnant still trusted and followed him. These believers were refined like silver and gold through the fire of their difficult circumstances. Determine to be part of God's remnant, that small part of the whole that is obedient to him. Obey no matter what the rest of the world does. This may mean trials and troubles at times: but as fire purifies gold and silver, you will be purified and made more like Christ.

9 And the LORD shall be King over all the earth.
    In that day it shall be—
    "The LORD *is* one,"
    And His name one.

10 All the land shall be turned into a plain from Geba to Rimmon south of Jerusalem. *Jerusalem* shall be raised up and inhabited in her place from Benjamin's Gate to the place of the First Gate and the Corner Gate, and *from* the Tower of Hananel to the king's winepresses.

11 *The people* shall dwell in it;
    And no longer shall there be utter destruction,
    But Jerusalem shall be safely inhabited.

12 And this shall be the plague with which the LORD will strike all the people who fought against Jerusalem:

    Their flesh shall dissolve while they stand on their
      feet,
    Their eyes shall dissolve in their sockets,
    And their tongues shall dissolve in their mouths.

13 It shall come to pass in that day
    That a great panic from the LORD will be among
      them.
    Everyone will seize the hand of his neighbor,
    And raise his hand against his neighbor's hand;
14 Judah also will fight at Jerusalem.

ANY MOMENT

14:1-2 The Bible speaks of the day of the Lord. What if you knew exactly when this would happen? Would you live differently? Christ could come at any moment. Study the Scriptures carefully and be sure you live as God intends for you to live—in obedience and spiritual readiness.

    And the wealth of all the surrounding nations
    Shall be gathered together:
    Gold, silver, and apparel in great abundance.

15 Such also shall be the plague
    On the horse *and* the mule,
    On the camel and the donkey,
    And on all the cattle that will be in those camps.
    So *shall* this plague *be*.

14:21 Zechariah was speaking to a people enduring hardships—they were being harassed by neighbors; they were discouraged over their small numbers and seemingly inadequate temple; and their worship was apathetic. But God said, "I am zealous for Jerusalem" (1:14). He promised to restore their land, their city, and their temple. Like other prophets, Zechariah blended prophecies of the present, near future, and final days into one sweeping panorama. Through his message we learn that our hope is found in God and his Messiah, who are in complete control of the world and its nations.

¹⁶And it shall come to pass *that* everyone who is left of all the nations which came against Jerusalem shall go up from year to year to worship the King, the LORD of hosts, and to keep the Feast of Tabernacles. ¹⁷And it shall be *that* whichever of the families of the earth do not come up to Jerusalem to worship the King, the LORD of hosts, on them there will be no rain. ¹⁸If the family of Egypt will not come up and enter in, they *shall have* no *rain;* they shall receive the plague with which the LORD strikes the nations who do not come up to keep the Feast of Tabernacles. ¹⁹This shall be the punishment of Egypt and the punishment of all the nations that do not come up to keep the Feast of Tabernacles.

²⁰In that day "HOLINESS TO THE LORD" shall be *engraved* on the bells of the horses. The pots in the LORD's house shall be like the bowls before the altar. ²¹Yes, every pot in Jerusalem and Judah shall be holiness to the LORD of hosts. Everyone who sacrifices shall come and take them and cook in them. In that day there shall no longer be a Canaanite in the house of the LORD of hosts.

MEGA *Themes*

GOD'S JEALOUSY God was angry at his people for neglecting his prophets through the years, and he was concerned that they not follow the careless and false leaders who exploited them. Disobedience was the root of their problems and the cause of their misery. God was jealous ("zealous") for his people's devotion.

God wants our devotion. To avoid Israel's ruin, don't walk in their steps. Don't reject God, follow false teachers, or lead others astray. Turn to God, faithfully obey his Word, and make sure you are leading others correctly. God calls you to complete loyalty to his Lordship.

1. Jealousy is usually considered a negative quality. How is God's jealousy a positive characteristic of his love?

2. What is it that God seems to desire so jealously from his people? Why do you think this is so important?

3. Describe how you are remaining faithful to God's perfect love. Also describe any areas of your life where you may be lacking in faithfulness.

4. What is your motivation for remaining faithful to God?

5. How do you plan to maintain that faithfulness throughout your life?

REBUILDING THE TEMPLE The Jews were discouraged. They were free from exile, but the temple was not completed. Zechariah encouraged them to rebuild it. God would both protect his workmen and also empower them by his Holy Spirit to carry out and complete his work.

More than the rebuilding of the temple was at stake—the people were staging the first act in God's wonderful drama of the end times. Those of us who believe in God must complete his work. To do so we must have the Holy Spirit's help. God will empower us to carry out his will in our relationships and daily tasks.

1. What did the men of Israel supply for the rebuilding of the temple? What did God supply?

2. How were the people responding to God's partnership with them in their task?

3. How does God want you to live for him? What is he supplying? What must you supply?

4. How are you responding to God's partnership in your life? List ways you could increase your productivity in the tasks God has called you to accomplish.

THE COMING KING The Messiah will come both to rescue people from sin and to reign as King. He will establish his kingdom, conquer all his enemies, and rule over all the earth. Everything will one day be under his loving and powerful control.

The Messiah came as a servant to die for us. He will return to earth as a victorious King. At that time, he will usher in peace throughout the world. Submit to his leadership now to be ready for the King's triumphant return.

1. Describe the King based on Zechariah.
2. In what ways is Christ's rule evident in lives today? Compare that evidence with how things will be when he returns in glory.
3. What evidence could someone find that Christ is King of your life?

GOD'S PROTECTION There was opposition to God's plan in Zechariah's day, and he prophesied future times of trouble. But God's word endures. God remembers his agreements with his people. God cares for his people and will deliver them from all who oppress them.

Although evil is still present, God's infinite love and personal care have been demonstrated through the centuries. God keeps his promises. Although our body may be destroyed, we need never fear our future and final destiny if we love and obey him.

1. What evidence is there in Zechariah that God's protection was present during times of trouble?
2. What potential trouble do you face in living a godly life in your world?
3. How would you describe the protection God has promised to you? How do you feel about this protection?
4. Complete this statement with appropriate phrases: "I need you, Lord, to provide me with your loving care and protection in the areas of: _____."

Mom, she did it again!" Tina's angry voice echoed throughout the house. "Mom!" ■ Tina had a little sister, Mary. She was really cute. Except she never learned. Mary was four, old enough to know better. She did know better, but she kept doing it. Because their house was small, Tina and Mary shared a room . . . and a closet. Mary had been told to keep out of Tina's clothes—but as often as she was told, Tina or her mother often found Mary in the bedroom, sitting on the floor, surrounded by Tina's clothes. Lectures hadn't helped; neither had spankings. Nothing seemed to deter Mary from playing in Tina's clothes. Tina wondered if Mary ever would learn. ■ God must have thought the same thing about his people. God had warned them repeatedly that he would punish them if they did not stop sinning—but they didn't repent, so God punished them. Israel was taken into captivity, and some years later so was Judah. All because they hadn't learned. ■ Then God brought his people back, forgiving them of their sin and offering them a fresh start. Certainly, they must have learned. ■ But they hadn't. God's people, rather than learn from the mistakes of their ancestors, chose to repeat their actions. Because they hadn't learned, Malachi came to warn them that God was watching—and he cared. ■ As you read, ask God to help you be aware of areas where you need to learn.

STATS

PURPOSE: To confront the people with their sins and to restore their relationship with God

AUTHOR: Malachi

TO WHOM WRITTEN: The Jews in Jerusalem and God's people everywhere

DATE WRITTEN: About 430 B.C.

SETTING: Malachi, Haggai, and Zechariah were postexilic prophets to Judah (the southern kingdom). Haggai and Zechariah rebuked the people for their failure to rebuild the temple. Malachi confronted them with their neglect of the temple and their false and profane worship.

KEY PEOPLE: Malachi, the priests

KEY PLACE: Jerusalem, the temple

SPECIAL FEATURES: Malachi's literary style displays a continual use of questions asked by God and his people (for example, see 3:7-8)

Mom, she did it again!" Tina's angry voice echoed throughout the house. "Mom!" ■ Tina had a little sister, Mary. She was really cute. Except she never learned. Mary was four, old enough to know better. She did know better, but she kept doing it. Because their house was small, Tina and Mary shared a room . . . and a closet. Mary had been told to keep out of Tina's clothes—but as often as she was told, Tina or her mother often found Mary in the bedroom, sitting on the floor, surrounded by Tina's clothes. Lectures hadn't helped; neither had spankings. Nothing seemed to deter Mary from playing in Tina's clothes. Tina wondered if Mary ever would learn. ■ God must have thought the same thing about his people. God had warned them repeatedly that he would punish them if they did not stop sinning—but they didn't repent, so God punished them. Israel was taken into captivity, and some years later so was Judah. All because they hadn't learned. ■ Then God brought his people back, forgiving them of their sin and offering them a fresh start. Certainly, they must have learned. ■ But they hadn't. God's people, rather than learn from the mistakes of their ancestors, chose to repeat their actions. Because they hadn't learned, Malachi came to warn them that God was watching—and he cared. ■ As you read, ask God to help you be aware of areas where you need to learn.

STATS

PURPOSE: To confront the people with their sins and to restore their relationship with God

AUTHOR: Malachi

TO WHOM WRITTEN: The Jews in Jerusalem and God's people everywhere

DATE WRITTEN: About 430 B.C.

SETTING: Malachi, Haggai, and Zechariah were postexilic prophets to Judah (the southern kingdom). Haggai and Zechariah rebuked the people for their failure to rebuild the temple. Malachi confronted them with their neglect of the temple and their false and profane worship.

KEY PEOPLE: Malachi, the priests

KEY PLACE: Jerusalem, the temple

SPECIAL FEATURES: Malachi's literary style displays a continual use of questions asked by God and his people (for example, see 3:7-8)

enemies, and rule over all the earth. Everything will one day be under his loving and powerful control.

The Messiah came as a servant to die for us. He will return to earth as a victorious King. At that time, he will usher in peace throughout the world. Submit to his leadership now to be ready for the King's triumphant return.

1. Describe the King based on Zechariah.
2. In what ways is Christ's rule evident in lives today? Compare that evidence with how things will be when he returns in glory.
3. What evidence could someone find that Christ is King of your life?

GOD'S PROTECTION There was opposition to God's plan in Zechariah's day, and he prophesied future times of trouble. But God's word endures. God remembers his agreements with his people. God

cares for his people and will deliver them from all who oppress them.

Although evil is still present, God's infinite love and personal care have been demonstrated through the centuries. God keeps his promises. Although our body may be destroyed, we need never fear our future and final destiny if we love and obey him.

1. What evidence is there in Zechariah that God's protection was present during times of trouble?
2. What potential trouble do you face in living a godly life in your world?
3. How would you describe the protection God has promised to you? How do you feel about this protection?
4. Complete this statement with appropriate phrases: "I need you, Lord, to provide me with your loving care and protection in the areas of: _____."

Malachi

CHAPTER 1 GOD LOVES HIS PEOPLE. The burden of the word of the LORD to Israel by Malachi.

² "I have loved you," says the LORD.
"Yet you say, 'In what way have You loved us?'
Was not Esau Jacob's brother?"
Says the LORD.
"Yet Jacob I have loved;
³ But Esau I have hated,
And laid waste his mountains and his heritage
For the jackals of the wilderness."

⁴ Even though Edom has said,
"We have been impoverished,
But we will return and build the desolate places,"

Thus says the LORD of hosts:

"They may build, but I will throw down;
They shall be called the Territory of Wickedness,
And the people against whom the LORD will have
    indignation forever.
⁵ Your eyes shall see,
And you shall say,
'The LORD is magnified beyond the border of Israel.'

⁶ "A son honors *his* father,
And a servant *his* master.
If then I am the Father,
Where *is* My honor?

And if I *am* a Master,
Where *is* My reverence?
Says the LORD of hosts
To you priests who despise My name.
Yet you say, 'In what way have we despised Your
    name?'

⁷ "You offer defiled food on My altar,
But say,
'In what way have we defiled You?'
By saying,
'The table of the LORD is contemptible.'

LEFTOVERS

1:2-8 God accused Israel of dishonoring him by offering imperfect sacrifices. Our life should be a living sacrifice to God (Romans 12:1). If we give God only our leftover time, money, and energy, we repeat the same sin as these worshipers who didn't want to bring anything valuable to God. What we give God reflects our true attitude toward him.

⁸ And when you offer the blind as a sacrifice,
Is it not evil?
And when you offer the lame and sick,
Is it not evil?
Offer it then to your governor!
Would he be pleased with you?
Would he accept you favorably?"
Says the LORD of hosts.

9 "But now entreat God's favor,
   That He may be gracious to us.
   While this is being *done* by your hands,
   Will He accept you favorably?"
   Says the LORD of hosts.
10 "Who *is there* even among you who would shut the
      doors,
   So that you would not kindle fire *on* My altar in vain?
   I have no pleasure in you,"
   Says the LORD of hosts,
   "Nor will I accept an offering from your hands.
11 For from the rising of the sun, even to its going
      down,

MESMERIZED
Last Sunday, Byron and John fidgeted their way through the morning worship service, mumbled their way through the songs, day dreamed their way through the prayers, and whispered and passed notes as the minister delivered his message. In short, they went through the motions of worshiping God, but they never actually thought about the one they were in church to honor.

What a shame, because the hymns and sermon were powerful reminders of the greatness of God—to everyone whose heart and mind was attentive.

That same Sunday afternoon, Byron and John rode their bikes over to the cinema at the mall to catch a new sci-fi flick. For two hours they were mesmerized, and they emerged into the bright sunlight enthusiastically buzzing about what they had just witnessed on the screen.

Bored with God in the morning . . . enthralled with Hollywood in the afternoon. That's how Byron and John spent last Sunday.

Why do we take worship so lightly? How can we be so moved by the things of this world and so unimpressed by the majesty of our God?

Read Malachi 1:6-14 to find out what God thinks about our worthless worship and half-hearted devotion.

My name *shall be* great among the Gentiles;
   In every place incense *shall be* offered to My name,
   And a pure offering;
   For My name shall be great among the nations,"
   Says the LORD of hosts.

12 "But you profane it,
    In that you say,
    'The table of the LORD is defiled;
    And its fruit, its food, *is* contemptible.'
13 You also say,
    'Oh, what a weariness!'
    And you sneer at it,"
    Says the LORD of hosts.
   "And you bring the stolen, the lame, and the sick;
    Thus you bring an offering!
    Should I accept this from your hand?"
    Says the LORD.
14 "But cursed *be* the deceiver
    Who has in his flock a male,

CHOSEN

1:11 A theme that runs through the Old Testament is affirmed in book—"My name *shall be* great among the Gentiles. . . . My name be great among the nations." God had a chosen people, the Jews, through whom he planned to save and bless the entire world. Today still wants to save and bless the world through his people, but now people are all those who believe in him—Jews and Gentiles. Our p offering to the Lord is our new life in Christ (see 2 Corinthians 2:14 Are you willing for God to use you in making his name great to the nations, beginning in your home and neighborhood?

And takes a vow,
   But sacrifices to the Lord what is blemished—
   For I *am* a great King,"
   Says the LORD of hosts,
   "And My name *is to be* feared among the nations.

CHAPTER 2 GOD WARNS HIS PRIESTS.

   "And now, O priests, this commandment is for you.
2 If you will not hear,
   And if you will not take *it* to heart,
   To give glory to My name,"
   Says the LORD of hosts,
   "I will send a curse upon you,
   And I will curse your blessings.
   Yes, I have cursed them already,
   Because you do not take *it* to heart.

3 "Behold, I will rebuke your descendants
   And spread refuse on your faces,
   The refuse of your solemn feasts;
   And *one* will take you away with it.
4 Then you shall know that I have sent this
      commandment to you,
   That My covenant with Levi may continue,"
   Says the LORD of hosts.
5 "My covenant was with him, *one* of life and peace,
   And I gave them to him *that he might* fear *Me;*
   So he feared Me
   And was reverent before My name.
6 The law of truth was in his mouth,
   And injustice was not found on his lips.
   He walked with Me in peace and equity,
   And turned many away from iniquity.

7 "For the lips of a priest should keep knowledge,
   And *people* should seek the law from his mouth;
   For he is the messenger of the LORD of hosts.
8 But you have departed from the way;
   You have caused many to stumble at the law.
   You have corrupted the covenant of Levi,"

HOLDING BACK

3:6-12 Malachi urged the people not to hold back their gifts to priests, their "tithes." Tithing began during Moses' time (Leviticus 27:30-34; Deuteronomy 14:22). The Levites received some of the because they couldn't have land (Numbers 18:20-21). During Ma day, the tithes were not used to support God's workers, so the Levi to go to work. God has given us everything. When we refuse to re him a part of what he has given, we rob him. Do you selfishly wa keep all you've been given, or are you willing to return the first p advancing God's kingdom?

Says the LORD of hosts.
⁹ "Therefore I also have made you contemptible and base
Before all the people,
Because you have not kept My ways
But have shown partiality in the law."

¹⁰ Have we not all one Father?
Has not one God created us?
Why do we deal treacherously with one another
By profaning the covenant of the fathers?
¹¹ Judah has dealt treacherously,
And an abomination has been committed in Israel and in Jerusalem,
For Judah has profaned
The LORD's holy *institution* which He loves:
He has married the daughter of a foreign god.
¹² May the LORD cut off from the tents of Jacob
The man who does this, being awake and aware,
Yet who brings an offering to the LORD of hosts!

¹³ And this is the second thing you do:
You cover the altar of the LORD with tears,
With weeping and crying;
So He does not regard the offering anymore,
Nor receive *it* with goodwill from your hands.
¹⁴ Yet you say, "For what reason?"
Because the LORD has been witness
Between you and the wife of your youth,
With whom you have dealt treacherously;
Yet she is your companion
And your wife by covenant.
¹⁵ But did He not make *them* one,
Having a remnant of the Spirit?
And why one?
He seeks godly offspring.
Therefore take heed to your spirit,
And let none deal treacherously with the wife of his youth.

¹⁶ "For the LORD God of Israel says
That He hates divorce,
For it covers one's garment with violence,"
Says the LORD of hosts.
"Therefore take heed to your spirit,
That you do not deal treacherously."

¹⁷ You have wearied the LORD with your words;
Yet you say,
"In what way have we wearied *Him?*"
In that you say,
"Everyone who does evil
Is good in the sight of the LORD,
And He delights in them,"
Or, "Where *is* the God of justice?"

CHAPTER **3** THE COMING OF THE MESSIAH.
"Behold, I send My messenger,
And he will prepare the way before Me.
And the Lord, whom you seek,
Will suddenly come to His temple,
Even the Messenger of the covenant,

In whom you delight.
Behold, He is coming,"
Says the LORD of hosts.

² "But who can endure the day of His coming?
And who can stand when He appears?

I see the offering plate passed every Sunday. I'm only a kid. Am I supposed to be giving my money to the church?

I WONDER . . .

Jesus talked about money more than he talked about anything else. That's because money, unlike any other possession, can take a strong foothold in our life. It can even control us.

Money itself is not evil. But the love of money leads to all sorts of problems (see 1 Timothy 6:10). In Malachi 3:8-10, God warned that refusing to give him tithes and offerings is actually stealing from him!

God doesn't want anything to take his place in our life. For many, money often becomes their god (especially those who don't know Christ).

The best way to keep from making money our god is to learn the joy of giving it away. Building this habit must begin when we're young.

Though not loaded with money, young people almost always have cash (from part-time jobs, gifts, and allowances) to spend. You probably spend your money on clothes, music, junk food, gas for the car (if you drive), and gifts for others. Mostly, though, you probably spend it on yourself.

God doesn't need our money. He owns everything! But we need to give it away. It's an incredible feeling to see our money go for something besides ourselves.

Here is a way to start giving your money back to God. Each time you get some, take 10 percent out and put it in an envelope that says "JESUS" on it. It doesn't matter if it's 50 cents from a $5 allowance or $10 from a $100 paycheck. Collect it for a month.

Next, decide where you want to give it away. Most churches support missionaries (people who have given their lives to spread the Good News of Jesus Christ). Maybe you could select a missionary and ask to receive his or her monthly prayer letter. By giving to a missionary (even if it's $7.23 a month!), you're furthering the cause of Christ here on earth—and you're making a wise investment in others' eternity!

Or you might want to support a child overseas. There are several good organizations who will give you the name of a needy child you can help support, usually for about $20.00 per month. This may be a larger investment than you want to make, but the fun of knowing you're helping a "real person" is worth it!

Of course, you can also give it directly to your church in the offering plate and let them decide how to use it.

At first, it may hurt to give money to something besides yourself. Eventually, however, you'll have such a good time giving that you will want to give more!

Remember, it doesn't matter how much you give. It only matters that you give what you can. See Luke 21:1-4 for a good illustration of this point.

DIVORCE

A high school sophomore reflects an increasingly common viewpoint: "I'll marry the first time for love, the second time for money, and the third time for companionship. That's what my dad did, so I guess I will, too." **W**e all know how prevalent divorce is in our society today. Sadly, practically every other student who reads this has seen his or her parents divorce. Once divorce was considered a social stigma—sort of a "Scarlet Letter" for our time. Now it's so commonplace that we barely even react to the news that another couple is calling it quits. **W**hy has divorce become an epidemic in our society? Is there hope for marriage in a modern world? What does God say about divorce—and marriage? **B**efore we discuss divorce, let's consider a couple of basic truths about marriage. First, marriage was God's idea. At the beginning of human history, God declared, "It is not good that man should be alone; I will make him a helper comparable to him" (Genesis 2:18). God made Adam and Eve to be husband and wife—one man for one woman—setting the parameters for marriage. Jesus added his stamp of approval by performing his first miracle at a wedding (John 2). Marriage is God's institution; it is "holy ground." No one should enter into it lightly, and no one should walk out of it lightly, either. **D**ivorce, however, is man's invention. When asked why Moses allowed divorce, Jesus replied: "Because of the hardness of your hearts . . . but from the beginning it was not so" (Matthew 19:8). God allows divorce. He controls, regulates, and contains it—but he does so as a concession, because of our sinfulness. Divorce was never "Plan A." **W**e are sinful, fallen people; God does know we will make mistakes—we will fail and "fall short of the glory of God" (Romans 3:23). Our fallen nature affects every area of our lives, including marriage. So God has allowed for divorce in some situations. (For more on the specifics of "biblical divorce," see Matthew 19 and 1 Corinthians 7.) Some marriage relationships become so badly damaged (through sexual immorality, desertion, abuse, or betrayal) that it's impossible to heal them. At those times, God has allowed for divorce. Even so, divorce is always painful, destructive, and damaging. That's why, in Malachi 2:16, God says he "hates divorce": even when it is permissible it is terribly destructive to persons made in God's image—an image that takes a real beating from divorce. **I**f all this makes you slightly hesitant about marriage—good. That is a healthy hesitation to have. Not because you should be terrified to the point of being paralyzed, but because you shouldn't rush into marriage. If a fuller understanding of the awesome implications of "two becoming one" causes you to approach the altar with prayer, respect for the holiness of marriage, and a godly perspective on the marriage covenant—great! Marriage is a high calling and should be treated as such. Never approach marriage with the attitude, "Oh well, if it doesn't work out, there's always divorce." Such a mind-set is a formula for marital meltdown. **I**n 1519 the Spanish conquistadors, headed by Hernán Cortés, landed at Veracruz, Mexico. His army, consisting of 500 men and 16 horses, seemed no match for the thousands of Aztec warriors standing between them and their goal of conquering the Aztec empire. Upon landing, Cortés sent a few of his men to do what seemed like a very stupid thing: burn all 10 of the ships they had sailed over on. In so doing, the Spaniards got their leader's message: Conquer or die. There was no turning back. **W**hen a man and woman say "I do," they are in effect burning their boats. The two become one, and the only way to fully make that transition is by focusing on the goal ahead: a godly marriage. If either one is constantly looking for a way out, the relationship is in serious trouble. Divorce may provide a sometimes necessary escape hatch, but it is never God's first choice for his children.

I AM THE LORD

I *do* **NOT** *change.*

For He *is* like a refiner's fire
And like launderers' soap.
³ He will sit as a refiner and a purifier of silver;
He will purify the sons of Levi,
And purge them as gold and silver,
That they may offer to the LORD
An offering in righteousness.

⁴ "Then the offering of Judah and Jerusalem
Will be pleasant to the LORD,
As in the days of old,
As in former years.
⁵ And I will come near you for judgment;
I will be a swift witness
Against sorcerers,
Against adulterers,

Against perjurers,
Against those who exploit wage earners and widows
    and orphans,
And against those who turn away an alien—
Because they do not fear Me,"
Says the LORD of hosts.

⁶ "For I *am* the LORD, I do not change;
Therefore you are not consumed, O sons of Jacob.
⁷ Yet from the days of your fathers
You have gone away from My ordinances
And have not kept *them.*
Return to Me, and I will return to you,"
Says the LORD of hosts.
"But you said,
'In what way shall we return?'

⁸ "Will a man rob God?
Yet you have robbed Me!
But you say,
'In what way have we robbed You?'
In tithes and offerings.
⁹ You are cursed with a curse,
For you have robbed Me,
Even this whole nation.
¹⁰ Bring all the tithes into the storehouse,
That there may be food in My house,
And try Me now in this,"
Says the LORD of hosts,
"If I will not open for you the windows of heaven
And pour out for you *such* blessing
That *there will* not *be room* enough *to receive it.*

¹¹ "And I will rebuke the devourer for your sakes,
So that he will not destroy the fruit of your ground,
Nor shall the vine fail to bear fruit for you in the
    field,"
Says the LORD of hosts;

MALACHI

served as a prophet to Judah about
430 B.C. He was the last of the
Old Testament prophets.

Climate of the times
The city of Jerusalem and the temple
had been rebuilt for almost a century,
but the people had become complacent
in their worship of God.

Main message
The people's relationship with God was broken
because of their sin, and they would soon be
punished. But the few who repented would
receive God's blessing, illustrated in his
promise to send a Messiah.

Importance of message
Hypocrisy, neglecting God, and careless living have
devastating consequences. Service and worship of
God must be the primary focus of our life, both now
and in eternity.

Contemporary prophets None

WHY WORSHIP?

3:13-15 These verses deal with the people's arrogant attitude toward God. When we say "What good does it do to worship God?" we really are saying "What good does it do for *me*?" Our focus is selfish. Our real question should be, "What good does it do for God?" We must worship God just because he is God and deserves to be worshiped.

12 And all nations will call you blessed,
For you will be a delightful land,"
Says the LORD of hosts.

13 "Your words have been harsh against Me,"
Says the LORD,
"Yet you say,
'What have we spoken against You?'

14 You have said,
'It is useless to serve God;
What profit *is it* that we have kept His ordinance,
And that we have walked as mourners
Before the LORD of hosts?

15 So now we call the proud blessed,
For those who do wickedness are raised up;
They even tempt God and go free.'"

FOUNDATION

4:4 These laws, given to Moses on Mount Horeb (Sinai), are the foundation of the nation's civil, moral, and ceremonial life (Exodus 20; Deuteronomy 4:5-6). We still must obey these moral laws; they apply to all generations.

16 Then those who feared the LORD spoke to one another,
And the LORD listened and heard *them;*
So a book of remembrance was written before Him
For those who fear the LORD
And who meditate on His name.

17 "They shall be Mine," says the LORD of hosts,
"On the day that I make them My jewels.
And I will spare them
As a man spares his own son who serves him."

18 Then you shall again discern
Between the righteous and the wicked,
Between one who serves God
And one who does not serve Him.

CHAPTER 4 THE GREAT JUDGMENT DAY.

"For behold, the day is coming,
Burning like an oven,
And all the proud, yes, all who do wickedly will be stubble.
And the day which is coming shall burn them up,"

JOY

4:6 Malachi gives us practical guidelines about commitment to G○ deserves the best we have to offer (1:7-10). We must be willing to change our wrong ways of living (2:1-2), to make family a priority (2:13-16), to be ready for God's refining process (3:3), to tithe (3 and to forget pride (3:13-15).

Malachi closes his message by pointing to the day of judgment those committed to God, it will be a day of joy, of ushering in eter○ God's presence. Those who have ignored God will be "stubble" to b burned up (4:1). To help people prepare for that day, God was to s prophet (John the Baptist). The New Testament begins with this pr○ calling the people to turn from their sins and turn toward God. Su○ commitment to God demands great sacrifice on our part, but we c○ sure it will be worth it all in the end.

Says the LORD of hosts,
"That will leave them neither root nor branch.

2 But to you who fear My name
The Sun of Righteousness shall arise
With healing in His wings;
And you shall go out
And grow fat like stall-fed calves.

3 You shall trample the wicked,
For they shall be ashes under the soles of your feet
On the day that I do *this*,"
Says the LORD of hosts.

4 "Remember the Law of Moses, My servant,
Which I commanded him in Horeb for all Israel,
With the statutes and judgments.

5 Behold, I will send you Elijah the prophet
Before the coming of the great and dreadful day of the LORD.

6 And he will turn
The hearts of the fathers to the children,
And the hearts of the children to their fathers,
Lest I come and strike the earth with a curse."

Who would you put on a list of the most influential people of all time? Think beyond singers, stars, or athletes. We're talking the real "heavyweights of history." People who took civilization by the scruff of the neck and shook it. Folks about whom we say, "Because of his/her presence, the world will never be the same." ■ Using that criteria, your list probably would feature Julius Caesar, Karl Marx, Martin Luther King, Jr., William Shakespeare, Adolf Hitler, Napoleon, Abraham Lincoln, Genghis Khan, Elvis Presley, Mohammed, Buddha, Alexander the Great, Mohandas Gandhi, or Henry Ford. ■ Those people—and many others—deserve to be on such a list. But if you're looking for one person who changed the world more than anyone, look at Jesus Christ. ■ Of course, naming a first-century carpenter and itinerant preacher "the most influential person of all time" probably won't sit well with some people. They may prefer to put Jesus on a list of influential "religious" figures. But here's why the founder of Christianity cannot be ignored: ■ Two thousand years ago, Jesus of Nazareth launched a spiritual revolution that is still going strong. He has been the motivation behind more songs and sermons, the inspiration underlying more works of charity, and the object of more affection than all the other great figures of history combined. And don't forget the millions of lives that have been transformed by his timeless touch. ■ Dive into the Gospel of Matthew. See for yourself how Jesus succeeded in turning ancient Israel on its ear. In the process, you'll also begin to see why he still rocks the planet.

STATS

PURPOSE: To prove that Jesus is the Messiah, the eternal King

AUTHOR: Matthew (Levi)

TO WHOM WRITTEN: Especially for the Jews

DATE WRITTEN: Probably between A.D. 60 and 65

SETTING: Matthew was a Jewish tax collector who became one of Jesus' disciples. This Gospel forms the connecting link between the Old and New Testaments because of its emphasis on the fulfillment of prophecy.

KEY PEOPLE: Jesus, Mary, Joseph, John the Baptist, disciples, religious leaders, Caiaphas, Pilate, Mary Magdalene

KEY PLACES: Bethlehem, Jerusalem, Capernaum, Galilee, Judea

NEW *Testament*

MEGA Themes

GOD'S LOVE God loves his people even when they neglect or disobey him. He has great blessings to bestow on those who are faithful to him. God's love never ends.

Because God loves us so much, he hates hypocrisy and careless living. This kind of living denies him the relationship he wants to have with us. What we give and how we live reflects the sincerity of our love for God. Live a life of love for God!

1. What do you learn about God's love in the book of Malachi?
2. Contrast the love of God experienced by those who are obedient with the love of God experienced by those who are disobedient.
3. What areas of your life are hindering you from completely enjoying God's love for you?
4. What is it about God's love that you want to know and experience more deeply? Commit yourself to remove hindrances and to actively seek more of God's love.

THE PRIESTS' SINS Malachi singled out the priests for condemnation. They knew what God required, yet their sacrifices were unworthy, their service was insincere, and they were lazy, arrogant, and insensitive. They had a casual attitude toward worshiping God and meeting his standards.

If religious leaders go wrong, how will the people be led? We all are leaders in some capacity. Don't neglect your responsibilities or be ruled by what is convenient. Neglect and insensitivity are acts of disobedience. God wants leaders who are faithful and sincere. You can make a difference in how others understand and respond to God.

1. What were the specific sins of the priests? (See 1:1—2:9)
2. What attitudes toward God are apparent in these sinful choices?
3. Why were the priests' sins especially harmful to the people?
4. What attitudes and actions enable leaders to have a positive impact on the church and community?
5. Which of these attitudes are areas of strength for you? Which ones are weak? How can you strengthen the weak areas?

THE PEOPLE'S SINS The people had not learned from their exile, nor had they listened to the prophets. Men were callously divorcing their faithful wives to marry younger, heathen women. This disobeyed God's commands about marriage and threatened the religious training of the children—but pride had hardened the people's hearts.

God deserves our total honor, respect, and faithfulness—but sin hardens us to our true condition. Don't let pride keep you from giving God your devotion, money, marriage, and family.

1. How do you feel toward people when you hear about their sins?
2. How does God see their sins?
3. Based on this study, how do you feel about the sins you have committed?
4. Explain your response to the statement: "Little sins are not that big of a deal."
5. What can you do to prepare yourself to live a life that brings God pleasure rather than grief?

THE LORD'S COMING God's love for his faithful people is demonstrated by the Messiah's coming to earth. The Messiah's purpose was, and is, to lead the people to the realization of all their fondest hopes. The day of his final coming will be a day of comfort and healing for a faithful few, and a day of judgment for those who reject him.

Christ's first coming brought purification to all those who believe in him. His second coming will expose and condemn those who are proud, insensitive, or unprepared. Yet God can heal and mend. Forgiveness is available now to all who come to Christ.

1. What did God accomplish through Jesus' first coming?
2. What differences has Jesus' coming made in the last 2,000 years?
3. What changes will take place in humanity when Christ returns?
4. As Christians, we know that Jesus will return. How should this knowledge affect our life in the present?

◣◣◣ WHY WORSHIP?

3:13-15 These verses deal with the people's arrogant attitude toward God. When we say "What good does it do to worship God?" we really are saying "What good does it do for *me*?" Our focus is selfish. Our real question should be, "What good does it do for God?" We must worship God just because he is God and deserves to be worshiped.

¹² And all nations will call you blessed,
  For you will be a delightful land,"
  Says the LORD of hosts.

¹³ "Your words have been harsh against Me,"
  Says the LORD,
  "Yet you say,
  'What have we spoken against You?'
¹⁴ You have said,
  'It is useless to serve God;
  What profit *is it* that we have kept His ordinance,
  And that we have walked as mourners
  Before the LORD of hosts?
¹⁵ So now we call the proud blessed,
  For those who do wickedness are raised up;
  They even tempt God and go free.'"

◣◣◣ FOUNDATION

4:4 These laws, given to Moses on Mount Horeb (Sinai), are the foundation of the nation's civil, moral, and ceremonial life (Exodus 20: Deuteronomy 4:5-6). We still must obey these moral laws; they apply to all generations.

¹⁶ Then those who feared the LORD spoke to one
    another,
  And the LORD listened and heard *them;*
  So a book of remembrance was written before Him
  For those who fear the LORD
  And who meditate on His name.

¹⁷ "They shall be Mine," says the LORD of hosts,
  "On the day that I make them My jewels.
  And I will spare them
  As a man spares his own son who serves him."
¹⁸ Then you shall again discern
  Between the righteous and the wicked,
  Between one who serves God
  And one who does not serve Him.

CHAPTER **4** THE GREAT JUDGMENT DAY.

"For behold, the day is coming,
  Burning like an oven,
  And all the proud, yes, all who do wickedly will be
    stubble.
  And the day which is coming shall burn them up,"

◣◣◣ JOY

4:6 Malachi gives us practical guidelines about commitment to God deserves the best we have to offer (1:7-10). We must be willing to change our wrong ways of living (2:1-2), to make family a priority (2:13-16), to be ready for God's refining process (3:3), to tithe (3:8 and to forget pride (3:13-15).

Malachi closes his message by pointing to the day of judgment. those committed to God, it will be a day of joy, of ushering in eterni God's presence. Those who have ignored God will be "stubble" to be burned up (4:1). To help people prepare for that day, God was to se prophet (John the Baptist). The New Testament begins with this prop calling the people to turn from their sins and turn toward God. Such commitment to God demands great sacrifice on our part, but we can sure it will be worth it all in the end.

  Says the LORD of hosts,
  "That will leave them neither root nor branch.
² But to you who fear My name
  The Sun of Righteousness shall arise
  With healing in His wings;
  And you shall go out
  And grow fat like stall-fed calves.
³ You shall trample the wicked,
  For they shall be ashes under the soles of your feet
  On the day that I do *this*,"
  Says the LORD of hosts.

⁴ "Remember the Law of Moses, My servant,
  Which I commanded him in Horeb for all Israel,
  With the statutes and judgments.
⁵ Behold, I will send you Elijah the prophet
  Before the coming of the great and dreadful day of
    the LORD.
⁶ And he will turn
  The hearts of the fathers to the children,
  And the hearts of the children to their fathers,
  Lest I come and strike the earth with a curse."

I AM THE LORD

I *do* **NOT** *change.*

MALACHI 3:6

For He *is* like a refiner's fire
And like launderers' soap.
3 He will sit as a refiner and a purifier of silver;
He will purify the sons of Levi,
And purge them as gold and silver,
That they may offer to the LORD
An offering in righteousness.

4 "Then the offering of Judah and Jerusalem
Will be pleasant to the LORD,
As in the days of old,
As in former years.
5 And I will come near you for judgment;
I will be a swift witness
Against sorcerers,
Against adulterers,

Against perjurers,
Against those who exploit wage earners and widows
and orphans,
And against those who turn away an alien—
Because they do not fear Me,"
Says the LORD of hosts.

6 "For I *am* the LORD, I do not change;
Therefore you are not consumed, O sons of Jacob.
7 Yet from the days of your fathers
You have gone away from My ordinances
And have not kept *them.*
Return to Me, and I will return to you,"
Says the LORD of hosts.
"But you said,
'In what way shall we return?'

8 "Will a man rob God?
Yet you have robbed Me!
But you say,
'In what way have we robbed You?'
In tithes and offerings.
9 You are cursed with a curse,
For you have robbed Me,
Even this whole nation.
10 Bring all the tithes into the storehouse,
That there may be food in My house,
And try Me now in this,"
Says the LORD of hosts,
"If I will not open for you the windows of heaven
And pour out for you *such* blessing
That *there will* not *be room* enough *to receive it.*

11 "And I will rebuke the devourer for your sakes,
So that he will not destroy the fruit of your ground,
Nor shall the vine fail to bear fruit for you in the
field,"
Says the LORD of hosts;

MALACHI

served as a prophet to Judah about 430 B.C. He was the last of the Old Testament prophets.

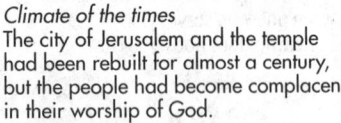

Climate of the times
The city of Jerusalem and the temple had been rebuilt for almost a century, but the people had become complacent in their worship of God.

Main message
The people's relationship with God was broken because of their sin, and they would soon be punished. But the few who repented would receive God's blessing, illustrated in his promise to send a Messiah.

Importance of message
Hypocrisy, neglecting God, and careless living have devastating consequences. Service and worship of God must be the primary focus of our life, both now and in eternity.

Contemporary prophets None

Matthew

CHAPTER 1 JESUS' FAMILY TREE.

The book of the genealogy of Jesus Christ, the Son of David, the Son of Abraham:

²Abraham begot Isaac, Isaac begot Jacob, and Jacob begot Judah and his brothers. ³Judah begot Perez and Zerah by Tamar, Perez begot Hezron, and Hezron begot Ram. ⁴Ram begot Amminadab, Amminadab begot Nahshon, and Nahshon begot Salmon. ⁵Salmon begot Boaz by Rahab, Boaz begot Obed by Ruth, Obed begot Jesse, ⁶and Jesse begot David the king.

David the king begot Solomon by her *who had been the wife* of Uriah. ⁷Solomon begot Rehoboam, Rehoboam begot Abijah, and Abijah begot Asa. ⁸Asa begot Jehoshaphat, Jehoshaphat begot Joram, and Joram begot Uzziah. ⁹Uzziah begot Jotham, Jotham begot Ahaz, and Ahaz begot Hezekiah. ¹⁰Hezekiah begot Manasseh, Manasseh begot Amon, and Amon begot Josiah. ¹¹Josiah begot Jeconiah and his brothers about the time they were carried away to Babylon.

¹²And after they were brought to Babylon, Jeconiah begot Shealtiel, and Shealtiel begot Zerubbabel. ¹³Zerubbabel begot Abiud, Abiud begot Eliakim, and Eliakim begot Azor. ¹⁴Azor begot Zadok, Zadok begot Achim, and Achim begot Eliud. ¹⁵Eliud begot Eleazar, Eleazar begot Matthan, and Matthan begot Jacob. ¹⁶And Jacob begot Joseph the husband of Mary, of whom was born Jesus who is called Christ.

¹⁷So all the generations from Abraham to David *are* fourteen generations, from David until the captivity in Babylon *are* fourteen generations, and from the captivity in Babylon until the Christ *are* fourteen generations.

¹⁸Now the birth of Jesus Christ was as follows: After His mother Mary was betrothed to Joseph, before they came together, she was found with child of the Holy Spirit. ¹⁹Then Joseph her husband, being a just *man*, and not wanting to make her a public example, was minded to put her away secretly. ²⁰But while he thought about these things, behold, an angel of the Lord appeared to him in a

◣◣◣〜〜〜 NO LIMITS

1:1-17 In the first 17 verses of Matthew we meet 46 people spanning 2,000 years. All were ancestors of Jesus, but they varied considerably in personality, spirituality, and experience. Some were heroes (and heroines) of faith—like Abraham, Isaac, Ruth, and David. Some had shady reputations—like Rahab and Tamar. Many were ordinary—like Hezron, Ram, and Achim. Others were evil—like Manasseh and Abijah. God's work has never been limited by human failures or sins; he works through ordinary people. God used all kinds of people to bring his Son into the world; he uses all kinds today to accomplish his will. And he wants to use you.

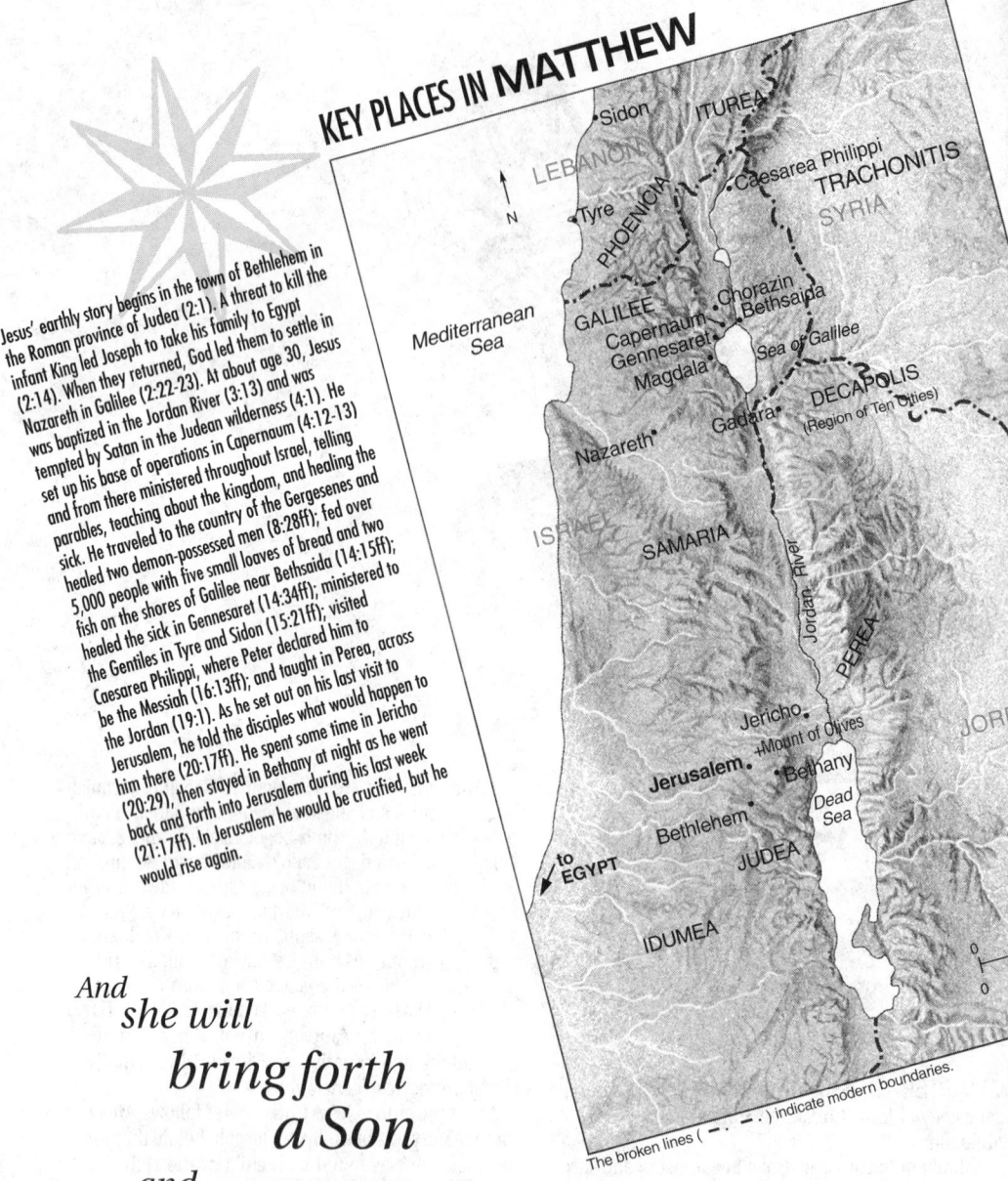

Jesus' earthly story begins in the town of Bethlehem in the Roman province of Judea (2:1). A threat to kill the infant King led Joseph to take his family to Egypt (2:14). When they returned, God led them to settle in Nazareth in Galilee (2:22-23). At about age 30, Jesus was baptized in the Jordan River (3:13) and was tempted by Satan in the Judean wilderness (4:1). He set up his base of operations in Capernaum (4:12-13) and from there ministered throughout Israel, telling parables, teaching about the kingdom, and healing the sick. He traveled to the country of the Gergesenes and healed two demon-possessed men (8:28ff); fed over 5,000 people with five small loaves of bread and two fish on the shores of Galilee near Bethsaida (14:15ff); healed the sick in Gennesaret (14:34ff); ministered to the Gentiles in Tyre and Sidon (15:21ff); visited Caesarea Philippi, where Peter declared him to be the Messiah (16:13ff); and taught in Perea, across the Jordan (19:1). As he set out on his last visit to Jerusalem, he told the disciples what would happen to him there (20:17ff). He spent some time in Jericho (20:29), then stayed in Bethany at night as he went back and forth into Jerusalem during his last week (21:17ff). In Jerusalem he would be crucified, but he would rise again.

The broken lines (– · – ·) indicate modern boundaries.

And *she will* ***bring forth a Son*** *and* YOU SHALL CALL HIS NAME

JESUS

for ***He will save His people*** *from their sins*

MATTHEW 1:21

dream, saying, "Joseph, son of David, do not be afraid to take to you Mary your wife, for that which is conceived in her is of the Holy Spirit. ²¹And she will bring forth a Son, and you shall call His name JESUS, for He will save His people from their sins."

²²So all this was done that it might be fulfilled which was spoken by the Lord through the prophet, saying: ²³ *"Behold, the virgin shall be with child, and bear a Son, and they shall call His name Immanuel,"* which is translated, "God with us."

²⁴Then Joseph, being aroused from sleep, did as the angel of the Lord commanded him and took to him his wife, ²⁵and did not know her till she had brought forth her firstborn Son. And he called His name JESUS.

CHAPTER **2** **WISE MEN VISIT BABY JESUS.** Now after Jesus was born in Bethlehem of Judea in the days of Herod the king, behold, wise men from the East came to Jerusalem, ²saying, "Where is He who has been born King of the Jews? For we have seen His star in the East and have come to worship Him."

³When Herod the king heard *this,* he was troubled, and all Jerusalem with him. ⁴And when he had gathered all the chief priests and scribes of the people together, he inquired of them where the Christ was to be born.

⁵So they said to him, "In Bethlehem of Judea, for thus it is written by the prophet:

⁶ *'But you, Bethlehem, in the land of Judah,*
Are not the least among the rulers of Judah;
For out of you shall come a Ruler
Who will shepherd My people Israel.'"

⁷Then Herod, when he had secretly called the wise men, determined from them what time the star appeared. ⁸And he sent them to Bethlehem and said, "Go and search carefully for the young Child, and when you have found *Him,* bring back word to me, that I may come and worship Him also."

⁹When they heard the king, they departed; and behold, the star which they had seen in the East went before them, till it came and stood over where the young Child was. ¹⁰When they saw the star, they rejoiced with exceedingly great joy. ¹¹And when they had come into the house, they saw the young Child with Mary His mother, and fell down and worshiped Him. And when they had opened their treasures, they presented gifts to Him: gold, frankincense, and myrrh.

¹²Then, being divinely warned in a dream that they should not return to Herod, they departed for their own country another way.

¹³Now when they had departed, behold, an angel of the Lord appeared to Joseph in a dream, saying, "Arise, take the young Child and His mother, flee to Egypt, and stay there until I bring you word; for Herod will seek the young Child to destroy Him."

AFRAID

2:16-18 Herod was afraid that this newborn King would one day take his throne. But Jesus wanted to be King of Herod's life. Jesus wanted to give Herod eternal life, not take away his present life. Today people often are afraid that Christ wants to take things away when, in reality, he wants to give them real freedom, peace, and joy.

¹⁴When he arose, he took the young Child and His mother by night and departed for Egypt, ¹⁵and was there until the death of Herod, that it might be fulfilled which was spoken by the Lord through the prophet, saying, *"Out of Egypt I called My Son."*

¹⁶Then Herod, when he saw that he was deceived by the wise men, was exceedingly angry; and he sent forth and put to death all the male children who were in Bethlehem and in all its districts, from two years old and under, according to the time which he had determined from the wise men. ¹⁷Then was fulfilled what was spoken by Jeremiah the prophet, saying:

¹⁸ *"A voice was heard in Ramah,*
Lamentation, weeping, and great mourning,
Rachel weeping for her children,

THE PHARISEES AND SADDUCEES

The Pharisees and Sadducees were the two major religious groups in Israel at the time of Christ. The Pharisees were more religiously minded, while the Sadducees were more politically minded. Although the groups disliked and distrusted each other, they became allies in their common hatred for Jesus.

PHARISEES

Positive Characteristics

- Were committed to obeying all of God's Word
- Were admired by the common people for their apparent piety
- Believed in a bodily resurrection and eternal life
- Believed in angels and demons

Negative Characteristics

- Behaved as though their own religious rules were just as important as God's rules for living
- Were often hypocritical, forcing others to try to live up to standards they themselves could not live up to
- Believed that salvation came from perfect obedience to the law and was not based on forgiveness of sins
- Became so obsessed with obeying their legal interpretations in every detail that they completely ignored God's message of mercy and grace
- Were more concerned with appearing to be good than with obeying God

SADDUCEES

Positive Characteristics

- Believed God's Word was limited to the first five books of the Bible: Genesis to Deuteronomy
- Were more practically minded than the Pharisees

Negative Characteristics

- Relied on logic while placing little importance on faith
- Did not believe all the Old Testament was God's Word
- Did not believe in a bodily resurrection or eternal life
- Did not believe in angels or demons
- Were often willing to compromise their values with the Romans and others in order to maintain their status and influential positions

SEX — WHY IS GOD SO NARROW-MINDED?

"The curves of your thighs are like jewels. . . . Your navel is a rounded goblet. . . . Your two breasts are like two fawns, twins of a gazelle. . . . This stature of yours is like a palm tree, and your breasts like its clusters. I said, 'I will go up to the palm tree, I will take hold of its branches.' Let now your breasts be like clusters of the vine." (Song of Solomon 7:1-9). **W**ow! What is writing like this doing in the Bible? We expect to find sexual messages in movies, music, and magazines—and even embarrassment. **T**he Song of Solomon has caused so much confusion, controversy, and even embarrassment. **T**he Song of Solomon is not the only place where the Bible talks about sex (for example, see 1 Corinthians 6; Galatians 5:16-25; Ephesians 5:1-3; Hebrews 13:4). But it is here that the Scriptures reach their highest, most beautiful and poetic affirmation of the goodness of sex as God's gift to men and women. Believe it: sex is God's invention—not Hollywood's or MTV's—which leads to several important observations:

- Sex is good. God's people haven't done a very good job in communicating this fact. We've treated this aspect of God's creation as if it were shameful or to be avoided. But God created sex, and he created us as sexual creatures; therefore, sex is good. Regardless of the dangers and trouble surrounding sex, this fact remains: Sex is part of God's creative plan for men and women.

- Sex is powerful. Of all the ways people have of expressing themselves to one another, sex is the most powerful. It involves a person's total being. When sex is kept in its proper context—marriage—it is a powerful vehicle for good, for bringing a husband and wife together as one. Unfortunately, when sex is expressed before or outside of marriage, it can be powerfully destructive. **T**hink of it like this: Say you give a six-year-old a hot new Ferrari and send him out to drive it in the Grand Prix. You know what will happen. A six-year-old isn't physically, mentally, or emotionally prepared to handle the car or the course. He'll crash and burn and get hurt badly. It's the same with people who are young and not married—they are not prepared mentally, emotionally, or spiritually for the experience of sex. They may think they're ready, but sex is powerful, and it requires a strong structure to support and contain it. **W**hich leads to our final observation.

- Sex is made for marriage. Period. Sex is such an explosive force between two people that it must be expressed in an environment of love, support, and commitment. Sex is 100 percent physical commitment. That's what is 100 percent emotional, financial, social, and spiritual commitment, the relationship will be unbalanced missing in sex outside of marriage—commitment. Especially physical commitment. Unless there will probably collapse, leading to pain, anger, shame, and much more. Those who decide to become sexually involved in spite of God's instructions shouldn't be surprised when, like our young Ferrari driver, they crash and burn. **S**ex, as the Song of Solomon says so beautifully, is God's idea. If you follow his leading—including waiting until marriage to have sex—you'll experience one of God's greatest gifts in a way that is fulfilling to you and pleasing to him.

Refusing to be comforted,
Because they are no more."

[19]Now when Herod was dead, behold, an angel of the Lord appeared in a dream to Joseph in Egypt, [20]saying, "Arise, take the young Child and His mother, and go to the land of Israel, for those who sought the young Child's life are dead." [21]Then he arose, took the young Child and His mother, and came into the land of Israel.

[22]But when he heard that Archelaus was reigning over Judea instead of his father Herod, he was afraid to go there. And being warned by God in a dream, he turned aside into the region of Galilee. [23]And he came and dwelt in a city called Nazareth, that it might be fulfilled which was spoken by the prophets, "He shall be called a Nazarene."

CHAPTER **3** JOHN THE BAPTIST PREACHES.

In those days John the Baptist came preaching in the wilderness of Judea, [2]and saying, "Repent, for the kingdom of heaven is at hand!" [3]For this is he who was spoken of by the prophet Isaiah, saying:

"The voice of one crying in the wilderness:
'Prepare the way of the LORD;
Make His paths straight.'"

[4]Now John himself was clothed in camel's hair, with a leather belt around his waist; and his food was locusts and wild honey. [5]Then Jerusalem, all Judea, and all the region around the Jordan went out to him [6]and were baptized by him in the Jordan, confessing their sins.

[7]But when he saw many of the Pharisees and Sadducees coming to his baptism, he said to them, "Brood of vipers! Who warned you to flee from the wrath to come? [8]Therefore bear fruits worthy of repentance, [9]and do not think to say to yourselves, 'We have Abraham as *our* father.' For I say to you that God is able to raise up children to Abraham from these stones. [10]And even now the ax is laid to the root of the trees. Therefore every tree which does not bear good fruit is cut down and thrown into the fire. [11]I indeed baptize you with water unto repentance, but He who is coming after me is mightier than I, whose sandals I am not worthy to carry. He will baptize you with the Holy Spirit and fire. [12]His winnowing fan *is* in His hand, and He will thoroughly clean out His threshing floor, and gather His wheat into the barn; but He will burn up the chaff with unquenchable fire."

[13]Then Jesus came from Galilee to John at the Jordan to be baptized by him. [14]And John *tried to* prevent Him, saying, "I need to be baptized by You, and are You coming to me?"

[15]But Jesus answered and said to him, "Permit *it to be so* now, for thus it is fitting for us to fulfill all righteousness." Then he allowed Him.

[16]When He had been baptized, Jesus came up immediately from the water; and behold, the heavens were opened to Him, and He saw the Spirit of God descending like a dove and alighting upon Him. [17]And suddenly a voice *came* from heaven, saying, "This is My beloved Son, in whom I am well pleased."

ACTIONS

3:8 John the Baptist called people to more than words or ritual; he told them to change their lives. God looks beyond our words and religious activities to see if our life backs up our words, and he judges our words by the actions that accompany them. Do your actions agree with your words?

CHAPTER **4** JESUS IS TEMPTED.

Then Jesus was led up by the Spirit into the wilderness to be tempted by the devil. [2]And when He had fasted forty days and forty nights, afterward He was hungry. [3]Now when the tempter came to Him, he said, "If You are the Son of God, command that these stones become bread."

[4]But He answered and said, "It is written, *'Man shall not live by bread alone, but by every word that proceeds from the mouth of God.'*"

[5]Then the devil took Him up into the holy city, set Him on the pinnacle of the temple, [6]and said to Him, "If You are the Son of God, throw Yourself down. For it is written:

I'm trying to understand how the Old and New Testaments relate to each other. Which one is more important?

I WONDER . . .

It's not that one is more important than the other. Instead, it's a question of timing.

Imagine being seven years old and your parents sitting you down and telling you all of the rules about driving a car. Not only would you have tuned them out after about two minutes, but ten years later, when it came time to drive, you wouldn't have remembered anything they said.

Timing is everything. Wise parents have figured this out; that's why they didn't give you all their rules as soon as you could talk. They waited until you were ready so that you would want to listen, the rules would make sense to you, and you would remember what they said.

The Old Testament was given to us for several reasons. After explaining Creation, its main purpose was to point the way to God's solution for the problem of mankind's sin. In Matthew 5:21-48, we see Jesus contrasting Old and New Testaments. Romans 7:7 tells us that the Old Testament Law was good because it showed us what sin was, and thus, showed us our need for a Savior.

The Old Testament points directly to Christ as the Savior that we needed. There are dozens of verses that tell the exact place of Jesus' birth, his sinless life, his death on a cross, his resurrection, and his return. Though the Old Testament was written from about 1450–430 B.C., it predicted minute details about the life of Jesus! This also serves to prove the authority of the Scriptures.

Also, the Old Testament is what helps the New Testament make sense. In Matthew 5, Jesus said he came to fulfill the law, not to destroy it. The Old Testament helps us understand why Jesus did what he did.

The Old Testament speaks of sacrifices (picturing Jesus as the ultimate sacrifice) and having faith in God's promise. This was how God prepared the way for Christ.

'He shall give His angels charge over you,'

and,

'In their hands they shall bear you up,
Lest you dash your foot against a stone.' "

⁷Jesus said to him, "It is written again, *'You shall not tempt the LORD your God.' "*

⁸Again, the devil took Him up on an exceedingly high mountain, and showed Him all the kingdoms of the world and their glory. ⁹And he said to Him, "All these things I will give You if You will fall down and worship me."

¹⁰Then Jesus said to him, "Away with you, Satan! For it is written, *'You shall worship the LORD your God, and Him only you shall serve.' "*

¹¹Then the devil left Him, and behold, angels came and ministered to Him.

¹²Now when Jesus heard that John had been put in prison, He departed to Galilee. ¹³And leaving Nazareth, He came and dwelt in Capernaum, which is by the sea, in the regions of Zebulun and Naphtali, ¹⁴that it might be fulfilled which was spoken by Isaiah the prophet, saying:

¹⁵ *"The land of Zebulun and the land of Naphtali,*
By the way of the sea, beyond the Jordan,
Galilee of the Gentiles:
¹⁶ *The people who sat in darkness have seen a great light,*
And upon those who sat in the region and shadow of death
Light has dawned."

¹⁷From that time Jesus began to preach and to say, "Repent, for the kingdom of heaven is at hand."

¹⁸And Jesus, walking by the Sea of Galilee, saw two brothers, Simon called Peter, and Andrew his brother, casting a net into the sea; for they were fishermen. ¹⁹Then He said to them, "Follow Me, and I will make you fishers of men." ²⁰They immediately left *their* nets and followed Him.

²¹Going on from there, He saw two other brothers, James *the son* of Zebedee, and John his brother, in the boat with Zebedee their father, mending their nets. He called them, ²²and immediately they left the boat and their father, and followed Him.

²³And Jesus went about all Galilee, teaching in their synagogues, preaching the gospel of the kingdom, and healing all kinds of sickness and all kinds of disease among the people. ²⁴Then His fame went throughout all Syria; and they brought to Him all sick people who were afflicted with various diseases and torments, and those who were demon-possessed, epileptics, and paralytics; and He healed them. ²⁵Great multitudes followed Him—from Galilee, and *from* Decapolis, Jerusalem, Judea, and beyond the Jordan.

CHAPTER 5 THE SERMON ON THE MOUNT. And

seeing the multitudes, He went up on a mountain, and when He was seated His disciples came to Him. ²Then He opened His mouth and taught them, saying:

▶ STRANGE

5:3-12 Jesus began his sermon with words that seem to contrad other. But God's way of living usually contradicts the world's. If you to live for God, you must be ready to say and do what seems stran the world. You must be willing to give when others take, to love wh others hate, to help when others abuse. In doing this, you will one receive everything, while the others will end up with nothing.

³ "Blessed *are* the poor in spirit,
For theirs is the kingdom of heaven.
⁴ Blessed *are* those who mourn,
For they shall be comforted.
⁵ Blessed *are* the meek,
For they shall inherit the earth.
⁶ Blessed *are* those who hunger and thirst for righteousness,
For they shall be filled.
⁷ Blessed *are* the merciful,
For they shall obtain mercy.
⁸ Blessed *are* the pure in heart,
For they shall see God.
⁹ Blessed *are* the peacemakers,
For they shall be called sons of God.
¹⁰ Blessed are those who are persecuted for righteousness' sake,
For theirs is the kingdom of heaven.

¹¹"Blessed are you when they revile and persecute you, and say all kinds of evil against you falsely for My sake. ¹²Rejoice and be exceedingly glad, for great *is* your reward in heaven, for so they persecuted the prophets who were before you.

¹³"You are the salt of the earth; but if the salt loses its flavor, how shall it be seasoned? It is then good for nothing but to be thrown out and trampled underfoot by men.

¹⁴"You are the light of the world. A city that is set on a hill cannot be hidden. ¹⁵Nor do they light a lamp and put it under a basket, but on a lampstand, and it gives light to all *who are* in the house. ¹⁶Let your light so shine before men, that they may see your good works and glorify your Father in heaven.

¹⁷"Do not think that I came to destroy the Law or the Prophets. I did not come to destroy but to fulfill. ¹⁸For assuredly, I say to you, till heaven and earth pass away, one jot or one tittle will by no means pass from the law till all is fulfilled. ¹⁹Whoever therefore breaks one of the least of these commandments, and teaches men so, shall be called least in the kingdom of heaven; but whoever does and teaches *them*, he shall be called great in the kingdom of heaven. ²⁰For I say to you, that unless your righteousness exceeds *the righteousness* of the scribes and Pharisees, you will by no means enter the kingdom of heaven.

▶ OUT OF CONTROL

5:21-22 Killing is a terrible sin, but *anger* is a great sin too becau also violates God's command to love. Anger in this case refers to a seething, brooding bitterness against someone. It is a dangerous em that always threatens to leap out of control and lead to violence, emotional hurt, increased mental stress, and other destructive results There is spiritual damage as well. Anger keeps us from developing a pleasing to God. Have you ever been proud that you didn't strike out say what was really on your mind? Self-control is good, but Christ wa us to practice thought-control as well. Jesus said we will be held accountable even for our attitudes.

21"You have heard that it was said to those of old, *'You shall not murder,* and whoever murders will be in danger of the judgment.' 22But I say to you that whoever is angry with his brother without a cause shall be in danger of the judgment. And whoever says to his brother, 'Raca!' shall be in danger of the council. But whoever says, 'You fool!' shall be in danger of hell fire. 23Therefore if you bring your gift to the altar, and there remember that your brother has something against you, 24leave your gift there before the altar, and go your way. First be reconciled to your brother, and then come and offer your gift. 25Agree with your adversary quickly, while you are on the way with him, lest your adversary deliver you to the judge, the judge hand you over to the officer, and you be thrown into prison. 26Assuredly, I say to you, you will by no means get out of there till you have paid the last penny.

27"You have heard that it was said to those of old, *'You shall not commit adultery.'* 28But I say to you that whoever looks at a woman to lust for her has already committed adultery with her in his heart. 29If your right eye causes you to sin, pluck it out and cast *it* from you; for it is more profitable for you that one of your members perish, than for your whole body to be cast into hell. 30And if your right hand causes you to sin, cut it off and cast *it* from you; for it is more profitable for you that one of your members perish, than for your whole body to be cast into hell.

31"Furthermore it has been said, 'Whoever divorces his wife, let him give her a certificate of divorce.' 32But I say to you that whoever divorces his wife for any reason except sexual immorality causes her to commit adultery; and whoever marries a woman who is divorced commits adultery.

33"Again you have heard that it was said to those of old, 'You shall not swear falsely, but shall perform your oaths to the Lord.' 34But I say to you, do not swear at all: neither by heaven, for it is God's throne; 35nor by the earth, for it is His footstool; nor by Jerusalem, for it is the city of the great King. 36Nor shall you swear by your head, because you cannot make one hair white or black. 37But let your 'Yes' be 'Yes,' and your 'No,' 'No.' For whatever is more than these is from the evil one.

38"You have heard that it was said, *'An eye for an eye and a tooth for a tooth.'* 39But I tell you not to resist an evil person. But whoever slaps you on your right cheek, turn the other to him also. 40If anyone wants to sue you and take away your tunic, let him have *your* cloak also. 41And whoever compels you to go one mile, go with him two. 42Give to him who asks you, and from him who wants to borrow from you do not turn away.

43"You have heard that it was said, *'You shall love your neighbor* and hate your enemy.' 44But I say to you, love your enemies, bless those who curse you, do good to those who hate you, and pray for those who spitefully use you and persecute you, 45that you may be sons of your Father in heaven; for He makes His sun rise on the evil and on the good, and sends rain on the just and on the unjust. 46For if you love those who love you, what reward have you? Do not even the tax collectors do the same? 47And if you greet your brethren only, what do you do more *than others?* Do not even the tax collectors do so? 48Therefore you shall be perfect, just as your Father in heaven is perfect.

CHAPTER **6** HELP OTHERS WITHOUT BRAGGING.

"Take heed that you do not do your charitable deeds before men, to be seen by them. Otherwise you have no reward from your Father in heaven. 2Therefore, when you do a charitable deed, do not sound a trumpet before you as the hypocrites do in the synagogues and in the streets, that they may have glory from men. Assuredly, I say to you, they have their reward. 3But when you do a charitable deed, do not let your left hand know what your right hand is doing, 4that your charitable deed may be in secret; and your Father who sees in secret will Himself reward you openly.

5"And when you pray, you shall not be like the hypocrites. For they love to pray standing in the synagogues

"Here's what I did..."

It was during a soccer game that I got to apply Matthew 5:39, about "turning the other cheek," in a very real way.

I was captain of our soccer team. The other team was out for blood—they took cheap shots every chance they got. The refs never saw any of it; I guess people don't realize how dirty girls can play. My team started taking matters into their own hands.

One time I was passed the ball and managed to have a clear break—only one person standing in my way. But she took a cheap shot, and instead of scoring, I was injured and taken out of the game. I was angry, but I started praying about it.

By halftime the other girls on my team were really down. But I told them not to seek revenge—not to take the attitude of "an eye for an eye," but to turn the other cheek, to play fair. I told them that's what I planned to do.

I went back into the game and made sure I played clean. My team followed my example. I scored two goals late in the game and our team tied, 2–2.

The most important thing to me wasn't the score of that game, though. It was the fact that playing clean really was better. Neither resisting nor returning violence was the better way—it really is best to play clean and fair so you can hold your head high. I think the whole team learned something that day. I know I did.

Susan
AGE 16

INCANTATION

6:7-8 Some people think that repeating the same words over and over—like a magic incantation—will ensure that God will hear them. It's not wrong to come to God with the same requests—Jesus encourages *persistent* prayer. But he condemns the shallow repetition of words that are not offered with a sincere heart. We can never pray too much if our prayers are honest and sincere. Before you start to pray, make sure you mean what you say.

and on the corners of the streets, that they may be seen by men. Assuredly, I say to you, they have their reward. ⁶But you, when you pray, go into your room, and when you have shut your door, pray to your Father who *is* in the secret *place;* and your Father who sees in secret will reward you openly. ⁷And when you pray, do not use vain repetitions as the heathen *do.* For they think that they will be heard for their many words.

⁸"Therefore do not be like them. For your Father knows the things you have need of before you ask Him. ⁹In this manner, therefore, pray:

Our Father in heaven,
Hallowed be Your name.
¹⁰ Your kingdom come.
Your will be done
On earth as *it is* in heaven.
¹¹ Give us this day our daily bread.
¹² And forgive us our debts,
As we forgive our debtors.
¹³ And do not lead us into temptation,
But deliver us from the evil one.
For Yours is the kingdom and the power and the
glory forever. Amen.

¹⁴"For if you forgive men their trespasses, your heavenly Father will also forgive you. ¹⁵But if you do not forgive men their trespasses, neither will your Father forgive your trespasses.

¹⁶"Moreover, when you fast, do not be like the hypo-

crites, with a sad countenance. For they disfigure their faces that they may appear to men to be fasting. Assuredly, I say to you, they have their reward. ¹⁷But you, when you fast, anoint your head and wash your face, ¹⁸so that you do not appear to men to be fasting, but to your Father who *is* in the secret *place;* and your Father who sees in secret will reward you openly.

¹⁹"Do not lay up for yourselves treasures on earth, where moth and rust destroy and where thieves break in and steal; ²⁰but lay up for yourselves treasures in heaven, where neither moth nor rust destroys and where thieves do not break in and steal. ²¹For where your treasure is, there your heart will be also.

²²"The lamp of the body is the eye. If therefore your eye

SUBTLE

6:13 Jesus is not implying that God leads us into temptation. He i simply asking for deliverance from Satan and his deceit. All Christi struggle with temptation. Sometimes it is so subtle that we don't ev realize what is happening to us. God has promised that he won't al to be tempted beyond our endurance (1 Corinthians 10:13). Ask G help you recognize temptation and to be strong enough to overcom and choose God's way.

is good, your whole body will be full of light. ²³But if your eye is bad, your whole body will be full of darkness. If therefore the light that is in you is darkness, how great *is* that darkness!

²⁴"No one can serve two masters; for either he will hate the one and love the other, or else he will be loyal to the one and despise the other. You cannot serve God and mammon.

²⁵"Therefore I say to you, do not worry about your life, what you will eat or what you will drink; nor about your body, what you will put on. Is not life more than food and

SEVEN REASONS NOT TO WORRY.

1 The same God who created life in you can be trusted with the details of your life. 6:25

2 Worrying about the future hampers your efforts for today. 6:26

3 Worrying is more harmful than helpful. 6:27

4 God does not ignore those who depend on him. 6:28-30

5 Worry shows a lack of faith and of understanding of God. 6:31-32

6 There are real challenges God wants us to pursue, and worrying keeps us from them. 6:33

7 Living one day at a time keeps us from being consumed with worry. 6:34

WHOEVER
HEARS THESE
SAYINGS OF MINE,
AND DOES THEM,
I WILL LIKEN HIM TO

A WISE MAN
WHO
BUILT
HIS HOUSE
ON THE
ROCK

MATTHEW 7:24

the body more than clothing? ²⁶Look at the birds of the air, for they neither sow nor reap nor gather into barns; yet your heavenly Father feeds them. Are you not of more value than they? ²⁷Which of you by worrying can add one cubit to his stature?

²⁸"So why do you worry about clothing? Consider the lilies of the field, how they grow: they neither toil nor spin; ²⁹and yet I say to you that even Solomon in all his glory was not arrayed like one of these. ³⁰Now if God so clothes the grass of the field, which today is, and tomorrow is thrown into the oven, *will He* not much more *clothe* you, O you of little faith?

³¹"Therefore do not worry, saying, 'What shall we eat?' or 'What shall we drink?' or 'What shall we wear?' ³²For after all these things the Gentiles seek. For your heavenly Father knows that you need all these things. ³³But seek first the kingdom of God and His righteousness, and all these things shall be added to you. ³⁴Therefore do not worry about tomorrow, for tomorrow will worry about its own things. Sufficient for the day *is* its own trouble.

CHAPTER 7 DON'T CRITICIZE
OTHERS. "Judge not, that you be not judged. ²For with what judgment you judge, you will be judged; and with the measure you use, it will be measured back to you. ³And why do you look at the speck in your brother's eye, but do not consider the plank in your own eye? ⁴Or how can you say to your brother, 'Let me remove the speck from your eye'; and look, a plank *is* in your own eye? ⁵Hypocrite! First remove the plank from your own eye,

and then you will see clearly to remove the speck from your brother's eye.

⁶"Do not give what is holy to the dogs; nor cast your pearls before swine, lest they trample them under their feet, and turn and tear you in pieces.

⁷"Ask, and it will be given to you; seek, and you will find; knock, and it will be opened to you. ⁸For everyone who asks receives, and he who seeks finds, and to him who knocks it will be opened. ⁹Or what man is there among you who, if his son asks for bread, will give him a stone? ¹⁰Or if he asks for a fish, will he give him a serpent? ¹¹If you then, being evil, know how to give good gifts to your children, how much more will your Father who is in heaven give good things to those who ask Him! ¹²Therefore, whatever you want men to do to you, do also to them, for this is the Law and the Prophets.

¹³"Enter by the narrow gate; for wide *is* the gate and broad *is* the way that leads to destruction, and there are many who go in by it. ¹⁴Because narrow *is* the gate and difficult *is* the way which leads to life, and there are few who find it.

¹⁵"Beware of false prophets, who come to you in sheep's clothing, but inwardly they are ravenous wolves. ¹⁶You will know them by their fruits. Do men gather grapes from thornbushes or figs from thistles? ¹⁷Even so, every good tree bears good fruit, but a bad tree bears bad fruit. ¹⁸A good tree cannot bear bad fruit, nor *can* a bad tree bear good fruit. ¹⁹Every tree that does not bear good fruit is cut down and thrown into the fire. ²⁰Therefore by their fruits you will know them.

²¹"Not everyone who says to Me, 'Lord, Lord,' shall enter the kingdom of heaven, but he who does the will of My Father in heaven. ²²Many will say to Me in that day, 'Lord, Lord, have we not prophesied in Your name, cast out demons in Your name, and done many wonders in Your name?' ²³And then I will declare to them, 'I never

"Here's what I did..."

I used to struggle a lot with doubt. Was God real? Did he really care about what happens to me? Is the Bible relevant? Then someone challenged me to actively try to apply a passage from the Bible every day for two weeks and see if that made any difference. I did. I read some of the psalms and found that they were wonderfully relevant. When I felt lonely and had no one to turn to, I found that David's words perfectly expressed my feelings. Another passage I came across reminded me that God has promised never to leave us. Then when I came across Jesus' words in Matthew 7:24-27, I realized that it's only through obeying and applying God's Word that we know he's real. His Word is the only solid thing we have to build our lives on. The Matthew passage, and my two-week experiment, motivated me to try to live out what I read more and more every day.

Laura
AGE 17

8:10-12 Jesus told the crowd that many religious Jews who should be in the kingdom would be excluded because of their lack of faith. They were so entrenched in their religious traditions that they could not accept Christ and his new message. We must be careful not to become so set in our religious habits that we expect God to work only in specified ways.

knew you; depart from Me, you who practice lawlessness!'

²⁴"Therefore whoever hears these sayings of Mine, and does them, I will liken him to a wise man who built his house on the rock: ²⁵and the rain descended, the floods came, and the winds blew and beat on that house; and it did not fall, for it was founded on the rock.

²⁶"But everyone who hears these sayings of Mine, and does not do them, will be like a foolish man who built his house on the sand: ²⁷and the rain descended, the floods came, and the winds blew and beat on that house; and it fell. And great was its fall."

²⁸And so it was, when Jesus had ended these sayings, that the people were astonished at His teaching, ²⁹for He taught them as one having authority, and not as the scribes.

CHAPTER 8 TWO MEN BELIEVE AND ARE HEALED.

When He had come down from the mountain, great multitudes followed Him. ²And behold, a leper came and worshiped Him, saying, "Lord, if You are willing, You can make me clean."

³Then Jesus put out *His* hand and touched him, saying, "I am willing; be cleansed." Immediately his leprosy was cleansed.

⁴And Jesus said to him, "See that you tell no one; but go your way, show yourself to the priest, and offer the gift that Moses commanded, as a testimony to them."

8:19-20 Following Jesus is not always an easy or comfortable road. Often it means great cost and sacrifice, with no earthly rewards or security. Jesus didn't have a place to call home. You may find that following Christ costs you popularity, friendships, leisure time, or treasured habits. But while the costs of following Christ may be high, the value of being Christ's disciple is an investment that lasts for eternity and yields incredible rewards.

⁵Now when Jesus had entered Capernaum, a centurion came to Him, pleading with Him, ⁶saying, "Lord, my servant is lying at home paralyzed, dreadfully tormented."

⁷And Jesus said to him, "I will come and heal him."

⁸The centurion answered and said, "Lord, I am not worthy that You should come under my roof. But only speak a word, and my servant will be healed. ⁹For I also am a man under authority, having soldiers under me. And I say to this *one*, 'Go,' and he goes; and to another, 'Come,' and he comes; and to my servant, 'Do this,' and he does *it*."

¹⁰When Jesus heard *it*, He marveled, and said to those who followed, "Assuredly, I say to you, I have not found such great faith, not even in Israel! ¹¹And I say to you that many will come from east and west, and sit down with Abraham, Isaac, and Jacob in the kingdom of heaven.

¹²But the sons of the kingdom will be cast out into outer darkness. There will be weeping and gnashing of teeth."

¹³Then Jesus said to the centurion, "Go your way; and as you have believed, *so* let it be done for you." And his servant was healed that same hour.

¹⁴Now when Jesus had come into Peter's house, He saw his wife's mother lying sick with a fever. ¹⁵So He touched her hand, and the fever left her. And she arose and served them.

¹⁶When evening had come, they brought to Him many who were demon-possessed. And He cast out the spirits with a word, and healed all who were sick, ¹⁷that it might be fulfilled which was spoken by Isaiah the prophet, saying:

*"He Himself took our infirmities
And bore our sicknesses."*

¹⁸And when Jesus saw great multitudes about Him, He gave a command to depart to the other side. ¹⁹Then a certain scribe came and said to Him, "Teacher, I will follow You wherever You go."

²⁰And Jesus said to him, "Foxes have holes and birds of the air *have* nests, but the Son of Man has nowhere to lay *His* head."

²¹Then another of His disciples said to Him, "Lord, let me first go and bury my father."

²²But Jesus said to him, "Follow Me, and let the dead bury their own dead."

²³Now when He got into a boat, His disciples followed Him. ²⁴And suddenly a great tempest arose on the sea, so that the boat was covered with the waves. But He was asleep. ²⁵Then His disciples came to *Him* and awoke Him, saying, "Lord, save us! We are perishing!"

²⁶But He said to them, "Why are you fearful, O you of little faith?" Then He arose and rebuked the winds and the sea, and there was a great calm. ²⁷So the men marveled, saying, "Who can this be, that even the winds and the sea obey Him?"

²⁸When He had come to the other side, to the country of the Gergesenes, there met Him two demon-possessed *men*, coming out of the tombs, exceedingly fierce, so that no one could pass that way. ²⁹And suddenly they cried out, saying, "What have we to do with You, Jesus, You Son of God? Have You come here to torment us before the time?"

³⁰Now a good way off from them there was a herd of many swine feeding. ³¹So the demons begged Him, saying, "If You cast us out, permit us to go away into the herd of swine."

³²And He said to them, "Go." So when they had come out, they went into the herd of swine. And suddenly the

9:11-12 The Pharisees constantly tried to trap Jesus, and they thou his association with these "low lifes" was the perfect opportunity. The were more concerned with criticism than encouragement, with their ov appearance of holiness than in helping people, with outward respectability than practical help. But God is concerned for all people, including the sinful and hurting ones. The Christian life is not a popula contest! We need to follow Jesus' example and share the Good News v the poor, lonely, and outcast—not just the good, talented, and popul

whole herd of swine ran violently down the steep place into the sea, and perished in the water.

³³Then those who kept *them* fled; and they went away into the city and told everything, including what *had happened* to the demon-possessed *men.* ³⁴And behold, the whole city came out to meet Jesus. And when they saw Him, they begged *Him* to depart from their region.

CHAPTER 9 JESUS HEALS A PARALYZED MAN.

So He got into a boat, crossed over, and came to His own city. ²Then behold, they brought to Him a paralytic lying on a bed. When Jesus saw their faith, He said to the paralytic, "Son, be of good cheer; your sins are forgiven you."

³And at once some of the scribes said within themselves, "This Man blasphemes!"

⁴But Jesus, knowing their thoughts, said, "Why do you think evil in your hearts? ⁵For which is easier, to say, '*Your* sins are forgiven you,' or to say, 'Arise and walk'? ⁶But that you may know that the Son of Man has power on earth to forgive sins"—then He said to the paralytic, "Arise, take up your bed, and go to your house." ⁷And he arose and departed to his house.

⁸Now when the multitudes saw *it,* they marveled and glorified God, who had given such power to men.

⁹As Jesus passed on from there, He saw a man named Matthew sitting at the tax office. And He said to him, "Follow Me." So he arose and followed Him.

¹⁰Now it happened, as Jesus sat at the table in the house, *that* behold, many tax collectors and sinners came and sat down with Him and His disciples. ¹¹And when the Pharisees saw *it,* they said to His disciples, "Why does your Teacher eat with tax collectors and sinners?"

¹²When Jesus heard *that,* He said to them, "Those who are well have no need of a physician, but those who are sick. ¹³But go and learn what *this* means: '*I desire mercy and not sacrifice.*' For I did not come to call the righteous, but sinners, to repentance."

¹⁴Then the disciples of John came to Him, saying, "Why do we and the Pharisees fast often, but Your disciples do not fast?"

¹⁵And Jesus said to them, "Can the friends of the bridegroom mourn as long as the bridegroom is with them? But the days will come when the bridegroom will be taken away from them, and then they will fast. ¹⁶No one puts a piece of unshrunk cloth on an old garment; for the patch pulls away from the garment, and the tear is made worse. ¹⁷Nor do they put new wine into old wineskins, or else the wineskins break, the wine is spilled, and the wineskins are ruined. But they put new wine into new wineskins, and both are preserved."

¹⁸While He spoke these things to them, behold, a ruler came and worshiped Him, saying, "My daughter has just died, but come and lay Your hand on her and she will live." ¹⁹So Jesus arose and followed him, and so *did* His disciples.

²⁰And suddenly, a woman who had a flow of blood for twelve years came from behind and touched the hem of His garment. ²¹For she said to herself, "If only I may touch His garment, I shall be made well." ²²But Jesus turned around, and when He saw her He said, "Be of good cheer, daughter; your faith has made you well." And the woman was made well from that hour.

²³When Jesus came into the ruler's house, and saw the flute players and the noisy crowd wailing, ²⁴He said to them, "Make room, for the girl is not dead, but sleeping."

TESTING

9:27-30 Jesus didn't respond immediately to the blind men's pleas. He waited to see how earnest they were. Not everyone who says he or she wants help really wants it badly enough to do something about it. Jesus may have waited and questioned these men to make their desire and faith stronger. If, in your prayers, it seems as if God is too slow in giving his answer, maybe he is testing you as he did the blind men. Do you believe God can help you? Do you *really* want his help?

And they ridiculed Him. ²⁵But when the crowd was put outside, He went in and took her by the hand, and the girl arose. ²⁶And the report of this went out into all that land.

²⁷When Jesus departed from there, two blind men followed Him, crying out and saying, "Son of David, have mercy on us!"

²⁸And when He had come into the house, the blind men came to Him. And Jesus said to them, "Do you believe that I am able to do this?"

They said to Him, "Yes, Lord."

²⁹Then He touched their eyes, saying, "According to

For over six months I've been praying that my dad would become a Christian. Why hasn't God answered my prayer?

I WONDER . . .

You have certainly been persistent. And you're doing exactly what Matthew 7:7-11 is talking about. You're "asking, seeking, and knocking."

God answers our prayers in three different ways: "Yes," "No," or "Wait." In our instant society, where everything happens when we want it, "Wait" answers are not the ones we're accustomed to hearing. Especially when it seems like the prayer is not being answered. Or is it?

God, in his perfect wisdom, knows the perfect time for people to respond to his call, turn from their sin, and come into a right relationship with him. If we try to manipulate circumstances apart from God's will, perhaps these people will say no instead of yes.

Perhaps there's no one in your dad's life right now who could help him grow. Maybe there are important questions still unanswered that would cause him to respond out of emotion, rather than with his will. Perhaps there are hurts or misconceptions about God and the church that still need to be worked through before he can begin to examine God's love for him.

Whatever the reason, the best thing you can do is to keep praying for him. Also, ask a Christian friend if his or her father would be able to start a friendship with your dad.

Even persistence in prayer will not always change the heart that is hard toward God. People have a will that can say no to any openings God's love may try to penetrate. Just continue your persistent prayer. Never give up.

Jesus forgave

the paralyzed man lowered on a bed through the roof ... Matthew 9:2-8

the woman caught in adultery ... John 8:3-11

the woman who anointed his feet with oil ... Luke 7:47-50

Peter, for denying he knew Jesus ... John 18:15-18, 25-27; 21:15-

the criminal on the cross ... Luke 23:39-43

the people who crucified him ... Luke 23:34

Jesus not only taught frequently about forgiveness, he also demonstrated his own willingness to forgive. Here are several examples that should help us recognize his willingness to forgive us also.

VALUE

10:29-31 Jesus said that God cares for the sparrows' every need. We are far more valuable to God than these little birds, so valuable that God sent his only Son to die for us (John 3:16). You are of great worth to God. Because he places such value on you, you need never fear personal threats or difficult trials. But don't think that because you are valuable to God he will take away all your troubles (see 10:16). The real test of value is how well something holds up under the wear, tear, and abuse of everyday life. Those who stand up for Christ in spite of their troubles truly have lasting value and will receive great rewards (see 5:11-12).

your faith let it be to you." [30]And their eyes were opened. And Jesus sternly warned them, saying, "See *that* no one knows *it*." [31]But when they had departed, they spread the news about Him in all that country.

[32]As they went out, behold, they brought to Him a man, mute and demon-possessed. [33]And when the demon was cast out, the mute spoke. And the multitudes marveled, saying, "It was never seen like this in Israel!"

[34]But the Pharisees said, "He casts out demons by the ruler of the demons."

[35]Then Jesus went about all the cities and villages, teaching in their synagogues, preaching the gospel of the kingdom, and healing every sickness and every disease among the people. [36]But when He saw the multitudes, He was moved with compassion for them, because they were weary and scattered, like sheep having no shepherd. [37]Then He said to His disciples, "The harvest truly *is* plentiful, but the laborers *are* few. [38]Therefore pray the Lord of the harvest to send out laborers into His harvest."

CHAPTER 10 JESUS SENDS OUT THE DISCIPLES.

And when He had called His twelve disciples to *Him*, He gave them power *over* unclean spirits, to cast them out, and to heal all kinds of sickness and all kinds of disease. [2]Now the names of the twelve apostles are these: first, Simon, who is called Peter, and Andrew his brother;

James the *son* of Zebedee, and John his brother; [3]Philip and Bartholomew; Thomas and Matthew the tax collector; James the *son* of Alphaeus, and Lebbaeus, whose surname was Thaddaeus; [4]Simon the Cananite, and Judas Iscariot, who also betrayed Him.

[5]These twelve Jesus sent out and commanded them, saying: "Do not go into the way of the Gentiles, and do not enter a city of the Samaritans. [6]But go rather to the lost sheep of the house of Israel. [7]And as you go, preach, saying, 'The kingdom of heaven is at hand.' [8]Heal the sick, cleanse the lepers, raise the dead, cast out demons. Freely you have received, freely give. [9]Provide neither gold nor silver nor copper in your money belts, [10]nor bag for *your* journey, nor two tunics, nor sandals, nor staffs; for a worker is worthy of his food.

[11]"Now whatever city or town you enter, inquire who in it is worthy, and stay there till you go out. [12]And when you go into a household, greet it. [13]If the household is worthy, let your peace come upon it. But if it is not worthy, let your peace return to you. [14]And whoever will not receive you nor hear your words, when you depart from that house or city, shake off the dust from your feet. [15]Assuredly, I say to you, it will be more tolerable for the land of Sodom and Gomorrah in the day of judgment than for that city!

[16]"Behold, I send you out as sheep in the midst of wolves. Therefore be wise as serpents and harmless as

DOUBTS

11:4-6 As John sat in prison, he felt some doubts about whether really was the Messiah. If John's purpose was to prepare people fo coming Messiah (3:3), and if Jesus really was that Messiah, then w John in prison instead of preaching to the crowds, preparing their

Jesus answered John's doubts by pointing to his acts of healing, curing the lepers, raising the dead, and preaching the gospel to th With so much evidence, Jesus' identity was obvious. If you sometir doubt your salvation, the forgiveness of your sins, or God's work i life, look at the evidence in Scripture and in your life. When you d don't turn away from Christ, turn *to* him.

doves. [17]But beware of men, for they will deliver you up to councils and scourge you in their synagogues. [18]You will be brought before governors and kings for My sake, as a testimony to them and to the Gentiles. [19]But when they deliver you up, do not worry about how or what you should speak. For it will be given to you in that hour what you should speak; [20]for it is not you who speak, but the Spirit of your Father who speaks in you.

[21]"Now brother will deliver up brother to death, and a father *his* child; and children will rise up against parents and cause them to be put to death. [22]And you will be hated by all for My name's sake. But he who endures to the end will be saved. [23]When they persecute you in this city, flee to another. For assuredly, I say to you, you will not have gone through the cities of Israel before the Son of Man comes.

[24]"A disciple is not above *his* teacher, nor a servant above his master. [25]It is enough for a disciple that he be like his teacher, and a servant like his master. If they have called the master of the house Beelzebub, how much more *will they call* those of his household! [26]Therefore do not fear them. For there is nothing covered that will not be revealed, and hidden that will not be known.

[27]"Whatever I tell you in the dark, speak in the light; and what you hear in the ear, preach on the housetops. [28]And do not fear those who kill the body but cannot kill the soul. But rather fear Him who is able to destroy both soul and body in hell. [29]Are not two sparrows sold for a copper coin? And not one of them falls to the ground apart from your Father's will. [30]But the very hairs of your head are all numbered. [31]Do not fear therefore; you are of more value than many sparrows.

[32]"Therefore whoever confesses Me before men, him I will also confess before My Father who is in heaven. [33]But whoever denies Me before men, him I will also deny before My Father who is in heaven.

[34]"Do not think that I came to bring peace on earth. I did not come to bring peace but a sword. [35]For I have come to *'set a man against his father, a daughter against her mother, and a daughter-in-law against her mother-in-law'*; [36]and *'a man's enemies will be those of his own household.'* [37]He who loves father or mother more than Me is not worthy of Me. And he who loves son or daughter more than Me is not worthy of Me. [38]And he who does not take his cross and follow after Me is not worthy of Me. [39]He who finds his life will lose it, and he who loses his life for My sake will find it.

[40]"He who receives you receives Me, and he who receives Me receives Him who sent Me. [41]He who receives a prophet in the name of a prophet shall receive a prophet's reward. And he who receives a righteous man in the name of a righteous man shall receive a righteous man's reward. [42]And whoever gives one of these little ones only a cup of cold *water* in the name of a disciple, assuredly, I say to you, he shall by no means lose his reward."

CHAPTER **11** JOHN'S QUESTIONS ABOUT JESUS.

Now it came to pass, when Jesus finished commanding His twelve disciples, that He departed from there to teach and to preach in their cities.

[2]And when John had heard in prison about the works of Christ, he sent two of his disciples [3]and said to Him, "Are You the Coming One, or do we look for another?"

[4]Jesus answered and said to them, "Go and tell John the things which you hear and see: [5]*The* blind see and *the* lame walk; *the* lepers are cleansed and *the* deaf hear; *the* dead are raised up and *the* poor have the gospel preached to them. [6]And blessed is he who is not offended because of Me."

[7]As they departed, Jesus began to say to the multitudes concerning John: "What did you go out into the wilderness to see? A reed shaken by the wind? [8]But what did you go out to see? A man clothed in soft garments? Indeed, those who wear soft *clothing* are in kings' houses. [9]But

---

My parents are quietly putting up with my new faith. Mom thinks it's "nice" and Dad won't talk to me about it. How do I make them see Jesus is a real person?

I WONDER . . .

There are many difficult sayings of Jesus in the New Testament. Matthew 10:34-39 is one of the toughest. What does Jesus mean when he says "a man's enemies will be those of his own household"?

If you have faced pressure and opposition from friends because of your new faith, you realize that your decision for Christ causes people to make decisions about you. Some will stay with you and support your decision because they are your true friends. Others will leave because they don't understand or because your values no longer encourage their life-style.

We also may find opposition at home. In these verses, Jesus is not telling us to be disobedient to our parents or to try to cause problems at home. He is just stating the fact that a person with different goals, values, purposes, perhaps even morals, may cause division. This is more than a fact, it is a promise! Rarely will the only Christian in a household go unchallenged.

Though it is uncommon for parents to be openly hostile toward someone in their home, it does happen. Put-downs can really hurt, especially if they come from someone you love.

The best course of action is to not try to make your parents see anything. Instead, just live your life in obedience to them as the Bible commands: "Children, obey your parents in the Lord, for this is right. 'Honor your father and mother,' which is the first commandment with promise: 'that it may be well with you and you may live long on the earth.'" (Ephesians 6:1-3).

It is not your role or responsibility to make them change. That is the job of the Holy Spirit: "And when He has come, He will convict the world of sin, and of righteousness, and of judgment" (John 16:8). You are to be God's representative in your home, hopefully to be a part of bringing your family to Christ.

Don't neglect your family because it does not yet accept your faith. But don't neglect the higher mission of keeping God as your number-one priority either.

Find some Christian friends who will pray for you and pray with you about your situation. Go to them for encouragement and when you need advice on how to respond as each difficult situation arises.

what did you go out to see? A prophet? Yes, I say to you, and more than a prophet. ¹⁰For this is *he* of whom it is written:

'Behold, I send My messenger before Your face,
Who will prepare Your way before You.'

¹¹"Assuredly, I say to you, among those born of women there has not risen one greater than John the Baptist; but he who is least in the kingdom of heaven is greater than he. ¹²And from the days of John the Baptist until now the kingdom of heaven suffers violence, and the violent take it by force. ¹³For all the prophets and the law prophesied until John. ¹⁴And if you are willing to receive *it*, he is Elijah who is to come. ¹⁵He who has ears to hear, let him hear!

MOUTH

Mrs. Rogers puts the groceries in the trunk, buckles four-year-old Richie in his seat, and heads for home.

Soon Richie is holding his plastic airplane out the open window, watching its propeller spin. Mrs. Rogers notices what Richie is up to. "Don't do that. Keep your hands—and your toys—inside the car!" Richie smiles and slowly obeys.

But soon the hand-held plane banks to the right—back out the window.

"Richie!" Mrs. Rogers screams. "I told you, 'No!'"

Startled, the little boy drops the plane and lets fly with a word that four-year-old boys have no business knowing.

Mrs. Rogers is shocked. "Richie! Where did you learn that word?"

"From Christi."

"What other words have you heard her say?"

Richie rolls off words that would make a sailor blush.

When Mrs. Rogers gets home, she marches into her 16-year-old daughter's bedroom. "Christie, Richie used some horrible language in the car today . . . and he said he learned it from you. You want to explain?"

"Gee, Mom," Christi responds nervously. "No way. Not me. I don't know why he would say something like that."

Obviously Christi is caught up in lying as well as profanity. She needs to read Matthew 12:33-37.

¹⁶"But to what shall I liken this generation? It is like children sitting in the marketplaces and calling to their companions, ¹⁷and saying:

'We played the flute for you,
    And you did not dance;
We mourned to you,
    And you did not lament.'

¹⁸For John came neither eating nor drinking, and they say, 'He has a demon.' ¹⁹The Son of Man came eating and drinking, and they say, 'Look, a glutton and a winebibber, a friend of tax collectors and sinners!' But wisdom is justified by her children."

²⁰Then He began to rebuke the cities in which most of His mighty works had been done, because they did not repent: ²¹"Woe to you, Chorazin! Woe to you, Bethsaida! For if the mighty works which were done in you had been done in Tyre and Sidon, they would have repented long ago in sackcloth and ashes. ²²But I say to you, it will be more tolerable for Tyre and Sidon in the day of judgment than for you. ²³And you, Capernaum, who are exalted to heaven, will be brought down to Hades; for if the mighty works which were done in you had been done in Sodom, it would have remained until this day. ²⁴But I say to you that it shall be more tolerable for the land of Sodom in the day of judgment than for you."

²⁵At that time Jesus answered and said, "I thank You, Father, Lord of heaven and earth, that You have hidden these things from *the* wise and prudent and have revealed them to babes. ²⁶Even so, Father, for so it seemed good in Your sight. ²⁷All things have been delivered to Me by My Father, and no one knows the Son except the Father. Nor does anyone know the Father except the Son, and *the one* to whom the Son wills to reveal *Him*. ²⁸Come to Me, all *you* who labor and are heavy laden, and I will give you rest. ²⁹Take My yoke upon you and learn from Me, for I am gentle and lowly in heart, and you will find rest for your souls. ³⁰For My yoke *is* easy and My burden is light."

CHAPTER **12** JESUS TALKS ABOUT THE SABBATH.
At that time Jesus went through the grainfields on the Sabbath. And His disciples were hungry, and began to pluck heads of grain and to eat. ²And when the Pharisees saw *it*, they said to Him, "Look, Your disciples are doing what is not lawful to do on the Sabbath!"

³But He said to them, "Have you not read what David did when he was hungry, he and those who were with him: ⁴how he entered the house of God and ate the showbread which was not lawful for him to eat, nor for those who were with him, but only for the priests? ⁵Or have you not read in the law that on the Sabbath the priests in the temple profane the Sabbath, and are blameless? ⁶Yet I say to you that in this place there is *One* greater than the temple. ⁷But if you had known what *this* means, 'I desire mercy and not sacrifice,' you would not have condemned the guiltless. ⁸For the Son of Man is Lord even of the Sabbath."

⁹Now when He had departed from there, He went into their synagogue. ¹⁰And behold, there was a man who had a withered hand. And they asked Him, saying, "Is it lawful to heal on the Sabbath?"—that they might accuse Him.

¹¹Then He said to them, "What man is there among you who has one sheep, and if it falls into a pit on the Sabbath, will not lay hold of it and lift *it* out? ¹²Of how much more value then is a man than a sheep? Therefore it is lawful to do good on the Sabbath." ¹³Then He said to the man, "Stretch out your hand." And he stretched *it* out, and it was restored as whole as the other. ¹⁴Then the Pharisees went out and plotted against Him, how they might destroy Him.

¹⁵But when Jesus knew *it*, He withdrew from there. And great multitudes followed Him, and He healed them all. ¹⁶Yet He warned them not to make Him known, ¹⁷that it might be fulfilled which was spoken by Isaiah the prophet, saying:

¹⁸ "Behold! My Servant whom I have chosen,
    My Beloved in whom My soul is well pleased!
    I will put My Spirit upon Him,
    And He will declare justice to the Gentiles.

19 *He will not quarrel nor cry out,*
   Nor will anyone hear His voice in the streets.
20 *A bruised reed He will not break,*
   And smoking flax He will not quench,
   Till He sends forth justice to victory;
21 *And in His name Gentiles will trust."*

22Then one was brought to Him who was demon-possessed, blind and mute; and He healed him, so that the blind and mute man both spoke and saw. 23And all the multitudes were amazed and said, "Could this be the Son of David?"

24Now when the Pharisees heard *it* they said, "This *fellow* does not cast out demons except by Beelzebub, the ruler of the demons."

25But Jesus knew their thoughts, and said to them: "Every kingdom divided against itself is brought to desolation, and every city or house divided against itself will not stand. 26If Satan casts out Satan, he is divided against himself. How then will his kingdom stand? 27And if I cast out demons by Beelzebub, by whom do your sons cast *them* out? Therefore they shall be your judges. 28But if I cast out demons by the Spirit of God, surely the kingdom of God has come upon you. 29Or how can one enter a strong man's house and plunder his goods, unless he first binds the strong man? And then he will plunder his house. 30He who is not with Me is against Me, and he who does not gather with Me scatters abroad.

31"Therefore I say to you, every sin and blasphemy will be forgiven men, but the blasphemy *against* the Spirit will not be forgiven men. 32Anyone who speaks a word against the Son of Man, it will be forgiven him; but whoever speaks against the Holy Spirit, it will not be forgiven him, either in this age or in the *age* to come.

33"Either make the tree good and its fruit good, or else make the tree bad and its fruit bad; for a tree is known by *its* fruit. 34Brood of vipers! How can you, being evil, speak good things? For out of the abundance of the heart the mouth speaks. 35A good man out of the good treasure of his heart brings forth good things, and an evil man out of the evil treasure brings forth evil things. 36But I say to you that for every idle word men may speak, they will give account of it in the day of judgment. 37For by your words you will be justified, and by your words you will be condemned."

38Then some of the scribes and Pharisees answered, saying, "Teacher, we want to see a sign from You."

39But He answered and said to them, "An evil and adulterous generation seeks after a sign, and no sign will be given to it except the sign of the prophet Jonah. 40For as Jonah was three days and three nights in the belly of the great fish, so will the Son of Man be three days and three nights in the heart of the earth. 41The men of Nineveh will rise up in the judgment with this generation and condemn it, because they repented at the preaching of Jonah; and indeed a greater than Jonah *is* here. 42The queen of the South will rise up in the judgment with this generation and condemn it, for she came from the ends of the earth to hear the wisdom of Solomon; and indeed a greater than Solomon *is* here.

43"When an unclean spirit goes out of a man, he goes through dry places, seeking rest, and finds none. 44Then he says, 'I will return to my house from which I came.' And when he comes, he finds *it* empty, swept, and put in order. 45Then he goes and takes with him seven other spirits more wicked than himself, and they enter and dwell there; and the last *state* of that man is worse than the first. So shall it also be with this wicked generation."

▰▰▰ EVIDENCE

12:38-40 The Pharisees were asking for another miracle, but they were not sincerely seeking to know Jesus. Jesus knew that they had already seen enough miracles to prove he was the Messiah. They just had to open their hearts. But the Pharisees had already decided not to believe in Jesus; more miracles would not change that. Many people have thought, *If I could just see a real miracle, then I could really believe in God.* But Jesus' response to the Pharisees applies to us also. We have plenty of evidence—Jesus' death, resurrection, and ascension, plus centuries of his work in the lives of believers around the world. Instead of looking for additional evidence or miracles, accept what God has already given and move forward. He may use your life as evidence to reach another person.

46While He was still talking to the multitudes, behold, His mother and brothers stood outside, seeking to speak with Him. 47Then one said to Him, "Look, Your mother and Your brothers are standing outside, seeking to speak with You."

48But He answered and said to the one who told Him, "Who is My mother and who are My brothers?" 49And He stretched out His hand toward His disciples and said, "Here are My mother and My brothers! 50For whoever does the will of My Father in heaven is My brother and sister and mother."

CHAPTER **13** A STORY ABOUT A FARMER. On the same day Jesus went out of the house and sat by the sea. 2And great multitudes were gathered together to Him, so that He got into a boat and sat; and the whole multitude stood on the shore.

3Then He spoke many things to them in parables, saying: "Behold, a sower went out to sow. 4And as he sowed, some *seed* fell by the wayside; and the birds came and devoured them. 5Some fell on stony places, where they did not have much earth; and they immediately sprang up because they had no depth of earth. 6But when the sun was up they were scorched, and because they had no root they withered away. 7And some fell among thorns, and the thorns sprang up and choked them. 8But others fell on good ground and yielded a crop: some a hundredfold, some sixty, some thirty. 9He who has ears to hear, let him hear!"

10And the disciples came and said to Him, "Why do You speak to them in parables?"

▰▰▰ FARMING

13:8 This parable should encourage spiritual "farmers"—those who teach, preach, and lead others. The farmer sowed good seed, but not all of his sowing brought high yield. Some seed did not sprout, and even the plants that grew had varying yields. Don't be discouraged if no one seems to be listening to you as you faithfully teach the Word. Belief cannot be forced to follow a mathematical formula. Rather, it is a miracle of God's Holy Spirit as he uses your words to move others to come to him.

¹¹He answered and said to them, "Because it has been given to you to know the mysteries of the kingdom of heaven, but to them it has not been given. ¹²For whoever has, to him more will be given, and he will have abundance; but whoever does not have, even what he has will be taken away from him. ¹³Therefore I speak to them in parables, because seeing they do not see, and hearing they do not hear, nor do they understand. ¹⁴And in them the prophecy of Isaiah is fulfilled, which says:

'Hearing you will hear and shall not understand,
And seeing you will see and not perceive;
¹⁵ *For the hearts of this people have grown dull.*
Their ears are hard of hearing,
And their eyes they have closed,
Lest they should see with their eyes and hear with
their ears,
Lest they should understand with their hearts and
turn,
So that I should heal them.'

¹⁶But blessed *are* your eyes for they see, and your ears for they hear; ¹⁷for assuredly, I say to you that many prophets and righteous *men* desired to see what you see, and did not see *it,* and to hear what you hear, and did not hear *it.*

¹⁸"Therefore hear the parable of the sower: ¹⁹When anyone hears the word of the kingdom, and does not understand *it,* then the wicked *one* comes and snatches away what was sown in his heart. This is he who received seed by the wayside. ²⁰But he who received the seed on stony places, this is he who hears the word and immediately receives it with joy; ²¹yet he has no root in himself, but endures only for a while. For when tribulation or persecution arises because of the word, immediately he stumbles. ²²Now he who received seed among the thorns is he who hears the word, and the cares of this world and the deceitfulness of riches choke the word, and he becomes unfruitful. ²³But he who received seed on the good ground is he who hears the word and understands *it,* who indeed bears fruit and produces: some a hundredfold, some sixty, some thirty."

²⁴Another parable He put forth to them, saying: "The kingdom of heaven is like a man who sowed good seed in his field; ²⁵but while men slept, his enemy came and sowed tares among the wheat and went his way. ²⁶But when the grain had sprouted and produced a crop, then the tares also appeared. ²⁷So the servants of the owner came and said to him, 'Sir, did you not sow good seed in your field? How then does it have tares?' ²⁸He said to them, 'An enemy has done this.' The servants said to him, 'Do you want us then to go and gather them up?' ²⁹But he said, 'No, lest while you gather up the tares you also uproot the wheat with them. ³⁰Let both grow together until the harvest, and at the time of harvest I will say to the reapers, "First gather together the tares and bind them in bundles to burn them, but gather the wheat into my barn." ' "

³¹Another parable He put forth to them, saying: "The kingdom of heaven is like a mustard seed, which a man took and sowed in his field, ³²which indeed is the least of all the seeds; but when it is grown it is greater than the herbs and becomes a tree, so that the birds of the air come and nest in its branches."

13:23 The four types of soil represent the different responses we have to God's message. We respond differently because we are in different states of readiness. Some people are hardened, others are shallow, others are contaminated by distracting cares, and some are receptive. How has God's Word taken root in your life? What kind are you?

³³Another parable He spoke to them: "The kingdom of heaven is like leaven, which a woman took and hid in three measures of meal till it was all leavened."

³⁴All these things Jesus spoke to the multitude in parables; and without a parable He did not speak to them, ³⁵that it might be fulfilled which was spoken by the prophet, saying:

"I will open My mouth in parables;
I will utter things kept secret from the foundation of
the world."

³⁶Then Jesus sent the multitude away and went into the house. And His disciples came to Him, saying, "Explain to us the parable of the tares of the field." ³⁷He answered and said to them: "He who sows the good seed is the Son of Man. ³⁸The field is the world, the good seeds are the sons of the kingdom, but the tares are the sons of the wicked *one.* ³⁹The enemy who sowed them is the devil, the harvest is the end of the age, and the reapers are the angels. ⁴⁰Therefore as the tares are gathered and burned in the fire, so it will be at the end of this age. ⁴¹The Son of Man will send out His angels, and they will gather out of His kingdom all things that offend, and those who practice lawlessness, ⁴²and will cast them into the furnace of fire. There will be wailing and gnashing of teeth. ⁴³Then the righteous will shine forth as the sun in the kingdom of their Father. He who has ears to hear, let him hear!

⁴⁴"Again, the kingdom of heaven is like treasure hidden in a field, which a man found and hid; and for joy over it he goes and sells all that he has and buys that field.

⁴⁵"Again, the kingdom of heaven is like a merchant seeking beautiful pearls, ⁴⁶who, when he had found one pearl of great price, went and sold all that he had and bought it.

⁴⁷"Again, the kingdom of heaven is like a dragnet that was cast into the sea and gathered some of every kind, ⁴⁸which, when it was full, they drew to shore; and they sat down and gathered the good into vessels, but threw the bad away. ⁴⁹So it will be at the end of the age. The angels will come forth, separate the wicked from among the just, ⁵⁰and cast them into the furnace of fire. There will be wailing and gnashing of teeth."

⁵¹Jesus said to them, "Have you understood all these things?"

They said to Him, "Yes, Lord."

⁵²Then He said to them, "Therefore every scribe instructed concerning the kingdom of heaven is like a householder who brings out of his treasure *things* new and old."

⁵³Now it came to pass, when Jesus had finished these parables, that He departed from there. ⁵⁴When He had come to His own country, He taught them in their synagogue, so that they were astonished and said, "Where did this *Man* get this wisdom and *these* mighty works? ⁵⁵Is this not the carpenter's son? Is not His mother called Mary? And His brothers James, Joses, Simon, and Judas? ⁵⁶And His sisters, are they not all with us? Where then did this *Man* get all these things?" ⁵⁷So they were offended at Him.

But Jesus said to them, "A prophet is not without honor except in his own country and in his own house." [58]Now He did not do many mighty works there because of their unbelief.

CHAPTER 14 HEROD KILLS JOHN THE BAPTIST.
At that time Herod the tetrarch heard the report about Jesus [2]and said to his servants, "This is John the Baptist; he is risen from the dead, and therefore these powers are at work in him." [3]For Herod had laid hold of John and bound him, and put *him* in prison for the sake of Herodias, his brother Philip's wife. [4]Because John had said to him, "It is not lawful for you to have her." [5]And although he wanted to put him to death, he feared the multitude, because they counted him as a prophet.

[6]But when Herod's birthday was celebrated, the daughter of Herodias danced before them and pleased Herod. [7]Therefore he promised with an oath to give her whatever she might ask.

[8]So she, having been prompted by her mother, said, "Give me John the Baptist's head here on a platter."

[9]And the king was sorry; nevertheless, because of the oaths and because of those who sat with him, he commanded *it* to be given to *her.* [10]So he sent and had John beheaded in prison. [11]And his head was brought on a platter and given to the girl, and she brought *it* to her mother. [12]Then his disciples came and took away the body and buried it, and went and told Jesus.

[13]When Jesus heard *it,* He departed from there by boat to a deserted place by Himself. But when the multitudes heard it, they followed Him on foot from the cities. [14]And when Jesus went out He saw a great multitude; and He was moved with compassion for them, and healed their sick. [15]When it was evening, His disciples came to Him, saying, "This is a deserted place, and the hour is already late. Send the multitudes away, that they may go into the villages and buy themselves food."

[16]But Jesus said to them, "They do not need to go away. You give them something to eat."

[17]And they said to Him, "We have here only five loaves and two fish."

[18]He said, "Bring them here to Me." [19]Then He commanded the multitudes to sit down on the grass. And He took the five loaves and the two fish, and looking up to heaven, He blessed and broke and gave the loaves to the disciples; and the disciples gave to the multitudes. [20]So they all ate and were filled, and they took up twelve baskets full of the fragments that remained. [21]Now those who had eaten were about five thousand men, besides women and children.

[22]Immediately Jesus made His disciples get into the boat and go before Him to the other side, while He sent the multitudes away. [23]And when He had sent the multitudes away, He went up on the mountain by Himself to pray. Now when evening came, He was alone there. [24]But the boat was now in the middle of the sea, tossed by the waves, for the wind was contrary.

[25]Now in the fourth watch of the night Jesus went to them, walking on the sea. [26]And when the disciples saw Him walking on the sea, they were troubled, saying, "It is a ghost!" And they cried out for fear.

[27]But immediately Jesus spoke to them, saying, "Be of good cheer! It is I; do not be afraid."

[28]And Peter answered Him and said, "Lord, if it is You, command me to come to You on the water."

◣▬▬▬▬◞GIVING IN

14:9 Herod did not want to kill John the Baptist, but he gave the order so he wouldn't be embarrassed in front of his guests. How easy it is to give in to crowd pressure, to let ourself be coerced into doing wrong. Don't place yourself in a position where it is too embarrassing to do what is right. Do what is right no matter how embarrassing or painful it may be.

[29]So He said, "Come." And when Peter had come down out of the boat, he walked on the water to go to Jesus. [30]But when he saw that the wind *was* boisterous, he was afraid; and beginning to sink he cried out, saying, "Lord, save me!"

[31]And immediately Jesus stretched out *His* hand and caught him, and said to him, "O you of little faith, why did you doubt?" [32]And when they got into the boat, the wind ceased.

[33]Then those who were in the boat came and worshiped Him, saying, "Truly You are the Son of God."

[34]When they had crossed over, they came to the land of Gennesaret. [35]And when the men of that place recognized Him, they sent out into all that surrounding region, brought to Him all who were sick, [36]and begged Him that they might only touch the hem of His garment. And as many as touched *it* were made perfectly well.

CHAPTER 15 THE RULES THAT COUNT.
Then the scribes and Pharisees who were from Jerusalem came to Jesus, saying, [2]"Why do Your disciples transgress the tradition of the elders? For they do not wash their hands when they eat bread."

[3]He answered and said to them, "Why do you also transgress the commandment of God because of your tradition? [4]For God commanded, saying, *'Honor your father and your mother';* and, *'He who curses father or mother, let him be put to death.'* [5]But you say, 'Whoever says to his father or mother, "Whatever profit you might have received from me *is* a gift *to God"*—[6]then he need not honor his father or mother.' Thus you have made the commandment of God of no effect by your tradition. [7]Hypocrites! Well did Isaiah prophesy about you, saying:

◣▬▬▬▬◞EYES

14:28 Peter was not testing Jesus, something we are told not to do (4:7). Instead he was the only one in the boat to react in faith. His impulsive request led him to experience a rather unusual demonstration of God's power. Peter started to sink because he took his eyes off Jesus and focused on the high waves around him. His faith wavered when he realized what he was doing. We may not walk on water, but we do walk through tough situations. If we focus on the waves of difficult circumstances around us without looking to Christ for help, we too may despair and sink. To maintain your faith in the midst of difficult situations, keep your eyes on Christ's power rather than on your inadequacies.

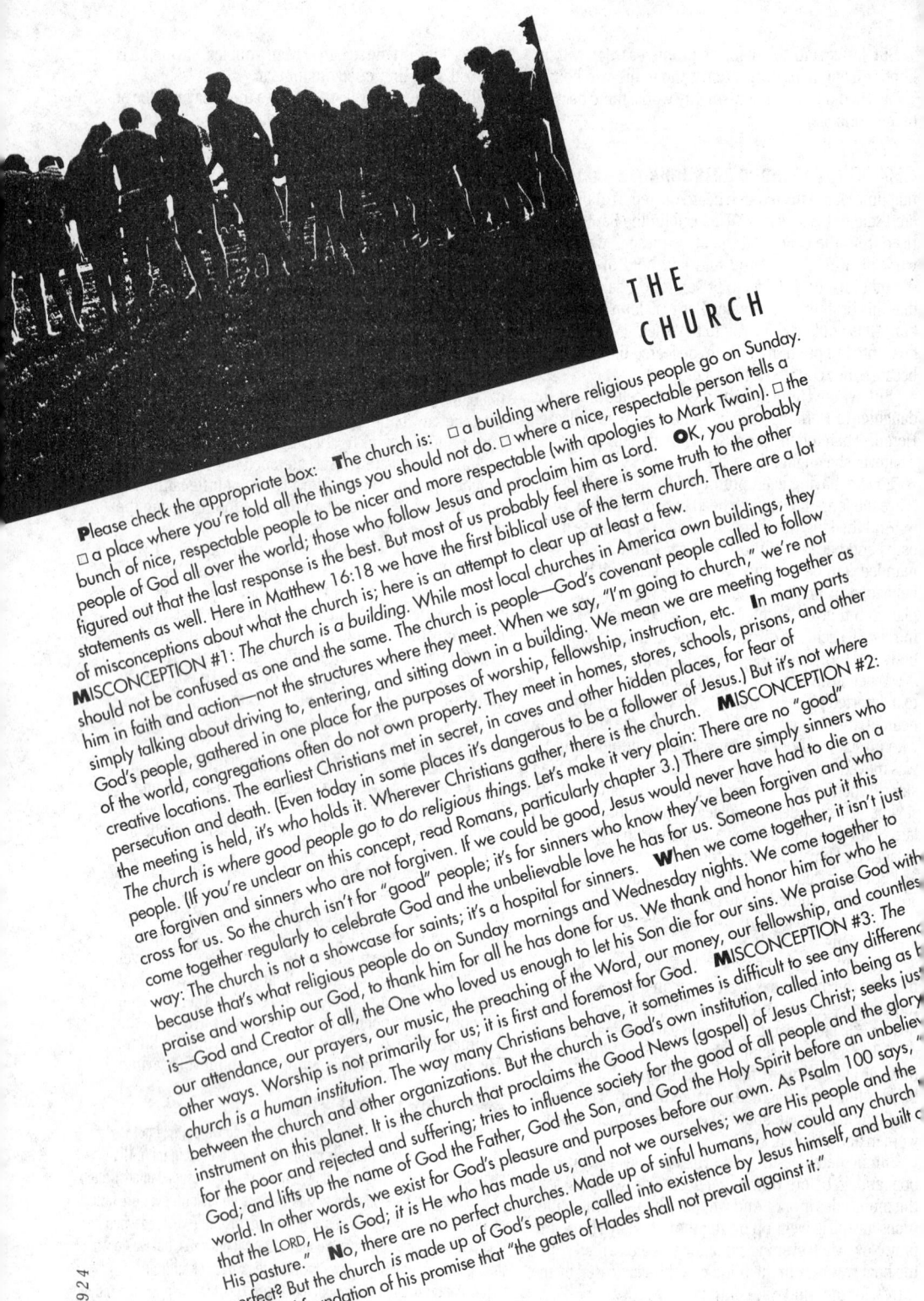

THE CHURCH

Please check the appropriate box: **T**he church is: ☐ a building where religious people go on Sunday. ☐ a place where you're told all the things you should not do. ☐ where a nice, respectable person tells a bunch of nice, respectable people to be nicer and more respectable (with apologies to Mark Twain). ☐ the people of God all over the world; those who follow Jesus and proclaim him as Lord. **O**K, you probably figured out that the last response is the best. But most of us probably feel there is some truth to the other statements as well. Here in Matthew 16:18 we have the first biblical use of the term *church*. There are a lot of misconceptions about what the church is; here is an attempt to clear up at least a few.

MISCONCEPTION #1: *The church is a building.* While most local churches in America own buildings, they should not be confused as one and the same. The church is people—God's covenant people called to follow him in faith and action—not the structures where they meet. When we say, "I'm going to church," we're not simply talking about driving to, entering, and sitting down in a building. We mean we are meeting together as God's people, gathered in one place for the purposes of worship, fellowship, instruction, etc. **I**n many parts of the world, congregations often do not own property. They meet in homes, stores, schools, prisons, and other creative locations. The earliest Christians met in secret, in caves and other hidden places, for fear of persecution and death. (Even today in some places it's dangerous to be a follower of Jesus.) But it's not where the meeting is held, it's who holds it. Wherever Christians gather, there is the church. **M**ISCONCEPTION #2: *The church is where good people go to do religious things.* Let's make it very plain: There are no "good" people. (If you're unclear on this concept, read Romans, particularly chapter 3.) There are simply sinners who are forgiven and sinners who are not forgiven. If we could be good, Jesus would never have had to die on a cross for us. So the church isn't for "good" people; it's for sinners who know they've been forgiven and who come together regularly to celebrate God and the unbelievable love he has for us. Someone has put it this way: The church is not a showcase for saints; it's a hospital for sinners. **W**hen we come together, it isn't just because that's what religious people do on Sunday mornings and Wednesday nights. We come together to praise and worship our God, to thank him for all he has done for us. We thank and honor him for who he is—God and Creator of all, the One who loved us enough to let his Son die for our sins. We praise God with our attendance, our prayers, our music, the preaching of the Word, our money, our fellowship, and countless other ways. Worship is not primarily for us; it is first and foremost for God. **M**ISCONCEPTION #3: *The church is a human institution.* The way many Christians behave, it sometimes is difficult to see any difference between the church and other organizations. But the church is God's own institution, called into being as his instrument on this planet. It is the church that proclaims the Good News (gospel) of Jesus Christ; seeks justice for the poor and rejected and suffering; tries to influence society for the good of all people and the glory of God; and lifts up the name of God the Father, God the Son, and God the Holy Spirit before an unbelieving world. In other words, we exist for God's pleasure and purposes before our own. As Psalm 100 says, that the LORD, He is God; *it is He* who has made us, and not we ourselves; we are His people and the sheep of His pasture." **N**o, there are no perfect churches. Made up of God's people, called into existence by Jesus himself, and built on the rock-solid foundation of his promise that "the gates of Hades shall not prevail against it."

8 '*These people draw near to Me with their mouth,*
  And honor Me with their lips,
  But their heart is far from Me.
9 *And in vain they worship Me,*
  Teaching as doctrines the commandments of men.' "

10When He had called the multitude to *Himself,* He said to them, "Hear and understand: 11Not what goes into the mouth defiles a man; but what comes out of the mouth, this defiles a man."

12Then His disciples came and said to Him, "Do You know that the Pharisees were offended when they heard this saying?"

13But He answered and said, "Every plant which My heavenly Father has not planted will be uprooted. 14Let them alone. They are blind leaders of the blind. And if the blind leads the blind, both will fall into a ditch."

15Then Peter answered and said to Him, "Explain this parable to us."

16So Jesus said, "Are you also still without understanding? 17Do you not yet understand that whatever enters the mouth goes into the stomach and is eliminated? 18But those things which proceed out of the mouth come from the heart, and they defile a man. 19For out of the heart proceed evil thoughts, murders, adulteries, fornications, thefts, false witness, blasphemies. 20These are *the things* which defile a man, but to eat with unwashed hands does not defile a man."

21Then Jesus went out from there and departed to the region of Tyre and Sidon. 22And behold, a woman of Canaan came from that region and cried out to Him, saying, "Have mercy on me, O Lord, Son of David! My daughter is severely demon-possessed."

23But He answered her not a word.

And His disciples came and urged Him, saying, "Send her away, for she cries out after us."

24But He answered and said, "I was not sent except to the lost sheep of the house of Israel."

25Then she came and worshiped Him, saying, "Lord, help me!"

26But He answered and said, "It is not good to take the children's bread and throw *it* to the little dogs."

27And she said, "Yes, Lord, yet even the little dogs eat the crumbs which fall from their masters' table."

28Then Jesus answered and said to her, "O woman, great *is* your faith! Let it be to you as you desire." And her daughter was healed from that very hour.

29Jesus departed from there, skirted the Sea of Galilee, and went up on the mountain and sat down there. 30Then great multitudes came to Him, having with them *the* lame, blind, mute, maimed, and many others; and they laid them down at Jesus' feet, and He healed them. 31So the multitude marveled when they saw *the* mute speaking, *the* maimed made whole, *the* lame walking, and *the* blind seeing; and they glorified the God of Israel.

32Now Jesus called His disciples to *Himself* and said, "I have compassion on the multitude, because they have now continued with Me three days and have nothing to eat. And I do not want to send them away hungry, lest they faint on the way."

33Then His disciples said to Him, "Where could we get enough bread in the wilderness to fill such a great multitude?"

34Jesus said to them, "How many loaves do you have?" And they said, "Seven, and a few little fish."

35So He commanded the multitude to sit down on the ground. 36And He took the seven loaves and the fish and gave thanks, broke *them* and gave *them* to His disciples; and the disciples *gave* to the multitude. 37So they all ate and were filled, and they took up seven large baskets full of the fragments that were left. 38Now those who ate were four thousand men, besides women and children. 39And He sent away the multitude, got into the boat, and came to the region of Magdala.

CHAPTER **16** THE LEADERS WANT A MIRACLE.

Then the Pharisees and Sadducees came, and testing Him asked that He would show them a sign from heaven. 2He answered and said to them, "When it is evening you say, '*It will be* fair weather, for the sky is red'; 3and in the morning, '*It will be* foul weather today, for the sky is red and threatening.' Hypocrites! You know how to discern the face of the sky, but you cannot *discern* the signs of the

◄▬▬▬▬▬▬▬▬ALL AROUND US

15:23 The disciples asked Jesus to get rid of the woman because she was bothering them with her begging. They showed no compassion for her or sensitivity to her needs. It is possible to become so occupied with spiritual matters that we miss real spiritual needs right around us, whether out of prejudice or simply because of the inconvenience they cause. Instead of being bothered, be aware of the opportunities that surround you. Be open to the beauty of God's message for all people, and make an effort not to shut out those who are different from you.

times. 4A wicked and adulterous generation seeks after a sign, and no sign shall be given to it except the sign of the prophet Jonah." And He left them and departed.

5Now when His disciples had come to the other side, they had forgotten to take bread. 6Then Jesus said to them, "Take heed and beware of the leaven of the Pharisees and the Sadducees."

7And they reasoned among themselves, saying, "*It is* because we have taken no bread."

8But Jesus, being aware of *it,* said to them, "O you of little faith, why do you reason among yourselves because you have brought no bread? 9Do you not yet understand, or remember the five loaves of the five thousand and how many baskets you took up? 10Nor the seven loaves of the four thousand and how many large baskets you took up? 11How is it you do not understand that I did not speak to you concerning bread?—*but* to beware of the leaven of the Pharisees and Sadducees." 12Then they understood that He did not tell *them* to beware of the leaven of bread, but of the doctrine of the Pharisees and Sadducees.

13When Jesus came into the region of Caesarea Philippi, He asked His disciples, saying, "Who do men say that I, the Son of Man, am?"

14So they said, "Some *say* John the Baptist, some Elijah, and others Jeremiah or one of the prophets."

15He said to them, "But who do you say that I am?"

¹⁶Simon Peter answered and said, "You are the Christ, the Son of the living God."

¹⁷Jesus answered and said to him, "Blessed are you, Simon Bar-Jonah, for flesh and blood has not revealed *this* to you, but My Father who is in heaven. ¹⁸And I also say to you that you are Peter, and on this rock I will build My church, and the gates of Hades shall not prevail against it. ¹⁹And I will give you the keys of the kingdom of heaven, and whatever you bind on earth will be bound in heaven, and whatever you loose on earth will be loosed in heaven."

PROTECT

16:21-22 Peter, Jesus' friend and devoted follower who had just eloquently proclaimed his Lord's true identity as the Christ, sought to protect him from the suffering he prophesied. Great temptations can come from those who love us and seek to protect us from something we must experience. Be cautious of advice from a friend who says, "Surely God doesn't want you to face this."

²⁰Then He commanded His disciples that they should tell no one that He was Jesus the Christ.

²¹From that time Jesus began to show to His disciples that He must go to Jerusalem, and suffer many things from the elders and chief priests and scribes, and be killed, and be raised the third day.

²²Then Peter took Him aside and began to rebuke Him, saying, "Far be it from You, Lord; this shall not happen to You!"

²³But He turned and said to Peter, "Get behind Me, Satan! You are an offense to Me, for you are not mindful of the things of God, but the things of men."

²⁴Then Jesus said to His disciples, "If anyone desires to come after Me, let him deny himself, and take up his cross, and follow Me. ²⁵For whoever desires to save his life will lose it, but whoever loses his life for My sake will find it. ²⁶For what profit is it to a man if he gains the whole world, and loses his own soul? Or what will a man give in exchange for his soul? ²⁷For the Son of Man will come in the glory of His Father with His angels, and then He will reward each according to his works. ²⁸Assuredly, I say to you, there are some standing here who shall not taste death till they see the Son of Man coming in His kingdom."

CHAPTER **17** JESUS SHINES LIKE THE SUN. Now after six days Jesus took Peter, James, and John his brother, led them up on a high mountain by themselves; ²and He was transfigured before them. His face shone like the sun, and His clothes became as white as the light. ³And behold, Moses and Elijah appeared to them, talking with Him. ⁴Then Peter answered and said to Jesus, "Lord, it is good for us to be here; if You wish, let us make here three tabernacles: one for You, one for Moses, and one for Elijah."

⁵While he was still speaking, behold, a bright cloud overshadowed them; and suddenly a voice came out of the cloud, saying, "This is My beloved Son, in whom I am well pleased. Hear Him!" ⁶And when the disciples heard *it*, they fell on their faces and were greatly afraid. ⁷But Jesus came and touched them and said, "Arise, and do

BELIEVE

17:22-23 Again Jesus predicted his death; but more important, told of his resurrection. Unfortunately, the disciples heard only the part and became discouraged. They couldn't understand why Jesus wanted to go back to Jerusalem and the trouble he'd find there. The disciples didn't fully comprehend the purpose of Jesus' death and resurrection until Pentecost (Acts 2). Don't get upset at yourself if y slow to understand everything about Jesus. After all, the disciples w with him, saw his miracles, and heard his words— and they still ha difficulty understanding. Despite their questions and doubts, howe they believed. We can do no less.

not be afraid." ⁸When they had lifted up their eyes, they saw no one but Jesus only.

⁹Now as they came down from the mountain, Jesus commanded them, saying, "Tell the vision to no one until the Son of Man is risen from the dead."

¹⁰And His disciples asked Him, saying, "Why then do the scribes say that Elijah must come first?"

¹¹Jesus answered and said to them, "Indeed, Elijah is coming first and will restore all things. ¹²But I say to you that Elijah has come already, and they did not know him but did to him whatever they wished. Likewise the Son of Man is also about to suffer at their hands." ¹³Then the disciples understood that He spoke to them of John the Baptist.

LITTLE KIDS

18:6 Children are trusting by nature. They trust adults, which he them learn about trusting God. Parents and others who influence y children are held accountable by God for how they affect these litt ability to trust. Jesus warned that anyone who turns little children from faith will receive severe punishment.

¹⁴And when they had come to the multitude, a man came to Him, kneeling down to Him and saying, ¹⁵"Lord, have mercy on my son, for he is an epileptic and suffers severely; for he often falls into the fire and often into the water. ¹⁶So I brought him to Your disciples, but they could not cure him."

¹⁷Then Jesus answered and said, "O faithless and perverse generation, how long shall I be with you? How long shall I bear with you? Bring him here to Me." ¹⁸And Jesus rebuked the demon, and it came out of him; and the child was cured from that very hour.

¹⁹Then the disciples came to Jesus privately and said, "Why could we not cast it out?"

²⁰So Jesus said to them, "Because of your unbelief; for assuredly, I say to you, if you have faith as a mustard seed, you will say to this mountain, 'Move from here to there,' and it will move; and nothing will be impossible for you. ²¹However, this kind does not go out except by prayer and fasting."

²²Now while they were staying in Galilee, Jesus said to them, "The Son of Man is about to be betrayed into the

KEEP TRACK

18:22 The rabbis taught that Jews should forgive three times tho offend them. Peter, in trying to be especially generous, asked Jesus seven (the "perfect" number) was enough times to forgive someone Jesus answered, "Seventy times seven," meaning that we shouldn't keep track of how many times we forgive someone. We should alwa forgive those who are truly repentant, no matter how many times t

hands of men, [23]and they will kill Him, and the third day He will be raised up." And they were exceedingly sorrowful.

[24]When they had come to Capernaum, those who received the *temple* tax came to Peter and said, "Does your Teacher not pay the *temple* tax?"

[25]He said, "Yes."

And when he had come into the house, Jesus anticipated him, saying, "What do you think, Simon? From whom do the kings of the earth take customs or taxes, from their sons or from strangers?"

[26]Peter said to Him, "From strangers."

Jesus said to him, "Then the sons are free. [27]Nevertheless, lest we offend them, go to the sea, cast in a hook, and take the fish that comes up first. And when you have opened its mouth, you will find a piece of money; take that and give it to them for Me and you."

CHAPTER **18** WHO IS THE GREATEST? At that time the disciples came to Jesus, saying, "Who then is greatest in the kingdom of heaven?"

[2]Then Jesus called a little child to Him, set him in the midst of them, [3]and said, "Assuredly, I say to you, unless you are converted and become as little children, you will by no means enter the kingdom of heaven. [4]Therefore whoever humbles himself as this little child is the greatest in the kingdom of heaven. [5]Whoever receives one little child like this in My name receives Me.

[6]"Whoever causes one of these little ones who believe in Me to sin, it would be better for him if a millstone were hung around his neck, and he were drowned in the depth of the sea. [7]Woe to the world because of offenses! For offenses must come, but woe to that man by whom the offense comes!

[8]"If your hand or foot causes you to sin, cut it off and cast *it* from you. It is better for you to enter into life lame or maimed, rather than having two hands or two feet, to be cast into the everlasting fire. [9]And if your eye causes you to sin, pluck it out and cast *it* from you. It is better for you to enter into life with one eye, rather than having two eyes, to be cast into hell fire.

[10]"Take heed that you do not despise one of these little ones, for I say to you that in heaven their angels always see the face of My Father who is in heaven. [11]For the Son of Man has come to save that which was lost.

[12]"What do you think? If a man has a hundred sheep, and one of them goes astray, does he not leave the ninety-nine and go to the mountains to seek the one that is straying? [13]And if he should find it, assuredly, I say to you, he rejoices more over that *sheep* than over the ninety-nine that did not go astray. [14]Even so it is not the will of your Father who is in heaven that one of these little ones should perish.

[15]"Moreover if your brother sins against you, go and tell him his fault between you and him alone. If he hears you, you have gained your brother. [16]But if he will not hear, take with you one or two more, that '*by the mouth of two or three witnesses every word may be established.*' [17]And if he refuses to hear them, tell *it* to the church. But if he refuses even to hear the church, let him be to you like a heathen and a tax collector.

[18]"Assuredly, I say to you, whatever you bind on earth will be bound in heaven, and whatever you loose on earth will be loosed in heaven.

[19]"Again I say to you that if two of you agree on earth concerning anything that they ask, it will be done for them by My Father in heaven. [20]For where two or three are gathered together in My name, I am there in the midst of them."

[21]Then Peter came to Him and said, "Lord, how often

I WONDER . . .

Is temptation a sin? If it is, I'm sinning all the time. It seems like thoughts are always coming into my mind to do things that are wrong.

If temptation were a sin, then Jesus was a sinner (see Matthew 4:1-11 for the story of when Satan tempted Jesus in the wilderness). Temptation is not a sin. According to Matthew 18:7-9, it's the natural consequence of living in this world.

What leads to sin is following the path temptation wants us to take. If taken far enough, the path will cause us to think and do what is wrong.

Though temptation always will be present, we do not have to wave the white flag and admit defeat. We have the power to resist, because the Holy Spirit lives in us.

God's Word also reminds us how to overcome temptation. First Corinthians 10:13 says, "No temptation has overtaken you except such as is common to man; but God *is* faithful, who will not allow you to be tempted beyond what you are able, but with the temptation will also make the way of escape, that you may be able to bear *it*."

Find the way of escape in this story:

At school a friend asks if you want to spend the night with some friends and watch videos. You check with your folks, assuring them there will be no R-rated videos. They give the OK. Everything is cool, so far.

Once you arrive, you look at the stack of videos and notice that half of them are R-rated. You get your friend alone and ask him what the deal is. He says the other guys picked out the videos. Besides, everyone (but you) has seen them before, so he didn't think you'd mind.

Do you stay and go against what your parents want, or do you go along with the group?

Let's say you stay. The next day Dad asks what movies you watched. Now you have to lie to stay out of trouble. So you lie. Unfortunately, your mom spoke with the mom of one of your friends on the phone and found out there were R-rated movies at the sleep-over. Now you're grounded until age 27!

Where were the escape hatches to the temptation to disobey your parents? When you found out that R-rated movies would be shown, you had two choices. You could have apologized to your friends, called your dad, and had him pick you up. Or you could have gone to a different part of the house and done something else.

God always provides a way of escape in every circumstance. We choose whether to take his way out or to do things we know are wrong.

If we stay close to God, we'll be more likely to resist and do what is right. We don't have to give in.

shall my brother sin against me, and I forgive him? Up to seven times?"

[22]Jesus said to him, "I do not say to you, up to seven times, but up to seventy times seven. [23]Therefore the kingdom of heaven is like a certain king who wanted to settle accounts with his servants. [24]And when he had begun to settle accounts, one was brought to him who owed him ten thousand talents. [25]But as he was not able to pay, his master commanded that he be sold, with his wife and children and all that he had, and that payment be made. [26]The servant therefore fell down before him, saying, 'Master, have patience with me, and I will pay you all.' [27]Then the master of that servant was moved with compassion, released him, and forgave him the debt.

DIVORCE

Annette and Mary are watching the evening soap opera "California Millionaires."

In this particular episode, police are investigating a possible murder at the Stanwick estate, Lance and Natasha are having an affair, and Sutherland is still thinking about having a sex-change operation. But as wild as those events are, they still are not the main plot of this week's show. No, the most disturbing revelation is that Gabrielle and Welborne Stanwick are divorcing.

"I can't believe it!" Annette laments as she clicks off the TV in disgust. "They were so perfect together. Now it's over."

"Yeah, I never thought we'd ever see them call it quits. I guess it just goes to show you that even the best marriages sometimes come to an end."

"Just like my aunt and uncle. They were married for 25 years and . . ."

"Ooh, don't tell me one of them had an affair?" Mary asks, an eager tone in her voice.

"No, they just grew apart over the years. . . ."

"That is so sad!" Mary says.

Mary is right. Divorce is sad. But what about her statement that some marriages have to end? Does God sanction divorce for reasons of incompatibility or "Well, we just don't love each other anymore"?

Read Matthew 19:1-12 to see what Jesus thinks about marriage, commitment, and divorce.

[28]"But that servant went out and found one of his fellow servants who owed him a hundred denarii; and he laid hands on him and took *him* by the throat, saying, 'Pay me what you owe!' [29]So his fellow servant fell down at his feet and begged him, saying, 'Have patience with me, and I will pay you all.' [30]And he would not, but went and threw him into prison till he should pay the debt. [31]So when his fellow servants saw what had been done, they were very grieved, and came and told their master all that had been done. [32]Then his master, after he had called him, said to him, 'You wicked servant! I forgave you all that debt because you begged me. [33]Should you not also have had compassion on your fellow servant, just as I had pity on you?' [34]And his master was angry, and delivered him to the torturers until he should pay all that was due to him.

[35]"So My heavenly Father also will do to you if each of you, from his heart, does not forgive his brother his trespasses."

CHAPTER **19** **MARRIAGE AND DIVORCE.** Now it came to pass, when Jesus had finished these sayings, *that* He departed from Galilee and came to the region of Judea beyond the Jordan. [2]And great multitudes followed Him, and He healed them there.

[3]The Pharisees also came to Him, testing Him, and saying to Him, "Is it lawful for a man to divorce his wife for *just* any reason?"

[4]And He answered and said to them, "Have you not read that He who made *them* at the beginning 'made *them male and female,*' [5]and said, '*For this reason a man shall leave his father and mother and be joined to his wife, and the two shall become one flesh*'? [6]So then, they are no longer two but one flesh. Therefore what God has joined together, let not man separate."

[7]They said to Him, "Why then did Moses command to give a certificate of divorce, and to put her away?"

[8]He said to them, "Moses, because of the hardness of your hearts, permitted you to divorce your wives, but from the beginning it was not so. [9]And I say to you, whoever divorces his wife, except for sexual immorality, and marries another, commits adultery; and whoever marries her who is divorced commits adultery."

[10]His disciples said to Him, "If such is the case of the man with *his* wife, it is better not to marry."

[11]But He said to them, "All cannot accept this saying, but only *those* to whom it has been given: [12]For there are eunuchs who were born thus from *their* mother's womb, and there are eunuchs who were made eunuchs by men, and there are eunuchs who have made themselves eunuchs for the kingdom of heaven's sake. He who is able to accept *it,* let him accept *it.*"

[13]Then little children were brought to Him that He might put *His* hands on them and pray, but the disciples rebuked them. [14]But Jesus said, "Let the little children come to Me, and do not forbid them; for of such is the kingdom of heaven." [15]And He laid *His* hands on them and departed from there.

[16]Now behold, one came and said to Him, "Good Teacher, what good thing shall I do that I may have eternal life?"

[17]So He said to him, "Why do you call Me good? No one *is* good but One, *that is,* God. But if you want to enter into life, keep the commandments."

[18]He said to Him, "Which ones?"

Jesus said, "'*You shall not murder,*' '*You shall not commit adultery,*' '*You shall not steal,*' '*You shall not bear false witness,*' [19]'*Honor your father and your mother,*' and, '*You shall love your neighbor as yourself.*'"

[20]The young man said to Him, "All these things I have kept from my youth. What do I still lack?"

[21]Jesus said to him, "If you want to be perfect, go, sell what you have and give to the poor, and you will have treasure in heaven; and come, follow Me."

[22]But when the young man heard that saying, he went away sorrowful, for he had great possessions.

[23]Then Jesus said to His disciples, "Assuredly, I say to you that it is hard for a rich man to enter the kingdom of heaven. [24]And again I say to you, it is easier for a camel to go through the eye of a needle than for a rich man to enter the kingdom of God."

²⁵When His disciples heard *it*, they were greatly astonished, saying, "Who then can be saved?"

²⁶But Jesus looked at *them* and said to them, "With men this is impossible, but with God all things are possible."

²⁷Then Peter answered and said to Him, "See, we have left all and followed You. Therefore what shall we have?"

²⁸So Jesus said to them, "Assuredly I say to you, that in the regeneration, when the Son of Man sits on the throne of His glory, you who have followed Me will also sit on twelve thrones, judging the twelve tribes of Israel. ²⁹And everyone who has left houses or brothers or sisters or father or mother or wife or children or lands, for My name's sake, shall receive a hundredfold, and inherit eternal life. ³⁰But many *who are* first will be last, and the last first.

CHAPTER 20 A STORY ABOUT A VINEYARD.

"For the kingdom of heaven is like a landowner who went out early in the morning to hire laborers for his vineyard. ²Now when he had agreed with the laborers for a denarius a day, he sent them into his vineyard. ³And he went out about the third hour and saw others standing idle in the marketplace, ⁴and said to them, 'You also go into the vineyard, and whatever is right I will give you.' So they went. ⁵Again he went out about the sixth and the ninth hour, and did likewise. ⁶And about the eleventh hour he went out and found others standing idle, and said to them, 'Why have you been standing here idle all day?' ⁷They said to him, 'Because no one hired us.' He said to them, 'You also go into the vineyard, and whatever is right you will receive.'

⁸"So when evening had come, the owner of the vineyard said to his steward, 'Call the laborers and give them *their* wages, beginning with the last to the first.' ⁹And when those came who *were hired* about the eleventh hour, they each received a denarius. ¹⁰But when the first came, they supposed that they would receive more; and they likewise received each a denarius. ¹¹And when they had received *it*, they complained against the landowner, ¹²saying, 'These last *men* have worked *only* one hour, and you made them equal to us who have borne the burden and the heat of the day.' ¹³But he answered one of them and said, 'Friend, I am doing you no wrong. Did you not agree with me for a denarius? ¹⁴Take *what is* yours and go your way. I wish to give to this last man *the same* as to you. ¹⁵Is it not lawful for me to do what I wish with my own things? Or is your eye evil because I am good?' ¹⁶So the last will be first, and the first last. For many are called, but few chosen."

¹⁷Now Jesus, going up to Jerusalem, took the twelve disciples aside on the road and said to them, ¹⁸"Behold, we are going up to Jerusalem, and the Son of Man will be betrayed to the chief priests and to the scribes; and they will condemn Him to death, ¹⁹and deliver Him to the Gentiles to mock and to scourge and to crucify. And the third day He will rise again."

²⁰Then the mother of Zebedee's sons came to Him with her sons, kneeling down and asking something from Him.

²¹And He said to her, "What do you wish?"

She said to Him, "Grant that these two sons of mine may sit, one on Your right hand and the other on the left, in Your kingdom."

²²But Jesus answered and said, "You do not know what you ask. Are you able to drink the cup that I am about to drink, and be baptized with the baptism that I am baptized with?"

They said to Him, "We are able."

²³So He said to them, "You will indeed drink My cup, and be baptized with the baptism that I am baptized with; but to sit on My right hand and on My left is not Mine to give, but *it is for those* for whom it is prepared by My Father."

²⁴And when the ten heard *it*, they were greatly displeased with the two brothers. ²⁵But Jesus called them to *Himself* and said, "You know that the rulers of the Gentiles lord it over them, and those who are great exercise authority over them. ²⁶Yet it shall not be so among you; but whoever desires to become great among you, let him be your servant. ²⁷And whoever desires to be first among you, let him be your slave— ²⁸just as the Son of Man did not come to be served, but to serve, and to give His life a ransom for many."

◤GOD'S GENEROSITY

20:15 This parable is a strong teaching about *grace*, God's generosity. We shouldn't begrudge those who turn to God in the last moments of life, because, in reality, *no one* deserves eternal life. Many people we don't expect to see in the kingdom may be there. The criminal who repented as he was dying (Luke 23:40-43) will be there, as well as the person who has believed and served God for many years. Do you resent God's gracious acceptance of the despised, the outcast, and the sinners who have turned to him for forgiveness? Are you ever jealous of what God has given to another person? Instead, focus on God's gracious benefits to you, and be thankful for what you have.

◤LEADERS

20:27 Jesus' description of leadership: serve people, don't use them. Jesus served others and gave his life away. A real leader appreciates others and realizes he's not above any job. Does something need to be done? Take the initiative and do it like a faithful servant.

²⁹Now as they went out of Jericho, a great multitude followed Him. ³⁰And behold, two blind men sitting by the road, when they heard that Jesus was passing by, cried out, saying, "Have mercy on us, O Lord, Son of David!"

³¹Then the multitude warned them that they should be quiet; but they cried out all the more, saying, "Have mercy on us, O Lord, Son of David!"

³²So Jesus stood still and called them, and said, "What do you want Me to do for you?"

³³They said to Him, "Lord, that our eyes may be opened." ³⁴So Jesus had compassion and touched their eyes. And immediately their eyes received sight, and they followed Him.

CHAPTER 21 JESUS RIDES INTO JERUSALEM. Now

when they drew near Jerusalem, and came to Bethphage, at the Mount of Olives, then Jesus sent two disciples, ²saying to them, "Go into the village opposite you, and

▶ BLANK CHECK

21:22 This is not a guarantee that we can get anything we want simply by asking Jesus. God does not grant requests that would hurt us or others, or that violate his own nature or will. Jesus' statement is not a blank check—our prayers must focus on the work of God's kingdom. Then we may go to him in peace and confidence, knowing he will respond to us in his love and wisdom.

immediately you will find a donkey tied, and a colt with her. Loose *them* and bring *them* to Me. ³And if anyone says anything to you, you shall say, 'The Lord has need of them,' and immediately he will send them."

⁴All this was done that it might be fulfilled which was spoken by the prophet, saying:

⁵ *"Tell the daughter of Zion,*
  'Behold, your King is coming to you,
  Lowly, and sitting on a donkey,
  A colt, the foal of a donkey.' "

⁶So the disciples went and did as Jesus commanded them. ⁷They brought the donkey and the colt, laid their clothes on them, and set *Him* on them. ⁸And a very great multitude spread their clothes on the road; others cut down branches from the trees and spread *them* on the road. ⁹Then the multitudes who went before and those who followed cried out, saying:

  "Hosanna to the Son of David!
  'Blessed is He who comes in the name of the Lord!'
  Hosanna in the highest!"

¹⁰And when He had come into Jerusalem, all the city was moved, saying, "Who is this?"
¹¹So the multitudes said, "This is Jesus, the prophet from Nazareth of Galilee."
¹²Then Jesus went into the temple of God and drove out all those who bought and sold in the temple, and overturned the tables of the money changers and the seats of those who sold doves. ¹³And He said to them, "It is written, *'My house shall be called a house of prayer,'* but you have made it a *'den of thieves.' "*

¹⁴Then *the* blind and *the* lame came to Him in the temple, and He healed them. ¹⁵But when the chief priests and scribes saw the wonderful things that He did, and the children crying out in the temple and saying, "Hosanna to the Son of David!" they were indignant ¹⁶and said to Him, "Do You hear what these are saying?"

And Jesus said to them, "Yes. Have you never read,

  'Out of the mouth of babes and nursing infants
  You have perfected praise' ?"

¹⁷Then He left them and went out of the city to Bethany, and He lodged there.
¹⁸Now in the morning, as He returned to the city, He was hungry. ¹⁹And seeing a fig tree by the road, He came to it and found nothing on it but leaves, and said to it, "Let no fruit grow on you ever again." Immediately the fig tree withered away.
²⁰And when the disciples saw *it*, they marveled, saying, "How did the fig tree wither away so soon?"
²¹So Jesus answered and said to them, "Assuredly, I say to you, if you have faith and do not doubt, you will not only do what was done to the fig tree, but also if you say

to this mountain, 'Be removed and be cast into the sea,' it will be done. ²²And whatever things you ask in prayer, believing, you will receive."

²³Now when He came into the temple, the chief priests and the elders of the people confronted Him as He was teaching, and said, "By what authority are You doing these things? And who gave You this authority?"
²⁴But Jesus answered and said to them, "I also will ask you one thing, which if you tell Me, I likewise will tell you by what authority I do these things: ²⁵The baptism of John—where was it from? From heaven or from men?"

And they reasoned among themselves, saying, "If we say, 'From heaven,' He will say to us, 'Why then did you not believe him?' ²⁶But if we say, 'From men,' we fear the multitude, for all count John as a prophet." ²⁷So they answered Jesus and said, "We do not know."

And He said to them, "Neither will I tell you by what authority I do these things.
²⁸"But what do you think? A man had two sons, and he came to the first and said, 'Son, go, work today in my vineyard.' ²⁹He answered and said, 'I will not,' but afterward he regretted it and went. ³⁰Then he came to the second and said likewise. And he answered and said, 'I go, sir,' but he did not go. ³¹Which of the two did the will of *his* father?"

They said to Him, "The first."

Jesus said to them, "Assuredly, I say to you that tax

▶ FAKING IT

21:30 The son who said he would obey and then didn't represent nation of Israel in Jesus' day. They said they wanted to do God's will they constantly disobeyed. It is dangerous to pretend to obey God w our heart is far from him, because God knows the intentions of our God isn't fooled. He knows when our actions don't match our words

collectors and harlots enter the kingdom of God before you. ³²For John came to you in the way of righteousness, and you did not believe him; but tax collectors and harlots believed him; and when you saw *it*, you did not afterward relent and believe him.

³³"Hear another parable: There was a certain landowner who planted a vineyard and set a hedge around it, dug a winepress in it and built a tower. And he leased it to vinedressers and went into a far country. ³⁴Now when vintage-time drew near, he sent his servants to the vinedressers, that they might receive its fruit. ³⁵And the vinedressers took his servants, beat one, killed one, and stoned another. ³⁶Again he sent other servants, more than the first, and they did likewise to them. ³⁷Then last of all he sent his son to them, saying, 'They will respect my son.' ³⁸But when the vinedressers saw the son, they said among themselves, 'This is the heir. Come, let us kill him and seize his inheritance.' ³⁹So they took him and cast *him* out of the vineyard and killed *him*.
⁴⁰"Therefore, when the owner of the vineyard comes, what will he do to those vinedressers?"
⁴¹They said to Him, "He will destroy those wicked men miserably, and lease *his* vineyard to other vinedressers who will render to him the fruits in their seasons."

[42]Jesus said to them, "Have you never read in the Scriptures:

'The stone which the builders rejected
Has become the chief cornerstone.
This was the LORD's doing,
And it is marvelous in our eyes'?

[43]"Therefore I say to you, the kingdom of God will be taken from you and given to a nation bearing the fruits of it. [44]And whoever falls on this stone will be broken; but on whomever it falls, it will grind him to powder."

[45]Now when the chief priests and Pharisees heard His parables, they perceived that He was speaking of them. [46]But when they sought to lay hands on Him, they feared the multitudes, because they took Him for a prophet.

CHAPTER 22 A STORY ABOUT A WEDDING. And

Jesus answered and spoke to them again by parables, and said: [2]"The kingdom of heaven is like a certain king who arranged a marriage for his son, [3]and sent out his servants to call those who were invited to the wedding; and they were not willing to come. [4]Again, he sent out other servants, saying, 'Tell those who are invited, "See, I have prepared my dinner; my oxen and fatted cattle *are* killed, and all things *are* ready. Come to the wedding." ' [5]But they made light of it and went their ways, one to his own farm, another to his business. [6]And the rest seized his servants, treated *them* spitefully, and killed *them*. [7]But when the king heard *about it*, he was furious. And he sent out his armies, destroyed those murderers, and burned up their city. [8]Then he said to his servants, 'The wedding is ready, but those who were invited were not worthy. [9]Therefore go into the highways, and as many as you find, invite to the wedding.' [10]So those servants went out into the highways and gathered together all whom they found, both bad and good. And the wedding *hall* was filled with guests.

[11]"But when the king came in to see the guests, he saw a man there who did not have on a wedding garment. [12]So he said to him, 'Friend, how did you come in here without a wedding garment?' And he was speechless. [13]Then the king said to the servants, 'Bind him hand and foot, take him away, and cast *him* into outer darkness; there will be weeping and gnashing of teeth.'

[14]"For many are called, but few *are* chosen."

[15]Then the Pharisees went and plotted how they might entangle Him in *His* talk. [16]And they sent to Him their disciples with the Herodians, saying, "Teacher, we know that You are true, and teach the way of God in truth; nor do You care about anyone, for You do not regard the person of men. [17]Tell us, therefore, what do You think? Is it lawful to pay taxes to Caesar, or not?"

[18]But Jesus perceived their wickedness, and said, "Why do you test Me, *you* hypocrites? [19]Show Me the tax money."

So they brought Him a denarius.

[20]And He said to them, "Whose image and inscription *is* this?"

[21]They said to Him, "Caesar's."

And He said to them, "Render therefore to Caesar the things that are Caesar's, and to God the things that are God's." [22]When they had heard *these words*, they marveled, and left Him and went their way.

[23]The same day the Sadducees, who say there is no

INVITED

22:1-14 In this culture, two invitations were expected when wedding dinners were given. The first invitation asked the guests to attend; the second announced that all was ready. Here the king, God, invited his guests three times—and each time they refused to come. God wants us to join him at his banquet, which will last for eternity. That's why he sends us invitations again and again. Have you accepted his invitation?

resurrection, came to Him and asked Him, [24]saying: "Teacher, Moses said that if a man dies, having no children, his brother shall marry his wife and raise up offspring for his brother. [25]Now there were with us seven brothers. The first died after he had married, and having no offspring, left his wife to his brother. [26]Likewise the second also, and the third, even to the seventh. [27]Last of all the woman died also. [28]Therefore, in the resurrection, whose wife of the seven will she be? For they all had her."

[29]Jesus answered and said to them, "You are mistaken, not knowing the Scriptures nor the power of God. [30]For in the resurrection they neither marry nor are given in marriage, but are like angels of God in heaven. [31]But concerning the resurrection of the dead, have you not read what was spoken to you by God, saying, [32]*I am the God of Abraham, the God of Isaac, and the God of Jacob'*? God is not the God of the dead, but of the living." [33]And when the multitudes heard *this*, they were astonished at His teaching.

[34]But when the Pharisees heard that He had silenced the Sadducees, they gathered together. [35]Then one of them, a lawyer, asked *Him a question*, testing Him, and saying, [36]"Teacher, which *is* the great commandment in the law?"

[37]Jesus said to him, " '*You shall love the LORD your God with all your heart, with all your soul, and with all your mind.'* [38]This is *the* first and great commandment. [39]And *the* second *is* like it: *'You shall love your neighbor as yourself.'* [40]On these two commandments hang all the Law and the Prophets."

[41]While the Pharisees were gathered together, Jesus asked them, [42]saying, "What do you think about the Christ? Whose Son is He?"

They said to Him, "*The Son* of David."

HEAVEN

22:29 The Sadducees asked Jesus what marriage would be like in eternity. Jesus said it was more important to understand God's power than know what heaven will be like. In every generation and culture, views about heaven or eternal life tend to be based upon images and experiences of present life. Jesus said these faulty views are caused by ignorance of God's Word. We must not make up our own ideas about eternity by trying to put it and God into human terms. We should concentrate more on our relationship with God than about what heaven will look like. Eventually we will find out, and it will be far beyond our greatest expectations.

⁴³He said to them, "How then does David in the Spirit call Him *'Lord,'* saying:

⁴⁴ *'The LORD said to my Lord,*
"Sit at My right hand,
Till I make Your enemies Your footstool" '?

⁴⁵If David then calls Him *'Lord,'* how is He his Son?" ⁴⁶And no one was able to answer Him a word, nor from that day on did anyone dare question Him anymore.

CHAPTER 23 JESUS WARNS THE PEOPLE. Then

Jesus spoke to the multitudes and to His disciples, ²saying: "The scribes and the Pharisees sit in Moses' seat. ³Therefore whatever they tell you to observe, *that* observe and do, but do not do according to their works; for they say, and do not do. ⁴For they bind heavy burdens, hard to bear, and lay *them* on men's shoulders; but they *themselves* will not move them with one of their fingers. ⁵But all their works they do to be seen by men. They make their phylacteries broad and enlarge the borders of their garments. ⁶They love the best places at feasts, the best seats in the synagogues, ⁷greetings in the marketplaces, and to be called by men, 'Rabbi, Rabbi.' ⁸But you, do not be called 'Rabbi'; for One is your Teacher, the Christ, and you are all brethren. ⁹Do not call anyone on earth your father; for One is your Father, He who is in heaven. ¹⁰And do not be called teachers; for One is your Teacher, the Christ. ¹¹But he who is greatest among you shall be your servant. ¹²And whoever exalts himself will be humbled, and he who humbles himself will be exalted.

¹³"But woe to you, scribes and Pharisees, hypocrites! For you shut up the kingdom of heaven against men; for you neither go in *yourselves,* nor do you allow those who are entering to go in. ¹⁴Woe to you, scribes and Pharisees, hypocrites! For you devour widows' houses, and for a pretense make long prayers. Therefore you will receive greater condemnation.

¹⁵"Woe to you, scribes and Pharisees, hypocrites! For you travel land and sea to win one proselyte, and when he is won, you make him twice as much a son of hell as yourselves.

¹⁶"Woe to you, blind guides, who say, 'Whoever swears by the temple, it is nothing; but whoever swears by the gold of the temple, he is obliged *to perform it.'* ¹⁷Fools and blind! For which is greater, the gold or the temple that sanctifies the gold? ¹⁸And, 'Whoever swears by the altar, it is nothing; but whoever swears by the gift that is on it, he is obliged *to perform it.'* ¹⁹Fools and blind! For which is greater, the gift or the altar that sanctifies the gift? ²⁰Therefore he who swears by the altar, swears by it and by all things on it. ²¹He who swears by the temple, swears by it and by Him who dwells in it. ²²And he who swears by heaven, swears by the throne of God and by Him who sits on it.

²³"Woe to you, scribes and Pharisees, hypocrites! For you pay tithe of mint and anise and cummin, and have neglected the weightier *matters* of the law: justice and mercy and faith. These you ought to have done, without leaving the others undone. ²⁴Blind guides, who strain out a gnat and swallow a camel!

◀━━━━━━━━━━■INSIDE

23:25-28 Jesus condemned the Pharisees and religious leaders f appearing saintly and holy but remaining full of corruption and gre the inside. Living our Christianity merely as a show for others is like washing a cup on the outside only. When we are clean on the inside, cleanliness on the outside won't be phony.

²⁵"Woe to you, scribes and Pharisees, hypocrites! For you cleanse the outside of the cup and dish, but inside they are full of extortion and self-indulgence. ²⁶Blind Pharisee, first cleanse the inside of the cup and dish, that the outside of them may be clean also.

²⁷"Woe to you, scribes and Pharisees, hypocrites! For you are like whitewashed tombs which indeed appear beautiful outwardly, but inside are full of dead *men's* bones and all uncleanness. ²⁸Even so you also outwardly appear righteous to men, but inside you are full of hypocrisy and lawlessness.

²⁹"Woe to you, scribes and Pharisees, hypocrites! Because you build the tombs of the prophets and adorn the monuments of the righteous, ³⁰and say, 'If we had lived in the days of our fathers, we would not have been partakers with them in the blood of the prophets.' ³¹Therefore you are witnesses against yourselves that you are sons of those who murdered the prophets. ³²Fill up, then, the measure of your fathers' *guilt.* ³³Serpents, brood of vipers! How can you escape the condemnation of hell? ³⁴Therefore, indeed, I send you prophets, wise men, and scribes: *some* of them you will kill and crucify, and *some* of them you will scourge in your synagogues and persecute from city to city, ³⁵that on you may come all the righteous blood shed on the earth, from the blood of righteous Abel to the blood of Zechariah, son of Berechiah, whom you murdered between the temple and the altar. ³⁶Assuredly, I say to you, all these things will come upon this generation.

³⁷"O Jerusalem, Jerusalem, the one who kills the prophets and stones those who are sent to her! How often I wanted to gather your children together, as a hen gathers her chicks under *her* wings, but you were not willing! ³⁸See! Your house is left to you desolate; ³⁹for I say to you, you shall see Me no more till you say, *'Blessed is He who comes in the name of the LORD!'* "

CHAPTER 24 JESUS TELLS ABOUT THE FUTURE.

Then Jesus went out and departed from the temple, and His disciples came up to show Him the buildings of the temple. ²And Jesus said to them, "Do you not see all these things? Assuredly, I say to you, not *one* stone shall be left here upon another, that shall not be thrown down."

³Now as He sat on the Mount of Olives, the disciples came to Him privately, saying, "Tell us, when will these things be? And what *will be* the sign of Your coming, and of the end of the age?"

⁴And Jesus answered and said to them: "Take heed that no one deceives you. ⁵For many will come in My name, saying, 'I am the Christ,' and will deceive many. ⁶And you will hear of wars and rumors of wars. See that you are not troubled; for all *these things* must come to pass, but the end is not yet. ⁷For nation will rise against nation, and kingdom against kingdom. And there will be famines, pestilences, and earthquakes in various places. ⁸All these *are* the beginning of sorrows.

9"Then they will deliver you up to tribulation and kill you, and you will be hated by all nations for My name's sake. 10And then many will be offended, will betray one another, and will hate one another. 11Then many false prophets will rise up and deceive many. 12And because lawlessness will abound, the love of many will grow cold. 13But he who endures to the end shall be saved. 14And this gospel of the kingdom will be preached in all the world as a witness to all the nations, and then the end will come.

15"Therefore when you see the 'abomination of desolation,' spoken of by Daniel the prophet, standing in the holy place" (whoever reads, let him understand), 16"then let those who are in Judea flee to the mountains. 17Let him who is on the housetop not go down to take anything out of his house. 18And let him who is in the field not go back to get his clothes. 19But woe to those who are pregnant and to those who are nursing babies in those days! 20And pray that your flight may not be in winter or on the Sabbath. 21For then there will be great tribulation, such as has not been since the beginning of the world until this time, no, nor ever shall be. 22And unless those days were shortened, no flesh would be saved; but for the elect's sake those days will be shortened.

23"Then if anyone says to you, 'Look, here is the Christ!' or 'There!' do not believe it. 24For false christs and false prophets will rise and show great signs and wonders to deceive, if possible, even the elect. 25See, I have told you beforehand.

26"Therefore if they say to you, 'Look, He is in the desert!' do not go out; or 'Look, He is in the inner rooms!' do not believe it. 27For as the lightning comes from the east and flashes to the west, so also will the coming of the Son of Man be. 28For wherever the carcass is, there the eagles will be gathered together.

29"Immediately after the tribulation of those days the sun will be darkened, and the moon will not give its light; the stars will fall from heaven, and the powers of the heavens will be shaken. 30Then the sign of the Son of Man will appear in heaven, and then all the tribes of the earth will mourn, and they will see the Son of Man coming on the clouds of heaven with power and great glory. 31And He will send His angels with a great sound of a trumpet, and they will gather together His elect from the four winds, from one end of heaven to the other.

32"Now learn this parable from the fig tree: When its branch has already become tender and puts forth leaves, you know that summer is near. 33So you also, when you see all these things, know that it is near—at the doors! 34Assuredly, I say to you, this generation will by no means pass away till all these things take place. 35Heaven and earth will pass away, but My words will by no means pass away.

36"But of that day and hour no one knows, not even the angels of heaven, but My Father only. 37But as the days of Noah were, so also will the coming of the Son of Man be. 38For as in the days before the flood, they were eating and drinking, marrying and giving in marriage, until the day that Noah entered the ark, 39and did not know until the flood came and took them all away, so also will the coming of the Son of Man be. 40Then two men will be in the

field: one will be taken and the other left. 41Two women will be grinding at the mill: one will be taken and the other left. 42Watch therefore, for you do not know what hour your Lord is coming. 43But know this, that if the master of the house had known what hour the thief

◣◣◣〜〜〜◖ FRAUDS

24:11 The Old Testament frequently mentions false prophets (see 2 Kings 3:13; Isaiah 44:25; Jeremiah 23:16; Ezekiel 13:2-3; Micah 3:5; Zechariah 13:2). False prophets were people who claimed to receive messages from God but preached a "health and wealth" message. They told the people what they wanted to hear, even when the nation was not following God as it should. We have false prophets today, too—popular leaders who spout a false gospel, telling people what they want to hear: "God wants you to be rich." "Do whatever your desires tell you." Or, "There is no such thing as sin or hell." Jesus said false teachers would come, and he warned his disciples—as he warns us—not to listen to their dangerous words.

would come, he would have watched and not allowed his house to be broken into. 44Therefore you also be ready, for the Son of Man is coming at an hour you do not expect.

45"Who then is a faithful and wise servant, whom his master made ruler over his household, to give them food in due season? 46Blessed is that servant whom his master, when he comes, will find so doing. 47Assuredly, I say to you that he will make him ruler over all his goods. 48But if that evil servant says in his heart, 'My master is delaying his coming,' 49and begins to beat his fellow servants, and to eat and drink with the drunkards, 50the master of that servant will come on a day when he is not looking for him and at an hour that he is not aware of, 51and will cut him in two and appoint him his portion with the hypocrites. There shall be weeping and gnashing of teeth.

CHAPTER **25** A STORY ABOUT TEN BRIDESMAIDS.
"Then the kingdom of heaven shall be likened to ten virgins who took their lamps and went out to meet the bridegroom. 2Now five of them were wise, and five were foolish. 3Those who were foolish took their lamps and took no oil with them, 4but the wise took oil in their vessels with their lamps. 5But while the bridegroom was delayed, they all slumbered and slept.

6"And at midnight a cry was heard: 'Behold, the bridegroom is coming; go out to meet him!' 7Then all those virgins arose and trimmed their lamps. 8And the foolish said to the wise, 'Give us some of your oil, for our lamps are going out.' 9But the wise answered, saying, 'No, lest there should not be enough for us and you; but go rather

◣◣◣〜〜〜◖ INVESTING

25:15 The master divided the money (talents) up among his servants according to their abilities— no one received more or less money than he could handle. If he failed in his master's assignment, his excuse could not be that he was overwhelmed. Failure could come only from laziness or hatred for the master. Talents, as used here, represent any kind of resource we are given. God gives us time, abilities, and other resources that he expects us to invest wisely until he returns. We are responsible to use well what God has given us. The issue is not how much we have, but what we do with what we have.

25:31-46 God will separate his obedient followers from pretenders and unbelievers. The real evidence of our belief is the way we act. To treat all persons we encounter as if they are Jesus is no easy task. What we do for others demonstrates what we really think about Jesus' words to us—feed the hungry, give the homeless a place to stay, visit the sick. How well do your actions separate you from pretenders and unbelievers?

to those who sell, and buy for yourselves.' ¹⁰And while they went to buy, the bridegroom came, and those who were ready went in with him to the wedding; and the door was shut.

¹¹"Afterward the other virgins came also, saying, 'Lord, Lord, open to us!' ¹²But he answered and said, 'Assuredly, I say to you, I do not know you.'

¹³"Watch therefore, for you know neither the day nor the hour in which the Son of Man is coming.

¹⁴"For *the kingdom of heaven is* like a man traveling to a far country, *who* called his own servants and delivered his goods to them. ¹⁵And to one he gave five talents, to another two, and to another one, to each according to his own ability; and immediately he went on a journey. ¹⁶Then he who had received the five talents went and traded with them, and made another five talents. ¹⁷And likewise he who *had received* two gained two more also. ¹⁸But he who had received one went and dug in the ground, and hid his lord's money. ¹⁹After a long time the lord of those servants came and settled accounts with them.

²⁰"So he who had received five talents came and brought five other talents, saying, 'Lord, you delivered to me five talents; look, I have gained five more talents besides them.' ²¹His lord said to him, 'Well *done,* good and faithful servant; you were faithful over a few things, I will make you ruler over many things. Enter into the joy of your lord.' ²²He also who had received two talents came and said, 'Lord, you delivered to me two talents; look, I have gained two more talents besides them.' ²³His lord said to him, 'Well *done,* good and faithful servant; you have been faithful over a few things, I will make you ruler over many things. Enter into the joy of your lord.'

²⁴"Then he who had received the one talent came and said, 'Lord, I knew you to be a hard man, reaping where you have not sown, and gathering where you have not scattered seed. ²⁵And I was afraid, and went and hid your talent in the ground. Look, *there* you have *what is* yours.'

²⁶"But his lord answered and said to him, 'You wicked and lazy servant, you knew that I reap where I have not sown, and gather where I have not scattered seed. ²⁷So you ought to have deposited my money with the bankers, and at my coming I would have received back my own with interest. ²⁸So take the talent from him, and give *it* to him who has ten talents.

²⁹"For to everyone who has, more will be given, and he will have abundance; but from him who does not have, even what he has will be taken away. ³⁰And cast the unprofitable servant into the outer darkness. There will be weeping and gnashing of teeth.'

³¹"When the Son of Man comes in His glory, and all the holy angels with Him, then He will sit on the throne of His glory. ³²All the nations will be gathered before Him, and He will separate them one from another, as a shepherd divides *his* sheep from the goats. ³³And He will set the sheep on His right hand, but the goats on the left. ³⁴Then the King will say to those on His right hand, 'Come, you blessed of My Father, inherit the kingdom prepared for you from the foundation of the world: ³⁵for I was hungry and you gave Me food; I was thirsty and you gave Me drink; I was a stranger and you took Me in; ³⁶I *was* naked and you clothed Me; I was sick and you visited Me; I was in prison and you came to Me.'

³⁷"Then the righteous will answer Him, saying, 'Lord, when did we see You hungry and feed *You,* or thirsty and give *You* drink? ³⁸When did we see You a stranger and take *You* in, or naked and clothe *You?* ³⁹Or when did we see You sick, or in prison, and come to You?' ⁴⁰And the King will answer and say to them, 'Assuredly, I say to you, inasmuch as you did *it* to one of the least of these My brethren, you did *it* to Me.'

⁴¹"Then He will also say to those on the left hand, 'Depart from Me, you cursed, into the everlasting fire prepared for the devil and his angels: ⁴²for I was hungry and you gave Me no food; I was thirsty and you gave Me no drink; ⁴³I was a stranger and you did not take Me in, naked and you did not clothe Me, sick and in prison and you did not visit Me.'

⁴⁴"Then they also will answer Him, saying, 'Lord, when did we see You hungry or thirsty or a stranger or naked or sick or in prison, and did not minister to You?' ⁴⁵Then He will answer them, saying, 'Assuredly, I say to you, inasmuch as you did not do *it* to one of the least of these, you did not do *it* to Me.' ⁴⁶And these will go away into everlasting punishment, but the righteous into eternal life."

CHAPTER 26 A STORY ABOUT TALENTS.

Now it came to pass, when Jesus had finished all these sayings, *that* He said to His disciples, ²"You know that after two days is the Passover, and the Son of Man will be delivered up to be crucified."

³Then the chief priests, the scribes, and the elders of the people assembled at the palace of the high priest, who was called Caiaphas, ⁴and plotted to take Jesus by trickery and kill *Him.* ⁵But they said, "Not during the feast, lest there be an uproar among the people."

⁶And when Jesus was in Bethany at the house of Simon the leper, ⁷a woman came to Him having an alabaster flask of very costly fragrant oil, and she poured *it* on His head as He sat *at the table.* ⁸But when His disciples saw *it,* they were indignant, saying, "Why this waste? ⁹For this fragrant oil might have been sold for much and given to *the* poor."

¹⁰But when Jesus was aware of *it,* He said to them, "Why do you trouble the woman? For she has done a good work for Me. ¹¹For you have the poor with you

26:40 Jesus used Peter's drowsiness to warn him about the kinds of temptation he would soon face. The way to overcome temptation is to alert to it and pray. Being alert involves being aware of the possibiliti of temptation, sensitive to the subtleties, and spiritually equipped to f it. Because temptation strikes where we are most vulnerable, we can' resist it alone. Prayer is essential because God's strength can shore up defenses and defeat Satan's power.

always, but Me you do not have always. [12]For in pouring this fragrant oil on My body, she did *it* for My burial. [13]Assuredly, I say to you, wherever this gospel is preached in the whole world, what this woman has done will also be told as a memorial to her."

[14]Then one of the twelve, called Judas Iscariot, went to the chief priests [15]and said, "What are you willing to give me if I deliver Him to you?" And they counted out to him thirty pieces of silver. [16]So from that time he sought opportunity to betray Him.

[17]Now on the first *day of the Feast* of Unleavened Bread the disciples came to Jesus, saying to Him, "Where do You want us to prepare for You to eat the Passover?"

[18]And He said, "Go into the city to a certain man, and say to him, 'The Teacher says, "My time is at hand; I will keep the Passover at your house with My disciples."'"

[19]So the disciples did as Jesus had directed them; and they prepared the Passover.

[20]When evening had come, He sat down with the twelve. [21]Now as they were eating, He said, "Assuredly, I say to you, one of you will betray Me."

[22]And they were exceedingly sorrowful, and each of them began to say to Him, "Lord, is it I?"

[23]He answered and said, "He who dipped *his* hand with Me in the dish will betray Me. [24]The Son of Man indeed goes just as it is written of Him, but woe to that man by whom the Son of Man is betrayed! It would have been good for that man if he had not been born."

[25]Then Judas, who was betraying Him, answered and said, "Rabbi, is it I?"

He said to him, "You have said it."

[26]And as they were eating, Jesus took bread, blessed and broke *it*, and gave *it* to the disciples and said, "Take, eat; this is My body."

[27]Then He took the cup, and gave thanks, and gave *it* to them, saying, "Drink from it, all of you. [28]For this is My blood of the new covenant, which is shed for many for the remission of sins. [29]But I say to you, I will not drink of this fruit of the vine from now on until that day when I drink it new with you in My Father's kingdom."

[30]And when they had sung a hymn, they went out to the Mount of Olives.

[31]Then Jesus said to them, "All of you will be made to stumble because of Me this night, for it is written:

'*I will strike the Shepherd,
And the sheep of the flock will be scattered.*'

[32]But after I have been raised, I will go before you to Galilee."

[33]Peter answered and said to Him, "Even if all are made to stumble because of You, I will never be made to stumble."

MATTHEW

More than any other disciple, Matthew had a clear idea of how much it would cost to follow Jesus, yet he did not hesitate a moment. When he left his tax-collecting booth, he guaranteed himself unemployment. For several of the other disciples, there was always fishing to return to, but for Matthew, there was no turning back.

Two changes happened to Matthew when he decided to follow Jesus. First, Jesus gave him a new life. He not only belonged to a new group; he belonged to the Son of God. He was not just accepting a different way of life; he was now an accepted person. For a despised tax collector, that change must have been wonderful! Second, Jesus gave Matthew a new purpose for his skills. When he followed Jesus, the only tool from his past job that he carried with him was his pen. From the beginning, God had made him a record keeper. Jesus' call eventually allowed him to put his skills to their finest work. Matthew was a keen observer, and he must have mentally recorded what he saw going on around him. The Gospel that bears his name came as a result.

Matthew's experience points out that each of us, from the beginning, is one of God's works in progress. Much of what God has for us he gives long before we are able to consciously respond to him. He trusts us with skills and abilities ahead of schedule. He has made us each capable of being his servant. When we trust him with what he has given us, we begin a life of real adventure. Matthew couldn't have known that God would use the very skills he had sharpened as a tax collector to record the greatest story ever lived. And God has no less meaningful a purpose for each of us. Have you recognized Jesus saying to you, "Follow Me"? What has been your response?

LESSONS: Jesus consistently accepted people from every level of society
Matthew was given a new life, and his God-given skills of record keeping and attention to detail were given new purpose
Having been accepted by Jesus, Matthew immediately tried to bring others into contact with Jesus

KEY VERSE: "As He passed by, He saw Levi the son of Alphaeus sitting at the tax office. And He said to him, 'Follow Me.' So he arose and followed Him" (Mark 2:14). Matthew's story is told in the Gospels. He is also mentioned in Acts 1:13.

UPS:
- Was one of Jesus' 12 disciples
- Responded immediately to Jesus' call
- Invited many friends to his home to meet Jesus
- Compiled the Gospel of Matthew
- Clarified for his Jewish audience Jesus' fulfillment of Old Testament prophecies

STATS:
- Where: Capernaum
- Occupation: Tax collector, disciple of Jesus
- Relatives: Father: Alphaeus
- Contemporaries: Jesus, Pilate, Herod, other disciples

26:69ff There were three stages to Peter's denial. First, he acted confused and said he didn't know what the girl was talking about. Second, using an oath he denied that he knew Jesus. Third, he began to curse and swear. Believers who deny Christ often begin doing so subtly by pretending not to know him. When opportunities to discuss religious issues come up, they walk away or pretend they don't know the answers. With only a little more pressure, they can be induced to flatly deny their relationship with Christ. If you find yourself subtly avoiding occasions to talk about Christ, watch out. You may be on the road to denying him.

³⁴Jesus said to him, "Assuredly, I say to you that this night, before the rooster crows, you will deny Me three times."

³⁵Peter said to Him, "Even if I have to die with You, I will not deny You!"

And so said all the disciples.

³⁶Then Jesus came with them to a place called Gethsemane, and said to the disciples, "Sit here while I go and pray over there." ³⁷And He took with Him Peter and the two sons of Zebedee, and He began to be sorrowful and deeply distressed. ³⁸Then He said to them, "My soul is exceedingly sorrowful, even to death. Stay here and watch with Me."

³⁹He went a little farther and fell on His face, and prayed, saying, "O My Father, if it is possible, let this cup pass from Me; nevertheless, not as I will, but as You *will*."

⁴⁰Then He came to the disciples and found them sleeping, and said to Peter, "What! Could you not watch with Me one hour? ⁴¹Watch and pray, lest you enter into temptation. The spirit indeed *is* willing, but the flesh *is* weak."

⁴²Again, a second time, He went away and prayed, saying, "O My Father, if this cup cannot pass away from Me unless I drink it, Your will be done." ⁴³And He came and found them asleep again, for their eyes were heavy.

⁴⁴So He left them, went away again, and prayed the third time, saying the same words. ⁴⁵Then He came to His disciples and said to them, "Are *you* still sleeping and resting? Behold, the hour is at hand, and the Son of Man is being betrayed into the hands of sinners. ⁴⁶Rise, let us be going. See, My betrayer is at hand."

⁴⁷And while He was still speaking, behold, Judas, one of the twelve, with a great multitude with swords and clubs, came from the chief priests and elders of the people. ⁴⁸Now His betrayer had given them a sign, saying, "Whomever I kiss, He is the One; seize Him." ⁴⁹Immediately he went up to Jesus and said, "Greetings, Rabbi!" and kissed Him.

⁵⁰But Jesus said to him, "Friend, why have you come?" Then they came and laid hands on Jesus and took Him. ⁵¹And suddenly, one of those *who were* with Jesus stretched out *his* hand and drew his sword, struck the servant of the high priest, and cut off his ear.

⁵²But Jesus said to him, "Put your sword in its place, for all who take the sword will perish by the sword. ⁵³Or do you think that I cannot now pray to My Father, and He will provide Me with more than twelve legions of angels? ⁵⁴How then could the Scriptures be fulfilled, that it must happen thus?"

⁵⁵In that hour Jesus said to the multitudes, "Have you come out, as against a robber, with swords and clubs to take Me? I sat daily with you, teaching in the temple, and you did not seize Me. ⁵⁶But all this was done that the Scriptures of the prophets might be fulfilled."

Then all the disciples forsook Him and fled.

⁵⁷And those who had laid hold of Jesus led *Him* away to Caiaphas the high priest, where the scribes and the elders were assembled. ⁵⁸But Peter followed Him at a distance to the high priest's courtyard. And he went in and sat with the servants to see the end.

⁵⁹Now the chief priests, the elders, and all the council sought false testimony against Jesus to put Him to death, ⁶⁰but found none. Even though many false witnesses came forward, they found none. But at last two false witnesses came forward ⁶¹and said, "This *fellow* said, 'I am able to destroy the temple of God and to build it in three days.'"

⁶²And the high priest arose and said to Him, "Do You answer nothing? What *is it* these men testify against You?" ⁶³But Jesus kept silent. And the high priest answered and said to Him, "I put You under oath by the living God: Tell us if You are the Christ, the Son of God!"

⁶⁴Jesus said to him, "*It is as* you said. Nevertheless, I say to you, hereafter you will see the Son of Man sitting at the right hand of the Power, and coming on the clouds of heaven."

⁶⁵Then the high priest tore his clothes, saying, "He has spoken blasphemy! What further need do we have of witnesses? Look, now you have heard His blasphemy! ⁶⁶What do you think?"

They answered and said, "He is deserving of death."

⁶⁷Then they spat in His face and beat Him; and others struck *Him* with the palms of their hands, ⁶⁸saying, "Prophesy to us, Christ! Who is the one who struck You?"

⁶⁹Now Peter sat outside in the courtyard. And a servant girl came to him, saying, "You also were with Jesus of Galilee."

⁷⁰But he denied it before *them* all, saying, "I do not know what you are saying."

⁷¹And when he had gone out to the gateway, another *girl* saw him and said to those *who were* there, "This *fellow* also was with Jesus of Nazareth."

⁷²But again he denied with an oath, "I do not know the Man!"

⁷³And a little later those who stood by came up and said to Peter, "Surely you also are *one* of them, for your speech betrays you."

⁷⁴Then he began to curse and swear, *saying*, "I do not know the Man!"

Immediately a rooster crowed. ⁷⁵And Peter remembered the word of Jesus who had said to him, "Before the rooster crows, you will deny Me three times." So he went out and wept bitterly.

CHAPTER 27 JUDAS HANGS HIMSELF. When morning came, all the chief priests and elders of the people plotted against Jesus to put Him to death. ²And when they had bound Him, they led Him away and delivered Him to Pontius Pilate the governor.

³Then Judas, His betrayer, seeing that He had been condemned, was remorseful and brought back the thirty

pieces of silver to the chief priests and elders, ⁴saying, "I have sinned by betraying innocent blood."

And they said, "What *is that* to us? You see *to it!*"

⁵Then he threw down the pieces of silver in the temple and departed, and went and hanged himself.

⁶But the chief priests took the silver pieces and said, "It is not lawful to put them into the treasury, because they are the price of blood." ⁷And they consulted together and bought with them the potter's field, to bury strangers in. ⁸Therefore that field has been called the Field of Blood to this day.

⁹Then was fulfilled what was spoken by Jeremiah the prophet, saying, *"And they took the thirty pieces of silver, the value of Him who was priced,* whom they of the children of Israel priced, ¹⁰*and gave them for the potter's field, as the* LORD *directed me."*

¹¹Now Jesus stood before the governor. And the governor asked Him, saying, "Are You the King of the Jews?"

Jesus said to him, "*It is as* you say." ¹²And while He was being accused by the chief priests and elders, He answered nothing.

¹³Then Pilate said to Him, "Do You not hear how many things they testify against You?" ¹⁴But He answered him not one word, so that the governor marveled greatly.

¹⁵Now at the feast the governor was accustomed to releasing to the multitude one prisoner whom they wished. ¹⁶And at that time they had a notorious prisoner called Barabbas. ¹⁷Therefore, when they had gathered together, Pilate said to them, "Whom do you want me to release to you? Barabbas, or Jesus who is called Christ?" ¹⁸For he knew that they had handed Him over because of envy.

¹⁹While he was sitting on the judgment seat, his wife sent to him, saying, "Have nothing to do with that just Man, for I have suffered many things today in a dream because of Him."

²⁰But the chief priests and elders persuaded the multitudes that they should ask for Barabbas and destroy Jesus. ²¹The governor answered and said to them, "Which of the two do you want me to release to you?"

They said, "Barabbas!"

²²Pilate said to them, "What then shall I do with Jesus who is called Christ?"

They all said to him, "Let Him be crucified!"

²³Then the governor said, "Why, what evil has He done?"

But they cried out all the more, saying, "Let Him be crucified!"

²⁴When Pilate saw that he could not prevail at all, but rather *that* a tumult was rising, he took water and washed *his* hands before the multitude, saying, "I am innocent of the blood of this just Person. You see *to it.*"

²⁵And all the people answered and said, "His blood *be* on us and on our children."

²⁶Then he released Barabbas to them; and when he had scourged Jesus, he delivered *Him* to be crucified.

²⁷Then the soldiers of the governor took Jesus into the Praetorium and gathered the whole garrison around Him. ²⁸And they stripped Him and put a scarlet robe on Him. ²⁹When they had twisted a crown of thorns, they put *it* on His head, and a reed in His right hand. And they bowed the

REGRETS

27:3-4 Jesus' formal accuser wanted to drop his charges, but the religious leaders refused to halt the trial. When Judas first betrayed Jesus, perhaps he was trying to force Jesus' hand to get him to lead a revolt against Rome. This did not work, of course. Whatever his reason, Judas changed his mind, but it was too late. Many of the plans we set into motion cannot be reversed. It is best to think of the potential consequences before we launch into an action we may later regret.

HASSLE

27:29 People still hassle Christians for their faith, but believers can take courage that Jesus himself was mocked terribly. Taunting may hurt our feelings, but we should never let it change our faith (see 5:11-12).

knee before Him and mocked Him, saying, "Hail, King of the Jews!" ³⁰Then they spat on Him, and took the reed and struck Him on the head. ³¹And when they had mocked Him, they took the robe off Him, put His *own* clothes on Him, and led Him away to be crucified.

³²Now as they came out, they found a man of Cyrene, Simon by name. Him they compelled to bear His cross. ³³And when they had come to a place called Golgotha, that is to say, Place of a Skull, ³⁴they gave Him sour wine mingled with gall to drink. But when He had tasted *it*, He would not drink.

³⁵Then they crucified Him, and divided His garments, casting lots, that it might be fulfilled which was spoken by the prophet:

"They divided My garments among them,
And for My clothing they cast lots."

³⁶Sitting down, they kept watch over Him there. ³⁷And they put up over His head the accusation written against Him:

THIS IS JESUS
THE KING OF THE JEWS.

³⁸Then two robbers were crucified with Him, one on the right and another on the left.

³⁹And those who passed by blasphemed Him, wagging their heads ⁴⁰and saying, "You who destroy the temple and build *it* in three days, save Yourself! If You are the Son of God, come down from the cross."

⁴¹Likewise the chief priests also, mocking with the scribes and elders, said, ⁴²"He saved others; Himself He cannot save. If He is the King of Israel, let Him now come down from the cross, and we will believe Him. ⁴³He trusted in God; let Him deliver Him now if He will have Him; for He said, 'I am the Son of God.'"

⁴⁴Even the robbers who were crucified with Him reviled Him with the same thing.

DREAD

27:46 Jesus was not questioning God; he was quoting the first line of Psalm 22—a deep expression of the anguish he felt when he took on the sins of the world and thus was separated from his Father. *This* was what Jesus dreaded as he prayed to God in the garden to take the cup from him (26:39). The physical agony was horrible, but even worse was the period of spiritual separation from God. Jesus suffered this double death so that we would never have to experience eternal separation from God.

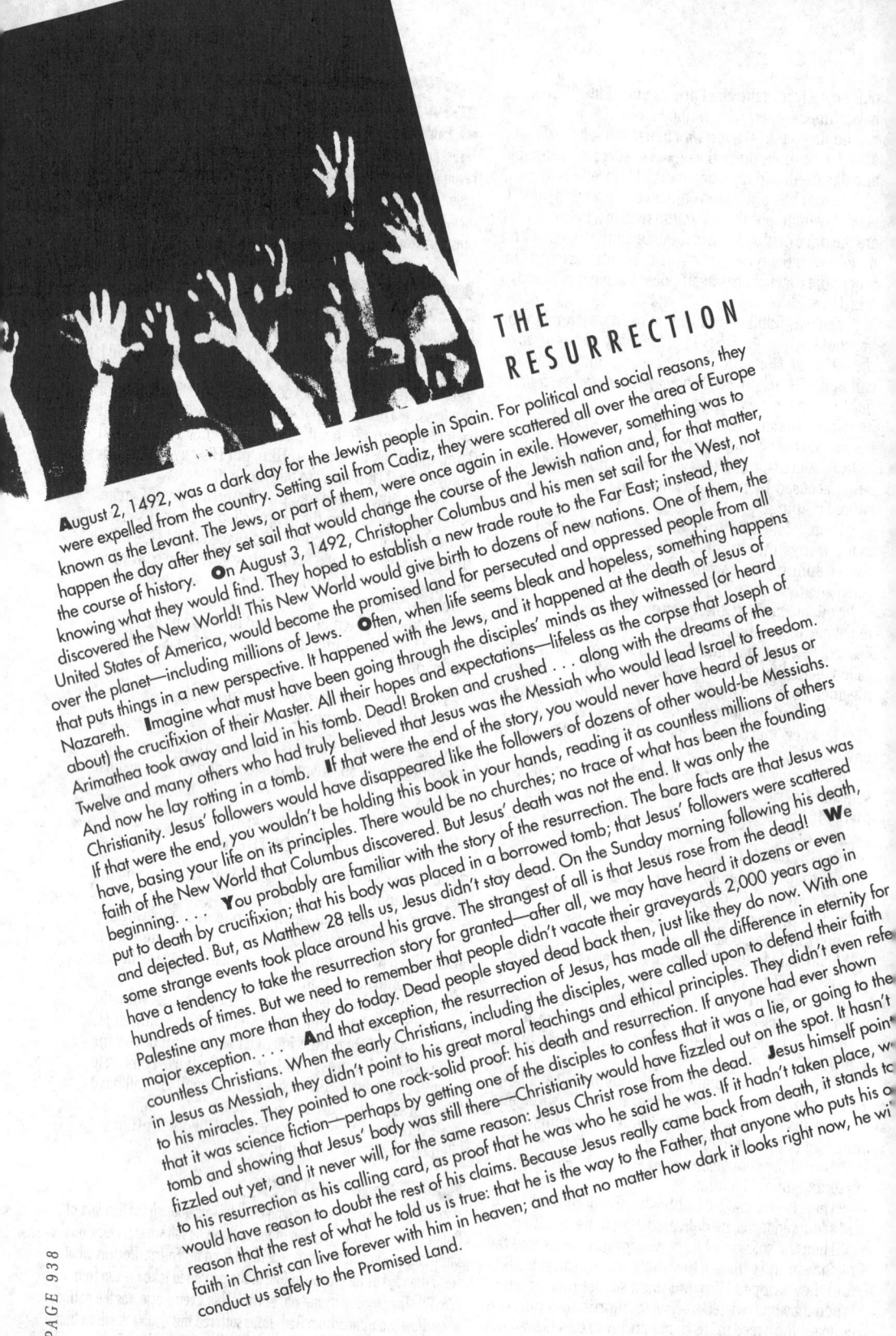

THE RESURRECTION

August 2, 1492, was a dark day for the Jewish people in Spain. For political and social reasons, they were expelled from the country. Setting sail from Cadiz, they were scattered all over the area of Europe known as the Levant. The Jews, or part of them, were once again in exile. However, something was to happen the day after they set sail that would change the course of the Jewish nation and, for that matter, the course of history. On August 3, 1492, Christopher Columbus and his men set sail for the West, not knowing what they would find. They hoped to establish a new trade route to the Far East; instead, they discovered the New World! This New World would give birth to dozens of new nations. One of them, the United States of America, would become the promised land for persecuted and oppressed people from all over the planet—including millions of Jews. Often, when life seems bleak and hopeless, something happens that puts things in a new perspective. It happened with the Jews, and it happened at the death of Jesus of Nazareth. Imagine what must have been going through the disciples' minds as they witnessed (or heard about) the crucifixion of their Master. All their hopes and expectations—lifeless as the corpse that Joseph of Arimathea took away and laid in his tomb. Dead! Broken and crushed . . . along with the dreams of the Twelve and many others who had truly believed that Jesus was the Messiah who would lead Israel to freedom. And now he lay rotting in a tomb. If that were the end of the story, you would never have heard of Jesus or Christianity. Jesus' followers would have disappeared like the followers of dozens of other would-be Messiahs. If that were the end, you wouldn't be holding this book in your hands, reading it as countless millions of others have, basing your life on its principles. There would be no churches; no trace of what has been the founding faith of the New World that Columbus discovered. But Jesus' death was not the end. It was only the beginning. . . . You probably are familiar with the story of the resurrection. The bare facts are that Jesus was put to death by crucifixion; that his body was placed in a borrowed tomb; that Jesus' followers were scattered and dejected. But, as Matthew 28 tells us, Jesus didn't stay dead. On the Sunday morning following his death, some strange events took place around his grave. The strangest of all is that Jesus rose from the dead! We have a tendency to take the resurrection story for granted—after all, we may have heard it dozens or even hundreds of times. But we need to remember that people didn't vacate their graveyards 2,000 years ago in Palestine any more than they do today. Dead people stayed dead back then, just like they do now. With one major exception. . . . And that exception, the resurrection of Jesus, has made all the difference in eternity for countless Christians. When the early Christians, including the disciples, were called upon to defend their faith in Jesus as Messiah, they didn't point to his great moral teachings and ethical principles. They didn't even refer to his miracles. They pointed to one rock-solid proof: his death and resurrection. If anyone had ever shown that it was science fiction—perhaps by getting one of the disciples to confess that it was a lie, or going to the tomb and showing that Jesus' body was still there—Christianity would have fizzled out on the spot. It hasn't fizzled out yet, and it never will, for the same reason: Jesus Christ rose from the dead. Jesus himself points to his resurrection as his calling card, as proof that he was who he said he was. If it hadn't taken place, we would have reason to doubt the rest of his claims. Because Jesus really came back from death, it stands to reason that the rest of what he told us is true: that he is the way to the Father, that anyone who puts his or her faith in Christ can live forever with him in heaven; and that no matter how dark it looks right now, he will conduct us safely to the Promised Land.

45Now from the sixth hour until the ninth hour there was darkness over all the land. 46And about the ninth hour Jesus cried out with a loud voice, saying, "Eli, Eli, lama sabachthani?" that is, *"My God, My God, why have You forsaken Me?"*

47Some of those who stood there, when they heard *that*, said, "This Man is calling for Elijah!" 48Immediately one of them ran and took a sponge, filled *it* with sour wine and put *it* on a reed, and offered it to Him to drink. 49The rest said, "Let Him alone; let us see if Elijah will come to save Him."

50And Jesus cried out again with a loud voice, and yielded up His spirit.

51Then, behold, the veil of the temple was torn in two from top to bottom; and the earth quaked, and the rocks were split, 52and the graves were opened; and many bodies of the saints who had fallen asleep were raised; 53and coming out of the graves after His resurrection, they went into the holy city and appeared to many.

54So when the centurion and those with him, who were guarding Jesus, saw the earthquake and the things that had happened, they feared greatly, saying, "Truly this was the Son of God!"

55And many women who followed Jesus from Galilee, ministering to Him, were there looking on from afar, 56among whom were Mary Magdalene, Mary the mother of James and Joses, and the mother of Zebedee's sons.

57Now when evening had come, there came a rich man from Arimathea, named Joseph, who himself had also become a disciple of Jesus. 58This man went to Pilate and asked for the body of Jesus. Then Pilate commanded the body to be given to him. 59When Joseph had taken the body, he wrapped it in a clean linen cloth, 60and laid it in his new tomb which he had hewn out of the rock; and he rolled a large stone against the door of the tomb, and departed. 61And Mary Magdalene was there, and the other Mary, sitting opposite the tomb.

62On the next day, which followed the Day of Preparation, the chief priests and Pharisees gathered together to Pilate, 63saying, "Sir, we remember, while He was still alive, how that deceiver said, 'After three days I will rise.' 64Therefore command that the tomb be made secure until the third day, lest His disciples come by night and steal Him *away*, and say to the people, 'He has risen from the dead.' So the last deception will be worse than the first."

65Pilate said to them, "You have a guard; go your way, make *it* as secure as you know how." 66So they went and made the tomb secure, sealing the stone and setting the guard.

CHAPTER 28 JESUS COMES BACK TO LIFE! Now after the Sabbath, as the first *day* of the week began to dawn, Mary Magdalene and the other Mary came to see the tomb. 2And behold, there was a great earthquake; for an angel of the Lord descended from heaven, and came and rolled back the stone from the door, and sat on it. 3His countenance was like lightning, and his clothing as white as snow. 4And the guards shook for fear of him, and became like dead *men*.

5But the angel answered and said to the women, "Do not be afraid, for I know that you seek Jesus who was crucified. 6He is not here; for He is risen, as He said. Come, see the place where the Lord lay. 7And go quickly and tell His disciples that He is risen from the dead, and indeed He is going before you into Galilee; there you will see Him. Behold, I have told you."

CHOICES

28:11-15 Jesus' resurrection was already causing a great stir in Jerusalem. A group of women was moving quickly through the streets, looking for the disciples to tell them the amazing news that Jesus was alive. At the same time, a group of religious leaders was plotting how to cover up the Resurrection. Today there is still a great stir over the Resurrection, and there are still only two choices—to believe that Jesus rose from the dead, or to be closed to the truth, denying it, ignoring it, or trying to explain it away.

8So they went out quickly from the tomb with fear and great joy, and ran to bring His disciples word.

9And as they went to tell His disciples, behold, Jesus met them, saying, "Rejoice!" So they came and held Him by the feet and worshiped Him. 10Then Jesus said to them, "Do not be afraid. Go *and* tell My brethren to go to Galilee, and there they will see Me."

11Now while they were going, behold, some of the guard came into the city and reported to the chief priests all the things that had happened. 12When they had assembled with the elders and consulted together, they gave a large sum of money to the soldiers, 13saying, "Tell them, 'His disciples came at night and stole Him *away* while we slept.' 14And if this comes to the governor's ears, we will appease him and make you secure." 15So they took the money and did as they were instructed; and this saying is commonly reported among the Jews until this day.

16Then the eleven disciples went away into Galilee, to the mountain which Jesus had appointed for them. 17When they saw Him, they worshiped Him; but some doubted.

18And Jesus came and spoke to them, saying, "All authority has been given to Me in heaven and on earth. 19Go therefore and make disciples of all the nations, baptizing them in the name of the Father and of the Son and of the Holy Spirit, 20teaching them to observe all things that I have commanded you; and lo, I am with you always, *even* to the end of the age." Amen.

COMMISSIONED

28:18-20 When someone is dying or leaving us, his last words are very important. Jesus left the disciples with these last words of instruction: they were under his authority; they were to make more disciples; they were to baptize and teach them to obey him; he would be with them always. Whereas in previous missions Jesus had sent his disciples only to the Jews (10:5-6), their mission from now on would be worldwide. Jesus is Lord of the earth, and he died for the sins of all those who trust him, everywhere.

We are to go—whether it is next door or to another country—and make disciples. It is not an option, but a command to all who call Jesus Lord. All of us are not evangelists, but we have all received gifts that we can use in helping to fulfill the great commission. As we obey, we have comfort in the knowledge that Jesus is always with us.

MEGA *Themes*

JESUS CHRIST, THE KING Jesus is revealed as the King of kings. His miraculous birth, his life and teaching, his miracles, and his triumph over death show us who he really is.

Jesus cannot be compared with any other person or power. He is the supreme ruler of time and eternity, heaven and earth, people and angels. We should give him his rightful place as King and Lord in our life.

1. In what ways is Jesus revealed as King in the book of Matthew?
2. In what ways did Jesus, though the King of kings, display humility in the book of Matthew?
3. What do you learn about the personal qualities of Jesus from these two lists? Why did so many people reject Jesus as King?
4. How does Jesus reign in the world today? What does it mean in terms of daily living for Jesus to be "the Lord" of your life?

THE MESSIAH Jesus was the Messiah, the One for whom the Jews had waited, who was to deliver them from Roman oppression. Yet, tragically, they didn't recognize him when he came. They were not ready to accept his kingship because it was not what they expected. They didn't understand that the true purpose of God's anointed deliverer was to die for all people, to free them from sin.

Because Jesus was sent by God, we can trust him with our life. It is worth everything we have to accept Christ and give ourself to him because he came to be our Messiah, our Savior.

1. In what ways did Jesus fulfill the prophecy of a coming Savior who would rescue the people?
2. How was Jesus' plan of deliverance different from what the people had anticipated? How was Jesus' deliverance actually greater than they could have imagined?

3. In what ways has Jesus delivered you?
4. Based on the fact that Jesus, the Messiah, has rescued you, what will you do to live for him?

KINGDOM OF GOD Jesus came to earth to begin his kingdom. His full kingdom will be realized at his return and will be made up of all those who have faithfully followed him.

The way to enter God's kingdom is by faith—by believing in Christ to save us from sin and change our life. Then we must do the work of his kingdom, helping prepare it for his return.

1. Matthew 5–7, known as the "Sermon on the Mount," introduces the values of Christ's kingdom. In accordance with these chapters, make a list of at least ten guidelines Jesus gave showing how he wants those who belong to the kingdom to live.
2. What would it mean for a person in your school to live by these kingdom guidelines?
3. Chapter 13 is filled with parables that Jesus used when teaching to help describe his kingdom. What do you learn about the kingdom of God from these parables? What is the importance of the kingdom of God?
4. In what ways are you living out the kingdom guidelines or values? In what areas do you need to become more obedient to Christ's call to kingdom values?

TEACHINGS Jesus taught the people using sermons, illustrations, and parables. He showed the true ingredients of faith and how to guard against an ineffective and hypocritical life.

Jesus' teachings show us how to prepare for life in his kingdom by living properly right now. His life was an example of his teachings, as our life should be.

1. What were the main purposes of Jesus' teachings?

2. How did different individuals and groups of people react to his teachings?
3. What seems to have caused some people to accept Jesus' teachings and others to reject them?
4. Describe the ways, both positive and negative, that people today respond to Jesus' teachings.
5. How are Jesus' teachings to be your authority in life? In what ways does this authority influence your decisions in your present life-style?

RESURRECTION When Jesus rose from the dead, he rose in power as the true King. In his victory over death, he established his credentials as King and his power and authority over evil.

The Resurrection shows that Jesus is all-powerful—that not even death could stop his plan of offering eternal life. People who believe in Jesus can hope for a resurrection like his. Our role is to live in that victory and share the message of his victory with those who do not yet know that "Jesus is alive!"

1. What difference does it make whether or not Jesus was resurrected?
2. What impact did Jesus' resurrection have on his disciples?
3. What impact has Jesus' resurrection made on mankind as a whole? On you specifically?

Has this ever happened to you? ■ Friends invite you to a just-released, critically acclaimed movie. ■ "It's supposed to be great," they insist. "You'll like it. Trust us." ■ So you go—with high expectations. Only the movie isn't great. It drags on and on. As far as excitement goes, this particular film ranks right up there with reading the phone book. ■ You keep thinking, *This has got to get better. Surely there's a car chase or a joke or some sort of surprise plot twist in the next scene.* But nothing happens— nothing at all. The most adventurous moment of the film comes at the end when two of the actors go to a fancy French restaurant and eat snails. It's gross, but at least they're finally doing something. ■ When the final credits roll, you leave the theater, vowing, "Never again!" ■ Guess what? You don't have to spend your time with stale stories, boring characters, or tedious plots! Instead, you can read one of the most exciting books in existence! And it's right here, on the next few pages. ■ You name it, and the Gospel of Mark has it—demons, death, and outrageous special effects (also called miracles), all served up in a swirling atmosphere of intrigue, jealousy, controversy, and murder. In short, this book is an action-packed biography of the most influential person in the history of the world. ■ Go for it! And when you're done, you will vow, "Never again . . . never again will I think of the Bible as a boring book!"

STATS

PURPOSE: To present Jesus' person, work, and teachings

AUTHOR: John Mark. He accompanied Paul on his first missionary journey (Acts 13:13).

TO WHOM WRITTEN: The Christians in Rome, where Mark wrote the Gospel, and believers everywhere

DATE WRITTEN: Between A.D. 55 and 65

SETTING: The Roman Empire. The empire, with its common language and excellent transportation and communication systems, was ripe to hear Jesus' message.

KEY PEOPLE: Jesus, the twelve disciples, Pilate, the Jewish religious leaders

KEY PLACES: Capernaum, Nazareth, Caesarea Philippi, Jericho, Bethany, Mount of Olives, Jerusalem, Golgotha

SPECIAL FEATURES: Mark was the first Gospel written. The other Gospels quote all but 31 verses of Mark. Mark records more miracles than does any other Gospel.

Mark

CHAPTER 1 PREPARING THE WAY FOR JESUS.

The beginning of the gospel of Jesus Christ, the Son of God. [2]As it is written in the Prophets:

"Behold, I send My messenger before Your face,
Who will prepare Your way before You."
[3] *"The voice of one crying in the wilderness:*
'Prepare the way of the LORD;
Make His paths straight.'"

[4]John came baptizing in the wilderness and preaching a baptism of repentance for the remission of sins. [5]Then all the land of Judea, and those from Jerusalem, went out to him and were all baptized by him in the Jordan River, confessing their sins.

[6]Now John was clothed with camel's hair and with a leather belt around his waist, and he ate locusts and wild honey. [7]And he preached, saying, "There comes One after me who is mightier than I, whose sandal strap I am not worthy to stoop down and loose. [8]I indeed baptized you with water, but He will baptize you with the Holy Spirit."

[9]It came to pass in those days *that* Jesus came from Nazareth of Galilee, and was baptized by John in the Jordan. [10]And immediately, coming up from the water, He saw the heavens parting and the Spirit descending upon Him like a dove. [11]Then a voice came from heaven, "You are My beloved Son, in whom I am well pleased."

[12]Immediately the Spirit drove Him into the wilderness. [13]And He was there in the wilderness forty days, tempted by Satan, and was with the wild beasts; and the angels ministered to Him.

[14]Now after John was put in prison, Jesus came to Galilee, preaching the gospel of the kingdom of God, [15]and saying, "The time is fulfilled, and the kingdom of God is at hand. Repent, and believe in the gospel."

[16]And as He walked by the Sea of Galilee, He saw Simon and Andrew his brother casting a net into the sea; for they were fishermen. [17]Then Jesus said to them, "Follow Me, and I will make you become fishers of men." [18]They immediately left their nets and followed Him.

[19]When He had gone a little farther from there, He saw James the *son* of Zebedee, and John his brother, who also *were* in the boat mending their nets. [20]And immediately He called them, and they left their father Zebedee in the boat with the hired servants, and went after Him.

[21]Then they went into Capernaum, and immediately on the Sabbath He entered the synagogue and taught. [22]And they were astonished at His teaching, for He taught them as one having authority, and not as the scribes.

[23]Now there was a man in their synagogue with an unclean spirit. And he cried out, [24]saying, "Let *us* alone! What have we to do with You, Jesus of Nazareth? Did You come to destroy us? I know who You are—the Holy One of God!" [25]But Jesus rebuked him, saying, "Be quiet, and come out of him!" [26]And when the unclean spirit had convulsed him and cried out with a loud voice, he came out of him. [27]Then they were all amazed, so that they questioned among themselves, saying, "What is this? What new doctrine *is* this? For with authority He commands even the unclean spirits, and they obey Him." [28]And immediately His fame spread throughout all the region around Galilee.

[29]Now as soon as they had come out of the synagogue, they entered the house of Simon and Andrew, with James and John. [30]But Simon's wife's mother lay sick with a fever, and they told Him about her at once. [31]So He came and took her by the hand and lifted her up, and immediately the fever left her. And she served them.

[32]At evening, when the sun had set, they brought to Him all who were sick and those who were demon-possessed. [33]And the whole city was gathered together at the door.

THRILLS

1:1 When you experience the excitement of a big event, you naturally want to tell someone. Telling the story can bring back that original thrill as you relive the experience. As you read Mark's first words, you can sense his excitement. Picture yourself in the crowd as Jesus heals and teaches. Imagine yourself as one of the disciples. Respond to Jesus' words of love and encouragement—and remember that he came for us who live today as well as for those who lived two thousand years ago.

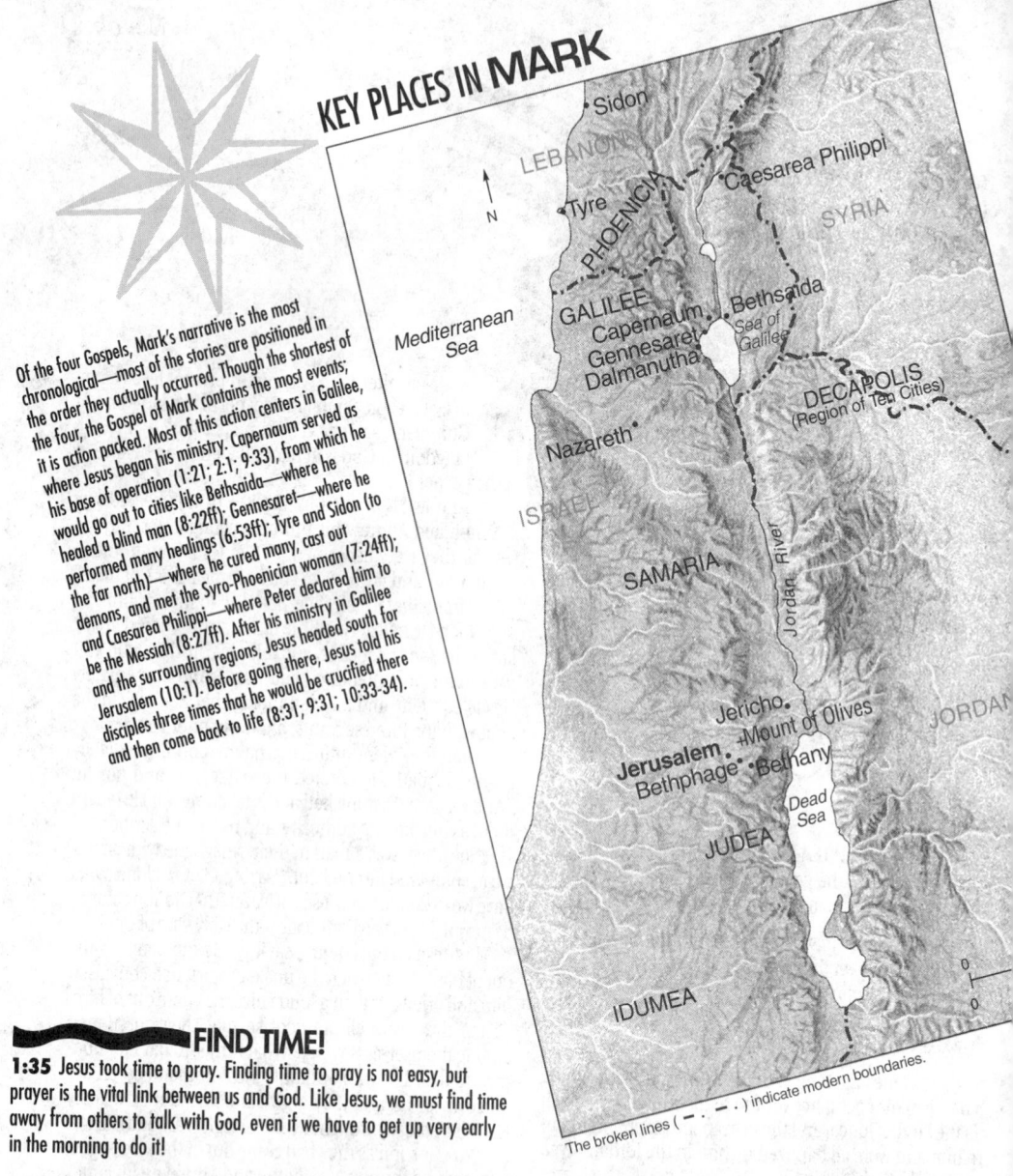

KEY PLACES IN MARK

Of the four Gospels, Mark's narrative is the most chronological—most of the stories are positioned in the order they actually occurred. Though the shortest of the four, the Gospel of Mark contains the most events; it is action packed. Most of this action centers in Galilee, where Jesus began his ministry. Capernaum served as his base of operation (1:21; 2:1; 9:33), from which he would go out to cities like Bethsaida—where he healed a blind man (8:22ff); Gennesaret—where he performed many healings (6:53ff); Tyre and Sidon (to the far north)—where he cured many, cast out demons, and met the Syro-Phoenician woman (7:24ff); and Caesarea Philippi—where Peter declared him to be the Messiah (8:27ff). After his ministry in Galilee and the surrounding regions, Jesus headed south for Jerusalem (10:1). Before going there, Jesus told his disciples three times that he would be crucified there and then come back to life (8:31; 9:31; 10:33-34).

The broken lines (— · — ·) indicate modern boundaries.

FIND TIME!

1:35 Jesus took time to pray. Finding time to pray is not easy, but prayer is the vital link between us and God. Like Jesus, we must find time away from others to talk with God, even if we have to get up very early in the morning to do it!

[34]Then He healed many who were sick with various diseases, and cast out many demons; and He did not allow the demons to speak, because they knew Him.

[35]Now in the morning, having risen a long while before daylight, He went out and departed to a solitary place; and there He prayed. [36]And Simon and those *who were* with Him searched for Him. [37]When they found Him, they said to Him, "Everyone is looking for You."

[38]But He said to them, "Let us go into the next towns, that I may preach there also, because for this purpose I have come forth."

[39]And He was preaching in their synagogues throughout all Galilee, and casting out demons.

[40]Now a leper came to Him, imploring Him, kneeling down to Him and saying to Him, "If You are willing, You can make me clean."

[41]Then Jesus, moved with compassion, stretched out *His* hand and touched him, and said to him, "I am willing; be cleansed." [42]As soon as He had spoken, immediately the leprosy left him, and he was cleansed. [43]And He strictly warned him and sent him away at once, [44]and said to him, "See that you say nothing to anyone; but go your way, show yourself to the priest, and offer for your cleansing those things which Moses commanded, as a testimony to them."

DON'T WAIT

2:14-15 The day that Levi met Jesus, he held a meeting at his house to introduce others to Jesus. Levi didn't waste any time starting to witness! Some people feel that new believers should wait for time, maturity, or training before they start telling others about Christ. But, like Levi, new believers can tell others about their faith right away with whatever knowledge, skill, or experience they already have.

45However, he went out and began to proclaim *it* freely, and to spread the matter, so that Jesus could no longer openly enter the city, but was outside in deserted places; and they came to Him from every direction.

CHAPTER 2 A HOLE IN THE ROOF.

And again He entered Capernaum after *some* days, and it was heard that He was in the house. 2Immediately many gathered together, so that there was no longer room to receive *them,* not even near the door. And He preached the word to them. 3Then they came to Him, bringing a paralytic who was carried by four *men.* 4And when they could not come near Him because of the crowd, they uncovered the roof where He was. So when they had broken through, they let down the bed on which the paralytic was lying.

5When Jesus saw their faith, He said to the paralytic, "Son, your sins are forgiven you."

6And some of the scribes were sitting there and reasoning in their hearts, 7"Why does this *Man* speak blasphemies like this? Who can forgive sins but God alone?"

8But immediately, when Jesus perceived in His spirit that they reasoned thus within themselves, He said to them, "Why do you reason about these things in your hearts? 9Which is easier, to say to the paralytic, '*Your* sins are forgiven you,' or to say, 'Arise, take up your bed and walk'? 10But that you may know that the Son of Man has power on earth to forgive sins"—He said to the paralytic, 11"I say to you, arise, take up your bed, and go to your house." 12Immediately he arose, took up the bed, and went out in the presence of them all, so that all were amazed and glorified God, saying, "We never saw *anything* like this!"

13Then He went out again by the sea; and all the multitude came to Him, and He taught them. 14As He passed by, He saw Levi the *son* of Alphaeus sitting at the tax office. And He said to him, "Follow Me." So he arose and followed Him.

15Now it happened, as He was dining in *Levi's* house, that many tax collectors and sinners also sat together with Jesus and His disciples; for there were many, and they followed Him. 16And when the scribes and Pharisees saw Him eating with the tax collectors and sinners, they said to His disciples, "How *is it* that He eats and drinks with tax collectors and sinners?"

17When Jesus heard *it,* He said to them, "Those who are well have no need of a physician, but those who are sick. I did not come to call *the* righteous, but sinners, to repentance."

18The disciples of John and of the Pharisees were fasting. Then they came and said to Him, "Why do the disciples of John and of the Pharisees fast, but Your disciples do not fast?"

19And Jesus said to them, "Can the friends of the bridegroom fast while the bridegroom is with them? As long as they have the bridegroom with them they cannot fast. 20But the days will come when the bridegroom will be taken away from them, and then they will fast in those days. 21No one sews a piece of unshrunk cloth on an old garment; or else the new piece pulls away from the old, and the tear is made worse. 22And no one puts new wine into old wineskins; or else the new wine bursts the wineskins, the wine is spilled, and the wineskins are ruined. But new wine must be put into new wineskins."

23Now it happened that He went through the grainfields on the Sabbath; and as they went His disciples began to pluck the heads of grain. 24And the Pharisees

I used to like to go to parties a lot before I became a Christian. Are parties bad?

I WONDER . . .

In answering this type of question, it's tough not to sound heavy handed. After all, teenage parties do not exactly have a great reputation.

The key word to remember is not *yes* or *no,* but *why*—your motive is the key.

If you were honest, you'd have to agree that many of the reasons people party are pretty selfish. Most parties cater to the notion that it's a person's right to have a good time, especially if it's not hurting anyone else.

If someone is living apart from God, why would he or she think anything different? The Bible agrees that if this life doesn't matter then "Let us eat and drink, for tomorrow we die!" (1 Corinthians 15:32).

The motive behind going to parties is what God is most concerned about. If it's to get drunk, take drugs, pick up the opposite sex, then God wouldn't want you at parties.

The motive might be to be seen with the "cool" people. Being with certain people sometimes may help you feel accepted and even popular, but God accepts you as you are—and his acceptance is more important than anyone else's.

Jesus isn't against parties. He went to parties, and was, in fact, the life of the party! But his motives were entirely different from the selfish ones described above. He went to show people that he accepted them, to communicate truth about the character of God, and to celebrate life (see Mark 2:13-17).

Should you do the same? Perhaps, but here are a few questions to consider:

- Have you grown sufficiently in your faith that you will not be tempted if there is pressure to drink (or whatever)?
- Do you know someone who will go with so you can encourage each other to stay clean?
- Are you going as a light or as a hammer? That is, do you genuinely want to help those in darkness, or do you want to pound on them to feel good about your "moral" life-style?
- Is there a chance that you could be found "guilty by association"? When others hear you were at the party, how will they know you didn't drink? Is it worth the hassle it may cause in making sure your reputation stays intact?
- What do your parents think about you attending that party? Would you have to not tell them in order to go? Remember, motive is the key. But even with good motives, be cautious. The results of such activities, even with the best of motives, may be more than you can handle.

said to Him, "Look, why do they do what is not lawful on the Sabbath?"

²⁵But He said to them, "Have you never read what David did when he was in need and hungry, he and those with him: ²⁶how he went into the house of God *in the days* of Abiathar the high priest, and ate the showbread, which is not lawful to eat except for the priests, and also gave some to those who were with him?"

²⁷And He said to them, "The Sabbath was made for man, and not man for the Sabbath. ²⁸Therefore the Son of Man is also Lord of the Sabbath."

CHAPTER 3 JESUS HEALS A CRIPPLED HAND. And

He entered the synagogue again, and a man was there who had a withered hand. ²So they watched Him closely, whether He would heal him on the Sabbath, so that they might accuse Him. ³And He said to the man who had the withered hand, "Step forward." ⁴Then He said to them, "Is it lawful on the Sabbath to do good or to do evil, to save life or to kill?" But they kept silent. ⁵And when He had looked around at them with anger, being grieved by the hardness of their hearts, He said to the man, "Stretch

◣ ANGER

3:5 Jesus was angry about the Pharisees' uncaring attitudes. Anger itself is not wrong. It depends on what makes us angry and what we do with our anger. Too often we express our anger in selfish and harmful ways. By contrast, Jesus expressed his anger by correcting a problem—healing the man's hand. Use your anger to find constructive solutions rather than to add to the problem by tearing people down.

out your hand." And he stretched *it* out, and his hand was restored as whole as the other. ⁶Then the Pharisees went out and immediately plotted with the Herodians against Him, how they might destroy Him.

⁷But Jesus withdrew with His disciples to the sea. And a great multitude from Galilee followed Him, and from Judea ⁸and Jerusalem and Idumea and beyond the Jordan; and those from Tyre and Sidon, a great multitude, when they heard how many things He was doing, came to Him. ⁹So He told His disciples that a small boat should be kept ready for Him because of the multitude, lest they should crush Him. ¹⁰For He healed many, so that as many as had afflictions pressed about Him to touch Him. ¹¹And the unclean spirits, whenever they saw Him, fell down before Him and cried out, saying, "You are the Son of God." ¹²But He sternly warned them that they should not make Him known.

¹³And He went up on the mountain and called to *Him* those He Himself wanted. And they came to Him. ¹⁴Then He appointed twelve, that they might be with Him and that He might send them out to preach, ¹⁵and to have power to heal sicknesses and to cast out demons: ¹⁶Simon, to whom He gave the name Peter; ¹⁷James the *son* of Zebedee and John the brother of James, to whom He gave the name Boanerges, that is, "Sons of Thunder"; ¹⁸Andrew, Philip, Bartholomew, Matthew, Thomas, James the *son* of Alphaeus, Thaddaeus, Simon the Cananite; ¹⁹and Judas Iscariot, who also betrayed Him. And they went into a house.

◣ READY

4:11-12 Some people do not understand God's truth because th[ey are] not ready for it. God reveals truth to people who will do somethin[g about] it. When you talk with people about God, be aware that they will [not] understand if they are not yet ready. Be patient, taking every cha[nce to] tell them more of the truth about God and praying that the Holy S[pirit] will open their minds and hearts, making them ready to receive th[e truth] and act on it.

²⁰Then the multitude came together again, so that they could not so much as eat bread. ²¹But when His own people heard *about this,* they went out to lay hold of Him, for they said, "He is out of His mind."

²²And the scribes who came down from Jerusalem said, "He has Beelzebub," and, "By the ruler of the demons He casts out demons."

²³So He called them to *Himself* and said to them in parables: "How can Satan cast out Satan? ²⁴If a kingdom is divided against itself, that kingdom cannot stand. ²⁵And if a house is divided against itself, that house cannot stand. ²⁶And if Satan has risen up against himself, and is divided, he cannot stand, but has an end. ²⁷No one can enter a strong man's house and plunder his goods, unless he first binds the strong man. And then he will plunder his house.

²⁸"Assuredly, I say to you, all sins will be forgiven the sons of men, and whatever blasphemies they may utter; ²⁹but he who blasphemes against the Holy Spirit never has forgiveness, but is subject to eternal condemnation"— ³⁰because they said, "He has an unclean spirit."

³¹Then His brothers and His mother came, and standing outside they sent to Him, calling Him. ³²And a multitude was sitting around Him; and they said to Him, "Look, Your mother and Your brothers are outside seeking You."

³³But He answered them, saying, "Who is My mother, or My brothers?" ³⁴And He looked around in a circle at those who sat about Him, and said, "Here are My mother and My brothers! ³⁵For whoever does the will of God is My brother and My sister and mother."

CHAPTER 4 A STORY ABOUT FOUR KINDS OF SOIL.

And again He began to teach by the sea. And a great multitude was gathered to Him, so that He got into a boat and sat *in it* on the sea; and the whole multitude was on the land facing the sea. ²Then He taught them many things by parables, and said to them in His teaching:

³"Listen! Behold, a sower went out to sow. ⁴And it happened, as he sowed, *that* some *seed* fell by the wayside; and the birds of the air came and devoured it. ⁵Some fell on stony ground, where it did not have much earth; and immediately it sprang up because it had no depth of earth. ⁶But when the sun was up it was scorched, and because it

◣ RESPONSES

4:14-20 The four soils represent four different ways people respo[nd to] God's Word. Usually we think Jesus was talking about four different [kinds] of people, but he may also have been talking about (1) different tim[e] phases in a person's life, or (2) how we willingly receive God's messa[ge in] some areas of our life and resist it in others. For example, you may b[e] open to God where your future is concerned, but closed concerning ho[w] you spend your money. You may respond like good soil to God's dem[and] for worship, but like rocky soil to his demand to give to those in need[.] Strive to be like good soil in every area of your life.

had no root it withered away. ⁷And some *seed* fell among thorns; and the thorns grew up and choked it, and it yielded no crop. ⁸But other *seed* fell on good ground and yielded a crop that sprang up, increased and produced: some thirtyfold, some sixty, and some a hundred."

⁹And He said to them, "He who has ears to hear, let him hear!"

¹⁰But when He was alone, those around Him with the twelve asked Him about the parable. ¹¹And He said to them, "To you it has been given to know the mystery of the kingdom of God; but to those who are outside, all things come in parables, ¹²so that

> 'Seeing they may see and not perceive,
> And hearing they may hear and not understand;
> Lest they should turn,
> And their sins be forgiven
>   them.' "

¹³And He said to them, "Do you not understand this parable? How then will you understand all the parables? ¹⁴The sower sows the word. ¹⁵And these are the ones by the wayside where the word is sown. When they hear, Satan comes immediately and takes away the word that was sown in their hearts. ¹⁶These likewise are the ones sown on stony ground who, when they hear the word, immediately receive it with gladness; ¹⁷and they have no root in themselves, and so endure only for a time. Afterward, when tribulation or persecution arises for the word's sake, immediately they stumble. ¹⁸Now these are the ones sown among thorns; *they are* the ones who hear the word, ¹⁹and the cares of this world, the deceitfulness of riches, and the desires for other things entering in choke the word, and it becomes unfruitful. ²⁰But these are the ones sown on good ground, those who hear the word, accept *it*, and bear fruit: some thirtyfold, some sixty, and some a hundred."

²¹Also He said to them, "Is a lamp brought to be put under a basket or under a bed? Is it not to be set on a lampstand? ²²For there is nothing hidden which will not be revealed, nor has anything been kept secret but that it should come to light. ²³If anyone has ears to hear, let him hear."

²⁴Then He said to them, "Take heed what you hear. With the same measure you use, it will be measured to you; and to you who hear, more will be given. ²⁵For whoever has, to him more will be given; but whoever does not have, even what he has will be taken away from him."

²⁶And He said, "The kingdom of God is as if a man should scatter seed on the ground, ²⁷and should sleep by night and rise by day, and the seed should sprout and grow, he himself does not know how. ²⁸For the earth yields crops by itself: first the blade, then the head, after that the full grain in the head. ²⁹But when the grain ripens, immediately he puts in the sickle, because the harvest has come."

JUDAS ISCARIOT

It is easy to forget that Jesus chose Judas to be his disciple. We may also miss the point that while Judas betrayed Jesus, all the disciples abandoned him. The disciples, including Judas, all had the wrong idea of Jesus' mission on earth. They expected Jesus to become a political leader. But when he kept talking about dying, they all felt a mixture of anger, fear, and disappointment. They couldn't understand why Jesus had asked them to follow him if his mission was going to fail.

We don't know exactly why Judas betrayed Jesus. But we can see that Judas let his own desires become so important that Satan was able to control him. He got paid to set up Jesus for the religious leaders.

He tried to undo the evil he had done by returning the money to the priests, but it was too late. How sad that Judas ended his life in despair without ever experiencing the gift of forgiveness God could give to even him through Jesus Christ.

In betraying Jesus, Judas made the greatest mistake in history. But just the fact that Jesus knew Judas would betray him doesn't mean that Judas was a puppet of God's will. Judas made the choice. God knew what that choice would be and made it part of the plan. Judas didn't lose his relationship with Jesus; rather, he had never found Jesus. He is called the "son of perdition" (John 17:12) because he was never saved.

Judas's life can help us if he makes us think again about our commitment to God. Is God's Spirit in us? Are we true disciples and followers, or uncommitted pretenders? We can choose disobedience and death, or we can choose repentance, forgiveness, hope, and eternal life. Judas's betrayal sent Jesus to the cross to guarantee that second choice, our only chance. Will we accept Christ's free gift, or—like Judas—betray him?

UPS:
• He was chosen as one of the 12 disciples; the only non-Galilean
• He kept the money bag for the expenses of the group
• He was able to recognize the evil in his betrayal of Jesus

DOWNS:
• He was greedy (John 12:6)
• He betrayed Jesus
• He committed suicide instead of seeking forgiveness

STATS:
• Where: probably from the town of Kerioth
• Occupation: disciple of Jesus
• Relatives: Father: Simon
• Contemporaries: Jesus, Pilate, Herod, the other 11 disciples

LESSONS: Evil plans and motives leave us open to being used by Satan for even greater evil

The consequences of evil are so devastating that even small lies and little wrongdoings have serious results

God's plan and purposes are worked out even in the worst possible events

KEY VERSES: "Then Satan entered Judas, surnamed Iscariot, who was numbered among the twelve. So he went his way and conferred with the chief priests and captains, how he might betray Him to them" (Luke 22:3-4).

Judas's story is told in the Gospels. He is also mentioned in Acts 1:17-19.

5:19-20 This man who had been demon-possessed became a living example of Jesus' power. He wanted to go with Jesus, but Jesus told him to go home and share his story there. If you have experienced Jesus' power, you, too, are a living example. Are you, like this man, enthusiastic about sharing the Good News with those around you? Just as we would tell others about a doctor who cured a physical disease, we should tell about Christ, who cures our sin.

³⁰Then He said, "To what shall we liken the kingdom of God? Or with what parable shall we picture it? ³¹*It is* like a mustard seed which, when it is sown on the ground, is smaller than all the seeds on earth; ³²but when it is sown, it grows up and becomes greater than all herbs, and shoots out large branches, so that the birds of the air may nest under its shade."

³³And with many such parables He spoke the word to them as they were able to hear *it*. ³⁴But without a parable He did not speak to them. And when they were alone, He explained all things to His disciples.

³⁵On the same day, when evening had come, He said to them, "Let us cross over to the other side." ³⁶Now when they had left the multitude, they took Him along in the boat as He was. And other little boats were also with Him. ³⁷And a great windstorm arose, and the waves beat into the boat, so that it was already filling. ³⁸But He was in the stern, asleep on a pillow. And they awoke Him and said to Him, "Teacher, do You not care that we are perishing?" ³⁹Then He arose and rebuked the wind, and said to the sea, "Peace, be still!" And the wind ceased and there was a great calm. ⁴⁰But He said to them, "Why are you so fearful? How *is it* that you have no faith?" ⁴¹And they feared exceedingly, and said to one another, "Who can this be, that even the wind and the sea obey Him!"

CHAPTER 5 JESUS HEALS A MAN WITH DEMONS.

Then they came to the other side of the sea, to the country of the Gadarenes. ²And when He had come out of the boat, immediately there met Him out of the tombs a man with an unclean spirit, ³who had *his* dwelling among the tombs; and no one could bind him, not even with chains, ⁴because he had often been bound with shackles and chains. And the chains had been pulled apart by him, and the shackles broken in pieces; neither could anyone tame him. ⁵And always, night and day, he was in the mountains and in the tombs, crying out and cutting himself with stones.

⁶When he saw Jesus from afar, he ran and worshiped Him. ⁷And he cried out with a loud voice and said, "What have I to do with You, Jesus, Son of the Most High God? I implore You by God that You do not torment me."

⁸For He said to him, "Come out of the man, unclean spirit!" ⁹Then He asked him, "What *is* your name?"

And he answered, saying, "My name *is* Legion; for we are many." ¹⁰Also he begged Him earnestly that He would not send them out of the country.

¹¹Now a large herd of swine was feeding there near the mountains. ¹²So all the demons begged Him, saying, "Send us to the swine, that we may enter them." ¹³And at once Jesus gave them permission. Then the unclean spirits went out and entered the swine (there were about two

*Go home to your friends and **tell them** WHAT GREAT THINGS THE LORD has done for you AND how He has had compassion on you.*

MARK 5:19

thousand); and the herd ran violently down the steep place into the sea, and drowned in the sea.

¹⁴So those who fed the swine fled, and they told *it* in the city and in the country. And they went out to see what it was that had happened. ¹⁵Then they came to Jesus, and saw the one *who had been* demon-possessed and had the legion, sitting and clothed and in his right mind. And they were afraid. ¹⁶And those who saw it told them how it happened to him *who had been* demon-possessed, and about the swine. ¹⁷Then they began to plead with Him to depart from their region.

¹⁸And when He got into the boat, he who had been demon-possessed begged Him that he might be with Him. ¹⁹However, Jesus did not permit him, but said to him, "Go home to your friends, and tell them what great things the Lord has done for you, and how He has had compassion on you." ²⁰And he departed and began to proclaim in Decapolis all that Jesus had done for him; and all marveled.

²¹Now when Jesus had crossed over again by boat to the other side, a great multitude gathered to Him; and He was by the sea. ²²And behold, one of the rulers of the synagogue came, Jairus by name. And when he saw Him, he fell at His feet ²³and begged Him earnestly, saying, "My little daughter lies at the point of death. Come and lay Your hands on her, that she may be healed, and she will

6:2-3 Jesus was teaching effectively and wisely, but the people of h hometown saw him as only a carpenter. "He's no better than we are—he's just a common laborer," they said. They were offended th others could be impressed by him and follow him. They rejected his authority because he was one of their peers. They thought they knew him, but their preconceived notions about who he was made it imposs for them to accept his message. Don't let prejudice blind you to truth. you learn more about Jesus, try to see him for who he really is.

live." [24]So *Jesus* went with him, and a great multitude followed Him and thronged Him.

[25]Now a certain woman had a flow of blood for twelve years, [26]and had suffered many things from many physicians. She had spent all that she had and was no better, but rather grew worse. [27]When she heard about Jesus, she came behind *Him* in the crowd and touched His garment. [28]For she said, "If only I may touch His clothes, I shall be made well." [29]Immediately the fountain of her blood was dried up, and she felt in *her* body that she was healed of the affliction. [30]And Jesus, immediately knowing in Himself that power had gone out of Him, turned around in the crowd and said, "Who touched My clothes?" [31]But His disciples said to Him, "You see the multitude thronging You, and You say, 'Who touched Me?'"

[32]And He looked around to see her who had done this thing. [33]But the woman, fearing and trembling, knowing what had happened to her, came and fell down before Him and told Him the whole truth. [34]And He said to her, "Daughter, your faith has made you well. Go in peace, and be healed of your affliction."

[35]While He was still speaking, *some* came from the ruler of the synagogue's *house* who said, "Your daughter is dead. Why trouble the Teacher any further?"

[36]As soon as Jesus heard the word that was spoken, He said to the ruler of the synagogue, "Do not be afraid; only believe." [37]And He permitted no one to follow Him except Peter, James, and John the brother of James. [38]Then He came to the house of the ruler of the synagogue, and saw a tumult and those who wept and wailed loudly. [39]When He came in, He said to them, "Why make this commotion and weep? The child is not dead, but sleeping."

[40]And they ridiculed Him. But when He had put them all outside, He took the father and the mother of the child, and those *who were* with Him, and entered where the child was lying. [41]Then He took the child by the hand, and said to her, "Talitha, cumi," which is translated, "Little girl, I say to you, arise." [42]Immediately the girl arose and walked, for she was twelve years *of age.* And they were overcome with great amazement. [43]But He commanded them strictly that no one should know it, and said that *something* should be given her to eat.

CHAPTER 6 REJECTED IN HIS HOMETOWN. Then

He went out from there and came to His own country, and His disciples followed Him. [2]And when the Sabbath had come, He began to teach in the synagogue. And many hearing *Him* were astonished, saying, "Where *did* this Man *get* these things? And what wisdom *is* this which is given to Him, that such mighty works are performed by His hands! [3]Is this not the carpenter, the Son of Mary, and brother of James, Joses, Judas, and Simon? And are not His sisters here with us?" So they were offended at Him.

[4]But Jesus said to them, "A prophet is not without honor except in his own country, among his own relatives, and in his own house." [5]Now He could do no mighty work there, except that He laid His hands on a few sick people and healed *them.* [6]And He marveled because

of their unbelief. Then He went about the villages in a circuit, teaching.

[7]And He called the twelve to *Himself,* and began to send them out two *by* two, and gave them power over

TEAMWORK

6:7 The disciples were sent out in pairs. Individually they could have reached more areas of the country, but this was not Christ's plan. One advantage in going out by twos was that they could strengthen and encourage each other, especially when they faced rejection. Our strength comes from God, but he meets many of our needs through others. As you serve Christ, don't try to go it alone.

unclean spirits. [8]He commanded them to take nothing for the journey except a staff—no bag, no bread, no copper in *their* money belts— [9]but to wear sandals, and not to put on two tunics.

[10]Also He said to them, "In whatever place you enter a

Now that I am a Christian, how should I act around my friends and family who are not believers?

I WONDER...

The most important thing you have going for you in both sets of relationships is that you already have a "relational bridge." Your friends and family knew what your life was like before you met Christ. Now they will have the chance to see you afterward.

In Mark 5:1-20, Jesus recognized that this was the case with the man he had just cleansed from demon possession. So he sent him back to his home instead of asking him to leave those who knew him best.

Another passage calls us Christ's ambassadors to our world (2 Corinthians 5:17-20). This means we are his hand-picked representatives! If people want to know what God is like, all they have to do is look at us.

God does not expect you to be perfect, but he does expect your faith to grow (Romans 10:17), and he expects you to try to live more like Jesus Christ would (Romans 12:1-2).

The people around you will be able to relate to your progress, not to perfection. Progress may be slow at first, but eventually, as you give areas of your life to Christ's control, changes will become noticeable. When this happens, you may find others starting to ask questions about your new faith.

When this happens, don't worry—although you may "feel" inadequate answering some of their questions, your responsibility is only to share what God has done for you and what you have learned, not to be the Bible expert. Sharing and living your faith as a new Christian is just as important (and biblical!) as being more mature in the faith or being a Bible scholar. God is not limited by our lack of knowledge.

Though new Christians sometimes face unique hardships, Jesus knows that, as with the Gadarene demoniac, your changed life may have a much greater impact on those with whom you have relational bridges already built than a stranger who may speak more eloquently!

house, stay there till you depart from that place. [11]And whoever will not receive you nor hear you, when you depart from there, shake off the dust under your feet as a testimony against them. Assuredly, I say to you, it will be more tolerable for Sodom and Gomorrah in the day of judgment than for that city!"

[12]So they went out and preached that *people* should repent. [13]And they cast out many demons, and anointed with oil many who were sick, and healed *them.*

[14]Now King Herod heard *of Him,* for His name had become well known. And he said, "John the Baptist is risen from the dead, and therefore these powers are at work in him."

[15]Others said, "It is Elijah."

LEGALISM

Perhaps you know someone like 17-year-old Neal.

A very opinionated churchgoer, he's got the Christian life all figured out (so he thinks). For Neal, there are no "gray areas." Everything is black and white, cut and dry. Certain deeds are expected, and most other activities simply are not acceptable for believers. And if you don't see things his way, Neal treats you like your relationship with the Lord is defective. Just look at some of his recent pronouncements:

- "Anybody who goes dancing is not walking with God."
- "How a girl who wears an outfit like that could call herself a Christian is beyond me!"
- "Going to a movie theater is no different than going into a bar. Both places are evil."
- "If you guys are serious about God, you'll be at youth group Wednesday night."

Is it any wonder that this outspoken junior has been nicknamed "Negative Neal"?

Legalism is the crazy idea that we can earn God's acceptance by strenuously following a lot of dos and don'ts. Legalistic people almost always feel either prideful ("I'm better than the people who do these things") or frustrated ("I can never measure up").

Is that what the Christian life is all about? A long list of rules and regulations? Not at all! Even if you don't know anyone as extreme as Neal, and even if you don't think you struggle with legalism, see what Jesus said in Mark 7:1-23.

And others said, "It is the Prophet, or like one of the prophets."

[16]But when Herod heard, he said, "This is John, whom I beheaded; he has been raised from the dead!" [17]For Herod himself had sent and laid hold of John, and bound him in prison for the sake of Herodias, his brother Philip's wife; for he had married her. [18]Because John had said to Herod, "It is not lawful for you to have your brother's wife." [19]Therefore Herodias held it against him and wanted to kill him, but she could not; [20]for Herod feared John, knowing that he *was* a just and holy man, and he protected him. And when he heard him, he did many things, and heard him gladly. [21]Then an opportune day came when Herod on his birthday gave a feast for his nobles, the high officers, and the chief *men* of Galilee. [22]And when Herodias' daughter herself came in and danced, and pleased Herod and those who sat with him, the king said to the girl, "Ask me whatever you want, and I will give *it* to you." [23]He also swore to her, "Whatever you ask me, I will give you, up to half my kingdom."

[24]So she went out and said to her mother, "What shall I ask?"

And she said, "The head of John the Baptist!"

[25]Immediately she came in with haste to the king and asked, saying, "I want you to give me at once the head of John the Baptist on a platter."

[26]And the king was exceedingly sorry; *yet,* because of the oaths and because of those who sat with him, he did not want to refuse her. [27]Immediately the king sent an executioner and commanded his head to be brought. And he went and beheaded him in prison, [28]brought his head on a platter, and gave it to the girl; and the girl gave it to her mother. [29]When his disciples heard *of it,* they came and took away his corpse and laid it in a tomb.

[30]Then the apostles gathered to Jesus and told Him all things, both what they had done and what they had taught. [31]And He said to them, "Come aside by yourselves to a deserted place and rest a while." For there were many coming and going, and they did not even have time to eat. [32]So they departed to a deserted place in the boat by themselves.

[33]But the multitudes saw them departing, and many knew Him and ran there on foot from all the cities. They arrived before them and came together to Him. [34]And Jesus, when He came out, saw a great multitude and was moved with compassion for them, because they were like sheep not having a shepherd. So He began to teach them many things. [35]When the day was now far spent, His disciples came to Him and said, "This is a deserted place, and already the hour *is* late. [36]Send them away, that they may go into the surrounding country and villages and buy themselves bread; for they have nothing to eat."

[37]But He answered and said to them, "You give them something to eat."

And they said to Him, "Shall we go and buy two hundred denarii worth of bread and give them *something* to eat?"

[38]But He said to them, "How many loaves do you have? Go and see."

And when they found out they said, "Five, and two fish."

[39]Then He commanded them to make them all sit down in groups on the green grass. [40]So they sat down in ranks, in hundreds and in fifties. [41]And when He had taken the five loaves and the two fish, He looked up to heaven, blessed and broke the loaves, and gave *them* to His disciples to set before them; and the two fish He divided among *them* all. [42]So they all ate and were filled. [43]And they took up twelve baskets full of fragments and of the fish. [44]Now those who had eaten the loaves were about five thousand men.

[45]Immediately He made His disciples get into the boat and go before Him to the other side, to Bethsaida, while He sent the multitude away. [46]And when He had sent them away, He departed to the mountain to pray. [47]Now when

evening came, the boat was in the middle of the sea; and He *was* alone on the land. ⁴⁸Then He saw them straining at rowing, for the wind was against them. Now about the fourth watch of the night He came to them, walking on the sea, and would have passed them by. ⁴⁹And when they saw Him walking on the sea, they supposed it was a ghost, and cried out; ⁵⁰for they all saw Him and were troubled. But immediately He talked with them and said to them, "Be of good cheer! It is I; do not be afraid." ⁵¹Then He went up into the boat to them, and the wind ceased. And they were greatly amazed in themselves beyond measure, and marveled. ⁵²For they had not understood about the loaves, because their heart was hardened.

⁵³When they had crossed over, they came to the land of Gennesaret and anchored there. ⁵⁴And when they came out of the boat, immediately the people recognized Him, ⁵⁵ran through that whole surrounding region, and began to carry about on beds those who were sick to wherever they heard He was. ⁵⁶Wherever He entered, into villages, cities, or the country, they laid the sick in the marketplaces, and begged Him that they might just touch the hem of His garment. And as many as touched Him were made well.

CHAPTER 7   A BUNCH OF HYPOCRITES. Then the

Pharisees and some of the scribes came together to Him, having come from Jerusalem. ²Now when they saw some of His disciples eat bread with defiled, that is, with unwashed hands, they found fault. ³For the Pharisees and all the Jews do not eat unless they wash *their* hands in a special way, holding the tradition of the elders. ⁴*When they come* from the marketplace, they do not eat unless they wash. And there are many other things which they have received and hold, *like* the washing of cups, pitchers, copper vessels, and couches.

⁵Then the Pharisees and scribes asked Him, "Why do Your disciples not walk according to the tradition of the elders, but eat bread with unwashed hands?"

⁶He answered and said to them, "Well did Isaiah prophesy of you hypocrites, as it is written:

'This people honors Me with their lips,
   But their heart is far from Me.
⁷ And in vain they worship Me,
   Teaching as doctrines the commandments of men.'

⁸For laying aside the commandment of God, you hold the tradition of men—the washing of pitchers and cups, and many other such things you do."

⁹He said to them, "*All too* well you reject the commandment of God, that you may keep your tradition. ¹⁰For Moses said, *'Honor your father and your mother'*; and, *'He who curses father or mother, let him be put to death.'* ¹¹But you say, 'If a man says to his father or mother, "Whatever profit you might have received from me *is* Corban"—' (that is, a gift *to God*), ¹²then you no longer let him do anything for his father or his mother, ¹³making the word of God of no effect through your tradition which you have handed down. And many such things you do."

¹⁴When He had called all the multitude to *Himself*, He said to them, "Hear Me, everyone, and understand: ¹⁵There is nothing that enters a man from outside which can defile him; but the things which come out of him, those are the things that defile a man. ¹⁶If anyone has ears to hear, let him hear!"

¹⁷When He had entered a house away from the crowd, His disciples asked Him concerning the parable. ¹⁸So He said to them, "Are you thus without understanding also? Do you not perceive that whatever enters a man from outside cannot defile him, ¹⁹because it does not enter his heart but his stomach, and is eliminated, *thus* purifying all foods?" ²⁰And He said, "What comes out of a man, that defiles a man. ²¹For from within, out of the heart of men, proceed evil thoughts, adulteries, fornications, murders, ²²thefts, covetousness, wickedness, deceit, lewdness, an evil eye, blasphemy, pride, foolishness. ²³All these evil things come from within and defile a man."

²⁴From there He arose and went to the region of Tyre and Sidon. And He entered a house and wanted no one to know *it*, but He could not be hidden. ²⁵For a woman whose young daughter had an unclean spirit heard about Him, and she came and fell at His feet. ²⁶The woman was a Greek, a Syro-Phoenician by birth, and she kept asking Him to cast the demon out of her daughter. ²⁷But Jesus said to her, "Let the children be filled first, for it is not good to take the children's bread and throw *it* to the little dogs."

²⁸And she answered and said to Him, "Yes, Lord, yet even the little dogs under the table eat from the children's crumbs."

²⁹Then He said to her, "For this saying go your way; the demon has gone out of your daughter."

³⁰And when she had come to her house, she found the demon gone out, and her daughter lying on the bed.

³¹Again, departing from the region of Tyre and Sidon, He came through the midst of the region of Decapolis to the Sea of Galilee. ³²Then they brought to Him one who was deaf and had an impediment in his speech, and they begged Him to put His hand on him. ³³And He took him aside from the multitude, and put His fingers in his ears, and He spat and touched his tongue. ³⁴Then, looking up to heaven, He sighed, and said to him, "Ephphatha," that is, "Be opened."

³⁵Immediately his ears were opened, and the impediment of his tongue was loosed, and he spoke plainly. ³⁶Then He commanded them that they should tell no one; but the more He commanded them, the more widely they proclaimed *it*. ³⁷And they were astonished beyond measure, saying, "He has done all things well. He makes both the deaf to hear and the mute to speak."

EXCUSES

7:10-11 The Pharisees used God as an excuse to avoid helping their families, especially their parents. They thought it was more important to put money in the temple treasury than to help their needy parents, although God's law specifically says to honor fathers and mothers (Exodus 20:12) and to care for those in need (Leviticus 25:35-43). We should give money and time to God, but we must never use God as an excuse to neglect our responsibilities. Helping those in need is one of the most important ways to honor God.

CHAPTER 8 ANOTHER MEALTIME MIRACLE.

In those days, the multitude being very great and having nothing to eat, Jesus called His disciples *to Him* and said to them, ²"I have compassion on the multitude, because they have now continued with Me three days and have nothing to eat. ³And if I send them away hungry to their own houses, they will faint on the way; for some of them have come from afar."

⁴Then His disciples answered Him, "How can one satisfy these people with bread here in the wilderness?"

⁵He asked them, "How many loaves do you have?"

And they said, "Seven."

⁶So He commanded the multitude to sit down on the ground. And He took the seven loaves and gave thanks,

broke *them* and gave *them* to His disciples to set before *them*; and they set *them* before the multitude. ⁷They also had a few small fish; and having blessed them, He said to set them also before *them*. ⁸So they ate and were filled, and they took up seven large baskets of leftover fragments. ⁹Now those who had eaten were about four thousand. And He sent them away, ¹⁰immediately got into the boat with His disciples, and came to the region of Dalmanutha.

¹¹Then the Pharisees came out and began to dispute with Him, seeking from Him a sign from heaven, testing Him. ¹²But He sighed deeply in His spirit, and said, "Why does this generation seek a sign? Assuredly, I say to you, no sign shall be given to this generation."

¹³And He left them, and getting into the boat again, departed to the other side. ¹⁴Now the disciples had forgotten to take bread, and they did not have more than one loaf with them in the boat. ¹⁵Then He charged them, saying, "Take heed, beware of the leaven of the Pharisees and the leaven of Herod."

¹⁶And they reasoned among themselves, saying, "*It is* because we have no bread."

¹⁷But Jesus, being aware of *it*, said to them, "Why do you reason because you have no bread? Do you not yet perceive nor understand? Is your heart still hardened? ¹⁸Having eyes, do you not see? And having ears, do you not hear? And do you not remember? ¹⁹When I broke the five loaves for the five thousand, how many baskets full of fragments did you take up?"

They said to Him, "Twelve."

²⁰"Also, when I broke the seven for the four thousand, how many large baskets full of fragments did you take up?"

And they said, "Seven."

²¹So He said to them, "How *is it* you do not understand?"

²²Then He came to Bethsaida; and they brought a blind man to Him, and begged Him to touch him. ²³So He took the blind man by the hand and led him out of the town. And when He had spit on his eyes and put His hands on him, He asked him if he saw anything.

²⁴And he looked up and said, "I see men like trees, walking."

²⁵Then He put *His* hands on his eyes again and made him look up. And he was restored and saw everyone clearly. ²⁶Then He sent him away to his house, saying, "Neither go into the town, nor tell anyone in the town."

²⁷Now Jesus and His disciples went out to the towns of Caesarea Philippi; and on the road He asked His disciples, saying to them, "Who do men say that I am?"

²⁸So they answered, "John the Baptist; but some *say,* Elijah; and others, one of the prophets."

²⁹He said to them, "But who do you say that I am?"

Peter answered and said to Him, "You are the Christ."

³⁰Then He strictly warned them that they should tell no one about Him.

³¹And He began to teach them that the Son of Man must suffer many things, and be rejected by the elders and chief priests and scribes, and be killed, and after three days rise again. ³²He spoke this word openly. Then Peter took Him aside and began to rebuke Him. ³³But when He had turned around and looked at His disciples, He rebuked Peter, saying, "Get behind Me, Satan! For you are not mindful of the things of God, but the things of men."

³⁴When He had called the people to *Himself*, with His disciples also, He said to them, "Whoever desires to come after Me, let him deny himself, and take up his cross, and follow Me. ³⁵For whoever desires to save his life will lose it, but whoever loses his life for My sake and the gospel's will

---

ＳUCCESS

You've heard of *A Tale of Two Cities*? Call this "A Tale of Two Sisters."

Karen, a senior, has a 4.0 grade-point average and is practically guaranteed a scholarship. She is president of her class and is both captain and number one seed on the girl's tennis team. Tan and very pretty, Karen dates Mitchell. Together they were voted by their class as "most likely to succeed." Karen's ambition? To marry Mitchell and be a stockbroker on Wall Street in New York City.

If Karen represents "the best of times," then to many, Alice, a sophomore, probably embodies "the worst of times." She struggles in school, making mostly Cs. She is not especially popular, nor is she very athletic. No, the truth is that Alice is painfully shy and average-looking. She has not been blessed with a boyfriend, voted into office, or had predictions of greatness bestowed upon her. Most of her free time goes to serving as a Big Sister to two youngsters at a local orphanage. Her goal in life? To be a social worker.

Do you know anyone like Karen? Like Alice? Which girl do you think is the most successful? By what standards does our society judge success and failure? What does Jesus say in Mark 9:33-37?

HE KNOWS

8:1-3 Do you ever feel that God is so busy with important concer[ns] he can't possibly be aware of your needs? Just as Jesus was concer[ned] about those people's need for food, he is concerned about our daily needs. At another time Jesus said, "Therefore do not worry, saying, shall we eat?' or 'What shall we drink?' or 'What shall we wear?'... your heavenly Father knows that you need all these things" (Matt[hew] 6:31-32). Do you have concerns that you think would not interest G[od]? There is no concern too large for him to handle, and no need too sm[all to] escape his interest.

YOU

8:29 Jesus asked the disciples who others thought he was; then he focused on them: "Who do you think I am?" It is not enough to know what others say about Jesus: you must know, understand, and accept yourself that he is the Messiah. You must move from curiosity to commitment and from admiration to adoration.

save it. [36]For what will it profit a man if he gains the whole world, and loses his own soul? [37]Or what will a man give in exchange for his soul? [38]For whoever is ashamed of Me and My words in this adulterous and sinful generation, of him the Son of Man also will be ashamed when He comes in the glory of His Father with the holy angels."

CHAPTER 9 THE TRANSFIGURATION. And He said to them, "Assuredly, I say to you that there are some standing here who will not taste death till they see the kingdom of God present with power."

[2]Now after six days Jesus took Peter, James, and John, and led them up on a high mountain apart by themselves; and He was transfigured before them. [3]His clothes became shining, exceedingly white, like snow, such as no launderer on earth can whiten them. [4]And Elijah appeared to them with Moses, and they were talking with Jesus. [5]Then Peter answered and said to Jesus, "Rabbi, it is good for us to be here; and let us make three tabernacles: one for You, one for Moses, and one for Elijah"— [6]because he did not know what to say, for they were greatly afraid.

[7]And a cloud came and overshadowed them; and a voice came out of the cloud, saying, "This is My beloved Son. Hear Him!" [8]Suddenly, when they had looked around, they saw no one anymore, but only Jesus with themselves.

[9]Now as they came down from the mountain, He commanded them that they should tell no one the things they had seen, till the Son of Man had risen from the dead. [10]So they kept this word to themselves, questioning what the rising from the dead meant.

[11]And they asked Him, saying, "Why do the scribes say that Elijah must come first?"

[12]Then He answered and told them, "Indeed, Elijah is coming first and restores all things. And how is it written concerning the Son of Man, that He must suffer many things and be treated with contempt? [13]But I say to you that Elijah has also come, and they did to him whatever they wished, as it is written of him."

[14]And when He came to the disciples, He saw a great multitude around them, and scribes disputing with them. [15]Immediately, when they saw Him, all the people were greatly amazed, and running to *Him*, greeted Him. [16]And He asked the scribes, "What are you discussing with them?"

[17]Then one of the crowd answered and said, "Teacher, I brought You my son, who has a mute spirit. [18]And wherever it seizes him, it throws him down; he foams at the mouth, gnashes his teeth, and becomes rigid. So I spoke to Your disciples, that they should cast it out, but they could not."

[19]He answered him and said, "O faithless generation, how long shall I be with you? How long shall I bear with you? Bring him to Me." [20]Then they brought him to Him. And when he saw Him, immediately the spirit convulsed him, and he fell on the ground and wallowed, foaming at the mouth.

[21]So He asked his father, "How long has this been happening to him?"

And he said, "From childhood. [22]And often he has thrown him both into the fire and into the water to destroy him. But if You can do anything, have compassion on us and help us."

[23]Jesus said to him, "If you can believe, all things *are* possible to him who believes."

[24]Immediately the father of the child cried out and said with tears, "Lord, I believe; help my unbelief!"

[25]When Jesus saw that the people came running together, He rebuked the unclean spirit, saying to it, "Deaf and dumb spirit, I command you, come out of him and enter him no more!" [26]Then *the spirit* cried out, convulsed him greatly, and came out of him. And he became as one dead, so that many said, "He is dead." [27]But Jesus took him by the hand and lifted him up, and he arose.

▶ POWER

9:23 Jesus' words do not mean that we can automatically obtain anything we want if we just think positively. Jesus meant that anything is *possible* with faith because nothing is too difficult for God. This is not a teaching on how to pray as much as a statement about God's power to overcome obstacles to his work. We cannot have everything we pray for as if by magic, but, with faith, we can have everything we need to serve God.

[28]And when He had come into the house, His disciples asked Him privately, "Why could we not cast it out?"

[29]So He said to them, "This kind can come out by nothing but prayer and fasting."

[30]Then they departed from there and passed through Galilee, and He did not want anyone to know *it*. [31]For He taught His disciples and said to them, "The Son of Man is being betrayed into the hands of men, and they will kill Him. And after He is killed, He will rise the third day." [32]But they did not understand this saying, and were afraid to ask Him.

[33]Then He came to Capernaum. And when He was in the house He asked them, "What was it you disputed among yourselves on the road?" [34]But they kept silent, for on the road they had disputed among themselves who *would be the* greatest. [35]And He sat down, called the twelve, and said to them, "If anyone desires to be first, he shall be last of all and servant of all." [36]Then He took a little child and set him in the midst of them. And when He had taken him in His arms, He said to them, [37]"Whoever receives one of these little children in My name receives Me; and whoever receives Me, receives not Me but Him who sent Me."

[38]Now John answered Him, saying, "Teacher, we saw someone who does not follow us casting out demons in Your name, and we forbade him because he does not follow us."

[39]But Jesus said, "Do not forbid him, for no one who works a miracle in My name can soon afterward speak evil of Me. [40]For he who is not against us is on our side. [41]For whoever gives you a cup of water to drink in My name, because you belong to Christ, assuredly, I say to you, he will by no means lose his reward.

[42]"But whoever causes one of these little ones who believe in Me to stumble, it would be better for him if a millstone were hung around his neck, and he were

9:43ff Jesus used startling language to stress the importance of cutting sin out of our life. Painful discipline is required of his true followers. Giving up a relationship, job, or habit that is against God's will may seem just as painful as cutting off a hand. Our high goal, however, is worth any sacrifice; Christ is worth any possible loss. Nothing should stand in the way of faith. We must be ruthless in removing sins from our life now, in order to avoid being stuck with them for eternity. Make your choices from an eternal perspective.

thrown into the sea. ⁴³If your hand causes you to sin, cut it off. It is better for you to enter into life maimed, rather than having two hands, to go to hell, into the fire that shall never be quenched— ⁴⁴where

'Their worm does not die
And the fire is not quenched.'

⁴⁵And if your foot causes you to sin, cut it off. It is better for you to enter life lame, rather than having two feet, to be cast into hell, into the fire that shall never be quenched— ⁴⁶where

'Their worm does not die
And the fire is not quenched.'

⁴⁷And if your eye causes you to sin, pluck it out. It is better for you to enter the kingdom of God with one eye, rather than having two eyes, to be cast into hell fire— ⁴⁸where

'Their worm does not die
And the fire is not quenched.'

⁴⁹"For everyone will be seasoned with fire, and every sacrifice will be seasoned with salt. ⁵⁰Salt *is* good, but if the salt loses its flavor, how will you season it? Have salt in yourselves, and have peace with one another."

CHAPTER 10 MARRIAGE AND DIVORCE. Then He arose from there and came to the region of Judea by the other side of the Jordan. And multitudes gathered to Him again, and as He was accustomed, He taught them again. ²The Pharisees came and asked Him, "Is it lawful for a man to divorce *his* wife?" testing Him.

³And He answered and said to them, "What did Moses command you?"

⁴They said, "Moses permitted *a man* to write a certificate of divorce, and to dismiss *her*."

⁵And Jesus answered and said to them, "Because of the hardness of your heart he wrote you this precept. ⁶But from the beginning of the creation, God *'made them male and female.'* ⁷ *'For this reason a man shall leave his father and mother and be joined to his wife,* ⁸ *and the two shall become one flesh';* so then they are no longer two, but one flesh. ⁹Therefore what God has joined together, let not man separate."

¹⁰In the house His disciples also asked Him again about the same *matter.* ¹¹So He said to them, "Whoever divorces his wife and marries another commits adultery against her. ¹²And if a woman divorces her husband and marries another, she commits adultery."

¹³Then they brought little children to Him, that He might touch them; but the disciples rebuked those who brought *them.* ¹⁴But when Jesus saw *it,* He was greatly displeased and said to them, "Let the little children come to Me, and do not forbid them; for of such is the kingdom of God. ¹⁵Assuredly, I say to you, whoever does not receive the kingdom of God as a little child will by no means enter it." ¹⁶And He took them up in His arms, laid *His* hands on them, and blessed them.

¹⁷Now as He was going out on the road, one came running, knelt before Him, and asked Him, "Good Teacher, what shall I do that I may inherit eternal life?"

¹⁸So Jesus said to him, "Why do you call Me good? No one *is* good but One, *that is,* God. ¹⁹You know the commandments: *'Do not commit adultery,' 'Do not murder,' 'Do not steal,' 'Do not bear false witness,'* 'Do not defraud,' *'Honor your father and your mother.' "*

BARRIERS

10:17-23 This young man wanted to be sure he would get eternc so he asked what he could *do.* Jesus lovingly addressed him with a challenge that brought out his true motives: "Sell whatever you hav give to the poor." Here was the barrier that could keep this young m out of the kingdom: his love of money. Money represented his pride accomplishment and self-effort. Ironically, the young man's attitude him from keeping the first commandment, to let nothing be more important than God (Exodus 20:3). He could not meet the one requirement Jesus gave—to turn his whole heart and life over to Ge The man came to Jesus wondering what he could do; he left seeing w he was unable to do. What barriers are keeping you from turning yo life over to Christ?

²⁰And he answered and said to Him, "Teacher, all these things I have kept from my youth."

²¹Then Jesus, looking at him, loved him, and said to him, "One thing you lack: Go your way, sell whatever you have and give to the poor, and you will have treasure in heaven; and come, take up the cross, and follow Me."

²²But he was sad at this word, and went away sorrowful, for he had great possessions.

²³Then Jesus looked around and said to His disciples, "How hard it is for those who have riches to enter the kingdom of God!" ²⁴And the disciples were astonished at His words. But Jesus answered again and said to them, "Children, how hard it is for those who trust in riches to enter the kingdom of God! ²⁵It is easier for a camel to go through the eye of a needle than for a rich man to enter the kingdom of God."

²⁶And they were greatly astonished, saying among themselves, "Who then can be saved?"

²⁷But Jesus looked at them and said, "With men *it is* impossible, but not with God; for with God all things are possible."

²⁸Then Peter began to say to Him, "See, we have left all and followed You."

²⁹So Jesus answered and said, "Assuredly, I say to you, there is no one who has left house or brothers or sisters or father or mother or wife or children or lands, for My sake and the gospel's, ³⁰who shall not receive a hundredfold now in this time—houses and brothers and sisters and mothers and children and lands, with persecutions—and in the age to come, eternal life. ³¹But many *who are* first will be last, and the last first."

³²Now they were on the road, going up to Jerusalem,

and Jesus was going before them; and they were amazed. And as they followed they were afraid. Then He took the twelve aside again and began to tell them the things that would happen to Him: ³³"Behold, we are going up to Jerusalem, and the Son of Man will be betrayed to the chief priests and to the scribes; and they will condemn Him to death and deliver Him to the Gentiles; ³⁴and they will mock Him, and scourge Him, and spit on Him, and kill Him. And the third day He will rise again."

³⁵Then James and John, the sons of Zebedee, came to Him, saying, "Teacher, we want You to do for us whatever we ask."

³⁶And He said to them, "What do you want Me to do for you?"

³⁷They said to Him, "Grant us that we may sit, one on Your right hand and the other on Your left, in Your glory."

³⁸But Jesus said to them, "You do not know what you ask. Are you able to drink the cup that I drink, and be baptized with the baptism that I am baptized with?"

³⁹They said to Him, "We are able."

So Jesus said to them, "You will indeed drink the cup that I drink, and with the baptism I am baptized with you will be baptized; ⁴⁰but to sit on My right hand and on My left is not Mine to give, but *it is for those* for whom it is prepared."

⁴¹And when the ten heard *it*, they began to be greatly displeased with James and John. ⁴²But Jesus called them to *Himself* and said to them, "You know that those who are considered rulers over the Gentiles lord it over them, and their great ones exercise authority over them. ⁴³Yet it shall not be so among you; but whoever desires to become great among you shall be your servant. ⁴⁴And whoever of you desires to be first shall be slave of all. ⁴⁵For even the Son of Man did not come to be served, but to serve, and to give His life a ransom for many."

⁴⁶Now they came to Jericho. As He went out of Jericho with His disciples and a great multitude, blind Bartimaeus, the son of Timaeus, sat by the road begging. ⁴⁷And when he heard that it was Jesus of Nazareth, he began to cry out and say, "Jesus, Son of David, have mercy on me!"

⁴⁸Then many warned him to be quiet; but he cried out all the more, "Son of David, have mercy on me!"

⁴⁹So Jesus stood still and commanded him to be called.

Then they called the blind man, saying to him, "Be of good cheer. Rise, He is calling you."

⁵⁰And throwing aside his garment, he rose and came to Jesus.

⁵¹So Jesus answered and said to him, "What do you want Me to do for you?"

The blind man said to Him, "Rabboni, that I may receive my sight."

⁵²Then Jesus said to him, "Go your way; your faith has made you well." And immediately he received his sight and followed Jesus on the road.

CHAPTER **11** **CROWDS WELCOME JESUS.** Now when they drew near Jerusalem, to Bethphage and Bethany, at the Mount of Olives, He sent two of His disciples; ²and He said to them, "Go into the village opposite you; and as soon as you have entered it you will find a colt tied, on which no one has sat. Loose it and bring *it*. ³And if anyone says to you, 'Why are you doing this?' say, 'The Lord has need of it,' and immediately he will send it here."

⁴So they went their way, and found the colt tied by the door outside on the street, and they loosed it. ⁵But some of those who stood there said to them, "What are you doing, loosing the colt?"

⁶And they spoke to them just as Jesus had commanded. So they let them go. ⁷Then they brought the colt to Jesus and threw their clothes on it, and He sat on it. ⁸And many spread their clothes on the road, and others cut down leafy branches from the trees and spread *them* on the road. ⁹Then those who went before and those who followed cried out, saying:

"Hosanna!
'Blessed is He who comes in the name of the Lord!'
10 Blessed is the kingdom of our father David
That comes in the name of the Lord!

"Here's what I did..."

In my school, people are popular only if they have the right looks, the right clothes, live in a certain neighborhood, play on the football team or are a cheerleader, or date a football player or cheerleader. The lines are pretty clearly drawn. And I'm on the other side of every one of those lines.

For a while it really bothered me. But when I tried to break into one of the cliques I found myself acting phony, and I couldn't stand it. I couldn't seem to help it, though; I wanted people to like me. I wanted to be popular.

Then, slowly, my viewpoint changed. The change started when my youth group studied the book of Mark. I really related to the disciples in chapters 9 and 10. They were trying to see who was more popular with Jesus, who would be considered the greatest. And Jesus said, "But many who are first will be last, and the last first." He also said that, in God's eyes, many who seem to be most important now are least important, and many who seem least important now are really most important (Mark 10:31).

I realized it didn't really matter whether kids in my school thought I was great; what matters is what God thinks of me. If I want him to think I'm great, I have to forget about the phoniness and just try to be friends with all kinds of people.

I've started doing that, and now I have lots of friends. I still wouldn't be considered one of the "popular" people, but that's OK now. I'm in touch with God, and because of that, I know I'm popular with one Person whose opinion really matters.

marita

AGE 16

11:14-15 Jesus became angry, but he did not sin in his anger. There is a place for righteous indignation. Christians should be upset about sin and injustice and should take a stand against them. Unfortunately, believers often are passive about these important issues and get angry over personal insults and petty irritations. Direct your anger toward the right issues.

Hosanna in the highest!"

[11]And Jesus went into Jerusalem and into the temple. So when He had looked around at all things, as the hour was already late, He went out to Bethany with the twelve.

[12]Now the next day, when they had come out from Bethany, He was hungry. [13]And seeing from afar a fig tree having leaves, He went to see if perhaps He would find something on it. When He came to it, He found nothing but leaves, for it was not the season for figs. [14]In response Jesus said to it, "Let no one eat fruit from you ever again."

And His disciples heard it.

[15]So they came to Jerusalem. Then Jesus went into the temple and began to drive out those who bought and sold in the temple, and overturned the tables of the money changers and the seats of those who sold doves.

[16]And He would not allow anyone to carry wares through the temple. [17]Then He taught, saying to them, "Is it not written, 'My house shall be called a house of prayer for all nations'? But you have made it a 'den of thieves.'"

[18]And the scribes and chief priests heard it and sought how they might destroy Him; for they feared Him, because all the people were astonished at His teaching. [19]When evening had come, He went out of the city.

[20]Now in the morning, as they passed by, they saw the fig tree dried up from the roots. [21]And Peter, remembering, said to Him, "Rabbi, look! The fig tree which You cursed has withered away."

[22]So Jesus answered and said to them, "Have faith in God. [23]For assuredly, I say to you, whoever says to this mountain, 'Be removed and be cast into the sea,' and does not doubt in his heart, but believes that those things he says will be done, he will have whatever he says. [24]Therefore I say to you, whatever things you ask when you pray, believe that you receive them, and you will have them.

[25]"And whenever you stand praying, if you have any-

WHAT JESUS SAID ABOUT LOVE

In Mark 12:28, a scribe asked Jesus which one of all the commandments was the most important to follow. Jesus mentioned two commandments, one from Deuteronomy 6:5, the other from Leviticus 19:18. Both had to do with love. Why is love so important? Jesus said that all of the commandments were given for two simple reasons--to help us love God and love others as we should.

What Else did Jesus Say about Love?	Reference
God loves us.	John 3:16
We are to love God.	Matthew 22:37
Because God loves us, he cares for us.	Matthew 6:25-34
God wants everyone to know how much he loves them.	John 17:23
God loves even those who hate him; we are to do the same.	Matthew 5:43-47; Luke 6:35
God seeks out even those most alienated from him.	Luke 15
God must be your first love.	Matthew 6:24; 10:37
You love God when you obey him.	John 14:21; 15:10
God loves Jesus his Son.	John 5:20; 10:17
Jesus loves God.	John 14:31
Those who refuse Jesus don't have God's love.	John 5:41-44
Jesus loves us just as God loves Jesus.	John 15:9
Jesus proved his love for us by dying on the cross so that we could live eternally with him.	John 3:14-15; 15:13-14
The love between God and Jesus is the perfect example of how we are to love others.	John 17:21-26
We are to love one another (John 13:34-35) and demonstrate that love.	Matthew 5:40-42; 10:42
We are not to love the praise of men (John 12:43), selfish recognition (Matthew 23:6), earthly belongings (Luke 16:19-31), or anything more than God.	Luke 16:13
Jesus' love extends to each individual.	John 10:11-15; Mark 10:21
Jesus wants us to love him through both the good and difficult times.	Matthew 26:31-35
Jesus wants our love to be genuine.	John 21:15-17

thing against anyone, forgive him, that your Father in heaven may also forgive you your trespasses. ²⁶But if you do not forgive, neither will your Father in heaven forgive your trespasses."

²⁷Then they came again to Jerusalem. And as He was walking in the temple, the chief priests, the scribes, and the elders came to Him. ²⁸And they said to Him, "By what authority are You doing these things? And who gave You this authority to do these things?"

²⁹But Jesus answered and said to them, "I also will ask you one question; then answer Me, and I will tell you by what authority I do these things: ³⁰The baptism of John—was it from heaven or from men? Answer Me."

³¹And they reasoned among themselves, saying, "If we say, 'From heaven,' He will say, 'Why then did you not believe him?' ³²But if we say, 'From men'"—they feared the people, for all counted John to have been a prophet indeed. ³³So they answered and said to Jesus, "We do not know."

And Jesus answered and said to them, "Neither will I tell you by what authority I do these things."

CHAPTER 12 A STORY ABOUT A FARM. Then He

began to speak to them in parables: "A man planted a vineyard and set a hedge around *it*, dug *a place for* the wine vat and built a tower. And he leased it to vine-dressers and went into a far country. ²Now at vintage-time he sent a servant to the vinedressers, that he might receive some of the fruit of the vineyard from the vine-dressers. ³And they took *him* and beat him and sent *him* away empty-handed. ⁴Again he sent them another ser-vant, and at him they threw stones, wounded *him* in the head, and sent *him* away shamefully treated. ⁵And again he sent another, and him they killed; and many others, beating some and killing some. ⁶Therefore still having one son, his beloved, he also sent him to them last, say-ing, 'They will respect my son.' ⁷But those vinedressers said among themselves, 'This is the heir. Come, let us kill him, and the inheritance will be ours.' ⁸So they took him and killed *him* and cast *him* out of the vineyard.

⁹"Therefore what will the owner of the vineyard do? He will come and destroy the vinedressers, and give the vineyard to others. ¹⁰Have you not even read this Scrip-ture:

'The stone which the builders rejected
Has become the chief cornerstone.
¹¹ This was the LORD's doing,
And it is marvelous in our eyes'? "

¹²And they sought to lay hands on Him, but feared the multitude, for they knew He had spoken the parable against them. So they left Him and went away.

¹³Then they sent to Him some of the Pharisees and the Herodians, to catch Him in *His* words. ¹⁴When they had come, they said to Him, "Teacher, we know that You are true, and care about no one; for You do not regard the person of men, but teach the way of God in truth. Is it lawful to pay taxes to Caesar, or not? ¹⁵Shall we pay, or shall we not pay?"

But He, knowing their hypocrisy, said to them, "Why

do you test Me? Bring Me a denarius that I may see *it*." ¹⁶So they brought *it*.

And He said to them, "Whose image and inscription *is* this?" They said to Him, "Caesar's."

¹⁷And Jesus answered and said to them, "Render to

◣◢◤MOTIVATIONS

11:24 Jesus, our example for prayer, once prayed, "All things are possible for You. . . . nevertheless, not what I will, but what You *will*" (Mark 14:36). Often when we pray, we are motivated by our own interests and desires. We like to hear that we can have anything. But Jesus prayed with God's interests in mind. When we pray, we are to express our desires, but we should want God's will above ours. Check yourself to see if your prayers are focusing on your interests or on God's.

Caesar the things that are Caesar's, and to God the things that are God's."

And they marveled at Him.

¹⁸Then *some* Sadducees, who say there is no resurrec-tion, came to Him; and they asked Him, saying: ¹⁹"Teacher, Moses wrote to us that if a man's brother dies, and leaves *his* wife behind, and leaves no children, his brother should take his wife and raise up offspring for his brother. ²⁰Now there were seven brothers. The first took a wife; and dying, he left no offspring. ²¹And the second took her, and he died; nor did he leave any offspring. And the third likewise. ²²So the seven had her and left no offspring. Last of all the woman died also. ²³Therefore, in the resurrection, when they rise, whose wife will she be? For all seven had her as wife."

²⁴Jesus answered and said to them, "Are you not there-fore mistaken, because you do not know the Scriptures nor the power of God? ²⁵For when they rise from the dead, they neither marry nor are given in marriage, but are like angels in heaven. ²⁶But concerning the dead, that they rise, have you not read in the book of Moses, in the *burning* bush *passage*, how God spoke to him, saying, *'I am the God of Abraham, the God of Isaac, and the God of Jacob'*? ²⁷He is not the God of the dead, but the God of the living. You are therefore greatly mistaken."

²⁸Then one of the scribes came, and having heard them reasoning together, perceiving that He had an-swered them well, asked Him, "Which is the first com-mandment of all?"

²⁹Jesus answered him, "The first of all the command-ments *is*: 'Hear, O Israel, the LORD our God, the LORD *is* one. ³⁰And you shall love the LORD your God with all your heart, with all your soul, with all your mind, and with all your strength.' This *is* the first commandment. ³¹And the second, like *it, is* this: 'You shall love your neighbor as yourself.' There is no other commandment greater than these."

◣◢◤IMAGE

12:17 The Pharisees and Herodians thought they had the perfect question to trap Jesus. But Jesus answered wisely, once again exposing their self-interest and wrong motives. Jesus said that the coin bearing the emperor's image should be given to the emperor. But whatever bears God's image—our life— belongs to God. Are you giving God all that is rightfully his? Make sure your life is given to God—you bear his image.

³²So the scribe said to Him, "Well *said*, Teacher. You have spoken the truth, for there is one God, and there is no other but He. ³³And to love Him with all the heart, with all the understanding, with all the soul, and with all the strength, and to love one's neighbor as oneself, is more than all the whole burnt offerings and sacrifices."

³⁴Now when Jesus saw that he answered wisely, He said to him, "You are not far from the kingdom of God."

But after that no one dared question Him.

³⁵Then Jesus answered and said, while He taught in the temple, "How *is it* that the scribes say that the Christ is the Son of David? ³⁶For David himself said by the Holy Spirit:

'The LORD said to my Lord,
"Sit at My right hand,
Till I make Your enemies Your footstool." '

³⁷Therefore David himself calls Him *'Lord'*; how is He *then* his Son?"

And the common people heard Him gladly.

³⁸Then He said to them in His teaching, "Beware of the scribes, who desire to go around in long robes, *love* greetings in the marketplaces, ³⁹the best seats in the synagogues, and the best places at feasts, ⁴⁰who devour widows' houses, and for a pretense make long prayers. These will receive greater condemnation."

⁴¹Now Jesus sat opposite the treasury and saw how the people put money into the treasury. And many *who were* rich put in much. ⁴²Then one poor widow came and threw in two mites, which make a quadrans. ⁴³So He called His disciples to *Himself* and said to them, "Assuredly, I say to you that this poor widow has put in more than all those who have given to the treasury; ⁴⁴for they all put in out of their abundance, but she out of her poverty put in all that she had, her whole livelihood."

CHAPTER 13 JESUS TELLS ABOUT THE FUTURE.

Then as He went out of the temple, one of His disciples said to Him, "Teacher, see what manner of stones and what buildings *are here!*"

²And Jesus answered and said to him, "Do you see these great buildings? Not *one* stone shall be left upon another, that shall not be thrown down."

³Now as He sat on the Mount of Olives opposite the temple, Peter, James, John, and Andrew asked Him privately, ⁴"Tell us, when will these things be? And what *will* be the sign when all these things will be fulfilled?"

⁵And Jesus, answering them, began to say: "Take heed that no one deceives you. ⁶For many will come in My name, saying, 'I am *He*,' and will deceive many. ⁷But when you hear of wars and rumors of wars, do not be troubled; for *such things* must happen, but the end *is* not yet. ⁸For nation will rise against nation, and kingdom against kingdom. And there will be earthquakes in various places, and there will be famines and troubles. These *are* the beginnings of sorrows.

⁹"But watch out for yourselves, for they will deliver you up to councils, and you will be beaten in the synagogues. You will be brought before rulers and kings for My sake, for a testimony to them. ¹⁰And the gospel must first be preached to all the nations. ¹¹But when they arrest *you* and deliver you up, do not worry beforehand, or premeditate what you will speak. But whatever is given you in that hour, speak that; for it is not you who speak, but the Holy Spirit. ¹²Now brother will betray brother to death, and a father *his* child; and children will rise up against parents and cause them to be put to death. ¹³And you will be hated by all for My name's sake. But he who endures to the end shall be saved.

¹⁴"So when you see the *'abomination of desolation,'*

spoken of by Daniel the prophet, standing where it ought not" (let the reader understand), "then let those who are in Judea flee to the mountains. ¹⁵Let him who is on the housetop not go down into the house, nor enter to take anything out of his house. ¹⁶And let him who is in the field not go back to get his clothes. ¹⁷But woe to those who are pregnant and to those who are nursing babies in those days! ¹⁸And pray that your flight may not be in winter. ¹⁹For *in* those days there will be tribulation, such as has not been since the beginning of the creation which God created until this time, nor ever shall be. ²⁰And unless the Lord had shortened those days, no flesh would be saved; but for the elect's sake, whom He chose, He shortened the days.

²¹"Then if anyone says to you, 'Look, here *is* the Christ!' or, 'Look, *He is* there!' do not believe it. ²²For false christs and false prophets will rise and show signs and wonders to deceive, if possible, even the elect. ²³But take heed; see, I have told you all things beforehand.

²⁴"But in those days, after that tribulation, the sun will

be darkened, and the moon will not give its light; 25the stars of heaven will fall, and the powers in the heavens will be shaken. 26Then they will see the Son of Man coming in the clouds with great power and glory. 27And then He will send His angels, and gather together His elect from the four winds, from the farthest part of earth to the farthest part of heaven.

28"Now learn this parable from the fig tree: When its branch has already become tender, and puts forth leaves, you know that summer is near. 29So you also, when you see these things happening, know that it is near—at the doors! 30Assuredly, I say to you, this generation will by no means pass away till all these things take place. 31Heaven and earth will pass away, but My words will by no means pass away.

32"But of that day and hour no one knows, not even the angels in heaven, nor the Son, but only the Father. 33Take heed, watch and pray; for you do not know when the time is. 34*It is* like a man going to a far country, who left his house and gave authority to his servants, and to each his work, and commanded the doorkeeper to watch. 35Watch therefore, for you do not know when the master of the house is coming—in the evening, at midnight, at the crowing of the rooster, or in the morning— 36lest, coming suddenly, he find you sleeping. 37And what I say to you, I say to all: Watch!"

CHAPTER **14** **A PLOT TO KILL JESUS.** After two days it was the Passover and *the Feast* of Unleavened Bread. And the chief priests and the scribes sought how they might take Him by trickery and put *Him* to death. 2But they said, "Not during the feast, lest there be an uproar of the people."

3And being in Bethany at the house of Simon the leper, as He sat at the table, a woman came having an alabaster flask of very costly oil of spikenard. Then she broke the flask and poured *it* on His head. 4But there were some who were indignant among themselves, and said, "Why was this fragrant oil wasted? 5For it might have been sold for more than three hundred denarii and given to the poor." And they criticized her sharply.

6But Jesus said, "Let her alone. Why do you trouble her? She has done a good work for Me. 7For you have the poor with you always, and whenever you wish you may do them good; but Me you do not have always. 8She has done what she could. She has come beforehand to anoint My body for burial. 9Assuredly, I say to you, wherever this gospel is preached in the whole world, what this woman has done will also be told as a memorial to her."

10Then Judas Iscariot, one of the twelve, went to the chief priests to betray Him to them. 11And when they heard *it*, they were glad, and promised to give him money. So he sought how he might conveniently betray Him.

12Now on the first day of Unleavened Bread, when they killed the Passover *lamb*, His disciples said to Him, "Where do You want us to go and prepare, that You may eat the Passover?"

13And He sent out two of His disciples and said to them, "Go into the city, and a man will meet you carrying a pitcher of water; follow him. 14Wherever he goes in, say

to the master of the house, 'The Teacher says, "Where is the guest room in which I may eat the Passover with My disciples?" ' 15Then he will show you a large upper room, furnished *and* prepared; there make ready for us."

16So His disciples went out, and came into the city, and

▶BETRAYED!

14:19 Judas, the very man who would betray Jesus, was at the table with the others. He had already determined to betray Jesus, but in cold-blooded hypocrisy he shared the fellowship of this meal. It is easy to become enraged or shocked by what Judas did, yet professing commitment to Christ and then denying him with one's life is also betraying him. It is denying Christ's love to disobey him; it is denying his truth to distrust him; it is denying his deity to reject his authority. Do your words and actions match? If not, consider a change of mind and heart that will protect you from making a terrible mistake.

found it just as He had said to them; and they prepared the Passover.

17In the evening He came with the twelve. 18Now as they sat and ate, Jesus said, "Assuredly, I say to you, one of you who eats with Me will betray Me."

19And they began to be sorrowful, and to say to Him one by one, "*Is* it I?" And another *said*, "*Is* it I?"

20He answered and said to them, "*It is* one of the twelve, who dips with Me in the dish. 21The Son of Man indeed goes just as it is written of Him, but woe to that

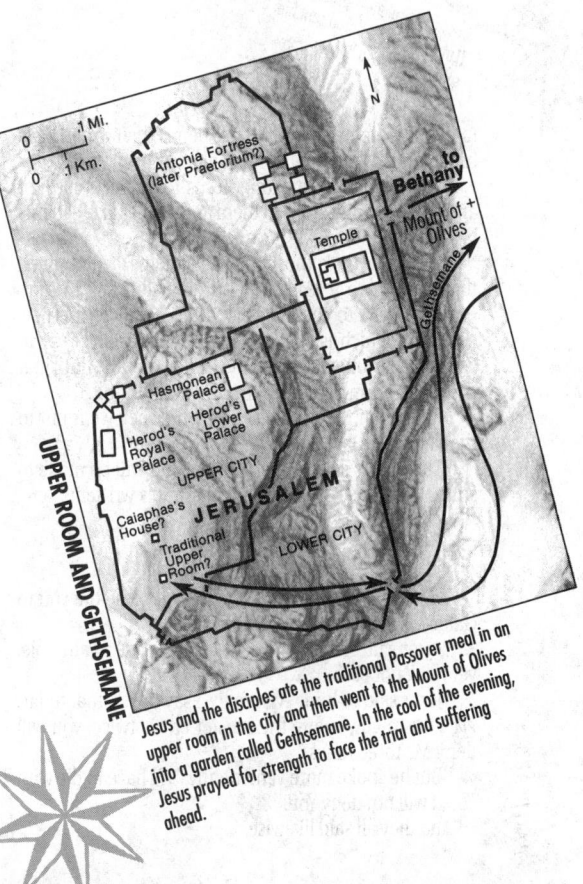

Jesus and the disciples ate the traditional Passover meal in an upper room in the city and then went to the Mount of Olives into a garden called Gethsemane. In the cool of the evening, Jesus prayed for strength to face the trial and suffering ahead.

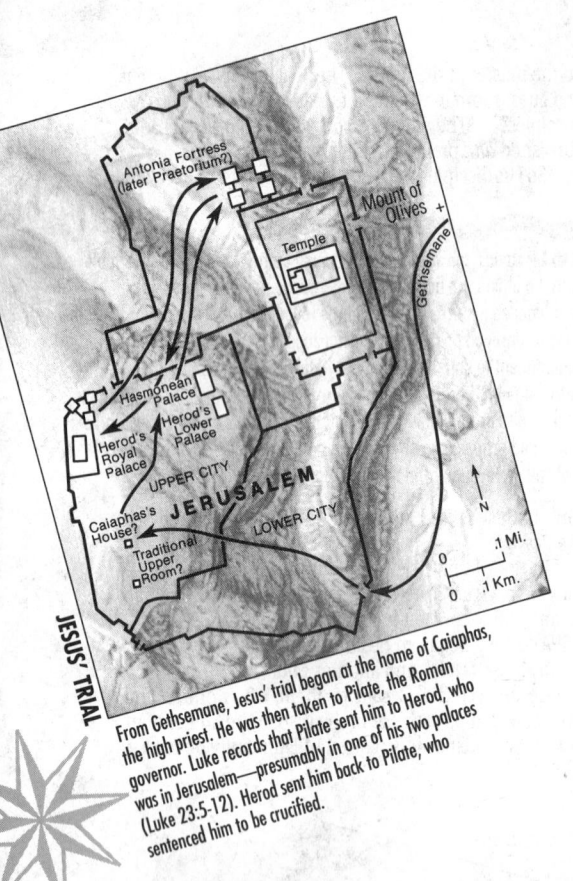

From Gethsemane, Jesus' trial began at the home of Caiaphas, the high priest. He was then taken to Pilate, the Roman governor. Luke records that Pilate sent him to Herod, who was in Jerusalem—presumably in one of his two palaces (Luke 23:5-12). Herod sent him back to Pilate, who sentenced him to be crucified.

NO EXCUSES

14:71 It is easy to get angry at the Jewish Sanhedrin for their inj▮ in condemning Jesus, but Peter and the rest of the disciples also contributed to Jesus' pain by deserting him (14:50). While most of ▮ not like the Jewish leaders, we are all like the disciples, for all of us ▮ been guilty of denying Christ as Lord in vital areas of our life. We m▮ pride ourself that we have not committed certain sins, but we are a▮ guilty of sin. Don't excuse yourself by pointing the finger at others ▮ sins seem worse than yours.

³²Then they came to a place which was named Gethsemane; and He said to His disciples, "Sit here while I pray." ³³And He took Peter, James, and John with Him, and He began to be troubled and deeply distressed. ³⁴Then He said to them, "My soul is exceedingly sorrowful, *even* to death. Stay here and watch."

³⁵He went a little farther, and fell on the ground, and prayed that if it were possible, the hour might pass from Him. ³⁶And He said, "Abba, Father, all things *are* possible for You. Take this cup away from Me; nevertheless, not what I will, but what You *will*."

³⁷Then He came and found them sleeping, and said to Peter, "Simon, are you sleeping? Could you not watch one hour? ³⁸Watch and pray, lest you enter into temptation. The spirit indeed *is* willing, but the flesh *is* weak."

³⁹Again He went away and prayed, and spoke the same words. ⁴⁰And when He returned, He found them asleep again, for their eyes were heavy; and they did not know what to answer Him.

⁴¹Then He came the third time and said to them, "Are you still sleeping and resting? It is enough! The hour has come; behold, the Son of Man is being betrayed into the hands of sinners. ⁴²Rise, let us be going. See, My betrayer is at hand."

⁴³And immediately, while He was still speaking, Judas, one of the twelve, with a great multitude with swords and clubs, came from the chief priests and the scribes and the elders. ⁴⁴Now His betrayer had given them a signal, saying, "Whomever I kiss, He is the One; seize Him and lead *Him* away safely."

⁴⁵As soon as he had come, immediately he went up to Him and said to Him, "Rabbi, Rabbi!" and kissed Him.

⁴⁶Then they laid their hands on Him and took Him. ⁴⁷And one of those who stood by drew his sword and struck the servant of the high priest, and cut off his ear.

⁴⁸Then Jesus answered and said to them, "Have you come out, as against a robber, with swords and clubs to take Me? ⁴⁹I was daily with you in the temple teaching, and you did not seize Me. But the Scriptures must be fulfilled."

⁵⁰Then they all forsook Him and fled.

⁵¹Now a certain young man followed Him, having a linen cloth thrown around *his* naked *body*. And the young men laid hold of him, ⁵²and he left the linen cloth and fled from them naked.

THE RIGHT THING

15:15 Although Jesus was innocent according to Roman law, Pilate caved in under political pressure. He abandoned what he knew was rig▮ He tried to give a decision that would please everyone while keeping himself safe. When we ignore God's statements of right and wrong and make decisions based on our audience, we fall into compromise and lawlessness. God promises to honor those who do right; not those who make everyone happy.

man by whom the Son of Man is betrayed! It would have been good for that man if he had never been born."

²²And as they were eating, Jesus took bread, blessed and broke *it*, and gave *it* to them and said, "Take, eat; this is My body."

²³Then He took the cup, and when He had given thanks He gave *it* to them, and they all drank from it. ²⁴And He said to them, "This is My blood of the new covenant, which is shed for many. ²⁵Assuredly, I say to you, I will no longer drink of the fruit of the vine until that day when I drink it new in the kingdom of God."

²⁶And when they had sung a hymn, they went out to the Mount of Olives.

²⁷Then Jesus said to them, "All of you will be made to stumble because of Me this night, for it is written:

'*I will strike the Shepherd,*
And the sheep will be scattered.'

²⁸"But after I have been raised, I will go before you to Galilee."

²⁹Peter said to Him, "Even if all are made to stumble, yet I *will* not *be*."

³⁰Jesus said to him, "Assuredly, I say to you that today, *even* this night, before the rooster crows twice, you will deny Me three times."

³¹But he spoke more vehemently, "If I have to die with You, I will not deny You!"

And they all said likewise.

⁵³And they led Jesus away to the high priest; and with him were assembled all the chief priests, the elders, and the scribes. ⁵⁴But Peter followed Him at a distance, right into the courtyard of the high priest. And he sat with the servants and warmed himself at the fire.

⁵⁵Now the chief priests and all the council sought testimony against Jesus to put Him to death, but found none. ⁵⁶For many bore false witness against Him, but their testimonies did not agree.

⁵⁷Then some rose up and bore false witness against Him, saying, ⁵⁸"We heard Him say, 'I will destroy this temple made with hands, and within three days I will build another made without hands.'" ⁵⁹But not even then did their testimony agree.

⁶⁰And the high priest stood up in the midst and asked Jesus, saying, "Do You answer nothing? What *is it* these men testify against You?" ⁶¹But He kept silent and answered nothing.

Again the high priest asked Him, saying to Him, "Are You the Christ, the Son of the Blessed?"

⁶²Jesus said, "I am. And you will see the Son of Man sitting at the right hand of the Power, and coming with the clouds of heaven."

⁶³Then the high priest tore his clothes and said, "What further need do we have of witnesses? ⁶⁴You have heard the blasphemy! What do you think?"

And they all condemned Him to be deserving of death.

⁶⁵Then some began to spit on Him, and to blindfold Him, and to beat Him, and to say to Him, "Prophesy!" And the officers struck Him with the palms of their hands.

⁶⁶Now as Peter was below in the courtyard, one of the servant girls of the high priest came. ⁶⁷And when she saw Peter warming himself, she looked at him and said, "You also were with Jesus of Nazareth."

⁶⁸But he denied it, saying, "I neither know nor understand what you are saying." And he went out on the porch, and a rooster crowed.

⁶⁹And the servant girl saw him again, and began to say to those who stood by, "This is one of them." ⁷⁰But he denied it again.

And a little later those who stood by said to Peter again, "Surely you are *one* of them; for you are a Galilean, and your speech shows *it*."

⁷¹Then he began to curse and swear, "I do not know this Man of whom you speak!"

⁷²A second time *the* rooster crowed. Then Peter called to mind the word that Jesus had said to him, "Before the rooster crows twice, you will deny Me three times." And when he thought about it, he wept.

CHAPTER **15** **PILATE QUESTIONS JESUS.** Immediately, in the morning, the chief priests held a consultation with the elders and scribes and the whole council; and they bound Jesus, led *Him* away, and delivered *Him* to Pilate. ²Then Pilate asked Him, "Are You the King of the Jews?"

He answered and said to him, "*It is as* you say."

³And the chief priests accused Him of many things, but He answered nothing. ⁴Then Pilate asked Him again,

saying, "Do You answer nothing? See how many things they testify against You!" ⁵But Jesus still answered nothing, so that Pilate marveled.

⁶Now at the feast he was accustomed to releasing one prisoner to them, whomever they requested. ⁷And there was one named Barabbas, *who was* chained with his

GUILTY

15:15 Who was guilty of Jesus' death? In reality, everyone was at fault. The disciples deserted him in fear. Peter denied that he even knew Jesus. Judas betrayed him. The crowds who had followed him stood by and did nothing. Pilate tried to blame the crowds. The religious leaders actively promoted Jesus' death. The Roman soldiers tortured him. If you were there watching these trials, what would your response have been?

fellow rebels; they had committed murder in the rebellion. ⁸Then the multitude, crying aloud, began to ask *him to do* just as he had always done for them. ⁹But Pilate answered them, saying, "Do you want me to release to you the King of the Jews?" ¹⁰For he knew that the chief priests had handed Him over because of envy.

¹¹But the chief priests stirred up the crowd, so that he should rather release Barabbas to them. ¹²Pilate answered and said to them again, "What then do you want me to do *with Him* whom you call the King of the Jews?"

¹³So they cried out again, "Crucify Him!"

¹⁴Then Pilate said to them, "Why, what evil has He done?"

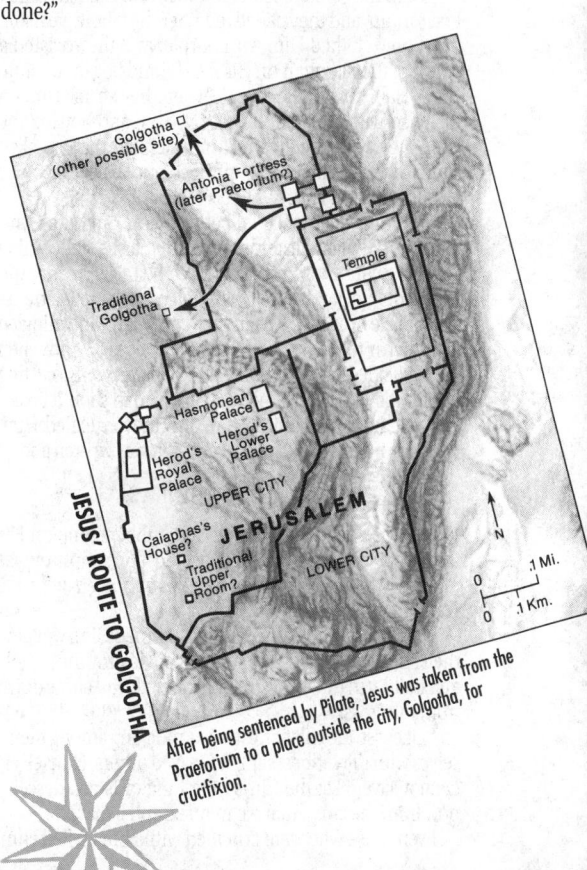

Golgotha (other possible site)

Antonia Fortress (later Praetorium?)

Traditional Golgotha

Temple

Hasmonean Palace

Herod's Lower Palace

Herod's Royal Palace

UPPER CITY

Caiaphas's House?

Traditional Upper Room?

JERUSALEM

LOWER CITY

N

0 .1 Mi.

0 .1 Km.

JESUS' ROUTE TO GOLGOTHA

After being sentenced by Pilate, Jesus was taken from the Praetorium to a place outside the city, Golgotha, for crucifixion.

WHY DID JESUS HAVE TO DIE?

The Problem
We have all done things that are wrong, and we have failed to obey God's laws. Because of this, we have been separated from God our Creator and deserve death. By ourselves we can do nothing to become reunited with God.

Why Jesus Could Help
Jesus was not only a man, he was God's unique Son. Because Jesus never disobeyed God and never sinned, only he can bridge the gap between the sinless God and sinful mankind.

The Solution
Jesus freely offered his life for us, dying on the cross in our place, taking all our wrongdoing upon himself, and saving us from the consequences of sin—including God's judgment and death. God in his love and his justice sent Jesus to take our place.

The Results
Jesus took our past, present, and future sins upon himself so that we could have new life. Because all our wrongdoing is forgiven, we are reconciled to God. Furthermore, Jesus' resurrection from the dead is the proof that his sacrifice on the cross in our place was acceptable to God, and his resurrection has become the source of new life for those who believe that Jesus is the Son of God. All who believe in him may have new life and live it in union with him.

But they cried out all the more, "Crucify Him!"

¹⁵So Pilate, wanting to gratify the crowd, released Barabbas to them; and he delivered Jesus, after he had scourged *Him*, to be crucified.

¹⁶Then the soldiers led Him away into the hall called Praetorium, and they called together the whole garrison. ¹⁷And they clothed Him with purple; and they twisted a crown of thorns, put it on His *head*, ¹⁸and began to salute Him, "Hail, King of the Jews!" ¹⁹Then they struck Him on the head with a reed and spat on Him; and bowing the knee, they worshiped Him. ²⁰And when they had mocked Him, they took the purple off Him, put His own clothes on Him, and led Him out to crucify Him.

²¹Then they compelled a certain man, Simon a Cyrenian, the father of Alexander and Rufus, as he was coming out of the country and passing by, to bear His cross. ²²And they brought Him to the place Golgotha, which is translated, Place of a Skull. ²³Then they gave Him wine mingled with myrrh to drink, but He did not take *it*. ²⁴And when they crucified Him, they divided His garments, casting lots for them to determine what every man should take.

²⁵Now it was the third hour, and they crucified Him. ²⁶And the inscription of His accusation was written above:

THE KING OF THE JEWS.

²⁷With Him they also crucified two robbers, one on His right and the other on His left. ²⁸So the Scripture was fulfilled which says, *"And He was numbered with the transgressors."*

²⁹And those who passed by blasphemed Him, wagging their heads and saying, "Aha! *You* who destroy the temple and build *it* in three days, ³⁰save Yourself, and come down from the cross!"

³¹Likewise the chief priests also, mocking among themselves with the scribes, said, "He saved others; Himself He cannot save. ³²Let the Christ, the King of Israel, descend now from the cross, that we may see and believe." Even those who were crucified with Him reviled Him.

³³Now when the sixth hour had come, there was darkness over the whole land until the ninth hour. ³⁴And at the ninth hour Jesus cried out with a loud voice, saying, "Eloi, Eloi, lama sabachthani?" which is translated, *"My God, My God, why have You forsaken Me?"*

³⁵Some of those who stood by, when they heard *that*, said, "Look, He is calling for Elijah!" ³⁶Then someone ran and filled a sponge full of sour wine, put *it* on a reed, and offered *it* to Him to drink, saying, "Let Him alone; let us see if Elijah will come to take Him down."

³⁷And Jesus cried out with a loud voice, and breathed His last.

³⁸Then the veil of the temple was torn in two from top to bottom. ³⁹So when the centurion, who stood opposite Him, saw that He cried out like this and breathed His last, he said, "Truly this Man was the Son of God!"

⁴⁰There were also women looking on from afar, among whom were Mary Magdalene, Mary the mother of James the Less and of Joses, and Salome, ⁴¹who also followed Him and ministered to Him when He was in Galilee, and many other women who came up with Him to Jerusalem.

⁴²Now when evening had come, because it was the Preparation Day, that is, the day before the Sabbath, ⁴³Joseph of Arimathea, a prominent council member, who was himself waiting for the kingdom of God, coming and taking courage, went in to Pilate and asked for the body

CRIMINALS

15:32-37 When James and John asked Jesus for the places of next to him in his kingdom, he told them they didn't know what the were asking (10:35-39). Here, where Jesus was preparing to inau his kingdom through his death, the places on his right and on his were taken by dying men—criminals. This illustrates that Jesus' d for *all* people. As Jesus explained to his two power-hungry disciple person who wants to be close to Jesus must be prepared to suffer as he himself was doing. The way to the kingdom is the way of the If we want the glory of the kingdom, we must be willing to be uni the crucified Christ.

of Jesus. ⁴⁴Pilate marveled that He was already dead; and summoning the centurion, he asked him if He had been dead for some time. ⁴⁵So when he found out from the centurion, he granted the body to Joseph. ⁴⁶Then he bought fine linen, took Him down, and wrapped Him in the linen. And he laid Him in a tomb which had been hewn out of the rock, and rolled a stone against the door of the tomb. ⁴⁷And Mary Magdalene and Mary *the mother* of Joses observed where He was laid.

CHAPTER **16** WOMEN VISIT JESUS' TOMB. Now when the Sabbath was past, Mary Magdalene, Mary *the mother* of James, and Salome bought spices, that they might come and anoint Him. ²Very early in the morning, on the first *day* of the week, they came to the tomb when the sun had risen. ³And they said among themselves,

"Who will roll away the stone from the door of the tomb for us?" ⁴But when they looked up, they saw that the stone had been rolled away—for it was very large. ⁵And entering the tomb, they saw a young man clothed in a long white robe sitting on the right side; and they were alarmed.

◆━━━━REMEMBERED
15:42-43 After Jesus died on the cross, Joseph of Arimathea asked for his body and then sealed it in a new tomb. Although an honored member of the Jewish Sanhedrin, Joseph was a secret disciple of Jesus. Not all the religious leaders hated Jesus. Joseph risked his reputation as a religious leader to give a proper burial to the One he followed. It is frightening to risk one's reputation even for what is right. If your Christian witness endangers your reputation, consider Joseph. Today he is well known in the Christian church. How many of the other members of the Jewish Supreme Court can you name?

EVIDENCE THAT JESUS ACTUALLY DIED AND AROSE

This evidence demonstrates Jesus' uniqueness in history and proves that he is God's Son. No one else was able to predict his own resurrection and then accomplish it.

Proposed Explanations for Empty Tomb	Evidence against These Explanations	References
Jesus was only unconscious and later revived.	A Roman soldier told Pilate Jesus was dead.	Mark 15:44-45
	The Roman soldiers did not break Jesus' legs because he had already died, and one of them pierced Jesus' side with a spear.	John 19:32-34
	Joseph of Arimathea and Nicodemus wrapped Jesus' body and placed it in the tomb.	John 19:38-40
The women made a mistake and went to the wrong tomb.	Mary Magdalene and Mary the mother of Jesus saw Jesus placed in the tomb.	Matthew 27:59-61 Mark 15:47 Luke 23:55
	On Sunday morning, Peter and John also went to the same tomb.	John 20:3-9
Unknown thieves stole Jesus' body.	The tomb was sealed and guarded by Roman soldiers.	Matthew 27:65-66
The disciples stole Jesus' body	The disciples were ready to die for their faith. Stealing Jesus' body would have been admitting their faith was meaningless.	Acts 12:2
	The tomb was guarded and sealed.	Matthew 27:65-66
The religious leaders stole Jesus' body to secure it.	If the religious leaders had taken Jesus' body, they would have produced it to stop the rumors of his resurrection.	None

OPPORTUNITIES

15:47 These women could do very little—they couldn't speak before the Sanhedrin in Jesus' defense; they couldn't appeal to Pilate; they couldn't stand against the crowds; they couldn't overpower the Roman guards. But they did what they could. They stayed at the cross when the disciples had fled; they followed Jesus' body to its tomb; and they prepared spices for his body. Because they used the opportunities they had, they were the first to witness the Resurrection. God blessed their devotion and diligence. As believers, we should take advantage of the opportunities we have and do what we *can* for Christ, instead of worrying about what we *cannot* do.

⁶But he said to them, "Do not be alarmed. You seek Jesus of Nazareth, who was crucified. He is risen! He is not here. See the place where they laid Him. ⁷But go, tell His disciples—and Peter—that He is going before you into Galilee; there you will see Him, as He said to you."

⁸So they went out quickly and fled from the tomb, for they trembled and were amazed. And they said nothing to anyone, for they were afraid.

⁹Now when *He* rose early on the first *day* of the week, He appeared first to Mary Magdalene, out of whom He had cast seven demons. ¹⁰She went and told those who had been with Him, as they mourned and wept. ¹¹And when they heard that He was alive and had been seen by her, they did not believe.

¹²After that, He appeared in another form to two of them as they walked and went into the country. ¹³And they went and told *it* to the rest, *but* they did not believe them either.

¹⁴Later He appeared to the eleven as they sat at the table; and He rebuked their unbelief and hardness of heart, because they did not believe those who had seen Him after He had risen. ¹⁵And He said to them, "Go into all the world and preach the gospel to every creature. ¹⁶He who believes and is baptized will be saved; but he who

DRIVING POWER

16:15 Jesus told his disciples to go into all the world telling everyon paid the penalty for sin and that those who believe in him can be for and live eternally with God. Christian disciples today are living in all of the world, telling this good news to people who haven't heard it. driving power that carries missionaries around the world and sets Ch church in motion is the faith that comes from the Resurrection. Do yc feel that you don't have the skill or determination to be a witness for Christ? You must personally realize that Jesus rose from the dead an for you today. As you grow in your relationship with him, he will prov you with both the opportunities and the inner strength to tell his mes

does not believe will be condemned. ¹⁷And these signs will follow those who believe: In My name they will cast out demons; they will speak with new tongues; ¹⁸they will take up serpents; and if they drink anything deadly, it will by no means hurt them; they will lay hands on the sick, and they will recover."

¹⁹So then, after the Lord had spoken to them, He was received up into heaven, and sat down at the right hand of God. ²⁰And they went out and preached everywhere, the Lord working with *them* and confirming the word through the accompanying signs. Amen.

MEGA Themes

JESUS CHRIST Jesus Christ alone is the Son of God. In Mark, Jesus demonstrates his divinity by overcoming disease, demons, and death. Although he had the power to be king of the earth, Jesus chose to obey the Father and die for us. Thus we see him in Mark as both Son of God and servant to man.

When Jesus rose from the dead, he proved that he was God, that he could forgive sin, and that he has the power to change our life. By trusting in Christ for forgiveness, we can begin a new life with him. As our guide, Jesus calls us to follow his example of obedience and service.

1. Which of Jesus' qualities do you see demonstrated in the Gospel of Mark?
2. Which of these qualities have you seen demonstrated in your church? Your youth group?

3. Which of these qualities have you experienced personally?
4. Which of Jesus' qualities do your non-Christian friends find it difficult to understand?
5. What could you do to be a living testimony of the gospel so that your friends could "read" your life to know Jesus?

SERVANT As the "Messiah," Jesus fulfilled the prophecies of the Old Testament by coming to earth. He did not come as a conquering king; he came as a servant. Jesus helped humankind by telling about God, showing compassion, and healing. But his ultimate act of service was giving his life as the sacrifice for sin.

Because of Jesus' example, we should be willing to serve God and others. Real greatness in Christ's kingdom is shown by love and sacrifice. We should not be motivated by ambition, love of power, or position. Instead, we should do God's work because we love him.

1. Read 10:45. How do you feel toward Jesus when you read this verse?
2. In what ways did Jesus display his servanthood in Mark? What do you learn about being a servant from the life of Jesus?
3. How do you feel about being a servant to others? What can you do to deal with any negative feelings you may have about being a servant?
4. What specific actions could you perform that would serve your family members? Your friends at school? Your friends at church? Someone in your community who is needy? A non-Christian who has not known Jesus' love?
5. From your list above, identify two specific actions you will choose to do in order to be a servant for Jesus' love.

MIRACLES Mark records more of Jesus' miracles than his sermons. Jesus was clearly a man of power and action, not just words. Jesus did miracles to confirm his message to the people and to teach the disciples his true identity as God.

The more convinced we become that Jesus is God, the more we will see his power and his love. Jesus' mighty works show us that he is able to save anyone, regardless of his or her past. His miracles of forgiveness bring healing, wholeness, and changed lives to those who trust him.

1. Why were miracles such an important part of Jesus' ministry?
2. What do you learn about Jesus from Mark's record of his miracles?
3. What displays of Jesus' power do you see today?
4. What testimony could you give to Jesus' ability to change lives through his miraculous power?

5. Are there situations in your life, or in the lives of your friends or family, that need Jesus' healing touch? Choose one or two, and ask God to bring his power into those situations.

SPREADING THE GOSPEL Jesus directed his public ministry to the Jews first. When the Jewish leaders opposed him, Jesus also went to the non-Jewish world, healing and preaching. Roman soldiers, Syrians, and other Gentiles heard the Good News. Many believed in Jesus and followed him. Jesus' final message to his disciples challenged them to go into all the world and preach the gospel of salvation.

Jesus crossed national, racial, and economic barriers to spread his Good News. Jesus' message of faith and forgiveness is for the whole world and not just for our church, neighborhood, or nation. We must reach out beyond our own people and needs to fulfill the worldwide vision of Jesus Christ so that people everywhere might hear this great message and be saved from sin and death.

1. How did Jesus show that God's love and grace are available to all types of people?
2. The book of Mark literally pivots on 8:29. Read 8:27-30 and consider these questions:
   a. What would people today say if they were asked about Jesus?
   b. How would you answer Jesus' question, "Who do you say that I am?"
   c. What does your life say about who Jesus is?
3. What key truth do people need to know about Jesus?
4. Which of your friends need to know this truth? What could you do and say to give them the Good News?
5. Choose one friend and identify two specific ways you will share the Good News with him or her.

*T*hey were two kids in love. In fact, they were *engaged.* As in "headed for the altar," "marital bliss." And M. & J. had big plans, and even bigger dreams. Then the roof caved in. M. found out she was pregnant. J. was hurt, confused, and ticked—he knew he wasn't the father. There was only one thing to do: call off the wedding. ■ But weird things started happening. M. claimed she'd been visited by a real-life angel, and that she'd been made pregnant by the Spirit of God! J. had heard some wild stories before, but *angels? Divine fertilization?* Come on! ■ Then J. started seeing angels! Surely it was all a dream . . . until the angel said (in a serious tone and with a straight face), "Hey, J., don't break off the engagement! The child inside M. really *is* the Savior of the world." J. gulped and mumbled, "Um, yeah . . . whatever you say." Soon M. could no longer hide her pregnancy. People stared. Rumors flew. M. and J. purposely kept a low profile. Together they wondered what it would be like to be parents—especially of such a special child. ■ Did M. realize that her little baby would incite a king to slaughter thousands of newborn infants? Did J. know that the child would one day speak such profound words or perform astounding miracles? Did these two realize their precious boy would die in a brutal manner? ■ Even if they *were* able to grasp any of that, did they truly believe that their murdered son would come back to life? ■ Read about M. & J. and their son—mainly about their son—in the following pages. The story is the Gospel of Luke. It's one you won't forget.

STATS

PURPOSE: To present an accurate account of the life of Christ and to present Christ as the perfect man and Savior

AUTHOR: Luke—a doctor (Colossians 4:14), a Greek and Gentile Christian. He is the only known Gentile author in the New Testament. He was a close friend and companion of Paul. He also wrote Acts, and the two books go together.

TO WHOM WRITTEN: Theophilus ("lover of God"), Gentiles, and people everywhere

DATE WRITTEN: About A.D. 60

SETTING: Luke wrote from Caesarea or from Rome

KEY PEOPLE: Jesus, Elizabeth, Zacharias, John the Baptist, Mary, the disciples, Herod the Great, Pilate, Mary Magdalene

KEY PLACES: Bethlehem, Galilee, Judea, Jerusalem

Luke

CHAPTER 1 | AN ANGEL VISITS ZACHARIAS. Inasmuch as many have taken in hand to set in order a narrative of those things which have been fulfilled among us, [2]just as those who from the beginning were eyewitnesses and ministers of the word delivered them to us, [3]it seemed good to me also, having had perfect understanding of all things from the very first, to write to you an orderly account, most excellent Theophilus, [4]that you may know the certainty of those things in which you were instructed.

[5]There was in the days of Herod, the king of Judea, a certain priest named Zacharias, of the division of Abijah. His wife *was* of the daughters of Aaron, and her name *was* Elizabeth. [6]And they were both righteous before God, walking in all the commandments and ordinances of the Lord blameless. [7]But they had no child, because Elizabeth was barren, and they were both well advanced in years.

[8]So it was, that while he was serving as priest before God in the order of his division, [9]according to the custom of the priesthood, his lot fell to burn incense when he went into the temple of the Lord. [10]And the whole multitude of the people was praying outside at the hour of incense. [11]Then an angel of the Lord appeared to him, standing on the right side of the altar of incense. [12]And when Zacharias saw *him*, he was troubled, and fear fell upon him.

[13]But the angel said to him, "Do not be afraid, Zacharias, for your prayer is heard; and your wife Elizabeth will bear you a son, and you shall call his name John. [14]And you will have joy and gladness, and many will rejoice at his birth. [15]For he will be great in the sight of the Lord, and shall drink neither wine nor strong drink. He will also be filled with the Holy Spirit, even from his mother's womb. [16]And he will turn many of the children of Israel to the Lord their God. [17]He will also go before Him in the spirit and power of Elijah, *'to turn the hearts of the fathers to the children,'* and the disobedient to the wisdom of the just, to make ready a people prepared for the Lord."

[18]And Zacharias said to the angel, "How shall I know this? For I am an old man, and my wife is well advanced in years."

[19]And the angel answered and said to him, "I am Gabriel, who stands in the presence of God, and was sent to speak to you and bring you these glad tidings. [20]But behold, you will be mute and not able to speak until the day these things take place, because you did not believe my words which will be fulfilled in their own time."

▰▰▰ CHECKED OUT

1:3 As a medical doctor, Luke knew the importance of a thorough checkup. He used his skills in observation and analysis to do a complete investigation of the stories about Jesus. His diagnosis? The gospel of Jesus Christ is true! You can read Luke's account of Jesus' life with confidence that it was written by a clear thinker and a thoughtful researcher. Because the gospel is founded on historical truth, our spiritual growth must involve careful, disciplined, thorough investigation of God's Word. If this kind of study is not part of your life, find a pastor, teacher, or book to help you get started and to guide you in this important part of Christian growth.

[21]And the people waited for Zacharias, and marveled that he lingered so long in the temple. [22]But when he came out, he could not speak to them; and they perceived that he had seen a vision in the temple, for he beckoned to them and remained speechless.

[23]So it was, as soon as the days of his service were completed, that he departed to his own house. [24]Now after those days his wife Elizabeth conceived; and she hid herself five months, saying, [25]"Thus the Lord has dealt with me, in the days when He looked on *me*, to take away my reproach among people."

[26]Now in the sixth month the angel Gabriel was sent by God to a city of Galilee named Nazareth, [27]to a virgin betrothed to a man whose name was Joseph, of the house of David. The virgin's name *was* Mary. [28]And having come

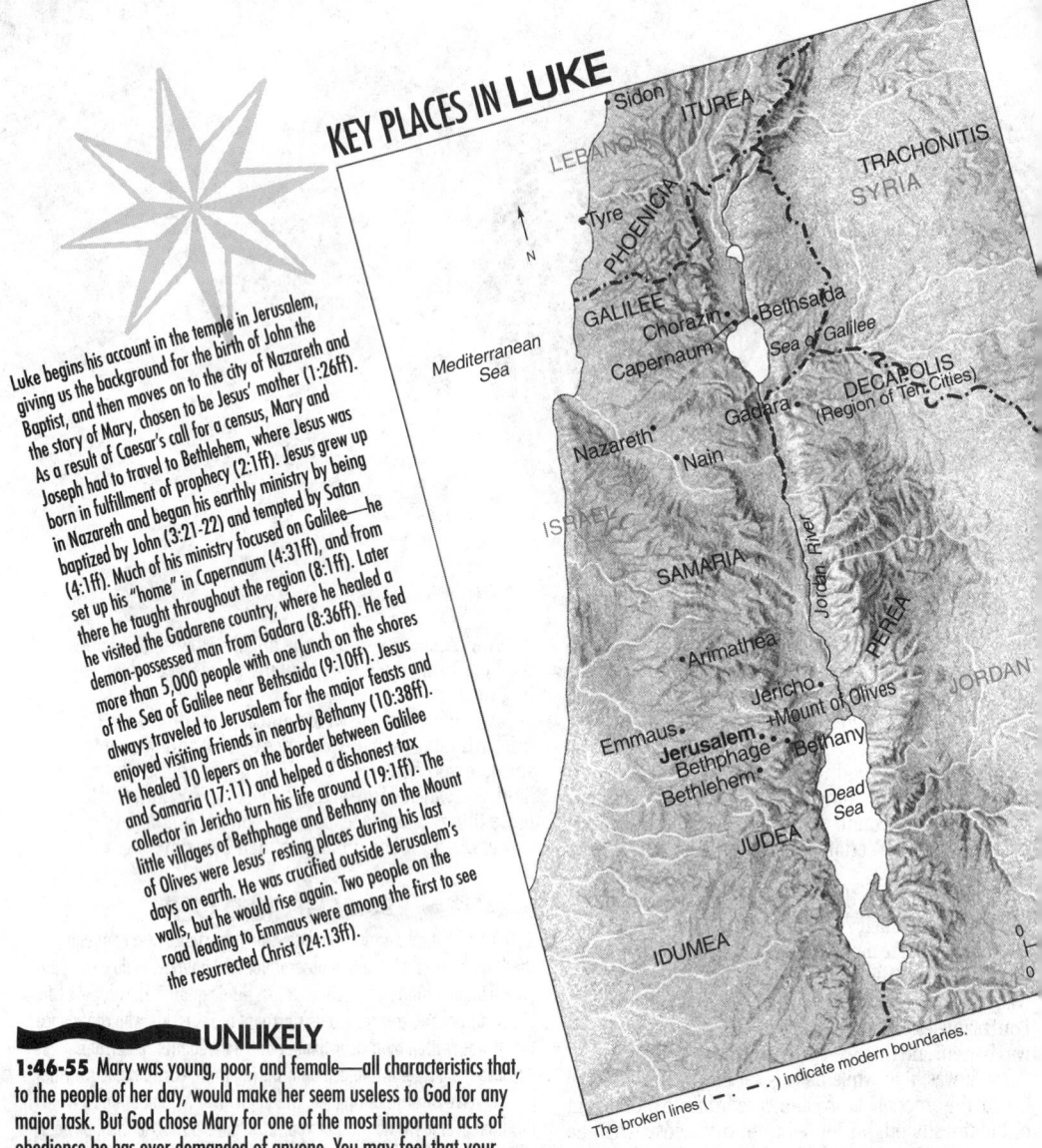

KEY PLACES IN LUKE

Luke begins his account in the temple in Jerusalem, giving us the background for the birth of John the Baptist, and then moves on to the city of Nazareth and the story of Mary, chosen to be Jesus' mother (1:26ff). As a result of Caesar's call for a census, Mary and Joseph had to travel to Bethlehem, where Jesus was born in fulfillment of prophecy (2:1ff). Jesus grew up in Nazareth and began his earthly ministry by being baptized by John (3:21-22) and tempted by Satan (4:1ff). Much of his ministry focused on Galilee—he set up his "home" in Capernaum (4:31ff), and from there he taught throughout the region (8:1ff). Later he visited the Gadarene country, where he healed a demon-possessed man from Gadara (8:36ff). He fed more than 5,000 people with one lunch on the shores of the Sea of Galilee near Bethsaida (9:10ff). Jesus always traveled to Jerusalem for the major feasts and enjoyed visiting friends in nearby Bethany (10:38ff). He healed 10 lepers on the border between Galilee and Samaria (17:11) and helped a dishonest tax collector in Jericho turn his life around (19:1ff). The little villages of Bethphage and Bethany on the Mount of Olives were Jesus' resting places during his last days on earth. He was crucified outside Jerusalem's walls, but he would rise again. Two people on the road leading to Emmaus were among the first to see the resurrected Christ (24:13ff).

The broken lines (- . - . - .) indicate modern boundaries.

UNLIKELY

1:46-55 Mary was young, poor, and female—all characteristics that, to the people of her day, would make her seem useless to God for any major task. But God chose Mary for one of the most important acts of obedience he has ever demanded of anyone. You may feel that your situation in life makes you an unlikely candidate for God's service. Don't limit God's choices. He can use you if you trust him.

in, the angel said to her, "Rejoice, highly favored *one*, the Lord *is* with you; blessed *are* you among women!"

²⁹But when she saw *him*, she was troubled at his saying, and considered what manner of greeting this was. ³⁰Then the angel said to her, "Do not be afraid, Mary, for you have found favor with God. ³¹And behold, you will conceive in your womb and bring forth a Son, and shall call His name JESUS. ³²He will be great, and will be called the Son of the Highest; and the Lord God will give Him the throne of His father David. ³³And He will reign over the house of Jacob forever, and of His kingdom there will be no end."

³⁴Then Mary said to the angel, "How can this be, since I do not know a man?"

³⁵And the angel answered and said to her, "*The* Holy Spirit will come upon you, and the power of the Highest will overshadow you; therefore, also, that Holy One who is to be born will be called the Son of God. ³⁶Now indeed, Elizabeth your relative has also conceived a son in her old age; and this is now the sixth month for her who was called barren. ³⁷For with God nothing will be impossible."

³⁸Then Mary said, "Behold the maidservant of the Lord! Let it be to me according to your word." And the angel departed from her.

³⁹Now Mary arose in those days and went into the hill country with haste, to a city of Judah, ⁴⁰and entered the house of Zacharias and greeted Elizabeth. ⁴¹And it happened, when Elizabeth heard the greeting of Mary, that

TIMING

3:23 Imagine the Savior of the world driving nails in some small-town carpenter's shop until he was 30 years old! Jesus patiently trusted the Father's timing for his life and ministry. Are you waiting and wondering what your next step should be? Don't jump ahead. Instead, like Jesus, trust God's timing and guidance.

for all the evils which Herod had done, ²⁰also added this, above all, that he shut John up in prison.

²¹When all the people were baptized, it came to pass that Jesus also was baptized; and while He prayed, the heaven was opened. ²²And the Holy Spirit descended in bodily form like a dove upon Him, and a voice came from heaven which said, "You are My beloved Son; in You I am well pleased."

²³Now Jesus Himself began *His ministry at* about thirty years of age, being (as was supposed) *the* son of Joseph, *the son* of Heli, ²⁴*the son* of Matthat, *the son* of Levi, *the son* of Melchi, *the son* of Janna, *the son* of Joseph, ²⁵*the son* of Mattathiah, *the son* of Amos, *the son* of Nahum, *the son* of Esli, *the son* of Naggai, ²⁶*the son* of Maath, *the son* of Mattathiah, *the son* of Semei, *the son* of Joseph, *the*

son of Judah, ²⁷*the son* of Joannas, *the son* of Rhesa, *the son* of Zerubbabel, *the son* of Shealtiel, *the son* of Neri, ²⁸*the son* of Melchi, *the son* of Addi, *the son* of Cosam, *the son* of Elmodam, *the son* of Er, ²⁹*the son* of Jose, *the son* of Eliezer, *the son* of Jorim, *the son* of Matthat, *the son* of Levi, ³⁰*the son* of Simeon, *the son* of Judah, *the son* of Joseph, *the son* of Jonan, *the son* of Eliakim, ³¹*the son* of Melea, *the son* of Menan, *the son* of Mattathah, *the son* of Nathan, *the son* of David, ³²*the son* of Jesse, *the son* of Obed, *the son* of Boaz, *the son* of Salmon, *the son* of Nahshon, ³³*the son* of Amminadab, *the son* of Ram, *the son* of Hezron, *the son* of Perez, *the son* of Judah, ³⁴*the son* of Jacob, *the son* of Isaac, *the son* of Abraham, *the son* of Terah, *the son* of Nahor, ³⁵*the son* of Serug, *the son* of Reu, *the son* of Peleg, *the son* of Eber, *the son* of Shelah, ³⁶*the son* of Cainan, *the son* of Arphaxad, *the son* of Shem, *the son* of Noah, *the son* of Lamech, ³⁷*the son* of Methuselah, *the son* of Enoch, *the son* of Jared, *the son* of Mahalalel, *the son* of Cainan, ³⁸*the son* of Enosh, *the son* of Seth, *the son* of Adam, *the son* of God.

THE SPIRIT OF THE LORD IS UPON ME

because HE HAS ANOINTED ME

TO PREACH THE GOSPEL to the poor

He has sent Me to heal the brokenhearted

TO PROCLAIM LIBERTY to the captives

and recovery of sight to THE BLIND

to set at liberty those who are oppressed

TO PROCLAIM THE ACCEPTABLE YEAR OF THE LORD.

And the glory of Your people Israel."

³³And Joseph and His mother marveled at those things which were spoken of Him. ³⁴Then Simeon blessed them, and said to Mary His mother, "Behold, this *Child* is destined for the fall and rising of many in Israel, and for a sign which will be spoken against ³⁵(yes, a sword will pierce through your own soul also), that the thoughts of many hearts may be revealed."

³⁶Now there was one, Anna, a prophetess, the daughter of Phanuel, of the tribe of Asher. She was of a great age, and had lived with a husband seven years from her virginity; ³⁷and this woman *was* a widow of about eighty-four years, who did not depart from the temple, but served *God* with fastings and prayers night and day. ³⁸And coming in that instant she gave thanks to the Lord, and spoke of Him to all those who looked for redemption in Jerusalem.

³⁹So when they had performed all things according to the law of the Lord, they returned to Galilee, to their *own* city, Nazareth. ⁴⁰And the Child grew and became strong in spirit, filled with wisdom; and the grace of God was upon Him.

⁴¹His parents went to Jerusalem every year at the Feast of the Passover. ⁴²And when He was twelve years old, they went up to Jerusalem according to the custom of the feast. ⁴³When they had finished the days, as they returned, the Boy Jesus lingered behind in Jerusalem. And Joseph and His mother did not know *it*; ⁴⁴but supposing Him to have been in the company, they went a day's journey, and sought Him among *their* relatives and acquaintances. ⁴⁵So when they did not find Him, they returned to Jerusalem, seeking Him. ⁴⁶Now so it was *that* after three days they found Him in the temple, sitting in the midst of the teachers, both listening to them and asking them questions. ⁴⁷And all who heard Him were astonished at His understanding and answers. ⁴⁸So when they saw Him, they were amazed; and His mother said to Him, "Son, why have You done this to us? Look, Your father and I have sought You anxiously."

⁴⁹And He said to them, "Why did you seek Me? Did you not know that I must be about My Father's business?" ⁵⁰But they did not understand the statement which He spoke to them.

⁵¹Then He went down with them and came to Nazareth, and was subject to them, but His mother kept all these things in her heart. ⁵²And Jesus increased in wisdom and stature, and in favor with God and men.

CHAPTER **3** **JOHN THE BAPTIST PREACHES.** Now in the fifteenth year of the reign of Tiberius Caesar, Pontius Pilate being governor of Judea, Herod being tetrarch of Galilee, his brother Philip tetrarch of Iturea and the region of Trachonitis, and Lysanias tetrarch of Abilene, ²while Annas and Caiaphas were high priests, the word of God came to John the son of Zacharias in the wilderness. ³And he went into all the region around the Jordan, preaching a baptism of repentance for the remission of sins, ⁴as it is written in the book of the words of Isaiah the prophet, saying:

"The voice of one crying in the wilderness:
   'Prepare the way of the LORD;
   Make His paths straight.
⁵ *Every valley shall be filled*
   And every mountain and hill brought low;
   The crooked places shall be made straight
   And the rough ways smooth;
⁶ *And all flesh shall see the salvation of God.'"*

⁷Then he said to the multitudes that came out to be baptized by him, "Brood of vipers! Who warned you to flee from the wrath to come? ⁸Therefore bear fruits worthy of repentance, and do not begin to say to yourselves, 'We have Abraham as *our* father.' For I say to you that God

▸ PARENTS

2:46-52 This is the first hint that Jesus realized he was God's Son. Even though Jesus knew his real Father, he did not reject his earthly parents. Jesus went back to Nazareth with them and lived under their authority for another 18 years. God's people do not despise human relationships or family responsibilities. If the Son of God obeyed his human parents, how much more should we honor our family members!

is able to raise up children to Abraham from these stones. ⁹And even now the ax is laid to the root of the trees. Therefore every tree which does not bear good fruit is cut down and thrown into the fire."

¹⁰So the people asked him, saying, "What shall we do then?"

¹¹He answered and said to them, "He who has two tunics, let him give to him who has none; and he who has food, let him do likewise."

¹²Then tax collectors also came to be baptized, and said to him, "Teacher, what shall we do?"

¹³And he said to them, "Collect no more than what is appointed for you."

¹⁴Likewise the soldiers asked him, saying, "And what shall we do?"

So he said to them, "Do not intimidate anyone or accuse falsely, and be content with your wages."

¹⁵Now as the people were in expectation, and all reasoned in their hearts about John, whether he was the Christ *or* not, ¹⁶John answered, saying to all, "I indeed baptize you with water; but One mightier than I is coming, whose sandal strap I am not worthy to loose. He will baptize you with the Holy Spirit and fire. ¹⁷His winnowing fan *is* in His hand, and He will thoroughly clean out His threshing floor, and gather the wheat into His barn; but the chaff He will burn with unquenchable fire."

¹⁸And with many other exhortations he preached to the people. ¹⁹But Herod the tetrarch, being rebuked by him concerning Herodias, his brother Philip's wife, and

▸ ON YOUR OWN

3:8 Many of John's hearers were shocked when he said that being Abraham's descendants was not enough. The religious leaders relied more on their family line than on their faith for their standing with God. For them, religion was inherited. But a relationship with God is not handed down from parents to children. Everyone has to find it on his or her own. Don't rely on someone else for your salvation. Put your faith in Jesus, and then exercise your faith by acting on it every day.

2:7 Although our first impression of Jesus is as a baby in a manger, it must not be our last. The Christ child in the manger makes a beautiful Christmas scene, but we cannot leave him there. This tiny, helpless baby lived an amazing life, died for us, ascended to heaven, and will return to earth as King of kings. He will rule the world and judge all people according to their decisions about him. Do you still picture Jesus as a baby in a manger—or is he your Lord? Make sure you don't underestimate Jesus. Let him grow up in your life.

And the hand of the Lord was with him.

[67]Now his father Zacharias was filled with the Holy Spirit, and prophesied, saying:

[68] "Blessed *is* the Lord God of Israel,
   For He has visited and redeemed His people,
[69] And has raised up a horn of salvation for us
   In the house of His servant David,
[70] As He spoke by the mouth of His holy prophets,
   Who *have been* since the world began,
[71] That we should be saved from our enemies
   And from the hand of all who hate us,
[72] To perform the mercy *promised* to our fathers
   And to remember His holy covenant,
[73] The oath which He swore to our father Abraham:
[74] To grant us that we,
   Being delivered from the hand of our enemies,
   Might serve Him without fear,
[75] In holiness and righteousness before Him all the
   days of our life.

[76] "And you, child, will be called the prophet of the
   Highest;
   For you will go before the face of the Lord to prepare
   His ways,
[77] To give knowledge of salvation to His people
   By the remission of their sins,
[78] Through the tender mercy of our God,
   With which the Dayspring from on high has visited us;
[79] To give light to those who sit in darkness and the
   shadow of death,
   To guide our feet into the way of peace."

[80]So the child grew and became strong in spirit, and was in the deserts till the day of his manifestation to Israel.

CHAPTER **2** **JESUS IS BORN.** And it came to pass in those days *that* a decree went out from Caesar Augustus that all the world should be registered. [2]This census first took place while Quirinius was governing Syria. [3]So all went to be registered, everyone to his own city.

[4]Joseph also went up from Galilee, out of the city of Nazareth, into Judea, to the city of David, which is called Bethlehem, because he was of the house and lineage of David, [5]to be registered with Mary, his betrothed wife, who was with child. [6]So it was, that while they were there, the days were completed for her to be delivered. [7]And she brought forth her firstborn Son, and wrapped Him in swaddling cloths, and laid Him in a manger, because there was no room for them in the inn.

[8]Now there were in the same country shepherds living out in the fields, keeping watch over their flock by night. [9]And behold, an angel of the Lord stood before them, and the glory of the Lord shone around them, and they were greatly afraid. [10]Then the angel said to them, "Do not be afraid, for behold, I bring you good tidings of great joy which will be to all people. [11]For there is born to you this day in the city of David a Savior, who is Christ the Lord. [12]And this *will be* the sign to you: You will find a Babe wrapped in swaddling cloths, lying in a manger."

[13]And suddenly there was with the angel a multitude of the heavenly host praising God and saying:

[14] "Glory to God in the highest,
   And on earth peace, goodwill toward men!"

[15]So it was, when the angels had gone away from them into heaven, that the shepherds said to one another, "Let us now go to Bethlehem and see this thing that has come to pass, which the Lord has made known to us." [16]And they came with haste and found Mary and Joseph, and the Babe lying in a manger. [17]Now when they had seen *Him,* they made widely known the saying which was told them concerning this Child. [18]And all those who heard *it* marveled at those things which were told them by the shepherds. [19]But Mary kept all these things and pondered *them* in her heart. [20]Then the shepherds returned, glorifying and praising God for all the things that they had heard and seen, as it was told them.

[21]And when eight days were completed for the circumcision of the Child, His name was called JESUS, the name given by the angel before He was conceived in the womb.

[22]Now when the days of her purification according to the law of Moses were completed, they brought Him to Jerusalem to present *Him* to the Lord [23](as it is written in the law of the Lord, *"Every male who opens the womb shall be called holy to the LORD"*), [24]and to offer a sacrifice according to what is said in the law of the Lord, *"A pair of turtledoves or two young pigeons."*

[25]And behold, there was a man in Jerusalem whose name was Simeon, and this man was just and devout, waiting for the Consolation of Israel, and the Holy Spirit was upon him. [26]And it had been revealed to him by the Holy Spirit that he would not see death before he had seen the Lord's Christ. [27]So he came by the Spirit into the temple. And when the parents brought in the Child Jesus, to do for Him according to the custom of the law, [28]he took Him up in his arms and blessed God and said:

[29] "Lord, now You are letting Your servant depart in
   peace,
   According to Your word;
[30] For my eyes have seen Your salvation
[31] Which You have prepared before the face of all peoples,
[32] A light to *bring* revelation to the Gentiles,

2:36 Although Simeon and Anna were very old, they still hoped the Messiah. Led by the Holy Spirit, they were among the first to b witness to Jesus. In the Jewish culture, elders were respected, so Si and Anna's prophecies carried extra weight. Our society, however, youthfulness over wisdom, and potential contributions by the elde often are ignored. As Christians, we should reverse those values wh we can. Encourage older people to share their wisdom and experie Listen carefully when they speak. Offer them your friendship and h them find ways to continue to serve God.

the babe leaped in her womb; and Elizabeth was filled with the Holy Spirit. ⁴²Then she spoke out with a loud voice and said, "Blessed *are* you among women, and blessed *is* the fruit of your womb! ⁴³But why *is* this *granted* to me, that the mother of my Lord should come to me? ⁴⁴For indeed, as soon as the voice of your greeting sounded in my ears, the babe leaped in my womb for joy. ⁴⁵Blessed *is* she who believed, for there will be a fulfillment of those things which were told her from the Lord."

⁴⁶And Mary said:

"My soul magnifies the Lord,
⁴⁷ And my spirit has rejoiced in God my Savior.
⁴⁸ For He has regarded the lowly state of His
      maidservant;
    For behold, henceforth all
      generations
      will call
      me
      blessed.
⁴⁹ For He who is
      mighty has
      done great
      things for me,
    And holy *is* His
      name.
⁵⁰ And His mercy *is* on
      those who fear
      Him
    From generation to
      generation.
⁵¹ He has shown strength
      with His arm;
    He has scattered *the*
      proud in the
      imagination of their
      hearts.
⁵² He has put down the mighty
      from *their* thrones,
    And exalted *the* lowly.
⁵³ He has filled *the* hungry with
      good things,
    And *the* rich He has sent away
      empty.
⁵⁴ He has helped His servant Israel,
    In remembrance of *His* mercy,
⁵⁵ As He spoke to our fathers,
    To Abraham and to his seed forever."

⁵⁶And Mary remained with her about three months, and returned to her house.

⁵⁷Now Elizabeth's full time came for her to be delivered, and she brought forth a son. ⁵⁸When her neighbors and relatives heard how the Lord had shown great mercy to her, they rejoiced with her.

⁵⁹So it was, on the eighth day, that they came to circumcise the child; and they would have called him by the name of his father, Zacharias. ⁶⁰His mother answered and said, "No; he shall be called John."

⁶¹But they said to her, "There is no one among your relatives who is called by this name." ⁶²So they made signs to his father—what he would have him called.

⁶³And he asked for a writing tablet, and wrote, saying, "His name is John." So they all marveled. ⁶⁴Immediately his mouth was opened and his tongue *loosed*, and he spoke, praising God. ⁶⁵Then fear came on all who dwelt around them; and all these sayings were discussed throughout all the hill country of Judea. ⁶⁶And all those who heard *them* kept *them* in their hearts, saying, "What kind of child will this be?"

MARY

Motherhood is a painful privilege. Young Mary of Nazareth had the unique role of being mother to the Son of God. Yet the pains and pleasures of her motherhood are understood by mothers everywhere. Mary was the only human present at Jesus' birth who also witnessed his death. She saw Jesus arrive as her baby son, and she watched him die as her Savior.

Until Gabriel's surprise visit, Mary's life was going well. She had recently become engaged to a local carpenter, Joseph, and was anticipating married life. But God had other plans for her. The angel greeted Mary as if she were the winner of a contest she had never entered; she found the angel's greeting puzzling and his presence frightening. What she heard next was the news almost every woman in Israel hoped to hear—that her child would be the Messiah, God's promised Savior. Mary did not doubt the message, but she wondered how she could be God's pregnant. Gabriel told her that the baby would be God's Son.

Mary's answer was one that God waits to hear from every person: "Behold the maidservant of the Lord! Let it be to me according to your word" (Luke 1:38). Later, her song of joy to Elizabeth shows us how well Mary knew God—her thoughts were filled with his words from the Old Testament.

Just days after his birth, Jesus was taken to the temple to be dedicated to God. There Joseph and Mary were met by two prophets, Simeon and Anna, who recognized the child as the Messiah and praised God. Simeon added some words for Mary that she must have remembered many times in the years that followed: "A sword will pierce through your own soul" (Luke 2:35).

We can imagine that even if she had known all she would suffer as Jesus' mother, Mary would have given the same response. Is your life as available to be used by God as Mary's was?

LESSONS: God's best servants are often plain people available to him
God's plans involve extraordinary events in the lives of ordinary people
A person's character is revealed by his or her response to the unexpected

KEY VERSE: "Behold the maidservant of the Lord! Let it be to me according to your word" (Luke 1:38).
Mary's story is told throughout the Gospels. She is also mentioned in Acts 1:14.

UPS:
• The mother of Jesus, the Messiah
• The one human who was with Jesus from birth to death
• Willing to be available to God
• Knew and applied God's Word

STATS:
• Where: Nazareth, Bethlehem
• Occupation: Homemaker
• Relatives: Husband: Joseph. Uncle and Aunt: Zacharias and Elizabeth. Children: Jesus, James, Joseph, Judas, and Simon, plus daughters.

CHAPTER 4 JESUS RESISTS TEMPTATION. Then Jesus, being filled with the Holy Spirit, returned from the Jordan and was led by the Spirit into the wilderness, ²being tempted for forty days by the devil. And in those days He ate nothing, and afterward, when they had ended, He was hungry.

³And the devil said to Him, "If You are the Son of God, command this stone to become bread."

⁴But Jesus answered him, saying, "It is written, *'Man shall not live by bread alone, but by every word of God.'"*

⁵Then the devil, taking Him up on a high mountain, showed Him all the kingdoms of the world in a moment of time. ⁶And the devil said to Him, "All this authority I will give You, and their glory; for *this* has been delivered to me, and I give it to whomever I wish. ⁷Therefore, if You will worship before me, all will be Yours."

⁸And Jesus answered and said to him, "Get behind Me, Satan! For it is written, *'You shall worship the LORD your God, and Him only you shall serve.'"*

⁹Then he brought Him to Jerusalem, set Him on the pinnacle of the temple, and said to Him, "If You are the Son of God, throw Yourself down from here. ¹⁰For it is written:

'He shall give His angels charge over you, To keep you,'

¹¹and,

'In their hands they shall bear you up, Lest you dash your foot against a stone.'"

¹²And Jesus answered and said to him, "It has been said, *'You shall not tempt the LORD your God.'"*

¹³Now when the devil had ended every temptation, he departed from Him until an opportune time.

¹⁴Then Jesus returned in the power of the Spirit to Galilee, and news of Him went out through all the surrounding region. ¹⁵And He taught in their synagogues, being glorified by all.

¹⁶So He came to Nazareth, where He had been brought up. And as His custom was, He went into the synagogue on the Sabbath day, and stood up to read. ¹⁷And He was handed the book of the prophet Isaiah. And when He had opened the book, He found the place where it was written:

⌐VULNERABLE

4:13 Christ's defeat of Satan was decisive but not final. Throughout his ministry, Jesus would confront Satan in many forms. Too often we see temptation as a once-and-for-all proposition. In reality, we need to be constantly on guard against the devil's ongoing attacks. Where are you most susceptible to temptation right now? How are you preparing to withstand it?

¹⁸ *"The Spirit of the LORD is upon Me,
Because He has anointed Me
To preach the gospel to the poor;
He has sent Me to heal the brokenhearted,
To proclaim liberty to the captives
And recovery of sight to the blind,*

JAMES

Jesus chose 3 of his 12 disciples for special training. James, his brother, John, and Peter made up this inner circle. Later, each played a key role among the first Christians. Peter became a great speaker; John became a great writer; James became the first of the 12 disciples to die for the faith.

James was older than his brother, John. Zebedee, their father, owned a fishing business where they worked along with Peter and Andrew, who also became disciples of Jesus. While Peter, Andrew, and John spent some time with John the Baptist, James stayed with the boats and nets. Later, when Jesus called them all, James was as eager as his partners to follow.

James liked the idea of being chosen as one of Jesus' disciples, but he misunderstood Jesus' purpose. He and his brother even tried asking Jesus for special positions in the kingdom they expected him to set up. Like all the disciples, James had a limited view of what Jesus was doing on earth. He hoped Jesus would start an earthly kingdom that would overthrow Rome and restore the nation of Israel.

More than anything, James wanted to be with Jesus. He didn't understand his leader, but he understood that Jesus was worth following. But when Jesus died and rose from the grave, James finally understood.

James was the first of many to die for the gospel. He was willing to die because he knew Jesus had conquered death. And he realized that death was only the doorway to eternal life. Our lives will be affected by what we think about death. Jesus promised eternal life to those willing to trust him. If we believe this promise, he will give us the courage to stand for him even during dangerous times.

LESSON: Many of Jesus' followers do not consider the loss of life too heavy a price to pay for following him

KEY VERSES: "Then James and John, the sons of Zebedee, came to Him, saying, 'Teacher, we want You to do for us whatever we ask.' And He said to them, 'What do you want Me to do for you?' They said to Him, 'Grant us that we may sit, one on Your right hand and the other on Your left, in Your glory'" (Mark 10:35-37).

James's story is told in the Gospels. He is also mentioned in Acts 1:13 and 12:2.

UPS:
- One of the 12 disciples
- One of a special inner circle of three with Peter and John
- First of the 12 disciples to be killed for his faith

DOWN:
- There are two outbursts from James that indicate struggles with temper (Luke 9:54) and selfishness (Mark 10:37). Both times, he and his brother, John, spoke as one.

STATS:
- Where: Galilee
- Occupation: Fisherman, disciple
- Relatives: Father: Zebedee. Mother: Salome. Brother: John.
- Contemporaries: Jesus, Pilate, Herod, other disciples

4:16 Jesus went to the synagogue "as His custom was." Even though he was the perfect Son of God, and his local synagogue left much to be desired, he attended services every week. Jesus' example makes most excuses for not attending church sound weak and self-serving. Make regular worship a part of your life.

> To set at liberty those who are oppressed;
> 19 To proclaim the acceptable year of the LORD."

[20]Then He closed the book, and gave *it* back to the attendant and sat down. And the eyes of all who were in the synagogue were fixed on Him. [21]And He began to say to them, "Today this Scripture is fulfilled in your hearing." [22]So all bore witness to Him, and marveled at the gracious words which proceeded out of His mouth. And they said, "Is this not Joseph's son?"

[23]He said to them, "You will surely say this proverb to Me, 'Physician, heal yourself! Whatever we have heard done in Capernaum, do also here in Your country.'" [24]Then He said, "Assuredly, I say to you, no prophet is accepted in his own country. [25]But I tell you truly, many widows were in Israel in the days of Elijah, when the heaven was shut up three years and six months, and there was a great famine throughout all the land; [26]but to none of them was Elijah sent except to Zarephath, *in the region* of Sidon, to a woman *who was* a widow. [27]And many lepers were in Israel in the time of Elisha the prophet, and none of them was cleansed except Naaman the Syrian."

[28]So all those in the synagogue, when they heard these things, were filled with wrath, [29]and rose up and thrust Him out of the city; and they led Him to the brow of the hill on which their city was built, that they might throw Him down over the cliff. [30]Then passing through the midst of them, He went His way.

[31]Then He went down to Capernaum, a city of Galilee, and was teaching them on the Sabbaths. [32]And they were astonished at His teaching, for His word was with authority. [33]Now in the synagogue there was a man who had a spirit of an unclean demon. And he cried out with a loud voice, [34]saying, "Let *us* alone! What have we to do with You, Jesus of Nazareth? Did You come to destroy us? I know who You are—the Holy One of God!"

[35]But Jesus rebuked him, saying, "Be quiet, and come out of him!" And when the demon had thrown him in *their* midst, it came out of him and did not hurt him. [36]Then they were all amazed and spoke among themselves, saying, "What a word this *is!* For with authority and power He commands the unclean spirits, and they come out." [37]And the report about Him went out into every place in the surrounding region.

[38]Now He arose from the synagogue and entered Simon's house. But Simon's wife's mother was sick with a high fever, and they made request of Him concerning her. [39]So He stood over her and rebuked the fever, and it left her. And immediately she arose and served them.

[40]When the sun was setting, all those who had any that were sick with various diseases brought them to Him; and He laid His hands on every one of them and healed them. [41]And demons also came out of many, crying out and saying, "You are the Christ, the Son of God!" And He, rebuking *them,* did not allow them to speak, for they knew that He was the Christ.

[42]Now when it was day, He departed and went into a deserted place. And the crowd sought Him and came to Him, and tried to keep Him from leaving them; [43]but He said to them, "I must preach the kingdom of God to the other cities also, because for this purpose I have been sent." [44]And He was preaching in the synagogues of Galilee.

CHAPTER 5 FISHING WITH JESUS.

So it was, as the multitude pressed about Him to hear the word of God, that He stood by the Lake of Gennesaret, [2]and saw two boats standing by the lake; but the fishermen had gone from them and were washing *their* nets. [3]Then He got into one of the boats, which was Simon's, and asked him to put out a little from the land. And He sat down and taught the multitudes from the boat.

[4]When He had stopped speaking, He said to Simon, "Launch out into the deep and let down your nets for a catch."

[5]But Simon answered and said to Him, "Master, we have toiled all night and caught nothing; nevertheless at Your word I will let down the net." [6]And when they had done this, they caught a great number of fish, and their net was breaking. [7]So they signaled to *their* partners in the other boat to come and help them. And they came and filled both the boats, so that they began to sink. [8]When Simon Peter saw *it,* he fell down at Jesus' knees, saying, "Depart from me, for I am a sinful man, O Lord!"

[9]For he and all who were with him were astonished at the catch of fish which they had taken; [10]and so also *were* James and John, the sons of Zebedee, who were partners with Simon. And Jesus said to Simon, "Do not be afraid. From now on you will catch men." [11]So when they had brought their boats to land, they forsook all and followed Him.

[12]And it happened when He was in a certain city, that behold, a man who was full of leprosy saw Jesus; and he fell on *his* face and implored Him, saying, "Lord, if You are willing, You can make me clean."

[13]Then He put out *His* hand and touched him, saying, "I am willing; be cleansed." Immediately the leprosy left him. [14]And He charged him to tell no one, "But go and show yourself to the priest, and make an offering for your cleansing, as a testimony to them, just as Moses commanded."

[15]However, the report went around concerning Him all the more; and great multitudes came together to hear, and to be healed by Him of their infirmities. [16]So He Himself *often* withdrew into the wilderness and prayed.

[17]Now it happened on a certain day, as He was teaching, that there were Pharisees and teachers of the law sitting by, who had come out of every town of Galilee, Judea, and Jerusalem. And the power of the Lord was *present* to heal them. [18]Then behold, men brought on a

TRY IT!

5:18-20 It wasn't the sick man's faith that impressed Jesus, but the faith of his friends. Jesus responded to their faith and healed the man. For better or worse, our faith affects others. We cannot make another person a Christian, but we can do much through our words, actions, and love to give him or her a chance to respond. Look for opportunities to bring your friends to the living Christ.

bed a man who was paralyzed, whom they sought to bring in and lay before Him. ¹⁹And when they could not find how they might bring him in, because of the crowd, they went up on the housetop and let him down with *his* bed through the tiling into the midst before Jesus.

²⁰When He saw their faith, He said to him, "Man, your sins are forgiven you."

²¹And the scribes and the Pharisees began to reason, saying, "Who is this who speaks blasphemies? Who can forgive sins but God alone?"

²²But when Jesus perceived their thoughts, He answered and said to them, "Why are you reasoning in your hearts? ²³Which is easier, to say, 'Your sins are forgiven you,' or to say, 'Rise up and walk'? ²⁴But that you may know that the Son of Man has power on earth to forgive sins"—He said to the man who was paralyzed, "I say to you, arise, take up your bed, and go to your house."

²⁵Immediately he rose up before them, took up what he had been lying on, and departed to his own house, glorifying God. ²⁶And they were all amazed, and they glorified God and were filled with fear, saying, "We have seen strange things today!"

²⁷After these things He went out and saw a tax collector named Levi, sitting at the tax office. And He said to him, "Follow Me." ²⁸So he left all, rose up, and followed Him.

²⁹Then Levi gave Him a great feast in his own house. And there were a great number of tax collectors and others who sat down with them. ³⁰And their scribes and the Pharisees complained against His disciples, saying, "Why do You eat and drink with tax collectors and sinners?"

³¹Jesus answered and said to them, "Those who are well have no need of a physician, but those who are sick. ³²I have not come to call *the* righteous, but sinners, to repentance."

³³Then they said to Him, "Why do the disciples of John fast often and make prayers, and likewise those of the Pharisees, but Yours eat and drink?"

³⁴And He said to them, "Can you make the friends of the bridegroom fast while the bridegroom is with them? ³⁵But the days will come when the bridegroom will be taken away from them; then they will fast in those days."

³⁶Then He spoke a parable to them: "No one puts a piece from a new gar- ment on an old one; otherwise the new makes a tear, and also the piece that was *taken* out of the new does not match the old. ³⁷And no one puts new wine into old

"Here's what I did..."

Even before I became a Christian, the Bible amazed me. I remember being floored the first time I read Luke 6:27-38. That's the passage about loving and doing good to your enemies. *How could anyone act like that?*

A year later, just before my freshman year in high school, I became a Christian. And that year I had the chance to find out firsthand how someone can follow Jesus' words.

I did well in shop class, so I decided to make a small bookcase for my mother for Christmas. I designed it myself. I worked on it a lot in my spare time, finally getting to the point where I put final touches on it and left it in the finishing room, which was always locked.

After school, when I went back to get the bookcase, it was gone. The shop teacher did some investigating and finally discovered that a student named Andy had stolen it. "We've had problems with Andy before," Mr. Petrako said. "Andy needs to learn a lesson. I've arranged to have him meet you after school to return your bookshelf." That's all he said, but I knew what he meant.

I didn't need any encouragement to "teach Andy a lesson." I was furious. And since I was a football player, big for my age, I wouldn't have any trouble beating someone up.

I waited for Andy, psyching myself up to face my enemy. Finally he walked in.

Something happened to me when I saw him. I had expected a hoodlum, but what I saw was just a boy, smaller and younger than me, who was obviously afraid to face the person he had hurt. When I saw Andy's scared face, all the hate just leaked out of me. Andy said, "Here's your bookshelf. I'm sorry." I had no words for him. I growled something, took the bookcase, and fled.

That night I felt very confused. *What happened? What took away my hate?* As I thought about these things, I remembered the passage in Luke. I read it again: "Love your enemies. . . . From him who takes away your goods do not ask *them* back."

Father God, I thought, *am I supposed to give the bookcase back to him? I can't! I made it for my mom!* I felt like God was asking me to respond to what I was reading. But how? Suddenly I knew. The next morning I went to school early and started work on an identical bookcase. For four days straight I stayed as long as shop was open.

When the bookcase was finished, I had Andy meet me after school in an empty shop class. I said, "Andy, I want to give you this. It's a gift from me to you, and from me to Jesus. I'd never be able to do this if it weren't for Jesus."

That's all I could say then. I didn't know how to share my faith. All I knew was that Jesus had touched my life and I wanted to share it.

Well, after that I got to know Andy. Seeing his family situation, I understood him better. I invited him to youth group on Thursday afternoons. When there was a retreat and Andy couldn't afford to go, my friends and I scraped up enough money for him. And at that retreat, Andy became a Christian.

It's hard to know who was more excited about God right then, me or Andy.

David AGE 17

6:13-16 Jesus picked ordinary men as his disciples. Today, God calls "ordinary" people to build his church, teach salvation, and serve others. Alone we may feel unqualified to serve Christ well. Together we are strong enough to serve God in any way. Ask for patience to accept differences and to build on the variety of strengths in your group.

wineskins; or else the new wine will burst the wineskins and be spilled, and the wineskins will be ruined. ³⁸But new wine must be put into new wineskins, and both are preserved. ³⁹And no one, having drunk old *wine*, immediately desires new; for he says, 'The old is better.'"

CHAPTER 6 PICKING WHEAT ON THE SABBATH.

Now it happened on the second Sabbath after the first that He went through the grainfields. And His disciples plucked the heads of grain and ate *them*, rubbing *them* in *their* hands. ²And some of the Pharisees said to them, "Why are you doing what is not lawful to do on the Sabbath?"

³But Jesus answering them said, "Have you not even read this, what David did when he was hungry, he and those who were with him: ⁴how he went into the house of God, took and ate the showbread, and also gave some to those with him, which is not lawful for any but the priests to eat?" ⁵And He said to them, "The Son of Man is also Lord of the Sabbath."

⁶Now it happened on another Sabbath, also, that He entered the synagogue and taught. And a man was there whose right hand was withered. ⁷So the scribes and Pharisees watched Him closely, whether He would heal on the Sabbath, that they might find an accusation against Him. ⁸But He knew their thoughts, and said to the man who had the withered hand, "Arise and stand here." And he arose and stood. ⁹Then Jesus said to them, "I will ask you one thing: Is it lawful on the Sabbath to do good or to do evil, to save life or to destroy?" ¹⁰And when He had looked around at them all, He said to the man, "Stretch out your hand." And he did so, and his hand was restored as whole as the other. ¹¹But they were filled with rage, and discussed with one another what they might do to Jesus.

¹²Now it came to pass in those days that He went out to the mountain to pray, and continued all night in prayer to God. ¹³And when it was day, He called His disciples to *Himself*; and from them He chose twelve whom He also named apostles: ¹⁴Simon, whom He also named Peter, and Andrew his brother; James and John; Philip and Bartholomew; ¹⁵Matthew and Thomas; James the *son* of Alphaeus, and Simon called the Zealot; ¹⁶Judas *the son* of James, and Judas Iscariot who also became a traitor.

¹⁷And He came down with them and stood on a level place with a crowd of His disciples and a great multitude of people from all Judea and Jerusalem, and from the seacoast of Tyre and Sidon, who came to hear Him and be healed of their diseases, ¹⁸as well as those who were tormented with unclean spirits. And they were healed. ¹⁹And the whole multitude sought to touch Him, for power went out from Him and healed *them* all.

²⁰Then He lifted up His eyes toward His disciples, and said:

"Blessed *are you* poor,
   For yours is the kingdom of God.
²¹ Blessed *are you* who hunger now,
   For you shall be filled.
Blessed *are you* who weep now,
   For you shall laugh.
²² Blessed are you when men hate you,
   And when they exclude you,
   And revile *you*, and cast out your name as evil,
   For the Son of Man's sake.
²³ Rejoice in that day and leap for joy!
   For indeed your reward *is* great in heaven,
   For in like manner their fathers did to the prophets.

²⁴ "But woe to you who are rich,
   For you have received your consolation.
²⁵ Woe to you who are full,
   For you shall hunger.
Woe to you who laugh now,
   For you shall mourn and weep.
²⁶ Woe to you when all men speak well of you,
   For so did their fathers to the false prophets.

²⁷"But I say to you who hear: Love your enemies, do good to those who hate you, ²⁸bless those who curse you, and pray for those who spitefully use you. ²⁹To him who strikes you on the *one* cheek, offer the other also. And from him who takes away your cloak, do not withhold *your* tunic either. ³⁰Give to everyone who asks of you. And from him who takes away your goods do not ask *them* back. ³¹And just as you want men to do to you, you also do to them likewise.

³²"But if you love those who love you, what credit is that to you? For even sinners love those who love them. ³³And if you do good to those who do good to you, what credit is that to you? For even sinners do the same. ³⁴And if you lend *to those* from whom you hope to receive back, what credit is that to you? For even sinners lend to sinners to receive as much back. ³⁵But love your enemies, do good, and lend, hoping for nothing in return; and your reward will be great, and you will be sons of the Most High. For He is kind to the unthankful and evil. ³⁶Therefore be merciful, just as your Father also is merciful.

³⁷"Judge not, and you shall not be judged. Condemn not, and you shall not be condemned. Forgive, and you will be forgiven. ³⁸Give, and it will be given to you: good measure, pressed down, shaken together, and running over will be put into your bosom. For with the same measure that you use, it will be measured back to you."

³⁹And He spoke a parable to them: "Can the blind lead the blind? Will they not both fall into the ditch? ⁴⁰A disci-

TOUGH LOVE

6:27 The Jews despised the Romans because they oppressed God's people, but Jesus told them to love these enemies. Such words turned many away from Christ. But Jesus wasn't talking about having affection for enemies; he was talking about an act of the will. You can't "fall into" this kind of love—it takes conscious effort. Loving our enemies means acting in their best interests. We can pray for them and we can think of ways to help them. Jesus loved the whole world, even though the world was in rebellion against God. He asks us to follow his example by loving our enemies.

ple is not above his teacher, but everyone who is perfectly trained will be like his teacher. ⁴¹And why do you look at the speck in your brother's eye, but do not perceive the plank in your own eye? ⁴²Or how can you say to your brother, 'Brother, let me remove the speck that *is* in your eye,' when you yourself do not see the plank that *is* in your own eye? Hypocrite! First remove the plank from your own eye, and then you will see clearly to remove the speck that is in your brother's eye.

⁴³"For a good tree does not bear bad fruit, nor does a bad tree bear good fruit. ⁴⁴For every tree is known by its own fruit. For *men* do not gather figs from thorns, nor do they gather grapes from a bramble bush. ⁴⁵A good man out of the good treasure of his heart brings forth good; and an evil man out of the evil treasure of his heart brings forth evil. For out of the abundance of the heart his mouth speaks.

⁴⁶"But why do you call Me 'Lord, Lord,' and not do the things which I say? ⁴⁷Whoever comes to Me, and hears My sayings and does them, I will show you whom he is like: ⁴⁸He is like a man building a house, who dug deep and laid the foundation on the rock. And when the flood arose, the stream beat vehemently against that house, and could not shake it, for it was founded on the rock. ⁴⁹But he who heard and did nothing is like a man who built a house on the earth without a foundation, against which the stream beat vehemently; and immediately it fell. And the ruin of that house was great."

CHAPTER 7 A MAN IS HEALED FAR AWAY. Now when He concluded all His sayings in the hearing of the people, He entered Capernaum. ²And a certain centurion's servant, who was dear to him, was sick and ready to die. ³So when he heard about Jesus, he sent elders of the Jews to Him, pleading with Him to come and heal his servant. ⁴And when they came to Jesus, they begged Him earnestly, saying that the one for whom He should do this was deserving, ⁵"for he loves our nation, and has built us a synagogue."

⁶Then Jesus went with them. And when He was already not far from the house, the centurion sent friends to Him, saying to Him, "Lord, do not trouble Yourself, for I am not worthy that You should enter under my roof. ⁷Therefore I did not even think myself worthy to come to You. But say the word, and my servant will be healed. ⁸For I also am a man placed under authority, having soldiers under me. And I say to one, 'Go,' and he goes; and to another, 'Come,' and he comes; and to my servant, 'Do this,' and he does *it*."

⁹When Jesus heard these things, He marveled at him, and turned around and said to the crowd that followed Him, "I say to you, I have not found such great faith, not even in Israel!" ¹⁰And those who were sent, returning to the house, found the servant well who had been sick.

¹¹Now it happened, the day after, *that* He went into a city called Nain; and many of His disciples went with Him, and a large crowd. ¹²And when He came near the gate of the city, behold, a dead man was being carried out, the only son of his mother; and she was a widow. And a large crowd from the city was with her. ¹³When the Lord saw her, He had compassion on her and said to her, "Do not weep." ¹⁴Then He came and touched the open coffin, and those who carried *him* stood still. And He said, "Young man, I say to you, arise." ¹⁵So he who was dead sat up and began to speak. And He presented him to his mother.

◣ NO POINTING

6:41 Jesus doesn't mean we should ignore wrongdoing, but we are not to be so worried about others' sins that we overlook our own. We often rationalize our sins by pointing out the same mistakes in others. What kinds of specks in others' eyes are the easiest for you to criticize? Remember your own planks when you feel like criticizing, and you may find you have less to say.

¹⁶Then fear came upon all, and they glorified God, saying, "A great prophet has risen up among us"; and, "God has visited His people." ¹⁷And this report about Him went throughout all Judea and all the surrounding region.

¹⁸Then the disciples of John reported to him concerning all these things. ¹⁹And John, calling two of his disciples to *him*, sent *them* to Jesus, saying, "Are You the Coming One, or do we look for another?"

²⁰When the men had come to Him, they said, "John the Baptist has sent us to You, saying, 'Are You the Coming One, or do we look for another?' " ²¹And that very hour He cured many of infirmities, afflictions, and evil spirits; and to many blind He gave sight.

²²Jesus answered and said to them, "Go and tell John the things you have seen and heard: that *the* blind see, *the* lame walk, *the* lepers are cleansed, *the* deaf hear, *the* dead are raised, *the* poor have the gospel preached to them. ²³And blessed is *he* who is not offended because of Me."

²⁴When the messengers of John had departed, He began to speak to the multitudes concerning John: "What did you go out into the wilderness to see? A reed shaken by the wind? ²⁵But what did you go out to see? A man clothed in soft garments? Indeed those who are gorgeously appareled and live in luxury are in kings' courts. ²⁶But what did you go out to see? A prophet? Yes, I say to you, and more than a prophet. ²⁷This is *he* of whom it is written:

'Behold, I send My messenger before Your face,
Who will prepare Your way before You.'

²⁸For I say to you, among those born of women there is not a greater prophet than John the Baptist; but he who is least in the kingdom of God is greater than he." ²⁹And when all the people heard *Him*, even the tax collectors justified God, having been baptized with the

◣ QUESTIONS

7:18-28 John was confused because the reports he received about Jesus were unexpected and incomplete. John's doubts were natural, and Jesus didn't rebuke him for them. Instead, Jesus responded in a way that John would understand by explaining that he had in fact accomplished the things the Messiah was supposed to accomplish. God also can handle our doubts, and he welcomes our questions. Do you have questions about Jesus—about who he is or what he expects of you? Admit them to yourself and to God, and begin looking for answers. Only as you admit your doubts can you begin to resolve them.

7:29-30 The wicked people heard John's message and repented. In contrast, the religious leaders rejected his words. Wanting to live their own way, they refused to listen to other ideas. Rather than trying to force your plans on God, try to discover his plan for you.

baptism of John. [30]But the Pharisees and lawyers rejected the will of God for themselves, not having been baptized by him.

[31]And the Lord said, "To what then shall I liken the men of this generation, and what are they like? [32]They are like children sitting in the marketplace and calling to one another, saying:

'We played the flute for you,
   And you did not dance;
We mourned to you,
   And you did not weep.'

[33]For John the Baptist came neither eating bread nor drinking wine, and you say, 'He has a demon.' [34]The Son of Man has come eating and drinking, and you say, 'Look, a glutton and a winebibber, a friend of tax collectors and sinners!' [35]But wisdom is justified by all her children."

[36]Then one of the Pharisees asked Him to eat with him. And He went to the Pharisee's house, and sat down to eat. [37]And behold, a woman in the city who was a sinner, when she knew that *Jesus* sat at the table in the Pharisee's house, brought an alabaster flask of fragrant oil, [38]and stood at His feet behind *Him* weeping; and she began to wash His feet with her tears, and wiped *them* with the hair of her head; and she kissed His feet and anointed *them* with the fragrant oil. [39]Now when the Pharisee who had invited Him saw *this*, he spoke to himself, saying, "This Man, if He were a prophet, would know who and what manner of woman *this is* who is touching Him, for she is a sinner."

[40]And Jesus answered and said to him, "Simon, I have something to say to you."

So he said, "Teacher, say it."

[41]"There was a certain creditor who had two debtors. One owed five hundred denarii, and the other fifty. [42]And when they had nothing with which to repay, he freely forgave them both. Tell Me, therefore, which of them will love him more?"

[43]Simon answered and said, "I suppose the *one* whom he forgave more."

And He said to him, "You have rightly judged." [44]Then He turned to the woman and said to Simon, "Do you see this woman? I entered your house; you gave Me no water for My feet, but she has washed My feet with her tears and wiped *them* with the hair of her head. [45]You gave Me no kiss, but this woman has not ceased to kiss My feet since the time I came in. [46]You did not anoint My head with oil, but this woman has anointed My feet with fragrant oil. [47]Therefore I say to you, her sins, *which are* many, are forgiven, for she loved much. But to whom little is forgiven, *the same* loves little."

[48]Then He said to her, "Your sins are forgiven."

[49]And those who sat at the table with Him began to say to themselves, "Who is this who even forgives sins?"

[50]Then He said to the woman, "Your faith has saved you. Go in peace."

CHAPTER 8 WOMEN GO WITH JESUS. Now it came to pass, afterward, that He went through every city and village, preaching and bringing the glad tidings of the kingdom of God. And the twelve *were* with Him, [2]and certain women who had been healed of evil spirits and infirmities—Mary called Magdalene, out of whom had come seven demons, [3]and Joanna the wife of Chuza, Herod's steward, and Susanna, and many others who provided for Him from their substance.

[4]And when a great multitude had gathered, and they had come to Him from every city, He spoke by a parable: [5]"A sower went out to sow his seed. And as he sowed, some fell by the wayside; and it was trampled down, and the birds of the air devoured it. [6]Some fell on rock; and as soon as it sprang up, it withered away because it lacked moisture. [7]And some fell among thorns, and the thorns sprang up with it and choked it. [8]But others fell on good ground, sprang up, and yielded a crop a hundredfold." When He had said these things He cried, "He who has ears to hear, let him hear!"

[9]Then His disciples asked Him, saying, "What does this parable mean?"

[10]And He said, "To you it has been given to know the mysteries of the kingdom of God, but to the rest *it is given* in parables, that

'Seeing they may not see,
   And hearing they may not understand.'

[11]"Now the parable is this: The seed is the word of God. [12]Those by the wayside are the ones who hear; then the devil comes and takes away the word out of their hearts, lest they should believe and be saved. [13]But the ones on the rock *are those* who, when they hear, receive the word with joy; and these have no root, who believe for a while and in time of temptation fall away. [14]Now the ones *that* fell among thorns are those who, when they have heard, go out and are choked with cares, riches, and pleasures of life, and bring no fruit to maturity. [15]But the ones *that* fell on the good ground are those who, having heard the word with a noble and good heart, keep *it* and bear fruit with patience.

[16]"No one, when he has lit a lamp, covers it with a vessel or puts *it* under a bed, but sets *it* on a lampstand, that those who enter may see the light. [17]For nothing is secret that will not be revealed, nor *anything* hidden that will not be known and come to light. [18]Therefore take heed how you hear. For whoever has, to him *more* will be

▬▬▬PIGS

8:33 The demons destroyed the swine (pigs) and hurt the herdsmen finances. But can pigs and money compare with a human life? A man been freed from the devil's power, but the villagers thought only abou their pocketbooks. People have always tended to value personal gain over other people. Throughout history many wars have been fought to protect economic interests. Much injustice and oppression, both at hom and abroad, is the direct result of some individual's or company's urge get rich. People continually are being sacrificed to money. Don't think more highly of "pigs" than of people. Think carefully about how your decisions will affect other human beings, and be willing to choose a simpler life-style if it would keep other people from being harmed.

given; and whoever does not have, even what he seems to have will be taken from him."

¹⁹Then His mother and brothers came to Him, and could not approach Him because of the crowd. ²⁰And it was told Him *by some,* who said, "Your mother and Your brothers are standing outside, desiring to see You."

²¹But He answered and said to them, "My mother and My brothers are these who hear the word of God and do it."

²²Now it happened, on a certain day, that He got into a boat with His disciples. And He said to them, "Let us cross over to the other side of the lake." And they launched out. ²³But as they sailed He fell asleep. And a windstorm came down on the lake, and they were filling *with water,* and were in jeopardy. ²⁴And they came to Him and awoke Him, saying, "Master, Master, we are perishing!"

Then He arose and rebuked the wind and the raging of the water. And they ceased, and there was a calm. ²⁵But He said to them, "Where is your faith?"

And they were afraid, and marveled, saying to one another, "Who can this be? For He commands even the winds and water, and they obey Him!"

²⁶Then they sailed to the country of the Gadarenes, which is opposite Galilee. ²⁷And when He stepped out on the land, there met Him a certain man from the city who had demons for a long time. And he wore no clothes, nor did he live in a house but in the tombs. ²⁸When he saw Jesus, he cried out, fell down before Him, and with a loud voice said, "What have I to do with You, Jesus, Son of the Most High God? I beg You, do not torment me!" ²⁹For He had commanded the unclean spirit to come out of the man. For it had often seized him, and he was kept under guard, bound with chains and shackles; and he broke the bonds and was driven by the demon into the wilderness.

³⁰Jesus asked him, saying, "What is your name?"

And he said, "Legion," because many demons had entered him. ³¹And they begged Him that He would not command them to go out into the abyss.

³²Now a herd of many swine was feeding there on the mountain. So they begged Him that He would permit them to enter them. And He permitted them. ³³Then the demons went out of the man and entered the swine, and the herd ran violently down the steep place into the lake and drowned.

³⁴When those who fed *them* saw what had happened, they fled and told *it* in the city and in the country. ³⁵Then they went out to see what had happened, and came to Jesus, and found the man from whom the demons had departed, sitting at the feet of Jesus, clothed and in his right mind. And they were afraid. ³⁶They also who had seen *it* told them by what means he who had been demon-possessed was healed. ³⁷Then the whole multitude of the surrounding region of the Gadarenes asked Him to depart from them, for they were seized with great fear. And He got into the boat and returned.

³⁸Now the man from whom the demons had departed begged Him that he might be with Him. But Jesus sent him away, saying, ³⁹"Return to your own house, and tell what great things God has done for you." And he went his way and proclaimed throughout the whole city what great things Jesus had done for him.

⁴⁰So it was, when Jesus returned, that the multitude welcomed Him, for they were all waiting for Him. ⁴¹And behold, there came a man named Jairus, and he was a ruler of the synagogue. And he fell down at Jesus' feet and begged Him to come to his house, ⁴²for he had an only daughter about twelve years of age, and she was dying.

But as He went, the multitudes thronged Him. ⁴³Now a woman, having a flow of blood for twelve years, who had spent all her livelihood on physicians and could not be healed by any, ⁴⁴came from behind and touched the border of His garment. And immediately her flow of blood stopped.

⁴⁵And Jesus said, "Who touched Me?"

When all denied it, Peter and those with him said, "Master, the multitudes throng and press You, and You say, 'Who touched Me?'"

⁴⁶But Jesus said, "Somebody touched Me, for I perceived power going out from Me." ⁴⁷Now when the woman saw that she was not hidden, she came trembling; and falling

---

There are so many things in my life that could pull me away from God. How can I make sure I will always be "good soil"?

I WONDER...

Skyscrapers must be carefully planned in order for them not to topple when a stiff wind hits. First, a huge hole is dug deep in the ground. Thousands of tons of concrete are poured, steel girders are welded into place, and everything is made to fit according to exact specifications. If the foundation is strong and straight, a strong building can be built on it.

The rest of the structure, however, must also be built strong, with the right materials fitted together in the right way, at the right time.

In Luke 8:9-18, Jesus tells a parable about the Word of God. He compares it to a seed being planted. Like the skyscraper, seeds need to be planted in the right kind of soil, at the right time. So it is with the Word of God. Only God knows when and how to plant his Spirit and life within each of us.

The first phase in your new life began when you accepted Christ's forgiveness and became a Christian: "For no other foundation can anyone lay than that which is laid, which is Jesus Christ" (1 Corinthians 3:11).

The second phase starts with the Word of God. If you study the Bible and have other Christians help you understand and apply it, your life in Christ will be strong. "Now if anyone builds on this foundation *with* gold, silver, precious stones, wood, hay, straw, each one's work will become clear" (1 Corinthians 3:12-13). If you are exposed to teaching that downplays God's Word, it is like building your life with wood, hay, and straw. It will collapse when problems or persecution from friends and family arise (see Matthew 7:21-28).

To build a solid Christian life, you should make sure that all you're hearing is lining up with what the Bible really says. You can do this by praying for direction, asking questions, and finding people who believe as you do that the Bible is God's blueprint for building a strong life.

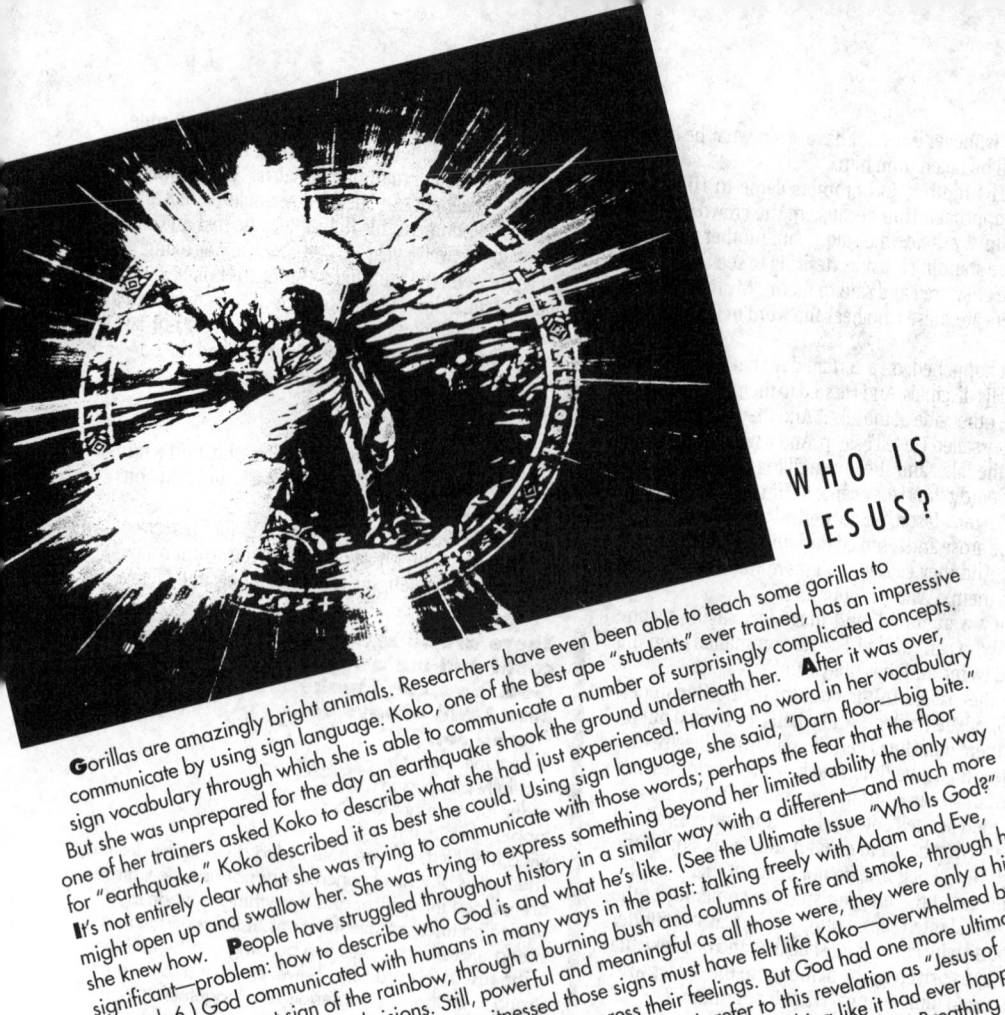

Gorillas are amazingly bright animals. Researchers have even been able to teach some gorillas to communicate by using sign language. Koko, one of the best ape "students" ever trained, has an impressive sign vocabulary through which she is able to communicate a number of surprisingly complicated concepts. But she was unprepared for the day an earthquake shook the ground underneath her. **A**fter it was over, one of her trainers asked Koko to describe what she had just experienced. Having no word in her vocabulary for "earthquake," Koko described it as best she could. Using sign language, she said, "Darn floor—big bite." **I**t's not entirely clear what she was trying to communicate with those words; perhaps the fear that the floor might open up and swallow her. She was trying to express something beyond her limited ability the only way she knew how. **P**eople have struggled throughout history in a similar way with a different—and much more significant—problem: how to describe who God is and what he's like. (See the Ultimate Issue "Who Is God?" in Isaiah 6.) God communicated with humans in many ways in the past: talking freely with Adam and Eve, through the covenant sign of the rainbow, through a burning bush and columns of fire and smoke, through his Law, and through miracles and visions. Still, powerful and meaningful as all those were, they were only a hint of the reality behind them. The people who witnessed those signs must have felt like Koko—overwhelmed by what they'd experienced but with no adequate way to express their feelings. But God had one more ultimate revelation to make: he came to our planet and became one of us. We refer to this revelation as "Jesus of Nazareth." **U**nderstandably, the coming of Jesus was an explosive event. Nothing like it had ever happened before, nor has it happened since. God—in human form—walking the same ground with us! Breathing our air, sharing our pain, laughing and bleeding just like we do, entering into all the exhilaration—and the anguish—of being human. Before this revelation, God had given us hints, glimpses, and whispers of who he was. Then he came in all his fullness. **B**ut Jesus was not what people expected. Even the Jewish authorities— the people who knew more about God than anyone—were totally unprepared for the way God came. They expected a strong political and military Messiah, one who would free his people from Rome. Instead, the Messiah came as a "suffering servant," proclaiming a kingdom that was not of this world. Like so many others the Jews were very confused as to who Jesus really was. Jesus himself knew that even his closest followers felt that uncertainty. He asked them point-blank: "Who do you say that I am?" Peter's response to this question, given here in Luke, was simple, direct, and tremendously powerful: "The Christ of God." **P**eter's answer, simple though it was, set off shock waves that have rippled down through history. If Jesus was—and is— indeed the Messiah, the Son of the living God, then God had entered into human history in a way he had never done before, and life on this planet could never be the same again. Countless millions of lives since then give testimony that that is exactly what has happened. Jesus of Nazareth was, and is, the unique Son of God: fully God, fully human, Lord of lords and King of kings. **T**hat same question Jesus asked his disciples confronts each of us today: Who do you say Jesus is? Be careful how you answer. It makes all the difference in eternity.

down before Him, she declared to Him in the presence of all the people the reason she had touched Him and how she was healed immediately.

⁴⁸And He said to her, "Daughter, be of good cheer; your faith has made you well. Go in peace."

⁴⁹While He was still speaking, someone came from the ruler of the synagogue's *house,* saying to him, "Your daughter is dead. Do not trouble the Teacher."

⁵⁰But when Jesus heard *it,* He answered him, saying, "Do not be afraid; only believe, and she will be made well." ⁵¹When He came into the house, He permitted no one to go in except Peter, James, and John, and the father and mother of the girl. ⁵²Now all wept and mourned for her; but He said, "Do not weep; she is not dead, but sleeping." ⁵³And they ridiculed Him, knowing that she was dead.

⁵⁴But He put them all outside, took her by the hand and called, saying, "Little girl, arise." ⁵⁵Then her spirit returned, and she arose immediately. And He commanded that she be given *something* to eat. ⁵⁶And her parents were astonished, but He charged them to tell no one what had happened.

CHAPTER 9 AN ASSIGNMENT FOR THE DISCIPLES.

Then He called His twelve disciples together and gave them power and authority over all demons, and to cure diseases. ²He sent them to preach the kingdom of God and to heal the sick. ³And He said to them, "Take nothing for the journey, neither staffs nor bag nor bread nor money; and do not have two tunics apiece.

⁴"Whatever house you enter, stay there, and from there depart. ⁵And whoever will not receive you, when you go out of that city, shake off the very dust from your feet as a testimony against them."

⁶So they departed and went through the towns, preaching the gospel and healing everywhere.

⁷Now Herod the tetrarch heard of all that was done by Him; and he was perplexed, because it was said by some that John had risen from the dead, ⁸and by some that Elijah had appeared, and by others that one of the old prophets had risen again. ⁹Herod said, "John I have beheaded, but who is this of whom I hear such things?" So he sought to see Him.

¹⁰And the apostles, when they had returned, told Him all that they had done. Then He took them and went aside privately into a deserted place belonging to the city called Bethsaida. ¹¹But when the multitudes knew *it,* they followed Him; and He received them and spoke to them about the kingdom of God, and healed those who had need of healing. ¹²When the day began to wear away, the twelve came and said to Him, "Send the multitude away, that they may go into the surrounding towns and country, and lodge and get provisions; for we are in a deserted place here."

¹³But He said to them, "You give them something to eat."

And they said, "We have no more than five loaves and two fish, unless we go and buy food for all these people." ¹⁴For there were about five thousand men.

Then He said to His disciples, "Make them sit down in groups of fifty." ¹⁵And they did so, and made them all sit down.

¹⁶Then He took the five loaves and the two fish, and looking up to heaven, He blessed and broke *them,* and gave *them* to the disciples to set before the multitude.

◼ RABBLE-ROUSER

9:7 People couldn't accept Jesus for who he was, so they tried to come up with other solutions. Many thought he was John the Baptist or another prophet come back to life. Some suggested he was Elijah, the great prophet who did not die but was taken to heaven in a whirlwind (2 Kings 2:1-11). Few found the correct answer, as Peter did (9:20). Many today find it no easier to accept Jesus as the fully human yet fully divine Son of God—they still are trying to find alternate explanations: he was a great prophet, a radical political leader, a self-deceived rabble-rouser. None of these explanations can account for Jesus' miracles or, especially, his glorious resurrection. In the end, the attempts to explain Jesus away are far more difficult to believe than the truth.

¹⁷So they all ate and were filled, and twelve baskets of the leftover fragments were taken up by them.

¹⁸And it happened, as He was alone praying, *that* His disciples joined Him, and He asked them, saying, "Who do the crowds say that I am?"

¹⁹So they answered and said, "John the Baptist, but some *say* Elijah; and others *say* that one of the old prophets has risen again."

²⁰He said to them, "But who do you say that I am?"

Peter answered and said, "The Christ of God."

²¹And He strictly warned and commanded them to tell this to no one, ²²saying, "The Son of Man must suffer many things, and be rejected by the elders and chief priests and scribes, and be killed, and be raised the third day."

²³Then He said to *them* all, "If anyone desires to come after Me, let him deny himself, and take up his cross daily, and follow Me. ²⁴For whoever desires to save his life will lose it, but whoever loses his life for My sake will save it. ²⁵For what profit is it to a man if he gains the whole world, and is himself destroyed or lost? ²⁶For whoever is ashamed of Me and My words, of him the Son of Man will be ashamed when He comes in His *own* glory, and *in His* Father's, and of the holy angels. ²⁷But I tell you truly, there are some standing here who shall not taste death till they see the kingdom of God."

²⁸Now it came to pass, about eight days after these sayings, that He took Peter, John, and James and went up on the mountain to pray. ²⁹As He prayed, the appearance

◼ ENDANGERED

9:24-25 If this life is most important to you, you will do everything you can to protect it. You will not want to do anything that might endanger your safety, health, or comfort. By contrast, if following Jesus is most important, you may find yourself in some very unsafe, unhealthy, and uncomfortable places. You will risk death, but you will not fear it because you know Jesus will raise you to eternal life. The person who is concerned only with this life has no such assurance. His earthly life may be longer, but it will most likely be marred by feelings of boredom and worthlessness.

of His face was altered, and His robe *became* white *and* glistening. ³⁰And behold, two men talked with Him, who were Moses and Elijah, ³¹who appeared in glory and spoke of His decease which He was about to accomplish at Jerusalem. ³²But Peter and those with him were heavy with sleep; and when they were fully awake, they saw His glory and the two men who stood with Him. ³³Then it happened, as they were parting from Him, *that* Peter said to Jesus, "Master, it is good for us to be here; and let us make three tabernacles: one for You, one for Moses, and one for Elijah"—not knowing what he said.

³⁴While he was saying this, a cloud came and overshadowed them; and they were fearful as they entered the cloud. ³⁵And a voice came out of the cloud, saying,

ENEMIES
The situation: Shannon is driving home from youth group on a stormy night. As she rounds a curve in the road, she sees someone walking along in the mud. It's Jenny. A hundred yards up the road, Shannon sees Jenny's car in the ditch.

Should she stop and help?

Maybe that seems like a stupid question, but consider . . .

The background:

Jenny's life is like a fairy tale . . . no exaggeration:

—Her family has some major bucks.

—She drives a brand new BMW convertible.

—She always looks like she just stepped off the cover of a fashion magazine.

—She dates a really handsome college sophomore.

—She makes straight A's.

—She has traveled all over the world.

As you might imagine, many people are jealous of Jenny's good fortune. Shannon is right there among them. But Shannon's feelings go beyond envy to include, shall we say, extreme dislike.

See, last year, Jenny made some really rude remarks about Shannon—behind her back. Then, two weeks later, she absolutely humiliated her at a big party—right in front of everyone! The two haven't spoken since, and when they're in the same room, everyone can feel the tension.

The solution:

Read Luke 10:25-37.

"This is My beloved Son. Hear Him!" ³⁶When the voice had ceased, Jesus was found alone. But they kept quiet, and told no one in those days any of the things they had seen.

³⁷Now it happened on the next day, when they had come down from the mountain, that a great multitude met Him. ³⁸Suddenly a man from the multitude cried out, saying, "Teacher, I implore You, look on my son, for he is my only child. ³⁹And behold, a spirit seizes him, and he suddenly cries out; it convulses him so that he foams *at the mouth;* and it departs from him with great difficulty, bruising him. ⁴⁰So I implored Your disciples to cast it out, but they could not."

⁴¹Then Jesus answered and said, "O faithless and perverse generation, how long shall I be with you and bear with you? Bring your son here." ⁴²And as he was still coming, the demon threw him down and convulsed *him.*

Then Jesus rebuked the unclean spirit, healed the child, and gave him back to his father.

⁴³And they were all amazed at the majesty of God.

But while everyone marveled at all the things which Jesus did, He said to His disciples, ⁴⁴"Let these words sink down into your ears, for the Son of Man is about to be betrayed into the hands of men." ⁴⁵But they did not understand this saying, and it was hidden from them so that they did not perceive it; and they were afraid to ask Him about this saying.

⁴⁶Then a dispute arose among them as to which of them would be greatest. ⁴⁷And Jesus, perceiving the thought of their heart, took a little child and set him by Him, ⁴⁸and said to them, "Whoever receives this little child in My name receives Me; and whoever receives Me receives Him who sent Me. For he who is least among you all will be great."

⁴⁹Now John answered and said, "Master, we saw someone casting out demons in Your name, and we forbade him because he does not follow with us."

⁵⁰But Jesus said to him, "Do not forbid *him,* for he who is not against us is on our side."

⁵¹Now it came to pass, when the time had come for Him to be received up, that He steadfastly set His face to go to Jerusalem, ⁵²and sent messengers before His face. And as they went, they entered a village of the Samaritans, to prepare for Him. ⁵³But they did not receive Him, because His face was *set* for the journey to Jerusalem. ⁵⁴And when His disciples James and John saw *this,* they said, "Lord, do You want us to command fire to come down from heaven and consume them, just as Elijah did?"

⁵⁵But He turned and rebuked them, and said, "You do not know what manner of spirit you are of. ⁵⁶For the Son of Man did not come to destroy men's lives but to save *them.*" And they went to another village.

⁵⁷Now it happened as they journeyed on the road, *that* someone said to Him, "Lord, I will follow You wherever You go."

⁵⁸And Jesus said to him, "Foxes have holes and birds of the air *have* nests, but the Son of Man has nowhere to lay *His* head."

⁵⁹Then He said to another, "Follow Me."

But he said, "Lord, let me first go and bury my father."

⁶⁰Jesus said to him, "Let the dead bury their own dead, but you go and preach the kingdom of God."

⁶¹And another also said, "Lord, I will follow You, but let me first go *and* bid them farewell who are at my house."

⁶²But Jesus said to him, "No one, having put his hand to the plow, and looking back, is fit for the kingdom of God."

MOUNTAINS

9:33 Peter, James, and John experienced a wonderful moment on the mountain, and they didn't want to leave. Sometimes we, too, have such an exciting experience we want to stay where we are—away from the reality and problems of our daily life. Knowing that struggles await us encourages us to retreat from reality. Yet staying on top of a mountain does not allow us to minister to others. Instead of becoming spiritual giants, we would soon become giants of self-centeredness. We need time of retreat and renewal, but only so we can return to minister to the world. Our faith must make sense off the mountain as well as on it.

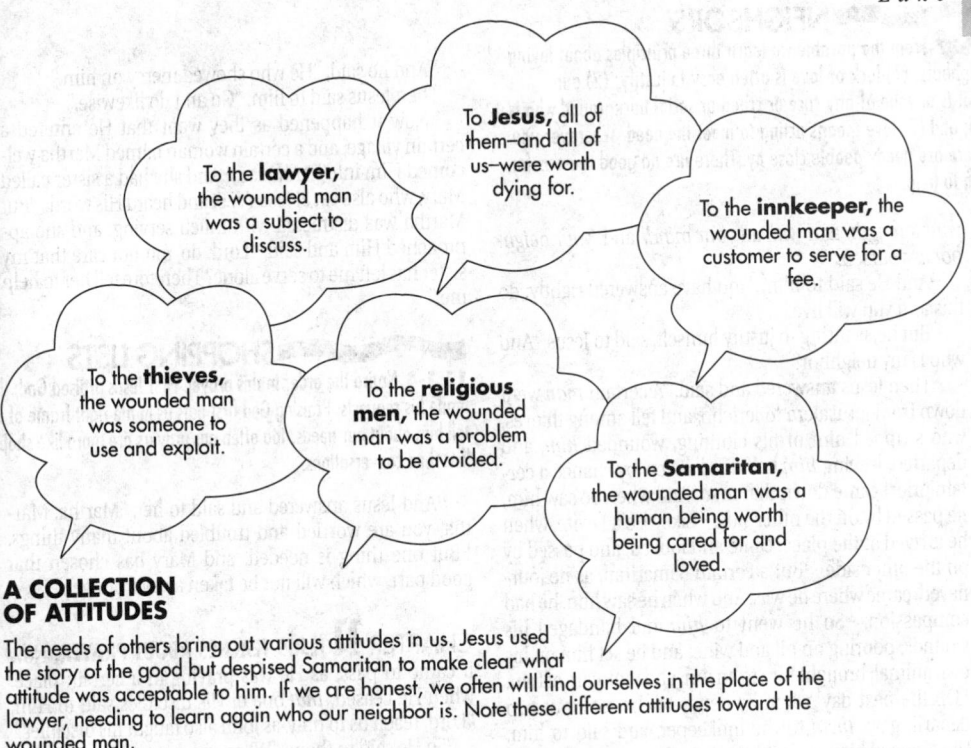

A COLLECTION OF ATTITUDES

The needs of others bring out various attitudes in us. Jesus used the story of the good but despised Samaritan to make clear what attitude was acceptable to him. If we are honest, we often will find ourselves in the place of the lawyer, needing to learn again who our neighbor is. Note these different attitudes toward the wounded man.

CHAPTER 10 JESUS SENDS OUT 70 MESSENGERS.

After these things the Lord appointed seventy others also, and sent them two by two before His face into every city and place where He Himself was about to go. ²Then He said to them, "The harvest truly *is* great, but the laborers *are* few; therefore pray the Lord of the harvest to send out laborers into His harvest. ³Go your way; behold, I send you out as lambs among wolves. ⁴Carry neither money bag, knapsack, nor sandals; and greet no one along the road. ⁵But whatever house you enter, first say, 'Peace to this house.' ⁶And if a son of peace is there, your peace will rest on it; if not, it will return to you. ⁷And remain in the same house, eating and drinking such things as they give, for the laborer is worthy of his wages. Do not go from house to house. ⁸Whatever city you enter, and they receive you, eat such things as are set before you. ⁹And heal the sick there, and say to them, 'The kingdom of God has come near to you.' ¹⁰But whatever city you enter, and they do not receive you, go out into its streets and say, ¹¹'The very dust of your city which clings to us we wipe off against you. Nevertheless know this, that the kingdom of God has come near you.' ¹²But I say to you that it will be more tolerable in that Day for Sodom than for that city.

¹³"Woe to you, Chorazin! Woe to you, Bethsaida! For if the mighty works which were done in you had been done in Tyre and Sidon, they would have repented long ago, sitting in sackcloth and ashes. ¹⁴But it will be more tolerable for Tyre and Sidon at the judgment than for you. ¹⁵And you, Capernaum, who are exalted to heaven, will be brought down to Hades. ¹⁶He who hears you hears Me, he who rejects you rejects Me, and he who rejects Me rejects Him who sent Me."

¹⁷Then the seventy returned with joy, saying, "Lord, even the demons are subject to us in Your name."

¹⁸And He said to them, "I saw Satan fall like lightning from heaven. ¹⁹Behold, I give you the authority to trample on serpents and scorpions, and over all the power of the enemy, and nothing shall by any means hurt you. ²⁰Nevertheless do not rejoice in this, that the spirits are subject to you, but rather rejoice because your names are written in heaven."

²¹In that hour Jesus rejoiced in the Spirit and said, "I thank You, Father, Lord of heaven and earth, that You have hidden these things from *the* wise and prudent and revealed them to babes. Even so, Father, for so it seemed good in Your sight. ²²All things have been delivered to Me by My Father, and no one knows who the Son is except the Father, and who the Father is except the Son, and *the one* to whom the Son wills to reveal *Him.*"

²³Then He turned to *His* disciples and said privately, "Blessed *are* the eyes which see the things you see; ²⁴for I tell you that many prophets and kings have desired to see what you see, and have not seen *it,* and to hear what you hear, and have not heard *it.*"

²⁵And behold, a certain lawyer stood up and tested Him, saying, "Teacher, what shall I do to inherit eternal life?"

²⁶He said to him, "What is written in the law? What is your reading *of it?*"

²⁷So he answered and said, " '*You shall love the* LORD *your God with all your heart, with all your soul, with all*

10:27-37 From the parable we learn three principles about loving our neighbors: (1) lack of love is often easy to justify; (2) our neighbor is anyone of any race or creed or social background who is in need; and (3) love means acting to meet the need. Wherever you live, there are needy people close by. There are no good reasons for refusing to help.

your strength, and with all your mind,' and *'your neighbor as yourself.'*"

²⁸And He said to him, "You have answered rightly; do this and you will live."

²⁹But he, wanting to justify himself, said to Jesus, "And who is my neighbor?"

³⁰Then Jesus answered and said: "A certain *man* went down from Jerusalem to Jericho, and fell among thieves, who stripped him of his clothing, wounded *him*, and departed, leaving *him* half dead. ³¹Now by chance a certain priest came down that road. And when he saw him, he passed by on the other side. ³²Likewise a Levite, when he arrived at the place, came and looked, and passed by on the other side. ³³But a certain Samaritan, as he journeyed, came where he was. And when he saw him, he had compassion. ³⁴So he went to *him* and bandaged his wounds, pouring on oil and wine; and he set him on his own animal, brought him to an inn, and took care of him. ³⁵On the next day, when he departed, he took out two denarii, gave *them* to the innkeeper, and said to him, 'Take care of him; and whatever more you spend, when I come again, I will repay you.' ³⁶So which of these three do you think was neighbor to him who fell among the thieves?"

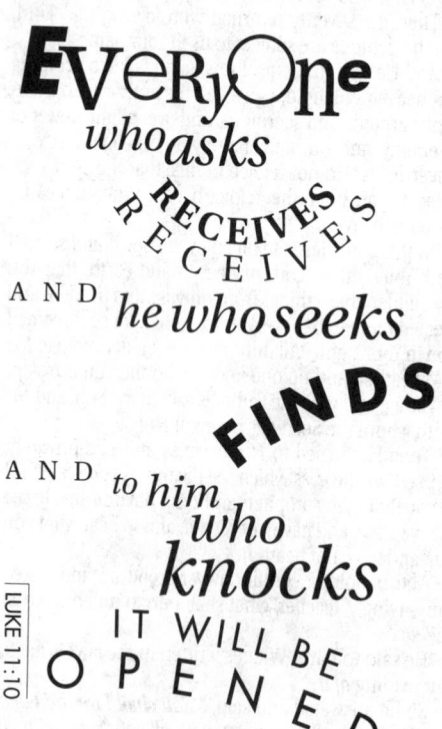

³⁷And he said, "He who showed mercy on him." Then Jesus said to him, "Go and do likewise."

³⁸Now it happened as they went that He entered a certain village; and a certain woman named Martha welcomed Him into her house. ³⁹And she had a sister called Mary, who also sat at Jesus' feet and heard His word. ⁴⁰But Martha was distracted with much serving, and she approached Him and said, "Lord, do You not care that my sister has left me to serve alone? Therefore tell her to help me."

SHOPPING LISTS

11:1-4 Notice the order in this prayer. First Jesus praised God; the made his requests. Praising God first puts us in the right frame of m tell him about our needs. Too often our prayers are more like shopp lists than conversations.

⁴¹And Jesus answered and said to her, "Martha, Martha, you are worried and troubled about many things. ⁴²But one thing is needed, and Mary has chosen that good part, which will not be taken away from her."

CHAPTER 11 JESUS TEACHES ABOUT PRAYER. Now it came to pass, as He was praying in a certain place, when He ceased, *that* one of His disciples said to Him, "Lord, teach us to pray, as John also taught his disciples."

²So He said to them, "When you pray, say:

Our Father in heaven,
Hallowed be Your name.
Your kingdom come.
Your will be done
On earth as *it is* in heaven.
³ Give us day by day our daily bread.
⁴ And forgive us our sins,
For we also forgive everyone who is indebted to us.
And do not lead us into temptation,
But deliver us from the evil one."

⁵And He said to them, "Which of you shall have a friend, and go to him at midnight and say to him, 'Friend, lend me three loaves; ⁶for a friend of mine has come to me on his journey, and I have nothing to set before him'; ⁷and he will answer from within and say, 'Do not trouble me; the door is now shut, and my children are with me in bed; I cannot rise and give to you'? ⁸I say to you, though he will not rise and give to him because he is his friend, yet because of his persistence he will rise and give him as many as he needs.

⁹"So I say to you, ask, and it will be given to you; seek, and you will find; knock, and it will be opened to you. ¹⁰For everyone who asks receives, and he who seeks finds, and to him who knocks it will be opened. ¹¹If a son asks for bread from any father among you, will he give him a stone? Or if *he asks* for a fish, will he give him a serpent instead of a fish? ¹²Or if he asks for an egg, will he offer him a scorpion? ¹³If you then, being evil, know how to give good gifts to your children, how much more will *your* heavenly Father give the Holy Spirit to those who ask Him!"

¹⁴And He was casting out a demon, and it was mute. So

it was, when the demon had gone out, that the mute spoke; and the multitudes marveled. ¹⁵But some of them said, "He casts out demons by Beelzebub, the ruler of the demons."

¹⁶Others, testing *Him*, sought from Him a sign from heaven. ¹⁷But He, knowing their thoughts, said to them: "Every kingdom divided against itself is brought to desolation, and a house *divided* against a house falls. ¹⁸If Satan also is divided against himself, how will his kingdom stand? Because you say I cast out demons by Beelzebub. ¹⁹And if I cast out demons by Beelzebub, by whom do your sons cast *them* out? Therefore they will be your judges. ²⁰But if I cast out demons with the finger of God, surely the kingdom of God has come upon you. ²¹When a strong man, fully armed, guards his own palace, his goods are in peace. ²²But when a stronger than he comes upon him and overcomes him, he takes from him all his armor in which he trusted, and divides his spoils. ²³He who is not with Me is against Me, and he who does not gather with Me scatters.

²⁴"When an unclean spirit goes out of a man, he goes through dry places, seeking rest; and finding none, he says, 'I will return to my house from which I came.' ²⁵And when he comes, he finds *it* swept and put in order. ²⁶Then he goes and takes with *him* seven other spirits more wicked than himself, and they enter and dwell there; and the last *state* of that man is worse than the first."

²⁷And it happened, as He spoke these things, that a certain woman from the crowd raised her voice and said to Him, "Blessed *is* the womb that bore You, and *the* breasts which nursed You!"

²⁸But He said, "More than that, blessed *are* those who hear the word of God and keep it!"

²⁹And while the crowds were thickly gathered together, He began to say, "This is an evil generation. It seeks a sign, and no sign will be given to it except the sign of Jonah the prophet. ³⁰For as Jonah became a sign to the Ninevites, so also the Son of Man will be to this generation. ³¹The queen of the South will rise up in the judgment with the men of this generation and condemn them, for she came from the ends of the earth to hear the wisdom of Solomon; and indeed a greater than Solomon *is* here. ³²The men of Nineveh will rise up in the judgment with this generation and condemn it, for they repented at the preaching of Jonah; and indeed a greater than Jonah *is* here.

³³"No one, when he has lit a lamp, puts *it* in a secret place or under a basket, but on a lampstand, that those who come in may see the light. ³⁴The lamp of the body is the eye. Therefore, when your eye is good, your whole body also is full of light. But when *your eye* is bad, your body also *is* full of darkness. ³⁵Therefore take heed that the light which is in you is not darkness. ³⁶If then your whole body *is* full of light, having no part dark, *the* whole *body* will be full of light, as when the bright shining of a lamp gives you light."

³⁷And as He spoke, a certain Pharisee asked Him to dine with him. So He went in and sat down to eat. ³⁸When the Pharisee saw *it*, he marveled that He had not first washed before dinner.

³⁹Then the Lord said to him, "Now you Pharisees make the outside of the cup and dish clean, but your inward part is full of greed and wickedness. ⁴⁰Foolish ones! Did not He who made the outside make the inside also? ⁴¹But rather give alms of such things as you have; then indeed all things are clean to you.

⁴²"But woe to you Pharisees! For you tithe the mint and

PRO JESUS

11:23 Jesus says, "He who is not with Me is against Me," while earlier he stated, "He who is not against us is on our side (9:50)." People who are neutral toward Christians are actually helping them more than hurting them because they are not setting up barriers. But while people can be neutral toward Christians, they cannot be neutral in their relationship with Jesus, or in the battle between Jesus and Satan. You can't be aloof or noncommittal, because there are only two sides. Since God has already won the battle, why be on the losing side? If you aren't actively for Christ, you are against him.

rue and all manner of herbs, and pass by justice and the love of God. These you ought to have done, without leaving the others undone. ⁴³Woe to you Pharisees! For you love the best seats in the synagogues and greetings in the marketplaces. ⁴⁴Woe to you, scribes and Pharisees, hypocrites! For you are like graves which are not seen, and the men who walk over *them* are not aware *of them*."

⁴⁵Then one of the lawyers answered and said to Him, "Teacher, by saying these things You reproach us also."

⁴⁶And He said, "Woe to you also, lawyers! For you load men with burdens hard to bear, and you yourselves do not touch the burdens with one of your fingers. ⁴⁷Woe to you! For you build the tombs of the prophets, and your fathers killed them. ⁴⁸In fact, you bear witness that you approve the deeds of your fathers; for they indeed killed them, and you build their tombs. ⁴⁹Therefore the wisdom of God also said, 'I will send them prophets and apostles, and *some* of them they will kill and persecute,' ⁵⁰that the blood of all the prophets which was shed from the foundation of the world may be required of this generation, ⁵¹from the blood of Abel to the blood of Zechariah who perished between the altar and the temple. Yes, I say to you, it shall be required of this generation.

⁵²"Woe to you lawyers! For you have taken away the key of knowledge. You did not enter in yourselves, and those who were entering in you hindered."

⁵³And as He said these things to them, the scribes and the Pharisees began to assail *Him* vehemently, and to cross-examine Him about many things, ⁵⁴lying in wait for Him, and seeking to catch Him in something He might say, that they might accuse Him.

MOTIVES

11:52 Jesus criticized the Pharisees harshly because they (1) washed their hands but not their hearts, (2) remembered to tithe but forgot justice, (3) loved people's praise, (4) made impossible religious demands, and (5) didn't accept the truth about Jesus and prevented others from believing it. They wrongly focused on outward appearances and ignored the condition of their hearts. We do the same when our service is motivated by a desire to be seen rather than from a pure heart and love for others. Others may be fooled, but God isn't. Don't be a Christian on the outside only. Bring your inner life under God's control; then your outer life will naturally reflect him.

CHAPTER 12 JESUS WARNS AGAINST HYPOCRISY.

In the meantime, when an innumerable multitude of people had gathered together, so that they trampled one another, He began to say to His disciples first *of all*, "Beware of the leaven of the Pharisees, which is hypocrisy. ²For there is nothing covered that will not be revealed, nor hidden that will not be known. ³Therefore whatever you have spoken in the dark will be heard in the light, and what you have spoken in the ear in inner rooms will be proclaimed on the housetops.

⁴"And I say to you, My friends, do not be afraid of those who kill the body, and after that have no more that they can do. ⁵But I will show you whom you should fear: Fear Him who, after He has killed, has power to cast into hell; yes, I say to you, fear Him!

◣ REAL VALUE

12:7 Our true value is God's estimate of our worth, not our peers'. Other people evaluate and categorize us according to how we perform, what we achieve, and how we look. But God's love gives us the real basis for our worth—we belong to him.

⁶"Are not five sparrows sold for two copper coins? And not one of them is forgotten before God. ⁷But the very hairs of your head are all numbered. Do not fear therefore; you are of more value than many sparrows.

⁸"Also I say to you, whoever confesses Me before men, him the Son of Man also will confess before the angels of God. ⁹But he who denies Me before men will be denied before the angels of God.

¹⁰"And anyone who speaks a word against the Son of Man, it will be forgiven him; but to him who blasphemes against the Holy Spirit, it will not be forgiven.

¹¹"Now when they bring you to the synagogues and magistrates and authorities, do not worry about how or what you should answer, or what you should say. ¹²For the Holy Spirit will teach you in that very hour what you ought to say."

¹³Then one from the crowd said to Him, "Teacher, tell my brother to divide the inheritance with me."

¹⁴But He said to him, "Man, who made Me a judge or an arbitrator over you?" ¹⁵And He said to them, "Take heed and beware of covetousness, for one's life does not consist in the abundance of the things he possesses."

¹⁶Then He spoke a parable to them, saying: "The ground of a certain rich man yielded plentifully. ¹⁷And he thought within himself, saying, 'What shall I do, since I have no room to store my crops?' ¹⁸So he said, 'I will do this: I will pull down my barns and build greater, and there I will store all my crops and my goods. ¹⁹And I will say to my soul, "Soul, you have many goods laid up for many years; take your ease; eat, drink, *and* be merry." ' ²⁰But God said to him, 'Fool! This night your soul will be required of you; then whose will those things be which you have provided?'

²¹"So *is* he who lays up treasure for himself, and is not rich toward God."

²²Then He said to His disciples, "Therefore I say to you, do not worry about your life, what you will eat; nor about the body, what you will put on. ²³Life is more than food, and the body *is more* than clothing. ²⁴Consider the ravens, for they neither sow nor reap, which have neither storehouse nor barn; and God feeds them. Of how much more value are you than the birds? ²⁵And which of you by worrying can add one cubit to his stature? ²⁶If you then are not able to do *the* least, why are you anxious for the rest? ²⁷Consider the lilies, how they grow: they neither toil nor spin; and yet I say to you, even Solomon in all his glory was not arrayed like one of these. ²⁸If then God so clothes the grass, which today is in the field and tomorrow is thrown into the oven, how much more *will He clothe* you, O *you* of little faith?

²⁹"And do not seek what you should eat or what you should drink, nor have an anxious mind. ³⁰For all these things the nations of the world seek after, and your Father knows that you need these things. ³¹But seek the kingdom of God, and all these things shall be added to you.

³²"Do not fear, little flock, for it is your Father's good pleasure to give you the kingdom. ³³Sell what you have and give alms; provide yourselves money bags which do not grow old, a treasure in the heavens that does not fail, where no thief approaches nor moth destroys. ³⁴For where your treasure is, there your heart will be also.

³⁵"Let your waist be girded and *your* lamps burning; ³⁶and you yourselves be like men who wait for their master, when he will return from the wedding, that when he comes and knocks they may open to him immediately. ³⁷Blessed *are* those servants whom the master, when he comes, will find watching. Assuredly, I say to you that he will gird himself and have them sit down *to eat*, and will come and serve them. ³⁸And if he should come in the second watch, or come in the third watch, and find *them* so, blessed are those servants. ³⁹But know this, that if the master of the house had known what hour the thief would come, he would have watched and not allowed his house to be broken into. ⁴⁰Therefore you also be ready, for the Son of Man is coming at an hour you do not expect."

⁴¹Then Peter said to Him, "Lord, do You speak this parable *only* to us, or to all *people?*"

⁴²And the Lord said, "Who then is that faithful and wise steward, whom *his* master will make ruler over his household, to give *them their* portion of food in due season? ⁴³Blessed *is* that servant whom his master will find so doing when he comes. ⁴⁴Truly, I say to you that he will make him ruler over all that he has. ⁴⁵But if that servant says in his heart, 'My master is delaying his coming,' and begins to beat the male and female servants, and to eat and drink and be drunk, ⁴⁶the master of that servant will come on a day when he is not looking for *him,* and at an hour when he is not aware, and will cut him in two and appoint *him* his portion with the unbe-

◣ LOYALTIES

12:51-53 In these strange and unsettling words, Jesus revealed that his coming often results in conflict. He demands a response, and close groups can be torn apart when some choose to follow him and others refuse to do so. There is no middle ground with Jesus. Loyalties must be declared and commitments made, sometimes to the severing of other relationships. Life is easiest when a family believes together in Christ, but this often does not happen. Are you willing to risk your family's disapproval to gain eternal life?

lievers. ⁴⁷And that servant who knew his master's will, and did not prepare *himself* or do according to his will, shall be beaten with many *stripes*. ⁴⁸But he who did not know, yet committed things deserving of stripes, shall be beaten with few. For everyone to whom much is given, from him much will be required; and to whom much has been committed, of him they will ask the more.

⁴⁹"I came to send fire on the earth, and how I wish it were already kindled! ⁵⁰But I have a baptism to be baptized with, and how distressed I am till it is accomplished! ⁵¹Do *you* suppose that I came to give peace on earth? I tell you, not at all, but rather division. ⁵²For from now on five in one house will be divided: three against two, and two against three. ⁵³Father will be divided against son and son against father, mother against daughter and daughter against mother, mother-in-law against her daughter-in-law and daughter-in-law against her mother-in-law."

⁵⁴Then He also said to the multitudes, "Whenever *you see* a cloud rising out of the west, immediately you say, 'A shower is coming'; and so it is. ⁵⁵And when you see the south wind blow, you say, 'There will be hot weather'; and there is. ⁵⁶Hypocrites! You can discern the face of the sky and of the earth, but how *is it* you do not discern this time?

⁵⁷"Yes, and why, even of yourselves, do you not judge what is right? ⁵⁸When you go with your adversary to the magistrate, make every effort along the way to settle with him, lest he drag you to the judge, the judge deliver you to the officer, and the officer throw you into prison. ⁵⁹I tell you, you shall not depart from there till you have paid the very last mite."

CHAPTER 13 JESUS TELLS THE PEOPLE TO REPENT.

There were present at that season some who told Him about the Galileans whose blood Pilate had mingled with their sacrifices. ²And Jesus answered and said to them, "Do you suppose that these Galileans were worse sinners than all *other* Galileans, because they suffered such things? ³I tell you, no; but unless you repent you will all likewise perish. ⁴Or those eighteen on whom the tower in Siloam fell and killed them, do you think that they were worse sinners than all *other* men who dwelt in Jerusalem? ⁵I tell you, no; but unless you repent you will all likewise perish."

⁶He also spoke this parable: "A certain *man* had a fig tree planted in his vineyard, and he came seeking fruit on it and found none. ⁷Then he said to the keeper of his vineyard, 'Look, for three years I have come seeking fruit on this fig tree and find none. Cut it down; why does it use up the ground?' ⁸But he answered and said to him, 'Sir, let it alone this year also, until I dig around it and fertilize *it*. ⁹And if it bears fruit, *well*. But if not, after that you can cut it down.'"

¹⁰Now He was teaching in one of the synagogues on the Sabbath. ¹¹And behold, there was a woman who had a spirit of infirmity eighteen years, and was bent over and could in no way raise *herself* up. ¹²But when Jesus saw her, He called *her* to *Him* and said to her, "Woman, you are loosed from your infirmity." ¹³And He laid *His* hands on her, and immediately she was made straight, and glorified God.

¹⁴But the ruler of the synagogue answered with indignation, because Jesus had healed on the Sabbath; and he said to the crowd, "There are six days on which men ought to work; therefore come and be healed on them, and not on the Sabbath day."

¹⁵The Lord then answered him and said, "Hypocrite! Does not each one of you on the Sabbath loose his ox or donkey from the stall, and lead *it* away to water it? ¹⁶So ought not this woman, being a daughter of Abraham, whom Satan has bound—think of it—for eighteen years, be loosed from this bond on the Sabbath?" ¹⁷And when He said these things, all His adversaries were put to shame; and all the multitude rejoiced for all the glorious things that were done by Him.

¹⁸Then He said, "What is the kingdom of God like? And to what shall I compare it? ¹⁹It is like a mustard seed, which a man took and put in his garden; and it grew and became a large tree, and the birds of the air nested in its branches."

²⁰And again He said, "To what shall I liken the kingdom of God? ²¹It is like leaven, which a woman took and hid in three measures of meal till it was all leavened."

²²And He went through the cities and villages, teaching, and journeying toward Jerusalem. ²³Then one said to Him, "Lord, are there few who are saved?"

And He said to them, ²⁴"Strive to enter through the narrow gate, for many, I say to you, will seek to enter and will not be able. ²⁵When once the Master of the house has risen up and shut the door, and you begin to stand outside and knock at the door, saying, 'Lord, Lord, open for us,' and He will answer and say to you, 'I do not know you, where you are from,' ²⁶then you will begin to say, 'We ate and drank in Your presence, and You taught in our streets.' ²⁷But He will say, 'I tell you I do not know you, where you are from. Depart from Me, all you workers of iniquity.' ²⁸There will be weeping and gnashing of teeth, when you see Abraham and Isaac and Jacob and all the prophets in the kingdom of God, and yourselves thrust out. ²⁹They will come from the east and the west, from the north and the south, and sit down in the kingdom of God. ³⁰And indeed there are last who will be first, and there are first who will be last."

SAVED

13:27 The people were eager to know who would be saved. Jesus explained that although many people know something about God, only a few have accepted his forgiveness. Just listening to his words or admiring his miracles is not enough—it is vital to turn from sin and trust in God to save us.

³¹On that very day some Pharisees came, saying to Him, "Get out and depart from here, for Herod wants to kill You."

³²And He said to them, "Go, tell that fox, 'Behold, I cast out demons and perform cures today and tomorrow, and the third *day* I shall be perfected.' ³³Nevertheless I must journey today, tomorrow, and the *day* following; for it cannot be that a prophet should perish outside of Jerusalem.

³⁴"O Jerusalem, Jerusalem, the one who kills the prophets and stones those who are sent to her! How

14:7-11 Jesus advised people not to rush for the best seats at a feast. People today are just as eager to raise their social status, whether by being with the right people, dressing for success, or driving the right car. Wanting a nice car or hoping to be successful in your career is not wrong in itself—it is wrong only when you want these things just to impress others. Whom do you try to impress? Don't aim for prestige; look for a place to serve. If God wants you to serve on a wider scale, he will invite you to take a higher place.

often I wanted to gather your children together, as a hen *gathers* her brood under *her* wings, but you were not willing! [35]See! Your house is left to you desolate; and assuredly, I say to you, you shall not see Me until *the time comes when you say, 'Blessed is He who comes in the name of the LORD!'"*

CHAPTER 14 HEALING ON THE SABBATH.

Now it happened, as He went into the house of one of the rulers of the Pharisees to eat bread on the Sabbath, that they watched Him closely. [2]And behold, there was a certain man before Him who had dropsy. [3]And Jesus, answering, spoke to the lawyers and Pharisees, saying, "Is it lawful to heal on the Sabbath?"

[4]But they kept silent. And He took *him* and healed him, and let him go. [5]Then He answered them, saying, "Which of you, having a donkey or an ox that has fallen into a pit, will not immediately pull him out on the Sabbath day?" [6]And they could not answer Him regarding these things.

[7]So He told a parable to those who were invited, when He noted how they chose the best places, saying to them: [8]"When you are invited by anyone to a wedding feast, do not sit down in the best place, lest one more honorable than you be invited by him; [9]and he who invited you and him come and say to you, 'Give place to this man,' and then you begin with shame to take the lowest place. [10]But when you are invited, go and sit down in the lowest place, so that when he who invited you comes he may say to you, 'Friend, go up higher.' Then you will have glory in the presence of those who sit at the table with you. [11]For whoever exalts himself will be humbled, and he who humbles himself will be exalted."

[12]Then He also said to him who invited Him, "When you give a dinner or a supper, do not ask your friends, your brothers, your relatives, nor rich neighbors, lest they also invite you back, and you be repaid. [13]But when you give a feast, invite *the* poor, *the* maimed, *the* lame, *the* blind. [14]And you will be blessed, because they cannot repay you; for you shall be repaid at the resurrection of the just."

[15]Now when one of those who sat at the table with Him heard these things, he said to Him, "Blessed *is* he who shall eat bread in the kingdom of God!"

[16]Then He said to him, "A certain man gave a great supper and invited many, [17]and sent his servant at supper time to say to those who were invited, 'Come, for all things are now ready.' [18]But they all with one *accord* began to make excuses. The first said to him, 'I have bought a piece of ground, and I must go and see it. I ask you to have me excused.' [19]And another said, 'I have bought five yoke of oxen, and I am going to test them. I ask you to

have me excused.' [20]Still another said, 'I have married a wife, and therefore I cannot come.' [21]So that servant came and reported these things to his master. Then the master of the house, being angry, said to his servant, 'Go out quickly into the streets and lanes of the city, and bring in here *the* poor and *the* maimed and *the* lame and *the* blind.' [22]And the servant said, 'Master, it is done as you commanded, and still there is room.' [23]Then the master said to the servant, 'Go out into the highways and hedges, and compel *them* to come in, that my house may be filled. [24]For I say to you that none of those men who were invited shall taste my supper.'"

[25]Now great multitudes went with Him. And He turned and said to them, [26]"If anyone comes to Me and does not hate his father and mother, wife and children, brothers and sisters, yes, and his own life also, he cannot be My disciple. [27]And whoever does not bear his cross and come after Me cannot be My disciple. [28]For which of you, intending to build a tower, does not sit down first and count the cost, whether he has *enough* to finish *it*— [29]lest, after he has laid the foundation, and is not able to finish, all who see *it* begin to mock him, [30]saying, 'This man began to build and was not able to finish.' [31]Or what king, going to make war against another king, does not sit down first and consider whether he is able with ten thousand to meet him who comes against him with twenty thousand? [32]Or else, while the other is still a great way off, he sends a delegation and asks conditions of peace. [33]So likewise, whoever of you does not forsake all that he has cannot be My disciple.

[34]"Salt *is* good; but if the salt has lost its flavor, how shall it be seasoned? [35]It is neither fit for the land nor for the dunghill, *but* men throw it out. He who has ears to hear, let him hear!"

CHAPTER 15 A STORY ABOUT A LOST SHEEP.

Then all the tax collectors and the sinners drew near to Him to hear Him. [2]And the Pharisees and scribes complained, saying, "This Man receives sinners and eats with them." [3]So He spoke this parable to them, saying:

[4]"What man of you, having a hundred sheep, if he loses one of them, does not leave the ninety-nine in the wilderness, and go after the one which is lost until he finds it? [5]And when he has found *it*, he lays *it* on his shoulders, rejoicing. [6]And when he comes home, he calls together *his* friends and neighbors, saying to them, 'Rejoice with me, for I have found my sheep which was lost!' [7]I say to you that likewise there will be more joy in heaven over one sinner who repents than over ninety-nine just persons who need no repentance.

14:34 Salt can lose its flavor. When it gets wet and then dries, nothing is left but a tasteless residue. Many Christians blend into the world to avoid the cost of standing for Christ. Jesus says if Christians lose their distinctive saltiness, they become worthless. Just as salt flavors and preserves food, we are to preserve the good in the world, keep it from spoiling, and bring new flavor to life. This requires planning, willing sacrifice, and unswerving commitment to Christ's kingdom. Being "salty" is not easy, but if a Christian fails in this function, he or she fails to represent Christ in the world. How salty are you?

8"Or what woman, having ten silver coins, if she loses one coin, does not light a lamp, sweep the house, and search carefully until she finds *it*? 9And when she has found *it*, she calls *her* friends and neighbors together, saying, 'Rejoice with me, for I have found the piece which I lost!' 10Likewise, I say to you, there is joy in the presence of the angels of God over one sinner who repents."

11Then He said: "A certain man had two sons. 12And the younger of them said to *his* father, 'Father, give me the portion of goods that falls *to me.*' So he divided to them *his* livelihood. 13And not many days after, the younger son gathered all together, journeyed to a far country, and there wasted his possessions with prodigal living. 14But when he had spent all, there arose a severe famine in that land, and he began to be in want. 15Then he went and joined himself to a citizen of that country, and he sent him into his fields to feed swine. 16And he would gladly have filled his stomach with the pods that the swine ate, and no one gave him *anything.*

17"But when he came to himself, he said, 'How many of my father's hired servants have bread enough and to spare, and I perish with hunger! 18I will arise and go to my father, and will say to him, "Father, I have sinned against heaven and before you, 19and I am no longer worthy to be called your son. Make me like one of your hired servants."'

20"And he arose and came to his father. But when he was still a great way off, his father saw him and had compassion, and ran and fell on his neck and kissed him. 21And the son said to him, 'Father, I have sinned against heaven and in your sight, and am no longer worthy to be called your son.'

22"But the father said to his servants, 'Bring out the best robe and put *it* on him, and put a ring on his hand and sandals on *his* feet. 23And bring the fatted calf here and kill *it*, and let us eat and be merry; 24for this my son was dead and is alive again; he was lost and is found.' And they began to be merry.

25"Now his older son was in the field. And as he came and drew near to the house, he heard music and dancing. 26So he called one of the servants and asked what these things meant. 27And he said to him, 'Your brother has come, and because he has received him safe and sound, your father has killed the fatted calf.' 28But he was angry and would not go in. Therefore his father came out and pleaded with him. 29So he answered and said to *his* father, 'Lo, these many years I have been serving you; I never transgressed your commandment at any time; and yet you never gave me a young goat, that I might make merry with my friends. 30But as soon as this son of yours

came, who has devoured your livelihood with harlots, you killed the fatted calf for him.'

31"And he said to him, 'Son, you are always with me, and all that I have is yours. 32It was right that we should make merry and be glad, for your brother was dead and is alive again, and was lost and is found.'"

OPPORTUNITY

15:30 In the story of the lost son, there is a contrast between the father's response and the older brother's reaction. The father was forgiving and overjoyed. The brother was unforgiving and bitter. The father forgave because he was joyful, and the son refused to forgive because he was bitter. The difference between bitterness and joy is our capacity to forgive. If you are refusing to forgive people, you are missing a wonderful opportunity of experiencing joy and sharing it with them.

CHAPTER **16** **A SHREWD MANAGER.** He also said to His disciples: "There was a certain rich man who had a steward, and an accusation was brought to him that this man was wasting his goods. 2So he called him and said to him, 'What is this I hear about you? Give an account of your stewardship, for you can no longer be steward.'

3"Then the steward said within himself, 'What shall I do? For my master is taking the stewardship away from me. I cannot dig; I am ashamed to beg. 4I have resolved

"Here's what I did..."

My mother and I had difficulty getting along. Often we would argue, sometimes over the stupidest things. After our fights, I'd feel real bad, but I didn't know what to do about it. I felt it was all her fault; she just didn't understand me; she was being totally unreasonable; etc.

Then I read in Luke 15:11-32 the parable about the lost son. And I began to realize that the younger son felt he had every right to take his inheritance and go off on his own. But it didn't get him anywhere, and finally he decided to go back home. His father gave him a big welcome and didn't say "I told you so" or anything like that.

I got to thinking about my own attitude with my mom. And I had to admit that I probably was at fault at least some of the time. Hard as it was, I had to apologize when I was wrong and ask forgiveness. (It was probably really hard for the lost son, too.)

I sat down and went over the past several arguments that weren't really resolved and wrote down the specifics on where I was wrong. Then I prayed hard that I could swallow my pride and go and ask my mom to forgi̶̶̶

I finally did. And my mom reacted very mu̶̶̶ ̶̶̶ was very forgiving. Since then, I've tried to co̶̶̶ attitude than on my mom's. And, amazingly, ̶̶̶ when we do argue, and I fall into the old patte̶̶̶ forgive me when I ask for it. (So does Mom—u̶̶̶

PAGE 990

16:18 Most religious leaders of Jesus' day permitted a man to divorce his wife for nearly any reason. Jesus' words about divorce went beyond Moses' (Deuteronomy 24:1-4). Stricter than any of the then-current schools of thought, they shocked his hearers (see Matthew 19:10) just as they shake today's readers. Jesus says in unmistakable terms that marriage is a lifetime commitment. As you think about marriage, remember that God intends it to be a permanent commitment.

what to do, that when I am put out of the stewardship, they may receive me into their houses.'

⁵"So he called every one of his master's debtors to *him,* and said to the first, 'How much do you owe my master?' ⁶And he said, 'A hundred measures of oil.' So he said to him, 'Take your bill, and sit down quickly and write fifty.' ⁷Then he said to another, 'And how much do you owe?' So he said, 'A hundred measures of wheat.' And he said to him, 'Take your bill, and write eighty.' ⁸So the master commended the unjust steward because he had dealt shrewdly. For the sons of this world are more shrewd in their generation than the sons of light.

⁹"And I say to you, make friends for yourselves by unrighteous mammon, that when you fail, they may receive you into an everlasting home. ¹⁰He who *is* faithful in *what is* least is faithful also in much; and he who is unjust in *what is* least is unjust also in much. ¹¹Therefore if you have not been faithful in the unrighteous mammon, who will commit to your trust the true *riches?* ¹²And if you have not been faithful in what is another man's, who will give you what is your own?

¹³"No servant can serve two masters; for either he will hate the one and love the other, or else he will be loyal to the one and despise the other. You cannot serve God and mammon."

¹⁴Now the Pharisees, who were lovers of money, also heard all these things, and they derided Him. ¹⁵And He said to them, "You are those who justify yourselves before men, but God knows your hearts. For what is highly esteemed among men is an abomination in the sight of God.

¹⁶"The law and the prophets *were* until John. Since that time the kingdom of God has been preached, and everyone is pressing into it. ¹⁷And it is easier for heaven and earth to pass away than for one tittle of the law to fail.

¹⁸"Whoever divorces his wife and marries another commits adultery; and whoever marries her who is divorced from *her* husband commits adultery.

¹⁹"There was a certain rich man who was clothed in purple and fine linen and fared sumptuously every day. ²⁰But there was a certain beggar named Lazarus, full of sores, who was laid at his gate, ²¹desiring to be fed with the crumbs which fell from the rich man's table. Moreover the dogs came and licked his sores. ²²So it was that the beggar died, and was carried by the angels to Abraham's bosom. The rich man also died and was buried. ²³And being in torments in Hades, he lifted up his eyes and saw Abraham afar off, and Lazarus in his bosom. ²⁴"Then he cried and said, 'Father Abraham, have mercy on me, and send Lazarus that he may dip the tip of his finger in water and cool my tongue; for I am tormented in this flame.' ²⁵But Abraham said, 'Son, remember that in your lifetime you received your good things, and likewise Lazarus evil things; but now he is comforted

and you are tormented. ²⁶And besides all this, between us and you there is a great gulf fixed, so that those who want to pass from here to you cannot, nor can those from there pass to us.'

²⁷"Then he said, 'I beg you therefore, father, that you would send him to my father's house, ²⁸for I have five brothers, that he may testify to them, lest they also come to this place of torment.' ²⁹Abraham said to him, 'They have Moses and the prophets; let them hear them.' ³⁰And he said, 'No, father Abraham; but if one goes to them from the dead, they will repent.' ³¹But he said to him, 'If they do not hear Moses and the prophets, neither will they be persuaded though one rise from the dead.'"

CHAPTER **17** **A STORY ABOUT A SERVANT.** Then He said to the disciples, "It is impossible that no offenses should come, but woe *to him* through whom they do come! ²It would be better for him if a millstone were hung around his neck, and he were thrown into the sea, than that he should offend one of these little ones. ³Take heed to yourselves. If your brother sins against you, rebuke him; and if he repents, forgive him. ⁴And if he sins against you seven times in a day, and seven times in a day returns to you, saying, 'I repent,' you shall forgive him."

⁵And the apostles said to the Lord, "Increase our faith."

⁶So the Lord said, "If you have faith as a mustard seed, you can say to this mulberry tree, 'Be pulled up by the roots and be planted in the sea,' and it would obey you. ⁷And which of you, having a servant plowing or tending sheep, will say to him when he has come in from the field, 'Come at once and sit down to eat'? ⁸But will he not rather say to him, 'Prepare something for my supper, and gird yourself and serve me till I have eaten and drunk, and afterward you will eat and drink'? ⁹Does he thank that servant because he did the things that were commanded him? I think not. ¹⁰So likewise you, when you have done all those things which you are commanded, say, 'We are unprofitable servants. We have done what was our duty to do.'"

¹¹Now it happened as He went to Jerusalem that He passed through the midst of Samaria and Galilee. ¹²Then as He entered a certain village, there met Him ten men who were lepers, who stood afar off. ¹³And they lifted up *their* voices and said, "Jesus, Master, have mercy on us!"

¹⁴So when He saw *them,* He said to them, "Go, show yourselves to the priests." And so it was that as they went, they were cleansed.

¹⁵And one of them, when he saw that he was healed, returned, and with a loud voice glorified God, ¹⁶and fell down on *his* face at His feet, giving Him thanks. And he was a Samaritan.

¹⁷So Jesus answered and said, "Were there not ten cleansed? But where *are* the nine? ¹⁸Were there not any

17:3-4 To rebuke does not mean to point out every sin we see; it means to bring sin to a person's attention with the purpose of restoring him or her to God and to fellow humans. When you feel you must rebuke another Christian for a sin, check your attitudes before opening your mouth. Do you love the person? Are you willing to forgive? Unless rebuke is tied to forgiveness, it will not help the sinning person.

found who returned to give glory to God except this foreigner?" ¹⁹And He said to him, "Arise, go your way. Your faith has made you well."

²⁰Now when He was asked by the Pharisees when the kingdom of God would come, He answered them and said, "The kingdom of God does not come with observation; ²¹nor will they say, 'See here!' or 'See there!' For indeed, the kingdom of God is within you."

²²Then He said to the disciples, "The days will come when you will desire to see one of the days of the Son of Man, and you will not see *it*. ²³And they will say to you, 'Look here!' or 'Look there!' Do not go after *them* or follow *them*. ²⁴For as the lightning that flashes out of one *part* under heaven shines to the other *part* under heaven, so also the Son of Man will be in His day. ²⁵But first He must suffer many things and be rejected by this generation. ²⁶And as it was in the days of Noah, so it will be also in the days of the Son of Man: ²⁷They ate, they drank, they married wives, they were given in marriage, until the day that Noah entered the ark, and the flood came and destroyed them all. ²⁸Likewise as it was also in the days of Lot: They ate, they drank, they bought, they sold, they planted, they built; ²⁹but on the day that Lot went out of Sodom it rained fire and brimstone from heaven and destroyed *them* all. ³⁰Even so will it be in the day when the Son of Man is revealed.

³¹"In that day, he who is on the housetop, and his goods *are* in the house, let him not come down to take them away. And likewise the one who is in the field, let him not turn back. ³²Remember Lot's wife. ³³Whoever seeks to save his life will lose it, and whoever loses his life will preserve it. ³⁴I tell you, in that night there will be two *men* in one bed: the one will be taken and the other will be left. ³⁵Two *women* will be grinding together: the one will be taken and the other left. ³⁶Two *men* will be in the field: the one will be taken and the other left."

³⁷And they answered and said to Him, "Where, Lord?"

So He said to them, "Wherever the body is, there the eagles will be gathered together."

CHAPTER **18** A STORY ABOUT A PERSISTENT WIDOW.

Then He spoke a parable to them, that men always ought to pray and not lose heart, ²saying: "There was in a certain city a judge who did not fear God nor regard man. ³Now there was a widow in that city; and she came to him, saying, 'Get justice for me from my adversary.' ⁴And he would not for a while; but afterward he said within himself, 'Though I do not fear God nor regard man, ⁵yet because this widow troubles me I will avenge her, lest by her continual coming she weary me.'"

⁶Then the Lord said, "Hear what the unjust judge said. ⁷And shall God not avenge His own elect who cry out day and night to Him, though He bears long with them? ⁸I tell you that He will avenge them speedily. Nevertheless, when the Son of Man comes, will He really find faith on the earth?"

⁹Also He spoke this parable to some who trusted in themselves that they were righteous, and despised others: ¹⁰"Two men went up to the temple to pray, one a Pharisee and the other a tax collector. ¹¹The Pharisee stood and prayed thus with himself, 'God, I thank You that I am not like other men—extortioners, unjust, adulterers, or even as this tax collector. ¹²I fast twice a week; I give tithes of all that I possess.' ¹³And the tax collector, standing afar off, would not so much as raise *his* eyes to heaven, but beat his breast, saying, 'God, be merciful to me a sinner!' ¹⁴I tell you, this man went down to his house justified *rather* than the other; for everyone who exalts himself will be humbled, and he who humbles himself will be exalted."

¹⁵Then they also brought infants to Him that He might touch them; but when the disciples saw *it*, they rebuked them. ¹⁶But Jesus called them to *Him* and said, "Let the little children come to Me, and do not forbid them; for of such is the kingdom of God. ¹⁷Assuredly, I say to you, whoever does not receive the kingdom of God as a little child will by no means enter it."

¹⁸Now a certain ruler asked Him, saying, "Good Teacher, what shall I do to inherit eternal life?"

I've always been taught to be independent and self-sufficient. My youth leader says this isn't right. What's wrong about being proud about doing your best?

I WONDER . . .

Have you ever known someone who thought he was so good in sports that he rarely listened to the coach? Although all coaches love to have players with great natural ability, most would settle for those with a few skills who are teachable. An athlete is much easier to mold than to motivate.

Being totally self-reliant is sort of like an athlete allowing the coach to give him advice only when he wants it. Before too long the athlete will start to deteriorate in talent and in the eyes of the coach. In the same way, we need to depend on God to lead us. And we should do what he says.

God wants us always to try to do our best. We should never do anything halfway. But there's a difference between doing our best and allowing God to do his best through us.

Taking the credit for everything we do is called pride—it's a dangerous thing. There is a good type of pride that comes from doing something well. Perhaps we've worked hard at something and everything has come out great. We feel good about ourselves, and that's OK. The problem comes when we take all the credit. That's the wrong kind of pride.

God wants us to recognize that he gave us our life and our talents. This shows humility and a deep respect for God.

The Pharisee in Luke 18:9-14 is a perfect example of someone with "bad pride." He was proud of his "holy" life. Although he acted like he was talking to God, he was really just talking to himself.

On the flip side is the tax collector. He had nothing to be proud of, especially as it related to his relationship with God. In humility, he asked God for mercy.

If we go through life with an I-can-make-it-OK-by-myself attitude, we're really saying to God, "I don't really need you after all." But God wants us to depend on him.

¹⁹So Jesus said to him, "Why do you call Me good? No one *is* good but One, *that is,* God. ²⁰You know the commandments: *'Do not commit adultery,' 'Do not murder,' 'Do not steal,' 'Do not bear false witness,' 'Honor your father and your mother.'* "

²¹And he said, "All these things I have kept from my youth."

²²So when Jesus heard these things, He said to him, "You still lack one thing. Sell all that you have and distribute to the poor, and you will have treasure in heaven; and come, follow Me."

²³But when he heard this, he became very sorrowful, for he was very rich.

CHILDREN

18:15-17 It was customary for a mother to bring her children to a rabbi for a blessing, and that is why these mothers gathered about Jesus. The disciples, however, thought the children were unworthy of the Master's time—less important than whatever else he was doing. But Jesus welcomed them because little children have the kind of faith and trust needed to enter God's kingdom. It is important to approach God with childlike attitudes of acceptance, faith, and trust.

²⁴And when Jesus saw that he became very sorrowful, He said, "How hard it is for those who have riches to enter the kingdom of God! ²⁵For it is easier for a camel to go through the eye of a needle than for a rich man to enter the kingdom of God."

²⁶And those who heard it said, "Who then can be saved?"

²⁷But He said, "The things which are impossible with men are possible with God."

²⁸Then Peter said, "See, we have left all and followed You."

²⁹So He said to them, "Assuredly, I say to you, there is no one who has left house or parents or brothers or wife or children, for the sake of the kingdom of God, ³⁰who shall not receive many times more in this present time, and in the age to come eternal life."

³¹Then He took the twelve aside and said to them, "Behold, we are going up to Jerusalem, and all things that are written by the prophets concerning the Son of Man will be accomplished. ³²For He will be delivered to the Gentiles and will be mocked and insulted and spit upon. ³³They will scourge *Him* and kill Him. And the third day He will rise again."

³⁴But they understood none of these things; this saying was hidden from them, and they did not know the things which were spoken.

³⁵Then it happened, as He was coming near Jericho, that a certain blind man sat by the road begging. ³⁶And hearing a multitude passing by, he asked what it meant. ³⁷So they told him that Jesus of Nazareth was passing by. ³⁸And he cried out, saying, "Jesus, Son of David, have mercy on me!"

³⁹Then those who went before warned him that he should be quiet; but he cried out all the more, "Son of David, have mercy on me!"

⁴⁰So Jesus stood still and commanded him to be

GIVE UP

18:26-30 Peter and the other disciples had paid a high price—leaving their homes and jobs—to follow Jesus. But Jesus reminded Peter that following him has its benefits as well as its sac[rifices.] Any believer who has had to give up something to follow Christ will [be] paid back in this life as well as in the next. If you give up friends, y[ou] find that God offers a secure relationship with himself now and fore[ver.] you give up your family's approval, you will gain the love of the fa[mily] of God. Don't dwell on what you have given up; think about what y[ou] have gained and give thanks for it. You can never outgive God.

brought to Him. And when he had come near, He asked him, ⁴¹saying, "What do you want Me to do for you?"

He said, "Lord, that I may receive my sight."

⁴²Then Jesus said to him, "Receive your sight; your faith has made you well." ⁴³And immediately he received his sight, and followed Him, glorifying God. And all the people, when they saw *it,* gave praise to God.

CHAPTER 19 JESUS GIVES ZACCHAEUS A NEW LIFE.

Then *Jesus* entered and passed through Jericho. ²Now behold, *there was* a man named Zacchaeus who was a chief tax collector, and he was rich. ³And he sought to see who Jesus was, but could not because of the crowd, for he was of short stature. ⁴So he ran ahead and climbed up into a sycamore tree to see Him, for He was going to pass that *way.* ⁵And when Jesus came to the place, He looked up and saw him, and said to him, "Zacchaeus, make haste and come down, for today I must stay at your house." ⁶So he made haste and came down, and received Him joyfully. ⁷But when they saw *it,* they all complained, saying, "He has gone to be a guest with a man who is a sinner."

⁸Then Zacchaeus stood and said to the Lord, "Look, Lord, I give half of my goods to the poor; and if I have taken anything from anyone by false accusation, I restore fourfold."

⁹And Jesus said to him, "Today salvation has come to this house, because he also is a son of Abraham; ¹⁰for the Son of Man has come to seek and to save that which was lost."

¹¹Now as they heard these things, He spoke another parable, because He was near Jerusalem and because they thought the kingdom of God would appear immediately. ¹²Therefore He said: "A certain nobleman went into a far country to receive for himself a kingdom and to return. ¹³So he called ten of his servants, delivered to them ten minas, and said to them, 'Do business till I come.' ¹⁴But his citizens hated him, and sent a delegation after him, saying, 'We will not have this *man* to reign over us.'

¹⁵"And so it was that when he returned, having received the kingdom, he then commanded these servants, to whom he had given the money, to be called to him, that he

UNPOPULAR

19:1-10 Tax collectors were among the most unpopular people in I[srael.] Jews by birth who chose to work for Rome were considered traitors. Besides, it was common knowledge that tax collectors made themselv[es] rich by gouging their fellow Jews. No wonder the crowds were displeas[ed] when Jesus went home with the tax collector Zacchaeus. But despite th[e] fact that Zacchaeus was both dishonest and a turncoat, Jesus loved him—and in response, the little tax collector was converted. In every society, certain groups of people are considered "untouchable" becaus[e of] their politics, immoral behavior, or life-style. We should not avoid thes[e] people. Jesus loves them, and they need to hear his Good News.

might know how much every man had gained by trading. ¹⁶Then came the first, saying, 'Master, your mina has earned ten minas.' ¹⁷And he said to him, 'Well *done,* good servant; because you were faithful in a very little, have authority over ten cities.' ¹⁸And the second came, saying, 'Master, your mina has earned five minas.' ¹⁹Likewise he said to him, 'You also be over five cities.'

²⁰"Then another came, saying, 'Master, here is your mina, which I have kept put away in a handkerchief. ²¹For I feared you, because you are an austere man. You collect what you did not deposit, and reap what you did not sow.' ²²And he said to him, 'Out of your own mouth I will judge you, *you* wicked servant. You knew that I was an austere man, collecting what I did not deposit and reaping what I did not sow. ²³Why then did you not put my money in the bank, that at my coming I might have collected it with interest?'

²⁴"And he said to those who stood by, 'Take the mina from him, and give *it* to him who has ten minas.' ²⁵(But they said to him, 'Master, he has ten minas.') ²⁶'For I say to you, that to everyone who has will be given; and from him who does not have, even what he has will be taken away from him. ²⁷But bring here those enemies of mine, who did not want me to reign over them, and slay *them* before me.'"

²⁸When He had said this, He went on ahead, going up to Jerusalem. ²⁹And it came to pass, when He drew near to Bethphage and Bethany, at the mountain called Olivet, *that* He sent two of His disciples, ³⁰saying, "Go into the village opposite *you,* where as you enter you will find a colt tied, on which no one has ever sat. Loose it and bring *it here.* ³¹And if anyone asks you, 'Why are you loosing *it?*' thus you shall say to him, 'Because the Lord has need of it.'"

³²So those who were sent went their way and found *it* just as He had said to them. ³³But as they were loosing the colt, the owners of it said to them, "Why are you loosing the colt?"

³⁴And they said, "The Lord has need of him." ³⁵Then they brought him to Jesus. And they threw their own clothes on the colt, and they set Jesus on him. ³⁶And as He went, *many* spread their clothes on the road.

³⁷Then, as He was now drawing near the descent of the Mount of Olives, the whole multitude of the disciples began to rejoice and praise God with a loud voice for all the mighty works they had seen, ³⁸saying:

" 'Blessed is the King who comes in the name of the
    LORD!'
Peace in heaven and glory in the highest!"

³⁹And some of the Pharisees called to Him from the crowd, "Teacher, rebuke Your disciples."

⁴⁰But He answered and said to them, "I tell you that if these should keep silent, the stones would immediately cry out."

⁴¹Now as He drew near, He saw the city and wept over it, ⁴²saying, "If you had known, even you, especially in this your day, the things *that make* for your peace! But now they are hidden from your eyes. ⁴³For days will come upon you when your enemies will build an embankment around you, surround you and close you in on every side, ⁴⁴and level you, and your children within you, to the

ground; and they will not leave in you one stone upon another, because you did not know the time of your visitation."

⁴⁵Then He went into the temple and began to drive out those who bought and sold in it, ⁴⁶saying to them, "It is written, *'My house is a house of prayer,'* but you have made it a *'den of thieves.'* "

⁴⁷And He was teaching daily in the temple. But the chief priests, the scribes, and the leaders of the people sought to destroy Him, ⁴⁸and were unable to do anything; for all the people were very attentive to hear Him.

CHAPTER **20** LEADERS CHALLENGE JESUS' AUTHORITY.

Now it happened on one of those days, as He taught the people in the temple and preached the gospel, *that* the chief priests and the scribes, together with the elders, confronted *Him* ²and spoke to Him, saying, "Tell us, by what authority are You doing these things? Or who is he who gave You this authority?"

³But He answered and said to them, "I also will ask you one thing, and answer Me: ⁴The baptism of John—was it from heaven or from men?"

⁵And they reasoned among themselves, saying, "If we say, 'From heaven,' He will say, 'Why then did you not believe him?' ⁶But if we say, 'From men,' all the people will stone us, for they are persuaded that John was a prophet." ⁷So they answered that they did not know where *it was* from.

⁸And Jesus said to them, "Neither will I tell you by what authority I do these things."

⁹Then He began to tell the people this parable: "A certain man planted a vineyard, leased it to vinedressers, and went into a far country for a long time. ¹⁰Now at vintage-time he sent a servant to the vinedressers, that they might give him some of the fruit of the vineyard. But the vinedressers beat him and sent *him* away empty-handed. ¹¹Again he sent another servant; and they beat him also, treated *him* shamefully, and sent *him* away empty-handed. ¹²And again he sent a third; and they wounded him also and cast *him* out.

¹³"Then the owner of the vineyard said, 'What shall I do? I will send my beloved son. Probably they will respect *him* when they see him.' ¹⁴But when the vinedressers saw him, they reasoned among themselves, saying, 'This is the heir. Come, let us kill him, that the inheritance may be ours.' ¹⁵So they cast him out of the vineyard and killed *him.* Therefore what will the owner of the vineyard do to them? ¹⁶He will come and destroy those vinedressers and give the vineyard to others."

And when they heard *it* they said, "Certainly not!"

¹⁷Then He looked at them and said, "What then is this that is written:

'The stone which the builders rejected
Has become the chief cornerstone'?

¹⁸Whoever falls on that stone will be broken; but on whomever it falls, it will grind him to powder."

¹⁹And the chief priests and the scribes that very hour sought to lay hands on Him, but they feared the people— for they knew He had spoken this parable against them.

²⁰So they watched *Him*, and sent spies who pretended to be righteous, that they might seize on His words, in order to deliver Him to the power and the authority of the governor. ²¹Then they asked Him, saying, "Teacher, we know that You say and teach rightly, and You do not show personal favoritism, but teach the way of God in truth: ²²Is it lawful for us to pay taxes to Caesar or not?"

²³But He perceived their craftiness, and said to them,

GIVING

The hot topic at school is what Kyla Whitfield will do with the huge inheritance she's getting as a result of her grandfather's death last week.

"How much do you think she'll end up getting?"

"Well, everyone says old man Whitfield was worth at least nine million dollars."

"Kyla gets it all?"

"No, I think they have to split it four ways."

"Oh my gosh! That's over two million dollars!"

"Well, she'll have to pay inheritance taxes on it first."

"But she'll still be a millionaire!"

"That's right."

"Oh, man! What I would do if I had a million dollars!"

"What would you do?"

"Spend most of it."

"On what?"

"I don't know . . . cars, a ski boat, whatever I wanted."

"What about giving?"

"What about it?"

"Would you give any of it away? You know, to other people, to your church, to charity?"

"Are you serious?"

That's a common response to the suggestion of giving. Unfortunately, even many Christians are that way.

What about you? Do you regularly give part of your money back to God? If not, why not? (By the way: "I will when I'm rich like Kyla" is a lousy excuse! See Luke 21:1-4.)

"Why do you test Me? ²⁴Show Me a denarius. Whose image and inscription does it have?"

They answered and said, "Caesar's."

²⁵And He said to them, "Render therefore to Caesar the things that are Caesar's, and to God the things that are God's."

²⁶But they could not catch Him in His words in the presence of the people. And they marveled at His answer and kept silent.

²⁷Then some of the Sadducees, who deny that there is a resurrection, came to *Him* and asked Him, ²⁸saying: "Teacher, Moses wrote to us *that* if a man's brother dies, having a wife, and he dies without children, his brother should take his wife and raise up offspring for his brother. ²⁹Now there were seven brothers. And the first took a wife, and died without children. ³⁰And the second took her as wife, and he died childless. ³¹Then the third took her, and in like manner the seven also; and they left

DUTY

20:20-26 Jesus turned his enemies' attempt to trap him into a powerful lesson: God's followers have legitimate obligations to both and the government. But what is important is to keep our priorities straight. When the two authorities conflict, our duty to God always c· before our duty to the government.

no children, and died. ³²Last of all the woman died also. ³³Therefore, in the resurrection, whose wife does she become? For all seven had her as wife."

³⁴Jesus answered and said to them, "The sons of this age marry and are given in marriage. ³⁵But those who are counted worthy to attain that age, and the resurrection from the dead, neither marry nor are given in marriage; ³⁶nor can they die anymore, for they are equal to the angels and are sons of God, being sons of the resurrection. ³⁷But even Moses showed in the *burning* bush *passage* that the dead are raised, when he called the Lord *'the God of Abraham, the God of Isaac, and the God of Jacob.'* ³⁸For He is not the God of the dead but of the living, for all live to Him."

³⁹Then some of the scribes answered and said, "Teacher, You have spoken well." ⁴⁰But after that they dared not question Him anymore.

⁴¹And He said to them, "How can they say that the Christ is the Son of David? ⁴²Now David himself said in the Book of Psalms:

'The LORD said to my Lord,
"Sit at My right hand,
⁴³   Till I make Your enemies Your footstool." '

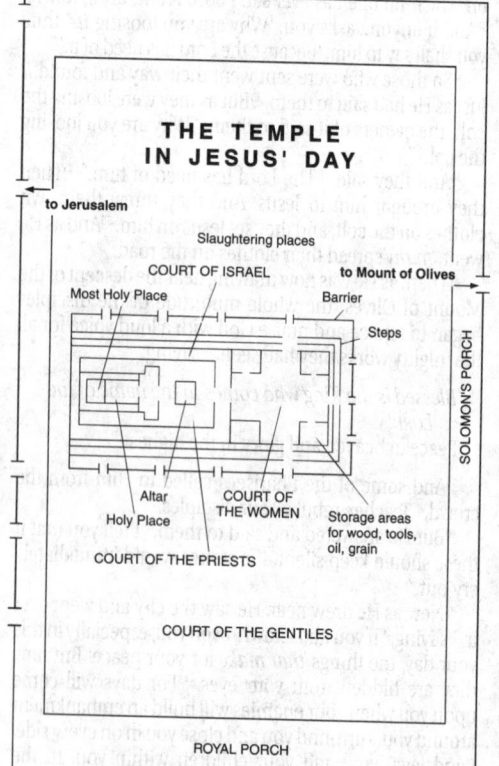

THE TEMPLE IN JESUS' DAY

to Jerusalem

Slaughtering places

COURT OF ISRAEL

to Mount of Olives

Most Holy Place

Barrier

Steps

SOLOMON'S PORCH

Altar

Holy Place

COURT OF THE WOMEN

Storage areas for wood, tools, oil, grain

COURT OF THE PRIESTS

COURT OF THE GENTILES

ROYAL PORCH

⁴⁴Therefore David calls Him *'Lord'*; how is He then his Son?"

⁴⁵Then, in the hearing of all the people, He said to His disciples, ⁴⁶"Beware of the scribes, who desire to go around in long robes, love greetings in the marketplaces, the best seats in the synagogues, and the best places at feasts, ⁴⁷who devour widows' houses, and for a pretense make long prayers. These will receive greater condemnation."

CHAPTER 21 THE WIDOW'S SMALL COINS.

And He looked up and saw the rich putting their gifts into the treasury, ²and He saw also a certain poor widow putting in two mites. ³So He said, "Truly I say to you that this poor widow has put in more than all; ⁴for all these out of their abundance have put in offerings for God, but she out of her poverty put in all the livelihood that she had."

⁵Then, as some spoke of the temple, how it was adorned with beautiful stones and donations, He said, ⁶"These things which you see—the days will come in which not *one* stone shall be left upon another that shall not be thrown down."

⁷So they asked Him, saying, "Teacher, but when will these things be? And what sign *will there be* when these things are about to take place?"

⁸And He said: "Take heed that you not be deceived. For many will come in My name, saying, 'I am *He,*' and, 'The time has drawn near.' Therefore do not go after them. ⁹But when you hear of wars and commotions, do not be terrified; for these things must come to pass first, but the end *will not come* immediately."

¹⁰Then He said to them, "Nation will rise against nation, and kingdom against kingdom. ¹¹And there will be great earthquakes in various places, and famines and pestilences; and there will be fearful sights and great signs from heaven. ¹²But before all these things, they will lay their hands on you and persecute *you,* delivering *you* up to the synagogues and prisons. You will be brought before kings and rulers for My name's sake. ¹³But it will turn out for you as an occasion for testimony. ¹⁴Therefore settle *it* in your hearts not to meditate beforehand on what you will answer; ¹⁵for I will give you a mouth and wisdom which all your adversaries will not be able to contradict or resist. ¹⁶You will be betrayed even by parents and brothers, relatives and friends; and they will put *some* of you to death. ¹⁷And you will be hated by all for My name's sake. ¹⁸But not a hair of your head shall be lost. ¹⁹By your patience possess your souls.

²⁰"But when you see Jerusalem surrounded by armies, then know that its desolation is near. ²¹Then let those who are in Judea flee to the mountains, let those who are in the midst of her depart, and let not those who are in the country enter her. ²²For these are the days of vengeance, that all things which are written may be fulfilled. ²³But woe to those who are pregnant and to those who are nursing babies in those days! For there will be great distress in the land and wrath upon this people. ²⁴And they will fall by the edge of the sword, and be led away captive into all nations. And Jerusalem will be trampled by Gentiles until the times of the Gentiles are fulfilled.

²⁵"And there will be signs in the sun, in the moon, and in the stars; and on the earth distress of nations, with perplexity, the sea and the waves roaring; ²⁶men's hearts failing them from fear and the expectation of those things which are coming on the earth, for the powers of the heavens will be shaken. ²⁷Then they will see the Son

THE TEMPLE

21:5 The temple the disciples were admiring was not Solomon's temple. That was destroyed by the Babylonians in the sixth century B.C. This temple was built by Zerubbabel after the return from exile in the sixth century B.C. It was a beautiful, imposing structure with a significant history, but Jesus said it would be completely destroyed. This happened in A.D. 70, when a Roman army burned Jerusalem. Now, as then, we can be sure of this: if God says something will happen, it will indeed take place!

of Man coming in a cloud with power and great glory. ²⁸Now when these things begin to happen, look up and lift up your heads, because your redemption draws near."

²⁹Then He spoke to them a parable: "Look at the fig tree, and all the trees. ³⁰When they are already budding, you see and know for yourselves that summer is now near. ³¹So you also, when you see these things happening, know that the kingdom of God is near. ³²Assuredly, I say to you, this generation will by no means pass away till all things take place. ³³Heaven and earth will pass away, but My words will by no means pass away.

³⁴"But take heed to yourselves, lest your hearts be weighed down with carousing, drunkenness, and cares of this life, and that Day come on you unexpectedly. ³⁵For it will come as a snare on all those who dwell on the face of the whole earth. ³⁶Watch therefore, and pray always that you may be counted worthy to escape all these things that will come to pass, and to stand before the Son of Man."

³⁷And in the daytime He was teaching in the temple, but at night He went out and stayed on the mountain called Olivet. ³⁸Then early in the morning all the people came to Him in the temple to hear Him.

CHAPTER 22 A PLAN TO KILL JESUS.

Now the Feast of Unleavened Bread drew near, which is called Passover. ²And the chief priests and the scribes sought how they might kill Him, for they feared the people.

³Then Satan entered Judas, surnamed Iscariot, who was numbered among the twelve. ⁴So he went his way and conferred with the chief priests and captains, how he might betray Him to them. ⁵And they were glad, and agreed to give him money. ⁶So he promised and sought opportunity to betray Him to them in the absence of the multitude.

⁷Then came the Day of Unleavened Bread, when the Passover must be killed. ⁸And He sent Peter and John,

BETRAYED

21:14-19 Jesus warned that in the coming persecutions his followers would be betrayed by their family members and friends. Christians of every age have had to face this possibility. It is reassuring to know that even when we feel completely abandoned, the Holy Spirit stays with us. He will comfort us, protect us, and give us the words we need. This assurance can give us the courage and hope to stand firm for Christ through all the difficult situations we face.

WRAPPED UP

22:24 The most important event in human history was about to take place, but the disciples were still arguing about their prestige in the kingdom! Looking back, we say, "This was no time to worry about status." But the disciples, wrapped up in their own concerns, did not perceive what Jesus had been trying to tell them about his approaching death and resurrection. What are your major concerns today? Twenty years from now will these worries look petty and inappropriate? Get your eyes off yourself and look for signs of the kingdom of God that is about to break into human history for the second time.

saying, "Go and prepare the Passover for us, that we may eat."

⁹So they said to Him, "Where do You want us to prepare?"

¹⁰And He said to them, "Behold, when you have entered the city, a man will meet you carrying a pitcher of water; follow him into the house which he enters. ¹¹Then you shall say to the master of the house, 'The Teacher says to you, "Where is the guest room where I may eat the Passover with My disciples?" ' ¹²Then he will show you a large, furnished upper room; there make ready."

¹³So they went and found it just as He had said to them, and they prepared the Passover.

¹⁴When the hour had come, He sat down, and the twelve apostles with Him. ¹⁵Then He said to them, "With *fervent* desire I have desired to eat this Passover with you before I suffer; ¹⁶for I say to you, I will no longer eat of it until it is fulfilled in the kingdom of God."

¹⁷Then He took the cup, and gave thanks, and said, "Take this and divide *it* among yourselves; ¹⁸for I say to you, I will not drink of the fruit of the vine until the kingdom of God comes."

¹⁹And He took bread, gave thanks and broke *it*, and gave *it* to them, saying, "This is My body which is given for you; do this in remembrance of Me."

²⁰Likewise He also *took* the cup after supper, saying, "This cup *is* the new covenant in My blood, which is shed for you. ²¹But behold, the hand of My betrayer *is* with Me on the table. ²²And truly the Son of Man goes as it has been determined, but woe to that man by whom He is betrayed!"

²³Then they began to question among themselves, which of them it was who would do this thing.

²⁴Now there was also a dispute among them, as to which of them should be considered the greatest. ²⁵And He said to them, "The kings of the Gentiles exercise lordship over them, and those who exercise authority over them are called 'benefactors.' ²⁶But not so *among* you; on the contrary, he who is greatest among you, let him be as the younger, and he who governs as he who serves. ²⁷For who *is* greater, he who sits at the table, or he who serves? *Is* it not he who sits at the table? Yet I am among you as the One who serves.

²⁸"But you are those who have continued with Me in My trials. ²⁹And I bestow upon you a kingdom, just as My Father bestowed *one* upon Me, ³⁰that you may eat and drink at My table in My kingdom, and sit on thrones judging the twelve tribes of Israel."

³¹And the Lord said, "Simon, Simon! Indeed, Satan has asked for you, that he may sift *you* as wheat. ³²But I have prayed for you, that your faith should not fail; and when you have returned to *Me*, strengthen your brethren."

³³But he said to Him, "Lord, I am ready to go with You, both to prison and to death."

³⁴Then He said, "I tell you, Peter, the rooster shall not crow this day before you will deny three times that you know Me."

³⁵And He said to them, "When I sent you without money bag, knapsack, and sandals, did you lack anything?"

So they said, "Nothing."

³⁶Then He said to them, "But now, he who has a money bag, let him take *it*, and likewise a knapsack; and he who has no sword, let him sell his garment and buy one. ³⁷For I say to you that this which is written must still be accomplished in Me: '*And He was numbered with the transgressors.*' For the things concerning Me have an end."

³⁸So they said, "Lord, look, here *are* two swords."

And He said to them, "It is enough."

³⁹Coming out, He went to the Mount of Olives, as He was accustomed, and His disciples also followed Him. ⁴⁰When He came to the place, He said to them, "Pray that you may not enter into temptation."

⁴¹And He was withdrawn from them about a stone's throw, and He knelt down and prayed, ⁴²saying, "Father, if it is Your will, take this cup away from Me; nevertheless not My will, but Yours, be done." ⁴³Then an angel appeared to Him from heaven, strengthening Him. ⁴⁴And being in agony, He prayed more earnestly. Then His sweat became like great drops of blood falling down to the ground.

⁴⁵When He rose up from prayer, and had come to His disciples, He found them sleeping from sorrow. ⁴⁶Then He said to them, "Why do you sleep? Rise and pray, lest you enter into temptation."

⁴⁷And while He was still speaking, behold, a multitude; and he who was called Judas, one of the twelve, went before them and drew near to Jesus to kiss Him. ⁴⁸But Jesus said to him, "Judas, are you betraying the Son of Man with a kiss?"

⁴⁹When those around Him saw what was going to happen, they said to Him, "Lord, shall we strike with the sword?" ⁵⁰And one of them struck the servant of the high priest and cut off his right ear.

⁵¹But Jesus answered and said, "Permit even this." And He touched his ear and healed him.

⁵²Then Jesus said to the chief priests, captains of the temple, and the elders who had come to Him, "Have you come out, as against a robber, with swords and clubs? ⁵³When I was with you daily in the temple, you did not try to seize Me. But this is your hour, and the power of darkness."

BITTER TEARS

22:62 Peter wept bitterly because he realized he had denied his Lord and because he had turned away from a dear friend who had loved and taught him for three years. Peter had said he would *never* deny Christ, but he went against all he had boldly promised. Unable to stand up for his Lord for even 12 hours, he had failed as a disciple and as a friend. need to be aware of our own breaking points and not become overconfident or self-sufficient. When we fail, we must remember that Christ can use those who recognize their failure. From this humiliating experience Peter learned much that would help him in the leadership responsibilities he soon would assume.

[54]Having arrested Him, they led *Him* and brought Him into the high priest's house. But Peter followed at a distance. [55]Now when they had kindled a fire in the midst of the courtyard and sat down together, Peter sat among them. [56]And a certain servant girl, seeing him as he sat by the fire, looked intently at him and said, "This man was also with Him."

[57]But he denied Him, saying, "Woman, I do not know Him."

[58]And after a little while another saw him and said, "You also are of them."

But Peter said, "Man, I am not!"

[59]Then after about an hour had passed, another confidently affirmed, saying, "Surely this *fellow* also was with Him, for he is a Galilean."

[60]But Peter said, "Man, I do not know what you are saying!"

Immediately, while he was still speaking, the rooster crowed. [61]And the Lord turned and looked at Peter. Then Peter remembered the word of the Lord, how He had said to him, "Before the rooster crows, you will deny Me three times." [62]So Peter went out and wept bitterly.

[63]Now the men who held Jesus mocked Him and beat Him. [64]And having blindfolded Him, they struck Him on the face and asked Him, saying, "Prophesy! Who is the one who struck You?" [65]And many other things they blasphemously spoke against Him.

[66]As soon as it was day, the elders of the people, both chief priests and scribes, came together and led Him into their council, saying, [67]"If You are the Christ, tell us."

But He said to them, "If I tell you, you will by no means believe. [68]And if I also ask *you*, you will by no means answer Me or let *Me* go. [69]Hereafter the Son of Man will sit on the right hand of the power of God."

[70]Then they all said, "Are You then the Son of God?"

So He said to them, "You *rightly* say that I am."

[71]And they said, "What further testimony do we need? For we have heard it ourselves from His own mouth."

CHAPTER 23 JESUS STANDS BEFORE PILATE.

Then the whole multitude of them arose and led Him to Pilate. [2]And they began to accuse Him, saying, "We found this *fellow* perverting the nation, and forbidding to pay taxes to Caesar, saying that He Himself is Christ, a King."

[3]Then Pilate asked Him, saying, "Are You the King of the Jews?"

He answered him and said, "*It is as* you say."

[4]So Pilate said to the chief priests and the crowd, "I find no fault in this Man."

[5]But they were the more fierce, saying, "He stirs up the people, teaching throughout all Judea, beginning from Galilee to this place."

[6]When Pilate heard of Galilee, he asked if the Man were a Galilean. [7]And as soon as he knew that He belonged to Herod's jurisdiction, he sent Him to Herod, who was also in Jerusalem at that time. [8]Now when Herod saw Jesus, he was exceedingly glad; for he had desired for a long *time* to see Him, because he had heard many things about Him, and he hoped to see some miracle done by Him. [9]Then he questioned Him with many words, but He answered him nothing. [10]And the chief priests and scribes stood and vehemently accused Him. [11]Then Herod, with his men of war, treated Him with contempt and mocked *Him*, arrayed Him in a gorgeous robe, and sent Him back to Pilate. [12]That very day Pilate and Herod became friends with each other, for previously they had been at enmity with each other.

[13]Then Pilate, when he had called together the chief priests, the rulers, and the people, [14]said to them, "You have brought this Man to me, as one who misleads the people. And indeed, having examined *Him* in your presence, I have found no fault in this Man concerning those things of which you accuse Him; [15]no, neither did Herod, for I sent you back to him; and indeed nothing deserving of death has been done by Him. [16]I will therefore chastise Him and release *Him*" [17](for it was necessary for him to release one to them at the feast).

There aren't very many Christians at my school, and I'm kind of embarrassed about admitting I am one. Do I have to come out and let the whole world know I've become a Christian?

I WONDER . . .

High school guys and girls wear letter jackets that tell the world they're athletes. Most people wear such jackets with pride. They have accomplished something, and they want other people to know it.

Identifying yourself as a Christian, however, is not always real popular. Peter found that out when he was confronted by the people who were trying to get warm around the fire (see Luke 22:54-62). Although he had been with Jesus for three years and was one of His best friends, Peter denied even knowing who Jesus was! He was afraid and embarrassed. But something happened during the next two months that convinced him he would never be ashamed of Jesus again (read about Peter in the first four chapters of the book of Acts).

As a new Christian, it is hard to identify yourself with Christ because you don't know him very well. It's like striking up a friendship with the new kid at school. You want to be his friend, but you hold back because you aren't sure how popular he's going to be.

Jesus understands our fears. It can be tough to admit we're his followers. He will patiently wait until we are confident in our relationship with him before we begin to speak out for him. But I can imagine he is kind of disappointed, too.

It takes most new Christians some time before they aren't embarrassed about admitting they're Christians. But at some point, something clicks that convinces them that Jesus Christ *is* alive. It could be the feeling of being forgiven, a miraculous answer to prayer, or a quiet realization that the Bible is accurate and everything Jesus said about himself is true!

However it happens, God doesn't expect you to get on the P.A. at school and make the "big announcement." He just expects you to be ready in case anyone asks you about your faith: "Always *be* ready to *give* a defense to everyone who asks you a reason for the hope that is in you, with meekness" (1 Peter 3:15).

WHY THE CROSS?

A youth pastor was talking to a group of junior highers about the cross of Christ, explaining how Jesus' death had provided for their individual forgiveness and salvation. "It's personal," he said. "Jesus didn't just die for people in general. He died for you." He paused to let the impact of the statement sink in. Suddenly one seventh-grade girl blurted out: "So?" "So?" As irreverent and inappropriate as that question seems, that seventh grader's response is sadly representative of how people think today. We know Jesus died on a cross for us; we just don't see the connection between that event 2,000 years ago and our lives today. What is the cross about? Why did Jesus have to die such a horrible death? I hope this short note may help you gain some insight into why Jesus had to die and why he died in such a gruesome way. The cross has inspired endless debates, wars, books, songs, and lives through the centuries.

All humans are sinners. We've broken God's laws, so we stand guilty before God and deserving of punishment. Sin has warped every aspect of human life; it has had such a radical effect on us that we stand in open rebellion and defiance of the God who made us and loves us. Think this is overstating the case? Consider this: God made himself vulnerable to human beings one time, and we murdered him. Because of our sinful nature, we are incapable of pleasing God or doing anything on our own to change the situation. We are, as Paul writes in Ephesians 2:5 and Colossians 2:13, dead in our sins—and dead people can't exactly help themselves. We desperately need help from someone who can please God, who can do something about the desperate state of human souls. Jesus, by virtue of his sinless life, is that Someone. But helping us is a terribly expensive process.

Again, we are guilty before God—we deserve his anger and punishment. But God took the wrath we deserve and poured it out on Jesus, on the cross. In some ways, it is beyond human understanding. Jesus took upon himself our sins—every mean, dishonest, disgusting thought or action—and was transformed from the perfect, holy, righteous Person he was into utter sin itself. Second Corinthians 5:21 tells us, "For He [God] made Him [Jesus] who knew no sin to be sin for us, that we might become the righteousness of God in Him." On the cross Jesus stood in the chasm between God and man, which would have created by our sins, and brought us back together by his blood. As horrible as the physical agony must have been, the spiritual agony of this transformation and punishment was worse. No wonder he screamed out, "My God, My God, why have You forsaken Me?" Jesus was deserted by God so that you and I never have to be. God, My God, why have You forsaken Me?" Jesus was deserted by God so that you and I never have to be.

That's the second fact you need to know. Jesus took your place on the cross and bore the terrible brunt of death of one righteous Man—the only righteous Man—pays for the sins of the world. Still, though we may sentence God could have imposed on you. He died for you. Take it personally. It's still a mystery how we not understand it, we can depend upon it for our salvation. It is the only way to peace with God and eternal life. It's fitting that God took the cross of Christ—the single darkest hour in the history of humanity—and turned it into the way of redemption for all people everywhere. That's the kind of God the Bible talks about. A God who loves you so much he would even die on a cross for you.

¹⁸And they all cried out at once, saying, "Away with this *Man*, and release to us Barabbas"— ¹⁹who had been thrown into prison for a certain rebellion made in the city, and for murder.

²⁰Pilate, therefore, wishing to release Jesus, again called out to them. ²¹But they shouted, saying, "Crucify *Him*, crucify Him!"

²²Then he said to them the third time, "Why, what evil has He done? I have found no reason for death in Him. I will therefore chastise Him and let *Him* go."

²³But they were insistent, demanding with loud voices that He be crucified. And the voices of these men and of the chief priests prevailed. ²⁴So Pilate gave sentence that it should be as they requested. ²⁵And he released to them the one they requested, who for rebellion and murder had been thrown into prison; but he delivered Jesus to their will.

²⁶Now as they led Him away, they laid hold of a certain man, Simon a Cyrenian, who was coming from the country, and on him they laid the cross that he might bear *it* after Jesus.

²⁷And a great multitude of the people followed Him, and women who also mourned and lamented Him. ²⁸But Jesus, turning to them, said, "Daughters of Jerusalem, do not weep for Me, but weep for yourselves and for your children. ²⁹For indeed the days are coming in which they will say, 'Blessed *are* the barren, wombs that never bore, and breasts which never nursed!' ³⁰Then they will begin *'to say to the mountains, "Fall on us!" and to the hills, "Cover us!" '* ³¹For if they do these things in the green wood, what will be done in the dry?"

³²There were also two others, criminals, led with Him to be put to death. ³³And when they had come to the place called Calvary, there they crucified Him, and the criminals, one on the right hand and the other on the left. ³⁴Then Jesus said, "Father, forgive them, for they do not know what they do."

And they divided His garments and cast lots. ³⁵And the people stood looking on. But even the rulers with them sneered, saying, "He saved others; let Him save Himself if He is the Christ, the chosen of God."

³⁶The soldiers also mocked Him, coming and offering Him sour wine, ³⁷and saying, "If You are the King of the Jews, save Yourself."

³⁸And an inscription also was written over Him in letters of Greek, Latin, and Hebrew:

THIS IS THE KING OF THE JEWS.

³⁹Then one of the criminals who were hanged blasphemed Him, saying, "If You are the Christ, save Yourself and us."

⁴⁰But the other, answering, rebuked him, saying, "Do you not even fear God, seeing you are under the same condemnation? ⁴¹And we indeed justly, for we receive the due reward of our deeds; but this Man has done nothing wrong." ⁴²Then he said to Jesus, "Lord, remember me when You come into Your kingdom."

⁴³And Jesus said to him, "Assuredly, I say to you, today you will be with Me in Paradise."

⁴⁴Now it was about the sixth hour, and there was dark-ness over all the earth until the ninth hour. ⁴⁵Then the sun was darkened, and the veil of the temple was torn in two. ⁴⁶And when Jesus had cried out with a loud voice, He said, "Father, *'into Your hands I commit My spirit.' "* Having said this, He breathed His last.

⁴⁷So when the centurion saw what had happened, he glorified God, saying, "Certainly this was a righteous Man!"

⁴⁸And the whole crowd who came together to that sight, seeing what had been done, beat their breasts and returned. ⁴⁹But all His acquaintances, and the women

NEW LIFE

23:34 Jesus asked God to forgive the people who were putting him to death— Jewish leaders, Roman politicians and soldiers, bystanders— and God answered that prayer by opening up the way of salvation even to Jesus' murderers. The Roman officer and soldiers who witnessed the crucifixion said, "Truly this was the Son of God" (Matthew 27:54). Soon many priests were converted to the Christian faith (Acts 6:7). Since we are all sinners, we all played a part in putting Jesus to death. The Good News is that God is gracious. He will forgive us and give us new life through his Son.

My church regularly does something called "Communion." What is it supposed to do for me?

I WONDER . . .

Have you ever saved something from a special event because you wanted to remember how great that moment was? Odds are you have. And if you ask your parents to take you through their "nostalgia boxes" sometime, they'll probably say things like: "This is the varsity letter I won my senior year for swimming." Or, "Here is the ring box from the ring your father gave me the day he proposed."

Certain items help us remember special moments in our life.

When Jesus was about to die, be resurrected, and return to heaven, he wanted to leave his followers something tangible to remember him by. He could have left a physical item like a robe or a cup. But people probably would begin to worship the object instead of God, and the object would be seen by just a few. So instead, he left an "act," something we could do.

Communion (the Lord's Supper, Eucharist) is that act—a word picture of what Jesus did on the cross. There, his body was broken and his blood was shed . . . for us. Luke 24:13-35 says that Jesus was recognized "in the breaking of bread" (verse 35). Communion helps us recognize who Jesus is and that he is with us as we worship.

Because Communion is celebrated by believers throughout the world, it is a unifying act. And because we retell the message of Christ's death, we are reminded that he is going to return someday to take us to heaven. (See also 1 Corinthians 11:23-26.)

Christians will always need those reminders. There are too many distractions that cause us to lose our focus on what really matters in this life. Communion briefly reminds us that real *life* revolves not around us, but around one incredible act of love at a certain time in history.

23:39-43 As this man was about to die, he turned to Christ for forgiveness, and Christ accepted him. This shows that our works don't save us—our faith in Christ does. It is never too late to turn to God. Even in his misery, Jesus had mercy on this criminal who decided to believe in him. Our life is much more useful and fulfilling if we turn to God early, but even those who repent at the very last moment will be with God in his kingdom.

who followed Him from Galilee, stood at a distance, watching these things.

⁵⁰Now behold, *there was* a man named Joseph, a council member, a good and just man. ⁵¹He had not consented to their decision and deed. *He was* from Arimathea, a city of the Jews, who himself was also waiting for the kingdom of God. ⁵²This man went to Pilate and asked for the body of Jesus. ⁵³Then he took it down, wrapped it in linen, and laid it in a tomb *that was* hewn out of the rock, where no one had ever lain before. ⁵⁴That day was the Preparation, and the Sabbath drew near.

⁵⁵And the women who had come with Him from Galilee followed after, and they observed the tomb and how His body was laid. ⁵⁶Then they returned and prepared spices and fragrant oils. And they rested on the Sabbath according to the commandment.

CHAPTER 24 JESUS IS ALIVE! Now on the first

day of the week, very early in the morning, they, and certain *other women* with them, came to the tomb bringing the spices which they had prepared. ²But they found the stone rolled away from the tomb. ³Then they went in and did not find the body of the Lord Jesus. ⁴And it happened, as they were greatly perplexed about this, that behold, two men stood by them in shining garments. ⁵Then, as they were afraid and bowed *their* faces to the earth, they said to them, "Why do you seek the living among the dead? ⁶He is not here, but is risen! Remember how He spoke to you when He was still in Galilee, ⁷saying, 'The Son of Man must be delivered into the hands of sinful men, and be crucified, and the third day rise again.'"

⁸And they remembered His words. ⁹Then they returned from the tomb and told all these things to the eleven and to all the rest. ¹⁰It was Mary Magdalene, Joanna, Mary *the mother* of James, and the other *women* with them, who told these things to the apostles. ¹¹And their words seemed to them like idle tales, and they did not believe them. ¹²But Peter arose and ran to the tomb; and stooping down, he saw the linen cloths lying by themselves; and he departed, marveling to himself at what had happened.

¹³Now behold, two of them were traveling that same day to a village called Emmaus, which was seven miles from Jerusalem. ¹⁴And they talked together of all these things which had happened. ¹⁵So it was, while they conversed and reasoned, that Jesus Himself drew near and went with them. ¹⁶But their eyes were restrained, so that they did not know Him.

¹⁷And He said to them, "What kind of conversation *is* this that you have with one another as you walk and are sad?"

¹⁸Then the one whose name was Cleopas answered and said to Him, "Are You the only stranger in Jerusalem,

and have You not known the things which happened there in these days?"

¹⁹And He said to them, "What things?"

So they said to Him, "The things concerning Jesus of Nazareth, who was a Prophet mighty in deed and word before God and all the people, ²⁰and how the chief priests and our rulers delivered Him to be condemned to death, and crucified Him. ²¹But we were hoping that it was He who was going to redeem Israel. Indeed, besides all this, today is the third day since these things happened. ²²Yes, and certain women of our company, who arrived at the tomb early, astonished us. ²³When they did not find His body, they came saying that they had also seen a vision of angels who said He was alive. ²⁴And certain of those *who were* with us went to the tomb and found *it* just as the women had said; but Him they did not see."

24:25-27 After the two disciples told Jesus they were puzzled, he answered them by going to Scripture and applying it to his ministry. When we are puzzled by questions or problems, we, too, can go to Scripture and find authoritative help. If we, like these two disciples, not understand what the Bible means, we can turn to other believers know the Bible and have the wisdom to apply it to our situation.

²⁵Then He said to them, "O foolish ones, and slow of heart to believe in all that the prophets have spoken! ²⁶Ought not the Christ to have suffered these things and to enter into His glory?" ²⁷And beginning at Moses and all the Prophets, He expounded to them in all the Scriptures the things concerning Himself.

²⁸Then they drew near to the village where they were going, and He indicated that He would have gone farther. ²⁹But they constrained Him, saying, "Abide with us, for it is toward evening, and the day is far spent." And He went in to stay with them.

³⁰Now it came to pass, as He sat at the table with them, that He took bread, blessed and broke *it*, and gave it to them. ³¹Then their eyes were opened and they knew Him; and He vanished from their sight.

³²And they said to one another, "Did not our heart burn within us while He talked with us on the road, and while He opened the Scriptures to us?" ³³So they rose up that very hour and returned to Jerusalem, and found the eleven and those *who were* with them gathered together, ³⁴saying, "The Lord is risen indeed, and has appeared to Simon!" ³⁵And they told about the things *that had happened* on the road, and how He was known to them in the breaking of bread.

³⁶Now as they said these things, Jesus Himself stood in the midst of them, and said to them, "Peace to you." ³⁷But they were terrified and frightened, and supposed they

24:45 Jesus opened these people's minds to understand the Scriptur The Holy Spirit does this in our life today when we study the Bible. Ha you ever wondered how to understand a difficult Bible passage? Besid reading surrounding passages, asking other people, and consulting reference works, pray that the Holy Spirit will open your mind to unde stand, giving you the needed insight to put God's Word into action in y life.

had seen a spirit. [38]And He said to them, "Why are you troubled? And why do doubts arise in your hearts? [39]Behold My hands and My feet, that it is I Myself. Handle Me and see, for a spirit does not have flesh and bones as you see I have."

[40]When He had said this, He showed them His hands and His feet. [41]But while they still did not believe for joy, and marveled, He said to them, "Have you any food here?" [42]So they gave Him a piece of a broiled fish and some honeycomb. [43]And He took *it* and ate in their presence.

[44]Then He said to them, "These *are* the words which I spoke to you while I was still with you, that all things must be fulfilled which were written in the Law of Moses and *the* Prophets and *the* Psalms concerning Me." [45]And He opened their understanding, that they might comprehend the Scriptures.

[46]Then He said to them, "Thus it is written, and thus it was necessary for the Christ to suffer and to rise from the dead the third day, [47]and that repentance and remission of sins should be preached in His name to all nations, beginning at Jerusalem. [48]And you are witnesses of these things. [49]Behold, I send the Promise of My Father upon you; but tarry in the city of Jerusalem until you are endued with power from on high."

[50]And He led them out as far as Bethany, and He lifted up His hands and blessed them. [51]Now it came to pass, while He blessed them, that He was parted from them and carried up into heaven. [52]And they worshiped Him, and returned to Jerusalem with great joy, [53]and were continually in the temple praising and blessing God. Amen.

MEGA Themes

JESUS CHRIST, THE SAVIOR
Luke describes how God's Son entered human history. Jesus lived as the perfect man. After a perfect ministry, he provided a perfect sacrifice for our sin so we could be saved.

Jesus is our perfect leader and Savior. He offers forgiveness to all who believe that what he says is true and accept him as Lord of their life.

1. How do you think Luke would answer this question: "What was Jesus like?"
2. What do you learn about Jesus in Luke 2:41-52?
3. Why is it so important that Jesus shared our human experiences, including all types of temptations?
4. Based on your responses to these questions, how would you describe Jesus to someone who had never heard of him?
5. What impact does this have on the person you are today? This is your testimony of who Jesus is in your life. Who do you know that needs to hear and understand your testimony?

HISTORY
Luke was a medical doctor and historian. He put great emphasis on dates and details, connecting Jesus to events and people in history.

Luke's devotion to accuracy gives us confidence in the reliability of the history of Jesus' life. Even more important, we can believe with certainty that Jesus is God.

1. What difference does it make whether or not Luke is historically accurate?
2. Why is it so important that Jesus actually lived, died, and rose again as opposed to this just being an allegory (symbolic story) that someone used to describe how much God loves us?
3. What historical facts clearly reveal that Jesus was both man and God?
4. How does the fact that Jesus was both man and God affect your relationship with him? How does it affect your life?

CARING FOR PEOPLE
Jesus was deeply interested in people and relationships. He showed warm concern for his followers and friends—men, women, and children.

Jesus' love for people is good news for everyone. His message is for all people in every nation. Each of us has an opportunity to respond to him in faith.

1. Jesus built his earthly ministry through personal relationships. What does this imply for how he wants you to minister to others?
2. What does it take for you to feel loved by someone? To trust that the person truly cares for you?
3. How would a person have to act to touch the people in your school with Christ's love?
4. What can you do to show Christ's love to the kids at your school?

HOLY SPIRIT
The Holy Spirit was present at Jesus' birth, baptism, ministry, and resurrection. As a perfect example for us, Jesus lived in dependence on the Holy Spirit.

The Holy Spirit was sent by God as confirmation of Jesus' authority. The Holy Spirit is given to enable people to live for Christ. By faith we can have the Holy Spirit's presence and power to witness and to serve.

1. In 4:1-20, what role did the Holy Spirit play in Jesus' life?
2. In what ways does the Spirit work in you during times of temptation or weariness, and during opportunities to do his ministry?
3. What do you think it means to be "full of the Spirit"?
4. How can you keep yourself daily filled with his Spirit?
5. What do you want to see the Holy Spirit do in your life? What will you do to keep yourself reliant on God's Spirit so that this will be accomplished?

Questions. Life is jam-packed with them. ■ *Dumb* questions: ■ "If the plural of goose is geese, shouldn't the plural of moose be meese?" ■ "Um, if God can do anything, can he make a rock so big that even he couldn't lift it?" ■ *Mysterious* questions: ■ "Gentlemen, we know that buttered bread usually falls butter-side-down and cats generally land feet-first. Now we will discover what happens when a piece of buttered bread is strapped to the back of a cat and both are tossed off a two-story building." ■ *Serious* questions: ■ "What will bring me long-lasting fulfillment?" ■ "How can I have a rich and satisfying life?" ■ Even people who don't (or won't) openly discuss serious issues have ideas about where to find happiness. Ray's formula for fulfillment includes partying and an active sex life. Anne thinks she'll find it in a 4.0 grade point average and a college scholarship. Kevin is banking on his athletic ability to do the trick. Sherry's relying on beauty and bucks. ■ *Nagging* questions: ■ "If happiness really *is* found in the things mentioned above, why are there people with 'awesome' sex lives, staggering IQs, truckloads of trophies, 'drop-dead' good looks, or bulging bank accounts who are unhappy?" ■ "Why don't more people consider what Jesus had to say about happiness and fulfillment?" ■ *Personal* questions: ■ "Have *you* ever really looked at and pondered Jesus' teachings in the Gospel of John?" ■ "What are you waiting for?"

STATS

PURPOSE: To prove conclusively that Jesus is the Son of God and that all who believe in him will have eternal life

AUTHOR: John, the apostle, son of Zebedee, brother of James, called a "Son of Thunder"

TO WHOM WRITTEN: New Christians and searching non-Christians

DATE WRITTEN: Probably A.D. 85–90

SETTING: Written after the destruction of Jerusalem in A.D. 70 and before John's exile to the island of Patmos

KEY PEOPLE: Jesus, John the Baptist, the disciples, Mary, Martha, Lazarus, Jesus' mother, Pilate, Mary Magdalene

KEY PLACES: Judean countryside, Samaria, Galilee, Bethany, Jerusalem

John

CHAPTER 1 GOD BECOMES A HUMAN. In the beginning was the Word, and the Word was with God, and the Word was God. [2]He was in the beginning with God. [3]All things were made through Him, and without Him nothing was made that was made. [4]In Him was life, and the life was the light of men. [5]And the light shines in the darkness, and the darkness did not comprehend it.

[6]There was a man sent from God, whose name *was* John. [7]This man came for a witness, to bear witness of the Light, that all through him might believe. [8]He was not that Light, but *was sent* to bear witness of that Light. [9]That was the true Light which gives light to every man coming into the world.

[10]He was in the world, and the world was made through Him, and the world did not know Him. [11]He came to His own, and His own did not receive Him. [12]But as many as received Him, to them He gave the right to become children of God, to those who believe in His name: [13]who were born, not of blood, nor of the will of the flesh, nor of the will of man, but of God.

[14]And the Word became flesh and dwelt among us, and we beheld His glory, the glory as of the only begotten of the Father, full of grace and truth.

[15]John bore witness of Him and cried out, saying, "This was He of whom I said, 'He who comes after me is preferred before me, for He was before me.'"

[16]And of His fullness we have all received, and grace for grace. [17]For the law was given through Moses, *but* grace and truth came through Jesus Christ. [18]No one has seen God at any time. The only begotten Son, who is in the bosom of the Father, He has declared *Him.*

[19]Now this is the testimony of John, when the Jews sent priests and Levites from Jerusalem to ask him, "Who are you?"

SO COMPLEX

1:3-5 Do you ever feel as though your life is so complex that God would never understand? Remember, God created the entire universe—nothing is too complex for him to understand. He created you, he is alive today, and his love is bigger than any problem you may face.

[20]He confessed, and did not deny, but confessed, "I am not the Christ."

[21]And they asked him, "What then? Are you Elijah?"

He said, "I am not."

"Are you the Prophet?"

And he answered, "No."

[22]Then they said to him, "Who are you, that we may give an answer to those who sent us? What do you say about yourself?"

[23]He said: "I *am*

'The voice of one crying in the wilderness:
"Make straight the way of the LORD," '

as the prophet Isaiah said."

[24]Now those who were sent were from the Pharisees. [25]And they asked him, saying, "Why then do you baptize if you are not the Christ, nor Elijah, nor the Prophet?"

KEY PLACES IN JOHN

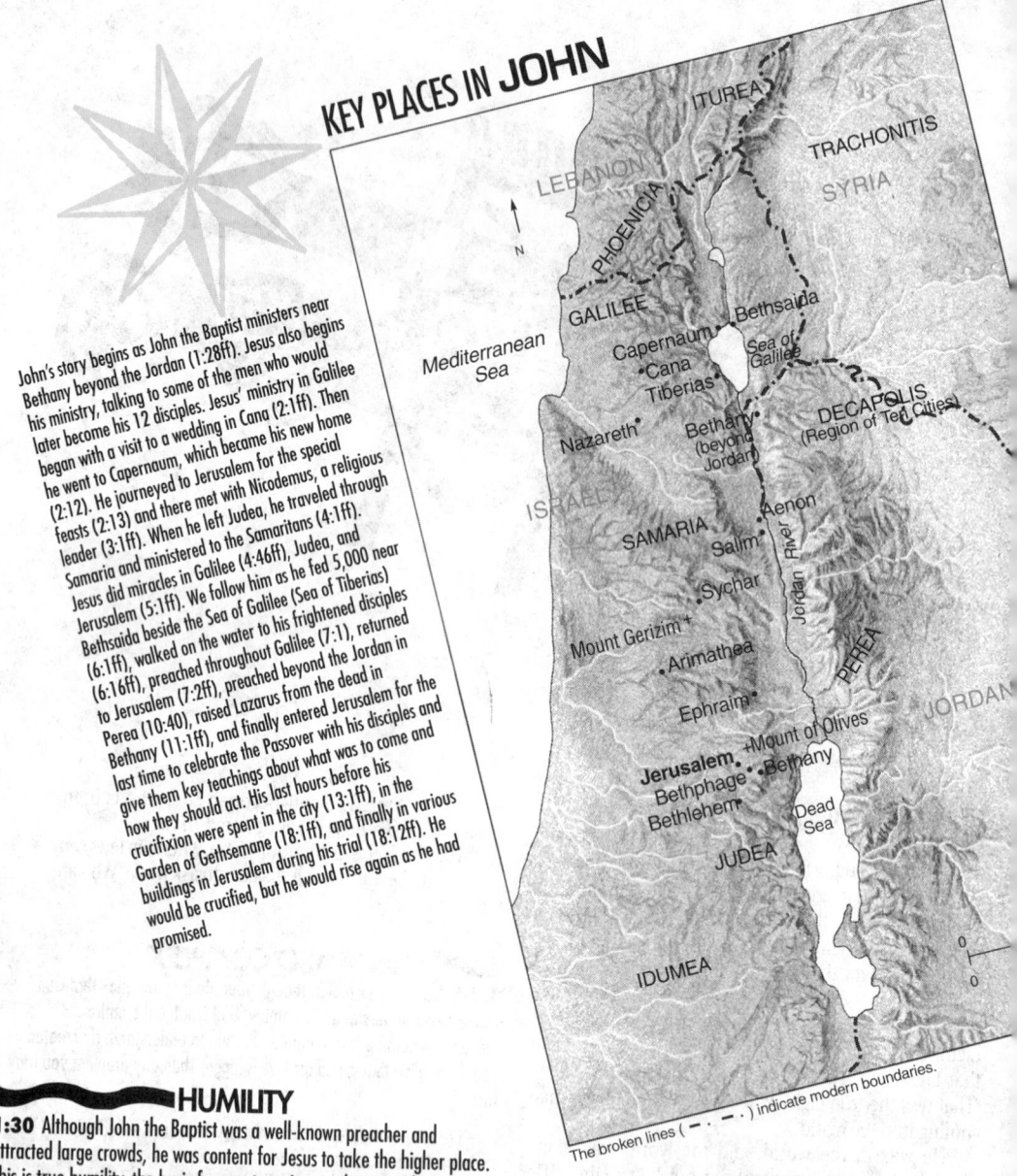

John's story begins as John the Baptist ministers near Bethany beyond the Jordan (1:28ff). Jesus also begins his ministry, talking to some of the men who would later become his 12 disciples. Jesus' ministry in Galilee began with a visit to a wedding in Cana (2:1ff). Then he went to Capernaum, which became his new home (2:12). He journeyed to Jerusalem for the special feasts (2:13) and there met with Nicodemus, a religious leader (3:1ff). When he left Judea, he traveled through Samaria and ministered to the Samaritans (4:1ff). Jesus did miracles in Galilee (4:46ff), Judea, and Jerusalem (5:1ff). We follow him as he fed 5,000 near Bethsaida beside the Sea of Galilee (Sea of Tiberias) (6:1ff), walked on the water to his frightened disciples (6:16ff), preached throughout Galilee (7:1), returned to Jerusalem (7:2ff), preached beyond the Jordan in Perea (10:40), raised Lazarus from the dead in Bethany (11:1ff), and finally entered Jerusalem for the last time to celebrate the Passover with his disciples and give them key teachings about what was to come and how they should act. His last hours before his crucifixion were spent in the city (13:1ff), in the Garden of Gethsemane (18:1ff), and finally in various buildings in Jerusalem during his trial (18:12ff). He would be crucified, but he would rise again as he had promised.

The broken lines (– · – · –) indicate modern boundaries.

⬛ HUMILITY

1:30 Although John the Baptist was a well-known preacher and attracted large crowds, he was content for Jesus to take the higher place. This is true humility, the basis for greatness in preaching, teaching, or any other work we do for Christ. When you are content to do what God wants you to do and let Jesus Christ be honored for it, God will do great things through you.

[26]John answered them, saying, "I baptize with water, but there stands One among you whom you do not know. [27]It is He who, coming after me, is preferred before me, whose sandal strap I am not worthy to loose."

[28]These things were done in Bethabara beyond the Jordan, where John was baptizing.

[29]The next day John saw Jesus coming toward him, and said, "Behold! The Lamb of God who takes away the sin of the world! [30]This is He of whom I said, 'After me comes a Man who is preferred before me, for He was before me.'

[31]I did not know Him; but that He should be revealed to Israel, therefore I came baptizing with water."

[32]And John bore witness, saying, "I saw the Spirit descending from heaven like a dove, and He remained upon Him. [33]I did not know Him, but He who sent me to baptize with water said to me, 'Upon whom you see the Spirit descending, and remaining on Him, this is He who baptizes with the Holy Spirit.' [34]And I have seen and testified that this is the Son of God."

[35]Again, the next day, John stood with two of his disciples. [36]And looking at Jesus as He walked, he said, "Behold the Lamb of God!"

[37]The two disciples heard him speak, and they followed Jesus. [38]Then Jesus turned, and seeing them following, said to them, "What do you seek?"

They said to Him, "Rabbi" (which is to say, when translated, Teacher), "where are You staying?"

³⁹He said to them, "Come and see." They came and saw where He was staying, and remained with Him that day (now it was about the tenth hour).

⁴⁰One of the two who heard John *speak*, and followed Him, was Andrew, Simon Peter's brother. ⁴¹He first found his own brother Simon, and said to him, "We have found the Messiah" (which is translated, the Christ). ⁴²And he brought him to Jesus.

Now when Jesus looked at him, He said, "You are Simon the son of Jonah. You shall be called Cephas" (which is translated, A Stone).

⁴³The following day Jesus wanted to go to Galilee, and He found Philip and said to him, "Follow Me." ⁴⁴Now Philip was from Bethsaida, the city of Andrew and Peter. ⁴⁵Philip found Nathanael and said to him, "We have found Him of whom Moses in the law, and also the prophets, wrote—Jesus of Nazareth, the son of Joseph."

⁴⁶And Nathanael said to him, "Can anything good come out of Nazareth?"

Philip said to him, "Come and see."

⁴⁷Jesus saw Nathanael coming toward Him, and said of him, "Behold, an Israelite indeed, in whom is no deceit!"

⁴⁸Nathanael said to Him, "How do You know me?"

Jesus answered and said to him, "Before Philip called you, when you were under the fig tree, I saw you."

⁴⁹Nathanael answered and said to Him, "Rabbi, You are the Son of God! You are the King of Israel!"

⁵⁰Jesus answered and said to him, "Because I said to you, 'I saw you under the fig tree,' do you believe? You will see greater things than these." ⁵¹And He said to him, "Most assuredly, I say to you, hereafter you shall see heaven open, and the angels of God ascending and descending upon the Son of Man."

CHAPTER 2 JESUS TURNS WATER INTO WINE.

On the third day there was a wedding in Cana of Galilee, and the mother of Jesus was there. ²Now both Jesus and His disciples were invited to the wedding. ³And when they ran out of wine, the mother of Jesus said to Him, "They have no wine."

⁴Jesus said to her, "Woman, what does your concern have to do with Me? My hour has not yet come."

⁵His mother said to the servants, "Whatever He says to you, do *it*."

⁶Now there were set there six waterpots of stone, according to the manner of purification of the Jews, containing twenty or thirty gallons apiece. ⁷Jesus said to them, "Fill the waterpots with water." And they filled them up to the brim. ⁸And He said to them, "Draw *some* out now, and take *it* to the master of the feast." And they took *it*. ⁹When the master of the feast had tasted the water that was made wine, and did not know where it came from (but the servants who had drawn the water knew), the master of the feast called the bridegroom. ¹⁰And he said to him, "Every man at the beginning sets out the good wine, and when the *guests* have well drunk, then the inferior. You have kept the good wine until now!"

¹¹This beginning of signs Jesus did in Cana of Galilee, and manifested His glory; and His disciples believed in Him.

¹²After this He went down to Capernaum, He, His mother, His brothers, and His disciples; and they did not stay there many days.

ANGER

2:15-16 Jesus was obviously angry at the merchants who exploited those who had come to God's house to worship. There is a difference between uncontrolled rage and righteous indignation— yet both are called anger. We must be very careful how we use the powerful emotion of anger. It is right to be angry about injustice and sin; it is wrong to be angry over small, personal offenses.

¹³Now the Passover of the Jews was at hand, and Jesus went up to Jerusalem. ¹⁴And He found in the temple those who sold oxen and sheep and doves, and the money changers doing business. ¹⁵When He had made a whip of cords, He drove them all out of the temple, with the sheep and the oxen, and poured out the changers' money and overturned the tables. ¹⁶And He said to those

"Here's what I did..."

It was an incredible weekend. A twister hit my town, and suddenly our house was ruined, my wrist was broken, and I lost my best friend.

I didn't know what to do, where to turn. It was too much to take in all at once. I felt depressed. Then I was angry; I felt ripped off. In all the confusion of adjusting to these disasters, I finally decided to open the Bible.

I started reading the Gospel of John. And as I thought about Jesus and all he gave up to come down to earth and live among us, my attitude started to change. I thought about verses 10-12 in the first chapter, how Jesus wasn't respected by the very people he came to help. If anybody had the right to feel self-pity, he did! But Jesus did it all for love, all for us.

The first 27 verses of chapter one opened my eyes to God's faithfulness and love. They made me realize that God would stand by me through everything, even this terrible time. I turned everything over to God and discovered a joy that was as incredible as everything that had happened to me in that one terrible weekend. I began to live the kind of Christian life I'd been missing so long when I was just going my own way. The following weeks were the happiest I'd ever felt, even though I still had to deal with the sorrow over losing my friend and our home. I found that the love of God was so much more real, and it gave me strength.

Barbara AGE 15

who sold doves, "Take these things away! Do not make My Father's house a house of merchandise!" ¹⁷Then His disciples remembered that it was written, *"Zeal for Your house has eaten Me up."*

¹⁸So the Jews answered and said to Him, "What sign do You show to us, since You do these things?"

¹⁹Jesus answered and said to them, "Destroy this temple, and in three days I will raise it up."

²⁰Then the Jews said, "It has taken forty-six years to build this temple, and will You raise it up in three days?" ²¹But He was speaking of the temple of His body. ²²Therefore, when He had risen from the dead, His disciples remembered that He had said this to them; and they believed the Scripture and the word which Jesus had said.

²³Now when He was in Jerusalem at the Passover, during the feast, many believed in His name when they saw the signs which He did. ²⁴But Jesus did not commit Himself to them, because He knew all *men*, ²⁵and had no need that anyone should testify of man, for He knew what was in man.

FOR

GOD

so loved the world
that He gave

HIS ONLY
BEGOTTEN
SON

THAT

WhoEver

believes in HIM

should not

perish

BUT

HAVE

EVERLASTING

EVERLASTING

LIFE

LIFE

CHAPTER 3 JESUS TALKS WITH NICODEMUS. There was a man of the Pharisees named Nicodemus, a ruler of the Jews. ²This man came to Jesus by night and said to Him, "Rabbi, we know that You are a teacher come from God; for no one can do these signs that You do unless God is with him."

³Jesus answered and said to him, "Most assuredly, I say to you, unless one is born again, he cannot see the kingdom of God."

⁴Nicodemus said to Him, "How can a man be born when he is old? Can he enter a second time into his mother's womb and be born?"

⁵Jesus answered, "Most assuredly, I say to you, unless one is born of water and the Spirit, he cannot enter the kingdom of God. ⁶That which is born of the flesh is flesh, and that which is born of the Spirit is spirit. ⁷Do not marvel that I said to you, 'You must be born again.' ⁸The wind blows where it wishes, and you hear the sound of it, but cannot tell where it comes from and where it goes. So is everyone who is born of the Spirit."

⁹Nicodemus answered and said to Him, "How can these things be?"

¹⁰Jesus answered and said to him, "Are you the teacher of Israel, and do not know these things? ¹¹Most assuredly, I say to you, We speak what We know and testify what We have seen, and you do not receive Our witness. ¹²If I have told you earthly things and you do not believe, how will you believe if I tell you heavenly things? ¹³No one has ascended to heaven but He who came down from heaven, *that is*, the Son of Man who is in heaven. ¹⁴And as Moses lifted up the serpent in the wilderness, even so must the Son of Man be lifted up, ¹⁵that whoever believes in Him should not perish but have eternal life. ¹⁶For God so loved the world that He gave His only begotten Son, that whoever believes in Him should not perish but have everlasting life. ¹⁷For God did not send His Son into the world to condemn the world, but that the world through Him might be saved.

¹⁸"He who believes in Him is not condemned; but he who does not believe is condemned already, because he

has not believed in the name of the only begotten Son of God. [19]And this is the condemnation, that the light has come into the world, and men loved darkness rather than light, because their deeds were evil. [20]For everyone practicing evil hates the light and does not come to the light, lest his deeds should be exposed. [21]But he who does the truth comes to the light, that his deeds may be clearly seen, that they have been done in God."

[22]After these things Jesus and His disciples came into the land of Judea, and there He remained with them and baptized. [23]Now John also was baptizing in Aenon near Salim, because there was much water there. And they came and were baptized. [24]For John had not yet been thrown into prison.

[25]Then there arose a dispute between *some* of John's disciples and the Jews about purification. [26]And they came to John and said to him, "Rabbi, He who was with you beyond the Jordan, to whom you have testified— behold, He is baptizing, and all are coming to Him!"

[27]John answered and said, "A man can receive nothing unless it has been given to him from heaven. [28]You yourselves bear me witness, that I said, 'I am not the Christ,' but, 'I have been sent before Him.' [29]He who has the bride is the bridegroom; but the friend of the bridegroom, who stands and hears him, rejoices greatly because of the bridegroom's voice. Therefore this joy of mine is fulfilled. [30]He must increase, but I *must* decrease. [31]He who comes from above is above all; he who is of the earth is earthly and speaks of the earth. He who comes from heaven is above all. [32]And what He has seen and heard, that He testifies; and no one receives His testimony. [33]He who has received His testimony has certified that God is true. [34]For He whom God has sent speaks the words of God, for God does not give the Spirit by measure. [35]The Father loves the Son, and has given all things into His hand. [36]He who believes in the Son has everlasting life; and he who does not believe the Son shall not see life, but the wrath of God abides on him."

CHAPTER 4 JESUS AND THE WOMAN AT A WELL.
Therefore, when the Lord knew that the Pharisees had heard that Jesus made and baptized more disciples than John [2](though Jesus Himself did not baptize, but His disciples), [3]He left Judea and departed again to Galilee. [4]But He needed to go through Samaria.

[5]So He came to a city of Samaria which is called Sychar, near the plot of ground that Jacob gave to his son Joseph. [6]Now Jacob's well was there. Jesus therefore, being wearied from *His* journey, sat thus by the well. It was about the sixth hour.

[7]A woman of Samaria came to draw water. Jesus said to her, "Give Me a drink." [8]For His disciples had gone away into the city to buy food.

[9]Then the woman of Samaria said to Him, "How is it that You, being a Jew, ask a drink from me, a Samaritan woman?"

JOHN THE BAPTIST

John the Baptist would be called unique. He wore odd clothes, ate strange food, and preached an unusual message. He would not have agreed with our habit of evaluating people by how they dress—or by how they act. He would have insisted that we listen to what he had to say.

John really wasn't interested in being unique. What he wanted to do more than anything was to obey God. And he wasn't afraid to ask others to do the same. John realized that he had a special role to play in the world. His job was to tell the world that the Savior was about to arrive. John was totally committed to his purpose.

This wild-looking man stood face-to-face with people and told them to repent. He told them the best way to get ready for the Savior was to be deeply sorry for their sins. Although John was preparing people to receive Jesus when he physically came to the world, John's message still applies today when we realize that Jesus wants to come into our life, too. We can't receive the Savior until we know we need him. We won't know we need him until we realize we are sinners.

Today, we still need to hear John's favorite word—repent! If you don't know what it means, you may not have done it. Repenting means that you are not only deeply sorry for your sinfulness but are also serious in wanting God's help to live his way. Until you have repented, you won't experience God's forgiveness or the strength he offers to live a life of obedience. Repentance may be the most important thing you think about today.

LESSONS: God does not guarantee an easy or safe life to those who serve him
Doing what God desires is the greatest possible life investment
Standing for the truth is more important than life itself

KEY VERSE: "Assuredly, I say to you, among those born of women there has not risen one greater than John the Baptist; but he who is least in the kingdom of heaven is greater than he" (Matthew 11:11).

John's story is told in all four Gospels. His coming was predicted in Isaiah 40:3 and Malachi 4:5ff; and he is mentioned in Acts 1:5,22; 10:37; 11:16; 13:24-25; 18:25; 19:3-4.

UPS:
• The God-appointed messenger to announce the arrival of Jesus
• A preacher whose theme was repentance
• A fearless confronter
• Known for his remarkable life-style
• Uncompromising

STATS:
• Where: Judea
• Occupation: Prophet
• Relatives: Father: Zacharias. Mother: Elizabeth. Distant cousin: Jesus.
• Contemporaries: Herod, Herodias

For Jews have no dealings with Samaritans. [10]Jesus answered and said to her, "If you knew the gift of God, and who it is who says to you, 'Give Me a drink,' you would have asked Him, and He would have given you living water."

[11]The woman said to Him, "Sir, You have nothing to draw with, and the well is deep. Where then do You get that living water? [12]Are You greater than our father Jacob, who gave us the well, and drank from it himself, as well as his sons and his livestock?"

[13]Jesus answered and said to her, "Whoever drinks of this water will thirst again, [14]but whoever drinks of the water that I shall give him will never thirst. But the water that I shall give him will become in him a fountain of

PREJUDICE It may be the nineties, but some people's attitudes show they are still living in the past.

Here's the story: Randy C. and Darnell T. are close friends. Randy is white; Darnell is black. When Darnell's parents went cross-country to a funeral, Darnell stayed for the week with Randy. No big deal, right?

Wrong. The first afternoon, Randy took Darnell to the neighborhood pool. Everyone glared at them, most started whispering, and some actually got out of the pool and left.

The second night of Darnell's stay, someone shattered the rear window in Mr. C.'s car. The third night, someone (or some ones) scrawled racial slurs on the C.'s garage door.

When school started, Randy's white friends avoided him. Randy finally confronted Keith, asked what his problem was, and got this reply: "Hey, look, Randy—you changed, not us. You're the one who's trying to be Mr. Civil Rights, OK?"

Randy was (and is) shocked.

Even at church, people are treating him weirdly. Says Randy, "What is going on?! I invited a friend to stay with me while his parents were gone. Would someone please tell me what in the world is wrong with that? So what if his skin is a different color? I don't understand why so many people are so full of hate."

Which person are you most like? Randy, Darnell, or Keith? Consider how Jesus treated people who were different from himself. (See John 4:1-42.)

water springing up into everlasting life."

[15]The woman said to Him, "Sir, give me this water, that I may not thirst, nor come here to draw."

[16]Jesus said to her, "Go, call your husband, and come here."

[17]The woman answered and said, "I have no husband."

Jesus said to her, "You have well said, 'I have no husband,' [18]for you have had five husbands, and the one whom you now have is not your husband; in that you spoke truly."

[19]The woman said to Him, "Sir, I perceive that You are a prophet. [20]Our fathers worshiped on this mountain, and you Jews say that in Jerusalem is the place where one ought to worship."

[21]Jesus said to her, "Woman, believe Me, the hour is coming when you will neither on this mountain, nor in

4:35 Sometimes Christians excuse themselves from witnessing by saying their family or friends aren't ready to believe. Jesus, however makes it clear that around us a continual harvest waits to be reaped. Don't let Jesus find you making excuses. Look around. You will find people ready to hear God's Word.

Jerusalem, worship the Father. [22]You worship what you do not know; we know what we worship, for salvation is of the Jews. [23]But the hour is coming, and now is, when the true worshipers will worship the Father in spirit and truth; for the Father is seeking such to worship Him. [24]God *is* Spirit, and those who worship Him must worship in spirit and truth."

[25]The woman said to Him, "I know that Messiah is coming" (who is called Christ). "When He comes, He will tell us all things."

[26]Jesus said to her, "I who speak to you am *He*."

[27]And at this *point* His disciples came, and they marveled that He talked with a woman; yet no one said, "What do You seek?" or, "Why are You talking with her?"

[28]The woman then left her waterpot, went her way into the city, and said to the men, [29]"Come, see a Man who told me all things that I ever did. Could this be the Christ?" [30]Then they went out of the city and came to Him.

[31]In the meantime His disciples urged Him, saying, "Rabbi, eat."

[32]But He said to them, "I have food to eat of which you do not know."

[33]Therefore the disciples said to one another, "Has anyone brought Him *anything* to eat?"

[34]Jesus said to them, "My food is to do the will of Him who sent Me, and to finish His work. [35]Do you not say, 'There are still four months and *then* comes the harvest'? Behold, I say to you, lift up your eyes and look at the fields, for they are already white for harvest! [36]And he who reaps receives wages, and gathers fruit for eternal life, that both he who sows and he who reaps may rejoice together. [37]For in this the saying is true: 'One sows and another reaps.' [38]I sent you to reap that for which you have not labored; others have labored, and you have entered into their labors."

[39]And many of the Samaritans of that city believed in Him because of the word of the woman who testified, "He told me all that I *ever* did." [40]So when the Samaritans had come to Him, they urged Him to stay with them; and He stayed there two days. [41]And many more believed because of His own word.

[42]Then they said to the woman, "Now we believe, not because of what you said, for we ourselves have heard *Him* and we know that this is indeed the Christ, the Savior of the world."

[43]Now after the two days He departed from there and went to Galilee. [44]For Jesus Himself testified that a prophet has no honor in his own country. [45]So when He came to Galilee, the Galileans received Him, having seen all the things He did in Jerusalem at the feast; for they also had gone to the feast.

[46]So Jesus came again to Cana of Galilee where He had made the water wine. And there was a certain nobleman whose son was sick at Capernaum. [47]When he heard that

Jesus had come out of Judea into Galilee, he went to Him and implored Him to come down and heal his son, for he was at the point of death. ⁴⁸Then Jesus said to him, "Unless you *people* see signs and wonders, you will by no means believe."

⁴⁹The nobleman said to Him, "Sir, come down before my child dies!"

⁵⁰Jesus said to him, "Go your way; your son lives." So the man believed the word that Jesus spoke to him, and he went his way. ⁵¹And as he was now going down, his servants met him and told *him*, saying, "Your son lives!"

⁵²Then he inquired of them the hour when he got better. And they said to him, "Yesterday at the seventh hour the fever left him." ⁵³So the father knew that *it was* at the same hour in which Jesus said to him, "Your son lives." And he himself believed, and his whole household.

⁵⁴This again *is* the second sign Jesus did when He had come out of Judea into Galilee.

CHAPTER 5 JESUS HEALS A SICK MAN.

After this there was a feast of the Jews, and Jesus went up to Jerusalem. ²Now there is in Jerusalem by the Sheep *Gate* a pool, which is called in Hebrew, Bethesda, having five porches. ³In these lay a great multitude of sick people, blind, lame, paralyzed, waiting for the moving of the water. ⁴For an angel went down at a certain time into the pool and stirred up the water; then whoever stepped in first, after the stirring of the water, was made well of whatever disease he had. ⁵Now a certain man was there who had an infirmity thirty-eight years. ⁶When Jesus saw him lying there, and knew that he already had been *in that condition* a long time, He said to him, "Do you want to be made well?"

⁷The sick man answered Him, "Sir, I have no man to put me into the pool when the water is stirred up; but while I am coming, another steps down before me."

⁸Jesus said to him, "Rise, take up your bed and walk." ⁹And immediately the man was made well, took up his bed, and walked.

And that day was the Sabbath. ¹⁰The Jews therefore said to him who was cured, "It is the Sabbath; it is not lawful for you to carry your bed."

¹¹He answered them, "He who made me well said to me, 'Take up your bed and walk.'"

¹²Then they asked him, "Who is the Man who said to you, 'Take up your bed and walk'?" ¹³But the one who was healed did not know who it was, for Jesus had withdrawn, a multitude being in *that* place. ¹⁴Afterward Jesus found him in the temple, and said to him, "See, you have been made well. Sin no more, lest a worse thing come upon you."

¹⁵The man departed and told the Jews that it was Jesus who had made him well.

¹⁶For this reason the Jews persecuted Jesus, and sought to kill Him, because He had done these things on the Sabbath. ¹⁷But Jesus answered them, "My Father has been working until now, and I have been working."

¹⁸Therefore the Jews sought all the more to kill Him, because He not only broke the Sabbath, but also said that God was His Father, making Himself equal with God. ¹⁹Then Jesus answered and said to them, "Most assuredly, I say to you, the Son can do nothing of Himself, but what He sees the Father do; for whatever He does, the Son also does in like manner. ²⁰For the Father loves the Son, and shows Him all things that He Himself does; and He will

BELIEVE IT!

4:50 This nobleman not only believed that Jesus could heal, he also obeyed Jesus by returning home and thus demonstrating his faith. It isn't enough for us to say we believe that Jesus can take care of our problems. We need to act as if he can. When you pray about a need or problem, live as though you believe Jesus can do what he says.

show Him greater works than these, that you may marvel. ²¹For as the Father raises the dead and gives life to *them*, even so the Son gives life to whom He will. ²²For the Father judges no one, but has committed all judgment to the Son, ²³that all should honor the Son just as they honor the Father. He who does not honor the Son does not honor the Father who sent Him.

²⁴"Most assuredly, I say to you, he who hears My word and believes in Him who sent Me has everlasting life, and shall not come into judgment, but has passed from death into life. ²⁵Most assuredly, I say to you, the hour is com-

TRAPPED

5:6 Jesus appropriately asked, "Do you want to be made well?" After 38 years, this man's problem had become a way of life. No one had ever helped him. He had no hope of ever being healed and no desire to help himself. No matter how trapped you feel in your infirmities, God can minister to your deepest needs. Don't let a problem or hardship cause you to lose hope. God may have special work for you to do in spite of your condition, or even because of it. Many have ministered effectively to hurting people because they have triumphed, with God's help, over their own hurts.

ing, and now is, when the dead will hear the voice of the Son of God; and those who hear will live. ²⁶For as the Father has life in Himself, so He has granted the Son to have life in Himself, ²⁷and has given Him authority to execute judgment also, because He is the Son of Man. ²⁸Do not marvel at this; for the hour is coming in which all who are in the graves will hear His voice ²⁹and come forth—those who have done good, to the resurrection of life, and those who have done evil, to the resurrection of condemnation. ³⁰I can of Myself do nothing. As I hear, I judge; and My judgment is righteous, because I do not seek My own will but the will of the Father who sent Me.

³¹"If I bear witness of Myself, My witness is not true. ³²There is another who bears witness of Me, and I know that the witness which He witnesses of Me is true. ³³You have sent to John, and he has borne witness to the truth. ³⁴Yet I do not receive testimony from man, but I say these things that you may be saved. ³⁵He was the burning and

CHOICES

5:19-23 Because of his unity with God, Jesus lived as God wanted him to live. Because of our identification with Jesus, we must live as he wants us to live. The questions "What would Jesus do?" and "What would Jesus have me do?" may help us make the right choices.

shining lamp, and you were willing for a time to rejoice in his light. ³⁶But I have a greater witness than John's; for the works which the Father has given Me to finish—the very works that I do—bear witness of Me, that the Father has sent Me. ³⁷And the Father Himself, who sent Me, has testified of Me. You have neither heard His voice at any time, nor seen His form. ³⁸But you do not have His word abiding in you, because whom He sent, Him you do not believe. ³⁹You search the Scriptures, for in them you think you have eternal life; and these are they which testify of Me. ⁴⁰But you are not willing to come to Me that you may have life.

⁴¹"I do not receive honor from men. ⁴²But I know you, that you do not have the love of God in you. ⁴³I have come in My Father's name, and you do not receive Me; if another comes in his own name, him you will receive. ⁴⁴How can you believe, who receive honor from one another, and do not seek the honor that *comes* from the only God? ⁴⁵Do not think that I shall accuse you to the Father; there is *one* who accuses you—Moses, in whom you trust. ⁴⁶For if you believed Moses, you would believe Me; for he wrote about Me. ⁴⁷But if you do not believe his writings, how will you believe My words?"

CHAPTER 6 JESUS FEEDS 5,000 PEOPLE.

After these things Jesus went over the Sea of Galilee, which is *the Sea* of Tiberias. ²Then a great multitude followed Him, because they saw His signs which He performed on those who were diseased. ³And Jesus went up on the mountain, and there He sat with His disciples.

⁴Now the Passover, a feast of the Jews, was near. ⁵Then Jesus lifted up *His* eyes, and seeing a great multitude coming toward Him, He said to Philip, "Where shall we buy bread, that these may eat?" ⁶But this He said to test him, for He Himself knew what He would do.

⁷Philip answered Him, "Two hundred denarii worth of bread is not sufficient for them, that every one of them may have a little."

⁸One of His disciples, Andrew, Simon Peter's brother, said to Him, ⁹"There is a lad here who has five barley loaves and two small fish, but what are they among so many?"

¹⁰Then Jesus said, "Make the people sit down." Now there was much grass in the place. So the men sat down, in number about five thousand. ¹¹And Jesus took the loaves, and when He had given thanks He distributed *them* to the disciples, and the disciples to those sitting down; and likewise of the fish, as much as they wanted. ¹²So when they were filled, He said to His disciples, "Gather up the fragments that remain, so that nothing is lost." ¹³Therefore they gathered *them* up, and filled twelve baskets with the fragments of the five barley loaves which were left over by those who had eaten. ¹⁴Then those men, when they had seen the sign that Jesus did, said, "This is truly the Prophet who is to come into the world."

¹⁵Therefore when Jesus perceived that they were about to come and take Him by force to make Him king, He departed again to the mountain by Himself alone.

¹⁶Now when evening came, His disciples went down to

the sea, ¹⁷got into the boat, and went over the sea toward Capernaum. And it was already dark, and Jesus had not come to them. ¹⁸Then the sea arose because a great wind was blowing. ¹⁹So when they had rowed about three or four miles, they saw Jesus walking on the sea and drawing near the boat; and they were afraid. ²⁰But He said to them, "It is I; do not be afraid." ²¹Then they willingly received Him into the boat, and immediately the boat was at the land where they were going.

²²On the following day, when the people who were standing on the other side of the sea saw that there was no other boat there, except that one which His disciples had entered, and that Jesus had not entered the boat with His disciples, but His disciples had gone away alone— ²³however, other boats came from Tiberias, near the place where they ate bread after the Lord had given thanks— ²⁴when the people therefore saw that Jesus was not there, nor His disciples, they also got into boats and came to Capernaum, seeking Jesus. ²⁵And when they found Him on the other side of the sea, they said to Him, "Rabbi, when did You come here?"

²⁶Jesus answered them and said, "Most assuredly, I say to you, you seek Me, not because you saw the signs, but because you ate of the loaves and were filled. ²⁷Do not labor for the food which perishes, but for the food which endures to everlasting life, which the Son of Man will give you, because God the Father has set His seal on Him."

²⁸Then they said to Him, "What shall we do, that we may work the works of God?"

²⁹Jesus answered and said to them, "This is the work of God, that you believe in Him whom He sent."

³⁰Therefore they said to Him, "What sign will You perform then, that we may see it and believe You? What work will You do? ³¹Our fathers ate the manna in the desert; as it is written, 'He gave them bread from heaven to eat.'"

³²Then Jesus said to them, "Most assuredly, I say to you, Moses did not give you the bread from heaven, but My Father gives you the true bread from heaven. ³³For the bread of God is He who comes down from heaven and gives life to the world."

³⁴Then they said to Him, "Lord, give us this bread always."

³⁵And Jesus said to them, "I am the bread of life. He who comes to Me shall never hunger, and he who believes in Me shall never thirst. ³⁶But I said to you that you

have seen Me and yet do not believe. [37]All that the Father gives Me will come to Me, and the one who comes to Me I will by no means cast out. [38]For I have come down from heaven, not to do My own will, but the will of Him who sent Me. [39]This is the will of the Father who sent Me, that of all He has given Me I should lose nothing, but should raise it up at the last day. [40]And this is the will of Him who sent Me, that everyone who sees the Son and believes in Him may have everlasting life; and I will raise him up at the last day."

[41]The Jews then complained about Him, because He said, "I am the bread which came down from heaven." [42]And they said, "Is not this Jesus, the son of Joseph, whose father and mother we know? How is it then that He says, 'I have come down from heaven'?"

[43]Jesus therefore answered and said to them, "Do not murmur among yourselves. [44]No one can come to Me unless the Father who sent Me draws him; and I will raise him up at the last day. [45]It is written in the prophets, '*And they shall all be taught by God.*' Therefore everyone who has heard and learned from the Father comes to Me. [46]Not that anyone has seen the Father, except He who is from God; He has seen the Father. [47]Most assuredly, I say to you, he who believes in Me has everlasting life. [48]I am the bread of life. [49]Your fathers ate the manna in the wilderness, and are dead. [50]This is the bread which comes down from heaven, that one may eat of it and not die. [51]I am the living bread which came down from heaven. If anyone eats of this bread, he will live forever; and the bread that I shall give is My flesh, which I shall give for the life of the world."

[52]The Jews therefore quarreled among themselves, saying, "How can this Man give us *His* flesh to eat?" [53]Then Jesus said to them, "Most assuredly, I say to you, unless you eat the flesh of the Son of Man and drink His blood, you have no life in you. [54]Whoever eats My flesh and drinks My blood has eternal life, and I will raise him up at the last day. [55]For My flesh is food indeed, and My blood is drink indeed. [56]He who eats My flesh and drinks My blood abides in Me, and I in him. [57]As the living Father sent Me, and I live because of the Father, so he who feeds on Me will live because of Me. [58]This is the bread which came down from heaven—not as your fathers ate the manna, and are dead. He who eats this bread will live forever."

[59]These things He said in the synagogue as He taught in Capernaum.

[60]Therefore many of His disciples, when they heard *this*, said, "This is a hard saying; who can understand it?" [61]When Jesus knew in Himself that His disciples complained about this, He said to them, "Does this offend you? [62]*What* then if you should see the Son of Man ascend where He was before? [63]It is the Spirit who gives life; the flesh profits nothing. The words that I speak to you are spirit, and *they* are life. [64]But there are some of you who do not believe." For Jesus knew from the beginning who they were who did not believe, and who would betray Him. [65]And He said, "Therefore I have said to you that no one can come to Me unless it has been granted to him by My Father."

[66]From that *time* many of His disciples went back and walked with Him no more. [67]Then Jesus said to the twelve, "Do you also want to go away?"

[68]But Simon Peter answered Him, "Lord, to whom shall we go? You have the words of eternal life. [69]Also we have come to believe and know that You are the Christ, the Son of the living God."

◣◣◣ THE SOURCE

6:67-68 After many of Jesus' followers had deserted him, he asked the 12 disciples if they were also going to leave. Peter responded, "To whom shall we go?" In his straightforward way, Peter answered for all of us—there is no other way. Jesus alone gives life. People look everywhere for eternal life and miss Christ, the only source. Stay with him, especially when you are confused or feel alone.

[70]Jesus answered them, "Did I not choose you, the twelve, and one of you is a devil?" [71]He spoke of Judas Iscariot, *the son* of Simon, for it was he who would betray Him, being one of the twelve.

CHAPTER **7** **JESUS' BROTHERS MAKE FUN OF HIM.**
After these things Jesus walked in Galilee; for He did not want to walk in Judea, because the Jews sought to kill Him. [2]Now the Jews' Feast of Tabernacles was at hand. [3]His brothers therefore said to Him, "Depart from here and go into Judea, that Your disciples also may see the works that You are doing. [4]For no one does anything in secret while he himself seeks to be known openly. If You do these things, show Yourself to the world." [5]For even His brothers did not believe in Him.

[6]Then Jesus said to them, "My time has not yet come, but your time is always ready. [7]The world cannot hate you, but it hates Me because I testify of it that its works are evil. [8]You go up to this feast. I am not yet going up to this feast, for My time has not yet fully come." [9]When He had said these things to them, He remained in Galilee.

[10]But when His brothers had gone up, then He also went up to the feast, not openly, but as it were in secret. [11]Then the Jews sought Him at the feast, and said, "Where is He?" [12]And there was much complaining among the people concerning Him. Some said, "He is good"; others said, "No, on the contrary, He deceives the people." [13]However, no one spoke openly of Him for fear of the Jews.

[14]Now about the middle of the feast Jesus went up into the temple and taught. [15]And the Jews marveled, saying, "How does this Man know letters, having never studied?"

[16]Jesus answered them and said, "My doctrine is not Mine, but His who sent Me. [17]If anyone wills to do His will, he shall know concerning the doctrine, whether it is from God or *whether* I speak on My own *authority*. [18]He who speaks from himself seeks his own glory; but He who seeks the glory of the One who sent Him is true, and no unrighteousness is in Him. [19]Did not Moses give you the

◣◣◣ TEST

7:16-18 Have you ever listened to religious speakers and wondered if they were telling the truth? Test them—(1) ask if their words agree with or contradict the Bible; and (2) ask if their words point to Christ or to themselves.

law, yet none of you keeps the law? Why do you seek to kill Me?"

20The people answered and said, "You have a demon. Who is seeking to kill You?"

21Jesus answered and said to them, "I did one work, and you all marvel. 22Moses therefore gave you circumcision (not that it is from Moses, but from the fathers), and you circumcise a man on the Sabbath. 23If a man receives circumcision on the Sabbath, so that the law of Moses should not be broken, are you angry with Me because I made a man completely well on the Sabbath? 24Do not judge according to appearance, but judge with righteous judgment."

25Now some of them from Jerusalem said, "Is this not He whom they seek to kill? 26But look! He speaks boldly, and they say nothing to Him. Do the rulers know indeed that this is truly the Christ? 27However, we know where this Man is from; but when the Christ comes, no one knows where He is from."

28Then Jesus cried out, as He taught in the temple, saying, "You both know Me, and you know where I am from; and I have not come of Myself, but He who sent Me is true, whom you do not know. 29But I know Him, for I am from Him, and He sent Me."

30Therefore they sought to take Him; but no one laid a hand on Him, because His hour had not yet come. 31And many of the people believed in Him, and said, "When the Christ comes, will He do more signs than these which this Man has done?"

32The Pharisees heard the crowd murmuring these things concerning Him, and the Pharisees and the chief priests sent officers to take Him. 33Then Jesus said to them, "I shall be with you a little while longer, and then I go to Him who sent Me. 34You will seek Me and not find Me, and where I am you cannot come."

35Then the Jews said among themselves, "Where does He intend to go that we shall not find Him? Does He intend to go to the Dispersion among the Greeks and teach the Greeks? 36What is this thing that He said, 'You will seek Me and not find Me, and where I am you cannot come'?"

37On the last day, that great day of the feast, Jesus stood and cried out, saying, "If anyone thirsts, let him come to Me and drink. 38He who believes in Me, as the Scripture has said, out of his heart will flow rivers of living water." 39But this He spoke concerning the Spirit, whom those believing in Him would receive; for the Holy Spirit was not yet given, because Jesus was not yet glorified.

40Therefore many from the crowd, when they heard this saying, said, "Truly this is the Prophet." 41Others said, "This is the Christ."

But some said, "Will the Christ come out of Galilee? 42Has not the Scripture said that the Christ comes from the seed of David and from the town of Bethlehem, where David was?" 43So there was a division among the people because of Him. 44Now some of them wanted to take Him, but no one laid hands on Him.

45Then the officers came to the chief priests and Pharisees, who said to them, "Why have you not brought Him?"

46The officers answered, "No man ever spoke like this Man!"

47Then the Pharisees answered them, "Are you also deceived? 48Have any of the rulers or the Pharisees believed in Him? 49But this crowd that does not know the law is accursed."

50Nicodemus (he who came to Jesus by night, being one of them) said to them, 51"Does our law judge a man before it hears him and knows what he is doing?"

52They answered and said to him, "Are you also from Galilee? Search and look, for no prophet has arisen out of Galilee."

53And everyone went to his own house.

CHAPTER 8 JESUS FORGIVES A GUILTY WOMAN.

But Jesus went to the Mount of Olives. 2Now early in the morning He came again into the temple, and all the people came to Him; and He sat down and taught them. 3Then the scribes and Pharisees brought to Him a woman caught in adultery. And when they had set her in the midst, 4they said to Him, "Teacher, this woman was caught in adultery, in the very act. 5Now Moses, in the law, commanded us that such should be stoned. But what do You say?" 6This they said, testing Him, that they might have something of which to accuse Him. But Jesus stooped down and wrote on the ground with His finger, as though He did not hear.

7So when they continued asking Him, He raised Himself up and said to them, "He who is without sin among you, let him throw a stone at her first." 8And again He stooped down and wrote on the ground. 9Then those who heard it, being convicted by their conscience, went out one by one, beginning with the oldest even to the last. And Jesus was left alone, and the woman standing in the midst. 10When Jesus had raised Himself up and saw no one but the woman, He said to her, "Woman, where are those accusers of yours? Has no one condemned you?"

11She said, "No one, Lord."

And Jesus said to her, "Neither do I condemn you; go and sin no more."

12Then Jesus spoke to them again, saying, "I am the light of the world. He who follows Me shall not walk in darkness, but have the light of life."

¹³The Pharisees therefore said to Him, "You bear witness of Yourself; Your witness is not true."

¹⁴Jesus answered and said to them, "Even if I bear witness of Myself, My witness is true, for I know where I came from and where I am going; but you do not know where I come from and where I am going. ¹⁵You judge according to the flesh; I judge no one. ¹⁶And yet if I do judge, My judgment is true; for I am not alone, but I *am* with the Father who sent Me. ¹⁷It is also written in your law that the testimony of two men is true. ¹⁸I am One who bears witness of Myself, and the Father who sent Me bears witness of Me."

¹⁹Then they said to Him, "Where is Your Father?"

Jesus answered, "You know neither Me nor My Father. If you had known Me, you would have known My Father also."

²⁰These words Jesus spoke in the treasury, as He taught in the temple; and no one laid hands on Him, for His hour had not yet come.

²¹Then Jesus said to them again, "I am going away, and you will seek Me, and will die in your sin. Where I go you cannot come."

²²So the Jews said, "Will He kill Himself, because He says, 'Where I go you cannot come'?"

²³And He said to them, "You are from beneath; I am from above. You are of this world; I am not of this world. ²⁴Therefore I said to you that you will die in your sins; for if you do not believe that I am *He,* you will die in your sins."

²⁵Then they said to Him, "Who are You?"

And Jesus said to them, "Just what I have been saying to you from the beginning. ²⁶I have many things to say and to judge concerning you, but He who sent Me is true; and I speak to the world those things which I heard from Him."

²⁷They did not understand that He spoke to them of the Father.

²⁸Then Jesus said to them, "When you lift up the Son of Man, then you will know that I am *He,* and *that* I do nothing of Myself; but as My Father taught Me, I speak these things. ²⁹And He who sent Me is with Me. The Father has not left Me alone, for I always do those things that please Him." ³⁰As He spoke these words, many believed in Him.

³¹Then Jesus said to those Jews who believed Him, "If you abide in My word, you are My disciples indeed. ³²And you shall know the truth, and the truth shall make you free."

³³They answered Him, "We are Abraham's descendants, and have never been in bondage to anyone. How *can* You say, 'You will be made free'?"

³⁴Jesus answered them, "Most assuredly, I say to you, whoever commits sin is a slave of sin. ³⁵And a slave does not abide in the house forever, *but* a son abides forever. ³⁶Therefore if the Son makes you free, you shall be free indeed.

³⁷"I know that you are Abraham's descendants, but you seek to kill Me, because My word has no place in you. ³⁸I speak what I have seen with My Father, and you do what you have seen with your father."

³⁹They answered and said to Him, "Abraham is our father."

Jesus said to them, "If you were Abraham's children, you would do the works of Abraham. ⁴⁰But now you seek to kill Me, a Man who has told you the truth which I heard from God. Abraham did not do this. ⁴¹You do the deeds of your father."

Then they said to Him, "We were not born of fornication; we have one Father—God."

◣▬▬▬▬▬▬**FREE**

8:34-35 Sin has a way of enslaving us, controlling us, dominating us, and dictating our actions. Jesus can free you from this slavery that keeps you from becoming the person that God created you to be. If sin is restraining, mastering, or enslaving you, Jesus can break its power over your life.

⁴²Jesus said to them, "If God were your Father, you would love Me, for I proceeded forth and came from God; nor have I come of Myself, but He sent Me. ⁴³Why do you not understand My speech? Because you are not able to listen to My word. ⁴⁴You are of *your* father the devil, and the desires of your father you want to do. He was a murderer from the beginning, and does not stand in the truth, because there is no truth in him. When he speaks a lie, he speaks from his own *resources,* for he is a liar and the father of it. ⁴⁵But because I tell the truth, you do not believe Me. ⁴⁶Which of you convicts Me of sin? And if I tell the truth, why do you not believe Me? ⁴⁷He who is of God hears God's words; therefore you do not hear, because you are not of God."

⁴⁸Then the Jews answered and said to Him, "Do we not say rightly that You are a Samaritan and have a demon?"

⁴⁹Jesus answered, "I do not have a demon; but I honor My Father, and you dishonor Me. ⁵⁰And I do not seek My *own* glory; there is One who seeks and judges. ⁵¹Most assuredly, I say to you, if anyone keeps My word he shall never see death."

⁵²Then the Jews said to Him, "Now we know that You have a demon! Abraham is dead, and the prophets; and You say, 'If anyone keeps My word he shall never taste death.' ⁵³Are You greater than our father Abraham, who is dead? And the prophets are dead. Who do You make Yourself out to be?"

⁵⁴Jesus answered, "If I honor Myself, My honor is nothing. It is My Father who honors Me, of whom you say that He is your God. ⁵⁵Yet you have not known Him, but I know Him. And if I say, 'I do not know Him,' I shall be a liar like you; but I do know Him and keep His word. ⁵⁶Your father Abraham rejoiced to see My day, and he saw *it* and was glad."

⁵⁷Then the Jews said to Him, "You are not yet fifty years old, and have You seen Abraham?"

⁵⁸Jesus said to them, "Most assuredly, I say to you, before Abraham was, I AM."

⁵⁹Then they took up stones to throw at Him; but Jesus hid Himself and went out of the temple, going through the midst of them, and so passed by.

CHAPTER 9 JESUS HEALS A BLIND MAN.

Now as *Jesus* passed by, He saw a man who was blind from birth. [2]And His disciples asked Him, saying, "Rabbi, who sinned, this man or his parents, that he was born blind?"

[3]Jesus answered, "Neither this man nor his parents sinned, but that the works of God should be revealed in him. [4]I must work the works of Him who sent Me while it is day; *the* night is coming when no one can work. [5]As long as I am in the world, I am the light of the world."

[6]When He had said these things, He spat on the ground and made clay with the saliva; and He anointed the eyes of the blind man with the clay. [7]And He said to him, "Go, wash in the pool of Siloam" (which is translated, Sent). So he went and washed, and came back seeing.

[8]Therefore the neighbors and those who previously had seen that he was blind said, "Is not this he who sat and begged?"

[9]Some said, "This is he." Others *said*, "He is like him." He said, "I am *he*."

[10]Therefore they said to him, "How were your eyes opened?"

[11]He answered and said, "A Man called Jesus made clay and anointed my eyes and said to me, 'Go to the pool of Siloam and wash.' So I went and washed, and I received sight."

WHAT'S HAPPENING?

9:2-3 A common belief in Jewish culture was that calamity or suffering was the result of some great sin. But Christ used this man's suffering to teach about faith and to glorify God. We live in a sinful world where good behavior is not always rewarded and bad behavior is not always punished. Therefore, innocent people sometimes suffer. If God took suffering away whenever we asked, we would follow him for comfort and convenience, not out of love and devotion. Regardless of the reasons for our suffering, Jesus has the power to help us deal with it. When you suffer from a disease, tragedy, or handicap, try not to ask, "Why did this happen to me?" or "What did I do wrong?" Instead, ask God to give you strength through the trial and offer you a deeper perspective on what is happening.

[12]Then they said to him, "Where is He?"
He said, "I do not know."

[13]They brought him who formerly was blind to the Pharisees. [14]Now it was a Sabbath when Jesus made the clay and opened his eyes. [15]Then the Pharisees also asked him again how he had received his sight. He said to them, "He put clay on my eyes, and I washed, and I see."

[16]Therefore some of the Pharisees said, "This Man is not from God, because He does not keep the Sabbath." Others said, "How can a man who is a sinner do such signs?" And there was a division among them.

[17]They said to the blind man again, "What do you say about Him because He opened your eyes?"
He said, "He is a prophet."

[18]But the Jews did not believe concerning him, that he had been blind and received his sight, until they called the parents of him who had received his sight. [19]And they asked them, saying, "Is this your son, who you say was born blind? How then does he now see?"

NEW FAITH

9:28,34 The man's new faith was severely tested by some of the authorities. He was cursed and evicted from the temple. You also m[ay] expect persecution when you follow Jesus. You may lose friends; yo[u] even lose your life. But no one can ever take away the eternal life [you] have been given by Jesus.

[20]His parents answered them and said, "We know that this is our son, and that he was born blind; [21]but by what means he now sees we do not know, or who opened his eyes we do not know. He is of age; ask him. He will speak for himself." [22]His parents said these *things* because they feared the Jews, for the Jews had agreed already that if anyone confessed *that* He *was* Christ, he would be put out of the synagogue. [23]Therefore his parents said, "He is of age; ask him."

[24]So they again called the man who was blind, and said to him, "Give God the glory! We know that this Man is a sinner."

[25]He answered and said, "Whether He is a sinner *or not* I do not know. One thing I know: that though I was blind, now I see."

[26]Then they said to him again, "What did He do to you? How did He open your eyes?"

[27]He answered them, "I told you already, and you did not listen. Why do you want to hear *it* again? Do you also want to become His disciples?"

[28]Then they reviled him and said, "You are His disciple, but we are Moses' disciples. [29]We know that God spoke to Moses; *as for* this *fellow*, we do not know where He is from."

[30]The man answered and said to them, "Why, this is a marvelous thing, that you do not know where He is from; yet He has opened my eyes! [31]Now we know that God does not hear sinners; but if anyone is a worshiper of God and does His will, He hears him. [32]Since the world began it has been unheard of that anyone opened the eyes of one who was born blind. [33]If this Man were not from God, He could do nothing."

[34]They answered and said to him, "You were completely born in sins, and are you teaching us?" And they cast him out.

[35]Jesus heard that they had cast him out; and when He had found him, He said to him, "Do you believe in the Son of God?"

[36]He answered and said, "Who is He, Lord, that I may believe in Him?"

[37]And Jesus said to him, "You have both seen Him and it is He who is talking with you."

[38]Then he said, "Lord, I believe!" And he worshiped Him.

[39]And Jesus said, "For judgment I have come into this world, that those who do not see may see, and that those who see may be made blind."

[40]Then *some* of the Pharisees who were with Him heard these words, and said to Him, "Are we blind also?"

[41]Jesus said to them, "If you were blind, you would have no sin; but now you say, 'We see.' Therefore your sin remains.

CHAPTER 10 JESUS: THE GOOD SHEPHERD.

"Most assuredly, I say to you, he who does not enter the sheepfold by the door, but climbs up some other way, the same is a thief and a robber. ²But he who enters by the door is the shepherd of the sheep. ³To him the doorkeeper opens, and the sheep hear his voice; and he calls his own sheep by name and leads them out. ⁴And when he brings out his own sheep, he goes before them; and the sheep follow him, for they know his voice. ⁵Yet they will by no means follow a stranger, but will flee from him, for they do not know the voice of strangers." ⁶Jesus used this illustration, but they did not understand the things which He spoke to them.

⁷Then Jesus said to them again, "Most assuredly, I say to you, I am the door of the sheep. ⁸All who *ever* came before Me are thieves and robbers, but the sheep did not hear them. ⁹I am the door. If anyone enters by Me, he will be saved, and will go in and out and find pasture. ¹⁰The thief does not come except to steal, and to kill, and to destroy. I have come that they may have life, and that they may have *it* more abundantly.

¹¹"I am the good shepherd. The good shepherd gives His life for the sheep. ¹²But a hireling, *he who is* not the shepherd, one who does not own the sheep, sees the wolf coming and leaves the sheep and flees; and the wolf catches the sheep and scatters them. ¹³The hireling flees because he is a hireling and does not care about the sheep. ¹⁴I am the good shepherd; and I know My *sheep*, and am known by My own. ¹⁵As the Father knows Me, even so I know the Father; and I lay down My life for the sheep. ¹⁶And other sheep I have which are not of this fold; them also I must bring, and they will hear My voice; and there will be one flock *and* one shepherd.

¹⁷"Therefore My Father loves Me, because I lay down My life that I may take it again. ¹⁸No one takes it from Me, but I lay it down of Myself. I have power to lay it down, and I have power to take it again. This command I have received from My Father."

¹⁹Therefore there was a division again among the Jews because of these sayings. ²⁰And many of them said, "He has a demon and is mad. Why do you listen to Him?" ²¹Others said, "These are not the words of one who has a demon. Can a demon open the eyes of the blind?"

²²Now it was the Feast of Dedication in Jerusalem, and it was winter. ²³And Jesus walked in the temple, in Solomon's porch. ²⁴Then the Jews surrounded Him and said to Him, "How long do You keep us in doubt? If You are the Christ, tell us plainly."

²⁵Jesus answered them, "I told you, and you do not believe. The works that I do in My Father's name, they bear witness of Me. ²⁶But you do not believe, because you are not of My sheep, as I said to you. ²⁷My sheep hear My voice, and I know them, and they follow Me. ²⁸And I give them eternal life, and they shall never perish; neither shall anyone snatch them out of My hand. ²⁹My Father, who has given *them* to Me, is greater than all; and no one is able to snatch *them* out of My Father's hand. ³⁰I and *My* Father are one."

³¹Then the Jews took up stones again to stone Him. ³²Jesus answered them, "Many good works I have shown you from My Father. For which of those works do you stone Me?"

³³The Jews answered Him, saying, "For a good work we do not stone You, but for blasphemy, and because You, being a Man, make Yourself God."

³⁴Jesus answered them, "Is it not written in your law, '*I said, "You are gods"* '? ³⁵If He called them gods, to whom the word of God came (and the Scripture cannot be broken), ³⁶do you say of Him whom the Father sanctified and sent into the world, 'You are blaspheming,' because I said, 'I am the Son of God'? ³⁷If I do not do the works of

BLIND

10:24 These leaders were waiting for the signs and answers *they* thought would convince them of Jesus' identity. Thus they couldn't hear the truth Jesus was giving them. Jesus tried to correct their mistaken ideas, but they clung to the wrong idea of what kind of Messiah God would send. Such blindness still keeps people away from Jesus. They want him on their own terms; they do not want him if it means changing their whole life.

My Father, do not believe Me; ³⁸but if I do, though you do not believe Me, believe the works, that you may know and believe that the Father *is* in Me, and I in Him." ³⁹Therefore they sought again to seize Him, but He escaped out of their hand.

⁴⁰And He went away again beyond the Jordan to the place where John was baptizing at first, and there He stayed. ⁴¹Then many came to Him and said, "John performed no sign, but all the things that John spoke about this Man were true." ⁴²And many believed in Him there.

CHAPTER **11** JESUS BRINGS LAZARUS TO LIFE.

Now a certain *man* was sick, Lazarus of Bethany, the town of Mary and her sister Martha. ²It was *that* Mary who anointed the Lord with fragrant oil and wiped His feet with her hair, whose brother Lazarus was sick. ³Therefore the sisters sent to Him, saying, "Lord, behold, he whom You love is sick."

⁴When Jesus heard *that*, He said, "This sickness is not unto death, but for the glory of God, that the Son of God may be glorified through it."

⁵Now Jesus loved Martha and her sister and Lazarus. ⁶So, when He heard that he was sick, He stayed two more days in the place where He was. ⁷Then after this He said to *the* disciples, "Let us go to Judea again."

⁸*The* disciples said to Him, "Rabbi, lately the Jews sought to stone You, and are You going there again?"

⁹Jesus answered, "Are there not twelve hours in the day? If anyone walks in the day, he does not stumble, because he sees the light of this world. ¹⁰But if one walks in the night, he stumbles, because the light is not in him." ¹¹These things He said, and after that He said to them, "Our friend Lazarus sleeps, but I go that I may wake him up."

TIMING

11:5-7 Jesus loved this family and often stayed with them. He knew their pain but did not respond immediately. His delay had a specific purpose. God's timing, especially his delays, may make us think he is not answering or is not answering the way we want. But he will meet all our needs according to his perfect schedule and purpose. Patiently await his timing.

11:33-38 John stresses that we have a God who cares. This contrasts with the Greek concept of God that was popular in his day—a God with no emotions and no messy involvement with humans. Here we see many of Jesus' emotions— compassion, indignation, sorrow, even frustration. Jesus often expressed deep emotion, and we must never be afraid to reveal our true feelings to him. He understands what we feel because he experienced emotions, too. Be honest, and don't try to hide anything from your Savior. He cares.

[12]Then His disciples said, "Lord, if he sleeps he will get well." [13]However, Jesus spoke of his death, but they thought that He was speaking about taking rest in sleep. [14]Then Jesus said to them plainly, "Lazarus is dead. [15]And I am glad for your sakes that I was not there, that you may believe. Nevertheless let us go to him." [16]Then Thomas, who is called the Twin, said to his fellow disciples, "Let us also go, that we may die with Him."

[17]So when Jesus came, He found that he had already been in the tomb four days. [18]Now Bethany was near Jerusalem, about two miles away. [19]And many of the Jews had joined the women around Martha and Mary, to comfort them concerning their brother.

[20]Now Martha, as soon as she heard that Jesus was coming, went and met Him, but Mary was sitting in the house. [21]Now Martha said to Jesus, "Lord, if You had been here, my brother would not have died. [22]But even now I know that whatever You ask of God, God will give You."

[23]Jesus said to her, "Your brother will rise again."

[24]Martha said to Him, "I know that he will rise again in the resurrection at the last day."

[25]Jesus said to her, "I am the resurrection and the life. He who believes in Me, though he may die, he shall live. [26]And whoever lives and believes in Me shall never die. Do you believe this?"

[27]She said to Him, "Yes, Lord, I believe that You are the Christ, the Son of God, who is to come into the world."

[28]And when she had said these things, she went her way and secretly called Mary her sister, saying, "The Teacher has come and is calling for you." [29]As soon as she heard *that*, she arose quickly and came to Him. [30]Now Jesus had not yet come into the town, but was in the place where Martha met Him. [31]Then the Jews who were with her in the house, and comforting her, when they saw that Mary rose up quickly and went out, followed her, saying, "She is going to the tomb to weep there."

[32]Then, when Mary came where Jesus was, and saw Him, she fell down at His feet, saying to Him, "Lord, if You had been here, my brother would not have died."

[33]Therefore, when Jesus saw her weeping, and the Jews who came with her weeping, He groaned in the spirit and was troubled. [34]And He said, "Where have you laid him?"

They said to Him, "Lord, come and see."

[35]Jesus wept. [36]Then the Jews said, "See how He loved him!"

[37]And some of them said, "Could not this Man, who opened the eyes of the blind, also have kept this man from dying?"

[38]Then Jesus, again groaning in Himself, came to the tomb. It was a cave, and a stone lay against it. [39]Jesus said, "Take away the stone."

Martha, the sister of him who was dead, said to Him, "Lord, by this time there is a stench, for he has been dead four days."

[40]Jesus said to her, "Did I not say to you that if you would believe you would see the glory of God?" [41]Then they took away the stone *from the place* where the dead man was lying. And Jesus lifted up *His* eyes and said, "Father, I thank You that You have heard Me. [42]And I know that You always hear Me, but because of the people who are standing by I said *this*, that they may believe that You sent Me." [43]Now when He had said these things, He cried with a loud voice, "Lazarus, come forth!" [44]And he who had died came out bound hand and foot with graveclothes, and his face was wrapped with a cloth. Jesus said to them, "Loose him, and let him go."

[45]Then many of the Jews who had come to Mary, and had seen the things Jesus did, believed in Him. [46]But some of them went away to the Pharisees and told them the things Jesus did. [47]Then the chief priests and the Pharisees gathered a council and said, "What shall we do? For this Man works many signs. [48]If we let Him alone like this, everyone will believe in Him, and the Romans will come and take away both our place and nation."

[49]And one of them, Caiaphas, being high priest that year, said to them, "You know nothing at all, [50]nor do you consider that it is expedient for us that one man should die for the people, and not that the whole nation should perish." [51]Now this he did not say on his own *authority*; but being high priest that year he prophesied that Jesus would die for the nation, [52]and not for that nation only, but also that He would gather together in one the children of God who were scattered abroad.

[53]Then, from that day on, they plotted to put Him to death. [54]Therefore Jesus no longer walked openly among the Jews, but went from there into the country near the wilderness, to a city called Ephraim, and there remained with His disciples.

[55]And the Passover of the Jews was near, and many went from the country up to Jerusalem before the Passover, to purify themselves. [56]Then they sought Jesus, and spoke among themselves as they stood in the temple, "What do you think—that He will not come to the feast?" [57]Now both the chief priests and the Pharisees had given a command, that if anyone knew where He was, he should report *it*, that they might seize Him.

CHAPTER **12** MARY ANOINTS JESUS' FEET. Then, six days before the Passover, Jesus came to Bethany, where Lazarus was who had been dead, whom He had raised from the dead. [2]There they made Him a supper; and Martha served, but Lazarus was one of those who sat

LOOK BACK

12:16 After Jesus' resurrection, the disciples understood many of the prophecies they had missed along the way. Jesus' words and actions took on new meaning and made more sense. In retrospect, they saw how Jesus had led them into a deeper and better understanding of his truth. Stop now and think about the events in your life leading up to where you are now. How has God led you to this point? As you grow older, you will look back and see God's involvement more clearly than you do now. Let this truth encourage you to live a life of faith today.

at the table with Him. ³Then Mary took a pound of very costly oil of spikenard, anointed the feet of Jesus, and wiped His feet with her hair. And the house was filled with the fragrance of the oil.

⁴But one of His disciples, Judas Iscariot, Simon's *son,* who would betray Him, said, ⁵"Why was this fragrant oil not sold for three hundred denarii and given to the poor?" ⁶This he said, not that he cared for the poor, but because he was a thief, and had the money box; and he used to take what was put in it.

⁷But Jesus said, "Let her alone; she has kept this for the day of My burial. ⁸For the poor you have with you always, but Me you do not have always."

⁹Now a great many of the Jews knew that He was there; and they came, not for Jesus' sake only, but that they might also see Lazarus, whom He had raised from the dead. ¹⁰But the chief priests plotted to put Lazarus to death also, ¹¹because on account of him many of the Jews went away and believed in Jesus.

¹²The next day a great multitude that had come to the feast, when they heard that Jesus was coming to Jerusalem, ¹³took branches of palm trees and went out to meet Him, and cried out:

"Hosanna!
'Blessed is He who
    comes in the name
    of the LORD!'
The King of Israel!"

¹⁴Then Jesus, when He had found a young donkey, sat on it; as it is written:

¹⁵ "Fear not, daughter of Zion;
Behold, your King is coming,
Sitting on a donkey's colt."

¹⁶His disciples did not understand these things at first; but when Jesus was glorified, then they remembered that these things were written about Him and *that* they had done these things to Him.

¹⁷Therefore the people, who were with Him when He called Lazarus out of his tomb and raised him from the dead, bore witness. ¹⁸For this reason the people also met Him, because they heard that He had done this sign. ¹⁹The Pharisees therefore said among themselves, "You see that you are accomplishing nothing. Look, the world has gone after Him!"

²⁰Now there were certain Greeks among those who came up to worship at the feast. ²¹Then they came to Philip, who was from Bethsaida of Galilee, and asked him, saying, "Sir, we wish to see Jesus."

²²Philip came and told Andrew, and in turn Andrew and Philip told Jesus.

²³But Jesus answered them, saying, "The hour has come that the Son of Man should be glorified. ²⁴Most assuredly, I say to you, unless a grain of wheat falls into the ground and dies, it remains alone; but if it dies, it produces much grain. ²⁵He who loves his life will lose it, and he who hates his life in this world will keep it for eternal life. ²⁶If anyone serves Me, let him follow Me; and where I am, there My servant will be also. If anyone serves Me, him *My* Father will honor.

²⁷"Now My soul is troubled, and what shall I say? 'Father, save Me from this hour'? But for this purpose I came to this hour. ²⁸Father, glorify Your name."

Then a voice came from heaven, *saying,*

MARY & MARTHA

Hospitality is an art. Making sure a guest is welcomed, warmed, and well fed requires creativity, organization, and teamwork. Mary and Martha's ability to accomplish these makes them the best sister hospitality team in the Bible. Jesus often stayed in their home.

For Mary, hospitality meant giving more attention to the guest himself than to his needs. She was more interested in her guest's words than in the cleanliness of her home or the timeliness of her meals. She let her sister Martha take care of those details. Mary was mainly a "responder." She did little preparation and lots of participation. She needed to learn that action often is appropriate and necessary.

Unlike her sister, Martha worried about details. She wished to please, to serve, to do the right thing—but she often succeeded in making everyone around her feel uncomfortable. Perhaps she was the oldest and felt specially responsible. So she tried too hard to have everything perfect. Mary's lack of cooperation bothered Martha so much that she finally asked Jesus to tell Mary to help. Jesus gently pointed out that Mary was actually doing her part.

Each sister had her own lesson to learn. Mary learned that worship sometimes involves service. Do people in your life know you care about them? Martha learned that obedient service often goes unnoticed. The last time she appears in the Gospels she is again serving a meal to Jesus and the disciples—this time without complaint. When was the last time you gladly served someone without being noticed?

LESSONS: Getting caught up in details can make us forget the main reasons for our actions.

There is a proper time to listen to Jesus and a proper time to work for him

KEY VERSE: "But Martha was distracted with much serving, and she approached Him and said, 'Lord, do You not care that my sister has left me to serve alone? Therefore tell her to help me' " (Luke 10:40).

Mary and Martha's story is told in Luke 10:38-42 and John 11:17-45.

UPS:
- Known as hospitable homeowners
- Friends of Jesus, they believed in him with growing faith
- Martha had a strong desire to do everything exactly right
- Mary had a deep concern for people's feelings

DOWNS:
- Martha expected others to agree with her priorities and was overly concerned with details
- Martha tended to feel sorry for herself when her efforts were not recognized
- Mary would let others do the work
- Mary tended to respond, not prepare

STATS:
- Where: Bethany
- Relative: Brother: Lazarus

12:37-38 Jesus had performed many miracles, but most people still didn't believe in him. Likewise, many today won't believe despite all God does. Don't be discouraged if your witness for Christ doesn't turn as many to him as you'd like. Your job is to continue as a faithful witness. You are not responsible for the decisions of others, but simply to reach out to others.

"I have both glorified *it* and will glorify *it* again."

²⁹Therefore the people who stood by and heard *it* said that it had thundered. Others said, "An angel has spoken to Him."

³⁰Jesus answered and said, "This voice did not come because of Me, but for your sake. ³¹Now is the judgment of this world; now the ruler of this world will be cast out. ³²And I, if I am lifted up from the earth, will draw all *peoples* to Myself." ³³This He said, signifying by what death He would die.

³⁴The people answered Him, "We have heard from the law that the Christ remains forever; and how *can* You say, 'The Son of Man must be lifted up'? Who is this Son of Man?"

³⁵Then Jesus said to them, "A little while longer the light is with you. Walk while you have the light, lest darkness overtake you; he who walks in darkness does not know where he is going. ³⁶While you have the light, believe in the light, that you may become sons of light." These things Jesus spoke, and departed, and was hidden from them.

³⁷But although He had done so many signs before them, they did not believe in Him, ³⁸that the word of Isaiah the prophet might be fulfilled, which he spoke:

"Lord, who has believed our report?
And to whom has the arm of the LORD been revealed?"

³⁹Therefore they could not believe, because Isaiah said again:

⁴⁰ "He has blinded their eyes and hardened their hearts,
Lest they should see with their eyes,
Lest they should understand with their hearts and turn,
So that I should heal them."

⁴¹These things Isaiah said when he saw His glory and spoke of Him.

⁴²Nevertheless even among the rulers many believed in Him, but because of the Pharisees they did not confess *Him*, lest they should be put out of the synagogue; ⁴³for they loved the praise of men more than the praise of God.

⁴⁴Then Jesus cried out and said, "He who believes in Me, believes not in Me but in Him who sent Me. ⁴⁵And he who sees Me sees Him who sent Me. ⁴⁶I have come *as a* light into the world, that whoever believes in Me should not abide in darkness. ⁴⁷And if anyone hears My words and does not believe, I do not judge him; for I did not come to judge the world but to save the world. ⁴⁸He who rejects Me, and does not receive My words, has that which judges him—the word that I have spoken will judge him in the last day. ⁴⁹For I have not spoken on My own *authority;* but the Father who sent Me gave Me a command, what I should say and what I should speak. ⁵⁰And I know that His command is everlasting life. Therefore, whatever I speak, just as the Father has told Me, so I speak."

CHAPTER 13 JESUS WASHES HIS DISCIPLES' FEET.

Now before the Feast of the Passover, when Jesus knew that His hour had come that He should depart from this world to the Father, having loved His own who were in the world, He loved them to the end.

²And supper being ended, the devil having already put it into the heart of Judas Iscariot, Simon's *son,* to betray Him, ³Jesus, knowing that the Father had given all things into His hands, and that He had come from God and was going to God, ⁴rose from supper and laid aside His garments, took a towel and girded Himself. ⁵After that, He

■■ ACTIVE LOVE

13:35 Love is not simply warm feelings; instead it is an attitude th reveals itself in action. How can we love others as Christ loves us? By helping when it's not convenient, by giving when it hurts, by devotin energy to others' welfare rather than our own, by absorbing hurts fr others without complaining or fighting back. This kind of loving is ha do. That is why people will notice when you do it and will know you a empowered by a supernatural source. The Bible has another beautifu description of love in 1 Corinthians 13.

poured water into a basin and began to wash the disciples' feet, and to wipe *them* with the towel with which He was girded. ⁶Then He came to Simon Peter. And *Peter* said to Him, "Lord, are You washing my feet?"

⁷Jesus answered and said to him, "What I am doing you do not understand now, but you will know after this."

⁸Peter said to Him, "You shall never wash my feet!"

JESUS
said to him,

JOHN 14:6

I AM THE WAY THE TRUTH AND THE LIFE NO ONE COMES TO THE FATHER EXCEPT THROUGH ME

Jesus answered him, "If I do not wash you, you have no part with Me."

⁹Simon Peter said to Him, "Lord, not my feet only, but also *my* hands and *my* head!"

¹⁰Jesus said to him, "He who is bathed needs only to wash *his* feet, but is completely clean; and you are clean, but not all of you." ¹¹For He knew who would betray Him; therefore He said, "You are not all clean."

¹²So when He had washed their feet, taken His garments, and sat down again, He said to them, "Do you know what I have done to you? ¹³You call Me Teacher and Lord, and you say well, for so I am. ¹⁴If I then, *your* Lord and Teacher, have washed your feet, you also ought to wash one another's feet. ¹⁵For I have given you an example, that you should do as I have done to you. ¹⁶Most assuredly, I say to you, a servant is not greater than his master; nor is he who is sent greater than he who sent him. ¹⁷If you know these things, blessed are you if you do them.

¹⁸"I do not speak concerning all of you. I know whom I have chosen; but that the Scripture may be fulfilled, *'He who eats bread with Me has lifted up his heel against Me.'* ¹⁹Now I tell you before it comes, that when it does come to pass, you may believe that I am *He*. ²⁰Most assuredly, I say to you, he who receives whomever I send receives Me; and he who receives Me receives Him who sent Me."

²¹When Jesus had said these things, He was troubled in spirit, and testified and said, "Most assuredly, I say to you, one of you will betray Me." ²²Then the disciples looked at one another, perplexed about whom He spoke.

²³Now there was leaning on Jesus' bosom one of His disciples, whom Jesus loved. ²⁴Simon Peter therefore motioned to him to ask who it was of whom He spoke.

²⁵Then, leaning back on Jesus' breast, he said to Him, "Lord, who is it?"

²⁶Jesus answered, "It is he to whom I shall give a piece of bread when I have dipped *it*." And having dipped the bread, He gave *it* to Judas Iscariot, *the son* of Simon. ²⁷Now after the piece of bread, Satan entered him. Then Jesus said to him, "What you do, do quickly." ²⁸But no one at the table knew for what reason He said this to him. ²⁹For some thought, because Judas had the money box, that Jesus had said to him, "Buy *those things* we need for the feast," or that he should give something to the poor.

³⁰Having received the piece of bread, he then went out immediately. And it was night.

³¹So, when he had gone out, Jesus said, "Now the Son of Man is glorified, and God is glorified in Him. ³²If God is glorified in Him, God will also glorify Him in Himself, and glorify Him immediately. ³³Little children, I shall be with you a little while longer. You will seek Me; and as I said to the Jews, 'Where I am going, you cannot come,' so now I say to you. ³⁴A new commandment I give to you, that you love one another; as I have loved you, that you also love one another. ³⁵By this all will know that you are My disciples, if you have love for one another."

³⁶Simon Peter said to Him, "Lord, where are You going?"

Jesus answered him, "Where I am going you cannot follow Me now, but you shall follow Me afterward."

³⁷Peter said to Him, "Lord, why can I not follow You now? I will lay down my life for Your sake."

³⁸Jesus answered him, "Will you lay down your life for My sake? Most assuredly, I say to you, the rooster shall not crow till you have denied Me three times.

CHAPTER **14** JESUS: THE WAY, TRUTH, AND LIFE.

"Let not your heart be troubled; you believe in God, believe also in Me. ²In My Father's house are many mansions; if *it were* not *so*, I would have told you. I go to prepare a place for you. ³And if I go and prepare a place for you, I will come again and receive you to Myself; that where I am, *there* you may be also. ⁴And where I go you know, and the way you know."

⁵Thomas said to Him, "Lord, we do not know where You are going, and how can we know the way?"

⁶Jesus said to him, "I am the way, the truth, and the life. No one comes to the Father except through Me.

◄▬▬▬▬▬▬A SURE WAY

14:6 Jesus says he is the *only* way to God the Father. Some people may argue that this is too narrow. In reality, it is wide enough for the whole world if the world chooses to accept it. Instead of worrying about how limited it sounds to have only one way, we should be saying, "Thank you God, for providing a sure way to get to you!"

⁷"If you had known Me, you would have known My Father also; and from now on you know Him and have seen Him."

⁸Philip said to Him, "Lord, show us the Father, and it is sufficient for us."

⁹Jesus said to him, "Have I been with you so long, and yet you have not known Me, Philip? He who has seen Me has seen the Father; so how can you say, 'Show us the Father'? ¹⁰Do you not believe that I am in the Father, and the Father in Me? The words that I speak to you I do not speak on My own *authority;* but the Father who dwells in Me does the works. ¹¹Believe Me that I *am* in the Father and the Father in Me, or else believe Me for the sake of the works themselves.

¹²"Most assuredly, I say to you, he who believes in Me, the works that I do he will do also; and greater *works* than these he will do, because I go to My Father. ¹³And whatever you ask in My name, that I will do, that the Father may be glorified in the Son. ¹⁴If you ask anything in My name, I will do *it*.

¹⁵"If you love Me, keep My commandments. ¹⁶And I will pray the Father, and He will give you another Helper, that He may abide with you forever— ¹⁷the Spirit of truth, whom the world cannot receive, because it neither sees Him nor knows Him; but you know Him, for He dwells with you and will be in you. ¹⁸I will not leave you orphans; I will come to you.

¹⁹"A little while longer and the world will see Me no more, but you will see Me. Because I live, you will live also. ²⁰At that day you will know that I *am* in My Father, and you in Me, and I in you. ²¹He who has My commandments and keeps them, it is he who loves Me. And he who loves Me will be loved by My Father, and I will love him and manifest Myself to him."

²²Judas (not Iscariot) said to Him, "Lord, how is it that You will manifest Yourself to us, and not to the world?"

²³Jesus answered and said to him, "If anyone loves Me,

he will keep My word; and My Father will love him, and We will come to him and make Our home with him. ²⁴He who does not love Me does not keep My words; and the word which you hear is not Mine but the Father's who sent Me.

²⁵"These things I have spoken to you while being present with you. ²⁶But the Helper, the Holy Spirit, whom the Father will send in My name, He will teach you all things, and bring to your remembrance all things that I said to you. ²⁷Peace I leave with you, My peace I give to you; not as the world gives do I give to you. Let not your heart be troubled, neither let it be afraid. ²⁸You have heard Me say to you, 'I am going away and coming *back* to you.' If you loved Me, you would rejoice because I said, 'I am going to the Father,' for My Father is greater than I.

ACCURATE

14:26 Jesus promised the disciples that the Holy Spirit would help them remember what he had been teaching them. This promise underscores the validity of the New Testament. The disciples were eyewitnesses of Jesus' life and teachings, and the Holy Spirit helped them remember without taking away their individual perspective. We can be confident that the Gospels are accurate records of what Jesus taught and did (see 1 Corinthians 2:10-14).

²⁹"And now I have told you before it comes, that when it does come to pass, you may believe. ³⁰I will no longer talk much with you, for the ruler of this world is coming, and he has nothing in Me. ³¹But that the world may know that I love the Father, and as the Father gave Me commandment, so I do. Arise, let us go from here.

CHAPTER 15 THE VINE AND THE BRANCHES.

"I am the true vine, and My Father is the vinedresser. ²Every branch in Me that does not bear fruit He takes away; and every *branch* that bears fruit He prunes, that it may bear more fruit. ³You are already clean because of the word which I have spoken to you. ⁴Abide in Me, and I in you. As the branch cannot bear fruit of itself, unless it abides in the vine, neither can you, unless you abide in Me.

⁵"I am the vine, you *are* the branches. He who abides in Me, and I in him, bears much fruit; for without Me you can do nothing. ⁶If anyone does not abide in Me, he is cast out as a branch and is withered; and they gather them and throw *them* into the fire, and they are burned. ⁷If you abide in Me, and My words abide in you, you will ask what you desire, and it shall be done for you. ⁸By this My Father is glorified, that you bear much fruit; so you will be My disciples.

⁹"As the Father loved Me, I also have loved you; abide in My love. ¹⁰If you keep My commandments, you will abide in My love, just as I have kept My Father's commandments and abide in His love.

¹¹"These things I have spoken to you, that My joy may remain in you, and *that* your joy may be full. ¹²This is My commandment, that you love one another as I have loved you. ¹³Greater love has no one than this, than to lay down one's life for his friends. ¹⁴You are My friends if you do whatever I command you. ¹⁵No longer do I call you servants, for a servant does not know what his master is doing; but I have called you friends, for all things that I heard from My Father I have made known to you. ¹⁶You did not choose Me, but I chose you and appointed you that you should go and bear fruit, and *that* your fruit should remain, that whatever you ask the Father in My name He may give you. ¹⁷These things I command you, that you love one another.

¹⁸"If the world hates you, you know that it hated Me before *it hated* you. ¹⁹If you were of the world, the world would love its own. Yet because you are not of the world, but I chose you out of the world, therefore the world hates you. ²⁰Remember the word that I said to you, 'A servant is not greater than his master.' If they persecuted Me, they will also persecute you. If they kept My word, they will keep yours also. ²¹But all these things they will do to you for My name's sake, because they do not know Him who sent Me. ²²If I had not come and spoken to them, they would have no sin, but now they have no excuse for their sin. ²³He who hates Me hates My Father also. ²⁴If I had not done among them the works which no one else did, they would have no sin; but now they have seen and also hated both Me and My Father. ²⁵But *this happened* that the word might be fulfilled which is written in their law, *'They hated Me without a cause.'*

²⁶"But when the Helper comes, whom I shall send to you from the Father, the Spirit of truth who proceeds from the Father, He will testify of Me. ²⁷And you also will bear witness, because you have been with Me from the beginning.

CHAPTER 16 THE HOLY SPIRIT.

"These things I have spoken to you, that you should not be made to stumble. ²They will put you out of the synagogues; yes, the time is coming that whoever kills you will think that he offers God service. ³And these things they will do to you because they have not known the Father nor Me. ⁴But these things I have told you, that when the time comes, you may remember that I told you of them.

"And these things I did not say to you at the beginning, because I was with you.

⁵"But now I go away to Him who sent Me, and none of you asks Me, 'Where are You going?' ⁶But because I have said these things to you, sorrow has filled your heart. ⁷Nevertheless I tell you the truth. It is to your advantage that I go away; for if I do not go away, the Helper will not come to you; but if I depart, I will send Him to you. ⁸And when He has come, He will convict the world of sin, and of righteousness, and of judgment: ⁹of sin, because they do not believe in Me; ¹⁰of righteousness, because I go to My Father and you see Me no more; ¹¹of judgment, because the ruler of this world is judged.

WARNINGS

16:1-16 In his last moments with his disciples, Jesus (1) warned about further persecution, (2) told them where he was going, when was leaving, and why, and (3) assured them they would not be left but that the Spirit would come. He knew what lay ahead, and he d want their faith shaken or destroyed. God wants you to know that are not alone in the world. You have the Holy Spirit to comfort you you truth, and help you.

¹²"I still have many things to say to you, but you cannot bear *them* now. ¹³However, when He, the Spirit of truth, has come, He will guide you into all truth; for He will not speak on His own *authority*, but whatever He hears He will speak; and He will tell you things to come. ¹⁴He will glorify Me, for He will take of what is Mine and declare *it* to you. ¹⁵All things that the Father has are Mine. Therefore I said that He will take of Mine and declare *it* to you.

¹⁶"A little while, and you will not see Me; and again a little while, and you will see Me, because I go to the Father."

¹⁷Then *some* of His disciples said among themselves, "What is this that He says to us, 'A little while, and you will not see Me; and again a little while, and you will see Me'; and, 'because I go to the Father'?" ¹⁸They said therefore, "What is this that He says, 'A little while'? We do not know what He is saying."

¹⁹Now Jesus knew that they desired to ask Him, and He said to them, "Are you inquiring among yourselves about what I said, 'A little while, and you will not see Me; and again a little while, and you will see Me'? ²⁰Most assuredly, I say to you that you will weep and lament, but the world will rejoice; and you will be sorrowful, but your sorrow will be turned into joy. ²¹A woman, when she is in labor, has sorrow because her hour has come; but as soon as she has given birth to the child, she no longer remembers the anguish, for joy that a human being has been born into the world. ²²Therefore you now have sorrow; but I will see you again and your heart will rejoice, and your joy no one will take from you.

²³"And in that day you will ask Me nothing. Most assuredly, I say to you, whatever you ask the Father in My name He will give you. ²⁴Until now you have asked nothing in My name. Ask, and you will receive, that your joy may be full.

²⁵"These things I have spoken to you in figurative language; but the time is coming when I will no longer speak to you in figurative language, but I will tell you plainly about the Father. ²⁶In that day you will ask in My name, and I do not say to you that I shall pray the Father for you; ²⁷for the Father Himself loves you, because you have loved Me, and have believed that I came forth from God. ²⁸I came forth from the Father and have come into the world. Again, I leave the world and go to the Father."

²⁹His disciples said to Him, "See, now You are speaking plainly, and using no figure of speech! ³⁰Now we are sure that You know all things, and have no need that anyone should question You. By this we believe that You came forth from God."

³¹Jesus answered them, "Do you now believe? ³²Indeed the hour is coming, yes, has now come, that you

will be scattered, each to his own, and will leave Me alone. And yet I am not alone, because the Father is with Me. ³³These things I have spoken to you, that in Me you may have peace. In the world you will have tribulation; but be of good cheer, I have overcome the world."

CHAPTER 17 JESUS PRAYS FOR HIMSELF. Jesus spoke these words, lifted up His eyes to heaven, and said: "Father, the hour has come. Glorify Your Son, that Your Son also may glorify You, ²as You have given Him authority over all flesh, that He should give eternal life to as many as You have given Him. ³And this is eternal life, that they may know You, the only true God, and Jesus Christ whom You have sent. ⁴I have glorified You on the earth. I have finished the work which You have given Me to do. ⁵And now, O Father, glorify Me together with Yourself, with the glory which I had with You before the world was.

⁶"I have manifested Your name to the men whom You have given Me out of the world. They were Yours, You gave them to Me, and they have kept Your word. ⁷Now they have known that all things which You have given Me are from You. ⁸For I have given to them the words which You have given Me; and they have received *them*, and have known surely that I came forth from You; and they have believed that You sent Me.

⁹"I pray for them. I do not pray for the world but for those whom You have given Me, for they are Yours. ¹⁰And all Mine are Yours, and Yours are Mine, and I am glorified in them. ¹¹Now I am no longer in the world, but these are in the world, and I come to You. Holy Father, keep through Your name those whom You have given Me, that they may be one as We *are*. ¹²While I was with them in the

"Here's what I did..."

One day I came home from school only to find a note saying that my mother had been rushed to the hospital! I called the hospital and discovered that she had a blood clot in her upper leg and would have to be hospitalized for a while.

Suddenly our household was thrown into chaos. Nothing seemed normal without Mom. Plus I was worried that this could be something serious, or lead to something serious.

Through this time, I read the Bible a lot. I memorized John 14:27: "Peace I leave with you, My peace I give to you; not as the world gives do I give to you. Let not your heart be troubled, neither let it be afraid." These words of Jesus' helped me not to freak out. Instead I gave the situation to God and trusted him to see me through it. Every time I started to worry, I repeated this verse to myself and felt calmer. Jesus understood what I was going through—and he was in control! The more I concentrated on this, the more peace I felt. It was strange to feel so peaceful even when there was plenty I could worry about. But I just kept reminding myself of this verse, and it helped me get through that difficult time.

Kris

AGE 15

17:18 Jesus didn't ask God to take believers *out* of the world, but instead to use them *in* the world. Because Jesus sends us into the world, we should not try to escape from the world or avoid all relationships with non-Christians. We are called to be salt and light (Matthew 5:13-16), and we are to do the work God sent us to do.

world, I kept them in Your name. Those whom You gave Me I have kept; and none of them is lost except the son of perdition, that the Scripture might be fulfilled. [13]But now I come to You, and these things I speak in the world, that they may have My joy fulfilled in themselves. [14]I have given them Your word; and the world has hated them because they are not of the world, just as I am not of the world. [15]I do not pray that You should take them out of the world, but that You should keep them from the evil one. [16]They are not of the world, just as I am not of the world. [17]Sanctify them by Your truth. Your word is truth. [18]As You sent Me into the world, I also have sent them into the world. [19]And for their sakes I sanctify Myself, that they also may be sanctified by the truth.

[20]"I do not pray for these alone, but also for those who will believe in Me through their word; [21]that they all may be one, as You, Father, *are* in Me, and I in You; that they also may be one in Us, that the world may believe that You sent Me. [22]And the glory which You gave Me I have given them, that they may be one just as We are one: [23]I in them, and You in Me; that they may be made perfect in one, and that the world may know that You have sent Me, and have loved them as You have loved Me.

[24]"Father, I desire that they also whom You gave Me may be with Me where I am, that they may behold My glory which You have given Me; for You loved Me before the foundation of the world. [25]O righteous Father! The world has not known You, but I have known You; and these have known that You sent Me. [26]And I have declared to them Your name, and will declare *it*, that the love with which You loved Me may be in them, and I in them."

CHAPTER 18 JESUS IS ARRESTED. When Jesus had spoken these words, He went out with His disciples over the Brook Kidron, where there was a garden, which He and His disciples entered. [2]And Judas, who betrayed Him, also knew the place; for Jesus often met there with His disciples. [3]Then Judas, having received a detachment *of troops*, and officers from the chief priests and Pharisees, came there with lanterns, torches, and weapons. [4]Jesus therefore, knowing all things that would come upon Him, went forward and said to them, "Whom are you seeking?"

[5]They answered Him, "Jesus of Nazareth."

Jesus said to them, "I am *He*." And Judas, who betrayed Him, also stood with them. [6]Now when He said to them, "I am *He*," they drew back and fell to the ground.

[7]Then He asked them again, "Whom are you seeking?" And they said, "Jesus of Nazareth."

[8]Jesus answered, "I have told you that I am *He*. Therefore, if you seek Me, let these go their way," [9]that the saying might be fulfilled which He spoke, "Of those whom You gave Me I have lost none."

[10]Then Simon Peter, having a sword, drew it and struck the high priest's servant, and cut off his right ear. The servant's name was Malchus.

[11]So Jesus said to Peter, "Put your sword into the sheath. Shall I not drink the cup which My Father has given Me?"

[12]Then the detachment *of troops* and the captain and the officers of the Jews arrested Jesus and bound Him. [13]And they led Him away to Annas first, for he was the father-in-law of Caiaphas who was high priest that year. [14]Now it was Caiaphas who advised the Jews that it was expedient that one man should die for the people.

[15]And Simon Peter followed Jesus, and so *did* another disciple. Now that disciple was known to the high priest, and went with Jesus into the courtyard of the high priest. [16]But Peter stood at the door outside. Then the other disciple, who was known to the high priest, went out and spoke to her who kept the door, and brought Peter in. [17]Then the servant girl who kept the door said to Peter, "You are not also *one* of this Man's disciples, are you?"

He said, "I am not."

[18]Now the servants and officers who had made a fire of coals stood there, for it was cold, and they warmed themselves. And Peter stood with them and warmed himself.

[19]The high priest then asked Jesus about His disciples and His doctrine.

[20]Jesus answered him, "I spoke openly to the world. I always taught in synagogues and in the temple, where the Jews always meet, and in secret I have said nothing. [21]Why do you ask Me? Ask those who have heard Me what I said to them. Indeed they know what I said."

[22]And when He had said these things, one of the officers who stood by struck Jesus with the palm of his hand, saying, "Do You answer the high priest like that?"

[23]Jesus answered him, "If I have spoken evil, bear witness of the evil; but if well, why do you strike Me?"

[24]Then Annas sent Him bound to Caiaphas the high priest.

[25]Now Simon Peter stood and warmed himself. Therefore they said to him, "You are not also *one* of His disciples, are you?"

He denied *it* and said, "I am not!"

[26]One of the servants of the high priest, a relative *of him* whose ear Peter cut off, said, "Did I not see you in the garden with Him?" [27]Peter then denied again; and immediately a rooster crowed.

[28]Then they led Jesus from Caiaphas to the Praetorium, and it was early morning. But they themselves did not go into the Praetorium, lest they should be defiled,

18:22-27 We can easily get angry at the Jewish council for their injustice in condemning Jesus, but Peter and the rest of the disciples contributed to Jesus' pain by deserting and denying him (Matthew 26:56). While most of us are not like the religious leaders, we all are the disciples, for all of us have been guilty of denying Christ as Lord in vital areas of our life. Don't excuse yourself by pointing at others whose sins seem worse than yours. Instead, come to Jesus for forgiveness and healing.

but that they might eat the Passover. [29]Pilate then went out to them and said, "What accusation do you bring against this Man?"

[30]They answered and said to him, "If He were not an evildoer, we would not have delivered Him up to you."

[31]Then Pilate said to them, "You take Him and judge Him according to your law."

Therefore the Jews said to him, "It is not lawful for us to put anyone to death," [32]that the saying of Jesus might be fulfilled which He spoke, signifying by what death He would die.

[33]Then Pilate entered the Praetorium again, called Jesus, and said to Him, "Are You the King of the Jews?"

[34]Jesus answered him, "Are you speaking for yourself about this, or did others tell you this concerning Me?"

[35]Pilate answered, "Am I a Jew? Your own nation and the chief priests have delivered You to me. What have You done?"

[36]Jesus answered, "My kingdom is not of this world. If My kingdom were of this world, My servants would fight, so that I should not be delivered to the Jews; but now My kingdom is not from here."

[37]Pilate therefore said to Him, "Are You a king then?"

Jesus answered, "You say *rightly* that I am a king. For this cause I was born, and for this cause I have come into the world, that I should bear witness to the truth. Everyone who is of the truth hears My voice."

[38]Pilate said to Him, "What is truth?" And when he had said this, he went out again to the Jews, and said to them, "I find no fault in Him at all.

[39]"But you have a custom that I should release someone to you at the Passover. Do you therefore want me to release to you the King of the Jews?"

[40]Then they all cried again, saying, "Not this Man, but Barabbas!" Now Barabbas was a robber.

CHAPTER **19** PILATE JUDGES JESUS. So then Pilate

took Jesus and scourged *Him*. [2]And the soldiers twisted a crown of thorns and put *it* on His head, and they put on Him a purple robe. [3]Then they said, "Hail, King of the Jews!" And they struck Him with their hands.

[4]Pilate then went out again, and said to them, "Behold, I am bringing Him out to you, that you may know that I find no fault in Him."

[5]Then Jesus came out, wearing the crown of thorns and the purple robe. And *Pilate* said to them, "Behold the Man!"

[6]Therefore, when the chief priests and officers saw Him, they cried out, saying, "Crucify *Him*, crucify *Him!*"

Pilate said to them, "You take Him and crucify *Him*, for I find no fault in Him."

[7]The Jews answered him, "We have a law, and according to our law He ought to die, because He made Himself the Son of God."

[8]Therefore, when Pilate heard that saying, he was the more afraid, [9]and went again into the Praetorium, and said to Jesus, "Where are You from?" But Jesus gave him no answer.

[10]Then Pilate said to Him, "Are You not speaking to me?

Do You not know that I have power to crucify You, and power to release You?"

[11]Jesus answered, "You could have no power at all against Me unless it had been given you from above. Therefore the one who delivered Me to you has the greater sin."

[12]From then on Pilate sought to release Him, but the Jews cried out, saying, "If you let this Man go, you are not Caesar's friend. Whoever makes himself a king speaks against Caesar."

◗ TRAGEDY

18:36-37 Pilate asked Jesus a straightforward question and Jesus answered clearly. He is a king, but one whose kingdom is not of this world. There seems to have been no question in Pilate's mind that Jesus spoke the truth and was innocent of any crime. It also seems apparent that while recognizing the truth, Pilate chose to reject it. It is a tragedy when we fail to recognize the truth. It is a greater tragedy when we recognize the truth but fail to heed it.

[13]When Pilate therefore heard that saying, he brought Jesus out and sat down in the judgment seat in a place that is called *The* Pavement, but in Hebrew, Gabbatha. [14]Now it was the Preparation Day of the Passover, and about the sixth hour. And he said to the Jews, "Behold your King!"

[15]But they cried out, "Away with *Him*, away with *Him!* Crucify Him!"

Pilate said to them, "Shall I crucify your King?"

The chief priests answered, "We have no king but Caesar!"

[16]Then he delivered Him to them to be crucified. Then they took Jesus and led *Him* away.

[17]And He, bearing His cross, went out to a place called *the Place* of a Skull, which is called in Hebrew, Golgotha, [18]where they crucified Him, and two others with Him, one on either side, and Jesus in the center. [19]Now Pilate wrote a title and put *it* on the cross. And the writing was:

JESUS OF NAZARETH,
THE KING OF THE JEWS.

[20]Then many of the Jews read this title, for the place where Jesus was crucified was near the city; and it was written in Hebrew, Greek, *and* Latin.

[21]Therefore the chief priests of the Jews said to Pilate, "Do not write, 'The King of the Jews,' but, 'He said, "I am the King of the Jews."'"

[22]Pilate answered, "What I have written, I have written."

[23]Then the soldiers, when they had crucified Jesus, took His garments and made four parts, to each soldier a part, and also the tunic. Now the tunic was without seam, woven from the top in one piece. [24]They said therefore among themselves, "Let us not tear it, but cast lots for it,

◗ FAMILY

19:25-27 Even while dying on the cross, Jesus was concerned about his family. He instructed John to care for Mary, his mother. Our families are precious gifts from God, and we should value and care for them under all circumstances. What can you do today to show your love to your family?

JESUS' APPEARANCES AFTER HIS RESURRECTION

The truth of Christianity rests heavily on the Resurrection. If Jesus rose from the grave, who saw him? How trustworthy were the witnesses? Those who claimed to have seen the risen Jesus went on to turn the world upside down. Most of them also died for being followers of Christ. People rarely die for halfhearted belief. These are people who saw Jesus risen from the grave:

Mary Magdalene	Mark 16:9-11; John 20:10-18
The other women at the tomb	Matthew 28:8-10
Peter in Jerusalem	Luke 24:34; 1 Corinthians 15:5
The two travelers on the road	Mark 16:12-13; Luke 24:13-35
Ten disciples behind closed doors	Mark 16:14; Luke 24:36-43; John 20:19-25
All the disciples, with Thomas (excluding Judas Iscariot)	John 20:26-31; 1 Corinthians 15:5
Seven disciples while fishing	John 21:1-14
Eleven disciples on the mountain	Matthew 28:16-20
A crowd of more than 500	1 Corinthians 15:6
Jesus' brother James	1 Corinthians 15:7
Those who watched Jesus ascend into heaven	Luke 24:44-49; Acts 1:3-8

---

whose it shall be," that the Scripture might be fulfilled which says:

> *"They divided My garments among them,*
> *And for My clothing they cast lots."*

Therefore the soldiers did these things.

[25]Now there stood by the cross of Jesus His mother, and His mother's sister, Mary the *wife* of Clopas, and Mary Magdalene. [26]When Jesus therefore saw His mother, and the disciple whom He loved standing by, He said to His mother, "Woman, behold your son!" [27]Then He said to the disciple, "Behold your mother!" And from that hour that disciple took her to his own *home.*

[28]After this, Jesus, knowing that all things were now accomplished, that the Scripture might be fulfilled, said, "I thirst!" [29]Now a vessel full of sour wine was sitting there; and they filled a sponge with sour wine, put *it* on hyssop, and put *it* to His mouth. [30]So when Jesus had received the sour wine, He said, "It is finished!" And bowing His head, He gave up His spirit.

[31]Therefore, because it was the Preparation *Day,* that the bodies should not remain on the cross on the Sabbath (for that Sabbath was a high day), the Jews asked Pilate that their legs might be broken, and *that* they might be taken away. [32]Then the soldiers came and broke the legs of the first and of the other who was crucified

with Him. [33]But when they came to Jesus and saw that He was already dead, they did not break His legs. [34]But one of the soldiers pierced His side with a spear, and immediately blood and water came out. [35]And he who has seen has testified, and his testimony is true; and he knows that he is telling the truth, so that you may believe. [36]For these things were done that the Scripture should be fulfilled, *"Not one of His bones shall be broken."* [37]And again another Scripture says, *"They shall look on Him whom they pierced."*

PROOF

20:29 Some people think they would believe in Jesus if they could se a definite sign or miracle. But Jesus says we are blessed if we can belie without seeing. We have all the proof we need in the words of the Bible and the testimony of believers. A physical appearance would not make Jesus any more real to us than he is while living within us.

[38]After this, Joseph of Arimathea, being a disciple of Jesus, but secretly, for fear of the Jews, asked Pilate that he might take away the body of Jesus; and Pilate gave *him* permission. So he came and took the body of Jesus. [39]And Nicodemus, who at first came to Jesus by night, also came, bringing a mixture of myrrh and aloes, about a hundred pounds. [40]Then they took the body of Jesus, and bound it in strips of linen with the spices, as the custom

of the Jews is to bury. [41]Now in the place where He was crucified there was a garden, and in the garden a new tomb in which no one had yet been laid. [42]So there they laid Jesus, because of the Jews' Preparation *Day*, for the tomb was nearby.

CHAPTER **20** PETER AND JOHN AT JESUS' TOMB.

Now the first *day* of the week Mary Magdalene went to the tomb early, while it was still dark, and saw *that* the stone had been taken away from the tomb. [2]Then she ran and came to Simon Peter, and to the other disciple, whom Jesus loved, and said to them, "They have taken away the Lord out of the tomb, and we do not know where they have laid Him."

[3]Peter therefore went out, and the other disciple, and were going to the tomb. [4]So they both ran together, and the other disciple outran Peter and came to the tomb first. [5]And he, stooping down and looking in, saw the linen cloths lying *there*; yet he did not go in. [6]Then Simon Peter came, following him, and went into the tomb; and he saw the linen cloths lying *there*, [7]and the handkerchief that had been around His head, not lying with the linen cloths, but folded together in a place by itself. [8]Then the other disciple, who came to the tomb first, went in also; and he saw and believed. [9]For as yet they did not know the Scripture, that He must rise again from the dead. [10]Then the disciples went away again to their own homes.

[11]But Mary stood outside by the tomb weeping, and as she wept she stooped down *and looked* into the tomb. [12]And she saw two angels in white sitting, one at the head and the other at the feet, where the body of Jesus had lain. [13]Then they said to her, "Woman, why are you weeping?"

She said to them, "Because they have taken away my Lord, and I do not know where they have laid Him."

[14]Now when she had said this, she turned around and saw Jesus standing *there*, and did not know that it was Jesus. [15]Jesus said to her, "Woman, why are you weeping? Whom are you seeking?"

She, supposing Him to be the gardener, said to Him, "Sir, if You have carried Him away, tell me where You have laid Him, and I will take Him away."

[16]Jesus said to her, "Mary!"

She turned and said to Him, "Rabboni!" (which is to say, Teacher).

[17]Jesus said to her, "Do not cling to Me, for I have not yet ascended to My Father; but go to My brethren and say to them, 'I am ascending to My Father and your Father, and *to* My God and your God.'"

[18]Mary Magdalene came and told the disciples that she had seen the Lord, and *that* He had spoken these things to her.

THOMAS

Even though some of Thomas's attitudes earned him the nickname "Doubter," we also need to respect his faith. Thomas expressed his doubts because he wanted to know the truth. He didn't hang on to his doubts but humbly believed when they were answered. Expressing doubts is a good way to clarify the truth.

The Bible doesn't tell us a lot about Thomas, but the brief glimpses are consistent. He tried hard to be faithful to what he knew, even though he didn't always feel like it. At one point, when it was clear to everyone that Jesus' life was in danger, only Thomas put into words what most were feeling: "Let us also go, that we may die with him" (John 11:16). He didn't hesitate to follow Jesus. Sometimes we have to go against our feelings in order to obey Christ.

We don't know why Thomas was missing the first time Jesus appeared to the disciples after the Resurrection. Whatever the reason, Thomas was reluctant to believe their story that Jesus was alive. Not even 10 friends could change his mind! But, because Thomas's doubt was honest, God didn't leave him in doubt.

We can doubt without having to live a doubting way of life. Doubt helps us clarify what we believe. Doubt works better at sharpening our mind than changing it. Doubts can help us ask good questions, seek for answers, push for decisions. But doubt was never meant to be a permanent condition. Doubt is one foot lifted, poised to step forward or back. There is no motion until the foot comes down.

When you experience doubt, take encouragement from Thomas. He didn't stay in his doubt but allowed Jesus to bring him to belief. Take encouragement also from the fact that countless other followers of Christ have struggled with doubts. The answers God gave them may be of great help. Don't settle into doubt, but move beyond it to decision and belief. Find another Christian with whom you can share your doubts. Silent doubts rarely find answers.

LESSONS: Jesus does not reject doubts that are honest and directed toward belief Better to doubt out loud than to disbelieve in silence

KEY VERSES: "Then [Jesus] said to Thomas, 'Reach your finger here, and look at My hands; and reach your hand here, and put it into My side. Do not be unbelieving, but believing.' And Thomas answered and said to Him, 'My Lord and my God!'" (John 20:27-28).

Thomas's story is told in the Gospels. He also is mentioned in Acts 1:13.

UPS:
- One of Jesus' 12 disciples
- Had a great capacity for intensity, both in doubt and belief
- Was a loyal and honest man

DOWNS:
- Along with the others, abandoned Jesus at his arrest
- Refused to believe the others' claims to have seen Christ and demanded proof
- Struggled with a pessimistic outlook

STATS:
- Where: Galilee, Judea, Samaria
- Occupation: Disciple of Jesus
- Contemporaries: Jesus, other disciples, Herod, Pilate

[19]Then, the same day at evening, being the first *day* of the week, when the doors were shut where the disciples were assembled, for fear of the Jews, Jesus came and stood in the midst, and said to them, "Peace *be* with you." [20]When He had said this, He showed them *His* hands and His side. Then the disciples were glad when they saw the Lord.

[21]So Jesus said to them again, "Peace to you! As the Father has sent Me, I also send you." [22]And when He had said this, He breathed on *them*, and said to them, "Receive the Holy Spirit. [23]If you forgive the sins of any, they are forgiven them; if you retain the *sins* of any, they are retained."

[24]Now Thomas, called the Twin, one of the twelve, was not with them when Jesus came. [25]The other disciples therefore said to him, "We have seen the Lord."

So he said to them, "Unless I see in His hands the print of the nails, and put my finger into the print of the nails, and put my hand into His side, I will not believe."

[26]And after eight days His disciples were again inside, and Thomas with them. Jesus came, the doors being shut, and stood in the midst, and said, "Peace to you!" [27]Then He said to Thomas, "Reach your finger here, and look at My hands; and reach your hand *here*, and put *it* into My side. Do not be unbelieving, but believing."

[28]And Thomas answered and said to Him, "My Lord and my God!"

[29]Jesus said to him, "Thomas, because you have seen Me, you have believed. Blessed *are* those who have not seen and *yet* have believed."

[30]And truly Jesus did many other signs in the presence of His disciples, which are not written in this book; [31]but these are written that you may believe that Jesus is the Christ, the Son of God, and that believing you may have life in His name.

CHAPTER **21** JESUS HELPS CATCH FISH. After these things Jesus showed Himself again to the disciples at the Sea of Tiberias, and in this way He showed *Himself*: [2]Simon Peter, Thomas called the Twin, Nathanael of Cana in Galilee, the *sons* of Zebedee, and two others of His disciples were together. [3]Simon Peter said to them, "I am going fishing."

They said to him, "We are going with you also." They went out and immediately got into the boat, and that night they caught nothing. [4]But when the morning had now come, Jesus stood on the shore; yet the disciples did not know that it was Jesus. [5]Then Jesus said to them, "Children, have you any food?"

They answered Him, "No."

[6]And He said to them, "Cast the net on the right side of the boat, and you will find *some*." So they cast, and now they were not able to draw it in because of the multitude of fish.

[7]Therefore that disciple whom Jesus loved said to Peter, "It is the Lord!" Now when Simon Peter heard that it was the Lord, he put on *his* outer garment (for he had removed it), and plunged into the sea. [8]But the other disciples came in the little boat (for they were not far from land, but about two hundred cubits), dragging the net with fish. [9]Then, as soon as they had come to land, they saw a fire of coals there, and fish laid on it, and bread. [10]Jesus said to them, "Bring some of the fish which you have just caught."

[11]Simon Peter went up and dragged the net to land, full of large fish, one hundred and fifty-three; and although there were so many, the net was not broken. [12]Jesus said to them, "Come *and* eat breakfast." Yet none of the disciples dared ask Him, "Who are You?"—knowing that it was the Lord. [13]Jesus then came and took the bread and gave it to them, and likewise the fish.

[14]This *is* now the third time Jesus showed Himself to His disciples after He was raised from the dead.

[15]So when they had eaten breakfast, Jesus said to Simon Peter, "Simon, *son* of Jonah, do you love Me more than these?"

He said to Him, "Yes, Lord; You know that I love You."

He said to him, "Feed My lambs."

[16]He said to him again a second time, "Simon, *son* of Jonah, do you love Me?"

He said to Him, "Yes, Lord; You know that I love You."

He said to him, "Tend My sheep."

[17]He said to him the third time, "Simon, *son* of Jonah, do you love Me?" Peter was grieved because He said to him the third time, "Do you love Me?"

And he said to Him, "Lord, You know all things; You know that I love You."

Jesus said to him, "Feed My sheep. [18]Most assuredly, I say to you, when you were younger, you girded yourself and walked where you wished; but when you are old, you will stretch out your hands, and another will gird you and carry *you* where you do not wish." [19]This He spoke, signifying by what death he would glorify God. And when He had spoken this, He said to him, "Follow Me."

[20]Then Peter, turning around, saw the disciple whom Jesus loved following, who also had leaned on His breast at the supper, and said, "Lord, who is the one who betrays You?" [21]Peter, seeing him, said to Jesus, "But Lord, what *about* this man?"

[22]Jesus said to him, "If I will that he remain till I come, what *is that* to you? You follow Me."

[23]Then this saying went out among the brethren that this disciple would not die. Yet Jesus did not say to him that he would not die, but, "If I will that he remain till I come, what *is that* to you?"

[24]This is the disciple who testifies of these things, and wrote these things; and we know that his testimony is true.

[25]And there are also many other things that Jesus did, which if they were written one by one, I suppose that even the world itself could not contain the books that would be written. Amen.

◄◄◄WHAT'S IT TO YOU?

21:21-22 Peter asked Jesus how John would die. Jesus replied ► Peter should not concern himself with that. We tend to compare our to others, whether to rationalize our own level of devotion to Christ question God's justice. Jesus responds to us as he did to Peter: "Wh *that* to you? You follow Me!"

of the Jews is to bury. ⁴¹Now in the place where He was crucified there was a garden, and in the garden a new tomb in which no one had yet been laid. ⁴²So there they laid Jesus, because of the Jews' Preparation *Day,* for the tomb was nearby.

CHAPTER 20 PETER AND JOHN AT JESUS' TOMB.

Now the first *day* of the week Mary Magdalene went to the tomb early, while it was still dark, and saw *that* the stone had been taken away from the tomb. ²Then she ran and came to Simon Peter, and to the other disciple, whom Jesus loved, and said to them, "They have taken away the Lord out of the tomb, and we do not know where they have laid Him."

³Peter therefore went out, and the other disciple, and were going to the tomb. ⁴So they both ran together, and the other disciple outran Peter and came to the tomb first. ⁵And he, stooping down and looking in, saw the linen cloths lying *there;* yet he did not go in. ⁶Then Simon Peter came, following him, and went into the tomb; and he saw the linen cloths lying *there,* ⁷and the handkerchief that had been around His head, not lying with the linen cloths, but folded together in a place by itself. ⁸Then the other disciple, who came to the tomb first, went in also; and he saw and believed. ⁹For as yet they did not know the Scripture, that He must rise again from the dead. ¹⁰Then the disciples went away again to their own homes.

¹¹But Mary stood outside by the tomb weeping, and as she wept she stooped down *and looked* into the tomb. ¹²And she saw two angels in white sitting, one at the head and the other at the feet, where the body of Jesus had lain. ¹³Then they said to her, "Woman, why are you weeping?"

She said to them, "Because they have taken away my Lord, and I do not know where they have laid Him."

¹⁴Now when she had said this, she turned around and saw Jesus standing *there,* and did not know that it was Jesus. ¹⁵Jesus said to her, "Woman, why are you weeping? Whom are you seeking?"

She, supposing Him to be the gardener, said to

Him, "Sir, if You have carried Him away, tell me where You have laid Him, and I will take Him away."

¹⁶Jesus said to her, "Mary!"

She turned and said to Him, "Rabboni!" (which is to say, Teacher).

¹⁷Jesus said to her, "Do not cling to Me, for I have not yet ascended to My Father; but go to My brethren and say to them, 'I am ascending to My Father and your Father, and *to* My God and your God.'"

¹⁸Mary Magdalene came and told the disciples that she had seen the Lord, and *that* He had spoken these things to her.

THOMAS

Even though some of Thomas's attitudes earned him the nickname "Doubter," we also need to respect his faith. Thomas expressed his doubts because he wanted to know the truth. He didn't hang on to his doubts but humbly believed when they were answered. Expressing doubts is a good way to clarify the truth.

The Bible doesn't tell us a lot about Thomas, but the brief glimpses are consistent. He tried hard to be faithful to what he knew, even though he didn't always feel like it. At one point, only when it was clear to everyone that Jesus' life was in danger, did Thomas put into words what most were feeling: "Let us also go, that we may die with him" (John 11:16). He didn't hesitate to follow Jesus. Sometimes we have to go against our feelings in order to obey Christ.

We don't know why Thomas was missing the first time Jesus appeared to the disciples after the Resurrection. Whatever the reason, Thomas was reluctant to believe their story that Jesus was alive. Not even 10 friends could change his mind! But, because Thomas's doubt was honest, God didn't leave him in doubt.

We can doubt without having to live a doubting way of life. Doubt helps us clarify what we believe. Doubt works better at sharpening our mind than changing it. Doubts can help us ask good questions, seek for answers, push for decisions. But doubt was never meant to be a permanent condition. Doubt is one foot lifted, poised to step forward or back. There is no motion until the foot comes down.

When you experience doubt, take encouragement from Thomas. He didn't stay in his doubt but allowed Jesus to bring him to belief. Take encouragement also from the fact that countless other followers of Christ have struggled with doubts. The answers God gave them may be of great help. Don't settle into doubt, but move beyond it to decision and belief. Find another Christian with whom you can share your doubts. Silent doubts rarely find answers.

LESSONS: Jesus does not reject doubts that are honest and directed toward belief. Better to doubt out loud than to disbelieve in silence.

KEY VERSES: "Then [Jesus] said to Thomas, 'Reach your finger here, and look at My hands; and reach your hand here, and put it into My side. Do not be unbelieving, but believing.' And Thomas answered and said to Him, 'My Lord and my God!'" (John 20:27-28).

Thomas's story is told in the Gospels. He also is mentioned in Acts 1:13.

UPS:
• One of Jesus' 12 disciples
• Had a great capacity for intensity, both in doubt and belief
• Was a loyal and honest man

DOWNS:
• Along with the others, abandoned Jesus at his arrest
• Refused to believe the others' claims to have seen Christ and demanded proof
• Struggled with a pessimistic outlook

STATS:
• Where: Galilee, Judea, Samaria
• Occupation: Disciple of Jesus
• Contemporaries: Jesus, other disciples, Herod, Pilate

MEGA *Themes*

JESUS CHRIST, SON OF GOD John shows us that Jesus is unique as God's special Son, yet he is fully God. Because Jesus is fully God, he is able to reveal God to us clearly and accurately.

Because Jesus is God's Son, we can perfectly trust what he says. By trusting him, we can gain an open mind to understand God's message and fulfill his purpose in our life.

1. What are the key points that John emphasizes in John 1:1-18?
2. What do you learn about God by looking at Jesus?
3. In what ways has knowing Christ made a difference in your life?
4. Based on John's Gospel and your life, what would you say this statement means: "Jesus Christ is God's perfect revelation of himself"?

ETERNAL LIFE Because Jesus is God, he lives forever. Before the world began, Jesus lived with God, and he will reign forever with God. In John, we see Jesus revealed in power and magnificence even before his resurrection.

Jesus offers eternal life to us. We are invited to live in a personal, eternal relationship with him that begins now. Although we must eventually age and die, by trusting Christ we can have a new life that lasts forever.

1. How does the idea of eternal life affect the way you view your earthly life?
2. What effect should the promise of eternal life in Jesus Christ have on the way you relate to non-Christians?
3. How can you be more faithful to the reality of eternal life in how you live your life now on earth?

BELIEVE John records eight specific signs or miracles that reveal the nature of Jesus' power and love. We see Christ's power over everything created, and we see his love for all people. These signs encourage us to believe in him.

Believing is active, living, and continuous trust in Jesus as God. When we believe in Jesus' life, words, death, and resurrection, and when we commit our life to him, he cleanses us from sin and empowers us to follow him. Jesus provides the cleansing and empowering; it is our role to respond in true belief.

1. What did John want to communicate about Jesus through the eight miracles he included in his book?

2. What did John want to communicate through the names or descriptions of Jesus?
3. What is the difference between knowing about Jesus and believing in him?
4. How did you come to believe in Jesus? What does it mean to you to be a "believer"?
5. What would you want to communicate about Jesus to your non-Christian friends? What could you do to begin to clearly communicate that message?

HOLY SPIRIT Jesus taught his disciples that after he went back to heaven, the Holy Spirit would come. Then the Holy Spirit would indwell, guide, counsel, and comfort all those who follow Jesus. Through the Holy Spirit, Christ's presence and power are multiplied in all who believe.

Through God's Holy Spirit we are drawn to him in faith. We must know the Holy Spirit to understand all that Jesus taught. We can experience Jesus' love and guidance as we allow the Holy Spirit to do his work in us.

1. In 14:15-31 and 16:5-16 Jesus teaches specifically about the Holy Spirit. List the key points of his teaching.
2. What resources are provided by the Holy Spirit?
3. Why do you think God gives his Holy Spirit to believers?
4. What can you do to develop a daily reliance on the Spirit so that you are able to enjoy his presence and blessings?

RESURRECTION On the third day after Jesus died, he rose from the dead. This was verified by his disciples and many eyewitnesses. This reality changed the disciples from frightened deserters to dynamic leaders in the new church. This fact is the foundation of the Christian faith.

We can be changed, as the disciples were, and have confidence that our bodies will one day be raised to live with Christ forever. The same power that raised Christ to life can give you the ability to follow Christ each day. God wants us to live in victory, not in fear or despair.

1. What makes the Resurrection so essential to Christian faith?
2. Describe how you might have felt if you had been one of the disciples who thought Jesus was dead and then saw him alive. What impact would this experience have had on your life?
3. What does it mean to live as a Christian who takes the Resurrection seriously?

*A*ssemble nine very different people: ■ The class cut-up who makes everything funny ■ The preppie rich kid with her very own BMW ■ The minority student from the not-so-nice part of town ■ The human computer who would rather do calculus problems than anything else ■ The mammoth football jock who loves to bash things—especially quarterbacks ■ The student whose recent "achievements" read like a sleazy novel ■ The school airhead who is not exactly headed for a career as a genetic scientist ■ The campus philosopher/political activist who *loves* to argue and *hates* shallow people ■ The quiet classmate who, for whatever reasons, never fits in ■ Now, give this diverse crowd a simple task to do . . . together. ■ Even if you could get them all in the same room, they'd *never* complete the assignment. What they'd most likely produce is nonstop arguing, bickering, and chaos! If they functioned as a team at all, it would be bumpy and very brief. ■ So, how do we explain the first-century church? How did *several hundred* radically different people accomplish the *complicated and time-consuming project* of taking Jesus' story all over the world? ■ How did they handle conflicts? What kept them going when hard times hit? What is it that those first Christians had that is lacking among believers today? ■ If you'd like the answers to those questions (and you'd like to see how you can help improve your own church), dive into the book of Acts.

STATS

PURPOSE: To give an accurate account of the birth and growth of the Christian church

AUTHOR: Luke

TO WHOM WRITTEN: Theophilus ("lover of God") and people everywhere

DATE WRITTEN: Between A.D. 63 and 70

SETTING: Acts is the link between Christ's life and the life of the church, between the Gospels and the Epistles

KEY PEOPLE: Peter, John, James, Stephen, Philip, Paul, Barnabas, Cornelius, James (Jesus' brother), Timothy, Lydia, Silas, Titus, Apollos, Agabus, Ananias, Felix, Festus, Agrippa, Luke

KEY PLACES: Jerusalem, Samaria, Lydda, Joppa, Antioch in Syria, Cyprus, Antioch in Pisidia, Iconium, Lystra, Derbe, Philippi, Thessalonica, Berea, Athens, Corinth, Ephesus, Caesarea, Malta, Rome

¹²Then they returned to Jerusalem from the mount called Olivet, which is near Jerusalem, a Sabbath day's journey. ¹³And when they had entered, they went up into the upper room where they were staying: Peter, James, John, and Andrew; Philip and Thomas; Bartholomew and Matthew; James *the son* of Alphaeus and Simon the Zealot; and Judas *the son* of James. ¹⁴These all continued with one accord in prayer and supplication, with the women and Mary the mother of Jesus, and with His brothers.

¹⁵And in those days Peter stood up in the midst of the disciples (altogether the number of names was about a hundred and twenty), and said, ¹⁶"Men *and* brethren, this Scripture had to be fulfilled, which the Holy Spirit spoke before by the mouth of David concerning Judas, who became a guide to those who arrested Jesus; ¹⁷for he was numbered with us and obtained a part in this ministry."

¹⁸(Now this man purchased a field with the wages of iniquity; and falling headlong, he burst open in the middle and all his entrails gushed out. ¹⁹And it became known to all those dwelling in Jerusalem; so that field is called in their own language, Akel Dama, that is, Field of Blood.)

²⁰"For it is written in the Book of Psalms:

'Let his dwelling place be desolate,
And let no one live in it';

and,

'Let another take his office.'

²¹"Therefore, of these men who have accompanied us all the time that the Lord Jesus went in and out among us, ²²beginning from the baptism of John to that day when He was taken up from us, one of these must become a witness with us of His resurrection."

²³And they proposed two: Joseph called Barsabas, who

CHAPTER **1** JESUS GOES UP TO HEAVEN.

The former account I made, O Theophilus, of all that Jesus began both to do and teach, ²until the day in which He was taken up, after He through the Holy Spirit had given commandments to the apostles whom He had chosen, ³to whom He also presented Himself alive after His suffering by many infallible proofs, being seen by them during forty days and speaking of the things pertaining to the kingdom of God.

⁴And being assembled together with *them,* He commanded them not to depart from Jerusalem, but to wait for the Promise of the Father, "which," *He said,* "you have heard from Me; ⁵for John truly baptized with water, but you shall be baptized with the Holy Spirit not many days from now." ⁶Therefore, when they had come together, they asked Him, saying, "Lord, will You at this time restore the kingdom to Israel?" ⁷And He said to them, "It is not for you to know times or seasons which the Father has put in His own authority. ⁸But you shall receive power when the Holy Spirit has come upon you; and you shall be witnesses to Me in Jerusalem, and in all Judea and Samaria, and to the end of the earth."

⁹Now when He had spoken these things, while they watched, He was taken up, and a cloud received Him out of their sight. ¹⁰And while they looked steadfastly toward heaven as He went up, behold, two men stood by them in white apparel, ¹¹who also said, "Men of Galilee, why do you stand gazing up into heaven? This *same* Jesus, who was taken up from you into heaven, will so come in like manner as you saw Him go into heaven."

CHANGED

1:3 Today there are still people who doubt Jesus' resurrection. But Jesus appeared to the apostles on many occasions after his resurrection, proving that he was alive. Look at the change the Resurrection made in the disciples' lives. At Jesus' death, they scattered. They were disillusioned and they feared for their lives. Then, after seeing the resurrected Christ, they grew fearless and risked everything to spread the Good News about him around the world. They faced imprisonment, beatings, rejection, and martyrdom, yet they never compromised their mission. These men would not have risked their lives for something they knew was a fraud. They knew Jesus was raised from the dead, and the early church was fired with their enthusiasm to tell others.

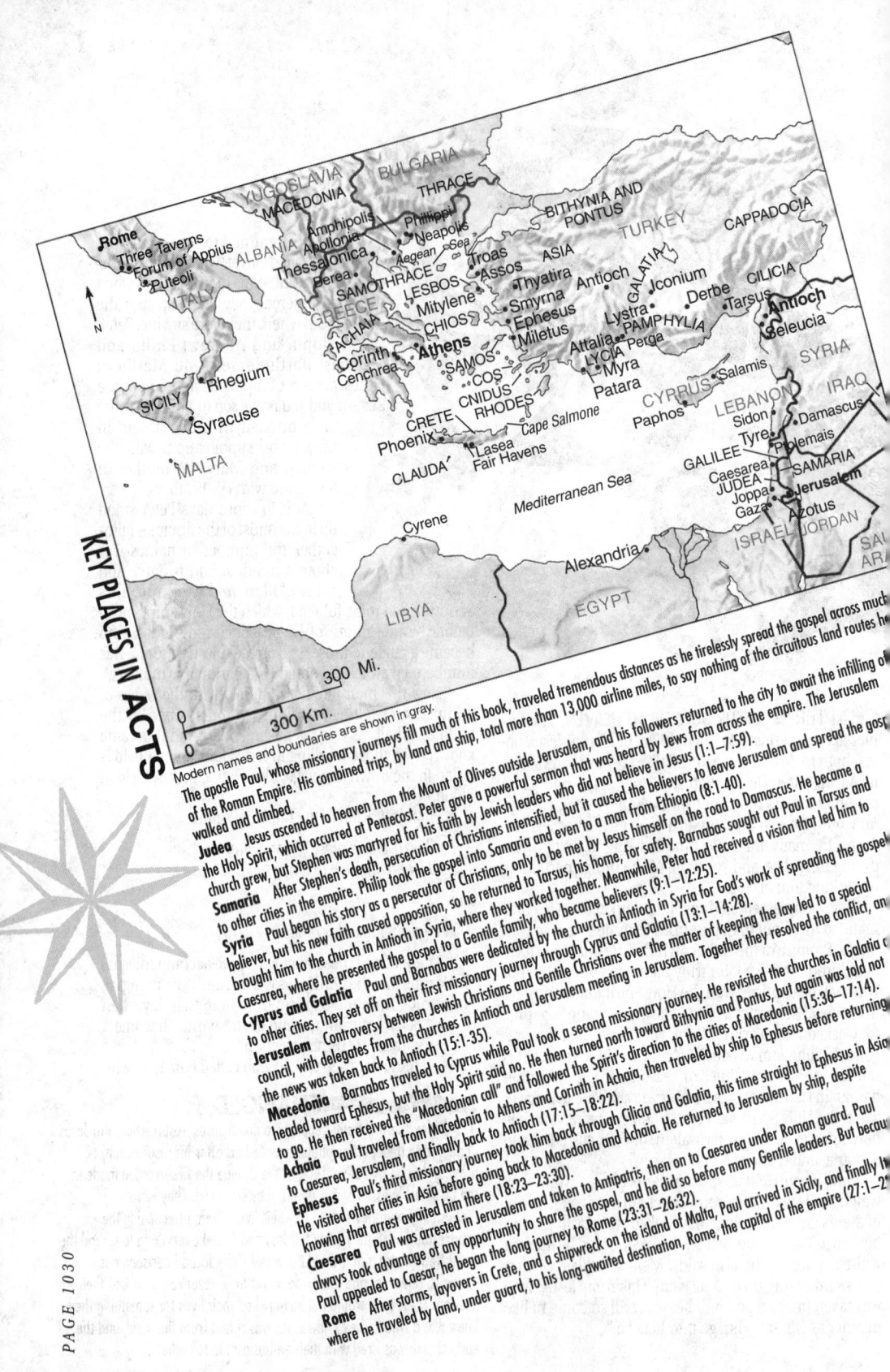

KEY PLACES IN ACTS

300 Mi.

300 Km.

Modern names and boundaries are shown in gray.

The apostle Paul, whose missionary journeys fill much of this book, traveled tremendous distances as he tirelessly spread the gospel across much of the Roman Empire. His combined trips, by land and ship, total more than 13,000 airline miles, to say nothing of the circuitous land routes he walked and climbed.

Judea Jesus ascended to heaven from the Mount of Olives outside Jerusalem, and his followers returned to the city to await the infilling of the Holy Spirit, which occurred at Pentecost. Peter gave a powerful sermon that was heard by Jews from across the empire. The Jerusalem church grew, but Stephen was martyred for his faith by Jewish leaders who did not believe in Jesus (1:1–7:59).

Samaria After Stephen's death, persecution of Christians intensified, but it caused the believers to leave Jerusalem and spread the gospel to other cities in the empire. Philip took the gospel into Samaria and even to a man from Ethiopia (8:1-40).

Syria Paul began his story as a persecutor of Christians, only to be met by Jesus himself on the road to Damascus. He became a believer, but his new faith caused opposition, so he returned to Tarsus, his home, for safety. Barnabas sought out Paul in Tarsus and brought him to the church in Antioch in Syria, where he presented the gospel to a Gentile family, who became believers (9:1–12:25). Meanwhile, Peter had received a vision that led him to Caesarea, where he presented the gospel to a Gentile family, who became believers (9:1–12:25).

Cyprus and Galatia Paul and Barnabas were dedicated by the church in Antioch in Syria for God's work of spreading the gospel to other cities. They set off on their first missionary journey through Cyprus and Galatia (13:1–14:28).

Jerusalem Controversy between Jewish Christians and Gentile Christians over the matter of keeping the law led to a special council, with delegates from the churches in Antioch and Jerusalem meeting in Jerusalem. Together they resolved the conflict, and the news was taken back to Antioch (15:1-35).

Macedonia Barnabas traveled to Cyprus while Paul took a second missionary journey. He revisited the churches in Galatia and headed toward Ephesus, but the Holy Spirit said no. He then turned north toward Bithynia and Pontus, but again was told not to go. He then received the "Macedonian call" and followed the Spirit's direction to the cities of Macedonia (15:36–17:14).

Achaia Paul traveled from Macedonia to Athens and Corinth in Achaia, then traveled by ship to Ephesus before returning to Caesarea, Jerusalem, and finally back to Antioch (17:15–18:22).

Ephesus Paul's third missionary journey took him back through Cilicia and Galatia, this time straight to Ephesus in Asia. He visited other cities in Asia before going back to Macedonia and Achaia. He returned to Jerusalem by ship, despite knowing that arrest awaited him there (18:23–23:30).

Caesarea Paul was arrested in Jerusalem and taken to Antipatris, then on to Caesarea under Roman guard. Paul always took advantage of any opportunity to share the gospel, and he did so before many Gentile leaders. But because Paul appealed to Caesar, he began the long journey to Rome (23:31–26:32).

Rome After storms, layovers in Crete, and a shipwreck on the island of Malta, Paul arrived in Sicily, and finally Italy, where he traveled by land, under guard, to his long-awaited destination, Rome, the capital of the empire (27:1–28:

was surnamed Justus, and Matthias. [24]And they prayed and said, "You, O Lord, who know the hearts of all, show which of these two You have chosen [25]to take part in this ministry and apostleship from which Judas by transgression fell, that he might go to his own place." [26]And they cast their lots, and the lot fell on Matthias. And he was numbered with the eleven apostles.

CHAPTER 2 THE HOLY SPIRIT COMES.

When the Day of Pentecost had fully come, they were all with one accord in one place. [2]And suddenly there came a sound from heaven, as of a rushing mighty wind, and it filled the whole house where they were sitting. [3]Then there appeared to them divided tongues, as of fire, and *one* sat upon each of them. [4]And they were all filled with the Holy Spirit and began to speak with other tongues, as the Spirit gave them utterance.

[5]And there were dwelling in Jerusalem Jews, devout men, from every nation under heaven. [6]And when this sound occurred, the multitude came together, and were confused, because everyone heard them speak in his own language. [7]Then they were all amazed and marveled, saying to one another, "Look, are not all these who speak Galileans? [8]And how *is it that* we hear, each in our own language in which we were born? [9]Parthians and Medes and Elamites, those dwelling in Mesopotamia, Judea and

BUT
YOU
SHALL
RECEIVE
POWER
WHEN
THE HOLY SPIRIT
has come upon you
AND
YOU
SHALL
BE WITNESSES
WITNESSES
WITNESSES
TO ME

ACTS 1.8

Cappadocia, Pontus and Asia, [10]Phrygia and Pamphylia, Egypt and the parts of Libya adjoining Cyrene, visitors from Rome, both Jews and proselytes, [11]Cretans and Arabs—we hear them speaking in our own tongues the wonderful works of God." [12]So they were all amazed and perplexed, saying to one another, "Whatever could this mean?"

[13]Others mocking said, "They are full of new wine."

[14]But Peter, standing up with the eleven, raised his voice and said to them, "Men of Judea and all who dwell in Jerusalem, let this be known to you, and heed my words. [15]For these are not drunk, as you suppose, since it is *only* the third hour of the day. [16]But this is what was spoken by the prophet Joel:

CHOOSE WELL

1:21-22 The apostles had to choose a replacement for Judas Iscariot. They outlined specific criteria for making the choice. When the "finalists" had been chosen, the apostles prayed, asking God to guide the selection process. This gives us a good example of how to proceed when we are making important decisions. Set up criteria consistent with the Bible, examine the alternatives, and pray for wisdom and guidance to reach a wise decision.

[17] '*And it shall come to pass in the last days, says God,*
That I will pour out of My Spirit on all flesh;
Your sons and your daughters shall prophesy,
Your young men shall see visions,
Your old men shall dream dreams.
[18] *And on My menservants and on My maidservants*
I will pour out My Spirit in those days;
And they shall prophesy.
[19] *I will show wonders in heaven above*
And signs in the earth beneath:
Blood and fire and vapor of smoke.
[20] *The sun shall be turned into darkness,*
And the moon into blood,
Before the coming of the great and awesome day of
the LORD.
[21] *And it shall come to pass*
That whoever calls on the name of the LORD
Shall be saved.'

[22]"Men of Israel, hear these words: Jesus of Nazareth, a Man attested by God to you by miracles, wonders, and signs which God did through Him in your midst, as you yourselves also know— [23]Him, being delivered by the determined purpose and foreknowledge of God, you have taken by lawless hands, have crucified, and put to death; [24]whom God raised up, having loosed the pains of death, because it was not possible that He should be held by it. [25]For David says concerning Him:

'*I foresaw the LORD always before my face,*
For He is at my right hand, that I may not be shaken.
[26] *Therefore my heart rejoiced, and my tongue was glad;*
Moreover my flesh also will rest in hope.
[27] *For You will not leave my soul in Hades,*
Nor will You allow Your Holy One to see corruption.
[28] *You have made known to me the ways of life;*
You will make me full of joy in Your presence.'

THE HOLY SPIRIT

Author Sheldon Vanauken has described a scene in which the characters in a drama sit around and discuss their play. The playwright's name is Smith. Some of the characters believe Smith exists; some don't. One of them recalls an earlier scene where a character named Smithson claimed that he was Smith, and that he had written himself into the play. After considerable debate over the likelihood of that happening, another character speaks: **"L**ook, do you know what's so impressive about all this? It's the idea of a sort of a trinity: Smith outside writing the play; and inside as a character; and inside each of us, too. I don't know whether it's true, but it's exactly the way it would be if it were. . . . This thing has the feel of something true. A sort of rightness."

No one can truly understand—much less explain—the Trinity, God in three persons. But Vanauken's analogy is a good attempt: an Author who writes characters into existence, then writes himself in as one of the players, and also is somehow in each of his characters. Historically, Christians have believed that God exists in three persons: the Father, Son, and Holy Spirit. The least understood of these three, though, is the Holy Spirit. So just who is the Holy Spirit and what does he do?

- **"He," not "it."** The New Testament always refers to the Holy Spirit as "he," not "it." The Spirit is personal, not merely a "force" or instrument. Just as God the Father and God the Son represent distinct personalities within the Trinity, so does the Spirit. We don't have any real point of reference to help us understand this since we don't know anyone else who is pure spirit. Still, it is true: the Holy Spirit is a person with intellect, feelings, will, and other personal characteristics.

- **Truly God.** The Holy Spirit is not in any way less than or inferior to the Father or the Son. One of the clearest statements of this reality is found in Matthew 28:19, where Jesus tells the disciples: "Go therefore and make disciples of all the nations, baptizing them in the name of the Father and of the Son and of the Holy Spirit." (Also check out John 14:16-26 and 15:26-27; 2 Corinthians 3:17 and 13:14.) The classic description of the Trinity is "one in essence, three in persons." The Holy Spirit is the third person described here, and he is just as much God as are the Father and the Son.

- **The Spirit's functions.** We can do little more here than simply list the roles that the Holy Spirit fulfills: he anoints and serves alongside the Messiah (Isaiah 48:16; 61:1; Luke 4:18-19); he ushers in the "last days" (Joel 2:28-32; Acts 2:14-36); he unifies the body of Christ (1 Corinthians 12:4-11; Ephesians 4:1-16); he gives new life (John 3:5-8); he convicts us of sin and enables us to repent and come to faith in Christ (John 16:8); he testifies to Jesus as the Messiah (John 14:26 and 16:14); he guides us into truth (John 16:13); he bears fruit in our life (Galatians 5:22-25); he gives us supernatural gifts (1 Corinthians 12–14); he prays for us (Romans 8:26); he is present in all Christians (Romans 8:9-11; 1 Corinthians 6:19). Even from this brief list you can begin to see how crucial the Spirit's role is in our life. Knowing this, it is understandable that Jesus calls the Holy Spirit the "Helper" or "Comforter" (John 15:26). **A**s characters in a divine so much that he "wrote himself into the play." And that now, having left the visible stage, he remains it is comforting for us to know that there is indeed an Author who knows and loves the people he created behind in an unseen—but no less real—way, guiding and strengthening his people.

29"Men *and* brethren, let *me* speak freely to you of the patriarch David, that he is both dead and buried, and his tomb is with us to this day. 30Therefore, being a prophet, and knowing that God had sworn with an oath to him that of the fruit of his body, according to the flesh, He would raise up the Christ to sit on his throne, 31he, foreseeing this, spoke concerning the resurrection of the Christ, that His soul was not left in Hades, nor did His flesh see corruption. 32This Jesus God has raised up, of which we are all witnesses. 33Therefore being exalted to the right hand of God, and having received from the Father the promise of the Holy Spirit, He poured out this which you now see and hear.

34"For David did not ascend into the heavens, but he says himself:

'The LORD said to my Lord,
" Sit at My right hand,
35   Till I make Your enemies Your footstool." '

36"Therefore let all the house of Israel know assuredly that God has made this Jesus, whom you crucified, both Lord and Christ."

37Now when they heard *this*, they were cut to the heart, and said to Peter and the rest of the apostles, "Men *and* brethren, what shall we do?"

38Then Peter said to them, "Repent, and let every one of you be baptized in the name of Jesus Christ for the remission of sins; and you shall receive the gift of the Holy Spirit. 39For the promise is to you and to your children, and to all who are afar off, as many as the Lord our God will call."

40And with many other words he testified and exhorted them, saying, "Be saved from this perverse generation." 41Then those who gladly received his word were baptized; and that day about three thousand souls were added *to them*. 42And they continued steadfastly in the apostles' doctrine and fellowship, in the breaking of bread, and in prayers. 43Then fear came upon every soul, and many wonders and signs were done through the apostles. 44Now all who believed were together, and had all things in common, 45and sold their possessions and goods, and divided them among all, as anyone had need. 46So continuing daily with one accord in the temple, and breaking bread from house to house, they ate their food with gladness and simplicity of heart, 47praising God and having favor with all the people. And the Lord added to the church daily those who were being saved.

CHAPTER **3** PETER AND JOHN HEAL A MAN. Now Peter and John went up together to the temple at the hour of prayer, the ninth *hour*. 2And a certain man lame from his mother's womb was carried, whom they laid daily at the gate of the temple which is called Beautiful, to ask alms from those who entered the temple; 3who, seeing Peter and John about to go into the temple, asked for alms. 4And fixing his eyes on him, with John, Peter said, "Look at us." 5So he gave them his attention, expecting to receive something from them. 6Then Peter said, "Silver and gold I do not have, but what I do have I give you: In the name of Jesus Christ of Nazareth, rise up and walk." 7And he took him by the right hand and lifted *him* up, and immediately his feet and ankle bones received strength. 8So he, leaping up, stood and walked and entered the temple with them—walking, leaping, and praising God. 9And all the people saw him walking and praising God. 10Then they knew that it was he who sat

My mom has said some pretty bad things to me over the years. Now that I'm a Christian, I know I should forgive her, but I can't. What should I do?

I WONDER . . .

The gap between knowing you need to forgive someone and actually being able to do it often seems like a vast canyon. You can see the other side, but getting there seems impossible.

Ever seen a shower drain plugged up with a two-month accumulation of hair? The water slowly seeps through the molding mass of greasy, soapy yuk. No amount of plunging can bring the glob up because it's too deep.

The next solution usually is to burn away the clog by applying something like Drāno. Sometimes this works if the buildup is not too severe. The last resort, of course, is to call a plumber. He'll come in with a narrow, hard, yet flexible piece of metal called a snake and drill through the clog until the water is flowing freely.

Unforgiveness is like a clogged drain. Sometimes it is fairly easy to unclog. Someone hurts us, we let them know they hurt us, they say they're sorry, we forgive them, and the whole episode is forgotten. But when unforgiveness collects from years of hurt it becomes similar to what a drain would look like after years of bathing your cat in the sink without cleaning out the drain! You might as well buy a new sink.

Likewise, our sin can collect and become a gross, yucky mass that eventually clogs our relationship with God. Until it is removed, we can't really receive anything meaningful from him. Jesus came to "unclog our pipes" so God's love and forgiveness could flow to us freely. He did nothing wrong—we were the transgressors—yet he died to open the way for that flow of love.

From what you wrote, your mom's sin against you has clogged your relationship. You may have every right not to forgive your mom, but you must put aside that right for a greater goal—you must "die" and open yourself to learning how you and your mom can love each other. Otherwise the clog will only get worse.

God took the initiative with us by humbling himself and forgiving all of our sin (to see the comparison of how much God has forgiven us and how much we must forgive others, see Matthew 18:21-34). You must do the same with the person who has wronged you.

The forgiveness must be from your heart and must not be dependent upon whether she feels sorry for what she has done. Forgiving someone is a gift you can offer. You can't make someone take a free gift, they must reach out and receive it. Though the canyon looks deep and treacherous, the reward on the other side is a clear conscience, times of wonderful refreshment (see Acts 3:19), and—hopefully—a renewed relationship.

3:19 When we repent, God promises not only to wipe away our sin, but also to bring spiritual refreshment. Repentance may seem painful at first because it is hard to give up certain sins. But God will give you a better way. As Hosea promised, "pursue the knowledge of the LORD. His going forth is established as the morning; He will come to us like the rain, like the latter *and* former rain to the earth" (Hosea 6:3). Do you feel a need to be refreshed?

begging alms at the Beautiful Gate of the temple; and they were filled with wonder and amazement at what had happened to him.

[11]Now as the lame man who was healed held on to Peter and John, all the people ran together to them in the porch which is called Solomon's, greatly amazed. [12]So when Peter saw *it*, he responded to the people: "Men of Israel, why do you marvel at this? Or why look so intently at us, as though by our own power or godliness we had made this man walk? [13]The God of Abraham, Isaac, and Jacob, the God of our fathers, glorified His Servant Jesus, whom you delivered up and denied in the presence of Pilate, when he was determined to let *Him* go. [14]But you denied the Holy One and the Just, and asked for a murderer to be granted to you, [15]and killed the Prince of life, whom God raised from the dead, of which we are witnesses. [16]And His name, through faith in His name, has made this man strong, whom you see and know. Yes, the faith which *comes* through Him has given him this perfect soundness in the presence of you all.

[17]"Yet now, brethren, I know that you did *it* in ignorance, as *did* also your rulers. [18]But those things which God foretold by the mouth of all His prophets, that the Christ would suffer, He has thus fulfilled. [19]Repent therefore and be converted, that your sins may be blotted out, so that times of refreshing may come from the presence of the Lord, [20]and that He may send Jesus Christ, who was preached to you before, [21]whom heaven must receive until the times of restoration of all things, which God has spoken by the mouth of all His holy prophets since the world began. [22]For Moses truly said to the fathers, *'The LORD your God will raise up for you a Prophet like me from your brethren. Him you shall hear in all things, whatever He says to you.* [23]*And it shall be that every soul who will not hear that Prophet shall be utterly destroyed from among the people.'* [24]Yes, and all the prophets, from Samuel and those who follow, as many as have spoken, have also foretold these days. [25]You are sons of the prophets, and of the covenant which God made with our fathers, saying to Abraham, *'And in your seed all the families of the earth shall be blessed.'* [26]To you first, God, having raised up His Servant Jesus, sent Him to bless you, in turning away every one *of you* from your iniquities."

CHAPTER **4** PETER AND JOHN'S COURAGE. Now as they spoke to the people, the priests, the captain of the temple, and the Sadducees came upon them, [2]being greatly disturbed that they taught the people and preached in Jesus the resurrection from the dead. [3]And they laid hands on them, and put *them* in custody until the next day, for it was already evening. [4]However, many of those who heard the word believed; and the number of the men came to be about five thousand.

[5]And it came to pass, on the next day, that their rulers, elders, and scribes, [6]as well as Annas the high priest, Caiaphas, John, and Alexander, and as many as were of the family of the high priest, were gathered together at Jerusalem. [7]And when they had set them in the midst, they asked, "By what power or by what name have you done this?"

[8]Then Peter, filled with the Holy Spirit, said to them, "Rulers of the people and elders of Israel: [9]If we this day are judged for a good deed *done* to a helpless man, by what means he has been made well, [10]let it be known to you all, and to all the people of Israel, that by the name of Jesus Christ of Nazareth, whom you crucified, whom God raised from the dead, by Him this man stands here before you whole. [11]This is the *'stone which was rejected by you builders, which has become the chief cornerstone.'* [12]Nor is there salvation in any other, for there is no other name under heaven given among men by which we must be saved."

[13]Now when they saw the boldness of Peter and John, and perceived that they were uneducated and untrained men, they marveled. And they realized that they had been with Jesus. [14]And seeing the man who had been healed standing with them, they could say nothing against it. [15]But when they had commanded them to go aside out of the council, they conferred among themselves, [16]saying, "What shall we do to these men? For, indeed, that a notable miracle has been done through them *is* evident to all who dwell in Jerusalem, and we cannot deny *it.* [17]But so that it spreads no further among the people, let us severely threaten them, that from now on they speak to no man in this name."

4:24-30 Notice how the believers prayed. First they praised God, th͟ they told God their specific problem and asked for his help. They did n͟ ask God to remove the problem, but to help them deal with it. This is a model for us to follow when we pray. We may ask God to remove our problems, and he may choose to do so, but we must recognize that oft͟ God will leave the problem in place and give us the strength to deal wit͟

[18]So they called them and commanded them not to speak at all nor teach in the name of Jesus. [19]But Peter and John answered and said to them, "Whether it is right in the sight of God to listen to you more than to God, you judge. [20]For we cannot but speak the things which we have seen and heard." [21]So when they had further threatened them, they let them go, finding no way of punishing them, because of the people, since they all glorified God for what had been done. [22]For the man was over forty years old on whom this miracle of healing had been performed.

[23]And being let go, they went to their own *companions* and reported all that the chief priests and elders had said to them. [24]So when they heard that, they raised their voice to God with one accord and said: "Lord, You *are* God, who made heaven and earth and the sea, and all that is in them, [25]who by the mouth of Your servant David have said:

'Why did the nations rage,
And the people plot vain things?
²⁶ *The kings of the earth took their stand,*
And the rulers were gathered together
Against the LORD and against His Christ.'

²⁷"For truly against Your holy Servant Jesus, whom You anointed, both Herod and Pontius Pilate, with the Gentiles and the people of Israel, were gathered together ²⁸to do whatever Your hand and Your purpose determined before to be done. ²⁹Now, Lord, look on their threats, and grant to Your servants that with all boldness they may speak Your word, ³⁰by stretching out Your hand to heal, and that signs and wonders may be done through the name of Your holy Servant Jesus."

³¹And when they had prayed, the place where they were assembled together was shaken; and they were all filled with the Holy Spirit, and they spoke the word of God with boldness.

³²Now the multitude of those who believed were of one heart and one soul; neither did anyone say that any of the things he possessed was his own, but they had all things in common. ³³And with great power the apostles gave witness to the resurrection of the Lord Jesus. And great grace was upon them all. ³⁴Nor was there anyone among them who lacked; for all who were possessors of lands or houses sold them, and brought the proceeds of the things that were sold, ³⁵and laid *them* at the apostles' feet; and they distributed to each as anyone had need.

³⁶And Joses, who was also named Barnabas by the apostles (which is translated Son of Encouragement), a Levite of the country of Cyprus, ³⁷having land, sold *it*, and brought the money and laid *it* at the apostles' feet.

CHAPTER 5 ANANIAS AND SAPPHIRA LIE TO GOD.

But a certain man named Ananias, with Sapphira his wife, sold a possession. ²And he kept back *part* of the proceeds, his wife also being aware *of it*, and brought a certain part and laid *it* at the apostles' feet. ³But Peter said, "Ananias, why has Satan filled your heart to lie to the Holy Spirit and keep back *part* of the price of the land for yourself? ⁴While it remained, was it not your own? And after it was sold, was it not in your own control? Why have you conceived this thing in your heart? You have not lied to men but to God."

⁵Then Ananias, hearing these words, fell down and breathed his last. So great fear came upon all those who heard these things. ⁶And the young men arose and wrapped him up, carried *him* out, and buried *him*.

⁷Now it was about three hours later when his wife came in, not knowing what had happened. ⁸And Peter answered her, "Tell me whether you sold the land for so much?"

She said, "Yes, for so much."

⁹Then Peter said to her, "How is it that you have agreed together to test the Spirit of the Lord? Look, the feet of those who have buried your husband *are* at the door, and they will carry you out." ¹⁰Then immediately she fell down at his feet and breathed her last. And the young men came in and found her dead, and carrying *her* out, buried *her* by her husband. ¹¹So great fear came upon all the church and upon all who heard these things.

¹²And through the hands of the apostles many signs and wonders were done among the people. And they were all with one accord in Solomon's Porch. ¹³Yet none of the rest dared join them, but the people esteemed them highly. ¹⁴And believers were increasingly added to the Lord, multitudes of both men and women, ¹⁵so that they brought the sick out into the streets and laid *them* on beds and couches, that at least the shadow of Peter passing by might fall on some of them. ¹⁶Also a multitude gathered from the surrounding cities to Jerusalem, bringing sick people and those who were tormented by unclean spirits, and they were all healed.

◣ ATTRACTIONS

5:14 What makes Christianity attractive? It is easy to be drawn to churches because of exciting programs, good speakers, beautiful facilities, or friendly people. Believers were attracted to the early church by God's power and miracles; the generosity, sincerity, honesty, and unity of the members; and the character of the leaders. We must be careful that our standards don't slip. God wants to add to his *church*, not just to programs or congregations.

¹⁷Then the high priest rose up, and all those who *were* with him (which is the sect of the Sadducees), and they were filled with indignation, ¹⁸and laid their hands on the apostles and put them in the common prison. ¹⁹But at night an angel of the Lord opened the prison doors and brought them out, and said, ²⁰"Go, stand in the temple and speak to the people all the words of this life."

²¹And when they heard *that*, they entered the temple early in the morning and taught. But the high priest and those with him came and called the council together,

"Here's what I did..."

I don't find it easy to witness. I haven't memorized a lot of verses, and I'm still working my way through the Bible. It's easy to tell myself that I can wait until I know more.

But when I read Acts 4:13, I realized I was kidding myself. The verse talks about the boldness of Peter and John, and says that the Jewish council noticed that they were uneducated and nonprofessionals. But they knew Jesus. In other words, you don't have to know the whole Bible or go to seminary to be able to share your faith. The main thing is to know Jesus and share what you know with other people. I'm finding that he gives me the boldness to open my mouth, if I ask him.

Kenneth
AGE 15

5:17-18 The apostles had power to do miracles, great boldness in preaching, and God's presence in their lives—yet they were not free from hatred and persecution. They were arrested and put in jail, beaten with rods and whips, and slandered by community leaders. Faith in God does not make troubles disappear; it makes troubles appear less fearsome because it puts them in the right perspective. You cannot expect everyone to react favorably when you share something as dynamic as your faith in Christ. Some will be jealous of you, frightened, or threatened. Expect some negative reactions. But remember that you must be more concerned about God's reactions than people's reaction.

with all the elders of the children of Israel, and sent to the prison to have them brought.

²²But when the officers came and did not find them in the prison, they returned and reported, ²³saying, "Indeed we found the prison shut securely, and the guards standing outside before the doors; but when we opened them, we found no one inside!" ²⁴Now when the high priest, the captain of the temple, and the chief priests heard these things, they wondered what the outcome would be. ²⁵So one came and told them, saying, "Look, the men whom you put in prison are standing in the temple and teaching the people!"

²⁶Then the captain went with the officers and brought them without violence, for they feared the people, lest they should be stoned. ²⁷And when they had brought them, they set *them* before the council. And the high priest asked them, ²⁸saying, "Did we not strictly command you not to teach in this name? And look, you have filled Jerusalem with your doctrine, and intend to bring this Man's blood on us!"

²⁹But Peter and the *other* apostles answered and said: "We ought to obey God rather than men. ³⁰The God of our fathers raised up Jesus whom you murdered by hanging on a tree. ³¹Him God has exalted to His right hand *to be* Prince and Savior, to give repentance to Israel and forgiveness of sins. ³²And we are His witnesses to these things, and *so* also *is* the Holy Spirit whom God has given to those who obey Him."

³³When they heard *this*, they were furious and plotted to kill them. ³⁴Then one in the council stood up, a Pharisee named Gamaliel, a teacher of the law held in respect by all the people, and commanded them to put the apostles outside for a little while. ³⁵And he said to them: "Men of Israel, take heed to yourselves what you intend to do regarding these men. ³⁶For some time ago Theudas rose up, claiming to be somebody. A number of men, about four hundred, joined him. He was slain, and all who obeyed him were scattered and came to nothing. ³⁷After this man, Judas of Galilee rose up in the days of the census, and drew away many people after him. He also perished, and all who obeyed him were dispersed. ³⁸And now I say to you, keep away from these men and let them alone; for if this plan or this work is of men, it will come to nothing; ³⁹but if it is of God, you cannot overthrow it—lest you even be found to fight against God."

⁴⁰And they agreed with him, and when they had called for the apostles and beaten *them*, they commanded that they should not speak in the name of Jesus, and let them go. ⁴¹So they departed from the presence of the council, rejoicing that they were counted worthy to suffer shame for His name. ⁴²And daily in the temple, and in every

house, they did not cease teaching and preaching Jesus *as* the Christ.

CHAPTER **6** SEVEN MEN WITH SPECIAL WORK.

Now in those days, when *the number of* the disciples was multiplying, there arose a complaint against the Hebrews by the Hellenists, because their widows were neglected in the daily distribution. ²Then the twelve summoned the multitude of the disciples and said, "It is not desirable that we should leave the word of God and serve tables. ³Therefore, brethren, seek out from among you seven men of *good* reputation, full of the Holy Spirit and wisdom, whom we may appoint over this business; ⁴but we will give ourselves continually to prayer and to the ministry of the word."

⁵And the saying pleased the whole multitude. And they chose Stephen, a man full of faith and the Holy Spirit, and Philip, Prochorus, Nicanor, Timon, Parmenas, and Nicolas, a proselyte from Antioch, ⁶whom they set before the apostles; and when they had prayed, they laid hands on them.

⁷Then the word of God spread, and the number of disciples multiplied greatly in Jerusalem, and a great

6:7 The gospel spread like ripples on a pond where, from a single center, each wave touches the next, spreading wider and farther. The gospel still spreads this way today. You don't have to change the worl single-handedly—it is enough just to be part of the wave, touching around you, who in turn will touch others until all have felt the movement. Don't ever feel that your part is insignificant or unimport

many of the priests were obedient to the faith.

⁸And Stephen, full of faith and power, did great wonders and signs among the people. ⁹Then there arose some from what is called the Synagogue of the Freedmen (Cyrenians, Alexandrians, and those from Cilicia and Asia), disputing with Stephen. ¹⁰And they were not able to resist the wisdom and the Spirit by which he spoke. ¹¹Then they secretly induced men to say, "We have heard him speak blasphemous words against Moses and God." ¹²And they stirred up the people, the elders, and the scribes; and they came upon *him*, seized him, and brought *him* to the council. ¹³They also set up false witnesses who said, "This man does not cease to speak blasphemous words against this holy place and the law; ¹⁴for we have heard him say that this Jesus of Nazareth will destroy this place and change the customs which Moses delivered to us." ¹⁵And all who sat in the council, looking steadfastly at him, saw his face as the face of an angel.

7:2ff Stephen wasn't really defending himself. Instead he took the offensive, seizing the opportunity to summarize his teaching about Jes Stephen was accusing these religious leaders of failing to obey God's laws—the laws they prided themselves in following so meticulously. Th was the same accusation that Jesus had leveled against them. When w witness for Jesus, we don't need to be on the defensive. Instead we should simply share our faith.

CHAPTER **7** **STEPHEN IS EXECUTED.** Then the high priest said, "Are these things so?"

²And he said, "Brethren and fathers, listen: The God of glory appeared to our father Abraham when he was in Mesopotamia, before he dwelt in Haran, ³and said to him, *'Get out of your country and from your relatives, and come to a land that I will show you.'* ⁴Then he came out of the land of the Chaldeans and dwelt in Haran. And from there, when his father was dead, He moved him to this land in which you now dwell. ⁵And *God* gave him no inheritance in it, not even *enough* to set his foot on. But even when *Abraham* had no child, He promised to give it to him for a possession, and to his descendants after him. ⁶But God spoke in this way: that his descendants would dwell in a foreign land, and that they would bring them into bondage and oppress *them* four hundred years. ⁷*'And the nation to whom they will be in bondage I will judge,'* said God, *'and after that they shall come out and serve Me in this place.'* ⁸Then He gave him the covenant of circumcision; and so *Abraham* begot Isaac and circumcised him on the eighth day; and Isaac *begot* Jacob, and Jacob *begot* the twelve patriarchs.

⁹"And the patriarchs, becoming envious, sold Joseph into Egypt. But God was with him ¹⁰and delivered him out of all his troubles, and gave him favor and wisdom in the presence of Pharaoh, king of Egypt; and he made him governor over Egypt and all his house. ¹¹Now a famine and great trouble came over all the land of Egypt and Canaan, and our fathers found no sustenance. ¹²But when Jacob heard that there was grain in Egypt, he sent out our fathers first. ¹³And the second *time* Joseph was made known to his brothers, and Joseph's family became known to the Pharaoh. ¹⁴Then Joseph sent and called his father Jacob and all his relatives to *him*, seventy-five people. ¹⁵So Jacob went down to Egypt; and he died, he and our fathers. ¹⁶And they were carried back to Shechem and laid in the tomb that Abraham bought for a sum of money from the sons of Hamor, *the father* of Shechem.

¹⁷"But when the time of the promise drew near which God had sworn to Abraham, the people grew and multiplied in Egypt ¹⁸till another king arose who did not know Joseph. ¹⁹This man dealt treacherously with our people, and oppressed our forefathers, making them expose their babies, so that they might not live. ²⁰At this time Moses was born, and was well pleasing to God; and he was brought up in his father's house for three months. ²¹But when he was set out, Pharaoh's daughter took him away and brought him up as her own son. ²²And Moses was learned in all the wisdom of the Egyptians, and was mighty in words and deeds.

²³"Now when he was forty years old, it came into his heart to visit his

STEPHEN

The book you hold in your hand is there today because thousands of Christians throughout history have given their lives to carry the gospel around the world. They died for the Good News. It is important for us to remember, though, that a person cannot give his life for the gospel until he has learned to live his life for the gospel. Stephen was just that kind of person.

One way God trains his servants is to have them do jobs that don't seem very important or glamorous. We meet Stephen in the New Testament when he is appointed with others to manage the distribution of food among Christians in Jerusalem. Because many people lost jobs and belongings when they became Christians, it became necessary for all Christians to share what they had with each other. Stephen and others were asked to make sure that the available food was handed out fairly. It was probably a job with more headaches than thank-yous.

Stephen also proved himself as a powerful speaker. When he was harassed in the temple by several troublemakers about his faith, he responded calmly and clearly. His logic devastated their arguments. Stephen was hauled before the official religious court, where he used a summary of the Jews' own history to show that Jesus was the Savior. The court was unable to answer him, so they decided to silence him. They stoned him to death while he prayed for their forgiveness. Stephen's final words show how much he had become like Jesus in a short time. His death had a lasting effect on a young Paul, who would later change from fiercely destroying the faith to radically defending it. Stephen's life is a continual challenge to Christians. Because he was the first to die for the faith, his sacrifice raises questions: How many risks do we take in being Jesus' followers? Would we be willing to die for him? Are we really willing to live for him?

LESSONS: Striving for excellence in small assignments prepares a person for greater responsibilities

Real understanding of God always leads to practical and compassionate actions

KEY VERSES: "And they stoned Stephen as he was calling on God and saying, 'Lord Jesus, receive my spirit.' Then he knelt down and cried out with a loud voice, 'Lord, do not charge them with this sin.' And when he had said this, he fell asleep" (Acts 7:59-60).

Stephen's story is told in Acts 6:3–8:2. He also is mentioned in Acts 11:19; 22:20.

UPS:
- One of seven leaders chosen to supervise food distribution to the needy in the early church
- Known for his spiritual qualities of faith, wisdom, grace, and power, and for the Spirit's presence in his life
- Outstanding leader, teacher, and debater
- First to give his life for the gospel

STATS:
- Church responsibilities: Deacon—distributing food to the needy
- Contemporaries: Paul, Caiaphas, Gamaliel, the apostles

brethren, the children of Israel. [24]And seeing one of *them* suffer wrong, he defended and avenged him who was oppressed, and struck down the Egyptian. [25]For he supposed that his brethren would have understood that God would deliver them by his hand, but they did not understand. [26]And the next day he appeared to two of them as they were fighting, and *tried to* reconcile them, saying, 'Men, you are brethren; why do you wrong one another?' [27]But he who did his neighbor wrong pushed him away, saying, '*Who made you a ruler and a judge over us?* [28]*Do you want to kill me as you did the Egyptian yesterday?*' [29]Then, at this saying, Moses fled and became a dweller in the land of Midian, where he had two sons.

[30]"And when forty years had passed, an Angel of the Lord appeared to him in a flame of fire in a bush, in the wilderness of Mount Sinai. [31]When Moses saw *it*, he marveled at the sight; and as he drew near to observe, the voice of the Lord came to him, [32]*saying, 'I am the God of your fathers—the God of Abraham, the God of Isaac, and the God of Jacob.*' And Moses trembled and dared not look. [33]*Then the* LORD *said to him, "Take your sandals off your feet, for the place where you stand is holy ground.* [34]*I have surely seen the oppression of My people who are in Egypt; I have heard their groaning and have come down to deliver them. And now come, I will send you to Egypt.*"'

[35]"This Moses whom they rejected, saying, '*Who made you a ruler and a judge?*' is the one God sent *to be* a ruler and a deliverer by the hand of the Angel who appeared to him in the bush. [36]He brought them out, after he had shown wonders and signs in the land of Egypt, and in the Red Sea, and in the wilderness forty years.

[37]"This is that Moses who said to the children of Israel, '*The* LORD *your God will raise up for you a Prophet like me from your brethren. Him you shall hear.*'

[38]"This is he who was in the congregation in the wilderness with the Angel who spoke to him on Mount Sinai, and *with* our fathers, the one who received the living oracles to give to us, [39]whom our fathers would not obey, but rejected. And in their hearts they turned back to Egypt, [40]saying to Aaron, '*Make us gods to go before us; as for this Moses who brought us out of the land of Egypt, we do not know what has become of him.*' [41]And they made a calf in those days, offered sacrifices to the idol, and rejoiced in the works of their own hands. [42]Then God turned and gave them up to worship the host of heaven, as it is written in the book of the Prophets:

'*Did you offer Me slaughtered animals and sacrifices during forty years in the wilderness,*
   O house of Israel?
[43]   *You also took up the tabernacle of Moloch,*
   And the star of your god Remphan,
   Images which you made to worship;
   And I will carry you away beyond Babylon.'

[44]"Our fathers had the tabernacle of witness in the wilderness, as He appointed, instructing Moses to make it according to the pattern that he had seen, [45]which our fathers, having received it in turn, also brought with Joshua into the land possessed by the Gentiles, whom God drove out before the face of our fathers until the days

of David, [46]who found favor before God and asked to find a dwelling for the God of Jacob. [47]But Solomon built Him a house.

[48]"However, the Most High does not dwell in temples made with hands, as the prophet says:

[49]   '*Heaven is My throne,*
   And earth is My footstool.
   What house will you build for Me? says the LORD,
   Or what is the place of My rest?
[50]   *Has My hand not made all these things?*'

[51]"*You* stiff-necked and uncircumcised in heart and ears! You always resist the Holy Spirit; as your fathers *did*, so *do* you. [52]Which of the prophets did your fathers not persecute? And they killed those who foretold the coming of the Just One, of whom you now have become the betrayers and murderers, [53]who have received the law by the direction of angels and have not kept *it.*"

[54]When they heard these things they were cut to the heart, and they gnashed at him with *their* teeth. [55]But he, being full of the Holy Spirit, gazed into heaven and saw the glory of God, and Jesus standing at the right hand of God, [56]and said, "Look! I see the heavens opened and the Son of Man standing at the right hand of God!"

[57]Then they cried out with a loud voice, stopped their ears, and ran at him with one accord; [58]and they cast *him* out of the city and stoned *him.* And the witnesses laid down their clothes at the feet of a young man named Saul. [59]And they stoned Stephen as he was calling on *God* and saying, "Lord Jesus, receive my spirit." [60]Then he knelt down and cried out with a loud voice, "Lord, do not charge them with this sin." And when he had said this, he fell asleep.

CHAPTER **8** **PHILIP AND AN ETHIOPIAN.** Now Saul was consenting to his death.

At that time a great persecution arose against the church which was at Jerusalem; and they were all scattered throughout the regions of Judea and Samaria, except the apostles. [2]And devout men carried Stephen *to his burial,* and made great lamentation over him.

[3]As for Saul, he made havoc of the church, entering every house, and dragging off men and women, committing *them* to prison.

[4]Therefore those who were scattered went everywhere preaching the word. [5]Then Philip went down to the city of Samaria and preached Christ to them. [6]And the multitudes with one accord heeded the things spoken by Philip, hearing and seeing the miracles which he did. [7]For unclean spirits, crying with a loud voice, came out of many who were possessed; and many who were para-

◣ PREPARING

8:4 Persecution forced the believers out of their homes in Jerusalem, but with them went the gospel. Often we have to become uncomfortab[le] before we'll move. Discomfort may be unwanted, but it is not unproductive, for out of our hurting God works his purposes. The next time you are tempted to complain about uncomfortable or painful circumstances, stop and ask if God may be preparing you for a special task.

lyzed and lame were healed. ⁸And there was great joy in that city.

⁹But there was a certain man called Simon, who previously practiced sorcery in the city and astonished the people of Samaria, claiming that he was someone great, ¹⁰to whom they all gave heed, from the least to the greatest, saying, "This man is the great power of God." ¹¹And they heeded him because he had astonished them with his sorceries for a long time. ¹²But when they believed Philip as he preached the things concerning the kingdom of God and the name of Jesus Christ, both men and women were baptized. ¹³Then Simon himself also believed; and when he was baptized he continued with Philip, and was amazed, seeing the miracles and signs which were done.

¹⁴Now when the apostles who were at Jerusalem heard that Samaria had received the word of God, they sent Peter and John to them, ¹⁵who, when they had come down, prayed for them that they might receive the Holy Spirit. ¹⁶For as yet He had fallen upon none of them. They had only been baptized in the name of the Lord Jesus. ¹⁷Then they laid hands on them, and they received the Holy Spirit.

¹⁸And when Simon saw that through the laying on of the apostles' hands the Holy Spirit was given, he offered them money, ¹⁹saying, "Give me this power also, that anyone on whom I lay hands may receive the Holy Spirit."

²⁰But Peter said to him, "Your money perish with you, because you thought that the gift of God could be purchased with money! ²¹You have neither part nor portion in this matter, for your heart is not right in the sight of God. ²²Repent therefore of this your wickedness, and pray God if perhaps the thought of your heart may be forgiven you. ²³For I see that you are poisoned by bitterness and bound by iniquity."

²⁴Then Simon answered and said, "Pray to the Lord for me, that none of the things which you have spoken may come upon me."

²⁵So when they had testified and preached the word of the Lord, they returned to Jerusalem, preaching the gospel in many villages of the Samaritans.

²⁶Now an angel of the Lord spoke to Philip, saying, "Arise and go toward the south along the road which goes down from Jerusalem to Gaza." This is desert. ²⁷So he arose and went. And behold, a man of Ethiopia, a eunuch of great authority under Candace the queen of the Ethiopians, who had charge of all her treasury, and had come to Jerusalem to worship, ²⁸was returning. And sitting in his chariot, he was reading Isaiah the prophet. ²⁹Then the Spirit said to Philip, "Go near and overtake this chariot."

³⁰So Philip ran to him, and heard him reading the prophet Isaiah, and said, "Do you understand what you are reading?"

³¹And he said, "How can I, unless someone guides me?" And he asked Philip to come up and sit with him. ³²The place in the Scripture which he read was this:

"He was led as a sheep to the slaughter;
And as a lamb before its shearer is silent,
So He opened not His mouth.

³³ *In His humiliation His justice was taken away,*
And who will declare His generation?
For His life is taken from the earth."

³⁴So the eunuch answered Philip and said, "I ask you, of whom does the prophet say this, of himself or of some other man?" ³⁵Then Philip opened his mouth, and begin-

---

Some kids at school (and even some teachers) give Christians a pretty tough time. This makes me not want to let anyone know I'm a believer. What should I do?

I WONDER . . .

Rejection comes with being a Christian, because our life and beliefs go against the flow of the rest of the world. Growing closer to God will naturally make you grow further away from the world.

Read Acts 7:54-60. Stephen took a stand for Christ that cost him much more than rejection from a few friends. It cost him his life. Read further, and in Acts 8 and 9 you will see what the results of a fearless faith can be.

Imagine being able to see all of history from beginning to end. You would understand so much more because you could see the whole picture. But only God can do that—so we have to trust him. We have to live on this earth without being able to see the future.

If Stephen had known what his death would accomplish, he would have died smiling. A man named Paul was one of the foremost persecutors of Christians. But Paul's life was turned around, and he became a follower of Christ. Paul had heard Stephen speak—and he had watched him die.

Paul didn't just become a church-only, pew-sitter type of follower. He traveled throughout the world, sharing the Good News about Christ. He also wrote nearly half of the books of the New Testament! Stephen's rejection helped bring Paul to Christ.

People are watching you and other Christians at school. They are seeing how you respond to rejection and verbal abuse. Within those crowded halls are people who want to believe in something true, something worth living for no matter what the cost. And when they find it, they may make an incredible impact in their world for Christ.

What do they learn from watching you?

---

ning at this Scripture, preached Jesus to him. ³⁶Now as they went down the road, they came to some water. And the eunuch said, "See, *here is* water. What hinders me from being baptized?"

³⁷Then Philip said, "If you believe with all your heart, you may."

And he answered and said, "I believe that Jesus Christ is the Son of God."

CRITICISM

8:24 Do you remember the last time a parent or friend strongly criticized you? Were you hurt? Angry? Defensive? Learn a lesson from Simon and his reaction to Peter's words. Simon exclaimed, "Pray to the Lord for me." When you are rebuked for a serious mistake, it is for your good. Admit your error and ask for prayer.

³⁸So he commanded the chariot to stand still. And both Philip and the eunuch went down into the water, and he baptized him. ³⁹Now when they came up out of the water, the Spirit of the Lord caught Philip away, so that the eunuch saw him no more; and he went on his way rejoicing. ⁴⁰But Philip was found at Azotus. And passing through, he preached in all the cities till he came to Caesarea.

CHAPTER 9 PAUL MEETS JESUS.

Then Saul, still breathing threats and murder against the disciples of the Lord, went to the high priest ²and asked letters from him to the synagogues of Damascus, so that if he found any who were of the Way, whether men or women, he might bring them bound to Jerusalem.

³As he journeyed he came near Damascus, and suddenly a light shone around him from heaven. ⁴Then he fell to the ground, and heard a voice saying to him, "Saul, Saul, why are you persecuting Me?"

⁵And he said, "Who are You, Lord?"

Then the Lord said, "I am Jesus, whom you are persecuting. It is hard for you to kick against the goads."

⁶So he, trembling and astonished, said, "Lord, what do You want me to do?"

Then the Lord said to him, "Arise and go into the city, and you will be told what you must do."

⁷And the men who journeyed with him stood speechless, hearing a voice but seeing no one. ⁸Then Saul arose from the ground, and when his eyes were opened he saw no one. But they led him by the hand and brought him into Damascus. ⁹And he was three days without sight, and neither ate nor drank.

¹⁰Now there was a certain disciple at Damascus named Ananias; and to him the Lord said in a vision, "Ananias."

And he said, "Here I am, Lord."

¹¹So the Lord said to him, "Arise and go to the street called Straight, and inquire at the house of Judas for one called Saul of Tarsus, for behold, he is praying. ¹²And in a vision he has seen a man named Ananias coming in and putting his hand on him, so that he might receive his sight."

¹³Then Ananias answered, "Lord, I have heard from many about this man, how much harm he has done to Your saints in Jerusalem. ¹⁴And here he has authority from the chief priests to bind all who call on Your name."

¹⁵But the Lord said to him, "Go, for he is a chosen vessel of Mine to bear My name before Gentiles, kings, and the children of Israel. ¹⁶For I will show him how many things he must suffer for My name's sake."

¹⁷And Ananias went his way and entered the house; and laying his hands on him he said, "Brother Saul, the Lord Jesus, who appeared to you on the road as you came, has sent me that you may receive your sight and be filled with the Holy Spirit." ¹⁸Immediately there fell from his eyes something like scales, and he received his sight at once; and he arose and was baptized.

¹⁹So when he had received food, he was strengthened. Then Saul spent some days with the disciples at Damascus.

PAGE 1040

DON'T WAIT

9:20 Immediately after receiving his sight, Paul went to the synag to tell the Jews about Jesus Christ. Some Christians counsel new bel to wait until they are thoroughly grounded in their faith before attempting to share the gospel. Paul took time alone to learn abou before beginning his worldwide ministry, but he did not wait to wit Although we should not rush into a ministry unprepared, we do not to wait before telling others what has happened to us.

²⁰Immediately he preached the Christ in the synagogues, that He is the Son of God.

²¹Then all who heard were amazed, and said, "Is this not he who destroyed those who called on this name in Jerusalem, and has come here for that purpose, so that he might bring them bound to the chief priests?"

²²But Saul increased all the more in strength, and confounded the Jews who dwelt in Damascus, proving that this *Jesus* is the Christ.

²³Now after many days were past, the Jews plotted to kill him. ²⁴But their plot became known to Saul. And they watched the gates day and night, to kill him. ²⁵Then the disciples took him by night and let *him* down through the wall in a large basket.

²⁶And when Saul had come to Jerusalem, he tried to join the disciples; but they were all afraid of him, and did not believe that he was a disciple. ²⁷But Barnabas took him and brought *him* to the apostles. And he declared to them how he had seen the Lord on the road, and that He had spoken to him, and how he had preached boldly at Damascus in the name of Jesus. ²⁸So he was with them at Jerusalem, coming in and going out. ²⁹And he spoke boldly in the name of the Lord Jesus and disputed against the Hellenists, but they attempted to kill him. ³⁰When the brethren found out, they brought him down to Caesarea and sent him out to Tarsus.

³¹Then the churches throughout all Judea, Galilee, and Samaria had peace and were edified. And walking in the fear of the Lord and in the comfort of the Holy Spirit, they were multiplied.

³²Now it came to pass, as Peter went through all *parts of the country,* that he also came down to the saints who dwelt in Lydda. ³³There he found a certain man named Aeneas, who had been bedridden eight years and was paralyzed. ³⁴And Peter said to him, "Aeneas, Jesus the Christ heals you. Arise and make your bed." Then he arose immediately. ³⁵So all who dwelt at Lydda and Sharon saw him and turned to the Lord.

³⁶At Joppa there was a certain disciple named Tabitha, which is translated Dorcas. This woman was full of good works and charitable deeds which she did. ³⁷But it happened in those days that she became sick and died. When they had washed her, they laid *her* in an upper room. ³⁸And since Lydda was near Joppa, and the disciples had heard that Peter was there, they sent two men to him, imploring *him* not to delay in coming to them. ³⁹Then Peter arose and went with them. When he had come, they

IMPACT

9:36-42 Dorcas had an enormous impact on her community by "good works and charitable deeds." When she died, the room was with mourners, people she had helped. When she was brought back life, the news raced through the town. God uses great preachers lik Peter and Paul, but he also uses those who have other gifts, like kindness. Make good use of the gifts God has given you.

brought *him* to the upper room. And all the widows stood by him weeping, showing the tunics and garments which Dorcas had made while she was with them. [40]But Peter put them all out, and knelt down and prayed. And turning to the body he said, "Tabitha, arise." And she opened her eyes, and when she saw Peter she sat up. [41]Then he gave her *his* hand and lifted her up; and when he had called the saints and widows, he presented her alive. [42]And it became known throughout all Joppa, and many believed on the Lord. [43]So it was that he stayed many days in Joppa with Simon, a tanner.

CHAPTER 10 A ROMAN CAPTAIN CALLS FOR PETER.

There was a certain man in Caesarea called Cornelius, a centurion of what was called the Italian Regiment, [2]a devout *man* and one who feared God with all his household, who gave alms generously to the people, and prayed to God always. [3]About the ninth hour of the day he saw clearly in a vision an angel of God coming in and saying to him, "Cornelius!"

[4]And when he observed him, he was afraid, and said, "What is it, lord?"

So he said to him, "Your prayers and your alms have come up for a memorial before God. [5]Now send men to Joppa, and send for Simon whose surname is Peter. [6]He is lodging with Simon, a tanner, whose house is by the sea. He will tell you what you must do." [7]And when the angel who spoke to him had departed, Cornelius called two of his household servants and a devout soldier from among those who waited on him continually. [8]So when he had explained all *these* things to them, he sent them to Joppa.

[9]The next day, as they went on their journey and drew near the city, Peter went up on the housetop to pray, about the sixth hour. [10]Then he became very hungry and wanted to eat; but while they made ready, he fell into a trance [11]and saw heaven opened and an object like a great sheet bound at the four corners, descending to him and let down to the earth. [12]In it were all kinds of four-footed animals of the earth, wild beasts, creeping things, and birds of the air. [13]And a voice came to him, "Rise, Peter; kill and eat."

[14]But Peter said, "Not so, Lord! For I have never eaten anything common or unclean."

[15]And a voice *spoke* to him again the second time, "What God has cleansed you must not call common." [16]This was done three times. And the object was taken up into heaven again.

[17]Now while Peter wondered within himself what this vision which he had seen meant, behold, the men who had been sent from Cornelius had made inquiry for Simon's house, and stood before the gate. [18]And they called and asked whether Simon, whose

PAUL

No person, apart from Jesus himself, shaped the history of Christianity as much as the apostle Paul. Paul was a leader in the frenzied persecution of Christians following Stephen's death. Eventually, Paul met Christ personally and his life was changed. However, Paul never lost his energy or intensity—it was redirected so that it was dedicated to Christ.

Paul was brought up in a very religious home. He was an expert in the Jewish Bible, the Old Testament. Convinced Christianity was dangerous to Judaism, Paul hated the Christian faith and persecuted Christians without mercy. At one point, Paul got permission to travel to Damascus to arrest Christians and bring them back to Jerusalem. His plans would have resulted in the death of many believers—but God had other plans. Paul was met on the road to Damascus by Jesus Christ . . . and Paul's life was never the same.

Paul became God's key tool in taking the gospel to non-Jewish people. Until Paul was converted, little had been done to carry Christ's message to the Gentiles. Paul and his missionary teams eventually carried the gospel across the entire Roman Empire.

Paul worked hard to convince the Jews that Gentiles were acceptable to God, but he spent even more time convincing Gentiles themselves that they were acceptable to God. People's lives were changed and challenged by meeting Christ through Paul. God did not waste any part of Paul—his background, his training, his citizenship, his mind, or even his weaknesses. He used them all. Are you willing to let God do the same for you? You will never know what he can do with you until you allow him to have all that you are!

LESSONS: The Good News is that forgiveness and eternal life are a gift of God's grace received by faith in Christ and available to all people Obedience results from a relationship with God, but obedience will never create or earn that relationship

God will use our past and present so that we may serve him with our future

KEY VERSES: "For to me, to live is Christ, and to die is gain. But if I live on in the flesh, this will mean fruit from my labor; yet what I shall choose I cannot tell. For I am hard-pressed between the two, having a desire to depart and be with Christ, which is far better. Nevertheless to remain in the flesh is more needful for you" (Philippians 1:21-24).

Paul's story is told in Acts 7:58–28:31 and throughout his New Testament letters.

UPS:
- Transformed by God from a persecutor of Christians to a preacher for Christ
- Preached for Christ throughout the Roman Empire on three missionary journeys
- Wrote letters, which became part of the New Testament, to various churches
- Was never afraid to face an issue head-on and deal with it
- Was sensitive to God's leading and, despite his strong personality, always did as God directed
- Often is called the apostle to the Gentiles

DOWNS:
- Witnessed and approved of Stephen's stoning
- Set out to destroy Christianity by persecuting Christians

STATS:
- Where: Born in Tarsus but became a world traveler for Christ
- Occupations: Trained as a Pharisee, learned the tentmaking trade, served as a missionary
- Contemporaries: Gamaliel, Stephen, the apostles, Luke, Barnabas, Timothy

surname was Peter, was lodging there.

[19]While Peter thought about the vision, the Spirit said to him, "Behold, three men are seeking you. [20]Arise therefore, go down and go with them, doubting nothing; for I have sent them."

[21]Then Peter went down to the men who had been sent to him from Cornelius, and said, "Yes, I am he whom you seek. For what reason have you come?"

[22]And they said, "Cornelius *the* centurion, a just man, one who fears God and has a good reputation among all the nation of the Jews, was divinely instructed by a holy angel to summon you to his house, and to hear words from you." [23]Then he invited them in and lodged *them*.

On the next day Peter went away with them, and some

PRIDE

Seventeen-year-old Leslie loves music and has always wanted to be a singer. Not just a member of the youth choir. No, Leslie wants to be big-time, performing in front of a packed auditorium of cheering fans.

Leslie is talented, she practices a lot, and every now and then she gets to do solos at church. But last night, she finally got the big break she's been hoping for. She sang three songs at a huge youth rally in a city 250 miles away. Over 2,000 young people. A big stage. Lights. Professional sound equipment. Top-notch technicians. A $300 honorarium. We're talking "big time"!

Well, it went great. The audience loved her. Afterward, a handful of youth pastors asked her, "How can I book you to sing for my group?" People complimented her like crazy, tossing around words and phrases like "wonderful," "beautiful," and "going places." Some even asked when her first album would be out. The killer was the group of younger kids who asked Leslie to autograph their Bibles!

The day after, Leslie is still basking in her sudden success.

The day after, Leslie is a victim of pride.

Why is success and/or adulation so difficult to handle? Where do our talents come from? What happens if we forget God and get a big head? See Acts 12:19-23.

brethren from Joppa accompanied him.

[24]And the following day they entered Caesarea. Now Cornelius was waiting for them, and had called together his relatives and close friends. [25]As Peter was coming in, Cornelius met him and fell down at his feet and worshiped *him*. [26]But Peter lifted him up, saying, "Stand up; I myself am also a man." [27]And as he talked with him, he went in and found many who had come together. [28]Then he said to them, "You know how unlawful it is for a Jewish man to keep company with or go to one of another nation. But God has shown me that I should not call any man common or unclean. [29]Therefore I came without objection as soon as I was sent for. I ask, then, for what reason have you sent for me?"

[30]So Cornelius said, "Four days ago I was fasting until this hour; and at the ninth hour I prayed in my house, and behold, a man stood before me in bright clothing, [31]and said, 'Cornelius, your prayer has been heard, and your alms are remembered in the sight of God. [32]Send therefore to Joppa and call Simon here, whose surname is Peter. He is lodging in the house of Simon, a tanner, by

EAGER

10:48 Cornelius wanted Peter to stay with him for several days. [A] new believer, Cornelius realized his need for teaching and fellowship[.] [Are] you that eager to learn more about Christ? Recognize your need to [relate] with more mature Christians, and then learn from them.

the sea. When he comes, he will speak to you.' [33]So I sent to you immediately, and you have done well to come. Now therefore, we are all present before God, to hear all the things commanded you by God."

[34]Then Peter opened *his* mouth and said: "In truth I perceive that God shows no partiality. [35]But in every nation whoever fears Him and works righteousness is accepted by Him. [36]The word which *God* sent to the children of Israel, preaching peace through Jesus Christ—He is Lord of all— [37]that word you know, which was proclaimed throughout all Judea, and began from Galilee after the baptism which John preached: [38]how God anointed Jesus of Nazareth with the Holy Spirit and with power, who went about doing good and healing all who were oppressed by the devil, for God was with Him. [39]And we are witnesses of all things which He did both in the land of the Jews and in Jerusalem, whom they killed by hanging on a tree. [40]Him God raised up on the third day, and showed Him openly, [41]not to all the people, but to witnesses chosen before by God, *even* to us who ate and drank with Him after He arose from the dead. [42]And He commanded us to preach to the people, and to testify that it is He who was ordained by God *to be* Judge of the living and the dead. [43]To Him all the prophets witness that, through His name, whoever believes in Him will receive remission of sins."

[44]While Peter was still speaking these words, the Holy Spirit fell upon all those who heard the word. [45]And those of the circumcision who believed were astonished, as many as came with Peter, because the gift of the Holy Spirit had been poured out on the Gentiles also. [46]For they heard them speak with tongues and magnify God. Then Peter answered, [47]"Can anyone forbid water, that these should not be baptized who have received the Holy Spirit just as we *have*?" [48]And he commanded them to be baptized in the name of the Lord. Then they asked him to stay a few days.

CHAPTER 11 WHY PETER PREACHES TO GENTILES.

Now the apostles and brethren who were in Judea heard that the Gentiles had also received the word of God. [2]And when Peter came up to Jerusalem, those of the circumcision contended with him, [3]saying, "You went in to uncircumcised men and ate with them!"

[4]But Peter explained *it* to them in order from the beginning, saying: [5]"I was in the city of Joppa praying; and

SHOCKED

11:2-18 When Peter brought the news of Cornelius's conversion to Jerusalem, the believers were shocked that he had eaten with G[entiles]. After they heard the whole story, however, they began praising Go[d] (11:18). Their reactions teach us how to handle disagreements with [other] Christians. Before judging the behavior of fellow believers, it is imp[ortant] to hear them out. The Holy Spirit may be using them to teach us something important.

in a trance I saw a vision, an object descending like a great sheet, let down from heaven by four corners; and it came to me. ⁶When I observed it intently and considered, I saw four-footed animals of the earth, wild beasts, creeping things, and birds of the air. ⁷And I heard a voice saying to me, 'Rise, Peter; kill and eat.' ⁸But I said, 'Not so, Lord! For nothing common or unclean has at any time entered my mouth.' ⁹But the voice answered me again from heaven, 'What God has cleansed you must not call common.' ¹⁰Now this was done three times, and all were drawn up again into heaven. ¹¹At that very moment, three men stood before the house where I was, having been sent to me from Caesarea. ¹²Then the Spirit told me to go with them, doubting nothing. Moreover these six brethren accompanied me, and we entered the man's house.

¹³And he told us how he had seen an angel standing in his house, who said to him, 'Send men to Joppa, and call for Simon whose surname is Peter, ¹⁴who will tell you words by which you and all your household will be saved.'

¹⁵And as I began to speak, the Holy Spirit fell upon them, as upon us at the beginning. ¹⁶Then I remembered the word of the Lord, how He said, 'John indeed baptized with water, but you shall be baptized with the Holy Spirit.' ¹⁷If therefore God gave them the same gift as *He gave* us when we believed on the Lord Jesus Christ, who was I that I could withstand God?"

¹⁸When they heard these things they became silent; and they glorified God, saying, "Then God has also granted to the Gentiles repentance to life."

¹⁹Now those who were scattered after the persecution that arose over Stephen traveled as far as Phoenicia, Cyprus, and Antioch, preaching the word to no one but the Jews only. ²⁰But some of them were men from Cyprus and Cyrene, who, when they had come to Antioch, spoke to the Hellenists, preaching the Lord Jesus. ²¹And the hand of the Lord was with them, and a great number believed and turned to the Lord.

²²Then news of these things came to the ears of the church in Jerusalem, and they sent out Barnabas to go as far as Antioch. ²³When he came and had seen the grace of God, he was glad, and encouraged them all that with purpose of heart they should continue with the Lord. ²⁴For he was a good man, full of the Holy Spirit and of faith. And a great many people were added to the Lord.

²⁵Then Barnabas departed for Tarsus to seek Saul. ²⁶And when he had found him, he brought him to Antioch. So it was that for a whole year they assembled with the church and taught a great many people. And the disciples were first called Christians in Antioch.

²⁷And in these days prophets came from Jerusalem to Antioch. ²⁸Then one of them, named Agabus, stood up and showed by

JOHN MARK

Mistakes can be effective teachers because the consequences have a way of making lessons painfully clear. But those who learn from their mistakes gain wisdom. John Mark, with the help of some time and encouragement, became a wise learner.

Mark was eager to do the right thing, but he had trouble staying with a task. In his Gospel, Mark mentions a young man (probably referring to himself) who fled in such fear during Jesus' arrest that he left his clothes behind. Mark's tendency to run showed up later when Paul and Barnabas took him as their assistant on their first missionary journey. Early in the trip, Mark left them and returned to Jerusalem. Paul didn't appreciate Mark's quitting. Two years later, Paul would not consider letting Mark try again. As a result, the team split up. Barnabas took Mark with him, and Paul chose Silas. Barnabas was patient with Mark, and the young man and Mark turned out to be a good investment. In fact, Paul and Mark were later reunited and the older apostle became a close friend of the young disciple.

Mark was able to watch closely the lives of three Christian leaders—Barnabas, Paul, and Peter. The material in Mark's Gospel seems to have come mostly from Peter. As his helper, Mark had a chance to hear Peter's stories of the years with Jesus over and over. Mark became one of the first to put Jesus' life into writing. He had someone who encouraged him to learn from his mistakes.

Barnabas played a key role in Mark's life. He stood beside the young man in his failure, giving him patient encouragement. Mark's experience can remind us to learn from our mistakes and to appreciate the patience of others. Is there a Barnabas in your life whom you need to thank for his or her encouragement to you?

LESSONS: Personal maturity usually comes from a combination of time and mistakes Effective living is not measured by what we accomplish so much as by what we overcome in order to accomplish Encouragement can change a person's life

KEY VERSE: "Only Luke is with me. Get Mark and bring him with you, for he is useful to me for ministry" (Paul writing to Timothy, 2 Timothy 4:11).

John Mark's story is told in Acts 12:23–13:13 and 15:36-39. He is also mentioned in Colossians 4:10; 2 Timothy 4:11; Philemon 24; 1 Peter 5:13.

UPS:
- Wrote the Gospel of Mark
- He and his mother provided their home as one of the main meeting places for the Christians in Jerusalem
- Persistent beyond his youthful mistakes
- Was an assistant and traveling companion to three of the greatest early missionaries

DOWNS:
- Probably the nameless young man described in the Gospel of Mark who fled in panic when Jesus was arrested
- Left Paul and Barnabas during the first missionary journey

STATS:
- Where: Jerusalem
- Occupation: Missionary-in-training, Gospel writer, traveling companion
- Relatives: Mother: Mary. Cousin: Barnabas.
- Contemporaries: Paul, Peter, Timothy, Luke, Silas

12:13-15 The prayers of the little group of believers were answered, even as they prayed. But when the answer arrived at the door, they didn't believe it. We should be people of faith who believe that God answers the prayers of those who seek his will. When you pray, believe you'll get an answer—and when the answer comes, don't be surprised!

the Spirit that there was going to be a great famine throughout all the world, which also happened in the days of Claudius Caesar. ²⁹Then the disciples, each according to his ability, determined to send relief to the brethren dwelling in Judea. ³⁰This they also did, and sent it to the elders by the hands of Barnabas and Saul.

CHAPTER 12 AN ANGEL LETS PETER OUT OF PRISON.

Now about that time Herod the king stretched out *his* hand to harass some from the church. ²Then he killed James the brother of John with the sword. ³And because he saw that it pleased the Jews, he proceeded further to seize Peter also. Now it was *during* the Days of Unleavened Bread. ⁴So when he had arrested him, he put *him* in prison, and delivered *him* to four squads of soldiers to keep him, intending to bring him before the people after Passover.

⁵Peter was therefore kept in prison, but constant prayer was offered to God for him by the church. ⁶And when Herod was about to bring him out, that night Peter was sleeping, bound with two chains between two soldiers; and the guards before the door were keeping the prison. ⁷Now behold, an angel of the Lord stood by *him*, and a light shone in the prison; and he struck Peter on the side and raised him up, saying, "Arise quickly!" And his chains fell off *his* hands. ⁸Then the angel said to him, "Gird yourself and tie on your sandals"; and so he did. And he said to him, "Put on your garment and follow me." ⁹So he went out and followed him, and did not know that what was done by the angel was real, but thought he was seeing a vision. ¹⁰When they were past the first and the second guard posts, they came to the iron gate that leads to the city, which opened to them of its own accord; and they went out and went down one street, and immediately the angel departed from him.

¹¹And when Peter had come to himself, he said, "Now I know for certain that the Lord has sent His angel, and has delivered me from the hand of Herod and *from* all the expectation of the Jewish people."

¹²So, when he had considered *this*, he came to the house of Mary, the mother of John whose surname was Mark, where many were gathered together praying. ¹³And as Peter knocked at the door of the gate, a girl named Rhoda came to answer. ¹⁴When she recognized Peter's voice, because of *her* gladness she did not open the gate, but ran in and announced that Peter stood before the gate. ¹⁵But they said to her, "You are beside yourself!" Yet she kept insisting that it was so. So they said, "It is his angel."

¹⁶Now Peter continued knocking; and when they opened *the* door and saw him, they were astonished. ¹⁷But motioning to them with his hand to keep silent, he declared to them how the Lord had brought him out of the prison. And he said, "Go, tell these things to James and to the brethren." And he departed and went to another place.

¹⁸Then, as soon as it was day, there was no small stir among the soldiers about what had become of Peter. ¹⁹But when Herod had searched for him and not found him, he examined the guards and commanded that *they* should be put to death.

And he went down from Judea to Caesarea, and stayed *there*.

²⁰Now Herod had been very angry with the people of Tyre and Sidon; but they came to him with one accord, and having made Blastus the king's personal aide their friend, they asked for peace, because their country was supplied with food by the king's *country*.

²¹So on a set day Herod, arrayed in royal apparel, sat on his throne and gave an oration to them. ²²And the people kept shouting, "The voice of a god and not of a man!" ²³Then immediately an angel of the Lord struck him, because he did not give glory to God. And he was eaten by worms and died.

13:1 What variety there is in the church! The only common thread among these five men was their deep faith in Christ. We must never exclude anyone whom Christ has called to follow him.

²⁴But the word of God grew and multiplied.

²⁵And Barnabas and Saul returned from Jerusalem when they had fulfilled *their* ministry, and they also took with them John whose surname was Mark.

CHAPTER 13 PAUL'S FIRST MISSIONARY JOURNEY.

Now in the church that was at Antioch there were certain prophets and teachers: Barnabas, Simeon who was called Niger, Lucius of Cyrene, Manaen who had been brought up with Herod the tetrarch, and Saul. ²As they ministered to the Lord and fasted, the Holy Spirit said, "Now separate to Me Barnabas and Saul for the work to which I have called them." ³Then, having fasted and prayed, and laid hands on them, they sent *them* away.

⁴So, being sent out by the Holy Spirit, they went down to Seleucia, and from there they sailed to Cyprus. ⁵And when they arrived in Salamis, they preached the word of God in the synagogues of the Jews. They also had John as *their* assistant.

⁶Now when they had gone through the island to Paphos, they found a certain sorcerer, a false prophet, a Jew whose name *was* Bar-Jesus, ⁷who was with the proconsul, Sergius Paulus, an intelligent man. This man called for Barnabas and Saul and sought to hear the word of God. ⁸But Elymas the sorcerer (for so his name is trans-

13:42-45 The Jewish leaders brought theological arguments against Paul and Barnabas, but the Bible tells us that the real reason for the denunciation was that "they were filled with envy." When we see others succeeding where we haven't or receiving the glory that we want, it's hard to be happy for them. Jealousy is our natural reaction. But it's tragic when our own jealous feelings make us try to stop God's work. If the work is God's work, rejoice in it—no matter who is doing it.

lated) withstood them, seeking to turn the proconsul away from the faith. [9]Then Saul, who also *is called* Paul, filled with the Holy Spirit, looked intently at him [10]and said, "O full of all deceit and all fraud, *you* son of the devil, *you* enemy of all righteousness, will you not cease perverting the straight ways of the Lord? [11]And now, indeed, the hand of the Lord *is* upon you, and you shall be blind, not seeing the sun for a time."

And immediately a dark mist fell on him, and he went around seeking someone to lead him by the hand. [12]Then the proconsul believed, when he saw what had been done, being astonished at the teaching of the Lord.

[13]Now when Paul and his party set sail from Paphos, they came to Perga in Pamphylia; and John, departing from them, returned to Jerusalem. [14]But when they departed from Perga, they came to Antioch in Pisidia, and went into the synagogue on the Sabbath day and sat down. [15]And after the reading of the Law and the Prophets, the rulers of the synagogue sent to them, saying, "Men *and* brethren, if you have any word of exhortation for the people, say on."

[16]Then Paul stood up, and motioning with *his* hand said, "Men of Israel, and you who fear God, listen: [17]The God of this people Israel chose our fathers, and exalted the people when they dwelt as strangers in the land of Egypt, and with an uplifted arm He brought them out of it. [18]Now for a time of about forty years He put up with their ways in the wilderness. [19]And when He had destroyed seven nations in the land of Canaan, He distributed their land to them by allotment.

[20]"After that He gave *them* judges for about four hundred and fifty years, until Samuel the prophet. [21]And afterward they asked for a king; so God gave them Saul the son of Kish, a man of the tribe of Benjamin, for forty years. [22]And when He had removed him, He raised up for them David as king, to whom also He gave testimony and said, *'I have found David* the *son* of Jesse, *a man after My own heart,* who will do all My will.' [23]From this man's seed, according to *the* promise, God raised up for Israel a Savior—Jesus— [24]after John had first preached, before His coming, the baptism of repentance to all the people of Israel. [25]And as John was finishing his course, he said, 'Who do you think I am? I am not *He.* But behold,

there comes One after me, the sandals of whose feet I am not worthy to loose.'

[26]"Men *and* brethren, sons of the family of Abraham, and those among you who fear God, to you the word of this salvation has been sent. [27]For those who dwell in Jerusalem, and their rulers, because they did not know Him, nor even the voices of the Prophets which are read every Sabbath, have fulfilled *them* in condemning *Him.* [28]And though they found no cause for death *in Him,* they asked Pilate that He should be put to death. [29]Now when they had fulfilled all that was written concerning Him, they took *Him* down from the tree and laid *Him* in a tomb. [30]But God raised Him from the dead. [31]He was seen for many days by those who came up with Him from Galilee to Jerusalem, who are His witnesses to the

BARNABAS

Think about the people who really matter in your life. Odds are that many of them are encouragers who have found ways to help you keep going. Good friends can tell when you are doing well and when you need to try harder. Mostly, they never give up on you! Everyone needs that kind of encouragement.

Among the first Christians, a man named Joseph was such an encourager that other believers nicknamed him "son of encouragement," or "Barnabas." Barnabas had an unusual ability to find people he could help. Whenever Barnabas encouraged Christians, the result was that others became believers!

Barnabas's actions were crucial to the early church. In a way, we can thank him for most of the New Testament. God used Barnabas's relationship with Paul at one point and with Mark at another to help these two men when either might have failed. Barnabas did wonders with encouragement.

We are surrounded by people we can encourage. Instead, we usually criticize. It may be important at times to show people where they are wrong, but we will be of greater help in the long run if we encourage people. They will accept our honest criticism if they know we want the best for them. Be prepared to encourage people today.

LESSONS: Encouragement is one of the most effective ways to help others

Sooner or later, true obedience to God will involve risk

There always is someone who needs encouragement

KEY VERSES: "When he came and had seen the grace of God, he was glad, and encouraged them all that with purpose of heart they should continue with the Lord. For he was a good man, full of the Holy Spirit and of faith. And a great many people were added to the Lord" (Acts 11:23-24).

Barnabas's story is told in Acts 4:36-37; 9:27–15:39. He also is mentioned in 1 Corinthians 9:6; Galatians 2:1,9,13; Colossians 4:10.

UPS:
- One of the first to sell possessions to help the Christians in Jerusalem
- First to travel with Paul as a missionary team
- Was an encourager, as his nickname shows, and thus one of the most quietly influential people in the early days of Christianity
- Called an apostle, although not one of the original Twelve

DOWN:
- Temporarily stayed aloof from Gentile believers until Paul corrected him

STATS:
- Where: Cyprus, Jerusalem, Antioch
- Occupation: Missionary, teacher
- Relatives: Sister: Mary. Cousin: John Mark.
- Contemporaries: Peter, Silas, Paul, Herod Agrippa I

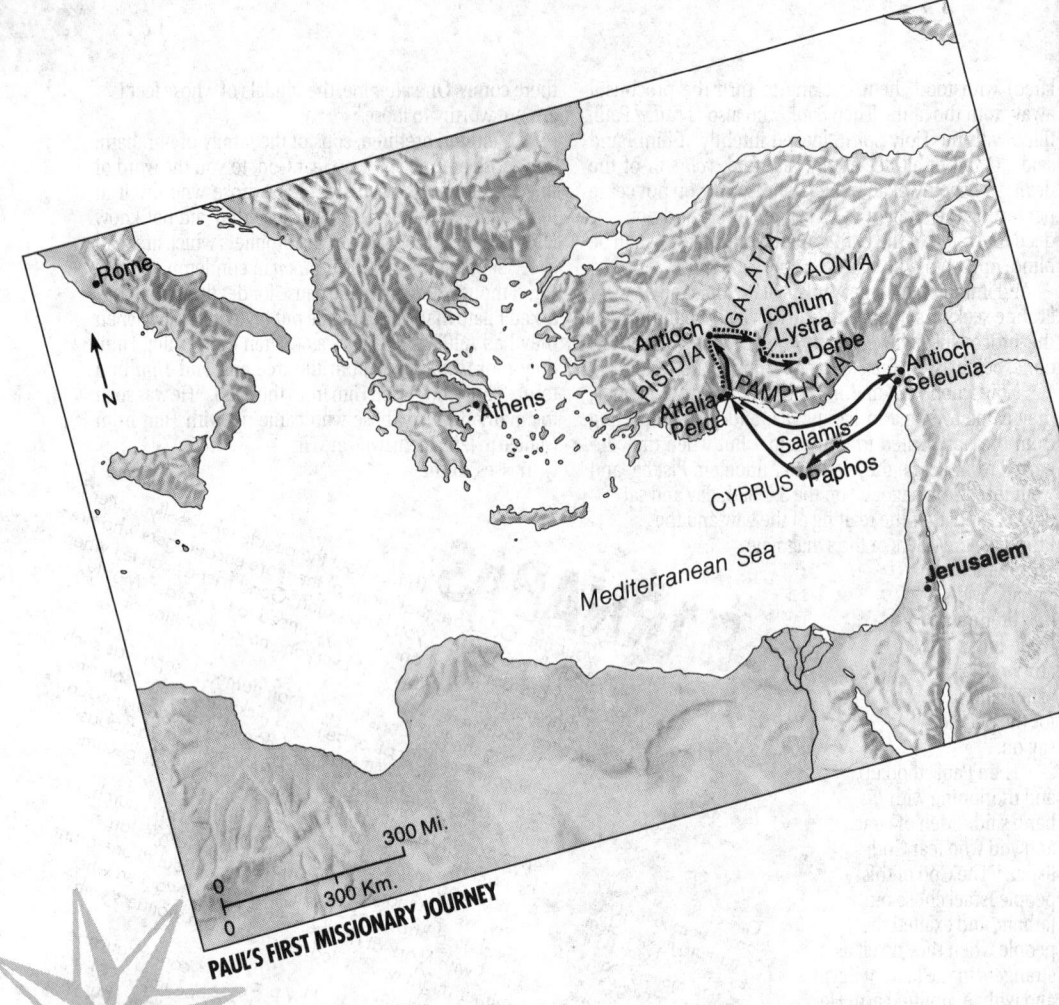

PAUL'S FIRST MISSIONARY JOURNEY

people. ³²And we declare to you glad tidings—that promise which was made to the fathers. ³³God has fulfilled this for us their children, in that He has raised up Jesus. As it is also written in the second Psalm:

'You are My Son,
Today I have begotten You.'

³⁴And that He raised Him from the dead, no more to return to corruption, He has spoken thus:

'I will give you the sure mercies of David.'

³⁵Therefore He also says in another *Psalm*:

'You will not allow Your Holy One to see corruption.'

³⁶"For David, after he had served his own generation by the will of God, fell asleep, was buried with his fathers, and saw corruption; ³⁷but He whom God raised up saw no corruption. ³⁸Therefore let it be known to you, brethren, that through this Man is preached to you the forgiveness of sins; ³⁹and by Him everyone who believes is justified from all things from which you could not be justified by the law of Moses. ⁴⁰Beware therefore, lest what has been spoken in the prophets come upon you:

⁴¹ 'Behold, you despisers,
Marvel and perish!
For I work a work in your days,
A work which you will by no means believe,
Though one were to declare it to you.'"

⁴²So when the Jews went out of the synagogue, the Gentiles begged that these words might be preached to them the next Sabbath. ⁴³Now when the congregation had broken up, many of the Jews and devout proselytes followed Paul and Barnabas, who, speaking to them, persuaded them to continue in the grace of God.

⁴⁴On the next Sabbath almost the whole city came together to hear the word of God. ⁴⁵But when the Jews saw the multitudes, they were filled with envy; and contradicting and blaspheming, they opposed the things spoken by Paul. ⁴⁶Then Paul and Barnabas grew bold and said, "It was necessary that the word of God should be spoken to you first; but since you reject it, and judge yourselves unworthy of everlasting life, behold, we turn to the Gentiles. ⁴⁷For so the Lord has commanded us:

'I have set you as a light to the Gentiles,
That you should be for salvation to the ends of the earth.'"

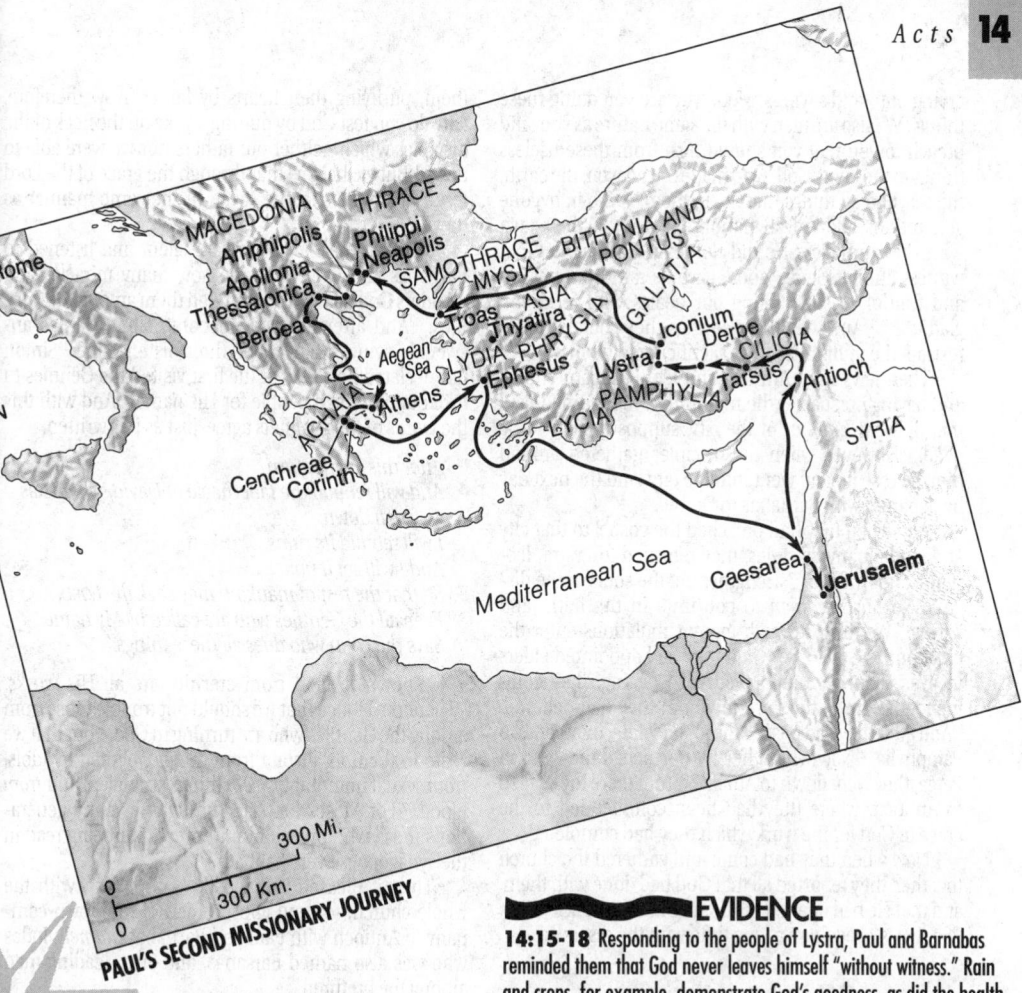

PAUL'S SECOND MISSIONARY JOURNEY

(Map labels: Rome, MACEDONIA, THRACE, Amphipolis, Philippi, Apollonia, Neapolis, Thessalonica, SAMOTHRACE, BITHYNIA AND PONTUS, MYSIA, ASIA, GALATIA, Beroea, Troas, Thyatira, PHRYGIA, Iconium, Derbe, CILICIA, Aegean Sea, LYDIA, Ephesus, Lystra, Tarsus, Antioch, Athens, PAMPHYLIA, ACHAIA, LYCIA, SYRIA, Cenchreae, Corinth, Mediterranean Sea, Caesarea, Jerusalem)

300 Mi.
0
300 Km.
0

⁴⁸Now when the Gentiles heard this, they were glad and glorified the word of the Lord. And as many as had been appointed to eternal life believed.

⁴⁹And the word of the Lord was being spread throughout all the region. ⁵⁰But the Jews stirred up the devout and prominent women and the chief men of the city, raised up persecution against Paul and Barnabas, and expelled them from their region. ⁵¹But they shook off the dust from their feet against them, and came to Iconium. ⁵²And the disciples were filled with joy and with the Holy Spirit.

CHAPTER **14** PAUL AND BARNABAS SEEN AS GODS.

Now it happened in Iconium that they went together to the synagogue of the Jews, and so spoke that a great multitude both of the Jews and of the Greeks believed. ²But the unbelieving Jews stirred up the Gentiles and poisoned their minds against the brethren. ³Therefore they stayed there a long time, speaking boldly in the Lord, who was bearing witness to the word of His grace, granting signs and wonders to be done by their hands.

⁴But the multitude of the city was divided: part sided with the Jews, and part with the apostles. ⁵And when a violent attempt was made by both the Gentiles and Jews, with their rulers, to abuse and stone them, ⁶they became

EVIDENCE

14:15-18 Responding to the people of Lystra, Paul and Barnabas reminded them that God never leaves himself "without witness." Rain and crops, for example, demonstrate God's goodness, as did the health and gladness people enjoyed because they had the food they needed. Later, Paul wrote that this evidence in nature and in people's lives leaves people without an excuse for unbelief (Romans 1:20). When in doubt about God, look around and you will see plenty of evidence that he is at work in our world.

aware of it and fled to Lystra and Derbe, cities of Lycaonia, and to the surrounding region. ⁷And they were preaching the gospel there.

⁸And in Lystra a certain man without strength in his feet was sitting, a cripple from his mother's womb, who had never walked. ⁹*This* man heard Paul speaking. Paul, observing him intently and seeing that he had faith to be healed, ¹⁰said with a loud voice, "Stand up straight on your feet!" And he leaped and walked. ¹¹Now when the people saw what Paul had done, they raised their voices, saying in the Lycaonian *language*, "The gods have come down to us in the likeness of men!" ¹²And Barnabas they called Zeus, and Paul, Hermes, because he was the chief speaker. ¹³Then the priest of Zeus, whose temple was in front of their city, brought oxen and garlands to the gates, intending to sacrifice with the multitudes.

¹⁴But when the apostles Barnabas and Paul heard this, they tore their clothes and ran in among the multitude,

crying out [15]and saying, "Men, why are you doing these things? We also are men with the same nature as you, and preach to you that you should turn from these useless things to the living God, who made the heaven, the earth, the sea, and all things that are in them, [16]who in bygone generations allowed all nations to walk in their own ways. [17]Nevertheless He did not leave Himself without witness, in that He did good, gave us rain from heaven and fruitful seasons, filling our hearts with food and gladness." [18]And with these sayings they could scarcely restrain the multitudes from sacrificing to them.

[19]Then Jews from Antioch and Iconium came there; and having persuaded the multitudes, they stoned Paul *and* dragged *him* out of the city, supposing him to be dead. [20]However, when the disciples gathered around him, he rose up and went into the city. And the next day he departed with Barnabas to Derbe.

[21]And when they had preached the gospel to that city and made many disciples, they returned to Lystra, Iconium, and Antioch, [22]strengthening the souls of the disciples, exhorting *them* to continue in the faith, and *saying,* "We must through many tribulations enter the kingdom of God." [23]So when they had appointed elders in every church, and prayed with fasting, they commended them to the Lord in whom they had believed. [24]And after they had passed through Pisidia, they came to Pamphylia. [25]Now when they had preached the word in Perga, they went down to Attalia. [26]From there they sailed to Antioch, where they had been commended to the grace of God for the work which they had completed. [27]Now when they had come and gathered the church together, they reported all that God had done with them, and that He had opened the door of faith to the Gentiles. [28]So they stayed there a long time with the disciples.

CHAPTER **15** A CHURCH CONFLICT. And certain *men* came down from Judea and taught the brethren, "Unless you are circumcised according to the custom of Moses, you cannot be saved." [2]Therefore, when Paul and Barnabas had no small dissension and dispute with them, they determined that Paul and Barnabas and certain others of them should go up to Jerusalem, to the apostles and elders, about this question.

[3]So, being sent on their way by the church, they passed through Phoenicia and Samaria, describing the conversion of the Gentiles; and they caused great joy to all the brethren. [4]And when they had come to Jerusalem, they were received by the church and the apostles and the elders; and they reported all things that God had done with them. [5]But some of the sect of the Pharisees who believed rose up, saying, "It is necessary to circumcise them, and to command *them* to keep the law of Moses."

[6]Now the apostles and elders came together to consider this matter. [7]And when there had been much dispute, Peter rose up and said to them: "Men and brethren, you know that a good while ago God chose among us, that by my mouth the Gentiles should hear the word of the gospel and believe. [8]So God, who knows the heart, acknowledged them by giving them the Holy Spirit, just as *He did* to us, [9]and made no distinction between us and

them, purifying their hearts by faith. [10]Now therefore, why do you test God by putting a yoke on the neck of the disciples which neither our fathers nor we were able to bear? [11]But we believe that through the grace of the Lord Jesus Christ we shall be saved in the same manner as they."

[12]Then all the multitude kept silent and listened to Barnabas and Paul declaring how many miracles and wonders God had worked through them among the Gentiles. [13]And after they had become silent, James answered, saying, "Men *and* brethren, listen to me: [14]Simon has declared how God at the first visited the Gentiles to take out of them a people for His name. [15]And with this the words of the prophets agree, just as it is written:

[16] 'After this I will return
And will rebuild the tabernacle of David, which has
    fallen down;
I will rebuild its ruins,
And I will set it up;
[17] So that the rest of mankind may seek the LORD,
Even all the Gentiles who are called by My name,
Says the LORD who does all these things.'

[18]"Known to God from eternity are all His works. [19]Therefore I judge that we should not trouble those from among the Gentiles who are turning to God, [20]but that we write to them to abstain from things polluted by idols, *from* sexual immorality, *from* things strangled, and *from* blood. [21]For Moses has had throughout many generations those who preach him in every city, being read in the synagogues every Sabbath."

[22]Then it pleased the apostles and elders, with the whole church, to send chosen men of their own company to Antioch with Paul and Barnabas, *namely,* Judas who was also named Barsabas, and Silas, leading men among the brethren.

[23]They wrote this *letter* by them:

The apostles, the elders, and the brethren,

To the brethren who are of the Gentiles in Antioch, Syria, and Cilicia:

Greetings.

[24] Since we have heard that some who went out from us have troubled you with words, unsettling your souls, saying, "*You must* be circumcised and keep the law"—to whom we gave no *such* commandment— [25]it seemed good to us, being assembled with one accord, to send chosen men to you with our beloved Barnabas and Paul, [26]men who have risked their lives for the name of our Lord Jesus Christ. [27]We have therefore sent Judas

◄YOUR ATTITUDE

15:23-29 This letter answered their questions and brought grea_ to the Gentile Christians in Antioch (15:31). Beautifully written, it a_ to the Holy Spirit's guidance and explains what should be done as ▮ the readers already knew it. It is helpful when people learn to be c_ not only in what they say, but also in how they say it. We may be c_ in our content, but we can lose our audience by our tone of voice o_ attitude.

and Silas, who will also report the same things by word of mouth. [28]For it seemed good to the Holy Spirit, and to us, to lay upon you no greater burden than these necessary things: [29]that you abstain from things offered to idols, from blood, from things strangled, and from sexual immorality. If you keep yourselves from these, you will do well.

Farewell.

[30]So when they were sent off, they came to Antioch; and when they had gathered the multitude together, they delivered the letter. [31]When they had read it, they rejoiced over its encouragement. [32]Now Judas and Silas, themselves being prophets also, exhorted and strengthened the brethren with many words. [33]And after they had stayed *there* for a time, they were sent back with greetings from the brethren to the apostles.

[34]However, it seemed good to Silas to remain there. [35]Paul and Barnabas also remained in Antioch, teaching and preaching the word of the Lord, with many others also.

[36]Then after some days Paul said to Barnabas, "Let us now go back and visit our brethren in every city where we have preached the word of the Lord, *and see* how they are doing." [37]Now Barnabas was determined to take with them John called Mark. [38]But Paul insisted that they should not take with them the one who had departed from them in Pamphylia, and had not gone with them to the work. [39]Then the contention became so sharp that they parted from one another. And so Barnabas took Mark and sailed to Cyprus; [40]but Paul chose Silas and departed, being commended by the brethren to the grace of God. [41]And he went through Syria and Cilicia, strengthening the churches.

CHAPTER 16 TIMOTHY IS PAUL'S HELPER. Then he

came to Derbe and Lystra. And behold, a certain disciple was there, named Timothy, *the* son of a certain Jewish woman who believed, but his father *was* Greek. [2]He was well spoken of by the brethren who were at Lystra and Iconium. [3]Paul wanted to have him go on with him. And he took *him* and circumcised him because of the Jews who were in that region, for they all knew that his father was Greek. [4]And as they went through the cities, they delivered to them the decrees to keep, which were determined by the apostles and elders at Jerusalem. [5]So the churches were strengthened in the faith, and increased in number daily.

[6]Now when they had gone through Phrygia and the region of Galatia, they were forbidden by the Holy Spirit to preach the word in Asia. [7]After they had come to Mysia, they tried to go into Bithynia, but the Spirit did not permit them. [8]So passing by Mysia, they came down to Troas. [9]And a vision appeared to Paul in the night. A man of Macedonia stood and pleaded with him, saying, "Come over to Macedonia and help us." [10]Now after he had seen the vision, immediately we sought to go to Macedonia, concluding that the Lord had called us to preach the gospel to them.

[11]Therefore, sailing from Troas, we ran a straight course to Samothrace, and the next *day* came to Neapolis, [12]and from there to Philippi, which is the foremost city of that part of Macedonia, a colony. And we were staying in that city for some days. [13]And on the Sabbath day we went out of the city to the riverside, where prayer was customarily made; and we sat down and spoke to the

BARRIERS

16:2-3 Timothy and his mother, Eunice, were from Lystra. Eunice had probably heard Paul's preaching during his first missionary journey (Acts 14:6-18). Timothy was the son of a Jewish mother and a Greek father—to the Jews, he was a half-breed, like a Samaritan. So Paul asked Timothy to be circumcised to erase some of the stigma he had with Jewish believers. Timothy was not required to be circumcised (the Jerusalem council had decided that—chapter 15), but he voluntarily did so to overcome barriers to his witness for Christ. Sometimes we must go beyond minimum requirements to help our audience receive our testimony.

women who met *there.* [14]Now a certain woman named Lydia heard *us.* She was a seller of purple from the city of Thyatira, who worshiped God. The Lord opened her heart to heed the things spoken by Paul. [15]And when she and her household were baptized, she begged *us,* saying, "If you have judged me to be faithful to the Lord, come to my house and stay." So she persuaded us.

[16]Now it happened, as we went to prayer, that a certain slave girl possessed with a spirit of divination met us, who brought her masters much profit by fortune-telling. [17]This girl followed Paul and us, and cried out, saying, "These men are the servants of the Most High God, who proclaim to us the way of salvation." [18]And this she did for many days.

But Paul, greatly annoyed, turned and said to the spirit, "I command you in the name of Jesus Christ to come out of her." And he came out that very hour. [19]But when her masters saw that their hope of profit was gone, they seized Paul and Silas and dragged *them* into the marketplace to the authorities.

[20]And they brought them to the magistrates, and said, "These men, being Jews, exceedingly trouble our city; [21]and they teach customs which are not lawful for us, being Romans, to receive or observe." [22]Then the multitude rose up together against them; and the magistrates tore off their clothes and commanded *them* to be beaten with rods. [23]And when they had laid many stripes on them, they threw *them* into prison, commanding the jailer to keep them securely. [24]Having received such a charge, he put them into the inner prison and fastened their feet in the stocks.

GOD'S WILL

16:6 We don't know how the Holy Spirit told Paul that he and his men were not to go into Asia. It may have been through a prophet, a vision, an inner conviction, or some other circumstance. To know God's will does not mean we must hear his voice. He leads in many ways. When seeking God's will: (1) make sure your plan is in harmony with God's Word; (2) ask mature Christians for their advice; (3) check your own motives (are you doing what you want or what you think God wants?); and (4) ask God to open and close doors of circumstances.

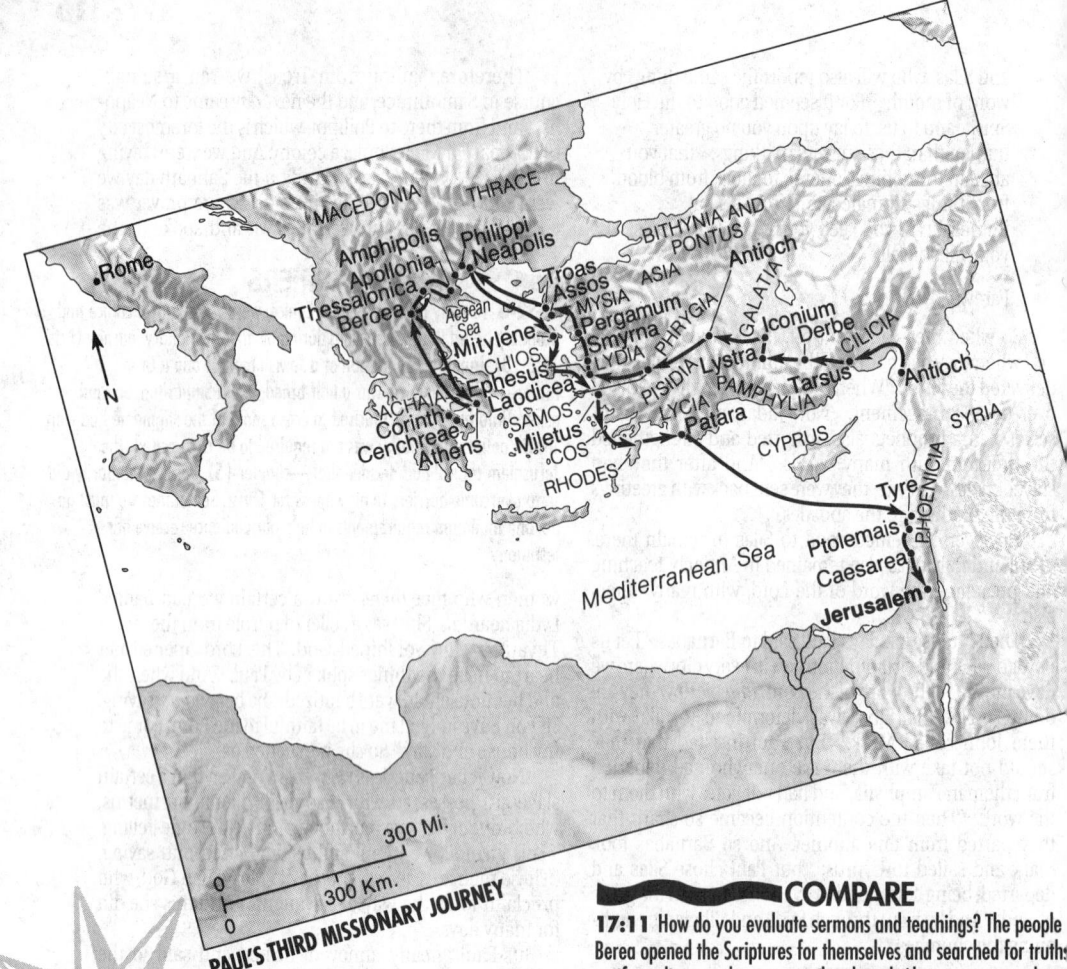

PAUL'S THIRD MISSIONARY JOURNEY

²⁵But at midnight Paul and Silas were praying and singing hymns to God, and the prisoners were listening to them. ²⁶Suddenly there was a great earthquake, so that the foundations of the prison were shaken; and immediately all the doors were opened and everyone's chains were loosed. ²⁷And the keeper of the prison, awaking

▶ IN THE DUNGEON

16:22-25 Paul and Silas were stripped, beaten, whipped, and placed in stocks in the inner dungeon. Despite this dismal situation, they praised God, praying and singing as the other prisoners listened. No matter what our circumstances, we should praise God. Others may come to Christ because of our example.

from sleep and seeing the prison doors open, supposing the prisoners had fled, drew his sword and was about to kill himself. ²⁸But Paul called with a loud voice, saying, "Do yourself no harm, for we are all here."

²⁹Then he called for a light, ran in, and fell down trembling before Paul and Silas. ³⁰And he brought them out and said, "Sirs, what must I do to be saved?"

³¹So they said, "Believe on the Lord Jesus Christ, and you will be saved, you and your household." ³²Then they spoke the word of the Lord to him and to all who were in

▶ COMPARE

17:11 How do you evaluate sermons and teachings? The people Berea opened the Scriptures for themselves and searched for truth verify or disprove the message they heard. Always compare what hear with what the Bible says. A preacher or teacher who gives Go message will never contradict or explain away anything in God's W

his house. ³³And he took them the same hour of the night and washed *their* stripes. And immediately he and all his family were baptized. ³⁴Now when he had brought them into his house, he set food before them; and he rejoiced, having believed in God with all his household.

³⁵And when it was day, the magistrates sent the officers, saying, "Let those men go."

³⁶So the keeper of the prison reported these words to Paul, saying, "The magistrates have sent to let you go. Now therefore depart, and go in peace."

³⁷But Paul said to them, "They have beaten us openly, uncondemned Romans, *and* have thrown *us* into prison. And now do they put us out secretly? No indeed! Let them come themselves and get us out."

³⁸And the officers told these words to the magistrates, and they were afraid when they heard that they were Romans. ³⁹Then they came and pleaded with them and brought *them* out, and asked *them* to depart from the city. ⁴⁰So they went out of the prison and entered *the house of* Lydia; and when they had seen the brethren, they encouraged them and departed.

CHAPTER **17** **PAUL VISITS TWO TOWNS.** Now when they had passed through Amphipolis and Apollonia, they came to Thessalonica, where there was a synagogue of the Jews. ²Then Paul, as his custom was, went in to them, and for three Sabbaths reasoned with them from the Scriptures, ³explaining and demonstrating that the Christ had to suffer and rise again from the dead, and *saying,* "This Jesus whom I preach to you is the Christ." ⁴And some of them were persuaded; and a great multitude of the devout Greeks, and not a few of the leading women, joined Paul and Silas.

⁵But the Jews who were not persuaded, becoming envious, took some of the evil men from the marketplace, and gathering a mob, set all the city in an uproar and attacked the house of Jason, and sought to bring them out to the people. ⁶But when they did not find them, they dragged Jason and some brethren to the rulers of the city, crying out, "These who have turned the world upside down have come here too. ⁷Jason has harbored them, and these are all acting contrary to the decrees of Caesar, saying there is another king—Jesus." ⁸And they troubled the crowd and the rulers of the city when they heard these things. ⁹So when they had taken security from Jason and the rest, they let them go.

¹⁰Then the brethren immediately sent Paul and Silas away by night to Berea. When they arrived, they went into the synagogue of the Jews. ¹¹These were more fair-minded than those in Thessalonica, in that they received the word with all readiness, and searched the Scriptures daily *to find out* whether these things were so. ¹²Therefore many of them believed, and also not a few of the Greeks, prominent women as well as men. ¹³But when the Jews from Thessalonica learned that the word of God was preached by Paul at Berea, they came there also and stirred up the crowds. ¹⁴Then immediately the brethren sent Paul away, to go to the sea; but both Silas and Timothy remained there. ¹⁵So those who conducted Paul brought him to Athens; and receiving a command for Silas and Timothy to come to him with all speed, they departed.

¹⁶Now while Paul waited for them at Athens, his spirit was provoked within him when he saw that the city was given over to idols. ¹⁷Therefore he reasoned in the synagogue with the Jews and with the *Gentile* worshipers, and in the marketplace daily with those who happened to be there. ¹⁸Then certain Epicurean and Stoic philosophers encountered him. And some said, "What does this babbler want to say?"

Others said, "He seems to be a proclaimer of foreign gods," because he preached to them Jesus and the resurrection.

¹⁹And they took him and brought him to the Areopagus, saying, "May we know what this new doctrine *is* of which you speak? ²⁰For you are bringing some strange things to our ears. Therefore we want to know what these things mean." ²¹For all the Athenians and the foreigners who were there spent their time in nothing else but either to tell or to hear some new thing.

SILAS

One word that doesn't fit in the lives of the first Christians is boring. There were just too many exciting things happening. Hundreds of people who had never heard of Jesus before were trusting him with their lives. Christian missionaries were taking hazardous journeys over land and sea. Even preaching the gospel was sometimes dangerous, since there was often resistance and hatred of the message. Right in the middle of all the excitement was a young man named Silas.

We first meet Silas when he is sent as a representative from Jerusalem, with Paul and Barnabas, to spread the official news that people did not have to become Jews before they became Christians. It was an important mission. Later, Silas joined Paul and Timothy as an effective traveling ministry team. Life continued to be exciting. Paul and Silas spent a night singing in a Philippian prison after being severely beaten. Another time, they were almost beaten in Thessalonica but were able to pull off a daring escape in the night. Then Paul left Silas and Timothy in Berea while he traveled on to Athens. Their job was to encourage the young believers in that new church. The team was reunited in Corinth. In each place they visited, they left behind a small group of Christians.

We don't know what eventually happened to Silas. He spent some time with Peter and is mentioned as the coauthor of 1 Peter. He continued to live the same faithful life that had made him a good choice to represent the church in Jerusalem. He was a helpful and encouraging member of Paul's team. Though he was never in the spotlight, his consistent life is a good model for us.

LESSONS: Partnership is a significant part of effective ministry

God never guarantees that his servants will not suffer

Obedience to God may mean giving up what makes us feel secure

KEY VERSES: "It seemed good to us . . . to send chosen men . . . who have risked their lives for the name of our Lord Jesus Christ. We have therefore sent Judas and Silas" (Acts 15:25-27).

Silas's story is told in Acts 15:22–19:10. He is also mentioned in 2 Corinthians 1:19; 1 Thessalonians 1:1; 2 Thessalonians 1:1; 1 Peter 5:12.

UPS:
• A leader in the Jerusalem church
• Represented the church in carrying the "acceptance letter" prepared by the Jerusalem council to the Gentile believers in Antioch
• Was closely associated with Paul from the second missionary journey on
• When imprisoned with Paul in Philippi, sang songs of praise to God
• Worked as a secretary for both Paul and Peter, using "Silvanus" as his pen name

STATS:
• Where: Roman citizen living in Jerusalem
• Occupation: One of the first career missionaries
• Contemporaries: Paul, Timothy, Peter, Mark, Barnabas

²²Then Paul stood in the midst of the Areopagus and said, "Men of Athens, I perceive that in all things you are very religious; ²³for as I was passing through and considering the objects of your worship, I even found an altar with this inscription:

TO THE UNKNOWN GOD.

Therefore, the One whom you worship without knowing, Him I proclaim to you: ²⁴God, who made the world and everything in it, since He is Lord of heaven and earth, does not dwell in temples made with hands. ²⁵Nor is He worshiped with men's hands, as though He needed anything, since He gives to all life, breath, and all things. ²⁶And He has made from one blood every nation of men to dwell on all the face of the earth, and has determined their preappointed times and the boundaries of their dwellings, ²⁷so that they should seek the Lord, in the hope that they might grope for Him and find Him, though He is not far from each one of us; ²⁸for in Him we live and move and have our being, as also some of your own poets have said, 'For we are also His offspring.' ²⁹Therefore, since we are the offspring of God, we ought not to think that the Divine Nature is like gold or silver or stone, something shaped by art and man's devising. ³⁰Truly, these times of ignorance God overlooked, but now commands all men everywhere to repent, ³¹because He has appointed a day on which He will judge the world in righteousness by the Man whom He has ordained. He has given assurance of this to all by raising Him from the dead."

WORTH IT

17:32-34 Paul's speech received a mixed reaction: some laughed, some kept searching for more information, and a few believed. Don't hesitate to tell others about Christ because you fear that some will not believe you. And don't expect a unanimously positive response to your witnessing. Even if only a few believe, it's worth the effort.

³²And when they heard of the resurrection of the dead, some mocked, while others said, "We will hear you again on this *matter.*" ³³So Paul departed from among them. ³⁴However, some men joined him and believed, among them Dionysius the Areopagite, a woman named Damaris, and others with them.

CHAPTER 18 PAUL WITH PRISCILLA AND AQUILA.

After these things Paul departed from Athens and went to Corinth. ²And he found a certain Jew named Aquila, born in Pontus, who had recently come from Italy with his wife Priscilla (because Claudius had commanded all the Jews to depart from Rome); and he came to them. ³So, because he was of the same trade, he stayed with them and worked; for by occupation they were tentmakers. ⁴And he reasoned in the synagogue every Sabbath, and persuaded both Jews and Greeks.

⁵When Silas and Timothy had come from Macedonia, Paul was compelled by the Spirit, and testified to the Jews *that* Jesus *is* the Christ. ⁶But when they opposed him and blasphemed, he shook *his* garments and said to them, "Your blood *be* upon your *own* heads; I *am* clean. From

DEBATABLE

18:27-28 Apollos was from Alexandria in Egypt, the second lar[ge] city in the Roman Empire, home of a great university. He was a sch[olar], orator, and debater. After his knowledge about Christ was more co[mplete], God greatly used his gifts to strengthen and encourage the church. Reason is a powerful tool in the right hands and the right situation[.] Apollos used his reasoning ability to convince many in Greece of t[he truth] of the gospel. You don't have to turn off your mind when you turn [to] Christ. You can use logic or debate to bring others to God.

now on I will go to the Gentiles." ⁷And he departed from there and entered the house of a certain *man* named Justus, *one* who worshiped God, whose house was next door to the synagogue. ⁸Then Crispus, the ruler of the synagogue, believed on the Lord with all his household. And many of the Corinthians, hearing, believed and were baptized.

⁹Now the Lord spoke to Paul in the night by a vision, "Do not be afraid, but speak, and do not keep silent; ¹⁰for I am with you, and no one will attack you to hurt you; for I have many people in this city." ¹¹And he continued *there* a year and six months, teaching the word of God among them.

¹²When Gallio was proconsul of Achaia, the Jews with one accord rose up against Paul and brought him to the judgment seat, ¹³saying, "This *fellow* persuades men to worship God contrary to the law."

¹⁴And when Paul was about to open *his* mouth, Gallio said to the Jews, "If it were a matter of wrongdoing or wicked crimes, O Jews, there would be reason why I should bear with you. ¹⁵But if it is a question of words and names and your own law, look *to it* yourselves; for I do not want to be a judge of such *matters.*" ¹⁶And he drove them from the judgment seat. ¹⁷Then all the Greeks took Sosthenes, the ruler of the synagogue, and beat *him* before the judgment seat. But Gallio took no notice of these things.

¹⁸So Paul still remained a good while. Then he took leave of the brethren and sailed for Syria, and Priscilla and Aquila *were* with him. He had *his* hair cut off at Cenchrea, for he had taken a vow. ¹⁹And he came to Ephesus, and left them there; but he himself entered the synagogue and reasoned with the Jews. ²⁰When they asked *him* to stay a longer time with them, he did not consent, ²¹but took leave of them, saying, "I must by all means keep this coming feast in Jerusalem; but I will return again to you, God willing." And he sailed from Ephesus.

²²And when he had landed at Caesarea, and gone up and greeted the church, he went down to Antioch. ²³After he had spent some time *there,* he departed and went over the region of Galatia and Phrygia in order, strengthening all the disciples.

²⁴Now a certain Jew named Apollos, born at Alexandria, an eloquent man *and* mighty in the Scriptures, came to Ephesus. ²⁵This man had been instructed in the way of the Lord; and being fervent in spirit, he spoke and taught accurately the things of the Lord, though he knew only the baptism of John. ²⁶So he began to speak boldly in the synagogue. When Aquila and Priscilla heard him, they took him aside and explained to him the way of God more accurately. ²⁷And when he desired to cross to

Achaia, the brethren wrote, exhorting the disciples to receive him; and when he arrived, he greatly helped those who had believed through grace; [28]for he vigorously refuted the Jews publicly, showing from the Scriptures that Jesus is the Christ.

CHAPTER **19** GOD SENDS THE HOLY SPIRIT. And it happened, while Apollos was at Corinth, that Paul, having passed through the upper regions, came to Ephesus. And finding some disciples [2]he said to them, "Did you receive the Holy Spirit when you believed?"

So they said to him, "We have not so much as heard whether there is a Holy Spirit."

[3]And he said to them, "Into what then were you baptized?"

So they said, "Into John's baptism."

[4]Then Paul said, "John indeed baptized with a baptism of repentance, saying to the people that they should believe on Him who would come after him, that is, on Christ Jesus."

[5]When they heard *this*, they were baptized in the name of the Lord Jesus. [6]And when Paul had laid hands on them, the Holy Spirit came upon them, and they spoke with tongues and prophesied. [7]Now the men were about twelve in all.

[8]And he went into the synagogue and spoke boldly for three months, reasoning and persuading concerning the things of the kingdom of God. [9]But when some were hardened and did not believe, but spoke evil of the Way before the multitude, he departed from them and withdrew the disciples, reasoning daily in the school of Tyrannus. [10]And this continued for two years, so that all who dwelt in Asia heard the word of the Lord Jesus, both Jews and Greeks.

[11]Now God worked unusual miracles by the hands of Paul, [12]so that even handkerchiefs or aprons were brought from his body to the sick, and the diseases left them and the evil spirits went out of them. [13]Then some of the itinerant Jewish exorcists took it upon themselves to call the name of the Lord Jesus over those who had evil spirits, saying, "We exorcise you by the Jesus whom Paul preaches." [14]Also there were seven sons of Sceva, a Jewish chief priest, who did so.

[15]And the evil spirit answered and said, "Jesus I know, and Paul I know; but who are you?"

[16]Then the man in whom the evil spirit was leaped on them, overpowered them, and prevailed against them, so that they fled out of that house naked and wounded. [17]This became known both to all Jews and Greeks dwelling in Ephesus; and fear fell on them all, and the name of the Lord Jesus was magnified. [18]And many who had believed came confessing and telling their deeds. [19]Also, many of those who had practiced magic brought their books together and burned *them* in the sight of all. And they counted up the value of them, and *it* totaled fifty thousand *pieces* of silver. [20]So the word of the Lord grew mightily and prevailed.

[21]When these things were accomplished, Paul purposed in the Spirit, when he had passed through Macedonia and Achaia, to go to Jerusalem, saying, "After I have been there, I must also see Rome." [22]So he sent into Macedonia two of those who ministered to him, Timothy and Erastus, but he himself stayed in Asia for a time.

[23]And about that time there arose a great commotion about the Way. [24]For a certain man named Demetrius, a silversmith, who made silver shrines of Diana, brought no small profit to the craftsmen. [25]He called them together with the workers of similar occupation, and said: "Men, you know that we have our prosperity by this trade. [26]Moreover you see and hear that not only at Ephesus, but throughout almost all Asia, this Paul has persuaded and turned away many people, saying that they are not gods which are made with hands. [27]So not only is

MAGIC CHARMS

19:13 Many Ephesians engaged in exorcism and occult practices for profit (see 19:18-19). The sons of Sceva were impressed by Paul's work, whose power to cast out demons came from God's Holy Spirit, not from witchcraft, and was obviously more powerful than theirs. They discovered, however, that no person can control or duplicate God's power. These men were calling upon the name without knowing the person. It is knowing Jesus, not reciting his name like a magic charm, that gives us the power to change people. Christ works his power only through those he chooses.

this trade of ours in danger of falling into disrepute, but also the temple of the great goddess Diana may be despised and her magnificence destroyed, whom all Asia and the world worship."

[28]Now when they heard *this*, they were full of wrath and cried out, saying, "Great *is* Diana of the Ephesians!" [29]So the whole city was filled with confusion, and rushed into the theater with one accord, having seized Gaius

I'm not the kind of person that can take everything at face value. I have to have more proof. Is it wrong to want to know the answers to questions I have about the Bible? I WONDER...

The Christians in Berea were complimented by Luke, the writer of Acts, because they "searched the Scriptures daily *to find out* whether these things [Paul and Silas's teachings] were so" (Acts 17:11).

Because being a Christian means accepting Christ's forgiveness by faith, some think we must believe everything just because another Christian said it. But getting your questions answered by studying the Bible is an important part of being a Christian. Although not every question can be answered, most of them can.

Some people are natural skeptics. They challenge everything in the Bible. But often they aren't looking for answers—just an argument. If, however, you have the prayerful heart of a seeker, God will help you unlock the secrets of his word. "Ask, and it will be given to you; seek, and you will find; knock, and it will be opened to you. For everyone who asks receives, and he who seeks finds, and to him who knocks it will be opened" (Matthew 7:7-8).

Keep asking your questions and looking for answers.

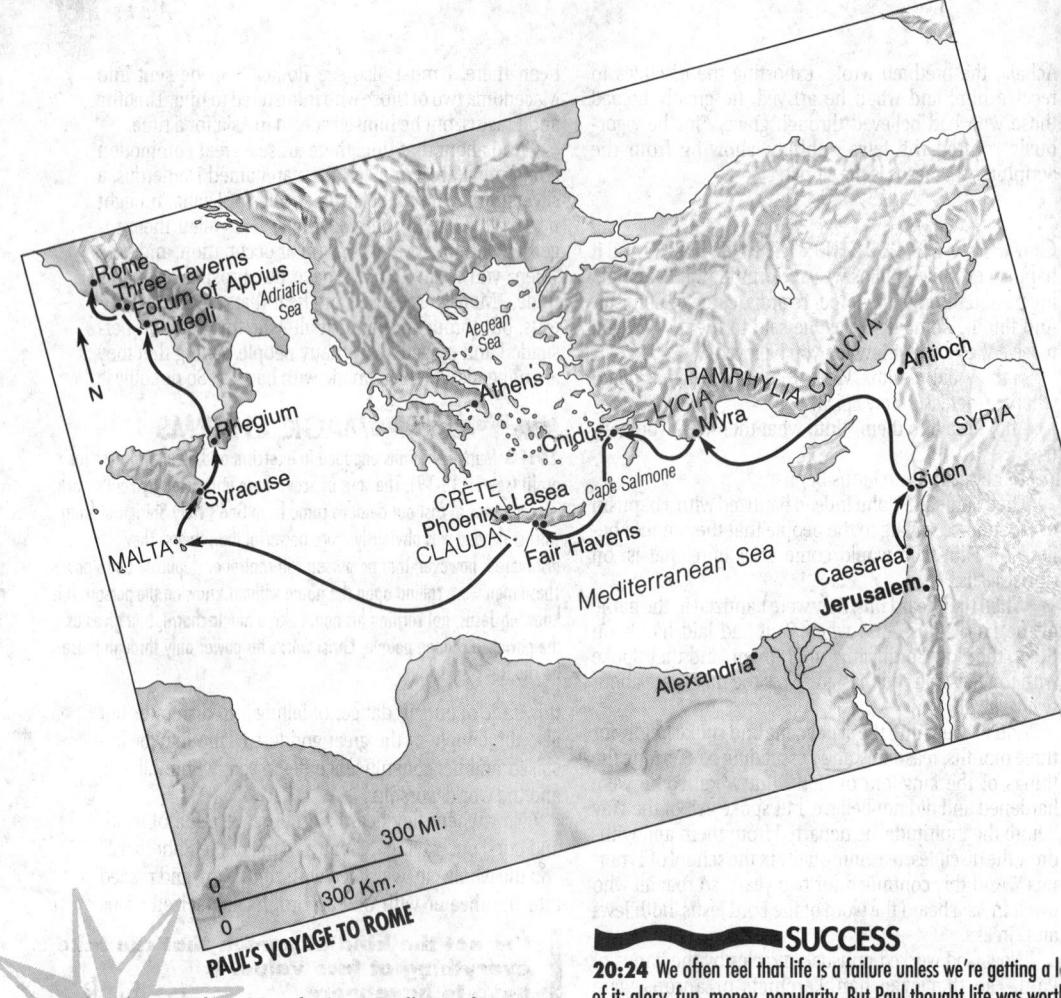

PAUL'S VOYAGE TO ROME

and Aristarchus, Macedonians, Paul's travel companions. ³⁰And when Paul wanted to go in to the people, the disciples would not allow him. ³¹Then some of the officials of Asia, who were his friends, sent to him pleading that he would not venture into the theater. ³²Some therefore cried one thing and some another, for the assembly was confused, and most of them did not know why they had come together. ³³And they drew Alexander out of the multitude, the Jews putting him forward. And Alexander motioned with his hand, and wanted to make his defense to the people. ³⁴But when they found out that he was a Jew, all with one voice cried out for about two hours, "Great *is* Diana of the Ephesians!"

³⁵And when the city clerk had quieted the crowd, he said: "Men of Ephesus, what man is there who does not know that the city of the Ephesians is temple guardian of the great goddess Diana, and of the *image* which fell down from Zeus? ³⁶Therefore, since these things cannot be denied, you ought to be quiet and do nothing rashly. ³⁷For you have brought these men here who are neither robbers of temples nor blasphemers of your goddess. ³⁸Therefore, if Demetrius and his fellow craftsmen have a case against anyone, the courts are open and there are proconsuls. Let them bring charges against one another.

SUCCESS

20:24 We often feel that life is a failure unless we're getting a lot of it: glory, fun, money, popularity. But Paul thought life was worth *nothing* unless he used it for God's work. What he put *into* life was more important than what he got out of it. Which is more important to you—what you get out of life, or what you put into it?

³⁹But if you have any other inquiry to make, it shall be determined in the lawful assembly. ⁴⁰For we are in danger of being called in question for today's uproar, there being no reason which we may give to account for this disorderly gathering." ⁴¹And when he had said these things, he dismissed the assembly.

CHAPTER **20** ON TO GREECE AND MACEDONIA.
After the uproar had ceased, Paul called the disciples to *himself*, embraced *them*, and departed to go to Macedonia. ²Now when he had gone over that region and encouraged them with many words, he came to Greece ³and stayed three months. And when the Jews plotted against him as he was about to sail to Syria, he decided to return through Macedonia. ⁴And Sopater of Berea accompanied him to Asia—also Aristarchus and Secundus of the Thessalonians, and Gaius of Derbe, and Timothy, and Tychicus and Trophimus of Asia. ⁵These men, going ahead, waited for us at Troas. ⁶But we sailed away from

Philippi after the Days of Unleavened Bread, and in five days joined them at Troas, where we stayed seven days. [7]Now on the first *day* of the week, when the disciples came together to break bread, Paul, ready to depart the next day, spoke to them and continued his message until midnight. [8]There were many lamps in the upper room where they were gathered together. [9]And in a window sat a certain young man named Eutychus, who was sinking into a deep sleep. He was overcome by sleep; and as Paul continued speaking, he fell down from the third story and was taken up dead. [10]But Paul went down, fell on him, and embracing *him* said, "Do not trouble yourselves, for his life is in him." [11]Now when he had come up, had broken bread and eaten, and talked a long while, even till daybreak, he departed. [12]And they brought the young man in alive, and they were not a little comforted.

[13]Then we went ahead to the ship and sailed to Assos, there intending to take Paul on board; for so he had given orders, intending himself to go on foot. [14]And when he met us at Assos, we took him on board and came to Mitylene. [15]We sailed from there, and the next *day* came opposite Chios. The following *day* we arrived at Samos and stayed at Trogyllium. The next *day* we came to Miletus. [16]For Paul had decided to sail past Ephesus, so that he would not have to spend time in Asia; for he was hurrying to be at Jerusalem, if possible, on the Day of Pentecost.

[17]From Miletus he sent to Ephesus and called for the elders of the church. [18]And when they had come to him, he said to them: "You know, from the first day that I came to Asia, in what manner I always lived among you, [19]serving the Lord with all humility, with many tears and trials which happened to me by the plotting of the Jews; [20]how I kept back nothing that was helpful, but proclaimed it to you, and taught you publicly and from house to house, [21]testifying to Jews, and also to Greeks, repentance toward God and faith toward our Lord Jesus Christ. [22]And see, now I go bound in the spirit to Jerusalem, not knowing the things that will happen to me there, [23]except that the Holy Spirit testifies in every city, saying that chains and tribulations await me. [24]But none of these things move me; nor do I count my life dear to myself, so that I may finish my race with joy, and the ministry which I received from the Lord Jesus, to testify to the gospel of the grace of God.

[25]"And indeed, now I know that you all, among whom I have gone preaching the kingdom of God, will see my face no more. [26]Therefore I testify to you this day that I *am* innocent of the blood of all *men.* [27]For I have not shunned to declare to you the whole counsel of God. [28]Therefore take heed to yourselves and to all the flock, among which the Holy Spirit has made you overseers, to shepherd the church of God which He purchased with His own blood. [29]For I know this, that after my departure savage wolves will come in among you, not sparing the flock. [30]Also from among yourselves men will rise up, speaking perverse things, to draw away the disciples after themselves. [31]Therefore watch, and remember that for three years I did not cease to warn everyone night and day with tears.

AQUILA & PRISCILLA

Some couples know how to make the most of life. They fit together, let each do his best, and form an effective team. Their combined efforts affect those around them. Aquila and Priscilla were such a couple. They are never mentioned apart from one another in the Bible.

Together, they loved God and people.

Priscilla and Aquila met Paul in Corinth while he was on his second missionary journey. They had just left Rome. Their home was as movable as the tents they made in their business. They invited Paul to stay with them, and he joined them in making tents. He helped them by sharing his wisdom about God.

Priscilla and Aquila made good use of what they learned from Paul. They listened and evaluated what they heard. For instance, when another preacher, Apollos, came to town, they listened to what he had to say. They realized he was a good speaker, but that there were important things he needed to learn. Instead of correcting Apollos in public, they quietly took him home with them and shared with him what he needed to know. Apollos had been preaching John the Baptist's message of repentance. Priscilla and Aquila told Apollos about Jesus' life, death, and resurrection, and how God's Spirit wanted to live in us. Apollos then used his great ability to tell the whole story!

This couple continued to use their home as a place for training and worship. Later, back in Rome, one of the churches met in their house. (The first Christians did not meet in church buildings, but in the homes of believers.) It is easy to imagine that anywhere Aquila and Priscilla lived would be a place of fellowship.

LESSONS: Couples can have an effective ministry together

The home is a valuable tool for evangelism

KEY VERSES: "Greet Priscilla and Aquila, my fellow workers in Christ Jesus, who risked their own necks for my life, to whom not only I give thanks, but also all the churches of the Gentiles" (Romans 16:3-4).

Their story is told in Acts 18. They are also mentioned in Romans 16:3-5; 1 Corinthians 16:19; 2 Timothy 4:19.

UPS:
- Outstanding husband-wife team who ministered in the early church
- Supported themselves by making tents while serving Christ
- Close friends of Paul
- Explained the full message of Christ to Apollos

STATS:
- Where: Originally from Rome; moved to Corinth, then Ephesus
- Occupation: Tentmakers
- Contemporaries: Emperor Claudius, Paul, Timothy, Apollos

[32]"So now, brethren, I commend you to God and to the word of His grace, which is able to build you up and give you an inheritance among all those who are sanctified. [33]I have coveted no one's silver or gold or apparel. [34]Yes, you yourselves know that these hands have provided for my necessities, and for those who were with me. [35]I have shown you in every way, by laboring like this, that you must support the weak. And remember the words of the Lord Jesus, that He said, 'It is more blessed to give than to receive.'"

[36]And when he had said these things, he knelt down and prayed with them all. [37]Then they all wept freely, and fell on Paul's neck and kissed him, [38]sorrowing most of all for the words which he spoke, that they would see his face no more. And they accompanied him to the ship.

CHAPTER 21 PAUL JOURNEYS TO JERUSALEM.

Now it came to pass, that when we had departed from them and set sail, running a straight course we came to Cos, the following *day* to Rhodes, and from there to Patara. [2]And finding a ship sailing over to Phoenicia, we went aboard and set sail. [3]When we had sighted Cyprus, we passed it on the left, sailed to Syria, and landed at Tyre; for there the ship was to unload her cargo. [4]And finding disciples, we stayed there seven days. They told Paul through the Spirit not to go up to Jerusalem. [5]When we had come to the end of those days, we departed and went on our way; and they all accompanied us, with wives and children, till *we were* out of the city. And we knelt down on the shore and prayed. [6]When we had taken our leave of one another, we boarded the ship, and they returned home.

[7]And when we had finished *our* voyage from Tyre, we came to Ptolemais, greeted the brethren, and stayed with them one day. [8]On the next *day* we who were Paul's companions departed and came to Caesarea, and entered the house of Philip the evangelist, who was *one* of the seven, and stayed with him. [9]Now this man had four virgin daughters who prophesied. [10]And as we stayed many days, a certain prophet named Agabus came down from Judea. [11]When he had come to us, he took Paul's belt, bound his *own* hands and feet, and said, "Thus says the Holy Spirit, 'So shall the Jews at Jerusalem bind the man who owns this belt, and deliver *him* into the hands of the Gentiles.'"

[12]Now when we heard these things, both we and those from that place pleaded with him not to go up to Jerusalem. [13]Then Paul answered, "What do you mean by weeping and breaking my heart? For I am ready not only to be bound, but also to die at Jerusalem for the name of the Lord Jesus."

[14]So when he would not be persuaded, we ceased, saying, "The will of the Lord be done."

[15]And after those days we packed and went up to Jerusalem. [16]Also some of the disciples from Caesarea went with us and brought with them a certain Mnason of Cyprus, an early disciple, with whom we were to lodge.

[17]And when we had come to Jerusalem, the brethren received us gladly. [18]On the following *day* Paul went in with us to James, and all the elders were present. [19]When he had greeted them, he told in detail those things which God had done among the Gentiles through his ministry. [20]And when they heard *it*, they glorified the Lord. And they said to him, "You see, brother, how many myriads of Jews there are who have believed, and they are all zealous for the law; [21]but they have been informed about you that you teach all the Jews who are among the Gentiles to forsake Moses, saying that they ought not to circumcise *their* children nor to walk according to the customs. [22]What then? The assembly must certainly meet, for they will hear that you have come. [23]Therefore do what we tell you: We have four men who have taken a vow. [24]Take them and be purified with them, and pay their expenses so that they may shave *their* heads, and that all may know that those things of which they were informed concerning you are nothing, but *that* you yourself also walk orderly and keep the law. [25]But concerning the Gentiles who believe, we have written *and* decided that they should observe no such thing, except that they should keep themselves from *things* offered to idols, from blood, from things strangled, and from sexual immorality."

[26]Then Paul took the men, and the next day, having been purified with them, entered the temple to announce the expiration of the days of purification, at which time an offering should be made for each one of them.

[27]Now when the seven days were almost ended, the Jews from Asia, seeing him in the temple, stirred up the whole crowd and laid hands on him, [28]crying out, "Men of Israel, help! This is the man who teaches all *men* everywhere against the people, the law, and this place; and furthermore he also brought Greeks into the temple and has defiled this holy place." [29](For they had previously seen Trophimus the Ephesian with him in the city, whom they supposed that Paul had brought into the temple.)

[30]And all the city was disturbed; and the people ran together, seized Paul, and dragged him out of the temple; and immediately the doors were shut. [31]Now as they were seeking to kill him, news came to the commander of the garrison that all Jerusalem was in an uproar. [32]He immediately took soldiers and centurions, and ran down to them. And when they saw the commander and the soldiers, they stopped beating Paul. [33]Then the commander came near and took him, and commanded *him* to be bound with two chains; and he asked who he was and

HE HAD TO

21:13-14 Paul knew that he would be imprisoned in Jerusalem. friends pleaded with him not to go there, but Paul knew God wante to. No one wants to face hardship or suffering, but a faithful discipl wants above all else to please God. When we really want to do God we must accept all that comes with it—even the pain. Then we can with Paul, "The will of the Lord be done."

what he had done. ³⁴And some among the multitude cried one thing and some another.

So when he could not ascertain the truth because of the tumult, he commanded him to be taken into the barracks. ³⁵When he reached the stairs, he had to be carried by the soldiers because of the violence of the mob. ³⁶For the multitude of the people followed after, crying out, "Away with him!"

³⁷Then as Paul was about to be led into the barracks, he said to the commander, "May I speak to you?"

He replied, "Can you speak Greek? ³⁸Are you not the Egyptian who some time ago stirred up a rebellion and led the four thousand assassins out into the wilderness?"

³⁹But Paul said, "I am a Jew from Tarsus, in Cilicia, a citizen of no mean city; and I implore you, permit me to speak to the people."

⁴⁰So when he had given him permission, Paul stood on the stairs and motioned with his hand to the people. And when there was a great silence, he spoke to *them* in the Hebrew language, saying,

CHAPTER 22 PAUL IS ARRESTED. "Brethren and

fathers, hear my defense before you now." ²And when they heard that he spoke to them in the Hebrew language, they kept all the more silent.

Then he said: ³"I am indeed a Jew, born in Tarsus of Cilicia, but brought up in this city at the feet of Gamaliel, taught according to the strictness of our fathers' law, and was zealous toward God as you all are today. ⁴I persecuted this Way to the death, binding and delivering into prisons both men and women, ⁵as also the high priest bears me witness, and all the council of the elders, from whom I also received letters to the brethren, and went to Damascus to bring in chains even those who were there to Jerusalem to be punished.

⁶"Now it happened, as I journeyed and came near Damascus at about noon, suddenly a great light from heaven shone around me. ⁷And I fell to the ground and heard a voice saying to me, 'Saul, Saul, why are you persecuting Me?' ⁸So I answered, 'Who are You, Lord?' And He said to me, 'I am Jesus of Nazareth, whom you are persecuting.'

⁹"And those who were with me indeed saw the light and were afraid, but they did not hear the voice of Him who spoke to me. ¹⁰So I said, 'What shall I do, Lord?' And the Lord said to me, 'Arise and go into Damascus, and there you will be told all things which are appointed for you to do.' ¹¹And since I could not see for the glory of that light, being led by the hand of those who were with me, I came into Damascus.

¹²"Then a certain Ananias, a devout man according to the law, having a good testimony with all the Jews who

dwelt *there*, ¹³came to me; and he stood and said to me, 'Brother Saul, receive your sight.' And at that same hour I looked up at him. ¹⁴Then he said, 'The God of our fathers has chosen you that you should know His will, and see the Just One, and hear the voice of His mouth. ¹⁵For you will be His witness to all men of what you have seen and heard. ¹⁶And now why are you waiting? Arise and be baptized, and wash away your sins, calling on the name of the Lord.'

◥◣◥◣◥◣◥◣ IN COMMON

22:3 By saying that at one time he was as zealous for God as any of his listeners, Paul was acknowledging their sincere motives in trying to kill him and recognizing that he would have done the same to Christian leaders a few years earlier. Paul always tried to find something he and his audience had in common before he launched into a full-scale defense of Christianity. When you witness for Christ, first identify yourself with your audience. They are much more likely to listen to you if they feel they have something in common with you.

¹⁷"Now it happened, when I returned to Jerusalem and was praying in the temple, that I was in a trance ¹⁸and saw Him saying to me, 'Make haste and get out of Jerusalem quickly, for they will not receive your testimony concerning Me.' ¹⁹So I said, 'Lord, they know that in every synagogue I imprisoned and beat those who believe on You. ²⁰And when the blood of Your martyr Stephen was shed, I also was standing by consenting to his death, and guarding the clothes of those who were killing him.' ²¹Then He said to me, 'Depart, for I will send you far from here to the Gentiles.'"

²²And they listened to him until this word, and *then* they raised their voices and said, "Away with such a *fellow* from the earth, for he is not fit to live!" ²³Then, as they

"Here's what I did..."

At my high school we have a Christian Bible study group called Saints' Battalion. A few months ago, Satanists on our campus formed a group they call Young Satanists of America. Before their own group meetings, held on the same day we have ours, they come into our meetings and bother us in every way they can. I know that in their meetings they put down Christianity and exalt Satan as a "philosophy."

We cannot ban them from coming to our meetings because our group has to be open to all. They still remain a problem. Our group and my church continue to pray about this problem. A passage that has really encouraged us is Acts 19:13-20. It talks about the power in the name of Jesus to cast out demons, and about how lots of people who heard about Christ burned their witchcraft books and turned to God. We use this passage to claim the power of Jesus, and we pray that many of the Young Satanists who come to our meetings will hear God's Word and turn to Christ.

Rick AGE 16

UNSUNG HEROES IN ACTS

When we think of the success of the early church, we often think of the work of the apostles. But the church could have died if it hadn't been for the "unsung" heroes, the men and women who through some small but committed act moved the church forward.

Hero	Reference	Heroic Action
LAME BEGGAR	3:9-12	After his healing, he praised God. With the crowds gathering to see what happened, Peter used the opportunity to tell many about Jesus.
FIVE DEACONS	6:2-5	Everyone knows Stephen, and many people know Philip, but there were five other men chosen to be deacons. They not only laid the foundation for service in the church, but their hard work gave the apostles more time to preach the gospel.
ANANIAS	9:10-19	He had the responsibility of being the first to demonstrate Christ's love to Saul (Paul) after his conversion.
CORNELIUS	10:30-35	His example showed Peter that the gospel was for all people, Jews and Gentiles.
RHODA	12:13-15	Her persistence brought Peter inside Mary's home, where he would be safe.
JAMES	15:13-21	He took command of the Jerusalem council and had the courage and discernment to make a decision that would affect literally millions of Christians over many generations.
LYDIA	16:13-15	She opened her home to Paul, from which he led many to Christ and founded a church in Philippi.
JASON	17:5-9	He risked his life for the gospel by allowing Paul to stay in his home. He stood up for what was true and right, even though he faced persecution for it.
PAUL'S NEPHEW	23:16-24	He saved Paul's life by telling officials of a plot to murder Paul.
JULIUS	27:1,43	He spared Paul's life when the other soldiers wanted to kill him.

cried out and tore off *their* clothes and threw dust into the air, [24]the commander ordered him to be brought into the barracks, and said that he should be examined under scourging, so that he might know why they shouted so against him. [25]And as they bound him with thongs, Paul said to the centurion who stood by, "Is it lawful for you to scourge a man who is a Roman, and uncondemned?"

[26]When the centurion heard *that*, he went and told the commander, saying, "Take care what you do, for this man is a Roman."

[27]Then the commander came and said to him, "Tell me, are you a Roman?"

He said, "Yes."

[28]The commander answered, "With a large sum I obtained this citizenship."

And Paul said, "But I was born *a citizen.*"

[29]Then immediately those who were about to examine him withdrew from him; and the commander was also afraid after he found out that he was a Roman, and because he had bound him.

[30]The next day, because he wanted to know for certain why he was accused by the Jews, he released him from *his* bonds, and commanded the chief priests and all their council to appear, and brought Paul down and set him before them.

IN THE HEAT

22:30 God used Paul's persecution as an opportunity for him to witness. Here even his enemies were creating a platform for him to address the entire Jewish council. If we are sensitive to the Holy Spirit's leading, we will notice increased opportunities to share our faith, even in the heat of opposition.

CHAPTER 23 Then Paul, looking earnestly at the council, said, "Men *and* brethren, I have lived in all good conscience before God until this day." ²And the high priest Ananias commanded those who stood by him to strike him on the mouth. ³Then Paul said to him, "God will strike you, *you* whitewashed wall! For you sit to judge me according to the law, and do you command me to be struck contrary to the law?".

⁴And those who stood by said, "Do you revile God's high priest?"

⁵Then Paul said, "I did not know, brethren, that he was the high priest; for it is written, *'You shall not speak evil of a ruler of your people.'*"

⁶But when Paul perceived that one part were Sadducees and the other Pharisees, he cried out in the council, "Men *and* brethren, I am a Pharisee, the son of a Pharisee; concerning the hope and resurrection of the dead I am being judged!"

⁷And when he had said this, a dissension arose between the Pharisees and the Sadducees; and the assembly was divided. ⁸For Sadducees say that there is no resurrection—and no angel or spirit; but the Pharisees confess both. ⁹Then there arose a loud outcry. And the scribes of the Pharisees' party arose and protested, saying, "We find no evil in this man; but if a spirit or an angel has spoken to him, let us not fight against God."

¹⁰Now when there arose a great dissension, the commander, fearing lest Paul might be pulled to pieces by them, commanded the soldiers to go down and take him by force from among them, and bring *him* into the barracks.

¹¹But the following night the Lord stood by him and said, "Be of good cheer, Paul; for as you have testified for Me in Jerusalem, so you must also bear witness at Rome."

¹²And when it was day, some of the Jews banded together and bound themselves under an oath, saying that they would neither eat nor drink till they had killed Paul. ¹³Now there were more than forty who had formed this conspiracy. ¹⁴They came to the chief priests and elders, and said, "We have bound ourselves under a great oath that we will eat nothing until we have killed Paul. ¹⁵Now you, therefore, together with the council, suggest to the commander that he be brought down to you tomorrow, as though you were going to make further inquiries concerning him; but we are ready to kill him before he comes near."

¹⁶So when Paul's sister's son heard of their ambush, he went and entered the barracks and told Paul. ¹⁷Then Paul called one of the centurions to *him* and said, "Take this young man to the commander, for he has something to tell him." ¹⁸So he took him and brought *him* to the commander and said, "Paul the prisoner called me to *him* and asked *me* to bring this young man to you. He has something to say to you."

¹⁹Then the commander took him by the hand, went aside, and asked privately, "What is it that you have to tell me?"

²⁰And he said, "The Jews have agreed to ask that you bring Paul down to the council tomorrow, as though they were going to inquire more fully about him. ²¹But do not yield to them, for more than forty of them lie in wait for him, men who have bound themselves by an oath that they will neither eat nor drink till they have killed him; and now they are ready, waiting for the promise from you."

²²So the commander let the young man depart, and commanded *him,* "Tell no one that you have revealed these things to me."

AMAZING!

23:23-24 The Roman commander ordered Paul to be sent to Caesarea. Jerusalem was the seat of Jewish government, but Caesarea was the area's Roman headquarters. God works in amazing and amusing ways. He could have gotten Paul to Caesarea in many ways, but he chose to use the Roman army to deliver Paul from his enemies. God's ways are not ours—we are limited, he is not. Don't ask him to respond your way. When God intervenes, anything can happen—often much more and much better than you could ever anticipate.

²³And he called for two centurions, saying, "Prepare two hundred soldiers, seventy horsemen, and two hundred spearmen to go to Caesarea at the third hour of the night; ²⁴and provide mounts to set Paul on, and bring *him* safely to Felix the governor." ²⁵He wrote a letter in the following manner:

²⁶   Claudius Lysias,

To the most excellent governor Felix:

Greetings.

²⁷   This man was seized by the Jews and was about to be killed by them. Coming with the troops I rescued him, having learned that he was a Roman. ²⁸And when I wanted to know the reason they accused him, I brought him before their council. ²⁹I found out that he was accused concerning questions of their law, but had nothing charged against him deserving of death or chains. ³⁰And when it was told me that the Jews lay in wait for the man, I sent him immediately to you, and also commanded his accusers to state before you the charges against him.

Farewell.

³¹Then the soldiers, as they were commanded, took Paul and brought *him* by night to Antipatris. ³²The next day they left the horsemen to go on with him, and returned to the barracks. ³³When they came to Caesarea and had delivered the letter to the governor, they also presented Paul to him. ³⁴And when the governor had read *it,* he asked what province he was from. And when he understood that *he was* from Cilicia, ³⁵he said, "I will hear you when your accusers also have come." And he commanded him to be kept in Herod's Praetorium.

CHAPTER 24 PAUL BEFORE FELIX. Now after five days Ananias the high priest came down with the elders and a certain orator *named* Tertullus. These gave evidence to the governor against Paul.

²And when he was called upon, Tertullus began his accusation, saying: "Seeing that through you we enjoy

great peace, and prosperity is being brought to this nation by your foresight, ³we accept *it* always and in all places, most noble Felix, with all thankfulness. ⁴Nevertheless, not to be tedious to you any further, I beg you to hear, by your courtesy, a few words from us. ⁵For we have found this man a plague, a creator of dissension among all the Jews throughout the world, and a ringleader of the sect of the Nazarenes. ⁶He even tried to profane the temple, and we seized him, and wanted to judge him according to our law. ⁷But the commander Lysias came by and with great violence took *him* out of our hands, ⁸commanding his accusers to come to you. By examining him yourself you may ascertain all these things of which we accuse him." ⁹And the Jews also assented, maintaining that these things were so.

¹⁰Then Paul, after the governor had nodded to him to speak, answered: "Inasmuch as I know that you have been for many years a judge of this nation, I do the more cheerfully answer for myself, ¹¹because you may ascertain that it is no more than twelve days since I went up to Jerusalem to worship. ¹²And they neither found me in the temple disputing with anyone nor inciting the crowd, either in the synagogues or in the city. ¹³Nor can they prove the things of which they now accuse me. ¹⁴But this I confess to you, that according to the Way which they call a sect, so I worship the God of my fathers, believing all things which are written in the Law and in the Prophets. ¹⁵I have hope in God, which they themselves also accept, that there will be a resurrection of *the* dead, both of *the* just and *the* unjust. ¹⁶This *being* so, I myself always strive to have a conscience without offense toward God and men.

¹⁷"Now after many years I came to bring alms and offerings to my nation, ¹⁸in the midst of which some Jews from Asia found me purified in the temple, neither with a mob nor with tumult. ¹⁹They ought to have been here before you to object if they had anything against me. ²⁰Or else let those who are *here* themselves say if they found any wrongdoing in me while I stood before the council, ²¹unless *it is* for this one statement which I cried out, standing among them, 'Concerning the resurrection of the dead I am being judged by you this day.'"

²²But when Felix heard these things, having more accurate knowledge of *the* Way, he adjourned the proceedings and said, "When Lysias the commander comes down, I will make a decision on your case." ²³So he commanded the centurion to keep Paul and to let *him* have liberty, and told him not to forbid any of his friends to provide for or visit him.

²⁴And after some days, when Felix came with his wife Drusilla, who was Jewish, he sent for Paul and heard him concerning the faith in Christ. ²⁵Now as he reasoned about righteousness, self-control, and the judgment to come, Felix was afraid and answered, "Go away for now; when I have a convenient time I will call for you." ²⁶Meanwhile he also hoped that money would be given him by Paul, that he might release him. Therefore he sent for him more often and conversed with him.

²⁷But after two years Porcius Festus succeeded Felix; and Felix, wanting to do the Jews a favor, left Paul bound.

CHAPTER 25 PAUL BEFORE FESTUS.

Now when Festus had come to the province, after three days he went up from Caesarea to Jerusalem. ²Then the high priest and the chief men of the Jews informed him against Paul; and they petitioned him, ³asking a favor against him, that he would summon him to Jerusalem—while *they* lay in ambush along the road to kill him. ⁴But Festus answered that Paul should be kept at Caesarea, and that he himself was going *there* shortly. ⁵"Therefore," he said, "let those who have authority among you go down with *me* and accuse this man, to see if there is any fault in him."

⁶And when he had remained among them more than ten days, he went down to Caesarea. And the next day, sitting on the judgment seat, he commanded Paul to be brought. ⁷When he had come, the Jews who had come down from Jerusalem stood about and laid many serious complaints against Paul, which they could not prove, ⁸while he answered for himself, "Neither against the law of the Jews, nor against the temple, nor against Caesar have I offended in anything at all."

⁹But Festus, wanting to do the Jews a favor, answered Paul and said, "Are you willing to go up to Jerusalem and there be judged before me concerning these things?"

¹⁰So Paul said, "I stand at Caesar's judgment seat, where I ought to be judged. To the Jews I have done no wrong, as you very well know. ¹¹For if I am an offender, or have committed anything deserving of death, I do not object to dying; but if there is nothing in these things of which these men accuse me, no one can deliver me to them. I appeal to Caesar."

¹²Then Festus, when he had conferred with the council, answered, "You have appealed to Caesar? To Caesar you shall go!"

¹³And after some days King Agrippa and Bernice came to Caesarea to greet Festus. ¹⁴When they had been there many days, Festus laid Paul's case before the king, saying: "There is a certain man left a prisoner by Felix, ¹⁵about whom the chief priests and the elders of the Jews informed *me*, when I was in Jerusalem, asking for a judgment against him. ¹⁶To them I answered, 'It is not the

custom of the Romans to deliver any man to destruction before the accused meets the accusers face to face, and has opportunity to answer for himself concerning the charge against him.' ¹⁷Therefore when they had come together, without any delay, the next day I sat on the judgment seat and commanded the man to be brought in. ¹⁸When the accusers stood up, they brought no accusation against him of such things as I supposed, ¹⁹but had some questions against him about their own religion and about a certain Jesus, who had died, whom Paul affirmed to be alive. ²⁰And because I was uncertain of such questions, I asked whether he was willing to go to Jerusalem and there be judged concerning these matters. ²¹But when Paul appealed to be reserved for the decision of Augustus, I commanded him to be kept till I could send him to Caesar."

²²Then Agrippa said to Festus, "I also would like to hear the man myself."

"Tomorrow," he said, "you shall hear him."

²³So the next day, when Agrippa and Bernice had come with great pomp, and had entered the auditorium with the commanders and the prominent men of the city, at Festus' command Paul was brought in. ²⁴And Festus said: "King Agrippa and all the men who are here present with us, you see this man about whom the whole assembly of the Jews petitioned me, both at Jerusalem and here, crying out that he was not fit to live any longer. ²⁵But when I found that he had committed nothing deserving of death, and that he himself had appealed to Augustus, I decided to send him. ²⁶I have nothing certain to write to my lord concerning him. Therefore I have brought him out before you, and especially before you, King Agrippa, so that after the examination has taken place I may have something to write. ²⁷For it seems to me unreasonable to send a prisoner and not to specify the charges against him."

CHAPTER 26 AGRIPPA WANTS TO HEAR PAUL.

Then Agrippa said to Paul, "You are permitted to speak for yourself."

So Paul stretched out his hand and answered for himself: ²"I think myself happy, King Agrippa, because today I shall answer for myself before you concerning all the things of which I am accused by the Jews, ³especially because you are expert in all customs and questions which have to do with the Jews. Therefore I beg you to hear me patiently.

⁴"My manner of life from my youth, which was spent from the beginning among my own nation at Jerusalem, all the Jews know. ⁵They knew me from the first, if they were willing to testify, that according to the strictest sect of our religion I lived a Pharisee. ⁶And now I stand and am judged for the hope of the promise made by God to our fathers. ⁷To this *promise* our twelve tribes, earnestly serving *God* night and day, hope to attain. For this hope's sake, King Agrippa, I am accused by the Jews. ⁸Why should it be thought incredible by you that God raises the dead?

⁹"Indeed, I myself thought I must do many things contrary to the name of Jesus of Nazareth. ¹⁰This I also did in Jerusalem, and many of the saints I shut up in prison, having received authority from the chief priests; and when they were put to death, I cast my vote against *them.* ¹¹And I punished them often in every synagogue and compelled *them* to blaspheme; and being exceedingly enraged against them, I persecuted *them* even to foreign cities.

¹²"While thus occupied, as I journeyed to Damascus with authority and commission from the chief priests, ¹³at midday, O king, along the road I saw a light from heaven, brighter than the sun, shining around me and those who journeyed with me. ¹⁴And when we all had fallen to the ground, I heard a voice speaking to me and saying in the Hebrew language, 'Saul, Saul, why are you persecuting Me? *It is* hard for you to kick against the goads.' ¹⁵So I said, 'Who are You, Lord?' And He said, 'I am Jesus, whom you are persecuting. ¹⁶But rise and stand on your feet; for I have appeared to you for this purpose, to make you a minister and a witness both of the things which you have seen and of the things which I will yet reveal to you. ¹⁷I will deliver you from the *Jewish* people, as well as *from* the Gentiles, to whom I now send you, ¹⁸to open their eyes, *in order* to turn *them* from darkness to light, and *from* the power of Satan to God, that they may receive forgiveness of sins and an inheritance among those who are sanctified by faith in Me.'

¹⁹"Therefore, King Agrippa, I was not disobedient to the heavenly vision, ²⁰but declared first to those in Damascus and in Jerusalem, and throughout all the region of Judea, and *then* to the Gentiles, that they should repent, turn to God, and do works befitting repentance. ²¹For these reasons the Jews seized me in the temple and tried to kill *me.* ²²Therefore, having obtained help from God, to this day I stand, witnessing both to small and great, saying no other things than those which the prophets and Moses said would come— ²³that the Christ would suffer, that He would be the first to rise from the dead, and would proclaim light to the *Jewish* people and to the Gentiles."

²⁴Now as he thus made his defense, Festus said with a loud voice, "Paul, you are beside yourself! Much learning is driving you mad!"

²⁵But he said, "I am not mad, most noble Festus, but speak the words of truth and reason. ²⁶For the king, before whom I also speak freely, knows these things; for I am convinced that none of these things escapes his attention, since this thing was not done in a corner. ²⁷King Agrippa, do you believe the prophets? I know that you do believe."

²⁸Then Agrippa said to Paul, "You almost persuade me to become a Christian."

FACTS

26:26 Paul was appealing to the *facts*—people were still alive who had heard Jesus and seen his miracles; the empty tomb could still be seen; and the Christian message was turning the world upside down (17:6). The history of Jesus' life and the early church are facts that are still open for us to examine. We can study eyewitness accounts of Jesus' life in the Bible as well as historical and archaeological records of the early church. Examine the events and facts as verified by many witnesses. Reconfirm your faith with the truth of these accounts.

²⁹And Paul said, "I would to God that not only you, but also all who hear me today, might become both almost and altogether such as I am, except for these chains."

³⁰When he had said these things, the king stood up, as well as the governor and Bernice and those who sat with them; ³¹and when they had gone aside, they talked among themselves, saying, "This man is doing nothing deserving of death or chains."

³²Then Agrippa said to Festus, "This man might have been set free if he had not appealed to Caesar."

CHAPTER 27 PAUL'S SHIP IS WRECKED. And

when it was decided that we should sail to Italy, they delivered Paul and some other prisoners to *one* named Julius, a centurion of the Augustan Regiment. ²So, entering a ship of Adramyttium, we put to sea, meaning to sail along the coasts of Asia. Aristarchus, a Macedonian of Thessalonica, was with us. ³And the next *day* we landed at Sidon. And Julius treated Paul kindly and gave *him* liberty to go to his friends and receive care. ⁴When we had put to sea from there, we sailed under *the shelter of* Cyprus, because the winds were contrary. ⁵And when we had sailed over the sea which is off Cilicia and Pamphylia, we came to Myra, *a city* of Lycia. ⁶There the centurion found an Alexandrian ship sailing to Italy, and he put us on board.

◀︎◀︎◀︎ EVEN BETTER

27:1—28:24 One of Paul's most important journeys was to Rome, but he didn't get there in quite the way he had expected. It turned out to be more of a legal journey than a missionary journey, thanks to a series of legal trials and transactions. These events resulted in Paul being delivered to Rome, where he told his story of the gospel in the most amazing places, including the palace of the emperor! Sometimes we feel frustrated because our plans don't work out the way we wanted them to. But God is never out of control! He knows how to work things out so that the results are even better than we expected. Trusting God with your plans is a surefire plan for success!

⁷When we had sailed slowly many days, and arrived with difficulty off Cnidus, the wind not permitting us to proceed, we sailed under *the shelter of* Crete off Salmone. ⁸Passing it with difficulty, we came to a place called Fair Havens, near the city *of* Lasea.

⁹Now when much time had been spent, and sailing was now dangerous because the Fast was already over, Paul advised them, ¹⁰saying, "Men, I perceive that this voyage will end with disaster and much loss, not only of the cargo and ship, but also our lives." ¹¹Nevertheless the centurion was more persuaded by the helmsman and the owner of the ship than by the things spoken by Paul. ¹²And because the harbor was not suitable to winter in, the majority advised to set sail from there also, if by any means they could reach Phoenix, a harbor of Crete opening toward the southwest and northwest, *and* winter there.

¹³When the south wind blew softly, supposing that they had obtained *their* desire, putting out to sea, they sailed close by Crete. ¹⁴But not long after, a tempestuous head wind arose, called Euroclydon. ¹⁵So when the ship

was caught, and could not head into the wind, we let *her* drive. ¹⁶And running under *the shelter of* an island called Clauda, we secured the skiff with difficulty. ¹⁷When they had taken it on board, they used cables to undergird the ship; and fearing lest they should run aground on the Syrtis *Sands,* they struck sail and so were driven. ¹⁸And because we were exceedingly tempest-tossed, the next *day* they lightened the ship. ¹⁹On the third *day* we threw the ship's tackle overboard with our own hands. ²⁰Now when neither sun nor stars appeared for many days, and no small tempest beat on *us,* all hope that we would be saved was finally given up.

²¹But after long abstinence from food, then Paul stood in the midst of them and said, "Men, you should have listened to me, and not have sailed from Crete and incurred this disaster and loss. ²²And now I urge you to take heart, for there will be no loss of life among you, but only of the ship. ²³For there stood by me this night an angel of the God to whom I belong and whom I serve, ²⁴saying, 'Do not be afraid, Paul; you must be brought before Caesar; and indeed God has granted you all those who sail with you.' ²⁵Therefore take heart, men, for I believe God that it will be just as it was told me. ²⁶However, we must run aground on a certain island."

²⁷Now when the fourteenth night had come, as we were driven up and down in the Adriatic *Sea,* about midnight the sailors sensed that they were drawing near some land. ²⁸And they took soundings and found *it* to be twenty fathoms; and when they had gone a little farther, they took soundings again and found *it* to be fifteen fathoms. ²⁹Then, fearing lest we should run aground on the rocks, they dropped four anchors from the stern, and prayed for day to come. ³⁰And as the sailors were seeking to escape from the ship, when they had let down the skiff into the sea, under pretense of putting out anchors from the prow, ³¹Paul said to the centurion and the soldiers, "Unless these men stay in the ship, you cannot be saved." ³²Then the soldiers cut away the ropes of the skiff and let it fall off.

³³And as day was about to dawn, Paul implored *them* all to take food, saying, "Today is the fourteenth day you have waited and continued without food, and eaten nothing. ³⁴Therefore I urge you to take nourishment, for this is for your survival, since not a hair will fall from the head of any of you." ³⁵And when he had said these things, he took bread and gave thanks to God in the presence of them all; and when he had broken *it* he began to eat. ³⁶Then they were all encouraged, and also took food themselves. ³⁷And in all we were two hundred and seventy-six persons on the ship. ³⁸So when they had eaten enough, they lightened the ship and threw out the wheat into the sea.

³⁹When it was day, they did not recognize the land; but they observed a bay with a beach, onto which they planned to run the ship if possible. ⁴⁰And they let go the anchors and left *them* in the sea, meanwhile loosing the rudder ropes; and they hoisted the mainsail to the wind and made for shore. ⁴¹But striking a place where two seas met, they ran the ship aground; and the prow stuck fast and remained immovable, but the stern was being broken up by the violence of the waves.

[42]And the soldiers' plan was to kill the prisoners, lest any of them should swim away and escape. [43]But the centurion, wanting to save Paul, kept them from *their* purpose, and commanded that those who could swim should jump *overboard* first and get to land, [44]and the rest, some on boards and some on *parts* of the ship. And so it was that they all escaped safely to land.

CHAPTER 28 PAUL IS SHIPWRECKED ON MALTA.

Now when they had escaped, they then found out that the island was called Malta. [2]And the natives showed us unusual kindness; for they kindled a fire and made us all welcome, because of the rain that was falling and because of the cold. [3]But when Paul had gathered a bundle of sticks and laid *them* on the fire, a viper came out because of the heat, and fastened on his hand. [4]So when the natives saw the creature hanging from his hand, they said to one another, "No doubt this man is a murderer, whom, though he has escaped the sea, yet justice does not allow to live." [5]But he shook off the creature into the fire and suffered no harm. [6]However, they were expecting that he would swell up or suddenly fall down dead. But after they had looked for a long time and saw no harm come to him, they changed their minds and said that he was a god.

[7]In that region there was an estate of the leading citizen of the island, whose name was Publius, who received us and entertained us courteously for three days. [8]And it happened that the father of Publius lay sick of a fever and dysentery. Paul went in to him and prayed, and he laid his hands on him and healed him. [9]So when this was done, the rest of those on the island who had diseases also came and were healed. [10]They also honored us in many ways; and when we departed, they provided such things as were necessary.

[11]After three months we sailed in an Alexandrian ship whose figurehead was the Twin Brothers, which had wintered at the island. [12]And landing at Syracuse, we stayed three days. [13]From there we circled round and reached Rhegium. And after one day the south wind blew; and the next day we came to Puteoli, [14]where we found brethren, and were invited to stay with them seven days. And so we went toward Rome. [15]And from there, when the brethren heard about us, they came to meet us as far as Appii Forum and Three Inns. When Paul saw them, he thanked God and took courage.

[16]Now when we came to Rome, the centurion delivered the prisoners to the captain of the guard; but Paul was permitted to dwell by himself with the soldier who guarded him.

[17]And it came to pass after three days that Paul called the leaders of the Jews together. So when they had come together, he said to them: "Men *and* brethren, though I have done nothing against our people or the customs of our fathers, yet I was delivered as a prisoner from Jerusalem into the hands of the Romans, [18]who, when they had examined me, wanted to let *me* go, because there was no cause for putting me to death. [19]But when the Jews spoke against *it*, I was compelled to appeal to Caesar, not that I had anything of which to accuse my nation. [20]For this reason therefore I have called for you, to see *you* and speak with *you*, because for the hope of Israel I am bound with this chain."

[21]Then they said to him, "We neither received letters from Judea concerning you, nor have any of the brethren who came reported or spoken any evil of you. [22]But we desire to hear from you what you think; for concerning this sect, we know that it is spoken against everywhere."

[23]So when they had appointed him a day, many came to him at *his* lodging, to whom he explained and solemnly testified of the kingdom of God, persuading them concerning Jesus from both the Law of Moses and the Prophets, from morning till evening. [24]And some were persuaded by the things which were spoken, and some disbelieved. [25]So when they did not agree among them-

◤ HEROES

28:31 The book of Acts shows the history of the Christian church and its expansion in ever-widening circles to Jerusalem, Antioch, Ephesus, and Rome—the most influential cities in the western world. Acts also shows the mighty miracles and testimonies of the heroes and martyrs of the early church—Peter, Stephen, James, Paul. All the ministry was prompted and held together by the Holy Spirit working in the lives of ordinary people—merchants, slaves, jailers, church leaders, men, women, Gentiles, Jews. Many unsung heroes of the faith continued the acts of the Holy Spirit, changing the world with a changeless message: Jesus Christ is Savior and Lord for all who call upon him. Today we can take part in the continuing story of the spread of the gospel, bringing that same message to our world so that others may hear and believe.

selves, they departed after Paul had said one word: "The Holy Spirit spoke rightly through Isaiah the prophet to our fathers, [26]saying,

'Go to this people and say:
"Hearing you will hear, and shall not understand;
And seeing you will see, and not perceive;
[27] For the hearts of this people have grown dull.
Their ears are hard of hearing,
And their eyes they have closed,
Lest they should see with their eyes and hear with
   their ears,
Lest they should understand with their hearts and
   turn,
So that I should heal them." '

[28]"Therefore let it be known to you that the salvation of God has been sent to the Gentiles, and they will hear it!" [29]And when he had said these words, the Jews departed and had a great dispute among themselves.

[30]Then Paul dwelt two whole years in his own rented house, and received all who came to him, [31]preaching the kingdom of God and teaching the things which concern the Lord Jesus Christ with all confidence, no one forbidding him.

WHAT ABOUT THOSE WHO'VE NEVER HEARD?

"**W**hat about the native in deep dark Africa? God wouldn't send him to hell for not accepting Christ when he's never even heard of him, would he? What about the millions of Hindus and Buddhists who are good moral people, but have never heard the gospel—God couldn't possibly send them to hell, could he?" **If** you've been following Jesus for very long, you've probably had a couple of discussions that deal with questions like these. What does God do with those who've never heard of Jesus? **The** Bible doesn't deal with that question directly. Instead, it talks about Jesus in rather exclusive terms. Take a look at Acts 4:12: "Nor is there salvation in any other, for there is no other name [other than Jesus Christ] under heaven given among men by which we must be saved." Because the Bible doesn't talk directly about the problem, we must proceed with humility and caution. Still, we aren't left totally in the dark. **F**irst, remember that God doesn't owe it to anybody to save him or her from hell and take that person to heaven for all eternity. He would be entirely justified in condemning everyone, for "all have sinned and fall short of the glory of God" (Romans 3:23). That's the nature of grace—we get what we don't deserve, instead of what we do deserve. Even if God arbitrarily chose whom to save and whom to condemn, he could not be accused of being unjust or unmerciful. **S**till, why would God condemn someone who has never heard of Christ for never claiming forgiveness through the cross of Christ? He wouldn't. Romans 1 (especially verses 18-20) makes it clear that God has created every one of us with the knowledge of our Creator. We have to try to suppress it. Psalm 19 begins, "The heavens declare the glory of God; and the firmament shows His handiwork. Day unto day utters speech, and night unto night reveals knowledge." Every person ever born has an innate knowledge that there is a Creator, someone bigger, smarter, and more powerful than we are, who put us here in this universe. Those who do not hear the message about Jesus are responsible for how they respond to the knowledge they do have about God. **So,** for anyone who has heard the Good News of Jesus—that God came to earth as a man named Jesus of Nazareth, and that he lived, died, and rose again so that through him we could have forgiveness of sins and his love, eternal life—salvation comes through faith in Jesus. For the person who's never heard of Jesus and his love, us, salvation comes based on the knowledge of our loving Creator, and responding to that knowledge with love, obedience, and worship. For all people, Christ is the only one who has opened the way for us to be restored to God. It is his act on the cross and his resurrection that enables any of us to approach our holy and all-righteous God. **W**e don't have all the answers to all the questions that confuse us about life and death, heaven and hell, and so on. But we can know the one who not only knows the truth, but is the Truth—and we know that he is loving, kind, and merciful. He will do what is right.

MEGA Themes

CHURCH BEGINNINGS Acts is the history of how Christianity was founded and organized and solved its problems. The community of believers began by faith in the risen Christ and in the power of the Holy Spirit, who enabled them to witness, love, and serve, and so reach their world for Christ.

New churches are continually being founded. By faith in Jesus Christ and in the power of the Holy Spirit, the church can be a vibrant agent for change. Acts gives important remedies for solving new problems we may face. God wants us to work together to bring his Good News to the world.

1. Read 2:42-47 and 4:32-37. Describe the relationships in these first gatherings.
2. What is similar and what is different about your church and these early gatherings?
3. What do you learn from 6:1-7 about how to deal with conflict in the church? What do you learn about the importance of servants in the church?
4. What can you do to help resolve a conflict or to serve in your church?

HOLY SPIRIT The church did not start or grow by its own power or enthusiasm. The disciples were empowered by God's Holy Spirit, the promised Helper sent by Jesus when he went to heaven.

The Holy Spirit's work demonstrated that Christianity is supernatural. Thus the church became more Holy Spirit–conscious than problem-conscious. By faith, any believer can experience the Holy Spirit's power to do Christ's work.

1. Summarize the various acts God performed through his Holy Spirit in chapters 1–5. What was God's purpose in acting so dramatically?
2. What were the key results of the Holy Spirit's work in the early church?
3. In what ways do you need to rely upon the Holy Spirit?

CHURCH GROWTH Acts presents the history of a dynamic, growing community of believers from Jerusalem to Syria, Africa, Asia, and Europe. In the first century, it spread from believing Jews to non-Jews in 39 cities and 30 countries or provinces.

When the Holy Spirit works, there is movement, excitement, and growth. He gives us the motivation and ability to get the gospel to the whole world. You can be an important part of this great world movement. Begin in your neighborhood and school to live for Christ and share the gospel with others.

1. How did the growth of the church in Acts accomplish Jesus' words in 1:8?
2. Look again at 1:8. What would be your Jerusalem? Judea? Samaria?
3. In what specific ways can you be used by God in each of the areas you listed above?

WITNESSING Peter, John, Philip, Paul, Barnabas, and thousands more told others about their new faith in Christ. By personal testimony, preaching, or defense before authorities, they shared the story with boldness and courage.

We are God's people, chosen to be part of his plan to reach the world. In love and by faith, we can have the Holy Spirit's help as we share the gospel. Witnessing also strengthens our faith.

1. In what ways did the early witnesses for Jesus share their message?
2. Looking back at your responses under church growth, what are some of the opportunities you have for being a witness for Christ?
3. What are you doing now to be a witness for Christ? What could you do to be more effective?

OPPOSITION Through imprisonment, beatings, plots, and riots, Christians were persecuted by both Jews and Gentiles. But the opposition became a catalyst, an energizer for the spread of Christianity. In the face of opposition it became evident that Christianity was not the work of humans, but of God.

God can work through any opposition. When you are treated harshly through ridicule, lies, or physical abuse from hostile unbelievers, realize that it is happening because of your faithful witness. Take every opportunity, even those that opposition brings, for communicating the Good News of Jesus Christ.

1. Describe how the various followers of Jesus responded to opposition and persecution.
2. How do you think these individuals felt when they were being threatened, ridiculed, beaten, even stoned? What motivated them to continue?
3. What potential opposition awaits you in your efforts to be a witness for Christ?
4. What are some possible responses that you might have when faced with this opposition?
5. How might God use the opposition you face to bring glory to himself and further his kingdom?

*I*magine you're out on an evening run when you happen upon your dream car. As you admire its beauty, you notice a key in the ignition . . . and unlocked doors. The car seems to say, "Take me out for a quick spin." You glance around. The street is deserted. ■ "But that would be stealing!" your conscience protests. "No way!" another voice blurts in. "You're not going to *keep* it." For an agonizingly long moment the inner voices battle—then adventure wins out. Your heart pounds as you slide into the driver's seat and the engine hums to life. ■ "This is awesome!" you say, slipping the car into gear. You intend to make one slow trip around the block—but the speedometer goes up to 160 mph, and when will you *ever* get another chance like this? You head for the open road. ■ What happens next is a blur. You remember the exhilaration of 143 mph, then flashing blue lights, cold steel handcuffs, being in court, and the judge's gavel pounding out a guilty verdict. The sentence: $10,000 and six months incarceration. You deserve punishment, but that's a severe penalty! ■ Then the judge does something curious. He removes his robe, whips out his checkbook, and pays your fine! Next he announces he will serve your jail sentence. Then he looks you in the eyes and says, "I love you." ■ This analogy isn't perfect, but it *does* help explain how God deals with sinful humanity. The very penalty he demands (death for sin), he provided (the death of Christ on the cross). If you'd like an even better explanation of God's perfect justice and his intense love for you, read the book of Romans.

STATS

PURPOSE: To introduce Paul to the Romans and to give a sample of his message before he arrives in Rome

AUTHOR: Paul

TO WHOM WRITTEN: The Christians in Rome and believers everywhere

DATE WRITTEN: About A.D. 57, from Corinth, as Paul was preparing for his visit to Jerusalem

SETTING: Apparently Paul had finished his work in the east, and he planned to visit Rome on his way to Spain after first bringing a collection to Jerusalem for the poor Christians there (15:22-28). The Roman church was mostly Jewish but also contained many Gentiles.

KEY PEOPLE: Paul, Phoebe

KEY PLACE: Rome

Romans

CHAPTER 1 PAUL WRITES WITH GOOD NEWS.

Paul, a bondservant of Jesus Christ, called *to be* an apostle, separated to the gospel of God ²which He promised before through His prophets in the Holy Scriptures, ³concerning His Son Jesus Christ our Lord, who was born of the seed of David according to the flesh, ⁴*and* declared *to be* the Son of God with power according to the Spirit of holiness, by the resurrection from the dead. ⁵Through Him we have received grace and apostleship for obedience to the faith among all nations for His name, ⁶among whom you also are the called of Jesus Christ;

⁷To all who are in Rome, beloved of God, called *to be* saints:

Grace to you and peace from God our Father and the Lord Jesus Christ.

⁸First, I thank my God through Jesus Christ for you all, that your faith is spoken of throughout the whole world. ⁹For God is my witness, whom I serve with my spirit in the gospel of His Son, that without ceasing I make mention of you always in my prayers, ¹⁰making request if, by some means, now at last I may find a way in the will of God to come to you. ¹¹For I long to see you, that I may impart to you some spiritual gift, so that you may be established— ¹²that is, that I may be encouraged together with you by the mutual faith both of you and me.

¹³Now I do not want you to be unaware, brethren, that I often planned to come to you (but was hindered until now), that I might have some fruit among you also, just as among the other Gentiles. ¹⁴I am a debtor both to Greeks and to barbarians, both to wise and to unwise. ¹⁵So, as much as is in me, *I am* ready to preach the gospel to you who are in Rome also.

GOOD NEWS

1:2-17 Paul was not ashamed because his message was *Good News.* It was powerful, it was for everyone, and it was part of God's revealed plan. When you are tempted to be ashamed, remember what the Good News is all about. If you focus on God and on what he is doing in the world rather than on your own inadequacy, your embarrassment will soon disappear.

¹⁶For I am not ashamed of the gospel of Christ, for it is the power of God to salvation for everyone who believes, for the Jew first and also for the Greek. ¹⁷For in it the righteousness of God is revealed from faith to faith; as it is written, *"The just shall live by faith."*

¹⁸For the wrath of God is revealed from heaven against all ungodliness and unrighteousness of men, who suppress the truth in unrighteousness, ¹⁹because what may be known of God is manifest in them, for God has shown *it* to them. ²⁰For since the creation of the world His invis-

NO EXCUSE

1:18-20 Paul answers a common objection: How could a loving God send anyone to hell, especially someone who has never heard the Good News of Jesus? In fact, says Paul, God has revealed himself to *all* people. Everyone knows what God requires, but no one lives up to it. If people suppress God's truth in order to live their own way, they have no excuse. They know the truth, and they will have to endure the consequences of ignoring it.

ible *attributes* are clearly seen, being understood by the things that are made, *even* His eternal power and Godhead, so that they are without excuse, [21]because, although they knew God, they did not glorify *Him* as God, nor were thankful, but became futile in their thoughts, and their foolish hearts were darkened. [22]Professing to be wise, they became fools, [23]and changed the glory of the incorruptible God into an image made like corruptible man—and birds and four-footed animals and creeping things.

[24]Therefore God also gave them up to uncleanness, in the lusts of their hearts, to dishonor their bodies among themselves, [25]who exchanged the truth of God for the lie, and worshiped and served the creature rather than the

Creator, who is blessed forever. Amen.

[26]For this reason God gave them up to vile passions. For even their women exchanged the natural use for what is against nature. [27]Likewise also the men, leaving the natural use of the woman, burned in their lust for one another, men with men committing what is shameful, and receiving in themselves the penalty of their error which was due.

[28]And even as they did not like to retain God in *their* knowledge, God gave them over to a debased mind, to do those things which are not fitting; [29]being filled with all unrighteousness, sexual immorality, wickedness, covetousness, maliciousness; full of envy, murder, strife, deceit, evil-mindedness; *they are* whisperers, [30]backbiters, haters of God, violent, proud, boasters, inventors of evil things, disobedient to parents, [31]undiscerning, untrustworthy, unloving, unforgiving, unmerciful; [32]who, knowing the righteous judgment of God, that those who practice such things are deserving of death, not only do the same but also approve of those who practice them.

CHAPTER **2** **GOD WILL JUDGE US ALL.** Therefore you are inexcusable, O man, whoever you are who judge, for in whatever you judge another you condemn yourself; for you who judge practice the same things. [2]But we know that the judgment of God is according to truth against those who practice such things. [3]And do you think this, O man, you who judge those practicing such things, and doing the same, that you will escape the judgment of God? [4]Or do you despise the riches of His goodness, forbearance, and longsuffering, not knowing that the goodness of God leads you to repentance? [5]But in accordance with your hardness and your impenitent heart you are treasuring up for yourself wrath in the day of wrath and revelation of the righteous judgment of God, [6]who *"will render to each one according to his deeds":* [7]eternal life to those who by patient continuance in doing good seek for glory, honor, and immortality; [8]but to those who are self-seeking and do not obey the truth, but obey unrighteousness—indignation and wrath, [9]tribulation and anguish, on every soul of man who does evil, of the Jew first and also of the Greek; [10]but glory, honor, and peace to everyone who works what is good, to the Jew first and also to the Greek. [11]For there is no partiality with God.

[12]For as many as have sinned without law will also perish without law, and as many as have sinned in the law will be judged by the law [13](for not the hearers of the law *are* just in the sight of God, but the doers of the law will be justified; [14]for when Gentiles, who do not have the law, by nature do the things in the law, these, although not having the law, are a law to themselves, [15]who show the work of the law written in their hearts, their conscience also bearing witness, and between themselves *their* thoughts accusing or else excusing *them*) [16]in the day when God will judge the secrets of men by Jesus Christ, according to my gospel.

[17]Indeed you are called a Jew, and rest on the law, and make your boast in God, [18]and know *His* will, and approve the things that are excellent, being instructed out of the law, [19]and are confident that you yourself are a guide to the blind, a light to those who are in darkness, [20]an instructor of the foolish, a teacher of babes, having the form of knowledge and truth in the law. [21]You, therefore, who teach another, do you not teach yourself? You who preach that a man should not steal, do you steal? [22]You who say, "Do not commit adultery," do you commit adultery? You who abhor idols, do you rob temples? [23]You who make your boast in the law, do you dishonor God through breaking the law? [24]For *"the name of God is blasphemed among the Gentiles because of you,"* as it is written.

[25]For circumcision is indeed profitable if you keep the law; but if you are a breaker of the law, your circumcision has become uncircumcision. [26]Therefore, if an uncircumcised man keeps the righteous requirements of the law, will not his uncircumcision be counted as circumcision? [27]And will not the physically uncircumcised, if he fulfills the law, judge you who, *even* with *your* written *code* and circumcision, *are* a transgressor of the law? [28]For he is not a Jew who *is one* outwardly, nor *is* circumcision that which *is* outward in the flesh; [29]but *he is* a Jew

who *is one* inwardly; and circumcision *is that* of the heart, in the Spirit, not in the letter; whose praise *is* not from men but from God.

CHAPTER **3** GOD REMAINS FAITHFUL.

What advantage then has the Jew, or what *is* the profit of circumcision? ²Much in every way! Chiefly because to them were committed the oracles of God. ³For what if some did not believe? Will their unbelief make the faithfulness of God without effect? ⁴Certainly not! Indeed, let God be true but every man a liar. As it is written:

"That You may be justified in Your words,
And may overcome when You are judged."

⁵But if our unrighteousness demonstrates the righteousness of God, what shall we say? *Is* God unjust who inflicts wrath? (I speak as a man.) ⁶Certainly not! For then how will God judge the world?

⁷For if the truth of God has increased through my lie to His glory, why am I also still judged as a sinner? ⁸And *why* not *say*, "Let us do evil that good may come"?—as we are slanderously reported and as some affirm that we say. Their condemnation is just.

⁹What then? Are we better *than they*? Not at all. For we have previously charged both Jews and Greeks that they are all under sin. ¹⁰As it is written:

"There is none righteous, no, not one;
¹¹ *There is none who understands;*
There is none who seeks after God.
¹² *They have all turned aside;*
They have together become unprofitable;

◤CUT OFF

3:23 Some sins seem bigger than others because their obvious consequences are much more serious. Murder, for example, seems much worse than hatred; adultery seems worse than lust. But this does not mean we can get away with some sins and not with others. All sin makes us sinners, and all sin cuts us off from our holy God. All sin, therefore, leads to death (because it disqualifies us from living with God), regardless of how great or small it seems. Don't minimize "little" sins or overrate "big" sins. All sins separate us from God—but they all can be forgiven.

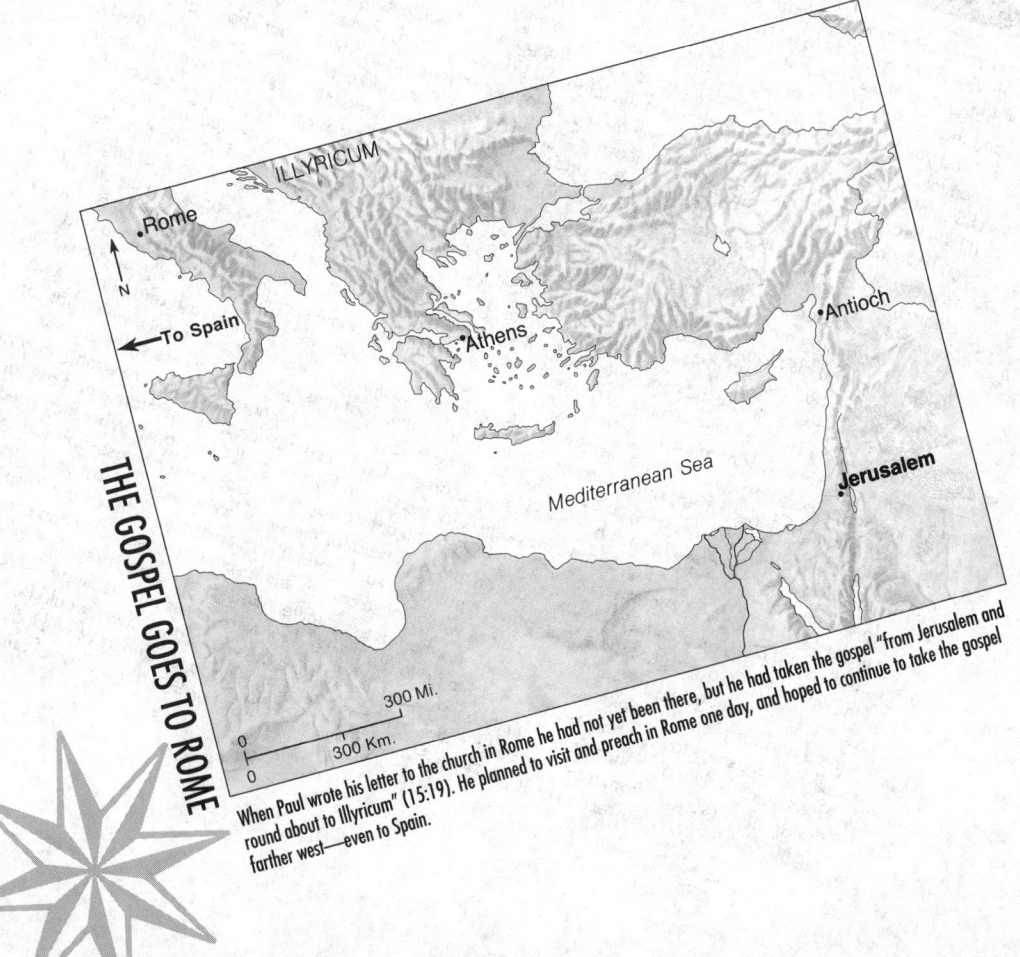

THE GOSPEL GOES TO ROME

ILLYRICUM

Rome

N

To Spain

Athens

Antioch

Mediterranean Sea

Jerusalem

300 Mi.

300 Km.

When Paul wrote his letter to the church in Rome he had not yet been there, but he had taken the gospel "from Jerusalem and round about to Illyricum" (15:19). He planned to visit and preach in Rome one day, and hoped to continue to take the gospel farther west—even to Spain.

HOMOSEXUALITY

If you're like most American teenagers, the day you get your driver's license and can take the car out for a drive—alone—is a day you dream (or dreamed) of. Before that, Mom, Dad, or the driving teacher rode "shotgun" to make sure you drove safely. But now, with your license, you're on your own. The thrill of freedom and the increased sense of responsibility make you feel more like an adult. No one will tell you when to stop or remind you to use your turn signal. It's up to you. **S**uppose you decide that, contrary to everything you've been told up to now, you want to drive on the left-hand side of the road. (Remember, we're talking about the U.S., not England or Hong Kong.) You will quickly encounter serious opposition to your choice of driving style (like a head-on collision). You can either learn from your observations and experiences, or you can insist that you have the right to drive however you wish, and whatever happens, happens. **W**hen it comes to driving, it's pretty obvious what the wisest choice is. Here in Romans 1, Paul addresses an issue that seems equally clear-cut, and yet men and women have struggled with it since Adam and Eve were evicted from Eden. The issue is homosexuality. **P**aul argues that all people everywhere are without excuse in knowing that there is a God. Proclaiming that nature itself reveals its Creator, Paul then begins a scathing rebuke against people who deny God and his plan for creation. These people, he writes, go against God's design for human sexuality, and in so doing will experience drastic consequences for their behavior. Like our fictional teenage driver, men and women who practice homosexuality experience tremendous opposition—socially, emotionally, physically, and spiritually. Yet they ignore all these warning signs. Sooner or later, though, they will crash and burn. **T**wo important messages need to be given on the subject of homosexuality. One is for our society, which has lost any meaningful idea of sin, righteousness, holiness, and truth. That message is that all life-styles are not acceptable. Some life-styles—such as alcoholism, or materialism . . . or homosexuality— are wrong; they are sinful. Those who engage in such behaviors should come to God in confession and repentance and ask for his forgiveness and healing. **T**he second message is for the church (meaning all Christians). What they need to understand is that while homosexuality is sin, it is not the unforgivable sin. God loves homosexuals just as much as he loves other sinners. Jesus' death on the cross paid for the sin of homosexuality, just as it paid for the sins of lying, greed, lust, hate, and pride. It is a place where those caught in the sin of homosexuality can come to be freed and forgiven. It is a place where believers who have committed the sins of hatred, prejudice, and self-righteousness toward homosexuals need to go to ask the Lord for forgiveness and healing. **H**omosexuals, like all sinners, stand guilty before God. If that were the whole story, there would be no hope for sinners of all kinds. The great message of Romans—and of the entire Bible—is that there is hope for sinners of all kinds. The life, death, and resurrection of Jesus Christ. He is the one who will set us free, regardless of our s

There is none who does good, no, not one."
13 *"Their throat is an open tomb;*
With their tongues they have practiced deceit";
"The poison of asps is under their lips";
14 *"Whose mouth is full of cursing and bitterness."*
15 *"Their feet are swift to shed blood;*
16 *Destruction and misery are in their ways;*
17 *And the way of peace they have not known."*
18 *"There is no fear of God before their eyes."*

19Now we know that whatever the law says, it says to those who are under the law, that every mouth may be stopped, and all the world may become guilty before God. 20Therefore by the deeds of the law no flesh will be justified in His sight, for by the law *is* the knowledge of sin.

21But now the righteousness of God apart from the law is revealed, being witnessed by the Law and the Prophets, 22even the righteousness of God, through faith in Jesus Christ, to all and on all who believe. For there is no difference; 23for all have sinned and fall short of the glory of God, 24being justified freely by His grace through the redemption that is in Christ Jesus, 25whom God set forth *as* a propitiation by His blood, through faith, to demonstrate His righteousness, because in His forbearance God had passed over the sins that were previously committed, 26to demonstrate at the present time His righteousness, that He might be just and the justifier of the one who has faith in Jesus.

27Where *is* boasting then? It is excluded. By what law? Of works? No, but by the law of faith. 28Therefore we conclude that a man is justified by faith apart from the deeds of the law. 29Or *is* He the God of the Jews only? *Is He* not also the God of the Gentiles? Yes, of the Gentiles also, 30since *there is* one God who will justify the circumcised by faith and the uncircumcised through faith. 31Do we then make void the law through faith? Certainly not! On the contrary, we establish the law.

CHAPTER 4 ABRAHAM BELIEVED GOD.

What then shall we say that Abraham our father has found according to the flesh? 2For if Abraham was justified by works, he has *something* to boast about, but not before God. 3For what does the Scripture say? *"Abraham believed God, and it was accounted to him for righteousness."* 4Now to him who works, the wages are not counted as grace but as debt.

5But to him who does not work but believes on Him who justifies the ungodly, his faith is accounted for righteousness, 6just as David also describes the blessedness of

the man to whom God imputes righteousness apart from works:

7 *"Blessed are those whose lawless deeds are forgiven,*
And whose sins are covered;
8 *Blessed is the man to whom the LORD shall not*
impute sin."

A GIFT

4:5 When some people learn we are saved through faith, they start to worry: "Do I have enough faith?" "Is my faith strong enough to save me?" These people miss the point. It is Jesus Christ who saves us, not *our* feelings or actions. He is strong enough to save us no matter how weak our faith is. Jesus offers us salvation as a gift because he loves us, not because we have earned it through our powerful faith. What, then, is the role of faith? Faith is believing and trusting in Jesus Christ, reaching out to accept his wonderful gift of salvation. Faith is effective whether it is great or small, timid or bold—because God loves us.

9*Does* this blessedness then *come* upon the circumcised *only,* or upon the uncircumcised also? For we say that faith was accounted to Abraham for righteousness. 10How then was it accounted? While he was circumcised, or uncircumcised? Not while circumcised, but while un-

"Here's what I did..."

During my freshman and sophomore years in high school, I led something of a double life. At home and at church, I was a "good Christian kid." I read my Bible, helped with Sunday school, and went to youth group. I really wanted to live a committed Christian life, but at school I was embarrassed to make it known that I was a Christian. I guess I was afraid of what people would think of me if they knew. When people said, "Come on, let's party," I'd feel torn. I loved God and knew he didn't approve of their idea of "party," but too often I just couldn't stand up to these people. I'd give in, then feel bad about myself for compromising what I knew was right.

The summer before my junior year, I knew things would have to change. That's when I read Romans 2:6-8. Verse 6 says God will give to each person as his deeds deserve. I got to thinking about what my deeds deserve, and it scared me. I realized how self-seeking I was. I really did want to please God, not hurt him or get him mad at me. I decided right then to make my goal eternal life that God promises "to those who by patient continuance in doing good seek for glory, honor, and immortality."

So I memorized that verse and decided to let people at school know I'm a Christian. It's made a big difference. For one thing, I met other Christians who were there all the time, but whom I hadn't bothered to get to know before. The last two years have been much better than the first two. I found that taking a stand against certain things didn't really cost me friends. In fact, because I've found other friends who know what friendship is about, I actually have more and better friends than before. But most of all I have a clear conscience; I know I'm trying to do God's will every day, at school as well as at church.

Lisa
AGE 18

To be forgiven for our sins, we must believe and confess that Jesus is Lord. Salvation comes through Jesus Christ. Romans 10:8-10

Jesus Christ died for sin. Romans 5:8

The penalty for our sin is death. Romans 6:23

Everyone has sinned. Romans 3:23

circumcised. [11]And he received the sign of circumcision, a seal of the righteousness of the faith which *he had while still* uncircumcised, that he might be the father of all those who believe, though they are uncircumcised, that righteousness might be imputed to them also, [12]and the father of circumcision to those who not only *are* of the circumcision, but who also walk in the steps of the faith which our father Abraham *had while still* uncircumcised.

OVERCOME

5:2-4 Paul tells us that in the future we will *become,* but until then we must *overcome.* This means we will experience difficulties that will help us grow. Problems we face will help develop our patience—which in turn will strengthen our character, deepen our trust in God, and give us greater confidence about the future. You probably find your patience tested in some way every day. Thank God for these opportunities to grow and deal with them in his strength (see also James 1:2-4; 1 Peter 1:6-7).

[13]For the promise that he would be the heir of the world *was* not to Abraham or to his seed through the law, but through the righteousness of faith. [14]For if those who are of the law *are* heirs, faith is made void and the promise made of no effect, [15]because the law brings about wrath; for where there is no law *there is* no transgression. [16]Therefore *it is* of faith that *it might be* according to grace, so that the promise might be sure to all the seed, not only to those who are of the law, but also to those who are of the faith of Abraham, who is the father of us all [17](as it is written, *"I have made you a father of many nations"*) in the presence of Him whom he believed—God, who gives life to the dead and calls those things which do not exist as though they did; [18]who, contrary to hope, in hope believed, so that he became the father of many nations, according to what was spoken, *"So shall your descen-*

dants be." [19]And not being weak in faith, he did not consider his own body, already dead (since he was about a hundred years old), and the deadness of Sarah's womb. [20]He did not waver at the promise of God through unbelief, but was strengthened in faith, giving glory to God, [21]and being fully convinced that what He had promised He was also able to perform. [22]And therefore *"it was accounted to him for righteousness."*

[23]Now it was not written for his sake alone that it was imputed to him, [24]but also for us. It shall be imputed to us who believe in Him who raised up Jesus our Lord from the dead, [25]who was delivered up because of our offenses, and was raised because of our justification.

CHAPTER **5** **FINDING PEACE AND JOY.** Therefore, having been justified by faith, we have peace with God through our Lord Jesus Christ, [2]through whom also we have access by faith into this grace in which we stand, and rejoice in hope of the glory of God. [3]And not only *that,* but we also glory in tribulations, knowing that tribulation produces perseverance; [4]and perseverance, character; and character, hope. [5]Now hope does not disappoint, because the love of God has been poured out in our hearts by the Holy Spirit who was given to us. [6]For when we were still without strength, in due time Christ died for the ungodly. [7]For scarcely for a righteous man will one die; yet perhaps for a good man someone would even dare to die. [8]But God demonstrates His own love toward us, in that while we were still sinners, Christ died for us. [9]Much more then, having now been justified

BEFORE

5:8 *While we were still sinners*—these are amazing words. God sent Jesus to die for us not because we were good enough, but because he loved us so much. Whenever you feel uncertain about God's love for y● remember that God loved you even before you turned to him.

by His blood, we shall be saved from wrath through Him. [10]For if when we were enemies we were reconciled to God through the death of His Son, much more, having been reconciled, we shall be saved by His life. [11]And not only *that,* but we also rejoice in God through our Lord Jesus Christ, through whom we have now received the reconciliation.

[12]Therefore, just as through one man sin entered the world, and death through sin, and thus death spread to all men, because all sinned— [13](For until the law sin was in the world, but sin is not imputed when there is no law. [14]Nevertheless death reigned from Adam to Moses, even over those who had not sinned according to the likeness of the transgression of Adam, who is a type of Him who was to come. [15]But the free gift *is* not like the offense. For if by the one man's offense many died, much more the grace of God and the gift by the grace of the one Man, Jesus Christ, abounded to many. [16]And the gift *is* not like *that which came* through the one who sinned. For the judgment *which came* from one *offense resulted* in condemnation, but the free gift *which came* from many offenses *resulted* in justification. [17]For if by the one man's offense death reigned through the one, much more those who receive abundance of grace and of the gift of righteousness will reign in life through the One, Jesus Christ.)

[18]Therefore, as through one man's offense *judgment* came to all men, resulting in condemnation, even so through one Man's righteous act *the free gift came* to all men, resulting in justification of life. [19]For as by one man's disobedience many were made sinners, so also by one Man's obedience many will be made righteous.

[20]Moreover the law entered that the offense might abound. But where sin abounded, grace abounded much more, [21]so that as sin reigned in death, even so grace might reign through righteousness to eternal life through Jesus Christ our Lord.

CHAPTER **6** **CHRIST BROKE SIN'S POWER.** What shall we say then? Shall we continue in sin that grace may abound? [2]Certainly not! How shall we who died to sin live any longer in it? [3]Or do you not know that as many of us as were baptized into Christ Jesus were baptized into His death? [4]Therefore we were buried with Him through baptism into death, that just as Christ was raised from the dead by the glory of the Father, even so we also should walk in newness of life.

[5]For if we have been united together in the likeness of His death, certainly we also shall be *in the likeness* of *His* resurrection, [6]knowing this, that our old man was crucified with *Him,* that the body of sin might be done away with, that we should no longer be slaves of sin. [7]For he who has died has been freed from sin. [8]Now if we died with Christ, we believe that we shall also live with Him, [9]knowing that Christ, having been raised from the dead, dies no more. Death no longer has dominion over Him. [10]For *the death* that He died, He died to sin once for all; but *the life* that He lives, He lives to God. [11]Likewise you also, reckon yourselves to be dead indeed to sin, but alive to God in Christ Jesus our Lord.

[12]Therefore do not let sin reign in your mortal body,

that you should obey it in its lusts. [13]And do not present your members *as* instruments of unrighteousness to sin, but present yourselves to God as being alive from the dead, and your members *as* instruments of righteousness to God. [14]For sin shall not have dominion over you, for you are not under law but under grace.

[15]What then? Shall we sin because we are not under law but under grace? Certainly not! [16]Do you not know that to whom you present yourselves slaves to obey, you are that one's slaves whom you obey, whether of sin *leading* to death, or of obedience *leading* to righteousness? [17]But God be thanked that *though* you were slaves of sin, yet you obeyed from the heart that form of doctrine to which you were delivered. [18]And having been set free from sin, you became slaves of righteousness. [19]I speak in human *terms* because of the weakness of your flesh. For just as you presented your members *as* slaves of uncleanness, and of lawlessness *leading* to *more* lawlessness, so now present your members *as* slaves *of* righteousness for holiness.

◣▬▬▬▬▬ SHARKS

7:9-11 If people feel fine without the law, why did God give it? Because sin is real and dangerous. Imagine a sunny day at the beach. You have just plunged into the surf and you've never felt better. Suddenly you notice a sign on the pier: "No swimming: Sharks in water." Your day is ruined. Is it the sign's fault? Are you angry with the people who put it up? Of course not. The law is like the sign. It is essential, and we are grateful for it—but it doesn't get rid of the sharks.

[20]For when you were slaves of sin, you were free in regard to righteousness. [21]What fruit did you have then in the things of which you are now ashamed? For the end of those things *is* death. [22]But now having been set free from sin, and having become slaves of God, you have your fruit to holiness, and the end, everlasting life. [23]For the wages of sin *is* death, but the gift of God *is* eternal life in Christ Jesus our Lord.

CHAPTER **7** **YOU CAN SERVE GOD.** Or do you not know, brethren (for I speak to those who know the law), that the law has dominion over a man as long as he lives? [2]For the woman who has a husband is bound by the law to *her* husband as long as he lives. But if the husband dies, she is released from the law of *her* husband. [3]So then if, while *her* husband lives, she marries another man, she will be called an adulteress; but if her husband dies, she is free from that law, so that she is no adulteress, though she has married another man. [4]Therefore, my brethren, you also have become dead to the law through the body of Christ, that you may be married to another—to Him who was raised from the dead, that we should bear fruit to God. [5]For when we were in the flesh, the sinful passions which were aroused by the law were at work in our members to bear fruit to death. [6]But now we have been delivered from the law, having died to what we were held by, so that we should serve in the newness of the Spirit and not *in* the oldness of the letter.

[7]What shall we say then? *Is* the law sin? Certainly not! On the contrary, I would not have known sin except

through the law. For I would not have known covetousness unless the law had said, *"You shall not covet."* [8]But sin, taking opportunity by the commandment, produced in me all *manner of evil* desire. For apart from the law sin *was* dead. [9]I was alive once without the law, but when the commandment came, sin revived and I died. [10]And the commandment, which *was* to *bring* life, I found to *bring* death. [11]For sin, taking occasion by the commandment, deceived me, and by it killed *me.* [12]Therefore the law *is* holy, and the commandment holy and just and good.

STRUGGLE

7:15 This is more than the cry of one desperate man—it describes the experience of any Christian struggling against sin. We must never underestimate the power of sin. Satan is a crafty tempter, and we have a great ability to make excuses. Instead of trying to overcome sin with human willpower, we must take hold of the tremendous power of Christ that is available to us. This is God's provision for victory over sin; he sends the Holy Spirit to live in us and give us power. And when we fall, he lovingly reaches out to us and helps us get up again.

[13]Has then what is good become death to me? Certainly not! But sin, that it might appear sin, was producing death in me through what is good, so that sin through the commandment might become exceedingly sinful. [14]For we know that the law is spiritual, but I am carnal, sold under sin. [15]For what I am doing, I do not understand. For what I will to do, that I do not practice; but what I hate, that I do. [16]If, then, I do what I will not to do, I agree with the law that *it is* good. [17]But now, *it is* no longer I who do it, but sin that dwells in me. [18]For I know that in me (that is, in my flesh) nothing good dwells; for to will is present with me, but *how* to perform what is good I do not find. [19]For the good that I will *to do,* I do not do; but the evil I will not *to do,* that I practice. [20]Now if I do what I will not *to do,* it is no longer I who do it, but sin that dwells in me.

[21]I find then a law, that evil is present with me, the one who wills to do good. [22]For I delight in the law of God according to the inward man. [23]But I see another law in my members, warring against the law of my mind, and bringing me into captivity to the law of sin which is in my members. [24]O wretched man that I am! Who will deliver me from this body of death? [25]I thank God—through Jesus Christ our Lord!

So then, with the mind I myself serve the law of God, but with the flesh the law of sin.

CHAPTER 8 THE HOLY SPIRIT FREES US FROM SIN.

There is therefore now no condemnation to those who are in Christ Jesus, who do not walk according to the flesh, but according to the Spirit. [2]For the law of the Spirit of life in Christ Jesus has made me free from the law of sin and death. [3]For what the law could not do in that it was weak through the flesh, God *did* by sending His own Son in the likeness of sinful flesh, on account of sin: He condemned sin in the flesh, [4]that the righteous requirement of the law might be fulfilled in us who do not walk according to the flesh but according to the Spirit. [5]For those who live according to the flesh set their minds on the things of the flesh, but those *who live* according to the Spirit, the things of the Spirit. [6]For to be carnally minded *is* death, but to be spiritually minded *is* life and peace. [7]Because the carnal mind *is* enmity against God; for it is not subject to the law of God, nor indeed can be. [8]So then, those who are in the flesh cannot please God.

[9]But you are not in the flesh but in the Spirit, if indeed the Spirit of God dwells in you. Now if anyone does not have the Spirit of Christ, he is not His. [10]And if Christ *is* in you, the body *is* dead because of sin, but the Spirit *is* life because of righteousness. [11]But if the Spirit of Him who raised Jesus from the dead dwells in you, He who raised Christ from the dead will also give life to your mortal bodies through His Spirit who dwells in you.

[12]Therefore, brethren, we are debtors—not to the flesh, to live according to the flesh. [13]For if you live according to the flesh you will die; but if by the Spirit you put to death the deeds of the body, you will live. [14]For as many as are led by the Spirit of God, these are sons of God. [15]For you did not receive the spirit of bondage again to fear, but you received the Spirit of adoption by whom we cry out, "Abba, Father." [16]The Spirit Himself bears witness with our spirit that we are children of God, [17]and if children, then heirs—heirs of God and joint heirs with Christ, if indeed we suffer with *Him,* that we may also be glorified together.

[18]For I consider that the sufferings of this present time are not worthy *to be compared* with the glory which shall be revealed in us. [19]For the earnest expectation of the creation eagerly waits for the revealing of the sons of God. [20]For the creation was subjected to futility, not willingly, but because of Him who subjected *it* in hope; [21]because the creation itself also will be delivered from the bondage of corruption into the glorious liberty of the children of God. [22]For we know that the whole creation groans and labors with birth pangs together until now. [23]Not only *that,* but we also who have the firstfruits of the Spirit, even we ourselves groan within ourselves, eagerly waiting for the adoption, the redemption of our body. [24]For we were saved in this hope, but hope that is seen is not hope; for why does one still hope for what he sees? [25]But if we hope for what we do not see, we eagerly wait for *it* with perseverance.

[26]Likewise the Spirit also helps in our weaknesses. For we do not know what we should pray for as we ought, but the Spirit Himself makes intercession for us with groanings which cannot be uttered. [27]Now He who searches the hearts knows what the mind of the Spirit *is,* because He

LONG-RANGE

8:28 God works out all things—not just isolated incidents—for good. This does not mean that all that happens to us is good. Evil i prevalent in our fallen world, but God is able to turn it around for long-range good. Note that God is not working to make us happy fulfill his purpose. Note also that this promise is not for everybody be claimed only by those who love God and are fitting into his pla Such people have a new perspective, a new mind-set. They trust i not life's treasures; they look to their security in heaven, not on ea they learn to accept pain and persecution rather than resent it, be brings them closer to God.

What then shall we say to these things?

If GOD IS FOR US who can be against us?

were accursed from Christ for my brethren, my countrymen according to the flesh, [4]who are Israelites, to whom *pertain* the adoption, the glory, the covenants, the giving of the law, the service *of God*, and the promises; [5]of whom *are* the fathers and from whom, according to the flesh, Christ *came*, who is over all, *the* eternally blessed God. Amen.

[6]But it is not that the word of God has taken no effect. For they *are* not all Israel who *are* of Israel, [7]nor *are they* all children because they are the seed of Abraham; but, *"In Isaac your seed shall be called."* [8]That is, those who *are* the children of the flesh, these *are* not the children of God; but the children of the promise are counted as the seed. [9]For this *is* the word of promise: *"At this time I will come and Sarah shall have a son."*

[10]And not only *this*, but when Rebecca also had conceived by one man, *even* by our father Isaac [11](for *the children* not yet being born, nor having done any good or

makes intercession for the saints according to *the will of God*.

[28]And we know that all things work together for good to those who love God, to those who are the called according to *His* purpose. [29]For whom He foreknew, He also predestined *to be* conformed to the image of His Son, that He might be the firstborn among many brethren. [30]Moreover whom He predestined, these He also called; whom He called, these He also justified; and whom He justified, these He also glorified.

[31]What then shall we say to these things? If God *is* for us, who *can be* against us? [32]He who did not spare His own Son, but delivered Him up for us all, how shall He not with Him also freely give us all things? [33]Who shall bring a charge against God's elect? *It is* God who justifies. [34]Who *is* he who condemns? *It is* Christ who died, and furthermore is also risen, who is even at the right hand of God, who also makes intercession for us. [35]Who shall separate us from the love of Christ? *Shall* tribulation, or distress, or persecution, or famine, or nakedness, or peril, or sword? [36]As it is written:

*"For Your sake we are killed all day long;
We are accounted as sheep for the slaughter."*

[37]Yet in all these things we are more than conquerors through Him who loved us. [38]For I am persuaded that neither death nor life, nor angels nor principalities nor powers, nor things present nor things to come, [39]nor height nor depth, nor any other created thing, shall be able to separate us from the love of God which is in Christ Jesus our Lord.

CHAPTER 9 GOD IS SOVEREIGN.

I tell the truth in Christ, I am not lying, my conscience also bearing me witness in the Holy Spirit, [2]that I have great sorrow and continual grief in my heart. [3]For I could wish that I myself

---

Since becoming a Christian, it seems like I am always fighting against certain thoughts and habits that I used to never give a second thought about. Why is this happening?

I WONDER...

Picture your life as a door. Before you became a Christian, your sins were like nails being pounded into the door and left there. When you asked Christ to forgive you, all of the nails you had collected were removed! Unfortunately, what was left was a door full of holes, not very pleasant to look at and not very useful.

But God began patching up the holes! More accurately, he began to heal the scars left by sin, making your life into a door that will look unscarred after years of constant pounding. We truly can become a new creation (see 2 Corinthians 5:17).

That is why it is so important for people to come to know Christ's forgiveness early in life. Because we inherited a sinful nature from Adam (Romans 5:12), time and wrong choices can pound some pretty large nails into our life. And those scars may take longer to heal. Paul knew this all too well, as you can see if you read his words in Romans 7:15–8:2. Like him, we all experience the tug to give in again to our sin nature, but our new nature moves us to resist.

So what you are experiencing is a new sensitivity to sin. Since sin wants to "drive a hole" in you and Christ wants to keep you unscarred by the effects of sin, it is no longer comfortable to ignore the constant pounding. Confessing your sin will always remove the nail.

This new sensitivity to sin means two things. First, it is a definite sign that God's Holy Spirit has truly entered your life (Romans 8:9). It is likely you would still be numb to the nails (sin) if you had rejected Christ's forgiveness. Second, it means that God is reminding you of his great love for you (Romans 8:38-39). Now your conscience advises you where you could stray off course. He does not want you to be left scarred by the consequences of your sin, so he begins at the source of it—your thoughts.

FOREVER TRYING

9:31-33 Sometimes we are like these people, trying to get right with God by keeping his laws. We may think church attendance, church work, giving offerings, and being nice will be enough. After all, we've played by the rules, haven't we? But Paul's words sting—this approach never succeeds. Paul explains that God's plan is not for those who try to earn his favor by being good; it is for those who realize they can never be good enough and so must depend on Christ. Only by putting our faith in what Jesus Christ has done will we be saved. If we do that, we will never be "put to shame" or be disappointed.

evil, that the purpose of God according to election might stand, not of works but of Him who calls), [12]it was said to her, *"The older shall serve the younger."* [13]As it is written, *"Jacob I have loved, but Esau I have hated."*

[14]What shall we say then? *Is there* unrighteousness with God? Certainly not! [15]For He says to Moses, *"I will have mercy on whomever I will have mercy, and I will have compassion on whomever I will have compassion."* [16]So then *it is* not of him who wills, nor of him who runs, but of God who shows mercy. [17]For the Scripture says to the Pharaoh, *"For this very purpose I have raised you up, that I may show My power in you, and that My name may be declared in all the earth."* [18]Therefore He has mercy on whom He wills, and whom He wills He hardens.

[19]You will say to me then, "Why does He still find fault? For who has resisted His will?" [20]But indeed, O man, who are you to reply against God? Will the thing formed say to him who formed *it*, "Why have you made me like this?" [21]Does not the potter have power over the clay, from the same lump to make one vessel for honor and another for dishonor?

[22]*What* if God, wanting to show *His* wrath and to make His power known, endured with much longsuffering the vessels of wrath prepared for destruction, [23]and that He might make known the riches of His glory on the vessels of mercy, which He had prepared beforehand for glory, [24]*even* us whom He called, not of the Jews only, but also of the Gentiles?

[25]As He says also in Hosea:

"I will call them My people, who were not My people,
And her beloved, who was not beloved."

[26] *"And it shall come to pass in the place where it was*
said to them,
'You are not My people,'
There they shall be called sons of the living God."

[27]Isaiah also cries out concerning Israel:

"Though the number of the children of Israel be as
the sand of the sea,
The remnant will be saved.
[28] *For He will finish the work and cut it short in*
righteousness,
Because the LORD will make a short work upon the
earth."

[29]And as Isaiah said before:

"Unless the LORD of Sabaoth had left us a seed,
We would have become like Sodom,
And we would have been made like Gomorrah."

[30]What shall we say then? That Gentiles, who did not pursue righteousness, have attained to righteousness, even the righteousness of faith; [31]but Israel, pursuing the law of righteousness, has not attained to the law of righteousness. [32]Why? Because *they did* not *seek it* by faith, but as it were, by the works of the law. For they stumbled at that stumbling stone. [33]As it is written:

"Behold, I lay in Zion a stumbling stone and rock of
offense,
And whoever believes on Him will not be put to
shame."

CHAPTER 10 SOME DON'T UNDERSTAND.

Brethren, my heart's desire and prayer to God for Israel is that they may be saved. [2]For I bear them witness that they have a zeal for God, but not according to knowledge. [3]For they being ignorant of God's righteousness, and seeking to establish their own righteousness, have not submitted to the righteousness of God. [4]For Christ *is* the end of the law for righteousness to everyone who believes.

SO CLOSE

10:8-12 Have you ever been asked, "How do I become a Christian These verses give you the beautiful answer—salvation is as close as own heart and mouth. People think it must be a complicated process it isn't. If they believe in their hearts and say with their mouths that Christ is the risen Lord, they will be saved.

[5]For Moses writes about the righteousness which is of the law, *"The man who does those things shall live by them."* [6]But the righteousness of faith speaks in this way, *"Do not say in your heart, 'Who will ascend into heaven?'"* (that is, to bring Christ down *from above*) [7]or, *"'Who will descend into the abyss?'"* (that is, to bring Christ up from the dead). [8]But what does it say? *"The word is near you, in your mouth and in your heart"* (that is, the word of faith which we preach): [9]that if you confess with your mouth the Lord Jesus and believe in your heart that God has raised Him from the dead, you will be saved. [10]For with the heart one believes unto righteousness, and with the mouth confession is made unto salvation. [11]For the Scripture says, *"Whoever believes on Him will not be put to shame."* [12]For there is no distinction between Jew and Greek, for the same Lord over all is rich to all who call upon Him. [13]For *"whoever calls on the name of the LORD shall be saved."*

[14]How then shall they call on Him in whom they have not believed? And how shall they believe in Him of whom they have not heard? And how shall they hear without a preacher? [15]And how shall they preach unless they are sent? As it is written:

"How beautiful are the feet of those who preach the
gospel of peace,
Who bring glad tidings of good things!"

[16]But they have not all obeyed the gospel. For Isaiah says, *"LORD, who has believed our report?"* [17]So then faith *comes* by hearing, and hearing by the word of God. [18]But I say, have they not heard? Yes indeed:

"Their sound has gone out to all the earth,
And their words to the ends of the world."

[19] But I say, did Israel not know? First Moses says:

"I will provoke you to jealousy by those who are not a
nation,
I will move you to anger by a foolish nation."

[20] But Isaiah is very bold and says:

"I was found by those who did not seek Me;
I was made manifest to those who did not ask for Me."

[21] But to Israel he says:

"All day long I have stretched out My hands
To a disobedient and contrary people."

CHAPTER **11** **GOD'S KINDNESS FOR ISRAEL.** I say
then, has God cast away His people? Certainly not! For I
also am an Israelite, of the seed of Abraham, *of* the tribe
of Benjamin. [2] God has not cast away His people whom
He foreknew. Or do you not know what the Scripture says
of Elijah, how he pleads with God against Israel, saying,
[3] *"LORD, they have killed Your prophets and torn down
Your altars, and I alone am left, and they seek my life"*?
[4] But what does the divine response say to him? *"I have
reserved for Myself seven thousand men who have not
bowed the knee to Baal."* [5] Even so then, at this present
time there is a remnant according to the election of
grace. [6] And if by grace, then *it is* no longer of works;
otherwise grace is no longer grace. But if *it is* of works, it
is no longer grace; otherwise work is no longer work.
[7] What then? Israel has not obtained what it seeks; but
the elect have obtained it, and the rest were blinded. [8] Just
as it is written:

"God has given them a spirit of stupor,
Eyes that they should not see
And ears that they should not hear,
To this very day."

[9] And David says:

"Let their table become a snare and a trap,
A stumbling block and a recompense to them.
[10] Let their eyes be darkened, so that they do not see,
And bow down their back always."

[11] I say then, have they stumbled that they should fall?
Certainly not! But through their fall, to provoke them to
jealousy, salvation *has come* to the Gentiles. [12] Now if their
fall *is* riches for the world, and their failure riches for the
Gentiles, how much more their fullness!
[13] For I speak to you Gentiles; inasmuch as I am an
apostle to the Gentiles, I magnify my ministry, [14] if by any
means I may provoke to jealousy *those who are* my flesh
and save some of them. [15] For if their being cast away *is*
the reconciling of the world, what *will* their acceptance
be but life from the dead?
[16] For if the firstfruit *is* holy, the lump *is* also *holy;* and
if the root *is* holy, so *are* the branches. [17] And if some of the
branches were broken off, and you, being a wild olive
tree, were grafted in among them, and with them became

a partaker of the root and fatness of the olive tree, [18] do
not boast against the branches. But if you do boast, *remember that* you do not support the root, but the root
supports you.
[19] You will say then, "Branches were broken off that I
might be grafted in." [20] Well *said.* Because of unbelief they
were broken off, and you stand by faith. Do not be
haughty, but fear. [21] For if God did not spare the natural
branches, He may not spare you either. [22] Therefore consider the goodness and severity of God: on those who fell,
severity; but toward you, goodness, if you continue in *His*
goodness. Otherwise you also will be cut off. [23] And they
also, if they do not continue in unbelief, will be grafted
in, for God is able to graft them in again. [24] For if you were
cut out of the olive tree which is wild by nature, and were
grafted contrary to nature into a cultivated olive tree,
how much more will these, who *are* natural *branches,* be
grafted into their own olive tree?

FREE

11:6 This great truth can be hard to grasp. Do you think it's easier for
God to love you when you're good? Do you secretly suspect God chose
you because you deserved to be chosen? Do you think some people's
behavior is so bad that God couldn't possibly save them? If you ever
think this way, you don't entirely understand the Good News that
salvation is a free gift. It cannot be earned, in whole or in part; it can
only be accepted with thankfulness and praise.

[25] For I do not desire, brethren, that you should be
ignorant of this mystery, lest you should be wise in your
own opinion, that blindness in part has happened to
Israel until the fullness of the Gentiles has come in. [26] And
so all Israel will be saved, as it is written:

"The Deliverer will come out of Zion,
And He will turn away ungodliness from Jacob;
[27] For this is My covenant with them,
When I take away their sins."

[28] Concerning the gospel *they are* enemies for your
sake, but concerning the election *they are* beloved for the
sake of the fathers. [29] For the gifts and the calling of God
are irrevocable. [30] For as you were once disobedient to
God, yet have now obtained mercy through their disobedience, [31] even so these also have now been disobedient,
that through the mercy shown you they also may obtain
mercy. [32] For God has committed them all to disobedience, that He might have mercy on all.
[33] Oh, the depth of the riches both of the wisdom and
knowledge of God! How unsearchable *are* His judgments
and His ways past finding out!

[34] "For who has known the mind of the LORD?
Or who has become His counselor?"
[35] "Or who has first given to Him
And it shall be repaid to him?"

[36] For of Him and through Him and to Him *are* all
things, to whom *be* glory forever. Amen.

CHAPTER **12** **GIVE YOUR LIFE TO GOD.** I beseech
you therefore, brethren, by the mercies of God, that you

BRAND NEW

12:2 Christians are called to "not be conformed to this world," with its behavior and customs that are usually selfish and often corrupting. Many Christians wisely decide that much worldly behavior is off-limits for them. Our refusal to conform to the world, however, must go even deeper than the level of behavior and customs—it must be firmly founded in our mind—"transformed by the renewing of your mind." It is possible to avoid most worldly customs and still be proud, covetous, selfish, stubborn, and arrogant. Only when our mind is renewed by the new attitude Christ gives us are we truly transformed. If our character is like Christ's, we can be sure our behavior will honor God.

present your bodies a living sacrifice, holy, acceptable to God, *which is* your reasonable service. [2]And do not be conformed to this world, but be transformed by the renewing of your mind, that you may prove what *is* that good and acceptable and perfect will of God.

[3]For I say, through the grace given to me, to everyone who is among you, not to think *of himself* more highly than he ought to think, but to think soberly, as God has dealt to each one a measure of faith. [4]For as we have many members in one body, but all the members do not have the same function, [5]so we, *being* many, are one body in Christ, and individually members of one another. [6]Having then gifts differing according to the grace that is given to us, *let us use them:* if prophecy, *let us prophesy* in proportion to our faith; [7]or ministry, *let us use it* in *our* ministering; he who teaches, in teaching; [8]he who exhorts, in exhortation; he who gives, with liberality; he who leads, with diligence; he who shows mercy, with cheerfulness.

GIFTS

12:4-8 God gives us gifts so we can build up his church. To use them effectively, we must (1) realize that all gifts and abilities come from God; (2) understand that not everyone has the same gifts; (3) know who we are and what we do best; (4) dedicate our gifts to God's service and not to our personal success; (5) be willing to spend our gifts generously, not holding back anything from God's service.

[9]*Let* love *be* without hypocrisy. Abhor what is evil. Cling to what is good. [10]*Be* kindly affectionate to one another with brotherly love, in honor giving preference to one another; [11]not lagging in diligence, fervent in spirit, serving the Lord; [12]rejoicing in hope, patient in tribulation, continuing steadfastly in prayer; [13]distributing to the needs of the saints, given to hospitality.

[14]Bless those who persecute you; bless and do not curse. [15]Rejoice with those who rejoice, and weep with those who weep. [16]Be of the same mind toward one another. Do not set your mind on high things, but associate with the humble. Do not be wise in your own opinion.

[17]Repay no one evil for evil. Have regard for good things in the sight of all men. [18]If it is possible, as much as depends on you, live peaceably with all men. [19]Beloved, do not avenge yourselves, but *rather* give place to wrath; for it is written, "Vengeance is Mine, I will repay," says the Lord. [20]Therefore

"If your enemy is hungry, feed him;
If he is thirsty, give him a drink;
For in so doing you will heap coals of fire on his head."

[21]Do not be overcome by evil, but overcome evil with good.

CHAPTER 13 OBEY THE GOVERNMENT.

Let every soul be subject to the governing authorities. For there is no authority except from God, and the authorities that exist are appointed by God. [2]Therefore whoever resists the authority resists the ordinance of God, and those who resist will bring judgment on themselves. [3]For rulers are not a terror to good works, but to evil. Do you want to be unafraid of the authority? Do what is good, and you will have praise from the same. [4]For he is God's minister to you for good. But if you do evil, be afraid; for he does not bear the sword in vain; for he is God's minister, an avenger to *execute* wrath on him who practices evil.

IN DEBT

13:8 Why is love for others considered something we owe? We ar permanently in debt to Christ for the lavish love he has poured out The only way we can even begin to repay this debt is by loving othe turn. Because Christ's love will always be infinitely greater than our will always have the obligation to love our neighbors.

[5]Therefore *you* must be subject, not only because of wrath but also for conscience' sake. [6]For because of this you also pay taxes, for they are God's ministers attending continually to this very thing. [7]Render therefore to all their due: taxes to whom taxes *are due,* customs to whom customs, fear to whom fear, honor to whom honor.

[8]Owe no one anything except to love one another, for he who loves another has fulfilled the law. [9]For the commandments, "You shall not commit adultery," "You shall not murder," "You shall not steal," "You shall not bear false witness," "You shall not covet," and if *there is* any other commandment, are *all* summed up in this saying, namely, "You shall love your neighbor as yourself." [10]Love does no harm to a neighbor; therefore love *is* the fulfillment of the law.

[11]And *do* this, knowing the time, that now *it is* high time to awake out of sleep; for now our salvation *is* nearer than when we *first* believed. [12]The night is far spent, the day is at hand. Therefore let us cast off the works of darkness, and let us put on the armor of light. [13]Let us walk properly, as in the day, not in revelry and drunkenness, not in lewdness and lust, not in strife and envy. [14]But put on the Lord Jesus Christ, and make no provision for the flesh, to *fulfill its* lusts.

CHAPTER 14 DON'T CRITICIZE OTHER CHRISTIANS.

Receive one who is weak in the faith, *but* not to disputes over doubtful things. [2]For one believes he may eat all

SELF-INVENTORY

14:1 Who is weak in faith and who is strong? We are all weak in son areas and strong in others. Our faith is strong in an area if we can survive contact with sin without falling into it. It is weak if we must avo certain activities or places in order to protect our spiritual life. We need take a self-inventory to find our weaknesses and strengths.

In areas of strength, we should not fear that we will be defiled by t world. Rather, from our position of strength we should lead the world. areas of weakness, however, we need to play it safe. If we have a stror faith but shelter it, we are not doing Christ's work in the world. If we ho a weak faith but expose it, we are being extremely foolish.

things, but he who is weak eats *only* vegetables. ³Let not him who eats despise him who does not eat, and let not him who does not eat judge him who eats; for God has received him. ⁴Who are you to judge another's servant? To his own master he stands or falls. Indeed, he will be made to stand, for God is able to make him stand.

⁵One person esteems *one* day above another; another esteems every day *alike*. Let each be fully convinced in his own mind. ⁶He who observes the day, observes *it* to the Lord; and he who does not observe the day, to the Lord he does not observe *it*. He who eats, eats to the Lord, for he gives God thanks; and he who does not eat, to the Lord he does not eat, and gives God thanks. ⁷For none of us lives to himself, and no one dies to himself. ⁸For if we live, we live to the Lord; and if we die, we die to the Lord. Therefore, whether we live or die, we are the Lord's. ⁹For to this end Christ died and rose and lived again, that He might be Lord of both the dead and the living. ¹⁰But why do you judge your brother? Or why do you show contempt for your brother? For we shall all stand before the judgment seat of Christ. ¹¹For it is written:

> *"As I live, says the LORD,*
> *Every knee shall bow to Me,*
> *And every tongue shall confess to God."*

¹²So then each of us shall give account of himself to God. ¹³Therefore let us not judge one another anymore, but rather resolve this, not to put a stumbling block or a cause to fall in *our* brother's way.

¹⁴I know and am convinced by the Lord Jesus that *there is* nothing unclean of itself; but to him who considers anything to be unclean, to him *it is* unclean. ¹⁵Yet if your brother is grieved because of *your* food, you are no longer walking in love. Do not destroy with your food the one for whom Christ died. ¹⁶Therefore do not let your good be spoken of as evil; ¹⁷for the kingdom of God is not eating and drinking, but righteousness and peace and joy in the Holy Spirit. ¹⁸For he who serves Christ in these things *is* acceptable to God and approved by men.

¹⁹Therefore let us pursue the things *which make* for peace and the things by which one may edify another. ²⁰Do not destroy the work of God for the sake of food. All things indeed *are* pure, but *it is* evil for the man who eats with offense. ²¹*It is* good neither to eat meat nor drink wine nor *do anything* by which your brother stumbles or is offended or is made weak. ²²Do you have faith? Have *it* to yourself before God. Happy *is* he who does not condemn himself in what he approves. ²³But he who doubts is condemned if he eats, because *he does* not *eat* from faith; for whatever *is* not from faith is sin.

CHAPTER **15** THINK OF OTHERS
FIRST. We then who are strong ought to bear with the scruples of the weak,

and not to please ourselves. ²Let each of us please *his* neighbor for *his* good, leading to edification. ³For even Christ did not please Himself; but as it is written, *"The reproaches of those who reproached You fell on Me."* ⁴For whatever things were written before were written for our learning, that we through the patience and comfort of the Scriptures might have hope. ⁵Now may the God of patience and comfort grant you to be like-minded toward one another, according to Christ Jesus, ⁶that you may with one mind *and* one mouth glorify the God and Father of our Lord Jesus Christ.

◄▬▬▬ SILENCE
14:23–15:6 We try to steer clear of actions forbidden by Scripture, of course. But when Scripture is silent, we should follow our conscience. When God shows us something is wrong for us, we should avoid it—but we should not look down on other Christians who exercise their freedom in those areas.

⁷Therefore receive one another, just as Christ also received us, to the glory of God. ⁸Now I say that Jesus Christ has become a servant to the circumcision for the truth of God, to confirm the promises *made* to the fathers, ⁹and that the Gentiles might glorify God for *His* mercy, as it is written:

> *"For this reason I will confess to You among the*
> *Gentiles,*
> *And sing to Your name."*

¹⁰And again he says:

> *"Rejoice, O Gentiles, with His people!"*

¹¹And again:

> *"Praise the LORD, all you Gentiles!*
> *Laud Him, all you peoples!"*

¹²And again, Isaiah says:

"Here's what I did..."

My boyfriend and I didn't have a very good relationship; we couldn't communicate much. I decided that it was time to break up. I tried to be as tactful as I could; I didn't want to hurt his feelings. His reaction was to call me a couple of names that were hurtful, demeaning, and completely untrue. Not only did he say these things to me, he said them to other people.

That enraged me. I thought of different ways to respond, to get even. But then I recalled a verse that tells us not to take revenge. I looked up Romans 12:19; it says, "Do not avenge yourselves, . . . for it is written, 'Vengeance is Mine, I will repay,' says the Lord." This helped me to remove any thoughts of revenge from my mind and to concentrate instead on forgiving him and praying for him. As I do this, concern for his spiritual life overshadows my feelings of anger and hurt.

Lavonne

AGE 16

15:17 Paul was not proud of what he had done, but of what God had done through him. Being proud of God's work is not a sin—it is worship. If you are not sure whether your pride is selfish or holy, ask yourself this question: Are you just as proud of what God is doing through other people as of what he is doing through you?

> *"There shall be a root of Jesse;*
> *And He who shall rise to reign over the Gentiles,*
> *In Him the Gentiles shall hope."*

¹³Now may the God of hope fill you with all joy and peace in believing, that you may abound in hope by the power of the Holy Spirit.

¹⁴Now I myself am confident concerning you, my brethren, that you also are full of goodness, filled with all knowledge, able also to admonish one another. ¹⁵Nevertheless, brethren, I have written more boldly to you on *some* points, as reminding you, because of the grace given to me by God, ¹⁶that I might be a minister of Jesus Christ to the Gentiles, ministering the gospel of God, that the offering of the Gentiles might be acceptable, sanctified by the Holy Spirit. ¹⁷Therefore I have reason to glory in Christ Jesus in the things *which pertain* to God. ¹⁸For I will not dare to speak of any of those things which Christ has not accomplished through me, in word and deed, to make the Gentiles obedient— ¹⁹in mighty signs and wonders, by the power of the Spirit of God, so that from Jerusalem and round about to Illyricum I have fully preached the gospel of Christ. ²⁰And so I have made it my aim to preach the gospel, not where Christ was named, lest I should build on another man's foundation, ²¹but as it is written:

> *"To whom He was not announced, they shall see;*
> *And those who have not heard shall understand."*

²²For this reason I also have been much hindered from coming to you. ²³But now no longer having a place in these parts, and having a great desire these many years to come to you, ²⁴whenever I journey to Spain, I shall come to you. For I hope to see you on my journey, and to be helped on my way there by you, if first I may enjoy your *company* for a while. ²⁵But now I am going to Jerusalem to minister to the saints. ²⁶For it pleased those from Macedonia and Achaia to make a certain contribution for the poor among the saints who are in Jerusalem. ²⁷It pleased them indeed, and they are their debtors. For if the Gentiles have been partakers of their spiritual things, their duty is also to minister to them in material things. ²⁸Therefore, when I have performed this and have sealed to them this fruit, I shall go by way of you to Spain. ²⁹But I know that when I come to you, I shall come in the fullness of the blessing of the gospel of Christ.

³⁰Now I beg you, brethren, through the Lord Jesus Christ, and through the love of the Spirit, that you strive together with me in prayers to God for me, ³¹that I may be delivered from those in Judea who do not believe, and that my service for Jerusalem may be acceptable to the saints, ³²that I may come to you with joy by the will of God, and may be refreshed together with you. ³³Now the God of peace *be* with you all. Amen.

CHAPTER **16** PAUL GREETS HIS FRIENDS. I commend to you Phoebe our sister, who is a servant of the church in Cenchrea, ²that you may receive her in the Lord in a manner worthy of the saints, and assist her in whatever business she has need of you; for indeed she has been a helper of many and of myself also.

³Greet Priscilla and Aquila, my fellow workers in Christ Jesus, ⁴who risked their own necks for my life, to whom not only I give thanks, but also all the churches of the Gentiles. ⁵Likewise *greet* the church that is in their house.

Greet my beloved Epaenetus, who is the firstfruits of Achaia to Christ. ⁶Greet Mary, who labored much for us. ⁷Greet Andronicus and Junia, my countrymen and my fellow prisoners, who are of note among the apostles, who also were in Christ before me.

⁸Greet Amplias, my beloved in the Lord. ⁹Greet Urbanus, our fellow worker in Christ, and Stachys, my beloved. ¹⁰Greet Apelles, approved in Christ. Greet those who are of the *household* of Aristobulus. ¹¹Greet Herodion, my countryman. Greet those who are of the *household* of Narcissus who are in the Lord.

¹²Greet Tryphena and Tryphosa, who have labored in the Lord. Greet the beloved Persis, who labored much in the Lord. ¹³Greet Rufus, chosen in the Lord, and his mother and mine. ¹⁴Greet Asyncritus, Phlegon, Hermas, Patrobas, Hermes, and the brethren who are with them. ¹⁵Greet Philologus and Julia, Nereus and his sister, and Olympas, and all the saints who are with them.

¹⁶Greet one another with a holy kiss. The churches of Christ greet you.

¹⁷Now I urge you, brethren, note those who cause divisions and offenses, contrary to the doctrine which you learned, and avoid them. ¹⁸For those who are such do not serve our Lord Jesus Christ, but their own belly, and by smooth words and flattering speech deceive the hearts of the simple. ¹⁹For your obedience has become known to all. Therefore I am glad on your behalf; but I want you to be wise in what is good, and simple concerning evil. ²⁰And the God of peace will crush Satan under your feet shortly.

The grace of our Lord Jesus Christ *be* with you. Amen.

²¹Timothy, my fellow worker, and Lucius, Jason, and Sosipater, my countrymen, greet you.

²²I, Tertius, who wrote *this* epistle, greet you in the Lord.

²³Gaius, my host and *the host* of the whole church, greets you. Erastus, the treasurer of the city, greets you, and Quartus, a brother. ²⁴The grace of our Lord Jesus Christ *be* with you all. Amen.

²⁵Now to Him who is able to establish you according to my gospel and the preaching of Jesus Christ, according to the revelation of the mystery kept secret since the world began ²⁶but now made manifest, and by the prophetic Scriptures made known to all nations, according to the commandment of the everlasting God, for obedience to the faith— ²⁷to God, alone wise, *be* glory through Jesus Christ forever. Amen.

MEGA Themes

SIN Sin means refusing to do God's will and failing to do all that God wants. Since Adam rebelled against God, it has become our nature to disobey God. Our sin cuts us off from God; sin causes us to want to live our own way rather than God's way. Because God is morally perfect, just, and fair, he is right to condemn sin.

Each person has sinned, either by rebelling against God or by ignoring his will. No matter what our background or how hard we try to live a good and moral life, we cannot earn salvation or remove our sin. Only Christ can save us.

1. Through Paul's writings to Rome, God reveals to us how destructive sin is in our world, how widespread it is in mankind, how fatal it is to individuals. Survey chapters 1, 3, and 5 and list the key teachings you find on the topic of sin.
2. What are some of the consequences of mankind's choices to rebel against God's will?
3. How does sin enslave a person?
4. Now read 7:14-25 to catch a glimpse of Paul's personal battle with sin. How does Paul overcome his weaknesses?
5. Check out your life in light of this study. What are the consequences of your sinful choices? At what points has sin enslaved you? Where can you identify with the feelings and thoughts of Paul?
6. How does an awareness of your sin lead you to a deeper reliance upon Jesus Christ?

SALVATION Our sin points out our need to be forgiven and cleansed. Although we don't deserve it, God in his kindness reaches out to love and forgive us. He provides the way for us to be saved. Christ's death paid the penalty for our sin.

It is good news that God saves us from our sin. But we must believe in Jesus Christ, that he forgave our sin, to enter into a wonderful new relationship with God.

1. Read Romans 3:23; 5:8; 6:23; and 10:9-10. How would you use these verses to explain what it means to receive salvation through Jesus Christ?
2. Describe your own personal response to the message of salvation. When did you first hear it? When did you first believe?
3. What difference has Christ's salvation made in your daily life?
4. How does knowing that God has forgiven your sins affect the way you live?

GROWTH By God's power, believers are made holy. This is known as "sanctification." It means we are set apart from sin, enabled to obey and to become more like Christ. When we are growing in our relationship with Christ, the Holy Spirit frees us from the demands of the law and from the fear of God's judgment.

Because we are free from sin's control, the law's demands, and fear of God's punishment, we can grow in our relationship with Christ. By trusting in the Holy Spirit and allowing him to help us, we can overcome sin and temptation. Without the Holy Spirit, we will be unable to conquer sin's power.

1. Rewrite 12:1-2 in your own words.
2. How has God transformed you?
3. In what areas of your life have you struggled—or are now struggling—with conformity to the world?
4. What should you do to submit more fully to God?

SOVEREIGNTY God oversees and cares about his people—past, present, and future. God's ways of dealing with people are always fair. Because God is in charge of all creation, he can save whomever he wills.

Because of God's mercy, both Jews and Gentiles can be saved—we all need to respond to God's mercy and accept his gracious offer of forgiveness. God is sovereign, so let him reign in your heart.

1. Contrast the life of the person who seeks to accept and live under God's rule with the person who ignores or rejects him as Lord.
2. Describe Jesus' lordship in your life. What does it mean to let him be Lord over your life?
3. What confidence do you have because of the sovereignty of God?

SERVICE When our purpose is to give credit to God for his love, power, and perfection in all we do, we can serve him properly. Serving God unifies all believers and enables them to be loving and sensitive to others.

None of us can be fully Christlike by himself or herself—it takes the entire body of Christ to fully express Christ. By actively and vigorously building up other believers, Christians can be a symphony of service to God.

1. Chapters 12–15 include various teachings on how to live with fellow believers as members of Christ's body. List a number of the ways we are to relate to each other to show that we are unified.
2. Who are the Christians with whom you are the closest? Why do you feel close to these people?
3. What Christians are hard for you to love? What could you do to get along better with them?
4. What acts of service could you do for those you listed in questions 2 and 3?

*F*ifteen-year-old Dicky just recently accepted Christ. Yesterday, he watched in total disbelief as two of the "leaders" of his church got into a shouting (and shoving!) match after Sunday services. Dicky quietly asks *you* why supposedly "mature" Christians act that way. What do you say? ■ Kim has discovered that a man and woman who are active in the church aren't really married, but are living together. "How can they do that? Why doesn't the preacher talk to them? Isn't that a sin?" Kim says, puzzled. What would you tell her? ■ Twelve-year-old Abby knows, as a Christian, that certain activities are wrong—drunkenness, premarital sex, lying, stealing, etc. But what about all those "gray areas" that God's Word *doesn't* address? Is it OK to dance, go to certain parties, or buy expensive clothes? What about her favorite videos on MTV and songs on the radio? And how does God feel about the movies she's watched recently? "I want to do what's right," she tells you, "but sometimes it's hard to know. Aren't there some guidelines from the Bible that can help?" How do you answer? ■ These questions are far from new. Christians (and churches) have struggled with immaturity, division, and immorality since the first hymn was sung. Fortunately, the apostle Paul's first letter to the Corinthians has some real and practical answers. If you're looking to live a godly life in a godless culture, or if you want to help someone else do so, keep reading.

STATS

PURPOSE: To identify problems in the Corinthian church, to offer solutions, and to teach the believers how to live for Christ in a corrupt society

AUTHOR: Paul

TO WHOM WRITTEN: The church in Corinth, and Christians everywhere

DATE WRITTEN: About A.D. 55, near the end of Paul's three-year ministry in Ephesus during his third missionary journey

SETTING: Corinth was a major cosmopolitan city, a seaport and major trade center—the most important city in Achaia. It was also filled with idolatry and immorality. The church was largely made up of Gentiles. Paul had established this church on his second missionary journey.

KEY PEOPLE: Paul, Timothy, members of Chloe's household

KEY PLACES: Worship meetings in Corinth

Corinthians

CHAPTER 1   PAUL: CHOSEN TO BE A MISSIONARY.

Paul, called *to be* an apostle of Jesus Christ through the will of God, and Sosthenes *our* brother,

²To the church of God which is at Corinth, to those who are sanctified in Christ Jesus, called *to be* saints, with all who in every place call on the name of Jesus Christ our Lord, both theirs and ours:

³Grace to you and peace from God our Father and the Lord Jesus Christ.

⁴I thank my God always concerning you for the grace of God which was given to you by Christ Jesus, ⁵that you were enriched in everything by Him in all utterance and all knowledge, ⁶even as the testimony of Christ was confirmed in you, ⁷so that you come short in no gift, eagerly waiting for the revelation of our Lord Jesus Christ, ⁸who will also confirm you to the end, *that you may be* blameless in the day of our Lord Jesus Christ. ⁹God *is* faithful, by whom you were called into the fellowship of His Son, Jesus Christ our Lord.

¹⁰Now I plead with you, brethren, by the name of our Lord Jesus Christ, that you all speak the same thing, and *that* there be no divisions among you, but *that* you be perfectly joined together in the same mind and in the same judgment. ¹¹For it has been declared to me concerning you, my brethren, by those of Chloe's *household*, that there are contentions among you. ¹²Now I say this, that each of you says, "I am of Paul," or "I am of Apollos," or "I am of Cephas," or "I am of Christ." ¹³Is Christ di-

vided? Was Paul crucified for you? Or were you baptized in the name of Paul?

¹⁴I thank God that I baptized none of you except Crispus and Gaius, ¹⁵lest anyone should say that I had baptized in my own name. ¹⁶Yes, I also baptized the household of Stephanas. Besides, I do not know whether I baptized any other. ¹⁷For Christ did not send me to

USEFUL

1:1 Paul was specially selected by God to preach about Jesus Christ. Each Christian has a task to do. One task may seem more spectacular than another, but all are necessary to carry out God's greater plans for the world (12:12-27). Be useful to God by using your gifts in his service. As you discover what he wants, be ready to serve.

baptize, but to preach the gospel, not with wisdom of words, lest the cross of Christ should be made of no effect.

¹⁸For the message of the cross is foolishness to those who are perishing, but to us who are being saved it is the power of God. ¹⁹For it is written:

"*I will destroy the wisdom of the wise,*
  And bring to nothing the understanding of the
    prudent."

²⁰Where *is* the wise? Where *is* the scribe? Where *is* the disputer of this age? Has not God made foolish the wisdom of this world? ²¹For since, in the wisdom of God, the world through wisdom did not know God, it pleased God through the foolishness of the message preached to save

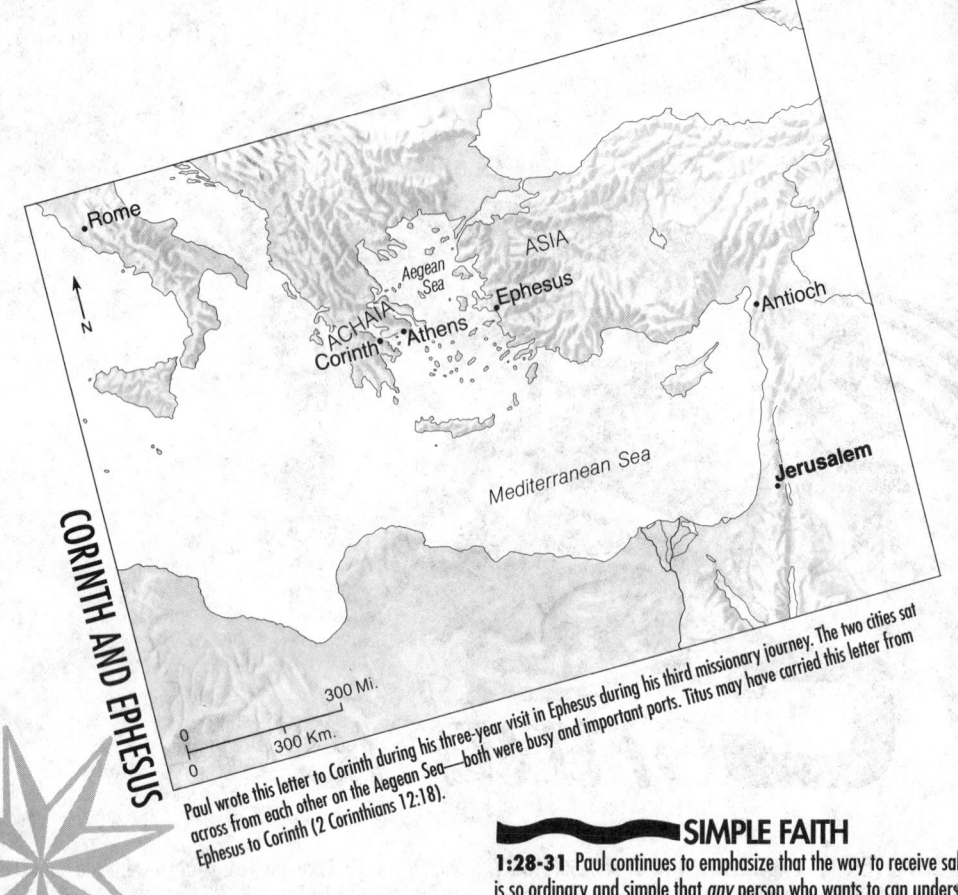

CORINTH AND EPHESUS

Paul wrote this letter to Corinth during his three-year visit in Ephesus during his third missionary journey. The two cities sat across from each other on the Aegean Sea—both were busy and important ports. Titus may have carried this letter from Ephesus to Corinth (2 Corinthians 12:18).

those who believe. ²²For Jews request a sign, and Greeks seek after wisdom; ²³but we preach Christ crucified, to the Jews a stumbling block and to the Greeks foolishness, ²⁴but to those who are called, both Jews and Greeks, Christ the power of God and the wisdom of God. ²⁵Because the foolishness of God is wiser than men, and the weakness of God is stronger than men.

²⁶For you see your calling, brethren, that not many wise according to the flesh, not many mighty, not many noble, *are called.* ²⁷But God has chosen the foolish things of the world to put to shame the wise, and God has chosen the weak things of the world to put to shame the things which are mighty; ²⁸and the base things of the world and the things which are despised God has chosen, and the things which are not, to bring to nothing the things that are, ²⁹that no flesh should glory in His presence. ³⁰But of Him you are in Christ Jesus, who became for us wisdom from God—and righteousness and sanctification and redemption— ³¹that, as it is written, *"He who glories, let him glory in the LORD."*

CHAPTER 2 THE HOLY SPIRIT GIVES US WISDOM.

And I, brethren, when I came to you, did not come with excellence of speech or of wisdom declaring to you the testimony of God. ²For I determined not to know anything among you except Jesus Christ and Him crucified.

◣◣▬ SIMPLE FAITH

1:28-31 Paul continues to emphasize that the way to receive sal is so ordinary and simple that *any* person who wants to can unders it. Skill does not get you into God's kingdom—simple faith does. planned it this way so no one could boast that his achievements he him secure eternal life. Salvation is totally from God through Jesus death, which allowed us to become perfect in God's eyes. There is we can do to become acceptable to God; we need only accept what has already done for us. He has done the work.

³I was with you in weakness, in fear, and in much trembling. ⁴And my speech and my preaching *were* not with persuasive words of human wisdom, but in demonstration of the Spirit and of power, ⁵that your faith should not be in the wisdom of men but in the power of God.

⁶However, we speak wisdom among those who are mature, yet not the wisdom of this age, nor of the rulers of this age, who are coming to nothing. ⁷But we speak the wisdom of God in a mystery, the hidden *wisdom* which God ordained before the ages for our glory, ⁸which none of the rulers of this age knew; for had they known, they would not have crucified the Lord of glory.

⁹But as it is written:

"Eye has not seen, nor ear heard,

◣◣▬ WHAT'S IN STORE?

2:9 We cannot imagine all that God has in store for us both in this and for eternity. He will create a new heaven and a new earth (Isaia 65:17; Revelation 21:1), and we will live with him forever. Until the Holy Spirit comforts and guides us. Knowing the future that awaits u should give us hope and courage to press on in this life, to endure hardship, and to avoid giving in to temptation. This world is not all t

Nor have entered into the heart of man
The things which God has prepared for those who
   love Him."

[10]But God has revealed *them* to us through His Spirit. For the Spirit searches all things, yes, the deep things of God. [11]For what man knows the things of a man except the spirit of the man which is in him? Even so no one knows the things of God except the Spirit of God. [12]Now we have received, not the spirit of the world, but the Spirit who is from God, that we might know the things that have been freely given to us by God.

[13]These things we also speak, not in words which man's wisdom teaches but which the Holy Spirit teaches, comparing spiritual things with spiritual. [14]But the natural man does not receive the things of the Spirit of God, for they are foolishness to him; nor can he know *them*, because they are spiritually discerned. [15]But he who is spiritual judges all things, yet he himself is *rightly* judged by no one. [16]For *"who has known the mind of the LORD that he may instruct Him?"* But we have the mind of Christ.

CHAPTER 3

And I, brethren, could not speak to you as to spiritual *people* but as to carnal, as to babes in Christ. [2]I fed you with milk and not with solid food; for until now you were not able *to receive it*, and even now you are still not able; [3]for you are still carnal. For where *there are* envy, strife, and divisions among you, are you not carnal and behaving like *mere* men? [4]For when one says, "I am of Paul," and another, "I *am* of Apollos," are you not carnal?

[5]Who then is Paul, and who *is* Apollos, but ministers through whom you believed, as the Lord gave to each one? [6]I planted, Apollos watered, but God gave the increase. [7]So then neither he who plants is anything, nor he who waters, but God who gives the increase. [8]Now he who plants and he who waters are one, and each one will receive his own reward according to his own labor.

[9]For we are God's fellow workers; you are God's field, *you are* God's building. [10]According to the grace of God which was given to me, as a wise master builder I have laid the foundation, and another builds on it. But let each one take heed how he builds on it. [11]For no other foundation can anyone lay than that which is laid, which is Jesus Christ. [12]Now if anyone builds on this foundation *with* gold, silver, precious stones, wood, hay, straw, [13]each one's work will become clear; for the Day will declare it, because it will be revealed by fire; and the fire will test each one's work, of what sort it is. [14]If anyone's work which he has built on *it* endures, he will receive a reward. [15]If anyone's work is burned, he will suffer loss; but he himself will be saved, yet so as through fire.

[16]Do you not know that you are the temple of God and *that* the Spirit of God dwells in you? [17]If anyone defiles the temple of God, God will destroy him. For the temple of God is holy, which *temple* you are.

[18]Let no one deceive himself. If anyone among you seems to be wise in this age, let him become a fool that he may become wise. [19]For the wisdom of this world is foolishness with God. For it is written, *"He catches the wise in their own craftiness"*; [20]and again, *"The LORD knows the thoughts of the wise, that they are futile."* [21]Therefore let no one boast in men. For all things are yours: [22]whether Paul or Apollos or Cephas, or the world or life or death, or things present or things to come—all are yours. [23]And you *are* Christ's, and Christ *is* God's.

I hear a lot about the New Age movement. Some of my friends say they are in it. How is this different from what I believe as a Christian?

I WONDER . . .

The most convenient religion is one you create yourself, and that is what the New Age movement does for people. It allows them to create their own rules concerning God, their behavior, and how to make it to the next life.

Because of this, *New Age* is impossible to define! But, generally, here is what most New-Agers believe:

- They believe that God is everywhere and in everybody. Because we are humans, we all have a unity of spirit that allows us to be brothers no matter what. God is not good or bad. In fact, each person is a god. He or she is the center of the universe. Morality, therefore, isn't important (since God is not seen as either good or bad). But the mind and intellect are very important, because, supposedly, a person has to think deep thoughts to understand these concepts.

- They believe that "salvation" comes through reincarnation. This means coming back to life again in the form of someone or something else, again and again, until you get it right. (Reincarnation is a lie; the Bible is very clear on this point. See Hebrews 9:27.)

There are so many strains within the New Age movement that it's impossible to outline them all. But the key is believing that there is no personal God, that humans are not sinful, and that the next life is assured in some form, no matter what you have done. This is a very convenient religion if you just want to do your own thing.

But listen to God: "Thus says the LORD: 'Cursed *is* the man who trusts in man and makes flesh his strength'" (Jeremiah 17:5). When people set their own beliefs and thoughts up as more important than what God thinks, they are actually being cursed by him!

Nearly every belief within the New Age movement allows you to become your own god. Eve was told by Satan that she would become like God if she ate of the fruit of the tree (Genesis 3:1-6). People are being told they can be god of their life if they would just look away from the one, true God.

The Bible must be our authority on what we are to believe about God, ourself, and what it takes to be saved from our sin. If it isn't, everyone can create a religion to suit his or her own desires. And that is a religion that will lead to destruction. Don't believe that? Just take a look at 1 Corinthians 1:19 "I will destroy the wisdom of the wise, and bring to nothing the understanding of the prudent."

There's only one place to find the real answers to who God is and what he's about: his holy Word, the Bible.

CHAPTER 4 CLIQUES IN THE CHURCH. Let a man

so consider us, as servants of Christ and stewards of the mysteries of God. [2]Moreover it is required in stewards that one be found faithful. [3]But with me it is a very small thing that I should be judged by you or by a human court. In fact, I do not even judge myself. [4]For I know of nothing against myself, yet I am not justified by this; but He who judges me is the Lord. [5]Therefore judge nothing before the time, until the Lord comes, who will both bring to light the hidden things of darkness and reveal the counsels of the hearts. Then each one's praise will come from God.

▲▲▲▲▲▲▲▲▲▲▲▲▲▲▲▲▲▲▲▲▲▲▲▲▲▲▲▲▲▲▲

DRUGS Scene 1: Lyle is having a massive argument with his parents. (They've just discovered a small amount of marijuana in his coat pocket.)

"Lighten up, OK? It's no big deal! It's just a little grass."

"'No big deal'? Listen here, that grass is illegal! You could go to jail for that grass!"

"Lyle, how could you do this to your father and me?"

"What? I'm not doing anything to you! It's my life!"

"That's right. It's your life. But you're gonna cut it short if you fill your body with drugs."

"Aw, come off of it! I don't 'fill my body with drugs.' I smoke a little harmless grass."

Scene 2: Gary looks nervously over his shoulder. No one is watching, so he pulls a pill bottle—containing anabolic steroids—out of his locker.

Quickly he turns and heads for the gym. Time to pump some serious iron.

Scene 3: With her parents out for the evening, Staci and her friend Kimberly search the workshop and garage for gas, paint thinner, or anything else with the right kind of fumes to get them high.

Drugs (no matter what kind) damage the human body. If you're a Christian, your body doesn't belong to you. God owns it, and he tells you to take care of it.

For that reason alone, you must resist the temporary thrill of a chemical high. See 1 Corinthians 6:19-20.

▼▼▼▼▼▼▼▼▼▼▼▼▼▼▼▼▼▼▼▼▼▼▼▼▼▼▼▼▼▼▼

[6]Now these things, brethren, I have figuratively transferred to myself and Apollos for your sakes, that you may learn in us not to think beyond what is written, that none of you may be puffed up on behalf of one against the other. [7]For who makes you differ *from another?* And what do you have that you did not receive? Now if you did indeed receive *it,* why do you boast as if you had not received *it?*

[8]You are already full! You are already rich! You have reigned as kings without us—and indeed I could wish you did reign, that we also might reign with you! [9]For I think that God has displayed us, the apostles, last, as men condemned to death; for we have been made a spectacle to the world, both to angels and to men. [10]We *are* fools for Christ's sake, but you *are* wise in Christ! We *are* weak, but you *are* strong! You *are* distinguished, but we *are* dishonored! [11]To the present hour we both hunger and thirst, and we are poorly clothed, and beaten, and homeless. [12]And we labor, working with our own hands. Being re-

◣JUDGING

4:5 It is tempting to judge fellow Christians, evaluating whether they are good followers of Christ. But only God knows a person's h and he is the only one with the right to judge. Paul's warning to th Corinthians should also warn us. We should help those who are sin (see 5:12-13), but we must not judge who is a better servant for C When you judge someone, you automatically consider yourself be and that is pride.

viled, we bless; being persecuted, we endure; [13]being defamed, we entreat. We have been made as the filth of the world, the offscouring of all things until now.

[14]I do not write these things to shame you, but as my beloved children I warn *you.* [15]For though you might have ten thousand instructors in Christ, yet *you do* not *have* many fathers; for in Christ Jesus I have begotten you through the gospel. [16]Therefore I urge you, imitate me. [17]For this reason I have sent Timothy to you, who is my beloved and faithful son in the Lord, who will remind you of my ways in Christ, as I teach everywhere in every church.

[18]Now some are puffed up, as though I were not coming to you. [19]But I will come to you shortly, if the Lord wills, and I will know, not the word of those who are puffed up, but the power. [20]For the kingdom of God *is* not in word but in power. [21]What do you want? Shall I come to you with a rod, or in love and a spirit of gentleness?

CHAPTER 5 SIN IN THE CHURCH. It is actually re-

ported *that there is* sexual immorality among you, and such sexual immorality as is not even named among the Gentiles—that a man has his father's wife! [2]And you are puffed up, and have not rather mourned, that he who has done this deed might be taken away from among you. [3]For I indeed, as absent in body but present in spirit, have already judged (as though I were present) him who has so done this deed. [4]In the name of our Lord Jesus Christ, when you are gathered together, along with my spirit, with the power of our Lord Jesus Christ, [5]deliver such a one to Satan for the destruction of the flesh, that his spirit may be saved in the day of the Lord Jesus.

[6]Your glorying *is* not good. Do you not know that a little leaven leavens the whole lump? [7]Therefore purge out the old leaven, that you may be a new lump, since you truly are unleavened. For indeed Christ, our Passover, was sacrificed for us. [8]Therefore let us keep the feast, not with old leaven, nor with the leaven of malice and wickedness, but with the unleavened *bread* of sincerity and truth.

[9]I wrote to you in my epistle not to keep company with sexually immoral people. [10]Yet *I* certainly *did* not *mean*

◣SEX

6:13 Sexual sin is a temptation we cannot escape. In movies and television, sex outside of marriage is treated as a normal—even desirable—part of life, while marriage is often shown as confinin joyless. We can even be looked down upon by others if suspected c being pure. But God does not forbid sexual sin just to be difficult. knows its power to destroy us physically and spiritually. No one sh underestimate the power of sexual sin. It has devastated countless and destroyed families, communities, and even nations. God wants protect us from damaging ourself and others, so he offers to fill us loneliness, our desires—with himself.

with the sexually immoral people of this world, or with the covetous, or extortioners, or idolaters, since then you would need to go out of the world. [11]But now I have written to you not to keep company with anyone named a brother, who is sexually immoral, or covetous, or an idolater, or a reviler, or a drunkard, or an extortioner—not even to eat with such a person.

[12]For what *have* I *to do* with judging those also who are outside? Do you not judge those who are inside? [13]But those who are outside God judges. Therefore *"put away from yourselves the evil person."*

CHAPTER **6** LAWSUITS.

Dare any of you, having a matter against another, go to law before the unrighteous, and not before the saints? [2]Do you not know that the saints will judge the world? And if the world will be judged by you, are you unworthy to judge the smallest matters? [3]Do you not know that we shall judge angels? How much more, things that pertain to this life? [4]If then you have judgments concerning things pertaining to this life, do you appoint those who are least esteemed by the church to judge? [5]I say this to your shame. Is it so, that there is not a wise man among you, not even one, who will be able to judge between his brethren? [6]But brother goes to law against brother, and that before unbelievers!

[7]Now therefore, it is already an utter failure for you that you go to law against one another. Why do you not rather accept wrong? Why do you not rather *let yourselves* be cheated? [8]No, you yourselves do wrong and cheat, and *you do* these things *to your* brethren! [9]Do you not know that the unrighteous will not inherit the kingdom of God? Do not be deceived. Neither fornicators, nor idolaters, nor adulterers, nor homosexuals, nor sodomites, [10]nor thieves, nor covetous, nor drunkards, nor revilers, nor extortioners will inherit the kingdom of God. [11]And such were some of you. But you were washed, but you were sanctified, but you were justified in the name of the Lord Jesus and by the Spirit of our God.

[12]All things are lawful for me, but all things are not helpful. All things are lawful for me, but I will not be brought under the power of any. [13]Foods for the stomach and the stomach for foods, but God will destroy both it and them. Now the body *is* not for sexual immorality but for the Lord, and the Lord for the body. [14]And God both raised up the Lord and will also raise us up by His power.

[15]Do you not know that your bodies are members of Christ? Shall I then take the members of Christ and make *them* members of a harlot? Certainly not! [16]Or do you not know that he who is joined to a harlot is one body *with her?* For *"the two,"* He says, *"shall become one flesh."* [17]But he who is joined to the Lord is one spirit *with Him.*

[18]Flee sexual immorality. Every sin that a man does is outside the body, but he who commits sexual immorality sins against his own body. [19]Or do you not know that your body is the temple of the Holy Spirit *who is* in you, whom you have from God, and you are not your own? [20]For you were bought at a price; therefore glorify God in your body and in your spirit, which are God's.

CHAPTER **7** QUESTIONS ABOUT MARRIAGE.

Now concerning the things of which you wrote to me:

It is good for a man not to touch a woman. [2]Nevertheless, because of sexual immorality, let each man have his own wife, and let each woman have her own husband. [3]Let the husband render to his wife the affection due her, and likewise also the wife to her husband. [4]The wife does not have authority over her own body, but the husband *does.* And likewise the husband does not have authority over his own body, but the wife *does.* [5]Do not deprive one another except with consent for a time, that you may give yourselves to fasting and prayer; and come together again so that Satan does not tempt you because of your lack of self-control. [6]But I say this as a concession, not as a commandment. [7]For I wish that all men were even as I

My Christian friends are dragging me down. How am I supposed to grow as a Christian if these friends aren't really trying to do anything with their faith?

I WONDER . . .

Because God is the one who called you "into the fellowship of His Son" (1 Corinthians 1:9), it's his responsibility, not yours, to make sure you grow in your faith. He has no intention of abandoning you.

Many people have been touched by divorce in one way or another. Kids of divorced parents are often determined to make sure that their own marriage is a success. They seek out positive role models to observe, and they pour through numerous resources about having a quality marriage. But, the opposite also can be true. Kids who grow up without a good model of what a family is supposed to look like can easily repeat their parents' mistakes.

Because your friends are acting like they have "divorced God," you are faced with a choice. Will you learn from their mistakes and search out people and other resources to help you succeed in your relationship with Christ? Or will you follow their lead and turn your back on God as well? If you're serious about giving God every chance to make himself real in your life, consider these suggestions:

First, pray for your friends and for an opportunity to talk to them about the situation. Don't worry about how much you've blown it by participating in whatever they've done. It's more important to think about your future than to dwell on the past. Next, go to one of your Christian friends, perhaps the leader of the group, and say something like: "I really want to give God a shot, but you're not helping much. I need your help. Can I count on you?" If this person says yes, it worked! If not, go to another friend and tell him the same thing. If no one responds, wait a week or two and start the process again, trusting that God has been working in their hearts. Or find some new friends you can count on. Maybe that's the answer God has for you.

Remember, God is faithful. He knows that you need friends and a group to hang around with. The last thing you need are people who are heading in the wrong direction.

AIDS:
WHAT WOULD
JESUS DO?

There are few more explosive topics in America than that of AIDS. Conservatives believe AIDS is God's judgment on certain sinners. Gay rights groups and others scream just as loudly that this is a medical issue, not a moral one. Who's right? And how should Christians respond to this overwhelming problem? In one sense, AIDS (Acquired Immune Deficiency Syndrome) is primarily a medical issue. The AIDS virus attacks the body's immune system, making the body defenseless against the diseases a healthy person's immune system would destroy. AIDS is an "equal opportunity" nightmare—it affects everyone: young, old, male, female, gay, or straight. But this is only a part of the picture. Since the majority of people in our country infected with AIDS are homosexual men and IV drug abusers who share needles, many people believe that AIDS must be a special judgment on those homosexuals and junkies. Many Christians and churches have jumped on the "judgment bandwagon," too, pointing to passages like Romans 1 or 1 Corinthians 6:9 as evidence of God's special displeasure on the sin of homosexuality. Is this a reasonable belief? Did God get "fed up" with gays and junkies and punish them with AIDS? There are a number of problems with this belief.

First, while male homosexuals make up the highest percentage of persons with AIDS in our culture, female homosexuals (lesbians) seldom contract it. Does this mean that God hates male gays, but female gays are OK? That is obviously inconsistent, and God is never inconsistent. As for drug abusers, those who don't use or share needles don't get it nearly as frequently. So does God only hate those drug abusers who inject drugs intravenously and share their needles with one another often contract the AIDS virus. Those who inject drugs and share needles? That's clearly illogical. If AIDS isn't a punishment from God, why has it hit the male gay community and IV drug abusers so hard? The answer is that gay men and IV drug abusers participate in activities that pass the virus from person to person very effectively. God hasn't singled out particular groups for special judgment; rather, those people engage in activities that are particularly risky in regard to the transmission of AIDS. God created the universe to run in accordance with natural laws, like gravity, inertia, etc. When you try to defy those laws, you lose. There are natural laws governing human behavior, too. One such law is that your body is not made for sexual promiscuity. Violate that law and you risk contracting AIDS or other you will—like it or not—encounter it. You may not like the law of gravity, but jump off a building and diseases (syphilis, gonorrhea, herpes, etc.). Likewise, your body was not made to handle large amounts of drugs. Continually inject them into your veins and you probably will experience a lot of physical problems— one of which may be AIDS. So it's not that God is using AIDS to "get" certain kinds of people. AIDS simply is a natural—though terrifying—result of human behavior that goes against God's design for our lives. Those who believe AIDS is a special divine judgment simply don't understand the reality of their own sin. As the psalmist wrote in Psalm 143:1-2, "Hear my prayer, O LORD, give ear to my supplications! In Your faithfulness answer me, and in Your righteousness. Do not enter into judgment with Your servant, for in Your sight no one living is righteous." A cure for AIDS is many years away; but even if it's not, the only reasonable, Christian response is to follow God's standards for sexual morality. Sex is made for marriage only—to be kept in the context of a faithful, monogamous relationship between husband and wife. Anything else is unbiblical, sinful and potentially fatal. Likewise, we must reaffirm God's ownership of our body by not abusing it with drugs. Paul writes in 1 Corinthians 6:19-20, "Do you not know that your body is the temple of the Holy Spirit who in you? . . . For you were bought at a price; therefore glorify God in your body and in your spirit, which a God's." Where we have failed to live up to this, we need to confess our sins, repent, and ask God's forgiv

Many Christians also need to confess their judgmental attitudes toward persons with AIDS. There is no re in Christianity for feelings of superiority or self-righteousness. Jesus had strong words for those who wer of spiritual pride, of thinking they were better than others. Our response toward anyone with this terribl disease should be concern, compassion, and a hand reaching out to ease his or her pain and distress.

Isn't that how Jesus deals with people, regardless of their sins?

myself. But each one has his own gift from God, one in this manner and another in that.

[8]But I say to the unmarried and to the widows: It is good for them if they remain even as I am; [9]but if they cannot exercise self-control, let them marry. For it is better to marry than to burn *with passion*.

[10]Now to the married I command, *yet* not I but the Lord: A wife is not to depart from *her* husband. [11]But even if she does depart, let her remain unmarried or be reconciled to *her* husband. And a husband is not to divorce *his* wife.

[12]But to the rest I, not the Lord, say: If any brother has a wife who does not believe, and she is willing to live with him, let him not divorce her. [13]And a woman who has a husband who does not believe, if he is willing to live with her, let her not divorce him. [14]For the unbelieving husband is sanctified by the wife, and the unbelieving wife is sanctified by the husband; otherwise your children would be unclean, but now they are holy. [15]But if the unbeliever departs, let him depart; a brother or a sister is not under bondage in such *cases*. But God has called us to peace. [16]For how do you know, O wife, whether you will save *your* husband? Or how do you know, O husband, whether you will save *your* wife?

[17]But as God has distributed to each one, as the Lord has called each one, so let him walk. And so I ordain in all the churches. [18]Was anyone called while circumcised? Let him not become uncircumcised. Was anyone called while uncircumcised? Let him not be circumcised. [19]Circumcision is nothing and uncircumcision is nothing, but keeping the commandments of God *is what matters.* [20]Let each one remain in the same calling in which he was called. [21]Were you called *while* a slave? Do not be concerned about it; but if you can be made free, rather use *it.*

COUPLES

7:9 Sexual pressure is not the best motive for getting married, but it is better to marry the right person than to burn with lust. Many new believers in Corinth thought that all sex was wrong, so engaged couples were deciding not to get married. In this passage, Paul is telling couples who wanted to marry that they should not deny their normal sexual drives by avoiding marriage. This does not mean, however, that people who have trouble controlling their thoughts should marry the first person who comes along. It is better to deal with the pressure of desire than to deal with an unhappy marriage.

[22]For he who is called in the Lord *while* a slave is the Lord's freedman. Likewise he who is called *while* free is Christ's slave. [23]You were bought at a price; do not become slaves of men. [24]Brethren, let each one remain with God in that *state* in which he was called.

[25]Now concerning virgins: I have no commandment from the Lord; yet I give judgment as one whom the Lord in His mercy *has made* trustworthy. [26]I suppose therefore that this is good because of the present distress—that *it is* good for a man to remain as he is: [27]Are you bound to a

HIGHLIGHTS OF 1 CORINTHIANS

The Meaning of the Cross, 1:18–2:16. Be considerate of one another because of what Christ has done for us. There is no place for pride or a know-it-all attitude. We are to have the mind of Christ.

The Story of the Last Supper, 11:23-29. The Last Supper is a time of reflection on Christ's final words to his disciples before he died on the cross; we must celebrate this in an orderly and correct manner.

The Poem of Love, 13:1-13. Love is to guide all we do. We have different gifts, abilities, likes, dislikes—but we are called, without exception, to love.

The Christian's Destiny, 15:42-58. We are promised by Christ, who died for us, that, just as he came back to life after death, our perishable bodies will be exchanged for heavenly bodies. Then we will live and reign with Christ.

NO PROBLEMS?

7:28 Many people think that finding the right boyfriend or girlfriend, and especially getting married, will solve all their problems. It does feel good to have someone special, someone who cares for you and whom you care for. But no relationship, even marriage, is a "cure for whatever ails you"! For example, here are a few of the problems even marriage won't solve: (1) loneliness, (2) sexual temptation, (3) satisfaction of one's deepest emotional needs, (4) elimination of life's difficulties. Marriage alone does not hold two people together, but commitment does—commitment to Christ and to each other despite conflicts and problems. Marriage can be great, but it isn't the solution to problems. There is only one reliable solution for anyone: trusting in Christ! Focus on Christ, not humans, to solve your problems.

wife? Do not seek to be loosed. Are you loosed from a wife? Do not seek a wife. [28]But even if you do marry, you have not sinned; and if a virgin marries, she has not sinned. Nevertheless such will have trouble in the flesh, but I would spare you.

[29]But this I say, brethren, the time *is* short, so that from now on even those who have wives should be as though they had none, [30]those who weep as though they did not weep, those who rejoice as though they did not rejoice, those who buy as though they did not possess, [31]and those who use this world as not misusing *it*. For the form of this world is passing away.

[32]But I want you to be without care. He who is unmarried cares for the things of the Lord—how he may please the Lord. [33]But he who is married cares about the things of the world—how he may please *his* wife. [34]There is a difference between a wife and a virgin. The unmarried woman cares about the things of the Lord, that she may be holy both in body and in spirit. But she who is married cares about the things of the world—how she may please *her* husband. [35]And this I say for your own profit, not that I may put a leash on you, but for what is proper, and that you may serve the Lord without distraction.

[36]But if any man thinks he is behaving improperly toward his virgin, if she is past the flower of youth, and thus it must be, let him do what he wishes. He does not sin; let them marry. [37]Nevertheless he who stands steadfast in his heart, having no necessity, but has power over his own will, and has so determined in his heart that he will keep his virgin, does well. [38]So then he who gives *her* in marriage does well, but he who does not give *her* in marriage does better.

[39]A wife is bound by law as long as her husband lives; but if her husband dies, she is at liberty to be married to whom she wishes, only in the Lord. [40]But she is happier if she remains as she is, according to my judgment—and I think I also have the Spirit of God.

MAKING CHOICES IN SENSITIVE ISSUES

All of us make hundreds of choices every day. Most choices have no right or wrong attached to them—like what to wear or what to eat. But we always face decisions that carry a little more weight. We don't want to do wrong, and we don't want to cause others to do wrong. So how can we make right decisions?

If I choose one course of action . . .

. . . am I motivated by a desire to help others to know Christ? (9:23; 10:33)

. . . will it help my witness for Christ? (9:19-22)

. . . will it help me do my best? (9:25)

. . . will it encourage someone else to sin? (10:32)

. . . is it against a specific command in Scripture and thus will cause me to sin? (10:12)

. . . will it glorify God? (10:31)

. . . will it be best and helpful? (10:23,33)

. . . will I be acting lovingly or selfishly? (10:28-31)

. . . will I be thinking only of myself, or do I truly care about the other person? (10:24)

CHAPTER **8** FOOD OFFERED TO IDOLS.

Now concerning things offered to idols: We know that we all have knowledge. Knowledge puffs up, but love edifies. ²And if anyone thinks that he knows anything, he knows nothing yet as he ought to know. ³But if anyone loves God, this one is known by Him.

⁴Therefore concerning the eating of things offered to idols, we know that an idol *is* nothing in the world, and that *there is* no other God but one. ⁵For even if there are so-called gods, whether in heaven or on earth (as there are many gods and many lords), ⁶yet for us *there is* one God, the Father, of whom *are* all things, and we for Him; and one Lord Jesus Christ, through whom *are* all things, and through whom we *live.*

⁷However, *there is* not in everyone that knowledge; for some, with consciousness of the idol, until now eat it as a thing offered to an idol; and their conscience, being weak, is defiled. ⁸But food does not commend us to God; for neither if we eat are we the better, nor if we do not eat are we the worse.

⁹But beware lest somehow this liberty of yours become a stumbling block to those who are weak. ¹⁰For if anyone sees you who have knowledge eating in an idol's temple, will not the conscience of him who is weak be emboldened to eat those things offered to idols? ¹¹And because of your knowledge shall the weak brother perish, for whom Christ died? ¹²But when you thus sin against the brethren, and wound their weak conscience, you sin against Christ. ¹³Therefore, if food makes my brother stumble, I will never again eat meat, lest I make my brother stumble.

CHAPTER **9** THE RIGHT OF AN APOSTLE.

Am I not an apostle? Am I not free? Have I not seen Jesus Christ our Lord? Are you not my work in the Lord? ²If I am not an apostle to others, yet doubtless I am to you. For you are the seal of my apostleship in the Lord.

³My defense to those who examine me is this: ⁴Do we have no right to eat and drink? ⁵Do we have no right to take along a believing wife, as *do* also the other apostles, the brothers of the Lord, and Cephas? ⁶Or *is it* only Barnabas and I *who* have no right to refrain from working? ⁷Who ever goes to war at his own expense? Who plants a vineyard and does not eat of its fruit? Or who tends a flock and does not drink of the milk of the flock?

⁸Do I say these things as a *mere* man? Or does not the law say the same also? ⁹For it is written in the law of Moses, *"You shall not muzzle an ox while it treads out the grain."* Is it oxen God is concerned about? ¹⁰Or does He say *it* altogether for our sakes? For our sakes, no doubt, *this* is written, that he who plows should plow in hope, and he who threshes in hope should be partaker of his hope. ¹¹If we have sown spiritual things for you, *is it* a great thing if we reap your material things? ¹²If others are partakers of *this* right over you, *are* we not even more?

Nevertheless we have not used this right, but endure all things lest we hinder the gospel of Christ. ¹³Do you not know that those who minister the holy things eat *of the things* of the temple, and those who serve at the altar partake of *the offerings of* the altar? ¹⁴Even so the Lord has commanded that those who preach the gospel should live from the gospel.

▶▬▬▬▬▬FREEDOM

8:10-13 Christian freedom does not mean "anything goes." It means that our salvation is not determined by legalism, good works, or rules, but by the free gift of God (Ephesians 2:8-9). Christian freedom is tied to Christian responsibility. New believers are sensitive to what is right or wrong. Some actions may be perfectly all right for us to do, but may harm a Christian brother or sister who is still young in the faith. We must be careful not to offend a sensitive or younger Christian or, by our example, to cause him or her to sin.

¹⁵But I have used none of these things, nor have I written these things that it should be done so to me; for it *would be* better for me to die than that anyone should make my boasting void. ¹⁶For if I preach the gospel, I have nothing to boast of, for necessity is laid upon me; yes, woe is me if I do not preach the gospel! ¹⁷For if I do this willingly, I have a reward; but if against my will, I have been entrusted with a stewardship. ¹⁸What is my reward then? That when I preach the gospel, I may present the gospel of Christ without charge, that I may not abuse my authority in the gospel.

"Here's what I did..."

For many years I had a problem with gossiping. I knew it was wrong, but I kept giving in to temptation. I prayed about it a lot. Then the Lord gave me two Scriptures that have helped me begin to conquer it.

The first is 1 Corinthians 10:13. That verse says that God will always provide a way to escape temptation's power. So I reminded myself of this whenever the temptation to pass on some juicy bit of news came my way. It helped some, but I still gave in more often than I wanted to.

Then God gave me something that's helped me even more. It's Psalm 141:3: "Set a guard, O LORD, over my mouth; keep watch over the door of my lips." That's exactly the prayer I started praying whenever I was tempted to gossip. This prayer-verse became my way to escape the temptation; whenever I take the time to pray it, I find I can keep my mouth shut. But I have to take a moment to refocus my thoughts on the prayer rather than on the temptation to say something, or I find myself giving in to temptation.

This experience has shown me just how practical the Bible can be. With God's power I can conquer anything!

Brooke AGE 18

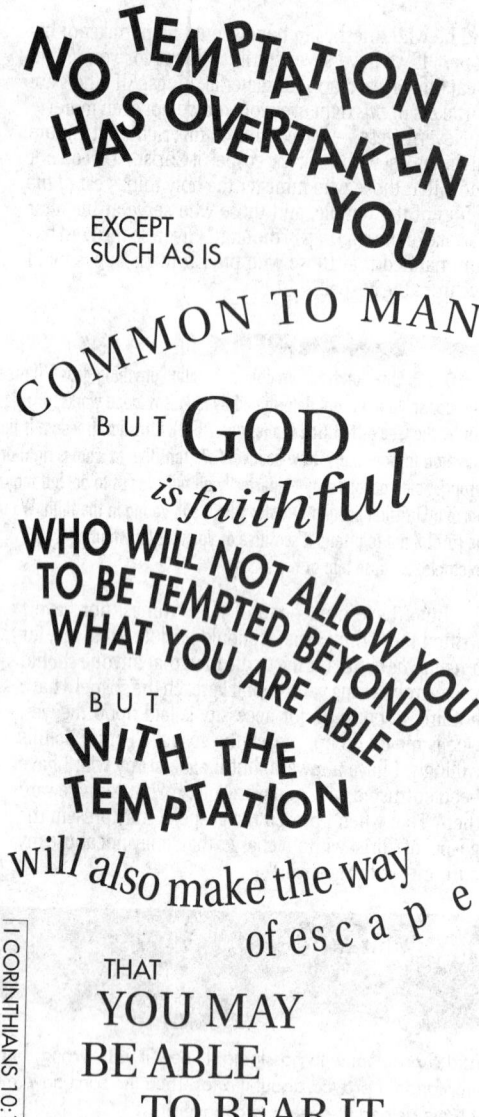

NO TEMPTATION HAS OVERTAKEN YOU EXCEPT SUCH AS IS COMMON TO MAN BUT GOD is faithful WHO WILL NOT ALLOW YOU TO BE TEMPTED BEYOND WHAT YOU ARE ABLE BUT WITH THE TEMPTATION will also make the way of escape THAT YOU MAY BE ABLE TO BEAR IT.

I CORINTHIANS 10:13

[19]For though I am free from all *men*, I have made myself a servant to all, that I might win the more; [20]and to the Jews I became as a Jew, that I might win Jews; to those *who are* under the law, as under the law, that I might win those *who are* under the law; [21]to those *who are* without law, as without law (not being without law toward God, but under law toward Christ), that I might win those *who are* without law; [22]to the weak I became as weak, that I might win the weak. I have become all things to all *men*, that I might by all means save some. [23]Now this I do for the gospel's sake, that I may be partaker of it with *you*.

[24]Do you not know that those who run in a race all run, but one receives the prize? Run in such a way that you may obtain *it*. [25]And everyone who competes *for the prize* is temperate in all things. Now they *do it* to obtain a perishable crown, but we *for* an imperishable *crown*. [26]Therefore I run thus: not with uncertainty. Thus I fight: not as *one who* beats the air. [27]But I discipline my body and bring *it* into subjection, lest, when I have preached to others, I myself should become disqualified.

CHAPTER 10 LESSONS ABOUT IDOL WORSHIP.

Moreover, brethren, I do not want you to be unaware that all our fathers were under the cloud, all passed through the sea, [2]all were baptized into Moses in the cloud and in the sea, [3]all ate the same spiritual food, [4]and all drank the same spiritual drink. For they drank of that spiritual Rock that followed them, and that Rock was Christ. [5]But with most of them God was not well pleased, for *their bodies* were scattered in the wilderness.

[6]Now these things became our examples, to the intent that we should not lust after evil things as they also lusted. [7]And do not become idolaters as *were* some of them. As it is written, *"The people sat down to eat and drink, and rose up to play."* [8]Nor let us commit sexual immorality, as some of them did, and in one day twenty-three thousand fell; [9]nor let us tempt Christ, as some of them also tempted, and were destroyed by serpents; [10]nor complain, as some of them also complained, and were destroyed by the destroyer. [11]Now all these things happened to them as examples, and they were written for our admonition, upon whom the ends of the ages have come.

[12]Therefore let him who thinks he stands take heed lest he fall. [13]No temptation has overtaken you except such as is common to man; but God *is* faithful, who will not allow you to be tempted beyond what you are able, but with the temptation will also make the way of escape, that you may be able to bear *it.*

[14]Therefore, my beloved, flee from idolatry. [15]I speak as to wise men; judge for yourselves what I say. [16]The cup of blessing which we bless, is it not the communion of the blood of Christ? The bread which we break, is it not the communion of the body of Christ? [17]For we, *though* many, are one bread *and* one body; for we all partake of that one bread.

[18]Observe Israel after the flesh: Are not those who eat of the sacrifices partakers of the altar? [19]What am I saying then? That an idol is anything, or what is offered to idols is anything? [20]Rather, that the things which the Gentiles sacrifice they sacrifice to demons and not to God, and I do not want you to have fellowship with demons. [21]You

TEMPTATION

10:13 In a culture filled with moral depravity and pressures, Paul ga[?] strong encouragement to the Corinthians about temptation. He said: (1) wrong desires and temptations happen to everyone, so don't feel you've been singled out; (2) others have resisted temptation, and so c[?] you; (3) any temptation can be resisted because God will help you resis[?] it. God helps you resist temptation by helping you recognize people an[?] situations that give you trouble. Run from anything you know is wrong[.] choose to do only what is right, pray for God's help, and seek friends w[?] love God and can offer help in times of temptation. Running from a tempting situation is the first step to victory (see 2 Timothy 2:22).

cannot drink the cup of the Lord and the cup of demons; you cannot partake of the Lord's table and of the table of demons. [22]Or do we provoke the Lord to jealousy? Are we stronger than He?

[23]All things are lawful for me, but not all things are helpful; all things are lawful for me, but not all things edify. [24]Let no one seek his own, but each one the other's *well-being.*

[25]Eat whatever is sold in the meat market, asking no questions for conscience' sake; [26]for *"the earth is the* LORD's, *and all its fullness."*

[27]If any of those who do not believe invites you *to dinner,* and you desire to go, eat whatever is set before you, asking no question for conscience' sake. [28]But if anyone says to you, "This was offered to idols," do not eat it for the sake of the one who told you, and for conscience' sake; for *"the earth is the* LORD's, *and all its fullness."* [29]"Conscience," I say, not your own, but that of the other. For why is my liberty judged by another *man's* conscience? [30]But if I partake with thanks, why am I evil spoken of for *the food* over which I give thanks?

[31]Therefore, whether you eat or drink, or whatever you do, do all to the glory of God. [32]Give no offense, either to the Jews or to the Greeks or to the church of God, [33]just as I also please all *men* in all *things,* not seeking my own profit, but the *profit* of many, that they may be saved.

CHAPTER **11** HONOR AND RESPECT IN WORSHIP.

Imitate me, just as I also *imitate* Christ.

[2]Now I praise you, brethren, that you remember me in all things and keep the traditions just as I delivered *them* to you. [3]But I want you to know that the head of every man is Christ, the head of woman *is* man, and the head of Christ *is* God. [4]Every man praying or prophesying, having *his* head covered, dishonors his head. [5]But every woman who prays or prophesies with *her* head uncovered dishonors her head, for that is one and the same as if her head were shaved. [6]For if a woman is not covered, let her also be shorn. But if it is shameful for a woman to be shorn or shaved, let her be covered. [7]For a man indeed ought not to cover *his* head, since he is the image and glory of God; but woman is the glory of man. [8]For man is not from woman, but woman from man. [9]Nor was man created for the woman, but woman for the man. [10]For this reason the woman ought to have *a symbol of* authority on *her* head, because of the angels. [11]Nevertheless, neither *is* man independent of woman, nor woman independent of man, in the Lord. [12]For as woman *came* from man, even so man also *comes* through woman; but all things are from God.

[13]Judge among yourselves. Is it proper for a woman to pray to God with her head uncovered? [14]Does not even nature itself teach you that if a man has long hair, it is a dishonor to him? [15]But if a woman has long hair, it is a glory to her; for *her* hair is given to her for a covering. [16]But if anyone seems to be contentious, we have no such custom, nor *do* the churches of God.

[17]Now in giving these instructions I do not praise *you,* since you come together not for the better but for the worse. [18]For first of all, when you come together as a church, I hear that there are divisions among you, and in part I believe it. [19]For there must also be factions among you, that those who are approved may be recognized among you. [20]Therefore when you come together in one place, it is not to eat the Lord's Supper. [21]For in eating, each one takes his own supper ahead of *others;* and one is hungry and another is drunk. [22]What! Do you not have houses to eat and drink in? Or do you despise the church of God and shame those who have nothing? What shall I say to you? Shall I praise you in this? I do not praise *you.*

THE BEST

10:33 Paul's criterion was not what he liked best, but what was best for those around him. There are several hurtful attitudes toward others: (1) being insensitive and doing what we want, no matter who is hurt by our actions; (2) being oversensitive and doing nothing, for fear that someone may be displeased; (3) being a "yes person" by going along with everything, trying to gain approval from people rather than from God. In this age of "me first" and "looking out for number one," Paul's startling statement is a good standard. When we make the good of others one of our primary goals, we develop a servant's heart.

[23]For I received from the Lord that which I also delivered to you: that the Lord Jesus on the *same* night in which He was betrayed took bread; [24]and when He had given thanks, He broke *it* and said, "Take, eat; this is My body which is broken for you; do this in remembrance of Me." [25]In the same manner *He* also *took* the cup after supper, saying, "This cup is the new covenant in My blood. This do, as often as you drink *it,* in remembrance of Me."

[26]For as often as you eat this bread and drink this cup, you proclaim the Lord's death till He comes.

[27]Therefore whoever eats this bread or drinks *this* cup of the Lord in an unworthy manner will be guilty of the body and blood of the Lord. [28]But let a man examine himself, and so let him eat of the bread and drink of the cup. [29]For he who eats and drinks in an unworthy manner eats and drinks judgment to himself, not discerning the Lord's body. [30]For this reason many *are* weak and sick among you, and many sleep. [31]For if we would judge ourselves, we would not be judged. [32]But when we are judged, we are chastened by the Lord, that we may not be condemned with the world.

EQUALS

11:3-4 Submission is a key element in the smooth functioning of any business, government, or family. God ordained submission in certain relationships to prevent chaos. We must understand, however, that submission is not surrender, withdrawal, or apathy. Nor does it mean inferiority. God created all people in his image; all have equal value. Submission is mutual commitment and cooperation.

Thus God calls for submission among *equals.* He did not make the man superior; he made a way for the man and woman to work together. Jesus Christ, although equal with God the Father, submitted to him to carry out the plan for salvation. Likewise, although equal to man under God, the wife should submit to her husband for the sake of their marriage and family. Submission between equals is submission by choice, not force. We serve God in these relationships through willing submission to others in our church, to our spouse, and to our government leaders.

³³Therefore, my brethren, when you come together to eat, wait for one another. ³⁴But if anyone is hungry, let him eat at home, lest you come together for judgment. And the rest I will set in order when I come.

CHAPTER 12 EVERYONE HAS SPECIAL ABILITIES.

Now concerning spiritual *gifts,* brethren, I do not want you to be ignorant: ²You know that you were Gentiles, carried away to these dumb idols, however you were led. ³Therefore I make known to you that no one speaking by the Spirit of God calls Jesus accursed, and no one can say that Jesus is Lord except by the Holy Spirit.

TEST THEM

12:3 Anyone can claim to speak for God, and the world is full of false teachers. Paul gives us a test to help us discern whether or not a messenger is really from God: does he or she confess Christ as Lord? Don't naively accept the words of all who claim to speak for God. Test their credentials by finding what they teach about Christ.

⁴There are diversities of gifts, but the same Spirit. ⁵There are differences of ministries, but the same Lord. ⁶And there are diversities of activities, but it is the same God who works all in all. ⁷But the manifestation of the Spirit is given to each one for the profit *of all:* ⁸for to one is given the word of wisdom through the Spirit, to another the word of knowledge through the same Spirit, ⁹to another faith by the same Spirit, to another gifts of healings by the same Spirit, ¹⁰to another the working of miracles, to another prophecy, to another discerning of spirits, to another *different* kinds of tongues, to another the interpretation of tongues. ¹¹But one and the same Spirit works all these things, distributing to each one individually as He wills.

BODY LIFE

12:14-17 Using the analogy of the body, Paul emphasizes the importance of each church member. If a seemingly insignificant part is taken away, the whole body becomes less effective (12:22). Thinking that your gift is more important than someone else's is spiritual pride. We should not look down on those who seem unimportant, and we should not be jealous of others who have impressive gifts. Instead, we must use the gifts we have been given and encourage others to use theirs. If we don't, the body of believers will be less effective.

¹²For as the body is one and has many members, but all the members of that one body, being many, are one body, so also *is* Christ. ¹³For by one Spirit we were all baptized into one body—whether Jews or Greeks, whether slaves or free—and have all been made to drink into one Spirit. ¹⁴For in fact the body is not one member but many.

¹⁵If the foot should say, "Because I am not a hand, I am not of the body," is it therefore not of the body? ¹⁶And if the ear should say, "Because I am not an eye, I am not of the body," is it therefore not of the body? ¹⁷If the whole body *were* an eye, where *would be* the hearing? If the whole *were* hearing, where *would be* the smelling? ¹⁸But now God has set the members, each one of them, in the

body just as He pleased. ¹⁹And if they *were* all one member, where *would* the body *be?*

²⁰But now indeed *there are* many members, yet one body. ²¹And the eye cannot say to the hand, "I have no need of you"; nor again the head to the feet, "I have no need of you." ²²No, much rather, those members of the body which seem to be weaker are necessary. ²³And those *members* of the body which we think to be less honorable, on these we bestow greater honor; and our unpresentable *parts* have greater modesty, ²⁴but our presentable *parts* have no need. But God composed the body, having given greater honor to that *part* which lacks it, ²⁵that there should be no schism in the body, but *that* the members should have the same care for one another. ²⁶And if one member suffers, all the members suffer with *it;* or if one member is honored, all the members rejoice with *it.*

²⁷Now you are the body of Christ, and members individually. ²⁸And God has appointed these in the church: first apostles, second prophets, third teachers, after that miracles, then gifts of healings, helps, administrations, varieties of tongues. ²⁹*Are* all apostles? *Are* all prophets? *Are* all teachers? *Are* all workers of miracles? ³⁰Do all have gifts of healings? Do all speak with tongues? Do all interpret? ³¹But earnestly desire the best gifts. And yet I show you a more excellent way.

CHAPTER 13 WHAT IS LOVE? Though I speak with

the tongues of men and of angels, but have not love, I have become sounding brass or a clanging cymbal. ²And though I have *the gift of* prophecy, and understand all mysteries and all knowledge, and though I have all faith, so that I could remove mountains, but have not love, I am nothing. ³And though I bestow all my goods to feed *the poor,* and though I give my body to be burned, but have not love, it profits me nothing.

⁴Love suffers long *and* is kind; love does not envy; love does not parade itself, is not puffed up; ⁵does not behave rudely, does not seek its own, is not provoked, thinks no evil; ⁶does not rejoice in iniquity, but rejoices in the truth; ⁷bears all things, believes all things, hopes all things, endures all things.

⁸Love never fails. But whether *there are* prophecies, they will fail; whether *there are* tongues, they will cease; whether *there is* knowledge, it will vanish away. ⁹For we know in part and we prophesy in part. ¹⁰But when that which is perfect has come, then that which is in part will be done away.

¹¹When I was a child, I spoke as a child, I understood as a child, I thought as a child; but when I became a man, I put away childish things. ¹²For now we see in a mirror, dimly, but then face to face. Now I know in part, but then I shall know just as I also am known.

¹³And now abide faith, hope, love, these three; but the greatest of these *is* love.

LOVE

13:4-7 Our society confuses love and lust. Unlike lust, God's kind of love is directed outward toward others, not inward toward ourself. It is utterly unselfish.

CHAPTER 14 PROPHECY AND TONGUES. Pursue love, and desire spiritual *gifts*, but especially that you may prophesy. ²For he who speaks in a tongue does not speak to men but to God, for no one understands *him;* however, in the spirit he speaks mysteries. ³But he who prophesies speaks edification and exhortation and comfort to men. ⁴He who speaks in a tongue edifies himself, but he who prophesies edifies the church. ⁵I wish you all spoke with tongues, but even more that you prophesied; for he who prophesies *is* greater than he who speaks with tongues, unless indeed he interprets, that the church may receive edification.

⁶But now, brethren, if I come to you speaking with tongues, what shall I profit you unless I speak to you either by revelation, by knowledge, by prophesying, or by teaching? ⁷Even things without life, whether flute or harp, when they make a sound, unless they make a distinction in the sounds, how will it be known what is piped or played? ⁸For if the trumpet makes an uncertain sound, who will prepare for battle? ⁹So likewise you, unless you utter by the tongue words easy to understand, how will it be known what is spoken? For you will be speaking into the air. ¹⁰There are, it may be, so many kinds of languages in the world, and none of them *is* without significance. ¹¹Therefore, if I do not know the meaning of the language, I shall be a foreigner to him who speaks, and he who speaks *will be* a foreigner to me. ¹²Even so you, since you are zealous for spiritual *gifts, let it be* for the edification of the church *that* you seek to excel.

¹³Therefore let him who speaks in a tongue pray that he may interpret. ¹⁴For if I pray in a tongue, my spirit prays, but my understanding is unfruitful. ¹⁵What is *the conclusion* then? I will pray with the spirit, and I will also pray with the understanding. I will sing with the spirit, and I will also sing with the understanding. ¹⁶Otherwise, if you bless with the spirit, how will he who occupies the place of the uninformed say "Amen" at your giving of thanks, since he does not understand what you say? ¹⁷For you indeed give thanks well, but the other is not edified.

¹⁸I thank my God I speak with tongues more than you all; ¹⁹yet in the church I would rather speak five words with my understanding, that I may teach others also, than ten thousand words in a tongue.

²⁰Brethren, do not be children in understanding; however, in malice be babes, but in understanding be mature.

²¹In the law it is written:

"With men of other tongues and other lips
 I will speak to this people;
 And yet, for all that, they will not hear Me,"

says the Lord.

²²Therefore tongues are for a sign, not to those who believe but to unbelievers; but prophesying is not for unbelievers but for those who believe. ²³Therefore if the whole church comes together in one place, and all speak with tongues, and there come in *those who are* uninformed or unbelievers, will they not say that you are out of your mind? ²⁴But if all prophesy, and an unbeliever or an uninformed person comes in, he is convinced by all, he is convicted by all. ²⁵And thus the secrets of his heart are revealed; and so, falling down on *his* face, he will worship God and report that God is truly among you.

²⁶How is it then, brethren? Whenever you come together, each of you has a psalm, has a teaching, has a tongue, has a revelation, has an interpretation. Let all things be done for edification. ²⁷If anyone speaks in a tongue, *let there be* two or at the most three, *each* in turn,

"Here's what I did..."

After a bad dating experience, I decided to find out what God wanted a dating relationship to be. I talked to my youth pastor and studied Scripture. This time, when I felt ready to date again, I made sure I went out with a Christian.

Jenny and I talked about God's will right from the beginning and adopted 1 Corinthians 13 as the basis for our relationship. Even though the romance didn't last forever, it was a very positive experience. We both tried to let verses 4-7 guide all our thoughts and actions toward each other, even when we broke up. I learned a lot from that. God's way really is so much better than any other way of running your life—or of having a relationship.

Sam AGE 16

and let one interpret. ²⁸But if there is no interpreter, let him keep silent in church, and let him speak to himself and to God. ²⁹Let two or three prophets speak, and let the others judge. ³⁰But if *anything* is revealed to another who sits by, let the first keep silent. ³¹For you can all prophesy one by one, that all may learn and all may be encouraged. ³²And the spirits of the prophets are subject to the prophets. ³³For God is not *the author* of confusion but of peace, as in all the churches of the saints.

³⁴Let your women keep silent in the churches, for they are not permitted to speak; but *they are* to be submissive, as the law also says. ³⁵And if they want to learn something, let them ask their own husbands at home; for it is shameful for women to speak in church.

³⁶Or did the word of God come *originally* from you?

REAL WORSHIP

14:26ff Everything done in worship services must be beneficial to the worshipers. This principle touches every aspect—singing, preaching, and the exercise of spiritual gifts. Those contributing to the service (singers, speakers, readers) must have love as their chief motivation, giving useful words or help that will strengthen the faith of other believers.

Or *was it* you only that it reached? ³⁷If anyone thinks himself to be a prophet or spiritual, let him acknowledge that the things which I write to you are the commandments of the Lord. ³⁸But if anyone is ignorant, let him be ignorant.

³⁹Therefore, brethren, desire earnestly to prophesy, and do not forbid to speak with tongues. ⁴⁰Let all things be done decently and in order.

CHAPTER 15 CHRIST ROSE FROM THE DEAD.

Moreover, brethren, I declare to you the gospel which I preached to you, which also you received and in which you stand, ²by which also you are saved, if you hold fast that word which I preached to you—unless you believed in vain.

◣ PROOF

15:5-8 There will always be people who will say that Jesus didn't rise from the dead. Paul assures us that many people saw Jesus after his resurrection, including more than 500 Christian believers. The Resurrection is a historical fact. Don't be discouraged by doubters who deny the Resurrection. Be filled with hope by the knowledge that one day you, and they, will stand before the living proof when Christ returns.

³For I delivered to you first of all that which I also received: that Christ died for our sins according to the Scriptures, ⁴and that He was buried, and that He rose again the third day according to the Scriptures, ⁵and that He was seen by Cephas, then by the twelve. ⁶After that He was seen by over five hundred brethren at once, of whom the greater part remain to the present, but some have fallen asleep. ⁷After that He was seen by James, then by all the apostles. ⁸Then last of all He was seen by me also, as by one born out of due time.

⁹For I am the least of the apostles, who am not worthy to be called an apostle, because I persecuted the church of God. ¹⁰But by the grace of God I am what I am, and His grace toward me was not in vain; but I labored more abundantly than they all, yet not I, but the grace of God *which was* with me. ¹¹Therefore, whether *it was* I or they, so we preach and so you believed.

¹²Now if Christ is preached that He has been raised from the dead, how do some among you say that there is no resurrection of the dead? ¹³But if there is no resurrection of the dead, then Christ is not risen. ¹⁴And if Christ is not risen, then our preaching *is* empty and your faith *is* also empty. ¹⁵Yes, and we are found false witnesses of God, because we have testified of God that He raised up Christ, whom He did not raise up—if in fact the dead do not rise. ¹⁶For if *the* dead do not rise, then Christ is not risen. ¹⁷And if Christ is not risen, your faith *is* futile; you are still in your sins! ¹⁸Then also those who have fallen asleep in Christ have perished. ¹⁹If in this life only we have hope in Christ, we are of all men the most pitiable.

²⁰But now Christ is risen from the dead, *and* has become the firstfruits of those who have fallen asleep. ²¹For since by man *came* death, by Man also *came* the resurrection of the dead. ²²For as in Adam all die, even so in Christ

all shall be made alive. ²³But each one in his own order: Christ the firstfruits, afterward those *who are* Christ's at His coming. ²⁴Then *comes* the end, when He delivers the kingdom to God the Father, when He puts an end to all rule and all authority and power. ²⁵For He must reign till He has put all enemies under His feet. ²⁶The last enemy *that* will be destroyed *is* death. ²⁷For *"He has put all things under His feet."* But when He says "all things are put under *Him*," *it is* evident that He who put all things under Him is excepted. ²⁸Now when all things are made subject to Him, then the Son Himself will also be subject to Him who put all things under Him, that God may be all in all.

²⁹Otherwise, what will they do who are baptized for the dead, if the dead do not rise at all? Why then are they baptized for the dead? ³⁰And why do we stand in jeopardy every hour? ³¹I affirm, by the boasting in you which I have in Christ Jesus our Lord, I die daily. ³²If, in the manner of men, I have fought with beasts at Ephesus, what advantage *is it* to me? If *the* dead do not rise, *"Let us eat and drink, for tomorrow we die!"*

³³Do not be deceived: "Evil company corrupts good habits." ³⁴Awake to righteousness, and do not sin; for some do not have the knowledge of God. I speak *this* to your shame.

³⁵But someone will say, "How are the dead raised up? And with what body do they come?" ³⁶Foolish one, what you sow is not made alive unless it dies. ³⁷And what you sow, you do not sow that body that shall be, but mere grain—perhaps wheat or some other *grain.* ³⁸But God gives it a body as He pleases, and to each seed its own body.

³⁹All flesh *is* not the same flesh, but *there is* one *kind of* flesh of men, another flesh of animals, another of fish, *and* another of birds.

⁴⁰*There are* also celestial bodies and terrestrial bodies; but the glory of the celestial *is* one, and the *glory* of the terrestrial *is* another. ⁴¹*There is* one glory of the sun, another glory of the moon, and another glory of the stars; for *one* star differs from *another* star in glory.

⁴²So also *is* the resurrection of the dead. *The body* is sown in corruption, it is raised in incorruption. ⁴³It is sown in dishonor, it is raised in glory. It is sown in weak-

◣ RESULTS

15:58 Paul said that because of the Resurrection, nothing we do is wasted. Sometimes we hesitate to do good because we don't see any results. But if we can maintain a heavenly perspective, we will understand that we don't often see the good that results from our efforts. Truly believing that Christ has won the ultimate victory will affect the way we live right now. Don't let discouragement over an apparent lack of results keep you from working. Do the good that you have opportunity to do, knowing that your work will have eternal results.

ness, it is raised in power. ⁴⁴It is sown a natural body, it is raised a spiritual body. There is a natural body, and there is a spiritual body. ⁴⁵And so it is written, *"The first man Adam became a living being."* The last Adam *became* a life-giving spirit.

⁴⁶However, the spiritual is not first, but the natural,

and afterward the spiritual. [47]The first man *was* of the earth, *made* of dust; the second Man *is* the Lord from heaven. [48]As *was* the man of dust, so also *are* those *who are made* of dust; and as *is* the heavenly *Man,* so also *are* those *who are* heavenly. [49]And as we have borne the image of the *man* of dust, we shall also bear the image of the heavenly *Man.*

[50]Now this I say, brethren, that flesh and blood cannot inherit the kingdom of God; nor does corruption inherit incorruption. [51]Behold, I tell you a mystery: We shall not all sleep, but we shall all be changed— [52]in a moment, in the twinkling of an eye, at the last trumpet. For the trumpet will sound, and the dead will be raised incorruptible, and we shall be changed. [53]For this corruptible must put on incorruption, and this mortal *must* put on immortality. [54]So when this corruptible has put on incorruption, and this mortal has put on immortality, then shall be brought to pass the saying that is written: *"Death is swallowed up in victory."*

[55] *"O Death, where is your sting?*
    O Hades, where is your victory?"

[56]The sting of death *is* sin, and the strength of sin *is* the law. [57]But thanks *be* to God, who gives us the victory through our Lord Jesus Christ.

[58]Therefore, my beloved brethren, be steadfast, immovable, always abounding in the work of the Lord, knowing that your labor is not in vain in the Lord.

CHAPTER **16** **GIVING AN OFFERING.** Now concerning the collection for the saints, as I have given orders to the churches of Galatia, so you must do also: [2]On the first *day* of the week let each one of you lay something aside, storing up as he may prosper, that there be no collections when I come. [3]And when I come, whomever you approve by *your* letters I will send to bear your gift to Jerusalem. [4]But if it is fitting that I go also, they will go with me.

[5]Now I will come to you when I pass through Macedonia (for I am passing through Macedonia). [6]And it may be that I will remain, or even spend the winter with you, that you may send me on my journey, wherever I go. [7]For I do not wish to see you now on the way; but I hope to stay a while with you, if the Lord permits.

[8]But I will tarry in Ephesus until Pentecost. [9]For a great and effective door has opened to me, and *there are* many adversaries.

[10]And if Timothy comes, see that he may be with you without fear; for he does the work of the Lord, as I also *do.* [11]Therefore let no one despise him. But send him on his journey in peace, that he may come to me; for I am waiting for him with the brethren.

GRAND FINALE

16:22 The Lord Jesus Christ is coming back to earth again. To Paul, this was a glad hope, the best he could look forward to. He was not afraid of seeing Christ—he could hardly wait! Do you share Paul's eager anticipation? Those who love Christ are looking forward to that wonderful time of his return (Titus 2:13).

[12]Now concerning *our* brother Apollos, I strongly urged him to come to you with the brethren, but he was quite unwilling to come at this time; however, he will come when he has a convenient time.

[13]Watch, stand fast in the faith, be brave, be strong. [14]Let all *that* you *do* be done with love.

[15]I urge you, brethren—you know the household of Stephanas, that it is the firstfruits of Achaia, and *that* they have devoted themselves to the ministry of the saints— [16]that you also submit to such, and to everyone who works and labors with *us.*

[17]I am glad about the coming of Stephanas, Fortunatus, and Achaicus, for what was lacking on your part they supplied. [18]For they refreshed my spirit and yours. Therefore acknowledge such men.

[19]The churches of Asia greet you. Aquila and Priscilla greet you heartily in the Lord, with the church that is in their house. [20]All the brethren greet you.

Greet one another with a holy kiss.

[21]The salutation with my own hand—Paul's.

[22]If anyone does not love the Lord Jesus Christ, let him be accursed. O Lord, come!

[23]The grace of our Lord Jesus Christ *be* with you. [24]My love *be* with you all in Christ Jesus. Amen.

MEGA Themes

LOYALTIES The Corinthians were rallying around various church leaders and teachers—Peter, Paul, and Apollos. These loyalties led to intellectual pride and divided the church.

Our loyalty to human leaders or human wisdom must never divide us into various groups. We must care for our fellow Christians, not fight with them. Your allegiance must be to Christ. Let him lead you.

1. How did Paul feel about the various groups who were giving their allegiance to him or Peter or Apollos?
2. What did Paul want to change about their attitude? Why?
3. Based on this passage, at what point does loyalty become a problem in the church?
4. Who are the key Christian leaders you respect? Describe the attitude you should have toward them.

IMMORALITY Paul received a report of uncorrected sexual sin in the church at Corinth. The people had grown indifferent to immorality. Others had misconceptions about marriage. We are to live morally because our body should be ready to serve God.

Christians must never compromise with sinful ideas and practices. You should not become just like those around you, even if everyone seems to disagree with your moral beliefs. You must live up to God's standard of morality and not go along with immoral behavior.

1. What specific immorality does Paul condemn in chapter 5?
2. Why is this type of immorality such an offense to God?
3. Why do you think the Corinthians were tolerating this behavior? How did Paul indicate that they should deal with this ongoing sin? How is this

different than the way they should respond to someone who was sinning but was not claiming to be a Christian? (See 5:9-11.)
4. How can you make an impact on your world without allowing the world to influence you?

FREEDOM Paul taught freedom of choice on practices not expressly forbidden in Scripture. Some believers thought that certain actions—like buying the meat of animals used in heathen rituals—were wrong. Others believed they could do such things without sinning because they were free from the law.

We are free in Christ, yet we must not abuse our Christian freedom by being inconsiderate and insensitive to others. We must never encourage others to do wrong by anything we do. Love should guide our behavior.

1. In chapter 8, Paul instructs the Corinthians on their freedom in Christ. What key principles do you find in this passage for dealing with areas of conduct that are "grays," not black or white?
2. What are some of the "gray areas" that Christians have different opinions about?
3. How could you as a Christian misuse your freedom in Christ and hurt someone else in these "gray" areas?
4. Identify specific ways that you could apply the principles of chapter 8 to your freedom in Christ.

WORSHIP Paul addressed disorder in worship. People were taking the Lord's Supper without first confessing sin. There was misuse of spiritual gifts and confusion over the role of women in the church.

Worship must be carried out properly and orderly. Everything we do to worship God should be done in a manner worthy of his high honor.

1. What concerns did Paul have concerning worship in the Corinthian church? What does this teach you about Paul's view of worship?

2. What actions or attitudes sometimes disrupt true worship in your church?
3. What actions and attitudes encourage true worship in your church?
4. What can you do in your church to help people's worship remain true?

RESURRECTION Some people denied that Christ rose from the dead. Others believed that people would not be physically resurrected. Christ's resurrection assures us that we will have a new, living body after we die. The fact of the Resurrection is the secret of Christian hope.

Because we will be raised again to life after we die, our life is not in vain. We must stay faithful to God in how we live and serve. And we should live today knowing that we will spend eternity with Christ. Eternal life has already begun!

1. Read chapter 15. According to Paul, what is the importance of the Resurrection?
2. What misconceptions did some of the Corinthians have regarding the resurrection of the dead? How did Paul correct those wrong ideas?
3. What would be different about life if Jesus had not risen from the dead?
4. How would you respond if asked to describe the difference Christ's resurrection has made in your own life?

Ministry ... or Madness?: A Quiz Just for You. ■ 1. At Bible club, it rains, a kid throws up on you, and one obnoxious six-year-old complains for *90 minutes* about watery punch. Do you: (a) Dump the watery punch on the obnoxious kid? (b) Wipe throw up *and* dump the punch on the obnoxious kid? (c) Retire from your Bible club career? (d) Pray (really hard!) for patience and kindness? ■ 2. Your youth group gives 400 hard-earned dollars to a family whose house just burned down. The family never even acknowledges the gift! Do you: (a) Break out your lecture on the importance of gratitude? (b) Think of all the ways *you* could have used the cash? (c) Ask for the money back? (d) Trust that God is in control? ■ 3. During a church mission trip, some older teens surround you and call you names, shove you, and make fun of the Christian message on your T-shirt. Do you: (a)"Do a Samson" (i.e., beat them up in the name of Jesus)? (b) Change your shirt? (c) Vow never to stand up for Christ again? (d) Consider it an honor to suffer for Christ? ■ 4. Second Corinthians discusses: (a) Living for the Lord when nothing seems to go right. (b) Why it *is* worth it (no matter what happens) to serve God and others. (c) The amazing truth that we can't outgive God. (d) The importance of telling others about Jesus Christ. (e) All of the above. ■ Being Christ's ambassador isn't crazy—it's the only way to find deep-down satisfaction! Tempted to give up? Second Corinthians is just what you need.

STATS

PURPOSE: To affirm Paul's own ministry, defend his authority as an apostle, and refute the false teachers in Corinth

AUTHOR: Paul

TO WHOM WRITTEN: The church in Corinth, and Christians everywhere

DATE WRITTEN: About A.D. 55–57, from Macedonia

SETTING: Paul had already written three letters to the Corinthians (two are now lost). In 1 Corinthians (the second of these letters), he used strong words to correct and teach. Most of the church had responded in the right spirit. There were, however, those who were denying Paul's authority and questioning his motives.

KEY PEOPLE: Paul, Timothy, Titus, false teachers

KEY PLACES: Corinth, Jerusalem

2 Corinthians

CHAPTER 1 PAUL: A MESSENGER OF GOD. Paul, an apostle of Jesus Christ by the will of God, and Timothy *our* brother,

To the church of God which is at Corinth, with all the saints who are in all Achaia:

²Grace to you and peace from God our Father and the Lord Jesus Christ.

³Blessed *be* the God and Father of our Lord Jesus Christ, the Father of mercies and God of all comfort, ⁴who comforts us in all our tribulation, that we may be able to comfort those who are in any trouble, with the comfort with which we ourselves are comforted by God. ⁵For as the sufferings of Christ abound in us, so our consolation also abounds through Christ. ⁶Now if we are afflicted, *it is* for your consolation and salvation, which is effective for enduring the same sufferings which we also suffer. Or if we are comforted, *it is* for your consolation and salvation. ⁷And our hope for you *is* steadfast, because we know that as you are partakers of the sufferings, so also *you will partake* of the consolation.

⁸For we do not want you to be ignorant, brethren, of our trouble which came to us in Asia: that we were burdened beyond measure, above strength, so that we despaired even of life. ⁹Yes, we had the sentence of death in ourselves, that we should not trust in ourselves but in God who raises the dead, ¹⁰who delivered us from so great a death, and does deliver us; in whom we trust that He will still deliver *us,* ¹¹you also helping together in prayer for us, that thanks may be given by many persons on our behalf for the gift *granted* to us through many.

¹²For our boasting is this: the testimony of our conscience that we conducted ourselves in the world in simplicity and godly sincerity, not with fleshly wisdom but by the grace of God, and more abundantly toward you. ¹³For we are not writing any other things to you than what you read or understand. Now I trust you will understand, even to the end ¹⁴(as also you have understood us in part), that we are your boast as you also *are* ours, in the day of the Lord Jesus.

¹⁵And in this confidence I intended to come to you before, that you might have a second benefit— ¹⁶to pass by way of you to Macedonia, to come again from Macedonia to you, and be helped by you on my way to Judea. ¹⁷Therefore, when I was planning this, did I do it lightly? Or the things I plan, do I plan according to the flesh, that with me there should be Yes, Yes, and No, No? ¹⁸But *as* God *is* faithful, our word to you was not Yes and No. ¹⁹For the Son of God, Jesus Christ, who was preached among you

COMFORT

1:3-4 Many think that when God comforts us, our hardships go away. If that were so, people would turn to God only to be relieved of pain and not out of love for him. Real comfort can also mean receiving strength, encouragement, and hope to deal with our hardships. The more we suffer, the more comfort God gives us (1:5). If you are feeling overwhelmed, allow God to comfort you. Remember, every trial you endure will later become an opportunity to minister to others suffering similar hardships.

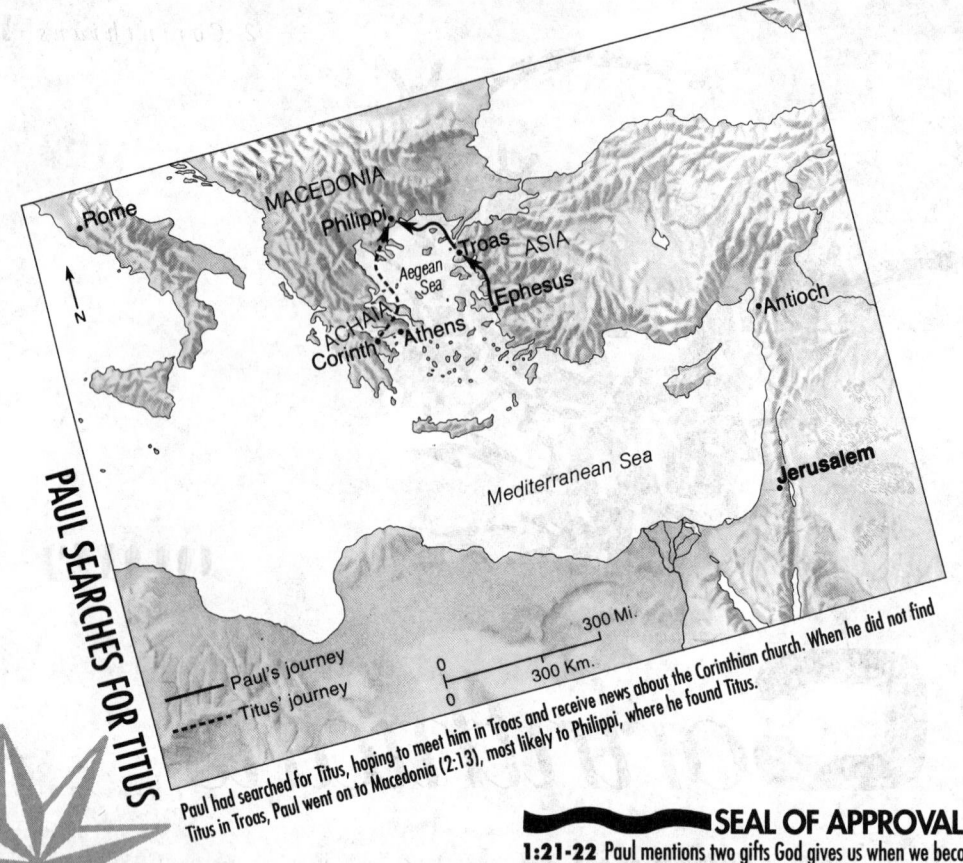

Paul had searched for Titus, hoping to meet him in Troas and receive news about the Corinthian church. When he did not find Titus in Troas, Paul went on to Macedonia (2:13), most likely to Philippi, where he found Titus.

Paul's journey
Titus' journey

by us—by me, Silvanus, and Timothy—was not Yes and No, but in Him was Yes. [20]For all the promises of God in Him *are* Yes, and in Him Amen, to the glory of God through us. [21]Now He who establishes us with you in Christ and has anointed us *is* God, [22]who also has sealed us and given us the Spirit in our hearts as a guarantee.

[23]Moreover I call God as witness against my soul, that to spare you I came no more to Corinth. [24]Not that we have dominion over your faith, but are fellow workers for your joy; for by faith you stand.

CHAPTER 2 FORGIVENESS AND ACCEPTANCE. But
I determined this within myself, that I would not come again to you in sorrow. [2]For if I make you sorrowful, then who is he who makes me glad but the one who is made sorrowful by me?

[3]And I wrote this very thing to you, lest, when I came, I should have sorrow over those from whom I ought to have joy, having confidence in you all that my joy is *the joy* of you all. [4]For out of much affliction and anguish of heart I wrote to you, with many tears, not that you should be grieved, but that you might know the love which I have so abundantly for you.

[5]But if anyone has caused grief, he has not grieved me, but all of you to some extent—not to be too severe. [6]This punishment which *was inflicted* by the majority *is* sufficient for such a man, [7]so that, on the contrary, you *ought* rather to forgive and comfort *him*, lest perhaps such a

SEAL OF APPROVAL

1:21-22 Paul mentions two gifts God gives us when we become believers: (1) a seal of ownership to show who our master is, and (2) Holy Spirit as a guarantee that we belong to him (Ephesians 1:13-1 With the privilege of belonging to God comes the responsibility of identifying ourself as a faithful representative and servant of our n Don't be ashamed to let others know you are his.

one be swallowed up with too much sorrow. [8]Therefore I urge you to reaffirm *your* love to him. [9]For to this end I also wrote, that I might put you to the test, whether you are obedient in all things. [10]Now whom you forgive any-thing, I also *forgive*. For if indeed I have forgiven any-thing, I have forgiven that one for your sakes in the presence of Christ, [11]lest Satan should take advantage of us; for we are not ignorant of his devices.

[12]Furthermore, when I came to Troas to *preach* Christ's gospel, and a door was opened to me by the Lord, [13]I had no rest in my spirit, because I did not find Titus my brother; but taking my leave of them, I departed for Macedonia.

[14]Now thanks *be* to God who always leads us in tri-umph in Christ, and through us diffuses the fragrance of His knowledge in every place. [15]For we are to God the

LIKE HIM

3:17-18 The glory that the Spirit imparts to the believer is great both in quality and longevity than that which Moses experienced. T glory gradually transforms the believer into Christlikeness. Becomin Christlike is a progressive experience (see Romans 8:29; Galatians Philippians 3:21; 1 John 3:2). The more closely we relate to him, th more we will be like him.

fragrance of Christ among those who are being saved and among those who are perishing. ¹⁶To the one *we are* the aroma of death *leading* to death, and to the other the aroma of life *leading* to life. And who *is* sufficient for these things? ¹⁷For we are not, as so many, peddling the word of God; but as of sincerity, but as from God, we speak in the sight of God in Christ.

CHAPTER 3 OUR SUCCESS COMES FROM GOD. Do

we begin again to commend ourselves? Or do we need, as some *others*, epistles of commendation to you or *letters* of commendation from you? ²You are our epistle written in our hearts, known and read by all men; ³clearly *you are* an epistle of Christ, ministered by us, written not with ink but by the Spirit of the living God, not on tablets of stone but on tablets of flesh, *that is*, of the heart.

⁴And we have such trust through Christ toward God. ⁵Not that we are sufficient of ourselves to think of anything as *being* from ourselves, but our sufficiency *is* from God, ⁶who also made us sufficient as ministers of the new covenant, not of the letter but of the Spirit; for the letter kills, but the Spirit gives life.

⁷But if the ministry of death, written *and* engraved on stones, was glorious, so that the children of Israel could not look steadily at the face of Moses because of the glory of his countenance, which *glory* was passing away, ⁸how will the ministry of the Spirit not be more glorious? ⁹For if the ministry of condemnation *had* glory, the ministry of righteousness exceeds much more in glory. ¹⁰For even what was made glorious had no glory in this respect, because of the glory that excels. ¹¹For if what is passing away *was* glorious, what remains *is* much more glorious.

¹²Therefore, since we have such hope, we use great boldness of speech— ¹³unlike Moses, *who* put a veil over his face so that the children of Israel could not look steadily at the end of what was passing away. ¹⁴But their minds were blinded. For until this day the same veil remains unlifted in the reading of the Old Testament, because the *veil* is taken away in Christ. ¹⁵But even to this day, when Moses is read, a veil lies on their heart. ¹⁶Nevertheless when one turns to the Lord, the veil is taken away. ¹⁷Now the Lord is the Spirit; and where the Spirit of the Lord *is*, there *is* liberty. ¹⁸But we all, with unveiled face, beholding as in a mirror the glory of the Lord, are being transformed into the same image from glory to glory, just as by the Spirit of the Lord.

CHAPTER 4 SATAN BLINDS, BUT GOD GIVES LIGHT. Therefore, since we have this ministry, as we have received mercy, we do not lose heart. ²But we have re-

nounced the hidden things of shame, not walking in craftiness nor handling the word of God deceitfully, but by manifestation of the truth commending ourselves to every man's conscience in the sight of God. ³But even if our gospel is veiled, it is veiled to those who are perishing, ⁴whose minds the god of this age has blinded, who do not believe, lest the light of the gospel of the glory of Christ, who is the image of God, should shine on them. ⁵For we do not preach ourselves, but Christ Jesus the Lord, and ourselves your bondservants for Jesus' sake. ⁶For it is the God who commanded light to shine out of darkness, who has shone in our hearts to *give* the light of the knowledge of the glory of God in the face of Jesus Christ.

⁷But we have this treasure in earthen vessels, that the excellence of the power may be of God and not of us. ⁸*We are* hard-pressed on every side, yet not crushed; *we are* perplexed, but not in despair; ⁹persecuted, but not forsaken; struck down, but not destroyed— ¹⁰always carrying about in the body the dying of the Lord Jesus, that the life of Jesus also may be manifested in our body. ¹¹For we who live are always delivered to death for Jesus' sake, that the life of Jesus also may be manifested in our mortal flesh. ¹²So then death is working in us, but life in you.

¹³And since we have the same spirit of faith, according to what is written, *"I believed and therefore I spoke,"* we also believe and therefore speak, ¹⁴knowing that He who

---

"Here's what I did..."

Last year I went through a very difficult time for a whole month. It was one thing after another; I wasn't sure I could take it. God saw me through it, but I still had lots of unresolved questions about why those things had to happen to me.

Not long afterward my friend's sister had a leukemia relapse. When I found out, I prayed and cried for a while. Then I decided to write her a note of encouragement. Later that night, I read 2 Corinthians 1:3-7 and it felt like God was speaking tender words of comfort right to me. I realized that there *was* a reason for the pain I had gone through not long before; it was so that I could relate to the pain of other people and offer true encouragement.

I was not only able to offer my friend's sister some sincere encouragement, but also my nagging questions over why God let me go through my pain were answered. Since then, whenever something painful happens to me I find it much easier to believe that there's a good reason for it.

Linda

AGE 17

◀━━━━FOCUS

4:5 The focus of Paul's preaching was Christ, not himself. When you witness, tell people about what Christ has done rather than about your abilities and accomplishments. People must be introduced to Christ, not to you. If you hear someone preaching about himself or his own ideas rather than Christ, beware—he is a false teacher.

TROUBLES

4:18 Our troubles should not diminish our faith or disillusion us. Instead, we should realize that there is a purpose in our suffering. Problems and human limitations have several benefits: (1) they help us remember Christ's suffering for us; (2) they help keep us from pride; (3) they help us look beyond this brief life; (4) they prove our faith to others; and (5) they give God the opportunity to demonstrate his great power. Don't resent your troubles—see them as opportunities!

raised up the Lord Jesus will also raise us up with Jesus, and will present *us* with you. [15]For all things *are* for your sakes, that grace, having spread through the many, may cause thanksgiving to abound to the glory of God.

[16]Therefore we do not lose heart. Even though our outward man is perishing, yet the inward *man* is being renewed day by day. [17]For our light affliction, which is but for a moment, is working for us a far more exceeding *and* eternal weight of glory, [18]while we do not look at the things which are seen, but at the things which are not seen. For the things which are seen *are* temporary, but the things which are not seen *are* eternal.

CHAPTER 5 WE WILL HAVE A NEW BODY. For we

know that if our earthly house, *this* tent, is destroyed, we have a building from God, a house not made with hands, eternal in the heavens. [2]For in this we groan, earnestly desiring to be clothed with our habitation which is from heaven, [3]if indeed, having been clothed, we shall not be found naked. [4]For we who are in *this* tent groan, being burdened, not because we want to be unclothed, but further clothed, that mortality may be swallowed up by life. [5]Now He who has prepared us for this very thing *is* God, who also has given us the Spirit as a guarantee.

MADE NEW

5:16-17 Christians are brand new people on the *inside*. The Holy Spirit gives them new life, and they are not the same any more. We are not reformed, rehabilitated, or reeducated—we are new creations, living in vital union with Christ (Colossians 2:6-7). We are not merely turning over a new leaf; we are beginning a new life under a new Master.

[6]So *we are* always confident, knowing that while we are at home in the body we are absent from the Lord. [7]For we walk by faith, not by sight. [8]We are confident, yes, well pleased rather to be absent from the body and to be present with the Lord.

[9]Therefore we make it our aim, whether present or absent, to be well pleasing to Him. [10]For we must all appear before the judgment seat of Christ, that each one may receive the things *done* in the body, according to what he has done, whether good or bad. [11]Knowing, therefore, the terror of the Lord, we persuade men; but we are well known to God, and I also trust are well known in your consciences.

[12]For we do not commend ourselves again to you, but give you opportunity to boast on our behalf, that you may have *an answer* for those who boast in appearance and not in heart. [13]For if we are beside ourselves, *it is* for God; or if we are of sound mind, *it is* for you. [14]For the love of Christ compels us, because we judge thus: that if One

died for all, then all died; [15]and He died for all, that those who live should live no longer for themselves, but for Him who died for them and rose again.

[16]Therefore, from now on, we regard no one according to the flesh. Even though we have known Christ according to the flesh, yet now we know *Him thus* no longer. [17]Therefore, if anyone *is* in Christ, *he is* a new creation; old things have passed away; behold, all things have become new. [18]Now all things *are* of God, who has reconciled us to Himself through Jesus Christ, and has given us the ministry of reconciliation, [19]that is, that God was in Christ reconciling the world to Himself, not imputing their trespasses to them, and has committed to us the word of reconciliation.

AMBASSADOR

5:20 An ambassador is an official representative from one countr another. As believers, we are Christ's ambassadors, sent with his me of peace to the world. An ambassador of reconciliation has an impo responsibility. We dare not take this responsibility lightly. How well you fulfilling your commission as Christ's ambassador?

[20]Now then, we are ambassadors for Christ, as though God were pleading through us: we implore *you* on Christ's behalf, be reconciled to God. [21]For He made Him who knew no sin *to be* sin for us, that we might become the righteousness of God in Him.

THEREFORE

IF aNYONE

IS IN CHRIST HE IS

A NEW CREATION

old things have passed away

BEHOLD

ALL THINGS HAVE BECOME NEW

2 CORINTHIANS 5:17

CHAPTER **6** **WHEN LIFE IS HARD, LEAN ON GOD.**
We then, *as* workers together *with Him* also plead with *you* not to receive the grace of God in vain. [2]For He says:

"*In an acceptable time I have heard you,*
And in the day of salvation I have helped you."

Behold, now *is* the accepted time; behold, now *is* the day of salvation.
[3]We give no offense in anything, that our ministry may not be blamed. [4]But in all *things* we commend ourselves as ministers of God: in much patience, in tribulations, in needs, in distresses, [5]in stripes, in imprisonments, in tumults, in labors, in sleeplessness, in fastings; [6]by purity, by knowledge, by longsuffering, by kindness, by the Holy Spirit, by sincere love, [7]by the word of truth, by the power of God, by the armor of righteousness on the right hand and on the left, [8]by honor and dishonor, by evil report and good report; as deceivers, and *yet* true; [9]as unknown, and *yet* well known; as dying, and behold we live; as chastened, and *yet* not killed; [10]as sorrowful, yet always rejoicing; as poor, yet making many rich; as having nothing, and *yet* possessing all things.
[11]O Corinthians! We have spoken openly to you, our heart is wide open. [12]You are not restricted by us, but you are restricted by your *own* affections. [13]Now in return for the same (I speak as to children), you also be open.
[14]Do not be unequally yoked together with unbelievers. For what fellowship has righteousness with lawlessness? And what communion has light with darkness? [15]And what accord has Christ with Belial? Or what part has a believer with an unbeliever? [16]And what agreement has the temple of God with idols? For you are the temple of the living God. As God has said:

"*I will dwell in them*
And walk among them.
I will be their God,
And they shall be My people."

[17]Therefore

"*Come out from among them*
And be separate, says the Lord.
Do not touch what is unclean,
And I will receive you."

[18] "*I will be a Father to you,*
And you shall be My sons and daughters,
Says the LORD *Almighty.*"

CHAPTER **7** **PAUL IS PROUD OF THE CHRISTIANS.**
Therefore, having these promises, beloved, let us cleanse ourselves from all filthiness of the flesh and spirit, perfecting holiness in the fear of God.
[2]Open *your hearts* to us. We have wronged no one, we have corrupted no one, we have cheated no one. [3]I do not say *this* to condemn; for I have said before that you are in our hearts, to die together and to live together. [4]Great *is* my boldness of speech toward you, great *is* my boasting on your behalf. I am filled with comfort. I am exceedingly joyful in all our tribulation.
[5]For indeed, when we came to Macedonia, our bodies had no rest, but we were troubled on every side. Outside *were* conflicts, inside *were* fears. [6]Nevertheless God, who comforts the downcast, comforted us by the coming of Titus, [7]and not only by his coming, but also by the consolation with which he was comforted in you, when he told us of your earnest desire, your mourning, your zeal for me, so that I rejoiced even more.
[8]For even if I made you sorry with my letter, I do not regret it; though I did regret it. For I perceive that the same epistle made you sorry, though only for a while. [9]Now I rejoice, not that you were made sorry, but that

---

I've been a Christian about nine months. Although I have made a lot of friends who are Christians, I still have quite a few who aren't. Should I still be hanging out with friends who aren't Christians?

I WONDER . . .

Find a quarter and two pennies. Place the quarter on a table. Put the two pennies about five inches below the quarter, one inch apart.

Now, pretend God is the quarter, you are the penny on the left, and your friend is the penny on the right. As you grow closer to God (move your penny up an inch or two), what happens to the distance between you and your friend? It gets wider! When only one person in a friendship moves closer to God, that's what happens to the relationship automatically!

There are degrees in friendships and stages we go through to make them stronger. But all friendships take time. And our closest friends affect us. Think about the friends you used to hang around with. You probably did the same things, used the same slang, laughed at the same type of jokes, etc.

Hanging around with old friends who aren't Christians will probably not help you become a stronger Christian. That's what 2 Corinthians 6:14 is about. If you spend all of your deeper friendship time with unbelievers, you'll tend to become like them and not move closer to God.

However, God doesn't want you to be totally isolated from those who aren't Christians. In fact, if you get to the point where you don't have any non-Christian friends, you're probably doing something wrong. If you're going to be Christ's representative to those who don't know him (see 2 Corinthians 5:18-20), you have to be around them! Just be careful, and remember that your goal is to point them to Christ.

"He who walks with wise *men* will be wise, but the companion of fools will be destroyed" (Proverbs 13:20). Especially in the early stages of your Christian life, you need to be around people who will be your friends and help you grow spiritually at the same time.

---

your sorrow led to repentance. For you were made sorry in a godly manner, that you might suffer loss from us in nothing. [10]For godly sorrow produces repentance *leading* to salvation, not to be regretted; but the sorrow of the world produces death. [11]For observe this very thing, that you sorrowed in a godly manner: What diligence it produced in you, *what* clearing *of yourselves, what* indigna-

7:11 It is difficult to hear that we have sinned, and even more difficult to get rid of sin. Paul praised the Corinthians for clearing up an especially troublesome situation. Do you tend to be defensive when confronted? Don't let pride keep you from admitting your sins. Accept confrontation as a tool for growth, and do all you can to correct problems that are pointed out to you.

tion, *what* fear, *what* vehement desire, *what* zeal, *what* vindication! In all *things* you proved yourselves to be clear in this matter. [12]Therefore, although I wrote to you, *I did* not *do it* for the sake of him who had done the wrong, nor for the sake of him who suffered wrong, but that our care for you in the sight of God might appear to you.

[13]Therefore we have been comforted in your comfort. And we rejoiced exceedingly more for the joy of Titus, because his spirit has been refreshed by you all. [14]For if in anything I have boasted to him about you, I am not ashamed. But as we spoke all things to you in truth, even so our boasting to Titus was found true. [15]And his affections are greater for you as he remembers the obedience of you all, how with fear and trembling you received him. [16]Therefore I rejoice that I have confidence in you in everything.

CHAPTER **8** GENEROUS GIVING PLEASES GOD.

Moreover, brethren, we make known to you the grace of God bestowed on the churches of Macedonia: [2]that in a great trial of affliction the abundance of their joy and their deep poverty abounded in the riches of their liberality. [3]For I bear witness that according to *their* ability, yes, and beyond *their* ability, *they were* freely willing, [4]imploring us with much urgency that we would receive

8:2 While on his third missionary journey, Paul was collecting mo the impoverished believers in Jerusalem. The churches in Macedon Philippi, Thessalonica, and Berea—gave money even though they poor, and they gave more than Paul expected. This was sacrificial g they were poor themselves, but they wanted to help. The point of g is not the amount we give, but why and how we give. God wants u give as these churches did—out of dedication to him, love for fell believers, the joy of helping those in need, and because it is right t so. How does your giving measure up?

the gift and the fellowship of the ministering to the saints. [5]And not *only* as we had hoped, but they first gave themselves to the Lord, and *then* to us by the will of God. [6]So we urged Titus, that as he had begun, so he would also complete this grace in you as well. [7]But as you abound in everything—in faith, in speech, in knowledge, in all diligence, and in your love for us—*see* that you abound in this grace also.

Affirm all you see that is good.
(7:4)

Be firm.
(7:9; 10:2)

Be accurate and honest.
(7:14; 8:21)

PRINCIPLES OF CONFRONTATION IN 2 CORINTHIANS

Sometimes rebuke is necessary, but it must be used with caution. The purpose of any rebuke, confrontation, or discipline is to help people, not hurt them.

Use discipline only when all else fails.
(13:2)

Know the facts.
(11:22-27)

Speak words that reflect Christ's message, not your own ideas.
(10:3,12-13; 12:19)

Be gentle after being firm.
(7:15; 13:11-13)

Follow up after the confrontation.
(7:13; 12:14)

[8]I speak not by commandment, but I am testing the sincerity of your love by the diligence of others. [9]For you know the grace of our Lord Jesus Christ, that though He was rich, yet for your sakes He became poor, that you through His poverty might become rich.

[10]And in this I give advice: It is to your advantage not only to be doing what you began and were desiring to do a year ago; [11]but now you also must complete the doing *of it;* that *there was* a readiness to desire *it,* so *there* also *may be* a completion out of what *you* have. [12]For if there is first a willing mind, *it is* accepted according to what one has, *and* not according to what he does not have.

[13]For I *do* not *mean* that others should be eased and you burdened; [14]but by an equality, *that* now at this time your abundance *may supply* their lack, that their abundance also may supply your lack—that there may be equality. [15]As it is written, *"He who gathered much had nothing left over, and he who gathered little had no lack."*

[16]But thanks *be* to God who puts the same earnest care for you into the heart of Titus. [17]For he not only accepted the exhortation, but being more diligent, he went to you of his own accord. [18]And we have sent with him the brother whose praise *is* in the gospel throughout all the churches, [19]and not only *that,* but who was also chosen by the churches to travel with us with this gift, which is administered by us to the glory of the Lord Himself and *to show* your ready mind, [20]avoiding this: that anyone should blame us in this lavish gift which is administered by us— [21]providing honorable things, not only in the sight of the Lord, but also in the sight of men.

[22]And we have sent with them our brother whom we have often proved diligent in many things, but now much more diligent, because of the great confidence which *we have* in you. [23]If *anyone inquires* about Titus, *he is* my partner and fellow worker concerning you. Or if our brethren *are inquired about, they are* messengers of the churches, the glory of Christ. [24]Therefore show to them, and before the churches the proof of your love and of our boasting on your behalf.

CHAPTER 9 GOD LIKES PEOPLE WHO GIVE HAPPILY.

Now concerning the ministering to the saints, it is superfluous for me to write to you; [2]for I know your willingness, about which I boast of you to the Macedonians, that Achaia was ready a year ago; and your zeal has stirred up the majority. [3]Yet I have sent the brethren, lest our boasting of you should be in vain in this respect, that, as I said, you may be ready; [4]lest if *some* Macedonians come with me and find you unprepared, we (not to mention you!) should be ashamed of this confident boasting. [5]Therefore I thought it necessary to exhort the brethren to go to you ahead of time, and prepare your generous gift beforehand, which *you had* previously promised, that it may be ready as *a matter of* generosity and not as a grudging obligation.

[6]But this *I say:* He who sows sparingly will also reap sparingly, and he who sows bountifully will also reap bountifully. [7]*So let* each one *give* as he purposes in his heart, not grudgingly or of necessity; for God loves a cheerful giver. [8]And God *is* able to make all grace abound toward you, that you, always having all sufficiency in all *things,* may have an abundance for every good work. [9]As it is written:

> *"He has dispersed abroad,*
> *He has given to the poor;*
> *His righteousness endures forever."*

[10]Now may He who supplies seed to the sower, and bread for food, supply and multiply the seed you have *sown* and increase the fruits of your righteousness, [11]while *you are* enriched in everything for all liberality, which causes thanksgiving through us to God. [12]For the

◣▬▬▬MORE TO GIVE

9:10 God gives us resources to use and invest for him. Paul used the illustration of seeds to explain that the resources God gives us are not to be hidden, foolishly devoured, or thrown away. Instead, they should be cultivated to produce more crops. When we invest what God has given us in his work, he will provide us with even more to give.

administration of this service not only supplies the needs of the saints, but also is abounding through many thanksgivings to God, [13]while, through the proof of this ministry, they glorify God for the obedience of your confession to the gospel of Christ, and for *your* liberal sharing with them and all *men,* [14]and by their prayer for you, who long for you because of the exceeding grace of God in you. [15]Thanks *be* to God for His indescribable gift!

CHAPTER 10 PAUL'S AUTHORITY.

Now I, Paul, myself am pleading with you by the meekness and gentleness of Christ—who in presence *am* lowly among you, but being absent am bold toward you. [2]But I beg *you* that when I am present I may not be bold with that confidence by which I intend to be bold against some, who think of us as if we walked according to the flesh. [3]For though we walk in the flesh, we do not war according to the flesh. [4]For the weapons of our warfare *are* not carnal but mighty in God for pulling down strongholds, [5]casting down arguments and every high thing that exalts itself against the knowledge of God, bringing every thought into captivity to the obedience of Christ, [6]and being ready to punish all disobedience when your obedience is fulfilled.

[7]Do you look at things according to the outward appearance? If anyone is convinced in himself that he is Christ's, let him again consider this in himself, that just as he *is* Christ's, even so we *are* Christ's. [8]For even if I should boast somewhat more about our authority, which the Lord gave us for edification and not for your destruction, I shall not be ashamed— [9]lest I seem to terrify you by letters. [10]"For *his* letters," they say, "*are* weighty and

◣▬▬▬WEAPONS

10:3-6 Christians must choose whose methods to use, God's or man's. Paul assures us that God's mighty weapons— prayer, faith, hope, love, God's Word, the Holy Spirit—are powerful and effective (see Ephesians 6:13-18)! When dealing with the pride that keeps people from a relationship with Christ, we may be tempted to use our own methods. But nothing can break down Satan's barriers like God's weapons.

powerful, but *his* bodily presence *is* weak, and *his* speech contemptible." [11]Let such a person consider this, that what we are in word by letters when we are absent, such *we will* also *be* in deed when we are present.

[12]For we dare not class ourselves or compare ourselves with those who commend themselves. But they, measuring themselves by themselves, and comparing themselves among themselves, are not wise. [13]We, however, will not boast beyond measure, but within the limits of the sphere which God appointed us—a sphere which especially includes you. [14]For we are not overextending ourselves (as though *our authority* did not extend to you), for it was to you that we came with the gospel of

SERVING GOD

"Tom, maybe you've got the dates mixed up," Jeff says.

"No way—the prison outreach is the same weekend."

"But what about Ben's ski party?"

"I guess I'll have to miss it."

"But, Tom, you can't! Everybody will be at Ben's—including every babe in the whole sophomore class! It's the party of the year!"

"Look, I wish I could go. But I promised to sing with the group at this prison thing."

"Can't you get out of it?"

Tom shakes his head. "Jeff, you just don't understand."

"Well, I say you're making a huge mistake. You'll regret it if you miss Ben's party."

Two weeks later "the" weekend has come and gone. Ben's party was every bit as fun as advertised. Great weather, great skiing—it was a certified blast!

And the prison outreach? Not quite so successful. Not only did the prisoners shower Tom's group with verbal abuse during the concert, but afterwards, during a meal stop on the way home, someone broke into the church van and stole the group's sound equipment!

Does it really pay to serve the Lord? Is the hardship encountered worth all the effort? Take it from the apostle Paul, a guy who should know. He endured unbelievable difficulties (2 Corinthians 4:8-10; 6:4-10; 11:23-28), and yet he was faithful to the end of his life.

Ask God to make you like that.

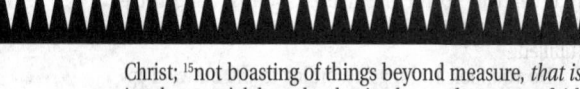

Christ; [15]not boasting of things beyond measure, *that is,* in other men's labors, but having hope, *that* as your faith is increased, we shall be greatly enlarged by you in our sphere, [16]to preach the gospel in the *regions* beyond you, *and* not to boast in another man's sphere of accomplishment.

[17]But *"he who glories, let him glory in the LORD."* [18]For not he who commends himself is approved, but whom the Lord commends.

CHAPTER 11 SMOOTH TALKERS & PHONY TEACHERS.

Oh, that you would bear with me in a little folly—and indeed you do bear with me. [2]For I am jealous for you with godly jealousy. For I have betrothed you to one husband, that I may present *you as* a chaste virgin to

Christ. [3]But I fear, lest somehow, as the serpent deceived Eve by his craftiness, so your minds may be corrupted from the simplicity that is in Christ. [4]For if he who comes preaches another Jesus whom we have not preached, or

SMOOTH TALK

11:3-4 The Corinthian believers fell for smooth talk and messages that sounded good and seemed to make sense. Today there are many teachings that seem to make sense. Don't believe anyone simply because he or she sounds like an authority or says things you like to hear. Read the Bible and check people's words against God's Word. The Bible should be your authoritative guide to all teaching.

if you receive a different spirit which you have not received, or a different gospel which you have not accepted—you may well put up with it!

[5]For I consider that I am not at all inferior to the most eminent apostles. [6]Even though *I am* untrained in speech, yet *I am* not in knowledge. But we have been thoroughly manifested among you in all things.

[7]Did I commit sin in humbling myself that you might be exalted, because I preached the gospel of God to you free of charge? [8]I robbed other churches, taking wages *from them* to minister to you. [9]And when I was present with you, and in need, I was a burden to no one, for what I lacked the brethren who came from Macedonia supplied. And in everything I kept myself from being burdensome to you, and so I will keep *myself.* [10]As the truth of Christ is in me, no one shall stop me from this boasting in the regions of Achaia. [11]Why? Because I do not love you? God knows!

[12]But what I do, I will also continue to do, that I may cut off the opportunity from those who desire an opportunity to be regarded just as we are in the things of which they boast. [13]For such *are* false apostles, deceitful workers, transforming themselves into apostles of Christ. [14]And no wonder! For Satan himself transforms himself into an angel of light. [15]Therefore *it is* no great thing if his ministers also transform themselves into ministers of righteousness, whose end will be according to their works.

[16]I say again, let no one think me a fool. If otherwise, at least receive me as a fool, that I also may boast a little. [17]What I speak, I speak not according to the Lord, but as it were, foolishly, in this confidence of boasting. [18]Seeing that many boast according to the flesh, I also will boast. [19]For you put up with fools gladly, since you *yourselves* are wise! [20]For you put up with it if one brings you into bondage, if one devours *you,* if one takes *from you,* if one exalts himself, if one strikes you on the face. [21]To *our* shame I say that we were too weak for that! But in whatever anyone is bold—I speak foolishly—I am bold also.

[22]Are they Hebrews? So *am* I. Are they Israelites? So *am* I. Are they the seed of Abraham? So *am* I. [23]Are they ministers of Christ?—I speak as a fool—I *am* more: in labors more abundant, in stripes above measure, in prisons more frequently, in deaths often. [24]From the Jews five times I received forty *stripes* minus one. [25]Three times I was beaten with rods; once I was stoned; three times I was shipwrecked; a night and a day I have been in the

deep; ²⁶*in* journeys often, *in* perils of waters, *in* perils of robbers, *in* perils of *my own* countrymen, *in* perils of the Gentiles, *in* perils in the city, *in* perils in the wilderness, *in* perils in the sea, *in* perils among false brethren; ²⁷in weariness and toil, in sleeplessness often, in hunger and thirst, in fastings often, in cold and nakedness— ²⁸besides the other things, what comes upon me daily: my deep concern for all the churches. ²⁹Who is weak, and I am not weak? Who is made to stumble, and I do not burn *with indignation?*

³⁰If I must boast, I will boast in the things which concern my infirmity. ³¹The God and Father of our Lord Jesus Christ, who is blessed forever, knows that I am not lying. ³²In Damascus the governor, under Aretas the king, was guarding the city of the Damascenes with a garrison, desiring to arrest me; ³³but I was let down in a basket through a window in the wall, and escaped from his hands.

CHAPTER **12** **PAUL'S PHYSICAL PROBLEMS.** It is doubtless not profitable for me to boast. I will come to visions and revelations of the Lord: ²I know a man in Christ who fourteen years ago—whether in the body I do not know, or whether out of the body I do not know, God knows—such a one was caught up to the third heaven. ³And I know such a man—whether in the body or out of the body I do not know, God knows— ⁴how he was caught up into Paradise and heard inexpressible words, which it is not lawful for a man to utter. ⁵Of such a one I will boast; yet of myself I will not boast, except in my infirmities. ⁶For though I might desire to boast, I will not be a fool; for I will speak the truth. But I refrain, lest anyone should think of me above what he sees me *to be* or hears from me.

⁷And lest I should be exalted above measure by the abundance of the revelations, a thorn in the flesh was given to me, a messenger of Satan to buffet me, lest I be exalted above measure. ⁸Concerning this thing I pleaded with the Lord three times that it might depart from me. ⁹And He said to me, "My grace is sufficient for you, for My strength is made perfect in weakness." Therefore most gladly I will rather boast in my infirmities, that the power of Christ may rest upon me. ¹⁰Therefore I take pleasure in infirmities, in reproaches, in needs, in persecutions, in distresses, for Christ's sake. For when I am weak, then I am strong.

¹¹I have become a fool in boasting; you have compelled me. For I ought to have been commended by you; for in nothing was I behind the most eminent apostles, though I am nothing. ¹²Truly the signs of an apostle were accomplished among you with all perseverance, in signs and wonders and mighty deeds. ¹³For what is it in which you were inferior to other churches, except that I myself was not burdensome to you? Forgive me this wrong!

¹⁴Now *for* the third time I am ready to come to you. And I will not be burdensome to you; for I do not seek yours, but you. For the children ought not to lay up for the parents, but the parents for the children. ¹⁵And I will very gladly spend and be spent for your souls; though the more abundantly I love you, the less I am loved.

¹⁶But be that *as it may,* I did not burden you. Nevertheless, being crafty, I caught you by cunning! ¹⁷Did I take advantage of you by any of those whom I sent to you? ¹⁸I urged Titus, and sent our brother with *him.* Did Titus take advantage of you? Did we not walk in the same spirit? Did *we* not *walk* in the same steps?

▶ PUT ON TRIAL

12:11-15 Paul is not merely revealing his feelings but defending his authority as an apostle of Jesus Christ. He was hurt that the church in Corinth was doubting and questioning him—but he was defending himself for the cause of the gospel, not to satisfy his ego. When you are "put on trial," do you think only about saving your reputation or are you more concerned about what people will think about Christ?

¹⁹Again, do you think that we excuse ourselves to you? We speak before God in Christ. But *we do* all things, beloved, for your edification. ²⁰For I fear lest, when I come, I shall not find you such as I wish, and *that* I shall be found by you such as you do not wish; lest *there be* contentions, jealousies, outbursts of wrath, selfish ambitions, backbitings, whisperings, conceits, tumults; ²¹lest, when I come again, my God will humble me among you, and I shall mourn for many who have sinned before and have not repented of the uncleanness, fornication, and lewdness which they have practiced.

CHAPTER **13** **CHECK UP ON YOURSELVES.** This *will be* the third *time* I am coming to you. *"By the mouth of two or three witnesses every word shall be established."* ²I have told you before, and foretell as if I were present the second time, and now being absent I write to those who have sinned before, and to all the rest, that if I come again I will not spare— ³since you seek a proof of Christ speaking in me, who is not weak toward you, but mighty in you. ⁴For though He was crucified in weakness, yet He lives by the power of God. For we also are weak in Him, but we shall live with Him by the power of God toward you.

⁵Examine yourselves *as to* whether you are in the faith. Test yourselves. Do you not know yourselves, that Jesus Christ is in you?—unless indeed you are disqualified. ⁶But I trust that you will know that we are not disqualified.

▶ CHECK-UP

13:5 Just as we get physical check-ups, Paul urges us to give ourselves spiritual check-ups. We should look for a growing awareness of Christ's presence and power in our life. Only then will we know if we are true Christians or impostors. If we're not taking active steps to grow closer to God, we are moving away from him.

⁷Now I pray to God that you do no evil, not that we should appear approved, but that you should do what is honorable, though we may seem disqualified. ⁸For we can do nothing against the truth, but for the truth. ⁹For we are glad when we are weak and you are strong. And this also we pray, that you may be made complete. ¹⁰Therefore I write these things being absent, lest being present I should use sharpness, according to the author-

ity which the Lord has given me for edification and not for destruction.

¹¹Finally, brethren, farewell. Become complete. Be of good comfort, be of one mind, live in peace; and the God of love and peace will be with you.

¹²Greet one another with a holy kiss.

¹³All the saints greet you.

¹⁴The grace of the Lord Jesus Christ, and the love of God, and the communion of the Holy Spirit *be* with you all. Amen.

MEGA *Themes*

TRIALS Paul experienced great suffering, persecution, and opposition in his ministry. He even struggled with a personal weakness—a "thorn in the flesh." Through it all, Paul affirmed God's faithfulness.

God is faithful. His strength is sufficient for any trial—and trials can keep us from becoming prideful and teach us dependence on God. We must look to God for comfort during trials. As he comforts us, we can learn to comfort others.

1. What are some of the feelings Paul expressed regarding his personal trial?
2. What truth had Paul learned from his suffering and persecution?
3. Based on Paul's example, what feelings can you expect when you encounter trials?
4. What attitude does God want you to have during trials? Why?
5. Describe a time when you encountered personal difficulty. How did you feel then? How do you feel about the experience now? What did you learn about God from that experience?

CHURCH DISCIPLINE Paul defends his role in church discipline. Neither immorality nor false teaching could be ignored. The church was to be neither too lax nor too severe in administering discipline. The church was to restore the corrected person when he or she repented.

The goal of discipline in the church should be correction, not vengeance. For churches to be effective, they must confront and solve problems, not ignore them. But in everything we must act in and on behalf of God's love.

1. In 2:5-11, we are given a glimpse into what church discipline should be about. What does this passage teach you about Paul?
2. What was Paul's motive for seeing the person disciplined?
3. What should the church's role be when dealing with members who refuse to repent of sin?

4. What does this teach you about how God wants you to deal with your personal sins?

HOPE Paul tried to encourage the Corinthians as they faced trials by reminding them that they would receive new bodies in heaven. This would be a great victory in contrast to their present suffering.

Knowing we will receive new bodies gives us hope. No matter what we face, we can keep going, for our faithful service will result in triumph.

1. Summarize the hope Paul gives to the Corinthians in 5:1-11.
2. Why did Paul use this part of his letter to communicate this hope to the Corinthians? (See 4:13-18.)
3. Under what circumstances would you most need to be reminded of your heavenly hope?
4. How should being reminded of that promise bring hope to you in your present circumstances?

GIVING Paul organized a collection of funds for the poor in the Jerusalem church. Many of the Asian churches gave money. Paul explains and defends his beliefs about giving, and he urges the Corinthians to follow through on their previous commitment.

We, too, should honor our financial commitments. Our giving must be generous, sacrificial, according to a plan, and based on need. Generosity helps the needy, enabling them to thank God. Giving is a part of our godliness.

1. What benefit had Paul received from the believers' giving? What benefit had the believers themselves received as a result of their giving?
2. What should Christians understand about giving money for God's work in the church? How could this be applied to giving other personal resources, such as time and service?
3. In what ways would God want you to continue what you are doing in your giving? How should you change what you are doing?

SOUND DOCTRINE False teachers were challenging Paul's ministry and authority as an apostle. Paul asserted his authority to preserve correct Christian doctrine. His sincerity, love for Christ, and concern for the people were his defense.

We should share Paul's concern for correct teaching in our churches. In so doing, we must also share his motivation—love for Christ and people—and we should be sincere.

1. Describe the common characteristics of those who were opposing Paul (chapters 10–11).

2. How was Paul responding to their opposition? Why do you think he was so concerned about their influence?

3. Contrast Paul's ministry with the actions of those who opposed him. What were the key differences?

4. How can you avoid being deceived by teachers of false doctrine?

5. We must not only know sound doctrine, but also live according to its truth. What areas of your daily life reflect sound doctrine?

*E*ver known a church like Matt's? Words like *different* and *strict* don't even begin to tell the story. Maybe Matt's best friend Randy gave the best description. He attended Matt's church for several months—then quit. Matt wanted to know why. ■ "I just don't like it, OK?" Randy finally said. "It's the 'don't church.' You guys have about fifty million rules—Don't date. Don't wear certain clothes. Don't go to the movies. Don't dance. Don't go to parties. Don't wear jewelry. Don't be friends with non-Christians. And the list just keeps going. I can't even *remember* all the rules, much less *follow* them! Besides, some people there act like they're *better* than people who go to other churches." ■ "But you said you *liked* our preacher—and the services." ■ "I guess I did—at first. But I came home feeling more and more guilty, and further away from God than ever. Sorry Matt, but if following all those rules is how I'm supposed to get close to God, I might as well forget it . . . . Hey, I want to be a good Christian—but I'll never be *that* good." ■ Almost 2,000 years ago there was another "don't church" of Christians trying to follow rules. In fact, a whole book of the Bible addresses trying to *earn* God's acceptance by doing "right" things. ■ Read Galatians. You'll find that anyone who thinks the Bible doesn't relate to modern times has never read it!

STATS

PURPOSE: To refute the Judaizers (who taught that Gentile believers must obey the Jewish law to be saved), and to call Christians to faith and freedom in Christ

AUTHOR: Paul

TO WHOM WRITTEN: The churches in southern Galatia founded on Paul's first missionary journey (including Iconium, Lystra, Derbe), and Christians everywhere

DATE WRITTEN: About A.D. 49, from Antioch, prior to the Jerusalem council (A.D. 50)

SETTING: The most pressing controversy of the early church was the relationship of new believers, especially Gentiles, to the Jewish laws. When this problem hit the converts and young churches Paul founded on his first missionary journey, Paul wrote to correct it. Later, at the council in Jerusalem, the conflict was officially resolved by the church leaders.

KEY PEOPLE: Paul, Peter, Barnabas, Titus, Abraham, false teachers

KEY PLACES: Galatia, Jerusalem

Galatians

¹⁰For do I now persuade men, or God? Or do I seek to please men? For if I still pleased men, I would not be a bondservant of Christ. ¹¹But I make known to you, brethren, that the gospel which was preached by me is not according to man. ¹²For I neither received it from man, nor was I taught *it*, but *it came* through the revelation of Jesus Christ.

TWISTED

1:7 Twisted truth is sometimes more difficult to spot than outright lies. The Judaizers were "perverting" or twisting the truth about Christ because they believed that all believers had to follow the Jewish laws in order to be saved. They claimed to follow him, but they denied that Jesus' work on the cross was sufficient for salvation. There will always be people who twist the Good News. Either they do not understand what the Bible teaches, or they are uncomfortable with the truth as it stands. How can we tell when people are twisting the truth? Find out what they teach about Jesus Christ. If their teaching does not match the truth in God's Word, then it is wrong.

¹³For you have heard of my former conduct in Judaism, how I persecuted the church of God beyond measure and *tried to* destroy it. ¹⁴And I advanced in Judaism beyond many of my contemporaries in my own nation, being more exceedingly zealous for the traditions of my fathers. ¹⁵But when it pleased God, who separated me from my mother's womb and called *me* through His grace, ¹⁶to reveal His Son in me, that I might preach Him among the Gentiles, I did not immediately confer with flesh and blood, ¹⁷nor did I go up to Jerusalem to those *who were* apostles before me; but I went to Arabia, and returned again to Damascus. ¹⁸Then after three years I went up to Jerusalem to see Peter, and remained with him fifteen days. ¹⁹But I saw none of the other apostles except James, the Lord's brother. ²⁰(Now *concerning* the things which I write to you, indeed, before God, I do not lie.) ²¹Afterward I went into the regions of Syria and Cilicia. ²²And I was unknown by face to the churches of Judea which *were* in Christ. ²³But they were hearing only, "He who formerly persecuted us now preaches the faith which he once *tried to* destroy." ²⁴And they glorified God in me.

BIG CHANGE

1:24 Paul's changed life brought many comments from people who saw or heard of him. His new life astonished them, and they glorified God because only God could have turned this zealous persecutor of Christians into a Christian himself. We may not have had as dramatic a change as Paul had, but our new life should glorify our Savior. When people look at us, do they recognize that God has made changes in us? If not, perhaps we are not living as we should.

CHAPTER 1 PAUL: CHRIST'S MISSIONARY. Paul, an apostle (not from men nor through man, but through Jesus Christ and God the Father who raised Him from the dead), ²and all the brethren who are with me,

To the churches of Galatia:

³Grace to you and peace from God the Father and our Lord Jesus Christ, ⁴who gave Himself for our sins, that He might deliver us from this present evil age, according to the will of our God and Father, ⁵to whom *be* glory forever and ever. Amen.

⁶I marvel that you are turning away so soon from Him who called you in the grace of Christ, to a different gospel, ⁷which is not another; but there are some who trouble you and want to pervert the gospel of Christ. ⁸But even if we, or an angel from heaven, preach any other gospel to you than what we have preached to you, let him be accursed. ⁹As we have said before, so now I say again, if anyone preaches any other gospel to you than what you have received, let him be accursed.

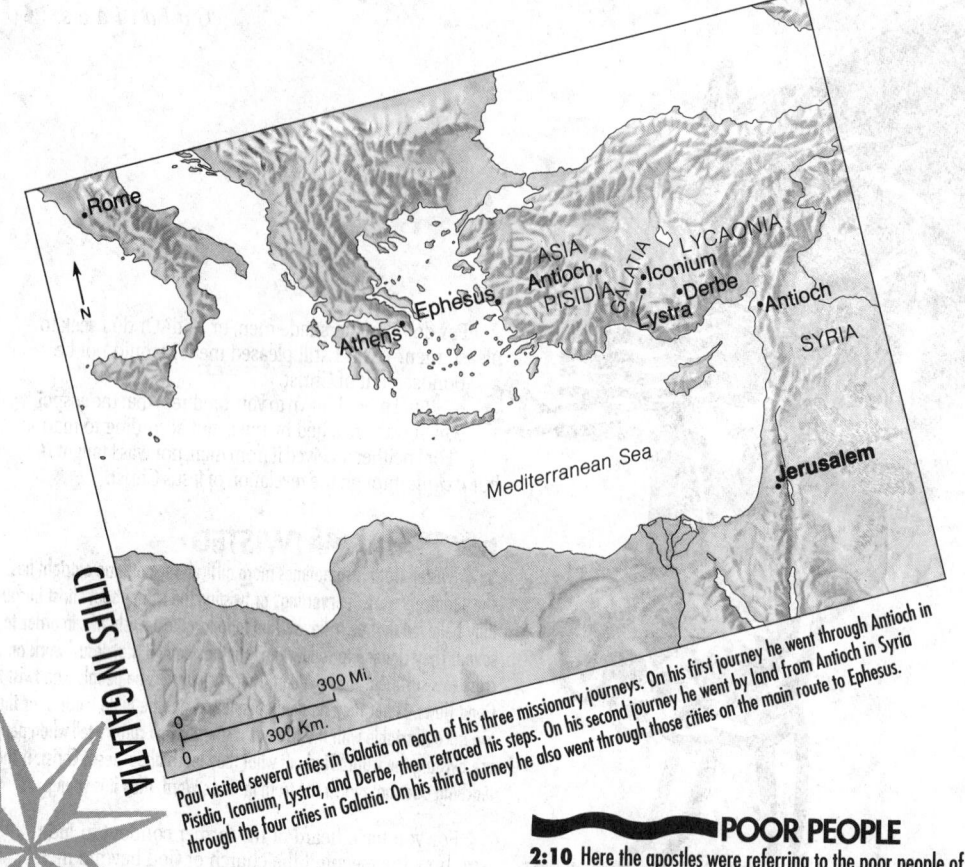

Paul visited several cities in Galatia on each of his three missionary journeys. On his first journey he went through Antioch in Pisidia, Iconium, Lystra, and Derbe, then retraced his steps. On his second journey he went by land from Antioch in Syria through the four cities in Galatia. On his third journey he also went through those cities on the main route to Ephesus.

CHAPTER 2 CHURCH LEADERS ACCEPTED PAUL.

Then after fourteen years I went up again to Jerusalem with Barnabas, and also took Titus with *me*. ²And I went up by revelation, and communicated to them that gospel which I preach among the Gentiles, but privately to those who were of reputation, lest by any means I might run, or had run, in vain. ³Yet not even Titus who *was* with me, being a Greek, was compelled to be circumcised. ⁴And *this occurred* because of false brethren secretly brought in (who came in by stealth to spy out our liberty which we have in Christ Jesus, that they might bring us into bondage), ⁵to whom we did not yield submission even for an hour, that the truth of the gospel might continue with you.

⁶But from those who seemed to be something—whatever they were, it makes no difference to me; God shows personal favoritism to no man—for those who seemed *to be something* added nothing to me. ⁷But on the contrary, when they saw that the gospel for the uncircumcised had been committed to me, as *the gospel* for the circumcised *was* to Peter ⁸(for He who worked effectively in Peter for the apostleship to the circumcised also worked effectively in me toward the Gentiles), ⁹and when James, Cephas, and John, who seemed to be pillars, perceived the grace that had been given to me, they gave me and Barnabas the right hand of fellowship, that we *should go* to the Gentiles and they to the circumcised. ¹⁰They desired

2:10 Here the apostles were referring to the poor people of Jerusale. While many Gentile converts were financially comfortable, the Jerusa church was suffering from a severe famine in Palestine (see Acts 11:28-30). Much of Paul's time was spent gathering funds for the Jew Christians (Acts 24:17; Romans 15:25-29; 1 Corinthians 16:1-4; 2 Corinthians 8). Believers caring for the poor is a constant theme of Scripture, but often we do nothing about it. Both in your own city and across the oceans, there are people who need help. What can you do show them God's love?

only that we should remember the poor, the very thing which I also was eager to do.

¹¹Now when Peter had come to Antioch, I withstood him to his face, because he was to be blamed; ¹²for before certain men came from James, he would eat with the Gentiles; but when they came, he withdrew and separated himself, fearing those who were of the circumcision. ¹³And the rest of the Jews also played the hypocrite with him, so that even Barnabas was carried away with their hypocrisy.

¹⁴But when I saw that they were not straightforward about the truth of the gospel, I said to Peter before *them* all, "If you, being a Jew, live in the manner of Gentiles and not as the Jews, why do you compel Gentiles to live as Jews? ¹⁵We *who are* Jews by nature, and not sinners of the Gentiles, ¹⁶knowing that a man is not justified by the works of the law but by faith in Jesus Christ, even we have believed in Christ Jesus, that we might be justified by faith in Christ and not by the works of the law; for by the works of the law no flesh shall be justified.

Ceremonial Law
This kind of law relates specifically to Israel's worship (for example, see Leviticus 1:1-13). Its primary purpose was to point forward to Jesus Christ. Therefore, these laws were no longer necessary after Jesus' death and resurrection. While we are no longer bound by ceremonial laws, the principles behind them—to worship and love a holy God—still apply. The Jewish Christians often accused the Gentile Christians of violating the ceremonial law.

Civil Law
This type of law dictated Israel's daily living (for example, see Deuteronomy 24:10-11). Because modern society and culture are so radically different, some of these guidelines cannot be followed specifically. But the principles behind the commands should guide our conduct. At times, Paul asked Gentile Christians to follow some of these laws, not because they had to, but to promote unity.

Moral Law
This sort of law is the direct command of God—for example, the Ten Commandments (Exodus 20:1-17). It requires strict obedience. It reveals the nature and will of God, and it still applies to us today. We are to obey this moral law, not to obtain salvation, but to live in ways pleasing to God.

WHAT IS THE LAW?

Part of the Jewish law included those laws found in the Old Testament. In the Old Testament there were three categories of law: ceremonial laws, civil laws, and moral laws. When Paul says that non-Jews (Gentiles) are no longer bound by these laws, he is not saying that the Old Testament laws do not apply to us today. He is saying certain types of laws may not apply to us.

---

[17]"But if, while we seek to be justified by Christ, we ourselves also are found sinners, *is* Christ therefore a minister of sin? Certainly not! [18]For if I build again those things which I destroyed, I make myself a transgressor. [19]For I through the law died to the law that I might live to God. [20]I have been crucified with Christ; it is no longer I who live, but Christ lives in me; and the *life* which I now live in the flesh I live by faith in the Son of God, who loved me and gave Himself for me. [21]I do not set aside the grace of God; for if righteousness *comes* through the law, then Christ died in vain."

CHAPTER 3 JEWISH LAW AND FAITH IN CHRIST.

O foolish Galatians! Who has bewitched you that you should not obey the truth, before whose eyes Jesus Christ was clearly portrayed among you as crucified? [2]This only I want to learn from you: Did you receive the Spirit by the works of the law, or by the hearing of faith? [3]Are you so foolish? Having begun in the Spirit, are you now being made perfect by the flesh? [4]Have you suffered so many things in vain—if indeed *it was* in vain?

[5]Therefore He who supplies the Spirit to you and works miracles among you, *does He do it* by the works of the law, or by the hearing of faith?— [6]just as Abraham *"believed God, and it was accounted to him for righteousness."* [7]Therefore know that *only* those who are of faith are sons of Abraham. [8]And the Scripture, foreseeing that God would justify the Gentiles by faith, preached the gospel to Abraham beforehand, *saying, "In you all the nations shall be blessed."* [9]So then those who *are* of faith are blessed with believing Abraham.

[10]For as many as are of the works of the law are under the curse; for it is written, *"Cursed is everyone who does not continue in all things which are written in the book of the law, to do them."* [11]But that no one is justified by the law in the sight of God *is* evident, for *"the just shall live by faith."* [12]Yet the law is not of faith, but *"the man who does them shall live by them."*

[13]Christ has redeemed us from the curse of the law, having become a curse for us (for it is written, *"Cursed is everyone who hangs on a tree"*), [14]that the blessing of Abraham might come upon the Gentiles in Christ Jesus, that we might receive the promise of the Spirit through faith.

¹⁵Brethren, I speak in the manner of men: Though *it is* only a man's covenant, yet *if it is* confirmed, no one annuls or adds to it. ¹⁶Now to Abraham and his Seed were the promises made. He does not say, "And to seeds," as of many, but as of one, *"And to your Seed,"* who is Christ. ¹⁷And this I say, *that* the law, which was four hundred and thirty years later, cannot annul the covenant that was confirmed before by God in Christ, that it should make the promise of no effect. ¹⁸For if the inheritance *is* of the law, *it is* no longer of promise; but God gave *it* to Abraham by promise.

¹⁹What purpose then *does* the law *serve?* It was added because of transgressions, till the Seed should come to whom the promise was made; *and it was* appointed

FREEDOM

Cindi storms up upstairs, slams her bedroom door, and flings herself onto the bed. Burying her face in a pillow, she lets out a yell of disgust.

Rolling over, she stares at the ceiling and begins thinking:

Ooooh. I can't believe them! They're like the Gestapo! Why don't they just go ahead and put bars around my room? They don't let me do anything. They ask me six million questions about everything. They hate all my friends. They make me dress like a street person.

Cindi glances at the calendar above her desk.

Nine more months—then I can go to college and do whatever I want. I'll be totally free. If I don't want to go to church, I won't have to. If I want to trash my room and leave it that way the whole semester, I can. I'll be able to go out when I want and see who I want without them totally humiliating me.

Oh, gosh, that is gonna be so great! No more missing out on life. There'll be parties, tons of awesome guys, and . . .

Cindi's daydream is shattered by a voice yelling:

"Cindi! Come pick up your shoes from out of the middle of the living room floor—now!"

Cindi groans and heads downstairs, mumbling, "Enjoy it now, Mom. Because in nine months, I'm out of here."

Is that freedom? Being able to do whatever you want? Or does real freedom have certain limits? See Galatians 5:16-25 to find out.

through angels by the hand of a mediator. ²⁰Now a mediator does not *mediate* for one *only,* but God is one.

²¹*Is* the law then against the promises of God? Certainly not! For if there had been a law given which could have given life, truly righteousness would have been by the law. ²²But the Scripture has confined all under sin, that the promise by faith in Jesus Christ might be given to those who believe. ²³But before faith came, we were kept under guard by the law, kept for the faith which would afterward be revealed. ²⁴Therefore the law was our tutor *to bring us* to Christ, that we might be justified by faith. ²⁵But after faith has come, we are no longer under a tutor.

²⁶For you are all sons of God through faith in Christ Jesus. ²⁷For as many of you as were baptized into Christ have put on Christ. ²⁸There is neither Jew nor Greek, there

DIFFERENCES

3:28 Our natural inclination is to feel uncomfortable around thos‹ are different from us and to spend time with those who resemble u‹ when we allow our differences to separate us from our fellow belie‹ we disregard clear biblical teaching. Make a point of seeking out ar‹ appreciating people who are different from you and your friends. Y‹ may find that you and they have a lot in common.

is neither slave nor free, there is neither male nor female; for you are all one in Christ Jesus. ²⁹And if you *are* Christ's, then you are Abraham's seed, and heirs according to the promise.

CHAPTER 4 PAUL'S CONCERN FOR THE GALATIANS.

Now I say *that* the heir, as long as he is a child, does not differ at all from a slave, though he is master of all, ²but is under guardians and stewards until the time appointed by the father. ³Even so we, when we were children, were in bondage under the elements of the world. ⁴But when the fullness of the time had come, God sent forth His Son, born of a woman, born under the law, ⁵to redeem those who were under the law, that we might receive the adoption as sons.

⁶And because you are sons, God has sent forth the Spirit of His Son into your hearts, crying out, "Abba, Father!" ⁷Therefore you are no longer a slave but a son, and if a son, then an heir of God through Christ.

BE OPEN

4:16 Paul did not gain great popularity when he criticized the Gala‹ for turning away from their first faith in Christ. Human nature hasn't changed much—we still get angry when we're scolded. But don't wr‹ off someone who challenges you. There may be truth in what he or s‹ says. Receive the challenge with humility; carefully think it over. If y‹ discover you need to change an attitude or action, take steps to do it.

⁸But then, indeed, when you did not know God, you served those which by nature are not gods. ⁹But now after you have known God, or rather are known by God, how *is it that* you turn again to the weak and beggarly elements, to which you desire again to be in bondage? ¹⁰You observe days and months and seasons and years. ¹¹I am afraid for you, lest I have labored for you in vain.

¹²Brethren, I urge you to become like me, for I *became* like you. You have not injured me at all. ¹³You know that because of physical infirmity I preached the gospel to you at the first. ¹⁴And my trial which was in my flesh you did not despise or reject, but you received me as an angel of God, *even* as Christ Jesus. ¹⁵What then was the blessing you *enjoyed?* For I bear you witness that, if possible, you would have plucked out your own eyes and given them

LOVE

5:14-15 When we are not motivated by love, we become critical of others. We stop looking for good in them and see only their faults. Soc‹ the unity of believers becomes broken. Have you talked behind someone's back? Have you focused on others' shortcomings instead of their strengths? Remind yourself of Jesus' command to love others as‹ love ourselves (Matthew 22:39). When you begin to feel critical of someone, make a list of that person's positive qualities. And don't say anything behind his back that you wouldn't say to his face.

to me. [16]Have I therefore become your enemy because I tell you the truth?

[17]They zealously court you, *but* for no good; yes, they want to exclude you, that you may be zealous for them. [18]But it is good to be zealous in a good thing always, and not only when I am present with you. [19]My little children, for whom I labor in birth again until Christ is formed in you, [20]I would like to be present with you now and to change my tone; for I have doubts about you.

[21]Tell me, you who desire to be under the law, do you not hear the law? [22]For it is written that Abraham had two sons: the one by a bondwoman, the other by a freewoman. [23]But he *who was* of the bondwoman was born according to the flesh, and he of the freewoman through promise, [24]which things are symbolic. For these are the two covenants: the one from Mount Sinai which gives birth to bondage, which is Hagar— [25]for this Hagar is Mount Sinai in Arabia, and corresponds to Jerusalem which now is, and is in bondage with her children— [26]but the Jerusalem above is free, which is the mother of us all. [27]For it is written:

> "*Rejoice, O barren,*
> *You who do not bear!*
> *Break forth and shout,*
> *You who are not in labor!*
> *For the desolate has many more children*
> *Than she who has a husband.*"

[28]Now we, brethren, as Isaac *was*, are children of promise. [29]But, as he who was born according to the flesh then persecuted him *who was born* according to the Spirit, even so *it is* now. [30]Nevertheless what does the Scripture say? *"Cast out the bondwoman and her son, for the son of the bondwoman shall not be heir with the son of the freewoman."* [31]So then, brethren, we are not children of the bondwoman but of the free.

CHAPTER **5** FREEDOM: CHRIST'S SPECIAL GIFT.

Stand fast therefore in the liberty by which Christ has made us free, and do not be entangled again with a yoke of bondage. [2]Indeed I, Paul, say to you that if you become circumcised, Christ will profit you nothing. [3]And I testify again to every man who becomes circumcised that he is a debtor to keep the whole law. [4]You have become estranged from Christ, you who *attempt to* be justified by law; you have fallen from grace. [5]For we through the Spirit eagerly wait for the hope of righteousness by faith. [6]For in Christ Jesus neither circumcision nor uncircumcision avails anything, but faith working through love.

[7]You ran well. Who hindered you from obeying the truth? [8]This persuasion does not *come* from Him who calls you. [9]A little leaven leavens the whole lump. [10]I have confidence in you, in the Lord, that you will have no other mind; but he who troubles you shall bear his judgment, whoever he is.

[11]And I, brethren, if I still preach circumcision, why do I still suffer persecution? Then the offense of the cross has ceased. [12]I could wish that those who trouble you would even cut themselves off!

[13]For you, brethren, have been called to liberty; only do not *use* liberty as an opportunity for the flesh, but through love serve one another. [14]For all the law is fulfilled in one word, *even* in this: *"You shall love your neighbor as yourself."* [15]But if you bite and devour one another, beware lest you be consumed by one another!

[16]I say then: Walk in the Spirit, and you shall not fulfill the lust of the flesh. [17]For the flesh lusts against the Spirit, and the Spirit against the flesh; and these are contrary to one another, so that you do not do the things that you wish. [18]But if you are led by the Spirit, you are not under the law.

[19]Now the works of the flesh are evident, which are:

I know that taking drugs is wrong, but the Bible doesn't talk about them. What should I say to someone if they ask me about drugs?

I WONDER . . .

There are some areas where the Bible is silent. A good example is R-rated movies. The Bible doesn't specifically forbid attending movies that contain vulgar language, violence, or sex. In such cases, it is essential to seek the wisdom of those who know God's Word well. By looking at a number of passages, it is obvious we should avoid those kind of movies.

Of course, there are many areas where the Bible is specific in its warnings. Homosexuality is a good example (see 1 Corinthians 6:9-10). Then there are areas that are "hidden" to a degree. Taking drugs falls into this category.

Originally the New Testament was written in Greek, a much more complicated language than English. Trying to translate a word from Greek to English often can only be done by a phrase.

In Galatians 5:20, Christians are warned against becoming involved in spiritism. The word *spiritism* (encouraging the activity of demons) actually comes from the Greek noun, *pharmakeia,* from which we get the word *pharmacy* (better known as a drug store!). When most of the Bible was translated, drug problems were not common, but there was "spiritism."

The connection is frightening. Spiritism (sorcery, witchcraft) actually happens when drugs are taken! These aren't the aspirin type of drugs, but the kinds that alter a person's emotions, reflexes, and brain waves.

To get even more specific, taking drugs is like opening your subconscious to demons! The connection between drugs and witchcraft is easily seen by going to the original Greek word.

Unknowingly, a person who takes drugs opens himself or herself to demonic influence. It's like an invitation to the spirit world to start influencing that person's life. That's why it's so dangerous.

Although many may laugh at this explanation, it's a message that must be given to those who are taking drugs.

Drugs also should be avoided because they harm our body. The Bible is very clear about our responsibility to take care of ourself. See 1 Corinthians 6:19-20; Romans 12:1-2; and 3 John 1:2-3.

5:22-23 The Spirit produces character traits, not specific actions. We can't go out and *do* these things, and we can't obtain them by trying to get them. If we want the fruit of the Spirit to develop in our life, we must recognize that all of these characteristics are found in Christ. The way to grow them is to know Christ, love him, remember him, imitate him (see John 15:4-5). The result will be that we will fulfill the intended purpose of the law—loving God and people. Which of these qualities most needs further development in your life?

adultery, fornication, uncleanness, lewdness, [20]idolatry, sorcery, hatred, contentions, jealousies, outbursts of wrath, selfish ambitions, dissensions, heresies, [21]envy, murders, drunkenness, revelries, and the like; of which I tell you beforehand, just as I also told *you* in time past, that those who practice such things will not inherit the kingdom of God.

EVERY PART

5:25 God is interested in every part of our life, not just the spiritual part. As we live by the Holy Spirit's power, we need to submit every aspect of our life to God— emotional, physical, social, intellectual, and vocational. Paul says, "You're saved, so live like it!" The Holy Spirit is the source of your new life, so walk with him. Don't let anything or anyone else determine your values and standards in any area of your life.

[22]But the fruit of the Spirit is love, joy, peace, longsuffering, kindness, goodness, faithfulness, [23]gentleness, self-control. Against such there is no law. [24]And those *who are* Christ's have crucified the flesh with its passions and desires. [25]If we live in the Spirit, let us also walk in the Spirit. [26]Let us not become conceited, provoking one another, envying one another.

CHAPTER **6** **WE REAP WHAT WE SOW.** Brethren, if a man is overtaken in any trespass, you who *are* spiritual restore such a one in a spirit of gentleness, considering yourself lest you also be tempted. [2]Bear one another's burdens, and so fulfill the law of Christ. [3]For if anyone thinks himself to be something, when he is nothing, he deceives himself. [4]But let each one examine his own work, and then he will have rejoicing in himself alone, and not in another. [5]For each one shall bear his own load.

[6]Let him who is taught the word share in all good things with him who teaches.

[7]Do not be deceived, God is not mocked; for whatever a man sows, that he will also reap. [8]For he who sows to his flesh will of the flesh reap corruption, but he who sows to the Spirit will of the Spirit reap everlasting life. [9]And let us not grow weary while doing good, for in due season we shall reap if we do not lose heart. [10]Therefore, as we have opportunity, let us do good to all, especially to those who are of the household of faith.

[11]See with what large letters I have written to you with my own hand! [12]As many as desire to make a good showing in the flesh, these *would* compel you to be circumcised, only that they may not suffer persecution for the cross of Christ. [13]For not even those who are circumcised keep the law, but they desire to have you circumcised

BUT
THE FRUIT
OF THE
SPIRIT
IS *Love*

GALATIANS 5:22-23

JOY

PEACE

LONGSUFFERING

kindness

GOODNESS

FAITHFULNESS

gentleness

SELF-CONTROL

that they may boast in your flesh. [14]But God forbid that I should boast except in the cross of our Lord Jesus Christ, by whom the world has been crucified to me, and I to the world. [15]For in Christ Jesus neither circumcision nor un-

LOOK AT JESUS

6:4 When you do your very best, you feel good about the results, there is no need to compare yourself with others. People make comparisons for many reasons. Some point out others' flaws in orde[r] feel better about themselves. Others simply want reassurance that [they] are doing well. When you are tempted to compare, look at Jesus Ch[rist]. His example will inspire you to do your very best, and his loving acceptance will comfort you when you fall short of your goals.

circumcision avails anything, but a new creation. [16]And as many as walk according to this rule, peace and mercy *be* upon them, and upon the Israel of God.

[17]From now on let no one trouble me, for I bear in my body the marks of the Lord Jesus.

[18]Brethren, the grace of our Lord Jesus Christ *be* with your spirit. Amen.

MEGA Themes

LAW A group of Jewish teachers were insisting that non-Jewish believers obey Jewish laws and traditions. These teachers believed that a person was saved by following the law of Moses (with emphasis on circumcision, the sign of the covenant) in addition to faith in Christ. Paul opposed them, showing that the law can't save anyone.

The law can't save us. It wasn't ever meant to be our salvation. It was intended to be a guide, to point out our need to be forgiven. Christ fulfilled the obligations of the law for us. We must turn to him to be saved. Christ alone can make us right with God. Then we should obey God in response to what he has done for us.

1. What error had the Jewish believers made concerning the role of the law?
2. What truth did Paul use to correct their error?
3. Based on Galatians, why are good works not enough to bring a person salvation?
4. How does the law point out our need for salvation?
5. How should you respond to the law now that you have been saved through Jesus Christ?

FAITH God's gracious gift to us saves us from God's judgment and the penalty for sin. We receive salvation by faith—trusting in Christ, not in anything else. Becoming a Christian is in no way based on our work, wise choices, or good character. We can only be right with God by believing in Christ.

Eternal life comes only through faith in Christ. You must never add to this truth or twist it. We are saved by faith and faith alone. Have you placed your whole trust and confidence in Christ? He alone can forgive you and bring you into relationship with God.

1. What does it mean to be saved by faith?
2. How would you answer a person who said: "I have been good, so I know God will let me into heaven"?
3. In spite of your sin, God gave you faith. What does this reveal to you about God?
4. How have you responded to God's offer of salvation?

5. During this past week, how have you lived your life by faith?

FREEDOM Galatians sets forth our freedom in Christ. We are not under the jurisdiction of Jewish laws and traditions, nor under the authority of Jerusalem. Faith in Christ brings true freedom from sin and from the futile attempt to be right with God by keeping the law.

We are free in Christ, free to serve him—but freedom is a privilege. Let us use our freedom to love and to serve, not to do wrong.

1. Finish these sentences:
   a) Christian freedom means _____
   b) Christian freedom does not mean _____
2. In what ways could your freedom in Christ be misused?
3. For what purpose has God given you freedom? How are you fulfilling that purpose in your life?

HOLY SPIRIT We become Christians through the work of the Holy Spirit. The Spirit brings new life, and even our faith is a gift from him. The Holy Spirit instructs us, guides us, leads us, and gives us power. He ends our bondage to evil desires; brings us love, joy, and peace; and changes us into the image of Christ.

When the Holy Spirit controls us, he produces his fruit in us. Through faith, we can have the Holy Spirit within us, strengthening and guarding us and helping us grow spiritually.

1. According to chapter 3, how does a person receive the Holy Spirit?
2. According to 5:16-26, what difference does the Holy Spirit bring to a person's life? What difference has the Holy Spirit made in your life?
3. Why do you need the Holy Spirit to be at work in your life?
4. What can you do to continue to "walk in the Spirit"?

An argument with a friend ■ A hug from Mom ■ A drive with
Dad ■ A note in your locker ■ A prayer before bedtime ■ Every event of every day
underlines this fundamental fact: *Life is made up of relationships.* We relate in a
"horizontal" way to other people; we relate in a "vertical" manner to our Creator. Pretty
basic stuff, right? ■ But here's where things get profound: Our problems, individual and
national, are due to *broken-down relationships.* It's because we fail to relate properly to
God and to each other that we lie, cheat, steal, murder, drink and drive, divorce, engage
in illicit sex, abort our babies, fight wars, pollute, buy and sell drugs, ignore the needy,
commit suicide, and all the other wrong things we do. ■ So what is the remedy for
ruptured relationships? In a nutshell: *Jesus Christ can repair our broken-down
relationships!* ■ First, Jesus pardons our sins, bringing us into a right relationship with
God. (Get this—by faith in Christ we are adopted into God's family! We become his
children . . . eternally!) Then Christ gives us the wisdom and the power to build stronger
horizontal ties—with parents, friends, bosses . . . even enemies! ■ Can your
relationships stand a little improving? Check out Ephesians. The first three chapters
explain how Jesus has made it possible for us to know God in a personal way. The rest of
the book provides practical tips for getting along with people. ■ Hey, it just might
change your life!

STATS

PURPOSE: To strengthen the Christian faith of the
believers in Ephesus by explaining the nature and
purpose of the church, the body of Christ

AUTHOR: Paul

TO WHOM WRITTEN: The church at Ephesus, and all
believers everywhere

DATE WRITTEN: About A.D. 60, from Rome, during Paul's
imprisonment there

SETTING: The letter was not written to confront any
heresy or problem. It was sent with Tychicus to
strengthen and encourage area churches. Paul spent
over three years with the Ephesian church; he was very
close to them. His last meeting with the Ephesian elders
was at Miletus (Acts 20:17-38)—a meeting filled with
great sadness because Paul was leaving them forever.
There are no specific references to people or problems
in the Ephesian church, so Paul may have intended this
letter to be read to all the area churches.

Ephesians

CHAPTER 1 **PAUL: A LOYAL FOLLOWER OF CHRIST.**
Paul, an apostle of Jesus Christ by the will of God,

To the saints who are in Ephesus, and faithful in Christ Jesus:

[2]Grace to you and peace from God our Father and the Lord Jesus Christ.

[3]Blessed *be* the God and Father of our Lord Jesus Christ, who has blessed us with every spiritual blessing in the heavenly *places* in Christ, [4]just as He chose us in Him before the foundation of the world, that we should be holy and without blame before Him in love, [5]having predestined us to adoption as sons by Jesus Christ to Himself, according to the good pleasure of His will, [6]to the praise of the glory of His grace, by which He made us accepted in the Beloved.

[7]In Him we have redemption through His blood, the forgiveness of sins, according to the riches of His grace [8]which He made to abound toward us in all wisdom and prudence, [9]having made known to us the mystery of His will, according to His good pleasure which He purposed in Himself, [10]that in the dispensation of the fullness of the

times He might gather together in one all things in Christ, both which are in heaven and which are on earth—in Him. [11]In Him also we have obtained an inheritance, being predestined according to the purpose of Him who works all things according to the counsel of His will, [12]that we who first trusted in Christ should be to the praise of His glory.

[13]In Him you also *trusted*, after you heard the word of truth, the gospel of your salvation; in whom also, having believed, you were sealed with the Holy Spirit of promise, [14]who is the guarantee of our inheritance until the redemption of the purchased possession, to the praise of His glory.

[15]Therefore I also, after I heard of your faith in the Lord Jesus and your love for all the saints, [16]do not cease to give thanks for you, making mention of you in my prayers: [17]that the God of our Lord Jesus Christ, the Father of glory, may give to you the spirit of wisdom and revelation in the knowledge of Him, [18]the eyes of your understanding being enlightened; that you may know what is the hope of His calling, what are the riches of the glory of His inheritance in the saints, [19]and what *is* the exceeding greatness of His power toward us who believe, according to the working of His mighty power [20]which He worked in Christ when He raised Him from the dead and seated *Him* at His right hand in the heavenly *places*, [21]far above all principality and power and might and dominion, and every name that is named, not only in this age but also in that which is to come.

[22]And He put all *things* under His feet, and gave Him *to be* head over all *things* to the church, [23]which is His body, the fullness of Him who fills all in all.

THE MYSTERY

1:4 Paul says that God "chose us in Him" to emphasize that salvation depends totally on God. We are not saved because we deserve it, but because God is gracious and freely gives salvation. We did not influence God's decision to save us; he did it according to his plan. Thus there is no way to take credit for your salvation or to find room for pride. The mystery of salvation originated in the timeless mind of God long before we existed. It is hard to understand how God could accept us, but because of Christ, we are holy and blameless in his eyes. God chose you, and when you belong to him through Jesus Christ, he looks at you as if you had never sinned.

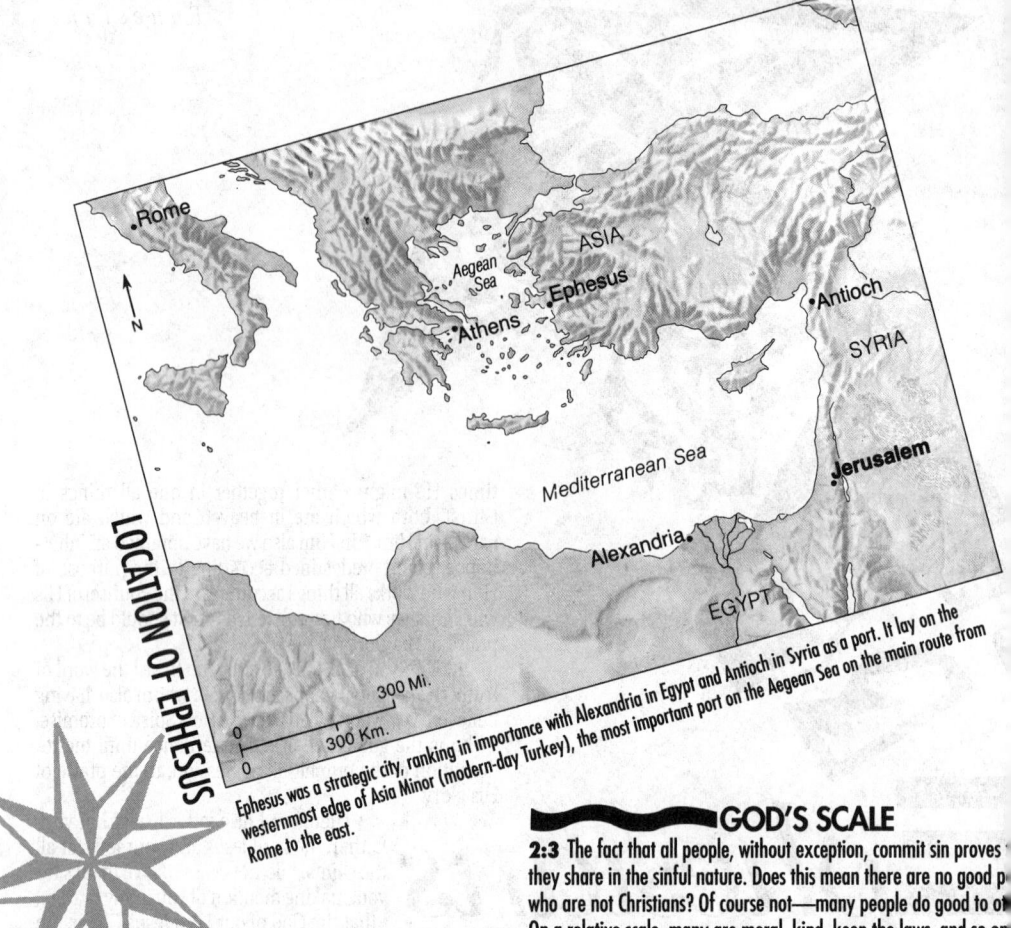

LOCATION OF EPHESUS

Ephesus was a strategic city, ranking in importance with Alexandria in Egypt and Antioch in Syria as a port. It lay on the westernmost edge of Asia Minor (modern-day Turkey), the most important port on the Aegean Sea on the main route from Rome to the east.

CHAPTER 2 OUR LIFE BEFORE AND AFTER CHRIST.

And you *He made alive*, who were dead in trespasses and sins, [2]in which you once walked according to the course of this world, according to the prince of the power of the air, the spirit who now works in the sons of disobedience, [3]among whom also we all once conducted ourselves in the lusts of our flesh, fulfilling the desires of the flesh and of the mind, and were by nature children of wrath, just as the others.

[4]But God, who is rich in mercy, because of His great love with which He loved us, [5]even when we were dead in trespasses, made us alive together with Christ (by grace you have been saved), [6]and raised *us* up together, and made *us* sit together in the heavenly *places* in Christ Jesus, [7]that in the ages to come He might show the exceeding riches of His grace in *His* kindness toward us in Christ Jesus. [8]For by grace you have been saved through faith, and that not of yourselves; *it is* the gift of God, [9]not of works, lest anyone should boast. [10]For we are His workmanship, created in Christ Jesus for good works, which God prepared beforehand that we should walk in them.

[11]Therefore remember that you, once Gentiles in the flesh—who are called Uncircumcision by what is called the Circumcision made in the flesh by hands— [12]that at that time you were without Christ, being aliens from the commonwealth of Israel and strangers from the cov-

GOD'S SCALE

2:3 The fact that all people, without exception, commit sin proves they share in the sinful nature. Does this mean there are no good pe who are not Christians? Of course not—many people do good to ot On a relative scale, many are moral, kind, keep the laws, and so on Comparing these people to criminals, we would say they are very g indeed. But on God's absolute scale, *no one* is good. Only through u our life to Christ's perfect life can we become good in God's sight.

enants of promise, having no hope and without God in the world. [13]But now in Christ Jesus you who once were far off have been brought near by the blood of Christ.

[14]For He Himself is our peace, who has made both one, and has broken down the middle wall of separation, [15]having abolished in His flesh the enmity, *that is,* the law of commandments *contained* in ordinances, so as to create in Himself one new man *from* the two, *thus* making peace, [16]and that He might reconcile them both to God in one body through the cross, thereby putting to death the enmity. [17]And He came and preached peace to you who were afar off and to those who were near. [18]For through Him we both have access by one Spirit to the Father.

PROUD

2:11-13 Jews and Gentiles alike could be guilty of spiritual pride—Jews for thinking their ceremonies elevated them above everyone else, Gentiles for forgetting the hopelessness of their cond apart from Christ. Spiritual pride blinds us to our own faults and magnifies the faults of others. Be careful not to become proud of yo salvation. Instead, humbly thank God for what he has done and encourage others who might be struggling in their faith.

[19]Now, therefore, you are no longer strangers and foreigners, but fellow citizens with the saints and members of the household of God, [20]having been built on the foundation of the apostles and prophets, Jesus Christ Himself being the chief corner*stone*, [21]in whom the whole building, being fitted together, grows into a holy temple in the Lord, [22]in whom you also are being built together for a dwelling place of God in the Spirit.

CHAPTER 3 SALVATION IS FOR EVERYONE.

For this reason I, Paul, the prisoner of Christ Jesus for you Gentiles— [2]if indeed you have heard of the dispensation of the grace of God which was given to me for you, [3]how that by revelation He made known to me the mystery (as I have briefly written already, [4]by which, when you read, you may understand my knowledge in the mystery of Christ), [5]which in other ages was not made known to the sons of men, as it has now been revealed by the Spirit to His holy apostles and prophets: [6]that the Gentiles should be fellow heirs, of the same body, and partakers of His promise in Christ through the gospel, [7]of which I became a minister according to the gift of the grace of God given to me by the effective working of His power.

[8]To me, who am less than the least of all the saints, this grace was given, that I should preach among the Gentiles the unsearchable riches of Christ, [9]and to make all see what *is* the fellowship of the mystery, which from the beginning of the ages has been hidden in God who created all things through Jesus Christ; [10]to the intent that now the manifold wisdom of God might be made known by the church to the principalities and powers in the heavenly *places*, [11]according to the eternal purpose which He accomplished in Christ Jesus our Lord, [12]in whom we have boldness and access with confidence through faith in Him. [13]Therefore I ask that you do not lose heart at my tribulations for you, which is your glory.

[14]For this reason I bow my knees to the Father of our Lord Jesus Christ, [15]from whom the whole family in heaven and earth is named, [16]that He would grant you, according to the riches of His glory, to be strengthened with might through His Spirit in the inner man, [17]that Christ may dwell in your hearts through faith; that you, being rooted and grounded in love, [18]may be able to comprehend with all the saints what *is* the width and length and depth and height— [19]to know the love of Christ which passes knowledge; that you may be filled with all the fullness of God.

[20]Now to Him who is able to do exceedingly abundantly above all that we ask or think, according to the power that works in us, [21]to Him *be* glory in the church by Christ Jesus to all generations, forever and ever. Amen.

CHAPTER 4 SPECIAL ABILITIES.

I, therefore, the prisoner of the Lord, beseech you to walk worthy of the calling with which you were called, [2]with all lowliness and gentleness, with longsuffering, bearing with one another in love, [3]endeavoring to keep the unity of the Spirit in the bond of peace. [4]*There is* one body and one Spirit, just as you were called in one hope of your calling; [5]one Lord, one faith, one baptism; [6]one God and Father of all, who *is* above all, and through all, and in you all.

[7]But to each one of us grace was given according to the measure of Christ's gift. [8]Therefore He says:

"When He ascended on high,
He led captivity captive,
And gave gifts to men."

[9](Now this, *"He ascended"*—what does it mean but that He also first descended into the lower parts of the earth? [10]He who descended is also the One who ascended far above all the heavens, that He might fill all things.)

[11]And He Himself gave some *to be* apostles, some prophets, some evangelists, and some pastors and teachers, [12]for the equipping of the saints for the work of

OUR LIFE BEFORE AND AFTER CHRIST

Before	After
Under God's curse	Loved by God
Doomed because of our sins	Shown God's mercy and given salvation
Went along with the crowd	Stand for Christ and truth
God's enemies	God's children
Enslaved to Satan	Free to love and serve Christ
Followed our evil thoughts and passions	Seated with Christ in glory
Under God's anger	Given undeserved favor
Spiritually dead	Given new spiritual life in Christ

MARRIAGE

Maria was 23 years old, bright, attractive—and headed for divorce. She and Danny had been married two years. Now she sat in her former youth pastor's office and dissolved into tears. "It's not working out," she choked out between sobs. "I don't know what happened. We were really in love, but we've lost something. I don't think we're going to make it. . . ." Tragically, this scene is repeated over and over. Why is it that two people who are "made for each other" so often end up looking for the escape hatch labeled "divorce"? Maybe a better question is: What does it take to keep a marriage from becoming a casualty? If marriage were just another human institution—like a corporation or a university—then getting out of it would be no more significant or painful than changing jobs or switching schools. Indeed, many people have tried to treat marriage that way, as something to enjoy when it's good or helpful and to terminate when it isn't. But those who have experienced a divorce will explain that a failed marriage is infinitely more painful. There's more to marriage than the human dimension. Marriage was God's holy and sacred idea. He performed the first "wedding" in the Garden of Eden (Genesis 2:18-25), thus setting up guidelines for all people to follow: marriage is for one man and one woman for life. There are valid reasons for sometimes breaking this pattern (for example, death or adultery). But the intended pattern is one man, one woman, for life. Unfortunately, in a fallen world it often is difficult to submit to God's standards, especially since his standards do not change. Marriage is a covenant between a husband and wife. A covenant is an agreement between two people (or groups) that has benefits for keeping the arrangement and penalties for breaking it. Our relationship to God is described in covenant language throughout Scripture. The marriage relationship is described as a covenant (Malachi 2:14-15), and is used as an illustration of our relationship with God (Hosea 1:2; Ephesians 5:22-33). Just as our relationship with God is built on his steadfast, unchanging love and commitment toward us, so a marriage relationship is designed to be solid, faithful, and committed. Therein lies another extremely important—but often overlooked—principle for a successful marriage: commitment. Marriage is based on commitment, not emotions. The emotional rush two people experience when they "fall in love" and when they decide to marry is wonderful. It also is a terribly inadequate basis for marriage. That "rush," as powerful and enjoyable as it may be, will undoubtedly wear off at some point. If that's what the relationship is based on—physical attraction, romantic ideals, passion—the flame may burn brightly, but it will not burn for long. Romance, sexual attraction, and passion are tremendous God-given elements of a love relationship. But do not mistake them for the foundation of a lifelong commitment. They are like icing on a cake. Icing makes the cake much sweeter, but a diet of 100 percent refined sugar doesn't make for good health. To survive the pressure and temptations that attack a marriage (as both husband and wife have to be totally committed to making it work. Even when the romance is gone (as sometimes will be in any marriage), when the money is tight, or the urge to run out is overwhelming, Christ must stand strong on the commitment they have made. Instead of allowing the stresses to divide them, they must cling that much more tightly together. "What God has joined together, let no one"—and no thing—"separate." Marriage, when seen from God's perspective, can be one of his greatest gifts to his children. It can also, as Maria and millions of others have unfortunately discovered, be a source of deep pain. Whether or not to marry—and what happens if you do marry—is up to you.

ministry, for the edifying of the body of Christ, [13]till we all come to the unity of the faith and of the knowledge of the Son of God, to a perfect man, to the measure of the stature of the fullness of Christ; [14]that we should no longer be children, tossed to and fro and carried about with every wind of doctrine, by the trickery of men, in the cunning craftiness of deceitful plotting, [15]but, speaking the truth in love, may grow up in all things into Him who is the head—Christ— [16]from whom the whole body, joined and knit together by what every joint supplies, according to the effective working by which every part does its share, causes growth of the body for the edifying of itself in love.

[17]This I say, therefore, and testify in the Lord, that you should no longer walk as the rest of the Gentiles walk, in the futility of their mind, [18]having their understanding darkened, being alienated from the life of God, because of the ignorance that is in them, because of the blindness of their heart; [19]who, being past feeling, have given themselves over to lewdness, to work all uncleanness with greediness.

[20]But you have not so learned Christ, [21]if indeed you have heard Him and have been taught by Him, as the truth is in Jesus: [22]that you put off, concerning your former conduct, the old man which grows corrupt according to the deceitful lusts, [23]and be renewed in the spirit of your mind, [24]and that you put on the new man which was created according to God, in true righteousness and holiness.

[25]Therefore, putting away lying, *"Let each one of you speak truth with his neighbor,"* for we are members of one another. [26]*"Be angry, and do not sin"*: do not let the sun go down on your wrath, [27]nor give place to the devil. [28]Let him who stole steal no longer, but rather let him labor, working with *his* hands what is good, that he may have something to give him who has need. [29]Let no corrupt word proceed out of your mouth, but what is good for necessary edification, that it may impart grace to the hearers. [30]And do not grieve the Holy Spirit of God, by whom you were sealed for the day of redemption. [31]Let all bitterness, wrath, anger, clamor, and evil speaking be put away from you, with all malice. [32]And be kind to one another, tenderhearted, forgiving one another, even as God in Christ forgave you.

CHAPTER **5** **LEARN WHAT PLEASES GOD.** Therefore be imitators of God as dear children. [2]And walk in love, as Christ also has loved us and given Himself for us, an offering and a sacrifice to God for a sweet-smelling aroma.

[3]But fornication and all uncleanness or covetousness, let it not even be named among you, as is fitting for saints; [4]neither filthiness, nor foolish talking, nor coarse jesting, which are not fitting, but rather giving of thanks. [5]For this you know, that no fornicator, unclean person, nor covetous man, who is an idolater, has any inheritance in the kingdom of Christ and God. [6]Let no one deceive you with empty words, for because of these things the wrath of God comes upon the sons of disobedience. [7]Therefore do not be partakers with them.

[8]For you were once darkness, but now *you are* light in the Lord. Walk as children of light [9](for the fruit of the Spirit *is* in all goodness, righteousness, and truth), [10]finding out what is acceptable to the Lord. [11]And have no fellowship with the unfruitful works of darkness, but

LITTLE BY LITTLE

4:17-24 People should be able to see a difference between Christians and non-Christians because of the way Christians live. Paul tells the Ephesians to leave behind the old life of sin now that they are followers of Christ. The Christian life is a process. Despite our new nature in Christ, we don't automatically have all good thoughts and attitudes. But if we keep listening to God, we will be changing all the time. As you look over the last year, do you see a process of change for the better in your thoughts, attitudes, and actions? Although change may be slow, it comes about if you trust God to change you. For more about our new nature as believers see Romans 6:6; 8:9; Galatians 5:16-26; and Colossians 3:3-8.

rather expose *them.* [12]For it is shameful even to speak of those things which are done by them in secret. [13]But all things that are exposed are made manifest by the light, for whatever makes manifest is light. [14]Therefore He says:

What does it mean to "grow as a Christian"?

I WONDER . . .

Spiritual growth is a lot like physical growth. To stay healthy and grow physically, we must eat the right foods, exercise, and get plenty of rest. You've heard that since you were a child. According to Scripture, especially in verses such as Ephesians 4:14-15, growing spiritually involves the same formula.

Christians must eat the right "spiritual food": God's Word. Many Christians are trying to survive on spiritual "fast food." That is, they watch Christian TV, read Christian magazines, and listen to Christian music, but they rarely give attention to God's Word. There is only one food that will nourish our soul—reading the Bible. Everything else is only meant to be supplementary.

Christians exercise through resisting temptation, enduring trials, serving others, and telling others about our faith. We need to be pushed to stay strong. This means exercise. Temptation and problems test our character; serving others stretches our faith; telling people about Christ strengthens our devotion.

Christians rest through worship. Our world has a tendency to tighten us, like a rubber band pulled to the limit. Unless we take time weekly (and daily!) to recognize and worship God, he won't have the opportunity to minister to our needs.

We need sleep, rest, and times of vacation to get our physical batteries recharged. In the same way, we need worship to keep us spiritually renewed.

Spiritual growth takes time—a lifetime! This means growing in a relationship, not just changing our behavior. Growing a strong Christian life means learning how to love the person of Jesus Christ more each day, staying close to him and getting to know him better.

"Awake, you who sleep,
Arise from the dead,
And Christ will give you light."

¹⁵See then that you walk circumspectly, not as fools but as wise, ¹⁶redeeming the time, because the days are evil.

¹⁷Therefore do not be unwise, but understand what the will of the Lord *is*. ¹⁸And do not be drunk with wine, in which is dissipation; but be filled with the Spirit, ¹⁹speaking to one another in psalms and hymns and spiritual songs, singing and making melody in your heart to the Lord, ²⁰giving thanks always for all things to God the Father in the name of our Lord Jesus Christ, ²¹submitting to one another in the fear of God.

²²Wives, submit to your own husbands, as to the Lord.

²³For the husband is head of the wife, as also Christ is head of the church; and He is the Savior of the body. ²⁴Therefore, just as the church is subject to Christ, so *let* the wives *be* to their own husbands in everything.

²⁵Husbands, love your wives, just as Christ also loved the church and gave Himself for her, ²⁶that He might sanctify and cleanse her with the washing of water by the word, ²⁷that He might present her to Himself a glorious church, not having spot or wrinkle or any such thing, but that she should be holy and without blemish. ²⁸So husbands ought to love their own wives as their own bodies; he who loves his wife loves himself. ²⁹For no one ever hated his own flesh, but nourishes and cherishes it, just as the Lord *does* the church. ³⁰For we are members of His body, of His flesh and of His bones. ³¹*"For this reason a man shall leave his father and mother and be joined to*

GOD'S ARMOR FOR US

We are engaged in a spiritual battle—all believers find themselves subject to Satan's attacks because they are no longer on Satan's side. Thus, Paul tells us to use every piece of God's armor to resist Satan's attacks and to stand true to God in the midst of them.

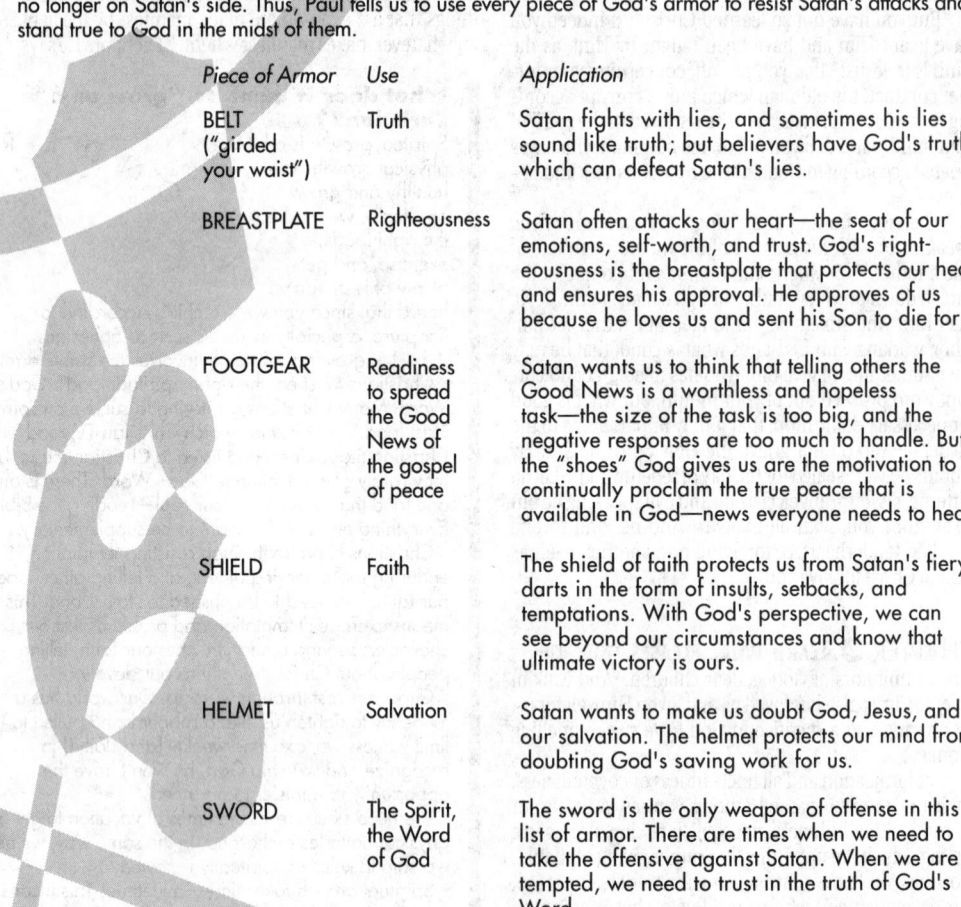

Piece of Armor	Use	Application
BELT ("girded your waist")	Truth	Satan fights with lies, and sometimes his lies sound like truth; but believers have God's truth, which can defeat Satan's lies.
BREASTPLATE	Righteousness	Satan often attacks our heart—the seat of our emotions, self-worth, and trust. God's righteousness is the breastplate that protects our heart and ensures his approval. He approves of us because he loves us and sent his Son to die for us.
FOOTGEAR	Readiness to spread the Good News of the gospel of peace	Satan wants us to think that telling others the Good News is a worthless and hopeless task—the size of the task is too big, and the negative responses are too much to handle. But the "shoes" God gives us are the motivation to continually proclaim the true peace that is available in God—news everyone needs to hear.
SHIELD	Faith	The shield of faith protects us from Satan's fiery darts in the form of insults, setbacks, and temptations. With God's perspective, we can see beyond our circumstances and know that ultimate victory is ours.
HELMET	Salvation	Satan wants to make us doubt God, Jesus, and our salvation. The helmet protects our mind from doubting God's saving work for us.
SWORD	The Spirit, the Word of God	The sword is the only weapon of offense in this list of armor. There are times when we need to take the offensive against Satan. When we are tempted, we need to trust in the truth of God's Word.

TAKE UP

THE WHOLE ARMOR OF GOD

THAT YOU MAY BE ABLE TO WITHSTAND *in the evil day* and having done all TO **STAND.**

EPHESIANS 6:13

might. [11]Put on the whole armor of God, that you may be able to stand against the wiles of the devil. [12]For we do not wrestle against flesh and blood, but against principalities, against powers, against the rulers of the darkness of this age, against spiritual *hosts* of wickedness in the heavenly *places*. [13]Therefore take up the whole armor of God, that you may be able to withstand in the evil day,

SPEAK OUT

5:10-14 It is important to avoid evil pleasures, but we must go even further. Paul instructs us to rebuke and expose them, for often our silence is interpreted as approval. God needs people who will take a stand for what is right. Wherever you are, lovingly speak out for what is true and right.

and having done all, to stand.

[14]Stand therefore, having girded your waist with truth, having put on the breastplate of righteousness, [15]and having shod your feet with the preparation of the gospel of peace; [16]above all, taking the shield of faith with which you will be able to quench all the fiery darts of the wicked one. [17]And take the helmet of salvation, and the sword of the Spirit, which is the word of God; [18]praying always with all prayer and supplication in the Spirit, being watchful to this end with all perseverance and supplication for all the saints— [19]and for me, that utterance may be given to me, that I may open my mouth boldly to

his wife, and the two shall become one flesh." [32]This is a great mystery, but I speak concerning Christ and the church. [33]Nevertheless let each one of you in particular so love his own wife as himself, and let the wife *see* that she respects *her* husband.

CHAPTER **6** FAMILY ADVICE. Children, obey your parents in the Lord, for this is right. [2]*"Honor your father and mother,"* which is the first commandment with promise: [3]*"that it may be well with you and you may live long on the earth."*

[4]And you, fathers, do not provoke your children to wrath, but bring them up in the training and admonition of the Lord.

[5]Bondservants, be obedient to those who are your masters according to the flesh, with fear and trembling, in sincerity of heart, as to Christ; [6]not with eyeservice, as men-pleasers, but as bondservants of Christ, doing the will of God from the heart, [7]with goodwill doing service, as to the Lord, and not to men, [8]knowing that whatever good anyone does, he will receive the same from the Lord, whether *he is* a slave or free.

[9]And you, masters, do the same things to them, giving up threatening, knowing that your own Master also is in heaven, and there is no partiality with Him.

[10]Finally, my brethren, be strong in the Lord and in the power of His

"Here's what I did..."

"Greg, what have you decided about going to the college we talked about? The deadline is coming up, isn't it?" Though my dad was trying to be casual, I could tell he wanted an answer.

"Yeah, I've decided. I don't want to go to that school, but you won't take that for an answer," I said.

"Greg," Dad began, but I could tell by his tone what he was going to say. We'd been through this too many times before. I didn't want to go; he wanted me to—and his pressuring me just made me angry.

I talked to my youth pastor about it the next day. "What do you think the Bible says about your situation?" Les asked me.

"Well, I know I'm not supposed to be angry at my dad, but I can't stand him pressuring me."

"Read Ephesians and let me know what you discover," Les suggested. So I read the book of Ephesians—and I saw that I can't always do what I want. Loving God means wanting to do *his* will, not mine. When I read Ephesians 6:1-3, I realized that God often chooses to work through my earthly parents. I tried to think through all the reasons Dad wanted me to go to that particular college and why I didn't want to go. Finally I decided it would be best to trust God and believe that he was leading me there.

God did bless my decision to attend this college. I am really growing in my faith here.

Greg AGE 19

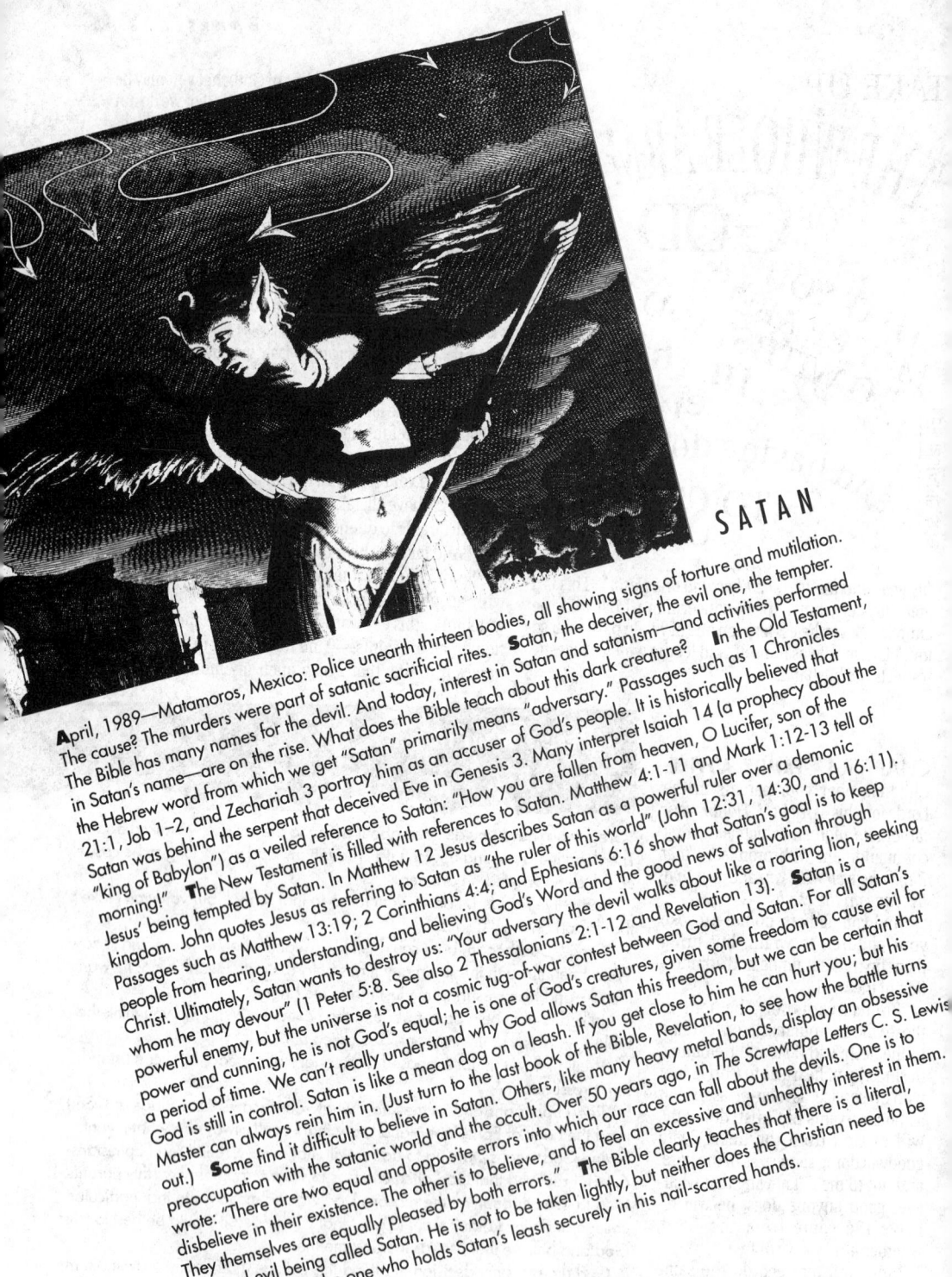

SATAN

April, 1989—Matamoros, Mexico: Police unearth thirteen bodies, all showing signs of torture and mutilation. The cause? The murders were part of satanic sacrificial rites. Satan, the deceiver, the evil one, the tempter. The Bible has many names for the devil. And today, interest in Satan and satanism—and activities performed in Satan's name—are on the rise. What does the Bible teach about this dark creature? In the Old Testament, the Hebrew word from which we get "Satan" primarily means "adversary." Passages such as 1 Chronicles 21:1, Job 1–2, and Zechariah 3 portray him as an accuser of God's people. It is historically believed that Satan was behind the serpent that deceived Eve in Genesis 3. Many interpret Isaiah 14 (a prophecy about the "king of Babylon") as a veiled reference to Satan: "How you are fallen from heaven, O Lucifer, son of the morning!" The New Testament is filled with references to Satan. Matthew 4:1-11 and Mark 1:12-13 tell of Jesus' being tempted by Satan. In Matthew 12 Jesus describes Satan as a powerful ruler over a demonic kingdom. John quotes Jesus as referring to Satan as "the ruler of this world" (John 12:31, 14:30, and 16:11). Passages such as Matthew 13:19; 2 Corinthians 4:4; and Ephesians 6:16 show that Satan's goal is to keep people from hearing, understanding, and believing God's Word and the good news of salvation through Christ. Ultimately, Satan wants to destroy us: "Your adversary the devil walks about like a roaring lion, seeking whom he may devour" (1 Peter 5:8. See also 2 Thessalonians 2:1-12 and Revelation 13). Satan is a powerful enemy, but the universe is not a cosmic tug-of-war contest between God and Satan. For all Satan's power and cunning, he is not God's equal; he is one of God's creatures, given some freedom to cause evil for a period of time. We can't really understand why God allows Satan this freedom, but we can be certain that God is still in control. Satan is like a mean dog on a leash. If you get close to him he can hurt you; but his Master can always rein him in. (Just turn to the last book of the Bible, Revelation, to see how the battle turns out.) Some find it difficult to believe in Satan. Others, like many heavy metal bands, display an obsessive preoccupation with the satanic world and the occult. Over 50 years ago, in The Screwtape Letters C. S. Lewis wrote: "There are two equal and opposite errors into which our race can fall about the devils. One is to disbelieve in their existence. The other is to believe, and to feel an excessive and unhealthy interest in them. They themselves are equally pleased by both errors." The Bible clearly teaches that there is a literal, personal evil being called Satan. He is not to be taken lightly, but neither does the Christian need to be afraid. We know the one who holds Satan's leash securely in his nail-scarred hands.

make known the mystery of the gospel, [20]for which I am an ambassador in chains; that in it I may speak boldly, as I ought to speak.

[21]But that you also may know my affairs *and* how I am doing, Tychicus, a beloved brother and faithful minister in the Lord, will make all things known to you; [22]whom I have sent to you for this very purpose, that you may know our affairs, and *that* he may comfort your hearts.

[23]Peace to the brethren, and love with faith, from God the Father and the Lord Jesus Christ. [24]Grace *be* with all those who love our Lord Jesus Christ in sincerity. Amen.

MEGA Themes

GOD'S PURPOSE FOR A LIVING CHURCH
According to God's eternal, loving plan, he directs, carries out, and sustains our salvation.

When we respond to Christ's love by trusting in him, his purpose becomes our mission. Have you committed yourself to fulfilling God's purpose? We should always be seeking to understand more of who God created us to be and what he wants us to do with our life.

1. What does God want to accomplish through his children (the body of Christ) working together?
2. What attitudes and actions are necessary for the body to function as it should? (Check Romans 12 and 1 Corinthians 12 for similar teaching on "Body Life.")
3. In what ways can these attitudes be displayed and these actions lived out in your church and among your Christian friends?
4. What do you think God wants to accomplish through you for other believers?

CHRIST, THE CENTER
Christ is exalted as the central meaning of the universe and the focus of history. He is the Head of his body, the church.

Because Christ is central to everything, his power must be central in us. Begin by placing all your priorities under his control. Your life decisions should be based on who you are as his disciple.

1. According to 1:3-15, what do we have in Christ?
2. According to 2:11-21, how does Christ change human relationships?
3. According to 4:11-16, what role does Christ play in the body?
4. Review your responses to questions 1–3. Why is it so important to make Jesus, in our heart and mind, the central focus of our life?
5. Where is your focus today? (At home, by yourself, with your best friends, at school, at church.) In what sense are you "on center" in your commitment to Christ? In what sense are you "off center"?

NEW FAMILY
Because God through Christ paid our penalty for sin and forgave us, we have been reconciled and brought near to him. We are a new society, a new family. Being united with Christ means that we are to treat each other as family members.

We are one family in Christ; so there should be no barriers, no divisions, and no discrimination. Because we all belong to him, we should live in harmony with one another. We have a responsibility toward each other as brothers and sisters in Christ.

1. Check out 2:11–3:13. What does God desire concerning relationships between Jews and Gentiles?
2. Who are the people in your community who do not relate well to each other because of difference in color, race, culture, social status, or other personal barriers?
3. From what people are you most separated or alienated in your personal life? What does this study teach you about those relationships?
4. What can you do to change those relationships because of your faith in Christ?

CHRISTIAN CONDUCT
Paul encourages all Christians to make wise, dynamic Christian living a goal.

God provides his Holy Spirit to enable us to live his way. To utilize his power, we must lay aside our evil desires and draw upon the power of his new life. Submit your will to Christ and seek to love with *his* love by the power of the Spirit.

1. Ephesians gives several specific commands to obey in following Christ (for instance 4:25—tell the truth!). Make a quick list of these commands.
2. Now consider each item on your list in light of this question: "How does doing this action relate to my loving God?"
3. Read 5:1-2. How does God's love become the motivation for Christian conduct?
4. As you look at your list from question one, which actions are areas of strength in your life? Which ones are weaknesses? How can you strengthen your areas of weaknesses so that your life is a greater "walk in the light"?

*T*ime for a little daydreaming: ■ Scenario #1—A high-powered attorney calls to inform you that a distant relative has left you her entire estate worth *several million bucks!* ■ Scenario #2—You ace all of your midterm exams! ■ Scenario #3—In the biggest game of the year, you score with one second left to give your school an upset victory. ■ Scenario #4—You learn that the most attractive member of the opposite sex (in your whole school!) likes you. ■ Some dreams, huh? So, do you think you could get *excited* about those situations? OK, let's daydream some more: ■ Scenario #5—Your dad accidentally throws away your term paper—the one you worked on for over a month—the one that is due *today.* ■ Scenario #6—You develop a huge pimple on the end of your nose the night before the most important date of your life. ■ Scenario #7—You've trained for months for track team tryouts. On the way to school, you get in a wreck and break your ankle. ■ Scenario #8—Your boyfriend/girlfriend dumps you—for your best friend! ■ OK, so these are more like nightmares. Is it possible to be *joyful* in bad situations like these? ■ Believe it or not, it *is* possible to be content—even in the midst of horrible, terrible circumstances. ■ Facing problems or trials? Get a fresh perspective. Read Philippians, Paul's letter to a group of Christians. The message is clear: Joy and contentment really *can* be ours . . . as long as we keep trusting God through life's hard times.

STATS

PURPOSE: To thank the Philippians and to strengthen them by showing that true joy comes from Jesus Christ

AUTHOR: Paul

TO WHOM WRITTEN: Christians at Philippi and all believers

DATE WRITTEN: About A.D. 61, from Rome, during Paul's imprisonment there

SETTING: Paul and his companions founded the church at Philippi on the second missionary journey (Acts 16:11-40). This was the first church established on the European continent. The Philippian church had sent a gift with Epaphroditus (one of their members) to be delivered to Paul (4:18).

KEY PEOPLE: Paul, Timothy, Epaphroditus, Euodias, Syntyche

KEY PLACE: Philippi

Philippians

CHAPTER 1 PAUL'S PRAYER: KEEP GROWING.

Paul and Timothy, bondservants of Jesus Christ,

To all the saints in Christ Jesus who are in Philippi, with the bishops and deacons:

[2]Grace to you and peace from God our Father and the Lord Jesus Christ.

[3]I thank my God upon every remembrance of you, [4]always in every prayer of mine making request for you all with joy, [5]for your fellowship in the gospel from the first day until now, [6]being confident of this very thing, that He who has begun a good work in you will complete *it* until the day of Jesus Christ; [7]just as it is right for me to think this of you all, because I have you in my heart, inasmuch as both in my chains and in the defense and confirmation of the gospel, you all are partakers with me of grace. [8]For God is my witness, how greatly I long for you all with the affection of Jesus Christ.

[9]And this I pray, that your love may abound still more and more in knowledge and all discernment, [10]that you may approve the things that are excellent, that you may be sincere and without offense till the day of Christ, [11]being filled with the fruits of righteousness which *are* by Jesus Christ, to the glory and praise of God.

[12]But I want you to know, brethren, that the things *which happened* to me have actually turned out for the furtherance of the gospel, [13]so that it has become evident to the whole palace guard, and to all the rest, that my chains are in Christ; [14]and most of the brethren in the Lord, having become confident by my chains, are much more bold to speak the word without fear.

[15]Some indeed preach Christ even from envy and strife, and some also from goodwill: [16]The former preach Christ from selfish ambition, not sincerely, supposing to

JOY SOURCE

1:4 This is the first of many times Paul uses the word *joy* in his letter. Here he says that the Philippians were a source of joy when he prayed. By helping Paul, they were helping Christ's cause. The Philippians were willing to be used by God for whatever task he had in store for them. When others think about you, are you a source of joy for them?

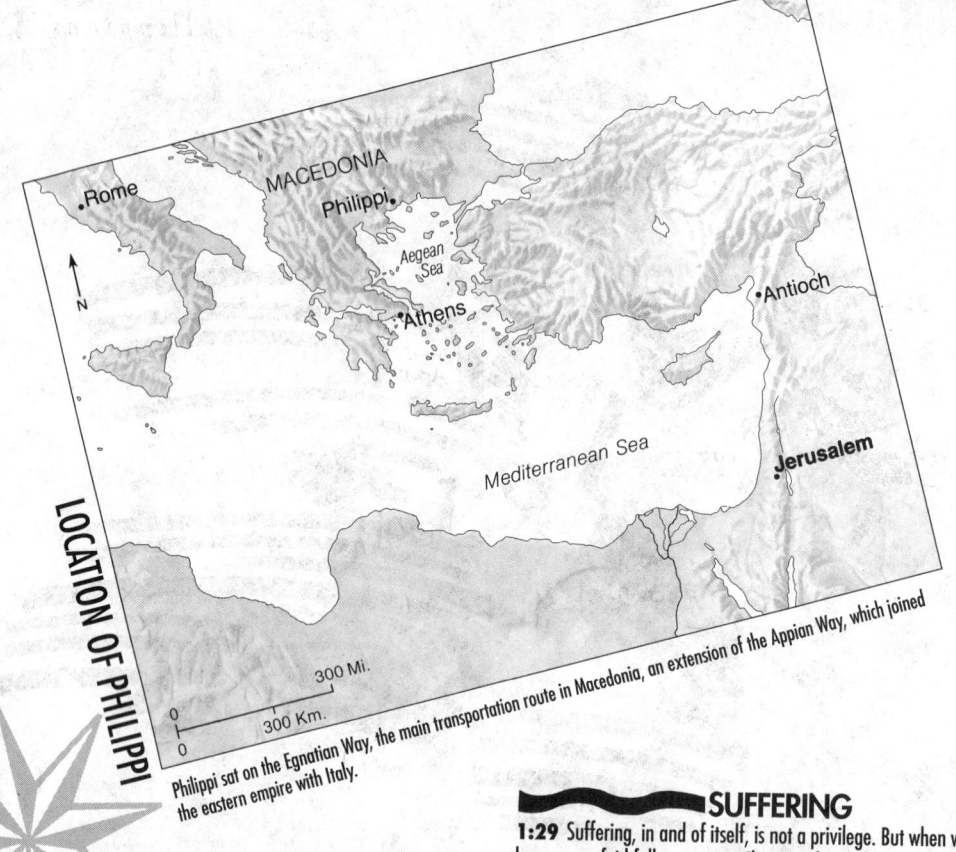

LOCATION OF PHILIPPI

MACEDONIA

•Rome

Philippi•

Aegean
Sea

•Athens

•Antioch

Mediterranean Sea

Jerusalem

N

300 Mi.

0

300 Km.

0

Philippi sat on the Egnatian Way, the main transportation route in Macedonia, an extension of the Appian Way, which joined the eastern empire with Italy.

add affliction to my chains; [17]but the latter out of love, knowing that I am appointed for the defense of the gospel. [18]What then? Only *that* in every way, whether in pretense or in truth, Christ is preached; and in this I rejoice, yes, and will rejoice.

[19]For I know that this will turn out for my deliverance through your prayer and the supply of the Spirit of Jesus Christ, [20]according to my earnest expectation and hope that in nothing I shall be ashamed, but with all boldness, as always, so now also Christ will be magnified in my body, whether by life or by death. [21]For to me, to live *is* Christ, and to die *is* gain. [22]But if *I* live on in the flesh, this *will mean* fruit from *my* labor; yet what I shall choose I cannot tell. [23]For I am hard-pressed between the two, having a desire to depart and be with Christ, *which is* far better. [24]Nevertheless to remain in the flesh *is* more needful for you. [25]And being confident of this, I know that I shall remain and continue with you all for your progress and joy of faith, [26]that your rejoicing for me may be more abundant in Jesus Christ by my coming to you again.

[27]Only let your conduct be worthy of the gospel of Christ, so that whether I come and see you or am absent, I may hear of your affairs, that you stand fast in one spirit, with one mind striving together for the faith of the gospel, [28]and not in any way terrified by your adversaries, which is to them a proof of perdition, but to you of salvation, and that from God. [29]For to you it has been granted on behalf of Christ, not only to believe in Him, but also to suffer for His sake, [30]having the same conflict which you saw in me and now hear *is* in me.

SUFFERING

1:29 Suffering, in and of itself, is not a privilege. But when we suffer because we faithfully represent Christ, we know that our message and example are having an effect and that God considers us worthy to represent him (see Acts 5:41). Suffering has these additional benefits: (1) it takes our eyes off of earthly comforts; (2) it weeds out superficial believers; (3) it strengthens the faith of those who endure; (4) it serves as an example to others who may follow us. Suffering for our faith doesn't mean we have done something wrong. In fact, the opposite is often true—it may verify that we have been faithful.

CHAPTER 2 A CHRISTLIKE ATTITUDE. Therefore if *there is* any consolation in Christ, if any comfort of love, if any fellowship of the Spirit, if any affection and mercy, [2]fulfill my joy by being like-minded, having the same love, *being* of one accord, of one mind. [3]*Let* nothing *be done* through selfish ambition or conceit, but in lowliness of mind let each esteem others better than himself. [4]Let each of you look out not only for his own interests, but also for the interests of others.

[5]Let this mind be in you which was also in Christ Jesus, [6]who, being in the form of God, did not consider it robbery to be equal with God, [7]but made Himself of no reputation, taking the form of a bondservant, *and* coming in the likeness of men. [8]And being found in appearance as a man, He humbled Himself and became obedient to *the point of* death, even the death of the cross. [9]Therefore God also has highly exalted Him and given Him the name which is above every name, [10]that at the name of Jesus every knee should bow, of those in heaven, and of those on earth, and of those under the

earth, [11]and *that* every tongue should confess that Jesus Christ *is* Lord, to the glory of God the Father.

[12]Therefore, my beloved, as you have always obeyed, not as in my presence only, but now much more in my absence, work out your own salvation with fear and trembling; [13]for it is God who works in you both to will and to do for *His* good pleasure.

[14]Do all things without complaining and disputing, [15]that you may become blameless and harmless, children of God without fault in the midst of a crooked and perverse generation, among whom you shine as lights in the world, [16]holding fast the word of life, so that I may rejoice in the day of Christ that I have not run in vain or labored in vain.

[17]Yes, and if I am being poured out *as a drink offering* on the sacrifice and service of your faith, I am glad and rejoice with you all. [18]For the same reason you also be glad and rejoice with me.

[19]But I trust in the Lord Jesus to send Timothy to you shortly, that I also may be encouraged when I know your state. [20]For I have no one like-minded, who will sincerely care for your state. [21]For all seek their own, not the things which are of Christ Jesus. [22]But you know his proven character, that as a son with *his* father he served with me in the gospel. [23]Therefore I hope to send him at once, as soon as I see how it goes with me. [24]But I trust in the Lord that I myself shall also come shortly.

[25]Yet I considered it necessary to send to you Epaphroditus, my brother, fellow worker, and fellow soldier, but your messenger and the one who ministered to my need; [26]since he was longing for you all, and was distressed because you had heard that he was sick. [27]For indeed he was sick almost unto death; but God had mercy on him, and not only on him but on me also, lest I should have sorrow upon sorrow. [28]Therefore I sent him the more eagerly, that when you see him again you may rejoice, and I may be less sorrowful. [29]Receive him therefore in the Lord with all gladness, and hold such men in esteem; [30]because for the work of Christ he came close to death, not regarding his life, to supply what was lacking in your service toward me.

CHAPTER **3** KNOW HIM. Finally, my brethren, rejoice in the Lord. For me to write the same things to you *is* not tedious, but for you *it is* safe.

[2]Beware of dogs, beware of evil workers, beware of the mutilation! [3]For we are the circumcision, who worship God in the Spirit, rejoice in Christ Jesus, and have no confidence in the flesh, [4]though I also might have confidence in the flesh. If anyone else thinks he may have confidence in the flesh, I more so: [5]circumcised the eighth day, of the stock of Israel, *of* the tribe of Benjamin, a Hebrew of the Hebrews; concerning the law, a Pharisee; [6]concerning zeal, persecuting the church; concerning the righteousness which is in the law, blameless.

[7]But what things were gain to me, these I have counted loss for Christ. [8]Yet indeed I also count all things loss for the excellence of the knowledge of Christ Jesus my Lord, for whom I have suffered the loss of all things, and count them as rubbish, that I may gain Christ [9]and be found in Him, not having my own righteousness, which *is* from the law, but that which *is* through faith in Christ, the righteousness which is from God by faith; [10]that I may know Him and the power of His resurrection, and the fellowship of His sufferings, being conformed to His death, [11]if, by any means, I may attain to the resurrection from the dead.

[12]Not that I have already attained, or am already perfected; but I press on, that I may lay hold of that for which Christ Jesus has also laid hold of me. [13]Brethren, I do not count myself to have apprehended; but one thing *I do*, forgetting those things which are behind and reaching forward to those things which are ahead, [14]I press toward the goal for the prize of the upward call of God in Christ Jesus.

[15]Therefore let us, as many as are mature, have this mind; and if in anything you think otherwise, God will reveal even this to you. [16]Nevertheless, to *the degree* that we have already attained, let us walk by the same rule, let us be of the same mind.

[17]Brethren, join in following my example, and note those who so walk, as you have us for a pattern. [18]For many walk, of whom I have told you often, and now tell you even weeping, *that they are* the enemies of the cross of Christ: [19]whose end *is* destruction, whose god *is their* belly, and *whose* glory *is* in their shame—who set their mind on earthly things. [20]For our citizenship is in heaven, from which we also eagerly wait for the Savior, the Lord Jesus Christ, [21]who will transform our lowly body that it may be conformed to His glorious body, according to the working by which He is able even to subdue all things to Himself.

Before I became a Christian, I put some real garbage through my mind. How do I clean up my thought life?

I WONDER . . .

Almost every school in America is equipped with computers. Most businesses remain competitive because they're able to access and store large amounts of information. Computers are serving nearly every segment of society. But they have one flaw—they are dependent on the programs and information put in them.

Your mind works like a computer. If it's programmed to think about crud, that's what will happen. If it's programmed to think about things that are healthy, you will think healthy thoughts. It's as simple as that.

The hard part comes in trying to keep out the unhealthy thoughts. It doesn't take much to pollute a mind.

So what's God's solution? Reprogram the mind! For this job, there are no shortcuts. The more exposure to things that have polluted us, whether from bad movies, magazines, TV, music, concerts, or just the everyday conversation of friends who don't care what they say, the longer it will take to clear our mind and reprogram it.

The reprogramming process begins when we realize that destructive thoughts and images are trying to get a foothold in our mind, and then kick them out. The next step, as we see from Philippians 4:8, is choosing to dwell on what is "true . . . noble . . . just . . . pure . . . lovely . . . of good report . . . [has] virtue and . . . praiseworthy."

CHAPTER **4** **THINK ABOUT THE GOOD.** Therefore,

my beloved and longed-for brethren, my joy and crown, so stand fast in the Lord, beloved.

[2]I implore Euodia and I implore Syntyche to be of the same mind in the Lord. [3]And I urge you also, true companion, help these women who labored with me in the gospel, with Clement also, and the rest of my fellow workers, whose names *are* in the Book of Life.

[4]Rejoice in the Lord always. Again I will say, rejoice!

SELF

Marie's favorite topic for discussion, her major concern, the number one thing on her mind is . . . Marie. Seriously, when we say she's stuck on herself, we're talking really stuck—super-glue style.

Just look:

- When Beth was extremely upset at not being asked to Homecoming, Marie responded by going on and on about her date.
- When anyone asks, "How was your weekend?" Marie gives a twenty-minute discourse. (Funny how she never asks anyone else that question.)
- When her favorite daytime TV show was interrupted last summer by a live news report about a four-alarm apartment fire, Marie got emotional. Not at the fact that people were dying and losing their home, but at the fact that she had to miss her program.
- When Marie's neighbor called, desperately needing a baby-sitter at the last minute, Marie wouldn't go, even though she had no other plans. She ended up going to work out at the health club.
- When Marie receives money (allowance, pay, or cash from an unexpected source), she immediately goes to the mall and buys something for herself.

[5]Let your gentleness be known to all men. The Lord *is* at hand.

[6]Be anxious for nothing, but in everything by prayer and supplication, with thanksgiving, let your requests be made known to God; [7]and the peace of God, which surpasses all understanding, will guard your hearts and minds through Christ Jesus.

[8]Finally, brethren, whatever things are true, whatever things *are* noble, whatever things *are* just, whatever things *are* pure, whatever things *are* lovely, whatever things *are* of good report, if *there is* any virtue and if *there is* anything praiseworthy—meditate on these things. [9]The things which you learned and received and heard and saw in me, these do, and the God of peace will be with you.

[10]But I rejoiced in the Lord greatly that now at last your care for me has flourished again; though you surely did care, but you lacked opportunity. [11]Not that I speak in regard to need, for I have learned in whatever state I am, to be content: [12]I know how to be abased, and I know how to abound. Everywhere and in all things I have learned both to be full and to be hungry, both to abound and to

suffer need. [13]I can do all things through Christ who strengthens me.

[14]Nevertheless you have done well that you shared in my distress. [15]Now you Philippians know also that in the beginning of the gospel, when I departed from Macedo-

NO WORRIES

4:6-18 Imagine never being "anxious" about anything! It seems an impossibility— we all have worries on the job, in our home, a ▮ But Paul's advice is to turn our worries into prayers. Do you want ▮ worry less? Then pray more! Whenever you start to worry, stop a▮

nia, no church shared with me concerning giving and receiving but you only. [16]For even in Thessalonica you sent *aid* once and again for my necessities. [17]Not that I seek the gift, but I seek the fruit that abounds to your account. [18]Indeed I have all and abound. I am full, having received from Epaphroditus the things *sent* from you, a

SECRET

4:23 In many ways the Philippian church was a model congrega▮ was made up of different kinds of people who were learning to wo▮ together. But Paul knew problems could arise, so he prepared the ▮ Philippians for possible difficulties. Though a prisoner in Rome, Pa▮ learned the true secret of joy and peace—imitating Christ and ser▮ others. By focusing on Christ we learn unity, humility, joy, and pea▮

sweet-smelling aroma, an acceptable sacrifice, well pleasing to God. [19]And my God shall supply all your need according to His riches in glory by Christ Jesus. [20]Now to our God and Father *be* glory forever and ever. Amen.

[21]Greet every saint in Christ Jesus. The brethren who are with me greet you. [22]All the saints greet you, but especially those who are of Caesar's household.

[23]The grace of our Lord Jesus Christ be with you all. Amen.

I CAN DO ALL tHiNGs THROUGH CHRIST WHO STRENGTHENS me.

PHILIPPIANS 4:13

MEGA Themes

HUMILITY Christ showed true humility when he laid aside his rights and privileges as God to become human. He poured out his life to pay the penalty we deserve. Laying aside self-interest is essential to all our relationships.

We are to take Christ's attitude in serving others. We must not be concerned about personal recognition. When we give up the need to receive credit and praise, we will be able to serve with joy, love, and kindness.

1. If a person was described to you as "humble," what would be your impression of that person? Positive or negative? Weak or strong? Unique or average?
2. How did Jesus display his attitude of humility?
3. If Jesus were to attend your school, how do you think people would respond to him as he humbly served others?
4. What would it mean for you to display humility toward kids at school?

SELF-SACRIFICE Christ suffered and died so that we might have eternal life. With courage and faithfulness, Paul sacrificed himself for the ministry, preaching the gospel even while he was in prison.

Christ gives us power to lay aside our personal needs and concerns. To utilize his power, we must imitate those leaders who deny themselves and serve others. We dare not be self-centered in view of such a self-sacrificing Savior.

1. What are the differences between a self-sacrificing person and a self-centered one?
2. What makes it difficult for a person to be self-sacrificing?
3. What was the connection between the self-sacrifice of Jesus and the self-sacrifice of Paul?
4. How could you overcome areas of self-centeredness through the help of Jesus and the work of his Spirit? What will you do to begin this work?

UNITY In every church, in every generation, there are problems that divide people (issues, loyalties, and conflicts). It is easy to turn against each other. Paul encouraged the Philippians to agree with one another, stop complaining, and work together.

As believers, we should fight against a common enemy, not each other. United in love, we become aware of Christ's strength. Always remember teamwork, consideration, and unselfishness. Keep your focus on the model of Jesus Christ.

1. What are some of the things that cause anger, hurt, and division among God's people?
2. What specific principles do you find in Philippians that could prevent or help resolve such conflict?
3. As you examine these principles, what truth is the key to maintaining unity in the body of believers?
4. What can you do to apply these principles in relationships with your Christian friends—specifically those in your church?

CHRISTIAN LIVING Paul shows us how to live a successful Christian life. We can become mature by being so identified with Christ that his attitude of humility and sacrifice rules us. Christ is both our source of power and our guide.

Developing our character begins with God's work in us, but it also requires discipline, obedience, and continual concentration on our part.

1. Read 3:1-16. If you had never heard of Paul before, what would be your impression of him after reading these verses? Do you agree or disagree with this statement: "Paul thought the Christian life was basically easy"? Explain your response based on Philippians.
2. Summarize the key points you find in Paul's testimony of himself and his life in Christ. What can you do to develop godly character?
3. Describe your life as a Christian. In what ways is your experience similar to Paul's? In what ways is it different?

JOY Believers can have profound contentment, serenity, and peace no matter what happens. This joy comes from knowing Christ personally and from depending on his strength rather than on our own.

Joy does not come from outward circumstances but from inner strength. As Christians, we must not rely on what we have or what we experience to give us joy, but on Christ within us. His joy is greater than life's trials.

1. Based on Paul's circumstances and the content of his letter to the Philippians, how do you think Paul would have described being "joyful"?
2. How can a Christian find joy in apparently unhappy circumstances?
3. If a Christian friend were to say to you, "How can I possibly find joy in the Lord when life seems so unfair?" what would you say?
4. How will you find joy in Jesus this week?

Will the Real Jesus Please Stand Up? ■ Sometimes it's hard to know what to think about Jesus Christ. ■ Christians say he is God with skin on—the second person of the Trinity and the carpenter from Nazareth all rolled into one. Others insist he never even existed. Still others regard Jesus as a troublesome politician with a messiah complex, who ended up being executed. Then there is the Hollywood Jesus—weak, wishy-washy, misguided, filled with contradictions, and surrounded by controversy. ■ How about the increasingly popular "New Age" Jesus who is but one of many ways to God? And don't forget some cults who claim that Christ is *now living on the earth* in the person of their leader! ■ So, was Jesus just a good man and great moral teacher? Or was he, as Islam teaches, a prophet like Moses, Buddha, and Mohammed? Was he just one of many gods? Was he truly divine, or was he just more than human, or was he simply one manifestation of a divine, universal force? ■ There are hundreds of conflicting ideas floating around about who Jesus is. But only one of the views can be true—which makes the others wrong . . . and extremely dangerous! ■ Don't fall for lies about Christ. Meet him as he really is. See for yourself how superior he is to everything and everyone else in the universe. See what it means to know him in a personal way. See all of this and more in the book of Colossians.

STATS

PURPOSE: To combat errors in the church and to show that believers have everything they need in Christ

AUTHOR: Paul

TO WHOM WRITTEN: The church at Colosse, a city in Asia Minor, and all believers everywhere

DATE WRITTEN: About A.D. 60, during Paul's imprisonment in Rome

SETTING: Paul had never visited Colosse—evidently the church had been founded by Epaphras and other converts from Paul's missionary travels. The church, however, had been infiltrated by religious relativism with some believers attempting to combine elements of heathenism and secular philosophy with Christian doctrine. Paul confronts these false teachings and affirms the sufficiency of Christ.

KEY PEOPLE: Paul, Timothy, Tychicus, Onesimus, Aristarchus, Mark, Epaphras

KEY PLACES: Colosse, Laodicea (4:15-16)

Colossians

CHAPTER 1 **PAUL: CHOSEN BY GOD.** Paul, an apostle of Jesus Christ by the will of God, and Timothy our brother,

²To the saints and faithful brethren in Christ *who are* in Colosse:

Grace to you and peace from God our Father and the Lord Jesus Christ.

³We give thanks to the God and Father of our Lord Jesus Christ, praying always for you, ⁴since we heard of your faith in Christ Jesus and of your love for all the saints; ⁵because of the hope which is laid up for you in heaven, of which you heard before in the word of the truth of the gospel, ⁶which has come to you, as *it has* also in all the world, and is bringing forth fruit, as *it is* also among you since the day you heard and knew the grace of God in truth; ⁷as you also learned from Epaphras, our dear fellow servant, who is a faithful minister of Christ on

◀▬▬CHANGED

1:6 Wherever Paul went, he preached the gospel—to Gentile audiences, to hostile Jewish leaders, and even to his Roman guards. Whenever people believed in the message he spoke, they were changed. God's Word is not just for our information, it is for our transformation! Becoming a Christian means beginning a whole new relationship with God, not just turning over a new leaf or determining to do right. New believers have a changed purpose, direction, attitude, and behavior. They no longer seek to serve themselves but to serve God. In what areas has hearing God's Word changed your life? Where should it do so?

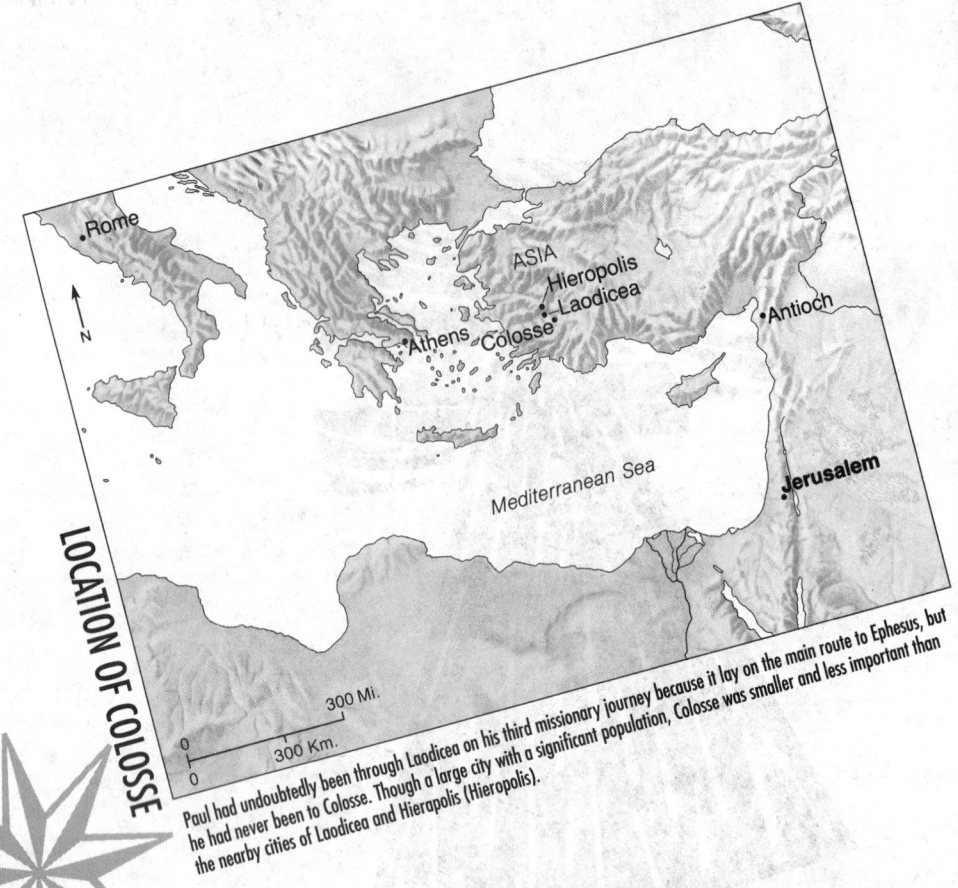

LOCATION OF COLOSSE

Paul had undoubtedly been through Laodicea on his third missionary journey because it lay on the main route to Ephesus, but he had never been to Colosse. Though a large city with a significant population, Colosse was smaller and less important than the nearby cities of Laodicea and Hierapolis (Hieropolis).

your behalf, [8]who also declared to us your love in the Spirit.

[9]For this reason we also, since the day we heard it, do not cease to pray for you, and to ask that you may be filled with the knowledge of His will in all wisdom and spiritual understanding; [10]that you may walk worthy of the Lord, fully pleasing *Him*, being fruitful in every good work and increasing in the knowledge of God; [11]strengthened with all might, according to His glorious power, for all patience and longsuffering with joy; [12]giving thanks to the Father who has qualified us to be partakers of the inheritance of the saints in the light. [13]He has delivered us from the power of darkness and conveyed *us* into the kingdom of the Son of His love, [14]in whom we have redemption through His blood, the forgiveness of sins.

[15]He is the image of the invisible God, the firstborn over all creation. [16]For by Him all things were created that are in heaven and that are on earth, visible and invisible, whether thrones or dominions or principalities or powers. All things were created through Him and for Him. [17]And He is before all things, and in Him all things consist. [18]And He is the head of the body, the church, who is the beginning, the firstborn from the dead, that in all things He may have the preeminence.

[19]For it pleased *the Father that* in Him all the fullness

▐ HOW TO PRAY

1:9-14 Sometimes we wonder how to pray for missionaries and leaders we have never met. Paul had never met the Colossians, bu faithfully prayed for them. His prayers teach us how to pray for ot whether we know them or not. We can request that they (1) unde God's will, (2) gain wisdom and spiritual understanding, (3) pleas honor God, (4) bear good fruit, (5) know God better and better, (6 filled with God's strength, (7) have great patience, (8) stay full of joy, and (9) always be thankful. All believers have these same bas needs. When you don't know how to pray for someone, remembe prayer pattern for the Colossians.

should dwell, [20]and by Him to reconcile all things to Himself, by Him, whether things on earth or things in heaven, having made peace through the blood of His cross.

▐ FOR THE BETTER

2:20-23 People should be able to see a difference between the Christians and non-Christians live. Still, we should not expect instan maturity of new Christians. The Christian life is a process. Although have a new nature, we don't automatically have all good thoughts attitudes when we become new people in Christ. But if we keep list to God, we will be changing all the time. As you look over the last what changes for the better have you seen in your thoughts and attitudes? Change may be slow, but your life will change significan you trust God to change you.

²¹And you, who once were alienated and enemies in your mind by wicked works, yet now He has reconciled ²²in the body of His flesh through death, to present you holy, and blameless, and above reproach in His sight— ²³if indeed you continue in the faith, grounded and steadfast, and are not moved away from the hope of the gospel which you heard, which was preached to every creature under heaven, of which I, Paul, became a minister.

²⁴I now rejoice in my sufferings for you, and fill up in my flesh what is lacking in the afflictions of Christ, for the sake of His body, which is the church, ²⁵of which I became a minister according to the stewardship from God which was given to me for you, to fulfill the word of God, ²⁶the mystery which has been hidden from ages and from generations, but now has been revealed to His saints. ²⁷To them God willed to make known what are the riches of the glory of this mystery among the Gentiles: which is Christ in you, the hope of glory. ²⁸Him we preach, warning every man and teaching every man in all wisdom, that we may present every man perfect in Christ Jesus. ²⁹To this *end* I also labor, striving according to His working which works in me mightily.

CHAPTER 2 A NEW LIFE IN CHRIST.

For I want you to know what a great conflict I have for you and those in Laodicea, and *for* as many as have not seen my face in the flesh, ²that their hearts may be encouraged, being knit together in love, and *attaining* to all riches of the full assurance of understanding, to the knowledge of the mystery of God, both of the Father and of Christ, ³in whom are hidden all the treasures of wisdom and knowledge.

⁴Now this I say lest anyone should deceive you with persuasive words. ⁵For though I am absent in the flesh, yet I am with you in spirit, rejoicing to see your *good* order and the steadfastness of your faith in Christ.

⁶As you therefore have received Christ Jesus the Lord, so walk in Him, ⁷rooted and built up in Him and established in the faith, as you have been taught, abounding in it with thanksgiving.

⁸Beware lest anyone cheat you through philosophy and empty deceit, according to the tradition of men, according to the basic principles of the world, and not according to Christ. ⁹For in Him dwells all the fullness of the Godhead bodily; ¹⁰and you are complete in Him, who is the head of all principality and power.

¹¹In Him you were also circumcised with the circumcision made without hands, by putting off the body of the sins of the flesh, by the circumcision of Christ, ¹²buried with Him in baptism, in which you also were raised with *Him* through faith in the working of God, who raised Him from the dead. ¹³And you, being dead in your trespasses and the uncircumcision of your flesh, He has made alive together with Him, having forgiven you all trespasses, ¹⁴having wiped out the handwriting of requirements that was against us, which was contrary to us. And He has taken it out of the way, having nailed it to the cross. ¹⁵Having disarmed principalities and powers, He made a public spectacle of them, triumphing over them in it.

¹⁶So let no one judge you in food or in drink, or regarding a festival or a new moon or sabbaths, ʸwhich are a shadow of things to come, but the substance is of Christ. ¹⁸Let no one cheat you of your reward, taking delight in *false* humility and worship of angels, intruding into those things which he has not seen, vainly puffed up by his fleshly mind, ¹⁹and not holding fast to the Head, from whom all the body, nourished and knit together by joints and ligaments, grows with the increase *that is* from God.

²⁰Therefore, if you died with Christ from the basic

I have been a Christian for about two months and I feel so far behind spiritually, compared to friends who have been Christians for a lot longer. Sometimes it gets pretty discouraging. How do I catch up?

I WONDER . . .

We live in a world that makes it nearly impossible not to compare ourselves with others.

Sometimes we even compare our life as a Christian to others. However, you must fight this urge and recognize two essential facts.

First, receiving forgiveness for our sin and asking Christ to come into our life is like a seed being planted in our heart (see 1 Corinthians 3:6). Any seed planted must first take root before it grows and blossoms.

Do you remember in first grade when you planted a seed in a clear plastic cup? If the seed was planted close enough to the edge, you would see that the roots would grow downward first; then a few days later a plant would appear above the dirt. It was miraculous!

The only difference between you and your friends is that they have had more time to spread their roots down deep. They have been "rooted and built up in Him and established in the faith" for a longer period of time.

When you took the first step of faith to trust Christ with your life, that was like the seed being planted. From this point it is up to you and God to nourish the seed and let the roots grow deep (see Colossians 2:6-7).

Your faith is nourished by rooting your new relationship with Christ. This means getting to know God better through reading and obeying his Word in the Bible (Romans 10:17). As with any relationship, time together helps you to appreciate God's character and will lead to a greater love for him (2 Peter 3:18).

Second, God doesn't compare one Christian to another. So you shouldn't, either. That would be like a father wanting his two-year-old son to throw a baseball as well as his nine-year-old. He can't!

As Christians, we never get to a point where we have arrived and are totally mature. Our love and appreciation for God can always grow deeper as he shows us new areas in our life to trust him with.

Enjoy these beginning stages of your faith by taking in all of the spiritual nourishment you can handle. Remember, the stronger and deeper your roots grow below the surface, the more beautiful and fruitful you will be as a Christian (see John 15:4-5).

3:11 Barriers of nationality, race, education, social standing, wealth, religion, and power should not apply in the Christian church. Christ breaks down all barriers and accepts all people who come to him. Nothing should keep us from telling others about Christ or accepting into our fellowship any and all believers (Ephesians 2:14-15). Christians should be in the business of building bridges, not walls.

principles of the world, why, as *though* living in the world, do you subject yourselves to regulations— 21"Do not touch, do not taste, do not handle," 22which all concern things which perish with the using—according to the commandments and doctrines of men? 23These things indeed have an appearance of wisdom in self-im-

LUST

Last year, thirteen-year-old Danny found a secret stash of pornographic magazines in his older brother's bedroom. Since then, he's developed a system. Each time his brother goes out for the evening, Danny sneaks one of the magazines into his own bedroom. There he'll stay for long hours fantasizing about being with each of the beautiful models. After a few days, he smuggles the much-studied magazine back into its place, whereupon he takes another one and repeats the process.

Each time he yields to these lustful temptations, Danny is overcome by a wave of guilt. After the short-term pleasure, Danny experiences only feelings of emptiness and loneliness. Even so, he rationalizes it this way:

"It's better to do what I'm doing than to be like my friends and actually go out and have sex! At least this way, I don't get myself or anybody else in trouble. Besides, I can't help it if I have a healthy sex drive. And anyway, I'm not sure I can stop."

What about Danny's ideas on lust? Are they sound arguments? Is it OK to stare at pictures (or real people) and imagine having sex with them? Take a look at Colossians 3:5 for God's thoughts on the issue.

posed religion, *false* humility, and neglect of the body, *but are* of no value against the indulgence of the flesh.

CHAPTER **3** **SOME RULES TO OBEY.** If then you were raised with Christ, seek those things which are above, where Christ is, sitting at the right hand of God. 2Set your mind on things above, not on things on the earth. 3For you died, and your life is hidden with Christ in God. 4When Christ *who is* our life appears, then you also will appear with Him in glory.

5Therefore put to death your members which are on the earth: fornication, uncleanness, passion, evil desire, and covetousness, which is idolatry. 6Because of these things the wrath of God is coming upon the sons of disobedience, 7in which you yourselves once walked when you lived in them.

8But now you yourselves are to put off all these: anger, wrath, malice, blasphemy, filthy language out of your mouth. 9Do not lie to one another, since you have put off the old man with his deeds, 10and have put on the new

AND **WHATEVER YOU DO, DO IT HEARTILY..**

KNOWING THAT FROM

THE LORD

you will receive

THE REWARD

FOR *you serve*

THE LORD CHRIST

FROM COLOSSIANS 3: 23-24

man who is renewed in knowledge according to the image of Him who created him, 11where there is neither Greek nor Jew, circumcised nor uncircumcised, barbarian, Scythian, slave *nor* free, but Christ *is* all and in all.

PEACE RULES

3:15 The word *rule* comes from athletics: Paul tells us to let God be "umpire" in our heart. Our heart is the center of conflict becau is where our feelings and desires clash—our fears and hopes, dis and trust, jealousy and love. How can we deal with these constant conflicts and live as God wants? Paul explains that we must decide between conflicting elements on the basis of peace. Ask yourself v choice will promote peace in our soul and in our families and chu

PERSIST

4:2 Have you ever grown tired of praying for something or som Paul says, "Continue earnestly." Vigilance demonstrates our faith God answers our prayers. Faith shouldn't die if the answers don't immediately, for the delay may be God's way of working his will i life. When you feel weary in your prayers, know that God is prese always listening, always acting—maybe not in ways you had hop in ways that he knows are best.

¹²Therefore, as *the* elect of God, holy and beloved, put on tender mercies, kindness, humility, meekness, longsuffering; ¹³bearing with one another, and forgiving one another, if anyone has a complaint against another; even as Christ forgave you, so you also *must do.* ¹⁴But above all these things put on love, which is the bond of perfection. ¹⁵And let the peace of God rule in your hearts, to which also you were called in one body; and be thankful. ¹⁶Let the word of Christ dwell in you richly in all wisdom, teaching and admonishing one another in psalms and hymns and spiritual songs, singing with grace in your hearts to the Lord. ¹⁷And *whatever* you do in word or deed, *do* all in the name of the Lord Jesus, giving thanks to God the Father through Him.

¹⁸Wives, submit to your own husbands, as is fitting in the Lord.

¹⁹Husbands, love your wives and do not be bitter toward them.

²⁰Children, obey your parents in all things, for this is well pleasing to the Lord.

²¹Fathers, do not provoke your children, lest they become discouraged.

²²Bondservants, obey in all things your masters according to the flesh, not with eyeservice, as menpleasers, but in sincerity of heart, fearing God. ²³And whatever you do, do it heartily, as to the Lord and not to men, ²⁴knowing that from the Lord you will receive the reward of the inheritance; for you serve the Lord Christ. ²⁵But he who does wrong will be repaid for what he has done, and there is no partiality.

CHAPTER 4 PAUL SAYS GOODBYE.

Masters, give your bondservants what is just and fair, knowing that you also have a Master in heaven.

²Continue earnestly in prayer, being vigilant in it with thanksgiving; ³meanwhile praying also for us, that God would open to us a door for the word, to speak the mystery of Christ, for which I am also in chains, ⁴that I may make it manifest, as I ought to speak.

⁵Walk in wisdom toward those *who are* outside, redeeming the time. ⁶*Let* your speech always *be* with grace, seasoned with salt, that you may know how you ought to answer each one.

⁷Tychicus, a beloved brother, faithful minister, and fellow servant in the Lord, will tell you all the news about me. ⁸I am sending him to you for this very purpose, that he may know your circumstances and comfort your hearts, ⁹with Onesimus, a faithful and beloved brother, who is *one* of you.

They will make known to you all things which *are* happening here.

¹⁰Aristarchus my fellow prisoner greets you, with Mark the cousin of Barnabas (about whom you received instructions: if he comes to you, welcome him), ¹¹and Jesus who is called Justus. These *are my* only fellow workers for the kingdom of God who are of the circumcision; they have proved to be a comfort to me.

◣ LIFELONG

4:2-8 The Christian is in a continuing education program. The more we know of Christ and his work, the more we will be changed to be like him. Because this process is lifelong, we must never stop learning and obeying. This should not be a justification for drifting along, but an incentive to find the rich treasures of growing in Christ. It takes practice, review, patience, and concentration to stay in line with his will.

¹²Epaphras, who is *one* of you, a bondservant of Christ, greets you, always laboring fervently for you in prayers, that you may stand perfect and complete in all the will of God. ¹³For I bear him witness that he has a great zeal for you, and those who are in Laodicea, and those in Hierapolis. ¹⁴Luke the beloved physician and Demas greet you. ¹⁵Greet the brethren who are in Laodicea, and Nymphas and the church that *is* in his house.

"Here's what I did..."

For a couple of years in high school, I didn't get along very well with my dad. I'm not sure why, now. It just seemed like everything he said irritated me. Dad seemed old-fashioned, too restrictive. I began to rebel, not openly, but more in my heart and on the sly. For instance, I would tell him that I'd do something he had asked me to, but then I never would get around to doing it. Then when he'd get angry, I'd tune him out. Or I would tell Dad I was going somewhere that I knew he'd approve, when I really was with friends he didn't like very much.

I knew things weren't great between us, but I didn't think much about it until our youth group was doing a study on relationships. When we talked about parents, we studied Colossians 3:20 and Ephesians 6:1-3. We talked about why we should obey our parents, and what it means to obey.

I felt cut to the heart. I realized that Dad was a good dad, and suddenly I understood that his restrictions were because he loved me. If I was honest with myself, a lot of them (not all, but a lot) made sense. I was being disobedient and rebellious. I cried some, knowing that I had been hurting my dad for a long time.

That evening I asked Dad to forgive me for all the ways I'd gone against him. It was hard to apologize, but it cleared the air. Dad took my apology well—he even admitted to some areas where he might have been too hard on me. That was the start of a much better father-son relationship, which has continued.

Brad
AGE 18

4:18 The Colossian church was facing pressure from a cultlike teaching that promised deeper spiritual life through secret knowledge. But Paul makes it clear in Colossians that Christ alone is the source of our spiritual life. He is the head of the body, the Lord of all. The path to deeper spiritual life is not through spiritual duties, special knowledge, or secrets; it is only through a clear connection with the Lord Jesus Christ. We must never let anything come between us and our Savior.

[16]Now when this epistle is read among you, see that it is read also in the church of the Laodiceans, and that you likewise read the epistle from Laodicea. [17]And say to Archippus, "Take heed to the ministry which you have received in the Lord, that you may fulfill it."

[18]This salutation by my own hand—Paul. Remember my chains. Grace *be* with you. Amen.

MEGA Themes

CHRIST IS GOD Jesus Christ is God in the flesh, Lord of all creation, and Lord of the new creation. He is the exact reflection of the invisible God. He is eternal, preexistent, all-powerful, and equal with the Father. Christ is supreme and complete.

Because Christ is supreme, our life must be Christ centered. To recognize Jesus as God means to regard our relationship with him as most vital and to make his interests our top priority. He must become the navigator of our life's voyage.

1. List the words and phrases that are used to describe Jesus Christ in chapters 1 and 2. What do you learn about Christ as God in these descriptions?
2. Why is it important to understand that Christ is both God and man?
3. Based on the fact that Christ is truly God, how should you respond to his lordship (control and leadership)?
4. How are you responding to his lordship in your life at the present? What can you do to be more submissive to Christ's role as your Lord?

CHRIST IS THE HEAD OF THE CHURCH

Because Christ is God, he is the head of the church, his true believers. Christ is the founder and leader of the church and the highest authority on earth. He requires first place in all our thoughts and activities.

To acknowledge Christ as our leader, we must welcome his leadership in all we do or think. No person, group, or church should have more loyalty from us than Christ.

1. What does this phrase mean: "Christ is the head of the church"?

2. If you were starting a local church, what kinds of things would you insist on in order to keep Christ as the central leader of that church?
3. Write a statement for yourself and other young people that challenges them to respond to Christ's headship of your local church.

UNION WITH CHRIST Because our sin has been forgiven and we have been reconciled to God, we have a union with Christ that can never be broken. In our faith connection with Christ, we identify with his death, burial, and resurrection.

We should live in constant contact and communication with God. When we do, we will be unified with Christ and with our fellow believers. We are a part of each other's "spiritual life-support system."

1. Read 2:6-15. What does it mean to have new life in Christ?
2. From what things were you set free when you were united with Christ?
3. Read 3:1-17. What things were you called to be and do when you were united to Christ?
4. In what specific ways has your union with Christ made a difference in your past? In your present? In your future?

MAN-MADE RELIGION False teachers were promoting a heresy that stressed man-made rules (legalism). They also sought spiritual growth by denying themselves personal contacts and by mysterious rules. This search created pride in their self-centered efforts.

We must not hold on to our own ideas and try to

blend them into Christianity. Nor should we let our hunger for a more fulfilling Christian experience cause us to trust in a teacher, group, or system of thought more than in Christ himself. Christ is our hope and our true source of wisdom. We must reject any teacher whose message is not based absolutely on the truth of Christ.

1. What lie was behind the legalism that the false teachers taught to the Colossians?

2. What is the danger of promoting a religion that is based on people's responsibility to save themselves with good works?

3. What are some current examples of the false teachings of legalism? Why are these harmful? How does this hinder non-Christians from understanding and accepting the gospel?

4. What can you do to make sure you don't get trapped by false teachings such as legalism?

*P*hobias are "phascinating" phenomena. Psychiatrists and psychologists have catalogued hundreds of them. Check out this list:

■ Anthophobia—the fear of flowers ■ Belonophobia—the fear of pins and needles

■ Decidophobia—the fear of making decisions ■ Mysophobia—the fear of dirt

■ Trichophobia—the fear of hair ■ Would you believe that some people are even terrified about *peanut butter sticking to the roof of their mouth?* That's called arachidutyrophobia. ■ You may not struggle with such odd fears, but you probably *do* worry about more common stuff. Every day, the media spotlights a different concern:

■ Is the environment damaged beyond repair? Will researchers ever find a cure for AIDS? How many people are infected without knowing it? ■ Are we on the brink of a worldwide economic collapse? How are we going to deal with a generation of drug-addicted babies? Can we confront and correct our country's epidemic of violent crimes? How has war affected our lives? ■ These are scary issues, but the Christian has real hope and genuine peace—even in uncertain times. ■ That's the message of this book: Be comforted, for no matter what happens, God is with us. Rest in the reassuring truth that Jesus Christ is coming back soon to . . . . ■ Aw, that's enough blabbering. Read it yourself. You won't believe your eyes.

STATS

PURPOSE: To strengthen the Thessalonian Christians in their faith and give them assurance of Christ's return

AUTHOR: Paul

TO WHOM WRITTEN: The church at Thessalonica and all believers everywhere

DATE WRITTEN: About A.D. 51 from Corinth; one of Paul's earliest letters

SETTING: The church at Thessalonica had been established only two or three years before this letter was written. The Christians needed to mature in their faith. Also, there was a misunderstanding about Christ's second coming—some thought he would return immediately, others wondered if the dead would experience a bodily resurrection at his return.

KEY PEOPLE: Paul, Timothy, Silas

KEY PLACE: Thessalonica

1Thessalonians

CHAPTER **1** **CHOSEN BY GOD.** Paul, Silvanus, and Timothy,

To the church of the Thessalonians in God the Father and the Lord Jesus Christ:

Grace to you and peace from God our Father and the Lord Jesus Christ.

[2]We give thanks to God always for you all, making mention of you in our prayers, [3]remembering without ceasing your work of faith, labor of love, and patience of hope in our Lord Jesus Christ in the sight of our God and Father, [4]knowing, beloved brethren, your election by God. [5]For our gospel did not come to you in word only, but also in power, and in the Holy Spirit and in much assurance, as you know what kind of men we were among you for your sake.

[6]And you became followers of us and of the Lord, having received the word in much affliction, with joy of the Holy Spirit, [7]so that you became examples to all in Macedonia and Achaia who believe. [8]For from you the word of the Lord has sounded forth, not only in Macedonia and Achaia, but also in every place. Your faith toward God has gone out, so that we do not need to say anything. [9]For they themselves declare concerning us what man-

ner of entry we had to you, and how you turned to God from idols to serve the living and true God, [10]and to wait for His Son from heaven, whom He raised from the dead, *even* Jesus who delivers us from the wrath to come.

CHAPTER **2** **PAUL'S FRIENDS.** For you yourselves know, brethren, that our coming to you was not in vain. [2]But even after we had suffered before and were spitefully treated at Philippi, as you know, we were bold in our God to speak to you the gospel of God in much conflict. [3]For our exhortation *did* not *come* from error or uncleanness, nor *was it* in deceit.

[4]But as we have been approved by God to be entrusted

S**EX** Melanie is confused about sex—not how (she learned that a long time ago), but when. Her mom tells her to wait. Her youth director gives her the same advice. But everywhere else the message is clearly, "Go for it!" Or, "If you're still a virgin, you're a total loser!"
- Friends at school tell her how great it is and how experienced they are.
- All the glamorous stars in TV shows and movies seem to be hopping from bed to bed—both on- and off-screen.
- In a health class lecture on birth control two weeks ago, the teacher stated, "Now, most normal young people are sexually active. I'm assuming you all are normal, so . . ."
- Melanie's boyfriend keeps telling her how much sex will strengthen their relationship.
- Almost every ad and billboard Melanie sees has a sexual twist or theme.
- A talk show featured live-in lovers talking about their "great" life-style.

"What am I supposed to think?" Melanie asks. "I feel like everybody else in the world is enjoying this really fantastic experience . . . and I'm like a nun or something. I want to wait, at least I think I do. Tell me, is it really worth saving yourself till marriage?"

The Bible says it's definitely wiser to wait until marriage for sex. Think hard about the message in 1 Thessalonians 4:1-8.

with the gospel, even so we speak, not as pleasing men, but God who tests our hearts. [5]For neither at any time did we use flattering words, as you know, nor a cloak for covetousness—God *is* witness. [6]Nor did we seek glory from men, either from you or from others, when we might have made demands as apostles of Christ. [7]But we were gentle among you, just as a nursing *mother* cherishes her own children. [8]So, affectionately longing for you, we were well pleased to impart to you not only the gospel of God, but also our own lives, because you had become dear to us. [9]For you remember, brethren, our labor and toil; for laboring night and day, that we might not be a burden to any of you, we preached to you the gospel of God.

[10]You *are* witnesses, and God *also,* how devoutly and justly and blamelessly we behaved ourselves among you who believe; [11]as you know how we exhorted, and comforted, and charged every one of you, as a father *does* his

own children, [12]that you would walk worthy of God who calls you into His own kingdom and glory.

[13]For this reason we also thank God without ceasing, because when you received the word of God which you heard from us, you welcomed *it* not *as* the word of men, but as it is in truth, the word of God, which also effec-

◤▬▬▬▬**OPPOSED**

2:14 Just as the Jewish Christians in Jerusalem were persecuted ▮ their own people, so the Gentile Christians in Thessalonica were persecuted by their fellow Gentiles. It is discouraging to face perse especially when it comes from your own people. But when we take stand for Christ, we will face opposition, disapproval, ridicule, and persecution from our neighbors, friends, and even family member

tively works in you who believe. [14]For you, brethren, became imitators of the churches of God which are in Judea in Christ Jesus. For you also suffered the same things from your own countrymen, just as they *did* from the Judeans, [15]who killed both the Lord Jesus and their own prophets, and have persecuted us; and they do not please God and are contrary to all men, [16]forbidding us to speak to the Gentiles that they may be saved, so as always to fill up *the measure of* their sins; but wrath has come upon them to the uttermost.

[17]But we, brethren, having been taken away from you for a short time in presence, not in heart, endeavored more eagerly to see your face with great desire. [18]Therefore we wanted to come to you—even I, Paul, time and again—but Satan hindered us. [19]For what *is* our hope, or joy, or crown of rejoicing? *Is it* not even you in the presence of our Lord Jesus Christ at His coming? [20]For you are our glory and joy.

CHAPTER **3** **A JOB WELL DONE.** Therefore, when we could no longer endure it, we thought it good to be left in Athens alone, [2]and sent Timothy, our brother and minister of God, and our fellow laborer in the gospel of Christ, to establish you and encourage you concerning your faith, [3]that no one should be shaken by these afflictions; for you yourselves know that we are appointed to this. [4]For, in fact, we told you before when we were with you that we would suffer tribulation, just as it happened, and you know. [5]For this reason, when I could no longer endure it, I sent to know your faith, lest by some means the tempter had tempted you, and our labor might be in vain.

[6]But now that Timothy has come to us from you, and brought us good news of your faith and love, and that you always have good remembrance of us, greatly desiring to see us, as we also *to see* you— [7]therefore, brethren, in all our affliction and distress we were comforted concerning you by your faith. [8]For now we live, if you stand fast in the Lord.

[9]For what thanks can we render to God for you, for all the joy with which we rejoice for your sake before our God, [10]night and day praying exceedingly that we may see your face and perfect what is lacking in your faith? [11]Now may our God and Father Himself, and our Lord

Jesus Christ, direct our way to you. ¹²And may the Lord make you increase and abound in love to one another and to all, just as we *do* to you, ¹³so that He may establish your hearts blameless in holiness before our God and Father at the coming of our Lord Jesus Christ with all His saints.

CHAPTER 4 HOW CAN I PLEASE GOD? Finally

then, brethren, we urge and exhort in the Lord Jesus that you should abound more and more, just as you received from us how you ought to walk and to please God; ²for you know what commandments we gave you through the Lord Jesus.

³For this is the will of God, your sanctification: that you should abstain from sexual immorality; ⁴that each of you should know how to possess his own vessel in sanctification and honor, ⁵not in passion of lust, like the Gentiles who do not know God; ⁶that no one should take advantage of and defraud his brother in this matter, because the Lord *is* the avenger of all such, as we also forewarned you and testified. ⁷For God did not call us to uncleanness, but in holiness. ⁸Therefore he who rejects *this* does not reject man, but God, who has also given us His Holy Spirit.

⁹But concerning brotherly love you have no need that I should write to you, for you yourselves are taught by God to love one another; ¹⁰and indeed you do so toward all the brethren who are in all Macedonia. But we urge you, brethren, that you increase more and more; ¹¹that you also aspire to lead a quiet life, to mind your own business, and to work with your own hands, as we commanded you, ¹²that you may walk properly toward those who are outside, and *that* you may lack nothing.

¹³But I do not want you to be ignorant, brethren, concerning those who have fallen asleep, lest you sorrow as others who have no hope. ¹⁴For if we believe that Jesus died and rose again, even so God will bring with Him those who sleep in Jesus.

¹⁵For this we say to you by the word of the Lord, that we who are alive *and* remain until the coming of the Lord will by no means precede those who are asleep. ¹⁶For the Lord Himself will descend from heaven with a shout, with the voice of an archangel, and with the trumpet of God. And the dead in Christ will rise first. ¹⁷Then we who are alive *and* remain shall be caught up together with them in the clouds to meet the Lord in the air. And thus we shall always be with the Lord. ¹⁸Therefore comfort one another with these words.

PRAY WITHOUT CEASING

Even though I know I'm going to heaven, I'm still afraid of dying. How can I quit being so afraid of death?

I WONDER . . .

Extreme fear of the unknown can cripple a person.

Unfortunately, death is an unknown for everyone, even for Christians.

What will we find on the other side? How is God going to take me? Will the people left behind be able to adjust? What if I die before I have a chance to get married or experience what I want to experience?

There are a lot of questions that don't have concrete answers. That can be frustrating. Someone once said that trying to explain to another person what God and heaven are like is similar to one dog telling another dog what it's like to be a human. It's impossible!

But death is not something that Christians have to fear, because—for them—death is not the end of the story. It is the gateway to a place of indescribable joy and beauty. It's the beginning of a new life!

Fear is a learned emotion. Through the years we are conditioned to fear certain things. Little kids aren't afraid of death because they don't understand it. Yet as they grow and see the response of adults and the media to death, they learn that it's something awful and to be avoided at all costs.

After we become Christians, we need to go through a relearning process about death. Paul, the author of half the books in the New Testament, said this about death, "For to me, to live *is* Christ, and to die *is* gain" (Philippians 1:21).

Paul had learned that death would actually put an end to the struggles he faced on earth. He looked forward to the day when he could see Christ face-to-face. In the meantime, though, he had work to do: winning people to Christ. Life wasn't a chore—it was a privilege!

Fear of dying doesn't disappear instantly. But as you spend time in the Bible and with other Christians who have the same hope you do, you will grow to realize that death is only a door to an eternity far better than your wildest dreams (see 1 Thessalonians 4:13-14).

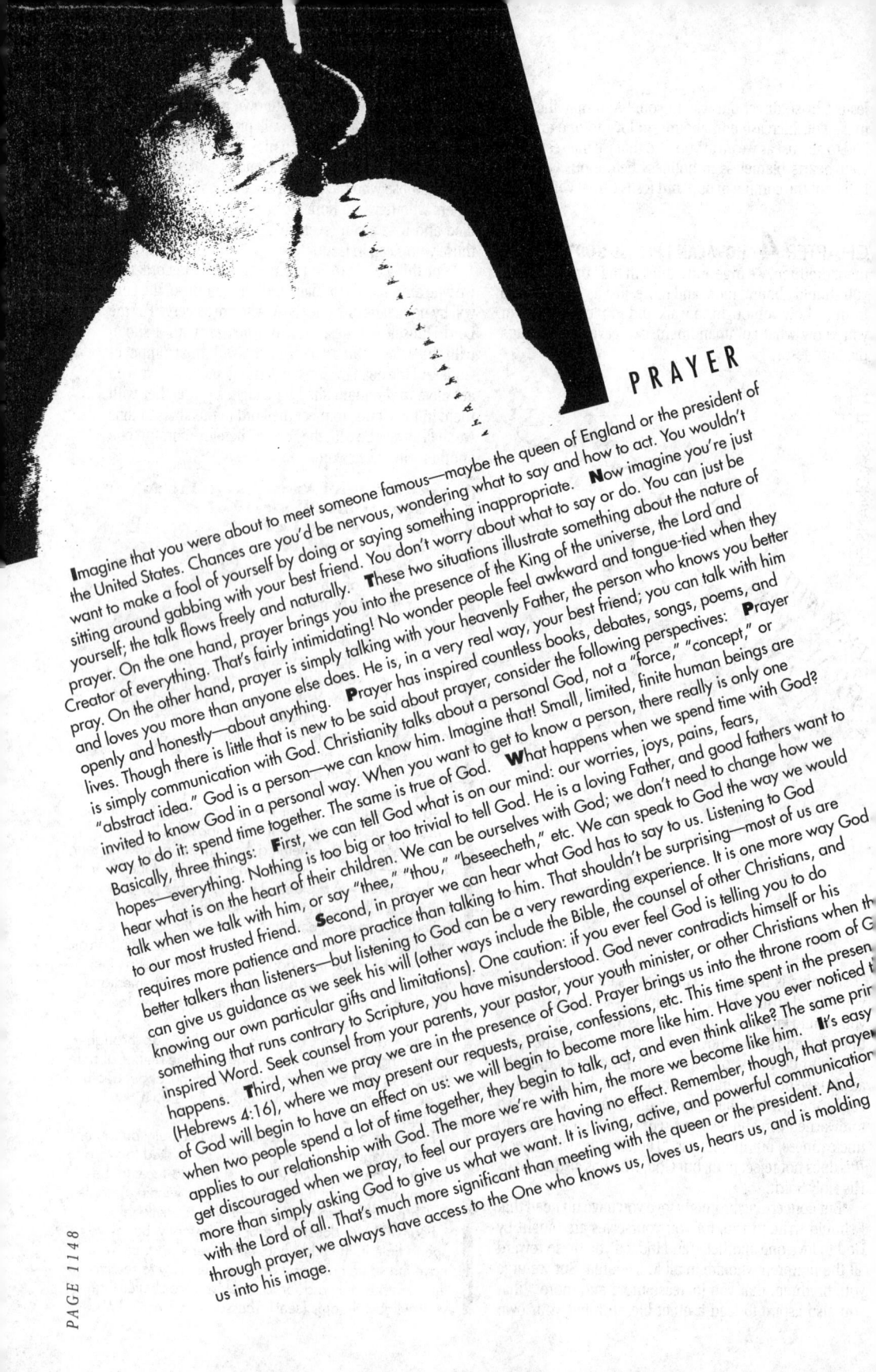

PRAYER

Imagine that you were about to meet someone famous—maybe the queen of England or the president of the United States. Chances are you'd be nervous, wondering what to say and how to act. You wouldn't want to make a fool of yourself by doing or saying something inappropriate. Now imagine you're just sitting around gabbing with your best friend. You don't worry about what to say or do. You can just be yourself; the talk flows freely and naturally. These two situations illustrate something about the nature of prayer. On the one hand, prayer brings you into the presence of the King of the universe, the Lord and Creator of everything. That's fairly intimidating! No wonder people feel awkward and tongue-tied when they pray. On the other hand, prayer is simply talking with your heavenly Father, your best friend; you can talk with him openly and honestly—about anything. Prayer has inspired countless books, debates, songs, poems, and lives. Though there is little that is new to be said about prayer, consider the following perspectives: Prayer is simply communication with God. Christianity talks about a personal God, not a "force," "concept," or "abstract idea." God is a person—we can know him. He is, in a very real way, your best friend. Prayer invited to know God in a personal way. When you want to get to know a person, there really is only one way to do it: spend time together. The same is true of God. What happens when we spend time with God? Basically, three things: First, we can tell God what is on our mind: our worries, joys, pains, fears, hopes—everything. Nothing is too big or too trivial to tell God. He is a loving Father, and good fathers want to hear what is on the heart of their children. We can be ourselves with God; we don't need to change how we talk when we talk with him, or say "thee," "thou," "beseecheth," etc. We can speak to God the way we would to our most trusted friend. Second, in prayer we can hear what God has to say to us. Listening to God requires more patience and more practice than talking to him. That shouldn't be surprising—most of us are better talkers than listeners—but listening to God can be a very rewarding experience. It is one more way God can give us guidance as we seek his will (other ways include the Bible, the counsel of other Christians, and knowing our own particular gifts and limitations). One caution: if you ever feel God is telling you to do something that runs contrary to Scripture, you have misunderstood. God never contradicts himself or his inspired Word. Seek counsel from your parents, your pastor, your youth minister, or other Christians when th happens. Third, when we pray we are in the presence of God. Prayer brings us into the throne room of G (Hebrews 4:16), where we may present our requests, praise, confessions, etc. This time spent in the presen of God will begin to have an effect on us: we will begin to become more like him. Have you ever noticed t when two people spend a lot of time together, they begin to talk, act, and even think alike? The same prin applies to our relationship with God. The more we're with him, the more we become like him. It's easy get discouraged when we pray, to feel our prayers are having no effect. Remember, though, that prayer more than simply asking God to give us what we want. It is living, active, and powerful communicatior with the Lord of all. That's much more significant than meeting with the queen or the president. And, through prayer, we always have access to the One who knows us, loves us, hears us, and is molding us into his image.

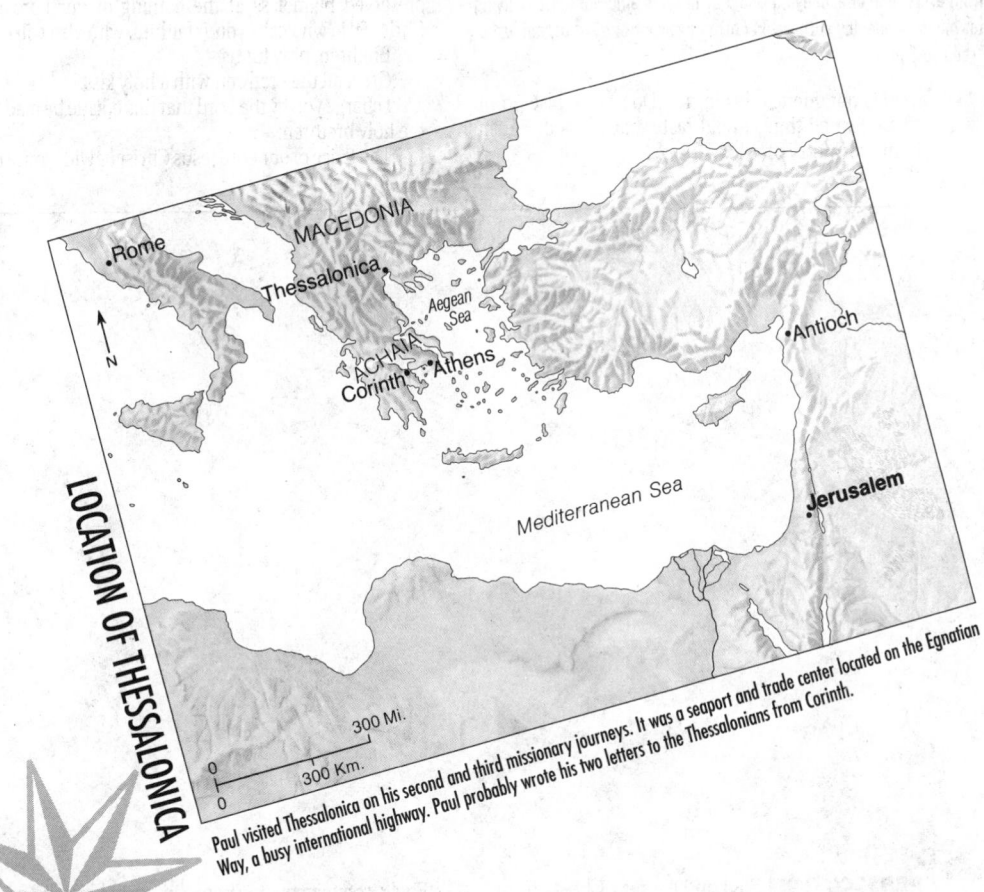

LOCATION OF THESSALONICA

300 Mi.

0

300 Km.

0

Paul visited Thessalonica on his second and third missionary journeys. It was a seaport and trade center located on the Egnatian Way, a busy international highway. Paul probably wrote his two letters to the Thessalonians from Corinth.

CHAPTER **5** **ARE YOU READY FOR CHRIST'S RE-TURN?** But concerning the times and the seasons, brethren, you have no need that I should write to you. [2]For you yourselves know perfectly that the day of the Lord so comes as a thief in the night. [3]For when they say, "Peace and safety!" then sudden destruction comes upon them, as labor pains upon a pregnant woman. And they shall not escape. [4]But you, brethren, are not in darkness, so that this Day should overtake you as a thief. [5]You are all sons of light and sons of the day. We are not of the night nor of darkness. [6]Therefore let us not sleep, as others *do*, but let us watch and be sober. [7]For those who sleep, sleep at night, and those who get drunk are drunk at night. [8]But let us who are of the day be sober, putting on the breastplate of faith and love, and *as* a helmet the hope of salvation. [9]For God did not appoint us to wrath, but to obtain salvation through our Lord Jesus Christ, [10]who died for us, that whether we wake or sleep, we should live together with Him.

[11]Therefore comfort each other and edify one another, just as you also are doing.

[12]And we urge you, brethren, to recognize those who labor among you, and are over you in the Lord and admonish you, [13]and to esteem them very highly in love for their work's sake. Be at peace among yourselves.

[14]Now we exhort you, brethren, warn those who are unruly, comfort the fainthearted, uphold the weak, be patient with all. [15]See that no one renders evil for evil to anyone, but always pursue what is good both for yourselves and for all.

THE FINISH LINE

5:9-11 As you near the end of a foot race, your legs ache, your throat burns, and your whole body cries out for you to stop. This is when friends and fans are most valuable. Their encouragement helps you push through the pain to the finish. In the same way, Christians are to encourage one another. A word of encouragement offered at the right moment can be the difference between finishing well and collapsing along the way. Look around you. Be sensitive to others' need for encouragement and offer supportive words or actions.

[16]Rejoice always, [17]pray without ceasing, [18]in everything give thanks; for this is the will of God in Christ Jesus for you.

5:23 The spirit, soul, and body are integral parts of a person. This expression is Paul's way of saying that God must be involved in *every* aspect of our life. It is wrong to think we can separate our spiritual life from everything else, obeying God only in some ethereal sense or living for him only one day each week. Christ must control *all* of us, not just a "religious" part.

¹⁹Do not quench the Spirit. ²⁰Do not despise prophecies. ²¹Test all things; hold fast what is good. ²²Abstain from every form of evil.

²³Now may the God of peace Himself sanctify you completely; and may your whole spirit, soul, and body be preserved blameless at the coming of our Lord Jesus Christ. ²⁴He who calls you *is* faithful, who also will do *it*.

²⁵Brethren, pray for us.

²⁶Greet all the brethren with a holy kiss.

²⁷I charge you by the Lord that this epistle be read to all the holy brethren.

²⁸The grace of our Lord Jesus Christ *be* with you. Amen.

MEGA Themes

PERSECUTION Paul and the new Christians at Thessalonica experienced persecution because of their faith in Christ. We can expect trials and troubles as well. We need to stand firm in our faith during our trials, being strengthened by the Holy Spirit.

The Holy Spirit helps us to remain strong in faith; he enables us to show genuine love to others and to maintain our moral character even when we are being persecuted, slandered, or oppressed.

1. How did the Thessalonians respond to pressure and opposition that came because of their faith in Christ?
2. During this persecution, where did they get their strength?
3. What pressures and/or opposition have you faced as a Christian? How did you feel when that happened? How have you responded to such situations?
4. What does it mean to "stand firm" when you are persecuted?
5. What can you do to prepare yourself so that you will stand firm throughout your life, even during intense persecution?

PAUL'S MINISTRY Paul expressed his concern for this church even while he was being slandered.

Paul's commitment to share the gospel in spite of difficult circumstances is an example that we should follow.

Paul not only gave his message, he also gave himself. In our ministries, we must become like Paul—faithful and bold, yet sensitive and self-sacrificing. Achieving such maturity results from years of commitment to God's will—the younger you begin, the deeper your growth will be.

1. What qualities do you see in Paul's wonderful example of godly ministry that enabled his message to be so powerful?
2. If you were Paul's companion in ministry, what would you most want to learn from him?
3. Who are the people closest to you who need to hear God's message? How will you follow Paul's example and do this?
4. What thoughts, attitudes, or actions do you have as a result of the hope that is within you in Christ? What can you do to comfort and encourage others with this truth?

BEING PREPARED No one knows when Christ will return. In the meantime, we are to live a moral and holy life, ever watching for his coming. Believers must not neglect their daily responsibilities, but always work and live as unto the Lord.

The gospel tells us not only what we should believe, but also how we must live. The Holy Spirit leads us in faithfulness, so we can avoid lust and fraud. Live as though you expect Christ's return at any time. Don't be caught unprepared.

1. Summarize the events of Christ's return as revealed in 1 Thessalonians.
2. What does it mean to be prepared for these events? Why is this so important? (Check Matthew 25 for Jesus' teaching.)
3. What are you doing to be ready for Christ's return?

A prominent author's best-selling new book has predicted that Christ is coming back in a few days. ■ Anne: "It's supposed to happen *this* weekend." ■ Sandra: "I guess I'm ready, but if it *does* happen, I'll never get my license—and I'll never get to . . . well, you know." ■ (Everyone but Pam giggles.) ■ Karen: "I think it's *great*. I've got a *huge* algebra test on Monday that I can't possibly pass. *Now* I can just relax and forget about it." ■ Sandra: "Right, and no more abuse from Steve Hampton and his atheist friends!" ■ Anne: "Omigosh, I never even thought about that. *That* will be the best!" ■ Pam: "You guys *cannot* be serious! You talk like you actually *believe* that stuff!" ■ Anne: "Of course we do! It all fits together, and it's in the Bible, Pam. It's going to be this weekend—you better get ready." ■ Jesus *is* coming back. And his return *will* radically change things. It *will* be great, just as the girls imagine. ■ But that doesn't mean we should start picking dates and sitting around waiting. The prospect of Christ's return should motivate us to action, not laziness. He is coming back, so let's live for him—and encourage others to do the same. ■ That's the message of 2 Thessalonians. Yes, the world is gross. Yes, the Christian life is hard. But Jesus is coming back soon to make everything right. So keep watching, waiting—and working. ■ (And by all means, study for your algebra exam!)

STATS

PURPOSE: To clear up the confusion about the second coming of Christ

AUTHOR: Paul

TO WHOM WRITTEN: The church at Thessalonica and all believers everywhere

DATE WRITTEN: About A.D. 51 or 52, a few months after 1 Thessalonians, from Corinth

SETTING: Many in the church were confused about the timing of Christ's return. Because of increasing persecution, they thought the Lord must return soon, so they interpreted Paul's first letter to say that the Second Coming would be at any moment. In light of this misunderstanding, some became lazy and disorderly.

KEY PEOPLE: Paul, Silas, Timothy

KEY PLACE: Thessalonica

SPECIAL FEATURES: This is a follow-up letter to 1 Thessalonians. In this epistle, Paul tells of various events that must precede the second coming of Christ.

2 *Thessalonians*

CHAPTER 1 PATIENCE IN SUFFERING. Paul, Silvanus, and Timothy,

To the church of the Thessalonians in God our Father and the Lord Jesus Christ:

²Grace to you and peace from God our Father and the Lord Jesus Christ.

³We are bound to thank God always for you, brethren, as it is fitting, because your faith grows exceedingly, and the love of every one of you all abounds toward each other, ⁴so that we ourselves boast of you among the churches of God for your patience and faith in all your persecutions and tribulations that you endure, ⁵*which is* manifest evidence of the righteous judgment of God, that you may be counted worthy of the kingdom of God, for which you also suffer; ⁶since *it is* a righteous thing with God to repay with tribulation those who trouble you, ⁷and to *give* you who are troubled rest with us when the Lord Jesus is revealed from heaven with His mighty angels, ⁸in flaming fire taking vengeance on those who do not know God, and on those who do not obey the gospel of our Lord Jesus Christ. ⁹These shall be punished with everlasting destruction from the presence of the Lord and from the glory of His power, ¹⁰when He comes, in that Day, to be glorified in His saints and to be admired among all those who believe, because our testimony among you was believed.

TROUBLES

1:5 As we live for Christ, we will experience troubles and hardships. Some say that troubles are a result of sin or lack of faith; Paul teaches that they may be a part of God's plan for believers. Our problems help us look upward and forward, not inward (Mark 13:35-36); help build strong character (Romans 5:3-4); and help us to be sensitive to others (2 Corinthians 1:3-5).

¹¹Therefore we also pray always for you that our God would count you worthy of *this* calling, and fulfill all the good pleasure of *His* goodness and the work of faith with power, ¹²that the name of our Lord Jesus Christ may be glorified in you, and you in Him, according to the grace of our God and the Lord Jesus Christ.

CHAPTER 2 THE ANTICHRIST. Now, brethren, concerning the coming of our Lord Jesus Christ and our gathering together to Him, we ask you, ²not to be soon shaken in mind or troubled, either by spirit or by word or by letter, as if from us, as though the day of Christ had

EVIL

2:3 Throughout history there have been antichrists— individuals who epitomized evil (see 1 John 2:18; 4:3; 2 John 7). Antichrists will occur until a "man of sin" arises just before the Second Coming. This evil individual will be Satan's tool—perhaps even Satan himself (2:9). This "son of perdition," the "lawless one," will be *the* Antichrist.

It is dangerous, however, to label certain individuals *antichrists* and try to predict Christ's coming based on those assumptions. Paul mentions the Antichrist, not necessarily to help us recognize him, but to urge us to ready ourselves for anything that might threaten our faith. If our faith is strong, we needn't fear what lies ahead. God is in control; he will be victorious. We must ready ourselves for Christ, spreading his Good News to help others be prepared also.

come. ³Let no one deceive you by any means; for *that Day will not come* unless the falling away comes first, and the man of sin is revealed, the son of perdition, ⁴who opposes and exalts himself above all that is called God or that is worshiped, so that he sits as God in the temple of God, showing himself that he is God.

⁵Do you not remember that when I was still with you I told you these things? ⁶And now you know what is restraining, that he may be revealed in his own time. ⁷For the mystery of lawlessness is already at work; only He who now restrains *will do so* until He is taken out of the

LAZINESS

Trip walks in the door, drops his books on the couch, and heads straight for the kitchen. Opening the pantry, he scans the shelves and scowls. "How come there's never anything to eat in this stupid house?" he mutters to no one in particular.

Grabbing a banana, he settles back in the recliner, remote control in hand. *Click . . . Click . . . Click.*

The phone rings. Trip doesn't budge.

A voice from the hallway: "Trip, can you get the phone? I've got shaving cream all over my hands."

Trip sits impassively, staring at the TV.

The phone continues to ring. The voice from the rear of the house gets louder. "Trip! Answer the phone!"

Just as the mystery caller gives up, Trip's mom staggers through the door, her arms loaded with grocery sacks.

Trip watches her struggle from his easy chair and greets her by saying, "I hope you bought something decent to eat."

"Go get the other sacks and I'll get supper started."

"Sheesh!" Trip complains as he grudgingly leaves his comfortable throne. "Why do I always have to do everything around here? You and Dad treat me like a slave!"

Are you a lazy person? See what the Bible says about individuals who are unwilling to pull their share of the load— 2 Thessalonians 3:6-13.

way. ⁸And then the lawless one will be revealed, whom the Lord will consume with the breath of His mouth and destroy with the brightness of His coming. ⁹The coming of the *lawless one* is according to the working of Satan, with all power, signs, and lying wonders, ¹⁰and with all unrighteous deception among those who perish, because they did not receive the love of the truth, that they might be saved. ¹¹And for this reason God will send them

strong delusion, that they should believe the lie, ¹²that they all may be condemned who did not believe the truth but had pleasure in unrighteousness.

¹³But we are bound to give thanks to God always for you, brethren beloved by the Lord, because God from the beginning chose you for salvation through sanctification

DON'T SAY NO

2:10-12 God gives people freedom to turn their back on him and believe Satan's lies. But if they say no to the truth, they will experie the consequences of their sin.

by the Spirit and belief in the truth, ¹⁴to which He called you by our gospel, for the obtaining of the glory of our Lord Jesus Christ. ¹⁵Therefore, brethren, stand fast and hold the traditions which you were taught, whether by word or our epistle.

¹⁶Now may our Lord Jesus Christ Himself, and our God and Father, who has loved us and given *us* everlasting consolation and good hope by grace, ¹⁷comfort your hearts and establish you in every good word and work.

CHAPTER 3 GOD MAKES US STRONG. Finally, brethren, pray for us, that the word of the Lord may run *swiftly* and be glorified, just as *it is* with you, ²and that we may be delivered from unreasonable and wicked men; for not all have faith.

ATTACKS

3:2-3 Beneath the surface of the routine of daily life, a fierce stru among invisible spiritual powers is being waged. Like the wind, the of evil powers can be devastating. Our main defense is prayer that will protect us from evil and that he will make us strong. (See also comments on Ephesians 6:10-19 concerning our armor for spiritual warfare.) The following guidelines can help you prepare for and sur satanic attacks: (1) take the threat of spiritual attack seriously; (2) for strength and help from God; (3) study the Bible to recognize Sat style and tactics; (4) memorize Scripture; (5) associate with those w speak the truth; and (6) practice what you are taught by spiritual le

³But the Lord is faithful, who will establish you and guard *you* from the evil one. ⁴And we have confidence in the Lord concerning you, both that you do and will do the things we command you.

⁵Now may the Lord direct your hearts into the love of God and into the patience of Christ.

⁶But we command you, brethren, in the name of our Lord Jesus Christ, that you withdraw from every brother who walks disorderly and not according to the tradition which he received from us. ⁷For you yourselves know how you ought to follow us, for we were not disorderly among you; ⁸nor did we eat anyone's bread free of charge,

WORK

3:6-10 There's a difference between leisure and laziness. Relaxat and recreation provide a necessary and much needed balance; but w it is time to work, Christians should be responsible. We should make most of our talent and time, doing all we can to provide for ourselv our families.

but worked with labor and toil night and day, that we might not be a burden to any of you, ⁹not because we do not have authority, but to make ourselves an example of how you should follow us.

¹⁰For even when we were with you, we commanded you this: If anyone will not work, neither shall he eat. ¹¹For we hear that there are some who walk among you in a disorderly manner, not working at all, but are busybodies. ¹²Now those who are such we command and exhort through our Lord Jesus Christ that they work in quietness and eat their own bread.

¹³But *as for* you, brethren, do not grow weary *in* doing good. ¹⁴And if anyone does not obey our word in this epistle, note that person and do not keep company with him, that he may be ashamed. ¹⁵Yet do not count *him* as an enemy, but admonish *him* as a brother.

¹⁶Now may the Lord of peace Himself give you peace always in every way. The Lord *be* with you all.

¹⁷The salutation of Paul with my own hand, which is a sign in every epistle; so I write.

¹⁸The grace of our Lord Jesus Christ *be* with you all. Amen.

MEGA Themes

PERSECUTION Paul encouraged the church to have patience in spite of troubles and hardships. God will bring victory to his faithful followers, and he will judge those who persecute them.

God promises to reward our faith with his power and to help us bear persecution. Suffering for our faith will strengthen us to serve Christ. God never will allow us to experience suffering apart from his power and presence.

1. How did the Thessalonians respond to persecution?
2. What did Paul say to encourage them?
3. What was the basis of Paul's belief that the Thessalonians could stand firm in their faith in spite of these painful experiences?
4. In what ways can Paul's words help you?

CHRIST'S RETURN Paul had said that Christ would come back at any moment, so some of the Thessalonian believers had stopped work to wait.

Christ will return and bring total victory to all who trust in him. If we stand firm and keep working, we will be ready. If we are ready, we don't have to be concerned about *when* he will return. Our life is already eternally secure in Christ.

1. What concerns did Paul express in chapter 3? What false ideas had developed about what it means to prepare for Christ's coming?
2. How did the promise of Christ's ultimate reign affect Paul's attitude toward life? How did he challenge the Thessalonians to live in light of Christ's coming?
3. How does thinking about the promise of Christ's ultimate reign affect your feelings? Thoughts? Actions?
4. What is your plan of preparation? How does this relate to Paul's prayer request in 3:5?

GREAT REBELLION Before Christ's return, there will be a great rebellion against God led by the man of lawlessness (the Antichrist). God will remove all the restraints on evil before he brings judgment on the rebels. The Antichrist will attempt to deceive many.

We should not be afraid when we see evil increase. God is in control, no matter how evil the world becomes. God guards us from satanic attack. We can have victory over evil by remaining faithful to God. Satan and all evil are subject to God.

1. What is the danger of the Antichrist?
2. In light of the fact that the Antichrist will impact the world and that evil is already present, how should we live?
3. How should you live in an evil world? How can this give you the confidence to endure even the dangers of the Antichrist?

PERSISTENCE Because church members had quit working and become disorderly and disobedient, Paul criticized them for their laziness. He told them to show courage and to live as Christians should.

We must never get so tired of doing right that we quit. We can be persistent by making the most of our time and talent. Our endurance will be rewarded.

1. Why is laziness so negative for a Christian?
2. In what areas do you struggle most with laziness? What does this tell you about the root of laziness?
3. Developing self-discipline is a learned quality. It is easy and natural to do only what we want to do. What does it take to develop self-discipline?
4. Outline a plan for developing self-discipline in one specific, weak area of your life.

*W*hat does it take to be a leader? Brains? Good looks? A magnetic personality? The ability to speak persuasively? A ruthless obsession for power? That's what the world says. ■ The world is wrong. Leadership is not about being tall, tan, and telegenic. Leadership has nothing to do with impressive résumés or rousing speeches. Leadership is far more than being wellborn or highly educated or multitalented. Jesus defined leadership as servanthood. It involves compassion, courage, and conviction. ■ So here's the shocker: *Anyone who takes the time to develop those qualities can be a leader.* ■ Even you. ■ "Who? Me?! You must be kidding. I don't have any special talents. Besides, I'm young and kind of shy. I could never lead anyone."

■ Funny you should say that. A young man by the name of Timothy once felt the exact same way. He found himself facing big responsibilities and even bigger challenges. He wondered what to do and whether he had what leadership requires. ■ Then he got the following letter from his friend and mentor, Paul. More than a mere letter, the Epistle of 1 Timothy is also an essay on leadership. ■ Hey, you may never be a major politician or the president of a big company, but you'll always have friends, relatives, neighbors, and acquaintances who need to be influenced. People you can (and should) influence for Christ. ■ So read about the character, compassion, courage, and conviction that leadership involves. ■ Then give it a try. Be a leader.

STATS

PURPOSE: To encourage and instruct Timothy

AUTHOR: Paul

TO WHOM WRITTEN: Timothy, young church leaders, and all believers everywhere

DATE WRITTEN: About A.D. 64, from Rome or Macedonia (possibly Philippi), probably just prior to Paul's final imprisonment in Rome

SETTING: Timothy was one of Paul's closest companions. Paul had sent him to the church at Ephesus to counter the false teaching that had arisen there (1 Timothy 1:3-4). Timothy probably served for a time as a leader in the church at Ephesus. Paul hoped to visit Timothy (3:14-15; 4:13), but in the meantime, he wrote this letter to give Timothy practical advice for the ministry.

KEY PEOPLE: Paul, Timothy

KEY PLACE: Ephesus

Timothy

CHAPTER 1 PAUL'S SON IN THE FAITH. Paul, an apostle of Jesus Christ, by the commandment of God our Savior and the Lord Jesus Christ, our hope,

²To Timothy, a true son in the faith:

Grace, mercy, *and* peace from God our Father and Jesus Christ our Lord.

³As I urged you when I went into Macedonia—remain in Ephesus that you may charge some that they teach no other doctrine, ⁴nor give heed to fables and endless genealogies, which cause disputes rather than godly edification which is in faith. ⁵Now the purpose of the commandment is love from a pure heart, *from* a good conscience, and *from* sincere faith, ⁶from which some, having strayed, have turned aside to idle talk, ⁷desiring to be teachers of the law, understanding neither what they say nor the things which they affirm.

ALLEGIANCE

1:3-11 The world is filled with people demanding our allegiance. Many would have us turn from Christ to follow them. Often their influence is subtle. How can you recognize false teaching before it does irreparable damage? (1) It stirs up questions and arguments instead of helping people come to Jesus (1:4). (2) It is often promoted by teachers whose motivation is to make a name for themselves (1:7). (3) It is contrary to the true teaching of the Scriptures (1:6-7; 4:1-3). Instead of listening to false teachers, we should learn what the Bible teaches and remain strong in our faith in Christ alone.

INNER TUGS

1:19 How can you keep a good conscience? Treasure your faith in Christ more than anything else and do what you know is right. Each time you deliberately ignore your conscience, you are hardening your heart. Soon your capacity to tell right from wrong will disappear. But when you walk with God, he is able to speak to you through your conscience, letting you know the difference between right and wrong. Be sure to act on those inner tugs to do what is right—then your conscience will remain clear.

[8]But we know that the law *is* good if one uses it lawfully, [9]knowing this: that the law is not made for a righteous person, but for *the* lawless and insubordinate, for

MATERIALISM

Jeremy and his girlfriend Blair can hardly wait until next Tuesday. That's the day when the winning numbers in the state lottery will be announced. Everybody is buzzing about the jackpot—now more than 100 million dollars!

"Just think if we won," Jeremy dreams out loud. "We'd be able—"

"I'm not even going to think about it," Blair interrupts. "I'll just get my hopes up, and then I'll be all disappointed."

"C'mon, Blair, why do you always have to be so negative?! We've got as much of a chance as anyone else. In fact, we've got 10 chances to win. It's got to happen to someone—it might as well be us. And if we do win, just think of all the stuff we could do, of all the things we could buy!"

"It would be great to be rich. You wouldn't have a care in the world. Imagine going into the mall and picking up whatever you want and not even having to look at the price tag."

"Yeah, or going to any car dealership, walking over to the car you want, and saying, 'I'll take it.' Imagine that!"

"That'd be awesome!" Blair exclaims.

The two dreamers sit thinking quietly for a few minutes. Finally Blair breaks the silence. "Jeremy, I still can't help feeling like we just poured 10 dollars down the drain!"

"Blair!"

See what God's Word says about the desire to get rich quick—1 Timothy 6:9-10.

the ungodly and for sinners, for *the* unholy and profane, for murderers of fathers and murderers of mothers, for manslayers, [10]for fornicators, for sodomites, for kidnappers, for liars, for perjurers, and if there is any other thing that is contrary to sound doctrine, [11]according to the glorious gospel of the blessed God which was committed to my trust.

[12]And I thank Christ Jesus our Lord who has enabled me, because He counted me faithful, putting *me* into the ministry, [13]although I was formerly a blasphemer, a persecutor, and an insolent man; but I obtained mercy because I did *it* ignorantly in unbelief. [14]And the grace of our Lord was exceedingly abundant, with faith and love which are in Christ Jesus. [15]This *is* a faithful saying and worthy of all acceptance, that Christ Jesus came into the world to save sinners, of whom I am chief. [16]However,

for this reason I obtained mercy, that in me first Jesus Christ might show all longsuffering, as a pattern to those who are going to believe on Him for everlasting life. [17]Now to the King eternal, immortal, invisible, to God who alone is wise, *be* honor and glory forever and ever. Amen.

[18]This charge I commit to you, son Timothy, according to the prophecies previously made concerning you, that by them you may wage the good warfare, [19]having faith and a good conscience, which some having rejected, concerning the faith have suffered shipwreck, [20]of whom are Hymenaeus and Alexander, whom I delivered to Satan that they may learn not to blaspheme.

CHAPTER 2 GUIDELINES FOR WORSHIP.

Therefore I exhort first of all that supplications, prayers, intercessions, *and* giving of thanks be made for all men, [2]for kings and all who are in authority, that we may lead a quiet and peaceable life in all godliness and reverence. [3]For this *is* good and acceptable in the sight of God our Savior, [4]who desires all men to be saved and to come to the knowledge of the truth. [5]For *there is* one God and one Mediator between God and men, *the* Man Christ Jesus, [6]who gave Himself a ransom for all, to be testified in due

MAKE PEACE

2:8 Besides being displeasing to God, it is difficult to pray when w[e] sinned or when we feel angry and resentful. That is why Jesus told [us to] interrupt worship, if necessary, to make peace with others (Matthe[w] 5:23-24). Our goal is to have a right relationship with God and als[o with] others.

time, [7]for which I was appointed a preacher and an apostle—I am speaking the truth in Christ *and* not lying—a teacher of the Gentiles in faith and truth.

[8]I desire therefore that the men pray everywhere, lifting up holy hands, without wrath and doubting; [9]in like manner also, that the women adorn themselves in modest apparel, with propriety and moderation, not with braided hair or gold or pearls or costly clothing, [10]but, which is proper for women professing godliness, with good works. [11]Let a woman learn in silence with all submission. [12]And I do not permit a woman to teach or to

GREAT EXPECTATIONS

3:1-13 The word *bishop* can refer to a pastor, church leader, or presiding elder. It is good to want to be a spiritual leader, but the standards are high. Paul lists some of the qualifications here. Do y[ou hold] a position of spiritual leadership, or would you like to be a leader s[ome] day? Check yourself against Paul's standard of excellence. Those w[ith] great responsibility must meet high expectations.

have authority over a man, but to be in silence. [13]For Adam was formed first, then Eve. [14]And Adam was not deceived, but the woman being deceived, fell into transgression. [15]Nevertheless she will be saved in childbearing if they continue in faith, love, and holiness, with self-control.

CHAPTER **3** **GUIDELINES FOR CHURCH LEADERS.**
This *is* a faithful saying: If a man desires the position of a bishop, he desires a good work. [2]A bishop then must be blameless, the husband of one wife, temperate, sober-minded, of good behavior, hospitable, able to teach; [3]not given to wine, not violent, not greedy for money, but gentle, not quarrelsome, not covetous; [4]one who rules his own house well, having *his* children in submission with all reverence [5](for if a man does not know how to rule his own house, how will he take care of the church of God?); [6]not a novice, lest being puffed up with pride he fall into the *same* condemnation as the devil. [7]Moreover he must have a good testimony among those who are outside, lest he fall into reproach and the snare of the devil.

[8]Likewise deacons *must be* reverent, not double-tongued, not given to much wine, not greedy for money, [9]holding the mystery of the faith with a pure conscience. [10]But let these also first be tested; then let them serve as deacons, being *found* blameless. [11]Likewise, *their* wives *must be* reverent, not slanderers, temperate, faithful in all things. [12]Let deacons be the husbands of one wife, ruling *their* children and their own houses well. [13]For those who have served well as deacons obtain for themselves a good standing and great boldness in the faith which is in Christ Jesus.

[14]These things I write to you, though I hope to come to you shortly; [15]but if I am delayed, *I write* so that you may know how you ought to conduct yourself in the house of God, which is the church of the living God, the pillar and ground of the truth. [16]And without controversy great is the mystery of godliness:

God was manifested in the flesh,
Justified in the Spirit,
Seen by angels,
Preached among the Gentiles,
Believed on in the world,
Received up in glory.

CHAPTER **4** **IGNORE FALSE TEACHERS: THEY LIE.** Now the Spirit expressly says that in latter times some will depart from the faith, giving heed to deceiving spirits and doctrines of demons, [2]speaking lies in hypocrisy, having their own conscience seared with a hot iron, [3]forbidding to marry, *and commanding* to abstain from foods which God created to be received with thanksgiving by those who believe and know the truth. [4]For every creature of God *is* good, and nothing is to be refused if it is received with thanksgiving; [5]for it is sanctified by the word of God and prayer.

[6]If you instruct the brethren in these things, you will be a good minister of Jesus Christ, nourished

TIMOTHY

Real leadership abilities are sometimes buried under a person's shyness. It takes a friend with understanding and patience to uncover those strengths. That's what happened between the apostle Paul and a young man named Timothy.

Timothy probably became a Christian when Paul visited his hometown of Lystra during his first missionary journey (Acts 14:8-20). Timothy's Jewish mother and grandmother had prepared him by teaching him from the Old Testament. By the time Paul visited Lystra again, Timothy was known as a growing Christian. When invited, Timothy jumped at the chance to travel with Paul and Silas.

Away from home, Timothy struggled with his shyness. Unfortunately, shy people are often written off as being unable to carry much responsibility. But Paul chose to give Timothy important responsibilities in the ministry. Paul even made Timothy his personal representative on several occasions. Sometimes Timothy failed on his missions, but Paul never gave up on him. Timothy became a "son" to Paul.

Our last pictures of Timothy come from the most personal letters in the New Testament: 1 and 2 Timothy. They were written by Paul in such a way that his deep friendship with Timothy is obvious; they had traveled, suffered, cried, and laughed together. The letters were intended to encourage and direct Timothy in Ephesus, where Paul had left him in charge of a young church (1 Timothy 1:3-4). These same letters have helped and encouraged countless other "Timothys" through the years. When you face a challenge that is beyond your abilities, read 1 and 2 Timothy. Remember, others have shared your experience.

LESSONS: Youthfulness should not be an excuse for ineffectiveness

Our inadequacies and inabilities should not keep us from being available to God

KEY VERSES: "For I have no one like-minded, who will sincerely care for your state. For all seek their own, not the things which are of Christ Jesus. But you know his [Timothy's] proven character, that as a son with his father he served with me in the gospel" (Philippians 2:20-22).

Timothy's story is told in Acts, starting in chapter 16. He is also mentioned in Romans 16:21; 1 Corinthians 1:1,19; 16:10-11; 2 Corinthians 1:1; 2:19-23; Colossians Philippians 1:1; 2:19-23; Colossians 1:1; 1 Thessalonians 1:1-10; 2:3-4; 3:2-6; 1 and 2 Timothy; Philemon 1; Hebrews 13:23.

UPS:
• Became a believer after Paul's first missionary journey and joined him for his other two journeys
• Was a respected Christian in his hometown
• Was Paul's special representative on several occasions
• Received two personal letters from Paul
• Probably knew Paul better than any other person, becoming like a son to him

DOWNS:
• Struggled with a timid and reserved nature
• Allowed others to look down on his youthfulness
• Was apparently unable to correct some of the problems in the church at Corinth when Paul sent him there

STATS:
• Where: Lystra
• Occupations: Missionary, church leader
• Relatives: Mother: Eunice; Grandmother: Lois; Greek father.
• Contemporaries: Paul, Silas, Luke, Mark, Peter, Barnabas

in the words of faith and of the good doctrine which you have carefully followed. [7]But reject profane and old wives' fables, and exercise yourself toward godliness. [8]For bodily exercise profits a little, but godliness is profitable for all things, having promise of the life that now is and of that which is to come. [9]This *is* a faithful saying and worthy of all acceptance. [10]For to this *end* we both labor and suffer reproach, because we trust in the living God, who is *the* Savior of all men, especially of those who believe. [11]These things command and teach.

[12]Let no one despise your youth, but be an example to the believers in word, in conduct, in love, in spirit, in faith, in purity. [13]Till I come, give attention to reading, to exhortation, to doctrine. [14]Do not neglect the gift that is in you, which was given to you by prophecy with the laying on of the hands of the eldership. [15]Meditate on these things; give yourself entirely to them, that your progress may be evident to all. [16]Take heed to yourself and to the doctrine. Continue in them, for in doing this you will save both yourself and those who hear you.

CHAPTER **5** **YOUR PART.** Do not rebuke an older man, but exhort *him* as a father, younger men as brothers, [2]older women as mothers, younger women as sisters, with all purity.

[3]Honor widows who are really widows. [4]But if any widow has children or grandchildren, let them first learn to show piety at home and to repay their parents; for this is good and acceptable before God. [5]Now she who is really a widow, and left alone, trusts in God and continues in supplications and prayers night and day. [6]But she who lives in pleasure is dead while she lives. [7]And these things command, that they may be blameless. [8]But if anyone does not provide for his own, and especially for those of his household, he has denied the faith and is worse than an unbeliever.

[9]Do not let a widow under sixty years old be taken into the number, *and not unless* she has been the wife of one man, [10]well reported for good works: if she has brought up children, if she has lodged strangers, if she has washed the saints' feet, if she has relieved the afflicted, if she has diligently followed every good work.

▬▬ YOUR FAMILY

5:8 Almost everyone has relatives, family of some kind. Family relationships are so important in God's eyes, Paul says, that a person who neglects his or her family responsibilities has denied the faith. Are you doing your part to meet the needs of those included in your family circle? Even your little brothers and sisters?

[11]But refuse *the* younger widows; for when they have begun to grow wanton against Christ, they desire to marry, [12]having condemnation because they have cast off their first faith. [13]And besides they learn *to be* idle, wandering about from house to house, and not only idle but also gossips and busybodies, saying things which they ought not. [14]Therefore I desire that *the* younger *widows* marry, bear children, manage the house, give no opportunity to the adversary to speak reproachfully. [15]For some

LET NO ONE **DESPISE** your youth, your youth, your youth, your youth, BUT BE AN EXAMPLE TO THE BELIEVERS IN WORD IN CONDUCT *in love* *in spirit* IN FAITH IN PURITY.

1 TIMOTHY 4:12

have already turned aside after Satan. [16]If any believing man or woman has widows, let them relieve them, and do not let the church be burdened, that it may relieve those who are really widows.

[17]Let the elders who rule well be counted worthy of double honor, especially those who labor in the word and doctrine. [18]For the Scripture says, *"You shall not muzzle an ox while it treads out the grain,"* and, "The laborer *is* worthy of his wages." [19]Do not receive an accusation against an elder except from two or three witnesses. [20]Those who are sinning rebuke in the presence of all, that the rest also may fear.

[21]I charge *you* before God and the Lord Jesus Christ and the elect angels that you observe these things with-

▬▬ MONEY CYCLE

6:6-10 Despite almost overwhelming evidence to the contrary, so people still believe money brings happiness. Rich people craving gr riches can be caught in an endless cycle that only ends in ruin and desperation. How can you avoid the love of money? Paul gives us s principles: (1) realize that one day riches will all be gone (6:7,17); content with what you have (6:8); (3) watch what you are willing t get more money (6:9-10); (4) love people and God's work more th money (6:11); (5) freely share what you have with others (6:18). also Proverbs 30:7-9.)

out prejudice, doing nothing with partiality. ²²Do not lay hands on anyone hastily, nor share in other people's sins; keep yourself pure.

²³No longer drink only water, but use a little wine for your stomach's sake and your frequent infirmities.

²⁴Some men's sins are clearly evident, preceding *them* to judgment, but those of some *men* follow later. ²⁵Likewise, the good works *of some* are clearly evident, and those that are otherwise cannot be hidden.

CHAPTER 6 MONEY ISN'T EVERYTHING. Let as

many bondservants as are under the yoke count their own masters worthy of all honor, so that the name of God and *His* doctrine may not be blasphemed. ²And those who have believing masters, let them not despise *them* because they are brethren, but rather serve *them* because those who are benefited are believers and beloved. Teach and exhort these things.

³If anyone teaches otherwise and does not consent to wholesome words, *even* the words of our Lord Jesus Christ, and to the doctrine which accords with godliness, ⁴he is proud, knowing nothing, but is obsessed with disputes and arguments over words, from which come envy, strife, reviling, evil suspicions, ⁵useless wranglings of men of corrupt minds and destitute of the truth, who suppose that godliness is a *means of* gain. From such withdraw yourself.

⁶Now godliness with contentment is great gain. ⁷For we brought nothing into *this* world, *and it is* certain we can carry nothing out. ⁸And having food and clothing, with these we shall be content. ⁹But those who desire to be rich fall into temptation and a snare, and *into* many foolish and harmful lusts which drown men in destruction and perdition. ¹⁰For the love of money is a root of all *kinds of* evil, for which some have strayed from the faith in their greediness, and pierced themselves through with many sorrows.

¹¹But you, O man of God, flee these things and pursue righteousness, godliness, faith, love, patience, gentleness. ¹²Fight the good fight of faith, lay hold on eternal life, to which you were also called and have confessed the good confession in the presence of many witnesses. ¹³I urge you in the sight of God who gives life to all things, and *before* Christ Jesus who witnessed the good confession before Pontius Pilate, ¹⁴that you keep *this* commandment without spot, blameless until our Lord Jesus Christ's appearing, ¹⁵which He will manifest in His own time, *He who is* the blessed and only Potentate, the King of kings and Lord of lords, ¹⁶who alone has immortality, dwelling in unapproachable light, whom no man has seen or can see, to whom *be* honor and everlasting power. Amen.

¹⁷Command those who are rich in this present age not to be haughty, nor to trust in uncertain riches but in the living God, who gives us richly all things to enjoy. ¹⁸Let *them* do good, that they be rich in good works, ready to give, willing to share, ¹⁹storing up for themselves a good foundation for the time to come, that they may lay hold on eternal life.

²⁰O Timothy! Guard what was committed to your trust, avoiding the profane *and* idle babblings and contradictions of what is falsely called knowledge— ²¹by professing it some have strayed concerning the faith.

Grace *be* with you. Amen.

YOU'RE RICH

6:17-19 Ephesus was a wealthy city, and the Ephesian church probably had many wealthy members. Paul advised Timothy to deal with a potential problem by teaching that the possession of riches carries great responsibility. Those who have money must be generous, not arrogant. They must be careful not to put their trust in money instead of in the living God. Even if we don't have material wealth, we can be rich in good works toward others. No matter how poor we are, we have something to share with someone.

I WONDER...

Trying to stay pure and not sin seems like a full-time job. How can anyone stay pure? Why would anyone want to?

Jesus talked a lot about the Pharisees. These men had created long lists of dos and don'ts about behavior of every kind. They wanted to be pure! Many of them were very, very good.

But in Matthew 5:20, Jesus made an incredible statement! "For I say to you, that unless your righteousness exceeds *the righteousness* of the scribes and Pharisees, you will by no means enter the kingdom of heaven."

Wow! If the Pharisees couldn't make it, who can?

Those who make it into the kingdom of heaven are not just pure on the outside, like the Pharisees. Anyone can make sure their behavior is correct (at least for a while).

Jesus was talking about being pure on the inside. This begins by accepting Christ's death on the cross as punishment for our sins. When we do this, we take on Christ's goodness, and, in God's eyes, we are pure and worthy of eternity in heaven! Now that's a pretty good deal!

It doesn't stop there, of course. God wants us to be like Jesus. This is a lifelong process of allowing God to mold us and change us (see 1 Timothy 6:11-12). It happens by staying close to Christ and living like he wants us to. It's what keeps the Christian life fun, interesting, and challenging.

A Christian who's really alive realizes that his eternity is settled. But he also genuinely wants to be more like the one who paid such a high price for his soul—Jesus. His motivation is not to parade his goodness in front of others, but rather to please God.

Staying pure and growing as a Christian are "full-time jobs." But they are also natural by-products of staying close to Christ.

MEGA Themes

SOUND DOCTRINE Paul instructed Timothy to preserve the Christian faith by teaching sound doctrine and modeling right living. Timothy had to oppose false teachers who were leading church members away from belief in salvation by faith in Jesus Christ alone.

We must know the truth to defend it. And the truth is that Christ came to save us. We should stay away from those who twist the words of the Bible for their own purposes. Therefore, we must study and know the Bible ourselves.

1. What do you consider to be the main points in the Bible concerning God and people, sin and salvation, life and death?
2. Why are these truths so important to the Bible's message?
3. Paul greatly opposed those who taught against the truth of the gospel. What did Paul tell Timothy to do about false teachers?
4. Based on this study, how should you respond to the message of a false teacher? What can you do to be able to discern the truth from error?

PUBLIC WORSHIP In public worship, prayer must be done with a proper attitude toward God and fellow believers.

Christian character must be evident in every aspect of worship. We must rid ourselves of any anger, resentment, or offensive attire that might disrupt worship or damage church unity. Christian unity begins with your own attitude and actions toward others.

1. What were Paul's instructions to Timothy about worship?
2. What aspects of public, congregational worship do you most enjoy? Least enjoy? How do you feel about worship overall?
3. What should be a Christian's attitude in worship?

What actions should be a part of worship services?
4. What steps can you take to deepen your worship as well as to encourage others in your church to do the same?

CHURCH LEADERSHIP Paul gives specific instructions concerning the qualifications for church leaders so that the church might honor God and run smoothly.

Church leaders must be wholly committed to Christ. If you are a new or young Christian, don't be anxious to become a leader in your church. Develop your Christian character first. Be sure to consider God, not your own ambition.

1. Describe the overall character of the persons who are qualified to serve in church leadership according to 3:1-16.
2. In what specific ways does Paul challenge Timothy to mature and develop personally?
3. How can a young person who is a Christian prepare now to be a man or woman of God later, as he or she matures?
4. Praise God for your areas of personal strength. Design a plan to work on your personal weaknesses so that, by his grace, you will be a godly leader throughout your life.

PERSONAL DISCIPLINE It takes discipline to be a leader in the church. Timothy, like all church leaders, had to guard his motives, minister faithfully, and live right. Any pastor must keep morally and spiritually fit.

To stay in good spiritual shape, you must discipline yourself to study God's Word and to live a godly life. Put your spiritual abilities to work!

1. What areas of personal discipline would Timothy have to develop as a result of what Paul told him?
2. How do you think Timothy felt as he read this letter? Read chapters 4 and 6 and describe how

you would have felt if this letter had been written to you.

3. What beginning steps can you take to deepen your faith?

4. How will the Holy Spirit of God help you to deal with the personal difficulties you may face as you attempt to step out?

CARING CHURCH The church has a responsibility to care for the needs of all its members, especially the sick, the poor, and the widowed. Caring for the family of believers demonstrates our Christlike attitude and genuine love. We are Christ's touch of love in one another's lives.

1. What did Paul think about the church's responsibility for reaching out to others?

2. Why is this so important for the church as Christ's body?

3. On a scale of A-B-C-D-F, give your church a grade in terms of Paul's descriptions of what it means to serve those in need.

4. Grade yourself on the above scale. What can you do to improve your grade? What can you do to get involved with your church to improve its grade?

*T*rivia is "unimportant matters." It's all that information that's often interesting but doesn't really matter much. For instance, did you know that:

■ Grasshoppers are approximately three times more nutritious than rib-eye steak?

■ Kangaroos can't jump when their tails are lifted off the ground? ■ France's King Louis XIV feared water so much that he never took a bath and rarely washed more than the tip of his nose? ■ It's impossible to sneeze with your eyes open? ■ Benjamin Franklin invented swim fins and the rocking chair? ■ Mozart wrote the tune "Twinkle, Twinkle, Little Star" when he was five? ■ Eating too many carrots can make your skin turn yellow?

■ Nine-hundred-and-twenty-eight average size fleas will fit inside a Ping-Pong ball?

■ Though amusing—and helpful for filling the silence in an awkward conversation—the facts just cited are worthless. They won't change your life. They're trivia. *Trivial* trivia.

■ Not so the book of 2 Timothy. ■ The apostle Paul's second letter to Timothy is serious stuff. History says that these were Paul's last words; he died shortly after penning them.

■ Perhaps the aged saint recognized that his time was running out. If so, it's not surprising that he talked about important matters. Consider carefully Paul's final thoughts. He is, after all, one of the most influential individuals in history. ■ And Paul's challenge to Timothy is just as appropriate 2,000 years later. ■ The bottom line? Second Timothy is no trivial pursuit!

STATS

PURPOSE: To give final instructions and encouragement to Timothy, a leader of the church at Ephesus

AUTHOR: Paul

TO WHOM WRITTEN: Timothy

DATE WRITTEN: About A.D. 66 or 67 from prison in Rome. After a year or two of freedom, Paul was arrested again and executed under Emperor Nero.

SETTING: Paul was virtually alone in prison; only Luke was with him. He wrote this letter to pass the torch to the new generation of church leaders. He also asked for visits from his friends, for his books, and especially the parchments—possibly parts of the Old Testament, the Gospels, and other biblical manuscripts.

KEY PEOPLE: Paul, Timothy, Luke, Mark, and others

KEY PLACES: Rome, Ephesus

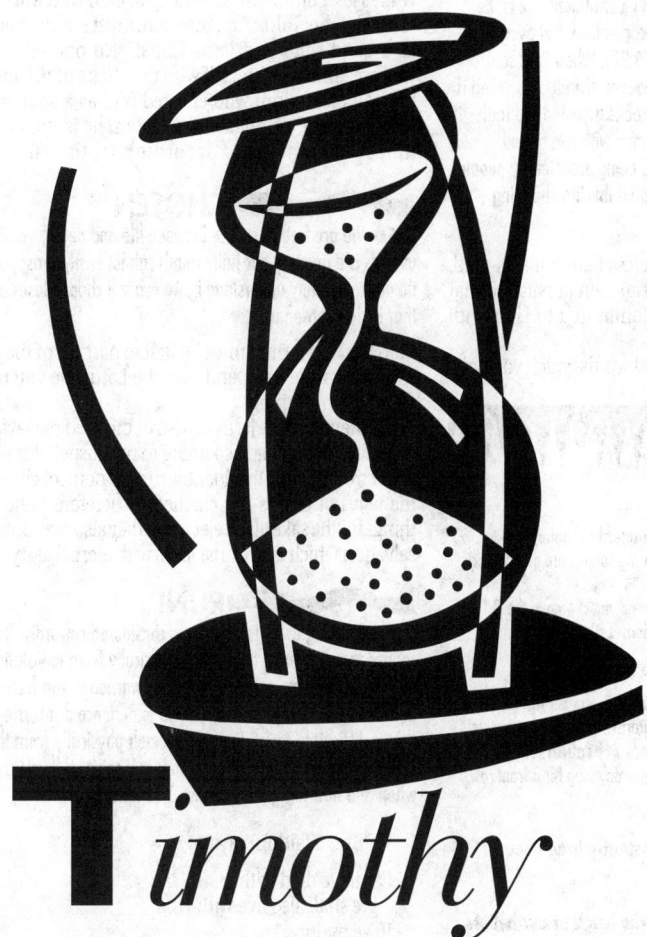

2 Timothy

CHAPTER 1 A LETTER TO ENCOURAGE TIMOTHY.
Paul, an apostle of Jesus Christ by the will of God, according to the promise of life which is in Christ Jesus,

²To Timothy, a beloved son:

Grace, mercy, *and* peace from God the Father and Christ Jesus our Lord.

³I thank God, whom I serve with a pure conscience, as *my* forefathers *did,* as without ceasing I remember you in my prayers night and day, ⁴greatly desiring to see you, being mindful of your tears, that I may be filled with joy, ⁵when I call to remembrance the genuine faith that is in you, which dwelt first in your grandmother Lois and your mother Eunice, and I am persuaded is in you also. ⁶Therefore I remind you to stir up the gift of God which is in you through the laying on of my hands. ⁷For God has not given us a spirit of fear, but of power and of love and of a sound mind.

⁸Therefore do not be ashamed of the testimony of our Lord, nor of me His prisoner, but share with me in the sufferings for the gospel according to the power of God, ⁹who has saved us and called *us* with a holy calling, not according to our works, but according to His own purpose and grace which was given to us in Christ Jesus before time began, ¹⁰but has now been revealed by the appearing of our Savior Jesus Christ, *who* has abolished death and brought life and immortality to light through the gospel, ¹¹to which I was appointed a preacher, an apostle, and a teacher of the Gentiles. ¹²For this reason I

BE BOLD

1:6-7 Timothy was experiencing great opposition to his message and to himself as a leader. Timothy's youth, his association with Paul, and his leadership had come under fire. Paul urged Timothy to be bold. When we allow people to intimidate us, we neutralize our effectiveness for God. The power of the Holy Spirit can help us overcome our fear of what some might say or do to us so we can continue to do God's work.

THE GOD-MAN

2:9 Paul was in chains because of the gospel he preached. When Paul said Jesus was God, he angered the Jews who had condemned Jesus for blasphemy, but many Jews became Christians (1 Corinthians 1:24); he angered the Romans who worshiped the emperor as God, but even some in Caesar's palace turned to Jesus (Philippians 4:22). When Paul said Jesus was man, he angered the Greeks who thought divinity was soiled if it had any contact with humanity; still many Greeks accepted the faith (Acts 11:20-21). The truth that Jesus is one person with two united natures has never been easy to accept, but it *is* being accepted by people every day. Are you one of those who has accepted this life-changing message?

also suffer these things; nevertheless I am not ashamed, for I know whom I have believed and am persuaded that He is able to keep what I have committed to Him until that Day.

¹³Hold fast the pattern of sound words which you have

*P*OPULAR MUSIC

It's guaranteed to be the most spectacular concert tour ever. The members of Oozing Tumors are getting back together for one last fling.

People line up to camp out for tickets—a week in advance! Among the O.T. faithful are three teenagers who happen to be Christians. Let's ask Em, Donny, and Brad a few questions.

"So you guys are pretty cranked, huh?"

Donny: "Oh, yeah! This is gonna be awesome! I saw O.T. on their last tour, and they were unbelievable. During the last song, the guitarist shattered nine guitars!"

"Isn't he the same guy who pulls the ears off rabbits?"

Em: "Only once . . . and he apologized later. I'd give anything for a front row seat. I want to see what he wears."

"You mean almost wears?" (Em giggles.)

"Does it bother you that these guys constantly brag about how many chicks they've slept with?"

Brad: "Oh, I just like their music."

"But should Christians support people who laugh at our beliefs and values?"

Em: "Whoa, dude! It's just a concert!"

What about popular music? Whether it's rock, metal, rap, country & western, or whatever? Read 2 Timothy 3:1-5, noting especially the end of verse five.

heard from me, in faith and love which are in Christ Jesus. ¹⁴That good thing which was committed to you, keep by the Holy Spirit who dwells in us.

¹⁵This you know, that all those in Asia have turned away from me, among whom are Phygellus and Hermogenes. ¹⁶The Lord grant mercy to the household of Onesiphorus, for he often refreshed me, and was not ashamed of my chain; ¹⁷but when he arrived in Rome, he sought me out very zealously and found *me.* ¹⁸The Lord grant to him that he may find mercy from the Lord in that Day—and you know very well how many ways he ministered *to me* at Ephesus.

CHAPTER 2 BE A GOOD SOLDIER. You therefore, my son, be strong in the grace that is in Christ Jesus. ²And the things that you have heard from me among many witnesses, commit these to faithful men who will be able to teach others also. ³You therefore must endure hardship as a good soldier of Jesus Christ. ⁴No one engaged in warfare entangles himself with the affairs of *this* life, that he may please him who enlisted him as a soldier. ⁵And also if anyone competes in athletics, he is not crowned unless he competes according to the rules. ⁶The

CHOSEN

2:10 We are free to choose between life and death, yet God has c us. This is a mystery our finite minds cannot easily grasp. But even i do not completely understand it, we can still choose Jesus and be g that he has chosen us.

hardworking farmer must be first to partake of the crops. ⁷Consider what I say, and may the Lord give you understanding in all things.

⁸Remember that Jesus Christ, of the seed of David, was raised from the dead according to my gospel, ⁹for which I suffer trouble as an evildoer, *even* to the point of chains; but the word of God is not chained. ¹⁰Therefore I endure all things for the sake of the elect, that they also may obtain the salvation which is in Christ Jesus with eternal glory.

RUN!

2:22 Running away is sometimes considered cowardly. But wise pe realize that removing themselves physically from temptation is often very wise. Timothy, a young man, was warned to run from anything produced evil thoughts. Perhaps you experience a recurring temptati that is difficult to resist. Remove yourself physically from the situatio Knowing when to run is as important in a spiritual battle as knowing when and how to fight. (See also 1 Timothy 6:11.)

¹¹ *This is* a faithful saying:

For if we died with *Him,*
We shall also live with *Him.*

¹² If we endure,
We shall also reign with *Him.*
If we deny *Him,*
He also will deny us.

¹³ If we are faithless,
He remains faithful;
He cannot deny Himself.

¹⁴Remind *them* of these things, charging *them* before the Lord not to strive about words to no profit, to the ruin of the hearers. ¹⁵Be diligent to present yourself approved

SUPERNATURAL

3:16 The Bible is not a collection of stories, fables, myths, or merely human ideas about God. It is not a human book. Through the Holy Spi God revealed his person and plan to godly men, who wrote down God message for his people (2 Peter 1:20-21). This process is known as *inspiration.* The writers wrote from their own personal, historical, and cultural contexts. Yet, though they used their own minds, talents, languages, and styles, they wrote what God wanted them to write. Scripture is completely trustworthy because God was in control of its writing. Its words are authoritative for our faith and life.

ALL SCRIPTURE IS GIVEN BY INSPIRATION OF GOD

AND

IS PROFITABLE

FOR DOCTRINE,
FOR REPROOF,
FOR CORRECTION,
FOR INSTRUCTION IN RIGHTEOUSNESS,

THAT the man of God may be complete,

THOROUGHLY
EQUIPPED FOR

EVERY GOOD WORK.

to teach, patient, [25]in humility correcting those who are in opposition, if God perhaps will grant them repentance, so that they may know the truth, [26]and *that* they may come to their senses *and escape* the snare of the devil, having been taken captive by him to *do* his will.

CHAPTER 3 BEING A CHRISTIAN CAN BE TOUGH.
But know this, that in the last days perilous times will come: [2]For men will be lovers of themselves, lovers of money, boasters, proud, blasphemers, disobedient to parents, unthankful, unholy, [3]unloving, unforgiving, slanderers, without self-control, brutal, despisers of good, [4]traitors, headstrong, haughty, lovers of pleasure rather than lovers of God, [5]having a form of godliness but denying its power. And from such people turn away! [6]For of this sort are those who creep into households and make captives of gullible women loaded down with sins, led away by various lusts, [7]always learning and never able to come to the knowledge of the truth. [8]Now as Jannes and Jambres resisted Moses, so do these also resist the truth: men of corrupt minds, disapproved concerning the faith; [9]but they will progress no further, for their folly will be manifest to all, as theirs also was.

[10]But you have carefully followed my doctrine, manner of life, purpose, faith, longsuffering, love, perseverance, [11]persecutions, afflictions, which happened to me at Antioch, at Iconium, at Lystra—what persecutions I endured. And out of *them* all the Lord delivered me. [12]Yes, and all who desire to live godly in Christ Jesus will suffer persecution. [13]But evil men and impostors will grow worse and worse, deceiving and being deceived. [14]But you must continue in the things which you have learned

A friend of mine stopped coming to church because he said that God had stopped answering his prayers. How do I answer him?

I WONDER . . .

Like Demas, who deserted Paul (see 2 Timothy 4:10), many Christians have a what-have-you-done-for-me-lately type of faith in God. They are willing to trust him in the good times, but when trouble hits they figure God has "checked out on them"—so they "check out on God."

Because we live in a society where we often can get what we want, when we want it, we may begin to think that God's only purpose is to meet our needs. Then when something doesn't work out—when we think that God hasn't come through for us—we turn away from him.

God is in the business of molding our character. One way he does this is by allowing us to go through tough times. When Paul wrote this letter, the church was going through intense persecution. Demas got tired of it and left. He wanted his comforts more than he wanted God's will.

Encourage your friend to change the what-have-you-done-for-me-lately attitude. Help him realize that God wants to build his character. His goal is not to make us feel good, but to develop us into the kind of people he wants.

to God, a worker who does not need to be ashamed, rightly dividing the word of truth. [16]But shun profane *and* idle babblings, for they will increase to more ungodliness. [17]And their message will spread like cancer. Hymenaeus and Philetus are of this sort, [18]who have strayed concerning the truth, saying that the resurrection is already past; and they overthrow the faith of some. [19]Nevertheless the solid foundation of God stands, having this seal: "The Lord knows those who are His," and, "Let everyone who names the name of Christ depart from iniquity."

[20]But in a great house there are not only vessels of gold and silver, but also of wood and clay, some for honor and some for dishonor. [21]Therefore if anyone cleanses himself from the latter, he will be a vessel for honor, sanctified and useful for the Master, prepared for every good work. [22]Flee also youthful lusts; but pursue righteousness, faith, love, peace with those who call on the Lord out of a pure heart. [23]But avoid foolish and ignorant disputes, knowing that they generate strife. [24]And a servant of the Lord must not quarrel but be gentle to all, able

3:16 The whole Bible is God's inspired Word. Because it is inspired and trustworthy, we should *read* it and *apply* it to our life. The Bible is our standard for testing everything else that claims to be true. It is our safeguard against false teaching and our source of guidance for how we should live. The Bible is our only source of knowledge about how we can be saved. God wants to show you what is true and equip you to live for him. How much time do you spend in God's Word? Read it regularly to discover God's truth and to become confident in your life and faith. Develop a plan for reading the whole Bible, not just the same familiar passages.

and been assured of, knowing from whom you have learned *them,* [15]and that from childhood you have known the Holy Scriptures, which are able to make you wise for salvation through faith which is in Christ Jesus. [16]All Scripture *is* given by inspiration of God, and *is* profitable for doctrine, for reproof, for correction, for instruction in righteousness, [17]that the man of God may be complete, thoroughly equipped for every good work.

CHAPTER **4** SHARE YOUR FAITH. I charge *you* therefore before God and the Lord Jesus Christ, who will judge the living and the dead at His appearing and His kingdom: [2]Preach the word! Be ready in season *and* out of season. Convince, rebuke, exhort, with all longsuffering and teaching. [3]For the time will come when they will not endure sound doctrine, but according to their own desires, *because* they have itching ears, they will heap up for themselves teachers; [4]and they will turn *their* ears away from the truth, and be turned aside to fables. [5]But you be watchful in all things, endure afflictions, do the work of an evangelist, fulfill your ministry.

[6]For I am already being poured out as a drink offering, and the time of my departure is at hand. [7]I have fought the good fight, I have finished the race, I have kept the faith. [8]Finally, there is laid up for me the crown of righteousness, which the Lord, the righteous Judge, will give to me on that Day, and not to me only but also to all who have loved His appearing.

[9]Be diligent to come to me quickly; [10]for Demas has forsaken me, having loved this present world, and has departed for Thessalonica—Crescens for Galatia, Titus for Dalmatia. [11]Only Luke is with me. Get Mark and bring him with you, for he is useful to me for ministry. [12]And Tychicus I have sent to Ephesus. [13]Bring the cloak that I left with Carpus at Troas when you come—and the books, especially the parchments.

[14]Alexander the coppersmith did me much harm. May the Lord repay him according to his works. [15]You also must beware of him, for he has greatly resisted our words.

[16]At my first defense no one stood with me, but all forsook me. May it not be charged against them. [17]But the Lord stood with me and strengthened me, so

4:10 Demas had been one of Paul's coworkers (Colossians 4:14; Philemon 24), but he deserted Paul because he "loved this present world." There are two ways to love the world. God loves the world created it and as it could be if it were rescued from evil. That is why sacrificed his Son to save the world (John 3:16). Others, like Demas the world as it is, sin and all. Do you love the world as it could be if justice were done, the hungry were fed, and people loved one anoth Or do you love what the world has to offer—wealth, power, pleasure—even if gaining it means hurting people and neglecting work God has given you to do?

that the message might be preached fully through me, and *that* all the Gentiles might hear. Also I was delivered out of the mouth of the lion. [18]And the Lord will deliver me from every evil work and preserve *me* for His heavenly kingdom. To Him *be* glory forever and ever. Amen!

[19]Greet Prisca and Aquila, and the household of Onesiphorus. [20]Erastus stayed in Corinth, but Trophimus I have left in Miletus sick.

[21]Do your utmost to come before winter.

Eubulus greets you, as well as Pudens, Linus, Claudia, and all the brethren.

[22]The Lord Jesus Christ be with your spirit. Grace be with you. Amen.

MEGA *Themes*

BOLDNESS In the face of opposition and persecution, Timothy was told to carry out his ministry unashamed and unafraid of the earthly consequences. Paul urged Timothy to use the gifts of preaching and teaching that the Holy Spirit had given him.

God honors our confident testimony even when we suffer. To get over our fear of what people might say or do, we must take our eyes off people and look only to God. People will disappoint us, God will always be faithful.

1. Why was boldness important in Timothy's ministry?

How did Paul challenge Timothy to find this boldness?

2. Describe a time in your life when you felt bold in your faith. Describe a time in your life when you felt timid about your faith.

3. What caused the difference between the time of boldness and the time of timidity?

4. What is your level of boldness for Christ at church? In your neighborhood? At home? In school? At social activities? In which areas is it most difficult for you to be boldly honest about your faith and life-style?

FAITHFULNESS Jesus was faithful to all of us when he died for our sins. Paul was a faithful minister even when he was in prison. Paul urged Timothy to maintain not only sound doctrine, but also loyalty, diligence, and endurance.

We can count on opposition, suffering, and hardship as we serve Christ. But that will show that our faithfulness is having an effect on others. As we trust Christ, he counts us worthy to suffer and will give us the strength we need to be steadfast.

1. How did Paul challenge Timothy to live out his faithfulness to God?

2. What reasons do you have for being faithful to God? What struggles do you face in trying to be faithful?

3. When you find yourself drifting away from God, what can you do to remember your commitment of faithfulness to God?

4. How are you being faithful today?

PREACHING AND TEACHING Paul and Timothy were active in preaching and teaching the Good News about Jesus Christ. Paul encouraged Timothy not only to carry the torch of truth but also to train others, passing on to them sound doctrine and enthusiasm for Christ's mission.

We must prepare people to pass on God's Word to others. Does your church carefully train others to teach? Each of us should look for ways to become better equipped to serve, as well as for ways to teach others what we have learned.

1. Why do you think Paul stressed to Timothy the importance of training others to carry out preaching and teaching?

2. How was Paul a good example of this?

3. Who are the preachers and teachers in your church? How are they training others? (Are they training others?)

4. What type of ministry training would you want to receive? Who could provide this training?

ERROR In the final days before Christ returns, there will be false teachers, spiritual dropouts, and heresy. The remedy for error is to have a solid program for teaching Christians.

Because of deception and false teaching, we must be disciplined and ready to reject error by knowing God's Word. Knowing the Bible is your sure defense against error and confusion.

1. What are the dangers of deceptive teachers?

2. According to 3:14-17, how does God use his Word to prevent his people from being deceived?

*I*n many of life's situations—whether from natural instinct, repeated instruction, or unpleasant experience—you know precisely what to do. ■ For instance: ■ If your clothing catches fire, drop to the ground and roll. ■ In case of emergency, call 911. ■ Never stare at the sun during an eclipse. ■ Always wash your hands after using the restroom and before eating. ■ On a romantic first date, never order pizza with extra garlic and onions. ■ Don't run while carrying sharp objects. ■ Never swim right after eating. ■ When attacked by a bear, fall face down and play dead. ■ Look both ways before crossing a street. ■ Make certain you know the price of an object before you agree to buy it. ■ Never sign *anything* until you read the fine print. ■ You've probably heard these rules before; no doubt you could handle each situation with ease. But what about the millions of other life circumstances where it's really *hard* to know what to do? ■ That's why the next book of the Bible is so important. The apostle Paul's epistle to Titus gives us plenty of practical advice for living a pure life in an impure world. Commitment, discipline, self-control, moral purity, solid relationships, civic duties—you'll learn about all those important topics and more. By the way—as you prepare to dive into this dynamite little letter, here's a reminder of one more famous rule of life (It's one our mom pounded into our head!): Never cross your eyes while reading; they might get stuck that way.

STATS

PURPOSE: To advise Titus in his responsibility of supervising the churches on the island of Crete

AUTHOR: Paul

TO WHOM WRITTEN: Titus, a Greek convert, who had become Paul's special representative to the island of Crete

DATE WRITTEN: About A.D. 64, around the same time 1 Timothy was written; probably from Macedonia when Paul traveled in between his Roman imprisonments

SETTING: Paul had sent Titus to organize and oversee the churches on Crete. This letter tells him how to do this job.

KEY PEOPLE: Paul, Titus

KEY PLACES: Crete, Nicopolis

SPECIAL FEATURE: Titus is very similar to 1 Timothy with its instructions to church leaders

Titus

CHAPTER 1 **PAUL IS SENT TO BRING FAITH.** Paul, a bondservant of God and an apostle of Jesus Christ, according to the faith of God's elect and the acknowledgment of the truth which accords with godliness, ²in hope of eternal life which God, who cannot lie, promised before time began, ³but has in due time manifested His word through preaching, which was committed to me according to the commandment of God our Savior;

⁴To Titus, a true son in *our* common faith:

Grace, mercy, *and* peace from God the Father and the Lord Jesus Christ our Savior.

⁵For this reason I left you in Crete, that you should set

NO LIE

1:1-2 The foundation of our faith is trust in God's character. Because he is truth, he is the source of all truth and cannot lie. The eternal life he has promised will be ours because he keeps his promises. Build your faith on the foundation of a trustworthy God who will not lie.

*I*NTEGRITY

When Dawn sticks her head into her youth pastor's office, it's plain to see she is troubled.

"Mike, can I talk to you?"

"Sure, Dawn. Come in."

"It's this whole youth group leadership team thing."

"What do you mean?"

"Well, you know Kelly, the girl who's been coming with me to church the last few weeks?"

"Yeah."

"Well, she told me that she wants to be on the team. She wants to be in charge of publicity for the youth group."

"That's great. We've been looking for someone to fill that—"

"No, that's not great! You don't know Kelly. She's pretty wild . . . I mean, she's not exactly living like a Christian."

"I see."

"Don't get me wrong. I really love Kelly, and I'm trying to be a good influence on her and everything. I just don't think it's a very good idea to have her out there in charge of publicizing our group. At least not while she's living like she is. People might get the wrong idea, you know?"

"I agree. So, are you going to talk to her?"

"Oh, I guess so. Any advice?"

"Sure. If I were you, I'd . . ."

Christians in leadership positions are expected to adhere to the highest standards of godly character. Read Titus 1:5-8; 2:11—3:8 for a quick glimpse at the integrity Christian leaders must possess.

in order the things that are lacking, and appoint elders in every city as I commanded you— [6]if a man is blameless, the husband of one wife, having faithful children not accused of dissipation or insubordination. [7]For a bishop must be blameless, as a steward of God, not self-willed, not quick-tempered, not given to wine, not violent, not greedy for money, [8]but hospitable, a lover of what is good, sober-minded, just, holy, self-controlled, [9]holding fast the faithful word as he has been taught, that he may be able, by sound doctrine, both to exhort and convict those who contradict.

SEE AND DO

2:6-8 Paul urged Titus to be a good example to those around him so that others might see his good works and imitate him. Titus's life would give his words greater impact. If you want someone to act a certain way, be sure to live that way yourself. Then you will earn the right to be heard.

[10]For there are many insubordinate, both idle talkers and deceivers, especially those of the circumcision, [11]whose mouths must be stopped, who subvert whole households, teaching things which they ought not, for the sake of dishonest gain. [12]One of them, a prophet of their own, said, "Cretans *are* always liars, evil beasts, lazy gluttons." [13]This testimony is true. Therefore rebuke them sharply, that they may be sound in the faith, [14]not giving heed to Jewish fables and commandments of men who turn from the truth. [15]To the pure all things are pure, but to those who are defiled and unbelieving nothing is pure; but even their mind and conscience are defiled.

SLAVE TO SIN

3:3 Following a life of pleasure and giving in to every sensual de leads to slavery. Many think freedom consists in doing anything th want. But this path leads to a slavish addiction to sensual gratifica person is no longer free, but is a slave to what his or her body dic (2 Peter 2:19). Christ frees us from the desires and control of sin. you been released?

[16]They profess to know God, but in works they deny Him, being abominable, disobedient, and disqualified for every good work.

CHAPTER **2** **SPECIAL GUIDELINES.** But as for you, speak the things which are proper for sound doctrine: [2]that the older men be sober, reverent, temperate, sound in faith, in love, in patience; [3]the older women likewise, that they be reverent in behavior, not slanderers, not given to much wine, teachers of good things— [4]that they admonish the young women to love their husbands, to love their children, [5]to be discreet, chaste, homemakers, good, obedient to their own husbands, that the word of God may not be blasphemed.

[6]Likewise, exhort the young men to be sober-minded, [7]in all things showing yourself *to be* a pattern of good works; in doctrine *showing* integrity, reverence, incorruptibility, [8]sound speech that cannot be condemned, that one who is an opponent may be ashamed, having nothing evil to say of you.

[9]*Exhort* bondservants to be obedient to their own masters, to be well pleasing in all *things*, not answering back, [10]not pilfering, but showing all good fidelity, that they may adorn the doctrine of God our Savior in all things.

TO THE PURE ALL THINGS ARE PURE, but to those who are defiled and unbelieving nothing is pure; BUT EVEN their mind and conscience are defiled.

TITUS GOES TO CRETE

Tradition says that after Paul was released from prison in Rome, he and Titus traveled together for a while. They stopped in Crete. When it was time for Paul to go, he left Titus behind to help the churches there.

¹¹For the grace of God that brings salvation has appeared to all men, ¹²teaching us that, denying ungodliness and worldly lusts, we should live soberly, righteously, and godly in the present age, ¹³looking for the blessed hope and glorious appearing of our great God and Savior Jesus Christ, ¹⁴who gave Himself for us, that He might redeem us from every lawless deed and purify for Himself *His* own special people, zealous for good works.

¹⁵Speak these things, exhort, and rebuke with all authority. Let no one despise you.

CHAPTER **3** **OBEY THE GOVERNMENT.** Remind them to be subject to rulers and authorities, to obey, to be ready for every good work, ²to speak evil of no one, to be peaceable, gentle, showing all humility to all men. ³For we ourselves were also once foolish, disobedient, deceived, serving various lusts and pleasures, living in malice and envy, hateful and hating one another. ⁴But when the kindness and the love of God our Savior toward man appeared, ⁵not by works of righteousness which we have done, but according to His mercy He saved us, through

ARGUMENTS

3:9-11 Paul warns Titus, as he warned Timothy, not to get involved in foolish and unprofitable disputes (2 Timothy 2:14). This does not mean that we should refuse to study, discuss, and examine different interpretations of difficult Bible passages. Paul is warning against petty quarrels, not honest discussion that leads to wisdom. When foolish arguments develop, it is best to either turn the discussion back to a track that is going somewhere or to politely excuse yourself.

the washing of regeneration and renewing of the Holy Spirit, ⁶whom He poured out on us abundantly through Jesus Christ our Savior, ⁷that having been justified by His grace we should become heirs according to the hope of eternal life.

⁸This is a faithful saying, and these things I want you to affirm constantly, that those who have believed in God should be careful to maintain good works. These things are good and profitable to men.

⁹But avoid foolish disputes, genealogies, contentions, and strivings about the law; for they are unprofitable and useless. ¹⁰Reject a divisive man after the first and second

admonition, [11]knowing that such a person is warped and sinning, being self-condemned.

[12]When I send Artemas to you, or Tychicus, be diligent to come to me at Nicopolis, for I have decided to spend the winter there. [13]Send Zenas the lawyer and Apollos on their journey with haste, that they may lack nothing. [14]And let our *people* also learn to maintain good works, to *meet* urgent needs, that they may not be unfruitful.

[15]All who *are* with me greet you. Greet those who love us in the faith.

Grace *be* with you all. Amen.

MEGA *Themes*

A GOOD LIFE The Good News of salvation is that we can't be saved by living a good life; we are saved only by faith in Jesus Christ. But the gospel transforms people's lives, so that they eventually perform good works. Our service won't save us, but we are saved to serve.

A good life is a witness to the gospel's power. As Christians, we must have commitment and discipline to serve. Each of us is to be a living servant; none of us is to consider himself or herself inactive.

1. Why do you think it is important for a Christian to live a good and pure life even though this is not the basis of salvation?
2. Describe a life that would be pleasing to God.
3. What areas of your life do you think are pleasing to God? In what areas of your life do you need to make changes in order to be more like the life you described in question 2?
4. Outline your personal plan for improving these areas for God's glory.

CHARACTER Titus's responsibility on Crete was to appoint pastors (elders) to maintain proper organization and discipline, so Paul listed the qualities that elders should have. Their conduct in their homes revealed their fitness for service in the church.

It's not enough to be educated or have a following to be Christ's kind of leader. You must have self-control, spiritual and moral fitness, and Christian character. Who you are is just as important as what you can do.

1. Summarize Paul's description of those who are qualified to serve as church leaders.
2. Describe the person you want to be when you are older. What will be your personal qualities? What will be your priorities? What will be the impact of your life? How will you be serving God?
3. What choices are you making now that will help you fulfill the above description one day?

CHURCH RELATIONSHIPS Church teaching was supposed to relate to various groups. Older Christians were to teach and to be examples to younger men and women. Every age and group has a lesson to learn and a role to play.

Right living and right relationship go along with right doctrine. Treat relationships with other believers as important parts of your relationship with God.

1. Summarize Paul's teaching on church relationships in 2:1-15.
2. What groups in your church seem to be the most "distant" in their personal relationships (young-old, wealthy-average-poor, liberal ideas—conservative ideas, traditional worshipers—nontraditional worshipers, etc.)?
3. What would Paul say to those groups if he were to write a letter to your church leaders about this distance? From your perspective, how could this gap be bridged?
4. What might you do to be a "bridge builder" in your church?

CITIZENSHIP Christians must be good citizens in society, not just in church. Believers must obey the government and work honestly.

How you fulfill your civic duties is a witness to the watching world. Your community life should reflect Christ's love as much as your church life does. You must guard against trying to separate your walk with God from the way you live each day.

1. Why is it important for Christians to obey the government?

2. Do you agree or disagree with this statement: "Being a good citizen involves more than just not breaking the law"? Explain your response.

3. What are the biggest issues facing your community? How would you apply this study to your role as a member of the community?

4. How can a Christian have an impact for Christ by simply being a citizen who contributes positively? How can you provide this impact in your community?

I could *never* forgive her!" ■ "He'll *never* get serious about God!" ■ "I wish things would work out, but they won't. My situation is *impossible!*" ■ Ever heard—or made—statements like those? If so, take this hint! Never say *never.* Many of the hard-to-believe things we declare "impossible!" eventually do come to pass . . . right before our embarrassed eyes. ■ Consider the Munich elementary school teacher who told ten-year-old Albert Einstein, "You will never amount to very much." ■ Or the misguided executive with the Decca Recording Company in the early '60s who decided *not* to offer a contract to an obscure musical group called The Beatles. ■ And you can be sure Simon Newcomb is red-faced in his grave. He's the guy who asserted in the 1800s that "flight by machines heavier than air is . . . utterly impossible." ■ Never say *never.* Don't end that friendship or relationship just because you've been wronged. Don't give up on that friend who claims to be an atheist. Don't throw in the towel on your dream. Don't write off your future just because you've made some bad choices in the past.

■ Never say *never.* The Gospel of Matthew states that same principle ("With God all things are possible"), and the book of Philemon illustrates it—describing how a poor slave and his rich master ended up as Christian brothers. You are about to read a story of betrayal and forgiveness, and of how Jesus Christ breaks down all barriers. ■ So before you say, "That's *impossible!*" Or, "That could *never* happen!" take five minutes to read Paul's postcard to Philemon.

STATS

PURPOSE: To convince Philemon to forgive—and accept as a brother in the faith—his runaway slave, Onesimus

AUTHOR: Paul

TO WHOM WRITTEN: Philemon, who probably was a wealthy member of the Colossian church

DATE WRITTEN: About A.D. 60, during Paul's first imprisonment in Rome, at about the same time the books of Ephesians and Colossians were written

SETTING: Slavery was very common in the Roman Empire. Evidently some Christians had slaves. Paul makes a radical statement by calling this slave Philemon's brother in Christ.

KEY PEOPLE: Paul, Philemon, Onesimus

KEY PLACES: Colosse, Rome

Philemon

ONESIMUS COMES HOME. Paul, a prisoner of Christ Jesus, and Timothy *our* brother,

To Philemon our beloved *friend* and fellow laborer, ²to the beloved Apphia, Archippus our fellow soldier, and to the church in your house:

³Grace to you and peace from God our Father and the Lord Jesus Christ.

⁴I thank my God, making mention of you always in my prayers, ⁵hearing of your love and faith which you have toward the Lord Jesus and toward all the saints, ⁶that the sharing of your faith may become effective by the acknowledgment of every good thing which is in you in Christ Jesus. ⁷For we have great joy and consolation in your love, because the hearts of the saints have been refreshed by you, brother.

GOOD DEAL

8-9 Because Paul was an elder and an apostle, he could have used his authority with Philemon, commanding him to deal kindly with his runaway slave. But Paul based his request not on his own authority, but on Philemon's Christian commitment. Paul wanted Philemon's heartfelt obedience. When you know something is right and you have the power to demand it, do you appeal to your authority or the other person's commitment? Here Paul provides a good example of how to deal with a possible conflict between Christian friends.

FORGIVEN

1Off Paul asked Philemon not only to forgive his runaway slave who had become a Christian, but to accept him as a brother. As Christians, we should forgive as we have been forgiven (Matthew 6:12; Ephesians 4:31-32). True forgiveness means that we treat the person we've forgiven as we would want to be treated. Is there someone you say you have forgiven, but who still needs your kindness?

[8]Therefore, though I might be very bold in Christ to command you what is fitting, [9]yet for love's sake I rather appeal to you—being such a one as Paul, the aged, and now also a prisoner of Jesus Christ— [10]I appeal to you for my son Onesimus, whom I have begotten while in my chains, [11]who once was unprofitable to you, but now is profitable to you and to me.

RECONCILIATION

As roommates (and total opposites), college freshmen Melanie and Laura had a very awkward relationship:

- Laura was short and stout; Melanie was tall and thin.
- Laura was refined and reserved; Melanie was loud and obnoxious.
- Laura was upper-class prep; Melanie was a middle-class freak.
- Laura was a conservative; Melanie was a liberal.
- Laura was a morning person; Melanie was a night owl.
- Laura was a Christian; Melanie clearly was not.

At the end of the fall semester, Melanie moved out of the dorm into an apartment. Right about that same time, Laura couldn't find her diamond pendant. She suspected Melanie, but she never said a word.

The following summer, Laura got a letter from Melanie. The first part of the letter told how she had come to Christ during a beach outreach. The second half was a confession. Melanie had indeed taken the pendant and pawned it for some needed cash. She was pleading for forgiveness.

Laura immediately wrote back—welcoming Melanie to the family of God, granting the requested forgiveness, and asking if the girls could get together first thing in the fall.

Could you have responded to Melanie as Laura did? Their story isn't a fairy tale. Read Philemon to see for yourself the amazing reconciliation that is possible in Jesus Christ.

[12]I am sending him back. You therefore receive him, that is, my own heart, [13]whom I wished to keep with me, that on your behalf he might minister to me in my chains

for the gospel. [14]But without your consent I wanted to do nothing, that your good deed might not be by compulsion, as it were, but voluntary.

[15]For perhaps he departed for a while for this *purpose*,

EQUALS

13-16 What a difference Onesimus's status as a Christian made in relationship to Philemon. He was no longer merely a servant, he was a brother. Now both Onesimus and Philemon were members of God's family—equals in Christ. A Christian's status as a member of God's family transcends all other distinctions among believers. Do you look down on any fellow Christians? Remember, they are your brothers, sisters, your equals before Christ (Galatians 3:28). How you treat your brothers and sisters in Christ's family reflects your true Christian commitment.

that you might receive him forever, [16]no longer as a slave but more than a slave—a beloved brother, especially to me but how much more to you, both in the flesh and in the Lord.

[17]If then you count me as a partner, receive him as *you would* me. [18]But if he has wronged you or owes anything,

IN THE FAMILY

25 Paul urged Philemon to be reconciled to his slave, receiving him brother and fellow member of God's family. *Reconciliation* means reestablishing a relationship. Christ has reconciled us to God and to others. Many barriers come between people—race, social status, sex, personality differences— but Christ can break down these barriers. Christ changed Onesimus's relationship to Philemon from slave to brother. Only in Christ can our most hopeless relationships be transformed into something wonderful.

put that on my account. [19]I, Paul, am writing with my own hand. I will repay—not to mention to you that you owe me even your own self besides. [20]Yes, brother, let me have joy from you in the Lord; refresh my heart in the Lord.

[21]Having confidence in your obedience, I write to you, knowing that you will do even more than I say. [22]But, meanwhile, also prepare a guest room for me, for I trust that through your prayers I shall be granted to you.

[23]Epaphras, my fellow prisoner in Christ Jesus, greets you, [24]as do Mark, Aristarchus, Demas, Luke, my fellow laborers.

[25]The grace of our Lord Jesus Christ *be* with your spirit. Amen.

MEGA Themes

FORGIVENESS Philemon was Paul's friend and Onesimus's owner. Paul asked Philemon not to punish Onesimus, but to forgive and restore him as a new Christian brother.

Christian relationships must be full of forgiveness and acceptance. Forgiving those who have wronged you is the appropriate response to Christ's forgiveness of you.

1. How would you have felt if you were Philemon before you received the letter? How would Paul's letter have changed your attitude? What verses in the letter would have had the most impact on your thinking?
2. How is Paul's request for Onesimus in verses 18-20 a reflection of what Christ has done for all of us?
3. As you reflect on this study and the people involved, what do you learn about the importance of forgiveness in Christian relationships? What is the basis of this forgiveness? How is this forgiveness lived out when someone has been wronged?
4. What difference does it make whether or not you forgive a Christian friend who wrongs you? If there is such a wrong that you have not forgiven, how can you go to that friend and make things right?

BARRIERS Slavery was widespread in the Roman Empire. Slavery was a barrier between people, but Christian love and fellowship can overcome such barriers.

In Christ we are one family. No walls of race, economic status, or political differences should separate believers. Let Christ work through you to remove barriers between Christian brothers and sisters. Take steps to act out the love of Christ in you.

1. What are some of the differences and prejudices that separate and alienate people from one another?
2. Why are such conflicts offensive to God?
3. In your community, what groups of people do not relate to each other simply because of external differences?
4. What can you do to demonstrate to your school or church that God is greater than all barriers?

RESPECT Paul was a friend of both Philemon and Onesimus. He had the authority as an apostle to tell Philemon what to do. Yet Paul chose to appeal to his friend in Christian love rather than to order him to do what he wished.

When dealing with people, tactful persuasion accomplishes a great deal more than commands. Remember to exhibit courtesy and respect in dealing with people.

1. What do you think it means to respect a person?
2. Who are the people you most respect? What are the qualities that lead you to respect them?
3. Which of these qualities do you most want to develop as you grow into an adult who can be respected by others?
4. What about now? What leads others to respect you as a young person?

*F*our Very Uncool Activities You Can Do: ■ 1. Wear a diaper to school and suck on a pacifier during all your classes. ■ 2. Treat yourself to a lunch of jars of baby food: strained carrots, creamed spinach, and milk (out of a baby bottle, of course). ■ 3. Drool all over yourself. ■ 4. Crawl from class to class. Anytime anything doesn't go your way, kick your legs, flail your arms, and cry uncontrollably. ■ Such behavior is uncool for a teenager—it's immature, the kind of things we expect *babies* to do. We would never tolerate such immaturity in an older person. ■ So why do we tolerate such infantile behavior in the spiritual realm? ■ The church has far too many "baby Christians." Some have only been believers in Christ a short time, so it's understandable that *they* might do silly or immature things. But for those Christians who have been in God's family for years and who still act like infants—well, there's just no excuse. ■ In the same way that little kids grow up physically, "baby" Christians need to grow up in their relationship with Christ. That's what Hebrews is all about—growing up spiritually. You should know up front that Hebrews contains some tough statements and some sobering challenges. It's a risky book to read—especially if you apply it. ■ Neglect its powerful message, and you face an even greater risk—remaining a spiritual infant. ■ You can't get more uncool than that.

STATS

PURPOSE: To present Christ's sufficiency and superiority

AUTHOR: Unknown. Paul, Luke, Barnabas, Apollos, Silas, Philip, Priscilla, and others have been suggested. Whoever the author was speaks of Timothy as "brother" (13:23).

TO WHOM WRITTEN: Hebrew Christians who may have been considering a return to Judaism, perhaps because of immaturity due to their lack of understanding of biblical truths. They seem to be "second-generation" Christians (2:3). And to all believers everywhere.

DATE WRITTEN: Probably before the destruction of the temple in Jerusalem in A.D. 70; the religious sacrifices and ceremonies are referred to, but not the temple's destruction

SETTING: These Jewish Christians were probably undergoing fierce persecution, socially and physically, from both Jews and from Romans. The people needed to be reassured that Christianity was true and that Jesus was the Messiah.

Hebrews

CHAPTER 1 JESUS CHRIST IS GOD'S SON. God, who at various times and in various ways spoke in time past to the fathers by the prophets, ²has in these last days spoken to us by *His* Son, whom He has appointed heir of all things, through whom also He made the worlds; ³who being the brightness of *His* glory and the express image of His person, and upholding all things by the word of His power, when He had by Himself purged our sins, sat down at the right hand of the Majesty on high, ⁴having become so much better than the angels, as He has by inheritance obtained a more excellent name than they.

⁵For to which of the angels did He ever say:

"*You are My Son,*
Today I have begotten You"?

And again:

"*I will be to Him a Father,*
And He shall be to Me a Son"?

⁶But when He again brings the firstborn into the world, He says:

"*Let all the angels of God worship Him.*"

⁷And of the angels He says:

"*Who makes His angels spirits*
And His ministers a flame of fire."

⁸But to the Son *He says:*

"*Your throne, O God, is forever and ever;*
A scepter of righteousness is the scepter of Your
kingdom.
⁹ *You have loved righteousness and hated lawlessness;*
Therefore God, Your God, has anointed You
With the oil of gladness more than Your companions."

¹⁰And:

▇▇▇▇▇▇ JESUS

1:2-3 Not only is Jesus God's "express image"; he is God himself—the very God who spoke in Old Testament times. Christ is eternal; he worked with the Father in creating the world (John 1:3; Colossians 1:16). He is the full revelation of God. You can have no clearer view of God than by looking at him. Jesus Christ is the complete expression of God in a human body.

2:9 God has put Jesus in charge of everything, and Jesus has revealed himself to us. We do not yet see Jesus reigning on earth, but we can picture him in his heavenly glory. When confused by tomorrow and anxious about the future, keep a clear view of Jesus Christ—who he is, what he has done, and what he is doing for you right now. This will give stability to your decisions day by day.

> "You, LORD, in the beginning laid the foundation of
>   the earth,
>   And the heavens are the work of Your hands.
> 11 They will perish, but You remain;
>   And they will all grow old like a garment;
> 12 Like a cloak You will fold them up,
>   And they will be changed.
>   But You are the same,
>   And Your years will not fail."

13But to which of the angels has He ever said:

> "Sit at My right hand,
>   Till I make Your enemies Your footstool"?

14Are they not all ministering spirits sent forth to minister for those who will inherit salvation?

CHAPTER 2 LISTEN CAREFULLY AND OBEY GOD.

Therefore we must give the more earnest heed to the things we have heard, lest we drift away. 2For if the word spoken through angels proved steadfast, and every transgression and disobedience received a just reward, 3how shall we escape if we neglect so great a salvation, which at the first began to be spoken by the Lord, and was confirmed to us by those who heard *Him*, 4God also

FOR IN THAT

HE HIMSELF
has suffered,
being
tempted,
He is able to aid
those
who
are
tempted.

bearing witness both with signs and wonders, with various miracles, and gifts of the Holy Spirit, according to His own will?

5For He has not put the world to come, of which we speak, in subjection to angels. 6But one testified in a certain place, saying:

> "What is man that You are mindful of him,
>   Or the son of man that You take care of him?
> 7 You have made him a little lower than the angels;
>   You have crowned him with glory and honor,
>   And set him over the works of Your hands.
> 8 You have put all things in subjection under his feet."

For in that He put all in subjection under him, He left nothing *that is* not put under him. But now we do not yet see all things put under him. 9But we see Jesus, who was made a little lower than the angels, for the suffering of death crowned with glory and honor, that He, by the grace of God, might taste death for everyone.

10For it was fitting for Him, for whom *are* all things and by whom *are* all things, in bringing many sons to glory, to make the captain of their salvation perfect through sufferings. 11For both He who sanctifies and those who are being sanctified *are* all of one, for which reason He is not ashamed to call them brethren, 12saying:

> "I will declare Your name to My brethren;
>   In the midst of the assembly I will sing praise to You."

13And again:

> "I will put My trust in Him."

And again:

> "Here am I and the children whom God has given Me."

14Inasmuch then as the children have partaken of flesh and blood, He Himself likewise shared in the same, that through death He might destroy him who had the power of death, that is, the devil, 15and release those who through fear of death were all their lifetime subject to bondage. 16For indeed He does not give aid to angels, but He does give aid to the seed of Abraham. 17Therefore, in all things He had to be made like *His* brethren, that He might be a merciful and faithful High Priest in things *pertaining* to God, to make propitiation for the sins of the people. 18For in that He Himself has suffered, being tempted, He is able to aid those who are tempted.

CHAPTER 3 JESUS: GREATER THAN MOSES.

Therefore, holy brethren, partakers of the heavenly calling, consider the Apostle and High Priest of our confes-

◣■TURN BACK

4:1-3 Some of the Jewish Christians who received this letter may been on the verge of turning back from their promised rest in Chris as the people in Moses' day turned back from the Promised Land. I cases, the difficulties of the present moment overshadowed the rea God's promise, and people stopped believing that God was able to f his promises. When we trust our own efforts instead of Christ, we to in danger of turning back. Our own efforts are never adequate; onl Christ can see us through.

sion, Christ Jesus, ²who was faithful to Him who appointed Him, as Moses also *was faithful* in all His house. ³For this One has been counted worthy of more glory than Moses, inasmuch as He who built the house has more honor than the house. ⁴For every house is built by someone, but He who built all things *is* God. ⁵And Moses indeed *was* faithful in all His House as a servant, for a testimony of those things which would be spoken *afterward*, ⁶but Christ as a Son over His own house, whose house we are if we hold fast the confidence and the rejoicing of the hope firm to the end.

⁷Therefore, as the Holy Spirit says:

"Today, if you will hear His voice,
⁸ *Do not harden your hearts as in the rebellion,*
In the day of trial in the wilderness,
⁹ *Where your fathers tested Me, tried Me,*
And saw My works forty years.
¹⁰ *Therefore I was angry with that generation,*
And said, 'They always go astray in their heart,
And they have not known My ways.'
¹¹ *So I swore in My wrath,*
'They shall not enter My rest.'"

¹²Beware, brethren, lest there be in any of you an evil heart of unbelief in departing from the living God; ¹³but exhort one another daily, while it is called *"Today,"* lest any of you be hardened through the deceitfulness of sin. ¹⁴For we have become partakers of Christ if we hold the beginning of our confidence steadfast to the end, ¹⁵while it is said:

"Today, if you will hear His voice,
Do not harden your hearts as in the rebellion."

¹⁶For who, having heard, rebelled? Indeed, *was it* not all who came out of Egypt, *led* by Moses? ¹⁷Now with whom was He angry forty years? *Was it* not with those who sinned, whose corpses fell in the wilderness? ¹⁸And to whom did He swear that they would not enter His rest, but to those who did not obey? ¹⁹So we see that they could not enter in because of unbelief.

CHAPTER **4** **GOD'S PROMISE OF REST.** Therefore, since a promise remains of entering His rest, let us fear lest any of you seem to have come short of it. ²For indeed the gospel was preached to us as well as to them; but the word which they heard did not profit them, not being mixed with faith in those who heard *it.* ³For we who have believed do enter that rest, as He has said:

"So I swore in My wrath,
'They shall not enter My rest,'"

although the works were finished from the foundation of the world. ⁴For He has spoken in a certain place of the seventh *day* in this way: *"And God rested on the seventh day from all His works"*; ⁵and again in this *place*: *"They shall not enter My rest."*

⁶Since therefore it remains that some *must* enter it, and those to whom it was first preached did not enter because of disobedience, ⁷again He designates a certain day, saying in David, *"Today,"* after such a long time, as it has been said:

"Today, if you will hear His voice,
Do not harden your hearts."

⁸For if Joshua had given them rest, then He would not afterward have spoken of another day. ⁹There remains therefore a rest for the people of God. ¹⁰For he who has entered His rest has himself also ceased from his works as God *did* from His.

¹¹Let us therefore be diligent to enter that rest, lest anyone fall according to the same example of disobedience. ¹²For the word of God *is* living and powerful, and sharper than any two-edged sword, piercing even to the division of soul and spirit, and of joints and marrow, and is a discerner of the thoughts and intents of the heart. ¹³And there is no creature hidden from His sight, but all things *are* naked and open to the eyes of Him to whom we *must give* account.

¹⁴Seeing then that we have a great High Priest who has

I have heard so many different opinions on what God is really like that I'm beginning to wonder if someone can ever know. Is there any way to know for sure?

Have you ever assembled a complicated jigsaw puzzle? If so, you know how important the picture on the box is. As you put the puzzle together, you use the picture as a reference, your guide.

But what if you had the wrong box top, and the picture didn't match the puzzle? The puzzle would be nearly impossible to assemble (at least until you realized the mistake).

People throughout the world are trying to put the "God puzzle" together. But often they are trying to match the pieces to the wrong picture!

God is not trying to hide. As Hebrews 1:1-3 tells us, God has clearly shown the world what he is like, through nature, through the Bible, and especially through Christ.

Jesus said it plainly, "I and My Father are one" (John 10:30).

Even when he was asked point-blank by Philip, he was straightforward in his reply. "Have I been with you so long, and yet you have not known Me, Philip? He who has seen Me has seen the Father; so how can you say, 'Show us the Father'?" (John 14:9).

It doesn't get more obvious than that! To know what God is like, all you have to do is look at Jesus.

People get their God-pictures from TV preachers; friends who say they believe in God, but never act like it; religious relatives; coaches who pray before games and then swear the paint off of the walls at halftime; and so forth. These are pictures of God that aren't anything like what he's really like. No wonder they can't put the puzzle together.

That's why it's so important not to settle for hearsay when it comes to finding out what God is like. Instead, look at the right picture—look at Christ.

passed through the heavens, Jesus the Son of God, let us hold fast *our* confession. [15]For we do not have a High Priest who cannot sympathize with our weaknesses, but was in all *points* tempted as *we are*, *yet* without sin. [16]Let us therefore come boldly to the throne of grace, that we may obtain mercy and find grace to help in time of need.

CHAPTER 5 JESUS CHRIST IS OUR HIGH PRIEST.

For every high priest taken from among men is appointed for men in things *pertaining* to God, that he may offer both gifts and sacrifices for sins. [2]He can have compassion on those who are ignorant and going astray, since he himself is also subject to weakness. [3]Because of this he is required as for the people, so also for himself, to offer *sacrifices* for sins. [4]And no man takes this honor to himself, but he who is called by God, just as Aaron *was*.

[5]So also Christ did not glorify Himself to become High Priest, *but it* was He who said to Him:

LET US
THEREFORE
COME
BOLDLY
TO THE
THRONE
OF **GRACE**

that we may obtain mercy

AND

find

grace

to help

in time

of need

"*You are My Son,*
Today I have begotten You."

[6]As *He* also *says* in another *place:*

"*You are a priest forever*
According to the order of Melchizedek";

[7]who, in the days of His flesh, when He had offered up prayers and supplications, with vehement cries and tears to Him who was able to save Him from death, and was heard because of His godly fear, [8]though He was a Son, *yet* He learned obedience by the things which He suffered. [9]And having been perfected, He became the author of eternal salvation to all who obey Him, [10]called by God as High Priest "*according to the order of Melchizedek,*" [11]of whom we have much to say, and hard to explain, since you have become dull of hearing.

[12]For though by this time you ought to be teachers, you need *someone* to teach you again the first principles of the oracles of God; and you have come to need milk and not solid food. [13]For everyone who partakes *only* of milk *is* unskilled in the word of righteousness, for he is a babe. [14]But solid food belongs to those who are of full age, *that is*, those who by reason of use have their senses exercised to discern both good and evil.

CHAPTER 6 COUNT ON GOD'S PROMISES.

Therefore, leaving the discussion of the elementary *principles* of Christ, let us go on to perfection, not laying again the foundation of repentance from dead works and of faith toward God, [2]of the doctrine of baptisms, of laying on of hands, of resurrection of the dead, and of eternal judgment. [3]And this we will do if God permits.

[4]For *it is* impossible for those who were once enlightened, and have tasted the heavenly gift, and have become partakers of the Holy Spirit, [5]and have tasted the good word of God and the powers of the age to come, [6]if they fall away, to renew them again to repentance, since they crucify again for themselves the Son of God, and put *Him* to an open shame.

[7]For the earth which drinks in the rain that often comes upon it, and bears herbs useful for those by whom it is cultivated, receives blessing from God; [8]but if it bears thorns and briers, *it is* rejected and near to being cursed, whose end *is* to be burned.

[9]But, beloved, we are confident of better things concerning you, yes, things that accompany salvation, though we speak in this manner. [10]For God *is* not unjust to forget your work and labor of love which you have shown toward His name, *in that* you have ministered to the saints, and do minister. [11]And we desire that each one of you show the same diligence to the full assurance of hope until the end, [12]that you do not become sluggish,

◼◼◼〰〰◼ EVIDENCE

6:7-8 Land that produces a good crop receives loving care, but l[and] that produces thorns and briers has to be burned off so that the fa[rmer] can start over. God condemns an unproductive Christian life. We ar[e] saved by works or conduct, but what we do is the *evidence* of our [faith?] Being productive for Christ is serious business.

but imitate those who through faith and patience inherit the promises.

¹³For when God made a promise to Abraham, because He could swear by no one greater, He swore by Himself, ¹⁴saying, *"Surely blessing I will bless you, and multiplying I will multiply you."* ¹⁵And so, after he had patiently endured, he obtained the promise. ¹⁶For men indeed swear by the greater, and an oath for confirmation *is* for them an end of all dispute. ¹⁷Thus God, determining to show more abundantly to the heirs of promise the immutability of His counsel, confirmed *it* by an oath, ¹⁸that by two immutable things, in which it *is* impossible for God to lie, we might have strong consolation, who have fled for refuge to lay hold of the hope set before *us.*

¹⁹This *hope* we have as an anchor of the soul, both sure and steadfast, and which enters the Presence *behind* the veil, ²⁰where the forerunner has entered for us, *even* Jesus, having become High Priest forever according to the order of Melchizedek.

CHAPTER 7 MELCHIZEDEK: JUSTICE AND PEACE.

For this Melchizedek, king of Salem, priest of the Most High God, who met Abraham returning from the slaughter of the kings and blessed him, ²to whom also Abraham gave a tenth part of all, first being translated "king of righteousness," and then also king of Salem, meaning "king of peace," ³without father, without mother, without genealogy, having neither beginning of days nor end of life, but made like the Son of God, remains a priest continually.

⁴Now consider how great this man *was,* to whom even the patriarch Abraham gave a tenth of the spoils. ⁵And indeed those who are of the sons of Levi, who receive the priesthood, have a commandment to receive tithes from the people according to the law, that is, from their brethren, though they have come from the loins of Abraham; ⁶but he whose genealogy is not derived from them received tithes from Abraham and blessed him who had the promises. ⁷Now beyond all contradiction the lesser is blessed by the better. ⁸Here mortal men receive tithes, but there he *receives them,* of whom it is witnessed that he lives. ⁹Even Levi, who receives tithes, paid tithes through Abraham, so to speak, ¹⁰for he was still in the loins of his father when Melchizedek met him.

¹¹Therefore, if perfection were through the Levitical priesthood (for under it the people received the law), what further need *was there* that another priest should rise according to the order of Melchizedek, and not be called according to the order of Aaron? ¹²For the priesthood being changed, of necessity there is also a change of the law. ¹³For He of whom these things are spoken belongs to another tribe, from which no man has officiated at the altar.

¹⁴For *it is* evident that our Lord arose from Judah, of which tribe Moses spoke nothing concerning priesthood. ¹⁵And it is yet far more evident if, in the likeness of Melchizedek, there arises another priest ¹⁶who has come, not according to the law of a fleshly commandment, but according to the power of an endless life. ¹⁷For He testifies:

"You are a priest forever
According to the order of Melchizedek."

¹⁸For on the one hand there is an annulling of the former commandment because of its weakness and unprofitableness, ¹⁹for the law made nothing perfect; on the other hand, *there is the* bringing in of a better hope, through which we draw near to God.

²⁰And inasmuch as *He was* not *made priest* without an oath ²¹(for they have become priests without an oath, but He with an oath by Him who said to Him:

"The Lord has sworn
And will not relent,
'You are a priest forever
According to the order of Melchizedek'"),

²²by so much more Jesus has become a surety of a better covenant.

²³Also there were many priests, because they were prevented by death from continuing. ²⁴But He, because He continues forever, has an unchangeable priesthood. ²⁵Therefore He is also able to save to the uttermost those who come to God through Him, since He always lives to make intercession for them.

²⁶For such a High Priest was fitting for us, *who is* holy, harmless, undefiled, separate from sinners, and has become higher than the heavens; ²⁷who does not need

◤━━━━━━━━PAID THE PRICE

7:25 What does it mean that Jesus is able to save "to the uttermost"? No one else can add to what Jesus did to save us; our past, present, and future sins are all forgiven. Jesus is with the Father as a sign that our sins are forgiven. If you are a Christian, remember that Christ has paid the price for your sins once and for all. (See also 9:24-28.)

daily, as those high priests, to offer up sacrifices, first for His own sins and then for the people's, for this He did once for all when He offered up Himself. ²⁸For the law appoints as high priests men who have weakness, but the word of the oath, which came after the law, *appoints* the Son who has been perfected forever.

CHAPTER 8 OUR NEW HIGH PRIEST. Now *this is*

the main point of the things we are saying: We have such a High Priest, who is seated at the right hand of the throne of the Majesty in the heavens, ²a Minister of the sanctuary and of the true tabernacle which the Lord erected, and not man.

³For every high priest is appointed to offer both gifts and sacrifices. Therefore *it is* necessary that this One also have something to offer. ⁴For if He were on earth, He would not be a priest, since there are priests who offer the gifts according to the law; ⁵who serve the copy and shadow of the heavenly things, as Moses was divinely instructed when he was about to make the tabernacle. For He said, *"See that you make all things according to the pattern shown you on the mountain."* ⁶But now He has obtained a more excellent ministry, inasmuch as He is also Mediator of a better covenant, which was established on better promises.

9:9-14 Though you know Christ, you may still be trying to make yourself good enough for God. But rules and rituals have never cleansed people's hearts. By Jesus' blood alone: (1) our conscience is cleared, (2) we are freed from death and can live to serve God, and (3) we are freed from sin's power. If you are carrying a load of guilt because you can't be good enough for God, take another look at Jesus' death and what it means for you.

[7]For if that first *covenant* had been faultless, then no place would have been sought for a second. [8]Because finding fault with them, He says: *"Behold, the days are coming, says the LORD, when I will make a new covenant with the house of Israel and with the house of Judah—* [9]*not according to the covenant that I made with their fathers in the day when I took them by the hand to lead them out of the land of Egypt; because they did not continue in My covenant, and I disregarded them, says the LORD.* [10]*For this is the covenant that I will make with the house of Israel after those days, says the LORD: I will put My laws in their mind and write them on their hearts; and I will be their God, and they shall be My people.* [11]*None of them shall teach his neighbor, and none his brother, saying, 'Know the LORD,' for all shall know Me, from the least of them to the greatest of them.* [12]*For I will be merciful to their unrighteousness, and their sins and their lawless deeds I will remember no more."*

[13]In that He says, *"A new covenant,"* He has made the first obsolete. Now what is becoming obsolete and growing old is ready to vanish away.

CHAPTER 9 OLD RULES ABOUT WORSHIP. Then indeed, even the first *covenant* had ordinances of divine service and the earthly sanctuary. [2]For a tabernacle was prepared: the first *part*, in which *was* the lampstand, the table, and the showbread, which is called the sanctuary; [3]and behind the second veil, the part of the tabernacle which is called the Holiest of All, [4]which had the golden censer and the ark of the covenant overlaid on all sides with gold, in which *were* the golden pot that had the manna, Aaron's rod that budded, and the tablets of the covenant; [5]and above it were the cherubim of glory overshadowing the mercy seat. Of these things we cannot now speak in detail.

[6]Now when these things had been thus prepared, the priests always went into the first part of the tabernacle, performing *the services.* [7]But into the second part the high priest *went* alone once a year, not without blood, which he offered for himself and *for* the people's sins *committed* in ignorance; [8]the Holy Spirit indicating this, that the way into the Holiest of All was not yet made manifest while the first tabernacle was still standing. [9]It *was* symbolic for the present time in which both gifts and sacrifices are offered which cannot make him who performed the service perfect in regard to the conscience— [10]*concerned* only with foods and drinks, various washings, and fleshly ordinances imposed until the time of reformation.

[11]But Christ came *as* High Priest of the good things to come, with the greater and more perfect tabernacle not made with hands, that is, not of this creation. [12]Not with the blood of goats and calves, but with His own blood He entered the Most Holy Place once for all, having obtained eternal redemption. [13]For if the blood of bulls and goats and the ashes of a heifer, sprinkling the unclean, sanctifies for the purifying of the flesh, [14]how much more shall the blood of Christ, who through the eternal Spirit offered Himself without spot to God, cleanse your conscience from dead works to serve the living God? [15]And for this reason He is the Mediator of the new covenant, by means of death, for the redemption of the transgressions under the first covenant, that those who are called may receive the promise of the eternal inheritance.

[16]For where there *is* a testament, there must also of necessity be the death of the testator. [17]For a testament *is* in force after men are dead, since it has no power at all while the testator lives. [18]Therefore not even the first

9:15 Value, in our human way of thinking, is not measured by how *many* people can have something good, but by how *few*. "Limited edition" means "valuable" because only a few can have it. God's gr▮ plan of redemption, however, is dramatically different. It is the mos▮ valuable of all treasures, yet it is available to all. The more who hav▮ and the more they use it, the greater its value! Exercise your faith b▮ sharing it and using it to serve God, and so increase its value.

covenant was dedicated without blood. [19]For when Moses had spoken every precept to all the people according to the law, he took the blood of calves and goats, with water, scarlet wool, and hyssop, and sprinkled both the book itself and all the people, [20]saying, *"This is the blood of the covenant which God has commanded you."*[21]Then likewise he sprinkled with blood both the tabernacle and all the vessels of the ministry. [22]And according to the law almost all things are purified with blood, and without shedding of blood there is no remission.

[23]Therefore *it was* necessary that the copies of the things in the heavens should be purified with these, but the heavenly things themselves with better sacrifices than these. [24]For Christ has not entered the holy places made with hands, *which are* copies of the true, but into heaven itself, now to appear in the presence of God for us; [25]not that He should offer Himself often, as the high priest enters the Most Holy Place every year with blood of another— [26]He then would have had to suffer often since the foundation of the world; but now, once at the end of the ages, He has appeared to put away sin by the sacrifice of Himself. [27]And as it is appointed for men to die once, but after this the judgment, [28]so Christ was offered once to bear the sins of many. To those who eagerly wait for Him He will appear a second time, apart from sin, for salvation.

10:25 To neglect Christian meetings is to give up the encouragem▮ and help of other Christians. We gather together to share our faith ▮ strengthen each other in the Lord. As we get closer to the time of Ch▮ return, we may face many spiritual struggles, tribulations, and even persecution. Anti-Christian forces will grow in strength. Difficulties s▮ never be excuses for missing church services. Rather, as difficulties ▮ we should make an even greater effort to be faithful in attendance▮

CHAPTER **10** FORGIVENESS: ONCE FOR ALL. For the law, having a shadow of the good things to come, *and* not the very image of the things, can never with these same sacrifices, which they offer continually year by year, make those who approach perfect. [2]For then would they not have ceased to be offered? For the worshipers, once purified, would have had no more consciousness of sins. [3]But in those *sacrifices there is* a reminder of sins every year. [4]For *it is* not possible that the blood of bulls and goats could take away sins.

[5]Therefore, when He came into the world, He said:

"Sacrifice and offering You did not desire,
But a body You have prepared for Me.
[6] In burnt offerings and sacrifices for sin
You had no pleasure.
[7] Then I said, 'Behold, I have come—
In the volume of the book it is written of Me—
To do Your will, O God.'"

[8]Previously saying, *"Sacrifice and offering, burnt offerings, and offerings for sin You did not desire, nor had pleasure in them"* (which are offered according to the law), [9]then He said, *"Behold, I have come to do Your will, O God."* He takes away the first that He may establish the second. [10]By that will we have been sanctified through the offering of the body of Jesus Christ once *for all.*

[11]And every priest stands ministering daily and offering repeatedly the same sacrifices, which can never take away sins. [12]But this Man, after He had offered one sacrifice for sins forever, sat down at the right hand of God, [13]from that time waiting till His enemies are made His footstool. [14]For by one offering He has perfected forever those who are being sanctified.

[15]But the Holy Spirit also witnesses to us; for after He had said before,

[16] *"This is the covenant that I will make with them after those days, says the LORD: I will put My laws into their hearts, and in their minds I will write them,"* [17]*then He adds,* "Their sins and their lawless deeds I will remember no more." [18]Now where there is remission of these, *there is* no longer an offering for sin.

[19]Therefore, brethren, having boldness to enter the Holiest by the blood of Jesus, [20]by a new and living way which He consecrated for us, through the veil, that is, His flesh, [21]and *having* a High Priest over the house of God, [22]let us draw near with a true heart in full assurance of faith, having our hearts sprinkled from an evil conscience and our bodies washed with pure water. [23]Let us hold fast the confession of *our* hope without wavering, for He who promised *is* faithful. [24]And let us consider one another in order to stir up love and good works, [25]not forsaking the assembling of ourselves together, as *is* the manner of some, but exhorting *one another,* and so much the more as you see the Day approaching.

[26]For if we sin willfully after we have received the knowledge of the truth, there no longer remains a sacrifice for sins, [27]but a certain fearful expectation of judgment, and fiery indignation which will devour the adversaries. [28]Anyone who has rejected Moses' law dies without mercy on the testimony of two or three witnesses. [29]Of how much worse punishment, do you suppose, will he be thought worthy who has trampled the Son of God underfoot, counted the blood of the covenant by which he was sanctified a common thing, and insulted the Spirit of grace? [30]For we know Him who said, *"Vengeance is Mine, I will repay,"* says the Lord. And again, *"The LORD will judge His people."* [31]It is a fearful thing to fall into the hands of the living God.

[32]But recall the former days in which, after you were illuminated, you endured a great struggle with sufferings: [33]partly while you were made a spectacle both by reproaches and tribulations, and partly while you became companions of those who were so treated; [34]for you had compassion on me in my chains, and joyfully accepted the plundering of your goods, knowing that you have a better and an enduring possession for yourselves in heaven. [35]Therefore do not cast away your confidence, which has great reward. [36]For you have need of endurance, so that after you have done the will of God, you may receive the promise:

[37] "For yet a little while,
And He who is coming will come and will not tarry.
[38] Now the just shall live by faith;
But if anyone draws back,
My soul has no pleasure in him."

[39]But we are not of those who draw back to perdition, but of those who believe to the saving of the soul.

I like the idea about having a personal faith in God. What I don't like is having to go to church. It seems boring and a waste of time. I have been to other churches and it all seems the same. Why can't there be a church with just kids my own age?

I WONDER . . .

Imagine growing up without a family. It's tough to think of life without at least one parent who really cares.

Now imagine growing up with just brothers and sisters in the house and no parents at all! For a day or two it may seem like heaven, but very soon you would see that it is chaos! Eventually you would miss not having someone take care of your basic needs.

Families are designed to take care of your daily needs and to give you the continual love and guidance you need as you are growing up. Because Mom and Dad have been around longer, they often know what to do when a tough circumstance comes up (as much as you may hate to admit it!).

In Hebrews 10:24-25, we are warned against neglecting our church meetings. Church is our spiritual family. If we stay away, we are left to try to survive by ourselves. If all we had around were other kids, church would be like a house with no adults. Pretty soon we would recognize that many of our needs were not being met.

The church, like the family, can often be underappreciated for the role it plays in our spiritual growth. Some Christians do not recognize its influence until years later, then they realize they would still be spiritual babies without the church's influence and love.

CHAPTER 11 GREAT HEROES OF THE FAITH. Now

faith is the substance of things hoped for, the evidence of things not seen. ²For by it the elders obtained a *good* testimony.

³By faith we understand that the worlds were framed by the word of God, so that the things which are seen were not made of things which are visible.

⁴By faith Abel offered to God a more excellent sacrifice than Cain, through which he obtained witness that he was righteous, God testifying of his gifts; and through it he being dead still speaks.

⁵By faith Enoch was taken away so that he did not see death, *"and was not found, because God had taken him"*; for before he was taken he had this testimony, that he

CONSISTENCY
Follow for six months the paths of Ramsey and Tyrone, two guys who made commitments to Christ in August at youth camp:

September: Both guys begin attending a midweek Bible study sponsored by a local church.

October: Both guys are taught how to have a morning devotional time and start digging into God's Word.

November: Ramsey shares his newfound faith in Christ with two friends on the football team. Tyrone, claiming a busy schedule, begins skipping Bible study.

December: Ramsey decides to nix his habit of weekend carousing with the boys. Tyrone is no longer reading his Bible.

January: Ramsey has signed up to go to a Christian discipleship conference over spring break. Tyrone doesn't want to go to the conference, and he acts weird whenever Ramsey tries to talk to him about spiritual matters.

February: Ramsey leads his girlfriend to Christ. Tyrone's girlfriend is pregnant and planning to get an abortion.

Why the difference in the two guys? Why was Ramsey able to be so consistent and why did Tyrone fall away? For a possible answer, read Hebrews 12:1-4.

pleased God. ⁶But without faith *it is* impossible to please *Him*, for he who comes to God must believe that He is, and *that* He is a rewarder of those who diligently seek Him.

⁷By faith Noah, being divinely warned of things not yet seen, moved with godly fear, prepared an ark for the saving of his household, by which he condemned the world and became heir of the righteousness which is according to faith.

⁸By faith Abraham obeyed when he was called to go out to the place which he would receive as an inheritance. And he went out, not knowing where he was going. ⁹By faith he dwelt in the land of promise as *in* a foreign country, dwelling in tents with Isaac and Jacob, the heirs with him of the same promise; ¹⁰for he waited for the city which has foundations, whose builder and maker *is* God.

¹¹By faith Sarah herself also received strength to conceive seed, and she bore a child when she was past the age, because she judged Him faithful who had promised. ¹²Therefore from one man, and him as good as dead,

▶ VISION

11:13-16 The people of faith listed here died without receiving God had promised, but they never lost their vision of heaven. Many Christians become frustrated and defeated because their needs, wa expectations, and demands were not immediately met when they believed in Christ. They become impatient and want to quit. Are you discouraged because your goal seems far away? Take courage from heroes of faith who lived and died without seeing the fruit of their on earth, yet continued to believe.

were born *as many* as the stars of the sky in multitude—innumerable as the sand which is by the seashore.

¹³These all died in faith, not having received the promises, but having seen them afar off were assured of them, embraced *them* and confessed that they were strangers and pilgrims on the earth. ¹⁴For those who say such things declare plainly that they seek a homeland. ¹⁵And truly if they had called to mind that *country* from which they had come out, they would have had opportunity to return. ¹⁶But now they desire a better, that is, a heavenly *country.* Therefore God is not ashamed to be called their God, for He has prepared a city for them.

¹⁷By faith Abraham, when he was tested, offered up Isaac, and he who had received the promises offered up his only begotten *son,* ¹⁸of whom it was said, *"In Isaac your seed shall be called,"* ¹⁹concluding that God *was* able to raise *him* up, even from the dead, from which he also received him in a figurative sense.

²⁰By faith Isaac blessed Jacob and Esau concerning things to come.

²¹By faith Jacob, when he was dying, blessed each of the sons of Joseph, and worshiped, *leaning* on the top of his staff.

²²By faith Joseph, when he was dying, made mention of the departure of the children of Israel, and gave instructions concerning his bones.

²³By faith Moses, when he was born, was hidden three months by his parents, because they saw *he was* a beautiful child; and they were not afraid of the king's command.

²⁴By faith Moses, when he became of age, refused to be called the son of Pharaoh's daughter, ²⁵choosing rather to suffer affliction with the people of God than to enjoy the passing pleasures of sin, ²⁶esteeming the reproach of Christ greater riches than the treasures in Egypt; for he looked to the reward.

²⁷By faith he forsook Egypt, not fearing the wrath of the king; for he endured as seeing Him who is invisible. ²⁸By faith he kept the Passover and the sprinkling of blood, lest he who destroyed the firstborn should touch them.

²⁹By faith they passed through the Red Sea as by dry *land, whereas* the Egyptians, attempting *to do* so, were drowned.

³⁰By faith the walls of Jericho fell down after they were encircled for seven days. ³¹By faith the harlot Rahab did not perish with those who did not believe, when she had received the spies with peace.

³²And what more shall I say? For the time would fail me to tell of Gideon and Barak and Samson and Jephthah, also *of* David and Samuel and the prophets: ³³who through faith subdued kingdoms, worked righteousness, obtained promises, stopped the mouths of lions, ³⁴quenched the violence of fire, escaped the edge of the sword, out of weakness were made strong, became val-

iant in battle, turned to flight the armies of the aliens. [35]Women received their dead raised to life again.

Others were tortured, not accepting deliverance, that they might obtain a better resurrection. [36]Still others had trial of mockings and scourgings, yes, and of chains and imprisonment. [37]They were stoned, they were sawn in two, were tempted, were slain with the sword. They wandered about in sheepskins and goatskins, being destitute, afflicted, tormented— [38]of whom the world was not worthy. They wandered in deserts and mountains, *in* dens and caves of the earth.

[39]And all these, having obtained a good testimony through faith, did not receive the promise, [40]God having provided something better for us, that they should not be made perfect apart from us.

CHAPTER **12** **LET GOD TRAIN YOU.** Therefore we also, since we are surrounded by so great a cloud of witnesses, let us lay aside every weight, and the sin which so easily ensnares *us,* and let us run with endurance the race that is set before us, [2]looking unto Jesus, the author and finisher of *our* faith, who for the joy that was set before Him endured the cross, despising the shame, and has sat down at the right hand of the throne of God.

[3]For consider Him who endured such hostility from sinners against Himself, lest you become weary and discouraged in your souls. [4]You have not yet resisted to bloodshed, striving against sin. [5]And you have forgotten the exhortation which speaks to you as to sons:

"*My son, do not despise the chastening of the LORD, Nor be discouraged when you are rebuked by Him;*
[6] *For whom the LORD loves He chastens, And scourges every son whom He receives.*"

[7]If you endure chastening, God deals with you as with sons; for what son is there whom a father does not chasten? [8]But if you are without chastening, of which all have become partakers, then you are illegitimate and not sons. [9]Furthermore, we have had human fathers who corrected *us,* and we paid *them* respect. Shall we not much more readily be in subjection to the Father of spirits and live? [10]For they indeed for a few days chastened *us* as seemed *best* to them, but He for *our* profit, that *we* may be partakers of His holiness. [11]Now no chastening seems to be joyful for the present, but painful;

nevertheless, afterward it yields the peaceable fruit of righteousness to those who have been trained by it.

[12]Therefore strengthen the hands which hang down, and the feeble knees, [13]and make straight paths for your

OUR COACH

12:12-13 God is not only a disciplining parent, he is also a demanding coach who pushes us to our limit and requires of us a disciplined life. Although we may not feel strong enough to push on to victory, we will be able to continue as we follow Christ and draw upon his strength. Then we can use our growing strength to help those around us who are weak and struggling.

feet, so that what is lame may not be *dislocated,* but rather be healed.

[14]Pursue peace with all *people,* and holiness, without which no one will see the Lord: [15]looking carefully lest anyone fall short of the grace of God; lest any root of bitterness springing up cause trouble, and by this many become

"Here's what I did..."

Money and material things used to be very important to me. I cared a lot about the clothes I wore. I liked it that my parents had a nice home and nice cars—and I wasn't very interested in people who didn't have nice clothes or nice things. I just didn't think I had much in common with people who didn't have as much money as I did.

Then I met Cathy. She attended my school, but I didn't know her because we hung around different groups. I got to know Cathy at a Christian camp. She and I were worlds apart in lots of ways. Her parents didn't have much money and she didn't care about fashion at all, but Cathy was the most caring person I had ever met. She knew how to listen, and that summer she turned out to be a good friend to me as I went through a rough time. Some other kids at the camp spread some untrue rumors about me, and it hurt me a lot. But Cathy was always there, to listen and encourage.

That fall when we returned to school, I began to see how shallow some of my other friendships were compared to what I'd experienced with Cathy. I began to do more things with her and her friends, and I found that I liked her friends, even though they weren't "cool." My old friends started making fun of me for hanging around Cathy, but that only showed me more that those people weren't true friends.

I asked Cathy once why she didn't seem to care about money. She said, "Sometimes I do care that I don't have nice clothes like you. But I found a Bible verse that says we're not to love money, but to be satisfied with what we have. I try to do that." She showed me the verse: Hebrews 13:5. What struck me was that she seemed to be more satisfied with what she had than I was, even though she owned much less. I knew she had something that I was just beginning to appreciate: the sense that God really was with her.

My attitude toward money and toward people started to change as I prayed that God would help me to be satisfied with what I had and not to care so much about externals. I saw that God—and true friends—look on the heart, not on whether you wear the latest fashions.

Katie
AGE 16

defiled; [16]lest there *be* any fornicator or profane person like Esau, who for one morsel of food sold his birthright. [17]For you know that afterward, when he wanted to inherit the blessing, he was rejected, for he found no place for repentance, though he sought it diligently with tears.

[18]For you have not come to the mountain that may be touched and that burned with fire, and to blackness and darkness and tempest, [19]and the sound of a trumpet and the voice of words, so that those who heard *it* begged that the word should not be spoken to them anymore. [20](For they could not endure what was commanded: *"And if so much as a beast touches the mountain, it shall be stoned or shot with an arrow."* [21]And so terrifying was the sight *that* Moses said, *"I am exceedingly afraid and trembling."*)

REPUTATION

There's a time-out on the floor, and the varsity cheerleaders are building a pyramid at midcourt. Their complicated stunt, however, is not the most fascinating thing taking place in Butler Gymnasium.

Far more interesting are the thoughts that fill the minds of those in the student section. What if you could crawl through each set of watching eyes into each churning brain? What would you discover?

Well, you'd find that most of the students, when they glance at Tammy (the girl at the apex of the pyramid), are thinking words like *conceited, snotty, snob, fake,* and *back-stabber.* Her reputation is, frankly, not the best.

Meanwhile the girl doing the splits out in front of the others, Amy, is regarded by almost everyone in the stands as "sweet," "nice," "friendly," "fun-to-be-with," and "likable."

Three quick questions:
1. Why would you suppose there is such a sharp contrast in reputations?
2. Do you know any people like Tammy and Amy?
3. How do other people regard you?
Read Hebrews 13 for a fast lesson in reputation making.

[22]But you have come to Mount Zion and to the city of the living God, the heavenly Jerusalem, to an innumerable company of angels, [23]to the general assembly and church of the firstborn *who are* registered in heaven, to God the Judge of all, to the spirits of just men made perfect, [24]to Jesus the Mediator of the new covenant, and to the blood of sprinkling that speaks better things than *that of* Abel.

[25]See that you do not refuse Him who speaks. For if they did not escape who refused Him who spoke on earth, much more *shall we not escape* if we turn away from Him who *speaks* from heaven, [26]whose voice then shook the earth; but now He has promised, saying, *"Yet once more I shake not only the earth, but also heaven."* [27]Now this, *"Yet once more,"* indicates the removal of those things that are being shaken, as of things that are made, that the things which cannot be shaken may remain.

[28]Therefore, since we are receiving a kingdom which cannot be shaken, let us have grace, by which we may serve God acceptably with reverence and godly fear. [29]For our God *is* a consuming fire.

CHAPTER 13 LIVE GOOD AND OBEDIENT LIVES.

Let brotherly love continue. [2]Do not forget to entertain strangers, for by so *doing* some have unwittingly entertained angels. [3]Remember the prisoners as if chained with them—those who are mistreated—since you yourselves are in the body also.

[4]Marriage *is* honorable among all, and the bed undefiled; but fornicators and adulterers God will judge.

[5]*Let your* conduct *be* without covetousness; *be* content with such things as you have. For He Himself has said, *"I will never leave you nor forsake you."* [6]So we may boldly say:

> *"The LORD is my helper;*
> *I will not fear.*
> *What can man do to me?"*

[7]Remember those who rule over you, who have spoken the word of God to you, whose faith follow, considering the outcome of *their* conduct. [8]Jesus Christ *is* the same yesterday, today, and forever. [9]Do not be carried about with various and strange doctrines. For *it is* good that the heart be established by grace, not with foods which have not profited those who have been occupied with them.

[10]We have an altar from which those who serve the tabernacle have no right to eat. [11]For the bodies of those animals, whose blood is brought into the sanctuary by the high priest for sin, are burned outside the camp. [12]Therefore Jesus also, that He might sanctify the people with His own blood, suffered outside the gate. [13]Therefore let us go forth to Him, outside the camp, bearing His reproach. [14]For here we have no continuing city, but we seek the one to come. [15]Therefore by Him let us continually offer the sacrifice of praise to God, that is, the fruit of *our* lips, giving thanks to His name. [16]But do not forget to do good and to share, for with such sacrifices God is well pleased.

[17]Obey those who rule over you, and be submissive, for they watch out for your souls, as those who must give account. Let them do so with joy and not with grief, for that would be unprofitable for you.

[18]Pray for us; for we are confident that we have a good conscience, in all things desiring to live honorably. [19]But I especially urge *you* to do this, that I may be restored to you the sooner.

[20]Now may the God of peace who brought up our Lord Jesus from the dead, that great Shepherd of the sheep, through the blood of the everlasting covenant, [21]make you complete in every good work to do His will, working in you what is well pleasing in His sight, through Jesus Christ, to whom *be* glory forever and ever. Amen.

[22]And I appeal to you, brethren, bear with the word of exhortation, for I have written to you in few words. [23]Know that *our* brother Timothy has been set free, with whom I shall see you if he comes shortly.

[24]Greet all those who rule over you, and all the saints. Those from Italy greet you.

[25]Grace *be* with you all. Amen.

UNCHANGING

13:1-21 We must keep our eyes on Christ, our ultimate leader, w unlike human leaders, will never change. He has been and will be t same forever. In a changing world we can trust our unchanging Lo

MEGA *Themes*

CHRIST IS SUPERIOR Hebrews reveals Jesus' true identity as God. Christ is the ultimate authority. He is greater than any religion or any angel, and superior to any Jewish leader (such as Abraham, Moses, or Joshua) or priest. Christ is the complete revelation of God.

Jesus alone can forgive your sin. He has secured your forgiveness and salvation by his death on the cross. With Christ you can find peace with God and real meaning for life. Without him, there is no hope for true life.

1. What was unique about Jesus Christ?
2. Why did the first-century Jews have difficulty accepting these truths about Jesus?
3. How do the majority of people in your school feel about being a Christian? What are their misconceptions about Jesus?
4. If you could explain one thing about Christ to those who do not understand him, what would you tell them?

HIGH PRIEST In the Old Testament, the high priest represented the Jews before God. Jesus Christ links us with God. There is no other way to reach God. Because Jesus Christ lived a sinless life, he is the perfect substitute to die for our sin. Christ is our perfect representative with God.

Jesus guarantees our access to God the Father. He intercedes for us so that we can boldly come to the Father with our needs. When we are weak we can come confidently to God for forgiveness and help. He never shuts us out or refuses to respond to our needs.

1. In Hebrews, what do you learn about the role of a high priest?
2. Based on 4:14-16 and 7:19-28, what are the ways that Jesus is the perfect High Priest?
3. What benefits do you have because Jesus is your High Priest?
4. What hurts, needs, or wants do you want to bring to God, your Father? How does Jesus, your High Priest, provide the way for you to present these to God? Express your needs to God and share with him your feelings about the perfect High Priest he has provided in Jesus.

SACRIFICE Christ's sacrifice was the ultimate fulfillment of all that the Old Testament sacrifices represented—God's forgiveness for sin. Because Christ was the perfect sacrifice, our sins have been completely forgiven—past, present, and future.

Christ removed sin that kept us from God's presence and fellowship. But we must accept Christ's sacrifice for us. By believing in him we are declared "not guilty," cleansed, and made whole. Christ's sacrifice provided the way for us to have eternal life.

1. What qualified Jesus to be the perfect, once-and-for-all fulfillment of the Old Testament sacrificial requirements?
2. What blessings do you have as a result of Jesus' sacrifice?
3. Contrast the difference for those who reject Christ's sacrifice and those who accept it (check 10:26-39).
4. What have you personally received from the one who sacrificed himself for your sins? What difference has Jesus' sacrifice made in your life?

FAITH Faith is confident trust in God. God's salvation is in his son Jesus, who is the only one who can save us from sin.

If you trust in Jesus Christ for your salvation, he will transform you completely. Then you should live a life of faith.

1. Rewrite 11:3 in your own words.
2. Explain what you think is meant by this statement: "Faith is not just knowing, it is doing."
3. Read chapter 11. What do you learn about the life of faith from the great men and women listed there?
4. If someone were to write a couple of verses describing your life of faith, what would they include?
5. In what ways would you like to see your faith grow? How do you develop this growth in faith?

MATURITY THROUGH ENDURANCE Faith enables Christians to face trials. Genuine faith includes the commitment to stay true to God when we are under fire. Endurance builds character and leads to victory.

You can have victory in your trials if you don't give up or turn your back on Christ. Stay true to Christ and pray for endurance. He will never grow tired of supporting you.

1. Hebrews 12 describes what it means to grow through endurance and discipline. Why is discipline necessary for growth?
2. Based on 12:1-5, what are the keys to endurance? How can you apply these principles to where you are in "the race" at this point in your life?
3. What are the main points of Hebrews' teaching concerning God's discipline?
4. If someone were to ask you, "Why should I take obedience to God so seriously?" how would you respond?

You've been feeling strange all week. At first you had trouble sleeping. Then came the headaches. Yesterday your teeth began hurting and your fingernails turned blue for several hours. This morning you realized it was time to consult your family doctor when, after a morning jog, your mom asked if you'd been sprayed by a skunk. ■ The doctor tries to hold her breath as she asks you questions. She nods knowingly as you tick off your symptoms. After looking in your eyes and noting your swollen eardrums, she orders some lab work. ■ A few hours later she returns to tell you, "Just what I suspected— you have an extremely high number of antibiomolecularsucrothyamin microbes in your liver." ■ "Huh?" you gulp. ■ "Oh, don't worry. You have a common ailment we call odoramonia. We'll put you on an antibiotic and get you eating a balanced diet, and you'll be fine." ■ Aren't doctors amazing? By examining us and noting our symptoms, they're usually able to diagnose our physical ailments and prescribe the proper treatment. ■ God does the same thing in our spiritual realm. ■ By looking at our actions (or lack of action) God can tell us exactly what attitudes and desires need healing. His Word gives detailed prescriptions for curing wrong behavior patterns. ■ Is your spiritual life on the sick side? Are you fighting worldly infections or possibly even the disease of disobedience?

■ Follow the advice of the Great Physician. No matter what your ailment, the Epistle of James has the cure.

STATS

PURPOSE: To expose unethical practices and to teach right Christian behavior

AUTHOR: James, Jesus' brother, a leader in the Jerusalem church

TO WHOM WRITTEN: First-century Jewish Christians residing in Gentile communities outside Palestine; all Christians everywhere

DATE WRITTEN: Probably A.D. 49, prior to the Jerusalem council held in A.D. 50

SETTING: This letter expresses James's concern for persecuted Christians who were once part of the Jerusalem church

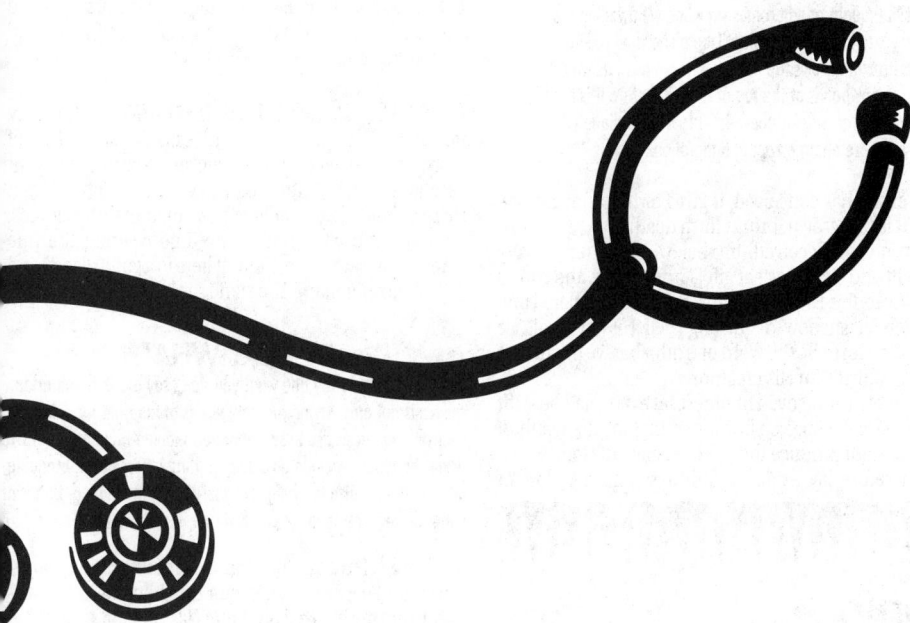

James

CHAPTER 1 **JAMES: A SERVANT OF GOD.** James, a bondservant of God and of the Lord Jesus Christ,

To the twelve tribes which are scattered abroad:

Greetings.

[2]My brethren, count it all joy when you fall into various trials, [3]knowing that the testing of your faith produces patience. [4]But let patience have *its* perfect work, that you may be perfect and complete, lacking nothing. [5]If any of you lacks wisdom, let him ask of God, who gives to all liberally and without reproach, and it will be given to him. [6]But let him ask in faith, with no doubting, for he who doubts is like a wave of the sea driven and tossed by the wind. [7]For let not that man suppose that he will receive anything from the Lord; [8]*he is* a double-minded man, unstable in all his ways.

[9]Let the lowly brother glory in his exaltation, [10]but the rich in his humiliation, because as a flower of the field he will pass away. [11]For no sooner has the sun risen with a burning heat than it withers the grass; its flower falls, and its beautiful appearance perishes. So the rich man also will fade away in his pursuits.

[12]Blessed *is* the man who endures temptation; for when he has been approved, he will receive the crown of life which the Lord has promised to those who love Him. [13]Let no one say when he is tempted, "I am tempted by God"; for God cannot be tempted by evil, nor does He Himself tempt anyone. [14]But each one is tempted when he is drawn away by his own desires and enticed. [15]Then,

ROUGH TIMES

1:2-4 We can't really know the depth of our character until we see how we react under pressure. It is easy to be kind when everything is going well, but can we still be kind when others are treating us unfairly? Instead of complaining about our struggles, we should see them as opportunities for growth. Thank God for promising to be with you in rough times. Ask him to help you solve your problems or give you the strength to endure them. Then be patient. God will not leave you; he will stay close by and help you grow.

◥◣◢◤SNOWBALL

1:12-15 Temptation comes from evil desires inside us, not from God. It begins with an evil thought and becomes sin when we dwell on the thought and allow it to become an action. Like a snowball rolling downhill, sin's destruction grows the more we let sin have its way. The best time to stop a snowball is at the top of the hill, before it is too big or moving too fast to control. See Matthew 4:1-11; 1 Corinthians 10:13; and 2 Timothy 2:22 for more about escaping temptation.

when desire has conceived, it gives birth to sin; and sin, when it is full-grown, brings forth death.

¹⁶Do not be deceived, my beloved brethren. ¹⁷Every good gift and every perfect gift is from above, and comes down from the Father of lights, with whom there is no variation or shadow of turning. ¹⁸Of His own will He brought us forth by the word of truth, that we might be a kind of firstfruits of His creatures.

¹⁹So then, my beloved brethren, let every man be swift to hear, slow to speak, slow to wrath; ²⁰for the wrath of man does not produce the righteousness of God.

²¹Therefore lay aside all filthiness and overflow of

O BEDIENCE

The First Church youth group has just heard a great talk about the importance of serving others. On the way home, three friends discuss the meeting:

"Andy is a great speaker! He always makes me laugh!"

"His talk was awesome."

"I know! I feel so convicted. I never do anything for my mom or dad."

"That was a cool idea he gave about doing a project down in the inner city."

"Yeah, wouldn't that be great? We should do that sometime."

Now, let's listen in on the conversation a few minutes later:

"So, what are you guys going to do this weekend?"

"Probably the same old stuff—go to a movie, sit around and be bored."

"That drives me nuts! How come there is nothing for kids our age to do? If I have to go to the mall one more time, I'm going to puke!"

"I agree!"

What's wrong with that conversation? Anything? Read over it again.

Less than 30 minutes after being challenged to serve others, these teens are complaining they don't have anything to do.

The point? Christians should never be bored! We always have opportunities to serve others. In fact, if we're not putting our faith into practice on a regular basis, the Bible says our religion isn't worth very much. See James 1:21-27.

wickedness, and receive with meekness the implanted word, which is able to save your souls.

²²But be doers of the word, and not hearers only, deceiving yourselves. ²³For if anyone is a hearer of the word and not a doer, he is like a man observing his natural face in a mirror; ²⁴for he observes himself, goes away, and immediately forgets what kind of man he was. ²⁵But he who looks into the perfect law of liberty and continues *in it*, and is not a forgetful hearer but a doer of the work, this one will be blessed in what he does.

²⁶If anyone among you thinks he is religious, and does

not bridle his tongue but deceives his own heart, this one's religion *is* useless. ²⁷Pure and undefiled religion before God and the Father is this: to visit orphans and widows in their trouble, *and* to keep oneself unspotted from the world.

CHAPTER **2** **NO SPECIAL TREATMENT.** My brethren, do not hold the faith of our Lord Jesus Christ, *the Lord* of glory, with partiality. ²For if there should come into your assembly a man with gold rings, in fine apparel, and there should also come in a poor man in filthy clothes, ³and you pay attention to the one wearing the fine clothes and say to him, "You sit here in a good place," and say to the poor man, "You stand there," or, "Sit here at my

◥◣◢◤SAY WHAT?

3:2-3 What you say and what you *don't* say are both important. Speech is not only saying the right words at the right time, but also controlling your desire to say what you shouldn't. Examples of wrong using the tongue include gossiping, putting others down, bragging, manipulating, false teaching, exaggerating, complaining, flattering, lying. Before you speak, ask, "Is it true, is it necessary, and is it kind

footstool," ⁴have you not shown partiality among yourselves, and become judges with evil thoughts?

⁵Listen, my beloved brethren: Has God not chosen the poor of this world *to be* rich in faith and heirs of the kingdom which He promised to those who love Him? ⁶But you have dishonored the poor man. Do not the rich oppress you and drag you into the courts? ⁷Do they not blaspheme that noble name by which you are called?

⁸If you really fulfill *the* royal law according to the Scripture, *"You shall love your neighbor as yourself,"* you do well; ⁹but if you show partiality, you commit sin, and are convicted by the law as transgressors. ¹⁰For whoever shall keep the whole law, and yet stumble in one *point*, he is guilty of all. ¹¹For He who said, *"Do not commit adultery,"* also said, *"Do not murder."* Now if you do not commit adultery, but you do murder, you have become a trans-

LET EVERY MAN BE SWIFT TO HEAR SLOW TO SPEAK SLOW TO WRATH

gressor of the law. [12]So speak and so do as those who will be judged by the law of liberty. [13]For judgment is without mercy to the one who has shown no mercy. Mercy triumphs over judgment.

[14]What *does it* profit, my brethren, if someone says he has faith but does not have works? Can faith save him? [15]If a brother or sister is naked and destitute of daily food, [16]and one of you says to them, "Depart in peace, be warmed and filled," but you do not give them the things which are needed for the body, what *does it* profit? [17]Thus also faith by itself, if it does not have works, is dead.

[18]But someone will say, "You have faith, and I have works." Show me your faith without your works, and I will show you my faith by my works. [19]You believe that there is one God. You do well. Even the demons believe—and tremble! [20]But do you want to know, O foolish man, that faith without works is dead? [21]Was not Abraham our father justified by works when he offered Isaac his son on the altar? [22]Do you see that faith was working together with his works, and by works faith was made perfect? [23]And the Scripture was fulfilled which says, *"Abraham believed God, and it was accounted to him for righteousness."* And he was called the friend of God. [24]You see then that a man is justified by works, and not by faith only.

[25]Likewise, was not Rahab the harlot also justified by works when she received the messengers and sent *them* out another way?

[26]For as the body without the spirit is dead, so faith without works is dead also.

CHAPTER 3 CONTROL WHAT YOU SAY.

My brethren, let not many of you become teachers, knowing that we shall receive a stricter judgment. [2]For we all stumble in many things. If anyone does not stumble in word, he *is* a perfect man, able also to bridle the whole body. [3]Indeed, we put bits in horses' mouths that they may obey us, and we turn their whole body. [4]Look also at ships: although they are so large and are driven by fierce winds, they are turned by a very small rudder wherever the pilot desires. [5]Even so the tongue is a little member and boasts great things.

See how great a forest a little fire kindles! [6]And the tongue *is* a fire, a world of iniquity. The tongue is so set among our members that it defiles the whole body, and sets on fire the course of nature; and it is set on fire by hell. [7]For every kind of beast and bird, of reptile and creature of the sea, is tamed and has been tamed by mankind. [8]But no man can tame the tongue. *It is* an unruly evil, full of deadly poison. [9]With it we bless our God and Father, and with it we curse men, who have been made in the similitude of God. [10]Out of the same mouth proceed blessing and cursing. My brethren, these things ought not to be so. [11]Does a spring send forth fresh *water* and bitter from the same opening? [12]Can a fig tree, my brethren, bear olives, or a grapevine bear figs? Thus no spring yields both salt water and fresh.

[13]Who *is* wise and understanding among you? Let him show by good conduct *that* his works *are done* in the meekness of wisdom. [14]But if you have bitter envy and self-seeking in your hearts, do not boast and lie against the truth. [15]This wisdom does not descend from above, but *is* earthly, sensual, demonic. [16]For where envy and self-seeking *exist,* confusion and every evil thing *are* there. [17]But the wisdom that is from above is first pure, then peaceable, gentle, willing to yield, full of mercy and good fruits, without partiality and without hypocrisy. [18]Now the fruit of righteousness is sown in peace by those who make peace.

I feel guilty more often now that I'm a Christian. Sometimes the guilt comes on for just little stuff that I used to never give a second thought about. When do I need to ask God for forgiveness?

I WONDER . . .

God's goal is not to overwhelm us with our sin so that we become discouraged. He knows when to point out sin in our life.

Some people are basically pretty "good" people when they come to faith in Christ. They don't have many destructive habits to overcome, and their parents have tried to teach them right from wrong. Others come with a lot of sin "baggage."

Although each person is unique, we're the same when it comes to our nature—we're sinners. In fact, we were born with a sinful nature. This is called "original sin." And throughout our life, we do all sorts of things that are wrong.

When we accept Christ as Savior, God declares us "not guilty." But this doesn't mean that we're perfect and don't sin anymore. We must daily deal with sin while we're still alive on earth. It's part of being human. Christians, like everyone, have two types of sin to deal with. Past sins and present sins.

As I said, when we become Christians, all of our past sins are wiped away. "As far as the east is from the west, so far has He removed our transgressions from us" (Psalm 103:12). That's a distance that can't be measured!

Ideally, having past sins removed should also take away our guilt feelings. We can put the past behind us. We're forgiven!

But what about present sin? One of the roles of the Holy Spirit is to remind us when we sin. He doesn't do this to condemn us, but to prompt us to confess it, forsake it, and move on. God has forgiven us for these present sins, too. We confess them to him to keep the communication channels open and to keep the relationship close. So we should talk to God about our life, and confess, whenever we need to. And remember, sins aren't limited to doing what is wrong. They also include not doing what is right.

The passage in James 4:17 is plain. "Therefore, to him who knows to do good and does not do *it,* to him it is sin."

If we know we should help someone stop gossiping; give our parents the whole truth, instead of only part of it; turn off the TV and spend time with God . . . and don't do it—we sin!

Let God, not others, do the convicting in your life and you'll be glad to confess your sins to him. He's eager to clear away the barriers between you and himself and start fresh.

CHAPTER 4 HOW CAN YOU GET CLOSE TO GOD?

Where do wars and fights come from among you? Do they not come from your desires for pleasure that war in your members? ²You lust and do not have. You murder and covet and cannot obtain. You fight and war. Yet you do not have because you do not ask. ³You ask and do not receive, because you ask amiss, that you may spend it on your pleasures. ⁴Adulterers and adulteresses! Do you not know that friendship with the world is enmity with God? Whoever therefore wants to be a friend of the world makes himself an enemy of God. ⁵Or do you think that the Scripture says in vain, "The Spirit who dwells in us yearns jealously"?

⁶But He gives more grace. Therefore He says:

◢ BUILD UP

4:11-12 Jesus summarized the law as loving God and your neighbor (Matthew 22:37-40), and Paul said that love demonstrated toward a neighbor fully satisfies the law (Romans 13:6-10). When we fail to love, we break God's law. Examine your attitude and actions. Do you build people up or tear them down? Instead of criticizing someone, remember God's law of love and say something good instead. If you make this a habit, your tendency to find fault with others will decrease and your ability to obey God will increase.

> "God resists the proud,
> But gives grace to the humble."

⁷Therefore submit to God. Resist the devil and he will flee from you. ⁸Draw near to God and He will draw near to you. Cleanse your hands, you sinners; and purify your hearts, you double-minded. ⁹Lament and mourn and weep! Let your laughter be turned to mourning and your joy to gloom. ¹⁰Humble yourselves in the sight of the Lord, and He will lift you up.

¹¹Do not speak evil of one another, brethren. He who speaks evil of a brother and judges his brother, speaks evil of the law and judges the law. But if you judge the law, you are not a doer of the law but a judge. ¹²There is one Lawgiver, who is able to save and to destroy. Who are you to judge another?

¹³Come now, you who say, "Today or tomorrow we will go to such and such a city, spend a year there, buy and sell, and make a profit"; ¹⁴whereas you do not know what will happen tomorrow. For what is your life? It is even a vapor that appears for a little time and then vanishes away. ¹⁵Instead you ought to say, "If the Lord wills, we shall live and do this or that." ¹⁶But now you boast in your arrogance. All such boasting is evil.

¹⁷Therefore, to him who knows to do good and does not do it, to him it is sin.

CHAPTER 5 A WARNING TO THE RICH. Come now,

you rich, weep and howl for your miseries that are coming upon you! ²Your riches are corrupted, and your garments are moth-eaten. ³Your gold and silver are corroded, and their corrosion will be a witness against you and will eat your flesh like fire. You have heaped up treasure in the last days. ⁴Indeed the wages of the laborers who mowed your fields, which you kept back by

◢ REARRANGED

4:13-16 It is good to have goals, but goals can disappoint us if [we] leave God out of them. There is no point in making plans as thoug[h God] does not exist because the future is in his hands. What would you [like to] be doing ten years from now? One year from now? Tomorrow? Ho[w would] you react if God steps in and rearranges your plans? Plan ahead, [but] hang on to your plans lightly. If you put God's desires at the cente[r of] your planning, you will not be disappointed.

fraud, cry out; and the cries of the reapers have reached the ears of the Lord of Sabaoth. ⁵You have lived on the earth in pleasure and luxury; you have fattened your hearts as in a day of slaughter. ⁶You have condemned, you have murdered the just; he does not resist you.

⁷Therefore be patient, brethren, until the coming of the Lord. See how the farmer waits for the precious fruit of the earth, waiting patiently for it until it receives the early and latter rain. ⁸You also be patient. Establish your hearts, for the coming of the Lord is at hand.

⁹Do not grumble against one another, brethren, lest you be condemned. Behold, the Judge is standing at the door! ¹⁰My brethren, take the prophets, who spoke in the name of the Lord, as an example of suffering and patience. ¹¹Indeed we count them blessed who endure. You have heard of the perseverance of Job and seen the end intended by the Lord—that the Lord is very compassionate and merciful.

¹²But above all, my brethren, do not swear, either by heaven or by earth or with any other oath. But let your "Yes" be "Yes," and your "No," "No," lest you fall into judgment.

¹³Is anyone among you suffering? Let him pray. Is anyone cheerful? Let him sing psalms. ¹⁴Is anyone among you sick? Let him call for the elders of the church, and let them pray over him, anointing him with oil in the name of the Lord. ¹⁵And the prayer of faith will save the sick, and the Lord will raise him up. And if he has committed

◢ TODAY!

4:14 Life is short no matter how long we live. Don't be deceived [into] thinking that you have lots of time to live for Christ, to enjoy your [loved] ones, or to do what you know you should. Live for God today! The[n no] matter when your life ends, you will have fulfilled God's plan for y[ou.]

sins, he will be forgiven. ¹⁶Confess your trespasses to one another, and pray for one another, that you may be healed. The effective, fervent prayer of a righteous man avails much. ¹⁷Elijah was a man with a nature like ours, and he prayed earnestly that it would not rain; and it did not rain on the land for three years and six months. ¹⁸And he prayed again, and the heaven gave rain, and the earth produced its fruit.

¹⁹Brethren, if anyone among you wanders from the truth, and someone turns him back, ²⁰let him know that he who turns a sinner from the error of his way will save a soul from death and cover a multitude of sins.

◢ HONESTY

5:12 A person with a reputation for exaggeration or lying often [can't] get anyone to believe him on his word alone. Christians should ne[ver] become like that. Always be honest so that others will believe you[r] yes or no. By avoiding lies, half-truths, and omissions of the truth, [you] will become known as a trustworthy person.

MEGA Themes

LIVING FAITH James wants believers to hear the truth *and* to do it. He contrasts empty faith ("claims without conduct") with faith that works. Commitment to love and to serve is evidence of true faith.

Living faith makes a difference. Make sure your faith results in action. Be alert to ways of putting your faith to work. Be certain that you not only "talk" the gospel, but that you "walk" the gospel as well.
1. Contrast "living faith" with "dead faith."
2. What would it mean to have a dead faith in your school? What would it mean to have a living faith in your school?
3. How are your vital signs? Identify evidence of life in your faith.
4. In what ways can you become more alive as a doer of God's Word in your school? With your friends? In your relationships at church? In response to the needy in your community?

TRIALS In the Christian life there are trials and temptations. Successfully overcoming these adversities produces maturity and strong character.

Don't resent troubles when they come. Pray for wisdom; God will supply all you need to face persecution or adversity. He will give you patience and keep you strong.
1. What attitude does James teach you to have concerning trials?
2. What trials and problems have you recently experienced?
3. How did you feel when you were facing these trials and problems? How did you feel toward God?
4. Describe how you can choose to respond with an appropriate attitude the next time you face a trial or problem. Why is developing such responses important for a Christian? (Check the results of enduring trials in chapter 1.)

LAW OF LOVE We are saved by God's gracious mercy, not by keeping the law. But Christ gave us a special command, "love your neighbor as yourself" (Matthew 19:19). We are to love and serve those around us.

Keeping the law of love shows that our faith is vital and real. To show love to others, we must root out our own selfishness. This begins by acting on what we know to be true about God's will in our life.
1. What does James teach in chapter 2 about the life of faith?
2. What would happen if every Christian in your community lived with the attitude and actions described in 2:2-16?
3. Why are the acts of giving to those in need and not showing favoritism important expressions of living faith?
4. What does it mean in your life (home, school, church) not to show favoritism? Who are the needy who can benefit from your resources (time, love, food, money, work)?

WISE SPEECH Wisdom shows itself in speech. We are responsible for the destructive results of our talk. The wisdom of God that helps control the tongue can help control all our actions.

Accepting God's wisdom will affect your speech because your words will reveal their godly source. Think of God and others before you speak, and allow God to strengthen your self-control.
1. Why does James devote so much of this book to the issue of controlling the tongue?
2. When did someone's words hurt you or a person you really care about? How did you feel? What were the results?
3. When did your words hurt another person? How did you feel? What were the results?
4. Taking the principles from James, what could have been done differently in those situations that would have led to positive communication?

WEALTH James teaches Christians not to compromise with worldly attitudes about wealth. Because the glory of wealth fades, Christians should store up God's treasures through sincere service. Christians must not show partiality to the wealthy or be prejudiced against the poor.

We all are accountable for how we use what we have. We should be generous toward others. We are to see one another as God sees us—created as equals in his image.
1. What does James think about rich people? What is it about these wealthy men in chapter 5 that causes James to react so strongly?
2. After studying James 2 and 5, what should be the Christian life-style of a person who is blessed with great wealth?
3. How can you make your possessions a part of your life of faith? Why is it important that you not separate what you have from your responsibility to God?

*E*ach year a few individuals compete in what may be the most grueling athletic competition of all: a bicycle race across the U.S. Consider the obstacles: blazing deserts, towering mountain ranges, inclement weather, 18- to 20-hour stretches of pedaling, flat tires, potholes, skin-scraping spills, inconsiderate motorists, and sheer fatigue. It's *amazing* anyone ever finishes. The fact that some complete the 2,000-plus mile trip in *just over a week* is downright unbelievable! ■ How do they do it? ■ With the help of carefully trained support teams. These support teams follow the cyclists in specially equipped recreational vehicles, providing whatever the rider needs—food, drink, a repair job, a replacement bike, medical attention, a rubdown, a short nap, coaching, or a few shouts of encouragement. These support teams make an otherwise impossible trip very possible. ■ The Christian life is similar to that grueling bicycle marathon. The occasional joys of gliding downhill are obscured by the more frequent times of having to churn our way up steep mountain peaks. We get weary. We feel like quitting. The finish line seems far, far away. ■ Fortunately God has given us a first-rate support team to help us go the distance. With the Holy Spirit, the Word of God, and other believers to encourage us, we can not only finish the race, we can *win!* ■ Find out more about your spiritual support team in the book that follows, the book called 1 Peter.

■ (But don't wait too long. The race has already started!)

STATS

PURPOSE: To offer encouragement to suffering Christians

AUTHOR: Peter

TO WHOM WRITTEN: Jewish Christians who had been driven out of Jerusalem and scattered throughout Asia Minor; all believers everywhere

DATE WRITTEN: About A.D. 62–64 from Rome

SETTING: Peter was probably in Rome when the great persecution under Emperor Nero began (Peter was eventually executed during the persecution). Throughout the Roman Empire, Christians were being tortured and killed for their faith, and the church in Jerusalem was being scattered throughout the Mediterranean world.

KEY PEOPLE: Peter, Silvanus (Silas), Mark

KEY PLACES: Jerusalem, Rome, and the regions of Pontus, Galatia, Cappadocia, Asia Minor, and Bithynia

*P*eter

CHAPTER 1 GOD'S MISSIONARY. Peter, an apostle of Jesus Christ,

To the pilgrims of the Dispersion in Pontus, Galatia, Cappadocia, Asia, and Bithynia, ²elect according to the foreknowledge of God the Father, in sanctification of the Spirit, for obedience and sprinkling of the blood of Jesus Christ:

Grace to you and peace be multiplied.

³Blessed *be* the God and Father of our Lord Jesus Christ, who according to His abundant mercy has begotten us again to a living hope through the resurrection of Jesus Christ from the dead, ⁴to an inheritance incorruptible and undefiled and that does not fade away, reserved in heaven for you, ⁵who are kept by the power of God through faith for salvation ready to be revealed in the last time.

⁶In this you greatly rejoice, though now for a little while, if need be, you have been grieved by various trials,

⁷that the genuineness of your faith, *being* much more precious than gold that perishes, though it is tested by fire, may be found to praise, honor, and glory at the revelation of Jesus Christ, ⁸whom having not seen you love. Though now you do not see *Him,* yet believing, you rejoice with joy inexpressible and full of glory, ⁹receiving the end of your faith—the salvation of *your* souls.

¹⁰Of this salvation the prophets have inquired and searched carefully, who prophesied of the grace *that would come* to you, ¹¹searching what, or what manner of time, the Spirit of Christ who was in them was indicating

LIVE IN HOPE

1:3-6 Do you need encouragement? Peter's words offer joy and hope in times of trouble, and he bases his confidence on what God has done for us in Christ Jesus. We're called into a *living* hope of eternal life (1:3). Our hope is not only for the future; eternal life begins when we believe in God and join his family. The eternal life we now have gives us hope and enables us to live with confidence in God.

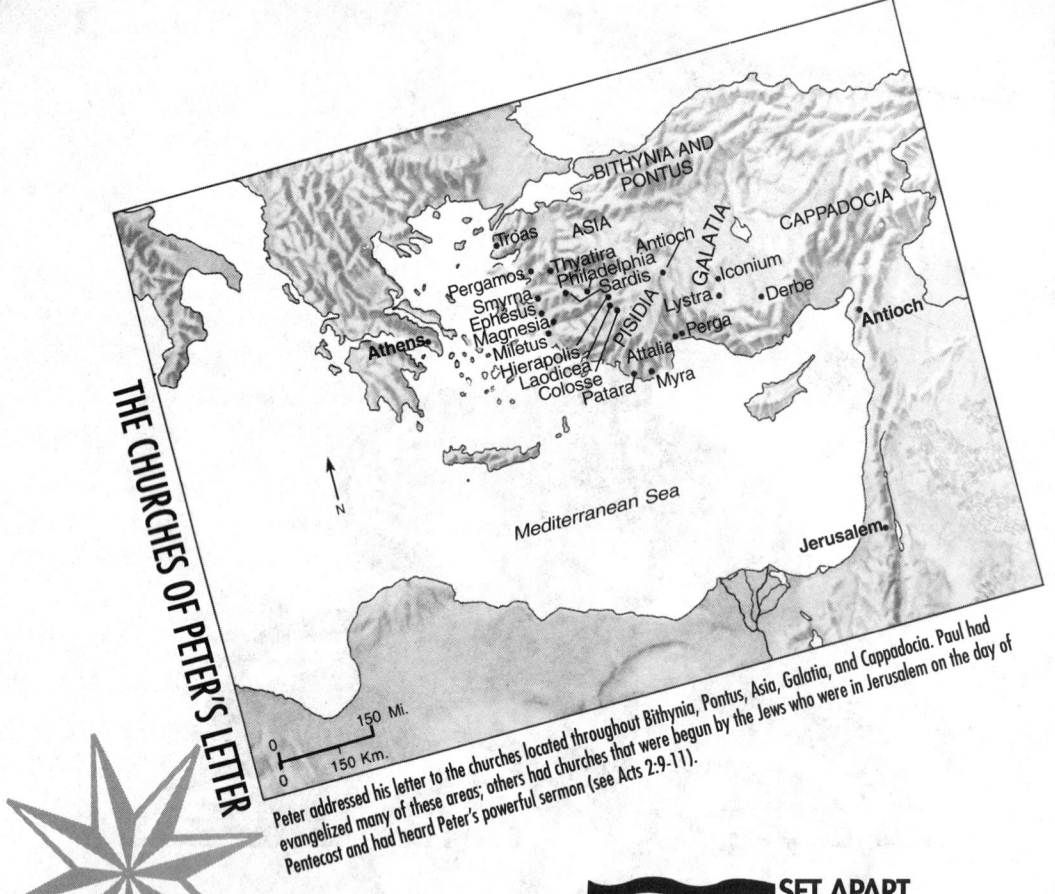

Peter addressed his letter to the churches located throughout Bithynia, Pontus, Asia, Galatia, and Cappadocia. Paul had evangelized many of these areas; others had churches that were begun by the Jews who were in Jerusalem on the day of Pentecost and had heard Peter's powerful sermon (see Acts 2:9-11).

when He testified beforehand the sufferings of Christ and the glories that would follow. ¹²To them it was revealed that, not to themselves, but to us they were min-

THE WORD OF THE LORD ENDURES ENDURES ENDURES FOREVER FOREVER FOREVER

SET APART

1:15-16 Peter tells us to be like our heavenly Father—holy in everything we do. Holiness means being totally devoted or dedicate God, set aside for his special use, and set apart from sin and its influ We're not to blend in with the crowd, yet we shouldn't be different be different. What makes us different are God's qualities in our life. focus and priorities must be his. All this is in direct contrast to our o ways (1:14). We cannot become holy on our own, but God gives us Holy Spirit to help us obey and to give us power to overcome sin. D use the excuse that you can't help slipping into sin. Ask all-powerful to free you from sin's grip.

istering the things which now have been reported to you through those who have preached the gospel to you by the Holy Spirit sent from heaven—things which angels desire to look into.

¹³Therefore gird up the loins of your mind, be sober, and rest *your* hope fully upon the grace that is to be brought to you at the revelation of Jesus Christ; ¹⁴as obedient children, not conforming yourselves to the former lusts, *as* in your ignorance; ¹⁵but as He who called you *is* holy, you also be holy in all *your* conduct, ¹⁶because it is written, *"Be holy, for I am holy."*

¹⁷And if you call on the Father, who without partiality judges according to each one's work, conduct yourselves throughout the time of your stay *here* in fear; ¹⁸knowing that you were not redeemed with corruptible things, *like* silver or gold, from your aimless conduct *received* by

radition from your fathers, [19]but with the precious blood of Christ, as of a lamb without blemish and without spot. [20]He indeed was foreordained before the foundation of the world, but was manifest in these last times for you [21]who through Him believe in God, who raised Him from the dead and gave Him glory, so that your faith and hope are in God.

[22]Since you have purified your souls in obeying the truth through the Spirit in sincere love of the brethren, love one another fervently with a pure heart, [23]having been born again, not of corruptible seed but incorruptible, through the word of God which lives and abides forever, [24]because

"All flesh is as grass,
And all the glory of man as the flower of the grass.
The grass withers,
And its flower falls away,
[25] *But the word of the LORD endures forever."*

Now this is the word which by the gospel was preached to you.

CHAPTER **2** A LIVING STONE FOR GOD'S HOUSE.
Therefore, laying aside all malice, all deceit, hypocrisy, envy, and all evil speaking, [2]as newborn babes, desire the pure milk of the word, that you may grow thereby, [3]if indeed you have tasted that the Lord *is* gracious.

[4]Coming to Him *as to* a living stone, rejected indeed by men, but chosen by God *and* precious, [5]you also, as living stones, are being built up a spiritual house, a holy priesthood, to offer up spiritual sacrifices acceptable to God through Jesus Christ. [6]Therefore it is also contained in the Scripture,

"Behold, I lay in Zion
A chief cornerstone, elect, precious,
And he who believes on Him will by no means be
*   put to shame."*

[7]Therefore, to you who believe, *He is* precious; but to those who are disobedient,

"The stone which the builders rejected
Has become the chief cornerstone,"

[8]and

"A stone of stumbling
And a rock of offense."

They stumble, being disobedient to the word, to which they also were appointed.

[9]But you *are* a chosen generation, a royal priesthood, a holy nation, His own special people, that you may proclaim the praises of Him who called you out of darkness into His marvelous light; [10]who once *were* not a people but *are* now the people of God, who had not obtained mercy but now have obtained mercy.

[11]Beloved, I beg *you* as sojourners and pilgrims, abstain from fleshly lusts which war against the soul, [12]having your conduct honorable among the Gentiles, that when they speak against you as evildoers, they may, by *your* good works which they observe, glorify God in the day of visitation.

[13]Therefore submit yourselves to every ordinance of man for the Lord's sake, whether to the king as supreme, [14]or to governors, as to those who are sent by him for the punishment of evildoers and *for the* praise of those who do good. [15]For this is the will of God, that by doing good you may put to silence the ignorance of foolish men— [16]as free, yet not using liberty as a cloak for vice, but as bondservants of God. [17]Honor all *people.* Love the brotherhood. Fear God. Honor the king.

It's hard to believe in anything you can't see. Why has God made it so difficult for people who would believe in him if they could only see him?
God is big, strong, powerful, and able to appear to anyone he wants. But if he did that, most people would feel forced or intimidated into following him, rather than loved into it. God wants us to respond out of love for him, not fear!

The truth is that people *can* see God . . . through the eyes of faith. This means taking God at his word—opening ourselves up to him. Some people say "seeing is believing." The truth is that "believing is seeing."

All of us believe in things we have never seen. A person in history. Gravity. The wind. Everyone has the capacity to believe things that aren't seen. The bottom line for most who say, "I can't believe in something I haven't seen," is "I won't believe in God, because I want to run my own life." God doesn't work that way. Each person must trust in Christ, acknowledging him as Savior.

Peter said that loving God, even though we have never seen him, will bring us "joy inexpressible" (1 Peter 1:8). Jesus said, "Blessed *are* those who have not seen and *yet* have believed" (John 20:29).

We live by faith, then we meet God.

I WONDER . . .

---

[18]Servants, *be* submissive to *your* masters with all fear, not only to the good and gentle, but also to the harsh. [19]For this *is* commendable, if because of conscience toward God one endures grief, suffering wrongfully. [20]For what credit *is it* if, when you are beaten for your faults, you take it patiently? But when you do good and suffer, if you take it patiently, this *is* commendable before God. [21]For to this you were called, because Christ also suffered for us, leaving us an example, that you should follow His steps:

[22] *"Who committed no sin,*
Nor was deceit found in His mouth";

[23]who, when He was reviled, did not revile in return; when He suffered, He did not threaten, but committed *Himself* to Him who judges righteously; [24]who Himself bore our sins in His own body on the tree, that we, having died to sins, might live for righteousness—by whose stripes you were healed. [25]For you were like sheep going astray, but have now returned to the Shepherd and Overseer of your souls.

PARTIES

It's prom time, and Courtney and Shelby are getting nervous.

Their problem?

Getting their dates, Terry and Peter, to forget the idea of an unchaperoned party in a hotel suite after the prom.

Maybe that situation seems simple to solve, but consider the facts:

- The girls are freshmen. Their dates are seniors and so are expected at the hotel.
- The party will feature an open bar and several available beds.
- Terry and Peter each have already kicked in $75 to pay for this private affair.
- A similar party last year featured some unbelievably wild activities.

"What are we gonna do?" Courtney pleads.

"Well, we could just tell our parents and let them get us out of this."

"Oh, right, Shelby! And get laughed out of school? We can't do that!"

"OK, what if we fake like we're sick or something?"

"Shelby!! And miss the whole prom? It's our first one—and I don't want it to be our last. Look, this whole mess isn't our fault. Let's just pray about it. Maybe God wants us to go and be good examples or something."

"OK," Shelby agrees.

The girls bow their heads.

Do Courtney and Shelby need to pray about such a decision? Especially when God's Word is pretty clear about Christians avoiding wild parties? See 1 Peter 4:3-6.

CHAPTER 3 ADVICE FOR HUSBANDS AND WIVES.

Wives, likewise, *be* submissive to your own husbands, that even if some do not obey the word, they, without a word, may be won by the conduct of their wives, [2]when

CUT DOWN

3:9 In our sinful world, it is acceptable to tear people down verbally or to get back at them if we feel hurt. Remembering Jesus' teaching to turn the other cheek (Matthew 5:39), Peter encourages his readers to pay back wrongs by praying for the offenders. In God's kingdom, revenge is unacceptable behavior. So is insulting a person, no matter how indirectly it is done. Rise above getting back at those who hurt you. Instead, pray for them.

they observe your chaste conduct *accompanied* by fear. [3]Do not let your adornment be *merely* outward—arranging the hair, wearing gold, or putting on *fine* apparel—[4]rather *let it be* the hidden person of the heart, with the incorruptible *beauty* of a gentle and quiet spirit, which is very precious in the sight of God. [5]For in this manner, in former times, the holy women who trusted in God also adorned themselves, being submissive to their own husbands, [6]as Sarah obeyed Abraham, calling him lord, whose daughters you are if you do good and are not afraid with any terror.

[7]Husbands, likewise, dwell with *them* with understanding, giving honor to the wife, as to the weaker vessel, and as *being* heirs together of the grace of life, that your prayers may not be hindered.

---

[8]Finally, all *of you be* of one mind, having compassion for one another; love as brothers, *be* tenderhearted, be courteous; [9]not returning evil for evil or reviling for reviling, but on the contrary blessing, knowing that you were called to this, that you may inherit a blessing. [10]For

"He who would love life
And see good days,

SPEAK UP

3:15 Some Christians believe that faith is a personal matter and should be kept to oneself. It is true that we shouldn't be boisterous or obnoxious in sharing our faith, but we should always be ready to answer, gently and respectfully, when asked about our beliefs, our life-style, or our Christian perspective. Will you tell others what God has done in your life?

Let him refrain his tongue from evil,
And his lips from speaking deceit.
[11] *Let him turn away from evil and do good;*
Let him seek peace and pursue it.
[12] *For the eyes of the LORD are on the righteous,*
And His ears are open to their prayers;
But the face of the LORD is against those who do evil.

[13]And who *is* he who will harm you if you become followers of what is good? [14]But even if you should suffer for righteousness' sake, *you are* blessed. *"And do not be afraid of their threats, nor be troubled."* [15]But sanctify the Lord God in your hearts, and always *be* ready to *give a* defense to everyone who asks you a reason for the hope that is in you, with meekness and fear; [16]having a good conscience, that when they defame you as evildoers, those who revile your good conduct in Christ may be ashamed. [17]For *it is* better, if it is the will of God, to suffer for doing good than for doing evil.

[18]For Christ also suffered once for sins, the just for the unjust, that He might bring us to God, being put to death in the flesh but made alive by the Spirit, [19]by whom also He went and preached to the spirits in prison, [20]who formerly were disobedient, when once the Divine longsuffering waited in the days of Noah, while *the* ark was being prepared, in which a few, that is, eight souls were saved through water. [21]There is also an antitype which now saves us—baptism (not the removal of the filth of the flesh, but the answer of a good conscience toward God), through the resurrection of Jesus Christ, [22]who has gone into heaven and is at the right hand of God, angels and authorities and powers having been made subject to Him.

CHAPTER 4 CONTINUE TO LOVE ONE ANOTHER.

Therefore, since Christ suffered for us in the flesh, arm

GOOD MARKS

4:16 It is not shameful to suffer for being a Christian. When Peter and John were persecuted for preaching the Good News, they rejoiced because such persecution was a mark of God's approval of their work (Acts 5:41). Don't seek out suffering, and don't try to avoid it. Instead, keep on doing what is right regardless of the suffering it might bring.

yourselves also with the same mind, for he who has suffered in the flesh has ceased from sin, [2]that he no longer should live the rest of *his* time in the flesh for the lusts of men, but for the will of God. [3]For we *have spent* enough of our past lifetime in doing the will of the Gentiles—when we walked in lewdness, lusts, drunkenness, revelries, drinking parties, and abominable idolatries. [4]In regard to these, they think it strange that you do not run with *them* in the same flood of dissipation, speaking evil of *you.* [5]They will give an account to Him who is ready to judge the living and the dead. [6]For this reason the gospel was preached also to those who are dead, that they might be judged according to men in the flesh, but live according to God in the spirit.

[7]But the end of all things is at hand; therefore be serious and watchful in your prayers. [8]And above all things have fervent love for one another, for *"love will cover a multitude of sins."* [9]*Be* hospitable to one another without grumbling. [10]As each one has received a gift, minister it to one another, as good stewards of the manifold grace of God. [11]If anyone speaks, *let him speak* as the oracles of God. If anyone ministers, *let him do it* as with the ability which God supplies, that in all things God may be glorified through Jesus Christ, to whom belong the glory and the dominion forever and ever. Amen.

[12]Beloved, do not think it strange concerning the fiery trial which is to try you, as though some strange thing happened to you; [13]but rejoice to the extent that you partake of Christ's sufferings, that when His glory is revealed, you may also be glad with exceeding joy. [14]If you are reproached for the name of Christ, blessed *are you,* for the Spirit of glory and of God rests upon you. On their part He is blasphemed, but on your part He is glorified. [15]But let none of you suffer as a murderer, a thief, an evildoer, or as a busybody in other people's matters. [16]Yet if *anyone suffers* as a Christian, let him not be ashamed, but let him glorify God in this matter.

[17]For the time *has come* for judgment to begin at the house of God; and if *it begins* with us first, what will *be* the end of those who do not obey the gospel of God? [18]Now

> *"If the righteous one is scarcely saved,*
> *Where will the ungodly and the sinner appear?"*

[19]Therefore let those who suffer according to the will of God commit their souls *to Him* in doing good, as to a faithful Creator.

CHAPTER **5** ADVICE FOR TEACHERS AND STUDENTS.

The elders who are among you I exhort, I who am a fellow elder and a witness of the sufferings of Christ, and also a partaker of the glory that will be revealed: [2]Shepherd the flock of God which is among you, serving as overseers, not by compulsion but willingly, not for dishonest gain but eagerly; [3]nor as being lords over those entrusted to you, but being examples to the flock; [4]and when the Chief Shepherd appears, you will receive the crown of glory that does not fade away.

[5]Likewise you younger people, submit yourselves to *your* elders. Yes, all of *you* be submissive to one another, and be clothed with humility, for

> *"God resists the proud,*
> *But gives grace to the humble."*

[6]Therefore humble yourselves under the mighty hand of God, that He may exalt you in due time, [7]casting all your care upon Him, for He cares for you.

[8]Be sober, be vigilant; because your adversary the devil walks about like a roaring lion, seeking whom he may devour. [9]Resist him, steadfast in the faith, knowing that the same sufferings are experienced by your

"Here's what I did..."

I attended a Christian school during junior high and the first year of high school. But after three years at Christian schools, I felt led to go back to a public school. I talked it over in depth with my parents. They supported me, but reminded me of how difficult it could be because of all the pressures to live for yourself, not for God.

They were right—the pressures and temptations were greater. I didn't know quite how to be a Christian in that atmosphere. I was afraid people would make fun of me once they found out I was a Christian, yet I was determined not to hide my faith. After all, I knew Jesus, the one person in this life who will never let me down. I wanted to share my faith with the new friends I was making.

I decided to adopt 1 Peter 3:15 as my key verse to get me through public school. It shows me how to live my life in that setting, among people who really need to hear some Good News.

This verse helps me keep in line in difficult situations. For instance, if I'm at a party and drinking only Coke, often someone will ask me why I'm not drinking any alcohol. I tell them that I don't need alcohol to help me have a good time, and that Jesus helps me to enjoy life and people just as they are. Most people respect me when I say that. (Even when they don't, as it says in 1 Peter 3:16-17, it's better that they mock me for doing something right than for making a fool of myself for getting drunk.)

First Peter 3:15 helps me overcome temptations like this and reminds me of my purpose for being in a public school: to be ready to tell people of the hope I have in Jesus.

Jenny AGE 16

5:5 Both young and old can benefit from Peter's instructions. Pride often keeps elders from trying to understand young people and young people from listening to their elders. Peter's instructions go both ways: he told both young and old to be humble, to serve each other. Young men should follow the leadership of older men, who should lead by example. Respect your elders, listen to those younger than you, and be humble enough to admit that you can learn from each other.

brotherhood in the world. [10]But may the God of all grace, who called us to His eternal glory by Christ Jesus, after you have suffered a while, perfect, establish, strengthen, and settle *you*. [11]To Him *be* the glory and the dominion forever and ever. Amen.

[12]By Silvanus, our faithful brother as I consider him, I have written to you briefly, exhorting and testifying that this is the true grace of God in which you stand.

[13]She who is in Babylon, elect together with *you*, greets you; and *so does* Mark my son. [14]Greet one another with a kiss of love.

Peace to you all who are in Christ Jesus. Amen.

MEGA Themes

SALVATION Salvation is a gracious gift from God. God chose us out of his love for us, Jesus died to pay the penalty for our sin, and the Holy Spirit cleansed us from sin when we believed. Eternal life is a wonderful privilege for those who trust in Christ.

Our safety and security are in God. If we experience joy in relationship with Christ now, how much greater will our joy be when he returns and we see him face-to-face! Such a hope should motivate us to serve Christ even more.

1. What are the blessings of our salvation that have been revealed to us through Jesus?
2. Why would this be such an important message for Jewish Christians who had been suffering for their faith?
3. What does it mean to you to be saved? Include your feelings, the present benefits, and your hope for the future.
4. How can you communicate this through your life to someone who is without Christ? Why is it important that others come to know Christ?

PERSECUTION Peter offers faithful believers comfort and hope. We should expect ridicule, rejection, and suffering because we are Christians. Persecution makes us stronger because it refines our faith. We can face persecution victoriously as Christ did, if we rely on him.

We don't have to be terrified by persecution. The fact that we will live eternally with Christ should give us the confidence, patience, and hope to stand firm even when we are persecuted. Suffering can glorify God.

1. Read 2:21-25. Describe Jesus' response to suffering.
2. How does Jesus' example provide encouragement and inspiration during suffering?
3. How do fellow believers provide encouragement and inspiration during suffering?
4. When you face ridicule or oppression for your faith, what are the specific ways that you can cope with this suffering?

GOD'S FAMILY We are privileged to belong to God's family, a community with Christ as the Founder and Foundation. Everyone in this community is related—we are all brothers and sisters, loved equally by God.

We must be devoted, loyal, and faithful to Christ, the foundation of our family. Through obedience, we show that we are his children. We must live differently from the society around us. Our relationships are to be patterned by what we see in Christ, not by what we see in the world.

1. List the specific teachings concerning Christian fellowship in 4:7-11.
2. Who are the people who have ministered Christ's love and grace to you? In what ways have they provided this love and grace?
3. Why is it necessary for you and other believers to be providers of his love to one another?
4. In what two ways will you become a part of God's love and grace in the life of fellow believers this week?

FAMILY LIFE Peter encouraged the wives of unbelievers to submit to the authority of their husband as a means of winning them to Christ. He urged all family members to treat others with sympathy, love, tenderness, and humility.

We must treat our families lovingly. Though it's never easy, willing service is the best way to influence our loved ones. To gain the needed strength, we must pray for God's help. Relationships with parents, brothers and sisters, and spouses are important aspects of Christian discipleship.

1. In 1 Peter, what principles do you find for a godly marriage?
2. How could 3:6 be misused by a domineering husband? What corrective does God's Word provide against misusing this husband-wife relationship? (Also check Ephesians 5.)
3. What qualities do you want in a marriage partner someday?
4. What qualities do you think your mate will desire in you? How can you develop those qualities so that you bring godliness and maturity to your marriage?

JUDGMENT God will judge everyone with perfect justice. He will punish evildoers and those who persecute his people; those who love God will be rewarded with life forever in his presence.

Because all are accountable to God, we can leave judgment of others to him. We must not hate or resent those who persecute us. We should realize that we will be held responsible for how we live each day.

1. What will happen to those without Christ when they face God's judgment?
2. What difference will having Jesus as your Lord make when you face God's judgment?
3. Review 1:14-25. If you will not be condemned because of Jesus, why should God's holiness continue to be your motivation for living a holy life?
4. What are the specific areas of your life that still need to become holy through obedience to Christ? How can this be accomplished?

We've all come face-to-face with life's ironies: ■ One man, noting the regularity (and certainty) of these quirks, decided to make a list. The result? The famous "Murphy's Laws." ■ Some of Murphy's more interesting observations: ■ If anything *can* go wrong it *will*. ■ "Broken" gadgets will operate perfectly in the presence of a repairman. ■ Saying "Watch this!" guarantees that the behavior you want others to witness will not happen. ■ A poorly thrown Frisbee will always come to rest under the exact center of a parked car. ■ Stored objects are never needed . . . until immediately after they are discarded. ■ The bowl that breaks is never the one that was already chipped. ■ The other line always moves faster. ■ If you put a napkin in your lap you will not spill; failure to use a napkin ensures spillage. ■ You will only be forced to wait when you do not have time to wait. ■ We nod and smile at those "laws" because we've lived them. They're amazingly true to life. How about some other laws of life? Perhaps not as humorous, but just as true—and much more life-changing: ■ Spiritual growth only happens when we get to know God and make the effort to serve him. ■ The world is full of people who will try to lead you astray. ■ Jesus Christ is coming back. ■ Would you like to know more about these critical principles? They're all contained in the book that follows, the Bible book we call 2 Peter.

STATS

PURPOSE: To warn Christians about false teachers and to exhort them to grow in their faith and knowledge of Christ

AUTHOR: Peter

TO WHOM WRITTEN: The church at large

DATE WRITTEN: About A.D. 67, three years after 1 Peter was written, possibly from Rome

SETTING: Peter knew that his time on earth was limited (1:13-14), so he was writing about what was on his heart, warning believers of what would happen when he was gone—especially about false teachers. He reminded believers of the unchanging truth of the gospel.

KEY PEOPLE: Peter, Paul

SPECIAL FEATURES: The date and destination are uncertain, and the authorship has been disputed. Because of this, 2 Peter was the last epistle admitted to the canon of the New Testament Scripture. Also, there are similarities between 2 Peter and Jude.

2Peter

CHAPTER **1** **STEPS TO SPIRITUAL GROWTH.** Simon Peter, a bondservant and apostle of Jesus Christ,

To those who have obtained like precious faith with us by the righteousness of our God and Savior Jesus Christ:

²Grace and peace be multiplied to you in the knowledge of God and of Jesus our Lord, ³as His divine power has given to us all things that *pertain* to life and godliness, through the knowledge of Him who called us by glory and virtue, ⁴by which have been given to us exceedingly great and precious promises, that through these you may be partakers of the divine nature, having escaped the corruption *that is* in the world through lust.

⁵But also for this very reason, giving all diligence, add to your faith virtue, to virtue knowledge, ⁶to knowledge self-control, to self-control perseverance, to perseverance godliness, ⁷to godliness brotherly kindness, and to brotherly kindness love. ⁸For if these things are yours and abound, *you will be* neither barren nor unfruitful in the

PERSEVERE!

1:5-9 Faith must be more than belief in certain facts; it must result in action, growth in Christian character, and the practice of moral discipline, or it will die (James 2:14-17). Peter lists several of faith's actions: learning to know God better, developing perseverance, doing God's will, loving others. These actions do not come automatically; they require hard work. They are not optional; all must be a continual part of the Christian life. We need to work on them all together, not one at a time. If it sounds tough, don't worry; God will help us to become what he wants us to be.

knowledge of our Lord Jesus Christ. ⁹For he who lacks these things is shortsighted, even to blindness, and has forgotten that he was cleansed from his old sins.

¹⁰Therefore, brethren, be even more diligent to make your call and election sure, for if you do these things you will never stumble; ¹¹for so an entrance will be supplied to you abundantly into the everlasting kingdom of our Lord and Savior Jesus Christ.

¹²For this reason I will not be negligent to remind you always of these things, though you know and are established in the present truth. ¹³Yes, I think it is right, as long as I am in this tent, to stir you up by reminding *you*, ¹⁴knowing that shortly I *must* put off my tent, just as our Lord Jesus Christ showed me. ¹⁵Moreover I will be careful to ensure that you always have a reminder of these things after my decease.

never came by the will of man, but holy men of God spoke *as they were* moved by the Holy Spirit.

CHAPTER **2** **BEWARE OF FALSE TEACHERS.** But there were also false prophets among the people, even as there will be false teachers among you, who will secretly bring in destructive heresies, even denying the Lord who

◥◥◥◥◥◥◥◥◥◥EFFORT

1:6 False teachers were saying that self-control was not needed b works do not help the believer anyway (2:19). It is true that works cannot save us, but it is absolutely false to think they are unimport We are saved so that we can grow to resemble Christ and so that w serve others. God wants to produce his character in us. But to do th demands effort from us. To grow spiritually, we must develop self-c

bought them, *and* bring on themselves swift destruction. ²And many will follow their destructive ways, because of whom the way of truth will be blasphemed. ³By covetousness they will exploit you with deceptive words; for a long time their judgment has not been idle, and their destruction does not slumber.

⁴For if God did not spare the angels who sinned, but cast *them* down to hell and delivered *them* into chains of darkness, to be reserved for judgment; ⁵and did not

▲▲▲▲▲▲▲▲▲▲▲▲▲▲▲▲▲▲

*C*ULTS A month ago, while on a city bus, Patricia picked up a discarded leaflet advertising a free music festival and complimentary vegetarian meal. She called her friend Elaine, and the two of them went to see what it was all about.

The whole afternoon Elaine was whispering, "Let's get out of here. This is weird!" But Patricia kept replying, "Lighten up, Elaine! You're too intense."

On the way home, Elaine made it clear what she thought. "Look, I don't care what you say. That group is some kind of cult or something."

"Why? Name one thing they did or said that was bad."

"Well, I don't know—they gave me the creeps."

"Aw, I think you're paranoid. Who knows? I just might go to one of their classes."

Patricia did go back. And now she's a full-fledged member of the "church," The Society of Enlightened Minds. The people there accept her and make her feel special.

Elaine's parents did some checking. Patricia's "church" doesn't accept the Bible; nor does it believe that Christ is God. It teaches that each of us is a god and that together, we can recreate the world.

With their popular, feel-good philosophies, dangerous cult groups are capturing millions of hungry hearts and uncritical minds. No wonder we are told in 2 Peter 2:17-22 to carefully consider the ideas that we hear every day. Read it and heed it!

▲▲▲▲▲▲▲▲▲▲▲▲▲▲▲▲▲▲▲▲▲▲▲▲▲▲

¹⁶For we did not follow cunningly devised fables when we made known to you the power and coming of our Lord Jesus Christ, but were eyewitnesses of His majesty. ¹⁷For He received from God the Father honor and glory when such a voice came to Him from the Excellent Glory: "This is My beloved Son, in whom I am well pleased." ¹⁸And we heard this voice which came from heaven when we were with Him on the holy mountain.

¹⁹And so we have the prophetic word confirmed, which you do well to heed as a light that shines in a dark place, until the day dawns and the morning star rises in your hearts; ²⁰knowing this first, that no prophecy of Scripture is of any private interpretation, ²¹for prophecy

THE DAY OF THE LORD WILL COME *as a thief...*

2 PETER 3:10-11

WHAT MANNER OF PERSONS OUGHT YOU TO BE IN HOLY CONDUCT AND GODLINESS?

spare the ancient world, but saved Noah, *one of* eight *people*, a preacher of righteousness, bringing in the flood on the world of the ungodly; ⁶and turning the cities of Sodom and Gomorrah into ashes, condemned *them* to destruction, making *them* an example to those who afterward would live ungodly; ⁷and delivered righteous Lot, *who was* oppressed by the filthy conduct of the wicked ⁸(for that righteous man, dwelling among them, tormented *his* righteous soul from day to day by seeing and hearing *their* lawless deeds)— ⁹*then* the Lord knows how to deliver the godly out of temptations and to reserve the unjust under punishment for the day of judgment, ¹⁰and especially those who walk according to the flesh in the lust of uncleanness and despise authority. *They are* presumptuous, self-willed. They are not afraid to speak evil of dignitaries, ¹¹whereas angels, who are greater in power and might, do not bring a reviling accusation against them before the Lord.

¹²But these, like natural brute beasts made to be caught and destroyed, speak evil of the things they do not understand, and will utterly perish in their own corruption, ¹³*and* will receive the wages of unrighteousness, *as* those who count it pleasure to carouse in the daytime. *They are* spots and blemishes, carousing in their own deceptions while they feast with you, ¹⁴having eyes full of adultery and that cannot cease from sin, enticing unstable souls. *They have* a heart trained in covetous practices, *and are* accursed children. ¹⁵They have forsaken the right way and gone astray, following the way of Balaam the *son* of Beor, who loved the wages of unrighteousness; ¹⁶but he was rebuked for his iniquity: a dumb donkey speaking with a man's voice restrained the madness of the prophet.

¹⁷These are wells without water, clouds carried by a tempest, for whom is reserved the blackness of darkness forever.

¹⁸For when they speak great swelling *words* of emptiness, they allure through the lusts of the flesh, through lewdness, the ones who have actually escaped from those who live in error. ¹⁹While they promise them liberty, they themselves are slaves of corruption; for by whom a person is overcome, by him also he is brought into bondage. ²⁰For if, after they have escaped the pollutions of the world through the knowledge of the Lord and Savior Jesus Christ, they are again entangled in them and overcome, the latter end is worse for them than the beginning. ²¹For it would have been better for them not to have known the way of righteousness, than having known *it*, to turn from the holy commandment delivered to them. ²²But it

has happened to them according to the true proverb: *"A dog returns to his own vomit,"* and, "a sow, having washed, to her wallowing in the mire."

CHAPTER **3** HOPE FOR GROWING CHRISTIANS.

Beloved, I now write to you this second epistle (in *both of* which I stir up your pure minds by way of reminder), ²that you may be mindful of the words which were spoken before by the holy prophets, and of the commandment of us, the apostles of the Lord and Savior, ³knowing

FREEDOM

2:19 Many people believe that freedom means doing anything you want. But no one is ever completely free in that way. If we refuse to follow God, we will follow our own sinful desires and become enslaved to what our body wants. If we submit our life to Christ, he will free us from slavery to sin. Christ frees us to serve him, and that will always result in our ultimate good.

this first: that scoffers will come in the last days, walking according to their own lusts, ⁴and saying, "Where is the promise of His coming? For since the fathers fell asleep, all things continue as *they were* from the beginning of creation." ⁵For this they willfully forget: that by the word of God the heavens were of old, and the earth standing out of water and in the water, ⁶by which the world *that*

"Here's what I did..."

I didn't want to break up with my girlfriend, but the more I prayed about the relationship, the more I saw that it was interfering with my relationship with God. My girlfriend wasn't a Christian; her values were completely different from mine. I cared about her, but it came down to a choice: either her or God.

The clincher came when I read 2 Peter 1:5-8. It says: "But also for this very reason, giving all diligence, add to your faith virtue, to virtue knowledge, to knowledge self-control, to self-control perseverance, to perseverance godliness, to godliness brotherly kindness, and to brotherly kindness love. For if these things are yours and abound, *you will be* neither barren nor unfruitful in the knowledge of our Lord Jesus Christ."

I didn't need anymore guidance; I knew I had to break up and concentrate on strengthening my relationship with the Lord. Though I felt bad after breaking up, I was confident that I had done the right thing and that the Lord still cared about me and my decisions.

I also was encouraged. God was showing me that I was slowly but surely becoming stronger spiritually. Every verse of that passage fit a part of my life. As I put God first and determined to obey him, I could see times when I put aside my own desires and how I was becoming more patient, etc. Yes, breaking up was hard, but knowing that I did it to obey God made all the difference.

Joel
AGE 16

then existed perished, being flooded with water. [7]But the heavens and the earth *which* are now preserved by the same word, are reserved for fire until the day of judgment and perdition of ungodly men.

[8]But, beloved, do not forget this one thing, that with the Lord one day *is* as a thousand years, and a thousand years as one day. [9]The Lord is not slack concerning *His* promise, as some count slackness, but is longsuffering toward us, not willing that any should perish but that all should come to repentance.

[10]But the day of the Lord will come as a thief in the night, in which the heavens will pass away with a great noise, and the elements will melt with fervent heat; both the earth and the works that are in it will be burned up. [11]Therefore, since all these things will be dissolved, what manner *of persons* ought you to be in holy conduct and godliness, [12]looking for and hastening the coming of the day of God, because of which the heavens will be dissolved, being on fire, and the elements will melt with fervent heat? [13]Nevertheless we, according to His promise, look for new heavens and a new earth in which righteousness dwells.

[14]Therefore, beloved, looking forward to these things, be diligent to be found by Him in peace, without spot and blameless; [15]and consider *that* the longsuffering of our Lord *is* salvation—as also our beloved brother Paul,

◤▬▬▬▬▬ANY DAY

3:14 We should not become lazy and complacent because Christ yet returned. Instead, our life should express our eager expectati coming. What would you like to be doing when Christ returns? Is t way you are living each day?

according to the wisdom given to him, has written to you, [16]as also in all his epistles, speaking in them of these things, in which are some things hard to understand, which untaught and unstable *people* twist to their own destruction, as *they do* also the rest of the Scriptures.

[17]You therefore, beloved, since you know *this* beforehand, beware lest you also fall from your own steadfastness, being led away with the error of the wicked; [18]but grow in the grace and knowledge of our Lord and Savior Jesus Christ.

To Him *be* the glory both now and forever. Amen.

MEGA *Themes*

DILIGENCE If our faith is real, it will be evident in our faithful behavior. If people are diligent in Christian growth, they won't backslide or be deceived by false teachers.

Growth is essential. It begins with faith and culminates in love for others. To keep growing, we need to know God, keep on following him, and remember what he taught us. It may not always be easy, but it will always be worthwhile.

1. According to chapter 1, what are the attitudes and actions that lead to maturity?
2. If a Christian friend were to ask you, "How are you growing?" what would be your response?

3. Based on this study, identify five practical steps to personal spiritual growth.
4. How and when will you apply these five steps to your relationship with God?

FALSE TEACHERS Peter warns the church to beware of false teachers. These teachers were proud of their position, promoted sexual sin, and advised against keeping the Ten Commandments. Peter countered them by pointing to the Spirit-inspired Scriptures as our authority.

Christians need discernment to resist false teachers. God can rescue us from their lies if we stay true to his Word, the Bible, and reject those who twist the truth. The truth is our best defense because it exposes the lies of those who try to deceive us.

1. Contrast the lives of the false teachers with the lives of those who follow God's truth.
2. Why can God's Word be trusted more than all teachers?
3. What false teaching have you heard about God and Jesus?
4. What would you say to someone who wanted to be certain not to fall into the deception of a false teacher?

CHRIST'S RETURN One day Christ will create a new heaven and earth where we will live forever. As Christians, our hope is in this promise. But with Christ's return comes his judgment on all who refuse to believe.

The cure for complacency, lawlessness, and heresy is found in the confident assurance that Christ will return. God is still giving unbelievers time to repent. To be ready, Christians must keep on trusting Christ and resist the pressure to give up waiting for his return.

1. What reason does Peter give for Christ's patience in waiting to return?
2. How does Peter say we should live in light of Christ's expected return?
3. How do most Christians view Christ's eventual return?
4. What difference does Christ's expected return make in your life?

*L*ove. ■ We can't touch it, count it, bottle it, or even see it. But who among us would argue that love isn't real? ■ Love. ■ It makes sane people do and say crazy things. It prompts snobby, selfish people to do noble things. It turns boring people into exciting, unpredictable creatures. What else on earth has that kind of power? ■ Love. ■ It can hurt like nothing else in the world. And yet, paradoxically, *not* loving is much more painful. ■ Love. ■ The most talked-about and sung-about and thought-about theme in all the world. And also the most misunderstood. ■ Love. ■ Would you like to know more about it and see it in a brand new light? Then read *1 John*, the most eloquent description of love ever penned. ■ Love. ■ It's not everything you think it is. It's more . . . much, much more.

STATS

PURPOSE: To reassure Christians in their faith and to counter false teachings

AUTHOR: The apostle John

TO WHOM WRITTEN: The letter is untitled and was written to no particular church. It was sent as a pastoral letter to several Gentile congregations. It was also written to all believers everywhere.

DATE WRITTEN: Probably between A.D. 85 and 90 from Ephesus

SETTING: John was an older man and perhaps the only surviving apostle at this time. He had not yet been banished to the island of Patmos, where he would live in exile. As an eyewitness of Christ, he wrote authoritatively to give this new generation of believers assurance and confidence in God and in their faith.

KEY PEOPLE: John, Jesus

SPECIAL FEATURES: John is the apostle of love, and love is mentioned throughout this letter. There are a number of similarities in vocabulary, style, and main ideas between this letter and John's Gospel. John uses brief statements and simple words, and he features sharp contrasts—light and darkness, truth and error, God and Satan, life and death, love and hate.

John

CHAPTER 1 JESUS CHRIST IS ETERNAL LIFE. That which was from the beginning, which we have heard, which we have seen with our eyes, which we have looked upon, and our hands have handled, concerning the Word of life— ²the life was manifested, and we have seen, and bear witness, and declare to you that eternal life which was with the Father and was manifested to us— ³that which we have seen and heard we declare to you, that you also may have fellowship with us; and truly our fellowship *is* with the Father and with His Son Jesus Christ. ⁴And these things we write to you that your joy may be full.

⁵This is the message which we have heard from Him and declare to you, that God is light and in Him is no darkness at all. ⁶If we say that we have fellowship with Him, and walk in darkness, we lie and do not practice the truth. ⁷But if we walk in the light as He is in the light, we have fellowship with one another, and the blood of Jesus Christ His Son cleanses us from all sin.

⁸If we say that we have no sin, we deceive ourselves, and the truth is not in us. ⁹If we confess our sins, He is

OVER & OVER

1:9 Confession frees us to enjoy fellowship with Christ. But some Christians do not understand confession. They feel guilty that they confess the same sins over and over, and then they wonder if they have forgotten something. Others believe that if they died with unconfessed sins, they would be lost forever. But *God wants to forgive us.* He allowed his beloved Son to die so he could pardon us. We don't need to confess the same sins all over again, and we don't need to be afraid that God will reject us if we don't keep our slate perfectly clear. Since our hope in Christ is secure, we should confess so that we can enjoy maximum fellowship and joy with Christ. And we must pray for strength to defeat the temptation the next time it appears.

2:9-11 Does this mean if you dislike anyone you aren't a Christian? These verses are not talking about disliking a disagreeable Christian brother or sister. There will always be people we will not like as well as others. John's words focus on the attitude that causes us to ignore or despise others, to treat them as irritants, competitors, or enemies. Fortunately, Christian love is not a feeling but a choice. We can choose to be concerned with people's well-being and to treat them with respect, whether or not we feel affection toward them. If we choose to love others, God will give us the necessary strength and will show us how to express our love.

faithful and just to forgive us *our* sins and to cleanse us from all unrighteousness. [10]If we say that we have not sinned, we make Him a liar, and His word is not in us.

LOVE   At a slumber party, Wendy makes the terrible mistake of being the first to fall asleep. A few hours later she is awakened by a funny smell and a damp feeling on her head. Staggering into the bathroom, she discovers her hair is filled with petroleum jelly, shaving cream, eggs, honey, and flour . . . all great products, but not exactly the sort of things you want to wear in your hair.

As she tries (in vain) to wash all the glop out, Wendy hears giggles and whispers coming from the living room.

Guess how Wendy feels?
(a) angry
(b) sad
(c) hurt
(d) rejected
(e) all of the above
You guessed it: (e) describes *exactly* how she feels.
Guess what Wendy wants to do?
(a) leave
(b) tell her friends off
(c) get back at them
(d) cry
(e) all of the above
That's right: (e) again. You are *so* smart!

So what does Wendy *actually* do? Here's the shocker: She prays and asks the Lord to give her the strength to love her friends in spite of what they have done. Later, when she has the chance to get back at them, she refuses.

Why is Wendy being so kind when her friends are being so mean? Because 1 John 4:7-21 is real to her. Check it out.

CHAPTER 2 LOVE GOD, NOT THIS WORLD. My little children, these things I write to you, so that you may not sin. And if anyone sins, we have an Advocate with the Father, Jesus Christ the righteous. [2]And He Himself is the propitiation for our sins, and not for ours only but also for the whole world.

[3]Now by this we know that we know Him, if we keep His commandments. [4]He who says, "I know Him," and does not keep His commandments, is a liar, and the truth

is not in him. [5]But whoever keeps His word, truly the love of God is perfected in him. By this we know that we are in Him. [6]He who says he abides in Him ought himself also to walk just as He walked.

[7]Brethren, I write no new commandment to you, but an old commandment which you have had from the beginning. The old commandment is the word which you heard from the beginning. [8]Again, a new commandment I write to you, which thing is true in Him and in you, because the darkness is passing away, and the true light is already shining.

[9]He who says he is in the light, and hates his brother, is in darkness until now. [10]He who loves his brother abides in the light, and there is no cause for stumbling in him. [11]But he who hates his brother is in darkness and walks in darkness, and does not know where he is going, because the darkness has blinded his eyes.

[12] I write to you, little children,
Because your sins are forgiven you for His name's sake.
[13] I write to you, fathers,
Because you have known Him *who is* from the beginning.
I write to you, young men,
Because you have overcome the wicked one.
I write to you, little children,
Because you have known the Father.
[14] I have written to you, fathers,

BEHOLD
WHAT MANNER
OF LOVE
THE
FATHER
has bestowed on us,
THAT
we should
be called
children
of GOD!

Because you have known Him *who is* from the beginning.

I have written to you, young men,
Because you are strong, and the word of God abides in you,
And you have overcome the wicked one.

¹⁵Do not love the world or the things in the world. If anyone loves the world, the love of the Father is not in him. ¹⁶For all that *is* in the world—the lust of the flesh, the lust of the eyes, and the pride of life—is not of the Father but is of the world. ¹⁷And the world is passing away, and the lust of it; but he who does the will of God abides forever.

¹⁸Little children, it is the last hour; and as you have heard that the Antichrist is coming, even now many antichrists have come, by which we know that it is the last hour. ¹⁹They went out from us, but they were not of us; for if they had been of us, they would have continued with us; but *they went out* that they might be made manifest, that none of them were of us.

²⁰But you have an anointing from the Holy One, and you know all things. ²¹I have not written to you because you do not know the truth, but because you know it, and that no lie is of the truth.

²²Who is a liar but he who denies that Jesus is the Christ? He is antichrist who denies the Father and the Son. ²³Whoever denies the Son does not have the Father either; he who acknowledges the Son has the Father also.

²⁴Therefore let that abide in you which you heard from the beginning. If what you heard from the beginning abides in you, you also will abide in the Son and in the Father. ²⁵And this is the promise that He has promised us—eternal life.

²⁶These things I have written to you concerning those who *try to* deceive you. ²⁷But the anointing which you have received from Him abides in you, and you do not need that anyone teach you; but as the same anointing teaches you concerning all things, and is true, and is not a lie, and just as it has taught you, you will abide in Him.

²⁸And now, little children, abide in Him, that when He appears, we may have confidence and not be ashamed before Him at His coming. ²⁹If you know that He is righteous, you know that everyone who practices righteousness is born of Him.

CHAPTER **3** WE ARE GOD'S CHILDREN.

Behold what manner of love the Father has bestowed on us, that we should be called children of

God! Therefore the world does not know us, because it did not know Him. ²Beloved, now we are children of God; and it has not yet been revealed what we shall be, but we know that when He is revealed, we shall be like Him, for we shall see Him as He is. ³And everyone who has this hope in Him purifies himself, just as He is pure.

⁴Whoever commits sin also commits lawlessness, and sin is lawlessness. ⁵And you know that He was manifested to take away our sins, and in Him there is no sin. ⁶Whoever abides in Him does not sin. Whoever sins has neither seen Him nor known Him.

⁷Little children, let no one deceive you. He who practices righteousness is righteous, just as He is righteous. ⁸He who sins is of the devil, for the devil has sinned from the beginning. For this purpose the Son of God was manifested, that He might destroy the works of the devil. ⁹Whoever has been born of God does not sin, for His seed remains in him; and he cannot sin, because he has been born of God.

¹⁰In this the children of God and the children of the devil are manifest: Whoever does not practice righteousness is not of God, nor *is* he who does not love his brother. ¹¹For this is the message that you heard from the

"Here's what I did..."

I was the master of rationalization—at least in some areas of my life. When I got into an argument with my parents, I always knew they were totally wrong. If I talked about someone behind her back, I told myself that it wasn't gossip, it was information the person really needed to know. When my boyfriend and I started having sex, I rationalized that it was OK because we loved each other, and didn't the Bible say that love was what it was all about?

Then I heard my pastor preach on 1 John 1:8-10, and suddenly I knew I was just fooling myself. God called these things—rebelliousness toward my parents, gossip, premarital sex—sins. I was kidding myself, but not God. The preacher said we are calling God a liar when we don't acknowledge our sins! That shook me up pretty bad.

I reread the passage after church, when I was alone in my room, and I cried. Not only because I'd been lying to myself and to God, but because this passage also talks about how willing God is to forgive us and cleanse us.

Before God that day, I owned up to the sins I had been rationalizing away. It was hard to do because I knew I had to be willing to change, not just to say "I'm sorry." Change would be hard, particularly in my relationship with my boyfriend. But verse 9 encouraged me that God would not only forgive, but also give me the strength to make a clean new start.

I did end up breaking up with my boyfriend; it proved impossible to start over in our physical relationship. The breakup hurt a lot. But underneath the pain, something felt very good, very right: I knew I was no longer lying to myself or to God. A new, clear conscience is helping me through the pain of change.

Tricia

AGE 16

3:8-9 We all have areas where temptation is strong and habits are hard to break. However, John is not talking about people who are working to overcome a particular sin; he is talking about people who make a practice of sinning and look for ways to justify it. Use these three steps to overcome prevailing sin: (1) seek the power of the Holy Spirit and God's Word; (2) stay away from tempting situations; and (3) seek the help of other Christians.

beginning, that we should love one another, [12]not as Cain *who* was of the wicked one and murdered his brother. And why did he murder him? Because his works were evil and his brother's righteous.

[13]Do not marvel, my brethren, if the world hates you. [14]We know that we have passed from death to life, because we love the brethren. He who does not love *his* brother abides in death. [15]Whoever hates his brother is a murderer, and you know that no murderer has eternal life abiding in him.

[16]By this we know love, because He laid down His life for us. And we also ought to lay down *our* lives for the brethren. [17]But whoever has this world's goods, and sees his brother in need, and shuts up his heart from him, how does the love of God abide in him?

[18]My little children, let us not love in word or in tongue, but in deed and in truth. [19]And by this we know that we are of the truth, and shall assure our hearts before Him. [20]For if our heart condemns us, God is greater than our heart, and knows all things. [21]Beloved, if our heart does not condemn us, we have confidence toward God. [22]And whatever we ask we receive from Him, because we keep His commandments and do those things that are pleasing in His sight. [23]And this is His commandment: that we should believe on the name of His Son Jesus Christ and love one another, as He gave us commandment.

◣◣◣ A TEST

4:20-21 It is easy to say we love God when it doesn't cost us anything more than weekly attendance at a religious service. But the real test of our love for God is how we treat the people right in front of us—our family members and fellow believers. We cannot truly love God while neglecting to love those who are created in his image.

[24]Now he who keeps His commandments abides in Him, and He in him. And by this we know that He abides in us, by the Spirit whom He has given us.

CHAPTER 4 WHAT'S TRUE AND WHAT'S NOT?

Beloved, do not believe every spirit, but test the spirits, whether they are of God; because many false prophets have gone out into the world. [2]By this you know the Spirit of God: Every spirit that confesses that Jesus Christ has come in the flesh is of God, [3]and every spirit that does not confess that Jesus Christ has come in the flesh is not of God. And this is the *spirit* of the Antichrist, which you have heard was coming, and is now already in the world.

[4]You are of God, little children, and have overcome them, because He who is in you is greater than he who is in the world. [5]They are of the world. Therefore they speak *as* of the world, and the world hears them. [6]We are of God. He who knows God hears us; he who is not of God does not hear us. By this we know the spirit of truth and the spirit of error.

[7]Beloved, let us love one another, for love is of God; and everyone who loves is born of God and knows God. [8]He who does not love does not know God, for God is love. [9]In this the love of God was manifested toward us, that God has sent His only begotten Son into the world, that we might live through Him. [10]In this is love, not that we loved God, but that He loved us and sent His Son *to be* the propitiation for our sins. [11]Beloved, if God so loved us, we also ought to love one another.

[12]No one has seen God at any time. If we love one another, God abides in us, and His love has been perfected in us. [13]By this we know that we abide in Him, and

I became a Christian at a big youth r[e] last fall. Afterwards, I felt great for a few days—I knew that having a relationship with God was something I wanted—but soon my good feelings went away. Did I lose God? Why didn't the good feelings stay around?

I WONDE[R]

Picture yourself meeting your favorite TV or music superstar face-to-face. It would be an experience th[at] you would likely never forget. Yet over time you wo[uld] forget the intensity of the emotion you once felt. W[ould it] mean that you did not actually meet this person? O[f] course not, but it does illustrate that our feelings oft[en] come and go based on current experience.

Asking Jesus Christ into your life is far better than meeting another human, famous or not! What you [have] begun is a lifelong relationship with God, who crea[ted] everything! He actually wants to live in you so that y[ou] will live forever *and* so others can see that he really [loves] them, too.

In John 14:23 Jesus says, "If anyone loves Me, he [will] keep My word; and My Father will love him, and W[e] will come to him and make Our home with him." Th[e] phrase *make Our home with him* actually means "b[uild] a mansion" in them. God wants to come into your l[ife] and make something extraordinary out of it. God h[as] begun a process of molding your character to beco[me] more like that of Jesus Christ. Within this lifelong pr[ocess] will be some good feelings, but more often we will n[ot] have, or want, continual, intense excitement.

The wonder of getting to know someone as loving [and] forgiving as Jesus Christ has similarities to other relationships you enjoy. There is the initial experienc[e of] meeting a person, followed by months and years of growing to appreciate his or her friendship and influence. Anything worthwhile takes time.

First John 5:10-12 assures us that "he who has H[im] has life." Once you have genuinely chosen to follow [in] Jesus Christ you can never lose him. He will always [be] there in your life to guide and love you, even in the midst of all our world may throw your way. This sho[uld] outweigh your tendency to base your relationship w[ith] God on your up-and-down feelings.

He in us, because He has given us of His Spirit. [14]And we have seen and testify that the Father has sent the Son *as* Savior of the world. [15]Whoever confesses that Jesus is the Son of God, God abides in him, and he in God. [16]And we have known and believed the love that God has for us. God is love, and he who abides in love abides in God, and God in him.

[17]Love has been perfected among us in this: that we may have boldness in the day of judgment; because as He is, so are we in this world. [18]There is no fear in love; but perfect love casts out fear, because fear involves torment. But he who fears has not been made perfect in love. [19]We love Him because He first loved us.

[20]If someone says, "I love God," and hates his brother, he is a liar; for he who does not love his brother whom he has seen, how can he love God whom he has not seen? [21]And this commandment we have from Him: that he who loves God *must* love his brother also.

CHAPTER 5 LOVE GOD AND OBEY HIM. Whoever believes that Jesus is the Christ is born of God, and everyone who loves Him who begot also loves him who is begotten of Him. [2]By this we know that we love the children of God, when we love God and keep His commandments. [3]For this is the love of God, that we keep His commandments. And His commandments are not burdensome. [4]For whatever is born of God overcomes the world. And this is the victory that has overcome the world—our faith. [5]Who is he who overcomes the world, but he who believes that Jesus is the Son of God?

[6]This is He who came by water and blood—Jesus Christ; not only by water, but by blood. And it is the Spirit who bears witness, because the Spirit is truth. [7]For there are three that bear witness in heaven: the Father, the Word, and the Holy Spirit; and these three are one. [8]And there are three that bear witness on earth: the Spirit, the water, and the blood; and these three agree as one.

[9]If we receive the witness of men, the witness of God is greater; for this is the witness of God which He has testified of His Son. [10]He who believes in the Son of God has the witness in himself; he who does not believe God has made Him a liar, because he has not believed the testimony that God has given of His Son. [11]And this is the testimony: that God has given us eternal life, and this life is in His Son. [12]He who has the Son has life; he who does not

have the Son of God does not have life. [13]These things I have written to you who believe in the name of the Son of God, that you may know that you have eternal life, and that you may *continue to* believe in the name of the Son of God.

[14]Now this is the confidence that we have in Him, that if we ask anything according to His will, He hears us. [15]And if we know that He hears us, whatever we ask, we know that we have the petitions that we have asked of Him.

[16]If anyone sees his brother sinning a sin *which does* not *lead* to death, he will ask, and He will give him

CAIN

and his brother Abel worshiped God. In some way, God let them know that Abel's worship was right and Cain's was wrong. God told Cain to start over. Cain got angry. God saw his anger and warned him to be careful. Though Cain was angry at God, he took it out on his brother. Then, instead of making things right with God by changing his attitude, he chose to kill his brother.

Anger is a powerful reaction. When something happens to us that we didn't expect, we get angry! It starts like a small hot flame and, unless it is put out, the flame can destroy a great deal. Cain's anger got out of control, but he wasn't in trouble until he acted out his anger in a wrong way. His attitude could have been corrected, but his actions couldn't. When we get angry, we're in the same danger.

Our anger may not result in murder, but we still act like Cain. We get angry. We see that we have a choice to make between right and wrong. And we often choose wrong. Being angry should remind us that we need God's help. Asking for his help to do the right thing may keep us from making mistakes we can't correct.

LESSONS: Anger is not sin. What causes our anger or what we do with our anger can be sinful.

What we offer to God must be from the heart, the best we are and have

The consequences of sin are sometimes for life

KEY VERSE: "If you do well, will you not be accepted? And if you do not do well, sin lies at the door. And its desire is for you, but you should rule over it" (Genesis 4:7).

Cain's story is told in Genesis 4:1-17. He is also mentioned in Hebrews 11:4; 1 John 3:12; Jude 1:11.

UPS:
• First human child
• First to follow in father's profession: farming

DOWNS:
• When disappointed, reacted out of anger and discouragement
• Took the negative choice even when a positive possibility was offered
• Was the first murderer

STATS:
• Where: Near Eden, which probably was located in the present-day countries of Iraq or Iran
• Occupations: Farmer at first, later a nomad
• Relatives: Parents: Adam and Eve. Brothers and sisters: Abel, Seth, and others not mentioned by name.

life for those who commit sin not *leading* to death. There is sin *leading* to death. I do not say that he should pray about that. [17]All unrighteousness is sin, and there is sin not *leading* to death.

[18]We know that whoever is born of God does not sin; but he who has been born of God keeps himself, and the wicked one does not touch him.

[19]We know that we are of God, and the whole world lies *under the sway of* the wicked one.

[20]And we know that the Son of God has come and has given us an understanding, that we may know Him who is true; and we are in Him who is true, in His Son Jesus Christ. This is the true God and eternal life.

[21]Little children, keep yourselves from idols. Amen.

MEGA *Themes*

SIN Even Christians sin. Sin requires God's forgiveness, which Christ's death provides. Determining to live according to God's biblical standards shows we are forgiven and that our life is being transformed.

We cannot deny our sinful nature or minimize the consequences of sin in our relationship with God. We must resist the attraction of sin, yet we must confess when we do sin. Sin is our fault—Christ is our redeemer.

1. What happened when the sinless Christ entered the sinful world?
2. What happens when the sinless Christ enters the life of a sinful person?
3. What does John say we should do about our sins?
4. What is happening in your life in terms of dealing with sin? Are you dealing with your sin with the action and attitude of 1:9? Explain.

LOVE Christ commands us to love others as he did. This love is evidence that we are truly saved. God is the creator of love; and he wants his children to love each other.

Love means putting others first. Love is action—showing others we care, not just saying it. To show love, we must give our time and money to meet the needs of others.

1. Describe God's love for you as described in 1 John.
2. Why is knowing and experiencing God's love essential to living a full life?
3. Who are the people you love most? How does your "love life" compare to your description of God's love? What are your strengths and weaknesses?
4. Whom do you have difficulty loving? How can you apply God's love to those relationships? Why should you do this?

FAMILY OF GOD We become God's children by believing in Christ. God's life in us enables us to love our fellow family members.

How we treat others shows who our Father is. Live as a faithful, loving family member. Remember whose child you are!

1. Who are the children of God according to 1 John?
2. What privileges do these children have? What responsibilities?
3. Complete this statement with specific responses from your own life: "Being a child of God enables me to _____."
4. How would those who know you describe your Father based on their knowledge of you as his child?

TRUTH AND ERROR False teachers encouraged believers to throw off moral restraints, teaching that the body does not matter. They also taught that Christ wasn't really a man and that we must be saved by having some special mystical knowledge. The result was that people became indifferent to sin.

God is truth and light, so the more we get to know him, the better we can keep focused on the truth. Don't be led astray by any teaching that denies Christ's deity or humanity. Check the message; test the claims.

1. Identify several false teachings that John was correcting in his letter.
2. What are our resources for discerning and dealing with false teachings?
3. How can you live so that others can see the difference between God's truth and the false messages in the world?
4. How would you describe your commitment to God's truth? What will you do this week? *Do* what you answered for question number 3.

ASSURANCE God is in control of heaven and earth. Because God's Word is true, we can have assurance of eternal life and victory over sin. By faith we can be certain of our eternal destiny with him.

Assurance of our relationship with God is a promise, but it is also a way of life. We build our confidence by trusting in God's Word and in Christ's provision for our sin.

1. If a young Christian were to ask you, "How can I be sure I am saved?" what would be your response?
2. How could you use 3:12-16 in your answer?
3. How do you know that *you* are saved? What impact does this assurance have in the way you are currently living?

*P*ractical jokes have been around a long time. Just read through the Old Testament; it's full of sneaky characters. There's Abraham, trying to pass off his wife Sarah as his sister—*twice*. There's Jacob donning a goatskin disguise to snatch his big brother's inheritance and blessing. (And that's just in the first half of the first book—Genesis!) ■ Most people have tried shocking or embarrassing someone with a joy buzzer or a whoopee cushion. Others have short-sheeted beds or done various phone pranks. Perhaps you have attempted a more complicated stunt—turning a friend's dresser drawers upside down, freezing your brother's underwear, toilet papering a house. (It's reported that some university pals lined a dorm mate's room with plastic and turned it into a giant aquarium—complete with a shark!) ■ As long as no one gets hurt, no laws are broken, and there's no property damage, pranks are no big deal. It's fun to fool people—or even be fooled. ■ Except in the spiritual dimension. There we can't afford to be deceived because our enemy, the devil, packs his pranks with disaster! ■ One of Satan's favorite methods of suckering us is to get us to listen to *false teaching*. This can come in many different forms, some very pleasing—but no matter how pleasant it may seem, false teaching is always deadly. ■ The book of 2 John warns us against false teaching. That's a warning we need to heed because the enemy's tricks aren't just for amusement—they're meant for destruction!

STATS

PURPOSE: To emphasize the basics of following Christ—truth and love—and to warn against false teachers

AUTHOR: The apostle John

TO WHOM WRITTEN: To "the elect lady" and her children (some think that the greeting refers instead to a local church) and to Christians everywhere

DATE WRITTEN: About the same time as 1 John, around A.D. 90, from Ephesus

SETTING: Evidently this woman and her family were involved in one of the churches that John was overseeing—they had developed a strong friendship. John was warning her of the false teachers that were becoming prevalent in some of the churches.

KEY PEOPLE: John, the elect lady, and her children

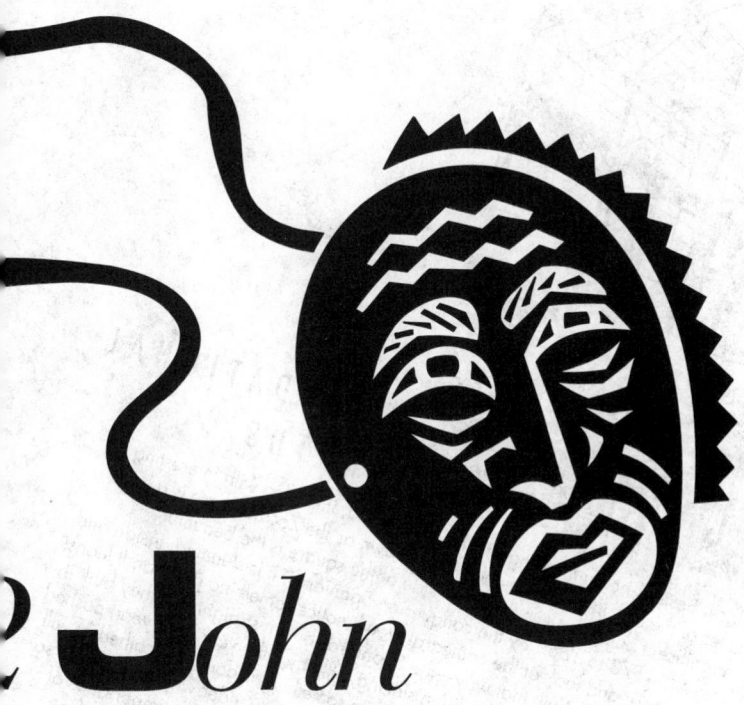

2 John

BEWARE OF FALSE TEACHERS. The Elder,

To the elect lady and her children, whom I love in truth, and not only I, but also all those who have known the truth, ²because of the truth which abides in us and will be with us forever:

³Grace, mercy, *and* peace will be with you from God the Father and from the Lord Jesus Christ, the Son of the Father, in truth and love.

⁴I rejoiced greatly that I have found *some* of your children walking in truth, as we received commandment from the Father. ⁵And now I plead with you, lady, not as though I wrote a new commandment to you, but that which we have had from the beginning: that we love one another. ⁶This is love, that we walk according to His commandments. This is the commandment, that as you have heard from the beginning, you should walk in it.

⁷For many deceivers have gone out into the world who do not confess Jesus Christ *as* coming in the flesh. This is a deceiver and an antichrist. ⁸Look to yourselves, that we do not lose those things we worked for, but *that* we may receive a full reward.

⁹Whoever transgresses and does not abide in the doctrine of Christ does not have God. He who abides in the doctrine of Christ has both the Father and the Son. ¹⁰If anyone comes to you and does not bring this doctrine, do not receive him into your house nor greet him; ¹¹for he who greets him shares in his evil deeds.

¹²Having many things to write to you, I did not wish *to do so* with paper and ink; but I hope to come to you and speak face to face, that our joy may be full.

¹³The children of your elect sister greet you. Amen.

SHOW LOVE

5-6 The love that Christians should have for one another is a recurrent New Testament theme. Yet love for one's neighbor is an old command first appearing in the third book of Moses (Leviticus 19:18). We can show love in many ways: by avoiding prejudice and discrimination; by accepting people; by listening, helping, giving, serving, and refusing to judge. Just knowing God's command is not enough. We must obey the command and put it into practice. (See also Matthew 22:37-39 and 1 John 2:7-8.)

FOUNDATIONAL TRUTHS

Mexico City is a fascinating place. Besides being the biggest city in the world, it is filled with interesting historical sights. At the very center of the city, in the historical district known as the Zocalo, there is a huge square plaza surrounded by magnificent buildings. On the north side of the square is the beautiful metropolitan cathedral, built from A.D. 1573 to 1667 by the conquering Spaniards. It is stunning, inside and out. **B**ut if you stand back in the square and look at the cathedral, you'll notice something peculiar. It leans. The entire building slopes to the right. It wasn't built that way—the Spaniards built it straight. But they built it on a dry lake bed (formerly Lake Texcoco). The church has been sinking, little by little, year after year, pushed into the soft ground by its own enormous weight. Sooner or later, unless something is done, the cathedral will crack and crumble into rubble just like many of the Aztec ruins nearby.

Do you wonder why John places so much emphasis on knowing the Bible? Well, he's not alone—many biblical authors stress the importance of knowing God's Word. In Psalm 119, the longest chapter in the Bible, all but three of the 176 verses refer specifically to God's Word. The writer uses various terms, such as law, instructions, rules—not exactly favorites for any of us—throughout this short letter. Why is knowing the Bible so important? And what in the world does this have to do with Mexico City's metropolitan cathedral? **J**ust this: Like any structure, your life needs a foundation. The bigger the structure, the stronger the foundation has to be. To build a skyscraper or a mass cathedral, you must build on a deep, lasting, rock-solid foundation. If you just want to pitch a tent or throw together a wooden shack, it doesn't really matter where you build. Any place will do. **L**ikewise, if you w to build a life worthy of God, a life that's big, bold, and reflective of his glory, you need a firm base from which to start. The only place to find such a support structure is in the Word of God. It is the only platfor will never buckle under the pressure of living for Christ in a very non-Christian world. When you spend reading the Bible—even when you don't feel like it—you're working on laying your solid foundation. But don't care what kind of life you're offering up to the Lord, sleep in or watch soap operas all day. If you want to have a life worthy of the hig surprised when your life's structure begins to sink and tilt. If you want to have a life worthy of the hig of following Jesus, start digging. You're already in the right place.

MEGA Themes

TRUTH Following God's Word, the Bible, is essential to Christian living because God is truth. Christ's true followers consistently obey his truth.

To be loyal to Christ's teaching we must know the Bible, but we must never twist the Bible's message to our own needs or purposes, nor encourage others who misuse it. We should be servants to the truth of the Word.

1. According to John, why is truth important?
2. How do we know truth?
3. Who are the enemies of the truth? What should be our response to these enemies?
4. How does your life compare with the enemies of the truth in your world?

LOVE Christ's command is for Christians to love one another. This is the basic ingredient of true Christianity.

To obey Christ fully, we must believe his command to love others. Helping, giving, and meeting needs puts love into practice. Love in deed is love indeed.

1. How does John connect love for one another with love for God?

2. What seems to be the connection between love and truth?
3. Identify the people in your life who do not know Christ and his love. What can you do for them that will be a witness concerning the reality of the truth and love of God?

FALSE LEADERS We must be wary of religious leaders who are not true to Christ's teachings. We should not give them a platform to spread false teachings.

Don't encourage those who are contrary to Christ. Politely remove yourself from association with false leaders. Be aware of what's being taught in the church.

1. How can you tell who is a false teacher?
2. What do you see as the main dangers of false teachings?
3. What passages of Scripture would you use to correct the error of these false teachers?
4. Why is it important, based on this study, to be a student of God's Word?
5. What steps are you taking to be led by the truth and to avoid error?

*I*t was over before it got started!" "Blink and you'll miss it." "Short, sweet, and to the point." ■ Those are just some of the expressions you might use to describe: ■ The 1896 war between the United Kingdom and Zanzibar. (It lasted a mere 38 minutes!) ■ Boxer Al Couture's 1946 knockout of opponent Ralph Walton in only 10 1/2 seconds (and that included a 10-second count by the referee)! ■ The 20-minute reign of King Dom Luis III of Portugal in 1908. ■ Montana's Roe River. (Its length? A measley 201 feet!) ■ The 10-yard-long (or should we say "10-yard-*short"*) McKinley Street in Bellefontaine, Ohio. ■ But just because things are brief or small or short doesn't mean they're unimportant. ■ Take 3 John for instance. With only 15 verses, it is one of the shortest books of the Bible—a quick contrast between godly living and worldly behavior. ■ In fact, this introduction is about as long as the book itself! So go ahead and read this warm, personal note from the apostle John to his friend Gaius. ■ When you do, another familiar expression may come to mind: ■ "Good things come in little packages."

STATS

PURPOSE: To commend Gaius for his hospitality and to encourage him in his Christian life

AUTHOR: The apostle John

TO WHOM WRITTEN: Gaius, a prominent Christian in one of the churches known to John, and all Christians everywhere

DATE WRITTEN: About A.D. 90, from Ephesus

SETTING: Church leaders traveled from town to town helping to establish new congregations. They depended on the hospitality of fellow believers. Gaius was one who welcomed them into his home.

KEY PEOPLE: John, Gaius, Diotrephes, Demetrius

3 John

HOSPITALITY PLEASES GOD. The Elder,

To the beloved Gaius, whom I love in truth:

²Beloved, I pray that you may prosper in all things and be in health, just as your soul prospers. ³For I rejoiced greatly when brethren came and testified of the truth *that is* in you, just as you walk in the truth. ⁴I have no greater joy than to hear that my children walk in truth.

⁵Beloved, you do faithfully whatever you do for the brethren and for strangers, ⁶who have borne witness of your love before the church. *If* you send them forward on their journey in a manner worthy of God, you will do well, ⁷because they went forth for His name's sake, taking nothing from the Gentiles. ⁸We therefore ought to receive such, that we may become fellow workers for the truth.

⁹I wrote to the church, but Diotrephes, who loves to have the preeminence among them, does not receive us. ¹⁰Therefore, if I come, I will call to mind his deeds which he does, prating against us with malicious words. And not content with that, he himself does not receive the brethren, and forbids those who wish to, putting *them* out of the church.

¹¹Beloved, do not imitate what is evil, but what is good. He who does good is of God, but he who does evil has not seen God. ¹²Demetrius has a *good* testimony from all, and from the truth itself. And we also bear witness, and you know that our testimony is true.

¹³I had many things to write, but I do not wish to write to you with pen and ink; ¹⁴but I hope to see you shortly, and we shall speak face to face.

Peace to you. Our friends greet you. Greet the friends by name.

OPEN HOUSE

5 In the church's early days, traveling prophets, evangelists, and teachers were helped on their way by people like Gaius who housed and fed them. Hospitality is a lost art in many churches today. We would do well to invite more people into our home for meals—fellow church members, young people, traveling missionaries, those in need, visitors. This is an active and much appreciated way to show your love. In fact, it probably is more important today than ever because of our individualistic, self-centered society. There are many lonely people who wonder if anyone cares whether they live or die. If you find such a lonely person, show him or her that *you* care!

THE NEW AGE MOVEMENT

Following Christ isn't easy. Consider John's words: "Beloved, do not imitate what is evil, but what is good. He who does good is of God, but he who does evil has not seen God." Imitate only what is good. In today's world, that's difficult! Now take a look at Luke 9:23, where Jesus tells us, "If anyone desires to come after Me, let him . . . take up his cross. . . . Whoever loses his life for My sake will save it." That's quite a price tag for following Jesus! Isn't there an easier path to God—one that doesn't make such tough demands on us?

Yes! At least, that's what those in the "New Age movement" say. And lots of people are listening. But are New Agers right? Just what is the New Age movement and what does it have to do with Jesus?

New religions researchers Bob and Gretchen Passantino describe the New Age movement as "the fastest growing alternative belief system" in the U.S. Alternative to what? To the Jewish-Christian tradition that most Americans have been raised in. J. Gordon Melton, another new religions expert, defines New Age as "a vision of a world transformed, a heaven on earth, a society in which the problems of today are overcome and a new existence emerges." New Agers believe that we stand on the threshold of a new era, a "new age," a major transitional shift into humanity's next evolutionary stage. Sound vague? Well, you're not alone. Even New Agers have difficulty defining who and what they are. But there are some general New Age principles that have been pinned down. The overriding philosophy of the New Age movement is the belief that "all is one." There is no distinction between right or wrong, male or female, good or bad. There isn't even a division between God and man. Everything is divine. This philosophy isn't new. It's been around for thousands of years and is called "pantheism." Pantheism is the basis for all Eastern mystical religions (Hinduism, Buddhism, Confucianism, etc.). But New Agers differ from these religions in that they see this unity from a positive and optimistic view. The New Age is kind of an "Eastern-religion-meets-American-positive-thinking." This blend of exotic religious thought and popular psychology attracts many people to New Age teachings. But there's a catch. A big one. If all is one, then there's no difference between right and wrong—or God and man. If there's no difference between God and man, the next logical step is that man is god. No one can tell me "no"; I can do whatever I want. After all, I'm god. (Sound farfetched? That's exactly what Shirley MacLaine, the "high priestess" of the New Age movement, claims in her autobiography, Out On A Limb. And she is not alone.)

The New Age movement is growing rapidly. The belief in the oneness of all things (along with things like ecological harmony, reincarnation, unlimited human potential) appeals to modern, "enlightened" people. The idea that I can be my own god is very seductive. However, history is littered with the atrocities committed by people who thought they answered to no one—Hitler, Pol Pot, Idi Amin, Saddam Hussein. In fact, this was Lucifer's sin, which resulted in his expulsion from heaven. Don't be deceived. There is only one true God—the God of Abraham, Moses, David, Peter, James, and John. He will not share his throne with anyone, and he has certain demands for his followers, like carrying your cross and losing your life for his sake. It's a high price, but Jesus promises us it is worth it. And he is worthy of our sacrificial commitment. The god of the New Age—the god that looks like us—doesn't ask anything of us. But that kind of god can't deliver us from our sins, show us how to love, or die on a cross for us. That god isn't real—he's a lie. Someone has said, "History is filled with men who would be gods; but only one God who would be man." His name is Jesus. Take up your cross and follow him.

ΜΕGΑ *Themes*

HOSPITALITY John wrote to encourage those who were kind to others. Genuine hospitality for traveling Christian workers was needed then and is still important.

Faithful Christian teachers and missionaries need our support. Whenever you can extend hospitality to others, it will make you a partner in their ministry.

1. Why is Christian hospitality important?
2. In what specific ways can you and your friends at church extend Christian hospitality?
3. How might your actions of hospitality enable you to become partners in God's work in and through others?
4. What attitudes are required in order to be truly hospitable? How are you doing in terms of these attitudes?
5. Develop a hospitality plan of action based on this study.

PRIDE Diotrephes not only refused to offer hospitality, but he set himself up as a church boss. Pride disqualified him as a real leader.

Christian leaders must shun pride and its effects on them. Be careful not to misuse your position of leadership. The best leaders are always the best servants.

1. What were Diotrephes' sinful actions?

2. Why does John label Diotrephes as prideful?
3. How can a person who is prideful learn to be more humble?
4. Do you struggle with sinful pride? If so, how can you apply your responses in number 3 to your pride?

FAITHFULNESS Gaius and Demetrius were commended for their faithful work in the church. They were held up as examples of faithful, selfless servants.

Don't take for granted Christian workers who serve faithfully. Be sure to encourage these workers so they won't grow weary of serving.

1. What do you learn about Gaius in 3 John?
2. What Christians do you know who live faithfully in their relationship with God? What qualities do you see in them that reflect faithfulness to God? How could you encourage them in their ministry and leadership?
3. Why is faithfulness such an essential quality in the Christian life?
4. What is currently reflecting faithfulness in your life? Identify the ways that your faithfulness, like that of Gaius and those you listed in number 2, makes a difference to others.

*I*s your faith fit for a (spiritual) fight? ■ What would you say if the school agnostic called the resurrection of Christ a myth? Or if a minister you respect admitted that he believes the Bible contains errors and contradictions? ■ What if your favorite teacher announced, "It is insensitive and downright *wrong* for one group of people to try to force its views on another group! Right and wrong is a relative concept, and we cannot legislate morality"? ■ Imagine meeting someone full of joy and peace, a person *seemingly* very much in touch with God. As you converse, this person tells you that she is content and fulfilled because of daily yoga exercises, meditation, and also because of an experience she recently had in which she journeyed back through her previous incarnations. She nods when you mention Jesus Christ and says, "If that works for you, great! But I found the truth another way." ■ If you haven't already had encounters like the ones just described, then just wait. Your time is definitely coming!

■ The fact of the matter is that our world is *full* of confused people who are eagerly spreading their confusing ideas. ■ Don't get caught off-guard! Get your Christian beliefs and behavior ready for spiritual battle by understanding what you believe and why. There's no better place to start your Bible Bootcamp Training than in Jude, the brief book that follows.

STATS

PURPOSE: To remind the church of the need for constant vigilance—to keep strong in the faith and defend it against heresy

AUTHOR: Jude, James's brother and Jesus' half brother

TO WHOM WRITTEN: Jewish Christians and all believers everywhere

DATE WRITTEN: About A.D. 65

SETTING: From the first century on, the church has been threatened by heresy and false teaching—we must always be on our guard

KEY PEOPLE: Jude, James, Jesus

Jude

TO CHRISTIANS EVERYWHERE. Jude, a bondservant of Jesus Christ, and brother of James,

To those who are called, sanctified by God the Father, and preserved in Jesus Christ:

²Mercy, peace, and love be multiplied to you.

³Beloved, while I was very diligent to write to you concerning our common salvation, I found it necessary to write to you exhorting you to contend earnestly for the faith which was once for all delivered to the saints. ⁴For certain men have crept in unnoticed, who long ago were marked out for this condemnation, ungodly men, who turn the grace of our God into lewdness and deny the only Lord God and our Lord Jesus Christ.

⁵But I want to remind you, though you once knew this, that the Lord, having saved the people out of the land of Egypt, afterward destroyed those who did not believe. ⁶And the angels who did not keep their proper domain, but left their own abode, He has reserved in everlasting chains under darkness for the judgment of the great day; ⁷as Sodom and Gomorrah, and the cities around them in a similar manner to these, having given themselves over to sexual immorality and gone after strange flesh, are set forth as an example, suffering the vengeance of eternal fire.

⁸Likewise also these dreamers defile the flesh, reject authority, and speak evil of dignitaries. ⁹Yet Michael the archangel, in contending with the devil, when he disputed about the body of Moses, dared not bring against him a reviling accusation, but said, "The Lord rebuke you!" ¹⁰But these speak evil of whatever they do not know; and whatever they know naturally, like brute beasts, in these things they corrupt themselves. ¹¹Woe to

DOCTRINE

4 Because people think theology is dry, they avoid studying the Bible. Those who refuse to learn correct doctrine, however, are susceptible to false teaching because they are not fully grounded in God's truth. We must understand the basic doctrines of our faith so that we can recognize false doctrines and prevent them from hurting us and others.

PERSEVERANCE

Cindy and Kate met way back in 8th grade. Not only did the girls become fast friends, but by the end of that school year Cindy had helped Kate find a personal relationship with Jesus Christ.

Throughout high school Cindy always did her best to help Kate grow in the Christian faith. It was sometimes comical—Cindy practically dragging Kate to retreats and youth functions. Had you known the girls in those years, you would have predicted that Cindy was destined to do great things for God. And you would have seriously doubted the long-term stability of Kate's faith.

Boy, would you have been wrong!

During their first year of college, Cindy got too physically involved with her boyfriend. When she had a baby out of wedlock, she married a non-Christian guy and dropped out of sight. Meanwhile, Kate has continued to mature in her walk with God. She's the one with the dynamic ministry on campus.

Yogi Berra said, "It ain't over till it's over." Another sports figure quipped, "The opera isn't over until the fat lady sings." The point? The Christian life is a long, long race.

Read about perseverance in the Epistle of Jude, and ask God to give you the grace and strength to hang in there for God all the days of your life.

them! For they have gone in the way of Cain, have run greedily in the error of Balaam for profit, and perished in the rebellion of Korah. [12]These are spots in your love feasts, while they feast with you without fear, serving *only* themselves. *They are* clouds without water, carried about by the winds; late autumn trees without fruit, twice dead, pulled up by the roots; [13]raging waves of the sea, foaming up their own shame; wandering stars for whom is reserved the blackness of darkness forever.

WATCH OUT!

10 False teachers were claiming that they possessed secret knowle[dge] that gave them authority. Their "knowledge" of God was mystical a[nd] beyond human understanding. In reality, the nature of God *is* bey[ond] our understanding. But God in his grace has chosen to reveal hims[elf to] us—in his Word, and supremely in Jesus Christ. Therefore, we mus[t] to know all we can about what God has revealed, even though we c[an't] fully comprehend God with our finite human mind. Beware of those [who] claim to have all the answers and who belittle what they do not understand.

[14]Now Enoch, the seventh from Adam, prophesied about these men also, saying, "Behold, the Lord comes with ten thousands of His saints, [15]to execute judgment on all, to convict all who are ungodly among them of all their ungodly deeds which they have committed in an ungodly way, and of all the harsh things which ungodly sinners have spoken against Him." [16]These are grumblers, complainers, walking accord-

NOW TO HIM

who is able to keep you from stumbling,

AND

TO PRESENT YOU

FAULTLESS

BEFORE THE PRESENCE OF

His glory

with exceeding joy

exceeding joy

exceeding joy

exceeding joy

ing to their own lusts; and they mouth great swelling *words,* flattering people to gain advantage. ¹⁷But you, beloved, remember the words which were spoken before by the apostles of our Lord Jesus Christ: ¹⁸how they told you that there would be mockers in the last time who would walk according to their own ungodly lusts. ¹⁹These are sensual persons, who cause divisions, not having the Spirit.

²⁰But you, beloved, building yourselves up on your most holy faith, praying in the Holy Spirit, ²¹keep yourselves in the love of God, looking for the mercy of our Lord Jesus Christ unto eternal life.

²²And on some have compassion, making a distinction; ²³but others save with fear, pulling *them* out of the fire, hating even the garment defiled by the flesh.

²⁴ Now to Him who is able to keep you from stumbling, And to present *you* faultless

Before the presence of His glory with exceeding joy,
²⁵ To God our Savior,
Who alone is wise,

QUICKSAND

23 In trying to find common ground with those to whom we witness, we must be careful not to fall into the quicksand of compromise. When reaching out to others, we must be sure that our own footing is safe and secure. Be careful not to become so much like non-Christians that no one can tell who you are or what you believe. Influence them for Christ—don't allow them to influence you to sin!

Be glory and majesty,
Dominion and power,
Both now and forever.
Amen.

MEGA *Themes*

FALSE TEACHERS Jude warns against false teachers and leaders who reject the lordship of Christ, undermine the faith of others, and lead people astray. These leaders and any who follow them will be punished.

We must stoutly defend Christian truth. Make sure that you avoid leaders and teachers who change the Bible to suit their own purposes. Genuine servants of God will faithfully portray Christ in their words and conduct.

1. How does Jude describe the false teachers?
2. What were the negative results of their teachings?
3. How were the Christians supposed to respond to teachings of error?
4. What safeguards can you build into your life to insure that you are not deceived by false teachings?
5. What are you doing to serve as a living testimony of the truth of God?

APOSTASY Jude warns against apostasy—turning away from Christ. We are to remember that God punishes rebellion against him. We must be careful not to drift away from a firm commitment to Christ.

Those who do not study God's Word are susceptible to apostasy. Christians must guard against any false teachings that would distract them from the truth preached by the apostles and written in God's Word.

1. Contrast those who are led by God with those who are living in rebellion.
2. What are the principles found in verses 20-23 for dealing with the rebellious?
3. How would you apply those principles to your life at school? In church? In your social life?
4. What confidence do you find in verses 24-25 that tells you God will remain faithful to you as you follow him? Take time to praise God for who he is and for how he keeps you in his love.

*F*airy tales always end perfectly. The frog turns into a prince, the unloved stepsister becomes a beloved bride, and mean and greedy people get paid back for the rotten things they've done. ■ Unfortunately, fairy tales aren't true. "Happily ever after"? No way! The real world doesn't work that way. ■ Or does it? ■ We are near the end of the Bible. One book left to read: Revelation. This strange vision of the apostle John's is one of the most discussed, mysterious, and controversial books ever written. It's labeled "prophecy" and "theology." And it's like a fairy tale. ■ *"A fairy tale"?!* ■ That's right. According to Revelation, those who have become God's children by faith in Christ will have the happiest of all endings: being in the very presence of God, enjoying an existence untouched by sorrow or death. ■ And every bad and wicked creature (including the devil himself) will "face the music." All injustices will be righted; all unforgiven sin will be judged. That, in a nutshell, is the message of Revelation: happiness and reward for the good, punishment and justice for all the guilty. A picture-perfect ending. ■ You must admit it *does* sound like a fairy tale. There is, however, one important difference: this too-good-to-be-true story is truer than anything that ever existed. It *is* going to happen. ■ You can count on it.

STATS

PURPOSE: To reveal the full identity of Christ and to give warning and hope to believers

AUTHOR: The apostle John

TO WHOM WRITTEN: Seven Asian churches, and all believers everywhere

DATE WRITTEN: About A.D. 95, from the island of Patmos

SETTING: Most scholars believe that the seven churches of Asia to whom John wrote were experiencing the persecution that took place under Emperor Domitian (A.D. 90–95). Apparently the Roman authorities had exiled John to the island of Patmos (off the coast of Asia). John, an eyewitness of the incarnate Christ, had a vision of the glorified Christ. God also revealed to him what is to take place in the future—judgment and the ultimate triumph of God over evil.

KEY PEOPLE: John, Jesus

KEY PLACES: Island of Patmos, the seven churches, the New Jerusalem

Revelation

CHAPTER 1 **A REVELATION ABOUT THE FUTURE.**
The Revelation of Jesus Christ, which God gave Him to show His servants—things which must shortly take place. And He sent and signified *it* by His angel to His servant John, [2]who bore witness to the word of God, and to the testimony of Jesus Christ, to all things that he saw. [3]Blessed *is* he who reads and those who hear the words of this prophecy, and keep those things which are written in it; for the time *is* near.

[4]John, to the seven churches which are in Asia:

Grace to you and peace from Him who is and who was and who is to come, and from the seven Spirits who are before His throne, [5]and from Jesus Christ, the faithful witness, the firstborn from the dead, and the ruler over the kings of the earth.

To Him who loved us and washed us from our sins in His own blood, [6]and has made us kings and priests to His God and Father, to Him *be* glory and dominion forever and ever. Amen.

[7]Behold, He is coming with clouds, and every eye will see Him, even they who pierced Him. And all the tribes of the earth will mourn because of Him. Even so, Amen.

[8]"I am the Alpha and the Omega, *the* Beginning and *the* End," says the Lord, "who is and who was and who is to come, the Almighty."

[9]I, John, both your brother and companion in the tribulation and kingdom and patience of Jesus Christ, was on the island that is called Patmos for the word of God and for the testimony of Jesus Christ. [10]I was in the Spirit on the Lord's Day, and I heard behind me a loud voice, as of a trumpet, [11]saying, "I am the Alpha and the Omega,

GREAT VISION

1:1 Jesus gave his message to John in a vision, allowing John to see and record certain future events as an encouragement to all believers. The vision includes many signs and symbols to effectively show what will happen. What John saw, in most cases, was indescribable, so he used illustrations to show what it was *like*. When reading this symbolic language, don't try to understand every detail—John didn't. Instead, let the imagery show you that Christ is the glorious, victorious Lord of all.

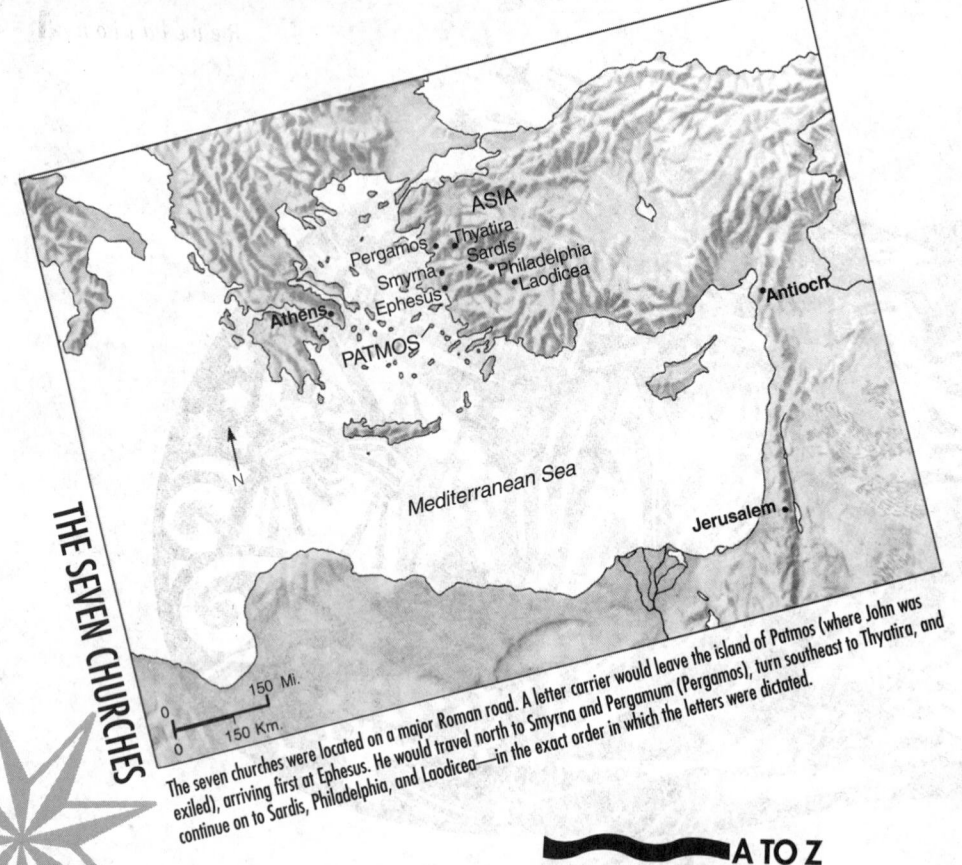

The seven churches were located on a major Roman road. A letter carrier would leave the island of Patmos (where John was exiled), arriving first at Ephesus. He would travel north to Smyrna and Pergamum (Pergamos), turn southeast to Thyatira, and continue on to Sardis, Philadelphia, and Laodicea—in the exact order in which the letters were dictated.

the First and the Last," and, "What you see, write in a book and send *it* to the seven churches which are in Asia: to Ephesus, to Smyrna, to Pergamos, to Thyatira, to Sardis, to Philadelphia, and to Laodicea."

¹²Then I turned to see the voice that spoke with me. And having turned I saw seven golden lampstands, ¹³and in the midst of the seven lampstands *One* like the Son of Man, clothed with a garment down to the feet and girded about the chest with a golden band. ¹⁴His head and hair *were* white like wool, as white as snow, and His eyes like a flame of fire; ¹⁵His feet *were* like fine brass, as if refined in a furnace, and His voice as the sound of many waters; ¹⁶He had in His right hand seven stars, out of His mouth went a sharp two-edged sword, and His countenance *was* like the sun shining in its strength. ¹⁷And when I saw Him, I fell at His feet as dead. But He laid His right hand on me, saying to me, "Do not be afraid; I am the First and the Last. ¹⁸I *am* He who lives, and was dead, and behold, I am alive forevermore. Amen. And I have the keys of Hades and of Death. ¹⁹Write the things which you have seen, and the things which are, and the things which will take place after this. ²⁰The mystery of the seven stars which you saw in My right hand, and the seven golden lampstands: The seven stars are the angels of the seven churches, and the seven lampstands which you saw are the seven churches.

A TO Z

1:8 Jesus is "the Alpha and the Omega" (the first and last letters Greek alphabet), the beginning and the end. Jesus is the eternal Lo and Ruler of the past, present, and future (see also 4:8; Isaiah 44:6 48:12-15). Without Christ you have nothing that is eternal, nothing can change your life, nothing that can save you from sin. Is Christ y reason for living, the "first and last" of your life? Honor the One wh the beginning and the end of all existence.

CHAPTER 2 JOHN WRITES TO SEVEN CHURCHES.

"To the angel of the church of Ephesus write,

'These things says He who holds the seven stars in His right hand, who walks in the midst of the seven golden lampstands: ²"I know your works, your labor, your patience, and that you cannot bear those who are evil. And you have tested those who say they are apostles and are not, and have found them liars; ³and you have persevered and have patience, and have labored for My name's sake and have not become weary. ⁴Nevertheless I have *this* against you, that you have left your first love. ⁵Remember therefore from where you have fallen; repent and do the first works, or else I will come to you quickly and remove your lampstand from its place—unless you repent. ⁶But this you have, that you hate the deeds of the Nicolaitans, which I also hate.

⁷"He who has an ear, let him hear what the Spirit says to the churches. To him who overcomes I will give to eat from the tree of life, which is in the midst of the Paradise of God." '

⁸"And to the angel of the church in Smyrna write,

'These things says the First and the Last, who was dead, and came to life: [9]"I know your works, tribulation, and poverty (but you are rich); and *I know* the blasphemy of those who say they are Jews and are not, but *are* a synagogue of Satan. [10]Do not fear any of those things which you are about to suffer. Indeed, the devil is about to throw *some* of you into prison, that you may be tested, and you will have tribulation ten days. Be faithful until death, and I will give you the crown of life.

[11]"He who has an ear, let him hear what the Spirit says to the churches. He who overcomes shall not be hurt by the second death." '

[12]"And to the angel of the church in Pergamos write,

'These things says He who has the sharp two-edged sword: [13]"I know your works, and where you dwell, where Satan's throne *is*. And you hold fast to My name, and did not deny My faith even in the days in which Antipas *was* My faithful martyr, who was killed among you, where Satan dwells. [14]But I have a few things against you, because you have there those who hold the doctrine of Balaam, who taught Balak to put a stumbling block before the children of Israel, to eat things sacrificed to idols, and to commit sexual immorality. [15]Thus you also have those who hold the doctrine of the Nicolaitans, which thing I hate. [16]Repent, or else I will come to you quickly and will fight against them with the sword of My mouth.

[17]"He who has an ear, let him hear what the Spirit says to the churches. To him who overcomes I will give some of the hidden manna to eat. And I will give him a white stone, and on the stone a new name written which no one knows except him who receives *it*." '

[18]"And to the angel of the church in Thyatira write,

'These things says the Son of God, who has eyes like a flame of fire, and His feet like fine brass: [19]I know your works, love, service, faith, and your patience; and *as* for your works, the last *are* more than the first. [20]Nevertheless I have a few things against you, because you allow that woman Jezebel, who calls herself a prophetess, to teach and seduce My servants to commit sexual immorality and eat things sacrificed to idols. [21]And I gave her time to repent of her sexual immorality, and she did not repent. [22]Indeed I will cast her into a sickbed, and those who commit adultery with her into great tribulation, unless they repent of their deeds. [23]I will kill her children with death, and all the churches shall know that I am He who searches the minds and hearts. And I will give to each one of you according to your works.

[24]"Now to you I say, and to the rest in Thyatira, as many as do not have this doctrine, who have not known the depths of Satan, as they say, I will put on you no other burden. [25]But hold fast what you have till I come. [26]And he who overcomes, and keeps My works until the end, to him I will give power over the nations—

[27]   'He shall rule them with a rod of iron;
       They shall be dashed to pieces like the potter's
          vessels'—

as I also have received from My Father; [28]and I will give him the morning star.

[29]"He who has an ear, let him hear what the Spirit says to the churches." '

CHAPTER 3 "And to the angel of the church in Sardis write,

'These things says He who has the seven Spirits of God and the seven stars: "I know your works, that you have a

SEX SIN

2:20 Why is sexual immorality serious? Sex outside marriage always hurts someone. It hurts God because it shows that we prefer to follow our own desires instead of God's Word. It hurts others because it violates the commitment so necessary to a marriage relationship. It hurts us because it often brings disease to our body and harms our personality. Sex sin has tremendous power to destroy families, communities, and even nations because it destroys the relationships upon which these institutions are built. God wants to protect us from hurting ourselves and others, so we should have no part in sexual immorality, even if our society says it's all right.

name that you are alive, but you are dead. [2]Be watchful, and strengthen the things which remain, that are ready to die, for I have not found your works perfect before God. [3]Remember therefore how you have received and

Because of my shyness and my family situation, I find it difficult to let people get close to me. As a Christian, I hear all the time how much God loves me. How close does God want to get with me?

I WONDER . . .

As close as you'll let him.

God knows everything about us, and yet he still wants to be a Father to us. Isn't that amazing? King David wrote about how close God wants to be.

"How precious also are Your thoughts to me, O God! How great is the sum of them! *If* I should count them, they would be more in number than the sand; when I awake, I am still with You" (Psalm 139:17-18).

Knowing how much God thinks about us (especially in light of how little we think of him) should give us an incredible feeling of worth. Our response to God's constant attentiveness, however, should never be out of obligation. God does not want us to come close to him only because we feel we have to.

Revelation 2:4 warns us not to allow our love for God to grow weaker. God wants us to progress and grow beyond our initial commitment to him, just like in a marriage where love should continue to grow. Unfortunately, this doesn't always happen. Many people who become Christians are really excited about their new relationship with God. But as problems come up, the excitement often wears off (just like what happens in some marriages!).

To maintain a growing relationship with God, the key word is time: daily time with him, time with others who know him, and time (in years) to grow to appreciate his love for you.

Though God is anxious for an intimate relationship with us, he will wait for the day when we'll experience for ourselves what loving him really means. And what a wonderful day that will be!

heard; hold fast and repent. Therefore if you will not watch, I will come upon you as a thief, and you will not know what hour I will come upon you. ⁴You have a few names even in Sardis who have not defiled their garments; and they shall walk with Me in white, for they are worthy. ⁵He who overcomes shall be clothed in white garments, and I will not blot out his name from the Book of Life; but I will confess his name before My Father and before His angels.

◣ YOUR CHOICE

3:20 Jesus is knocking on the door of our heart every time we sense that we should turn to him. He wants to have fellowship with us, and he wants us to open up to him. Jesus is patient and persistent in trying to get through to us—not breaking and entering, but knocking. He allows us to decide whether or not to open our life to him. Do you intentionally keep Christ's life-changing presence and power on the other side of the door?

⁶"He who has an ear, let him hear what the Spirit says to the churches." '

⁷"And to the angel of the church in Philadelphia write,

'These things says He who is holy, He who is true, *"He who has the key of David, He who opens and no one shuts, and shuts and no one opens":* ⁸I know your works. See, I have set before you an open door, and no one can shut it; for you have a little strength, have kept My word, and have not denied My name. ⁹Indeed I will make *those*

REVELATION 3:20

BEHOLD
I STAND
AT THE
DOOR
AND
KNOCK
K K N O C K
K N O C K K
N O C K
C K

If anyone hears My voice and opens the door, I will come in to him and dine with him and he with Me.

of the synagogue of Satan, who say they are Jews and are not, but lie—indeed I will make them come and worship before your feet, and to know that I have loved you. ¹⁰Because you have kept My command to persevere, I also will keep you from the hour of trial which shall come upon the whole world, to test those who dwell on the earth. ¹¹Behold, I am coming quickly! Hold fast what you have, that no one may take your crown. ¹²He who overcomes, I will make him a pillar in the temple of My God, and he shall go out no more. I will write on him the name of My God and the name of the city of My God, the New Jerusalem, which comes down out of heaven from My God. And *I will write on him* My new name.

¹³"He who has an ear, let him hear what the Spirit says to the churches." '

¹⁴"And to the angel of the church of the Laodiceans write,

'These things says the Amen, the Faithful and True Witness, the Beginning of the creation of God: ¹⁵"I know your works, that you are neither cold nor hot. I could wish you were cold or hot. ¹⁶So then, because you are lukewarm, and neither cold nor hot, I will vomit you out of My mouth. ¹⁷Because you say, 'I am rich, have become wealthy, and have need of nothing'—and do not know that you are wretched, miserable, poor, blind, and naked— ¹⁸I counsel you to buy from Me gold refined in the fire, that you may be rich; and white garments, that you may be clothed, *that* the shame of your nakedness may not be revealed; and anoint your eyes with eye salve, that you may see. ¹⁹As many as I love, I rebuke and chasten. Therefore be zealous and repent. ²⁰Behold, I stand at the door and knock. If anyone hears My voice and opens the door, I will come in to him and dine with him, and he with Me. ²¹To him who overcomes I will grant to sit with Me on My throne, as I also overcame and sat down with My Father on His throne.

²²"He who has an ear, let him hear what the Spirit says to the churches." ' "

CHAPTER **4** THE GLORIOUS THRONE. After these things I looked, and behold, a door *standing* open in heaven. And the first voice which I heard *was* like a trumpet speaking with me, saying, "Come up here, and I will show you things which must take place after this." ²Immediately I was in the Spirit; and behold, a throne set in heaven, and *One* sat on the throne. ³And He who sat there was like a jasper and a sardius stone in appearance; and *there was* a rainbow around the throne, in appearance like an emerald. ⁴Around the throne *were* twenty-four thrones, and on the thrones I saw twenty-four elders sitting, clothed in white robes; and they had crowns of gold on their heads. ⁵And from the throne proceeded lightnings, thunderings, and voices. Seven lamps of fire

◣ NO FEAR

4:1 Chapters 4 and 5 are a glimpse into Christ's glory. Here we se the throne room of heaven. God is orchestrating all the events tha will record. The world is not spinning out of control; the God of cre will carry out his plans as Christ initiates the final battle with the fo evil. John shows us heaven before showing us earth so we will not frightened by future events.

were burning before the throne, which are the seven Spirits of God.

[6]Before the throne *there was* a sea of glass, like crystal. And in the midst of the throne, and around the throne, *were* four living creatures full of eyes in front and in back. [7]The first living creature *was* like a lion, the second living creature like a calf, the third living creature had a face like a man, and the fourth living creature *was* like a flying eagle. [8]*The* four living creatures, each having six wings, were full of eyes around and within. And they do not rest day or night, saying:

"Holy, holy, holy,
Lord God Almighty,
Who was and is and is to come!"

[9]Whenever the living creatures give glory and honor and thanks to Him who sits on the throne, who lives forever and ever, [10]the twenty-four elders fall down before Him who sits on the throne and worship Him who lives forever and ever, and cast their crowns before the throne, saying:

[11]"You are worthy, O Lord,
To receive glory and honor and power;
For You created all things,
And by Your will they exist and were created."

CHAPTER 5 THE SEALED SCROLL AND THE LAMB.

And I saw in the right *hand* of Him who sat on the throne a scroll written inside and on the back, sealed with seven seals. [2]Then I saw a strong angel proclaiming with a loud voice, "Who is worthy to open the scroll and to loose its seals?" [3]And no one in heaven or on the earth or under the earth was able to open the scroll, or to look at it.

[4]So I wept much, because no one was found worthy to open and read the scroll, or to look at it. [5]But one of the elders said to me, "Do not weep. Behold, the Lion of the tribe of Judah, the Root of David, has prevailed to open the scroll and to loose its seven seals."

[6]And I looked, and behold, in the midst of the throne and of the four living creatures, and in the midst of the elders, stood a Lamb as though it had been slain, having seven horns and seven eyes, which are the seven Spirits of God sent out into all the earth. [7]Then He came and took the scroll out of the right hand of Him who sat on the throne.

[8]Now when He had taken the scroll, the four living creatures and the twenty-four elders fell down before the Lamb, each having a harp, and golden bowls full of incense, which are the prayers of the saints. [9]And they sang a new song, saying:

"You are worthy to take the scroll,
And to open its seals;
For You were slain,
And have redeemed us to God by Your blood
Out of every tribe and tongue and people and
    nation,
[10] And have made us kings and priests to our God;
And we shall reign on the earth."

[11]Then I looked, and I heard the voice of many angels around the throne, the living creatures, and the elders; and the number of them was ten thousand times ten thousand, and thousands of thousands, [12]saying with a loud voice:

"Worthy is the Lamb who was slain
To receive power and riches and wisdom,
And strength and honor and glory and blessing!"

◢ ALL TYPES

5:9-10 People from every nation are praising God before his throne. The gospel is not limited to a specific culture, race, or country. Anyone who comes in repentance and faith is accepted by God and will be part of his kingdom. Don't allow prejudice or bias to stop you from sharing Christ with others. Christ welcomes all types of people into his kingdom.

[13]And every creature which is in heaven and on the earth and under the earth and such as are in the sea, and all that are in them, I heard saying:

"Blessing and honor and glory and power
Be to Him who sits on the throne,
And to the Lamb, forever and ever!"

[14]Then the four living creatures said, "Amen!" And the twenty-four elders fell down and worshiped Him who lives forever and ever.

CHAPTER 6 BREAKING THE SEALS ONE BY ONE.

Now I saw when the Lamb opened one of the seals; and I heard one of the four living creatures saying with a voice like thunder, "Come and see." [2]And I looked, and behold, a white horse. He who sat on it had a bow; and a crown was given to him, and he went out conquering and to conquer.

[3]When He opened the second seal, I heard the second living creature saying, "Come and see." [4]Another horse, fiery red, went out. And it was granted to the one who sat on it to take peace from the earth, and that *people* should kill one another; and there was given to him a great sword.

[5]When He opened the third seal, I heard the third living creature say, "Come and see." So I looked, and behold, a black horse, and he who sat on it had a pair of scales in his hand. [6]And I heard a voice in the midst of the four living creatures saying, "A quart of wheat for a denarius, and three quarts of barley for a denarius; and do not harm the oil and the wine."

[7]When He opened the fourth seal, I heard the voice of the fourth living creature saying, "Come and see." [8]So I looked, and behold, a pale horse. And the name of him who sat on it was Death, and Hades followed with him.

◢ GOD'S TIME

6:9-11 The martyrs are eager for God to bring justice to the earth, but they are told to wait. Those who suffer and die for their faith will not be forgotten, nor do they die in vain. Rather, they will be singled out by God for special honor. We may wish for justice immediately, as these martyrs did, but we must be patient. God works on his own timetable, and he promises justice. No suffering for the sake of God's kingdom is wasted effort.

THE ONLY WAY

7:10 **People try many methods to remove the guilt of sin—good works, intellectual pursuits, and even placing blame on others. The crowd in heaven, however, praises God, saying that salvation comes from him and from the Lamb. Salvation from sin's penalty can come only through Jesus Christ. Have you had the guilt of sin removed in the only way possible?**

And power was given to them over a fourth of the earth,
to kill with sword, with hunger, with death, and by the
beasts of the earth.
9When He opened the fifth seal, I saw under the altar
the souls of those who had been slain for the word of God
and for the testimony which they held. 10And they cried
with a loud voice, saying, "How long, O Lord, holy and
true, until You judge and avenge our blood on those who
dwell on the earth?" 11Then a white robe was given to
each of them; and it was said to them that they should
rest a little while longer, until both *the number of* their
fellow servants and their brethren, who would be killed
as they *were,* was completed.
12I looked when He opened the sixth seal, and behold,
there was a great earthquake; and the sun became black
as sackcloth of hair, and the moon became like blood.
13And the stars of heaven fell to the earth, as a fig tree
drops its late figs when it is shaken by a mighty wind.
14Then the sky receded as a scroll when it is rolled up, and
every mountain and island was moved out of its place.
15And the kings of the earth, the great men, the rich men,
the commanders, the mighty men, every slave and every
free man, hid themselves in the caves and in the rocks of
the mountains, 16and said to the mountains and rocks,
"Fall on us and hide us from the face of Him who sits on
the throne and from the wrath of the Lamb! 17For the
great day of His wrath has come, and who is able to
stand?"

CHAPTER **7** **THE 144,000 CHOSEN BY GOD.** After
these things I saw four angels standing at the four corners of the earth, holding the four winds of the earth, that
the wind should not blow on the earth, on the sea, or on
any tree. 2Then I saw another angel ascending from the
east, having the seal of the living God. And he cried with
a loud voice to the four angels to whom it was granted to
harm the earth and the sea, 3saying, "Do not harm the
earth, the sea, or the trees till we have sealed the servants
of our God on their foreheads." 4And I heard the number
of those who were sealed. One hundred *and* forty-four
thousand of all the tribes of the children of Israel *were*
sealed:

5 of the tribe of Judah twelve thousand *were* sealed;
of the tribe of Reuben twelve thousand *were* sealed;
of the tribe of Gad twelve thousand *were* sealed;
6 of the tribe of Asher twelve thousand *were* sealed;
of the tribe of Naphtali twelve thousand *were* sealed;
of the tribe of Manasseh twelve thousand *were*
sealed;
7 of the tribe of Simeon twelve thousand *were* sealed;
of the tribe of Levi twelve thousand *were* sealed;
of the tribe of Issachar twelve thousand *were* sealed;
8 of the tribe of Zebulun twelve thousand *were* sealed;

THE NAMES OF JESUS

JESUS' NAME	REFERENCE
A AND Ω THE BEGINNING AND THE END	1:8
LORD	1:8
THE ALMIGHTY	1:8
Son of Man	1:13
THE FIRST AND THE LAST	1:17
Son of GOD	2:18
WITNESS	3:14
CREATOR	4:11
Lion of the tribe of Judah	5:5
ROOT OF DAVID	5:5
Lamb	5:6
Shepherd	7:17
CHRIST	12:10
FAITHFUL FAITHFUL FAITHFUL FAITHFUL AND TRUE	19:11
THE WORD OF GOD	19:13
KING of KINGS	19:16
LORD of LORDS	19:16
THE BRIGHT AND MORNING STAR	22:16

Scattered among the vivid images of the book of Revelation is a large collection of names for Jesus. Each one tells something of his character and highlights a particular aspect of his role within God's plan of redemption.

were burning before the throne, which are the seven Spirits of God.

⁶Before the throne *there was* a sea of glass, like crystal. And in the midst of the throne, and around the throne, *were* four living creatures full of eyes in front and in back. ⁷The first living creature *was* like a lion, the second living creature like a calf, the third living creature had a face like a man, and the fourth living creature *was* like a flying eagle. ⁸*The* four living creatures, each having six wings, were full of eyes around and within. And they do not rest day or night, saying:

"Holy, holy, holy,
 Lord God Almighty,
 Who was and is and is to come!"

⁹Whenever the living creatures give glory and honor and thanks to Him who sits on the throne, who lives forever and ever, ¹⁰the twenty-four elders fall down before Him who sits on the throne and worship Him who lives forever and ever, and cast their crowns before the throne, saying:

¹¹ "You are worthy, O Lord,
 To receive glory and honor and power;
 For You created all things,
 And by Your will they exist and were created."

CHAPTER **5** THE SEALED SCROLL AND THE LAMB.

And I saw in the right *hand* of Him who sat on the throne a scroll written inside and on the back, sealed with seven seals. ²Then I saw a strong angel proclaiming with a loud voice, "Who is worthy to open the scroll and to loose its seals?" ³And no one in heaven or on the earth or under the earth was able to open the scroll, or to look at it.

⁴So I wept much, because no one was found worthy to open and read the scroll, or to look at it. ⁵But one of the elders said to me, "Do not weep. Behold, the Lion of the tribe of Judah, the Root of David, has prevailed to open the scroll and to loose its seven seals."

⁶And I looked, and behold, in the midst of the throne and of the four living creatures, and in the midst of the elders, stood a Lamb as though it had been slain, having seven horns and seven eyes, which are the seven Spirits of God sent out into all the earth. ⁷Then He came and took the scroll out of the right hand of Him who sat on the throne.

⁸Now when He had taken the scroll, the four living creatures and the twenty-four elders fell down before the Lamb, each having a harp, and golden bowls full of incense, which are the prayers of the saints. ⁹And they sang a new song, saying:

"You are worthy to take the scroll,
 And to open its seals;
 For You were slain,
 And have redeemed us to God by Your blood
 Out of every tribe and tongue and people and
     nation,
¹⁰ And have made us kings and priests to our God;
 And we shall reign on the earth."

¹¹Then I looked, and I heard the voice of many angels

around the throne, the living creatures, and the elders; and the number of them was ten thousand times ten thousand, and thousands of thousands, ¹²saying with a loud voice:

"Worthy is the Lamb who was slain
 To receive power and riches and wisdom,
 And strength and honor and glory and blessing!"

▌ALL TYPES

5:9-10 People from every nation are praising God before his throne. The gospel is not limited to a specific culture, race, or country. Anyone who comes in repentance and faith is accepted by God and will be part of his kingdom. Don't allow prejudice or bias to stop you from sharing Christ with others. Christ welcomes all types of people into his kingdom.

¹³And every creature which is in heaven and on the earth and under the earth and such as are in the sea, and all that are in them, I heard saying:

"Blessing and honor and glory and power
 Be to Him who sits on the throne,
 And to the Lamb, forever and ever!"

¹⁴Then the four living creatures said, "Amen!" And the twenty-four elders fell down and worshiped Him who lives forever and ever.

CHAPTER **6** BREAKING THE SEALS ONE BY ONE.

Now I saw when the Lamb opened one of the seals; and I heard one of the four living creatures saying with a voice like thunder, "Come and see." ²And I looked, and behold, a white horse. He who sat on it had a bow; and a crown was given to him, and he went out conquering and to conquer.

³When He opened the second seal, I heard the second living creature saying, "Come and see." ⁴Another horse, fiery red, went out. And it was granted to the one who sat on it to take peace from the earth, and that *people* should kill one another; and there was given to him a great sword.

⁵When He opened the third seal, I heard the third living creature say, "Come and see." So I looked, and behold, a black horse, and he who sat on it had a pair of scales in his hand. ⁶And I heard a voice in the midst of the four living creatures saying, "A quart of wheat for a denarius, and three quarts of barley for a denarius; and do not harm the oil and the wine."

⁷When He opened the fourth seal, I heard the voice of the fourth living creature saying, "Come and see." ⁸So I looked, and behold, a pale horse. And the name of him who sat on it was Death, and Hades followed with him.

▌GOD'S TIME

6:9-11 The martyrs are eager for God to bring justice to the earth, but they are told to wait. Those who suffer and die for their faith will not be forgotten, nor do they die in vain. Rather, they will be singled out by God for special honor. We may wish for justice immediately, as these martyrs did, but we must be patient. God works on his own timetable, and he promises justice. No suffering for the sake of God's kingdom is wasted effort.

of the tribe of Joseph twelve thousand *were* sealed; of the tribe of Benjamin twelve thousand *were* sealed.

⁹After these things I looked, and behold, a great multitude which no one could number, of all nations, tribes, peoples, and tongues, standing before the throne and before the Lamb, clothed with white robes, with palm branches in their hands, ¹⁰and crying out with a loud voice, saying, "Salvation *belongs* to our God who sits on the throne, and to the Lamb!" ¹¹All the angels stood around the throne and the elders and the four living creatures, and fell on their faces before the throne and worshiped God, ¹²saying:

"Amen! Blessing and glory and wisdom,
Thanksgiving and honor and power and might,
Be to our God forever and ever.
Amen."

¹³Then one of the elders answered, saying to me, "Who are these arrayed in white robes, and where did they come from?"

¹⁴And I said to him, "Sir, you know."

So he said to me, "These are the ones who come out of the great tribulation, and washed their robes and made them white in the blood of the Lamb. ¹⁵Therefore they are before the throne of God, and serve Him day and night in His temple. And He who sits on the throne will dwell among them. ¹⁶They shall neither hunger anymore nor thirst anymore; the sun shall not strike them, nor any heat; ¹⁷for the Lamb who is in the midst of the throne will shepherd them and lead them to living fountains of waters. And God will wipe away every tear from their eyes."

CHAPTER **8** THE SEVENTH SEAL IS BROKEN.

When He opened the seventh seal, there was silence in heaven for about half an hour. ²And I saw the seven angels who stand before God, and to them were given seven trumpets. ³Then another angel, having a golden censer, came and stood at the altar. He was given much incense, that he should offer *it* with the prayers of all the saints upon the golden altar which was before the throne. ⁴And the smoke of the incense, with the prayers of the saints, ascended before God from the angel's hand. ⁵Then the angel took the censer, filled it with fire from the altar, and threw *it* to the earth. And there were noises, thunderings, lightnings, and an earthquake.

⁶So the seven angels who had the seven trumpets prepared themselves to sound.

⁷The first angel sounded: And hail and fire followed, mingled with blood, and they were thrown to the earth. And a third of the trees were burned up, and all green grass was burned up.

⁸Then the second angel sounded: And *something* like a great mountain burning with fire was thrown into the sea, and a third of the sea became blood. ⁹And a third of the living creatures in the sea died, and a third of the ships were destroyed.

¹⁰Then the third angel sounded: And a great star fell from heaven, burning like a torch, and it fell on a third of the rivers and on the springs of water. ¹¹The name of the star is Wormwood. A third of the waters became wormwood, and many men died from the water, because it was made bitter.

¹²Then the fourth angel sounded: And a third of the sun was struck, a third of the moon, and a third of the stars, so that a third of them were darkened. A third of the day did not shine, and likewise the night.

MAKE SURE

8:6 The trumpet blasts have three purposes: (1) to warn that judgment is certain, (2) to call the forces of good and evil to battle, and (3) to announce the return of the King, the Messiah. These warnings urge us to make sure our faith is firmly fixed on Christ.

¹³And I looked, and I heard an angel flying through the midst of heaven, saying with a loud voice, "Woe, woe, woe to the inhabitants of the earth, because of the remaining blasts of the trumpet of the three angels who are about to sound!"

CHAPTER **9**

Then the fifth angel sounded: And I saw a star fallen from heaven to the earth. To him was given the key to the bottomless pit. ²And he opened the bottomless pit, and smoke arose out of the pit like the smoke of a great furnace. So the sun and the air were darkened because of the smoke of the pit. ³Then out of the smoke locusts came upon the earth. And to them was given power, as the scorpions of the earth have power. ⁴They were commanded not to harm the grass of the earth, or any green thing, or any tree, but only those men who do not have the seal of God on their foreheads. ⁵And they were not given *authority* to kill them, but to torment them *for* five months. Their torment *was* like the torment of a scorpion when it strikes a man. ⁶In those days men will seek death and will not find it; they will desire to die, and death will flee from them.

⁷The shape of the locusts was like horses prepared for battle. On their heads were crowns of something like gold, and their faces *were* like the faces of men. ⁸They had hair like women's hair, and their teeth were like lions' *teeth.* ⁹And they had breastplates like breastplates of iron, and the sound of their wings *was* like the sound of chariots with many horses running into battle. ¹⁰They had tails like scorpions, and there were stings in their tails. Their power *was* to hurt men five months. ¹¹And they had as king over them the angel of the bottomless pit, whose name in Hebrew *is* Abaddon, but in Greek he has the name Apollyon.

¹²One woe is past. Behold, still two more woes are coming after these things.

¹³Then the sixth angel sounded: And I heard a voice from the four horns of the golden altar which is before God, ¹⁴saying to the sixth angel who had the trumpet, "Release the four angels who are bound at the great river Euphrates." ¹⁵So the four angels, who had been prepared for the hour and day and month and year, were released to kill a third of mankind. ¹⁶Now the number of the army of the horsemen *was* two hundred million; I heard the number of them. ¹⁷And thus I saw the horses in the vision: those who sat on them had breastplates of fiery red,

9:20-21 These people were so hardhearted that even plagues did not drive them to God. People don't usually fall into immorality and evil suddenly—they slip into it a little at a time until they are entangled in their wicked ways. Any person who allows sin to take root in his life can find himself in this predicament. Temptation entertained today becomes sin tomorrow, a habit the next day, then death and separation from God forever (see James 1:15). To think you could never become this evil is the first step toward a hard heart. Acknowledge your need to confess your sin to God.

hyacinth blue, and sulfur yellow; and the heads of the horses *were* like the heads of lions; and out of their mouths came fire, smoke, and brimstone. ¹⁸By these three *plagues* a third of mankind was killed—by the fire and the smoke and the brimstone which came out of

SEEK THE TRUTH

"Dana, are you still planning to talk to Rhonda?"

"I've got to. Those people she's been hanging around are weird. My mom even thinks they're a cult!"

"So why don't her parents say something? I mean, my folks would kill me if I came home spouting all that junk!"

"Oh, Mr. and Mrs. Jordan don't care what she does. He's all wrapped up in his business, and she's got some pretty strange religious ideas herself. Their basic attitude is, 'Whatever makes you happy, Rhonda.'"

"What do you think she'll say?"

"I don't know."

"What are you going to say?"

"I'm going to tell her that what she's been hearing from those people isn't true. I'll show her what the Bible says about false teachers. And I'll challenge her to quit seeking some kind of ooey-gooey feeling and start seeking the truth."

We need more people like Dana—people who cling doggedly to the truth and who encourage others to do the same. Would you have the courage to confront a friend who was caught up in a false religion? Would you know what to say? As you read Revelation, notice the constant emphasis on seeking the truth.

their mouths. ¹⁹For their power is in their mouth and in their tails; for their tails *are* like serpents, having heads; and with them they do harm.

²⁰But the rest of mankind, who were not killed by these plagues, did not repent of the works of their hands, that they should not worship demons, and idols of gold, silver, brass, stone, and wood, which can neither see nor hear nor walk. ²¹And they did not repent of their murders or their sorceries or their sexual immorality or their thefts.

CHAPTER 10 AN ANGEL WITH A BOOK TO EAT. I saw still another mighty angel coming down from heaven, clothed with a cloud. And a rainbow *was* on his head, his face *was* like the sun, and his feet like pillars of fire. ²He had a little book open in his hand. And he set his right foot on the sea and *his* left *foot* on the land, ³and cried with a loud voice, as *when* a lion roars. When he cried out, seven thunders uttered their voices. ⁴Now

when the seven thunders uttered their voices, I was about to write; but I heard a voice from heaven saying to me, "Seal up the things which the seven thunders uttered, and do not write them."

⁵The angel whom I saw standing on the sea and on the land raised up his hand to heaven ⁶and swore by Him who lives forever and ever, who created heaven and the things that are in it, the earth and the things that are in it, and the sea and the things that are in it, that there should be delay no longer, ⁷but in the days of the sounding of the seventh angel, when he is about to sound, the mystery of God would be finished, as He declared to His servants the prophets.

⁸Then the voice which I heard from heaven spoke to me again and said, "Go, take the little book which is open in the hand of the angel who stands on the sea and on the earth."

⁹So I went to the angel and said to him, "Give me the little book."

And he said to me, "Take and eat it; and it will make your stomach bitter, but it will be as sweet as honey in your mouth."

¹⁰Then I took the little book out of the angel's hand and ate it, and it was as sweet as honey in my mouth. But when I had eaten it, my stomach became bitter. ¹¹And he said to me, "You must prophesy again about many peoples, nations, tongues, and kings."

CHAPTER 11 TWO WITNESSES. Then I was given a reed like a measuring rod. And the angel stood, saying, "Rise and measure the temple of God, the altar, and those who worship there. ²But leave out the court which is outside the temple, and do not measure it, for it has been given to the Gentiles. And they will tread the holy city underfoot *for* forty-two months. ³And I will give *power* to my two witnesses, and they will prophesy one thousand two hundred and sixty days, clothed in sackcloth."

⁴These are the two olive trees and the two lampstands standing before the God of the earth. ⁵And if anyone wants to harm them, fire proceeds from their mouth and devours their enemies. And if anyone wants to harm them, he must be killed in this manner. ⁶These have power to shut heaven, so that no rain falls in the days of their prophecy; and they have power over waters to turn them to blood, and to strike the earth with all plagues, as often as they desire.

⁷When they finish their testimony, the beast that ascends out of the bottomless pit will make war against them, overcome them, and kill them. ⁸And their dead

CARPE DIEM

10:4 Throughout history people have wanted to know what would happen in the future, and God reveals some of it in this book. But J was stopped from revealing certain parts of his vision. An angel also the prophet Daniel that some things he saw were not to be revealed to everyone (Daniel 12:9), and Jesus told his disciples that the time the end is known by no one but God (Mark 13:32-33). God has reve all we need to know to live for him now. In our desire to be ready f end, we must not place more emphasis on speculation about the las than on living for God while we wait.

bodies *will lie* in the street of the great city which spiritually is called Sodom and Egypt, where also our Lord was crucified. ⁹Then *those* from the peoples, tribes, tongues, and nations will see their dead bodies three-and-a-half days, and not allow their dead bodies to be put into graves. ¹⁰And those who dwell on the earth will rejoice over them, make merry, and send gifts to one another, because these two prophets tormented those who dwell on the earth.

¹¹Now after the three-and-a-half days the breath of life from God entered them, and they stood on their feet, and great fear fell on those who saw them. ¹²And they heard a loud voice from heaven saying to them, "Come up here." And they ascended to heaven in a cloud, and their enemies saw them. ¹³In the same hour there was a great earthquake, and a tenth of the city fell. In the earthquake seven thousand people were killed, and the rest were afraid and gave glory to the God of heaven.

¹⁴The second woe is past. Behold, the third woe is coming quickly.

¹⁵Then the seventh angel sounded: And there were loud voices in heaven, saying, "The kingdoms of this world have become *the kingdoms* of our Lord and of His Christ, and He shall reign forever and ever!" ¹⁶And the twenty-four elders who sat before God on their thrones fell on their faces and worshiped God, ¹⁷saying:

"We give You thanks, O Lord God Almighty,
　The One who is and who was and who is to come,
　Because You have taken Your great power and
　　reigned.
¹⁸　The nations were angry, and Your wrath has come,
　And the time of the dead, that they should be judged,
　And that You should reward Your servants the
　　prophets and the saints,
　And those who fear Your name, small and great,
　And should destroy those who destroy the earth."

¹⁹Then the temple of God was opened in heaven, and the ark of His covenant was seen in His temple. And there were lightnings, noises, thunderings, an earthquake, and great hail.

CHAPTER **12** THE WOMAN AND THE DRAGON.

Now a great sign appeared in heaven: a woman clothed with the sun, with the moon under her feet, and on her head a garland of twelve stars. ²Then being with child, she cried out in labor and in pain to give birth.

³And another sign appeared in heaven: behold, a great, fiery red dragon having seven heads and ten horns, and seven diadems on his heads. ⁴His tail drew a third of the stars of heaven and threw them to the earth. And the dragon stood before the woman who was ready to give birth, to devour her Child as soon as it was born. ⁵She bore a male Child who was to rule all nations with a rod of iron. And her Child was caught up to God and His throne. ⁶Then the woman fled into the wilderness, where she has a place prepared by God, that they should feed her there one thousand two hundred and sixty days.

⁷And war broke out in heaven: Michael and his angels fought with the dragon; and the dragon and his angels fought, ⁸but they did not prevail, nor was a place found for them in heaven any longer. ⁹So the great dragon was cast out, that serpent of old, called the Devil and Satan, who deceives the whole world; he was cast to the earth, and his angels were cast out with him.

¹⁰Then I heard a loud voice saying in heaven, "Now salvation, and strength, and the kingdom of our God, and the power of His Christ have come, for the accuser of our brethren, who accused them before our God day and night, has been cast down. ¹¹And they overcame him by the blood of the Lamb and by the word of their testimony, and they did not love their lives to the death. ¹²Therefore rejoice, O heavens, and you who dwell in them! Woe to the inhabitants of the earth and the sea! For the devil has come down to you, having great wrath, because he knows that he has a short time."

¹³Now when the dragon saw that he had been cast to the earth, he persecuted the woman who gave birth to the male *Child*. ¹⁴But the woman was given two wings of a great eagle, that she might fly into the wilderness to her place, where she is nourished for a time and times and half a time, from the presence of the serpent. ¹⁵So the serpent spewed water out of his mouth like a flood after the woman, that he might cause her to be carried away by the flood. ¹⁶But the earth helped the woman, and the earth opened its mouth and swallowed up the flood which the dragon had spewed out of his mouth. ¹⁷And the dragon was enraged with the woman, and he went to make war with the rest of her offspring, who keep the commandments of God and have the testimony of Jesus Christ.

CHAPTER **13** THE TWO STRANGE BEASTS. Then I

stood on the sand of the sea. And I saw a beast rising up out of the sea, having seven heads and ten horns, and on his horns ten crowns, and on his heads a blasphemous name. ²Now the beast which I saw was like a leopard, his feet were like *the feet of* a bear, and his mouth like the mouth of a lion. The dragon gave him his power, his throne, and great authority. ³And *I saw* one of his heads as if it had been mortally wounded, and his deadly wound was healed. And all the world marveled and followed the beast. ⁴So they worshiped the dragon who gave authority to the beast; and they worshiped the beast, saying, "Who *is* like the beast? Who is able to make war with him?"

⁵And he was given a mouth speaking great things and blasphemies, and he was given authority to continue for

CREATURES

13:1ff Satan (the dragon) has two evil accomplices: (1) the beast out of the sea (13:1ff) and (2) the beast out of the earth (13:11ff). Together, the three form an unholy trinity in direct opposition to the holy Trinity of God, Christ, and the Holy Spirit.

When Satan tempted Jesus in the wilderness, he wanted Jesus to show his power (see Matthew 4:1-11). Satan wanted to rule the world through Jesus, but Jesus refused to do what Satan asked. Thus Satan turns to the fearsome beasts of Revelation, giving them special powers. This unholy trinity—the dragon, the beast out of the sea, and the false prophet (see 16:13)—unite in a desperate attempt to overthrow God. To find out what becomes of them, read Revelation 19:19-21 and 20:10.

forty-two months. ⁶Then he opened his mouth in blasphemy against God, to blaspheme His name, His tabernacle, and those who dwell in heaven. ⁷It was granted to him to make war with the saints and to overcome them. And authority was given him over every tribe, tongue, and nation. ⁸All who dwell on the earth will worship him, whose names have not been written in the Book of Life of the Lamb slain from the foundation of the world.

⁹If anyone has an ear, let him hear. ¹⁰He who leads into captivity shall go into captivity; he who kills with the sword must be killed with the sword. Here is the patience and the faith of the saints.

¹¹Then I saw another beast coming up out of the earth, and he had two horns like a lamb and spoke like a dragon. ¹²And he exercises all the authority of the first beast in his presence, and causes the earth and those who dwell in it to worship the first beast, whose deadly wound was healed. ¹³He performs great signs, so that he even makes fire come down from heaven on the earth in the sight of men. ¹⁴And he deceives those who dwell on the earth by those signs which he was granted to do in the sight of the beast, telling those who dwell on the earth to make an image to the beast who was wounded by the sword and lived. ¹⁵He was granted *power* to give breath to the image of the beast, that the image of the beast should both speak and cause as many as would not worship the image of the beast to be killed. ¹⁶He causes all, both small and great, rich and poor, free and slave, to receive a mark on their right hand or on their foreheads, ¹⁷and that no one may buy or sell except one who has the mark or the name of the beast, or the number of his name.

¹⁸Here is wisdom. Let him who has understanding calculate the number of the beast, for it is the number of a man: His number *is* 666.

CHAPTER 14 THE LAMB AND A GREAT CHOIR.

Then I looked, and behold, a Lamb standing on Mount Zion, and with Him one hundred *and* forty-four thousand, having His Father's name written on their foreheads. ²And I heard a voice from heaven, like the voice of many waters, and like the voice of loud thunder. And I heard the sound of harpists playing their harps. ³They sang as it were a new song before the throne, before the four living creatures, and the elders; and no one could learn that song except the hundred *and* forty-four thousand who were redeemed from the earth. ⁴These are the ones who were not defiled with women, for they are virgins. These are the ones who follow the Lamb wherever He goes. These were redeemed from *among* men, *being* firstfruits to God and to the Lamb. ⁵And in their mouth was found no deceit, for they are without fault before the throne of God.

⁶Then I saw another angel flying in the midst of heaven, having the everlasting gospel to preach to those who dwell on the earth—to every nation, tribe, tongue, and people— ⁷saying with a loud voice, "Fear God and give glory to Him, for the hour of His judgment has come; and worship Him who made heaven and earth, the sea and springs of water."

▶ PASSED OUT

14:14-17 This is an image of judgment: Christ is separating the faithful from the unfaithful like a farmer harvesting his crops. This a time of joy for the Christians who have been persecuted and martyred— they will receive their long awaited reward. Christians should not fear the last judgment. Jesus said, "Most assuredly, I sa you, he who hears My word and believes in Him who sent Me has everlasting life, and shall not come into judgment, but has passed death into life" (John 5:24).

⁸And another angel followed, saying, "Babylon is fallen, is fallen, that great city, because she has made all nations drink of the wine of the wrath of her fornication."

⁹Then a third angel followed them, saying with a loud voice, "If anyone worships the beast and his image, and receives *his* mark on his forehead or on his hand, ¹⁰he himself shall also drink of the wine of the wrath of God, which is poured out full strength into the cup of His indignation. He shall be tormented with fire and brimstone in the presence of the holy angels and in the presence of the Lamb. ¹¹And the smoke of their torment ascends forever and ever; and they have no rest day or night, who worship the beast and his image, and whoever receives the mark of his name."

¹²Here is the patience of the saints; here *are* those who keep the commandments of God and the faith of Jesus.

¹³Then I heard a voice from heaven saying to me, "Write: 'Blessed *are* the dead who die in the Lord from now on.'"

"Yes," says the Spirit, "that they may rest from their labors, and their works follow them."

¹⁴Then I looked, and behold, a white cloud, and on the cloud sat *One* like the Son of Man, having on His head a golden crown, and in His hand a sharp sickle. ¹⁵And another angel came out of the temple, crying with a loud voice to Him who sat on the cloud, "Thrust in Your sickle and reap, for the time has come for You to reap, for the harvest of the earth is ripe." ¹⁶So He who sat on the cloud thrust in His sickle on the earth, and the earth was reaped.

¹⁷Then another angel came out of the temple which is in heaven, he also having a sharp sickle.

¹⁸And another angel came out from the altar, who had power over fire, and he cried with a loud cry to him who had the sharp sickle, saying, "Thrust in your sharp sickle and gather the clusters of the vine of the earth, for her grapes are fully ripe." ¹⁹So the angel thrust his sickle into the earth and gathered the vine of the earth, and threw *it* into the great winepress of the wrath of God. ²⁰And the winepress was trampled outside the city, and blood came out of the winepress, up to the horses' bridles, for one thousand six hundred furlongs.

CHAPTER 15

Then I saw another sign in heaven, great and marvelous: seven angels having the seven last plagues, for in them the wrath of God is complete.

²And I saw *something* like a sea of glass mingled with fire, and those who have the victory over the beast, over his image and over his mark *and* over the number of his name, standing on the sea of glass, having harps of God.

[3]They sing the song of Moses, the servant of God, and the song of the Lamb, saying:

"Great and marvelous *are* Your works,
Lord God Almighty!
Just and true *are* Your ways,
O King of the saints!
[4] Who shall not fear You, O Lord, and glorify Your
name?
For *You* alone *are* holy.
For all nations shall come and worship before You,
For Your judgments have been manifested."

[5]After these things I looked, and behold, the temple of the tabernacle of the testimony in heaven was opened. [6]And out of the temple came the seven angels having the seven plagues, clothed in pure bright linen, and having their chests girded with golden bands. [7]Then one of the four living creatures gave to the seven angels seven golden bowls full of the wrath of God who lives forever and ever. [8]The temple was filled with smoke from the glory of God and from His power, and no one was able to enter the temple till the seven plagues of the seven angels were completed.

CHAPTER 16 SEVEN BOWLS OF WRATH. Then I

heard a loud voice from the temple saying to the seven angels, "Go and pour out the bowls of the wrath of God on the earth."

[2]So the first went and poured out his bowl upon the earth, and a foul and loathsome sore came upon the men who had the mark of the beast and those who worshiped his image.

[3]Then the second angel poured out his bowl on the sea, and it became blood as of a dead *man;* and every living creature in the sea died.

[4]Then the third angel poured out his bowl on the rivers and springs of water, and they became blood. [5]And I heard the angel of the waters saying:

"You are righteous, O Lord,
The One who is and who was and
who is to be,
Because You have judged these
things.
[6] For they have shed the blood of
saints and prophets,
And You have given them blood
to drink.
For it is their just due."

[7]And I heard another from the altar saying, "Even so, Lord God Almighty, true and righteous *are* Your judgments."

[8]Then the fourth angel poured out his bowl on the sun, and power was given to him to scorch men with fire. [9]And men were scorched with great heat, and they blasphemed the name of God who has power over these plagues; and they did not repent and give Him glory.

[10]Then the fifth angel poured out his bowl on the throne of the beast, and his kingdom became full of darkness; and they gnawed their tongues because of the pain. [11]They blasphemed the God of heaven because of their pains and their sores, and did not repent of their deeds.

READY OR NOT

16:15 Christ will return unexpectedly (1 Thessalonians 5:1-6), so we must be ready when he returns. We can prepare ourselves by resisting temptation and by being committed to God's moral standards. In what ways does your life show your readiness for Christ's return?

[12]Then the sixth angel poured out his bowl on the great river Euphrates, and its water was dried up, so that the way of the kings from the east might be prepared. [13]And I saw three unclean spirits like frogs *coming* out of the mouth of the dragon, out of the mouth of the beast, and out of the mouth of the false prophet. [14]For they are spirits of demons, performing signs, *which* go out to the kings of the earth and of the whole world, to gather them to the battle of that great day of God Almighty.

[15]"Behold, I am coming as a thief. Blessed *is* he who watches, and keeps his garments, lest he walk naked and they see his shame."

[16]And they gathered them together to the place called in Hebrew, Armageddon.

[17]Then the seventh angel poured out his bowl into the air, and a loud voice came out of the temple of heaven, from the throne, saying, "It is done!" [18]And there were noises and thunderings and lightnings; and there was a great earthquake, such a mighty and great earthquake as had not occurred since men were on the earth. [19]Now the great city was divided into three parts, and the cities of the nations fell. And great Babylon was remembered before God, to give her the cup of the wine of the fierceness

"Here's what I did..."

I struggle with apathy. I guess you can say I'm not very self-disciplined. This affects both my schoolwork and my Christian life: I have trouble applying myself to what I need to do if I don't feel like doing it at the moment.

In my youth group we studied 2 Timothy and one verse has really challenged me directly: verse 15 of chapter 2. It says, "Be diligent to present yourself approved to God, a worker who does not need to be ashamed, rightly dividing the word of truth." These words remind me that my actions and attitudes are significant, and someday I'll have to answer to God for them. Revelation tells about when that will happen (14:7). That helps me make an extra effort to do the right thing, whether it's reading my Bible regularly or turning off the TV and opening a textbook.

Sue AGE 15

of His wrath. [20]Then every island fled away, and the mountains were not found. [21]And great hail from heaven fell upon men, *each hailstone* about the weight of a talent. Men blasphemed God because of the plague of the hail, since that plague was exceedingly great.

CHAPTER 17 A DRUNKEN WOMAN.

Then one of the seven angels who had the seven bowls came and talked with me, saying to me, "Come, I will show you the judgment of the great harlot who sits on many waters, [2]with whom the kings of the earth committed fornication, and the inhabitants of the earth were made drunk with the wine of her fornication."

[3]So he carried me away in the Spirit into the wilderness. And I saw a woman sitting on a scarlet beast *which was* full of names of blasphemy, having seven heads and ten horns. [4]The woman was arrayed in purple and scarlet, and adorned with gold and precious stones and pearls, having in her hand a golden cup full of abominations and the filthiness of her fornication. [5]And on her forehead a name *was* written:

MYSTERY,
BABYLON THE GREAT,
THE MOTHER OF HARLOTS
AND OF THE ABOMINATIONS
OF THE EARTH.

[6]I saw the woman, drunk with the blood of the saints and with the blood of the martyrs of Jesus. And when I saw her, I marveled with great amazement.

[7]But the angel said to me, "Why did you marvel? I will tell you the mystery of the woman and of the beast that carries her, which has the seven heads and the ten horns. [8]The beast that you saw was, and is not, and will ascend out of the bottomless pit and go to perdition. And those who dwell on the earth will marvel, whose names are not written in the Book of Life from the foundation of the world, when they see the beast that was, and is not, and yet is.

◣◣◣◣◣ IN CHARGE

17:17 No matter what happens, we must trust that God is still in charge, that his plans will happen just as he says. He even uses people opposed to him to execute his will. Although he allows evil to permeate this present world, the new earth will never know sin.

[9]"Here *is* the mind which has wisdom: The seven heads are seven mountains on which the woman sits. [10]There are also seven kings. Five have fallen, one is, *and* the other has not yet come. And when he comes, he must continue a short time. [11]The beast that was, and is not, is himself also the eighth, and is of the seven, and is going to perdition.

[12]"The ten horns which you saw are ten kings who have received no kingdom as yet, but they receive authority for one hour as kings with the beast. [13]These are of one mind, and they will give their power and authority to the beast. [14]These will make war with the Lamb, and the Lamb will overcome them, for He is Lord of lords and King of kings; and those *who are* with Him *are* called, chosen, and faithful."

[15]Then he said to me, "The waters which you saw, where the harlot sits, are peoples, multitudes, nations, and tongues. [16]And the ten horns which you saw on the beast, these will hate the harlot, make her desolate and naked, eat her flesh and burn her with fire. [17]For God has put it into their hearts to fulfill His purpose, to be of one mind, and to give their kingdom to the beast, until the words of God are fulfilled. [18]And the woman whom you saw is that great city which reigns over the kings of the earth."

CHAPTER 18 THE FALL OF BABYLON.

After these things I saw another angel coming down from heaven, having great authority, and the earth was illuminated with his glory. [2]And he cried mightily with a loud voice, saying, "Babylon the great is fallen, is fallen, and has become a dwelling place of demons, a prison for every foul spirit, and a cage for every unclean and hated bird! [3]For all the nations have drunk of the wine of the wrath of her fornication, the kings of the earth have committed fornication with her, and the merchants of the earth have become rich through the abundance of her luxury."

[4]And I heard another voice from heaven saying, "Come out of her, my people, lest you share in her sins, and lest you receive of her plagues. [5]For her sins have reached to heaven, and God has remembered her iniquities. [6]Render to her just as she rendered to you, and repay her double according to her works; in the cup which she has mixed, mix double for her. [7]In the measure that she glorified herself and lived luxuriously, in the same measure give her torment and sorrow; for she says in her heart, 'I sit *as* queen, and am no widow, and will not see sorrow.' [8]Therefore her plagues will come in one day—death and mourning and famine. And she will be utterly burned with fire, for strong *is* the Lord God who judges her.

[9]"The kings of the earth who committed fornication and lived luxuriously with her will weep and lament for her, when they see the smoke of her burning, [10]standing at a distance for fear of her torment, saying, 'Alas, alas, that great city Babylon, that mighty city! For in one hour your judgment has come.'

[11]"And the merchants of the earth will weep and mourn over her, for no one buys their merchandise anymore: [12]merchandise of gold and silver, precious stones and pearls, fine linen and purple, silk and scarlet, every kind of citron wood, every kind of object of ivory, every kind of object of most precious wood, bronze, iron, and marble; [13]and cinnamon and incense, fragrant oil and frankincense, wine and oil, fine flour and wheat, cattle and sheep, horses and chariots, and bodies and souls of men. [14]The fruit that your soul longed for has gone from you, and all the things which are rich and splendid have

◣◣◣◣◣ GREED GUARD

18:11-19 God's people should not live for money. Instead, they should keep on guard constantly against greed, which is always ready ➤ take over their life. Money will be worthless in eternity, and God calls greed sinful.

gone from you, and you shall find them no more at all. [15]The merchants of these things, who became rich by her, will stand at a distance for fear of her torment, weeping and wailing, [16]and saying, 'Alas, alas, that great city that was clothed in fine linen, purple, and scarlet, and adorned with gold and precious stones and pearls! [17]For in one hour such great riches came to nothing.' Every shipmaster, all who travel by ship, sailors, and as many as trade on the sea, stood at a distance [18]and cried out when they saw the smoke of her burning, saying, 'What *is* like this great city?'

[19]"They threw dust on their heads and cried out, weeping and wailing, and saying, 'Alas, alas, that great city, in which all who had ships on the sea became rich by her wealth! For in one hour she is made desolate.'

[20]"Rejoice over her, O heaven, and *you* holy apostles and prophets, for God has avenged you on her!"

[21]Then a mighty angel took up a stone like a great millstone and threw *it* into the sea, saying, "Thus with violence the great city Babylon shall be thrown down, and shall not be found anymore. [22]The sound of harpists, musicians, flutists, and trumpeters shall not be heard in you anymore. No craftsman of any craft shall be found in you anymore, and the sound of a millstone shall not be heard in you anymore. [23]The light of a lamp shall not shine in you anymore, and the voice of bridegroom and bride shall not be heard in you anymore. For your merchants were the great men of the earth, for by your sorcery all the nations were deceived. [24]And in her was found the blood of prophets and saints, and of all who were slain on the earth."

CHAPTER **19** AN ALLELUIA CHORUS. After these

things I heard a loud voice of a great multitude in heaven, saying, "Alleluia! Salvation and glory and honor and power *belong* to the Lord our God! [2]For true and righteous *are* His judgments, because He has judged the great harlot who corrupted the earth with her fornication; and He has avenged on her the blood of His servants *shed* by her." [3]Again they said, "Alleluia! Her smoke rises up forever and ever!" [4]And the twenty-four elders

◀▬▬▬▬▬TRUE WORSHIP

19:1-10 Praise is the heartfelt response to God by those who love him. The more you get to know God and realize what he has done, the more you will respond with praise. Praise is at the heart of true worship. Let your praise of God flow out of your realization of who he is and how much he loves you.

and the four living creatures fell down and worshiped God who sat on the throne, saying, "Amen! Alleluia!" [5]Then a voice came from the throne, saying, "Praise our God, all you His servants and those who fear Him, both small and great!"

[6]And I heard, as it were, the voice of a great multitude, as the sound of many waters and as the sound of mighty thunderings, saying, "Alleluia! For the Lord God Omnipotent reigns! [7]Let us be glad and rejoice and give Him glory, for the marriage of the Lamb has come, and His wife has made herself ready." [8]And to her it was granted to be arrayed in fine linen, clean and bright, for the fine linen is the righteous acts of the saints.

[9]Then he said to me, "Write: 'Blessed *are* those who are called to the marriage supper of the Lamb!'" And he said

THE BEGINNING AND THE END

The Bible records for us the beginning of the world and the end of the world. The story of mankind, from beginning to end—from the fall into sin to the redemption of Christ and God's ultimate victory over evil—is found in the pages of the Bible.

GENESIS
The sun is created
Satan is victorious
Sin enters the human race
People run and hide from God
Tears are shed, with sorrow for sin
The garden and earth are cursed
The fruit from the tree of life is not to be eaten
People are doomed to death
Paradise is lost

REVELATION
The sun is not needed
Satan is defeated
Sin is banished
People are invited to live with God forever
The curse is removed
No more sin, no more tears or sorrow
God's city is glorified, the earth is made new
God's people may eat from the tree of life
Paradise is regained
Death is defeated, believers live forever with God

to me, "These are the true sayings of God." [10]And I fell at his feet to worship him. But he said to me, "See *that you do* not *do that!* I am your fellow servant, and of your brethren who have the testimony of Jesus. Worship God! For the testimony of Jesus is the spirit of prophecy."

[11]Now I saw heaven opened, and behold, a white horse. And He who sat on him *was* called Faithful and True, and in righteousness He judges and makes war. [12]His eyes *were* like a flame of fire, and on His head *were* many crowns. He had a name written that no one knew except Himself. [13]He *was* clothed with a robe dipped in blood, and His name is called The Word of God. [14]And the armies in heaven, clothed in fine linen, white and clean, followed Him on white horses. [15]Now out of His mouth

---

*D*ESPAIR

Blood, violence, murder, mayhem, images of doom and gloom.

What have we got here? Some kind of horror movie?

No, just another edition of the nightly news.

With smiling faces and playful banter, the channel 2 news anchors recite one horror story after another: the ongoing drug war, tensions in the Middle East, 18 killed in a school bus tragedy, a psychotic killer on the loose, alarming new predictions about AIDS, a devastating flood in India, the growing nightmare of pollution, the possible consequences of the greenhouse effect.

As Wes turns off the TV, he sighs.

"I'm telling you," he mutters to himself, "this world is totally messed up. What's the point? I mean, what do I have to live for? The way things are going, we won't even make it to the year 2000."

Is it any wonder the guy's depressed? The human race does seem bent on self-destruction. Is there any hope in a world that seems to be spinning out of control?

Yes! One of the greatest, most encouraging passages in the whole Bible is found right at the end. Read Revelation 21 and 22 for a fascinating and faith-building look at what the future holds for those who know Christ. (If you don't know Christ as your Savior, now is a perfect time to ask him to forgive your sins and to give you eternal life.)

---

goes a sharp sword, that with it He should strike the nations. And He Himself will rule them with a rod of iron. He Himself treads the winepress of the fierceness and wrath of Almighty God. [16]And He has on *His* robe and on His thigh a name written:

KING OF KINGS
AND LORD OF LORDS.

[17]Then I saw an angel standing in the sun; and he cried with a loud voice, saying to all the birds that fly in the midst of heaven, "Come and gather together for the supper of the great God, [18]that you may eat the flesh of kings, the flesh of captains, the flesh of mighty men, the flesh of horses and of those who sit on them, and the flesh of all *people,* free and slave, both small and great."

[19]And I saw the beast, the kings of the earth, and their armies, gathered together to make war against Him who sat on the horse and against His army. [20]Then the beast was captured, and with him the false prophet who

worked signs in his presence, by which he deceived those who received the mark of the beast and those who worshiped his image. These two were cast alive into the lake of fire burning with brimstone. [21]And the rest were killed with the sword which proceeded from the mouth of Him who sat on the horse. And all the birds were filled with their flesh.

CHAPTER **20** THE 1,000 YEARS. Then I saw an angel coming down from heaven, having the key to the bottomless pit and a great chain in his hand. [2]He laid hold of the dragon, that serpent of old, who is *the* Devil and Satan, and bound him for a thousand years; [3]and he cast him into the bottomless pit, and shut him up, and set a seal on him, so that he should deceive the nations no more till the thousand years were finished. But after these things he must be released for a little while.

[4]And I saw thrones, and they sat on them, and judgment was committed to them. Then *I saw* the souls of those who had been beheaded for their witness to Jesus and for the word of God, who had not worshiped the beast or his image, and had not received *his* mark on their foreheads or on their hands. And they lived and reigned with Christ for a thousand years. [5]But the rest of the dead did not live again until the thousand years were finished. This *is* the first resurrection. [6]Blessed and holy *is* he who has part in the first resurrection. Over such the second death has no power, but they shall be priests of God and of Christ, and shall reign with Him a thousand years.

[7]Now when the thousand years have expired, Satan will be released from his prison [8]and will go out to deceive the nations which are in the four corners of the earth, Gog and Magog, to gather them together to battle, whose number *is* as the sand of the sea. [9]They went up on the breadth of the earth and surrounded the camp of the saints and the beloved city. And fire came down from God out of heaven and devoured them. [10]The devil, who deceived them, was cast into the lake of fire and brimstone where the beast and the false prophet *are.* And they will be tormented day and night forever and ever.

[11]Then I saw a great white throne and Him who sat on it, from whose face the earth and the heaven fled away. And there was found no place for them. [12]And I saw the dead, small and great, standing before God, and books were opened. And another book was opened, which is *the Book* of Life. And the dead were judged according to their works, by the things which were written in the

NO CONTEST

20:9 This is not a typical battle where the outcome is in doubt du the heat of the conflict. Here there is no contest. Two mighty forces evil—those of the beast (19:19) and of Satan (20:8)—unite to d battle against God. The Bible uses just two verses to describe each battle—the evil beast and his forces are captured and thrown into lake of fire (19:20-21), and fire from heaven consumes Satan and attacking armies (20:9-10). There will be no doubt, no worry, and second thoughts for believers about whether they have chosen the side. If you choose God, you will experience this tremendous victor Christ.

books. [13]The sea gave up the dead who were in it, and Death and Hades delivered up the dead who were in them. And they were judged, each one according to his works. [14]Then Death and Hades were cast into the lake of fire. This is the second death. [15]And anyone not found written in the Book of Life was cast into the lake of fire.

CHAPTER 21 A NEW HEAVEN AND NEW EARTH.

Now I saw a new heaven and a new earth, for the first heaven and the first earth had passed away. Also there was no more sea. [2]Then I, John, saw the holy city, New Jerusalem, coming down out of heaven from God, prepared as a bride adorned for her husband. [3]And I heard a loud voice from heaven saying, "Behold, the tabernacle of God *is* with men, and He will dwell with them, and they shall be His people. God Himself will be with them *and be* their God. [4]And God will wipe away every tear from their eyes; there shall be no more death, nor sorrow, nor crying. There shall be no more pain, for the former things have passed away."

[5]Then He who sat on the throne said, "Behold, I make all things new." And He said to me, "Write, for these words are true and faithful."

[6]And He said to me, "It is done! I am the Alpha and the Omega, the Beginning and the End. I will give of the fountain of the water of life freely to him who thirsts. [7]He who overcomes shall inherit all things, and I will be his God and he shall be My son. [8]But the cowardly, unbelieving, abominable, murderers, sexually immoral, sorcerers, idolaters, and all liars shall have their part in the lake which burns with fire and brimstone, which is the second death."

[9]Then one of the seven angels who had the seven bowls filled with the seven last plagues came to me and talked with me, saying, "Come, I will show you the bride, the Lamb's wife." [10]And he carried me away in the Spirit to a great and high mountain, and showed me the great city, the holy Jerusalem, descending out of heaven from God, [11]having the glory of God. Her light *was* like a most precious stone, like a jasper stone, clear as crystal. [12]Also she had a great and high wall with twelve gates, and twelve angels at the gates, and names written on them, which are *the names* of the twelve tribes of the children of Israel: [13]three gates on the east, three gates on the north, three gates on the south, and three gates on the west.

[14]Now the wall of the city had twelve foundations, and on them were the names of the twelve apostles of the Lamb. [15]And he who talked with me had a gold reed to measure the city, its gates, and its wall. [16]The city is laid out as a square; its length is as great as its breadth. And he measured the city with the reed: twelve thousand furlongs. Its length, breadth, and height are equal. [17]Then he measured its wall: one hundred *and* forty-four cubits, *according* to the measure of a man, that is, of an angel. [18]The construction of its wall was *of* jasper; and the city *was* pure gold, like clear glass. [19]The foundations of the wall of the city *were* adorned with all kinds of precious stones: the first foundation *was* jasper, the second sapphire, the third chalcedony, the fourth emerald, [20]the fifth

sardonyx, the sixth sardius, the seventh chrysolite, the eighth beryl, the ninth topaz, the tenth chrysoprase, the eleventh jacinth, and the twelfth amethyst. [21]The twelve gates *were* twelve pearls: each individual gate was of one pearl. And the street of the city *was* pure gold, like transparent glass.

[22]But I saw no temple in it, for the Lord God Almighty and the Lamb are its temple. [23]The city had no need of the sun or of the moon to shine in it, for the glory of God illuminated it. The Lamb *is* its light. [24]And the nations of those who are saved shall walk in its light, and the kings of the earth bring their glory and honor into it. [25]Its gates shall not be shut at all by day (there shall be no night

ETERNITY IS . . .

21:3-4 Have you ever wondered what eternity will be like? The "holy city, the New Jerusalem" is described as the place where God will "wipe away every tear from their eyes." Forevermore, there will be no death, pain, sorrow, or crying. What a wonderful truth! No matter what you are going through, it's not the last word—God has written the final chapter, and it includes eternal joy for those who love him. We do not know as much as we would like, but it is enough to know that eternity with God will be more wonderful than we can imagine.

there). [26]And they shall bring the glory and the honor of the nations into it. [27]But there shall by no means enter it anything that defiles, or causes an abomination or a lie, but only those who are written in the Lamb's Book of Life.

CHAPTER 22 THE RIVER OF LIFE. And he showed

me a pure river of water of life, clear as crystal, proceeding from the throne of God and of the Lamb. [2]In the middle of its street, and on either side of the river, *was* the tree of life, which bore twelve fruits, each *tree* yielding its fruit every month. The leaves of the tree *were* for the healing of the nations. [3]And there shall be no more curse, but the throne of God and of the Lamb shall be in it, and His servants shall serve Him. [4]They shall see His face, and His name *shall be* on their foreheads. [5]There shall be no night there: They need no lamp nor light of the sun, for the Lord God gives them light. And they shall reign forever and ever.

[6]Then he said to me, "These words *are* faithful and true." And the Lord God of the holy prophets sent His angel to show His servants the things which must shortly take place.

[7]"Behold, I am coming quickly! Blessed *is* he who keeps the words of the prophecy of this book."

[8]Now I, John, saw and heard these things. And when I heard and saw, I fell down to worship before the feet of the angel who showed me these things.

[9]Then he said to me, "See *that you do* not *do that*. For I am your fellow servant, and of your brethren the prophets, and of those who keep the words of this book. Wor-

EYEWITNESS

22:8-9 Hearing or reading an eyewitness account is the next best thing to seeing the event yourself. John witnessed the events reported in Revelation and wrote them down so we could "see" and believe as he did. If you have read this far, you have "seen." Have you also believed?

ship God." [10]And he said to me, "Do not seal the words of the prophecy of this book, for the time is at hand. [11]He who is unjust, let him be unjust still; he who is filthy, let him be filthy still; he who is righteous, let him be righteous still; he who is holy, let him be holy still."

[12]"And behold, I am coming quickly, and My reward *is* with Me, to give to every one according to his work. [13]I am the Alpha and the Omega, *the* Beginning and *the* End, the First and the Last."

YOU ARE INVITED

22:17 When Jesus met the Samaritan woman at the well, he told her of the living water that he could supply (John 4:10-15). This image is used again as Christ invites anyone to come and drink of the water of life. The gospel is unlimited in scope—all people, everywhere, may come. Salvation cannot be earned, but God gives it freely. We live in a world desperately thirsty for living water, and many are dying of thirst. But it's still not too late. Let us invite everyone to come and drink.

[14]Blessed *are* those who do His commandments, that they may have the right to the tree of life, and may enter through the gates into the city. [15]But outside *are* dogs and sorcerers and sexually immoral and murderers and idolaters, and whoever loves and practices a lie.

[16]"I, Jesus, have sent My angel to testify to you these things in the churches. I am the Root and the Offspring of David, the Bright and Morning Star."

[17]And the Spirit and the bride say, "Come!" And let him who hears say, "Come!" And let him who thirsts come. Whoever desires, let him take the water of life freely.

GOD WINS!

22:21 Revelation closes human history as Genesis opened it—i paradise. But there is one distinct difference: in Revelation, evil is forever. Genesis describes Adam and Eve walking and talking with Revelation describes people worshiping him face-to-face. Genesis describes a garden with an evil serpent; Revelation describes a pe city with no evil.

The book of Revelation ends with an urgent request: "Come, L Jesus!" In a world of problems, persecution, evil, and immorality, calls us to endure in our faith. Our efforts to better our world are important, but their results cannot compare with the transformatio will bring about when he returns. He alone controls human history forgives sin, and he will recreate the earth and bring lasting peace

Revelation is above all a book of hope. It shows that no matter happens on earth, God is in control. It promises that evil will not la forever, and it depicts the wonderful reward that is waiting for all who believe in Jesus Christ as Savior and Lord.

[18]For I testify to everyone who hears the words of the prophecy of this book: If anyone adds to these things, God will add to him the plagues that are written in this book; [19]and if anyone takes away from the words of the book of this prophecy, God shall take away his part from the Book of Life, from the holy city, and *from* the things which are written in this book.

[20]He who testifies to these things says, "Surely I am coming quickly."

Amen. Even so, come, Lord Jesus!

[21]The grace of our Lord Jesus Christ *be* with you all. Amen.

MEGA *Themes*

GOD'S SOVEREIGNTY God is sovereign. He is greater than any power in the universe, and not to be compared with any leader, government, or religion. He controls history for the purpose of uniting true believers in loving fellowship with him.

Though Satan's power may temporarily increase, we are not to be led astray. God is all-powerful. Satan is not equivalent to God. God is supreme, in control, and will safely bring his family into eternal life. God cares for us; we can trust him with our life.

1. In what ways is God revealed as sovereign in Revelation?
2. How does God's sovereignty offer security to you?

3. Based on your security in God, what plans, dreams, worries, and/or problems can you bring to him today? How does trusting God with both hopes and fears enable you to experience his sovereignty?

CHRIST'S RETURN Christ came to earth as a "Lamb," the symbol of his perfect sacrifice for our sin. He will return as the triumphant "Lion," the rightful ruler and conqueror. Christ will defeat Satan, settle accounts with all those who rejected him, and bring his faithful people into eternity.

Assurance of Christ's return gives suffering Christians the strength to endure. We can look forward to Christ's return as King and Judge. Because no one knows the time when Christ will appear, we must be ready at all times by keeping our faith strong.

1. Contrast the nature of Christ's first coming with his second coming.
2. What impact did Christ's first coming have on the world? On you?
3. What impact will Christ's second coming have on the world? On you?
4. How can the reality of Christ's second coming have a positive impact on you now?

GOD'S FAITHFUL PEOPLE John wrote to encourage the church not to worship the Roman emperor. He warns all God's faithful people to be devoted only to Christ. Revelation identifies the faithful people and what they should be doing until Christ returns.

Take your place in the ranks of God's faithful people: believe in Christ. Victory is sure for those who resist temptation and make loyalty to Christ their top priority.

1. What were some of the problems facing the churches in chapters 2 and 3? How were they to correct those problems?
2. Which of these churches can you identify with? How would you apply the command for correction?
3. What is the reward of those who endure faithfully?
4. Why is the cost of being a Christian worth it? Explain how this motivates you to grow in Christ rather than just surrendering to your weaknesses.

JUDGMENT One day God's anger toward sin will be fully and completely unleashed. Satan will be defeated; false religion will be destroyed. God will reward the faithful with eternal life, but all who refuse to believe in him will face eternal punishment.

God's final judgment will put an end to evil and injustice. We must be certain of our commitment to Christ if we want to escape this great final judgment. No one who is uncommitted to Christ will escape God's punishment. All who belong to Christ will receive their full reward based on what Christ has done.

1. What will happen in the final judgment? (chapter 20)
2. Whose names are written in the Book of Life?
3. How does knowledge of this final judgment affect the way you live your life? The way you view death?
4. What would you like to communicate to your friends about the final judgment? How can you do this?

HOPE One day God will create a new heaven and a new earth. All believers will live with God forever in perfect peace and security. Those who have already died will be raised to life. These promises for the future bring us hope.

Our greatest hope is that what Christ promises will be true. When we have confidence in our final destination, we will be able to follow Christ with unwavering dedication no matter what we must face. Because we belong to him, there is no room for despair.

1. What will God do after the final judgment?
2. What is your ultimate hope in Christ?
3. When do you find yourself most needing to rely on this ultimate hope? How does "final hope" provide hope in the present?
4. What would you like to communicate to your friends about the final hope? How can you do this?

BIBLE READING PLAN

INTRODUCTION
We usually think of the Bible as one book. That's logical because it looks like one book and claims to come from one Author. We also speak of it as God's Word. But when we read and study the Bible, we discover that it is actually an entire library between two covers. Not one book, but 66 (39 in the Old Testament; 27 in the New Testament)! Each book has its own style and uniqueness—yet each book contributes to the message God wants to get across with the whole Bible. What's more, though we use the word *book*, some parts of the Bible are letters (like Paul's letter to the Romans) or collections (like the Psalms). Still, the overall message of the Bible is one message because it has one main Author—God. The reason the styles throughout the Bible vary is because God teamed up with dozens of people to write his Word.

HOW THIS PLAN IS DIFFERENT
There are many plans to help you read through the Bible library. You can even start at page one and read straight through. The approach taken here, however, is designed to help you get a flavor of the whole Bible by reading selections from it throughout a year. You will be reading the best-known stories and many important lessons. Some parts of the Bible offer so much help that they can be read every day. Among these are the Gospels, Psalms, and Proverbs. One way or another, you need to read God's Word!

BEFORE YOU BEGIN
Notice that each day's reading has a title and a question. These are important application questions that will help you as you read. Always pray before you read and ask God to help you understand, apply, and obey his Word. And remember, this is only the start of the great adventure of reading God's Word and getting to know him.

BIBLE JOURNEY 365 GREAT STORIES AND LESSON

Numbers 14:5-45 A Majority That Was Wrong
How often are your decisions based on peer pressure?
Numbers 21:4-9 Another Hard Lesson
What can you do to avoid repeating mistakes?
Numbers 22:5-38 Balaam and His Donkey
What happens when you do what you know you shouldn't do?
Deuteronomy 29:1-29 Moses Reviews God's Actions
How do you keep track of what God has done for you?
Deuteronomy 30:1-20 Moses Challenges the People
How do you show that you love God?
Deuteronomy 31:1-8 Moses Appoints New Leaders
If you were Joshua, who would be "Moses" in your life?
Deuteronomy 34:1-12 The Death of Moses
How would you most like to be remembered?
Joshua 1:1-18 God Takes Over
Which of these qualities would you most need to be like Joshua?
Joshua 2:1-24 Spies Visit Jericho
What persons has God used in your life unexpectedly?
Joshua 3:1-17 The Invasion of Canaan
How would you illustrate God's guidance in your life?
Joshua 5:13–6:27 The Battle of Jericho
How serious are you about having God use you?
Joshua 7:1-26 Ultimate Consequences
What strongly negative or positive consequences have you experienced?
Joshua 10:1-15 The Longest Day
How do you know God is powerful?
Joshua 23:1-16 Joshua Warns the Leaders
Which of Joshua's warnings do you most need to obey?
Joshua 24:1-31 Joshua's Last Words
How can you get hope from history?
Judges 4:4-24 Judge Deborah
How do people know that you care about them?
Judges 6:1-40 Gideon Becomes a Judge
What examples of obedience can be found in your life?
Judges 7:1-25 Gideon and the Midianites
In what area of your life do you need to trust God more?
Judges 13:1-25 The Birth of Samson
In which part of your life do you need more discipline?
Judges 14:1-20 Samson's Riddle
How carefully do you consider the wisdom of your parents?
Judges 15:1-20 Samson and the Jawbone
What proof do you have that mistakes usually don't correct themselves?
Judges 16:1-21 Samson and Delilah
In what situations do you find yourself flirting with disaster?
Judges 16:22-31 Samson's Death
How well do you understand God's patience?
Ruth 1:1-22 Ruth and Naomi—A Friendship
How do difficulties affect your friendships?
Ruth 2:1-23 Ruth Meets Boaz
When have you found your reputation to be an advantage?
Ruth 3:1-18 Ruth Finds a Husband
What unexpected methods has God used in your life?

Ruth 4:1-22 A Happy Ending
What future reasons could there be for obeying God today?
1 Samuel 1:1-28 A Serious Prayer
What promises have you made to God lately that you have kept?
1 Samuel 3:1-21 God Calls Samuel
When you read God's Word, what do you expect him to say to you?
1 Samuel 8:1-5 Samuel's Disappointing Sons
What positive lessons have you learned from your parents' mistakes?
1 Samuel 8:6-22 The People Want a King
What has God taught you about being responsible for your own choices?
1 Samuel 9:1-21 Saul and the Lost Donkeys
What is God's part in your daily decisions?
1 Samuel 10:1-27 Saul Becomes King
How do you evaluate people?
1 Samuel 14:1-23 A Son to Make a Father Proud
What would it mean to have a friend like Jonathan?
1 Samuel 16:1-13 Samuel Appoints David
What people do you appreciate for something other than how they look?
1 Samuel 17:1-31 David and Goliath's Challenge
How does your confidence in God affect your decision to accept challenges?
1 Samuel 17:32-58 David Kills Goliath
What "giants" need to be defeated in your life?
1 Samuel 18:1-30 Trouble between Saul and David
How do you treat your friends who succeed?
1 Samuel 20:1-42 David and Jonathan
How much can your friends trust you?
1 Samuel 24:1-22 David Spares Saul's Life
Do you treat others the way you want to be treated?
1 Samuel 25:1-42 David and Abigail
How does God keep you from making big mistakes?
1 Samuel 28:1-25 Saul and the Occult
What kinds of things could be considered "occult practices"? How would God feel about your involvement in such things?
2 Samuel 5:1-12 David Becomes King over All Israel
How could you become a person who is more pleasing to God, as David was?
2 Samuel 9:1-13 The King's Kindness
What promises need to be kept in your life?
2 Samuel 11:1-27 David and Bathsheba
How often are you tempted to correct one sin by committing another?
2 Samuel 12:1-25 David and Nathan
Which of your friends love you enough to correct you?
2 Samuel 13:1-19 Family Consequences of Sin
What actions do you take to avoid temptation?
2 Samuel 13:20-39 Family Revenge
Are you more likely to have committed David's sin or Absalom's?
2 Samuel 15:1-37 Family Betrayal
Who helps you keep your motives clear?

2 Samuel 18:1-18 The Death of Absalom
In what situations are you most likely to lose control?

1 Kings 1:5-27 Conflict over the Throne
What happens when you don't make good decisions?

1 Kings 1:28-53 David Gives Solomon the Crown
When things in your world get confusing, how do you know God is still in control?

1 Kings 3:1-15 Solomon's Wisdom
Which of Solomon's choices would you have made?

1 Kings 3:16-28 Solomon Solves a Problem
In what situation in your life do you presently need God's wisdom?

1 Kings 6:1-38 Solomon Builds the Temple
What can you learn from Solomon about making and carrying out plans?

1 Kings 10:1-13 Solomon and the Queen of Sheba
When are you tempted to try to impress people?

1 Kings 12:1-24 Solomon's Unwise Son
Who are the people you know will give you good advice?

1 Kings 17:1-24 God Takes Care of Elijah
How do obeying and trusting God go together in your life?

1 Kings 18:16-46 Elijah versus the Priests of Baal
How would you describe your attitude toward God's power today?

1 Kings 19:1-21 Spiritual Burnout
When was the last time you felt sorry for yourself?

1 Kings 21:1-29 The Stolen Vineyard
How important is justice in your life?

1 Kings 22:29-40 The Death of King Ahab
When are you tempted to think that you can hide from God?

2 Kings 2:1-12 Elijah's Chariot
When you make a commitment, how far will you go to carry it out?

2 Kings 2:13-25 Elisha's Miracles
How would someone else know that you have a deep respect for God?

2 Kings 5:1-27 The Healing of Naaman
What "small" things have you refused to do for God?

2 Kings 11:1-21 The King Who Was Seven Years Old
Who were your best examples in childhood?

2 Kings 22:1–23:3 Discovery of the Lost Book
What happens in your life when the Bible is a "lost book"?

Ezra 3:7-13 Rebuilding the Temple
How do you feel when you're working on a large, important project?

Nehemiah 2:1-20 Nehemiah Returns to Jerusalem
What relationships in your past need to be rebuilt?

Nehemiah 5:1-19 Nehemiah's Concern for the Poor
How do you express your concern for the poor?

Nehemiah 8:1-18 Reading God's Word
What are your expectations when you open God's Word?

Esther 1:1-22 The Fall of a Queen
How often do you take the important people in your life for granted?

Esther 2:1-23 A Strange Way to Become Queen
When have difficult or confusing events in your life actually been a preparation for something you would later experience?

Esther 3:1-15 The Jews in Danger
In what situations are you tempted to compromise your faith?

Esther 4:1-17 The Queen Decides to Help
In what ways has your faith cost you?

Esther 5:1-14 Esther Risks Her Life
When was the last time you did something scary to obey God?

Esther 6:1–7:10 God Protects His People
When is it helpful to remember that God is still in control of the world?

Job 1:1-22 The Testing of Job
In what situations do you most quickly question God's care?

Job 2:1-13 Job and His Friends
How do you normally respond to someone else's pain? How should you respond?

Job 38:1-41 God Speaks to Job
What things around you remind you of God's greatness?

Job 42:1-17 The Rest of Job's Story
What difference does it make to know and remember that God always has the last word?

Psalm 1:1-6 Two Kinds of Lives
What kind of person do you really want to be?

Psalm 8:1-9 The Value of Humans
How do you know you have worth?

Psalm 23:1-6 A Sheep's Song
What is the most comforting phrase to you in this psalm?

Psalm 51:1-19 A Confession
What examples of repentance have been part of your life?

Psalm 103:1-22 What God Is Like
Which picture in this psalm helps you understand God better?

Psalm 139:1-24 How Well God Knows Us
What do you feel when you read this psalm?

Psalm 145:1-21 God for All People and Time
Which of God's qualities do you most need today?

Proverbs 4:1-27 Wise Words about Life
What priority have you given finding wisdom?

Proverbs 5:1-23 Wise Words about Sex
How do these words match what you hear around you every day?

Ecclesiastes 12:1-14 A Summary of Life
In what way can you remember your Creator today?

Isaiah 6:1-13 God Chooses Isaiah
When did you last realize your continuing need for God's forgiveness?

Isaiah 53:1-12 The Suffering Servant
How would you describe what Jesus did for you?

Jeremiah 1:1-9 God Calls a Prophet
What is your reaction to the possibility of God using your life?

Jeremiah 36:1-32 The Book Burning
How much risk is involved in your relationship with God?

Jeremiah 38:1-13 Jeremiah in the Dungeon
What part of your life compares in any way with Jeremiah's time in the dungeon?

Ezekiel 37:1-14 A Valley of Dry Bones
What can you do to better understand God's plan for the world?

Daniel 1:1-21 Coping with Pressure to Conform
How might Daniel react to the pressure situations in your life?

Daniel 2:1-24 A King's Dream
What do you do in seemingly hopeless situations?

Daniel 2:25-49 The Meaning of the Dream
Who gets the credit when things go right in your life?

Daniel 3:1-30 Three Friends in a Furnace
What examples can you give of God's protection in your life?

Daniel 5:1-30 The Writing on the Wall
What reasons would God have for passing judgment on the society in which you live?

NEW TESTAMENT

You will be reading various parts of the four Gospels in order to have a fairly chronological biography of Jesus' life.

Luke 1:1-4; John 1:1-18 Beginnings
Have you personally received Jesus as your Savior and become a child of God?

Luke 1:5-25 The Angel and Zacharias
How would you react to an angel's visit?

Luke 1:26-56 Mary and Elizabeth
What gives you joy in your life?

Luke 1:57-80 John the Baptist Is Born
When did you last say thank you to your parents?

Matthew 1:1-25 A Family Tree
Which of these people have you read about in the Old Testament?

Luke 2:1-20 Jesus Is Born!
What does Christmas mean to you?

Luke 2:21-39 Jesus' First Trip to Church
How would you react to holding Jesus when he was a baby?

Matthew 2:1-12 Foreign Visitors
What gifts have you ever given Christ?

Matthew 2:13-23 Escape and Return
How has knowing God brought excitement into your life?

Luke 2:41-52 Jesus in the Temple Again
What four words would summarize your teenage years?

Mark 1:1-13 Baptism and Temptation
What are your most difficult temptations? Compare them to Jesus' temptations.

John 1:19-34 John the Baptist and Jesus
To whom did you last talk about Christ?

John 1:35-51 Jesus' First Disciples
How would someone know that you're a disciple of Jesus?

John 2:1-25 Jesus and Surprises
How has Christ been unpredictable in your life?

John 3:1-21 Jesus and Nicodemus
When did you first meet Jesus? How?

John 3:22-36; Luke 3:19-20 John Gets into Trouble
When has knowing Christ ever gotten you into trouble?

John 4:1-42 Jesus Changes a Town
In what ways has Jesus affected your town?

John 4:43-54 Jesus Preaching and Healing
Why do you believe in Christ?

Luke 4:16-30 Jesus Rejected
How would Jesus be received in your church next Sunday?

Mark 1:16-39 Jesus Calls People to Follow
What specific things have you left behind to follow Christ?

Luke 5:1-39 Miracles and Questions
How do Jesus' miracles affect you today?

John 5:1-47 Jesus Demonstrates He Is God's Son
What do you find most attractive about Jesus?

Mark 2:23–3:19 Jesus and Disciples
How would Jesus treat your personal traditions?

Matthew 5:1-16 Jesus Gives the Beatitudes
Which of these attitudes most needs to be in your life today?

Daniel 6:1-28 Daniel and the Lions
When do you pray regularly?

Jonah 1:1–2:10 Bending God's Directions
When did you last try to avoid doing what you knew God wanted you to do?

Jonah 3:1–4:11 Wrong Motives
About what things do you complain to God?

Matthew 5:17-30 Jesus on Law, Anger, and Lust
How do Jesus' views compare with yours?

Matthew 5:31-48 Jesus on Relationships
What part of your life could be most radically changed by these words?

Matthew 6:1-18 Jesus on Doing Good Things
How do your public and private lives compare?

Matthew 6:19-34 Jesus on Money and Worry
In what ways are money and worry related in your life?

Matthew 7:1-12 Jesus on Criticizing and Praying
Which one are you most persistent in doing? Why?

Matthew 7:13-29 How Jesus Looks at Us
What is your foundation in life?

Luke 7:1-17 Jesus and Foreigners
What is your attitude toward foreigners? How can you show them God's love?

Matthew 11:1-30 Jesus Describes John
How would you want Jesus to summarize your life?

Luke 7:36–8:3 Jesus and Women
How would you have fit into the group that followed Jesus?

Matthew 12:22-50 Troubles for Jesus
When are you tempted to have Jesus prove himself to you?

Mark 4:1-29 Jesus Seeks, Seeds, and Weeds
What kind of soil is your life right now?

Matthew 13:24-43 More of Jesus' Parables
How concerned are you about the eternal fates of the people you know?

Matthew 13:44-52 Even More Parables
How and where did you find the hidden treasure?

Luke 8:22-56 Jesus in Control
Which of these examples gives you greatest comfort?

Matthew 9:27-38 The Concerns of Jesus
How do you picture Jesus caring for you?

Mark 6:1-13 Some Don't Listen; Some Need to Hear
How clear an idea do you have of what God wants you to do?

Matthew 10:16-42 Jesus Prepares His Disciples
In what ways do Jesus' words speak to the fears you have?

Mark 6:14-29 Herod Kills John the Baptist
How do you most want to be like John the Baptist?

Matthew 14:13-36 Jesus: Cook, Water Walker, Healer
Would you have been more likely to step out with Peter or to stay in the boat? Why?

John 6:22-40 Jesus Is the Bread from Heaven
How is Jesus "bread" to you?

John 6:41-71 Jesus Criticized and Deserted
How do you react when you hear critical or derogatory comments about Jesus?

Mark 7:1-37 Jesus Teaches and Creates Purity
What would God have to do to improve the purity of your life?

Matthew 15:32–16:12 Jesus Feeds and Warns
How do you evaluate what you hear?

Matthew 25:1-30 Parables about Being Prepared
With which of the people in these two stories do you identify most?

Matthew 25:31-46 Jesus on the Final Judgment
What people in your life are you treating in ways you would want to treat Christ?

Luke 22:1-13 Preparing the Last Supper
How do you prepare yourself for Communion?

John 13:1-20 Jesus Washes His Disciples' Feet
What is the greatest service someone has done for you? How do you serve others?

John 13:21-38 A Sad Prediction
How well do you feel Christ knows you?

John 14:1-14 Jesus Is the Way
How would you rate your present level of understanding of Christ and his teachings?

John 14:15-31 Jesus Promises the Helper
How have you experienced the Helper?

John 15:1-16 Jesus on the Vine and the Branches
What kind of fruit has God produced in you?

John 15:17–16:4 Jesus Warns about Troubles
What have you learned recently about loving others?

John 16:5-33 Jesus on the Holy Spirit and Prayers
Where in these verses do you find peace of heart and mind?

John 17:1-26 Jesus Prays
Where do you find yourself in this prayer?

Mark 14:26-52 A Repeated Prediction
What practical prayer problems do you need to work on?

John 18:1-24 Jesus Betrayed and Abandoned
How close have you come to Peter's denial of Christ?

Matthew 26:57-75 Trial and Denial
In what ways has being a follower of Jesus complicated your life?

Matthew 27:1-10 The Religious Trial and Judas's Death
When you think of sin's consequences, what personal examples come to mind?

Luke 23:1-12 Two Political Trials
In what ways did your childhood and background prepare you to respond to Jesus?

Mark 15:6-24 Sentencing and Torture
Was there a time you chose to do the wrong thing on purpose? Why? What happened?

Luke 23:32-49 Jesus Crucified
What do you feel when you read the description of the Crucifixion?

Matthew 27:57-66 Jesus' Body Laid in a Guarded Tomb
What have you seen people do in their resistance to Christ?

John 20:1-18 Jesus Is Alive!
What makes Easter an important celebration in your life?

Matthew 28:8-15 Reactions to the Resurrection
What would be your first words to Jesus if he appeared to you?

Luke 24:13-43 Appearances of Jesus
Would you recognize Jesus if you saw him today? How?

John 20:24–21:14 More Appearances of Jesus
How has Christ answered your doubts?

John 21:15-25 Jesus Talks with Peter
What difference would it make to you to read these verses with your name in the place of Simon Peter's?

Matthew 28:16-20 Jesus Gives the Great Commission
What are you doing specifically to obey Christ's words?

Luke 24:44-53 Jesus Says Farewell
How do you find Christ opening your mind as you read the Bible?

Acts 1:1-11 The Departure of Jesus
What one thing would you be sure to do if you knew Jesus was coming back today?

Acts 1:12-26 First Things First
What is your idea of the right amount of time for prayer?

Acts 2:1-13 An Amazing Gift
What is the main purpose of any gift God might have given you?

Acts 2:14-40 Peter's First Sermon
How would you put this sermon into your own words?

Acts 2:41–3:11 Daily Life in the Early Church
What part of these early days would you have enjoyed the most?

Acts 3:12–4:4 Peter's Second Sermon
If you were given three minutes to tell the story of your spiritual life, what would you say?

Acts 4:5-22 Hostile Reactions
What excuses are you most likely to use to keep from sharing your faith?

Acts 4:23-37 Praying and Sharing
When was the last time you shared something with someone else?

Acts 5:1-16 Strange Events
How often are you tempted to take God lightly?

Acts 5:17-42 Arrested!
How do you react when you are treated unfairly?

Acts 6:1-15 Stephen: Special Servant
What specific responsibilities do you have in your local church?

Acts 7:1-29 History Review I
How familiar are you becoming with "his story" in history?

Acts 7:30-60 History Review II
In what ways would you want to be more like Stephen?

Acts 8:1-25 Benefits of Persecution
Which difficulties in your life has God used to help you grow spiritually?

Acts 8:26-40 Unexpected Appointment
What have you done about baptism?

Acts 9:1-19 Paul Meets Jesus
What unusual events has God used to catch your attention?

Acts 9:20-31 Paul's New Life
What are three ways that Christ has changed your life?

Acts 9:32-42 God Uses Peter
This past week, what special ability did you use to meet someone's need?

Acts 10:1-23 Peter Sees a Lesson
What lessons has God had to repeat in your life?

Acts 10:24-48 Peter Learns a Lesson
How has God helped you change your mind about some attitudes?

Acts 11:1-18 Gentiles Get a Chance
On which of your prejudices is God still working?

Acts 11:19-29 Christians Helping One Another
What do you do when you hear stories of extreme poverty or hardship among Christians in other parts of the world?

Acts 12:1-25 A Great Escape and Capital Punishment
How do you react when God answers your prayers?

Acts 13:1-12 Paul and Barnabas: Travel Preaching
What Christians do you know who might help you discover more clearly how God wants you to invest your time and abilities?

Acts 14:1-28 Response and Reaction
How does the gospel act like Good News in your life?

Acts 15:1-21 A Church Conference
How important is it for you to talk problems over with other Christians?

Hebrews 12:1-13 Our Turn
Which of these directions would have a significant impact on your faith?

James 1:2-27 Tough Times, Happy People
In what difficulty could you use the "James plan" right now?

James 2:1-13 Valuing Other People
Which tendencies do you have to watch out for in how you treat others?

James 3:1-12 Words as Weapons
How sharp would others consider your tongue?

1 Peter 2:1-25 Living Stones
Which would you choose as the biggest personal challenge in these verses?

1 Peter 3:1-22 Relationships and Pain
How willing are you to carry out your relationships God's way, even when there are difficulties?

2 Peter 1:2-21 Knowing God
How would you answer someone who asked you what it means to know God?

1 John 1:1-10 The Way of Forgiveness
What part does confession have in your life?

1 John 3:1-24 God Is Love
How can you tell if your love is growing?

1 John 5:1-21 The Life God Gives
How do you know that you have eternal life?

2 John 4-6; 3 John 5-8; Jude 17-25 Family Matters
How often do you go out of your way to meet the needs of other Christians?

Revelation 1:1-20 Jesus the King
How would you describe your mental picture of Jesus?

Revelation 21:1-27 Everything Made New
What difference do you think you will most notice between the new world and the old?

Revelation 22:1-21 Life in the New City
When was the last time you were excited about heaven?

FOLLOW-UP FOR NEW CHRISTIANS

"We also rejoice in God through our Lord Jesus Christ, through whom we have now received the reconciliation" (Romans 5:11).

You have just helped someone become a new Christian or you have been given the responsibility to do the follow-up of a new Christian . . . so now what do you do?

First of all, you can be excited about this opportunity. Second, you need to be serious about this responsibility. Read Romans 5:11 again. You have the privilege of helping someone grow in his or her new relation ship with your friend Jesus Christ. Here are some ways you can help a new Christian and Jesus grow closer. Remember, we all need FRIENDS:

F*ollow up with your new Christian friend by getting together regularly.* Get together within 48 hours after your friend receives Christ, and at least once a week during the next six weeks (Matthew 28:20).

R*einforce what Christ has done in your friend's life.* Do this by looking at Scriptures that affirm God's commitment to Christians (John 14:20; Hebrews 13:5; Colossians 2:13-14; 1 John 5:13; Galatians 5:25).

I*nvolve your friend in a Bible-teaching church.* Take your friend with you and help answer any of his or her questions (Hebrews 10:24-25).

E*xhibit Christ in your life through your actions and words.* You don't have to be perfect, just someone who wants to obey and please God (Colossians 3:17).

N*urture your friend's spiritual growth.* A new Christian is like a newborn baby who needs spiritual food and care. Try using the 14 appointments with God included in this section (1 Peter 2:2-3).

D*o things together.* Spending time together will give you opportunities to encourage your friend and put your faith into practice (Acts 14:21-22).

S*tand by your friend in both the good and bad times.* Your friend will fall down spiritually. Get ready to help him or her get up and go again (Ephesians 4:11-16).

You have recently trusted Jesus Christ to be your Savior . . . so now what do you do?

First of all, you must know that through Christ you have become friends with God. Read Romans 5:11. Remember:

- You realized that your sin was keeping you from a relationship with God;

- You understood that Jesus Christ died on the cross to pay the penalty for your sin and that he rose again from the dead;
- You prayed, asking Jesus to forgive your sins and be your Savior.

Next, please understand that you have begun an exciting and lasting friendship. As in any relationship, getting to know someone takes time—it doesn't just happen by itself. (Make sure you have a friend who has been a Christian for a while who can help you grow in your new faith. If no one has contacted you, you should go back to the person who helped you become a Christian and ask for help.)

You can grow closer to God just like you grow closer to people. God created you to have a relationship with him, to be his very own son or daughter. Now that you're his child and friend, he will patiently help you get to know him better and better.

Here are some ideas you can use to help you and God become close friends. Remember, all it takes is TIME:

Talk to God through prayer. To help you learn how to talk to God, the 14 appointments with God include ideas for prayer. Give them a try. God will listen when you talk to him.

Investigate God's Word. Decide on a time and place to read the Bible each day. The schedule for 14 appointments with God will help you know what to read. This will help you grow.

Make it practical. One of the best ways to learn is by doing. The 14-appointment schedule includes action steps to help you make your friendship with God active and practical.

Express your thoughts. You know how important it is to show appreciation to a friend. As you finish your daily time with God, tell him thank you. During the next 14 appointments with God, try to keep a personal journal. Simply write down your thoughts, your questions, and, most important of all, why you're thankful to God!

Finally, to get to know God better, try using the following "14 Appointments with God." These appointments are great ways to spend some time with God and find out more about who he is and who he wants you to be.

14 APPOINTMENTS WITH GOD

APPOINTMENT 1
It's Guaranteed
■ ASSURANCE

You recently became a Christian. Have you had any doubts about whether or not Jesus really came into your life? Do you wonder if you'll really go to heaven someday?

Talk to God: "Father, thank you for giving me a relationship with you. Jesus, thank you for giving me life. Please teach me and help me learn more about you. Amen."

Investigate God's Word: Read 1 John 5:11-13. Memorize verse 13.

Make it practical: Check out "I Wonder"—1 John 5:10-12, page 1216, or "Here's What I Did"—Matthew 7:24-27, page 915. How can you put the ideas presented here into action
in your own life?

Express your thoughts: In your journal, write a description of when, where, and how you became a Christian. Say thanks to God!

APPOINTMENT 2
Part of the Family
■ GOD, OUR FATHER

Everyone knows what it's like to not feel totally accepted by others. Did you know that when you became a Christian, God adopted you into his family and accepted you unconditionally?

Talk to God: "Dear God, thanks for making me part of your family. You accept me. That's awesome! Amen."

Investigate God's Word: Ephesians 1:3-8. Memorize verse 5.

Make it practical: "I Wonder"—Hebrews 1:1-3, page 1183, or "Here's What I Did"—Mark 10:31, page 955.

Express your thoughts: In your journal, make a list of what you like about being part of God's family. Don't forget to thank him.

APPOINTMENT 3
New Life in Christ
■ GROWTH

OK, now that you're a new Christian, what's next? Well, the best relationships are those that grow and deepen. It's the same way in your relationship with Jesus Christ. It's time for growth.

Talk to God: "Lord, help me to let my roots sink down into you. Thanks for helping me grow. Amen."

Investigate God's Word: Colossians 2:6-7. Memorize the first part of verse 7.

Make it practical: "I Wonder"—Colossians 2:6-7, page 1139, or "Here's What I Did"—2 Peter 1:5-8, page 1209.

Express your thoughts: Think of one way that you'd like to grow spiritually, share it with one friend, and write it in your journal. Then ask God to help you do what you've decided to do.

APPOINTMENT 4
Time to Talk
■ PRAYER

You know how good friends love to talk with each other. God, our heavenly Father, is ready for a heart-to-heart talk all the time. Conversation with God is a must!

Talk to God: "God, I'm so glad we can talk anytime. Thank you that you'll listen to my needs. Help me learn to listen to you. Amen."

Investigate God's Word: Philippians 4:6-7. Memorize verse 6.

Make it practical: "I Wonder"—1 Kings 3:3-14, page 323, or "Here's What I Did" —Ecclesiastes 5:1-7, page 615.

Express your thoughts: Commit yourself to spending at least three minutes in prayer every day. In your journal, keep a record of your prayer requests and answers. Tell God thanks for those answers.

APPOINTMENT 5
Dig In
■ BIBLE

When you get something new, you often receive an instruction manual. With your new life in Christ, you need God's instruction manual, the Bible. God communicates to us through his Word.

Talk to God: "Dear God, thank you for showing me what you're like through your Word. Help me to read it, study it, and obey it. Amen."

Investigate God's Word: 2 Timothy 3:14-17. Memorize verse 16.

Make it practical: "Here's What I Did"—Isaiah 41:10, page 665.

Express your thoughts: Commit yourself to spending five minutes a day reading the Bible. As a result of something you read, write down in your journal something you will do. Ask God to help you.

APPOINTMENT 6
Jesus Did It All
■ JESUS, OUR SAVIOR

Friendships get stronger when you really get to know the other person. You have trusted Christ to be your Savior and to give you new life. Really get to know who he is and what he has done! It's incredible!

Talk to God: "Jesus, you are so powerful! I'm thankful that you hold everything together, including me! Amen."

Investigate God's Word: Colossians 1:15-23. Memorize verse 17.

Make it practical: "I Wonder"—Judges 17:6, page 239.

Express your thoughts: Ask a friend to tell you what he or she really likes about Jesus. In your journal, write a note to Jesus about what you really appreciate about him.

APPOINTMENT 7
Solid Rock
■ OBEDIENCE

A good foundation is essential for a house to stand strong. Jesus wants you to realize that obeying God will give your life a solid foundation.

Talk to God: "Dear God, you know what's best for me. Help me to be strong and obey you in each area of my life. Amen."

Investigate God's Word: Luke 6:46-49. Memorize the first part of verse 47.

Make it practical: "I Wonder"—Joshua 24:14-15, page 215, or "Here's What I Did"—Ephesians 6:1-3, page 1127.

Express your thoughts: In your journal, list one area of your life where you are obeying God and one where you are not. Say thanks to God for helping you to want to obey.

APPOINTMENT

8

You Have Insight
◼ HOLY SPIRIT

Nobody in this world knows you better than you know yourself. Nobody knows God like God's Spirit knows God. As a new Christian, you have been given God's Holy Spirit. He will give you insight into what God is like and what he wants you to do.

Talk to God: "Thank you, God, for giving me your Spirit. You know me so well, and I will trust your Spirit to help me know more about you. Amen."

Investigate God's Word: 1 Corinthians 2:9-16. Memorize verse 12.

Make it practical: "I Wonder"—Romans 7:15–8:2, page 1075, or "Here's What I Did"—Isaiah 7:9, page 639.

Express your thoughts: In your journal, write down one question that you'd like the Holy Spirit to help you with. Now take a couple of minutes and just listen to God. Tell him thanks.

APPOINTMENT

9

Don't Give In
◼ TEMPTATION

The Bible says in 1 Peter 5:8 that our enemy Satan is like a lion that wants to rip us apart. Satan will tempt us to disobey God, but God will show us a way out!

Talk to God: "Dear God, you know the temptations I struggle with. Thank you that you have promised me a way to escape. Amen."

Investigate God's Word: 1 Corinthians 10:13. Memorize verse 13.

Make it practical: "I Wonder"—Matthew 18:7-9, page 927, or "Here's What I Did"—1 Peter 3:15, page 1203.

Express your thoughts: List the three temptations that Satan really uses on you. Now thank God ahead of time that he will show you how to not give in next time.

APPOINTMENT

10

I'm Sorry
◼ FORGIVENESS

As a child in God's family, you'll still mess up. But God's love for you is so great that he will forgive you! He can do that because he loves you!

Talk to God: "Dear God, I confess to you my sin of _____. I admit that it was wrong. Thank you that Jesus died on the cross to forgive me for this sin. Amen."

Investigate God's Word: 1 John 1:8-10. Memorize verse 9.

Make it practical: "I Wonder"—James 4:17, page 1195, or "Here's What I Did"—Lamentations 3:21-23, page 751.

Express your thoughts: Write down ways that you have disobeyed God recently. Look at each one and confess it through prayer. Cross out each sin. Let this remind you of God's loving forgiveness. Be sure to thank him!

APPOINTMENT

11

Worship Him
◼ CHURCH

Christians are part of the body of Christ, which is called his church. Be sure you get together with other believers, members of the "body." It's an opportunity to love God and each other.

Talk to God: "Dear God, thank you for your body of believers, the church. Teach me how to get involved with other Christians and really worship you. Amen."

Investigate God's Word: Hebrews 10:22-25. Memorize verse 25.

Make it practical: "I Wonder"—Hebrews 10:24-25, page 1187.

Express your thoughts: Go with some friends or family to church this week. List two ways you worshiped God.

APPOINTMENT

12

*I Gotta
Tell You
Something*

■ WITNESSING

If you have a close friend, you can't keep from talking about that person. When you love someone, you can hardly contain yourself! Let your love for Christ motivate you to tell others about him.

Talk to God: "Lord, you have changed my life. Give me the courage and opportunities to tell others about you. Amen."

Investigate God's Word: Romans 1:16-17. Memorize verse 16.

Make it practical: "I Wonder"—Luke 22:54-62, page 997, or "Here's What I Did"—Acts 4:13, page 1035.

Express your thoughts: Write down the name of one person who needs to know Jesus Christ. Start praying for that person to become a Christian. Ask a Christian friend to pray with you for the person and to help you learn how to share your faith with him or her.

APPOINTMENT

13

*Do You
Remember*

■ BIBLE
MEMORY

To fight a battle you need powerful equipment. The Holy Spirit will use the power of God's Word like a sword to defeat Satan. So a great strategy is to memorize Scripture! What verses have you already learned?

Talk to God: "Lord, I need your power! Help me to memorize Scripture verses. I know this will help me live for you. Amen."

Investigate God's Word: Ephesians 6:10-17. Memorize verse 17.

Make it practical: "I Wonder"—Philippians 4:8, page 1133, or "Here's What I Did"—Isaiah 46:4, page 669.

Express your thoughts: Review your memory verses from the past 12 days. In your journal, write down your favorite verse.

APPOINTMENT

14

Be like Christ

■ SPIRITUAL
GOAL

You've been a Christian for a short time now, and you're learning that you have a lifelong relationship with Christ. So what's your long-range plan? Becoming like Christ is the ultimate goal.

Talk to God: "Dear Jesus, more than anything else I want to become more like you. Thanks that you'll be patient and help me. Amen."

Investigate God's Word: Colossians 3:10-11. Memorize verse 10.

Make it practical: "I Wonder"—Jeremiah 29:11-13, page 719, or "Here's What I Did"—Micah 4:6-13, page 859.

Express your thoughts: Make a list of at least five ways you want to become more like Jesus. Spend time asking God to help you. Remind yourself to read this part of your journal in one month to check on your spiritual growth.

LIFE CHANGER INDEX

(Look up notes by referring to Scripture location or page number.)

BACKSLIDING
Selected passages

BALANCED LIFE
Selected passages

BELIEVING IN GOD
Selected passages

BOREDOM
Selected passages

CARING FOR OTHERS
Selected passages

CHANGE
Selected passages

FREEDOM
*Selected
passages*

Notes

FRIENDSHIPS
*Selected
passages*

Notes

FREEDOM
Selected passages

Notes

FRIENDSHIPS
Selected passages

Notes

PREJUDICE
*Selected
passages*

Notes

PRIDE
*Selected
passages*

Notes

PROBLEMS
*Selected
passages*

INDEX TO THE MORAL DILEMMAS

(Look up notes by referring to Scripture location or page number.)

INDEX TO "I WONDER"

(Look up notes by referring to Scripture location or page number.)

INDEX TO THE MORAL DILEMMAS

(Look up notes by referring to Scripture location or page number.)

INDEX TO THE ULTIMATE ISSUES

(Look up notes by referring to Scripture location or page number.)

INDEX TO THE CHARTS

(Look up charts by referring to Scripture location or page number.)

INDEX TO THE PERSONALITY PROFILES

(Look up profiles by referring to Scripture location or page number.)

INDEX TO THE MAPS

(Look up maps by referring to Scripture location or page number.)

INDEX TO "HERE'S WHAT I DID"

(Look up notes by referring to Scripture location or page number.)

"WHERE TO FIND IT" INDEX

TEACHING PARABLES

GOSPEL PARABLES